THE BASEBALL TIMELINE

BURT SOLOMON

18

MAJOR LEAGUE BASEBALL™

THE BASEBALL TIMELINE

IN ASSOCIATION WITH MAJOR LEAGUE BASEBALL

BURT SOLOMON

DK

LONDON, NEW YORK, DELHI, JOHANNESBURG,
MUNICH, PARIS, and SYDNEY

London, New York, Sydney, Delhi,
Paris, Munich, Johannesburg

Design: NewEarthMedia
Editor: Bob Woods
Senior Art Editor: Michelle Baxter
Editorial Director: LaVonne Carlson
Art Director: Tina Vaughan
Publisher: Sean Moore
Production Directors: David Proffit and Chris Avgherinos
DTP Designer: Megan Clayton
Editorial Consultant and Picture Research: Shoreline Publishing Group

MAJOR LEAGUE BASEBALL

MAJOR LEAGUE BASEBALL
Timothy J. Brosnan, Executive Vice President, Business
Don Hintze, Vice President, Publishing
Rich Pilling, Manager, MLB Photos
Paul Cunningham, Photo Editor
Mike McCormack, Editor
Erin Whiteside, Assistant Editor

Major League Baseball Properties, Inc.
245 Park Avenue, New York, NY 10167

First American Edition, 2001
2 4 6 8 10 9 7 5 3 1
Published in the United States
by DK Publishing, Inc.
95 Madison Avenue
New York, New York 10016

"A Stonesong Press Book"

Library of Congress Cataloging-in-Publication Data
Solomon, Burt.
The baseball timeline / Burt Solomon.
p. cm.
Includes index
ISBN 0-7894-7132-9 (alk. paper)
1. Baseball–United States–History–Miscellanea. I. Title.
GV863.A1 S693 2001
796.357'0973–dc21 00-065812

Reproduced by Colourscan, Singapore
Printed and bound in the United States of America

See our complete catalog at

www.dk.com

CONTENTS

1956 WORLD SERIES
AMERICAN LEAGUE VS NATIONAL LEAGUE
GAME 5
ENTER AT GATE 2
MEZZANINE BOX SEAT
RAIN CHECK

INTRODUCTION

GEORGE BERNARD SHAW called baseball "America's tragedy" and observed: "When a man asks you to come and see baseball played twice, it sets you to asking yourself why you went to see it played once."

Journalist Walter "Red" Smith might have been thinking of Shaw when he said: "Baseball is a dull game only to those with dull minds." He called it the "meat-and-potatoes sport" and observed: "Ninety feet between home plate and first base may be the closest man has ever come to perfection."

Philosophical musings like those were beyond most of us when I was growing up. It was a time when baseball was more than a game—it was the only game. We watched college football and basketball with mild curiosity and transient interest simply to bridge the gap between baseball seasons. Professional football was irrelevant. Baseball was the game we cared about, the one we listened to and later watched, the sport we adapted for the streets with broomsticks and rubber balls— "Spaldeens" and tennis balls—in place of bats and baseballs.

It was Joe DiMaggio and Hank Greenberg, Mel Ott and Carl Hubbell, Dolf Camilli and Pee Wee Reese whom we imitated, whose images we collected on Play Ball cards. Later, when the color line was belatedly broken, Jackie Robinson and Larry Doby, then Willie Mays and Henry Aaron, were among those who fired our imaginations.

Succeeding generations found their own heroes: Roberto Clemente, Carl Yastrzemski, Rod Carew, Nolan Ryan, Tom Seaver, Reggie Jackson, and Pete Rose, whose rise and fall are worthy of a Shakespearean protagonist. Today's young fans believe that the likes of Frank Thomas, Ken Griffey Jr., Barry Bonds, and Greg Maddux can match the exploits of Babe Ruth, Walter Johnson, and Lou Gehrig—and then some. That is one of the things that binds the generations of fans—the notion that the heroes of your generation are better than those of any other generation. Another is the eagerness of those of all ages to debate their heroes' merits.

Jimmie Foxx was one of baseball's all-time great power hitters.

But baseball fans really compose one seamless generation, one that lives the entire continuity of the sport all at once. Baseball fans tend to root in the present, look forward to the future, and dwell in the past. Nostalgia is as much a part of the sport as the sound of wood on horsehide. Memories of old ballparks, old players, and old games, filtered and enhanced through memory, are part of what gives baseball its magic, the mystique that reaches beneath and beyond the rules and mechanics of the game. Those memories give the game its enigmatic quality, the preternatural aspect that is reflected in W. P. Kinsella's *Shoeless Joe* and the film version, *Field of Dreams.* It is what inspires the many songs and poems, books, and plays that have focused on the sport. It is what brings strangers together in the discussion of even the most minor of plays, the most obscure of players, and the most trivial of facts.

This most American of sports possesses you the first time you are introduced to it and never lets you go. Baseball and I have broken up many times, but I always return to it. It is in the nature of the game and it is in the psyche of the fan. This book is the culmination of that lifelong on-again, off-again romance.

The Baseball Timeline is for browsers and readers, for serious, casual, and new fans. Unlike conventional histories, it is a book you can read from any starting point, backward or forward, from top to bottom or in reverse. It was designed and created to enable the reader to visit or revisit the landmark events of the sport in the context of the world and the United States at any particular time. It was written in a format that will stir memories and introduce new-old events. It might even settle a few bets. In addition to the important on-field highlights, it details births, deaths, and trades; the peripheral events; the humor and the unusual; and the role of baseball in the arts. You will find nail-biting no-hitters; titanic home runs; great plays and zany misplays; and memorable, forgettable, and despicable characters. You may cry over Lou Gehrig and Roberto Clemente, cheer for Jackie Robinson and Hank Greenberg, groan over Jim Piersall and Albert Belle, fume over Cap Anson and Ben Chapman. It is history—with the accent on the personalities that made the game.

The Baseball Timeline is intended to augment, not replace, the many fine histories of baseball and baseball reference books. It is a volume I hope will find its way to the TV-viewing room, night tables, and other reading sites, perhaps even into broadcast booths and sports desks; it is a book to have on hand while you watch, talk, or think about baseball, not a work to store on a shelf.

When I began this project, my goal was to produce an error-free book. By the time I finished, I realized that despite the wealth of books and articles about the sport—or perhaps because of it—there often is conflict on facts, dates, and language. Even within a given work, authors contradict themselves. I encountered one book in which the same event was listed under two different dates only paragraphs apart. Even something as basic as Lou Gehrig's farewell address appears in print in a variety of versions. Box scores and narratives for the same game by the same author sometimes fail to jibe. In a number of books, writers bemoan the difficulty in determining proper dates, particularly for trades and other transactions. Perhaps the most disturbing piece of information I encountered in my quest for accuracy was a remark by the celebrated sportswriter Fred Lieb in his *Baseball As I Have Known It.* He noted that his contemporaries did their own scoring and "made out their own box scores for the use of their papers. Sometimes the *Press, Tribune,* and *Morning Sun* would have different hit totals."

To resolve these difficulties, I established a sort of "factual pecking order." Members of the Society for American Baseball Research—who often devote endless hours to a single subject—generally were accorded a high credibility, as were publications of the teams themselves. Information from biographers, who focus on one subject, generally was given precedence over histories. Newspaper accounts, particularly in the *New York Times* and especially for dates, were given high credence. (I know from my philosophy classes that an event cannot be reported before it occurs.) I also consulted *The Baseball Encyclopedia,* which, like all of us, is not error-free. But it is like your first high school crush—you love it despite the zits.

Other books I found particularly valuable and that I commend to readers who want more of America's pastime include the aforementioned Fred Lieb memoir, Harold Seymour's three-volume history, Jules Tygiel's *Baseball's Great Experiment: Jackie Robinson and His Legacy*; Eliot Asinof's *Eight Men Out*; Peter C. Bjarkman's *Encyclopedia of Major League Baseball—American League* and *Encyclopedia of Major League Baseball—National League*; James Mote's *Everything Baseball* (a compendium of the movies, plays, novels, poems, songs, and works of art inspired by the sport); *Baseball by the Books: A History and Complete Bibliography of Baseball Fiction* by Andy McCue; Daniel E. Ginsburg's *The Fix Is In: A History of Baseball Gambling and Game Fixing Scandals*; and Jerry Lansche's *Glory Fades Away-The 19th Century World Series Rediscovered.*

This marks the second edition of *The Baseball Timeline*. At this writing it is the intention of the publisher and the Stonesong Press to revise and update *The Baseball Timeline* periodically. I invite all readers to submit corrections and suggested additions—with documentation in both cases—to me in care of:

THE STONESONG PRESS,
11 EAST 47TH STREET,
NEW YORK, NY
10017.

Please note that while submission doesn't guarantee inclusion, all submissions will be considered.

Without Paul Fargis, president of the Stonesong Press, there would be no book. *The Baseball Timeline* was his idea, and he generously assigned the task of realizing the concept to me. Through more than two years of mostly solitary labor—sometimes of love, other times of pain—Paul was always supportive and encouraging, asking the right questions, making the correct suggestions, and applauding at just the right moments.

Whitey Ford is 2-0 in the World Series, with a 0.00 ERA.

NY
NY

Also on the list of those "without whom this book..." is the staff at the Katonah Village Library in Westchester County, New York, particularly Van Kozelka, who hunted for and borrowed books for me from libraries all over the country, and research librarians Virginia Fetscher and Helen Olson, who assisted me in tracking down information and put up with my long stretches on their microfilm viewer.

I am a writer who still regards an electric typewriter as high-tech. Through his patience and expertise, Ken Kurzweil helped guide me through the modern world of computers, online services, the Internet, and a variety of other mystifying technological developments.

I discovered the amazing David W. Smith, president of Retrosheet, in the final stages of my writing, but his unstinting help in resolving conflicts and providing facts was invaluable. He is assembling play-by-play accounts of every baseball game in history through 1983 and shared his information and his personal knowledge without reservation. Retrosheet will be an essential resource to future writers and researchers.

My profound thanks to the superb staff of the National Baseball Hall of Fame Library Research Department, which responded promptly and well to my late-hour fact-checking needs. I would especially like to thank Scot E. Mondore, associate researcher; Joshua Eisenberg and Daniel Messeloff, library interns; and Richard Gannon, research assistant. Seamus Kearny and his Society for American Baseball Research on-line system opened up many opportunities for tracking down information. SABR members (referred to as SABR-ites in this book) were responsive with their time and knowledge. Particularly helpful in providing answers to my questions were Patric J. Doyle, David Pietrusza, Merritt Clifton, Neal McCabe, Andy McCue, Gary Plunkitt, Russ Lake, Gary Collard, Troy Soos, Joe Naiman, Clifford Otto and David Trautman of the Citadel, Howard Pollack, MD, David S. Vincent, Sandra Vigil, and Patrick Lethert.

A variety of people I have never met in person were incredibly generous. Robert S. Fuchs took time from writing his own book, *Memories of a Baseball Fan: Judge Fuchs and His Boston Braves,* to answer my inquiries about his father, Emil Fuchs, onetime owner of the Boston Braves.

Glen Serra of the Atlanta Braves was the first to respond to my inquiries to major league teams, telephoning to see how he could help and providing many valuable leads into the team's history. John Olguin, the Los Angeles Dodgers' archivist, responded to my questions with a handwritten letter crammed with information. Ty Yomo, an Oakland Athletics intern assigned to my inquiry by Dave Perron, director of public affairs and community relations, researched questions about the team's past and Charles O. Finley. An anonymous Chicago White Sox employee photocopied original box scores, and a nameless counterpart for the Pittsburgh Pirates actually hand-copied box scores of a 1920 tripleheader. Others who provided information and leads and whose names I know include Mark Bastion of the New York Mets, Adam Levin and Matt Roebuck of the Boston Red Sox; Stephanie Seavers of the San Diego Padres; Bill Stetka and Isaac Fryman of the Baltimore Orioles; Dave Fanucchi of the St. Louis Cardinals; Suzanne Reichart of the Chicago White Sox; Ted Werner and Thurman Brooks of the Atlanta Braves; Kitty Wilkerson and Dana Wilcox of the Texas Rangers; Trey Wilkinson of the Houston Astros; Kelly Lippincott of the Cincinnati Reds; Connie Bell of the Detroit Tigers; Eric Radovich of the Seattle Mariners; Mike Selleck of the Oakland Athletics; Peter Hirdt and Matthew Malm of the Elias Sports Bureau (who resolved the "mystery" of the date of the Adcock-Gomez fight); Glenn Wilburn of the National League; John Neves of the New York Yankees; John Kehl of the Colorado Rockies and James Carpenter of the Cleveland Indians; Brad Smith of the Minnesota Twins; and Blake Rhodes of the San Francisco Giants.

The editor of my college newspaper, Jack Clary, who has written more books about sports than many people have read, offered invaluable guidance at the outset on how to organize my research. Howard Berk,

EASTON

a former New York Yankee and major league baseball executive, provided an almost daily dose of baseball conversation. Young Jonathan Schecter, who someday will write a book of his own, spent a day tracking down key data for me. Peter Krawchuk brought *The Baseball Timeline* to the attention of a number of baseball dignitaries. Amanda Cohen at KDKA Radio in Pittsburgh; Marty Appel at the Topps Co.; Michele J. Herwig at the Babe Ruth Birthplace and Baseball Center; Bill Williams of Hillerich & Bradsby; Lisa Hum at the University of Michigan's Bentley Historical Library; and the University of Southern California Sports Information Office also were responsive. The staff of the Bedford Hills Free Library helped during the preparation of the proposal for this book, as did Jackie Russo of the National Baseball Hall of Fame in Cooperstown, New York. A number of people—including Wynn Lowenthal, David Sribnik, and Chris Fargis—lent me books from their personal collections.

Libraries who sent books to the Katonah Village Library for my use were Babson Library/Springfield College (Massachusetts); Bronxville Public Library (New York); Buffalo and Erie County Public Library (New York); Emma Clark Memorial Library (Setauket, New York); Field Library (Peekskill, New York); Free Library of Philadelphia; Greenburgh Public Library (New York); James Prendergast Library Association (Jamestown, New York); Memphis/Shelby County Public Library and Information Center (Tennessee); Mid-York Library System (Utica, New York); Mount Vernon Public Library (New York); New Rochelle Public Library (New York); New York State Library (Albany, New York); North Castle Public Library (New York); Pennsylvania State University Libraries; Scarsdale Public Library (New York); Southwest Wisconsin Library System (Fennimore, Wisconsin); State University of New York at Brockport/Drake Memorial Library; University of Massachusetts (Amherst); West Hartford Public Library (Connecticut); Woodbridge Public Library (New Jersey); and Worchester Public Library (Massachusetts).

Rickey Henderson of the Oakland A's tries to avoid being tagged out by the Yankees's Ranady Velarde.

The *New York Times* as it is for most projects, was an invaluable source of facts in baseball and peripheral events. Secondary sources that were helpful in my research included *Chronicle of America, The New York Public Library Book of Chronologies, The Timeline Book of the Arts,* the *Timetables of History,* and *What Happened When—A Chronology of Life and Events in America.*

Last but not least was the assistance of my immediate family: My son Robert assisted with the year-end statistics, and my daughter, Carrie, provided encouragement. My aunt Elsie Adler and my cousin Paul Adler (who made a key introduction); my sister and brother-in-law, Betty and Steve Sribnik; and my old friends Milton Skolsky and Jim Mauceri provided moral and other support at the times I needed it most. I also would like to acknowledge two outstanding attorneys and good friends—Dominic J. Calabrese and Karen Akst Schecter.

FOREWORD TO THE NEW EDITION

Most of the "thank yous" for the original edition of *The Baseball Timeline* are herewith renewed and extended.

Once again, without Paul Fargis of the Stonesong Press, there would be no book. And without the constant prodding and encouragement of Ellen Scordato, managing editor of the Stonesong Press, there might not be a new edition.

Thanks to the readers who submitted suggestions and corrections. They include Scott M. Bushnell, Robert J. Levy (who generously shared the fruits of his own extensive research), Andy McCue, and Stewart Venit.

Thanks to Wendy Bloom and the research staff of the Mount Kisco Library, in my new hometown, as well as to Santo Labombarda of Elias Sports Bureau, and Eric Enders and Bill Francis of the Baseball Hall of Fame Library.

And to Erwin Hersch, Bob Brutting, and Chris Kearin of the late lamented Mt. Kisco Book Company, one of the best of the independent bookshops.

And to my boss and friend Bonnie Riscica Slusarczyk, the librarian at Pleasantville High School, for her understanding and assistance, and to my PHS colleague and friend Drew Marino, for the stimulating baseball talk.

Burt Solomon

How to Use This Book

THE BASEBALL TIMELINE is a year-by-year chronicle of America's national past time.

Part 1 explores the sport's roots in the 18th and early 19th centuries. **Part 2**, which begins in 1845, traces baseball's development from an amateur activity to a professional sport. **Part 3** covers baseball in the 20th century—from the freewheeling era of Ty Cobb and Babe Ruth to the recordbreaking years of Hank Aaron and Mark McGwire. **Part 4** is a portrait of baseball as it enters its third century—and a new millennium.

Each annual section is divided into four parts: Pre-Season (from the beginning of the calendar year to Opening Day), Season (from Opening Day to the end of the regular season), Regular Season Wrap-Up (the World Series), and Post-Season (through the end of the calendar year).

A comprehensive index guides you quickly to specific dates and pages, and a bibliography lists the best books on baseball.

These quotes and excerpts are some of the most interesting things people have said and written about baseball. They offer insight into many of baseball's most colorful characters.

Move through baseball's history year by year.

At the start of each year, this list of headlines reminds you of key events occurring in the world at large.

These headings separate each year's season into four phases.

1891

JULY 31
Giants' pitcher Amos Rusie, 20, becomes the youngest to toss a no-hitter.

NEWS

JAMES NAISMITH INVENTS BASKETBALL IN CANADA

FIRST WOMEN'S CHRISTIAN TEMPERANCE UNION MEETING HELD

Carnegie Hall opens in New York with Peter Illich Tchaikovsky as guest conductor

Thomas Edison patents the motion picture camera

THOMAS HARDY'S *TESS OF THE D'UBERVILLES* AND OSCAR WILDE'S *THE PICTURE OF DORIAN GRAY* ARE PUBLISHED

UNIVERSITY OF CHICAGO FOUNDED

GOLD RUSH ON PIKE'S PEAK

First full-service ad agency in U.S. opens in New York City

PRE-SEASON

MARCH:

Players begin returning to their original teams after the collapse of the Players League.

Albert Spalding retires as president of the Chicago White Stockings; he is replaced by James A. Hart, former manager of Louisville and Milwaukee.

MARCH 4:

Clarence "Dazzy" Vance is born in Orient, Iowa.

APRIL 20:

Dave Bancroft is born in Sioux City, Iowa.

THE SEASON

APRIL 22:

In the first game at the third Polo Grounds, Boston beats the New York Giants, 4-3.

MAY 1:

Cleveland's League Park opens with 10,000 fans on hand to see pitcher Denton "Cy" Young beat Cincinnati, 12-3.

MAY 3:

Eppa Rixey is born in Culpeper, Virginia.

JUNE 22:

Brooklyn's Tom Lovett no-hits the Giants, 4-0. He walks three batters and fans four. Amos Rusie is the losing pitcher.

JULY 31:

The Giants' Amos Rusie throws a no-hitter against the Bridegrooms, winning 6-0, with eight walks and four strikeouts. At 20 years and two months old, Rusie is the youngest to throw a no-hitter and the first to toss one against Brooklyn. Adonis Bill Terry is the losing pitcher.

AUGUST 26:

John J. McGraw debuts with the Baltimore Orioles in the AA. He plays shortstop, makes an error, and has a hit as the Orioles defeat the Columbus Buckeyes, 6-5.

SEPTEMBER 4:

Responding to writers who claim it's time for him to quit, Chicago's 39-year-old player-manager Cap Anson wears a false white beard against Boston. It doesn't help him at the plate – he is hitless in three at-bats. The White Stockings beat Boston, 5-3.

OCTOBER 4:

In his first start, Ted Breitenstein of the Browns (AA) no-hits Louisville, 8-0. He is the first to debut with a no-hitter.

REGULAR SEASON WRAP-UP:

Boston's Beaneaters, win the NL pennant, its Reds take the AA flag. But the Beaneaters decline a playoff, so for the first time since 1883, baseball has no Championships.

POST-SEASON

OCTOBER 14:

Larry Corcoran, who pitched three no-hitters and won 177 games, dies at age 32 in Newark, New Jersey. In his first five seasons with the Chicago White Stockings, Corcoran won 43, 31, 27, 34, and 35 games. His career ERA was 2.36.

NOVEMBER 11:

Walter "Rabbit" Maranville is born in Springfield, Massachusetts.

DECEMBER 17:

The AA folds. The Baltimore Orioles, St. Louis Browns, Louisville Colonels, and Washington Senators will be absorbed into the NL.

The gray date bars introduce the most significant days in each season's history.

BEST OF YEAR STATISTICS:

Statistics have long been a part of the fascination of baseball. In this book, many of the statistics are obvious. But if you're a newcomer to the sport, or to the art of baseball statistics, here's a little background detail to help you catch up.

Home Runs, Hits, Stolen Bases, Wins, Strikeouts, and Saves are simply totals of what a player has done for the season. But some of the other statistics are figured by formulas that are not so straightforward.

Batting Average is the total number of base hits divided by the number of times a player has been at bat.

Slugging Average is the total number of bases gained on all base hits, divided by a player's time at bat.

Runs Batted In are the total number of points scored as the result of the player's hits.

Winning Percentage is used to gauge the percentage of games a pitcher wins. It's the number of games won divided by the total number of decisions.

Awards

Most Valuable Player has a checkered history. In 1911, automobile manufacturer Hugh Chalmers agreed to present the **Chalmers Award** at the conclusion of the season to the Most Valuable Player in each league. The decision for this honor was to be made by a committee of baseball writers – one writer from each club city in each league. That award was given through 1914. In 1922 the American League Trophy Committee drafted MVP rules for the AL, picked by one baseball writer from each of the AL cities. The rules proved to be complicated and unpopular.

In 1924 the National League made its own rules for an MVP, still using sportswriters

Sidebars provide interesting baseball-related information

The corner date bar shows you where you are chronologically at a glance.

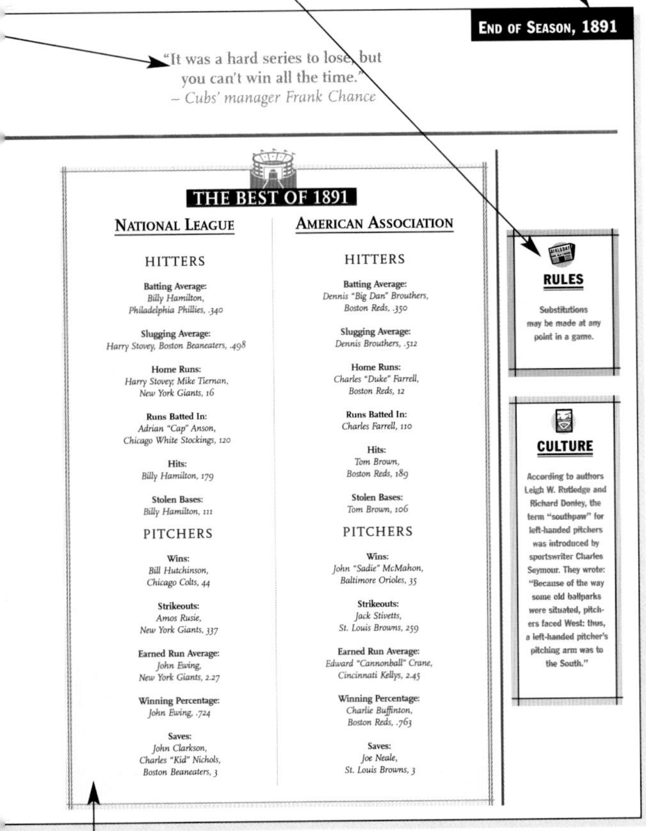
End of Season, 1891
"It was a hard series to lose, but you can't win all the time."
– Cubs' manager Frank Chance
THE BEST OF 1891
National League
American Association
HITTERS
Batting Average: Billy Hamilton, Philadelphia Phillies, .340
Slugging Average: Harry Stovey, Boston Beaneaters, .498
Home Runs: Harry Stovey; Mike Tiernan, New York Giants, 16
Runs Batted In: Adrian "Cap" Anson, Chicago White Stockings, 120
Hits: Billy Hamilton, 179
Stolen Bases: Billy Hamilton, 111
PITCHERS
Wins: Bill Hutchinson, Chicago Colts, 44
Strikeouts: Amos Rusie, New York Giants, 337
Earned Run Average: John Ewing, New York Giants, 2.27
Winning Percentage: John Ewing, .724
Saves: John Clarkson, Charles "Kid" Nichols, Boston Beaneaters, 3
HITTERS
Batting Average: Dennis "Big Dan" Brouthers, Boston Reds, .350
Slugging Average: Dennis Brouthers, .512
Home Runs: Charles "Duke" Farrell, Boston Reds, 12
Runs Batted In: Charles Farrell, 110
Hits: Tom Brown, Boston Reds, 189
Stolen Bases: Tom Brown, 106
PITCHERS
Wins: John "Sadie" McMahon, Baltimore Orioles, 35
Strikeouts: Jack Stivetts, St. Louis Browns, 259
Earned Run Average: Edward "Cannonball" Crane, Cincinnati Kellys, 2.45
Winning Percentage: Charlie Buffinton, Boston Reds, .763
Saves: Joe Neale, St. Louis Browns, 3
RULES
Substitutions may be made at any point in a game.
CULTURE
According to authors Leigh W. Rutledge and Richard Donley, the term "southpaw" for left-handed pitchers was introduced by sportswriter Charles Seymour. They wrote: "Because of the way some old ballparks were situated, pitchers faced West: thus, a left-handed pitcher's pitching arm was to the South."

A Best of Season box at the end of each annual section gives the season's top stats and lists major award winners.

THROUGHOUT THIS BOOK you'll find extra information provided outside the main text. This information is organized into several broad categories, marked with the following symbols and colors for instant recognition:

Equipment
Notes new equipment and changes in how equipment is used.

Rules Changes
Describes how the rules change from season to season.

Team Changes
Recounts how the rosters changed, and what teams moved where.

Culture
Highlights the movies, songs, plays, and books written about baseball.

History
Features historical facts, records, statistics and anecdotes here.

Trivia
Explains how players and teams got their nicknames and other fun facts.

League changes
Follows the various leagues as they came and went, and how they realigned themselves. Includes information about the Negro Leagues, All-American Girls Professional Baseball League and Little League.

to pick the winner. The AL award was officially voted out at a special league meeting in 1929. The National League followed suit with the AL's decision, but agreed to continue its award through the 1929 season. In an effort to standardize MVP voting, the Baseball Writers Association of America, in its annual winter meeting on December 11, 1930, decided to appoint two committees (one in each league) to elect Most Valuable Players. One MVP in each league has been chosen by Association members since 1931.

Cy Young Award was the brainchild of Commissioner Ford Frick. It is now given to the best pitcher in each league. The pitcher is chosen by the Baseball Writers Association of America. At its inception in 1956, the award was given to only one pitcher in the Major Leagues. But from 1967 on, after Frick retired, pitchers from both leagues were honored.

Rookie of the Year is awarded by the Baseball Writers Association of America to the individual player from each league who has the best rookie season pitching, hitting, or fielding during his first year of eligibility. From 1949 on a player has been selected from each league.

Manager of the Year was first awarded by the Baseball Writers Association of America in 1983. It is given to the Major League manager from each league who accomplishes more than was expected from his team.

This symbol marks which players have been elected to the National Baseball Hall of Fame in Cooperstown, New York.

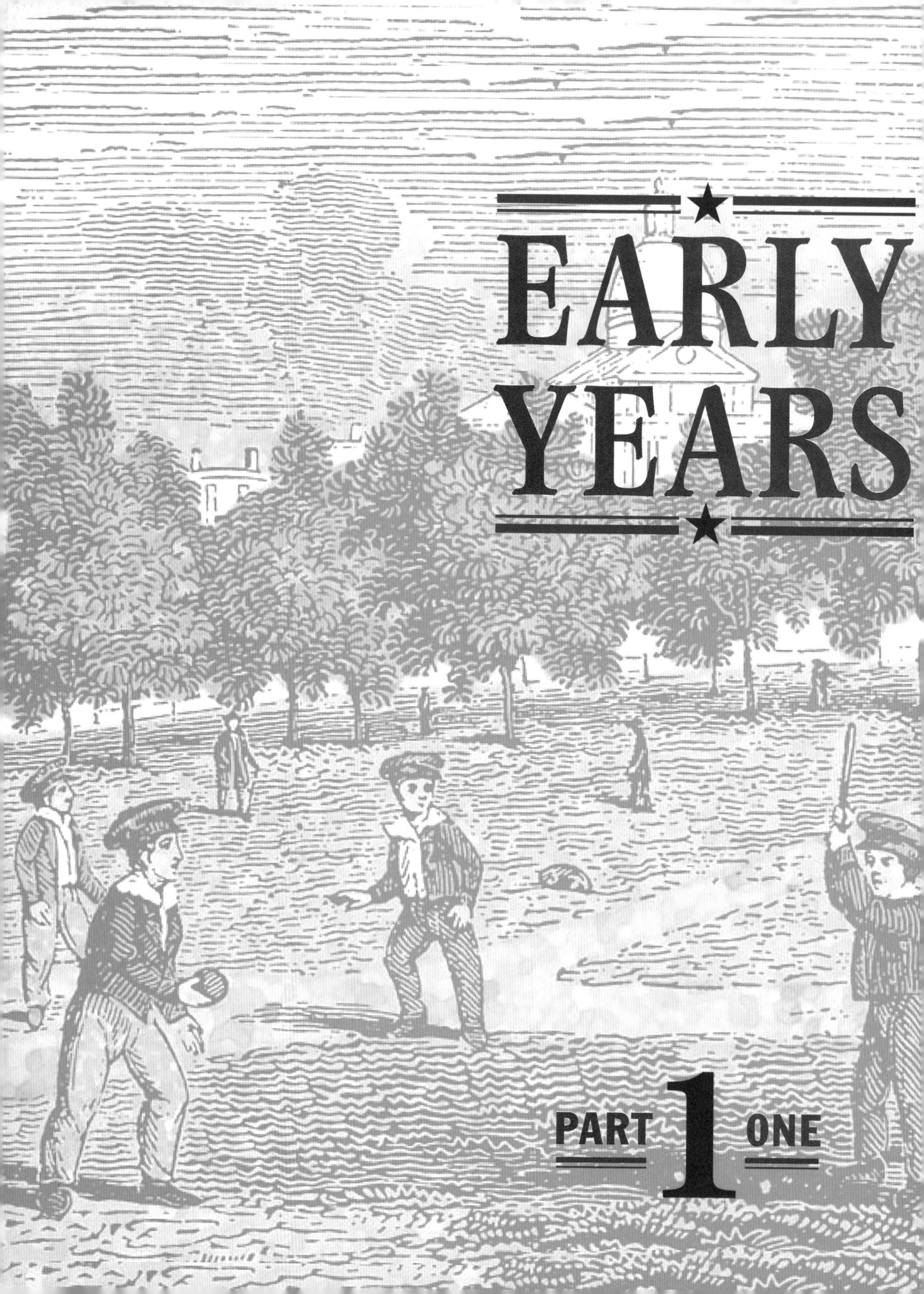

EARLY YEARS

PART 1 ONE

1778-1844

NEWS

CAPTAIN COOK DISCOVERS SANDWICH ISLANDS (1778)

George Washington becomes first U.S. President (1789)

ELI WHITNEY INVENTS COTTON GIN (1794)

ERIE CANAL OPENS (1825)

LONGFELLOW PUBLISHES *VOICES OF THE NIGHT* (1839)

Alas, Abner Doubleday did *not* invent baseball.

1778

The diary of a soldier found at Valley Forge, Pennsylvania, refers to a game of "base" played by the troops.

1818

In *Northanger Abbey,* Jane Austen writes: "...Catherine, who had by nature nothing heroic about her, should prefer cricket, baseball, riding on horseback, and running about the country, at the age of fourteen, to books, or at least books of information..."

1820

APRIL 17:

Alexander Cartwright is born in New York City.

1834

Robin Carver's *Book of Sports* includes printed rules for baseball. A woodcut in the book shows boys playing the game on the Boston Common. The rules are the same as for the British game of rounders, which appeared in 1829 in *The Boy's Own Book* in London.

1835

JANUARY 10:

William "Harry" Wright is born in Sheffield, England.

1837

DECEMBER 26:

Morgan G. Bulkeley is born in East Haddam, Connecticut.

1839

As legend has it, Abner Doubleday invents baseball in Cooperstown, New York. At the time, however, Doubleday is a cadet at the U.S. Military Academy at West Point, New York. There is no credible evidence that he visited Cooperstown this year or that he had anything to do with the creation of the game. In his diaries he stakes no claim to creating the game.

HISTORY

From the time baseball was reputedly invented in 1839, until the first rules were written in 1845, no official documents were kept.

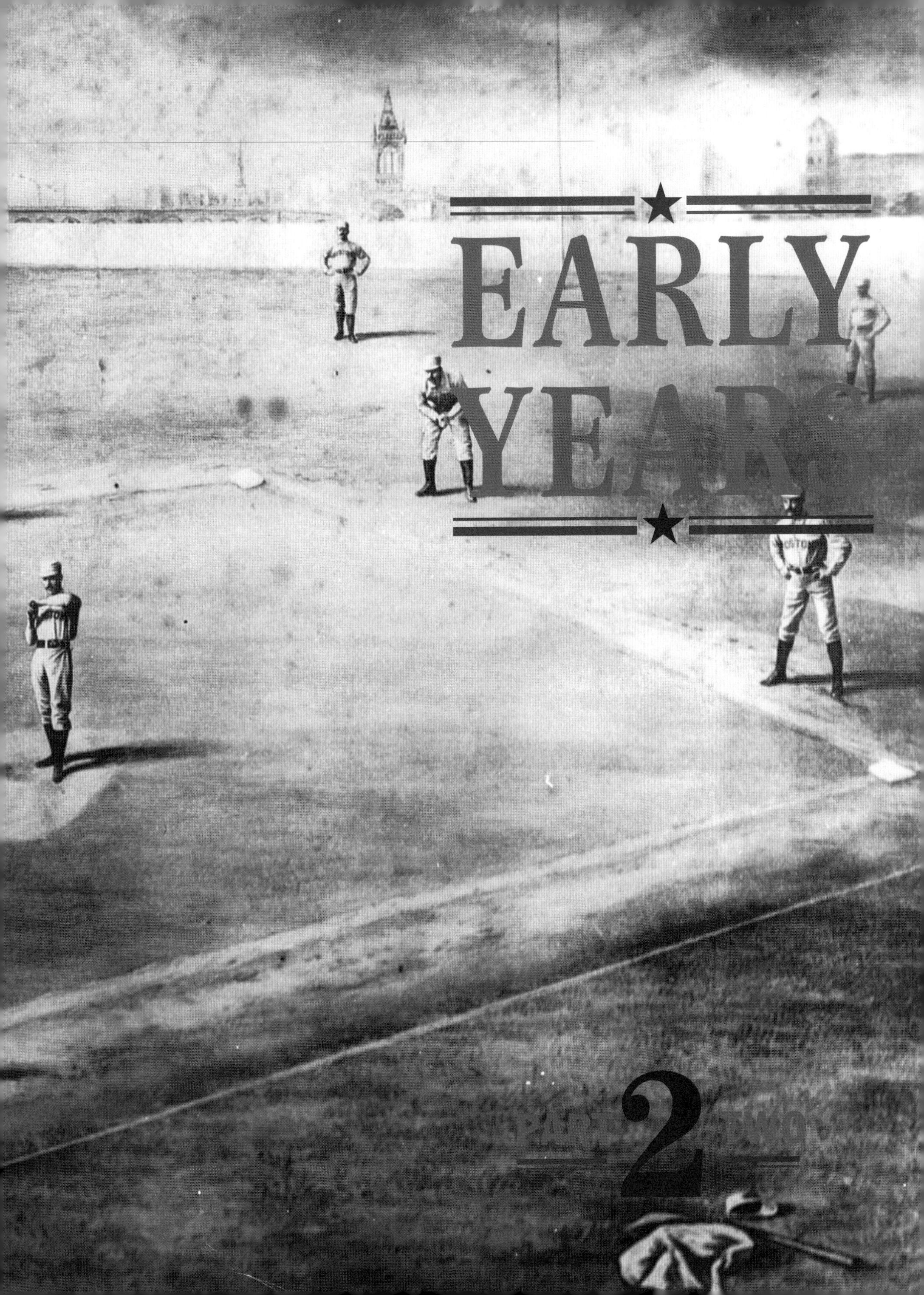

EARLY YEARS

PART 2 TWO

1845-75

1845
September 13,
Alexander Cartwright,
the father of baseball,
presents the first set of
rules for the game.

NEWS

1845: TEXAS BECOMES 28TH STATE

1849: Discovery of gold at Sutter's Mill begins California Gold Rush

1851: HARRIET BEECHER STOWE'S *UNCLE TOM'S CABIN* IS PUBLISHED

1859: CHARLES DARWIN'S *ORIGIN OF SPECIES* IS PUBLISHED

1861: Civil War Begins at Fort Sumter

1865: LEE SURRENDERS TO GRANT AT APPOMATTOX

1865: President Abraham Lincoln Assassinated

1869: PRESIDENT JOHNSON IMPEACHED BUT ACQUITTED

1871: P.T. BARNUM'S "GREATEST SHOW ON EARTH" OPENS IN NEW YORK

1875: Edison invents duplicating machine

1845

SEPTEMBER 13:

Alexander Cartwright presents the first set of baseball rules, 20 in number. 1) Members must strictly observe the time agreed upon for exercise and be punctual in their attendance. 2) When assembled for practice, the President, or Vice President in his absence, shall appoint an umpire, who shall keep the game in a book provided for that purpose, and note all violations of the By-Laws and Rules during the time of exercise. 3) The presiding officer shall designate two members as captains, who shall retire and make the match to be played, observing at the same time the players put opposite each other should be as nearly equal as possible; the choice of the two sides to be then tossed for, and the first in hand to be decided in a like manner. 4) The bases shall be from "home" to second base, 42 paces; from first base to third base, 42 paces, equidistant. 5) No stump match shall be played on a regular day of exercise. 6) If there should not be a sufficient number of members of the club present at the time agreed upon to commence exercise, gentlemen not members may be chosen in to make up the match, which shall not be broken up to take in members that may afterwards appear; but in all cases, members shall have the preference, when present at the making of the match. 7) If members appear after the game is commenced they may be chosen in if mutually agreed upon. 8) The game to consist of 21 counts, or aces; but at the conclusion of an equal number of hands must be played. 9) The ball must be pitched, and not thrown, for the bat. 10) A ball knocked out of the field, or outside the range of the first or third base, is foul. 11) Three balls being struck at and missed and the last one caught is a hand out; if not caught is considered fair, and a striker is bound to run. 12) A ball being struck or tipped and caught either flying or on the first bound is a hand out. 13) A player running the base shall be out, if the ball is in the hands of an adversary on the base, or the runner is touched with it before he makes his base; it being understood, however, that in no instance is a ball to be thrown at him. [Note: This is a major departure from the rules of "town ball."] 14) A player running who shall prevent an adversary from catching or getting the ball before making his base, is a hand out. 15) Three hands out, all out. 16) Players must take their strike in a regular turn. 17) All disputes and differences relative to the game, to be determined by the umpire, from which there is no appeal. 18) No ace or base can be made on a foul strike. 19) A runner cannot be put out in making one base, when a balk is made by the pitcher. 20) But one base allowed when a ball bounds out of the field when struck.

SEPTEMBER 23:

The Knickerbocker Base Ball Club is formed and Alexander Cartwright's 20 rules are adopted.

OCTOBER 21:

The New York Ball Club and a Brooklyn team face off at the Elysian Fields in Hoboken. New York wins, 24-4.

The New York Ball Club meets the Brooklyn team on the grounds of the Star Club, Myrtle Avenue in Brooklyn. New York wins the game, 37-19.

Spirit of the Times describes baseball as "the national pastime," writing: "We feel a degree of old Knickerbocker pride at the continued prevalence of Base Ball as the National game in the region of Manhattanese."

1846

JUNE 19:

At the Elysian Fields in Hoboken, New Jersey, the New York Ball Club trounces the Knickerbockers 23-1 in four innings. (Some sources list the final score as 21-1.) Under existing "Cartwright/Knickerbocker" rules, 21 runs or "aces" win a game. The game is played with nine men on a side on a diamond infield with bases 90 feet apart. Cartwright serves as the umpire. Daniel Okrent and Steve Wulf note: "There is some reason to believe that the Knickerbockers lost on purpose to encourage the other team to actively pursue this new sport. For one thing, Cartwright, one of their best players, only served as the umpire."

JULY:

The American poet Walt Whitman writes in the Brooklyn Eagle: "In our sundown perambulations, of late, through the outer parts of Brooklyn, we have observed several parties of youngsters playing 'base,' a certain game of ball."

1847

JANUARY 28:

George Wright, the younger brother of Harry Wright, is born in Yonkers, New York. Harry will play just two games of professional baseball, while George will play 627 over a five-year career.

1848

OCTOBER 17:

William "Candy" Cummings is born today in Ware, Massachusetts.

1849

JUNE:

The Knickerbockers, a New York team, are the first to wear uniforms for a game. Their attire is composed of straw hats, white shirts, and blue trousers. (One source reports this as happening in 1851.)

1850

SEPTEMBER 2:

Albert Goodwill Spalding is born in Byron, Illinois.

Alexander Cartwright, the true father of baseball.

Baseball is played on the Boston Common in 1834.

HISTORY

A *New York Morning News* account of the October 21, 1845, game, discovered at the New York Historical Society by Harvard graduate student Edward L. Widmer, refers to a game played before October 21. Widmer also found information on the October 21 game, as did sports historian Melvin L. Adelman. An October 24 boxscore was also discovered by Adelman.

CULTURE

"The Baseball Polka," a song by J.R. Blodgett, makes its debut in 1857.

HISTORY

In what some characterize as the first post-season championship series, in the fall of 1857, the Brooklyn Atlantics win two of three from the Brooklyn Eckfords.

1851

JUNE 17:

In baseball's first recorded extra-inning game, the Knickerbockers beat the Washington Club, 22-20, in 10 innings. The game is played in Hoboken, New Jersey.

1852

APRIL 11:

Adrian Constantine "Cap" Anson is born in Marshalltown, Iowa.

JUNE 27

At the Red House Grounds at 106th St. and Second Ave. in Harlem, New York, the Gothams (formerly the Washington Club) defeat the Knickerbockers, 21-16, in 16 innings.

SEPTEMBER 1:

James "Orator Jim" O'Rourke is born in Bridgeport, Connecticut.

1853

APRIL:

William Cauldwell, the editor and proprietor of the *Sunday Mercury* in New York City, publishes what is reportedly the first printed coverage of baseball games.

JULY 16:

The *New York Clipper* publishes what is believed – at the time – to be the first tabulated boxscore of a baseball game. It details a 21-12 victory by the Knickerbockers over the Gotham Club on July 5, 1854

OCTOBER 26:

New York's archrival Knickerbockers and Gotham Club play a baseball game that turns into a 12-12 standoff and ends after 12 innings because of darkness. It is the first recorded game of baseball to end in a tie. The Knickerbockers had led after 9 innings of play, 11-9, but under the current rules the game had to be continued.

DECEMBER 11:

Charles "Old Hoss" Radbourn is born in Rochester, New York.

1856

DECEMBER 25:

James Francis "Pud" Galvin is born in St. Louis, Missouri.

1857

JANUARY 1:

Tim Keefe is born in Cambridge, Massachusetts.

JANUARY 22:

In New York City, the first formal baseball convention is held, with 25 different teams represented.

MARCH 10:

The National Association of Baseball Players is formed at a meeting in New York City at 298 Bowery. Twenty-two teams are represented, and William H. Van Cott of the Gothams is elected president.

JULY 1:

Roger Connor is born in Waterbury, Connecticut.

AUGUST 22

A future player and manager comes into the world. Edward Hugh "Ned" Hanlon is born in Montville, Connecticut.

OCTOBER 7:

Moses Fleetwood Walker is born in Mount Pleasant, Ohio.

DECEMBER 31

Michael "King" Kelly is born in Troy, New York.

1858

MAY 8:

Dennis "Dan" Brouthers is born in Sylvan Lake, New York.

JULY 20:

A financial precedent is established today that will become a major feature of the game. Admission is charged for the first time for a baseball game. Some 1,500 spectators pay 50 cents a head to see an all-star game played between two teams from New York and Brooklyn at the Fashion Race Course in Newtown, Long Island. The New York All-Stars win the game, 22-18

1859

MAY 31:

A professional baseball team is organized today in the city of Philadelphia. It is decided that the new team will play its home games at the St. George Cricket Club.

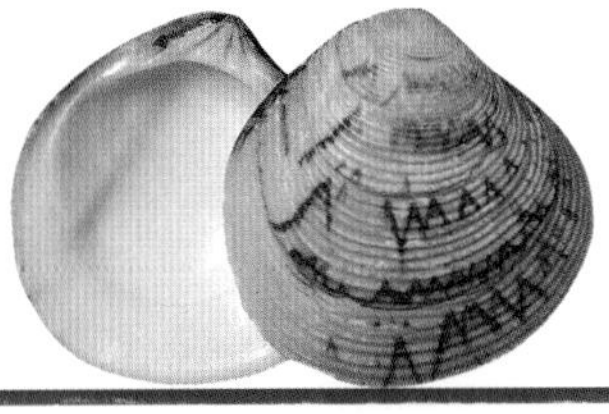

Candy Cummings claims clamshells cultivated the curveball.

JULY 1:

Spectators gather together and observe history being made as Amherst College defeats Williams College , 66-32, in the first inter-collegiate baseball game ever played.

JULY 4:

Mickey Welch is born in Brooklyn, New York.

AUGUST 15:

Charles A. Comiskey is born in Chicago, Illinois.

OCTOBER 17:

William "Buck" Ewing is born in Hoaglands, Ohio.

OCTOBER 26:

Frank Selee is born in Amherst, New Hampshire.

NOVEMBER 11:

John "Bid" McPhee is born in Massena, New York. McPhee will begin an 18-year career in 1882.

1860

MARCH 3:

John Montgomery "Monte" Ward is born in Bellefonte, Pennsylvania.

MARCH 5:

Big Sam Thompson is born in Danville, Indiana.

JULY 2:

The Excelsiors of Brooklyn begin the first ever baseball tour. In Albany, New York, they beat a team of local players, 24-6.

1861

July 1:

John Clarkson is born in Cambridge, Massachusetts.

1862

MAY 15:

The Union Baseball Grounds, located in Brooklyn, the first enclosed park with an admission charge, opens. It includes a special section for gamblers and fences six feet high set 500 feet from home plate. For the first time "The Star-Spangled Banner" is played before the game begins.

DECEMBER 23:

Cornelius Alexander McGillicuddy (Connie Mack) is born in East Brookfield, Massachusetts.

DECEMBER 25:

On Christmas Day, an estimated 40,000 spectators watch two teams of Union soldiers play a baseball game at Hilton Head, South Carolina.

1863

JANUARY 6:

Byron "Ban" Johnson is born in Cincinnati, Ohio.

JUNE 29:

Wilbert "Uncle Robbie" Robinson is born in Bolton, Massachusetts.

1864

JUNE:

A.J. Reach leaves the Athletics of Philadelphia to play for Brooklyn, where he will receive a salary. Reportedly, he becomes the first professional baseball player. Reach, who was born in London in 1840, played for five years with the Athletics before moving to New York.

JULY 24:

Tommy McCarthy is born in Boston.

DECEMBER 14:

Baseball's National Association adopts a key rule: outs are recorded only when a ball is caught on a fly, not on the first bounce.

1865

SEPTEMBER 28:

In what may be the first fixed baseball game, the Brooklyn Eckfords beat the New York Mutuals, 23-11. The Mutuals were up by 5-4 after four innings, when a series of errors and passed balls opened the door for the Eckfords. Three Mutuals players – third baseman Ed Duffy, catcher William Wansley, and shortstop Thomas Devyr – are involved in the conspiracy. Wansley is charged with six passed balls in the game and is hitless in five at-bats. Behind the fix is a New York gambler named Kane McLoughlin, who the previous night paid Wansley $100. Wansley, in turn, paid Duffy and Devyr. Ed Duffy and William Wansley are banned from baseball, but the Mutuals convince the National Association

RULES

Two basic rules are changed at the January 22, 1857 convention: Games will now be nine innings long and can end after five innings. Previously a game ended when one team scored 21 runs.

RULES

It was determined in 1858 that a ball must be caught on a fly to constitute an out; previously, an out was recorded if the ball was caught on one bounce.

TRIVIA

In 1860, the Philadelphia baseball team, organized the previous year, begins using the nickname Athletics. Still in use today, it is the oldest team nickname in baseball.

1871
In what is believed to be the first use of a pinch hitter, Pete Norton of the Washington Olympics bats for his injured teammate Doug Allison and strikes out.

1872
The National Association decides a baseball must weigh between five and five and a half ounces and its circumference must be between nine and nine and a half inches.

CULTURE

Henry Chadwick's *Beadle's Dime Baseball Player* is published in 1860.

RULES

In 1862, the year that General Ulysses S. Grant wins the Battle of Shiloh, baseball institutes a rules change: runners must touch all bases in order to score.

HISTORY

In 1864, William "Candy" Cummings is credited with throwing the first curveball. By some accounts this occurred in 1865. According to historian David Quentin Voigt, Cummings learned to throw a curve by "snapping his wrist and the second finger of the right hand..." It was, says Voigt, the result of Cummings's observation that clamshells curve when thrown.

of Amateur Baseball Players to drop charges against Devyr.

OCTOBER 20:

The Athletics of Philadelphia score nearly 300 runs in a double header against two different opponents. In the morning, the Athletics beat Williamsport, 101-8, and in the afternoon overwhelm the Alerts of Danville, Pennsylvania, 162-11. Al Reach scores 34 times on the day's double-header.

1866

FEBRUARY 16:

Billy Hamilton is born in Newark, New Jersey.

OCTOBER 1:

In the first intracity baseball game in official league (championship) play, the Athletics of Philadelphia beat the Atlantics of Brooklyn. The final lopsided score of the game is 32-12.

NOVEMBER 20:

Kenesaw Mountain Landis is born in Millville, Ohio.

NOVEMBER 26:

Hugh Duffy is born in Cranston, Rhode Island.

1867

MARCH 29:

Denton True "Cy" Young is born in Gilmore, Ohio.

JUNE 12:

Harry Wright of Cincinnati hits seven home runs in a game against the Holt Club of Newport, Kentucky.

JULY 12:

The National Baseball Club of Washington, D.C., known as the Senators, begins a 3,000-mile, $6,000 tour with a 90-10, seven-inning victory against a team in Columbus, Ohio.

AUGUST 4:

Jake Beckley is born in Hannibal, Missouri.

OCTOBER 30:

Big Ed Delahanty is born in Cleveland.

DECEMBER 11:

The National Association of Baseball Players opens its annual convention in the city of Philadelphia. The two-day event is attended by 237 delegates.

1868

MAY 10:

Ed Barrow is born in a covered wagon in Springfield, Illinois.

DECEMBER 4:

Jesse "The Crab" Burkett is born in Wheeling, West Virginia.

DECEMBER 9:

The National Association of Baseball Players holds its annual meeting and okays the use of professionals. Previous rules had prohibited play for pay.

1869

APRIL 2:

Hugh Jennings is born in Pittston, Pennsylvania.

APRIL 17:

The Cincinnati Enquirer reports: "The baseball season for 1869 opened yesterday by a game between the first nine of the Cincinnati Club and the field. The playing on both sides was very poor. There was quite a large number of spectators present, but the enthusiasm of last summer was lacking."

MAY 4:

The Red Stockings of Cincinnati make their debut with a 45-9 win over Great Western.

JUNE 14:

The Red Stockings, on a 17-game win streak, play the New York Mutuals at the Union Grounds in Brooklyn. Some 8,000 spectators see Cincinnati prevail 4-2. (One source indicates the crowd numbered 20,000 fans.)

JULY 5:

The Atlantics of Brooklyn and the Athletics of Philadelphia combine for 99 runs – the most ever by two professional teams – in a game at the Capitoline Grounds in New York. With 15,000 on hand, Brooklyn wins, 51-48.

AUGUST 27:

The winning streak of the Cincinnati Red Stockings is snapped. With the score tied, 17-17, against the Troy Haymakers, Carl McVey of Cincinnati foul-tips a

1875
First baseman Charlie Waitt of the St. Louis Brown Stockings is the first player to wear a glove in a baseball game. His "mitt" is a fingerless, tight-fitting model.

The lineup for for the 1869 Cincinnati Red Stockings, baseball's first professional team.

HISTORY

In 1863, Ned Cuthbert of the Philadelphia Keystones is believed to be the first player ever to steal a base. He takes second without the batter putting the ball into play in a game against the Brooklyn Atlantics.

HISTORY

IN 1865, at the Capitoline Grounds in Brooklyn, Eddie Cuthbert of the Keystone Club of Philadelphia executes the first recorded example of the headfirst slide during a steal of third base against the Brooklyn Atlantics. Disputing Cuthbert's 1863 feat, some accounts report this as the first known stolen base. This decade also saw what is believed to be the first slide into a base. The slider was outfielder Bob Addy of the Forest City Club of Rockford, Illinois.

1874
With a record of 43-17, the Boston Red Stockings finish at the top of the National Association for the third consecutive year.

1875
Jim "Deacon" White of the Boston Red Stockings becomes the first player to catch in the modern position.

HISTORY

In 1868, baseball uniforms are more informal. Knickers replace long trousers. Players wear less formal shirts. Red stockings are introduced.

In 1863, Union prisoners play baseball at a Confederate army camp.

pitch. Troy maintains it is strike three and leaves the field, enabling a gambler friendly with the players to avoid paying off bets.

The Red Stockings embark on a tour of the United States, playing in New York, Boston, Washington, D.C., San Francisco, Omaha, Chicago, and Cleveland. They compile a record of 57-0, with one disputed tie against the Troy club. Although records are sketchy, George Wright presumably hits 59 home runs and bats above .500.

SEPTEMBER 4:

Charles "Kid" Nichols is born in Madison, Wisconsin.

SEPTEMBER 18:

Baseball may be segregated, but the teams still find ways to play each other. For example, the Pythians of Philadelphia, a team of all black players, beat the City Items, an all-white team, 27-17. It is said to be the first game ever between a black team and a white one.

NOVEMBER 20:

Clark Griffith is born in Stringtown, Missouri.

1870

JANUARY 16:

Jimmy Collins is born in Buffalo, New York.

JUNE 14:

With an amazing 27 straight wins this season, the Cincinnati Red Stockings come to Brooklyn to play the Atlantics at the Capitoline Grounds before a crowd estimated at between 12,000 and 15,000. And their winning streak ends 8-7, in a bizarre fashion. With the score tied 5-5 after nine innings, Cincinnati's Harry Wright and Aaron Champion

1872
In 1872, a second baseman named John J. "Bud" Fowler signs with the professional baseball team in New Castle. A native of Cooperstown, New York, Fowler becomes the first black professional baseball player.

decide to continue play. The Red Stockings score twice in the top of the 11th. In the bottom of the frame a fan jumps on Cal McVey's back as he tries to field a ball hit by Joe Start into right field. Start gets a triple and scores on a Bob Ferguson single. Ferguson drives in the tying run and then scores the winner on a throwing error, inflicting the first loss in 130 games on Cincinnati.

JULY 23:

The Mutuals of New York blank Chicago, 9-0, in what is reportedly only the sixth shutout ever. As a result of the whitewash, "Chicagoed" becomes the popular term for holding the opposition scoreless.

AUGUST 16:

Fred Goldsmith demonstrates to writer Henry Chadwick that a baseball curves. Posts are set between the plate and the mound at 20-foot intervals; Goldsmith's pitch travels to the right of the first and to the left of the second. Chadwick credits Goldsmith with the first curveball until he learns of Candy Cummings's earlier achievement.

FOLLOWING THE RED STOCKINGS-ATLANTICS GAME ON JUNE 14, 1870, CINCINNATI'S AARON CHAMPION TELLS A LOCAL NEWSPAPER: "THE FINEST GAME EVER PLAYED. OUR BOYS DID NOBLY BUT FORTUNE WAS AGAINST US. THOUGH BEATEN, NOT DISGRACED."

IN *THE NATIONAL PASTIME*, GEORGE BULKELEY OFFERS A DIFFERENT VERSION OF EVENTS: "SHORTLY BEFORE HE DIED... CAL (MCVEY) TOLD A NEWSMAN THAT HE REMEMBERED THE PLAY VERY WELL AND THAT NO ONE CLIMBED HIS BACK. HE SAID THAT HE ENCOUNTERED SOME DIFFICULTY IN DIGGING THE BALL OUT OF THE CROWD, BUT THAT NO ONE DELIBERATELY INTERFERED WITH HIM."

AUGUST 23:

George Stacey Davis is born today in Cohoes, New York.

November :

Because stockholders cut back expenses for the club, baseball's Wright brothers – Harry and George – announce they will leave the Cincinnati Red Stockings to play for Boston and will call their team the Red Stockings.

NOVEMBER 20:

The Cincinnati Red Stockings team officially disbands.

DECEMBER 31:

Tom Connolly is born in Manchester, England.

1871

JANUARY 20:

At a meeting in Boston's Parker House today, the National Association Boston Red Stockings are born.

MARCH 17:

At Collier's Saloon in New York City, the National Association

HISTORY

In 1866, Candy Cummings reportedly becomes the first pitcher to throw a curveball in actual competition. Contemporary baseball writer Henry Chadwick, known as the Father of Baseball, verifies the story but, at other times, he credited an anonymous pitcher in Syracuse with being the first.

1872
With a record of 39-8, the Boston Red Stockings capture first place in the National Association.

1873
For the second consecutive year, the Boston Red Stockings top the National Association of Professional Baseball Players. Boston compiles a 43-16 record.

HISTORY

Professional baseball is "born" in 1869, when attorney Aaron B. Champion raises money to back the Cincinnati Red Stockings. Harry Wright, the father of professional baseball, is the owner, and his brother George, the only Cincinnatian on the team, is the shortstop. The team is comprised of nine players and one sub, and they are outfitted in shirts, knee-length pants, and red stockings. According to historian David Quentin Voigt, the Red Stockings are not the first professional team, but the first that is "all salaried."

HISTORY

In 1870, the Rockfords of Illinois, the only team to defeat Washington during that team's 1867 tour, begins a $7,000 swing of its own through the East.

of Professional Baseball Players is formed. Organized by Henry Chadwick, it is baseball's first professional association. Ten teams are represented at the meeting; nine begin the season. The Eastern division will be composed of the Boston Red Stockings, the New York Mutuals, the Philadelphia Athletics, the Washington Olympics, and the Troy (New York) Haymakers. Playing in the West will be the Chicago White Stockings, the Cleveland Forest Citys, the Fort Wayne Kekiongas, and the Rockford (Illinois) Forest Citys. James W. Kerns of Troy (Philadelphia) is elected president of the National Association.

MARCH 19:

Joseph Jerome McGinty, later known as Iron Man Joe McGinnity, is born in Rock Island, Illinois.

MAY 30:

Amos "The Hoosier Thunderbolt" Rusie is born in Mooresville, Indiana.

DECEMBER 9:

Joe Kelley is born in Cambridge, Massachusetts.

1872

MARCH 3:

William Henry "Wee Willie" Keeler is born in Brooklyn.

MARCH 8:

The New York Times, writing about contemporary baseball players, describes them as "worthless, dissipated gladiators; not much above the professional pugilist in morality and respectability."

OCTOBER 3:

Fred "Cap" Clarke is born in Winterset, Iowa.

1873

JANUARY 16:

Jimmy Collins is born in Niagara Falls, New York.

APRIL 7:

The McGraws have a son who will grow up to become one of baseball's most influential figures. John J. McGraw is born in Truxton, New York.

NOVEMBER 4:

Rhoderick "Bobby" Wallace is born in Pittsburgh.

1874

FEBRUARY 22:

Bill Klem is born in Rochester, New York.

FEBRUARY 24:

Honus Wagner is born in Mansfield, Pennsylvania.

JUNE 5:

Jack Chesbro is born in North Adams, Massachusetts.

SEPTEMBER 5:

Napoleon Lajoie is born in Woonsocket, Rhode Island.

1875

MAY 29:

Joseph L. McElroy Mann of Princeton University no-hits the team from fellow Ivy Leaguer Yale University, 2-0, in New Haven. Two errors by Princeton allow the only two Yale base runners. According to George L. Moreland, the author of *Balldom*, it is the first no-hit game ever played.

JULY 28:

The Philadelphia Athletics' Joe Borden, who calls himself Josephus the Phenomenal, no-hits the visiting ballclub from Chicago, 4-0. The game proves to be the only no-hitter in the five-year history of the National Association.

AUGUST 31:

Eddie Plank is born in Gettysburg, Pennsylvania.

DECEMBER 17:

At William A. Hulbert's home in Chicago, he and Albert Spalding create the constitution and bylaws for a new league – an organization of teams, not players. To be known as the National League of Professional Base Ball Clubs, it will ban gambling, drunkenness, and disorderly conduct; have paid umpires; and sell tickets for 50 cents.

1874
According to historian David Quentin Voigt, in 1874 Henry Chadwick publishes Chadwick's Base Ball Manual. The publication includes such terms as assists, balks, fungoes, grounders, popups, double plays, passed balls, blanked, and white-washed (the last two for shutouts).

1875
William A. Hulbert, president of the Chicago team in the National Association of Professional Baseball Players, signs the game's best pitcher – Albert G. Spalding (below) – who had been with Boston. Spalding then helps Hulbert sign three other stars: Jim "Deacon" White, Ross Barnes, and Carl McVey, who will join Chicago for the 1876 season.

ACCORDING TO HISTORIAN DAVID QUENTIN VOIGT IN HIS *BASEBALL: AN ILLUSTRATED HISTORY*, HARRY WRIGHT WAS "A BASEBALL GENIUS, A MASTER OF STRATEGY AND TACTICS, BUT WITH THAT VITAL 'SOMETHING EXTRA' THAT GENIUSES POSSESS... HE INVENTED DRILLS, INCLUDING BACKUP DRILLS FOR INFIELDERS AND OUTFIELDERS." WRIGHT'S CONTEMPORARY, WRITER HENRY CHADWICK, DUBBED HIM THE FATHER OF PROFESSIONAL BASEBALL.

HISTORY

The June 14, 1870, Red Stockings-Atlantics game marks two firsts. Brooklyn's Bob Ferguson, normally a right-handed hitter, bats from the left side against George Wright, becoming the first known switch hitter. And, in the 10th inning, Cincinnati executes the first recorded double play when shortstop George Wright deliberately drops a pop fly and throws to third baseman Fred Waterman for one out. Waterman relays the ball to second baseman Charlie Sweasy for the second out.

HISTORY

In 1875, the Boston Red Stockings, with a record of 71-8, top the National Association for the fourth straight season. Pitcher Albert Spalding compiles a record of 57-5. He also bats .318. Boston has eight of the association's top 20 hitters.

1876

Albert Spalding introduces a new uniform concept. Players wear different colored hats to designate their positions. The *Chicago Tribune* is less than complimentary, describing the team as a "Dutch bed of tulips."

NEWS

SITTING BULL, GALL, CRAZY HORSE, AND SEVERAL CHEYENNE LEADERS DEFEAT CUSTER AT THE BATTLE OF THE LITTLE BIG HORN IN MONTANA

Mark Twain publishes *The Adventures of Tom Sawyer*

COLORADO BECOMES A STATE

RUTHERFORD B. HAYES ELECTED PRESIDENT

Morgan Bulkeley was the first NL president.

PRE-SEASON

JANUARY 11:

Elmer Flick is born in Bedford, Ohio.

FEBRUARY 2:

During a 70-mile-per-hour gale in New York City, owners of four Eastern teams – G.W. Thompson of Philadelphia, Nathaniel T. Apollonio of Boston, William H. Cammeyer of Brooklyn, and Morgan Bulkeley of Hartford – meet at the Grand Central Hotel to follow up on the January talk in Louisville. The result is a new league – the National League of Professional Baseball Clubs. The eight-team circuit will consist of the Boston Red Stockings managed by Harry Wright, the Chicago White Stockings managed by Albert G. Spalding, the Cincinnati Redlegs managed by Charles H. Gould, the Hartford Dark Blues managed by Robert V. Ferguson, the Louisville Grays managed by John C. Chapman, the Philadelphia Athletics managed by Alfred H. Wright, the Brooklyn Mutuals of New York managed by William H. Cammeyer, and the St. Louis Brown Stockings, or Browns, managed by S. Mason Graffen. Morgan Bulkeley of Hartford is elected president and Nicholas E. Young, secretary. The owners agree to play a 70-game schedule between April 22 and October 21 of this year; a pennant worth at least $100 will be awarded. Tickets will be 50 cents. Rules include: a pitcher's mound must be 45 feet from home plate; a pitcher's arm must not go above his waist; a runner may return to base safely on a foul and run on a foul caught on the fly; a ball that is hit fair and rolls foul will be foul. There is to be no liquor at games, no betting by players, and written contracts with no raiding of other teams' rosters.

APRIL 12:

Vic Willis is born in Cecil County, Maryland.

THE SEASON

APRIL 22:

Philadelphia (25th and Jefferson Streets) is the site of the first NL game, with Boston beating the hometown Athletics, 6-5, before a crowd of some 3,000. Losing pitcher Alonzo "Lon" Knight throws the first pitch in NL history to George Wright, who grounds out, shortstop Davy Force to first baseman Wes Fisler. Orator Jim O'Rourke of the Red Stockings singles to left off Knight with two out in the first inning for the initial hit. His teammate Tim McGinley scores the first run on the first RBI – registered by John Manning. Every event is a first for the NL, including stolen base (Tim Murnane, Boston) and double play (Philadelphia center fielder Dave Eggler throws a runner out at the plate after catching a fly). Joe Borden is the winning pitcher. It is not a crisply played game: Philadelphia commits 12 errors and Boston seven.

APRIL 25:

The Chicago White Stockings debut with the NL's first shutout, 4-0, over Louisville in Kentucky. Albert Spalding is the winning pitcher and has three hits.

APRIL 27:

Albert Spalding throws another shutout, becoming the

JUNE 14
Philadelphia's George Hall becomes the first major leaguer to hit for the cycle.

Noting that attendance is up – with many women in the crowd – whenever handsome Tony Mullane pitches, the Cincinnati owner schedules him to throw every Tuesday at League Park and designates it as Ladies' Day, beginning a long baseball tradition.

first pitcher to begin a major league career with two shutouts.

APRIL 29:

In Boston, the Red Stockings and the Hartford Blues play the NL's first extra-inning game. Boston wins in 10 innings by a score of 3-2.

MAY 2:

In Cincinnati, Chicago's second baseman Ross Barnes hits an inside-the-park home run in the fifth inning against William "Cherokee" Fisher. It is the NL's first home run, and Chicago wins the game, 15-9.

MAY 23:

Joe Borden of Boston beats Cincinnati, 8-0. Oliver Perry Caylor of the *Cincinnati Enquirer* is serving as the official scorer, and he records two hits for the Redlegs.

MAY 25:

Philadelphia and Louisville play 14 innings to a 2-2 tie, the first in NL history.

JUNE 3:

Outfielder-first baseman Art Allison makes his debut for Louisville in an 8-1 win over the New York Mutuals. His brother, Doug, is a catcher for Hartford, and the Allisons become the first siblings to play in the major leagues.

JUNE 6:

Boston manager Harry Wright inserts himself into the lineup today, playing right field against Louisville. His brother George is playing at shortstop for the Red Stockings, and the Wrights become the first siblings to play in the same game. Louisville wins it, 3-0.

JUNE 14:

With a single, double, triple, and home run, Philadelphia's George Hall becomes the first major leaguer to hit for the cycle.

JUNE 17:

Philadelphia's George Hall hits two home runs and scores five in a nine-inning game – the first player with both marks.

JUNE 27:

Philadelphia's Dave Force becomes the first major leaguer with six hits in a nine-inning game.

JUNE 29:

St. Louis executes the major leagues' first triple play.

Shortstop Dickey Pearce, who starts the triple play, also is credited with playing shortstop in what has become the traditional position, and with inventing the bunt – then known as the "tricky hit."

JULY 15:

In St. Louis, George Washington Bradley of the Brown Stockings pitches the first no-hitter in major league history, beating the Hartford Dark Blues, 2-0. In the loss, Bradley issues a walk to Tom York, and his teammates commit three errors behind him.

JULY 25:

For the second time in less than a week, Chicago's Cal McVey has six hits in a ball game. Playing today at home, the White Stockings wipe out Cincinnati, 23-2, recording 26 hits. Al Spalding is the winning pitcher.

JULY 27:

The White Stockings beat the visiting club from Cincinnati, 17-3, and set a major league record with 88 runs in four games. Ross Barnes has six of Chicago's 23 hits; Al Spalding is the winner.

AUGUST 21:

Trailing the Brown Stockings by 7-6 in the ninth inning in St. Louis, Chicago leaves the field to protest an umpire's call. St. Louis is awarded a 9-0 forfeit – the first in major league history. The dispute begins when St. Louis's Mike McGreary starts for home from third on a grounder by teammate Ned Cuthbert. The ball strikes McGreary and goes foul. Chicago claims interference, but the umpire rules that the contact was incidental and the run scores. Captain Albert Spalding leads his team off the field, producing the forfeit.

SEPTEMBER 26:

In Chicago, the White Stockings win the first NL pennant by six games, clinching with a 7-6 victory over the Hartford Dark Blues. Chicago finishes with a record of 52-14, followed by Hartford, St. Louis, Boston, Louisville, New York, Philadelphia, and Cincinnati. Chicago's Ross Barnes is the NL's top batter at .429. George Hall of the Philadelphia Athletics wins major league baseball's first home run title with five. The estimated National League attendance in its premier season is 343,750.

HISTORY

According to Glenn Dickey, subsequent research by Hall of Fame librarian Lee Allen indicates that walks were scored as hits and that Borden, in fact, pitched a no-hitter. But it is not officially credited as such.

LEAGUE

In January in Louisville, Colonel John A. Joyce, Charles A. Fowle, and Charles E. Chase meet secretly with William A. Hulbert and Albert Spalding. The formation of a new league is discussed; Hulbert and Spalding urge the three invitees to drop out of the National Association and join a new circuit. A committee is formed to contact teams in the East.

DECEMBER 7
The New York and Philadelphia teams are expelled from the National League.

LEAGUE

Financial troubles strike the New York Mutuals and the Philadelphia Athletics. The owners of the two teams cancel the season's last Western trip. As a result, they are expelled from the NL.

POST-SEASON

OCTOBER 13:

George Edward "Rube" Waddell is born in Bradford, Pennsylvania.

OCTOBER 19:

Mordecai Peter Centennial "Three Finger" Brown is born in Nyesville, Indiana.

DECEMBER 7:

In Cleveland, the NL holds its first annual meeting. The Athletics of Philadelphia and the Mutuals of New York are formally expelled. The two teams had, without league permission, elected to forgo playing their final games in the west, citing the runaway by the White Stockings and the poor attendance at their games. President Morgan Bulkeley is not interested in a second term and does not attend. William A. Hulbert is unanimously elected to succeed him. Hulbert presides over the expulsion of Philadelphia and New York, which leaves just six teams to compete next season. The result of all this will deprive the populated areas around both of those cities of having their own baseball teams again until 1883.

THE BEST OF 1876

NATIONAL LEAGUE

HITTERS

Batting Average:
Ross Barnes, Chicago White Stockings, .429

Slugging Average:
Ross Barnes, .590

Home Runs:
George Hall, Philadelphia Athletics, 5

Runs Batted In:
James "Deacon" White, Chicago White Stockings, 60

Hits:
Ross Barnes, 138

PITCHERS

Wins:
Albert Spalding, Chicago White Stockings, 47

Strikeouts:
Jim Devlin, Louisville Grays, 122

Earned Run Average:
George Bradley, St. Louis Brown Stockings, 1.23

Winning Percentage:
Albert Spalding, .783

Saves:
Jack Manning, Boston Red Caps, 5

1877

OCTOBER 1, 1877

FEBRUARY 20
The first minor league, the Internaltional Association, is formed.

NEWS

PRESIDENT HAYES SENDS IN ARMY TO BREAK UP VIOLENT NATIONAL RAILROAD STRIKE

FIRST SOUND RECORDING MADE BY THOMAS EDISON

British Queen Victoria proclaimed Empress of India

Samurai revolt suppressed in Japan

Federal troops called in to end great railroad strike

ANTI-CHINESE VIOLENCE IN SAN FRANCISCO

Nez Percé tribes battle with U.S. troops in Northwest

BRITAIN ANNEXES SOUTH AFRICAN REPUBLIC

German Robert Koch develops way to fix and strain bacteria

RECONSTRUCTION ENDS IN THE SOUTH

PRE-SEASON

FEBRUARY 20:

Baseball's first minor league, known as the International Association, is formed in Pittsburgh. The new league will be composed of the Maple Leafs of Guelph (Toronto), the London Tecumsahs (Toronto), the Pittsburgh Alleghenies, the Columbus Buckeyes (Ohio), the Lynn Live Oaks (Massachusetts), the Rochester Hop Bitters (New York), and the Manchesters of Manchester (New Hampshire).

THE SEASON

APRIL 11:

Harvard baseball captain Fred Thayer designs the first-ever catcher's mask. It is to be worn by teammate Jim Tyng in a game against the Live Oaks of Lynn, Massachusetts.

SEPTEMBER 9:

Frank Chance is born in Fresno, California.

OCTOBER 1:

The young National League has a scandal. The *Louisville Courier-Journal* reports a fix involving the Grays.

After compiling a 27-12 record, the first-place Grays lose eight straight games. Boston wins 13 of 15 to beat out the Grays. Louisville president Charles E. Chase receives an anonymous telegram warning him of fixed games. Grays' outfielder George Bechtel is suspended after teammate Jim Devlin accuses him of offering $500 to

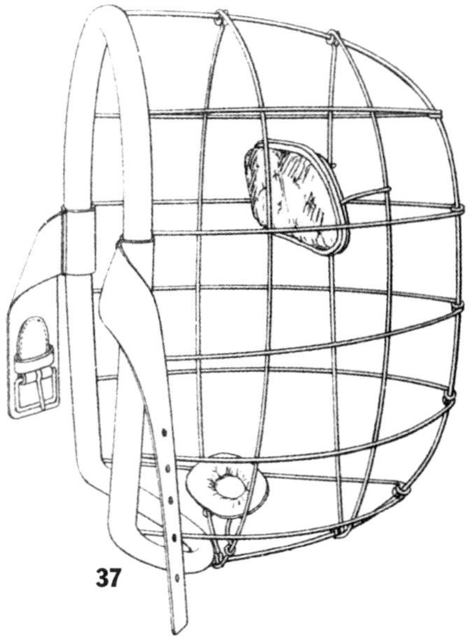

EQUIPMENT

Syracuse Stars' catcher Pete Hotaling becomes the first professional to wear a mask.

LEAGUE

A loose grouping of baseball teams is formed under the League Alliance. The teams include Buffalo, Indianapolis, Memphis, Milwaukee, Minneapolis, Providence, and St. Paul. Also included are the Athletics of Philadelphia and the Mutuals of New York, teams expelled from the NL. The League Alliance has no formal schedule.

Harvard captain Fred Thayer designed the first catcher's mask. It was worn by his teammate Jim Tyng.

RULES

Home plate is moved inside the baseball diamond. Fifteen-inch-square canvas bases are approved.

EQUIPMENT

Boston pitcher Will White becomes the first to wear eyeglasses during a game.

throw a game. Despite indications that Bechtel's name may have been forged on the offer, he is suspended for drunkenness.

POST-SEASON

OCTOBER 30:

Louisville suspends Jim Devlin, Al Nichols, Bill Craver, and NL home run king George Hall for "crooked play." Devlin, a pitcher, lost 13 of his last 20 games, blaming his poor performance on boils. Hall is charged with giving Devlin $100 for dumping an exhibition game and a regular season contest. There is no concrete proof of the allegations, but Hall admits to throwing exhibitions on August 30 and September 3. Hall and Devlin confess to intentionally losing to Cincinnati on September 16 and Indianapolis on September 24. The players become known as the Louisville Four.

DECEMBER:

This month at the NL's annual meeting the Louisville Four are banned from baseball for life. St. Louis, which had signed the players for next season, withdraws from the NL, and Hartford folds. New teams for next year will play in Milwaukee, Indianapolis, and Providence. With no reason revealed, all Cincinnati games are declared null and void. Because the Reds' games no longer count, Boston is declared the 1877 league champion by three games over Louisville.

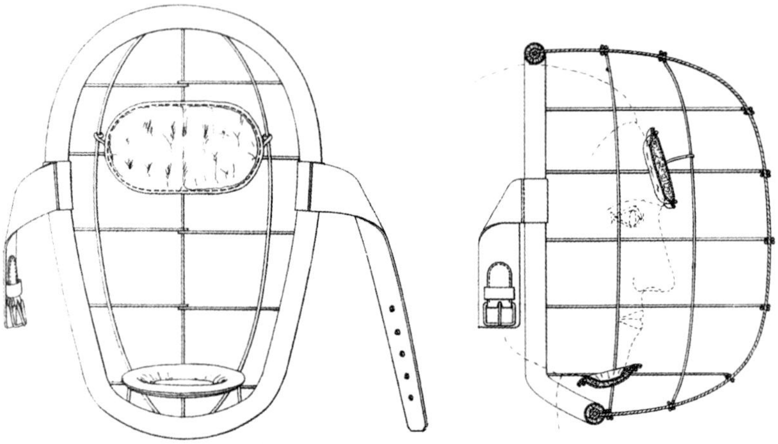

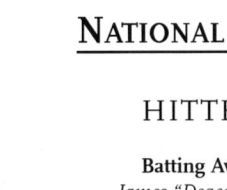

THE BEST OF 1877

NATIONAL LEAGUE

HITTERS:

Batting Average:
James "Deacon" White, Boston Red Caps, .387

Slugging Average:
James White, .545

Home Runs:
Lipman "Lip" Pike, Cincinnati Red Stockings, 4

Runs Batted In:
James White, 49

Hits:
James White, 103

PITCHERS:

Wins:
Tommy Bond, Boston Red Caps, 40

Strikeouts:
Tommy Bond, 170

Earned Run Average:
Tommy Bond, 2.11

Winning Percentage:
Tommy Bond, .702

Saves:
Cal McVey, Chicago White Stockings, 2

1878

JULY 20
The Providence Grays' John Montgomery Ward throws a 3-0 shutout against the Hoosiers.

NEWS

Milk delivered in bottles for first time

U.S. SUPREME COURT RULES RACE SEPARATION ON TRAINS UNCONSTITUTIONAL

THOMAS EDISON PATENTS THE GRAMOPHONE

FIRST TELEPHONE INSTALLED IN THE WHITE HOUSE

Russo-Turkish wars end, Ottomans surrender to Russians

LARGEST YELLOW DIAMOND DISCOVERED; BOUGHT BY TIFFANY

Chile and Bolivia nearly go to war in dispute over control of nitrate deposits used in making fertilizers and explosives

YELLOW FEVER KILLS 14,000 IN GULF STATES; SMALLPOX HITS DAKOTA

THE SEASON

MAY 8:

Playing against the Boston Red Caps, the Providence Grays' Paul Hines makes a shoestring catch in left center field and steps on third base. Under this year's rules, because both runners had passed third base, they are out, and Hines becomes the first player to execute an unassisted triple play.

JULY 20:

John Montgomery Ward of the Providence Grays shuts out the Indianapolis Hoosiers, 3-0, in his first major league start.

SEPTEMBER 17:

Andrew "Rube" Foster is born in Calvert, Texas.

THE BEST OF 1878

NATIONAL LEAGUE

HITTERS

Batting Average: *Paul Hines, Providence Grays, .358*

Slugging Average: *Paul Hines, .486*

Home Runs: *Paul Hines, 4*

Runs Batted In: *Paul Hines, 50*

Hits: *Joe Start, Chicago White Stockings, 100*

PITCHERS

Wins: *Tommy Bond, Boston Red Caps, 40*

Strikeouts: *Tommy Bond, 182*

Earned Run Average: *John Montgomery Ward, Providence Grays, 1.51*

Winning Percentage: *Tommy Bond, .678*

Saves: *Tom Healey, Providence Grays/Indianapolis Hoosiers, 1*

LEAGUE

The NL will operate with eight teams in 1879 after two seasons with six teams. Indianapolis and Milwaukee are dropped, and Buffalo, Cleveland, Syracuse, and Troy are added.

TRIVIA

Cincinnati pitcher Will White and catcher James "Deacon" White become baseball's first brother battery. Will wins 30 games and loses 21; Deacon bats .314.

HISTORY

Under Harry Wright, the Cincinnati Reds win the NL pennant at 41-19, four games ahead of second-place Boston.

1879

NEWS

GERMAN CHANCELLOR OTTO BISMARCK NEGOTIATES MILITARY ALLIANCE BETWEEN GERMANY AND AUSTRIA-HUNGARY

THOMAS EDISON INVENTS ELECTRIC LIGHT BULB

ZULU WAR AGAINST BRITISH COLONIAL RULE IN SOUTH AFRICA

U.S. ECONOMIST HENRY GEORGE WRITES *PROGRESS AND POVERTY*

Russian scientist Ivan Pavlov makes dogs salivate in study on learned behavior in humans

ST. PATRICK'S CATHEDRAL OPENS IN NEW YORK CITY

Henry Ibsen's *A Doll's House* first performed in Copenhagen

MARCH 27:

Miller Huggins is born in Cincinnati.

JUNE 11:

Roger Bresnahan is born in Toledo, Ohio.

SEPTEMBER 29:

Baseball's controversial reserve clause is born. NL owners, led by Boston's Arthur Soden, debate players' salaries, which are characterized as too high. They seek to limit competitive pay for players, with some arguing for fixed amounts. Under a secret agreement, five players on each team will be "reserved" – off-limits to all other clubs. The reserve clause will be in effect for the 1880 season. The owners inform the newspapers that they have agreed upon a uniform contract with no salary advances.

OCTOBER 1:

News of the secret reserve clause leaks. O.P. Caylor, sports editor of the *Cincinnati Enquirer*, reports: "It appears that all signed a written agreement... each club should name five men in their club who should be held inviolate; that is, no club would have a right to approach them or sign them without the consent of said club. The delegates all selected their five men; they were put in writing, together with the agreements, and the delegates all attached their names. Just who were chosen it is decidedly difficult to find out. All the delegates believe that this rule will solve the problem of how to reduce wages, and feel confident it will be lived up to."

THE BEST OF 1879

NATIONAL LEAGUE

HITTERS:

Batting Average:
Paul Hines, Providence Grays, .357

Slugging Average:
John O'Rourke, Boston Red Caps, .521

Home Runs:
Long Charley Jones, Boston Red Caps, 9

Runs Batted In:
John O'Rourke, Charley Jones, 62

Hits:
Paul Hines, 146

PITCHERS

Wins:
John Montgomery Ward, Providence Grays, 47

Strikeouts:
John Montgomery Ward, 239

Earned Run Average:
Tommy Bond, Boston Red Caps, 1.96

Winning Percentage:
John Montgomery Ward, .734

Saves:
John Montgomery Ward; Bobby Mathews, Providence Grays; Charles "Curry" Foley, Boston Red Caps, 1

1880

AUGUST 19, 1880

MAY 1
Cincinnati's Mike "King" Kelly hits baseball's first opening day home run.

NEWS

British factory workers begin to play soccer

THE BOERS IN SOUTH AFRICA DECLARE THEIR INDEPENDENCE FROM BRITAIN

BUILDING OF PANAMA CANAL BEGINS

James Garfield, turning back Ulysses S. Grant's reelection bid, becomes U.S. President

William Gladstone becomes British Prime Minister, taking place of Benjamin Disraeli

GAME CALLED "BINGO" IS DEVELOPED

Diamond miner De Beers opens in South Africa

CANNED FRUITS, MEATS FIRST APPEAR IN STORES

Russian novelist Fyodor Dostoyevsky's *The Brothers Karamazov* is published

PRE-SEASON

APRIL 12:

Adrian "Addie" Joss is born in Woodland, Wisconsin.

APRIL 18:

Sam Crawford is born in Wahoo, Nebraska.

THE SEASON

MAY 1:

Cleveland's League Park opens with 10,000 fans on hand to see Denton "Cy" Young win a game over Cincinnati, 12-3.

In Cincinnati, Mike "King" Kelly hits baseball's first opening day home run as his Chicago White Stockings defeat the Red Stockings, 4-3. Cincinnati's player-manager John Clapp also hits a home run, but the first belongs to Kelly.

JUNE 10:

Boston's Charley Jones becomes the first major leaguer to hit two home runs in a single game.

JUNE 12:

At Worcester, the Ruby Legs' John Lee Richmond pitches major league baseball's first perfect game, defeating the visiting Cleveland Blues, 1-0. It also is the first no-hitter by a left-hander. Richmond strikes out five. Jim McCormick gets the loss.

JUNE 17:

For the second time in five days, an NL pitcher throws a perfect game as 20-year-old John Montgomery Ward of the Providence Grays tops the visiting Buffalo Bisons, 5-0. The loser is Jim "Pud" Galvin.

JULY 8:

At home, the Chicago White Stockings, behind pitcher Larry Corcoran, beat the Providence Grays, 5-4, for their 21st consecutive win.

JULY 27:

Joe Tinker is born in Muscotah, Kansas.

AUGUST 12:

Christy Mathewson is born in Factoryville, Pennsylvania.

AUGUST 19:

In Chicago, the White Stockings' Larry Corcoran no-hits the Boston Red Caps, 6-0. White Stockings first baseman Cap Anson records 21 putouts.

RULES

A third strike must be caught on the fly; previously a catcher could catch a third strike on a bounce. A walk is reduced from nine to eight balls.

LEAGUE

The Worcester Ruby Legs replace the Syracuse Stars. The Metropolitans of New York begin play as an independent team, with most of their games in Brooklyn and New Jersey. Owner John B. Day, a tobacco wholesaler, puts up the money and partner James Mutrie provides the expertise. After a bootblack suggests a new locale to Day – at 110th Street and Sixth Avenue in Manhattan – he and Mutrie lease part of the Polo Grounds.

CULTURE

The Fairport Nine **is published, a novel by Noah Brooks.**

TRIVIA

Chicago shortstop Johnny Peters becomes the first "player to be named later" in a trade. After the season, he goes to Providence in return for the earlier acquisition of catcher Lew Brown.

AUGUST 20:

For the second day in a row, an NL pitcher throws a no-hitter. Today's hero is Jim "Pud" Galvin of the Buffalo Bisons, who no-hits the Worcester Ruby Legs, 1-0. Galvin's no-hitter is the last from a pitching distance of 45 feet – the NL rule since 1876.

SEPTEMBER 2:

Two Boston department stores – Jordan Marsh and R.H. White – face off at Nantasket Beach's Sea Foam House in Hull, Massachusetts, in the first baseball game played under artificial light. Illumination is provided by the Northern Electric Light Company; two engines and three generators power 36 lamps on three wooden towers. The game ends in a 16-16 tie.

T.J. Keefe

SEPTEMBER 15:

In Cincinnati, Chicago clinches the NL pennant with a 5-2 win over the Reds. Larry Corcoran is the winning pitcher and also hits a double.

SEPTEMBER 29:

The Metropolitans beat the Washington Nationals, 4-2, in five innings at the Polo Grounds, in the first professional game ever played in Manhattan.

POST-SEASON

OCTOBER 4:

The NL outlaws Sunday baseball and the sale of beer at games. Cincinnati objects to the Sunday ban and is expelled by NL president William Hulbert.

According to historian Lee Allen, the sale of liquor was the public reason, but the truth may have been the opposition of Cincinnati's president William H. Kennett to the reserve clause. Detroit becomes the NL's new franchise.

THE BEST OF 1880

NATIONAL LEAGUE

HITTERS

Batting Average:
George Gore, Chicago White Stockings, .360

Slugging Average:
George Gore, .463

Home Runs:
Harry Stovey, Worcester Ruby Legs; Orator Jim O'Rourke, Boston Red Caps, 6

Runs Batted In:
Adrian "Cap" Anson, Chicago White Stockings, 74

Hits:
Abner Dalrymple, Chicago White Stockings, 126

PITCHERS

Wins:
Jim McCormick, Cleveland Blues, 45

Strikeouts:
Larry Corcoran, Chicago White Stockings, 268

Earned Run Average:
Tim Keefe, Troy Trojans, 0.86

Winning Percentage:
Fred Goldsmith, Chicago White Stockings, .875

Saves:
Lee Richmond, Worcester Ruby Legs, 3

1881

SEPTEMBER 10
Troy's Roger Connor hits the first grand slam home run in major league history.

NEWS

PRESIDENT GARFIELD ASSASSINATED; CHESTER A. ARTHUR SWORN IN AS PRESIDENT

EARPS AND CLANTONS BATTLE IN SHOOTOUT AT THE O.K. CORRAL IN TOMBSTONE, ARIZONA

BILLY THE KID KILLED BY PAT GARRETT

AMERICAN RED CROSS FOUNDED BY CLARA BARTON

BOOKER T. WASHINGTON FOUNDS TUSKEGEE INSTITUTE

Alexander II, Czar of Russia, assassinated at age 62

TCHAIKOVSKY, BRAHMS DEBUT NEW MUSIC

Supreme Court rules Civil War income tax of 1861 was unconstitutional

GERMANY OPERATES ELECTRIC STREETCAR

Boers and British at war in South Africa's Transvaal

PRE-SEASON

After the expulsion of the Cincinnati Reds from the NL, O.P. Caylor, sports editor of the *Cincinnati Enquirer*, writes: "We respectfully suggest that while the league is in the missionary field, having eliminated beer and Sunday games from the Cincinnati grounds, they turn their attention to Chicago and prohibit the admission to the Lake Street Grounds of the great number of prostitutes who patronize the games up there." Caylor organizes the Cincinnati Reds, a team that is independent of the NL. Alfred H. Spink founds another independent club, the St. Louis Browns.

THE SEASON

MAY 14:

Big Ed Walsh is born in Plains, Pennsylvania.

JUNE 25:

In Chicago, George "Piano Legs" Gore looks more like fleet-footed Mercury as he steals seven bases against the visiting Providence Grays. Gore, who gets three hits in the White Stockings' 12-8 victory, steals second base five times and third base twice.

JULY 21:

Johnny Evers is born in Troy, New York.

AUGUST 21:

In an early example of Jim Crow in baseball, the Louisville Eclipses bar the visiting Cleveland Whites from playing their black catcher, Moses Fleetwood Walker.

SEPTEMBER 10:

In Albany, Roger Connor of Troy hits the major leagues' first grand slam home run. It comes off Lee Richmond of Worcester. Troy wins, 8-7.

SEPTEMBER 27:

In a rainstorm in Chicago, 12 dedicated fans watch their hometown heroes beat Troy, 10-8. It is the smallest paid major league "crowd" ever.

Chicago wins the NL pennant by nine games over second-place Providence.

POST-SEASON

OCTOBER 10:

Hustling Horace Phillips, manager of the Rochester Hop

FORMER PLAYER AND MANAGER ALBERT SPALDING, NOW IN THE SPORTING GOODS BUSINESS, WRITES: "PROFESSIONAL BASEBALL IS ON THE WANE. SALARIES MUST COME DOWN, OR THE INTEREST OF THE PUBLIC MUST BE INCREASED IN SOME WAY. IF ONE OR THE OTHER DOES NOT HAPPEN, BANKRUPTCY STARES EVERY TEAM IN THE FACE."

Bitters, suggests to Alfred H. Spink that a new league should include teams in Cincinnati, St. Louis, Louisville, Pittsburgh, Baltimore, and Philadelphia. A meeting is scheduled in Pittsburgh, but Phillips loses his job and does not attend. Instead, three Cincinnatians – journalists O.P. Caylor and Frank Wright and brewer Justus Thorner – meet. They contact former National Association pitcher Al Pratt and businessman Denny McKnight and also send telegrams describing a successful meeting to Chris Von Der Ahe of St. Louis, Billy Sharsig of Philadelphia, and J.H. Park of Louisville. The three wire back expressing a desire to join the new enterprise, and thus baseball's American Association is born.

NOVEMBER 2:

The new American Association of Baseball Clubs – a rival to the NL – is formed in St. Louis. Representatives from Brooklyn, Cincinnati, Columbus, St. Louis, Philadelphia, and Pittsburgh attend. They elect Denny McKnight the league's first president. Admission is set at 25 cents (the NL charges 50 cents), Sunday baseball will be allowed, and beer drinking will be okay at games. The New York Giants, however, opt not to join. The American Association fields teams in Brooklyn, Cincinnati, Louisville, Philadelphia, Pittsburgh, and St. Louis. It becomes known as the Beer and Whiskey League – not for any type of imbibing at games, but because many of the team owners were brewers or saloon owners.

DECEMBER 20:

Branch Rickey is born in Stockdale, Ohio.

Rickey would grow up and spend 59 years of his life in baseball, as a player, manager, and general manager. Highly regarded for establishing the St. Louis Cardinals' farm system, he was hired in 1946 as GM of the Brooklyn Dodgers when Larry McPhail went into the army. That season, Rickey made a move that would forever change the game: signing Jackie Robinson to the Dodgers' minor league franchise in Montreal. A year later, Robinson became the first black player in the modern major leagues.

RULES

The pitching distance is increased from 45 feet to 50 feet from home plate.

LEAGUE

The National League begins its season with teams in eight cities: Boston (Red Caps), Buffalo (Bisons), Chicago (White Stockings), Cleveland (Blues), Detroit (Wolverines), Providence (Grays), Troy (Trojans), and Worcester (Ruby Legs).

THE BEST OF 1881

NATIONAL LEAGUE

HITTERS

Batting Average:
Adrian "Cap" Anson, Chicago White Stockings, .399

Slugging Average:
Dennis "Big Dan" Brouthers, Buffalo Bisons, .541

Home Runs:
Dennis Brouthers, 8

Runs Batted In:
Adrian Anson, 82

Hits:
Adrian Anson, 137

PITCHERS

Wins:
Larry Corcoran, Chicago White Stockings; Jim Whitney, Boston Red Caps, 31

Strikeouts:
George Derby, Detroit Wolverines, 212

Earned Run Average:
George "Stump" Weidman, Detroit Wolverines, 1.80

Winning Percentage:
Charles "Old Hoss" Radbourn, Providence Grays, .694

Saves:
Bobby Mathews, Providence Grays/Boston Red Caps, 2

1882

JULY 18
Louisville pitcher Tony Mullane throws both right-handed and left-handed in a game.

NEWS

TRIPLE ALLIANCE AMONG GERMANY, AUSTRIA-HUNGARY, AND ITALY IS SIGNED

THOMAS EDISON DESIGNS THE FIRST HYDROELECTRIC PLANT IN WISCONSIN

U.S. bans Chinese immigration for 10 years

ROBERT KOCH DISCOVERS TUBERCULOSIS BACILLUS

William Vanderbilt eliminates mail trains from Chicago, saying, "The public be damned."

OUTLAW JESSE JAMES SHOT IN THE BACK

John D. Rockefeller's Standard Oil dominates petroleum industry

ITALY INVADES ETHIOPIA

JUMBO THE ELEPHANT IN P.T. BARNUM'S CIRCUS

Italian author Carlo Collodi writes children's classic *Pinocchio*

PRE-SEASON

The National League's Detroit Wolverines introduce color-coded uniforms. All belts, ties, and pants are white. Pitchers wear light blue; catchers, scarlet; first basemen, scarlet and white; second basemen, orange and black; third basemen, gray and white; shortstops, maroon; left fielders, white; center fielders, red and black; right fielders, gray; first substitutes, green; and second substitutes, brown. The coding system ends in June.

For the 1882 season, NL teams will be permitted to wear colored uniforms. Chicago wears white; Boston, red; Providence, light blue; Cleveland, navy; Troy, green; Buffalo, gray; Worcester, brown, and Detroit, old gold.

THE SEASON

MAY 2:

On the American Association's first day, the St. Louis Brown Stockings beat the Louisville Eclipse at home, 9-7.

JUNE 20:

In Chicago, Larry Corcoran of the NL White Stockings demonstrates he is one of baseball's first "good-hitting pitchers." In a 13-3 victory over Worcester, Corcoran hits the first grand slam home run in team history and adds a double and two singles.

JUNE 24:

Umpire Dick Higham, the first to wear a mask, is banned for life after a graphologist retained by Detroit Wolverine owner William Thompson identifies Higham's handwriting in a letter implicating him in a conspiracy with gamblers.

JULY 18:

In Baltimore, the Louisville Eclipse's Tony Mullane – known as the Apollo of the Box – pitches three innings right-handed, as usual, and then throws left-handed in the fourth. His ambidextrous display is in vain – Louisville loses the game, 9-8, to the Orioles.

JULY 24:

Chicago sets a major league scoring record with a 35-4 win over the Cleveland Blues in the Windy City. In his only pitching appearance of the year, Cleveland out-

EQUIPMENT

Outfielder Paul Hines of the Providence Grays becomes the first player to wear sunglasses in the field.

TRIVIA

With his team coming to bat in the seventh inning, Brother Jasper, Manhattan College's baseball coach, supposedly instructs the student body to stand up and stretch, creating the baseball tradition of the Seventh Inning Stretch. The practice spread from college games to the professionals during exhibition games between Manhattan College and the New York Giants at the Polo Grounds. Manhattan College's teams are known as the Jaspers in honor of the brother.

According to historian Lee Allen: "If Hulbert made the National League possible, Mills, The Bismarck of Baseball, made organized baseball possible."

HISTORY

Cincinnati of the AA executes three triple plays this season, with Will White on the mound for all of them. The pitcher participates in the second and third triple plays.

LEAGUE

John Day is playing both sides of the street. He enters his New York Metropolitans in the AA and his new team, the New York Gothams, in the NL. He then loads his Gothams with former Troy stars, including first baseman Roger Connor, catcher William "Buck" Ewing, and pitcher Mickey Welch. He further strengthens the Gothams by buying John Montgomery Ward from the Providence Grays.

fielder Dave Rowe goes all the way, though yielding 29 hits – including 10 doubles – and seven walks.

AUGUST 17:

Providence Grays' pitcher Charles "Old Hoss" Radbourn, playing right field, hits a home run in the bottom of the ninth to defeat the Detroit Wolverines, 1-0, in an NL game. John Montgomery Ward is the game's winning pitcher.

SEPTEMBER 11:

Today in the AA, Louisville's Tony Mullane no-hits Cincinnati, 2-0. It is the first no-hitter at the 50-foot pitching distance to home.

SEPTEMBER 19:

Guy Hecker of Louisville in the AA no-hits Pittsburgh, 3-1, at home.

SEPTEMBER 20:

Not to be outdone by the rival AA, the NL has a no-hitter today as Chicago's Larry Corcoran mows down visiting Worcester, 5-0. It is the second no-hitter of Corcoran's career, and he becomes the majors' first pitcher to accomplish that feat.

SEPTEMBER 29:

At home, Chicago beats Buffalo, 11-5, and clinches the NL pennant.

SEPTEMBER 30:

In Chicago, a 16-year-old substitute first baseman helps the White Stockings to a 6-5 victory over the Buffalo Bisons. The youngster, Milton Scott, gets two hits in five at-bats and scores a run. Larry Corcoran goes all the way for his 10th consecutive victory.

This is Milt Scott's only 1882 appearance. In 1884, the Chicago-born Scott (known as Mikado Milt) hits .247 for Detroit. He splits time during the 1885 season between the AA Detroit and Pittsburgh teams and finishes up his career at age 20 with Baltimore in the AA. His four-year batting average is .228. Scott dies in Baltimore in 1938 at the age of 72.

POST-SEASON

OCTOBER 1:

Because the AA has a rule against playing NL ballclubs, the league's champion Cincinnati Red Stockings releases all its players and then re-signs them as a "new" team.

OCTOBER 6:

In Cincinnati with 2,700 fans on hand, the Reds Stockings (led by player-manager Charles "Pop" Snyder) face off against the NL pennant-winners, the Chicago White Stockings (managed by Adrian "Cap" Anson) in a post-season "World Series." The Red Stockings' bespectacled pitcher Will White pitches a 4-0 eight-hitter. The losing pitcher is Fred Goldsmith.

OCTOBER 7:

Visiting Chicago bounces back in game two with a 2-0 win behind Larry Corcoran, who fans six and allows only three hits. Yesterday's winner, Will White, is today's losing pitcher despite allowing only four hits. After the game, AA president Denny McKnight, who had banned interleague play, wires the Red Stockings threatening to expel its re-signed players. As a result, the series ends after today's game.

In December, the National League fines the Cincinnati franchise $100 and issues a reprimand for having played in the "World Series" against Chicago and in an exhibition baseball game against Cleveland. Even so, the Red Stockings are not expelled from the American Association.

In Providence, Rhode Island, the National League begins its seventh annual convention. The franchises in Troy (which drew only 25 fans at its last ball game of the season) and Worcester both resign from the league. Meanwhile, John B. Day of New York and Alfred J. Reach of Philadelphia apply for membership for their city's ballclubs and are admitted into the league and will begin playing games next season. (Franchises representing the two cities had been expelled from the National League in 1876.) Abraham Gilbert Mills, an attorney and Civil War veteran, is elected to succeed Arthur Soden as the league president.

DECEMBER 14:

The American Association is the majors' first league to hire a full-time staff of permanent umpires. They will begin work next year.

SEPTEMBER 19
Louisville pitcher Guy Hecker throws a no-hitter in defeating Pittsburgh, 3-1.

SEPTEMBER 30
Milton Scott, only 16, is two-for-five in a 6-5 White Stockings win over the Bisons.

THE BEST OF 1882

National League

HITTERS

Batting Average:
Dennis "Big Dan" Brouthers, Buffalo Bisons, .368

Slugging Average:
Dennis Brouthers, .547

Home Runs:
George Wood, Detroit Wolverines, 7

Runs Batted In:
Adrian "Cap" Anson, Chicago White Stockings, 83

Hits:
Dennis Brouthers, 129

PITCHERS

Wins:
Jim McCormick, Cleveland Blues, 36

Strikeouts:
Charles "Old Hoss" Radbourn, Providence Grays, 201

Earned Run Average:
Larry Corcoran, Chicago White Stockings, 1.95

Winning Percentage:
Larry Corcoran, .692

Saves:
John Montgomery Ward, Providence Grays, 1

American Association

HITTERS

Batting Average:
Louis "Pete" Browning, Louisville Eclipse, .378

Slugging Average:
Louis Browning, .510

Home Runs:
Oscar Walker, St. Louis Brown Stockings, 7

Hits:
Warren "Hick" Carpenter, Cincinnati Red Stockings, 120

PITCHERS

Wins:
Will "Whoop-La" White, Cincinnati Red Stockings, 40

Strikeouts:
Tony Mullane, Louisville Eclipse, 170

Earned Run Average:
John "Denny" Driscoll, Pittsburgh Alleghenys, 1.21

Winning Percentage:
Will White, .769

Saves:
Ed Fusselbach, St. Louis Brown Stockings, 1

RULES

Seven balls now constitute a walk; previously a base on balls was awarded after eight.

LEAGUE

The NL begins its season with teams in eight cities: Boston, Buffalo, Chicago, Cleveland, Detroit, Providence, Troy, and Worcester. The American Association has teams in the cities of Baltimore (Orioles), Cincinnati (Red Stockings), Louisville (Eclipse), Philadelphia (Athletics), Pittsburgh (Alleghenys), and St. Louis (Brown Stockings).

1883

NEWS

BROOKLYN BRIDGE IS OFFICIALLY OPENED BY U.S. PRESIDENT CHESTER A. ARTHUR

FIRST U.S. VAUDEVILLE THEATER OPENS IN BOSTON

KARL MARX DIES AT AGE 64

VOLCANO ERUPTS ON KRAKATOA; SEISMIC SEA WAVES CREATE A RISE IN THE ENGLISH CHANNEL

ORIENT EXPRESS MAKES FIRST TRIP BETWEEN PARIS AND CONSTANTINOPLE

HIRAM MAXIM INVENTS AUTOMATIC MACHINE GUN

Robert Louis Stevenson's novel *Treasure Island* is published

PRE-SEASON

FEBRUARY 17:

NL president A.G. Mills calls a "harmony conference." The NL, American Association, and Northwestern League (minors) participate and work out a "tripartite agreement" that becomes the first National Agreement – a system for ruling baseball. One of its provisions is the reserve clause covering 11 players per team. In addition, the contracts of 18 players signed with two or more teams are settled. An arbitration committee will settle disputes.

MARCH 12:

The NL and the AA make peace. Raiding for players is no longer allowed.

THE SEASON

MAY 1:

Some 12,000 people, including United States President Ulysses S. Grant, come out to the Polo Grounds today to watch the New York Gothams get a win against the Boston Beaneaters, 7-5, in a National League baseball game.

In their first game, the Gothams field four future Hall of Famers: first baseman Roger Connor, catcher William "Buck" Ewing, center fielder John Montgomery Ward, and pitcher "Smiling" Mickey Welch.

MAY 22:

In Chicago, Billy "The Evangelist" Sunday makes his major league debut, and it is sinful – in baseball terms. Sunday fans four times in four at-bats against Boston's Jim Whitney. But Chicago wins, 4-3, behind the pitching of Larry Corcoran.

MAY 24:

Heavyweight boxing champion John L. Sullivan is throwing baseballs today instead of punches. Before 4,000 fans at New York's Polo Grounds, the Boston Strong Boy is paid $1,200 and is the winning pitcher in an exhibition game between a team of former major league players and the American Association's New York Metropolitans. Sullivan was once considered a professional baseball prospect, but opted for bare-knuckle boxing instead.

MAY 30:

Cincinnati plays a double header – in two different cities. In the morning it loses in New York, 1-0, then travels to Philadelphia, where it wins an afternoon game, 10-9.

JUNE 2:

In a game under artificial lights in Fort Wayne, Indiana, the hometown team beats Quincy, 19-11, in seven innings.

JULY 25:

In Cleveland, Providence Grays' Charles "Old Hoss" Radbourn pitches an 8-0 no-hitter. Hugh Daily is the game's losing pitcher.

From The Baseball Hall of Fame 50th Anniversary Book*: "The (Providence) Grays pitching ace for several years was Radbourn, a 25-year-old rookie for Buffalo in 1880 before shuffling off to Providence. He won 31 in 1882, 49 the next year, and an incredible 60 for the 1884 season, including 26 wins in the final 27 games.... Because of Old Hoss's contentious nature, his catcher was described by one writer as an unsung*

SEPTEMBER 13
Cleveland's one-armed pitcher Hugh Daily no-hits Philadelphia in a 1-0 win.

martyr for putting up with the 'erratic, ill-tempered, and capricious Lord Radbourn...without a murmur.' The pitcher went to Boston for the 1886 season and won 20 games or more for four seasons before his overworked right arm quit."

AUGUST 21:

Providence, behind Charles "Old Hoss" Radbourn, beats Philadelphia, 28-0. Philadelphia commits 27 errors, leading to 21 unearned runs. Philadelphia pitcher Art Hagan does his part with 11 errors, including five wild pitches. There is something of an excuse for Philadelphia's shoddy fielding: prior to 1888, walks, wild pitches, and passed balls were scored as errors and were included in the pitiful total of 27 today.

SEPTEMBER 12:

There's another league on the horizon. Henry Van Noye Lucas and Al Spink form the Union Association in Pittsburgh. The new circuit will not honor the reserve clause of the NL and AA. Teams in the Union Association will be the Altoona Pride, Baltimore Unions, Boston Unions, Chicago Unions, Cincinnati Outlaw Reds, Philadelphia Keystones, St. Louis Unions, and Washington Unions.

SEPTEMBER 13:

In Philadelphia, Cleveland's Hugh Daily, a one-armed pitcher, throws a 1-0 no-hitter against Philadelphia. John Coleman is the game's losing pitcher.

Born Harry Criss, Daily had part of his left arm amputated when he was a youngster. Known as One-Arm, he pitched six seasons, compiling a 73-87 record. Daily used an adjustable protective pad at the elbow of his left arm.

SEPTEMBER 27:

Boston beats Cleveland, 4-1, to wrap up the NL pennant. After the American Association champion Philadel-phia Athletics proceed to lose their first eight post-season exhibition games, the team's manager, Lew Simmons, cancels the "World Series" with the National League's pennant winners, the Boston Beaneaters.

Adrian "Cap" Anson played with the Cubs for 22 years, finishing with a .334 career average.

LEAGUE

The former Worcester franchise in the NL will become the Philadelphia Quakers.

RULES

Sidearm pitching is now legal; a pitcher may deliver the ball in any manner except overhand. A runner now can return safely to base after a foul ball (fly or tip). A foul ball caught on a fly is an out. The NL now regulates only stockings, not uniforms: Boston will wear red; Buffalo, gray; Chicago, white; Cleveland, blue; Providence, light blue; Detroit, brown; Philadelphia, blue and white checks; and New York, crimson and black.

THE BEST OF 1883

NATIONAL LEAGUE

HITTERS

Batting Average:
Dennis "Big Dan" Brouthers, Buffalo Bisons, .374

Slugging Average:
Dennis Brouthers, .572

Home Runs:
William "Buck" Ewing, New York Gothams, 10

Runs Batted In:
Jack Burdock, Boston Beaneaters, 88

Hits:
Dennis Brouthers, 159

PITCHERS

Wins:
Charles "Old Hoss" Radbourn, Providence Grays, 49

Strikeouts:
Jim Whitney, Boston Beaneaters, 345

Earned Run Average:
Jim McCormick, Cleveland Blues, 1.84

Winning Percentage:
Jim McCormick, .700

Saves:
George "Stump" Weidman, Detroit Wolverines; Jim Whitney, 2

AMERICAN ASSOCIATION

HITTERS

Batting Average:
Cyrus "Ed" Swartwood, Pittsburgh Alleghenys, .356

Slugging Average:
Harry Stovey, Philadelphia Athletics, .504

Home Runs:
Harry Stovey, 14

Hits:
Cyrus Swartwood, 147

PITCHERS

Wins:
Will White, Cincinnati Red Stockings, 43

Strikeouts:
Tim Keefe, New York Metropolitans, 361

Earned Run Average:
Will White, 2.09

Winning Percentage:
Tony Mullane, St. Louis Browns, .700

Saves:
Bob Barr, Pittsburgh Alleghenys; Tony Mullane, 1

1884

APRIL 18
A rivalry is born as New York and Brooklyn meet for the first time as major league teams.

NEWS

GEORGE EASTMAN PRODUCES PHOTOGRAPHIC PAPER

FIRST SKYSCRAPER BUILT IN CHICAGO; IT IS 10 STORIES HIGH

FIRST UNDERGROUND TRAIN SYSTEM OPENS IN LONDON

Gold discovered in the Transvaal in Southern Africa

MISSISSIPPI ESTABLISHES FIRST U.S. STATE COLLEGE FOR WOMEN

GROVER CLEVELAND ELECTED PRESIDENT

Mark Twain's *Huckleberry Finn* is published

FIRST ROLLER COASTER OPENS AT CONEY ISLAND

Ottmar Mergenthaler invents Linotype machine for typesetting

GERMANY TAKES OVER SOUTHWEST AFRICA

PRE-SEASON

The NL begins playing ball with teams in Boston, Buffalo, Chicago, Cleveland, Detroit, New York, Philadelphia, and Providence. The AA is now a 12-team league, with teams in Baltimore, Brooklyn, Cincinnati,Columbus, Indianapolis, Louisville, New York City, Philadelphia, Pittsburgh, Richmond (which lasts only 42 games), St. Louis, and Toledo. The Union Association schedules 128 games for its teams in Altoona, Baltimore, Boston, Chicago, Cincinnati, Philadelphia, St. Louis, and Washington. Over the course of the 1884 season, the Union Association also will operate ball clubs in Milwaukee, Pittsburgh, St. Paul, Kansas City, and Wilmington.

FEBRUARY 10:

Billy Evans is born in Chicago.

THE SEASON

APRIL 12:

The Brooklyn Trolley-Dodgers – in their first-ever major league game – lose to the visiting Cleveland Blues in an American Association contest.

APRIL 18:

New York and Brooklyn meet for the first time as major league teams, beginning one of baseball's classic rivalries. The visiting Metropolitans win, 8-0.

APRIL 25:

John Henry "Pop" Lloyd is born in Palatka, Florida.

MAY 1:

Moses Fleetwood Walker becomes the first black to play major league ball when he catches for the Toledo Blue Stockings against the Louisville Eclipse in the AA.

A white fan composed a verse to Walker: "There was a catcher named Walker, who behind the bat is a corker. He throws to a base with ease and with grace, and steals 'round the bags like a stalker."

MAY 5:

Charles "Chief" Bender is born in Crow Wing County, Minnesota.

MAY 24:

Al Atkinson of the Philadelphia Athletics in the American Association no-hits

LEAGUE

The National League schedule is expanded to 112 games.

EQUIPMENT

Philadelphia Keystones' (Union Association) rookie left-handed catcher Jack Clements becomes the first player to wear a chest protector in a game. At the turn of the century, Roger Bresnahan popularized the device.

RULES

Overhand pitching is legalized. Walks are reduced from seven to six balls.

The Louisville Slugger was originally called the Falls City Slugger.

LEAGUE

During the season, the Union Association experiences franchise shifts. Altoona resigns in May, followed by Philadelphia in August. They are replaced by Kansas City and Wilmington. Cleveland drops out of the NL after the 1884 season.

HISTORY

After 46 games in which he hit .263 but made 37 errors, the major leagues' first black player, Moses Fleetwood Walker, is released by the Toledo Blue Stockings.

the visiting Pittsburgh Alleghenys. The final score is 10-1.

MAY 29:

Ed Morris of the AA Columbus Buckeyes no-hits the visiting Alleghenys, 5-0.

MAY 30:

Chicago's Edward "Ned" Williamson becomes the first major leaguer to hit three home runs in a game. Chicago beats visiting Buffalo, 11-10 and 12-2. Williamson is aided by a rule change that makes balls over the fence homers instead of doubles.

JUNE 5:

In an AA game, Frank Mountain of Columbus no-hits Washington, 12-0.

JUNE 27:

The White Stockings' Larry Corcoran becomes the first pitcher with three career no-hitters when he stops the visiting Providence Grays, 6-0, in Chicago.

JULY 7:

Hugh "One-Arm" Daily of the Chicago Browns strikes out 19 Boston Reds' batters and allows only one hit in a Union Association game. Daily loses a 20th strikeout when Browns' catcher Ed Crane drops the ball.

JULY 16:

After the Providence Grays lose to the Boston Beaneaters, 5-2, the team decides to suspend pitcher Charles "Old Hoss" Radbourn for his "insubordination." Although he is 24-8, Radbourn has lost four times in the last two weeks.

JULY 22:

Problems continue for the Grays. Pitcher Charlie Sweeney, 17-8, misses practice because he is drunk. He starts against Philadelphia and, with the Grays ahead, 6-2, manager Frank Bancroft brings in Joe "Cyclone" Miller. Sweeney refuses to leave the mound and is suspended. The Grays play the final two innings with only eight players, losing, 10-6, on eight unearned runs in the ninth inning.

Sweeney is kicked off the team and jumps to St. Louis in the Union Association, where he goes 24-7. Providence is left with only one pitcher – Old Hoss Radbourn. The slight right-hander begins what is one of the most remarkable "iron man" feats in all of baseball history. From July 23 on, he pitches in nine straight games, winning seven, tying one, and losing one. He takes a "day off," playing right field, and returns to pitch six more consecutive games. He plays shortstop for a single game, then pitches in 20 more straight contests, winning 10 before having his 20-game win streak snapped.

THE BROTHERHOOD OF PROFESSIONAL BASE BALL PLAYERS PREAMBLE READS: "PROFESSIONAL BASEBALL PLAYERS, RECOGNIZING THE IMPORTANCE OF THE UNITED EFFORT AND IMPRESSED WITH THE NECESSITE IN OUR BEHALF, DO FORM OURSELVES THIS DAY INTO AN ORGANIZATION TO BE KNOWN AS THE BROTHERHOOD OF PROFESSIONAL BASE BALL PLAYERS."

AUGUST 4:

Buffalo's James "Pud" Galvin no-hits Detroit, 18-0, striking out seven. Frank Meinke is the loser. It is Galvin's second career no-hitter and the most one-sided ball game in all of major league history.

AUGUST 6:

Chicago's Cap Anson hits three consecutive home runs today to pace Chicago to a 13-4 win over Cleveland. Anson sets a major league record with five homers in two games. The winner is Larry Corcoran.

AUGUST 15:

Louisville's Guy Hecker becomes the first pitcher to hit three home runs in a game and the

MAY 30
Chicago's Ned Williamson becomes the first to hit three home runs in a game.

AUGUST 15
Guy Hecker of Louisville is the first pitcher to hit three homers in a game.

only player to score seven runs in a contest.

AUGUST 26:

Dick Burns of the Cincinnati Outlaw Reds no-hits the visiting Kansas City Unions, 3-1.

SEPTEMBER 5:

Providence's Old Hoss Radbourn sits out his first game since July 23. He has accounted for 18 of the club's 20 wins in a current unbeaten streak.

OCTOBER 4:

In an AA game, the Brooklyn Trolley-Dodgers' 31-year-old rookie pitcher Sam Kimber no-hits Toledo for 11 innings. The ball game is called because of darkness and ends in a 0-0 tie. Tony Mullane allows only four hits for the Blue Stockings. Kimber's masterpiece is the first nine innings-plus no-hitter in the major leagues.

The Providence Grays beat the Buffalo Bisons, 4-1, clinching the NL pennant.

OCTOBER 15:

Providence's Old Hoss Radbourn finishes a mythic season by shutting out Philadelphia, 8-0, for his 60th win and 11th shutout of the year. He pitches 679 innings and 73 complete games, and compiles a 60-12 won-lost record with a 1.38 ERA. Radbourn earns a salary of $3,000 this season.

OCTOBER 23:

As a result of a challenge issued by manager Jim Mutrie of the first-place New York Metropolitans of the AA to the NL champion Providence Grays, the teams begin a three-game series. The pennant-winning St. Louis Maroons of the Union Association are bypassed. With AA rules, Providence wins, 6-0, at the Polo Grounds in New York. Winning pitcher Old Hoss Radbourn strikes out nine, yielding two hits; Tim Keefe is the loser. The 2,500 fans in attendance will receive a steel engraving of key players.

OCTOBER 24:

Providence, on an Old Hoss Radbourn three-hitter, beats New York again, 3-1. Jerry Denny hits a three-run homer in the fifth – the first round-tripper in World Series history. Tim Keefe loses his second straight. Cold weather in New York holds the attendance to 1,000, and darkness ends the game after seven innings.

OCTOBER 25:

The temperature drops and so does the crowd – to 500 – as Providence bombs New York, 11-2, in the final game of the post-season series. Old Hoss Radbourn is the winning pitcher – for the third straight time.

POST-SEASON

NOVEMBER 19:

In New York , the NL holds its ninth annual meeting. Because he opposes the admission of St. Louis from the Union Association and the pardoning of players who jumped to the new league, NL president Abraham G. Mills resigns after two years in office and will be replaced by secretary Nick Young.

RULES

One key difference in the rules: In the AA, a batter hit by a pitch is awarded first base; in the NL he is not.

Moses Walker played in the majors in 1884.

TRIVIA

Outfielder Harry Wheeler defines "well-traveled." In 1884, he becomes the only player to appear with five teams in a season. He plays five games with the St. Louis Browns in the AA; and 14 games with the Kansas City Unions, 20 games with the Chicago Browns, 17 games with the Pittsburgh Stogies, and 17 games with the Baltimore Monumentals, all in the Union Association. Perhaps his .244 average and 32 errors explain his mobility and the fact that he never again played in the major leagues.

THE BEST OF 1884

National League

HITTERS

Batting Average:
Mike "King" Kelly, Chicago White Stockings, .354

Slugging Average:
Dennis "Big Dan" Brouthers, Buffalo Bisons, .563

Home Runs:
Edward "Ned" Williamson, Chicago White Stockings, 27

Runs Batted In:
Bill Phillips, Cleveland Blues, 46

Hits:
Orator Jim O'Rourke, Buffalo Bisons; Ezra Sutton, Boston Beaneaters, 162

PITCHERS

Wins:
Charles "Old Hoss" Radbourn, Providence Grays, 60

Strikeouts:
Charles Radbourn, 441

Earned Run Average:
Charles Radbourn, 1.38

Winning Percentage:
Charles Radbourn, .833

Saves:
John Morrill, Boston Beaneaters, 2

American Association

HITTERS

Batting Average:
Dave Orr, New York Metropolitans, .354

Slugging Average:
Long John Reilly, Cincinnati Red Stockings, .551

Home Runs:
John Reilly, 11

Hits:
John Reilly, Dave Orr, 162

PITCHERS

Wins:
Guy Hecker, Louisville Eclipse, 52

Strikeouts:
Guy Hecker, 385

Earned Run Average:
Guy Hecker, 1.80

Winning Percentage:
Ed Morris, Columbus Buckeyes, .723

Saves:
Frank Mountain, Columbus Buckeyes; Hank O'Day, Toledo Blue Stockings; Thomas "Oyster" Burns, Baltimore Orioles, 1

Union Association

HITTERS

Batting Average:
Fred Dunlap, St. Louis Maroons, .412

Slugging Average:
Fred Dunlap, .621

Home Runs:
Fred Dunlap, 13

Hits:
Fred Dunlap, 185

PITCHERS

Wins:
Bill Sweeney, Baltimore Monumentals, 40

Strikeouts:
Hugh "One Arm" Daily, Chicago Browns/Pittsburgh Stogies/Washington Nationals, 483

Earned Run Average:
Jim McCormick, Cincinnati Outlaw Reds, 1.54

Winning Percentage:
Billy Taylor, St. Louis Maroons, .862

Saves:
Billy Taylor, 4

1885

OCTOBER 14
Game one of a championship series between Chicago and St. Louis ends in a tie.

NEWS

KARL BENZ BUILDS THE FIRST GASOLINE ENGINE FOR A MOTOR CAR

CONGRESS OF BERLIN GIVES CONGO TO BELGIUM AND NIGERIA TO ENGLAND

American Telephone & Telegraph (AT&T) incorporates

STATUE OF LIBERTY ARRIVES IN NEW YORK ABOARD THE FRENCH SHIP *ISERE*

Louis Pasteur administers first anti-rabies vaccine to a nine-year-old schoolboy

CANADIAN PACIFIC RAILWAY IS COMPLETED

Gilbert & Sullivan's opera *The Mikado* opens in London

FIRST MODERN BICYCLE IS BUILT

Honoring ornithologist John Audubon, National Audubon Society is founded in U.S.

PRE-SEASON

JANUARY 10:

The St. Louis Unions and the Cleveland Spiders merge into a new franchise named the St. Louis Maroons. Owned by Henry V. Lucas, organizer of the Union Association, the Maroons are admitted to the NL. Before the month is out, the Union Association is down to two baseball teams and folds.

THE SEASON

JULY 27:

Chicago's John Clarkson no-hits the Grays in Providence, 4-0, in an NL game. Old Hoss Radbourn is the losing pitcher.

AUGUST 29:

Philadelphia's Charles Ferguson no-hits visiting Providence, 1-0, striking out eight batters. Frederick "Dupee" Shaw takes the loss.

SEPTEMBER 4:

In Chicago, the White Stockings' starting pitcher, right-hander Jim McCormick, tops the Buffalo Bisons, 12-4, for his 14th consecutive win of the season.

SEPTEMBER 19:

In Chicago, John Clarkson of the White Stockings two-hits Boston, 10-3, for his 50th win of the season.

SEPTEMBER 30:

At home at West Side Park, the White Stockings clinch the NL pennant with a 2-1 win over New York.

OCTOBER 7:

Dupee Shaw of Providence no-hits Buffalo, 4-0, in a five-inning NL game.

OCTOBER 14:

In Chicago, 2,000 fans turn out to see Cap Anson's NL champion White Stockings meet the AA pennant-winning St. Louis Browns, managed by Charles Comiskey, in a "championship series." Pitcher Bob Caruthers, with 40 wins, starts for St. Louis; 53-game winner John Clarkson pitches for Chicago. After eight innings, the game is called because of darkness with the score tied, 5-5.

OCTOBER 15:

At Sportsman's Park in St. Louis, Chicago wins game two of the championship series by a 9-0 forfeit. Angered by umpire

RULES

Six balls now constitute a walk, down from seven the previous season. The American Association decrees the catcher must handle a third strike without a bounce.

LEAGUE

The NL begins its season with the founding franchise members Boston (Beaneaters) and Chicago (White Stockings), plus Buffalo (Bisons), Detroit (Wolverines), New York (Giants), Philadelphia (Quakers), Providence (Grays), and St. Louis (Maroons).

OCTOBER 24
The White Stockings-Browns NL-AA series ends tied at three games apiece.

LEAGUE

The NL's New York team acquires a nickname that will endure as long as the franchise. Cheering for his team during a game, manager Jim Mutrie exclaims, "These are my big fellows! These are my Giants!"

EQUIPMENT

Art Irwin of the Providence Grays, suffering two broken fingers, pads a buckskin glove for protection and comes up with the first known fielder's glove.

LEAGUE

The NL and AA set maximum pay for players at $2,000 with no bonuses.

David F. Sullivan's calls, manager Charles Comiskey threatens to take his Browns off the field. After Sullivan reverses his call several times on another play, some 200 fans storm the field, forcing the White Stockings to leave with police escort. The umpire calls a forfeit when he gets back to his hotel room. At the time, Chicago was ahead, 5-4.

By some accounts, the forfeit is awarded to Chicago when the Browns leave the field. Jerry Lansche in Glory Fades Away *attributes it to fans on the field. According to Lansche, David Sullivan acknowledged he had a bad day.*

OCTOBER 16

With a new umpire – Harry McCaffrey – okayed by Cap Anson, the White Stockings and Browns face off in St. Louis for game three before 3,000 fans. The Browns are awarded every close call and win, 7-4.

Once again, a dispute among sources: William Medart is listed by one source as the new game-three umpire. Jerry Lansche identifies the arbiter as Harry McCaffrey.

OCTOBER 17:

In St. Louis, there is a 45-minute delay in starting the game because of a dispute about umpires. William Medart, a St. Louis fan, is called from his seat to ump, and the Browns beat the White Stockings, 3-2. In the ninth inning with Chicago at bat, behind 3-2, Jim McCormick is standing on first when Browns' first sacker Charles Comiskey "playfully" tags him. Medart calls McCormick out, precipitating another ruckus. James "Bug" Holliday, 17 years old, fouls out to end the game.

Holliday, a St. Louis native, becomes the only amateur ever to play in a World Series game, when he starts in place of John Clarkson in right field. Holliday goes 0-4 with an error. He returns to the majors in 1889 and plays 10 years with Cincinnati, batting .316.

OCTOBER 22:

After a five-day delay for the Chicago "City Series," the scene shifts to a neutral site – Recreation Park in Pittsburgh. The White Stockings top the Browns, 9-2. Honest John Kelly, imported to umpire, halts the game after seven because of darkness.

After sportswriter William Voltz suggests a "protective association of baseball players" to aid the injured or needy, John Montgomery Ward and eight Giant teammates – spurred by the $2,000 salary ceiling – form a local chapter of the Brotherhood of Professional Base Ball Players. Ward is elected president and Tim Keefe, secretary. Detroit is the first team to sign up for the Brotherhood. Subsequently Chicago, Kansas City, Boston, Philadelphia, and Washington join the fold.

OCTOBER 23:

The championship series takes to the road again. Game six is played in Cincinnati, and the White Stockings beat the Browns, 9-2, despite 10 errors.

OCTOBER 24:

In Cincinnati, the Browns manhandle the White Stockings, 13-4, to tie the series at three games each. In the series there are more errors than hits – 102 to 96.

A special committee rules the series a tie, but Cap Anson, who bats .423, claims the championship. The Browns' owner, Chris Von Der Ahe, publicly says the series is deadlocked, but otherwise claims his team is the champion. Chicago president Albert Spalding protests: "Does anyone suppose that if there had been so much at stake that I should have consented to the games being played in American Association cities upon their grounds, and under the authority of their umpires?" By publicly acknowledging a tie, the owners avoid paying the players their share of $1,000 in prize money. In October, $500 is returned to the owner of each team.

POST-SEASON

After the 1885 major league season, two National League franchises, the Buffalo Bisons and Providence Grays drop out. They will be replaced by two new teams, the Washington Senators and Kansas City Cowboys.

THE BEST OF 1885

NATIONAL LEAGUE

HITTERS

Batting Average:
Roger Connor, New York Giants, .371

Slugging Average:
Dennis "Big Dan" Brouthers, Buffalo Bisons, .543

Home Runs:
Abner Dalrymple, Chicago White Stockings, 11

Runs Batted In:
Adrian "Cap" Anson, Chicago White Stockings, 114

Hits:
Roger Connor, 169

PITCHERS

Wins:
John Clarkson, Chicago White Stockings, 53

Strikeouts:
John Clarkson, 308

Earned Run Average:
Tim Keefe, New York Giants, 1.58

Winning Percentage:
Mickey Welch, New York Giants, .800

Saves:
Edward "Ned" Williamson, Nathaniel "Fred" Pfeffer, Chicago White Stockings, 2

AMERICAN ASSOCIATION

HITTERS

Batting Average:
Louis "Pete" Browning, Louisville Colonels, .362

Slugging Average:
Dave Orr, New York Metropolitans, .543

Home Runs:
Harry Stovey, Philadelphia Athletics, 13

Hits:
Louis Browning, 174

PITCHERS

Wins:
Bob Caruthers, St. Louis Browns, 40

Strikeouts:
Ed Morris, Pittsburgh Alleghenys, 298

Earned Run Average:
Bob Caruthers, 2.07

Winning Percentage:
Bob Caruthers, .755

Saves:
Thomas "Oyster" Burns, Baltimore Orioles, 3

HISTORY

The tradition of spring training in the South begins when Cap Anson takes his Chicago White Stockings to Hot Springs, Arkansas, to get into shape for the season.

TRIVIA

In 1885, the waiters at the Argyle Hotel in Babylon, New York, form a baseball team – the Cuban Giants – and tour the East. According to historian Jules Tygiel, they are the "first all-black team to achieve wide-spread recognition" and "chattered gibberish on the field to pass as Cubans."

1886

NEWS

HAYMARKET RIOT AND BOMBING FOLLOWS BITTER LABOR BATTLES FOR 8-HOUR WORKDAY IN CHICAGO

GERONIMO, LEADER OF THE APACHE NATION, SURRENDERS

STATUE OF LIBERTY IS DEDICATED IN NEW YORK

American Federation of Labor (AFL) is formed by 25 craft unions

ATLANTA PHARMACIST CREATES COCA-COLA, CONTAINING COCA LEAVES AND KOLA NUT, AS "HEADACHE TONIC"

Gold-mining town of Johannesburg is founded in South Africa

BRITAIN IMPOSES "HOME RULE" ON IRELAND

Richard Sears establishes mail-order house in Minneapolis

PRE-SEASON

MARCH 13:

John Franklin "Home Run" Baker is born in Trappe, Maryland.

MARCH 17:

The Sporting News, known as "the Bible of Baseball," is founded in St. Louis, Missouri.

APRIL 6:

"Smokey" Joe Williams is born in Seguin, Texas.

THE SEASON

MAY 1:

Al Atkinson, who was out of the major leagues in 1885, returns and throws a 3-2 no-hitter today for the Philadelphia Athletics against the New York Metropolitans in an AA game. It is Atkinson's second career no-hitter.

JUNE 16:

The first black organized baseball league, the Southern League of Colored Base Ballists, begins play with the Memphis Eclipse beating the New Orleans Unions, 3-1.

JULY 1:

White Stockings' pitcher Jim McCormick rings up his 16th consecutive win by topping New York, 7-3, today in Chicago.

JULY 24:

In an AA game, Brooklyn's Adonis Bill Terry no-hits St. Louis, 1-0.

AUGUST 7:

Bill McKechnie is born in Wilkinsburg, Pennsylvania.

SEPTEMBER 26:

Chris Von Der Ahe, owner of the AA St. Louis Browns, writes to Chicago White Stocking president A. G. Spalding, "... I therefore take the opportunity of challenging your team, on behalf of the Browns, for a series of contests to be known as The World's Championship Series." He proposes either five, seven, or nine games to be played on the respective home fields only. Spalding accepts the challenge, wants a nine-game series, but settles for seven (the first time this format is used). Other conditions: the seventh game will be played on a neutral site; winner takes all and pays the umpires, and, in the event of a four-game sweep, game five will be an exhibition contest.

OCTOBER 6:

Baltimore's Matt Kilroy no-hits Pittsburgh, 6-0, in an AA game.

OCTOBER 9:

The White Stockings clinch their second straight National League pennant with a 12-3, seven-inning win in Boston. John Clarkson is credited with the win.

OCTOBER 16:

William Harridge is born in Chicago.

OCTOBER 18:

The Brooklyn Trolley-Dodgers of the AA and New York Giants of the NL meet in the first of four post-season matches. Brooklyn wins, 7-2, at home.

Championship Series, game one. In Chicago, 5,000 fans see the White Stockings top the Browns, 6-0, on John Clarkson's five-hitter. Dave Foutz is the losing pitcher.

OCTOBER 19:

Championship Series, game two. The St. Louis Browns demolish the White Stockings, 12-0. James "Tip" O'Neill drives in four runs with two inside-

OCTOBER 19
Tip O'Neill hits two inside-the-park homers in game two of the Championship Series.

MOTHER, MAY I SLUG THE UMPIRE, MAY I SLUG HIM RIGHT AWAY, SO HE CANNOT BE HERE, MOTHER, WHEN THE CLUBS BEGIN TO PLAY? LET ME CLASP HIS THROAT, DEAR MOTHER, IN A DEAR, DELIGHTED GRIP, WITH ONE HAND, AND WITH THE OTHER BAT HIM SEVERAL IN THE LIP.
– *CHICAGO TRIBUNE*, AUGUST 15

the-park home runs and is the first player with two round-trippers in championship play. It also is the first time three umpires (John Kelly, John McQuaid, and Joe Quest) are used in the Series. Bob Caruthers allows one hit and strikes out eight. Jim McCormick gets the loss.

OCTOBER 20:

Championship Series, game three. The White Stockings beat the Browns, 11-4 in Chicago. George Gore and Mike "King" Kelly homer for Chicago; John Clarkson is the winning pitcher. Bob Caruthers is tagged with the loss.

OCTOBER 21:

Championship Series, game four. Today at St. Louis's Sportsman's Park, the Browns beat the White Stockings, 8-5, in a game called after seven. Dave Foutz is the winning pitcher; John Clarkson gets the loss. In the fifth, Clarkson intentionally walks James "Tip" O'Neill; it is the first intentional pass in series history and one of the first ever in baseball. Rumors of dumping (called "hippodroming") mar the game and the Series.

OCTOBER 22:

Championship Series, game five. Nat Hudson and the Browns win, 10-3, at Sportsman's Park. Ned Williamson, normally a shortstop, starts and loses for Chicago.

OCTOBER 23:

The *Chicago News* charges: "Admitting that baseball is a business conducted for pecuniary profit, there still can be no palliation for the offense of brazenly giving away a game as the game was given away yesterday in St. Louis... Yesterday the Chicagoes started in with a seeming determination to prevent at the very outset every possibility of winning."

Championship Series, game six: Play at Sportsman's Park begins at 2:18 in an attempt to complete the game before dark. Behind Bob Caruthers, the Browns beat the White Stockings, 4-3, in 10 innings and win the Series. John Clarkson, despite nine strikeouts, is the loser. With Albert "Doc" Bushong at bat, Clarkson uncorks a pitch over the head of catcher Mike Kelly, and Curt Welch – who had singled – slides home with the winning run. It becomes known as the "$15,000 slide" – the winners' share.

POST-SEASON

DECEMBER 9:

Walter S. Brown forms the National Colored Baseball League with representatives from Boston, Baltimore, Louisville, Pittsburgh, Washington, and Philadelphia, and investors from Chicago and Cincinnati.

DECEMBER 18:

Tyrus Raymond Cobb is born in The Narrows, Georgia.

William Hoy's deafness led to a signal system.

RULES

A walk is again upped from six to seven balls. Umpires may put a new ball into play at any time instead of waiting for an inning to end. Bases are put inside the playing field, in fair territory.

HISTORY

Baltimore pitcher Matt Kilroy finishes the season with 513 strikeouts in 68 games. He wins 29 and loses 34 for the last-place team. Guy Hecker of Louisville, who topped the AA in pitching in 1884 with 52 wins, this season leads the league in batting – .341 – and becomes the first and only player to lead the same league in pitching and batting.

THE BEST OF 1886

NATIONAL LEAGUE

HITTERS

Batting Average:
Mike "King" Kelly, Chicago White Stockings, .388

Slugging Average:
Dennis "Big Dan" Brouthers, Detroit Wolverines, .581

Home Runs:
Dennis Brouthers; Abram "Hardy" Richardson, Detroit Wolverines, 11

Runs Batted In:
Adrian "Cap" Anson, Chicago White Stockings, 147

Hits:
Abram Richardson, 189

PITCHERS

Wins:
Charles "Lady" Baldwin, Detroit Wolverines; Tim Keefe, New York Giants, 42

Strikeouts:
Charles Baldwin, 323

Earned Run Average:
Henry Boyle, St. Louis Maroons, 1.76

Winning Percentage:
John "Jocko" Flynn, Chicago White Stockings, .800

Saves:
Charles Ferguson, 2

AMERICAN ASSOCIATION

HITTERS

Batting Average:
Louis "Pete" Browning, Louisville Colonels, .340

Slugging Average:
Dave Orr, New York Metropolitans; Bob Caruthers, St. Louis Browns, .527

Home Runs:
Harry Stovey, Philadelphia Athletics; John "Bid" McPhee, Cincinnati Red Stockings; Dave Orr, 7

Hits:
Dave Orr, 193

PITCHERS

Wins:
Dave Foutz, St. Louis Browns; Ed Morris, Pittsburgh Alleghenys, 41

Strikeouts:
Matt Kilroy, Baltimore Orioles, 513

Earned Run Average:
Dave Foutz, 2.11

Winning Percentage:
Dave Foutz, .719

Saves:
Morris; William "Bones" Ely, Louisville Colonels; Dave Foutz; Nat Hudson, St. Louis Browns; Joe Strauss, Louisville Colonels, 1

1887

APRIL 16
The Orioles' Mike Griffin is the first to homer in his first major league at-bat.

NEWS

QUEEN VICTORIA CELEBRATES HER GOLDEN JUBILEE

SHERLOCK HOLMES FIRST APPEARS IN PRINT

GERMANY, AUSTRIA-HUNGARY, AND FRANCE END TRIPLE ALLIANCE

U.S. SENATE APPROVES NAVAL BASE LEASE OF PEARL HARBOR

Polish philologist Lazarus Ludwig Zemenhof invents new international language, Esperanto

ITALY GOES TO WAR AGAINST ETHIOPIA

Interstate Commerce Act passed

YELLOWSTONE NATIONAL PARK IS CREATED

Thomas Edison invents the record player

PRE-SEASON

FEBRUARY 14:

Mike "King" Kelly, last year's batting champion at .388, is sold by the White Stockings to Boston for $10,000. Kelly gets his own valentine – a $2,000 contract for 1887 and a $3,000 bonus "for the use of his picture."

FEBRUARY 26:

Grover Cleveland "Pete" Alexander is born in Elba, Nebraska.

THE SEASON

APRIL 16:

On the AA's fourth opening day, the Baltimore Orioles' Mike Griffin becomes the first player ever to homer in his initial major league at-bat. Later in the day, Cincinnati's George "White Wings" Tebeau duplicates the very same feat.

APRIL 21:

Joe McCarthy is born in Philadelphia.

MAY 2:

Eddie Collins is born in Millerton, New York.

MAY 6:

In Pittsburgh, the National Colored Baseball League begins play, with the New York Gothams defeating the Keystones, 11-8, before some 1,200 fans. Besides the Pittsburgh and New York ballclubs, the league begins play with the Baltimore Lord Baltimores, the Boston Resolutes, the Cincinnati Browns, the Louisville Fall City, the Philadelphia Pythians, and the Washington Capitol Citys, but it folds within weeks.

JULY 9:

The White Stockings' John Clarkson beats the Philadelphia Quakers, 5-3, for his 11th consecutive win.

JULY 14:

The International League's directors ban contracts with black players; those already playing will not be affected. However, Bud Fowler – the first black professional baseball player – is released by Binghamton despite batting .350 with 35 stolen bases. According to *The Sporting Life*, Fowler is "one of the best general players in the country and if he had a white face

HISTORY

In what may be the first "farm team" arrangement, Cincinnati signs a working agreement with the minor league club in Emporia, Kansas.

RULES

It will take four strikes – up from last year's three – for an out; five balls constitute a walk. The strike zone is defined as shoulders to knees. The batter no longer can request a high or low pitch. A batter hit by a pitch is awarded first base. Walks are scored as hits.

JULY 23
Fred Chapman, still four months shy of 15, pitches for the Philadelphia Athletics.

LEAGUE

The St. Louis Maroons and Kansas City Blues are out of the NL; the Indianapolis Hoosiers and Pittsburgh Alleghenyes – the latter from the AA – are in. The Cleveland Spiders replace Pittsburgh in the AA.

HISTORY

The Browns' James "Tip" O'Neill finishes the season at .492. However, his average is inflated because walks count as hits in 1887. His "adjusted" average – by modern rules – is still an outstanding .435. Sam Thompson of Detroit drives in a record 166 runs.

would be playing with the best of them."

JULY 23:

Fred Chapman, who turns 15 in November, pitches for the Philadelphia Athletics against the Cleveland Spiders in an AA game and becomes the youngest ever to play in the majors. The game ends in a forfeit, and there is no winning pitcher. Chapman goes five, allowing eight hits and two walks, while fanning four. It is his only major league game; he ends his brief career with a 7.20 ERA.

AUGUST 24:

Harry Hooper is born in Bell Station, California.

From The Baseball Hall of Fame 50th Anniversary Book: *"In 1909, a stocky, one-time pitcher and civil engineer from California, Harry Hooper, came to Boston. According to Hooper, he was persuaded to move East in 1909 by John J. Taylor, the Red Sox owner who dangled the possibility of Hooper practicing his profession while playing some ball. He quickly established himself as a fielding star, covering the turf in left." Wrote the* Philadelphia Inquirer *of Hooper: "Harry B. Hooper, right-fielder of the Boston Red Sox and one of the original 'Speed Boys' who will be the first man to toe the plate in the big fracas, is one of the very best men in the country to lead off a batting order."*

OCTOBER 6:

The Philadelphia Quakers beat the New York Giants, 6-3, to close their season with 16 consecutive wins.

OCTOBER 10:

Championship Series, game one. Today at Sportsman's Park in St. Louis, the Browns beat the Wolverines, 6-1, on Bob Caruthers's four-hitter. The losing pitcher is Charlie "Pretzels" Getzien. Braving the day's rain and cold are 12,000 fans.

OCTOBER 11:

Championship Series, game two. Detroit wins, 5-3. Pete Conway is the winning pitcher; Dave Foutz takes the loss.

OCTOBER 12:

The Giants' John Montgomery Ward marries actress Helen Dauvray. The popular performer convinces Stearns and Von Der Ahe to underwrite an $800 Tiffany trophy. To be known as the Dauvray Cup, it will go to the Series' victor; individual gold medallions commissioned by Dauvray will be presented to the winning players.

Championship Series, game three. A capacity crowd of 9,000 fans fills Recreation Park to see the Wolverines narrowly beat the visiting Browns, 2-1, in 12. Charlie Getzien is the winning pitcher; Bob Caruthers, the loser.

JERRY LANSCHE, AUTHOR OF *GLORY FADES AWAY*, DESCRIBES THE 1887 PLAYOFFS AS THE "SERIES THAT WENT ON FOREVER."

OCTOBER 13:

Championship Series, game four. Detroit, on a two-hitter by Charles "Lady" Baldwin, beats the Browns, 8-0, in Pittsburgh. Charles "Silver" King is charged with the loss. Wolverines' pitchers now have recorded 20 consecutive shutout innings.

Baldwin is known as "Lady" because he doesn't smoke, drink, or curse. But he can pitch, although he fell to 13-10 in 1887 from 42-13 in 1886. In his six-year career in

OCTOBER 6
The Philadelphia Quakers end the season with their 16th consecutive win.

OCTOBER 26
The 15-game Championship Series between the Browns and Wolverines ends.

the majors, he is 73-41 with a 2.85 ERA.

OCTOBER 14:

Championship Series, game five. Today at Washington Park in Brooklyn, a sellout crowd of 10,000 – including an estimated 2,000 women – sees St. Louis win, 5-2. Bob Caruthers is the winner; Pete Conway is the loser.

OCTOBER 15:

Championship Series, game six. At the Polo Grounds in New York City, with only 3,000 on hand, Detroit wins, 9-0, behind Charlie Getzien, who yields his first hit to Tip O'Neill with two out in the ninth. The loser is Dave Foutz.

OCTOBER 16:

No rest for the weary. At least not the weary Browns. With an open date from the Series, owner Chris Von Der Ahe schleps his team to Brooklyn for an exhibition game against the Trolley-Dodgers. Brooklyn wins, 10-3, before 5,000 fans.

OCTOBER 17:

Championship Series, game seven. At the Philadelphia Base Ball Grounds, Detroit beats St. Louis, 3-1, behind the pitching of Lady Baldwin; Bob Caruthers is the loser. Chris Von Der Ahe tells the *St. Louis Post-Dispatch*, "I will put in Caruthers today and tomorrow and the next day, and the day after that and every day until he can't pitch any more, and after that I don't know what I'm going to do."

OCTOBER 18:

Championship Series, game eight. It's north to Boston, where Detroit wins again, 9-2, with Sam Thompson contributing two homers. The winning pitcher is Charlie Getzien. The loser for the second consecutive day is Bob Caruthers, who says, "I can win from them every other day, but I'm not made of iron. I'm a man, and I can't do the work."

OCTOBER 19:

Championship Series, game nine. Only 500 fans turn up in Philadelphia, where the Wolverines win, 4-2. Silver King gets the loss; Pete Conway is the winner.

OCTOBER 21:

Championship Series, game 10. Rain postponed yesterday's scheduled game and the teams meet twice today. In a morning game at Washington's Capitol Park Grounds, which is also known as Swampdoodle Grounds, St. Louis bounces back with an 11-4 victory. Bob Caruthers gets the win. Loser Charlie Getzien allows 19 hits.

Championship Series, game 11. Following a train trip to Baltimore, the Wolverines prevail, 13-3, at Union Park, for their eighth win and the championship, but the games go on. The winner is Lady Baldwin on a three-hitter; Dave Foutz gets the loss.

OCTOBER 22:

Championship Series, game 12. Back in Brooklyn, a small crowd (variously estimated as 200, 500, or 800) sees the Browns win a meaningless game (the remaining series contests are considered exhibitions), 5-1. Swirling winds and cold end the game after six and a half innings. Silver King gets the win, Pete Conway the loss.

OCTOBER 24:

Championship Series, game 13. Back home in Detroit, 4,000 watch the champion Wolverines win, 6-3. Lady Baldwin is the winner; Bob Caruthers is the loser.

OCTOBER 25:

Championship Series, game 14. With Halloween less than a week away, 378 fans see the Wolverines beat the Browns, 4-3. Charlie Getzien gets the win; Silver King is the loser.

OCTOBER 26:

Championship Series, game 15. Admission is a quarter, but only 800 hardy souls are at Sportsman's Park as the Browns win, 9-2. The overworked Bob Caruthers is the winner. Lady Baldwin gets the loss. The game ends after six; three extra games are canceled because of impending winter.

St. Louis owner Chris Von Der Ahe expresses his unhappiness with his team's play by giving the players no money for the post-season. Consequently, the Browns appear in 16 games (including one exhibition) and earn nothing for their effort.

POST-SEASON

NOVEMBER 6:

Walter Johnson is born in Humboldt, Kansas.

HISTORY

Frederick Stearns, owner of the NL champion Detroit Wolverines, challenges Chris Von Der Ahe and the three-time AA pennant-winning Browns to a best of 15 World Series.

TRIVIA

St. Louis Browns' first baseman and manager Charles Comiskey becomes the first player to be paid for a product endorsement when he lends his name to Menell's Penetrating Oil.

HISTORY

With 137 homers between 1880 and 1897, Roger Connor becomes baseball's all-time home run leader, BR (Before Ruth).

TRIVIA

Thomas "Toad" Ramsey of the Louisville Colonels, who twice has fanned 17 in one game, is believed to be the originator of the knuckleball, which he described as a "deep curve."

THE BEST OF 1887

NATIONAL LEAGUE

HITTERS

Batting Average:
Sam Thompson, Detroit Wolverines, .372

Slugging Average:
Sam Thompson, .571

Home Runs:
Billy O'Brien, Washington Statesmen, 19

Runs Batted In:
Sam Thompson, 166

Hits:
Sam Thompson, 203

Stolen Bases:
John Montgomery Ward, New York Giants, 111

PITCHERS

Wins:
John Clarkson, Chicago White Stockings, 38

Strikeouts:
John Clarkson, 237

Earned Run Average:
Dan Casey, Philadelphia Quakers, 2.86

Winning Percentage:
Charlie "Pretzels" Getzien, Detroit Wolverines, .690

Saves:
Eight players with 1 each

AMERICAN ASSOCIATION

HITTERS

Batting Average:
James "Tip" O'Neill, St. Louis Browns, .435

Slugging Average:
James O'Neill, .691

Home Runs:
James O'Neill, 14

Hits:
James O'Neill, 225

Stolen Bases:
Hugh Nicol, Cincinnati Red Stockings, 138

PITCHERS

Wins:
Matt Kilroy, Baltimore Orioles, 46

Strikeouts:
Thomas "Toad" Ramsey, Louisville Colonels, 355

Earned Run Average:
Elmer Smith, Cincinnati Red Stockings, 2.94

Winning Percentage:
Bob Caruthers, St. Louis Browns, .763

Saves:
Adonis Bill Terry, Brooklyn Trolley-Dodgers, 3

1888

JUNE 3, 1888

MAY 18
The baseball poem "Casey at the Bat" makes its stage debut in New York City.

NEWS

JACK THE RIPPER MURDERS SIX WOMEN IN LONDON

NIKOLA TESLA CONSTRUCTS AN ELECTRIC MOTOR

George Eastman perfects box camera

J.B. DUNLOP INVENTS PNEUMATIC TIRE

HEINRICH HERTZ IDENTIFIES RADIO WAVES

BENJAMIN HARRISON DEFEATS GROVER CLEVELAND TO TAKE OVER WHITE HOUSE

SCULPTOR AUGUSTE RODIN FINISHES *THE THINKER*

EDWARD BELLAMY WRITES SCIENCE-FICTION NOVEL *LOOKING BACKWARD*

Death of German Emperor Wilhelm I ends 27-year reign

PRE-SEASON

APRIL 4:

Tristram "Tris" Speaker is born in Hubbard, Texas.

THE SEASON

APRIL 18:

The AA's John Gaffney alters the way umpires work games. Previously, an umpire worked behind either the pitcher or catcher. Gaffney, the highest paid at $2,500, moves behind the plate for all calls except with runners on base, when he moves behind the pitcher.

APRIL 29:

Quakers' pitcher Charles Ferguson dies in Philadelphia, 12 days after his 25th birthday. A 30-game winner in 1886, he was a 20-game winner in each of his three other major league seasons.

MAY 18:

At Wallack's Theatre in New York City, Ernest L. Thayer's baseball poem "Casey at the Bat" makes its stage debut with actor William De Wolfe Hopper reading the work.

Thayer's poem begins with the familiar: "The outlook wasn't brilliant for the Mudville nine that day; The score stood four to two with but one inning more to play." It concludes with the poignant: "Oh! somewhere in this favored land the sun is shining bright; The band is playing somewhere, and somewhere hearts are light, And somewhere men are laughing, and somewhere children shout; But there is no joy in Mudville, mighty Casey has struck out."

MAY 23:

Zack Wheat is born in Hamilton, Missouri.

MAY 27:

Brooklyn's Adonis Bill Terry no-hits visiting Louisville, 4-0, in an AA game. It is Terry's second career no-hitter.

JUNE 3:

Arguably the most popular piece of baseball writing ever, "Casey at the Bat," by 25-year-old Ernest L. Thayer, is published today in the *San Francisco Examiner*. Thayer receives $5 for his poem, which is attributed to "Phin."

RULES

It's back to three strikes for an out. Walks will no longer count as hits and they will not be official at-bats. A batter gets a hit if the ball strikes a base runner.

TRIVIA

Chris Von Der Ahe cleans house and the Browns begin the season missing many old standbys. Sold to Brooklyn at the end of last season are pitcher Bob Caruthers for $8,250, pitcher Dave Foutz for $5,500, and catcher Albert "Doc" Bushong for $5,000. The Browns also sell outfielder Curt Welch to the Athletics for $3,000 and trade shortstop Bill Gleason to Philadelphia for second baseman James "Chippy" McGarr.

Baseball's popularity rises in U.S. cities.

JULY 13
Pittsburgh pitchers record the majors' first-ever double-header shutout.

LEAGUE

In June, the Louisville Colonels of the American Association stage the first player walkout in major league history. Their work stoppage, led by Pete Browning and Guy Hecker, protests the tactics of owner Mordecai Davidson, who fines players $100 for an error, changes managers too frequently to suit his team, and slams his players in the press. Davidson also managed three games, losing two of them. The AA takes over the Louisville franchise and refunds half the fine money. The walkout ends after two days.

LEAGUE

Owner Chris Von Der Ahe of the Browns and John B. Day of the Giants agree that the first team with six victories will win the 1888 Championship.

JUNE 6:

Kansas City's Henry Porter no-hits the Orioles, 4-0, in Baltimore.

JUNE 21:

The White Stockings' George Van Haltren pitches a six inning, 1-0, no-hitter against visiting Pittsburgh.

JULY 13:

Pittsburgh pitchers Harry Staley and Pud Galvin whitewash Boston, 4-0 and 6-0. It is the first-ever doubleheader shutout in major league history.

JULY 19:

Newark of the International League – led by George Stovey – is scheduled to play an exhibition game in New Jersey against the Chicago White Stockings. Stovey, who is black and the league's top pitcher, is close to being acquired by the New York Giants through the efforts of John Montgomery Ward, with the approval of owner John Day and manager Jim Mutrie. Also scheduled to play is Moses Fleetwood Walker, who, with Stovey, forms baseball's first black battery. Chicago manager Cap Anson refuses to put his players on the field. Stovey then complains of illness and removes himself from the game, and Walker is benched. It is the second time Anson has protested playing against Walker. Four years ago, Walker played despite Anson's protests.

Following today's events, the Giants decide not to purchase Stovey, who goes on to a 34-14 record with Newark and hits .255. Stovey plays the rest of his career with the Cuban Giants, New York Gothams, and the Cuban X-Giants.

JULY 26:

Philadelphia's Ed Seward no-hits visiting Cincinnati, 12-2, in an AA game.

JULY 31:

Gus Weyhing of Philadelphia no-hits visiting Kansas City, 4-0, in an AA game.

AUGUST 10:

Giants' pitcher Tim Keefe beats Pittsburgh, 2-1, in New York for his 19th consecutive win. Keefe's streak began on June 23 with a 7-6 victory over Philadelphia.

AUGUST 14:

In New York, Gus Krock five-hits the Giants, and the White Stockings snuff out Tim Keefe's streak, 4-2. That night, with Keefe, his teammates, Chicago players, and Civil War hero General William Tecumsah Sherman in attendance, actor William De Wolfe Hopper again reads the baseball poem "Casey at the Bat" at Wallack's Theatre in New York City.

SEPTEMBER 6:

Urban "Red" Faber is born in Cascade, Iowa.

SEPTEMBER 27:

The Giants' Ed "Cannonball" Crane pitches a seven-inning, 3-0, no-hitter against Washington.

OCTOBER 16:

Championship Series, game one. The Browns, winner of four consecutive AA pennants, meet the NL champion Giants at the Polo Grounds. New York wins, 2-1, on Tim Keefe's three-hitter. The losing pitcher is Charles "Silver" King, who yields only two hits.

OCTOBER 17:

Championship Series, game two. St. Louis wins behind pitcher Elton "Icebox" Chamberlain's five-hitter, 3-0. The loser, Mickey Welch, also allows only five hits.

OCTOBER 18:

Championship Series, game three. A Polo Grounds crowd of 5,850 fans sees the Giants triumph, 4-2. Tim Keefe strikes out 11 and allows five hits. Silver King, the loser, now has pitched 16 innings, allowed seven hits, and has two losses.

OCTOBER 19:

Championship Series, game four. In freezing drizzle, the Giants beat the Browns, 6-3, before 3,062 hardy fans at Brooklyn's Washington Park. Edward "Cannonball" Crane strikes out eight and gets the win. Icebox Chamberlain is the losing pitcher.

OCTOBER 20:

Championship Series, game five. The weather is sunny and clear and 9,124 turn up at the Polo Grounds to root the Giants to a 6-4, eight-inning win. Tim Keefe gets the victory and is 3-0 in the series. Silver King is charged with his third loss.

OCTOBER 22:

Championship Series, game six. Today in Philadelphia, the

Cincinnati Red Stockings fans followed the game with a scorecard.

Giants win, 12-5, in eight. Mickey Welch allows three hits and fans seven. Buck Ewing and Monte Ward have three RBI each. The loser is Icebox Chamberlain.

OCTOBER 23:

Controversy follows Chris Von Der Ahe home. Charges that umpires John Kelly and John Gaffney had wagered on the Giants are attributed to the Browns' owner and reported by the Associated Press. Both umpires threaten to sit out the rest of the Series. Von Der Ahe claims he was misquoted and affirms the honesty of the umpires.

OCTOBER 24:

Championship Series, game seven. The Browns, behind Silver King, win, 7-5, at home in another eight-inning game ended by darkness. Cannonball Crane is the losing pitcher.

OCTOBER 25:

Championship Series, game eight. The Giants win, 11-3, in Sportsman's Park and take the series. Tim Keefe is the winner with a five-hitter. In 35 innings, he compiles an ERA of 0.51. Icebox Chamberlain is the loser. The three remaining games will be exhibitions, and four Giants will miss them. Monte Ward and Cannonball Crane leave for Australia on a world baseball tour; Willard Brown and Buck Ewing go home.

OCTOBER 26:

Championship Series game nine. Only 711 fans turn up today at Sportsman's Park for a game that does not count. The Browns win, 14-11, on James "Tip" O'Neill's three-run homer in the 10th. Jim Devlin is the winner; Bill George is credited with the loss.

OCTOBER 27:

Championship Series, game 10. Today's game is played in St. Louis for the benefit of the players, but only 400 fans show. The Browns win, 18-7, with home runs from Tommy McCarthy and Tip O'Neill. The winning pitcher is Icebox Chamberlain.

OCTOBER 28:

Championship Series, game eleven. The Browns and Silver King win, 6-0, at Sportsman's Park with 3,000 attending another players' benefit contest.

The Giants earn $200 each – the winner's share – plus $28 from the first benefit and another $100 from the second. Von Der Ahe calling his team "chumps," once again gives his players nothing, keeping $1,200 for winning the pennant and the proceeds from the benefit games. The Browns now have played 27 post-season games over two seasons and received no money in return. Giants' manager Jim Mutrie nixes future extended Series: "If I ever engage in another World Series, the ball will stop rolling just as soon as the series is decided."

POST-SEASON

NOVEMBER 21-22:

NL owners meet in New York City and approve a graded system for paying ball players.

DECEMBER 25:

In the first known indoor baseball game ever played, the Downtowners beat the Uptowners, 6-1, before a crowd of 2,000 fans in the main building of the Philadelphia State Fairgrounds. Six major league players participate in the historic contest.

CULTURE

John Montgomery Ward's *Baseball: How to Become a Player* is published.

CULTURE

***Angela, or the Umpire's Revenge*, a musical by John Philip Sousa, features songs such as "The Umpire and the Dude" and "He Stands in the Box with the Ball in His Hands."**

TRIVIA

The 1888 Giants field six future Hall of Famers: first baseman Roger Connor, shortstop John Montgomery Ward, outfielder Orator Jim O'Rourke, catcher William "Buck" Ewing, pitcher Tim Keefe, and pitcher Michael "Smiling Mickey" Welch. The Browns have only manager-first baseman Charles Comiskey and outfielder Tommy McCarthy.

THE BEST OF 1888

NATIONAL LEAGUE

HITTERS

Batting Average:
Adrian "Cap" Anson, Chicago White Stockings, .344

Slugging Average:
Jimmy Ryan, Chicago White Stockings, .515

Home Runs:
Jimmy Ryan, 16

Runs Batted In:
Adrian Anson, 84

Hits:
Jimmy Ryan, 182

Stolen Bases:
William "Dummy" Hoy, Washington Statesmen, 82

PITCHERS

Wins:
Tim Keefe, New York Giants, 35

Strikeouts:
Tim Keefe, 333

Earned Run Average:
Tim Keefe, 1.74

Winning Percentage:
Tim Keefe, .745

Saves:
George Wood, Philadelphia Quakers, 2

AMERICAN ASSOCIATION

HITTERS

Batting Average:
James "Tip" O'Neill, St. Louis Browns, .335

Slugging Average:
Long John Reilly, Cincinnati Red Stockings, .501

Home Runs:
John Reilly, 13

Runs Batted In:
John Reilly, 103

Hits:
James O'Neill, 177

Stolen Bases:
Walter "Arlie" Latham, St. Louis Browns, 109

PITCHERS

Wins:
Charles "Silver" King, St. Louis Browns, 45

Strikeouts:
Ed Seward, Philadelphia Athletics, 272

Earned Run Average:
Charles King, 1.64

Winning Percentage:
Nat Hudson, St. Louis Browns, .714

Saves:
John "Pop" Corkhill, Cincinnati Red Stockings, Brooklyn Trolley-Dodgers; Bob Gilks, Cleveland Blues; Tony Mullane, Cincinnati Red Stockings, 1

1889

MAY 2
Controversial Browns' owner Chris Von Der Ahe feuds with player "Yank" Robinson.

NEWS

U.S. DECLARES OKLAHOMA OPEN TO WHITE SETTLEMENT; WITHIN 24 HOURS, CLAIMS ARE STAKED BY 50,000 SETTLERS FOR 2 MILLION ACRES

2,200 PEOPLE DIE IN JOHNSTOWN, PENNSYLVANIA, FLOOD

SOUTH DAKOTA, NORTH DAKOTA, WASHINGTON, AND MONTANA BECOME STATES

Herman Hollerith patents first data-processing computer

Gustave Eiffel builds Eiffel Tower

VAN GOGH FINISHES *THE STARRY NIGHT*

The *Wall Street Journal* begins publication

BARNARD COLLEGE OPENS

PRE-SEASON

FEBRUARY:

New York City officials announce their plans to raze the Polo Grounds, home of baseball's Giants.

THE SEASON

MAY 2:

Browns' owner Chris Von Der Ahe, who draws controversy like some players draw walks, is in the center of another one. This time he targets second baseman William "Yank" Robinson, whose dirty flannel uniform offends his boss. Robinson sends the clubhouse boy to his hotel for a fresh set. But the ticket taker refuses to let the youngster back into the ballpark and is cursed by Robinson. Von Der Ahe fines Robinson $25 for his actions and the brouhaha between the two is on. Robinson leaves the park, Von Der Ahe threatens him with suspension and blacklisting, and the Browns refuse to board a train for Kansas City for the next game. Finally, manager Charles Comiskey convinces the owner to bring back Robinson.

"LOVING THE SPOTLIGHT, (CHRIS VON DER AHE) INSISTED ON PERSONALLY LEADING HIS TEAM TO THE RAILROAD DEPOT EVERY TIME THEY LEFT TOWN..."

– *FROM* BASEBALL: AN ILLUSTRATED HISTORY

RULES

Four balls now constitute a walk; previously it took five.

TRIVIA

Albert Spalding acquires the Reach sporting goods company.

JUNE 19
Dummy Hoy is the first outfielder to throw out three runners at the plate in a game.

CULTURE

Boston's Mike "King" Kelly is the subject of a song, "Slide, Kelly, Slide," recorded by Maggie Cline. According to Michael Gershman, it becomes the first nationally popular baseball song. At the ballpark, fans serenade Kelly with the song. The lyrics include:
"Your running's
a disgrace
Stay there, hold
your base!
If someone doesn't
steal you,
and your batting
doesn't fail you,
They'll take you to
Australia:
Slide, Kelly, slide!"

The wooden grandstand at Washington Park burns, which leaves the Brooklyn Bridegrooms without a home field until Decoration Day. The damage is estimated at $18,000.

JUNE 19:

Washington's William Hoy is the first outfielder to throw three runners out at the plate in a single game.

Hoy was left deaf and mute from meningitis at the age of three. He played in the majors for 14 years, hitting .288 with 40 home runs and 726 RBI, and in 1901 became the first to hit two grand slam homers in a single game. From the baseball mythology department, Hoy claimed to have caught a fly ball in the minor leagues in 1886 while riding a horse.

The Boston Beaneaters' Mike "King" Kelly was pictured on an early version of a baseball card.

JUNE 22:

The Louisville Colonels of the AA set a major league record with their 26th consecutive loss.

JULY 8:

After playing 25 ball games on Staten Island, the Giants are back in Manhattan at the new 15,000-seat Polo Grounds located at 155th Street and Eighth Avenue. A crowd of 9,000 fans greets the Giants, who respond with a 7-5 win over the visiting Alleghenys.

JULY 13:

Stan Coveleski is born Stanley Anthony Kowalewski in Shamokin, Pennsylvania.

JULY 14:

The chapters of the Brotherhood of Professional Baseball Players assemble for a meeting today in New York City. During the procedings, John Montgomery Ward of the New York Giants announces that ball players will form their own baseball league, although it will be in partnership with franchise owners. The representatives are instructed to begin raising money in order to fund their new league.

JULY 16:

Joseph Jefferson "Shoeless Joe" Jackson is born in Pickens County, South Carolina.

JULY 28:

Wilber "Bullet" Rogan is born in Oklahoma City, Oklahoma.

SEPTEMBER 6:

The Browns come to Brooklyn for a key three-game AA series with the Trolley-Dodgers. A crowd of 16,974 gathers for a 4 P.M. start. The Browns lead, 4-2, in the ninth, when umpire Fred Goldsmith rejects the claim of St. Louis manager Charles Comiskey that it is too dark to play. Comiskey pulls his team from the field and Brooklyn is awarded a forfeit win. St. Louis owner Chris Von Der Ahe alleges that all close calls go to Brooklyn because the crowd is really a mob, there are not enough police, and the umpires are intimidated. He vows his team will play no more games in Brooklyn.

SEPTEMBER 7:

While a crowd estimated between 15,000 and 20,000 waits at Ridgewood

OCTOBER 18
New York's Giants and Trolley-Dodgers square off in game one of the World Series.

Park, Chris Von Der Ahe, Comiskey, and the Browns remain in their hotel. Umpire Fred Goldsmith awards another forfeit to Brooklyn.

SEPTEMBER 8:

Today's scheduled ball game between the Browns and the Trolley-Dodgers is not played.

SEPTEMBER 17:

The Philadelphia Athletics' owner, H.C. Pennypacker disbands his team and releases his players, including 30-game winner Gus Weyhing. The AA takes over the franchise.

SEPTEMBER 23:

AA owners meet and consider the controversy between the Browns and the Trolley-Dodgers. They reverse the forfeit of September 6, awarding St. Louis a victory; uphold the forfeit of September 7, awarding Brooklyn a victory; take no action on the unplayed game of September 8; and fire umpire Fred Goldsmith.

OCTOBER 5:

The Giants beat Cleveland while fifth-place Pittsburgh tops Boston and 49-game winner John Clarkson, giving New York the NL pennant. It is the first flag ever decided on the final day of the season.

OCTOBER 9:

Richard "Rube" Marquard is born in Cleveland.

There are questions about Marquard's actual birth year. Some sources cite 1887. Fred Schuld of the Society for Baseball Research unearthed a birth certificate for a male Marquard born on October 9, 1886. Larry D. Mansch writes in the 1996 National Pastime*: "It is remotely possible that this child was an older brother who did not live long. Given that the birthdate is exactly the same as Rube's, however, and since there is never again a mention of an older brother, that seems unlikely. The logical conclusion is that the 1886 birthday is Rube's, and Rube was three years older than he always claimed."*

OCTOBER 11:

John Montgomery Ward meets with Giants' owner John Day and informs him that the players have financing for eight franchises and have planned to launch the Brotherhood League for the 1890 season.

OCTOBER 14:

Brooklyn wins the AA pennant by beating Columbus, 6-1, while Cincinnati is beating St. Louis, 8-3. Brooklyn's Adonis Bill Terry pitches a five-hitter for his 22nd win and smacks a triple and single.

OCTOBER 18:

World Series, game one. Today at New York's Polo Grounds, Brooklyn manager Bill "Gunner" McGunnigle leads his Trolley-Dodgers against Jim Mutrie's New York Giants. With 8,848 attending (they pay 50 cents for regular admission and a quarter for the grandstand), Brooklyn wins, 12-10. Danny Richardson homers for the Giants, Hub Collins for Brooklyn. With darkness falling and Brooklyn batting last in the eighth, fans wander onto the field of play. Umpire Bob Ferguson calls the game at the end of the inning; if he had taken such action earlier, the score would have reverted to 10-8 with the Giants winning. New York protests to no avail. Adonis Terry gets the victory and Tim Keefe is the losing pitcher.

This is the first meeting between the Giants and Trolley-Dodgers in what will become one of the most enduring and hottest rivalries in all of baseball.

OCTOBER 19:

World Series, game two. In Brooklyn, with a crowd of 16,172 on hand, the Giants get a win over the Trolley-Dodgers, 6-2. Ed "Cannonball" Crane gets the win; Bob Caruthers is the game's losing pitcher.

OCTOBER 22:

World Series, game three. Back at the Polo Grounds after an off-day and a rainout, the Trolley-Dodgers win, 8-7, in another game called after eight. Once again there is controversy as Brooklyn stalls to keep the game from going into the ninth. Mickey Hughes is the winning pitcher; Mickey Welch takes the loss. John "Pop" Corkhill homers for Brooklyn; Orator Jim O'Rourke hits a three-run shot for New York. The Giants' manager, Jim Mutrie, complains about the stalling tactics: "The Brooklyns played like schoolboys. I would rather lose a game than win as they did this afternoon."

LEAGUE

While the White Stockings and all-star teams are on their world tour, Indianapolis president John T. Brush wins approval of a salary classification plan. Players are rated – based on personal habits – from A to E, and salaries are fixed from $1,500 to $2,500. The owners refuse to meet with players to discuss the "Brush Plan." A Class A player will receive $2,500. A Class E player will receive $1,500 and is expected to do chores, like sweeping up. Boston owner Arthur Soden intends to use his players at the turnstiles. Monte Ward, president of the Brotherhood of Professional Baseball Players, helps to avert a players' strike, but the seeds of the Players League are planted.

> "Players have been bought, sold, or exchanged as though they were sheep, instead of American citizens."
> – *Monte Ward*

TRIVIA

Brooklyn has two nicknames: Trolley-Dodgers and Bridegrooms, the latter because several players are married but supposedly abstain from sex.

OCTOBER 23:

World Series, game four. In sub-40-degree weather and heavy winds in Brooklyn, the Trolley-Dodgers win, 10-7, in six innings. At one point, the Giants threaten to leave the field in protest of calls by umpires Tom Lynch and John Gaffney. Thomas "Oyster" Burns hits a home run for the Trolley-Dodgers when left-fielder Jim O'Rourke heads for the clubhouse in the darkness and a ground ball becomes a home run. With the ball impossible to see, Brooklyn scores three in the sixth. Adonis Terry gets the win. Cannonball Crane is tagged with the game's loss.

Giants' owner John B. Day warns Brooklyn owner Charles H. Byrne: "The games will begin at 2:30 o'clock hereafter or my team will not play." He also protests the umpiring and the intentional delays. He tells Byrne: "This kind of ballplaying and umpiring is enough to kill the game... I will not allow my team to compete against a club that insists on playing dirty ball." Byrne agrees to an earlier starting time.

OCTOBER 24:

World Series, game five. The Giants win, 11-3, at Washington Park today behind Cannonball Crane, who fans seven. The big bats for the Giants are Danny Richardson with an inside-the-park homer and pitcher Crane with a two-run homer. Willard Brown also has an inside-the-park round-tripper. Bob Caruthers is the game's losing pitcher.

OCTOBER 25:

World Series, game six: At the Polo Grounds, the Giants beat the Trolley-Dodgers, 2-1, in 11. Hank O'Day gets the win; Adonis Bill Terry is the loser.

OCTOBER 26:

World Series, game seven. New York tops visiting Brooklyn, 11-7. Orator Jim O'Rourke and Danny Richardson homer for the Giants. George "Germany" Smith loses a grand slam for Brooklyn. He hits a drive into the left-field seats and, as he trots around the bases, O'Rourke jumps the fence, retrieves the ball, and fires it home, and Smith is tagged out. The winner is Cannonball Crane; the loser, Tom Lovett.

OCTOBER 28:

World Series, game eight. The Giants decline Brooklyn's offer to postpone the game because of a muddy field and win, 16-7. Cannonball Crane gets the victory despite homers by the Trolley-Dodgers' Dave Foutz (a pop fly that goes for four bases when Mike Slattery slips in the outfield) and Oyster Burns. Adonis Bill Terry is the losing pitcher.

OCTOBER 29:

World Series, game nine. Before 3,057 at the Polo Grounds, the Giants win their first World Championship with a 3-2 win. Hank O'Day gets the win; Adonis Bill Terry again is the loser. The Giants score the winning run in the seventh when Mike Slattery scores from second base on a third strike to Buck Ewing that goes over the head of Brooklyn catcher Doc Bushong. Jim Mutrie and the fans chant, "We are the people!"

POST-SEASON

NOVEMBER 7:

John Montgomery Ward organizes a meeting to discuss the formation of the Players League.

NOVEMBER 14:

Cincinnati and Brooklyn leave the AA and join the NL.

DECEMBER 16:

The Players League is organized by John Montgomery Ward. It consists of the Boston Reds, Brooklyn Wonders, Buffalo Bisons, Chicago Pirates, Cleveland Infants, New York Giants, Philadelphia Quakers, and Pittsburgh Burghers. There will be three-year contracts at 1888 salarys, with guaranteed money the first year and no subsequent cuts. The reserve rule is out. Rules include a pitching distance of 51 feet (compared to 45 feet in the NL and AA) and the use of two umpires, dressed in white, per game. One investor is a catcher named Cornelius McGillicuddy (Connie Mack), who lays out $500. Owners and players will share profits. The Players League manifesto states: "By a combination among themselves, stronger than the strongest trust, the owners were able to enforce the most arbitrary measures, and the players had either to submit or get out of the profession in which he had spent years attaining proficiency."

OCTOBER 29
The New York Giants win their first World Championship, beating the Trolley-Dodgers.

DECEMBER 16
John Montgomery Ward officially organizes the eight-team Players League.

THE BEST OF 1889

NATIONAL LEAGUE

HITTERS

Batting Average:
Dennis "Big Dan" Brouthers, Boston Beaneaters, .373

Slugging Average:
Roger Connor, New York Giants, .528

Home Runs:
Sam Thompson, Philadelphia Quakers, 20

Runs Batted In:
Roger Connor, 130

Hits:
Jack Glasscock, Indianapolis Hoosiers, 205

Stolen Bases:
Jim Fogarty, Philadelphia Quakers, 99

PITCHERS

Wins:
John Clarkson, Boston Beaneaters, 49

Strikeouts:
John Clarkson, 284

Earned Run Average:
John Clarkson, 2.73

Winning Percentage:
John Clarkson, .721

Saves:
Bill Sowders Boston Beaneaters/ Pittsburgh Alleghenys, 3

AMERICAN ASSOCIATION

HITTERS

Batting Average:
Tommy Tucker, Baltimore Orioles, .372

Slugging Average:
Harry Stovey, Philadelphia Athletics, .525

Home Runs:
Stovey; James "Bug" Holliday, Cincinnati Red Stockings, 19

Runs Batted In:
Harry Stovey, 119

Hits:
Tommy Tucker, 196

Stolen Bases:
Billy Hamilton, Kansas City Cowboys, 111

PITCHERS

Wins:
Bob Caruthers, Brooklyn Bridegrooms, 40

Strikeouts:
Mark "Fido" Baldwin, Columbus Buckeyes, 368

Earned Run Average:
Jack Stivetts, St. Louis Browns, 2.25

Winning Percentage:
Bob Caruthers, .784

Saves:
Tony Mullane, Cincinnati Red Stockings, 5

1890

NEWS

MASSACRE OF NATIVE AMERICANS BY THE U.S. ARMY AT WOUNDED KNEE, SOUTH DAKOTA

SHERMAN ANTI-TRUST ACT BEGINS THE FEDERAL EFFORT TO CURB BUSINESS MONOPOLIES

William II becomes Kaiser of Germany, forces Bismarck to resign

FIRST MOVING-PICTURE SHOWS APPEAR IN NEW YORK CITY

GLOBAL INFLUENZA EPIDEMIC

Idaho and Wyoming become states

MISSISSIPPI IMPEDES BLACK VOTE WITH POLL TAX AND LITERACY TESTS

EMILY DICKINSON'S FIRST VOLUME OF POETRY IS POSTHUMOUSLY PUBLISHED

JACOB RIIS WRITES *HOW THE OTHER HALF LIVES*

PRE-SEASON

JANUARY 11:

Max Carey is born Maximilian Carnarius in Terre Haute, Indiana.

The Players League makes an offer to Giants' owner John B. Day: $25,000 and 50 percent of its New York franchise to serve as league president. With five teams in New York, Day threatens to sell his team. But Albert Spalding convinces NL owners to step in. John Brush forgives a debt of $25,000 for the sale of some Indianapolis players to the Giants. Spalding and Arthur Soden lend Day $25,000 each, and Philadelphia's Alfred J. Reach and Brooklyn Bridegrooms shareholder Ferdinand A. Abell float $6,250 apiece. Day declines the offer. According to baseball historian Lee Allen, "Had he joined, he might have put the National League out of business."

In March, the Giants get a boost in their struggle with the Players League franchise in New York with the acquisition from Indianapolis of Amos Rusie, Jesse Burkett, Handsome Henry Boyle, Dick Buckley, Joseph "Pete" Sommers, Jack Glasscock, Jerry Denny, Charles Bassett, and Mort Scanlon. Boyle never plays major league baseball again.

FEBRUARY 3:

Larry MacPhail is born in Cass City, Michigan.

FEBRUARY 20:

Edgar "Sam" Rice is born in Morocco, Indiana.

THE SEASON

APRIL 19:

The Players League begins its season with all eight teams in action. On opposite ends of Coogan's Hollow, the NL's "real" Giants lose to the Philadelphia Phillies, 4-0, with William "Kid" Gleason outpitching 18-year-old Amos Rusie. The Players League Giants also lose to Philadelphia–the Quakers – 12-11, with Tim Keefe pitching for New York. In another Players League inaugural today, the Buffalo Bisons record the greatest opening day winning margin with a 23-2 victory over the Cleveland Infants.

Fifty-five percent of NL players (12 from the New York Giants) and 17 percent of AA players jump to the eight teams in the Players League. On the rosters of the new league are 14 future Hall of Fame players: Jake Beckley, Dan Brouthers, Charles Comiskey, Roger Connor, Ed Delahanty, Hugh Duffy, Buck Ewing, Pud Galvin, Tim Keefe, Mike "King" Kelly, Connie Mack, Orator Jim O'Rourke, Charles "Old Hoss" Radbourn, and John Montgomery Ward.

MAY 3:

Brooklyn and New York meet as NL rivals for the first time. Before 3,774 fans at Washington Park, the Bridegrooms prevail, 7-3. The winning pitcher is Bob Caruthers.

MAY 8:

Wee Willie McGill starts today for the Cleveland Infants against the Buffalo Bisons in a Players League game. McGill, a virtual infant himself at only 16 years and six months old, yields seven hits, walks seven, strikes out 10, and singles in a 14-5 complete-game victory.

SEPTEMBER 1
Brooklyn sweeps a rare tripleheader against the visiting Pittsburgh Alleghenys.

McGill is 11-9, with a 4.12 ERA, in 1890. In seven years in the AA and NL, he compiles an overall record of 71-74 with a 4.59 ERA. His career ends in 1896 at age 22.

MAY 12:

The New York Giants' Mike Tiernan hits a 13th-inning homer to beat Charles "Kid" Nichols and the Boston Beaneaters, 1-0. The ball travels over the center-field fence of the Polo Grounds into the adjacent Brotherhood Park, and Tiernan is cheered in both parks. Winning pitcher Amos Rusie allows four hits and one walk, and fans 10. Nichols yields three hits and two walks, and strikes out 13. *The New York Times* calls it "the finest contest ever played between two professional teams and will go down on record as such."

JULY 21:

Charles "Silver" King of the Brooklyn Wonders pitches the only no-hitter in the Players League but loses, 1-0, in eight. The Chicago Pirates score on errors in the seventh.

JULY 30:

Charles Dillon "Casey" Stengel is born in Kansas City, Missouri.

AUGUST 16:

In an NL game, Chicago third baseman Tom Burns and catcher Malachi Kittredge hit grand slams in the fifth inning against Pittsburgh's Bill Phillips. The Colts push 13 runs across in the frame and go on to win the game, 18-5. Phillips becomes the only pitcher to yield two grand slam homers in an inning.

SEPTEMBER 1:

Brooklyn and Pittsburgh work overtime on Labor Day. In the first tripleheader ever – one game in the morning and two in the afternoon – the Bridegrooms beat the visiting Alleghenys, 10-9, 3-2, and 8-4, at Washington Park. The trio of winning Brooklyn pitchers are Bob Caruthers, Tom Lovett, and Adonis Terry.

SEPTEMBER 15:

In an American Association game today, the Rochester Bronco's Ledell "Cannonball" Titcomb no-hits the visiting Syracuse Stars, 7-0. Charles "Count" Campau of the Browns leads the AA in home runs with 10 on the year.

OCTOBER 3:

In a game called because of darkness after seven, Chicago's John "Pat" Luby beats the Giants, 3-2, for his 17th consecutive win. Amos Rusie is the losing pitcher.

OCTOBER 9:

The NL meets in New York City. Before the meeting, discussions take place between Albert Spalding of the NL and representatives of the Players League. Among them are Albert Johnson, Wendell Goodwin, and E.B. Talcott. With the National League owners smelling victory, a formal meeting is scheduled for October 22.

With the better teams and the better performers in the Players League, there is little interest in the upcoming World Series. The Philadelphia Evening Bulletin *notes: "There is scarcely enough interest in the Series to induce the people to read the scores."*

Giants' pitcher Amos Rusie led the NL with 345 strikeouts in 1890.

RULES

A sacrifice fly is not a charged time at bat. A batter can be called out for deliberately fouling off pitches.

OCTOBER 17
The Brooklyn Bridegrooms and Louisville Cyclones open the World Series.

OCTOBER 28
After seven games, the Series – at 3-3-1 – is canceled due to winter weather.

LEAGUE

After a cyclone devastates Louisville, the NL team changes its name from the Colonels to the Cyclones.

LEAGUE

The Brooklyn Bridegrooms and Cincinnati Reds switch from the AA to the NL, which also drops the Washington Senators. In the AA, Kansas City folds; the Rochester Hop Bitters, Syracuse Stars, Toledo Maumees, and Brooklyn Gladiators are added. Brooklyn moves to Baltimore during the season. The Players League will have franchises in Boston, Brooklyn, Buffalo, Chicago, Cleveland, New York, Philadelphia, and Pittsburgh.

OCTOBER 17:

World Series, game one. The Brooklyn Bridegrooms, who won the AA pennant last year, are the NL's champion in 1890 and the first team to win consecutive pennants in two different leagues. After a postponement because of rain, Brooklyn meets the AA pennant-winning Louisville Cyclones in Kentucky. An over-capacity crowd of 5,563 sees the Bridegrooms win, 9-0, in a game that's ended after eight because of darkness. The winner is Adonis Bill Terry, who allows only two hits. Scott Stratton is charged with the loss.

OCTOBER 18:

World Series, game two. Louisville loses to visiting Brooklyn, 5-3. Winner Tom Lovett allows six hits and strikes out seven. Ed Daily is the loser.

OCTOBER 20:

World Series, game three. In freezing, 30-degree weather, a small turnout of 1,253 sees a 7-7 tie, called after eight because of darkness.

OCTOBER 21:

World Series, game four. In poor weather, Louisville and Phillip "Red" Ehret win, 5-4. Tom Lovett is the losing pitcher.

OCTOBER 25:

World Series, game five. After an open day and two straight rainouts, the Bridegrooms win today, 7-2, in Brooklyn. Tom Lovett gets the win; Ed Daily is the loser. Thomas "Oyster" Burns hits a two-run homer in the first inning for Brooklyn.

> THE NEW YORK DAILY TRIBUNE DESCRIBES BROOKLYN'S WASHINGTON PARK FIELD AS "FULL OF MALARIA, MUD, AND WATER."

OCTOBER 27:

World Series, game six. After a Sunday hiatus, Louisville wins, 9-8, behind Scott Stratton in Brooklyn. Adonis Bill Terry is the loser. Louisville's Ed Daily gets the first-ever series fine – $25 for "ungentlemanly talk" to umpire Wesley Curry.

OCTOBER 28:

World Series, game seven. Louisville overcomes six errors to beat the Bridegrooms, 6-2. Red Ehret pitches a four-hitter; the loser is Tom Lovett. The Series stands at 3-3-1, and the remaining games are canceled because of impending winter weather.

Before the seventh game, Brooklyn manager Bill "Gunner" McGunnigle and Louisville skipper Jack Chapman agree to resolve the championship in the spring. Because of conflict between the two leagues, it never happens and the title remains undecided.

POST-SEASON

OCTOBER:

It is becoming quite apparent that the end is near for the beleaguered Players League. Allan W. Thurman, a director of the American Association's Columbus franchise, comes forward to offer a peace plan that he contends will transform major league baseball into two eight-team leagues; the teams will all be placed in large cities. Two Players League officials – Wendell Goodwin of the Brooklyn Wonders and Eddie Talcott of the New York Giants – counter Thurman's proposal by offering to merge their teams with the competing National League in New York, the Giants and Bridegrooms, respectively. Unaware of the National League's problems and considering that its own money is drying up, the Players League proposes a plan for a truce. Albert Spalding, Chicago president and chairman of the NL's "war committee," emulates Ulysses S. Grant and demands unconditional surrender.

After the Players League finally collapses in December, ballplayers return to their original teams. The Pittsburgh franchise, however, deviates from the others by signing second baseman Louis Bierbauer, who had originally belonged to the Philadelphia Phillies and played for the Brooklyn Wonders in the Players League in 1890. Pittsburgh is accused of "pirating." They keep both Bierbauer and the nickname.

THE BEST OF 1890

NATIONAL LEAGUE

HITTERS

Batting Average:
Jack Glasscock, New York Giants, .336

Slugging Average:
Mike Tiernan, New York Giants, .495

Home Runs:
Walt Wilmot, Chicago Colts, 14

Runs Batted In:
Thomas "Oyster" Burns, Brooklyn Bridegrooms, 128

Hits:
Jack Glasscock; Sam Thompson, Philadelphia Phillies, 172

Stolen Bases:
Billy Hamilton, Philadelphia Phillies, 102

PITCHERS

Wins:
Bill Hutchinson, Chicago Colts, 42

Strikeouts:
Amos Rusie, New York Giants, 341

Earned Run Average:
Billy Rhines, Cincinnati Reds, 1.95

Winning Percentage:
Tom Lovett, Brooklyn Bridegrooms, .732

Saves:
Dave Foutz, Brooklyn Bridegrooms; William "Kid" Gleason, Philadelphia Phillies; Bill Hutchinson, 2

AMERICAN ASSOCIATION

HITTERS

Batting Average:
William "Chicken" Wolf, Louisville Colonels, .363

Slugging Average:
Denny Lyons, Philadelphia Athletics, .531

Home Runs:
Charles "Count" Campau, St. Louis Browns, 10

Hits:
William Wolf, 197

Stolen Bases:
Tommy McCarthy, St. Louis Browns, 83

PITCHERS

Wins:
John "Sadie" McMahon, Philadelphia Phillies/Baltimore Orioles, 36

Strikeouts:
John McMahon, 291
Earned Run Average: Scott Stratton, Louisville Colonels, 2.36

Winning Percentage:
Scott Stratton, .708

Saves:
Herb Goodall, Louisville Colonels, 4

PLAYERS LEAGUE

HITTERS

Batting Average:
Louis "Pete" Browning, Cleveland Infants; Dave Orr, Brooklyn Wonders, .373

Slugging Average:
Roger Connor, New York Giants, .548

Home Runs:
Roger Connor, 13

Runs Batted In:
Abram "Hardy" Richardson, Boston Reds, 146

Hits:
Hugh Duffy, Chicago Pirates, 191

Stolen Bases:
Harry Stovey, Boston Reds, 97

PITCHERS

Wins:
Mark "Fido" Baldwin, Chicago Pirates, 34

Strikeouts:
Mark Baldwin, 211

Earned Run Average:
Charles "Silver" King, 2.69

Winning Percentage:
Bill Daley, Boston Reds, .720

Saves:
Hank O'Day, New York Giants; George "Old Wax Finger" Hemming, Cleveland Infants/Brooklyn Wonders, 3

HISTORY

Boston, with players like Dan Brouthers, Mike "King" Kelly, and Charles "Old Hoss" Radbourn on its roster, wins the Players League pennant by six and a half games over Brooklyn. John Montgomery Ward of the Players League offers an olive branch – or is it a white flag? He invites NL owners to discuss peace between the rival circuits. Players League attendance actually tops that of the NL. According to authors Lee Lowenfish and Tony Lupien, "One estimate said it was 913,000 to 850,000 in the final count."

1891

JULY 31
Giants' pitcher Amos Rusie, 20, becomes the youngest to toss a no-hitter.

NEWS

JAMES NAISMITH INVENTS BASKETBALL IN CANADA

FIRST WOMEN'S CHRISTIAN TEMPERANCE UNION MEETING HELD

Carnegie Hall opens in New York with Peter Illich Tchaikovsky as guest conductor

Thomas Edison patents the motion picture camera

THOMAS HARDY'S *TESS OF THE D'UBERVILLES* AND OSCAR WILDE'S *THE PICTURE OF DORIAN GRAY* ARE PUBLISHED

UNIVERSITY OF CHICAGO FOUNDED

GOLD RUSH ON PIKE'S PEAK

First full-service ad agency in U.S. opens in New York City

PRE-SEASON

MARCH:

Players begin returning to their original teams after the collapse of the Players League.

Albert Spalding retires as president of the Chicago White Stockings; he is replaced by James A. Hart, former manager of Louisville and Milwaukee.

MARCH 4:

Clarence "Dazzy" Vance is born in Orient, Iowa.

APRIL 20:

Dave Bancroft is born in Sioux City, Iowa.

THE SEASON

APRIL 22:

In the first game at the third Polo Grounds, Boston beats the New York Giants, 4-3.

MAY 1:

Cleveland's League Park opens with 10,000 fans on hand to see pitcher Denton "Cy" Young beat Cincinnati, 12-3.

MAY 3:

Eppa Rixey is born in Culpeper, Virginia.

JUNE 22:

Brooklyn's Tom Lovett no-hits the Giants, 4-0. He walks three batters and fans four. Amos Rusie is the losing pitcher.

JULY 31:

The Giants' Amos Rusie throws a no-hitter against the Bridegrooms, winning 6-0, with eight walks and four strikeouts. At 20 years and two months old, Rusie is the youngest to throw a no-hitter and the first to toss one against Brooklyn. Adonis Bill Terry is the losing pitcher.

AUGUST 26:

John J. McGraw debuts with the Baltimore Orioles in the AA. He plays shortstop, makes an error, and has a hit as the Orioles defeat the Columbus Buckeyes, 6-5.

SEPTEMBER 4:

Responding to writers who claim it's time for him to quit, Chicago's 39-year-old player-manager Cap Anson wears a false white beard against Boston. It doesn't help him at the plate – he is hitless in three at-bats. The White Stockings beat Boston, 5-3.

OCTOBER 4:

In his first start, Ted Breitenstein of the Browns (AA) no-hits Louisville, 8-0. He is the first to debut with a no-hitter.

REGULAR SEASON WRAP-UP:

Boston's Beaneaters, win the NL pennant, its Reds take the AA flag. But the Beaneaters decline a playoff, so for the first time since 1883, baseball has no Championships.

POST-SEASON

OCTOBER 14:

Larry Corcoran, who pitched three no-hitters and won 177 games, dies at age 32 in Newark, New Jersey. In his first five seasons with the Chicago White Stockings, Corcoran won 43, 31, 27, 34, and 35 games. His career ERA was 2.36.

NOVEMBER 11:

Walter "Rabbit" Maranville is born in Springfield, Massachusetts.

DECEMBER 17:

The AA folds. The Baltimore Orioles, St. Louis Browns, Louisville Colonels, and Washington Senators will be absorbed into the NL.

THE BEST OF 1891

NATIONAL LEAGUE

HITTERS

Batting Average:
Billy Hamilton, Philadelphia Phillies, .340

Slugging Average:
Harry Stovey, Boston Beaneaters, .498

Home Runs:
Harry Stovey; Mike Tiernan, New York Giants, 16

Runs Batted In:
Adrian "Cap" Anson, Chicago White Stockings, 120

Hits:
Billy Hamilton, 179

Stolen Bases:
Billy Hamilton, 111

PITCHERS

Wins:
Bill Hutchinson, Chicago Colts, 44

Strikeouts:
Amos Rusie, New York Giants, 337

Earned Run Average:
John Ewing, New York Giants, 2.27

Winning Percentage:
John Ewing, .724

Saves:
John Clarkson, Charles "Kid" Nichols, Boston Beaneaters, 3

AMERICAN ASSOCIATION

HITTERS

Batting Average:
Dennis "Big Dan" Brouthers, Boston Reds, .350

Slugging Average:
Dennis Brouthers, .512

Home Runs:
Charles "Duke" Farrell, Boston Reds, 12

Runs Batted In:
Charles Farrell, 110

Hits:
Tom Brown, Boston Reds, 189

Stolen Bases:
Tom Brown, 106

PITCHERS

Wins:
John "Sadie" McMahon, Baltimore Orioles, 35

Strikeouts:
Jack Stivetts, St. Louis Browns, 259

Earned Run Average:
Edward "Cannonball" Crane, Cincinnati Kellys, 2.45

Winning Percentage:
Charlie Buffinton, Boston Reds, .763

Saves:
Joe Neale, St. Louis Browns, 3

RULES

Substitutions may be made at any point in a game.

CULTURE

According to authors Leigh W. Rutledge and Richard Donley, the term "southpaw" for left-handed pitchers was introduced by sportswriter Charles Seymour. They wrote: "Because of the way some old ballparks were situated, pitchers faced West: thus, a left-handed pitcher's pitching arm was to the South."

1892

OCTOBER 15
Cincinnati pitcher Bumpus Jones throws a no-hitter in his major league debut.

NEWS

VIOLENT STRIKE AT CARNEGIE STEEL MILLS IN PENNSYLVANIA

SUNDAY SCHOOL TEACHER LIZZIE BORDEN ARRESTED IN MASSACHUSETTS FOR MURDERING HER PARENTS WITH AN AXE

Ellis Island opens as New York City's immigration center

FIRST AUTOMATIC TELEPHONE SWITCHBOARD IS BUILT

WALT WHITMAN DIES AT AGE 72

GROVER CLEVELAND ELECTED PRESIDENT

AMERICAN SCHOOL OF OSTEOPATHY OPENS IN MISSOURI

German Gottlieb Daimler invents the carburetor

SIERRA CLUB FOUNDED TO PROTECT ENVIRONMENT

PRE-SEASON

Brooklyn's Tom Lovett, who won 53 games over the past two years, refuses a salary cut and becomes the first player to hold out for the entire season. Along with reduced rosters, owners are offering players contracts with large salary cuts, in some cases as much as 40%.

THE SEASON

MAY 9:

Edward "Ned" Hanlon becomes manager of the Baltimore Orioles, replacing interim manager Jack Waltz (2-6). Waltz had replaced George Van Haltren (1-10).

Under Hanlon, the Orioles begin rebuilding. They acquire shortstop Hughie Jennings from Louisville and outfielder Joe Kelley from Pittsburgh in return for Van Haltren.

JUNE 10:

The Orioles' Wilbert Robinson gets 7 hits in 7 at-bats – a major league record – as Baltimore routs the St. Louis Browns, 25-4. Robinson sets another record by driving in 11 runs with his 6 singles and a double.

JULY 1:

George Bechel of the *Chicago Evening News* knocks Jimmy Ryan of the Colts in print. They argue after a game and Ryan lands several punches. According to authors Art Ahrens and Eddie Gold, it is the first instance of a sportswriter being assaulted.

JULY 12:

Alexander Cartwright, who is credited with organizing baseball's very first team – the Knickerbockers – and with formulating the game's rules, dies in Hawaii at age 72.

AUGUST 6:

In Boston, Jack Stivetts no-hits Brooklyn, 11-0. He gives up five walks, and three Brooklyn batters reach base by error. Ed Stein is the game's losing pitcher.

AUGUST 12:

Ray Schalk is born in Harvell, Illinois.

AUGUST 22:

Louisville pitcher Alexander "Ben" Sanders no-hits visiting Baltimore, 6-2, issuing three walks. Louisville commits four errors. John "Sadie" McMahon is the losing pitcher.

OCTOBER 15:

On the last day of the season, Cincinnati's Charles "Bumpus" Jones makes his major league debut with a 7-1 no-hitter against visiting Pittsburgh. He is the second to pitch a no-hitter in his first major league start. Mark Baldwin is tagged with the loss.

The no-hitter is Jones' only 1892 appearance – and the last no-hitter ever at the 51-foot pitching distance.

REGULAR SEASON WRAP-UP:

The Cleveland Spiders (93-56 overall) win the first half of the split season. The second-half winners are the Boston Beaneaters (102-48). There are charges that Boston purposely lost in the second half, after salaries were cut, and Mike "King" Kelly, John Clarkson, and Harry Stovey are released. The popular Kelly is named team captain. A number of the clubs' owners want to see Boston declared the champion on its superior record, but the Spiders demand a playoff. A best-of-nine format is agreed upon.

OCTOBER 24
The Beaneaters' 8-3 win over the Spiders gives Boston the World Championship.

OCTOBER 17:

World Series, game one. In Cleveland, the Spiders – who are managed by Oliver "Patsy" Tebeau – and the Beaneaters – under Frank Selee – battle through 11 innings without a run. Boston's "Happy Jack" Stivetts allows only four hits; Cleveland starter Denton True "Cy" Young yields five hits.

OCTOBER 18:

World Series, game two. A crowd of 7,000 is at League Park to see the Beaneaters beat the Spiders, 4-3. The winner is Harry Staley, the loser is John Clarkson.

OCTOBER 19:

World Series, game three. Boston wins again, 3-2, at League Park. The winning pitcher is Jack Stivetts, who allows eight hits. Cy Young is tagged with the game's loss.

OCTOBER 21:

World Series, game four. The Series moves to Boston, where Charles "Kid" Nichols shuts out the Spiders, 4-0, allowing seven hits and striking out eight. George Cuppy is the losing pitcher. Hugh Duffy hits a two-run homer.

OCTOBER 22:

World Series, game five. The Boston Beaneaters top the Cleveland Spiders, 12-7. The winning pitcher is Jack Stivetts; the game's losing pitcher is John Clarkson. Tommy Tucker hits a home run for Boston; John Clarkson hits one for Cleveland.

OCTOBER 24:

World Series, game six. Today the Boston Beaneaters win again, this time by a a score of 8-3. The victory gives Boston the World Championship. Beaneaters' starting pitcher Kid Nichols is credited with the Series-sealing victory. Nichols strikes out eight Cleveland hitters and helps his own cause by batting in two runs. The losing pitcher is Cy Young. Charlie Bennett smacks a home run for Boston. The hitting star of the Series, however, is Hugh Duffy, who bats .462 with nine RBI for the victors. Following the Series, Boston president Arthur Soden divides the $1,000 winners' share among his 13 players; each gets $76.92, or $12.82 per game.

THE BEST OF 1892

National League

HITTERS

Batting Average:
Dennis "Big Dan" Brouthers, Brooklyn Bridegrooms, .335

Slugging Average:
Ed Delahanty, Philadelphia Phillies, .495

Home Runs:
James "Bug" Holliday, Cincinnati Reds, 13

Runs Batted In:
Dennis Brouthers, 124

Hits:
Dennis Brouthers, 197

Stolen Bases:
John Montgomery Ward, Brooklyn Bridegrooms, 88

PITCHERS

Wins:
Bill Hutchinson, Chicago Colts, 37

Strikeouts:
Bill Hutchinson, 316

Earned Run Average:
Denton "Cy" Young, Cleveland Spiders, 1.93

Winning Percentage:
Cy Young, .750

Saves:
Gus Weyhing, Philadelphia Phillies, 3

RULES

Free substitution will be allowed (previously a player could be replaced only for injury). Rosters are cut from 15 to 13 players.

LEAGUE

Because of the expanded number of teams, the season will be split: part one will conclude on July 15, the second half in October. The schedule will be between 140 and 154 games. Where local laws allow it, Sunday baseball (a staple of the disbanded AA) will be allowed for the first time.

1893

AUGUST 16
Baltimore's Bill Hawke is the first to throw a no-hitter from the new mound distance.

NEWS

FINANCIAL PANIC LEADS TO FOUR-YEAR DEPRESSION

AMERICAN BUSINESSMEN AND LAWYERS IN HAWAII STAGE A REVOLT, BACKED BY U.S. TROOPS

HENRY FORD BUILDS HIS FIRST CAR

WORLD EXHIBITION IN CHICAGO

ZULU REVOLT SUPPRESSED IN SOUTH AFRICA

SOCIALIST EUGENE VICTOR DEBS FOUNDS AMERICAN RAILWAY UNION

LAOS BECOMES FRENCH PROTECTORATE

Governor John Altgeld frees three convicted for Haymarket riot

NEW ZEALAND GRANTS WOMEN SUFFRAGE

PRE-SEASON

JANUARY:

C.C. Van Cott purchases the New York Giants from John B. Day.

MARCH 7:

In New York, NL owners meet and consider a proposal from W.R. Lester, sports editor of the *Philadelphia Record.* Lester wants the pitching mound moved to a distance of 65 feet from home plate. He also proposes 93 feet between bases. A 12-inch by 4-inch rubber slab also will replace the pitcher's box.

MARCH 24:

George Sisler is born in Manchester, Ohio.

MAY 8:

Edd Roush is born in Oakland City, Indiana.

THE SEASON

JULY 22:

Jesse "Pop" Haines is born in Clayton, Ohio.

AUGUST 16:

Baltimore's Bill Hawke is the first to pitch a no-hitter at the 60-foot, 6-inch distance; he beats Washington, 5-0, walking two and fanning six. George Stephens is the loser.

AUGUST 18:

Burleigh Grimes is born in Emerald, Wisconsin.

SEPTEMBER 18:

Cincinnati is the setting for the first wedding at home plate, where groundskeeper Louis Rapp and Rosie Smith exchange vows. It's the brainchild of Reds' business manager Frank Bancroft, who made another lasting contribution to baseball tradition: He procured for Cincinnati the right to host the first game of the year. That custom held until 1994.

SEPTEMBER 23:

Big doings in the city of Cincinnati. Five days ago a wedding, today a seven-inning perfect game as Elton "Icebox" Chamberlain beats Boston, 6-0.

POST-SEASON

NOVEMBER 21:

After the Western League folds, representatives of the Detroit, Grand Rapids, Indianapolis, Kansas City, Milwaukee, Minneapolis, Sioux City, and Toledo franchises meet to revive the circuit, and elect Ban Johnson their new president.

DECEMBER:

National League owners want to do something special in the post-season beginning at the end of next season. They decide that the winner of a best-of-seven playoff between the first- and second-place teams in the NL in 1894 will receive a two-foot-tall silver loving cup, valued at $800. The trophy will be named after the donor – who also happens to be the originator of the idea – sportsman and Pittsburgh Pirates' president William Chase Temple. It is further agreed upon that permanent possession of the playoff cup will be awarded to the first team to win the series three times. Too bad they didn't have a playoff this season, when the Pirates, perhaps benefitting from the move of the pitcher's mound 10 1/2 feet back from home plate, raised their batting average 63 points and finished in second place.

Ned Hanlon was a hard-nosed manager from 1889 to 1907; he led the Orioles in 1893.

THE BEST OF 1893

National League

HITTERS

Batting Average:
Billy Hamilton, Philadelphia Phillies, .380

Slugging Average:
Ed Delahanty, Philadelphia Phillies, .583

Home Runs:
Ed Delahanty, 19

Runs Batted In:
Ed Delahanty, 146

Hits:
Sam Thompson, Philadelphia Phillies, 222

Stolen Bases:
Tom Brown, Louisville Colonels, 66

PITCHERS

Wins:
Frank Killen, Pittsburgh Pirates, 36

Strikeouts:
Amos Rusie, New York Giants, 208

Earned Run Average:
Ted Breitenstein, St. Louis Browns, 3.18

Winning Percentage:
Hank Gastright, Pittsburgh Pirates/ Boston Beaneaters, .750

Saves:
Five players with 2 each

LEAGUE

After appearing in only seven games for the Giants – and batting .313 – outfielder Wee Willie Keeler goes from the Giants to the Bridegrooms.

RULES

The original intent is to set the pitcher's mound 60 feet from home plate. But a mistake is made on the handwritten instructions, and six inches are inadvertently added. The pitching mound thus becomes and remains 60 feet, six inches away. It is allegedly the speed of Amos "The Hoosier Thunderbolt" Rusie's overhand pitches that precipitates the increase in distance.

1894

JUNE 30
In his major league debut, Louisville's Fred Clarke has a record five hits.

NEWS

COLUMBUS WORLD'S FAIR IN CHICAGO DESTROYED BY FIRE

U.S. AND CHINA SIGN TREATY PREVENTING CHINESE LABORERS FROM ENTERING U.S.

REPUBLIC OF HAWAII ESTABLISHED

HERSHEY'S CHOCOLATE BAR MAKES ITS DEBUT

First polio epidemic breaks out in Vermont

STRIKE OF PULLMAN RAILROAD CAR WORKERS

UNEMPLOYED WORKERS MARCH ON WASHINGTON

ALFRED DREYFUS COURT-MARTIALED IN FRANCE ON TREASON CHARGES

FIRST U.S. OPEN GOLF TOURNAMENT IS HELD

PRE-SEASON

FEBRUARY 10:

Herb Pennock is born in Kennett Square, Pennsylvania.

FEBRUARY 28:

Baltimore pitcher Edgar McNabb shoots his mistress, who is the married actress Louise Kellogg, and then kills himself in a Pittsburgh hotel. Ms. Kellogg survives, but is paralyzed from the waist down. In 1893, his only year in the majors, McNabb was 8-7 with a 4.12 ERA.

THE SEASON

MAY 15:

A trash fire breaks out in the right-field bleachers of the Congress Street Park in Boston in the third inning of a game with Baltimore, even while the Orioles' John McGraw is fighting with Tommy Tucker, who spiked him at third base. The fire devastates the grandstand, bleachers, and 170 homes, causing $1 million in damages, but luckily no one is killed.

MAY 30:

In Boston, the Beaneaters' Bob Lowe becomes the first player to hit four home runs in a single game. Lowe's homers are all hit over the fence off Cincinnati's Elton "Icebox" Chamberlain. Boston wins the game, 20-11.

According to historian Glenn Dickey, after Lowe's fourth homer, fans "showered him with silver, reportedly $160 worth."

JUNE 2:

Brooklyn's Ed Stein pitches a six-inning no hitter today and beats Chicago, 1-0.

JUNE 16:

In a game against Princeton, two Yale baseball players – George Case and Dutch Carter – invent the squeeze play. Eight years later it is used in the major leagues.

JUNE 30:

Louisville's Fred Clarke makes a memorable major league debut, with a first-game record five hits – four singles and a triple.

JULY 25:

At Chicago's West Side Grounds, George Decker hits one of the earliest "tape-measure" home runs, a drive estimated to travel 520 feet. With Jimmy Ryan scoring six runs, Chicago trounces Pittsburgh, 24-6.

AUGUST 3:

Harry Heilmann is born in San Francisco.

AUGUST 5:

Fire breaks out in Chicago's West Side Park in the sixth inning while the Colts' Adrian "Cap" Anson is batting. Some 10,000 fans panic. Chicago's George Decker, Jimmy Ryan, and Walt Wilmot use their bats to force open a barbed-wire fence – constructed to segregate bleacher fans – and help 1,600 escape, but hundreds are injured in the blaze. The cause is variously reported as a cigar stub put into garbage or a plumber's stove. The game is called after six innings, with Chicago and pitcher Clark Griffith winning, 8-1.

AUGUST 7:

The Colts' Bill Dahlen is hitless in six at-bats today to end his record consecutive game hitting streak at 42 games. But Chicago beats Cincinnati, 13-11, in 10 innings.

Wee Willie Keeler, who finishes his season at .361 – making him a .300-plus hitter in his first three major league seasons – says, "I have already written a treatise and it reads like this: 'Keep your eye clear and hit 'em where they ain't; that's all!'"

Dahlen's streak is the second-longest in NL history.

Boston outfielder Jimmy Bannon – a 23-year-old known as Foxy Grandpa – hits a grand slam homer against Boston. He is the first player with grand slams in consecutive games – yesterday's also coming against Boston.

AUGUST 21:

The Boston Beaneaters set a major league record by scoring 43 runs against Cincinnati in a doubleheader played today.

AUGUST 31:

In an eight-inning game at home in the Huntingdon Avenue Grounds, the Philadelphia Phillies' Billy Hamilton steals seven bases against Washington, tying a major league record. Hamilton swipes second base five times and steals third base two times.

SEPTEMBER 3:

With his team under .500, at 53-55, Pittsburgh manager Al Buckenberger resigns and is replaced by Connie Mack .

SEPTEMBER 9:

In Chicago, Bill Dahlen extends his second major hit streak of the season to 28 games. Still, Cleveland beats Chicago, 9-5.

REGULAR SEASON WRAP-UP:

The pennant-winning and favored Orioles (89-39 under Ned Hanlon) will meet the second-place Giants (88-44 under manager John Montgomery Ward) in Baltimore for the Temple Cup.

Hugh Duffy of the Boston Beaneaters hits .440 – the highest batting average ever under modern rules. The jewels in his batting crown include: a .690 slugging average, 18 homers, 145 RBI, 15 triples, and 51 doubles. But his team finishes in third place.

Philadelphia's outfield finishes the season with a cumulative batting average of .400 – the best ever. Sam Thompson bats .404; Ed Delahanty, .400; and Billy Hamilton, "only" .399. The next best will be the Detroit Tigers outfield

Billy Hamilton was a member of Philadelphia's ".400" club in 1894.

RULES

The National League institutes a $100 fine for "vulgar, indecent, or improper language." On February 26, the NL makes a bunt hit foul a strike.

LEAGUE

The Western League, still the minors, comprises the Detroit Cream, Grand Rapids Rustlers, Indianapolis Hoosiers, Kansas City Blues, Milwaukee Brewers, Minneapolis Millers, Sioux City Huskers, and Toledo White Stockings.

EQUIPMENT

With the retirement of the last "hardliner," the Louisville Colonels' third baseman Jerry Denny, all major league players are now wearing fielder's gloves.

OCTOBER 7
The Giants beat the Orioles, 16-3, in game four of the Temple Cup for a series sweep.

DECEMBER 19
Future baseball commissioner Ford Frick is born in Wawaka, Indiana.

LEAGUE

The Baltimore Orioles obtain outfielder Wee Willie Keeler (.317 in 27 games) and first baseman Dennis "Dan" Brouthers (.337 in 77 games) from the Brooklyn Bridegrooms for third baseman Bill Shindle (.261) and outfielder George Treadway (.260).

TRIVIA

Brooklyn teams at various times have been known as the Trolley-Dodgers, the Gladiators, Ward's Wonders (after John Montgomery Ward, their 1892 and 1893 manager), and Foutz's Follies (after the present manager). In 1894 they are the Bridegrooms.

Medal in honor of Baltimore's Temple Cup win in '94.

of 1925 (Harry Heilmann, Ty Cobb, Al Wingo) at .380.

OCTOBER 4:

Temple Cup, game one. Behind a seven-hitter by Amos Rusie, the Giants win, 4-1, in a game marked by several skirmishes. The loser is Charles "Duke" Esper, who yields 13 hits.

OCTOBER 5:

Temple Cup, game two. The visiting Giants win, 9-6. Results of the ball game in progress are telegraphed to Ford's Theatre in Washington. Police are needed when the Giants' Eddie Burke gets into a pre-game altercation with a spectator and fans pour onto the field. The winner is Jouett Meekin; William "Kid" Gleason is tagged with the loss.

OCTOBER 6:

Temple Cup, game three. In the new Polo Grounds in New York, 22,000 are on hand to see the Giants, behind Amos Rusie, defeat the Orioles, 4-1. George Hemming is the loser. The game is marked by mishaps: during the top of the seventh, a horse charges onto the field; the Giant outfielders scramble to safety but several fans suffer minor injuries. In addition, a section of the bleachers collapses with no injuries.

OCTOBER 7:

Temple Cup, game four. The Giants beat the Orioles, 16-3, at the Polo Grounds and sweep the series. Jouett Meekin is the winner and knocks in three runs. The loser is Bill Hawke. After the game, Monte Ward tells the fans, "My friends, we'll all drink from the Temple Cup together." The Giants, led by Jack Doyle's .588, bat .389 as a team. The Orioles hit only .201. Rusie allows one earned run in 18 innings.

POST-SEASON

NOVEMBER 8:

Mike "King" Kelly, arguably baseball's first superstar, dies of pneumonia in Boston, although alcohol reportedly is a factor. It is only six weeks before his 37th birthday. Kelly played in just 20 games for the New York Giants in 1893, hitting .269. His lifetime average for 16 years is .308. Kelly's coffin lies in Boston's Elk Hall where 3,000 fans pay their final respects.

THE BEST OF 1894

NATIONAL LEAGUE

HITTERS

Batting Average:
Hugh Duffy, Boston Beaneaters, .440

Slugging Average:
Hugh Duffy, .690

Home Runs:
Hugh Duffy, 18

Runs Batted In:
Hugh Duffy, 145

Hits:
Hugh Duffy, 237

Stolen Bases:
Billy Hamilton, Philadelphia Phillies, 98

PITCHERS

Wins:
Amos Rusie, New York Giants, 36

Strikeouts:
Amos Rusie, 195

Earned Run Average:
Amos Rusie, 2.78

Winning Percentage:
Jouett Meekin, New York Giants, .786

Saves:
Tony Mullane, Baltimore Orioles/ Cleveland Spiders, 4

1895

FEBRUARY 6
Future Hall of Famer George Herman "Babe" Ruth is born in Baltimore, Maryland.

NEWS

GEORGE EASTMAN PRODUCES THE HAND-HELD KODAK CAMERA

GEORGE WESTINGHOUSE DESIGNS GENERATING SYSTEM AND WINS CONTRACT TO BUILD POWER STATION AT NIAGARA FALLS

C. Gillette invents safety razor

GUGLIELMO MARCONI INVENTS RADIO TELEGRAPHY

Wilhelm Roentgen discovers X-rays

FIRST AUTO RACE IN U.S. TAKES PLACE BETWEEN CHICAGO AND MILWAUKEE

DIESEL ENGINE INVENTED

Oscar Wilde's plays *An Ideal Husband* and *The Importance of Being Earnest* premiere in London

PRE-SEASON

JANUARY 17:

Andrew Freedman buys 2,380 shares – the controlling interest – in the New York Giants for an estimated $50,000, paying less than half of their par value.

Andrew Freedman might be described as the George Steinbrenner of his day. In a nine-month period, he hired George Davis as manager (16-17) and fired him after two months, sacked replacement "Dirty Jack" Doyle in five weeks (32-31), and hired actor Harvey Watkins to finish the season (18-17).

FEBRUARY 6:

George Herman "Babe" Ruth is born in Baltimore.

APRIL 16:

The *Detroit Free Press* runs a baseball story featuring a headline that reads: "STROUTHERS' TIGERS SHOWED UP VERY NICELY." The same page includes a section titled, "Notes of the Detroit Tigers of 1895." This is the first known instance of Detroit's baseball team being called Tigers. Previously, the team had been called the Detroits, Wolverines, and Creams.

THE SEASON

JUNE 23:

Before a game with visiting Cleveland, the entire Chicago Colts team is arrested for "aiding and abetting the forming of a noisy crowd on a Sunday." The bust is the work of Reverend W.W. Clark and the Sunday Observance League. After Chicago owner Jim Hart posts bond, the game goes on with a crowd of 10,000 on hand; Chicago beats Cleveland, 13-4, and Clark Griffith gets the win.

George Weiss is born in New Haven, Connecticut.

SEPTEMBER 10:

George "Highpockets" Kelly is born in San Francisco.

REGULAR SEASON WRAP-UP:

In Cleveland, the pennant-winning Baltimore Orioles (87-43, managed by Ned Hanlon) will meet the second place Spiders (84-46, under Oliver "Patsy" Tebeau) for the Temple Cup.

LEAGUE

Charles Comiskey buys the Western League's Sioux City franchise and moves it to St. Paul, Minnesota.

RULES

The pitcher's rubber is increased to 24 inches long by six inches wide. The bat diameter is increased from two and a half inches to two and three-quarter inches. Only catchers and first baseman may wear oversized mitts. Clubs can no longer pay players' fines. A foul tip is a strike.

OCTOBER 2
In game one of the Temple Cup, the Spiders' Cy Young beats the Giants.

OCTOBER 8
Cleveland's game five win, behind Cy Young, gives the Spiders the Temple Cup.

CULTURE

***A Runaway Colt*, a play based on the life of Cap Anson and starring the Chicago manager-first baseman, runs for three weeks in Syracuse and briefly on Broadway.**

RULES

The infield fly rule is instituted. It is a fair fly ball that can be caught by an infielder with ordinary effort, when there are runners on first and second or first, second, and third and there are less than two outs. The batter is out when the umpire declares an infield fly, and the ball does not have to be caught. The runners are no longer forced to run but they may run if they wish, at the risk of being put out.

OCTOBER 2:

Temple Cup, game one. Cleveland wins with two runs in the bottom of the ninth. The winning pitcher is Cy Young, who had 35 victories in the regular season. John "Sadie" McMahon is the loser. Former Giants' pitcher Timothy Keefe is one of the umpires.

OCTOBER 3:

Harry Wright, the Father of Professional Baseball, dies at age 60 in Atlantic City, New Jersey. An English-born cricket player, Wright organized the first fully professional team – the 1869 Cincinnati Red Stockings. As a player, he was hitless in seven at-bats over two seasons. At his death, he was chief of the NL's umpires.

Temple Cup, game two. With a sellout crowd of 10,000 fans rooting them on today, Cleveland gets the win over Baltimore, 7-2, behind a George Cuppy five-hitter. The loser is rookie Billy Hoffer. Fans bombard the Orioles with bottles and garbage during the game.

OCTOBER 5:

Temple Cup, game three. At League Park, the Spiders score three runs in the first and win, 7-1. Cy Young wins his second game with a seven-hitter. Sadie McMahon is tagged with the loss. As the Spiders depart for Baltimore, manager Patsy Tebeau tells them, "We'll be back Wednesday morning, no need to take more than one shirt."

OCTOBER 7:

Temple Cup, game four. In Baltimore, the Orioles avoid a sweep with a 5-0 win, behind Charles "Duke" Espy's five-hitter. Nig Cuppy is the loser. Baltimore fans retaliate – and then some – for the treatment of their team in Cleveland; as the Spiders leave their hotel, they are pelted with rocks and vegetables. During the first inning, pieces of brick are thrown at them and, after the game, they are besieged by 1,500 fans, bombarded with vegetables, rocks, sticks, and bricks, and need a police escort.

OCTOBER 8:

Temple Cup, game five. For the second year in a row, the pennant-winning Orioles come up short in their latest quest for the Temple Cup. Cleveland beats Baltimore, 5-2, behind Cy Young. Billy Hoffer is the game's losing pitcher.

THE BEST OF 1895

NATIONAL LEAGUE

HITTERS

Batting Average:
Jesse Burkett, Cleveland Spiders, .409

Slugging Average:
Sam Thompson, Philadelphia Phillies, .654

Home Runs:
Sam Thompson, 18

Runs Batted In:
Sam Thompson, 165

Hits:
Jesse Burkett, 225

Stolen Bases:
Billy Hamilton, Philadelphia Phillies, 97

PITCHERS

Wins:
Denton "Cy" Young, Cleveland Spiders, 35

Strikeouts:
Amos Rusie, New York Giants, 201

Earned Run Average:
Al Maul, Washington Senators, 2.45

Winning Percentage:
Bill Hoffer, Baltimore Orioles, .838

Saves:
Charles "Kid" Nichols, Boston Beaneaters; Ernie Beam, Philadelphia Phillies; Tacky Tom Parrott, Cincinnati Reds, 3

1896

JULY 12
The Phillies' Ed Delahanty hits four inside-the-park homers against the Colts.

NEWS

Supreme Court case *Plessy v. Ferguson* approves racial segregation under "separate but equal" doctrine

FIRST MODERN OLYMPIC GAMES ARE HELD IN ATHENS

BEGINNING OF KLONDIKE GOLD RUSH IN CANADA

UTAH BECOMES A STATE

WILLIAM McKINLEY DEFEATS WILLIAM JENNINGS BRYAN AND IS ELECTED U.S. PRESIDENT

OTTOMANS MASSACRE 3,000 ARMENIANS

NOBEL PRIZES FOR PEACE, SCIENCE, AND LITERATURE ESTABLISHED

French physicist Antoine Henri Becquerel discovers radioactivity in uranium

PRE-SEASON

JANUARY 18:

Bill McGowan is born in Wilmington, Delaware.

FEBRUARY:

Future Red Sox manager and Yankees' general manager Ed Barrow discovers Honus Wagner in the town of Mansfield, Pennsylvania, reportedly throwing coal and rocks with kids in a railroad yard. He signs Wagner (who played for six teams in the Ohio State League in 1895) for his Paterson, New Jersey, team in the Atlantic League and pays him $125 per month.

THE SEASON

APRIL 27:

Rogers Hornsby is born in Winters, Texas.

MAY 3:

With an overflow 17,231 at Chicago's West Side Grounds, the umpires determine that a ball hit into the crowd will be a ground-rule triple. Chicago and St. Louis respond with nine three-baggers. Bill Dahlen hits three to lead the Colts to a 16-7 win.

MAY 28:

Warren Giles is born in Tiskilwa, Illinois.

JULY 12:

Today in Chicago, Philadelphia's Ed Delahanty hits four homers – all inside-the-park – and bats in seven runs against Adonis Bill Terry. Despite Delahanty's hitting – which includes a single – the Colts go on to beat the Phillies, 9-8. Virgil "Ned" Garvin is the losing pitcher.

SEPTEMBER 21:

Connie Mack resigns after three years as Pittsburgh's manager, effective at the end of the year.

Pittsburgh finishes the season in sixth place with a record of 66-63. Mack then becomes the manager of the Milwaukee franchise in the Western League.

REGULAR SEASON WRAP-UP:

In Baltimore, the Orioles (90-29, managed by Ned Hanlon), winners of three straight pennants, will meet the second-place Cleveland Spiders (80-48, managed by Patsy Tebeau) for the Temple Cup.

RULES

Home teams must have at least 12 balls on hand for the start of games. Only uniformed personnel – players, manager, and team president – are allowed on the bench during play.

LEAGUE

Philadelphia owner John Rogers buys Fall River (New England League) outfielder Phil Geier for $1,500 and gets a throw-in named Napoleon Lajoie. Lajoie plays 39 games in 1896 for Philadelphia, hits .326 with four homers, and goes on to a Hall of Fame career. Geier plays for five teams in five years, averaging .249 and hitting a total of two homers.

Scorecard from the 1896 Temple Cup series

OCTOBER 8
With a 5-0 victory in Cleveland, the Orioles sweep the Temple Cup series in four games.

HISTORY

Giants' pitcher Amos Rusie, who was 23–23 last season after 35 wins in 1894, holds out for the entire season over a $200 dispute with owner Andrew Freedman.

HISTORY

The Orioles, who attempted to sign heavyweight boxing champion Gentleman Jim Corbett for $10,000 in 1894, settle for his brother Joe, a pitcher and sparring partner. With Washington last year, Joe Corbett was 0-2. He is 3-0 for Baltimore this season and in 1897 is 24-8.

OCTOBER 2:

Temple Cup, game one. The Orioles win, 7-1, on Bill Hoffer's five-hitter. Losing pitcher Cy Young suffers a severe wrist injury when struck by John McGraw's line drive. Cleveland's manager-first baseman Patsy Tebeau hurts his back and is out for the playoffs.

OCTOBER 3:

Temple Cup, game two. Baltimore wins, 7-2, before 3,200 at home. Joe Corbett pitches a seven-hitter. The losing pitcher is Bobby Wallace.

OCTOBER 5:

Temple Cup, game three. The Orioles top the Spiders, 6-2, and are within a win of the Temple Cup. Bill Hoffer gets the victory; George "Nig" Cuppy, the loss.

OCTOBER 8:

Temple Cup, game four. After exhibition games in Newark, Scranton, Wilkes-Barre, and Cantonville, the Orioles and the Spiders get back to business. In Cleveland before a sparse 1,200 in cold weather, the Orioles complete a sweep of the playoffs with a 5-0 victory. Joe Corbett is the winning pitcher; Nig Cuppy gets the loss.

The Orioles, celebrated for their aggressiveness and fortitude, are described by historian Lee Allen: "It was a dirty team in a pugnacious league, a team that filled the atmosphere with tobacco juice, oaths, and flying fists. There was no trick in the book unknown to the Orioles. They did not invent rowdiness, perhaps, but no team in league history developed it into such a precise science."

POST-SEASON

OCTOBER 14:

Oscar Charleston is born in Indianapolis, Indiana.

OCTOBER 30:

Bill Terry is born in Atlanta.

NOVEMBER 8:

Stanley "Bucky" Harris is born in Port Jervis, New York.

DECEMBER 15:

Baseball's first pitching machine is demonstrated today; it is the brainchild of a Princeton University professor named Charles E. Hinton.

THE BEST OF 1896

NATIONAL LEAGUE

HITTERS

Batting Average:
Jesse Burkett, Cleveland Spiders, .410

Slugging Average:
Ed Delahanty, Philadelphia Phillies, .631

Home Runs:
Scrappy Bill Joyce, Washington Senators/ New York Giants, 14

Runs Batted In:
Ed Delahanty, 126

Hits:
Jesse Burkett, 240

Stolen Bases:
Joe Kelley, Baltimore Orioles, 87

PITCHERS

Wins:
Charles "Kid" Nichols, Boston Beaneaters; Frank Killen, Pittsburgh Pirates, 30

Strikeouts:
Denton "Cy" Young, Cleveland Spiders, 140

Earned Run Average:
Billy Rhines, Cincinnati Reds, 2.45

Winning Percentage:
Bill Hoffer, Baltimore Orioles, .781

Saves:
Cy Young, 3

1897

JUNE 19
The Baltimore Orioles' Wee Willie Keeler hits in his 44th consecutive game.

NEWS

68 KLONDIKE MINERS RETURN TO SEATTLE ON SS PORTLAND

R. Ross discovers malaria bacillus

New York Sun runs famous *"Yes, Virginia, there is a Santa Claus"* editorial

SEVERE EARTHQUAKE IN ASSAM, INDIA, IS FELT ACROSS EUROPE

J.J. THOMSON DISCOVERS THE ELECTRON

FIRST U.S. SUBWAY LINE OPENS IN BOSTON

John Philip Sousa debuts his popular march *The Stars and Stripes Forever*

BRAM STOKER'S VAMPIRE TALE, *DRACULA*, IS PUBLISHED

PRE-SEASON

FEBRUARY 5:

Charles "Old Hoss" Radbourn dies today at the age of 42 in his Bloomington, Illinois, billiards parlor. In 11 years, he was 311-194 (with 60 wins in 1884) with a 2.67 ERA.

MARCH 5:

Dave Foutz, who resigned as Brooklyn's manager at the end of last season, dies at age 40 of asthma in Waverly, Maryland. In 11 years he compiled a 147-66 record, with a 2.84 ERA and the second-best percentage ever – .690. He won 33 games in 1885 and 41 in 1886.

APRIL 10:

Royce "Ross" Youngs is born in Shiner, Texas.

THE SEASON

JUNE 29:

Chicago sets a major league record for runs scored in a single game when it defeats the visiting Louisville Colonels, 36-7, on 30 hits. The Colts score at least once in every single inning. Barry McCormick has six hits; winning pitcher Jim "Nixey" Callahan gets five hits.

JUNE 18:

Before his home fans, Chicago's player-manager Cap Anson singles in the fourth inning against Baltimore for his 3,000th career hit. Anson is the first player to reach that plateau. Chicago scores three in the fourth for a 6-3 win.

Anson's 3,000 total includes 59 walks, counted as hits in 1897. He gets additional hits after July 18, although The Baseball Encyclopedia *credits him with a career total of exactly 3,000.*

JUNE 19:

Baltimore's Wee Willie Keeler hits in his 44th consecutive game. Honus Wagner debuts in the NL as a center fielder for the Louisville Colonels and singles against Washington's James "Doc" McJames in his first at-bat.

JULY 27:

Raleigh "Biz" Mackey is born in Eagle Pass, Texas. Mackey plays 24 years, batting .322, and is ranked by many observers as the greatest of the Negro Leagues' catchers. He died in 1959 in Los Angeles.

RULES

No error will be charged for failure to complete a double play unless a runner takes an extra base. No error for a catcher who throws wildly on a stolen base attempt unless the runner advances.

LEAGUE

The Orioles obtain outfielder Jake Stenzel (.361, 57 stolen bases) from Pittsburgh for outfielder Walter "Steve" Brodie (.297, 25 stolen bases) and third baseman Jim Donely (.328, 38 stolen bases). (Note: John McGraw biographer Charles C. Alexander uses "Donely"; *The Baseball Encyclopedia* lists him as "Donnelly.")

SEPTEMBER 18
Cleveland pitcher Cy Young throws a no-hitter in beating the Reds, 6-0.

HISTORY

In his first full major league season, Philadelphia's Napoleon Lajoie hits .361 and leads the NL with nine homers and a .569 slugging average; he earns $1,800.

AUGUST 13:

After seven seasons, Chicago pitcher Clark Griffith throws his first major league shutout, beating Cincinnati, 2-0. Griffith makes a point of avoiding shutouts, in fact, because he considers them bad luck. On one occasion, Griffith supposedly told a rookie catcher to drop a pop fly and allow a run to score.

AUGUST 27:

Roger Bresnahan makes his major league debut today as a pitcher for the Washington Senators. The right-hander shuts out the St. Louis Browns by a score of 3-0.

Bresnahan is 4-0 with a 3.95 ERA in 1897, but goes on to a Hall of Fame career as a catcher.

AUGUST 30:

A pitcher appearing in the outfield wearing a bathrobe, the ejection of a key player, and dwindling daylight combine to cost the Chicago Colts a victory. With his team behind 7-5 in the top of the ninth, Chicago player-manager Cap Anson is thumbed by umpire Bob Emslie for arguing too strenuously about the lack of daylight. After the Colts rally for five runs, the regular left fielder goes to first to replace Anson. Then pitcher Danny Friend, who already has showered and is wearing his street clothes, is summoned to play left. Friend dons his Chicago baseball cap, slips on a bathrobe, and trots onto the field. Giants' manager Bill Joyce protests, and as he and Emslie argue the ump decides it is too dark to continue. The top of the ninth is canceled, the score reverts to 7-5, and the Giants win the game.

SEPTEMBER 18:

Cleveland Spiders' pitcher Cy Young no-hits the visiting Cincinnati Reds, 6-0, walking one and fanning three; the Spiders have three errors. Billy Rhines is the losing pitcher.

OCTOBER 3:

Cap Anson makes his last major league appearances in a doubleheader against St. Louis. In game one, Chicago loses, 10-9, but the 45-year-old Anson hits two round-trippers, becoming the oldest player to homer in the major leagues. Although in game two he is hitless in three at-bats, Chicago still wins, 7-1.

Wee Willie Keeler hit a league-best .424 in 1897.

REGULAR SEASON WRAP-UP:

Boston, managed by Frank Selee, wins the pennant with a record of 93-39. Second-place Baltimore, led by Ned Hanlon, is 90-40. Each team boasts three 20-game winners: Boston has Charles "Kid" Nichols (31-11), Fred Klobedanz (26-7), and Ted Lewis (21-12); Baltimore's staff is Joe Corbett (24-8), Bill Hoffer (22-11), and Jerry Nops (20-6).

OCTOBER 4:

Temple Cup, game one. In Boston, the Beaneaters beat the visiting Orioles, 13-12. Ted Lewis gets the win; Jerry Nops is charged with the loss.

OCTOBER 5:

Temple Cup, game two. Baltimore wins a second slugfest, 13-11, in Boston with three Orioles homering – Henry "Heinie" Reitz, William "Boileryard" Clarke, and winning pitcher Joe Corbett.

OCTOBER 6:

Temple Cup, game three. The Orioles beat the Beaneaters, 8-3. Baltimore now has 60 runs and 85 hits in Cup play. The winner is Bill Hoffer; Ted Lewis gets the loss. The *New York Times* describes the game redundantly as "dull and uninteresting."

OCTOBER 9:

Temple Cup, game four. After two exhibition games in Massachusetts, the Orioles and Giants resume cup play in Baltimore, where the Orioles pound out 14 hits in a 12-11 win. The winner is Jerry Nops; Jack Stivetts gets the loss.

OCTOBER 11:

Temple Cup, game five. The Orioles top the Beaneaters, 9-3, for their second straight cup. The winner is Bill Hoffer; Charles "Piano Legs" Hickman, the loser.

POST-SEASON

DECEMBER:

Baltimore sends infielder "Dirty Jack" Doyle (.354, 62 stolen bases), second baseman Henry "Heinie" Reitz (.289, 23 stolen bases), and pitcher Morris "Doc" Amole (4-4, 2.57 ERA) to Washington for first baseman Dennis "Dan" McGann (.322 in 43 games in 1896) and second baseman Gene DeMontreville (.341, 30 stolen bases).

THE BEST OF 1897

NATIONAL LEAGUE

HITTERS

Batting Average:
"Wee" Willie Keeler, Baltimore Orioles, .424

Slugging Average:
Napoleon Lajoie, Philadelphia Phillies, .569

Home Runs:
Hugh Duffy, Boston Beaneaters, 11

Runs Batted In:
George Davis, New York Giants, 134

Hits:
Willie Keeler, 239

Stolen Bases:
Bill Lange, Chicago Colts, 73

PITCHERS

Wins:
Charles "Kid" Nichols, Boston Beaneaters, 31

Strikeouts:
James "Doc" McJames, Washington Senators, 156

Earned Run Average:
Amos Rusie, New York Giants, 2.54

Winning Percentage:
Fred Klobedanz, Boston Beaneaters, .788

Saves:
Charles Nichols, 3

LEAGUE

After this year's Baltimore-Boston series, won by the second-place team for the third time in four years, the owners junk the play-off system, and with it goes the Temple Cup. The only dissenter is Orioles' manager Ned Hanlon. The cup is returned to William Chase Temple and today resides at the Baseball Hall of Fame in Cooperstown, New York.

1898

JULY
5
Lizzie Arlington becomes the first woman to play in organized baseball.

NEWS

U.S. battleship *Maine* blown up in Havana harbor, killing 260; Spanish-American War ensues

U.S. ANNEXES THE INDEPENDENT REPUBLIC OF HAWAII

RUSSIAN SOCIAL DEMOCRATIC LABOUR PARTY FOUNDED ON MARXIST PRINCIPLES

Paris Metro system opens

DREYFUS IS ACQUITTED IN FRANCE

FIVE BOROUGHS OF NEW YORK CITY ARE UNIFIED TO CREATE SINGLE CITY

MOTORCAR PRODUCTION IN U.S. RISES FROM 100 A YEAR AGO TO 1,000

Bubonic plaque breaks out in China and India

FIRST PHOTOGRAPHS TAKEN WITH FLASHBULB

PRE-SEASON

JANUARY 4:

Charles H. Byrne, one-third owner of the Brooklyn Bridegrooms and team president, dies. The club's secretary and former office boy, Charles Ebbets, becomes president. Gambler Ferdinand Abell and Orioles' owners Harry Von Der Horst and Ned Hanlon buy Byrne's shares of the Brooklyn team.

FEBRUARY 1:

After 22 years – 19 as its player-manager – 45-year-old Cap Anson is released by Chicago. The team finished in ninth place at 59-73 in 1897; Anson hit .285.

THE SEASON

APRIL 16:

Approximately 100 in a crowd of 4,000 are injured when fire breaks out during the second inning of a game between the Browns and the visiting Chicago Orphans in Sportsman's Park in St. Louis. The blaze destroys the grandstand and left-field bleachers in a half-hour. A lit cigar on tarpaulins is the suspected cause.

APRIL 21:

In the second inning in a game today against the visiting Giants, Phillies' pitcher Bill Duggleby comes to bat for the first time in the major leagues and hits a grand slam.

No player hits a grand slam again in his first game until Bobby Bonds does so in 1968. But Duggleby remains the only one to accomplish the feat in his first at-bat.

APRIL 22:

In only his second major league start, Orioles' pitcher Jim Hughes no-hits Boston, 8-0, in Baltimore, walking two and fanning three. Ted Lewis is the loser. On April 18, Hughes shut out the Senators, 9–0.

In the second no-hitter of the day, Cincinnati's Ted Breitenstein beats visiting Pittsburgh, 11-0. He walks one and strikes out two. Charlie Hastings is the losing pitcher. It's Breitenstein's second career no-hitter; he is the first to pitch no-hitters in two major leagues. In 1891, he pitched a no-hitter for St. Louis in the American Association.

JUNE 7:

Owner and new president Charles Ebbets becomes the Brooklyn Bridegrooms' new manager. His self-appointment follows the firing of Bill Barnie (15-20) and the resignation of his successor, outfielder Mike Griffin (1-3). Ebbets manages wearing a silk hat. Brooklyn goes 38-68 and finishes in 10th place.

JULY 5:

Lizzie Arlington (real name, Lizzie Stroud) reportedly becomes the first woman to play in organized baseball when she pitches an inning for Reading in the Eastern League. According to another account, Arlington, who was taught by Boston pitcher Jack Stivetts, was hired by Atlantic League president Ed Barrow to play in exhibition games.

From Baseball: An Illustrated History, *by Geoffrey C. Ward and Ken Burns: "In 1883, two Philadelphia promoters, who did not dare use their real names, fielded a pair of women's teams: the Red Stockings and the Blue Stockings. The players, their bill claimed, 'were selected with tender solicitude*

AUGUST 21
Chicago pitcher Walter Thornton no-hits the Brooklyn Bridesgrooms to gain a 2-0 win.

from 200 applicants, variety actresses and ballet girls being positively barred.' To boost attendance, women were admitted free – until 500 of them turned up for a game in Camden, New Jersey. After that, they were charged the children's price: fifteen cents. By the 1890s, barnstorming 'bloomer girls' played up and down the country – sometimes including a man or two wearing women's clothes. And in 1898, Ed Barrow, the president of the Atlantic League, sought to boost receipts for his Reading, Pennsylvania, men's team by advertising that a young pitcher named Lizzie Arlington would actually appear with his club. More than a thousand fans turned out to see her, including 200 women. She pitched just part of the ninth inning and gave up two hits and a walk – but nobody scored a run against her. 'Miss Arlington,' said the local newspaper, 'might do as a pitcher among amateurs, but the sluggers of the Atlantic League would soon put her out of business. But, f or a woman, she is a success.'"

JULY 8:

Philadelphia's Francis "Red" Donahue no-hits Boston, 5-0. Donahue allows two walks and strikes out one. The losing pitcher is Vic Willis.

AUGUST 21:

In the nightcap of a twinbill, Chicago's Walter Thornton no-hits the Bridegrooms, 2-0, striking out three and walking three.

SEPTEMBER 9:

Frankie Frisch is born in the Bronx, New York.

SEPTEMBER 18:

Brooklyn and New York meet on a Sun-day for the first time, but in Weehawken, New Jersey, to play legally. Some 4,000 fans show up, and the Giants win, 7-3.

REGULAR SEASON WRAP-UP:

Frank Selee's Boston Beaneaters win the pennant with a 102-47 record. The Orioles finish second. Orioles' "Wee" Willie Keeler, with 206 singles, is the only player ever to top the 200 mark in one-base hits.

POST-SEASON

OCTOBER 9:

Joe Sewell is born in Titus, Alabama.

THE BEST OF 1898

NATIONAL LEAGUE

HITTERS

Batting Average:
"Wee" Willie Keeler, Baltimore Orioles, .385

Slugging Average:
John Anderson, Brooklyn Bridegrooms/ Washington Senators, .494

Home Runs:
Jimmy Collins, Boston Beaneaters, 15

Runs Batted In:
Napoleon Lajoie, Philadelphia Phillies, 127

Hits:
Willie Keeler, 216

Stolen Bases:
Ed Delahanty, Philadelphia Phillies, 58

PITCHERS

Wins:
Charles "Kid" Nichols, Boston Beaneaters, 31

Strikeouts:
James "Cy" Seymour, New York Giants, 239

Earned Run Average:
Clark Griffith, Chicago Orphans, 1.88

Winning Percentage:
Edward "Ted" Lewis, Boston Beaneaters, .765

Saves:
Charles Nichols, 4

LEAGUE

Cincinnati owner John T. Brush, author of the controversial salary cap plan, comes up with a new scheme targeting players. He instigates a Purification Plan to counter obscene or indecent language during play. No "dirty mouth" cases reach the owners' Board of Discipline during 1898, and it is disbanded at the end of the year.

HISTORY

NL teams contribute to a fund to make up the salary lost by Amos Rusie during his season-long holdout and he will return to baseball and the Giants for the 1898 season.

1899

NEWS

SPANISH-AMERICAN WAR ENDS; SPAIN CEDES PHILIPPINES, PUERTO RICO, AND GUAM TO THE UNITED STATES AND APPROVES INDEPENDENCE FOR CUBA

The Hague Conference establishes the Permanent Court of International Justice

Horatio Alger dies

ASPIRIN IS PATENTED BY FELIX HOFFMANN

Brazos River in Texas floods 12 miles wide, causing $10 million in damage

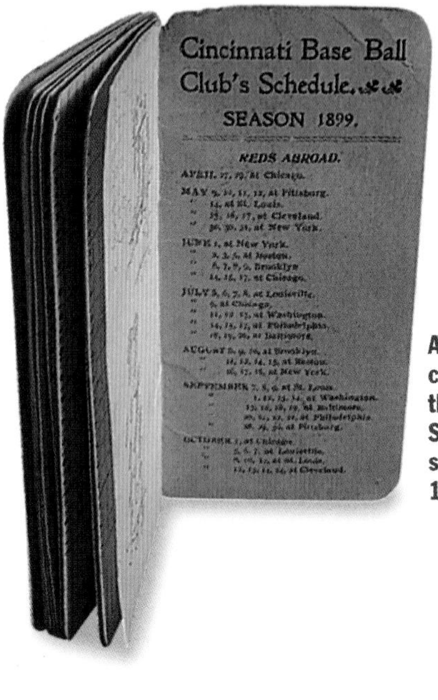

A booklet containing the Red Stockings' schedule for 1899

PRE-SEASON

APRIL 3:

Big doings in St. Louis: Brothers Frank De Haas Robison and Matthew Stanley Robison buy the Browns. They already own the NL's Cleveland Spiders.

THE SEASON

APRIL 30:

The largest baseball crowd ever to date – 27,489 – turns up at West Side Grounds to watch the Chicago Orphans beat the visiting St. Louis Perfectos, 4-0. Pitcher James "Nixey" Callahan allows 12 hits, but gets the victory.

MAY 14:

Earle Combs is born in Pebworth, Kentucky.

MAY 22:

Brooklyn – with a new nickname, the Superbas – beats the Louisville Colonels in Kentucky, 5–2, on a Jack Dunn eight-hitter, and moves into first place.

MAY 25:

Louisville's Charles "Deacon" Phillippe no-hits the visiting Giants, 7-0, yielding two walks and fanning one. Ed Doheny is the losing pitcher.

Only 64 games into the season, with the Giants at 29-35, club owner Andrew Freedman fires another manager – John Day – and replaces him with Fred Hoey, who has never managed before.

AUGUST 7:

Boston's Vic Willis no-hits Washington, 7-1, on the road. Willis walks four and strikes out five; Boston commits three errors. Bill Dinneen is the losing pitcher.

AUGUST 30:

Hazen Shirley "Kiki" Cuyler is born in Harrisville, Michigan.

SEPTEMBER 9:

Waite Hoyt is born in Brooklyn.

SEPTEMBER 17:

In Chicago, the new American Association of Baseball Clubs is formed today, with Milwaukee's H.D. Quinn as temporary president. Among the participants are Adrian "Cap" Anson, Chris Von Der Ahe, and Alfred H. Spink. The league's platform is: "Honest competition, no syndicate baseball, no reserve rule, to respect all contracts, and popular prices." The Association's Eastern Division will be composed of teams in Chicago, Detroit, Milwaukee, and St. Louis. The West will be made up of franchises in Baltimore, New York, Philadelphia, and Washington, D.C.

SEPTEMBER 18:

Nothing lasts forever, not even Cleveland's record losing streak. After 24 consecutive losses, the Spiders beat Washington.

Scheduling and the transfer of their best players to St. Louis were factors in the Spiders' 24 straight losses. After July 1, the team had only six home games (41 for the season). In their streak, they lost 21 times on the road. The Spiders, managed by Lave Cross (38 games) and Joe Quinn, finish last, 80 games behind Brooklyn, at 20-134. Their best streak is two wins in a row – one time. On the last day of their pitiful season, the inept Spiders start a 19-year-old cigarstand employee by the name of Eddie Kolb against Cincinnati. Kolb traded a box of cigars to manager Joe Quinn in

OCTOBER 8
Three teams play in one doubleheader: Chicago vs. Cleveland, then Chicago vs. Louisville.

return for the starting assignment. He pitches eight innings, gives up 18 hits, walks five, strikes out one, makes an error, gets a hit in four at-bats, and loses, 19-3. The team is dissolved after the season.

SEPTEMBER 27:

Jay Parker starts for Pittsburgh in today's game against Chicago, faces two batters, and walks both of them. After Parker is relieved, both runners score. The game ends in a 7-7 tie. This is Parker's only major league appearance and, since he allowed two runs without retiring a batter, his lifetime ERA is infinity.

OCTOBER 8:

Three teams play in one doubleheader today in Chicago. Game one pits Chicago against Cleveland. Jack "Brakeman" Taylor pitches his first major league shutout and his 39th complete game of the season in a 13-0 Chicago win. In the afternoon, Chicago beats Louisville, 7-3, in a game called because of darkness after five. Highlights include a Sam Mertes inside-the-park homer by Bill "Little Eva" Lange, after which he steals third and home.

REGULAR SEASON WRAP-UP:

Napoleon Lajoie hits .379 for Philadelphia and earns the NL's maximum $2,400. Boston's Charles "Kid" Nichols completes the decade with 297 wins. In 10 years in the majors, he has won 30 or more games seven times, 20 or more the other three seasons.

POST-SEASON

OCTOBER 11:

W.F.C. Golt of Indianapolis introduces a motion to change the name of the Western League to the American League. The motion carries.

OCTOBER 26:

William Julius "Judy" Johnson is born in Snow Hill, Maryland.

(Judy Johnson's birthday also is reported to be October 20, 1900.)

NOVEMBER 11:

Harold "Pie" Traynor is born in Framingham, Massachusetts.

DECEMBER 6:

John Bertrand "Jocko" Conlan is born in Chicago.

THE BEST OF 1899

National League

HITTERS

Batting Average:
Ed Delahanty, Philadelphia Phillies, .410

Slugging Average:
Ed Delahanty, .582

Home Runs:
John "Buck" Freeman, Washington Senators, 25

Runs Batted In:
Ed Delahanty, 137

Hits:
Ed Delahanty, 238

Stolen Bases:
Jimmy Sheckard, Baltimore Orioles, 77

PITCHERS

Wins:
Jim Hughes, Brooklyn Superbas; Iron Man Joe McGinnity, Baltimore Orioles, 28

Strikeouts:
Frank "Noodles" Hahn, Cincinnati Reds, 145

Earned Run Average:
Al Orth, Philadelphia Phillies, 2.49

Winning Percentage:
Jim Hughes, .824

Saves:
Sam Leever, Pittsburgh Pirates, 3

RULES

The modern-day balk rule is instituted.

LEAGUE

The Robisons oust president Chris Von Der Ahe and shift the best Spiders' players to their St. Louis team. Among those making the move are pitcher Cy Young (25–13) and outfielder Jesse Burkett (.341). St. Louis, dubbed the Perfectos by their new owners, acquires the nickname Cardinals. William McHale of the *St. Louis Republic* comes up with the name when the team changes its uniform trim from brown to cardinal red. According to one account, he heard a woman describe the uniforms as "a lovely shade of cardinal..." The Robison brothers make another change: Sportsman's Park becomes League Park.

Sprite
3:23
Coca-Cola
EXPRESS MAIL
UNITED STATES POSTAL SERVICE
AT BAT AVG. BALL STRIKE OUT
CUBS
REDS
Budweiser
3:23
Marlboro
SHARP
375
NATIONAL LEAGUE

1900s

PART 3 THREE

1900

MARCH 6
Robert Moses "Lefty" Grove is born in Lonaconing, Maryland.

APRIL 23
Sunny Jim Bottomley is born today in Oglesby, Illinois.

NEWS

WILLIAM MCKINLEY RE-ELECTED PRESIDENT; THEODORE ROOSEVELT IS VICE PRESIDENT

1.3 MILLION TELEPHONES IN USE IN UNITED STATES

HURRICANE STRIKES GALVESTON, TEXAS, KILLS 6,000

Brownie box camera debuts from Eastman Kodak for $1

U.S. population reaches 75.9 million

Boxer Rebellion breaks out in China

FREUD'S *THE INTERPRETATION OF DREAMS* IS PUBLISHED

First Davis Cup tennis tournament is organized by Harvard's Dwight Davis

PRE-SEASON

JANUARY 19:

Boston catcher Marty Bergen, reportedly depressed by the death of his son in 1898, chops his family – including a three-year-old son and a six-year-old daughter – to death with an axe and then commits suicide in Brookfield, Massachusetts. He was 28 years old and played 72 games with Boston last season. Billy Hamilton is the only one of Bergen's teammates to attend the funeral.

JANUARY 29:

The AL is formed in Chicago. Charles Comiskey gets approval to move his team from St. Paul to Chicago, where they will be known as the White Stockings, a name originally used for the NL's Chicago franchise.

FEBRUARY 11:

Baltimore sells third baseman-manager John McGraw (.391), infielder Bill Keister (.329), and catcher Wilbert Robinson to the Cardinals (.284). In the deal, McGraw and Robinson win a major concession: the reserve clause will be omitted from their contracts.

APRIL 2:

The AL's White Stockings, in their first game as a Chicago franchise, beat the University of Illinois, 10-9, in an exhibition game at Champaign. Roy Patterson is the winning pitcher.

THE SEASON

APRIL 19:

In Boston, the Phillies win 19-17 in the NL's highest scoring opening day game. Boston ties the game with nine runs in the ninth. Philadelphia, once up 16-4, scores two in the 10th for the win.

APRIL 21:

The Chicago White Stockings make their regular season AL debut in cold and rainy weather, losing to the Milwaukee Brewers, 5-4, in 10 innings.

APRIL 22:

The White Stockings win for the first time, beating Milwaukee, 5-3, behind the pitching of Roger Denzer.

MAY 5:

The Orphans' Jimmy Ryan hits his 20th career leadoff homer against the visiting Cincinnati Reds and Frank "Noodles" Hahn. Chicago wins, 4-3.

JUNE 9:

The Protective Association of Professional Base Ball is formed in New York City at a meeting attended by three representatives of each NL team. Charles "Chief" Zimmer is elected president; Clark Griffith and Hugh Jennings are the vice presidents. This first meeting is addressed by Daniel Harris, representing the head of the American Federation of Labor, Samuel Gompers.

JUNE 19:

In Chicago Clark Griffith duels George "Rube" Waddell and the Pirates for 14 innings. Griffith pitches a complete game as Chicago wins, 1-0; Waddell fans 12.

JULY 4:

At the West Side Grounds, about 1,000 of the 10,000 fans at the game fire pistols to celebrate July 4. No injuries are reported. Meanwhile, Chicago beats Philadelphia, 5-4, in 12 innings.

JULY 7:

Boston's Charles "Kid" Nichols beats Chicago, 11-4, for his 300th career win. At 30, he is the youngest pitcher to reach the 300 mark.

APRIL 26 Lewis "Hack" Wilson is born in Elwood City, Pennsylvania.

OCTOBER 16 Leon "Goose" Goslin is born in Salem, New Jersey.

OCTOBER 31 Robert "Cal" Hubbard is born in Keytesville, Missouri.

DECEMBER 20 Charles "Gabby" Hartnett is born in Woonsocket, Rhode Island.

DECEMBER 28 Ted Lyons is born in Lake Charles, Louisiana.

JULY 12:

Cincinnati's Frank "Noodles" Hahn no-hits the visiting Phillies, 4-0. Hahn walks two and strikes out eight; there is one error. Wahoo Sam Crawford homers for the Reds. Bill Bernhard is the loser.

JULY 13:

The Phillies' third baseman, Harry Wolverton, has three triples among his five hits in a 23-8 win over the Pirates.

JULY 17:

The Giants' Christy Mathewson, acquired from Norfolk of the North Carolina League, makes his major league debut, relieving in the fifth inning against Brooklyn at Washington Park with the score tied, 5-5. The results are less than glowing: two walks, three hit batters, five runs. Ed Doheny relieves Mathewson after four; the Superbas win the game, 13-7.

After pitcher Christy Mathewson goes 0-3 with a 5.08 ERA, the Giants return him to Norfolk and seek a return of his purchase money. He subsequently is drafted for $100 by the Cincinnati Reds.

AUGUST 18:

With the St. Louis Cardinals at a lackluster 42-50, the team's manager, Oliver "Patsy" Tebeau, quits and is quickly replaced by the club's secretary, Louie Heilbroner. According to biographer Charles C. Alexander, Heilbroner is the manager in name only, while the third baseman, John McGraw, actually is running the team on the ball field.

SEPTEMBER 19:

St. Louis Cardinals' catcher Wilbert Robinson today throws the ball at umpire Jim Gaffney's legs. The ump then swings his mask at Robinson's head, misses, and promptly ejects him. When Cardinals' manager John McGraw refuses to replace Robinson on the field, Gaffney awards a forfeit to Brooklyn.

REGULAR SEASON WRAP-UP:

Brooklyn, under manager Ned Hanlon, wins the NL pennant with an 82-54 record.

The Chicago White Stockings become the AL's first pennant winner by virtue of a 12-4 victory gained on September 12 over the Cleveland Blues.

POST-SEASON

OCTOBER 13:

AL president Ban Johnson accepts most of the terms and conditions set by the Players Protective Association. No players will be traded, farmed out, or sold without their consent.

NOVEMBER 13:

Baltimore will join the AL and play next season in the East, along with teams in Buffalo, Philadelphia, and Washington. The West will comprise Chicago, Cleveland, Detroit, and Milwaukee.

DECEMBER 10:

In December, the NL owners – represented by Arthur Soden, John Brush, and Colonel John I. Rogers – meet with attorney Harvey Leonard Taylor for the Players Protective Association. The key agenda item is contract revision, which the owners reject. They also ignore Ban Johnson and the AL.

DECEMBER 15:

The Giants reacquire Christy Mathewson from the Reds for pitcher Amos Rusie. Rusie did not play in 1900; Mathewson had been sent by the Giants to the minors.

THE BEST OF 1900

NATIONAL LEAGUE

HITTERS

Batting Average:
Honus Wagner, Pittsburgh Pirates, .381

Slugging Average:
Honus Wagner, .573

Home Runs:
Herman "Germany" Long, Boston Beaneaters, 12

Runs Batted In:
Elmer Flick, Philadelphia Phillies, 110

Hits:
"Wee" Willie Keeler, Brooklyn Superbas, 204

Stolen Bases:
Patsy Donovan, St. Louis Cardinals; George Van Haltren, New York Giants, 45

PITCHERS

Wins:
"Iron Man" Joe McGinnity, Brooklyn Superbas, 29

Strikeouts:
George "Rube" Waddell, Pittsburgh Pirates, 130

Earned Run Average:
George Waddell, 2.37

Winning Percentage:
Jesse Tannehill, Pittsburgh Pirates, .769

Saves:
Frank Kitson, Brooklyn Superbas, 4

1901

JANUARY 28
The American League meets in Chicago and declares itself a major league.

MARCH 15
Boston Beaneaters' third baseman Jimmy Collins defects to the Boston Somersets.

NEWS

PRESIDENT McKINLEY ASSASSINATED IN BUFFALO; THEODORE ROOSEVELT ASSUMES OFFICE

WALL STREET PANIC SINKS STOCK MARKET

J.P. MORGAN CREATES WORLD'S LARGEST CORPORATION, U.S. STEEL

QUEEN VICTORIA DIES

Eugene Debs organizes U.S. Socialist Party

OKLAHOMA LAND RUSH BEGINS

THE COMMONWEALTH OF AUSTRALIA IS FORMED

Booker T. Washington publishes *Up from Slavery*

ANIMATOR WALT DISNEY IS BORN IN CHICAGO

PRE-SEASON

JANUARY 28:

In Chicago's Grand Pacific Hotel, the American League declares itself a major league. It will play a 140-game schedule; rosters will be set at 14 players two weeks after the start of the season; the Players Protective Association is recognized.

FEBRUARY 12:

Ban Johnson, AL president, on his league's new status, "If we had waited for the National League to do something for us, we would have remained a minor league forever. The American League will be the principal organization of the country within a very short time. Mark my prediction!"

FEBRUARY 20:

Benjamin H. Shibe, a partner in A.J. Reach Co. – a manufacturer of baseballs – is revealed as the local backer, half-owner, and president of the American League's Philadelphia Athletics. Connie Mack is a 25 percent owner of the franchise. Mack also manages the A's from 1901-50, retiring at age 87.

FEBRUARY 25-28:

The NL Rules Committee meets at the Fifth Avenue Hotel in New York City. It decides that the catcher must position himself within 10 feet of the batter.

In February, NL owners Arthur Soden, John Brush, and James B. Hart meet with Charles "Chief" Zimmer, who was instructed not to bring lawyer Henry Taylor with him. The owners recognize the Players Protective Association, make some concessions, and get Zimmer to agree to oust players who jump to the AL.

MARCH 2:

Negro Leaguer George "Mule" Suttles is born in Brockton, Alabama. Suttles, who died in Newark, New Jersey, in 1968, was an outfielder-first baseman who played for 22 years and batted .329 for his career.

MARCH 11:

The *Cincinnati Enquirer* reports that a Cherokee Indian named Chief Charlie Tokohoma has been signed by John McGraw of the Orioles. "Tokohoma" is, in reality, a black second baseman named Charlie Grant. McGraw's plans fall apart when Charles Comiskey recognizes Grant as a member of the Columbia Giants, a black team that plays in Chicago.

MARCH 15:

Jimmy Collins, rated the best third baseman in baseball, jumps the NL and the Boston Beaneaters to sign with the AL and the Boston Somersets. Owner Charles W. Somers gives the 28-year-old Collins – who hit .304 in 1900– a guaranteed $4,000.

MARCH 20:

AL teams announce their rosters. Of the 185 players, 111 jumped from the NL. Included are such stars as Napoleon Lajoie, Charles "Chick" Fraser, Lave Cross, and Bill Barnhart (Philadelphia Athletics); Cy Young – who gets $3,500 – plus his catcher Lou Criger, Jimmy Collins, Charles "Chick" Stahl, and Ted Lewis (Boston Somersets); John McGraw, Roger Bresnahan, Iron Man Joe McGinnity, Wilbert Robinson, Cy Seymour, Steve Brodie, and Mike Donlin (Baltimore Orioles); Hugh Duffy and John "Jiggs" Donahue (Milwaukee Brewers); Norman

APRIL 18
On opening day, Brooklyn's Jimmy Sheckard hits three triples.

APRIL 26
The Philadelphia Athletics make their AL debut at Columbia Park

THE ORIOLES' JOHN MCGRAW SAYS, "THE ATHLETICS ARE GOING TO BE THE WHITE ELEPHANTS OF THE AMERICAN LEAGUE." OWNER-MANAGER CONNIE MACK TAKES THE WHITE ELEPHANT AS THE TEAM SYMBOL, AND IT IS STILL THE SYMBOL OF THE OAKLAND ATHLETICS TODAY.

"Kid" Elberfeld (Detroit Tigers); Clark Griffith, Fielder Jones, and William "Dummy" Hoy (Chicago White Stockings).

Griffith represents a "double steal" for Chicago owner Charles Comiskey: he takes the star pitcher from the NL's Chicago franchise and appropriates their nickname as well.

MARCH 20-21:

The AL decrees that the catcher must be within 10 feet of home plate.

APRIL 3:

The *Cincinnati Enquirer* reports that "Indian" Grant will not be joining McGraw and the Baltimore Orioles.

Lave Cross joins the AL's Philadelphia Athletics and becomes the first to play for four teams in one city. Previously, he was a member of the Athletics in the AA, the Phillies in the NL, and the Quakers in the Players League.

THE SEASON

APRIL 18:

Brooklyn's Jimmy Sheckard becomes the first player to hit three triples in an opening day game. Sheckard also scores four times as visiting Brooklyn downs Philadelphia, 12-7.

APRIL 24:

With three other scheduled games rained out, the honor of playing the AL's first official game belongs to Cleveland and Chicago. The game is played in Chicago with a crowd of more than 10,000 on hand. Cleveland right fielder Ollie Pickering is the AL's first batter. Chicago and pitcher Roy Patterson go on to win, 8-2.

In Boston, Wolfie Jacobs announces rules decisions to fans via a megaphone.

APRIL 25:

At Detroit's Bennett Field, the Tigers and the Milwaukee Brewers make their AL bows, with 8,000 fans on hand. The Brewers hold a 13-3 lead after seven and a half innings, but Detroit scores one in the bottom of the eighth and 10 in the ninth for a 14-13 win. The ninth inning rally is led by first baseman Frank "Pop" Dillon, who has two doubles and drives in the winning run. Dillon has a record four two-base hits in the game.

Cleveland's Ervin Beck hits the AL's first homer against Chicago's John Skopec.

APRIL 26:

After two days of rain-outs, the Athletics make their AL debut at Columbia Park in Philadelphia before a crowd of 10,524. Washington spoils the opening with a 5-1 win despite three hits and an RBI by the Athletics' Napoleon Lajoie.

RULES

The modern infield fly rule is adopted; players are no longer able to "trap" pop-ups. In the NL, the first two foul balls are strikes; in the AL, all fouls are strikes.

Ban Johnson was the AL's first president.

MAY 23
Cleveland, down 13-5, sets an AL record in rallying to beat Washington, 14-13.

In Baltimore, AL president Ban Johnson throws out the first ball as the Orioles host Boston, after postponements for rain and wet grounds. Baltimore wins, 10-6, behind nine-hit pitching by Iron Man Joe McGinnity, who is fighting malaria. The loser, Win Kellum, yields 11 hits, including two triples to "Turkey Mike" Donlin.

LEAGUE

The NL consists of the Boston Beaneaters, Brooklyn Superbas, Chicago Orphans, Cincinnati Reds, New York Giants, Philadelphia Phillies, Pittsburgh Pirates, and St. Louis Cardinals. American League teams are the Baltimore Orioles, Boston Somersets, Chicago White Stockings, Cleveland Blues, Detroit Tigers, Milwaukee Brewers, Philadelphia Athletics, and Washington Nationals.

APRIL 27:

The Cleveland Blues win for the first time, beating the White Stockings in Chicago, 10-4, behind pitcher William Hart.

APRIL 28:

In Chicago, the White Stockings avenge yesterday's loss by banging out 23 hits – all singles – in beating the Blues, 13-1. Charles "Bock" Baker, in his first major league start, allows all 23 hits.

APRIL 30:

At Philadelphia's Columbia Park, Boston beats the visiting Athletics, 8-6, in 10 innings. The game marks the American League's first extra-innings game, as well as the first-ever win for the Somersets.

MAY 1:

Dummy Hoy and Herm McFarland, Chicago teammates, hit the first grand slam home runs in the AL, and Detroit makes a record 12 errors.

MAY 2:

In Chicago, the White Stockings and player-manager Clark Griffith lose the first forfeit in the AL. In the top of the ninth Detroit takes the lead; Griffith and his team stall, hoping rain will end the game. Instead, umpire Tom Connolly awards the Tigers a 9-0 forfeit.

MAY 4:

In the bottom of the 10th in a game against Cincinnati, fire breaks out in St. Louis's Robison Field. Cincinnati owner John T. Brush, in a wheelchair, is carried to safety by fans. The cause of the fire is a cigarette thrown into the garbage.

St. Louis plays one home game at Sportsman's Park before returning to Robison Field.

MAY 8:

Boston has a successful AL home debut at the Huntington Avenue Grounds. With an overflow crowd of 11,500 on hand, the Somersets thump the Athletics, 12-4, on 19 hits. The Boston attack is led by John "Buck" Freeman with a homer, a triple, and a single. The winning pitcher is Cy Young, who allows 11 hits; Bill Bernhard is the loser.

MAY 8:

Norman Thomas "Turkey" Stearnes is born in Nashville, Tennessee.

MAY 9:

Earl Moore of the Cleveland Blues no-hits the visiting Chicago White Stockings into the 10th inning when Sam Mertes singles. The White Stockings go on to win the game, 4-2, on only two hits.

It takes police with drawn guns to protect umpire Hank O'Day from the wrath of Cardinals' fans after a game their team loses. Outside the ballpark, the assault continues in the form of rock throwing.

MAY 15:

In the AL's first shutout, the Washington Nationals beat the Boston Somersets, 4-0.

MAY 23:

In Cleveland, 1,250 fans see the Blues accomplish an AL record comeback. Behind 13-5 to the Washington Nationals with two out in the 9th, the batboys are packing equipment when Cleveland scores nine runs for a 14-13 win. The Blues bang out six singles and two doubles; the Senators walk one, hit a batter, and commit a passed ball.

The Athletics' Napoleon Lajoie becomes the first player known to be walked intentionally with the bases loaded.

JUNE 9:

In Cincinnati, the visiting Giants pound out a major league record 31 hits. With two out in the ninth and New York up 25-13, some fans have seen enough and swarm onto the field; umpire Bob Emslie calls a forfeit. The Giants are led by Al Selbach, who is six for seven, with two doubles and four runs. The winning pitcher is Bill Phyle; Bill Phillips is credited with the loss.

JUNE 21:

The Superbas slaughter the visiting Reds, 21-2, at Washington

JULY 12
Boston ace Cy Young notches his 300th career win with a 5-3 victory over the A's.

Park. Cincinnati pitcher Harley "Doc" Parker goes the distance, ending up with the worst statistical line of any 20th-century pitcher: 26 hits and 21 runs in eight innings.

According to statistician and Society for American Baseball Research member Joseph Cardello, Parker gave up trying to retire the Brooklyn batters and allowed them to hit the ball in the hope his fielders would put an end to the debacle. Parker is sent to the minors on June 22, never to return.

JUNE 24:

There's no running on Brooklyn catcher James "Deacon" McGuire today. The veteran guns down five Chicago baserunners. The Superbas register a 2-1 win on a Willie Keeler single and a Bill Dahlen sacrifice fly that drives him in.

JULY 12:

Boston Beaneater pitcher Cy Young beats the Philadelphia Athletics, 5-3, in gaining his 300th career win. The right-handed Young gives up seven hits. In the loss, Philadelphia's Napoleon Lajoie steals two bases.

JULY 15:

The Giants' Christy Mathewson no-hits St. Louis, 5-0. The 22-year-old walks four and strikes out four; the Giants make one error. The losing pitcher is Willie Sudhoff.

JULY 16:

Boston's Cy Young wins his 12th consecutive game with a 10-8 victory over the Blues in Cleveland.

JULY 20:

Henry "Heinie" Manush is born in Tuscumbia, Alabama.

JULY 31:

There's turbulent air in Cincinnati as 26 batters are struck out in 14 innings in a game with Chicago. "Long" Tom Hughes of the Orphans registers 15 of the strikeouts; Frank "Noodles" Hahn of the Reds racks up the other 11. Cincinnati wins, 5-4.

AUGUST 5:

Orioles' rookie first baseman James "Burt" Hart is out trying to stretch a double into a triple. He throws his glove at umpire John Haskell and then punches him. AL president Ban Johnson lives up to his name and bans the six-foot, three-inch, 200-pound Burt Hart for life. Hart hit .311 in 58 games for Baltimore.

AUGUST 7:

Brewers' manager Hugh Duffy, angered over a ninth-inning call by Al Mannassau, expresses himself by punching the umpire. In addition to losing his temper, he loses the game. Ban Johnson doesn't live up to his name and the veteran Duffy is spared a lifetime suspension.

AUGUST 21:

In a game against Detroit, the Orioles' Joe McGinnity is ejected for spitting in the face of umpire Tommy Connolly. The aptly nicknamed Norman "The Tabasco Kid" Elberfeld uncharacteristically tries to play peacemaker and, for his efforts, he is floored by Baltimore's Mike Donlin. Elberfeld, McGinnity, Baltimore's Bill Keister, and a fan are all arrested. Judge Harry Goldman, who happens to own shares in the Orioles, dismisses the charges against the players – but fines the fan $100.

McGinnity is permanently suspended by AL president Ban Johnson, but the pitcher apologizes to Connolly and the punishment is reduced to 12 days.

It is a bad day for umpires, and this time Jack Haskell is the target of players' wrath. Chicago White Stockings pitcher Jack Katoll throws the ball at him, and his teammate, shortstop Frank Shugart, punches the arbiter. A riot ensues and the police are summoned. The players claim Haskell instigated the incident by using his mask as a weapon, but AL president Ban Johnson suspends the two anyway.

AUGUST 24:

This time it is umpire Pongo Joe Cantillon who is under attack by Boston fans. Somerset players Chick Stahl and Parson Ted Lewis come to his rescue.

SEPTEMBER 3:

Baltimore Orioles pitcher Iron Man Joe McGinnity earns his nickname, throwing both ends of a double header against the Milwaukee Brewers, winning the first game, 10-0, and losing the second, 6-1.

LEAGUE

In May, Chicago buys pitcher Rube Waddell from the Pirates. Waddell is 0-2 at the time. On the strength of a nine-run second inning and a 10-run third, the Boston Somersets thump the Philadelphia Athletics, 23-12.

TRIVIA

Baseball fans get a new food and America gets a new culinary term. Concessionaire Harry M. Stevens introduces frankfurters to the Polo Grounds in New York; cartoonist Tad Dorgan provides a newspaper sketch, and for the first known time dubs them "hot dogs."

"The only thing Cy Young didn't win was the Cy Young Award."
– *Announcer Joe Torre, 1986*

SEPTEMBER 12
For the second time in 10 days, Joe McGinnity pitches both games of a double header.

HISTORY

The only 1901 post-season action is a series between the Chicago White Stockings and an AL all-star team – the All-American Series. The teams split their games.

LEAGUE

The AL outdraws the NL head-to-head in Chicago, but overall NL attendance for the 1901 season tops AL attendance, 1,920,031 to 1,683,584.

SEPTEMBER 12:

Joe McGinnity again pitches both ends of a double header; Baltimore beats Philadelphia, 4-3, in the opener and loses, 5-4, in the nightcap.

SEPTEMBER 14:

In Boston, the Somersets' Cy Young racks up his 30th win of the season with a 12-1 victory over Washington. Young has only nine losses.

SEPTEMBER 15:

Cleveland spares itself possible further humiliation when the second game of a double header against the Tigers today is shortened to seven innings so the Blues can make a train. At the time, Detroit leads, 21-0. Ed Siever gets the win.

SEPTEMBER 21:

At the West Side Grounds, the Chicago Orphans beat the Boston Beaneaters in a 17-inning game with no extra-base hits. Long Tom Hughes goes all the way for the 1-0 win, striking out 13. Clarence Childs singles in the winning run.Despite a loss today to Philadelphia on the road, the Chicago White Stockings win the AL's first pennant.

REGULAR SEASON WRAP-UP:

The White Stockings finish ahead of Boston by four games. Clark Griffith is 24-7, rookie Roy Patterson is 20-16, and Fielder Jones tops Chicago's batters with a .311 average.

The NL pennant goes to the Pittsburgh Pirates by seven and a half games over Philadelphia. Deacon Phillippe and Jack Chesbro are 20-game winners for Pittsburgh; Honus Wagner hits .353.

SEPTEMBER 24:

Brooklyn's Jimmy Sheckard hits a grand slam homer as the Superbas continue a two-day assault on Cincinnati pitching with a 16-2 win. It is Sheckard's second consecutive game with a grand slam, tying the 1894 record of Jimmy Bannon of Boston. Paced by grand slams by Sheckard and Joe Kelley, Brooklyn won yesterday's game against the Reds, 25-6, on 26 hits.

SEPTEMBER 25:

In Boston, the Somersets' Cy Young wins his league-best 33rd game of the season by downing Chicago, 5-2. Young finishes the year 33-10, with a 1.62 ERA.

POST-SEASON

DECEMBER 11:

At the NL owners' annual meeting, opponents of the Giants' Andrew Freedman and his allies advance Albert Spalding for president. The pro-Freedman forces nominate present president Nick Young. The owners cast 25 ballots; Spalding and Freedman are deadlocked at four votes each. Freedman and his group leave the room and a 26th ballot is taken; Spalding is declared the winner, 4-0.

DECEMBER 16:

New York Giants' owner Andrew Freedman is granted a court injunction that keeps Albert Spalding from assuming his duties. Spalding resigns the job he held only in name, and Henry Clay Pulliam is elected to the position as a compromise candidate. Freedman ultimately decides to sell his stake in the Giants and leave baseball altogether.

SEPTEMBER 14
With a 12-1 win over Washington, Cy Young records his 30th win of the season.

SEPTEMBER 21
Chicago's Long Tom Hughes goes all the way in a 17-inning, 1-0 win over Boston.

THE BEST OF 1901

NATIONAL LEAGUE

HITTERS

Batting Average:
Jesse Burkett, St. Louis Cardinals, .382

Slugging Average:
Jimmy Sheckard, Brooklyn Dodgers, .536

Home Runs:
Sam Crawford, Cincinnati Reds, 16

Runs Batted In:
Honus Wagner, Pittsburgh Pirates, 126

Hits:
Jesse Burkett, 228

Stolen Bases:
Honus Wagner, 49

PITCHERS

Wins:
Wild Bill Donovan, Brooklyn Dodgers, 25

Strikeouts:
Frank "Noodles" Hahn, Cincinnati Reds, 239

Earned Run Average:
Jesse Tannehill, Pittsburgh Pirates, 2.18

Winning Percentage:
Jack Chesbro, Pittsburgh Pirates, .677

Saves:
Jack Powell, St. Louis Cardinals, 3

AMERICAN LEAGUE

HITTERS

Batting Average:
Napoleon Lajoie, Philadelphia Athletics, .422

Slugging Average:
Napoleon Lajoie, .635

Home Runs:
Napoleon Lajoie, 14

Runs Batted In:
Napoleon Lajoie, 125

Hits:
Napoleon Lajoie, 229

Stolen Bases:
Frank Isbell, Chicago White Stockings, 52

PITCHERS

Wins:
Denton "Cy" Young, Boston Somersets, 33

Strikeouts:
Cy Young, 158

Earned Run Average:
Cy Young, 1.62

Winning Percentage:
Clark Griffith, Chicago White Stockings, .774

Saves:
Bill Hoffer, Cleveland Blues, 3

EQUIPMENT

J.F. Hillerich makes a bat for Napoleon Lajoie with two knobs, enabling him to hit for power without giving up his split-hands grip.

LEAGUE

In August, the idea of "syndicate baseball" is born at Andrew Freedman's New Jersey estate. The Giants' boss hosts fellow owners Arthur Soden of Boston, John T. Brush of Cincinnati, Frank Robison of St. Louis, and others. They propose dumping the National Agreement. Under their plan, a central NL office, not individual teams, will own all players and assign them to teams on an annual basis. In addition, preferred and common stock in franchises will be sold and controlled by a board of regents.

1902

"Frank Selee will devote his strongest efforts on the new Cubs."
– *Chicago Daily News*

NEWS

20TH CENTURY LIMITED TRAIN TRAVELS FROM NEW YORK TO CHICAGO IN RECORD 16 HOURS

JELL-O IS INTRODUCED

U.S. unemployment at 20-year low

ENRICO CARUSO MAKES FIRST PHONOGRAPH RECORD

U.S. will control Panama Canal "perpetually"

U.S. BUYS VIRGIN ISLANDS

BOER WAR ENDS; BRITAIN CONTROLS SOUTH AFRICA

Flatiron Building opens in New York City

MICHIGAN WINS FIRST ROSE BOWL, BEATING STANFORD, 49-0

PRE-SEASON

MARCH 7:

An impoverished James Francis "Pud" Galvin dies at age 45 in Pittsburgh. In 14 seasons, Galvin won 361 games and had an ERA of 2.87.

MARCH 27:

The *Chicago Daily News* writes of the NL's Chicago team: "Frank Selee will devote his strongest efforts on the team work of the new Cubs, this year." It is the first use of the nickname; until now the team has been called the Colts and the Orphans. But it will take three years for the name Cubs to come into common usage in the league.

THE SEASON

APRIL 19:

The Reds' Bob Ewing makes an inauspicious debut in a 9-5 losing effort to visiting Chicago. He walks five batters in the fifth inning and 10 in the game.

Ewing goes on to a respectable career, winning 125 games against 118 losses, with an ERA of 2.49. In 2,301 1/3 innings, he walks 614.

APRIL 26:

Cleveland's Addie Joss one-hits St. Louis, 3-0, in his major league debut. Joss also knocks in two runs with a seventh inning double.

APRIL 29:

The Orioles' John McGraw is hit by pitches from Boston's Bill Dinneen five times today. And each time, umpire Jack Sheridan refuses to award him first base. In the ninth inning, when he is hit for the fifth time, McGraw sits down in the batter's box and refuses to follow orders to get off the field. Sheridan becomes the target of a near-riot after the game. Ban Johnson suspends McGraw for five days.

MAY 21:

Earl Howard Averill is born in Snohomish, Washington.

MAY 22:

Al Simmons is born Aloys (in some references, Aloysius) Szymanski in Milwaukee.

JUNE 3:

St. Louis Cardinals' outfielder Mike O'Neill raps the NL's first-ever pinch-hit grand slam homer. It comes against Charles "Togie" Pittinger of Boston.

JUNE 4:

Napoleon Lajoie makes his Cleveland debut with one hit in three at bats as his new team defeats Boston, 4-3.

JUNE 15:

Jay Clarke hits eight homers in a Texas League game. His Corsicana team defeats Texarkana, 51-3. Because Sunday baseball is not allowed in Corsicana, the game is played on a small, nonleague field in Ennis, Texas. The 19-year-old Clarke is only one gun in Corsicana's arsenal: the team hits 21 homers, and seven players have at least five hits; Clarke is one of three players who go eight for eight. In his entire nine-year Major League career, Clarke hits only six home runs, and has a lifetime .254 batting average.

According to The Sporting News' Baseball: *"Some historians claim Clarke hit only three homers in the game (the typographical similarity of an 8 and a 3 cited in various ways for an alleged mix-up). The latest studies support the credibility of the*

JUNE 4
Cleveland rookie Napoleon Lajoie goes one-for-three in his NL debut.

JULY 23
John McGraw gets his first win as Giants' manager, 4-1 over the Superbas.

eight-homer feat." Some telegraphers cannot believe the score is 51-3 and transmit it as 5-3.

JUNE 18:

Amid rumors that the Orioles will be dropped from the AL next season, manager John McGraw meets in New York with the Giants' owner, Andrew Freedman.

JUNE 22:

In a game neither pitcher deserves to lose, Chicago's Bobby Lowe hits an RBI single in the bottom of the 19th inning against Charles "Deacon" Phillippe to defeat Pittsburgh, 3-2. Jack "Brakeman" Taylor goes all the way for Chicago and gets the win. Phillippe, also a complete game pitcher, is charged with the loss.

JUNE 24:

Cleveland's Napoleon Lajoie hits a grand slam – the first in team history – against St. Louis in a 12-4 win. The winning pitcher of the game is Bill Bernhard.

JUNE 27:

Andrew Freedman, who is in the process of selling his team to John T. Brush, hires John McGraw to manage the Giants.

JUNE 28:

Baltimore's John McGraw and Joe Kelley clash with umpires Tom Connolly and Jimmy Johnstone at Oriole Park. In the eighth inning, Connolly ejects McGraw and is bumped and cursed by Kelley. Connolly calls a forfeit. McGraw and Kelley receive indefinite suspensions.

John McGraw later "explains" his behavior on June 28 in mixed metaphors: "No man likes to be ordered off the earth like a dog in the presence of his friends. Ballplayers are not a lot of cattle to have the whip cracked over them."

JUNE 30:

Cleveland becomes the first team in AL history with three consecutive home runs. In the sixth inning in game one of today's doubleheader against St. Louis, Napoleon Lajoie, Charles "Piano Legs" Hickman, and Bill Bradley accomplish the feat. Cleveland wins the game, 17-2. In game two, which ends in a 3-3 tie after 15, Lajoie is thumbed when his apparent game-winning double in the 10th inning to score Elmer Flick is called foul.

JULY 9:

After two days of negotiations with the Orioles that result in the purchase of his stock in the team for $6,500, John McGraw "officially" signs to manage the Giants. McGraw actually inked the contract on July 5 and told reporters yesterday that he was headed for New York. He will replace Heinie Smith (5-27), who in turn followed Horace Fogel (18-23). According to biographer Charles C. Alexander, McGraw receives an $11,000 annual salary and a four-year pact.

JULY 16:

Joseph C. France, acting for Giants' owner Andrew Freedman, buys 201 of the 400 shares of the Orioles for $50,000. He releases Iron Man Joe McGinnity, Dan McGann, Roger Bresnahan, and Jack Cronin and signs them for the Giants. Joe Kelley goes to Cincinnati as the Reds' manager, along with Cy Seymour.

JULY 17:

The Orioles, with only five players left – including Wilbert Robinson – forfeit to St. Louis in Baltimore. Ban Johnson steps in, revokes the franchise, and takes over the team, borrowing players from other teams. Wilbert Robinson becomes the manager.

JULY 18:

The makeshift Orioles beat the Browns.

JULY 19:

The Giants, in their first game under new manager John J. McGraw, lose to the Phillies, 4-3. Herman "Ham" Iburg is the winner; newly acquired Iron Man Joe McGinnity's the losing pitcher.

JULY 23:

John McGraw gets his first win as Giants' manager as New York beats the Superbas, 4-1, in Brooklyn. Luther Taylor, a deaf player known as Dummy, gets the win.

AUGUST 9:

The Reds are sold for $150,000 by John T. Brush to George B. Cox, Max and Julius Fleischman (manufacturers of yeast), and August "Garry" Hermann.

LEAGUE

John McGraw, owner Andrew Freedman's 12th manager in eight years, cuts 11 players from the Giants' roster.

LEAGUE

Last year's AL Milwaukee Brewers (48-49, last place) are this year's St. Louis Browns and will play home games in Sportsman's Park. The American Association, now a minor league, opens the season under its first president, Thomas J. Hickey, with teams in Columbus, Milwaukee, Toledo, St. Paul, Minneapolis, Kansas City, Indianapolis, and Louisville. The NL offers an amalgamation plan under which it would absorb four AL teams; AL president Ban Johnson declines.

"I threw the ball so hard I tore a couple of boards off the grandstand. One of the fellows said that the stand looked like a cyclone struck it."
– Denton True Young, on how he got his nickname, Cy

LEAGUE

The St. Louis Browns instigate an exodus of stars from the NL Cardinals to their own team. The players are the NL's 1901 batting champion, outfielder Jesse Burkett (.382); outfielder Emmett Heidrick (.339); shortstop Bobby Wallace (.322); and pitchers Jack Harper (23-13), Jake Powell (19-19), and Willie Sudhoff (17-11).

TRIVIA

In his brief stint as Giants manager, Horace Fogel perhaps will be best remembered for an ill-conceived experiment. He moved 20-game winner Christy Mathewson to first base. Mathewson played there for three games before returning to the mound.

AUGUST 12:

John T. Brush becomes managing director of the Giants.

SEPTEMBER 4:

Chicago's David "Alex" Hardy becomes the first "modern" pitcher to throw a shutout in his major league debut. Hardy beats Brooklyn, 1-0. The Canadian-born Hardy has only a brief career: He plays for two years with a 4-3 record and a 4.34 ERA.

SEPTEMBER 6:

In St. Louis, Boston's Cy Young beats the Browns, 6-5, for his 30th win of the season.

SEPTEMBER 7:

Brooklyn and New York play a "home-and-home" double-header. In the morning the teams meet at Brooklyn's Washington Park, where the Giants win, 6-4, before 9,300 fans. In the afternoon, game two is played before 23,628 fans at the Polo Grounds; Brooklyn wins, 3-0.

SEPTEMBER 9:

John T. Brush buys the New York Giants for $200,000 from Andrew Freedman, marking the exit from baseball of one of its most outrageous characters.

SEPTEMBER 13:

Shortstop Joe Tinker, second baseman Johnny Evers, and first baseman Frank Chance all appear together for first time on the Chicago Cubs. Herman "Germany" Schaefer is the team's third baseman.

SEPTEMBER 15:

Two days after making their major league debut, the first Tinker-to-Evers-to-Chance double play is executed. The twin killing occurs in a game against visiting Cincinnati at West Side Grounds, where only 260 fans see history made. Chicago and pitcher Carl "The Human Icicle" Lundgren win the game, 6-3.

SEPTEMBER 20:

In Chicago, James "Nixey" Callahan pitches the AL's second no-hitter, beating Detroit, 3-0. He strikes out two and walks two; his team commits one error. Aloysius "Wish" Egan is the losing pitcher. Prior to the game, Callahan was in jail after assaulting a hotel bellhop for "poor room service."

SEPTEMBER 23:

At age 35, Boston's Cy Young wins his 32nd game of the season, topping Washington, 14-1. Young is now 32-11, with 41 complete games in 43 starts.

OCTOBER 4:

The Pirates, with a huge 27-game lead on Brooklyn and the NL pennant clinched, are at home seeking a record 103 wins. Their opponent is fourth-place Cincinnati, 33 1/2 games out of first place. The day is cold and rainy, the field muddy, and only 1,200 fans show up. With no incentive to play, Cincinnati wants a cancellation; Pittsburgh owner Barney Dreyfuss declines. In protest, Reds' player-manager Joe Kelley makes a mockery of the game. He puts three left-handed fielders in his infield and sends three players who have never pitched to the mound – first baseman Jake Beckley starts and is relieved by outfielder Mike Donlin; outfielder Cy Seymour finishes up. Cincinnati's best pitcher, Frank "Noodles" Hahn, plays first. Behind the plate is rookie pitcher Harry "Rube" Vickers, who sets a major league record with six passed balls. Players take the field smoking cigars, including Kelley, who goes to bat with a stogie in his mouth and ignores umpire Hank O'Day's order to lose it. When the travesty ends, the Pirates have a win; Dreyfuss refunds the gate receipts to fans.

REGULAR SEASON WRAP-UP:

The AL pennant is won by Philadelphia, managed by Connie Mack, with an 83-53 record, five games over second place St. Louis. The Athletics have two 20-game winners – Rube Waddell (24-7) and Eddie Plank (20-15).

The Pirates, managed by Fred Clarke, win the NL flag. They boast three 20-game winners – Jack Chesbro (28-6), Jesse Tannehill (20-6), and Deacon Phillippe (20-9). Chesbro has 31 complete games in 33 starts. Their top hitter is Clarence "Ginger" Beaumont at a league-leading .357.

POST-SEASON

DECEMBER:

NL owners hold their annual meeting in New York City and elect Harry Pulliam president. A committee is appointed to pursue peace with the AL.

The rare Honus Wagner "tobacco card" today fetches more than a half million dollars.

THE BEST OF 1902

NATIONAL LEAGUE

HITTERS

Batting Average:
Clarence "Ginger" Beaumont, Pittsburgh Pirates, .357

Slugging Average:
Honus Wagner, Pittsburgh Pirates, .467

Home Runs:
Tommy Leach, Pittsburgh Pirates, 6

Runs Batted In:
Honus Wagner, 91

Hits:
Clarence Beaumont, 194

Stolen Bases:
Honus Wagner, 42

PITCHERS

Wins:
Jack Chesbro, Pittsburgh Pirates, 28

Strikeouts:
Vic Willis, Boston Braves, 225

Earned Run Average:
Jack "Brakeman" Taylor, Chicago Cubs, 1.33

Winning Percentage:
Jack Chesbro, .824

Saves:
Vic Willis, 3

AMERICAN LEAGUE

HITTERS

Batting Average:
Ed Delahanty, Washington Nationals, .376

Slugging Average:
Ed Delahanty, .590

Home Runs:
Ralph "Socks" Seybold, Philadelphia Athletics, 16

Runs Batted In:
John "Buck" Freeman, Boston Somersets, 121

Hits:
Charles "Piano Legs" Hickman, Boston Somersets/Cleveland Blues, 194

Stolen Bases:
Tully "Topsy" Hartsel, Philadelphia Athletics, 47

PITCHERS

Wins:
Denton "Cy" Young, Boston Somersets, 32

Strikeouts:
George "Rube" Waddell, Philadelphia Athletics, 210

Earned Run Average:
Ed Siever, Detroit Tigers, 1.91

Winning Percentage:
Bill Bernhard, Philadelphia Athletics/Cleveland Blues, .783

Saves:
Jack Powell, St. Louis Browns, 2

LEAGUE

In April, Napoleon Lajoie is enjoined by Pennsylvania Supreme Court Justice William P. Potter from playing with the Philadelphia Athletics. Lajoie has a three-year contract to play with the NL's Phillies. Also affected are Chick Fraser, Bill Bernhard, Elmer Flick, and Ed Delahanty. To circumvent the injunction, which applies only within Pennsylvania, AL president Ban Johnson arranges for the transfer of Lajoie's contract to Cleveland in June. Bernhard and Flick also go to Cleveland; Delahanty joins the Washington Senators; Fraser remains in the NL with Philadelphia. Jack Harper, who jumped to the Browns from the Cardinals, fares better than Lajoie in court. A St. Louis city circuit court denies a Cardinals' request for an injunction.

1903

NEWS

WRIGHT BROTHERS' FLYING MACHINE STAYS ALOFT FOR 12 SECONDS AND TRAVELS 120 FEET AT KITTY HAWK, NORTH CAROLINA

HENRY FORD ESTABLISHES AUTO COMPANY WITH $100,000; FIRST MODEL A SELLS FOR $850

Pope Leo XIII dies

Pepsi-Cola is introduced

AT 12 MINUTES, *THE GREAT TRAIN ROBBERY* IS THE LONGEST FILM EVER

ANTOINE BECQUEREL AND THE CURIES WIN NOBEL PRIZE FOR PHYSICS

Caffeine-free Sanka introduced in Germany

JACK LONDON'S *THE CALL OF THE WILD* IS PUBLISHED

PRE-SEASON

JANUARY 9:

Gambler Frank Farrell and former New York City police commissioner Big Bill Devery buy the Baltimore Orioles for $18,000. They intend to move the team to New York.

JANUARY 9-10:

The National and American Leagues hold a "peace conference" in the St. Nicholas Hotel in Cincinnati. Representing the NL are president Harry Pulliam; Frank DeHaas Robison, president of the St. Louis Cardinals; James A. Hart, owner of the Chicago Cubs; and August "Garry" Hermann, president of the Cincinnati Reds. On the AL side are president Ban Johnson; Charlie Somers and Henry Killilea of the Boston Pilgrims; and Charles Comiskey, president of the Chicago White Stockings. The parties agree to two eight-team leagues. The AL will have a franchise in New York, but will steer clear of Pittsburgh. Baseball will be governed by a three-man National Commission consisting of the two league presidents and Reds' president Garry Hermann. The two circuits will be separate and equal, have coordinated schedules and common contracts; they will refrain from raiding one another's teams' rosters. The reserve clause will be in effect in both the leagues; options won by the Players Protective Association are canceled. They also agree to a post-season playoff between pennant winners.

A total of 16 players are in dispute. The owners decide that nine will belong to the AL: Ed Delahanty (Washington), Sam Crawford (Detroit), Alonzo "Lefty" Davis (New York), Norman "Kid" Elberfeld (Detroit), Wee Willie Keeler (New York), William "Wid" Conroy (New York), Wild Bill Donovan (Detroit), Napoleon Lajoie (Cleveland), and Dave Fultz (New York). Seven will belong to NL teams: Vic Willis (Boston), Tommy Leach (Pittsburgh), Harry Smith (Pittsburgh), Rudy Hulswitt (Philadelphia), Sam "Sandow" Mertes (New York), Frank Bowerman (New York), and Christy Mathewson (New York). The distribution of players – they remain with their current teams – is regarded as a victory for the AL.

JANUARY 12:

George "Win" Mercer, who was to be player-manager for the Tigers in the 1903 season, replacing Frank Dwyer, commits suicide in San Francisco's Occidental Hotel by inhaling gas. Mercer, whose suicide is attributed to "women and gambling," is only 28 years old.

FEBRUARY 12:

Charles "Chick" Hafey is born in Berkeley, California. 🏛

FEBRUARY 21:

Tom Yawkey is born Thomas Austin in Detroit. 🏛

MARCH 1:

The Rules Committee decrees that the pitcher's "box" (mound) may be no higher than 15 inches.

MARCH 12:

The Greater New York Club of the American League is officially admitted into the American League. The new team, managed by Clark Griffith, will play home games at Hilltop Park, a site leased by the AL 10

APRIL 20
"Chief" Bender makes his major league debut for the Athletics with a 10-7 win over Boston.

MAY 7
The New York-Boston rivalry begins as the Pilgrims beat the Highlanders, 6-2.

years ago from the New York Institute for the Blind. It is located on Broadway between 165th and 168th Streets and bounded by 11th Avenue and Fort Washington Road. The grandstand holds 6,000; three other sections can accommodate an additional 10,000.

To make the American League's New York team competitive with the NL's Giants, a roster is fashioned with "names" from other teams. From the White Stockings comes player-manager Clark Griffith, who is joined by Jack Chesbro, Jesse Tannehill, Wee Willie Keeler, Dave Fultz, Alfonso "Lefty" Davis, Wid Conroy, Herman Long, Jimmy Williams, Herman McFarland, Lou Wiltse, and Handsome Harry Howell. The team's players will wear white uniforms with black stockings and red jackets.

APRIL 6:

Gordon Stanley "Mickey" Cochrane is born in Bridgewater, Massachusetts.

APRIL 16:

Paul "Big Poison" Waner is born in Harrah, Oklahoma.

THE SEASON

APRIL 20:

Charles "Chief" Bender makes his major league debut for the Athletics, replacing Eddie Plank in the third inning and beating Boston, 10-7. In the morning game of a doubleheader, Rube Waddell beats Boston, 9-4.

APRIL 22:

The AL's New York team makes its debut in Washington with a 3-1 defeat before a crowd of 11,950. Jack Chesbro gets the loss.

APRIL 23:

The New York losing streak ends at one; Handsome Harry Howell beats the Nationals, 7-2, in Washington for the AL franchise's first-ever win.

APRIL 30:

The 69th Regiment Band serenades 16,243 fans, and the AL's president, Ban Johnson, throws out the ceremonial first ball as the New York Highlanders (who got their nickname only yesterday) make their home debut. Spirits remain high as the Highlanders beat Washington, 6-2. Jack Chesbro avenges his opening day loss to the Nationals with the win today.

MAY 6:

It's butterfingers time in Chicago's West Side Park, where the White Stockings and the Tigers combine for an AL record 18 errors. Despite committing a record-tying 12, Chicago wins the game, 10-9; Patsy Flaherty gets the victory. The losing pitcher is Mal Eason.

MAY 7:

The Boston-New York AL rivalry begins today at Huntington Avenue Grounds, where the Pilgrims defeat the visiting Highlanders, 6-2. Bill Dinneen is the winning pitcher. Albert "Hobe" Ferris of Boston homers.

MAY 11:

Charlie Gehringer is born in Fowlerville, Michigan.

The first and second home runs in the New York Highlanders' history are hit today at Detroit's Bennett Field. The first homer comes off the bat of John Henry Ganzel; teammate Wid Conroy connects for the second roundtripper, and New York wins the game, 8-2.

MAY 17:

James Thomas "Cool Papa" Bell is born in Starkville, Mississippi.

Playing in Columbus, Ohio, because of the ban on Sunday baseball in Cleveland, the Blues and pitcher Addie Joss defeat the Highlanders, 9-2.

MAY 31:

Chicago uses 17 singles, three St. Louis walks, and six errors by the Cardinals to defeat the visitors, 17-4. The winning pitcher is Jake Weimer.

JUNE 8:

Charles "Deacon" Phillippe whitewashes the Boston Beaneaters, 4-0, giving the Pirates six consecutive shutouts. The previous five were: June 2, Charles "Deacon" Phillippe over New York, 7-0; June 3, Sam Leever over New York, 5-0; June 4, Irvin "Kaiser" Wilhelm, over Boston 5-0; June 5, Ed Doheny over Boston, 9-0; and June 6, Charles "Deacon" Phillippe over Boston, 4-0.

JUNE 16:

Player-manager Clark Griffith pitches the Highlanders' first

THE NEW NATIONAL AGREEMENT, WHICH ALSO IS SIGNED BY THE NATIONAL ASSOCIATION OF PROFESSIONAL MINOR LEAGUES, AIMS TO "PERPETUATE BASEBALL AS THE NATIONAL GAME OF AMERICA, AND TO SURROUND IT WITH SUCH SAFEGUARDS AS TO WARRANT ABSOLUTE CONFIDENCE IN ITS INTEGRITY AND METHODS; AND TO PROMOTE AND AFFORD PROTECTION TO SUCH PROFESSIONAL BASEBALL LEAGUES AND ASSOCIATIONS AS MAY DESIRE TO OPERATE WITHIN ITS PROVISIONS."

"I do not like living in the east and will not report."
– Pitcher Henry Schmidt

LEAGUE

The Pacific Coast League (minor league) is formed.

RULES

The AL will now count foul balls as strikes; the rule has been in force in the NL since 1901.

HISTORY

Andrew "Rube" Foster forms the black Chicago American Giants.

shutout, topping his old teammates, the White Sox, 1-0.

JUNE 19:

Henry Louis Gehrig is born in New York City. He weighs nearly 14 pounds at birth.

JUNE 22:

Carl Hubbell is born in Carthage, Missouri. (Also reported as Red Oak.)

JUNE 28:

In St. Louis, the Boston Pilgrims whitewash the Browns in both games of a double-header. The shutouts are the second and third in a row for Boston. Cy Young allows five hits and beats Francis "Red" Donahue, 1-0, in the opener. In the nightcap, Long Tom Hughes tops Jack Powell, 3-0, also on five hits. The Browns have managed but a single run in their last six games.

JULY 2:

Big Ed Delahanty leaves the Washington Nationals in Detroit after being suspended for rules violations and boards a New York Central Railroad train. While the train is crossing the International Bridge over Niagara Falls without Delahanty on board, he is killed. According to some accounts, a conductor ordered him off at Fort Erie for drunk and disorderly behavior and he fell through a drawbridge into the falls. One of five brothers who played in the major leagues, Delahanty had a lifetime batting average of .346.

Left-handed pitcher Jack Doscher makes his major league bow for the Chicago Cubs today against the Philadelphia Phillies. His father, Herm Doscher, was a major league third baseman from 1879 to 1882 with ballclubs in Troy and Cleveland. The Doschers become the first father and son to play in the major leagues.

JULY 4:

Ed Delahanty's body is discovered, but the exact circumstances of his death will remain a mystery.

AUGUST 1:

Today in Boston, the Giants' pitcher "Iron Man" Joe McGinnity starts and wins both ends of a double-header, 4-1 and 5-2. McGinnity allows six hits and one walk in each game.

The Athletics' Rube Waddell limits the Highlanders to four hits – all singles by Kid Elberfeld – but he loses, 3-2. Elberfeld becomes the first player with all of his team's hits when there are four or more.

AUGUST 3:

Brooklyn reaches 1,000 wins as an NL team with a 7-4 win against Philadelphia. Henry Schmidt throws a five-hitter; Jimmy Sheckard backs him with a homer.

Schmidt, just a rookie, is 21-13 with a 3.83 ERA and five shutouts. He returns his unsigned contract for 1904 from his home in Texas with a note saying, "I do not like living in the east and will not report." And he doesn't report – ever.

AUGUST 6:

During a game between Philadelphia and Brooklyn, the left-field bleachers at Baker Bowl collapse, killing 12 and injuring 232. The accident is caused when a crowd of fans move in the stands to watch either a fire or a fight outside the ballpark. Philadelphia will play its home games at Columbia Park.

AUGUST 8:

A week after beating Boston in both ends of a doubleheader, the Giants' "Iron Man" Joe McGinnity duplicates the feat against the Brooklyn Superbas, winning, 6-1 and 4-3. He allows a total of 13 hits and four walks.

AUGUST 17:

AL president Ban Johnson prohibits betting in his circuit's ballparks.

AUGUST 18:

Philadelphia (NL) experiences its ninth consecutive postponement. The streak of delays began on August 10.

AUGUST 27:

Philadelphia pitchers issue 17 walks to visiting Brooklyn.

AUGUST 28:

The Browns and Blues escape disaster when their train derails in Ohio. Cleveland star Napoleon Lajoie suffers a sprained knee and facial cuts. The Browns' Bill Sudhoff incurs a sprained wrist and cuts, while his St. Louis teammate Emmett "Snags" Heidrick is bruised and lacerated.

SEPTEMBER 5
The Pilgrims' Patsy Dougherty sets a record by hitting three triples in a 12-1 win.

AUGUST 31:

For the third time in a month, "Iron Man" Joe McGinnity pitches and wins both games of a doubleheader. Today's victim at the Polo Grounds is Philadelphia by scores of 4-1 and 9-2. It is the fifth time in McGinnity's career that he has won both games of a doubleheader – a major league record. The Giant right-hander allows a total of 11 hits and four walks and strikes out 13. The *New York Times* reports, "... no signs of fatigue – in fact, he seemed fresh enough to tackle the visitors for a third contest if that were necessary." The losing pitchers today are Chick Fraser and Bill Duggleby.

SEPTEMBER 5:

In Boston, the Pilgrims' Patsy Dougherty hits an AL record three triples and adds two singles to lead his team over the Athletics, 12-1, in eight innings.

SEPTEMBER 14:

In St. Louis, the Giants' 21-year-old right-hander Leon "Red" Ames makes his major league debut with an abbreviated no-hitter against the Cardinals, 5-0. Ames fans seven and walks two in the second game of a doubleheader, shortened to five innings by darkness.

SEPTEMBER 16:

The owners of the Pittsburgh Pirates and the Boston Pilgrims – Barney Dreyfuss and Henry Killilea – agree to a post-season world championship between their pennant-winning teams. The series will have a best of nine games format. AL president Ban Johnson tells Killilea, "You must beat them."

SEPTEMBER 17:

The Boston Pilgrims officially win the AL pennant, scoring in every inning to defeat the Cleveland Blues.

SEPTEMBER 18:

At Chicago's West Side Grounds with 2,000 attending, Philadelphia's Chick Fraser no-hits the Cubs, 10-0, in game two of a doubleheader. Fraser walks five and strikes out four; Chicago makes four errors. The losing pitcher is George "Peaches" Graham.

Pitching is not peachy for Graham. The losing end of Fraser's no-hitter is his only major league pitching appearance. He ends his brief career 0-1 with a 5.40 ERA, but fares a little better as a catcher, playing seven years and hitting .265. His son, Jack, plays in the majors in 1946 and 1949, batting .231.

REGULAR SEASON WRAP-UP:

Managed by third baseman Jimmy Collins, the Boston Pilgrims win the pennant with a record of 91-47, 14 1/2 games over the Athletics. The team has three 20-game winners: Cy Young, Bill Dinneen, and Long Tom Hughes.

Pittsburgh, under player-manager Fred Clarke (who hits .351) finishes at 91-49 – six and a half ahead of the Giants – for their third straight NL pennant. They have two 20-game winners: Deacon Phillippe and Sam Leever. Honus Wagner hits .355.

OCTOBER 1:

World Series, game one. The first modern World Series begins today with the Boston Pilgrims meeting the Pittsburgh Pirates at the Huntington Avenue Grounds in Boston. Cy Young retires Pirates' center fielder Clarence "Ginger" Beaumont on a fly ball to begin play. But the Pirates win, 7-3, with Deacon Phillippe besting Young. In the seventh inning, the Pirates' Jimmy Sebring hits the series' first homer; he also knocks in four runs. His teammate Tommy Leach has four hits. Phillippe limits Boston to six hits, issues no walks, and strikes out 10. Attendance is 16,242.

OCTOBER 2:

World Series, game two. Boston ties the Series with a 3-0 win at home. Bill Dinneen pitches a three-hitter and the first World Series shutout. He walks two and strikes out 11. Boston's right-fielder Patsy Dougherty hits two home runs. The attendance is 9,415.

OCTOBER 3:

World Series, game three. In Boston with 18,801 fans in attendance, the Pirates beat the Pilgrims, 4-2, behind Deacon Phillippe's four-hitter. Long Tom Hughes lasts only two innings and gets the loss.

OCTOBER 6:

World Series, game four. The Series moves to Exposition

HISTORY

"Iron Man" Joe McGinnity sets a modern major league record with 434 innings pitched this season. He also completes 44 of his 48 starts.

TRIVIA

Journalist Henry Chadwick writes that baseball was developed from the British game of rounders.

The New York Highlanders played their home games at Hilltop Park.

WILSON WHISKEY
C·C·A
THIS IS THE CIGAR MAKERS'
BLUE
LABEL
HOOT MON!
C.M.C.
GARTERS FOR MEN
HOSE SUPPORTERS
STAINILGO
EMERSON SHOE

Program from the first modern World Series, in which the Boston Pilgrims beat the Pittsburgh Pirates

HISTORY

The AL fares well in three other post-season meetings: The Athletics beat the Phillies four games to three; Cleveland tops Cincinnati in five of seven games, and the White Stockings and Cubs split 14 games.

TRIVIA

"Iron Man" Joe McGinnity's nickname is not the result of his iron-man pitching feats. It derives instead from his off-season occupation and a remark he made to a writer while he was pitching in the minor leagues: "I'm an iron man. I work in a foundry."

Park in Pittsburgh, where 7,600 fans turn out to see the Pirates win, 5-4, and go up in games three to one. Deacon Phillippe wins his third complete game, stopping the Pilgrims in the ninth with the tying run on second, three runs in, and only one out. The loser is Bill Dinneen. The Pirates' Honus Wagner and Clarence "Ginger" Beaumont have three hits each.

OCTOBER 7:

World Series, game five. Boston comes back with an 11-2 victory in Pittsburgh on a six-hitter by starter Cy Young. And Boston's Patsy Dougherty, who had two homers in game one, has two triples today. His teammates Jimmy Collins and Chick Stahl also triple, and Cy Young adds two hits of his own. The game's losing pitcher is Bill Kennedy. Attendance is 12,322.

OCTOBER 8:

World Series, game six. Boston, behind Bill Dinneen, wins today's game, 6-3, in Pittsburgh. Sam Leever is the losing pitcher. Ginger Beaumont has four of Pittsburgh's 10 hits, as well as two stolen bases. Attendance is 11,556.

OCTOBER 10:

World Series, game seven. After a day's delay because of cold weather, the Series resumes in Pittsburgh, with Cy Young besting Deacon Phillippe, 7-3. A plethora of triples results from a ground rule awarding three bases for fair balls hit into the crowd. Jimmy Collins, John "Buck" Freeman, Chick Stahl, Fred Parent, and Albert "Hobe" Ferris have three-baggers for the Pilgrims. Bill "Kitty" Bransfield of the Pirates has three hits. Attendance is 17,038.

OCTOBER 13:

World Series, game eight. After a two-day delay (no Sunday baseball followed by a rainout), baseball's first modern World Championship goes to the Pilgrims with a 3-0 victory in Boston. Bill Dinneen goes all the way for his third victory. He limits Pittsburgh to four hits, striking out seven and walking two. Deacon Phillippe records his fifth complete game, allowing eight hits in a losing effort. A half-hour delay results from a scuffle between the two teams. Pirates' player-manager Fred Clarke objects to a pitch from Dinneen and bunts down the first base line. Boston first sacker George "Candy" LaChance hits Clarke with the throw. The benches empty and fans from center field pour onto the field. Eventually, umpires Tommy Connolly and Hank O'Day restore order. The attendance is 7,455. The World Series share for each Boston player is $1,182. Pittsburgh management waives its portion of the loser's share; each Pirate gets $1,316.25.

POST-SEASON

OCTOBER 14:

The Pittsburgh Pirates' pitcher Ed Doheny, age 28, is committed to a mental institution after attacking a doctor and nurse. Doheny was 16-8 this past season. Although he lives 13 more years, Doheny will never play again in the majors. In nine years, he was 75-83 with a 3.75 ERA.

NOVEMBER 2:

Travis Jackson is born in Waldo, Arkansas.

DECEMBER 6:

Tony Lazzeri is born in San Francisco.

DECEMBER 12:

The Chicago Cubs acquire pitcher Mordecai "Three Finger" Brown (9-13, 2.60 ERA) and catcher Jack O'Neill (.236) from the Cardinals for pitcher Jack "Brakeman" Taylor (21-14, 2.45 ERA) and catcher Larry McLean (.000 in one game). In another December deal, the Highlanders obtain pitcher Long Tom Hughes (20-7, 2.57 ERA) from the Pilgrims for pitcher Jesse Tannehill (15-15, 3.27 ERA).

DECEMBER 17:

At their annual meeting in Chicago's Auditorium Annex, AL owners adopt a 154-game schedule.

DECEMBER 18:

Today Ban Johnson is rewarded by the American League's owners with a $5,000 Christmas bonus and a salary increase from $7,500 to $10,000. In *Total Baseball*, David Voigt writes: "Johnson reigned as the most powerful president in major league history. As the AL's entrenched 'czar,' Johnson used his powers to safeguard his league against any NL treachery.... [He] imposed his standards on owners and players."

OCTOBER 13
Boston wins game eight and the Series, behind a complete-game shutout from Bill Dineen.

DECEMBER 17
American League owners approve the new 154-game regular season schedule.

THE BEST OF 1903

NATIONAL LEAGUE

HITTERS

Batting Average:
Honus Wagner, Pittsburgh Pirates, .355

Slugging Average:
Fred Clarke, Pittsburgh Pirates, .532

Home Runs:
Jimmy Sheckard, Brooklyn Superbas, 9

Runs Batted In:
Sam Mertes, New York Giants, 104

Hits:
Clarence "Ginger" Beaumont, Pittsburgh Pirates, 209

Stolen Bases:
Frank Chance, Chicago Cubs; Jimmy Sheckard, 67

PITCHERS

Wins:
Joe McGinnity, New York Giants, 31

Strikeouts:
Christy Mathewson, New York Giants, 267

Earned Run Average:
Sam Leever, Pittsburgh Pirates, 2.06

Winning Percentage:
Sam Leever, .781

Saves:
Carl Lundgren, Chicago Cubs; Roscoe Miller, New York Giants, 3

AMERICAN LEAGUE

HITTERS

Batting Average:
Napoleon Lajoie, Cleveland Blues, .355

Slugging Average:
Napoleon Lajoie, .533

Home Runs:
John "Buck" Freeman, Boston Pilgrims, 13

Runs Batted In:
John Freeman, 104

Hits:
Patsy Dougherty, Boston Pilgrims, 195

Stolen Bases:
Harry "Deerfoot" Bay, Cleveland Blues, 45

PITCHERS

Wins:
Cy Young, Boston Pilgrims, 28

Strikeouts:
George "Rube" Waddell, Philadelphia Athletics, 302

Earned Run Average:
Earl Moore, Cleveland Blues, 1.77

Winning Percentage:
Cy Young, .757

Saves:
Bill Dinneen, Boston Pilgrims; Al Orth, Washington Nationals; Jack Powell, St. Louis Browns; George Mullin, Detroit Tigers; Cy Young, 2

TRIVIA

Boston owner Henry J. Killilea makes Pittsburgh owner Barney Dreyfuss pay his way into the ballpark for the World Series.

HISTORY

Prior to the start of the World Series, Pilgrims' catcher Lou Criger is approached by a gambler who offers to bribe him and teammate Cy Young. Criger refuses and reports the offer to AL president Ban Johnson.

1904

"My team will have nothing to do with the American League."
– *Giants' manager John McGraw*

NEWS

THEODORE ROOSEVELT IS ELECTED PRESIDENT

RUSSIA AND JAPAN GO TO WAR

New York City subway opens after four years of construction

HENRY FORD SETS AUTO SPEED RECORD, 91.37 MPH

Roosevelt establishes "Big Stick" policy, extends Monroe Doctrine

AMERICAN TOBACCO COMPANY FOUNDED

Panama Canal Zone becomes U.S. property

ST. LOUIS WORLD'S FAIR OPENS

Helen Keller graduates from Radcliffe College

Hudson Tunnel connects Manhattan and New Jersey

PRE-SEASON

JANUARY 23:

The New York Highlanders acquire pitcher Al "The Curveless Wonder" Orth (10-22, 4.34 ERA) from the Washington Nationals for pitcher Long Tom Hughes (20-7, 2.57 ERA) and Bill Wolfe 6-9, 2.97 ERA).

MARCH 10:

New York Giants players leave Mobile, Alabama, ahead of the law after a judge issues a warrant for their arrest for beating a local umpire unconscious during an exhibition game. The players were goaded by manager John McGraw.

THE SEASON

APRIL 17:

Brooklyn's management figures a way around the laws banning Sunday baseball. Fans are admitted free to the game at Washington Park but must buy a program. In their first Sunday home game, the Superbas beat the Boston Beaneaters by a score of 9–1.

APRIL 25:

Boston's Cy Young and Philadelphia's George "Rube" Waddell face off and the Athletics win, 2-0. Young yields no hits in the final two innings.

APRIL 26:

Ty Cobb makes his professional debut, playing center field and batting seventh for the Augusta Tourists in the Class C South Atlantic (Sally) League. He singles and doubles in four at-bats against George Engel of Columbia in an 8-7 losing effort. Biographer Charles Alexander credits Cobb with two for four, based on the boxscore of the game. In his *My Life in Baseball*, Cobb claims he hit an inside-the-park homer.

APRIL 30:

Boston's Cy Young relieves George Winter in the third inning, retires 21 Nationals in a row, and extends his consecutive no-hit inning string to nine.

MAY 3:

Charles "Red" Ruffing is born in Granville, Illinois.

MAY 5:

Cy Young pitches baseball's first perfect game since the pitching mound was moved to 60 feet 6 inches, defeating the Athletics in Boston, 3-0. The 37-year-old right-hander also becomes the first to pitch no-hitters in two different centuries. In today's masterpiece, he strikes out eight and allows only six balls out of the infield in an 83-minute game seen by 10,267. Rube Waddell, the losing pitcher and fittingly the last out of the game, earlier in the year had taunted Young with: "How did you like that one, you hayseed." Waddell fanned six and allowed 10 hits today. A's manager Connie Mack describes it as the finest ball game he'd ever seen.

MAY 11:

Cy Young's consecutive no-hit streak reaches 23 today against the Tigers. Detroit breaks the streak in the sixth but the Boston Pilgrims win, 1-0, in 15 innings.

MAY 21:

Boston Pilgrims' shortstop Bill O'Neill can't find the handle. In a forgettable performance, he commits six errors today in 13 innings.

MAY 24:

The Detroit Tigers play a "home" game in Grand Rapids, Michigan, beating

APRIL 25
Rival aces Cy Young and Rube Waddell square off, with the Athletics winning, 2-0.

MAY 11
Cy Young pitches his 23rd consecutive no-hit inning before Detroit breaks the streak.

TRIVIA

"Husky Hans," by William J. Hartz, is a song about Honus Wagner.

RULES

The height of the pitcher's mound may not exceed 15 inches.

HISTORY

In January, Giants' manager John McGraw is hauled in for gambling and resisting arrest.

Rube Waddell leads the majors in strikeouts, with 349 for the season.

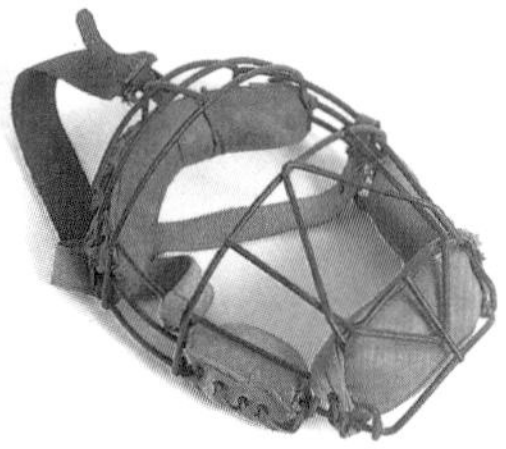

Early catcher's mask

THE ATHLETICS' RUBE WADDELL, WHO SETS A MAJOR LEAGUE RECORD WITH 349 STRIKEOUTS, IS KNOWN FOR HIS WILD AND ECCENTRIC BEHAVIOR AS WELL AS HIS PITCHING PROWESS. BRANCH RICKEY OBSERVES: "WHEN WADDELL HAD CONTROL – AND SOME SLEEP – HE WAS UNBEATABLE."

the Washington Nationals by a final score of 5-4. A crowd of approximately 6,000 fans turns out.

MAY 27:

The New York Giants' first baseman, Dan McGann, steals a record five bases today. He ends up finishing the season with a career-high 42 stolen bases.

MAY 30:

Today in Cincinnati, the Chicago Cubs' first baseman Frank Chance takes a beating in both ends of a doubleheader split. In the first game, which is won by the Reds, Chance is hit by pitches three times. In a Cubs 5-2 victory in the nightcap, Chance is hit two more times. The day's final damage report: a cut forehead and a black eye.

Throughout his playing days, Chance paid a high price for crowding the plate. The many beanings he incurred throughout his 17-year career in the major leagues impaired his hearing. From that point onward, his general health began to deteriorate. It's debatable as to whether the bean balls also may have contributed to his early death.

JUNE 5:

With the team at 23-18, the Chicago White Sox replace their manager, Jimmy "Nixey" Callahan, with Fielder Jones.

JUNE 11:

The Mertes Curse strikes again. For the second time in his career, Sam "Sandow" Mertes breaks up a no-hitter in extra innings. In New York, Mertes hits a single with one out in the 10th inning to foil the no-hit bid of the Cubs' Robert Wicker. It is the only hit Wicker allows, and the Cubs beat the Giants, 1-0, in 12. The game's only run scores when Frank Chance doubles and is driven in by a Johnny Evers single. The game also marks the finale of Joe McGinnity's winning streak at 14.

JUNE 12:

Bill "Willie" Foster, the younger half-brother of Andrew "Rube" Foster, is born in Calvert, Texas.

JUNE 13:

Chicago, with Frank Chance hitting for the cycle, beats the Giants and Christy Mathewson, 3-2, at the Polo Grounds. Mordecai "Three Finger" Brown gets the win.

JUNE 21:

The *Boston Herald* reports a June 18 trade sending outfielder Patsy Dougherty (.272) to New York for infielder Bob Unglaub (.211). The *Herald* headline reads: "DOUGHERTY AS A YANKEE." This may be the first time the nickname is applied to the New York Highlanders.

JULY 4:

The Highlanders' Jack Chesbro wins his 14th consecutive game – an AL record.

JULY 5:

Philadelphia snaps the 18-game win streak of the visiting Giants with a 10-inning, 6-5 win.

JULY 13:

The Blues' second baseman Napoleon "Nap" Lajoie connects for three triples today – which sets an American League record – in leading his Cleveland ballclub over the New York Highlanders, 16-3.

JULY 20-23:

The warfare between AL president Ban Johnson and Giants' manager John McGraw continues, and this time the World Series is at stake. Describing the AL as a "minor league," McGraw says, "The Giants will not play a post-season series with the American League champions. Ban Johnson has not been on the level with me personally, and the American League management has been crooked more than once." Johnson fires back, "No thoughtful patron of baseball can weigh seriously the wild vaporings of this discredited player who was canned out of the American League." And McGraw adds, "My team will have nothing to do with the American League and nothing will make me change my mind."

AUGUST 11:

The Cardinals' player-manager Charles "Kid" Nichols, now 35 years old, strikes out 15 hitters in a 17-inning, 4-3 win over Brooklyn today.

AUGUST 17:

Boston's Jesse Tannehill no-hits the visiting White Sox, 6-0, allowing one walk and fanning four. Tannehill's brother Lee, Chicago's third baseman, fares no better than his teammates. Ed Walsh is the game's losing pitcher today.

JULY 13
The Blues' Nap Lajoie sets a major league record by hitting three triples in a game.

SEPTEMBER 30
White Sox pitcher Doc White becomes the first to pitch six shutouts in a month.

SEPTEMBER 12:

The New York Giants' left-handed pitcher George "Hooks" Wiltse wins his 12th consecutive game. With today's victory, Wiltse sets a rookie major league record for consecutive wins to begin a season.

SEPTEMBER 22:

Orator Jim O'Rourke, 54 years old, catches game one of a doubleheader for the New York Giants, becoming the oldest to play a full game. He manages a hit in four at-bats and scores a run as the Giants clinch the NL pennant with a victory against the visiting Cincinnati Reds.

SEPTEMBER 30:

White Sox pitcher Guy "Doc" White whitewashes the Highlanders, becoming the first pitcher to hurl six shutouts in a month. It also is his fifth consecutive shutout of the year.

OCTOBER 2:

Today in Chicago, the New York Highlanders register a score against Doc White of the White Sox, thereby putting to an end the left-handed pitcher's string of consecutive scoreless innings at 45.

OCTOBER 7:

At Hilltop Park in New York, Jack Chesbro beats Boston and Norwood Gibson, 3-2, for his 41st victory of the season, giving the Highlanders a half game lead in the AL pennant race. Charles "Chuck" Klein is born in Indianapolis.

OCTOBER 10:

With the Highlanders trailing the Pilgrims by a game and a half, the teams face off in a doubleheader on the last day of the season before a crowd of 28,540 at New York's Hilltop Park. The Highlanders, needing both games for the pennant, start their 41-game winner Jack Chesbro against Big Bill Dinneen. In the ninth, with the game tied 2-2, Boston's Lou Criger gets an infield hit, moves to second on a Dinneen sacrifice, and goes on to third on a groundout by Albert "Kip" Selbach. With Fred Parent at bat, Chesbro then uncorks a wild two-strike pitch over catcher John "Red" Kleinow's head to score Criger; Boston wins, 3-2, clinching its second straight pennant. Dinneen pitches his 37th consecutive complete game (an AL record) for the win. The Highlanders win a now-meaningless second game, 1-0, with Ambrose Puttmann besting George Winter.

REGULAR SEASON WRAP-UP:

Despite the previous agreement between the two leagues, there will be no World Series in 1904. The Giants' owner John T. Brush and manager John J. McGraw announce on October 12 that they refuse to meet the AL pennant winners, the Boston Pilgrims. Brush says the Giants won't agree "to a contest with a victorious club in a minor league." NL president Harry Pulliam supports the Giants. The Pilgrims claim the championship and *The Sporting News* declares them the league champions.

The salvos between the two leagues continue. Brush says, "We are content when our season is ended to rest upon our laurels. The club that wins from the clubs that represent the cities of Boston, Brooklyn, New York, Philadelphia, Pittsburgh,Cincinnati, Chicago, and St. Louis, the eight largest and most important cities in America, in a series of 154 games, is entitled to the honor of champions of the United States without being called upon to contend with or recognize clubs from minor leagues. Neither the players nor the manager of the Giants nor myself desires any greater glory than to win the pennant in the National League, that is the greatest honor that can be obtained in baseball." Highlanders' manager Clark Griffith fires back, "Brush's statement is not a surprise to us. He always was a sure-thing fellow, and his remarks indicate that he is hiding behind a bush. McGraw knows well that almost any team in the American League can beat the Giants, so it is no wonder to me that he is fighting shy of a series with the Yankees. Of course, we have not yet won the pennant, but I am confident that we will."

POST-SEASON

NOVEMBER 2:

Arthur Newbold and James Potter together agree to purchase "the lease and effects" of the Philadelphia Phillies National League baseball franchise today at a sheriff's sale. They will own the club a year.

HISTORY

The Giants are the NL winners with a record of 106-47, 13 games ahead of Chicago.

LEAGUE

The National and American Leagues expand their schedules to 154 games.

HISTORY

The Cardinals' Jack "Brakeman" Taylor and Vic Willis of Boston (NL) set a major league record this season with 39 consecutive complete games.

THE BEST OF 1904

NATIONAL LEAGUE

HITTERS

Batting Average:
Honus Wagner, Pittsburgh Pirates, .349

Slugging Average:
Honus Wagner, .520

Home Runs:
Harry Lumley, Brooklyn Superbas, 9

Runs Batted In:
Bill Dahlen, New York Giants, 80

Hits:
Clarence "Ginger" Beaumont, Pittsburgh Pirates, 185

Stolen Bases:
Honus Wagner, 53

PITCHERS

Wins:
Joe McGinnity, New York Giants, 35

Strikeouts:
Christy Mathewson, New York Giants, 212

Earned Run Average:
Joe McGinnity, 1.61

Winning Percentage:
Joe McGinnity, .814

Saves:
Joe McGinnity, 5

AMERICAN LEAGUE

HITTERS

Batting Average:
Napoleon Lajoie, Cleveland Blues, .381

Slugging Average:
Napoleon Lajoie, .554

Home Runs:
Harry "Jasper" Davis, Philadelphia Athletics, 10

Runs Batted In:
Napoleon Lajoie, 102

Hits:
Napoleon Lajoie, 211

Stolen Bases:
Elmer Flick, Cleveland Blues, 42

PITCHERS

Wins:
Jack Chesbro, New York Highlanders, 41

Strikeouts:
George "Rube" Waddell, Philadelphia Athletics, 349

Earned Run Average:
Addie Joss, Cleveland Blues, 1.59

Winning Percentage:
Jack Chesbro, .774

Saves:
Casey Paten, Washington Nationals, 3

1905

APRIL 26
Cubs' outfielder Jack McCarthy throws out three Pirates' runners at the plate.

NEWS

RUSSIAN SAILORS MUTINY ON RUSSIAN BATTLESHIP *POTEMKIN*

NORWAY AND SWEDEN SEPARATE

Nickelodeons open across the U.S.

EINSTEIN FORMULATES HIS SPECIAL THEORY OF RELATIVITY

PRESIDENT ROOSEVELT MEDIATES END TO RUSSIAN-JAPANESE WAR

New York City restaurateur introduces pizza

THE INDUSTRIAL WORKERS OF THE WORLD ("WOBBLIES") IS FOUNDED

PANAMA CANAL CONSTRUCTION BEGINS

JAPAN DECLARES KOREA ITS PROTECTORATE

U.S. NOW HAS 77,988 REGISTERED AUTOMOBILES

PRE-SEASON

JANUARY 16:

The Boston Pilgrims get outfielder Jesse "Thc Crab" Burkett (.273 and two homers) from the St. Louis Browns for outfielder George Stone (.000 in two games in 1903).

Outfielder Frank Huelsman is baseball's traveling man. He begins the day with the Washington Nationals (on loan from the Browns). St. Louis reclaims him and trades him to Boston, which then sends him back to Washington to complete a trade for outfielder George Stone. Today's transactions represent Huelsman's fourth trade in eight months. On May 30 of last year he was sold by the White Sox to the Tigers. On June 16, Detroit sold him to St. Louis. And on July 14, he was sent by the Browns on loan along with infielder-outfielder Hunter Hill to the Senators for infielder Charlie Moran.

Washington is the last stop in Huelsman's career. He plays in 126 games for the Senators, hitting .271. Lifetime, he is at .258 for three years.

FEBRUARY:

The Browns acquire catcher Branch Rickey, who was not in the majors last season, from the White Sox for catcher Frank Roth (.258, one homer).

APRIL:

Sportsman's Park, the first concrete, double-deck baseball stadium, opens in St. Louis.

THE SEASON

APRIL 26:

In Pittsburgh, Chicago outfielder Jack McCarthy throws out three Pirates' runners at the plate. He is the only major leaguer to do so. The Cubs win, 2-1.

APRIL 29:

Christy Mathewson shows cracks in his public image. In Philadelphia, while a two-player fight is taking place on the field, Mathewson is the target of abuse from a kid selling lemonade. Mathewson responds by punching the youngster with what a Philadelphia writer describes as a "brutal blow." The youngster has a cut lip and loosened teeth. After the game, which the Giants win, 10-3, the

LEAGUE

The Cleveland Blues change their name to the Naps, in honor of their star Napoleon Lajoie.

TRIVIA

The Tigers pay the rent for their spring training facilities in Augusta, Georgia, by assigning pitcher Eddie Cicotte to play for the local team.

LEAGUE

Another borrowed player this year is catcher Charles "Gabby" Street, who is loaned to Boston by Cincinnati for three games and then returned.

"I am now convinced that base ball did not originate from rounders."
– *Albert G. Spalding*

JUNE 13
Giants' pitcher Christy Mathewson hurls a 1-0 no-hitter against the Cubs.

JUNE 24
Ed Reulbach tosses an 18-inning complete game in Chicago's 2-1 win at St. Louis.

CULTURE

Archibald "Moonlight" Graham appears in W.P. Kinsella's novel *Shoeless Joe* and in the film version, *Field of Dreams*, in which he is portrayed by Burt Lancaster. In addition to his one appearance with the Giants, Graham played for Plattsburgh in the Vermont-and-New York Northern League. In 1906 with Scranton, he led the New York State League with a .336 average. Graham did not appear in early editions of *The Baseball Encyclopedia*. Following the release of *Field of Dreams* in 1982, he was added.

team is menaced by the crowd. According to historian Dr. Harold Seymour, "This episode was not in keeping with the accepted stereotype of Mathewson and somehow got painted out during the process of portraying him as a paragon of virtue."

MAY 19:

At the Polo Grounds, Giants' manager John McGraw is ejected by Jimmy Johnstone during a game against the Pirates after arguing with opposing manager Fred Clarke and the umpires. McGraw claims Dreyfuss tried to make a $10,000 bet with him and then welshed. Dreyfuss protests; McGraw telephones NL president Harry Pulliam and insults him. Pulliam slaps McGraw with a 15-day suspension and a $150 fine.

MAY 29:

Brooklyn's Elmer Stricklett, a sore-armed minor leaguer last season, shows the Giants a pitch they've never seen and strikes out five in a 4-3 victory in game two of a Polo Grounds double header. The Giants won the morning opener, 7-2.

Stricklett's "mystery pitch" is the spitball, and he may have been the first to use it in the majors. George Hildebrand, who had a season in the majors as a player and later umpired, is the probable discoverer – by accident – of the spitball. In 1902, as a minor league outfielder, he noticed the result of dew on a thrown baseball. Hildebrand taught the pitch to Stricklett, who in turn passed it on to two future Hall of Famers – Jack Chesbro and Big Ed Walsh.

JUNE 5:

John McGraw and owner John T. Brush get an injunction in a Boston court against the fine and suspension levied on the Giants' manager by Harry Pulliam.

JUNE 13:

The Giants' Christy Mathewson no-hits the Cubs, 1-0, in Chicago's West Side Grounds. It is Mathewson's second career no-hitter, and two errors – by shortstop Bill Dahlen and second baseman Billy Gilbert – prevent him from throwing a perfect game. Mathewson registers two strikeouts. The losing pitcher is Mordecai "Three Finger" Brown.

IN HIS *SPALDING'S GUIDE*, ALBERT G. SPALDING SAYS, "HAVING READ THE WRITINGS OF MR. [HENRY] CHADWICK [SPORTS JOURNALIST] THAT OUR AMERICAN GAME OF BASE BALL ORIGINATED FROM ROUNDERS, AND HAVING BEEN TAUNTED WITH THIS STATEMENT AROUND THE WORLD, GENERALLY SPOKEN IN DERISION OF OUR GAME, I AM NOW CONVINCED THAT BASE BALL DID NOT ORIGINATE FROM ROUNDERS, ANY MORE THAN CRICKET ORIGINATED FROM THAT ASININE PASTIME." HE CALLS FOR THE ESTABLISHMENT OF A NATIONAL COMMITTEE TO UNCOVER THE ORIGINS OF BASEBALL. WHEN THE PANEL IS ESTABLISHED, IT IS CHAIRED BY FORMER NL PRESIDENT A.G. MILLS.

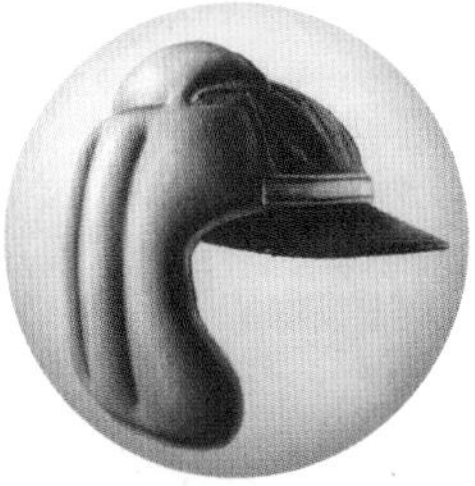

After a beaning, Giants' Roger Bresnahan wears a "pneumatic head protector."

JULY 4
Cy Young out-duels Rube Waddell over 20 innings in the second end of a double header.

Brooklyn president Charles Ebbets, manager Patsy Donovan, and pitcher Mal Eason are arrested for playing Sunday baseball. Visiting Cincinnati isn't spared; police also haul in manager Ned Hanlon and pitcher Chick Fraser. The case is dismissed because Brooklyn's "contribution plan" is not covered under existing law.

JUNE 24:

In St. Louis, the Cubs beat the Cardinals, 2-1, on Ed Reulbach's 18-inning complete game. The loser is Jack "Brakeman" Taylor. Chicago first baseman Frank Chance has a busy day with 27 putouts and two assists.

JUNE 29:

Archibald "Moonlight" Graham plays in his only major league game as an outfielder for the New York Giants. At Brooklyn's Washington Park against the Superbas, Graham is a late-inning substitute for right fielder George Brown. He does not bat and handles no balls in the field. The Giants win, 11-1. Graham will be portrayed by actor Burt Lancaster in *Field of Dreams.*

JULY 1:

Frank Owen of the Chicago White Sox becomes the first AL pitcher to pitch and win complete games in both ends of a doubleheader. Owen tops the Browns, 3-2 and 3-0, allowing a total of seven hits and three walks.

A suspension imposed by Ban Johnson on White Sox outfielder James "Ducky" Holmes causes a rift between the AL president and his longtime ally Charles Comiskey. Holmes, no stranger to abusive language (he was the center of an 1898 controversy when he used an ethnic slur to Giants' owner Andrew Freedman), is again suspended for bad language in a run-in with umpire Frank "Silk" O'Loughlin. Johnson explains, "The language that Holmes used to O'Loughlin merited the punishment I gave him."

O'Loughlin, who called a record seven no-hitters, was tough to argue with. He would tell protesting players, "I have never missed one in my life and it's too late to start now. The Pope for religion, O'Loughlin for base ball. Both infallible."

JULY 4:

In the longest major league game to date, Boston's 38-year-old Cy Young goes head-to-head with Philadelphia's Rube Waddell for 20 innings in game two of a doubleheader. The Athletics win on an error, a hit batter, two hits, and a force-out. Young, the losing pitcher, allows 13 hits and no walks, while striking out four. Waddell yields 15 hits and four walks, while striking out 11. Philadelphia also won the opener, 5-2, with Waddell making an appearance in that game as well.

JULY 8:

Boston and Philadelphia combine for 26 doubles in an AL doubleheader. The Athletics have 14; Boston's total includes five by Albert "Hobe" Ferris.

JULY 22:

The Philadelphia Athletics' right-handed pitcher Weldon Henley no-hits the St. Louis Browns, 6-0, in game one of a doubleheader in St. Louis. Henley strikes out five and walks three; Philadelphia makes one error. The losing pitcher in the game is Barney Pelty.

Giants' pitcher Christy Mathewson posted an NL-best 31-9 record in 1905.

AUGUST 19
Ty Cobb, just 18, is sold to the Detroit Tigers for a total of $900.

SEPTEMBER 8
Pittsburgh leaves an NL-record 18 runners on base in losing, 8-3, to Cincinnati.

EQUIPMENT

During the 1905 season, Cleveland catcher Jay Clarke secretly wears soccer shin guards under his uniform pants. It is the first step toward shin protectors for catchers.

JULY 25:

Leo Durocher is born in West Springfield, Massachusetts, according to his biographer, Gerald Eskenazi. His Dodger bio, however, lists the date as July 27, 1906, and *The Baseball Encyclopedia* goes with July 27, 1905. All agree on his birthplace.

AUGUST 1:

The Peerless Leader, Frank Chance, is the new manager of the Chicago Cubs. He replaces Frank Selee, who is suffering from tuberculosis. Under Selee, Chicago is 37-28. In their first game under Chance, the Cubs blow a 5-0 lead against visiting Philadelphia and lose at home, 7-6, in 11 innings.

AUGUST 15:

The Athletics' Rube Waddell pitches an abbreviated no-hitter, beating the Browns, 2-0, in five innings.

AUGUST 19:

Ty Cobb, 18 years old, is sold to the Detroit Tigers by Augusta of the South Atlantic (Sally) League. The Tigers pay $700 plus an additional $200 because the season is not over for Cobb, who will report to his new team at the end of the month.

AUGUST 24:

In Philadelphia, Chicago's Ed Reulbach is the winner in another marathon pitcher's duel. The Cubs' right-hander pitches all 20 innings in a 2-1 victory over Philadelphia. Player-manager Frank Chance singles in Jack McCarthy with the winning run. Thomas "Tully" Sparks, who also pitches a complete game, is the hard-luck loser. On June 24, Reulbach pitched an 18-inning complete-game victory.

AUGUST 25:

Ty Cobb finishes his abbreviated season with Augusta. His final stats include a .326 batting average, 40 stolen bases, and 13 errors.

AUGUST 30:

Center fielder Ty Cobb makes his major league debut with the Tigers at home in Bennett Field. In his first at-bat, hitting in the fifth spot, he doubles off New York's Jack Chesbro in a 5-3 Tigers' win. Cobb also walks and is caught stealing. The winning pitcher for Detroit is George Mullin.

Detroit Free Press writer Joe S. Jackson analyzes the major league prospects of Sally League batting champion Ty Cobb, "He won't pile up anything like that in this league . . . If he gets away with a .275 mark he will be satisfying everybody."

> THE DAY AFTER THE TINKER-EVERS FIGHT, TINKER SAYS, "LOOK, EVERS, IF YOU AND I TALK TO EACH OTHER, WE'RE ONLY GOING TO BE FIGHTING ALL THE TIME. SO DON'T TALK TO ME, AND I WON'T TALK TO YOU. YOU PLAY YOUR POSITION AND I'LL PLAY MINE, AND LET IT GO AT THAT." EVERS RESPONDS, "THAT SUITS ME." ACCORDING TO HISTORIAN MICHAEL GERSHMAN, THEY DO NOT SPEAK TO EACH OTHER FOR 33 YEARS.

SEPTEMBER 1:

On a train from New York to Boston, Athletics' pitchers Rube Waddell and Andy Coakley get into a fight over straw hats. Waddell injures his shoulder in the scrap. Waddell misses seven starts and a shot at 30 wins; he ends the season at 26-11. Rumors circulate that Waddell received money from gamblers and deliberately injured himself; there is no proof.

Honus Wagner of the Pirates reportedly becomes the first professional athlete to endorse a commercial product when he signs a contract with J.F. Hillerich & Son. Under the agreement, the bat maker obtains permission to use Wagner's autograph on its Louisville Slugger bats. Wagner is the first player with his signature on his bat.

SEPTEMBER 27
Boston's Bill Dinneen no-hits the White Sox, 2-0, in game one of a doubleheader.

OCTOBER 14
Behind Christy Mathewson's third shutout, the Giants are World Champions.

SEPTEMBER 6:

In game two of a double header in Detroit, White Sox pitcher Frank Smith no-hits the Tigers, 15-0. It is the most one-sided no-hitter ever. Smith strikes out eight and walks three. Jimmy Wiggs gets the loss.

SEPTEMBER 8:

The Pirates leave 18 runners on base – an NL record – in a game against Cincinnati. Little surprise: the Pirates lose the game, 8-3.

SEPTEMBER 14:

It's Tinker to Evers and back again, but they're exchanging punches, not baseballs. Cubs' teammates Joe Tinker and Johnny Evers get into a fistfight at second base during an exhibition game in Indiana. They are separated by other players. The source of the hostility: Evers took a taxi from their hotel and left Tinker and others behind.

SEPTEMBER 27:

The White Sox are on the short end of a no-hitter in game one of a doubleheader in Boston. In the 2-0 win, Bill Dinneen issues two walks and strikes out six. Frank Owen takes the loss.

REGULAR SEASON WRAP-UP:

Under the fiery John McGraw, the Giants, with a record of 105-48, win their second straight NL pennant, beating Pittsburgh by nine games. The pitching staff is anchored by 31-8 Christy Mathewson; Mike Donlin is the league's top hitter at .356, and the team steals 291 bases.

Athletics' manager Connie Mack leads his team to the AL pennant, two games ahead of Chicago. Philadelphia boasts three 20-game winners: Rube Waddell (26-11), Eddie Plank (25-12), and Andy Coakley (20-7).

OCTOBER 9:

World Series, game one. In Philadelphia, the Giants win the opening game, 3-0, on the strength of Christy Mathewson's four-hit pitching. Eddie Plank yields 10 hits and takes the loss. The Athletics sport black uniforms and white hose.

OCTOBER 10:

World Series, game two. At the Polo Grounds, Philadelphia strikes back as Charles "Chief" Bender matches Mathewson's game one performance with a four-hit, 3-0 shutout of his own. Briscoe "The Human Eyeball" Lord drives in two runs for Philadelphia. Joe McGinnity takes the loss.

OCTOBER 12:

World Series, game three. After a postponement for rain, Christy Mathewson pitches his second shutout and the Giants convert nine hits into nine runs, routing the Athletics, 9-0, in Philadelphia. Mathewson again limits Philadelphia to only four hits. Andy Coakley, with his teammates committing five errors behind him, gets the loss. John McGraw has three hits and four RBI. Bill Dahlen steals home in the fifth inning – a World Series first.

Richard "Rick" Ferrell is born in Durham, North Carolina.

OCTOBER 13:

World Series, game four. The goose eggs keep multiplying. In New York, Iron Man Joe McGinnity shuts out the Athletics, 1-0, allowing five hits. Eddie Plank holds the Giants to just four hits, allowing only an unearned run in the fourth inning.

OCTOBER 14:

World Series, game five. At the Polo Grounds, Christy Mathewson pitches his third series shutout, beating Philadelphia, 2-0, to clinch the World Championship. Every game in the series is a shutout. Chief Bender, who allows the Giants only five hits, is tagged with the loss. Mathewson's World Series totals include three shutout wins, 18 strikeouts, 14 hits allowed, and only one walk.

POST-SEASON

NOVEMBER 21:

Freddie Lindstrom is born in Chicago.

DECEMBER 15:

In an off-season deal, the Pittsburgh Pirates send three position players to the Boston Beaneaters in exchange for right-handed pitcher Vic Willis (11-29, 3.21 ERA). Boston receives outfielder-infielder George "Del" Howard (.292), infielder Dave Brain (.247), and pitcher Vivan "Vive" Lindaman, who did not play in the majors in 1905. Willis would go on to win at least 20 games in each of the next four seasons.

EQUIPMENT

A.J. Reach Co. develops a "pneumatic head protector" and, after being beaned, Giants' catcher Roger Bresnahan experiments with it. According to historian Dr. Harold Seymour, it "resembled a football helmet sliced in half and covered the side of the head exposed to the pitches."

THE BEST OF 1905

NATIONAL LEAGUE

HITTERS

Batting Average:
James "Cy" Seymour, Cincinnati Reds, .377

Slugging Average:
James Seymour, .559

Home Runs:
Fred Odwell, Cincinnati Reds, 9

Runs Batted In:
James Seymour, 121

Hits:
James Seymour, 219

Stolen Bases:
Art Devlin, New York Giants; Billy Maloney, Chicago Cubs, 59

PITCHERS

Wins:
Christy Mathewson, New York Giants, 31

Strikeouts:
Christy Mathewson, 206

Earned Run Average:
Christy Mathewson, 1.27

Winning Percentage:
Christy Mathewson, .795

Saves:
Claude Elliott, New York Giants, 6

AMERICAN LEAGUE

HITTERS

Batting Average:
Elmer Flick, Cleveland Naps, .306

Slugging Average:
Elmer Flick, .466

Home Runs:
Harry Davis, Philadelphia Athletics, 8

Runs Batted In:
Harry Davis, 83

Hits:
George Stone, St. Louis Browns, 187

Stolen Bases:
Danny Hoffman, Philadelphia Athletics, 46

PITCHERS

Wins:
George "Rube" Waddell, Philadelphia Athletics, 27

Strikeouts:
George Waddell, 287

Earned Run Average:
George Waddell, 1.48

Winning Percentage:
George Waddell, .730

Saves:
Bill Wolfe, Washington Nationals; Jim Buchanan, St. Louis Browns, 2

1906

"It was a hard series to lose, but you can't win all the time."
– Cubs' manager Frank Chance

NEWS

EARTHQUAKE DEVASTATES SAN FRANCISCO; 452 DIE, 225,000 LEFT HOMELESS; $350 MILLION IN DAMAGE

W.K. KELLOGG INTRODUCES CORN FLAKES

THEODORE ROOSEVELT WINS NOBEL PEACE PRIZE FOR MEDIATING RUSSIAN-JAPANESE WAR

HARRY K. SHAW KILLS ARCHITECT STANFORD WHITE OVER EVELYN NESBIT

Sonar is invented

Caffeine replaces cocaine in Coca-Cola

CUBA OCCUPIED BY U.S. TROOPS

SUSAN B. ANTHONY DIES

21 DEAD IN ATLANTA RACE RIOTS

FIRST RADIO BROADCAST OF VOICE AND MUSIC

PRE-SEASON

JANUARY 20:

The Giants sign pitcher Henry Mathewson, younger brother of their ace Christy. He pitches in only three games over two years. He completes his brief career with an 0-1 record with a 4.91 ERA.

MARCH 16:

Lloyd "Little Poison" Waner is born in Harrah, Oklahoma.

THE SEASON

APRIL 12:

Boston Beaneaters' rookie outfielder Johnny Bates becomes the first player of the 20th century to hit a home run in his initial major league at-bat.

APRIL 16:

It's a bad day in Cincinnati for the Chicago Cubs' celebrated double-play combination. First, Johnny Evers and Frank Chance are ejected during a 3-0 loss. Then, after the game, the third member of the trio – Joe Tinker – gets into a fight with a fan outside the ballpark.

APRIL 28:

Cubs' player-manager Frank Chance steals home in the bottom of the ninth inning to give his team a 1-0 win over the Reds.

MAY 1:

Philadelphia's Johnny Lush no-hits Brooklyn, 1-0, striking out 11 and walking three. His teammates commit one error. The losing pitcher is Mal Eason.

Lush, now 20, was a first baseman-outfielder with Philadelphia in 1904 – the youngest regular player in the majors in the 20th century. He pitches for seven years, compiling a 66-85 record with a 2.68 ERA.

MAY 6:

The Pirates become the first team to use a tarpaulin to cover the infield at Exhibition Field when it rains.

MAY 7:

Tigers' pitcher Wild Bill Donovan shows legs to go with his arm. In the fifth inning of today's game against Cleveland, he singles, then steals second, third, and – on a double steal – home. He also triples and pitches the Tigers to an 8-3 victory.

MAY 8:

Athletics' manager Connie Mack finds himself shorthanded in the sixth inning against Boston and sends pitcher Charles "Chief" Bender to the outfield. Bender responds with two homers (one inside the park).

MAY 25:

Martin Dihigo is born in Matanzas, Cuba. *The Negro Leagues Book* cites May 25, 1906 as Dihigo's birthdate; *The Baseball Encyclopedia* lists it as 1905.

At its Huntington Avenue Grounds, Boston beats the White Sox, 3-0, behind Jesse Tannehill's two-hitter to end the team's 20-game losing streak. Catcher Bob Peterson drives in all three runs. The losing streak was the AL's longest ever and the third worst in major league history. Nineteen of the 20 defeats were at home.

JUNE 7:

In rare subpar performances by two of baseball's best, Christy Mathewson and Joe McGinnity

JULY 7
Future Negro League legend Leroy "Satchel" Paige is born in Mobile, Alabama.

LEAGUE

St. Louis Browns' shortstop Bobby Wallace, at $6,000, is baseball's highest paid player.

get rocked by the Cubs for 11 first-inning runs. In the worst performance of his career, Mathewson surrenders nine tallies. Chicago beats the Giants, 19–0, behind a three-hitter by Jack "The Giant Killer" Pfiester, who today lives up to his nickname.

JUNE 11:

Beaneaters' third baseman Dave Brain commits five errors – a major league record for a nine-inning game – and his teammates add six more.

JUNE 19:

The Beaneaters beat the Cardinals, 6-3, to end their 19-game losing streak – which is the fifth longest of all time.

JULY 3:

One way to make a point: When it begins drizzling during the sixth inning in Cleveland, Detroit infielder Herman "Germany" Schaefer appears on the field in a raincoat.

Schaefer may have been an earlier incarnation of Jim Piersall. Among his stunts: after a pinch-hit homer in Chicago, he slid into every base. He also accomplished what most fans think is impossible; he "stole" first base. In a game against Cleveland, Schaefer takes off from first to second base, trying to draw a throw from catcher Jay "Nig" Clarke that would let teammate Davy Jones score from third. Clarke doesn't throw, so on the next pitch, Schaefer runs back to first. He yells to Clarke that he's going back to second base; this time the catcher does throw and Jones scores.

JULY 4:

There are no batting fireworks today as the Cubs' Mordecai "Three Finger" Brown and the Pirates Albert "Lefty" Leifeld match one-hitters. Brown's is just a little bit better; he and the Cubs win, 1-0.

JULY 7:

Leroy "Satchel" Paige is born in Mobile, Alabama.

The actual year of Paige's birth has never been conclusively determined, but the record books list 1906.

In Only the Ball Was White, *Robert Peterson writes that when Bill Veeck signed Paige he "hired a private detective to inspect Mobile's birth records. On the basis of the detective's findings, Veeck announced that Paige could not have been born later than 1899."*

JULY 14:

The Giants buy outfielder James "Cy" Seymour (.257 in 79 games) from the Reds for $12,000. Seymour was last season's NL batting champion with a .377 average.

Joe H. Jackson of the *Detroit Free Press* dubs Ty Cobb the "Georgia Peach." While the nickname is generally attributed to Grantland Rice, Cobb biographer Charles C. Alexander writes that Jackson used the sobriquet earlier.

A Windy City writer introduces another nickname to baseball history. Charles Dryden of the *Chicago Tribune* covers today's victory by the White Sox under the headline:

HITLESS WONDERS RALLY AND TURN AN APPARENT NEW YORK VICTORY INTO DEFEAT

JULY 18:

Ty Cobb leaves the Tigers on the road and returns to Detroit. Manager Bill Armour reports only that the outfielder is suffering from an undisclosed "stomach trouble."

JULY 20:

In St. Louis, Brooklyn pitcher Mal Eason no-hits the Cardinals, 2-0. The right-handed Eason was on the short end of Johnny Lush's May 11 no-hitter. Eason fans five batters and walks three; Brooklyn commits one error. The losing pitcher is Gus Thompson.

JULY 22:

With all putouts and no assists, the Cincinnati Reds defeat the Pittsburgh Pirates, 10-3, behind pitcher George "Long Bob" Ewing.

JULY 27:

Joe H. Jackson of the *Detroit Free Press* reports that Ty Cobb is in a sanitarium. Cobb undergoes surgery, possibly for an ulcer.

AUGUST 1:

It's close but no cigar and no no-hitter for Brooklyn's Harry McIntire. Pitching against the Pirates, McIntire takes a no-hitter into the 11th, when Claude Richey breaks it up with a single. Pittsburgh goes on to win on four hits, 1-0, in 13.

AUGUST 23
Roy Patterson's 4-1 win over the Senators marks Chicago's 19th straight victory.

SEPTEMBER 1
The Athletics prevail over the Pilgrims, 4-1, in a 24-inning marathon in Boston.

AUGUST 6:

Jimmy Johnstone calls Art Devlin of the Giants out at the plate in a 3-2 Cubs victory. After he ejects manager John McGraw, Johnstone becomes the target of a bottle barrage from Polo Grounds fans.

AUGUST 7:

John McGraw strikes again. After his disputed call against the Giants yesterday, umpire James Johnstone finds himself "locked out" of the Polo Grounds. When he shows up for today's game between the Giants and Cubs, he is barred from entering by the gatekeeper and told that police inspector James Sweeney cannot ensure his safety. The incident is the work of McGraw; neither Sweeney nor the city police have knowledge of it. Inside the ballpark, the second umpire, Bob Emslie, refuses to work without Johnstone. McGraw designates Giant infielder Sammy Strang as umpire, and the Cubs refuse to play. Strang then awards his teammates a victory by forfeit. Meanwhile, on the outside, umpire Johnstone awards the Cubs a 9-0 forfeit.

AUGUST 8:

With NL president Harry Pulliam backing James Johnstone and assigning him to today's game, Giants' owner John T. Brush allows the umpire into the Polo Grounds. The umpires are applauded by the fans, and this time the game is settled on the field with Chicago winning, 3-2, behind Mordecai "Three Finger" Brown and Ed Reulbach. John McGraw and Art Devlin are not in uniform. Yesterday's forfeit stands as a Cubs victory.

AUGUST 9:

In Brooklyn, the Cubs' Jack "Brakeman" Taylor goes all the way for a 5-3 win, setting a major league record with his 187th consecutive complete game. Taylor's streak began on June 20, 1901, encompasses 1,727 innings, and includes one 19-inning and one 18-inning game. He also had appeared 15 times in relief, but those games do not count in his streak.

AUGUST 13:

The Brooklyn Superbas, the victims in Jack "Brakeman" Taylor's record-breaking complete game four days ago, kayo him in the third inning today, ending his streak.

AUGUST 23:

The White Sox and Roy Patterson beat the Senators, 4-1; it is Chicago's 19th consecutive win.

AUGUST 24:

In game two of a doubleheader, Cincinnati's Jake Weimer pitches a seven-inning no-hitter, winning, 1-0, on a run in the final frame. Brooklyn took the opener, 6-4, with Jim Pastorius getting the win.

AUGUST 29:

Jimmy Dygert and Rube Waddell of the Athletics combine on a five-inning no-hitter against the White Sox. Philadelphia wins, 4-3.

Jimmy Collins is suspended for leaving on a holiday without permission and Chick Stahl is named acting manager of the Pilgrims. Collins's team is at 35-79 and down in the AL standings.

AUGUST 30:

Highlanders' rookie Judd "Slow Joe" Doyle gets off to a fast start, pitching and winning shutouts in his first two major league starts. Today, he whitewashes Washington, 5-0. In his first start, on August 25, he shut out Cleveland, 2-0.

Unfortunately for Doyle, he subsequently lives up to his name, going 2-2 for the year and finishing his five-year career at 22-22.

SEPTEMBER 1:

In a 24-inning, four-hour, 47-minute epic contest – the longest to date in major league history – at Boston's Huntington Avenue Grounds, the Athletics beat the Pilgrims, 4-1. With some 18,000 fans on hand, the teams battle through 20 scoreless innings; with two out in the 24th inning, triples by Ralph "Socks" Seybold and Danny Murphy produce three runs for Philadelphia. Winning pitcher Jack Coombs and loser Joe Harris both pitch complete games. Coombs gives up 15 hits and six walks, while fanning 18. Harris allows 16 hits and two walks and strikes out 14. Thirty-one of the hits in the

LEAGUE

Stanley Robison, president of the Cardinals, proposes a World Series format that would enable all 16 major league teams to participate. He tells the *Toledo News-Bee*, "The regular season in both leagues will end on September 1 or soon thereafter. Then the American League clubs will start out, each playing two games in the National League city. When that series has been completed the National League clubs take to the road, each playing two games in each American League city."

OCTOBER 4
The Cubs' 4-0 win over the Pirates is Chicago's record 116th victory of the season.

OCTOBER 9
Chicago's Cubs and White Sox square off in the first intracity World Series.

CULTURE

It's not the kind of work that earns Grantland Rice sportswriting immortality, but he pens a paean to the White Sox for the October *Chicago Inter Ocean*:

What city's in the baseball eye?

Chicago.

Who'll win the pennant by and by?

Chicago.

What team threw down the clan of Mack?

Chicago.

Who soon will hurl Clark Griffith back?

Chicago.

Who's got 'em all upon the rack?

Chicago.

game are singles – 16 by the A's. Joe Harris, a hard-luck pitcher, is now 2-21 after beginning the season with a major league record 14 straight losses. When the umpires for today's game in Chicago are stricken with food poisoning and are unable to work, like a sandlot game they pick one guy from each side to officiate. Cardinals' catcher Peter Noonan and Cubs' pitcher Carl Lundgren are chosen. On "Three Finger" Brown's five-hitter, the Cubs win, 8-1; it marks Chicago's 14th consecutive victory.

SEPTEMBER 3:

In St. Louis, Ty Cobb returns to the Tiger lineup playing center field and has a single and stolen base against the Browns' Barney Pelty. But he misplays a Charley Hemphill fly ball into a home run and the Browns win, 1-0, in a game halted after seven innings by rain.

SEPTEMBER 4:

The New York Highlanders, behind Walter Clarkson and Al Orth, sweep a doubleheader from Boston. It is a major league record five twin bill sweeps in six days for the Highlanders. It also is their second double header shutout in 10 days. They beat Washington in twin bills on August 30 and 31 and September 1, and Philadelphia yesterday.

SEPTEMBER 12:

From now on it's strictly managing for John McGraw, who plays his last game for the Giants today at third base.

SEPTEMBER 13:

In St. Louis, the Cubs' Mordecai "Three Finger" Brown beats the Cardinals, 6-2, for his 11th consecutive win.

SEPTEMBER 17:

For the third time this season, Tigers' manager Bill Armour sends a pinch-hitter in for Ty Cobb; today George Mullin triples. On April 24, Sam Crawford singled and on May 30 Fred Payne singled, all batting for the Georgia Peach.

SEPTEMBER 19:

In Boston, the visiting Cubs behind Ed Reulbach win, 3-1, and clinch the NL pennant.

SEPTEMBER 24:

In the second game of a doubleheader in Brooklyn, the Cardinals' Ulysses Simpson Grant "Stoney" McGlynn pitches no-hit ball for seven innings. The game is called because of darkness with the score tied at 1-1.

SEPTEMBER 26:

As the days grow short, abbreviated no-hitters multiply. In Philadelphia, Albert "Lefty" Leifield of the Pirates no-hits the Philadelphia Phillies in an abbreviated second game of a doubleheader. The contest only lasts six innings and Pittsburgh wins, 8-0.

OCTOBER 1:

In Philadelphia, the Cubs Ed Reulbach rings up his 12th straight win, 4-3, in the nightcap of a doubleheader. The game is called after six innings due to darkness. In the opener, the Cubs' Carl Lundgren wins a 4-0 two-hitter.

OCTOBER 3:

Arthur Soden and his associates sell the NL Boston Beaneaters and their ballpark to brothers George B. and John S.C. Dovey of Kentucky and John P. Harris for $75,000. The team now will be known as the Doves in honor of their new owners. Manager Fred Tenney, who negotiated the deal, remains as manager despite a 49-102 record and a last-place finish.

OCTOBER 4:

In Pittsburgh, the Cubs beat the Pirates, 4-0, for their record 116th victory of the season, as well as the highest winning percentage of all time. Jack Pfeister gets the win, his 20th of the season, and pitcher Carl Lundgren plays nine innings at second base.

OCTOBER 6:

Ty Cobb and teammate Ed Siever, who had cursed him for not hustling in the field, get into a fight. Cobb knocks Siever down and kicks him in the head.

REGULAR SEASON WRAP-UP:

The Chicago Cubs, under Frank Chance, are runaway winners in the NL, finishing 20 games ahead of the New York Giants. Paced by Mordecai "Three Finger" Brown, Jack Pfiester, and Ed Reulbach, they boast a team ERA of 1.76. Their crosstown

OCTOBER 12
After being shut out the day before, the Cubs blank the White Sox in game four of the Series.

OCTOBER 14
Game six goes to "the Hitless Wonders," and the White Sox win the World Series.

rivals, the White Sox, beat the Highlanders by three games with a record of 93-58. Managed by Fielder Jones, they have only a .228 team batting average and seven homers; their top hitter is Frank Isbell at .279, hence their nickname, the Hitless Wonders.

OCTOBER 9:

World Series, game one. In an all-Chicago matchup, the first modern World Series intracity faceoff, the White Sox are the visiting team and beat the Cubs, 2-1. Frank Isbell singles in player-manager Fielder Jones in the sixth inning for the game-winning run. Nick Altrock goes all the way, allowing four hits, walking one, and striking out three, for the win. Despite yielding only four hits and a walk while fanning seven, Mordecai "Three Finger" Brown gets the loss. Attendance is 12,693.

OCTOBER 10:

World Series, game two. It is the Cubs' turn to be the visiting team, and they bounce back with a 7-1 victory. Ed Reulbach no-hits the White Sox into the seventh inning, when John "Jiggs" Donahue singles. Reulbach ends up with a one-hitter, yielding six walks, for the win. The loser is Guy "Doc" White, who lasts only three innings. Attendance is 12,595.

OCTOBER 11:

World Series, game three. Big Ed Walsh two-hits the Cubs, striking out 12, and the White Sox win, 3-0. The White Sox manage only four hits, but one is a sixth-inning triple by George "Whitey" Rohe, driving in all the game's runs. Jack Pfiester strikes out nine, but gets the loss. Attendance is 13,667.

OCTOBER 12:

World Series, game four. The Cubs come back with a shutout of their own. Three Finger Brown allows two hits and wins, 1-0. Johnny Evers singles in player-manager Frank Chance in the seventh inning for the only run, making a loser of Nick Altrock. Attendance is 18,385.

In the year of the great earthquake that destroyed his parents' home, future Hall of Fame shortstop Joe Cronin is born in San Francisco.

OCTOBER 13:

World Series, game five. The Cubs are the home team today, but, despite six White Sox errors, Big Ed Walsh pitches his team to an 8-6 victory, with two and two-thirds innings of relief from Doc White and a 12-hit attack. Frank Isbell of the White Sox hits a series record four doubles, scores three times, and has two RBI. The Cubs' losing pitcher is Jack Pfiester. Attendance is 23,257.

OCTOBER 14:

World Series, game six. The Hitless Wonders from Chicago are the World Champions of baseball by virtue of today's 8-3 win over the Cubs. Left-hander Doc White gets a complete-game win, allowing the Cubs seven hits. The White Sox overcome three errors by banging out 14 hits and kayoing losing pitcher Mordecai "Three Finger" Brown in the second inning. The White Sox offense is led by substitute shortstop George Davis and Jiggs Donahue, who each drive in three runs, and Edgar Hahn, who records four hits. Attendance is 19,249.

AFTER THE WORLD SERIES LOSS, CUBS MANAGER FRANK CHANCE IS PHILOSOPHICAL, OBSERVING, "IT WAS A HARD SERIES TO LOSE, BUT YOU CAN'T WIN ALL THE TIME."

POST-SEASON

OCTOBER 20:

William "Buck" Ewing dies in Cincinnati, three days after his 47th birthday. Ewing played 18 years in the majors – hitting .303 – and managed for seven seasons.

DECEMBER:

The New York Highlanders buy catcher Wesley Branch "The Mahatma" Rickey (.284, three home runs) from the St. Louis Browns.

THE BEST OF 1906

NATIONAL LEAGUE

HITTERS

Batting Average:
Honus Wagner, Pittsburgh Pirates, .339

Slugging Average:
Harry Lumley,
Brooklyn Superbas, .477

Home Runs:
Tim Jordan, Brooklyn Superbas, 12

Runs Batted In:
Harry Steinfeldt,
Chicago Cubs; Jim Nealon,
Pittsburgh Pirates, 83

Hits:
Harry Steinfeldt, 176

Stolen Bases:
Frank Chance, Chicago Cubs, 57

PITCHERS

Wins:
Joe McGinnity, New York Giants, 27

Strikeouts:
Fred Beebe, Chicago Cubs/St. Louis Cardinals, 171

Earned Run Average:
Mordecai "Three Finger" Brown, Chicago Cubs, 1.04

Winning Percentage:
Ed Reulbach,
Chicago Cubs, .826

Saves:
George Ferguson,
New York Giants, 6

AMERICAN LEAGUE

HITTERS

Batting Average:
George Stone, St. Louis Browns, .358

Slugging Average:
George Stone, .501

Home Runs:
Harry Davis,
Philadelphia Athletics, 12

Runs Batted In:
Harry Davis, 96

Hits:
Napoleon Lajoie, Cleveland Naps, 214

Stolen Bases:
John Anderson, Washington Nationals;
Elmer Flick, Cleveland Naps, 39

PITCHERS

Wins:
Al Orth, New York Highlanders, 27

Strikeouts:
George "Rube" Waddell,
Philadelphia Athletics, 196

Earned Run Average:
Guy "Doc" White, Chicago White Sox, 1.52

Winning Percentage:
Eddie Plank,
Philadelphia Athletics, .760

Saves:
Otto Hess, Cleveland Naps;
Charles "Chief" Bender,
Philadelphia Athletics, 3

1907

"We both hated to lose.
And we'd both do anything to win."
– *Pete Rose on Ty Cobb*

NEWS

President Roosevelt halts Japanese immigration

J.P. MORGAN INTERVENES IN WALL STREET DISASTER, STOPS RUN ON BANKS

OKLAHOMA BECOMES THE 46TH STATE

Second Sunday in May designated Mother's Day

CONGRESS BANS CORPORATE CONTRIBUTIONS TO NATIONAL POLITICAL CAMPAIGNS

The first canned tuna is packed in San Pedro, California

PARIS HOSTS THE FIRST EXHIBITION OF CUBIST ART

Great Britain joins with France and Russia to form the Triple Entente

PRE-SEASON

MARCH 4:

Brooklyn pays $40,000 – plus $12,000 in interest – to Baltimore. The money was supposed to go to the Orioles when the team dropped out of the National League.

MARCH 16:

After Ty Cobb gets into a fight with a black groundskeeper and his wife, then with his Detroit teammate Charley "Boss" Schmidt, Tigers' manager Hugh Jennings offers the Georgia Peach to Cleveland for outfielder Elmer Flick. Cleveland manager Napoleon Lajoie turns down the trade.

Cobb and Schmidt go at it again before spring training ends. Schmidt, a solidly built catcher, takes offense at a newspaper article that implies Cobb can whip him and other team members. Schmidt thrashes Cobb, who ends up with a broken nose and swollen eyes. He misses the next two exhibition games.

MARCH 28:

Charles "Chick" Stahl, player-manager of the Boston Pilgrims, commits suicide by drinking four ounces of carbolic acid in a hotel room in West Baden, Indiana. Three days earlier, the 34-year-old Stahl had asked to be replaced as Boston's skipper. His last words to teammate Jimmy Collins are, "Boys, I couldn't help it; it drove me to it." In 1986, information surfaced that alleged the married Stahl was a father-to-be with another woman.

MARCH 29:

On his 40th birthday, Cy Young is named acting manager of the Boston Pilgrims.

APRIL 2:

Lucius "Luke" Appling is born in High Point, North Carolina.

APRIL 6:

Ace Cy Young will stick to the thing he does best – pitching. He informs Boston's owners that he will manage the team only until a permanent replacement for the late Chick Stahl can be found.

THE SEASON

APRIL 11:

Snow falls before the opening day game at the Polo Grounds in New York, and is removed from the field. Apparently it still is within reach of Giants fans in the roped-off sections of the outfield. Throughout the game, they hurl snowballs and cushions onto the field. There are no New York City police inside the ballpark on the orders of the police commissioner. Instead, private cops are on duty but cannot control the crowd – which numbers 17,000. After Philadelphia goes up, 3-0, fans storm the playing field, and umpire Bill Klem awards the Phillies a 9-0 forfeit – the only one on an opening day in modern baseball history.

The AL's Boston Pilgrims begin their season with a new name – the Red Sox.

APRIL 17:

Boston honors Cy Young's request. After only six games (3-3), George Huff is named the team's manager and Young returns to full-time duty on the mound.

APRIL 18:

It's the end of the line after 11 years in the majors for outfielder-infielder John "Buck"

MAY 8
In his no-hitter against Cincinnati, Francis "Big Jeff" Pfeffer strikes out three and walks one.

AUGUST 2
Walter "Big Train" Johnson makes his major league debut with the Senators.

HISTORY

Frank Navin, the team's one-time bookkeeper, buys a half-interest in the Detroit Tigers for $40,000 from William Hoover Yawkey, the uncle of Tom Yawkey.

EQUIPMENT

In the September-October 1995 issue of The SABR Bulletin, Michael J. Kahoe – who played from 1895 to 1909 – is identified as the first to wear shin guards, five years before Bresnahan. The same article says Pete Hotaling was the first to use a catcher's mask. Hotaling, who was principally an outfielder, played from 1879 to 1888.

Freeman, a two-time home run champion and a five-time .300 hitter. Boston releases the 35-year-old Freeman today after he hits just .182 in four games.

MAY 1:

Boston has its fourth manager in less than two months. Bob Unglaub is named to lead the Red Sox when George Huff resigns after eight games and a 2-6 record.

MAY 8:

Francis "Big Jeff" Pfeffer of the Boston Doves no-hits visiting Cincinnati, 6-0. He walks one, and fans three, and Boston makes one error. The loser is Del Mason.

MAY 21:

Polo Grounds fans are out of control – again. The Cubs top the Giants and Christy Mathewson, 3-0, to take over first place. The loss doesn't sit well with an estimated 10,000 fans who swarm onto the playing field and hurl objects at umpires Hank O'Day and Bob Emslie. Pinkerton guards fire shots into the air to disperse the crowd, and players ring the umpires to protect them from the angry mob. Fortunately, no one is seriously injured in the chaos.

MAY 26:

Chicago's Big Ed Walsh pitches an abbreviated no-hitter against the New York Giants, winning 8-1, in five innings.

JUNE 6:

Bill Dickey is born in Bastrop, Louisiana.

JUNE 7:

The Red Sox send third baseman and former manager Jimmy Collins (.291 in 41 games) to the Athletics for infielder John "Schoolboy" Knight (.222 in 38 games). The 37-year-old Collins was Boston's manager from 1901 through last season, winning two pennants and one World Series.

JUNE 12:

The Tigers capitalize on 11 New York errors for a 14-6 win.

JUNE 17:

It's the fourth managerial change for the Red Sox, and it's only early June. Deacon Jim McGuire, AKA Old Reliable, becomes Boston's new manager. The 43-year-old, who still catches on occasion, succeeds Bob Unglaub, whose record was 9-20.

JUNE 21:

At the West Side Grounds in Chicago, Mordecai "Three Finger" Brown beats the visiting Cardinals for his 10th straight win. Brown gets help from his catcher Johnny Kling, who throws out four would-be Cardinal base stealers at second.

JUNE 28:

New York catcher Branch Rickey isn't as skillful as Johnny Kling and gets little help holding runners from pitchers Earl Moore and Lew Brockett. With Rickey behind the plate, Washington steals an American League record 13 bases and beats the Highlanders, 16-5.

JULY 8:

In Brooklyn, unruly fans throw bottles at Cubs manager Frank Chance as "Three Finger" Brown is pitching Chicago to a 5-0 victory. Chance responds in kind, throwing bottles back and cutting the leg of a fan. It takes three policemen and an armored car to get him safely out of Washington Park.

JULY 14:

A.B. "Happy" Chandler is born in Corydon, Kentucky.

JULY 16:

With the Philadelphia Athletics' Rube Waddell on the mound, the Tigers' Ty Cobb steals home for the first time.

JULY 27:

Boston Red Sox manager Deacon McGuire sends himself up to pinch-hit and smacks a home run. At age 43, he becomes the oldest player ever to pinch-hit a homer.

AUGUST 2:

Walter Johnson makes his major league debut, pitching for the Washington Senators against the visiting Detroit Tigers. Ty Cobb greets the 19-year-old right-hander with a bunt single, one of his two against Johnson, who pitches into the eighth and leaves for a pinch-hitter with his team behind, 2-1. He yields six hits – including three bunts – strikes out three, walks one, and is charged with the loss. Sam Crawford's inside-the-park homer gives the Tigers a 3-2 win.

AUGUST 7
Ed Karger pitches seven perfect innings in an abbreviated game, winning it 4-0.

SEPTEMBER 9
Cy Young and Rube Waddell duel for 13 scoreless innings in a game that ends tied.

TY COBB, IN HIS *MY LIFE IN BASEBALL*, WRITES THAT WHEN THE TIGERS MET WALTER JOHNSON, WE "KNEW WE'D MET THE MOST POWERFUL ARM EVER TURNED LOOSE IN A BALL PARK."

AUGUST 7:

In his second major league start, Walter Johnson wins his first game with a 7-2 four-hitter over Cleveland. Johnson, signed out of the Western Association for a $100 bonus, train fare, and $350 per month, is dubbed the Big Train by sportswriter Grantland Rice, supposedly because of the sound of his fastball.

AUGUST 11:

St. Louis's Ed Karger is perfect in an abbreviated game, no-hitting Boston for seven innings and winning, 4-0.

AUGUST 23:

The Pirates' Howie Camnitz pitches the season's third abbreviated no-hitter. Camnitz shuts down the Giants, 1-0, in the second game of a doubleheader called after five innings.

SEPTEMBER 8:

Walter "Buck" Leonard is born in Rocky Mount, North Carolina.

SEPTEMBER 9:

Cy Young of the Red Sox and Rube Waddell of the A's pitch scoreless ball and walk no one in a 13-inning tie.

SEPTEMBER 12:

In Philadelphia, outfielder Tris Speaker makes his major league debut for the Red Sox.

SEPTEMBER 20:

In Pittsburgh, Pirates' rookie Nick Maddox no-hits Brooklyn, 2-1, allowing three walks and striking out five while his team makes two errors. The Superbas' run scores on wild throws by Maddox and Honus Wagner. The losing pitcher, Elmer Stricklett, allows only two hits – both by Fred Clarke. On September 13, in his first start, Maddox shut out the Cardinals, 4-0.

SEPTEMBER 23:

In Chicago, the Cubs beat Philadelphia, 4-1, in a game shortened to seven and a half innings by rain, and capture the NL pennant. Ed Reulbach is the winning pitcher in relief of Three Finger Brown. In the fifth inning, the Cubs execute a triple play.

SEPTEMBER 27:

Leading the Athletics by percentage points, the Tigers come to Philadelphia for a crucial three-game series. Today, Friday, Wild Bill Donovan and Detroit beat Eddie Plank, 5-4.

SEPTEMBER 30:

After two days off – rain on Saturday and no Sunday baseball in Philadelphia – the Athletics and Tigers resume with a doubleheader. Some 24,000 faithful fans jam Columbia Park, which has only 15,000 seats. The opener matches the Tigers' Wild Bill Donovan and the Athletics' Jimmy Dygert. The teams battle 17 innings to a 9-9 tie; the game is called because of darkness and there is no nightcap. The Athletics blow a golden opportunity and a 7-1 lead after six innings. Rube Waddell relieves Dygert in the second, and Eddie Plank comes on for him.
Ty Cobb sends the game into extra innings by hitting a two-run homer in the ninth and also has a single and double. In the 14th inning, a policeman steps in front of Detroit's center fielder Sam Crawford and prevents him from catching Harry Davis's fly. Umpire Tom Connolly upholds the Tigers' claim of interference, the Athletics pour onto the field, and there is an altercation involving Donovan and Claude Rossman of the Tigers, and Waddell (not in uniform) and Monte Cross of Philadelphia.

SEPTEMBER 29:

The Phillies' George McQuillan begins his major league career by tossing 32 consecutive shutout innings, a major league record for a rookie.

OCTOBER 2:

In New York, Phillies' third baseman Eddie Grant has a big day against two

TRIVIA

Ty Cobb gets his first commercial endorsement – Coca-Cola.

EQUIPMENT

On opening day at the Polo Grounds, the Giants' Roger Bresnahan appears wearing "cricket leg guards" – the first overt use of shin guards by a major league catcher. The shin guards protect Bresnahan when he is hit with a fifth-inning foul tip. When Bresnahan wears his shin guards against Pittsburgh in May (some claim this was their first appearance), Pirates' manager Fred Clarke claims they are illegal and files a protest. NL president Harry Pulliam okays the new equipment.

OCTOBER 12
The Cubs complete a sweep of the Tigers in the World Series with a a 2-0 shutout.

NOVEMBER 4
Charles Ebbets becomes the majority stockholder of the Brooklyn Superbas.

TRIVIA

The Brooklyn Superbas introduce new checkered uniforms for 1907

HISTORY

Pittsburgh's rookie pitcher Nick Maddox went 5-1 with an 0.83 ERA in 1907. But he faded fast, lasting only four years and compiling a 43-20 record with a 2.29 ERA.

of baseball's best pitchers. Batting against Rube Marquard and Christy Mathewson in a doubleheader, Grant collects seven hits in seven at-bats.

OCTOBER 3:

The Red Sox snap a 16-game losing streak by beating the St. Louis Browns in Boston, 1-0. It is the second major losing streak in two years for Boston; last year they lost 20 in a row.

OCTOBER 5:

After sweeping Washington in a four-game series, the Tigers beat the Browns, 10-2, drop a double header to St. Louis, and win the AL pennant with a 92-58 record. The Athletics finish at 88-57.

Harvey "Rube" Vickers of the Athletics pitches five perfect innings and shuts down Washington, 4-0. The game, the nightcap of a doubleheader, is curtailed by darkness.

REGULAR SEASON WRAP-UP:

The 1907 World Series will match the Cubs and Tigers. Chicago, under Frank Chance, wins the NL pennant by 17 games over the Pirates. The Cubs' staff has five outstanding pitchers: Orval Overall, Three Finger Brown, Carl Lundgren, Ed Reulbach, and Jack Pfiester. Chance is their top hitter, with a .293 batting average.

The Tigers are managed by Hugh Jennings and led by 20-year-old Ty Cobb, with a .350 average. Sam Crawford bats .323, and Wild Bill Donovan, Ed Killian, and George Mullin all are 20-game winners.

OCTOBER 8:

World Series, game one. The series opens in Chicago with a 12-inning, 3-3 tie. The Cubs, trailing in the bottom of the ninth, score the tying run on a third-strike passed ball by Tiger catcher Charles "Boss" Schmidt, who has an all-around bad day, with the Cubs stealing seven bases. Wild Bill Donovan goes all the way for Detroit and fans 12; Chicago uses Orval Overall and Ed Reulbach, who pitches the final three innings. Attendance is 24,377.

OCTOBER 9:

World Series, game two. With a crowd of 21,901 fans attending in Chicago, the Cubs top the Tigers, 3-1, behind Jack Pfiester's complete-game nine-hitter. George Mullin takes the loss. Jimmy Slagle singles in Joe Tinker with the winning run.

OCTOBER 10:

World Series, game three. Ed Reulbach limits the Tigers to six hits in a 5-1 victory. The Cubs' 10-hit attack is paced by Johnny Evers, who has three, including two doubles. Ed Siever is charged with the loss. Attendance in Chicago is 13,114.

OCTOBER 11:

World Series, game four. The scene shifts to Detroit, but the outcome is the same: the Cubs, behind pitcher Orval Overall's tidy five-hitter, win, 6-1. Wild Bill Donovan allows seven hits – one is a two-run single to Overall in the fifth inning. Attendance is 11,300.

OCTOBER 12:

World Series, game five. In Detroit, with a 2-0 shutout today, the Cubs sweep the Tigers (with one tie). Three Finger Brown pitches a seven-hitter; George Mullin takes the loss. Keys to the Cubs' victory include a team ERA of 0.75 (limiting AL batting champion Ty Cobb to four hits and a .200 average) and 18 stolen bases. Harry Steinfeldt leads Chicago with .471.

POST-SEASON

OCTOBER 22:

Jimmie "Double X" Foxx, AKA "The Beast," is born in Sudlersville, Maryland.

NOVEMBER 4:

With borrowed money, Brooklyn Superbas' president Charles Ebbets becomes the team's majority stockholder by buying out F.A. Abel, Ed Hanlon, and the estate of the late Harry Van Der Horst. Ebbets was 24 when he first went to work for the team's original owners, Abel, Charles Byrne, and Joseph Doyle. Ebbets did everything from selling peanuts in the stands to assisting Byrne in the front office, and bought stock in the team as he toiled away. By the time Byrne died, in 1897, Ebbets owned 10 percent – enough to get himself elected team president. He immediately began planning to build a new ballpark.

THE BEST OF 1907

NATIONAL LEAGUE

HITTERS

Batting Average:
Honus Wagner, Pittsburgh Pirates, .350

Slugging Average:
Honus Wagner, .513

Home Runs:
Dave Brain, Boston Doves, 10

Runs Batted In:
Sherry Magee,Philadelphia Phillies, 85

Hits:
Clarence "Ginger" Beaumont, Boston Doves, 187

Stolen Bases:
Honus Wagner, 61

PITCHERS

Wins:
Christy Mathewson, New York Giants, 24

Strikeouts:
Christy Mathewson, 178

Earned Run Average:
Jack Pfiester, Chicago Cubs, 1.15

Winning Percentage:
Ed Reulbach, Chicago Cubs, .810

Saves:
Joe McGinnity, New York Giants, 4

AMERICAN LEAGUE

HITTERS

Batting Average:
Ty Cobb, Detroit Tigers, .350

Slugging Average:
Ty Cobb, .473

Home Runs:
Harry Davis, Philadelphia Athletics, 8

Runs Batted In:
Ty Cobb, 116

Hits:
Ty Cobb, 212

Stolen Bases:
Ty Cobb, 49

PITCHERS

Wins:
Guy "Doc" White, Chicago White Sox; Addie Joss, Cleveland Naps, 27

Strikeouts:
George "Rube" Waddell, Philadelphia Athletics, 232

Earned Run Average:
Big Ed Walsh, Chicago White Sox, 1.60

Winning Percentage:
Wild Bill Donovan, Detroit Tigers, .862

Saves:
Bill Dinneen, Boston Red Sox/St. Louis Browns; Ed Walsh; Long Tom Hughes, Washington Nationals, 4

HISTORY

In July, the Mills Commission, investigating the origins of baseball, receives a letter from Abner Graves, a 71-year-old mining engineer, who claims he witnessed Abner Doubleday designing a baseball diamond, explaining the rules to young boys, and naming the game Baseball. He states, "The present game of Baseball was designed and named by Abner Doubleday in Cooperstown, New York, in 1839." Graves seems to be blessed with a remarkable memory; he was five years old in 1839. Separately, an old trunk is found and opened in a farmhouse in Fly Creek, New York, three miles from Cooperstown. In it is an old baseball. Stephen C. Clark buys it for $5 and puts it on display at the Village Club in Cooperstown, and it supposedly inspires the idea for a Hall of Fame in the upstate New York town.

1908

"The first scheme for playing Baseball...was devised by Abner Doubleday."
– *Mills Commission report*

NEWS

William Howard Taft elected president, defeating William Jennings Bryan

FORMER PRESIDENT GROVER CLEVELAND DIES

Model T automobile on market sells for $850

***LUSITANIA* SETS TRANSATLANTIC SPEED RECORD**

Jack Johnson defeats Tommy Burns; becomes first black heavyweight champ

FEDERAL BUREAU OF INVESTIGATION FOUNDED AS ARM OF JUSTICE DEPARTMENT

***Christian Science Monitor*, founded by Mary Baker Eddy, first published**

President Roosevelt visits Panama; first sitting president to travel abroad

PRE-SEASON

FEBRUARY 7:

The St. Louis Browns purchase George "Rube" Waddell (19-13, 2.15 ERA) from the Athletics for $5,000.

APRIL 2:

Who invented baseball? The Mills Commission, established to answer the question, settles on – Abner Doubleday. In its final report, the seven-man commission states: "The first scheme for playing Baseball, according to the best evidence to date, was devised by Abner Doubleday at Cooperstown, N.Y., in 1839." The commission finds "no traceable connection whatever with 'Rounders' or any other foreign game." It concludes, "... a circumstantial statement by a reputable gentleman, according to which the first known diagram of the diamond, indicating positions for the players was drawn by Abner Doubleday in Cooperstown, N.Y., in 1839."

Logic and evidence seemed to play little if any part in the work of the Mills Commission, which included former NL president A.G. Mills, former U.S. Senator from Maryland Arthur P. Gorman, and former Connecticut governor Morgan C. Bulkeley (also a former NL president). It seems to have totally disregarded the fact that Doubleday was a cadet at West Point when he supposedly was in Cooperstown inventing the sport. In 200 Years of Sport in America, *Wells Twombly writes: "The Doubleday diaries suggest that instead of going home to Cooperstown, New York, in the summer of 1839, he stayed on duty at West Point."*

"NO ONE, OF COURSE, INVENTED BASEBALL."
– HENRY CHADWICK

APRIL 6:

Ernesto Natali "Ernie" Lombardi is born in Oakland, California.

APRIL 13:

Ground is broken for the Philadelphia Athletics' brand-new stadium, to become known as Shibe Park.

THE SEASON

APRIL 17:

A renovated Bennett Field, enlarged to 10,500 seats, opens today with the Detroit Tigers meeting visiting Cleveland. With 14,051 fans – an over-capacity crowd – on hand, the visiting Cleveland Naps beat the Tigers, 9-3, in 12 innings, despite a three-hit, two-RBI day from Ty Cobb.

APRIL 20:

Sports journalist and historian Henry Chadwick, known as the Father of Baseball, dies at age 83 in Brooklyn.

MAY 2:

In Detroit today, Ty Cobb is called out by umpire Frank "Silk" O'Loughlin while trying to stretch a double into a triple and then ejected for arguing. It is Cobb's first ejection.

JUNE 2:

In Chicago, Cubs' outfielder Jimmy Sheckard has a close call during a game

APRIL 17
The Cleveland Naps host the Detroit Tigers in their renovated park, Bennett Field.

JULY 4
Giants' pitcher Hooks Wiltse tosses a 10-inning no-hitter against the Athletics.

ACCORDING TO HIS BIOGRAPHER, CHARLES C. ALEXANDER, IT IS IN 1908 THAT TY COBB'S REPUTATION FOR SHARPENING HIS SPIKES BEGINS. THE STORY BEGINS IN NEW YORK, WHERE TIGERS SUBS ARE FILING THEIR SPIKES AS THE HIGHLANDERS TAKE THE FIELD. SPORTSWRITERS THEN ATTRIBUTE THE PRACTICE TO COBB, BECAUSE, ALEXANDER WRITES: "IT SERVED HIS PURPOSES ... IF OPPOSING BASEMEN REALLY BELIEVED THAT HE REGULARLY SHARPENED HIS SPIKES." HE CONTINUES: "THAT YARN BECAME THE MOST DURABLE ITEM IN THE VAST AMOUNT OF COBBIAN FOLKLORE... COBB LET IT STAND UNTIL WELL AFTER HIS RETIREMENT."

with the Pirates when a bottle of ammonia explodes into his eyes. Prompt action saves his eyesight. The Pirates win the game, 6-2.

JUNE 7:

For the second consecutive game, the Tigers victimize the Red Sox with a triple play.

JUNE 24:

With his team in sixth place at 24-32, the New York Highlanders' first and only manager, Clark Griffith, resigns after a tirade from owner Frank Farrell. He is replaced by shortstop Norman "Kid" Elberfeld.

JUNE 30:

Cy Young of the Red Sox, at 41 years old, becomes the oldest pitcher to throw a no-hitter, when he shuts down New York today, 8-0, at their Hilltop Park. He walks the leadoff hitter Harry Niles, who is then caught stealing by catcher Lou Criger, and retires every other Highlanders' batter. It is the third career no-hitter for Young, who strikes out three and also hits two singles and a double, driving in four runs. Walter "Rube" Manning is the losing pitcher.

JULY 4:

The Giants' George "Hooks" Wiltse pitches a 10-inning no-hitter against visiting Philadelphia, winning 1-0 in the morning game of a doubleheader at the Polo Grounds. The losing pitcher is George McQuillan, who yields the game's only run on an error. Wiltse allows no walks, strikes out six, and misses a perfect game when he hits the 27th batter of the game with a pitch.

Wiltse overshadows another pitching gem, Mordecai "Three Finger" Brown's fourth straight shutout. Brown beats the Pirates in Pittsburgh, 2-0, in the opener of a doubleheader. Ed Reulbach and the Cubs win the nightcap as well, 8-3.

JULY 17:

In Chicago, "Three Finger" Brown outduels Christy Mathewson, 1-0, on a fifth-inning inside-the-park homer by Joe Tinker.

JULY 22:

Brooklyn first baseman Tim Jordan hits the first home run to clear the fence in Pittsburgh in nine

TRIVIA

***Baseball Magazine* makes its debut.**

JULY 25
A record crowd of 25,000 jams the Polo Grounds as the Pirates beat the Giants, 7-2.

CULTURE

"Between You and Me," a song supposedly by Johnny Evers and Joe Tinker, is recorded.

CULTURE

In his 1989 book, *Everything Baseball*, James Mote lists 67 recordings of "Take Me Out to the Ballgame."

years. However, it's Brooklyn's only run scored in a 2-1 loss.

JULY 25:

The largest crowd ever at the Polo Grounds – 25,000 – see Honus Wagner and the Pirates top the Giants, 7-2. Wagner has five hits in five at-bats.

JULY 29:

The Browns' Rube Waddell fans 16 of his former Philadelphia teammates to set an AL record.

AUGUST 6:

The Cardinals' Johnny Lush no-hits Brooklyn for the second time in his career. Today's no-hitter is shortened to six innings by rain, and the final is 2-0 for St. Louis. An error with the bases loaded by Superbas' first sacker Tim Jordan provides the Cardinals with the winning margin today.

AUGUST 9:

After a four-day absence to get married, Ty Cobb returns to the Tigers' lineup against Washington and singles and triples in a victory.

AUGUST 20:

Alfonso Lopez is born in Tampa, Florida.

AUGUST 21:

Senators' catcher Charles "Gabby" Street becomes the latest to catch a ball dropped 504 feet from the top of the Washington Monument.

AUGUST 22:

The Athletics' Connie Mack buys outfielder Joe Jackson from the Greenville Spinners in the South Atlantic (Sally) League.

AUGUST 28:

With the Red Sox at 53-62, Fred Lake is appointed the team's new manager, replacing James "Deacon" McGuire.

SEPTEMBER 2:

In Philadelphia, Frank "Fiddler" Corridon is in tune, going 17 innings without issuing a walk, to beat Brooklyn, 2-1.

SEPTEMBER 3:

The New York Giants offer a record $11,000 for left-hander Richard "Rube" Marquard after their scouts watch him pitch a perfect game for Indianapolis in the minor leagues.

Rube Marquard, who won 28 games with Indianapolis, gets off to a slow start with the Giants, winning only nine games and losing 18 in his first three seasons, and becomes known as "McGraw's $11,000 lemon." In 1911, he turns things around and goes on to a Hall of Fame career.

Hal Chase, one of the best fielding first baseman ever but a man with shadowy morals, jumps the New York Highlanders to play with Stockton in the "outlaw" California State League. Chase reportedly is angered by a news story casting aspersions on his character and by being passed over for manager when Clark Griffith was replaced. Commenting on his departure, Chase, who is hitting .257, says, "I feel that I could not do myself justice under such conditions and therefore I have decided to quit. I never had managerial ideas." He adds: "I am not satisfied to play under a management that sees fit to give out a story detrimental to my character and honesty."

SEPTEMBER 4:

In Pittsburgh, the Cubs' "Three Finger" Brown and the Pirates' Vic Willis are locked in a 0-0 game going into the bottom of 10th. With two out and the bases loaded, the Pirates' Owen "Chief" Wilson singles to drive in Fred Clarke with the winning run. Warren Gill, the runner on first, thinking the game is over, leaves the field without touching second base – a common practice in 1908. The Cubs' Johnny Evers calls for the ball, touches second and claims the inning is over on a force out. The rules support Evers but umpire Hank O'Day doesn't see the play.

This game eerily presages events of September 23, with some of the same cast of characters. A key to future events is Hank O'Day's realization that he made a mistake and his determination to make the right call if the play ever occurs again.

SEPTEMBER 5:

Brooklyn's George "Nap" Rucker no-hits visiting Boston, 6-0, fanning 14 and allowing no walks. His team makes three errors behind him. The losing pitcher is Patsy Flaherty.

SEPTEMBER 7:

The Big Train is more like a steamroller to the Highlanders. Walter Johnson, in his first full year, shuts

SEPTEMBER 23
The Giant's Fred Merkle commits an infamous baserunning error in a crucial game.

out New York for the third straight time, 4-0. The Senators' right-hander allows only two hits, walks none, and fans five, beating Jack Chesbro. Back on September 4, he six-hit the Highlanders, 3-0, beating Chesbro then, too. Then, on September 5, Johnson was even better, pitching a four-hit, 6-0 shutout over Walter Manning. There was no game scheduled yesterday.

SEPTEMBER 8:

W.W. Aulick writes in today's *New York Times* about Walter Johnson: "We are grievously disappointed in this man Johnson of Washington. He and his team had four games to play with the champion Yankees. Johnson pitched the first game and shut us out. Johnson pitched the second game and shut us out. Johnson pitched the third game and shut us out. Did Johnson pitch the fourth game and shut us out? He did not. Oh, you quitter!"

SEPTEMBER 11:

Walter Johnson continues his "iron man" demonstration, topping the Athletics, 5-4, after beating them yesterday by a 3-2 score.

SEPTEMBER 18:

In St. Louis, Rube Waddell and the Browns beat Walter Johnson and the Senators, 2-1, in 10 innings on a bunt. In 58 innings, Johnson won five games, allowing only eight runs to score.

Cleveland's Bob Rhoades no-hits visiting Boston, 2-1, fanning two and walking two; his teammates commit two errors. The losing pitcher is Frank Arellanes.

SEPTEMBER 20:

Frank Smith of the White Sox no-hits the Athletics, 1-0, in Chicago. Eddie Plank, who allows only four hits, loses the game in the bottom of the ninth when Frank Isbell singles, goes to second on a passed ball, moves to third on a wild pitch, and scores on a fielder's choice. The White Sox commit one error; Smith walks one and fans two in his second career no-hitter.

Rube Waddell of the Browns fans 17 Washington batters in a 10-inning game.

SEPTEMBER 23:

The Giants, in first place by percentage points, face the second-place Cubs at the Polo Grounds. With Jack Pfiester on the mound and the score tied, 1-1, with two out in the bottom of the ninth, the Giants have Harry "Moose" McCormick on third base and Fred Merkle on first. Al Bridwell singles, scoring McCormick; Merkle, believing the game is over, heads for the clubhouse without touching second base. Center fielder Arthur "Solly" Hofman throws the ball in, and Cubs' substitute Floyd Kroh tries to retrieve it. Coach Joe McGinnity fights him for the ball, which may have gone into the stands. Cubs' second baseman Johnny Evers comes up with a baseball and touches second base. This time home plate umpire Hank O'Day calls the base runner out. (According to some accounts, umpire Bob Emslie actually made the call after being briefed by O'Day. Another source has Emslie missing the play and O'Day making the call.) The call is not communicated to the fans, who swarm on the field to celebrate the Giants' "victory." Instead, O'Day rules the game a 1-1 tie.

A footnote to the play that becomes known as the "Merkle boner" and haunts the player the rest of his career comes from sportswriter Tom Meany: Historian Lee Allen tells him he heard that Giants' manager John McGraw hid Merkle in the Shelbourne Hotel in Brighton Beach. According to the story, he took Merkle back to the deserted Polo Grounds and had him touch second base so McGraw would be able to swear that he did so on September 23, 1908.

SEPTEMBER 24:

Chicago Cubs' manager Frank Chance puts his team on the Polo Grounds playing field at 1:30 p.m., supposedly to continue yesterday's game, and calls for a forfeit, but he is ignored. In the regularly scheduled 4 p.m. game, the Giants win, 5-4.

Cleveland's 10-game winning streak comes to an end, 2-1, on a three-hitter by the Senators' pitcher Walter Johnson.

SEPTEMBER 25:

Cardinals' president Frank De Haas Robison dies at the age of 54 today in Cleveland, Ohio, of apoplexy. With his brother, Matthew

AFTER THE SEPTEMBER 23 GAME, CHRISTY MATHEWSON VOWS: "IF THIS GAME GOES TO CHICAGO BY ANY TRICK OR ARGUMENT, YOU CAN TAKE IT FROM ME THAT IF WE LOSE THE PENNANT THEREBY, I WILL NEVER PLAY PROFESSIONAL BASEBALL AGAIN." THE GIANTS LOSE THE PENNANT AND MATHEWSON PITCHES FOR EIGHT MORE SEASONS.

OCTOBER 7
Wild Bill Donovan two-hits the White Sox, 7-0, to boost the Tigers into the World Series.

HISTORY

Detroit plays only 153 games, winning 90 and losing 63. Cleveland plays 154, ending with a 90-64 record, a half-game behind.

Stanley Robison, De Haas bought the Cardinals in 1898.

SEPTEMBER 26:

On the road in Washington Park, the Cubs' Ed Reulbach pitches shutouts in both ends of a doubleheader, beating Brooklyn 5-0 and 3-0. He allows a total of eight hits and five walks on the day, while fanning 10. The losing pitchers are Irvin "Kaiser" Wilhelm and Jim Pastorius.

SEPTEMBER 29:

Big Ed Walsh of the White Sox almost matches pitcher Ed Reulbach's iron man feat. Walsh wins both games from the Red Sox today in Boston, allowing one run, seven hits, and a walk with 15 strikeouts. Chicago wins by scores of 5-1 and 2-0.

OCTOBER 1:

At the West Side Grounds in Chicago, Ed Reulbach whitewashes Cincinnati, 6-0 – his fourth straight shutout, matching teammate Three Finger Brown's 1908 feat.

OCTOBER 2:

At Cleveland's League Park, Addie Joss pitches a 1-0 perfect game against the visiting Chicago White Sox. He joins Cy Young as the only modern-era pitchers with perfect games. Joss strikes out three and lowers his season ERA to 1.16. Big Ed Walsh is the game's hard-luck loser, striking out 15 and allowing only four hits in eight innings. Cleveland scores the game's only run in the third inning when Joe Birmingham singles, steals second base, goes to third base on a wild throw, and scores when catcher Ossee Schreckengost can't handle a pitch from Walsh (supposedly a spitball). The game's last out is John Anderson pinch-hitting for Walsh.

OCTOBER 3:

The NL's president Harry Pulliam holds a hearing on the September 23 game between the Giants and Cubs and rules the game should be replayed on October 8 at the Polo Grounds.

OCTOBER 4:

At the West Side Grounds, Three Finger Brown beats the visiting Pirates, 5-2, to clinch a tie for the NL pennant. An unidentified woman in the crowd of 30,247 delivers a baby during the ball game.

OCTOBER 5:

The NL board of directors – comprised of Garry Herrman of Cincinnati, Charles Ebbets of Brooklyn, and George B. Dovey of Boston – hears the "Merkle episode." The Giants claim they should be awarded a 2-1 victory. The Cubs seek a forfeit and a victory, charging interference by Joe McGinnity. The NL upholds the umpires and NL president Pulliam: the game is a 1-1 tie and will be replayed on October 8.

While the Cubs are making headlines in New York, White Sox pitcher Big Ed Walsh beats the Tigers, 6-1, for his 40th win of the year, bringing his team within a half-game of Detroit.

OCTOBER 7:

With 27,000 fans watching in Chicago, the Tigers' Wild Bill Donovan two-hits the White Sox, 7-0, to clinch the AL pennant for Detroit. Guy "Doc" White is the losing pitcher. Ty Cobb has a two-run triple and two singles. Teammates Sam Crawford and Matty McIntyre have four and three hits, respectively.

OCTOBER 8:

The Polo Grounds is packed with 35,000 people and the Cubs, in town for the make-up game, require police protection in order to get into and out of New York City. The teams begin the day tied at 98-55. The Cubs win, 4-2, and clinch the pennant on Three Finger Brown's ninth straight victory over Giants' ace Christy Mathewson. The streak dates back to July 12, 1905. Brown gets the victory in relief of Jack Pfiester and finishes his season at 29-9. Joe Tinker's triple is the key blow for Chicago.

Before the game, umpires Bill Klem and Jimmy Johnstone are approached by Giants' team physician, Dr. Joseph M. Creamer, who allegedly tells him: "Bill, you'll be set for life if the Giants win. Tammany Hall [New York City's political machine] has assured me of that." Creamer supposedly presses money into Klem's hand – by some accounts a sum of $2,500 (Charles C. Alexander puts the

OCTOBER 10 The Cubs rally in the ninth inning to win game one of the World Series with the Tigers.

OCTOBER 14 The Cubs beat the Tigers, 2-0, in game five to win their second straight World Series.

sum at $5,000) – in an envelope, saying: "You know who is behind me and you needn't be afraid of anything." Klem declines the offer.

REGULAR SEASON WRAP-UP:

It's Chicago and Detroit in the World Series again. The Cubs, managed by Frank Chance, have two 20-game winners – Three Finger Brown and Ed Reulbach. Johnny Evers at an even .300 is their top hitter.

The Detroit Tigers, managed by Hughie Jennings, are paced by Ty Cobb's league-leading .324; Sam Crawford hits .311. The team has one 20-game winner, rookie Ed Summers.

OCTOBER 10:

World Series, game one. The Series begins on a rainy day in Detroit with 10,812 in attendance. The Cubs win, 10-6, on six straight hits and five runs in the top of the ninth. The big hits in the rally are two-run singles by Solly Hofman and Johnny Kling. Three Finger Brown gets the win with two innings of relief. The loser is reliever Ed Summers, who blows a 6-5 lead in the game's very last frame.

OCTOBER 11:

World Series, game two. Behind starter Orval Overall's four-hitter, the Chicago Cubs make it two in a row with a 6-1 win in the Windy City. With Wild Bill Donovan pitching for the Detroit Tigers, the game is scoreless until Joe Tinker's eighth-inning home run with Solly Hofman on base begins a six-run rally. Attendance is 17,760.

OCTOBER 12:

World Series, game three. Today, back in Chicago, the Tigers get a complete game from George Mullin and four hits from Ty Cobb – plus two RBI and two stolen bases – to beat the Cubs and Jack Pfiester, 8-3. Attendance is 14,543.

OCTOBER 13:

World Series, game four. Three Finger Brown four-hits the Tigers, 3-0, in Detroit to put the Cubs one win away from the championship. Harry Steinfeldt and Solly Hofman hit RBI singles in the third to give Brown all the runs he needs. The losing pitcher is Ed Summers. Official attendance is 12,907.

OCTOBER 14:

World Series, game five. The Cubs close out the Tigers in Detroit for their second consecutive World Series title. Orval Overall limits Detroit to three hits while fanning 10 for a 2-0 victory. The losing pitcher is Wild Bill Donovan. Johnny Evers and Frank Chance each have three hits and an RBI for the bulk of Chicago's offensive output. Attendance is 6,210. The Cubs are led by Frank Chance with a .421 batting average and two wins each by Three Finger Brown and Orval Overall. Cobb hits .368 for Detroit with two stolen bases.

Journalists, unhappy with their seats for game five of the World Series, form the Baseball Writers Association of America.

POST-SEASON

OCTOBER 24:

Billy Murray introduces "Take Me Out to the Ballgame," the song that becomes baseball's anthem. It features music by Albert Von Tilzer and words by Jack Norworth (who has never seen a game).

NOVEMBER 26:

Vernon "Lefty" Gomez is born in Rodeo, California.

DECEMBER 12:

The Giants trade catcher Roger Bresnahan (.283) to the Cardinals for catcher George "Admiral" Schlei (.220), outfielder John "Red" Murray (.282), and pitcher Arthur "Bugs" Raymond (15-25, 2.03 ERA). The next season, Bresnahan – famous as the battery mate of Christy Mathewson – will become player-manager of the Cardinals. J.W. McConaughy of the *New York Evening Journal* writes of Bresnahan: "In a hot game when things begin to go wrong, he is a composite of ginger and bad language. In his clumsy shinguards and wind-pad, his head in a wire cage, through which at intervals comes a stream of reproof and comment as he fusses around the plate, he suggests a grotesque overgrown hen trying to get the family in out of the rain." He will be elected to the Hall of Fame in 1945.

HISTORY

Among the year's statistical highlights: White Sox pitcher Big Ed Walsh pitches 464 innings, a major league record that still stands. The New York Highlanders (or Yankees as they are often called) lose 103 games to finish in last place 39 1/2 games behind the Detroit Tigers.

THE BEST OF 1908

NATIONAL LEAGUE

HITTERS

Batting Average:
Honus Wagner, Pittsburgh Pirates, .354

Slugging Average:
Honus Wagner, .542

Home Runs:
Tim Jordan, Brooklyn Superbas, 12

Runs Batted In:
Honus Wagner, 109

Hits:
Honus Wagner, 201

Stolen Bases:
Honus Wagner, 53

PITCHERS

Wins:
Christy Mathewson, New York Giants, 37

Strikeouts:
Christy Mathewson, 259

Earned Run Average:
Christy Mathewson, 1.43

Winning Percentage:
Ed Reulbach, Chicago Cubs, .774

Saves:
Christy Mathewson; Mordecai "Three Finger" Brown, Chicago Cubs, 5

AMERICAN LEAGUE

HITTERS

Batting Average:
Ty Cobb, Detroit Tigers, .324

Slugging Average:
Ty Cobb, .475

Home Runs:
Sam Crawford, Detroit Tigers, 7

Runs Batted In:
Ty Cobb, 108

Hits:
Ty Cobb, 188

Stolen Bases:
Patsy Dougherty, Chicago White Sox, 47

PITCHERS

Wins:
"Big" Ed Walsh, Chicago White Sox, 42

Strikeouts:
Ed Walsh, 269

Earned Run Average:
Addie Joss, Cleveland Naps, 1.16

Winning Percentage:
Ed Walsh, .727

Saves:
Ed Walsh, 6

1909

FEBRUARY 17
Cleveland acquires Cy Young from Boston for two pitchers and cash.

NEWS

CONGRESS PASSES THE 16TH AMENDMENT IMPOSING AN INCOME TAX; STATES MUST STILL RATIFY

ROBERT E. PEARY AND MATTHEW HENSON REACH THE NORTH POLE

Orville Wright flies for a record one hour and 40 minutes

NATIONAL ASSOCIATION FOR THE ADVANCEMENT OF COLORED PEOPLE (NAACP) IS FOUNDED

CONGRESS PASSES THE UNITED STATES COPYRIGHT LAW

Oil baron John D. Rockefeller becomes the world's first billionaire

The first synthetic plastic, Bakelite, is invented by Leo Baekeland

PRE-SEASON

JANUARY 19:

Charles Comiskey, owner of the Chicago White Sox, buys a parcel of land at 35th Street and Shields from Roxanna Bowen and plans to build a new ballpark there.

FEBRUARY 4:

John Clarkson, who compiled a 326-177 record and a 2.81 ERA in 12 years, dies at age 47 in Belmont, Massachusetts. Clarkson won 53 games with the Chicago White Stockings in 1885 and 49 for the Boston Beaneaters in 1889.

FEBRUARY 17:

Cleveland acquires 41-year-old pitcher Cy Young (21-11) from the Red Sox for pitchers Charlie Chech (11-7) and Jack Ryan (1-1) plus $12,500.

FEBRUARY 26:

Israel Durham and two partners purchase the Phillies from Alfred Reach and John Rogers. Durham becomes the team's president.

FEBRUARY 27:

Another great career comes to an end. The Giants release Iron Man Joe McGinnity, who was 11-7 last season. The 37-year-old righthander was 247-144 with an ERA of 2.64 in his 10-year career.

MARCH 1:

Construction begins today on a new stadium for the Pittsburgh Pirates in the Oakland section near Schenley Park.

MARCH 2:

Mel "Master Melvin" Ott is born in Gretna, Louisiana.

THE SEASON

APRIL 12:

Shibe Park, the new ballpark for the Philadelphia Athletics, opens today with 30,162 fans on hand to see their hometown team top the Red Sox, 8-1, on Eddie Plank's six-hitter. The new ballpark, located at 21st and Lehigh, cost $500,000 (estimates in various sources range from $300,000 to $1 million) to build, is the first concrete and steel stadium, and features a French Renaissance pavilion. Historian Lee Allen describes Shibe as having "walls of brick and terra cotta trim, and a mansard roof of green slate." Late in the game Athletics'

HISTORY

Who is the only player to finish his career with a 1.000 average in batting and fielding, as well as a 1.000 winning percentage as a pitcher? It's John Kull of the Athletics, described by Connie Mack as "the man with a million-dollar arm." The 27-year-old pitcher appears in one game, wins it, gets a hit in his only at-bat, and cleanly handles his only fielding chance.

APRIL 15
Giants' pitcher Red Ames nearly tosses an opening day no-hitter against Brooklyn.

Honus Wagner swung a hot bat for the Pirates.

catcher Mike "Doc" Powers complains of stomach pains after hitting the wall chasing a pop foul. After the game, he undergoes surgery.

APRIL 15:

On opening day, the Giants' Leon "Red" Ames no-hits Brooklyn for nine innings. His no-hitter is ruined by Charles "Whitey" Alperman's hit in the tenth. Ames ends up allowing seven hits and losing, 3-0, in 13. Into the eighth, Brooklyn's Irvin "Kaiser" Wilhelm also is pitching a no-hitter.

APRIL 19:

Former Giants' team physician Joseph M. Creamer, charged with trying to bribe umpires Bill Klem and Jimmy Johnstone before last year's key game with the Cubs, is barred for life from all major league ballparks.

APRIL 20:

Pittsburgh's new stadium will be named Forbes Field in honor of General John "Old Ironsides" Forbes, who founded the city and was a hero of the French and Indian Wars. Team owner Barney Dreyfuss gets 100,000 suggestions in a poll and declines to affix his own name to the new ballpark.

APRIL 26:

Following three operations, Athletics' catcher Mike "Doc" Powers dies at 38 of gangrene in Philadelphia. He is the first major leaguer to die of on-field injuries.

MAY 3:

The controversial Hal Chase returns to the New York Highlanders. He is reinstated after being

JUNE 30
Forbes Field opens in Pittsburgh, with the Pirates losing to the Cubs, 3-2.

fined $200 for playing in the "outlaw" California State League, and receives a silver loving cup from his teammates.

MAY 10:

It's minor league baseball, but it's an impressive performance. Fred Toney of Winchester pitches a 17-inning no-hit game, defeating Lexington, 1-0, in the Blue Grass League. The 21-year-old strikes out 19 and walks only one.

Toney comes to the majors in 1911 with the Cubs. In 1917, while with Cincinnati, he pitches a no-hitter in one of the classic pitching duels in history. He plays for 12 years, compiling a 137-102 record with a 2.69 ERA.

JUNE 18:

Some 3,000 people turn out at the League Park in Cincinnati to see a startling innovation – night baseball. The game, between the Elks of Cincinnati and those of Newport, Kentucky, is the brainchild of George Cahill of Holyoke, Massachusetts, the inventor of portable lights mounted on steel towers. Among the attendees are the Reds and Phillies, who remain after their own game to watch the experiment. Cincinnati's Elks win the game, 8-5.

FORBES FIELD ALSO HAS GARGANTUAN DIMENSIONS: 360 FEET (LEFT FIELD), 462 FEET (CENTER FIELD) AND 376 FEET (RIGHT FIELD). THE FORBES FIELD 60TH ANNIVERSARY PICTURE ALBUM SAYS THAT BARNEY DREYFUSS "HATED CHEAP HOME RUNS AND VOWED HE'D HAVE NONE IN HIS PARK."

JUNE 28:

Only four months after buying the Phillies, team president Israel Durham dies in Atlantic City, New Jersey.

JUNE 30:

Forbes Field, a $2 million steel and concrete stadium, opens with a crowd of 30,338 on hand. The Cubs beat the Pirates, 3-2. Forbes, one of two concrete and steel stadiums, features three decks, electric lights, telephones, and maids in the ladies' room. With Shibe Park, it is the only ballpark with a visitors' dressing room.

JULY 4:

Maybe he thinks it is April 1. The Pirates' Honus Wagner comes to bat with a "torpedo" – a form of fireworks – shaped like a bat. It explodes when he swings at the first pitch.

JULY 5:

Frank Selee dies in Denver at age 49. Although he never played major league baseball, Selee managed in the NL for 16 years with Boston and Chicago, winning five pennants and compiling a .598 winning percentage.

JULY 7:

William Jennings Bryan "Billy" Herman is born in New Albany, Indiana.

JULY 8:

Experiments continue with night baseball. In a Central League game, Grand Rapids beats Zanesville, 11-10.

JULY 16:

Ed Summers of the Tigers pitches 18 shutout innings against the Senators, and all he gets for his effort is tired. The game ends in a 0-0 tie when it is called because of darkness. Summers allows seven hits and only one walk, fanning 10. Tiger stars Ty Cobb and Sam Crawford each are 0 for seven. Bill Gray starts for Washington.

JULY 17:

At Cleveland, Smoky Joe Wood of the Red Sox comes in from the bullpen to strike out 10 batters in four innings. Boston wins, 6-4.

JULY 19:

Cleveland shortstop Neal Ball executes the first unassisted triple

HISTORY

Brooklyn catcher Bill Bergen manages 48 hits in 346 at-bats over 112 games for an average of .139, the lowest ever by a regular player. Bergen is no stranger to microscopic batting averages. After a career high of .227 in 1903, he hits .182 in 1904, .190 in 1905, .159 in 1906, .159 in 1907, and .175 in 1908. Bergen lasts for 11 years, never again topping .200 and ending with a lifetime average of .170 with two homers.

SEPTEMBER 16
William Howard Taft becomes the first U.S. President to attend a baseball game.

CULTURE

***The Short-Stop*, a "young adult" novel by Zane Grey, is published.**

play in the modern major leagues. With runners on first and second in the second inning, Red Sox second baseman Ambrose "Amby" McConnell hits a liner to Ball, who gets Heinie Wagner at second and then tags Jake Stahl. Ball then hits an inside-the-park homer in the bottom of the inning to lead Cleveland to a 6-1 win in the opener of a double header. Ball was sold to Cleveland in May by the Highlanders. Boston wins game two, 3-2.

JULY 24:

Brooklyn's George "Nap" Rucker strikes out 16 Cardinals, winning 1-0.

JULY 28:

National League president Henry Pulliam shoots himself in the head in his room at the New York Athletic Club. Because of the nature of his wounds, the 40-year-old Pulliam could not be moved to the hospital and dies the following day. In February at a banquet for NL owners, Pulliam suffered a breakdown, saying: "My days as a baseball man are numbered. The National League doesn't want me as president anymore." Pulliam was granted an indefinite leave of absence and replaced by John A. Heydler.

> IN 1955, TY COBB TELLS *THE SPORTING NEWS*, "I AM NOW 68 YEARS OLD. I STILL RESENT THE CHARGE OF BRUTAL AND INTENTIONAL SPIKING. THIS INCIDENT, REMEMBER, HAPPENED IN 1909. THIS IS 1955, AND TO THIS DAY, IN MEETING SOME YOUNG BOY INTERESTED IN BASEBALL AND WHOSE FATHER I MIGHT HAVE MET, I HAVE BEEN TOLD, 'OH, YOU'RE THE MAN WHO SPIKED BAKER.'"

AUGUST 3:

All NL games are canceled for the funeral of Henry Pulliam.

AUGUST 4:

At Shibe Park, umpire Tim Hurst calls the Athletics' Eddie Collins out on strikes in a game against the White Sox. Collins argues and steps on the umpire's shoes. Hurst tells Collins, a Columbia University graduate: "I don't like college boys" and spits in his face. Hurst needs police protection from the fans at the end of the game. AL president Ban Johnson fires Hurst from the umpiring staff. In 1897, the overly aggressive Hurst was dismissed from the NL for throwing a beer stein back into the stands and hitting the wrong fan, and once he fired a gun in the air to quiet a crowd. Hurst, who said of umpiring, "The pay is good, it keeps you out in the fresh air and sunshine and you can't beat the hours," once followed New York Highlanders' manager Clark Griffith into the dugout and decked him. On another occasion, George Moriarty – himself later an umpire – argues a strike call, insisting it was worse than the previous pitch, which was a ball. Hurst agrees and makes both pitches strikes.

AUGUST 10:

The Cubs' Ed Reulbach beats visiting Brooklyn, 8-1, at the West Side Grounds for his 14th consecutive win.

AUGUST 17:

Unable to cope with the inexperience of his team, second baseman Napoleon Lajoie resigns as Cleveland's manager. The team is at 57-57.

AUGUST 18:

Walter "Arlie" Latham is appointed by Giants' manager John McGraw as baseball's first full-time coach.

Latham, whose nickname is the Freshest Man on Earth, plays in four games this season and, at the age of 49, becomes the oldest player to steal a base.

AUGUST 22:

Jim "Deacon" McGuire, a coach under Napoleon

SEPTEMBER 18
A record crowd of 35,409 fills Shibe Park to witness the A's 2-0 shutout of the Tigers.

SEPTEMBER 30
The White Sox's win over the Athletics gives the Tigers the AL pennant

Lajoie, is named to succeed him as Cleveland's manager. McGuire was the manager of the Boston Red Sox for two seasons and also managed Washington in the NL in 1898.

AUGUST 24:

At Bennett Field in Detroit, Ty Cobb attempts to steal third during an intentional walk to Sam Crawford. Athletics' catcher Paddy Livingston gets the ball to third on time, but Cobb hook slides to his left and spikes third baseman Frank Baker on the hand and arm when he tries a barehanded tag. Despite protests by Philadelphia, Cobb remains in the game and Detroit wins, 7-6. Athletics' manager Connie Mack complains to AL president Ban Johnson about Cobb's dirty play. Johnson warns that Cobb "must stop this sort of playing or he will have to quit the game." The next day Johnson backs off his warning.

SEPTEMBER 11:

The Red Sox buy one-time 41-game winner Jack Chesbro (0-4) from the Highlanders for the waiver price.

Zack Wheat has the misfortune of making his major league debut against the Giants' Christy Mathewson, who horse collars him as New York beats Brooklyn, 4-0, in game one of a double header. Wheat fares better in game two, collecting two hits against Arthur "Bugs" Raymond in a 10-1 Brooklyn victory.

SEPTEMBER 12:

Bill Dinneen, who compiled a 170-176 record in 12 years in the majors, becomes an AL umpire. Dinneen umpires for 29 years, working 45 World Series games.

SEPTEMBER 16:

President William Howard Taft becomes the first U.S. president to attend a baseball game, when he joins 27,000 fans in Chicago to see Christy Mathewson and the Giants beat Three Finger Brown and the Cubs, 2-1.

SEPTEMBER 17:

Former major leaguer Herman "Germany" Long dies at age 43 in Denver. A shortstop who also played the other infield positions and the outfield, Long played 16 years and is the only major league player with more than 1,000 errors in his career (he had 1,096).

SHADES OF EARL WEAVER: REPORTEDLY, AFTER ATTENDING A GAME BETWEEN THE PIRATES AND CUBS, PRESIDENT WILLIAM HOWARD TAFT COMMENTS, "SATURDAY'S GAME WAS A FUN ONE, BUT SEVERAL TIMES WHEN A HIT MEANT A RUN, THE BATTER WAS ORDERED TO BUNT. I BELIEVE THEY SHOULD HIT IT OUT. I LOVE THE GAME WHEN THERE IS PLENTY OF SLUGGING."

Long played from 1899 to 1904, batted .278, and stole a total of 534 bases.

SEPTEMBER 18:

The biggest crowd in major league history to date – 35,409 – turns out at Shibe Park to see the Athletics battle the visiting Tigers. They are not disappointed as the Athletics' Charles "Chief" Bender beats Wild Bill Donovan, 2-0.

SEPTEMBER 30:

The Tigers back into the pennant, clinching despite a loss today to Boston, because the White Sox eliminate the second-place Athletics.

REGULAR SEASON WRAP-UP:

The World Series will match the Detroit Tigers and the Pittsburgh Pirates. The Tigers, under Hughie Jennings, win their third straight pennant with a record of 98-54, three and a half games over the A's. Cobb wins the Triple Crown, batting .377, driving in 107 runs, and hitting nine homers – all inside the park. The team has three 20-game winners: George Mullin (29-8), Ed Willett, and Ed

CULTURE

His Last Game, **a one-reel silent film, focuses on an all-Indian baseball team. It is described by writer James Mote as the "earliest-known dramatic photoplay relating to baseball."**

"We also play a little rough in this league, Mr Cobb."
– Honus Wagner to Ty Cobb

Summers. The Pirates, under Fred Clarke, win 110 games, beating the Cubs by six and a half despite Chicago's 104 victories – a record for second place. Honus Wagner leads the NL in batting (.339) for the fourth straight year; Howie Camnitz and Vic Willis are 20-game winners.

OCTOBER 8:

World Series, game one. A crowd of 29,264 jams Forbes Field and sees the Pirates top the Tigers, 4-1, behind a six-hitter by Charles "Babe" Adams. Player-manager Fred Clarke's solo homer is one of only five hits yielded by loser George Mullin, whose teammates make four errors.

Game one features a confrontation between future Hall of Famers Ty Cobb and Honus Wagner. What is legend and what is fact has become blurred with the years. The story goes that Cobb, on first base, shouted down to shortstop Wagner, "Get ready, I'm coming down." Wagner responds, "I'll be waiting" – and he is. He tags Cobb in the face, cutting his lip and loosening three teeth. (By some accounts he knocked out his teeth.)

According to Fred Lieb, Wagner tells Cobb, "We also play a little rough in this league, Mr. Cobb." In Superstars, Stars and Just Plain Heroes, *Nathan Salant quotes Wagner's explanation, "I didn't cut his lip on purpose, but I knew he'd be coming in hard, and I wasn't about to let him nail me. Besides, if he made it once, he'd run a thousand times, and we wanted to win that World Series badly because of the way we played in 1903."*

OCTOBER 9:

World Series, game two. The Tigers beat the Pirates, 7-2, at Forbes Field, where attendance is 30,915. In the third inning, while Vic Willis is in his windmill windup, Ty Cobb steals home as part of a three-run rally. Howie Camnitz gets the loss; Wild Bill Donovan holds the Pirates to five hits for the victory.

OCTOBER 11:

World Series, game three. At Bennett Field in Detroit, the Pirates beat the Tigers, 8-6, on a five-run first inning. Honus Wagner is the big bat with three hits and three RBI, as well as three stolen bases. The Tigers rally for two in the ninth, but fall short. The winner is Nick Maddox; Ed Summers is charged with the loss. Attendance is 18,277.

OCTOBER 12:

World Series, game four. George Mullin five-hits the Pirates and strikes out 10 in a 5-0 win at Bennett Field. Ty Cobb and Oscar Stanage each drive in two runs. Al "Lefty" Leifeld gets the loss. Pittsburgh commits six errors. Attendance is 17,036.

OCTOBER 13:

World Series, game five. It's back to Pittsburgh, where the Pirates prevail, 8-4, despite homers by the Tigers' Davy Jones and Sam Crawford. Fred Clarke's three-run homer in the seventh is the big hit for the Pirates, breaking a 3-3 tie. Babe Adams allows six hits for the win. Ed Summers gets the loss. Attendance is 21,706.

OCTOBER 14:

World Series, game six. George Mullin gets his second series win, 5-4, allowing seven hits. Vic Willis, who lasts five innings, is charged with the loss. Attendance in Detroit is 10,535.

OCTOBER 16:

World Series, game seven. Pirates righthander Babe Adams becomes the first rookie to pitch and win three complete World Series games. Today in Detroit, Adams six-hits the Tigers, 8-0, to win the World Championship for Pittsburgh. Honus Wagner and John "Dots" Miller each drive in two runs. Wild Bill Donovan gets the loss. Attendance is 17,562. Wagner outhits Cobb in the Series .333 (six RBI, six stolen bases) to .231 (six RBI, two stolen bases). The Pirates tie a World Series record with 18 stolen bases.

POST-SEASON

NOVEMBER 1:

Patsy Donovan, former Brooklyn manager, becomes skipper of the Boston Red Sox. He replaces Fred Lake, who led the Red Sox to an 88-63 third-place finish, and will manage the Braves next season.

NOVEMBER 26:

Now he gets second-guessed by the press. Former Philadelphia sportswriter Horace Fogel, with financial support from Charles P. Taft – the president's brother – buys the Phillies. Fogel will be the team's president.

OCTOBER 11
Honus Wagner picks up 3 RBIs in the Pirates' 8-6 World Series win over the Tigers

OCTOBER 16
The Pirates take the World Series as rookie pitcher Babe Adams gets his third win.

THE BEST OF 1909

National League

HITTERS

Batting Average:
Honus Wagner, Pittsburgh Pirates, .339

Slugging Average:
Honus Wagner, .489

Home Runs:
John "Red" Murray, New York Giants, 7

Runs Batted In:
Honus Wagner, 100

Hits:
Larry Doyle, New York Giants, 172

Stolen Bases:
Bob Bescher, Cincinnati Reds, 54

PITCHERS

Wins:
Mordecai "Three Finger" Brown, Chicago Cubs, 27

Strikeouts:
Orval Overall, Chicago Cubs, 205

Earned Run Average:
Christy Mathewson, New York Giants, 1.14

Winning Percentage:
Samuel "Howie" Camnitz, Pittsburgh Pirates; Christy Mathewson, .806

Saves:
Mordecai Brown, 7

American League

HITTERS

Batting Average:
Ty Cobb, Detroit Tigers, .377

Slugging Average:
Ty Cobb, .517

Home Runs:
Ty Cobb, 9

Runs Batted In:
Ty Cobb, 107

Hits:
Ty Cobb, 216

Stolen Bases:
Ty Cobb, 76

PITCHERS

Wins:
George Mullin, Detroit Tigers, 29

Strikeouts:
Frank "Piano Mover" Smith, Chicago White Sox, 177

Earned Run Average:
Harry Krause, Philadelphia Athletics, 1.39

Winning Percentage:
George Mullin, .784

Saves:
Frank Arellanes, Boston Red Sox, 8

1910

"I wasn't going to get killed playing in on Lajoie."
– John "Red" Corriden

William Howard Taft is the first U.S. president to throw out the ceremonial first pitch at a ball game.

NEWS

U.S. POPULATION TOPS 91 MILLION

Boy Scouts of America chartered; Camp Fire Girls organized

FIRST CELEBRATION OF FATHER'S DAY

MANN ACT IS PASSED, MAKING CHILD PROSTITUTION A FEDERAL OFFENSE

MARK TWAIN DIES AT AGE 75

UNION OF SOUTH AFRICA IS FORMED AS DOMINION OF GREAT BRITAIN

REVOLUTION BEGINS IN MEXICO; PRESIDENT DIAZ OVERTHROWN

Britain's Edward VII dies; his son succeeds and is crowned George V

Trans-Andean railroad links Chile and Argentina

PRE-SEASON

JANUARY 16:

Jay Hanna "Dizzy" Dean is born in Lucas, Arkansas.

There are a variety of names and several birthdates for Dizzy Dean. His biographer, Vince Staten, consulted the 1910 census book for Tomlinson Township, Logan County, Arkansas, for the facts. The result makes Dean older by one year than generally recorded. Staten also was able to establish that Dean's real name was Jay Hanna – not Jerome Herman or other variations. And he was able to pinpoint his place of birth, as well.

MARCH 17:

The cornerstone is laid in Chicago for the new stadium for the White Sox.

THE SEASON

APRIL 14:

William Howard Taft, the 27th President of the United States, becomes the first to inaugurate a baseball season by throwing out the first ball. In Washington, D.C., President Taft, who last season also was the first to attend a game, makes the ceremonial toss, and Senators, pitcher Walter Johnson makes the catch. Johnson then pitches a one-hitter against the Athletics, winning, 3-0. The only hit for Philadelphia is a Frank Baker double.

APRIL 20:

Cleveland's Addie Joss no-hits the White Sox, 1-0, in Chicago. The game's only run scores on an Art Kruger single and a Terry Turner double. Joss, who pitched a no-hitter in 1908, today walks two and strikes out two while his teammates commit a single error. Guy "Doc" White is the losing pitcher.

APRIL 21:

Cleveland plays its first game in renovated League Park, which now has a 40-foot wall in right field. A crowd of 19,869 fills the new stands, which have a capacity of 21,000, to see the Tigers win, 5-0, behind Ed Willett. The cost of renovation is estimated at $300,000.

MAY 2:

In Pittsburgh, President William Howard Taft takes in another ballgame. The Chief Executive watches as the Pirates beat the Cubs, 5-2.

MAY 4:

So who's watching the White House? President Taft continues as baseball's number one fan. With the Cardinals at home at Robison Field, while the Browns are playing at Sportsman's Park, the president shuttles between both stadiums so he can remain nonpartisan.

MAY 12:

The Athletics' Charles "Chief" Bender no-hits the Cleveland Naps, 4-0, walking one and fanning four. Fred Link is the losing pitcher.

JUNE 23:

Giants' third baseman Art Devlin and two others are arrested after assaulting a heckler in Washington Park in Brooklyn. The Giants win, 8-2.

JUNE 27:

In the last game at their 39th Street Grounds, the Chicago White Sox lose to visiting Cleveland, 7-2.

JUNE 28:

The Cubs' Joe Tinker becomes the first major leaguer to steal

JULY 19
Cy Young, at age 43, beats the Senators, 5-4, for his record 500th career victory.

AUGUST 4
The Athletics' Jack Coombs and Ed Walsh of the White Sox pitch to a 0-0, 16-inning tie.

home twice in one game. The baseball larceny takes place at Chicago's West Side Grounds, where the Cubs and Mordecai "Three Finger" Brown beat Cincinnati, 11-1.

JULY 1:

The new $750,000 White Sox Park opens today with some 28,000 fans on hand. The Browns, behind Barney Pelty, spoil the debut with a 2-0 win. White Sox Park will be renamed Comiskey Park.

JULY 10:

With the Cubs in town to play the Giants, Franklin P. Adams of the *New York Evening Mail* pens a poem – "Baseball's Sad Lexicon" – that will build a reputation for Chicago's double play combination that far exceeds their actual on-field accomplishments.

The year this poem was published is a matter of some debate. Some sources say it first appeared in 1908 or 1912; the most credible information pegs it as 1910.

JULY 19:

In game two of a doubleheader in Washington today, 43-year-old Cy Young beats the Senators, 5-4, in 11 innings to register his record 500th career victory. Young has won 287 games in the NL and 213 in the AL.

JULY 25:

Outfielder Shoeless Joe Jackson, unhappy with Philadelphia because of the ridicule of his teammates, is traded by the Athletics to the Naps for outfielder Briscoe "The Human Eyeball" Lord (.219). Jackson appeared in only five games each for Philadelphia in 1908 and 1909, and in none this year.

JULY 31:

Detroit beats Chicago 6-5 at the new White Sox Park. In the fourth inning Chicago's Lee Tannehill hits a grand slam homer and Ty Cobb hits a home run against Big Ed Walsh in the fifth.

In attendance is a six-year-old fan named James T. Farrell, who will go on to write the Studs Lonigan trilogy. Baseball and the White Sox figure prominently in the young protagonist's life.

Leonard "King" Cole of the Cubs might be a merrier soul if he'd been able to pitch two more innings. Cole no-hits the Cardinals, 4-0, in a game called after seven because of the train schedule out of Chicago.

AUGUST 4:

The Athletics' Jack Coombs and Big Ed Walsh of the White Sox battle 16 innings to a 0-0 tie in a game called because of darkness. Walsh yields just six hits; Coombs allows only three hits and strikes out 18 batters.

AUGUST 13:

Today Brooklyn and Pittsburgh play to an 8-8 tie. The two teams also tie in eight statistical categories for the game. Each has 38 at-bats, 13 hits, three walks, five strikeouts, one hit batter, two errors, 12 assists, and one passed ball.

AUGUST 24:

The old catch-a-ball-from-the-top-of-the-Washington-Monument stunt rides again. White Sox pitcher Big Ed Walsh throws 23 baseballs from the top of the famous monument to his battery mate, catcher Billy Sullivan, at a speed estimated at 110 miles per hour. Sullivan manages to hang on to three of the balls.

AUGUST 27:

The new White Sox Park is the scene of the first night game ever in an AL stadium. But the game, which attracts 20,000 spectators, matches two amateur teams under temporary lights developed by George Cahill. The ballpark is lit with 137,000 candle power arc lights. Charles Comiskey sponsors the event.

SEPTEMBER 24:

First baseman Hal Chase is today named the Highlanders' new manager, replacing George Stallings. With the Highlanders at 78-59 and in second place, Stallings accuses Chase of dumping games. Owners Frank Farrell and AL president Ban Johnson support Chase, and Stallings was fired yesterday. Johnson takes a parting shot at Stallings, accusing him of trying "to besmirch the character of a sterling player. Anybody who knows Hal Chase knows that he is not guilty of the accusations."

SEPTEMBER 25:

The Athletics' Jack Coombs extends his consecutive shutout innings streak to 53. Coombs shuts out the White Sox in the last

EQUIPMENT

A new baseball with a cork center – described as a "rabbit ball" – is used in the National League.

LEAGUE

In December, New Yorker William Hepburn Russell and publishers Louis and George Page buy the NL Boston franchise from John Dovey. The team had been known as the Doves, for their previous owners, John and his late brother George. Now they will become the Rustlers in honor of Russell.

Members of the Cleveland Indians model the bulky wool sweaters that served as warm-up gear in this era.

White Sox owner Charles Comiskey calls Ty Cobb "the greatest player of all time," adding, he "plays ball with his whole anatomy – his head, his arms, his hands, his legs, his feet."

EQUIPMENT

A baseball with a cork center – invented by Athletics' owner Benjamin S. Shibe – is patented by sporting goods manufacturer Alfred J. Reach.

six innings of the opener of today's doubleheader. In game two, he pitches two additional innings, with Chicago finally scoring to end the skein.

OCTOBER 2:

In Cincinnati, the Cubs wrap up the NL pennant with a triple play – left fielder Jimmy Sheckard to catcher Johnny Kling to first baseman Jimmy Archer – and an 8-4 win.

OCTOBER 4:

The Athletics' Eddie "Cocky" Collins steals his 81st base of the season.

OCTOBER 5:

Earle Mack becomes the first major leaguer to play for his father when he makes his major league debut as a catcher for the Athletics, managed by Connie Mack. He handles pitchers Eddie Plank and Jack Coombs. At bat, he singles and triples, but Philadelphia still loses to the Highlanders, 7-4.

OCTOBER 9:

With Ty Cobb holding a lead in the AL batting race, he sits out the last game against the White Sox. Cleveland's Napoleon Lajoie, in second place, faces St. Louis in a doubleheader. Browns' manager Jack O'Connor orders rookie third baseman John "Red" Corriden to play deep when Lajoie bats. In game one, Lajoie hits a triple and three bunt singles (one to shortstop Bobby Wallace, two to Corriden). St. Louis wins the game, 5-4. In game two, he lays down four more bunt singles, and in his fifth at-bat an error by Corriden deprives him of another hit. Cleveland wins, 3-0. O'Connor explains that Lajoie "outguessed us. We figured he did not have the nerve to bunt every time." Lajoie gets messages of congratulations from eight of Cobb's teammates.

OCTOBER 13:

AL president Ban Johnson holds hearings on the "Lajoie incident." Red Corriden asserts he played deep to avoid injury and that it was not deliberately done to help Lajoie. "I wasn't going to get killed playing in on Lajoie," he says. Johnson accepts his testimony, but holds up the Chalmers Award, an automobile, given to the American League batting champion.

According to Ty Cobb biographer Charles C. Alexander, Red Corriden was telling the truth. Manager Jack O'Connor really did tell him to play deep to avoid injury.

OCTOBER 15:

Browns' owner Robert Lee Hedges fires manager Jack O'Connor. His dismissal is said to be related to the Lajoie-Cobb controversy, although finishing 47-107 in last place may not have helped his case. By some accounts, O'Connor hated Cobb and allegedly offered official scorer E.V. Parrish a suit of clothes to change Lajoie's last at-bat from an error to a hit. Parrish declined. Also discharged is pitching coach Harry Howell, who is charged with delivering O'Connor's offer to the official scorer. Ban Johnson calculates the final averages as Cobb, .384944; Lajoie, .384084, and the Chalmers Automobile Co. gives both players cars. Johnson subsequently blackballs O'Connor and Howell from baseball for life.

In 1981 The Sporting News *reported that, in the calculation of Cobb's average, one game was used twice, and the final numbers should be Lajoie, .383; and Cobb, .382. The official records were not changed.* The Baseball Encyclopedia *records the averages as Cobb, .385; Lajoie, .384.*

REGULAR SEASON WRAP-UP:

Connie Mack's Athletics finish at 102-48, 14 1/2 games ahead of the Highlanders. Second baseman Eddie Collins leads the offense with a .322 average and 81 stolen bases. The pitching staff is headed by Jack Coombs at 31-9 with 13 shutouts, and Charles "Chief" Bender, 23-5.
The Cubs, managed by Frank Chance, compile a 104-50 record, beating the Giants by 13 games. The staff has two 20-game winners, "Three Finger" Brown (25-3) and rookie Leonard "King" Cole (20-4.) The Cubs' leading hitters are Arthur "Solly" Hofman at .325 and Frank "Wildfire" Schulte at .301 with a league-leading 10 homers.

It is a strong offensive year for the NL. A record 214 homers are hit and the cumulative batting average

OCTOBER 4
Eddie "Cocky" Collins of the Athletics steals his 81st base – tops in the majors this season.

OCTOBER 23
The Athletics beat the Cubs, 9-2, in game five to win the World Championship.

rises to .257 from last year's .244. But the AL Chicago White Sox record the worst team batting average in the history of baseball – a paltry .211.

OCTOBER 17:

World Series, game one. The Fall Classic opens in Philadelphia with a 4-1 win by the Athletics. Chief Bender allows three hits in nine innings for the win; Orval Overall is the losing pitcher. Frank Baker paces the Philadelphia attack with two doubles, a single, and two RBIs.

OCTOBER 18:

World Series, game two. Jack Coombs pitches nine strong innings, yielding eight hits, for a 9-3 win in Philadelphia. A six-run rally in the seventh inning sends the Cubs and "Three Finger" Brown to defeat. Every Philadelphia batter has at least one hit.

OCTOBER 20:

World Series, game three. Jack Coombs, the winner of game two, does it again today, allowing six hits in a 12-5 victory. A five-run third inning featuring a homer by Danny Murphy salts the game away. Coombs helps himself with three RBI on three hits. The losing pitcher is Harry McIntire, who pitches only a third of an inning.

OCTOBER 21:

The Giants beat the Highlanders today, 6-3, at the Polo Grounds to win the New York City Series, two games to one with a tie. The two New York teams finished in second place in their respective leagues in 1910.

OCTOBER 22:

World Series, game four. At home, the Chicago Cubs stay alive with a dramatic 10-inning come-from-behind win against the Athletics, 4-3. Down three games to none and trailing today 3-2 in the ninth inning with one out, the Cubs tie on a Frank Chance triple. They win in the 10th on Jimmy Sheckard's RBI single. The winning pitcher is "Three Finger" Brown, who hurls two innings in relief of "King" Cole. "Chief" Bender gets the loss.

OCTOBER 23:

World Series, game five. Behind Jack Coombs's third Series win, the Athletics top the Cubs, 9-2, in Chicago for the World Championship. Eddie Collins has three hits and two RBI; the Athletics score five runs in the eighth. Three Finger Brown is charged with the loss. In winning the Series, Philadelphia uses only Coombs and Bender. Eddie Collins is their top hitter at .429; Frank Baker hits .409. Frank Chance and "Wildfire" Schulte each hit .353 for the Cubs.

POST-SEASON

NOVEMBER 27:

The Detroit Tigers, led by George Mullin and including Ty Cobb, travel to Cuba to play exhibition games. Some 15,000 are on hand today as the Tigers with Mullin on the mound beat Alemnadres, 4-0.

NOVEMBER 29:

Gonazalez beats the Tigers today, 3-0. How good is catcher Bruce Petway, who played last season in the U.S. with the Negro League team, the Chicago Leland Giants? In today's game, Cobb walks and tries to steal second. Petway gets the ball to John Henry Lloyd so quickly, the shortstop waits for Cobb, avoids his spikes, and puts the tag on him.

DECEMBER 13:

Former major league first baseman Dan McGann shoots himself to death in Louisville, Kentucky, at the age of 33. He played 13 years in the major leagues, from 1895 to 1908, with several different teams. For his career, he hit .285 and stole 282 bases. He played with the Giants in 1905, and in the World Series went 4-for-17 with seven strikeouts.

DECEMBER:

John A. Heydler, who has been serving as the National League's president, declines to serve another term. When his replacement is considered by the league's hierarchy, a deadlock develops between the candidacies of John Montgomery Ward and Robert W. Brown. Ban Johnson, a member of the National Commission, declares that he will never serve with Ward. According to Giants' owner John T. Brush, the only important role the league president plays is supervision of the umpires. Accordingly, he offers Thomas J. Lynch, known as King of the Umpires, as a compromise candidate, and he is approved by the league.

LEAGUE

Horace Fogel, the sportswriter turned owner, lobbies for a name change for his team. He wants the Phillies to be known as the Live Wires. The idea goes nowhere.

CULTURE

***The Bride and the Pennant*, a "young adult" novel by Frank Chance of the Cubs, is published. SABR-ite Andy McCue speculates that it was ghostwritten by journalist High Fullerton. *Won in the Ninth*, a young adult book by Christy Mathewson, also makes its debut. It is ghostwritten by John Wheeler and features such characters as Hans "Honus" Hagner, Johnny Everson, and Hal Case.**

THE BEST OF 1910

NATIONAL LEAGUE

HITTERS

Batting Average:
Sherry Magee, Philadelphia Phillies, .331

Slugging Average:
Sherry Magee, .507

Home Runs:
Frank "Wildfire" Schulte, Chicago Cubs; Fred Beck, Boston Doves, 10

Runs Batted In:
Sherry Magee, 123

Hits:
Honus Wagner, Bobby Byrne, Pittsburgh Pirates, 178

Stolen Bases:
Bob Bescher, Cincinnati Reds, 70

PITCHERS

Wins:
Christy Mathewson, New York Giants, 27

Strikeouts:
Earl Moore, Philadelphia Phillies, 185

Earned Run Average:
George McQuillan, Philadelphia Phillies, 1.60

Winning Percentage:
Leonard "King" Cole, Chicago Cubs, .833

Saves:
Mordecai "Three Finger" Brown, Chicago Cubs, 7

AMERICAN LEAGUE

HITTERS

Batting Average:
Ty Cobb, Detroit Tigers, .385

Slugging Average:
Ty Cobb, .554

Home Runs:
Garland "Jake" Stahl, Boston Red Sox, 10

Runs Batted In:
Sam Crawford, Detroit Tigers, 120

Hits:
Napoleon Lajoie, Cleveland Naps, 227

Stolen Bases:
Eddie "Cocky" Collins, Philadelphia Athletics, 81

PITCHERS

Wins:
Jack Coombs, Philadelphia Athletics, 31

Strikeouts:
Walter Johnson, Washington Senators, 313

Earned Run Average:
Big Ed Walsh, Chicago White Sox, 1.27

Winning Percentage:
Charles "Chief" Bender, Philadelphia Athletics, .821

Saves:
Ed Walsh, 5

1911

NEWS

146 DIE IN TRIANGLE SHIRTWAIST FACTORY FIRE IN NEW YORK CITY

Carnegie Corporation is established

Antitrust laws break up John D. Rockefeller's Standard Oil Co.

NORWAY'S ROALD AMUNDSEN IS FIRST TO REACH SOUTH POLE

Revolution in China ends 267-year Qing dynasty

American explorer Hiram Bingham discovers lost Incan city of Macchu-Pichu

THOMAS MANN'S *DEATH IN VENICE* IS PUBLISHED

Irving Berlin's "Alexander's Ragtime Band" begins popularization of ragtime music

PRE-SEASON

JANUARY 1:

Henry "Hank" Greenberg is born in New York City.

FEBRUARY 14:

The Giants and the Phillies become the first teams with pinstripes on their uniforms.

MARCH 24:

Cardinals' owner and president Matthew Stanley Robison dies unexpectedly in Cleveland. His sister-in-law, Mrs. Frank de Hass Robison, is the main heir and inherits the Cardinals, becoming the first woman to own a major league team.

APRIL 4:

Automobile manufacturer Hugh Chalmers agrees to present the Chalmers Award at the conclusion of the season to the Most Valuable Player in each league.

THE SEASON

APRIL 12:

In the first game at Griffith Stadium in Washington, D.C., the Senators beat the visiting Red Sox, 8-5. It is two years to the day that Boston helped Philadelphia inaugurate Shibe Park. The Red Sox lost that opener too.

APRIL 14:

Cleveland pitcher Adrian "Addie" Joss dies of meningitis in Toledo, Ohio, two days after his 31st birthday. In nine years with Cleveland, he was 160-97 with a spectacular 1.88 ERA.

A nighttime fire razes the Polo Grounds after the second Giants' game of the season, in which they bow to the Phillies and Earl Moore, 2-0. Damage is estimated at $250,000; concessionaire Harry M. Stevens loses $25,000 in food and supplies.

Two other significant fires occur in 1911: The grandstand at the Senators' ballpark burns and the facility remains closed for three weeks, and the Mills Commission's evidence on the origins of baseball is destroyed in a blaze.

APRIL 15:

The New York Giants play at Hilltop Park, home of the AL Highlanders, and beat Brooklyn, 6-3.

HISTORY

Andrew "Rube" Foster forms the black Chicago American Giants.

RULES

Ban Johnson, seeking to speed up American League games, prohibits warm-up pitches. Home teams will wear white uniforms.

JULY 4
The White Sox end Ty Cobb's record hitting streak at 40 consecutive games.

HISTORY

In 1911, Cubs' second baseman Johnny Evers suffers a nervous breakdown and misses most of the season. He appears in only 46 games, batting .226.

LEAGUE

Connie Mack of the Athletics trots out his "$100,000 infield" – John "Stuffy" McInnis at first base, Eddie "Cocky" Collins at second, Jack Barry at shortstop, and Frank Baker at third base.

The Senators' Walter Johnson strikes out four Red Sox batters in the fifth inning today. (How is that possible? The catcher failed to hold onto the third strike pitch, so a batter reached first base safely despite the called strike.) His victims are Ray Collins, Larry Gardner, Harry Hooper, and George "Duffy" Lewis. Visiting Boston beats Washington 6-2.

MAY 13:

At Detroit, Ty Cobb hits a grand slam homer off Ed Karger in the third inning – the first of his career – in a wild and woolly game won in 10 innings by the Red Sox, 13-11. The big hit for Boston is a grand slam by "Duffy" Lewis. Down 10-1 after five innings, Boston wins on 20 hits. Detroit has 14.

In New York, the Giants stage a monster first-inning rally against the Cardinals, scoring 10 runs before an out is made; they end up with 13 runs all-told in the frame and win, 19-5, on 12 hits and 11 walks. Christy Mathewson is relieved after one inning by Richard "Rube" Marquard, who strikes out 11. Fred Merkle hits a home run for New York.

MAY 14:

In their first Sunday home game, the Cleveland Naps defeat the New York Highlanders, 16-3, before a crowd of nearly 16,000 spectators. Cleveland's George Stovall leads the offense with four hits.

JUNE 18:

The Tigers, trailing the White Sox 13-1 after four and a half innings, use a four-run fifth as a springboard. Detroit goes on to win, 16-15, with three in the bottom of the ninth. Detroit has 21 hits to Chicago's 16. Ty Cobb scores the winning run when Sam Crawford's drive goes over the head of center fielder Frank "Ping" Bodie. The winning pitcher is Clarence Mitchell; Big Ed Walsh takes the game's loss.

JUNE 27:

In Boston, the enforcement of the rule change banning warm-up pitches results in a fluke home run. With Ed Karger on the mound for the Red Sox and some of his fielders thinking he is warming up, Philadelphia's Stuffy McInnis hits the second pitch. The ball travels just over second base, but with center fielder Tris Speaker not yet in position, McInnis runs it into an inside-the-park homer. Umpire Ben Egan rules it a legal hit and the Athletics go on to win the game, 7-3.

JUNE 28:

The new Polo Grounds, a horseshoe-shaped structure, opens.

JULY 4:

Big Ed Walsh of the Chicago White Sox halts Ty Cobb's 20th-century record hitting streak at 40 consecutive games.

JULY 10:

In the third inning in St. Louis today, Philadelphia left fielder Sherry Magee is ejected for arguing a third strike and throwing his bat in the air. In response, he throws a punch at rookie umpire Bill Finneran, who is hospitalized with a broken jaw. Magee, the NL's top hitter in 1910, is suspended for the rest of the season and fined $200 by the league's president, Thomas Lynch. Yet with Philadelphia in a pennant race and its roster decimated by injuries, Lynch "commutes" Magee's suspension after 36 days and allows him to play again.

In Philadelphia, during a game with the Cubs, Bill Klem reputedly becomes the first umpire to eject a fan. The reported dialogue between the two:

Klem: "Sir, you did not buy that seat to insult ballplayers."

Fan: "Go ump the game, you big fathead."

Klem: "You are gone now, my friend. Officer, throw that man out."

JULY 19:

The Cardinals avert a tragedy, and a complaint from manager Roger Bresnahan may have been the reason. The Pullman car carrying the team from Washington to Boston is repositioned because Bresnahan claims it is too close to the engine and the noise is keeping his team awake. Shortly thereafter, the train crashes into a viaduct and plunges down an 18-foot embankment just west of the city of Bridgeport, Connecticut, killing 14 and injuring 47. The coach that took the place of the Cardinals' Pullman is damaged beyond

OCTOBER 4
Christy Mathewson shuts out the Dodgers to clinch the NL pennant for the Giants.

recognition. The Cardinals escape injury and help in the rescue effort.

JULY 21:

Pirates' owner Barney Dreyfuss buys a battery – and it doesn't come cheap. He pays St. Paul $22,500 for pitcher Marty O'Toole and $5,000 for his catcher Bill Kelly – reportedly record amounts. O'Toole pitched in one game for Cincinnati in 1908; Kelly appeared in two for St. Louis in 1910. Neither pays dividends for the Pirates. Kelly spends three years with the team, appearing in a total of only 102 games. O'Toole hangs on for three-plus seasons, winning 25 and losing 35 games.

JULY 24:

An American League all-star team – including Walter Johnson, Hal Chase, and Smoky Joe Wood – plays the Cleveland Naps to raise money for the widow of Addie Joss. The All-Stars win, 5-3.

JULY:

Cy Young is sold by Cleveland to the Boston Rustlers for the waiver price. The 44-year-old Young is 3-4. (The specific date is not available.)

JULY 29:

Boston's 21-year-old right-hander Smoky Joe Wood no-hits the visiting Browns, 5-0. In his last start, also against the Browns, Wood took a no-hitter into the ninth when Burt Shotton singled with two outs. Today, in game one of a doubleheader, he finishes the job, walking two and fanning 12; Boston commits one error. Tris Speaker hits a home run. Joe Lake gets the loss.

AUGUST 3:

Brooklyn's Eddie Zimmerman, Ross "Tex" Erwin, and Zack Wheat homer in the fifth inning to spark a 5-3 win over the Cubs in Chicago. The three homers represent half of the season's total for those three players.

AUGUST 7:

Even the great players have a nemesis, and for the Giants' Christy Mathewson it's Joe Tinker. The Chicago shortstop hits a double, triple, and single in four at-bats, and scores three times – including stealing home. The Cubs beat the Giants, 8-6, in Chicago. Mordecai "Three Finger" Brown gets the win.

AUGUST 27:

Big Ed Walsh of the White Sox no-hits the Red Sox, 5-0. Walsh walks one and strikes out eight while his teammates are flawless in the field. The losing pitcher is Ray Collins.

SEPTEMBER 7:

The old order changeth. Philadelphia's 24-year-old rookie right-hander, Grover Cleveland Alexander, beats 44-year-old Cy Young and Boston, 1-0.

SEPTEMBER 21:

Today in Chicago, Philadelphia's Grover Cleveland Alexander whitewashes the Cubs; it is his fourth consecutive shutout. The streak began on September 7 against Boston and continued through September 13 against Brooklyn, and September 17 against Cincinnati.

SEPTEMBER 22:

Starter Cy Young and the Rustlers beat Pittsburgh, 1-0. It is the 511th – and final – major league win for the 44-year-old Young. Charles "Babe" Adams is the losing pitcher.

SEPTEMBER 24:

In St. Louis, the Cardinals end the 41 consecutive shutout inning string of Grover Cleveland Alexander with a run in the sixth inning.

SEPTEMBER 26:

At Shibe Park, the Athletics clinch their second consecutive AL pennant with an 11-5 win over the Tigers, who held a 12-game lead over Philadelphia in May. The A's get two homers and two doubles from Frank Baker.

SEPTEMBER 28:

After the Highlanders top visiting St. Louis 18-12, the *New York Times* calls the Browns a "minor league team masquerading in major league livery." The Highlanders steal six bases in the second inning off catcher Jim "Little Nemo" Stephens, who is replaced by Jay Clarke. New York bangs out 29 hits and steals 15 bases (including four each by Hal Chase and William "Birdie" Cree). The losing pitcher in the game is Earl Hamilton.

OCTOBER 4:

Christy Mathewson shuts out the Dodgers to clinch the pennant for the New York Giants. Second baseman Laughing Larry Doyle, 25 years old,

EQUIPMENT

The livelier baseball, used in the NL last season, is introduced this season to the AL.

TRIVIA

During the 1911 season, rookie umpire Ralph Frary ejects all the players on Brooklyn's bench. Enraged fans make him the target of a bottle barrage and he has to leave. After the season, Frary quits as an umpire.

> "I give Charlie Faust full credit for winning the pennant for me."
> *– Giants' manager John McGraw*

TRIVIA

The "Mendoza line" is the figurative boundary in the batting averages between those batters hitting above and below .200. It is named for shortstop Mario Mendoza. But maybe it should be the "Bergen line" instead. Catcher Bill Bergen of the Dodgers completed his 11-year major league career in 1911 with an average of .170 – the lowest in history. Bergen appeared in 947 games from 1904 to 1911 with Cincinnati and Brooklyn and hit a total of two homers. By comparison, Mendoza was a weak hitter, compiling a "torrid" .215 with four homers in nine seasons with the Pirates, Mariners, and Rangers between 1974 and 1982.

exults, "Goddamn! It's great to be young and a New York Giant!"

OCTOBER 5:

Baseball's National Commission sells the film rights to the World Series for $3,500. But the deal is cancelled when the players seek a cut of the rights money.

OCTOBER 6:

In his last major league game, Cy Young of the Boston Rustlers loses to Brooklyn and Eddie Dent. It is Young's 313th career loss to go with 511 wins.

OCTOBER 7:

In their last game at the Huntington Avenue Grounds in Boston, the Red Sox beat Washington, 8-1.

Today, Charles Victor "Victory" Faust makes his major league debut pitching the top of the ninth at the Polo Grounds against the Boston Rustlers, who deliberately make three outs. Despite the fact that there already are three outs in the home half of the inning, Faust is allowed to bat. He hits a comebacker and circles the bases while the Rustlers throw the ball around. But, as he heads for home, he is tagged out by Boston catcher Bill Rariden.

OCTOBER 11:

Baseball's first Most Valuable Player awards are announced. The newly established Chalmers Award goes to the AL's Ty Cobb (.420, 144 RBI, 83 stolen bases, .621 slugging average), and the NL's Frank "Wildfire" Schulte (.300, 121 RBI, 21 homers). Cobb, who missed winning the Triple Crown (batting average, RBIs, and home runs) by one homer, beats out Chicago pitcher Big Ed Walsh. Schulte wins over Christy Mathewson.

OCTOBER 12:

One of baseball's strangest sagas climaxes when the Giants send "Victory" Faust to the mound again against the Dodgers for his second major league pitching appearance. He pitches one inning, is hit by a pitch in the ninth, steals second base and third, and scores on a Buck Herzog infield out. But it happens because the Dodgers are playing along with a sad joke.

Who is Charles Faust and what is the joke? A six-foot, two-inch non-athlete who irrationally believed he would star for the Giants, Faust wires manager John McGraw offering his services. When his offer is ignored, he shows up at the Planter's Hotel in St. Louis and claims he has the word of a fortune teller that he will bring the team good luck. The Giants, with Faust on the bench, win four in a row from the Cardinals and McGraw allows him to travel with the team and warm up before games. Then he allows him to make two pitching appearances. When the Giants win the NL pennant, McGraw says, "I give Charlie Faust full credit for winning the pennant for me – the National League pennant of 1911." Faust is institutionalized in 1914 and dies in 1915 at the age of 34 in Fort Steilacoom, Washington. His two appearances, however, are part of baseball's official records.

REGULAR SEASON WRAP-UP:

By winning 20 of their last 24 games, the Giants under John McGraw finish 99-54 and beat the Cubs by seven and a half games. The team steals a record 347 bases, including 61 by Josh Devore. Christy Mathewson (26-13) and Richard "Rube" Marquard (24-7, 237 strikeouts) lead the pitching staff. The top hitter is John "Chief" Meyers at .332; Larry Doyle hits .310.

The Athletics at 101-50 win their second straight AL pennant, beating Detroit by 13 1/2 games. Under Connie Mack, the team hits a record .296 and has two 20-game winners, Jack Coombs (28-12) and Eddie Plank (23-8). Eddie "Cocky" Collins bats .365; Frank Baker hits .334 with a league-leading 11 homers.

OCTOBER 14:

World Series, game one. In New York, Christy Mathewson limits the Athletics to six hits, beating Charles "Chief" Bender (who allows only five hits and strikes out 11), 2-1. The Giants score the lead run in the seventh inning on a Josh Devore single.

Bill Dinneen, who pitched the first World Series shutout back in 1903, today becomes the first former player to umpire in the Fall Classic.

OCTOBER 16:

World Series, game two. In Philadelphia, Eddie Plank evens the

OCTOBER 6
Cy Young, now with the Boston Rustlers, pitches his final game in the major leagues.

OCTOBER 26
Routing the Giants, 13-2, in game six, the Athletics win the World Championship.

Series with a five-hit, 3-1 win. Frank Baker hits a two-run home run off losing pitcher "Rube" Marquard in the sixth inning to break a 1-1 tie.

OCTOBER 17:

World Series, game three. In New York, Jack Coombs and Christy Mathewson battle through 11 innings, with the Athletics prevailing, 3-2. Coombs allows only three hits; Mathewson nine. Frank Baker ties the game with a ninth-inning homer – his second of the Series – and he earns the nickname Home Run. The winning run scores on a single by Harry "Jasper" Davis.

OCTOBER 24:

World Series, game four. After six days of rain, the Series resumes today in Philadelphia, with the Athletics winning, 4-2, on a seven-hitter by "Chief" Bender. Christy Mathewson gets the loss. The Athletics' attack is paced by Frank Baker, Danny Murphy, and Jack Barry, who each hit two doubles.

OCTOBER 25:

World Series, game five. The Giants stay alive in New York with a 10-inning, 4-3 win. James "Doc" Crandall gets the win with three innings of scoreless relief. Eddie Plank, who pitches only two-thirds of an inning, is charged with the loss. Reuben "Rube" Oldring hits a three-run homer for the Athletics. Fred Merkle drives in Larry Doyle and the winning run in the bottom of the 10th with a sacrifice fly.

According to Fred Lieb (an original member of the Base Ball Writers Association), umpire Bill Klem later stated that Doyle failed to touch home plate, but no one on the Athletics called for the ball. "I stood there waiting for an Athletics' protest," Klem said, "but none came." He insisted he never gave a "safe" sign, but Philadelphia catcher Jack Lepp had left the playing field.

OCTOBER 26:

World Series, game six. "Chief" Bender four-hits the Giants in a 13-2 rout, giving the Athletics the World Championship. Philadelphia mounts a 13-hit attack and scores seven unearned runs against three Giants' pitchers, with Leon "Red" Ames getting tagged with the loss. Philadelphia allows only 1.29 earned runs in the Series; the Giants staff posts an outstanding 2.83 ERA in a losing cause. Frank Baker is the hitting star at .375, with two homers and five RBI. Larry Doyle bats .304 to lead New York.

POST-SEASON

OCTOBER 27:

Clark Griffith buys a 10 percent interest in the Washington Senators – making him the franchise's single largest shareholder – and becomes the team's manager. He replaces Jimmy McAleer, who had finished the 1911 season with a seventh-place, 64-90 record.

NOVEMBER 21:

Prince Hal's reign is short. After a sixth-place finish at 76-76, Hal Chase resigns as the manager of the New York Highlanders and is replaced by Harry Wolverton, who wears a sombrero and smokes cigars. Chase, who also managed the team for 14 games in 1910 and was 10-4, will remain with the ballclub as a player.

William Hepburn Russell, owner of the Boston Rustlers, dies and the team is put up for sale. Before the year is out, the Boston franchise is bought by former major leaguer John Montgomery Ward, former policeman James E. Gaffney, and John Carroll. Gaffney, connected to New York's Tammany Hall political machine, which has an Indian as its symbol, honors his roots by calling the team the Braves, a name that will endure.

NOVEMBER 24:

Joe "Ducky" Medwick is born in Carteret, New Jersey.

DECEMBER 1:

Walter "Smokey" Alston is born in Venice, Ohio.

DECEMBER 21:

Joshua "Josh" Gibson is born in Buena Vista, Georgia.

Gibson will grow up to become a superstar in the Negro Leagues and what some baseball critics have said was the greatest catcher of all time, even though he was never allowed to showcase his incredible talents in the majors. Nonetheless, he was elected to the Hall of Fame in 1972. His Cooperstown plaque at credits him with "almost 800 home runs."

HISTORY

Cleveland Indians outfielder Shoeless Joe Jackson hits .408 and doesn't win the AL batting title. He finishes second to Ty Cobb's .420.

TRIVIA

The song "Gee! It's a Wonderful Game," with words by sportswriter Ring Lardner and music by Chicago White Stockings' pitcher Harris "Doc" White, makes its debut.

"I know I am a better ball player – so why should inferiors criticize superiors."
– Ty Cobb, to theater critic Allen Johnson

TRIVIA

In November, Ty Cobb tours in George Ade's play *The College Widow,* portraying football player Billy Bolton. Cobb makes his debut in Newark, New Jersey, then plays Asheville, North Carolina, Atlanta, and Nashville. He is rumored to be earning $10,000 for the tour. After Allen G. Johnson, theater critic and sportswriter for the *Birmingham News,* pans him, Cobb responds, "I am a better actor than you are, a better sports editor than you are, a better dramatic critic than you are. I make more money than you do, and I know I am a better ball player – so why should inferiors criticize superiors." Cobb quits the play in mid-January 1912, vowing "never again."

THE BEST OF 1911

NATIONAL LEAGUE

HITTERS

Batting Average:
Honus Wagner, Pittsburgh Pirates, .334

Slugging Average:
Frank "Wildfire" Schulte, Chicago Cubs, .534

Home Runs:
Frank Schulte, 21

Runs Batted In:
Frank Schulte, 121

Hits:
Roy "Doc" Miller, Boston Rustlers, 192

Stolen Bases:
Bob Bescher, Cincinnati Reds, 81

PITCHERS

Wins:
Grover Cleveland Alexander, Philadelphia Phillies, 28

Strikeouts:
Richard "Rube" Marquard, New York Giants, 237

Earned Run Average:
Christy Mathewson, New York Giants, 1.99

Winning Percentage:
Richard Marquard, .774

Saves:
Mordecai "Three Finger" Brown, Chicago Cubs, 13

Most Valuable Player (Chalmers Award):
Frank "Wildfire" Schulte, Chicago Cubs

AMERICAN LEAGUE

HITTERS

Batting Average:
Ty Cobb, Detroit Tigers, .420

Slugging Average:
Ty Cobb, .621

Home Runs:
Frank "Home Run" Baker, Philadelphia Athletics, 11

Runs Batted In:
Ty Cobb, 144

Hits:
Ty Cobb, 248

Stolen Bases:
Ty Cobb, 83

PITCHERS

Wins:
Jack Coombs, Philadelphia Athletics, 28

Strikeouts:
Big Ed Walsh, Chicago White Sox, 255

Earned Run Average:
Sylveanus "Vean" Gregg, Cleveland Naps, 1.81

Winning Percentage:
Charles "Chief" Bender, Philadelphia Athletics, .773

Saves:
Eddie Plank, Philadelphia Athletics; Ed Walsh; Charley "Sea Lion" Hall, Boston Red Sox, 4

Most Valuable Player (Chalmers Award):
Ty Cobb, Detroit Tigers

1912

"Call it Ebbets Field, Charlie... it's your monument."
– *Unnamed journalist*

NEWS

Arizona and New Mexico become states

TITANIC SINKS AFTER STRIKING AN ICEBERG; 1,513 DIE, 711 RESCUED

U.S. MARINES ARE SENT INTO CUBA

WOODROW WILSON ELECTED PRESIDENT, DEFEATING TEDDY ROOSEVELT AND WILLIAM HOWARD TAFT IN THREE-PARTY RACE

U.S. TROOPS OCCUPY TIENTSIN, CHINA

CONGRESS SETS AN 8-HOUR WORKDAY FOR ALL FEDERAL WORKERS

Jim Thorpe wins decathlon and pentathlon at Olympics

Universal Pictures is founded in Hollywood

PRE-SEASON

JANUARY 2:

Charles H. Ebbets, Dodgers' president and major stockholder, announces the team will build a new concrete and steel, 18,000-seat stadium on 4.5 acres the team purchased for some $100,000 in the Pigtown section of Brooklyn.

MARCH 4:

Charlie Ebbets wields a silver spade to break ground in Brooklyn for the Dodgers' new $650,000 ballpark, which is scheduled to be called Washington Park after the team's original field. A journalist tells Ebbets: "Call it Ebbets Field, Charlie. You put yourself into hock to build it and it's your monument."

MARCH 9:

Joseph "Arky" Vaughan is born in Clifty, Arkansas.

APRIL 9:

Snow buffets Boston as the Red Sox play their first game – an open house exhibition against Harvard University – in their brand new stadium, Fenway Park. The Red Sox win the game, 2–0.

THE SEASON

APRIL 11:

In what is scheduled to be the last opening day at Washington Park in Brooklyn, 30,000 are on hand to see today's game against the Giants. With New York ahead, 18-3, fans spill onto the field and the game is called after six innings because of darkness. Balls hit into the crowd are called ground-rule doubles and the Giants collect 13 of them. Richard "Rube " Marquard gets the win.

Cincinnati's new Redlands Field opens today.

APRIL 12:

The fabled double-play combination of Tinker to Evers to Chance makes its last appearance together today, with Ed Lennox anchoring at third base. The Reds beat the visiting Cubs, 3-2.

APRIL 20:

After rain washes out the scheduled debut of Fenway Park on April 17, an April 18 game, and an April 19 Patriots' Day doubleheader, the Red Sox finally get to play in their new home.

TRIVIA

Fenway Park is named by Red Sox owner John I. Taylor after the Fenway section of Boston.

APRIL 26
Red Sox first baseman Hugh Bradley becomes the first to homer over Fenway's left-field wall.

Boston's Tris Speaker was the 1912 AL MVP.

Boston Mayor John F. "Honey Fitz" Fitzgerald throws out the first ball. The Red Sox debut is a successful one as Tris Speaker drives in Steve Yerkes to beat New York, 7-6, in 11 innings. The Sea Lion – Charles Hall – bests the Hippo, James Vaughn, who is the game's losing pitcher.

Detroit opens Navin Field, its new steel and concrete ballpark. A crowd of 24,384, including AL president Ban Johnson, watches the Tigers beat Cleveland, 6-5, in 11. Ty Cobb has two singles and two stolen bases – including one of home on the front end of a double steal with Sam Crawford in the first inning. It is the second double steal in that frame for the Tigers. George Mullin wins his own game with an RBI single.

At the Polo Grounds, the Giants' Richard "Rube" Marquard relieves Jeff Tesreau in the ninth inning, when Brooklyn overcomes a 2-0 deficit and goes ahead 3-2. Marquard quells the rally and the Giants' catcher Art Wilson hits a two-run homer in the bottom of the ninth for a 4-3 win. Tesreau gets the win. The game features an altercation: Brooklyn manager Bill Dahlen and 240-pound umpire Charles "Cy" Rigler get into a fistfight over a foul call. The scuffle is broken up by Giants' coach Wilbert Robinson.

The game has some ramifications for "Rube" Marquard. Under today's scoring rules, the victory would have gone to Marquard, not Tesreau. And Marquard would have added another game to his consecutive-win streak, finishing with 20 instead of 19, giving him the all-time record instead of a tie with Tim Keefe (1888).

APRIL 26:

Red Sox first baseman Hugh Bradley becomes the first of many to home run over the left-field wall in Fenway Park.

MAY 13:

A prank with a long echo: A Western Union operator named Lou Proctor transmits the box score of a Browns-Red Sox game and inserts his name as pinch hitter (going hitless in one at-bat). The box score is picked up and published by *The Sporting News* and years later Proctor appears in early editions of *The Baseball Encyclopedia.*

MAY 14:

The Cubs' Heinie Zimmerman extends his consecutive game hitting streak to 23 with a single and double against the visiting Phillies. The Cubs win the contest, 2-0. Zimmerman's hitting streak will end the following day, May 15.

MAY 15:

At New York's Hilltop Park, Ty Cobb attacks a fan and triggers one of baseball's most bizarre chains of events. The fan, Claude Lucker, is missing one hand and part of his other as a result of a workplace accident. He has been heckling Cobb As Lucker recounts the story, "He struck me with his fists on the forehead and over the left eye and knocked me down. Then he jumped on me and spiked me in the left leg, and kicked me in the side, after which he booted me behind the left ear. I was down and Cobb was kicking me when someone in the crowd shouted, 'Don't kick him! He has no hands!' Cobb answered, 'I don't care if he has no feet!'" Lucker

JUNE 13
Giants' pitcher Christy Mathewson marks his 300th career victory with a 3-2 win over the Cubs.

later claims he was not the fan riding Cobb. Plate umpire Fred Westervelt ejects Cobb.

MAY 16:

Cobb has been suspended. Today's game is rained out and the Detroit Tigers meet in Philadelphia, voting to strike on May 18 if Cobb is not permitted to play.

MAY 18:

With 19 players on strike and Cobb suspended, the Tigers avoid a $1,000 fine by fielding a replacement team against the Athletics in Philadelphia. With 20,000 on hand to see the spectacle, the Athletics trample the Tigers, 24-2. Drafted to pitch is 20-year-old seminary student Aloysius J. Travers, who calls, "Let's play ball" to start the game. Also appearing are 42-year-old manager Hugh Jennings, who goes 0-for-one as a pinch hitter, coach James "Deacon" McGuire (age 46) as catcher, and coach Joe Sugden (age 41) at first base. McGuire, who becomes the oldest player to catch a major league game, also has three putouts and three assists. The coaches each single and score. The lineup is filled out with local semiprofessionals.

Travers, who becomes a priest, pitches a complete game. His major league career statistics include an 0-1 record, 15.75 ERA, 26 hits yielded, seven walks, and one strikeout. He is 0-for-three at bat. William "Ed" Irvin, around 30 years old, also makes his only professional appearance, playing third base and hitting two triples and making one error. Appearing at third base is Billy Maharg, a key player in the impending Black Sox scandal of 1919. (There is some dispute over Maharg's true identity. The Baseball Encyclopedia *lists his real name as William Joseph Graham, who also appeared in one game for the Phillies in 1916. Others insist they are two different people. Fred Lieb wrote: "One of them was Joe Maharg, a name when read backwards gives the real name Graham, a gambler and preliminary fighter who later was a go-between in the Black Sox scandal.")*

MAY 20:

With no game scheduled yesterday and today's game rained out, Ban Johnson travels to Philadelphia and threatens the Tigers with lifetime suspensions. Ty Cobb asks his teammates to end their strike and they agree to play.

As the result of a court decision in St. Louis, complete control of the Cardinals ballclub is now in the hands of Mrs. Schuyler F. Britton.

MAY 21:

AL president Ban Johnson fines each Tigers' striker $100 – $150 for each day they stayed out. Ty Cobb remains suspended. The Tigers beat Washington, 2-0.

MAY 26:

Ty Cobb completes his suspension, is fined $50, and returns to the Detroit lineup. He singles in four at-bats in a 6-2 victory over the White Sox.

JUNE 13:

The Giants' Christy Mathewson beats the Cubs, 3-2, for his 300th career victory.

JUNE 20:

In Boston, the Braves and Giants combine for 17 runs in the ninth inning. Leading 14-2, the Giants add seven runs in the top of the ninth. The Braves counter with an impressive 10-run rally of their own, but come up short and lose, 21-12. The Giants also steal 11 bases, a modern record.

JUNE 26:

Smoky Joe Wood of the Red Sox beats Walter Johnson and the Senators with a three-hitter, 3-0. Johnson allows only four hits – including a triple to Tris Speaker – and fans 10.

The Senators acquire six-foot, four-inch, 215-pound left-handed pitcher James "Hippo" Vaughn (2-8) from the Highlanders for the waiver price.

JUNE 29:

Red Sox catcher Forrest "Hick" Cady has two hits in a single at-bat against the Highlanders today, but only one counts. With runners at first and second in the second inning, Cady singles. But umpire Frank "Silk" O'Loughlin calls a balk, allowing one runner to score and negating Cady's single. He gets another at-bat and this time he doubles. Boston wins, 13-6. In the first game of the day's doubleheader, Boston also beat the Highlanders, 6-0.

LEAGUE

John Montgomery Ward, who has been many things in baseball, including player, manager, team president, and union organizer, now plays scout. He discovers Walter "Rabbit" Maranville in New Bedford, Massachusetts, and buys him for the Braves for $2,200.

JULY 4
On his 32nd birthday, the Tigers' George Mullin no-hits the Browns, 7-0.

TRIVIA

Today's Yankees' owner, George Steinbrenner, may be one of a kind, but he is not the first with that surname in major league baseball. Eugene Gass Steinbrenner plays with the Phillies, appearing as a second baseman in three games, going two-for-nine with a double, knocking in a run, and fanning three times.

JULY 3:

At the Polo Grounds, "Rube" Marquard beats Brooklyn and Nap Rucker, 2-1, for his record-tying 19th consecutive win. His streak, which began on April 11 with an 18-3 win over Brooklyn, ties the 1888 mark of Tim Keefe. The game also marks the 15th straight victory for the Giants. They extend their streak to 16 in game two of today's doubleheader.

According to James Mote's Everything Baseball, *"Rube" Marquard appears on the stage of Hammerstein's Theatre in New York City that night with Blossom Seeley in a skit titled* Breaking the Record, or The 19th Straight. *Part of the routine is the song "The Marquard Glide," with music by Seeley and Thomas J. Gray and words by Marquard and Seeley.*

JULY 4:

It's a triple celebration today for the Tigers' George Mullin: Independence Day, his 32nd birthday, and a 7-0 no-hitter against the Browns. Mullin fans five and walks five; the Tigers make one error. He also hits a double and two singles, and drives in two runs. Willie Adams gets the loss. Ty Cobb celebrates in his own way, stealing second, third, and home in the fifth inning – the fourth time in his career he has accomplished that baserunning feat.

JULY 7:

Concerned about legal challenges to the reserve clause, major league owners consider splitting players' salaries into two components: 75 percent for services and 25 percent for "reserving" for the following season.

JULY 8:

Today in Chicago, the Cubs' rookie right-handed pitcher Jimmy Lavender beats the New York Giants, 7-2, snapping "Rube" Marquard's consecutive game winning streak at 19. Marquard is off form today, giving up six runs in six innings, before being relieved by right-hander Jeff Tesreau in the seventh inning. In the span of the last 20 games, Marquard has allowed a total of 49 runs.

The Cubs' famous double-play combo (from left): Joe Tinker, Johnny Evers, and Frank Chance

AUGUST 23
Walter Johnson's 8-1 victory over the Tigers is his 16th straight win.

JULY 16:

Tris Speaker of the Red Sox extends his hitting streak to 30 consecutive games.

JULY 18:

When is a stolen base more potent than 21 hits? Philadelphia's Clifford "Gavvy" Cravath steals home in the 11th inning today to beat the Chicago Cubs, who collect 21 hits in a losing effort.

JULY 22:

The Chicago White Sox purchase pitcher Ed Cicotte for the waiver price from the Red Sox, with whom he was 1-3.

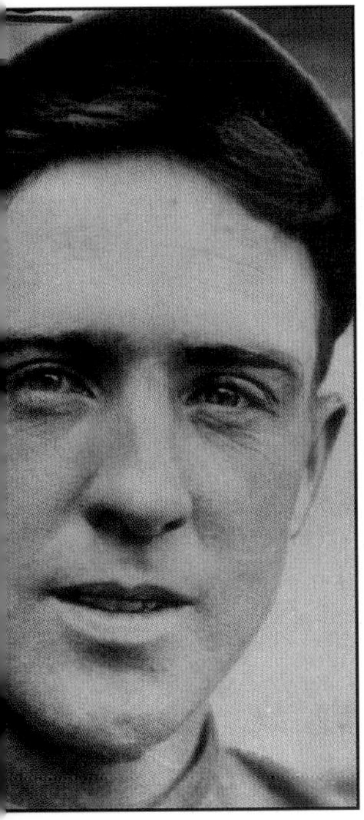

JULY 31:

John Montgomery Ward resigns as president of the Boston Braves and sells his stock to co-owner James Gaffney.

AUGUST 1:

"Rube" Marquard is fined by the Giants for pitching in a semi-professional game on his day off.

AUGUST 6:

The Fraternity of Professional Baseball Players of America is chartered today in New York. The president is former major leaguer David Lewis "Swarthy Dave" Fultz. A total of 288 players join the fraternity.

AUGUST 12:

Three men attack Ty Cobb on his way to the Detroit railroad station. Cobb tries to defend himself with the pistol he regularly travels with, but the gun jams and he is cut on the shoulder by a knife. However, he catches one of his assailants and pistol-whips him. Apparently unfazed, Cobb travels on to Syracuse and gets two hits in an exhibition game that day.

AUGUST 14:

At Fenway Park, Tris Speaker extends his consecutive game hitting streak to 20. Earlier this season Speaker hit in 30 consecutive games. In game two today, Smoky Joe Wood shuts out the St. Louis Browns, 8-0, for his 25th win of the year. Speaker puts together three major batting streaks in 1912 – 30 games once and 20 games twice.

AUGUST 20:

Today Walter Johnson pitches eight and two-thirds innings in relief and beats the Indians, 4-2, for his 15th consecutive victory, breaking Jack Chesbro's 1904 record. Vean Gregg gets the loss. In the nightcap, Johnson's teammate Jay Cashion no-hits Cleveland, 2-0, in a game abbreviated to six innings.

AUGUST 23:

Walter Johnson beats the Tigers, 8-1, for his 16th straight win.

AUGUST 26:

The Browns end Walter Johnson's winning streak when a runner put on base by Long Tom Hughes scores with one out in the seventh inning.

AUGUST 30:

Earl Hamilton of the Browns no-hits the Tigers, 5-1, in Detroit. He allows two walks, striking out three. St. Louis makes three errors. Jean Dubuc is the losing pitcher.

SEPTEMBER 2:

In game two of a doubleheader in New York, Smoky Joe Wood wins his 30th game, beating the Highlanders, 1-0. It is Wood's 13th consecutive win and his eighth shutout of the season.

SEPTEMBER 6:

Two of baseball's hardest throwers, Boston's Smoky Joe Wood and Washington's Walter Johnson, face off before a crowd of 30,000 at Fenway Park. Wood allows six hits, strikes out nine, and wins 1-0 – his 14th straight victory. Johnson yields five hits and fans five. With two out in the sixth, back-to-back doubles by Tris Speaker and Duffy Lewis produce the game's only run.

In Philadelphia, the Giants' Jeff Tesreau no-hits the Phillies, 3-0. He allows two walks and strikes out two; the Giants com-

TRIVIA

Several books are published: *Baseball Joe on the School Nine* and *Baseball Joe of the Silver Stars* by Lester Chadwick (a pen name of Edward Stratemeyer, who also wrote Hardy Boys, Nancy Drew, and Bobsey Twins books); *Pitching in a Pinch* by Christy Mathewson (John Wheeler is the ghostwriter).

"If Casey Stengel were alive today, he'd be spinning in his grave."
– *Ralph Kiner, 1988*

mit two errors. The losing pitcher is Eppa Rixey.

SEPTEMBER 7:

The Athletics' Eddie "Cocky" Collins sets a major league record with six stolen bases on catcher Brad Kocher in today's 9-7 win over the Tigers. The game features another Ty Cobb "episode." After he hits and loses a single when umpire Tom Connolly calls him out for leaving the batter's box, Cobb refuses to go to his position. In the ensuing argument Tigers' manager Hughie Jennings and reserve Oscar "Ossie" Vitt are ejected.

Former major league pitcher Arthur "Bugs" Raymond dies two days after being beaten and kicked in the head during an altercation at a sandlot baseball game in his native Chicago. In 1911, Raymond was banned then reinstated by the National Commission, but dropped out of baseball when Giant manager John McGraw refused to let him play because of his excessive drinking. Raymond, who was 30 years old, pitched six years in the majors with the Tigers, Cardinals, and Giants, compiling a 45-57 record and a 2.49 ERA. His best season was 1909, when he was 18-12 with a 2.47 ERA for the New York Giants.

SEPTEMBER 15:

In St. Louis, Smoky Joe Wood of the Red Sox beats the Browns, 2-1 for his 16th straight win, tying Walter Johnson's record established earlier this year. The game, the nightcap of a doubleheader, is called after eight innings because of darkness. Wood also scores the winning run in the eighth on a wild pitch by loser Earl Hamilton. It is Wood's 33rd victory of the season.

SAYS WALTER JOHNSON: "CAN I THROW HARDER THAN JOE WOOD? LISTEN, MY FRIEND, THERE'S NO MAN ALIVE WHO CAN THROW HARDER THAN JOE WOOD."

SEPTEMBER 17:

Outfielder Charles Dillon "Casey" Stengel makes his major league debut with Brooklyn today. Playing against the Pirates in Pittsburgh, Stengel hits safely four times – including a single in his first at bat – walks, and steals three bases in a 7-3 Dodger victory.

According to biographer Robert W. Creamer, Stengel's lifelong nickname originated soon after his debut. Following several losing hands in a clubhouse poker game, Stengel won a pot and an unidentified teammate remarked, "About time you took a pot, Kansas City" (Stengel's home town). It was shortened to Casey, the name by which he became known. In his first week as a major leaguer, Stengel batted .478 with 11 hits and nine RBI.

SEPTEMBER 18:

While the Boston Red Sox are rained out in Cleveland, the White Sox beat the Athletics in the opener of a doubleheader, clinching the AL pennant for Boston.

SEPTEMBER 20:

In Detroit's Navin Field, the Tigers end Smoky Joe Wood's 16-game win streak with a 6-4 victory over the Red Sox. Wood allows seven hits, walks five, and fans eight. Joe Lake, the winning pitcher in relief of starter William "Tex" Covington, fans three and walks two.

SEPTEMBER 22:

Philadelphia's Eddie Collins becomes the third player in the majors this season to steal second, third, and home against Browns' catchers Walter Alexander and Jim Stephens. The feat previously was accomplished by Ty Cobb and Joe Jackson. He also ties his own major league record – set September 11 – with six stolen bases in a single game.

SEPTEMBER 26:

The Giants sweep the Braves in a Polo Grounds doubleheader to wrap up the NL pennant.

SEPTEMBER 28:

What have you done for us lately? After seven-plus seasons, four pennants, two World Series titles, and 753 wins, manager Frank Chance is fired by Cubs' owner Charles Webb Murphy. The Cubs finish in third this season with a record of 91-59.

SEPTEMBER 15
Matching Walter Johnson, Smoky Joe Wood notches his 16th straight win of the year.

OCTOBER 3
Smoky Joe Wood beats the Athletics, 17-5, for his 34th win – best in the majors this year.

According to Baseball Hall of Fame director Ken Smith, on September 12, Murphy announced, "Frank Chance is through as manager."

OCTOBER 3:

At Shibe Park, Joe Wood beats the Athletics, 17-5, for his 34th win of the season. He allows eight hits, strikes out six, and walks two. Duffy Lewis hits a homer for Boston.

OCTOBER 5:

The Highlanders play their last ball game at Hilltop Park, beating Washington, 8-6, with Hal Chase providing a three-run home run. After 10 years at Hilltop, the Highlanders next year will play in the Giants' Polo Grounds.

Brooklyn plays its last home game in Washington Park, bowing to the Giants, 1-0, with 10,000 in attendance. Pat Ragan gets the game's loss.

REGULAR SEASON WRAP-UP:

The Giants, under John McGraw, win their second straight pennant with a record of 103-48, finishing 10 games ahead of Pittsburgh. "Rube" Marquard (26-11) and Christy Mathewson (23-12) are the strong arms of the pitching staff. The top hitters are John "Chief" Meyers at .358 and Larry Doyle with a .330 average.

Managed by Jake Stahl, the Red Sox win the AL pennant with a record of 105-47, 14 games ahead of the second-place Senators. The ace of the staff is Smoky Joe Wood at .345 with an ERA of 1.91. Boston also has two 20-game winners – Hugh Bedient and Thomas "Buck" O'Brien. The team's top hitter is Tris Speaker at .383.

The New York Highlanders, who are managed by Harry Wolverton, bring up the rear of the AL at 50-102, 55 games out of first place. One area in which the Highlanders excelled was steals of home plate – a record 18, including one by pitcher Jack Warhop.

OCTOBER 8:

World Series, game one. In New York, Smoky Joe Wood beats the Giants and Jeff Tesreau, 4-3. Wood fans 11 and allows eight hits. The Red Sox have six hits, including a double by Harry Hooper and a triple by Tris Speaker. Attendance is 35,730.

OCTOBER 9:

World Series, game two. In Boston, the Red Sox and Giants play an 11-inning, 6-6 tie, called because of darkness. Christy Mathewson goes all the way for New York, allowing 10 hits while his teammates make five errors behind him. Boston uses three pitchers: Ray Collins, Charley "Sea Lion" Hall, and Hugh Bedient. Attendance at the game is 30,148.

OCTOBER 10:

World Series, game three. In Boston, the Giants' starter "Rube" Marquard beats the Red Sox and Tom "Buck" O'Brien, 2-1. An outstanding catch by Josh Devore on Forrest "Hick" Cady's drive with two on and two out preserves the victory. Devore runs into the clubhouse after the catch; many fans who can't see the play think the Red Sox won the game. Attendance is 34,624.

OCTOBER 11:

World Series, game four. At the Polo Grounds, Smoky Joe Wood fans eight, topping the Giants and Jeff Tesreau, 3-1. Boston's offense is paced by Wood with two hits and an RBI; Tris Speaker with a double; and Larry Gardner with a triple and single. Today's attendance is 36,502.

OCTOBER 12:

World Series, game five. Back in Boston, Christy Mathewson retires 17 in a row, allows only five hits, and comes up on the short end of a 2-1 score. The winning pitcher is Hugh Bedient, who three-hits the Giants and gets all his run support in the third inning on a Larry Doyle error and back-to-back triples by Harry Hooper and Steve Yerkes. Today's attendance is 34,683.

OCTOBER 14:

World Series, game six. With 30,622 fans at the Polo Grounds, Rube Marquard yields seven hits in beating the Red Sox and Thomas "Buck" O'Brien, 5-2. The Giants get all their runs in the first inning; Fred Merkle and Charles "Buck" Herzog hit back-to-back RBI doubles.

The Red Sox reportedly beat up their teammate and losing pitcher Buck O'Brien after the game.

OCTOBER 16
An error by Giants' fielder Fred Snodgrass leads the Red Sox to a World Series clincher.

OCTOBER 15:

World Series, game seven. In Boston, the Giants explode for six runs in the first, kayo Smoky Joe Wood, and roll to an 11-4 win behind Jeff Tesreau. Larry Doyle hits a two-run home run for New York; Larry Gardner reaches the seats with no one on for Boston. Attendance is 32,694.

OCTOBER 16:

World Series, game eight. At Fenway Park, Boston scores twice in the bottom of the 10th to beat the Giants, 3-2, and win the Series. The pivotal plays are an error by center fielder Fred Snodgrass and a misplay by Giants first baseman Fred Merkle. In the top of the 10th, Merkle drives in the go-ahead run and the Giants enter the bottom of the inning up 2-1. Snodgrass drops a Clyde Engle fly ball for a two-base error, then makes an outstanding catch on Harry Hooper's drive. Tris Speaker's foul pop fly falls between Merkle, Christy Mathewson, and catcher Chief Meyers. Given a reprieve, Speaker drives in Engle to tie the score. Steve Yerkes, who had walked, moves to third on the hit. Larry Gardner's sacrifice fly scores Yerkes with the winning run. Joe Wood, with three innings of relief, gets the win. Mathewson goes all the way and gets the loss. Today's attendance is 17,034.

"IT GIVES ONE THE CHANCE TO 'SMILE OUT LOUD' UNDER GOD'S CLEAR SKY AND TO TAKE IN LIFE-GIVING BREATHS OF FRESH AIR EVERY TIME ONE EMPTIES THE LUNGS WITH A LUSTY CHEER."

– Entertainer Lillian Russell

New York Times *headline: SOX CHAMPIONS ON MUFFED FLY; SNODGRASS DROPS EASY BALL, COSTING TEAMMATES $29,514.*

POST-SEASON

OCTOBER 22:

With four years remaining on his contract, Cardinals' manager Roger Bresnahan is fired in a disagreement with the team's new owner. St. Louis finished in sixth place with a 63-90 record.

NOVEMBER 4:

Miller Huggins, the Cardinals' second baseman, is named the team's new manager for next season.

NOVEMBER 26:

Giants' owner John T. Brush dies in his private railroad car near St. Louis. Brush's widow and daughter inherit the team. Mrs. Brush's son-in-law by a previous marriage, Harry N. Hempstead, takes over operations.

DECEMBER 15:

After 11 years with the team, shortstop Joe Tinker (.282) is traded by the Cubs to Cincinnati along with pitcher Grover Lowdermilk (0-1, 9.69 ERA) and catcher Harry Chapman (.250). In return, Chicago obtains pitcher Bert Humphries (9-11, 3.23 ERA), infielder-outfielder Pete Knisely (.328 in 21 games), infielder John "Red" Corriden (.203 with Detroit), infielder Art Phelan (.243, three homers), and outfielder Mike Mitchell (.283, four homers).

DECEMBER 15
After 11 years with the team, the Cubs trade shortstop Joe Tinker to the Cincinnati Reds.

THE BEST OF 1912

NATIONAL LEAGUE

HITTERS

Batting Average:
Henry "Heinie" Zimmerman, Chicago Cubs, .372

Slugging Average:
Henry Zimmerman, .571

Home Runs:
Henry Zimmerman, 14

Runs Batted In:
Henry Zimmerman, 103

Hits:
Henry Zimmerman, 207

Stolen Bases:
Bob Besher, Cincinnati Reds, 67

PITCHERS

Wins:
Richard "Rube" Marquard, New York Giants; Larry Cheney, Chicago Cubs, 26

Strikeouts:
Grover Cleveland Alexander, Philadelphia Phillies, 195

Earned Run Average:
Charles "Jeff" Tesreau, New York Giants, 1.96

Winning Percentage:
Claude Hendrix, Pittsburgh Pirates, .727

Saves:
Harry "Slim" Sallee, St. Louis Cardinals, 6

Most Valuable Player (Chalmers Award):
Larry Doyle, New York Giants

AMERICAN LEAGUE

HITTERS

Batting Average:
Ty Cobb, Detroit Tigers, .410

Slugging Average:
Ty Cobb, .586

Home Runs:
Frank "Home Run" Baker, Philadelphia Athletics; Tris Speaker, Boston Red Sox, 10

Runs Batted In:
Frank Baker, 133

Hits:
Ty Cobb, 227

Stolen Bases:
Clyde Milan, Washington Senators, 88

PITCHERS

Wins:
"Smoky" Joe Wood, Boston Red Sox, 34

Strikeouts:
Walter Johnson, Washington Senators, 303

Earned Run Average:
Walter Johnson, 1.39

Winning Percentage:
Joe Wood, Boston Red Sox,.872

Saves:
Big Ed Walsh, Chicago White Sox, 10

Most Valuable Player (Chalmers Award):
Tris Speaker, Boston Red Sox

1913

"The trouble with baseball today is that most players are in (it) for the money."
– *Ty Cobb*

NEWS

First automobile rolls off Ford assembly line

792-FOOT WOOLWORTH BUILDING, WORLD'S TALLEST SKYSCRAPER, OPENS IN NEW YORK

467 PERISH IN DAYTON, OHIO, FLOOD

16TH AMENDMENT ESTABLISHES INCOME TAX

U.S. SENATORS WILL BE ELECTED BY POPULAR VOTE, PER THE 17TH AMENDMENT

U.S. DEPARTMENT OF LABOR IS FOUNDED

Nijinsky's *Rites of Spring* ballet premieres in Paris

Duchamp's *Nude Descending a Staircase* first shown

Football coach Knute Rockne introduces forward pass

PRE-SEASON

JANUARY 7:

Johnny "The Big Cat" Mize is born in Demorest, Georgia.

JANUARY 8:

The Peerless Leader comes to New York. Frank Chance is signed to a three-year contract to manage the Highlanders, who finished last in 1912. Chance, who won four pennants (1906, 1907, 1908, and 1910) and two World Series as manager of the Cubs, is lured out of retirement in California by owners Frank Farrell and Bill Devery.

JANUARY 15:

The Philadelphia Phillies are bought by William H. Locke, who becomes the team's president.

MARCH 4:

The New York Highlanders begin spring training in Bermuda, becoming the first team to train outside the U.S. Their opponents for exhibition games will be the International League's Jersey City Skeeters.

MARCH 8:

The National and American Leagues will have competition. The Federal League announces it will play as a major league next season with a 120-game schedule. As an "outlaw" league, the new organization will be free to raid the existing teams for players. The Federal League will operate franchises in Chicago (Chi-Feds), St. Louis (Terriers), Brooklyn (Tip-Tops), Baltimore (Terrapins), Kansas City (Packers), Pittsburgh (Rebels), Buffalo (Buffeds), and Indianapolis (Hoosiers). As a result of the new league's incursion into existing areas, New York will have four teams and Chicago three. Among the Federal League's backers are oilman Harry Sinclair, Chicago restaurateur Charles Weeghman, and Brooklyn bakery executive Robert W. Ward.

MARCH 28:

A player is traded for the use of a ballpark. The St. Louis Browns' Clyde "Buzzy" Wares is "traded" for the right to use a spring training stadium in Montgomery, Alabama. In return for the rent due, the Browns assign Wares to the minor league team in Montgomery. Wares does return to the Browns and appears in 10 games in 1913, hitting .286.

APRIL 5:

Ebbets Field hosts its first game, an exhibition between the Dodgers and the Giants, attended by 25,000. Genevieve Ebbets, daughter of Brooklyn's owner and president Charles Ebbets, throws out the first ball. Casey Stengel hits an inside-the-park home run in the fifth and the Dodgers, behind the pitching of Nap Rucker, win the game, 3-2.

THE SEASON

APRIL 9:

On a cold, windy day, thousands attend the dedication of and the first official game at the new $750,000 Ebbets Field. The Phillies, behind Tom Seaton, win 1-0; the only run scores in the first when outfielder Benny "Earache" Meyer drops a fly ball. Nap Rucker gets the loss. Attendance is some 10,000 fans.

APRIL 10:

The New York Highlanders become the New York Yankees. But the results are familiar. In Washington,

APRIL 10
The New York Highlanders, now the New York Yankees, lose to Washington, 2-1.

APRIL 25
Ty Cobb signs a one-year, $12,000 contract, declaring, "This is my last holdout."

Walter Johnson and the Senators beat the Yankees, 2-1, after President Woodrow Wilson throws out the first ball. The loser is George McConnell.

The Tigers' season begins without Ty Cobb, who holds out in Augusta, Georgia. Cobb, who has won six straight batting titles and hit .400 for two consecutive seasons, is seeking $15,000. Until yesterday, when he disbanded the team, he was barnstorming with his All Georgians. According to the *New York Times*, the Senators' owner Clark Griffith offers the Tigers $100,000 for Cobb's rights.

APRIL 17:

After beating the Yankees on opening day in Washington, D.C., the Senators travel north for New York's first game ever at the Polo Grounds – and Chance Day, honoring their new manager. The Senators spoil the Yankees' festivities with a 9-3 win.

APRIL 25:

Declaring "this is my last holdout," Ty Cobb signs a one-year $12,000 contract. His salary is prorated to $11,322.55 for the previous two weeks' worth of games he missed. Cobb, who was suspended under the guidelines of baseball's National Commission, even becomes a political issue in Washington. A Georgia politician leads the effort for a resolution to investigate baseball for anti-trust violations.

The Giants come calling at Ebbets Field for the very first time in the regular season. Casey Stengel's two-run home run breaks a 2-2 tie and gives Brooklyn a 5-3 victory.

APRIL 29:

It looks like the White Sox against the Cubs at Wrigley Field. But it isn't an experiment in inter-league play. It's Cincinnati, whose uniforms were left behind in St. Louis's Pennsylvania Station, wearing White Sox uniforms. The Cubs are not distracted, beating the Reds/White Sox, 7-1.

APRIL 30:

At Navin Field, 6,732 fans give Ty Cobb a two-minute ovation when he returns to the lineup against Chicago. He singles and drives in a run, but the White Sox win the game, 6-5, in 12 innings.

> SPORTSWRITER GRANTLAND RICE CONCLUDES A POEM ABOUT THE "BIG TRAIN," ST. LOUIS PITCHER WALTER JOHNSON, WITH: "HOW DO THEY KNOW WHAT JOHNSON'S GOT? NOBODY'S SEEN IT YET."

MAY 10:

Yet another "major" circuit, the United States League, is formed.

MAY 12:

The United States League is out of business after only two days in existence.

MAY 14:

In St. Louis, the Browns end Walter Johnson's 56 consecutive scoreless inning streak in the fourth inning. The Senators win, 10-5.

MAY 18:

In Detroit with a crowd of 24,466 on hand, Ty Cobb spoils a Walter Johnson shutout by stealing home. But the Senators and Johnson win, 2-1.

MAY 22:

The Reds acquire infielder Henry "Heinie" Groh (.000 in four games), pitcher Leon "Red" Ames (2-1), outfielder Josh Devore (.190 in 16 games), and $20,000 from the Giants for pitcher Art Fromme (1-4) and infielder Eddie Grant (.213 in 27 games).

HISTORY

During spring training, Boston's great pitcher Smoky Joe Wood slips on wet grass while fielding a bunt and injures his thumb. He spends several weeks wearing a cast. He tries pitching through the pain, but has lost his blazing speed. In 1915, at age 26, the pain becomes too much and he quits baseball, coming back two years later as an outfielder and occasional pitcher for Cleveland.

MAY 30
The Red Sox Harry Hooper leads off both ends of a doubleheader with home runs.

TRIVIA

***The Girl and the Pennant*, by Ida Johnson Young and Christy Mathewson, starring Florence Reed, is a play about a female team owner.**

MAY 30:

The Red Sox Harry Hooper leads off both games of a Decoration Day doubleheader against the Senators with home runs – a major league first.

JUNE 1:

The troubled and troublesome Hal Chase (.212) is on the move again. The New York Yankees send the first baseman to the Chicago White Sox for infielder Rollie Zeider (.350) and first baseman William "Babe" Borton (.275).

The day before, Hal Chase had mocked manager Frank Chance and was told by catcher Jeff Sweeney, "Get out. You'll never wear this uniform again." To further complicate matters, Chance tells two local sportswriters, Fred Lieb of the New York Press *and Heywood Broun of the* New York Tribune, *that Chase is "throwing games on me." When stories of the accusation appear in the newspapers, the Yankees' co-owner, Frank Farrell, takes exception. The* Tribune*'s Broun responds, "... he told me a lot more than I wrote in the paper."*

JUNE 4:

Tris Speaker's hitting streak is ended at 22 games by Ed Cicotte and the White Sox.

JUNE 7:

Hal Chase returns to New York in a White Sox uniform, gets a mixed reception at the Polo Grounds, and gets two hits in four at-bats. But the Yankees end their 13-game losing streak with a 3-2 victory.

JUNE 17:

The Cubs' Henry "Heinie" Zimmerman is thumbed by an umpire for the third time in five days. Chicago beats the visiting Phillies, 4-0.

JUNE 30:

Giants' manager John McGraw gets into a shoving match with Philadelphia Phillies' pitcher Addison "Ad" Brennan after an 11-inning, 11-10 New York win. Fans join the fracas.

JULY 3:

The Senators' Walter Johnson scatters 15 hits and still shuts out the Red Sox, 1-0, in 15 innings. Johnson sets a major league record for most hits allowed in a shutout. Ray Collins is the losing pitcher.

JULY 4:

Smoky Joe Wood's fastball has lost some of its bite, but his bat is still potent. The Red Sox pitcher sets a pitchers' record by hitting two doubles in an inning against the visiting Athletics.

JULY 12:

At Navin Field in Detroit, Ty Cobb plays second base for the Tigers in a 16-9 loss to the Athletics. He commits three errors in five chances and is described by E.A. Batchelor of the *Detroit Free Press* as "the worst second baseman living or dead."

JULY 20:

The Senators buy five-time 20-game winner George Mullin (1-6) from the Tigers.

JULY 25:

The Senators' Walter Johnson comes out of the bullpen and strikes out 16 Browns batters in 11 innings. Browns' pitcher Carl Weilman sets a major league record by striking out a total of six times in 15 innings.

AUGUST 2:

The Federal League holds a secret meeting in Indianapolis to discuss expansion from six to eight teams. The league's president, John T. Powers, is fired and replaced with James A. Gilmore. Former Phillies owner Horace Fogel, who was bounced from the NL, announces his plans for the two teams, in Philadelphia and New York.

AUGUST 13:

The Cubs acquire pitcher Jim "Hippo" Vaughn from Kansas City in the American Association for pitcher Lew Richie (2-4). Vaughn was 6-11 last season with the New York Highlanders and Washington Senators.

AUGUST 14:

The Chicago Cubs trade their one-time ace, 33-year-old pitcher Ed Reulbach (1-3), to Brooklyn for pitcher Eddie Stack (4-4) and cash.

AUGUST 30:

Today in Philadelphia, with the Phillies leading the New York Giants, 8-6, in the top of the ninth inning, fans begin distracting the Giants' batters by waving hats, papers, and handkerchiefs. As a result, umpire William Brennan declares a forfeit victory for the Giants.

JULY 25
Working in relief, Walter Johnson strikes out 16 Browns in 11 innings.

AUGUST 31:

Ray Dandridge is born in Richmond, Virginia.

SEPTEMBER 2:

National League president Thomas Lynch overturns umpire William Brennan's forfeit call on August 30, and the Phillies get the victory.

The NL board overturns Lynch's decision and orders the game to be resumed on October 2 before a doubleheader at the Polo Grounds.

SEPTEMBER 6:

The Browns, vying against the Yankees for seventh place, name Branch Rickey their new manager, replacing Jimmy Austin. At the helm for only eight games (2-6), Austin had replaced George Stovall (50-84).

SEPTEMBER 14:

In Chicago, the Cubs' Larry Cheney allows 14 hits and manages to shut out the Giants, 7-0. He sets an NL record for most hits in a shutout.

SEPTEMBER 29:

Walter Johnson wins his 36th game of the season by beating the Athletics, 1-0. The Big Train completes a banner year: in addition to his consecutive shutout inning record, he throws 346 innings, 29 complete games, and 11 shutouts, striking out 243 and compiling a 1.09 ERA. He loses only seven times all year.

OCTOBER 2:

In a game that took two months to complete, the Phillies retire two Giants batters in a "suspended" ninth inning and win, 8-6. The Giants and Phillies then split the regularly scheduled doubleheader.

OCTOBER 4:

Is it baseball or is it farce? In Boston, on the last day of the season, the Red Sox and Senators have nothing at stake and decide to fool around a little. The Senators' 43-year-old manager Clark Griffith pitches an inning and faces 44-year-old coach Jack Ryan. Players are allowed to inflate their averages, and the umpires, getting into the spirit of the game, allow four outs in one of the innings. Walter Johnson plays center field, but comes in to pitch in the ninth inning, yielding a double, a triple, and two runs. The Senators win, 10-9.

REGULAR SEASON WRAP-UP:

The Giants, under John McGraw, dominate the NL with a 101-51 record, 12 1/2 games ahead of Philadelphia. The ballclub has three 20-game winners: Christy Mathewson (25-11), Rube Marquard (23-10) and Jeff Tesreau (22-13), and the staff ERA is a league-best 2.43. John "Chief" Meyers at .312 and Art Fletcher with .297 are the top hitters.

Connie Mack's Athletics compile a 96-57 record, beating out the Senators by six and a half games. The leading hitters are Eddie "Cocky" Collins (.345), Frank Baker (.336 and a league-leading 12 homers and 126 RBI), and John "Stuffy" McInnis (.326). The ace of the staff is Charles "Chief" Bender at 21-10.

OCTOBER 7:

World Series, game one. Today at the Polo Grounds, the Athletics beat the Giants, 6-4, behind the hitting of Frank Baker, who smacks a two-run fifth-inning homer and two other hits for three RBI. Chief Bender pitches a complete game, yielding 11 hits for the win. Rube Marquard, who lasts five, is the game's losing pitcher.

OCTOBER 8:

World Series, game two. In Philadelphia, Christy Mathewson and Eddie Plank match nine shutout innings. Mathewson singles in the winning run in a three-run 10th inning and gets the win, 3-0.

OCTOBER 9:

World Series, game three. Back at the Polo Grounds, Bullet Joe Bush pitches the Athletics to an 8-2 win, defeating Jeff Tesreau. Wally Schang homers for Philadelphia and, for the second time in the series, Eddie Collins has three hits.

OCTOBER 10:

World Series, game four. Chief Bender wins his second game of the Series, beating the Giants and Al Demaree, 6-5, in Philadelphia. Fred Merkle hits a three-run home run for New York but is countered by Wally Schang's three RBI.

OCTOBER 11:

World Series, game five. Eddie Plank outduels Christy

HISTORY

Walter Johnson's ERA for 1913 is a matter of dispute. His 1.09 official ERA ignores two runs allowed in a farcical game on October 4. With those runs, he finishes at 1.14. The two runs are relevant, because in 1968, Bob Gibson of the Cardinals compiles a 1.12 ERA.

HISTORY

Walter Malmquist completes his season at .477 for York in the Nebraska State League. It is the highest batting average ever in organized baseball, yet Malmquist never makes it to the major leagues.

NOVEMBER 17
The Dodgers hire a new manager, Wilbert Robinson, and rename the team the Robins.

DECEMBER 6
In the first game of a world tour, the White Sox beat the Giants, 9-4, in Tokyo.

CULTURE

"Jake, Jake (The Yiddisha Ballplayer)," a song by Irving Berlin, makes its debut.

Mathewson, allowing the Giants only two hits in a 3-1 victory, giving the Athletics this year's World Championship. Mathewson is good, allowing only six hits, but Plank is better. He yields singles to Mathewson and Larry McLean and faces only 29 batters. The Athletics, who win the series for the third time in four years, are paced by Frank Baker's .450 (seven RBI) and Eddie Collins's .421. Larry McLean hits .500 (in 12 at bats) for the Giants.

POST-SEASON

NOVEMBER 17:

Brooklyn fires manager Bill Dahlen after a 64-84, sixth-place finish. He is replaced by pitching coach Wilbert Robinson. In honor of their new manager, the Dodgers will be known as the Robins.

NOVEMBER 18:

A group of White Sox and Giants players begin a tour of Japan, Ceylon, Australia, Egypt, Italy, France, and England. Underwritten by Charles Comiskey, the tour will feature a special exhibition baseball game for King George of England.

DECEMBER 6:

The White Sox beat the Giants, 9-4, at Keio University in Tokyo, in the first game of their world tour.

DECEMBER 9:

Brooklyn reportedly offers Cincinnati $35,000 for shortstop Joe Tinker, who hit .317 this season. Tinker is sold to Brooklyn along with infielder Dick Egan (.282) for $6,500. Tinker demands $2,000 as part of the deal. When refused, he jumps to Chicago in the Federal League for the 1914 season. Egan joins Brooklyn.

John K. Tener is elected to a four-year term as president of the NL, replacing Thomas Lynch. He will earn $25,000 a year. A former congressman, governor of Pennsylvania, and major league pitcher, Tener is a native of County Tyrone, Ireland. He is the first former player to hold a league presidency. Tener pitched in the majors from 1888 to 1890, compiling a 25-31 record with a 4.30 ERA. Tener will force Charles Webb Murphy to sell his share of the Cubs to Charles B. Taft. As consolation, Murphy receives $503,500.

DECEMBER 12:

Cubs owner Charles Webb Murphy fires manager-second baseman Johnny Evers. Under Evers, the Cubs finished in third at 88-65 and Evers hit .284

DECEMBER 24:

Louis "Chief" Sockalexis dies of heart disease today at the age of 42 in Burlington, Maine. A Penobscot Indian, born in Old Town, Maine, and the first Native American to play in the major leagues, Sockalexis was once described by John McGraw as the greatest natural baseball talent he'd ever seen. In his brief, 94-game career (1897 to 1899) as an outfielder with the Cleveland Spiders, Sockalexis had a .313 batting average, with three home runs and 55 RBI.

In his playing days, from 1891 to 1906, John McGraw was a career .334 hitter.

THE BEST OF 1913

National League

HITTERS

Batting Average:
Jake Daubert, Brooklyn Dodgers, .350

Slugging Average:
Clifford "Gavvy" Cravath, Philadelphia Phillies, .568

Home Runs:
Clifford Cravath, 19

Runs Batted In:
Clifford Cravath, 128

Hits:
Clifford Cravath, 179

Stolen Bases:
Max Carey, Pittsburgh Pirates, 61

PITCHERS

Wins:
Tom Seaton, Philadelphia Phillies, 27

Strikeouts:
Tom Seaton, 168

Earned Run Average:
Christy Mathewson, New York Giants, 2.06

Winning Percentage:
Bert Humphries, Chicago Cubs, .800

Saves:
Larry Cheney, Chicago Cubs, 11

Most Valuable Player (Chalmers Award):
Jake Daubert, Brooklyn Dodgers

American League

HITTERS

Batting Average:
Ty Cobb, Detroit Tigers, .390

Slugging Average:
"Shoeless" Joe Jackson, Cleveland Naps, .551

Home Runs:
Frank "Home Run" Baker, Philadelphia Athletics, 12

Runs Batted In:
Frank Baker, 126

Hits:
Joe Jackson, 197

Stolen Bases:
Clyde Milan, Washington Senators, 75

PITCHERS

Wins:
Walter Johnson, Washington Senators, 36

Strikeouts:
Walter Johnson, 243

Earned Run Average:
Walter Johnson, 1.09

Winning Percentage:
Walter Johnson, .837

Saves:
Charles "Chief" Bender, Philadelphia Athletics, 13

Most Valuable Player (Chalmers Award):
Walter Johnson, Washington Senators

LEAGUE

In November, the Federal League denies membership to former Phillies owner Horace Fogel, who was expelled from the NL. Fogel threatens to start a fourth major league.

1914

"Wrigley Field is a Peter Pan of a ballpark... It's never grown up [or] old."
– Sportswriter E. M. Swift

NEWS

WORLD WAR I BREAKS OUT IN EUROPE

U.S. Marines occupy Vera Cruz; Mexico severs relations with U.S.

FORD SETS AN EIGHT-HOUR, $5 WORKDAY, TWICE THE NATIONAL AVERAGE

JAMES JOYCE PUBLISHES *DUBLINERS*

EDGAR RICE BURROUGHS PUBLISHES *TARZAN OF THE APES*

MARGARET SANGER COINS TERM "BIRTH CONTROL"

After 10 years of construction Panama Canal opens

Gandhi begins non-violent protest of British rule

Last known passenger pigeon dies in Cincinnati Zoo

PRE-SEASON

JANUARY 6:

Baseball's National Commission recognizes the Fraternity of Professional Baseball Players of America and agrees to 11 conditions including: teams will pay for uniforms; there will be no discrimination against members of the Fraternity; and outfield fences will be painted green to provide a better background for batters.

JANUARY 18:

The *New York Times* reports the Federal League has offered Ty Cobb $15,000 a year for five years. Last year, Cobb held out for $15,000 from the Tigers and settled for $12,000, making him baseball's highest paid player. The *Times* continues: "He has assured president Navin of the Tigers that he will sign a contract for next year."

FEBRUARY 1:

The Chicago White Sox and New York Giants play a 10-inning, 3-3, tie in Cairo, Egypt. The first baseball game played on the African continent, it is part of their world tour.

FEBRUARY:

(There is no specific date available.) The last link to the legend is gone. The Cubs trade second baseman Johnny Evers (.284) to the Braves for infielder Bill Sweeney (.257) and cash. Evers receives $25,000 and decides not to jump to the Federal League. Evers was the last of the Tinker to Evers to Chance double-play combination with the Cubs.

FEBRUARY 9:

Bill Veeck Jr. is born in Chicago.

FEBRUARY 26:

The White Sox and Giants play for King George in London, going 11 innings. A Tom Daly homer wins for Chicago, which takes the "international series" 24-20, with two ties. The teams played on all inhabited continents except South America.

FEBRUARY 27:

Twenty-one days after celebrating his 19th birthday, George Herman Ruth leaves St. Mary's Industrial School and joins the Baltimore Orioles, owned and managed by Jack Dunn.

MARCH 6:

The Federal League offers Red Sox outfielder Tris Speaker a three-year $100,000 contract to manage its Brooklyn franchise. Speaker subsequently re-signs with the Red Sox for a reported $11,000.

APRIL 1:

One of baseball's greatest and most eccentric pitchers, George "Rube" Waddell, dies of tuberculosis in San Antonio, Texas,

APRIL 13
The Federal League debuts with the Buffalo Buffeds losing to the Baltimore Terrapins.

APRIL 22
The Orioles' Babe Ruth makes his pitching debut in the majors, a 6-0 win over the Bisons.

at age 37. In 13 years, Waddell had a career win-loss record of 191-145 with a 2.16 ERA. In *Baseball Anecdotes,* Daniel Okrent and Steve Wulf write, "During his time with Philadelphia, Waddell would periodically disappear from the club to join a minstrel show, to wrestle alligators, to chase fires. At one point [Connie] Mack paid the pitcher's entire $2,200 salary in one-dollar bills, hoping this might make it last longer."

THE SEASON

APRIL 13:

The Federal League debuts with the Baltimore Terrapins defeating the visiting Buffalo Buffeds, 3-2, in Oriole Park. Attendance is a healthy 27,140.

APRIL 22:

Babe Ruth, who previously played one inning in the field, makes his pitching debut today with the Orioles. He beats the Buffalo Bisons, 6-0, allowing six hits, and has two singles in his four at-bats.

The first batter to face Babe Ruth is Joe McCarthy, who will be the Bambino's manager on the Yankees some 17 years later. McCarthy walks.

APRIL 23:

The first baseball game to be played at new Weeghman Park – which was built at a cost of $250,000 – is a matchup between the Chicago Whales and the visiting Kansas City Packers in a Federal League game. Art Wilson hits two home runs, which help power the Whales to a 9-1 win. Packers' pitcher Claude Hendrix comes away with the victory, tossing a five-hitter. Attendance at the game is 21,000. Weeghman Park will later be renamed Wrigley Field. Two years later, in 1916, the ballpark will become the celebrated confines of the Chicago Cubs.

RULES

A batter is awarded three bases if a player throws his glove or cap to stop a hit ball.

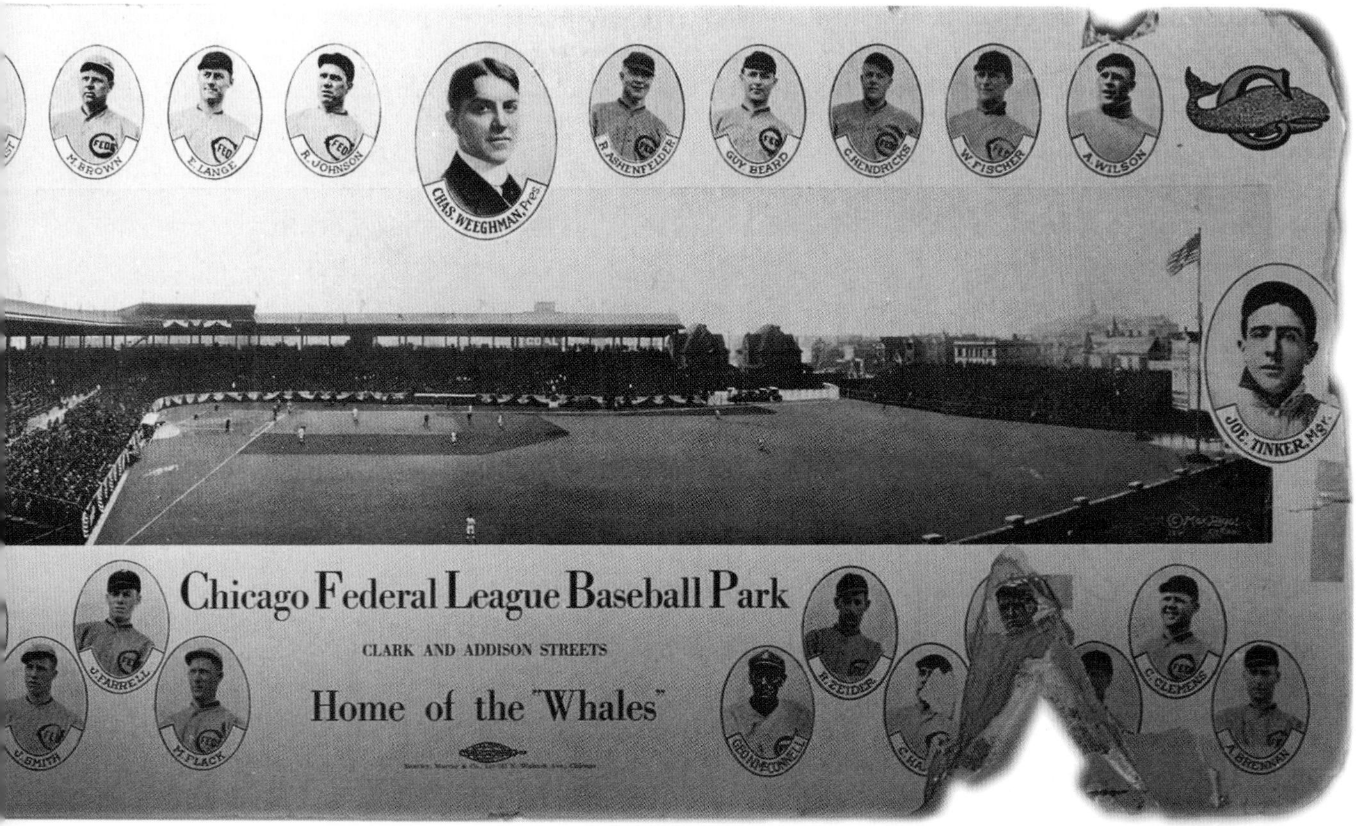

Weeghman Park, home of the Whales, opened in Chicago in 1914.

JUNE 9
The Pirates' Honus Wagner becomes the first modern player with 3,000 hits.

LEAGUE

The Federal League begins play with 172 former AL and NL players, including such established stars as Mordecai "Three-Finger" Brown (who becomes manager of the St. Louis team), George Stovall, Joe Tinker, Edd Roush, Ed Reulbach, George Mullin, Russ Ford, Howie Camnitz, Arthur "Solly" Hofman, Tom Seaton, Jack Quinn, Ad Brennan, Mickey Doolin, Otto Knabe, Bill McKechnie, and Fielder Jones. Brooklyn owner Charles Ebbets holds on to his stars, explaining, "I have assumed the burden of the biggest payroll I have ever been called upon to meet. The Federal League wanted my stars – well, so did I."

"I HAVE OBSERVED THAT BASEBALL IS NOT UNLIKE WAR."
– TY COBB

MAY 18:

At Detroit's Navin Field, Ty Cobb is hit in the ribs by a pitch from Boston's Hubert "Dutch" Leonard. In his next at bat, Cobb drags a bunt down the first base line. When Leonard comes over to cover, Cobb rips the pitcher's stockings with his spikes. Cobb plays for two more days with a broken rib before leaving the lineup.

MAY 30:

In St. Louis, the Tigers – without Ty Cobb, out with a broken rib – meet the Browns in a doubleheader. The teams combine for a record low 11 hits for the two games. In the opener, the Tigers with four hits beat the Browns, 2-1, on a one-hitter by Harry Coveleski. The loser is Earl Hamilton. The Browns win the nightcap, 2-0, on a Carl Weilman three-hitter (Sam Crawford gets two of them). The losing pitcher is Miles "Alex" Main, who also yields three hits.

MAY 31:

In Chicago, Joe Benz of the White Sox no-hits the Cleveland Naps, 6-1. He walks two and strikes out six; his team commits three errors. Abe Bowman is the losing pitcher.

JUNE 9:

In Philadelphia, Pittsburgh's Honus Wagner gets his 3,000th hit, becoming the first modern player to reach that plateau. Adrian "Cap" Anson had 3,000 hits in the 19th century. The Phillies win the game, 3-1.

JUNE 20:

Giants' manager John McGraw tells *Literary Digest*: "I believe that worrying over Bugs Raymond took five years off my life."

JULY 4:

Baseball folklore has it that the team in first place on July 4 wins the pennant. By that standard, the Boston Braves are out of the running. They drop two today to Brooklyn, 7-5 and 4-3, falling 15 games behind the first-place Giants. Braves' manager George Stallings says, "I've got 16 pitchers and they're all rotten."

JULY 9:

The Boston Red Sox buy pitchers George Herman "Babe" Ruth and Ernie Shore, along with catcher Ben Egan, from the Baltimore Orioles of the International League for $8,000.

JULY 11:

Babe Ruth makes his major league debut in Fenway Park before a crowd of 11,087. The 19-year-old left-handed pitcher strikes out the first batter he faces – Jack Graney – and goes seven innings against Cleveland, allowing eight hits. He leaves for pinch hitter George "Duffy" Lewis in the seventh. The Red Sox go on to win the game, 4-3, but Ruth is not involved in the decision.

JULY 17:

Pittsburgh's Charles "Babe" Adams does a lot of work with no reward. He pitches all 21 innings against Brooklyn today, allowing no walks, but the Pirates lose, 3-1.

JULY 19:

In Cincinnati, the Braves beat the Reds, 3-2, behind Paul Strand. The victory helps Boston climb out of last place.

JULY 20:

The Braves beat the Pirates, 1-0, and "soar" into sixth place.

JULY 21:

The Braves win again, 6-0 over Pittsburgh, moving into fourth place.

JULY 22:

The Fraternity of Professional Baseball Players of America flexes its muscles. Under the leadership of Dave Fultz, approximately 500 players threaten to strike. The issue is the demotion of first baseman Clarence Kraft of Brooklyn. The Robins assigned Kraft to the Newark team in the AA minor International League. However, baseball's National Commission awards him to Nashville in the Southern Association, an A league. Under the agreement with the brotherhood, a player cannot be required to go to a lower level when a team in a higher league wants him. The dispute is settled without a strike when Brooklyn owner Charles Ebbets pays Nashville $2,500

JULY 11
Babe Ruth, purchased by the Red Sox two days ago, makes his debut at Fenway Park.

and Kraft is finally permitted to go to Newark in the higher-rated league.

AUGUST 1:

The Braves top the Cardinals, 4-3, reaching the .500 mark. But they still linger in fourth, behind the Giants, Cubs, and Cardinals.

AUGUST 3:

Yankees' catcher Les Nunamaker cuts down three Tiger runners attempting to steal second base in the second inning. Nunamaker is the only catcher to accomplish that feat in the 20th century.

AUGUST 5:

The Red Sox send Babe Ruth to their minor league team in Providence.

AUGUST 8:

Tris Speaker executes an unassisted double play against the Tigers, his second of the season – a record for outfielders. His previous one was against the Athletics on April 21.

AUGUST 10:

The Braves beat the Reds, 3-1, moving into second place, six and a half games behind the Giants.

AUGUST 14:

Brooklyn first baseman Jake Daubert, hampered by an ankle injury, finds a way to help his team, putting down a record six sacrifice bunts in a doubleheader against Philadelphia at Ebbets Field. Four of Daubert's sacrifices are in the nightcap. Brooklyn wins twice, 8-4 and 13-5.

SEPTEMBER 2:

The Braves take two from the Phillies, 7-5 and 12-3, while the Robins are beating the Giants in Brooklyn. The Braves move ahead of the Giants into first place by one game.

SEPTEMBER 5:

In Canada, Babe Ruth, playing for Providence, hits his first professional home run – with two on – and pitches a one-hitter. The Babe's homer is hit against Ellis Johnson of Toronto in the first game of a doubleheader. Ruth played in 46 minor league games, but this was his only home run.

SEPTEMBER 7:

At Fenway Park, the Braves draw more than 74,000 fans for a morning-afternoon doubleheader against the New York Giants. Boston wins the opener, 5-4, then loses, 10-1.

SEPTEMBER 8:

The Braves beat the Giants, 5-4, to regain first place, after having dropped back to third place.

SEPTEMBER 9:

The Braves' George Davis, a student at Harvard Law School, no-hits Philadelphia, 7-0, in Boston. He walks five and fans four; the Braves commit two errors. Ben Tincup takes the loss.

SEPTEMBER 10:

But did it answer? After being ejected by umpire Mal Eason for swearing, Braves' shortstop Johnny Evers comes up with a novel explanation. He claims he was talking to the ball, not Eason. Evers gets a three-day suspension.

SEPTEMBER 15:

After an ongoing dispute with owners Frank Farrell and Bill Devery over the quality of his players and the Hal Chase trade, Frank Chance resigns as Yankees' manager. Before returning to California, Chance tries to take a punch at Devery. Under Chance, the Yankees were 61-76 this season after a seventh-place finish in 1913.

SEPTEMBER 16:

Roger Peckinpaugh, the Yankees' 23-year-old shortstop, will manage the team for the remaining 17 games. He becomes the youngest manager in baseball history.

SEPTEMBER 19:

In a Federal League game in Brooklyn, Ed "Doc" Lafitte of the Tip-Tops no-hits the visiting Kansas City Packers, 6-2. A former Tiger, Lafitte walks seven batters. Reportedly, he is a descendant of the 19th-century pirate Jean Lafitte.

SEPTEMBER 20:

Cleveland rookie Guy "Alabama Blossom" Morton loses to the Athletics, 4-1, his 13th consecutive loss at the start of his career. Despite a respectable 3.02 ERA, Morton is 1-13 in 1914. He overcomes his rocky start to pitch in the majors for 11 years and compile a winning record – 98-88 – with a 3.13 ERA.

SEPTEMBER 22:

In Detroit, Ray Collins of the Red Sox pitches two complete-

LEAGUE

The Federal League lineup for 1914 is the Baltimore Terrapins, Brooklyn Tip-Tops, Buffalo Buffeds, Chicago Chi-Feds, Indianapolis Hoosiers, Kansas City Packers, Pittsburgh Rebels, and St. Louis Terriers.

SEPTEMBER 27
Cleveland's Nap Lajoie joins Honus Wagner as a member of the 3,000-hits club.

"I've got 16 pitchers and they're all rotten."
– Braves' manager George Stallings

LEAGUE

Connie Mack's fears are partially realized when pitchers Eddie Plank and Chief Bender jump to the Federal League.

game victories over the Tigers in a doubleheader, becoming the eighth pitcher in the century to accomplish the feat. Collins wins the opener, 5-3 on a four-hitter. In the nightcap, shortened to eight innings because of darkness, he allows 12 hits and wins, 5-0. He walks only one batter in each of the games.

SEPTEMBER 27:

In a twinbill today against the Yankees, Cleveland's Napoleon Lajoie doubles for his 3,000th career hit, becoming the second modern player ever to reach 3,000. Lajoie has 2,051 hits in a Cleveland uniform. Earlier in the year, Honus Wagner broke the ice with his 3,000th career hit. Cleveland wins the game, 5-3, with rookie Guy Morton breaking his 13-game losing streak and registering his first-ever major league win. The Yankees win game two.

SEPTEMBER 29:

The Braves beat the Cubs, 7-6, to win the NL pennant.

REGULAR SEASON WRAP-UP:

The Miracle Braves, managed by George Stallings, win the pennant with 34 wins in their final 44 games. They end the season at 94-59, 10 1/2 games ahead of the Giants. Dick Rudolph at 27-10 and Bill James with 26-7 are the team's top pitchers. The top hitter among the regulars is Joe Connolly with a .306 average.

Connie Mack's Athletics win their fourth AL pennant in five years. They finish at 99-53, eight and a half games ahead of the Boston Red Sox. Although seven pitchers have double figures in victories, the team has no 20-game winner. Eddie Collins leads the ballclub at .344. Frank Baker leads the AL with nine homers and hits .319.

The Indianapolis Hoosiers, managed by Bill Phillips, win the first Federal League pennant, but will not participate in post-season play. They finish at 88-65, a game and a half ahead of the Chicago Whales. Their top hitter is Benny Kauff at a league-leading .370. Frederick "Cy" Falkenberg is the ace of the staff at 25-16.

OCTOBER 9:

World Series, game one. In Philadelphia, Dick Rudolph

ACCORDING TO DANIEL OKRENT AND STEVE WULF, MANAGER GEORGE STALLINGS WAS "A GRADUATE OF VIRGINIA MILITARY INSTITUTE, A MEDICAL STUDENT AT THE COLLEGE OF PHYSICIANS AND SURGEONS IN BALTIMORE, A CHALLENGER OF ORTHODOXY WHO WAS THE FIRST MANAGER TO PLAY PLATOON BASEBALL, USING LEFTY/RIGHTY TANDEMS IN BOTH LEFT AND RIGHT FIELDS. HE ALSO WAS A MONOMANIAC OF STAGGERING PROPORTIONS."

SEPTEMBER 29
The Boston Braves top the Chicago Cubs, 7-6, to clinch the National League pennant.

OCTOBER 9
In game one of the World Series, Hank Gowdy hits a single, double, and triple.

five-hits the Athletics and the Braves win, 7-1. Charles "Chief" Bender fails to go the distance for the first time in 10 post-season starts and gets the loss. Hank Gowdy paces the Braves' attack with a single, double, triple, and walk.

OCTOBER 10:

World Series, game two. In Philadelphia, Boston's Bill James two-hits Philadelphia, 1-0. Eddie Plank, who allows only seven hits, is the losing pitcher. The Braves score the game's only run in the top of the ninth when Amos Strunk misplays Charlie Deal's fly ball. Les Mann then singles Deal home.

OCTOBER 12:

World Series, game three. Bill James gets his second consecutive Series win with two innings of relief in the Braves' 12-inning, 5-4 victory in Boston. Bullet Joe Bush pitches well – allowing eight hits in 12 innings – but his wild throw gives the Braves the winning run. Hank Gowdy again is the big hitter with a homer and two doubles.

OCTOBER 13:

World Series, game four. The Braves complete the Miracle

Boston Braves catcher Hank Gowdy had five hits in 11 at-bats – .545 – in the 1914 World Series.

OCTOBER 13
The Boston Braves complete a four-game World Series sweep of the Philadelphia A's.

DECEMBER 31
Col. Jacob Ruppert and Capt. Tillinghast L'Hommedieu buy the New York Yankees.

TRIVIA

According to historian Lee Allen in *The American League Story*, Babe Ruth acquired his nickname in Orioles training camp when veteran players were riding him. Baltimore scout Sam Steinman warned, "You'd better be careful; he's one of Jack Dunn's babes." Dunn was the team's owner.

of 1914, beating Philadelphia, 3-1, in Boston to sweep the World Series. Dick Rudolph pitches a complete-game seven-hitter for the win. Bob Shawkey is the loser. The game's big blow is Johnny Evers's two-run single in the fifth. The unlikely hitting star of the series is catcher Hank Gowdy, a .243 batter during the season. In the four games of the fall classic, he hits .545 with five extra-base hits, including a homer. The Braves also steal nine bases in the four games. Johnny Evers bats .438. The Braves staff compiles a 1.15 ERA.

POST-SEASON

OCTOBER 14:

A dispute erupts over the rights to George Sisler, who is a senior at the University of Michigan. In 1911, after signing with Akron in the Central League, Sisler decided on college instead. Akron then assigned the youngster's contract to Columbus and then the Pittsburgh Pirates, without paying anything to Sisler. Detroit Judge George B. Codd, representing Sisler, today writes to baseball's National Commission seeking to have him declared a free agent. According to the commission's attorney, Sisler's contract is invalid. The National Commission eventually votes 2-1 to award Sisler to the Browns. AL President Ban Johnson and Garry Herrman are the majority; National League president John Tener dissents. Barney Dreyfuss issues a 12,000-word response: "An outsider, some person not affiliated with either league, should be placed at the head of the National Commission. The finding in the Sisler case is a freak of baseball legislation."

NOVEMBER 1:

Connie Mack, reportedly motivated by unhappiness with the World Series results and concerned about raids by the Federal League, begins selling off players. The first to go is the one-time ace of his staff, Jack Coombs, who fell to 0-1, with a 4.50 ERA, in 1914. Coombs is shipped to Brooklyn.

NOVEMBER 25:

Joseph Paul DiMaggio is born in Martinez, California.

NOVEMBER 28:

After Walter Johnson "slumps" to 28-18 with a 1.72 ERA in 371 2/3 innings pitched, 33 complete games, and nine shutouts, Senators' president Benjamin Minor Jr. gives him an ultimatum – accept a salary of $12,500 or go back to last year's $10,000.

DECEMBER 1:

The Braves buy Allston Golf Club near Boston University and will build a stadium on the site.

DECEMBER 4:

The Federal League announces that Walter Johnson has accepted an offer of $20,000 annually for three years plus a $10,000 bonus from the Chicago Whales. Senators' manager Clark Griffith talks Walter Johnson into accepting $12,500 per year and a three-year pact to remain in Washington. Johnson also gets to keep the $10,000 bonus; the Senators will reimburse the Whales for that amount.

DECEMBER 8:

The Chicago White Sox buy second baseman Eddie "Cocky" Collins from the Athletics for $50,000. Collins, a .300 hitter for six straight seasons, hit .344 in 1914 with two homers and 58 stolen bases. Regarded as baseball's best position player, the 27-year-old Collins gets a $15,000 bonus in the deal.

"Players who jump for the dough,

Bandits and crooks, every one.

Baseball's a pleasure, you know.

Players should play for the fun.

Magnates don't care for the mon'

They can't be tempted with gold,

They're in the game for the fun –

That is why Collins was sold."

– Ring Lardner

DECEMBER 31:

The Colonel and the Captain are now in command of the New York Yankees. New York City brewery owner Colonel Jacob Ruppert and Spanish-American war veteran and engineer Captain Tillinghast L'Hommedieu buy the New York Yankees from Frank Farrell and Bill Devery. The price tag is $460,000. Rupert will retain his ownership in the club until 1939, when Edward G. Barrow takes over.

THE BEST OF 1914

NATIONAL LEAGUE

HITTERS

Batting Average:
Jake Daubert, Brooklyn Robins, .329

Slugging Average:
Sherry Magee, Philadelphia Phillies, .509

Home Runs:
Clifford "Gavvy" Cravath, Philadelphia Phillies, 19

Runs Batted In:
Sherry Magee, 103

Hits:
Sherry Magee, 171

Stolen Bases:
George J. Burns, New York Giants, 62

PITCHERS

Wins:
Grover Cleveland Alexander, Philadelphia Phillies, 27

Strikeouts:
Grover Cleveland Alexander, 214

Earned Run Average:
"Spittin' Bill" Doak, St. Louis Cardinals, 1.72

Winning Percentage:
Bill James, Boston Braves, .788

Saves:
Leon "Red" Ames, Cincinnati Reds; Harry "Slim" Sallee, St. Louis Cardinals, 6

Most Valuable Player (Chalmers Award):
Johnny Evers, Boston Braves

AMERICAN LEAGUE

HITTERS

Batting Average:
Ty Cobb, Detroit Tigers, .368

Slugging Average:
Ty Cobb, .513

Home Runs:
Frank "Home Run" Baker, Philadelphia Athletics, 9

Runs Batted In:
Sam Crawford, Detroit Tigers, 104

Hits:
Tris Speaker, Boston Red Sox, 193

Stolen Bases:
Frederick "Fritz" Maisel, New York Yankees, 74

PITCHERS

Wins:
Walter Johnson, Washington Senators, 28

Strikeouts:
Walter Johnson, 225

Earned Run Average:
Hubert "Dutch" Leonard, Boston Red Sox, 1.01

Winning Percentage:
Charles "Chief" Bender, Philadelphia Athletics,.850

Saves:
George "Hooks" Dauss, Detroit Tigers; John "Jim" Shaw, Washington Senators; Jack Bentley, Washington Senators; Albert "Roy" Mitchell, St. Louis Browns; Urban "Red" Faber, Chicago White Sox, 4

Most Valuable Player (Chalmers Award):
Eddie Collins, Philadelphia Athletics

FEDERAL LEAGUE

HITTERS

Batting Average:
Bennie Kauff, Indianapolis Hoosiers, .370

Slugging Average:
Louis "Steve" Evans, Brooklyn Tip-Tops, .556

Home Runs:
William "Duke" Kenworthy, Kansas City Packers; Edward "Dutch" Zwilling, Chicago Chi-Feds, 15

Runs Batted In:
Frank LaPorte, Indianapolis Hoosiers, 107

Hits:
Bennie Kauff, 211

Stolen Bases:
Bennie Kauff, 75

PITCHERS

Wins:
Claude Hendrix, Chicago Chi-Feds, 29

Strikeouts:
Frederick "Cy" Falkenberg, Indianapolis Hoosiers, 236

Earned Run Average:
Adam Johnson, Chicago Chi-Feds, 1.58

Winning Percentage:
Russ Ford, Buffalo Buffeds, .769

Saves:
Russ Ford, 6

1915

"I'd say he was the smartest hitter that ever lived."
– *Branch Rickey, on George Sisler*

NEWS

GERMAN U-BOAT SINKS *LUSITANIA* OFF IRELAND; 1,198 DROWN

U.S. Marines march into Haiti; it becomes U.S. protectorate

BOOKER T. WASHINGTON DIES

Congress establishes Coast Guard

VICTOR TALKING MACHINE CO. MANUFACTURES PHONOGRAPH

ALEXANDER GRAHAM BELL AND DR. THOMAS WATSON MAKE FIRST TRANS-AMERICA TELEPHONE CALL, FROM NEW YORK TO SAN FRANCISCO

LEO FRANK LYNCHED IN GEORGIA

D.W. Griffith's *The Birth of a Nation* stars Lillian Gish and Wallace Reid

German U-Boats blockade Britain

Franz Kafka's *The Metamorphosis* is published

PRE-SEASON

JANUARY 5:

The Federal League files an anti-trust suit against major league baseball, charging violations of the Sherman Anti-Trust Act. Presiding over the case in U.S. district court in Chicago is Judge Kenesaw Mountain Landis. The suit is spurred by Chicago owners Charles Weeghman and James A. Gilmore

The Athletics buy Napoleon Lajoie from Cleveland. A .300 hitter 15 times and a .400 batter once, Lajoie slumped to .258 last season – a drop of nearly 80 points from his 1913 batting average. Lajoie returns to Philadelphia 13 years after his contract was transferred from the Athletics to the Cleveland Indians.

JANUARY 7:

The Yankees buy first baseman Wally Pipp (.161 in 12 games) from the Detroit Tigers for the waiver price of $7,500.

JANUARY 11:

The sale of the New York Yankees by Frank Farrell and Bill Devery to Colonel Jacob Ruppert and Captain Tillinghast L'Hommedieu for $460,000 is finalized today.

Ruppert describes the Yankees as an "orphan ball club" and installs Wild Bill Donovan as the team's manager for the 1915 season.

MARCH 13:

In a variation on catching a ball dropped from the top of the Washington Monument, Brooklyn manager Wilbert Robinson intends to field one released from an airplane at Daytona Beach, Florida. Ruth Law flies a Wright Model B to an altitude of 525 feet and a grapefruit is dropped instead of a baseball. It utterly splatters on impact; Robinson is floored and yells, "I'm killed! I'm dead! My chest's split open! I'm covered with blood!" The responsible parties are believed to be Brooklyn's assistant trainer John Kelley and outfielder Casey Stengel.

MARCH 20:

Ground is broken for Boston's Braves Field. The ball park will open later this year, with a seating capacity of 40,000.

THE SEASON

APRIL 14:

The Athletics' Herb Pennock comes within an out of pitching an opening day no-hitter in Philadelphia. Harry Hooper of the Red Sox breaks it up with a bouncer over Pennock's head. It is the only hit he gives up and Philadelphia wins the game, 2-0.

APRIL 15:

The Giants' Richard "Rube" Marquard no-hits the Brooklyn Robins, 2-0, at the Polo Grounds. He walks two and fans two; the Giants make one error. The losing pitcher is George "Nap" Rucker. Marquard had jumped briefly to the Federal League, but returned to the Giants without appearing in a Federal game.

APRIL 22:

The Yankees wear pinstriped uniforms for the first time.

APRIL 24:

The Pittsburgh Rebels' Frank Allen no-hits the visiting St. Louis Terriers, 2-0, in a Federal League game. Allen will end up starting 41 games this season and go 23-12 with a 2.51 ERA.

MAY 6
Red Sox pitcher Babe Ruth hits his first major league homer – a feat that took 18 at-bats.

JUNE 11
Yankees' pitcher "Slim" Caldwell is the first to hit consecutive pinch-hit homers.

MAY 6:

Boston pitcher Babe Ruth hits his first major league home run after 18 major league at-bats. At the Polo Grounds, Ruth sends a pitch from the Yankees' Jack Warhop into the second deck in right field. A crowd of 5,000 see the blow. The Yankees win, 5-3, in 13; Ruth gets the loss. The winning pitcher is Edwin "Cy" Pieh.

MAY 9:

On a freezing day in Cleveland, 7,000 fans turn out to salute their longtime hero on Nap Lajoie Day. Now with the Athletics, Lajoie is hitless in the game which the Indians win, 6-0, on a Guy Morton six-hitter.

MAY 15:

Chicago's Claude Hendrix no-hits the visiting Pittsburgh Rebels, 10-0, in a Federal League game.

JUNE 2:

Babe Ruth, back at the Polo Grounds, homers again off Jack Warhop – but this one is deeper into the second deck than his May 6 shot. And the outcome is different – Ruth wins this game, 7-1, pitching a five-hitter.

JUNE 11:

It takes 29 innings and two days for the Reds to beat the Robins, but they do it today, 1-0, in 15 innings. Yesterday's game between the two teams ended in a 2-2 tie after 14 innings.

Yankees' pitcher Ray "Slim" Caldwell becomes the first player ever to hit consecutive pinch-hit home runs, after hitting one on June 10.

JUNE 12:

The Yankees' Ray Caldwell hits a home run today in a regular at-bat against the St. Louis Browns. It is his third round-tripper in three days.

JUNE 13:

The Athletics sell pitcher Herb Pennock (3-6) to the Red Sox for the waiver price.

JUNE 17:

The Cubs' George Washington "Zip" Zabel pitches the longest relief stint in major league history. In a game against the visiting Robins, Zabel is called in from the bullpen with two out in the first and goes 18 1/3 innings, allowing 15 hits, two runs, and one walk while striking out six. He is rewarded when Vic Saier hits a homer in the bottom of the 19th for a 4-3 win. Jeff Pfeffer, who goes 19, allows 15 hits and eight walks while striking out six, and is tagged with the loss.

JUNE 23:

Ty Cobb steals home against the Browns in a 4-2 Tiger victory. It is Cobb's fifth steal of home this month.

In Philadelphia, Athletics' rookie Bruno "Boon" Haas walks a record 16 batters and allows 15 runs and 11 hits, compounding his troubles by uncorking three wild pitches. Surprisingly, he goes the distance, striking out four. Not surprisingly, he loses to the Yankees, 15-7. Haas pitches 14 1/3 innings in six games, yielding 28 walks and 23 hits with an ERA of 11.93. His future lies in another sport: He becomes a National Football League halfback.

JUNE 24:

George Sisler graduates today from the University of Michigan and signs a contract with the St. Louis Browns, where he will be managed by his college coach, Branch Rickey.

JUNE 28:

In Chicago, St. Louis Browns' rookie first baseman George Sisler pitches three scoreless innings of relief against the White Sox – his major league pitching debut. But the White Sox win the game, 4-2.

JULY 2:

Connie Mack continues to sell off players. Jack Barry (.222), the shortstop in the Athletics' "$100,000 Infield," goes to the Red Sox for $8,000.

JULY 3:

George Sisler gets his first complete game victory as a Brown, beating the Indians, 3-1.

JULY 7:

The Athletics sell pitcher Bob Shawkey (6-6) to the Yankees for $18,000. He will become one of their mainstays.

After 16 innings of scoreless pitching in the second game of a doubleheader, Brooklyn and Boston end up in a tie as darkness ends the contest. Brooklyn's Shufflin' Phil Douglas goes all the way for Brooklyn; Bill James and George Davis share the pitching for the

LEAGUE

Among the players jumping to the Federal League for the 1915 season are William "Babe" Borton, Big Ed Konetchy, Hugh Bedient, Lee Magee, George "Hooks" Wiltse, and the two Philadelphia Athletics stars, Eddie Plank and Charles "Chief" Bender. The Buffalo Buffeds change their name to the Blues; a contest for a new name for the Chicago team produces the Whales. The Indianapolis Hoosiers, financed by oilman Harry Sinclair, move to Newark, New Jersey, and become the Peppers.

JULY 29
Honus Wagner, 41, becomes the oldest player to hit a grand slam homer.

LEAGUE

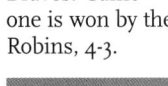

In August, the Giants sell outfielder-infielder Fred Snodgrass (.194 in 103 games) to the Braves. In the 1912 World Series, Snodgrass dropped a routine fly, an error that helped the Red Sox defeat the Giants.

Braves. Game one is won by the Robins, 4-3.

JULY 14:

With rain threatening, White Sox pitcher Urban "Red" Faber tries to make a game official by deliberately getting himself picked off base against the Athletics. Philadelphia, with a conflicting goal, doesn't play along and Faber ends up stealing his way around the bases, including home. The game is played for the full nine innings and Chicago wins it by two runs.

JULY 21:

At Sportsman's Park in St. Louis, Babe Ruth wallops a gargantuan home run against the Browns' Big Bill James. The ball clears the right-field stands, travels across Grand Avenue and breaks the plate-glass window of an automobile showroom. *The Sporting Life* even calls it "the longest home run ever witnessed at the local American League park." But Ruth is not done. He also has two doubles and a single, scores a run, drives in two, and pitches a five-hitter for a 4-2 Red Sox victory.

JULY 29:

Honus Wagner, now 41, hits an eighth-inning grand slam home run to deep center at Forbes Field against Brooklyn's Jeff Pfeffer. He becomes the oldest player ever to hit a grand slam. The Pirates win, 8-2.

AUGUST 8:

In Cincinnati today, Phillies' outfielder Clifford "Gavvy" Cravath ties a major league record with four doubles in a 14-7 Phillies' victory.

AUGUST 16:

In a Federal League game, Miles "Alex" Main of the Kansas City Packers no-hits the visiting Buffalo Blues, 5-0.

AUGUST 18:

The St. Louis Browns acquire outfielder William "Baby Doll" Jacobson (.215) from the Detroit Tigers for pitchers Bill James (7-10) and Grover Lowdermilk (9-17).

How does a six-foot, three-inch, 215-pound athlete become known as Baby Doll? Jacobson hit a home run for Mobile in a Southern League opening day game. The band played "Oh You Beautiful Doll," and the next day's newspaper published his photo as "Baby Doll."

Braves Field opens with a crowd variously estimated at between 42,000 and 46,000 for a game between Boston and St. Louis; 6,000 fans are turned away. The Braves make their debut in their new ballpark a successful one with a 3-1 victory. Dick Rudolph gets the win.

AUGUST 21:

The White Sox obtain Shoeless Joe Jackson (.331) from the Indians for outfielders Robert "Braggo" Roth (.250) and Larry Chappell (.000 in three games), along with pitcher Ed Klepfer (1-0) plus $31,500 in cash.

AUGUST 31:

The Cubs' Jimmy Lavender no-hits the Giants, 2-0, in the Polo Grounds. He strikes out eight and walks one; Chicago makes only a single error. The losing pitcher is the Russian-born Alexander "Rube" Schauer.

The Giants sell their one-time ace "Rube" Marquard (9-8) to Brooklyn for the waiver price of $7,500. Marquard had been unclaimed on waivers and due to report to Newark in the International League. He arranged his own sale to Brooklyn.

SEPTEMBER 7:

Big Dave Davenport of the St. Louis Terriers no-hits the visiting Chicago Whales, 3-0, in a Federal League game.

SEPTEMBER 9:

Albert Goodwill Spalding dies in San Diego a week after his 55th birthday. Spalding was player-manager of Chicago in the NL in 1876 and 1877. In 1876, he compiled a 48-13 pitching record with a 1.75 ERA, and Chicago finished the season in first place.

SEPTEMBER 10:

Rogers Hornsby makes his major league debut, replacing Artie Butler at shortstop for the Cardinals in the seventh inning, with the Reds leading, 7-0. Hornsby is hitless in two at-bats against Charles "King" Lear. The 19-year-old Hornsby hits .246 in 18 games.

SEPTEMBER 11:

Eddie Plank, pitching with the St. Louis Terriers in the Federal League, beats

SEPTEMBER 29
Phillies' pitcher Grover Cleveland Alexander one-hits the Braves for his 31st win of the year.

Newark Peppers, 12-5, for his 300th career win. He is the first left-handed pitcher to win 300 games.

SEPTEMBER 16:

At Fenway Park, it's Ty Cobb versus Boston and the Red Sox fans. With 22,000 looking on, Cobb takes a close pitch from Carl Mays. Cobb is angered because George "Rube" Foster and Mays have been throwing at him all game. In the eighth inning, after two close pitches from Mays, Cobb flings his bat at the submarine-ball pitcher, calling him a "yellow dog." With the very next pitch, Mays hits Cobb on the wrist, and fans begin tossing bottles at the Tiger star. When Cobb catches a fly for the final out in a 6-1 Detroit win, he is surrounded by throngs of fans. As he walks to the clubhouse, a bottle nicks him. Two police officers and his teammates brandishing bats escort him safely off the field.

SEPTEMBER 24:

In Philadelphia, only 300 fans are on hand as Ty Cobb steals his record 90th base of the season.

SEPTEMBER 29:

In Boston, Grover Cleveland Alexander one-hits the Braves, 5-0, for his 31st win of the year, and the Phillies clinch the NL pennant. Sherry Magee's single in the fourth, a walk, and an error account for Boston's only base runners. Alexander strikes out four in pitching his 12th shutout and fourth one-hitter of the season. Gavvy Cravath gets Alexander all the runs he needs with a three-run homer in the first. The game's losing pitcher is Dick Rudolph.

OCTOBER 5:

In Cleveland, Ty Cobb steals his 96th and final base of the season, but the Indians beat the Tigers, 5-0.

OCTOBER 6:

In New York, Hubert "Dutch" Leonard pitches the Red Sox to a 2-0 win over the Yankees and the team's 100th victory of the season.

REGULAR SEASON WRAP-UP:

Manager Pat Moran's Phillies win their first National League pennant, finishing at 90-62, seven games ahead of the Braves. Grover Alexander is the NL's dominant pitcher at 31-10, with a 1.22 ERA and 12 shutouts. Erskine Mayer wins 21 games. Gavvy Cravath hits a major league record 24 homers, drives in 115 runs, and bats .285. Fred Luderus has Philadelphia's top average – .315.

Under manager Bill Carrigan, the Red Sox win the AL pennant with 101-50 record. The Tigers are in second, two and a half games behind. George "Rube" Foster and Ernie Shore are each 19-8. In his first full season, Babe Ruth is 18-8 and hits four homers. Tris Speaker bats .322.

In the Federal League, the Chicago Whales, under Joe Tinker, edge the St. Louis Terriers by .001. (Chicago played 152 games, St. Louis 154) Max Flack hits .314; Edward "Dutch" Zwilling hits 13 homers. George McConnell, at 25-10, is the top pitcher. Once again, the Federal League has no post-season play.

Other statistics of note: Walter Johnson's 27 victories for the fourth-place Senators – it is his sixth consecutive year with 20 or more victories. Ty Cobb, at .369, wins his ninth straight AL batting title and steals a record 96 bases. George Sisler completes his first season as a pitcher-first baseman-outfielder, batting .285 with three home runs, a 4-4 record, and a 2.83 ERA.

OCTOBER 8:

World Series, game one. This afternoon at Philadelphia's Baker Bowl, the Phillies, behind Grover Cleveland Alexander, beat the Boston Red Sox and Ernie Shore, 3-1. Alexander allows eight hits; Shore only five. A Gavvy Cravath groundout in the eighth drives in the key run; the Phillies score two runs in the frame without hitting a ball out of the infield. George "Duffy" Lewis has two hits for Boston. Babe Ruth makes his World Series debut pinch-hitting for Shore in the ninth inning and grounds out to first baseman Fred Luderus. The attendance is 19,343.

Ernie Shore is the only pitcher to lose a World Series game to the Phillies until Dennis Leonard of the Royals drops the opener of the 1980 Fall Classic.

CULTURE

"Alibi Ike," a short story by Ring Lardner, is published.

TRIVIA

With the release of Napoleon Lajoie, Cleveland needs a nickname to replace the Naps. A Cleveland newspaper runs a contest and the winning entry is the Indians in honor of the first Native American in the major leagues, the late Louis Sockalexis.

OCTOBER 9
Woodrow Wilson is the first president to throw out the first ball at a World Series.

LEAGUE

The owners of the Baltimore Terrapins file suit under the Sherman Anti-Trust Act; it is unsuccessful.

OCTOBER 9:

World Series, game two. In Philadelphia, Boston wins, 2-1, with George "Rube" Foster yielding three hits, striking out eight and facing only 30 batters to beat Erskine Mayer. Foster wins his own game with a ninth-inning RBI single scoring Larry Gardner. He also has a double and another single. Attendance is 20,306, including Woodrow Wilson, who is the first president to attend the World Series and who throws out the ceremonial first ball.

OCTOBER 11:

World Series, game three. In Boston, the Red Sox beat the Phillies, 2-1. Hubert "Dutch" Leonard is the winner with a three-hitter; Grover Cleveland Alexander takes the loss, despite yielding only six hits. Duffy Lewis drives in Harry Hooper in the bottom of the ninth with two out to win the game. Lewis has three hits; Tris Speaker has two hits, including a triple. Attendance is 42,300.

OCTOBER 12:

World Series, game four. In Boston, the Red Sox make it three in a row as Ernie Shore beats George Chalmers, 2-1, with 41,096 on hand. Once again, Duffy Lewis drives in Dick Hoblitzell with the winning run – this time with a sixth-inning double.

OCTOBER 13:

World series, game five. In Boston, the Red Sox win the World Championship today with a 5-4 victory over the Phillies. The winning pitcher is George "Rube" Foster. Erskine Mayer gets the start when Grover Cleveland Alexander comes up with a sore arm. Eppa Rixey relieves Mayer in the third and is tagged with the loss. The Series' only homers are hit today: two by Harry Hooper and one each by Duffy Lewis of Boston and Fred Luderus of the Phillies. Official attendance is 20,306. Duffy Lewis hits .444 with five RBI; Harry Hooper hits .350 with two homers. George Foster goes 2-0 and the Red Sox staff has a 1.84 ERA. Fred Luderus tops Phillies batters with .438 with six RBI.

POST-SEASON

DECEMBER 4:

Former Giants' owner Andrew Freedman, who fired 16 managers in seven years, dies at age 55. Never married, Freedman leaves an estate of $7 million.

DECEMBER 22:

In Cincinnati, the National, American, and Federal Leagues sign a "peace treaty." The NL and AL owners pay $600,000 to be distributed to the owners of the eight Federal League franchises. As part of the agreement, the Federal's antitrust suit will be dropped and two of the league's owners can purchase NL and AL franchises. Philip de Catesby Ball, who owns the St. Louis Terriers, buys the Browns from Robert Hedges, John E. Bruce, and associates. The Ward family, owners of the Brooklyn Tip-Tops, get a reported $400,000. Immunity is granted to the jumpers, who are reinstated. As a result of the peace treaty, the Federal League ceases to exist after two seasons.

DECEMBER 23:

The Federal League's leading hitter moves to the NL. The Giants buy Benny Kauff from the Brooklyn Tip-Tops for $35,000. In two seasons in the Federal League, Kauff hit .370 (eight homers) and .342 (12 homers). In 1912, he appeared in five games with the Yankees. The Giants also purchase outfielder Edd Roush (.298) today from the Newark Peppers of the Federal League for $7,500.

THE REDS' RUBE BRESSLER ON GROVER CLEVELAND ALEXANDER: "NO FUSSING AROUND OUT THERE, NO STALLING, NO WASTED MOTION, NO CATCHERS AND INFIELDERS ALWAYS RUNNING OUT TO THE MOUND TO TELL HIM HE'S IN TROUBLE, AND JUST MAKING MATTERS WORSE."

OCTOBER 11
In game two of the World Series, 42,300 watch as the Red Sox beat the Phillies, 2-1.

OCTOBER 13
The Red Sox win game five of the World Series vs. the Phillies for the World Championship.

THE BEST OF 1915

NATIONAL LEAGUE

HITTERS

Batting Average:
Larry Doyle, New York Giants, .320

Slugging Average:
Clifford "Gavvy" Cravath, Philadelphia Phillies, .510

Home Runs:
Clifford Cravath, 24

Runs Batted In:
Clifford Cravath, 115

Hits:
Larry Doyle, 189

Stolen Bases:
Max Carey, Pittsburgh Pirates, 36

PITCHERS:

Wins:
Grover Cleveland Alexander, Philadelphia Phillies, 31

Strikeouts:
Grover Cleveland Alexander, 241

Earned Run Average:
Grover Cleveland Alexander, 1.22

Winning Percentage:
Grover Cleveland Alexander, .756

Saves:
John "Rube" Benton, Cincinnati Reds, New York Giants; Tom E. Hughes, Boston Braves, 5

AMERICAN LEAGUE

HITTERS

Batting Average:
Ty Cobb, Detroit Tigers, .369

Slugging Average:
Jack Fournier, Chicago White Sox, .491

Home Runs:
Robert "Braggo" Roth, Chicago White Sox, Cleveland Indians, 7

Runs Batted In:
Bobby Veach, Sam Crawford, Detroit Tigers, 112

Hits:
Ty Cobb, 208

Stolen Bases:
Ty Cobb, 96

PITCHERS:

Wins:
Walter Johnson, Washington Senators, 27

Strikeouts:
Walter Johnson, 203

Earned Run Average:
"Smoky" Joe Wood, Boston Red Sox, 1.49

Winning Percentage:
Joe Wood, .750

Saves:
Carl Mays, Boston Red Sox, 7

FEDERAL LEAGUE

HITTERS

Batting Average:
Benny Kauff, Brooklyn Tip-Tops, .342

Slugging Average:
Benny Kauff, .509

Home Runs:
Hal Chase, Buffalo Blues, 17

Runs Batted In:
Edward "Dutch" Zwilling, Chicago Whales, 94

Hits:
Jack Tobin, St. Louis Terriers, 184

Stolen Bases:
Benny Kauff, 55

PITCHERS:

Wins:
George McConnell, Chicago Whales, 25

Strikeouts:
Dave Davenport, St. Louis Terriers, 229

Earned Run Average:
Earl Moseley, Newark Peppers, 1.91

Winning Percentage:
George McConnell, .714

Saves:
Hugh Bedient, Buffalo Blues, 10

1916

"The fact is, we're a better ball club, and McGraw knows it."
– Robins manager Wilbert Robinson

NEWS

WOODROW WILSON RE-ELECTED PRESIDENT, BEATS CHARLES EVANS HUGHES

TOMMY GUN INVENTED

GENERAL JOHN J. PERSHING PURSUES PANCHO VILLA INTO MEXICO

William Boeing opens his first airplane factory

BOY SCOUTS OF AMERICA INCORPORATED UNDER FEDERAL LEGISLATION

JEANNETTE RANKIN OF MONTANA IS FIRST WOMAN ELECTED TO CONGRESS

Authors Henry James and Jack London die

Battle of Verdun claims nearly 700,000 lives

West Indian black nationalist Marcus Garvey moves to U.S.

Margaret Sanger opens birth-control clinic

PRE-SEASON

JANUARY 8:

A syndicate that includes Governor David I. Walsh buys the Boston Braves from James Gaffney.

JANUARY 16:

Charles Weeghman buys the Cubs from Charles B. Taft at dinner in the Majestic Club in the Great Northern Hotel in Chicago. Among the minority shareholders is chewing gum manufacturer William Wrigley Jr., who invests $50,000. The deal is consummated on January 20. The new owner will move the team from its present ballpark, the West Side Grounds, to Weeghman Park.

FEBRUARY 10:

The Phillies buy pitcher Charles "Chief" Bender (4-16) from the Baltimore Terrapins of the Federal League. Last season, with the Philadelphia Athletics, Bender was 21-10.

The St. Louis Browns go to market and return with 11 members of the St. Louis Terriers in the Federal League. They buy pitcher Eddie Plank, first baseman William "Babe" Borton, catcher Harry Chapman, pitcher James "Doc" Crandall, third baseman Charlie Deal, pitcher Bob Groom, catcher Grover "Slick" Hartley, shortstop Ernie Johnson, outfielder Armando Marsans, outfielder Ward Miller, and outfielder Jack Tobin.

The Federal League fire sale continues. The Cubs buy 11 players from the Chicago Whales. They are pitcher Mordecai "Three Finger" Brown, catcher Clem Clemens, shortstop Mickey Doolan, catcher Bill Fischer, outfielder Max Flack, pitcher Claude Hendrix, outfielder Les Mann, pitcher George McConnell, pitcher Dykes Potter, shortstop Joe Tinker, and, finally, infielder Rollie Zeider.

FEBRUARY 15:

Connie Mack of the Athletics sells third baseman Frank "Home Run" Baker to the Yankees for $37,500. Baker did not play in the majors in 1915 to protest the sale of his teammates Eddie Collins and Jack Barry by Mack. Instead, Baker played semiprofessional ball in Upland, New York. In 1914 with the Athletics, he hit .319 with a league-leading nine home runs and 97 RBI.

FEBRUARY 21:

Charles W. Somers sells the Cleveland Indians to Jim Dunn.

MARCH 31:

The Brooklyn Robins introduce new checkered uniforms that they will wear at home and on the road. The design is described as a variation on the team's "cross-hatched" uniforms of 1907, with wider spacing.

APRIL 6:

After being passed on by most other major league teams, the shadowy Hal Chase (.291, 17 homers) is signed to a three-year, $25,000 contract by the Cincinnati Reds.

THE SEASON

APRIL 12:

The Indians acquire one of baseball's premier players – outfielder Tris Speaker – from the Boston Red Sox. Speaker hit .322 last season, his seventh straight season at more than .300. In return, Boston gets pitcher Sad Sam Jones (4-9, 3.65 ERA), minor league infielder Fred Thomas, and $55,000.

APRIL 12
The Indians make a deal with the Red Sox to acquire outfielder Tris Speaker.

JUNE 21
Red Sox pitcher George Foster no-hits the Yankees, 2-0, in just an hour and 31 minutes.

At the Polo Grounds, Walter Johnson and the Senators beat the Yankees, 3-2, in 11. It is the third opening day win for Johnson and the Senators over New York. The game's losing pitcher is Ray Caldwell.

APRIL 20:

The Cubs play at Weeghman Park (at Clark and Addison) for the first time, beating the Reds, 7-6, in 11 innings. Vic Saier singles in the winning run. The Reds' Johnny Beall hits the first NL homer in the ballpark, which was a Federal League stadium last season. Attendance is 20,000.

Weeghman Park becomes known as Cubs Park and, in 1926, the name will be changed to Wrigley Field.

APRIL 27:

Enos "Country" Slaughter is born in Roxboro, North Carolina.

MAY 6:

George Cutshaw of the Robins beats the Phillies, 3-2, with a home run in the 11th inning that lands near the foul line, bounces onto the wall at Ebbet's Field, "climbs" to the top, and drops over it.

MAY 9:

Pitchers for the Tigers and Athletics issue 30 walks in a game won by Philadelphia, 16-2. It is the most walks in any game of any length. Athletics' pitchers are responsible for 18 of the bases on balls. Carl Ray alone issues a dozen.

MAY 14:

At Robison Field in St. Louis, batting against Edward "Jeff" Pfeffer of the Brooklyn Robins, Rogers Hornsby hits his first major league home run.

MAY 26:

In a demonstration of how not to run the bases, the Giants' Benny Kauff today is picked off three times in one game.

JUNE 1:

Babe Ruth pitches his second consecutive shutout as the Boston Red Sox beat the Senators, 1-0. Walter Johnson ends up the game's losing pitcher.

JUNE 5:

It's three straight shutouts for Babe Ruth as the Red Sox beat the Indians, 5-0.

JUNE 13:

Babe Ruth gets another streak going, this time as a hitter. In a 5-3 victory over the Browns, he hits a home run for the third consecutive game.

JUNE 16:

Tom Hughes of the Braves no-hits the Pirates, 2-0, in Boston. He is the third to pitch a no-hitter in each league. On August 30, 1910, while with the New York Yankees, he no-hit Cleveland for nine innings, yielded a hit in the 10th, and lost in the 11th, 5-0. Today he finishes the game in high style, striking out Honus Wagner. Hughes records seven strikeouts and walks two. The losing pitcher is Erv Kantlehner, whose throwing error in the first inning gives Boston a run. Walter "Rabbit" Maranville adds the second run, scoring on the front end of a double steal.

JUNE 21:

George Foster of the Red Sox no-hits the Yankees at Fenway Park, 2-0, in a bristling hour-and-31-minute game. Foster strikes out three and walks three, and Boston commits no errors. Bob Shawkey takes the loss for New York. Harry Hooper has three hits for Boston.

JUNE 26:

New York City police officers invade the stands at the Polo Grounds and arrest three fans for petty larceny. Their crime? Keeping balls hit into the stands.

The Cleveland Indians use numbers on their uniforms on an experimental basis in a home game against the White Sox. The numbers, which are worn on uniform sleeves and are difficult to see, correspond with information in the scorecards. Cleveland outfielder Jack Graney is the first player to appear with a number.

JUNE 28:

It's a big day for the Cardinals' young infielder Rogers Hornsby in his first full season in the major leagues. He has three singles and two doubles.

JULY 14:

At Fenway Park, the Red Sox and Browns battle 17 innings to a scoreless tie. Ernie Koob goes all the way for the Browns. He blows an opportunity

TRIVIA

The movie *Somewhere in Georgia* is released. It features Ty Cobb and Elsie McLeod, from a script by sportswriter Grantland Rice. Cobb plays a bank clerk from Georgia who is also – what else? – a Detroit Tiger. *Kill the Umpire*, a silent short film starring Eddie Lyons, also appears.

SEPTEMBER
4
Christy Mathewson and Mordecai Brown face each other in their final appearances.

Babe Ruth is 23-12 with a league-best 1.75 ERA in 1916.

to win the game in the 15th when he tries to score what would be the winning run on a Ward Miller hit, misses third base, and is called out. Carl Mays pitches 15 innings for Boston and Hubert "Dutch" Leonard the final two.

JULY 20:

The Giants send their longtime ace Christy Mathewson (3-4) to Cincinnati along with outfielder Edd Roush (.188) and infielder Bill McKechnie (.246) in return for infielder Charles "Buck" Herzog (.267) and infielder-outfielder Wade "Red" Killefer (.244). The transaction is designed to give the 35-year-old Mathewson the opportunity to become the Reds' manager.

AUGUST 9:

The Athletics, behind Bullet Joe Bush, beat the Tigers, 7-1, and snap their 20-game losing streak.

AUGUST 12:

George L. Moreland's *Sporting Records* reports that new Cubs owner Charles Weeghman will be the first to allow fans to keep balls hit into the stands. Until now, fans at all major league parks often ended up in scuffles with one another or with security guards who were instructed to retrieve the balls. According to Jim Charlton, the policy was put into effect on April 29.

AUGUST 15:

At Fenway Park today, Babe Ruth and Walter Johnson face off in another pitchers' duel. The Red Sox and Ruth win, 1-0, in 13 innings.

AUGUST 20:

The Giants send first baseman Fred Merkle (.237) across town to the Brooklyn Robins for catcher Lew McCarty (.313).

AUGUST 26:

The Athletics' pitcher Joe Bush no-hits Cleveland, 5-0, in Philadelphia. He walks one and fans seven, while Philadelphia plays errorless ball. Stan Coveleski is the game's losing pitcher.

AUGUST 28:

The Giants obtain first baseman Henry "Heinie" Zimmerman (.291) and shortstop Michael "Mickey" Doolan (.214) from the Cubs for second baseman Larry Doyle (.268), third baseman Herb Hunter (.250), and outfielder Merwin Jacobson, who hasn't played in the majors this season. Zimmerman has been under a 10-day suspension, imposed by manager Joe Tinker for "laying down on the job."

AUGUST 30:

What a difference a day makes for Boston's pitcher Hubert "Dutch" Leonard, who no-hits the St. Louis Browns, 4-0, yielding only two walks and striking out three in an hour and 35 minutes. Yesterday in game one of a doubleheader, the Browns knocked out Leonard in the first inning, getting two runs on two hits, a walk, a hit batter, and a wild pitch. He was relieved by Babe Ruth. Today the loser for St. Louis is Carl Weilman.

SEPTEMBER 4:

Two pitching legends face off in the final game for each. On the mound for the Reds in game two of a doubleheader is the great right-hander Christy Mathewson. Opposing him for the Cubs is their right-handed star Mordecai "Three Finger" Brown. The game is not an artistic tri-

SEPTEMBER 23
Grover Cleveland Alexander records victories in both ends of a doubleheader.

umph for either man. Mathewson goes all the way and yields 15 hits in a 10-8 victory and records his 373rd career win. Brown also pitches a complete game, gives the Reds 19 hits, and takes the loss. He finishes up his career with 239 wins.

SEPTEMBER 8:

Wally Schang of the Athletics becomes the first major leaguer to hit home runs from both sides of the plate in the same game.

SEPTEMBER 9:

Babe Ruth beats Walter Johnson for the fifth straight time. The Red Sox top the Senators, 2-1.

SEPTEMBER 12:

The Red Sox will have a new manager for 1917. The team's owner, Joe Lannin, today announces the retirement of Bill Carrigan, effective at the end of the current season.

SEPTEMBER 16:

The Reds and Fred Toney snap Zack Wheat's consecutive game hitting streak at 29 in the nightcap of today's doubleheader. The Robins and Reds have to end the second game in a 1-1 tie after 12 innings.

SEPTEMBER 17:

Young Browns' left-handed pitcher George Sisler beats Walter Johnson and the Senators, 1-0. Sisler allows only six hits. In his second full season, big Red Sox left-hander Babe Ruth is a 20-game winner. In Chicago, before a record crowd of 40,000, Ruth beats the White Sox, 6-2.

SEPTEMBER 23:

In Philadelphia, the Phillies' Grover Cleveland Alexander ties three major league records with complete-game doubleheader victories over the Reds. The Phillies win, 7-4 and 4-0. In the doubleheader, Alexander allows only a single walk. In game two of the twinbill, he records his 16th shutout of the season and his fifth against the Reds.

SEPTEMBER 24:

At Cleveland, the Indians' Marty Kavanaugh hits the first pinch-hit grand slam home run in American League history – a ball that goes through a hole in the outfield fence. Kavanaugh is batting in place of pitcher Joe Boehling against Red Sox pitcher Dutch Leonard.

SEPTEMBER 30:

At the Polo Grounds with 38,000 in attendance, the Giants win their 26th straight in the first game of a doubleheader, beating the Braves, 4-0, behind John "Rube" Benton's one-hitter. The only hit comes in the eighth by Braves' first baseman Ed Konetchy. Dick Rudolph takes the loss for the Braves. All of the victories in the skein, which began on September 7 with a Ferdie Schupp win over the Robins, 4-1, have been at home. On September 28, Schupp took a no-hitter into the seventh with Konetchy the spoiler in a one-hit, 6-0, Giants win. In game two, which is held up by rain, the Braves score five runs in the seventh to beat the Giants, 8-3, and snap the winning streak. George Tyler is the winning pitcher, beating Slim Sallee. The 26 in a row topped the mark of 21 set by the Cubs in 1880. During the streak, which included a 1-1 tie with the Pirates on September 18, the Giants climbed from last to fourth place. Among the 26 games are doubleheader victories on September 9 by right-hander William "Pol" Perritt.

At Fenway Park today, 21-year-old Babe Ruth shuts out the New York Yankees, 3-0, to record his 23rd win of the season. It also is his ninth shutout of the season.

OCTOBER 1:

The idle Red Sox clinch the AL pennant.

OCTOBER 2:

The Phillies' Grover Cleveland Alexander shuts out the Braves, 2-0, on three hits in the first game of a doubleheader. It is Alexander's 16th shutout of the season, a modern major league record. In 1876, St. Louis' pitcher George Washington Bradley also had 16 shutouts.

OCTOBER 3:

In the fifth inning of today's game against Brooklyn, Giants' manager John McGraw shouts to his team, "You bunch of quitters!" He then leaves the field for the clubhouse. The Robins win the game, 9-6, and capture their first ever NL pennant. The fiery McGraw says after the game: "I do not say my players did not try to win, but they refused to obey my orders... It was too much for me and I lost my patience. Such base-

TRIVIA

William Graham – who may or may not be Billy Maharg – appears in one game in the outfield for the Phillies. He is the only amateur in the replacement lineup of the Tigers on May 18, 1912, to appear again in a major league game.

OCTOBER 7
In game one of the World Series, the Red Sox nip the Brooklyn Robins, 6-5.

LEAGUE

In July, James C. Jones and a syndicate buy the Cardinals from Helene Robison Britton for $250,000.

ball disgusted me and I left the bench." Wilbert Robinson responds: "That's a joke. The fact is, we're a better ball club, and McGraw knows it..."

REGULAR SEASON WRAP-UP:

Brooklyn, managed by Uncle Wilbert Robinson, wins its first NL pennant with a record of 94-60, two and a half games ahead of the Phillies. Jake Daubert (.316) and Zack Wheat (.312) are the leading hitters. Jeff Pfeffer tops the pitchers with 25-11 and a 1.92 ERA. The staff includes veterans "Rube" Marquard and Jack Coombs, both 13-game winners.

The Red Sox, 91-63 under Bill Carrigan, beat the White Sox by two games. Babe Ruth, 21 years old, is 23-12 with a league-leading 1.75 ERA and nine shutouts – an AL record for left-handed pitchers. Larry Gardner, at .308, is the team's leading hitter.

The once-mighty Athletics drop a record 117 games and suffer through a 20-game losing streak. Their pitcher Jack Nabors loses 20 straight during the season. Ty Cobb is dethroned as batting champion, despite a .371 average; Tris Speaker of the Cleveland Indians hits a blistering .386.

OCTOBER 7:

World Series, game one. In Boston, the Red Sox edge the Robins, 6-5. Ernie Shore wins despite a four-run ninth-inning rally by Brooklyn. Carl Mays comes on with two out and two on and earns a huge save when he gets the last out on shortstop Everett Scott's fine play on Jack Daubert's grounder. "Rube" Marquard is the losing pitcher. Hal Janvrin and Tillie Walker have two hits apiece for Boston. Attendance is 36,117.

OCTOBER 9:

World Series, game two. In Boston, with Babe Ruth going all the way and allowing only six hits, the Red Sox beat the Robins, 2-1, in 14. It is the longest game in Series history, and Ruth's stint is the longest complete game pitching win ever in the fall classic. He strikes out four and walks three. The winning run is scored by Mike McNally on pinch hitter Del Gainor's single. Hy Myers has a home run for Brooklyn and Sherry Smith takes the loss. Attendance is 41,373.

OCTOBER 10:

World Series, game three. In Brooklyn, Jack Coombs outpitches Carl Mays and the Robins win, 4-3. Jeff Pfeffer relieves Coombs with one out in the seventh and sets down eight consecutive batters for the save. Coombs, who appeared with the Athletics in 1910 and 1911, is the first to pitch for American and National League teams' games in the Series. Larry Gardner homers for Boston. Attendance is 21,087.

OCTOBER 11:

World Series, game four. In Brooklyn, with Larry Gardner's three-run home run in the second inning the big hit, the Red Sox beat the Robins, 6-2. Winning pitcher Dutch Leonard throws a three-hitter. Rube Marquard takes the loss for Brooklyn. All the Robins' runs are scored in the first inning. Attendance is 21,662.

OCTOBER 12:

World Series, game five. Prior to the game, Red Sox manager Bill Carrigan says this is his last game. The Red Sox go out and give him his second World Championship with a 4-1 victory on Ernie Shore's complete game three-hitter. Jeff Pfeffer is the loser. A World Series record crowd of 42,620 attends the game. Shore wins two games and Babe Ruth registers a 0.64 ERA. Duffy Lewis bats .353 for Boston. Casey Stengel leads the Robins with .364.

POST-SEASON

Branch Rickey is hired by the Cardinals for a front office position at $15,000 a year, making him baseball's highest paid executive.

OCTOBER 30:

Leon Day is born in Alexandria, Virginia.

DECEMBER 4:

The day after Boston newspapers report the sale of the World Champion Red Sox, the deal is official. Broadway producer Harry Frazee and Hugh Ward acquire the ball club from Joe Lannin.

In December, at their winter meetings, the owners unanimously decide they will cut ball players' salaries almost in half.

OCTOBER 12
Boston wins game five of the World Series, giving the Red Sox the World Championship.

DECEMBER 4
Broadway producer Harry Frazee and Hugh Ward purchase the Boston Red Sox.

THE BEST OF 1916

NATIONAL LEAGUE

HITTERS

Batting Average:
Hal Chase, Cincinnati Reds, .339

Slugging Average:
Zack Wheat, Brooklyn Robins, .461

Home Runs:
Fred "Cy" Williams, Chicago Cubs; Dave Robertson, New York Giants, 12

Runs Batted In:
Henry "Heinie" Zimmerman, Chicago Cubs, New York Giants, 83

Hits:
Hal Chase, 184

Stolen Bases:
Max Carey, Pittsburgh Pirates, 63

PITCHERS

Wins:
Grover Cleveland Alexander, Philadelphia Phillies, 33

Strikeouts:
Grover Cleveland Alexander, 167

Earned Run Average:
Grover Cleveland Alexander, 1.55

Winning Percentage:
Tom L. Hughes, Boston Braves, .842

Saves:
Leon "Red" Ames, St. Louis Cardinals, 7

AMERICAN LEAGUE

HITTERS

Batting Average:
Tris Speaker, Cleveland Indians, .386

Slugging Average:
Tris Speaker, .502

Home Runs:
Wally Pipp, New York Yankees, 12

Runs Batted In:
Del Pratt, St. Louis Browns, 103

Hits:
Tris Speaker, 211

Stolen Bases:
Ty Cobb, Detroit Tigers, 68

PITCHERS

Wins:
Walter Johnson, Washington Senators, 25

Strikeouts:
Walter Johnson, 228

Earned Run Average:
Babe Ruth, Boston Red Sox, 1.75

Winning Percentage:
Eddie Cicotte, Chicago White Sox, .682

Saves:
Bob Shawkey, New York Yankees, 8

TRIVIA

Baseball books: *You Know Me Al* by Ring Lardner, *Baseball Joe on the Giants* by Lester Chadwick, *First Base Faulkner* by Christy Mathewson.

1917

"You can't hit the ball with the bat on your shoulder."
– *Bill Byron, the Singing Ump*

NEWS

U.S. DECLARES WAR ON GERMANY, ENTERS WORLD WAR I

PUERTO RICO BECOMES U.S. TERRITORY

Selective Service Act, drafting men into military, passed

WOMEN WIN RIGHT TO VOTE IN NEW YORK STATE

U.S. TROOPS IN COMBAT IN FRANCE

U.S. BUYS VIRGIN ISLANDS FROM DENMARK

CZAR NICHOLAS II ABDICATES; COMMUNISTS TAKE CONTROL OF RUSSIAN GOVERNMENT

MARY PICKFORD STARS IN THE LITTLE PRINCESS

Literacy test required for all immigrants to the U.S.

PRE-SEASON

JANUARY 5:

Jack Barry replaces Bill Carrigan as manager of the Boston Red Sox.

JANUARY 15:

Henry Mathewson, the younger brother of Christy, commits suicide in Factoryville, Pennsylvania, at the age of 31. Mathewson pitched briefly for the New York Giants in 1906, appearing in two games and going 0-1 with 10 innings pitched, and again in 1907, when he pitched one inning and had no decisions.

FEBRUARY 17:

A group called the St. Louis Stock Co. announces it intends to purchase the Cardinals.

FEBRUARY 24:

The Indians buy Smoky Joe Wood from the Boston Red Sox for $15,000. A 34-game winner in 1912 but plagued by injuries, Wood did not play in 1916 after a long holdout.

FEBRUARY 25:

The Chicago White Sox buy first baseman Arnold "Chick" Gandil (.259) from the Indians for $3,500.

MARCH 31:

During a pre-season trip north, the Tigers and Giants meet in Dallas for the second game in an exhibition series. Ty Cobb arrives from a round of golf just before game time and is heckled by the Giants' shortstop Art Fletcher and second baseman Charles "Buck" Herzog. After a single, Cobb warns Herzog that he is coming down, then slides in tearing the second baseman's pants and spiking him. They begin fighting, then Fletcher joins in, and a major brawl erupts. The umpires, other players, and Dallas police intervene. When order is restored umpire Bill Brennan ejects Cobb. Chapter two takes place in the Oriental Hotel where Herzog invites himself to Cobb's room. After clearing the room, Cobb awaits his adversary, who shows up with Henry "Heinie" Zimmerman. Tiger trainer Harry Tuthill is the "referee" as Cobb badly thrashes Herzog.

APRIL 1:

Ty Cobb and Giants' manager John McGraw face off in the hotel lobby, but this time only words are exchanged.

THE SEASON

APRIL 14:

The White Sox' Eddie Cicotte no-hits the Browns, 11-0, in Sportsman's Park, St. Louis. Cicotte walks three and fans five. Chicago commits one error. The losing pitcher is Earl Hamilton.

APRIL 24:

Yankees' left-hander George Mogridge no-hits the Red Sox, 2-1, in Boston. It is the first winning no-hitter by a Yankees' pitcher. Mogridge strikes out three and yields three walks; the Yankees commit three errors. The losing pitcher is Hubert "Dutch" Leonard. The game takes one minute more than two hours.

MAY 1:

Johnny Berardino is born in Los Angeles. In 11 years as an infielder with the Cardinals, Browns, and Indians, Berardino hit only .249. He enjoyed greater success in his next career – as an actor in the soap opera *General Hospital*.

MAY 2:

Weeghman Park in Chicago is the scene of one of history's

APRIL 24
George Mogridge becomes the first Yankees' pitcher to win a no-hitter.

MAY 7
Red Sox pitcher Babe Ruth hurls a shutout against Walter Johnson and the Senators.

most remarkable pitching duels. Reds' right-hander Fred Toney and the Cubs' left-hander Jim "Hippo" Vaughn match nine no-hit innings. At the end of nine, the score is 0-0. Toney has issued two walks; Vaughn has allowed two Reds runners via bases on balls and one on an error. In the 10th, Reds' shortstop Larry Kopf singles off Vaughn. Greasy Neale flies out to Cy Williams; Hal Chase lifts a fly ball to Williams who muffs it and Kopf goes to third base. Kopf scores when Vaughn throws home late on Jim Thorpe's swinging bunt. Toney sets down the Cubs in the 10th, striking out the last two batters – Larry Doyle and Cy Williams – to complete a 1-0 no-hitter.

Two players who gained fame in football played the outfield for the Reds in the classic Toney-Vaughn matchup – Jim Thorpe and Greasy Neale. Thorpe arguably was America's greatest all-around athlete of all time. Neale became a National Football League coach and is a member of the Pro Football Hall of Fame.

MAY 5:

Ernie Koob of the Browns no-hits the Chicago White Sox, 1-0. The losing pitcher is Eddie Cicotte, who pitched a no-hitter against the Browns just 20 days ago. In today's game, a first-inning single by George "Buck" Weaver is changed to an error after the game by a group of sportswriters who review the play.

MAY 6:

In game two of a doubleheader, the White Sox are no-hit for the second time in two days. This time it is the Browns' Bob Groom, who beats Chicago and Joe Berry, 4-0. Groom also pitched two innings of no-hit ball as a reliever in game one today.

MAY 7:

Babe Ruth pitches a shutout and drives in the game's only run on a sacrifice fly as the Red Sox top Walter Johnson and the Senators, 1-0.

JUNE 2:

Braves' catcher Hank Gowdy becomes the first major leaguer to enlist in the military during World War I. He travels by train from Cincinnati to Columbus, Ohio, to sign up.

JUNE 6:

At Redland Field in Cincinnati, Bill Byron, also known as the Singing Ump because he hums between pitches, thumbs Giants' manager John McGraw and third baseman Hans Lobert, along with four Reds' players.

JUNE 8:

After a sixth-inning argument with umpires Bill Byron and Ernie Quigley over a non-call, John McGraw and Art Fletcher are ejected. After the Reds' Jim Thorpe singles in the winning run, McGraw confronts Byron, who allegedly makes a remark about the manager being "run out of Baltimore." The pugnacious McGraw takes exception to the remark by bloodying Byron's lip. McGraw follows the umpire toward the runway, throwing more punches. Players, fans, and police get involved in the melee. Reds' groundskeeper Marty Schwab tries to intervene and is assaulted by Giants' catcher Bill Rariden. McGraw calls Byron's comments an "infamous lie."

According to contemporary reports, Bill Byron, the Singing Ump, was crooning, "To the clubhouse you must go, you must go, you must go, my fair manager." Another of Byron's favorite ditties is: "You'll have to learn before you get older, you can't hit the ball with the bat on your shoulder."

JUNE 13:

The punch costs John McGraw a 16-day suspension and a $500 fine from NL president John K. Tener.

JUNE 14:

In the *New York Globe*, McGraw charges NL president John K. Tener with a bias in favor of the Phillies. McGraw later retracts his accusation.

JUNE 23:

At Fenway Park, Babe Ruth is ejected by umpire Clarence "Brick" Owens after facing and walking the leadoff hitter for the Senators, Ray Morgan. He is relieved by Ernie Shore. Chester "Pinch" Thomas, the catcher, leaves with Ruth and is replaced by Sam Agnew. Morgan is caught stealing and Shore retires the next 26

LEAGUE

With a year to go on his contract, Giants' manager John McGraw gets a renewal at $40,000 plus a percentage of the team's profits, making him the highest-paid man in baseball.

TRIVIA

Baseball Joe in the World Series **by Lester Chadwick,** ***Second Base Sloan*** **by Christy Mathewson, and** ***Guarding the Keystone Sack*** **by Burt L. Standish are all published.**

JUNE 30
Ty Cobb's grand slam home run is considered to that date the longest-ever homer in Sportsman's Park to that date.

HISTORY

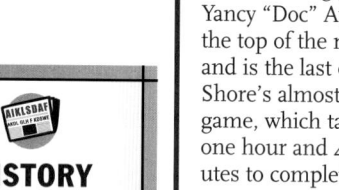

Before the end of the season, 37-year-old Tiger outfielder Wahoo Sam Crawford pinch-hits against the Indians, grounds out, and leaves the team, heading for California. He never plays again in the majors, ending up 36 hits short of the 3,000 plateau. He finishes his career at .309 with 1,525 RBI, 312 triples, and a record consecutive game streak of 472. But Crawford doesn't abandon baseball; he plays four years with Los Angeles in the Pacific Coast League, hitting .300 three times.

batters in a row as Boston wins, 4-0. Mike Menosky pinch-hits for losing pitcher Yancy "Doc" Ayers in the top of the ninth and is the last out of Shore's almost perfect game, which takes one hour and 40 minutes to complete.

JUNE 27:

Braves catcher Hank Gowdy begins his military service.

JUNE 30:

Ty Cobb may be more respected for his speed than his power, but today in St. Louis he shows he can ride the ball as well. In game two of a doubleheader against the Browns, Cobb hits an opposite-field grand slam homer. The ball clears the left-field bleachers and is considered the longest ever in Sportsman's Park – exceeding Babe Ruth's 1916 homer. Cobb also triples in a 5-3 Tiger win. Cobb has a single and double in a Tiger loss in the opening game.

JULY 1:

Two months after his no-hitter against the Cubs, the Reds' Fred Toney continues his pitching mastery, beating the Pirates with two three-hitters in 4-1 and 5-1 doubleheader wins. He sets a major league record for fewest hits allowed in a doubleheader.

In the first Sunday baseball game in Brooklyn at which admission is being charged, the Robins edge the Phillies, 3-2. Robins' owner Charles Ebbets donates part of the gate to a charity, the Militia of Mercy, and to circumvent the ban on Sunday baseball, arranges a pre-game concert. Technically, fans pay for the concert and see the game free, but it doesn't deter the police, who arrest Ebbets and his manager, Wilbert Robinson.

JULY 3:

Honus Wagner resigns as Pirates' manager after five games (the team is 1-4) and is replaced by Hugo Bezdek. Wagner explains, "I wasn't ready for it. I just couldn't get mad at anybody." Wagner succeeded James "Nixey" Callahan, who was 20-40 in his career.

JULY 6:

The Chicago White Sox put a stop to Ty Cobb's consecutive game hitting streak, halting it at 35.

JULY 10:

Today in St. Louis, the Yankees' Ray Caldwell comes out of the bullpen and pitches 9 2/3 hitless innings. The Yankees eventually beat the Browns with two runs in the 17th inning, 7-5.

JULY 12:

The Braves sell 35-year-old Johnny Evers (.193 in 24 games) – the longtime middleman in the Cubs' great double-play combination – to the Phillies today.

JULY 17:

Lou Boudreau is born in Harvey, Illinois.

JULY 25:

The Pirates buy first baseman George "Highpockets" Kelly (.000 in 11 games) from the New York Giants for the waiver price.

AUGUST 4:

The Pirates sell George "Highpockets" Kelly (.087 in eight games) back to the Giants for the waiver price.

AUGUST 19:

It's a raid! Manager John McGraw, pitcher Christy Mathewson, and the owners of the New York Giants are arrested at the Polo Grounds for playing the first Sunday baseball game there – against the Reds.

AUGUST 22:

The Robins, who seem to specialize in marathon games, play another one – a 22-inning affair in Brooklyn which they win, 6-5, against the Pirates. Robins' batters bang out 28 hits. It is the third straight extra-inning game between the two teams. Two Pittsburgh players set records: Carson Bigbee comes to bat 11 times with six hits and pitcher Elmer Jacobs works 16 2/3 innings of relief.

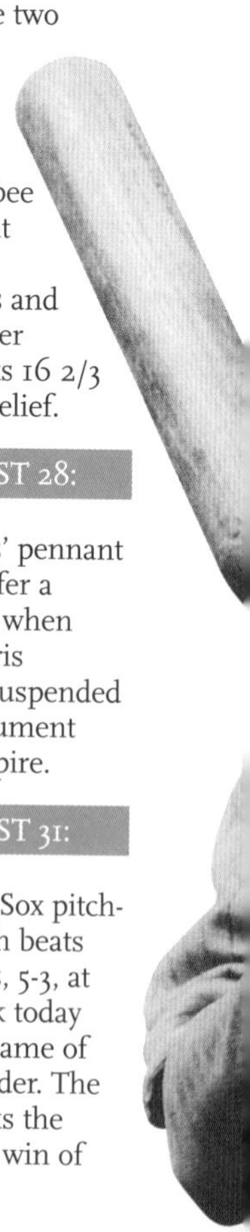

AUGUST 28:

The Indians' pennant chances suffer a severe blow when outfielder Tris Speaker is suspended after an argument with an umpire.

AUGUST 31:

Boston Red Sox pitcher Babe Ruth beats the Athletics, 5-3, at Fenway Park today in the first game of a doubleheader. The victory marks the Babe's 20th win of the season.

OCTOBER 6
In Chicago, the White Sox edge the Giants, 2-1, in game one of the World Series.

SEPTEMBER 3:

Today in Brooklyn, the Philadelphia Phillies' Grover Cleveland Alexander records complete game victories pitching in both ends of a doubleheader against the Brooklyn Robins. Alexander allows a major league record-tying one walk in the two games. Philadelphia wins the opening game by a score of 5-0, the nightcap by 9-3.

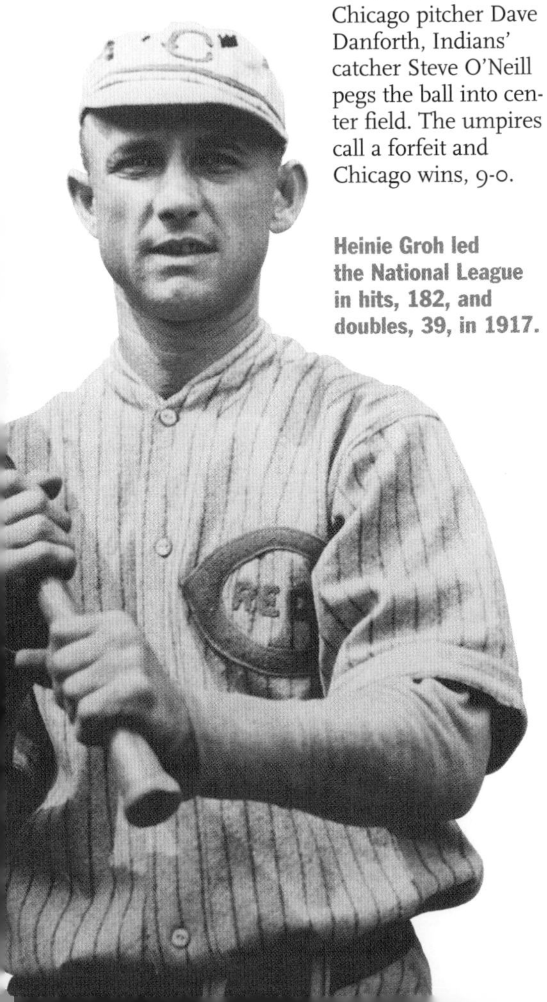

SEPTEMBER 9:

In Chicago, Cleveland does just about everything short of holding its collective breath and turning blue. After Indians' outfielder Jack Graney is called out for interfering with the White Sox third baseman, in the bottom of the 10th, the Indians argue for 10 minutes. When they finally take the field, they throw their gloves down and roll on the ground. After Frederick "Fritz" Coumbe strikes out Chicago pitcher Dave Danforth, Indians' catcher Steve O'Neill pegs the ball into center field. The umpires call a forfeit and Chicago wins, 9-0.

Heinie Groh led the National League in hits, 182, and doubles, 39, in 1917.

SEPTEMBER 21:

In Boston, the White Sox, behind pitcher Urban "Red" Faber, beat the Red Sox to clinch the AL pennant.

SEPTEMBER 25:

Johnny Sain is born in Havana, Arkansas. He has the distinction of throwing the last pitch ever to Babe Ruth and the first pitch to Jackie Robinson.

REGULAR SEASON WRAP-UP:

The White Sox, managed by Clarence "Pants" Rowland, win the AL pennant with a 100-54 record, nine games ahead of the Red Sox. Eddie Cicotte leads the pitching staff at 28-12 with a 1.53 ERA. Oscar "Happy" Felsch (.308) and Shoeless Joe Jackson (.301) are the club's top hitters.

John McGraw leads the Giants back to the top of the NL at 98-56, 10 games over the Phillies. Ferdie Schupp at 21-7 is their pitching ace; Benny Kauff (.308) and George Burns (.302) the top hitters.

For the Red Sox, Babe Ruth continues to shine. He finishes the season at 24-13 with a 2.01 ERA and bats .325. At 30-13, Grover Cleveland Alexander of the Phillies has his third straight 30-win season. He also leads the NL for the third consecutive time in ERA (1.86) and shutouts (eight).

OCTOBER 6:

World Series, game one. In Chicago, Ed Cicotte allows seven hits and outpitches Harry "Slim" Sallee as the White Sox beat the Giants, 2-1. Happy Felsch hits a fourth-inning home run and John "Shano" Collins has three hits for the White Sox.

OCTOBER 8:

Danny Murtagh is born in Chester, Pennsylvania.

OCTOBER 7:

World Series, game two. In Chicago, Urban "Red" Faber pitches the White Sox to their second straight over the Giants, 7-2. The losing pitcher is Fred Anderson. Faber gives the Giants eight hits and the Sox put the game away with a five-run fourth inning. A light note: Red Faber steals second base, only to find teammate George "Buck" Weaver already there.

OCTOBER 10:

World Series, game three. Back in New York, the Giants

EQUIPMENT

NL batting champion Edd Roush uses the heaviest bat in the history of baseball – 48 ounces.

TRIVIA

Eddie Cicotte of the White Sox had a bonus clause in his contract that would earn him $10,000 for 30 wins. When he reaches 28, owner Charles Comiskey orders manager Clarence "Pants" Rowland to hold him out of games, and Cicotte fails to reach 30. His resentment becomes a factor in the 1919 Black Sox scandal.

RULES

Earned run averages are now official statistics in both leagues.

HISTORY

In October, six-foot, five-inch Joe Williams of the New York Lincoln Giants pitches against the New York Giants and holds them hitless while striking out 20 in 10 innings. The Giants score a single run off the Negro Leagues' star to win the game, 1-0. Ross Youngs tells Williams: "That was a hell of a game, Smokey," and the name sticks.

rebound behind the five-hit shutout pitching of Rube Benton and beat the White Sox and Ed Cicotte, 2-0. A triple by Dave Robertson and a double by Walter Holke are the big hits in the Giants' two-run fourth inning.

OCTOBER 11:

World Series, game four. In New York, the Giants tie the Series at two games with a 5-0 win. Ferdie Schupp is the winning pitcher. Red Faber takes the loss for Chicago. Benny Kauff provides most of the offense with two home runs – one with a runner on.

OCTOBER 13:

World Series, game five. In Chicago, behind Red Faber, the White Sox go up 3-2 in games with an 8-5 win. The losing pitcher for the Giants is Slim Sallee. The Giants get 12 hits, the White Sox 14. A key hit is Eddie Collins' single in a three-run eighth-inning Chicago rally.

OCTOBER 15:

World Series, game six. The White Sox become World Series champions for the second time. Today in New York, Red Faber tops Rube Benton, 4-2, for the title. Faber finishes the Series with a 3-1 record. The key play occurs in the fourth inning with no score. Eddie Collins is on third base and Joe Jackson on first for the White Sox. Happy Felsch hits back to pitcher Benton. Collins breaks for home plate and Benton throws to third baseman Heinie Zimmerman. Neither catcher Bill Rariden, Benton, nor first baseman Walter Holke covers the plate, and Zimmerman chases Collins home with a run. Chick Gandil then singles in two runs and Chicago has all the runs Faber will need. Afterward, Zimmerman will demand to know, "Who the hell was I going to throw the ball to, Klem [the home plate umpire]?" The Series' leading hitter is Dave Robertson of the Giants at .500; teammate Bill Rariden bats .385. The winning White Sox are led by Eddie Collins (.409, three stolen bases), George "Buck" Weaver (.333), and Shoeless Joe Jackson (.304).

POST-SEASON

OCTOBER 25:

Miller Huggins resigns as manager of the Cardinals to become the Yankees' skipper. Yankees' co-owner Jacob Ruppert prevails over his partner Tillinghast L'Hommedieu Huston – who wants Wilbert Robinson – and signs Huggins to a two-year contract. St. Louis was 82-70 under Huggins this past season and finished in third place.

ACCORDING TO JOURNALIST FRANK GRAHAM, AFTER THE FINAL GAME OF THE SERIES, WHITE SOX MANAGER PANTS ROWLAND STOPS JOHN MCGRAW TO TELL HIM, "MR. MCGRAW, I'M GLAD WE WON, BUT I'M SORRY YOU HAD TO BE THE ONE TO LOSE." MCGRAW RESPONDS, "GET AWAY FROM ME, YOU ______ ______ BUSHER!"

DECEMBER 11:

The Phillies trade 30-game winner Grover Cleveland Alexander (30-13, 1.86 ERA, 201 strikeouts, eight shutouts) to the Cubs along with catcher Bill Killefer (.274). In return they receive catcher Bill "Pickles" Dillhoefer (.126), as well as pitcher Mike Prendergast (3-6, 3.35 ERA) and $55,000.

DECEMBER 26:

The Cubs trade Cy Williams (.241, five homers), a former NL home run champ, to the Phillies for George "Dode" Paskert (.251, four homers).

DECEMBER 31:

Minor league manager Jack Hendricks is hired by the Cardinals to replace Miller Huggins as manager.

OCTOBER 15
The Chicago White Sox become the World Champions for the second time.

DECEMBER 11
The Phillies trade 30-game winner Grover Cleveland Alexander to the Cubs.

THE BEST OF 1917

National League

HITTERS

Batting Average:
Edd Roush, Cincinnati Reds, .341

Slugging Average:
Rogers Hornsby, St. Louis Cardinals, .484

Home Runs:
Clifford "Gavvy" Cravath, Philadelphia Phillies; Dave Robertson, New York Giants, 12

Runs Batted In:
Henry "Heinie" Zimmerman, New York Giants, 102

Hits:
Henry "Heinie" Groh, Cincinnati Reds, 182

Stolen Bases:
Max Carey, Pittsburgh Pirates, 46

PITCHERS

Wins:
Grover Cleveland Alexander, Philadelphia Phillies, 30

Strikeouts:
Grover Cleveland Alexander, 201

Earned Run Average:
Grover Cleveland Alexander, 1.86

Winning Percentage:
Ferdie Schupp, New York Giants, .750

Saves:
Harry "Slim" Sallee, New York Giants, 4

American League

HITTERS

Batting Average:
Ty Cobb, Detroit Tigers, .383

Slugging Average:
Ty Cobb, .571

Home Runs:
Wally Pipp, New York Yankees, 9

Runs Batted In:
Bobby Veach, Detroit Tigers, 103

Hits:
Ty Cobb, 225

Stolen Bases:
Ty Cobb, 55

PITCHERS

Wins:
Eddie Cicotte, Chicago White Sox, 28

Strikeouts:
Walter Johnson, Washington Senators, 188

Earned Run Average:
Eddie Cicotte, 1.53

Winning Percentage:
Ewell "Reb" Russell, Chicago White Sox, .750

Saves:
Dave Danforth, Chicago White Sox, 9

HISTORY

In the Western Association, Ernie "Crazy Snake" Calbert hits 43 home runs for Muskogee – the most in baseball to date. The highest modern major league total through 1917 was 24 by the Phillies' Gavvy Cravath in 1915. In the 19th century, Ned Williamson hit 27 for Chicago in 1884 and John "Buck" Freeman had 25 for Washington in 1899. Despite his power display, Crazy Snake never makes it to the big leagues.

1918

"I throw as hard as I can, when I think that I have to throw as hard as I can."
– *Walter Johnson*

NEWS

EDDIE RICKENBACKER SHOOTS DOWN 26 ENEMY PLANES

WORLD WAR I ENDS AT 11 A.M. ON NOVEMBER 11

GERMANY'S KAISER WILHELM ABDICATES THRONE

UP TO HALF A MILLION PEOPLE DIE IN INFLUENZA EPIDEMIC

U.S. breaks diplomatic ties with Bolshevik government in Russia

SELECTIVE SERVICE DRAFT BEGINS

Daylight Savings Time okayed by President Wilson

PRESIDENT WILSON OFFERS 14-POINT PEACE PLAN

British women over 30 given right to vote

PRE-SEASON

JANUARY 9:

Pittsburgh obtains outfielder Casey Stengel (.257) and second baseman George Cutshaw (.259) from Brooklyn for pitchers Burleigh Grimes (3-16) and Al Mamaux (2-11) and shortstop Chuck Ward (.236).

JANUARY 11:

The Philadelphia Athletics send first baseman Stuffy McInnis (.303) – one of the team's "$100,000 Infield" – to the Boston Red Sox for third baseman Larry Gardner (.265), outfielder Clarence "Tilly" Walker (.246), and catcher Forrest "Hick" Cady (.152).

JANUARY 15:

Babe Ruth signs a $7,000 contract with the Boston Red Sox for the 1918 season

JANUARY 22:

The Browns and the Yankees swing a seven-player trade. Going to the Browns are second baseman Elmer "Joe" Gedeon (.239), catcher Les Nunamaker (.261), third baseman Frederick "Fritz" Maisel (.198), and pitchers Norman "Nick" Cullup (5-9, 3.32 ERA) and Urban Shocker (8-5, 2.62 ERA). The Yankees receive pitcher Eddie Plank (5-6, 1.79 ERA), second baseman Del Pratt (.247), and $15,000.

Plank to Yanks: "No thanks." Eddie Plank, who won 327 games – the most ever by a left-handed pitcher – is 42 years old at the time of the trade. He refuses to report, turns down a three-year contract from the Yankees, and then retires.

FEBRUARY 11:

Ed Barrow is named manager of the Boston Red Sox, succeeding Jack Barry. Boston was 90-62 last season under Barry and finished in second place. Barrow was president of the International League.

APRIL 7:

Bobby Doerr is born in Los Angeles.

THE SEASON

APRIL 15:

The New York Yankees break Walter Johnson's opening day jinx, defeating the Big Train, 6-3, in Washington, D.C., with Allan Russell pitching.

APRIL 18:

Indians' center fielder Tris Speaker pulls off an unassisted double play – the fifth of his career. Against the Detroit Tigers, with two runners on base, he traps a ball hit to shallow center field, runs to the infield, tags Ossie Vitt at second base, and forces Herbert "Babe" Ellison coming from first. The Indians win the game, 6-2, behind Stan Coveleski.

APRIL 27:

After setting a modern National League record by beginning the season with nine straight losses, the Brooklyn Robins end the "schneid" by beating the undefeated New York Giants 5-3, behind Larry Cheney, who fans seven and drives in the winning run.

APRIL 29:

Tris Speaker is making the unusual routine. Today against the White Sox he executes his sixth career unassisted double play and the second in eleven days. With Eddie Collins on second and Shoeless Joe Jackson on first, Speaker traps a ball

APRIL 18
Indians' outfielder Tris Speaker pulls off the fifth unassisted double play of his career.

MAY 24
The Indians outlast the Yankees in 19 innings – the most innings ever at the Polo Grounds.

in short center field, speeds to second where he tags Collins, and then steps on the base to force Jackson. The White Sox win anyway, 8-4.

MAY 4:

The Yankees set a major league record with eight sacrifices – six bunts and two flies – against the Red Sox and Babe Ruth.

MAY 6:

In New York, Babe Ruth plays first base and bats sixth in the lineup for the Red Sox. It marks the first time he has appeared as anything but a pitcher or pinch hitter. After watching him hit a home run, the Yankees' owner, Colonel Jacob Ruppert, offers to buy Ruth. Owner Harry Frazee declines to sell his star player.

MAY 14:

Sunday baseball is okayed to be played in Washington, D.C.

MAY 15:

The Senators' Walter Johnson records the longest shutout victory in history, pitching 18 innings to beat the White Sox, 1-0. Claude "Lefty" Williams goes the distance for Chicago, allowing the winning run on a wild pitch. Johnson gives up 10 hits and one walk while fanning nine. Williams yields only eight hits, walks two, and strikes out three.

Former major league player and one-time manager of the St. Louis Cardinals and Spiders Oliver Wendell "Patsy" Tebeau commits suicide in a St. Louis saloon. He is 54 years old and describes himself in a note as "a very unhappy and miserable man." A local newspaper headline reads:

PATSY TEBEAU ACTS AS HIS OWN UMPIRE.

MAY 20:

Cleveland's Tris Speaker is hit in the head with a pitch from Boston's Carl Mays. Mays calls it accidental; Speaker insists that the beaning was intentional.

MAY 23:

Because of the Great War, the U.S. government issues a "work or fight" order. According to U.S. provost-marshal general Enoch H. Crowder, baseball players will have until July 1 to find essential work or become eligible for induction. Film actors, among others, are exempted from the order; however, baseball players are regarded as nonessential.

FRANK "PING" BODIE ON SHARING HOTEL ACCOMMODATIONS WITH BABE RUTH: "I NEVER SEE HIM. I ROOM WITH HIS SUITCASE." THIS REMARK WAS ATTRIBUTED TO OTHER RUTH ROOMMATES THROUGH THE YEARS.

MAY 24:

In the longest game by innings in Polo Grounds history, the Indians beat the Yankees, 3-2, in 19. Stan Coveleski goes all the way for the win, giving up 12 hits and six walks; George Mogridge takes the loss. Former pitcher Smoky Joe Wood, now an outfielder-infielder, hits two home runs for Cleveland, including the game winner. Yankees' third baseman Frank "Home Run" Baker handles an AL extra-inning record 11 assists.

JUNE 3:

Hubert "Dutch" Leonard of the Red Sox no-hits the Tigers, 5-0, today in Detroit. Leonard's no-hitter comes one year to the day after teammate Ernie Shore's no-hitter for the Red Sox in relief of Babe Ruth. For Leonard, who strikes out four and walks one, it is the second career no-hitter. Babe Ruth hits a home run into the right-field bleachers. The losing

LEAGUE

Among the major league players who spend all or part of the 1918 season in military uniform are Grover Cleveland Alexander, Cubs; Bob Shawkey and Wally Pipp, Yankees; Harry Heilmann, Tigers; Casey Stengel, Pittsburgh; Hank Gowdy and Rabbit Maranville, Braves; George Kelly, John "Rube" Benton, and Jesse Barnes, Giants; Eddie Collins and Red Faber, White Sox; Sam Rice, Senators; Jeff Pfeffer, Robins; Herb Pennock, Hubert "Dutch" Leonard, Jack Barry, and George "Duffy" Lewis, Red Sox.

JUNE 13
Red Sox pitcher Dutch Leonard records his third straight shutout in three starts.

LEAGUE

When play concludes for the 1918 season, the owners cut all players from their rosters to save money on the balance of the salaries due and agree not to sign each other's free agents. Brooklyn's Jake Daubert sues and settles out of court. Senators' outfielder Burt Shotton also files suit and is waived by Washington. One journalist reports "something or other turned him Bolsheviki." Shotton is signed by the Cardinals for the 1919 season.

pitcher for the Tigers is George "Hooks" Dauss.

JUNE 13:

Red Sox pitcher Dutch Leonard continues to overpower AL batters. Today he beats the White Sox, 6-0, for his third consecutive shutout in three starts.

JUNE 16:

Casey Stengel makes his return to Ebbets Field in a Pirates' uniform. During his first at-bat, he tips his cap to the Brooklyn crowd and a sparrow flies out. The Robins win the game, 1-0, when Hy Meyers steals home on the front end of a double steal.

JUNE 25:

Jake Beckley dies in Kansas City, Missouri, at age 50. The former first baseman played 20 years in the major leagues and hit .308, and is fourth all-time in triples, hitting 243 in his career.

JULY 3:

Harvey Fred Bluhm, a right-handed batter, pinch-hits for the Red Sox. But his name does not appear in some box scores and for many years the AL has no record of his at-bat. Forty years later, proof surfaces of Bluhm's existence and his single appearance. Today he has a line in the *Baseball Encyclopedia* that lists one at-bat and a string of subsequent zeroes.

JULY 8:

In Fenway Park, Babe Ruth hits a home run against Cleveland but gets credit for only a triple. Ruth comes to bat with a runner on first base in the bottom of the 10th inning and hits a drive into the right-field seats. Under 1918 rules, the game is over only when the winning run crosses home plate. The Red Sox win, 1-0.

In Philadelphia, the Tigers' Ty Cobb steals home twice against the Athletics' pitcher Scott Perry and catcher Cy Perkins.

JULY 9:

Brooklyn's Larry Cheney pitches his way into the NL record book with five wild pitches in a game against the Cardinals. St. Louis also gets 12 hits and beats the Robins, 6-4.

JULY 16:

It's another home-run-that-isn't for Babe Ruth. He comes to bat in the bottom of the ninth inning against the Browns' Lefty Leifeld and hits one out of the park. The winning run scores ahead of him, the Red Sox win, 2-1, and Ruth gets another triple and an RBI.

JULY 17:

In Chicago, the Cubs and Phillies set a major league record for fielding – they play the longest errorless game ever. In 21 innings, the Cubs win, 2-1, with George "Lefty" Tyler going all the way for the victory. Tyler fans eight and walks one. His opponent, John "Mule" Watson, also pitches a complete game, striking out five and walking four. The winning run scores on a Max Flack single, one of his five in the game.

JULY 23:

Harold "Pee Wee" Reese, the Little Colonel, is born in Ekron, Kentucky.

JULY 25:

The Senators' Walter Johnson shuts out the Browns for 15 innings on four hits, winning 1-0. In the first 11 innings, the Browns managed only one hit, a George Sisler triple.

The first game of a doubleheader with the Braves is targeted by Hal Chase and Lee Magee of the Reds for a fix. Each puts up $500 for one-third of the winnings by gamblers, who claim Pete Schneider will throw the game, but the pitcher asks manager Christy Mathewson not to start him today. Magee slows down on the bases in front of Edd Roush, on his way to an inside-the-park homer, Roush shouts, "Run, you son-of-a-bitch!" The Reds win anyway, 4-2; Magee scores the lead run on a grounder that breaks shortstop Johnny Rawlings's nose.

Magee stops payment on his check; Chase doesn't. NL president John Heydler later learns of Magee's involvement in the plot. After the 1919 season, Magee is released by the Cubs following private hearings with Heydler.

JULY 27:

Word comes from the White House: There is "no necessity at all for stopping or curtailing the baseball schedule." Earlier the secretary of war, Newton D. Baker, had indicated the baseball season should end September 2 with the World Series to follow. Both leagues vote to shorten this year's season anyway.

AUGUST 29
With a 1-0 blanking of the Reds, the Cubs clinch the National League pennant.

AUGUST 1:

The Braves' Art Nehf pitches 20 shutout innings against the Pirates and ends up the losing pitcher when Pittsburgh wins, 2-0, in the 21st inning.

AUGUST 6:

After five years in office, John K. Tener resigns as president of the NL.

At the Polo Grounds, Hal Chase is at work again; he tries to bribe Giants' pitcher Bill "Pol" Perritt.

AUGUST 9:

Reds' manager Christy Mathewson suspends first baseman Hal Chase for the remainder of the season without pay for "indifferent playing." Chase was hitting .301 at the time.

AUGUST 13:

In a statistician's dream – or is it a nightmare? – a game between the Brooklyn Robins and Pittsburgh Pirates today is called because of darkness. The score is knotted, 8-8, and each team has 38 at-bats, 13 hits, 12 assists, two errors, five strikeouts, three walks, one hit batter, and one passed ball.

AUGUST 26:

After the Pacific Coast League folds, both the Yankees and White Sox claim pitcher Jack Quinn, who plays with Chicago this season and was with the Yankees from 1909 through 1912. Quinn is awarded to the Yankees.

AUGUST 28:

Indians outfielder Tris Speaker assaults umpire John Connolly over a call at home plate. Speaker, who is hitting .318 with 33 doubles, is suspended by the league for the rest of the season.

AUGUST 29:

In Chicago, the Cubs, behind pitcher Lefty Tyler, beat the Reds, 1-0, to sew up the NL pennant.

AUGUST 30:

Theodore Samuel Williams is born in San Diego.

The New York Giants and Brooklyn Robins complete a game in only 57 minutes – the fastest nine innings ever. The Giants win the game, 1-0, beating Jack Coombs.

AUGUST 31:

In game one of a doubleheader, Babe Ruth beats the Athletics, 6-1, which clinches the pennant for the Boston Red Sox.

SEPTEMBER 1:

It's Ty Cobb versus George Sisler – on the mound. Cobb pitches two innings of relief for the Tigers against the Browns and Sisler hits a double against him. Sisler pitches one scoreless inning in relief and the Browns win the game, 6-2.

Knowing that the season originally was shortened to September 1, but apparently unaware that the owners had decided to play all the way through Labor Day (September 2), Cleveland players are under the impression they have no more games. Having been eliminated from the AL's pennant race, they refuse to travel to St. Louis to play Sunday (September 1) as well as Monday (September 2). The Browns demand a forfeit and a $1,000 per-game fine.

REGULAR SEASON WRAP-UP:

With Ed Barrow as manager, the Red Sox win their third pennant in four years. They finish at 75-51 in the abbreviated season, two and a half games ahead of Cleveland. Carl Mays is the big winner at 21-12; Babe Ruth finishes at 13-7, hits .300, and has 11 of his team's 15 homers. Clarence "Tilly" Walker also hits .300.

The Cubs, under Fred Mitchell, are 84-45, 10 1/2 games ahead of the Giants. Jim "Hippo" Vaughn is 22-10 and rookie shortstop Charlie Hollocher, at .316, has the team's top batting average.

SEPTEMBER 5:

World Series, game one. In Chicago, the Red Sox beat the Cubs, 1-0, behind Babe Ruth's complete-game six-hitter. Ruth walks one and strikes out four. The losing pitcher is Hippo Vaughn, who yields only six hits and three walks and fans six. The game is marked by a fight precipitated when Red Sox coach Heinie Wagner takes exception to insults by Vaughn, charges the Cubs' dugout, and takes on the team. Attendance is 19,274.

According to Michael Gershman, "The Star Spangled Banner" was played by a military band in the seventh inning of the game, starting a World Series

LEAGUE

With Scott Perry successfully pitching for the Athletics, the Braves exercise what they believe is a prior claim for him. The National Commission's Gary Herrman and NL president John Tener vote with the Braves; AL president Ban Johnson supports the Athletics, who go to court. Tener threatens to cancel the World Series, but is overruled by the owners. A cash settlement finally resolves the dispute and Perry stays with Philadelphia. After going 21-19 in 1918, Perry pitches three more seasons and never has a winning record.

SEPTEMBER 11
The Boston Red Sox win the World Series with a 2-1 win over the Cubs in game six.

DECEMBER 10
National League owners select John Heydler to replace John Tener as league president.

HISTORY

After "war reductions," the Red Sox each receive $890 (down from $1,102.51); the Cubs get $535 (reduced from $671.09). The National Commission reneges on a promise to give the winners diamond lapel World Series pins.

TRIVIA

During spring training, Red Sox outfielder Harry Hooper (a future Hall of Famer) suggests to new manager Ed Barrow that he make an everyday player out of pitcher Babe Ruth. Barrow rejects the idea, but Hooper persists and Ruth debuts as a first baseman on May 6.

tradition that has seen the national anthem played at every baseball game since.

SEPTEMBER 6:

World Series, game two. In Chicago, the Cubs and George "Lefty" Tyler beat the Red Sox and Joe Bush, 3-1, with 20,040 on hand. Tyler drives in two runs with a second inning single. On the mound, he walks four and strikes out two. In the ninth inning Boston's Amos Strunk and George Whiteman triple for Boston's only run. Joe Bush walks three. Boston coach Heinie Wagner and Hippo Vaughn are again involved in a fight and pitcher Bush and the Cubs' Lester Mann also go at it.

SEPTEMBER 7:

World Series, game three. In Chicago, Carl Mays allows Chicago seven hits and Boston wins, 2-1. Hippo Vaughn goes all the way for the losers. Mays walks one, strikes out four. Vaughn issues one base on balls and fans seven. Each pitcher allows seven hits. An Everett Scott single in the fourth inning drives in Stuffy McInnis with the deciding run. In the bottom of the ninth with two out, the Cubs' Charlie Pick is out in a rundown after trying to score from second base on a passed ball. Attendance is 27,054.

SEPTEMBER 9:

World Series, game four. In Boston, 22,183 see Babe Ruth win his second game, beating the Cubs and Shufflin' Phil Douglas, 3-2. Ruth extends his consecutive scoreless inning string to 29 2/3 – a World Series record. The streak, which began in the 1916 World Series, ends when the Cubs score twice in the eighth. Boston scores the winning run in the eighth on a passed ball and a wild throw. Ruth walks six and strands six Cubs runners.

SEPTEMBER 10:

World Series, game five. In Boston, while 24,694 fans wait, the threat of a players' strike holds up the start of the game. Under a plan by outgoing NL president John K. Tener, players' shares were cut to less than $1,000 for the winners and less than $500 for the losers. The Red Sox and Cubs want $1,500 for each winning player and $1,000 for each member of the losing team. While the teams remain in their dressing rooms, Boston's Harry Hooper and Chicago's Les Mann meet with baseball's National Commission under the stands. After Gary Herrmann reminds them they have contracts, the protest is ended and the teams take the field one hour late. Former Boston mayor John F. "Honey Fitz" Fitzgerald announces to the fans, "The players have agreed to play for the sake of the public and the wounded soldiers in the stands." The Cubs win the game, 3-0, as Hippo Vaughn allows only five hits and outpitches Sad Sam Jones. Both pitchers go all the way.

SEPTEMBER 11:

World Series, game six. In Boston, Carl Mays three-hits the Cubs and Boston wins the World Series with a 2-1 victory. George Tyler takes the loss. The Red Sox score both of their runs in the third inning on an error by outfielder Max Flack. Attendance is 15,238.

POST-SEASON

SEPTEMBER 25:

Phil Rizzuto is born in New York City.

OCTOBER 5:

Former major league infielder Eddie Grant, an infantry battalion captain, is killed in action at Argonne Forest, France, at age 35. A Harvard graduate, Grant played 10 years with the Indians, Phillies, Reds, and Giants. He retired in 1916 with a lifetime batting average of .249. Known as Harvard Eddie in baseball, Grant is the only major leaguer killed in action in World War I.

NOVEMBER 3:

Bob Feller is born in Van Meter, Iowa.

DECEMBER 10:

Today John Heydler is selected by the National League owners as their president, replacing John K. Tener. Heydler gets a three-year term at $12,000 per annum.

DECEMBER 31:

William "Kid" Gleason is named the new manager of the Chicago White Sox. He will replace outgoing skipper Clarence "Pants" Rowland. Under Rowland this past season, Chicago finished with a record of 57-67, which landed the ball club in sixth place.

THE BEST OF 1918

NATIONAL LEAGUE

HITTERS

Batting Average:
Zack Wheat, Brooklyn Robins, .335

Slugging Average:
Edd Roush, Cincinnati Reds, .455

Home Runs:
Clifford "Gavvy" Cravath, Philadelphia Phillies, 8

Runs Batted In:
Sherry Magee, Cincinnati Reds, 76

Hits:
Charlie Hollocher, Chicago Cubs, 161

Stolen Bases:
Max Carey, Pittsburgh Pirates, 58

PITCHERS

Wins:
James "Hippo" Vaughn, Chicago Cubs, 22

Strikeouts:
James Vaughn, 148

Earned Run Average:
James Vaughn, 1.74

Winning Percentage:
Claude Hendrix, Chicago Cubs, .731

Saves:
Fred Toney, Cincinnati Reds, New York Giants; Joe Oeschger, Philadelphia Phillies; Wilbur Cooper, Pittsburgh Pirates; Fred Anderson, New York Giants, 3

AMERICAN LEAGUE

HITTERS

Batting Average:
Ty Cobb, Detroit Tigers, .382

Slugging Average:
Babe Ruth, Boston Red Sox, .555

Home Runs:
Babe Ruth; Clarence "Tilly" Walker, Philadelphia Athletics, 11

Runs Batted In:
Bobby Veach, Detroit Tigers, 78

Hits:
George Burns, Philadelphia Athletics, 178

Stolen Bases:
George Sisler, St. Louis Browns, 45

PITCHERS

Wins:
Walter Johnson, Washington Senators, 23

Strikeouts:
Walter Johnson, 162

Earned Run Average:
Walter Johnson, 1.27

Winning Percentage:
Sam Jones, Boston Red Sox, .762

Saves:
George Mogridge, New York Yankees, 7

HISTORY

In December, in France, where they are officers in the Chemical Warfare Service training soldiers, Ty Cobb and Christy Mathewson are involved in a gas chamber mishap. Cobb has minimal exposure to the gas. Mathewson, who had resigned as Reds' manager with 10 days to go in the season to enlist, inhales a larger amount. Some attribute Mathewson's later bout with tuberculosis and his death at age 45 in 1925 to the accident.

1919

NEWS

Prohibition ratified by Congress, despite Woodrow Wilson's veto

FORMER PRESIDENT THEODORE ROOSEVELT DIES

PEACE CONFERENCE CONVENES IN PARIS

Communist Labor Party founded in U.S

PRESIDENT WILSON SUFFERS STROKE

SENATE VOTES DOWN TREATY OF VERSAILLES

MASSACHUSETTS GOVERNOR CALVIN COOLIDGE PUTS DOWN BOSTON POLICE STRIKE

Mechanical rabbit ushers in modern greyhound racing

BRITISH SCIENTIST ERNEST RUTHERFORD SPLITS ATOM

PRE-SEASON

JANUARY 8:

James "Orator Jim" O'Rourke dies today in Bridgeport, Connecticut, at age 68. O'Rourke, who played every position except pitcher in his 19-year career, batted .310. From 1881 to 1884, he managed the Buffalo Bisons in the NL, and in 1893 he served as the skipper of the Washington Senators.

JANUARY 14:

A syndicate headed by stockbroker Charles A. Stoneham, New York City magistrate Francis X. McQuade, and manager John J. McGraw buys the Giants for more than $1 million from Harry N. Hempstead. McGraw will remain as manager while functioning also as a vice president. Stoneham has questionable business ties to gambler Arnold Rothstein in a "bucket shop" – an operation that takes stock orders and doesn't execute them.

JANUARY 26:

Branch Rickey replaces Jack Hendricks as manager of the Cardinals. Rickey will continue as the team's president and will maintain his current salary increase of $15,000 per year. Under Hendricks, St. Louis finished last in the league in 1918 with a record of 51-78.

JANUARY 30:

NL president John Heydler holds a hearing on charges that Hal Chase attempted to bribe a teammate in a game last season and was throwing games. Chase is present with three attorneys, clerk, and stenographer. Christy Mathewson is with the military in France and unable to testify in person; he submits an affidavit. Chase maintains that the money he gave pitcher Jimmy Ring was merely a gift.

JANUARY 31:

Jack Roosevelt Robinson is born in Cairo, Georgia.

FEBRUARY 1:

Brooklyn trades its first baseman, Jake Daubert (.301), to the Reds for outfielder Tommy Griffith (.265). Daubert, a former NL Most Valuable Player and a two-time batting champion, had sued Brooklyn for one month's pay he lost because of the shortened season.

FEBRUARY 2:

With Christy Mathewson on his way home from Europe, the Reds trade first baseman Hal Chase (.301) to the Giants for catcher Bill Rariden (.224).

FEBRUARY 5:

Without Christy Mathewson's first-hand testimony, NL president John Heydler finds there is insufficient evidence against Hal Chase and clears him. Heydler states: "In justice to Chase, I feel bound to state that both the evidence and the records of the games to which reference was made, fully refute this accusation." He states that Chase "acted in a foolish and careless manner both on the field and among the players..."

FEBRUARY 25:

Merrill Monford "Monte" Irvin is born in Columbia, Alabama.

APRIL 3:

It's a press agent's delight: In Jacksonville, Florida, Yankees' outfielder Frank "Ping"

JANUARY 26
Branch Rickey replaces Jack Hendricks as manager of the St. Louis Cardinals.

MAY 20
Babe Ruth hits his first career grand slam, off Browns' pitcher Dave Davenport.

Bodie faces off against Percy the ostrich in a spaghetti-eating contest. After 11 servings each, Percy passes out and Ping prevails.

APRIL 12:

A District of Columbia court awards the Baltimore Terrapins of the now-defunct Federal League triple damages of $240,000. Terrapins' principals Ned Hanlon and Harvey Goldman had been left out of the "peace settlement" with organized baseball.

THE SEASON

APRIL 23:

The Senators' Walter Johnson shuts out the Athletics, 1-0, in 13 innings on opening day. It is his record fifth opening day shutout.

MAY 11:

In the first Yankees' Sunday home ball game, Walter Johnson of the Senators pitches 12 scoreless innings, at one stretch retiring 28 Yanks in a row and allowing only two hits. Matching Johnson is Jack Quinn in a 0-0 game. One of Johnson's principal victims is George Halas, who strikes out twice and is retired in three other at-bats. Halas makes his mark in the NFL as the owner and longtime coach of the Chicago Bears.

BABE RUTH TELLS SPORTSWRITER GRANTLAND RICE: "I MAY BE A PITCHER, BUT FIRST OFF I'M A HITTER. I COPIED MY SWING AFTER JOE JACKSON'S. HIS IS THE PERFECTEST."

Walter Johnson's pitching feat is overshadowed by Hod Eller of the Reds, who no-hits the Cardinals, 6-0, in St. Louis, striking out eight and walking three; his teammates play errorless baseball. Frank "Jakie" May gets the loss.

MAY 12:

The Yankees and Senators play their second consecutive unresolved baseball marathon. Before 2,000 fans at the Polo Grounds, the teams go 15 innings and end up tied, 4-4. Walter Johnson allows two singles and a walk; at one point he retires 28 straight. Jack Quinn allows nine hits. The Yankees are up 3-1 in the eighth, but Joe Judge hits a home run and an error permits a second run to tie the game. Yesterday, the Yankees and Senators went 12 innings in a game called because of darkness with no score.

MAY 15:

It's better late than never for the Reds. At Ebbets Field, they break a 0-0 tie with 10 runs off Brooklyn's Al Mamauz in the 13th inning and win the game, 10-0.

MAY 20:

Red Sox pitcher Babe Ruth hits his first career grand slam today; the bomb comes against Dave

Joe Jackson, according to Babe Ruth, had the "perfectest" swing.

LEAGUE

Cardinals' president Branch Rickey buys the Houston franchise in the Texas League, beginning the creation of the first pioneering, extensive minor league farm system. In the 1900s, John T. Brush owned the major league Cincinnati Reds and Indianapolis in the Western League, but did not expand on his baseball holdings.

JUNE 23
The Phillies' Clifford Cravath ties a major league record by hitting four doubles.

LEAGUE

The White Sox represent a lot of Charles Comiskey's money: Shoeless Joe Jackson was purchased for $65,000, Eddie Collins for $50,000, and Happy Felsch for $12,000. After the 1909 season, Comiskey also invested $500,000 to increase the seating capacity of his ballpark to 33,000 seats. Yet he is tightfisted with his players, a trait that will be a factor in baseball's greatest scandal.

Davenport of the Browns in St. Louis. Boston wins, 6-4.

JUNE 23:

The Phillies' Clifford "Gavvy" Cravath ties the major league record for doubles in a game for the second time in his career, banging out four two-baggers today. He previously accomplished the feat on August 8, 1915.

JUNE 27:

The Athletics reacquire shortstop Jack Barry (.241), an original member of the "$100,000 Infield," along with outfielder Amos Strunk (.272). In return, Philadelphia sends outfielder Robert "Braggo" Roth (.323) and shortstop Maurice "Red" Shannon (.271) to the Red Sox. Barry refuses to return to Philadelphia and retires. He completes his 11-year career in the majors with a .243 batting average.

JULY 1:

The Brooklyn Robins' first baseman Ed Konetchy goes 5-for-5 today against the Phillies, giving him a major league record-tying 10 consecutive hits the last two days. Brooklyn wins, 9-4.

JULY 7:

The Phillies steal eight bases in the ninth inning against the Giants' catcher Miguel Gonzalez in the second game of a doubleheader. Gonzalez matches the unenviable mark of Steve O'Neill in 1915.

JULY 9:

Yankees' shortstop Roger Peckinpaugh hits in his 29th consecutive game. But New York loses, 2-0, to Cleveland, ending pitcher Bob Shawkey's 10-game winning streak.

The Chicago White Sox move into first place in the AL.

JULY 12:

Following a 5-0 loss to the White Sox in Chicago, Carl Mays says he will never pitch again for the Red Sox. He states, "I have pitched the best ball of my life, but I am not winning... The team just doesn't win when I'm pitching, so I'm going home to Pennsylvania." Mays is 5-11 this season.

JULY 18:

At League Park in Cleveland, Babe Ruth hits a grand slam home run in the top of the ninth inning to beat the Indians, 8-7. It is the third grand slam of the season for Ruth and it breaks the Red Sox nine-game losing streak. It also produces a change of managers for Cleveland. With the Indians up 7-4 and Ruth coming to bat, center fielder Tris Speaker – who in effect runs the team – signals for a pitching change. Manager Lee Fohl misunderstands and brings in the wrong pitcher – Frederick "Fritz" Coumbe – to relieve Elmer Myers. Ruth hits Coumbe's second pitch – a slow curve – over the right-field wall. Immediately after the game, Fohl leaves the dugout and resigns. Speaker becomes manager in name as well as in practice. Fohl departs with a 44-34 record.

JULY 21:

In Detroit, Boston's Babe Ruth clears the right-field fence with the longest homer ever at Navin Field.

JULY 29:

The Yankees acquire the unhappy Carl Mays for pitchers Allan Russell (5-5) and Bob McGraw (1-0), plus $40,000. AL president Ban Johnson intervenes and orders Mays back to Boston. The Yankees refuse. Johnson instructs his umpires to prevent Mays from playing; the Yankees will go to court.

In Boston, Babe Ruth hits a two-out homer in the bottom of the ninth inning off Hubert "Dutch" Leonard with Robert "Braggo" Roth on base. It is not enough to win the game against the Tigers, but it is Ruth's ninth homer in the month of July – tying an AL record – and his 16th of the young season. Previously, he had two doubles. Detroit wins the game, 10-8.

AUGUST 2:

Phillies first baseman Fred Luderus appears today in his 479th consecutive game, surpassing the major league record set by Eddie Collins. Luderus's streak began on June 2, 1916.

NL owners hold a special meeting in New York City and vote to shorten the season to September 1.

AUGUST 3:

The Yankees seek an injunction from New York City judge Robert F. Wagner against Ban Johnson in the Carl Mays case. Tigers' owner Frank Navin threatens to

AUGUST 24
Indians' pitcher Ray Caldwell is struck by lightning, but recovers and beats the A's.

keep his Tigers off the field against the Yankees if Mays is allowed to stay. The Yankees have the support of owners Harry Frazee of the Red Sox and Charles Comiskey of the White Sox. The five others support Ban Johnson.

AUGUST 6:

What a way to lose! In Chicago, the Cubs' Grover Cleveland Alexander loses, 2-0, to the Braves when a fly ball off the bat of rival pitcher Ray Keating finds a hole in the wire fence in center field and goes through for a home run. Alexander gets little offensive support; the Cubs manage only three hits.

Judge Robert F. Wagner grants the Yankees a temporary injunction; additional briefs are to be filed. The Yankees' owners, Col. Jacob Ruppert and Capt. Tillinghast L'Hommedieu Huston, instruct manager Miller Huggins to schedule Mays to pitch.

AUGUST 9:

Despite the controversy and court actions, Carl Mays debuts as a Yankees pitcher, defeating the visiting Indians, 6-4.

The Phillies obtain outfielder Casey Stengel (.293) from the Pirates for infielder-outfielder George "Possum" Whitted (.249). Stengel, whose demand for a raise is turned down by Phillies' owner William Baker, goes home to Kansas City and embarks on a barnstorming tour for the remainder of the season.

AUGUST 15:

Babe Ruth hits a home run over the right-field bleachers against Erskine Mayer in Comiskey Park today, but his Red Sox lose to the White Sox, 7-6. The *Chicago Tribune* describes it as "the most thrilling base hit that Chicago fans have seen since the days of Captain Anson."

AUGUST 24:

Lightning strikes Indians' pitcher Ray Caldwell – literally – during his windup. He recovers and pitches Cleveland to a 2-1 victory over the Athletics.

AUGUST 31:

At least they had each other to talk to. Manager Wilbert Robinson and the batboy are the only ones left on the Brooklyn bench thanks to the thumb of umpire Bill Klem, who's heard enough from the Robins in the seventh inning. To make it worse for Robinson – and the batboy – the Giants score three times in the frame and win, 4-3. And, as a final blow, Robins' pitcher Burleigh Grimes is spiked at first base and will end up missing the rest of the season.

SEPTEMBER 8:

Babe Ruth hits his 25th homer of the season, matching the major league record set by John "Buck" Freeman in 1899.

SEPTEMBER 10:

At the Polo Grounds, the Indians' Ray Caldwell no-hits the Yankees, 3-0. The Yankees have only two base runners – one on a walk and the other by error; Caldwell strikes out five. Carl Mays gets the loss. Joe Harris has a home run for Cleveland.

SEPTEMBER 11:

After appearing in both games of yesterday's doubleheader against the Chicago Cubs, Heinie Zimmerman is out of the lineup in today's game. Fred Toney is on the mound for New York and allegedly is approached by Zimmerman with a bribe offer at the end of the first. Toney goes two innings, allowing two hits and no runs, then asks to be removed. The Giants win the game. That evening John "Rube" Benton is offered "easy money" by Zimmerman and the Cubs' Charles "Buck" Herzog to dump tomorrow's game.

SEPTEMBER 12:

After Rube Benton beats the Cubs, he is approached by Heinie Zimmerman in a bar at night and, according to *The Sporting News*, Zimmerman tells him, "You poor fish, don't you know there was $400 waiting for you to lose that game today?"

SEPTEMBER 16:

The Reds beat the Giants, 4-3, behind Walter "Dutch" Ruether, to clinch the NL pennant.

SEPTEMBER 18:

The World Series fix is born in a room in Boston's Hotel Buckminster, when White Sox first baseman Arnold "Chick" Gandil tells bookmaker-gambler Joseph

HISTORY

Hal Chase may change his teams, but not his ways. Now with the Giants, Chase enlists his new teammate Henry "Heinie" Zimmerman and together they try to bribe fellow Giants John "Rube" Benton, Lee Magee, Fred Toney, and Jean Dubuc.

HISTORY

The next target for Hal Chase and Heinie Zimmerman is teammate Benny Kauff, who is offered $125 for each game he throws. Zimmerman is quietly suspended by McGraw, but Chase remains with the team.

SEPTEMBER 24
Babe Ruth sets a new major league home run record, hitting his 28th of the season.

"I think we can put it [the World Series] in the bag."
– Arnold "Chick" Gandil

LEAGUE

Because of the world war, major league owners cut the season to 140 games, reduce rosters to 21, and will begin spring training two weeks later than usual.

"Sport" Sullivan, "I think we can put it [the World Series] in the bag." He asks Sullivan for $80,000. Some sources indicate the amount was $100,000. Eliot Asinof, author of the definitive book *Eight Men Out,* puts it at $80,000.

SEPTEMBER 19:

Arnold "Chick" Gandil is busy soliciting his teammates for the World Series fix. He recruits Charles "Swede" Risberg. They are overheard by Fred McMullen, who demands that he be included. Claude "Lefty" Williams at first is not interested, but then agrees to join the conspiracy when he learns it will go forward with or without him. Eddie Cicotte will participate for $10,000 upfront.

SEPTEMBER 20:

In game one of a Fenway Park doubleheader, Babe Ruth drives a pitch from the White Sox' Lefty Williams over the left-field wall. It is Ruth's 27th homer of the season, tying Edward "Ned" Williamson's major league record, set in 1884. Many of Williamson's homers were hit over a wall only 200 feet from home plate.

Gandil and his fellow plotters – Ed Cicotte, Happy Felsch, Shoeless Joe Jackson, Fred McMullin, Swede Risberg, and Buck Weaver – meet at the Hotel Ansonia in New York and decide to see if gambler-bookmaker Joseph "Sport" Sullivan delivers the cash.

Former major league outfielder James "Cy" Seymour dies penniless at age 46 in New York City. In 16 years, Seymour – whose career ended in 1913 – batted .304 and stole 222 bases.

SEPTEMBER 21:

The Cubs' Grover Cleveland Alexander spins a 58-minute five-hitter, beating the Boston Braves, 3-0.

The trend toward fast-paced games continues. Brooklyn and Cincinnati complete today's game in only 55 minutes, with the Robins winning, 3-1. Losing pitcher Harry "Slim" Sallee throws only 65 pitches, an NL record.

Ed Cicotte briefs William "Sleepy Bill" Burns, a gambler and former major league pitcher. Cicotte agrees to involve Burns in the fix. Burns, operating independently of Sport Sullivan, brings in Billy Maharg, described by author Eliot Asinof as a "third-rate character" and an "ex-fighter," to proceed with the fix.

SEPTEMBER 23:

Sleepy Bill Burns and Billy Maharg offer to meet with gambler Arnold Rothstein and former world featherweight champion Abe Attell at Jamaica Race Track. Rothstein turns down their proposal and without him, Burns and Maharg drop their fix.

SEPTEMBER 24:

Babe Ruth breaks Ned Williamson's home run mark when he hits his 28th of the season, a ninth-inning drive over the right-field roof of the Polo Grounds into Manhattan Field. The *New York Times* describes the blast as the "longest ever made at the Polo Grounds." The historic homer is hit off a slow curve from the Yankees' Bob Shawkey. The teams split a doubleheader. Nearly 5,000 fans see Ruth set the record in 139 games.

The White Sox are officially in the World Series. By defeating the Browns, 6-5, Chicago mathematically eliminates the Indians and wins the AL pennant.

At Navin Field, the Tigers meet the Indians in a game with significance for Detroit. Cleveland has clinched second place, but the Detroit players can earn approximately $500 each – coming from World Series moneys – if they beat out the Yankees for third place. Ty Cobb gets one hit in four at-bats and the Tigers win, 9-5, on 18 hits. Tris Speaker of the Indians has two triples and a single. This game, played against the backdrop of the impending World Series, gets little attention at the time. But later it will have serious implications for the reputations of Cobb and Speaker and for the integrity of baseball.

Abe Attell tells Sleepy Bill Burns that Arnold Rothstein has reconsidered and will provide $100,000 for the fix. But Rothstein's name cannot be used. He shows Burns, Chick Gandil, and Billy Maharg a telegram from Rothstein. The Rothstein telegram later is disclosed to be a fake.

SEPTEMBER 26:

Sport Sullivan discusses the fix with Arnold Rothstein, whose level of interest

SEPTEMBER 29
Arnold Rothstein decides to finance the fix of the World Series.

OCTOBER 1
The "fixed" World Series between the White Sox and Reds opens in Cincinnati.

seems different three days after he rejected the Burns-Maharg proposal. He sends Nat Evans, one of his partners, to talk to the Chicago players.

SEPTEMBER 27:

In Washington, Babe Ruth adds to his newly set home run record with his 29th of the season today. However, the Senators sweep a doubleheader, 7-5 and 4-1.

SEPTEMBER 28:

With a game to go, Hal Chase leaves the Giants. When Chase is revealed to be missing from his New York hotel, McGraw lies that the first baseman is not well and has returned to California. In the spring of 1920, when questioned about Zimmerman and Chase, McGraw responds, "I cannot talk of the matter. If anything is to be said, it must come from the players. As far as the Giants are concerned, Chase and Zimmerman are through." According to McGraw biographer Charles C. Alexander, his "genuine fondness for a man whom he and his wife had known for thirteen years apparently kept him from acting on what, by his own account, he strongly suspected as early as August. " McGraw later tells *The Sporting News*: "In my opinion Chase deliberately threw us down. I never was more deceived by a player than by Chase."

Sport Sullivan and Nat Evans meet with Chick Gandil in Chicago amid growing suspicion between the gamblers and the White Sox. Lefty Williams wants out; Joe Jackson demands $20,000.

The Giants, who completed a game in a record 57 minutes last year, take only 51 today to put away the Phillies, 6-1, in the first game of a doubleheader at the Polo Grounds. The winning pitcher is Jesse Barnes on a five-hitter; Lee Meadows gets the loss.

SEPTEMBER 29:

Arnold Rothstein decides to finance the World Series fix. The plan calls for Nat Evans to deliver $40,000 to Sport Sullivan for distribution to the White Sox "eight." An additional $40,000 will be put in the safe at the Hotel Congress in Chicago for the players if the fix is successful. Sullivan siphons off $29,000 and bets it on the Reds; he gives Chick Gandil only $10,000. Ed Cicotte finds the $10,000 he demanded under his pillow and sews it into the lining of his jacket.

Rothstein bets $90,000 with oilman Harry Sinclair. His bets total $270,000 and drive down the odds from 8-5 on Chicago to even money. In Cincinnati, the players, minus Joe Jackson, meet in Ed Cicotte's room with William "Sleepy" Burns and Rothstein "associate" Abe Attell. The players are told they will receive $20,000 after each loss. But word is leaking out; a newspaper man tells Gandil he's heard rumors of a fix.

REGULAR SEASON WRAP-UP:

Cincinnati manager Pat Moran is the first manager to win pennants with two different teams; in 1915, he was the pilot of the NL champion Phillies. The Reds finish at 99-44, nine games ahead of the Giants. Harry "Slim" Sallee (21-7) and Horace "Hod" Eller (20-9) are the top pitchers. Center fielder Edd Roush leads the team and the NL in batting with a .321 average.

William "Kid" Gleason wins a pennant in his first year as a manager, leading the White Sox to an 88-52 record and beating the Indians by three and a half games. Eddie Cicotte is 29-7 with a 1.82 ERA and Lefty Williams at 23-11 top the Chicago staff. Shoeless Joe Jackson (.351) and Eddie "Cocky" Collins (.319) are the top hitters.

The once-mighty Philadelphia Athletics lose 104 games and finish last for the fifth straight season. Ty Cobb wins his 12th batting title with a .384 average.

OCTOBER 1:

World Series, game one. In Cincinnati, before the game Joe Jackson asks manager Kid Gleason to bench him; his request is denied. In the bottom of the first, Chicago's starting pitcher Eddie Cicotte signals the fix is on by hitting the leadoff batter, Maurice Rath, with the first pitch. Arnold Rothstein responds by betting an additional $100,000 on Cincinnati. Cicotte makes a bad throw in the fourth on a routine double play ball; the Reds score five runs in the inning to go up 6-1. They

HISTORY

NL president John Heydler obtains a copy of a $500 check from a Boston gambler to Hal Chase as payment for an allegedly fixed game.

"If we can't win for Cicotte and Williams, we're not gonna win for no bushers."
– *Chick Gandil*

go on to wallop the White Sox, 9-1. First baseman Chick Gandil commits an error. Walter "Dutch" Ruether is the winning pitcher; Cicotte is the losing pitcher. Attendance is 30,511.

Abe Attell does not deliver $20,000 as promised to Bill Burns and Billy Maharg; the former boxer claims all of the money is tied up in bets. J. G. Taylor Spink, publisher of *The Sporting News*, informs Ban Johnson of the rumors and suspicions surrounding the Series. At 11 p.m. White Sox owner Charles Comiskey and manager Kid Gleason discuss the possibility that the Series is fixed. After midnight, Comiskey talks to NL president John Heydler. Then, at 3 a.m. Comiskey expresses his concerns to AL president Ban Johnson who responds, "That is the yelp of a beaten cur."

OCTOBER 2:

With Lefty Williams present, Chick Gandil tells Abe Attell, Bill Burns, and Billy Maharg he wants $20,000. Attell insists there will be no money until after the game, but he leaves a Texas oil lease as security.

According to Grantland Rice, during game two, his sportswriting colleague Ring Lardner was "pounding his typewriter furiously. He kept humming, I'm Forever Blowing Bubbles. His bitter parody of that song, dedicated to Williams, opened with, 'I'm forever blowing ball games.'"

World Series, game two. In Cincinnati, the Reds go up two games to none, with a 4-2 win, before a crowd of 30,511. Slim Sallee is the game's winning pitcher. Lefty Williams, who walks three men in the fourth and gives up a two-run triple to Larry Kopf, leading to three Reds' runs, is tagged with the loss. Shortstop Swede Risberg makes an error. After the game, Chick Gandil is beaten up by manager Kid Gleason; catcher Ray Schalk attacks Lefty Williams under the grandstands.

Gandil is getting suspicious of the promises the players have been receiving, after Bill Burns and Billy Maharg seek $40,000 from Abe Attell and get $10,000.

OCTOBER 3:

Chick Gandil tells Sleepy Bill Burns the fix is on for game three. He says, referring to Dickie Kerr, the starting pitcher for the game, "If we can't win for Cicotte and Williams, we're not gonna win for no busher." Burns and Billy Maharg then bet all their money on the Reds.

World Series, game three. In Chicago, Dickie Kerr pitches a three-hitter and the White Sox get their first win, 3-0. Kerr walks one and fans four. A second-inning double by Chick Gandil produces two runs. The losing pitcher is Ray Fisher. Attendance is 29,126.

Burns and Maharg go back to Abe Attell for $20,000 for the players to ensure a loss in game four. Attell expresses his distrust for the eight White Sox. The players claim they will not dump any more games. Burns is turned down for a $1,000 fee and threatens to reveal the conspiracy.

OCTOBER 4:

Sport Sullivan panics when another gambler wants to bet on the White Sox. Chick Gandil tells Sullivan the fix is off. Sullivan then offers $20,000 prior to game four and another $20,000 before game five if the White Sox agree to resume dumping. Gandil takes the $20,000 and distributes $5,000 each to Happy Felsch, Joe Jackson, Swede Risberg, and Lefty Williams. Fred McMullen and Buck Weaver get nothing.

World Series, game four. In Chicago, the Reds, behind Jimmy

Cincinnati World Series ticket

OCTOBER 9
The Reds win game eight of the World Series, beating the White Sox, 10-5.

Ring's three-hitter, beat Ed Cicotte and the White Sox, 2-0. Cicotte's two errors in the fifth inning open the door for both of the Reds' runs. Attendance is 34,363. On one play, Cicotte gets his glove in the way of a throw to the plate by Shoeless Joe Jackson and diverts it.

OCTOBER 6:

World Series, game five. In Chicago, with Hod Eller pitching a three-hitter, the Reds win again, 5-0, defeating Chicago's Lefty Williams. Once again, the White Sox fielding is shoddy – second baseman Eddie Collins, first baseman Chick Gandil, and shortstop Swede Risberg all commit errors. Attendance at the game is 34,379.

OCTOBER 7:

World Series, game six. In Cincinnati, Dickie Kerr goes 10 innings to beat the Reds, 5-4, overcoming errors by shortstop Swede Risberg and center fielder Happy Felsch. Chicago's Chick Gandil singles in Buck Weaver with the winning run in the top of the 10th. The losing pitcher is Jimmy Ring. Attendance is 32,006.

The players do not get the promised $20,000; Sport Sullivan doesn't show up to meet them.

OCTOBER 8:

World Series, game seven. In Cincinnati, the White Sox stay alive by beating the Reds, 4-1, behind Eddie Cicotte's seven-hitter. This time Cincinnati's fielding is flawed; the Reds commit four errors. The losing pitcher is Slim Sallee. Joe Jackson singles in John "Shano" Collins with the lead run. Attendance is 13,923 fans.

Eddie Cicotte, it should be noted, was the top pitcher in the AL in 1919, with a 29-7 record, an .806 winning percentage, 306 2/3 innings pitched, and 30 complete games.

OCTOBER 9:

World Series, game eight. Back in Chicago, the Reds wrap up the game and the Series early; they score four runs in the first against Lefty Williams, who retires only one batter. The Reds coast to a 10-5 victory and Williams gets his third loss of the series. Hod Eller strikes out six and goes all the way for the win despite a Joe Jackson homer.

CINCINNATI OUTFIELDER AND HALL OF FAMER EDD ROUSH REFLECTS ON THE 1919 WORLD SERIES: "ONE THING THAT'S ALWAYS OVERLOOKED IN THE WHOLE MESS IS THAT WE COULD HAVE BEATEN THEM NO MATTER WHAT THE CIRCUMSTANCES!" ACCORDING TO SOME BASEBALL HISTORIANS, ROUSH NOTIFIED CINCINNATI MANAGEMENT OF BRIBE ATTEMPTS AND BELIEVED THAT SOME OF HIS TEAMMATES WERE PLAYING LESS THAN THEIR BEST. THE UNANSWERED AND PROBABLY UNANSWERABLE QUESTION FOR THE BASEBALL AGES IS: WERE THE REDS DOING A WORSE JOB OF DUMPING THAN THE WHITE SOX?

HISTORY

Outfielder Joe Wilhoit of Wichita Wolves in the Class A Western League sets an organized baseball record in 1919 when he hits in 69 consecutive games. Wilhoit plays parts of four seasons – including six games with the Red Sox in 1919 – and bats .257. Over the 61 games, he has 151 hits and an average of .505. He plays in the major leagues with the Braves, Pirates, Giants and Red Sox, hitting only .257 in a total of 283 games.

OCTOBER 15
Charles Comiskey offers a $20,000 reward for clues about a World Series fix.

DECEMBER 26
Red Sox owner Harry Frazee signs a secret deal to sell Babe Ruth to the Yankees.

LEAGUE

Because of the World War, major league owners cut the season to 140 games, reduce rosters to 21, and will begin spring training two weeks later than usual.

Swede Risberg commits an error. The series is not marked by crisp fielding: the White Sox commit 12 errors, the Reds 11. Dickie Kerr, not involved in the fix, has a 1.41 ERA to go with his two wins. Alfred "Greasy" Neale paces the Red regulars with .317. For Chicago, Joe Jackson bats .375 and Buck Weaver .324. Catcher Ray Schalk chips in at .304.

POST-SEASON

OCTOBER 10:

Shoeless Joe Jackson asks for a meeting with owner Charles Comiskey. After waiting in vain for two hours, he goes home to Georgia. Sport Sullivan and Nat Evans retrieve $40,000 from the Congress Hotel safe. In Chick Gandil's room they distribute: $15,000 to Swede Risberg, $5,000 to Fred McMullin (who had only two Series at-bats) and $35,000 to Gandil.

OCTOBER 15:

Charles Comiskey offers a reward of $20,000 for a "single clue" about a World Series fix. Shoeless Joe Jackson writes to the White Sox owner, but the letter is ignored.

Detectives hired by Comiskey report back: Chick Gandil has purchased a home, a car, and jewelry.

OCTOBER 23:

Today from Augusta, Georgia, Ty Cobb corresponds with his pitcher Hubert "Dutch" Leonard about the Tigers-Indians game on September 24. Cobb writes (in part), "[Smoky Joe] Wood and myself were considerably disappointed in our business proposition, as we had $2,000 to put into it and the other side quoted us $1,400, and when we finally secured that much money it was about 2 o'clock and they refused to deal with me, as they had men in Chicago to take up the matter with and they had no time, so we completely fell down and of course we feel badly over it... It was quite a responsibility and I don't care for it again, I can assure you."

Joe Wood also writes to Leonard (in part): "Enclosed please find certified check for sixteen hundred and thirty dollars. The only bet West could get down was $600 against $240 (10-7). Cobb did not get up a cent. He told us and I believed him. Could have put some 5-2 on Detroit, but did not, as that would make us put up $1,000 to win $400. We won the $420. I gave West $30, leaving $390 or $30 for each of us... We would have won $1,750 for the $2,500 if we could have placed it."

OCTOBER 25:

Judge Robert F. Wagner rules that AL clubs can conduct their business without interference from league president Ban Johnson and he awards a permanent injunction to the Yankees in the Carl Mays case.

OCTOBER 29:

Baseball's National Commission withholds the third place share of World Series moneys from the Yankees because the team used Carl Mays. Frank Navin, whose Tigers were beaten out for third by the Yankees, claims the nine games Mays won for New York should be disallowed.

NOVEMBER 5:

Yankees' players receive the third-place share of World Series money directly from team owners Jacob Ruppert and Tillinghast L'Hommedieu Huston.

DECEMBER 26:

Red Sox owner Harry Frazee – mired in losses from his theater business, which forced him to sell off his team's better players – and Yankees' co-owner Jacob Ruppert sign a secret agreement for the sale of Babe Ruth to New York. The terms read, "in consideration of the sum of twenty-five thousand dollars and other good and valuable consideration." The deal, of course, was eventually consummated, though the Babe went to New York for $125,000, plus a $300,000 mortgage on Fenway Park. And the "Curse of the Bambino" was on. Writes Frederick Ivor-Campbell in *Total Baseball* of Boston's plight after the deed was done: "The Red Sox were embarked on a fifteen year sojourn in the second division that even a 1923 change of ownership was powerless to end. In the 11 years from 1922 through 1932 the Sox emerged from last place only twice. In 1932 they reached their nadir, losing 111 games and finishing 64 games out of first."

"Enclosed please find certified check for sixteen hundred and thirty dollars."
– Smoky Joe Wood, writing to Dutch Leonard

THE BEST OF 1919

NATIONAL LEAGUE

HITTERS

Batting Average:
Edd Roush, Cincinnati Reds, .321

Slugging Average:
Henry "Hy" Myers, Brooklyn Robins, .436

Home Runs:
Clifford "Gavvy" Cravath, Philadelphia Phillies, 12

Runs Batted In:
Henry Myers, 73

Hits:
Ivan "Ivy" Olson, Brooklyn Robins, 164

Stolen Bases:
George J. Burns, New York Giants, 40

PITCHERS

Wins:
Jesse Barnes, New York Giants, 25

Strikeouts:
James "Hippo" Vaughn, Chicago Cubs, 141

Earned Run Average:
Grover Cleveland Alexander, Chicago Cubs, 1.72

Winning Percentage:
Walter "Dutch" Ruether, Cincinnati Reds, .760

Saves:
Oscar Tuero, St. Louis Cardinals, 4

AMERICAN LEAGUE

HITTERS

Batting Average:
Ty Cobb, Detroit Tigers, .384

Slugging Average:
Babe Ruth, Boston Red Sox, .657

Home Runs:
Babe Ruth, 29

Runs Batted In:
Babe Ruth, 114

Hits:
Ty Cobb; Bobby Veach, Detroit Tigers, 191

Stolen Bases:
Eddie "Cocky" Collins, Chicago White Sox, 33

PITCHERS

Wins:
Ed Cicotte, Chicago White Sox, 29

Strikeouts:
Walter Johnson, Washington Senators, 147

Earned Run Average:
Walter Johnson, 1.49

Winning Percentage:
Ed Cicotte, .806

Saves:
Allan Russell, New York Yankees/Boston Red Sox; Jim Shaw, Washington Senators, 5

TRIVIA

In early August, Giants' manager John McGraw finds a new way to stir up controversy. After completing a series against the Reds in Cincinnati, he offends the city's German-American population by saying, "We beat you today and we'll be glad to get out of the home of the Huns." He then gets into a fight with a policeman over the remark.

1920

"One of the most selfish... men ever to put on a baseball uniform."
– *Harry Frazee, on Babe Ruth*

NEWS

U.S. WOMEN WIN RIGHT TO VOTE

REPUBLICAN TICKET OF WARREN HARDING AND CALVIN COOLIDGE DEFEATS DEMOCRATS JAMES M. COX AND FRANKLIN DELANO ROOSEVELT

PROHIBITION ENACTED IN THE U.S.

League of Nations formed; Senate rejects U.S. membership

RUSSIAN CIVIL WAR ENDS

NICOLA SACCO AND BARTOLOMEO VANZETTI INDICTED FOR MURDER

Atlantic City, New Jersey, hosts the first Miss America Beauty Pageant

MAN O' WAR WINS THE PREAKNESS AND BELMONT STAKES

F. Scott Fitzgerald's *This Side of Paradise* is published

PRE-SEASON

JANUARY 3:

The secret agreement reached on December 26, 1919, selling Babe Ruth to the New York Yankees, is made public. Boston Red Sox owner and Broadway producer Harry Frazee, strapped for cash, gets more than $400,00 cash and credit ($125,000 cash, $300,000 loan). The Babe's sale price is more than twice the amount previously paid for a ballplayer's contract.

At the time of Babe Ruth's departure, the Red Sox had won 15 pennants and six World Series. They haven't won another World Series since. Some fans attribute this to the "Curse of the Bambino."

JANUARY 5:

Frazee attempts to explain why he sold Babe Ruth to the Yankees. "We were fast becoming a one-man team," he says. He accuses Ruth of being "one of the most selfish and inconsiderate men ever to put on a baseball uniform." Frazee is responding to fans who are upset with the transaction and are threatening to boycott the Red Sox games. Frazee fares somewhat better with Boston sportswriters, who assume Ruth had peaked in 1919. One newspaper cartoon, however, comments on the Ruth deal by picturing landmarks Faneuil Hall and the Boston Public Library with "for sale" signs hanging on them.

JANUARY 6:

Early Wynn is born in Hartford, Alabama.

FEBRUARY 3:

Rube Foster, the manager of the Chicago American Giants, and the owners of Negro teams in the midwest meet in Kansas City to form the Negro National Baseball League. The eight-team league is comprised of the Kansas City Monarchs, the Kansas City American Giants, the Indianapolis ABCs, the Chicago Giants, the St. Louis Giants, the Detroit Stars, the Dayton Marcos, and the Cuban Stars.

FEBRUARY 8:

Babe Ruth asks the Red Sox for $15,000 of the money the team received from the Yankees for his contract. He later reports on Harry Frazee's response, "The son of a bitch wouldn't even see me."

FEBRUARY 9:

Baseball bans all "freak deliveries" – including spitballs, applying grease, or sandpapering the ball. Seventeen current pitchers are "grandfathered," or exempted from the new rule.

Frank Shellenback, who pitched for the White Sox in 1918 and in the minors in 1919, is inadvertently left off the "grandfathered" list and never makes it back to the majors. The Pacific Coast league allows him to throw spitballs and he wins 295 games in his 19-year career.

FEBRUARY 13:

Shoeless Joe Jackson holds out; he returns his unsigned contract to the Chicago White Sox and demands more money before reporting to spring training camp.

MARCH 8:

The *New York Times* reports that Babe Ruth swings a 54-ounce bat. "The average player is content to do his hitting with a stick weighing from 36 to 45 ounces," the *Times* notes.

JANUARY 3
It is officially announced that Babe Ruth has been sold to the Yankees.

JULY 19
Babe Ruth hits his 30th and 31st home runs of the season, against the White Sox.

MARCH 20:

In Jacksonville, Florida, the Robins beat the Yankees, 5-1, in an exhibition game. Babe Ruth strikes out twice and, in the ninth inning, jumps into the left-field bleachers after a fan who has been heckling him. Yankees' pitcher Ernie Shore, Ruth's former Red Sox teammate, restrains him.

THE SEASON

APRIL 26:

Red Sox shortstop Everett Scott sets a major league record when he appears in his 534th consecutive game. Scott, who surpasses the record of 533 set by the Phillies' Fred Luderus, began his streak on June 20, 1916.

MAY 1:

The Robins and Braves play a 26-inning, 1-1 tie, the longest major league game to end deadlocked. Leon Cadore of the Dodgers and Joe Oeschger of the Braves pitch the entire game. It is a particularly bad day for Tony Boeckel and Charlie Pick of the Braves; each goes 0-for-11 in the game.

MAY 2:

In the Negro National Baseball League's first game, the Indianapolis ABCs beat the Chicago Giants, 4-2, today in Indianapolis. The Phillies beat the Robins, 3-1, in 13 innings at Brooklyn.

MAY 3:

The Robins lose to Braves, 2-1, in 19 innings. In their last two meetings, the teams have played 45 innings. Brooklyn has played 58 innings in three days – equivalent to six and a half games.

MAY 14:

The Senators' Walter Johnson beats the Tigers, 9-8, for his 300th career victory.

MAY 17:

The *New York Times* reports today that the Giants will evict the Yankees from the Polo Grounds at the conclusion of the 1920 season.

MAY 20:

Under an agreement between the Giants and AL president Ban Johnson, the eviction notice is rescinded and the Yankees can play at the Polo Grounds beyond the current season.

MAY 24:

Betting and bookmaking activities at Cubs games are targeted by Chicago police. Disguised as farmers, sailors, and soldiers, and in other costumes, they bust 24 bleacher fans. On the field, Grover Cleveland Alexander shuts out the Phillies, 6-0.

JUNE 8:

The Giants acquire shortstop Dave "Beauty" Bancroft (.298) from the Phillies for shortstop Art Fletcher (.257), pitcher Bill Hubbell (0-1), and $100,000.

JUNE 23:

The majors' record consecutive game streak of Phillies' first baseman Fred Luderus ends at 533.

JUNE 26:

At Cincinnati, Reds' pitcher Dolf Luque attacks umpire Bill Klem, claiming Klem used "vicious language." The *New York Times* reports Luque "dealt Bill Klem several hard blows about the head." Earlier, fans threw pop bottles at Klem after a safe call at the plate favoring the St. Louis Cardinals, who win the game, 5-0.

JULY 1:

The Senators' Walter Johnson celebrates his son's fifth birthday by no-hitting the Red Sox in Boston, 1-0. Johnson strikes out 10 and issues no walks. An error by Stanley "Bucky" Harris with two out in the ninth spoils the perfect game bid. A great play by first baseman Joe Judge on a Harry Hooper liner with two out in the final frame preserves Johnson's no-hitter. Harry Harper is the losing pitcher.

JULY 10:

Cleveland's Tris Speaker collects a major league record 11 straight hits.

JULY 19:

Babe Ruth hits his 30th and 31st homer's of the season today against the White Sox', Dickie Kerr. New York and Chicago split a doubleheader.

AUGUST 8:

In the shortest game in AL history – one hour and 13 minutes – the Tigers' Howard Ehmke beats the Yankees, 1-0.

AUGUST 16:

At the Polo Grounds in New York, Yankees' pitcher Carl Mays hits Cleveland shortstop Ray Chapman in the head with one of his submarine pitches. In the clubhouse, Chapman regains conscious-

RULES

Batters will be credited with a sacrifice fly when a runner scores from third base. Runs batted in are now an official statistic

TRIVIA

New York's Commerce High School baseball team travels to Chicago to play against Lane Tech at Weeghman Field. On the train from New York is Supreme Court justice and former President William Howard Taft. With Commerce ahead, 8-6, 17-year-old Lou Gehrig adds to the lead with a ninth-inning bases-loaded homer to right field that clears the ballpark. Playing third base for Lane is another future Hall of Famer, Fred Lindstrom. Some 10,000 attend the game.

SEPTEMBER 29
Babe Ruth hits his 54th home run of the year, breaking his own major league record.

EQUIPMENT

Was there a lively baseball in 1920? Whenever home run totals soar, speculation begins about a rabbit ball. *The Baseball Encyclopedia* states: "To take advantage of the rising popularity of a young star named Babe Ruth, the ball was made much livelier." According to another account, it happened by accident when the manufacturers of American League balls switched to Australian yarn, which could be wound tighter, resulting in more bounce. In any event, Babe Ruth made the home run the offensive weapon in modern baseball.

ness briefly, saying, "Tell Mays not to worry."

AUGUST 17:

Ray Chapman dies of his injuries at the age of 29; he is the only fatality as the result of being hit by a pitch in the history of major league baseball.

AUGUST 24:

The Giants again reverse fields, refusing to extend the Yankees' lease for the Polo Grounds. The AL holds a special meeting in Philadelphia and decides the Yankees will have their own ballpark. Co-owner Jacob Ruppert indicates three sites are under consideration, all within "a few minutes ride from Times Square." The new stadium will have a seating capacity in excess of 50,000.

AUGUST 31:

In Chicago, Cubs' president William L. Veeck receives a telegram informing him of heavy betting on the Phillies in today's game with the Cubs, and warning him of rumors that the game is fixed. He replaces scheduled starting pitcher Claude Hendrix with Grover Cleveland Alexander, but the Cubs lose anyway, 3-0.

Hendrix is released over the winter and never plays again in the majors. Cook County (Illinois) district attorney MacClay Hoyne and a grand jury looking into the events surrounding the Cubs-Phillies game are led to the Black Sox scandal. Phillies manager Gavvy Cravath comments, "I don't know why they gotta bring a thing like this up just because we win one. We're liable to win a game any time."

SEPTEMBER 2:

The *Chicago Herald and Examiner* reports that the August 31 Phillies-Cubs game was fixed and that $50,000 was bet on Philadelphia to win.

SEPTEMBER 7:

The grand jury of Cook County (Illinois) convenes to investigate gambling in baseball. In addition to investigating the August 31 Phillies-Cubs game, presiding Judge Charles McDonald recommends that the grand jury look at the 1919 White Sox-Reds World Series, won by Cincinnati, five games to three.

SEPTEMBER 9:

The baseball field in Cooperstown, New York, where Abner Doubleday allegedly "invented" baseball in 1839 – far from a historic certainty – is named in his honor. To mark the occasion NL president John Heydler umpires a game between two local teams.

SEPTEMBER 17:

The Cardinals bang out a record 12 consecutive hits over two innings in a 9-4 win over the Braves. It sounds impossible, but, with one out on the fourth inning, the Cardinals score eight runs on 10 straight hits. The last two hitters – Milt Stock and Austin Henry – are retired trying to stretch hits. In the fifth, John "Doc" Lavan leads off with a double and Cliff Heathcote singles for the ninth and 10th consecutive hits.

SEPTEMBER 21:

Assistant Illinois state attorney Hartley Replogle announces he will subpoena players, owners, managers, and gamblers to testify before the grand jury. White Sox owner Charles A. Comiskey is among the first to testify. He tells the grand jury, "If any of my players are not honest, I'll fire them no matter who they are, and if I can't get honest players to fill their places, I'll close the gates of the park that I have spent a lifetime to build and in which, in the declining years of my life, I take the greatest measure of pride and pleasure."

SEPTEMBER 22:

The Cook County grand jury hearings begin.

Bob Lemon is born in San Bernardino, California.

SEPTEMBER 24:

New York Giants' pitcher John "Rube" Benton tells the grand jury that the Cubs' Buck Herzog and the Giants' Hal Chase had offered him $800 to throw a game. He testifies that Hal Chase won $40,000 betting on the 1919 World Series. Benton implicates Chick Gandil, Happy Felsch, Lefty Williams, and Eddie Cicotte.

SEPTEMBER 28:

Pitcher Eddie Cicotte admits to the grand jury he "sold out the other boys... sold them out for $10,000... I threw the game..." Cicotte is referring to game one of the 1919 World Series, which the Reds won, 9-1. Shoeless Joe Jackson also testifies for nearly two hours and

OCTOBER
3
The Browns' George Sisler sets a major league record with his 257th hit of the year.

implicates Chick Gandil and Swede Risberg. Charles Comiskey is not in court to hear his two players. Instead, he remains in his office and issues suspensions for his eight "Black Sox." In his letter to the players, Comiskey remarks: "Until there is a finality to this investigation, it is due to the public that I take this action even though it costs Chicago the pennant."

SEPTEMBER 29:

On the last day of the season, in the first game of a doubleheader, Babe Ruth hits his 54th home run – a major league record. Ruth's record homer is served up by Athletics' pitcher Dave Keefe in the ninth inning of a 7-3 Yankees' win. In the second game of the twin bill, Ruth doubles as the Yankees win again, 9-4, in 11 innings. He ends the season with an all-time high slugging average of .847. Only one other team in the AL hits more than 44 home runs.

SEPTEMBER 30:

The *Chicago Herald and Examiner* reports: "As [Shoeless Joe] Jackson departed from the Grand Jury room, a small boy clutched at his sleeve and tagged along after him. 'Say it ain't so, Joe,' he pleaded, 'Say it ain't so.' 'Yes, kid, I'm afraid it is,' Jackson replied. 'Well, I never would've thought it,' the boy said."

OCTOBER 2:

Jim Bagby wins his 31st game of the season and the Indians clinch the AL pennant with a 10-1 victory over the Tigers today, while the second-place White Sox beat the Browns, 10-7. Bagby contributes a bases-loaded triple in the seventh to aid his own cause.

At Forbes Field, the Pirates and visiting Reds play baseball's last tripleheader. Pittsburgh first baseman Clyde Barnhart hits in each of the three games. The Reds win, 13-4 and 7-3, then lose, 6-0.

OCTOBER 3:

The Browns' George Sisler collects his 257th hit of the season – a major league record – in a 16-7 win over the visiting White Sox in the final game of the season.

OCTOBER 5:

World Series, game one. In Brooklyn, the Cleveland Indians win, 3-1, behind Stan Coveleski's five-hit, complete-game pitching. The loser is "Rube" Marquard. Indians' catcher Steve O'Neill has two RBI.

Starting for the Indians at shortstop is Joe Sewell, who will be 22 years old in four days and has fewer than 100 games of professional experience. Back on August 17, when Ray Chapman dies after being hit with a pitch, Sewell is playing in the minors at New Orleans. On Labor Day, Chapman's replacement, Harry Lunte, is injured, and Sewell is brought up to play shortstop for the Indians in the heat of a pennant race. He appears in 22 regular season games, batting .329. In the Series, Sewell faces perhaps unprecedented pressure for a player of his age and experience. He bats only .174 and makes six errors, but rebounds to play 14 years with a .312 lifetime average and is inducted into the Hall of Fame in 1977.

New York Giants' manager John McGraw testifies for the second time before the grand jury. He describes the activities of his former players, first baseman Hal Chase and third baseman Heinie Zimmerman. According to McGraw, they attempted to bribe their teammates to throw ball games. Zimmerman, a Triple

HISTORY

New York Yankees' third baseman Frank "Home Run" Baker sits out the entire 1920 season to care for his wife, who is terminally ill. Baker hit .293 with 10 homers in 1919.

George Sisler led the majors with a .407 average in 1920.

OCTOBER 12
With a 3-0 shutout of the Robins, the Indians clinch the World Championship.

"If any one of my players are not honest, I'll fire them."
– *Charles Comiskey*

CULTURE

Babe Ruth appears with Ruth Taylor in the silent film *Headin' Home.*

TRIVIA

***The Redheaded Outfield and Other Stories*, by Zane Grey, includes the title story (first published in 1915) about a minor league team in a pivotal game. According to Joseph M. Overfield, the fictional outfielders were modeled after Larry Gilboy, Billy Clymer, and Romer Grey (Zane's brother) of the Eastern League's 1897 Buffalo Bisons. *The Home-Run King*, a young-adult novel ostensibly by Babe Ruth, also makes its debut.**

Crown winner with the Cubs in 1912, called himself the Great Zim. He was suspended by McGraw in 1919 after offering teammate pitcher Fred Toney a bribe in a September 11 game against the Cubs.

OCTOBER 6:

World Series, game two. The Robins' Burleigh Grimes pitches a seven-hit shutout, besting Jim Bagby, 3-0, in Brooklyn.

OCTOBER 7:

World Series, game three. The Robins' Sherry Smith goes the distance and three-hits the Indians, 2-1. Losing pitcher Ray Caldwell is kayoed in a Brooklyn two-run first inning.

OCTOBER 9:

World Series, game four. In Cleveland, the Indians win, 5-1, on a Stan Coveleski five-hitter. Tris Speaker and Bill Wambsganss have two hits and two runs each. The losing pitcher is Leon Cadore.

OCTOBER 10:

World Series, game five. Bill Wambsganss executes an unassisted triple play – the first in World Series history – in the fifth inning in Cleveland. Elmer Smith hits the first Series grand slam homer, and winning pitcher Jim Bagby launches a two-run round-tripper in an 8-1 Indians' victory. Burleigh Grimes is tagged with the loss.

OCTOBER 11:

World Series, game six. John "Duster" Mails, who played for Brooklyn in 1915 and 1916, comes back to haunt the Robins with a 1-0 three-hitter. Sherry Smith pitches a seven-hitter, but loses. The game's only run is scored in the sixth on a Tris Speaker single and a George Burns double.

OCTOBER 12

The Indians' Stan Coveleski shuts out the Robins, 3-0, on five hits. It is his third World Series win and his third five-hitter, sealing the championship for the Indians, five games to two. Burleigh Grimes gets the loss. Cleveland's pitchers finish the Series with a microscopic 0.89 ERA. Six regulars hit .300 and Elmer Smith has six RBI. Zack Wheat leads Brooklyn with .333.

POST-SEASON

OCTOBER 22:

The Black Sox scandal shatters baseball. Eight members of the Chicago White Sox are indicted for throwing the 1919 World Series. The "Eight Men Out" are Shoeless Joe Jackson, Buck Weaver, Eddie Cicotte, Lefty Williams, Swede Risberg, Happy Felsch, Chick Gandil, and Fred McMullin. Also indicted are New York gambler Arnold Rothstein, former world featherweight champion Abe Attell, and former New York Giants first baseman Hal Chase, who was involved in previous gambling scandals. Jackson, one of the games' greatest players and an illiterate, received $5,000 of a promised $20,000 bribe. He batted .375 in the 1919 series and .382 for the 1920 season. Teammate Eddie Cicotte won 29 games in the now-tainted 1919 season and then 21 games this year.

OCTOBER 29:

Ed Barrow, who managed the Red Sox to a pennant and World Series win in 1918, upset by the sale of Babe Ruth, joins the exodus to New York. He becomes the Yankees' general manager. Last season Boston finished 72-81 and in fifth place.

NOVEMBER 12:

The major league owners name Kenesaw Mountain Landis, a U.S district court judge and an ardent fan, to preside over baseball. Landis gets a seven-year term and a $50,000 salary.

NOVEMBER 21:

Stan "The Man" Musial is born in Donora, Pennsylvania.

DECEMBER 15:

The Red Sox trade pitcher Waite Hoyt (6-6, 4.38 ERA), pitcher Harry Harper (5-14, 3.04 ERA), catcher Wally Schang (.305, four homers) and infielder Mike McNally (.256) to the Yankees for pitcher Herbert "Hank" Thormahlen (9-6, 4.14 ERA), catcher Herold "Muddy" Ruel (.268), third baseman Derrill "Del" Pratt (.314) and outfielder Sammy Vick (.220).

Brooklyn trades pitcher Richard "Rube" Marquard (10-7, 3.23 ERA) to the Reds for pitcher Walter "Dutch" Ruether (16-12, 2.47 ERA). Marquard was arrested for scalping World Series tickets, and after he is found guilty, Brooklyn's Charles Ebbets unloads him.

DECEMBER 18:

Ty Cobb, on his 34th birthday, signs a one-year contract with the Detroit Tigers.

NOVEMBER 12
Major league owners name Kenesaw Mountain Landis the first commissioner.

DECEMBER 18
Ty Cobb, on his 34th birthday, signs a one-year contract with the Detroit Tigers.

THE BEST OF 1920

NATIONAL LEAGUE

HITTERS

Batting Average:
Rogers Hornsby, St. Louis Cardinals, .370

Slugging Average:
Rogers Hornsby, .559

Home Runs:
Fred "Cy" Williams, Chicago Cubs, 15

***Runs Batted In:**
Rogers Hornsby, 94

Hits:
Rogers Hornsby, 218

Stolen Bases:
Max Carey, Pittsburgh Pirates, 52

PITCHERS

Wins:
Grover Cleveland Alexander, Chicago Cubs, 27

Strikeouts:
Grover Cleveland Alexander, 173

Earned Run Average:
Grover Cleveland Alexander, 1.91

Winning Percentage:
Burleigh Grimes, Brooklyn Robins, .676

Saves:
Bill Sherdell, St. Louis Cardinals, 6

AMERICAN LEAGUE

HITTERS

Batting Average:
George Sisler, St. Louis Browns, .407

Slugging Average:
Babe Ruth, New York Yankees, .847

Home Runs:
Babe Ruth, 54

***Runs Batted In:**
Babe Ruth, 137

Hits:
George Sisler, 257

Stolen Bases:
Sam Rice, Washington Senators, 63

PITCHERS

Wins:
Jim Bagby, Cleveland Indians, 31

Strikeouts:
Stan Coveleski, Cleveland Indians, 133

Earned Run Average:
Bob Shawkey, New York Yankees, 2.45

Winning Percentage:
Jim Bagby, .721

Saves:
Dickie Kerr, Chicago White Sox;
Urban Shocker, St. Louis Browns, 5

**RBI statistics were compiled for the first time in 1920. To arrive at RBI statistics before that, the totals were compiled after the fact by historians of the game who pieced together the stats.*

HISTORY

The venue may change, but the behavior is consistent. Hal Chase is accused of trying to bribe Salt Lake City pitcher Sider Baum, and the former major league first baseman is banished from all Pacific Coast League stadiums.

HISTORY

The 1920 World Series produces two statistical oddities: Brooklyn pitcher Clarence Mitchell, who lines into Bill Wambsganss's unassisted triple play, also hits into a double play – accounting for five outs in two at-bats. And Cleveland pitcher Stan Coveleski wins three World Series games with a total of only 261 pitches.

1921

"Landis cleaned it up, and Babe Ruth glorified it."
– Tommy Henrich, on baseball

NEWS

SACCO AND VANZETTI CONVICTED OF MURDER

Striking coal miners and U.S. troops clash in West Virginia

WILLIAM HOWARD TAFT APPOINTED CHIEF JUSTICE

Armistice Day becomes legal holiday

FRANKLIN D. ROOSEVELT STRICKEN BY POLIO

AGATHA CHRISTIE BEGINS CAREER AS MYSTERY WRITER

Unknown Soldier is buried in Arlington National Cemetery

Rudolph Valentino stars in **The Sheik** *and* **Four Horsemen of the Apocalypse**

Chanel No. 5 is world's best-selling perfume

PRE-SEASON

JANUARY 12:

The National Agreement is ratified by the major league baseball owners. The commissioner is given far-ranging powers including "to investigate, either upon complaint or upon his own initiative, any act, transaction, or practice... suspected to be detrimental to the best interests of the national game of baseball." He then can fine or blacklist clubs, owners, and players for such conduct. The owners also agree that the commissioner will be the final arbiter of disputes, that they will abide by his decisions, and that they will refrain from public criticism. Philip deCatesby Ball of the Browns is the only owner who refuses to sign the agreement.

Judge Kenesaw Mountain Landis assumes the position of commissioner of baseball. He replaces the three-man National Commission that has governed the sport since the 1903 merger of the National and American Leagues.

FEBRUARY 5:

The Yankees buy 10 acres of land at 161st Street and River Avenue in the Bronx from the estate of William Waldorf Astor for $600,000. The property will be the site of their new ballpark.

FEBRUARY 23:

Shortstop Walter "Rabbit" Maranville (.260) goes from the Braves to the Pirates. In return, the Braves get outfielder Billy Southworth (.284, two homers), outfielder Fred Nicholson (.360, four homers), infielder Walter Barbare (.274), and $15,000.

MARCH 4:

Outfielder Harry Hooper (.312, seven homers) goes to the White Sox from the Red Sox in exchange for outfielders John "Shano" Collins (.303, one homer) and Harry "Nemo" Leibold (.220).

MARCH 9:

The Cardinals sign Rogers Hornsby to a three-year contract with an annual salary of $18,500 – the highest in NL history. Hornsby led the league in batting with .370 last season and drove in 94 runs.

MARCH 12:

Judge Kenesaw Mountain Landis suspends Shoeless Joe Jackson, Oscar "Happy" Felsch, Eddie Cicotte, Claude "Lefty" Williams, Arnold "Chick" Gandil, Charles "Swede" Risberg, George "Buck" Weaver, and Fred McMullen – the eight Black Sox players.

MARCH 24:

Judge Landis bans Phillies' infielder Eugene Paulette for life. Paulette was charged with associating with a gambler while playing for the Cardinals in 1919. He allegedly accepted a loan from a St. Louis gambler and instead of repaying it, offered to throw a game for additional money. Paulette denies any guilt. According to Landis, Paulette "offered to betray his team." Paulette, who hit .269 in six years with the Giants, Browns, Cardinals, and Phillies, was instructed to report to Landis again. He failed to do so and never returned to the majors.

APRIL 7:

The bans keep coming from the commissioner's office. Today, Judge Landis rules the Giants' Benny Kauff "permanently ineligible." On February 20 of last year, Kauff and his brother were indicted for automobile theft, possession

JANUARY 12
Judge Kenesaw Mountain Landis becomes baseball's first commissioner.

JUNE 14
With two homers today, Babe Ruth has a total of seven roundtrippers in his last five games.

of stolen vehicles, and other charges. The criminal case against Kauff is still pending.

APRIL 13:

On opening day at the Polo Grounds, the Yankees' Babe Ruth enjoys his first five-hit day – two doubles and three singles – as New York routs the Athletics, 11-1.

Giants' owner Charles Stoneham allows gambler Arnold Rothstein – a key figure in the Black Sox scandal – to sit in his box at the Polo Grounds and draws the wrath of Commissioner Landis. Stoneham gets off by promising that it won't happen again.

APRIL 23:

Warren Spahn is born in Buffalo, New York.

MAY 7:

Babe Ruth slams a home run into center field off Walter Johnson, a drive deemed to be the longest ever hit in Washington. The Yankees' Bob Meusel hits for the cycle. The Yankees edge the Senators, 6-5.

MAY 16:

A fan named Reuben Berman is ejected from the Polo Grounds for refusing to return a foul ball hit into the stands. He, in turn, sues the club for $20,000.

MAY 17:

Boston Red Sox shortstop Everett Scott plays in his 700th consecutive game.

MAY 20:

Hal Newhouser is born in Detroit.

MAY 25:

In St. Louis, Babe Ruth belts a 500-foot home run – the longest ever hit in Sportsman's Park. It is his 13th of the season, but the Browns beat the Yankees, 7-6.

JUNE 1:

Umpires begin rubbing down baseballs with mud before games in order to cut glare and improve the grip. The mud comes from a New Jersey farm owned by Philadelphia Athletics coach Lena Blackburne.

JUNE 2:

Reds' outfielder Pat Duncan hits the first-ever home run out of Redland Field in Cincinnati. The ball travels over the left-field wall and is only the fifth career homer for Duncan.

JUNE 6:

The Yankees' Babe Ruth hits a home run off Cleveland's Jim Bagby in the third inning of today's game. It is the 120th career homer for the 26-year-old Ruth, the most ever by a player in the 20th century. The previous modern-day record was held by Clifford "Gavvy" Cravath at 119. The Indians win, 8-6.

JUNE 8:

After being arrested for speeding on New York City's Riverside Drive, Babe Ruth is fined $100 and held in custody until 4 p.m. With game time set for 3:15, Ruth decidedly has a problem. His uniform is delivered to the police station and Ruth arrives at the Polo Grounds to cheers with his team trailing, 3-2. The Yankees go on to win the game, 4-3, with no contribution from Ruth.

JUNE 13:

At the Polo Grounds, Babe Ruth gives another demonstration of his batting power and his pitching prowess. Against the Tigers, Ruth pitches the first five innings of an 11-8 win, strikes out Ty Cobb, and gets the victory. And he hits two homers against Howard Ehmke, marking the fourth straight day he has reached the seats. Ruth's second home run to right center field carries 460 feet.

JUNE 14:

Babe Ruth continues his assault on the Tigers' pitching staff. Today, he hits two against George "Hooks" Dauss, setting an AL record with a homer in five straight games. The Babe has a total of seven in the last five contests.

JUNE 23:

In Philadelphia, the Athletics and Tigers combine for a record eight home runs. Philadelphia wins the game, 15-9.

TRIVIA

The Cardinals introduce the logo that will remain the team's symbol to the present day: two cardinals perched on a bat. Branch Rickey gets the idea from decorations made by a St. Louis church worker named Allie May Schmidt.

Baseball's first commissioner, Judge Kenesaw Mountain Landis

JULY 21
Joe Sewell has five of the Indians' 22 hits in a 17-8 demolition of the Yankees.

LEAGUE

Branch Rickey continues to build the Cardinals' farm system, adding Syracuse of the International League to Houston (purchased in 1919) and Fort Smith, Arkansas, of the Western Association (1920).

HISTORY

In May, Benny Kauff is acquitted of criminal charges in his auto theft case. Judge Landis denies him reinstatement. Kauff gets a temporary injunction against his ban, but Judge Edward O. Whitaker denies a permanent injunction because Kauff's contract has expired. The case eventually is settled out of court, but Kauff never returns to the majors.

JUNE 27:

The trial of eight White Sox players and 10 gamblers (including former major league first baseman Hal Chase) begins today in Chicago. Hugo Friend is the presiding judge.

Among the key developments in the Black Sox trials: A New York criminal attorney claims the Abe Attell named in the indictment is not the former world featherweight champion and Attell does not appear; Hal Chase is released on a legal technicality; Eddie Cicotte, Lefty Williams, and Shoeless Joe Jackson retract their confessions, and White Sox owner Charles Comiskey actually pays for topflight defense attorneys for his accused players.

JULY 1:

The Giants and Phillies swap six players. The Giants get outfielder Casey Stengel (.305), infielder Johnny Rawlings (.291), and pitcher Cecil "Red" Causey (33). The Phillies get infielder Joseph "Goldie" Rapp (.215 in 58 games) outfielder Lee King (.223) and outfielder-infielder Lance Richbourg, who was not in the majors at the time of the trade.

JULY 5:

Judge Hugo Friend turns down a defense motion to dismiss the indictments in the Black Sox case and jury selection begins.

JULY 6:

With his home run today – the 137th of his career – Babe Ruth becomes the major leagues' all-time home run leader. The previous record holder – with 136 – was Roger Connor, who played from 1880 through 1897.

JULY 9:

Pirates fans may keep baseballs hit into the stands as far as Pittsburgh's director of public safety Robert J. Alderdice is concerned. After threat of a lawsuit, the commissioner rules that policemen will no longer get involved. Ballpark employees still are free to attempt to retrieve baseballs.

JULY 21:

The Indians hit nine doubles in a 17-8 victory over the Yankees, who bang out seven two-base hits of their own. The teams set a record for doubles in one game. George Uhle is the winning pitcher and the Indians' Joe Sewell has five of his team's 22 hits in the game.

JULY 23:

The grand jury confessions and waivers of immunity of Eddie Cicotte, Shoeless Joe Jackson, and Lefty Williams are missing from the files of the Illinois state attorney. The players repudiate their confessions. Jackson, who is illiterate, says he didn't know what he was signing and wants to withdraw his confession.

Ban Johnson charges that Arnold Rothstein paid $10,000 to get rid of the files. According to writers Donald Dewey and Nicholas Acocella, Arnold Rothstein arranged for Charles Comiskey's attorney – Alfred Austrian – to steal the documents from the state attorney's office. Eliot Asinof attributes the action to defense attorney William Fallon, also known as "The Great Mouthpiece." In a 1924 suit by Shoeless Joe Jackson for $18,000 in back pay, the confessions resurface – in the possession of Charles Comiskey's attorney, George B. Hudnall.

JULY 25:

The New York Giants acquire outfielder Emil "Irish" Meusel (.353) from the Phillies for three players and $30,000. Going to Philadelphia are pitcher Jesse Winters, who has appeared in no games this season, outfielder Curt Walker (.286), and catcher Butch Henline (.000 in one game).

JULY 29:

The state makes its final argument in the Black Sox case and demands five-year sentences plus $2,000 fines for each of the eight players. The defense argues that the players' contracts didn't require that they try to win games.

JULY 31:

The Phillies' Goldie Rapp has his 23-game hitting streak snapped by the Chicago Cubs. Rapp sets a major league record for rookies with his streak.

AUGUST 2:

Judge Hugo Friend instructs the Black Sox jury that in order to reach a guilty verdict there must be proof that games were thrown plus an intention to defraud the public. After only two hours of deliberation, the eight Black Sox are acquitted on charges of throwing the 1919 World Series. The jurors lift

SEPTEMBER 5
With seven strikeouts against the Yankees, Walter Johnson passes Cy Young's "K" record.

the players onto their shoulders and march them around the courtroom. Chick Gandil says, "I guess that will learn Ban Johnson he can't frame an honest bunch of ballplayers." The jurors then retire to an Italian restaurant with the players they just acquitted.

AUGUST 3:

Despite their acquittal yesterday, the eight White Sox players will not be allowed to play baseball. Judge Landis and AL president Ban Johnson issue separate statements to that effect today. Swede Risberg comments, "I am entirely innocent and the jury has proved that."

AUGUST 4:

Judge Landis bans the Black Sox for life. He says, in part, "They can't come back... the doors are closed to them for good. The most scandalous chapter in the game's history is closed."

AUGUST 5:

Radio station KDKA in Pittsburgh broadcasts the first play-by-play coverage of a baseball game. Harold Arlin announced the game from a ground-level box at Forbes Field. The Pirates beat the Phillies, 8-5. Arlin, an electrical engineer, also was the first full-time radio announcer in the world.

AUGUST 19:

Ty Cobb gets his 3,000th career hit and, at 34, is the youngest player to reach that level. The historic hit comes against Boston Red Sox right-hander Elmer Myers.

AUGUST 25:

The Indians and Yankees brawl after three hit batters. Coming in with his team down, 11-1, in the eighth, Yankees' pitcher Harry Harper hits Charlie Jamieson in the ribs, Bill Gardner on the wrist, and Steve O'Neill in the back. O'Neill fires the ball back at him and charges the mound. The benches empty and the ruckus is on. Yankees' right fielder Bob Meusel makes four errors in the contest, which Cleveland wins, 15-1, to move into first place past New York.

AUGUST 30:

For the first time in major league history, there are two triple plays in one day. And in both games, the team executing the fielding gem loses the game. In New York, the Cubs execute a triple play against the Giants and lose, 5-3. And the Braves pull a triple killing against the Reds and lose, 6-4.

SEPTEMBER 1:

Red Sox shortstop Everett Scott plays in his 800th consecutive ball game.

SEPTEMBER 5:

Walter Johnson strikes out seven Yankees to pass Cy Young's previous mark of 2,796.

SEPTEMBER 15:

At the Polo Grounds, Babe Ruth hits his 55th home run of the season as the Yankees beat the Browns twice, 10-6 and 13-5.

SEPTEMBER 24:

Tigers' player-manager Ty Cobb, angered by two calls by Billy Evans in a 5-1 loss to Walter Johnson and the Senators in Washington, goes to the umpires' dressing room. He challenges Evans and the two agree to have it out without informing or involving AL president Ban Johnson. Cobb wins a bloody fight in front of players, some fans, and his son, Ty Jr. The

CULTURE

Chewing gum manufacturer William Wrigley Jr. is now the sole owner of the Chicago Cubs.

Walter Johnson of the Washington Senators

Eddie Collins, second baseman on the 1919 White Sox and one of its "clean" players, describes the team: "They were the best. There never was a ball club like that one."

HISTORY

The Chicago American Giants win the Negro National League pennant with a 41-21 record.

HISTORY

The Athletics, once the AL's dominant team, finish last for the eighth straight season. The streak of cellar finishes began after the 1914 pennant-winning season.

game's second umpire, George Hildebrand, reports the incident to Ban Johnson, who takes no action. However, Commissioner Landis suspends Cobb indefinitely as a player, but not as a manager.

SEPTEMBER 26:

At the Polo Grounds today, the Yankees are again in first place and Babe Ruth bombs Cleveland with his 57th and 58th home runs of the season, a double and a walk. New York wins, 8-7, increasing its lead over the Indians to two and a half games.

OCTOBER 1:

At the Polo Grounds, the Yankees win their first-ever AL pennant by defeating the Athletics, 5-3, in the first game of a doubleheader while the Indians are losing to the White Sox. The victory also evens New York's all-time record at 1,412-1,412. In game two, Babe Ruth comes in to pitch with the Yankees up, 6-0, in the eighth inning and drives in his 167th run of the season, topping a record of 166 RBI set by Sam Thompson of Detroit in the NL in 1887. On the mound, Ruth yields six runs, then throws three shutout innings. The Yankees win the game in the 11th inning, 7-6.

OCTOBER 2:

The pennant may be won, but Babe Ruth continues his relentless assault on AL pitchers and the record book. At the Polo Grounds today in the last game of the season, he hits his 59th home run of the year. It comes off Curt Fullerton in the third inning with two on base and lands in the upper right-field stands. The Yankees beat the Red Sox, 7-6. Bill Piercy gets the win; Fullerton is the losing pitcher. Ruth finishes the season with a .378 average and an .846 slugging average, 171 RBI, 144 walks, 177 runs, 457 total bases, and 119 extra-base hits.

OCTOBER 5:

World Series, game one. The Yankees and the Giants begin the first intra-New York City championship. Because both teams play at the Polo Grounds, there is no traveling involved, but these post-season matchups come to be known as the Subway Series. Behind Carl Mays's five-hitter, the Yankees win, 3-0. In the first inning, Babe Ruth singles in centerfielder Elmer Miller with the first ever Yankees' World Series run. In the fifth inning, third baseman Mike McNally steals home. In the sixth inning Bob Meusel triples in a run but is out for missing first base. Frankie Frisch has four hits for the Giants. The losing pitcher is Shufflin' Phil Douglas.

Game one of the 1921 World Series was the first to be broadcast by radio. Play-by-play bulletins are (see p. 247) relayed to a wireless receiver at the Electrical Show in New York City's 71st Regiment Armory and to radio station WJZ in New Jersey. The sports editor of the Sunday Call *in Newark, Sandy Hunt, telephones the reports from the Polo Grounds. Tommy Cowan is the "relay" man. KDKA in Pittsburgh, with a direct wire from New York, broadcasts play-by-play by sportswriter Grantland Rice.*

OCTOBER 6:

World Series, game two. Waite Hoyt's two-hitter lifts the Yankees to a 3-0 victory over the Giants. A leadoff single by Johnny Rawlings in the third inning and another by Frankie Frisch with one out in the ninth are all the offense the Giants can generate. Babe Ruth walks in the fifth, steals second and then third, injuring his elbow. The Yankees score twice in the eighth, including Bob Meusel's steal of home. Art Nehf, the losing pitcher for the Giants, allows the Yankees only three hits.

OCTOBER 7:

World Series, game three. The Giants bounce back with a 13-5 win highlighted by an eight-run seventh inning. The Giants' uprising includes back-to-back bases-loaded walks issued by Bob Shawkey. The Giants get 20 hits against four Yankees' pitchers; George Burns and Frank Snyder lead with four each. The Giants' Ross Youngs doubles and triples to become the first player to get two hits in a single inning in the Series. The winning pitcher is Jesse Barnes in relief of Fred Toney. Jack Quinn takes the loss for the Yankees.

OCTOBER 9:

World Series, game four. The Giants even the Series with a 4-2 win behind a complete game seven-hitter by Shufflin' Phil Douglas. Carl Mays is

OCTOBER 2
Babe Ruth ends his first season in pinstripes with his record-setting 59th home run.

OCTOBER 13
The Giants beat the Yankees, 1-0, in game eight to win the World Series.

the losing pitcher. Babe Ruth homers for the Yankees; George Burns drives in two runs with a double for the Giants. Mays allows three runs in the eighth.

After today's game, sportswriter Fred Lieb tells Yankees' co-owner Tillinghast L'Hommedieu Huston that he saw Carl Mays's wife signal the pitcher during the game about a payoff. Commissioner Landis's investigation produces no evidence, but Yankees' manager Miller Huggins believes the story. In Baseball As I Have Known It, *Lieb writes that in 1928 Huston told him about players dumping ball games in 1921 and 1922, but offered no specific details.*

OCTOBER 10:

World Series, game five. The Yankees forge ahead again, three games to two, on a 3-1 victory behind Waite Hoyt, who allows 10 hits. Art Nehf, who yields only six hits, is tagged with the loss. Babe Ruth, playing with an infected elbow and leg and knee injuries, leads off the fourth with a bunt base hit and scores on a Bob Meusel double.

OCTOBER 11:

World Series, game six. With Babe Ruth out of the lineup, the Yankees fall, 8-5. Jesse Barnes, who gets the win in relief of Fred Toney, strikes out 10 Yankees. Bob Shawkey, who comes on for Harry Harper in the second, is the loser. Frank Snyder and Wilson "Chick" Fewster – with one on – homer for the Giants. Bob Meusel has a two-run homer for the Yankees.

OCTOBER 12:

World Series, game seven. Babe Ruth remains sidelined and the Giants edge the Yankees, 2-1. Shufflin' Phil Douglas allows eight Yankees hits in a complete-game performance and beats Carl Mays, who yields six hits to the Giants. An RBI double by Frank Snyder is the game's difference.

OCTOBER 13:

World Series, game eight. The Giants win, 1-0, to take the Series five games to three. The game's only run scores in the first on an error by Yankees' shortstop Roger Peckinpaugh. Art Nehf goes all the way, yielding four hits. Waite Hoyt, who takes the loss, gives the Giants only six. Babe Ruth makes his only appearance in three games, pinch hitting in the ninth inning. He grounds out. Emil "Irish" Meusel leads the Giants with a .345 average and seven RBI. Babe Ruth hits .313 with one homer. Waite Hoyt allows no earned runs in 27 innings, striking out 18, but is only 21.

POST-SEASON

OCTOBER 16:

In violation of a 1912 rule about post-season play, Babe Ruth and other major league stars begin a barnstorming tour that includes exhibition games in the New York cities of Buffalo, Jamestown, and Elmira.

OCTOBER 21:

After Commissioner Landis issues suspensions, Yankees' co-owner Captain Tillinghast L'Hommedieu Huston convinces Babe Ruth to end his barnstorming tour. With half of the schedule remaining, the tour ends in Scranton, Pennsylvania.

NOVEMBER 19:

Roy Campanella is born in Philadelphia.

DECEMBER 5:

Commissioner Kenesaw Mountain Landis suspends Babe Ruth and his teammates Bob Meusel and Bill Piercy for six weeks of the 1922 season for participating in an "illegal post-season barnstorming tour." The three also are fined $3,362 each, equivalent to the loser's share of the 1921 World Series money, and will lose six weeks' worth of salary. Ruth, Meusel, and Piercy had been warned by Judge Landis that they were in violation of a 1912 rule banning post-season exhibition games by World Series participants. He accuses the players of "mutinous defiance," but he does not penalize Yankees' pitcher Tom Sheehan because he was not on the World Series roster.

DECEMBER 6:

The New York Giants acquire third baseman Henry "Heinie" Groh (.331 in 97 games) from the Cincinnati Reds for catcher Miguel "Mike" Gonzalez (.375 in 13 games), outfielder George Burns (.299, four homers), and $150,000 in cash. The deal allowed Frankie Frisch to move to second base, which solidified the Giants' infield for its defense of the league championship the following season.

HISTORY

Smoky Joe Wood, who became an outfielder after injuring his pitching arm, plays 66 games as an outfielder with the Indians. He drives in 60 runs in 194 at bats – the most ever for a player with fewer than 200 plate appearances. Wood also hits .366 with four home runs.

> "Every time I stepped up to the plate with a bat in my hands, I felt sorry for them."
> – *Rogers Hornsby, on pitchers*

HISTORY

In June, Judge Landis swings the ax again. The Reds' 32-year-old pitcher Ray Fisher is banned for life despite an offense that, at worst, seems to be a technicality. After having his original salary of $5,500 cut by $1,000 in 1920, Fisher gets approval from his manager Pat Moran to apply for a coaching job at the University of Michigan. He is successful and asks for his release from the Reds. The team offers him a raise but Moran wants a two-year contract. When he is refused, he accepts the college job and Garry Herrmann, president of the Reds, promises to put him on the voluntary retired list. Fisher hears rumors of a ban and, after an "outlaw league" contacts him, asks Judge Landis about his status and gets no answer. Then word of the ban comes down. According to historian Harold Seymour, "No explanation was given, no charges were made, no hearing was offered." Thirty years later, Fisher's files, containing his contract, were released.

THE BEST OF 1921

NATIONAL LEAGUE

HITTERS

Batting Average:
Rogers Hornsby, St. Louis Cardinals, 397

Slugging Average:
Rogers Hornsby, .639

Home Runs:
George L. Kelly, New York Giants, 23

Runs Batted In:
Rogers Hornsby, 126

Hits:
Rogers Hornsby, 235

Stolen Bases:
Frankie Frisch, New York Giants, 49

PITCHERS

Wins:
Burleigh Grimes, Brooklyn Robins; Wilbur Cooper, Pittsburgh Pirates, 22

Strikeouts:
Burleigh Grimes, 136

Earned Run Average:
Bill Doak, St. Louis Cardinals, 2.59

Winning Percentage:
Bill Doak, .714

Saves:
Lou North, St. Louis Cardinals, 7

AMERICAN LEAGUE

HITTERS

Batting Average:
Harry Heilmann, Detroit Tigers, .394

Slugging Average:
Babe Ruth, New York Yankees, .846

Home Runs:
Babe Ruth, 59

Runs Batted In:
Babe Ruth, 171

Hits:
Harry Heilmann, 237

Stolen Bases:
George Sisler, St. Louis Browns, 35

PITCHERS

Wins:
Urban Shocker, St. Louis Browns; Carl Mays, New York Yankees, 27

Strikeouts:
Walter Johnson, Washington Senators, 143

Earned Run Average:
Urban "Red" Faber, Chicago White Sox, 2.48

Winning Percentage:
Carl Mays, .750

Saves:
Carl Mays; Jim Middleton, Detroit Tigers, 7

1922

NEWS

REBECCA FULTON BECOMES FIRST FEMALE U.S. SENATOR

MORE THAN 50 AFRICAN-AMERICANS ARE LYNCHED IN U.S. THIS YEAR

LINCOLN MEMORIAL DEDICATED IN WASHINGTON, D.C.

TEAPOT DOME SCANDAL ROCKS NATION'S CAPITAL

Skywriting introduced to U.S.

JAMES JOYCE'S ULYSSES PUBLISHED

SINN FEIN PARTY ESTABLISHES IRISH REPUBLICAN ARMY

INSULIN FIRST USED TO TREAT DIABETES

WILLIAM RANDOLPH HEARST ADDS NEW YORK DAILY MIRROR TO HIS NEWSPAPER STABLE

PRE-SEASON

JANUARY 14:

Benjamin "Uncle Ben" Shibe, an American League pioneer owner, dies at age 84. He was president and half-owner of the Philadelphia Athletics.

JANUARY 17:

The appellate court rejects Benny Kauff's application for an injunction to restrain Commissioner Kenesaw Mountain Landis and NL president John Heydler from keeping him out of baseball. It is the end of the line for Kauff, who was declared ineligible by Landis in April 1921, despite his acquittal on auto theft charges. Says Landis: "I read every line of the testimony, and the acquittal smells to high heaven. That acquittal was one of the worst miscarriages of justice that ever came under my observation."

FEBRUARY 18:

The Boston Braves obtain pitcher Richard "Rube" Marquard (17-14, 3.39 ERA) from the Reds for infielder Larry Kopf (.218, one home run) and pitcher Jack Scott (15-13, 3.70 ERA).

MARCH 5:

In Hot Springs, Arkansas, Babe Ruth signs a three-year contract with the Yankees for a salary in excess of $50,000 per year. He becomes the highest-paid baseball player ever. When Ruth and Yankees' co-owner Captain Tillinghast Lihommedieu Huston reached an impasse on terms, they agreed to settle the matter by a coin toss. Ruth called tails and tails it was. He receives $500 for each home run he hits and the Yankees have a two-year option on his services. Ruth still is under suspension for playing in unauthorized barnstorming games.

THE SEASON

APRIL 12:

The Yankees begin their season without Babe Ruth and Bob Meusel and lose the season opener to the Senators in Washington, 6-5. President Warren Harding throws out the first ball.

APRIL 14:

Adrian "Cap" Anson dies in Chicago, three days after his 70th birthday. In 22 years, all with Cincinnati, he

HISTORY

After turning down Charles Comiskey's offer of $4,500, Dickie Kerr, the man who stayed clean in the Black Sox scandal, signs with a semiprofessional team in Texas for $5,000. Commissioner Landis suspends Kerr, who does not return to the major leagues until 1925. That season he pitches in only 12 games for the White Sox and goes 0-1, and his major league career ends. Kerr, who was 13-7 in 1919, 21-9 in 1920, and 19-17 in 1921, won two games in the tainted 1919 World Series. His major league career spans only four seasons.

APRIL 30
White Sox rookie pitcher Charlie Robertson pitches a perfect game.

hit .329 with a high of .399 in 1881. He also managed in the NL for 20 years in the 19th century.

APRIL 22:

The Browns' Ken Williams hits three home runs against the White Sox with George Sisler on base each time. Williams is the first modern American Leaguer with three round-trippers in a game. The Browns beat the visiting White Sox, 10-7.

APRIL 30:

Chicago White Sox rookie hurler Charlie Robertson pitches a perfect game against the Tigers, winning 2-0, at Navin Field in Detroit. The 26-year-old righthander is the third modern era pitcher with a perfect game. The others are Cy Young and Addie Joss. The Tigers' Ty Cobb and Harry Heilmann charge that Robertson, who strikes out six Detroit batters, is doctoring the ball. The White Sox score both their runs thanks to an Earl Sheely single in the second inning. Johnny Mostil, playing in left field for the first time – instead of his customary center field position – preserves the perfect game with a running catch in the second inning. With two out in the bottom of the ninth, Tigers' manager Cobb sends Johnny Bassler in to pinch-hit for losing pitcher Herman Pillette, and Robertson retires him.

The perfect game is Charlie Robertson's moment of baseball glory. In his eight-year major league career, he never records a winning season and concludes with a lifetime record of 49-80 with an ERA of 4.44. His no-hitter is his second White Sox victory – his season record is 14-15.

The Indians' Bill Wambsganss, who executed the only unassisted triple play in World Series history, is involved in another today, but this time he gets help. In the third inning against the Browns, with runners on first base and second, Wally Gerber lines to Wambsganss, who steps on second base and throws to first for the third out. The Indians, trailing at the time by 5-1, lose to the Browns, 11-9.

MAY 1:

Robins' 25-year-old rookie Harry "Pop" Shriver makes his major league debut with a 2-0 shutout of the Phillies. The Brooklyn righthander is the first NL pitcher to debut with a shutout.

Although his moment of brilliance was not as bright as Charlie Robertson's, Harry Shriver also fails to live up to the promise of today's performance. He finishes the season at 4-6 with an ERA of 2.99 and pitches only four innings in 1923 – the sum of his major league career.

MAY 5:

Ground is broken and construction begins today for Yankee Stadium at 161st Street and River Avenue in the Bronx. The White Construction Co. is building the ballpark, a job estimated to take 284 days at a cost of $2.3 million.

MAY 7:

The Giants' Jesse Barnes no-hits the Phillies, 6-0, at the Polo Grounds. Only a walk mars Barnes's pitching performance. He strikes out five and the Giants play errorless ball. Lee Meadows is the losing pitcher.

MAY 8:

Sam Breadon buys the stock of J.C. Jones and acquires controlling interest in the Cardinals. A former automobile dealer, Breadon originally invested $200 in the team as a favor to a friend.

MAY 11:

Nestor Chylak is born in Peckville, Pennsylvania.

MAY 15:

On a rainy day at the Polo Grounds, Ty Cobb hits a grounder to Yankees' shortstop Everett Scott, who misplays the ball in the mud. Cobb reaches base safely. Fred Lieb, scorer for the Associated Press, is stationed beneath the overhang because of the rain and scores the play a hit for Cobb. Today's official scorer, John Kieran of the *New York Tribune,* is in the press section at ground level behind home plate. He calls the play an error on Scott. The two do not confer.

At the end of the season, the disputed hit puts Cobb at .400. At that time, Fred Lieb reverses his call and says Kieran's "error on Scott" should be the proper call. The official statistician of the AL uses Lieb's call, giving Cobb 211 hits in 526 – .401. Cobb still finishes second to George

HISTORY

Frank Baker's career home run total is a matter of dispute. *The Baseball Encyclopedia* credits him with 96. Some statisticians maintain, with scoring changes, he should be credited with 93. He led the AL in homers for four straight seasons, with a personal all-time high of 12 in 1913.

JUNE
12
In beating the Phillies, 14-7, the Cardinals collect a record 10 hits in a row.

Sisler's .420. According to Cobb biographer Charles C. Alexander, AL president Ban Johnson is "unable to authenticate any ruling besides the AP's." The Baseball Writers Association of America protests, asserting that the League has no right to reverse Kieran, but Johnson won't back off. Cobb takes his own potshot, claiming that New York writers subtracted three hits from his season total and added two at-bats.

MAY 20:

The Indian's Tris Speaker hits his first major league grand slam home run. It comes against Red Sox pitcher Bill Piercy in a 5-2 Cleveland victory.

The suspensions of Yankees Babe Ruth and Bob Meusel end today. Ruth is named the team captain, but neither player gets a hit in a Yankees' loss to the Browns, 8-2. The game takes a strange turn in the ninth inning, with New York ahead 2-1 and Sad Sam Jones pitching. Covering first base on a routine putout, Jones drops the ball. Some of the 40,000 fans at Yankee Stadium think Jones held onto the ball and that the game is over, and they swarm onto the field. When order is restored, the Browns resume batting, score seven runs, and win the game.

MAY 22:

Frank "Home Run" Baker of the Yankees hits the final home run of his career. It comes against Urban Shocker of the St. Louis Browns. Babe Ruth responds to the booing and jeering of hometown fans at the Polo Grounds with his first home run of the year. The Yankees edge the Browns, 4-3.

MAY 25:

Less than a week after returning to action, Babe Ruth will be facing another suspension. At the Polo Grounds, Ruth is thrown out at second base by Senators' center fielder while trying to turn a base hit into a double. Ruth throws dirt into the face of umpire George Hildebrand and then goes after a fan. Ruth is ejected and the Yankees win, 6-4. Afterward, according to the *New York Times*, Ruth says, "They can boo and hoot me all they want. That doesn't matter to me. But when a fan calls insulting names from the grandstand and becomes abusive I don't intend to stand for it. This fellow today... called me a lowdown bum and other names that got me mad..." As to umpire Hildebrand, Ruth declares, "Furthermore, I didn't throw any dust in Hildebrand's face. It didn't go into his face, only on his sleeve." For his conduct, Babe Ruth is fined $200 and suspended for one game by AL president Ban Johnson. He also loses the captaincy of the Yankees – a position he held for six games.

The major leagues win a big victory and the Baltimore Terrapins of the now-defunct Federal League take a big loss in a suit against organized baseball when the U.S. Supreme Court – by a 9-0 vote – rules that the sport is not interstate commerce. Justice Oliver Wendell Holmes writes that baseball "is not interstate business in the sense of the Sherman Act."

MAY 30:

The Cubs and Cardinals trade outfielders between games of a doubleheader against each other in Chicago. The Cubs acquire Cliff Heathcote (.245); Max Flack (.222) goes to the Cardinals. Each was hitless in game one, played in the morning. In game two, an afternoon contest, Flack, now a Cardinal, goes one for four. Heathcote in a Cub uniform gets two hits in four at-bats. The Cubs win both games, 4-1 and 3-1. Flack and Heathcote become the first players ever to play for two teams on the same day.

JUNE 12:

In Philadelphia, the Cardinals beat the Phillies, 14-7, on a record 10 hits in a row in a seven-run sixth inning. And it could have been worse. The Cardinals' George "Specs" Toporcer pinch-hits for Dixie Walker and homers. But he is out for passing a base runner and gets credit for a single – one of the 10 straight hits.

JUNE 19:

Babe Ruth is once again on the sidelines. American League president Ban Johnson suspends the Bambino for "vulgar and vicious language." Earlier in the day, in a game against the Indians, umpire Bill Dinneen ejected Ruth for arguing a call at second base. The Indians win the game, 3-2, extending a Yankees' losing streak to eight games.

HISTORY

Ty Cobb, despite hitting .401, finishes second to George Sisler's .420. The Tigers under his tutelage hit .305 as a team, second to the Browns' .313. Years later, Cobb observes, "In all modesty, I could teach hitting."

LEAGUE

The St. Louis Browns protest the trade of Joe Dugan from Boston to New York and the impact it will have on the pennant race. In 1921, Dugan hit .295 with 10 home runs. In response, Commissioner Kenesaw Mountain Landis institutes a June 15 deadline for future trades.

LEAGUE

Baseball historian Bill Felber ranks the 1922 Browns among the best teams never to win a pennant. The roster included George Sisler, who hit a major league-leading .420; Ken Williams, who led the AL with 39 homers and the major leagues with 155 RBI; Jack Tobin (.331); Hank Severeid (.321); and Marty McManus (.317). As a team, the Browns hit .313 (tops in the AL) and lead in slugging (.455), stolen bases (132), ERA (3.38), and strikeouts (534). Urban Shocker records 24 wins. And, at 93-61, the Browns had their best season ever. But they finished in second place, one game behind New York.

JUNE 20:

An apparently unrepentant Babe Ruth continues to heap criticism on umpire Bill Dinneen. AL president Ban Johnson tacks another two days onto Ruth's suspension. It is his fourth of the season and has cost him $1,500 in pay.

JUNE 28:

At Griffith Stadium in Washington, D.C., Walter Johnson whitewashes the Yankees, 1-0. It is his third consecutive shutout. Waite Hoyt allows only two hits over eight innings. In the ninth, Earl Smith doubles in the game's only run. Johnson allows only seven hits – including Babe Ruth's two singles – and strikes out nine. It is the 95th career shutout for Johnson.

JULY 7:

Pirates' outfielder Max Carey is a total mystery to Giant pitchers today. In a 22-inning game which the Giants win, 9-8, Carey comes to the plate nine times and gets six hits plus three walks.

JULY 13:

Cardinals' pitcher Bill Doak makes a fielding mistake and it costs him a place in the record book. In the seventh inning, the Phillies' Curt Walker hits a bouncer to Cardinals' first baseman Jack Fournier and Doak fails to cover the base. Walker is credited with an infield hit, spoiling Doak's no-hit bid. The Cardinals win, 1-0.

JULY 20:

At Sportsman's Park in St. Louis, Rogers Hornsby hits a two-out, three-run home run in the ninth inning to beat the visiting Braves, 7-6. It is Hornsby's 25th round-tripper of the season, setting a modern NL record.

JULY 23:

With an RBI today, Cubs' first baseman Oscar "Ray" Grimes sets a major league record. Grimes now has driven in at least one run in 17 consecutive games. His total during the streak is 27.

The trade winds blow from Boston to New York again. This time it sweeps third baseman Jumping Joe Dugan (.287 in 84 games) and outfielder Elmer Smith (.286 in 73 games) to the Yankees. In return the Red Sox get outfielder Wilson "Chick" Fewster (.242 in 44 games), outfielder Elmer Miller (.267 in 51 games), shortstop Johnny Mitchell (no hits in four games), $50,000, and a player to be named later.

JULY 25:

The Braves end the 17-game consecutive RBI streak of the Cubs' Ray Grimes.

JULY 26:

It's another baseball brawl – but this time between teammates on a road trip. In the preliminary, Yankees' outfielder Bob Meusel and catcher Wally Schang trade blows in the dugout. The main event features Babe Ruth – who seems unable to avoid trouble this season – and first baseman Wally Pipp. Ruth is unhappy with Pipp's fielding and warns, "We'll settle this after the game." But all the hostilities are forgotten after the Yankees beat the Browns, 11-6. The combatants seem to have thrived on the animosity. Ruth has two home runs and Pipp one. Schang adds a two-run triple. Little Miller Huggins warns his Yankees' players, "I'm running a ball club, not a fight club. Hereafter, if there is any fighting, you'll pay for it in fines and suspensions."

AUGUST 1:

After being castigated by manager John J. McGraw following a loss to the Pirates at the Polo Grounds, today Giants' pitcher Shufflin' Phil Douglas disappears. He is eventually found unconscious in a Manhattan apartment by detectives hired by McGraw and brought to the 135th Street police station. From there he is taken to the West End Sanitarium and sedated. His clothing is confiscated.

AUGUST 2:

Browns' outfielder Ken Williams homers in his sixth consecutive game, setting a major league record. Williams has hit one homer per game since July 28.

AUGUST 5:

After being released from the West End Sanitarium and before reporting to the Polo Grounds, Shufflin' Phil Douglas gets drunk. The game is postponed because of rain, but Douglas's troubles are multiplying. He finds a bill from the team for $224.30 for the sanitarium and learns that McGraw has fined him $100 plus five days' salary.

JUNE 28
Walter Johnson blanks the Yankees, 1-0, for his third consecutive shutout.

AUGUST 8
Rabbit Maranville comes to bat 13 times in a doubleheader, tying an ML record.

Former major league outfielder-infielder Tommy McCarthy dies at age 59 in Boston. McCarthy batted .292 and stole 467 bases in 13 major league seasons.

AUGUST 8:

The Pirates' Rabbit Maranville ties a major league record by coming to bat 13 times in a doubleheader. The Pirates collect a major league record 46 hits to sweep the Phillies, 19-8 and 7-3.

After returning to the Polo Grounds two days ago and threatening reporters, today Shufflin' Phil Douglas writes a letter that will have a profound impact on his career and life. He tells outfielder Leslie Mann of the Cardinals, "I want to leave here, but I want some inducement. I don't want this guy [manager John McGraw] to win the pennant and I feel if I stay here I win it for him." Mann gives the letter to Cardinals' manager Branch Rickey, who notifies Commissioner Kenesaw Mountain Landis.

AUGUST 14:

At Fenway Park, Lizzie Murphy plays two innings at first base in an exhibition game against the Red

Rogers Hornsby was a career .358 hitter.

"You should be ashamed of yourself."
– Umpire Tom Connolly, to Babe Ruth

HISTORY

The Yankees and Giants will meet in the second consecutive Subway Series. The Yankees, under Miller Huggins, win their second straight pennant, finishing at 94-60. Babe Ruth has 35 homers in 110 games, finishing second to Ken Williams. He also hits .315 and leads the league in slugging with .672. Wally Pipp bats .329. The pitching staff is led by Joe Bush (26-7) and Bob Shawkey (20-12). Manager John McGraw leads the Giants to a 93-61 season, seven games ahead of the Reds. Frank Snyder at .343 and Emil "Irish" Meusel at .331 are the top hitters. Casey Stengel hits .368 in 84 games. The Giants have no 20-game winners; Art Nehf is their top pitcher at 19-13. The Athletics finish last in the AL for the seventh consecutive year.

Sox and reportedly becomes the first woman to compete against a major league team.

AUGUST 18:

After his disappearance last month and the bizarre aftermath, including his letter written to the Cardinals' Leslie Mann, Shufflin' Phil Douglas of the Giants is banned for life by Commissioner Landis. Douglas asserts he telephoned Mann with a request to destroy the letter; Mann says the call never took place. Says Commissioner Kenesaw Mountain Landis, who traveled to Pittsburgh to meet with manager John McGraw and Douglas: "He will never play another game in Organized Baseball and not a league will knowingly admit him to its parks." After learning he is banned, reportedly Douglas asked the commissioner, "Is this all true, Judge, that I'm through for good." "Yes, Douglas, it is," replies Landis. McGraw comments, "We have the goods on Douglas. He will never play another game in organized baseball... Without exception, he is the dirtiest ballplayer I have ever seen."

AUGUST 23:

George Kell is born in Swifton, Arkansas.

AUGUST 25:

At Chicago's Wrigley Field, the Cubs and Phillies play the highest scoring game in major league history. The Cubs use a 10-run second inning and a 14-run fourth to beat the Phillies, 26-23. The Cubs bang out 25 hits – including home runs by Lawrence "Hack" Miller and Bob O'Farrell. The Phillies amass 26 hits. There are 25 walks and 16 runners left on base. After four innings, the Cubs were ahead, 25-6. After the Phillies score six runs in the ninth and have the bases loaded, Earnest "Tiny" Osborne strikes out the Phils' DeWitt "Bevo" LeBourveau to end the game, which took an amazingly quick three hours and one minute. The winning pitcher is Tony Kaufmann; Jimmy Ring gets the loss.

AUGUST 30:

It's another ejection for Babe Ruth. At the Polo Grounds, he homers in his first at-bat. The second time up, he is called out on strikes by umpire Tom Connolly and then tossed from the game for abusive language. Ruth started for the stands to confront a heckler and Connolly, outweighed by some 100 pounds, stopped him. "You should be ashamed of yourself," Connolly tells the Yankees' slugger.

Connolly's scolding may have had an impact on Babe Ruth; it is the last time he was ejected from a baseball game in his career. Connolly umpired until 1931 and never ejected another ballplayer.

SEPTEMBER 1:

Babe Ruth receives his fifth suspension of the year when Ban Johnson sidelines him for three games for his behavior on August 30.

SEPTEMBER 5:

Babe Ruth hits his last regular season home run as a Yankee at the Polo Grounds. Next year the Yankees will be playing in their own new ballpark. Ruth whacks his round-tripper against Red Sox pitcher Herb Pennock, who also was on the mound on May 1, 1920, when Ruth hit his first Polo Grounds homer as a Yankee. The Red Sox sweep the doubleheader, 4-3 and 6-5.

SEPTEMBER 9:

The Browns win their most one-sided game ever, a 16-0 bombing of the Tigers. Bill "Baby Doll" Jacobson paces the attack with three triples and Elam Vangilder is the winning pitcher.

SEPTEMBER 10:

A crowd estimated at 40,000 packs the Polo Grounds to watch the Yankees in their last regular season appearance at the ballpark. Another 25,000 ticket-seekers are turned away. The Yankees sweep the Athletics, 10-3 and 2-1, behind Bullet Joe Bush and Waite Hoyt.

SEPTEMBER 13:

The Browns' pennant hopes suffer a severe setback when their .400 hitting first baseman George Sisler badly sprains the ligaments in his right arm. Sisler, who throws and bats left-handed, is injured making a catch on a ball hit by Ty Cobb.

SEPTEMBER 15:

Phillies' catcher Walter "Butch" Henline homers three times, becoming the first modern National Leaguer to accomplish the feat. The Phillies defeat the visiting Cardinals, 10-9.

SEPTEMBER 15
The Phillies' Butch Henline is the first modern NLer to homer three times in a game.

SEPTEMBER 16:

As the Yankees-Browns pennant race goes down to the wire, a crucial meeting between the two ballclubs at Sportsman's Park in St. Louis turns ugly. With 18,000 looking on, Urban Shocker of the Browns and Bob Shawkey of New York are locked in a pitchers' duel. Then, in the ninth inning, Lawton "Whitey" Witt and Bob Meusel both go after a ball hit by Eddie Foster. A bottle is thrown from the stands, hits Witt between the eyes and breaks, drawing blood and knocking him unconscious. As police restrain fans, someone yells, "We'll get you too, Meusel." His Yankees' teammates carry Witt off the field and New York goes on to win, 2-1. The respectable fans of St. Louis, according to contemporary reports, began cheering for the Yankees. George Sisler comments: "The bottle throwing had taken the heart out of the Browns."

SEPTEMBER 17:

In St. Louis, the Yankees begin the day one and a half games ahead of the Browns. Behind Hub Pruett, the Browns beat the Yankees and Waite Hoyt, 5-1. Babe Ruth homers for New York; Ken Williams for St. Louis. Despite his injured arm, George Sisler extends his consecutive game hitting streak to 41, topping Ty Cobb's 1911 AL record of 40.

SEPTEMBER 18:

In the third game of this pivotal series in St. Louis, the Yankees see their pennant hopes slipping away as they trail the Browns, 2-1, in the ninth inning. Frank "Dixie" Davis walks the Yankee's Wally Schang, then throws a wild pitch. Hub Pruett, yesterday's winning pitcher, relieves him. Mike McNally bunts and then catcher Hank Severeid throws wildly to third. After a walk to Everett Scott loads the bases, Urban Shocker is called in to pitch. Whitey Witt steps to the plate, his head bandaged as a result of the September 16 bottle-throwing incident. And, in an ending worthy of a Hollywood script, he singles in two runs to win the game, 3-2. The Yankees now hold a game-and-a-half lead over the Browns, whose fans remain in foul humor. They accost a New York journalist after the game.

SEPTEMBER 20:

In game one of an Ebbets Field doubleheader, Burleigh Grimes and the Robins stop Rogers Hornsby's consecutive game hitting streak at 33. Grimes three-hits the Cardinals for a 6-1 win. In game two, Hornsby homers twice.

SEPTEMBER 24:

And one for your brother! The Cardinals' Rogers Hornsby hits his 41st home run of the year against the New York Giants' Jesse Barnes. Later in the game he smacks number 42 against Virgil Barnes, Jesse's brother. The Cardinals top the Giants, 10-6.

SEPTEMBER 30:

It was a rough road for the Yankees and Babe Ruth, but they clinch the AL pennant today by beating the Red Sox, 3-1, behind the pitching of Joe Bush and Waite Hoyt.

OCTOBER 1:

In a last-game effort to reach the coveted .400 mark, St. Louis's Rogers Hornsby gets three hits in five at-bats today. He finishes the season at .401 as the visiting Cardinals beat the Cubs, 71. Hornsby – with 42 homers and 152 RBI – becomes baseball's first Triple Crown winner since Ed Delahanty in 1899. He also sets an NL record for hits in a season – 250 – topping the mark set by Wee Willie Keeler in 1897.

OCTOBER 4:

World Series, game one. In the first game of a best-of-seven format, the Giants get off first with a 3-2 win. The Giants score all their runs in the eighth inning on a two-run single by Emil "Irish" Meusel and a sacrifice fly by Ross Youngs. Babe Ruth's sixth-inning single scores Joe Dugan with the Yankee's first run. The winning pitcher is Wilfred "Rosy" Ryan in relief of Art Nehf; Joe Bush is the losing pitcher.

Game one of the 1922 World Series is the first to be broadcast play-by-play. Grantland Rice does the announcing for WJZ in Newark, New Jersey, and the game also is carried by WGY in Schenectady, New York, and WBZ in Springfield, Massachusetts.

OCTOBER 5:

World Series, game two. At 4:45 P.M., the sun shining, an estimated 45 more minutes of daylight, and

HISTORY

The Chicago American Giants, with a record of 36-23, win the Negro National League pennant.

OCTOBER 8
For the second year, the Giants beat the Yankees in the Subway World Series.

DECEMBER 12
Colonel Jacob Ruppert buys out his partner and becomes sole owner of the Yankees.

the score tied 3-3 after ten innings, umpire George Hildebrand puts the ball in his pocket and calls the game "on account of darkness." Commissioner Kenesaw Mountain Landis is besieged by fans, who also pour onto the field, forcing Hildebrand to make a hasty exit. Hildebrand explains to Judge Landis, "There was a temporary haze on the field." The commissioner orders the day's gate receipts – $120,544 – donated to charity. Prior to the controversy, Yankees' pitcher Bob Shawkey gave up three runs in the first inning on a three-run homer by Irish Meusel. The Yankees pecked away, scoring on a Wally Pipp RBI single in the first, an Aaron Ward homer in the fourth, and Bob Meusel's double in the eighth. Shawkey and Giant pitcher Jesse Barnes each went the distance and allowed eight hits.

OCTOBER 6:

World Series, game three. The Giants win again, 3-0, on a complete-game four-hitter by Jack Scott. The losing pitcher is Waite Hoyt, who goes seven and is relieved by Sad Sam Jones. There are no home runs hit today.

OCTOBER 7:

World Series, game four. The Giants continue to dominate their crosstown rivals, beating the Yankees today, 4-3. The Giants get all their runs in the fifth, coming back from a 2-0 deficit. Hugh McQuillan limits the Yankees to eight hits – including a bases-empty homer by Aaron Ward – and goes all the way for the win. The losing pitcher is Carl Mays.

OCTOBER 8:

World Series, game five. The Giants close out the Yankees and win the World Series with a 5-3 victory today. Art Nehf pitches a complete-game five-hitter, beating Joe Bush. The Giants score three in the bottom of the eighth, a rally sparked by George Kelly's RBI single. Giant third baseman Heinie Groh hits .474 and second baseman Frankie Frisch hits .471 for the series. Babe Ruth is a disappointing .118 with no home runs and no hits in the last three games of the Series.

In the eighth inning of game five, Miller Huggins orders Joe Bush to intentionally walk George Kelly. Fans and sportswriters are able to hear Bush screaming four-letter words at the manager. Bush is later accused of "allowing" Kelly to hit the single that wins the game and the series.

POST-SEASON

OCTOBER 12:

Pitcher Lefty O'Doul (0-0, 3.38 ERA) is sent by the Yankees to the Red Sox to complete a July 24 trade that brought Joe Dugan to New York.

OCTOBER 27:

Ralph Kiner is born in Santa Rita, New Mexico.

NOVEMBER 5:

The Indians sell Jim Bagby, who won 31 games in 1920, to the Pirates for the waiver price. Last season, Bagby slumped to 4-5 with an ERA of 6.32.

NOVEMBER 6:

Morgan G. Bulkeley, the first president of the NL, dies at the age of 84. In addition to his baseball activities, Bulkeley was governor of Connecticut and a U.S. senator from that state.

NOVEMBER 7:

Former major league outfielder Sam Thompson dies at age 62 in Detroit. In his 15-year career, Big Sam hit .331

NOVEMBER 27:

Outfielder Austin McHenry, who hit .303 in 64 games for the St. Louis Cardinals this past season, dies at the age of 27 of a brain tumor in Jefferson, Ohio. McHenry is the second Cardinals' player to pass away this year. On February 23, catcher William "Pickles" Dillhoefer died of pneumonia, also at age 27, in St. Louis.

DECEMBER 12:

The Captain sells to the Colonel. An agreement is reached today for Yankees' co-owner Captain Tillinghast L'Hommedieu Huston to sell his share of the ballclub to the team's other owner, Colonel Jacob Ruppert, for $1.5 million. At this point, all the pieces are coming together for the Yankees. Along with Babe Ruth, Ruppert had brought over Ed Barrow from Boston to manage the team, and made deals for pitcher Waite Hoyt and catcher Wally Schang. While the Yankees came up just short this year and last, in 1923, with Ruppert in full control, they would finally win it all.

THE BEST OF 1922

National League

HITTERS

Batting Average:
Rogers Hornsby, St. Louis Cardinals, .401

Slugging Average:
Rogers Hornsby, .722

Home Runs:
Rogers Hornsby, 42

Runs Batted In:
Rogers Hornsby, 152

Hits:
Rogers Hornsby, 250

Stolen Bases:
Max Carey, Pittsburgh Pirates, 51

PITCHERS

Wins:
Eppa Rixey, Cincinnati Reds, 25

Strikeouts:
Dazzy Vance, Brooklyn Robins, 134

Earned Run Average:
Wilfred "Rosy" Ryan, New York Giants, 3.01

Winning Percentage:
Pete Donohue, Cincinnati Reds, .667

Saves:
Claude Jonnard, New York Giants, 5

American League

HITTERS

Batting Average:
George Sisler, St. Louis Browns, .420

Slugging Average:
Babe Ruth, New York Yankees, .672

Home Runs:
Ken Williams, St. Louis Browns, 39

Runs Batted In:
Ken Williams, 155

Hits:
George Sisler, 246

Stolen Bases:
George Sisler, 51

PITCHERS

Wins:
Ed Rommel, Philadelphia Athletics, 27

Strikeouts:
Urban Shocker, St. Louis Browns, 149

Earned Run Average:
Urban "Red" Faber, Chicago White Sox, 2.80

Winning Percentage:
Joe Bush, New York Yankees, .788

Saves:
Sam Jones, New York Yankees, 8

Most Valuable Player:
George Sisler, St. Louis Browns

TRIVIA

Babe Ruth loved the Polo Grounds' short right field – 257 feet and 259 feet to the upper deck. He said, "I cried when they took me out of the Polo Grounds." In 1921, Ruth had 32 homers in only 255 at-bats playing at home.

1923

"I'd give a year of my life if I can hit a home run in this first game."
– *Babe Ruth*

NEWS

PRESIDENT WARREN HARDING DIES AT 57

CALVIN COOLIDGE IS NEW PRESIDENT

HITLER'S ATTEMPT TO OVERTHROW GERMAN GOVERNMENT FAILS

200,000 attend Ku Klux Klan convention in Kokomo, Indiana

OKLAHOMA UNDER MARTIAL LAW TO MEET KKK TERRORISM

WILLIAM JENNINGS BRYAN ATTACKS EVOLUTION

***TIME* MAGAZINE MAKES ITS DEBUT**

Evangelist Aimee Semple McPherson opens $1.5 Million temple in Los Angeles

Maidenform bras introduced

PRE-SEASON

JANUARY 1:

"Wee" Willie Keeler dies in Brooklyn at age 50. The outfielder compiled a lifetime batting average of .343 over 19 years and stole 495 bases. Keeler, who stood five feet, four and a half inches and weighed 140 pounds, swung a 30 1/2-inch bat, reportedly the shortest ever used in the major leagues.

JANUARY 3:

The Yankees acquire left-handed pitcher and future Hall of Famer Herb Pennock (10-17, 4.32 ERA) from the Red Sox in return for outfielder Elisha "Camp" Skinner (.182), infielder Norm McMillan (.256), pitcher George Murray (4-2, 3.97 ERA), and $50,000.

FEBRUARY 2:

Albert "Red" Schoendienst is born in Germantown, Illinois.

FEBRUARY 10:

The Red Sox trade pitcher Al Russell (6-7, 5.01 ERA) and catcher Herold "Muddy" Ruel (.255 with no homers) to the Senators for outfielders Howard Shanks (.283 with one homer in 84 games) and Ed Goebel (.271 with one homer in 37 games), and catcher Val Picinich (.229 with no homers in 76 games).

MUDDY RUEL IS BELIEVED TO BE THE FIRST TO DESCRIBE A CATCHER'S EQUIPMENT AS "THE TOOLS OF IGNORANCE."

FEBRUARY 11:

The Boston Braves are purchased for $350,000 from George Washington Grant and associates by Judge Emil Fuchs, James McDonough, and former Giants' pitching great Christy Mathewson, who becomes the team's president.

Fuchs was the youngest deputy attorney general in the state of New York and also was attorney for the Giants and for manager John McGraw. According to his son, Robert S. Fuchs, he "purchased the Braves for one reason only – to bring Christy Mathewson, one of the most brilliant gentlemen of all times, back to baseball."

FEBRUARY 15:

The Robins acquire first baseman Jack Fournier (.295, 10 homers) from the Cardinals for outfielder Henry "Hy" Myers (.317, six homers) and first baseman Ray Schmandt (.269, two home runs). Fournier threatens to quit baseball rather than join the Brooklyn club.

APRIL 17
The St. Louis Cardinals wear numbers on their uniforms for the first time.

APRIL 18
Yankee Stadium – the House that Ruth Built – opens with a New York win over the Red Sox.

THE SEASON

APRIL 17:

In the longest opening day game ever played in the NL, the Phillies and Robins battle to a 14-inning, 5-5 tie in Brooklyn.

The Cardinals wear uniform numbers for the first time in a regular season game, but bow to the Reds, 3-2, in 11 innings in Cincinnati today. The numbers correspond to a player's position in the batting order.

APRIL 18:

This season, Babe Ruth is available on opening day and he makes his presence felt at the opening of the new Yankee Stadium. A crowd of 74,200 crams into the new ballpark in the Bronx and another 25,000 are turned away. They see New York governor Al Smith throw out the first ball and then cheer Ruth's three-run homer in the third inning. Ruth's blast over the right-field fence comes on a 2-2 slow curve from Boston's Howard Ehmke with Whitey Witt on third and Joe Dugan on first. Prior to the game, the Bambino is quoted as saying: "I'd give a year of my life if I can hit a home run in this first game in this new park." It is Ruth's 199th career homer. But the honor of the first hit at the stadium goes to Red Sox first baseman George Burns, who singles in the second and is erased trying to steal. The Yankees win the game, 4-1, on a Bob Shawkey three-hitter.

In the *Evening Telegram*, Fred Lieb dubs the new Yankee Stadium the House that Ruth Built. It is a three-tier modern ballpark, constructed at a cost of some $2.5 million. Situated across the Harlem River from the Polo Grounds on the site of an old lumberyard at 161st Street and River Avenue in the Bronx,

"The House that Ruth Built" opens in the Bronx.

"I think I've just seen another Babe Ruth."
– Yankees' scout, on Lou Gehrig

CULTURE

Rumors are circulating about a late August fistfight in the Polo Grounds clubhouse between Cardinals' manager Branch Rickey and second baseman Rogers Hornsby. According to accounts, the fight was broken up by Burt Shotton, St. Louis coach and Sunday manager (Rickey doesn't work on the Sabbath). The disagreement began when Rickey gave a batter a take sign and Hornsby was stranded on third base and swore at the manager. Rickey comments that it "amounted to nothing more than a passing incident and had been forgotten."

The catcher's mitt is a basic "tool of ignorance."

it took 11 months to complete. In addition to Al Smith's inaugural pitch, opening day festivities included the playing of the National Anthem by the 7th Regiment Band under conductor John Philip Sousa.

In an intercollegiate game, Columbia University left-hander Lou Gehrig strikes out 17 Williams College batters.

APRIL 20:

In Chicago, the Cubs hit six homers today in a 12-11 win over the Pirates; the team now has 12 homers in two days. Today's home run hitters are Charles "Gabby" Hartnett (two), Gustaf "Barney" Friberg (two), Arnold "Jigger" Statz, and Cliff Heathcote. Hartnett's second homer wins the game for the Cubs in the ninth. The Pirates' bats are not silent; Charlie Grimm and Harold "Pie" Traynor homer for Pittsburgh.

APRIL 26:

Yankees' scout Paul Krichell watches Lou Gehrig power two home runs against Rutgers University in New Jersey and tells general manager Ed Barrow, "I think I've just seen another Babe Ruth."

APRIL 29:

One day after scout Paul Krichell sees Columbia's Lou Gehrig hit a homer some 450 feet against New York University, the 20-year-old signs a Yankee contract. He will receive a salary of $2,000 for four months plus a $1,500 bonus.

MAY 2:

Yankees' shortstop Everett Scott plays in his 1,000th consecutive major league game. His streak began on June 20, 1916, when he was with the Red Sox. The previous record holder was Fred Luderus of the Phillies with 533. Scott's landmark game is played in Washington, D.C., where he is presented with a gold medal by secretary of the navy Edwin Denby. In the game itself, Senators' pitcher Walter Johnson creates his own special occasion by ringing up his 100th career shutout, a three-hit, 3-0 victory over Bob Shawkey and the Yankees.

MAY 7:

In Philadelphia, the Phillies' Phil Weinert decks Casey Stengel of the Giants in the fourth inning after hitting him with a pitch in the second. Stengel throws his bat at Weinert and attacks him. With Stengel getting the best of the scrap, Phillies' manager Art Fletcher pries him loose and two police officers escort him from the field. NL president John Heydler suspends Stengel for 10 days.

MAY 11:

At Baker Bowl in Philadelphia, the Phillies and Cardinals combine for a NL record 10 home runs and a major league record 79 total bases in a game won by Philadelphia, 20-14. Three of the 10 homers belong to the Phillies' Cy Williams. The other home run hitters are the Phillies' Johnny Mokan (two) and Frank Parkinson (one); for the Cardinals, Les Mann (two), losing pitcher Bill Sherdel (one), and Eddie Dyer (one). A record 23 players hit safely in the game; 12 get extra-base hits, and a dozen walks are issued. The winning pitcher is Charles "Petie" Behan.

While the Cardinals and Phillies are demonstrating power in the major leagues, outfielder Pete Schneider of Vernon in the Pacific Coast League hits five home runs – including two grand slams – and a double to drive in 14 runs against Salt Lake City in a 35-11 victory. Schneider pitched in the major leagues from 1914 through 1919 with the Reds and Yankees (one year), compiling an unimpressive 58-86 record with a respectable ERA of 2.62.

MAY 21:

In New York, Jacob Ruppert completes the purchase of Captain Tillinghast Huston's share of the Yankees for $1.5 million. Huston, who originally invested $230,000 in the Yankees, leaves with a profit of 650 percent. Colonel Ruppert wires his team in Chicago: "I now am the sole owner of the Yankees. Miller Huggins is my manager." Huggins and his team are locked in a 15-inning struggle with the White Sox, and road secretary Mark Roth is concerned about the team missing its train. "Take it easy. I'll get us out of here," says Babe Ruth, who then homers to give New York and Herb Pennock a 3-1 victory.

APRIL 20
The Chicago Cubs hit six home runs in a 12-11 win over the Pittsburgh Pirates.

JULY 22
Walter Johnson is the first pitcher to reach the 3,000 career strikeouts mark.

MAY 27:

At the Polo Grounds, the Phillies' Cy Williams homers against the Giants' Wilfred "Rosy" Ryan. It is Williams's 15th homer in May – an NL record – and his 18th of the season, the most ever by an NL player by this date.

JUNE 15:

Rogers Hornsby leaves the Cardinals for five days to visit his ailing mother.

JUNE 30:

When you're hot, you're hot. Brooklyn's Jimmy Johnston has eight consecutive hits today in a double-header against the Phillies in Philadelphia. Johnston hits a homer, three doubles, and four singles, and is 24 for his last 34 at-bats. The Robins win game one, 10-4. The Phillies take the nightcap, 6-2.

JULY 1:

Against the Giants, Johnston is cooled down, going hitless in two official at-bats. The infielder goes on to hit .325 for the entire ML season with four home runs. In a 13-year career, he compiles a lifetime average of .294 with 22 home runs.

JULY 7:

In Cleveland, Red Sox manager Frank Chance punishes pitcher Francis "Lefty" O'Doul, and the Indians salt the wounds. In the sixth inning, O'Doul relieves the injured Bill Piercy. He then faces 16 batters, walking six and giving up 13 runs. Chance refuses to relieve him until he gets the third out. The Indians win, 27-3, setting a major league record for most runs in a game. Nine Indians score two or more runs.

Chance was angry at O'Doul for breaking curfew and had fined him $200. After seeing O'Doul admire himself in a mirror, Chance vows, "I'm going to leave that looking-glass so-and-so out there if it takes him all day to get 'em out." O'Doul fares better as a hitter. After the 1923 season, he becomes a full-time outfielder and leads the NL in batting twice, including a .398 season in 1929.

JULY 11:

An Ohio group led by Bo Quinn and E.M. Schoenborn will purchase the Boston Red Sox from Harry Frazee for $1.5 million. Frazee, a Broadway producer, will be remembered in baseball as the man who sold Babe Ruth and other stars to cover his theatrical expenses.

JULY 17:

Did he get the idea from Frank Chance or is it a trend? Ten days after Chance refused to relieve pitcher Lefty O'Doul, Yankee manager Miller Huggins follows suit with Carl Mays and once again, the Indians are happy to cooperate. Angered by Mays's attitude and a spring training argument, Huggins leaves Mays on the mound for all nine innings as Cleveland pounds him for 20 hits and 13 runs. Shortstop Everett Scott and first baseman Wally Pipp protest by coming out of the game. The Indians win, 13-0.

JULY 18:

In Detroit, Del Pratt lines to Yankees' right-fielder Elmer Smith with Harry Heilmann running on the play. Smith trots in from right field, reaching first base before Heilmann can return for a rare unassisted double play by an outfielder. It is the only one in Yankee history.

JULY 22:

Walter Johnson today becomes the first pitcher to reach the 3,000 career strikeout mark. Johnson strikes out five for the game and beats the Indians, 3-1.

JULY 26:

James Hoyt Wilhelm is born in Huntersville, North Carolina.

With the Reds trailing the Giants, 6-2, in the eighth, Cincinnati pitcher Adolfo Luque takes exception to remarks from the New York bench and leaves the mound to attack Casey Stengel. He slugs Stengel and is restrained by New York's Ross Youngs, who was the batter. Luque is taken off by police. But Reds' right fielder Edd Roush renews the dispute, and when the police turn their attention to him, Luque grabs a bat and again heads for the Giants' dugout. He is intercepted and removed to the clubhouse. Stengel and Luque are ejected; Roush remains.

SEPTEMBER 4:

Sad Sam Jones has reason to smile today. The Yankees' right-hander no-hits the

HISTORY

After hitting .420 in 1922, George Sisler will miss the entire 1923 season. The Browns' first baseman is having problems with his eyesight as a result of a sinus condition. Sisler returns to baseball in 1924 and has some outstanding seasons, but never again reaches his pre-1923 levels.

TRIVIA

***The Sun Field*, by noted sportswriter Heywood Broun, is published. According to SABR-ite Andy McCue, it is "the first novel with serious baseball content aimed at an adult audience."**

SEPTEMBER 14
Boston Red Sox first baseman George Burns turns an unassisted triple play.

SEPTEMBER 17
The Giants' George Kelly becomes the first MLer to homer in three consecutive at-bats.

TRIVIA

William Carlos Williams publishes the poem "The Crowd at the Ball Game."

LEAGUE

Player prices are escalating. The White Sox buy third baseman Willie Kamm from San Francisco in the Pacific Coast League for $125,000. Kamm is a solid player with a .281 average for 13 years, but hardly a star. His best season is 1928 when he hits .308 with one homer. The Orioles' Jack Dunn, who sold Babe Ruth to the Red Sox for $2,500, gets a lot more for pitcher Jack Bentley. The left-hander, who played with the Senators from 1913 to 1916, brings $65,000 from the Giants. Bentley's best season with New York is 1924, when he is 16-5.

Athletics, 2-0, in Philadelphia, allowing only two base runners – on a walk and an error. With two out in the ninth inning, A's shortstop Clarence "Chick" Galloway asserts, "I'm gonna break it up if I can." He bunts down the third base line. Jones fields the ball and throws him out to end the game. The losing pitcher is Bob Hasty.

SEPTEMBER 7:

In Philadelphia today, Howard Ehmke of the Red Sox no-hits the Athletics, 4-0. It is the second time in less than a week that Philadelphia has gone hitless. Ehmke gets some help in the seventh inning when opposing pitcher Bill "Slim" Harriss hits a drive to the outfield wall and is called out on appeal for missing first base. A scoring decision in the eighth inning also keeps the no-hitter alive. Left fielder Mike Menosky drops a line drive. The scorer rules it is a hit, then changes it to an error. Ehmke strikes out one. Harriss is the losing pitcher in a game that takes only one hour and 34 minutes to play.

SEPTEMBER 11:

In New York, Red Sox pitcher Howard Ehmke bids for his second straight no-hitter but comes up short in the first inning on a controversial call. Yankees' outfielder Lawton "Whitey" Witt hits a grounder to Boston third baseman Howard Shanks, who misplays the ball. Official scorer Fred Lieb rules it a hit and refuses to change it to an error under pressure. Ehmke then retires the next 27 Yankees in a row and wins the game, 3-0.

Umpire Tom Connolly asserts Shanks should have had the ball, but AL president Ban Johnson supports the right of Lieb to make the call and Ehmke misses a chance for two straight no-hitters.

SEPTEMBER 14:

Red Sox first baseman George Burns executes an unassisted triple play in the second inning of a game against the Indians. With runners on first and second, Burns snares a liner hit by Frank Brower, tags Walter "Rube" Lutzke, who was on first base, and beats Riggs Stephenson to second base.

SEPTEMBER 16:

At Wrigley Field, Commissioner Kenesaw Mountain Landis and NL president John A. Heydler witness a nasty spectacle. In the eighth inning, umpire Charles Moran calls the Cubs' Earl "Sparky" Adams out at second base. Fans pelt the umpire with bottles. Giant outfielder Emil "Irish" Meusel and infielder Barney Friberg are hit with bottles and Judge Landis shakes his cane at the crowd with no effect. The game is delayed for 10 minutes, and when it resumes, the Giants win, 10-6. But after the game Giants' manager John McGraw and the umpires get a police escort off the field.

SEPTEMBER 17:

At Wrigley Field, Giants' first baseman George Kelly becomes the first major leaguer to homer in three consecutive innings. Kelly victimizes Cubs' pitchers in the third, fourth, and fifth. New York wins, 13-6.

SEPTEMBER 20:

The Yankees win their third straight AL pennant by beating the Browns, 4-3. They lead the Detroit Tigers by 18 games after today's action.

SEPTEMBER 27:

The Red Sox will have a new manager for 1924. According to an announcement today by new owner Bob Quinn, Frank Chance will not return. Boston is mired in last place in the American League.

Rogers Hornsby is fined $500 and suspended for the five remaining games of the season by Cardinals' manager Branch Rickey. According to team owner Sam Breadon, Hornsby was capable of playing yesterday against the Robins. Hornsby asserts he has a knee injury and sat out the game. Breadon holds a press conference to address rumors that Rogers Hornsby will be moved to the Giants. Says the teams' owner: "The Cardinals positively will not trade him... If he declines to play with St. Louis next year, he will not play anyplace in organized baseball."

At Fenway Park, 20-year-old Lou Gehrig hits his first major league home run. It comes against ex-Yankee Bill Piercy in an 8-3 New York victory over Boston.

SEPTEMBER 28:

The pennant may be clinched, but Yankee bats are booming. Today they beat the Red Sox, 24-4, on 30 hits. Howard Ehmke,

OCTOBER 10
In the first World Series game ever played at Yankee Stadium, the Giants win, 5-4.

"Casey Stengel just can't keep from being Casey Stengel."
– Commissioner Landis

who came within a controversial call of no-hitting the Yankees 17 days ago, is mauled today. He goes six innings, giving up 21 hits and 17 runs. In the sixth, 16 Yankees come to the plate against him.

With Art Nehf's 3-0 shutout of the Brooklyn Robins, the Giants clinch their third straight NL pennant, setting up a Subway Series for the third year in a row.

OCTOBER 6:

On the last day of the season, Braves' shortstop Ernie Padgett executes the first unassisted triple play in modern NL history. In Boston, in the fourth inning of a double header nightcap, Padgett snares a line drive hit by Walter Holke, doubles up James "Cotton" Tierney at second base, and tags Cliff Lee for the third out. Boston wins the game, 4-1, in five innings to sweep the double header. Joe Batchelder takes the win; Phil "Lefty" Weinert is the losing pitcher.

REST OF SEASON

WRAP-UP: For the third straight year, the two New York teams will meet in the World Series. The Giants, under John McGraw, get there with a 95-58 record, finishing four and a half games ahead of the Reds. The Giants have no 20-game winner, but plenty of offense, including Frank Frisch (.348), Ross Youngs (.336), George Kelly (.307), and Dave Bancroft (.304). Handsome Hugh McQuillan is their most effective pitcher with a 3.41 ERA and a 15-14 record.

The Yankees, managed by Miller Huggins, finish 16 games ahead of the Tigers with a 98-54 record. Babe Ruth has a Ruthian year, but he isn't the whole show: Wally Pipp hits .304; Lawton "Whitey" Witt, 314; and Bob Meusel, .313. Four ex-Red Sox – Sam Jones (21-8), Herb Pennock (19-6), Joe Bush (19-15) and Waite Hoyt (17-9) – and ex-Athletic Bob Shawkey (16-11) comprise the Yankees' staff. In 13 games, Lou Gehrig hits .423.

OCTOBER 10:

World Series, game one. At Yankee Stadium, the Giants pick up where they left off last fall, beating the Yankees. Today's 5-4 win marks the eighth straight for the Giants over the Yankees (with one tie). Casey Stengel wins the game with an inside-the-park home run to left center field off losing pitcher Joe Bush with two out in the top of the ninth inning. Stengel loses his shoe while rounding the bases. Wilfred "Rosy" Ryan is the winning pitcher with seven innings in relief of John "Mule" Watson. Today's game is the first World Series contest to be broadcast nationally on the radio.

OCTOBER 11:

World Series, game two. Behind complete-game pitching by Herb Pennock and three home runs, the Yankees break the Giants' string and win, 4-2, at the Polo Grounds. Babe Ruth hits two bases-empty homers and in the ninth inning sends a drive 475 feet to center field, where it is caught by Casey Stengel. Aaron Ward adds a home run for the Yankees; Irish Meusel reaches the seats for the Giants. Pennock allows eight hits en route to the win. The losing pitcher is Hugh McQuillan.

OCTOBER 12:

World Series, game three. At Yankee Stadium, the Giants' Art Nehf locks up with Sad Sam Jones in a pitching classic. In the seventh inning, Casey Stengel homers into the right-field bleachers for the games' only run. It is one of only four hits Jones yields on the way to a 1-0 defeat. Nehf allows the Yankees only six hits. This time Stengel keeps both shoes on. But he thumbs his nose as he rounds the bases. Yankees' owner Jacob Ruppert protests the gesture; Commissioner Landis comments: "Casey Stengel just can't keep from being Casey Stengel."

LEAGUE

In September, the Giants obtain outfielder Lewis "Hack" Wilson from Portsmouth for $11,000 and minor league players. Wilson, who has been ripping up the Virginia League, appears in three games in 1923 for New York, hitting .200 with two singles.

Casey Stengel

OCTOBER 15
The Yankees top the Giants in game six of the Series for their first World Championship.

"The paths of glory lead but to the Braves."
– *Casey Stengel*

HISTORY

The Kansas City Monarchs win the Negro National League pennant with a 57-33 record. The Eastern Colored League pennant is won by Hilldale, which finishes at 32-17.

HISTORY

Babe Ruth rebounds in a big way from his disappointing 1922 season. His 1923 stats include 41 home runs (tying for the major league lead), 151 runs, 131 RBI, 170 walks, a .393 batting average, and a slugging percentage of .764.

OCTOBER 13:

World Series, game four. At the Polo Grounds today, the Yankees beat the Giants, 8-4. Bob Shawkey is the winner – despite allowing 13 hits – with a save from Herb Pennock. A six-run second inning propels the Yankees to the victory. Jack Scott, the first of five pitchers, takes the loss for the Giants. Ross Youngs of the Giants has the game's only homer.

OCTOBER 14:

World Series, game five. Back across the Harlem River at Yankee Stadium, the Yankees bomb the Giants, 8-1. Joe Dugan paces the attack with a three-run homer – one of his four hits. Joe Bush goes all the way for the win, allowing only three hits – all to Irish Meusel. Jack Bentley is the losing pitcher.

OCTOBER 15:

World Series, game six. It took three tries, but the Yankees finally win a World Series from the Giants. At the Polo Grounds today, Herb Pennock – with a save by Sad Sam Jones – beats the Giants, 6-4. The Yankees score five of their runs in the top of the eighth with the tying and lead runs walked in on eight pitches by loser Art Nehf. He had limited the Yankees to two hits over the first seven. Babe Ruth homers into the upper deck in right field for the Yankees; Frank Snyder hits one for the Giants. Babe Ruth ends the series with three home runs and a .368 average. Casey Stengel hits .417 with two game-winning home runs.

POST-SEASON

OCTOBER 22:

Lee Fohl is named manager of the Boston Red Sox. He replaces Frank Chance, who led the Red Sox to a last-place finish with a 61-91 record. Fohl managed the Indians from 1915 through 1919 and the Browns from 1921 through part of this past season. The Browns were 52-49 in 1923 when he was replaced as manager by Jimmy Austin.

OCTOBER 25:

Bobby Thomson is born in Glasgow, Scotland. In 1951, Thomson, playing for the Giants, will hit one of the most famous homers ever.

NOVEMBER 12:

The Giants trade Series hero Casey Stengel (.339, five homers) to the Braves along with shortstop Dave Bancroft (.304, one home run) and outfielder Bill Cunningham (.271, five homers). In return, New York gets outfielder Billy Southworth (.319, six homers) and pitcher Joe Oeschger (5-15, 5.68 ERA). Bancroft is named Boston's manager, replacing Fred Mitchell. Stengel supposedly says of the trade: "The paths of glory lead but to the Braves."

DECEMBER 9:

Former major league pitcher and manager Wild Bill Donovan dies in a train wreck in Forsyth, New York. The 47-year-old Donovan, skipper of New Haven in the Eastern League, is on his way to baseball's winter meetings in Chicago when the accident occurs. Surviving the wreck is his boss, George Weiss. Donovan had a lifetime record of 186-139 with an ERA of 2.69, in stints with Washington, Brooklyn, Detroit, and the Yankees. He managed the Yankees from 1916 through 1917 and the Phillies for the 1921 season.

DECEMBER 11:

The Yankees sell pitcher Carl Mays to the Reds for $7,500. The submarine-ball right-hander was only 5-2 with a 6.20 ERA in 23 games this past season. In past years he was a big winner for New York. In 1920 he won 26 games, and in 1921 led the American League with 27 victories. Yankees' manager Miller Huggins tells Reds' president Garry Herrmann, "I may be sending you the best pitcher I have, but I warn you that Carl is a troublemaker and always will be a hard man to sign."

DECEMBER 13:

Larry Doby is born in Camden, South Carolina.

DECEMBER 16:

Representatives of the Brooklyn Royal Giants, the Lincoln Giants of New York, Bacharach Giants, Baltimore Black Sox, and the Hilldale Club meet in Philadelphia and form the Eastern Colored League. Four of the six teams are owned by whites. The clubs will be successful in obtaining many of the better players from the competing Negro National League.

NOVEMBER 12
The New York Giants trade World Series hero Casey Stengel to the Boston Braves.

DECEMBER 16
At a meeting in Philadelphia, the six-team Eastern Colored League is formed.

THE BEST OF 1923

National League

HITTERS

Batting Average:
Rogers Hornsby, St. Louis Cardinals, 384

Slugging Average:
Rogers Hornsby, .627
Home Runs: Fred "Cy" Williams, Philadelphia Phillies, 41

Runs Batted In:
Emil "Irish" Meusel, New York Giants, 125

Hits:
Frankie Frisch, New York Giants, 223

Stolen Bases:
Max Carey, Pittsburgh Pirates, 51

PITCHERS

Wins:
Dolf Luque, Cincinnati Reds, 27

Strikeouts:
Dazzy Vance, Brooklyn Robins, 197

Earned Run Average:
Dolf Luque, 1.93

Winning Percentage:
Dolf Luque, .771

Saves:
Claude Jonnard, New York Giants, 5

American League

HITTERS

Batting Average:
Harry Heilmann, Detroit Tigers, .403

Slugging Average:
Babe Ruth, New York Yankees, .764

Home Runs:
Babe Ruth, 41

Runs Batted In:
Babe Ruth, 131

Hits:
Charlie Jamieson, Cleveland Indians, 222

Stolen Bases:
Eddie "Cocky" Collins, Chicago White Sox—47

PITCHERS

Wins:
George Uhle, Cleveland Indians, 26

Strikeouts:
Walter Johnson, Washington Senators, 130

Earned Run Average:
Stan Coveleski, Cleveland Indians, 2.76

Winning Percentage:
Herb Pennock, New York Yankees, .760

Saves:
Allan Russell, Washington Senators, 9

Most Valuable Player:
Babe Ruth, New York Yankees

HISTORY

In the Pacific Coast League, Paul Strand of Salt Lake City completes the season with 325 hits, a record for organized baseball, and hits .394. Last year, Strand had 289 hits. The hit totals are tempered somewhat by the fact that PCL teams play a 194-game season – 40 more than the major leagues. A pitcher-outfielder, Strand played with the Red Sox from 1913 to 1915, never hitting higher than .167. He will get a final big league shot next season with the A's, batting .228 in 47 games.

1924

NEWS

CALVIN COOLIDGE ELECTED PRESIDENT

AMERICA HAS 2.5 MILLION RADIOS

Price of a Ford falls to $280

J. EDGAR HOOVER BECOMES ACTING DIRECTOR OF FBI

LEOPOLD AND LOEB CONVICTED OF "THRILL" MURDER, SENTENCED TO LIFE

WOODROW WILSON DIES AT AGE 67

LENIN DIES

Congress grants citizenship to native-born Indians

HITLER SENTENCED TO FIVE YEARS IN JAIL FOR FAILED PUTSCH

IBM IS NEW NAME OF TABULATING COMPANY

The Thief of Bagdad *stars Douglas Fairbanks and Anna May Wong*

PRE-SEASON

JANUARY 7:

The Yankees buy the contract of outfielder Earle Combs from the Louisville Colonels, with whom he hit .380 with 241 hits last year under manager Joe McCarthy.

FEBRUARY 16:

Braves' infielder Tony Boeckel is killed at the age of 31 in an automobile accident in Torrey Pines, California. Boeckel hit .298 with seven homers last season.

FEBRUARY 17:

Before he has the opportunity to manage the White Sox, new manager Frank Chance is taken ill. Owner Charles Comiskey names coach Johnny Evers acting manager.

FEBRUARY 21:

Cardinals' manager Branch Rickey and star Rogers Hornsby bury the hatchet. They meet with reporters from St. Louis newspapers, and Hornsby says, "There is no longer any misunderstanding between us. I want to have the best year in baseball I have ever had and I want the Cardinals club to have the best year it has ever had."

MARCH 7:

Cincinnati Reds' manager Pat Moran dies at age 48 in Orlando, Florida, of Bright's disease. Moran has been Cincinnati's skipper for the past five years and led the team to its 1920 World Series win against the Black Sox. He also managed the Phillies for four seasons and played in the major leagues for 14 years as a catcher, hitting .235.

THE SEASON

APRIL 23:

The Chicago Cubs begin regular radio coverage of their home games with Hal Totten broadcasting via WMAQ.

MAY 11:

Moses Fleetwood Walker dies in Cleveland at age 67. Walker, a catcher, was one of the first black professional baseball players and the first major leaguer and, to date, the last. In 1884, he appeared in 42 games for Toledo in the American Association, batting .263. Pitcher Tony Mullane, who played with Fleetwood Walker at Toledo in 1884, was quoted as saying, "He was the best catcher I ever worked with, but I disliked a Negro and whenever I had to pitch to him I used anything I wanted without looking at his signals."

MAY 14:

At Yankee Stadium, on Babe Ruth Day, the Bambino is presented with the AL's League Award as the Most Valuable Player of 1923. The Yankees' World Championship banner is unfurled, but the Browns spoil the day with an 11-1 victory. Ruth is limited to a single.

MAY 16:

William A. "Candy" Cummings, the purported inventor of the curveball, dies at age 75 in Toledo, Ohio. Cummings pitched in the NL in 1876 and 1877, compiling a 21-22 record with a 2.78 ERA.

MAY 23:

Walter Johnson limits the visiting White Sox to one hit and strikes out 14 batters in a 1-0 Senators' victory. It is Johnson's fourth shutout of the young season. A

Jack Bentley, the losing pitcher in game seven, says, "The good Lord just couldn't bear to see a fine fellow like Walter Johnson lose again."

fourth-inning single by Harry Hooper is Chicago's only hit.

JUNE 13:

At Navin Field in Detroit, the Yankees win, 9-0, on a forfeit when umpire Billy Evans calls the game for what *The Sporting News* describes as a "life-threatening situation for players, umps and police." The Yanks are leading, 10-6, in the top of the ninth. After just missing Babe Ruth with a pitch, Tigers' hurler Bert "King" Cole hits Bob Meusel in the back. Meusel rushes the mound but is restrained by umpire Emmett "Red" Ormsby. Ty Cobb, never known to shy from combat, charges onto the field and confronts Ruth. The two superstars square off and swear at each other; Ruth has to be restrained. Meusel and Ruth are ejected, and an estimated 1,000 of the 18,000 fans on hand pour onto the field. Police escort the Yankees and umpires off the field but are unable to restore order. There are reports of guns and clubs among the crowd.

According to author Mark Gallagher, Babe Ruth told Bob Meusel he saw Ty Cobb call for Bert Cole to hit him. Meusel and Cole are fined $100 and suspended for 10 days. Ruth is fined $100. Cobb goes unpunished. Babe Ruth once said of the Georgia Peach, "Ty Cobb is a jerk."

JUNE 16:

First baseman George "Highpockets" Kelly homers today against the Reds. He now has hit a home run in six straight games, which ties a major league record. Kelly, whose streak began on June 11, has seven homers in the six games. Abner Graves, 90 years old, the man whose letter helped "establish" Abner Doubleday as the inventor of baseball, shoots his wife to death and is institutionalized. He dies in confinement.

JULY 17:

Jesse Haines of the Cardinals no-hits the Braves, 5-0, in St. Louis. It marks the first no-hitter for the Cardinals in the modern era. Haines strikes out five and walks three; St. Louis commits two errors. The losing pitcher is Tim McNamara.

JULY 21:

The Indians' George Burns hits two homers and two doubles today against Boston. The Red Sox win, 16-12. Burns becomes the first major leaguer to have four extra-base hits in a game twice in one season. On June 19, he had three doubles and a homer.

Walter Johnson had an AL-best 6 shutouts in '24.

SEPTEMBER 22
Senators' pitcher Walter Johnson registers his 13th straight win.

TRIVIA

Many years after the fact, AL president Ban Johnson reveals the possibility that the 1903 World Series – the first modern championship – between Boston and Pittsburgh may have been rigged. Last year Lou Criger, a catcher for the 1903 Boston Beaneaters, thought he was dying and told Johnson he got an offer of $12,000 from a gambler in the Hotel Monongahela to dump the series. He said the gambler claimed an oil millionaire had bet $50,000 on Boston. Criger reportedly turned down the offer. Boston won the series five games to three. Criger made three errors, but Honus Wagner committed six. Criger recovered from his illness and survived until 1934, when he died at age 62 in Tucson, Arizona.

AUGUST 1:

Brooklyn's Dazzy Vance strikes out seven straight Cubs batters to set a major league record. The Robins get the win, 4-0, and record only three assists – two of them by Vance.

AUGUST 25:

In Washington, Walter Johnson of the Senators hurls a seven-inning no-hitter against the Browns in a game shortened by rain. The Big Train records his sixth shutout of the season – and 107th of his career – walking two and striking out two. The losing pitcher is Frank "Dixie" Davis. The game was to be the opener of a doubleheader; the nightcap is postponed.

AUGUST 28:

The Senators overcome two homers by Babe Ruth to beat the Yankees, 11-6. With the victory, Washington takes over first place from New York.

SEPTEMBER 4:

Brooklyn beats the Braves, 4-1, behind Clarence "Dazzy" Vance, and 9-1 with Walter "Dutch" Ruether pitching. The two victories today give Brooklyn an NL-record four doubleheader sweeps in four days. Prior to today's two wins, the Robins topped the Phillies in twinbills on September 1, 2, and 3.

SEPTEMBER 7:

At Ebbets Field on Sunday, some 7,000 fans without tickets force their way into a crucial game between the Robins and the Giants. Many use crowbars and rip heavy gates off their hinges. Some 40 police battle the crowd and have to call for 150 reinforcements. The day began with the Giants in first place, one-half game ahead of Brooklyn; it ends with New York up by a game and a half on an 8-7 victory. The Robins' three-run rally in the bottom of the ninth falls short.

SEPTEMBER 15:

Frank Chance dies at age 47 in Los Angeles, following brain surgery he underwent in an attempt to cure chronic headaches that resulted from numerous beanings. The Peerless Leader hit .296 in his 17-year major league career. He managed the Cubs to four pennants and two World Series championships and also managed both the Yankees and Red Sox.

SEPTEMBER 16:

The Cardinals' Sunny Jim Bottomley single-handedly wrecks the Brooklyn Robins at Ebbets Field. The first baseman drives in a major league record 12 runs in a 17-3 victory. The previous record holder was the present Brooklyn manager Wilbert Robinson with the Orioles in 1892. Bottomley has six hits in a row and tallies 13 total bases. He played a role in every one of St. Louis's 13 runs. The Cardinals worked over five Robins' pitchers (Welton "Rube" Erhardt, John "Bonnie" Hollingsworth, Art Decatur, Gomer "Tex" Wilson, Jim Roberts) for 18 hits. Willie Sherdel is the winning pitcher for St. Louis.

The anatomy of a 12-RBI game: Jim Bottomley began routinely with a two-run single against Rube Erhardt in the first inning. In the second, he doubled in a run against Bonnie Hollingsworth. He did his major damage against Art Decatur, knocking in four runs with a fourth-inning homer and two more against the pitcher with a two-run homer in the sixth. Against Tex Wilson in the seventh, he drove in two more with a single. And he capped his record day with an RBI single against Jim Roberts in the ninth inning.

SEPTEMBER 20:

The Cubs' 37-year-old Grover Cleveland Alexander wins his 300th career game, a 7-3 triumph against the Giants in 12 innings at the Polo Grounds. The only other modern-day pitchers to reach the 300-win level are Christy Mathewson, Walter Johnson, and Eddie Plank.

SEPTEMBER 22:

Walter Johnson and the Senators beat the Red Sox, 8-3. It is the 13th win in a row for the Big Train.

SEPTEMBER 27:

The Giants beat the Phillies, 5-1, to win the NL pennant, but the drama takes place before the game off the field. New York outfielder Jimmy O'Connell – in collusion with coach Patrick "Cozy" Dolan – tells Phillies' shortstop John "Heinie" Sand, "I'll give you $500 if you don't bear down too hard." Sand answers, "Nothing doing," and informs

Rogers Hornsby explains how he hit .424: "I hustled on everything I hit."

his manager, Art Fletcher, who in turn notifies Commissioner Kenesaw Mountain Landis.

SEPTEMBER 29:

With Frederick "Firpo" Marberry hurling six innings of relief, the Senators beat the Red Sox in Boston, 4-2, to clinch their first-ever AL pennant. Under 27-year-old player-manager Stanley "Bucky" Harris, known as the Boy Wonder, the Senators finish two games ahead of the Yankees. After 18 years, the great Walter Johnson will get to pitch in his first World Series. The Big Train, now 36 years old, is 23-7 and tops the AL in ERA (2.72) and strikeouts (158).

SEPTEMBER 30:

Phillies' manager Art Fletcher and Heinie Sand meet with the commissioner. Landis also summons Frankie Frisch, Ross Youngs, and George Kelly, implicated by Jimmy O'Connell, who admits his role to the commissioner and to reporters. Frisch, Youngs, and Kelly maintain they knew nothing of the plot until today.

OCTOBER 1:

Commissioner Landis bans Jimmy O'Connell and Cozy Dolan from participation in the World Series and exonerates Frankie Frisch, Ross Youngs, and George Kelly. O'Connell insists, "They're making a goat out of me. I've been a damned fool. They were all in on it and they deserted me when they found I was caught." AL president Ban Johnson describes Landis as a "wild-eyed nut," wants the World Series canceled, and boycotts it because the three other players were cleared. Landis responds, "Keep your shirt on."

OCTOBER 4:

World Series, game one. At a packed Griffith Stadium in Washington, the visiting Giants beat the Senators and Walter "Big Train" Johnson, 4-3, in 12 innings. Left-hander Art Nehf gets a complete-game victory. Johnson, who takes the loss, strikes out 12 Giants, but loses in the 12th inning when Ross Youngs gets a single with the bases loaded. Both George Kelly and Bill Terry hit home runs for New York.

WEAF in New York and WCAP in Washington, D.C., carry live radio coverage of the series by Graham McNamee.

OCTOBER 5:

World Series, game two. In Washington, the Senators rebound with a 4-3 win on Roger Peckinpaugh's RBI double in the bottom of the ninth. Tom Zachary gets the win with a save from Firpo Marberry. Jack Bentley is the loser. Goose Goslin and player-manager Bucky Harris hit home runs.

OCTOBER 6:

World Series, game three. In New York, the Giants beat the Senators, 6-4. Wilfred "Rosy" Ryan is the winning pitcher and hits a home run. The loser is starting pitcher Firpo Marberry, who only lasts for three innings.

OCTOBER 7:

World Series, game four. In New York, the Senators, paced by Goose Goslin's four hits – including a three-run home run – beat the Giants, 7-4. The winning pitcher is George Mogridge, with a save by Firpo Marberry. Virgil Barnes is tagged with the loss.

Commissioner Landis meets with Jimmy O'Connell and Cozy Dolan and sticks with his ban. Neither O'Connell nor Dolan ever returns to baseball.

OCTOBER 8:

World Series, game five. In New York, the Giants, behind Jack Bentley, beat Walter Johnson and the Senators, 6-2. Bentley hits a two-run homer; Goose Goslin has a solo home run for Washington.

OCTOBER 9:

World Series, game six. In Washington, Tom Zachary goes all the way, limiting the Giants to seven hits for a 2-1 victory. The Senators manage only four hits, but Art Nehf gets the loss when Bucky Harris singles in two runs in the fifth inning.

Jake Daubert dies at age 40 in Cincinnati. Daubert played first base for 15 seasons with Brooklyn and Cincinnati, batting .303. He twice led the NL in batting.

OCTOBER 10:

World Series, game seven. Playing in Washington, the Senators win a 12-inning struggle, 4-3, for the World Championship. The winning pitcher is

HISTORY

John McGraw's Giants win their fourth straight pennant with a record of 93-60, one and a half games ahead of Brooklyn. It is McGraw's 10th pennant. With Ross Youngs (.356), Frankie Frisch (.328), and George Kelly (.324) as leaders, the team compiles a .300 batting average. Once again, the Giants have no 20-game winners. Under rookie manager Stanley "Bucky" Harris, the Senators go 92-62. Walter Johnson is 23-7 with a 2.72 ERA. Leon "Goose" Goslin hits .344 (129 RBI), Sam Rice .334, and Joe Judge .324.

OCTOBER 10
The White Sox and Giants begin a world exhibition tour of Europe.

CULTURE

Two silent films debut: *The Battling Orioles*, starring Glenn Tryon; and *Hit and Run*, starring Hoot Gibson and former major leaguer Mike Donlin.

HISTORY

The Kansas City Monarchs (55-22) of the Negro National League defeat Hilldale (47-22) in the Negro League World Series, five games to four with one tie.

Walter Johnson, who pitches the final four innings in relief. Bucky Harris hits a home run with no one on. Jack Bentley becomes the losing pitcher when catcher Hank Gowdy drops his mask, gets his foot caught in it, and messes up a Muddy Ruel foul. Ruel then doubles, and a one-out grounder by Earl McNeely bounces over third baseman Fred Lindstrom's head to score the winning run. Roger Peckinpaugh leads the victorious Senators with .417. Goose Goslin has three homers for the series. Bill Terry hits .429 for New York in limited at-bats.

OCTOBER 10:

The White Sox and owner Charles Comiskey and the Giants, with their manager John McGraw, embark on another world exhibition tour. This time they will play in London, Dublin, Glasgow, Berlin, Paris, and Rome.

POST-SEASON

OCTOBER 27:

The Pirates obtain first baseman George Grantham (.316 with 12 homers), pitcher Vic Aldridge (15-12, 3.50 ERA), and first baseman Al Niehaus from the Cubs for first baseman Charlie Grimm (.288, two homers), shortstop Walter "Rabbit" Maranville (.266, two homers), and pitcher Wilbur Cooper (20-14, 3.28 ERA and a league-leading four shutouts). Niehaus was not in the major leagues last season.

DECEMBER 11:

The AL approves the "Charles Ebbets plan" for the World Series, presented to the NL yesterday. Under the new format, games one, two, six, and seven will be played in the NL team's city; games three, four, and five will be home contests for the AL representative. The leagues will alternate positions each year.

White Sox second baseman Eddie "Cocky" Collins is named the team's player-manager for the 1925 season. He replaces acting manager Johnny Evers. Collins had handled the team for 27 games (14-13) last season. Evers had two stints (10-11 and 41-61) as the team's skipper after Frank Chance took ill. Ed Walsh also managed the team for three games. With four managers, the team finished in last place, with a 66-87 record.

> "I WILL CONCEDE [ROGERS] HORNSBY IS A MOST VALUABLE PLAYER TO HIMSELF."
>
> *– MVP voter Jack Ryder*

The Indians trade pitcher Stan Coveleski (15-16, 4.04 ERA) to the Senators for pitcher Byron Speece (2-1, 2.65 ERA) and outfielder Carr Smith (.200 in five games). Coveleski was a hero of the 1920 World Series when he won three games for Cleveland.

DECEMBER 17:

The New York Yankees trade three pitchers to the St. Louis Browns for one pitcher. Coming to the Yankees is Urban Shocker (16-13, 4.17 ERA). Shocker, a right-hander, has been a 20-game winner for four straight seasons. The Yankees traded Shocker to the Browns in 1918, according to manager Miller Huggins, "because I was foolish." The Browns get right-hander Joe Bush (17-16, 3.57 ERA), who has had difficulties with Huggins; right-hander Milt Gaston (5-3, 4.50 ERA), and left-hander Joe Giard, who did not play in the major leagues in 1924.

DECEMBER 11
The AL approves Charles Ebbets' format for playing World Series games.

THE BEST OF 1924

National League

HITTERS

Batting Average:
Rogers Hornsby, St. Louis Cardinals, .424

Slugging Average:
Rogers Hornsby, .696

Home Runs:
Jack Fournier, Brooklyn Robins, 27

Runs Batted In:
George Kelly, New York Giants, 136

Hits:
Rogers Hornsby, 227

Stolen Bases:
Max Carey, Pittsburgh Pirates, 49

PITCHERS

Wins:
Dazzy Vance, Brooklyn Robins, 28

Strikeouts:
Dazzy Vance, 262

Earned Run Average:
Dazzy Vance, 2.16

Winning Percentage:
Emil Yde, Pittsburgh Pirates, .842

Saves:
Frank "Jakie" May, Cincinnati Reds, 6

Most Valuable Player:
Dazzy Vance, Brooklyn Robins

American League

HITTERS

Batting Average:
Babe Ruth, New York Yankees, .378

Slugging Average:
Babe Ruth, .739

Home Runs:
Babe Ruth, 46

Runs Batted In:
Leon "Goose" Goslin, Washington Senators, 129

Hits:
Sam Rice, Washington Senators, 216

Stolen Bases:
Eddie "Cocky" Collins, Chicago White Sox, 42

PITCHERS

Wins:
Walter Johnson, Washington Senators, 23

Strikeouts:
Walter Johnson, 158

Earned Run Average:
Walter Johnson, 2.72

Winning Percentage:
Walter Johnson, .767

Saves:
Frederick "Firpo" Marberry , Washington Senators, 15

Most Valuable Player:
Walter Johnson, Washington Senators

HISTORY

Clarence "Dazzy" Vance (28-6, 2.16 ERA) is named the NL's Most Valuable Player, beating out Rogers Hornsby, who hit .424 with 25 homers and 152 RBI. Vance wins because Jack Ryder of Cincinnati leaves Hornsby completely off his ballot. He tells *The Sporting News*, "I will concede Hornsby is a most valuable player to himself, but not to his team. On that basis I couldn't give him a solitary vote."

1925

"I'm going for home runs for the first time in my career."
– Ty Cobb, before hitting three

NEWS

IT'S CLARENCE DARROW FOR THE DEFENSE AND WILLIAM JENNINGS BRYAN FOR THE PROSECUTION IN TENNESSEE'S "MONKEY TRIAL"; TEACHER JOHN SCOPES CONVICTED FOR TEACHING EVOLUTION; BRYAN DIES FIVE DAYS LATER

Walter Chrysler founds an automobile company

TOTAL SOLAR ECLIPSE IN JANUARY IS THE FIRST ONE IN 300 YEARS

F. SCOTT FITZGERALD PUBLISHES *THE GREAT GATSBY*

A YEAR OF CLASSIC SILENT FILMS:

THE PHANTOM OF THE OPERA, STARRING LON CHANEY;

GO WEST, STARRING BUSTER KEATON;

THE GOLD RUSH, STARRING CHARLIE CHAPLIN;

THE FRESHMAN, STARRING HAROLD LLOYD

PRE-SEASON

MARCH 4:

John Montgomery Ward, one of baseball's most fascinating characters, succumbs to pneumonia in Augusta, Georgia, one day after his 65th birthday. Largely responsible for the organization of the Brotherhood of National League Players, Ward also was a driving force behind the Players' League. After his playing career, which spanned 17 years, Ward was president of the Boston Braves, business manager for the Brooklyn Tip Tops in the Federal League, and a highly successful lawyer.

MARCH 15:

Brooklyn manager Wilbert Robinson becomes the first member of his newly established Bonehead Club. And he's the last. Uncle Wilbert set up the "club" as a vehicle for fining his players $10 for mistakes. Today he gives the umpires the wrong lineup, pays his $10, and disbands the Bonehead Club.

APRIL 7:

Babe Ruth collapses in a train station in Asheville, North Carolina. He is unconscious again on a train outside Washington, D.C. In New York City, he is taken to St. Vincent's Hospital.

THE SEASON

APRIL 14:

Broadcasting from the roof of Weeghman Stadium, Chicago radio station WGN airs the opening day game between the Cubs and Pirates; Quin Ryan is the announcer. It is the first regular-season game carried on radio. Cubs fans at home and those in the crowd of 38,000 at the ballpark are not disappointed. Grover Cleveland Alexander doubles and singles in beating Pittsburgh, 8-2.

In St. Louis, the Indians spoil the Browns' home opener by scoring 12 runs in the eighth inning to defeat the Browns, 21-14 – the most combined runs in an AL game. The Browns commit five errors in the fateful eighth. First baseman George Sisler commits four errors in the game.

There's an unfamiliar figure in right field for the Yankees on opening day in New York. It's Ben Paschal, filling in for the ailing Babe Ruth. With 50,000 fans on hand, Paschal provides a reasonable imitation of Ruth, hitting a home run in the Yankees 5-1 victory over the Senators.

APRIL 17:

Babe Ruth undergoes surgery for an intestinal abscess at St. Vincent's Hospital in New York City. It becomes known as the "belly ache heard 'round the world."

APRIL 18:

As his team prepares to meet the Giants in the season opener, Brooklyn Robins' owner Charlie Ebbets dies at age 65. He leaves an estate estimated at $1,275,811. After a moment of silence prior to the game, the Giants beat the Robins, 7-1, in the ballpark that bears Charlie Ebbets's name. Ed McKeever becomes the team's new president.

APRIL 21:

All NL games are postponed to honor Charlie Ebbets, who is being buried in Greenwood Cemetery today in Brooklyn.

APRIL 29:

A second tragedy strikes the Brooklyn Robins. Ed McKeever, the new president of

APRIL 14
Filling in for the ailing Babe Ruth, Ben Paschal homers, and the Yanks beat the Senators, 5-1.

MAY 17
The Cleveland Indians' Tris Speaker joins the 3,000-hits club.

the team, dies of an illness he contracted standing in the cold rain at Charles Ebbets's funeral. Manager Wilbert Robinson assumes the additional responsibilities of team president.

MAY 5:

Age is not hindering Tigers' player-manager Ty Cobb. The 38-year-old hits three home runs in a 14-8 win over the Browns in Sportsman's Park, St. Louis. With six hits – including a double – he ties a modern major league record and sets a record for total bases – 16. The previous record holder was Edward "Patsy" Gharrity of the Senators, who had 13 in a 1919 game. Cobb's homers come in the first inning against Joe Bush, in the second against Elam Vangilder, and in the eighth off Milt Gaston. Others with three homers in a game are George Kelly of the Giants, Ken Williams of the Browns, and Cy Williams and Walter Henline of the Phillies. Before the game, Cobb tells a reporter, "I'll show you something today. I'm going for home runs for the first time in my career."

Everett Scott, the New York Yankees' shortstop, plays in his 1,307th straight game. Scott's streak began back on June 20, 1916, when he was a member of the Boston Red Sox.

MAY 6:

Ty Cobb hits two more home runs (off Dave Danforth and Chester Falk) and has six RBI today against the Browns. With three yesterday, he ties the modern major league record of five round-trippers in two games and equals the 1884 mark of Adrian "Cap" Anson. Two other drives just miss going out of the park. His single in the first inning today also gives him nine consecutive hits. The Tigers win, 11-4.

Yankees' shortstop Everett Scott is benched by manager Miller Huggins, ending his consecutive game streak at 1,307. Pee Wee Wanninger replaces him in the lineup. Miller says he made the substitution because Scott "was not feeling well." Scott is unhappy with the benching. He says, "It seems funny that it should happen the day after we win and I make two hits. Not that I care about the record. When I passed the 1,000 mark, I lost interest in the matter." Scott's streak began on June 20, 1916, and covered parts of 10 seasons. The Athletics win the game, 6-2.

MAY 7:

Against the Browns, Cobb misses another homer by about a foot. He concludes the series in St. Louis by going 12 for 19, with 29 total bases.

At Forbes Field in Pittsburgh, Pirates' shortstop Glenn Wright pulls off an unassisted triple play in the ninth inning against the Cardinals. With Rogers Hornsby on first base and Jimmy Cooney on second base, Jim Bottomley hits a line drive to Wright. The shortstop steps on second to get Cooney and tags Hornsby for the third out. The Cardinals win, 10-9.

The rain gods must be angry. The Phillies experience their eighth straight postponement. Today's game was scheduled in New York against the Giants.

MAY 8:

The NL is marking its 50th season. In Boston, the Braves and Cubs – the last "charter members" of the NL – meet in what president John Heydler designates the "golden jubilee" game. The Braves win the historic game, 5-2.

MAY 11:

It has been done from the top of the Washington Monument; it's been done from an airplane – sort of. Now White Sox catcher Ray Schalk catches a baseball dropped from the top of Chicago's Tribune Tower, 460 feet above ground level.

MAY 12:

Lawrence Peter "Yogi" Berra is born today in St. Louis.

MAY 17:

The Indians' Tris Speaker collects his 3,000th hit. The 37-year-old Speaker gets the landmark hit against the Senators' Tom Zachary and adds two more. But Washington wins, 2-1.

Tom Zachary throws an even more memorable pitch two years later. It is off the left-hander – then with the Senators – that Babe Ruth hits his historic 60th homer.

MAY 29:

In Pittsburgh, the Pirates hit a modern record eight triples against the Cardinals in a 15-5 win. The

EQUIPMENT

Balls with cushioned cork centers are introduced.

RULES CHANGE

The minimum distance for home runs is increased from 235 feet to 250 feet.

JUNE 2
The Yankees' Lou Gehrig fills in at first base for the injured Wally Pipp.

CULTURE

***Life's Greatest Game*, a movie about baseball, premieres.**

HISTORY

Hilldale of the Eastern Colored League defeats the Kansas City Monarchs five games to one in the Negro Leagues World Series.

Cardinals' newly acquired Bob O'Farrell also triples to give the two teams a record nine. Pirate three-baggers are hit by Clyde Barnhart (two), Max Carey (two), Earl Moore, Hazen "Kiki" Cuyler, Glenn Wright, and Harold "Pie" Traynor. Earl Smith homers for Pittsburgh, Rogers Hornsby goes deep for St. Louis. The winning pitcher is "Jughandle" Johnny Morrison. Clyde "Pea Ridge" Day gets the loss.

MAY 30:

Rogers Hornsby becomes the Cardinals' player-manager. He replaces Branch Rickey, who was fired as manager by club owner Sam Breadon. Rickey will remain as vice president and will continue to supervise St. Louis's farm system. So far this season the Cardinals are 13-25 and in last place. Playing in Pittsburgh, St. Louis loses a morning game, 4-1, and an afternoon contest, 15-5 – despite Hornsby's two homers in the nightcap.

JUNE 1:

At Yankee Stadium, there are two significant lineup changes for the Yankees today. Babe Ruth returns and Lou Gehrig replaces Wally Pipp at first base after pinch-hitting for Paul "Pee Wee" Wanninger in the eighth inning. The Yankees were 15-25 and in seventh place without Ruth. He plays six innings before his fatigue gets the best of him. He just misses a home run on a drive that goes foul, makes one outstanding fielding play, and is thrown out in a play at the plate. Despite all the big doings, the Senators win the game, 5-3.

JUNE 2:

Lou Gehrig starts at first base for the Yankees after Wally Pipp is hit in the head during batting practice by Charlie Caldwell Jr. He comes up with a headache and is hospitalized. "You're my first baseman today and from now on," manager Miller Huggins tells the 21-year-old Gehrig. Batting sixth, Gehrig gets three hits in five at-bats – including a double – off George Mogridge and losing pitcher Allan Russell. Alex Ferguson gets credit for the Yankees' 8-5 win over the Senators.

JUNE 3:

Eddie "Cocky" Collins of the visiting White Sox gets his 3,000th career hit, a single off the Tigers' Harry "Rip" Collins. Chicago tops Detroit, 12-7.

JUNE 15:

In Philadelphia, the Athletics score 13 runs in the bottom of the eighth inning and beat the Indians, 17-15. Al Simmons weighs in with a single and a three-run home run. Jimmy Dykes adds a triple. The A's get nine hits and four walks in the big inning. The beneficiary is Tom Glass, who allows a run and seven hits in three innings, and gets the win. The losing pitcher is George Uhle, one of four pitchers used in the eighth. Joe Sewell and Glenn Myatt homer for Cleveland. This is to be Tom Glass's only major league win. His career consists of two games and a total of five innings.

JUNE 17:

The Tigers humiliate the Yankees in New York, 19-1. It is the worst beating in New York history and the most runs scored in Yankee Stadium by a visiting team.

JUNE 24:

Young Lou Gehrig records his first big league steal – and it is a big one. He swipes home on the front end of a double steal, with catcher Wally Schang taking second.

JULY 1:

The Giants' Lewis "Hack" Wilson has 12 total bases in a game against the Phillies. Wilson connects for two homers and two doubles in a 16-7 New York victory.

JULY 3:

Brooklyn infielder Milt Stock gets four hits today. It is Stock's fourth consecutive game with four hits – a streak that began on June 30.

JULY 4:

Yankees' left-hander Herb Pennock matches Lefty Grove pitch for pitch – and then some. The Yankees and Pennock beat Grove and the Athletics, 1-0, in 15 innings. Pennock allows only four hits and no walks. He retires the first 18 A's batters in a row and then the final 21.

JULY 6:

Bill Killefer is replaced as Cubs' manager by Walter "Rabbit" Maranville. Under Killefer, the Cubs are 33-42. At Ebbets Field, the Cubs win their first game under Maranville, beating the Robins, 10-5. That

JULY 20
Brooklyn Robins' pitcher Dazzy Vance whiffs 17 Cardinals in a 10-inning, 4-3 win.

night, Maranville is arrested after an altercation with a hack driver.

JULY 9:

The Pirates' Harold "Pie" Traynor sets a major league record for third basemen by starting four double plays.

JULY 15:

The NL meets in New York City, and one of the principal topics is the "rabbit ball." The owners hear from Columbia University professor Harold A. Fales, who has studied the 1914, 1923, and 1925 balls, and detects only a slight difference. Fales also finds the 1925 ball is larger and heavier, and because the seams are smoother they give the pitcher less control. He concludes, "The elasticity of the ball for small heights of fall, namely 13.5, is practically the same." The livelier response is said to be due to pitching changes, the use of more new balls in a game, and better stitching. The NL plans no change in the balls, but its president John A. Heydler will hold discussions with AL president Ban Johnson. In addition, rosin bags will be placed behind the pitchers mound by the umpires – a practice of the Southern Association.

JULY 20:

The Robins' Dazzy Vance dazzles the Cardinals, striking out 17 in a 10-inning, 4-3 victory.

AUGUST 9:

Babe Ruth steps aside for a pinch hitter. In today's game, Yankees' manager Miller Huggins sends Bobby Veach up to hit for Ruth, explaining that the slugger had wrenched his back. Veach flies out, and the Yanks lose, 4-3, to the visiting White Sox.

AUGUST 17:

The Senators acquire outfielder Bobby Veach from the Yankees on waivers. Veach, who came to New York in a May 9 trade, is hitting .353 in 56 games.

AUGUST 29:

Babe Ruth is instructed not to suit up for the game, is suspended indefinitely, and is smacked with a $5,000 fine by Yankees' manager Miller Huggins for arriving late at the Yankees' locker room. Ruth tells Huggins, "If you weighed 50 more pounds, I'd punch you." Huggins responds, "If I weighed 50 pounds more, I'd have punched you."

SEPTEMBER 1:

In chapter two of the Ruth-Huggins dispute, the Babe goes directly to Yankees' owner Colonel Jacob Ruppert to argue his case. Huggins has beaten him to the boss and has the support of the Colonel and general manager Ed Barrow. At the Ruppert Brewery, the Colonel says the fine and suspension stand. "I told Ruth, as I tell you in front of him, that he went too far. I told him Miller Huggins is in absolute command of the ball club and that I stand behind Huggins to the very limit." Ruth goes on to Yankee Stadium to apologize, but Huggins will have no part of it. Ruth is reduced to watching the game from Colonel Ruppert's box. The Yankees beat the Red Sox, 2-1, without him, and Ruth tells the press, "No, I don't want to do any more talking. It only gets me in bad. I did too much of it with those reporters in St. Louis and Chicago."

SEPTEMBER 3:

Cubs' owner Bill Veeck Sr. replaces manager Rabbit Maranville – after eight weeks – with George Gibson, the third pilot of the season. Maranville, who has a drinking problem, is ousted after dumping spittoon contents on players during a train trip. The Cubs are 23-30 under Maranville, and finish the year in last place.

Browns' slugger Ken Williams is beaned and will miss the rest of the year. In 102 games, Williams was hitting .331 with 25 homers and 105 RBI.

SEPTEMBER 6:

A contrite Babe Ruth apologizes to manager Miller Huggins in front of his Yankees' teammates.

SEPTEMBER 7:

Babe Ruth finally goes back to work as the Yankees meet the Red Sox. He gets one hit in a 5-1 loss.

SEPTEMBER 8:

Babe Ruth hits his 300th home run; the landmark round-tripper comes off Chester "Buster" Ross of the Red Sox in a 7-4 Yankee win.

SEPTEMBER 13:

The Robins' Dazzy Vance no-hits the Phillies, 10-1, in

CULTURE

John Philip Sousa writes "The National Game March."

OCTOBER 7
On the opening day of the World Series, pitching great Chrisy Mathewson dies.

"If you weighed 50 more pounds, I'd punch you."
– Babe Ruth to Miller Huggins

HISTORY

Tigers' rookie Al Wingo finishes with a .370 batting average, yet is the low man in Detroit's outfield. Harry Heilmann bats .393 and Ty Cobb .378.

HISTORY

Second baseman Tony Lazzeri of Salt Lake City in the Pacific Coast League finishes the season with 60 home runs – the first player in organized baseball to reach that number. Lazzeri adds 222 RBI, but the PCL schedule is 197 games long.

game one of a doubleheader in Brooklyn. Vance one-hits the Phillies on September 8 and sets a record for fewest hits in two consecutive games. Today he gives up an unearned run in the second inning when Philadelphia's Nelson "Chicken" Hawks hits a fly ball that is dropped by Robins' left fielder Jimmy Johnston for a two-base error. Hawks scores on Barney Friberg's sacrifice fly. Vance strikes out nine batters. The losing pitcher is Clarence Mitchell. The Phillies win the nightcap, 7-3.

SEPTEMBER 21:

In Pittsburgh, against the Phillies, the Pirates' Kiki Cuyler ties an NL record today with his 10th consecutive hit. Pittsburgh wins, 9-7.

SEPTEMBER 22:

In what must rank as one of the most counterproductive batting days ever, Robins' pitcher Burleigh Grimes hits into a triple play and two double plays. The Robins lose to the Cubs, 3-2, in 12 innings.

In game one of a doubleheader at Yankee Stadium, New York outfielder Ben Paschal becomes the first ALer to hit two inside-the-park home runs in a single game. The Yankees beat the White Sox, 11-6. Chicago rebounds in game two, however, for a 4-2 victory.

SEPTEMBER 27:

The Cardinals split a doubleheader with the visiting Boston Braves. Player-manager Rogers Hornsby hits his 38th and 39th homers of the season and adds a triple, double, and single to finish the at .403. It is the second consecutive .400 season for Hornsby and his third in four years.

OCTOBER 2:

Leo Durocher makes a quiet major league debut today with the New York Yankees in Philadelphia. Durocher pinch-hits for pitcher Garland Braxton in the eighth inning against Stan Baumgartner and flies out to Walter French in right field. The Athletics win, 10-0.

OCTOBER 4:

In the last game of the season for both teams, Browns' player-manager George Sisler and Tigers' player-manager Ty Cobb take the mound against each other. Cobb pitches one perfect inning; Sisler two scoreless innings. The Tigers win the game, 11-6, but end the season in fourth place. The Browns finish third.

OCTOBER 7:

Baseball loses one of its genuine heroes. Christy Mathewson dies at age 45 in Saranac Lake, New York. Mathewson suffered from tuberculosis for five years, possibly as the result of being gassed in a training accident while serving as a U.S. Army captain during World War I. During the infamous 1919 World Series, he publicly expressed doubt that the White Sox were playing to win. Mathewson won 373 games – the third highest ever – in 17 years and compiled a lifetime ERA of 2.13. He won 30 or more games four times and was a nine-time 20-game winner. At the time of his death, he was a part owner of the Boston Braves.

World Series, game one. At Forbes Field, the Senators beat the Pirates, 4-1, on Walter Johnson's five-hitter. Johnson strikes out 10 and goes the distance. The losing pitcher is Lee Meadows. Washington's Joe Harris hits a home run in his first World Series at-bat – the first player to accomplish that feat. Pie Traynor homers for Pittsburgh. In the fifth inning, Washington's Sam Rice drives in two with a single to give Johnson all the runs he needs.

OCTOBER 8:

World Series, game two. In Pittsburgh, the Pirates bounce back to beat the Senators, 3-2. Kiki Cuyler's home run after two errors by shortstop Roger Peckinpaugh leads to two runs for the Pirates in the eighth inning. Vic Aldridge is the winning pitcher; Stan Coveleski takes the loss. Washington's Joe Judge and Pittsburgh's Glenn Wright also homer.

OCTOBER 9:

Through a mistake by the Giants, the Cubs draft outfielder Hack Wilson for $5,000 from the Toledo Mud Hens in the American Association. Wilson, who hit .295 with 10 homers for the Giants in 1924, was sent to the minors this year. (He slumped to .239 in 62 games with New York.) The Giants erroneously leave his name off the reserve list, and Wilson becomes eli-

OCTOBER 10
In game three of the World Series, the Senators win, 4-3, on a controversial call.

OCTOBER 15
The Pirates win game seven of the Series, 9-7, and become World Champions.

gible for the post-season draft. The Cubs' new manager, Joe McCarthy recommends him and he is quickly snapped up by Chicago.

Commissioner Kenesaw Mountain Landis rejects the Giants' protest, and the Cubs have a man who will become one of baseball's most-feared sluggers.

OCTOBER 10:

World Series, game three. In Washington, D.C., the Senators top the Pirates, 4-3. Alex Ferguson is the winning pitcher with a save by Firpo Marberry. Ray Kremer gets the loss. Goose Goslin has a homer for the winners, but a controversial call in the bottom of the eighth preserves the Senators' lead and ultimately the victory. With Marberry pitching and Washington up, 4-3, Earl Smith of the Pirates hits a long drive to center field. Sam Rice goes over the railing and into the stands, emerging with the ball; Smith is called out.

OCTOBER 11:

World Series, game four. In Washington, the Senators beat the Pirates, 4-0, on a complete-game six-hitter by Walter Johnson. Emil Yde is the loser. A four-run third inning, highlighted by back-to-back home runs by Goose Goslin and Joe Harris, provides all the scoring.

OCTOBER 12:

World Series, game five. In Washington, the Pirates get back on the winning track, 6-3. Vic Aldridge goes all the way for the win; Stan Coveleski is charged with the loss. Joe Harris homers for the Senators.

OCTOBER 13:

Joe McCarthy is officially named the new manager of the Cubs, replacing George Gibson, who was 12-14. The Cubs finished last in 1925. McCarthy has no major league managing or playing experience. From 1919 to 1925, he managed Louisville in the American Association.

World Series, game six. Playing back in Pittsburgh, the Pirates even the series with a 3-2 win. Ray Kremer pitches a complete game, holding Washington to six hits. Alex Ferguson is the losing pitcher. Goose Goslin homers for the Senators; Eddie Moore's fifth-inning home run is the margin of victory for the Pirates. In the ninth Joe Harris doubles off a temporary screen in center field, just missing a home run, and the Senators fall short.

OCTOBER 15:

World Series, game seven. In Pittsburgh, the Pirates are the World Champions on the strength of today's 9-7 win over the Senators. Rain, fog, and mud make the field almost unplayable, but Commissioner Kenesaw Mountain Landis orders the game to begin and then refuses to suspend the game. Ray Kremer is the winner for the second consecutive game, this time in relief. Walter Johnson is the losing pitcher. Roger Peckinpaugh of the Senators hits the game's only home run. A called ball on what reportedly should have been the third strike to Kiki Cuyler and a controversial ruling on his shot down the right-field line lead to two Pirates runs in the eighth with two out. The Pirates become the first team to overcome a 3-1 deficit in games and win the World Series.

After the game Senators' manager Bucky Harris gets heat from AL president Ban Johnson for allowing Walter Johnson to pitch the entire game. Johnson says, "You sacrificed a World's Championship for our league through your display of mawkish sentiment." According to Johnson biographer Jack Kavanagh, Goose Goslin later recalls Cuyler's game-winning hit, "The umpires couldn't see it. It was too dark and foggy. It wasn't fair at all. It was foul by two feet. I know because the ball hit in the mud and stuck there."

POST-SEASON

NOVEMBER 9:

Brooklyn buys infielder Walter "Rabbit" Maranville from the Cubs for the waiver price. Maranville hit only .233 this past season in 75 games.

DECEMBER 30:

The Phillies receive pitchers Jack Bentley (11-9, 5.04) and Wayland Dean (10-7, 4.64) from the New York Giants for pitcher Jimmy Ring (14-16, 4.37 ERA).

HISTORY

1925 was a disappointing year for Babe Ruth. In addition to health problems, he was embroiled in a serious dispute with manager Miller Huggins, and there were some who thought the great slugger was through. His statistics gave them ammunition: In 98 games, he managed only 25 home runs, 66 RBI, and a .290 batting average.

"If I weighed 50 pounds more,
I'd have punched you."
– *Miller Huggins to Babe Ruth*

HISTORY

The Pirates break the Giants' four-year stranglehold on the NL. Under Bill McKechnie, Pittsburgh is 95-58, eight and a half games ahead of New York. The team batting average is .307, with seven regulars batting .300 or more, led by Kiki Cuyler at .357 and Max Carey at .343. An NL record four players have 100 or more RBI – Glenn Wright, Pie Traynor, Cuyler, and Clyde Barnhart. Shortstop Wright is the first NL player with 100 RBI in each of his first two years (121 and 111). The team has no 20-game winners; Lee Meadows tops the staff at 19-10. The Senators, managed by Bucky Harris, win their second straight AL pennant. They are 96-55, eight and a half games over the Athletics. Walter Johnson (207) is a 20-game winner for the 12th time and bats .433 – a record for pitchers with 75 or more at-bats. The top hitters are Sam Rice at .350 and Goose Goslin with .334.

THE BEST OF 1925

National League

HITTERS

Batting Average:
Rogers Hornsby, St. Louis Cardinals, .403

Slugging Average:
Rogers Hornsby, .756

Home Runs:
Rogers Hornsby, 639

Runs Batted In:
Rogers Hornsby, 143

Hits:
Jim Bottomley, St. Louis Cardinals, 227

Stolen Bases:
Max Carey, Pittsburgh Pirates, 4

PITCHERS

Wins:
Dazzy Vance, Brooklyn Robins, 22

Strikeouts:
Dazzy Vance, 221

Earned Run Average:
Dolf Luque, Cincinnati Reds, 2.63

Winning Percentage:
*Bill "Wee Willie" Sherdel,
St. Louis Cardinals, .714*

Saves:
*"Jughandle" Johnny Morrison,
Pittsburgh Pirates;
Guy Bush, Chicago Cubs, 4*

Most Valuable Player:
Rogers Hornsby, St. Louis Cardinals

American League

HITTERS

Batting Average:
Harry Heilmann, Detroit Tigers, .393

Slugging Average:
Ken Williams, St. Louis Browns, .613

Home Runs:
Bob Meusel, New York Yankees, 33

Runs Batted In:
Bob Meusel, 138

Hits:
Al Simmons, Philadelphia Athletics, 253

Stolen Bases:
Johnny Mostil, Chicago White Sox, 43

PITCHERS

Wins:
*Eddie Rommel, Philadelphia Athletics;
Ted Lyons, Chicago White Sox, 21*

Strikeouts:
*Robert "Lefty" Grove,
Philadelphia Athletics, 116*

Earned Run Average:
Stan Coveleski, Washington Senators, 2.84

Winning Percentage:
Stan Coveleski, .800

Saves:
*Frederick "Firpo" Marberry,
Washington Senators, 15*

Most Valuable Player:
Roger Peckingpaugh, Washington Senators

1926

"Get the ball up there faster than he can get his bat around."
– Walter Johnson on Ty Cobb

NEWS

U.S. CELEBRATES ITS 150TH BIRTHDAY

RICHARD BYRD, FLOYD BENNETT CIRCLE THE NORTH POLE BY AIR

Gertrude Ederle is first woman to swim the English Channel

Ford introduces the 40-hour, five-day work week

LIQUID FUEL ROCKET DEVELOPED BY ROBERT GODDARD

SCREEN IDOL RUDOLPH VALENTINO DIES AT AGE 31

CARL SANDBURG PUBLISHES *ABRAHAM LINCOLN, THE PRAIRIE YEARS*

A.A. MILNE'S FIRST WINNIE THE POOH BOOK IS PUBLISHED

Josef Stalin names himself dictator of the Soviet Union

PRE-SEASON

FEBRUARY 1:

The Reds buy first baseman Wally Pipp (.230, three home runs) from the Yankees for $7,500. Pipp was replaced in the Yankees' starting lineup last year by Lou Gehrig.

FEBRUARY 24:

Eddie Plank dies in Gettysburg, Pennsylvania, at age 51. In 17 years, the left-handed pitcher won 327 games (10th highest) while losing 193, with an ERA of 2.34. His 69 shutouts rank fifth on the all-time list.

APRIL 3:

The Washington Senators announce that play-by-play coverage of all of their road games will be broadcast on station WRC beginning with the April 21 contest with the Athletics at Shibe Park in Philadelphia.

THE SEASON

APRIL 13:

Thirty-eight-year-old Walter Johnson thrills an opening day crowd of 25,000 in Washington, D.C., by pitching and winning a 15-inning game, 1-0. Johnson allows just six hits and strikes out 12 in beating Philadelphia and Ed Rommel. The Athletics' pitcher yields nine hits, walks five, and strikes out one. Manager Bucky Harris scores the winning run after his single is followed by a Goose Goslin double and a Joe Harris single. It is Johnson's ninth victory in 14 Opening Day starting assignments. In his 21-year career, Walter Johnson is involved in 64 1-0 games, winning 38 of them and losing 26.

APRIL 20:

It's a big day for the Babe. He has five of the Yankees' 22 hits, along with eight RBI and five runs scored in an 18-5 rout of the Senators. His hits include a two-run home run against Walter Johnson.

APRIL 27:

Tigers' manager Ty Cobb makes the right move. He puts outfielder Ty Cobb into the starting lineup for the first time this year. Cobb responds with a single, double, triple, two runs, four RBI, and an outstanding catch. The Tigers triumph over the White Sox, 8-7.

HISTORY

Ty Cobb earns $50,000 in 1926, second only to Babe Ruth's $80,000.

TRIVIA

Weeghman Field in Chicago is renamed Wrigley Field.

MAY
1
Satchel Paige debuts for the Chattanooga Black Lookouts in the Negro Southern League.

The Cardinals acquired ace Grover Cleveland Alexander from the Cubs.

Mel Ott, who is just 17 years and six months old, makes his major league debut for the Giants.

MAY 1:

Right-handed pitcher Leroy "Satchel" Paige debuts for the Chattanooga Black Lookouts in the Negro Southern League. The 20-year-old beats the Birmingham Black Barons, 5-4.

MAY 8:

The wooden bleachers along the left-field line in Boston's Fenway Park are destroyed by a fire. The insurance is paid, but the bleachers are never replaced.

MAY 21:

White Sox first baseman Earl Sheeley sets a major league record for most extra-base hits in two consecutive games. Today, Sheeley hits three doubles and a homer in an 8-7 win over the Red Sox in Boston. With his hits today, he also has seven consecutive extra-base hits tying a major league record. He flies out in his last at-bat. Yesterday, Sheeley had three doubles in his last three at-bats as Chicago topped Boston, 13-4.

MAY 26:

The Yankees win their 16th straight, beating the Red Sox, 9-8. The streak breaks the team record of 15 set in 1906. Today's win completes a four-game sweep of Boston.

MAY 28:

The Athletics end the Yankees' winning streak with a 2-1 victory in the first game of a doubleheader. For good measure, they take the nightcap as well, 6-5.

JUNE 5:

The *Sun* strikes back, and the Robins pay the price. After the *New York Sun* criticizes Brooklyn because pitcher Jesse Petty is not among their highest-paid players, manager Wilbert Robinson telephones to complain. From this date forward, Robinson's Robins (so named in his honor) are called Dodgers by the *Sun*.

JUNE 8:

Babe Ruth, written off by some after his mediocre 1925 season, demonstrates his old power – and then some. The Bambino launches a 602-foot home run – his longest ever in regular season play – out of Detroit's Navin Field in an 11-9 Yankees' victory. The ball, hit off Ulysses Simpson Grant "Lil" Stoner, lands outside the ballpark two blocks away, an estimated 800 feet from home plate. Ruth pays a youngster $20 for returning the ball.

JUNE 22:

One of baseball's greatest pitchers changes addresses. The Cardinals acquire Grover Cleveland Alexander from the Cubs for the waiver price. Cleveland appeared in only seven games for the Cubs this year, winning three and losing three. He was a 30-

JUNE 24
Rogers Hornsby gets his 2,000th career hit – a grand slam that beats Pittsburgh, 6-2.

game winner three times and a 20-game winner five times with the Cubs.

JUNE 24:

Rogers Hornsby collects his 2,000th career hit, a bases-loaded home run that beats the Pirates, 6-2.

JUNE 27:

In St. Louis, in his first appearance in a Cardinals' uniform, Grover Cleveland Alexander four-hits his former teammates, the Cubs, 3-2 in the first game of a doubleheader; Billy Southworth homers for St. Louis. The Cubs win the night-cap, 5-0. Game two is marred by a barrage of bottles from fans when umpire Charlie Moran calls catcher interference on a pop-up by the Reds' Sparky Adams.

JULY 3:

Ty Cobb, age 39, walks against Cleveland's George Uhle, steals second, moves to third on an out, and steals home.

JULY 22:

Reds' outfielder Curt Walker becomes the first player in 16 years to hit two triples in an inning. Walker hits his three-baggers in the second inning of a 13-1 victory over the Braves. Two other Cincinnati players triple in the 11-run second.

JULY 25:

In Cincinnati, the Braves beat the Reds, 8-4, but... In the third inning, Reds' third baseman Ralph "Babe" Pinelli is provoked by Braves' third base coach Art Devlin, and the two exchange punches. Players from both teams pour onto the field and Cincinnati police intervene. Devlin suffers a cut cheek and a bruised eye. Pinelli is ejected. One arrest is made: Braves' reserve outfielder Frank Wilson is nabbed for punching a policeman. In the fourth inning, hostilities resume when Boston outfielder Jimmy Welsh crashes into Reds' catcher Val Picinich. Picinich is ejected and the police are summoned again before play can resume.

AUGUST 11:

Indians' centerfielder Tris Speaker doubles against Chicago's Joe Edwards in the third inning; it is the 700th two-bagger of his career. The White Sox beat the Indians, 7-2. Speaker finishes his career with an all-time high 792 doubles.

At Ebbets Field, Brooklyn's Babe Herman falls one short of the major league record for consecutive hits. Ironically, it is Kiki Cuyler of the Pirates – the co-holder of the record, along with Brooklyn's Ed Konetchy – who catches Herman's fly ball after nine straight hits. Herman singles and doubles in his first two at-bats to reach nine straight. The Robins beat Pittsburgh, 4-2.

AUGUST 13:

The Robins buy one of baseball's premier base stealers, Max Carey (.222), from the Pirates. Pitcher Charles "Babe" Adams and outfielder Carson Bigbee are released unconditionally by the Pirates.

The departure of Adams, Bigbee and Carey, in what is known as "the ABC affair," is the result of a convoluted feud in the ranks of the Pirates. The trouble begins in 1925 when the players refuse to vote coach Fred Clarke a share of World Series money. Pittsburgh manager Bill McKechnie intervenes and manages to get Clarke $1,000, but Clarke returns it. Subsequently, McKechnie and Clarke have a major flare-up. This season, when Carey slumps, Clarke recommends that he be benched. Carey then petitions to have Clarke fired, but he fails. Sam Dreyfuss, running the team while his father, Barney, is in Europe, unloads the three players. Carey goes after being suspended without pay. McKechnie is fired and replaced by Donie Bush.

AUGUST 15:

It is the kind of play that has earned Brooklyn a reputation for bizarre baseball: Brooklyn outfielder Babe Herman doubles with the bases loaded against the Braves and ends up with one run batted in and a double play. With Hank DeBerry on third, Dazzy Vance on second, and Chick Fewster on first, Herman hits a George Mogridge pitch off the right-field wall. DeBerry scores. Herman, head down, passes Fewster, who has slowed down between second and third. Vance goes back to third and he and Herman end up occupying the bag at the same time. Fewster resumes running and joins his teammates. Herman is called out for pass-

TRIVIA

In 1926, left-handed pitcher Carl Hubbell tries out with the Detroit Tigers. It is part of baseball lore that the Tiger coaches –or Ty Cobb himself – advise him to forget throwing a screwball to protect his arm. Ty Cobb biographer Charles S. Alexander denies that the player-manager slighted Hubbell or released him. He writes, "Hubbell remained under a Detroit contract at Toronto and was released only after Cobb left the organization. Cobb always insisted that he urged Navin [the Tigers' owner] to keep Hubbell until he developed control of his strangely breaking pitch..." Ken Smith reports Cobb as saying, "I know Hubbell will verify that he never threw a screwball in my presence. I still don't think he had one until a year or two after I lost sight of him." Smith writes, "Hubbell... cannot recall Cobb ever seeing him pitch."

"I gave (Grover Cleveland Alexander) the ball and told him to get Lazerri."
– Rogers Hornsby

CULTURE

***Along Came Ruth*, a song by Irving Berlin, has special lyrics by Christy Walsh, Addy Britt, and Harry Link.**

HISTORY

Outfielder John "Moose" Clabaugh finds it's a little tougher in the big leagues. In 14 at-bats this season with the Robins, he hits .071 with no home runs. With Tyler of the East Texas League this season, Clabaugh hits 62 home runs. His 11 games with Brooklyn constitute his entire major league career.

ing Fewster, who is out for being on third illegally.

AUGUST 21:

Ted Lyons of the Chicago White Sox no-hits the Red Sox before 7,000 fans in Boston, 6-0. Lyons walks one and fans two; Chicago makes one error. The losing pitcher is Slim Harriss.

AUGUST 22:

After three consecutive rainouts, the A's Connie Mack and Tom Shibe go to court and receive an injunction allowing them to play a Sunday game. Lefty Grove tops the White Sox, 3-2.

The courts later decide that Sunday baseball is illegal in Philadelphia, and the ban is not overturned until 1934.

AUGUST 28:

The Cleveland Indians' Emil "Dutch" Levsen beats the Boston Red Sox, 6-1 and 5-1, in both games of a doubleheader. Levsen, a right-hander, is the 24th – and last – pitcher to win two complete games in a single day. Levsen allows the Red Sox batters four hits in each game and strikes out none on the day.

SEPTEMBER 3:

Mel Ott goes three-for-three with a stolen base in five innings of the Giants' 17-3 win against the Braves.

SEPTEMBER 5:

The New York Giants come up with an NL record 12 runs in the fifth inning of a game against the Boston Braves.

SEPTEMBER 18:

At Cleveland's Dunn Field, managers Miller Huggins (five feet, six and a half inches and some 140 pounds) of the Yankees and Tris Speaker (five feet, 11 inches and 193 pounds) of the Indians get involved in a physical confrontation as Cleveland wins its fourth in a row over New York. Despite today's 3-1 loss, the Yankees maintain a two-and-a-half game lead over the Indians. George Uhle is today's winning pitcher.

SEPTEMBER 19:

Edwin Donald "Duke" Snider is born in Los Angeles.

The Cardinals tie the Reds for first place by thumping the Phillies in both ends of a doubleheader. In the first game, the Cards score 12 runs in the third inning en route to a 23-3 blowout. Every Cardinal hits safely in the inning except Billy Southworth, who is robbed of an extra-base hit. In game two, the Cardinals continue the offensive onslaught, winning 10-2. Locked in a pennant race with the Indians, the Yankees take the field at League Park in Cleveland for the final game of a six-game series. Cleveland has won four of the first five, and this is a must-win game for New York. With 31,000 on hand, Lou Gehrig and Babe Ruth pace the Yankees to an 8-3 win. Gehrig weighs in with a home run, three doubles, and five RBI. Ruth has a homer (his 43rd of the season) and scores three runs. Dutch Ruether pitches into the ninth. The Yanks leave Cleveland three and a half games ahead of the Indians.

SEPTEMBER 24:

At the Polo Grounds, the Cardinals win their first-ever NL pennant by beating the Giants, 6-4. Charles "Flint" Rhem and Bill Sherdel pitch for St. Louis.

SEPTEMBER 25:

The Yankees sweep the Browns in a doubleheader in St. Louis to clinch the AL pennant and set up a World Series meeting with Cardinals. In game one, the Yanks win, 10-2, behind Herb Pennock. In game two, with Waite Hoyt pitching, New York triumphs, 10-4. Babe Ruth has three home runs – including a grand slam – to finish the season with a major league-leading 47.

SEPTEMBER 26:

With the pennant race decided in yesterday's doubleheader, the Yankees and Browns play a twin bill in record time – two hours and seven minutes. In game one, the Browns win, 6-1, in one hour and 12 minutes. The Yankees take game two, 6-2, in only 55 minutes.

SEPTEMBER 30:

Robin Roberts is born in Springfield, Illinois.

OCTOBER 1:

The legend of Babe Ruth and 11-year-old Johnny Sylvester is born. Ruth visits the youngster in a hospital in Essex, New Jersey, where the boy is reportedly near death from blood poisoning. Ruth

AUGUST 28
Cleveland's Dutch Levsen beats the Red Sox in both ends of a doubleheader.

OCTOBER 6
In game four of the World Series vs. St. Louis, Babe Ruth hits three home runs.

promises young Johnny he will hit a home run for him.

OCTOBER 2:

World Series, game one. In New York, Yankees' lefty Herb Pennock goes all the way and three-hits the Cardinals, 2-1. In the sixth inning, Lou Gehrig singles in Babe Ruth with what proves to be the winning run. Sunny Jim Bottomley has two of the Cards' three hits. The losing pitcher is Bill Sherdel.

OCTOBER 3:

World Series, game two. In New York, Grover Cleveland Alexander pitches a complete-game four-hitter and the Cardinals top the Yankees, 6-2. Alexander retires the last 21 Yankees in a row, fanning 12 of them. Urban Shocker takes the loss. Billy Southworth hits a three-run home run in the seventh inning and Tommy Thevenow hits a solo homer for St. Louis.

OCTOBER 5:

World Series, game three. A crowd of 37,708 turn out to see the Cardinals in their first World Series game in St. Louis, and they are treated to a Jesse Haines five-hit, complete-game shutout. The Cardinals beat Dutch Ruether and the Yankees, 4-0. Haines hits a two-run home run into the rightfield bleachers in the fourth inning.

OCTOBER 6:

World Series, game four. The Babe gives St. Louis a firsthand view of Ruthian power: he connects for a World Series record three round-trippers. In the first inning, Ruth hits a homer over the right-field roof of Sportsman's Park against Flint Rhem. In the third inning he hits number two over the right center-field roof against Rhem. And he victimizes Hi Bell in the sixth inning, launching a 3-2 pitch into the centerfield bleachers with a runner on. In the fifth and eighth innings Ruth is walked. The Yankees win the game, 10-5, with Waite Hoyt going all the way and yielding 14 hits. The losing pitcher is Art Reinhart. Johnny Sylvester is reportedly listening to the game on the radio in his hospital room as Ruth breaks a World Series record for homers in one game.

OCTOBER 7:

Johnny Sylvester is reported to be improving. According to the *New York Times*, "Physicians say that the boy's return to health began when he learned the news of Ruth's three homers... His fever began to abate at once, and the favorable course was hastened today after he had listened to the radio returns, clutching the autographed baseballs which he received by air mail on Wednesday night."

World Series, game five. In St. Louis, the Yankees win, 3-2, in 10 innings behind Herb Pennock's complete game. The Yankees are behind, 2-1, in the ninth inning when Lou Gehrig doubles to right field. Following a Tony Lazzeri bunt, Ben Paschal's single drives in Gehrig with the tying run. In the 10th inning, Lazzeri's sacrifice fly with the bases loaded against loser Bill Sherdel scores Mark Koenig and gives the Yankees their winning margin.

OCTOBER 9:

World Series, game six. Back at Yankee Stadium, the Cardinals tie the series with a 10-2 win. Grover Cleveland Alexander goes all the way and allows eight hits for his second straight win. Bob Shawkey is the loser. Cardinals' third baseman Les Bell has three hits – including a two-run home run – and four RBI.

OCTOBER 10:

World Series, game seven. In New York, the Cardinals beat the Yankees, 3-2, to claim the World Championship – and they do it in dramatic fashion. The Cardinals hold a 3-2 lead with two out in the seventh inning; the Yankees have the bases loaded. With Tony Lazzeri at bat, Cardinals manager Rogers Hornsby summons Grover Cleveland Alexander from the bullpen. Lazzeri hits a foul into the left-field stands and then is fanned by Alexander to end the inning. In the ninth, Babe Ruth, who had homered earlier, walks. With Bob Meusel at bat, Ruth tries to steal second base and is out on a throw from catcher Bob O'Farrell to second baseman Rogers Hornsby to end the game. The winning pitcher is Jesse Haines; the loser is Waite Hoyt. The Cardinals score all three of their runs, which were unearned, in a fourth-inning rally triggered by a dropped fly by New York left-fielder Bob Meusel.

HISTORY

The Chicago American Giants of the Negro National League beat the Bacharach Giants of the Eastern Colored League, five games to three with one tie, in the Negro Leagues World Series.

TRIVIA

How single-minded is the Cardinals' player-manager Rogers Hornsby? He does not attend his mother's funeral, which is held in Texas between the end of the regular season and the beginning of the World Series. He explains, "I've got a job to do here; getting this club primed for our games with the Yankees. Mother would have understood."

"Less than a foot made the difference between a hero and a bum."
– *Grover Cleveland Alexander*

TRIVIA

Under Rogers Hornsby, the Cardinals compile a record of 89-65 and finish two games over the Reds. The top hitter is Les Bell at .325. Hornsby hits .317, Sunny Jim Bottomley drives in 120 runs. Flint Rhem at 20-7 is the ace of the staff. The New York Yankees, managed by Miller Huggins, are back on top with a 91-63 record, three games up on the Indians. Babe Ruth (.372, 47 homers, 145 RBI, .737 slugging average) and Lou Gehrig (.313, 16 homers, 107 RBI) are a potent one-two punch. Herb Pennock leads the pitchers with 23-11. The Tigers finish sixth – 79-75 – despite an outfield composed of Henry "Heinie" Manush (.378), Harry Heilmann (.367), and Bob Fothergill (.367). Their player-manager Ty Cobb, nearly 40 years old, appears in only 79 games for the Tigers, but hits .339 and strikes out only two times. The Senators' Firpo Marberry sets modern major league records by appearing in 64 games and recording 22 saves.

According to Flint Rhem – as reported by Charles C. Alexander in Rogers Hornsby *– Grover Cleveland Alexander was sleeping in the bullpen when the call from manager Hornsby came. He "staggered a little, handed me the pint, hitched up his britches, and walked as straight as he could to the mound." Alexander on his face-off with Tony Lazerri: "Less than a foot made the difference between a hero and a bum.*

POST-SEASON

OCTOBER 21:

Edward "Whitey" Ford is born in New York City.

NOVEMBER 3:

Ty Cobb announces his resignation as manager of the Detroit Tigers. Under Cobb, the team finished in sixth place with a record of 79-75.

NOVEMBER 11:

The Chicago White Sox drop Eddie Collins as their manager and replace him with catcher Roy Schalk, who will continue to play. Collins also is released as a player despite hitting .344. The White Sox under his leadership were 81-72 and finished fifth.

NOVEMBER 29:

Today Tris Speaker announces his resignation as manager of the Cleveland Indians. The team finished in second, behind the Yankees, and had a record of 88-66. Speaker, who was earning $35,000 a year, says he is taking "a vacation from baseball I expect will last the rest of my life."

Why did two of baseball's greats – Ty Cobb and Tris Speaker – resign their managerial posts within four weeks of one another? The reason can be traced to a game between the two teams on September 15, 1919. Pitcher Hubert "Dutch" Leonard, then with the Tigers, sends two letters to AL president Ban Johnson and claims they show that the game was fixed for Detroit to win. He claims he, Cobb, Speaker, and the Indians' Joe Wood met beneath the Navin Field grandstands in New York and arranged for the Tigers to win the game and finish in third place. Ban Johnson and Tiger owner Frank Navin buy the letters for $20,000. Leonard hates Cobb and tells writer Damon Runyon, "I'll have my revenge." The AL owners vote to refer the matter to Commissioner Kenesaw Mountain Landis. After studying the matter, Judge Landis announces that Cobb and Speaker are being "permitted to resign." Wood retired after the 1922 season.

DECEMBER 16:

Commissioner Kenesaw Mountain Landis gets a new seven-year contract; his salary is $65,000.

DECEMBER 20:

The Cardinals and Giants engineer a blockbuster trade. Second baseman and manager Rogers Hornsby (.317, 11 homers) goes from St. Louis to New York. In return, the Cardinals receive second baseman Frankie Frisch (.314) and pitcher Jimmy Ring (11-10, 4.57). Hornsby, one of baseball's top hitters, has batted more than .400 three times, including .424 in 1924 – the highest average ever. Hornsby had demanded a three-year contract after the Cardinals' World Series win this year and gets a trade instead.

Commissioner Landis meets with Ty Cobb, Tris Speaker, and Smoky Joe Wood, who was on the 1919 Indians. Cobb admits writing one of the letters and insists it was a business proposition, not a fix. Wood backs Cobb, and Speaker claims a bet was made on a horse, not baseball. Their accuser, Dutch Leonard, does not attend. According to sportswriter Fred Lieb, "Ballplayers who knew of Cobb's terrible temper told me that Leonard was afraid to come to the hearing for fear that Cobb would tear him apart physically."

AL president Ban Johnson voices his outrage over the Cobb-Speaker affair and declares he will allow neither to have any future association with his circuit.

DECEMBER 22:

Ty Cobb and Tris Speaker deny they conspired to fix a baseball game.

DECEMBER 24:

Cleared of Dutch Leonard's "fixing" charges, Tris Speaker and Ty Cobb decide to play again in 1927.

DECEMBER 28:

Bob O'Farrell replaces Rogers Hornsby as manager of the St. Louis Cardinals.

THE BEST OF 1926

NATIONAL LEAGUE

HITTERS

Batting Average:
Eugene "Bubbles" Hargrave, Cincinnati Reds, 353

Slugging Average:
Fred "Cy" Williams, Chicago Cubs, .568

Home Runs:
Hack Wilson, Chicago Cubs, 21

Runs Batted In:
Jim Bottomley, St. Louis Cardinals, 120

Hits:
Eddie Brown, Boston Braves, 201

Stolen Bases:
Hazen "Kiki" Cuyler, Pittsburgh Pirates, 35

PITCHERS

Wins:
Lee Meadows, Pittsburgh Pirates; Ray Kremer, Pittsburgh Pirates, 20

Strikeouts:
Clarence "Dazzy" Vance, Brooklyn Robins, 140

Earned Run Average:
Ray Kremer, 2.61

Winning Percentage:
Ray Kremer, .769

Saves:
Lloyd "Chick" Davies, New York Giants, 6

Most Valuable Player:
Bob O'Farrell, St. Louis Cardinals

AMERICAN LEAGUE

HITTERS

Batting Average:
Henry "Heinie" Manush, Detroit Tigers, .378

Slugging Average:
Babe Ruth, New York Yankees, .737

Home Runs:
Babe Ruth, 47

Runs Batted In:
Babe Ruth, 145

Hits:
George Burns, Cleveland Indians, 216

Stolen Bases:
Johnny Mostil, Chicago White Sox, 35

PITCHERS

Wins:
George Uhle, Cleveland Indians, 27

Strikeouts:
Lefty Grove, Philadelphia Athletics, 194

Earned Run Average:
Lefty Grove, 2.51

Winning Percentage:
George Uhle, .711

Saves:
Frederick "Firpo" Marberry, Washington Senators, 22

Most Valuable Player:
George Burns, Cleveland Indians

CULTURE

***Around the Bases (The Collegians)*, a silent film starring George Lewis and Eddie Phillips, makes its premiere.**

HISTORY

Bill Diester of Salina in the Southwestern League finishes the season with a batting average of .444 – the highest in organized baseball in the 20th century. Yet Diester never makes it to the major leagues.

1927

"A more determined athlete than George Herman Ruth never lived."
– *Paul Gallico, writer*

NEWS

LINDBERGH FLIES SOLO FROM NEW YORK TO PARIS

TELEVISION DEMONSTRATED IN NEW YORK CITY

President Coolidge announces, "I do not choose to run"

CBS FORMED

MOUNT RUSHMORE DEDICATED

Holland Tunnel opens, connecting New York with New Jersey

***The Jazz Singer*, starring Al Jolson, is the first feature-length talking film**

DEMPSEY-TUNNEY HEAVYWEIGHT TITLE FIGHT IS BROADCAST ON THE RADIO

***FUNNY FACE, SHOW BOAT* DEBUT ON BROADWAY**

PRE-SEASON

JANUARY 1:

The Robins release Zack Wheat. The outfielder spent 18 consecutive seasons with Brooklyn. He hit .300 or better 13 times, leading the NL in 1918 with a .335 average. Last year he hit .290.

JANUARY 9:

The Phillies, Giants, and Robins complete a three-team trade. New York gets outfielder George Harper (.314 in 56 games) and 33-year-old pitcher Burleigh Grimes (12-13, 3.71 ERA). Going to Brooklyn is catcher Walter "Butch" Henline (.283 in 99 games). Philadelphia receives pitcher Jack Scott (13-15, 4.34 ERA) and second baseman Lafayette "Fresco" Thompson (.625 in two games).

JANUARY 12:

Commissioner Kenesaw Mountain Landis has another scandal to handle. Banned Black Sox player Charles "Swede" Risberg has charged that the 1917 White Sox bribed the Tigers with $1,000 to dump four games. He fingers Chicago manager Clarence "Pants" Rowland as the mastermind. He also implicates Ray Schalk and Eddie Collins, who were not involved in the Black Sox scandal. Risberg also charges the White Sox were to intentionally lose other games so that the Tigers would finish third. Says Risberg, "I heard that the bosses of baseball said they wanted to clean the game up and I told them my piece to help them." Another banned Black Sox, Chick Gandil, corroborates Risberg's story. Judge Landis summons 29 players. There is an admission that money was collected, but the players assert it was a gift to Detroit's pitchers for beating the Red Sox three out of four games. Collins and Schalk admit participating and Tiger pitchers acknowledge receiving money. But Collins insists it is a common practice. Today, the commissioner issues his ruling. He clears the involved parties, stating, "It was an act of impropriety, reprehensible and censurable, but not an act of criminality. Henceforth there is a new rule in baseball: Anyone who gives a gift to an opposing player for any reason will receive a one-year ban."

Rogers Hornsby also comes under Commissioner Landis's scrutiny when a Cincinnati bookie named Frank L. Moore charges the slugger with betting $92,000 on horses, losing, and reneging. Hornsby denies the charges. Moore sues and loses. Landis admonishes Hornsby but does not impose any type of punishment.

JANUARY 27:

Commissioner Kenesaw Mountain Landis clears Tris Speaker, Ty Cobb, and all others who were named in the alleged attempt to fix a Tiger-Indians game on September 24, 1919. Judge Landis says, "These players have not been, nor are they now, found guilty of fixing a ball game. By no decent system of justice could such a finding be made."

JANUARY 31:

Tris Speaker signs with the Senators for a reported $35,000. After the Indians hired Jack McAllister to replace Speaker as manager, the team cleared him to sign with any team.

FEBRUARY 9:

Ty Cobb officially signs to play with the Athletics. The announcement was made last night at the annual dinner of the

FEBRUARY 9
The Tigers' Ty Cobb officially signs to play with the Philadelphia Athletics.

APRIL 12
In Philadelphia, the Giants' Bill Terry hits the first-ever opening day grand slam.

Philadelphia chapter of the Baseball Writers Association.

The Giants reacquire outfielder Edd Roush (.323, seven homers) from the Reds 11 years after trading him away. In return the Reds receive infielder George Kelly (.303, 13 homers) and cash. Roush has hit .300 or better for the past 10 consecutive seasons. Kelly has hit .300 or higher six straight years.

MARCH 2:

Babe Ruth becomes the highest paid baseball player in history with the announcement of a new three-year contract for a reported $70,000 per season. Yankees' owner Colonel Jacob Ruppert says, "The Babe is a sensible fellow." The official signing is March 4.

MARCH 9:

White Sox outfielder Johnny Mostil tries to commit suicide by slashing himself with a razor. Supposedly, he is depressed about a jaw ailment. But the true cause is the discovery by teammate Urban "Red" Faber that Mostil is having an affair with Faber's wife. Mostil appears in only 13 games in 1927, but plays two more seasons with Chicago – with Faber as his teammate. He completes a 10-year career with a .301 batting average.

UMPIRE BILLY EVANS SAYS IN A NEWSPAPER COLUMN, "ONLY A MISERABLE THIRST FOR VENGEANCE ACTUATED LEONARD'S ATTACK ON COBB AND SPEAKER... HE DECIDED TO DRAG DOWN WITH HIM THOSE WHOM HE BELIEVED HAD CAST HIM ASIDE... IT IS A CRIME THAT MEN OF THE STATURE OF TY AND TRIS SHOULD BE BLACKENED BY A MAN OF THIS CALIBER WITH CHARGES THAT EVERY BASEBALLER KNOWS TO BE UTTERLY FALSE."

MARCH 19:

Richie Ashburn is born in Tilden, Nebraska.

APRIL 9:

After a January 31 ruling by Commissioner Landis that Rogers Hornsby cannot own stock in the Cardinals and play for New York, the new Giant sells his shares for $100,000 and gets his legal costs reimbursed. Cardinals' owner Sam Breadon, ordered by the NL to buy out Hornsby, comes up with $86,000; the Giants ante up $12,000; the other teams each contribute $2,000.

THE SEASON

APRIL 12:

The Giants' Bill Terry starts his season in top form. On opening day in Philadelphia, he hits a fifth-inning grand slam homer off the Phillies' Hal Carlson. It is the first base-loaded home run ever on opening day. The Giants win 15-7. A crowd of 72,000 packs Yankee

TRIVIA

Baseball has a field day at the movies: *Casey at the Bat*, starring Wallace Beery in the title role, Zasu Pitts, and Sterling Holloway; *The Bush Leaguer*, starring Monte Blue and William Demarest; *Slide, Kelly, Slide*, starring Joe E. Brown with the Indians' Lew Fonseca in a small role; *The Babe Comes Home*, starring Babe Ruth, as baseball player Babe Dugan, and Anna Q. Nilsson; *College*, starring Buster Keaton.

MAY 30
At Forbes Field, Cubs' shortstop Jimmy Cooney pulls off an unassisted triple play.

TRIVIA

Babe Ruth was as bad with names as he was great with the bat. During spring training, the uncle of Johnny Sylvester – to whom Ruth promised a home run in last year's World Series – visits the Bambino and informs him that the youngster is doing well. Ruth sends his regards to the youngster and, after the uncle leaves, asks reporters, "Who the hell is Johnny Sylvester?"

Stadium to see a game against visiting Philadelphia. The Yankees knock out Robert "Lefty" Grove and win, 8-3, behind Waite Hoyt. The game features 13 future Hall of Famers: for Philadelphia, Ty Cobb, Eddie Collins, Zack Wheat, Lefty Grove, Jimmie Foxx, Al Simmons, Mickey Cochrane, and manager Connie Mack; for the Yankees, Babe Ruth, Lou Gehrig, Waite Hoyt, Herb Pennock, and manager Miller Huggins.

APRIL 15:

Babe Ruth hits a bases-empty homer against Howard Ehmke of the visiting Athletics in the first inning; it is his first of the year. The Yankees win, 6-3.

APRIL 19:

With Ty Tyson handling the microphone, the Detroit Tigers begin broadcasting their home games today on radio station WWJ as they meet the Indians at Navin Field.

MAY 7:

The Yankees' Lou Gehrig hits a grand slam homer off Ted Lyons today, the first ball hit into the new right-field pavilion at Comiskey Park. The Yankees beat the White Sox, 8-0.

MAY 14:

Tragedy strikes Baker Bowl in Philadelphia. During the seventh inning of a Phillies-Cardinals game, a full section of the right-field stands collapses. Some 50 fans are injured and one dies of a heart attack. The game goes on and the Phillies win, 12-4. Until Baker Bowl is repaired, the Phillies will play all their home games at the Athletics' Shibe Park.

The Cubs' Guy Bush and the Braves' Charlie Robertson lock up in an extra-inning pitchers' duel. Bush pitches 18 innings without relief, gives up 11 hits and eight walks, strikes out five, and wins, 7-2. Robertson goes 17 1/3 innings. Jimmy Cooney drives in the lead run and teammate Earl "Sparky" Adams has four hits.

MAY 17:

The Cubs win another marathon. Bob Smith of the Braves goes 22 innings only to lose to the Cubs, 4-3, in Boston. Smith yields 20 hits, walks nine, and strikes out five. Bob Osborne, who pitches the final 14 in relief, gets the win when Charlie Grimm singles in Hack Wilson. The Braves have 15 hits.

MAY 20:

At Ebbets Field, fans shower umpire Pete McLaughlin with bottles as the Cubs beat the Robins, 7-5, behind Tony Kaufmann.

MAY 21:

For the second straight day, Robins' fans attack an umpire at Ebbets Field. Today's target is Frank Wilson, who needs a police escort after the Cubs sweep Brooklyn, 6-4 and 11-6, in a doubleheader.

MAY 22:

The Yankees are in high spirits in Cleveland as they beat the Indians, 7-2, with Babe Ruth hitting his 10th home run of the young season. Ruth's homer is described as a popup that goes over the fence. The Yankees, who wear Indian headdresses during the game, now lead the AL by four and a half games.

MAY 23:

At Wrigley Field, Hack Wilson's monster home run is overshadowed by peripheral events. In the fifth inning, Wilson launches the first homer ever to hit the center-field ground level scoreboard. The Cubs score seven in the eighth inning to beat the Braves, 14-8. Umpire Jim Sweeney is showered with bottles after thumbing Cubs' third baseman Howard Freigau. In the evening, Wilson is arrested in a friend's apartment for drinking beer in violation of the Prohibition Act.

MAY 30:

At Forbes Field, Cubs' shortstop Jimmy Cooney pulls off an unassisted triple play in the fourth inning against the Pirates. With runners on first and second, Paul Waner lines to Cooney, who steps on second base to get brother Lloyd Waner and then tags Clyde Barnhart as he comes down from first. The Cubs win the game, 7-6, in 10 innings. Cooney himself was on the victim's end of an unassisted triple play when he was caught off second base by the Pirates' Glen Wright in 1925. The Cubs win today's second game, 6-5, in 10 innings.

MAY 31:

For the second consecutive day, there is an unassisted triple play in baseball. At Detroit's Navin Field,

"Who is this Baby Ruth? And what does she do?"
– George Bernard Shaw

Tigers' first baseman Johnny Neun preserves a 1-0 victory over the Indians in the ninth inning by snaring a Homer Summa line drive, tagging Charlie Jamieson who was on first, and then outrunning Glenn Myatt to second. The winning pitcher is Harry "Rip" Collins; the loser is Garland Buckeye.

Babe Ruth homers for the fourth consecutive game in the fifth inning of the nightcap of a doubleheader in Shibe Park. Ruth, who hits his 15th against Jack Quinn and 16th off Howard Ehmke, finishes May with 12 round-trippers. They Yankees lose the opener, 10-3. The Athletics' Jimmie Foxx hits his first major league homer; it comes off Urban Shocker.

JUNE 7:

Eight days after executing an unassisted triple play, shortstop Jimmy Cooney (.242) is sent by the Cubs, along with pitcher Tony Kaufmann (3-3), to the Phillies in return for pitcher Hal Carlson (4-5).

JUNE 11:

In Cleveland, Babe Ruth hits his 19th and 20th home runs against left-hander Garland Buckeye. The Yankees win, 6-4.

JULY 4:

At Yankee Stadium, 74,000 turn up for a doubleheader with the Senators. They see Babe Ruth go five for seven, but he is overshadowed by Lou Gehrig, who hits two home runs – including a grand slam – and passes Ruth for the home run lead. The Yankees sweep, 12-1 and 21-1, and now hold first place by 11 1/2 games.

JULY 5:

With Lou Gehrig at 28 homers and Babe Ruth at 25, the New York Telegram headlines: THE ODDS FAVOR GEHRIG TO BEAT OUT RUTH IN HOME RUN DERBY.

JULY 9:

In Detroit, Babe Ruth rocks Navin Field with homers number 28 and 29 against Ken Holloway. Ruth adds two doubles in a Yankee 19-7 victory.

JULY 18:

At Navin Field in Detroit, before what were for 22 years his hometown fans, Ty Cobb of the Athletics doubles off Harry Heilmann's glove in the first inning against Sam Gibson for his 4,000th career hit. The Tigers win the game, 5-3, against Lefty Grove.

JULY 24:

Babe Ruth hits his 31st home run of the season and his first of 1927 at Comiskey Park; he now has homered in every AL park. The homer, off Tommy Thomas, breaks a 12-day drought for the Bambino. The Yankees win the game, 3-2.

JULY 27:

At the Polo Grounds, 18-year-old Mel Ott of the Giants hits his first career home run, an inside-the-park shot, against Hal Carlson of the Cubs.

AUGUST 2:

On the 20th anniversary of his first major league game, Walter Johnson is honored by the Washington Senators with a "day." But the Tigers spoil the party by defeating Washington and Johnson, 7-6. Johnson's first major league opponent was Detroit, and they won that game too, 3-2.

AUGUST 16:

At Comiskey Park, Babe Ruth hits a home run against Tommy Thomas. It is Ruth's 37th of the season, but he trails teammate Lou Gehrig, who has 38. The Yankees win the game, 8-1.

AUGUST 22:

The Braves' Ed Brown sets an NL record by appearing in his 534th consecutive game. The previous record holder was Fred Luderus, who played with the Cubs and the Phillies.

Babe Ruth hit a record 60 home runs in 1927.

SEPTEMBER 30
At "The House that Ruth Built," the Babe hits his 60th home run of the season.

HISTORY

Babe Ruth's 60 home runs are more than the total of any AL team. The closest to 60 are the Athletics, who hit 56. The Yankees bang out 158, including 47 by Lou Gehrig. How did Ruth get to his historic 60 home runs? An incredible September – in which he hit 17 – put Ruth at 60. He hit four in April, 12 in May, and nine each in June, July, and August.

SEPTEMBER 3:

In the midst of their offensive mayhem, the Yankees experience a lull. For the first (and only) time this year they are shut out. Lefty Grove limits the Bronx Bombers to three singles – two by Babe Ruth – and the Athletics win, 1–0.

SEPTEMBER 4:

At Shibe Park in Philadelphia, Babe Ruth hits his 400th career home run and his 44th of the year. The landmark homer comes against George "Rube" Walberg in a 12-2 Yankees' win.

SEPTEMBER 6:

Babe Ruth and the Yankees come to Fenway Park for a doubleheader. In game one, Ruth hits his 45th and 46th home runs of the year against Tony Welzer, and the Yankees win, 14-2. One of Ruth's round-trippers clears the center-field fence and is reportedly the longest ever hit at Fenway. In game two, the Red Sox win, 5-2, despite Ruth's 47th home run, hit against Jack Russell.

SEPTEMBER 7:

Babe Ruth follows up on his three-homer day at Fenway Park with two more. Against Danny MacFayden, the Bambino hits his 48th and later cracks number 49 against Slim Harriss. The Yankees win, 12-10, and Ruth now has eight home runs at Fenway Park.

SEPTEMBER 10:

The Yankees beat the Browns for the 21st time this year, setting an AL record for most wins against one team in a season. Eleven of those victories came in Sportsman's Park in St. Louis. Today's score is 1-0.

SEPTEMBER 11:

Back at Yankee Stadium, Babe Ruth continues his home run barrage. Today he hits number 50, this one against Milt Gaston of the Browns. The Yankees lose nonetheless, 6-2.

SEPTEMBER 13:

A big day for the Yankees and the Babe. In a doubleheader against the Indians, Ruth hits his 51st home run against Willis Hudlin and his 52nd off Joe Shaute. The Yankees win both games by the score of 5-3 and clinch the AL pennant in their 139th game of the season. In addition, Waite Hoyt wins his 20th game.

SEPTEMBER 18:

At Yankee Stadium, New York sweeps Chicago in a doubleheader, 2-1 and 5-1. In the nightcap, against Ted Lyons, Babe Ruth hits his 54th home run of the year. Lou Gehrig weighs in with his third grand slam home run of the season.

SEPTEMBER 22:

At Yankee Stadium, Babe Ruth homers against the Tigers' Ken Holloway for his 56th of the season. Earl Combs hits three consecutive triples, and the Yankees win, 8-7.

Tommy Lasorda is born in Norristown, Pennsylvania.

SEPTEMBER 24:

The Yankees beat the Tigers, 6-0, at Yankee Stadium. It is New York's 104th win of the year, breaking a record set by the 1912 Boston Red Sox.

SEPTEMBER 27:

Babe Ruth homers with the bases loaded against Lefty Grove of the Athletics. It is Ruth's 57th of the season. The Yankees win, 74.

SEPTEMBER 29:

Babe Ruth ties his own major league record for home runs with number 59 today in the first inning of a Yankee win over the Senators, 15-4. In the first inning at Yankee Stadium, Ruth launches number 58 with no one on base against Hod Lisenbee. After hitting a triple, Ruth smacks number 59, a grand slam homer, in the fifth inning against Paul Hopkins. It was the seventh bases-loaded homer of the year for New York. In his final at-bat of the game, Ruth sends Leon "Goose" Goslin to the wall to make a catch.

SEPTEMBER 30:

Babe Ruth scales unprecedented home run heights. With 10,000 hometown fans looking on at Yankee Stadium, the Bambino hits a 1-1 knee-high fastball from left-hander Tom Zachary into the right-field bleachers for his 60th home run of the season. Ruth breaks his own record of 59, established in 1921. Today's blast comes with the score tied 2-2 with one out in the eighth inning and Mark Koenig – who had tripled – on base. Zachary calls, "foul ball," but Ruth's drive is fair by 10 feet. The Yankees salute Ruth by pounding their bats on the dugout floor, and when he returns to right field,

After hitting his historic home run, Babe Ruth reportedly says, "Sixty, count 'em, 60. Let's see some son-of-a-bitch match that." On another occasion, the Bambino observes, "If I'd just tried for them dinky singles, I could've batted around .600."

he salutes the fans, military-style. The ball is caught by Joe Forner of Manhattan, a baseball fan for 35 years. Ruth previously had singled twice. The Yankees, in an anticlimax, beat the Senators, 4-2, for their 109th win of the year.

Years later, Tom Zachary reflects on serving up Babe Ruth's 60th homer: "If you really want to know the truth, I'd rather have thrown at his big, fat head."

In 1927, Philadelphia manager Connie Mack testifies against 26-year-old Harry Donnelly, who was arrested for heckling the Athletics at Shibe Park. Mack, who had the fan arrested, claims Donnelly was responsible for errors by outfielder Zack Wheat and infielder Sammy Hall in a Philadelphia loss. He also says Donnelly is responsible for the release of outfielder Good Time Bill Lamar. Donnelly is held on $500 bail and charged with disturbing the peace.

A footnote to the September 30 game is the last appearance of the great Walter Johnson. The Big Train pinch-hits for pitcher Tom Zachary in the ninth inning and flies out to Ruth in right field. Johnson, 39 years old, finishes his distinguished 21-year career – all spent with Washington – with a record of 416-279, an ERA of 2.17, 3,508 strikeouts, and an all-time high 110 shutouts. At bat, he hits a lifetime .236 with 24 home runs. Next season, Johnson will manage the Newark team in the International League.

OCTOBER 1:

The Yankees beat Washington, 4-3, for their 110th victory of 1927. Babe Ruth, however, does not hit a home run.

OCTOBER 4:

The Yankees wage psychological warfare against the Pirates before the start of the World Series. At Forbes Field, during batting practice, New York puts on an awesome display of power hitting, led by Babe Ruth, who hits four straight over the fence. On hand are Pittsburgh's Waner brothers, themselves no slouches with the bat. Paul led the NL with a .380 average and Lloyd hit .355. After watching the Yankees, Lloyd remarks to his brother, "Jesus, they're big, aren't they?"

OCTOBER 5:

World Series, game one. At Forbes Field, the Yankees, behind Waite Hoyt and relief help from Wilcy Moore, beat the Pirates, 5-4. The losing pitcher is Ray Kremer. The Yankees score a run in the first inning on a Babe Ruth single – one of his three hits – and a

An idol of baseball fans everywhere, Babe Ruth was especially popular with kids.

"Ruth made a grave mistake when he gave up pitching."
– Tris Speaker

HISTORY

For the second consecutive season, the Chicago American Giants of the Negro National beat the Bacharach Giants of the Eastern Colored League, five games to three, for the Negro Leagues World Championship.

Lou Gehrig triple. In the third, New York scores three runs on one hit. Paul Waner of the Pirates has three hits.

OCTOBER 6:

World Series, game two. In Pittsburgh, the Yankees make it two in a row with a 6-2 victory. George Pipgras goes all the way, limiting the Pirates to seven hits. Vic Aldrich takes the loss. Mark Koenig has three hits for New York and Lou Gehrig hits a key double in the third inning.

OCTOBER 7:

World Series, game three. At Yankee Stadium, New York's Murderers Row flexes its muscles in an 8-1 victory. Babe Ruth homers with two runners on in the seventh inning. In the first inning, Lou Gehrig tripled in two runs to give winner Herb Pennock all the support he would need. Pennock pitches a complete game three-hitter and retires 22 in a row. Pie Traynor's single in the eighth with one out breaks up the no-hitter. Lee Meadows is the loser.

OCTOBER 8:

World Series, game four. In New York, the Yankees win, 4-3, to sweep the Pirates and win the World Series. William "Wilcy" Moore pitches a complete game, yielding ten hits, for the win. Ruth hits a two-run, fifth-inning home run – his second of the series. After striking out Lou Gehrig and Bob Meusel with the bases loaded in the bottom of the ninth, loser Johnny Miljus faces Tony Lazzeri and throws a wild pitch, allowing Earle Combs – who had faked breaking for the plate – to score from third with the winning run. Babe Ruth finishes the series with a .400 batting average, two home runs, and seven RBI. Mark Koenig bats .500.

POST-SEASON

OCTOBER 17:

AL president Ban Johnson, whose power has been eroding steadily, resigns today. The investigation he spurred of Ty Cobb and Tris Speaker helped to promote his downfall. In July, when instructed by the owners to call a special meeting, Johnson anticipated he would be fired and submitted the resignation effective this date to Yankee owner Jacob Ruppert. Johnson has been on the job 27 years, from the very inception of the league. Ernest Sargent Barnard, president of the Indians for six years and a former sports editor, is elected to succeed Johnson. William Harridge becomes the AL secretary. Harridge has served as a private secretary to Johnson for 15 years.

OCTOBER 22:

Ross Youngs dies of Bright's disease, a kidney ailment, at the age of 30, in San Antonio, Texas. The Giants' outfielder hit .306 in 1926 in only 95 games and did not play in 1927. His lifetime batting average was .322.

NOVEMBER 7:

Bill McKechnie becomes the new manager of the Cardinals, replacing Bob O'Farrell. Under O'Farrell in 1927, St. Louis was 92-61 and finished second to the pennant-winning Pirates.

NOVEMBER 17:

A group headed by Alva Bradley and John Sherwin Sr. buys the Indians from Jim Dunn's widow and others. Dunn died in 1922.

NOVEMBER 28:

Outfielder Kiki Cuyler (.309) is shipped by the Pirates to the Cubs in exchange for catcher Earl "Sparky" Adams (.292) and outfielder Pete Scott (.314). Cuyler, a genuine star, is unloaded as aftermath of an August 8 game, when manager Donie Bush benched him and fined him $50 for not sliding in a play at second base. For the rest of the season, Cuyler played only sparingly.

DECEMBER 2:

The Browns obtain outfielder Henry "Heinie" Manush (.298) and first baseman Luzerne "Lu" Blue (.260) from the Tigers for shortstop Clarence "Chick" Galloway (.265), pitcher Elam Vangilder (10-12, 4.79 ERA), and outfielder Harry Rice (.287).

DECEMBER 14:

The Senators buy first baseman George Sisler (.327) from the Browns for $25,000. Sisler spent 12 seasons with the Browns and hit .407 in 1920 and .420 in 1922.

DECEMBER 15:

For the second consecutive day, the St. Louis Browns unload one of their stars. Today, slugger Ken Williams (.323, 17 homers) is sold to the Boston Red Sox for $10,000.

OCTOBER 8
The Yankees complete a sweep of the Pirates and win the World Series.

THE BEST OF 1927

NATIONAL LEAGUE

HITTERS

Batting Average:
Paul Waner, Pittsburgh Pirates, .380

Slugging Average:
Charles "Chick" Hafey, St. Louis Cardinals, .590

Home Runs:
Fred "Cy" Williams, Philadelphia Phillies, 30

Runs Batted In:
Paul Waner, 131

Hits:
Paul Waner, 237

Stolen Bases:
Frankie Frisch, St. Louis Cardinals, 48

PITCHERS

Wins:
Charlie Root, Chicago Cubs, 26

Strikeouts:
Clarence "Dazzy" Vance, Brooklyn Robins, 184

Earned Run Average:
Ray Kremer, Pittsburgh Pirates, 2.47

Winning Percentage:
Larry Benton, Boston Braves/ New York Giants, .708

Saves:
Bill "Wee Willie" Sherdel, St. Louis Cardinals, 6

Most Valuable Player:
Paul Waner, Pittsburgh Pirates

AMERICAN LEAGUE

HITTERS

Batting Average:
Harry Heilmann, Detroit Tigers, .398

Slugging Average:
Babe Ruth, New York Yankees, .772

Home Runs:
Babe Ruth, 60

Runs Batted In:
Lou Gehrig, New York Yankees, 175

Hits:
Earl Combs, New York Yankees, 231

Stolen Bases:
George Sisler, St. Louis Browns, 27

PITCHERS

Wins:
Waite Hoyt, New York Yankees; Ted Lyons, Chicago White Sox, 22

Strikeouts:
Lefty Grove, Philadelphia Athletics, 174

Earned Run Average:
Wilcy Moore, New York Yankees, 2.28

Winning Percentage:
Waite Hoyt, .759

Saves:
Moore; Garland Braxton, Washington Senators, 13

Most Valuable Player:
Lou Gehrig, New York Yankees

HISTORY

Manager Miller Huggins leads his "Murderers Row" to a 110-44 record, 19 games ahead of the star-studded Athletics. Babe Ruth, with 60 homers, 164 RBI, and a .356 average, and Lou Gehrig, at .373 with 47 homers and 175 RBI, are the heart of the fearsome lineup. Earle Combes hits .356, Bob Meusel .337, and Tony Lazzeri .309. Waite Hoyt is the top pitcher, with a 22-7 record. The Pirates, managed by Donie Bush, finish 94-60, one and a half games ahead of the Cardinals. Paul Waner leads the NL with .380, brother Lloyd hits .355, and Pie Traynor .342. Carmen Hill is the team's big winner at 22-11. The Cubs draw 1,159,168 fans – the first NL team to top a million. Ty Cobb, at age 40 and now with the A's, plays in 134 games, bats .357 with five homers and 93 RBI, and steals 22 bases.

1928

MAY 19
Charlie Root's sacrifice fly is the difference in the Cubs' 3-2 win over the Braves.

NEWS

HERBERT HOOVER ELECTED PRESIDENT, DEFEATING AL SMITH

Automakers Chrysler and Dodge merge

AMELIA EARHART IS FIRST WOMAN TO FLY THE ATLANTIC

WGY IN SCHENECTADY, NEW YORK, BEGINS FIRST SCHEDULED TELECASTS

The animated film STEAMBOAT WILLIE *introduces Mickey Mouse*

MARGARET MEAD PUBLISHES *COMING OF AGE IN SAMOA*

THE FIRST EDITION OF THE *OXFORD ENGLISH DICTIONARY* IS PUBLISHED

IN THE MIDST OF PROHIBITION, DOCTORS WRITE PRESCRIPTIONS FOR WHISKEY

PRE-SEASON

JANUARY 10:

The Braves acquire second baseman Rogers Hornsby (.361, 26 homers, 125 RBI) from the Giants for catcher James "Shanty" Hogan (.288, three homers) and outfielder Jimmy Welsh (.288, nine homers). Hornsby had been involved in a trial concerning allegedly unpaid gambling debts, but cleared. The trade is made "in the best interests of the New York Giants."

JANUARY 21:

The St. Louis Cardinals buy the Rochester minor league franchise in the International League and transfer all of the Syracuse players to the new farm team.

FEBRUARY 1:

Hughie Jennings dies at age 58 in Scranton, Pennsylvania. From 1907 through 1909, he managed the Tigers to the AL pennant, losing in three World Series. His playing career spanned 17 years and he compiled a lifetime batting average of .312 with a career high .401 in 1896. Jennings played all infield positions and the outfield.

FEBRUARY 11:

The Giants get pitcher Vic Aldridge (15-10, 4.25 ERA) from the Pirates for pitcher Burleigh Grimes (19-8, 3.54 ERA).

THE SEASON

MAY 14:

The New York Giants' tough guy manager John McGraw tangles with a car. The car wins. McGraw is struck while crossing a street outside Wrigley Field in Chicago as he tries to hail a taxicab. McGraw assumes responsibility for the accident and does not get the name of the driver. He is struck in the right leg, and X-rays reveal a break that will put him on crutches and sideline him for the next six weeks.

MAY 19:

At Wrigley Field, the Cubs beat the Braves, 3-2, to extend their winning streak to 13 straight – all at home. Hack Wilson homers and pitcher Charlie Root drives in the winning run with a sacrifice fly.

MAY 23:

Rogers Hornsby takes over as manager of the Braves 31 games into the season, with the team at 11-20. He replaces Jack Slattery. Owner Judge Emil Fuchs asks Hornsby what kind of team he has. Hornsby replies, "Mostly bums."

MAY 27:

The Braves buy George Sisler (.245) from the Senators for $7,500. Sisler was obtained by Washington from the Browns only last December for $25,000. The Senators give up on Sisler too soon. He hits .340 for the Braves in 118 games and goes on to bat .331, .326, and .309 in the final three years of his career.

JUNE 12:

Today in Chicago's Comiskey Park, Lou Gehrig outshines Babe Ruth at the plate. The Iron Horse bats four times and hits two homers and two triples, driving in six runs. Ruth has one homer and scores four times in a 15-7 Yankee victory. Gehrig homers with one on in the first inning, triples in the third, hits a three-run home run in the sixth and triples again in the

"He was frank to the point of being cruel, and subtle as a belch."
– Writer Lee Allen on Rogers Hornsby

JULY 10
The Senators' Milt Gaston gives up 14 hits, but still manages a 9-0 shutout of the Indians.

eighth. The Pirates set a major league record when seven players get at least three hits each in a game against the Phillies. Pittsburgh wins, 15-4, in Philadelphia.

JUNE 15:

The aging Ty Cobb, playing in Cleveland, doubles in Athletics' teammate Lefty Grove in the eighth inning against George Grant. He moves to third on a grounder and steals home, sliding under the mitt of catcher Luke Sewell. It is Cobb's 35th career steal of home and his last. The Athletics beat the Indians, 12-5.

JUNE 21:

At Wrigley Field, after a ninth-inning groundout in game two of a twin bill, the Cubs' Hack Wilson goes into the stands and attacks milkman Edward Young, who has been heckling him. Teammates Charles "Gabby" Hartnett and Joe Kelly intervene. The Cubs lose, 4-1, to the Cards, after taking the opener, 2-1.

NL president John Heydler slaps Wilson with a $100 fine. In court, Judge Francis P. Allgretti imposes a $1 fine on the milkman.

JUNE 25:

In Philadelphia, Fred Lindstrom's hot bat helps New York to a 12-4, 8-2 doubleheader sweep of the Phillies. Lindstrom ties a major league record with nine hits in the twinbill. One month ago today, Lindstrom had two doubles and two homers in a game.

JULY 4:

Despite a doubleheader split against the Senators, the Yankees hold first place by 12 games with a record of 53-17. This is the largest July 4 lead ever by an eventual pennant winner. The Yankees drop the opener, 5-2, and rebound, 5-4.

The White Sox pressure manager Ray Schalk into resigning with the team at 32-42. He is replaced by coach Russell "Lena" Blackburne.

JULY 10:

In the second game of a doubleheader in Washington, D.C., Milt Gaston pitches an astonishing shutout against the Indians. The Senators' right-hander yields 14 hits (including two doubles and a triple) and walks two, yet allows no runs. Sam Rice homers for Washington, which wins, 9-0. The loser is Jake Miller.

JULY 21:

In the fifth inning at Shibe Park, 20-year-old Jimmie Foxx of the Athletics hits a pitch from the Browns' Johnny Ogden over the left-field stands. Estimated at 450 feet, it is the first ball ever hit out of Shibe without bouncing on the roof. In the eighth inning, teammate Al Simmons hits a homer into the upper deck of the right-field stands. The A's win game one of a doubleheader, 8-2, then take the nightcap, 7-3. Every Philadelphia player

Lefty Grove won a league-high 24 games for the A's in 1928.

"I have only one superstition. I make sure to touch all the bases when I hit a home run."
– *Babe Ruth*

TRIVIA

Warming Up, **a baseball film, stars Richard Dix, Jean Arthur, and former major leaguer Mike Donlin.**

had at least one hit in each game of the twinbill.

JULY 26:

In Detroit, in game one of a doubleheader, the Tigers and Yankees battle into the 12th inning, tied 1-1. The Yankees score 11 runs in the top of the 12th to win the game, 12-1. Outfielder Bob Meusel hits for the cycle for a modern major league-record third time. In the second game, the Tigers win, 13-10.

JULY 27:

In Chicago, a major chapter in baseball comes to an end. The Athletics' Ty Cobb, back from a wrist injury – the result of being hit by a pitch nine days ago – starts for the last time in a regular season game. After singling and doubling, he is hit in the chest by a pitch from White Sox right-hander George "Sarge" Connally and leaves the game with a bad bruise. Cobb exits hitting .332. He is 41 years old.

JULY 28:

The Giants' Carl Hubbell makes his major league debut and is kayoed by the Pirates in the second inning. Hubbell records his first major league win, shutting out the Phillies on August 11.

JULY 29:

At Cleveland's Dunn Field, the Indians turn the tables on the Yankee sluggers and pound out 27 hits to beat New York, 24-6. It is the most runs ever scored against the Yankees. The Indians build an insurmountable lead with eight runs in the first and nine in the second. They hit an AL record of 24 singles in the game. Johnny Hodapp becomes the second player in history to have two hits in an inning twice in one game (Max Carey was the first in 1925). He and Luke Sewell have five hits each.

AUGUST 1:

In Sportsman's Park in St. Louis, Babe Ruth hits his 42nd home run of the season, a shot off Alvin "General" Crowder that carries over the right-field roof and onto Grand Avenue. Ruth is now 27 games ahead of his own record-setting 1927 pace. The Yankees win the game, 12-1, and pitcher Hank Johnson connects for five hits in five at-bats.

AUGUST 23:

It's a great day for pitcher Tom Zachary (6-9). He no longer has to face Babe Ruth. Zachary, the pitcher who served up Ruth's historic 60th home run last season, is purchased by the Yankees on waivers from the Senators.

SEPTEMBER 1:

In Washington, D.C., Republican presidential candidate Herbert Hoover shows up at the Senators-Yankee game to pose with Babe Ruth. Ruth declines. "Nothing doing. I'm for Al Smith."

SEPTEMBER 3:

Pinch-hitting for Athletics' shortstop Joe Boley against the Senators' Irving "Bump" Hadley, Ty Cobb hits a double – his 724th career two-bagger. It also is Cobb's career 4,191st hit – and his last.

SEPTEMBER 7:

The Yankee pennant laugher is now a nail-biter. Philadelphia wins a doubleheader at home from Boston today while the Yankees are losing twice to the Senators. The Yankees' 13-game lead has evaporated, and they are now tied for first with the Athletics. In game one of the Philadelphia-Boston doubleheader, A's pitcher Ray Benge is far from sharp. He yields 11 hits and three walks but manages to shut out the Red Sox, 4-0.

SEPTEMBER 8:

The Athletics keep the heat on the Yankees, taking their second straight doubleheader from the Red Sox in two days. The Yankees beat the Senators in a single contest and trail Philadelphia by a half-game. The two teams meet tomorrow for a doubleheader in New York. Tickets are in such demand, there is a near riot at the 42nd Street outlet and $2 seats are going for $25.

SEPTEMBER 9:

With 85,265 in attendance at Yankee Stadium and an estimated 5,000 or more watching from nearby rooftops, the Yankees take two from the Athletics to regain first place. It is the largest baseball crowd ever. In game one, George Pipgras shuts out Philadelphia, 3-0, beating Jack Quinn. Waite Hoyt wins the nightcap, 7-3, on a Bob Meusel grand slam homer against losing pitcher Ed Rommel in the eighth inning. But the Yankees' elation is tempered by tragic

SEPTEMBER 3
Ty Cobb's double is his 4,191st career hit – and his last. He will retire in two weeks.

SEPTEMBER 29
The Tigers and Yankees combine for an AL-record 45 hits in a 19-10 New York win.

news. Their 38-year-old teammate Urban Shocker is dead of a heart ailment and pneumonia in Denver. Born Urbain Jacques Shockcor, the right-hander pitched only two innings this season. Last year, with the Yankees he was 18-6 and his lifetime stats include 188-117 won-loss record with a 3.17 ERA in 13 years.

SEPTEMBER 11:

At Yankee Stadium, with the score tied 3-3 in the bottom of the eighth inning, Babe Ruth hits a two-run homer against the Athletics' Lefty Grove for a 5-3 New York victory. Hank Johnson is the winning pitcher as the Yankees sweep a four-game series against Philadelphia and go up two and a half games. Today also is Ty Cobb's final game. He pinch-hits for Jimmy Dykes against Johnson and pops up to shortstop Mark Koenig behind third base.

SEPTEMBER 17:

In Cleveland, where the Athletics are meeting the Indians, Ty Cobb says, "Never again will I be an active player." He tells a group of writers he will retire after the season because, "I'm just baseball tired and want to quit."

Cobb retires having played in 3,034 games. His lifetime batting average is the best ever – .367 – and he has 1,961 RBI, 2,245 runs saved, 892 stolen bases, 297 triples, and only 357 strikeouts. Despite bad legs and a cataract in his right eye, he hits .323 in his 24th and final season. Also retiring is the Grey Eagle, Tris Speaker, regarded by many as the greatest center fielder of all time. Speaker spends the past season with Cobb on the Athletics, batting .267 in 64 games. He leaves baseball with a lifetime average of .345 and hit .300 or better 18 times in his 22 years.

SEPTEMBER 20:

At the Polo Grounds, the Cardinals hold on to a two-game lead against the Giants by splitting a doubleheader before a crowd of nearly 50,000 fans. In game one, the Cardinals win, 8-5, on George Harper's three home runs. Game two goes to the second-place Giants, 7-4.

SEPTEMBER 24:

The tough economic times are taking their toll on baseball along with the rest of U.S. society. Only 404 turn up in Detroit to see the Tigers play the Red Sox.

SEPTEMBER 28:

The Yankees beat the Tigers, 11-6, and clinch the AL pennant. Babe Ruth hits his 53rd home run.

SEPTEMBER 29:

The Cardinals wrap up the National League pennant with a 3-1 victory over the Braves. The winning pitcher is Bill Sherdel with relief help from Flint Rhem.

The Yankees and Tigers combine for an AL-record 45 hits in nine innings. Detroit accounts for 28 of the safeties and beats New York, 19-10.

SEPTEMBER 30:

In the final game of the season, with the AL batting title on the line, Leon "Goose" Goslin (.379) and the Senators meet Henry "Heinie" Manush (.377) and the Browns in St. Louis. Going into the ninth, Goslin retains the batting lead with a homer in four at-bats; Manush has a triple and single in his four trips to the plate. Goslin can win the championship by giving way to a pinch hitter, but elects to take his chances. He hits a two-strike pop single to end up with a league-leading .379. Washington wins the game, 9-1.

OCTOBER 4:

World Series, game one. At Yankee Stadium, New York's Waite Hoyt three-hits the Cardinals, 4-1. The first Cardinal hit – a George Harper single – comes in the fifth inning with one out. Sunny Jim Bottomley has the other two Cardinals' hits – a home run and a single. Bob Meusel of the Yankees homers in the fourth inning with a man on base.

OCTOBER 5:

World Series, game two. Again at Yankee Stadium, New York wins its second straight, 9-3, knocking out Grover Cleveland Alexander in the third inning. Lou Gehrig provides the spark with a first-inning, three-run homer against the scoreboard. George Pipgras pitches a complete-game four-hitter for New York. Alexander takes the loss.

OCTOBER 7:

World Series, game three. The scene shifts to Sportsman's Park in St. Louis, but the script remains the same. The Yankees win their third straight, 7-3. Tom Zachary adds a positive note to his career with a complete-game, nine-hit victory.

TRIVIA

***Elmer the Great*, a play by Ring Lardner and George M. Cohan and starring Walter Huston, opens.**

Rabbit Maranville on alcohol consumption in baseball: "There is much less drinking now than there was before, because I quit drinking on May 5, 1927."

HISTORY

With the demise of the Eastern Colored League in the spring, there is no Negro Leagues World Series in 1928. In the Negro National League, the St. Louis Stars win the first half of the season; the Chicago American Giants, the second.

Lou Gehrig hits two home runs against losing pitcher Jesse Haines. In the first inning, he hits one onto the right-field roof and in the fourth connects for an inside-the-park homer with one on.

OCTOBER 9:

World Series, game four. Yesterday it was Lou Gehrig. Today it is Babe Ruth and Lou Gehrig and Cedric Durst. The Yankees sweep their second consecutive World Series, beating the Cardinals, 7-3, at Sportsman's Park. Babe Ruth matches his 1926 series power show with three home runs. In the fourth inning, he hits a leadoff homer against losing pitcher Bill Sherdel. In the seventh, Sherdel seemingly strikes out Ruth, but the home plate umpire rules a "quick pitch." Ruth then homers. And, with Grover Cleveland Alexander on the mound, he hits a third, also with the bases empty. Gehrig and Durst add solo homers while Waite Hoyt goes all the way for the win, giving the Cardinals 11 hits. Once again, Gehrig is overshadowed by Ruth. Gehrig hits .545 with four homers and nine RBI. But Ruth hits an all-time high .625, with three home runs and four RBI. Cumulatively, the two Yankees' sluggers have 16 hits, seven homers, and 13 RBI. The Yankees outscore the Cardinals, 27-10.

POST-SEASON

OCTOBER 15:

Walter Johnson will be back in a Senators' uniform in 1929 – as the team's manager. The Big Train signs a three-year contract and will take over for Stanley "Bucky" Harris, who led Washington to a 75-79, fourth-place finish this season.

OCTOBER 29:

The Phillies get outfielder Francis "Lefty" O'Doul (.319, eight homers) and cash from the Giants for outfielder Freddy Leach (.304, 13 homers).

NOVEMBER 3:

A bond issue to build the first municipally funded stadium is approved in Cleveland.

NOVEMBER 6:

Arnold Rothstein dies at the age of 46, two days after being shot while playing poker in the Park Central Hotel in New York City. Rothstein was alleged to be the promoter of the 1919 Black Sox scandal, and when the FBI searched his files after his death, they discovered affidavits testifying that he had paid out $80,000 for the infamous fix.

NOVEMBER 7:

Rogers Hornsby (.387, 21 homers) is on the move again. The Braves, who acquired Hornsby in January, ship him to the Cubs, despite the fact he led the majors in batting and the NL in slugging. In return for Hornsby, the Braves get $200,000 and five players. They are pitcher Harry "Socks" Seibold, who has not played in the major leagues since 1919; pitcher Percy Jones (10-6, 4.03 ERA), catcher Lou Legett, not in the majors in 1928; infielder Freddie Maguire (.279, one homer), and pitcher Bruce Cunningham, not in the big leagues prior to the trade. Following the trade of Hornsby, Boston Braves' owner Judge Emil Fuchs installs himself as the team's manager. Fuchs explains, "The time has gone when a manager has to chew tobacco and talk from the side of his mouth. I don't think our club can do any worse with me as manager than it has done the last few years." Coach Johnny Evers makes most of the game decisions.

NOVEMBER 21:

Billy Southworth replaces Bill McKechnie as manager of the Cardinals. Under McKechnie, the Cards won the 1928 pennant and were swept in the World Series by the Yankees.

DECEMBER 1:

At the annual major league meeting in Chicago, NL president John Heydler proposes a "designated hitter," a 10th player who would bat in place of the pitcher. Heydler argues that it will speed up the game and eliminate weak-hitting pitchers. Among supporters is Giants' manager John McGraw. The NL votes to approve the idea, the AL says no, and the current system remains in place.

DECEMBER 8:

The Braves buy Rabbit Maranville (.240) from the Cardinals.

DECEMBER 19:

The Tigers acquire player-manager Bucky Harris (.204) from the Senators for infielder Jack Warner (.214). Harris is named manager, replacing George Moriarty.

OCTOBER 9
With a 7-3 win over the Cardinals, the Yankees sweep their second straight World Series.

DECEMBER 1
NL president John Heydler proposes using a "designated hitter" to bat for the pitcher.

THE BEST OF 1928

NATIONAL LEAGUE

HITTERS

Batting Average:
Rogers Hornsby, Boston Braves, .387

Slugging Average:
Rogers Hornsby, .632

Home Runs:
Hack Wilson, Chicago Cubs;
"Sunny" Jim Bottomley, St. Louis Cardinals, 31

Runs Batted In:
Jim Bottomley, 136

Hits:
Fred Lindstrom, New York Giants, 231

Stolen Bases:
Hazen "Kiki" Cuyler, Chicago Cubs, 37

PITCHERS

Wins:
Larry Benton, New York Giants;
Burleigh Grimes, Pittsburgh Pirates, 25

Strikeouts:
Dazzy Vance, Brooklyn Robins, 200

Earned Run Average:
Dazzy Vance, 2.09

Winning Percentage:
Larry Benton, .735

Saves:
Bill "Wee Willie" Sherdel, St. Louis Cardinals;
Hal Haid, St. Louis Cardinals, 5

Most Valuable Player:
"Sunny" Jim Bottomley, St. Louis Cardinals

AMERICAN LEAGUE

HITTERS

Batting Average:
Leon "Goose" Goslin, Washington Senators, .379

Slugging Average:
Babe Ruth, New York Yankees, .709

Home Runs:
Babe Ruth, 54

Runs Batted In:
Babe Ruth, Lou Gehrig, New York Yankees, 142

Hits:
Henry "Heinie" Manush, St. Louis Browns, 241

Stolen Bases:
Charles "Buddy" Myer,
Boston Red Sox, 30

PITCHERS

Wins:
Lefty Grove, Philadelphia Athletics;
George Pipgras, New York Yankees, 24

Strikeouts:
Lefty Grove, 183

Earned Run Average:
Garland Braxton, Washington Senators, 2.51

Winning Percentage:
Alvin "General" Crowder,
St. Louis Browns, .808

Saves:
Waite Hoyt, New York Yankees, 8

Most Valuable Player:
Gordon "Mickey" Cochrane, Detroit Tigers

HISTORY

Miller Huggins leads the Yankees to a 101-53 record and another AL pennant, two and a half games over the Athletics. Babe Ruth hits .323 with 54 homers, 142 RBI, and a .709 slugging percentage. Lou Gehrig hits .374; Tony Lazzeri, .332; Mark Koenig, .319; and Earle Combs, .310. George Pipgras at 24-13 and Waite Hoyt at 23-7 top the pitchers. The Cardinals, managed by Bill McKechnie, finish at 95-59, two games ahead of the Giants. Charles "Chick" Hafey bats .337; Sunny Jim Bottomley, .325; Frankie Frisch, .300; and George Harper, .305. The team has two 20-game winners: Wee Willie Sherdel (21-10) and Jesse Haines (20-8).

1929

APRIL 27
Dodgers' pitcher Clise Dudley is the first to hit a home run off the first pitch he sees.

NEWS

STOCK MARKET CRASHES; BLACK TUESDAY CREATES PANIC

SEVEN DIE IN CHICAGO'S ST. VALENTINE'S DAY MASSACRE; CAPONE GANG SUSPECTED

Commander Richard Byrd first to fly over South Pole

Buck Rogers comic strip debuts

One millionth Ford Model A rolls off assembly line

Police raid Margaret Sanger's birth-control clinic in New York City

"BELIEVE IT OR NOT," BY ROBERT RIPLEY APPEARS IN NEWSPAPERS

NEW YORK'S MUSEUM OF MODERN ART OPENS

MOVIE INDUSTRY PRESENTS ITS FIRST ACADEMY AWARDS; *WINGS* NAMED BEST FILM

AMOS AND ANDY GO NATIONAL ON THE RADIO

PRE-SEASON

JANUARY 11:

Helen Ruth, the Babe's estranged wife, dies in a fire in Watertown, Massachusetts, where she was living with dentist Edward Kinder.

FEBRUARY 28:

The Indians acquire outfielder Bibb Falk (.290, 1 homer) from the White Sox for catcher Martin Autry (.300 in 22 games, one homer).

MARCH:

Commissioner Kenesaw Mountain Landis "frees" ten minor league players in the farm systems of the Athletics, Pirates, Tigers, and Senators. Among the liberated is catcher Rick Ferrell, who subsequently is signed by the Browns for $25,000. Ferrell goes on to a Hall of Fame career.

THE SEASON

APRIL 16:

Earl Averill of the Indians makes his major league debut with a home run in his first at-bat. He is first AL player to accomplish the feat. His homer comes off the Tigers' Earl Whitehill in a game won by Cleveland, 5-4, in 11 innings.

The Yankees become the first team to permanently add numbers to the backs of players' uniforms. Today's opening day game was postponed twice by rain, enabling the Indians to become the first team to actually wear numbers on the field, but Cleveland used them on an experimental basis. Except for Yankee pitchers, the numbers correspond to a player's spot in the batting order – Babe Ruth becomes number 3, Lou Gehrig number 4 – but will not change if the batting order does. They will be worn on both home and road uniforms. New York beats the Red Sox, 7-3, with George Pipgras the winning pitcher. The only other Yankee to play, besides the starters, is relief pitcher Fred Heimach, who wears number 17. In his first at-bat in the first inning, Ruth hits a home run against Red Ruffing. Ruth throws a kiss and tips his hat to Claire Merritt Hodgson Ruth, the widow he wed yesterday. Gehrig hits a home run later in the game against reliever Milt Gaston.

APRIL 27:

Dodgers' relief pitcher Elzie "Clise" Dudley becomes the first major leaguer to hit a home run off the first pitch he sees. Nonetheless, the Phillies beat Brooklyn, 8-3.

"Gehrig thought Ruth was a big-mouth and Ruth thought Gehrig was cheap."
– *Tony Lazerri*

MAY 4
Lou Gehrig smacks three home runs in the Yankees' 11-9 win over the Tigers.

APRIL 28:

With the way now cleared by the voters of the state of Massachusetts, the Red Sox play the first-ever Sunday baseball game in Boston, losing to the Philadelphia Athletics, 7-3. Eddie Rommel is the winning pitcher; Charles "Red" Ruffing takes the loss. Despite the threat of rain, 22,000 fans turn out, while a church near Fenway Park protests the game.

MAY 4:

In Detroit, Lou Gehrig hits three home runs as the Yankees beat the Tigers, 11-9. Gehrig's three in a game are the first in the American League since the Iron Horse himself performed the feat in 1927. In the first inning, Babe Ruth, Gehrig, and Bob Meusel homer back-to-back-to-back – the first consecutive round-trippers in the AL since that Yankees' threesome did it in 1925.

Yankees' skipper Miller Huggins, flanked by Babe Ruth (l) and Lou Gehrig.

MAY 24
George "The Bull" Uhle pitches 20 innings for the Tigers in a 6-5 win over the White Sox.

TRIVIA

Today's Yankees' lineup and numbers are: Earle Combs, CF, number 1; Mark Koenig, 3B, number 2; Babe Ruth, RF, number 3; Lou Gehrig, 1B, number 4; Bob Meusel, LF, number 5; Tony Lazzeri, 2B, number 6; Leo Durocher, SS, number 7; Johnny Grabowski, C, number 8; George Pipgras, P, number 14.

MAY 5:

In their first Sunday home game, the Braves lose to the Pirates, 7-2. The Braves were scheduled to play Boston's first Sunday game, but their home opener on April 21 was rained out and the distinction went to the Red Sox.

MAY 8:

The Giants' Carl Hubbell no-hits the Pirates, 11-0. Hubbell walks only one and strikes out four; the Giants make three errors. The losing pitcher is Jesse Petty.

MAY 13:

George "The Miracle Man" Stallings dies in Haddock, Georgia, at age 61. Stallings managed the 1914 Miracle Braves to the pennant and a World Series championship. In 13 years as a manager, it was his only first-place finish. As a player, he appeared in only seven games over a three-year period, had 20 at-bats, and hit .200.

At Cleveland's League Park, the Yankees meet the Indians, marking the first time opposing teams have worn uniform numbers in a game. The Indians – who had used numerals on an experimental basis – put up bigger numbers on the scoreboard and defeat New York, 4-3. In the sixth inning, Yankees' catcher Bill Dickey has three assists.

MAY 18:

The Robins' Babe Herman and Johnny Frederick bang out five hits apiece in a 20-16 romp over the Phillies in game one of a doubleheader in Philadelphia. Frederick also scores five runs. In game two, won by the Phillies, 8-6, despite a Robins' triple play, Frederick scores three more times to set a major league record with eight runs over two consecutive games. The teams combine for 63 hits on the day.

MAY 19:

The career of White Sox's outfielder Johnny Mostil – a lifetime .300 hitter – ends today when he breaks his ankle. Mostil survived a suicide attempt in 1927.

During a cloudburst at Yankee Stadium, fans in right field – known as Ruthville – stampede toward the exit, killing two and injuring 62. Babe Ruth pays a hospital visit to the injured fans.

MAY 24:

At Comiskey Park, the Tigers' George "The Bull" Uhle pitches 20 innings against the White Sox. He is removed for a pinch runner, and gets credit for Detroit's 6-5 victory. Ted Lyons goes all 21 innings for Chicago and gets the loss.

MAY 25:

Pitcher Dizzy Dean signs a contract with the Houston Buffaloes of the AAA Texas League, a Cardinals' farm team. Dean will receive $100 a month.

Much about Dizzy Dean's background is an amalgam of fact and fiction. In his film biography, The Pride of St. Louis, *the nickname is attributed to a heckling White Sox coach. There are also other explanations. In* Ol' Diz, *Vince Staten traces it to an army experience. According to the biographer's source, Dean was practicing pitching while on KP by throwing potatoes. When he explained what he was doing, a sergeant described him as a "dizzy son of a gun."*

MAY 26:

At the Polo Grounds, in the bottom of the sixth inning, with the score 2-2, the Giants' Pat Crawford, pinch-hitting for pitcher Frank "Dutch" Henry, hits a grand slam home run against Boston's Harry "Socks" Seibold. The Giants come up with nine runs in the inning. In the top of the seventh, the Braves' Lester Bell pinch-hits for pitcher Art Delaney and hits a grand slam home run against Carl Hubbell. It is the only time opposing pinch hitters have hit grand slam homers in the same game. The Giants go on to win, 15-8.

JUNE 4:

Harry H. Frazee, the former owner of the Red Sox, dies. The *Boston Traveler* reports, "Funeral services will be held tomorrow for Harry Frazee, who sold Babe Ruth to the Yankees for $137,000."

JUNE 7:

Babe Ruth enters St. Vincent's Hospital in New York for treatment of a chest cold, and is diagnosed with a heart murmur. He is ordered to rest.

JUNE 19:

Babe Ruth returns to the Yankees lineup and goes hitless in his one at-bat.

JULY 10
The Phillies' Chick Klein goes deep four times in a 9-6 win over the Pirates.

JUNE 28:

The Cubs defeat the Cardinals at Sportsman's Park, 9-5, and move into first place. Hack Wilson, pitcher Pat Malone, and Rogers Hornsby homer in the second inning for the Cubs. Wilson hits a second in the game and Earl Grace also homers. Malone gets the complete-game victory.

JULY 5:

The Polo Grounds is the first major league ballpark to use a public address system.

JULY 6:

The Cardinals end an 11-game losing streak with an exclamation point! In Philadelphia's Baker Bowl, after dropping the opener of a twinbill, 10-6 (despite 15 hits), the Cardinals come back with a 28-6 rout of the Phillies. The 28 runs break the modern major league record of 27 set by the Indians against the Boston Red Sox on July 7, 1923. In 1874, the New York Mutuals of the old National Association scored 38 against Chicago. In their 28-run barrage, St. Louis gets 28 hits, including a bases-loaded home run from Sunny Jim Bottomley, who had two in game one. The Cardinals score 10 in the first and 10 in the fifth. St. Louis's Chick Hafey also hits a grand slam homer – one of his five hits; he has four RBI. Taylor Douthit also has five hits. Denny Southern has a round-tripper for Philadelphia. The beneficiary of the record offensive output is winning pitcher Fred Frankhouse, who has four hits of his own. Every Cardinal who played had a hit; eight players had two or more. The losing pitcher is Claude Willoughby.

The Detroit Stars of the Negro National League lose their home field when Mack Park burns. The team will have to play its home games at Hamtramck Stadium.

JULY 9:

The Cardinals' Charles "Chick" Hafey gets his NL-record 10th consecutive hit today against the Phillies. In the eighth inning, Phil Collins stops the streak. The Cardinals win the game, 7-4, in 10 innings.

JULY 10:

The Phillies' Chuck Klein raps out four home runs in a 10-inning game against the Pirates. The Phillies win, 9-6.

According to *The Biographical History of Baseball*, Phillies' owner William Baker installed a screen in right field at Baker Field (named after him) to make home runs more difficult to hit. Reportedly, it was to keep his own star, Chuck Klein, from breaking Babe Ruth's record and, consequently, to keep Klein's salary down.

AUGUST 3:

Brooklyn's Clarence "Dazzy" Vance is dazzling the Cubs–with the tattered sleeve on his right arm, not his pitches. The Cubs protest that their batters are being distracted, but they still manage to pound the Robins,12-2. Hal Carlson gets the win without the aid of his shirt.

AUGUST 4:

A ninth-inning rally to remember in New York: With two out and the Yankees ahead, 6-5, the Indians come up with nine runs and go on to win, 14-6.

AUGUST 10:

In Philadelphia, in the second game of a doubleheader, Grover Cleveland Alexander beats the Phillies in an 11-9, 11-inning game for his 373rd win, tying Christy Mathewson's NL mark. Alexander comes in to pitch in the eighth inning with the Phillies ahead, 9-8. St. Louis ties the game in the ninth and scores two in the top of the 10th. Alexander pitches four shutout innings for the win. At age 42, he is now in his 19th year of major league baseball. Only Cy Young (511) and Walter Johnson (416) have more victories than Alexander and Mathewson.

AUGUST 11:

At Cleveland's League Park, Babe Ruth hits Willis Hudlin's first pitch in the second inning over the right-field wall and onto Lexington Avenue. It is Ruth's 500th career home run and his 30th of the year. Ruth is on a hot streak, with six round-trippers in his last seven games. Ruth's 500 represent more than twice as many as Cy Williams of the Phillies, who holds second place on the all-time list with 237. The Yankees lose the game to the Indians, 6-5.

LEAGUE

In 1929, the Eastern Colored League is reorganized as the American Negro League.

CULTURE

***Fast Company* opens, starring Jackie Oakie in a film version of Ring Lardner and George M. Cohan's play, *Elmer the Great*.**

SEPTEMBER 19
The Indians' Joe Sewell plays in his 115th consecutive game without striking out.

"A manager has his cards dealt to him, and he must play them."
– *Miller Huggins*

AUGUST 25:

In a Giants-Pirates game at the Polo Grounds, home plate umpire Cy Rigler is wired for sound so that the fans can hear his calls. He has a microphone in his mask and wires inside his uniform. Metal plates are affixed to his shoes, and he stands on a metal sheet. The Giants win the game, 10-5.

SEPTEMBER 2:

A total of 81,000 fans watch a morning-afternoon doubleheader in Chicago between the Cubs and the St. Louis Cardinals. With 38,000 in attendance, the Cubs win the morning game, 11-7. They are victorious again in the afternoon, 12-10, with 43,000 on hand. The Cubs' Rogers Hornsby thrills the throngs by hitting two homers on the day, while Hack Wilson adds one.

SEPTEMBER 18:

The Cubs back into the NL pennant, losing today to the Giants and Carl Hubbell, 7-3, at Wrigley Field. But the second-place Pirates lose the opener of their doubleheader with the Braves, 5-4, giving Chicago the pennant.

SEPTEMBER 19:

Indians' third baseman Joe Sewell plays in his 115th consecutive game without striking out – which sets a major league record. He doesn't do as well in the field, though, making a key error as the Red Sox beat the Indians, 3-2.

In 152 games (578 at-bats) this year, Sewell fans only four times. He becomes the hardest batter in history to strike out. In 14 years and 7,132 at-bats, he strikes out only 114 times – one for every 62.6 turns.

SEPTEMBER 20:

Yankees' manager Miller Huggins is admitted to St. Vincent's Hospital in New York City. He is running a fever of 105 degrees. Coach Art Fletcher is designated to handle the team in Huggins's absence.

SEPTEMBER 24:

Tom Zachary, the pitcher who yielded Babe Ruth's record-setting 60th home run in 1927 and now is his Yankees' teammate, wins his 12th game without a single loss. Zachary finishes the season at 12-0, the best record ever for an undefeated pitcher. His ERA is 2.48.

SEPTEMBER 25:

Miller Huggins dies of blood poisoning in New York City at age 50. The Yankees were informed of their manager's death during a game at Fenway Park. After the fifth inning, the Yankees and Red Sox line up at home plate to salute Huggins. The Yankees go on to win the game, 11-10, in 11 innings.

SEPTEMBER 26:

The AL postpones all of today's scheduled games to honor the late Miller Huggins.

In the Negro National League, the Kansas City Monarchs win both halves of the season. The Baltimore Black Sox also win both halves of the American Negro League's season.

OCTOBER 5:

The Giants and Phillies meet in a doubleheader at Baker Bowl in Philadelphia. The day begins with the Giants' Mel Ott and the Phillies' Chuck Klein tied for the NL home run leadership with 42. In the first game, Klein hits a home run and Ott singles and is walked once. Klein sets an NL record, topping Rogers Hornsby's 42 homers in a season. To protect Klein's lead, Phillies pitchers intentionally walk Ott five times – in the

A's manager Connie Mack won five World Series.

OCTOBER 8
In game one of the World Series, 35-year-old Howard Ehmke is the A's starter.

OCTOBER 11
The Cubs win game three, 3-1, but the A's lead the Series, two games to one.

first, fourth, sixth, eighth, and ninth innings – including once with the bases loaded. Another of Hornsby's records falls today. Frank "Lefty" O'Doul gets six hits for a season total of 254, passing Hornsby's 1922 total of 250. The major league mark is held by George Sisler, who had 257 in 1920. The Phillies win the opener, 5-4. The Giants take the second game, 12-3.

OCTOBER 6:

After being walked five times yesterday by the Phillies, Mel Ott fails to homer today against the Braves and finishes second to Chuck Klein for the NL homer title.

REGULAR SEASON WRAP-UP:

The Athletics, managed by Connie Mack, finish at 104-46 – 18 games ahead of the Yankees – for their first pennant since 1914. Robert "Lefty" Grove (20-6) and George Earnshaw (24-8) are the top pitchers. Grove has an ERA of 2.81 – the only pitcher in the majors under 3.00 this season. The starting lineup is intimidating; it includes Al Simmons (.365 and 157 RBI), Mickey Cochrane (.331), Jimmie Foxx (.354), Edmund "Bing" Miller (.335), George "Mule" Haas (.313), and utilityman Jimmy Dykes (.327). Joe McCarthy leads the Cubs to a 98-54 record, 10 over the Pirates. The team batting average is .303. Rogers Hornsby bats .380 with 39 homers and 149 RBI. He is followed by Hazen "Kiki" Cuyler at .360, Jackson "Riggs" Stephenson at .362, and Hack Wilson at .345 with 39 homers and 159 RBI. Pat Malone at 22-10 is the NL's only 20-game winner. With owner Judge Emil Fuchs managing, the Braves finish in last place with a 56-98 record. Last year, with Jack Slattery and Rogers Hornsby splitting the season as managers, they finished seventh, with a 50-103 record. Mel Ott of the Giants, at 20, becomes the youngest player ever to hit 40 or more homers.

OCTOBER 8:

World Series, game one. In Chicago, Athletics' manager Connie Mack bypasses 24-game winner George Earnshaw and 20-game winner Lefty Grove. Instead, he picks 35-year-old Howard Ehmke as his starter today. Ehmke, who has pitched only 55 innings and is 7-2 in the regular season, responds with a complete-game eight-hitter, and the A's beat the Cubs, 3-1. He strikes out 13, setting a World Series record. Jimmie Foxx homers in the seventh with the bases empty against loser Charlie Root. Edmund "Bing" Miller drives in the A's second and third runs with a ninth-inning single.

According to Daniel Okrent and Steve Wulf, Ehmke was scheduled to be dropped from the Athletics, but convinced Connie Mack to keep him by stating, "I have always wanted to pitch in the World Series. Mr. Mack, there is one great game left in this old arm." Mack instructs Ehmke to learn all he can about the Cubs' hitters because, "You are my opening pitcher for the World Series."

OCTOBER 9:

World Series, game two. In Chicago, the Athletics, powered by a three-run homer by Jimmie Foxx and a two-run blast by Al Simmons, beat the Cubs again, 9-3. George Earnshaw gets the win, with a save by Lefty Grove. Pat Malone takes the loss for Chicago.

After catcher Mickey Cochrane is chastened by the commissioner for his heckling, he greets a Cubs' batter with, "Hello, sweetheart. We're gonna serve tea this afternoon."

OCTOBER 11:

World Series, game three. Playing in Philadelphia, the Cubs bounce back, 3-1, on a complete-game nine-hitter by Guy Bush. George Earnshaw also goes the distance, yielding only six hits and fanning 10, but takes the loss on two unearned runs. Kiki Cuyler's single in the sixth inning drives in two runs for the Cubs. It is the first win by an NL team in 11 World Series games.

OCTOBER 12:

World Series, game four. In Philadelphia, it's a parade of pitchers as the Athletics come back from an 8-0 deficit with 10 runs in the eighth to win, 10-8. The A's rally is helped by outfield misplays by Hack Wilson, who loses two balls in the sun – one for an inside-the-park homer scoring three runs. Four pitchers appear for Philadelphia; Ed

> "The secret to my success was clean living and a fast-moving outfield."
> – *Pitcher Lefty Gomez*

Rommel gets the win with a save by Lefty Grove. The Cubs use five pitchers, with John "Sheriff" Blake taking the loss. Al Simmons hits a bases-empty home run; George "Mule" Haas hits an inside-the-park, three-run homer – one of the balls Wilson loses. Charlie Grimm has a solo homer for the Cubs.

OCTOBER 14:

World Series, game five. In Philadelphia, the Athletics score three runs in the bottom of the ninth to win the game, 3-2, and the World Series. Mule Haas hits a two-run home run to tie the score. With two out, Al Simmons doubles and Bing Miller drives him in with the game-winning run. George "Rube" Walberg, who pitches five and a third innings in relief of Howard Ehmke, gets the win. Pat Malone, who goes all the way, is the loser for the Cubs. Jimmy Dykes paces Philadelphia with .421. Bing Miller bats .368 and Jimmie Foxx .350. Charlie Grimm at .389 is Chicago's top hitter.

The Tigers sell outfielder Harry Heilmann (.344, 15 homers) to the Reds. In 15 years with Detroit, the 35-year-old has hit .300 or better 11 times, and led the AL in batting four times, including a high of .403 in 1923.

POST-SEASON

OCTOBER 16:

The Reds acquire their second outstanding but aging outfielder in two days. Today they purchase 33-year-old Bob Meusel (.261, 10 homers) from the Yankees. In 10 years with New York, he hit .300 or better seven times and appeared in six World Series.

OCTOBER 23:

Bob Shawkey, the Yankees' fourth choice for the job, becomes the team's new manager. Owner Jacob Ruppert and general manager Ed Barrow previously failed to sign Donie Bush, Eddie Collins, and Art Fletcher – who guided the Yankees in their final 11 games last year after the death of Miller Huggins. The Yankees finished second in 1929, 16 games behind the A's.

OCTOBER 30:

Charles "Gabby" Street is named the new manager of the Cardinals, replacing Bill McKechnie. Street handled the team for one game in 1929, between Billy Southworth and McKechnie's stints, and won it. It is his only managerial experience to date.

NOVEMBER 14:

Iron Man Joe McGinnity dies in Brooklyn at the age of 58. McGinnity pitched in the major leagues for 10 years, winning 247 and losing 144, with an ERA of 2.64. In 1903 he won 31 games and came back in 1904 with 35 wins and an ERA of 1.61.

The Yankees buy pitcher Vernon "Lefty" Gomez from the San Francisco Seals at a price estimated between $35,000 and $50,000.

DECEMBER 11:

The Cardinals send Grover Cleveland Alexander (9-8, 3.89 ERA), the hero of the 1926 World Series, to the Phillies along with catcher Harry McCurdy, who did not play in the majors in 1929. In return, they get pitcher Bob McGraw (5-5, 5.73 ERA) and outfielder Homer Peel (.269).

In December, after major league baseball drops its Most Valuable Player awards, *The Sporting News* creates its own.

> "THERE IS NOTHING IN BASEBALL I DISLIKE. I'LL STAY IN THE GAME AS LONG AS MY MIND IS CLEAR. WHEN I REACH THE STAGE WHEN I DON'T KNOW MY BUSINESS, OR TRADE A .300 HITTER FOR A .200 HITTER, THEN YOU'LL KNOW I'M UNFIT."
> – *Connie Mack, who managed the Athletics until he was 87 years old.*

OCTOBER 14
The A's score three runs in the bottom of the ninth to win the World Series.

NOVEMBER 14
The Yankees acquire future Hall of Famer Lefty Gomez from the San Francisco Seals.

THE BEST OF 1929

NATIONAL LEAGUE

HITTERS

Batting Average:
Francis "Lefty" O'Doul, Philadelphia Phillies, .398

Slugging Average:
Rogers Hornsby, Chicago Cubs, .679

Home Runs:
Chuck Klein, Philadelphia Phillies, 43

Runs Batted In:
Lewis "Hack" Wilson, Chicago Cubs, 159

Hits:
O'Doul, 254

Stolen Bases:
Hazen "Kiki" Cuyler, Chicago Cubs, 43

PITCHERS

Wins:
Pat Malone, Chicago Cubs, 22

Strikeouts:
Malone, 166

Earned Run Average:
Bill Walker, New York Giants, 3.09

Winning Percentage:
Charlie Root, Chicago Cubs, .760

Saves:
Guy Bush, Chicago Cubs;
Johnny Morrison, Brooklyn Robins, 8

Most Valuable Player:
Rogers Hornsby, Chicago Cubs

AMERICAN LEAGUE

HITTERS

Batting Average:
Lew Fonseca, Cleveland Indians, .369

Slugging Average:
Babe Ruth, New York Yankees, .697

Home Runs:
Ruth, 46

Runs Batted In:
Al Simmons, Philadelphia Athletics, 157

Hits:
Dale Alexander, Detroit Tigers, 215

Stolen Bases:
Charlie Gehringer, Detroit Tigers, 28

PITCHERS

Wins:
George Earnshaw, Philadelphia Athletics, 24

Strikeouts:
Lefty Grove, Philadelphia Athletics, 170

Earned Run Average:
Grove, 2.81

Winning Percentage:
Grove, .769

Saves:
Frederick "Firpo" Marberry,
Washington Senators, 11

Most Valuable Player:
No award.

1930

APRIL 20
Dizzy Dean, pitching for the minor league St. Joseph Saints, makes his professional debut.

NEWS

U.S. POPULATION REACHES 122.7 MILLION

Former U.S. President and Supreme Court Chief Justice William Howard Taft dies

BLONDIE COMIC STRIP MAKES ITS DEBUT

MARLENE DIETRICH AND EMIL JANNINGS STAR IN *THE BLUE ANGEL*

DASHIELL HAMMETT PUBLISHES *THE MALTESE FALCON*

ASTRONOMERS DISCOVER THE NINTH PLANET, PLUTO

VIRGINIA WOOLF PUBLISHES THE ESSAY "A ROOM OF ONE'S OWN"

GRANT WOOD PAINTS *AMERICAN GOTHIC*

URUGUAY DEFEATS ARGENTINA, 4-2, IN SOCCER'S FIRST WORLD CUP

PRE-SEASON

JANUARY 8:

Babe Ruth meets with Yankees' owner Colonel Jacob Ruppert and general manager Ed Barrow to discuss a new contract. No progress is made.

FEBRUARY 2:

The Reds buy shortstop Leo Durocher (.246) from the Yankees for the waiver price of $10,000.

FEBRUARY 16:

The Cardinals attempt to send catcher Gus Mancuso to their International League Rochester team, but Commissioner Kenesaw Mountain Landis blocks the move.

MARCH 8:

Babe Ruth reports to spring training. He has been seeking $85,000 a year for three years, while Yankee owner Jacob Ruppert has been offering $80,000 for two years.

MARCH 10:

After accepting Colonel Jacob Ruppert's offer, Babe Ruth today signs a contract worth $160,000 over the next two years.

APRIL 1:

Gabby tops Gabby in an April Fool's Day stunt. Cubs' catcher Charles Gabby Hartnett hangs on to a baseball dropped from the Goodyear blimp from an altitude of 550 feet. He tops the record set by Senators' catcher Charles "Gabby" Street, who, in 1908, caught a ball dropped 504 feet from atop the Washington Monument.

APRIL 9:

The Braves acquire baseball's last legal spitball pitcher, 35-year-old Burleigh Grimes (17-7, 3.13 ERA) in return for pitcher Percy Lee Jones (7-15, 4.64 ERA) and cash.

THE SEASON

APRIL 20:

Dizzy Dean makes his professional debut, pitching for the St. Joseph Saints in the Western League against the Denver Bears. He allows four hits and three runs – all unearned – strikes out eight, and walks one in a 4-3, 10-inning win.

APRIL 27:

Chicago White Sox first baseman John "Bud" Clancy could have left his glove home today. In a game against the Browns in St. Louis, Clancy plays all the way and records no putouts or assists. He sets an AL record for idleness; the fewest chances in a nine-inning game. It is a mark that may be equaled but never can be beaten.

MAY 1:

In Boston, a high fever keeps Indians' shortstop Joe Sewell out of the lineup against the Red Sox, ending his consecutive game streak at 1,103. It is the first game Sewell has missed since 1922 and only the third since 1920, when he broke into the majors. The Indians win without him, 8-5.

MAY 2:

The Des Moines Demons in the Class A Western League reportedly become the first team to play in a ballpark with permanent lights. The Demons defeat the Wichita Aviators tonight, 13-6, with baseball commissioner Kenesaw Mountain Landis and American League president E.S. Bernard among the 12,000 in attendance. NBC radio broadcasts the game nationally. The *New York Times*

"I may not have been the greatest pitcher ever, but I was amongst 'em."
– Jay Hanna "Dizzy" Dean

MAY 21
Babe Ruth, at age 35, enjoys his first three-homer regular-season game.

reports, "In the opinion of many fans, the contest was viewed as clearly as a game played under daylight conditions."

Writer William B. Mead asserts that the Independence Producers of Kansas hosted Muskogee in a Western Association (Class C) night game on April 28 – four days before the Des Moines-Wichita game. The Producers won the game, 12-2.

MAY 5:

In his first major league start, the Yankees' Lefty Gomez pitches a complete game and beats the White Sox, 4-1. He allows five hits and no walks and strikes out six. Urban "Red" Faber is the losing pitcher. Gomez lost his major league debut after coming on in relief against the Senators on April 29.

MAY 6:

The Yankees acquire pitcher Charles "Red" Ruffing (0-3) from the Red Sox in return for outfielder Cedric Durst (.158) and $50,000. Ruffing, who was 9-22 last season with a 4.86 ERA, is a good hitting pitcher, batting .307 last season and .273 this year.

SOMEONE POINTS OUT TO BABE RUTH THAT HE MAKES MORE MONEY THAN PRESIDENT HERBERT HOOVER. "WHY NOT?" THE BABE RETORTS. "I HAD A BETTER YEAR THAN HE DID."

MAY 11:

In Cleveland, the Indians pound out 27 hits, scoring in every inning except the eighth, to beat the Athletics, 25-7. And Cleveland does it without a homer. For Indians' outfielder Bibb Falk five is today's lucky number – he has five hits, five runs, and five RBI in the first five innings.

MAY 12:

Cleveland pitcher Milt Shoffner balks three times in the third inning – a major league record – as the Indians lose to the Athletics, 13-7.

MAY 18:

In a game at Braves Field in Boston, the Yankees beat the Red Sox, 11-0. The game is marked by a Babe Ruth homer against Ed Morris that clears the right-field bleachers and is reported as the longest ever at this ballpark.

MAY 21:

Babe Ruth may be 35 years old, but his swing is as vigorous as ever today in the opener of a doubleheader at Shibe Park in Philadelphia. The Bambino hits first- and third-inning home runs off George Earnshaw and a third round-tripper against Lefty Grove in the eighth. It is Ruth's first three-homer regular-season game, but the Yankees lose, 15-7.

MAY 26:

White Sox left-hander Pat Caraway strikes out Indians' shortstop Joe Sewell twice today. Sewell will fan only one more time this year in 353 at-bats.

MAY 30:

It's trade time for pitcher Waite Hoyt (2-2) as a Yankee. Hoyt has an argument with manager Bob Shawkey in which he is told, "You'll pitch the way I tell you to, or you won't pitch for me at all." A two-time 20-game winner, Hoyt is then sent to the Tigers, along with shortstop Mark Koenig (.230). In return, New York gets pitcher Owen "Ownie" Carroll (0-5), outfielder Harry Rice (.305), and shortstop George "Yats" Wuestling (.000 in four games).

JUNE 3:

It's the end of a long, glorious, and often bumpy road for Grover Cleveland Alexander. He is released today by the Philadelphia Phillies after going 0-3 in nine games with an

TRIVIA

In April, the Negro Leagues' Kansas City Monarchs become the first team to play a night game.

JULY
5
The first Negro League game at Yankee Stadium is played.

TRIVIA

The film *Hot Curves; They Learned About Women* (remade in 1949 as *Take Me Out to the Ball Game*), starring Benny Rubin and Rex Lease, is released.

Pirates' third baseman Pie Traynor hit .300 or better 10 times.

ERA of 9.14. Alexander won 373 games in his 20-year career and registered three consecutive 30-win seasons.

JUNE 13:

The Senators send outfielder Leon "Goose" Goslin (.271) to the Browns for outfielder Henry "Heinie" Manush (.328) and pitcher Alvin "General" Crowder (3-7).

Writer Tom Simon notes that this is the only time in major league history that former batting champions were traded for one another.

JUNE 16:

Burleigh Grimes (3-5) is on the move again. For the second time this year he is traded – this time from the Boston Braves to the Cardinals for pitchers Fred Frankhouse (2-3) and Bill "Wee Willie" Sherdel (3-2).

JULY 2:

In game two of a doubleheader in New York, Chicago White Sox outfielder Carl Reynolds hits home runs in the first, second, and third innings against the Yankees. He becomes the second player ever to homer in three consecutive innings. Chicago wins the game, 15-4.

JULY 5:

The first Negro League game played at Yankee Stadium draws a crowd of 20,000. The New York Lincoln Giants split a doubleheader with the Baltimore Black Sox.

JULY 17:

According to his biographer Charles C. Alexander, Rogers Hornsby – in a letter dated today – writes Commissioner Kenesaw Mountain Landis, "I wish to inform you that I do not in the future intend to have anything to do with gamblers, bookmakers, horse races or bets, etc. I also wish you to know that I do not play cards or shoot craps; and intend taking no part in any of these enterprises." The letter, apparently written in response to continuing rumors about Hornsby's gambling, was found by the son of Leslie O'Connor, secretary to Judge Landis.

JULY 18:

The White Sox buy outfielder Bob "Fats" Fothergill (.259) from the Tigers. Fothergill has hit .300 or better in every one of his eight major league seasons.

JULY 21:

At Ebbets Field, the Robins and Cardinals set a major league record with four pinch-hit home runs in a doubleheader. In game one, the Robins' Harvey Hendrick hits a three-run pinch-hit homer to win the

JULY 25
The Athletics pull off two triple steals in a 14-1 thumping of the Indians.

game, 9-8. In the seventh, the Cardinals' Sunny Jim Bottomley homered as a pinch hitter to give St. Louis a 5-4 lead. In the eighth, pinch hitter George Puccinelli hit a three-run homer to give the Cardinals a temporary lead. In game two, Brooklyn's Hal Lee hit the record-setting homers as a pinch hitter in the second inning. His three-run round-tripper put the Robins ahead, 8-5, but the Cardinals prevail, 17-10. The home runs by Lee and Puccinelli are their first major league hits.

JULY 23:

In game two of a doubleheader in Philadelphia, 48 total bases on 27 hits are not enough for the Phillies as they lose to the Pirates, 16-15, in 13 innings. Don Hurst has two homers for the Phillies, and the 48 total bases tie a major league record, but a Pie Traynor homer in the 13th gives the Pirates the win. In game two, Traynor hits a ninth-inning home run to give the Pirates a 2-1 win and a sweep of the doubleheader.

JULY 25:

A triple steal is a baseball rarity, but the Athletics execute it twice today against the Indians. The triple steals are pulled off in the first and fourth innings of a 14-1 Philadelphia victory.

JULY 26:

In Philadelphia, the Cubs' Hack Wilson wrecks the Phillies with three home runs and five RBI. The Cubs win, 16-2.

JULY 27:

In Cincinnati, the Reds' Ken Ash comes in to relieve in the fifth inning and throws one pitch to the Cubs' Charlie Grimm, who hits into a triple play. Ash leaves for a pinch hitter, Cincinnati goes on to win, 6-5, and Ash gets the victory – on one pitch.

JULY 31:

At Boston, the spotlight is on Lou Gehrig. The Iron Horse knocks in eight runs on a grand slam home run and two doubles as the Yankees outhit the Red Sox, 14-13. It is Gehrig's second grand slam of the season and the fifth by Yankee hitters in five weeks (the others are by Tony Lazzeri, Jimmy Reese, Bill Dickey, and Harry Rice). Two days ago, Gehrig had six RBI in a game.

AUGUST 3:

The Phillies' Chuck Klein extends his consecutive game hitting streak to 26 in the opener of a doubleheader in Boston. It is the second time this season he has hit in 26 straight games. In game two of today's doubleheader, Klein's streak is snapped. The Phillies sweep the Braves, 11-5 and 4-1.

AUGUST 6:

Gene Rye of Waco in the Texas League hits three home runs in one inning. Going into the eighth, Beaumont leads, 6-2, but Waco comes up with 18 runs. Rye hits a homer with the bases empty, a two- run shot, and a grand slam.

AUGUST 14:

Earl Weaver is born in St. Louis.

AUGUST 18:

At Wrigley Field, Hack Wilson hits his 42nd homer of the year and the Cubs beat the Phillies, 17-3. Pat Malone also hits a homer and gets the win.

AUGUST 19:

The Browns' Goose Goslin hits three consecutive home runs.

AUGUST 31:

At the Polo Grounds in Manhattan, the Giants' Mel Ott hits three consecutive home runs. Even so, New York loses to the visiting Boston Braves, 14-10.

HISTORY

The St. Louis Stars, winners of the first half of the Negro National League season, defeat the Detroit Stars – second half winners – in a playoff to win the pennant.

Slugger Hack Wilson hit a major-league best 56 home runs in 1930.

Branch Rickey on Dizzy Dean:
"If there were one more like him in all of baseball, just one more, as God is my judge, I'd get out of the game."

The Giants' Bill Terry was the last NLer to hit .400 in a season.

SEPTEMBER 1:

In game two of a doubleheader, the Indians' Wes Ferrell beats the Browns, 9-5, for his 13th consecutive win. In game one, the Indians win, 13-8, on a grand slam homer by Dick Porter.

SEPTEMBER 15:

A strange tale unfolds in Brooklyn. With four teams in a tight pennant race, the Cardinals come to Brooklyn for a three-game series with the Robins. St. Louis pitcher Flint Rhem, scheduled to start tomorrow, disappears.

SEPTEMBER 16:

The Red Sox acquire outfielder Gene Rye from Waco. Earlier this year, Rye hit three home runs in an inning with Waco. Rye, whose real name is Eugene Rudolph Mercantelli, plays with the Red Sox in 1931. He appears in 17 games, bats 39 times, and hits .179 – seven singles – with no homers. He never again appears in the major leagues.

SEPTEMBER 17:

In game one of a doubleheader against the Senators, the Indians' Earl Averill hits three consecutive home runs and misses a fourth on an apparent "bad call." The Indians win, 13-7. Averill leads off game two with another homer, but Washington wins, 6-4. Averill has a major league record 11 RBI in the doubleheader. On July 12, Averill had eight RBI in a game.

Flint Rhem reappears in a condition described as "unbecoming a major league player." The pitcher, who has a drinking problem, claims he was kidnapped by several men, forced to imbibe bootleg liquor, and warned not to pitch against Brooklyn.

SEPTEMBER 19:

Flint Rhem takes the mound for the Cardinals today and beats the Phillies, 9-3. Rhem, a 20-game winner in 1926, sticks in the majors for six more seasons, ending his career at 105-97 and a 4.20 ERA.

Flint Rhem's roommate Bill Hallahan remarks, "Imagine kidnapping Flint Rhem and making him take a drink."

SEPTEMBER 23:

Rogers Hornsby is named manager of the Cubs for the 1931 season. The second-place Cubs are 90-64 under Joe McCarthy, who led the team to the 1929 NL pennant.

SEPTEMBER 26:

Behind 37-year-old pitcher Jesse "Pop" Haines, the Cardinals win the NL pennant with a 10-5 victory over the Pirates.

SEPTEMBER 27:

Joe McCarthy decides not to wait for the end of the season and resigns as manager of the Chicago Cubs with four games to go. Rogers Hornsby will handle the team for the final contests.

At Wrigley Field, the Cubs' Hack Wilson slams his 56th homer of the year – an NL record. Gabby Hartnett also homers as the Cubs beat the Reds, 13-8, for Pat Malone's 20th win.

SEPTEMBER 28
Hack Wilson's two RBI, in the Cubs' 13-11 win over the Reds, gives him a season record 190.

OCTOBER 1
In game one of the World Series, the A's top the visiting Cardinals, 5-2.

SEPTEMBER 28:

For the second consecutive day Hack Wilson sets a significant record. At Wrigley Field, on the last day of the season, he drives in two runs against the Reds in a 13-11 Cubs' win. They are Wilson's 189th and 190th of the year – a major league record.

After 885 games at first base, the Yankees' Lou Gehrig plays the outfield and Babe Ruth returns to the mound. The Yankees defeat the Red Sox in the season finale, 9-3, at Fenway Park. Ruth goes all the way, allowing 11 hits, and two walks, and striking out three.

In St. Louis, Cardinals' right-hander Dizzy Dean makes his major league debut against the Pirates, allowing one run and three hits, walking three, and striking out five in a 3-1 victory. He also bunts a ball into left field for a single and steals home in the third inning. The losing pitcher is Larry French. Dean's post-game comment: "Those bums got three hits off'n me."

REGULAR SEASON WRAP-UP:

The Athletics, managed by Connie Mack, win their second straight AL pennant with a 102-52 record, eight games ahead of the Senators. Lefty Grove (28-5) and George Earnshaw (22-13) lead the pitching staff. Al Simmons is the team's and league's top hitter at .381. Jimmie Foxx bats .335 with 37 homers and 156 RBI. Mickey Cochrane bats .357.

AL pitchers have a combined 4.65 ERA and throw 36 shutouts – the fewest ever. AL teams bat .288.

Managed by Gabby Street, the Cardinals finish at 92-62, two games over the Cubs in the NL. The team has seven regulars hitting over .300: Jim Bottomley, Frank Frisch, Charley Gelbart, George Watkins, Taylor Douthit, Charles "Chick" Hafey, and Jimmie Wilson. The Cardinals score the most runs ever in the NL – 1,004. Wild Bill Hallahan is the top pitcher at 15-9.

NL pitchers have a 4.97 ERA and a cumulative batting average of .303. The Giants, who finish in third, set a major league record with a team batting average of .319. In addition to .400 hitter Bill Terry, the team has eight .300 hitters: Fred Lindstrom (.379), Mel Ott (.349), Travis Jackson (.339), Shanty Hogan (.339), Freddie Leach (.327), Edward "Doc" Marshall (.309), Ethan Allen (.307), and Bob O'Farrell (.301).

DURING A BARNSTORMING TOUR, NEGRO LEAGUES' STAR LEROY "SATCHEL" PAIGE FANS 22 MAJOR LEAGUERS IN ONE GAME. PAIGE PLAYED WITH THE BIRMINGHAM BLACK BARONS AND BALTIMORE BLACK SOX DURING 1930. IN ONE CONTEST, HE FACES HACK WILSON AND BABE HERMAN. AFTER THE GAME, WILSON TELLS PAIGE, "IT STARTS LIKE A BASEBALL AND WHEN IT GETS TO THE PLATE IT LOOKS LIKE A MARBLE." PAIGE RESPONDS, "YOU MUST BE TALKIN' ABOUT MY SLOW BALL. MY FAST BALL LOOKS LIKE A FISH EGG."

1930 is a big year for sluggers. In the AL, Babe Ruth wins his fifth consecutive home run crown with 49. He adds 150 runs, 153 RBI, 136 walks, a .359 batting average, and a .697 slugging percentage. Once again, Lou Gehrig plays in the shadow of Ruth despite 41 homers, 174 RBI and a .379 batting average. The AL's Al Simmons leads the league with a .381 batting average.

In the National League, the Giants' Bill Terry hits .401 with 254 hits. The Cubs' Hack Wilson tops the Babe's home run total with an NL record 56, plus an all-time record 190 runs. He bats .356 and compiles a .723 slugging average while walking 105 times. The NL average is .303.

OCTOBER 1:

World Series, game one. In Philadelphia, Lefty Grove outpitches Burleigh Grimes, and the Athletics beat the Cardinals in the opener, 5-2. Grimes limits the A's to five hits, but each was for

HISTORY

Playing for Baltimore in the International League, first baseman Joe Hauser finishes the season with 62 home runs. Hauser played with the A's and Indians from 1922 through 1929. His best year was 1924, when he hit 27 homers for the A's and he totaled 79 for his sixth season. Despite his 62 this season, he does not get another shot at the majors.

"He could throw a lamb chop past a wolf."
– *Writer Bugs Baer on Lefty Grove*

LEAGUE

Movie and drugstore chain owner Lucille Thomas buys the Wichita franchise in the Western League, and is ahead of her time. She moves the team – to Tulsa, Oklahoma.

extra bases –including solo home runs by Al Simmons and Mickey Cochrane.

OCTOBER 2:

World Series, game two. In Philadelphia, George Earnshaw pitches a complete game six-hitter and the Athletics take today's game, 6-1. Earnshaw strikes out eight and walks only one; losing pitcher Flint Rhem is knocked out in the fourth. Mickey Cochrane homers for the A's; George Watkins has a home run for St. Louis.

OCTOBER 4:

World Series, game three. In St. Louis, Wild Bill Hallahan shuts out Philadelphia, 5-0, on seven hits. George "Rube" Walberg is the losing pitcher. Taylor Douthit homers for the Cardinals. The A's 47- year-old Jack Quinn pitches the final two innings, becoming the oldest pitcher to finish a series game. He gives up three hits and three runs.

Quinn was 9-7 with a 4.42 ERA in the regular season. He stays in the majors for three more years, concluding a 23-year career in 1933 at 247-217 with a 3.27 ERA.

OCTOBER 5:

World Series, game four. In St. Louis, Jesse Haines beats the Athletics, 3-1, on a four-hitter, holding them hitless over the final six innings. Lefty Grove takes the loss. An error by third baseman Jimmy Dykes leads to two Cardinals' runs in the fourth inning.

OCTOBER 6:

World Series, game five. In St. Louis, the Athletics beat the Cardinals, 2-0, on a ninth-inning two-run homer by Jimmie Foxx against Burleigh Grimes, who pitches a complete game five-hitter and loses. Lefty Grove gets the win in relief of George Earnshaw. The Cardinals are limited to just three hits. Cardinals' outfielder Ray Blades records seven putouts.

OCTOBER 8:

World Series, game six. In Philadelphia, George Earnshaw pitches a complete game five-hitter as the Athletics beat the Cardinals, 7-1, to win the 1930 World Series. Wild Bill Hallahan, who lasts only two innings, gets the loss. Al Simmons homers and Jimmy Dykes adds a two-run round-tripper. Al Simmons bats .364 with two homers for Philadelphia; Jimmie Foxx hits .333, and George Earnshaw is 2-0 with a 0.72 ERA. Charlie Gelbart hits .353 for St. Louis.

POST-SEASON

OCTOBER 14:

Joe McCarthy signs a four-year contract to manage the New York Yankees.

The Phillies get pitcher James "Jumbo" Elliott (10-7, 3.95 ERA), pitcher Clise Dudley (2-4, 6.35 ERA), outfielder Hal Lee (.162, one homer), and $25,000 from Brooklyn for outfielder Francis "Lefty" O'Doul (.383, 22 homers) and second baseman Lafayette "Fresco" Thompson (.282, four homers).

OCTOBER 24:

The Cleveland Indians release infielder Joe Sewell (.289).

DECEMBER 9:

At the Commodore Hotel in New York City, American League owners hold their annual meeting and reelect Ernest S. Bernard to a five-year term as their president.

Andrew "Rube" Foster, the founder of the Negro National Baseball League and an overpowering pitcher, dies at age 52 in Kankakee, Illinois. Foster spent the last four years in the Illinois State Mental Institution at Kankakee. Though he was not well-known among white baseball fans until his induction into the Hall of Fame in 1981, his contributions were recognized by the 3,000 who attended his funeral.

DECEMBER 11:

The Baseball Writers Association of America, in its annual winter meeting, decides to appoint two committees (one in each league) to elect Most Valuable Players.

DECEMBER 12:

In New York City, at the annual major league meetings, baseball's rules committee cancels the sacrifice fly rule. Under the rule, a hitter was not charged with an official at-bat when he advanced a runner with a fly ball. The rule had been reinstated in 1920. The committee also decreed that balls which bounce into the stands will now be ground-rule doubles, not home runs.

OCTOBER 8
George Earnshaw five-hits the Cardinals for a 7-1 win, and the A's take the World Series.

OCTOBER 14
Joe McCarthy signs a four-year contract to manage the New York Yankees.

THE BEST OF 1930

NATIONAL LEAGUE

HITTERS

Batting Average:
Bill Terry, New York Giants, .401

Slugging Average:
Lewis "Hack" Wilson, Chicago Cubs, .723

Home Runs:
Hack Wilson, 56

Runs Batted In:
Hack Wilson, 190

Hits:
Bill Terry, 254

Stolen Bases:
Hazen "Kiki" Cuyler, Chicago Cubs, 37

PITCHERS

Wins:
Pat Malone, Chicago Cubs;
Ray Kremer, Pittsburgh Pirates, 20

Strikeouts:
Wild Bill Hallahan, St. Louis Cardinals, 177

Earned Run Average:
Clarence "Dazzy" Vance, Brooklyn Robins, 2.61

Winning Percentage:
Fred Fitzsimmons, New York Giants, .731

Saves:
Herman "Hi" Bell, St. Louis Cardinals, 87

AMERICAN LEAGUE

HITTERS

Batting Average:
Al Simmons, Philadelphia Athletics, .381

Slugging Average:
Babe Ruth, New York Yankees, .732

Home Runs:
Babe Ruth, 49

Runs Batted In:
Lou Gehrig, New York Yankees, 174

Hits
Johnny Hoddap, Cleveland Indians, 225

Stolen Bases:
Marty McManus, Detroit Tigers, 23

PITCHERS

Wins:
Lefty Grove, Philadelphia Athletics, 28

Strikeouts:
Lefty Grove, 209

Earned Run Average:
Lefty Grove, 2.54

Winning Percentage:
Lefty Grove, .848

Saves:
Lefty Grove, 9

LEAGUE

Major league baseball gives the go-ahead to the Baseball Writers Association to conduct balloting next year for the Most Valuable Players in both the AL and NL.

1931

"A homer a day
will boost my day."
– *Josh Gibson*

NEWS

DEPRESSION CAUSES UNEMPLOYMENT FOR 4 TO 5 MILLION AMERICANS

"THE STAR SPANGLED BANNER" OFFICIALLY BECOMES U.S. NATIONAL ANTHEM

NBC IN NEW YORK BEGINS FIRST REGULARLY SCHEDULED TELEVISION BROADCASTS

EMPIRE STATE BUILDING, THE WORLD'S TALLEST, OPENS IN NYC

Twinkies introduced

Al Capone sent to prison for tax evasion

Two gangster films and two horror movies: Little Caesar, starring Edward G. Robinson; Public Enemy, starring James Cagney; Dracula, starring Bela Lugosi; Frankenstein, starring Boris Karloff

PRE-SEASON

JANUARY 4:

Former major league first baseman Roger Connor dies in Waterbury, Connecticut, at age 73. In 18 years, he batted .317 and is fifth all-time in triples with 233. His best season came in 1885, when Connor hit .371.

JANUARY 6:

The Yankees sign infielder Joe Sewell (.289), released after last season by the Cleveland Indians.

JANUARY 31:

Ernie Banks is born in Dallas.

MARCH 27:

E. S. Bernard, president of the American League since 1927, dies at age 56 at the Mayo Clinic in Rochester, Minnesota.

MARCH 28:

Byron Bancroft "Ban" Johnson, the man who guided the AL from its birth until 1927, dies at age 67 at St. John's Hospital in St. Louis.

APRIL 2:

In an exhibition game with the Yankees in Chattanooga, the Lookouts send their new signee – Verne "Jackie" Mitchell, reportedly the first female professional pitcher – to the mound. The 17-year-old strikes out Babe Ruth and Lou Gehrig, then walks Tony Lazzeri. The Yankees win the game, 14-4.

Are Ruth and Gehrig faking? Some sportswriters maintain they are. In any event, the contract of Jackie Mitchell – who was taught to pitch by Clarence "Dazzy" Vance – is voided within a week by Commissioner Kenesaw Mountain Landis, who regards baseball as too rough for women. Mitchell goes on to barnstorm with the House of David, a popular freelance team.

THE SEASON

APRIL 24:

Cubs' player-manager Rogers Hornsby hits three straight homers and knocks in eight runs to power his team past the Pirates in Pittsburgh, 10-6.

APRIL 25:

A third major baseball figure dies. Garry Herrmann, chairman of the National Commission and retired president of the Reds, dies today in Cincinnati.

APRIL 26:

A baserunning mistake costs the Yankees' Lou Gehrig a home run. In a game against the Senators in Washington, D.C., Lyn Lary is on first base when Gehrig hits a ball into the right centerfield stands. The ball bounces out again and Senators' outfielder Sam Rice tosses it toward the infield. Lary sees the throw, thinks the ball was caught, and heads to the dugout after rounding third. Gehrig keeps on going and is called out for passing the base runner. He is credited with a triple. Gehrig and Babe Ruth finish the season tied for the AL lead with 46 homers each. Lynn Lary's sloppy baserunning costs Gehrig his only opportunity to beat out Ruth head-to-head for a home run crown. The Yankees also lose the game, 9-7.

APRIL 29:

Wes Ferrell, pitching for the Indians against the Browns, carries a no-hitter into the eighth inning. Then his bid for baseball immortality is almost spoiled by a grounder to shortstop

APRIL 2 In an exhibition game, Jackie Mitchell – a female pitcher – fans Ruth and Gehrig.

JULY 12 The largest crowd ever at Sportsman's Park sees the Cards and Cubs split two games.

AUGUST 5 The Cardinals' Jim Bottomley gets 10 hits in a doubleheader with the Pirates.

Bill Hunnefield, whose throw pulls first baseman Lew Fonseca off the bag and is scored an error. The ball is hit by his brother Rick, the Browns' catcher. Ferrell allows three walks, striking out eight and wins his no-hitter, 9-0. It is the first AL no-hitter since 1926. The Indians make three errors. Sam Gray gets the loss.

MAY 6:

Willie Mays is born in Westfield, Alabama.

MAY 7:

In St. Louis, an odd call by umpire Charley Evans triggers a Cardinals' protest. Cubs' leftfielder Jackson "Riggs" Stephenson misplays a ball hit by Sunny Jim Bottomley. The ball goes into the crowd and Evans calls Bottomley out, claiming that the fans had verbally interfered with Stephenson. The Cubs win the game, 4-1. NL president John A. Heydler denies the appeal of the Cardinals, who claim Evans misinterpreted the rules. The game result stands.

MAY 17:

The White Sox obtain infielder-outfielder Lew Fonseca (.370), the 1929 AL batting champion, from the Indians for third baseman Willie Kamm (.254).

MAY 27:

In a special meeting in Chicago, AL owners elect William Harridge president to succeed the late E. S. Bernard. Harridge has been with the AL for 20 years as private secretary to Ban Johnson and as league secretary.

JUNE 30:

The Athletics buy pitcher Waite Hoyt (3-8) from the Tigers.

JULY 2:

The Yankees pound the Tigers, 13-1, in Detroit. For the 11th consecutive game, Babe Ruth has an RBI. He has a total of 18 for the 11 games.

JULY 11:

The Giants get 28 hits against the Phillies and win, 23-8, in Philadelphia.

JULY 12:

The Cardinals learn that a record crowd may be good for the gate, but it can wreak havoc with the game. The largest crowd in the history of Sportsman's Park – 45,715 – turns out for a Cardinals-Cubs doubleheader. By 1 p.m., fans are wandering around the field, overwhelming the ushers. Police and firemen are needed to clear 8,000 fans, but a throng remains in the outfield. The ground rules are altered – balls hit into the crowd will be doubles. As a result, the Cardinals account for 23 two-base hits on the day and the Cubs 10. Game one goes to the Cubs, 7-5, on a Hack Wilson homer. The Cardinals bounce back in the nightcap, 17-13. Paul Derringer gets the win; Ed Baecht is charged with the loss. Clarence "Footsie" Blair homers for Chicago. For Chicago, three doubles are hit by Charles "Gabby" Hartnett and Elwood "Woody" English; for St. Louis, by James "Ripper" Collins and Gus Mancuso.

The Giants' Mel Ott, now in his sixth year in the majors, hits his 100th career home run. At 22 years, four months, and 10 days old, he is the youngest to reach that plateau.

JULY 24:

Brooklyn's Floyd "Babe" Herman hits for the cycle for the second time in 10 weeks. Herman last accomplished the feat on May 18. Despite Herman's heavy hitting, the Pirates win today's game, 8-7.

JULY 28:

It's a big inning and a big game for a big man. White Sox outfielder Bob "Fats" Fothergill (5 feet 10 inches – and 230 pounds) hits a homer and a triple in an 11-run eighth inning. He adds two doubles as Chicago beats the Yankees, 14-12.

AUGUST 5:

Pinch hitter Dave Harris of the Senators – the 27th batter to face Tigers' Tommy Bridges today – hits a bloop single to spoil a perfect game. The Tigers win, 13-0.

Sunny Jim Bottomley of the Cardinals has 10 hits in today's doubleheader against the Pirates. In game one, which the Cardinals lose, 5-4, Bottomley has four hits. In game two, he is six for six – a double and five singles – and the Cardinals win, 16-2.

AUGUST 8:

The Senators' Bobby Burke no-hits the Red Sox, 5-0, in Washington, D.C.

RULES CHANGE

A home run is determined fair or foul by where it leaves the playing field. Previously, the call was made by where it left the umpire's sight.

EQUIPMENT

Al Simmons of the Athletics, the AL's two-time batting champion, stands 5 feet 11 inches tall, but swings a 38-inch bat – the longest bat ever manufactured by Louisville Slugger.

AUGUST 18
Lou Gehrig, the Iron Horse, appears in his 1,000th consecutive ballgame.

HISTORY

The St. Louis Stars win both halves of the Negro National League season.

TRIVIA

Chick Hafey, who leads the NL – with Bill Terry – at .349, is the first batting champion ever who wears eyeglasses.

Burke walks five and strikes out eight; the Senators play errorless ball. Joe Cronin has a two-run triple; Charles "Buddy" Myer also hits a three-bagger. The loser is William "Wilcy" Moore.

AUGUST 18:

Lou Gehrig appears in his 1,000th consecutive game; the Yankees lose to the Tigers, 5-4.

AUGUST 21:

Babe Ruth hits his 600th career home run. The landmark drive is struck off George Blaeholder of the Browns in Sportsman's Park. Ruth's homer bounces off a car parked on Grand Avenue outside the stadium and is exchanged for an autographed replacement plus cash. Ruth's blast is followed by Lou Gehrig's 34th homer of the season. The Yankees beat the Browns, 11-7.

AUGUST 23:

In St. Louis, Lefty Grove's 16-game winning streak is snapped as the result of a fly ball misjudged by Athletics' left fielder Jim Moore in the third inning. The misjudged fly hit by Oscar Melillo follows a Fred Schulte single, giving the Browns the game's only run. Instead of setting an AL record, Grove shares the existing one with Smoky Joe Wood and Walter Johnson. The winning pitcher is Dick Coffman, who yields three hits. Grove, who allows seven hits, has a 15-minute temper tantrum after the game. Grove recalled, "I went in and tore the clubhouse up. Wrecked the place, tore those stall lockers off the wall and everything else. Threw everything I could get my hands on, giving Al Simmons hell all the while." Grove wins his next six games and never forgives Al Simmons, who was sidelined by injuries, for not being in left field for the game.

SEPTEMBER 1:

At Yankee Stadium, Lou Gehrig hits home runs in both games of a doubleheader against the Red Sox, extending his consecutive-game homer streak to six. Gehrig now shares a major league record with George Kelly (1924) and Ken Williams (1922). In game one, which the Yankees win, 11-3, Gehrig hits his 39th homer of the year against Milt Gaston in the seventh inning. In game two, he unloads a grand slam – his third in five days – against Ed Morris and the Yankees win again, 5-1. Gehrig has seven RBI for the day. Since he began his home run streak on August 28, Gehrig has 21 RBI.

SEPTEMBER 9:

The Yankees, Giants, and Robins – New York's three teams – agree to play a series of exhibition games to help the unemployed of the Depression. In the first game, played today, Babe Ruth hits a home run and the Yankees beat the Giants, 7-2. The game draws 60,000 fans and raises $59,000. The exhibition games ultimately raise $100,000.

SEPTEMBER 13:

In game one of a doubleheader in Chicago, Cubs' player-manager Rogers Hornsby sends himself in to pinch-hit with the bases loaded in the bottom of the 11th and the score tied 7-7. He responds with a grand slam homer to beat the Braves. In game two, the Cubs win again, 8-1, on a Guy Bush one-hitter.

SEPTEMBER 16:

The Giants lose to the Reds, 7-3 and 4-3, ensuring the Cardinals the pennant. Later today, St. Louis beats the Phillies, 6-3, on Wild Bill Hallahan's 18th win.

SEPTEMBER 19:

The Athletics' Lefty Grove beats the White Sox, 2-1, for his 30th win of the season.

SEPTEMBER 20:

For the first time since 1912, Gabby Street appears in a major league game. The 48-year-old Cardinals' manager goes hitless in one at-bat, but shows his old catching skills when he throws out Babe Herman on an attempted steal. The Cardinals beat the Robins, 6-1.

SEPTEMBER 27:

The Robins and Giants meet in a doubleheader at Ebbets Field that marks the last face-off between two old rivals – New York Giants' manager John J. McGraw and Brooklyn skipper Wilbert Robinson. Brooklyn wins the opener, 12-3, and the nightcap is called because of darkness after three with no score. McGraw finishes their rivalry with a 197-190 edge; there are five ties.

Lefty Grove has an uncharacteristic outing in his last start of the season. He

SEPTEMBER 13
Cubs' player-manager Rogers Hornsby puts himself in to pinch-hit – a grand slam homer.

OCTOBER 6
Phillies' pitcher George Earnshaw throws a shutout in game four of the World Series.

lasts only three innings against the Yankees, giving up eight hits and five runs. New York wins, 13-1, and Grove is tagged with only his fourth loss of the year; he has 31 wins.

REGULAR SEASON WRAP-UP:

The 1931 World Series will rematch last year's participants, the Cardinals and the Athletics. Connie Mack's Athletics, at 107-45, are the first AL team to win 100 games or more three consecutive seasons. Philadelphia finishes 13 1/2 games ahead of the Yankees. Al Simmons is the AL's top hitter at .390. Jimmie Foxx has 30 homers, Mickey Cochrane hits .349, and George "Mule" Haas .323. The pitching staff is formidable with Lefty Grove (31-4), George Earnshaw (21-7), and George "Rube" Walberg (20-12).

Gabby Street leads the Cardinals to a 101-53 record, 13 games ahead of the NL Giants. Chick Hafey hits .349; Frankie Frisch bats .311 – his 11th straight .300 season.

The Cardinals have no 20-game winner, but, for the first time, neither does the entire National League. Wild Bill Hallahan is 19-9, Paul Derringer 18-8, and 38-year-old Burleigh Grimes 17-9.

OCTOBER 1:

World Series, game one. In St. Louis, Lefty Grove scatters 12 hits and the Athletics beat the Cardinals, 6-2. Al Simmons's two-run homer is the big hit. Paul Derringer takes the loss. John "Pepper" Martin collects three hits for the Cardinals.

OCTOBER 2:

World Series, game two. Cardinals' pitcher Wild Bill Hallahan three-hits the Athletics in St. Louis, winning 2-0. George Earnshaw loses the contest, despite yielding only eight hits. Pepper Martin has two hits – including a double, two stolen bases, and scores twice.

OCTOBER 5:

World Series, game three. In Philadelphia, Cardinals' pitcher Burleigh Grimes bests Lefty Grove, allowing only two hits in a 5-2 victory. Al Simmons hits his second two-run homer of the series. Grimes helps his cause by knocking in two runs with a fourth-inning single.

OCTOBER 6:

World Series, game four. George Earnshaw spins a two-hit, 3-0 win over the St. Louis Cardinals in Philadelphia. Jimmie Foxx homers and Al Simmons doubles in a run for the A's. Pepper Martin has two more hits for St. Louis. Syl Johnson gets the loss.

OCTOBER 7:

World Series, game five. Wild Bill Hallahan gives up nine hits, but he's stingy with runs in a 5-1 Cardinals' win in Philadelphia. Pepper Martin has a two-run home run among his three hits and four RBI. Waite Hoyt lasts only six innings and absorbs the loss. The Cards now lead the Series, three games to two.

HISTORY

Negro Leagues' star Josh Gibson reportedly hits 75 home runs for the Homestead Grays this season.

Josh Gibson is credited with "almost 800 home runs" in his career.

"He was built along the lines of a beer keg and not unfamiliar with its contents."
– Writer Shirley Povich on Hack Wilson

HISTORY

Indians' pitcher Wes Ferrell hits nine homers for the season.

TRIVIA

The Class of 1931 produced four members of the 500-plus home run club – players who cumulatively hit 2,220 round-trippers in their big league careers. Born in 1931 were Willie Mays (660 homers), Mickey Mantle (536), Ernie Banks (512), and Eddie Mathews (512). All four also are members of the Hall of Fame.

PRESIDENT HERBERT HOOVER ATTENDS GAME FOUR AND, AFTER BEING BOOED, HEARS THE FANS CHANT, "WE WANT BEER! WE WANT BEER!"

OCTOBER 9:

World Series, game six. Back in St. Louis, Lefty Grove five-hits the Cardinals, 8-1. The Athletics KO loser Paul Derringer in the fifth, scoring four runs on two hits, an error and four walks.

OCTOBER 10:

World Series, game seven. Burleigh Grimes goes eight and two-thirds innings, Wild Bill Hallahan closes out the Athletics, and the Cardinals win the World Series with a 4-2 victory in St. Louis. George Watkins has a two-run homer in the third inning over the right-field pavilion for the Cardinals. George Earnshaw gets the loss. Pepper Martin leads all hitters with a .500 average; he also steals five bases, knocks in five, and scores five times. Bill Hallahan – with a 0.49 ERA – and Burleigh Grimes each win two. Lefty Grove has 16 strikeouts and George Earnshaw 20 in a losing cause. Al Simmons hits .333 with two homers; Jimmie Foxx has a .348 batting average.

POST-SEASON

OCTOBER 13:

Eddie Mathews is born in Texarkana, Texas.

OCTOBER 20:

Mickey Charles Mantle, named after his father's hero Mickey Cochrane, is born in Spavinaw, Oklahoma.

OCTOBER 23:

After 18 years, Uncle Wilbert Robinson is ousted as Brooklyn's manager, a team known as the Robins in his honor. He is replaced by Max Carey. Last season, the Robins finished fourth at 79-73. Carey has no managerial experience.

Jim Bunning is born in Southgate, Kentucky.

OCTOBER 26:

Owner, player, and manager Charles A. Comiskey dies at age 72 in Eagle River, Wisconsin. Comiskey had owned the White Sox since 1901, when the AL began. From 1883 to 1894, he managed in the American Association, the Players League, and the NL. He played major league ball for 13 years in the nineteenth century, hitting .264 with 29 homers. He leaves an estate estimated at more than $1.5 million to his son, J. Louis Comiskey.

NOVEMBER 6:

Jack Chesbro, who holds the all-time record for wins in a season – 41 with the 1904 New York Highlanders – dies today at the age of 57 in Conway, Massachusetts. In his 11-year career, Chesbro was 199-131 with a 2.68 ERA.

NOVEMBER 12:

The Yankees acquire their first farm team when owner Jacob Ruppert buys the Newark Bears of the International League from newspaper publisher Paul Block.

DECEMBER 1:

One year after his record-breaking season – in which he hit .356 with 56 home runs, 190 RBI, and a .723 slugging average – outfielder Lewis "Hack" Wilson (.261, 13 homers) is traded by the Chicago Cubs, along with pitcher Arthur "Bud" Teachout (1-2, 5.72 ERA), to the St. Louis Cardinals. Coming to the Cubs in the deal is pitcher Burleigh Grimes (17-9, 3.65 ERA), who is being traded for the third time in two years. Only a year ago, Wilson led the major leagues in home runs and runs batted in; his slugging percentage was the high in the NL. Wilson, who got along with manager Joe McCarthy but not with his successor, Rogers Hornsby, is known to suffer from alcohol problems that may be contributing to his precipitous decline. Consider that his RBI total drops a precipitous two-thirds, to just 61 on the year.

DECEMBER 9:

Because of the economic strains that all Americans, including ballplayers, are suffering through during the Depression, major league rosters are cut from 25 to 23.

OCTOBER 10
With a 4-2 win in St. Louis in game seven, the Cardinals are the World Champions.

OCTOBER 20
The Mantles of Spavinaw, Oklahoma, celebrate the birth of their son Mickey.

THE BEST OF 1931

NATIONAL LEAGUE

HITTERS

Batting Average:
Chick Hafey, St. Louis Cardinals; Bill Terry, New York Giants, .349

Slugging Average:
Chuck Klein, Philadelphia Phillies, .584

Home Runs:
Chuck Klein, 31

Runs Batted In:
Chuck Klein, 121

Hits:
Lloyd Waner, Pittsburgh Pirates, 214

Stolen Bases:
Frankie Frisch, St. Louis Cardinals, 28

PITCHERS

Wins:
"Wild" Bill Hallahan, St. Louis Cardinals, James "Jumbo" Elliott, Philadelphia Phillies, Henry "Heinie" Meine, Pittsburgh Pirates, 19

Strikeouts:
Bill Hallahan, 159

Earned Run Average:
Bill Walker, New York Giants, 2.26

Winning Percentage:
Paul Derringer, St. Louis Cardinals, .692

Saves:
Jack Quinn, Brooklyn Robins, 15

Most Valuable Player:
Frankie Frisch, St. Louis Cardinals

AMERICAN LEAGUE

HITTERS

Batting Average:
Al Simmons, Philadelphia Athletics, .390

Slugging Average:
Babe Ruth, New York Yankees, .700

Home Runs:
Babe Ruth; Lou Gehrig, New York Yankees, 46

Runs Batted In:
Lou Gehrig, 184

Hits
Lou Gehrig, 211

Stolen Bases:
Ben Chapman, New York Yankees, 61

PITCHERS

Wins:
Robert "Lefty" Grove, Philadelphia Athletics, 31

Strikeouts:
Lefty Grove, 175

Earned Run Average:
Lefty Grove, 2.06

Winning Percentage:
Lefty Grove, .886

Saves:
William "Wilcey" Moore, Boston Red Sox, 10

Most Valuable Player:
Lefty Grove, Philadelphia Athletics

1932

JANUARY 26
Cubs' owner William Wrigley dies, and his son Philip inherits the team.

NEWS

13 Million Americans Unemployed

FRANKLIN DELANO ROOSEVELT DEFEATS HERBERT HOOVER, PLEDGES A "NEW DEAL"

KIDNAPPED LINDBERGH BABY FOUND DEAD

AMELIA EARHART IS FIRST WOMAN TO FLY SOLO ACROSS ATLANTIC

Radio City Music Hall opens in New York City

Skippy peanut butter and Fritos are introduced

BUCK ROGERS COMES TO THE RADIO

IRVING BERLIN'S *FACE THE MUSIC* AND COLE PORTER'S *THE GAY DIVORCEE* ARE ON STAGE

BABE DIDRIKSON WINS GOLD AT L.A. OLYMPICS

PRE-SEASON

JANUARY 23:

The Dodgers acquire outfielder Hack Wilson (.261, 13 homers) from the Cardinals for minor league pitcher Bob Parham and $45,000. At one time Wilson was one of baseball's most feared right-handed hitters.

JANUARY 26:

William Wrigley, owner of the Cubs, dies at age 70 of a stroke in Phoenix, Arizona. His 37-year-old son, Philip K. Wrigley, inherits the team. Says Philip Wrigley, "I don't know much about baseball, and I don't care much for it, either."

FEBRUARY 5:

Pirates owner Barney Dreyfuss dies at age 66 of pneumonia following surgery. Dreyfuss is predeceased by his 36-year-old son, Sam, who was to head up the team, but himself succumbed to pneumonia earlier in the year.

FEBRUARY 12:

Yankees' owner Jacob Ruppert appoints 38-year-old George Weiss to head the team's new farm system. Weiss was vice president and general manager of the Baltimore Orioles in the International League.

MARCH 14:

The Reds obtain outfielder Floyd "Babe" Herman (.313, 18 homers), catcher Ernie Lombardi (.294, four homers), and third baseman Wally Gilbert (.266) from the Dodgers for infielder Tony Cuccinello (.315), catcher Clyde Sukeforth (.256), and infielder Joe Stripp (.324, three homers).

MARCH 16:

In St. Petersburg, Florida, Babe Ruth signs a one-year contract for $75,000, plus a percentage of exhibition games' profits. Supposedly, Ruth accepted a blank contract with the amount filled in by owner Jacob Ruppert.

APRIL 11:

The Cardinals trade the 1931 NL batting champion Charles "Chick" Hafey (.349, 16 homers) to the Reds. In return, St. Louis gets outfielder-infielder Harvey Hendrick (.315, one homer) and pitcher Benny Frey (8-12, 4.92 ERA).

THE SEASON

APRIL 23:

The Yankees extend their consecutive game streak with homers to eight and defeat the Athletics, 16-5. The streak began on opening day, April 12, with a Babe Ruth round-tripper against the A's in Philadelphia.

MAY 11:

In St. Louis, the Cardinals' Wild Bill Hallahan is living up to his nickname. After walking 10 against the Cubs on May 1, he uncorks three wild pitches in the 12th inning today against the Dodgers. The last NL pitcher to throw three wild pitches in an inning was Jacob Weimer of the Cubs – in 1903. Brooklyn beats St. Louis, 6-3.

MAY 20:

The Pirates' Paul Waner hits four doubles, tying a major league record held by many players.

MAY 30:

The Yankees unveil a new permanent monument to their late manager Miller Huggins. Located in centerfield at Yankee Stadium, it

"I don't know much about baseball, and I don't care much for it, either."
– *Cubs' owner Philip Wrigley*

JUNE 3
Lou Gehrig becomes the first player in the 20th century to hit four home runs in a game.

reads: "As a tribute to a splendid character who made priceless contributions to baseball and on this field brought glory to the New York club of the American League." The Yankees then beat the Red Sox twice today, 7-5 and 13-3.

A disputed call leads to a fistfight in the runway in Cleveland. Home plate umpire George Moriarty calls a 2-2 pitch from White Sox pitcher Milt Gaston ball three. The batter, Earl Averill of the Indians, hits the next pitch for a triple that wins the game. As they leave the field, Gaston confronts Moriarty, who decks him. White Sox manager Lew Fonseca and catcher Charlie Berry gang up on the umpire, kicking and punching him. Moriarty is later hospitalized for a broken hand (from hitting Gaston), bruises, and spike wounds. Will Harridge, AL president, suspends Gaston for 10 days.

JUNE 3:

In Philadelphia, Lou Gehrig hits four home runs in a game against the Athletics – the first 20th-century player to accomplish that feat – and narrowly misses a fifth. He also drives in six runs. The Yankees bang out 50 total bases – a major league record – and 23 hits to beat Philadelphia, 20-13. In addition to Gehrig's onslaught, Earle Combs, Tony Lazzeri (grand slam), and Babe Ruth (15th of the season) homer to establish a record for the most by a team. Gehrig's bid for a fifth homer comes in the ninth when he sends an Eddie Rommel pitch to the deepest part of Shibe Park, where it is caught at the fence by A's left-fielder Al Simmons. Three of Gehrig's homers are hit against George Earnshaw, the fourth off Larry Mahaffey. He also ties an AL record with 16 total bases.

Despite Gehrig's on-field heroics, the headlines tomorrow will feature John McGraw. The Giants' manager resigns after 32 years because of ill health. The sudden announcement is made at the Polo Grounds after a doubleheader with the Phillies is rained out. In his tenure as Giants' skipper, the fiery McGraw won three World Series and nine NL pennants. McGraw, the only manager to win four straight pennants, will be succeeded by first baseman Bill Terry.

JUNE 14:

The Yankees' Ben Chapman steals home on the front end of a rare triple steal as New York beats the Indians, 7-6.

JUNE 15:

Unhappy with his salary, Dizzy Dean jumps the Cardinals, leaving the team in Philadelphia and heading back to St. Louis. Claiming he was underage when he signed his contract, he petitions the commissioner for free-agent status. The Cardinals produce a copy of Dean's marriage certificate, showing that he actually is a year older – 22 – than believed. Dean biographer Vince Staten writes: "This was the first time Diz's true age was ever reported, but the discrepancy somehow eluded the press and his age continued to be reported incorrectly even in his obituaries." After he is denied free agency, Dean finally rejoins the team.

JUNE 19:

Marty McManus is named the new manager of the Red Sox, replacing John "Shano" Collins, who resigned yesterday with the team at 11-44.

McManus finishes the season with Boston in last place and manages them to a seventh-place finish in 1933. In the 1940s, he manages the Kenosha Comets in the All-American Girls Professional Baseball League.

JUNE 30:

In Philadelphia, Chuck Klein of the Phillies homers twice against the Dodgers. The homers are his 23rd and 24th of the season, the most by any NL player by the end of June. The Phillies win, 9-3.

JULY 4:

It's fisticuffs, not fireworks, at Griffith Stadium. In the seventh inning, Carl Reynolds crashes into Yankee catcher Bill Dickey, jarring the ball loose. Dickey responds with a right hand that breaks Reynolds's jaw in two places. Both players are ejected. There are extenuating circumstances in Dickey's behavior. Reynolds returns to home plate after the collision to make sure he touched it. Dickey hears him coming,

TRIVIA

With manager Wilbert Robinson gone, Brooklyn reverts to its old nickname – the Dodgers. The team had been dubbed the Robins in honor of Robinson.

HISTORY

In 1932, the Negro National League goes out of business.

JULY
31
A crowd of 80,184 is on hand for the opener at Cleveland's new Municipal Stadium.

TRIVIA

The movie *Fireman, Save My Child* stars Joe E. Brown as a firefighter/baseball player.

thinks Reynolds is returning to fight, turns, and hits him. The Yankees drop the doubleheader, 5-3 and 12-6. Dickey, who was hitting .360, is fined $1,000 and suspended 30 days.

JULY 6:

In Chicago's Carlos Hotel, a 21-year-old dancer named Violet Popovich Valli shoots Cubs' shortstop Billy Jurges with a .25 caliber pistol. Jurges is hit in the left side and left hand. His assailant then turns the gun on herself. According to one source, she intended suicide and Jurges was wounded trying to stop her. Both survive. Jurges misses three weeks, and Ms. Valli uses her notoriety as part of her act, billing herself as Violet "I Did It For Love" Popovich.

JULY 9:

Yankees' outfielder Ben Chapman hits three homers – two of them inside-the-park – as New York beats the Detroit Tigers, 14-9, at Yankee Stadium.

JULY 10:

The Athletics come to Cleveland with only 15 players, including two pitchers. When rookie Lew Krausse lasts less than an inning, manager Connie Mack is left with a choice of 35-year-old Ed Rommel or no one. Rommel pitches 18 innings of relief against the Indians, serving up 29 hits and 14 runs. But he is the winning pitcher when the A's eke out an 18-17 win on an RBI by Eric "Boob" McNair. The Indians' Johnny Burnett gets a record nine hits. Jimmie Foxx of the A's hits his 31st, 32nd, and 33rd homers, knocks in eight runs with six hits, and accounts for 16 total bases, tying an AL record. The losing pitcher is Wes Ferrell.

JULY 15:

Charles "Red" Lucas of the Reds completes 250 consecutive innings without being relieved. The streak actually began back on August 13 of last season.

JULY 31:

The first game at Cleveland's new Municipal Stadium will be hard to equal. With a crowd of 80,184 on hand, the Athletics' Lefty Grove beats the Indians' Mel Harder, 1-0. Grove allows only four hits. In the eighth inning, Max Bishop, who had walked, scores the winning run on a Mickey Cochrane single. Harder allows five hits; relief pitcher Oral Hildebrand allows one. The stadium, built at a cost of $2.64 million, has 78,129 permanent seats. Ohio Governor George White throws out the first ball as Commissioner Kenesaw Mountain Landis, AL president Will Harridge, and former Indians' stars Napoleon Lajoie, Cy Young, Charles "Chief" Zimmer, Tris Speaker, Elmer Flick, and Bill Wambsganss witness the festivities.

AUGUST 2:

Dennis "Big Dan" Brouthers dies at age 74 in East Orange, New Jersey. One of baseball's first power hitters, first baseman Brouthers played 19 years and compiled a lifetime batting average of .342 – ninth best all-time.

The Cubs fire manager Rogers Hornsby with the team at 53-46 in second place and replace him with first baseman Charlie Grimm. In front of reporters, team president William Veeck Sr. says, "There has been no quarrel, has there, Rog?" Hornsby replies, "I guess we won't call it a quarrel. Only a big difference of opinion about the ball club and the way it should be handled." Hornsby owes several of his players money, borrowed to cover his gambling losses. After Hornsby is fired as Cubs' manager, baseball Commissioner Kenesaw Mountain Landis levies no discipline on him regarding charges he bet on horses.

AUGUST 4:

Swinging his bat instead of his fist, Bill Dickey returns to action in Chicago after his 30-day suspension for breaking Carl Reynolds's jaw. Dickey hits a grand slam homer and three singles as the Yankees beat the White Sox, 15-3.

AUGUST 13:

Charles "Red" Ruffing shuts out Washington for 10 innings and wins the game, 1-0, on his own home run. Ruffing allows three hits and strikes out 10. Tommy Thomas, who also pitches a complete game, gets the loss. Is this why he's known as "Sloppy"?

SEPTEMBER 12
The Dodgers' Johnny Frederick sets a major league record with his sixth pinch-hit homer.

Dodgers' pitcher Hollis Thurston serves up six home runs to the Giants. He atones somewhat with four hits of his own as Brooklyn manages to outslug the Giants, 18-9, in game one of a doubleheader. The Giants come back with a 4-3 win in the nightcap.

AUGUST 14:

The Dodgers' Jack Quinn, 49 years old, becomes the oldest pitcher to win a major league game when he defeats the Giants.

AUGUST 31:

At Wrigley Field, Kiki Cuyler of the Cubs hits a three-run homer with two out in the bottom of the ninth inning to beat the Giants, 10-9. It is Cuyler's fourth home run in five games, and his fifth base hit today. The victory is the Cubs' 12th in a row.

SEPTEMBER 2:

The Cubs make it 13 in a row before 45,000 at Wrigley Field. Kiki Cuyler hits his fifth home run in six games. Teammate Mark Koenig adds a round-tripper of his own in an 8-5 victory over the visiting Cardinals.

SEPTEMBER 3:

Dizzy Dean and the Cardinals snap the Cubs' winning streak at 14 games with a 3-0 victory in game two of a doubleheader, after Chicago wins the day's opener.

SEPTEMBER 7:

Babe Ruth, hitting .341, is hospitalized with pains in his right side. He requires no surgery, is treated with ice packs, and will be back with the Yankees in five days.

SEPTEMBER 12:

At Ebbets Field, the Dodgers' Johnny Frederick hits his sixth pinch-hit homer of the season – a major league record. Frederick's round-tripper with Glenn Wright on base in the bottom of the ninth beats the Cubs, 4-3.

SEPTEMBER 13:

The Yankees, without the ailing Babe Ruth, clinch the AL pennant by beating the Indians, 9-3. Skipper Joe McCarthy thus becomes the first manager to win pennants in both leagues.

SEPTEMBER 20:

At Wrigley Field, Kiki Cuyler's seventh-inning triple with the bases loaded gives the Cubs a 5-2 win over the Pirates in the opener of a doubleheader and clinches the NL pennant. Guy Bush rings up his 19th win. Billy Herman becomes the 10th rookie with 200 hits in a season.

SEPTEMBER 21:

Jimmie Foxx, in pursuit of Babe Ruth's record 60 homers, slams his 54th of the season against the Yankees at Shibe Park. Ruth is back in the lineup after his illness, and gets one hit in four at-bats. The A's win the game, 8-5.

SEPTEMBER 25:

In Washington, Jimmie Foxx hits his 58th homer of the season. Foxx also has two singles in his three at-bats against the Senators' Alvin "General" Crowder. Washington wins, 2-1, and Crowder gets his 15th straight and 26th victory of the season. The losing pitcher is Merritt "Sugar" Cain.

According to historian Glenn Dickey, Jimmie Foxx lost two home runs to rainouts and had three other drives hit wire netting on the fence in St. Louis' Sportsman's Park for ground-rule doubles.

REGULAR SEASON WRAP-UP:

Joe McCarthy leads his Yankees to a 107-47 record, 13 games over the Athletics. The Yankees are the only team to go through a full season without being shut out. Babe Ruth, 37 years old, hits .341 with 41 homers, but, for the first time in seven years, fails to lead the league. Lou Gehrig bats .349, hits 34 homers, and bats in 151 runs. Tony Lazzeri (.300), Earle Combs (.321), and Bill Dickey (.310) make it hard to pitch around Ruth and Gehrig. Vernon "Lefty" Gomez leads the Yanks' pitching staff with a 24-7 record.

The AL's batting champion is Dale Alexander, traded by the Tigers to the Red Sox in June; he is the first major leaguer to lead a batting title while playing for two teams in a season.

Charlie Grimm goes 27-18 after replacing Rogers Hornsby as Cubs' manager. The team finishes at 90-64, four games over the Pirates in the NL. Lon Warneke paces the pitchers at 22-6. Riggs Stephenson is the top hitter with .324. Other .300 hitters are Billy Herman (.314), manager Grimm (.307), and Johnny Moore (.305).

HISTORY

Cole's American Giants of Chicago defeat the Nashville Elite Giants, four games to three, for the Negro Southern League pennant.

"I believe the greatest team I ever saw was the 1932 Yankees."
– *Cubs' Billy Herman*

HISTORY

Left-handed pitcher Hub "Shucks" Pruett retires after a 1-5 season with the Braves and a lifetime record of only 29-48 (4.63 ERA). But, when he pitched for the Browns from 1922 to 1924, Pruett had an uncanny knack for handling Babe Ruth. The first 11 times he batted against Pruett, Ruth struck out eight times, walked twice, and hit a comebacker to the pitcher. In 14 games, Ruth batted 33 times against Pruett. In 25 official at-bats, he struck out 14 times, hit two homers, and had five other hits, finishing at .280.

SEPTEMBER 28:

Connie Mack begins paring the highest payroll in baseball history. He sells three of the Athletics' stars – outfielder Al Simmons (.322, 35 homers, 151 RBI), outfielder George "Mule" Haas (.305, six homers), and infielder Jimmy Dykes (.265, seven homers) to the Chicago White Sox for $150,000.

World Series, game one. At Yankee Stadium, New York beats the Cubs, 12-6, on eight hits. In the fourth, Lou Gehrig follows a Babe Ruth single with a two-run home run. Bill Dickey and Earle Combs each drive in two runs.Charles "Red" Ruffing goes the distance, allowing 10 hits and fanning 10 for the win. Guy Bush, who retired the first nine Yankees, gets the loss. The official attendance is 41,459.

SEPTEMBER 29:

World Series, game two. In New York, behind Lefty Gomez's nine-hit complete-game pitching, the Yankees make it two in a row, with a 5-2 win. Lou Gehrig has three hits. Lon "The Arkansas Hummingbird" Warneke gets the loss for the Cubs.

OCTOBER 1:

World Series, game three. In Chicago, the Yankees, paced by two homers each by Babe Ruth and Lou Gehrig, beat the Cubs, 7-5. In the fifth inning, with the score at 4-4, Babe Ruth, who has been taunted all day, gestures to the Cubs' bench and to pitcher Charlie Root. He then hits a two-strike pitch for a homer into deep center field. Ruth crosses the plate, winks to Gehrig, and says, "You do the same thing." Root dusts him, but Gehrig homers on the next pitch. Kiki Cuyler and Gabby Hartnett reach the seats for the Cubs. George Pipgras gets the win with an inning of relief from Herb Pennock. Charlie Root gets the loss.

Joe DiMaggio makes his professional debut playing shortstop for the San Francisco Seals in the Pacific Coast League. He triples off the left-field wall against pitcher Ted Pillette of the San Francisco Missions. Signed on the recommendation of his older brother Vince, the 17-year-old DiMaggio replaces shortstop Augie Galan, who is missing the last three games of the season with permission.

AFTER GESTURING AND HITTING HIS FIFTH-INNING HOMER, RUTH CROWS ABOUT HIS TORMENTORS. "DID MR. RUTH CHASE THOSE GUYS INTO THE DUGOUT? MR. RUTH SURE DID!"

OCTOBER 2:

World Series, game four. In Chicago, the Yankees sweep the Cubs by banging out 19 hits in a 13-6 win today. New York now has won 12 straight World Series games. Tony Lazzeri is the Yankees' big gun with two two-run homers. Teammate Earle Combes, who scores four times, also hits a home run; Frank Demaree hits one out for the Cubs. William "Wilcy"Moore gets the win with five and a third innings of relief. Jakie May is charged with the loss. The Yankees score 37 runs to the Cubs' 19. Gehrig hits .529 with three homers and eight RBI. Ruth is at .333 with two homers and six RBI. Dickey hits .438. Riggs Stephenson bats .444 for the Cubs.

In *Baseball for the Love of It*, by Anthony J. Connor, Hall of Famer Billy Herman is quoted: "I believe the greatest team I ever saw was the 1932 Yankees. An all-star at every position."

POST-SEASON

OCTOBER 24:

Branch Rickey signs Rogers Hornsby to a one-year, $15,000

OCTOBER 2
The Yankees complete a devastating sweep of the Cubs, winning game four, 13-6.

OCTOBER 24
Branch Rickey signs Rogers Hornsby to a one-year contract for $15,000.

contract for 1933. With the Cubs this past season, before being discharged as player-manager, Hornsby appeared in only 19 games, batting .224.

DECEMBER 12:

In a complicated three-team transaction, outfielder-infielder Freddie Lindstrom (.271, 15 homers), who had demanded a trade rather than play for new Giants' manager Bill Terry, ends up with the Pirates. Outfielder George "Kiddo" Davis (.309, five homers) and pitcher Glenn Spencer (4-8, 4.97 ERA) go to the Giants. And outfielders Gus Dugas (.237, three home runs) and Charles "Chick" Fullis (.298, one home run) wind up with the Phillies.

DECEMBER 14:

Outfielders Leon "Goose" Goslin (.299, 17 homers) and Fred Schulte (.294, nine home runs) are sent to the Browns along with pitcher Walter "Lefty" Stewart (14-19, 4.61 ERA). In return, St. Louis gets two outfielders, Sammy West (.287, six homers) and Carl Reynolds (.305, nine homers), plus pitcher Lloyd Brown (15-12, 4.44ERA) and $20,000 in cash.

DECEMBER 17:

The St. Louis Cardinals trade their longtime first baseman Sunny Jim Bottomley (.296, 11 homers) to the Cincinnati Reds for outfielder Estel Crabtree (.274, two homers) and pitcher Owen Carroll (10-19, 4.50 ERA).

Lou Gehrig congratulates Babe Ruth after the Bambino's "Called Shot" in the World Series.

LEAGUE

The White Sox buy third baseman Willie Kamm from San Francisco in the Pacific Coast League for $125,000. Kamm's best season is 1928, when he hits .308 with one homer. The Orioles' Jack Dunn, who sold Babe Ruth to the Red Sox for $2,500, gets more for pitcher Jack Bentley. The left-hander, who played with the Senators from 1913-16, brings $65,000 from the Giants. Bentley's best season is 1924, when he is 16–5.

THE BEST OF 1932

NATIONAL LEAGUE

HITTERS

Batting Average:
Francis "Lefty" O'Doul, Brooklyn Dodgers, .368

Slugging Average:
Chuck Klein, Philadelphia Phillies, .646

Home Runs:
Chuck Klein; Mel Ott, New York Giants, 38

Runs Batted In:
Frank "Don" Hurst, Philadelphia Phillies, 143

Hits:
Chuck Klein, 226

Stolen Bases:
Chuck Klein, 20

PITCHERS

Wins:
Lon Warneke, Chicago Cubs, 22

Strikeouts:
Dizzy Dean, St. Louis Cardinals, 191

Earned Run Average:
Lon Warneke, 2.37

Winning Percentage:
Lon Warneke, .786

Saves:
Jack Quinn, Brooklyn Dodgers, 8

Most Valuable Player
Chuck Klein, Philadelphia Phillies

AMERICAN LEAGUE

HITTERS

Batting Average:
Dale Alexander, Detroit Tigers/ Boston Red Sox, .367

Slugging Average:
Jimmie Foxx, Philadelphia Athletics, .749

Home Runs:
Jimmie Foxx, 58

Runs Batted In:
Jimmie Foxx, 169

Hits:
Al Simmons, Philadelphia Athletics, 216

Stolen Bases:
Ben Chapman, New York Yankees, 38

PITCHERS

Wins:
Alvin "General" Crowder, Washington Senators, 26

Strikeouts:
Charles "Red" Ruffing, New York Yankees, 190

Earned Run Average:
Lefty Grove, Philadelphia Athletics, 2.84

Winning Percentage:
Johnny Allen, New York Yankees, .810

Saves:
Fredrick "Firpo" Marberry, Washington Senators, 13

Most Valuable Player
Jimmie Foxx, Philadelphia Athletics

1933

"I expected a cut, but $25,000 is no cut, that's an amputation."
– *Babe Ruth*

NEWS

FDR INAUGURATED

FRANCES PERKINS IS FIRST WOMAN EVER IN CABINET

PROHIBITION REPEALED

AMERICA'S BANKS START REOPENING

NATIONAL RECOVERY ADMINISTRATION LAUNCHED TO IMPROVE ECONOMY

***U.S.S. Ranger*, first American aircraft carrier, is christened**

WOULD-BE ASSASSIN MISSES FDR

SOVIET UNION RECOGNIZED BY U.S.

***King Kong* stars Fay Wray and a mechanical ape; *Duck Soup* stars the Marx Brothers**

Spam is invented, ushering in processed food era

PRE-SEASON

JANUARY 2

William "Kid" Gleason, the manager of the Black Sox, dies at age 66. Gleason managed the White Sox for five years and produced only one pennant-winner – in 1919. He played in the majors for 22 years as an infielder, hitting .261.

FEBRUARY 25:

Tom Yawkey buys the Red Sox from Bob Quinn for $1 million. Yawkey inherited $7 million on February 21, his 30th birthday. He is the adopted son of William Yawkey, his uncle and one-time part-owner of the Tigers.

MARCH 22:

In St. Petersburg, Florida, after another heated contract dispute, Babe Ruth signs for $52,000. Although he was seeking $60,000, the Babe remains baseball's highest-paid player and meets the signing deadline of March 29 set by Yankee owner Colonel Jacob Ruppert. According to biographer Robert Creamer, Ruth originally was offered $50,000 and responded, "I expected a cut, but $25,000 is no cut, that's an amputation."

"BASEBALL WAS IN HIS BLOOD: HIS ADOPTIVE FATHER, A MINING AND LUMBER MAGNATE, HAD BEEN A PARTOWNER OF THE DETROIT TIGERS – AND AS A 10-YEAR-OLD HE HAD CHASED GROUND BALLS HIT BY TY COBB."

–*FROM* BASEBALL: AN ILLUSTRATED HISTORY

LEAGUE

Commissioner Kenesaw Mountain Landis starts the year by taking a 40 percent pay cut because of the continuing national Depression.

HISTORY

A.G. Gus Greenlee, owner of the Pittsburgh Crawfords, launches a second Negro National League; it lasts for more than 12 years.

MAY 6
The Tigers' Hank Greenberg hits the first of what will be 331 career home runs.

TRIVIA

The film *Elmer the Great* stars Joe E. Brown. It's a remake of the 1929 movie *Fast Company*, a Ring Lardner story based on Big Ed Walsh.

HISTORY

The leading vote getter for the 1933 All-Star team is Al Simmons of the White Sox with 346,291; Chuck Klein of the Phillies is second with 342,283, and 38-year-old Babe Ruth is sixth with 320,518. A box seat sells for $1.65, grandstand admission is $1.10, and the bleachers cost 55 cents. Baseball owners say they will make the All-Star Game an annual event.

THE SEASON

APRIL 23:

Former major league pitcher Tim Keefe dies at the age of 76 in Cambridge, Massachusetts. Keefe compiled a record of 342-225 with a 2.62 ERA in his 14-year career, which began in 1880 with the NL's Troy Trojans. In 1886, he won 42 games for the Giants.

APRIL 25:

What will he do for an encore? Yankees' rookie Russ Van Atta makes his major league debut, shutting out the Senators on five hits, 16-0. Van Atta also has four singles in four at-bats. Teammate Earle Combs is five for five. Bad blood, which began last year when Bill Dickey broke Carl Reynolds's jaw, continues. Washington second baseman Charles "Buddy" Myer spikes Lou Gehrig at first base. Ben Chapman then retaliates by going out of the basepath to spike Myer while breaking up a double play at second. Players, fans, and police get involved, with Yankee pitcher Vernon "Lefty" Gomez wielding a bat. Fred "Dixie" Walker beats up Myer. New York manager Joe McCarthy is decked. Police, unable to quell the brawl at first, finally restore order and five fans are arrested. But two notables remain spectators; Babe Ruth and Lou Gehrig never leave the Yankees' dugout, where they are observed laughing at the spectacle. Myer, Chapman, and Walker are ejected. On the way to the locker room, Chapman gets into another fight – this time with pitcher Earl Whitehall, whose teammates join in. Finally, order is restored. AL president Will Harridge dispenses $100 fines and five-day suspensions to the combatants.

Van Atta pitches another shutout in 1933 and finishes his rookie year at 12-4. He cuts his pitching hand in the off-season and struggles through six additional seasons, ending his career with the St. Louis Browns. His lifetime statistics are 33-41 with a 5.60 ERA.

MAY 6:

The Tigers' Hank Greenberg hits a home run against Earl Whitehill of the Senators in the bottom of the eighth inning. It is the first major league homer for Greenberg, who has only two hits in 14 career at-bats.

MAY 7:

The Reds send shortstop Leo Durocher (.216) to the Cardinals along with pitchers Jack Ogden and Frank "Dutch" Henry. Neither pitcher has appeared in 1933 games. In return, Cincinnati gets pitchers Paul Derringer (0-2) and Allyn Stout (0-0), along with infielder Earl "Sparky" Adams (.167).

MAY 14:

In heavy rain at Ebbets Field, Hack Wilson hits the Dodgers' first grand slam pinch-hit homer. Wilson hits his round-tripper against Ad Liska of the Phillies. The Dodgers win the game, 8-6.

MAY 16:

Washington third baseman Cecil Travis makes his major league debut with a modern record five singles in his first five at-bats. The Senators beat the Indians, 11-10, in 12 innings in Washington, D.C., with Travis hitless his final two at-bats. The winning pitcher is Alvin "General" Crowder; the loser is Mel Harder.

MAY 18:

As part of the Century of Progress Exhibition (World's Fair), the *Chicago Tribune* will sponsor an "all star" game between the National and American Leagues. The game is the brainchild of *Tribune* sports editor Arch Ward, and will benefit the Association of Professional Baseball Players. Fans will vote on the players.

JUNE 8:

Philadelphia slugger Jimmie Foxx homers in his first three at-bats against the Yankees today. With a homer in his last at-bat yesterday, Foxx has four consecutive round-trippers. The Athletics beat the Yankees, 14-0.

JUNE 9:

Jimmie Foxx smashes another homer today – his fifth in three games – but the Yankees defeat the Athletics, 7-6.

The Big Train pulls into Cleveland's Municipal Stadium. With the Indians in fifth place at 26-25, Roger Peckinpaugh is dismissed as manager and will be replaced by Walter Johnson. Bibb Falk will serve as a one-game interim manager.

JULY 6
In the very first All-Star Game, at Comiskey Park, the AL tops the NL, 4-2

JUNE 16:

The Giants obtain last year's NL batting champion, Francis "Lefty" O'Doul (.252), and pitcher William "Watty" Clark (2-4), a 20-game winner last year, from the Dodgers. In return, Brooklyn gets first baseman Sam Leslie (.321).

JUNE 28:

In a doubleheader at Baker Bowl in Philadelphia, the Cubs' Billy Herman has five hits, but sets a major league record with his glove. He has 16 put-outs at second base in the doubleheader – 11 in game one. The Cubs sweep the Phillies, 9-5 and 8-3.

JULY 2:

In game one of a Polo Grounds doubleheader, Carl Hubbell pitches an 18-inning, six-hit shutout to beat the St. Louis Cardinals, 1-0. Hubbell strikes out 12 and issues no walks. St. Louis's James "Tex" Carleton matches Hubbell for 17 innings, giving way to Jesse Haines, who yields the run – on a single by Hughie Critz – and gets the loss. Game two also features spectacular pitching. The Giants' Roy Parmelee strikes out 13 Cardinals' batters and beats Dizzy Dean, 1-0, on a fourth-inning home run off the bat of Johnny Vergez.

JULY 4:

The A's Jimmie Foxx has four homers in a doubleheader against the visiting Red Sox. Philadelphia sweeps, 14-4 and 9-1.

JULY 6:

Baseball holds its first All-Star Game, and Babe Ruth leads the AL to a 4-2 win before a crowd of 47,595 at Comiskey Park. In the "Game of the Century," AL players wear their own team uniforms. The senior circuit players wear gray uniforms created by Albert Spalding on an order from NL president John Heydler. "National League" is lettered on the uniform fronts. John McGraw makes his last field appearance and manages the NL from the bench, wearing a brown business suit. In the third inning, Ruth hits a two-run homer against the Cardinals' Wild Bill Hallahan. Frankie Frisch homers for the NL. The Yankees' Vernon "Lefty" Gomez is the game's first pitcher, knocks in the first run, and is the first winning pitcher.

JULY 19:

It's brother versus brother as Boston meets Cleveland. Red Sox catcher Rick Ferrell homers off Indians' pitcher Wes

TRIVIA

***Lose With a Smile,* a book by Ring Lardner, is published.**

The National League had common uniforms in the first All-Star Game.

"During the reign of Hubbell, first base itself is a marathon route."
– Sportswriter Heywood Broun

HISTORY

Dale Alexander's career ends with the 1933 season, in which he hit .281 for 94 games. The Red Sox first baseman, the AL batting champion in 1932 at .367, hit better than .300 in each of his four years. But earlier in 1933, after Alexander injures himself in a game against the Athletics, Boston team physician "Doc" Woods uses a diathermy heat lamp on him, causing third degree burns that become gangrenous. He appears in only 94 games, and his career is over. In five years, he bats .331 with 459 RBI.

Ferrell, his brother. Wes also hits a home run in the game. It marks the only time the Ferrells homered in the same game.

JULY 20:

In Chicago, the Cubs' Babe Herman drives in eight runs – for the second time this season – with three homers and a single as Chicago beats the Phillies, 10-1. The winning pitcher is Lyle "Bud" Tinning.

JULY 22:

The Cardinals' Rogers Hornsby doubles against the Braves in St. Louis. It is his last hit in the NL.

JULY 24:

With the team at 46-45, the Cardinals fire manager Charles "Gabby" Street and replace him with second baseman Frankie Frisch.

JULY 25:

The Cardinals unconditionally release second baseman Rogers Hornsby. After slumping to .224 in only 19 games last season, Hornsby is hitting .325 in 46 games this year.

JULY 26:

Rogers Hornsby clears waivers and is signed by the Browns. He inks a three-year contract with an annual salary of $15,000 as the Browns' player-manager. He replaces interim skipper Allan Sothoron who was 2-6.

Oakland Oaks' pitcher Ed Walsh, the son of former major league pitcher Big Ed Walsh, holds 18-year-old Joe DiMaggio hitless in five at bats and snaps his hitting streak at 61 consecutive games. DiMaggio, playing with the San Francisco Seals, has his ninth-inning line drive caught one-handed by Harlin Pool. During the streak, DiMaggio batted .398. DiMaggio finishes his season with a .340 batting average, 28 home runs, 169 RBI, and 32 assists in 187 games.

JULY 30:

In St. Louis, Dizzy Dean fans 17 – a modern major league record – in an 8-2 win over the visiting Cubs. His catcher, Jimmy Wilson, has a record 18 putouts. Dean allows six hits and walks one. He strikes out the side in the final two frames and the Cardinals win game two, 6-5. Afterward, Dean says, "Heck, if anybody told me I was settin' a record, I'd of got me some more strikeouts."

AUGUST 2:

For the second time in his career, Athletics' catcher Gordon "Mickey" Cochrane hits for the cycle as Philadelphia beats the Yankees, 16-3. Cochrane also hit for the cycle on July 22, 1932.

AUGUST 3:

For the first time in 308 games, the Yankees are shut out, and the Athletics' Lefty Grove does the job, five-hitting New York and winning, 7-0. The last time the Yankees were whitewashed was August 2, 1931, when William "Wilcy" Moore of the Red Sox held them scoreless. The 308-game streak is a major league record.

AUGUST 14:

The Athletics' Jimmie Foxx continues to wreak havoc on AL pitchers. Today he hits for the cycle and bats in nine runs in an 11-5 Philadelphia victory over the Cleveland Indians.

AUGUST 17:

Yankees' first baseman Lou Gehrig plays in his 1,308th consecutive game today, breaking the record of one-time Yankee Everett Scott. Gehrig, who never has missed a spring training, exhibition (more than 200), regular season, or World Series (19) game since 1925, is presented with a silver statuette by AL president Will Harridge after the first inning at Sportsman's Park. Gehrig gets two hits in five at-bats, but the Browns go on to beat the Yankees, 7-6, in 10 innings.

SEPTEMBER 2:

Marv Throneberry is born in Collierville, Tennessee.

SEPTEMBER 11:

The Athletics' Johnny Marcum whitewashes the White Sox, 8-0, to become the second AL pitcher and the fourth in the major leagues to begin a career with two consecutive shutouts. In his major league debut on September 7, Marcum beat the Indians, 6-0.

Marcum's first two starts represent 25 percent of his career shutouts. In seven years, he is 65-63, with a 4.66 ERA and eight shutouts.

SEPTEMBER 13:

The White Sox send 85 years' worth of pitchers to the mound in a doubleheader

SEPTEMBER 30
The Cubs' Babe Herman hits for the cycle for the third time in his career.

OCTOBER 6
Carl Hubbell wins his second game of the World Series, as the Giants prevail, 2-1.

against the Athletics. In game one, 41-year-old Sad Sam Jones starts and Chicago wins, 3-2. Urban "Red" Faber, 44 years old, starts the nightcap, and Philadelphia prevails, 4-2.

First baseman Joe Hauser hits 69 homers for Minneapolis in the American Association. Hauser, who hit 63 in 1930 with Baltimore in the International League, is the only player in organized baseball to top 60 homers two times.

SEPTEMBER 30:

At Sportsman's Park, the Cubs' Babe Herman hits for the cycle for the third time in his career. Behind Herman's slugging, the Cubs beat the Cardinals and Dizzy Dean, 12-2. Guy Bush gets his 20th win.

OCTOBER 1:

With the Yankees out of the pennant race, 38-year-old Babe Ruth returns to the mound to face his old team, the Red Sox, before 25,000 at Yankee Stadium. The Yankees win, 6-5, as Ruth homers (his 34th of the year). He pitches a complete game, allowing five runs, 12 hits, and three walks, and gets the victory. The Yankees have 18 outfield putouts. Ruth's pitching record with the Yankees is 5-0. The losing pitcher is Bob Kline.

In the last game of the season, Senators' coach Nick Altrock pinch-hits for Johnny Kerr and is retired by the Athletics George "Rube" Walberg. At 57 years and 16 days old, Altrock becomes the oldest player to appear in a major league game.

REGULAR SEASON WRAP-UP:

The Senators, with a "rookie" manager – Joe Cronin – finish at 99-53, seven games ahead of the Yankees in the AL. The team has four .300 hitters in its starting lineup: Henry "Heinie" Manush (.336), Joe Kuhel (.322), Cronin (.309), and Buddy Myer (.302). The top pitchers are Alvin "General" Crowder (24-15) and Earl Whitehill (22-8).

The Giants, managed by Bill Terry, finish five games ahead of the Pirates with a record of 91-61. Terry, at .322, is the team's only .300 hitter. Carl Hubbell has a 23-12 record with a 1.66 ERA and 10 shutouts. For the first time, baseball has Triple Crown winners in both leagues in the same year (and in the same city) – Jimmie Foxx of the Athletics (AL) and Chuck Klein of the Phillies (NL).

OCTOBER 3:

World Series, game one. In New York, Carl Hubbell five-hits the Senators, striking out 10, and the Giants win the game, 4-2; both Senators' runs are unearned. Mel Ott hits a two-run homer. The losing pitcher is Walter "Lefty" Stewart, who lasts only two innings.

OCTOBER 4:

World Series, game two. Harold "Prince Hal" Schumacher pitches a five-hit complete game and the Giants make it two in a row with a 6-1 victory at the Polo Grounds. Washington's lone tally comes on a Goose Goslin homer in the third. Lefty O'Doul drives in two runs with a pinch-hit single. The losing pitcher is Alvin "General" Crowder.

OCTOBER 5:

World Series, game three. In Washington, D.C., Earl Whitehill keeps the Senators alive with a five-hit shutout and Washington wins, 4-0, defeating Freddie Fitzsimmons. The big hits are first-inning doubles by Goose Goslin and Fred Schulte.

William Veeck Sr., president of the Cubs, dies of leukemia.

OCTOBER 6:

World Series, game four. Carl Hubbell masters the Senators again, going 11 innings, allowing eight hits, and winning the game, 2-1, in Washington. Travis Jackson scores the winning run on a single by John "Blondy" Ryan. Bill Terry homers in the fourth. The loser is Monte Weaver, who pitches 10 1/3 outstanding innings.

OCTOBER 7:

World Series, game five. Dolf Luque allows no earned runs in four and a third innings of relief; the Giants win the game, 4-3, and the World Series on a Mel Ott home run with two out and two strikes in the top of the 10th. Jack Russell gets the loss. Earlier, Washington's Fred Schulte buoyed the hometown fans with a game-tying three-run homer in the sixth. Hubbell allows no earned runs in his two wins; Mel Ott is the top Giant hitter

HISTORY

Cole's American Giants of Chicago beat out the Pittsburgh Crawfords to win the Negro National League first half. The second half of the season is not completed. Author Robert Peterson notes that "W.A. (Gus) Greenlee, league president, awarded the pennant to his club, the Pittsburgh Crawfords. This was, of course, disputed by the American Giants."

HISTORY

Chuck Klein of the Phillies sets an NL record by accumulating 200 hits for five straight seasons.

LEAGUE

Total attendance at major league ballparks dips to 6.3 million.

HISTORY

In November, Pennsylvania voters approve an amendment that would make Sunday baseball legal.

with .389, four RBI and two homers. Schulte leads the Senators with .333.

The Giants' victory in five games is costly. A crowd of 50,000 was expected at the Polo Grounds if there had been a game six, and the lost revenue is estimated at $100,000.

POST-SEASON

OCTOBER 22:

Browns' owner Philip deCatesby Ball dies of septicemia in St. John's hospital in St. Louis on his 69th birthday. Ball had owned the team since the days of the old Federal League.

NOVEMBER 7:

Leland "Larry" MacPhail, 43 years old, becomes general manager of the Reds.

NOVEMBER 21:

Outfielder Chuck Klein (.368, 28 homers, 120 RBI) becomes the only player traded after a Triple Crown season. The Phillies send the slugging outfielder to the Cubs in exchange for pitcher Ted Kleinhans (not in majors in 1933), infielder Mark Koenig (.284, three homers), outfielder Harvey Hendrick (.291, four homers), and $65,000.

DECEMBER 12:

The Tigers acquire catcher Gordon "Mickey" Cochrane (.322, 15 homers) from the Athletics for $100,000 and catcher Johnny Pasek (.246).

The Athletics send pitcher George Earnshaw (5-10, 5.97 ERA) and catcher Johnny Pasek – acquired earlier today – to the White Sox for catcher Charlie Berry (.255, two homers) and $20,000.

The Philadelphia Athletics send pitcher Lefty Grove to the Red Sox, along with pitcher George "Rube" Walberg and second baseman Max Bishop (.294, four home runs). Boston sends $125,000 to Connie Mack plus pitcher Bob Kline (7-8, 4.54 ERA) and infielder Harold "Rabbit" Warstler (.217)

DECEMBER 20:

The Tigers make their second major acquisition in eight days, trading outfielder John "Rocky" Stone (.280, 11 homers) to the Senators for outfielder Leon "Goose" Goslin (.297, 10 homers).

"Being traded is like celebrating your 100th birthday. It might not be the happiest occasion in the world, but consider the alternatives."

– Joe Garagiola

THE BEST OF 1933

NATIONAL LEAGUE

HITTERS

Batting Average:
Chuck Klein, Philadelphia Phillies, .368

Slugging Average:
Chuck Klein, .602

Home Runs:
Chuck Klein, 28

Runs Batted In:
Chuck Klein, 120

Hits:
Chuck Klein, 223

Stolen Bases:
John "Pepper" Martin, St. Louis Cardinals, 26

PITCHERS

Wins:
Carl Hubbell, New York Giants, 23

Strikeouts:
Dizzy Dean, St. Louis Cardinals, 199

Earned Run Average:
Carl Hubbell, 1.66

Winning Percentage:
Ben Cantwell, Boston Braves, .667

Saves:
"Fidgety Phil" Collins, Philadelphia Phillies, 6

Most Valuable Player:
Carl Hubbell, New York Giants

AMERICAN LEAGUE

HITTERS

Batting Average:
Jimmie Foxx, Philadelphia Athletics, .356

Slugging Average:
Jimmie Foxx, .703

Home Runs:
Jimmie Foxx, 48

Runs Batted In:
Jimmie Foxx, 163

Hits:
Henry "Heinie" Manush, Washington Senators, 221

Stolen Bases:
Ben Chapman, New York Yankees, 27

PITCHERS

Wins:
Lefty Grove, Philadelphia Athletics;
Alvin "General" Crowder, Washington Senators, 24

Strikeouts:
Lefty Gomez, New York Yankees, 163

Earned Run Average:
Monte Pearson, Cleveland Indians, 2.33

Winning Percentage:
Lefty Grove, .750

Saves:
Jack Russell, Washington Senators, 13

Most Valuable Player:
Jimmie Foxx, Philadelphia Athletics

TRIVIA

George and Ira Gershwin debut their song "I Know a Foul Ball."

1934

"John McGraw... was a man in every old-fashioned sense of the word."
– Umpire Bill Klem

NEWS

"BABY FACE" NELSON, "PRETTY BOY" FLOYD, BONNIE AND CLYDE, JOHN DILLINGER SLAIN IN SEPARATE ENCOUNTERS WITH LAWMEN

CONGRESS APPROVES INDEPENDENCE FOR THE PHILIPPINES

FORMER MAJOR LEAGUER BILLY SUNDAY HOLDS REVIVAL MEETING IN NEW YORK CITY

Federal Communications Commission, Securities and Exchange Commission formed in Washington

DIONNE QUINTUPLETS BORN IN CANADA

NATIONAL LABOR RELATIONS BOARD IS CREATED

Dust Bowl blows 300 million tons of topsoil into Atlantic

ISLAND OFF SAN FRANCISCO BECOMES ALCATRAZ PRISON

PRE-SEASON

JANUARY 5:

A four-alarm fire razes rehabilitation construction begun by Tom Yawkey at Fenway Park. The blaze takes five hours to control. It is the second fire at Fenway; the first occurred in May 1926.

The Yankees release one-time ace pitcher Herb Pennock (7-4, 5.54 ERA) and third baseman Joe Sewell (.273, two homers). Sewell ends his career with a .312 batting average for 14 years.

JANUARY 15:

Babe Ruth takes a $17,000 pay cut, but remains baseball's highest-paid player at $35,000. The Yankees' original offer was $25,000. Ruth hit .301 in 1933, with 34 homers and 103 RBI.

The Boston Red Sox sign Herb Pennock, who previously pitched for Boston from 1916 to 1922.

JANUARY 18:

In a *St. Louis Star-Times* article, Dizzy Dean predicts he and his brother, Paul, will lead the Cardinals to the NL pennant:"How are they going to stop us? Paul's going to be a sensation. He'll win 18 or 20 games. I'll count 20 to 25 for myself. I won 20 last season, and I know I'll pass that figure."

JANUARY 24:

In a conversation about the season's prospects with Roscoe McGowen of the *New York Times*, New York Giants' manager Bill Terry asks, "Brooklyn? Is Brooklyn still in the league?"

FEBRUARY 5:

Hank Aaron is born in Mobile, Alabama.

FEBRUARY 22:

George "Sparky" Anderson is born in Bridgewater, South Dakota.

FEBRUARY 23:

Dodgers' coach Casey Stengel is named the team's manager, replacing Max Carey. Stengel gets a two-year contract at $12,000 per annum. Under Carey, the Dodgers were 64-88 and in sixth place last season. Stengel comments, "Darned if I don't know a few things about baseball, and I think I can teach baseball."

FEBRUARY 25:

The fiery John J. McGraw dies of prostate cancer at age 60 in New Rochelle, New York. McGraw stepped down as Giants' manager in 1932 after leading the team to nine World Series and winning three championships. In his 33 years as a manager, he was 2,784-1,959. His playing career spanned 16 years, and he hit .333, while stealing 436 bases.

Irish playwright George Bernard Shaw, given to making observations about baseball, once said, "In Mr. McGraw I at last discovered the real and most authentic most remarkable man in America." Umpire Bill Klem, who had legendary clashes with McGraw on the field but remained friendly with him until a final break in 1928, said, "John McGraw off the field was a man in every old-fashioned sense of the word. He helped his friends; he fought for his rightful due with words, fists or whatever came readily to hand; his charity knew neither restraint nor publicity."

MARCH 20:

The world's greatest female athlete, Mildred "Babe" Didrikson, pitches one inning for the Athletics in an exhibi-

FEBRUARY 23
Casey Stengel is named the new manager of the Brooklyn Dodgers.

APRIL 17
Despite a fire in January, the renovated Fenway Park opens in Boston.

tion game against the Dodgers and walks one batter.

APRIL 8:

As part of their City Series, Philadelphia's Athletics and Phillies play the first legal Sunday baseball game in the City of Brotherly Love's history. The exhibition game has been made possible when Pennsylvania Governor Gifford Pinchot signs a bill making Sunday baseball a local option.

DIZZY DEAN SAYS, "IT AIN'T BRAGGING IF YOU CAN BACK IT UP." HE ALSO PREDICTS, "ME 'N PAUL'LL WIN 45 GAMES THIS YEAR." PAUL WINS 19 GAMES; DIZZY WINS 30.

Voters had approved a Sunday baseball referendum last November.

THE SEASON

APRIL 17:

The rebuilt Fenway Park opens with the Red Sox hosting the Senators. Washington wins, 6-5, in 11 innings. On hand is George Wright, nineteenth-century NL star with Boston and Providence. The celebrated left-field wall at Fenway makes its "debut" today. Previously, there was a

RULES

The NL and AL now will use the same baseball. Previously, the official balls of the two leagues had different stitching.

In 1934, Dizzy Dean became the last NL pitcher to win 30 games.

MAY 6
The Red Sox hit four consecutive triples in a 12-run inning in their 14-4 win over Detroit.

HISTORY

The three New York teams agree to ban radio broadcasts of their games

LEAGUE

According to writer Bob Rathgaber, Reds' general manager Larry MacPhail was interested in hiring Babe Ruth to manage the team for the 1934 season, but Yankees' owner Colonel Jacob Ruppert refused to give the Bambino his release.

HISTORY

Lou Gehrig hits .363, with 49 homers and 165 RBI. Mickey Cochrane is named the AL's Most Valuable Player.

10-foot embankment, known as Duffy's Cliff, and a wooden wall in centerfield. It has been torn down, replaced with an 18-foot concrete wall, topped with a wooden railroad tie framework and covered with tin. The entire structure measures 37 feet, 2 inches.

On opening day in Cleveland, Browns' manager Rogers Hornsby employs an infield shift against left-handed batters Earl Averill and Hal Trosky. The Indians win anyway, 5-2.

Lon "The Arkansas Hummingbird" Warneke of the Cubs carries a no-hitter into the ninth inning on opening day in Cincinnati. With one out, Adam Comorosky singles and many in the crowd of 30,427 boo their home team player. Warneke fans 13, finishing with a one-hitter and a 6-0 win.

The legendary Walter "Red" Barber makes his debut as the Cincinnati Reds radio broadcaster.

APRIL 21:

Washington's Morris "Moe" Berg sets an AL record for catchers today – 117 games without an error.

APRIL 22:

For the second time in the young season, Cubs' pitcher Lon Warneke just misses a no-hitter. Today, a fifth-inning double by the Cardinals' James "Ripper" Collins ruins the effort. Warneke settles for a one-hitter and a 15-2 victory in St. Louis. The Cubs get 22 hits – including homers by Chuck Klein and Charles "Gabby" Hartnett – against Dizzy and Paul Dean.

APRIL 28:

The Tigers' Leon "Goose" Goslin sets a major league record by grounding into four consecutive double plays today against the visiting Indians. But the Tigers win, 4-1.

APRIL 29:

In their first-ever legal Sunday home game, the Phillies lose to the Dodgers, 8-7. The winning pitcher is Phil Page; Frank Pearce gets the loss.

In their first Sunday home game ever, the Pirates fare better than the Phillies. Pittsburgh beats Cincinnati, 9-5.

Luis Aparicio is born in Maracaibo, Venezuela.

MAY 1:

The game's last legal spitballer, Burleigh Grimes of the Cards, wins his 270th career game. Grimes comes out of the bullpen as the Cardinals beat the Reds, 3-2, in 11 innings. It is Grimes's last victory.

MAY 6:

The Red Sox hit four consecutive triples in a 12-run fourth inning against the visiting Tigers and win, 14-4. Carl Reynolds, Julius "Moose" Solters, Rick Ferrell, and William "Bucky" Walters hit the three-baggers against Frederick "Firpo" Marberry. In their second at-bats in the inning, Reynolds and Solters single, Ferrell walks, and Walters doubles.

MAY 10:

At Yankee Stadium, Lou Gehrig sits at his own request after five innings because of illness. But before he goes to the bench, Gehrig hits two homers – including a grand slam – and two doubles, driving in seven runs. The Yankees beat the White Sox, 13-3.

MAY 13:

Lou Gehrig hits a grand slam homer against Lloyd Brown of the Indians. On August 31, 1931, Gehrig also hit a bases-loaded homer against Brown, then with the Senators.

MAY 15:

The Cardinals release 40-year-old pitcher Burleigh Grimes (2-1).

Grimes is signed by the Yankees on May 28; he is 1-2 with New York, which releases him on August 1. On August 5, the Pirates sign Grimes and he matches his Yankees' record of 1-2. Grimes ends his 19-year career with a 270-212 record and a 3.53 ERA.

MAY 16:

The Phillies acquire pitcher Syl Johnson (0-0 in two games) and outfielder Johnny Moore (.190) from the Reds for pitcher Ted Kleinhans (0-0 in five games) and outfielder Edward "Wes" Schulmerich (.250). Moore blossoms with the Phillies, hitting .330 for 1934 and better than .300 in the three following years.

MAY 17:

Chuck Klein returns to Philadelphia for the first time in a Cub uniform and hits two homers as Chicago beats Philadelphia, 10-3.

JUNE 25
Lou Gehrig hits for the cycle as the Yankees beat the White Sox, 11-2.

MAY 22:

Lou Gehrig drives in the Yankees' lone run in a 5-1 loss to Cleveland. For the second time in his career, Gehrig has at least one RBI in 10 consecutive games. On this streak, he bats in a total of 22.

MAY 26:

Only 11 days after they acquired him from the Cardinals, the Pirates sell pitcher Burleigh Grimes (1-2 with Pittsburgh, 3-3 on the season) to the Yankees.

JUNE 1:

In Pittsburgh, feuding over money for his brother Paul, Dizzy Dean complains of a sore arm. Manager Frankie Frisch tells him, "If you don't want to pitch, go home."

JUNE 2:

After telling Frankie Frisch, "My arm's getting better fast," Dizzy Dean – with relief from brother Paul – beats the Pirates, 13-4.

JUNE 5:

Dodgers' outfielder Ralph "Buzz" Boyle gets four hits in game one of today's doubleheader against the Phillies to extend his consecutive-game hitting streak to 25. Boyle's streak is snapped in the nightcap when he strikes out pinch-hitting for Hack Wilson – his only at-bat in the game.

JUNE 6:

Yankees' outfielder Myril Hoag has six singles in six at-bats as the Yankees spank the Red Sox, 15-3.

JUNE 13:

Braves' shortstop Billy Urbanski ties a major league record for the most trips to the plate without an official at-bat – six. Urbanski walks four times today and executes two successful sacrifices.

Urbanski has one other "zero" next to his name. The Linoleumville, New York, native played all of the 1933 season – appearing in 144 games and batting 566 times – without a home run.

JUNE 14

The Phillies buy third baseman William "Bucky" Walters (.216) from the Red Sox. Walters is 0-0 with a 1.29 ERA on the mound this season for Philadelphia. In 1935, he becomes a pitcher and is a 20-game winner three times in his career.

JUNE 25:

The Reds buy pitcher Clarence "Dazzy" Vance (1-1) from the Cardinals for the waiver price.

Lou Gehrig hits for the cycle as the Yankees beat the White Sox, 11-2, behind Johnny Broaca. The rookie pitcher doesn't fare as well at the plate; he fans five straight times, tying a major league record.

Broaca, who has a 12-9 rookie season, plays five years in the majors and makes the list of worst hitting pitchers ever – he manages 23 hits in 254 at-bats for a career average of .091. A Yale graduate, he twice interrupts his career to try boxing and then quits baseball after the 1939 season.

JUNE 27:

In St. Louis, the Cardinals beat the Giants, 8-7, on a Bill DeLancey homer in the bottom of the ninth. Dizzy Dean pitches eight and two-thirds, allowing the tying run in the ninth before he is replaced by Jim

LEAGUE

Larry MacPhail, general manager of the Reds, introduces season ticket plans. And, when the official scorer rules an error, the scoreboard at Crosley Field will inform fans by flashing an "E."

Pitcher Carl Hubbell had 253 career wins.

JULY 4
Satchel Paige wins two games – a no-hitter in Pittsburgh and a 1-0 shutout in Chicago.

HISTORY

According to the eyewitness testimony of Jack Marshall of the Chicago Giants – reported in Robert Peterson's *Only the Ball Was White* – Josh Gibson hit a fair ball out of Yankee Stadium in 1934. "Josh hit the ball over the triple deck next to the bullpen in left field. Over and out!" If accurate, it makes Gibson the only player ever to accomplish the feat.

TRIVIA

During the 1934 season, the Reds employ young Scotty Rustun – out of the University of Cincinnati – as a public relations man. His real name is James "Scotty" Reston, and he goes on to become a Pulitzer Prize-winning columnist for the *New York Times.*

Mooney, who becomes the pitcher of record. However, official scorer Martin J. Haley of the St. Louis Globe-Democrat credits Dean with the victory.

JUNE 28:

NL president John Heydler changes a scoring decision that had resulted in the Cardinals' Bill Hallahan getting a victory against the Dodgers on June 23. Because he was the pitcher of record when St. Louis scored the winning run, Dizzy Dean gets the victory.

JUNE 29:

In the second inning of an exhibition game against the Norfolk Tars, Lou Gehrig is hit in the head by a pitch from Ray White after Babe Ruth singles. Gehrig, who had homered in the first, is hit on the crown and is unconscious for five minutes. Manager Joe McCarthy laments, "My God, there goes the pennant!" Gehrig is taken to the hospital and diagnosed with a concussion, but no fracture. His consecutive game streak is in jeopardy as Gehrig is expected to miss some games.

JUNE 30:

The seemingly indestructible Lou Gehrig

POPULAR POET EDGAR A. GUEST SALUTES HANK GREENBERG'S DECISION NOT TO PLAY ON YOM KIPPUR WITH ONE OF HIS RHYMES THAT APPEARS IN NEWSPAPERS THROUGHOUT THE COUNTRY. FOCUSING ON TWO IRISHMEN NAMED MURPHY AND MULROONEY, IT READS, IN PART: "BUT UPON THE JEWISH NEW YEAR WHEN HANK GREENBERG CAME TO BAT AND MADE TWO HOMERS OFF PITCHER RHODES – THEY CHEERED LIKE MAD FOR THAT. CAME YOM KIPPUR – HOLY FAST DAY WORLD-WIDE OVER TO THE JEWS, AND HANK GREENBERG TO HIS TEACHING AND THE OLD TRADITION TRUE SPENT THE DAY AMONG HIS PEOPLE AND HE DIDN'T COME TO PLAY, SAID MURPHY TO MULROONEY, 'WE SHALL LOSE THE GAME TODAY! WE SHALL MISS HIM IN THE INFIELD AND SHALL MISS HIM AT THE BAT, BUT HE'S TRUE TO HIS RELIGION – AND I HONOR HIM FOR THAT!'"

JULY 13
In Detroit, Babe Ruth hits his 700th career home run, off Tommy Bridges.

JULY 31
Dizzy Dean pitches all 18 innings in an 8-6 Cardinals' win over the Reds.

leaves the hospital, travels by steamboat to Washington, D.C., and is in the lineup when the Yankees meet the Senators. He triples three times in three at-bats – once to each field, but the game is washed out by squalls in the fifth inning while the Senators are at bat and trailing.

JULY 4:

It's two victories in one day for Leroy "Satchel" Paige – in different cities. Pitching for the Pittsburgh Crawfords, he no-hits the visiting Homestead Grays, 4-0, in a Negro National League game. He then drives to Chicago where he defeats the American Giants, 1-0, in 12 innings.

JULY 5:

At Yankee Stadium, Lou Gehrig hits two homers – including his fourth grand slam of the year, singles twice, and bats in seven runs as New York tops Washington, 8-3.

JULY 10:

At the Polo Grounds in New York, the AL All-Stars win, 9-7, despite home runs by the Cardinals' Frankie Frisch and Joe Medwick and an eye-popping pitching performance by the Giants' Carl Hubbell. The left-hander, facing an awesome lineup, strikes out Babe Ruth, Lou Gehrig, Jimmie Foxx, Al Simmons, and Joe Cronin in succession. The AL comes back from a 4-0 deficit with a six-run fifth inning. Earl Averill of the Indians has a triple, a double, and three RBI. The winning pitcher is the Indians Mel Harder; the loser Van Lingle Mungo of the Dodgers.

JULY 13:

With almost every swing a new record, Babe Ruth hits his 700th career home run today in Detroit's Navin Field. Before some 21,000 eye witnesses, Ruth drives a 3-2 pitch from Tommy Bridges in the third inning 480 feet over the right-field fence. Earle Combs is on base and the game is scoreless at the time. As Ruth circles the bases, he yells, "I want that ball! I want that ball!" He gets that ball – for $20, an autographed replacement, and a box seat for the rest of the game for Lennie Bielski, the youngster who retrieves it. The Yankees win, 4-2, behind a six-hitter by Charles "Red" Ruffing and move into first place. Gehrig, whose consecutive game streak is at 1,426, leaves the game in the second inning with back problems. In the first inning Gehrig singles and stumbles while running. He moves up on Ben Chapman's hit and is doubled off second on a Bill Dickey liner. After taking the field, he requests a replacement and comes out for Jack Saltzgaver.

JULY 14:

For the second consecutive day, Lou Gehrig singles to right in the first inning and is replaced by a pinch runner – keeping his consecutive game streak going. Gehrig, in the lineup as a shortstop, leads off with a single against the Tigers' Vic Sorrell and is replaced by Robert "Red" Rolfe

JULY 17:

At League Park in Cleveland, Indians' pitcher Oral Hildebrand walks Babe Ruth twice. They are Ruth's 1,999th and 2,000th career walks – the most ever issued to a player.

JULY 18:

In Cleveland, Babe Ruth is hit on the right leg by a line drive off the bat of Lou Gehrig, is carried off the field and taken to the hospital by ambulance. The Yankees lose the game as well, 15-14, on three Indian runs in the bottom of the ninth. Earl Averill drives in the winning run. The teams set an AL record for a nine-inning game when 22 players (12 Yankees) hit safely. Ruth misses a week as a result of his injury. He says, "I'm going to get out of this game before I'm carried out."

JULY 24:

Yankees' outfielder Earle Combs fractures his skull and lapses into a coma when he crashes headfirst into the center-field wall in Sportsman's Park in St. Louis. He also tears a muscle in his right shoulder. The Browns beat the Yankees, 4-2. Combs, who was batting .319, recovers but is lost for the season. He plays only one more year in the majors.

JULY 31:

Dizzy is busy in Cincy. Dizzy Dean pitches all 18 innings in an 8-6 victory over the Reds and Tony Freitas.

AUGUST 4:

In game two of a doubleheader in Philadelphia, the Giants' Mel Ott ties a major league record by scoring six runs. The Giants also set

TRIVIA

According to writer Michael Gershman, a Brooklyn fan known only as "Abie the Truck Driver" gave the Dodgers their other nickname – the Bums. In his *Diamonds – The Evolution of the Ballpark*, Gershman writes that Abie would yell from his seat in the upper deck on the third baseline, "Ya bum, ya." Offered free tickets by manager Wilbert Robinson, he supposedly said, "You can keep the pass. I can't stand it anymore. They're still bums!" The Dodger "bum" was given physical characteristics by cartoonist Willard Mullin.

CULTURE

Dizzy and Daffy, a Warner Brothers short subject, stars the Dean brothers, who also do a one-week vaudeville turn at New York City's Roxy Theatre.

AUGUST 25
Tigers' rookie pitcher Schoolboy Rowe beats the Senators, 4-2, for his 16th straight win.

HISTORY

Hack Wilson's drinking is taking its toll on his perceptions as well as his skills. Wilson, whose home run output has dropped from a high of 56 in 1930 to nine in 1933, is hung over in the outfield during a game at Philadelphia's Baker Bowl this season. His Dodgers' teammate Walter "Boom Boom" Beck is driven from the mound by the Phillies. In anger, he throws the ball into right field, hitting the tin fence. Wilson looks up, thinks it's been hit, fields it, and rifles a throw back into the infield. Wilson plays the last seven games of his career with the Phillies this season, hitting only .100.

a modern NL record when they score 11 runs on 11 hits in the ninth inning against Reggie Grabowski. The Giants win, 21-4, but Grabowski isn't the loser. The "honor" goes to Roy "Snipe" Hansen. Ott does the major damage with two homers, a double and single, and four RBI. He also walks and is hit by a pitch. Travis Jackson also homers for New York, and Hal Schumacher gets the win.

The Tigers acquire pitcher Alvin "General" Crowder (4-10) on waivers from the Senators. Crowder topped the AL in victories in 1932 and 1933.

AUGUST 8:

Baseball loses another of its legendary and colorful characters when Uncle Wilbert Robinson dies of a brain hemorrhage in Atlanta at age 71. Robinson managed for 19 seasons, compiling a 1,399-1,398 record. He managed Brooklyn to the World Series in 1916 and 1920. In 17 years as a player, he hit .273.

AUGUST 9:

The Cardinals sign Elmer Dean, the older brother of Dizzy and Paul, to work as a ballpark vendor. Elmer Dean lasts some three days, and returns to his original job – selling peanuts at the home games of the Houston Buffaloes, a Cardinals' minor league team.

AUGUST 12:

Fenway says farewell to the Babe. Realizing that this probably will be Babe Ruth's final game in Boston, 41,766 turn out for a doubleheader with the Yankees. In game one, the 39-year-old Bambino hits a single and a double in five at-bats, but misplays a Billy Werber line drive into a triple. Boston wins, 6-4. Ruth walks twice in the nightcap and is hitless in one official at-bat. He leaves the game in the sixth, tipping his hat to the fans. The Yankees win, 7-1.

Dizzy and Daffy drive the manager batty. After the Dean brothers lose both ends of a doubleheader, they refuse to go from St. Louis to Detroit by train for an exhibition game; Dizzy is fined $100 and Paul $50 by manager Frank Frisch. When Frisch refuses to rescind the fines, Dizzy declares, "Then me 'n Paul are through with the Cardinals." The Deans then refuse to take the field for a game. Frisch asks for their uniforms and Dizzy rips his to shreds. Then he destroys another one for the benefit of a photographer. He is suspended for 10 days, but Frisch reduces it to seven. In an August 20 hearing, Commis-sioner Kenesaw Mountain Landis up-holds the suspensions.

AUGUST 18:

Roberto Clemente is born in Carolina, Puerto Rico.

AUGUST 24:

Dizzy Dean returns to the Cardinals and five-hits the Giants, 5-0, for his 22nd win of the season.

AUGUST 25:

The Tigers' Lynwood "Schoolboy" Rowe is making his rookie season one for the record books. Today, in Washington, D.C., he beats the Senators, 4-2, for his 16th consecutive victory, putting him in the fine company of Walter Johnson, Smoky Joe Wood, and Lefty Grove. Rowe also drives in the winning run with a ninth-inning single.

AUGUST 29:

The A's beat the Tigers, 13-5, to snap Schoolboy Rowe's 16-game winning streak.

SEPTEMBER 10:

With the Tigers in the thick of a pennant race, Hank Greenberg is faced with the tough choice of observing the Jewish high holy day of Rosh Hashanah or playing baseball. A Detroit newspaper consults a leading rabbi, who says Greenberg can play because the Jewish New Year is a happy occasion. Greenberg hits two homers today against Gordon Rhodes to beat the Red Sox, 2-1. HAPPY NEW YEAR, HANK, headlines the *Detroit Free Press* in Yiddish and English.

SEPTEMBER 13:

The Ford Motor Company buys the radio rights to the World Series for $100,000.

SEPTEMBER 14:

The Cardinals, locked in a pennant race with the Giants, are in New York to play the Dodgers. Dizzy Dean pays a visit to the Polo Grounds, bringing a black cat into the Giants' dugout and pointing it at second baseman Hughie Critz. Dean tells John Lardner of the New York Post, "That got him. This

SEPTEMBER 16
Brothers Dizzy and Paul Dean sweep the Giants, 5-3 and 3-1, in a doubleheader.

SEPTEMBER 21
Paul Dean no-hits the Dodgers – walking one and fanning six – in a 3-0 Cardinals win.

will get 'em all." He sets the cat free in the New York bullpen.

SEPTEMBER 16:

The Deans do in the Giants in New York. Before 62,573 at the Polo Grounds, the Cardinals sweep a doubleheader. In the opener, Dizzy Dean gets the win in a 5-3 game; the Cardinals score four runs in the seventh when Dizzy is lifted for a pinch hitter. In game two, Paul Dean bests Carl Hubbell, 3-1, in 11 innings. The key hit is a homer by John "Pepper" Martin. The Giants remain three and a half games ahead of the Cardinals.

SEPTEMBER 18:

Today is Yom Kippur, the Jewish Day of Atonement and the highest of the holy days. Hank Greenberg sits out the game. His father, David Greenberg, tells the *New York Evening Post* that Yom Kippur is different, and "I put my foot down and Henry obeyed." The Tigers beat the visiting Yankees, 2-0. The Browns' Louis "Bobo" Newsom no-hits the Red Sox for nine innings, only to lose, 2-1, in the 10th. Newsom's no-hitter is ruined by a Roy Johnson single in the 10th that follows two walks. Newsom is tough to hit, but wild; he walks seven and strikes out nine.

ABOUT THE DODGERS' REVENGE ON BILL TERRY, JOHN KIERAN OF THE *NEW YORK TIMES* WRITES, "WHY, MISTER TERRY, OH!, WHY DID YOU EVER CHORTLE THE QUERY THAT MADE BROOKLYN HOT? JUST FOR THE CRACK THAT YOU THOUGHT WAS SO CLEVER, NOW YOU STAND TEETERING RIGHT ON THE SPOT! VAIN WAS YOUR HOPE THEY FORGAVE OR FORGOT ; NOW THAT YOU'RE WEARY AND BOWED WITH FATIGUE, HERE IS THE DRAMA AND THIS IS THE PLOT : BROOKLYN, DEAR FELLOWS, IS STILL IN THE LEAGUE."

Browns' manager Rogers Hornsby fines his pitchers $50 if they throw a strike on an 0-2 count. Newsom once argued with an umpire to call a pitch a ball so he could avoid the fine.

SEPTEMBER 21:

In game two of a doubleheader at Ebbets Field, Paul Dean no-hits the Dodgers, 3-0. Dean walks one and strikes out six; the Cardinals make no errors. The losing pitcher is Ray Benge. The victory is Paul Dean's 18th of 1934. In the opener, Dizzy Dean had three-hit Brooklyn, 13-0, beating Tom Zachary for his 27th win of the season. The Dean brothers set a major league record for the fewest hits allowed in a doubleheader.

Before the game, Dizzy Dean is almost right when he predicts to St. Louis writers, "Zachary and Benge will be pitching against one-hit Dean and no-hit Dean." Afterward, he allegedly comments on brother Paul's no-hitter,

HISTORY

The 1934 All-Star Game truly was a game of stars – 17 of the 18 starters ultimately were elected to the Hall of Fame. The AL Hall of Famers were Charlie Gehringer, Henry "Heinie" Manush, Babe Ruth, Lou Gehrig, Jimmie Foxx, Al Simmons, Joe Cronin, Bill Dickey, and Vernon "Lefty" Gomez. The NL starters who made the Hall were Frankie Frisch, Harold "Pie" Traynor, Joe Medwick, Hazen "Kiki" Cuyler, Bill Terry, Travis Jackson, Charles "Gabby" Hartnett, and Carl Hubbell. The odd man out was Braves center fielder Wally Berger, himself no slouch. In 11 years, Berger batted .300, had 242 homers, and knocked in 100 runs four times.

SEPTEMBER 30
Dizzy Dean wins his 30th game of the year and seals the NL pennant for the Cards.

HISTORY

The Philadelphia Stars–second half winners –defeat the first half winners, Cole's American Giants of Chicago, four games to three, for the Negro National League pennant.

CULTURE

***Death on the Diamond* by Cortland Fitzsimmons is published. It involves the murders of three Cardinals players. According to SABR-ite Andy McCue, it's "perhaps the first adult baseball mystery." Later that same year it's released as a movie, starring Robert Young and Mickey Rooney.**

"If I had known what Paul was gonna do, I would have pitched one, too." Dean biographer Vince Staten writes, "There is no evidence that Diz said that. No next-day game stories carry that quote, either in the New York or St. Louis papers." He did tell a New York Herald-Tribune *reporter, "If someone only told me, we'd both had a no-hitter."*

SEPTEMBER 24:

A small crowd of 4,000 is unaware they are seeing Babe Ruth at Yankee Stadium for the last time as a player. Ruth walks in the first inning and is replaced by pinch runner Myril Hoag. The Yankees lose, 5-0, to the Red Sox.

SEPTEMBER 28:

Dizzy Dean shuts out the Reds, 4-0, tightening the National League pennant race.

SEPTEMBER 29:

Washington, D.C., fans witness another "last." In the opener of a doubleheader, Babe Ruth hits a homer against Syd Cohen. It is his 659th, his last as a Yankee, and the 708th of his career. The Yankees lose, 8-5, and bounce back to take the nightcap, 9-6.

The Cardinals beat the Reds, 6-1, on a Paul Dean 11-hitter, while the Giants are losing to the Dodgers, 5-1, at the Polo Grounds. St. Louis moves into first place, one game ahead of New York with one game to play.

SEPTEMBER 30:

Babe Ruth takes the field at Griffith Stadium in Washington, D.C., wearing Yankee pinstripes for the last time; it is his 2,084th game with New York. In attendance are his wife, Claire, and his daughter, Dorothy. Washington fans present the Babe with a scroll of appreciation, and a band from St. Mary's Industrial School – his alma mater – plays. After going hitless in three at-bats, with a walk, Ruth comes to bat for the final time as a Yankee. With a 2-0 count, Washington player-manager Joe Cronin calls for strikes so Ruth will have a final opportunity to hit. Ruth then flies out to center fielder Jake Powell and leaves the field crying. Gehrig gets three hits in four at-bats to wrap up the Triple Crown. The Senators go on to win the game, 5-3, with Orville Armbrust getting the win.

Thus, an awesome chapter in baseball history ends. From 1925 through 1934, the combination of Ruth and Gehrig produced 772 homers – an average of 77-plus per season. The two homered in the same game 72 times, back-to-back 16 times, and they averaged a cumulative 274 RBI per year. Gehrig biographer Ray Robinson describes them as the "most fearsome 1-2 punch in history."

The Dodgers have their revenge on Bill Terry for his demeaning preseason remark. Not only is Brooklyn still in the league, they beat the Giants today at the Polo Grounds, 8-5. It is Brooklyn's second victory in a row over New York and knocks the Giants out of the pennant race.

It's 30 on the 30th for Dizzy Dean and a pennant for the St. Louis Cardinals. At Sportsman's Park before a crowd of 35,274, Dean loads the bases in the ninth inning; he then fans Clyde Manion and Frederick "Ted" Petosky; Earl "Sparky" Adams fouls out to end the game and the Cardinals have a 9-0 victory and the NL pennant. Pitching on two days' rest, he becomes baseball's first 30-game winner since Grover Cleveland Alexander in 1917. It also is his seventh shutout of the year.

REGULAR SEASON WRAP-UP:

Gordon "Mickey" Cochrane leads the Tigers to the AL pennant in his rookie season as manager. The Tigers, at 101-53, beat the Yankees by seven games and become the first "Western" team to take the AL pennant since 1920. Lynwood "Schoolboy" Rowe (24-8) and Tommy Bridges (22-11) are the top pitchers. The Tigers have a team batting average of .300. Charlie Gehringer (.356), Hank Greenberg (.339), and player-manager Mickey Cochrane (.320) are the leading hitters. The Tigers infield accumulates 462 RBI. First baseman Greenberg leads with 139, second baseman Gehringer has 127, shortstop Billy Rogell 100, and third baseman Marv Owen, 96.

According to historian John C. Hawkins, Mickey Cochrane almost didn't get the job. The first choice of Tigers' owner Frank Navin to succeed Stanley "Bucky" Harris was Babe Ruth. Navin

OCTOBER 9
The Cardinals win game seven of the World Series, 11-0, behind Dizzy Dean's six-hitter.

invited Ruth to Detroit to meet with him. Instead, Ruth took his family on a trip to Hawaii, telling Navin he'd see him later. Navin then turned to his catcher, Cochrane.

By going 21-7 in September while the Giants are 14-13, the Cardinals under manager Frankie Frisch win the NL pennant. They finish at 95-58, two games ahead of New York. Dizzy Dean is 30-7; brother Paul 19-11. James "Ripper" Collins is the leading hitter at .333 with 35 homers and 128 RBI. Joe Medwick bats .319 and Frisch .305.

OCTOBER 3:

World Series, game one. In Detroit, Dizzy Dean allows eight hits and beats the Tigers, 8-3. Joe Medwick has four hits including a homer and the Tigers' infield makes things tough for losing pitcher Alvin "General" Crowder by committing five errors. Hank Greenberg homers for the losers.

Leo Durocher demonstrates that no remark is too vile for him. In the third inning with the Cardinals leading 3-1, runners on second and third, and Hank Greenberg batting, Durocher calls to pitcher Dizzy Dean, "Don't waste your fastball. Throw the son of a bitch a ham sandwich. He won't touch it." Dean strikes out Greenberg.

OCTOBER 4:

World Series, game two. Schoolboy Rowe teaches the Cardinals about his stuff; he allows seven hits in 12 innings as the Tigers win, 3-2, in Detroit. Rowe allows no hits over the first seven innings. Goose Goslin singles in the winning run after losing pitcher Bill Walker issues bases on balls to Gehringer and Greenberg.

OCTOBER 5:

World Series, game three. In St. Louis, the Cardinals win, 4-1, behind a complete-game eight-hitter by Paul Dean. The Tigers get five walks but strand thirteen base runners. Tommy Bridges goes four and gets the loss. John "Pepper" Martin is today's hitting star with a double and triple; he scores twice.

OCTOBER 6:

World Series, game four. The Tigers give winning pitcher Elden Auker strong offensive support, banging out thirteen hits in a 10-4 win in St. Louis. Hank Greenberg has three safeties and three RBI; Billy Rogell drives in four runs. The losing pitcher is Bill Walker in relief.

In the fourth inning Dizzy Dean enters the game as a pinch runner. Going into second, he is hit in the head by Billy Rogell's throw and carried off the field on a stretcher. Dean says, "The doctors X-rayed my head and found nothing."

OCTOBER 7:

World Series, game five. The Tigers make it two in a row in St. Louis. Tommy Bridges goes all the way, allowing the Cardinals seven hits, in a 3-1 win. Dizzy Dean, back from yesterday's head injury, is the loser. Charlie Gehringer's leadoff homer in the sixth is the winner. Bill DeLancey homers for St. Louis.

OCTOBER 8:

World Series, game six. In Detroit, Paul Dean drives in the winning run with a seventh-inning single and seven-hits the Tigers for a 4-3 victory. Schoolboy Rowe gets the loss.

OCTOBER 9:

World Series, game seven. The Cardinals win the World Series on a 17-hit, 11-0 Dizzy Dean six-hitter. But the game in Detroit is marred by a near riot. In the sixth inning, the Cardinals' Joe Medwick slides high into third baseman Marvin Owen. The two go at it, the benches empty. When order is restored and Medwick returns to left field, he is pelted with garbage, bottles, and seat cushions by Tigers' fans. Time out is called and the field is cleared four times. Ultimately, baseball Commissioner Kenesaw Mountain Landis, who is at the game, orders Medwick to the bench for his own safety. Medwick is replaced by Charles "Chick" Fullis, leaving with 11 hits, one short of the series record. The losing pitcher is Elden Auker, the first of six Detroit pitchers. Dizzy Dean finishes the series with two wins and a 1.73 ERA. Joe Medwick, .379, is St. Louis' top hitter. The Tigers' Charlie Gehringer matches Medwick. Fielding is not crisp: the Cardinals commit 15 errors, the Tigers 12.

According to Daniel Okrent and Steve

HISTORY

Nineteen-year-old Joe DiMaggio of the San Francisco Seals finishes second in the Pacific Coast League batting race because he will not accept a cheap hit. DiMaggio and Oscar "Ox" Eckhardt enter the final game of the season neck-and-neck. DiMaggio gets three hits on bunts with the infield back and then hits a fly to center field that should be caught but is allowed to drop for a hit. Stating, "I don't want to lead the league if I don't deserve to," he goes to the official scorer and has the double changed to an error. Eckhardt finishes at .399 to DiMaggio's .398

OCTOBER 26
The Boston Red Sox acquire shortstop Joe Cronin from the Washington Senators.

HISTORY

Burleigh Grimes, the last of the legal spitball pitchers, hangs up his glove and dries his fingers. Grimes was only 4-5 with a 6.11 ERA this year with the Cardinals, Pirates, and Yankees. In his 19-year career, he is 270-212 with a 3.53 ERA. Grimes lost none of his nastiness as he aged. Earlier this season, the Tigers' Leon "Goose" Goslin hit a homer against Grimes. While Goslin was waiting in the on-deck circle for a later at-bat, Grimes threw a pitch at him.

TRIVIA

Negro Leagues star Josh Gibson, now catching for the Pittsburgh Crawfords, is recorded as hitting 69 home runs this season.

Wulf, umpire Bill Klem is fined $50, for "using abusive language," by Commissioner Landis and never works a Word Series again.

POST-SEASON

OCTOBER 26:

The Boston Red Sox acquire shortstop Joe Cronin (.284, seven homers) from the Washington Senators in exchange for shortstop Lyn Lary (.241, two homers) and $225,000 in cash (although according to some accounts the amount is actually $250,000).

NOVEMBER 21:

The New York Yankees buy Joe DiMaggio, the sensational young outfielder, from the San Francisco Seals in the Pacific Coast League. It is just four days before DiMaggio's 20th birthday. The price tag is debatable, variously estimated at between $25,000 and $50,000. Despite showing great promise in the minor leagues, DiMaggio had become devalued because of torn tendons in his left knee. In addition to paying the Seals cash, the Yankees assign infielder Edward "Doc" Farrell, pitcher Floyd Newkirk, pitcher Jim Densmore, first baseman Les Powers, and outfielder Ted Norbert to play in San Francisco. Actually, DiMaggio will end up playing another season in the Bay Area, finally reporting to the Yankees in 1936.

NOVEMBER 22:

The Chicago Cubs send outfielder Babe Herman (.304, 14 home runs) along with pitchers Guy Bush (18-10, 3.83 ERA) and Jim Weaver (13-9, 4.18 ERA) to the Pittsburgh Pirates. In return, they get outfielder Freddie Lindstrom (.290, four homers) and pitcher Larry French (12-18, 3.58 ERA).

DECEMBER 13:

The Cincinnati Reds buy minor league first baseman Johnny Mize from the St. Louis Cardinals. However, Mize is returned to St. Louis because it is determined by Reds' physicians that he has a bad knee. Nonetheless, he makes his major league debut with the Cardinals in 1936.

DECEMBER 19:

Albert William Kaline is born in Baltimore, Maryland.

THE 1934 CHAMPION CARDINALS ARE KNOWN AS THE GAS HOUSE GANG. THE ORIGIN OF THE NICKNAME IS HAZY. IN 1932, WARREN BROWN OF THE *CHICAGO HERALD-EXAMINER* DESCRIBED PEPPER MARTIN AS "A REFUGEE FROM A GASWORKS." DURING THIS YEAR'S WORLD SERIES, JOE WILLIAMS OF THE *NEW YORK WORLD-TELEGRAM* WROTE, "I PICKED THE TIGERS, BUT THE CARDINALS HAVE GOT ME WORRIED. THEY LOOKED LIKE A BUNCH OF BOYS FROM THE GAS HOUSE DISTRICT WHO HAD CROSSED THE RAILROAD TRACKS FOR A GAME OF BALL WITH NICE KIDS." SIX DAYS LATER, THE *WORLD-TELEGRAM* USES THE PHRASE "GAS HOUSE GANG."

NOVEMBER 21
The New York Yankees purchase Joe DiMaggio from the San Francisco Seals.

THE BEST OF 1934

NATIONAL LEAGUE

HITTERS

Batting Average:
Paul Waner, Pittsburgh Pirates, .362

Slugging Average:
James "Ripper" Collins, St. Louis Cardinals, .615

Home Runs:
Mel Ott, New York Giants, 35

Runs Batted In:
Mel Ott, 135

Hits:
Paul Waner, 217

Stolen Bases:
John "Pepper" Martin, St. Louis Cardinals, 23

PITCHERS

Wins:
Dizzy Dean, St. Louis Cardinals, 30

Strikeouts:
Dizzy Dean, 195

Earned Run Average:
Carl Hubbell, New York Giants, 2.30

Winning Percentage:
Dizzy Dean, .811

Saves:
Carl Hubbell, 8

Most Valuable Player:
Dizzy Dean, St. Louis Cardinals

AMERICAN LEAGUE

HITTERS

Batting Average:
Lou Gehrig, New York Yankees, .363

Slugging Average:
Lou Gehrig, .706

Home Runs:
Lou Gehrig, 49

Runs Batted In:
Lou Gehrig, 165

Hits
Charlie Gehringer, Detroit Tigers, 214

Stolen Bases:
Bill Werber, Boston Red Sox, 40

PITCHERS

Wins:
Vernon "Lefty" Gomez, New York Yankees, 26

Strikeouts:
Lefty Gomez, 158

Earned Run Average:
Lefty Gomez, 2.33

Winning Percentage:
Lefty Gomez, .839

Saves:
Jack Russell, Washington Senators, 7

Most Valuable Player:
Gordon "Mickey" Cochrane, Detroit Tigers

HISTORY

A team of major leaguers, managed by Connie Mack, tours Japan. Included are such stars as Babe Ruth, Lou Gehrig, Lefty Gomez, Charlie Gehringer, Earl Averill, and Jimmie Foxx. On the roster is a journeyman catcher named Moe Berg, a Phi Beta Kappa graduate who is fluent in 12 languages. (A teammate supposedly says, "He can speak 10 languages, but he can't hit in any of them.") Berg's role on the trip has been the subject of much conjecture. It is fairly certain that he used his knowledge of the language and customs to spy on the Japanese. According to some accounts, photographs he took from the roof of St. Luke's International Hospital were used in Jimmy Doolittle's 1942 "30 Seconds Over Tokyo" bombing raid on the Japanese capital.

1935

APRIL 16
40-year-old Babe Ruth makes his National League debut with the Boston Braves.

NEWS

SOCIAL SECURITY ACT SIGNED BY FDR

WILL ROGERS DIES IN PLANE CRASH

CIO labor union formed by John Lewis

BRUNO HAUPTMANN CHARGED WITH KIDNAPPING LINDBERGH BABY

U.S. SENATOR HUEY LONG ASSASSINATED IN NEW ORLEANS

Alcoholics Anonymous founded in Ohio

MOBSTER DUTCH SCHULTZ GUNNED DOWN IN NEW JERSEY

NOTORIOUS MA BARKER SLAIN BY FBI

MONOPOLY BOARD GAME MAKES ITS DEBUT

FIRST HOWARD JOHNSON'S RESTAURANT OPENS

PRE-SEASON

JANUARY 26:

Bob Uecker is born in Milwaukee.

FEBRUARY 19:

After winning the Triple Crown in 1934, Lou Gehrig asks for $35,000. He settles for $30,000 – a raise of $7,000. He is now the highest-paid player in baseball.

FEBRUARY 26:

The Yankees hold a press conference at the Ruppert Brewery in New York to announce the unconditional release of Babe Ruth. Ruth, who returned from a world tour on February 20, will be signing with the Braves as a player, assistant manager, and vice president. Yankee owner Jacob Ruppert asserts he is getting no money for allowing Ruth to go to the Braves. Boston owner Judge Emil Fuchs says that, as vice president, Ruth will be used in an advisory capacity, "He'll be consulted on trades and so forth." Ruppert adds, "A vice president signs checks. Everybody knows that." In his final season with the Yankees, the Babe batted .288 with 22 homers and 84 RBI.

FEBRUARY 27:

As expected, Babe Ruth signs with the Braves in a triple capacity. He will earn $25,000.

THE SEASON

APRIL 16:

After 21 years in the American League, Babe Ruth makes his National League debut. Playing for the Braves against the Giants, he hits a home run and a single against Carl Hubbell of the Giants. It is the 709th career homer for the 40-year-old Ruth. The Braves win the game, 4-2.

With Babe Ruth gone, the New York spotlight falls exclusively on Lou Gehrig. Named the Yankees' first captain since Everett Scott in 1925, Gehrig leads his team onto the field at Yankee Stadium on opening day. There is a new number 3, a lefthanded batter in right field, but no one is mistaking George "Twinkletoes" Selkirk for his predecessor. The Yankees lose to the Red Sox, 1-0.

APRIL 21:

In Boston, Babe Ruth homers against the Dodgers' Ray Benge. It is his second NL and 710th career home run.

MAY 5:

It's the Babe versus Dizzy for the first time. And Dean prevails, fanning Ruth once and getting him to ground out twice.

MAY 8:

The Reds' leaden-footed catcher Ernie Lombardi keeps rolling snakes eyes, but it's the Phillies who come up the losers. Lombardi doubles in the sixth, seventh, eighth, and ninth innings against four different pitchers as Cincinnati flattens the Phillies, 15-4. Lombardi also has a single.

MAY 21:

In Chicago, Babe Ruth homers against James "Tex" Carleton of the Cubs. It is his 711th round-tripper.

The Senators buy pitcher Louis "Bobo" Newsom (16-20, 4.01 ERA) for $40,000, reportedly a record.

MAY 23:

Rain in Cincinnati delays the first major league night game.

Indians' manager Walter Johnson shows he can be

"To understand him, you had to understand this: He wasn't human."
– Joe Dugan on Babe Ruth

MAY 24
The Reds beat the Phillies, 2-1, in the first night game in the major leagues.

tough. He sends catcher Glenn Myatt (.083 in 10 games) and third baseman Willie Kamm (.333 in six games) packing because they are a bad influence on the team's young players. Myatt signs on with the Giants; Kamm's career is over.

MAY 24:

A crowd of 20,422 is on hand at Crosley Field to see a major league first – night baseball. Big league night baseball, essentially the brainchild of new Reds' general manager Larry MacPhail, is realized through the work of General Electric. The company installs 614 bulbs of 1,500 watts each that provide 921,000 watts of light. Crosley Field is illuminated when President Franklin Delano Roosevelt pushes a button in the White House. NL president Ford Frick, substituting for the ailing Commissioner Kenesaw Mountain Landis, throws out the first ball. The festivities include fireworks and four drum and bugle corps. The players get a six-minute warm-up to acclimate to the artificial light. The game, almost an anticlimax, begins with Lou Chiozza of the Phillies leading off against Paul Derringer and grounding out to shortstop Billy Myers. Myers gets the first hit under the lights, a double in the bottom of the first. The game is played with no errors and the Reds beat the Phillies, 2-1. Derringer gets the win; Joe Bowman is charged with the loss. Veteran Bill Klem is the home plate umpire.

HOW INTENSE WAS TY COBB? NOTED SPORTSWRITER GRANTLAND RICE REMEMBERED A DINNER HE HAD – "IT MUST HAVE BEEN IN 1935" – WITH COBB AT THE DETROIT ATHLETIC CLUB. THEY WERE JOINED BY JAY CLARKE, A FORMER INDIANS' CATCHER. RICE REMARKED ON CLARKE'S "PHANTOM" TAGS AT HOME PLATE AND HOW UMPIRES WERE FOOLED INTO CALLING A BASERUNNER OUT. AS RICE RELATED IT, CLARKE LAUGHED AND SAID, "I MISSED YOU AT LEAST 10 TIMES AT THE PLATE, TY – TIMES WHEN YOU WERE CALLED OUT." COBB BECAME ENRAGED, CURSING AND SHAKING CLARKE. HE SHOUTED, "YOU COST ME 10 RUNS – RUNS I EARNED." RICE PULLED COBB OFF CLARKE AND SETTLED HIM DOWN. THAT'S HOW INTENSE TY COBB WAS.

TRIVIA

At Ebbets Field, a pint-size, teenage shortstop from Brooklyn tries out for the Dodgers. Manager Casey Stengel dismisses him, saying, "You're too small. You'll get hurt. Go on, get outa here. Go get a shoebox." The youngster was Phil Rizzuto.

Crosley Field hosted the majors' first night game.

TRIVIA

Tom Zachary and Charlie Root arguably are the pitchers most identified with Babe Ruth homers. But it is George "Rube" Walberg who yielded the most to the Bambino – 17.

RULES

As a result of Lefty Gomez's six-inning stint in the All-Star game, the NL is successful in bringing about an All-Star Game rule change. From now on, no pitcher can go more than three innings unless a game goes into extra innings.

MAY 25:

The NL gets a taste of what Babe Ruth used to be. At Forbes Field, Ruth slugs two-run homers in the first (against Charles "Red" Lucas) and third innings (against Guy Bush), singles in the fifth, and hits a solo round-tripper in the seventh (against Bush). The last shot – the 714th of his career – clears the right-field grandstand, 600 feet away from the plate, clears the roof, and soars out of the ballpark.It is the longest ever hit at Forbes. The ball goes over the heads of a group of youngsters on the corner of Boquet and Joncire and into a construction lot. Henry "Wiggy" Diorio retrieves the ball and Ruth autographs it for him at Schenley Hotel. The Pirates win the game, 11-7.

MAY 31:

Babe Ruth goes out, not with a bang but a grounder. In his last major league at-bat, the Bambino bats against the Phillies' Jim Bivin and grounds out to first baseman Dolf Camilli of the Phillies. He leaves the game and is replaced in left field by Hal Lee.

SENATORS' OWNER CLARK GRIFFITH PREDICTS, "NIGHT BASEBALL IS A PASSING FAD." HE ADDS, "THERE IS NO CHANCE OF NIGHT BASEBALL EVER BECOMING POPULAR. . . HIGH-CLASS BASEBALL CANNOT BE PLAYED UNDER ARTIFICIAL LIGHTS." FRANK NAVIN, OWNER OF THE TIGERS, FORECASTS, "NIGHT BASEBALL WILL BE THE BEGINNING OF THE END FOR THE MAJOR LEAGUES." BROADCASTER RED BARBER IS MORE PRESCIENT, "AS SOON AS THE LIGHTS CAME ON, I KNEW THEY WERE THERE TO STAY."

JUNE 1:

At Yankee Stadium, New York sets a major league record for home runs with no one on base – six. Connecting for solo homers are Bill Dickey (twice), Frank Crosetti, Ben Chapman, George Selkirk and Robert "Red" Rolfe. The one Red Sox homer is hit by Baldomero "Mel" Almedo with a runner on, but it is not enough as the Yankees beat the Red Sox, 7-2.

JUNE 2:

It's the end of the road – and what a road – for Babe Ruth. Unhappy with the role to which the Braves have relegated him and batting .181, the Bambino announces his retirement. He leaves baseball as its greatest power hitter with 714 career home runs and a .690 slugging average. According to Roger Kahn, Babe Ruth earned $1,076,474 for playing baseball – plus endorsements and other income.

JUNE 3:

The Indians score an AL record seven runs in the 14th inning to beat the Red Sox, 11-4.

MAY 31
In his last major league at-bat, with the Braves, Babe Ruth hits a ground-ball out.

JULY 5
Brothers Tony and Al Cuccinello hit homers – Tony for the Dodgers, Al for the Giants.

JUNE 5:

In Pittsburgh, Dizzy Dean turns petulant when his Cardinals' teammates make two errors leading to four unearned runs. Dean begins lobbing the ball and the Pirates tally four more times, leading to a dispute with Joe "Ducky" Medwick. Dean reportedly tells Medwick, "I'll punch you in your Hungarian beezer." He and brother Paul advance on the outfielder, who takes up a bat and warns, "Keep coming, brothers Dean. Come on, both of you. I'll separate you real good." The Cardinals get between them. Medwick subsequently hits a grand slam, returns to the dugout, and spits water all over Dean's shoes, telling him, "see if you can hold that lead, gutless."

JUNE 6:

The Indians' veteran players go public about their dissatisfaction with manager Walter Johnson. They place an ad in today's newspapers fingering the Big Train as the cause of the dissension on the team.

JUNE 8:

The League Park crowd in Cleveland is supportive of Indians' manager Walter Johnson in his controversy with his players. The scorecards contain an article favoring the Big Train. Mel Harder pitches Cleveland to a 3-2 win over the Browns.

JUNE 11:

In St. Louis, Dizzy Dean is the target of the hometown fans, who throw lemons at him when he takes the mound against the Cubs. After crying, Dean composes himself and six-hits Chicago for a 13-2 win.

JUNE 28:

The Indians' Earl Averill has his consecutive game streak ended at 673 when he is injured by fireworks and is unable to play today.

JULY 5:

At the Polo Grounds, Tony Cuccinello of the Dodgers hits a home run against the Giants. His brother Al Cuccinello answers with a home run for the Giants. The Dodgers win the game, 14-4.

JULY 8:

In Cleveland, the American League wins its third straight All-Star Game, 3-1. Lefty Gomez of the Yankees pitches six innings, gives up three hits, and is the winning pitcher. Jimmie Foxx drives in three with a two-run homer and a single. Bill Walker is the losing pitcher.

Despite having 110 RBI by the All-Star break, Tigers' first baseman Hank Greenberg is not picked for the AL squad. The AL's first basemen for the game are Lou Gehrig and Jimmie Foxx.

JULY 10:

The first major league home run in a night game is hit by the Reds' Babe Herman against the Dodgers. The Reds win, 15-2.

JULY 28:

Slightly more than a year after his life-threatening skull fracture, 36-year-old Yankee outfielder Earle Combs retires. He was hitting .282 in 89 games this season. Combs, who has a lifetime batting average of .325, will become a Yankee coach.

JULY 31:

The sixth night game held at Cincinnati's Crosley Field is a chaotic affair. Almost incidental is the Reds 4-3 victory over the Cardinals in 10 innings. An overflow crowd spills on to the field during the game. In the fourth inning, fans are removed from the outfield and many then crowd along the sidelines and behind the plate, talking to the players, making it necessary to protect the Reds and Cardinals and their equipment. In the eighth inning with one out, the Cardinals ahead, 2-1, and the Reds' Sammy Byrd on first base, a nightclub singer identified as Kitty Burke grabs a bat from Babe Herman and steps up to the plate. Paul Dean, pitching for St. Louis, throws her an under-hand toss. She hits it back to Dean, who throws her out at first. Cardinals' manager Frankie Frisch argues – in vain – that the out should count. The Cardinals later claim that the unrestrained crowd made it impossible for the umpires to make impartial calls.

AUGUST 1:

Judge Emil Fuchs and associates sell the Boston Braves to Charles F. Adams, owner of the Boston Bruins hockey team.

AUGUST 5:

Lou Gehrig, suffering a back ailment, gives way to pinch hitter Myril Hoag in the

TRIVIA

Three baseball movies premiere: *Alibi Ike* starring Joe E. Brown as a Cubs rookie and 19-year-old Olivia De Havilland, based on a story by Ring Lardner; *Dizzy and Daffy* starring the Dean brothers; and *Swell-Head*, starring Wallace Ford.

LEAGUE

The Indians sign 16-year-old right-handed pitcher Bob Feller for a $1 million bonus.

"No one can tell you how to hit home runs. You either have the natural strength and reflexes, or you don't."
– *Hank Greenberg*

fourth inning of today's game against the Red Sox in Boston. Jack Saltgaver takes Gehrig's place in the field. The Yanks win, 10-2.

The fans might support Cleveland manager Walter Johnson, but management doesn't. Indians' president Alva Bradley announces Johnson has been allowed to "resign" and is being replaced by Steve O'Neill. Johnson was informed of the decision on July 29. Cleveland was 46-48 under the Big Train.

AUGUST 14:

He learned hitting along with pitching. Tigers' pitcher Lynwood "Schoolboy" Rowe has a double, a triple, three singles, and three RBI in an 18-2 Tiger victory over the Senators.

AUGUST 26:

White Sox first baseman Henry "Zeke" Bonura, regarded as one of baseball's slowest runners, steals home against the Yankees. Chicago wins, 9-8, in 15 innings.

AUGUST 31:

Frank Robinson is born in Beaumont, Texas.

Vern Kennedy of the White Sox no-hits the Indians, 5-0. Kennedy helps his own cause with a bases-loaded triple. He walks four and strikes out five; the White Sox make no errors. The losing pitcher is Willis Hudlin.

SEPTEMBER 7:

At Fenway Park, the Indians execute a triple play with an unusual beginning. With Oral Hildebrand on the mound and the bases loaded in the ninth inning, Joe Cronin hits a line drive off the head of Indians' third baseman Odell Hale. The ball rebounds to shortstop Bill Knickerbocker who gets one runner for the second out and throws to second baseman Roy Hughes to complete the triple killing. The Indians, who led the game 5-1 going into the ninth, hold on for a 5-3 win.

SEPTEMBER 12:

The Cardinals' Joe Medwick has his 28-game consecutive hit streak snapped today by the Giants. The streak began on August 17 against the Giants; Medwick hits .358 in the 28 games.

SEPTEMBER 17:

Dodgers' outfielder Len Koenecke is killed in a fight on a chartered plane over Toronto, Canada. Koenecke was cut by

IN *THE HISTORY OF AMERICAN LEAGUE BASEBALL SINCE 1901*, GLENN DICKEY WRITES, "THERE HAS NEVER BEEN ANOTHER PLAYER LIKE BABE RUTH. SOME MAY ARGUE THAT TY COBB WAS THE BETTER PLAYER, BUT THERE IS ONE SIGNIFICANT DIFFERENCE BETWEEN THE TWO: COBB PLAYED THE EXISTING GAME BETTER THAN ANYBODY ELSE, BUT RUTH COMPLETELY CHANGED THE GAME. BASEBALL WAS NOT THE SAME AFTER RUTH."

LEAGUE

Bob Quinn assumes ownership of the Boston Braves from Charles Adams – who is part owner of the Suffolks Downs racetrack – after the season. Kenesaw Mountain Landis frowns on associations between gambling and baseball, and Adams, essentially given his choice between baseball and horses, apparently decides not to test the commissioner's resolve, and chooses the ponies.

SEPTEMBER 12
The Cardinals' Joe Medwick's 28-game hitting streak is snapped by the Giants.

SEPTEMBER 29
The Cubs' Augie Galan completes the season without having hit into a double play.

Brooklyn yesterday because of discipline problems, despite a respectable .283 average. Despondent over his release, he boards an American Airlines plane from St. Louis, but, appearing drunk, he knocks down a stewardess, Eleanor Woodward, and is ordered off the plane. He then charters a three-seater to Buffalo. In mid-air, he reaches for the controls and gets into a fight with Irwin Davis, a friend of pilot William J. Mulqueeney. The pilot joins the fray and, after some 10 to 15 minutes, hits Koenecke with a fire extinguisher. Mulqueeney then lands the damaged plane on a racetrack near Toronto. Koenecke was 31 years old.

SEPTEMBER 21:

The Tigers take two from the visiting Browns, 6-2 and 2-0, clinching the AL pennant. The winning pitchers are Tommy Bridges and Elden Auker.

SEPTEMBER 22:

The Cubs beat the Pirates, 2-0, for their 18th consecutive win.

SEPTEMBER 27:

The Cubs win two from the Cardinals today in Sportsman's Park to extend their winning streak to 21 consecutive games and wrap up the NL pennant. Bill Lee wins his 20th game in the opener, 6-2, aided by Fred Lindstrom's four RBI. The Cubs' 5-3 victory in the nightcap clinches the National League pennant.

SEPTEMBER 29:

Despite a victory over the Giants today, the Braves finish with the most losses ever – 115. They win only 38 and finish 61 1/2 games behind the first-place Cubs. The Braves are 25-50 at home and 12-65 on the road.

Cubs' left fielder Augie Galan completes his 154th game of the season today without ever hitting into a double play – setting a modern major league record. The Cardinals beat the Cubs, 2-1. However, Galan did hit into a triple play in the 11th inning of a game against the Reds, won by Cincinnati, 8-4, in 12 innings on April 21. In his 16-year career, Galan bats 5,937 times and hits into 72 double plays.

REGULAR SEASON WRAP-UP:

With a record of 100-54, the Cubs, managed by Charlie Grimm, win the NL pennant by four games over the Cardinals. NL Most Valuable Player Charles "Gabby" Hartnett hits .344. Other .300 hitters are Billy Herman (.341), Stan Hack (.311), Frank Demaree (.325), and Augie Galan (.314). The top pitchers are Bill Lee (20-6) and Lon Warneke (20-13). The Pirates' Arky Vaughan hits .385 to become the second shortstop in the 20th century to lead the NL in batting; the first was Honus Wagner, also of Pittsburgh.

Gordon "Mickey" Cochrane manages the Tigers to a 93-58 record and their second straight AL pennant – three games up on the Yankees. Hank Greenberg hits .328 with 36 homers and 170 RBI. Other .300 hitters are Charlie Gehringer (.330), Pete Fox (.321), and Cochrane (.319). Tommy Bridges, at 21-10, is the team's only 20-game winner.

OCTOBER 2:

World Series, game one. In Detroit, Lon Warneke four-hits the Tigers, 3-0; Augie Galan drives in two runs and Gabby Hartnett one. The losing pitcher is Lynwood "Schoolboy" Rowe, who allows seven hits but sets up a Cubs' two-run first inning with his own error.

From Baseball: The Biographical Encyclopedia*: "St. Louis sportswriter J. Roy Stockton dubbed Lon Warneke 'the Arkansas Hummingbird' – after what Stockton termed his 'darting form of delivery.' That delivery was good enough to earn the big right-hander the National League lead in victories three times and in shutouts twice. Yet Warneke might never have made it to the major leagues had it not been for catcher Zack Taylor's advice. Taylor counseled Warneke to watch the plate instead of his feet, noting that Warneke 'keeps lookin' at his dogs instead of the hitter.' Once that flaw was corrected, there was no stopping Warneke. In high school, Warneke's diamond experience was limited to first base. He became a pitcher by throwing batting practice for Houston of the Texas League."*

OCTOBER 3:

World Series, game two. Tigers' Hank Greenberg answers with his bat; he hits a two-run homer off

TRIVIA

"I Can't Get to First Base with You," by Eleanor (Mrs. Lou) Gehrig and Fred Fischer, includes the lyric, "You got me crying, alibiing, making me blue, I can't get to first base with you."

LEAGUE

At baseball's winter meetings, held in December, Ford Frick gets a new two-year contract as NL president. The AL turns down night baseball.

Guy Bush, who served up the last of Babe Ruth's homers, recalled later, "I never saw a ball hit so hard before or since. He was fat and old, but he still had that great swing. I can't forget the last one he hit off me. It's probably still going."

HISTORY

The Pittsburgh Crawfords are the 1935 Negro National League champions, defeating the New York Cubans, four games to three. Five future Hall of Fame members are on the Crawfords' 1935 roster; only one – Satchel Paige – will ever play in the major leagues. The others are Oscar Charleston, Judy Johnson, Cool Papa Bell, and Josh Gibson.

Charlie Root – one of his tormentors – in the first inning of an 8-3 Tigers' victory in Detroit. The Tigers' Tommy Bridges pitches a complete-game six-hitter for the win. Root takes the loss. The bad news: Greenberg breaks his wrist during the game.

OCTOBER 4:

World Series, game three. In Chicago, with Greenberg injured, Marv Owen moves to first base and Herman "Flea" Clifton takes his spot at third. Despite the shifts, the Tigers win, 6-5, in 11 innings on a single by Joyner "Jo-Jo" White scoring Marv Owen. Schoolboy Rowe gets the win with four innings of relief. Larry French is charged with the loss. Frank Demaree homers for the Cubs.

OCTOBER 5:

World Series, game four. In Chicago, the Detroit Tigers win their third in a row, 2-1. Consecutive errors by left fielder Augie Galan and shortstop Billy Jurges in the sixth inning give the Tigers the winning run. Alvin "General" Crowder allows only five hits and gets the win. James "Tex" Carleton is charged with the loss.

OCTOBER 6:

World Series, game five. In Chicago, the Cubs keep their championship hopes alive with a 3-1 victory. A Billy Herman triple followed by Chuck Klein's homer produce two runs in the third. The winning pitcher, Lon Warneke, pitches six shutout innings, but has to depart with a sore shoulder, and Bill Lee finishes the game. The losing pitcher is Schoolboy Rowe.

OCTOBER 7:

World Series, game six. The Tigers beat the Cubs, 4-3, in Detroit to take their first-ever World Championship. Leon "Goose" Goslin singles in Mickey Cochrane with the winning run in the ninth with two out. Billy Herman hits a two-run homer for the Cubs in the fifth. The winning pitcher is Tommy Bridges, who goes the distance despite allowing 12 hits. Larry French, who also yields 12 hits, gets the loss. Hank Greenberg remains sidelined with a broken wrist on Yom Kippur, the Jewish Day of Atonement. Pete Fox leads all hitters with .385; Gehringer hits .375. Each has four RBI. Billy Herman and Chuck Klein at .333 are Chicago's leading series hitters.

POST-SEASON

OCTOBER 27:

Dizzy Dean is the winner and loser in an exhibition game in Los Angeles. He pitches three innings for a minor league team. With his side trailing 2-0, he takes the mound for the major league team, which wins the game, 12-4. Starting pitcher Newt Kimball failed to complete the required minimum for the victory so it goes to Dean.

NOVEMBER 6:

Billy Sunday dies in Chicago at age 72. The world-famous evangelist played major league baseball from 1883 to 1890 with Chicago, Pittsburgh, and Philadelphia in the National League. An outfielder with a .248 lifetime average, Sunday used baseball metaphors in his sermons.

NOVEMBER 9:

Bob Gibson is born in Omaha.

NOVEMBER 13:

Tigers' owner Frank Navin dies of a heart attack while horseback riding in Detroit. After Navin's estate is settled, Walter O. Briggs becomes sole owner of the Tigers.

DECEMBER 10:

Connie Mack's cash register rings up another sale and one of baseball's top sluggers is heading north. Mack sends first baseman Jimmie Foxx (.346, 36 homers, 115 RBI) and pitcher Johnny Marcum (17-12, 4.08) to the Boston Red Sox. In return, the Athletics get pitcher Gordon Rhodes (2-10, 5.41 ERA), minor league catcher George Savino, and $150,000 in cash.

The Tigers buy outfielder Al Simmons (.267, 16 homers, 79 RBI) from the White Sox for $75,000 in cash.

DECEMBER 17:

The Red Sox obtain outfielder Henry "Heinie" Manush (.273, four homers) from the Senators for outfielders Roy Johnson (.315, three homers) and Carl Reynolds (.270, six homers).

DECEMBER 30:

Sandy Koufax (born Sanford Braun) is born in Brooklyn, New York.

OCTOBER 7
The Tigers beat the Cubs, 4-3, and Detroit wins its first-ever World Championship.

THE BEST OF 1935

NATIONAL LEAGUE

HITTERS

Batting Average:
Joseph "Arky"Vaughan, Pittsburgh Pirates, .385

Slugging Average:
Joseph Vaughan, .607

Home Runs:
Wally Berger, Boston Braves, 34

Runs Batted In:
Wally Berger, 130

Hits:
Billy Herman, Chicago Cubs, 227

Stolen Bases:
Augie Galan, Chicago Cubs, 22

PITCHERS

Wins:
Dizzy Dean, St. Louis Cardinals, 28

Strikeouts:
Dizzy Dean, 190

Earned Run Average:
Darrell "Cy" Blanton, 2.58

Winning Percentage:
Big Bill Lee, Chicago Cubs, .769

Saves:
Emil "Dutch" Leonard, Brooklyn Dodgers, 8

Most Valuable Player:
Charles "Gabby" Hartnett, Chicago Cubs

AMERICAN LEAGUE

HITTERS

Batting Average:
Charles "Buddy" Myer, Washington Senators, .349

Slugging Average:
Jimmie Foxx, Philadelphia Athletics, .636

Home Runs:
Jimmie Foxx; Hank Greenberg, Detroit Tigers, 36

Runs Batted In:
Hank Greenberg, 170

Hits
Joe Vosmik, Cleveland Indians, 216

Stolen Bases:
Bill Werber, Boston Red Sox, 29

PITCHERS

Wins:
Wes Ferrell, Boston Red Sox, 25

Strikeouts:
Tommy Bridges, Detroit Tigers, 163

Earned Run Average:
Lefty Grove, Boston Red Sox, 2.70

Winning Percentage:
Elden Auker, Detroit Tigers, .720

Saves:
Jack Knott, St. Louis Browns, 7

Most Valuable Player:
Hank Greenberg, Detroit Tigers

1936

"If Joe played in Fenway Park... he would have had 1,000 homers."
– Henry Kissinger on DiMaggio

NEWS

FDR SWAMPS ALF LANDON IN PRESIDENTIAL ELECTION; WINS 46 OF 48 STATES FOR SECOND TERM

HOOVER DAM OPENS ON ARIZONA-NEVADA BORDER

***LIFE* MAGAZINE DEBUTS**

Bruno Hauptmann executed for kidnapping and murder of Lindbergh baby

ENGLAND'S KING GEORGE V DIES

***SWING TIME* STARS FRED ASTAIRE AND GINGER ROGERS**

Margaret Mitchell's *Gone with the Wind* and Dale Carnegie's *How to Win Friends and Influence People* are published

THE SPANISH CIVIL WAR BEGINS

PRE-SEASON

JANUARY 4:

Once again, the Athletics trade established players for fringe players and cash. Going to the Red Sox are outfielder Roger "Doc" Cramer (.332, three homers) and infielder Eric "Boob" McNair (.270, four homers). In exchange, Philadelphia gets pitcher Henry Johnson (2-1, 5.52 ERA) and second baseman Al Niemiec, who hit .219 in 1934, his only major league season.

JANUARY 6:

Giants' owner Charles Stoneham dies in Hot Springs, Arkansas, of Bright's disease. His 32-year-old son, Horace, will assume ownership of the team.

JANUARY 30:

When quality is lacking, try distraction. After 115 losses last season, the Boston Braves come up with a program. They poll fans for a new team name; Bees is picked to replace Braves. The new name lasts through the 1940 season.

FEBRUARY 2:

The first Hall of Fame results are announced. In voting by the Baseball Writers' Association, the first Hall "class" is composed of Ty Cobb, Babe Ruth, Honus Wagner, Christy Mathewson, and Walter Johnson. Failing to be named on 75 percent of the ballots and not elected are Napoleon Lajoie, Tris Speaker, Cy Young, and Rogers Hornsby. A separate vote is conducted for pre-1900 players, but no one is chosen.

MARCH 1:

A nickname is created that lasts a lifetime. Dodgers' infielder-outfielder Stanley Bordagaray turns up at spring training camp in Daytona Beach, Florida, with a new look. He has a Vandyke beard and a handlebar mustache and is wearing a beret. Casey Stengel takes a look at his player and comments that it "looked like a little French waiter joined the club." But he tells Bordagaray, "Go shave it off before someone throws a ball at it and kills you." From that day on Bordagaray is known as Frenchy.

According to SABR-ite Neal McCabe, Bordagaray actually was nicknamed Frenchy as a child by his mother.

MARCH 9:

Hank Greenberg is a holdout as the Tigers begin spring training in Lakeland, Florida. Greenberg holds out for two weeks, then signs for $25,000.

MARCH 21:

First baseman Sunny Jim Bottomley (.258, one homer) is traded by the Reds to the Browns for infielder Johnny Burnett (.223).

APRIL 7:

The Yankees announce that heralded rookie Joe DiMaggio suffered a burned leg while receiving a diathermy treatment from team doctor Harry G. Jacobi. Last year with the San Francisco Seals, DiMaggio hit .398, had 34 homers, and drove in 154 runs; he was the Pacific Coast League's Most Valuable Player.

THE SEASON

APRIL 14:

On opening day in St. Louis, the Cardinals' Eddie Morgan becomes the first to hit a pinch-hit home run in his first major league at-bat. Morgan connects on the very first pitch he sees in the seventh inning. The Cubs win, 12-7.

MAY 3
The much-heralded Joe DiMaggio makes his Yankees debut, with a single in his first at-bat.

MAY 11
The Giants' Mel Ott drives in eight runs in a 13-12 victory over the Phillies.

MAY 3:

At Yankee Stadium, 25,530 anxious fans see 21-year-old Joe DiMaggio make his belated major league debut. Batting third and wearing number 9 against the Browns, DiMaggio singles to left field off Jack Knott in his first at-bat. DiMaggio adds a triple and another single in six at-bats; he scores three times and drives in a run. DiMaggio had 12 hits in 20 at-bats in spring training, but missed the start of the season because of a burned leg. The Yankees win today's game, 14-5; Lou Gehrig has four hits and bats in two runs. The winning pitcher is Johnny Murphy. Knott gets the loss.

MAY 10:

At Yankee Stadium, Joe DiMaggio hits his first major league homer – a 400-foot drive against George Turbeville. He also has three RBI and makes an outstanding catch in a 7-2 Yankee win over the Athletics.

MAY 11:

At Baker Bowl in Philadelphia, the Giants' Mel Ott drives in eight runs in a 13-12 victory over the Phillies.

MAY 14:

The AL is learning what the Pacific Coast League already knows about Joe DiMaggio. Today he has three doubles and a single as the Yankees beat the Browns, 6-1, in St. Louis.

MAY 21:

Chuck Klein goes home. The outfielder (.294) is traded back to Philadelphia, where he enjoyed his best years, along with pitcher Fabian Kowalik (0-2) and $50,000. In return, the Cubs get outfielder Ethan Allen (.296) and pitcher Curt Davis (2-4).

MAY 24:

The visiting Yankees smash the A's, 25-2, at Shibe Park with Tony Lazzeri doing most of the damage. Batting in the eighth spot, the Yankee second baseman hits three homers – including two grand slams – and a triple, driving in an AL record 11 runs. He also ties the major league record for extra-base hits in a game – four. His two-run triple in the eighth inning just misses being a homer. He hits his homers against George Turbeville in the second and Malton "Red" Bullock in the fifth. The 32-year-old Lazzeri now has seven homers in his last four games and six in his last three. Overshadowed by Lazzeri's offensive outburst are Joe DiMaggio, who hits a homer, double, and single, and Ben Chapman, with two doubles and five walks. Frank Crosetti adds another Yankees' round-tripper. The winning pitcher is Monte Pearson; Turbeville gets the loss. The Yankees complete a three-game weekend with 52 runs on 49 hits, including 13 homers.

JUNE 14:

The Yankees trade center fielder Ben Chapman (.266) to the Senators for outfielder Jake Powell (.290). The departure of Chapman opens center field for rookie Joe DiMaggio, who has been playing left field.

JUNE 17:

The Yankees' Charles "Red" Ruffing sets a hitting record for AL pitchers today with 10 total bases. In the opener of a doubleheader, Ruffing has four hits – including two homers – and beats the Indians, 15-4. In game 2, Monte Pearson has four hits and four RBI while pitching the Yankees to a 12-2 win. New York has 19 hits in each game.

JUNE 24:

In Chicago, Joe DiMaggio hits a two-run homer against Ray Phillips and a three-run blast off Russell "Red" Evans as part of a 10-run Yankee fifth inning. DiMaggio is the third player in AL history with two homers in an inning. He also has two doubles in the game. Jake Powell hits a grand slam homer between DiMaggio's two round- trippers. The Yankees win, 18-11.

JUNE 29:

Harmon Killebrew is born in Payette, Idaho.

JULY 2:

Indians' reserve outfielder Bruce Campbell is inserted in the lineup to replace the injured Earl Averill in a doubleheader against the visiting Browns. Campbell responds with a seven-for-seven day. He has six hits in six at-bats in the opener and is one for one in the nightcap. The Indians win both games, 14-6 and 4-2.

JULY 6:

Bob Feller pitches in an exhibition game against the Cardinals

TRIVIA

Because too many baseballs are being hit onto Lansdowne Street and breaking windows, the Boston Red Sox top the leftfield wall at Fenway Park with a 23-foot screen.

HISTORY

In May, at Griffith Stadium, the Senators' Jake Powell runs into Hank Greenberg at first base. Greenberg suffers a broken wrist and appears in only 12 games in 1936.

HISTORY

The Washington Elite Giants win the Negro National League first half. The Pittsburgh Crawfords are the top team in the second half. No playoff is held between the two leaders.

Bob Feller was still in high school when he signed with Cleveland.

at Cleveland's League Park with 12,000 on hand. The 17-year-old gets the first batter he faces – Ambrose "Brusie" Ogrodowski – on a bunt. Leo Durocher works the count to 2-2 and makes believe he is hiding behind the water cooler. When he returns to the plate, he goes down swinging, making him Feller's first ever major league strikeout victim. Feller works three innings and fans eight – including Durocher twice – with his blazing fastball.

JULY 7:

The NL scores its first win in All-Star Game competition, 4-3, at Braves Field, despite a Lou Gehrig homer. Augie Galan homers for the NL. With Joe "Ducky" Medwick singling in the winning run in the fifth, Dizzy Dean gets the victory. Lefty Grove is the loser. Joe DiMaggio becomes the first rookie to play in an All-Star Game; he is hitless in five at-bats and makes an error in right field.

JULY 10:

Phillies' slugger Chuck Klein today becomes the fourth major leaguer to hit four homers in a game. Klein's homers lead the Phillies past the Pirates, 9-6, in 10 innings at Forbes Field, a tough stadium for longball hitters. Klein's shots are hit in the first, fifth, seventh, and tenth innings, and all go into the right-field seats. Klein has six RBI and just misses a homer in the second when right fielder Paul Waner catches his drive at the wall. William "Bucky" Walters gets the win. Bill Swift, who yields Klein's tie-breaking bases-empty home run in the 10th, is charged with the loss.

JULY 17:

Jimmie Foxx of the Athletics hits a Ruthian home run. It soars over the upper deck roof in Comiskey Park's left field and out onto the street.

JULY 19:

Bob Feller makes his official major league debut, pitching one inning of relief against the Senators in Washington, D.C. He allows no hits and no runs, walking two. Officially, Feller records no strikeouts. But in his autobiography, he writes that he fanned John "Buddy" Lewis and that the Senators' third baseman corroborates his recollection. However, it does not appear in the box score.

JULY 21:

With three safeties today against the Giants, the Cardinals' Joe "Ducky" Medwick extends his consecutive hit streak to 10, tying an NL record. Medwick got his hits over three games. The Giants win today's game on a 10th-inning homer by Dick Bartell.

JULY 23:

Don Drysdale is born in Van Nuys, California.

JULY 30:

The Red Sox become the first to fly as a team, when they travel by air from St. Louis to Chicago, accompanied by AL president Will Harridge. Five players skip the flight. Previously groups of players have traveled by plane.

AUGUST 23:

In Cleveland's League Park, Bob Feller makes his first major league start, striking out the first eight Browns to face him. He opens the game by fanning Lyn Lary on three pitches and makes the Browns' shortstop the final out of the game as well as his 15th strikeout victim. Feller allows only six hits and walks four, and the Indians win, 4-1. The losing pitcher is Earl Caldwell.

AUGUST 25:

The Boston Bees humiliate the Cardinals in a doubleheader, knocking St. Louis out of first place. In game one, the Bees build on an 11-run first inning – which includes a record seven doubles – to beat the Cardinals, 20-5. In the nightcap, the Bees bang out 25 hits in a 5-4 victory.

AUGUST 27:

After the Dodgers make four errors behind him in a 6-3 loss to the Pirates, Van Lingle Mungo is upset by what he regards as lack of support. He jumps the team in Pittsburgh and returns to Brooklyn. Following a conversation with Dodger president Steve McKeever, Mungo rejoins the team.

JULY 10
Phillies' Chuck Klein becomes the fourth major leaguer to hit four homers in a game.

SEPTEMBER 13
Cleveland's teen pitcher Bob Feller fans 17 A's – tying the NL and setting an AL mark.

AUGUST 28:

Yankee pitchers continue to flex their muscles. In game two of a doubleheader at Yankee Stadium, pitcher Johnny Murphy has five hits and five RBI in five at-bats; he also scores three times. Two of Murphy's hits come in an 11-run second. The Yankees win, 19-4, after taking the opener, 14-5.

SEPTEMBER 9:

The Yankees sweep the Indians, 11-3 and 12-9, to wrap up their eighth AL pennant. It is New York's 138th game of the season – the earliest clinching in AL history. Lou Gehrig hits a grand slam homer.

SEPTEMBER 11:

Once again, Connie Mack is short of pitchers on a road trip, and today it is Horace "Hod" Lisenbee who pays the price. The 37-year-old right-hander labors without relief for nine innings against the White Sox in Comiskey Park, yielding 26 hits and losing, 17-2. Lisenbee ties a record set by seminarian Aloysius Travers, who pitched one game for the Tigers in 1912 and gave up 26 hits. The winning pitcher today is Monte Stratton. Minter "Jackie" Hayes homers for Chicago.

SEPTEMBER 13:

Teenager Bob Feller continues to overpower adults. He ties a major league record and sets an AL mark by striking out 17 batters. In the first game of a doubleheader at Cleveland's Municipal Stadium, Rapid Robert limits Philadelphia to two hits and strikes out every batter except pinch hitter Charlie Moss, who gets one of Feller's walks. Feller's 17th strikeout victim is George Puccinelli, who takes a called third strike. The Athletics' starting pitcher, Randy Gumpert, at age 18, is not much older than Feller. The Indians beat the Athletics, 5-2.

His rookie season over, Feller returns home to Van Meter, Iowa, to graduate from high school.

SEPTEMBER 22:

The Tigers bounce the Browns, 12-0 and 14-0, in the most one-sided doubleheader shutout sweep ever. Elden Auker and Tommy Bridges get the wins.

SEPTEMBER 23:

The Indians' Hal Trosky hits his 42nd homer of the year in a 17-8 victory over the White Sox. A bright spot for Chicago is Luke Appling, who hits a homer, a double, and two singles to finish the season at .388, sewing up the AL batting title. Bob Feller, who fans 10 in the game, finds himself in the center of a controversy. Lee Kayser, president of Des Moines in the Western League, charges Feller was illegally signed by Cleveland and is his team's property.

Appling's .388 is the highest batting average by a shortstop in this century, and he is the first White Sox batter to lead the AL in hitting. The Dodgers' Ernest "Babe" Phelps hits .367, the highest ever for a catcher with 300 at-bats in a season.

SEPTEMBER 25:

The Cardinals' Joe "Ducky" Medwick doubles against Ray Davis in today's 3-2 loss at Cincinnati. It is Medwick's 64th two-bagger of the season, an NL record.

SEPTEMBER 26:

The Giants' Carl Hubbell beats the Phillies, 5-4, for his 16th consecutive victory. It also is the 26th win of the year for King Carl, who is two shy of Richard "Rube" Marquard's 1912 major league record. Hubbell began his streak on July 17, but with five games to go this season, he is unlikely to extend it this year.

SEPTEMBER 27:

At Sportsman's Park in St. Louis, Walter Alston of the Cardinals replaces Johnny Mize at first base. He strikes out against Lon Warneke in his only major league at-bat and makes one error in two chances. The Cubs win the game, 6-3.

Alston goes on to fashion a Hall of Fame career as a manager, spending 23 years with the Dodgers and winning five World Championships and seven pennants.

SEPTEMBER 28:

Outfielder Henry "Heinie" Manush (.291 in 82 games) is released by the Red Sox. Manush is a 10-time .300 hitter.

REGULAR SEASON WRAP-UP:

The Yankees, at 102-51 under Joe McCarthy, run away with the AL pennant, beating the Tigers by 19 1/2 games. Six regulars hit .300 or better: Lou Gehrig (.354 with 49 homers and 152 RBI), Robert

TRIVIA

Bob Feller throws out the first ball at the Illinois State Amateur Baseball Championship in Illinois. A 10-year-old obtains Feller's autograph on the ball. In 1948, the youngster, Robin Roberts, makes his major league debut with the Phillies.

"I want to thank the good Lord for making me a Yankee."
– Joe DiMaggio

HISTORY

Lou Gehrig has a record 14 homers against the Indians in 1936. His favorite victims are Lloyd Brown (four) and Johnny Allen (three).

"Red" Rolfe (.319), George Selkirk (.308), Jake Powell (.306), Joe DiMaggio (.323), and Bill Dickey (.362). Five Yankees have 100 or more RBI: DiMaggio, Tony Lazzeri, Dickey, Selkirk, and Gehrig. Charles "Red" Ruffing is the top pitcher at 20-12. Bill Terry's Giants finish at 92-62, five games ahead of the Cardinals and Cubs, who tie for second in the NL. Carl Hubbell is the Giants' ace at 26-6. Mel Ott hits .328 with 33 homers and 135 RBI. The team's only other regular at .300 is Joe Moore with .301.

SEPTEMBER 30:

World Series, game one. The Subway Series opens in the rain at the Polo Grounds. Carl Hubbell seven-hits the Yankees, winning, 6-1. The Yankees' lone run is a homer into the upper deck in right field by George Selkirk in his first ever series at-bat. The loss ends the Yankees' 12-game series winning streak. Dick Bartell homers for the Giants. Red Ruffing gets the loss.

OCTOBER 2:

World Series, game two. The Yankees flex their muscles at the Polo Grounds, overwhelming the Giants, 18-4, on 17 hits, with President Franklin D. Roosevelt in attendance. The record 18-run outburst is highlighted by a bases-loaded homer by Tony Lazzeri and a three-run shot by Bill Dickey; each has five RBI. Every starter has at least one hit and scores at least once (Frank Crosetti tallies a record four runs). Vernon "Lefty" Gomez goes all the way for the win, allowing six hits. Hal Schumacher gets the loss.

OCTOBER 3:

World Series, game three. The teams cross the river into the Bronx, where the Yankees win again, 2-1, behind the pitching of Bump Hadley. Frank Crosetti tallies in Jake Powell with the winning run in the eighth and Fred Fitzsimmons gets the loss. Lou Gehrig homers for the Yankees, Jimmy Ripple for the Giants.

OCTOBER 4:

World Series, game four. At Yankee Stadium, Lou Gehrig hits a two-run homer and Monte Pearson limits the Giants to seven hits in a 5-2 win. Carl Hubbell pitches seven innings and gets the loss.

OCTOBER 5:

World Series, game five. The Giants stay alive with a 5-4 win in 10 innings at Yankee Stadium. Hal Schumacher goes all the way, despite 10 Yankee hits, and gets the win. Pat Malone, in relief of Red Ruffing, is the loser. Bill Terry's sacrifice fly gives the Giants the winning run. George Selkirk homers for the Yankees.

OCTOBER 6:

World Series, game six. Yankee power is the difference in a 17-hit, 13-4 victory over the Giants for the World Championship. A seven-run ninth inning in which the Yankees get five hits and four walks ices the game at the Polo Grounds. Jake Powell hits a two-run home run for the Yankees; Joe Moore and Mel Ott homer with no one on for the Giants. Lefty Gomez gets the win; Fred Fitzsimmons is charged with the loss. The Yankees' Jake Powell leads all hitters with .455; Red Rolfe bats .400. Gehrig (five RBI) and Selkirk have two homers each. Dick Bartell hits .381 for the Giants.

POST-SEASON

OCTOBER 8:

The Arkansas Hummingbird becomes a Cardinal. Pitcher Lon Warneke (16-13, 3.44 ERA) is traded to St. Louis by the Cubs for first baseman James "Ripper" Collins (.292, 13 homers) and pitcher Roy Parmelee (11-11, 4.56 ERA).

NOVEMBER 5:

Former spitball pitcher Burleigh Grimes is named manager of the Dodgers, replacing Casey Stengel.

NOVEMBER 7:

Donald L. Barnes, a 42-year-old loan company owner, buys the Browns from the estate of Phil Ball. He pays $325,000, and also receives 80 percent ownership of the San Antonio Missions in the Texas League.

NOVEMBER 29:

The Red Sox sign free-agent catcher Johnny Peacock for $10,000. Peacock was "freed" from the Reds' organization by Commissioner Landis.

DECEMBER 10:

Despite the fact that Bob Feller was still in high school when he was signed by Indians' scout Cy Slapnicka, Commissioner Landis awards the young fireballer to the Indians in the dispute with a Western League team. Des Moines gets cash compensation.

SEPTEMBER 30
The Giants top the Yankees, 6-1, in game one of the Subway Series.

OCTOBER 6
A 17-hit, 13-4 victory by the Yankees gives the team another World Championship.

THE BEST OF 1936

NATIONAL LEAGUE

HITTERS

Batting Average:
Paul Waner, Pittsburgh Pirates, .373

Slugging Average:
Mel Ott, New York Giants, .588

Home Runs:
Mel Ott, 33

Runs Batted In:
Joe "Ducky" Medwick, St. Louis Cardinals, 138

Hits:
Joe Medwick, 223

Stolen Bases:
John "Pepper" Martin, St. Louis Cardinals, 23

PITCHERS

Wins:
Carl Hubbell, New York Giants, 26

Strikeouts:
Van Lingle Mungo, Brooklyn Dodgers, 238

Earned Run Average:
Carl Hubbell, 2.31

Winning Percentage:
Carl Hubbell, .813

Saves:
Dizzy Dean, St. Louis Cardinals, 11

Most Valuable Player:
Carl Hubbell, New York Giants

AMERICAN LEAGUE

HITTERS

Batting Average:
Luke Appling, Chicago White Sox, .388

Slugging Average:
Lou Gehrig, New York Yankees, .696

Home Runs:
Lou Gehrig, 49

Runs Batted In:
Hal Trosky, Cleveland Indians, 162

Hits
Earl Averill, Cleveland Indians, 232

Stolen Bases:
Lynn Lary, St. Louis Browns, 37

PITCHERS

Wins:
Tommy Bridges, Detroit Tigers, 23

Strikeouts:
Tommy Bridges, 175

Earned Run Average:
Robert "Lefty" Grove, Boston Red Sox, 2.81

Winning Percentage:
Monte Pearson, New York Yankees, .731

Saves:
Perce "Pat" Malone, New York Yankees, 9

Most Valuable Player:
Lou Gehrig, New York Yankees

LEAGUE

At the winter meetings in December, AL owners reverse a 1935 decision and give the Browns permission to play night games next season. They also effect a rule change: AL batters now will need a minimum of 400 at-bats to win a batting championship.

1937

NEWS

AIRSHIP *HINDENBERG* BURNS AT LAKEHURST, NEW JERSEY, AFTER TRANSATLANTIC FLIGHT; 37 DIE

GOLDEN GATE BRIDGE DEDICATED IN CALIFORNIA

OIL MAGNATE, PHILANTHROPIST JOHN D. ROCKEFELLER DIES

WALT DISNEY'S *SNOW WHITE AND THE SEVEN DWARFS* PREMIERES

John Steinbeck publishes *Of Mice and Men*

Pablo Picasso paints his cubist masterpiece, *Guernica*

Frank Lloyd Wright completes *"Falling Water"*

Amelia Earhart and her aircraft disappear

George Gershwin dies at age 38

PRE-SEASON

JANUARY:

Cy Young, Tris Speaker, Connie Mack, Napoleon "Larry" Lajoie, Byron "Ban" Johnson, John J. McGraw, and George Wright are elected to the Hall of Fame. Tris Speaker, a center-field paragon, played 22 years, batting .345 with 3,514 hits, 792 doubles, 223 triples, and 1,882 runs. He hit .300 or more 18 times. Speaker also managed for six seasons, leading the Indians to the 1920 World Series championship. Cy Young pitched in the majors for 22 years, compiling astonishing statistics, including a 511-316 record with a 2.63 ERA, 750 complete games, 76 shutouts, and 7,356 innings. He pitched in the 1903 World Series for the Boston Pilgrims and was 2-1. Connie Mack, an AL pioneer, is still actively managing. After managing Pittsburgh from 1894 to 1896, he took over as skipper of the Philadelphia Athletics and remained there to the present day. His Athletics have won nine pennants and five World Series. Mack played 11 seasons of major league ball, hitting .245. McGraw managed the New York Giants from 1902 to 1932, winning nine pennants and three World Series. As a player, he spent 16 seasons in the majors, batting .333 and stealing 436 bases. He died in 1934. Lajoie, an infielder for 21 seasons, batted .338 with 3,244 hits, 658 doubles, and 382 stolen bases. His career high was .422 for the 1901 Athletics. A three-time batting champion, he hit .300 or more 16 times. Lajoie managed Cleveland from 1905 to 1909. Wright, a shortstop, was the first player signed when his brother, Harry Wright, put together the professional Cincinnati Red Stockings in 1876. In seven seasons, he batted .256. On August 21, Wright will die at the age of 90. Johnson was the driving force in elevating the American League to a major circuit. A former journalist, he was the AL's president from 1901 to 1927. Johnson passed away in 1931.

APRIL 3:

Dizzy Dean is the center of an ugly incident during spring training in Tampa. Dean confronts Jack Miley of the New York *Daily News* in the lobby of the Tampa Terrace Hotel and complains about a critical article. Dean takes a swing at Miley. Paul Dean, followed by other Cardinal players, attacks the journalist, who is punched in the eye. The following day, Miley writes, "If the Cards haven't any more punch than they showed in that little impromptu battle... they'll finish the season in the International League."

APRIL 4:

The Senators buy outfielder Al Simmons (.327, 13 homers) from the Tigers for $15,000.

APRIL 14:

Commissioner Kenesaw Mountain Landis "liberates" another minor league player, and this one gets rich quick. Landis rules that the Indians deliberately kept Tommy Henrich from moving up from the minors to the majors; he declares the outfielder-first baseman a free agent. The Yankees shock baseball by signing Henrich for $25,000; he is temporarily assigned to the Newark Bears in the International League.

Former major league player and manager Edward Hugh "Ned"

Renowned rhymer Ogden Nash once celebrated Cy Young in verse: "Y is for Young, The Magnificent Cy; People batted against him, But I never knew why."

Hanlon dies in Baltimore, at the age of 79. Hanlon managed for 19 years, leading the Baltimore Orioles to three first-place finishes and the Brooklyn Superbas to two. An outfielder, he batted .260 in 13 seasons.

THE SEASON

APRIL 20:

For the second season in a row, the Yankees' Joe DiMaggio misses opening day. DiMaggio is in New York's Lenox Hill Hospital for the removal of his tonsils and adenoids and will be out for six games.

Tigers' outfielder Gerald "Gee" Walker becomes the first player to hit for the cycle on opening day. He has four hits including a second-inning homer as Detroit beats Cleveland, 4-3.

MAY 1:

Joe DiMaggio begins his season today with three hits as the Yankees defeat the Red Sox and George "Rube" Walberg, 3-2.

MAY 9:

Reds' catcher Ernie Lombardi and second baseman Alex Kampouris gun down the Phillies, 21-10. Kampouris drives in eight runs with three homers. Lombardi has six hits in six at-bats.

MAY 13:

Carl Hubbell beats the Cardinals for his 21st consecutive win, tying the record of Richard "Rube" Marquard, but Dizzy Dean steals the spotlight. After a balk is called on him, Dean leaves the mound and returns only when the crowd begins to chant for him. He resumes pitching – at, not to, the Giants. In the ninth inning, he knocks down Jimmy Ripple on consecutive pitches. Ripple bunts to second baseman Jimmy Brown, who throws to Johnny Mize. Dean comes over to cover and Ripple bumps into him precipitating a bench-emptying incident.

Another chapter in the legend of Dizzy Dean: According to historian Glenn Dickey, after Dean strikes out Vince DiMaggio three times, the Boston Bees' rookie hits a foul pop-up. Dean yells for catcher Ambrose "Brusie" Ogrodowski to drop the ball. Ogrodowski does and Dean fans DiMaggio for the fourth time.

MAY 18:

Brooks Robinson is born in Little Rock, Arkansas.

MAY 25:

In the fifth inning at Yankee Stadium, Tigers' manager-catcher Mickey Cochrane is hit in the right temple with a 3-2 fastball that tails in on him from Irving "Bump" Hadley. Cochrane, who had homered in the second, suffers a triple skull fracture and is removed on a stretcher to St. Elizabeth's Hospital. The game goes on and the Yankees win, 4-3.

Yankees' catcher Bill Dickey recalls Cochrane's beaning in Nathan Salant's Superstars, Stars and Just Plain Heroes, *"The next pitch was a fastball that sailed high and inside, and it struck him on the left side of the head. It made a sickening thud, and it dropped straight off his head on to the plate. He dropped to the ground like he'd been shot. I thought he was dead. God, it was awful. I saw his eyes rolling, and I thought he was dead." Cochrane is in and out of a coma for 10 days. His 13-year playing career ends as a result of the injury.*

MAY 26:

Indians' teammates Billy Sullivan and Bruce Campbell connect for pinch-hit homers today against the Athletics. It marks the first time two AL pinch hitters have homered in a game. Sullivan's hit in the sixth inning with two on, ties the score at 4-4. Campbell hits his round-tripper in the ninth and the Indians go on to win, 8-6.

MAY 27:

Carl Hubbell beats the Reds in Cincinnati, 3-2, and extends his winning streak to 24–over two years. Hubbell comes out of the bullpen to relieve Hal Schumacher in the bottom of the eighth with the score tied, 2-2. Mel Ott hits a ninth inning homer and Hubbell retires the side on pop-ups for the win. Hubbell has added eight consecutive wins to the streak of 16 he began on July 17, 1936. The losing pitcher is Lee Grissom.

MAY 31:

Carl Hubbell's amazing consecutive game winning streak ends today at 24. In game

LEAGUE

In February, under H.G. Hall, president of the Chicago American Giants, the Negro American League formed. The league lasts until 1960.

one of a doubleheader, the Dodgers and Fred Frankhouse beat the Giants and Hubbell, 10-3. The last time Hubbell lost a game was on July 13, 1936, 1-0, to the Cubs.

JUNE 1:

Bill Dietrich of the White Sox no-hits the Browns, 8-0, in Chicago. Dietrich walks two and fans five; Chicago makes one error. The losing pitcher is Elon "Chief" Hogsett. Umpiring the game is Bill Dinneen, who pitched a no-hitter himself for the Red Sox in 1905.

JUNE 5:

The St. Louis Cardinals sign 16-year-old pitcher Stan Musial to his first professional contract.

The consecutive-game streak of Pirates' first baseman Gus Suhr ends today at 822, when he misses a game to attend his mother's funeral. Suhr's streak began on September 11, 1931.

JUNE 6:

Umpire John "Ziggy" Sears awards the Cardinals a forfeit win over the Phillies in game two of today's doubleheader in Philadelphia. With St. Louis ahead, 8-2, the Phillies go into a fifth-inning stall – hoping to have the Sunday curfew wipe out the game – and won't come out of it. The Cardinals, behind Lon Warneke, won the opener, 7–2.

JUNE 11:

The Red Sox trade their brother battery to the Senators. Pitcher Wes Ferrell (3-6) and his brother, catcher Rick Ferrell (.308), are sent to Washington along with outfielder Baldomero "Mel" Almada (.236). Boston gets outfielder Ben Chapman (.262) and the well-traveled pitcher Louis "Bobo" Newsom (3-4). It is Newsom's 10th move since 1935.

JUNE 13:

In St. Louis, Joe DiMaggio smacks three consecutive homers against the Browns in game two of a doubleheader. New York and St. Louis tie, 8-8. In the opener, the Yankees score seven runs in the top of the ninth for a 16-9 win.

JUNE 25:

At Wrigley Field, Augie Galan of the Cubs homers batting left-handed. In his next at-bat, he hits a home run batting right-handed. He is the first NL player to hit "switch" homers in a game. The Cubs beat the Dodgers, 11-2, on a five-hitter by James "Tex" Carleton.

JULY 5:

In the nightcap of a Yankee Stadium doubleheader, Joe DiMaggio hits his first career grand slam homer in the sixth inning against George "Rube" Walberg of the Red Sox. It also is DiMaggio's 20th homer of the year. The Yankees win, 8-4, after beating Boston, 15-0, in the opener.

JULY 7:

With squads selected by rival managers Joe McCarthy of the Yankees and Bill Terry of the Giants – as directed by Commissioner Kenesaw Mountain Landis – the AL beats the NL, 8-3, in the All-Star Game played in Washington's Griffith Stadium. Franklin Delano Roosevelt, the first President to attend an All-Star Game, throws out the ceremonial first ball. For the third time, Lefty Gomez gets the win. In the third inning, with losing pitcher Dizzy Dean pitching, Joe DiMaggio singles and Lou Gehrig parks a 3-2 pitch in the right-field stands. Earl Averill then breaks Dean's right big toe with a line drive. Gehrig also doubles and has four RBI for the AL; Joe Medwick has four hits for the NL.

The injury has serious consequences for Dean, who rushes his return and develops arm trouble while compensating for his broken toe. He never again is the same pitcher, slumping to 13-10 this season. He pitches for five more seasons, winning a total of only 16 games.

JULY 20:

Maybe it's his predilection for playing the ponies – or his team's 25-52 record. But whatever, the reason, the Browns fire manager Rogers Hornsby and replace him with first baseman Sunny Jim Bottomley. Of his gambling, Hornsby says, "Aw, they always bring that up. That's the theme song, so let 'em sing it if they want to."

JULY 25:

In St. Louis, Senators' center fielder Baldomero "Mel" Almada sets a record

HISTORY

After being fired by the Browns in July, Rogers Hornsby retires from baseball. In 20 games with the Browns this season, he hit .321. The 41-year-old Hornsby has the highest lifetime batting average of any right-handed hitter – .358. In 1944, he "unretires" briefly to play in Mexico.

JUNE 25
Cubs' switch-hitter Augie Galan is the first NLer to homer from both sides of the plate.

AUGUST 25
"Rapid Robert" Feller strikes out 16 Red Sox in the Indians' 8-1 home win.

by scoring nine times in a doubleheader against the Browns. In game one, Almada collects three hits – including a double – in five at-bats and scores four runs. The Senators win, 16-10. Wes Ferrell gets the win; Lou Koupal gets the loss. Almada is 3-4, including a double and stolen base, and scores five more times in the nightcap. The Senators win, 15-5, behind Jimmy DeShong. Jim Walkup gets the loss.

AUGUST 1:

Joe DiMaggio picks up in August where he left off in July. He hits his 31st homer of the season as the Yankees romp over the Browns, 14-5. It is DiMaggio's third homer in three days and puts him one game ahead of Babe Ruth's 1927 record pace. Lou Gehrig hits for the cycle for the second time in his career.

AUGUST 3:

At Yankee Stadium, 66,767 turn out for Lou Gehrig Appreciation Day. Headline entertainer George M. Cohan presents the Iron Horse with a pocket watch commemorating his 1936 Most Valuable Player Award. In game one, Gehrig responds to the salute with a three-run homer. Joe DiMaggio also hits a three-run homer, and Tony Lazzeri blasts a solo shot in a 7-2 Yankee win over the White Sox. In the nightcap, Bill Dickey hits a grand slam homer, Tony Lazzeri launches a solo shot, and the Yankees win the game, 5-3.

AUGUST 4:

Yankees' catcher Bill Dickey hits his second grand slam homer in two days to tie a major league record. Today's blow is struck against Vern Kennedy of the Browns in the third inning of a 10-9 Yankees' win. Babe Ruth is the only other Yankee with grand slams in consecutive games.

The Cardinals' Joe "Ducky" Medwick hits four doubles today; the second time this year he has had four extra-base hits in a game. On May 12, Medwick hit two doubles and two homers in one game. St. Louis defeats visiting Boston, 7-6.

AUGUST 6:

Roy Johnson of the Boston Bees leads off today's game with a homer against James "Tex" Carleton of the Cubs. The Bees' second batter, Harold "Rabbit" Warstler, follows suit. It is the first time in modern baseball that a game has begun with back-to-back homers. But the Cubs sweep the Bees, 12-6 and 6-2.

AUGUST 14:

The Tigers maul the Browns with 36 runs on 40 hits in a doubleheader at Navin Field – a major league record. Detroit's Pete Fox puts serious wear and tear on home plate by scoring eight times. In game one, the Tigers win, 16-1, on a five-hitter by Elden Auker, who hits two homers and drives in five runs. In the nightcap, Charlie Gehringer has two homers and six RBI, and Cletus "Boots" Poffenberger pitches in a 20-7 Detroit win. Other Tigers homering in the doubleheader are Rudy York, Gerald "Gee"Walker, Fox, and Leon "Goose" Goslin.

AUGUST 25:

At League Park in Cleveland, Bob Feller of the Indians strikes out 16 and four-hits the Red Sox, 8-1. Feller fans everyone in Boston's lineup except Ben Chapman. Joe Cronin, who is victimized twice, takes a called strike and says to umpire Lou Kolls, "If I can't see it, how did you see it?" Louis "Bobo" Newsom gets the loss.

AUGUST 27:

Fred Frankhouse of the Dodgers pitches an eight-inning no-hitter, beating the Reds, 5-0, at Ebbets Field. With two out in the eighth the game is curtailed because of rain.

AUGUST 31:

One of Babe Ruth's home run records falls. Tigers' 24-year-old rookie Rudy York hits his 17th and 18th homers in August, breaking the Babe's one-month total of 17 (September 1927). York's home runs – his 29th and 30th of the year – are hit against losing pitcher Pete Appleton and help the Tigers beat the Senators, 12-3, in Washington, D.C. York also has two singles and drives in seven runs. The winning pitcher is Alfred "Roxie" Lawson.

SEPTEMBER 2:

For the second time this season, two batters lead off a game with back-to-back homers. Louis "Boze" Berger and Mike Kreevich of the White Sox hit round-trippers against Johnny

HISTORY

Joe DiMaggio has 15 homers in July – a record for the month.

"He could throw strikes at midnight."
– Billy Herman on Carl Hubbell

SEPTEMBER 19
Hank Greenberg is the first to hit a home run into Yankee Stadium's center-field bleachers.

HISTORY

The Homestead Grays win the Negro National League championship. In the Negro American League, the Kansas City Monarchs defeat the Chicago American Giants, four games to one.

Marcum of the Red Sox at Fenway Park. Chicago sweeps a doubleheader, 4-2 and 10-8.

SEPTEMBER 17:

Orlando Cepeda is born in Ponce, Puerto Rico.

SEPTEMBER 18:

Larry MacPhail resigns as general manager of the Reds.

SEPTEMBER 19:

Hank Greenberg of the Tigers becomes the first player ever to hit a home run into the center-field bleachers of Yankee Stadium. Detroit wins, 8-1. On May 22, a Greenberg homer to center field off Wes Ferrell cleared Fenway Park.

SEPTEMBER 23:

The Yankees lose to the Browns, 9-5, today at Yankee Stadium in their 142nd game of the year, but back into the AL pennant when the Tigers lose to the Red Sox.

SEPTEMBER 29:

Giants' rookie Cliff Melton wins his 20th game, beating the Phillies, 6-3, in a doubleheader at Baker Bowl. He is the first "true" rookie – no major league experience at all – to win 20 since Grover Cleveland Alexander in 1911. Melton had a bittersweet major league debut earlier in the year, fanning 13 Boston Bees, but losing, 3-1.

SEPTEMBER 30:

Indians' pitcher Johnny Allen beats the White Sox, 6-4, for his 15th straight win this season and 17th dating back to July 10, 1936. In the second game of a doubleheader, Bob Feller wins his ninth of the year.

OCTOBER 2:

The Bees' 34-year-old "true" rookie Jim Turner wins his 20th game of the season, beating the visiting Phillies, 7-1.

OCTOBER 3:

Joe DiMaggio hits a grand slam homer against Joe Gonzales of the Red Sox in the seventh inning today. It is DiMaggio's third of the season.

The winning streak of Indians' pitcher Johnny Allen is ended at 15 (17 over two seasons) by the Tigers, who beat the right-hander, 1-0, on a Whistlin' Jake Wade one-hitter in Detroit. In the first inning, Pete Fox doubles and Hank Greenberg drives in the game's only run; it is his 183rd RBI of the season. The sole hit for Cleveland is a Hal Trosky single in the seventh inning. Allen finishes the season at 15-1.

The Bees' 30-year-old rookie Lou Fette beats the Phillies, 6-0, in Boston for his 20th win of the year. He is the third "true" rookie to record his 20th win in four days – all against the Phillies.

OCTOBER 4:

The Dodgers ship four players to the Cardinals for shortstop Leo Durocher (.203). St. Louis receives infielders Jim Bucher (.253, four homers) and Joe Stripp (.243), along with outfielder Johnny Cooney (.293) and pitcher Roy Henshaw (5-12, 5.07 ERA).

REGULAR SEASON WRAP-UP:

For the second straight year, Joe McCarthy's Yankees have 102 wins. This year they finish 13 games ahead of the Tigers. The Yankees present an awesome lineup that includes Joe DiMaggio (.346, 46 homers, 167 RBI), Lou Gehrig (.351, 37 homers, 159 RBI), and Bill Dickey (.332, 29 homers, 133 RBI). The Yankees also have the AL's only 20-game winners– Vernon "Lefty" Gomez (21-11) and Charles "Red" Ruffing (20-7).

The Giants, under Bill Terry, finish at 95-57, three games ahead of the Cubs. The team has three regulars at .300 or more – Jimmy Ripple (.317), Joe "Jo-Jo" Moore (.310), and Dick Bartell (.306). Carl Hubbell at 22-8 and Cliff Melton at 20-9 are the top pitchers. The Pirates' Paul Waner gets 219 hits; it is the eighth time he has topped 200, setting a modern NL record.

OCTOBER 6:

World Series, game one. The second consecutive Subway Series begins at Yankee Stadium with Vernon "Lefty" Gomez six-hitting the Giants, 8-1. The Yankees explode for seven runs in the sixth inning; Joe DiMaggio and George Selkirk each drive in two runs with bases-loaded singles. Tony Lazzeri homers for the Yankees' eighth run. The losing pitcher is Carl Hubbell.

OCTOBER 7:

World Series, game two. Charles "Red" Ruffing seven hits the Giants, 8-1, at Yankee

OCTOBER 25
The Boston Bees sign Casey Stengel as their manager for the 1938 season.

Stadium. The Yankees have 12 hits; Ruffing has three of them and drives in three runs. Cliff Melton gets the loss.

OCTOBER 8:

World Series, game three. The scene shifts to the Polo Grounds, but the script remains the same. Behind a combined five-hitter by winner Monte Pearson and a save by relief pitcher Johnny Murphy, the Yankees top the Giants, 5-1. The Giants make it tough for loser Hal Schumacher, committing four errors. Bill Dickey has a triple for the Bronx Bombers.

OCTOBER 9:

World Series, game four. The Giants are breathing, but barely. Carl Hubbell goes all the way, allowing the Yankees six hits in a 7-3 victory. The Giants score six runs in the second; Henry "Hank" Leiber has two hits in the inning. Lou Gehrig homers for the Yankees. Bump Hadley is charged with the loss.

OCTOBER 10:

World Series, game five. Lefty Gomez, one of baseball's worst-hitting pitchers, drives in the winning run with a fifth-inning single and holds the Giants to eight hits in a 4-2 victory, giving the New York Yankees their second consecutive World Championship. Cliff Melton is tagged with the loss. Joe DiMaggio and Myril Hoag homer with the bases empty for the Yankees. Mel Ott has a two-run homer for the Giants. Gomez finishes the series 2-0 with a 1.50 ERA. Tony Lazzeri leads all hitters at .400. Joe Moore at .391 is the Giants' top hitter.

POST-SEASON

OCTOBER 15:

Tony Lazzeri is released by the Yankees. Lazzeri will sign with the Cubs, whose owner, Phil Wrigley, asked New York general manager Ed Barrow to make the second baseman available. In 12 years with the Yankees, Lazzeri hit .293 with 169 homers. He is the only second baseman ever to drive in 100-plus runs seven times. Lazzeri's release paves the way for Newark Bears' second sacker Joe "Flash" Gordon to join the Yankees.

OCTOBER 20:

Juan Marichal is born in Laguna Verde, Dominican Republic.

COULD HE REALLY SEE INTO THE FUTURE? SPORTSWRITER PAUL GALLICO STATES IN HIS BOOK *FAREWELL TO SPORT*: "FIFTY YEARS FROM NOW, NOT A RECORD IN THE BOOKS WILL BE LEFT STANDING. I BELIEVE WE HAVE GONE ONLY A LITTLE WAY TOWARD THE PEAK OF POSSIBLE ACHIEVEMENT IN ANY SPORT."

OCTOBER 25:

The Boston Bees sign Casey Stengel as their 1938 manager. He replaces Bill McKechnie, who compiled a 79-73 record and finished fifth this season.

NOVEMBER 19:

Sunny Jim Bottomley is unconditionally released by the Browns, ending his 16 year career as a player and his less-than-a-year stint as a manager. After replacing Rogers Hornsby in mid-season, Bottomley managed the Browns to a 21-56 record and a last-place finish. He hit .239 in 65 games. Bottomley leaves baseball with a .310 lifetime average.

DECEMBER 2:

The White Sox and Tigers complete a six-player deal. Chicago gets third baseman Marv Owen (.288), outfielder Gerald "Gee" Walker (.335, 18 homers), and minor league catcher Mike Tresh. In return, the Tigers acquire outfielder Fred "Dixie" Walker (.302, nine homers), infielder Tony Piet (.235, four homers), and pitcher Lloyd "Vern" Kennedy (14-13, 4.63 ERA).

LEAGUE

A federal court awards $7,500 to David Levy, whose skull was fractured in a scuffle with Yankee Stadium ushers when he tried to retrieve a foul ball hit by Lou Gehrig in August 1934. As a result, major league clubs decide fans can keep balls hit into the stands.

LEAGUE

In December, the Red Sox acquire the contract of outfielder Ted Williams (.291, 23 homers) from the San Diego Padres of the Pacific Coast League for $35,000 plus outfielder Dominic Dallessandro (.231 in 68 games) and infielder Al Niemiec (not in majors in 1937).

THE BEST OF 1937

NATIONAL LEAGUE

HITTERS

Batting Average:
Joe "Ducky" Medwick, St. Louis Cardinals, .374

Slugging Average:
Joe Medwick, .641

Home Runs:
Joe Medwick; Mel Ott, New York Giants, 31

Runs Batted In:
Joe Medwick, 154

Hits:
Joe Medwick, 237

Stolen Bases:
Augie Galan, Chicago Cubs, 23

PITCHERS

Wins:
Carl Hubbell, New York Giants, 22

Strikeouts:
Carl Hubbell, 159

Earned Run Average:
Jim Turner, Boston Bees, 2.38

Winning Percentage:
Carl Hubbell, .733

Saves:
Cliff Melton, New York Giants;
Mace Brown, Pittsburgh Pirates, 7

Most Valuable Player:
Joe Medwick, St. Louis Cardinals

AMERICAN LEAGUE

HITTERS

Batting Average:
Charlie Gehringer, Detroit Tigers, .371

Slugging Average:
Joe DiMaggio, New York Yankees, .673

Home Runs:
Joe DiMaggio, 46

Runs Batted In:
Hank Greenberg, Detroit Tigers, 183

Hits
Roy "Beau" Bell, St. Louis Browns, 218

Stolen Bases:
Bill Werber, Philadelphia Athletics;
Ben Chapman, Washington Senators/
Boston Red Sox, 35

PITCHERS

Wins:
Vernon "Lefty" Gomez, New York Yankees, 21

Strikeouts:
Lefty Gomez, 194

Earned Run Average:
Lefty Gomez, 2.33

Winning Percentage:
Johnny Allen, Cleveland Indians, .938

Saves:
Clint Brown, Chicago White Sox, 18

Most Valuable Player:
Charlie Gehringer, Detroit Tigers

1938

"A ballplayer's got to be kept hungry to become a big leaguer."
– *Joe DiMaggio*

NEWS

GERMANY OCCUPIES AUSTRIA

SUPERMAN DEBUTS IN ACTION COMICS

TEFLON AND FIBERGLASS HIT THE MARKET

ORSON WELLES CREATES PANIC WITH SCIENCE-FICTION RADIO SHOW, *WAR OF THE WORLDS*, ABOUT A MARTIAN LANDING

ROOSEVELT SIGNS MINIMUM-WAGE LAW

"WRONG WAY" CORRIGAN FLIES TO IRELAND

At the movies, *Angels with Dirty Faces*, *Jezebel*, *The Lady Vanishes*, *Boys' Town*, and *The Adventures of Robin Hood* are popular

Folk singer Woody Guthrie takes his show on the road

First Xerox image is made

PRE-SEASON

JANUARY 1:

Grover Cleveland Alexander, Alexander J. Cartwright Jr., and Henry Chadwick are elected to the Hall of Fame. Alexander pitched in the majors for 20 years with the Phillies, Cubs, and Cardinals, from 1911 to 1930. He compiled a 373-208 record with an ERA of 2.56. Alexander pitched 5,189 2/3 innings and recorded 90 shutouts. In three World Series, Alexander was 3-2. Cartwright, who died in 1892, is credited with creating the basic rules of modern baseball. He was the driving force behind the Knickerbocker Base Ball Club in 1845. With discovering gold as his goal, Cartwright left New York for California in 1849, teaching baseball along the way. Chadwick, known as the Father of Baseball for his promotional efforts on behalf of the sport, was a journalist who traveled to Brooklyn from England as a young man. After watching a game in 1856, he successfully worked on behalf of newspaper coverage of the game and issued an annual guide. Chadwick passed away in 1908.

On the day he is elected to the Hall of Fame, Grover Cleveland Alexander reportedly is being paid to appear at a flea circus.

JANUARY 10:

Willie "Stretch" McCovey is born in Mobile, Alabama.

JANUARY 18:

Curt Flood is born in Houston.

JANUARY 19:

Larry MacPhail becomes the general manager and executive vice president of the Brooklyn Dodgers.

JANUARY 21:

After a 30-minute meeting with Yankees' owner Jacob Ruppert and general manager Ed Barrow, Joe DiMaggio rejects a $25,000 contract and begins a holdout that keeps him in San Francisco when spring training begins. DiMaggio earned $15,000 last season, when he hit .346, with 46 homers, and 151 RBI. In his rookie season, he was paid $8,000. He is seeking $45,000. Barrow points out to Joe DiMaggio that the $45,000 he is demanding is more than Lou Gehrig earns. DiMaggio

TRIVIA

Henry Chadwick is the only writer in the Hall of Fame proper. Others are enshrined in the Writers' Wing.

APRIL 16
The Cardinals trade ace Dizzy Dean to the Cubs for a pair of pitchers and an outfielder.

responds, "It's too bad that Gehrig is so underpaid."

MARCH 3:

Dan Casey, in his mid-70s, who has been claiming to be the prototype of the ill-fated slugger in Ernest L. Thayer's "Casey at the Bat," appears on the popular *We the People* radio program to tell his story. According to Casey, he pitched for Philadelphia at the Huntingdon Avenue Grounds, which was known as Mudville. He offers details of a game against the Giants in which his play paralleled the poetic Casey's.

The date Dan Casey provides for his monumental strikeout was an off day for Philadelphia. A Dan Casey is listed in The Baseball Encyclopedia. *He pitched for the Philadelphia Quakers from 1886 to 1889, but he was hardly "mighty" – his lifetime batting average was .162 with one home run.*

MARCH 6:

The Dodgers obtain first baseman Dolf Camilli (.339, 27 homers) from the Phillies for outfielder Ed Morgan (.188) and $45,000. Several sources put the figure at $50,000.

MARCH 7:

Steve McKeever, part owner of the Dodgers, dies at age 83. His shares in the team go to his daughter, Dearie (Mrs. James) Mulvey.

MARCH 8:

Lou Gehrig follows Joe DiMaggio's lead and rejects the Yankees' contract offer. Gehrig, who hit .351 with 37 homers and 159 RBI in 1937, is offered $39,000 – a $3,000 raise over last season's salary.

A dispute over the rights to an 18-year-old second baseman turns bizarre during spring training. The Giants' Bill Nowak is "kidnapped" from a hotel in Baton Rouge, Louisiana, and taken to the Indians' training camp. Nowak never makes it to the major leagues.

MARCH 12:

Lou Gehrig signs his Yankees' contract for $39,000. Joe DiMaggio continues his holdout.

MARCH 21:

The Red Sox send 19-year-old Ted Williams to their Minneapolis Millers farm team. Boston bought Williams from San Diego in the Pacific Coast League in December 1937 for $35,000, plus outfielder Dom Dallessandro and second baseman Al Niemiec.

Williams is jeered by Red Sox outfielders Roger "Doc" Cramer, Joe Vosmik, and Ben Chapman with remarks like "good-bye, busher." He sends them a message through clubhouse man Johnny Orlando: "Tell 'em I'll be back, and tell them I'm going to wind up making more money in this game than all three of them put together."

Commissioner Kenesaw Mountain Landis "frees" 74 Cardinals' minor leaguers and slaps St. Louis with a fine. Among the players cut loose is outfielder Pete Reiser.

MARCH 27:

In an exhibition game against the Cubs, White Sox shortstop Luke Appling breaks his leg on a slide and will miss half of the season.

MARCH 29:

Captain Tillinghast L'Hommedieau Huston, former co-owner of the Yankees, dies at age 71 on Butler Island near Brunswick, Georgia.

APRIL 16:

Who woulda thunk it? The Cardinals trade Dizzy Dean (13-10, 2.69 ERA) to the Cubs for pitchers Curt Davis (10-5, 4.08 ERA) and Clyde Shoun (7-7, 5.61 ERA), plus outfielder Tuck Stainback (.231) and $185,000. Dean has not been the same dominant pitcher since he returned too soon last year from his broken toe.

THE SEASON

APRIL 18:

For the third straight year, Joe DiMaggio is missing from the Yankees' opening day lineup. New York loses, 8-4, to the Red Sox in Boston.

APRIL 19:

In Philadelphia, two rookies debut with a bang. The Dodgers' Ernie Koy homers against the Phillies in his first major league at-bat. Later in the game, Philadelphia's Emmett "Heinie" Mueller returns the favor, homering the first time he comes to the plate. The veterans aren't idle either: Dolf Camilli and Harry "Cookie" Lavagetto homer for Brooklyn; Chuck Klein for the Phillies. The Dodgers win, 12-5; Luke "Hot Potato"

APRIL 24
Dizzy Dean, now a Cub, beats his old team, the Cardinals, 5-0, giving up just four hits.

Hamlin gets the win. The loss belongs to Wayne LaMaster.

APRIL 20:

Bob Feller one-hits the Browns, 9-0. A sixth-inning bunt by catcher Billy Sullivan is the only hit. Sullivan apologizes after the game, and umpire Ed Rommel, who made the safe call, also says he is sorry, but that the call was correct and it stands.

Joe DiMaggio agrees to the Yankees' original offer of $25,000 and heads for New York from San Francisco by train. Owner Jacob Ruppert continues his hard-line stance, stating, "His pay will be $25,000, no more, no less, and it won't start until McCarthy [the Yankees' manager] says it should." DiMaggio is the highest-paid third-year player ever and the third-highest paid in baseball today.

APRIL 24:

After defeating the Reds for his first win as a Cub, Dizzy Dean limits the Cardinals to four hits, beating his old teammates, 5-0, in Chicago. Sportswriter Grantland Rice asks Dizzy Dean about his arm. Dean responds, "Well, Grant, it ain't what it was... but then, what the hell is?"

Senators' owner Clark Griffith tells Sam Lacy of the *Washington Tribune*, "There are few big league magnates who are not aware of the fact that the time is not far off when colored players will take their places besides those of other races in the major leagues. However, I'm not sure that time has arrived yet." Griffith forecasts, "A lone Negro in the game will face caustic comments. He will be made the target of cruel, filthy epithets. Of course, I know the time will come when the ice will have to be broken. Both by the organized game and by the colored player who is willing to volunteer and thus become a sort of martyr to the cause."

APRIL 30:

Joe DiMaggio makes his 1938 debut after a 12 game holdout that cost him $2,000. During his absence the Yankees were 6-6. In the field, after singling in his first at-bat, DiMaggio crashes into second baseman Joe Gordon and injures his head. Both are knocked unconscious in the outfield and hospitalized overnight.

MAY 2:

Yankees' manager Joe McCarthy makes a lineup shift that signals a changing of the guard. Lou Gehrig is dropped to sixth in the order and Joe DiMaggio is moved into the cleanup position. Gehrig breaks an 0-for-11 slump with a single and DiMaggio homers as the Yankees beat the Senators, 3-2, in Washington.

MAY:

(Specific date not available.) The Pirates buy outfielder Henry "Heinie" Manush (.235) from the Brooklyn Dodgers for the waiver price.

MAY 5:

At Wrigley Field, Wayne LaMaster of the Phillies is tagged with a loss without pitching a complete

TRIVIA

For a period during the 1930s, John Forsythe worked at Ebbets Field. Forsythe, who goes on to star in films and on TV in *Bachelor Father*, *Dynasty*, and as the voice of Charlie in *Charlie's Angels*, is variously reported to have been the public address announcer and a broadcaster.

> "We're not trying to beat you, we're just trying to get a base hit."
> – *Casey Stengel to Johnny Vander Meer*

official at-bat. While pitching to the Cubs' Stan Hack, LaMaster comes up with a sore arm and is relieved by Tommy Reis. Hack walks – the base on balls is charged to LaMaster – and scores the first tally in a four-run first inning. The Cubs add 12 runs off Hal Kelleher in the eighth and win the game, 21-2; LaMaster gets the loss. Al Epperly is the winner. The big Chicago hitters are Joe Marty with four hits, four runs, and four RBI, and Augie Galan with a homer, triple, and four RBI.

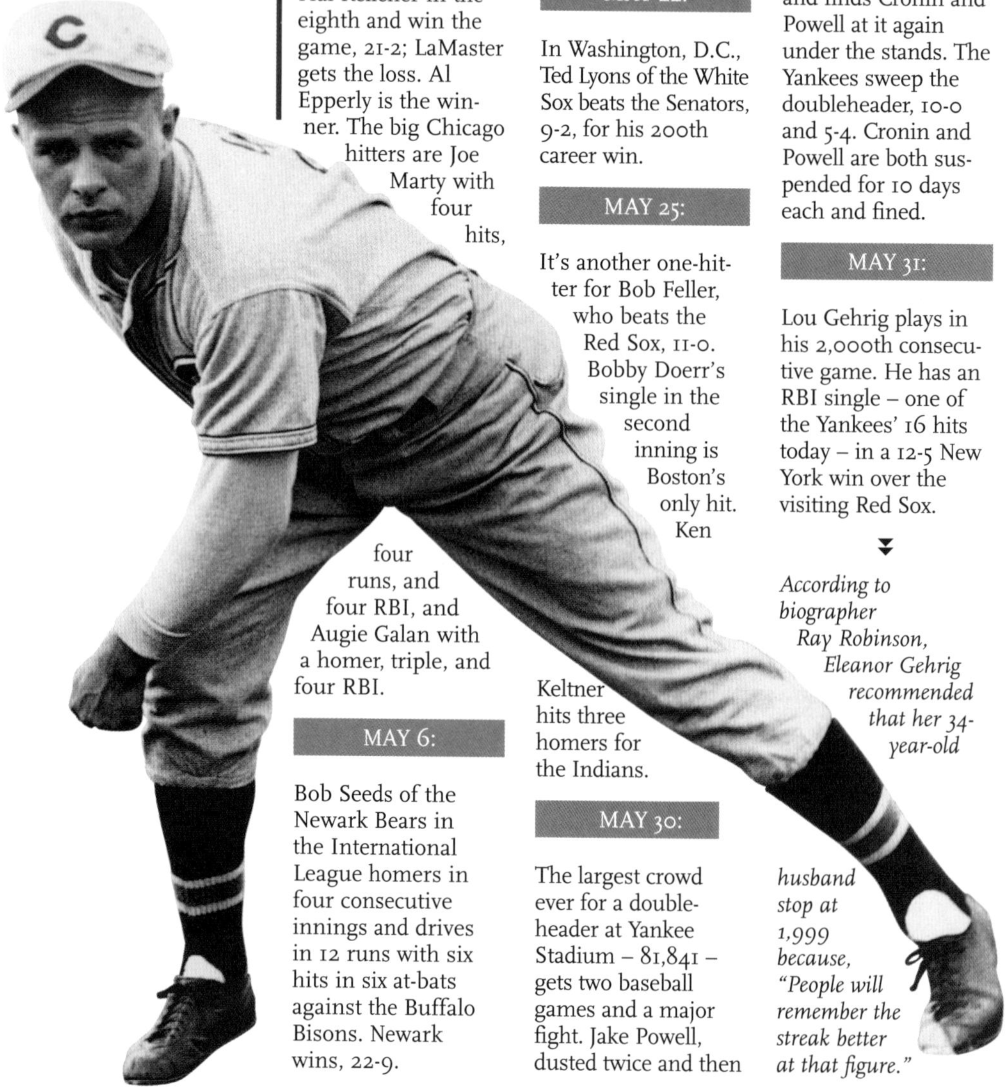

Cincinnati's Johnny Vander Meer tossed two consecutive no-hitters.

MAY 6:

Bob Seeds of the Newark Bears in the International League homers in four consecutive innings and drives in 12 runs with six hits in six at-bats against the Buffalo Bisons. Newark wins, 22-9.

MAY 7:

Bob Seeds hits three more homers against Buffalo in a 14-8 win. Known as "Suitcase Bob," he plays with five major league teams between 1930 and 1940, hitting .277 with 28 home runs in 615 games.

MAY 22:

In Washington, D.C., Ted Lyons of the White Sox beats the Senators, 9-2, for his 200th career win.

MAY 25:

It's another one-hitter for Bob Feller, who beats the Red Sox, 11-0. Bobby Doerr's single in the second inning is Boston's only hit. Ken Keltner hits three homers for the Indians.

MAY 30:

The largest crowd ever for a doubleheader at Yankee Stadium – 81,841 – gets two baseball games and a major fight. Jake Powell, dusted twice and then hit by Boston's Archie McKain, goes after him. When player-manager Joe Cronin intervenes, he and Powell slug it out. Both are ejected by umpire Cal Hubbard, who then notices the Yankees' dugout is empty. He hustles into the runway, followed by the Red Sox, and finds Cronin and Powell at it again under the stands. The Yankees sweep the doubleheader, 10-0 and 5-4. Cronin and Powell are both suspended for 10 days each and fined.

MAY 31:

Lou Gehrig plays in his 2,000th consecutive game. He has an RBI single – one of the Yankees' 16 hits today – in a 12-5 New York win over the visiting Red Sox.

According to biographer Ray Robinson, Eleanor Gehrig recommended that her 34-year-old husband stop at 1,999 because, "People will remember the streak better at that figure."

JUNE 7:

In the second inning at Fenway Park, umpire Bill McGowan directs Indians' pitcher Johnny Allen to cut the tattered sleeves off his undershirt because they are distracting the batters. Allen refuses and storms off the field. The Indians go on to win the game, 7-5. Allen is fined $250 by Indians' manager Ossie Vitt, but team president Alva Bradley buys the undershirt from the pitcher for that same amount. It is exhibited at the Higbee Co. department store and then shipped to the Hall of Fame.

JUNE 11:

Reds' left-hander Johnny Vander Meer no-hits the Boston Bees, 3-0, in Cincinnati. Vander Meer allows three walks and strikes out four; the Reds make no errors. Vander Meer retires the final batter, Ray Mueller, pinch-hitting for Elbie Fletcher, on a ground ball to third baseman Lew Riggs. Danny McFayden is the losing pitcher.

JUNE 13:

The Reds obtain infielder turned pitcher William "Bucky" Walters (4-8) from the

JUNE 16
Browns' pitchers intentionally walk Jimmie Foxx six at-bats in a row.

JULY 4
In their debut at new Shibe Park, the Phillies split a doubleheader with the Boston Bees.

Phillies for pitcher Al Hollingsworth (2-2), catcher Virgil "Spud" Davis (.167), and $50,000.

JUNE 15:

It was supposed to be remembered as the first major league night game outside Cincinnati, but Johnny Vander Meer changes all that with an unprecedented pitching feat at Ebbets Field. The Reds' left-hander becomes the first pitcher with two consecutive no-hitters, when he beats the Dodgers tonight, 6-0. Vander Meer is wild, walking eight, but he fans seven and the Reds play errorless ball. Vander Meer comes close to losing his no-hitter with one out in the ninth when he walks Ernest "Babe" Phelps, Harry "Cookie" Lavagetto, and Dolf Camilli on 18 pitches. After a visit from manager Bill McKechnie, he settles down. Ernie Koy grounds to third baseman Lew Riggs, who forces Phelps at home. Leo Durocher then flies out to Harry Craft in short centerfield and Vander Meer is in the record books. Max Butcher is the losing pitcher.

Johnny Vander Meer was at one time the property of the two teams he no-hits this season. The Dodgers lost his services through an administrative error; the Bees sold him in 1936 to Nashville in the Southern Association.

Billy Williams is born in Whistler, Alabama.

JUNE 16:

It's called pitching around him. Browns' pitchers pay slugger Jimmie Foxx the ultimate compliment – they don't let him hit. Foxx collects six consecutive walks from four St. Louis pitchers (Les Tietje, Ed Linke, Ed Cole, and Russ Van Atta) in nine innings, tying a major league and setting an AL record. It doesn't help; the Red Sox win the game, 12-8. The winning pitcher is Johnny Marcum; Linke gets the loss.

JUNE 19:

In Boston, with one out in the fourth inning, Debs Garms of the Bees singles, thus ending Johnny Vander Meer's consecutive no-hit innings string at 21 2/3 and foiling his bid for a third straight no-hitter. But the Reds win, 14-1.

Boston manager Casey Stengel distracts Vander Meer by switching from the third base coaching box to first base as the Bees are coming to bat in the fourth. He walks in front of the Reds' pitcher and tells him, "We're not trying to beat you, we're just trying to get a base hit."

The Babe makes a return to baseball – kind of. After signing with the Dodgers for $15,000 as a coach, Babe Ruth is in the third base box today at Ebbets Field. The Dodgers win the opener of a doubleheader, 6-2; the Cubs take the nightcap, 4-3.

JUNE 21:

Mike "Pinky" Higgins of the Red Sox sets a major league record by rapping out 12 consecutive hits. He also walks twice, reaching base safely 14 straight times. Higgins's streak began with a double, three singles, and a walk in Chicago two days ago. There was no scheduled game yesterday. In today's doubleheader in Detroit, Higgins has four hits – including a double – in four at-bats in the opener. In game two, he again is 4-4. The previous record-holder was Tris Speaker, with 11 in 1920. Boston wins the opener, 8-3. The Tigers capture the nightcap, 5-4.

JUNE 22:

The Tigers' Vern Kennedy fans Pinky Higgins in his first at-bat today, ending his consecutive hit streak at 12.

At Comiskey Park, Hank Steinbacher, a substitute White Sox outfielder, gets a start and has six consecutive hits – including a double – in six at-bats. Chicago beats the Senators, 16-3.

JUNE 30:

After 51 years, the Phillies say good-bye to Baker Bowl – with a 14-1 loss to the Giants. The winning pitcher is Clydell "Slick" Castleman; Claude Passeau gets the loss. The Giants' Hank Leiber hits the last home run ever at the ballpark.

JULY 4:

At Griffith Stadium in Washington, game one of a doubleheader is held up for 15 minutes while fans, unhappy with an umpire's call, bombard the field with vegetables and glass bottles. When the game resumes, the Yankees beat the Senators, 10-5. Lou Gehrig drives in three runs.

The Phillies debut at Shibe Park, the new home they share with

CULTURE

The movie *Rawhide* stars Smith Bellow, and Lou Gehrig, as himself.

Former Tiger Harry Heilmann says, "Hank Greenberg hits the ball harder than Babe Ruth, Jimmie Foxx, or Lou Gehrig."

HISTORY

Hank Greenberg sets one record: He homers 39 times this season in Briggs Stadium in Detroit, the most ever in a ballpark in one season.

the Athletics. They lose the opener of a doubleheader to the Bees, 10-5, and come back to beat Boston, 10-2, in the nightcap.

JULY 6:

The NL wins the All-Star Game, 4-1, at Crosley Field. NL pitchers Johnny Vander Meer and Bill Lee – both of the Reds – and the Pirates' Mace Brown allow the AL only seven hits. Vander Meer is the winning pitcher; the Yankees' Vernon "Lefty" Gomez takes the loss. The AL commits four errors.

JULY 14:

Red Sox pitcher Lefty Grove, 38 years old, injures his pitching arm on a throw to first after fielding a bunt. He presently has 14 wins.

JULY 26:

The Tigers' Hank Greenberg homers in his last two at-bats today as the Tigers down the Senators, 6-1, in Detroit.

JULY 27:

By homering in his first two at-bats today, Hank Greenberg of the Tigers joins a select list of players with four consecutive round-trippers. The Tigers once again defeat the visiting Senators, 9-4.

JULY 30:

Hank Greenberg hits his ninth home run of the week, tying a record set by Babe Ruth. Greenberg's Tigers beat the visiting Athletics, 9-2.

JULY 31:

In Chicago, Yankees' outfielder Jake Powell goes on the radio after the Yankees beat the White Sox, 7-3, in 15 innings. Among his remarks, Powell says he'd like to "hit every colored person in Chicago over the head with a club." He is suspended for 10 days for his remark.

Daniel Okrent and Steve Wulf claim, "When Powell returned to New York, he went up to the top of Harlem, alone and after dark. Working southward, he stopped in every saloon he came across, introducing himself as Jake Powell, apologizing for his foolish words, and buying everyone a round of drinks."

AUGUST 2:

Brooklyn general manager Larry MacPhail, the man who brought night baseball to the major leagues, has a new idea. He introduces dandelion-yellow colored baseballs at Ebbets Field today in game one of a doubleheader against the Cardinals. The balls are being tested – with the approval of NL president Ford Frick – to see if they are easier to follow and safer than the regulation ball. The Cardinals' Johnny Mize has no trouble with the new ball – described as a "stitched lemon"; he hits a home run against Freddie Fitzsimmons, but the Dodgers win, 6-2. The balls were created by Frederick Rah. The reaction to Rah? Blah! Playing with a white baseball, the Dodgers win the nightcap, as well, 9-3.

AUGUST 6:

Tigers' owner Walter Briggs fires his ailing manager, Mickey Cochrane, and replaces him with Delmar "Del" Baker. Baker managed the Tigers for 54 games in the middle of last season, when Cochrane was recovering from a triple skull fracture.

AUGUST 11:

The U.S. Olympic baseball team arrives in Plymouth, England. The team will play a five-game "test series" against British professionals. The U.S. nine will participate in five additional games against teams from Yorkshire, Lancashire, London, Birmingham, and the Royal Air Force. England wins the "Test Match," four games to one. The U.S. wins all the five exhibition games. Because of World War II, the Olympic Games were canceled.

AUGUST 20:

Lou Gehrig hits a grand slam homer – the major league record 23rd of his career – and bats in six runs against the Athletics' Lee "Buck" Ross. The Yankees win the game, 11-3.

AUGUST 27:

Monte Pearson no-hits the Indians, 13-0, in the nightcap of a doubleheader at Yankee Stadium. It also is his 10th consecutive victory and the first no-hitter at Yankee Stadium. Pearson walks two batters – who are erased by double plays – and faces only 27 batters. He fans seven, and New York plays errorless ball behind him. John Humphries is the losing pitcher.

The Yankees win the opener as well, 8-7, largely due to Joe DiMaggio's three consecutive triples.

AUGUST 30:

Henry "Heinie" Manush is returning to the majors. The outfielder, who played 17 games with the Dodgers earlier this year and hit .235, is purchased by the Pirates from the Toronto Maple Leafs in the International League.

AUGUST 31:

Despite a 12-6 loss to the visiting Tigers today, the Yankees end up with a 28-8 record for the month. The 28 victories are the most ever for an AL team in one month. Hank Greenberg paces the Tigers with his 46th homer. He now is six games and six days ahead of Babe Ruth's record pace.

Greenberg shows his bruises, saying, "I was hit by pitched balls. How do I know what for? They don't send letters along with each ball..."

SEPTEMBER 7:

It's Joe Cronin Day at Fenway Park, but Jimmie Foxx steals the spotlight with eight RBI in an 11-4 victory over the visiting Yankees.

SEPTEMBER 9:

Hank Greenberg hits his 47th homer of the season in an 11-5 Tigers' victory over the Indians in Cleveland.

SEPTEMBER 10:

Frankie Frisch is fired as Cardinals' manager and replaced by Miguel "Mike" Gonzalez. St. Louis is 63-72 under Frisch.

SEPTEMBER 11:

In Detroit, Hank Greenberg hits two homers against White Sox pitcher Ted Lyons. The home runs are Greenberg's 48th and 49th of the season, and Detroit sweeps a doubleheader, 10-1 and 5-3.

SEPTEMBER 15:

New York Giants' pitcher Cliff Melton becomes the only pitcher to yield consecutive home runs to brothers. Lloyd and Paul Waner do the damage in the fifth inning of today's game, pacing visiting Pittsburgh to a 7-2 win.

Gaylord Perry is born in Williamston, North Carolina.

SEPTEMBER 17:

Hank Greenberg hits two homers today – his 52nd and 53rd – against the Yankees' Monte Pearson. Greenberg is two games ahead of Babe Ruth's 1927 pace. The *New York Sun* reports, "Pearson was under orders to pitch to Greenberg today." The Tigers beat the Yankees, 7-3.

Cubs' pitcher Bill Lee has it when he needs it. Despite giving up 13 hits today, he whitewashes the Giants, 4-0. It is Lee's third consecutive shutout.

SEPTEMBER 18:

The Yankees drop two to the Browns in St. Louis but win the AL pennant when second-place Boston is rained out of a doubleheader. The Yankees become the first team in history to win 10 pennants.

SEPTEMBER 21:

A hurricane cuts short today's game at Braves Field. The umpires decide it is time to call the game when Bees' first baseman Elbie Fletcher's pop fly is blown into the right-field seats.

SEPTEMBER 22:

At Shibe Park, Bill Lee and the Cubs beat the Phillies, 4-0. It is Lee's fourth consecutive shutout.

SEPTEMBER 23:

Hank Greenberg continues his pursuit of Babe Ruth. In game one of a doubleheader, he hits his 55th and 56th homers of the season, both off the Indians' Earl Whitehill. Greenberg now holds the major league season record for most games with two home runs – 10. Game two is called after seven innings because of darkness – without Greenberg hitting a homer.

SEPTEMBER 27:

With five games to go, Hank Greenberg is now within two home runs of Babe Ruth's record 60. Greenberg hits two homers today in the nightcap of a doubleheader against the Browns' Bill Cox. The game is called at the end of five innings because of darkness. The Tigers win, 10-2, and Greenberg has four RBI. Detroit also won the opener, 5-4.

At Yankee Stadium, on the 15th anniversary of his first major league home run, Lou Gehrig homers against the Senators' pitcher Emil "Dutch" Leonard. It stands as Gehrig's 29th homer

HISTORY

The Homestead Grays are the champions of the Negro National League. In the Negro American League, the Memphis Red Sox and the Atlanta Black Crackers win the first and second halves, respectively. Memphis wins the first two games of the playoff, but the series is not completed.

Walter "Buck" Leonard, who played first base for the Homestead Grays from 1934 to 1948 in the Negro Leagues, says, "We are not disorganized, just unrecognized."

TRIVIA

In 1949, *The Stratton Story*, about Monty Stratton, is released. It stars James Stewart as the pitcher and June Allyson as his wife.

of the year and the 493rd – and last – of his career.

The Pirates come to Chicago for a crucial series, one and a half games ahead of the Cubs. Behind Dizzy Dean, the Cubs top the Pirates, 2-1. Dean's record goes to 7-1.

SEPTEMBER 28:

In the bottom of the ninth, with darkness falling, the Cubs and Pirates are tied, 5-5. Chicago's catcher-manager Charles "Gabby" Hartnett hits a two-strike pitch for what comes to be known as the "homer in the gloaming" against reliever Mace Brown for a 6-5 win. Charlie Root is the winning pitcher. It is the Cubs' ninth straight win.

In St. Louis, Hank Greenberg just misses but comes away empty. Batting against left-hander Howard Mills, he walks twice, drives a foul ball onto the left-field roof, strikes out, and pops up. Yesterday, Greenberg went homerless against Bobo Newsom.

SEPTEMBER 29:

Time is running out on Greenberg as he singles, pops up twice, and flies out in a 6-2 Tigers' victory

One of Hank Greenberg's two home runs on September 27 is a 440-foot, inside-the-park drive. Home plate umpire Bill McGowan calls Greenberg safe on a close play. In his autobiography, Greenberg writes, "The catcher had me out by a mile." He recounts how, 40 years later, he has a letter from that Browns catcher, Sam Harshaney, requesting a picture of the play so he can show his grown sons that Greenberg was out. Greenberg responds, "I'm sorry I have no picture, but you are absolutely right. I was out by a mile and had no business being called safe. So you can tell your boys that their dad stopped Hank Greenberg from getting home run number 57."

over the Browns. The Cubs beat the Pirates, 10-1, for their 10th straight win.

OCTOBER 1:

In St. Louis, in the opener of a doubleheader, the Cubs get a complete game from Charlie Root, plus four hits from Billy Herman to beat the Cardinals, 10-3, and wrap up the NL pennant.

OCTOBER 2:

One record is set today at Cleveland Stadium, another is not. On the last day of the season, Bob Feller strikes out 18 Tigers en route to a 4-1 loss in game one of a doubleheader. And Hank Greenberg does not hit a home run in either game, ending his season with 58 – two shy of Babe Ruth's 1927 record. Greenberg gets a double in four at-bats against Feller and has three singles – one traveling 420 feet – and a walk in the nightcap. Feller, who had shared the single-game strikeout record – 17 – with Dizzy Dean, fans Chet Laabs in the ninth inning on a called third strike for his 18th K of the day. Feller walks seven and gives up seven hits today, finishing the season with 240

SEPTEMBER 28
At twilight, the Cubs' Gabby Hartnett hits the famed "homer in the gloaming."

OCTOBER 9
The Yankees become the first team to win three consecutive World Championships.

strikeouts. The winning pitcher is Harry Eisenstat.

In his autobiography, Greenberg recalls the end of the Babe Ruth chase. As the nightcap is about to be called after seven innings because of darkness, umpire George Moriarty tells Greenberg, "I'm sorry, Hank. But this is as far as I can go." Greenberg responds, "That's all right, George. This is as far as I can go, too."

REGULAR SEASON WRAP-UP:

The Yankees are 99-53, winning their third pennant in a row under Joe McCarthy. They beat the Tigers by nine and a half games. Red Ruffing (21-7) is one of the AL's two 20-game winners. Joe DiMaggio (.324, 32 homers, 140 RBI), Bill Dickey (.313, 27 homers, 115 RBI), and Lou Gehrig (.295, 29 homers, 114 RBI) are the Yankees' big guns. Robert "Red" Rolfe bats .311.

The AL is a hitters' circuit, with 30 hitters at .300 or better and a cumulative batting average of .281. Jimmie Foxx of the Red Sox, who had 58 homers with the 1932 A's, hits 50 this season, becoming the first to hit 50 for two different teams.

The Cubs, under Gabby Hartnett – who took over from Charlie Grimm – finish 89-63 in the NL. Stan Hack at .320 is their top hitter, followed by Carl Reynolds at .302. Bill Lee leads the pitchers with a 22-9 record.

OCTOBER 5:

World Series, game one. In Chicago, Charles "Red" Ruffing scatters nine hits and issues no walks as the Yankees beat the Cubs, 3-1. Bill Dickey has four singles in four at-bats. Bill Lee is charged with the loss.

OCTOBER 6:

World Series, game two. Two of the game's great characters, Vernon "Lefty" Gomez and Dizzy Dean, face off in Chicago. Gomez, with relief help from Johnny Murphy and two-run homers by Frank Crosetti and Joe DiMaggio, wins, 6-3. Dean holds the Yankees to five hits and two runs in the first seven innings until his arm acts up.

OCTOBER 8:

World Series, game three. Monte Pearson five-hits the Cubs, 5-2, at Yankee Stadium. Joe Gordon and Bill Dickey homer for the Yankees, Joe Marty for the Cubs. All three are hit with the bases empty. Claiborne "Clay" Bryant gets the loss.

OCTOBER 9:

World Series, game four. Behind Red Ruffing's eight-hit pitching, the Yankees beat the Cubs in New York, 8-3, wrap up the Series, and become the first team ever with three consecutive World Championships. Ruffing helps his own cause with a two-run single in the second inning. Frank Crosetti's triple and Tommy Henrich's homer are the big blows. Ken O'Dea hits a two-run homer. In a losing effort, Joe Marty hits .500 and Phil Cavarretta .462. For the Yankees, Joe Gordon and Bill Dickey finish at .400. Red Ruffing compiles a 1.50 ERA with his two victories.

POST SEASON

OCTOBER 12:

Shortstop Leo Durocher is named manager of the Dodgers for the 1939 season. He replaces Burleigh Grimes, whose Dodgers were 69-80 and finished in seventh place.

NOVEMBER 2:

Jimmie Foxx tops Bill Dickey and Hank Greenberg for the AL's Most Valuable Player Award, becoming the first player ever to be so honored three times.

Lucky Charlie Weeghman, former owner of the Cubs, dies of a stroke at age 64 in New York City. Among Weeghman's innovations was allowing fans to keep balls hit into the stands and a weekly "ladies' day" discount.

NOVEMBER 28:

White Sox pitcher Monty Stratton must have his right leg amputated at the knee after shooting himself while hunting rabbits in Texas. The surgery is necessary to halt the spread of gangrene and save Stratton's life. The right-hander was a 15-game winner in each of the last two seasons.

DECEMBER 29:

Washington outfielder Al Simmons (.302, 21 homers), whose price tag was $75,000 three years ago, is sold by the Senators to the Boston Bees for $3,000.

LEAGUE

In December, AL president Will Harridge gets a 10-year contract. The Reds get approval to play their season opener one day earlier than the rest of the NL. The early opening day is approved as recognition of the 1869 Red Stockings, the first all professional baseball team.

"I guess they just didn't want him to beat Babe Ruth's record."
– Billy Rogell on Hank Greenberg's 119 walks

THE BEST OF 1938

NATIONAL LEAGUE

HITTERS

Batting Average:
Ernie Lombardi, Cincinnati Reds, .342

Slugging Average:
Johnny Mize, St. Louis Cardinals, .614

Home Runs:
Mel Ott, New York Giants, 36

Runs Batted In:
Joe "Ducky" Medwick, St. Louis Cardinals, 122

Hits:
Frank McCormick, Cincinnati Reds, 209

Stolen Bases:
Stan Hack, Chicago Cubs, 16

PITCHERS

Wins:
"Big Bill" Lee, Chicago Cubs, 22

Strikeouts:
Claiborne "Clay" Bryant, Chicago Cubs, 135

Earned Run Average:
Bill Lee, 2.66

Winning Percentage:
Bill Lee, .710

Saves:
Dick Coffman, New York Giants, 12

Most Valuable Player:
Ernie Lombardi, Cincinnati Reds

AMERICAN LEAGUE

HITTERS

Batting Average:
Jimmie Foxx, Boston Red Sox, .349

Slugging Average:
Jimmie Foxx, .704

Home Runs:
Hank Greenberg, Detroit Tigers, 58

Runs Batted In:
Jimmie Foxx, 175

Hits:
Joe Vosmik, Boston Red Sox, 201

Stolen Bases:
Frank Crosetti, New York Yankees, 27

PITCHERS

Wins:
Charles "Red" Ruffing, New York Yankees, 21

Strikeouts:
Bob Feller, Cleveland Indians, 240

Earned Run Average:
Lefty Grove, Boston Red Sox, 3.08

Winning Percentage:
Charles Ruffing, .75

Saves:
Johnny Murphy, New York Yankees, 11

Most Valuable Player:
Jimmie Foxx, Boston Red Sox

1939

MAY 22, 1939

"It would not be fair to the boys... for me to try going on."
– *Lou Gehrig*

NEWS

HITLER CONQUERS CZECHOSLOVAKIA, ATTACKS POLAND

BRITAIN, FRANCE DECLARE WAR ON GERMANY; FDR DECLARES U.S. NEUTRALITY

NEW YORK WORLD'S FAIR OPENS

Pan Am begins regular air passenger service between U.S. and Europe

SIGMUND FREUD, FATHER OF PSYCHOANALYSIS, DIES

AL CAPONE PAROLED FROM PRISON FOR GOOD BEHAVIOR

GONE WITH THE WIND WINS THE OSCAR OVER *THE WIZARD OF OZ*

John Steinbeck's *The Grapes of Wrath* is published

General Electric invents fluorescent lighting

PRE-SEASON

JANUARY13 :

Colonel Jacob Ruppert, owner of the Yankees for the past 25 years, dies in New York of phlebitis at age 71. A lifelong bachelor, Ruppert leaves the team to his estate.

FEBRUARY 6:

Yankees' general manager Ed Barrow assumes the presidency of the team.

APRIL 1:

Phil Niekro is born in Blaine, Ohio.

THE SEASON

APRIL 18:

Walter "Red" Barber broadcasts today's Dodgers-Giants game, marking the first time a regular-season Brooklyn game is heard on the radio. The Giants beat the Dodgers, 7-3, on 13 hits.

APRIL 20:

After two rainouts, the Yankees open against the Red Sox at Yankee Stadium. Charles "Red" Ruffing seven-hits Boston, 2-0, beating Robert "Lefty" Grove. One of the seven hits is a 407-foot double to right-center field by Boston's 20-year-old rookie Ted Williams, who is making his major league debut. Ruffing fans Williams in his first two at-bats. Bill Dickey homers for the Yankees, and Lou Gehrig extends his consecutive-game streak to 2,123, although he is hitless in four at-bats and lines into two double plays.

APRIL 21:

Ted Williams begins his long love-hate relationship with Boston's fans when he debuts at Fenway Park today against the Athletics. Williams scores the game's first run on a passed ball by catcher Frank Hayes in a 9-2 Boston win.

APRIL 23:

Ted Williams begins to acclimate himself to the contours of Fenway Park. He hits his first major league home run and has four hits in five at-bats in a 12-8 loss to the Athletics.

APRIL 29:

In Washington, Joe DiMaggio tears a leg muscle in the muddy outfield at Griffith Stadium going after a Bobby Estalella liner. He will be lost to the Yankees for five weeks.

APRIL 30:

Lou Gehrig plays in his 2,130th consecutive game – and goes hitless – against the Senators' Joe Krakauskas. Gehrig's play has so deteriorated that he is congratulated by teammate Johnny Murphy when he makes a routine play. Gehrig, who has only four hits and a .143 average this season, boards the train for Detroit with his team after the game.

MAY 2:

The Iron Horse has worn down. After his astonishing major league record of 2,130 consecutive games, Lou Gehrig takes himself out of the lineup at Briggs Stadium, telling the team's manager, Joe McCarthy, he can no longer play. "It would not be fair to the boys, to Joe, or to the baseball public for me to try going on," Gehrig explains. The 35-year-old Gehrig is suffering from unexplained weakness and sluggishness. After carrying the scorecard out to the umpires and getting an ovation from the Detroit crowd of 11,379, he sits on the bench for the first time as Ellsworth "Babe" Dahlgren takes his place at first base.

MAY 2
After playing in 2,130 consecutive games, Lou Gehrig takes himself out of the lineup.

MAY 4
Red Sox rookie Ted Williams has the first of many two-home-run games.

Gehrig was Dahlgren's boyhood hero and he urges, "Come on, Lou. You better get out there! You've put me in a terrible spot." Gehrig responds, "Go on out there, Babe, and knock in some runs." In the top of the seventh, Dahlgren tries again to convince Gehrig to play. Gehrig answers that the team is "doing fine." Dahlgren is doing fine, driving in three runs with a homer and double. The Yankees win, 22-2.

One of the Tigers' pitchers in the game against the Yankees is 19-year-old Fred Hutchinson, who makes his major league debut, yielding eight runs, four hits, and five walks in two-thirds of an inning.

MAY 4:

In Detroit, Ted Williams hits two homers in a game for the first time in his career. One of Williams's homers – against Bob Harris – is the first ever to clear the right-field roof at Briggs Stadium. The Red Sox win, 7-6.

MAY 13:

The Browns and Tigers complete a 10-player trade that is heavy on movement and light on statistics. Going to St. Louis are infielder Mark Christman (.250), outfielder Chet Laabs (.313), and pitchers Lloyd "Vern" Kennedy (0-3), Alfred "Roxie" Lawson (1-1), George Gill (0-1), and Bob Harris (1-1). The Tigers get infielder Ralph "Red" Kress (.279), outfielder Roy "Beau" Bell (.219), and pitchers Louis "Bobo" Newsom (3-1) and Jim Walkup (0-1).

MAY 14:

Bob Feller's parents travel to Chicago from Van Meter, Iowa, to see him pitch in a Mother's Day game. In the third inning, a foul off the bat of Marv Owen hits Feller's mother, breaks her glasses, and causes a cut requiring six stitches over her right eye. After checking his mother, Feller fans Owen; the Indians win, 9-4.

MAY 16:

It's lights at night for the first time in the AL. Shibe Park becomes the third major league stadium with lights, and 15,109 fans turn up to see the hometown Athletics meet the Indians. Despite a Frank Hayes homer, the Indians win, 8-3, in 10 innings. Johnny Humphries is the winning pitcher; Roy Parmelee is credited with the loss.

MAY 17:

NBC's experimental television station, WXBS in New York, airs the first baseball game ever on television, a college match-up between Princeton and Columbia at Baker Field. Princeton wins, 2-1, in 10 innings. Bill Stern is the sportscaster.

MAY 29:

The Cubs acquire pitcher Claude Passeau (2-4) from the Phillies for outfielder Joe Marty (.132) and pitchers Ray Harrell (0-2) and Walter "Kirby" Higbe (2-1). By one account, Philadelphia also receives $50,000.

JUNE 1:

The Phillies play their first-ever night game and lose to the Pirates, 5-2, at Shibe Park. Gilbert "Gib" Brack of the Phillies and Wilbur "Bill" Brubaker of the Pirates hit homers. Truett "Rip" Sewell is the winning pitcher. Newly acquired Kirby Higbe gets the loss.

JUNE 6:

At the Polo Grounds, the Giants tie the one-game home run record with seven.

> LEFTY GOMEZ TO LOU GEHRIG: "HELL, LOU, IT TOOK THEM 15 YEARS TO GET YOU OUT OF THE BALL GAME. SOMETIMES THEY GET ME OUT IN 15 MINUTES." JOE MCCARTHY SAYS, "LOU JUST TOLD ME HE FELT IT WOULD BE BEST FOR THE CLUB IF HE TOOK HIMSELF OUT OF THE LINEUP. I ASKED HIM IF HE REALLY FELT THAT WAY. HE TOLD ME HE WAS SERIOUS. HE FEELS BLUE. HE IS DEJECTED."

HISTORY

Dodgers' outfielder Pete Reiser learns how tough it is to break into the majors with only eight teams in each league. Despite a homer in his first spring training at-bat and a 1.000 batting average (10-for-10), the Dodgers ship the 20-year-old back to the minors.

After being given a replica of his Hall of Fame plaque, Grover Cleveland Alexander says, "You know I can't eat tablets or nicely framed awards. Neither can my wife. But they don't think of things like that."

Five of the homers are hit with two out in the fourth inning. The home run hitters are Joe "Jo-Jo" Moore (two), Mel Ott, Harry Danning, Frank Demaree, Burgess Whitehead, and pitcher Manny Salvo – who legs out an inside-the-park round-tripper. The Giants win the game, 17-3, on 20 hits.

Joe DiMaggio returns to action after being injured and hits a home run, double, and single in a 7-2 Yankees' win over the White Sox.

In Williamsport, Pennsylvania, Carl Stotz and George Bebble form the Little League.

JUNE 12:

The Phillies release 1933 Triple Crown-winner Chuck Klein (.191 in 35 games), and he is signed by the Pirates.

JUNE 12:

The Baseball Hall of Fame is officially dedicated in Cooperstown, New York. A crowd of 11,000 gathers on the site where Abner Doubleday allegedly "invented" baseball 100 years ago. The ceremonies include the induction of George Sisler, Adrian "Cap" Anson, Eddie Collins, Charles Comiskey, William "Candy" Cummings, William "Buck" Ewing, Wee Willie Keeler, Charles "Old Hoss" Radbourn, and Albert G. Spalding. With Commissioner Kenesaw Mountain Landis as master of ceremonies, 10 living Hall of Fame members are present: Babe Ruth, Connie Mack, Honus Wagner, Napoleon Lajoie, Walter Johnson, George Sisler, Tris Speaker, Grover Cleveland Alexander, Cy Young, and Eddie Collins. Cobb, who is angry at Landis, does not attend the ceremony to avoid having his picture taken with the commissioner, but shows up later. In a game on Doubleday Field, Honus Wagner's team defeats Eddie Collins's nine, 4-2. Landis tells the gathering, "Nowhere other than at its birthplace, could this museum be appropriately situated. To the pioneers who were the moving spirits of this game in its infancy and to the players who have been nominated into the Hall of Fame by the Baseball Writers Association, we pay just tribute. But I should like to dedicate this museum to all America." The Hall is supported by money from Stephen C. Clark of Cooperstown.

Sisler, a first baseman whose career was hampered by a sinus infection in 1923 that permanently impaired his vision, has a .340 lifetime average for 15 years,

TRIVIA

The April 20 Yankees-Red Sox game marks the only time Lou Gehrig and Ted Williams play against one another.

Original Baseball Hall of Fame inductees

JUNE 12
The Baseball Hall of Fame is dedicated in Cooperstown, New York.

JUNE 20
It is reported that Lou Gehrig is suffering from a disease that will end his baseball career.

along with 100 homers, 2,812 hits, and 375 stolen bases. Originally a pitcher, he hit .407 in 1920 and .420 in 1922. He also batted .300 or better 11 times. Anson, regarded by many as the best of the 19th-century players, also is noted for his virulent racism. He played 22 years with the Chicago White Stockings/ Colts in the NL, batting .329 and collecting 3,000 hits. The two-time batting champion died in 1922. Collins, a second baseman, is a graduate of Columbia University. He played 25 seasons with the Athletics and White Sox, batting .333 with 743 stolen bases. In the 18 years in which he appeared in at least 100 games, he hit .300 or better 17 times. Comiskey was the owner of the White Sox from 1900 until his death in 1931. He played for 13 years as a first baseman, batting .264, and managed for 12 years – from 1883 to 1894 – compiling a .608 winning percentage, third best all-time. Cummings is the reputed inventor of the curveball. He played two seasons in the NL with the Hartford Dark Blues and the Cincinnati Reds, compiling a 21-22 record. Previously, he was 124-72 in National Association play. Cummings died in 1924. Ewing, principally a catcher, is rated among the all-time greats at that position. He played 18 seasons from 1880 to 1897, batting .303 with 36 stolen bases. In 1883, with the Giants, he led the NL in homers with 10. Ewing died in 1906. Radbourn, a graduate of Illinois Wesleyan University, pitched 11 years in the nineteenth century, compiling a record of 311-194, with a 2.67 ERA. He won 49 games in 1883 and 60 the following year. His record includes 489 complete games and 35 shutouts. Radbourne died in 1897. Spalding is being honored as the "organizational genius of baseball's pioneer days." Spalding, who died in 1915, pitched for two years in the NL, with a 48-13 record, and was 207-56 prior to 1875 in National Association play. He was baseball's first 200-game winner and formed the A.G. Spalding and Brothers sporting goods company. Keeler played 19 seasons, batting .343 with 2,947 hits and 495 stolen bases. He hit .424 in 1897 and batted .300 in his first 15 seasons. Keeler passed away in 1923. John J. McGraw once said of Keeler, "With the possible exception of Ty Cobb, Willie Keeler was the greatest player of all time..."

Lou Gehrig (l) at his farewell ceremony at Yankee Stadium

Lou Gehrig plays in a night exhibition game against the Blues at Ruppert Field in Kansas City and tomorrow will check into the Mayo Clinic in Rochester, Minnesota. In his one at-bat tonight, he grounds out to second baseman Gerry Priddy. After having trouble with, but catching, a line drive, he leaves the game in the third inning.

JUNE 18:

Lou Brock is born El Dorado, Arkansas.

JUNE 20:

The word on Lou Gehrig is out and it is not good. Dr. Harold C. Harbein of the Mayo Clinic reports, "This is to certify that Mr. Lou Gehrig has been under examination at the Mayo Clinic from June 13 to June 19, 1939, inclusive. After a careful and complete examination, it was found that he is suffering from amyotrophic lateral sclerosis. This type of illness involves the motor pathways and cells of the central nervous system and, in lay terms, is known as a form of chronic poliomyelitis – infantile paralysis. The nature of this trouble makes it such that Mr. Gehrig will be unable to continue his active participation as a baseball player inasmuch as it is advisable that he conserve his muscular energy. He could, however, continue in some executive capacity."

"Today I consider myself the luckiest man on the face of the earth."
– Lou Gehrig

According to Ray Robinson's biography, Yankee general manager Ed Barrow tells Eleanor Gehrig, "It was about time for Lou to get himself another job."

JUNE 27:

Boston and Brooklyn, which seem to specialize in extra-inning, unresolved games, play another one. This time it goes 23 innings – five hours and 15 minutes – in Boston and ends tied at 2 when called because of darkness. Brooklyn's Whitlow Wyatt puts in nearly two games' worth of work, pitching the first 16 innings. The two teams bang out 33 hits, and four pitchers issue 12 walks. In 1920, Boston and Brooklyn played a 26-inning tie.

JUNE 28:

Even without Babe Ruth and now Lou Gehrig, the Yankees show they still are the Bronx Bombers, dismantling the Athletics in a Philadelphia doubleheader. The Yankees score 33 runs, hit 13 home runs, and accumulate 53 total bases. The Yankee power display is highlighted by a record eight homers in the opening game. Reaching the Shibe Park seats are Joe DiMaggio (two), Babe Dahlgren (two), Bill Dickey, Joe Gordon, Tommy Henrich, and George Selkirk. The Yankees win the opener, 23-2. The nightcap provides little relief for the beleaguered Athletics. The Yankees hit five more homers – by Gordon (two), DiMaggio, Dahlgren, and Frank Crosetti – and beat Philadelphia, 10-0.

JULY 4:

Yankee Stadium echoes with the cheers of 61,808 fans who come to honor their stricken star on Lou Gehrig Day. Present to pay tribute to their teammate are former Yankees Babe Ruth, Waite Hoyt, Tony Lazzeri, Herb Pennock, Wally Pipp (replaced by Gehrig at the start of the record streak), Bob Meusel, Earle Combs (now a Yankees' coach), Mark Koenig, Joe Dugan, George Pipgras (umpiring the game), Benny Bengough, Wally Schang, and Everett Scott (who once held the consecutive-game record). His teammates present him with a trophy inscribed with a poem by John Kieran of the *New York Times*. It describes Gehrig as an "idol of cheering millions..." Gehrig, who nearly collapsed on his arrival at the stadium, is the center of a rectangle formed by the current Yankees and Senators. Manager Joe McCarthy tells Gehrig's replacement Babe Dahlgren, "Catch him if he starts to go down." The Yankees lose the opener to the Senators, 3-2, and, after the ceremony, win the nightcap, 11-1.

After introductions by present and former New York City mayors Fiorello La Guardia and James J. Walker, Gehrig gives one of the sports world's most memorable speeches: "Fans, for the past two weeks, you have been reading about a bad break I got. Yet today I consider myself the luckiest man on the face of the earth. I have been in ballparks for 17 years and I have never received anything but kindness and encouragement from you fans. Look at these grand men. Which of you wouldn't consider it the highlight of his career just to associate with them for even one day? Sure, I'm lucky. Who wouldn't consider it an honor to have known Jacob Ruppert? Also, the builder of baseball's greatest empire, Ed Barrow? To have spent six years with that wonderful little fellow, Miller Huggins? Then to have spent the next nine years with that outstanding leader, that smart student of psychology, the best manager in baseball today, Joe McCarthy? Sure, I'm lucky. When the New York Giants, a team you would give your right arm to beat and vice versa, sends you a gift, that's something. When everybody down to the groundskeepers and those boys in white coats remember you with trophies, that's something. When you have a wonderful mother-in-law who takes sides with you in squabbles against her own daughter, that's something. When you have a father and mother who work all their lives so that you can have an education and build your body, it's a blessing. When you have a wife who has been a tower of strength and shown more courage than you dreamed existed, that's the finest I know. So I close in saying that I might have had a bad break, but I have an awful lot to live for."

Jim Tabor of the Red Sox packs a season's worth of offense into today's doubleheader against the Athletics

TRIVIA

Baseball has had two pitchers named Jim Walkup, and both were born in Havana, Arkansas. James Huey Walkup, born on November 3, 1895, was 0-0 with the Tigers in 1927. He died on June 12, 1990, in Duncan, Oklahoma. James Elton Walkup was born December 14, 1909, and was 16-38 in six years with the Browns and Tigers. *The Baseball Encyclopedia* indicates no kinship between the two.

in Philadelphia. In one afternoon's work he has four homers, 19 total bases, seven runs, and 11 RBI. The two teams combine for 65 base hits in the doubleheader – 35 by Boston. In game one, the Red Sox win, 17-7, on homers by Tabor, Ted Williams, Joe Cronin, and Bobby Doerr. Ben Chapman, Indian Bob Johnson, and Frank Hayes hit home runs for the Athletics. The winning pitcher is Joe Heving; Henry "Cotton" Pippen gets the loss. In the nightcap, Tabor hits three homers – two with the bases loaded – and bats in nine runs. The Red Sox sweep the doubleheader, with an 18-12 victory. The winner is Denny Galehouse; Alfred "Chubby" Dean is the loser.

JULY 11:

In recognition of baseball's "centennial year," the AL decides to appoint 66-year-old Connie Mack to manage its All-Star squad instead of 1938 pennant-winner, Joe McCarthy. But Mack takes ill and McCarthy takes the helm. He starts six of his own players, and manages the AL to a 3-1 victory at Yankee Stadium. Bob Feller's sharp relief work saves a victory for Tommy Bridges. Bill Lee is the losing pitcher. Joe DiMaggio hits a home run in the fifth.

JULY 15:

At the Polo Grounds, Giants' shortstop Billy Jurges and umpire George Magerkurth exchange punches and spittle. An argument develops when the Giants claim a homer by the Reds' Harry Craft into the left-field upper deck was foul. Magerkurth, a magnet for trouble, is umping at first and is not involved in the call, but he and Jurges go at it anyway. Magerkurth says, "Take your ugly puss out of my face and I won't be spitting in it." Jurges responds, "Yeah and I'll spit right in your ugly puss." Magerkurth decks Jurges with one punch, precipitating a free-for-all. The Reds win, 8-4. Each is fined $250 and suspended for 10 days.

JULY 17:

Chuck Klein returns to Philadelphia in the uniform of the Pirates and smacks two home runs in a 7-4 Pittsburgh victory.

JULY 18:

J. Louis Comiskey, owner of the White Sox, dies at age 56 in Eagle River, Wisconsin. With player-manager Joe Cronin solid at shortstop, the Red Sox sell Harold "Pee Wee" Reese to the Dodgers for $75,000. Reese had starred at short with the Louisville Colonels in the American Association.

JULY 23:

Boston Red Sox rookie Ted Williams is stricken with appendicitis, but decides to forego surgery.

JULY 25:

The Dodgers buy outfielder Fred "Dixie" Walker (.305) from the Tigers for the waiver price.

New York Yankees' right-hander Richard "Atley" Donald beats the Browns, 5-1, tying a rookie record with his 12th consecutive win at the start of a season. The 28-year-old holds St. Louis hitless for five and two-thirds innings and ends up throwing a five-hitter. Joe DiMaggio hits a 450-foot homer into the center-field bleachers at Yankee Stadium, and Robert "Red" Rolfe also homers. The Athletics and Indians score an AL record 14 runs in the ninth inning. The teams enter the final frame tied, 3-3. The Indians open with nine runs, paced by pinch hitter Jeff Heath's double and triple. The Athletics respond with five runs, but fall short.

JULY 26:

Paced by Bill Dickey's three consecutive homers, the Yankees tie a major league record by scoring in every inning against the visiting Browns. Charles "Red" Ruffing limits St. Louis to three hits while the Yankees are banging out 20 safeties in a 14-1 victory.

AUGUST 6:

Just as every comedian wants to play Hamlet, it appears every slugger wants to play pitcher. Today Jimmie Foxx of the Red Sox takes a turn on the mound, retiring all three batters he faces, including one by strikeout. The Tigers beat the Red Sox, 10-1.

AUGUST 13:

In a game called after eight innings, the Yankees pummel the Athletics, 21-0, tying the AL record for the most lopsided shutout victory. Joe DiMaggio and Babe Dahlgren hit two homers each and Red Ruffing pitches a four-hitter. Hal Pippen is the game's losing pitcher. The Giants go on a home run spree. For

HISTORY

In Chicago, more than 25,000 fans show up to see Monty Stratton, who lost a leg in a 1938 hunting accident, pitch for the White Sox in a May exhibition game against the Cubs. The White Sox beat the Cubs, 4-1.

the second time this season, New York has seven homers in one game. In the opener of a Polo Grounds doubleheader against the Phillies, home runs are hit by Frank Demaree (two), Joe Moore, Bob Seeds, Zeke Bonura, Alex Kampouris, and pitcher Bill Lohrman. Phillies' rookie Bill Kerksieck serves up four round-trippers in the fourth inning – to Bonura, Kampouris, Lohrman and Moore – and six in the game. The Giants win, 11-2.

AUGUST 14:

A crowd of 30,000 attend the first night game at Comiskey Park and see the White Sox beat the visiting Browns, 5-2, on a Johnny Rigney three-hitter.

AUGUST 19:

Ted Williams hits his first major league grand slam homer in an 8-6 Red Sox victory over the Senators.

AUGUST 22:

Carl Yastrzemski is born in Southampton, New York.

AUGUST 25:

Robert "Red" Rolfe scores twice in each game of the Yankees' doubleheader wins against the Browns. He sets an AL record with runs in his 17th and 18th consecutive games. Rolfe has 30 runs in the streak. The Yankees win, 11-0 and 8-2.

AUGUST 26:

WXBS makes history with the telecast of a major league baseball game – a Dodgers-Reds faceoff in the opener of an Ebbets Field doubleheader. Red Barber describes the action for the owners of the approximately 400 television sets in New York. He also conducts the first-ever post-game, on-field interviews – with opposing managers Leo Durocher and Bill McKechnie. One camera is placed at ground level behind the catcher and another in the upper deck behind the Reds' dugout on the third-base side of the field. The *New York Times* reports: "At times it was possible to catch a fleeting glimpse of the ball as it sped from the pitcher's hand toward home plate." The broadcast includes commercials for Ivory Soap, Mobil Oil, and Wheaties. The Reds win the opener, 5-2, on a William "Bucky" Walters two-hitter. Luke Hamlin gets the loss.

AUGUST 27:

Jimmy Powers writes in the New York *Daily News*, "I have seen personally at least 10 colored ball players I know who are big leaguers. I am positive that if Josh Gibson were white, he would be a major league star."

AUGUST 31:

The Reds buy outfielder Al Simmons (.282) from the Boston Bees.

SEPTEMBER 3:

The Yankees and Red Sox play a game of "who can trump whom" at Fenway Park. The Yankees score two in the top of the eighth inning to take a 7-5 lead. It is nearly 6:30, the time of Boston's Sunday curfew. If the Red Sox do not get to bat in the bottom of the eighth, the entire inning is canceled and the score reverts to 5-5. The Yankees try to make out to end the half-inning – George Selkirk and Joe Gordon trot home. Boston issues intentional walks and generally stalls. The fans get in the spirit of the day and litter the playing field with garbage. Finally umpire Cal Hubbard ends the fiasco by awarding the Yankees a forfeit win. The Red Sox protest. AL president Will Harridge orders the game replayed and fines managers Joe McCarthy and Joe Cronin. The rescheduled game is rained out, however, and is never replayed.

SEPTEMBER 8:

"Rapid Robert" Feller beats the Browns, 12-1, in St. Louis, for his 20th win, becoming the youngest modern-era player to reach that mark.

REGULAR SEASON WRAP-UP:

Joe McCarthy's Yankees, once again packed with power, finish at 106-45 and waltz to the AL pennant, 17 games ahead of the Red Sox. Joe DiMaggio leads the majors with a .381 average along with 30 homers and 126 RBI. Charlie Keller (.334), Red Rolfe (.329), George Selkirk (.306), and Bill Dickey (.302) are the big guns. Lou Gehrig's replacement, Babe Dahlgren, hits .235 with 15 homers and 89 RBI. Red Ruffing, 21-7, is the Yankees' ace. Fireman Johnny Murphy, the prototype of the modern relief pitcher, operates full-time out of the bullpen and records 19 saves.

RULES CHANGE

After the July 15 dispute between Giants' shortstop Billy Jurges and umpire George Magerkurth, NL president Ford Frick has nets installed on the foul poles in all ballparks to make the fair-foul call easier for umpires.

> "If Josh Gibson were white, he would be a major league star."
> – *Sportswriter Jimmy Powers*

HISTORY

The Homestead Grays are first in the Negro National League, but lose the pennant to the Baltimore Elite Giants in a playoff. In the Negro American League, the Kansas City Monarchs beat the St. Louis Stars in a playoff to win the pennant.

Bill McKechnie manages the Reds to 97-57 record in the NL, four and a half ahead of the Cardinals. He is the first manager to lead three different franchises to the World Series (the 1925 Pirates and the 1928 Cardinals before the Reds). Frank McCormick at .332 with 128 RBI and Ival Goodman at .323 are the top hitters. Bucky Walters (27-11) and Paul Derringer (25-7) are the team's leading pitchers.

OCTOBER 4:

World Series, game 1. At Yankee Stadium, Red Ruffing allows only 4 hits to beat starter Paul Derringer and the Reds, 2-1. Derringer, who yields only 6 hits, goes into the bottom of the eighth tied, 1-1. Charlie Keller then triples to right-center field, Joe DiMaggio is intentionally walked, and Bill Dickey singles in the winning run.

OCTOBER 5:

World Series, game 2. Monte Pearson two-hits the Reds at Yankee Stadium and New York wins, 4-0. Pearson carries a no-hitter into the eighth when Ernie Lombardi singles with one out. Babe Dahlgren has a homer and double against losing pitcher Bucky Walters.

OCTOBER 7:

World Series, game 3. In Cincinnati, Irving "Bump" Hadley pitches 8 innings in relief of Vernon "Lefty" Gomez and the Yankees win, 7-3. The Reds' 10 singles are no match for the Yanks' 5 hits – including 4 homers. Charlie Keller smacks a pair of 2-run homers, Joe DiMaggio homers with one on, and Bill Dickey has a solo shot. Eugene "Junior" Thompson gets the loss.

OCTOBER 8:

World Series, game four. In Cincinnati, in the top of the 10th with the score tied 4-4 and Charlie Keller on first, Joe DiMaggio singles to left field, where Ival Goodman mishandles the ball. Keller heads for home plate as the throw hits catcher Ernie Lombardi in the groin. As Lombardi collapses, Keller crashes into him, enabling DiMaggio to score as well. The Yankees go on to win the game, 7-4, and the series in a four-game sweep. It is a major league record four consecutive World Championships for the Yankees. The winning pitcher is Johnny Murphy; Bucky Walters gets the loss. Charlie Keller and Bill Dickey hit homers for New York. Keller leads all hitters with .438, three homers, and six RBI, followed by DiMaggio at .313. Frank McCormick hits .400 for the Reds and Lombardi becomes the target of criticism for "snoozing."

> ANOTHER SEER IS HEARD FROM. YANKEES' GENERAL MANAGER ED BARROW PREDICTS, "NIGHT BASEBALL IS A PASSING ATTRACTION WHICH WILL NOT LIVE LONG ENOUGH TO MAKE IT WISE FOR THE NEW YORK CLUB TO SPEND $250,000 FOR A LIGHTING SYSTEM. AS LONG AS I HAVE ANYTHING TO SAY ABOUT THE RUNNING OF THE YANKEES, THEY WILL NOT PLAY NIGHT BALL IN THE STADIUM."

POST-SEASON

DECEMBER 8:

Lou Gehrig, who has remained with the Yankees as the team captain, is elected unanimously to the Hall of Fame after the Baseball Writers Association waives the usual five year waiting period.

Gehrig's number 4 is retired by the Yankees; it is the first time any team has retired a number. Gehrig also is appointed by Mayor Fiorello La Guardia to the New York City Parole Commission.

DECEMBER 10:

Dom DiMaggio follows his older brothers Joe and Vince to the major leagues. The Boston Red Sox buy the contract of the bespectacled outfielder from the San Francisco Seals for $40,000 plus two players to be named later.

"Lou Gehrig... seemed so durable that many of us thought he could have played forever."
– Former Yankee George Selkirk

THE BEST OF 1939

NATIONAL LEAGUE

HITTERS

Batting Average:
Johnny Mize, St. Louis Cardinals, .349

Slugging Average:
Johnny Mize, .626

Home Runs:
Johnny Mize, 28

Runs Batted In:
Frank McCormick, Cincinnati Reds, 128

Hits:
Frank McCormick, 209

Stolen Bases:
Lee Handley, Pittsburgh Pirates;
Stan Hack, Chicago Cubs, 17

PITCHERS

Wins:
William "Bucky" Walters, Cincinnati Reds, 27

Strikeouts:
Bucky Walters; Claude Passeau,
Philadelphia Phillies/Cincinnati Reds, 137

Earned Run Average:
Bucky Walters, 2.29

Winning Percentage:
Paul Derringer, Cincinnati Reds, .781

Saves:
Bob Bowman, Clyde Shoun, St. Louis Cardinals, 9

Most Valuable Player:
Bucky Walters, Cincinnati Reds

AMERICAN LEAGUE

HITTERS

Batting Average.
Joe DiMaggio, New York Yankees, .381

Slugging Average:
Jimmie Foxx, Boston Red Sox, .694

Home Runs:
Jimmie Foxx, 35

Runs Batted In:
Ted Williams, Boston Red Sox, 145

Hits
Robert "Red" Rolfe, New York Yankees, 213

Stolen Bases:
George Case, Washington Senators, 51

PITCHERS

Wins:
Bob Feller, Cleveland Indians, 24

Strikeouts:
Bob Feller, 246

Earned Run Average:
Lefty Grove, Boston Red Sox, 2.54

Winning Percentage:
Lefty Grove, .789

Saves:
Johnny Murphy, New York Yankees, 19

Most Valuable Player:
Joe DiMaggio, New York Yankees

1940

APRIL 16
Indians' pitcher Bob Feller is the first to throw a no-hitter on opening day.

NEWS

GERMANY TAKES PARIS; FRANCE SURRENDERS

FDR DEFEATS WENDELL WILLKIE FOR UNPRECEDENTED THIRD TERM

BATTLE OF BRITAIN BEGINS

30 million American homes have radios

First successful helicopter flight in the U.S.

***For Whom the Bell Tolls,* by Ernest Hemingway, and *Native Son,* by Richard Wright, are published**

PREHISTORIC CAVE PAINTING DISCOVERED IN FRANCE

LEON TROTSKY STABBED AND KILLED IN MEXICO

Frank Sinatra joins Tommy Dorsey Band

PRE-SEASON

JANUARY 1:

Commissioner Kenesaw Mountain Landis cancels a December 9 trade that would have sent outfielder Wally Moses to the Tigers from the Athletics in return for second baseman Benny McCoy and pitcher George "Slick" Coffman. Landis determines that McCoy was "hidden" in the minor leagues by the Tigers and he declares him a free agent. McCoy then signs with the Athletics for a $10,000 bonus.

JANUARY 14:

Commissioner Landis grants free agency to 91 players in the Tigers' system, including 87 minor leaguers – talent estimated to be worth $500,000. In addition, the Tigers must pay $50,000 compensation to 14 players. The Tigers were judged by the commissioner to be concealing the movement of players within their farm system. In addition to Benny McCoy, declared a free agent earlier this month, the players affected by Landis's decision include outfielder Roy Cullenbine and pitcher Lloyd "Dutch" Dietz.

JANUARY 30:

The Yankees sell minor league outfielder Walt Judnich to the Browns for $7,500 as part of AL president Will Harridge's "socialistic" plan.

FEBRUARY 8:

The Browns buy another $7,500 player – pitcher Elden Auker (9-10, 5.36 ERA) – from the Red Sox.

FEBRUARY 29:

A federal district judge clears the way for Grace Comiskey, widow of J. Louis Comiskey, to retain the White Sox. She has been engaged in a legal battle with the First National Bank of Chicago over the estate of her late husband.

MARCH 3:

The Bees sell outfielder Debs Garms (.298, two homers) to the Pirates.

MARCH 6:

Willie Stargell is born in Earlsboro, Oklahoma.

MARCH 26:

The Phillies sign free agent Chuck Klein (.284, 12 homers), who split last season between Philadelphia and Pittsburgh. It is his third stint with the Phillies.

THE SEASON

APRIL 14:

For the fourth time in the last five seasons, the Yankees open the season without Joe DiMaggio. The Yankee Clipper injured his right knee yesterday during an exhibition game against the Dodgers and will be out of the lineup for 15 days.

APRIL 16:

In 47-degree weather at Comiskey Park, the Indians' Bob Feller pitches modern baseball's first opening day no-hitter, beating the White Sox, 1-0. It also is the first career no-hitter for Feller, who fans eight and walks five. The Indians commit one error. In the fourth inning, catcher Ralston "Rollie" Hemsley triples in Jeff Heath – who had singled – with the game's only run. With his parents and his sister, Marguerite, cheering him on, Feller gets Taft Wright to ground out, sealing the no-hitter. Eddie Smith is the game's losing pitcher.

President Franklin D. Roosevelt throws out the first ball at opening day at Griffith Stadium and hits *Washington Post* photographer Irving Schlossberg.

APRIL 23:

The Ohio River floods and causes the Reds to cancel today's and tomorrow's games with the Cardinals. The river is seven feet above flood stage and expected to reach eight feet at Cincinnati's Crosley Field.

APRIL 30:

The flood has subsided at Crosley Field – and 10,544 fans show up – but the Reds may be wishing it hadn't. The visiting Dodgers' James "Tex" Carleton no-hits Cincinnati, 3-0. The win also is Brooklyn's ninth straight, tying the modern record for a season opening. Carleton strikes out four and issues two walks; the Dodgers make three errors. It is the first start as a Dodger for Carleton, who spent last year in the minor leagues. Pete Coscararts homers with two on in the fifth for all of Brooklyn's runs. Jim Turner is the day's losing pitcher.

MAY 5:

In St. Louis today, the Cardinals and Brooklyn use a record 39 players – 22 for the Dodgers – in a nine-inning game. The Dodgers score four runs in the final frame edging over the Cards for a 9-6 win. The old record of 37 players was set in two games involving the Cardinals – in 1928 against the Phillies and in 1937 against the Cubs.

MAY 7:

In St. Louis, the Cardinals bomb the Dodgers, 18-2, on 20 hits – 13 of them for extra bases – and a National League record-tying seven home runs. Eddie Lake (two), Johnny Mize (two), Stu Martin, Joe "Ducky" Medwick, and Don Padgett wreak havoc on Brooklyn's pitching staff. The Dodgers do have a fast way to get out of town. After the game, the team flies from St. Louis to Chicago on two planes, becoming the first full team to travel by commercial airliner.

MAY 8:

DiMaggio gets traded to the Pirates – but it's outfielder Vince, Joe's older brother, who makes the move, not Joe. In return for the elder DiMaggio (.250), the Reds get outfielder Johnny Rizzo (.179).

MAY 9:

The Dodgers travel home to Brooklyn, New York, by air.

MAY 11:

The Yankees are in an unaccustomed position – looking up from last place – after losing, 9-8, to the Red Sox. It is New York's eighth straight loss at home, and leaves them at 6-8.

MAY 13:

Because of a scheduling snafu, Reds' coach Jim Wilson and Cardinals' pitcher Lon Warneke serve as umpires when their teams meet today at Crosley Field in Cincinnati. The teams have a game to make up because of a flooded-out April 23 contest. Today is selected by the teams and just about everyone is notified except the NL, which doesn't assign umpires. Larry Goetz, a Cincinnati resident and an NL umpire, is tracked down and agrees to come in. The game is in progress when umpire Larry Goetz arrives. No one goes home feeling cheated when Goetz calls the game because of darkness after 14 innings with the score tied 8-8. Johnny Mize of the Cardinals has three homers; Billy Werber of the Reds, four doubles.

Today's events provide good training for Warneke, who umpires in the NL for six years when his playing days are finally over.

MAY 24:

Night baseball comes to Sportsman's Park in St. Louis, but the hometown nine lose the game, 3-2, to Cleveland and Bob Feller, who also hits his first major league home run.

MAY 30:

The Giants' Carl Hubbell is the model of efficiency against the Dodgers at Ebbets Field. He one-hits Brooklyn on 87 pitches and faces only 27 batters. In the second inning, Johnny Hudson walks and is erased trying to steal. The Giants win the opener, 7-0, and take the nightcap, 12-5.

JUNE 4:

In the first night game at Forbes Field, the Pirates beat the visiting Bees, 14-2.

Meanwhile, the Cardinals are appearing under the lights in St. Louis for the first time, as well. With 23,500 in atten-

LEAGUE

The Browns are foundering, and visiting AL teams have trouble earning back their expenses when they visit St. Louis. AL president Will Harridge urges the other teams to "go a little socialistic for their own good." Each team sells the Browns a player for $7,500.

HISTORY

No one is elected to the Hall of Fame in 1940.

HISTORY

Joe DiMaggio comes close to confrontation with Commissioner Kenesaw Mountain Landis. DiMaggio, after hitting .381 in 1939, consults a friend about his $32,000 salary for this season. The friend happens to be gambler and fight manager Joe Gould, who receives no money for his advice. Landis learns of Gould's role and investigates the relationship, finding this is not a case of consorting with gamblers. Sportswriter Bob Considine comments, "The big league bosses are afraid that the ball players will smarten up enough to hire fast-talking tough bargaining agents to speak for them. And if that ever comes to pass the ball clubs would have to pay all the blokes what they're actually worth."

dance, the Cardinals bow to the Dodgers, 10-1. Pete Coscarart's three-run home run highlights a five-run first inning. The Cardinals' hurler Joe Medwick thrives under the lamps, with five hits in five at-bats.

The Giants also join the trend to night baseball by constructing lights at the Polo Grounds.

JUNE 6:

The Boston Bees sign 19-year-old left-handed pitcher Warren Edward Spahn.

JUNE 7:

With the Cardinals at 15-29, 15 1/2 games out of first place, manager Ray Blades is fired and replaced by Billy Southworth, who managed the Cardinals for part of the 1929 season.

JUNE 8:

Is he a fireman or an arsonist? In Brooklyn, Dodgers' pitcher Carl Doyle comes out of the bullpen to face the Reds. He goes four innings, yielding 16 hits and 14 runs. Cincinnati wins, 23-2, on 27 hits. Harry Craft has a homer, triple, double, and two singles, batting in seven runs.

JUNE 12:

Dodgers obtain outfielder Joe "Ducky" Medwick (.304) along with pitcher Curt Davis (0-4) from the Cardinals for outfielder Ernie Koy (.229), minor league first baseman Bert Haas, pitcher Carl Doyle (0-0), minor league pitcher Sam "Subway" Nahem, and $125,000.

JUNE 13:

The Indians rebel against manager Oscar "Ossie" Vitt. They complain about his "dugout demeanor, criticism, and disparaging conduct." Eleven members of the team meet with owner Alva Bradley to air their grievances; they want Vitt fired.

JUNE 14:

First baseman John "Buddy" Hassett of the Boston Bees gets four hits against the Cubs at Braves Field and becomes the seventh NL player with 10 consecutive hits. Hassett's streak extends over three games. Boston beats Chicago, 4-2

JUNE 16:

Twenty-one Indians withdraw their call for the resignation of Ossie Vitt, saying the action is in "the best interest of the team." The Indians sweep a doubleheader from the Athletics, 4-2 and 4-3.

JUNE 18:

Dodger outfielder Joe "Ducky" Medwick is beaned by his former Cardinals' teammate Bob Bowman in the nightcap of a doubleheader at Ebbets Field. Medwick, traded to Brooklyn only six days ago, is carried off on a stretcher and hospitalized for observation. Medwick and Bowman had quarreled before the game and Dodgers' president Larry MacPhail accuses the pitcher of purposely hitting Medwick in the head. St. Louis manager Billy Southworth removes Bowman from the game and he is escorted off the field by police. The Cardinals win, 7-5.

Hostility between the Dodgers and Cardinals persists for more than a year. Medwick returns, but never quite regains his "pre-beaning" consistency.

JULY 2:

The Red Sox score 14 runs in the seventh inning against the Athletics, becoming the second AL team to accomplish that feat. Philadelphia scores twice in its half of the inning for a combined AL record of 16 runs. Ted Williams has no hits in the game, but sets a modern record by batting three times in one inning; he walks twice and grounds out. Boston wins the game, 15-9.

JULY 9:

In St. Louis, the NL wins the first ever shutout in an All-Star Game, 4-0. Five pitchers combine for the three-hit whitewash: Paul Derringer (the game's winner), Bucky Walters, Whitlow Wyatt, Larry French, and Carl Hubbell (who gets the save). Red Ruffing gives up a three-run homer in the first to Max West and is tagged with the loss.

JULY 19:

At Wrigley Field, Cubs' pitcher Claude Passeau is hit in the back by the Dodgers' Hugh Casey in the eighth inning; he responds by flinging his bat at the mound and a fight ensues. After, Passeau and Brooklyn outfielder Joe "Muscles" Gallagher are ejected. The Cubs, with a first-inning grand slam from Hank Leiber and an eighth-inning two-run homer from Bill "Swish" Nicholson,

AUGUST 24
Slugger Ted Williams takes to the mound for two innings of mop-up in a 21-1 loss.

win, 11-4. Passeau gets credit for his 11th victory of the season.

JULY 23:

Commissioner Kenesaw Mountain Landis declares pitcher Larry Jansen a free agent and fines the Red Sox $500 for improper contract procedures.

AUGUST 2:

In Detroit, Red Sox player-manager Joe Cronin hits for the cycle as Boston wins, 12-9, on 14 hits. Among Cronin's four hits in five at-bats is an eighth-inning homer against Archie McKain. Jimmie Foxx hits his 23rd home run of the year and Dominic DiMaggio adds another round-tripper. Jack Wilson gets the victory; Tom Seats is the losing pitcher.

AUGUST 3:

Reds' catcher Willard Hershberger commits suicide in a Boston hotel room by cutting his throat. The 30-year-old Hershberger fails to show up for today's game at Braves Field and is found by a friend, Cincinnati businessman Dan Cohen. Hershberger had been playing in place of the injured Ernie Lombardi and hitting .309. His suicide is attributed to blaming himself for calling the wrong pitches in a loss to the Giants on July 31. There were signs of trouble. Manager Bill McKechnie, noticing his "depressed mental condition," had tried talking to him, but to no avail.

AUGUST 5:

In St. Louis, Silent John Whitehead of the Browns quiets the Tigers, 4-0, with an abbreviated no-hitter. Rain curtails the game after six innings.

AUGUST 17:

Ted Williams raps Boston sportswriters and fans and asks the Red Sox to trade him to the Tigers.

AUGUST 18:

New York *Daily News* sports editor Jimmy Powers has an explanation for the Yankees' poor play and their present fifth-place standing. He attributes the poor play to a "mass polio epidemic" contracted from Lou Gehrig. Lou Gehrig sues Powers for $1 million. Bill Dickey, who was Gehrig's roommate, also files suit.

His current salary of $12,500 is "peanuts," according to Boston's Ted Williams.

AUGUST 24:

Now pitching for the Red Sox, number 9. Ted Williams, who had asked for a trade to the Tigers, pitches two innings against them today. Red Sox pitcher Jim Bagby completes the switch, playing in Williams's left-field spot. Hurling the eighth and ninth innings, Williams allows three hits and a run and strikes out slugger Rudy York on three pitches with a sidearm curve. The Tigers win, 12-1, at Fenway Park; Tommy Bridges gets the win. Catching Williams is Joe Glenn, who was the receiver for Babe Ruth's last pitch, in 1933.

SEPTEMBER 8:

The Cardinals' Johnny Mize hits his 38th, 39th, and 40th homers of the season against the Pirates in the opener of a doubleheader to become the first player with three homers in a game four times in his career. Mize had three homers on May 13 and twice in 1938 games. Despite Mize's power hitting, the Pirates still beat the Cardinals twice, 16-14 and 9-4.

SEPTEMBER 16:

Browns' reserve second baseman Johnny Lucadello becomes the second AL player to hit switch homers in a game. The two homers are the first of his career and his only round-trippers of the season. Wally Schang of the Athletics was the first in 1916.

Umpire George Magerkurth, six feet, three inches tall, weighing in at 245 pounds, is decked by a 190-pound fan – one of the hundreds on the field – after a Dodgers' loss to the Reds, 4-3, in 10 innings in Brooklyn. The fan is arraigned. This is not the first incident of fan-umpire trouble in New York. In July, with 68,000-plus at Yankee Stadium, umpire Joe Rue was bombarded with bottles after a foul call.

SEPTEMBER 21:

The Pirates' Deb Garms gets five hits today against the Reds to win the NL batting championship with a .355 average.

SEPTEMBER 22:

In Detroit, a crowd of 56,771 sees Bob Feller hit a homer and defeat the Tigers, 10-5, for his 27th win of the season. The Indians bang out four more homers – by Hal Trosky, Roy Weatherly, Ben Chapman, and Ken Keltner.

TRIVIA

The Cardinals' farm system now includes more than 600 players.

LEAGUE

The Cubs send sore-armed Dizzy Dean down to Tulsa, their Class AA Texas League farm team, in the hope that a warm climate will benefit him.

TRIVIA

What team had the same batting average at the beginning and end of a game? The White Sox, no-hit on opening day. Each player begins the game at .000 and ends the game with the same average.

Thomas Wolfe writes in *You Can't Go Home Again*, published posthumously this year: "What visions burn, what dreams possess him Seeker of the night? The faultless velvet of the diamond, The mounting roar of 80,000 voices And Gehrig coming to bat..."

Jimmie Foxx batted his 500th career homer in 1940.

SEPTEMBER 24
Jimmie Foxx hits his 500th career home run in the Red Sox sweep of a doubleheader.

SEPTEMBER 24:

Jimmie Foxx hits his 500th career homer, and it comes against his former team, the A's, in Philadelphia. Foxx's homer off George Caster in the sixth inning is followed by round-trippers by Ted Williams, Joe Cronin, and Jim Tabor. The Red Sox collect seven extra-base hits and 25 total bases in the inning and sweep the twin-bill, 16-8 and 4-3.

SEPTEMBER 26:

Jimmy Powers and the New York *Daily News* extend "our apologies to Lou Gehrig and the Yankees." Powers says, "Gehrig has no communicable diseases and was not suffering from the mysterious polio germ that supposedly played havoc with the Yankee ball club." Powers adds that "hurting his feelings was far from my mind."

SEPTEMBER 27:

After four consecutive years at Yankee Stadium, the AL pennant will fly elsewhere. The Yankees are eliminated from the pennant race when they lose, 6-2, to the Athletics and their former farmhand, Johnny Babich. Municipal Stadium in Cleveland is packed with 45,553 fans who come to see the first-place Tigers meet the second-place Indians. The prospects are good for the home team with 27-game winner Bob Feller opposing 30-year-old Floyd Giebell, just called up from the Buffalo Bisons of the International League, where he was 15-17. Feller pitches a two-hitter and loses, 2-0, on a homer by Rudy York with one on, giving the Tigers the AL pennant. The Tigers become the targets of garbage-throwing fans, who pelt them with vegetables and eggs. Tigers' catcher George "Birdie" Tebbetts, working in the bullpen, is knocked out by a basket of tomatoes thrown from the upper deck in left field by "fan" Armen Guerra. Umpire George Pipgras says, "I thought Tebbetts was dead. I thought they had killed him."

REGULAR SEASON WRAP-UP:

Under Bill McKechnie, the Reds run away with the NL pennant, compiling a 100-53 record and beating the Dodgers by 12 games. The team has two 20-game winners, William "Bucky" Walters (22-10) and Paul Derringer (20-12). Frank McCormick hits .309. Myron "Mike" McCormick bats .300, and Ernie Lombardi finishes at .319.

The Tigers, under Del Baker, break the Yankees' stranglehold on the AL pennant. They finish at 90-64, edging the Indians by one game. The Yankees are in third, two back. Louis "Bobo" Newsom leads the pitching staff with 21-5. Hank Greenberg bats .340 with 41 homers and 150 RBI. Close behind is Rudy York with .316, thirty three homers, and 134 RBI. Barney McCoskey (.340) and Charlie Gehringer (.313) add bite to the Tigers' dangerous lineup.

OCTOBER 2:

World Series, game one. In Cincinnati, Bobo Newsom eight-hits the Reds and the visiting Tigers win the opener, 7-2. Bruce Campbell hits a two-run home run and Detroit scores five runs in the second inning. Paul Derringer gets the loss.

OCTOBER 3:

World Series, game two. William "Bucky" Walters three-hits the Tigers, 5-3, at Crosley Field, with help from a two-run Jimmy Ripple homer in the third inning. Lynwood "Schoolboy" Rowe is the losing pitcher.

OCTOBER 4:

World Series, game three. Playing before a home crowd of 52,877, the Tigers beat the Reds, 7-4. Rudy York and Mike "Pinky" Higgins hit two-run homers in the seventh to put the Tigers ahead for good. Hank Greenberg hits a two-run triple. Tommy Bridges gets the win; Jim Turner takes the loss.

OCTOBER 5:

World Series, game four. With Paul Derringer limiting the Tigers to 5 hits, the Reds win, 5-2, to even the series. Paul "Dizzy" Trout, the first of four Tigers' pitchers, gets the loss.

OCTOBER 6:

World Series, game five. In Detroit, Hank Greenberg's three-run homer and Bobo Newsom's three-hit pitching lead the

TRIVIA

Dickie Kerr, one of the honest 1919 White Sox, is managing the Daytona Beach team in the Florida State League, where he has a 19-year-old pitcher named Stan Musial (18-5). Kerr recognizes Musial's hitting talent and uses him in the outfield in 57 games. Musial is earning $100 a month and has a pregnant wife. Kerr invites Musial to live with his family. In August, after an injury, Musial becomes a full-time position player. The Musials name their son Richard after Kerr, and when he is an established star, Stan buys a home in Houston for his former skipper.

TRIVIA

As a New York City parole officer, Lou Gehrig hears the parole violation case of 19-year-old Rocco Barbella and sends him to reform school. As Rocky Graziano, Barbella becomes the world's middleweight world champion.

CULTURE

In *The Kid From Tomkinsville,* a novel by John R. Tunis, pitcher Roy Tucker becomes an outfielder when his pitching career is cut short by an injury.

Tigers to an 8-0 win. The Tigers pound out 13 hits against four Reds pitchers. Eugene "Junior" Thompson gets the loss.

Bobo Newsom dedicates the victory to his father, who died several days ago. He says, "It was the hardest game I ever wanted to win." His catcher Billy Sullivan tells him, "Bobo, your dad would have liked this."

OCTOBER 7:

World Series, game six. Back in Cincinnati, the series is knotted again on Bucky Walters's five-hit, 4-0 win over the Tigers and Schoolboy Rowe. Walters also homers with no one on in the eighth.

OCTOBER 8:

World Series, game seven. In Cincinnati, the Reds win their first World Series since 1919 with a 2-1 victory on Paul Derringer's seven-hit pitching. Bobo Newsom, who also allows only seven hits, is the hard-luck loser when he gives up two runs in the bottom of the seventh on doubles by Frank McCormick and Jimmy Ripple, and Billy Myers's sacrifice fly. Billy Werber of the Reds leads all hitters with .370. Greenberg bats .357 with six RBI. Walters and Derringer account for all the Reds' wins. Newsom compiles a 1.38 ERA and is 2-1.

> IN HIS AUTOBIOGRAPHY, TED WILLIAMS RECALLS, "THAT WAS...THE YEAR I GOT BOOED FOR MAKING AN ERROR AND THEN FOR STRIKING OUT, AND THE UNFAIRNESS OF IT HIT ME. I VOWED THAT DAY I'D NEVER TIP MY HAT AGAIN."

POST-SEASON

OCTOBER 17:

George Davis passes away in Philadelphia, Pennsylvania, at the age of 70.

NOVEMBER 4:

The Dodgers acquire catcher Arnold "Mickey" Owen (.264) from the Cardinals for catcher Gus Mancuso (.229), minor league pitcher John Pintar, and $65,000 in cash.

NOVEMBER 11:

The Dodgers acquire a new pitcher to go along with their new catcher. They obtain Walter "Kirby" Higbe (14-19, 3.72 ERA) from the Phillies for pitchers Vito Tamulis (8-5, 3.09 ERA) and Bill Crouch, along with catcher Thompson "Mickey" Livingston plus $100,000. Crouch and Livingston did not play in the major leagues in 1940.

NOVEMBER 12:

Roger Peckinpaugh becomes manager of the Indians for the second time. He replaces Ossie Vitt, who was the center of a player revolt, and finished 89-65 in second place. Peckinpaugh previously managed Cleveland from 1928 through 51 games of the 1933 season.

DECEMBER 3:

The Browns buy pitchers Denny Galehouse (6-6, 5.18 ERA) and Frederick "Fritz" Ostermueller (5-9, 4.95 ERA) from the Red Sox for $30,000.

DECEMBER 10:

The Pirates release outfielder Paul "Big Poison" Waner (.290, one homer).

DECEMBER 15:

Billy Hamilton dies at age 74 in Worcester, Massachusetts. He played in the majors for 14 years, twice leading the NL in batting. His lifetime average was .344, and he stole 915 bases.

DECEMBER 20:

Connie Mack buys the controlling interest in the Athletics.

THE BEST OF 1940

National League

HITTERS

Batting Average:
Debs Garms, Pittsburgh Pirates, .355

Slugging Average:
Johnny Mize, St. Louis Cardinals, .636

Home Runs:
Johnny Mize, 43

Runs Batted In:
Johnny Mize, 137

Hits:
Stan Hack, Chicago Cubs;
Frank McCormick, Cincinnati Reds, 191

Stolen Bases:
Linus "Lonny" Frey, Cincinnati Reds, 22

PITCHERS

Wins:
William "Bucky" Walters, Cincinnati Reds, 22

Strikeouts:
Walter "Kirby" Higbe, Philadelphia Phillies, 137

Earned Run Average:
Bucky Walters, 2.48

Winning Percentage:
Fred Fitzsimmons, Brooklyn Dodgers, .889

Saves:
Mace Brown, Pittsburgh Pirates;
Joe Beggs, Cincinnati Reds;
Walter "Jumbo" Brown, New York Giants, 7

Most Valuable Player:
Frank McCormick, Cincinnati Reds

American League

HITTERS

Batting Average:
Joe DiMaggio, New York Yankees, .352

Slugging Average:
Hank Greenberg, Detroit Tigers, .670

Home Runs:
Hank Greenberg, 41

Runs Batted In:
Hank Greenberg, 150

Hits:
Raymond "Rip" Radcliff, St. Louis Browns;
Barney McCoskey, Detroit Tigers;
Roger "Doc" Cramer, Boston Red Sox, 200

Stolen Bases:
George Case, Washington Senators, 35

PITCHERS

Wins:
Bob Feller, Cleveland Indians, 27

Strikeouts:
Bob Feller, 261

Earned Run Average:
Bob Feller, 2.61

Winning Percentage:
Lynwood "Schoolboy" Rowe, Detroit Tigers, .842

Saves:
John "Al" Benton, Detroit Tigers, 17

Most Valuable Player:
Hank Greenberg, Detroit Tigers

HISTORY

The Homestead Grays win the Negro National League pennant; the Kansas City Monarchs take the Negro American League flag.

1941

"I'm tickled to death it's over."
– Joe DiMaggio on his hitting streak

NEWS

JAPAN ATTACKS PEARL HARBOR; U.S. DECLARES WAR ON JAPAN, GERMANY, ITALY

Germany invades Soviet Union

FDR, CHURCHILL DRAFT ATLANTIC CHARTER

PENICILLIN PRODUCED BY U.S. COMPANIES

Literary giants James Joyce, F. Scott Fitzgerald, Virginia Woolf die

FEDERAL COMMUNICATIONS COMMISSION LICENSES FIRST TWO COMMERCIAL TV STATIONS: NBC AND CBS IN NEW YORK

MOVIEGOERS ARE WATCHING *THE MALTESE FALCON* AND *CITIZEN KANE*

Mount Rushmore sculptor John Gutzon dies

TREASURY BONDS ISSUED

PRE-SEASON

JANUARY 2:

Babe Ruth supports America's mobilization efforts by purchasing $50,000 worth of defense bonds – the legal limit for one person.

FEBRUARY 25:

Ellsworth "Babe" Dahlgren (.264, 12 homers), the man who replaced Lou Gehrig, is sold by the Yankees to the Braves. Dahlgren had played in every Yankee game since May 2, 1939.

MARCH 4:

There's another Comiskey at the helm of the White Sox. After winning her court case, Grace Comiskey is elected president of the team, and her daughter, Dorothy Rigney, is named secretary.

MARCH 8:

Philadelphia Phillies' pitcher Hugh Mulcahy swaps his baseball flannels for an army uniform when he becomes the first major leaguer to be drafted into the service. Mulcahy was 13-22 with a 3.60 ERA last season.

APRIL 14:

Pete Rose is born in Cincinnati, Ohio.

THE SEASON

APRIL 20:

The Dodgers become the first of any major league team to wear batting helmets – caps with a protective plastic liner. The helmets have been invented by Johns Hopkins surgeons George Barnett and Walter Dandy. The helmets were designed after the "beanball wars" of 1940, and 25 experimental models preceded the selection of the ones the Dodgers wear today.

APRIL 23:

At Yankee Stadium, rookie Phil Rizzuto's first major league home run gives New York a 4-2 win over the Red Sox in 11 innings. Rizzuto's round-tripper is hit against Charlie Wagner with George Selkirk on base.

APRIL 26:

Cubs fans are greeted by the sound of music – a pre-game program by Roy Nelson after Wrigley Field becomes the first ballpark with an organ. The music doesn't help the Cubs; they lose to Max Lanier and the Cardinals, 6-2.

MAY 1:

Dodgers' president Larry MacPhail reports he has applied for a patent on the Brooklyn Safety Cap introduced into play by the team on April 20. MacPhail asserts he is not interested in making money but in making it possible for other teams to use the caps.

In the first night game at Griffith Stadium in Washington, D.C., the Yankees defeat the Senators, 6-5.

MAY 6:

Hank Greenberg says good-bye in style, hitting two homers and batting in three runs in a 7-4 victory over the Yankees at Briggs Stadium. Tomorrow, Greenberg – the first major league starter to be drafted – will report to Fort Custer, Michigan, for basic training as a private.

Because he is 30 years old and the selective service laws prohibit drafting anyone over the age of 28, Hank Greenberg – now a sergeant– is discharged on December 5. He subsequently enlists in the Army Air Corps and attains the rank of captain.

MAY 6
The day before leaving for the army, Hank Greenberg hits two home runs.

JUNE 2
Exactly 16 years after becoming a Yankees' starter, Lou Gehrig dies of ALS.

MAY 7:

Outfielder Lloyd "Little Poison" Waner goes from the Pirates to the Braves in exchange for pitcher Nick Strincevich (0-0).

MAY 12:

The Boston Bees are once again the Boston Braves after five years. From 1876 to 1907, the team was known as the Beaneaters; from 1907 to 1912, they were the Doves.

MAY 14:

Dizzy Dean, who won 30 games in 1934, retires from baseball after an 0-0 start with an 18.00 ERA for the Cubs. He writes Chicago general manager Jim Gallagher: "I feel as though I can be of no benefit to the club as a pitcher this year... The only hope I have is that maybe complete rest of the arm for a while will do something for it."

Roy Stockton of the St. Louis Post-Dispatch *writes, "Baseball is mourning the passing of Dizzy Dean from the major league scene, and it does well to mourn. There will never be another Dizzy. They broke the mold when he was born. There will be other great pitchers, but no Dizzy Dean."*

MAY 19:

At Wrigley Field, Dodger manager Leo Durocher tries an unusual but futile form of protest. After a galling loss to the Cubs, 14-1, Durocher claims the Cubs were over the 25-player roster limit. The Cubs score nine runs in the second inning, highlighted by a grand slam homer by pitcher Claude Passeau against Hugh Casey.

MAY 20:

Robert "Lefty" Grove defeats the Tigers, 4-2, for his 20th consecutive home game win – the first major leaguer with a streak that long in his home park.

MAY 24:

Joe DiMaggio singles against Earl Johnson of the Red Sox with runners on second and third in the seventh and the Yankees trailing, 6-5. The Yankees win the game, and DiMaggio extends his consecutive-game hitting streak to 10.

The Braves have a double dose of poison. After trading for Lloyd "Little Poison" Waner on May 7, Boston signs Paul "Big Poison" Waner (.171), who was released earlier in the month by the Dodgers.

MAY 25:

The Dodgers' Pete Reiser, beaned by Isaac "Ike" Pearson of the Phillies last month, strikes back. He hits a grand slam home run against Pearson at Ebbets Field; the Dodgers win the game, 8-4.

With Joe DiMaggio early in his record hitting streak, Red Sox pitcher Lefty Grove surrenders a single to him. Grove becomes one of two pitchers who yielded a hit to DiMaggio in his streak and ahome run to Babe Ruth in 1927 (on September 27) – one of his record 60. Ted Lyons of the White Sox is the other pitcher with the distinction.

MAY 27:

In Washington, D.C., Joe DiMaggio has four hits in five at-bats, drives in three runs, and scores three runs in a 10-8 Yankees' victory over the Senators. DiMaggio now has hit in 12 consecutive games.

MAY 28:

In a night game at Griffith Stadium, the Yankees' George Selkirk hits a pinch-hit grand slam homer and the Yankees win, 6-5. Joe DiMaggio triples against Sid Hudson.

JUNE 1:

Mel Ott hits his 400th homer and drives in his 1,500th run in the Giants' win, 3-2, over the Reds.

JUNE 2:

At his home in Riverdale, New York, 16 years to the day after he stepped into the Yankee starting lineup, and 17 days before his 38th birthday, Lou Gehrig dies of ALS (amyotrophic lateral sclerosis). Gehrig had been fighting the disease

HISTORY

For the second consecutive year, no one is voted into the Hall of Fame.

Joe D gets yet another hit.

for two years. The Yankees are informed when they arrive today in Detroit.

JUNE 4:

Lou Gehrig's funeral is held in Christ Episcopal Church in Riverdale, the Bronx. Attending are American League president Will Harridge, Yankee manager Joe McCarthy, Babe Ruth, Billy Dickey, Arthur Huggins (brother of the late Yankees' manager Miller Huggins), and many other baseball notables. The Reverend Gerald V. Barry tells the mourners why there is no eulogy: "We need none, because you all knew him."

JUNE 7:

Joe DiMaggio's streak is getting serious. The Yankee Clipper gets three hits against three pitchers in St. Louis; he now has hit in 22 consecutive games. Charlie Keller hits a grand slam homer in the Yankees' 11-7 win over the Browns.

JUNE 8:

The Yankees sweep the Browns, 9-3 and 8-3, in a doubleheader. Joe DiMaggio has four hits in eight at-bats, including three homers, four runs, and seven RBI. His hitting streak is at 24 straight games.

TRIVIA

Among the skills of White Sox shortstop Luke Appling is his ability to foul off pitches. In the spring of 1941, after hitting .348 in 1940, he holds out for $20,000 but ends up signing for Chicago's original offer – $17,500. Appling reportedly decides to get even. According to a 1991 story in the *Chicago Tribune*, Appling's teammate, Bob Kennedy, counted 400 foul balls from spring training to the first two weeks of the season before manager Jimmy Dykes convinced him to stop.

"JOE HASN'T BEEN THE GREATEST HITTER THAT BASEBALL HAS KNOWN, EITHER. HE'LL NOT MATCH TY COBB'S LIFETIME AVERAGE, HE'LL NEVER THREATEN BABE RUTH'S HOME-RUN RECORD, NOR WILL HE EVER GRIP THE IMAGINATION OF THE CROWDS AS THE BABE DID. BUT YOU DON'T RATE A GREAT BALLPLAYER ACCORDING TO HIS SEPARATE SPECIAL TALENTS. YOU MUST RANK HIM OFF THE SUM TOTAL OF HIS COMPONENT PARTS, AND ON THIS BASIS THERE HAS NOT BEEN DURING JOE'S BIG-LEAGUE EXISTENCE A RIVAL CLOSE TO HIM."

– *Red Smith,* New York Herald Tribune

JUNE 12:

The Braves break up the set. A little more than a month after reuniting the Waner brothers, Boston sends Lloyd Waner (.412 in 19 games) to the Reds for pitcher Johnny Hutchings (0-0 in eight games). Paul Waner remains with the Braves.

JUNE 17:

Batting against Johnny Rigney of the White Sox, Joe DiMaggio singles off the shoulder of shortstop Luke Appling; his hitting streak is at 30. Chicago beats New York, 8-7.

JUNE 19:

With three hits in three at-bats – including a home run – against the White Sox, Joe DiMaggio extends his consecutive-game hitting streak to 32. The Yankees win, 7-2.

JUNE 21:

At Fenway Park, the Browns beat the Red Sox, 13-9, to end Lefty Grove's 20-game winning streak. Grove began the streak on May 3, 1938.

Grove's streak is dead, but DiMaggio's lives. He singles off the Tigers' Paul "Dizzy" Trout to extend his skein to 34, but Detroit wins, 7-2.

White Sox pitcher Ted Lyons describes Stan Musial's odd, coiled stance as looking like "a kid peeking around the corner to see if the cops were coming."

JUNE 24:

Joe DiMaggio's hitting streak comes perilously close to ending today against the Browns at Yankee Stadium. DiMaggio enters the eighth inning, hitless in three at bats against St. Louis's Bob Muncrief. In his final at-bat, DiMaggio singles, and his streak is alive at 36 games. Browns' manager Luke Sewell explains why he didn't have DiMaggio walked. "That wouldn't have been fair – to him or me. Hell, he's the greatest player I ever saw." The Yankees win, 9-1.

JUNE 25:

Former rivals and now unlikely friends, 40-year-old Babe Ruth and 54-year-old Ty Cobb meet in the first of a series of charity golf matches. Cobb describes it as the "Has Beens' Golf Tournament of Nowhere in Particular." Playing at the Commonwealth Country Club in West Newton, Massachusetts, for the benefit of underprivileged kids, Cobb beats Ruth, 80-83, and receives a trophy from actress Bette Davis. Ruth and Cobb play again on June 27 on Long Island for the benefit of the USO (United Service Organization), and the match ends in a tie. On June 29, in Grosse Point, Michigan, Cobb finishes 15 over to Ruth's 19 over.

JUNE 26:

Keeping DiMaggio's streak going is becoming a team effort for the Yankees. DiMaggio is hitless today going into the eighth inning, when he is scheduled to bat fourth. Robert "Red" Rolfe walks, and manager Joe McCarthy okays a bunt for Tommy Henrich to keep from hitting into a double play. The strategy succeeds and DiMaggio doubles off Elden Auker. The Yankees win, 4-1, and move into first place, and the streak is now at 38 games.

JUNE 28:

At Shibe Park, Athletics' pitcher Johnny Babich is a man with a plan. He walks Joe DiMaggio in his first at-bat. The next time up, on a three-ball count, the Yankee Clipper rockets an outside pitch between Babich's legs for a single. He adds a double, tying Cobb for the second longest hitting streak ever in the AL – 40 games. The Yankees win the game, 7-4.

JUNE 29:

One streak goes on, another dies. In a doubleheader against the Senators, Joe DiMaggio ties and then breaks George Sisler's AL consecutive game hitting streak. In the opener, DiMaggio is one-for-four with a long double against Emil "Dutch" Leonard to tie Sisler at 41; the Yankees win, 9-4. In the second game, he has a single off Walt Masterson in the seventh, his only hit in six at-bats, to break the record. After two lineouts and a fly ball, DiMaggio is brushed back by Arnold "Red" Anderson; he responds with a line drive to left for a hit. The Yankees' consecutive-game home run streak ends at 25.

JULY 1:

In the fourth inning of the second game of a doubleheader against the Red Sox at Yankee Stadium, Joe DiMaggio singles against Jack Wilson to tie Wee Willie Keeler's major league record consecutive game hit streak at 44. Keeler set the record in 1897. The Yankees win, 7-2 and 9-2; the nightcap is shortened by rain. On a close call, official scorer Dan Daniel of the *New York World-Telegram* rules that DiMaggio's ball – to third baseman Jim Tabor, who makes a bad throw – is a hit. Daniel says, "Damn you, DiMaggio, I gave you a hit this time, but everything has to be clean from now on."

JULY 2:

Joe DiMaggio now stands alone. With a three-run homer against Boston's Dick Newsome – after being robbed of hits in his first two at-bats – he sets a major league consecutive game hitting streak record – 45. In 95-degree weather, 52,832 attend the game at Yankee Stadium and see the Yankees win, 8-4. After today's game Lefty Gomez tells DiMaggio, "You not only broke Keeler's

TRIVIA

Brooklyn Dodgers' president Larry MacPhail enters the army as a lieutenant colonel, assisting Under Secretary of War Robert Patterson.

Ted Williams demonstrates the sweet swing that helped him hit .406 this season.

"I believe there isn't a record in the books that will be harder to break than Joe's 56 games. It may be the greatest batting achievement of all." – *Ted Williams*

JULY 8
Ted Williams' three-run homer in the bottom of the ninth gives the AL the All-Star Game win.

TRIVIA

Robert Russell Bennett's *Symphony in D, for Dodgers* is described by Donald Dewey and Nicholas Acocella as "the most elaborate music ever inspired by baseball." It consists of four movements: *Allegro con brio* (Brooklyn wins), *Andante lamentosa* (Brooklyn loses), *Scherzo* (Larry MacPhail tries to give Cleveland the Brooklyn Bridge for Bob Feller), and *Finale* (The Giants Come to Town). Less elaborate is "Joltin' Joe DiMaggio," recorded by Les Brown and his band with Betty Bonney on the vocal, which climbs to number 12 on the pop charts. Also on the airwaves are "Connie Mack Is the Grand Old Name" by George M. Cohan, and "Dodgers Fan Dance" by Harry James and Jack W. Matthias.

record, you even used his formula – you hit 'em where they ain't."

JULY 6:

The Yankees unveil a centerfield monument to Lou Gehrig. It reads: "A man, a gentleman and a great ballplayer whose amazing record of 2,130 consecutive games should stand for all time. This memorial is a tribute from the Yankee players to their beloved captain and teammate." The Yankees sweep the Athletics, 8-4 and 3-1. Joe DiMaggio extends his hitting streak to 48 games on six hits in nine at-bats, including four RBI. The Yankees now lead the Indians by three and a half games at the All-Star break.

JULY 8:

The AL wins the All-Star Game, 7-5, at Briggs Stadium in Detroit on a dramatic home run by Ted Williams. With two out and two on base in the bottom of the ninth, Williams homers on a 2-1 pitch from Claude Passeau. Williams's game-winner overshadows a pair of two-run homers by the Pirates' Arky Vaughan. Joe and Dom DiMaggio become the first brothers to play in the same All-Star Game; Dom singles, Joe hits a double. Eddie Smith gets the win.

JULY 13:

In Chicago, two streaks are extended: Joe DiMaggio hits in his 52nd and 53rd consecutive games and the Yankees win their 13th and 14th in a row. In the opener, DiMaggio has three singles (two against Ted Lyons) and scores twice in an 8-1 win. In the nightcap, he singles against Thornton Lee in an 11-inning, 1-0 New York victory.

JULY 16:

Joe DiMaggio makes it 56 straight on his record-setting hitting streak. Today he hits a double and two singles – one in the opening frame – against the Indians in Cleveland; the Yankees win, 10–3.

JULY 17:

Joe DiMaggio's record hitting streak is stopped at 56 by Indians' pitchers Al Smith and Jim Bagby with the help of excellent fielding by third baseman Ken Keltner. Before 67,000 in Cleveland, Keltner throws out DiMaggio after an outstanding stop in the seventh. In the eighth, with the bases loaded and Bagby pitching, DiMaggio grounds into a double play to shortstop Lou Boudreau. The Yankees go on to win the game, 4-3, with Johnny Murphy saving the game for Lefty Gomez.

Joe DiMaggio on the end of his 56-game hitting streak: "I'm tickled to death it's over." In the 56 games, which began on May 15 against the White Sox at Yankee Stadium, DiMaggio bats .408 with 91 hits, including 15 homers, and bats in 55 runs. He ends up five games short of his own 1933 Pacific Coast League consecutive-game hitting streak. In his next game, on July 18 against Bob Feller, DiMaggio begins a second streak that reaches 16 – and 72 out of 73 games.

JULY 20:

Joe DiMaggio is off on a new tear; he hits a homer and two doubles as the Yankees beat the Tigers in Detroit, 12-6, in 17 innings.

JULY 22:

The University of Michigan's Dick Wakefield, the 20-year-old son of former major league catcher Howard Wakefield, becomes baseball's first "bonus baby" when the Tigers sign him for $52,000 and a car. He appears in seven games in 1941, hitting .143 with no homers and no RBI.

JULY 25:

At Fenway Park, 41-year-old Lefty Grove wins his career 300th game – in his third try – as the Red Sox beat the Indians, 10-6. Grove, who joins Cy Young, Walter Johnson, Christy Mathewson, Grover Cleveland Alexander, and Eddie Plank in the modern era "300 Club," gives up 12 hits, strikes out six, and walks one. Jimmie Foxx breaks a 6-6 tie with a triple against losing pitchers Al Milnar and Jim Tabor, then hits his second home run of the game.

JULY 30:

Michael "Smiling Mickey" Welch, a 300-game winner, dies in Concord, New Hampshire, at age 82. Welch pitched for the Troy Trojans and the New York Giants from 1880 to 1892, compiling a 308-209 record with a 2.71 ERA. In 1885 with New York, he won 44 games.

JULY 31:

The Browns and Red Sox play a three-hour-and-11-minute, nine-

JULY 25
Pitcher Lefty Grove, 41, notches his 300th career win as the Red Sox beat the Indians.

SEPTEMBER 17
Stan Musial, just 20, goes two-for-four in his major league debut with the Cardinals.

inning game, the longest in AL history; St. Louis wins, 16-11.

AUGUST 1:

It's a shutout, but far from a masterpiece for Lefty Gomez. He walks 11 – a major league record for a shutout – and yields five hits, but the Browns strand 15 runners. New York wins, 9-0, at Yankee Stadium.

AUGUST 4,

"I got it!" Mickey Owen of the Dodgers becomes the first catcher ever to handle three foul popups in a single inning. It happens today in the third at Ebbets Field in an 11-6 win over the visiting Giants.

AUGUST 10:

The Cardinals' pennant chances are significantly reduced when Enos Slaughter breaks his collarbone in an outfield collision with teammate Terry Moore at Sportsman's Park and will be lost for the rest of the season.

AUGUST 20:

The Cardinals' outfield suffers its second serious injury in 10 days. Center fielder Terry Moore is beaned by pitcher Art Johnson of the Braves and will be out until September 14.

AUGUST 24:

The band that will become a fixture at Ebbets Field under the name the Dodger Sym-Phony debuts during a Brooklyn-St. Louis doubleheader. The Cardinals win the opening game, 7-3; the Dodgers come back behind Whitlow Wyatt for a 3-2 victory in the second game.

AUGUST 27:

At Braves Field, Chicago's Charlie Root beats Boston, 6-4, to become the first pitcher to win his 200th game in a Cubs' uniform. Root singles in a three-run ninth-inning rally.

AUGUST 30:

The Cardinals' Lon "The Arkansas Hummingbird" Warneke no-hits the Reds, 2-0, today in Cincinnati; the victory propels St. Louis into first place. Warneke walks one batter and strikes out two; Frank "Creepy" Crespi and Jimmy Brown make errors behind him. The losing pitcher is Elmer Riddle.

SEPTEMBER 4:

At Fenway Park, the Yankees, on a Richard "Atley" Donald five-hitter, beat the Red Sox, 6-3, for their 91st win and the AL pennant. It is New York's 136th game and the earliest clinching date ever.

SEPTEMBER 13:

In St. Louis, the Cardinals face the Dodgers in the third game of a crucial series, which began with Brooklyn in first place by one and a half games. The Dodgers won the opener, 6-4, in 11 innings and the Cardinals took the second game, 4-3. Today Whitlow Wyatt of the Dodgers and Mort Cooper of the Cardinals are the opposing pitchers. The Cardinals have the game's big opportunity with runners on second and third in the second inning. Wyatt strikes out Gus Mancuso, and then retires Jimmy Brown. Cooper cruises into the eighth inning, allowing no hits until Fred "Dixie" Walker doubles off the right-field screen. Billy Herman then doubles Walker home and the Dodgers win the rubber match, 1-0.

SEPTEMBER 15:

In Cincinnati, the Dodgers and Reds match zeroes for 16 innings. In the top of the 17th, Brooklyn scores five times and the Reds come back with one run. Hugh Casey, in relief, gets the victory after Johnny Allen goes 15 innings.

SEPTEMBER 16:

Lloyd Waner is 35 years old, but the Reds' outfielder still knows how to make contact; he bats in his 77th consecutive game without striking out. The Reds beat the visiting Dodgers, 4-3.

SEPTEMBER 17:

In St. Louis, 20-year-old Stan Musial makes his major league debut in game two of a doubleheader against the Braves, before only 3,585 fans. Musial has two hits in four at-bats and bats in two runs. He was hitting .326 with the Rochester Red Wings in the International League. Musial appears in 12 games and offers a preview of coming attractions, hitting .426 with seven RBI.

SEPTEMBER 23:

In Pittsburgh, Stan Musial hits his first major league home run in a 9-0 Cardinals' win in the nightcap of a doubleheader.

SEPTEMBER 25:

With a 6-0 win over the Braves and a Cardinals' loss to the Pirates, the Dodgers clinch their first pennant in 21 years. Pete

TRIVIA

James Thurber's short story, "You Could Look It Up," appears in the *Saturday Evening Post.* The story of a midget pinch hitter, it supposedly inspires Bill Veeck to try the stunt in 1951.

HISTORY

The Homestead Grays beat the New York Cubans, three games to one, to take the Negro National League pennant. According to author Robert Peterson, the Negro American League did not publish standings, and "in later years, the Monarchs were referred to as 1941 champions."

SEPTEMBER 28
Ted Williams, with a homer and two singles, finishes the season with a .4057 average.

"Ain't I the best hitter you ever saw?"
– *Ted Williams*

TRIVIA

The war between the Dodgers and umpire George Magerkurth continues. At Brooklyn's victory parade, fans carry a coffin marked "Magerkurth" down the streets. Earlier in the year, Hugh Casey gets called for a balk and fires three straight pitches at Magerkurth. The following day, manager Leo Durocher knocks down Associated Press writer Ted Meier for asking about the incident.

LEAGUE

After the season, the AL lends the troubled St. Louis Browns $25,000.

Reiser hits a two-run homer, Dixie Walker adds a bases-loaded triple, and Whitlow Wyatt pitches a five-hitter for his 22nd win. Cardinals' manager Billy Southworth extends his congratulations, calling this "the greatest pennant race in history."

SEPTEMBER 26:

Bob Feller one-hits the Browns, 3-2, for his 25th win. The only hit is a fifth-inning bunt by Rick Ferrell. It is Feller's fifth career one-hitter.

SEPTEMBER 28:

Ted Williams begins the day at .39955 for 143 games. With the pennant race decided, Williams can sit out a doubleheader against the Athletics – manager Joe Cronin offers him the option – and "back into" a .400 average. Williams responds, "I don't care to be known as a .400 hitter with a lousy average of .39955. I'm going to be a .400 hitter." And then he delivers. In the opener, the Splendid Splinter hits a homer and two singles; the Red Sox win, 12-11. The tension mounts and Williams comes through with a double and three singles in the nightcap, called after eight innings because of darkness. He finishes the season at .4057, becoming the AL's first .400 hitter since Harry Heilmann (.403) in 1923 and the first in the majors since Bill Terry (.401) in 1930. Williams adds 37 homers, 120 RBI, 133 runs, and 145 walks – and he's only 23 years old. The nightcap, won by the A's, 7-1, marks the final major league game for Lefty Grove, who is charged with the loss.

Ted Williams, after getting three hits in the nightcap, asks the press, "Ain't I the best hitter you ever saw?" He has some additional remarks about his fabulous season: "If I was being paid $30,000 a year, the least I could do was hit .400." and "There never was a .400 hitter who wasn't lucky." Williams recalls in his autobiography that when he came to bat for the first time that day, home plate umpire Bill McGowan dusted the plate, and "without looking up said, 'To hit .400, a batter has got to be loose. He has got to be loose.'"

At Ebbets Field, the Dodgers beat the Phillies, 5-1, for their 100th win of 1941. It is Philadelphia's 111th loss of the season, which, mercifully, ends today.

REGULAR SEASON WRAP-UP:

The Dodgers, managed by the fiery Leo Durocher, take their first pennant since 1920. They finish at 100-54, two and a half games ahead of the Cardinals. The team is led by Dolf Camilli (.285, 34 homers, 120 RBI) and .343 hitter Pete Reiser (at 22, the youngest NL batting champ ever). Kirby Higbe at 22-9 and Whitlow Wyatt at 22-10 are the top pitchers. Cardinals' pitcher Howie Krist (10-0) sets an NL record for most wins without a loss.

Joe McCarthy's Yankees run away with the pennant, finishing at 101-53, 17 games ahead of the Red Sox. The Yankees have no 20-game winners and don't need any: Joe DiMaggio hits .357 with 30 homers and 125 RBI; Charlie Keller has 33 homers and 122 RBI; Tommy Henrich, 31 homers and 85 RBI; and Joe Gordon, 24 homers and 87 RBI. Rookie shortstop Phil Rizzuto hits .307. The Indians' Jeff Heath becomes the first AL player to top the 20 mark in homers (24), triples (20), and doubles (32); he also hits .340.

OCTOBER 1:

World Series, game one. The subway travels between the Bronx and Brooklyn for the first Subway Series. At Yankee Stadium, the New York Yankees, behind five-hit pitching by Charles "Red" Ruffing, beat the Dodgers, 3-2. It is Ruffing's fifth consecutive Series win. Leo Durocher tries to con the Yankees by warming up three pitchers before the game: Whitlow Wyatt, Kirby Higbe, and Curt Davis. He selects Davis, who ends up as the losing pitcher. Joe Gordon of the Yankees homers.

OCTOBER 2:

World Series, game two. Whitlow Wyatt gets the start one day late and responds with a nine-hit, 3-2 win at Yankee Stadium, snapping New York's string of 10 consecutive series wins. Dolf Camilli singles in Dixie Walker with the winning run in the sixth. Spurgeon "Spud" Chandler goes five innings and is pegged with the loss.

OCTOBER 4:

World Series, game three. At Ebbets Field, 40-year-old Dodger Freddie Fitzsimmons becomes the oldest pitcher to start a Series game. Fitzsimmons

OCTOBER 1
The latest Subway Series begins with a 3-2 Yankees' win over the visiting Dodgers.

OCTOBER 6
It's "wait 'til next year" again for Brooklyn, as the Yanks win game five – and the Series.

pitches well, but has the misfortune to be opposed by Marius Russo, who is equally effective. In the seventh, with neither team on the scoreboard, Russo hits a line drive off of Fitzsimmons's left knee. The ball caroms to shortstop Harold "Pee Wee" Reese, who catches it on the fly. Fitzsimmons' injury forces him out of the game. The Yankees score twice against losing pitcher Hugh Casey and win, 2-1. Russo gets the win.

OCTOBER 5:

World Series, game four. With a 4-3 lead in the ninth inning at Ebbets Field, the Dodgers' Hugh Casey strikes out Tommy Henrich on a 3-2 pitch for what should be the final out of the game. The ball gets by catcher Mickey Owen, and Henrich is safe at first. Joe DiMaggio singles, Charlie Keller doubles in two runs, and Bill Dickey walks. Joe Gordon follows with a double, scoring Keller and Dickey; the Yankees have four runs and now lead, 7-4. Reliever Johnny Murphy, who had come on in the eighth, closes out the Dodgers in the ninth, putting them at a 3-1 disadvantage in games. Murphy gets the win; Casey the loss. Pete Reiser has a two-run homer.

OCTOBER 6:

World Series, game five. With their golden opportunity gone with the muffed third strike, the Dodgers bow out, 3-1, giving the Yankees the World Series. Ernie Bonham limits Brooklyn to four hits. Whitlow Wyatt allows six hits, but it isn't good enough. After Tommy Henrich homers in the fifth inning, Wyatt decks Joe DiMaggio, who flies out to Pete Reiser and then goes after the pitcher. The dugouts empty and the umpires intervene. The victory is the Yankees 32nd in their last 36 World Series games and their fifth World Championship in six years. The team compiles a 1.80 ERA; four pitchers win games. Joe Gordon leads all hitters at .500 with five RBI. Charlie Keller hits .389 with 5 RBI. Joe Medwick tops Brooklyn's starters with only .235.

POST-SEASON

NOVEMBER 25:

Lou Boudreau, the Indians' 24-year-old shortstop, is named the team's player-manager. He succeeds Roger Peckinpaugh, who now becomes Cleveland's general manager, replacing Cy Slapnicka. The Indians finished in fourth in 1941 with a record of 75-79.

DECEMBER 1:

Dodgers' pitcher Fred Fitzsimmons demonstrates that a baseball really does curve. The test is conducted with three posts set in a straight line. Fitzsimmons's curve goes to the right of the first post, to the left at the second, and back to the right of post three.

DECEMBER 2:

Mel Ott replaces Bill Terry as manager of the Giants. Last year under Terry, New York was 74-79 and finished in fifth place. Terry will head the Giants' farm system.

DECEMBER 7:

Robert "Lefty" Grove announces that he will retire. Grove spent the past eight seasons with the Red Sox after nine years with the Athletics. He completes his career with a 300-141 record, a 3.06 ERA, and 2,266 strikeouts.

DECEMBER 8:

At the AL meeting beginning today, owners were expected to approve the transfer of the St. Louis Browns to Los Angeles. The bombing of Pearl Harbor and the entry of the U.S. into the World War II derails any action.

DECEMBER 9:

Two days after the attack on Pearl Harbor, Bob Feller enlists in the navy.

Two years to the day after a canceled transaction, the A's trade outfielder Wally Moses (.301, four homers). He goes to the White Sox in return for outfielder Mike Kreevich (.232) and pitcher Jack Hallett (5-5, 6.03 ERA).

DECEMBER 11:

The Giants obtain first baseman Johnny Mize (.317, 16 homers, 100 RBI) from the Cardinals for pitcher Bill Lohrman (9-10, 4.02 ERA), catcher James "Ken" O'Dea (.213, three homers), first baseman Johnny McCarthy (.325 in 14 games), and $50,000.

DECEMBER 12:

The Pirates trade infielder Joseph "Arky" Vaughan (.316, six homers) to the Dodgers for pitcher Luke "Hot Potato" Hamlin (8-8, 4.24 ERA), outfielder Jimmy Wasdell (.298), catcher Ernest Phelps (.233), and infielder Pete Coscarat (.129).

TRIVIA

Since the dramatic turn of events in game four, there has been unresolved speculation about why the pitch got by Mickey Owen, who set an NL record in 1941 with 476 chances and no errors. Much of that speculation centers on the possibility that Hugh Casey surprised his catcher with a spitball. Durocher denied it; Pee Wee Reese described it as "a little wet slider."

TRIVIA

The Cubs, the last team to play night games at home, could have been playing under the lights by the 1942 season. Owner Phil Wrigley actually had light towers shipped to Chicago for installation for the 1942 season, but Pearl Harbor and World War II altered his plans. Instead, the light towers were sent to the Great Lakes Naval Air Station in Illinois.

THE BEST OF 1941

NATIONAL LEAGUE

HITTERS

Batting Average:
Pete Reiser, Brooklyn Dodgers, .343

Slugging Average:
Pete Reiser, .558

Home Runs:
Dolf Camilli, Brooklyn Dodgers, 34

Runs Batted In:
Dolf Camilli, 120

Hits:
Stan Hack, Chicago Cubs, 186

Stolen Bases:
Danny Murtaugh, Philadelphia Phillies, 18

PITCHERS

Wins:
John "Whitlow" Wyatt,
Walter "Kirby" Higbe, Brooklyn Dodgers, 22

Strikeouts:
Johnny Vander Meer, Cincinnati Reds, 202

Earned Run Average:
Elmer Riddle, Cincinnati Reds, 2.24

Winning Percentage:
Elmer Riddle, .826

Saves:
Walter "Jumbo" Brown, New York Giants, 8

Most Valuable Player:
Dolf Camilli, Brooklyn Dodgers

AMERICAN LEAGUE

HITTERS

Batting Average:
Ted Williams, Boston Red Sox, .406

Slugging Average:
Ted Williams, .735

Home Runs:
Ted Williams, 37

Runs Batted In:
Joe DiMaggio, New York Yankees, 125

Hits:
Cecil Travis, Washington Senators, 218

Stolen Bases:
George Case, Washington Senators, 33

PITCHERS

Wins:
Bob Feller, Cleveland Indians, 25

Strikeouts:
Bob Feller, 260

Earned Run Average:
Thornton Lee, Chicago White Sox, 2.37

Winning Percentage:
Vernon "Lefty" Gomez, New York Yankees, .750

Saves:
Johnny Murphy, New York Yankees, 15

Most Valuable Player:
Joe DiMaggio, New York Yankees

1942

NEWS

JAPANESE TAKE MANILA

5,200 AMERICANS DIE ON BATAAN DEATH MARCH

GENERAL DOOLITTLE LEADS FIRST AIR ATTACK ON JAPAN, KNOWN AS "30 SECONDS OVER TOKYO"

U.S. wins two crucial Pacific battles: Coral Sea and Midway

U.S. RATIONS GASOLINE, SUGAR, AND COFFEE

ACTRESS CAROLE LOMBARD DIES IN PLANE CRASH

BING CROSBY CROONS *WHITE CHRISTMAS*

GENERAL FOODS SENDS INSTANT COFFEE TO GI'S

***CASABLANCA* WINS OSCAR FOR BEST PICTURE**

NAPALM IS INVENTED

PRE-SEASON

JANUARY 6:

Bob Feller reports for naval duty at Norfolk, Virginia, saying, "I can throw a few strikes for Uncle Sam... I always wanted to be on the winning side and this time I know I'm with a winner." In the past three seasons, the 23-year-old Feller won 24, 27, and 25 games and led the AL in strikeouts three consecutive times.

JANUARY 15:

President Franklin Delano Roosevelt gives Commissioner Kenesaw Mountain Landis the go-ahead to play ball despite the war. FDR says the final decision about the baseball season rests with Landis and the owners. He adds "so what I am going to say is solely a personal and not official point of view. I honestly feel that it would be best for the country to keep baseball going... they [Americans] ought to have a chance for recreation and for taking their minds off their work even more than before... if 300 teams use 5,000 or 6,000 players, these players are a definite recreational asset to at least 20,000,000 of their fellow citizens – and that in my judgment is thoroughly worthwhile."

FEBRUARY 3:

Major league owners, meeting at the Hotel Roosevelt in New York City, respond to President Roosevelt's suggestion for more night games and give the okay for 11 teams with lights to play 14 night games per season; twice as many as previously allowed. The Washington Senators get special permission for 21 games. The owners also vote to hold two All-Star Games for the benefit of various war causes. The first will be played at the Polo Grounds; the second will pit major leaguers against an armed forces all-star team and will take place in Cleveland. And they approve a night curfew that will prevent an inning from beginning after 12:50 a.m.

FEBRUARY 5:

The Yankees trade minor league outfielder Tommy Holmes to the Braves for first baseman John "Buddy" Hassett (.296, one homer) and outfielder Gene "Rowdy" Moore (.272, five homers).

> "It would be best for the country to keep baseball going."
>
> *– President Franklin D. Roosevelt*

TRIVIA

World War II spawns a baseball tradition. Richard Goldstein reports in *Spartan Seasons*, "Before World War II, 'The Star Spangled Banner' had been played at ballparks only on special occasions, such as opening day and the World Series. Now it would be heard prior to every game."

FEBRUARY 7:

Catcher Ernie Lombardi (.264, 10 homers), who has been with Cincinnati for 10 years, is sold to the Braves.

MARCH 10:

In Sarasota, Florida, Ted Williams asks for a military deferment.

MARCH 12:

After originally being asked to take a pay cut – despite a .357 batting average with 30 home runs and a league-leading 125 RBI – Joe DiMaggio receives a $6,250 raise, to $43,750.

MARCH 18:

Jackie Robinson and pitcher Nate Moreland work out for White Sox manager Jimmy Dykes in Pasadena, California. Despite complimentary remarks from Dykes about Robinson – "He's worth $50,000 of anybody's money" – no offer is made to either of the black players.

THE SEASON

MAY 2:

The Browns' Elden Auker has a painful complete game stint against the Red Sox at Fenway Park. He allows 17 hits and 11 runs in nine innings and gets the loss, 11-10, on a Ted Williams homer in the ninth inning.

MAY 12:

The lights are on at Ebbets Field and the Polo Grounds, but the playing fields are unused. It is part of a test to see if the lights would assist Nazi submarines operating in the Atlantic Ocean off New York. The following week, word comes down from New York City's police commissioner Lewis Valentine: the Giants and Dodgers are asked to cancel their remaining night games.

MAY 13:

The Braves' Jim Tobin hits three consecutive homers and hurls a five-hitter to beat the Cubs, 6-5, at Braves Field. Tobin, who homered with a man on base as a pinch hitter against the Cubs yesterday, today hits solo round-trippers in the fifth and seventh and a two-run shot in the eighth that wins the game. He is the only modern era pitcher with three homers in a game and sets a record for total bases by a pitcher with 12. The losing pitcher is Hi Bithorn.

MAY 14:

Atanasio "Tony" Perez is born in Ciego De Avila, Cuba.

MAY 19:

The Cubs sell first baseman Ellsworth "Babe" Dahlgren for the second time in six days. On May 13, with a .214 average, he was purchased conditionally by the Browns and, after going hitless in two games, returned to Chicago. Today he is shipped to the Dodgers.

MAY 22:

Ted Williams is sworn into the U.S. Navy. He will remain with the Red Sox while awaiting his call to report for active duty.

JUNE 1:

The Chicago Cubs acquire first baseman Jimmie Foxx (.270) after he is released by the Boston Red Sox.

JUNE 15:

In the major league's first-ever twilight game, Claude Passeau and the Cubs beat the Dodgers, 6-0, at Ebbets Field. Attendance for the game is 15,159.

JUNE 19:

The Braves' Paul Waner singles against Pirates' pitcher Truett "Rip" Sewell for his 3,000th career hit. Waner, 39 years old, is the seventh player and the third NL player to reach that plateau. The Braves drop the game, 7-6, in 11 innings.

On June 17, Waner had what should have been his 3,000th hit – a ball hit off the glove of Reds' shortstop Eddie Joost, who made a diving play. But Waner refused to accept the ball from umpire John "Beans" Reardon and convinced the official scorer to reverse his call.

JUNE 21:

White Sox pitcher Ted Lyons beats the visiting Red Sox, 6-5, for his 250th career win. Dick Newsome is the losing pitcher.

JUNE 27:

Gene Stack (born Eugene Stackowiach), a pitcher for the White Sox who never appeared in a major league game, dies after a mound appearance for an army team at Michigan City, Indiana. Stack was the first roster player in uniform for service in World War II.

JULY 6:

At the Polo Grounds in New York, the AL wins the All-Star

AUGUST 3
Rogers Hornsby is the year's lone inductee into the Baseball Hall of Fame.

Game, 3-1, paced by first-inning homers by Lou Boudreau and Rudy York. Mort Cooper – the losing pitcher – and catcher Walker Cooper make up the only starting brother battery in All-Star history. Joe DiMaggio makes history of his own; he is the first to play every inning in seven consecutive All-Star Games. Spurgeon "Spud" Chandler hurls four innings and allows two hits for the win. Mickey Owen homers for the NL.

JULY 7:

The AL plays Mickey Cochrane's Service All-Stars – composed mainly of major leaguers in the military – in Cleveland for the benefit of the Ball and Bat and Army-Navy relief. The AL wins, 5-0.

JULY 19:

At Sportsman's Park, Dodgers' center fielder Pete Reiser runs headfirst into the wall while chasing an Enos Slaughter drive in the 11th inning. Reiser manages a throw to shortstop Harold "Pee Wee" Reese before going down, bleeding from the ears with a concussion. Slaughter circles the bases for an inside-the-park home run and a 7-6 Cardinals' win.

JULY 21:

The irrepressible Leroy "Satchel" Paige finds a new way to make a ballgame intriguing. Pitching for the Kansas City Monarchs against the Homestead Grays at Forbes Field, Paige intentionally walks three batters to load the bases and pitch to one of baseball's great hitters, Josh Gibson. Paige then tells Gibson what pitches he will throw – and proceeds to strike him out.

JULY 22:

Ted Williams is fined $250 by manager Joe Cronin for "loafing." Williams apologizes.

AUGUST 1:

The Brooklyn Dodgers beat the Chicago Cubs and their starter, Johnny Schmitz, 9-6, for the team's 71st victory in the first 100 games of the season. The Dodgers now lead the Cardinals by nine full games in the NL standings.

AUGUST 3:

Rogers Hornsby enters the Hall of Fame alone. Hornsby played 23 seasons, hitting .358 (second best of all time), with a slugging average of .577, 301 homers, and 2,930 hits. He hit .400 or better three times (including .424 in 1924) and .300 or better 15 times. He was the NL's batting champion seven times and appeared in two World Series.

Satchel Paige was the ace of the Kansas City Monarchs.

AUGUST 23
Babe Ruth, now 47, and Walter Johnson, 56, hook up in an Army-Navy Relief Fund game.

CULTURE

The Pride of the Yankees **stars Gary Cooper as Lou Gehrig and Teresa Wright as Eleanor Gehrig; also appearing as themselves are Babe Ruth, Bill Dickey, and Mark Koenig.** ***It Happened in Flatbush*** **stars Lloyd Nolan as manager of the Dodgers;** ***Moonlight in Havana,*** **with William Frawley, is about a catcher who becomes a singer.**

AUGUST 6:

As pressure – from organized labor, the New York State Legislature, and a Citizens' Committee to End Jim Crow – builds on major league baseball to end discrimination against blacks, *The Sporting News* blames "agitators, ever ready to seize an issue that will redound to their profit and self-aggrandizement" and incredibly concludes that they should stop making "an issue of a question on which both sides would prefer to be left alone."

AUGUST 8:

Pitchers Whitlow Wyatt of the Dodgers and Manny Salvo of the Braves go at each other after the teams exchange beanballs. The Braves win the game, 2-0.

AUGUST 14:

Yankees' shortstop Phil Rizzuto and second baseman Joe Gordon execute seven double plays – an AL record – against the Athletics. New York wins, 11-2.

AUGUST 23:

Babe Ruth, 47 years old, and Walter Johnson, 56 years old, briefly return to the playing field to help raise money for the Army-Navy Relief Fund. With 69,136 on hand at Yankee Stadium, Ruth bats against Johnson between games of a regularly scheduled doubleheader. He hits the fifth pitch into the lower right-field stands and ends his at-bat with a foul shot into the upper deck. As the fans cheer, he circles the bases, tips his hat, and leaves the field. The event raises $80,000. The Senators win the opener of the doubleheader, 7-6; the Yankees take the nightcap, 3-0, when it is called after five and a half innings because of darkness.

Babe Ruth continues to live on the fringes of the game he saved. His one consuming ambition, to manage the New York Yankees, remains unfulfilled. Yankees' owner Jacob Ruppert offered him the opportunity to manage the Newark Bears in the International League, but not the "big club." Reportedly, Ruppert told him, "You can't take care of yourself. How can I be sure you can take care of my best players? Newark, Ruth, or nothing." Ruth chose nothing.

FORMER MAJOR LEAGUER FRANCIS "LEFTY" O'DOUL WORKS WITH GARY COOPER ON *THE PRIDE OF THE YANKEES,* TRYING TO TEACH THE RIGHT-HANDED ACTOR HOW TO BAT AND THROW LEFT-HANDED. O'DOUL CRITIQUES HIS STUDENT: "HE THREW THE BALL LIKE AN OLD WOMAN TOSSING A HOT BISCUIT."

AUGUST 30:

In four months, the market value of Louis "Bobo" Newsom (11-17) has dropped some $15,000. The Senators, who bought Newsom for $40,000 at the end of March, in turn sell him to the Dodgers for a reported price of $25,000. Newsom wires the Dodgers: "Congratulations on buying pennant. Will report tomorrow in fine shape, rarin' to go."

SEPTEMBER 11:

Seeking his 20th win of the season, Cardinals' right-hander Mort Cooper takes the mound against the Dodgers in Herman "Coaker" Triplett's uniform – with number 20 on the back. He hurls a 3-0, three-hitter.

Mort Cooper believes in flaunting his stuff. The big right-hander has been changing his uniform number from game to game to match the victory he is seeking.

SEPTEMBER 13:

A bad inning creates a lifelong nickname. Cubs' shortstop Len Merullo commits four errors in one inning at Braves Field on the day his son, Leonard Merullo Jr., is born. The senior Merullo

SEPTEMBER 30
In game one of the World Series, the visiting Yankees beat the Cardinals, 7-4.

dubs his new son Boots. The Braves win the opener, 11-6; the Cubs come back, 12-8.

SEPTEMBER 14:

The Yankees win their 13th American League pennant with an 8-3 win over the Indians in the 145th game of the season. Ernie Bonham gets his 20th win; Joe DiMaggio hits a home run and three singles.

SEPTEMBER 25:

U.S. Navy-bound Larry French leaves with a flourish. The Dodgers' left-hander one-hits the Phillies, 6-0, facing only 27 batters. The lone hit is a second-inning single by Nick Etten, who is erased on a double play.

French never returns to the majors after the war. He finishes his career at 197-171 with a 3.44 ERA.

SEPTEMBER 26:

Kids who bring 10 pounds of scrap metal for the war effort are admitted free to today's double-header between the Giants and Braves at the Polo Grounds, but the goodwill gesture backfires. In the bottom of the eighth, with rookie Warren Spahn, in his first major league start, trailing the Giants 5-2, youngsters swarm onto the field making play impossible. Umpire John "Ziggy" Sears awards the Braves a 9-0 forfeit win. Under the rules, Spahn gets credit for a complete game, but he is not awarded the victory. He finishes his first season at 0-0 with a 5.74 ERA in four games.

SEPTEMBER 28:

Phillies' left fielder Danny Litwhiler is a bright spot in his team's dismal 42-109 season. Litwhiler completes 151 games today without making an error and sets a major league record for outfielders. Litwhiler had 308 putouts and nine assists in his errorless year. He also hit a respectable .271 with nine homers.

REGULAR SEASON WRAP-UP:

The Cardinals, under Billy Southworth, are a hot team coming into the World Series. In order to beat out the Dodgers by two games, St. Louis wins 43 of their last 51 games and 21 of 26 in September. They finish at 106-48. Not a powerful team, the Cardinals are led by Enos Slaughter at .318 with 13 homers and young Stan Musial, .315 with 10. The top pitchers are Mort Cooper (22-7, 1.78 ERA) and rookie Johnny Beazley (21-6, 2.13 ERA). With the exception of pitcher Harry Gumpert, every member of the NL pennant-winning Cardinals is a product of the team's farm system created by Branch Rickey.

The Yankees, managed by Joe McCarthy, finish nine games ahead of the Red Sox with a record of 103-51. Joe Gordon hits .322, with 18 homers and 103 RBI. Joe DiMaggio hits .305 with 21 homers and 114 RBI – an off year by his standards.

SEPTEMBER 30:

World Series, game one. In St. Louis, Charles "Red" Ruffing bests Mort Cooper in a 7-4 Yankees' win. Ruffing, who has a no-hitter until Terry Moore's two-out single in the eighth, becomes the first pitcher to win seven World Series games. Cooper takes the loss, undermined by four Cardinals' errors.

OCTOBER 1:

World Series, game two. The Cardinals get only six hits against righty Ernie Bonham, but win, 4-3, behind Johnny Beazley. A two-run homer by Charlie Keller puts the Yankees even in the top of the eighth, but in the bottom of the frame Stan Musial singles in Enos Slaughter, who had doubled.

OCTOBER 3:

World Series, game three. Ernie White shuts out the Yankees on six hits at Yankee Stadium and the Cardinals win, 2-0. It is the first time the Yankees have been shut out in series play since 1926. Spurgeon "Spud" Chandler gets the loss. The game is marked by a fracas involving the Yankees' Joe Gordon and Frank Crosetti and umpire Bill Summers. Crosetti pushes Summers during the game's confrontation.

OCTOBER 4:

World Series, game four. The Cardinals move to within a win of the championship with a 9-6 win at Yankee Stadium, overcoming a Charlie Keller three-run homer. Max Lanier, the Cardinals' fourth pitcher of the day, gets the win. Richard

HISTORY

The Kansas City Monarchs, the Negro American League pennant winners, sweep the Homestead Grays of the Negro National League in four games for the championship. The Grays actually won game four, but it was discounted after a protest because they used three Newark Eagles' players.

OCTOBER 5
The Cardinals win game five of the Series, 4-2, and capture the World Championship.

NOVEMBER 4
Yankees' Joe Gordon is the AL MVP – despite Ted Williams having won the Triple Crown.

HISTORY

Pittsburgh catcher Ernest "Babe" Phelps retires from baseball after 11 years because of a fear of flying. Phelps hit .284 with nine homers in 95 games in 1942. His lifetime average is .310, and he is 34 years old.

CULTURE

Dan Parker of the *New York Daily Mirror* writes "Leave Us Go Root for the Dodgers, Rodgers." Parker's "poem" is set to music. It concludes:

Leave us make noise for the boisterous boys On the BMT. Summer or winter or any season, Flatbush fanatics don't need no reason. Leave us go root for the Dodgers, Rodgers That's the team for me.

"Atley" Donald gets the loss in relief of starter Hank Borowy.

OCTOBER 5:

World Series, game five. The Cardinals, on the strength of Johnny Beazley's seven-hitter, complete the upset of the Yankees with a 4-2 win to take the series. It is the first time since 1926 that the Yankees have failed to win a World Series. Red Ruffing gets the loss at Yankee Stadium with a crowd of 69,052 on hand. Enos Slaughter hits a solo homer and George "Whitey" Kurowski adds a two-run shot for St. Louis. Phil Rizzuto homers with no one on for New York. In what is essentially a pitchers' series, the star is Johnny Beazley, 2-0 with a 2.50 ERA. Jimmy Brown leads the Cardinals' batters with .300. Robert "Red" Rolfe hits .353 for New York.

POST-SEASON

OCTOBER 29:

Branch Rickey, the architect of the Cardinals' farm system, resigns as the team's vice president.

NOVEMBER 1:

Branch Rickey is named president of the Dodgers, replacing Larry MacPhail, who is in the military. The 60-year-old Rickey will earn $40,000 a year, plus bonuses.

MacPhail once said of Rickey: "There but for the grace of God, goes God."

ROGERS HORNSBY SAYS, "BASEBALL IS MY LIFE. IT'S THE ONLY THING I KNOW AND CARE ABOUT." AND ON ANOTHER OCCASION: "I DON'T LIKE TO SOUND EGOTISTICAL, BUT EVERY TIME I STEPPED UP TO THE PLATE WITH A BAT IN MY HANDS, I COULDN'T HELP BUT FEEL SORRY FOR THE PITCHER."

NOVEMBER 4:

Despite his Triple Crown season, Ted Williams is passed over again for the AL Most Valuable Player award. The winner is the Yankees' Joe Gordon with a .322 batting average, 18 homers, and 103 RBI. By contrast, Williams hits .356 with 36 homers and 137 RBI, along with a slugging average of .648 – all major league highs. Last year, despite hitting .406, Williams finished second to Joe DiMaggio for the MVP Award.

NOVEMBER 6:

Not only did the Yankees lose the World Series, they will be without the services of their shortstop when the 1943 season begins. Frank Crosetti is suspended for the first 30 days of next season and fined $250 for pushing umpire Bill Summers in game three of the Series. Yankees' second baseman Joe Gordon is fined $250, but gets no suspension.

NOVEMBER:

The minor leagues are shrinking. The 1941 season began with 41 leagues; by the start of the 1942 season, the number was 31. At the conclusion of this past season, there are only 26.

DECEMBER 6:

Former pitcher Amos "The Hoosier Thunderbolt" Rusie dies in Seattle, Washington, at the age of 71. In 10 years in the major leagues, Rusie compiled a 246-174 record, winning 30 games or more four times and 20 games or more four times. He struck out 341 batters during the 1890 season and won 36 games in 1894.

DECEMBER 29:

New York Yankees' pitcher Charles "Red" Ruffing is inducted into the armed services. The 38-year-old right-hander, who is missing four toes on his left foot as a result of a mining accident, will perform non-combat duties while serving with the Army Air Corps. He was 14-7 in 1942, with a 3.21 ERA.

THE BEST OF 1942

NATIONAL LEAGUE

HITTERS

Batting Average:
Ernie Lombardi, Boston Braves, .330

Slugging Average:
Johnny Mize, New York Giants, .521

Home Runs:
Mel Ott, New York Giants, 30

Runs Batted In:
Johnny Mize, 110

Hits:
Enos Slaughter, St. Louis Cardinals, 188

Stolen Bases:
Pete Reiser, Brooklyn Dodgers, 20

PITCHERS

Wins:
Mort Cooper, St. Louis Cardinals, 22

Strikeouts:
Johnny Vander Meer, Cincinnati Reds, 186

Earned Run Average:
Mort Cooper, 1.78

Winning Percentage:
Larry French, Brooklyn Dodgers, .789

Saves:
Hugh Casey, Brooklyn Dodgers, 13

Most Valuable Player:
Mort Cooper, St. Louis Cardinals

AMERICAN LEAGUE

HITTERS

Batting Average:
Ted Williams, Boston Red Sox, .356

Slugging Average:
Ted Williams, .648

Home Runs:
Ted Williams, 36

Runs Batted In:
Ted Williams, 137

Hits:
Johnny Pesky, Boston Red Sox, 205

Stolen Bases:
George Case, Washington Senators, 44

PITCHERS

Wins:
Cecil "Tex" Hughson, Boston Red Sox, 22

Strikeouts:
Cecil Hughson; Louis "Bobo" Newsom, Washington Senators, 113

Earned Run Average:
Ted Lyons, Chicago White Sox, 2.10

Winning Percentage:
Ernie Bonham, New York Yankees, .808

Saves:
Johnny Murphy, New York Yankees, 11

Most Valuable Player:
Joe Gordon, New York Yankees

TRIVIA

Warren Spahn plays under Boston manager Casey Stengel. At the close of his illustrious career, he again plays for Stengel, with the Mets. Spahn notes, "I played for Casey before and after he was a genius." In his "pre-genius" period, Stengel farms out Spahn when he refuses to dust off the Dodgers' Harold "Pee Wee" Reese. In *Where Have You Gone, Vince DiMaggio?*, Spahn recalls: "I threw in front of Reese, behind him, only I didn't get one under his chin. Casey was furious. He came out to the mound and cursed me out. He was right. I guess I wasn't ready for the big leagues."

1943

JANUARY 25
After 13 years with the club, the Yankees sell pitcher Lefty Gomez to the Braves.

NEWS

30 DIE IN DETROIT RACE RIOTS

Italy surrenders to Allies; new government declares war on Germany

EISENHOWER NAMED SUPREME COMMANDER FOR INVASION OF EUROPE

U.S., SOVIET UNION, AND BRITAIN MEET AT TEHERAN TO PLAN INVASION STRATEGY

MOVIEGOERS WATCH *FOR WHOM THE BELL TOLLS*

THE PENTAGON, THE WORLD'S LARGEST OFFICE BUILDING, IS COMPLETED

LSD's hallucinogenic properties discovered by accident

JEWS IN POLAND'S WARSAW GHETTO RESIST THE NAZIS' ADVANCE

PRE-SEASON

JANUARY 3:

John Alexander "Bid" McPhee dies in San Diego, California, at the age of 83. McPhee was regarded as the best second baseman of the 19th century. He played for 14 seasons without a glove, before donning one for the 1896 season.

JANUARY 5:

Major League owners and Commissioner Kenesaw Mountain Landis hold an emergency joint meeting in Chicago and create procedural changes necessitated by the war. Opening day will be April 21 – eight days later than usual – and the season will end October 3 instead of September 26, but the schedule will remain 154 games. Instead of using the customary Florida and California sites, spring training will be as close to home as possible to reduce train travel. Teams will train east of the Mississippi and North of the Potomac and Ohio Rivers. The two St. Louis teams will use camps in Missouri. Joseph B. Eastman, director of the Office of Defense Transportation, commends baseball, saying, "I am greatly pleased by the action which the major leagues have taken to reduce their travel requirements for the coming season."

JANUARY 19:

Outfielder Paul Waner (.258, one homer) and outfielder-first baseman Johnny Cooney (.207) are unconditionally released by the Braves. Both are subsequently signed by the Dodgers for the 1943 season.

JANUARY 22:

The Yankees acquire first baseman Nick Etten (.264, eight homers) from the Phillies for catcher Tom Padden, pitcher Al Gerheauser, and $10,000. Padden and Gerheauser were not in the majors last season.

The Baseball Encyclopedia *has the Phillies acquiring pitcher Al Gettel and first baseman Ed Levy. Other sources do not include those two. Levy played for New York in 1944 and Gettel in 1945; the* Encyclopedia *doesn't indicate if and how they gained their return to the Yankees' ballclub.*

JANUARY 25:

The Yankees sell longtime ace Vernon "Lefty" Gomez (6-4, 4.28 ERA) to the Braves. In 13 years with the Yankees, he was 189-101. The Braves release Gomez before he ever appears in a game for them. He then signs with the Senators, pitches and loses one game, and is again released, ending his career.

Cardinals' outfielder Enos Slaughter is called to serve on active duty with the Army Air Corps.

FEBRUARY 2:

Outfielder Al Simmons (last in the majors in 1941 with the Athletics hitting .125 with one homer) is signed by the Boston Red Sox.

FEBRUARY 16:

Joe DiMaggio is drafted into the army.

FEBRUARY 18:

William Cox buys the Phillies for $80,000.

Bill Veeck Jr. offers to buy the Phillies from Gerry Nugent. If successful, he plans to fill his roster with players from the Negro Leagues. Veeck later explains why his plan failed. "Out of my long respect

"There is something uniquely American about hitting one out of the park."
– *Sportswriter Dick Young*

FEBRUARY 20
The All-American Girls Softball League is launched by Branch Rickey and Phil Wrigley.

for Judge Landis, I felt he was entitled to prior notification of what I intended to do." After his meeting with the baseball commissioner, Veeck learns the NL has taken over the Phillies. The team is then sold by NL president Ford Frick to William Cox for less than half of Veeck's offering price. Some baseball experts question Veeck's claim.

FEBRUARY 20:

Dodgers' president Branch Rickey and Cubs' owner Phil Wrigley launch the All-American Girls Softball League with the Racine Belles, Wisconsin; Kenosha Comets, Wisconsin; Rockford Peaches, Illinois, and South Bend Blue Sox, Indiana. The teams play a split season. Racine at 20-15 wins the first half, Kenosha – 33-21 – the second. Racine wins the championship. Later, the women's league will switch from softball to baseball.

FEBRUARY 25:

A want ad appears in today's issue of the *Sporting News*; it reads: "Cardinal Organization Needs Players. If you are a free agent and have previous professional experience, we may be able to place you to your advantage on one of our clubs. We have positions open in our AA, B, and D classification clubs. If you believe you can qualify for one of these good baseball jobs, tell us about yourself."

FEBRUARY 26:

The Cardinals buy infielder-outfielder Debs Garms, the NL batting champ in 1940 at .355, from the Sacramento Solons in the Pacific Coast League.

FEBRUARY 28:

A total of 2,431 minor league players are either in military service or have retired since October 10, 1940, and the manpower drain is having its impact. The Texas League suspends operations for the duration of the war. Baseball now has only nine minor leagues in operation: the International League, Pacific Coast League, American Association, Piedmont League, Southern Association, Eastern League, Interstate League, Appalachian League, and Pony League.

MARCH 3:

After going 21-6 with a 2.13 ERA and two World Series wins, Cardinals' pitcher Johnny Beazley is commissioned a second lieutenant in the Army Air Corps. Pitching under orders from a superior before he was properly prepared, he injures his arm and never regains his pre-war form. After his discharge, he pitches in the majors from 1946 to 1949, winning a total of only nine games.

MARCH 6:

Former major league third baseman Jimmy Collins dies at age 73 in Buffalo, New York. Collins played, mostly in Boston, for 14 major league years in the late 19th and early 20th centuries, finishing at .294.

MARCH 9:

The Dodgers acquire outfielder Lloyd Waner (.261, one homer) and infielder Alban "Al" Glossop (.225, four homers) from the Phillies for first baseman Ellsworth "Babe" Dahlgren (.169 in 36 games with three different teams).

MARCH 13:

A new, official baseball, manufactured by A.G. Spalding, will be used for the 1943 season. The interior is made of reclaimed cork and balata instead of rubber and cork. The new ball is said to have the resiliency of the 1939 version.

THE SEASON

APRIL 23:

Amid complaints that the new balata balls are 25 percent less resilient than the old ones because of rubber cement, the Spalding Co. maintains they were not tested fairly in play because of bad weather.

APRIL 27:

The Giants obtain hard-hitting and slow-running catcher Ernie Lombardi (.330 with 11 homers in 1942) from the Braves for catcher Hugh Poland (.083) and infielder Cornelius "Connie" Ryan (.185).

MAY 9:

Home run production increases somewhat after the introduction of another new baseball, following 11 shutouts in 29 games and many low-scoring contests. Today, AL hitters hit six homers in four doubleheaders, but NL batters manage only one in eight games.

EQUIPMENT

The American Heritage Dictionary **defines "balata," now used in baseballs, as, "The nonelastic rubber obtained from the latex of the South American tree *Manilkara bidentata*." It says nothing about resiliency.**

HISTORY

There are no Hall of Fame inductees in 1943.

TRIVIA

During the fourth inning of the second game of a June doubleheader at Griffith Stadium between the Senators and the visiting Athletics, a DC-3 buzzes the playing field, wigwagging its wings. The plane is piloted by John "Buddy" Lewis of the Army Air Corps – and formerly a star outfielder-third baseman for the Senators.

MAY 21:

In Washington, D.C., the White Sox take only one hour and 29 minutes – the quickest nine innings ever in the AL – to beat the Senators, 1-0.

JUNE 1:

Pirates' pitcher Truett "Rip" Sewell introduces a new blooper pitch, named the "eephus" by his teammate Maurice Van Robays. Sewell throws the ball between 18 to 25 feet in the air and it crosses home plate on its descent.

JUNE 5:

The Giants' Carl Hubbell one-hits the Pirates, 5-1, in Pittsburgh for his 250th career win.

JUNE 13:

Aided by 11 walks from their former teammate, pitcher Ken Chase, plus 18 hits, the Senators beat the Red Sox, 16-5, in the opener of a doubleheader. The Senators get 13 walks in the game. Chase doesn't even set a record for wildness; that "distinction" goes to Bruno Hass with 16 in a 19-15 game.

JUNE 17:

The Red Sox player-manager, Joe Cronin, makes the most of his dwindling at-bats. He ties a major league record with a pair of three-run pinch-hit homers in a doubleheader today against the Athletics at Fenway Park. Cronin also had a three-run pinch-hit homer yesterday, giving him three in three games. In the opener today, Cronin pinch-hits for Lou Lucier in the seventh and connects off Russ Christopher; the Red Sox win, 5-4. In the nightcap, he hits for Mike Ryba and homers against Don Black in the eighth inning; the A's hold on to win, 8-7.

JUNE 23:

With race riots raging in Detroit, 350 armed troopers are at Briggs Stadium for a Tigers-Indians doubleheader. The teams split: Detroit wins the opener, 3-1, behind Hal Newhouser; then Jeff Heath's 11th-inning home run gives Cleveland the win in the nightcap, 9-6.

JULY 10:

At Ebbets Field, the Dodgers protest the three-day suspension of pitcher Louis "Bobo" Newsom by team manager Leo Durocher. Durocher claims he suspended Newsom for ignoring instructions on how to pitch to Vince DiMaggio before a double. The players believe it is because Newsom griped about a Durocher favorite, catcher Bobby Bragan. Joseph "Arky" Vaughan and Joe Medwick turn in their uniforms and Fred "Dixie" Walker offers his as well. After 10 minutes, the Dodgers – minus Vaughan and Newsom – take the field. Vaughan, after a discussion with team president Branch Rickey, joins them. The Dodgers then thrash the Pirates, 23-6.

JULY 13:

In the first night All-Star Game – played at Shibe Park – Bobby Doerr's three-run homer against Mort Cooper in the second inning is the key hit in a 5-3 AL victory. Cooper gets the loss; Emil "Dutch" Leonard the win. Johnny Vander Meer, who is not involved in the decision, fans six in two and two-thirds innings. DiMaggio has a single, triple, and home run – but it's Vince of the Pirates, playing for the NL.

JULY 15:

Brooklyn bounces Bobo to Browns. Bobo Newsom (9-4), the focus of a Dodger player rebellion five days ago, is traded to the Browns for a pair of pitchers, Frederick "Fritz" Ostermueller (0-2) and Archie McKain (1-1).

JULY 23:

The Dodgers' outfield makes the record book, tying a major league mark with 18 putouts. Whitlow Wyatt has the Reds hitting the ball in the air as he pitches a 2-0, four-hitter. Luis Olmo has eight of the putouts.

JULY 28:

Babe Ruth continues to make charity appearances. Today at Yankee Stadium, he manages a team of old-time Yankees against Ted Williams's University of North Carolina Pre-Flight Cloudbusters, a squad of former major leaguers. The game raises $30,000 for the Red Cross. Williams's team wins, 11-5. Ruth appears as a pinch hitter against Johnny Sain and walks. Earlier in the month, he participated in a benefit in Boston, where his all-star team of servicemen beat the Braves, 9-8, on a three-run homer by Ted Williams. Ruth pinch-hit in the eighth and flied out to right field. Prior to the game Williams and Ruth faced off in

JUNE 5
Carl Hubbell earns his 250th career win with a 5-1 Giants' win over the Pirates.

AUGUST 13
White Sox shortstop Luke Appling collects his 2,000th career hit, against the Red Sox.

a home run contest. Williams hit three; Ruth, on an injured knee, none.

The new owner of the Phillies, 36-year-old lumberman William D. Cox, fires the team's manager, Stanley "Bucky" Harris. He hires Freddie Fitzsimmons to take over the 38-52, last-place team. The Phillies threaten to boycott over their manager's dismissal, but a personal appeal from Harris prevents it. But Harris does not go quietly: He tells the press that owner Cox is betting on Phillies' games – to win. Landis learns of Harris's charges from a reporter and the commissioner begins an investigation.

AUGUST 4:

Catcher Roy Campanella of the Baltimore Elite Giants and pitcher Dave Barnhill of the New York Cubans were to try out with the Pirates at Forbes Field today. However, Pirates owner William Benswanger cancels the session by mail.

AUGUST 13:

White Sox shortstop Lucius "Luke" Appling gets his 2,000th career hit today in a game against the Red Sox.

IN APRIL, BRAVES' MANAGER CASEY STENGEL IS HIT BY A BOSTON TAXI AND WILL BE LOST TO THE TEAM FOR 45 GAMES. AFTER THE SEASON, DAVE EGAN OF THE *BOSTON RECORD* WRITES, "THE MAN WHO DID THE MOST FOR BASEBALL IN BOSTON IN 1943 WAS THE MOTORIST WHO RAN STENGEL DOWN TWO DAYS BEFORE THE OPENING GAME AND KEPT HIM AWAY FROM THE BRAVES FOR TWO MONTHS."

AUGUST 14:

Former infielder-outfielder and manager Joe Kelley dies in Baltimore at age 71. Kelley played 17 years from 1891 to 1908, hitting .317 with 194 triples. In 1896, he stole 87 stolen bases.

AUGUST 24:

At Comiskey Park, the Athletics lose, 6-4, to the White Sox in the bottom of the ninth. It is Philadelphia's 20th consecutive loss, tying the 1906 Red Sox for the AL record. In the nightcap, the A's finally win one on an 8-1, eight-hitter by Roger Wolff. Philadelphia's last victory was on August 6 against the Yankees; Wolff was the winner in that game too.

AUGUST 31:

The Browns sell the peripatetic Bobo Newsom (1-6) to the Senators.

SEPTEMBER 6:

With the war thinning the ranks of qualified baseball players, the Athletics send a teenager to the mound. Carl Scheib, 16 years and eight months old, makes his major league debut today, pitching two-thirds

TRIVIA

***Ladies' Day* stars Eddie Albert as a pitcher for the Brooklyn Sox, Lupe Velez, and Max Baer as a catcher.**

HISTORY

The Homestead Grays of the Negro National League defeat the Birmingham Black Barons of the Negro American League, four games to three, for the championship. The Harrisburg-St. Louis Stars of the Negro NL were suspended after nine games for going on a barnstorming tour against Dizzy Dean's major leaguers.

"Branch Rickey believes there should be no limit on salaries – provided they are paid to a club president."
– Sportswriter Dan Parker

of an inning in the second game of a doubleheader against the Yankees. Philadelphia bows, 11-2; Scheib gets the loss.

Woody Williams of the Reds ties an NL record today with his 10th consecutive hit as the Reds sweep the Cubs, 10-1 and 3-1 in Chicago.

SEPTEMBER 19:

Joe Morgan is born in Bonham, Texas.

REGULAR SEASON WRAP-UP:

The Yankees, under Joe McCarthy, win their seventh pennant in eight years. They finish 98-56, 13 1/2 games ahead of the Senators. Spud Chandler is the ace of the staff at 20-4, with a 1.64 ERA. Much of the Yankee power has gone to war. Bill Dickey, in limited duty, hits .351. Next is Billy Johnson at .280. Charlie Keller hits .271 with 31 homers and 86 RBI.

The Cardinals, managed by Billy Southworth, also run away with the pennant, finishing at 105-49, 18 games up on the Reds. Stan Musial bats .357 with 13 homers and 81 RBI. Walker Cooper bats .318 and brother Mort is the staff's only 20-game winner (21-8, 2.30 ERA). The Giants Ace Adams pitches in a record 70 games – 67 in relief. His 11 relief wins are a record.

OCTOBER 5:

World Series, game one. Spurgeon "Spud" Chandler seven-hits the Cardinals in New York for a 4-2 win. Joe Gordon homers for New York. Max Lanier gets the loss.

OCTOBER 6:

World Series, game two. Mort Cooper goes the route allowing six hits in a 4-3 Cardinals' victory at Yankee Stadium. The clubhouse mood is sobered, however, by the news of the death of Robert Cooper, Mort and Walker's father. Ernie Bonham gets the loss. Ray Sanders hits a two-run homer and Marty Marion has a solo shot for the Cardinals.

OCTOBER 7:

World Series, game three. The Yankees beat the Cardinals, 6-2, in New York. Hank Borowy gets the win with eight innings of strong pitching, and Johnny Murphy gets the save. Billy Johnson delivers the big blow – a three-run triple in the eighth inning. The loss goes to pitcher Alpha Brazle.

OCTOBER 10:

World Series, game four. Marius Russo limits the Cardinals to

Stan Musial was a lifetime .331 hitter.

seven hits in nine innings to lead the Yankees to a 2-1 win in St. Louis. Harry Brecheen gets the loss in relief of starter Max Lanier. Russo's double followed by a Frank Crosetti sacrifice fly accounts for the game's winning run.

OCTOBER 11:

World Series, game five. Spud Chandler baffles the Cardinals, and the Yankees win the game, 2-0, to close out the Series. Chandler scatters 10 hits and the Cardinals leave 11 runners on base. Cooper starts strong with five straight strikeouts but becomes the losing pitcher when he yields a two-out sixth-inning homer to Bill Dickey with Charlie Keller on base for the game's only runs. Murry Dickson, on a 10-day pass from the army, pitches two-thirds of an inning of scoreless relief for the Cardinals. Chandler finishes with 2-0 and a microscopic 0.50 ERA. Billy Johnson is the Yankees' top hitter at .300. Marty Marion hits .357 for the Cardinals.

POST-SEASON

OCTOBER 15:

Al Simmons is released by the Red Sox after hitting only .203 in 40 games with one homer and 12 RBI. The future Hall of Famer, in a sad decline, moves one step closer to oblivion.

OCTOBER 25:

After a salary dispute with team president Branch Rickey, Dodger manager Leo Durocher signs to manage again in 1944. Durocher, whose Dodgers were 81-72 in third place, will receive $20,000 plus an attendance bonus. For every 100,000 fans Brooklyn draws, above 600,000, Durocher gets an additional $5,000. During Durocher's salary debate, Dan Parker of the *New York Daily Mirror* writes, "Branch Rickey believes there should be no limit on salaries – provided they are paid to a club president."

NOVEMBER 6:

The White Sox buy outfielder Hal Trosky from the Indians. Trosky has been in retirement for the past two seasons because of migraine headaches. The AL's 1936 RBI leader, Trosky is five days short of his 31st birthday.

NOVEMBER 15:

Commissioner Landis summons William Cox to a hearing in New York City on gambling charges, including allegations that he bet on his Phillies to win.

NOVEMBER 18:

Phillies' owner William Cox writes to Commissioner Landis, "I have... decided to devote all my time to my war-essential business. I have today submitted to the chairman of the board of the club my resignation as president and director thereof. I have as you know, what to me is a large investment in the club, and I shall dispose of that investment, in its entirety, as soon as I can find a satisfactory purchaser. In view of my resignation... I do not see that any useful purpose would be served by my attending any further hearings before you."

NOVEMBER 23:

William D. Cox is barred for life from baseball for betting on the Phillies to win. It is estimated that he wagered $25 to $100 per game. Cox first denies the charges, then admits he bet items like dinners. Landis reveals Cox's November 3 admission that he "placed through a bookmaker approximately 15 or 20 bets of from $25 to $100 per game on Philadelphia to win." On the same day Cox is booted, announcement is made of the sale of the Phillies to Robert R. M. Carpenter Sr., who is chairman of the board of DuPont, for $400,000. His 28-year-old son, Robert Carpenter Jr., will operate the team.

After a November 22 radio statement in which he admits to making small "and sentimental bets before I learned of the rule against it," William Cox recants his admission of gambling and asks for his originally scheduled December 4 hearing with the commissioner. The friendly bets, he alleges, were for items such as hats, cigars, and dinners, but did not involve baseball game results. Nonetheless, Judge Landis refuses to reopen the case and, therefore, the ban on Cox stands.

DECEMBER 13:

Ferguson Jenkins is born in Chatham, Ontario, Canada. Jenkins will grow up to have a Hall of Fame baseball career, which begins with the Philadelphia Phillies in 1965. In his 19-year career, he was 284-226 with a 3.34 ERA.

HISTORY

Controversy follows the Dodgers like the BMT subway follows the tracks. Among the 1943 "highlights": After lining out, second baseman Billy Herman throws a ball into the dugout and hits his own manager, Leo Durocher, between the eyes. Herman is angered at being given two take signs with the count at 2-0. In another incident, umpire George Barr calls a balk on Johnny Allen. The pitcher nearly chokes Barr with his own tie – leading to the end of cravats for umpires. And the Cardinals' mild-mannered Stan Musial goes after Brooklyn pitcher Les Webber.

TRIVIA

According to Richard Goldstein in his *Spartan Seasons,* Nazi propaganda minister Joseph Goebbels announced, "There are fresh atrocities in the United States. The Yankees, not content with their pious interference all over the world, are beating up their own cardinals in St. Louis."

THE BEST OF 1943

NATIONAL LEAGUE

HITTERS

Batting Average:
Stan Musial, St. Louis Cardinals, .357

Slugging Average:
Stan Musial, .562

Home Runs:
Bill "Swish" Nicholson, Chicago Cubs, 29

Runs Batted In:
Bill Nicholson, 128

Hits:
Stan Musial, 220

Stolen Bases:
Joseph "Arky" Vaughan, Brooklyn Dodgers, 20

PITCHERS

Wins:
Elmer Riddle, Cincinnati Reds; Truett "Rip" Sewell, Pittsburgh Pirates; Mort Cooper, St. Louis Cardinals, 21

Strikeouts:
Johnny Vander Meer, Cincinnati Reds, 174

Earned Run Average:
Howie Pollet, St. Louis Cardinals, 1.75

Winning Percentage:
Mort Cooper, .724

Saves:
Les Webber, Brooklyn Dodgers, 10

Most Valuable Player:
Stan Musial, St. Louis Cardinals

AMERICAN LEAGUE

HITTERS

Batting Average:
Luke Appling, Chicago White Sox, .328

Slugging Average:
Rudy York, Detroit Tigers, .527

Home Runs:
Rudy York, 34

Runs Batted In:
Rudy York, 118

Hits:
Dick Wakefield, Detroit Tigers, 200

Stolen Bases:
George Case, Washington Senators, 61

PITCHERS

Wins:
Paul "Dizzy" Trout, Detroit Tigers; Spurgeon "Spud"Chandler, New York Yankees, 20

Strikeouts:
Allie Reynolds, Cleveland Indians, 151

Earned Run Average:
Spud Chandler, 1.64

Winning Percentage:
Spud Chandler, .833

Saves:
Gordon Maltzberger, Chicago White Sox, 14

Most Valuable Player:
Spurgeon "Spud" Chandler, New York Yankees

1944

"We've got to keep baseball on a high standard for... the youngsters."
– *Kenesaw Mountain Landis*

NEWS

ALLIES INVADE FRANCE

PARIS IS LIBERATED

U.S. FORCES WITHSTAND LAST NAZI OFFENSIVE IN BATTLE OF THE BULGE

Circus fire kills 167 in Hartford, Connecticut

GLENN MILLER'S PLANE IS LOST BETWEEN PARIS AND LONDON

Theatergoers flock to Tennessee Williams's The Glass Menagerie, *Leonard Bernstein's* On the Town

HARVARD SCIENTISTS BUILD FIRST COMPUTER

CONGRESS PASSES GI BILL

FDR ELECTED TO FOURTH TERM

PRE-SEASON

JANUARY 27:

Construction magnates Lou Perini, Guido Rugo, and Joseph Maney – known as the Three Little Steam Shovels – purchase the Boston Braves. Perini becomes 50% owner of the team.

Casey Stengel resigns as manager of the Braves. The team finished in sixth place last season; Stengel managed only 117 games because of a broken leg.

FEBRUARY 28:

Pitcher Joseph Frank "Joe" Wood, son of the great Smoky Joe Wood, signs with the Red Sox. Joe Wood's career lasts only three games; he is 0-1 with a 6.52 ERA. His father's pitching career, cut short by injury, encompassed 11 years; he was 116-57 with a 2.03 ERA.

MARCH 13:

Denton "Cy" Young's "secret" is out. His middle name is True, not Tecumseh, as generally thought

MARCH 17:

Clarence "Cito" Gaston is born in San Antonio, Texas.

MARCH 29:

Denny McLain is born in Chicago.

MARCH 31:

Rogers Hornsby, 48 years old, is the manager of the Vera Cruz Blues in the Mexican League. Trailing in a game, 14-13, he pinch hits a grand slam homer for a 17-14 victory. The next morning Jorge Pasquel, owner of the Blues and other teams in the League, tells him, "Mr. Hornsby, that was a nice hit yesterday, but it would have been better if we hadn't won the game." Hornsby quits and returns to the U.S.

APRIL 20:

Elmer John Gedeon, who played five games in 1939 as an outfielder for the Senators and hit .200, is killed five days before his 27th birthday when his Army Air Corps plane is shot down over St. Pol, France. He is the first major leaguer killed in World War II.

THE SEASON

APRIL 27:

The Braves' Jim "Abba Dabba" Tobin no-hits the Dodgers, 2-0, before only 1,984 fans in Boston. The 31-year-old knuckle-

TRIVIA

As a result of another one of those fan contests – this one promoted by the new team president Robert Carpenter Jr., – the Phillies will have a new name, the Blue Jays. The winning name was selected from 623 suggestions. The team never officially drops Phillies, and that more familiar name is restored in 1946.

Ogden Nash writes: "D is for Dean, The grammatical Diz, When they asked, Who's tops? Said correctly, I is."

LEAGUE

The All-American Girls Professional Baseball League adds the Minneapolis Millerettes and the Milwaukee Chicks. It decreases the size of the ball by a half-inch to 11 1/2 inches and increases the distance between bases from 65 feet to 68 feet – both in midyear. The second-half winners, the Milwaukee Chicks, beat the Kenosha Comets for the championship.

HISTORY

The Negro National League's Homestead Grays defeat the Birmingham Black Barons of the Negro American League, four games to one, to capture the championship.

baller also homers over the left-field wall in the eighth inning, becoming the first pitcher with a home run in his no- hit game. Tobin walks two and strikes out six; the Braves play errorless ball. Frederick "Fritz" Ostermueller gets the loss.

In St. Louis, the Browns beat the Indians, 5-2, for their seventh straight win to open the season, tying the Yankees' AL record. Only 960 fans are on hand to cheer the Browns on. St. Louis puts the game away with a four-run sixth inning, highlighted by a Don Gutteridge triple and a Vern Stephens double. The winning pitcher is Steve Sundra; Allie Reynolds gets the loss.

APRIL 28:

The Browns now own the AL record for consecutive wins to start a season. Behind the pitching of Nelson Potter, they defeat the Indians for their eighth straight win, 5-1.

APRIL 29:

The Browns and Jack Kramer beat the Indians, 3-1, to extend St. Louis's record winning streak to nine games. They now hold a three-and-a-half-game lead over the Senators.

APRIL 30:

How many games does a team win when it scores 30 runs in a double-header? One, if it's the Giants. With 58,068 at the Polo Grounds, the Giants dismantle the Dodgers, 26-8 – two runs short of the major league scoring record. First baseman Phil Weintraub has a homer, a triple, two doubles, and 11 RBI. Catcher Ernie Lombardi weighs in with seven RBI on three hits. And manager Mel Ott has two hits and five walks, scoring six times (to tie a major league record). Dodger pitchers issue a record-tying 17 walks – six consecutively in the second inning. Dodger manager Leo Durocher is thumbed in the sixth by all three umpires. But, in game two, the Dodgers beat the Giants, 5-4, in a game shortened to seven innings by darkness. Hal Gregg gets his first major league win. Brooklyn's Joe Medwick is hit in the groin by a bottle.

MAY 2:

Ted Williams is commissioned a second lieutenant in the Marine Air Corps and is awarded his wings.

MAY 4:

The last bastion of segregated seating in the major leagues – Sportsman's Park in St. Louis – has a new ticket policy. The Browns and Cardinals announce that "Negroes" now will be allowed to buy grandstand tickets. Previously, blacks were restricted to the bleachers.

MAY 7:

The Cubs' poor start takes its toll. Two days ago, Jimmy Wilson (1-9) was dropped as manager. Roy Johnson (0-1) replaces him as a one-day interim. And today, Charlie Grimm returns for his second stint as Chicago's skipper. In his first go-round, Grimm won pennants in 1932 and 1935.

Supposedly, a Cubs scout delivers a report to Grimm on a pitcher who allowed only one foul fly out of the infield. Grimm responds, "Forget the pitcher. Send the guy who hit the foul fly. We need hitters."

MAY 15:

The Reds' Clyde Shoun no-hits the Braves, 1-0, in Cincinnati. He misses a perfect game when he walks Jim Tobin – a no-hit pitcher in his last start – in the third inning. Chuck Aleno's fifth-inning homer gives Shoun, who has one strike-out, the win. Tobin is the losing pitcher.

MAY 23:

Night baseball returns to Ebbets Field after a two-year blackout because of the war. The Dodgers, wearing satin uniforms, beat the Giants, 3-2.

JUNE 3:

A crowd of 9,171 fans at the Polo Grounds for a game with the Pirates gets word over the public-address system that the Allies have invaded Europe. But after cheers and a prayer, the disappointed fans learn the bulletin is a mistake. According to writer Richard Goldstein, "Joan Ellis, a young teletype operator in the London bureau of the Associated Press, deciding to get in a little practice at her machine, had punched out 'Flash – Eisenhower's Headquarters Announce Allied Landings France,' just to see

JULY 10
Original Commissioner Kenesaw Mountain Landis is inducted into the Hall of Fame.

what it would look like. The dispatch had been transmitted inadvertently to AP's New York office..."

JUNE 6:

As Allied Forces invade the beaches of Normandy, France, on the long-awaited D-Day, baseball cancels its two-game schedule today so Americans cans spend the day at home or church as urged by President Franklin Delano Roosevelt. The International League, American Association, Eastern League, and other minor circuits also cancel their games.

The Dodgers obtain second baseman Eddie Stanky (.240) from the Cubs for pitcher Bob Chipman (3-1).

JUNE 10:

The Reds' Joe Nuxhall, only 15 years old, makes his major league debut. He starts off well enough, getting the Cardinals' George Fallon to ground out. Then, in two-thirds of an inning, he yields two singles, five walks, and five runs and uncorks a wild pitch. Mort Cooper five-hits the Reds, 18-0. It could have been worse – the Cardinals strand a major league record-tying 18 runners.

Nuxhall is a month and a half from his 16th birthday and the youngest of the wartime "babies." He says, "I felt fine warming up on the sidelines. It didn't get to me until I went out to the mound to start the ninth inning." He finishes the season with an ERA of 67.50. But he overcomes this rocky start to pitch 16 years in the major leagues with a winning record of 135-117, and a respectable ERA of 3.90.

JUNE 12:

The Giants' Mel Ott hits two homers against the Dodgers in a 15-9 win. He now has 14 in three weeks. New York's Phil Weintraub also homers twice.

The Giants buy baseball's tallest pitcher, six-foot, nine-inch, 225-pound Johnny Gee (0-0) from the Pirates. In his three previous seasons with Pittsburgh, Gee is a combined 5-8.

JUNE 22:

The Braves' Jim Tobin pitches a five-inning, 7-0 no-hitter against the Phillies in the nightcap of a Braves Field doubleheader. The game is called because of darkness. Tobin pitched a full no-hitter on April 27 against the Dodgers.

JUNE 26:

In a format reminiscent of a sandlot game, the Yankees, Giants, and Dodgers play a unique game against each other at the Polo Grounds to raise money for war bonds. One team plays an inning against each of the other two, then retires to the dugout for an inning. Each team plays six of the nine innings. More than 50,000 fans are on hand and $6.5 million is raised. The final score is Dodgers 5, Yankees 1, Giants 0.

JULY 4:

Historic Oriole Park in Baltimore burns to the ground. The wooden structure, built in 1914 for the Baltimore Terrapins of the Federal League, was the current home of the International League's Baltimore Orioles.

JULY 10:

Judge Kenesaw Mountain Landis, baseball's first and – to date – only commissioner, is inducted into the Hall of Fame. Landis, who is credited with helping to save baseball after the 1920 Black Sox scandal, supervises the game in autocratic style. A former federal judge, he banned 15 players – including the eight Black Sox – in his first year as commissioner.

JULY 11:

The NL beats the AL in the All-Star Game played this year at Pittsburgh's Forbes Field. Phil Cavaretta leads the NL offense with a triple, single, and three walks – getting on base a record five consecutive times. The winning pitcher is Ken Raffensberger; Cecil "Tex" Hughson gets the loss.

TRIVIA

Rolfe Humphries publishes his poem "Polo Grounds."

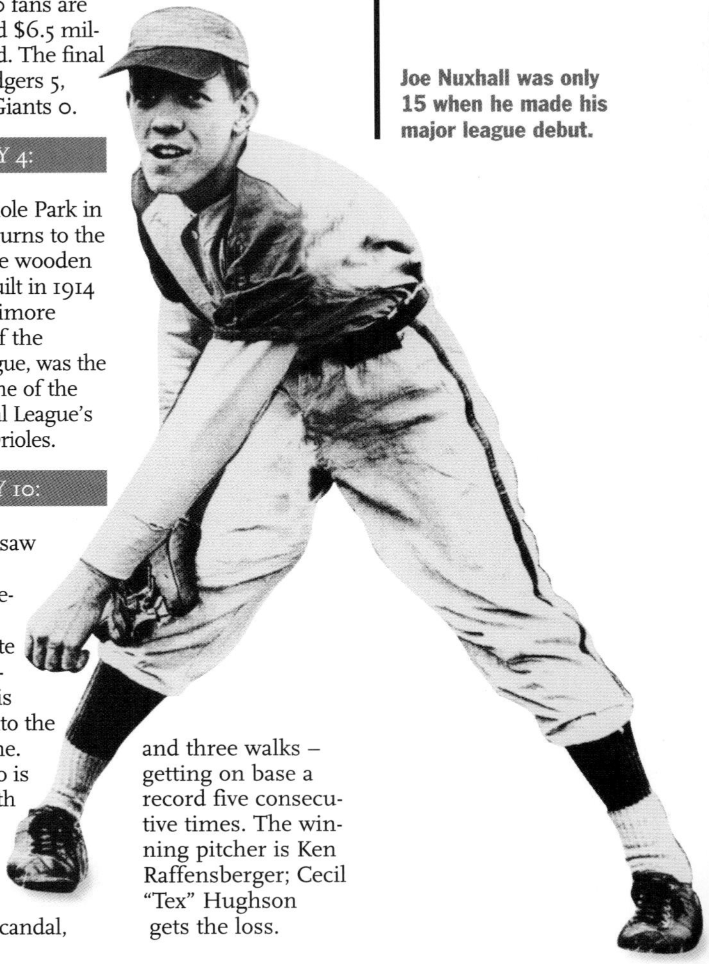

Joe Nuxhall was only 15 when he made his major league debut.

OCTOBER 1
In beating the Yankees, 4-1, the St. Louis Browns capture their first-ever AL pennant.

TRIVIA

The Office of War Information has a ban on mentioning weather during radio broadcasts. During a one-hour rain delay, unexplained to the radio listeners, Dizzy Dean finally says, "If you folks don't know what's holdin' up this game, just stick your heads out of the window."

JULY 16:

On the strength of eight unearned runs, the Dodgers beat the Braves, 8-5, in Boston, ending their 16-game losing streak – the longest in Brooklyn history. Curt Davis gets the win; the loser is Al Javery.

JULY 20:

Browns' pitcher Nelson Potter becomes the first pitcher ejected from a game for expressly violating the ban on spitballs when umpire Cal Hubbard catches him in the act. Spitballs were outlawed 25 years ago. As a result, Potter is fined and suspended for 10 days.

JULY 23:

In the nightcap of a Polo Grounds doubleheader, Giants' manager Mel Ott apparently deduces that one run is less destructive than four – he intentionally walks Cubs' slugger Bill "Swish" Nicholson with the bases loaded, forcing in a run. Nicholson already has four homers on the day. The bizarre strategy works and the Giants edge the Cubs, 12-10. Ott may have learned from the Phillies, who once did the same thing to him. In the opener, Nicholson had one homer and the Cubs won, 7-4. In the nightcap, prior to the intentional walk, Nicholson had three consecutive homers. Ott has a homer in game one; he and Nicholson are tied for the NL lead with 23.

JULY 28:

Walter Alston, whose major league playing career consists of one at-bat in 1936, is signed to manage the Dodgers' Trenton farm team.

AUGUST 3:

Sixteen-year-old high school student Tommy Brown makes his major league debut at shortstop for the Dodgers in the first game of a doubleheader against the Cubs. Brown, who is four months short of 17, doubles, scores a run, and commits an error.

Peoria Pennant

AUGUST 10:

The Braves' Charles "Red" Barrett gives a demostration in pitching efficiency, beating the Reds, 2-0, on a record 58 pitches; the game takes one hour and 15 minutes to play.

AUGUST 16:

In St. Louis, the Cardinals beat the Giants, 5-0, for their 80th win of the season – the earliest any modern team has tallied that many victories. Fred Schmidt is the winning pitcher.

AUGUST 17:

The Yankees' Johnny Lindell joins a long list of record holders when he hits four doubles in a 10-3 win over the Indians. Lindell hits his doubles consecutively, drives in two runs, and scores twice.

SEPTEMBER 14:

Joe DiMaggio is discharged from the Army Air Corps and will rejoin the Yankees for the 1945 season.

SEPTEMBER 16:

Jack Kramer one-hits the White Sox, 9-0, and the Browns take over first place.

SEPTEMBER 25:

After today's action, the Browns and Tigers are tied for first place. The Browns, behind Nelson Potter, beat the Red Sox, 3-0, while the Tigers are losing to the Athletics, 2-1.

SEPTEMBER 29:

The Browns continue driving toward their first ever pennant by sweeping the Yankees today. They win the opener, 4-1, behind Jack Kramer's pitching and a two-run homer by George McQuinn in the eighth. In the nightcap, Nelson Potter six-hits New York, 1-0.

SEPTEMBER 30:

The Browns continue to beat up the Yankees. Today Denny Galehouse shuts out New York, 2-0.

OCTOBER 1:

In St. Louis, with a sell-out crowd of 37,815 on hand, the Browns, after 43 years, win their first-ever pennant by beating the Yankees for the fourth straight time, 5-2. Sig Jakucki pitches a six-hitter; Chet Laabs and Vern Stephens homer. The Browns are in when Emil "Dutch" Leonard and the Senators beat Paul "Dizzy" Trout and the Tigers, 4-1.

REGULAR SEASON WRAP-UP:

Billy Southworth's Cardinals' 105-49, 14 1/2 games ahead of the Pirates – become

OCTOBER 9
With today's 3-1 win, the all-St. Louis World Series goes to the Cardinals in six games.

the first NL team with 100 wins in three consecutive years. In their runaway race, St. Louis wins 73 of their first 120 games. The big hitters are Stan Musial (.347), Johnny Hopp (.336), and Walker Cooper (.317). Mort Cooper is a 20-game winner for the third straight year with 22-7. The Giants' Ace Adams pitches in 65 games, becoming the first 20th-century player to appear in 60 games in three consecutive seasons.

The Cinderella Browns, under Luke Sewell, are 89-65, one game up on the Tigers. Their team batting average is only .252 with 72 homers. Vern Stephens provides much of the offense with .293, 20 homers and 109 RBI. Mike Kreevich is at .301. The Browns have no 20-game winners; Nelson Potter is 19-7. For the AL runner-ups, the Tigers, Hal Newhouser (29-9) and Paul "Dizzy" Trout (27-14) account for 56 of their team's 88 wins.

OCTOBER 4:

World Series, game one. With the two St. Louis teams facing off for the World Championship, Sportsman's Park will be the site of all games. The Cardinals are the home team today, but the Browns win, 2-1, on only two hits – one is a fourth-inning two-run shot by George McQuinn into the right-field stands. Denny Galehouse holds the Cardinals to seven hits for the win. Mort Cooper gets the loss. Attendance is 33,242.

Tony LaRussa is born in Tampa, Florida.

OCTOBER 5:

World Series, game two. The Cardinals' Sylvester "Blix" Donnelly pitches four shutout innings of relief, striking out seven to get a 3-2 win in 11 innings. James "Ken" O'Dea's pinch-hit single drives in the winning run. Bob Muncrief gets the loss.

OCTOBER 6:

World Series, game three. Jack Kramer allows seven hits and strikes out 10 for a Browns' "home" game win over the Cardinals, 6-2. Losing pitcher Ted Wilks is victimized by five straight singles in the third inning by Gene Moore, Vern Stephens, George McQuinn, Al Zarilla, and Mark Christman.

OCTOBER 7:

World Series, game four. Stan Musial hits a two-run homer and a double while Harry Brecheen scatters nine hits in a 5-1 Cardinal victory. Sig Jakucki gets the loss.

OCTOBER 8:

World Series, game five. Mort Cooper allows seven hits, strikes out 12, and outduels Denny Galehouse in a 2-0 Cardinal win. Galehouse strikes out 10 and allows only six hits, but two are homers by Ray Sanders and Danny Litwhiler.

OCTOBER 9:

World Series, game six. The Cardinals, on strong pitching by Max Lanier and Ted Wilks, beat the Browns, 3-1, to win the all-St. Louis World Series. Lanier limits the Browns to three hits in five and a third innings for the victory; Wilks pitches hitless relief. The loser is Nelson Potter. The Browns' pitching staff is outstanding with a 1.49 ERA; their offense betrays them with 12 runs for the series. The Browns' bats are particularly silent over the final three games, scoring only two runs. The Cardinals' pitchers compile a 1.96 ERA. The Browns' George McQuinn leads all hitters at .438. For the Cardinals, Emil Verban bats a "quiet" .412 and Walker Cooper finishes at .318.

POST-SEASON

NOVEMBER 1:

General manager Branch Rickey, attorney Walter O'Malley, and businessman Andrew J. Schmitz buy 25% of the Dodgers from the estate of Steve McKeever.

NOVEMBER 17:

Tom Seaver is born in Fresno, California.

NOVEMBER 25:

Judge Kenesaw Mountain Landis, baseball's first and only commissioner, dies at St. Luke's Hospital in Chicago, five days after his 78th birthday, of a heart attack. In accordance with his wishes, there will be no funeral.

DECEMBER 4:

Former catcher and manager Roger Bresnahan dies in Toledo, Ohio, at 65. He played 17 years, hitting .280. His best season was 1903, when he hit .350 with the Giants. He also managed for five years with the Cardinals and Cubs.

DECEMBER 22:

Steve Carlton is born in Miami, Florida.

HISTORY

The Navy beats the Army, eight games to two with one tie, in the armed services World Series. Among the players are Johnny Mize, Phil Rizzuto, Johnny Beazley, Pee Wee Reese, Dom DiMaggio, Virgil Trucks, Lynwood "Schoolboy" Rowe, Johnny Vander Meer, Hugh Casey, and Joe Grace.

LEAGUE

The war does not seem to be affecting baseball attendance. The major leagues draw 8,976,902 for 1944 – the best since 1941 (10,250,208). The Tigers top all teams with 923,000. The majors also raise $329,555 for the National War Fund and American Red Cross in 16 games – one hosted by each team. Players, umpires, and club officials, along with fans, pay their way into these benefit games. The AL accounts for $205,740; the NL $122,270. The Yankees top all teams with $34,587.

THE BEST OF 1944

NATIONAL LEAGUE

HITTERS

Batting Average:
Fred "Dixie" Walker, Brooklyn Dodgers, .357

Slugging Average:
Stan Musial, St. Louis Cardinals, .549

Home Runs:
Bill "Swish" Nicholson, Chicago Cubs, 33

Runs Batted In:
Bill Nicholson, 122

Hits:
Stan Musial; Phil Cavarretta, Chicago Cubs, 197

Stolen Bases:
Johnny Barrett, Pittsburgh Pirates, 28

PITCHERS

Wins:
William "Bucky" Walters, Cincinnati Reds, 23

Strikeouts:
Bill Voiselle, New York Giants, 161

Earned Run Average:
Ed Heusser, Cincinnati Reds, 2.38

Winning Percentage:
Ted Wilks, St. Louis Cardinals, .810

Saves:
Ace Adams, New York Giants, 13

Most Valuable Player:
Marty Marion, St. Louis Cardinals

AMERICAN LEAGUE

HITTERS

Batting Average:
Lou Boudreau, Cleveland Indians, .327

Slugging Average:
Bobby Doerr, "Indian Bob" Johnson, Boston Red Sox, .528

Home Runs:
Nick Etten, New York Yankees, 22

Runs Batted In:
Vern Stephens, St. Louis Browns, 109

Hits:
George "Snuffy" Stirnweiss, New York Yankees, 205

Stolen Bases:
George Stirnweiss, 55

PITCHERS

Wins:
Hal Newhouser, Detroit Tigers, 29

Strikeouts:
Hal Newhouser, 187

Earned Run Average:
Paul "Dizzy" Trout, Detroit Tigers, 2.12

Winning Percentage:
Cecil "Tex" Hughson, Boston Red Sox, .783

Saves:
George Caster, St. Louis Browns; Gordon Maltzberger, Chicago White Sox; "Jittery Joe" Berry, Philadelphia Athletics, 12

Most Valuable Player:
Hal Newhouser, Detroit Tigers

NEWS

HITLER KILLS HIMSELF IN HIS BERLIN BUNKER

WAR ENDS IN EUROPE

FDR dies at Warm Springs, Georgia; Harry S. Truman inaugurated as President

ATOM BOMBS DROPPED ON HIROSHIMA, NAGASAKI

JAPANESE SURRENDER ABOARD U.S.S. *MISSOURI*

U.S. Senate ratifies United Nations charter

B-25 BOMBER CRASHES INTO 78TH, 79TH FLOORS OF EMPIRE STATE BUILDING; 14 DIE

***George Orwell publishes* Animal Farm**

AFRICAN-AMERICAN MAGAZINE *EBONY* FIRST APPEARS ON NEWSSTANDS

PRE-SEASON

JANUARY 22:

Cardinals' star Stan Musial enlists in the army. The Cardinals recall infielder Albert "Red" Schoendienst from their Rochester Red Wings farm team.

JANUARY 25:

The Yankees are purchased by Larry MacPhail, Dan Topping, and Del Webb for $2.8 million from the heirs of Colonel Jacob Ruppert. The Yankees' farm system, including teams in Newark and Kansas City, are part of the transaction. General manager Ed Barrow will continue to operate the team. MacPhail, who brought night baseball to the majors, was a baseball executive with the Reds and Dodgers. Topping is the heir to a fortune and a businessman. Webb is in the construction business in Arizona.

FEBRUARY 10:

The Philadelphia Blue Jays sign 37-year-old free agent Jimmie Foxx, who hit only .050 in 15 games – with no homers – for the Cubs last season. The greater they are, the harder they fall.

FEBRUARY 15:

Billy Southworth Jr., a highly decorated bomber pilot, is killed at age 27 when his B-29 Superfortress crashes into Flushing Bay, New York, shortly after takeoff from Mitchell Field. The son of Cardinals' manager Billy Southworth, he wore a team cap during 25 missions over Europe. The younger Southworth was an outfielder with the Toronto Maple Leafs in the International League in 1940 when he became the first player in major league baseball to enlist.

FEBRUARY 21:

Less than a month after the sale of the Yankees and the announcement that Ed Barrow would remain as general manager, the front office undergoes a shake-up. Co-owner Larry MacPhail becomes president and general manager. The 76-year-old Barrow is kicked upstairs to become chairman of the board, a position that takes him out of the action.

MARCH 6:

Harry O'Neill, who caught one game for the Athletics in 1939, is killed at Iwo Jima,

LEAGUE

The All-American Girls Professional Baseball League adds two more teams – the Grand Rapids Chicks and the Fort Wayne Daisies. In midyear, the pitching distance is increased from 40 feet to 42 feet. The Rockford Peaches (67-43) are the league champions.

HISTORY

Umpire Ernie Stewart is fired after five years in the AL, for attempting to organize a union.

The Giants host General Dwight D. Eisenhower at a game against the Braves in June. As he leaves after the sixth inning, he asks Giants' owner Horace Stoneham, "What the hell has happened to the pitching since I went away to the war?"

Marianasis, at the age of 27. He is the second – and last – major leaguer killed in World War II.

MARCH 14:

AL president Will Harridge tells the *St. Louis Post-Dispatch* that his umpires are being briefed on the way Pete Gray of the Memphis Chicks catches the ball in case the one-armed outfielder makes it to the major leagues.

One-armed Pete Gray appeared in 77 games for the Browns in 1945.

APRIL 2:

Don Sutton is born in Clio, Alabama.

THE SEASON

APRIL 17:

On opening day at Braves Field, Giants' player-manager Mel Ott writes a new chapter in the NL record book. Ott, who doubles, walks twice, and scores three times in an 11-6 Giants' win, sets six records: 1,026 extra-base hits, 2,076 total bases, 1,778 RBI, 1,787 runs, 1,631 walks and 20 years with one team.

For want of a bow, a game is lost. With two runners on base and the Pirates' Jim Russell at bat, teammate Frankie Zak calls time out from first base to tie his shoe. Reds' pitcher William "Bucky" Walters pitches anyway and Russell hits a home run. Because of Zak's time-out the homer is erased and the Reds win, 7-6.

From The Sporting News Selects Baseball's Greatest Players: *"[Mel Ott] was a living, breathing oxymoron, a diminutive 5-9, 170-pound boy wonder who dared to challenge Babe Ruth for home run-hitting superiority in New York City. When he lifted his famous right leg and lashed into another pitch, Giants fans stationed in the Polo Grounds' short right-field bleachers braced – a ritual they enjoyed for 22 glorious seasons...." One writer said that Ott "...squared away to the pitcher as if he was going to beat a rug."*

APRIL 18:

Pete Gray, who lost his right arm in a childhood truck accident, is called up from the minors by the Browns and makes his major league debut today against the Tigers. The 30-year-old outfielder has a single – against Les Mueller – in four at bats as the Browns beat the Tigers, 7-1, at Sportsman's Park. Gray plays left field, and in his first at-bat, against Hal Newhouser, grounds out. He also strikes out and is robbed of an extra-base hit by Roger "Doc" Cramer.

Gray bats from the left side of the plate. In the field, he catches the ball, flips it while dropping his glove, catches it again, and throws it with his bare hand. Last year with the Memphis Chicks, he hit .333, had five homers, and stole 68 bases. He fielded an outstanding .983.

APRIL 19:

At Yankee Stadium, Red Sox player-manager Joe Cronin catches his spikes rounding second

MAY 13
Red Sox rookie pitcher "Boo" Ferriss runs his scoreless-innings streak to 22.

base, breaking his leg. The 38-year-old Cronin is carried out on a stretcher and retires as an active player. Cronin was at .375 (three for eight) this season and finishes his career with a .301 batting average for 20 years.

APRIL 24:

U.S. Senator and former Kentucky Governor Albert B. "Happy" Chandler is unanimously elected baseball's second commissioner on the first ballot of owners. The 46-year-old Chandler gets a seven-year contract with an annual salary of $50,000.

From Baseball: An Illustrated History*: "Judge Landis's replacement as baseball commissioner was a jovial, gregarious Kentucky politician... who once said he took the job because the $50,000 salary was such a big improvement over the $10,000 he'd recently been making as a United States senator.... Reporters called him 'the Mahatma,' because, one wrote, he reminded them of a combination of 'God, your father, and a Tammany Hall leader.'"*

APRIL 29:

Dave "Boo" Ferriss of the Red Sox overcomes a rocky start to beat the Athletics, 2-0, for his first major league win. Ferriss throws 10 straight balls and walks the bases loaded in the first inning, but goes on to pitch a five-hitter. He has three hits of his own in the game.

MAY 6:

Dave "Boo" Ferriss of the Red Sox starts his second major league game and pitches his second shutout, beating the Yankees, 5-0.

MAY 13:

Against the Tigers today, Red Sox rookie Dave Ferriss extends his consecutive scoreless innings streak to 22. He fans Rudy York four consecutive times on called strikes. Boston wins, 8-2 in Detroit.

MAY 20:

Pete Gray has a big day for the Browns in a Sportsman's Park doubleheader against the Yankees. Gray has four hits in eight at-bats, makes several outstanding catches among his 10 outfield putouts, and scores the winning run in a 5-2 Browns' victory in the nightcap. The Browns win the opener, 10-1.

MAY 23:

The Cardinals trade their three-time 20-game winner Mort Cooper (2-0) to the Braves for pitcher Charles "Red" Barrett (2-3) and $60,000. Cooper had repeatedly threatened to leave the Cardinals over salary disputes.

MAY 27:

Dave "Boo" Ferriss of the Red Sox one-hits the White Sox in the opener of a doubleheader and teammate Emmett O'Neill holds Chicago to two hits in the nightcap. Boston wins, 7-0 and 2-1, at Fenway Park.

JUNE 3:

The Browns' Alvis "Tex" Shirley lowers his ERA, but gains nothing more. He pitches 13 shutout innings against the Athletics today, but the game ends in a 0-0 tie.

JUNE 9:

At Ebbets Field, manager Leo Durocher confronts a fan named John Christian near the Dodgers' dugout. They argue over the language Christian has directed toward the Dodgers. Christian ends up with a broken jaw and files charges against Durocher and private cop Joe Moore. The two are released on bail. Through the intervention of entertainer Danny Kaye, a friend of Durocher's, Christian drops civil charges in return for a settlement of approximately $7,000. Durocher is acquitted of criminal charges.

JUNE 15:

The Dodgers send outfielder-pitcher Ben Chapman (.136 in 13 games; 3-3 in 10 games) to the Blue Jays for catcher-infielder Johnny Peacock (.203).

Pitcher Dave Ferriss of the Red Sox defeats the Senators, 6-5, in the opener of a doubleheader; the rookie right-hander now has beaten every AL team on his first try.

JUNE 16:

The Braves acquire outfielder Joe "Ducky" Medwick (.304) and pitcher Ewald Pyle (0-0) from the Giants for catcher Clyde Kluttz (.296).

JUNE 21:

The Athletics and Tigers battle to a 1-1, 24-inning tie.

HISTORY

Due to wartime travel restrictions, no All-Star Game is played in 1945. Instead there will be a series of interleague games. On July 10, the White Sox meet the Cubs, the Yankees play the Giants, and the Reds and Indians face off. On July 11, it is the Braves and Red Sox, the Browns and Cardinals, the Blue Jays and Athletics, and the Dodgers and Senators. Detroit and Pittsburgh will not participate because of travel distances.

> "Every time I sign a ball... I thank my luck I wasn't born Coveleski or Wambganss or Peckinpaugh."
> – *Hall of Famer Mel Ott*

JUNE 29:

The Blue Jays name newly acquired veteran Ben Chapman their manager. He will replace Fred Fitzsimmons, who had Philadelphia at 18-51.

JULY:

The Hall of Fame inducts Roger Bresnahan, Dennis "Dan" Brouthers, Frederick C. Clarke, James J. Collins, Ed Delahanty, Hugh Duffy, Hugh Jennings, Michael "King" Kelly, James O'Rourke, and Wilbert Robinson. However, because of wartime restrictions, no ceremonies are held. Bresnahan, a catcher, played for 17 years and batted .280. His best season was 1903 when he batted .350 for the Giants. In 1905, he hit .313 for New York in the World Series. Bresnahan died in 1944. Big Dan Brouthers played first base for 19 years and compiled a lifetime average of .342, with 2,296 hits and 235 stolen bases. A four-time NL batting champion, he played from 1879 to 1904 and died in 1932. Cap Clarke played 21 years, batting .312, with 220 triples and 506 stolen bases. He batted .300 or better 11 times. Clarke also managed for 19 years, leading the Pirates to two pennants and a World Series championship. Collins, a third baseman, batted .294 in his 14-year career. A five-time .300 hitter, he died in 1943. Delahanty, who died in a 1903 accident, was an infielder-outfielder who batted .346 in 16 years, with 2,597 hits and 455 stolen bases. He hit .400 or better three times – including .410 for the 1899 Phillies – and .300 or better nine times. Duffy, an outfielder, hit an all-time high .438 with the 1894 Boston Beaneaters. In 17 seasons, he compiled a .324 lifetime average with 583 stolen bases. Jennings, a shortstop-first baseman, batted .312 in 17 seasons and stole 359 bases. In 1896, he batted .401 for the Baltimore Orioles. Jennings died in 1928. King Kelly, who played all positions, batted .308 in his 16-year career. He hit .354 in 1884 and .388 in 1886 with the Chicago White Stockings. Kelly died in 1894. O'Rourke, another all-position player, hit .300 or better 11 times in his 19-year career and compiled a .310 lifetime mark. He died in 1919. Uncle Wilbert Robinson, a colorful catcher, hit .273 in 17 years. He managed the 1902 Orioles and, as Brooklyn's manager from 1914 to 1931, led the team to two pennants. He died in 1934.

Sportswriter Tom Meany wrote of Robinson in the 1937 Saturday Evening Post, *"Robbie was a rule-of-thumb manager, a gentle Falstaff, who could get more out of less material than any manager before or since."*

JULY 1:

Hank Greenberg returns to the Tigers and homers in the eighth inning against Charley Gassaway of the Athletics at Briggs Stadium. The Tigers win the game, 9-5, and take the nightcap as well. It is the first homer for Greenberg in four years, one month, and 24 days. The first major leaguer to return from the war, he served from May 7, 1941, until June 14, 1945.

JULY 4:

Playing against the Yankees, the Indians become the first team in ML history to go through a full game without an assist. Cleveland wins the opener, 4-2, and drops the nightcap, 3-2.

JULY 6:

With three hits in each game of a doubleheader against the visiting Pirates, the Braves' Tommy Holmes extends his consecutive-game hit streak to 34, surpassing Rogers Hornsby's 32 in 1922. The Braves win, 13-5 and 14-8.

JULY 8:

Outfielder Floyd "Babe" Herman, 42 years old, returns to the majors after an 8-year hiatus and rejoins the Dodgers. In his first at-bat, he pinch hits against the Reds, singles to right, trips on first base, and falls, but scrambles back safely on his hands and knees. In the opener of today's doubleheader, Dodgers' manager Leo Durocher gets into an argument with umpire Lynton "Dusty" Boggess. The fans respond by bombarding Boggess with fruit and bottles.

JULY 12:

In the opener of a doubleheader at Wrigley Field, the Braves' Tommy Holmes is held hitless, ending his hitting streak at 37 games. Behind pitcher Hank Wyse, the Cubs win their 11th game in a row. In the nightcap,

JULY 12 The Cubs hold the Braves' Tommy Holmes hitless, ending his streak at 37 games.

AUGUST 1 Mel Ott of the Giants hits his 500th career home run, off Braves' Johnny Hutchings.

the Braves win, ending the Cubs' win streak and beating Claude Passeau, who had won nine in a row. The teams split.

JULY 16:

Charles "Red" Ruffing, 41 years old and 30 pounds overweight, returns to the Yankees after two and a half years in the armed forces. Ruffing last pitched in 1942 when he was 14-7. The Yankees win, 13-4

JULY 19:

Umpire George Magerkurth punches Dayton restaurateur Thomas J. Longo, who had been riding him during a Reds-Braves game in Cincinnati. He avoids a lawsuit with a letter of apology and the payment of $100 for medical expenses.

JULY 21:

The Detroit Tigers' Les Mueller pitches 19 2/3 innings as Detroit and the Athletics tie 1-1 in a 24-inning game at Shibe Park. Darkness ends the contest. The Tigers' Rudy York ties an AL record with 34 chances at first base; teammate Bob Swift catches the entire game without an error.

The Yankees' Red Ruffing still has his stuff; he hurls six shutout innings against the Athletics. Ruffing compiles a 7-3 record with a 2.89 ERA in the remainder of the 1945 season.

JULY 27:

The Cubs buy pitcher Hank Borowy (10-5) from the Yankees for $97,000 after he clears waivers. (Some writers put the figure at $97,500.) Larry MacPhail explains why he sells the team's top pitcher, "A hundred thousand dollars." He adds, "This was a good chance to sell a pitcher who never has been a winner in the last month or so of a season." Borowy responds with action; he wins 11 games for the Cubs, leading them to the NL pennant.

AUGUST 1:

The Giants' Mel Ott homers against Johnny Hutchings of the visiting Braves for his 500th career home run. New York wins the game, 9-2.

AUGUST 8:

A line drive by Hank Greenberg knocks out Red Sox pitcher Jim Wilson and fractures his skull, necessitating two hours of surgery. Wilson recovers and pitches for 11 more years, struggling to a lifetime 86-89, with a 4.01 ERA.

AUGUST 13:

Branch Rickey, Walter O'Malley, and John L. Smith buy the controlling interest in the Brooklyn Dodgers.

AUGUST 14:

Robert "Bert" Shepard, a combat pilot who lost his right leg below the knee when his plane was downed over Germany, makes his major league debut, pitching in relief against the Red Sox. He goes five and a third innings and gives up three hits, a walk, and one run, while fanning two. He is hitless in three at-bats. The Red Sox win the game, 15-4. Authors Donald Dewey and Nicholas Acocella describe Shepard's appearance, his only one, as a "public relations gesture."

AUGUST 20:

Tommy Brown of the Dodgers hits a home run against Elwin "Preacher" Roe of the Pirates at Ebbets Field. At 17 years, eight months, and 14 days old, Brown becomes the youngest major leaguer ever to homer. His round-tripper is the only run against Roe, who wins, 11-1, aided by 11 Dodgers' errors.

AUGUST 24:

After 43 months of naval service, Bob Feller is back and so is his fastball. Before 46,477 fans at Municipal Stadium, he pitches a four-hitter against the Tigers and strikes out 12 en route to a 4-2 win. Feller, who was discharged on August 22, spent nearly four years in the Navy, including 20 months at sea. He holds the Tigers hitless through six and two-thirds innings. Pat Seerey

LEAGUE

Baseball sets an attendance record with 10,951,502.

Hal Newhouser was voted the American League MVP in 1945.

TRIVIA

The Naughty Nineties, starring Bud Abbott and Lou Costello, introducing a classic baseball comedy routine.

Costello: What's the name of the first baseman?
Abbott: Who is on first.
Costello: Well, what are you asking me for?
Abbott: I'm not asking you – I'm telling you. Who is on first.
Costello: I'm asking you – who's on first?
Abbott: That's the man's name.
Costello: That's whose name?
Abbott: Yes.
Costello: Well, go ahead, tell me!
Abbott: Who.
Costello: The guy on first.
Abbott: Who.
Costello: The first baseman.
Abbott: Who is on first.
Costello: Have you got a first baseman on first?
Abbott: Certainly.
Costello: Well, all I'm trying to find out is what's the guy's name on first base.
Abbott: Oh, no, no, What is on second base.

hits a two-run homer for the Indians. The games' losing pitcher is Hal Newhouser.

AUGUST 28

Dodgers' president Branch Rickey and scout Clyde Sukeforth meet with Jackie Robinson. The topic: the possibility of Robinson breaking baseball's color barrier. Robinson asks, "Mr. Rickey, do you want a ballplayer who's afraid to fight back?" Then Rickey responds, "I want a player with the guts not to fight back."

AUGUST 30:

In Pittsburgh, the Cubs' Stan Hack singles against Preacher Roe for his 2,000th career hit. The Pirates win the game, 6-4.

SEPTEMBER 1:

In Boston, the Blue Jays' Vince DiMaggio hits a grand slam home run against Elmer Singleton, tying a major league record with four in a season. DiMaggio previously had grand slams on May 20, June 2, and June 27. Philadelphia wins, 8-3.

SEPTEMBER 4:

After being activated by the Yankees, 42-year-old batting practice pitcher Paul Schreiber relieves Al Gettel in the sixth inning of today's game against Detroit at Yankee Stadium. He works three and a third innings, walking two, allowing no hits, and striking out Paul Richards. The Yankees lose, 10-0. Schreiber's last major league appearance was in 1923 for the Dodgers. In 1931, he pitched for Allentown in the Eastern League.

Schreiber appears in two games, pitches four and a third innings for an 0-0 record and an ERA of 3.98.

SEPTEMBER 7:

Hen's teeth are as rare as Senators' homers. Washington's Joe Kuhel hits an inside-the-park homer against Bob Muncrief of the Browns today at Griffith Stadium. It is the first and only round-tripper at home this season for Washington.

The Senators hit only 27 homers for the season; Harlond Clift leads the team with eight. Visiting players have almost equal difficulty generating enough power to reach the seats at Griffith Stadium. Only six are hit against the Senators at home, and two of those are by the Tigers' Rudy York.

SEPTEMBER 9:

In Pittsburgh, the Blue Jays' Jimmie Foxx homers in the opener of a doubleheader. It is his sixth of the season and the 533rd of his career. The Pirates win, 4-3. In the nightcap, Foxx homers against the Pirates' Johnny Lanning; it is his 534th and final career homer. Philadelphia wins, 14-3.

Athletics' pitcher Dick Fowler, discharged from the Canadian army nine days ago, no-hits the Browns, 1-0, at Shibe Park. It is the first no-hitter for the A's since 1916 and the first in the AL since Bob Feller's in 1940. Fowler, making his first start after three relief appearances, walks four and fans six; Philadelphia makes no errors. The losing pitcher is John "Ox" Miller," who allows only 5 hits. The Athletics score the game's only run in the bottom of the 9th when Hal Peck triples and Irv Hall singles.

SEPTEMBER 14:

The Dodgers sweep the Cardinals, 7-3 and 6-1, then board a train from St. Louis to Chicago. After midnight the train is wrecked and a fire breaks out. The engineer is killed, but none of the Dodgers'players is injured.

SEPTEMBER 15:

The Dodgers, who survived a train wreck en route to Chicago, are defeated twice by the Cubs, 12-5 and 7-6.

SEPTEMBER 17:

Cubs' slugger Bill Nicholson shows he has a glove as well as a bat. He handles 10 putouts, setting a record for right fielders, in a 4-0 loss to the Dodgers at Wrigley Field.

SEPTEMBER 30:

A huge grand slam home run by Hank Greenberg in the ninth inning against Nelson Potter's 1-0 screwball gives the Tigers a 6-3 win over the Browns and clinches the pennant for Detroit. The game, played on a rain-soaked field at Sportsman's Park, also marks the final major league at-bat for Pete Gray, who hits into a fielder's choice against Hal Newhouser in the 8th inning. The Tigers began the day with a one-game lead over the Senators, who had completed their sea-

SEPTEMBER 30
Hank Greenberg's ninth-inning grand slam gives Detroit a win – and the AL pennant.

OCTOBER 1
The Cubs shut out the Tigers, 9-0, in game one of the World Series.

son. Game 2 is rained out after an inning. In Philadelphia, Dodgers' second baseman Eddie Stanky walks for the 148th time this season – an NL record, breaking Jimmy Sheckard's 1911 mark. In cold weather, only 2,241 fans see Brooklyn beat Philadelphia, 4-1.

REGULAR SEASON WRAP-UP:

The Tigers, bolstered by the return of Hank Greenberg (.311, 13 homers and 60 RBI in 78 games), win the pennant by a game and a half over the Senators. Managed by Steve O'Neill, Detroit is 88-65. Hal Newhouser, at 25-9 with a 1.81 ERA, is the ace of the staff. Roy Cullenbine and Rudy York each have 18 home runs.

The Cubs, under Charlie Grimm, are 98-56 and beat the Cardinals by three games. The mid-season acquisition of Hank Borowy bolsters the pitching staff; he is 11-2. Hank Wyse is the only 20-game winner (22-10). NL batting champion Phil Cavarretta (.355), Stan Hack (.323), and Don Johnson (.302) are the Cubs' top hitters.

Pete Gray, the one-armed outfielder, appears in 77 games for the St. Louis Browns, hitting .218 with six doubles and two triples. Tommy Holmes of the Braves bats .352 and fans only nine times. The Blue Jays' Andy Karl sets an NL record with 167 innings of relief pitching.

OCTOBER 1:

Rod Carew is born in Gatun, Panama.

OCTOBER 3:

World Series, game one. Hank Borowy pitches a complete game six-hitter as the Cubs bounce the Tigers, 9-0, in Detroit. Losing pitcher Hal Newhouser gives up seven runs in 3 innings. Phil Cavarretta hits a homer and scores 3 runs; Bill Nicholson triples and has 3 RBI.

OCTOBER 4:

World Series, game two. Hank Greenberg's three-run homer in the fifth inning against losing pitcher Hank Wyse powers the Tigers past the Cubs, 4-1. Virgil "Fire" Trucks, out of the navy less than a week, limits Chicago to seven hits and pitches a complete game.

OCTOBER 5:

World Series, game three. Claude Passeau is brilliant in limiting the Tigers to one hit – a Rudy York single in the second – and the Cubs top the Tigers, 3-0, in Detroit. The only other Tiger base runner is Bob Swift, on a sixth-inning walk. A fourth-inning double by Harry "Peanuts" Lowrey, followed by a Bill Nicholson single, gives Passeau all the runs he needs. The losing pitcher is Frank "Stubby" Overmire.

OCTOBER 6:

World Series, game four. The Tigers score four runs in the fourth inning against Ray Prim, and Paul "Dizzy" Trout allows only five hits in a 4-1 Tigers' win in Chicago.

OCTOBER 7:

World Series, game five. Behind Hank Greenberg's three doubles and Hal Newhouser's seven-hit, nine-strikeout pitching, the Tigers get an 8-4 win in Chicago. The losing pitcher is Hank Borowy.

Abbott and Costello entered baseball lore with their hilarious "Who's on First" routine.

TRIVIA

Are the Cubs victims of the Billy Goat Curse? During the 1945 World Series, a tavern owner named Billy Sianis brings his goat to Wrigley Field and is denied admission. He puts a hex on the team, which some fans believe is responsible for the failure of the Cubs to ever again win a pennant. According to a 1994 article by Paul Sullivan of the *Chicago Tribune*, "The Billy Goat Curse was removed twice by Sianis' nephew, Sam. It supposedly was removed in 1984... Then one month ago, a 'ringer' goat from Wisconsin was paraded around Wrigley Field after a record 12-game home losing streak. The streak was snapped, but at least until further notice, the curse lives on."

OCTOBER 8:

World Series, game six. At Wrigley Field in Chicago, the Cubs outlast the Tigers, 8-7, in 12 innings. Bill Schuster scores the winning run when Stan Hack's bouncer gets past Hank Greenberg in left field. With the Cubs leading 5-3 in the seventh, starter Claude Passeau is hit on the finger by a Jimmy Outlaw liner and has to leave the game. Greenberg homers in the eighth, one of the Tigers' 13 hits. The Cubs have 15. The winner is Hank Borowy – the Cubs' fourth pitcher – with four innings of shut-out ball. The Tigers' fifth pitcher, Dizzy Trout, gets the loss. Writer Charles Einstein calls it "the worst game of baseball ever played in this country."

OCTOBER 10:

World Series, game seven. The Tigers explode for five runs in the first inning. The Cubs' Hank Borowy, pitching on one day's rest, cannot retire a batter. Hank Greenberg, playing with an injured wrist, sets up the rally with a surprise sacrifice bunt. From there, the Tigers coast to a 9-3 win and the World Series championship. Hal Newhouser scatters 10 hits and strikes out 10 for the win. The Cubs' Phil Cavarretta leads all batters with a .423 average. Roger "Doc" Cramer hits .379 for Detroit, and Hank Greenberg, at .304, has two homers and seven RBI.

POST-SEASON

OCTOBER 15:

Jim Palmer is born in New York City.

OCTOBER 23:

Branch Rickey stuns baseball – and the world at large – with the announcement that he has signed Jack Roosevelt Robinson.

Robinson is to play with the Dodgers' Montreal farm team in the International League next season. He will become the first black player in major league baseball in the 20th century. He will receive a bonus of $3,500 and a salary of $600 per month. Robinson, 26, who played with the Kansas City Monarchs in the Negro League in 1945, hitting .387, is a former UCLA football star and was a lieutenant in the army.

NOVEMBER 1:

Of Jackie Robinson, *The Sporting News* states: "Jackie Robinson, at 26, is reported to possess baseball abilities which, if he were white, would make him eligible for a trial with, let us say, the Brooklyn Dodgers' Class B farm at Newport News, if he were six years younger." The "Bible of Baseball" predicts that "the waters of competition in the International League will flood far over his head."

Joe Williams writes in *The Sporting News*, "It is no secret that players of suspected Negro parentage have appeared in big league games. They were presented as Indians, Cubans, Mexicans, and you name it."

In his 1983 classic, Baseball's Great Experiment: Jackie Robinson and His Legacy, *Jules Tygiel writes: "Despite the generally accepted notion that some blacks had passed as white to enter organized baseball, no proven instances of this phenomenon exist." Tygiel also reports that Tigers' first baseman Rudy York, "alone among the southern players, publicly deviated from the consensus. York, from Catersville, Georgia, said... 'I wish him all the luck in the world and hope he makes good.'"*

NOVEMBER 6:

Billy Southworth resigns as manager of the Cardinals (95-59, second place) and is inked to manage the Braves in 1946. He replaces Del Bissonette (25-34). Eddie Dyer will succeed Southworth as the Cardinals' skipper.

NOVEMBER 10:

Sportswriter Sam Lacey writes in the *Baltimore Afro-American*: "Baseball has given employment to known epileptics, kleptomaniacs, and a generous scattering of saints and sinners. A man who is totally lacking in character has turned out to be a star in baseball. A man whose skin is white or red or yellow has been acceptable. But a man whose character may be of the highest and whose ability may be Ruthian has been barred completely from the sport because he is colored."

THE BEST OF 1945

NATIONAL LEAGUE

HITTERS

Batting Average:
Phil Cavarretta, Chicago Cubs, .355

Slugging Average:
Tommy Holmes, Boston Braves, .577

Home Runs:
Tommy Holmes, 28

Runs Batted In:
Fred "Dixie" Walker, Brooklyn Dodgers, 124

Hits:
Tommy Holmes, 224

Stolen Bases:
Albert "Red" Schoendienst, St. Louis Cardinals, 26

PITCHERS

Wins:
Charles "Red" Barrett, Boston Braves/St. Louis Cardinals, 23

Strikeouts:
Elwin "Preacher" Roe, Pittsburgh Pirates, 148

Earned Run Average:
Hank Borowy, Chicago Cubs 2.13

Winning Percentage:
Harry Brecheen, St. Louis Cardinals, .789

Saves:
Ace Adams, New York Giants; Andy Karl, Philadelphia Blue Jays, 15

Most Valuable Player:
Phil Cavarretta, Chicago Cubs

AMERICAN LEAGUE

HITTERS

Batting Average:
George "Snuffy" Stirnweiss, New York Yankees, .309

Slugging Average:
George Stirnweiss, .476

Home Runs:
Vern Stephens, St. Louis Browns, 24

Runs Batted In:
Nick Etten, New York Yankees, 111

Hits:
George Stirnweiss, 195

Stolen Bases:
George Stirnweiss, 33

PITCHERS

Wins:
Hal Newhouser, Detroit Tigers, 25

Strikeouts:
Hal Newhouser, 212

Earned Run Average:
Hal Newhouser, 1.81

Winning Percentage:
Hal Newhouser, .735

Saves:
Jim Turner, New York Yankees, 10

Most Valuable Player:
Hal Newhouser, Detroit Tigers

HISTORY

The Cleveland Buckeyes of the Negro American League sweep the Homestead Grays of the Negro National League in four games to win the championship.

1946

"Those who did not return by opening day are now out."
– *Happy Chandler on "jumpers"*

NEWS

U.S. CONDUCTS A-BOMB TESTS ON BIKINI ATOLL IN THE PACIFIC

ATOMIC ENERGY COMMISSION FORMED

TRUMAN DECLARES INDEPENDENCE FOR PHILIPPINES

Mother Cabrini canonized

FRANK CAPRA'S *IT'S A WONDERFUL LIFE* STARS JAMES STEWART AND DONNA REED

Dr. Benjamin Spock's *The Common sense Book of Baby and Child Care* is published

JUAN PERON IS ELECTED PRESIDENT OF ARGENTINA

THE NUREMBERG TRIALS CONDEMN 12 NAZIS TO DEATH, INCLUDING HERMANN GOERING

AS RELATIONS BETWEEN THE U.S.AND THE U.S.S.R. CHILL, WINSTON CHURCHILL COINS THE TERM "IRON CURTAIN"

PRE-SEASON

JANUARY 12:

It's Mr. Splendid Splinter. Ted Williams is discharged from the Marine Air Corps after three years away from baseball.

JANUARY 23:

After nearly four years in the Army Air Corps, the Cardinals' Enos Slaughter is a civilian again.

JANUARY 25:

The Red Sox sign Ted Williams to a three-year contract.

FEBRUARY 8:

Joe "Ducky" Medwick (.290, three homers in 92 games) is unconditionally released by the Braves.

FEBRUARY 18:

After rejecting the Giants' $5,000 offer, outfielder Danny Gardella (.272, 18 homers) goes to Vera Cruz and signs a one-year contract with a two-year option to play in the Mexican League. He reportedly gets $8,000 plus a $5,000 bonus. Dodger outfielder Luis Olmo (.313, 10 homers in 1945) also heads south for a three-year contract at an annual $10,000.

FEBRUARY 26:

Back from his tour with the Marine Air Corps, Ted Williams hits the first spring training pitch he sees for a home run.

MARCH 3:

The Browns sign outfielder Joe Medwick.

MARCH 9:

Ted Williams is given an offer of $500,000 to jump over to the Mexican League.

MARCH 12:

Reportedly, aspiring 20-year-old pitcher Fidel Castro tries out for the Washington Senators. He is not signed, and returns home to Cuba to pursue other interests.

MARCH 21:

U.S. baseball players appear in Mexican League games.

APRIL 5:

The Browns release Joe Medwick before he plays a regular-season game. Medwick signs with Brooklyn; it is his second stint with the Dodgers.

APRIL 8:

James "Catfish" Hunter is born in Hertford, North Carolina.

THE SEASON

APRIL 15:

Giants' player-manager Mel Ott, once known as Master Melvin and now 37 years old, homers against Oscar Judd of the Phillies today at the Polo Grounds. It is Ott's 511th career home run – and his last. The Giants win, 8-4. He bats only 68 times in 1946 without another homer and four times in 1947.

APRIL 16:

In Cincinnati for the Reds-Cubs opener, Commissioner A.B. "Happy" Chandler announces that all players who jumped to play in the Mexican League are now suspended. He says, "Those who did not return by opening day are now out." Chandler had offered "jumpers" a grace period until opening day; they now face suspensions of up to five years.

In Washington, D.C., Ted Williams shows his pre-war power with a mammoth homer. The Red Sox top the Senators, 6-3.

APRIL 18:

In opening day in the International League, Jackie Robinson

APRIL 16
On opening day, Ted Williams, in his first game back from the war, hits a home run.

APRIL 18
Jackie Robinson is in the lineup for the Montreal Royals on their opening day.

becomes the first black player in modern organized baseball when he takes the field for the Montreal Royals against the Jersey City Giants at Roosevelt Stadium in New Jersey. A crowd of 25,000 is on hand to witness the historic moment. Robinson grounds out against Warren Sandell in his first at-bat. In his next turn, he hits a 335-foot homer. He adds three more hits, and ends up with four RBI, four runs, as well as two stolen bases. Robinson has one bad moment; he makes a throwing error attempting a double play in the fifth. The Royals win, 14-1.

Robert F. Murphy holds a press conference to announce the formation of the American Baseball Guild, registered yesterday in Massachusetts. The goal of the guild is "a square deal for players, the men who make possible big dividends and high salaries for stockholders and club executives." The guild will seek minimum salaries of $6,500, the resolution of salary disputes by impartial arbitration, and 50% of the proceeds of a player sale to the athlete himself.

BILL VEECK ONCE SAID, "NOBODY IN BASEBALL IS MORE AWARE OF THE FACT THAT A BALL CLUB MUST SELL BASEBALL, AND WIN GAMES. THERE IS NO SUBSTITUTE FOR THAT. BUT YOU DON'T SELL YOUR BASEBALL WITHOUT DRESSING IT UP IN BRIGHT COLORED PAPER AND RED RIBBONS."

APRIL 23:

The Dodgers' Ed Head no-hits Boston, 5-0, at Ebbets Field. Head issues 3 walks and strikes out 2; the Dodgers commit one error. The losing pitcher is Mort Cooper.

APRIL 28:

White Sox pitcher Ted Lyons beats the Browns, 4-3, for his 260th career win. It is Lyons's last major league win. He appears in only five games, ending up at 1-4. In 21 years, he is 260-230 with a 3.67 ERA.

APRIL 30:

Bob Feller no-hits the Yankees, 1-0, before a crowd of 38,112 at Yankee Stadium. Catcher Frank "Blimp" Hayes homers against Floyd "Bill" Bevens in the ninth to win the game for Feller. Feller fans 11 and walks 5 in fashioning his second career no-hitter. Appearing in center field for Cleveland is Bob Lemon, who has one hit in four at-bats. In the ninth inning, George Stirnweiss reaches first on a Les Fleming error and goes to second on a Tommy Henrich sacrifice. Joe DiMaggio grounds out, moving Stirnweiss to third. Charlie Keller

LEAGUE

With the war over and the stars returning, baseball faces another threat – this one from south of the border. Mexican millionaire Jorge Pasquel and his brothers – Alfonso, Bernardo, Mario, and Gerardo – begin flashing big money to attract major league stars to their Mexican League. Talking becomes a punishable offense. Giants' owner Horace Stoneham fires pitcher Sal Maglie, second baseman George Hausmann, and first baseman-outfielder Roy Zimmerman for talking to Mexican League representatives. Zimmerman's major league career ends. Hausmann returns to the Giants in 1949, Maglie is back in 1950.

LEAGUE

Others headed for Mexico include Browns' shortstop Vern Stephens, Dodgers' catcher Arnold "Mickey" Owen, White Sox pitcher Alex Carrasquel, and Giants' pitchers Sal Maglie and Ace Adams. Stephens (.307, 14 homers) reportedly gets a $15,000 bonus and a five-year, $175,000 contract.

LEAGUE

In February, the Montreal Royals sign a second black player – 27-year-old pitcher John Wright, who has been with the Newark Eagles, Toledo Crawfords, and Homestead Grays in the Negro Leagues.

grounds out to give Feller the first no-hitter ever against New York in Yankee Stadium. Feller also is the first to no-hit the Yankees since Ray Caldwell of the Indians in 1919.

MAY 3:

The Boston Red Sox announce that Fenway Park will have lights in time for the 1947 season.

The Pasquel brothers are a hot topic. Rumors of offers and turn-downs flit through the major leagues. Dodgers' rookie infielder Stan Rojek reportedly rejects a $10,000 proposition from the Mexican League and remains at home.

MAY 6:

After 11 consecutive hits – tying Tris Speaker's major league record – Johnny Pesky of the Red Sox grounds out against the Browns' Al Milnar. Pesky began his streak on May 3 and collected his 11 hits over two days.

MAY 8:

Johnny Pesky of the Red Sox scores 6 runs today against the White Sox, tying a major league record. Boston wins, 14-10.

MAY 10:

The largest weekday crowd ever at Yankee Stadium – 64,183 including 6,756 for Ladies' Day – turn out to see the Yankees host the Red Sox. Despite a homer by Joe DiMaggio, Boston wins, 5-4. The winning pitcher is Earl Johnson; Joe Page is the loser.

MAY 11:

The Giants beat the Braves, 5-1, in the first night game at Braves Field. The ball game draws the largest crowd at that park in 13 years – 35,945.

At Yankee Stadium, 52,011 see Ernie Bonham pitch a two-hitter, and Tommy Henrich – with a homer, double and single – knocks in both runs in a 2-0 victory. The Yankee win ends the Red Sox 15-game winning streak.

MAY 13:

The Yankees become the first major league team to fly regularly. The team departs from La Guardia Airport in New York today on the Yankee Mainliner, a United Airlines four-engine plane, to Lambert Field in St. Louis, a four-and-a-half-hour trip. Charles "Red" Ruffing and four teammates are excused from the flight and head for St. Louis by train.

MAY 18:

Reginald Martinez "Reggie" Jackson is born in Wyncote, Pennsylvania.

The Tigers acquire third baseman George Kell (.299) from the Athletics for outfielder William "Barney" McCoskey (.198).

MAY 19:

The Red Sox reacquire third baseman Mike "Pinky" Higgins (.217 in 18 games) in a cash transaction.

MAY 21:

Yankees' manager Joe McCarthy does not join his team at Briggs Stadium in Detroit following a run-in with pitcher Joe Page. Coach Johnny Neun fills in.

MAY 22:

At Ebbets Field, the Dodgers beat the Cubs, 2-1, in a 13-inning game marked by two fights. Cubs' shortstop Len Merullo and Dodger second baseman Eddie Stanky are the combatants in one encounter. And Brooklyn manager Leo Durocher gets his uniform shirt torn off by Chicago pitcher Claude Passeau.

MAY 23:

Cardinals' pitchers Max Lanier and Fred Martin and second baseman Lou Klein accept contracts with the Mexican League.

The fight starts before the game today at Ebbets Field. The main event pits Dodger outfielder Fred "Dixie" Walker against Len Merullo – a veteran of yesterday's hostilities – during batting practice. Brooklyn wins the game, 2-1, in 11 innings.

MAY 24:

In Boston, Yankees' president Larry MacPhail announces the resignation of the team's manager, Joe McCarthy. McCarthy wires management from his farm in Tonawanda, New York, stating, "It is with extreme regret that I must request that you accept my resignation as manager of the Yankee Baseball Club, effective immediately. My doctor advises me that my health will seriously be jeopardized if I continue." McCarthy, reportedly suffering from gall bladder problems, managed the Yankees for 15 years, winning

MAY 28
The first night game ever played at Yankee Stadium draws a crowd of 49,917.

eight pennants and seven World Series championships. Bill Dickey is then named the Yankees' new manager.

MAY 25:

Cardinals' manager Eddie Dyer tells Sid Keener of the *St. Louis Star-Times* that Stan Musial, Enos Slaughter, Terry Moore, and George "Whitey" Kurowski have turned down "fabulous offers" from the Mexican League. According to some sources, Musial's rejected offer was a five-year $130,000 contract.

MAY 26:

Dave "Boo" Ferriss of the Red Sox one-hits the White Sox in the opener of a doubleheader and teammate Emmett O'Neill holds Chicago to two hits in the nightcap. Ferriss and O'Neill tie the 1934 record of Paul and Dizzy Dean – three hits in a doubleheader.

MAY 28:

The first night game at Yankee Stadium draws 49,917 on a cold Tuesday night. General Electric president Charles E. Wilson throws out the first ball. Bill Dickey makes his debut as Yankees' manager, but the Senators spoil the night with a 2-1 victory.

MAY 30:

At Ebbets Field on Memorial Day, the Braves' Carvel "Bama" Rowell hits and breaks the Bulova clock on top of the scoreboard, sending glass down on Dodgers' outfielder Fred "Dixie" Walker. Bulova promises Rowell a watch for his home run. He receives it 41 years later, in 1987.

JUNE 7:

The Pirates are the first target of Robert Murphy and his American Baseball Guild. Murphy, who has been trying to organize the team, sets today as a strike deadline. With coaches and trainers voting, the team approves a strike, 20-16, but because there is not a two-thirds majority, there will be no action. When the team takes the field, 15,000 fans boo. The Pirates then beat the Giants.

JUNE 9:

The usually easygoing Giants' Mel Ott becomes the first manager to be ejected from both ends of a doubleheader. The Pirates sweep the Giants, 2-1 and 5-1. With 66,545 turning out for a game with the Indians at Yankee Stadium, the Yankees top the 1 million attendance mark – the first time any major league team attracts a crowd of that size.

JUNE 13:

The largest class ever – 11 – is inducted into the Hall of Fame. The honorees are the celebrated Cubs' double-play combination Joe Tinker, Johnny Evers, and Frank Chance, along with Eddie Plank, George "Rube" Waddell, Jack Chesbro, Big Ed Walsh, Iron Man Joe McGinnity, Jesse Burkett, Clark Griffith, and Thomas McCarthy. Evers and Tinker are alive for the honor; Frank Chance died in 1924 at the age of 47. Tinker played 15 years, batting .263 with 336 stolen bases; Evers hit .270 in 18 seasons and stole 324 bases; Chance played 17 years and hit .296 with 405 stolen bases. Plank, a left-hander, was 327-193 with a 2.34 ERA and 60 shutouts in 17 seasons, mostly with the Athletics. He also hurled 412 complete games. Plank, who played from 1901 to 1917, died in 1926. Waddell, a true eccentric, broke his health fighting a Kentucky flood in 1912 and died in an institution in 1914. In 13 seasons, he was 191-145, with a 2.16 ERA and 50 shutouts. He was a 20-game winner four times. Chesbro is modern baseball's biggest single-season winner with a 41-12 mark in 1904 with the New York Highlanders. A four-time 20-game winner, he compiled a lifetime mark of 199-131 in 11 years with a 2.68 ERA and 35 shutouts. Chesbro died in 1931. Big Ed Walsh, described as a "man who could strut while standing still," has the all-time best career ERA – 1.82. In 14 seasons – 13 with the White Sox – he was 195-126 and recorded 57 shutouts. In 1908, he was 40-15. Iron Man McGinnity pitched only 10 years in the majors, but was 247-144 with a 2.64 ERA, 314 complete games and 32 shutouts. In 1904, he was 35-8 for the Giants. He twice won 30 games and was a 20-game winner in six other seasons. He died in 1929. Burkett, an outfielder known as the Crab because of his personality, played 16 years, batting .339 with 2,853 hits and 389 stolen bases. His career lasted from 1890 to 1905. Griffith,

CULTURE

The *Great McGraw* takes to the radio airwaves. It's the biography of the Giants' manager, with Pat O'Brien in the title role.

LEAGUE

For many of the 23 U.S. players signed by Pasquel, Mexico's promise is greater than its fulfillment and, spurred by an amnesty offer from Commissioner A.B. "Happy" Chandler, come home. Vern Stephens leaves after a few games in the Mexican League and rejoins the Browns. Mickey Owen also leaves, but does not play again in the majors until 1949.

JUNE 21
Bill Veeck is among a group that purchases the Cleveland Indians, for $1.6 million.

LEAGUE

The All-American Girls Professional Baseball League adds the Muskegon Lassies (Michigan) and the Peoria Redwings (Illinois). The size of the ball is reduced a half-inch to 11 inches, the distance between base paths is lengthened from 68 feet to 72 feet, and the pitcher's mound moved back from 42 feet to 43 feet. "Limited" sidearm is allowed in addition to underhand pitching. The Racine Belles, 74-38, are the league champions.

TRIVIA

The Braves create the first major league team yearbook. Called *Braves' Sketch Book*, it sells approximately 22,000 copies.

TINKER, EVERS, AND CHANCE ARE NOT WITHOUT THEIR DETRACTORS. GIANTS' MANAGER JOHN MCGRAW ONCE HELD A PRESS CONFERENCE TO ANNOUNCE, "YOU NEWSPAPERMEN HAVE DONE VERY WELL BY TINKER, EVERS, AND CHANCE. IN FACT, YOU HAVE BUILT UP A FAKE." AND, HISTORIAN GLENN DICKEY WROTE IN 1979, "TINKER TO EVERS TO CHANCE WAS AN OVERRATED COMBINATION. THEY SHOULD HAVE TAKEN F.P.A. [FRANKLIN P. ADAMS, THE AUTHOR OF THE POEM THAT CELEBRATED THE TRIO] INTO THE HALL OF FAME WITH THEM." DANIEL OKRENT AND STEVE WULF POINT OUT, "THE THREE MEN COMBINED FOR ONLY 56 DOUBLE PLAYS SCORED 4-6-3 OR 6-4-3."

the owner of the Washington Senators, pitched for 20 seasons between 1891 and 1914, compiling a 240-144 record with a 3.31 ERA. He managed from 1901 to 1920 and led the 1901 White Stockings to a first-place finish. McCarthy, an outfielder, played in the majors for 13 seasons – 1884 to 1896 – batting .292 with 467 stolen bases. His best season was 1894 when he hit .349 for the Boston Beaneaters.

Johnny Evers, who has had his "moments" with Joe Tinker, says, "I'm glad we made it together. Chance should have been elected long ago. I wish he were alive to feel as happy about it as I do. I'm glad for Tinker too." Joe McGinnity at one point in his career was hitting one of every 19 batters he faced and was accused by then NL president Harry Pulliam of "attempting to make the ballpark a slaughterhouse." Connie Mack once said of Waddell, "Rube had the greatest combination of speed and a deep, fast-breaking curve I ever saw. He almost had Johnson's speed, but [Walter] Johnson hasn't his curve. Nor has anyone else."

JUNE 21
Eddie Waitkus and Marv Rickert hit back-to-back inside-the-park homers for the Cubs.

JULY 6
Dodgers' manager Leo "The Lip" Durocher utters his famous "nice guys finish last" line.

JUNE 15:

The Braves obtain second baseman Billy Herman (.288 in 47 games) from the Dodgers for catcher Stew Hofferth (.235 in 1945).

JUNE 21:

A syndicate headed by Bill Veeck, son of former Cubs' president William L. Veeck, buys the Indians from Alva Bradley for $1.6 million. Veeck, a 32-year-old Marine combat veteran, is the major shareholder in the syndicate, which includes comedian Bob Hope and former White Sox executive Harry Grabiner.

JUNE 23:

At the Polo Grounds, Eddie Waitkus and Marv Rickert of the Cubs hit back-to-back, inside-the-park home runs in the fourth inning, becoming the first major leaguers to accomplish the feat. The Giants win the game, 15-10; the Cubs come back with a 9-4 win in the nightcap.

JUNE 24:

Baseball loses a round in court. Former major leaguer Al Niemiec gets a favorable ruling from Judge Lloyd Black of the Washington state federal district court. Niemiec sued the Seattle Rainiers under the Veterans Act, which guarantees returning serviceman their pre-war jobs. After serving with the navy, Niemiec was given his unconditional release by Seattle on April 21, 1946. Judge Black states, "Youth must be served, but not at the expense of men who have worn the uniform and contrary to the law." The 25-year-old Niemiec is awarded all of his 1946 pay.

Nine Spokane Indians players (Class B Western International League) die when their bus tragically plunges into a ravine. The bus was enroute to Bremerton, Washington, after a game in Salem, Oregon. Among the dead is first baseman Vic Picetti, regarded as a can't-miss major league prospect. Before the crash, infielder Jack Lohrke is called up to AAA San Diego Padres in the Pacific Coast League and leaves the team bus during a food break 175 miles from Spokane, earning him the career-long nickname Lucky.

Lucky Lohrke joins the Giants in 1947 and hits .240. He plays seven years in the majors with New York and the Phillies, hitting .242.

JUNE 29:

Charles "Red" Ruffing suffers a broken kneecap when he is hit by a line drive hit off the bat of the Athletics' Hank Majeski. Recovering from that injury is difficult at any age; Ruffing, at 42, faces almost insurmountable odds. The Athletics win the game, 2-0.

JULY 6:

Dodgers' skipper Leo Durocher is talking to announcer Walter "Red" Barber, with writer Frank Graham and others listening, prior to a game with the Giants. Barber remarks, "But Ott's a nice guy." Durocher responds, "A nice guy! I've been in baseball a long time. Do you know a nicer guy in the world than Mel Ott? He's a nice guy. In last place. Where am I? In first place. I'm in first place. The nice guys are over there in last place, not in this dugout." The "nice guys" beat Brooklyn, 7-6, on an RBI by former Dodger Goodwin "Goody" Rosen.

Not long after threatening to hit manager Eddie Dyer between the eyes with the baseball when he comes out to remove him from a game, pitcher Sylvester "Blix" Donnelly (1-2) is sold to the Phillies.

LEAGUE

The Dodgers sign two Negro League stars – 25-year-old catcher Roy Campanella of the Baltimore Elite Giants and 19-year-old pitcher Don Newcombe of the Newark Eagles. The players are assigned to the Nashua Dodgers in the New England League, where they will be managed by Walter Alston.

In the '46 All-Star Game, Ted Williams homered on a "blooper" pitch.

HISTORY

Pitcher Eddie Klepp, who is white, plays this season with the all-black Cleveland Buckeyes. Klepp has to stay and eat alone in white hotels. He is subjected to hazing by fans and, during spring training, harassment by Birmingham, Alabama, city officials.

LEAGUE

In June, the threatened five-year suspensions for the Mexican League jumpers become a reality. Commissioner Happy Chandler imposes the ban on those who violated 1946 contracts. Players who broke the reserve clause receive three-year suspensions.

JULY 7:

A New York newspaper headline reads: "NICE GUYS FINISH LAST – LEO." The quote will be forever associated with Leo Durocher, a win-at-any-cost manager. Durocher puts a different spin on his comments: "I called off his players' names as they came marching up the steps behind him, `Walker, Cooper, Mize, Marshall, Kerr, Gordon, Thomson. Take a good look at them. All nice guys. They'll finish last. Nice Guys. Finish last.' " Despite the explanations, Durocher later uses *Nice Guys Finish Last* as the title of his autobiography.

JULY 8:

A steering committee to "consider and test all matters of Major League interest" is set up by the NL and AL. Chaired by Larry MacPhail of the Yankees, the committee is composed of the league presidents, Tom Yawkey of the Red Sox, Sam Breadon of the Cardinals, and Philip Wrigley of the Cubs.

JULY 9:

The All-Star Game resumes after a one-year wartime hiatus with the American League winning, 12-0, at Fenway Park. Ted Williams mauls NL pitching before 34,906 hometown fans. He has two home runs (tying a record), a record-setting 5 RBI, and 2 singles. Williams hits his second homer against Truett "Rip" Sewell's unique "blooper" or "eephus" pitch. Charlie Keller also homers and Bob Feller gets the win. Claude Passeau is the loser.

SENATORS' MANAGER BUCKY HARRIS ONCE REMARKED ON FACING BOB FELLER: "YOU GO UP THERE AND HIT WHAT YOU SEE. IF YOU CAN'T SEE IT, COME ON BACK."

Pittsburgh outfielder Maurice Van Robays explains how he came up with the name for Sewell's blooper pitch: "An eephus ain't nothin', and that's what that ball is."

JULY 14:

In game one of a doubleheader against the Indians at Fenway Park, Ted Williams hits three homers – including a 400-foot grand slam against Steve Gromek – and a single, driving in 8 runs and scoring 4 times. Williams overshadows Indians' player-manager Lou Boudreau, who hits a homer and 4 doubles. The Red Sox win, 11-10. In the nightcap, after Williams doubles, Boudreau unveils a new defense when Williams comes to bat. Six players are stationed on the right side of the diamond. The left fielder moves to the conventional shortstop position. The third baseman is positioned to the right of second. The shortstop shifts to the spot of the second baseman, who moves into short right field. First baseman Jimmy Wasdell is deep on the foul line; the right and center fielders are in their normal places. In his first at-bat against the "Boudreau shift," Williams takes a look at the defense, steps out of the batter's box, and laughs. Then he doubles down the right field line. The next time up, he grounds out to Boudreau at short. Lou Boudreau explains, "We had to do something."

The Braves' 25-year-old left-hander Warren Spahn gets his first major league win, beating the Pirates, 4-1. Spahn debuted in 1942, then entered the armed forces.

JULY 16:

In St. Louis, the Cardinals beat the Brooklyn Dodgers, 5-4, on a ninth-inning 3 run pinch-hit homer by Erv Dusak. The win gives St. Louis a 4 game sweep; they now trail Brooklyn by a half-game.

JULY 9
The All-Star Game resumes after a one-year hiatus due to World War II.

AUGUST 20
"Rapid Robert" Feller's fastball is clocked at a healthy record 98.6 miles per hour.

JULY 19:

It gets lonely on the White Sox bench as umpire Red Jones thumbs 14 players. The Red Sox win the game, 9-2.

Ted Williams wrecks the Browns in a doubleheader at Fenway Park. In game one, Williams warms up with three hits in four at-bats as Dave Ferriss pitches a 5-0, five-hitter for his 15th win. In the nightcap, the Splendid Splinter really goes to work. In the second inning he hits a 1-1 pitch from Cliff Fannin for his 27th homer of the year. In the third inning, he triples, and in the fifth, he singles. He then adds a double, hitting for the cycle. The Red Sox win, 5-0, and Williams concludes his day with seven consecutive hits. Joe Dobson gets the win; Fannin is the loser.

Lew Flick of the Little Rock Travelers in the Southern Association has nine consecutive hits in 10 at-bats in a 19-inning ball game against the Memphis Chicks. His teammate Major "Kerby" Farrell has eight hits in the game, won by the Chicks, 8-6. Flick appears in 20 games with the Athletics over two seasons; he has fewer hits – seven – in 20 games than he does today. Farrell fares somewhat better. He plays a season each with the Braves and White Sox, batting .262. He manages the 1957 Indians to a sixth-place finish.

JULY 27:

Red Sox slugger Rudy York hits grand slam homers against relief pitcher Alvis "Tex" Shirley in the second and fifth innings and drives in 10 runs in a 13-6 win over the St. Louis Browns. York is the first player with two grand slams against the same pitcher in a game. With 10 RBI in the first five innings, York has two other opportunities to bat in runs. With a runner on in the seventh, he fans and he grounds into a double play in the ninth with two runners on base.

JULY 31:

For the second time in their careers, Bobby Doerr of the Red Sox breaks up a Bob Feller no-hit bid. Feller, pitching on two days' rest, hits a two-run triple, one-hits the Red Sox, 4-1, and wins his 20th game of the season. It is his seventh career one-hitter. Doerr previously broke up a Feller no-hit bid in May 1938.

AUGUST 6:

Tony Lazzeri, who appeared in seven World Series in his 14-year career, dies in San Francisco at age 42. Lazzeri had a lifetime average of .292 with 178 homers. He spent 12 years with the Yankees, one with the Cubs, and split his final season between the Dodgers and Giants.

AUGUST 7:

Bill Benswanger, son-in-law of the late Barney Dreyfuss, sells the Pirates to a group headed by banker Frank McKinney, real estate businessman John Galbreath, film/recording star Bing Crosby, and Tom Johnson. The Dreyfuss family, which had owned the team for 46 years, gets less than $2.5 million.

AUGUST 9:

For the first time, the entire major league schedule is played at night under artificial lighting systems.

AUGUST 11:

In Cincinnati, Stan Musial has eight hits in nine at-bats in a twinbill to lead the Cardinals past the Reds , 15-4 and 7-3.

AUGUST 12:

With four hits in four at-bats today against the Cubs, Stan Musial has 12 hits over three consecutive games. Musial's hitting and Alpha Brazle's three-hit pitching give the Cardinals a 5-0 win over the Cubs in Chicago.

AUGUST 14:

For the first time in modern major league history, separate admissions are charged for each game of a doubleheader. The Giants and Dodgers play a day-night doubleheader at Ebbets Field. Brooklyn wins, 8-4 and 2-1.

AUGUST 20:

Just how rapid is Robert? Prior to today's Indians-Senators game in Washington, D.C., Bob Feller's fastball is clocked by the U.S. Army's Sky Screen Chronograph. Reportedly accurate to one-10,000th of a second, the test machine measures Feller's fastball at 98.6 miles per hour. The former record was 94 mph by Richard "Atley" Donald.

The Pirates vote today on whether to recognize the American Baseball Guild as

CULTURE

Blues singer Brownie McGhee writes "Baseball Boogie" in honor of Jackie Robinson.

HISTORY

The Negro National League's Newark Eagles beat the Kansas City Monarchs of the Negro American League four games to three for the championship.

CULTURE

The Walt Disney film *Make Mine Music* features Jerry Colonna's voice in a rendition of "Casey at the Bat."

"In my opinion, Greenberg's surge is one of baseball's greatest achievements..."
– Sportswriter Grantland Rice, on Hank Greenberg

CULTURE

***Rhubarb*, by H. Allen Smith, is a novel about a cat that inherits a baseball team.**

HISTORY

Jackie Robinson comes up big in his first season in the minors. He leads the International League in batting with .349 and all second basemen in fielding. He hits 25 doubles, eight triples, three homers, scores 113 times, bats in 65 runs, and steals 40 bases. His Montreal Royals beat the American Association champion Louisville in the Little World Series. Robinson is a box-office attraction as well: Montreal draws a record 412,744 at home and 399,047 on the road.

their bargaining agent. With 12 players failing to show for the vote, the guild loses, 15-3, and is all but defunct. Guild founder Robert Murphy says, "The players have been offered an apple, but they could have had an orchard."

AUGUST 25:

Roland "Rollie" Fingers is born in Steubenville, Ohio.

AUGUST 26:

At Fenway Park, as Ted Williams prepares to bat against the "Boudreau shift," three-foot-tall Marco Songini runs out onto the field and occupies the empty third baseman's position. The umpires chase him off the field, the game resumes, and the Red Sox win, 5-1.

AUGUST 31:

The Dodgers are in another fight. Today it's Eddie Stanky, after a spiking incident at second base, against Goodwin "Goody" Rosen of the Giants at the Polo Grounds. The Giants go on to win the game, 2-1.

SEPTEMBER 8:

Yankees' manager Bill Dickey makes his last appearance as an active player, hitting a pinch-hit single for Al Gettel in the eighth inning. The Yankees lose two, 2-1 and 9-8, both in extra innings. Dickey finishes the season at .261 in 54 games and his playing career with a .313 average for 17 years.

SEPTEMBER 11:

At Ebbets Field, the Reds and Dodgers play the longest scoreless tie ever – 4 hours and 40 minutes and 19 innings. The game is ended because of darkness. The Reds come within a good throw of winning in the top of the ninth. Dain Clay tries to score from second on a single by Bert Haas, but Fred "Dixie" Walker's throw to catcher Bruce Edwards cuts him down. The Reds' Johnny Vander Meer pitches 15 innings, allowing seven hits and fanning 14; Harry Gumbert allows one hit over the final four frames. The Dodgers use four pitchers – Hal Gregg, Hugh Casey, Art Herring, and Hank Behrman. The game will be replayed on September 20.

SEPTEMBER 12:

Bill Dickey resigns as Yankees' skipper after 105 games (57-48). Coach Johnny Neun – the team's third manager this year – will finish the season.

SEPTEMBER 13:

So much for your shift! In Cleveland, Ted Williams, not known for his speed, hits a first-inning inside-the-park homer to left field past Pat Seerey, beating the "Boudreau shift" and the Indians, 1–0, to clinch the AL pennant for the Red Sox. It is Boston's first flag in 28 years. Cecil "Tex" Hughson is the winning pitcher. Charles "Red" Embree gets the loss, despite yielding only two hits. The game attracts only 3,295. Williams recalls in his autobiography, "Someone said, 'Is that the easiest homer you ever got?' And I said, 'Hell no, it was the hardest. I had to run.'"

SEPTEMBER 20:

Red Ruffing, sidelined most of the year with a broken kneecap, is released by the Yankees.

In a replay of the 19-inning scoreless tie of September 11, the Dodgers beat the Reds, 5-3. Dixie Walker hits a three-run homer.

SEPTEMBER 21:

In the last game ever at Cleveland's League Park, the Tigers beat the Indians, 5-3, in 11 innings.

SEPTEMBER 22:

Catcher Larry "Yogi" Berra and infielder Bobby Brown make their major league debuts with the Yankees in a doubleheader at Yankee Stadium against the Athletics. Berra has a two-run homer and Brown, playing shortstop, has a single. The two rookies were brought up today from the Newark Bears in the International League. The Yankees win both games, 4-3 and 7-4.

SEPTEMBER 24:

Hank Greenberg, thought by some to be finished, booed by fans, and benched on August 22, hits three homers for the Tigers in a doubleheader sweep against the Browns, 4-3 and 10-1. The 35-year-old Greenberg now has 41 homers for the season.

The "washed up" Greenberg finishes the 1946 season at .277 and leads the AL with 44 homers and 127 RBI. Grantland Rice writes in the New York Sun*: "In my opinion, Greenberg's surge is one of baseball's greatest achievements when you consider all the angles involved – the four years away from action, Greenberg's age, the handicap he faced*

SEPTEMBER 22
Larry "Yogi" Berra makes his major league debut for the Yankees.

OCTOBER 3
The Cardinals' 8-4 over the Dodgers sends St. Louis to the World Series.

in moving after such a power hitter as Williams has become."

SEPTEMBER 25:

A total of 12,800 fans take advantage of free admission to today's game offered by Indians' owner Bill Veeck. But the White Sox beat the Indians, 4-1.

SEPTEMBER 27:

Bob Feller comes out of the Indians' bull-pen, works five innings, and fans six. Strikeout number six – Jimmy Outlaw – gives Feller 343 to date for the season. Cleveland wins, 9-8, with Bob Kuzava getting the victory.

SEPTEMBER 30:

The Braves obtain third baseman Bob Elliott (.263, five homers) and catcher Hank Camelli (.208) from the Pirates for second baseman Billy Herman (.298, three homers), pitcher Elmer Singleton (0-1, 3.74 ERA), infielder William "Whitey" Wietelmann (.205), and pitcher Stan Wentzel (no record).

OCTOBER 1:

The Dodgers and Cardinals, who finished the season in a first-place tie at 96-58, meet in the NL's first-ever playoff – a best two-of-three affair. The Cardinals win the first game, 4-2, in St. Louis. Stan Musial hits a key triple; Joe Garagiola drives in two runs with three hits in four at-bats. Howie Pollet is the winner with an eight-hitter; Ralph Branca gets the loss.

While the Cardinals and Dodgers are resolving the NL pennant, the Red Sox are warming up with an exhibition game against a team of AL all-stars. Ted Williams is hit in the right elbow with a sidearm curve from the Senators' Milton "Mickey" Haefner in the fifth inning. In My Turn at Bat, Williams remembers, "I saw it coming and I kind of held up waiting for it to break. It hit me right on the tip of my right elbow. Shoosh, the elbow went up like a balloon. It turned blue. The World Series was to begin three days later, but I couldn't take batting practice for two days."

OCTOBER 3:

At Ebbets Field, the Dodgers score three in the bottom of the ninth, but come up short as the Cardinals win, 8-4, to take the NL pennant. Relief pitcher Harry Brecheen fans Eddie Stanky and Howie Schultz to end the game and the Dodgers' hopes. Murry Dickson, who hits a triple, is the winning pitcher; Joe Hatten gets the loss. In two games, the Cardinals have 25 hits.

Leo Durocher, commenting on stories that he will be moving to the Giants, says he will be with the Dodgers "until the day I die."

REGULAR SEASON WRAP-UP:

The Red Sox under Joe Cronin are 104-50, 12 games ahead of Detroit. Ted Williams hits .342 with 38 homers and 123 RBI. Johnny Pesky (.335) and Dominic DiMaggio (.316) are the team's other top hitters. Dave "Boo" Ferriss is 25-6; Cecil "Tex" Hughson has a record of 20-11.

The Cardinals edge the Dodgers in a playoff, finishing 98-58, two ahead of Brooklyn. Eddie Dyer's team is led by Stan Musial with .365, 16 homers, and 103 RBI. George "Whitey" Kurowski hits .301 and Enos Slaughter finishes at .300 with 18 homers

LEAGUE

In December, the owners vote to return the All-Star Game to the fans, who will select the position players; managers will pick pitchers.

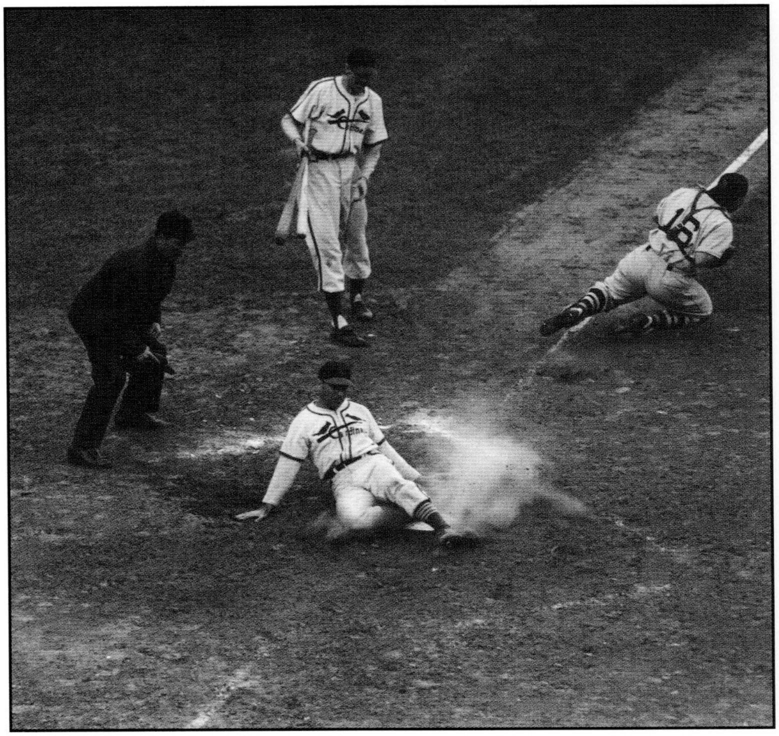

Enos Slaughter slides into home with the run that gives the Cardinals the World Championship.

"The only people who seemed to recognize that giving Robinson a chance was right, or even fair, were (Branch) Rickey and me."
– Commissioner Happy Chandler, on Jackie Robinson

and 130 RBI. Howie Pollet is the Cardinals' ace at 21-10.

The Pirates' Ralph Kiner becomes the first NL rookie to lead the league in homers. For the first time since 1917, the third-place Yankees have no .300 hitter in their lineup. The majors attract an unprecedented 18,534,444 fans. Among the other 1946 records are two by catchers and one by a base runner: Pete Reiser sets an NL mark with seven steals of home; the Pirates' Al Lopez catches his league record 1,861st game, and Warren "Buddy" Rosar of the A's becomes the first catcher to make no errors in more than 100 (117) games.

HISTORY

Bill Kennedy, pitching for Rocky Mount in the Coastal Plains League (one source reports the Western Carolinas League), strikes out 456 and compiles a record of 28-3 with a 1.03 ERA. Like many minor league "phenoms," Kennedy is mediocre, at best, in his eight-year career in the majors. He breaks in with the Indians in 1948 and also pitches for the Browns, completing the season at 8-8, 5.21 ERA. Lifetime, he is 15-28 with a 4.71 ERA, striking out 256 in 464 2/3 innings.

OCTOBER 6:

World Series, game one. A crowd of 36,218 at Sportsman's Park sees the Red Sox beat the Cardinals, 3-2, in 10 innings on a Rudy York home run. Earl Johnson, in relief of Tex Hughson, gets the win. Howie Pollet pitches a complete game, allowing seven hits, but is the loser. The Red Sox tie the game in the ninth after a bad hopper by Mike "Pinky" Higgins gets by Marty Marion, and Glenn Russell and Tom McBride single.

OCTOBER 7:

World Series, game two. At Sportsman's Park in St. Louis, Harry Brecheen pitches a four-hit, 3-0 victory, driving in one of the Cardinals' runs. Maurice "Mickey" Harris goes seven and gets the loss.

OCTOBER 9:

World Series, game three. Dave "Boo" Ferriss shuts out the Cardinals on six hits at Fenway Park and Rudy York hits a three-run homer in the first inning. The Red Sox win, 4-0; it is the 50th shutout in series history. Murry Dickson is charged with the loss. Bobby Doerr has two hits, including a double.

OCTOBER 10:

World Series, game four. The Cardinals pound six Red Sox pitchers for a series record 20 hits in a 12-3 victory at Fenway Park. Enos Slaughter has a solo homer among his four hits. George "Whitey" Kurowoski and Joe Garagiola also have four hits each. Bobby Doerr homers in a losing effort. George "Red" Munger scatters nine hits for a complete game victory. Starter Tex Hughson is tagged with the loss.

OCTOBER 11:

World Series, game five. After a 20-hit barrage in game 4, the Cardinals manage only four hits today, losing, 6-3, to Joe Dobson at Fenway Park. Pinky Higgins's seventh-inning double scores Dominic DiMaggio with the go-ahead run. Leon Culberson homers for Boston and Johnny Pesky has three hits. The losing pitcher is Alpha Brazle, who relieves Howie Pollet in the first.

OCTOBER 13:

World Series, game six. Back in St. Louis, Harry Brecheen allows seven hits, beating Boston and Mickey Harris, 4-1. The Cardinals score three runs in the third as they tie the series at three games apiece.

OCTOBER 15:

World Series, game seven. In the bottom of the eighth inning, Enos Slaughter scores from first base on a double by Harry Walker to left center field. Centerfielder Leon Culberson fields the ball and throws to shortstop Johnny Pesky, who hesitates on the relay home. Slaughter's run gives the Cardinals a 4-3 victory and the 1946 World Championship. Dom DiMaggio had tied the score for Boston in the bottom of the eighth with a two-run double. But he sprained his ankle doing so and was replaced by Culberson, setting up the ninth-inning dramatics. Harry Brecheen is the winning pitcher with two innings of relief. Bob Klinger is the loser. Brecheen, who was a .500 pitcher in the regular season, is 3-0 with an 0.45 ERA in the series. Harry Walker hits .412 for St. Louis. Bobby Doerr tops Boston with .409. Ted Williams, hampered by an elbow injury, is limited to five singles and one RBI; he hits .200.

POST-SEASON

OCTOBER 19:

The Yankees acquire pitcher Allie Reynolds (1-15, 3.88 ERA) from the Indians for second baseman Joe Gordon (.210, 11 homers), who was the AL's Most Valuable Player in 1942, and third baseman Eddie Bockman (.083 in four games).

Reynolds would start out poorly with the Yankees, but finished strong, going 19-8 in 1947. "Don't just throw the ball," veteran hurler Spud Chandler advised during his early slump. "Think about

OCTOBER 15
The Cardinals win the World Series with a thrilling 4-3 victory in game seven.

NOVEMBER 14
Finally... Ted Williams is named the American League's Most Valuable Player.

what you're doing. Change speeds. Set hitters up. Think, think, think." His advice apparently worked.

NOVEMBER 5:

Bucky Harris is named manager of the Yankees for 1947, a move he had denied that he would make. Charlie Dressen, rumored for the job, breaks his contract as a Dodger coach to join Harris's staff. Johnny Neun, the interim Yankee manager after Joe McCarthy and Bill Dickey, will manage the Reds in 1947.

NOVEMBER 14:

Ted finally gets one. After being bypassed for Joe DiMaggio and Joe Gordon, Williams is named the AL's Most Valuable Player. Tigers' pitcher Hal Newhouser is second in the voting.

NOVEMBER 16:

Baseball Commissioner A.B. "Happy" Chandler meets with Arthur Mann, assistant to Branch Rickey, in Cincinnati. Mann carries a message from Rickey to Chandler; he wants the commissioner to warn manager Leo Durocher about the people with whom he's associating.

IN THE 1946 WORLD SERIES, TED WILLIAMS BATS AGAINST THE "DYER SHIFT," DESCRIBED IN HIS AUTOBIOGRAPHY AS "A LITTLE DIFFERENT FROM BOUDREAU'S. HE LET MARTY MARION STAY AT SHORTSTOP AND MOVED HIS THIRD BASEMAN, WHITEY KUROWSKI, AROUND BEHIND SECOND AND JUST SHADED EVERYBODY ELSE TO THE RIGHT. IN OTHER WORDS, HE LEFT TWO MEN, THE LEFT-FIELDER AND THE SHORTSTOP, ON THE LEFT SIDE OF SECOND BASE INSTEAD OF JUST ONE."

Chandler chides Durocher about his relationships in a meeting at the Claremont Country Club in Berkeley, California. He cites Durocher's association with "undesirables," including his friend, actor George Raft, casino owner Benjamin "Bugsy" Siegel, and other gamblers.

NOVEMBER 21:

Long-time Yankees' general manager Ed Barrow, 78 years old, resigns from his most recent position, chairman of the board. Although he is reportedly resigning because of friction with part-owner and president Larry MacPhail, Barrow says, "We are parting on very friendly terms. When a man gets to be as old as I am, well, I'm afraid he's getting pretty old." The Yankees won 14 pennants under his guidance.

DECEMBER 6:

Red Ruffing, released in September by the Yankees, signs with the White Sox.

DECEMBER 10:

Walter Johnson, a member of the Hall of Fame's "first class" in 1936, dies at age 59. In 21 years, the Big Train was 416-279 with a 2.17 ERA.

LEAGUE

The players make significant strides in their benefits at a meeting of the Major League Baseball Policy Committee in New York. The committee itself will be replaced by an executive council consisting of the Commissioner, AL and NL presidents, and one owner and one player representative from each league. In addition, the committee decides on a $5,000 minimum salary ($500 less than promised during the threat of a players' union); no pay cuts in excess of 25%; spring training expense allowances of $25 per week; injured players will receive a full season's salary, as well as hospital and medical expenses, and player contracts mailed by February 1. In addition, spring training will not begin before February 15 in 1947 and March 1 in 1948. There also is a proposal to expand the schedule to 168 games in 1947.

THE BEST OF 1946

NATIONAL LEAGUE

HITTERS

Batting Average:
Stan Musial, St. Louis Cardinals, .365

Slugging Average:
Stan Musial, .587

Home Runs:
Ralph Kiner, Pittsburgh Pirates, 23

Runs Batted In:
Enos Slaughter, St. Louis Cardinals, 130Hits:

Hits:
Musial, 228

Stolen Bases:
Pete Reiser, Brooklyn Dodgers, 34

PITCHERS

Wins:
Howie Pollet, St. Louis Cardinals, 21

Strikeouts:
Johnny Schmitz, Chicago Cubs, 135

Earned Run Average:
Howie Pollet, 2.10

Winning Percentage:
Murry Dickson, St. Louis Cardinals, .714

Saves:
Ken Raffensberger, Philadelphia Phillies, 6

Most Valuable Player:
Stan Musial, St. Louis Cardinals

AMERICAN LEAGUE

HITTERS

Batting Average:
James "Mickey" Vernon, Washington Senators, .353

Slugging Average:
Ted Williams, Boston Red Sox, .667

Home Runs:
Hank Greenberg, Detroit Tigers, 44

Runs Batted In:
Hank Greenberg, 127

Hits:
Johnny Pesky, Boston Red Sox, 208

Stolen Bases:
George Case, Cleveland Indians, 28

PITCHERS

Wins:
Hal Newhouser, Detroit Tigers; Bob Feller, Cleveland Indians, 26

Strikeouts:
Bob Feller, 348

Earned Run Average:
Hal Newhouser, 1.94

Winning Percentage:
Dave "Boo" Ferriss, Boston Red Sox, .806

Saves:
Bob Klinger, Boston Red Sox, 9

Most Valuable Player:
Ted Williams, Boston Red Sox

1947

"He hits the ball a mile.
Throws like a rifle."
– *Walter Johnson, on Josh Gibson*

NEWS

COLD WAR HEATS UP

MARSHALL PLAN WILL AID RECONSTRUCTION OF EUROPE

Chuck Yeager flies an airplane faster than sound

Northeast buffeted by blizzard; nearly 80 die; New York City gets 25.8 inches of snow

TEXAS EXPLOSION KILLS NEARLY 500

DESIGNER CHRISTIAN DIOR INTRODUCES THE "NEW LOOK"

Tennessee Williams's A Streetcar Named Desire *and Arthur Miller's* All My Sons *debut on Broadway*

DEFENSE DEPARTMENT AND CENTRAL INTELLIGENCE AGENCY ARE CREATED

PRE-SEASON

JANUARY 7:

The Yankees' Joe DiMaggio undergoes surgery in New York to remove a bone spur on his left heel.

JANUARY 18:

Hank Greenberg, an institution in Detroit since 1933, is dealt to the Pirates for $75,000. Greenberg hit .277 last year and led the AL in homers with 44 and RBI with 127. After obtaining Greenberg, the Pirates shorten the distance to the left-field fence in Forbes Field to take advantage of his right-handed power. The area becomes known as Greenberg's Gardens. The sale price for Greenberg varies according to the source; some say it may have been as low as between $10,000 and $25,000. According to *The Baseball Encyclopedia*, it was $75,000.

JANUARY 19:

Yankees' president Larry MacPhail says, "We did not claim Greenberg because Detroit would not let us have him on waivers. All we would have accomplished by claiming him was to keep Greenberg on the Detroit club or some other American League club other than New York."

JANUARY 20:

Catcher Josh Gibson, who may have been baseball's greatest player, dies at age 35 of a brain tumor in Pittsburgh. Gibson was known as the "black Babe Ruth." From 1930 to 1946, he played with the Homestead Grays and the Pittsburgh Crawfords in the Negro Leagues, hitting .362.

Wrote Robert Peterson in the New York Times: *"The old fan can bring to mind Josh Gibson... at Yankee Stadium during a Negro League double-header in 1934 and... propelling the ball over the third tier next to the left-field bullpen, the only fair ball ever hit out of the Stadium."*

JANUARY 31:

Nolan Ryan is born in Refugio, Texas.

FEBRUARY 1:

After a joint session at New York City's Waldorf-Astoria Hotel, the American and National Leagues reveal the creation of a pension plan for players. Making the announcement is

LEAGUE

In January, the Dodgers release John Wright, who was signed after Jackie Robinson. Wright, who never makes it to the majors, goes back to the Homestead Grays, where he pitches for two more seasons.

TRIVIA

The Red Sox create the "Green Monster" in Fenway Park, painting over advertisements for Lifebuoy Soap and Gem Blades on the high left-field wall.

> Johnny Evers was "a bundle of nerves with the best brain in baseball."
> – *Sportswriter Hugh Fullerton*

Commissioner A.B. "Happy" Chandler, with player reps, the Yankees' Johnny Murphy and the Dodgers' Fred "Dixie" Walker, on hand. Players with five years in the majors will receive $50 per month at the age of 50. For each year of subsequent service, retirees will receive an additional $10 per month to a maximum of $100 for 10-year veterans. Players, coaches, and trainers on active status on opening day are eligible, and war service counts toward retirement years. The plan calls for a yearly pool of $650,000, with 80 percent coming from the teams. The remainder will be made up by players' dues, All-Star Game receipts, $150,000 in World Series broadcast rights, and a minimum series pool of $250,000.

FEBRUARY 3:

Ted Williams, the AL's Most Valuable Player in 1946, joins the ranks of baseball's salary elite, signing a $70,000 contract.

MARCH 1:

The Brooklyn Catholic Youth Organization, under the leadership of the Reverend Vincent J. O'Keefe, announces a mass boycott of the Dodgers and will pull 125,000 youngsters out of the team's *Knothole Gang*, a pregame TV show. They charge that manager Leo Durocher is "undermining the moral training of Brooklyn's Roman Catholic youth." Among their objections is Durocher's marriage to actress Laraine Day before the one-year wait stipulated in the California divorce from her previous husband. She also had been divorced in Mexico with no restrictions. Father O'Keefe writes, "The present manager of the Brooklyn Baseball team is not the kind of leader we want for your youth to idealize and imitate."

MARCH 3:

In his column in the *Brooklyn Eagle* – ghostwritten by team traveling secretary Harold Parrott – Leo Durocher says former Dodgers' general manager Larry MacPhail "tried to drive a wedge between myself and all these things I hold dear."

MARCH 9:

A new chapter in the Leo Durocher saga unfolds in Havana, Cuba, where the Dodgers and Yankees are in spring training. Connie Immerman, an acquaintance of mobster Charles "Lucky" Luciano, and Memphis Engelberg, a racing handicapper, are in a box behind the Yankee dugout for the second day in a row. Durocher, who has been chastised by Commissioner Happy Chandler for his shady associations, points them out to Dick Young of the *New York Daily News* and Milt Gross of the *New York Post*. He is variously reported as saying, "Look at that. If I had those guys in my box, I'd be kicked out of baseball." He asks, "Are there two sets of rules? One applying to managers and one to club owners?" Dick Young pursues Yankee co-owner Larry MacPhail, who claims they are not in his box but in seats across the aisle. When Young persists in asking if they are his guests, MacPhail replies, "What are you – the F.B.I.?" MacPhail subsequently calls Durocher a liar and alleges that Immerman and Engelberg were guests of the Dodgers. He files charges against Durocher with the commissioner for "conduct detrimental to baseball."

MARCH 24:

Commissioner Chandler holds a four-hour hearing at the Sarasota Terrace Hotel. Leo Durocher admits playing occasional card games – for money – with Kirby Higbe.

MARCH 28:

Hall of Famer Johnny Evers, the most celebrated middleman in baseball history, dies at age 65 in Albany, New York. Sportswriter Hugh Fullerton once described Johnny Evers as "a bundle of nerves with the best brain in baseball."

Commissioner A.B. Happy Chandler holds a meeting with Larry MacPhail and Branch Rickey. The subject: Leo Durocher. There is no love lost between Chandler and Durocher. The commissioner once said, "He would hold the lamp while his mother was cutting wood."

APRIL 3:

As the Yankees complete spring training at St. Petersburg, Florida, Joltin' Joe DiMaggio, who had surgery on his heel in March, works out for the first time, wearing a special

LEAGUE

The All-American Girls Professional Baseball League legalizes sidearm pitching and adds no teams this season. The Grand Rapids Chicks win the championship.

TRIVIA

In an exhibition game, Dallas introduces a new version of the "Boudreau shift." When Ted Williams comes to bat, only the pitcher and catcher remain in position. The seven other players climb into the right-field stands and sit down.

FEBRUARY
3
Ted Williams, last year's AL MVP, signs a new contract with the Red Sox, for $70,000.

shoe. He will remain in Florida while the team heads north.

APRIL 9:

Back in Brooklyn, Branch Rickey receives a call from Happy Chandler. Leo Durocher is suspended for one year for "an accumulation of unpleasant incidents in which he has been involved which the Commissioner construes as detrimental to baseball." Chandler isn't finished. He fines the Yankees and Dodgers $2,000 each – "because their officials engaged in public controversy damaging to baseball" – and Dodgers' road secretary Harold Parrott is docked $500 for ghostwriting the controversial "Durocher Says" column. Charlie Dressen, now a Yankees' coach, gets a 30-day suspension for failing to keep a verbal agreement with the Dodgers for this season. Chandler's statement also says, "Durocher has not measured up to the standards expected or required of managers of our baseball teams...Club owners, managers, players and all others connected with baseball have been heretofore warned that associating with... notorious gamblers

FROM *BASEBALL: THE BIOGRAPHICAL ENCYCLOPEDIA*, ON LEO DUROCHER: "IRONICALLY, DUROCHER DIDN'T GET TO MANAGE (JACKIE) ROBINSON IN THE PLAYER'S ROOKIE YEAR. IN ONE OF THE MOST CONTROVERSIAL DECISIONS BY ANY COMMISSIONER, A.B. 'HAPPY' CHANDLER SUSPENDED DUROCHER FOR A YEAR. THE CHARGES WERE VAGUE AND IMPLIED MORAL TURPITUDE ON DUROCHER'S PART FOR ASSOCIATING WITH GAMBLERS AND FOR MARRYING ACTRESS LARAINE DAY IN MEXICO BEFORE HER CALIFORNIA DIVORCE WAS FINAL."

HISTORY

Before Jackie Robinson, the last black to play in the majors was Moses Fleetwood Walker with Toledo in the American Association in 1884.

TRIVIA

In a May 3 deal, the Pirates get the player who may have the longest name ever in baseball – Calvin Coolidge Julius Caesar Tuskahoma McLish. A baseball wag suggests Al Gionfriddo was included in the trade because the Dodgers needed someone to carry the $100,000 back from Pittsburgh.

In "Line-Up for Yesterday," by Ogden Nash:
"E is for Evers, His Jaw in advance; Never afraid To Tinker with Chance."

Jackie Robinson broke baseball's "color barrier" in 1947.

will not be tolerated... All parties to this controversy are silenced from the time this order is issued."

Durocher's reaction to the suspension: "For what?" In 1975, Durocher writes in his autobiography: "To this day, if you ask me why I was suspended, I could not tell you."

APRIL 10:

It takes Yankees' president Larry MacPhail one day to violate the Commissioner's gag order. Although he has been warring with Durocher, he claims Leo should not have been suspended.

The Dodgers meet their Montreal Royals farm team – with Jackie Robinson – in an Ebbets Field exhibition game. During the sixth inning, Branch Rickey distributes a statement to the press. It reads: "The Brooklyn Dodgers today purchased the contract of Jackie Roosevelt Robinson from the Montreal Royals. He will report immediately."

APRIL 14:

The Yankees release relief pitcher Johnny Murphy (4-2, 3.40 ERA, seven saves). One of the first relief specialists, Murphy pitched 12 years for New York; his record is 93-53 with 104 saves. Later in the day, Murphy is signed by the Red Sox.

THE SEASON

APRIL 15:

At Ebbets Field, 25,623 fans (an estimated 14,000 of them black) see an unprecedented sight. Jackie Robinson, the first black player in a major league uniform in modern times, takes first base as the Braves come to bat. In his first at-bat, Robinson faces Johnny Sain and grounds out to third baseman Bob Elliott. In his second turn, he grounds out to short and flies out to left in his third at-bat. With the Dodgers down, 3-2, in the seventh and a runner on, Robinson lays down a sacrifice bunt and is safe on Earl Torgeson's wild throw. He scores the go-ahead run on a Pete Reiser double. Under interim manager Clyde Sukeforth, the Dodgers win, 5-3. Robinson handles 11 chances flawlessly at first. Lost in all the excitement of Robinson's appearance is the major league debut of Edwin "Duke" Snider, who hits a single batting for Dixie Walker.

Said Robinson after the game of Sain's pitches: "If they're all like this, I'm going to have a tough time making this league."

APRIL 17:

Jackie Robinson beats out a bunt against pitcher Glenn Elliott for his first major league hit. The Dodgers beat the Braves, 12-6, at Ebbets Field.

APRIL 18:

At the Polo Grounds, Jackie Robinson hits his first major league homer. Dave Koslo throws the historic pitch in a 10-4 Giants' victory.

Johnny Beazley (7-5, 4.46 ERA), unable to regain his pre-war

APRIL 15
Jackie Robinson becomes the first black player in modern major league history.

APRIL 27
On Babe Ruth Day, 58,339 gather at Yankee Stadium to pay tribute.

brilliance, is sold by the Cardinals to the Braves.

APRIL 19:

After coach Clyde Sukeforth manages the Dodgers as an interim for two games – winning both – scout Burt Shotton takes over at the Polo Grounds. A la Connie Mack, Shotton manages from the bench wearing street clothes.
The Giants spoil his debut with a 4-3 victory; Bill Rigney and Johnny Mize homer for the winners.

Former AL umpire George Moriarty writes to Commissioner Chandler, "Judge Landis had convenient hiding places for his ideals. If the populace was not looking, he had little compunction about defending the underdog, but if the spotlight were turned on in full focus, he would defend anyone to the last camera."

APRIL 20:

After a pinch-hitting appearance yesterday, Joe DiMaggio returns to the Yankees' lineup in the first game of a doubleheader against the Athletics in Philadelphia. DiMaggio hits a three-run home run, and the Yankees win, 6-2. He sits out the second game, which the Yankees also win, 3-2.

APRIL 22:

At Ebbets Field, Jackie Robinson is the target of taunts and insults from the Phillies' dugout, led by manager Ben Chapman. Robinson answers in the eighth inning by singling and scoring the game's only run on Gene Hermanski's hit. Hal Gregg pitches a one-hitter for the Dodgers.

In Jackie Robinson: A Biography, *Arnold Rampersad writes: "Chapman's campaign brought Jack crashing down. Particularly pressing was the fact that it occurred at home, in New York City, and from a Northern team – not St. Louis, which he had feared, or Louisville or Baltimore, which he had endured in 1946. 'I felt tortured and I tried just to play ball and ignore the insults,' he would recall, in language overheated by his ghostwriter. 'But it was really getting to me. What did the Phillies want from me? What, indeed, did Mr. Rickey expect of me? I was, after all, a human being....' But Jack remembered his pact with Rickey, and his unspoken pact with his people, to do what was necessary to make the experiment work. In a 1-0 Dodgers victory, he singled, moved to third on an error, and scored on a hit by Gene Hermanski. (But on that same day, after 47 chances as a major leaguer, Jack also made his first error, in the eighth inning.) To his further relief, the next two games also went to the Dodgers for a sweep of the series. Gradually Jack pulled out of his gloom."*

Yankees' president Larry MacPhail continues to talk. "So far as any evidence developed at the Sarasota and St. Petersburg hearings is concerned, there was nothing to justify even a five-minute suspension of Durocher." In his biography of Leo Durocher, The Lip, Gerald Eskenazi quotes the Commissioner's son, A.B. Chandler II, 45 years after the fact. Eskenazi writes: "Dad didn't have trouble with his conscience over suspending Leo. My dad signed 34 death warrants when he was governor. That's something to lose sleep over."

APRIL 24:

The Giants' Johnny Mize hits three homers against the Braves' Johnny Sain. Mize becomes the first major leaguer to hit three homers in a game on five occasions. The Braves win the game, 14-5.

APRIL 27:

It's Babe Ruth Day throughout baseball, and 58,339 fans gather at Yankee Stadium the House That Ruth Built – to say goodbye to their no-longer-robust hero. Among the attendees are baseball commissioner Happy Chandler, NL president and former sportswriter Ford Frick, and Francis Cardinal Spellman of New York. The 52-year-old Babe, suffering from throat cancer and speaking in a hoarse voice, tells the crowd, "Thank you very much, ladies and gentlemen. You know how bad my voice sounds. Well, it feels just as bad... There's been so many lovely things said about me, I'm glad I had the opportunity to thank everybody. Thank you." In the game that follows, Sid Hudson of

TRIVIA

Bill Voiselle, who lives in Ninety-Six, South Carolina, wears number 96 and is the only player with his hometown on the back of his uniform.

CULTURE

Baseball is the subject of two poems: Robert Francis's "The Base Stealer" and "Night Game" by Rolfe Humphries.

Asked about his secret for pitching, the irascible Lefty Grove replies, "No secret. They tell me to pitch, and I say gimme the ball."

HISTORY

Danny Gardella, one of the major leaguers who jumped to the outlaw Mexican League, is back in the U.S., but unable to play with any sanctioned team. He signs on with the semiprofessional Gulf Oilers, a team scheduled to play the Negro League Cleveland Buckeyes. But members of the Buckeyes refuse to play because they are worried that competing against Gardella will hurt their own chances of getting a shot at the majors.

the Senators beats the Yankees and Spurgeon "Spud" Chandler, 1-0.

Afterward Ruth tells his former teammate Joe Dugan, "Joe, I'm gone. I'm gone, Joe."

MAY 2:

Bob Feller pitches his 10th career one-hitter, beating the Red Sox, 2-0. The suspense ends quickly when Johnny Pesky singles in the first inning. It is Feller's third consecutive shutout. After meeting yesterday with him in Cincinnati, Commissioner Happy Chandler declines to make public how Larry MacPhail has been punished for insubordination.

MAY 3:

The Dodgers send five players – pitchers Walter "Kirby" Higbe (2-0), Hank Behrman (0-2), Cal McLish (0-0), infielder Gene Mauch (.300), and catcher Homer "Dixie" Howell (.276) to the Pirates for $100,000 and outfielder Al Gionfriddo (.000 in one game).

MAY 8:

The Associated Press reports that a strike by the Cardinals against Jackie Robinson has been averted by the intervention of NL president Ford Frick and St. Louis owner Sam Breadon. Frick says, "I didn't have to talk to the players myself. Mr. Breadon did the talking to them. From what Breadon told me afterward the trouble was smoothed over. I don't know what he said to them, who the ringleader was, or any other details."

MAY 9:

Stanley Woodward, sports editor of the *New York Herald-Tribune*, publishes a report of the alleged strike against Robinson. He credits NL president Ford Frick and Sam Breadon, owner of the Cardinals, with aborting the plot. The Dodgers also make public threatening letters Robinson has been receiving.

The St. Louis "strike" remains a matter of controversy. Breadon and Cardinals' manager Eddie Dyer denied the report. A number of living members of the Cardinals insist there never was a strike threat. Bob Broeg of the St. Louis Post-Dispatch *writes in* The National Pastime, *"The story about the Cardinals' planned 'rebellion'... is a barnyard vulgarism. Some players grumbled about having to play on the same field with a black, just as did some of the Dodgers. Maybe here and there one popped off about how he didn't care to play against Robinson, but no one paid attention to it. Certainly not the captain of the Cardinals, Terry Moore, nor his infield alter ego, Marty Marion."*

MAY 10:

New York Post columnist Jimmy Cannon describes Jackie Robinson as "the loneliest man I have ever seen in sports."

MAY 17:

The Red Sox-Browns game at Fenway Park today is delayed after a "bombing mission" by a seagull. With St. Louis pitcher Ellis Kinder on the mound, the bird swoops in and drops a smelt on the mound. It misses Kinder, but creates a time-out for cleanup. Despite the distraction, the Browns win, 4-2.

MAY 18:

Hal Chase, banned from baseball for life in 1919, dies of beriberi in Colusa, California, at the age of 64. Prince Hal was involved in the Black Sox scandal and other shady activities but was a good enough player to make Babe Ruth's All-Time Greatest Team. He was regarded as a paragon of fielding at first base, but some observers believe that reputation masked his average of 28-plus errors a year.

As published in Richard Scheinin's Field of Screams, *Chase acknowledged to an interviewer that he knew about the Black Sox fix but denied he was part of it. He stated, "My best proof is that I am flat on my back without a dime... I wasn't satisfied with what club owners paid me. Like others, I had to have a bet on the side and we used to bet with the other team and the gamblers who sat in the boxes. You note that I am not in the Hall of Fame. Some of the old-timers said I was one of the greatest fielding first basemen of all time... I am an outcast, and I haven't a good name. I'm a loser, just like all gamblers are..." In* Baseball: The Golden Years, *Harold Seymour minces no words about Chase, describing him as "a malignant genius... Until somebody worse can be found, he will serve as the archetype of all crooked ball players...*

his defects of character more than match his playing skill."

MAY 20:

The Athletics' Warren "Buddy" Rosar makes an error after setting a major league record for a catcher with 147 error-free games.

MAY 22:

It's conflict with the commissioner and turmoil with his team for Yankees' president Larry MacPhail. He fines Joe DiMaggio $100 for not posing for U.S. Army Signal Corps photographers; the Yankee Clipper was taking batting practice at the time. DiMaggio has been slapped with other fines for such "transgressions" as missing banquets. MacPhail relents and offers to return fines he's collected to DiMaggio, who has the money sent to the Damon Runyon Cancer Fund.

JUNE 2:

Are the defensive shifts – first introduced by Indians' manager Lou Boudreau last season–taking their toll on Ted Williams? He is batting .271 and former major league slugger Al Simmons says, "Well, that's the end of Williams – he can't hit to left field."

JUNE 4:

The last rites of the Roman Catholic Church are administered to an unconscious Pete Reiser in the Dodger clubhouse after he crashes into the wall at Ebbets Field in the fifth inning, chasing a ball hit by the Pirates' Cully Rickard. Reiser fractures his skull and dislocates both shoulders, but he holds on to the ball. The Dodgers win, 9-4.

JUNE 9:

The Cardinals' Albert "Red" Schoendienst sets an NL record for futility. He comes to bat 12 times in a doubleheader against the Phillies without a hit. The Cardinals win the opener, 4-2; the Phillies take the nightcap, 2-1, in 15 innings.

JUNE 13:

In the first night game at Fenway Park, a crowd of 34,510 sees the Red Sox beat the White Sox, 5-3. Dave "Boo" Ferriss is the winning pitcher; Frank Papish gets the loss. With lights on at Fenway, 14 of the 16 major league teams are playing night baseball. The holdouts are the Tigers and the Cubs.

Pitcher Mort Cooper (2-5) is reunited with his brother, catcher Walker Cooper, when he is traded by the Braves to the Giants in exchange for pitcher Bill Voiselle (1-4) and cash.

JUNE 14:

Dodgers' outfielder Pete Reiser is discharged from the hospital.

JUNE 15:

The Red Sox front office looks good. Two days after first baseman Jake Jones comes to Boston from the White Sox for Rudy York, he plays a key role in a doubleheader win against his old team. Jones homers in a 7-3 Red Sox victory in the opener. In the nightcap, he has a grand slam homer and a two-run single in an 84 win.

JUNE 18:

The Reds' Ewell "The Whip" Blackwell no-hits the Braves, 6-0, in Cincinnati. Blackwell walks four and strikes out three; the Reds make no errors. Norman "Babe" Young produces all of Cincinnati's runs with a pair of three-run homers. Ed Wright is the losing pitcher.

JUNE 22:

Eddie Stanky singles through Ewell "The Whip" Blackwell's legs with one out in the ninth to spoil the pitcher's bid for a second consecutive no-hitter in the opener of a doubleheader at Crosley Field. After Al Gionfriddo flies out, Jackie Robinson singles for the only other hit against Blackwell. The Reds win, 4-0. The Dodgers win the second game, 9-8. According to Jules Tygiel, after Stanky's hit, "Blackwell unleashed a stream of racial epithets at Robinson...."

JUNE 24:

Jackie Robinson steals home plate against the Pirates' Frederick "Fritz" Ostermueller in a 4-2 Brooklyn win. It is Robinson's first time stealing home in the majors.

JUNE 28:

The Giants' Walker Cooper ties a major league record when he homers in his sixth consecutive game. Cooper has a total of seven in the six games, beginning on June 22. The Giants beat the Phillies, 14-6.

JULY 5:

A little more than two months after Jackie Robinson debuts with the Dodgers, Larry Doby becomes the first black player in the AL after his contract is

HISTORY

In August, the hometown Maynard Midgets win the first Little League World Series, played in Williamsport, Pennsylvania.

LEAGUE

In October, Danny Gardella, who jumped to the Mexican League and was banned from the majors, is working as a $36-a-week hospital orderly. He retains attorney Frederic Augustus Johnson and sues major league baseball. The case is heard by Southern District federal court judge John Bright.

"Trying to lift Carl Hubbell's screwball was like a guy trying to hit fungoes out of a well."
– *Frankie Frisch*

HISTORY

In the Negro Leagues World Series, the New York Cubans of the National League beat the Cleveland Buckeyes of the American League, four games to one.

TRIVIA

The seagull is not the only creature to cause chaos. A Dodgers-Cubs game at Ebbets Field is called this season because of an intrusion by swarms of gnats.

purchased by the Indians from the Newark Eagles of the Negro National League, where the 22-year-old is hitting .414. Appearing as a pinch hitter for Cleveland pitcher Bryan Stephens in the seventh inning with two men on base, Doby strikes out against Earl Harrist of the White Sox. Chicago wins, 6-5. Doby was personally escorted to Comiskey Park by Indians' owner Bill Veeck.

According to Bill Veeck in his autobiography, after he signed Larry Doby, he received a telegram from Satchel Paige reading: IT TIME FOR ME TO COME? Veeck says he wired back: ALL THINGS IN DUE TIME.

JULY 8:

The Yankees' Frank "Spec" Shea becomes the first rookie to win an All-Star Game as the AL triumphs, 2-1, at Chicago's Wrigley Field. The losing pitcher is Johnny Sain, whose errant pickoff throw sets up the winning run, singled in by Stan Spence. The game's only homer is hit by Johnny Mize.

JULY 10:

The Indians' Don Black no-hits the Philadelphia A's, 3-0, in the rain-delayed first game of a doubleheader in Cleveland. Black walks six and strikes out five; Cleveland commits no errors. Bill McCahan is the losing pitcher.

JULY 11:

The Yankees buy pitcher Louis "Bobo" Newsom (4-6) from the Senators for the waiver price. It is Newsom's 13th uniform change and his seventh different team.

JULY 17:

The Yankees extend their winning streak to 19 with a doubleheader sweep over the Indians. Begun on June 29, the 19-game streak equals the AL mark set by the 1906 Chicago White Sox. In game one, Louis "Bobo" Newsom gets his 200th career win and George McQuinn hits a two-run homer in a 3-1 victory. Billy Johnson's three RBI lead New York and Vic Raschi to a 7-2 win.

The Browns buy the contracts of two Negro League players, infielder Hank Thompson and outfielder Willard Brown, from the Kansas City Monarchs. Thompson was hitting .344. They also option the rights to Monarchs' infielder Lorenzo Davis.

JULY 18:

In Detroit, Fred Hutchinson of the Tigers two-hits the Yankees, 8-0, ending New York's record-tying winning streak at 19. Hutchinson faces only 28 batters, striking out nine and allowing no walks. The only Yankee hits are a second-inning single off the bat of Joe DiMaggio and a seventh-inning bunt by George "Snuffy" Stirnweiss. Despite the loss, the Yankees lead the AL by 10 1/2 games.

Ted Williams hits two homers and – for the first time in his career – has five hits in five at-bats, yet the visiting Red Sox lose to the Browns, 9-8.

JULY 20:

For the first time in modern major league baseball, two black players appear in the same lineup. Second baseman Hank Thompson and 36-year-old right fielder Willard "Home Run" Brown, formerly of the Kansas City Monarchs, take the field together against the visiting Red Sox today for the Browns, who win two, 4-3 and 7-6.

JULY 21:

Two great southpaws, Robert "Lefty" Grove and Carl Hubbell, are inducted into the Hall of Fame along with Gordon "Mickey" Cochrane and Frankie Frisch. Grove, who gave new meaning to "fiery," pitched 17 years with the Athletics and Red Sox, compiling a 300-141 record with a 3.06 ERA, 2,266 strikeouts, and 35 shutouts. He was 31-4 in 1931 and appeared in three World Series. Hubbell pitched for 16 seasons, all with the New York Giants, and was 253-154 with a 2.97 ERA and 36 shutouts. He was a 20-game winner for five consecutive seasons from 1933 through 1937. Frisch, an infielder known as the Fordham Flash, played 19 seasons and batted .316 with 419 stolen bases. He was a .300 hitter for 11 consecutive seasons from 1921 through 1931. He appeared in eight World Series and managed the 1934 Cardinals to the World Championship. Cochrane, a catcher, had his 13-year career ended by beaning in 1937. He batted .320 and hit .300 or better nine times. He

JULY 18
Fred Hutchinson's two-hitter in Detroit's 8-0 win snaps the Yankees' win streak at 19.

AUGUST 16
Pirates' slugger Ralph Kiner hits three consecutive homers in a 12-7 win over the Cardinals.

appeared in five World Series with the Athletics and Tigers. Cochrane managed Detroit from 1934 to 1938, winning two AL pennants and one World Series.

Frankie Frisch on his fellow Hall of Fame inductee Carl Hubbell: "Trying to lift Carl Hubbell's screwball was like a guy trying to hit fungoes out of a well."

JULY 22:

The Tigers Roy Columbine walks in his 22nd straight game, a major league record.

JULY 23:

Ewell Blackwell of the Cincinnati Reds tops the Dodgers, 5-4, for his 16th straight win.

JULY 27:

Red Sox first baseman James "Jake" Jones gets a 60-foot triple today against the Browns. Umpire Cal Hubbard awards Jones three bases when St. Louis pitcher Fred Sanford throws his glove at the ball, trying to keep it rolling foul.

JULY 30:

The Giants snap the Whip. In 10 innings, New York beats the Reds and Ewell "The Whip" Blackwell, 5-4, ending his winning streak at 16 games.

AUGUST 3:

Vic Willis dies in Elkton, Maryland, at age 71. In his 13-year pitching career, he was 248-204 with an ERA of 2.63 and 1,651 strikeouts.

AUGUST 9:

Another first for baseball as the racial barriers continue to come down. Larry Doby of the Indians and Hank Thompson of the Browns are in the lineup when their teams meet in the opener of a doubleheader in Cleveland. It is the first time in baseball that blacks have opposed each other in a modern major league game. Thompson has three singles and two walks; Doby, who comes in for defense, has a base on balls. The Indians sweep, 5-2 and 5-4.

AUGUST 11:

In St. Louis, the Browns' Willard "Home Run" Brown lives up to his nickname when he hits an inside-the-park round-tripper against Hal Newhouser. Brown, who is pinch-hitting for catcher Joe Schultz in the second game of a doubleheader, is the first black to homer in the AL. The Tigers win the game, 3-1.

AUGUST 16:

The Pirates' Ralph Kiner hits three consecutive homers in a 12-7 win over St. Louis. Kiner, who homered in his last at-bat yesterday, ties a record with four in a row.

AUGUST 23:

The Browns drop Hank Thompson (.256 in 27 games) and Willard Brown (.179, one homer in 21 games). Earlier in the month they relinquished their option on Piper Davis after he decided not to go to a minor league team.

AUGUST 26:

Branch Rickey and the Dodgers continue to make history. Dan Bankhead, a 27-year-old who has been with the Memphis Red Sox and was signed August 24, becomes the first

LEAGUE

Major league baseball sells the radio rights to the World Series for $475,000.

Larry Doby was the AL's first black player.

Red Barber's call of Al Gionfriddo's dramatic catch: "Belted! It's a long one, deep into left center. Back goes Gionfriddo, back, back, back, back, back... He makes a one-handed catch in front of the bullpen! Ooooh, doctor!"

LEAGUE

Cardinals' owner Sam Breadon, in poor health and saddled with income tax problems, sells the team to real estate magnate Fred Saigh and former U.S. Postmaster General Robert Hannegan for $60,000.

black pitcher in the modern major leagues. He relieves Hal Gregg in a game against the Pirates. His hitting is more impressive than his pitching. He becomes the first NL pitcher ever to homer in his first at-bat when he drills one against Frederick "Fritz" Ostermueller. On the mound he works three and a third innings, yielding 10 hits and eight runs. The Dodgers lose, 16-3. St. Louis honors Larry "Yogi" Berra, its hometown-boy-made-good, with a night at Sportsman's Park. Berra tells the crowd, "I want to thank all you people for making this night necessary."

SEPTEMBER 3:

Bill McCahan of the Athletics, on the losing end of Don Black's no-hitter in July, spins one of his own today, beating the Senators, 3-0. McCahan strikes out two and walks none; first baseman Ferris Fain commits a throwing error. The losing pitcher is Ray Scarborough.

SEPTEMBER 11:

In the second game of a doubleheader, Pittsburgh's Ralph Kiner homers three consecutive times – the second time this season he has accomplished the feat. Kiner had a homer in the opener, tying a major league record with four in a doubleheader. Kiner hit two yesterday; he now has six in his last three games, tying a record he already shares with Tony Lazzeri. The Pirates sweep the Braves, 4-3 and 10-8.

SEPTEMBER 17:

The Sporting News, which only last year disparaged his abilities, names Jackie Robinson its Rookie of the Year for 1947.

SEPTEMBER 22:

The Cardinals' Stan Musial has his fifth five-hit game of the season, tying Ty Cobb's record. St. Louis and Chicago split a doubleheader.

SEPTEMBER 23:

Brooklyn salutes its new hero on Jackie Robinson Day at Ebbets Field, one day after the Dodgers clinch their first pennant in six years. The Dodgers beat the Giants, 6-1.

SEPTEMBER 27:

In Philadelphia, Bobby Thomson connects to give the Giants their major league record 221st home run of the season. Despite the home run record, the Giants lose to the Phillies, 10-7, and finish in fourth place, 13 games behind the Dodgers. The major contributors to the Giants total of 221 homers are Johnny Mize (51), Willard Marshall (36), Walker Cooper (35), and Bobby Thomson (29).

SEPTEMBER 28:

Browns' broadcaster Dizzy Dean, 36 years old, comes down from the booth to the mound to start against the White Sox today. Dean, who claims he "could beat nine out of 10 who call themselves pitchers today," then hurls four scoreless innings, allowing three hits and a walk. He has one hit in one at-bat, but is not involved in the decision. Dean, who earns a dollar for his efforts, says, "I think I still could pitch well enough to win up here, but I don't intend to try."

SEPTEMBER 29:

Former Yankees' skipper Joe McCarthy is coming out of retirement and will manage the Red Sox in 1948. McCarthy gets a two-year contract estimated at $50,000 annually. He succeeds Joe Cronin, who becomes the general manager, replacing Eddie Collins. The Red Sox finished in third (83-71), this past season, Cronin's 13th at the helm. He led Boston to the AL pennant in 1946. McCarthy won eight pennants and seven World Series championships with the Yankees, and one flag with the Cubs in 1929. McCarthy is asked how he will handle the temperamental Ted Williams. He responds, "A manager who cannot get along with a .400 hitter ought to have his head examined."

REGULAR SEASON WRAP-UP:

The Yankees, under Stanley "Bucky" Harris, beat the Tigers by 12 games, with a 97-57 record. Joe DiMaggio (.315, 20 homers, 97 RBI) and George McQuinn (.304) are the leading hitters. The team has no 20-game winners; Allie Reynolds is 19-8. Burt Shotton, who took over from the suspended Leo Durocher, manages the Dodgers to the NL pennant, five games ahead of the Cardinals. The Dodgers compile a 94-60 record. Pete Reiser at .309 and Dixie Walker at .306 are the top batters. Ralph Branca's 21-12 tops the staff. Jackie Robinson finishes his rookie year at .297

SEPTEMBER 11
For the second time this season, Ralph Kiner homers three consecutive times.

OCTOBER 6
The Yankees take game seven of the Subway Series with the Dodgers, 5-2.

with a league-leading 29 stolen bases. Ted Williams is the first AL player to capture two Triple Crowns. Teammate Johnny Pesky becomes the first to lead the AL in hits in his first three seasons. Harry Walker of the Phillies leads the NL in batting; Dixie Walker led the NL in 1944 – they are the first brothers to win batting titles.

SEPTEMBER 30:

World Series, game one. Today at Yankee Stadium, Spec Shea, with a save by Joe Page, beats the Dodgers and Ralph Branca, 5-3. The Yankees, who have only four hits in the game, score five times in the fifth, after Branca retires the first 12.

OCTOBER 1:

World Series, game two. Allie Reynolds and the Yankees dominate the Dodgers, 10-3, at Yankee Stadium. The Yankees bang out 15 hits, including a Tommy Henrich homer. Dixie Walker's solo round-tripper is one of nine hits allowed by Reynolds, who fans 12. Vic Lombardi is the losing pitcher.

OCTOBER 2:

World Series, game three. On the strength of a six-run second inning, the Dodgers edge the Yankees, 9-8, at Ebbets Field. Each team has 13 hits; the Yankees' include a two-run homer by Joe DiMaggio. In the seventh inning, Yogi Berra hits a solo shot against Ralph Branca; it is the first ever World Series pinch-hit homer. Hugh Casey, with two and two-thirds innings of shutout relief, gets the win. Starter Bobo Newsom is the loser.

The Pirates release Hank Greenberg (.249, 25 homers, 74 RBI) for the purpose of retirement. Greenberg finishes his 13-year career with a .313 average, a .605 slugging average, 331 homers, and 1,276 RBI. He missed three-plus seasons while serving in the army.

OCTOBER 3:

World Series, game four. At Ebbets Field, Yankees' pitcher Floyd "Bill" Bevens enters the ninth inning working on a no hitter and holding on to a 2-1 lead. He gets Bruce Edwards on a flyout; Carl Furillo walks. John "Spider" Jorgensen fouls out and Al Gionfriddo runs for Edwards. With Pete Reiser batting, Gionfriddo steals second on a 2-1 pitch. Bevens throws a third ball and then Reiser gets an intentional walk. Eddie Miksis runs for Reiser, and then manager Burt Shotton sends Harry "Cookie" Lavagetto in to hit for Eddie Stanky. Lavagetto doubles off the left-field wall, scoring Gionfriddo and Miksis. The Yankees lose, 3-2, and Bevens misses the opportunity for the first World Series no-hitter. For the second straight game, Hugh Casey is the game's winner in relief.

OCTOBER 4:

World Series, game five. Rookie Spec Shea four-hits the Dodgers and drives in a run, and Joe DiMaggio homers in a 2-1 Yankee victory at Ebbets Field. With two out in the bottom of the ninth and a runner on second, Shea fans yesterday's hero, Cookie Lavagetto, to end the game. Rex Barney gets the loss.

OCTOBER 5:

World Series, game six. The Dodgers bounce back with an 8-6 win at Yankee Stadium to tie the series. In the sixth inning with two on, Al Gionfriddo robs Joe DiMaggio of a 415-foot extra-base hit near the left-field bullpen, snuffing a potentially big inning. As he nears second base, DiMaggio kicks the dirt. Burt Shotton had substituted Gionfriddo for Eddie Miksis to start the sixth. The teams use a record 38 players – including 10 pitchers. Ralph Branca gets the win; Joe Page is charged with the loss.

After leaving game six with a cracked rib, Yankee outfielder Johnny Lindell is berated by co-owner and president Larry MacPhail.

OCTOBER 6:

World Series, game seven. The Yankees win, 5-2, and take the World Series on five strong innings of relief by winning pitcher Joe Page, who allows one hit and retires 15 in a row. The Yankees trail 2-1 in the fourth when Bobby Brown hits a two-run pinch-hit double and Tommy Henrich singles in the go-ahead run. The losing pitcher is starter Hal Gregg. Carl Furillo, in a losing cause, leads all hitters with .353. Henrich tops the Yankees with .323 and five RBI. Despite hitting .231, DiMaggio has two homers and five RBI. Spec Shea wins two games. Jackie Robinson finishes his first World Series with a .259

TRIVIA

A poll ranks Jackie Robinson behind singer Bing Crosby as the most-admired man in the United States.

"Home run hitters drive Cadillacs; singles hitters drive Fords."
– *Ralph Kiner*

LEAGUE

In April, Red Sox owner Tom Yawkey and Yankees' co-owner Dan Topping have dinner in New York City and, in the course of the evening, agree on a trade: Boston will get Joe DiMaggio; Ted Williams will come to New York. In the morning, Topping calls Yawkey to confirm the deal. The difference in the ages of the two stars – DiMaggio is four years older – becomes an issue. Yawkey asks that the Yankees throw in their "little left-fielder" Yogi Berra; the deal collapses. The idea of DiMaggio batting in Fenway Park with its short left field and Williams taking aim at the right-field porch in Yankee Stadium has intrigued baseball fans for years. Would either – or both – have been able to break Babe Ruth's single season record? When the question of Williams hitting 60 is suggested to Joe McCarthy, he says: "Lou Gehrig didn't."

average, three RBI, two stolen bases, and no errors at first base.

After the game, manager Bucky Harris throws Larry MacPhail out of the victory celebration in retaliation for his conduct toward Johnny Lindell after game six of the Series. The Dodgers vote a full share of World Series money to manager Leo Durocher; Commissioner Happy Chandler says no.

The Yankees' $10,000 Victory Dinner at New York's Biltmore Hotel is the scene of wild doings–mostly by team president Larry MacPhail. He begins by warning the press, "Stay away or get punched." Then he belts his former Dodger road secretary. And, for an encore, he fires Yankee farm system director George Weiss. Co-owner Dan Topping pushes MacPhail into the kitchen, saying, "I have taken enough. Come with me and we will settle this thing once and for all." MacPhail returns from the kitchen after quitting his job. Mrs. MacPhail describes her husband as "a mighty sick, nervous man."

POST-SEASON

OCTOBER 7:

It doesn't take long for the other shoe to drop. Dan Topping and Del Webb announce they have purchased Larry MacPhail's one-third share of the Yankees for $2 million. Topping will become the team's new president. George Weiss, fired last night by MacPhail, is reinstated and promoted to general manager. MacPhail issues a terse statement, "I have this day resigned as president, treasurer and general manager of the Yankees."

NOVEMBER 17:

The Red Sox and Browns complete an eight-player trade. Coming to Boston are shortstop Vern Stephens (.279, 15 homers, 83 RBI) and pitcher Jack Kramer (11-16, 4.97 ERA). For its part of the deal, St. Louis gets $310,000 plus pitchers Jim Wilson (0-0), Al Widmar (0-0), and minor leaguer Joe Ostrowksi, as well as catcher Roy Partee (.231), infielder Eddie Pellagrini (.203, four homers), and minor league outfielder Pete Layden.

NOVEMBER 18:

The Red Sox and Browns liked trading so much yesterday, they do it again today, swapping five players. Boston obtains pitcher Ellis Kinder (8-15, 4.49 ERA) and infielder Billy Hitchcock (.222). The Browns get $65,000 and infielder Sam Dente (.232), pitcher Clem Dreisewerd (4-1, 4.18 ERA in 1946), as well as minor league third baseman Bill Sommers. In two days, the Browns receive $375,000 in cash.

NOVEMBER 27:

Joe DiMaggio edges Ted Williams for the AL's Most Valuable Player Award. It is the third for DiMaggio, who hit .315 with 20 home runs and 97 runs batted in. Williams, the Triple Crown winner, finishes second when one of the voting writers – Mel Webb – doesn't list him at all on his ballot. A 10th-place vote would have given Williams the MVP Award. Also, Jackie Robinson is the winner of the first-ever Rookie of the Year Award.

DECEMBER 6:

Leo Durocher, his "sentence" completed, is signed by the Dodgers to manage the team in 1948. Branch Rickey states: "The 1947 contract of Leo Durocher has been renewed for 1948 by the Brooklyn Baseball Club." Burt Shotton, who filled in for Durocher and led the team to the NL pennant, says, "I'm giving Durocher his job back."

DECEMBER 7:

Johnny Bench is born in Oklahoma City.

DECEMBER 8:

The Dodgers send Fred "Dixie" Walker (.306, nine homers), to the Pirates along with pitchers Hal Gregg (4-5, 5.87 ERA), and Vic Lombardi (12-11, 2.99 ERA). Brooklyn gets third baseman Billy Cox (.274, 15 home runs), pitcher Elwin "Preacher" Roe (4-15, 5.25 ERA), and infielder Gene Mauch (.300 in 16 games). According to Jules Tygiel, while Jackie Robinson and Dixie Walker "maintained good relations throughout the season," it was an "unnatural pairing." Branch Rickey was to send Walker to the Pirates on June 4, but Pete Reiser's injury that evening caused him to postpone the deal.

DECEMBER 26:

Carlton Fisk is born in Bellows Falls, Vermont.

THE BEST OF 1947

NATIONAL LEAGUE

HITTERS

Batting Average:
Harry "The Hat" Walker, St. Louis Cardinals/Philadelphia Phillies, .363

Slugging Average:
Ralph Kiner, Pittsburgh Pirates, .639

Home Runs:
Ralph Kiner; Johnny Mize, New York Giants, 51

Runs Batted In:
Johnny Mize, 138

Hits:
Tommy Holmes, Boston Braves, 191

Stolen Bases:
Jackie Robinson, Brooklyn Dodgers, 29

PITCHERS

Wins:
Ewell Blackwell, Cincinnati Reds, 22

Strikeouts:
Ewell Blackwell, 193

Earned Run Average:
Warren Spahn, Boston Braves, 2.33

Winning Percentage:
Larry Jansen, New York Giants, .808

Saves:
Hugh Casey, Brooklyn Dodgers, 18

Most Valuable Player:
Bob Elliott, Boston Braves

Rookie of the Year:
Jackie Robinson, Brooklyn Dodgers

AMERICAN LEAGUE

HITTERS

Batting Average:
Ted Williams, Boston Red Sox, .343

Slugging Average:
Ted Williams, .634

Home Runs:
Ted Williams, 32

Runs Batted In:
Ted Williams, 114

Hits:
Johnny Pesky, Boston Red Sox, 207

Stolen Bases:
Bob Dillinger, St. Louis Browns, 34

PITCHERS

Wins:
Bob Feller, Cleveland Indians, 20

Strikeouts:
Bob Feller, 196

Earned Run Average:
Spurgeon "Spud" Chandler, New York Yankees, 2.46

Winning Percentage:
Allie Reynolds, New York Yankees, .704

Saves:
Joe Page, New York Yankees; Eddie Klieman, Cleveland Indians, 17

Most Valuable Player:
Joe DiMaggio, New York Yankees

1948

"When I was playing, they threew at you to see what kind of man you were."
– *Lou Boudreau*

NEWS

Truman defeats Dewey

U.S. MOUNTS MASSIVE BERLIN AIRLIFT AFTER COMMUNISTS SEAL ROUTES BETWEEN EAST AND WEST GERMANY

ALGER HISS INDICTED FOR PERJURY

Polaroid camera patented

SUPREME COURT RULES PUBLIC-FUNDED RELIGIOUS EDUCATION VIOLATES FIRST AMENDMENT

TRUMAN SIGNS SELECTIVE SERVICE ACT

12 TOP COMMUNISTS ACCUSED OF ADVOCATING OVERTHROW OF U.S. GOVERNMENT

Bernard Baruch introduces "Cold War" to the vocabulary

MILTON BERLE, PERRY COMO, ED SULLIVAN HAVE TELEVISION SHOWS

PRE-SEASON

JANUARY 30:

Herb Pennock, general manager of the Phillies, dies in New York City at age 53. The left-hander pitched in the majors for 22 years, compiling a 240-162 record with a 3.61 ERA. Pennock appeared in five World Series and had a 5-0 record with a 1.95 ERA.

New York Yankees' manager Miller Huggins called Herb Pennock the greatest left-hander in the history of baseball. "If you were to cut that bird's head open," Huggins said, "the weakness of every batter in the league would fall out." Wrote Jack Conway of the New York Daily Mirror *in defense of Pennock during contract negotiations with Yankees owner Colonel Jacob Ruppert: "The Yankees' can get along without Herb Pennock like an automobile without its gasoline, like a hunk of liver without its rasher of bacon, like a mud-turtle without its shell. Pennock is the best left-hander in the business, not excluding the phenomenal Lefty Grove, who is not yet matured. If Colonel Ruppert thinks the Yankees can get along without Herbie, he is kidding himself. Herbie wants $20,000 and he's cheap at that price."*

FEBRUARY 14:

Former major league pitcher Mordecai "Three Finger" Brown dies in Terre Haute, Indiana, at the age of 71. In 14 seasons, Brown was 239-129 with the third best ERA of all time – 2.06. He also had five World Series wins.

Brown actually had four fingers. At the age of seven, he lost his index finger above the knuckle in a farm accident that also left his pinkie useless. He also had a mangled middle finger. Brown said, "It gives me a bigger dip."

FEBRUARY 24:

The Yankees get pitcher Ed Lopat (16-13, 2.81 ERA) from the White Sox for catcher Aaron Robinson (.297, five homers), pitcher Bill Wight (1-0, 1.00 ERA), and minor league pitcher Fred Bradley.

FEBRUARY 27:

Less than a month after his death, Herb Pennock is elected to the Hall of Fame. Also ticketed for Cooperstown is Harold "Pie" Traynor.

MARCH 6:

The Dodgers trade Eddie Stanky (.252, three homers) to the Braves, opening second base for Jackie Robinson. In return, Brooklyn gets first baseman Ray Sanders (not in the majors in 1947), infielder/outfielder Carvel "Bama" Rowell (.276, five home runs), and $40,000.

MARCH 27:

After investing $100,000 in the Cleveland Indians, Hank Greenberg joins Bill Veeck as second vice president of the team.

Prior to an exhibition game in Orlando between Philadelphia and Washington, Athletics' owner manager Connie Mack, age 85, and Senators' owner Clark Griffith, age 78, stage a footrace. After entering the field in an ambulance, Mack and Griffith race from third base to home plate–and finish in a tie.

APRIL 7:

The Phillies acquire first baseman Dick Sisler (.203 in 46 games), son of Hall of Famer George Sisler,

MARCH 6
The Dodgers send Eddie Stanky to the Braves, opening second base for Jackie Robinson.

APRIL 19
On opening day, Boston hits back-to-back-to-back homers, yet the A's prevail, 5-4.

from the Cardinals for infielder Ralph LaPointe (.308 in 30 games) and $30,000.

APRIL 12:

The Yankees release their one-time ace, Spurgeon "Spud" Chandler (9-5, 2.46 ERA). Chandler had a career year in 1943 –20-4, 1.64 ERA – prior to entering the armed services. After his return, he reached his pre-war level only once, winning 20 in 1946. In 11 years, Chandler is 109-43 with a 2.84 ERA.

THE SEASON

APRIL 19:

The Red Sox come out bombing on opening day. In the second inning against the Athletics' Phil Marchildon, Boston's Stan Spence, Vern Stephens, and Bobby Doerr hit consecutive homers. It's the only time a team has hit three straight on

Babe Ruth's Number 3 was retired on June 13.

The AL MVP of '48, Lou Boudreau hit .355 with 18 homers and 106 RBI.

MAY 20
Joe DiMaggio hits for the cycle and drives in six runs in the Yankees' 13-2 win in Chicago.

TRIVIA

Despite the retirement of Hank Greenberg, the Pirates keep the shortened left field previously known as Greenberg's Garden. But it is renamed Kiner's Korner.

CULTURE

***The Babe Ruth Story* premieres in New York City on July 26. The ailing Babe Ruth makes his last public appearance at the opening. The film stars William Bendix in the title role, along with Claire Trevor, Charles Bickford, Sam Levene, and William Frawley.**

Opening Day. But the Athletics come back to win, 5-4, in 11 innings.

The Dodgers return first baseman Ray Sanders to the Braves and accept $60,000 instead to complete the March 6 trade of Eddie Stanky.

APRIL 21:

Joe DiMaggio launches a 450-foot homer, one of the longest ever at Griffith Stadium in Washington, D.C. Still, the Senators beat the Yankees, 6-3.

And when he's wild... The Reds' Johnny Vander Meer, the only pitcher with consecutive no-hitters, walks 12 in a 5-2 loss to the St. Louis Cardinals. George "Red" Munger pitches a five-hitter for the victory.

APRIL 23:

The Yankees host the Red Sox on the 25th anniversary of the opening of Yankee Stadium. Boston was the first visiting team to play at the House That Ruth Built. With the ailing Babe Ruth in the dugout, the Seventh Regiment Band plays "The Star Spangled Banner." The World Championship flag is unfurled and Joe DiMaggio is presented with his Most Valuable Player Award. With Joe McCarthy, who was so much a part of the Yankees' glory of the past 25 years, now managing the Red Sox, Boston ruins the day with a 4-0 victory.

APRIL 25:

Larry Doby of the Indians fans five times to tie a major league record. The Indians win, 7-4, on two home runs by Ken Keltner and one by Eddie Robinson. Bob Muncrief is the game's winner.

APRIL 29:

At Shibe Park in Philadelphia, Ted Williams hits his 200th career home run in an 11-5 victory over the Athletics.

The Reds snap reliever Ted Wilks's streak of 77 consecutive pitching appearances without a loss. Cincinnati beats Wilks and St. Louis, 5-4, in 14 innings. Rookie Hank Sauer, who had tied the game with an eighth-inning homer, wins it with an RBI single. Wilks last lost on September 3, 1945; he has 12 wins in his 77 appearances.

MAY 8:

Larry Doby finds the range, launching a 408-foot homer over a 35-foot wall at Griffith Stadium. It is estimated to be longer than a 1922 Babe Ruth homer to the same spot. The Indians' Gene Bearden, who suffered a fractured skull and cracked knee with the navy in the South Pacific during World War II, makes his first major league start, three hitting the Senators, 6-1.

> "AGE IS A QUESTION OF MIND OVER MATTER. IF YOU DON'T MIND, AGE DON'T MATTER."
> – *Satchel Paige*

MAY 20:

In Chicago, the big man has a big day. Before only 5,001 paid admissions, Joe DiMaggio drives in six runs by hitting for the cycle with two homers, a triple, a double, and a single. DiMaggio comes close to another extra-base hit but left fielder Ralph Hodgin catches his drive at the wall. DiMaggio's outburst is part of a 22-hit (38 total bases) Yankee attack that sinks the White Sox, 13-2. Johnny Lindell also homers. Vic Raschi is the winning pitcher; Orval Grove gets the loss.

At Ebbets Field, Stan Musial homers, doubles twice, singles, and bats in two runs as the Cardinals and Howie Pollet beat the Dodgers, 13-4. Enos Slaughter has a double and two singles. The loser is Joe

JUNE 30
Cleveland pitcher Bob Lemon no-hits the Tigers, 2-0 – the AL's first-ever night no-hitter.

Hatten. Musial concludes the visit to Brooklyn with 11 hits in 15 at-bats for a .733 average. Slaughter hits .500.

While Joe DiMaggio and Stan Musial are banging the ball, the Indians are walking the bases. Red Sox pitchers Maurice "Mickey" Harris and Maurice "Mickey" McDermott issue a record-tying 18 bases on balls in nine innings. The Indians win the game, 13-4.

JUNE 5:

In Chicago, the Phillies' Richie Ashburn singles to extend his consecutive game hitting streak to 23, tying the major league rookie record. The Phillies win, 6-5. Ashburn is hitting .439 for the streak.

JUNE 6:

In St. Louis, Phillies' pitcher Charlie Bicknell lives out a pitcher's nightmare. In the sixth inning today, he yields 18 total bases, including four homers – by Erv Dusak, Albert "Red" Schoendienst, Enos Slaughter, and Vernal "Nippy" Jones. The Cardinals win the opener of a double-header, 11-1. In game two, the Cardinals ride an Alpha Brazle five-hitter to a 2-0 win. Schoendienst takes a page from the Stan Musial slugger's manual. He ends the day with five doubles and a homer, on the heels of three doubles yesterday.

It must be the air. While the Cardinals are hitting four homers in an inning, at Fenway Park the Red Sox smack three in a row in one frame against the Tigers, becoming the first team to accomplish the feat twice in the same season. Boston had three in an inning on April 19. Today's home run hitters are Ted Williams, Stan Spence, and Vern Stephens. The Red Sox sweep, 5-4 and 12-4.

JUNE 11:

Umpire Cal Hubbard becomes the target of debris at Yankee Stadium after he ejects Larry "Yogi" Berra for arguing calls on Tommy Byrne's pitches. One fan runs in from right field and throws a beer can at Hubbard; it misses.

JUNE 13:

The Yankees mark their silver anniversary by retiring Babe Ruth's number 3 in ceremonies attended by 49,641 at Yankee Stadium. With broadcaster Mel Allen as master of ceremonies, Will Harridge officially retires Ruth's number; the Babe's uniform will be sent to the Hall of Fame. On hand are members of the 1923 team, the first Yankees' World Champions and the first to play at the stadium. Babe Ruth, wearing his familiar number, carries a bat to home plate as the crowd sings "Auld Lang Syne" to him. The 1923 Yankees and representatives of later teams then play a two-inning Old-Timers' Game. The 1948 Yankees then beat Cleveland, 5-3, in the regulation game.

Members of the 1923 team on hand for the ceremonies, in addition to Ruth, are Waite Hoyt, Bob Meusel, Jumping Joe Dugan, Wally Pipp, Bullet Joe Bush, George Pipgras, Lawton "Whitey" Witt, Sad Sam Jones, Wally Schang, Carl Mays, Fred "Bootnose" Hoffman, Mike McNally, Henry "Hinkey" Haines, Oscar Roettger, and Elmer Smith.

JUNE 15:

The lights finally go on at Briggs Stadium – the last AL ballpark to host a night game. A crowd of 54,480 turns out to watch the Tigers play the Athletics under the $40,000 system. Hal Newhouser throws a two-hitter; Dick Wakefield and Pat Mullin hit eighth-inning homers, and the Tigers win, 4-1. The A's Barney McCoskey is carried out on a stretcher after crashing into the left-field wall.

JUNE 30:

Cleveland's Bob Lemon no-hits the Tigers, 2-0, at Briggs Stadium. It is the AL's first-ever night no-hitter. Lemon has a close call in the third inning when Dale Mitchell runs down a line drive by George Kell near the left-field line. Lemon fans two and walks three; the Indians play errorless ball. Art Houtteman is the loser.

LEAGUE

The All-American Girls Professional Baseball League adds two Illinois teams – the Chicago Colleens and the Springfield Sallies. The ball is reduced from 11 inches to 10 3/8 inches and the pitching distance is increased from 43 feet to 50 feet. Overhand pitching replaces sidearm delivery. The Rockford Peaches (74-49) are the league champions.

Babe Ruth autographed ball

JULY
4
The Red Sox explode for 14 runs in the seventh inning of a 20-8 rout of the A's.

TRIVIA

Today at Ebbets Field, Stan Musial approaches the plate and a Dodgers' fan supposedly says, "Here comes that man again." And his Stan the Man nickname is born. Maybe.

HISTORY

Outfielder Bob Crues of Amarillo in the Class C West Texas-New Mexico League completes his season with a .404 batting average, 69 homers, 254 RBI, and 228 hits in 140 games. He had two homers and 32 RBI in four previous seasons as a pitcher. Crues, who spent three years in military service and is 30 years old, never makes it to the major leagues.

After the game, Indians' second baseman Joe Gordon says, "Let that be a lesson to you other pitchers. If you pitch the way Lemon did tonight, you'll very seldom lose."

JULY 1:

The Dodgers' Roy Campanella makes his major league debut, hitting a double in his first at-bat and adding two singles. He also catches for Ralph Branca in a 6-4 loss to the Giants.

From The Baseball Hall of Fame 50th Anniversary Book*: "Buck Leonard first saw [Campanella] in 1946...catching batting practice for the Baltimore Elite Giants. [He] digested the complete curriculum of a ball player, mastering the art of swatting curves, guiding pitchers, and coping with all deliveries."*

JULY 3:

Dick Lane of Muskegon in the Fort Wayne Central League hits five homers in one game today. Three of his round-trippers are struck against Fort Wayne's player manager Walter "Boom-Boom" Beck, a former major leaguer. Lane homers in the first, fourth (twice), seventh, and eighth, and bats in 10 runs.

ROGER KAHN WRITES IN *HOW THE WEATHER WAS*: "THERE IS A CURIOUS DERIVATIVE OF GRESHAM'S LAW THAT APPLIES TO AMERICAN HEROES. JUST AS BAD MONEY DRIVES OUT GOOD, SO HEROIC FANCY DRIVES OUT HEROIC FACT, AND WE ARE OFTEN LEFT STANDING IN A FOREST OF CHOPPED-DOWN CHERRY TREES WONDERING WHAT OUR MAN ACTUALLY WAS LIKE. THE GREATER THE HERO, THE MORE PREVALENT THE FICTIONS. SINCE RUTH WAS THE MOST POPULAR OF BASEBALL HEROES, MOVIE COMPANIES, CARELESS WRITERS, AND GLIB STORYTELLERS HAVE BUSIED THEMSELVES WITH THE OBFUSCATION OF FACT."

JULY 4:

The Red Sox specialize in offensive explosions against Philadelphia on July 4. On Independence Day in 1939, Boston scored 35 runs in a doubleheader against the Athletics. The following year, it was 19 in a single game against the A's. And today at Fenway Park, they bang the A's around in the seventh inning, sending 19 to the plate and scoring 14 runs – tying a modern major league record. The game was tied, 5-5, going into the seventh. Charlie Harris allows 12 of the runs, retiring only one of the 14 batters he faces. Ted Williams bats three times, walking twice and grounding out. Boston wins, 20-8.

After being ejected in a Dodgers-Giants game at Ebbets Field, Leo Durocher gets a message: Branch Rickey wants his resignation.

JULY 7:

After many years of dominant pitching in the Negro Leagues where he became a living legend, Satchel

JULY
9
Satchel Paige, a 42-year-old rookie, makes his major league debut, with the Indians.

Paige is signed by Bill Veeck and will wear the uniform of the Cleveland Indians. Today is Paige's birthday – reportedly his 42nd – and he is the oldest rookie in major league history. *The Sporting News*, which once belittled Jackie Robinson, calls Paige's signing "a travesty on baseball."

JULY 9:

Satchel Paige makes his major league debut, relieving Bob Lemon in the fifth inning at Municipal Stadium in Cleveland. Paige becomes the first black pitcher in AL history. He yields a single to the first batter he faces, Chuck Stevens of the Browns, but settles down to allow only one more hit and no runs, before Larry Doby pinch-hits for him in the sixth inning.

JULY 10:

In the nightcap of a twi-night doubleheader against the Athletics, Satchel Paige comes out of the bullpen in the sixth inning with Indians up, 5-3, and two runners on. He retires the side, then yields a two-run homer to Hank Majeski in the following frame. Larry Doby hits a two-run homer in the eighth and the Indians add another run to forge ahead again. Paige retires Philadelphia in the final two innings of the game for his first major league win.

JULY 12:

Herb Pennock and Harold "Pie" Traynor are inducted into the Hall of Fame. Pennock, a left-hander who died earlier this year, pitched for 22 years and was 240-162 with a 3.61 ERA and 35 shutouts. In five World Series with the Athletics and Yankees, he was 5-0 with a 1.95 ERA. Traynor, a third baseman, played all of his 17 years with the Pirates. His career average was .320, with a high of .366 in 1930. Traynor appeared in two World Series.

JULY 13:

At Sportsman's Park, the AL makes it 11 wins in 15 All-Star Games, defeating the NL, 5-2. Vic Raschi pitches shutout ball in the fourth, fifth, and sixth innings and gets the win. He also singles in two runs in the fourth. Stan Musial hits a two-run homer; Walter "Hoot" Evers hits a solo shot for the AL. Johnny Schmitz is charged with the loss.

JULY 14:

The Sporting News criticizes Bill Veeck for signing Satchel Paige, arguing, "To sign a hurler at Paige's age is to demean the standards of baseball in the big circuits... Were Satchel white, he would not have drawn a second thought from Veeck." In his autobiography, *Veeck As in Wreck*, the controversial baseball entrepreneur responds: "If Satch were white, of course, he would have been in the majors 25 years earlier."

JULY 16:

Yesterday's enemy is today's hero. Leo Durocher of the Brooklyn Dodgers is now Leo Durocher of the New York Giants. He replaces manager Mel Ott, who is 37-38. Durocher will be succeeded by Burt Shotton, who led the Dodgers to the 1947 NL pennant.

The Phillies fire manager Ben Chapman, who last year led some of the most vicious verbal assaults against the Dogers' Jackie Robinson. The Phillies currently are 37-41. Allen "Dusty" Cooke will handle the team on an interim basis.

JULY 17:

Leo Durocher debuts as the Giants' manager in Pittsburgh, and Bobby Thomson makes him a 6-5 winner by smacking a pinch-hit single.

JULY 18:

In Philadelphia, White Sox outfielder Pat Seerey hits four homers in an 11-inning game against the Athletics. Seerey's homers are struck in the fourth, fifth, sixth, and 11th innings and he knocks in seven runs in a 12-11 Chicago victory. He walks and fouls out in his other at-bats. Seerey is the fifth player with four homers in a game and joins modern players Lou Gehrig (1932) and Chuck Klein (1936) in the record book. In 1945, he hit three homers in a game. The winning pitcher is Howie Judson; Lou Brissie gets the loss. The A's win the second game, abbreviated to five innings by curfew, 6-1.

JULY 24:

Pat Seerey is in the record books again, becoming the first to strike out seven times in a doubleheader.

TRIVIA

According to Negro Leagues pitcher Max Manning, Satchel Paige got his nickname when he "invented a contraption to carry four satchels at a time while working on a railroad station in Mobile."

LEAGUE

In October, the Homestead Grays beat the Birmingham Black Barons in five games in the final Negro League World Series. The Negro National League goes out of business after the 1948 season, and the remaining franchises form a new 10-team Negro American League.

AUGUST 16
Babe Ruth, 53, dies in New York City after a two-year battle with throat cancer.

CULTURE

***Flashing Spikes* by Frank O'Rourke is a novel with a character said to be patterned after Swede Risberg of the 1919 Black Sox.**

LEAGUE

The All-American Girls Professional Baseball League draws one million fans for the season.

JULY 26:

After Allen "Dusty" Cooke handles the team for 12 games (6-6), Eddie Sawyer takes over as the Phillies' manager. Sawyer had been with the Toronto Maple Leafs in the International League.

JULY 27:

Leo Durocher returns to Ebbets Field in a Giants uniform for the first time, with a crowd of 33,932 on hand. The Giants collect 17 hits and beat the Dodgers, 13-4. Sheldon Jones gets the win; Elwin "Preacher" Roe is the losing pitcher.

Hall of Fame shortstop Joe Tinker dies on his 68th birthday in Orlando, Florida. Tinker is destitute and in ill health – having lost a leg to diabetes – at the time of his death. Elected to the Hall of Fame with his two teammates in 1946, Tinker batted .263 over his 15-year career.

AUGUST 1:

In Cleveland, Lou Boudreau of the Indians steals home against the Red Sox battery – pitcher Maurice "Mickey" Harris and catcher Matt Batts. Boston manager Joe McCarthy comes out to argue the call with the umpire and then kicks Batts in the rear. Despite 70,000 witnesses, McCarthy denies he did it.

AUGUST 3:

At the age of 42 or so and with his glory years behind him, Satchel Paige makes his first major league start with a crowd of 72,434 packing Cleveland Stadium. Paige goes seven strong innings against the Senators and gets the 5-3 win. Jim Hegan hits a homer and Eddie Klieman finishes the game for Cleveland, which moves into a four-way tie for first.

AUGUST 12:

In game two of a doubleheader, the Indians rap out 26 hits to beat the Browns, 26-3; 14 players hit safely for Cleveland, a major league record.

AUGUST 13:

With Satchel Paige scheduled to pitch, a crowd of 50,013 packs Comiskey Park and another 15,000 are turned away. Paige responds with a five-hitter, beating Chicago, 5-0, with his first complete game and fourth straight win. It is Paige's 12th game and his second start; he is 5-1 and has drawn a total of 201,829 fans in his appearances.

AUGUST 16:

Babe Ruth, who single-handedly changed the nature of baseball to a game of power and was its greatest gate attraction, dies this evening at 8 p.m. at Memorial Hospital in New York City at age 53 after a two-year battle with throat cancer. His wife, Claire, and his two adopted daughters are at his bedside. Ruth leaves a stack of records that includes the highest slugging percentage ever (.691), the most career homers (714), the most home runs in a season (60), and the most lifetime walks (2,056).

Robert Creamer cites statistics that dramatize the impact of the Babe on baseball: He was the first player to hit 30, 40, 50, and 60 homers. From 1926 to 1931, he averaged 50-plus home runs per year and 46.8 from 1920 to 1931.

AUGUST 17:

Babe Ruth's body is on display at Yankee Stadium, and an estimated 100,000 people pass by to pay their respects. The flag on Main Street in Cooperstown, New York, is flown at half-mast, and the lights in all ballparks are dimmed in tribute. The family receives condolences from President Harry S. Truman and former president Herbert Hoover, among others.

The Yankees' Tommy Henrich ties one of Ruth's records by hitting his fourth grand slam home run of the year.

AUGUST 19:

Francis Cardinal Spellman celebrates a funeral mass for Babe Ruth at St. Patrick's Cathedral in New York. Some 6,000 mourners are on hand. Ruth is buried at the Gate of Heaven Cemetery in Mount Pleasant, New York.

It is hot in New York, and pallbearer Joe Dugan tells Waite Hoyt, "I'd give a hundred dollars for a cold beer." Hoyt responds, "Joe, so would the Babe." The story is told with some variations, but sources agree on the basics.

AUGUST 20:

With 78,382 at Cleveland Stadium, Satchel Paige three-

AUGUST 29
Jackie Robinson hits for the cycle in game one of a doubleheader against the Cardinals.

hits the White Sox, 3-0, for his second consecutive shutout. It also is the Indians' fourth straight shutout. Larry Doby drives in the winning run.

AUGUST 21:

After shutting out the White Sox into the ninth inning, Bob Lemon walks Pat Seerey and yields home runs to Aaron Robinson and Dave Philley. Cleveland's bid for five consecutive shutouts and its string of 47 straight scoreless innings ends – as does the team's eight-game winning streak. The final score is 3-2.

AUGUST 22:

The Dodgers execute a rare triple steal against the Braves in the fifth inning at Ebbets Field. Jackie Robinson is the lead runner, stealing home. The game features eight stolen bases. The Braves win, 4-3, on an eighth-inning homer.

AUGUST 25:

Bob Lemon and the Indians beat the Boston Red Sox, 9-0; Cleveland moves into first place. It is Lemon's eighth shutout of the year and his 17th win.

AUGUST 26:

Umpire John "Jocko" Conlan triggers a near-riot at Wrigley Field when he calls a third-inning drive by Phil Cavarretta a ground-rules double instead of a homer. With the ball at his feet, the Braves' Jeff Heath pretends it is lost in the vines on the left-field wall and Conlan makes the controversial call. For 20 minutes, fans throw bottles, straw hats, and other debris on the field and Conlan berates a cop for inaction. When order is restored, the Cubs' Harry "Peanuts" Lowrey hits a three-run triple and Chicago wins, 5-2. The Cubs had won the opener, 5-1.

AUGUST 29:

In St. Louis, Jackie Robinson takes the Cardinals to the cleaners before a crowd of 33,826. He hits for the cycle, scores three runs, drives in two, and steals a base. The Dodgers win, 12-7, and take the nightcap, 6-4, moving into first place by .003 over the Braves.

SEPTEMBER 1:

The Indians sign outfielder Orestes "Minnie" Minoso, who played with the New York Cubans in 1946 and 1947.

SEPTEMBER 9:

The Dodgers' Rex Barney no-hits the Giants, 2-0, at the Polo Grounds. It is the first no-hitter against the Giants since Jimmy Lavender's in 1915. Barney walks three and fans four; the Dodgers commit two errors. Gil Hodges and Carl Furillo drive in the Brooklyn runs. The losing pitcher is Monte Kennedy.

SEPTEMBER 13:

Indians' pitcher Don Black, 32 years of age, suffers a cerebral hemorrhage while batting against the Browns in the second inning. He is rushed to a hospital where he is in critical condition. Black, who was 2-2 at the time, recovers, but his career is over.

SEPTEMBER 16:

In Detroit, Joe DiMaggio hits his 300th career home run, joining Babe Ruth, Lou Gehrig, Mel Ott, Jimmie Foxx, Rogers Hornsby, Chuck Klein, and Hank Greenberg in the 300 Club.

SATCHEL PAIGE ON THE ROOKIE OF THE YEAR AWARD: "I DECLINED THE HONOR. I WASN'T SURE WHICH YEAR THOSE GENTLEMEN HAD IN MIND."

LEAGUE

In November, Danny Gardella's appeal goes to the Second Circuit Appellate Federal Court, New York Southern District, where it will be heard by three judges, including Learned Hand.

LEAGUE

In February, John Bright, the federal judge hearing Danny Gardella's lawsuit against major league baseball, dies. He is replaced by Henry W. Goddard, who dismisses the case.

"Spahn and Sain
and pray for rain."
– *Anonymous*

TRIVIA

The bat Babe Ruth leans on while staring toward the outfield in the famous Associated Press photo taken June 13 by Nat Fein belongs to the day's starting pitcher, Bob Feller. In his autobiography, Feller writes that Indians' first baseman Eddie Robinson selected the bat at random from the rack for the frail Ruth to use for support.

SEPTEMBER 22:

In Boston, Stan Musial has five hits in five at-bats for the fourth time this season, setting an NL record and tying the major league mark of Ty Cobb. Musial hits his 38th homer of the season, a double, and three singles, driving in two runs in an 8-2 Cardinals' victory, snapping the Braves' eight-game win streak. Alpha Brazle gets the win; Warren Spahn is charged with the loss. Enos Slaughter suffers a broken nose when he is hit by a line drive off the bat of teammate Vernal "Nippy" Jones.

SEPTEMBER 24:

With seven games left in the season, the Red Sox, Yankees, and Indians are in a three-way tie for first at 91-56.

SEPTEMBER 26:

The Indians forge into first place. Joe Gordon hits a two-run homer –his 31st of the season–and Bob Feller wins his sixth consecutive game, 4-1, against the Tigers. The Yankees and Red Sox split two games against each other.

In Boston, the Braves beat the Giants, 3-2, to clinch their first NL pennant since 1914.

BABE RUTH REMAINED DISAPPOINTED THROUGHOUT HIS NON-PLAYING DAYS BY HIS INABILITY TO FIND A MEANINGFUL JOB IN BASEBALL. IN *THE BABE RUTH STORY* (WRITTEN WITH BOB CONSIDINE), HE SAYS: "IT'S HARD TO BE ON THE OUTSIDE OF SOMETHING YOU LOVE. JUST LOOKING IN DOESN'T HELP."

Bob Elliott's three-run home run gives Boston pitchers Vern Bickford and Nelson Potter all the support they need. The Giants manage only five hits.

SEPTEMBER 28:

It's Good Old Joe Early Night in Cleveland. Who is Joe Early? He's a night watchman who writes Indians' owner Bill Veeck to ask why the average fan never gets a special day. Never one to miss a promotional opportunity, Veeck sets up a tribute to the 26-year-old World War II veteran and a crowd of 60,405 turns out. Early receives an outhouse, livestock, clothing, a convertible, appliances, and other gifts. He becomes something of a local media celebrity. Veeck also has $30,000 worth of orchids flown in and they are distributed free to the first 20,000 women at the ballpark. When the fun is over, Gene Bearden wins his 18th game, 11-0 over the White Sox, and Dale Mitchell hits a home run. The Yankees and Red Sox lose, giving the Indians a two-game lead with four to play.

OCTOBER 2:

Larry Doby collects four hits and Gene Bearden wins his 19th game, beating the Tigers, 8-0. The Red Sox eliminate the Yankees from pennant contention with a 5-1 victory.

OCTOBER 3:

On the last day of the season, the Indians hold a Bill Veeck Day, drawing 74,181 fans. They go home disappointed after the Tigers win, 7-1, on a Hal Newhouser five-hitter. Bob Feller is the losing pitcher. With today's crowd, the Indians set a one-season attendance record of 2,620,627. Meanwhile, at Fenway Park, Detroit beats the Yankees, 10-5, despite two doubles, two singles, and three RBI by Joe DiMaggio. Cleveland and Boston end the season tied at 96-58, necessitating a playoff game to decide the pennant.

OCTOBER 4:

At Fenway Park in a one-game playoff, the Indians send rookie Gene Bearden to the mound against Denny Galehouse of the Red Sox. Bearden, supported by two homers and two singles from player-manager Lou Boudreau, wins, 8-3. Bearden allows only one earned run, fanning six and walking

OCTOBER 4
In a one-game playoff for the AL pennant, the Indians beat the Red Sox, 8-3.

OCTOBER 11
The Indians take game six in Boston, 4-3, to capture the World Championship.

five; he serves up a homer to Bobby Doerr. Ken Keltner homers for the Indians. Galehouse is kayoed in the fourth and gets the loss. It is the first pennant for Cleveland since 1920.

The Phillies trade former NL batting champion Harry "The Hat" Walker (.292, two homers) to the Cubs for former home run king Bill "Swish" Nicholson (.261, 19 homers).

The Yankees fire manager Stanley "Bucky" Harris. The Yankees finished third in the AL at 94-60 last season. In 1947, his only other year with New York, the team won the World Series.

REGULAR SEASON WRAP-UP:

The Braves, under Billy Southworth, are 91-61, six and a half games ahead of his former team, the Cardinals. His pitching staff is based on the principle of "Spahn and Sain and pray for rain." Johnny Sain is 24-15, Warren Spahn is 15-12. Tommy Holmes (.325), Alvin Dark (.322), Eddie Stanky (.320), Jeff Heath (.319, 20 homers, 76 RBI), and Mike McCormick (.303) are the top average hitters. Bob Elliott has 23 home runs and 100 RBI.

With their victory over Boston in the playoffs, Lou Boudreau's Indians finish at 97-58, winning the pennant by one game. Boudreau hits .355 with 18 homers and 106 RBI; Dale Mitchell hits .336, and Larry Doby, .301. Joe Gordon has 32 homers, a record for a second baseman. Bob Lemon (20-14), rookie Gene Bearden (20-7), and Bob Feller (19-15) anchor the staff.

The Giants' Johnny Mize and the Pirates' Ralph Kiner share the NL home run lead with 40 each. Last year, they tied at 51 and are the only players to twice share a home run crown.

OCTOBER 6:

World Series, game one. In Boston, Bob Feller makes his first World Series appearance, limits the Braves to two hits, and loses a 1-0 heartbreaker on a controversial call. In the eighth inning, Feller apparently picks Phil Masi off second base on a play he has used before with shortstop Lou Boudreau. But Masi is called safe and scores the game's only run on Tommy Holmes's single. Johnny Sain, who allows four hits, is the winner.

OCTOBER 7:

World Series, game two. Bob Lemon scatters eight hits, beating the Braves, 4-1, in Boston. The Indians score two fourth-inning runs, knocking starter Warren Spahn out of the box; he gets the loss.

OCTOBER 8:

World Series, game three. Indians' left-hander Gene Bearden continues his dazzling rookie performances with a five-hit, 5-0 win over the Braves in Cleveland. He also doubles – one of his two hits – in the third and scores the lead run on an error by Alvin Dark. Vern Bickford gets the loss.

OCTOBER 9:

World Series, game four. A World Series record crowd of 81,897 sees the hometown Indians make it three in a row, with a 2-1 victory by Steve Gromek. Johnny Sain, pitching on two days' rest, gets the loss despite allowing only five hits to Gromek's seven. Larry Doby homers for Cleveland; Marv Rickert for the Braves.

OCTOBER 10:

World Series, game five. The Braves stay alive with a 12-hit, 11-5 victory today in Cleveland before another record crowd–86,288. Bob Elliott hits a three-run homer in the first and a solo shot in the third, driving in four runs. Bill Salkeld also homers for the Braves; Dale Mitchell and Jim Hegan for the Indians. The game is tied 5-5 in the seventh, when five Braves singles result in six runs. Warren Spahn gets the win in relief of starter Nelson Potter. Indians' starter Bob Feller goes six and a third and gets tagged with the game's loss. Satchel Paige becomes the first African-American ball player to pitch in the World Series, allowing no hits and no walks in his two-thirds of an inning of work.

OCTOBER 11:

World Series, game six. In Boston, the Indians top the Braves, 4-3, to take the World Series. Bob Lemon gets the win, with a save and one and two-thirds innings of relief from Gene Bearden. Joe Gordon homers for Cleveland. Bill Voiselle is the losing pitcher. Earl Torgeson of the Braves has the

LEAGUE

Branch Rickey makes another kind of deal. He trades a player for a broadcaster. He brings Ernie Harwell of the Atlanta Crackers to Brooklyn to team with Walter "Red" Barber and Connie Desmond. As compensation, the Crackers get catcher Cliff Dapper, who played in eight games for the Dodgers in 1942.

"I respect anybody who lasts over one year as manager."
– *Casey Stengel*

LEAGUE

In January, Commissioner A.B. Chandler fines the Yankees and White Sox $500 each for signing high school players.

top average – .389; his teammate Bob Elliott hits .333 with two homers and 5 RBI. But strong pitching by Bob Lemon (2-0, 1.65 ERA) and timely hitting by Jim Hegan (.211, but five RBI), Larry Doby (.318), and Lou Boudreau (three RBI) do it for Cleveland. Johnny Sain is only 1-1 for Boston, but has a 1.06 ERA.

POST-SEASON

OCTOBER 12:

The Yankees appoint 58-year-old Casey Stengel as their manager and sign him to a two-year contract. Stengel previously managed the Dodgers and Braves, never finishing higher than fifth place. He had more success this season, leading the Oakland Oaks to the Pacific Coast League championship.

NOVEMBER 4:

Former major league outfielder Alvin "Jake" Powell shoots himself to death in a Washington, D.C., police station. The controversial Powell was 40 years old. He played 11 years with the Senators, Yankees, and Phillies, batting .271. He hit .455 with the Yankees in the 1936 World Series.

THE DAY BEFORE HE DIES, BABE RUTH TELLS CONNIE MACK, "THE TERMITES HAVE GOT ME."

NOVEMBER 10:

The Tigers send pitcher Billy Pierce (3-0, 6.34 ERA) and $10,000 to the White Sox for catcher Aaron Robinson (.252, eight homers).

NOVEMBER 11:

The Yankees' Joe DiMaggio again undergoes surgery at Johns Hopkins Hospital in Baltimore for bone spurs on his right heel.

NOVEMBER 23:

Another of baseball's great power hitters, Lewis "Hack" Wilson, dies in Baltimore, at the age of 48, of sclerotic liver and pulmonary edema – a likely consequence of alcohol abuse. Wilson had been admitted to Baltimore City Hospital, identified only as a "white male... appearing acutely ill." Wilson, a man of peculiar build – 5 feet, 6 inches, 190 pounds, an 18-inch neck and only size six feet – hit 244 homers and batted .307. His career year was 1930 with the Cubs, when he hit 56 home runs and drove in an all-time high 190 runs. The following year, he had only 13 home runs and 61 RBI.

NOVEMBER 26:

After Hack Wilson's body remains unclaimed, NL president Ford Frick steps in and pays $350 for a coffin and funeral service.

DECEMBER 14:

The Indians acquire pitcher Early Wynn (8-19, 5.82 ERA) and first baseman James "Mickey" Vernon (.242, three homers) – a former AL batting champion – from the Senators. In return, Washington gets first baseman Eddie Robinson (.254, 16 homers) and a pair of pitchers, Joe Haynes (9-10, 3.97 ERA) and Eddie Klieman (3-2, 2.60 ERA).

First baseman Eddie Waitkus (.295, seven homers) and pitcher Hank Borowy (5-10, 4.89) come to the Phillies from the Cubs in exchange for pitchers Walter "Monk" Dubiel (9-10, 3.89 ERA) and Emil "Dutch" Leonard (11-18, 2.51 ERA). The Phillies also purchase pitcher Ken Trinkle (4-5, 3.18 ERA) from the Giants.

DECEMBER 15:

The Dodgers give up on Pete Reiser (.236). They ship the outfielder Myron "Mike" McCormick (.303).

THE BEST OF 1948

NATIONAL LEAGUE

HITTERS

Batting Average:
Stan Musial, St. Louis Cardinals, .376

Slugging Average:
Stan Musial, .702

Home Runs:
Ralph Kiner, Pittsburgh Pirates; Johnny Mize, New York Giants, 40

Runs Batted In:
Stan Musial, 131

Hits:
Stan Musial, 230

Stolen Bases:
Richie Ashburn, Philadelphia Phillies, 32

PITCHERS

Wins:
Johnny Sain, Boston Braves, 24

Strikeouts:
Harry Brecheen, St. Louis Cardinals, 149

Earned Run Average:
Harry Brecheen, 2.24

Winning Percentage:
Harry Brecheen, .741

Saves:
Harry Gumbert, Cincinnati Reds, 17

Most Valuable Player:
Stan Musial, St. Louis Cardinals

Rookie of the Year:
Alvin Dark, Boston Braves

AMERICAN LEAGUE

HITTERS

Batting Average:
Ted Williams, Boston Red Sox, .369

Slugging Average:
Ted Williams, .615

Home Runs:
Joe DiMaggio, New York Yankees, 39

Runs Batted In:
Joe DiMaggio, 155

Hits:
Bob Dillinger, St. Louis Browns, 207

Stolen Bases:
Bob Dillinger, 28

PITCHERS

Wins:
Hal Newhouser, Detroit Tigers, 21

Strikeouts:
Bob Feller, Cleveland Indians, 164

Earned Run Average:
Gene Bearden, Cleveland Indians, 2.43

Winning Percentage:
Jack Kramer, Boston Red Sox, .783

Saves:
Russ Christopher, Cleveland Indians, 17

Most Valuable Player:
Lou Boudreau, Cleveland Indians

TRIVIA

Bowman Gum Company issues a set of 48 baseball cards. Its competitor, the Topps Company, markets Magic Photos, which include 19 baseball cards among their 252 subjects.

1949

"A great ball player... a great man... a great American...."
– *Inscription on Babe Ruth's plaque*

NEWS

SOVIETS TEST ATOM BOMB

ECUADOR EARTHQUAKE KILLS NEARLY 5,000

BERLIN AIRLIFT ENDS AFTER BREAKING SOVIET BLOCKADE

KONRAD ADENAUER NEW GERMAN CHANCELLOR

11 U.S. COMMUNIST LEADERS FOUND GUILTY OF TREASON

U.S. and 11 other nations form NATO

COMMUNISTS TAKE POWER IN CHINA

UN's permanent headquarters open in New York City

STEELWORKERS STRIKE, WIN PENSIONS

Theatergoers see Richard Rodgers and Oscar Hammerstein's *South Pacific*, Arthur Miller's *Death of a Salesman*, Jule Styne's *Gentlemen Prefer Blondes*

PRE-SEASON

FEBRUARY 7:

The Yankees' Joe DiMaggio becomes the first player to earn $100,000 for a season. DiMaggio, who last year batted .320 with 39 homers and 155 RBI, originally was offered $90,000 plus an attendance clause. His friend, saloonkeeper Toots Shor, advises him to take a flat $100,000, and Yankees' owners Dan Topping and Del Webb agree.

FEBRUARY 10:

Will it be only three more years for Ted Williams? He tells a sports editor in Miami he plans to retire after the 1951 baseball season.

FEBRUARY 10:

The Gardella case lives and goes to trial.

MARCH 2:

After his first workout, Joe DiMaggio, who underwent surgery for bone spurs in his right heel November 11, 1948, again experiences pain and again checks into Johns Hopkins Hospital in Baltimore. Surgeon George Bennett advises no surgery and DiMaggio returns to camp.

APRIL 11:

Joe DiMaggio's heel acts up once more, and he is forced to leave an exhibition game in Texas.

APRIL 12:

Joe DiMaggio goes back to Baltimore's Johns Hopkins Hospital, where he is diagnosed with "immature calcium deposits in tissues adjacent to the heel bone." He will miss 65 games because of the bone spur.

THE SEASON

APRIL 19:

On opening day, the Yankees unveil a granite monument honoring Babe Ruth. It stands in center field next to plaques for Lou Gehrig and Miller Huggins and reads: "A great ball player/A great man/A great American..." On hand are 40,075 fans and Mrs. Claire Ruth, New York Governor Thomas E. Dewey, and Mayor William O'Dwyer. A recuperating Joe DiMaggio watches from the Yankees' dugout. After the ceremonies the Yankees – under new skipper Casey Stengel – beat the Senators, 3-2, on a two-out homer by Tommy Henrich in the bottom of the ninth.

Stengel refines "platooning" to a baseball high art, shuffling outfielders like Hank Bauer and Gene Woodling and infielders Billy Johnson and Bobby Brown in and out of the lineup and moving other players around. Ironically, as a player, Stengel had objected to being platooned. "They said I couldn't hit left-handers and they'd pull me out as soon as a lefthander appeared. But how was I expected to hit them when I never faced them?"

APRIL 20:

In Boston, Phillies' third baseman Willie "Puddin' Head" Jones ties a major league record with four consecutive doubles in a 6-5 loss to the Braves.

APRIL 30:

With his team ahead, 3-2, Cubs' center fielder Andy Pafko attempts a game-ending catch on a line drive hit by Glenn "Rocky" Nelson of the Cardinals. Umpire Al Barlick rules it was a trap, not a catch. Pafko, holding the ball, argues while Nelson circles the base for an inside-the-park homer. The Cardinals win the game.

APRIL 20
Phillies' Willie "Puddin' Head" Jones ties an ML record with four consecutive doubles.

MAY 22
Pitcher Don Newcombe makes his first start for the Dodgers, shutting out the Reds, 3-0.

MAY 6:

In Philadelphia, diminutive left-hander Bobby Shantz pitches nine innings of no-hit relief against the Tigers. The five-foot, six-inch, 139-pound Shantz gives up a run in the top of the 13th. But he gets the victory, when Wally Moses hits a two-run homer in the bottom of the inning for a 5-4 win.

MAY 10:

Former Cardinals' owner Sam Breadon dies of cancer at age 72. Breadon, who owned the Cardinals from 1920 to 1947, originally invested $200 in the team and received $3 million when he sold it in 1947 to Robert Hannegan and Fred Saigh. He is credited with introducing Sunday doubleheaders on the theory that people want a full afternoon of diversion on their day off, and he also was an advocate of night baseball.

MAY 22:

The Dodgers' Don Newcombe makes his first major league start, shutting out the Reds, 3-0, in Cincinnati.

MAY 31:

Indians' fan Charley Lupica climbs a flagpole, settles down on a platform, and maintains he isn't coming down until the team – presently in seventh place – moves into first.

JUNE 2:

The Phillies shell the Reds with five homers in a 10-run eighth inning at Shibe Park, tying a major league record. Catcher Andy Seminick reaches the seats twice (three times for the game) and outfielder Del Ennis, third baseman Willie "Puddin' Head" Jones, and pitcher Elwood "Schoolboy" Rowe once each. The final is 12-3, with Curt Simmons getting the win. The loser is Ken Raffensberger.

JUNE 5:

Commissioner Happy Chandler extends amnesty to 18 players who jumped to the outlaw Mexican League. The players, who received five-year suspensions in 1946, are notified by mail that they must apply for reinstatement in writing and that approval will be automatic. Chandler's action comes after the owners are threatened with anti-trust lawsuits. But, he states, "The threat of compulsion by a court having been ended, I feel justified in tempering justice with mercy in dealing with all of these players."

JUNE 9:

In a game noted for its statistical oddity rather than its significance, the Phillies beat the Pirates, 4-3, in 18 innings in Pittsburgh. Each team ends the game with 68 at-bats, 16 hits, 21 assists and three errors.

JUNE 12:

After 13 years as the Cubs' manager – and three pennants – Charlie Grimm steps down – or up – to become a team vice president, and is replaced by Frankie Frisch. In Grimm's last games at the helm, the Cubs split a doubleheader with the Braves for a 19-31 record.

JUNE 13:

Mordecai "Three Finger" Brown, Charlie Gehringer, and Charles "Kid" Nichols are inducted into the Hall of Fame. Brown, who died last year, owns the third best career ERA mark – 2.06. In 14 years, he was 239-129 with 57 shutouts. From 1906 to 1911, he won 20 games or more each season, including a 27-9 mark in 1909. He pitched in four World Series for the Cubs. Nichols, who pitched for 15 seasons between 1890 and 1906, was a 30-game winner seven times and a 20-game winner in four other years. His lifetime mark is 361-208 with a 2.94 ERA, 532 complete games, and 48 shutouts. Gehringer played his entire 19-year career as a second baseman for the Tigers, batting .320 with 1,427 RBI. In 1937, he was the AL's leading hitter at .371 and batted .321 in three World Series.

Gehringer was known as the Mechanical Man. Hall of Fame teammate Mickey Cochrane once said: "Charlie says 'hello' on opening day, 'good-bye' on closing day and in between hits .350." Yankees' pitcher Lefty Gomez stated: "He's in a rut. Gehringer goes two-for-five on opening day and stays that way all season."

JUNE 14:

Philadelphia Phillies first baseman Eddie Waitkus is shot with a .22 rifle in Room 1297A of the Edgewater Beach Hotel in Chicago by 19-year-old Ruth Ann Steinhagen. The young woman, who is obsessed with Waitkus, had created

CULTURE

Moviegoers see a lot of baseball: *Take Me Out to the Ballgame*, a musical starring Gene Kelly, Frank Sinatra, and Jules Munshin as the double-play combo "O'Brien to Ryan to Goldberg"; *It Happens Every Spring*, starring Ray Milland; *The Stratton Story*, starring James Stewart as major leaguer Monty Stratton, who loses his leg in an accident, and June Allyson; *The Kid From Cleveland*, starring Rusty Tamblyn and George Brent (also appearing are Indians' owner Bill Veeck, pitcher Satchel Paige, and other team members).

HISTORY

The Baltimore Elite Giants sweep the Chicago American Giants in four games to win the Negro American League Championship.

JUNE 24
The Yankees sign an Oklahoma high school star named Mickey Charles Mantle.

LEAGUE

In the All-American Girls Professional Baseball League, the size of the ball is reduced from 10 3/8 inches to 10 inches. In midseason, the pitching distance is increased from 50 feet to 55 feet. The Grand Rapids Chicks overcome a 57-54 record to win the league championship.

HISTORY

Jackie Robinson, Don Newcombe, Roy Campanella, and Larry Doby are the first African-Americans to appear in a major league All-Star Game. Joe and Dominic DiMaggio, the first brothers to hit safely in an All-Star Game, do it again. Each has a single and a double in four at-bats.

a shrine – including news photos – dedicated to Waitkus in her bedroom. She explains: "As time went on I just became nuttier and nuttier about the guy and I knew I would never get to know him in a normal way... and if I can't have him, nobody else can. And I then decided I would kill him..." Waitkus is taken to Illinois Masonic Hospital with a bullet in the muscles near his spine and a collapsed right lung.

In sandlot spirit, the Red Sox allow a "courtesy runner" for Indians' player-manager Lou Boudreau after he is hit by a Joe Dobson pitch.

JUNE 24:

The Yankees sign high school star Mickey Charles Mantle for $1,000. Scout Tom Greenwade inks the 17-year-old Mantle.

Greenwade says afterward: "The first time I saw Mantle I knew how Paul Krichell felt when he first saw Lou Gehrig. He knew that as a scout he'd never have another moment like it."

JUNE 27:

After 65 days in seclusion, Joe DiMaggio tests his ailing heel in the Mayor's Trophy exhibition game against the Giants at Yankee Stadium. He is hitless in four at-bats, but plays the full nine innings. In the pre-game home run contest, he parks one in the left-field seats.

JUNE 28:

The Yankees travel to Boston in first place, leading the third-place Red Sox by five and a half games and with Joe DiMaggio back in the lineup. He warms up with a second-inning single against Maurice "Mickey" McDermott and scores on Hank Bauer's three-run homer. In the third inning, after a Phil Rizzuto single, DiMaggio drives a homer over the left-field screen. Joe Page finishes up and the Yankees win, 5-4.

JUNE 29:

Joe DiMaggio puts an exclamation point on yesterday's statement. Boston takes a 7-1 lead, but in the fifth DiMaggio hits a three-run home run. Gene Woodling ties the game for New York with a bases-loaded double in the seventh. With two out in the eighth, Joe DiMaggio hits an Earl Johnson pitch over the left-field wall and out of Fenway Park. Manager Casey Stengel steps onto the field and bows to DiMaggio and the Boston fans give the Yankee Clipper an ovation. Joe Page pitches three scoreless innings in relief and the Yankees win, 9-7.

JUNE 30:

Joe DiMaggio puts the finishing touch on a legendary series, smashing a 3-2 pitch from Mel Parnell off the left-field light tower with George Stirnweiss and Tommy Henrich on base. The ball is hit so hard, it caroms back to second base. The Yankees win, 6-3, to sweep the series.

In his remarkable return, DiMaggio gets five hits in 11 at-bats for a .455 average and adds four home runs and nine RBI. During the June 30 game, a plane flies over Fenway hauling a banner that reads: THE GREAT DiMAGGIO!

JULY 5:

The Giants sign outfielder Monte Irvin and infielder Hank Thompson, their first black players. Irvin was with the Newark Eagles last season; Thompson with the Kansas City Monarchs after playing in 27 games for the Browns in 1947 and batting .256. The Giants also sign pitcher Ford Smith, who played with the Kansas City Monarchs. All three players go to the AAA Jersey City Giants in the International League.

JULY 6:

The Reds' new catcher Walker Cooper hits three homers and three singles, drives in 10, and scores five times as Cincinnati beats the visiting Cubs, 23-4, at Crosley Field.

JULY 8:

Monte Irvin and Hank Thompson debut for the Giants at Ebbets Field. Don Newcombe is on the mound for the Dodgers when the Giants' starting second baseman Hank Thompson comes to bat; it is the first time in modern major league history that a black pitcher has faced a black hitter. Newcombe prevails, keeping Thompson hitless for the game, won by Brooklyn, 4-3. Irvin walks in a pinch-hitting appearance.

JULY 12:

The AL wins an All-Star Game slugfest at Ebbets Field, 11-7. The AL overcomes two-run homers by Stan

Shoeless Joe Jackson of the 1919 Black Sox claims in an article by Furman Bisher that appears in *Sport Magazine*: "I can say that my conscience is clear and I will stand on my record in that World Series."

Musial and Ralph Kiner with a 13-hit attack and a great catch by Ted Williams on Don Newcombe's liner to left-field in the second inning with the bases loaded. Virgil Trucks gets the win; Newcombe is the loser.

JULY 18:

Mr. Robinson goes to Washington. After black singer-actor Paul Robeson declares that American blacks would not fight against the Soviet Union if war breaks out, Branch Rickey convinces Jackie Robinson to testify before the House Un-American Activities Committee. Robinson uses the occasion to speak out against racial discrimination, pointing out, "I'm not fooled because I've had a chance open to very few Negro Americans." Then he tells the representatives, "I've got too much invested for my wife and child and myself in the future of this country, and I and other Americans of many races and faiths have too much invested in our country's welfare, for any of us to throw it away for a siren song sung in bass." (Paul Robeson is an operatic bass.) That night Robinson steals home as the Dodgers beat the Cubs, 3-0.

Author Jules Tygiel describes Robinson's testimony as "one of the more embarrassing moments of his career." Tygiel reports that shortly before his death, Robinson still defended his testimony, but expressed respect for Robeson because "I believe he was sincerely trying to help his people."

AUGUST 7:

Game one of today's Yankees-Browns doubleheader has the makings of an NL-style beanball war. In his next at-bat after hitting a three-run home run, Yogi Berra is plunked on the thumb by former Yankees Dick Starr and has to leave the game. Relief pitcher Karl Drews, another former Yankee, hits Tommy Henrich on the elbow, then gets Berra's substitute, Gus Niarhos, and Jerry Coleman. Yankees' pitcher Tommy Byrne retaliates by shaving Starr in the fifth and Drews in the seventh. Joe DiMaggio hits a three-run homer and the Yankees win, 20-2. Game two ends in a 2-2 tie.

AUGUST 9:

With his brother Joe watching from center field, the Yankees snap Dominic DiMaggio's consecutive game hitting streak at 34. Dom falls 22 games short of the major league record set by Joe. Vic Raschi, with the help of a shoestring catch of a sinking liner by Joe DiMaggio in the eighth inning, shuts down Dominic although the Red Sox win, 6-3, on two-run home runs by Ted Williams and George "Birdie" Tebbetts. Hank Bauer has two homers for New York. Ellis Kinder gets the win.

AUGUST 21:

At Shibe Park, the Giants are awarded a forfeit win against the Phillies. With the Giants leading, 4-2, and one out in the top of the ninth, Joe Lafata hits a liner to Richie Ashburn in center. Second base umpire George Barr rules it a trap by Ashburn and the fans go berserk, pelting the field with debris and making it impossible for play to continue.

AUGUST 22:

The Yankees buy first baseman Johnny Mize (.263) from the Giants.

AUGUST 26:

In an Appalachian League game, visiting Pulaski defeats Bluefield, 11-7, ending the Blue-Grays 34-game home winning streak.

SEPTEMBER 13:

Ralph Kiner of the Pirates homers in his first two at-bats today. Kiner had two home runs in his last game on September 11 in his final plate appearances, tying him for the major league record with four consecutive homers. It is the second time in his career that Kiner has hit four home runs in a row; the first was in 1947.

SEPTEMBER 15:

Pirates' pitcher Ernie Bonham dies in Pittsburgh while undergoing an emergency appendectomy. Bonham, 36 years old, was 7-4 with the Pirates at the time of his hospitalization. His best season was in 1942 when he won 21 and lost five for the New York Yankees with six shutouts. The players' pension fund provides no money to Bonham's widow.

SEPTEMBER 18:

The Yankee Clipper's health woes continue to plague him. This time, Joe DiMaggio contracts pneumonia and will be out of the lineup for a week.

LEAGUE

In 1949, Commissioner Happy Chandler sells the radio and television rights to the World Series to the Gillette Safety Razor Co. for $1 million per year.

RULES

Major league owners approve the installation of warning tracks – cinder paths around the outfield – in all ballparks to cut down on the growing incidence of players crashing into fences

CULTURE

NBC television airs *The Ballad of Satchel Paige*, also known as *Destination Freedom*.

In his autobiography, Bill Veeck notes the hostility of what he describes as baseball's "Old Guard" to his stunts. He writes: "The others, like Clark Griffith, looked upon my little entertainments as a disgrace to the game and insult to their persons – although I never noticed any of them, Mr. Griffith in particular, looking quite that insulted when I handed them their share of the receipts."

CULTURE

***It Happens Every Spring*, by Valentine Davies, is published. *Strike Three!*, by Clair Bee, also appears. It is the first of the Chip Hilton books to focus on baseball.**

RULES

In December, the Major League Rules Committee redesigns the strike zone for 1950, making it smaller. A strike is now defined as a ball over the plate between the batter's armpits and the top of his knees.

SEPTEMBER 19:

The Pirates' Ralph Kiner homers against the Giants' Kirby Higbe at Forbes Field. It is Kiner's 50th of the season, and he becomes the first NL player to reach that level two times. The Giants win the game, 6-4, thanks to Dave Williams's two-run homer in the 10th. Sheldon "Available" Jones gets the win; Harry Gumbert is the losing pitcher.

SEPTEMBER 25:

Mel Parnell wins his 25th game of the season and the Red Sox beat the Yankees, 4-1, to move into a tie with New York for first place. On July 4, the Yankees were ahead by 12 games.

SEPTEMBER 25:

Charlie Lupica has been on a platform 20 feet above ground level since May 31 and the Indians still are not in first place. Owner Bill Veeck, who had Lupica's flagpole moved to Municipal Stadium, convinces him that fourth place is close enough. He schedules ceremonies at the ballpark and Lupica returns to terra firma.

Veeck also holds a "funeral service" for the 1948 pennant. The flag is removed from the pole and transported in a horse-drawn hearse, taken to center field and buried in a pine coffin.

SEPTEMBER 26:

The Boston Red Sox take over first place with a 7-6 victory over the Yankees; Bobby Doerr squeeze bunts Johnny Pesky home from third in the eighth inning with what proves to be the winning run.

SEPTEMBER 27:

Mike Schmidt is born in Dayton, Ohio.

SEPTEMBER 30:

Ralph Kiner clears the scoreboard clock in left field at Forbes Field for his 54th homer of the season. It also is Kiner's 16th of the month. The Pirates beat the Reds, 3-2.

OCTOBER 1:

On Joe DiMaggio Day at Yankee Stadium, 69,551 salute the Yankee Clipper – who is back from a bout with pneumonia – prior to a critical game with the first-place Boston Red Sox. DiMaggio donates all his gifts to charity and tells the fans, "I'd like to thank the Good Lord for making me a Yankee." With the Yankees needing two wins for the pennant, Allie Reynolds opposes Boston's Mel Parnell. The Yankees fall behind, 4-0, in the third inning. In the fourth, DiMaggio hits a double as the Yankees draw closer. In the fifth, DiMaggio hits a key single. In the eighth inning, Johnny Lindell hits a home run into the lower left-field stands to give the Yankees a 5-4 lead. Joe Page completes six and two-thirds innings of one-hit relief pitching and Boston and New York are again tied for first place.

OCTOBER 1:

Outfielder Sam Jethroe is acquired by the Braves from the Dodgers' Montreal Royals farm team.

OCTOBER 2:

The pennant is on the line, and 70,000 fans turn out at Yankee Stadium to see the game that will decide it. Vic Raschi starts for New York against Ellis Kinder. The Yankees score in the first inning on Phil Rizzuto's triple and Tommy Henrich's grounder. A solo homer by Henrich and a three-run triple by Jerry Coleman give the Yankees a five-run lead. The Red Sox fight back in the ninth, scoring three runs. After a Bobby Doerr triple, an exhausted Joe DiMaggio leaves the game. Berra goes to the mound to confer with his pitcher and is told by the irascible Raschi, "Give me the ball and get out of here." Raschi then gets Birdie Tebbetts out on a foul pop to Henrich, and the pennant will fly again over Yankee Stadium. Coach Bill Dickey is so excited, he KO's himself hitting his head on the dugout roof. Ted Williams loses a batting title and a shot at an unprecedented third Triple Crown. Williams is hitless in two official at-bats while the Tigers' George Kell has two hits in three plate appearances. Kell finishes the season with an average of .3429 – compared to Williams's .34275 – and wins the AL batting title.

The Dodgers beat the Phillies, 9–7, in 10 innings at Shibe Park on the last day of the season to clinch the NL pennant by just one game over the Cardinals. The Dodgers win when Harold "Pee Wee" Reese scores on a single by Edwin "Duke" Snider, who is driven in by a Luis Olmo single. The winning

SEPTEMBER 19
With today's home run, Ralph Kiner becomes the first NLer to reach 50 two times.

OCTOBER 2
The Yankees and Dodgers clinch their respective pennants and will meet in the Series.

pitcher is Jack Banta in relief of Don Newcombe and Rex Barney. Ken Heintzelman is the losing pitcher.

On the last day of the season, the St. Louis Browns provide plenty of work for their pitching staff. In the opener of a doubleheader, they use a different pitcher every inning against the White Sox, trotting out Ned Garver, Joe Ostrowski, Cliff Fannin, Tom Ferrick, Karl Drews, Bill Kennedy, Al Papai, Charles "Red" Embree, and Dick Starr. It doesn't help the seventh-place Browns; they lose to Chicago, 4-3. Kennedy gets the loss. In the nightcap, they go with one pitcher, 20-year-old Eddie Albrecht, called up from Pine Bluff in the Class C Cotton State League, where he won 29 games. Albrecht one-hits Chicago for five innings, walking four and fanning one. The game is called because of darkness after the fifth and Albrecht gets a 5-3 win. Albrecht pitches in one other game – in 1950 – losing it and ending his brief career at 1-1.

REGULAR SEASON WRAP-UP:

The Dodgers and Yankees approach the series after razor-thin pennant victories and with identical 97-57 records. Casey Stengel, in his first year as the Yankees' manager, finishes one game ahead of the Red Sox. An injury-riddled Joe DiMaggio hits .346 in only 76 games. No other regular hits .300. Vic Raschi is the top pitcher at 21-10, and Joe Page has a league-leading 27 saves.

The Dodgers, managed by Burt Shotton, beat the Cardinals by a single game. Jackie Robinson leads the NL with a .342 average, with 16 homers and 124 RBI. Carl Furillo bats .322 with 18 homers and 106 RBI. Gil Hodges knocks in 115 runs. The team has no 20-game winners; Don Newcombe is 17-8.

OCTOBER 5:

World Series, game one. After a one-year hiatus, New York City has another Subway Series. The opener at Yankee Stadium is a pitching classic, with the Yankees' Allie Reynolds and the Dodgers' Don Newcombe matching zeroes for eight innings. In the bottom of the ninth, Tommy Henrich leads off with a homer on a 2-0 count to win the game. It is only the fifth hit allowed by Newcombe, who strikes out 11 Yankees. Reynolds gives up only two hits, along with two walks, and strikes out nine.

OCTOBER 6:

World Series, game two. For the second consecutive game at Yankee Stadium, the pitchers dominate. Elwin "Preacher" Roe outduels Vic Raschi and the Dodgers win, 1-0. In the second inning, Gil Hodges singles in Jackie Robinson with the game's only run. Roe gives up six hits.

OCTOBER 7:

World Series, game three. At Ebbets Field, the Yankees overcome three Dodgers' home runs – by Harold "Pee Wee" Reese, Luis Olmo, and Roy Campanella – for a 4-3 win. Johnny Mize's pinch-hit single drives in two Yankees' runs in a three-run ninth. Joe Page gets the victory in relief of Tommy Byrne. Starter Ralph Branca is charged with the loss.

OCTOBER 8:

World Series, game four. Allie Reynolds is perfect, retiring the 10 batters he faces in relief of Eddie Lopat, and the Yankees top the Dodgers, 6-4, at Ebbets Field. Don Newcombe gets his second loss of the Series, and now the Yankees are one victory away from another World Championship.

After a district court judge rules there is no cause for compulsory reinstatement for three Mexican League jumpers, Danny Gardella reaches an out-of-court settlement with baseball commissioner Happy Chandler. His suspension is rescinded and he receives a cash settlement, which he splits with his attorney Frederic Augustus Johnson.

The 27-year-old Danny Gardella is sold to the St. Louis Cardinals by the Giants; he plays only one game with the Cardinals in 1950, going hitless in one at-bat. His co-plaintiff, Max Lanier, had returned to the Cardinals during the season and is 5-4 in 15 games. Lanier pitches four more seasons. The third party to the suit, pitcher Fred Martin, also returned to St. Louis during 1949 and was 6-0 in 21 games. He completes his career with a 4-2 season in 1950.

OCTOBER 9:

World Series, game five. The Yankees break in front early today and withstand a

TRIVIA

Johnny Mize is the first cousin of Claire Hodgson Ruth, the Babe's second wife.

HISTORY

Left-hander Lou Brissie wins 16 games for the Athletics, following 14 wins last season. Brissie suffered severe shrapnel wounds in combat in Italy in 1944, and when he plays, he wears specially constructed gear to protect his left leg, which has exposed bone and nerves.

TRIVIA

During game five, lights are turned on for the first time during a World Series game.

OCTOBER 9
The Yankees win the latest Subway Series with a 10-6 win over the Dodgers.

NOVEMBER 21
Bill Veeck sells the Cleveland Indians to a syndicate for $2.2 million.

four-run Dodger seventh at Ebbetts Field to win the game, 10-6, and the World Series. Joe DiMaggio hits a solo home run for the Yankees, while Jerry Coleman drives in three runs. Gil Hodges has a three-run shot for Brooklyn. Vic Raschi gets the win, with a save by Joe Page. Dodgers' starter Rex Barney gets the loss. Allie Reynolds finishes with no earned runs and 14 strikeouts in 12 1/3 innings. Yankees' third baseman Bobby Brown leads all hitters with a .500 average and five RBI. Pee Wee Reese hits .316. Joe DiMaggio has a home run and single in 18 at bats.

Warren Spahn led the NL in wins in 1949, with 21.

POST-SEASON

OCTOBER 19:

The White Sox acquire second baseman Jacob "Nellie" Fox (.255 in 88 games) from the Athletics for catcher Joe Tipton (.204, three home runs in 67 games).

NOVEMBER 21:

Bill Veeck sells the Indians for $2.2 million to a syndicate headed by insurance executive Ellis Ryan.

DECEMBER 13:

The St. Louis Browns again get a bundle of cash while completing a four-for-two player trade with the Philadelphia Athletics. Going to Philadelphia in the deal are third baseman Bob Dillinger (.324) and outfielder Paul Lehner (.229, three home runs). In return, the Browns receive $100,000 in cash, along with third baseman Frank Gustine (.226 with the Chicago Cubs), infielder Billy DeMars, outfielder Ray Coleman, and minor league outfielder Ray Ippolitto. Niether DeMars nor Coleman appeared in the majors leagues in 1949.

DECEMBER 14:

The Giants get a double-play combination from the Braves in return for four players. Coming to New York are shortstop Alvin Dark (.276, three homers) and second baseman Eddie Stanky (.285, one home run). Heading for Boston are outfielder-infielder Sid Gordon (.284, 26 homers, 90 RBI), outfielder Williard Marshall (.307, 12 homers), shortstop John "Buddy" Kerr (.209), and pitcher Samuel "Red" Webb (1-1, 4.03 ERA).

DECEMBER 24:

Pitching great Grover Cleveland Alexander, a Hall of Fame inductee in 1938 and the winner of 373 games during his 20-year career in the major leagues – from 1911 to 1930 – is found unconscious in an alley in Hollywood, California. He is suffering from alcoholism and epilepsy and is missing an ear. He will survive the incident and live for nearly another year.

THE BEST OF 1949

NATIONAL LEAGUE

HITTERS

Batting Average:
Jackie Robinson, Brooklyn Dodgers, .342

Slugging Average:
Ralph Kiner, Pittsburgh Pirates, .658

Home Runs:
Ralph Kiner, 54

Runs Batted In:
Ralph Kiner, 127

Hits:
Stan Musial, St. Louis Cardinals, 207

Stolen Bases:
Jackie Robinson, 37

PITCHERS

Wins:
Warren Spahn, Boston Braves, 21

Strikeouts:
Warren Spahn, 151

Earned Run Average:
Dave Koslo, New York Giants, 2.50

Winning Percentage:
Preacher Roe, Brooklyn Dodgers, .714

Saves:
Ted Wilks, St. Louis Cardinals, 9

Most Valuable Player:
Jackie Robinson, Brooklyn Dodgers

Rookie of the Year:
Don Newcombe, Brooklyn Dodgers

AMERICAN LEAGUE

HITTERS

Batting Average:
George Kell, Detroit Tigers, .343

Slugging Average:
Ted Williams, Boston Red Sox, .650

Home Runs:
Ted Williams, 43

Runs Batted In:
Ted Williams; Vern Stephens, Boston Red Sox, 159

Hits:
Dale Mitchell, Cleveland Indians, 203

Stolen Bases:
Bob Dillinger, St. Louis Browns, 20

PITCHERS

Wins:
Mel Parnell, Boston Red Sox, 25

Strikeouts:
Virgil "Fire" Trucks, Detroit Tigers, 153

Earned Run Average:
Mel Parnell, 2.77

Winning Percentage:
Ellis Kinder, Boston Red Sox, .793

Saves:
Joe Page, New York Yankees, 27

Most Valuable Player:
Ted Williams, Boston Red Sox

Rookie of the Year:
Roy Sievers, St. Louis Browns

TRIVIA

Ted Williams and Willie Mays in the same outfield? The Red Sox have the opportunity to buy Mays's contract from the Birmingham Black Barons for $5,000. They pass. Mays and Mantle in the same outfield? The Yankees also miss their chance. According to *The Biographical History of Baseball*, they send traveling secretary Bill McCorry to look at Mays, and he contradicts the report of scout Joe Press by claiming Mays can't hit a curve. Years later, McCorry reportedly told John Drebinger of the *New York Times*: "I got no use for him or any of them. I wouldn't arrange a berth on the train for any of them."

1950

"Attendance did not warrant our continuance of a Newark club."
– Yankees' GM George Weiss

NEWS

NORTH KOREA INVADES SOUTH KOREA

TRUMAN ORDERS U.S. TROOPS TO KOREA; DOUGLAS MACARTHUR COMMANDS UN FORCES

JOSEPH STALIN DIES

U.S. population tops 150 million

ALGER HISS GUILTY OF PERJURY

CBS GETS LICENSE TO BROADCAST COLOR TV

Television viewers watch The Gene Autry Show, The George Burns and Gracie Allen Show, Beat the Clock, Your Hit Parade, You Bet Your Life, The Jack Benny Show, What's My Line

CHARLES SCHULZ'S PEANUTS COMIC STRIP PREMIERES

PRE-SEASON

JANUARY 12:

The Newark Bears, once the crown jewel of the Yankees' farm system, are sold to the Chicago Cubs, who will move the team to Springfield, Massachusetts. The Yankees had owned the Bears since 1932. The team finished last in the International League in 1949. Yankees' general manager George Weiss explains: "Attendance did not warrant our continuance of a Newark club...."

JANUARY 31:

The Pirates sign high school pitcher Paul Pettit for a $100,000 bonus – the largest ever. Even before he inks his contract with Pittsburgh, the 18-year-old Pettit is signed to a $100,000 film deal by producer Frederick Stephani.

FEBRUARY 7:

Boston's Ted Williams becomes the highest-paid baseball player of all time when the Red Sox give him a new $125,000 contract.

FEBRUARY 11:

Hazen "Kiki" Cuyler dies in Ann Arbor, Michigan, at age 50. A Red Sox coach, Cuyler played 18 years in the majors, hitting .321. His best season was 1929 when he batted .360 for the Cubs. Cuyler was an outstanding outfielder and base runner.

APRIL 1:

The Hollywood Stars of the Pacific Coast League appear in a new style uniform today for their game with the Portland Beavers. They wear T-shirt uniform tops and striped shorts, which manager Fred Haney says will be cooler and help his team to run faster. He doesn't mention what it will be like to slide.

According to historian David Quentin Voigt, Branch Rickey also tries to introduce shorts, but doesn't get very far.

THE SEASON

APRIL 18:

Sam Jethroe becomes the first black player to wear a Boston Braves' uniform when he debuts against the Giants today at the Polo Grounds. Jethroe has two hits – including a homer – in four at-bats, scores twice, and bats in two runs. The Braves win, 11-4. Jethroe spent seven years with the Cleveland Buckeyes in the Negro League, batting .340.

In the first night opener in St. Louis, the Cardinals beat the Pirates, 4-2, on pitcher Gerry Staley's six-hitter. Stan Musial and Albert "Red" Schoendienst homer.

Scrawny Yankees' rookie Alfred "Billy" Martin makes his debut and sets a record. At Fenway Park, the second baseman is the first major leaguer with two hits in an inning in his first game. Martin doubles then singles in the eighth as the Yankees come from nine runs down, scoring nine times in the frame against a record five different pitchers. Joe DiMaggio has a single, double, and triple as the Yankees beat Boston, 15-10.

APRIL 23:

At Braves Field, for the first time a game begun in daylight is finished under the lights. But the home team is the loser, as the Phillies beat the Braves, 6-5, in the second game of a doubleheader.

MAY 6:

The Braves beat the Reds, 15-11, on home runs by Luis Olmo, Earl Torgeson, Bob

APRIL 18
In his ML debut, the Yankees' Billy Martin sets a record with two hits in an inning.

MAY 9
Ralph Kiner hits his second grand slam in four days and drives in seven runs.

Elliott, Willard Marshall, and Sid Gordon. The Braves now have 13 home runs in three games, breaking a record set by the 1947 Giants; Gordon and Marshall were members of that team.

MAY 9:

Ralph Kiner of the Pirates hits a grand slam home run and drives in seven runs in a 10-5 victory over the Dodgers. It is Kiner's second grand slam in the last four days, the first one coming on May 6.

MAY 11:

After making errors in both games of a doubleheader, Ted Williams is booed by Fenway Park fans. He responds with what is described as an "insulting gesture."

MAY 13:

The Red Sox release Lorenzo "Piper" Davis, their first black minor leaguer. Davis, who hit .378 last year with the Birmingham Black Barons, was playing for Boston's Scranton farm team in the Class A Eastern League and is the club's leading hitter. The Red Sox paid $7,500 for Davis's contract; if they kept him until May 15 they would be required to pay an additional $7,500 in cash to Birmingham. That is the ostensible reason given for his release. The team doesn't provide Davis with a train ticket to return to Alabama.

MAY 14:

Yankees' rookie Billy Martin is farmed out to the Kansas City Blues but not before he has an argument with general manager George Weiss about his demotion.

MAY 18:

It must be the glove. Cardinals' third baseman Tom Glaviano has a game at Ebbets Field that will live on in his nightmares. In the ninth inning, with St. Louis leading Brooklyn, 8-5 – after a four-run Dodgers' rally in the eighth – Campanella hits a bases-loaded grounder to Glaviano, who throws wide to second, allowing a run to score. Eddie Miksis grounds to Glaviano; he throws wildly to the plate and another run scores, leaving the bases full and the score, 8-7. Pee Wee Reese's grounder goes through Glaviano's legs and the tying and winning runs score. Glaviano's math: three errors equal four runs plus one loss, 9-8.

At the Polo Grounds, history is made when opposing teams hit grand slam homers in the same inning. In the top of the sixth, Cubs' catcher Albert "Rube" Walker hits a grand slam. In the Giants' half of the inning, Monte Irvin answers with one of his own. Rain curtails the game after six innings; the Giants win the game, 10-4.

JUNE 1:

The Boston Braves' Sid Gordon hits two homers – including a grand slam – and drives in seven runs in a 10-6 win over the visiting Pirates.

JUNE 6:

The Red Sox release 33-year-old third baseman Ken Keltner. He spent 12 seasons with the Indians and is best remembered for his fielding plays that helped end Joe DiMaggio's record hitting streak. Keltner was hitting .321 in 13 games for Boston.

JUNE 7:

The Red Sox beat the Browns, 20-4, at Fenway Park on 23 hits – including six homers and 42 total bases.

Alex Pompez, chief Caribbean scout for the Giants, recommends the team sign 23-year-old, right-handed pitcher Fidel Castro.

JUNE 8:

The Red Sox set a major league record for runs, bashing the Browns, 29-4, on 28 hits at Fenway Park. The magnitude of the beating is reflected in the statistics. Boston sets single-game records for most runs, most extra base hits (17), most total bases (60). They set a two-game record for most runs (49) and most hits (51). Ted Williams has two homers and five RBI; Walt Dropo hits two round-trippers and drives in seven; Bobby Doerr connects three times and has eight RBI. Winning pitcher Chuck Stobbs chips in with two hits. Cliff Fannin gets the loss.

The Browns fire hypnotist David Tracy, hired to break the "loser's syndrome." Under Dr. Tracy's spell the Browns yield 49 runs in two games with the Red Sox and are in last place.

JUNE 14:

At Ebbets Field, with the Dodgers leading, 19-12, the game is halted because of a curfew. The Pirates' 19-year-old first baseman Dale Coogan hits his first major

LEAGUE

The All-American Girls Professional Baseball League adds the Kalamazoo Lassies and loses the Muskegon Lassies for the 1950 season. There are no major rules changes. The Rockford Peaches, 67-44, win the league championship.

league home run, a three-run shot against Ralph Branca, in the first inning. The game will resume on August 1.

JUNE 20:

Joe DiMaggio collects his 1,999th career hit against Bob Lemon in Cleveland, batting in two runs. In the seventh inning, he gets number 2,000 – an RBI single – against Marino "Chick" Pieretti, who gives DiMaggio the ball. The Yankees win, 8-2.

JUNE 23:

The Yankees and Tigers combine for a major league record 11 home runs in a slugfest won by Detroit, 10-9, before a Briggs Stadium crowd of 51,400. Walter "Hoot" Evers wins the shootout with a ninth-inning inside-the-park homer, his second round-tripper of the game. Four Tigers homer in the fourth inning: pitcher Paul "Dizzy" Trout – with the bases loaded, Gerry Priddy, Vic Wertz, and Evers. For the Yankees, Hank Bauer hits two homers and Yogi Berra, Jerry Coleman, Joe DiMaggio, and Tommy Henrich hit one each.

Joe McCarthy resigns as manager of the Red Sox, who are at 31-28, and is replaced by Steve O'Neill. In his two years at the helm, the 63-year-old McCarthy led the Red Sox to two second-place finishes. He is retiring from baseball.

Indians' first baseman Luscious "Luke" Easter launches a 3-0 pitch from the Senators' Joe Haynes 477 feet into the upper deck of right field at Cleveland Stadium – the longest shot ever at the ballpark. The Indians win the game, 14-3.

JUNE 24:

Giants' catcher Wes Westrum, who has 11 career homers prior to this season, hits three today plus a triple in leading the Giants to a 12-2 win over the Reds.

JUNE 25:

The Pirates' Ralph Kiner hits for the cycle – including two homers – and drives in eight runs as Pittsburgh beats the Dodgers, 16-11.

JULY 1:

In Boston, Edward "Whitey" Ford, 6-3 with the Kansas City Blues, makes an inauspicious major league debut. He relieves Tommy Byrne and pitches four and two-thirds innings, giving up seven hits, six walks, and five earned runs. Tommy Byrne gets the loss in a 13-4 Boston win.

JULY 2:

In front of a home crowd of 78,187 at Cleveland Stadium, Bob Feller beats the Tigers, 5-3, for his 200th career win.

JULY 3:

Casey Stengel shuffles his lineup and Joe DiMaggio ends up at first base – the first and only time in his major league career he does not play the outfield. He handles 13 chances without an error, but is hitless in four at-bats. The Yankees lose, 7-2, to the Senators.

JULY 4:

The Braves' Sid Gordon hits a grand slam homer against the Phillies; it is his fourth of the season, tying him for the major league record. The Braves beat the Phillies, 12-9.

JULY 11:

At Comiskey Park, the NL wins the annual All-Star Game, 4-3, in 14 innings. But the game is overshadowed by Boston's Ted Williams's disastrous crash into the left-field wall in the first inning, breaking his left elbow. Larry Jansen pitches five innings, allowing one hit and fanning six; Ewell Blackwell gets the win. Albert "Red" Schoendienst wins the game with a 14th-inning homer after Ralph Kiner sends it into extra innings with a ninth-inning round-tripper. Ted Gray gets the loss.

JULY 12:

Following his injury in yesterday's All-Star Game, Ted Williams faces the possibility that his career may be over. His left elbow is shattered and he will undergo surgery tomorrow for the removal of bone chips and possibly his radius as well. If his radius is removed, Williams will be finished.

JULY 13:

The news is good for Ted Williams and for baseball. After some 75 minutes of surgery on his left elbow and the removal of seven bone chips, Williams may be able to return before the end of the season.

JULY 17:

Whitey Ford gets his first major league win, 4-3, over the Chicago White Sox

CULTURE

At the movies, *The Jackie Robinson Story* stars Jackie Robinson and Ruby Dee. *Kill the Umpire* stars William Bendix, Una Merkel, and William Frawley.

JULY 2
Cleveland pitcher Bob Feller gets his 200th career win with a 5-3 victory over the Tigers.

AUGUST 26
Roy Campanella hits three consecutive two-run homers against the Reds.

at Yankee Stadium, with relief help from Tom Ferrick.

JULY 25:

Philadelphia's Whiz Kids move into first place on the strength of double shutouts against the Cubs. In the opener, Emory "Bubba" Church whitewashes Chicago, 7-0. In game two, it's Robin Roberts, with a 1-0 victory.

JULY 27:

The Dodgers snap Musial's 30-game hit streak. Ironically, Musial is the only Cardinal hitless as St. Louis raps five Dodger pitchers in a 13-3 win.

Phillies outfielder Del Ennis drives in seven runs in two innings in a 13-3 win over the Cubs in Philadelphia. Ennis hits a bases-loaded double in the seventh inning and a grand slam homer in the eighth.

AUGUST 1:

Curt Simmons of the Phillies is the first major league player drafted for the Korean War. The 21-year-old left-hander has a 17-8 record with a 3.40 ERA when he leaves the team to report.

The Dodgers and Pirates resume their suspended game of June 14. Pittsburgh first baseman Dale Coogan, who homered in the first inning, is now playing for the Indianapolis Indians in the American Association. The Dodgers score two additional runs and win the game, 21-12.

At Braves Field, Vern Bickford no-hits the visiting Dodgers, 7-0. Bickford walks four and strikes out three in the majors' first no-hitter in nearly two years. The Braves play errorless ball behind him. Carl Erskine is the game's losing pitcher.

AUGUST 2:

In Cleveland, the AL's leading hitter, Larry Doby, hits three consecutive homers against the Senators. Bob Lemon pitches an 11-0, three-hitter for his ninth consecutive win and his 17th of the season. Joe Gordon also hits a home run.

AUGUST 26:

Maybe pitching around him would have helped the Reds. Brooklyn's catcher Roy Campanella hits three consecutive homers – each with Gil Hodges on base – against Reds' pitcher Ken Raffensberger in Cincinnati. The Dodgers win, 7-5.

AUGUST 31:

Dodgers' first baseman Gil Hodges ties a major league record with 17 total bases in a game. Hodges hits four home runs – the fourth 20th-century player to accomplish the feat – and a single, driving in nine runs at Ebbets Field. The Dodgers wallop the Braves, 19-3. Hodges hits a two-run homer off losing pitcher Warren Spahn in the second inning, another two-run shot off Norman Roy in the third, a third round-tripper with one on against Bob Hall in the sixth, and a three-run drive off Johnny Antonelli in the eighth. Carl Erskine gets the win. A crowd of 14,226 at Ebbetts Field witnesses Hodges's history-making game.

SEPTEMBER 5:

Curt Simmons ships out for Korea.

SEPTEMBER 6:

Don Newcombe's attempt to emulate Iron Man Joe

HISTORY

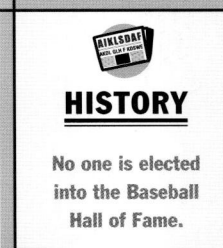

No one is elected into the Baseball Hall of Fame.

Robin Roberts won 20 games for the 1950 Phillies – the Whiz Kids.

SEPTEMBER 10
Joe DiMaggio hits three 400-foot-plus home runs in an 8-1 Yankees' win over the Senators.

CULTURE

***Behold, Thy Brother* by Murrell Edmunds is published. So is *The Sunlit Field* by Lucy Kennedy. Andy McCue speculates that this "may be the first baseball novel written by a woman for an adult audience."**

McGinnity by starting and winning both ends of a doubleheader comes up short. The Dodgers' right-hander three-hits the Phillies, 2-0, in the opener, but he fails to finish the nightcap. With Brooklyn trailing 2-0, Newcombe comes out for a pinch hitter in the seventh. The Dodgers score three runs in the ninth, and reliever Dan Bankhead gets the win.

SEPTEMBER 10:

Joe DiMaggio hits three 400-foot-plus homers against the Senators in an 8-1 Yankees' victory. DiMaggio becomes the first player to hit three home runs in Griffith Stadium.

SEPTEMBER 15:

Ted Williams returns to the Red Sox lineup for the first time since breaking his elbow on July 11 in the All-Star Game.

In Detroit, Johnny Mize hits three homers and drives in six runs in a 9-7 loss to the Tigers. It is the sixth three-homer game for Mize's career, a major league record.

SEPTEMBER 16:

At Briggs Stadium, Joe DiMaggio hits his 30th homer and

According to Daniel Okrent and Steve Wulf in their *Baseball Anecdotes*, after working in a flea circus, Grover Cleveland Alexander "got by on the handouts of friends. Foremost among the latter was Sam Breadon, the old owner of the Cardinals. The checks Alexander got came with National League of Professional Baseball Clubs imprinted... and Alexander thought it was an official pension. In fact, it was Breadon's money, passed through National League accounts so that the old pitcher wouldn't know it was charity."

Whitey Ford pitches the Yankees to an 8-1 victory, putting them back into first place by a half-game. The Yankees score seven runs in the ninth, giving Ford his seventh consecutive win without a loss.

SEPTEMBER 18:

At Ebbets Field, Ron Northey of the Cubs hits a pinch-hit grand slam homer against Dan Bankhead. It is the third of Northey's third career, setting a major league record. He previously pinch-hit grand slams in 1947 and 1948 for the Cardinals. The Cubs beat the Dodgers, 9-7.

SEPTEMBER 21:

In the first inning of the second game of a doubleheader against the Athletics, the Indians tie a modern major league record with 14 runs. Jim Hegan hits a grand slam homer and five Cleveland players score two or more runs, tying an American League record. The Indians win, 21-2. In the opener, Bob Feller pitched a two-hitter, beating Philadelphia, 7-0.

SEPTEMBER 25:

Yankees' rookie Whitey Ford beats Washington for his

OCTOBER 1
The "Whiz Kids" Phillies are going to the World Series after a win over the Dodgers.

ninth consecutive win since being called up to New York from the minor leagues.

SEPTEMBER 26:

In Boston, Jim Konstanty of the Phillies comes out of the bullpen for his 71st pitching appearance of the year – a major league record. The Phillies beat the Braves, 8-7.

SEPTEMBER 27:

In Philadelphia, Whitey Ford relieves and loses for the first time, 8-7, breaking his nine-game winning streak.

SEPTEMBER 29:

While the Yankees and Red Sox are rained out in Boston, Cleveland beats the Tigers, assuring New York of its second straight pennant.

OCTOBER 1:

With a one-game lead going into the last game of the season, the first-place Phillies face the second-place Dodgers at Ebbets Field. Each team sends its ace pitcher to the mound: It's Robin Roberts for Philadelphia and Don Newcombe for Brooklyn. A home run by Pee Wee Reese in the sixth inning ties the score and the Dodgers lose a chance to end the game when center fielder Richie Ashburn guns down Cal Abrams trying to score on a single hit by Duke Snider. In the top of the ninth Dick Sisler hits a Newcombe pitch for a three-run homer. Roberts retires the Dodgers in the bottom of the 10th, getting the final batter, pinch hitter Tommy Brown, on a pop-up to first baseman Eddie Waitkus. The Phillies win the pennant and Roberts – on his seventh try – gets his 20th win, a five-hitter.

White Sox shortstop Luke Appling, completing 20 years in the majors, gets his 2,749th and final career hit. His teammate, outfielder Gus Zernial, hits four homers in today's doubleheader.

REGULAR SEASON WRAP-UP:

Casey Stengel leads the Yankees to their second pennant in two years, with a record of 98-56, two games over the Tigers. The team has four .300 hitters – Phil Rizzuto (.324), Yogi Berra (.322, 28 homers, 124 RBI), Hank Bauer (.320), and Joe DiMaggio (.301, 32 homers, 122 RBI). Vic Raschi (21-8) is the ace of the staff. Rookie Whitey Ford, recalled from the minors in late season, wins nine of his first 10 decisions and compiles a 2.81 ERA.

Philadelphia's Whiz Kids, managed by Eddie Sawyer, finish two games ahead of the Dodgers at 91-63. Del Ennis is the big gun with a .311 average, 31 homers, and 126 RBI. Richie Ashburn bats .303. Robin Roberts paces the pitchers with a 20-11 record. Jim Konstanty, in 74 relief appearances, is 16-7 with 22 saves. Eddie Waitkus returns to baseball after being shot last year by a deranged fan; he plays in all 154 games, batting .284 and earning the league's Comeback Player of the Year Award.

OCTOBER 4:

World Series, game one. Philadelphia's Whiz Kids have a surprise starter for the Yankees at Shibe Park. They send their 33-year-old bespectacled relief pitcher, Jim Konstanty to the mound to oppose the Yankees' Vic Raschi. It is Konstanty's first start since 1948; since then he's appeared in 133 games in relief. He holds the Yankees to five hits, but Raschi is more effective with a two-hitter. Bobby Brown doubles in the fourth inning, moves to third on a Hank Bauer fly, and scores on Jerry Coleman's fly ball. The Yankees win the game, 1-0.

OCTOBER 5:

World Series, game two. In yet another pitching gem in Philadelphia, Allie Reynolds allows the Phillies 10 hits, beating Robin Roberts, 2-1, in 10 innings on a Joe DiMaggio home run.

OCTOBER 6:

World Series, game three. The Phillies continue to play just well enough to lose. At Yankee Stadium for the first time, Philadelphia drops another one-run game. Jerry Coleman singles in Gene Woodling in the bottom of the ninth to beat the Phillies and Russ Meyer, 3-2. Tom Ferrick gets the win in relief of starter Eddie Lopat. A Granny Hamner error with the bases loaded and two out in the eighth inning enabled the Yankees to tie the game.

OCTOBER 7:

World Series, game four. Rookie hurler Whitey Ford holds the Phillies to seven hits and Allie Reynolds

HISTORY

Would they do it now? Billy Goodman, a player without a position for the Red Sox, is in contention for the AL batting title. He has been filling in for injured left fielder Ted Williams, but with the return of the Splendid Splinter, manager Steve O'Neill is looking for a place to play Goodman. Third baseman Johnny Pesky volunteers to sit out for Goodman when Williams returns. Goodman beats out George Kell with a .354 average, becoming the first to win a batting title without being a regular position player.

> "I'm not quitting because I'm too old. I'm quitting because I think people want me to."
> – *Connie Mack, upon his retirement*

gets the final out, as the Yankees win, 5-2, to sweep the series. Bob Miller gets the loss. The Yankees – with a Yogi Berra homer and a Bobby Brown triple – score three runs in the fifth. Philadelphia rallies for two in the ninth, but Reynolds then strikes out Stan Lopata to end the game and the Series. Jerry Coleman, who hits .286, gets the Babe Ruth Award as the series' Most Valuable Player. Gene Woodling of the Yankees and Granny Hamner share hitting honors at .429. The Phillies pitching staff allows 2.27 earned runs; the Yankees are better at an intimidating 0.73.

HISTORY

The Negro American League, now divided into an Eastern and Western Division, has no playoffs this season. The Indianapolis Clowns win the Eastern Division first half and the New York Cubans lead the second half standings. In the Western Division, the Kansas City Monarchs take both halves.

POST-SEASON

OCTOBER 18:

The Grand Old Man of Baseball, Connie Mack, retires after 67 years in baseball – 50 as owner-manager of the Philadelphia Athletics. The 87-year-old Mack will retain the title of team president, but day-to-day business will be handled by general manager Arthur Ehlers. Jimmy Dykes will take over as manager. Mack, who managed wearing a business suit, led the A's to nine pennants and five World Series championships, but his teams also finished last 17 times. He was one of the "pioneer" members of the Hall of Fame, being inducted in 1937. In his last game at the helm, October 1, the Athletics lost, 5-3, to the Senators at Shibe Park. Mack says: "I'm not quitting because I'm too old. I'm quitting because I think people want me to."

OCTOBER 26:

The battle between Walter O'Malley and Branch Rickey for control of the Broolyn Dodgers ends today. Rickey resigns and sells up to 25% of his holdings in the club to the 47-year-old O'Malley, the former team attorney. The price is estimated at $1.5 million.

NOVEMBER 1:

Lucius "Luke" Appling hangs up his spikes after 20 years at shortstop for the White Sox. Appling leaves with a lifetime average of .310, with a high of .388 in 1936. Old Aches and Pains will manage Chicago's minor league team in Memphis next season.

NOVEMBER 4:

Hall of Fame pitcher Grover Cleveland Alexander dies at age 63 in St. Paul, Nebraska. According to writer Nathan Salant: "The coroner's report is rumored to have read, in part: 'Based on the condition of this man's liver, he has been dead for 10 years.'" Alexander, the third winningest pitcher ever, with 373, was inducted into the Hall of Fame in 1938. In his 20-year career, he compiled a 2.56 ERA and pitched 90 shutouts. He was the star of the 1926 World Series, pitching for the Cardinals.

NOVEMBER 10:

Former major league catcher Al Lopez is named manager of the Indians, replacing Lou Boudreau.

NOVEMBER 27:

The Red Sox sign 33-year-old shortstop Lou Boudreau (.269, one homer in 81 games). Boudreau has been released by the Indians at his own request after 13 years.

DECEMBER 11:

The major league owners, in a surprise move, will not renew the contract of their second commissioner, A.B. Happy Chandler. Chandler's current pact expires on April 30, 1952, and expectations were that it would be renewed. Yet fearing that he would not be reelected, Chandler calls for a vote of confidence before the owners' annual winter meetings. The commissioner needs 12 votes to be retained; Chandler receives only nine for, seven against, which is three short of the mandatory three quarters. He will end up resigning and accepting a year's pay as severance. Thirty-two years later, he will be elected to the Baseball Hall of Fame in Cooperstown. Among his opponents are representatives of the Cardinals, the Phillies, the Yankees, and the Cubs.

DECEMBER 26:

Baseball's lame duck commissioner A.B. Happy Chandler announces that the Gillette Safety Razor Co. will pay $6 million over six years for the television rights to broadcast the annual All-Star Game. Gillette previously had purchased the radio rights for the game through 1956 for $1.37 million. A large portion of the proceeds will be contributed to the baseball players' pension fund.

THE BEST OF 1950

NATIONAL LEAGUE

HITTERS

Batting Average:
Stan Musial, St. Louis Cardinals, .346

Slugging Average:
Stan Musial, .596

Home Runs:
Ralph Kiner, Pittsburgh Pirates, 47

Runs Batted In:
Del Ennis, Philadelphia Phillies, 126

Hits:
Duke Snider, Brooklyn Dodgers, 199

Stolen Bases:
Sam Jethroe, Boston Braves, 35

PITCHERS

Wins:
Warren Spahn, Boston Braves, 21

Strikeouts:
Warren Spahn, 191

Earned Run Average:
Jim Hearn, St. Louis Cardinals/New York Giants, 2.49

Winning Percentage:
Sal Maglie, New York Giants, .818

Saves:
Jim Konstanty, Philadelphia Phillies, 22

Most Valuable Player:
Jim Konstanty, Philadelphia Phillies

Rookie of the Year:
Sam Jethroe, Boston Braves

AMERICAN LEAGUE

HITTERS

Batting Average:
Billy Goodman, Boston Red Sox, .354

Slugging Average:
Joe DiMaggio, New York Yankees, .585

Home Runs:
Al Rosen, Cleveland Indians, 37

Runs Batted In:
Walt Dropo, Boston Red Sox;
Vern Stephens, Boston Red Sox, 144

Hits:
George Kell, Detroit Tigers, 218

Stolen Bases:
Dominic DiMaggio, Boston Red Sox, 15

PITCHERS

Wins:
Bob Lemon, Cleveland Indians, 23

Strikeouts:
Bob Lemon, 170

Earned Run Average:
Early Wynn, Cleveland Indians, 3.20

Winning Percentage:
Vic Raschi, New York Yankees, .724

Saves:
Mickey Harris, Washington Senators, 15

Most Valuable Player:
Phil Rizzuto, New York Yankees

Rookie of the Year:
Walt Dropo, Boston Red Sox

1951

NEWS

CHINESE RED ARMY ENTERS KOREAN CONFLICT

Truman fires MacArthur

22nd Amendment limits U.S. Presidents to two terms in office

KOREAN TRUCE TALKS BEGIN

MISSOURI RIVER FLOODS CAUSE $1 BILLION IN DAMAGES

CBS airs first commercial color telecast

STATE OF WAR WITH GERMANY OFFICIALLY ENDS

48 Nations Sign Peace Treaty with Japan

FIRST COMMERCIAL ELECTRONIC DIGITAL COMPUTER DEMONSTRATED

At the movies, A Streetcar Named Desire *stars Marlon Brando, Vivien Leigh, and Kim Hunter;* An American in Paris *stars Gene Kelly and Leslie Caron;* The African Queen *stars Humphrey Bogart and Katharine Hepburn*

PRE-SEASON

JANUARY 9:

Ted Williams will be recalled to active duty with the Marine Corps to serve in the Korean War. Williams missed the 1943, 1944, and 1945 baseball seasons serving in World War II.

FEBRUARY 25:

Negro Leagues pitching star "Smokey" Joe Williams dies in New York City at the age of 64. In 1914, with the American Giants, he was 41-3 and often struck out 20 batters in a game. According to author Robert Peterson: "His last manager, Cum Posey of the Grays, said only Walter Johnson and perhaps Lefty Grove and Satchel Paige, could match Williams's fastball."

For some years, Williams's date of death was erroneously reported as March 12, 1946. According to the Baseball Hall of Fame, a family member filled out a questionnaire and provided the wrong information.

MARCH 25:

Hall of Fame second baseman Eddie "Cocky" Collins dies at age 63 in Boston. Collins, one of the honest members of the Black Sox, played 25 years, hitting .333 with 3,313 hits and 743 stolen bases. He batted .328 in six World Series. Vice president of the Red Sox since 1933, Collins also managed the White Sox from 1924 to 1926.

MARCH 26:

Yankees' rookie Mickey Mantle, age 19, hits a home run estimated at 660 feet out of Bovard Stadium at the University of Southern California. The Yankees beat USC, 15-1, in an exhibition game. Mantle bats in seven runs and has four hits – including a pair of two-run homers and a bases-loaded triple – in five at-bats.

Among the USC players are pitcher Charley Ane, who becomes an outstanding professional football player with the Detroit Lions; future major leaguer Bob Lillis; and twin brothers Hal and Stan Charnofsky, who will become Yankees' farmhands.

APRIL 1:

The Indians acquire infielder George "Snuffy" Stirnweiss (.216) – the 1945 AL batting champion – and shortstop Merrill Combs (.245) from the St. Louis Browns for $35,000 and infielder Fred Marsh, who appeared in one major league game in 1949.

APRIL 14:

For the second time, the Selective Service System classifies Mickey Mantle 4-F because of osteomyelitis, a bone condition in his leg.

APRIL 15:

Mickey Mantle has a homer and three singles in an exhibition game against the Dodgers at Ebbets Field. He finishes spring training with a .402 average, nine homers and 31 RBI.

THE SEASON

APRIL 17:

At Yankee Stadium, Mickey Mantle makes his major league debut playing right field against the Red Sox. He singles in four at-bats as New York wins 5-0 behind Vic Raschi. His first chance in right field is a Walt Dropo fly ball.

APRIL 30:

The Indians, Athletics, and White Sox execute a seven-player, three-way trade. At the end of

MARCH 26
In an exhibition game, Yankees' rookie Mickey Mantle hits a homer estimated at 660-feet.

MAY 12
Flu-bitten Stan Musial manages a three-run, game-winning homer against the Red.

the day, pitcher Lou Brissie (0-2) is with Cleveland; outfielder Gus Zernial (.105 in four games), outfielder Dave Philley (.240 in seven games), pitcher Sam Zoldak (no appearances in 1951), and catcher Ray Murray (1.000 in one game) belong to the Athletics; outfielders Orestes "Minnie" Minoso (.429 in eight games) and Paul Lehner (.208 in 23 games) join the Chicago White Sox.

MAY 1:

At Comiskey Park, batting left-handed against Randy Gumpert, switch-hitting Mickey Mantle hits his first major league home run – a 450-foot drive. Minnie Minoso makes his White Sox debut, becoming the team's first black player, and homers against Vic Raschi. The Yankees win the game, 8-3.

MAY 3:

Gil McDougald, the less-celebrated of the Yankees' rookies, ties a major league record by driving in six runs in a single inning. Today at Sportsman's Park, McDougald hits a two-run triple and a grand slam homer during an 11-run ninth inning against the Browns. New York wins, 17-3.

GIANTS' ANNOUNCER RUSS HODGES CALLS BOBBY THOMSON'S HOME RUN: "BRANCA THROWS. THERE'S A LONG FLY. IT'S GONNA BE – I BELIEVE – THE GIANTS WIN THE PENNANT! THE GIANTS WIN THE PENNANT! THE GIANTS WIN THE PENNANT! BOBBY HIT THAT BALL INTO THE LOWER DECK OF THE LEFTFIELD STANDS. THE GIANTS WIN THE PENNANT AND THEY'RE GOING CRAZY. I DON'T BELIEVE IT, I DON'T BELIEVE IT, I WILL NOT BELIEVE IT!"
DODGERS' ANNOUNCER WALTER "RED" BARBER CALLS BOBBY THOMSON'S HOME RUN: "IT'S IN THERE FOR THE PENNANT."

MAY 6:

Despite walking eight batters, Pirates' pitcher Cliff Chambers no-hits the Braves, 3-0, in Boston. Chambers strikes out four; the Pirates make no errors. The losing pitcher is George Estock, who gives up eight hits. In game one of the doubleheader, Warren Spahn shuts out Pittsburgh, 6-0.

MAY 10:

The Indians sign Johnny Vander Meer (3-4, 3.79 ERA), the only pitcher with two consecutive no-hitters. They also send outfielder Allie Clark (.300 in three games) and infielder Lou Klein to the Athletics for outfielder Sam Chapman (.169). Chapman hit 23 homers last season; Klein was out of the majors in 1950.

MAY 12:

Even the flu can't stop Stan Musial. Weakened by illness, Musial returns to action in game two of a doubleheader in Cincinnati and hits a three-run homer in the eighth inning to lift the

HISTORY

Yankees' pitcher Whitey Ford is enlisted in the army for two years of service.

TRIVIA

Bill Sharman becomes the only player ever ejected without playing in a game. His future lies in another sport: He teams in the backcourt with Bob Cousy on the great Boston Celtics' teams from 1951 to 1961 and is elected to the Basketball Hall of Fame.

LEAGUE

The All-American Girls Professional Baseball League loses the Racine Belles. There are no major playing rules changes for the 1951 season. In a new format, the second half winners, the South Bend Blue Sox (38-14) beat the first half leaders, the Grand Rapids Chicks (40-13), for the league championship.

Cardinals to an 8-6 victory. The Reds won the opener, 7-2.

MAY 15:

At Fenway Park, Ted Williams homers against Howie Judson of the White Sox; it is the 300th of his career. Chicago beats Boston, 9-7.

MAY 16:

Mickey Mantle hits his first of many Yankee Stadium home runs. Mantle's blow comes off Dick Rozek of the Indians in the ninth with one on. The Yankees win, 11-3.

MAY 20:

Richie Ashburn has four hits in each end of today's doubleheader as his Phillies sweep the Pirates, 17-0 and 12-4, in Pittsburgh.

MAY 25:

Willie Mays – hitting .477, with eight homers and 30 RBI with the Minneapolis Milers in the American Association – joins the Giants in Philadelphia for a night game with the Phillies. Mays is fanned by Emory "Bubba" Church in his first at-bat, is hitless in five trips to the plate and makes three good plays in the field. New York wins the game, 8-5.

MAY 28:

After going hitless in his first twelve at-bats, Willie Mays hits a home run off Warren Spahn of the Braves at the Polo Grounds. Says Spahn, "For the first sixty feet it was a hell of a pitch."

MAY 30:

Yankees' phenom Mickey Mantle is struggling. He strikes out five consecutive times today in a doubleheader against the Red Sox and tells manager Casey Stengel, "Put somebody in there who can hit. I can't!" The Yankees lose both games, 11-10 and 9-4; Ted Williams hits his 15th homer of the year.

JUNE 4:

Today, after losing eleven straight and thirty of thirty six to left-hander Eddie Lopat, the Indians are ready to try anything. With the Yankees in Cleveland, the Indians declare Beat Eddie Lopat Night and distribute 15,000 rabbits' feet. They trot out a black cat and four live rabbits – presumably luckier than the ones who lost their feet. Something works: Cleveland scores five in the first inning – including a three-run homer by Bob Kennedy – to beat the Yankees, 8-2, and extend their current winning streak to nine games. It is their first win over Lopat since June 17, 1949.

JUNE 20:

Indians' second baseman Bobby Avila, with only one career homer prior to today's game against the Red Sox, hits three plus a double and a single. Cleveland beats Boston, 14-8, at Fenway Park.

JULY 1:

Bob Feller no-hits the Tigers, 2-1, fanning five and walking three; the Indians make two errors behind him. It is his third career no-hitter. The losing pitcher is Bob Cain. Luke Easter drives in both of the Cleveland runs. The Tigers spoil the shutout, but not the no-hitter, in the fourth inning when Johnny Lipon reaches first on an error by shortstop Ray Boone, steals second, and moves to third on a wild pickoff throw. He then scores on a fly ball. Feller becomes baseball's third pitcher with three no-hitters.
Red Sox second baseman Bobby Doerr singles against Ed Lopat of the Yankees for his 2,000th career hit.

JULY 3:

Bill Veeck completes the necessary acquisition of stock to assume ownership of the Browns from the DeWitt brothers.

Former Dodgers' pitcher Hugh Casey deliberately shoots himself to death with a shotgun at age 37 in Atlanta. He reportedly was depressed over marital problems. In his nine-year career, Casey was 75-41 with an ERA of 3.45. It was Casey's third-strike pitch in the 1941 World Series that got by catcher Arnold "Mickey" Owen, igniting a Yankees' rally and ending the Dodgers' chances of victory.

Adolfo "Dolf" Luque dies in Havana, Cuba, at age 66. Known as the Pride of Havana, he was one of the major league's first successful Cuban-born players. In 20 years, he was 193-179 with a 3.24 ERA. His best year was 1923 with the Reds, when he led the league in wins (27), ERA (1.93) and shutouts (six).

MAY 15
Ted Williams's home run – the 300th of his career – helps beat Chicago, 9-7.

JULY 10
In Detroit, the NL wins the All-Star Game, 8-3, on the strength of four home runs.

JULY 4:

"The Giants is dead," pronounces Dodgers' manager Charlie Dressen. "They'll never bother us again." Dressen's boast comes after Brooklyn sweeps a doubleheader, 6-5 and 4-2, to increase its first-place lead to six and a half games.

JULY 6:

Former Giants Willard Marshall and Walker Cooper homer for the Braves in the top of the third at the Polo Grounds. The Giants answer in the bottom of the inning with homers by Wes Westrum, Bobby Thomson, and Don Mueller and go on to win the game, 12-10.

JULY 9:

Harry Heilmann, a three-time AL batting champion and the radio broadcaster for the Tigers, dies in Southfield, Michigan, of lung cancer at age 56. In 17 years, the outfielder hit .342 with a high of .403 in 1923. He hit .393 or better in three other years.

JULY 10:

In Detroit, the NL wins the All-Star Game, 8-3, for its first back-to-back victories. Stan Musial, Bob Elliott, Ralph Kiner, and Gil Hodges homer for the NL; Vic Wertz and George Kell for the AL. Kiner becomes the first player to homer in three consecutive All-Star Games. Sal Maglie is the winning pitcher; Ed Lopat gets the loss.

JULY 12:

Yankees' right-hander Allie Reynolds no-hits the Indians, 1-0, in a Cleveland night game. Bob Feller, who pitched his own no-hitter 11 days ago, is the losing pitcher. A seventh-inning homer by Gene Woodling accounts for the game's only run. Reynolds fans four and walks three;

CULTURE

***The Big Out*, written by Arnold Hano, is published**

Bobby Thomson's "shot heard 'round the world."

Walter "Red" Smith comments during the 1951 season: "Rooting for the Yankees is like rooting for U.S. Steel."

TRIVIA

Bill Veeck, who brought 42-year-old Leroy "Satchel" Paige to the majors, offers a contract to another Negro League star, 48-year-old James "Cool Papa" Bell, to play for the Browns. Bell declines.

the Yankees make one error. Reynolds, a former Cleveland Indian, retires the last 17 batters in a row.

JULY 14:

The Red Sox and White Sox battle through 36 innings on two consecutive nights to earn a split. In last night's contest, Chicago won, 5-4, in 17 innings. Today the teams go 19 with Boston winning, 3-2. Maurice "Mickey" McDermott of the Red Sox pitches 17 innings but is not involved in the decision. Red Sox third baseman Vern Stephens has no putouts in 18 1/3 innings. The two contests are the longest AL night games.

JULY 15:

Budding superstar Mickey Mantle has not lived up to his press clippings and is sent to the Yankees' minor league team in Kansas City. Mantle has been fanned 52 times.

A.B. "Happy" Chandler completes his term as baseball commissioner after failing in 1950 to get sufficient support from the owners for a contract renewal. Chandler was elected on April 24, 1945. Sportswriter Walter "Red" Smith notes, "Happy left office for reasons of health; that is, the owners got sick of him."

JULY 18:

Ralph Kiner "moiders dem Bums." In the first inning at Ebbets Field, the Pirates' slugger hits a grand slam homer against Phil Haugstad. In the fourth inning, with Dan Bankhead on the mound, Kiner hits another with a runner on. In the eighth, with the score tied, 12-12, Kiner muscles an Erv Palica pitch for a solo homer. The Pirates win, 13-12.

JULY 21:

With the Cubs at 34-45, Frankie Frisch is out as manager. First baseman Phil Cavarretta replaces him.

JULY 23:

Two members of baseball's "500 home run club" – Jimmie Foxx and Mel Ott–are inducted into the Hall of Fame. Foxx, who played 20 years and batted .325, hit 534 homers with a slugging average of .609, and 1,921 RBI. Foxx's power is evidenced in three seasons: in 1932, he hit .364 with 58 homers and 151 RBI; in 1933, it was .356, 48, and 163; and in 1938, he batted .349 with 50 homers and 175 RBI. He played mostly at first base. Ott, an outfielder known as Master Melvin, debuted with the Giants at the age of 17. He spent his entire 22-year career with the team, totaling 511 homers. His lifetime average is .304 and he amassed 1,861 RBI, 1,859 runs, and 1,708 walks. He appeared in three World Series and managed the Giants from 1942 to 1948.

Vernon "Lefty" Gomez's description of Jimmie Foxx: "He has muscles in his hair."

JULY 26:

The Dodgers' Jim Russell becomes the first player to switch hit homers in a game twice in his career. Russell's first left-handed/right-handed homers were hit while he was with the Braves on June 7, 1948.

JULY 28:

Red Sox outfielder Clyde Vollmer hits a grand slam homer in the 16th inning to beat Bob Feller and the Indians, 8-4, at Fenway Park. Vollmer, in the middle of a torrid hitting streak, had tied the game in the 15th with an RBI single. On July 26, he hit three homers in one game, including the winning shot. In his last 24 games, Vollmer has 13 homers – including two grand slams and 30 hits. In his six major league seasons previously he has a total of 23 round-trippers.

JULY 30:

Even the greatest can have their lapses. In a game against the visiting Tigers, with George Kell on second base, Joe DiMaggio catches a fly ball hit by Steve Souchek. Thinking it is the third out, DiMaggio trots in from center field with the ball while Kell scores. But the Yankees win, 5-4.

JULY 31:

Clyde Vollmer doubles against the Browns in an 8-6 Red Sox loss. He finishes the month with 31 hits in 104 at bats (.298), 13 homers, four doubles, and a triple. Vollmer bats .251 in 1951 with career highs in homers (22) and RBI (85).

AUGUST 11:

The Dodgers beat Boston, 8-1, in the opener of a doubleheader, while the Giants are being shut out by the Phillies, 4-0. Brooklyn is in first place, 13 1/2 games ahead of New York.

JULY 15
Struggling rookie Mickey Mantle – 52 Ks – is sent down to the minors, in Kansas City.

AUGUST 15
Indians' slugger Al Rosen hits his fourth grand slam of the season.

The Dodgers have 49 games left to play; the Giants have 44.

AUGUST 13:

The Dodgers hold Musical Depreciation Night at Ebbets Field; everyone with a musical instrument is admitted free. Some 2,000 music makers – including one with a piano – turn up. The Dodgers drum out the Braves, 7-6.

AUGUST 15:

Al Rosen hits a grand slam homer as part of a huge seven-run Indians' first inning. It is Rosen's fourth grand slam of the year; he is the ninth player to accomplish the feat. Cleveland racks up its 13th consecutive win, 9-4.

In an early installment in his series of greatest catches ever made, with the score tied, 1-1, rookie Willie Mays runs down a 330-foot drive by Carl Furillo at the Polo Grounds, wheels, and throws out Billy Cox trying to score from third. The Giants win, 3-1. Dodgers' manager Charlie Dressen says, "When he does it again I'll believe it."

AUGUST 19:

Browns' owner Bill Veeck trots out a midget to pinch-hit in the first inning of the opener in today's doubleheader against the Tigers at Sportsman's Park. Before today's game, Veeck has a birthday cake wheeled onto the field. Public address announcer Bernie Ebert tells the 18,000 fans, "Ladies and gentlemen, as a special birthday present to our manager Zack Taylor, the management is presenting him with a brand-new Brownie." (Taylor's birthday actually is July 27.) Eddie Gaedel, three feet, seven inches tall and 65 pounds, pops out of the cake wearing turned up slippers. Most on hand think that is the end of the stunt, but Veeck isn't through. In the nightcap, the Browns start Frank Saucier in center field in place of regular Jim Delsing. When Saucier is due to bat in the first inning, Gaedel reports instead, wearing a Browns' uniform with 1/8 on the back. Umpire Ed Hurley yells, "Hey, what's going on here?" Manager Taylor shows him Gaedel's contract and the midget's name on the active list. Tiger catcher Bob Swift goes to the mound to confer with pitcher Bob Cain. Gaedel crouches at the plate, giving Cain a strike zone that Veeck has measured at one and a half inches. After two fastballs, Cain is laughing. He throws two more balls, Gaedel walks and is replaced by pinch runner Delsing. The Tigers win the game, 6-2.

AUGUST 20:

AL president Will Harridge negates Eddie Gaedel's contract with the Browns, stating, "I feel his participation in an American League championship game comes under the heading of conduct detrimental to baseball." Harridge orders Eddie Gaedel's at-bat stricken from the records and bars him from further play. Gaedel protests, "This is a conspiracy against the little people... Now that someone has finally taken a direct step to help us short guys, Harridge is ruining my baseball career."

Despite Will Harridge's ruling, Gaedel 45 years later still has a line in the authoritative Baseball Encyclopedia. *It reads: "Gaedel, Edward Carl BR TL 3'7" 065 pounds" and lists his one at-bat.*

AUGUST 21:

Baseball owners elect a new commissioner. He is Major General Emmett "Rosey"

BASEBALL SUPERSTITION IS THAT NO ONE TALKS ABOUT A NO-HITTER IN PROGRESS. ALLIE REYNOLDS SAYS: "I REALLY KNOCKED THESE GUYS OFF THE BENCH. I WALKED IN AT THE END OF THE SEVENTH, SAT NEXT TO ED LOPAT, AND SAID, 'HEY, PAL, DO YOU THINK I CAN PITCH A NO-HITTER?'"

LEAGUE

In July, Brooklyn Congressman Emanuel Cellar, chairman of the House Judicial Subcommittee on Monopolies, opens an investigation of major league baseball. However, authors Lee Lowenfish and Tony Lupien observe in retrospect, "It was evident that the committee had no desire to upset baseball's applecart."

> "Now that someone has finally taken a direct step to help us short guys, Harridge is ruining my baseball career.."
> – *Eddie Gaedel*

TRIVIA

In 1951, Topps introduces its first baseball cards – in five sets. The most popular have red and black backs and can be used to play a baseball game. Among the notables included are future Hall of Famers Richie Ashburn, Yogi Berra, Bob Feller, Monte Irvin, Ralph Kiner, Phil Rizzuto, Enos Slaughter, Duke Snider, and Warren Spahn.

O'Donnell. But President Harry S. Truman overrules the move because O'Donnell is needed in his present job – as commander of bombers in Korea.

AUGUST 24:

So, what to do for an encore? After sending midget Eddie Gaedel to bat five days ago, Bill Veeck finds the answer. He enlists 1,115 fans to "manage" his Browns in a ball game against the Athletics at Sportsman's Park. The rest of the paid attendance of 3,925 are spectators. Manager Zack Taylor is relegated to a box seat while fans vote yes or no via placards to determine how to position the infield, set lineups, and change pitchers. The fans bench catcher Matt Batts and insert Sherman Lollar and Hank Arft into the lineup. Lollar gets three hits, including the game-winning homer, in a 5-3 win. Arft knocks in two runs. After five of the first six Athletics batters hit safely against starter Ned Garver, the placard asks: SHALL WE WARM UP A NEW PITCHER? The fans say no; Garver settles down and then holds the Athletics to only two more hits. Despite the placards, the game takes only two hours and 11 minutes to complete.

Let's hope we meet again on September 24. Yankees' outfielder Gene Woodling hits a two-run home run against the Indians' Early Wynn. Woodling homered off Wynn on June 24 and again on July 24. The game also marks the return from the minors of Mickey Mantle, who is in right field in the Yankees' 2-0 victory.

AUGUST 28:

Howie Pollet's three-hitter ends the Giants' 16-game winning streak. The Pirates win, 2-0. During the 16 games – the longest streak in the NL since 1935 – the Giants cut into the Dodgers' lead, from 13 1/2 games to six. The Giants begin their winning streak on August 12.

AUGUST 30:

The Yankees acquire the Braves' one-time pitching mainstay Johnny Sain (5-13) in return for pitcher Lew Burdette (0-0) and $50,000.

SEPTEMBER 1:

The Giants' Don Mueller strokes three homers today against the Dodgers at the Polo Grounds, giving him five in two days.

Former NL umpire Bill Klem dies at the age of 77 in Miami.

SEPTEMBER 3:

Johnny Sain pays immediate dividends for the Yankees. In the opening game of a doubleheader in Philadelphia, Sain doubles and five-hits the Athletics, 3-1. The nightcap goes to the Athletics, 3-2.

SEPTEMBER 13:

For the first time since 1883, a team plays a doubleheader against two different opponents. In a day game, rescheduled because of rain yesterday, the Giants lose to the Cardinals, 6-4. They then lose again, 2-0, in the regularly scheduled night game with the Braves.

SEPTEMBER 14:

At Fenway Park, Bob Nieman of the Browns becomes the first ever to hit homers in his first two major league at-bats. Both homers come off the Red Sox Maurice "Mickey" McDermott with one runner on base. Nieman also has a bunt single in the ninth off Ellis Kinder. But homers by Boston's Walt Dropo, Ted Williams, and Dominic DiMaggio offset Nieman's efforts and the Red Sox win, 9-6.

The Yankees edge into first place by percentage points with a 5-1 win over the visiting Indians. Allie Reynolds allows five hits to beat Bob Feller. The Yankees turn the game around in the fifth when Mickey Mantle doubles, Yogi Berra is walked intentionally, and Joe DiMaggio legs out a triple.

SEPTEMBER 17:

In the bottom of the ninth inning, with the score tied 1-1, Joe DiMaggio on third base, and Phil Rizzuto at bat, Bob Lemon fires a high inside fastball. Rizzuto drops a perfect squeeze bunt, scoring DiMaggio, and the Yankees win, 2-1. Eddie Lopat gets his 20th win; Bob Lemon is charged with the loss.

From Baseball: The Biographical Encyclopedia*: "...Rizzuto did what he did best. He pulled off a masterful squeeze bunt to break a 1-1 tie in the ninth and bring home Joe DiMaggio with the winning run."*

SEPTEMBER 1
The Giants' Don Mueller's three home runs give him five in two days.

SEPTEMBER 30
Jackie Robinson's bat and glove are the difference in a 9-8 Dodgers win.

SEPTEMBER 19:

Outfielder Dino Restelli (.184), who looked like the second coming of Babe Ruth for several weeks last season, is sold by the Pittsburgh Pirates to the Senators for the waiver price. Restelli had 12 home runs in 72 games in 1950.

SEPTEMBER 20:

Ford Frick, NL president and former journalist, is elected to a seven-year term as baseball's third commissioner after more than 50 ballots at the Palmer House in Chicago. Frick wins when his rival for the job, Cincinnati general manager Warren Giles, withdraws. The 56-year-old Frick, who has been NL president since 1934, will earn $65,000 per year.

SEPTEMBER 27:

Warren C. Giles is elected president of the NL. The 56-year-old Giles succeeds the new Commissioner, Ford Frick.

At Braves Field, umpire Frank Dascoli ejects catcher Roy Campanella, pitcher Elwin "Preacher" Roe, and the Dodgers' bench in a dispute over a play at the plate. Among those thumbed is outfielder Bill Sharman, just called up from Fort Worth in the Texas League. The Braves win, 4-3, on the disputed run scored by Bob Addie.

SEPTEMBER 28:

Allie Reynolds's second no-hitter of the season defeats the Red Sox, 8-0, and clinches at least a tie for the AL pennant for the Yankees. Reynolds gets his no-hitter the hard way – he has to face Ted Williams twice in the ninth inning with two out. Williams hits a pop foul to the first base side of the infield, but catcher Yogi Berra drops the ball. Williams tells him, "You had your chance. You blew it." But Reynolds is equal to the task. He throws a hard fastball and Williams pops it up foul again. Berra waves off first baseman Joe Collins and this time he holds it for the final out. Reynolds fans nine and walks four. Collins and Gene Woodling homer for New York. Mel Parnell is the losing pitcher. The Yankees clinch the pennant with an 11-3 victory behind Vic Raschi in game two. The Yankees score seven runs in the second inning and later, Joe DiMaggio hits a three-run homer against Chuck Stobbs. It is the 361st career home run for the Yankee Clipper and his last in regular season play. The pennant is New York's 18th and Stengel's third in his first three years as the manager.

SEPTEMBER 30:

Jackie Robinson's heroics at bat and in the field keep the Dodgers alive and force a playoff for the NL pennant. At Shibe Park, the Dodgers rally from 5-1 and 8-5 deficits, scoring three runs in the eighth to send the game into extra innings. Robinson makes a diving catch in the 12th inning to prevent a Phillies' run and is knocked groggy. But he recovers to hit a Robin Roberts pitch into the upper center-field stands in the 14th, giving Brooklyn a 9-8 win. The Giants beat the Braves, 3-2, in Boston. Larry Jansen retires 22 Braves in a row and earns the win. The Giants and Dodgers end the regular season with 96-58 records and will meet in a three-game playoff.

Ned Garver of the last-place Browns beats the White Sox, 9-5, for his 20th win of the season.

OCTOBER 1:

At Ebbets Field, the Giants and Dodgers meet in game one of the NL playoff. Brooklyn wins the coin toss and elects to open at home. Bobby Thomson's two-run homer against Ralph Branca lifts the Giants to a 3-1 victory. Monte Irvin also homers. Jim Hearn gets the win.

OCTOBER 2:

Clem Labine shuts out the Giants at the Polo Grounds, 10-0, to even the playoffs. After the game, a reporter asks Giants' manager Leo Durocher what happened. Durocher responds, " Does anybody else have a bright question?"

OCTOBER 3:

David Mark Winfield is born in St. Paul, Minnesota.

At the Polo Grounds, the Giants' Sal Maglie and the Dodgers' Don Newcombe are the starters in the rubber game of the playoffs. The Dodgers take a 4-1 lead into the ninth inning. Alvin Dark and Don Mueller single back-to-back to open the home half of the ninth. Monte Irvin pops up to first baseman Gil Hodges. Lockman doubles in

CULTURE

At the movies, *Angels in the Outfield* stars Paul Douglas and Janet Leigh, with Joe DiMaggio and Ty Cobb in cameo roles. *Rhubarb*, the story of a cat who inherits a baseball team, is based in the 1946 novel. *The Brooklyn Loons* stars Ray Milland and Jan Sterling.

Leo Durocher goes to a three-man rotation – Sal Maglie, Larry Jansen, and Jim Hearn – for the pennant stretch drive. When asked who he will pitch tomorrow, Durocher responds: "I want to win today. Tomorrow? It might rain."

HISTORY

Red Sox outfielder Charlie Maxwell hits his first three career homers in 1951. All are against Cleveland Indians and all against future Hall of Famers: Bob Feller, Bob Lemon, and Satchel Paige. Maxwell finishes his career in 1964 with 148 career homers – 40 were hit on Sundays.

Dark; Mueller moves to third, injuring his ankle on the slide. After Mueller is removed on a stretcher, Clint Hartung enters the game as a pinch runner. With Bobby Thomson coming to bat and Willie Mays on deck, manager Charlie Dressen calls the bullpen, where he has Carl Erskine and Ralph Branca warming up. Bullpen coach Clyde Sukeforth tells him, "Take Ralph Branca. Erskine's wild." Dressen takes Branca. On a one-strike pitch, Bobby Thomson hits the "shot heard 'round the world," a home run into the left-field stands and the NL pennant.

The eloquent Walter "Red" Smith of the *New York Herald-Tribune* writes: "The art of fiction is dead. Reality has strangled invention. Only the utterly impossible, the inexpressibly fantastic, can ever be plausible again."

REGULAR SEASON WRAP-UP:

The Yankees at 98-56 beat the Indians by five games for Casey Stengel's third pennant in three years. No regular bats .300; Hank Bauer hits .296; Yogi Berra collects 27 homers and drives in 88 runs. Rookie Gil McDougald hits .306. The heralded Mickey Mantle finishes his season with a .267 average, 13 homers, and 65 RBI in 96 games. Eddie Lopat (21-9) and Vic Raschi (21-10) lead the pitching staff.

ACCORDING TO LEO DUROCHER'S BIOGRAPHER, GERALD ESKENAZI, WHEN MAYS LEARNS HE HAS BEEN CALLED UP TO THE GIANTS, HE SAYS, "I'M NOT COMING." DUROCHER ASKS HIM WHAT HE'S HITTING WITH MINNEAPOLIS, AND MAYS REPLIES, ".477." DUROCHER RESPONDS, "WELL, DO YOU THINK YOU CAN HIT TWO FIFTY FOR ME" MAYS REPORTS TO THE GIANTS.

The Giants, managed by Leo Durocher, are in the series with a 98-59 record. Monte Irvin bats .312 with 24 homers and 121 RBI. Alvin Dark finishes at .303 and playoff hero Bobby Thomson hits .293 with 32 homers and 101 RBI. Sal Maglie is 23-6, Larry Jansen, 23-11.

The Dodgers' pitcher Preacher Roe has the highest winning percentage ever for a 20-game winner – .880. The NL has seven 20-game winners, the AL six; the most in the majors in 31 years. Ned Garver wins 20 and loses 12 for the last-place Browns, who win only 52 games.

OCTOBER 4:

World Series, game one. The Yankees and Giants renew an old Subway Series rivalry. The Giants draw first blood with a Dave Koslo seven-hitter, winning at Yankee Stadium, 5-1. Alvin Dark hits a three-run homer; Monte Irvin

OCTOBER 16
The Yankees edge the Giants, 4-3, in game six to capture the World Championship.

DECEMBER 11
The Yankee Clipper – Joe DiMaggio – retires after 13 seasons with the Yankees.

has four hits and steals home. Allie Reynolds is the losing pitcher.

OCTOBER 5:

World Series, game two. Eddie Lopat baffles the Giants, allowing only five hits – three to Monte Irvin – in a 3-1 victory at Yankee Stadium. Joe Collins homers for the Yankees. Larry Jansen is the losing pitcher.

In the fifth inning of game two, Mickey Mantle suffers an injury that will have career-long consequences, tearing ligaments in his right knee when his spikes catch on a sprinkler in right center field of Yankee Stadium. Mantle is carried off the field and requires surgery.

OCTOBER 6:

World Series, game three. At the Polo Grounds, the Giants beat the Yankees, 6-2, with a five-run fifth-inning rally. Eddie Stanky sparks the rally when he steals second base, kicking the ball out of Phil Rizzuto's glove. Carroll "Whitey" Lockman hits a three-run homer in the frame. Gene Woodling homers for the Yankees. Jim Hearn gets the win; Vic Raschi is charged with the loss.

OCTOBER 8:

World Series, game four. The Series resumes after a rain-out yesterday. Allie Reynolds scatters eight hits in a 6-2 Yankees' victory at the Polo Grounds. The Yankees rap out 12 hits, including a two-run homer and a single by Joe DiMaggio, who drives in three runs. It is DiMaggio's eighth post-season homer. Sal Maglie is the loser.

Bill Veeck, whose father fired Rogers Hornsby as Cubs' manager in 1932, hires him to lead the Browns for the 1952 season. Hornsby replaces Zack Taylor, who finished in last place with a 52-102 record.

OCTOBER 9:

World Series, game five. The Yankees capitalize on 12 hits to bury the Giants at the Polo Grounds, 13-1. Rookie Gil McDougald hits a grand slam homer – the third ever in World Series play – and Phil Rizzuto has a two-run round-tripper. Eddie Lopat coasts to the win, allowing five hits. Larry Jansen is charged with the loss.

OCTOBER 16:

World Series, game six. At the stadium, the Yankees withstand a ninth inning two-run rally by the Giants to win the game, 4-3, and the World Series. Bob Kuzava comes out of the bullpen with the bases loaded and no outs. He snuffs out the Giants, preserving the win for Vic Raschi. Hank Bauer's bases-loaded triple in the sixth inning is the big blow and he makes a game-ending tumbling catch of Sal Yvars's line drive. In his final at-bat, Joe DiMaggio doubles to right against Larry Jansen. The Giants' starter, Dave Koslo, gets the loss. Monte Irvin has 11 hits in the series – one short of the record – and leads all batters with .458. Alvin Dark hits .417 for the Giants. Phil Rizzuto, with .320, wins the Babe Ruth Award.

After the Yankees win the championship, Joe DiMaggio, who batted .261 with a homer and five RBI, tells the press, "I've played my last game."

POST-SEASON

NOVEMBER 16:

Boston's new manager, Lou Boudreau, who replaced Steve O'Neill on October 22, creates a stir; he states that Ted Williams is available for a trade. In December, Boudreau backs off; Williams will stay with the Red Sox.

NOVEMBER 20:

Henry Aaron, 17 years old, signs to play with the all-black Indianapolis Clowns.

DECEMBER 5:

Shoeless Joe Jackson, banned for life from baseball for his role in the Black Sox scandal, dies of a heart attack in Greenville, South Carolina, at age 62. Jackson, regarded as one of baseball's best, was a liquor store owner at the time of his death. In 13 years, Jackson compiled a .356 average – third best ever – and hit .408 in 1911.

DECEMBER 11:

Joe DiMaggio makes official what he said after the final game of the World Series – he is retiring. In 13 years, DiMaggio hit .325, had a slugging average of .579, with 361 homers and 1,537 RBI. He struck out only 369 times in 6,821 at-bats. In 1951, his performance slipped. By the season's end he was only at .263 with 12 homers and 71 RBI.

TRIVIA

It has been suggested that Bill Veeck got the idea of using a midget from the James Thurber story "You Could Look It Up." But in his autobiography, *Veeck As in Wreck*, he writes: "I didn't steal the idea from Thurber, I stole it from John J. McGraw... He would always swear to my father that one day before he retired he was going to send his gnome up to bat." McGraw was referring to Eddie Morrow, whom he regarded as his "good-luck charm."

"That's an easy one. Ted Williams, without question."
– Joe DiMaggio, when asked who was the best hitter he's seen

TRIVIA

According to Roger Kahn, Ralph Branca is met by his fiancée, Ann Mulvey, and Fordham University priest Frank Rowley after the Bobby Thomson-home run game. Branca says: "Why me? I don't smoke. I don't drink. I don't run around. Baseball is my whole life. Why me?" Father Rowley answers: "God chose you because He knew you had faith and strength enough to bear this cross."

THE BEST OF 1951

National League

HITTERS

Batting Average:
Stan Musial, St. Louis Cardinals, .355

Slugging Average:
Ralph Kiner, Pittsburgh Pirates, .627

Home Runs:
Ralph Kiner, 42

Runs Batted In:
Monte Irvin, New York Giants, 121

Hits:
Richie Ashburn, Philadelphia Phillies, 221

Stolen Bases:
Sam Jethroe, Boston Braves, 35

PITCHERS

Wins:
Larry Jansen, New York Giants; Sal Maglie, New York Giants, 23

Strikeouts:
Don Newcombe, Brooklyn Dodgers; Warren Spahn, Boston Braves, 164

Earned Run Average:
Chet Nichols, Boston Braves, 2.88

Winning Percentage:
Elwin "Preacher" Roe, Brooklyn Dodgers, .880

Saves:
Ted Wilks, St. Louis Cardinals, Pittsburgh Pirates, 13

Most Valuable Player:
Roy Campanella, Brooklyn Dodgers

Rookie of the Year:
Willie Mays, New York Giants

American League

HITTERS

Batting Average:
Ferris Fain, Philadelphia Athletics, .344

Slugging Average:
Ted Williams, Boston Red Sox, .556

Home Runs:
Gus Zernial, Chicago White Sox, Philadelphia Athletics, 33

Runs Batted In:
Gus Zernial, 129

Hits:
George Kell, Detroit Tigers, 191

Stolen Bases:
Orestes "Minnie" Minoso, Cleveland Indians/Chicago White Sox, 31

PITCHERS

Wins:
Bob Feller, Cleveland Indians, 22

Strikeouts:
Vic Raschi, New York Yankees, 164

Earned Run Average:
Saul Rogovin, Detroit Tigers/Chicago White Sox, 2.78

Winning Percentage:
Bob Feller, .733

Saves:
Ellis Kinder, Boston Red Sox, 14

Most Valuable Player:
Lawrence "Yogi" Berra, New York Yankees

Rookie of the Year:
Gil McDougald, New York Yankees

1952

NEWS

PRESIDENT TRUMAN SIGNS KOREAN GI BILL

DWIGHT EISENHOWER ELECTED PRESIDENT, BEATING ADLAI STEVENSON

IKE FULFILLS HIS VOW AND GOES TO KOREA

Flying-saucer sightings, panty raids sweep country

S.S. *UNITED STATES* SETS TRANSATLANTIC SPEED MARK

A good year for literature: Ralph Ellison's The Invisible Man, *Ernest Hemingway's* The Old Man and the Sea, *John Steinbeck's* East of Eden; *E.B. White's* Charlotte's Web

ROCKY MARCIANO BEATS "JERSEY" JOE WALCOTT TO EARN HEAVYWEIGHT TITLE

Ralph Ellison's the *Invisible man* is published

AMERICAN BANDSTAND DEBUTS

PRE-SEASON

JANUARY 1:

Former major league pitcher Hiram "Hi" Bithorn is shot to death by police while fleeing arrest in El Mante, Mexico, where he is playing ball in the Mexican Winter League. Bithorn, Puerto Rican by birth, pitched in the majors for four years before developing a sore arm. His record was 34-31 with a 3.16 ERA. Bithorn was an 18-game winner for the Cubs in 1943.

JANUARY 17:

Tigers' owner Walter Briggs Sr. dies. His son Walter "Spike" Briggs Jr. assumes the team presidency.

JANUARY 28:

Cardinals' owner Fred Saigh is sentenced to 15 months in prison and fined $15,000 after a no-contest plea on income-tax evasion charges.

FEBRUARY 14:

At least he won't be the target of further Bill Veeck stunts. Bob Cain (121-12, 4.56 ERA), who pitched to midget Eddie Gaedel last season, is traded to the Browns along with first baseman Dick Kryhoski (.287, 12 homers) and pitcher Gene Bearden (3-4, 4.64 ERA) – 1948's rookie sensation. Coming to the Tigers are first baseman Bennie Taylor (.258, three home runs), outfielder Cliff Mapes (.262, nine home runs) and pitcher Dick Littlefield (1-1, 8.38 ERA).

FEBRUARY 26:

Dodgers pitcher Don Newcombe is drafted for two years of military service.

MARCH 6:

The *New York Times* reports that architect Norman Bel Geddes has been in discussions about designing a new baseball stadium for Brooklyn

APRIL 8:

The Giants obtain third baseman Bob Elliott (.285, 15 home runs, 70 RBI) from the Braves for pitcher Sheldon "Available" Jones (6-11, 4.26 ERA) and $50,000. Elliott was the NL's Most Valuable Player of the 1947 season.

THE SEASON

APRIL 23:

The Indians' starter Bob Feller and the Browns' newly acquired Bob Cain match one-hitters, set-

LEAGUE

The All-American Girls Professional Baseball League begins play minus the Peoria Redwings and the Kenosha Comets. There are no major rules changes. The South Bend Blue Sox (64-45) win the league championship.

APRIL 30
Ted Williams whallops a two-run homer– then departs to serve in the Marine Corps.

ting an AL record for the fewest hits in a game by two teams. In the first inning, St. Louis's Bob Young triples and scores the game's only run when Al Rosen misplays a Marty Marion ground ball. Cain yields a fifth-inning single to Luke Easter. Feller, who now has pitched four career one-hitters against the Browns, gets the loss. Cain, who was the losing pitcher when Feller no-hit Detroit last season, gets the win.

The Giants' James "Hoyt" Wilhelm, a 28-year-old rookie and a Purple Heart winner at the Battle of the Bulge, hits a fourth-inning homer off Dick Hoover of the Braves in his first major league at-bat and wins his first major league game in relief, 9-5.

APRIL 29:

What a difference five days make. Al Rosen, whose error cost the Indians and Bob Feller a 1-0 loss on April 23, hits three homers and bats in seven runs in a 21-9 victory over the Athletics today. The Indians' Jim Fridley is six for six.

APRIL 30:

In his last at-bat before reporting for duty with the Marine Corps, 33-year-old Ted Williams hits a two-run home run against Paul "Dizzy" Trout for one of his two safeties today. It is Williams's 324th career round-tripper. Williams is making his first start since pulling a muscle on Opening Day and is serenaded with "Auld Lang Syne" by the fans. The Red Sox win, 5-3, before a crowd of 24,764 at Fenway Park.

MAY 2:

Ted Williams reports at Camp Willow Grove, Pennsylvania, for active duty as a Marine fighter pilot.

MAY 3:

The Yankees send their Golden Boy, outfielder Jackie Jensen (.105 in seven games), and onetime rookie star pitcher Frank "Spec" Shea (5-5, 4.33 ERA) to the Senators in a six-player deal. Also on their way to Washington are outfielder Archie Wilson (.500 in three games) and minor league infielder Jerry Snyder. The Yankees get outfielder Irv Noren (.245 in 12 games) and infielder Tom Upton (.198 in 1951).

MAY 13:

The Pirates' 19-year-old farmhand Ron Neccai of the Bristol

THE LEGENDARY FIRST BASEMAN WALTER "BUCK" LEONARD, ONE OF THE NEGRO LEAGUE'S GREATEST PLAYERS, TURNS DOWN AN OFFER FROM BILL VEECK TO PLAY WITH THE BROWNS. THE 44-YEAR-OLD LEONARD, WHO SPENT 15 YEARS WITH THE HOMESTEAD GRAYS, EXPLAINS HE "DIDN'T WANT TO EMBARRASS ANYONE OR HURT THE CHANCES OF THOSE WHO MIGHT FOLLOW."

TRIVIA

Red Sox pitcher Al Benton, now 41 years old, becomes the only pitcher to face both Babe Ruth and Mickey Mantle in the majors. As a member of the Athletics, Benton pitched to Ruth during the 1934 season.

MAY 15
Tigers's pitcher Virgil "Fire" Trucks no-hits the Senators in a 1-0 Detroit victory.

Twins no-hits the Welch Miners and strikes out an unbelievable 27 batters. The Twins win the Class D Appalachian League game, 7-0.

MAY 15:

The Tigers' Virgil "Fire" Trucks no-hits the Senators, 1-0, at Briggs Stadium, fanning seven and walking one; Detroit makes three errors. The Tigers and Trucks win with two out in the bottom of the ninth on a Vic Wertz homer run against Erwin "Bob" Porterfield.

MAY 20:

Casey Stengel sends Mickey Mantle to center field and installs him in the number three spot in the batting order. Mantle responds by hitting two singles – batting left-handed –against Ken Holcombe. Then he turns around and hits two more right-handed against Chuck Stobbs. Johnny Sain pitches a six-hitter and the Yankees beat the White Sox, 3-1.

MAY 21:

Ron Neccai strikes out 24 in a game against Kingsport. He gets a brief shot with the Pirates this season, appearing in 12 games, going 1-6. He strikes out 31, while walking 32 in 54 $\frac{2}{3}$ innings and has an ERA of 7.08. He never plays in the majors again.
In the bottom of the first inning at Ebbets Field, Reds' pitcher Ewell Blackwell retires Billy Cox and then the roof falls in. The Dodgers score a major league record 15 runs. Blackwell is knocked out of the game, showers, and returns to his hotel; the Dodgers still are batting. The Dodgers send 21 batters to the plate – 19 straight reach base – and record 15 RBI. They score 12 of the runs with two out. After Blackwell, the Reds use Eldred "Bud" Byerly, Herman Wehmeier, and Frank Smith in the 59-minute inning. Pee Wee Reese reaches base three times. Winning pitcher Chris Van Cuyk has more hits than any other Dodger in the game – four. Bobby Morgan hits a pair of two-run homers and Duke Snider has one with a runner on. Homer "Dixie" Howell homers for the Reds' lone run. The final is 19-1.
Players on the Reds' bench harass Dodgers' rookie Joe Black by singing "Ol' Black Joe." He responds by firing head-high, inside fastballs at seven consecutive Cincinnati batters. The singing stops.

MAY 24:

Jimmy Piersall of the Red Sox and Billy Martin of the Yankees get into a fistfight in the runway between the Boston dugout and the clubhouse. Piersall angered Martin either by making fun of his nose or by making believe he was shooting a film – a reference to Martin breaking his ankle during a commercial shoot in March. Martin lands two punches before Yankees' coach Bill Dickey, Boston's Oscar Melillo, and others break it up. Piersall heads to the clubhouse to change his bloody and torn uniform and gets into another fight – this time with teammate Maurice "Mickey" McDermott.

MAY 28:

Dodgers' fans cheer a Giant. During his last at-bat prior to reporting for duty at Fort Eustis, Virginia, Willie Mays gets an ovation from Brooklyn fans at Ebbets Field. He is hitless in four at-bats, but the Giants beat the Dodgers and Billy Loes, 6-2.

MAY 29:

The Boston Braves offer to buy the contract of 18-year-old Henry Aaron from the Indianapolis Clowns. Under the terms of the proposal, the Clowns will receive $2,500 plus an additional $7,500 if Aaron remains with the Braves' organization for 30 days. Aaron will receive $350 per month to play for Eau Claire (Wisconsin) in the Northern League. The Chicago Defender describes Aaron as the "best prospect seen in the Negro League since Willie Mays."

JUNE 3:

Two infield fixtures, shortstop Johnny Pesky (.149, .313 last season) and third baseman George Kell (.296), are changing addresses in a blockbuster trade. Pesky goes to the Tigers along with first baseman Walt Dropo (.265), third baseman Fred Hatfield (.320 in 19 games), pitcher Bill Wight (2-1), and outfielder Don Lenhardt (.295) – who hit a grand slam homer yesterday. Kell moves to the Red Sox with pitcher Paul "Dizzy" Trout (1-5), shortstop Johnny Lipon (.221),

LEAGUE

In May, the House Judicial Subcommittee on Monopolies, chaired by Brooklyn Congressman Emanuel Cellar, reports on its investigation of baseball's reserve clause: "Experience points to no feasible substitute to protect the integrity of the game or to guarantee a comparatively even competitive struggle."

Ted Williams, who is flying combat missions in Korea, is quoted as saying: "I expect to be killed, of course."

and outfielder Walter "Hoot" Evers (1.000 in one game).

JUNE 9:

After a conflict over charges that owner Bill Veeck was meddling, Rogers Hornsby is fired as manager of the Browns and replaced with shortstop Marty Marion. Under Hornsby, the Browns were 22-29.

JUNE 10:

Sabath "Sam" Mele of the White Sox has a three-run homer and a bases-loaded triple – batting in six runs – in a 12-run fourth against the Athletics in Philadelphia. Chicago wins, 15-4.

JUNE 11:

Hank Aaron reports to the Braves' farm team in Eau Claire (Wisconsin) in the Northern League.

It must be the tides in Boston Harbor. At Fenway Park, the Browns take a 9-5 lead into the bottom of the ninth with Satchel Paige pitching. Lead off hitter Jim Piersall warns Paige he will bunt and does, beating it out. While Paige is facing Walter "Hoot" Evers, Piersall mimics his pitching motion. Then he imitates a seal. Evers walks and Piersall moves to second, where he continues his mimicry, jumping and whistling. Paige walks George Kell. Piersall goes to third, calling, "Oink, oink, oink." Billy Goodman walks. Ted Lepcio singles bringing up Sammy White, who hits a grand slam to give Boston an 11-9 win. White joins in the insanity – he crawls the last 15 feet and kisses home plate.

JUNE 14:

On this date 68 years ago, Boston Beaneaters' pitcher Jim Whitney struck out 18 Providence Grays in a 15-inning NL game. Today, pitching at home for the same franchise, now the Boston Braves, Warren Spahn fans 18 Cubs in a 15-inning game. He allows six hits but Chicago wins the game, 3-1.

JUNE 15:

The Cardinals, trailing the Giants, 11-0, after four innings in the opener of a Polo Grounds doubleheader, come back to win, 14-12, setting an NL comeback record. The Giants score five runs in the second inning and six in the third. The Cardinals score seven runs in the fifth, three in the seventh, two in the eighth, and two in the ninth – on a Solly Hemus homer. The game ends with the bases loaded for the Giants. Tommy Glaviano, Enos Slaughter, and Solly Hemus (two) homer for St. Louis; Hank Thompson and Wes Westrum for New York. The winning pitcher is Bill Werle; Max Lanier is tagged with the loss. The nightcap is a tame affair; starter Dave Koslo five-hits the Cardinals, 3-0, on Westrum's three-run homer.

JUNE 18:

In Boston, Warren Spahn's luck continues bad. The Braves' left-hander fans 11 – on the heels of 18 strikeouts in his last start – and loses, 3-1, to the Reds.

JUNE 19:

Brooklyn's Carl Erskine no-hits the Cubs, 5-0, at Ebbets Field. Erskine walks one – relief pitcher Willard Ramsdell, the game's only base runner – and fans one; the Dodgers play errorless ball. Erskine overcomes a rain delay and halts the Dodgers' four-game losing streak. The losing pitcher is Warren Hacker.

JUNE 21:

Stenographer-shortstop Eleanor Engle is signed by team president, Dr. Jay Smith, to play ball with the Harrisburg Senators in the Class B Inter-State League. She gets to participate in one infield practice, but National Association president George Trautman, who governs the minors, nixes her contract, with the support of Commissioner Ford Frick. Future pioneers are warned that signing female players will be met with "severe penalties."

Ted Williams played in only six games in 1952 before reporting for duty with the Marines.

JUNE 15
The Cardinals trail the Giants, 11-0, in the fourth inning, but rally to win, 14-12.

JULY 8
The National League wins a rain-shortened, five-inning All-Star Game, 3-2.

Engle, 24 years old, never gets her shot.

JULY 1:

At Braves Field, the Giants beat the Braves, 3-1, but the game is almost incidental to the fisticuffs. In the first inning Earl Torgeson takes a cut and hits Giants' catcher Sal Yvars with his backswing. They argue, and following Torgeson's single, Yvars breaks the bat. After the Giants' turn at bat, Torgeson punches Yvars in the New York dugout. Torgeson and Braves' pitcher Vern Bickford are ejected; Yvars remains in the game.

JULY 5:

Right-handed pitcher Fred Hutchinson is named manager of the Tigers, replacing Robert "Red" Rolfe. Detroit is 23-49.

JULY 8:

The NL wins the All-Star Game, 3-2, in five innings at Philadelphia's Shibe Park. It is the first All-Star Game to be curtailed because of weather. Hank Sauer hits a two-run homer in the bottom of the fourth for the winning run. Jackie Robinson also homers. Bob Rush gets the win; Bob Lemon is the loser. Bobby Shantz strikes out Carroll "Whitey" Lockman, Jackie Robinson, and Stan Musial in the fifth. Lon Warneke, who works the right-field line, is the first ever to play and then umpire in an All-Star Game. He pitched in the 1933, 1934, and 1936 games.

JULY 12:

At Yankee Stadium Browns' catcher Clint Courtney – who played one game for New York in 1951 – goes to war with his former teammates. In the second inning, he kicks the ball out of Billy Martin's glove in a play at second base. In the sixth, he slides hard into Yogi Berra at the plate. In the eighth, on an attempted steal, he slides in spikes high and Martin tags him in the face. When Courtney comes after Martin, he gets decked twice. The two continue to fight as both dugouts empty and two umpires are knocked down. When calm is restored, Courtney is ejected; Martin is not. The Yankees win, 5-4.

Bad blood between Martin and Courtney – known as Scrap Iron – dates back to 1947. During that season in the Arizona-Texas League, Courtney spiked Martin's friend Eddie LeNieve.

JULY 15:

At Yankee Stadium, Al Rosen of the Indians swipes home as the lead runner on a rare triple steal. Cleveland gets home runs from Luke Easter – recalled from the Indianapolis Indians – and Harry "Suitcase" Simpson to beat the Yankees, 4-3.

The Tigers' Walt Dropo singles, doubles, and triples in the nightcap of a doubleheader against the Senators, giving him 13 hits in three games, tying an AL record. Dropo had four consecutive singles in the opener and five hits last night against the Yankees, tying him Mike "Pinky" Higgins's record of 12 consecutive hits. Dropo fouled out in the seventh inning to end his streak. Since July 4, Dropo is hitting .524. The Senators win both games, 8-2 and 9-8.

JULY 19:

Red Sox general manager Joe Cronin announces that outfielder Jimmy Piersall will miss the rest of the season on doctors' advice. Piersall, with no recollection of his bizarre behavior toward Satchel Paige on June 11, is admitted to a sanitarium.

The first African-American to play in the Georgia State League is a 12-year-old batboy named Joe Relford. With Statesboro leading visiting Fitzgerald by 13-0 in the eighth, the fans start calling for the batboy. With the okay of umpire Ed Kubrik, manager Charlie Ridgeway sends Relford in to bat for .330 hitter Ray Nichting. Relford grounds out and goes to center field, where he makes a running catch. Relford is the youngest player ever in a professional baseball game.

JULY 20:

The Georgia State League fires the umpire and suspends manager Charlie Ridgeway for five days, adding a $50 fine. But it doesn't end there; Ridgeway is replaced and Joe Relford is fired by their team.

JULY 21:

Outfielders Harry Heilmann and Paul Waner are inducted into the Hall of Fame. Heilmann, who died last year, hit .342 in 15 years with the Tigers and two with the

TRIVIA

A fan with a Brooklyn accent reportedly was responsible for the Big Poison and Little Poison nicknames of Paul and Lloyd Waner. According to Michael Gershman and others, the anonymous fan said, "Every time you look up those Waner boys are on base; it's always the little poyson on third and the big poyson on first." Or something like that. Another Brooklyn fan was said to have remarked that "Waite Hurt got hoit."

"Man, I'm a hundred years old and I can still strike these guys out."
– *Satchel Paige, age approximately 46*

CULTURE

At the movies, *The Pride of St. Louis* stars Dan Dailey as Dizzy Dean, Joanne Dru as Patricia Dean, and Richard Crenna as Paul Dean; *The Winning Team* stars Ronald Reagan as Grover Cleveland Alexander, Frank Lovejoy as Rogers Hornsby, and Doris Day as Alexander's wife.

Reds. He led the AL in batting four times – including 1923 when he hit .403; he exceeded .390 in each of the other seasons. For 12 seasons, from 1919 to 1930, he hit over .300. Waner, a three-time NL batting champion, hit .309 or more for 12 consecutive seasons beginning as a rookie with the Pirates in 1926. In his 20-year career, he compiled a .333 average with 603 doubles and 190 triples.

Pitcher Burleigh Grimes told The Sporting News *in 1955: "I saw a lot of good hitters but I never saw a better one than Paul Waner... I may have got Waner out but I never fooled him."*

JULY 28:

Rogers Hornsby does not remain unemployed for long. The Reds fire manager Luke Sewell (39-59) and replace him with Hornsby, who will take over on August 5 after he finishes looking at Cincinnati's minor league players. In the interim, coach Earle Brucker will handle the team.

AUGUST 2:

Shufflin' Phil Douglas, banned from baseball for life in one of the game's oddest scandals, dies of a stroke at age 62 in Sequatchie Valley, Tennessee. In 1922, the year he was banished, he was 11-4 with a league-leading 2.63 ERA for the Giants. In his nine-year career, he was 93-93 with a 2.80 ERA.

AUGUST 6:

The Browns' ageless Satchel Paige – approximately 46 – becomes the oldest pitcher ever to pitch a complete game when he defeats the Tigers and Virgil Trucks, 1-0, in 12 innings. Paige says, "Man, I'm a hundred years old, and I can still strike these guys out."

AUGUST 8:

Bob Neighbors, a shortstop who played in seven games for the 1939 Browns, is killed in North Korea at the age of 34. He is the first and only major leaguer to die in action in the Korean War. Neighbors hit .182 in his brief career.

AUGUST 14:

The Browns and Tigers complete an eight-player trade that they began negotiating on August 11 and continued through yesterday. Detroit gets pitcher Ned Garver (7-10), outfielder Jim Delsing (.255), pitcher Dave Madison (4-2), and minor league pitcher Bill Black. Heading for St. Louis are first baseman Vic Wertz (.246), outfielder Don Lenhardt (.295), and pitchers Marlin Stuart (3-2) and Dick Littlefield (0-3).

RALPH KINER RECALLS THE LAST PLACE (42-112) PIRATES: "OUR BACKUP CATCHER WAS A FOOTBALL STAR NAMED VIC JANOWICZ; AND WE HAD THE O'BRIEN BROTHERS, BOTH OF WHOM WERE ALL-AMERICANS IN BASKETBALL. WE HAD GOOD FOOTBALL PLAYERS, GREAT BASKETBALL PLAYERS, BUT PRECIOUS FEW BASEBALL PLAYERS."

AUGUST 16:

The rain gods are merciful. At Ebbets Field, the Dodgers beat the Phillies 15-0 in a game called with one out in the seventh inning because of precipitation.

AUGUST 20:

Harvey Haddix, on leave from army service makes his major league debut with the Cardinals with a five-hit, seven-and-a-half-inning, rain-shortened victory over the Braves, 7-2.

Pitchers for Batavia and visiting Bradford of the Pony League pitch a double no-hitter. Bradford's Frank Etchberger fans six, walks five, and wins, 1-0. Batavia's Jim Mitchell

AUGUST 20 Harvey Haddix, on leave from the army, makes his major league debut, with the Cardinals.

SEPTEMBER 7 With a grand slam at Griffith Stadium, Johnny Mize has now homered in every ML park.

strikes out seven, walks one, and hits one batter. The walk, in the eighth inning, is followed by a sacrifice, a wild pitch, and an error, leading to the game's only run.

AUGUST 23:

The Giants have two hitters and two ejections in one at-bat at the Polo Grounds. Home plate umpire Augie Donatelli calls a second strike on the Giants' Bob Elliott, who gets ejected for kicking dirt on him. Elliott is replaced by Bobby Hofman, who takes a called third strike and is thumbed by Donatelli for protesting too strenuously.

AUGUST 25:

Virgil Trucks of the Tigers no-hits New York, 1-0, at Yankee Stadium. He becomes the third in major league history to pitch two no-hitters in one season. The 33-year-old Trucks walks Mickey Mantle in the third and fans eight; the Tigers make two errors. Trucks almost loses his no-hitter in the third inning when a scoring decision is reversed twice. Phil Rizzuto grounds to Johnny Pesky. The ball gets stuck in his glove and the throw to first baseman Walt Dropo is late. The Tigers argue in vain that Rizzuto is out. The official scorer calls it an error, then reverses it to a hit. Finally it is deemed an error. Pesky says, "I just messed it up." The Tigers score the game's only run in the seventh when Dropo doubles and Steve Souchock singles. Bill Miller gets the loss.

While Virgil Trucks is pitching his second no-hitter of the season, minor league pitcher Bill Bell is hurling his third. Bell, a Pirates' farmhand pitching for Bristol, no-hits Bluefield. In consecutive starts, he pitched no-hitters against Kingsport (May 22) and Bluefield (May 26).

AUGUST 26:

Bill Bell's Bristol teammate, Frank Ramsay, no-hits Bluefield, 1-0. It is the third time this season that Bluefield has been no-hit by Bristol pitchers. The Bristol staff has five no-hitters overall for the season.

AUGUST 30:

Joseph "Arky" Vaughan drowns in Eagleville, California, at age 40, when his fishing boat capsizes. Primarily a shortstop, Vaughan hit .318 in his 14-year career with the Pirates and Dodgers

SEPTEMBER 2:

The Senators' Jose "Mike" Fornieles makes his major league debut with one-hitter, beating the Athletics, 5-0. Fornieles never lives up to the promise of his debut. While he pitches for 12 years, his record is only 63-64 with a 3.96 ERA.

SEPTEMBER 7:

Johnny Mize, one of the great pure hitters in baseball history, reaches a milestone at Griffith Stadium today when he hits a grand slam homer over the right-field wall against Walt Masterson. Mize, whose grand slam gives the Yankees a 5-1 win, now has hit a home run in every major league ballpark in the country.

SEPTEMBER 14:

In Cleveland, Eddie Lopat and the Yankees win, 7-1. It is Lopat's 35th career win against the Indians. The Yankees, now in first by two and a half games, also put a stop to Mike Garcia's streak of 28 shutout innings. The game draws 73,609.

SEPTEMBER 15:

Who invented baseball? It was not Abner Doubleday, nor was it Alexander Cartwright. According to *Smena* it was the Russians. The *New York Times* publishes material from the Soviet publication which describes "beizbol" as a "beastly battle, a bloody fight with mayhem and murder." The nature of the game is reflected by team names like Tigrov and Piratov. The publication notes, "It is well known that in Russian villages they played lapta, of which beizbol is an imitation. It was played in Russian villages when the United States was not even marked on the maps."

SEPTEMBER 21:

In their last game ever in Boston, the Braves – who will play in Milwaukee next season – lose to the Dodgers, 8-2. With the win, Brooklyn is assured of at least a tie for the NL pennant. Joe Black pitches a three-hitter in his first major league start and his 55th game of the year. The losing pitcher is Jim Wilson. Roy Campanella hits the last ever homer at

HISTORY

In the home stretch, the Indians under Al Lopez are using their three top pitchers – Bob Lemon, Early Wynn, and Mike Garcia – as their only starters, and in relief as well. Comments Casey Stengel: "Well, I always heard it couldn't be done, but sometimes it don't always work."

"You get smart only when you begin getting old."
– *Allie Reynolds*

Braves Field, before a crowd of 8,822 – which is the second largest in the ballpark this season.

SEPTEMBER 23:

The Dodgers beat the Phillies, 5-4, to sew up the NL pennant.

SEPTEMBER 26:

The Yankees clinch the AL pennant with a 5-2, 11-inning victory over the Athletics in Philadelphia. In the eighth inning, an Irv Noren homer ties the score at 2-2. The Yankees win on Billy Martin's two-out, two-run single in the 11th inning. Johnny Sain gets the win in relief of Eddie Lopat. Since September 14, when the Yankees beat the Indians, 7-1, in Cleveland, each team has lost only one game.

SEPTEMBER 27:

The Pirates' Ralph Kiner hits his 37th homer of the season today, ending in a tie with Hank Sauer of the Cubs for the NL lead. Kiner becomes the first player to lead the NL in homers for seven straight years.

The Boston Braves, soon to be an extinct species of baseball team, beat the Dodgers and Joe Black, 11-3, at Ebbets Field. Virgil Jester gets the last NL win for a Boston pitcher.

SEPTEMBER 28:

On the last day of the 1952 season, Robin Roberts of the Phillies beats the Giants, 7-4, before a sparse crowd of 5,933 at the Polo Grounds. The win marks Roberts's 28th victory of the year; he is the first pitcher since Dizzy Dean in 1935 to reach that level. Roberts yields nine hits, fans six, and walks one, finishing his season at 28-7 with an ERA of 2.59, 330 innings pitched, and 30 complete games; he wins 17 of his last 18 decisions. The Phillies get home runs from Willie Jones and Bill Nicholson. Hank Thompson homers for the Giants. Jack Harshman is the losing pitcher.

In their last game as a Boston team, the Braves tie the Dodgers, 5-5, at Ebbets Field in a game called after 12 innings because of darkness.

SEPTEMBER 29:

Former minor league pitcher Stan Musial makes his major league mound debut at Sportsman's Park.

Joe DiMaggio is flanked by pitchers Allie Reynolds (l) and Vic Raschi.

SEPTEMBER 27
Ralph Kiner becomes the first player to lead the NL in homers seven straight seasons.

OCTOBER 1
After a three-year hiatus, the Dodgers and Yankees meet in another Subway Series.

After starter Harvey Haddix walks the first Cubs' batter, he moves to right field, Hal Rice shifts to center field, and Musial comes in to pitch. Frankie Baumholtz grounds to third baseman Solly Hemus, who mishandles the ball. Everyone then returns to his original position and the Cubs go on to win, 3-0. Haddix gets the loss; Paul Minner is the winner. Musial has one hit in three at-bats, finishing at .336 to win the league's batting title. Baumholtz finishes second, at .326.

REGULAR SEASON WRAP-UP:

The Yankees, 95-59, win their fourth straight AL pennant under Casey Stengel, finishing two games ahead of the Indians. Allie Reynolds is 20-8. Mickey Mantle bats .311 with 23 homers and 87 RBI. Yogi Berra hits 30 homers and drives in 98 runs, while batting .273.

The Dodgers, managed by Charlie Dressen, finish at 96-57, four and a half games ahead of the Giants. The team has no 20-game winners, but Joe Black is 15-4 with 15 saves. Jackie Robinson is Brooklyn's top average hitter with .308. Duke Snider bats .303 with 21 homers and 92 RBI. Gil Hodges drives in 102 runs with 32 homers and a batting average of .254.

"PLAYERS VIOLATED THE NIGHTS ON MR. STENGEL ONCE IN A WHILE," SAID BILLY MARTIN, ONE OF THE YANKEES' WELL-PUBLICIZED VIOLATORS, "BUT...IF YOU'RE IN A PENNANT RACE, YOU CAN PUT UP WITH ANY KIND OF CHARACTER EXCEPT A MAN THAT'S LAZY."

OCTOBER 1:

World Series, game one. After a three-year hiatus, the Yankees-Dodgers subway rivalry resumes. Joe Black goes all the way at Ebbets Field, limiting the Yankees to six hits in a 4-2 victory. All the Dodgers' scoring is on home runs – Jackie Robinson and Harold "Pee Wee" Reese hit solo shots; Duke Snider homers with one on. Gil McDougald has a round-tripper for the Yankees. Allie Reynolds gets the loss. Black made only two starts – with 54 relief appearances – during the regular season. He is the first black pitcher to win a World Series game.

OCTOBER 2:

World Series, game two. Vic Raschi three-hits the Dodgers and Billy Martin hits a double and a three-run homer, driving in three runs. The Yankees win, 7-1, at Ebbets Field. Raschi holds Brooklyn hitless in every inning except the third. Carl Erskine gets the loss.

OCTOBER 3:

World Series, game three. At Yankee Stadium, Elwin "Preacher" Roe holds the Yankees to five hits and Yogi Berra's passed ball scores two runs in the top of the ninth. Berra and Johnny Mize – as a pinch hitter – have solo homers for New York. Eddie Lopat pitches eight and two-thirds strong innings, but is tagged with the 5-3 loss.

OCTOBER 4:

World Series, game four. Allie Reynolds overpowers the Dodgers at Yankee Stadium, allowing four hits – all singles – and striking out 10 in a 2-0 victory. The Yankees have four hits – but they include a Johnny Mize three-run homer and a Mickey Mantle triple. Joe Black pitches well but gets the loss.

OCTOBER 5:

World Series, game five. Carl Erskine pitches all the way as the visiting Dodgers win, 6-5, in 11 innings. The winning run scores on a Duke Snider single; Erskine retires the final 19 batters en route to the

CULTURE

The Natural**, by Bernard Malamud, is a novel with some elements of the Eddie Waitkus shooting case. Ernest Hemingway's *The Old Man and the Sea* is not a baseball novel, but the protagonist reflects: "I would like to take the great DiMaggio fishing. They say his father was a fisherman."**

LEAGUE

Major league attendance is down for the second year in a row. The NL drops by 904,854; the AL is down 588,788.

HISTORY

Pitcher Bill Thomas ends his career with 383 wins – the most ever in the minor leagues. But he never gets a chance to play in the major leagues.

win. Snider also has a two-run homer; Johnny Mize has a round-tripper with two on for the Yankees. Johnny Sain pitches six innings in relief of starter Ewell Blackwell and is pegged with the loss.

OCTOBER 6:

World Series, game six. The Dodgers return to Ebbets Field needing only one win in the remaining two games for the World Championship. They don't get it today. Vic Raschi, with a save by Allie Reynolds, stops Brooklyn, 3-2. Yogi Berra and Mickey Mantle homer for the Yankees; Duke Snider has two for the Dodgers – all are solo shots. Billy Loes gets the loss.

OCTOBER 7:

World Series, game seven. The Yankees frustrate the Dodgers one more time, winning, 4-2, for their fourth straight World Championship, under Casey Stengel. Allie Reynolds gets the win with three innings of relief; Bob Kuzava comes out of the bullpen and retires the final eight batters for the save. With two on and two out, Jackie Robinson pops up a 3-2 pitch that first baseman Joe Collins loses. Billy Martin charges in from second base and makes a running catch near the mound to end the game and the series. Both Gene Woodling and Mickey Mantle hit homers for New York. Joe Black is tagged with the loss. Duke Snider is gallant in defeat with a .345 average, four homers, and eight RBI. Johnny Mize bats .400 with three homers and four RBI and gets the Babe Ruth Award. Mickey Mantle (.345, two homers), Gene Woodling (.348), and Pee Wee Reese (.345) come up big at bat. Allie Reynolds (1.77 ERA) and Vic Raschi (1.59 ERA) account for all four wins.

POST-SEASON

NOVEMBER 21:

Fred McMullen, one of the eight Black Sox banned for life from baseball for fixing the World Series, dies in the U.S. marshall's office – where he had been working – in Los Angeles. McMullin was 61 years old. A reserve infielder, McMullin made only two pinch-hitting appearances in the 1919 series and hit a single.

NOVEMBER 30:

Jackie Robinson ignites a controversy. Appearing on the NBC-TV program *Youth Want to Know,* he accuses the Yankees of prejudice. Responding to a question from a young participant, Robinson says, "Yes. There isn't a single Negro on the team now and there are very few in the entire Yankees' farm system." He blames the team's executives, adding, "It seems to me that the Yankees' front office has used racial prejudice in its dealings with Negro ballplayers. I may be wrong, but the Yankees will have to prove it to me."

Yankees' general manager George Weiss responds that there are "numerous" blacks in the system. "It has always been our hope that one of these shall prove good enough to make it with the Yankees. But we do not intend under any circumstances to bring one up just for exploitation."

DECEMBER 2:

The Pirates pluck a gem when they buy pitcher Elroy Face from the Dodgers' Montreal Royals AAA farm team. Face will end up spending 14 seasons with Pittsburgh as a workhorse out of the bullpen. In 1959, he wins a league-best 18 games as a reliever, and in 1962 he records 28 saves and an ERA of 1.88 in 91 innings of work.

DECEMBER 4:

The Tigers send pitcher Virgil Trucks (5-19, 3.97 ERA) – who pitched two no-hitters this season – to the Browns along with outfielder Johnny Groth (.284, four homers) and pitcher Hal White (1-8, 3.69 ERA). In return, Detroit gets outfielder Bob Nieman (.289, 18 homers), outfielder-catcher J.W. Porter (.250 in 33 games), and infielder Owen "Red" Friend, who did not play in the majors in 1952.

DECEMBER 18:

It's post-season turmoil in the Cleveland Indians' front office. Today the Indians undergo a dramatic management shake-up. After the ballclub's stockholders vote "no confidence" in team president Ellis Ryan, who has been in the job since 1950. As a result, Ryan sells all of his shares of stock in the team to a group headed by Myron H. "Mike" Wilson Jr. Wilson will become the team's eighth president and serve until 1962.

THE BEST OF 1952

NATIONAL LEAGUE

HITTERS

Batting Average:
Stan Musial, St. Louis Cardinals, .336

Slugging Average:
Stan Musial, .538

Home Runs:
Ralph Kiner, Pittsburgh Pirates; Hank Sauer, Chicago Cubs, 37

Runs Batted In:
Hank Sauer, 121

Hits:
Stan Musial, 194

Stolen Bases:
Harold "Pee Wee" Reese, Brooklyn Dodgers, 30

PITCHERS

Wins:
Robin Roberts, Philadelphia Phillies, 28

Strikeouts:
Warren Spahn, Boston Braves, 183

Earned Run Average:
Hoyt Wilhelm, New York Giants, 2.43

Winning Percentage:
Hoyt Wilhelm, .833

Saves:
Alpha Brazle, St. Louis Cardinals, 16

Most Valuable Player:
Hank Sauer, Chicago Cubs

Rookie of the Year:
Joe Black, Brooklyn Dodgers

AMERICAN LEAGUE

HITTERS

Batting Average:
Ferris Fain, Philadelphia Athletics, .327

Slugging Average:
Larry Doby, Cleveland Indians, .541

Home Runs:
Larry Doby, 32

Runs Batted In:
Al Rosen, Cleveland Indians, 105

Hits:
Jacob "Nellie" Fox, Chicago White Sox, 192

Stolen Bases:
Orestes "Minnie" Minoso, Chicago White Sox, 22

PITCHERS

Wins:
Bobby Shantz, Philadelphia Athletics, 24

Strikeouts:
Allie Reynolds, New York Yankees, 160

Earned Run Average:
Allie Reynolds, 2.06

Winning Percentage:
Bobby Shantz, .774

Saves:
Harry Dorish, Chicago White Sox, 11

Most Valuable Player:
Bobby Shantz, Philadelphia Athletics

Rookie of the Year:
Harry Byrd, Philadelphia Athletics

CULTURE

Television viewers see *You Could Look It Up*, starring Ward Bond, based on James Thurber's short story.

1953

MARCH 18
NL owners approve the move of the Braves to Milwaukee, after 77 years in Boston.

NEWS

TRUCE DECLARED IN KOREA

ETHEL AND JULIUS ROSENBERG ARE FIRST U.S. CIVILIANS EXECUTED FOR ESPIONAGE

Chuck Yeager flies Bell X-1A at more than 1,000 mph

OREGON SENATOR WAYNE MORSE SETS FILIBUSTER RECORD – 22 HOURS AND 26 MINUTES

In the theater, Arthur Miller's The Crucible, *William Inge's* Picnic, *Robert Wright and George Forrest's* Kismet

JOSIP TITO BECOMES PRESIDENT OF YUGOSLAVIA

EDMUND HILARY ANDTENZING NORGAY ARE FIRST TO REACH THE TOP OF MT. EVEREST

JAMES BALDWIN'S *GO TELL IT ON THE MOUNTAIN* IS PUBLISHED

PRE-SEASON

JANUARY 8:

Bruce Sutter is born in Lancaster, Pennsylvania.

JANUARY 27:

The Athletics trade the 1952 AL batting champion Ferris Fain (.327, two home runs, 59 RBI) and minor league second baseman Bob Wilson to the White Sox for first baseman Eddie Robinson (.296, 22 home runs, 10 RBI), shortstop Joe DeMaestri (.226 in 81 games), and outfielder Ed McGhee, who did not play in the majors in 1952.

FEBRUARY 16:

The Braves, Dodgers, Phillies, and Reds complete a complex four-cornered trade. When the day's wheeling and dealing is done, first baseman Joe Adcock (.278, 13 home runs with the Reds) and outfielder-infielder Jim Pendleton (Brooklyn's farm system in 1952) are with the Braves, infielder Everett "Rocky" Bridges (.196 with the Dodgers) and cash go to the Reds, first baseman Earl Torgeson (.230, five homers with the Braves) is a member of the Phillies, and Russ Meyer (13-14, 3.14 ERA with the Phillies) will be pitching for the Dodgers.

FEBRUARY 19:

It's a close call for Ted Williams, but he escapes without injury when his F-9 Panther jet fighter is hit by enemy fire in Korea. He crash-lands the burning plane, which explodes after Williams exits.

FEBRUARY 20:

Anheuser-Busch buys the Cardinals from Fred Saigh for $3.75 million, including the assumption of $1.25 million in debts. Saigh, who has been convicted of income tax evasion, claims he had an offer of $4.1 million but declined it so the Cardinals would remain in St. Louis. August A. Busch Jr. becomes the team's new president.

MARCH 11:

Fred Toney, who pitched a 10-inning no-hitter for the Reds in 1917, dies at age 64 in Nashville. Toney, who was six feet, six inches, and weighed 245 in his playing days, was 137-102 with a 2.69 ERA in 12 years. He was indicted and acquitted on draft-dodging charges during World War I.

MARCH 16:

The AL owners reject Bill Veeck's proposed move of the Browns from St. Louis to Baltimore. The "reason" is not enough time before the start of the season.

MARCH 18:

It's bye-bye Boston for the Braves. Lou Perini gets unanimous approval from NL owners, meeting at the Vinoy Park Hotel in St. Petersburg, Florida, to move the team to Milwaukee. The Braves had played in Boston for 77 years. The American Association Brewers will get a cash settlement for the territorial rights and will move to Toledo. The Braves reportedly lost $700,000 last season. It is the first NL franchise shift since 1900.

APRIL 9:

Less than two months after purchasing the Cardinals, Anheuser-Busch buys Sportsman's Park from the financially strapped Bill Veeck of the St. Louis Browns for $800,000; the ballpark will be renamed Budweiser Park.

The Cincinnati Reds – once known as the Red Stockings – are

"No man in the history of baseball had as much power as Mickey Mantle."
– *Billy Martin*

APRIL 17
Mickey Mantle hits a home run out of Griffith Stadium, calculated at 565 feet.

now the Redlegs, according to an announcement today by general manager Gabe Paul. Despite the Cold War and hostility toward the Soviet Union, fans do not take to the new name. Sportswriter Tom Swope notes: "We were Reds before they were."

APRIL 11:

Hall of Fame pitcher Charles "Kid" Nichols dies at the age of 83 in Kansas City, Missouri. Nichols was 361-208 in his 15-year career with a 2.94 ERA. Inducted into the Hall of Fame in 1948, Nichols was a seven-time 30-game winner and pitched 532 complete games. He also managed the Cardinals in 1904 and part of 1905.

THE SEASON

APRIL 13:

On opening day in Cincinnati, the Braves play their first game as Milwaukee's team and beat the Redlegs, 2-0. Max Surkont pitches a three-hitter for the win; rookie Bill Bruton has Milwaukee's first hit.

APRIL 14:

In the return of major league baseball to Milwaukee after more than 50 years, the Braves beat the visiting Cardinals, 3-2, in 10 innings on a homer by rookie Bill Bruton at County Stadium. Bruton tripled earlier to give the Braves a 2-0 lead. Warren Spahn gets the win; Gerry Staley is charged with the loss. Despite cold, damp weather and only 27,982 permanent seats, a crowd of 34,357 turns out to cheer on their new home team.

BRANCH RICKEY OF THE BASEMENT-DWELLING PIRATES OFFERS NL HOMER CHAMPION RALPH KINER A 25 PERCENT SALARY CUT. RICKEY EXPLAINS: "WE WOULD HAVE FINISHED LAST WITHOUT YOU."

APRIL 16:

In Pittsburgh, the Pirates beat the Phillies, 14-12, with Philadelphia second baseman Connie Ryan collecting two doubles and four singles in six at-bats. The Phillies score nine runs in the top of the fifth and the Pirates answer with six; the 15-run total ties a modern NL record.

APRIL 17:

Mickey Mantle hits a 565-foot home run in Griffith Park against left-hander Chuck Stobbs. In the top of the fifth, batting right-handed, Mantle drives a Stobbs fastball over the 50-foot wall in left center field at the 391-foot marker into the backyard of a house on 434 Oakdale Street. The distance is calculated by Yankees' publicist Arthur "Red" Patterson. The ball is retrieved by 10-year-old Donald Dunaway, who returns it for an undisclosed amount of cash and Mantle's autograph on a replacement. Mantle later displays another weapon in his arsenal – speed – when he beats out a bunt for a single. Eddie Lopat is the winner, 7-3; Stobbs gets the loss.

APRIL 28:

In St. Louis, Mickey Mantle hits another tape measure homer. Batting right-handed, Mantle catches all of a Bob Cain pitch and drives it over the scoreboard for a three-run homer. The game marks the resumption of hostilities between Browns' backstop Clint Courtney and the Yankees. With the score tied, 6-6, in the top of the 10th, Gil McDougald crashes into Courtney, jars the ball loose, and scores the go-ahead run. When Courtney comes to bat in the bottom of the frame, he warns catcher Yogi Berra he will retaliate. And he does, going into second base spikes high and slashing shortstop Phil Rizzuto on the right leg. Billy Martin, who fought Courtney in 1952, goes after him again and decks him.

LEAGUE

In February, the Athletics change the name of their home field from Shibe Park to Connie Mack Stadium in honor of their longtime owner and manager.

CULTURE

In the movies, baseball is featured in *The Kid from Left Field*, starring Dan Dailey and Billy Chapin; *The Big Leaguer*, starring Edward G. Robinson and Jeff Richards, with Carl Hubbell as a Giants' scout, directed by Robert Aldrich.

Casey Stengel says, "John McGraw was a great man in New York and he won a lot of pennants. But Stengel is in town now, and he's won a lot of pennants, too."

Ralph Kiner averaged 35 home runs in his 10-year major league career.

A 17-minute fight follows involving players from both teams; umpire John Stevens suffers a dislocated collarbone. With only three cops on duty, the fans begin pelting the Yankees with bottles. When order is restored, six players are ejected. The AL fines Courtney $250 and Browns' shortstop Billy Hunter $150. Martin, McDougald, Joe Collins, and Allie Reynolds get lesser fines.

APRIL 29:

Joe Adcock launches an epic homer of his own. The Braves' slugger becomes the first to hit a home run into the center-field bleachers of the Polo Grounds since its 1923 remodeling – which lengthened the distance. Adcock's blow comes off Jim Hearn in the third inning and is estimated at 475 feet; it clears a 5-foot wire fence and lands 10 rows deep. Lynwood "Schoolboy" Rowe in a 1933 exhibition game and Luke Easter in a Negro League game also reached the bleachers. The Braves win, 3-2; Warren Spahn gets the victory, Hoyt Wilhelm the loss.

MAY 6:

Browns' rookie Bobo Holloman no-hits the visiting Athletics, 6-0, in his first major league start, walking five and striking out three. He also drives in three runs with two singles. The losing pitcher is Morrie Martin.

According to Bill Veeck's autobiography, Holloman was due to be returned to the minors to save a $25,000 payment if he remained with the Browns past June 15. He convinces manager Marty Marion to give him a start and responds with a no-hitter. Veeck keeps him with the Browns, explaining, "I don't think it's wise to send a man back to the minor leagues right after he's become immortal... it looks as if you're punishing him for throwing a no-hitter." The no-hitter is Holloman's only complete game – and one of three wins – in his only major league season.

MAY 10:

Billy Loes pitches a shutout and Roy Campanella drives in five runs with a double and a homer to beat the Phillies, 5-0. The Dodgers sweep the three-game series and take over first place in the NL.

Even as a peacemaker, Jimmy Piersall seems beset with trouble. He tries to keep teammate Billy Goodman away from an umpire in a game against the Yankees. Goodman's ribs are bruised and he will miss three weeks.

MAY 12:

Boston fans used to serenade him with "He's better than his brother Joe, Dominic DiMaggio." Now they might be singing "So long, it's been good to know yuh." The 36-year-old center fielder, known as the Little Professor for his eyeglasses, retires after 11 seasons. He has a .298 lifetime average, 87 homers, and a reputation as one of the premier glovemen of his time.

APRIL 29
Braves' Joe Adcock is the first to homer into the center-field stands at the Polo Grounds.

JUNE 10
Jimmy Piersall ties an AL record with a double and five singles in the Red Sox 11-2 win.

MAY 15:

George Brett is born in Glen Dale, West Virginia.

MAY 16:

White Sox manager Paul Richards makes an unorthodox lineup change, with right-hander Ewell Blackwell on the mound in Yankee Stadium, Chicago trailing, 3-1, and the bases loaded in the ninth inning. He sends left-handed pitcher Tommy Byrne to bat for right-handed Vern Stephens, who has 10 career grand slam homers. When the groans subside, Byrne hits a grand slam of his own against his former teammates, and Chicago comes away with a 5-3 victory.

At Milwaukee, the Phillies' starter Curt Simmons gives up a leadoff single to Bill Bruton, then retires the next 27 Braves in order for a one-hit, 3-0 win. He also ends the Braves' six-game winning streak.

MAY 18:

The Dodgers tie a record for unproductivity by stranding 18 runners today against former teammate Clarence "Bud" Podbielan. Podbielan gives them plenty of opportunity to leave runners on base – he allows six hits and walks 13 in a 2-1 win for the Redlegs.

MAY 20:

On the basis of attendance, the Braves' move from Boston to Milwaukee seems to be paying off. Today, in their 13th home game, the Braves reach 281,278 in attendance – more than their full-season total attendance in Boston last year.

MAY 25:

At Forbes Field, the Pirates' Ralph Kiner homers in the fifth against Al Corwin of the visiting Giants. It is his 300th career homer, and he is the 12th player to reach that total. New York wins the game, 6-3.

In Milwaukee, Braves' starting pitcher Max Surkont sets a modern major league record when he strikes out eight consecutive Cincinnati batters in the nightcap of a doubleheader. The Braves beat the Redlegs, 10-3.

MAY 27:

Hall of Fame outfielder Jesse "The Crab" Burkett passes away in Worcester, Massachusetts, at the age of 84. In 16 seasons, Burkett batted .339 with highs of .409 in 1895 and .410 in 1896. He also pitched in 23 games, with a 3-11 record. He was inducted into the Hall of Fame in 1946.

PRODIGIOUS HOME RUN HITTER RALPH KINER HAD MANY FANS, BUT BRANCH RICKEY WAS NOT ONE OF THEM: "RALPH KINER HAS SO MANY OTHER WEAKNESSES THAT IF YOU HAD EIGHT RALPH KINERS ON AN AMERICAN ASSOCIATION TEAM, IT WOULD FINISH LAST."

JUNE 4:

Branch Rickey decides to see if the Pirates can finish last without Ralph Kiner (.270). He ships the seven-time NL home run leader to the Cubs along with pitcher Howie Pollet (1-1), catcher Joe Garagiola (.233), and outfielder George "Catfish" Metkovich (.146). In return, the Pirates get $150,000 plus outfielder Gene Hermanski (.150), third baseman George Freese (.000 with the Tigers), first baseman-outfielder Preston Ward (.230), pitcher Bob Schultz (0-2), and catchers Maurice "Toby" Atwell (.230) and Bob Addis (.167).

JUNE 10:

In St. Louis, Jimmy Piersall of the Red Sox hits a double and five singles, tying an AL record for consecutive hits in a nine-inning game, as Boston beats the Browns, 11-2. In game two, Piersall is hitless in five at-bats and gets dusted by Satchel Paige, the tar-

LEAGUE

The All-American Girls Professional Baseball League loses the Battle Creek Belles and adds the Muskegon Belles. The distance between base paths is lengthened from 72 feet to 75 feet. Pitching distance is increased from 55 feet to 56 feet.

LEAGUE

The Negro American League is reduced to four teams.

Branch Rickey's philosophy of deal-making: "Trade a player a year too early rather than a year too late."

LEAGUE

The Indianapolis Clowns of the Negro American League sign Toni Stone to play second base for a reported $12,000. According to Robert Peterson, Ms. Stone "played four to six innings in about 50 of the Clowns' 175 games." She batted .243.

get of his ridicule last season. The Red Sox complete the sweep, 3-2.

JUNE 14:

The Yankees sweep a doubleheader from the Indians in Cleveland, 6-2 and 3-0, extending their winning streak to 18 games. The Yankees, who began the streak on May 27 and have 15 road victories in the 18 wins, now lead Cleveland by 10 1/2 games. Yogi Berra has a homer in the opener and a triple in the nightcap.

JUNE 15:

The Browns end two streaks with one victory. Behind the combined six-hit pitching of winning pitcher Duane Pillette and reliever Satchel Paige, they beat the Yankees, 3-1, snapping New York's 18-game winning streak and ending their own skein of 14 losses. Johnny Mize collects his 2,000th career hit and drives in the Yankees' only run against Pillette. The Yankees fall one shy of the AL record set by the 1919 White Sox.

JUNE 17:

At Fenway Park, the Red Sox bang out 20 hits and defeat the Tigers, 17-1. Dick Gernert hits two homers and drives in four runs. Tom Umphlett has four hits and Billy Goodman three. The winning pitcher is Willard Nixon; Dick Marlowe is charged with the loss.

JUNE 18:

The Red Sox continue their assault on Tigers' pitching, scoring a modern major league record 17 runs in the seventh inning and winning, 23-3. Boston sends 23 batters to bat in 47 minutes against three Detroit pitchers – Steve Gromek, who yields nine runs; Dick Weik, four runs; and Earl Harrist, four runs. They bang out 14 hits in the inning for another record. Gene Stephens has three safeties (two singles and a double), and Sammy White scores three times to set marks of their own. The Red Sox collect 27 hits in the game, but the only homers are by Dick Gernert and Walt Dropo. Sammy White and Billy Goodman each hit safely four times. Detroit also commits five errors. Ned Garver, out before the seventh inning, gets the loss. The winning pitcher is Ellis Kinder. In two consecutive games, the Red Sox have outscored the Tigers, 40-4, and have 47 hits against Detroit pitching.

JUNE 24:

Seventeen-year-old pitcher Joey Jay signs with the Braves, becoming the first player to make it from the Little Leagues to the major leagues.

JUNE 25:

In Philadelphia, 18-year-old Al Kaline makes his major league debut for the Tigers, replacing center fielder Jim Delsing for defense.

JULY 6:

Mickey Mantle hits a pinch-hit grand slam home run over the roof in left-center field of Connie Mack Stadium in Philadelphia.

JULY 7:

The bus transporting the Yankees players from Connie Mack Stadium to the railroad station in the city of Philadelphia is involved in an accident. Pitcher Allie Reynolds suffers a back injury that will cause him chronic pain.

JULY 8:

Tigers' rookie Al Kaline singles against White Sox pitcher Luis Aloma for his first major league hit. Chicago wins, 14-4.

JULY 9:

In Philadelphia, pitcher Robin Roberts's streak of 28 consecutive complete games ends when Bob Miller is summoned from the bullpen to relieve him in the eighth inning of today's game against the Dodgers. Roberts had yielded 11 hits and five earned runs in his seven and a third innings of work. The Phillies go on to win, 6-5, and Miller gets credit for the victory. Roberts's streak began on August 28, 1952, with a 10-6 win over the Cardinals. He pitched his 28th complete game on July 5 of this season, beating Pittsburgh, 2-0. Dodgers' starter Johnny Podres also is KO'd, but Jim Hughes gets the loss.

JULY 10:

Ralph Branca, the man who served "the pitch" to Bobby Thomson in 1951, is a Dodger no more. Brooklyn sells Branca (0-0 in 7 games) to the Tigers for the waiver price.

JULY 11:

The Giants' Al Worthington whitewashes the Dodgers,

JUNE 25
Al Kaline, only 18, makes his major league debut, with the Detroit Tigers.

JULY 6
Mickey Mantle sends a pinch-hit grand slam over the roof at Connie Mack Stadium.

6-0, joining a select list of pitchers with shutouts in their first two major league starts. On July 6, Worthington shut out the Phillies, also by a 6-0 score.

JULY 22:

The Detroit Tigers unconditionally release four-time 20-game winner Hal Newhouser (0-1, 7.06 ERA in seven games).

JULY 27:

Edward G. Barrow, Charles "Chief" Bender, Thomas Connolly, Dizzy Dean, Bill Klem, Al Simmons, Roderick "Bobby" Wallace, and William "Harry" Wright are inducted into the Hall of Fame. As general manager, Barrow was the main architect of the great Yankees' teams of 1921 to 1945, winning 14 pennants and 10 World Series. In 1918, he was manager of the World Champion Red Sox. Bender pitched 16 years and compiled a 210-127 record with a 2.46 ERA and 41 shutouts. He pitched from 1903 to 1925 and appeared in five World Series for the Athletics. Connolly umpired in the NL from 1898 to 1900 and in the AL from 1901 to 1931, calling eight World Series. Dean enjoyed a brief but brilliant career, cut short by a sore arm. In 12 years, he was 150-83 with a 3.02 ERA and 26 shutouts. In 1934 he was 30-7 with a 2.66 ERA and seven shutouts. Klem was an NL umpire from 1905 to 1940, working 18 World Series. He died in 1951. Outfielder Simmons played 20 seasons, batting .334 with 307 homers and 1,827 RBI. In 1930 and 1931 he was the AL's top batter, with averages of .381 and .390. Bobby Wallace, an outstanding shortstop in the field, played from 1894 to 1918 and compiled a career average of .266. Harry Wright organized the first fully professional team – the 1869 Cincinnati Red Stockings. He was a manager for 18 years and introduced many strategies and tactics that persist in modern baseball. Wright, who led the 1877 and 1878 Boston Red Caps and the 1890 Phillies to NL first-place finishes, died in 1895.

Dean tells the assemblage: "The Good Lord

BILL KLEM, WHO CLAIMED, "I NEVER CALLED ONE WRONG," WORKED MORE WORLD SERIES GAMES THAN ANY OTHER UMPIRE – 108 – AND AT AGE 68 WAS THE OLDEST UMPIRE TO WORK IN THE MAJOR LEAGUES. HE ONCE TOLD A PLAYER WHO CALLED HIM "BILL," "MR. KLEM, TO YOU, AND DON'T YOU EVER FORGET IT!" KLEM CLAIMED HE KNEW IT WAS TIME TO RETIRE WHEN, IN 1941, HE CALLED A RUNNER OUT ON A CLOSE PLAY AT SECOND AND THOUGHT HE WAS RIGHT. "I ALMOST WEPT. FOR THE FIRST TIME IN MY CAREER I ONLY 'THOUGHT' A MAN WAS OUT." HE RETIRED AFTER THAT GAME.

CULTURE

***The Southpaw*, by Mark Harris, is the first of four novels featuring Henry "Author" Wiggen.**

> "The players can do more for themselves than any outside representative."
> – *NL president Warren Giles*

RULES

In November, the owners restore the sacrifice fly rule: a hitter is not charged with an at-bat if he scores a runner with a fly ball.

was good to me. He gave me a strong body, a good right arm, and a weak mind." Dean once said of himself: "I may not have been the greatest pitcher ever, but I was amongst 'em."

JULY 29:

Ted Williams is back in a Red Sox uniform after five and a half months and 39 combat missions in Korea. A crowd of 19,083 welcomes him home to Fenway Park, but Williams doesn't play today against the Chicago White Sox.

JULY 30:

Boston University buys Braves Field for $500,000.

AUGUST 1:

In Milwaukee, Warren Spahn is almost perfect against the Phillies. The only base runner against Spahn is Richie Ashburn with an infield hit in the fourth inning. The Braves and Spahn win, 5-0; it is the 31st shutout of his career.

AUGUST 4.

The Yankees' Vic Raschi sets an AL record for pitchers with seven RBI – on three hits. He beats the Tigers, 15-0.

> IN 1989, CONNIE MACK RECALLED CHARLES ALBERT "CHIEF" BENDER: "IF I HAD ALL THE MEN I'VE EVER HANDLED AND THEY WERE IN THEIR PRIME AND THERE WAS ONE GAME I WANTED TO WIN ABOVE ALL OTHERS, ALBERT WOULD BE MY MAN."

AUGUST 6:

Ted Williams returns to action – in baseball. He pinch-hits for Tom Umphlett against the Browns and pops up.

AUGUST 9:

Ted Williams is getting his stroke back. At Fenway Park, he pinch-hits for Johnny Lipon in the eighth inning and hits a homer off a 3-1 pitch from Mike Garcia of the Indians.

AUGUST 21:

Major league players hire an attorney, New Yorker Jonas Norman Lewis, to represent them. NL president Warren Giles says, "The players can do more for themselves than any outside representative, no matter how able that outsider may be. By delegating someone else to negotiate for them, the players are surrendering a privilege that has been very valuable to them." In August, Commissioner Ford Frick notifies Lewis that he is not welcome at the owners' meeting.

AUGUST 30:

The Braves turn Forbes Field into home run haven in a doubleheader against the Pirates. In game one, Milwaukee hits an NL record eight round-trippers to defeat Pittsburgh, 19-4. Jim Pendleton has three, Eddie Mathews two, and Johnny Logan, Del Crandall, and Jack Dittmer, one each. Johnny Antonelli gets the win; Johnny Lindell is the loser. In the nightcap, the Braves' Mathews, Joe Adcock, Logan, and Sid Gordon homer in an 11-5 victory to set an NL doubleheader record of 12 round-trippers. On September 3, Milwaukee hits four more homers to give them an NL record 16 in four games.

SEPTEMBER 1:

The Cardinals hit five homers with the bases empty – tying a major league record – and lose to the Dodgers, who counter with 17 hits for a 12-5 win. Elwin "Preacher" Roe throws gopher balls to Stan Musial, Harry Elliott, Eldon "Rip" Repulski, and Steve Bilko (twice).

SEPTEMBER 6:

A Dodgers-Giants brawl at the Polo Grounds has major consequences for Brooklyn's Carl Furillo. Roy Campanella homers for the Dodgers in the second inning. When Furillo, the NL's leading hitter, steps to the

SEPTEMBER 1
Despite five solo home runs off Cardinals' bats, the Dodgers get the win, 12-5.

SEPTEMBER 17
Ernie Banks goes 0-for-3 in his major league debut, with the Chicago Cubs.

plate, Giants' manager Leo Durocher yells to pitcher Ruben Gomez, "Stick it in his ear." The next pitch hits Furillo in the wrist. He then charges the mound as Durocher shouts, "Crybaby, crybaby" and challenges Furillo, who goes into the dugout after his former manager. In the melee, Furillo's hand is stepped on, fracturing the metacarpal bone and shelving him for the rest of the regular season. The Dodgers win the game, 6-3.

SEPTEMBER 8:

The Cubs buy the contract of 22-year-old shortstop Ernie Banks from the Kansas City Monarchs in the Negro American League for $10,000 in cash.

SEPTEMBER 9:

Mickey Mantle blows a bubble, gets a rebuke and endorsement money. The Yankees' center fielder is photographed blowing a bubble during a game against the White Sox, which upsets manager Casey Stengel and pleases the Bowman Gum Co.

SEPTEMBER 12:

The Dodgers beat the Braves and Bob Buhl, 5-2, in Milwaukee to clinch the NL pennant. It is the earliest ever for an NL team to wrap up the flag.

Mickey Mantle joins the select few who just miss hitting a fair ball out of Yankee Stadium. Batting right-handed, he drives a pitch from Billy Hoeft of the Tigers deep to left field. The ball is still ascending when it lands 80 feet high and 425 feet deep. The Yankees win, 13-4.

SEPTEMBER 13:

Pitcher Bob Trice becomes the first black to play for the Athletics.

SEPTEMBER 14:

The Yankees come back from a 5-0 deficit to beat the Indians, 8-5, clinching their fifth consecutive AL pennant. Yogi Berra has a two-run homer; Billy Martin bats in four runs.

SEPTEMBER 17:

Ernie Banks makes his major league debut at Wrigley Field, going hitless in three at-bats, scoring once, and making an error at shortstop. The Phillies beat the Cubs, 16-4. Ernie Banks begins his streak of 424 consecutive games played with his major league debut.

After 197 games (51 in 1952), Rogers Hornsby is out as manager of the Reds. Under Hornsby, the team compiled a 64-82 record this season. He will be replaced for the final eight games by Colonel Buster Mills.

SEPTEMBER 19:

Mel Parnell of the Red Sox shuts out the Yankees for the fourth time this season. He is the first pitcher since Walter Johnson in 1908 to whitewash New York. Today's score is 3-0.

SEPTEMBER 20:

In St. Louis, Ernie Banks hits a home run – the first of his major league career – against Gerry Staley. The Cardinals beat the Cubs, 11-6.

SEPTEMBER 27:

It's the last game ever for the St. Louis Browns, who will be playing in Baltimore as the Orioles next season. In true Browns' tradition they lose – for the 100th time this season – to the White Sox, 2-1, in 11 innings. Billy Pierce is the winning pitcher; Duane Pillette gets the loss.

REGULAR SEASON WRAP-UP:

The Yankees and Casey Stengel win their fifth consecutive pennant with a 99-52 record, eight and a half games ahead of the Indians. Whitey Ford, out of the army, finishes 18-6. Gene Woodling has the top batting average – .306. Hank Bauer is second at .304. Yogi Berra hits 27 homers and drives in 108 runs; Mickey Mantle bats .295 with 21 homers and 92 RBI.

The Dodgers bring a power-packed lineup into the Series. Under Charlie Dressen, they run away with the NL pennant, compiling a record of 105-49, and finishing 13 games ahead of the Braves. They are the first NL team with two players at 40-plus homers. Roy Campanella hits 41 – the most ever by a catcher – bats .312, and tops the NL with 142 RBI. Duke Snider hits 42 homers, bats .336, and has 126 RBI. Gil Hodges (.302, 31 homers, 122 RBI) and Jackie Robinson (.329, 95 RBI) add punch to the lineup. During the season, the Dodgers homer in a record 24 consecutive games. The top winner is Carl Erskine at 20-6. The Senators have the AL's top hitter, James

CULTURE

Robert Francis' poem "Pitcher" is published

"I always thought the pitcher had the advantage. It's like serving in tennis."
– *Allie Reynolds*

CULTURE

On television, CBS airs *Death on the Diamond* (not based on the 1934 movie), with Ralph Bellamy as a murdered player. *0 for 37* stars Arthur O'Connell, Eva Marie Saint, and James Broderick.

TRIVIA

Among the Marine pilots with whom Ted Williams flies in Korea is future astronaut and U.S. Senator John Glenn.

"Mickey" Vernon, and the top pitcher, Erwin "Bob" Porterfield, but finish fifth with a .500 record. Ellis Kinder of the Red Sox sets a major league record by pitching in 69 games. The Cardinals' Harry "Peanuts" Lowrey sets a major league record with 22 pinch hits.

SEPTEMBER 29:

Bill Veeck, one of the game's genuine characters and a madcap innovator, is out of baseball. At the Commodore Hotel in New York City, the AL announces the sale of Veeck's controlling interest in the St. Louis Browns to a group led by Baltimore Mayor Tom D'Alesandro and attorney Clarence Miles for $2,475,000. The new owners receive approval to move the franchise to Baltimore for the 1954 season. It is the first franchise shift in the AL since 1903, when the Baltimore Orioles moved to New York and became the Highlanders; the Browns had been in St. Louis for 52 years. The AL twice had refused Veeck permission to move the team to Maryland.

SEPTEMBER 30:

World Series, game one. The Yankees begin with a bang; Billy Martin triples with the bases loaded in the first inning at Yankee Stadium, kayoing Dodgers' starter Carl Erskine. Brooklyn claws its way back, tying the game, 6-6, in the sixth. Joe Collins homers in the seventh and the Yankees go on to win, 9-6. Johnny Sain, in relief of Allie Reynolds, gets the win. Brooklyn reliever Clem Labine is charged with the loss. Yogi Berra homers for the Yankees; Jim "Junior" Gilliam, Gil Hodges, and George "Shotgun" Shuba (with one on) for the Dodgers.

OCTOBER 1:

World Series, game two. Yesterday the hitters, today the pitchers. Eddie Lopat scatters nine hits, beating the Dodgers and Preacher Roe, 4-2. Mickey Mantle's two-run homer in the eighth inning breaks a 2-2 tie and gives New York its winning margin. Billy Martin also hits a home run for the Yankees.

OCTOBER 2:

World Series, game three. Back in Brooklyn, Carl Erskine sets a series record with 14 strikeouts – including Mickey Mantle four times – and six-hits the Yankees, 3-2. Vic Raschi gets the loss, yielding a home run to Roy Campanella.

OCTOBER 3:

World Series, game four. Duke Snider is the big gun in a 7-3 win for the Dodgers at Ebbets Field. He hits a homer and two doubles, driving in four runs while winning pitcher Billy Loes and reliever Clem Labine hold the Yankees in check. Whitey Ford fails to survive the first inning and gets the loss. Duke Snider has a homer and two doubles, driving in four runs. Gil McDougald hits a two-run homer for the Yankees.

OCTOBER 4:

World Series, game five. The Yankees beat the Dodgers, 11-7, in a slugfest at Ebbets Field featuring six homers – including a grand slam by Mickey Mantle in the third. The teams combine for a series record 47 total bases. Jim McDonald gets the win for New York; Johnny Podres is the loser. In addition to Mantle's grand slam against Russ Meyer, homers are hit by Gene Woodling, Billy Martin (with one on), and Gil McDougald (with two on) for the Yankees; Billy Cox (with two on) and Junior Gilliam connect for Brooklyn.

OCTOBER 5:

World Series, game six. The Yankees win their fifth consecutive World Championship with a 4-3 win at Yankee Stadium. Billy Martin drives in Hank Bauer with the winning run in the bottom of the ninth, making a winner of Allie Reynolds in relief of Whitey Ford. Clem Labine gets the loss. Carl Furillo hits a two-run homer. In what is a hitters' series, Billy Martin bats .500 with two homers and five RBI, Yogi Berra bats .429, and Mickey Mantle has two homers and seven RBI. Gil Hodges leads the Dodgers with .364, followed by Carl Furillo's .333.

POST-SEASON

OCTOBER 14:

Charlie Dressen asks for more; the Dodgers show him the door. Dressen, who led the Dodgers to two straight NL pennants, demands a multiyear contract. The Dodgers offer him a one-year deal and, when he refuses, he is no longer the manager.

OCTOBER 5
With a 4-3 win over the Dodgers, the Yankees win their fifth straight World Championship.

NOVEMBER 9
The Supreme Court says baseball is not a business and not subject to antitrust laws.

NOVEMBER 9:

The U.S. Supreme Court speaks and baseball likes what it hears: it is a sport, not a business, and is not subject to the nation's antitrust laws. By a 7-2 vote, the Court finds no cause to overturn a 1922 ruling antitrust exemption and allows the reserve clause to remain in effect. The case concerned George Toolson, a Yankees' minor leaguer who refused to be demoted to Binghamton in the Eastern League from Newark in the International League. The bottom line on today's decision is that baseball cannot be challenged as an illegal monopoly in the courts, and the reserve clause – preventing players from dealing with teams other than their current ones – is safe unless Congress acts.

NOVEMBER 24:

After Pee Wee Reese turns down the job to continue playing, 42-year-old Walter "Smokey" Alston is signed to a one-year contract to manage the Dodgers. For the past four years, Alston was the manager of Brooklyn's Montreal Royals farm team in the International League.

NOVEMBER 30:

In Springfield, Missouri, Mickey Mantle undergoes surgery for the removal of torn cartilage in his right knee.

DECEMBER 2:

In Atlanta, team representatives attend the first meeting of the Major League Baseball Players Association and elect Bob Feller their first president.

DECEMBER 9:

The Red Sox obtain outfielder Jackie Jensen (.266, 10 homers, 84 RBI) and his fear of flying from the Senators for pitcher Maurice "Mickey" McDermott (18-10, 3.01 ERA) and outfield- er Tommy Umphlett (.283, 3 homers).

DECEMBER 15:

Hall of Famer Ed Barrow dies at age 85 in Port Chester, New York. While Barrow was general manager of the Yankees the team won 14 pennants and 10 World Series. He is credited with making an everyday player out of Babe Ruth. Barrow was inducted into the Hall of Fame earlier this year.

"THEY WERE WAITING TO SEE IF I COULD TURN WHITE, BUT I COULDN'T DO IT."

–Vic Power

DECEMBER 16:

Vic Power, arguably the most talented black player in the Yankees' farm system, will never wear pinstripes. The Yankees trade the 22-year-old, Puerto Rican-born minor league outfielder-infielder to the Athletics as part of an 11-player swap. Leaving the Yankees' organization with Power are first baseman Don Bollweg (.297, six homers), outfielder Bill Renna (.314 in six games), and three other minor leaguers: pitcher John Gray, catcher Jim Robertson, and third baseman Jim Finigan. Philadelphia sends the Yankees first baseman Eddie Robinson (.247, 22 homers, 102 RBI), pitcher Harry Byrd (11-20, 5.51 ERA), outfielder Carmen Mauro (.244), infielder Loren Babe (.230), and first baseman Tom Hamilton (.196).

DECEMBER 17:

AL owners okay a sale and leaseback arrangement for Yankee Stadium. The House That Ruth Built will be purchased for $6.5 million by Chicago industrialist Arnold Johnson, who will rent it back to the team. The Yankees also sell Johnson their territorial rights to Kansas City and Blues' Stadium in that city.

DECEMBER 26:

How much is Pirates' infielder Danny O'Connell (.294, seven homers) worth? The Braves believe it's $100,000 and six players. They send that amount to Pittsburgh along with pitcher Max Surkont (11-5, 4.18 ERA), outfielder-infielder Sid Gordon (.274, 19 homers), outfielder Sam Jethroe (not in the majors in 1953), catcher Fred Walters (not in the majors in 1953), and minor league pitchers Curt Raydon and Larry LaSalle.

HISTORY

Al Rosen of the Indians leads the AL in home runs (43), RBI (145), and slugging percentage (.613) while batting .336. He also leads the league in double plays and assists. Historian/statistician Bill James writes it was "probably the greatest season that any third baseman ever had."

TRIVIA

Twelve players were on the roster for all five of the Yankees' consecutive World Series wins. They are Hank Bauer, Yogi Berra, Jerry Coleman, Joe Collins, Ralph Houk, Eddie Lopat, Johnny Mize, Vic Raschi, Allie Reynolds, Phil Rizzuto, Charlie Silvera, and Gene Woodling. Houk and Silvera are reserve catchers with one and two Series at-bats, respectively, and no hits.

THE BEST OF 1953

National League

HITTERS

Batting Average:
Carl Furillo, Brooklyn Dodgers, .344

Slugging Average:
Edwin "Duke" Snider, Brooklyn Dodgers; Eddie Mathews, Milwaukee Braves, 627.

Home Runs:
Eddie Mathews, 47

Runs Batted In:
Roy Campanella, Brooklyn Dodgers, 142

Hits:
Richie Ashburn, Philadelphia Phillies, 205

Stolen Bases:
Bill Bruton, Milwaukee Braves, 26

PITCHERS

Wins:
Warren Spahn, Milwaukee Braves; Robin Roberts, Philadelphia Phillies, 23

Strikeouts:
Robin Roberts, 198

Earned Run Average:
Warren Spahn, 2.10

Winning Percentage:
Carl Erskine, Brooklyn Dodgers, .769

Saves:
Alpha Brazle, St. Louis Cardinals, 18

Most Valuable Player:
Roy Campanella, Brooklyn Dodgers

Rookie of the Year:
Jim "Junior" Gilliam, Brooklyn Dodgers

American League

HITTERS

Batting Average:
James "Mickey" Vernon, Washington Senators, .337

Slugging Average:
Al Rosen, Cleveland Indians, .613

Home Runs:
Al Rosen, 43

Runs Batted In:
Al Rosen, 145

Hits:
Harvey Kuenn, Detroit Tigers, 209

Stolen Bases:
Orestes "Minnie" Minoso, Chicago White Sox, 25

PITCHERS

Wins:
Erwin "Bob" Porterfield, Washington Senators, 22

Strikeouts:
Walter "Billy" Pierce, Chicago White Sox, 186

Earned Run Average:
Eddie Lopat, New York Yankees, 2.42

Winning Percentage:
Eddie Lopat, .800

Saves:
Ellis Kinder, Boston Red Sox, 27

Most Valuable Player:
Al Rosen, Cleveland Indians

Rookie of the Year:
Harvey Kuenn, Detroit Tigers

1954

"Most of what I know about style I learned from Roberto Clemente."
– *Director John Sayles*

NEWS

FRENCH DEFEATED IN DIEN BIEN PHU, VIETNAM

FIRST H-BOMB EXPLODED

Army-McCarthy hearings held

SENATE CONDEMNS SENATOR JOSEPH McCARTHY

SUPREME COURT RULES PUBLIC SCHOOL SEGREGATION UNCONSTITUTIONAL

Children receive Salk polio vaccine

PUERTO RICAN NATIONALISTS WOUND FIVE U.S. CONGRESSMEN

Moviegoers enjoy On the Waterfront, *starring Marlon Brando and Eva Marie Saint, and* A Star Is Born, *starring Judy Garland and James Mason. On television,* Father Knows Best, Lassie, *and* The Tonight Show *debut*

WILLIAM GOLDING'S NOBEL PRIZE-WINNING NOVEL, *LORD OF THE FLIES*, IS PUBLISHED

PRE-SEASON

JANUARY 5:

Walter "Rabbit" Maranville dies in New York City at age 63. In 23 years, the shortstop batted .258 and hit 28 home runs. In his career, Maranville played for the Braves, Cubs, Dodgers, Pirates, and Cardinals.

JANUARY 14:

Joe DiMaggio marries Marilyn Monroe in San Francisco.

FEBRUARY 1:

The Giants send 1951 playoff hero, outfielder Bobby Thomson (.288, 26 homers, 106 RBI) to the Braves along with catcher Sammy Calderone (.222 in 35 games). In return, they receive pitcher Johnny Antonelli (12-12, 3.18 ERA), catcher Edward "Ebba" St. Clair (.200 in 33 games), infielder Billy Klaus (.000 in two games), and $50,000 in cash.

FEBRUARY 2:

Mickey Mantle is hospitalized in Springfield, Missouri, for surgery on a cyst behind his right knee. The Yankees' star had knee surgery last November.

FEBRUARY 19:

The Brooklyn Dodgers sign Roberto Clemente to a minor league contract. He receives a $10,000 signing bonus and will be paid $5,000 for the season.

FEBRUARY 23:

The Yankees sell Vic Raschi (13-6, 3.33 ERA), a member of six World Series champions, to the St. Louis Cardinals for $85,000. Raschi, who never missed a starting assignment and was 120-50 with New York, had refused a 25 percent pay cut and reportedly told Yankees' general manager George Weiss, "You have a very short memory."

MARCH 1:

Ted Williams fractures his left collarbone on the first day of spring training. He suffers the injury diving for a ball hit by teammate Walter "Hoot" Evers at Payne Park in Sarasota, Florida. The fracture is at the junction of the middle third and outer clavicle. Williams misses 36 games as a result of the injury.

MARCH 13:

The Braves' Bobby Thomson breaks his ankle sliding into sec-

RULES

Players no longer may leave gloves on the field between innings.

APRIL 15
Rookie Hank Aaron gets his first major league hit in a 7-6 Braves' win over the Cardinals.

MAY 2
Stan "The Man" Musial launches five home runs in a doubleheader against the Giants.

LEAGUE

The All-American Girls Professional Baseball League begins its season with no franchise changes. The ball size is decreased from 10 inches to nine inches and then increased at mid-season to nine and a quarter inches. Base paths are lengthened from 75 feet to 85 feet. The pitcher's mound is moved back from 56 feet to 60 feet. The league champions are the Kalamazoo Belles, only 48-49 in season play. The league, which commenced play in 1943, folds after the 1954 season.

ond base in an exhibition game against the Yankees. He will be out for four months and is replaced in the Milwaukee lineup by young outfielder Henry Aaron.

APRIL 11:

The Yankees acquire Enos "Country" Slaughter (.291, six home runs, 89 RBI), who, along with Stan Musial and Terry Moore, made up one of baseball's great outfields. In return for Slaughter, who will be 38 years old later this month, the Cardinals get four minor leaguers: outfielder Bill Virdon, pitcher Mel Wright, catcher Harold R. "Hal" Smith, and outfielder Emil Tellinger.

Slaughter recalls leaving the Cardinals: "You get a few handshakes and walk away from 20 years of your life. I cried like a baby."

THE SEASON

APRIL 13:

After 51 years, the Orioles are back in the major leagues. In Detroit, the transplanted St. Louis Browns have changed uniforms but not their losing ways. With Mrs. John J. McGraw, widow of the Orioles' Hall of Fame player-manager, on hand, Baltimore loses, 3-0, to the Tigers. Steve Gromek gets the win; Don Larsen is charged with the loss.

Willie Mays returns to the Giants after two years of army service – during which he injured an ankle – and spoils Walter Alston's debut as Dodgers' manager with a two-run homer in the sixth inning. The Giants win, 4-3, at the Polo Grounds. For the first time in 15 years Red Barber is not behind the mike for Brooklyn; the new broadcasting team is Andre Baruch and Vin Scully.

They're seeing doubles at Crosley Field in Cincinnati. Extra seats are set up to accommodate an overflow opening day crowd. As a result of the temporary reconfiguration, 12 ground-rule doubles and one conventional two-bagger are hit. Jim Greengrass of the Redlegs joins Frank Dillon of the 1901 Tigers as the only players with four two-baggers on the first day of the season. Eddie Mathews hits two homers for the Braves, and after his second, Cincinnati's Joe Nuxhall beans Andy Pafko. The game marks Hank Aaron's major league debut; he is hitless in five at-bats. It also is the first game in which the defense must remove its gloves from the field at the end of a half-inning. The Redlegs beat the Braves, 9-8.

APRIL 14:

In Detroit, the Orioles win their first game, beating the Tigers, 3-2, behind pitcher Duane Pillette.

APRIL 15:

In Milwaukee, rookie Hank Aaron gets his first major league hit. He ends the day with two hits in five at-bats as the Braves beat the Cardinals, 7-6.

The Orioles play in Baltimore for the first time before a crowd of 46,354 at Memorial Stadium, including Vice President Richard M. Nixon. The Orioles beat the White Sox as Bob Turley pitches a seven-hitter and fans nine. He gets home run support from Vern Stephens and Clint Courtney. The losing pitcher is Virgil Trucks. The game is preceded by a 90-minute, three-and-a-half-mile-long parade featuring 20-plus bands and 32 floats, drawing 500,000 spectators.

APRIL 17:

At Wrigley Field, the Cubs and Cardinals battle for three hours and 43 minutes – the longest nine-inning game ever in the NL. The Cubs prevail, 23-13. The teams combine for 35 hits, including five homers: Eldon "Rip" Repulski, Sal Yvars, and Tom Alston for St. Louis; Ransom Jackson and Hal Jeffcoat for Chicago. The winning pitcher is Jim Brosnan; Gerry Staley, one of the Cardinals' six pitchers, gets the loss.

Another team's color barrier falls. In Milwaukee, Chuck Harmon bats for Reds' pitcher Harold "Corky" Valentine in the seventh inning, becoming Cincinnati's first African-American player. Harmon pops up.

APRIL 21:

Today at Memorial Stadium in Baltimore, Bob Turley of the Orioles takes a no-hitter into the ninth inning against the Indians. With one out, Al Rosen singles and Larry Doby homers; Turley, despite 14 strikeouts, loses his no-hitter and the game, 2-1.

After a trip to Korea to entertain the troops, Marilyn Monroe tells Joe DiMaggio, "Joe, Joe, you've never heard such cheering." He responds, "Yes, I have."

APRIL 23:

In St. Louis, Braves rookie Hank Aaron, playing in his seventh game, homers in the seventh inning with the bases empty against the Cardinals' Vic Raschi. It is Aaron's first major league home run.

MAY 2:

In St. Louis, Stan Musial slams five home runs in a doubleheader against the Giants. But the Cardinals only manage a split, winning the opener, 10-6, and bowing in the nightcap, 9-7. In the opener, Musial hits two homers against Johnny Antonelli – a solo shot in the third inning and a two-run round-tripper in the fifth. In the eighth, he reaches losing pitcher Jim Hearn with two men on base. Alpha Brazle gets the win in the nightcap, he victimizes Hoyt Wilhelm twice. Larry Jansen is the winning pitcher; Royce Lint gets the loss. Musial sets a record with 21 total bases and ties a major league record with five homers in two consecutive games. He has nine RBI for the day.

MAY 15:

After sitting out six weeks with a broken collarbone, Ted Williams returns to action with a steel pin in his shoulder. He is hitless in two trips against the Orioles in Baltimore.

MAY 16:

It takes Ted Williams only one game and two at-bats to regain his form. After being held hitless in two at-bats yesterday in Baltimore, he moves on to Detroit for a doubleheader and savages Tigers' pitching for eight hits – including two homers, a double, and nine RBI – in nine at-bats.

MAY 22:

Charles "Chief" Bender dies at age 70 in Philadelphia. Inducted into the Hall of Fame last year, Bender pitched in the majors for 16 years, compiling a 210-127 record with a 2.46 ERA. He competed in five World Series with the Athletics, going 6-4.

MAY 23:

The White Sox get infielder George Kell (.258) from the Red Sox for infielder Grady Hatton (.000 in one game) and $100,000.

MAY 24:

First there was the Williams shift, now Stan Musial faces an oddball alignment. Redlegs manager George "Birdie" Tebbetts makes shortstop Roy McMillan a fourth outfielder when Musial comes to bat. It's irrelevant as Musial, perhaps distracted, is fanned by Art Fowler. Cincinnati wins, 4-2.

MAY 28:

At the Polo Grounds, Davey Williams, Alvin Dark, Monte Irvin, and Billy Gardner homer against the Dodgers' Ben Wade in the eighth, tying a major league record for most homers in one inning. The Giants score six runs in the frame and win the game, 17-6.

JUNE 1:

The Indians obtain first baseman Vic Wertz (.202 in 29 games) from the Orioles for pitcher Bob Chakales (2-0). In another roster move, Baltimore releases pitcher Dave Koslo (0-1) today.

JUNE 3:

Hank Thompson hits three homers and drives in eight runs and Willie Mays hits two round-trippers, batting in five, to account for all the Giants' scoring in a 13-8 win against the Cardinals.

JUNE 4:

Ted Williams will be lost to the Red Sox for three weeks because of pneumonia.

JUNE 12:

The Braves' Jim Wilson no-hits the Phillies, 2-0, in Milwaukee. He fans six and walks two; the Braves play errorless ball. The losing pitcher is Robin Roberts.

Bob Feller beats the Red Sox and records his 2,500th career strikeout. Don Mossi retires the last three batters. The Indians improve to 35-17, moving into first place – where they remain for the rest of the season – a half-game ahead of Chicago.

JUNE 23:

The Red Sox and Orioles struggle through nearly five hours and 17 innings of unaesthetic baseball. Baltimore wins, 8-7. The Red Sox use 22 players and strand 21 runners. The Orioles use 20 players and leave 17 on base.

JULY 1:

Yankees' infielder Bobby Brown retires at age 29 to become a hospital intern. Brown has been pursuing his medical

CULTURE

***The Year the Yankees Lost the Pennant*, by Douglas Wallop, is about an aging Washington Senators' fan who sells his soul to the devil to become superstar Joe Hardy. The book eventually became the stage and film musical *Damn Yankees*.**

Casey Stengel, who managed Al Lopez with the Dodgers, describes the Indians' skipper: "Sure he's smart. I taught him, didn't I?"

studies during the off-season. Signed by the Yankees in 1946, Brown played for eight seasons – with parts of two years out for military service – hitting .279. He was especially proficient in post-season play, batting .439 in four World Series. Brown goes on to become a prominent cardiologist and then president of the AL.

CULTURE

The film *Roogie's Bump*, starring Robert Marriott and Ruth Warrick, features Dodgers Roy Campanella, Billy Loes, Carl Erskine, and Russ Meyer.

JULY 6:

The Indians set an AL record by scoring eight runs in the first inning before a batter is retired. Before the Orioles can get out of the opening frame, Cleveland sends 16 men to the plate and scores 11 runs. Bill Glynn has a homer and a single; Wally Westlake, a triple, and Larry Doby, two hits. Cleveland wins the game, 11-3.

JULY 12:

The Major League Baseball Players Association is formed in Cleveland, where representatives of all 16 major league teams meet for three and a half hours and draw up by-laws and a constitution. Attorney J. Norman Lewis is being paid $30,000 per year to negotiate with the owners. According to Lewis, the association is not a union and players will not pay dues. The association and Lewis will seek revisions in the players' pension plan.

JULY 13:

In Cleveland, the AL wins the highest scoring All-Star Game ever, 11-9, on 17 hits. Al Rosen drives in five runs with a pair of homers; Ray Boone and Larry Doby hit one each for the winners. Rosen and Boone hit back-to-back homers – the first ever in All-Star play – in the third inning; Ted Kluszewski and David "Gus" Bell each homer with one on for the NL. Dean Stone gets the win; Gene Conley is charged with the loss.

The dean of American sportswriters, Grantland Rice, dies at the age of 73 in New York City.

JULY 18:

There are wild doings in St. Louis where the Phillies are awarded a 9-0 forfeit win over the Cardinals by umpire Ralph "Babe" Pinelli. After an 11-10 Phillies' win in 10 innings, the nightcap of today's doubleheader begins at 6:48 P.M. By the fifth inning of the game, with Philadelphia up, 8-1, it is getting dark and Cardinals' manager Eddie Stanky goes into a stall hoping to get the game called before it is official. An argument between St. Louis catcher Sal Yvars and Phillies' first baseman Earl Torgeson – precipitated by Cardinals' pitcher Ellis "Cot" Deal – degenerates into a melee and Pinelli calls the forfeit. Stanky gets a five-day suspension and a $100 fine from NL president Warren Giles. Yvars and Torgeson get docked two days each.

JULY 22:

Casey Stengel shakes well before using. When he's done, Mickey Mantle is at his minor league position, shortstop, and Phil Rizzuto shifts to second base, which he's never played in the majors. Mantle hits a game-winning homer in the tenth inning and the Yankees beat the White Sox, 3-2.

JULY 24:

Perhaps inspired by his successful unorthodox lineup changes two days ago, Casey Stengel introduces a new defense in the eighth inning after removing his shortstop, Phil Rizzuto, for a pinch hitter. He shifts Mickey Mantle from center to the infield. For right-handed hitters, Mantle plays second and Willie Miranda is at short. For left-handed hitters, Mantle and Miranda switch positions. All the movement doesn't help; the Yankees lose to the Indians, 5-4.

JULY 31:

Milwaukee Braves' first baseman Joe Adcock flexes his muscles. In a game against the Dodgers at Ebbets Field, Adcock hits four home runs (he is the seventh player ever to accomplish the feat) and a double. His 18 total bases set a major league record; he ties the mark for most extra base hits – five – and for the most homers in two games – five. Adcock hits a bases-empty home run against Don Newcombe in the second inning, a double in the third and a three-run homer off Erv Palica in the fifth; a two-run shot off Pete Wojey in the seventh, and a solo round-tripper against Johnny Podres in the 9th. Eddie Mathews hits two homers and Andy Pafko one for Milwaukee. Don Hoak, Gil Hodges, and Albert "Rube" Walker hit round-trip-

JULY 6
The Indians score a record eight runs in the first inning in an 11-3 romp over Baltimore.

JULY 31
Braves' slugger Joe Adcock becomes the seventh player to hit four homers in a game.

pers for Brooklyn. Milwaukee wins the slugfest, 15-7.

AUGUST 1:

Joe Adcock continues on his batting tear against the Dodgers. He has a double in two at-bats and then is hit in the head by Clem Labine and leaves the game. Braves' pitcher Gene Conley knocks Jackie Robinson down in the fourth and sixth innings. Robinson and Braves' third baseman Eddie Mathews get into an altercation. Milwaukee wins its 10th straight game, 14-6; Conley gets the victory.

Starting with today's game, Red Sox manager Lou Boudreau will have Ted Williams second in the lineup so he can accumulate enough plate appearances to qualify for the AL batting title.

AUGUST 8:

At Ebbets Field, the Dodgers score 12 runs with two out and no one on – a major league record – against the Redlegs. Brooklyn has seven hits and seven walks, tallying 13 runs in all – 12 unearned – in the eighth inning en route to a 20-7 victory. The game features homers by Roy Campanella, Jim Gilliam, and Don Hoak. Carl Erskine gets the win; Karl Drews is the losing pitcher.

> IN HIS BOOK *THE TUMULT AND THE SHOUTING*, GRANTLAND RICE WRITES: "BABE RUTH'S RECORD OF 60 HOME RUNS IN ONE YEAR MAY BE BROKEN, ALTHOUGH PERSONALLY I HOPE IT STANDS FOR ETERNITY... BUT IT IS A SURE THING THAT COBB'S MARK OF 4,191 BASE HITS WILL NEVER BE APPROACHED."

AUGUST 9:

Bill Dickey, Walter "Rabbit" Maranville, and Bill Terry are inducted into the Hall of Fame. Dickey, the Yankees' catcher for 17 seasons, batted .313 with a high of .362 in 1936. He hit .300 or better 11 times and drove in 1,209 runs. Dickey appeared in eight World Series, batting .255 and amassing 24 RBI. Shortstop Maranville, a speedster and an outstanding gloveman, batted .258 in 23 seasons, stealing 291 bases. He hit .308 in two World Series with the Braves and Cardinals. Maranville, only five feet, five inches tall, died earlier this year. Bill Terry, like Dickey, spent his full career with one team. In 14 years with the Giants, the first baseman hit .341 with a high of .401 in 1930. He batted better than .300 10 times and appeared in three World Series, averaging .295. He managed the Giants from 1932 to 1941, winning three pennants and one World Series.

New York World-Telegram *sportswriter Dan Daniel wrote in 1939 of Dickey: "You have to watch this man, day in and day out, to appreciate him to the full... before you are able to realize how completely he dominates his field."*

AUGUST 21:

The Indians' pennant express is rolling. They beat the Orioles, 4-1, today to move four and a half games ahead of the Yankees. The game features a fourth-inning triple play started by pitcher Bob Lemon when he snares a Jim Fridley line drive. Larry Doby hits a bases-loaded triple to up his RBI total to 100.

AUGUST 22:

The Yankees buy relief pitcher Jim Konstanty (2-3) from the Phillies. Konstanty was the NL's Most Valuable Player in 1950, the first relief pitcher to win the award.

SEPTEMBER 5:

Rookie Hank Aaron breaks his ankle.

Joe Bauman, playing for the Roswell Rockets in the Class C Longhorn League, hits his 70th, 71st, and 72nd homers of the season. Bauman finishes his 138-game season at .400, with a .916 slugging average and 224 RBI. Four

CULTURE

"Say Hey (The Willie Mays Song)" is recorded by the Treniers, with Willie Mays singing background and Quincy Jones directing the orchestra. "Baseball, Baseball," written by David Kapp, Allan Roberts, and Albon Timothy, is recorded by Jane Morgan.

years of military service and two years as a holdout minimize his chances for a major league shot – and he never does get one. According to former sportswriter Bob Rives, Bauman's 72 homers translate to 85 in a full major league season.

SEPTEMBER 6:

Master manipulator Casey Stengel uses 10 pinch hitters – including pitcher Tommy Byrne for shortstop Phil Rizzuto – in a Yankee Stadium game against the Red Sox. But he manages only a split. The Yankees and Jim Konstanty win the opener, 6-5, on a home run pinch hit by Joe Collins – one of five in the game. Boston takes the nightcap, 8-7.

Cuban-born outfielder Carlos Paula becomes the first black player to become a member of the Senators.

SEPTEMBER 10:

Joe Adcock homers off Billy Loes of the Dodgers – his record ninth homer at Ebbets Field this season.

SEPTEMBER 11:

For the second time this season, Joe Adcock of the Braves is hit by a Dodgers' pitcher. This time he is lost for the remainder of the season, suffering a broken right hand when struck by a pitch from Don Newcombe. On August 1, after a four-homer game the previous day, he was beaned by Clem Labine.

SEPTEMBER 12:

After five straight World Championships, the Yankees

Yogi Berra won his first of three American League Most Valuable Player Awards in 1954.

Johnny Mize comments: "Rabbit Maranville was working with kids for the *Journal-American* when he died in January of '54. The next summer he was voted into the Hall of Fame. Why did his record get so much better after he died?"

will be home watching the 1954 fall classic on television. The Indians take two from New York today at Cleveland Stadium increasing their first-place lead to eight and a half games. With 84,587 attending, the Indians top the Yankees in the opener, 4-1, on Bob Lemon's 22nd win, a six-hitter. Al Rosen's seventh-inning two-run double is the key hit. In the nightcap, Early Wynn pitches a three-hitter for his 21st victory, beating New York, 3-2. Yogi Berra's homer for the Yankees is offset by a three-run fifth inning highlighted by three singles and a Wally Westlake double. The Indians are now 104-40.

SEPTEMBER 14:

Paul Richards joins the Orioles, replacing Jimmy Dykes as manager and Arthur Ehlers as general manager. Baltimore was 54-100 this past season, finishing in seventh place.

Bob Lemon pitches Cleveland to a 6-3 win over the Tigers, ensuring at least a tie for the AL pennant. It is Lemon's 23rd win of the season. Bobby Avila breaks a 2-2 tie with a seventh-inning grand slam home run.

SEPTEMBER 18:

In heavy rain in Detroit, the Indians wrap up the AL pennant with a 3-2 victory behind Early Wynn. Dale Mitchell delivers a seventh-inning pinch-hit homer; Jim Hegan also has a round-tripper. It is Cleveland's ninth consecutive win and their 107th victory of the season.

SEPTEMBER 22:

The Indians beat the White Sox, 3-1, for their 110th win of the season, tying the AL record set by the 1927 Yankees. Don Mossi is the winning pitcher with a five-hitter.

The Dodgers' Karl Spooner makes his major league debut, striking out 15 – including six in a row in the seventh and eighth innings. The 23-year-old left-hander is the first player to ring up that strikeout total in his first game. The Dodgers defeat the Giants, 3-0.

SEPTEMBER 25:

In Cleveland, the Indians set an AL record with their 111th win – an 11-1 thrashing of the Tigers on the next-to-last day of the season. Early Wynn has a no-hitter into the ninth, when Fred Hatfield singles and Steve Souchock triples. George Zuverink gets the loss. The 1906 Cubs hold the all-time record with 116 wins.

SEPTEMBER 26:

The Dodgers' Karl Spooner makes his second major league start and pitches his second shutout, striking out 12 in a 1-0 victory over the Pirates. Spooner has 27 strikeouts in his two games.

In Philadelphia, the Phillies' Richie Ashburn plays in his 730th consecutive game. In the final contest of the year, the Phillies lose, 3-2, to the Giants. Ashburn's streak began back on June 7, 1950.

The Philadelphia Athletics, who have been in the AL since its inception in 1901, play their final game. The franchise will be relocated to Kansas City for the 1955 season. The A's close on an upbeat note at Yankee Stadium, beating New York, 8-6, for Art Ditmar's first major league win. Tommy Byrne gets the loss. The Yankees, mathematically eliminated from the pennant race, start catcher Yogi Berra at third, first baseman Bill "Moose" Skowron at second, and center fielder Mickey Mantle at shortstop.

Willie Mays, his teammate Don Mueller, and the Dodgers' Duke Snider are locked in a tight battle for the NL batting race on the last day of the season. Playing against the Phillies, Mays has a single, double, and triple in four official at-bats (he walks once). Mueller has two hits in six at-bats in the Giants' 3-2 win in 11 innings. Duke Snider is held hitless by the Pirates. Mays, who has 41 homers and 110 RBI, finishes at .345, becoming the first Giant since Bill Terry (.401) in 1930 to win the NL batting title. Mueller's final average is .342, Snider's .341.

REGULAR SEASON WRAP-UP:

Cleveland, under Al Lopez, looks unbeatable after winning the AL pennant with a modern-day best 111-43 (.721) regular season record. Despite 103 wins, the Yankees finish eight games out. The Indians have four outstanding pitchers: Bob Lemon (23-7), Early Wynn (23-11), Mike Garcia (19-8), and Bob Feller (13-3) and excellent relievers in Don Mossi and Ray

HISTORY

Giants' farmhand Bob Lennon hits 64 homers for Nashville in the Southern Association. Like many minor league sluggers, Lennon has a brief and unspectacular shot at the majors. He pinch-hits three times for the New York Giants without a hit this season, has 10 hits in 55 at-bats with no homers in 1956, and concludes his big league career as a Cub in 1957 with three hits – including a homer and double – in 21 plate appearances.

"I caught it the way a football end catches a long leading pass. Then I spun and threw."
– Willie Mays, on "The Catch"

TRIVIA

On television, *Baseball Blues* stars Frank Lovejoy, with Frankie Frisch and Vernon "Lefty" Gomez.

Narleski. The staff ERA is 2.78. Bobby Avila, the AL batting champion, hits .341; Larry Doby has 32 homers, 126 RBI, and a .272 average. Al Rosen bats .300 with 24 homers and 102 RBI.

The Giants, under Leo Durocher, finish at 97-57, beating their crosstown archrivals, the Dodgers, by five games. Willie Mays is the dominant hitter with a league-leading .345 with 41 homers and 110 RBI. Don Mueller bats .342; Hank Thompson has 26 homers and Alvin Dark 20. Johnny Antonelli, at 21-7, is New York's ace.

The Braves set an attendance record with 2,131,388. Ted Williams returns to baseball after serving parts of the 1952 and 1953 seasons in Korea; he compiles a slugging average of .635, bats .345, and hits 29 home runs. The Cardinals' Eldon "Rip" Repulski sets a major league record by getting two or more hits in 10 consecutive games.

WROTE ARNOLD HANO IN *A DAY IN THE BLEACHERS*, REMARKING ON THE OTHER ASPECT OF MAYS'S "CATCH" IN GAME ONE OF THE '54 WORLD SERIES: "BUT THE THROW!... THIS WAS THE THROW OF A GIANT, THE THROW OF A HOWITZER MADE HUMAN."

SEPTEMBER 29:

World Series, game one. At the Polo Grounds, Willie Mays delights the hometown fans and stuns the Indians when he makes a spectacular running catch of Vic Wertz's 440-foot shot with his back to the plate in the eighth inning. Mays's catch, with two runners on, keeps the score tied at 2-2. The Giants go on to win, 5-2, in the 10th on a three-run pinch-hit home run off the bat of James "Dusty" Rhodes. Marv Grissom gets the win in relief; Bob Lemon goes all the way for the loss.

SEPTEMBER 30:

World Series, game two. Johnny Antonelli scatters eight hits and the Giants win, 3-1, on only four safeties – including another homer by Dusty Rhodes. Al Smith homers for the visiting Indians. The losing pitcher is Early Wynn.

OCTOBER 1:

World Series, game three. In Cleveland, the Giants make it three in a row with a 6-2 victory behind Ruben Gomez, with a save from Hoyt Wilhelm. Dusty Rhodes pinch-hits for Monte Irvin in the third inning and drives in two key runs with a bases-loaded single. Vic Wertz homers for the Indians; Mike Garcia is the losing pitcher.

OCTOBER 2:

World Series, game four. The Giants sweep the Indians with a 7-4 victory in Cleveland. The new World Champions use 10 hits to defeat Bob Lemon, the first of five Indians' pitchers. Hank Majeski homers for Cleveland. The winning pitcher is Don Liddle. The key to the series is pitching: the Giants allow 1.46 earned runs, the Indians 4.84. Dusty Rhodes hits .667 with two homers and seven RBI. Alvin Dark bats .412 and Don Mueller .389. Mays knocks in three runs and has a .286 average. Vic Wertz is all of Cleveland's offense with a .500 batting average, one homer, and three RBI.

Hoyt Wilhelm relieves Giants' starter Don Liddle in the seventh inning, and his knuckleball is at its dancing best. In the eighth, his pitches become too evasive for catcher Wes Westrum. According to author Charles Einstein, Leo Durocher asks Westrum if he wants a new pitcher. Westrum responds, "No. I want a new catcher. If somebody's going to set a record for passed balls in the World Series, I don't want it to be me."

SEPTEMBER 29
In game one of the Indians-Giants World Series, Willie Mays makes "The Catch."

OCTOBER 2
The Giants complete a four-game Series sweep of the Indians with a 7-4 win in Cleveland.

Durocher brings on Johnny Antonellii to finish the game.

POST-SEASON

OCTOBER 5:

Marilyn Monroe files for divorce from Joe DiMaggio in California.

OCTOBER 6:

Negro League player-manager Oscar Charleston dies in Philadelphia nine days short of his 58th birthday. Charleston played first base and the outfield for 26 years with a variety of teams, including the Homestead Grays and the Pittsburgh Crawfords, hitting an estimated .350, and was considered by John J. McGraw as the best player in the Negro Leagues.

OCTOBER 19:

Hall of Famer Hugh Duffy, who compiled the highest single season average ever, dies at age 87 in Boston. In 1894, Duffy hit .438 with the NL Boston Beaneaters. In his 17 years of major league ball, he hit .324. Inducted into the Hall of Fame in 1945, Duffy also managed for eight seasons.

NOVEMBER 4:

The family of Connie Mack – who is now 91 years old – sells the Athletics to 47-year-old Chicago businessman Arnold Johnson for $604,000. The deal means that Philadelphia will lose its AL team; the owners had rejected the proposal of a local group on October 28. Johnson, who previously bought Kansas City territorial rights – along with Yankee Stadium – from New York, plans to move the team in time for next season. Connie Mack's sons, Earle and Roy, act on behalf of the family.

NOVEMBER 8:

AL owners, meeting in New York City, approve the transfer of the Athletics from Philadelphia to Kansas City. The vote is 6-2, with Clark Griffith of Washington and Hank Greenberg of Cleveland dissenting. Johnson agrees to sell Yankee Stadium. The transfer of the Athletics is the third franchise shift in 20 months. The Athletics will play at Municipal Stadium, the former home of the Yankees' minor league Kansas City Blues. Plans call for the facility to be expanded from 17,000 to 36,000 seats.

NOVEMBER 16:

Former NL home run champion Ralph Kiner (.285, 22 homers, 73 RBI) is traded to the Indians by the Cubs for pitcher Sam Jones (not in the majors in 1954), minor league outfielder Galeward "Gale" Wade, and $60,000.

NOVEMBER 18:

The Yankees and Orioles trade nine players. Coming to New York are pitchers Bob Turley (14-15, 3.46 ERA) and Don Larsen (3-21, 4.37 ERA), along with shortstop Billy Hunter (.243). In return Baltimore gets pitchers Harry Byrd (9-7, 2.99 ERA) and Jim McDonald (4-1, 3.17 ERA), catcher Gus Triandos (.000 in two games), outfielder Gene Woodling (.250, three homers), shortstop Willie Miranda (.250), and minor league catcher Hal W. Smith.

NOVEMBER 22:

The Pirates draft outfielder Roberto Clemente from the Dodgers' farm system. Clemente hit .257 with Brooklyn's Montreal Royals farm team in the International League.

DECEMBER 1:

The Yankees and Orioles exchange nine more players to complete their November 18 trade, making it the largest transaction in baseball history. New York gets first baseman Dick Kryhoski (.260), outfielder Jim Fridley (.246, four homers), pitcher Mike Blyzka (1-5, 4.69 ERA), and minor league catcher Darrell Johnson. Reporting to Baltimore are outfielder Bill Miller (0-1, 6.35 ERA), minor league infielder Kal Segrist, second baseman Don Leppert, and outfielder Ted Del Guercio, and a player to be named later. When the two-part trade is completed, the Yankees have eight new players and the Orioles nine.

DECEMBER 13:

The Dodgers offer $14,000 to 19-year-old left-handed pitcher Sanford "Sandy" Koufax.

The Dodgers send third baseman Billy Cox (.235, two homers) and pitcher Elwin "Preacher" Roe (3-4, 5.00 ERA) to the Pirates for $50,000 and minor leaguers John Kancse and Harry Schwegeman.

DECEMBER 26:

Osborne "Ozzie" Smith is born in Mobile, Alabama.

THE BEST OF 1954

NATIONAL LEAGUE

HITTERS

Batting Average:
Willie Mays, New York Giants, .345

Slugging Average:
Willie Mays, .667

Home Runs:
Ted Kluszewski, Cincinnati Redlegs, 49

Runs Batted In:
Ted Kluszewski, 141

Hits:
Don Mueller, New York Giants, 212

Stolen Bases:
Bill Bruton, Milwaukee Braves, 34

PITCHERS

Wins:
Robin Roberts, Philadelphia Phillies, 23

Strikeouts:
Robin Roberts, 185

Earned Run Average:
Johnny Antonelli, New York Giants, 2.30

Winning Percentage:
Johnny Antonelli, .750

Saves:
Jim Hughes, Brooklyn Dodgers, 24

Most Valuable Player:
Willie Mays, New York Giants

Rookie of the Year:
Wally Moon, St. Louis Cardinals

AMERICAN LEAGUE

HITTERS

Batting Average:
Roberto "Bobby" Avila, Cleveland Indians, .341

Slugging Average:
Ted Williams, Boston Red Sox, .613

Home Runs:
Larry Doby, Cleveland Indians, 32

Runs Batted In:
Larry Doby, 126

Hits:
Jacob "Nellie" Fox, Chicago White Sox;
Harvey Kuenn, Detroit Tigers, 201

Stolen Bases:
Jackie Jensen, Boston Red Sox, 22

PITCHERS

Wins:
Bob Lemon, Cleveland Indians;
Early Wynn, Cleveland Indians, 23

Strikeouts:
Bob Turley, Baltimore Orioles, 185

Earned Run Average:
Mike Garcia, Cleveland Indians, 2.64

Winning Percentage:
Sandalio "Sandy" Consuegra, Chicago White Sox, .842

Saves:
Johnny Sain, New York Yankees, 22

Most Valuable Player:
Lawrence "Yogi" Berra, New York Yankees

Rookie of the Year:
Bob Grim, New York Yankees

NEWS

EISENHOWER OKAYS USE OF NUCLEAR WEAPONS IN WAR

U.S., Britain, France, USSR attend Geneva Conference

SOUTH EAST ASIA TREATY ORGANIZATION (SEATO) FORMED

AFL, CIO UNIONS MERGE

Disneyland opens in California

ACTOR JAMES DEAN DIES IN AUTO CRASH; *REBEL WITHOUT A CAUSE* AND *EAST OF EDEN* RELEASED

TELEVISION VIEWERS TUNE IN TO *THE HONEYMOONERS, THE LAWRENCE WELK SHOW, THE MICKEY MOUSE CLUB, THE $64,000 QUESTION, GUNSMOKE*

HITS: "MAYBELLINE," "ROCK AROUND THE CLOCK"

PRE-SEASON

JANUARY 29:

Under the terms of his agreement with the AL, Arnold Johnson sells Yankee Stadium. The buyer is John William Cox, who purchases both the stadium and the grounds, selling the latter to the Knights of Columbus and willing the ballpark to Rice University in Texas.

THE SEASON

APRIL 12:

The Athletics debut in Kansas City with a 6-2 win over the Tigers at Municipal Stadium with a crowd of 32,844 on hand. Connie Mack, 92 years old, and AL president Will Harridge are among the baseball notables attending. Former president Harry S. Truman throws out the first ball. Prior to the game, a parade for the Athletics draws some 200,000 spectators. Bill Wilson hits Kansas City's first-ever homer in the eighth inning, and Bob Wilson of the Tigers also hits a round-tripper. The winning pitcher is Alex Kellner with three innings in relief of starter Ewell Blackwell. Ned Garver gets the loss.

APRIL 13:

At Yankee Stadium, the visiting Senators suffer the most lopsided opening day defeat in history: 19-1. (This is the Yankees' opening day; Washington actually had its home debut on April 11, beating the Orioles, 12-5.) Whitey Ford pitches a two-hitter, hits three singles, and drives in four runs. Mickey Mantle, Yogi Berra, and Bill Skowron homer for the Yankees. Mantle and Bob Cerv each drive in four runs.

APRIL 14:

One day short of eight years since Jackie Robinson's debut with the Dodgers, the Yankees finally have their first black player. He is 26-year-old Elston Howard, a catcher-outfielder. Howard breaks into the lineup at Fenway Park when leftfielder Irv Noren is ejected over a call at the plate Howard plays three innings, singles and drives in a run. The Red Sox win the game, 8-4.

The New York Yankees are the 13th of 16 major league teams to field a black player. The holdouts are the Red Sox, Tigers, and Phillies.

MAY
1
Bob Feller, 36, pitches his ML-record 12th career one-hitter and blanks Boston, 2-0.

CULTURE

On stage, theater-goers delight in *Damn Yankees*, by Richard Adler and Jerry Ross, the musical version of Douglass Wallop's *The Year the Yankees Lost the Pennant.*

APRIL 16:

In St. Louis, the Cubs get consecutive homers from Ransom "Randy" Jackson, Ernie Banks, and Dee Fondy in the second inning, but lose, 12-11, in 11 innings on a bloop single by Wally Moon.

APRIL 17:

The Pirates' 20-year-old outfielder Roberto Clemente makes his major league debut against the Dodgers at Forbes Field and singles once in four at-bats against Johnny Podres. Brooklyn wins, 10-3.

Young Al Kaline has a big day against the Athletics in Detroit. He hits two homers in the sixth inning, adds a third among his four consecutive hits, and drives in six runs. The Tigers romp, 16-0, and Steve Gromek gets the win.

APRIL 21:

The Dodgers beat the Phillies, 14-4, at Ebbets Field, for their 10th consecutive win – a major league record at the start of a season.

APRIL 23:

The wind is blowing out at Municipal Stadium in Kansas City and so are the baseballs – off White Sox bats. Chicago ties a modern league record for runs in a game with a 29-6 blowout of the Athletics. White Sox catcher Sherman Lollar ties a mark with two hits in an inning twice today – the second and sixth. He also has two of Chicago's seven homers and drives in five runs. Bob Nieman adds two more, along with seven RBI. Pitcher Jack Harshman, Walt Dropo, and Minnie Minoso also homer. Minoso drives in five runs. The winning pitcher is Harshman; Bobby Shantz is tagged with the loss.

APRIL 27:

With 81-year-old Hall of Famer Honus Wagner in attendance, the Pirates unveil a statue of him in Schenley Park outside Forbes Field.

MAY 1:

In the twilight of his great career, 36-year-old Bob Feller pitches his major league record 12th career one-hitter. The victim today is Boston, 2-0. Sammy White's seventh-inning single spoils Feller's no-hit bid. In the nightcap, the Indians' 21-year-old rookie Herb Score fans 16, holds the Red Sox to four hits, and wins, 2-1. Score strikes out the first nine Boston batters.

MAY 5:

Dodgers' left-hander Tommy Lasorda makes his first major league start, going against the Cardinals in Brooklyn. He ties an NL record with three wild pitches in the first inning, gets spiked by Wally Moon, and argues with his catcher, Roy Campanella, about the calls and the target he is getting. The Dodgers go on to win, 4-3.

MAY 11:

Today the Dodgers' winning streak is snapped at 11 by an Ernie Banks grand slam homer – the first of his career. The Cubs win, 10-8, at Wrigley Field. Dee Fondy hits a three-run homer in the fifth inning for Chicago.

The Yankees ship two veterans, outfielder Enos Slaughter (.111 in 10 games) and pitcher Johnny Sain (0-0 in three games), to the Athletics for pitcher John "Sonny" Dixon (0-0, 16.20 ERA) and cash.

MAY 12:

For the first time in 38 years, Wrigley Field – a hitter's paradise – is the scene of a no-hitter. The Cubs' Sad Sam Jones – AKA Toothpick – no-hits the Pirates, 4-0. Jones becomes the first black pitcher to throw a major league no-hitter. The game has a precarious finish for the 29-year-old Jones. He walks the bases loaded in the ninth, then strikes out Dick Groat, Roberto Clemente, and Frank J. Thomas. Jones walks eight and strikes out six; the Cubs are errorless behind him. The losing pitcher is Nelson "Nellie" King.

MAY 13:

Mickey Mantle bombs the Tigers from both sides of the plate at Yankee Stadium in a 5-2 win. He is the second AL player ever with "switch homers" in a game. The first was Johnny Lucadello with the 1940 Browns. Batting left-handed, Mantle hits a 400-foot first-inning drive into the right center field bleachers with Andy Carey on base. After an RBI single in the third, Mantle slams a 430-foot homer into the right center field bleachers on a 2-0 pitch from Gromek. In the eighth inning, with Bob Miller on the mound, Mantle turns around and slams a right-handed shot into right center field. He drives in all of New York's runs in a 5-2 victory.

MAY 27:

Norm Zauchin of the Red Sox hits three homers and a double and drives in 10 runs in the first five innings of a 16-0 trouncing of the Senators.

MAY 28:

After a 17-19 start, the Cardinals fire manager Eddie Stanky and replace him with Harry "The Hat" Walker. His brother, Fred "Dixie" Walker, succeeds him as manager of the Rochester Red Wings in the International League.

MAY 30:

The Dodgers' Don Newcombe hits two homers for the second time this year and beats the Giants, 10-8. On May 26, Newcombe had a triple, stole home, and batted in two runs against the Pirates.

JUNE 5:

Mickey Mantle launches a pitch from Billy Pierce over the left-field upper deck at Comiskey Park, a home run estimated at more than 500 feet. The teams split a double header.

FORMER YANKEES' MANAGER JOE MCCARTHY TOLD MAURY ALLEN IN *WHERE HAVE YOU GONE, JOE DIMAGGIO?*: "HE DID EVERYTHING SO EASILY. THAT'S WHY THEY NEVER APPRECIATED HIM AS MUCH AS THEY SHOULD. YOU NEVER SAW HIM MAKE A GREAT CATCH. YOU NEVER SAW HIM FALL DOWN OR GO DIVING FOR A BALL. HE DIDN'T HAVE TO. HE JUST KNEW WHERE THE BALL WAS HIT AND HE WENT AND GOT IT. THAT'S WHAT YOU'RE SUPPOSED TO DO. THE IDEA IS TO CATCH THE BALL. THE IDEA ISN'T TO MAKE EXCITING CATCHES." TEAMMATE BILL DICKEY ECHOED THE REMARKS TO ALLEN: "I THINK DIMAGGIO WAS UNDERESTIMATED AS A PLAYER. HE DID THINGS SO EASILY, PEOPLE DIDN'T REALIZE HOW GOOD HE WAS."

JUNE 8:

The Dodgers make a roster move, swapping left-handers within the organization. Pitcher Sandy Koufax is activated after 30 days on the disabled list. To make room for him, pitcher Tommy Lasorda is farmed out to the Montreal Royals in the International League.

Lasorda's playing days with the Dodgers are over after 13 innings of work in parts of two seasons and no decisions. He is 0-4 with the Athletics in 1956 before turning to managing.

JUNE 9:

The Dodgers send 1952 Rookie of the Year Joe Black (1-0 in six games) to the Redlegs for outfielder-infielder Bob Borkowski (.167 in 25 games) and a cash payment.

JUNE 19:

Leo Durocher replaces Willie Mays, who is hitting .279, with Carroll "Whitey" Lockman in today's starting lineup. The Braves beat the Giants, 8-7.

CULTURE

***Fear Strikes Out*, by Jim Piersall, with Al Hirschberg, is the autobiography of the talented and troubled outfielder. *Man on Spikes*, by Eliot Asinof, is a worthy and neglected novel about a minor leaguer trying for the majors after 16 years. *The Only Game in Town*, a novel by Charles Einstein, is also published.**

JUNE 21:

Mickey Mantle becomes the first ever to hit a homer to straightaway center field in Yankee Stadium. Mantle's blow clears the 30-foot hitters' backdrop and lands in the ninth row, an estimated 486 feet from home plate. New York beats Kansas City, 6-2.

JUNE 24:

The Senators' 19-year-old rookie Harmon Killebrew hits his first major league home run – off Billy Hoeft – in an 18-7 loss to the Detroit Tigers at Griffith Stadium.

JUNE 27:

The baseball world is stunned by the death of 25-year-old Red Sox first baseman Harry Agganis at Santa Maria Hospital in Cambridge, Massachusetts, of a blood clot after he is hospitalized with pneumonia. An All-American football player at Boston University, Agganis – known as the Golden Greek – was signed by Boston for an estimated $35,000. In his rookie year, he hit .251 with 11 homers. This season he was hitting .313 in 25 games. Teammate Sammy White says, "Harry was not only a talented athlete with the strength of Hercules, the competitive spirit and courage of a lion, he was a leader and at the same time a follower of all that was good."

JULY 5:

Today Crosley Field in Cincinnati is the scene of another baseball fight, but this one involves managers only. Redlegs' manager George "Birdie" Tebbetts comes out of the dugout to protest to umpire John "Jocko" Conlan about delaying tactics by Cardinals' catcher Bill Sarni and manager Harry Walker. Walker leaves his bench and exchanges angry words with Tebbetts. They exchange punches and wrestle each other to the ground as players from both teams get involved. When they are separated, Walker has a bruised forehead and Tebbetts a bloody nose and abrasions on his mouth. The Redlegs score twice in the ninth to win the game, 5-4. NL President Warren Giles fines each manager $100 and Bill Sarni $25.

JULY 6:

It's not exactly a preview of coming attractions when Sandy Koufax makes his first major league start. Pitching against the Pirates today in Pittsburgh, Koufax goes four and two-thirds innings, allowing three hits and eight walks, while fanning four. He is not involved in the decision as the Pirates beat the Dodgers, 4-1.

JULY 8:

The Athletics' light-hitting shortstop Joe DeMaestri gets six hits in six at-bats in an 11-8 loss to the Tigers in 11 innings.

JULY 9:

Arch Ward, the founder of baseball's All-Star Game, dies. The sports editor of the *Chicago Tribune*, Ward also created the Chicago College All-Star Football Game and the professional All-America Football Conference.

JULY 12:

At County Stadium in Milwaukee, the 22nd All-Star Game is delayed 30 minutes so representatives of baseball can attend the Chicago funeral of Arch Ward. With the score tied, 5-5, in the bottom of the 10th, Stan Musial hits the first pitch from Frank Sullivan for a homer and an NL victory. Earlier Mickey Mantle hit a 430-foot three-run homer over the center-field fence against Robin Roberts. The winning pitcher is Gene Conley.

JULY 14:

The Indians sign two-time AL batting champion Ferris Fain (.264 in 58 games). The first baseman recently was released by the Tigers.

JULY 18:

In the second inning, Giants' pitcher Ruben Gomez hits Joe Adcock on the wrist with a pitch. The Braves' six-foot, four-inch, 210-pound first baseman, who has been a prime target for NL pitchers, takes off after Gomez (six feet, 170 pounds), who hits him in the leg with the ball. Adcock chases Gomez off the mound and into the dugout. Umpire Bill Jackowski ejects both. Adcock is fined $100; Gomez is fined $250 and gets a three-game suspension.

JULY 19:

Pirates' pitcher Vern Law pitches 18 innings against the Braves, striking out 12, allowing nine hits, and walking only three. The

JUNE 24
The Senators' rookie Harmon Killebrew, 19, hits his first major league home run.

AUGUST 15
With today's homer, Braves' pitcher Warren Spahn has a home run in every NL ballpark.

Pirates win, 4-3, but Law is not involved in the decision.

JULY 22:

Pee Wee Reese gets a cake and a serenade from Dodgers' fans at Ebbets Field, then celebrates his 36th birthday with two doubles in an 8-4 win over the Braves.

JULY 23:

In the top of the ninth inning today, Yankees' pinch hitter Bob Cerv homers against Kansas City's Alex Kellner. The Athletics bring in Tom A. Gorman, and Elston Howard hits another pinch-hit home run. Cerv and Howard become the first AL players to pinch-hit homers in the same half-inning, but Kansas City holds on to win, 8-7.

JULY 25:

Joe DiMaggio, J. Franklin "Home Run" Baker, Charles "Gabby" Hartnett, Ted Lyons, Ray Schalk, and Dazzy Vance are inducted into the Hall of Fame. Considered by many the finest all-around player of his time, DiMaggio played 13 seasons with the Yankees, on 10 pennant and nine World Series winners. He batted .325 with 361 home runs and 1,537 RBI, and was the AL's Most Valuable Player three times. He twice led the AL in batting – with a high of .381 in 1939. Baker played 13 years with the Athletics and Yankees, batting .307 with 96 homers. The third baseman was the AL's home run champion for four years from 1911 to 1914. He appeared in six World Series, hitting .363 with three homers (two in 1911). Hartnett, called the "perfect catcher" by manager Joe McCarthy, played 20 seasons – 19 with the Cubs – and batted .297. In 1937 he hit .354. Hartnett was the Cubs' player-manager from 1938 to 1940, winning one pennant. Ted Lyons, who pitched in the majors until he was 45 years old, compiled a 260-230 record with a 3.67 ERA in 21 years – all with the White Sox. He was a 20-game winner three times, and twice – in 1925 and 1927 – was the AL's big winner. Schalk, an outstanding catcher, was one of the honest players on the 1919 Black Sox team. In 18 years – 17 with the White Sox – he hit .253 and appeared in two World Series. He caught a major league record four no-hitters, including Charlie Robertson's 1922 perfect game. Vance, who won his first major league game at age 31, pitched 16 seasons and had a record of 197-140 with an ERA of 3.24 and 2,045 strikeouts. He won 20 games three times and was 28-6 with a 2.16 ERA in 1924. He led the NL in strikeouts for seven consecutive seasons.

In his Summer of '49, *David Halberstam writes of the time DiMaggio was asked why he played so hard with his team so far ahead in the pennant race. DiMaggio responded, "Because there might be somebody out there who's never seen me play."*

JULY 30:

The Yankees send pitcher Eddie Lopat (4-8) to the Orioles for the waiver price. Lopat was 113-59 in seven-plus seasons with New York and 4-1 in five World Series.

AUGUST 2:

At Wrigley Field, the Cubs' Ernie Banks hits his fourth grand slam homer of the season. The Cubs and Bob Rush beat the Pirates, 12-4.

AUGUST 4:

Ernie Banks is making the Pirates' pitching staff wish they'd never seen the inside of Wrigley Stadium. Today he homers against Lino Donoso, Max Surkont, and Dick Littlefield in an 11-10 win.

AUGUST 10:

Stan Musial doubles against the Braves' Lew Burdette for his 1,000th extra base hit. It also is Musial's 529th career two-base hit. Visiting St. Louis wins, 7-2.

AUGUST 11:

Ted Williams lines a single off the Yankees' Bob Turley in the first inning for his 2,000th career hit. Regardless, the Yankees beat the visiting Red Sox, 5-3.

AUGUST 15:

The Braves' Warren Spahn reaches an unusual milestone for a pitcher. With today's home run against the Cardinals' Mel Wright in St. Louis, Spahn has hit a round-tripper in every NL ball ballpark during his 21-year career.

AUGUST 20:

Dodgers owner Walter O'Malley makes a prediction to New York City mayor Robert F. Wagner about his team and

HISTORY

The Dodgers' sensational young left-hander Karl Spooner injures his arm in spring training when he comes in to relieve in an exhibition game against the Cardinals. In *Where Have You Gone, Vince DiMaggio?*, Spooner remembers, "What a mistake. I really thought I was set to go. I just wasn't ready. What else can I say? I felt something pop almost as soon as I got out there. Afterwards it really started to hurt. In those days they called it tendonitis. It was really a rotator cuff. And you know what that means, you're finished." Spooner struggles through an 8-6 season with a 3.65 ERA and never pitches again in the majors, although he gets a shot with the Cardinals in 1959 spring training.

the Giants, "It's unlikely that one club or the other will move. You'll find that the two will move."

AUGUST 26:

Indians first baseman Vic Wertz is stricken with polio. He is batting .253 with 14 homers and 55 RBI when he becomes ill.

Wertz is not paralyzed and returns to play in 136 games in 1956 and remains in the majors until 1963.

AUGUST 31:

Today's Orioles-Indians game turns into a strikeout clinic. Cleveland left-hander Herb Score fans 13. Hal "Skinny" Brown relieves Bill Wight and strikes out 10 in eight no-hit innings. Before his departure, Wight yields five hits, two walks, and five runs in the first, enough for a 5-1 Indians' victory.

SEPTEMBER 2:

Ernie Banks drills a 2-1 pitch from Paul LaPalme with two men on base into left field for his 40th homer of the season – a major league record for shortstops. The previous mark of 39 was set by Vern Stephens with the Red Sox in 1949. The Cubs beat up on the Cardinals, 12-2. Other homers are hit by Ransom Jackson and Walker Cooper of the Cubs and Wally Moon of the Cardinals. The winning pitcher is Paul Minner; Tom Poholsky is credited with the loss.

Mickey Mantle hits his 36th homer of the year to lead the Yankees over the Senators, 4-2. Today also marks second baseman Billy Martin's return from the military.

SEPTEMBER 5:

The Dodgers' Don Newcombe homers in an 11-4 victory over the Phillies. It is Newcombe's seventh of the year, an NL record for pitchers.

SEPTEMBER 7:

The Indians' Early Wynn five-hits the Orioles, 6-0, for his 200th career win. Larry Doby hits two home runs.

Whitey Ford one-hits the Athletics, 2-1, at Yankee Stadium. He sets an AL record with back-to-back one-hitters. Jim Finigan's double in the seventh with two out spoils today's no-hit bid. On September 2, Ford one-hit the Senators,

IN HIS AUTOBIOGRAPHY, TED WILLIAMS REFLECTS ON HIMSELF AND JOE DIMAGGIO: "IT IS PROBABLY MY MISFORTUNE THAT I HAVE BEEN AND WILL INEVITABLY BE COMPARED WITH JOE DIMAGGIO... IN MY HEART I HAVE ALWAYS FELT I WAS A BETTER HITTER THAN JOE, WHICH WAS ALWAYS MY FIRST CONSIDERATION, BUT I HAVE TO SAY THAT HE WAS THE GREATEST BALLPLAYER OF OUR TIME. HE COULD DO IT ALL."

4-2. Carlos Paula had the game's only hit in the 7th inning.

SEPTEMBER 8:

In Milwaukee, the Dodgers beat the second-place Braves, 10-2, to move 17 games ahead and clinch the NL pennant.

SEPTEMBER 14:

The Indians' Herb Score breaks Grover Cleveland Alexander's rookie strikeout mark when he fans Roy Sievers for his 235th of the year. The Senators win the game, 3-2, beating reliever Ray Narleski.

SEPTEMBER 16:

Robin Yount is born in Danville, Illinois.

Mickey Mantle suffers a hamstring injury on a bunt. He will appear only twice more this season – as a pinch hitter.

SEPTEMBER 17:

Brooks Robinson makes his major league debut at third base for the Orioles and gets two hits in four at-bats against the visiting Senators in a 3-1 victory.

SEPTEMBER 18:

At Yankee Stadium, New York beats the Red Sox, 3-2, on a Bob Grim three-hitter, to sweep the three-game series and move two games up on the second-place Indians.

Willie Mays homers at Ebbets Fields against the Dodgers. It is his ninth round-tripper in Brooklyn, matching Adcock's 1954 mark. Brooklyn wins, 7-5.

SEPTEMBER 19:

Ernie Banks hits his major league record fifth grand slam homer of the season. But it's not enough as the Cardinals beat the Cubs, 6-5, in 12 innings. A homer by Eldon "Rip" Repulski off Jim Davis provides the winning run for St. Louis.

Another flagpole sitter – Braves' fan Bill Sherwood – alights after 89 days. He originally had pledged to remain on the pole until the Braves won seven straight games. They won six consecutively three times, but never seven.

SEPTEMBER 20:

Willie Mays becomes the seventh player ever to hit 50 homers in a season. Mays reaches the mark with two-run homers in each game of a doubleheader against the Pirates at the Polo Grounds. He joins Babe Ruth, Ralph Kiner, Jimmie Foxx, Hank Greenberg, Hack Wilson, and Johnny Mize in the "50" club. The two homers also give Mays seven in six games, tying a major league record. The Giants win, 11-1 and 14-8.

SEPTEMBER 21:

Frank Lane steps down as general manager of the White Sox. In seven years, he made 241 deals involving a total of 353 ball players.

SEPTEMBER 25:

Leo Durocher resigns as manager of the Giants to accept a job in broadcasting, and Willie Mays hits his 51st homer of the season as the Giants beat the Phillies, 5-2, in the opener of a doubleheader. The Phillies win the nightcap, 3-1, ending the game with a triple play.

Playing with a sore wrist, 20-year-old Al Kaline is hitless in one at-bat against the Indians but concludes his season at .340, becoming the youngest batting champion ever by one day over Ty Cobb in 1907. The Tigers win the game, 6-2.

Dodgers' Hall of Fame shortstop Pee Wee Reese played in seven World Series.

"If one can be certain of anything in baseball, it is that we shall not look upon his like again."
– *Sportswriter Roger Kahn, on Jackie Robinson*

In St. Louis, the Cardinals' Wally Moon homers against Chet Nichols, bringing the NL's total to an all-time high of 1,263. The Cardinals beat the Braves, 8-5.

REGULAR SEASON WRAP-UP:

The Dodgers waltz to the pennant by 13 1/2 games ahead of the Braves. Under Walter Alston the team is 98-55 and power-laden. Roy Campanella hits .318 with 32 homers and 107 RBI; Snider .309, 42 homers, and 136 RBI; Gil Hodges .289, 27 homers, and 102 RBI; and Carl Furillo .314, 26 homers, and 95 RBI. Don Newcombe tops the pitching staff at 20-5 and wields a mean bat, with a .359 average and seven homers.

The Yankees, under Casey Stengel, are 96-58 for their sixth flag in seven years. They finish three games ahead of the Indians. Yogi Berra hits .272 with 27 homers and 108 RBI. Mickey Mantle is at .306 with 37 round-trippers and 99 RBI. Bill Skowron hits .319. Whitey Ford leads the pitchers with an 187 record.

1954 is a boom year for rookies. The ranks include future Hall of Famers Sandy Koufax, Ernie Banks, Brooks Robinson, Roberto Clemente, and Harmon Killebrew, along with one "might have been" – Herb Score, who sets a rookie strikeout record with 245. The AL has no 20-game winners and only three with 18 victories: Whitey Ford, Frank Sullivan of the Red Sox, and Bob Lemon of the Indians.

SEPTEMBER 28:

World Series, game one. At Yankee Stadium, New York beats Brooklyn, 6-5, in a game marked by five homers and Jackie Robinson's eighth-inning steal of home. For the Yankees, Elston Howard hits a two-run homer and Joe Collins hits two – a solo and a two-run shot. Carl Furillo and Duke Snider hit round-trippers for the Dodgers. Whitey Ford gets the win with a save from Bob Grim. Don Newcombe is charged with the loss. September 28 is the earliest start for a series since 1918.

SEPTEMBER 29:

World Series, game two. Tommy Byrne five-hits the Dodgers, 4-2, today at Yankee Stadium. Byrne sparks a four-run fourth with a two-run single. Billy Loes is the loser.

SEPTEMBER 30:

World Series, game three. The Dodgers collect 11 hits – including a two-run home run by Roy Campanella – to beat the Yankees, 8-3, at Ebbets Field. Campanella totals three hits and three RBI and Johnny Podres gets a complete-game victory. Mickey Mantle homers for the Yankees. Bob Turley gets the loss.

OCTOBER 1:

World Series, game four. Roy Campanella, Gil Hodges (with one on), and Duke Snider (with two on) homer in an 8-5 victory for the Dodgers at Ebbets Field. Gil McDougald hits a bases-empty homer for New York. Clem Labine gets the win with four and a third innings of relief. Yankees' starter Don Larsen is the loser.

OCTOBER 2:

World Series, game five. Bob Grim puts the Yankees in a hole by yielding a two-run homer to Sandy Amoros and two solo round-trippers to Duke Snider in the first five innings. Homers by Bob Cerv and Yogi Berra bring the Yankees close, but they fall short, 5-3. Roger Craig gets the win with a save from Clem Labine. The Dodgers now are just one win away from their first World Championship.

OCTOBER 3:

World Series, game six. Today at Yankee Stadium, Whitey Ford four-hits the Dodgers, 5-1, to knot the series. The Yankees score all their runs in the first inning, with Bill Skowron's three-run homer the big blow. Karl Spooner, who lasts only a third of an inning, is charged with the loss.

OCTOBER 4:

World Series, game seven. Next year is today for the Dodgers, who win the team's first-ever World Championship with a 2-0 Johnny Podres five-hitter. Gil Hodges drives in both runs. In the sixth inning, left fielder Sandy Amoros makes a running catch on a Yogi Berra drive and doubles up Gil McDougald to snuff out a Yankees' rally. Tommy Byrne is the losing pitcher. Duke Snider is the batting star with .320, a record-tying four homers, and seven

SEPTEMBER 28
Game one of the Yankees-Dodgers World Series features Jackie Robinson stealing home.

OCTOBER 4
No more waiting 'til next year! The Dodgers win their first World Championship.

RBI. Johnny Podres has two wins and a 1.00 ERA. Hank Bauer (.429) and Yogi Berra (.417) lead New York. Mickey Mantle is held to .200 with one homer and a single RBI.

POST-SEASON

OCTOBER 9:

Former major league pitcher Howie Fox is knifed to death in a barroom fight in San Antonio, Texas. He was 34 years old. In nine major league seasons, he was 43-72. He last pitched in the majors in 1954 with the Orioles and was 1-2.

OCTOBER 18:

Ralph Kiner, who led the NL in home runs for seven consecutive years, is calling it a career. Kiner, who hit 18 homers and batted .243 in 113 games for the Indians in 1955, has the best home run ratio – 7.1 percent – of all time. In 10 years, he batted .279 with 369 homers.

OCTOBER 20:

Branch Rickey retires as Pirates' general manager after the team finishes last five consecutive times.

OCTOBER 25:

Larry Doby (.291, 26 homers, 100 RBI), who broke the AL's color line in 1947 with the Indians, is traded by Cleveland to the White Sox for outfielder Jim Busby (.239, seven homers with Washington and Chicago) and shortstop Alfonso "Chico" Carrasquel (.256, 11 homers).

OCTOBER 26:

Joe L. Brown – son of movie star Joe E. Brown – is named general manager of the Pirates, replacing the retired Branch Rickey.

OCTOBER 27:

Hall of Famer Clark Griffith dies at age 85 in Washington, D.C. Known as the Old Fox, Griffith was a player, manager, and the owner of the Washington Senators. As a major league pitcher, he was 240-144 with a 3.31 ERA over 20 years. He won 20 games or more six consecutive seasons. He managed for 20 years, leading the 1901 Chicago White Stockings to the AL pennant. He began his association with the Senators in 1912 as part owner and manager. Griffith was inducted into the Hall of Fame in 1946. Ownership of the Senators goes to his adopted son, Calvin R. Griffith.

NOVEMBER 4:

Denton True "Cy" Young dies at age 88 in New Comerstown, Ohio. Young, inducted into the Hall of Fame in 1937, won 511 games – more than any other pitcher in history – and lost a record 316. He compiled a 2.63 ERA over 22 years, pitching 7,356 innings and striking out 2,796. He had a record 750 complete games and pitched 76 shutouts.

NOVEMBER 8:

The Senators trade first baseman James "Mickey" Vernon (.301, 14 homers), a two-time AL batting champion, pitchers Erwin "Bob" Porterfield (10-17, 4.45 ERA) and John Schmitz (7-10, 3.71 ERA), along with outfielder Tom Umphlett (.217) to Boston. In return, the Red Sox send Washington pitchers Dick Brodowski (1-0, 5.63 ERA) and Truman "Tex" Clevenger (did not play in 1955), outfielder Karl Olson (.250 in 26 games), minor league pitcher Al Curtis, and minor league outfielder Neil Chrisley.

DECEMBER 6:

Hall of Fame shortstop John "Honus" Wagner dies at age 81 in Carnegie, Pennsylvania. Wagner played 21 years – 18 of them with Pittsburgh. He finished his celebrated career batting .327 with 643 doubles, 252 triples, and 722 stolen bases. He hit 101 home runs, with never more than 10 in a single season. He was the National League's batting champion eight times and batted .300 or better 16 times – including 15 seasons in a row. Wagner retired after the 1917 season and was inducted into the Hall of Fame in 1936.

DECEMBER 16:

Following the resignation of Frank Lane, who became general manager of the Cardinals, Chuck Comiskey – grandson of Charles Comiskey – and former pitcher John D. Rigney will share the general manager's duties for the White Sox. Rigney is the son-in-law of the late Charles Comiskey.

DECEMBER 18:

Boston fans get good news; the Red Sox will stay home despite rumors that the franchise will be moved to San Francisco. General manager Joe Cronin brands reports of a move as untrue.

CULTURE

Television audiences see *Fear Strikes Out*, based on Jimmy Piersall's autobiography, starring Tab Hunter and Mona Freeman. *How Charlie Faust Won a Pennant for the Giants*, starring Lee Marvin, recounts the bizarre role of the Giants' mascot during the 1911 season. *Man on Spikes*, starring Warren Stevens, is based on Eliot Asinof's outstanding novel. *Rookie of the Year* stars John Wayne and his son Patrick Wayne.

THE BEST OF 1955

NATIONAL LEAGUE

HITTERS

Batting Average:
Richie Ashburn, Philadelphia Phillies, .338

Slugging Average:
Willie Mays, New York Giants, .659

Home Runs:
Willie Mays, 51

Runs Batted In:
Edwin "Duke" Snider, Brooklyn Dodgers, 136

Hits:
Ted Kluszewski, Cincinnati Redlegs, 192

Stolen Bases:
Bill Bruton, Milwaukee Braves, 25

PITCHERS

Wins:
Robin Roberts, Philadelphia Phillies, 23

Strikeouts:
Sam Jones, Chicago Cubs, 198

Earned Run Average:
Bob Friend, Pittsburgh Pirates, 2.83

Winning Percentage:
Don Newcombe, Brooklyn Dodgers, .800

Saves:
Jack Meyer, Philadelphia Phillies, 16

Most Valuable Player:
Roy Campanella, Brooklyn Dodgers

Rookie of the Year:
Bill Virdon, St. Louis Cardinals

AMERICAN LEAGUE

HITTERS

Batting Average:
Al Kaline, Detroit Tigers, .340

Slugging Average:
Mickey Mantle, New York Yankees, .611

Home Runs:
Mickey Mantle, 37

Runs Batted In:
Ray Boone, Detroit Tigers;
Jackie Jensen, Boston Red Sox, 116

Hits:
Al Kaline, 200

Stolen Bases:
Jim Rivera, Chicago White Sox, 25

PITCHERS

Wins:
Bob Lemon, Cleveland Indians;
Ed "Whitey" Ford, New York Yankees;
Frank Sullivan, Boston Red Sox, 18

Strikeouts:
Herb Score, Cleveland Indians, 245

Earned Run Average:
Walter "Billy" Pierce, Chicago White Sox, 1.97

Winning Percentage:
Tommy Byrne, New York Yankees, .762

Saves:
Ray Narleski, Cleveland Indians, 19

Most Valuable Player:
Lawrence "Yogi" Berra, New York Yankees

Rookie of the Year:
Herb Score, Cleveland Indians

1956

NEWS

EISENHOWER RE-ELECTED, DEFEATING ADLAI STEVENSON

Campus violence erupts as first African-American student enrolls at University of Alabama

NASSER ELECTED PRESIDENT OF EGYPT

Elvis Presley becomes headline performer

128 DIE IN MID-AIR COLLISION OVER GRAND CANYON

FIRST TRANSATLANTIC TELEPHONE CABLE SYSTEM LAID

MONACO'S PRINCE RAINIER MARRIES GRACE KELLY

ALLEN GINSBERG'S BEAT CLASSIC *HOWL* IS PUBLISHED

Melbourne hosts summer olympic games

PRE-SEASON

JANUARY 23:

Billy Evans dies in Miami. A Hall of Famer who umpired in the AL for 21 years, he perhaps is best remembered for a 1921 fist-fight with Ty Cobb.

JANUARY 24:

Mickey Mantle, 24 years old, gets a $10,000 pay increase and will earn $30,000 for the 1956 season.

JANUARY 31:

George "Buck" Weaver, one of the 8 Black Sox banned from baseball for life, collapses and dies at age 65 on the streets of Chicago's South Side. Weaver, who hit .324 in the tainted 1919 World Series with 11 hits, maintained his innocence and was punished principally because he did not inform on his seven teammates. In the nine years before his expulsion, Weaver hit .272. According to sportswriter Fred Lieb, Weaver met with Commissioner Kenesaw Mountain Landis to discuss his case. Weaver admitted attending two meetings with the gamblers and his teammates, but maintained he received no money and played his best. Landis responds, "If you attended two such meetings, you knew everything that was going on; and if you did not so inform your club, I hold you as guilty as the actual plotters and the men who took money for throwing the Series."

FEBRUARY 8:

Connie Mack (Cornelius Alexander McGillicuddy), the Grand Old Man of Baseball, dies at 3:20 p.m. today at the age of 93 in Philadelphia. Mack, the longtime owner and manager of the Philadelphia Athletics, was the last of the AL pioneers. He was elected to the Hall of Fame in 1937.

FEBRUARY 24:

Eddie Murray is born in Los Angeles.

FEBRUARY 29:

Charles McGhee, Matthew Baxter, and Nate Dolin sell 55 percent of the stock of the Cleveland Indians to William R. Daley, Ignatius O'Shaugnessy, and present general manager Hank Greenberg. The price tag is $3,961,800.

MARCH 2:

Former major league first baseman Fred Merkle dies at age 67 in Daytona Beach,

LEAGUE

Baseball establishes the Cy Young Award, which will go to the best pitcher in the majors after each season.

CULTURE

On Broadway, *The Hot Corner* stars Sam Levene and Don Murray.

Florida. Despite a respectable 16-year career in which he hit .273 and stole 20 or more bases eight times, he is best remembered for his "boner." In 1909 with the Giants, he failed to touch second base in a critical game against the Cubs in a confusing play, negating the winning run and ultimately costing his team the NL pennant.

THE SEASON

APRIL 17:

Mickey Mantle hits 1,000 feet-plus worth of homers today as the Yankees top the Senators, 10-4, on opening day in Washington. With President Dwight D. Eisenhower – who threw out the first ball – looking on, Mantle cracks two homers in excess of 500 feet each against Camilo Pascual. The second of Mantle's homers may be the longest ever hit into the right-field bleachers at Griffith Park. Mantle has four RBI in the game.

In the clubhouse after the game, coach Bill Dickey says: "Mantle's got more power than any hitter I ever saw, including the Babe."

Don Drsydale makes his major league debut with the Brooklyn Dodgers on opening day. He relieves in the ninth inning, walking one and fanning one while allowing no hits or runs.

APRIL 19:

Dodgers' owner Walter O'Malley demonstrates his unhappiness with the "cramped" conditions at Ebbets Field by scheduling seven "home" games at Roosevelt Stadium in Jersey City, New Jersey. With 12,214 fans on hand, the Dodgers play the first of the seven games today and beat the Phillies, 5-4, in 10 innings. Catcher Roy Campanella gets his 1,000th career hit in the game; it is struck off losing pitcher Murry Dickson. Clem Labine gets the win on Al "Rube" Walker's game-winning sacrifice fly.

APRIL 28:

Redlegs' rookie outfielder Frank Robinson homers against Paul Minner of the Cubs in Cincinnati. It is the 20-year-old Robinson's first career homer. The Reds win, 9-1.

MAY 2:

Some days you're just better off staying in bed. Cubs' third baseman Don Hoak has one of those days against the Giants at Wrigley Field. Hoak fans six times against six different pitchers in a 17-inning loss to New York, 6-5. The Giants use 25 players in the game and the Cubs use 23.

MAY 12:

Carl Erskine of the Dodgers no-hits the Giants, 3-0, at Ebbets Field. It is Erskine's second career no-hitter; his first was in 1952 against the Cubs. Today Erskine walks Willie Mays and Alvin Dark and strikes out three. The Dodgers are perfect in the field. Jackie Robinson, Edwin "Duke" Snider, and Roy Campanella drive in all of the Dodgers' runs. Al Worthington is the losing pitcher.

Before the game, Carl Erskine reads a newspaper article quoting Giants' scout Tom Sheehan as saying Erskine is through. Jackie Robinson plays with the newspaper stuffed into his uniform. After Erskine's no-hitter, Robinson shoves the newspaper at Sheehan.

MAY 13:

The Dodgers buy Sal "The Barber" Maglie (0-0 in two games) from the Indians.

MAY 14:

The Dodgers sell pitcher Billy Loes (0-1), a great talent largely wasted, to the Orioles for $20,000.

MAY 16:

Wally Moon of the Cardinals hits the first major league home run at the Dodgers' second home, Roosevelt Stadium in Jersey City, but Brooklyn wins the game, 5-3.

MAY 17:

The Pirates obtain outfielder Bill Virdon (.211 in 24 games) from the Cardinals for outfielder Bobby Del Greco (.200 in 14 games) and pitcher Dick Littlefield (0-0 in six games).

MAY 18:

In Chicago, Mickey Mantle homers from both sides of the plate for the third time in his career – a major league record. Mantle has four hits

APRIL 28
Cincinnati's Frank Robinson connects on the first of what will be 586 career home runs.

in four at-bats including a double. Mantle hits the first of today's homers against Billy Pierce of the White Sox 12 rows deep into the upper deck at Comiskey Park. Mantle hits his left-handed round-tripper into the right-field seats against Millard "Dixie" Howell; it is his 15th of the season. Yogi Berra hits his 12th; both are ahead of Babe Ruth's record 1927 pace. The Yankees win, 8-7, in 10 innings.

MAY 19:

Who needs hits when you're being walked? The Indians parlay 11 walks – three with the bases loaded – and two hits against the Senators' Camilo Pascual into a 5-1 win. Herb Score is brilliant for Cleveland, allowing Washington only three hits and fanning 15.

MAY 20:

Senators' pitcher Chuck Stobbs aims at the plate but pitches the ball 17 rows into the stands some 30 feet off on the first base side. Stobbs comments, "I wanted to dig a hole and hide under the mound."

MAY 21:

The Orioles and White Sox swing a six-player trade. Going to Baltimore are third baseman George Kell (.313 in 21 games), outfielder Bob Nieman (.300 in 14 games), and pitchers Jose "Mike" Fornieles (0-1) and Clifford "Connie" Johnson (0-1). Chicago gets outfielder Dave Philley (.205 in 32 games) and pitcher Jim Wilson (4-2).

"UNQUESTIONABLY, (AL) SIMMONS WAS THE WORST LOOKING OF ALL TOP HITTERS," WROTE ARTHUR DALEY IN THE *NEW YORK TIMES* OF THE HALL OF FAMER. "HIS STYLE WAS ATROCIOUS... HE SHOULD HAVE BEEN A SUCKER FOR AN OUTSIDE PITCH. HE WASN'T... CURVES SHOULD HAVE TROUBLED HIM. THEY DIDN'T. IN FACT, HE WAS THE DEADLIEST CLUTCH HITTER ON THE GREAT ATHLETICS TEAMS."

MAY 26:

Hall of Fame outfielder Al Simmons dies four days after his 54th birthday in Milwaukee. Born Aloys Szymanski, he batted .334 with 307 homers in his 20-year major league career. He had career highs of .390 in 1931 and .381 in 1930. In four World Series, he hit .329. Simmons was inducted into the Hall of Fame in 1953.

Redlegs' pitchers Johnny Klippstein, Hershell Freeman, and Joe Black combine to hold the Braves hitless into the 10th inning. Black then yields a two-out double to Jack Dittmer and three more hits in the 11th, when Frank Torre hits an RBI single for a 2-1 Braves win. Klippstein does the bulk of the no-hit pitching for Cincinnati, going seven innings and allowing a second-

TRIVIA

The Yankees' Don Larsen, known for his love of nightlife, runs his car into a tree in the morning hours. Manager Casey Stengel notes: "The man was either out too late or up too early." He also is quoted as saying: "He was probably mailing a letter."

MAY 28
Dale Long's home run gives him an ML-record eight homers in eight straight games.

inning run on a Torre sacrifice fly. Freeman pitches one and Black the final three.

MAY 27:

Cubs' reliever Jim Davis becomes the fourth pitcher ever – and the first in 40 years – to strike out four batters in one inning. In the sixth inning of the opener of a doubleheader in St. Louis, Davis yields a double to Wally Moon, who then steals third. Davis, a knuckleball pitcher, fans Hal R. Smith and Jackie Brandt. He then strikes out pitcher Lindy McDaniel, but the ball gets away from catcher Hobie Landrith. McDaniel is safe at first and Moon scores. He then retires Don Blasingame on a called third strike. The Cardinals win, 11-9, and then take the nightcap, 12-2.

AL President Will Harridge marks his 25th year in office. None of those who appointed him are still alive.

MAY 28:

Dale Long of the Pirates homers in the fourth inning against Carl Erskine in Forbes Field, giving him eight round-trippers in eight consecutive games – a major

EQUIPMENT

Ed Rommel becomes the first umpire to wear eyeglasses while umpiring a game. He works the Yankees-Senators game at Griffith Stadium.

IN THE APRIL ISSUE OF *BASEBALL DIGEST*, GEORGE BARTON OF THE *MINNEAPOLIS TRIBUNE* REPORTS ON A CONVERSATION WITH ABE ATTELL, ALLEGEDLY ONE OF THE PARTIES TO THE 1919 WORLD SERIES FIX. AMONG ATTELL'S ALLEGATIONS: "[BUCK] WEAVER REFUSED TO BE A PARTY OF THE FIX BUT WAS SWORN TO SECRECY BY [CHICK] GANDIL AND [SWEDE] RISBERG, WHO THREATENED HIM, WITH PHYSICAL VIOLENCE IF HE TIPPED OFF THE DEAL..." ATTELL ALSO IS QUOTED AS SAYING: "I'M THE GUY WHO SWUNG THE DEAL WITH GANDIL AND RISBERG, WHO HANDLED OTHER PLAYERS IN ON THE FIX. THEY ASSURED ME THEY HAD FIXED CICOTTE, WILLIAMS, JACKSON, FELSCH, AND MCMULLIN, BUT COULDN'T REACH WEAVER... I WAS THE PAYOFF MAN, AND YOU GENTLEMEN MAY REST ASSURED BUCK DID NOT ACCEPT A PENNY OF THE LOOT." DANIEL E. GINSBURG, AUTHOR OF *THE FIX IS IN*, WRITES: "VIRTUALLY ALL CONTEMPORARY OBSERVERS ACCEPTED THE IDEA THAT WEAVER PLAYED TO THE BEST OF HIS ABILITY... IT IS ALSO GENERALLY ACKNOWLEDGED THAT WEAVER DID NOT RECEIVE ANY MONEY FROM THE GAMBLERS AND PLAYED NO PART IN THROWING THE WORLD SERIES."

MAY 31
The Milwaukee Braves go deep five times in a 15-8 rout of the Chicago Cubs.

league record. Long began his streak on May 19 against Jim Davis of the Cubs. Today's drive, into the right-center field stands, ties the game and Pittsburgh goes on to beat the Dodgers, 3-2, on a Bob Friend two-hitter. Erskine gets the loss.

MAY 29:

Dale Long is hitless in four at-bats against Brooklyn's Don Newcombe, ending his consecutive game homer streak at eight. The visiting Dodgers top the Pirates, 10-1.

MAY 30:

Mickey Mantle misses driving the first home run out of Yankee Stadium by 18 inches. Batting left-handed against the Senators' Pedro Ramos with a 2-2 count and two men on base, Mantle launches a home run that hits the right-field upper deck facade 370 feet from home plate and 117 feet high. It is calculated that if it hadn't struck the facade, the ball would have traveled 600 feet. The Yankees win the game, 4-3. They also win the nightcap, 12-5, with Mantle homering against Camilo Pascual for his 20th of the season and his 16th in May. Mantle is hitting .425 with 50 RBI.

At Wrigley Field, the Cubs and visiting Braves face off in a doubleheader marked by homers and an ugly beanball incident. The teams combine for a doubleheader record 15 round-trippers. In game one, Eddie Mathews, Hank Aaron, Joe Adcock, and Bobby Thomson (two) homer for the Braves; Gene Baker, pitcher Omar "Turk" Lown, Hobie Landrith, and Dee Fondy for the Cubs, who win, 10-9. After Mathews, Aaron, and Thomson homer consecutively in the first inning, Russ Meyer brushes back Bill Bruton and then hits him in the head. Bruton goes after him and both are ejected. Meyer yields three runs in two-thirds of an inning. Jim Brosnan gets the win; Dave Jolly is the loser. In the nightcap, Meyer returns and gives up four more runs in an inning. Bobby Thomson has two more homers for Milwaukee; teammates Aaron and Mathews hit one each. Harry Chiti and Ernie Banks homer for the Cubs. The Braves win, 11-9, with Ray Crone getting the win. Warren Hacker is the loser.

MAY 31:

The Braves continue to maul Cubs pitchers at Wrigley Field, with five more homers today. Joe Adcock hits 2 and Del Crandall, Bill Bruton, and Eddie Mathews add one each. The Braves tie their own major league record of 16 home runs in 4 games and set a new mark of 14 in 3 contests. Milwaukee wins, 15-8.

JUNE 14:

The Giants and Cardinals complete a nine-player deal. New York gets second baseman Albert "Red" Schoendienst (.314), outfielder Jackie Brandt (.286), catcher Bill Sarni (.291), pitcher Dick Littlefield (0-2), and infielder Bobby Stephenson (.243 in 1955). Going to St. Louis are shortstop Alvin Dark (.252), outfielder-first baseman Carroll "Whitey" Lockman (.272), catcher Ray Katt (.228), and pitcher Don Liddle (1-2).

JUNE 15:

Paul Richards, general manager and field skipper of the Orioles, comes up with a proposal that would put Frank "Trader" Lane to shame. Richards offers to trade all 25 of his players to Kansas City for 25 Athletics. The deal doesn't happen because Athletics' general manager Parke Carroll cannot reach owner Arnold Johnson before the expiration of today's trading deadline.

Richards was a free-spender. According to Donald Dewey and Nicholas Acocella, an observer noted: "Paul was the only man in baseball who had an unlimited budget and exceeded it."

JUNE 17:

Joe Adcock continues to thrive at Ebbets Field. The Braves' first baseman hits three homers today in a twin bill against the Dodgers, giving him a record 13 at the ballpark this season. One of his round-trippers, hit off Ed Roebuck, clears an 87-foot wall 350 feet from home plate. Milwaukee sweeps Brooklyn, 5-4 and 3-1.

JUNE 18:

Despite an 18-mph wind blowing in, Mickey Mantle clears Tiger Stadium with a

CULTURE

***The Great American Pastime*, a movie about the Little Leagues, stars Tom Ewell, Anne Francis, and Ruby Dee.**

LEAGUE

The value of baseball's TV rights is soaring. In July, Commissioner Ford Frick announces that NBC will pay $16.25 million for the All-Star Game and World Series for five years.

home run. Hitting left-handed against Paul Foytack, Mantle hits a drive that goes over the 94-foot roof 380 feet from home, traveling more than 500 feet. The only other player to hit a fair ball out of Tiger Stadium is Ted Williams. The Yankees win, 7-4.

JULY 1:

Mickey Mantle hits "switch" homers for the fourth time in his career. In game two at Yankee Stadium, Mantle bats right-handed against the Senators' Dean Stone and hits his 28th of the season. In the bottom of the 9th, he homers left-handed against Eldred "Bud" Byerly to give the Yankees an 8-6 win. New York also won the opener, 3-2.

JULY 7:

Stan Musial is the Player of the Decade in a poll of 260 players and journalists conducted by *The Sporting News*. Joe DiMaggio finishes second and Ted Williams is third.

JULY 8:

The Giants pound out seven home runs – including four in one inning – to beat the Pirates, 16-1. In the fourth inning, Willie Mays, Hank Thompson, Daryl Spencer, and Wes Westrum hit round-trippers. Spencer, Mays, and Westrum hit second home runs in the game.

LEE ALLEN WROTE OF CONNIE MACK IN *THE AMERICAN LEAGUE STORY*: "HE DIFFERED FROM OTHER MANAGERS IN THE AMERICAN LEAGUE BECAUSE HE NEVER WORE A UNIFORM, NEVER APPEARED ON THE FIELD BUT CONDUCTED HIS CAMPAIGN ENTIRELY FROM THE BENCH, SELDOM SHOUTED AT AN UMPIRE, AND NEVER SEEMED TO BE UPSET ABOUT THE RESULT OF A SINGLE GAME. HE WAS CERTAINLY THE FIRST OF THE MANAGERS TO MARK DOWN WHAT HAPPENED ON EVERY BALL THAT WAS PITCHED, AND PROBABLY THE FIRST TO HOLD DAILY MEETINGS AT WHICH WERE DISCUSSED THE PREVIOUS DAY'S MISTAKES."

JULY 10:

At Griffith Stadium, the NL wins the All-Star Game, 7-3, with a two-run homer by Willie Mays and a solo shot by Stan Musial. The NL is up 5-0, when the AL stages a sixth-inning mini-rally with a 2-run homer by Ted Williams followed by a round-tripper by Mickey Mantle. The winning pitcher is Bob Friend; Billy Pierce takes the loss.

JULY 14:

Boston's Mel Parnell no-hits the White Sox, 4-0, at Fenway Park. He is the first Red Sox pitcher since Howard Ehmke in 1923 to pitch a no-hitter. Parnell faces 28 batters, allowing one walk and fanning four. The losing pitcher is Jim McDonald.

JULY 17:

In the second game of a doubleheader at Fenway Park, Ted Williams homers against Tom A. Gorman of the Athletics for his 400th career round-tripper. Williams stares angrily at the press box and spits in the direction of the journalists. The Red Sox register a 1-0 win after a 10-0 victory in the opener. Red Sox general manager Joe Cronin is honored prior to the game.

JULY 21:

The Pirates and Roberto Clemente end the 13-game winning streak of the Cardinals' Brooks Lawrence. Clemente hits a three-run homer in a 4-3 Pittsburgh victory.

Pee Wee Reese singles for his 2,000th career hit. It is Reese's second hit in a 13-6 loss to the Cardinals. Dodgers' second baseman Jim Gilliam has 12 assists, tying the major league record set in 1892 by John Montgomery Ward.

Casey Stengel walks into the Yankees' dugout, empty except for one player, and sits down beside him, saying, "Nobody knows this, but one of us has just been traded to Kansas City." Outfielder Bob Cerv is reportedly the player, but he wasn't traded until October, after the season ended.

JULY 23:

Joe Cronin and Hank Greenberg are inducted into the Hall of Fame. Greenberg, a two-time AL Most Valuable Player, hit .313 with 1,276 RBI and 311 homers in only nine full seasons. He has a 6.4 home run percentage, averages nearly an RBI a game, and ranks fifth all-time with a .605 slugging average. Cronin played shortstop for the Pirates, Senators, and Red Sox for 20 years. He hit .301 with 170 homers and batted .300 or better 11 times.

Greenberg tells the crowd at Cooperstown: "I'm also glad Joe Cronin was named too. He was one of the greatest ballplayers and toughest competitors I ever saw." Cronin returns the compliment: "Hank is the greatest right-handed hitter I ever saw."

JULY 24:

Walter O'Malley clears the first hurdle in his quest for a new ballpark at Atlantic and Flatbush Avenues in Brooklyn when New York State approves forming the Brooklyn Sports Authority.

JULY 25:

Carl Furillo hits the first Dodgers' home run at Roosevelt Stadium in Jersey City in a 2-1 victory over the Redlegs.

AUGUST 7:

Before a Red Sox-Yankees games, Boston's Jackie Jensen is restrained by teammate Mel Parnell and coach Paul Schreiber from going after a fan in the right-field stands. Jensen explains: "I thought he got too personal in things he was saying about my wife." Jensen is married to world-class diver Zoe Ann Olson.

During the game, Ted Williams misplays a wind blown fly ball from Mickey Mantle and is booed by fans at Fenway Park. He then makes an over-the-shoulder catch on a Yogi Berra drive and spits twice toward his "jeering section" – fans and sportswriters – as he makes his way to the dugout. The Yankees join in, ragging Williams from the bench. He comes out on the field and spits two more times – the second toward the Yankees. With the bases loaded in the bottom of the 11th, Williams draws a walk from Tommy Byrne, forcing in the game's only run. As he heads toward first base, he flips his bat 40 feet in the air.

Williams is fined $5,000 by general manager Joe Cronin, but he is unrepentant. "I'm not a bit sorry for what I did. I was right and I'd spit again at the same fans who booed me today. Some of them are the worst in the world. Nobody's going to stop me from spitting." The next night, Williams homers against the Orioles and gets a big hand from the Fenway Park fans. He recalls: "When I crossed home plate I made a big display of clapping my hand over my mouth."

Satchel Paige, some 50 years old, can still pack them in. Pitching for the Miami Marlins of the International League at the Orange Bowl, Paige attracts a crowd of 57,000 – the largest ever in the minors – hits a double, and beats the Columbus Jets, 6-2.

AUGUST 11:

At Ebbets Field, Stan Lopata of the Phillies hits a two-run homer in the second inning, which snaps Don Newcombe's scoreless inning streak at 39 2/3. Brooklyn wins the game, 5-2.

AUGUST 18:

The Redlegs and the Braves combine for an NL record 10 home runs in a regulation night game. The Reds do most of

HISTORY

Three minor league players hit 60 homers or more in 1956. The top slugger was Dick Stuart with 66 for Lincoln in the Western League. Ken Guettler hits 62 for Shreveport in the Texas League. And Edward "Frosty" Kennedy has 60 for Plainview in the Southwestern League. Only Stuart makes it to the majors, playing 10 years and hitting 228 homers. His fielding – or lack thereof – earns him the nickname Dr. Strangeglove.

"Close don't count in baseball. Close only counts in horseshoes and hand grenades."
– *Frank Robinson*

the heavy lifting – with eight homers – in a 13-4 win, and Bob Thurman hits three plus a double.

AUGUST 22:

Paul Molitor is born today in St. Paul, Minnesota.

Mickey Mantle comes close again at Yankee Stadium. This time, batting right-handed, he rockets a home run some 20 rows into the upper left-field stands against Paul LaPalme of the White Sox. The baseball comes within 20 feet of completely clearing the ballpark.

AUGUST 23:

Jacob "Nellie" Fox of the White Sox has yet another day illustrating why he should be in the Hall of Fame. He has seven straight hits in today's doubleheader against the Yankees. In the second game, Mickey Mantle hits a home run, a triple, and a bunt single, but New York loses, 6-4.

AUGUST 25:

The Yankees reacquire outfielder Enos "Country" Slaughter (.278) from the Athletics for approximately $50,000. It's Old-Timers' Day at Yankee Stadium, and 38-year-old Phil Rizzuto is summoned to meet with general manager George Weiss and Casey Stengel. Rizzuto is "consulted" about a cut the Yankees must make to create a roster spot for Enos Slaughter, purchased earlier in the day. Weiss then tells Rizzuto he is the one who is going. At the time of his unconditional release, Rizzuto is hitting .231 in 31 games. He has been the anchor of the Yankees infield since joining the team in 1941. In 13 years, he batted .273.

SEPTEMBER 9:

Cleveland celebrates Bob Feller Day. As part of the festivities, Indians' president Mike Wilson presents the 37-year-old pitcher with a new car.

SEPTEMBER 11:

Bob Lemon has a landmark day against the Orioles. He beats Baltimore, 3-1, for his 200th career and his 19th of the season. And he hits his 36th career homer, placing

Mickey Mantle won the Triple Crown in 1956.

SEPTEMBER 11
Frank Robinson connects for his 38th homer of the season, tying a rookie record.

SEPTEMBER 11
Bob Lemon's 3-1 win over the Orioles gives the Cleveland ace his 200th career victory.

him among the top three pitchers of all time.

Frank Robinson of the Redlegs homers against the Giants' Steve Ridzik in an 11-5 Cincinnati victory. It is Robinson's 38th of the season, tying the rookie record set by Wally Berger in 1930.

SEPTEMBER 12:

The Dodgers and Braves enter today's game at Ebbets Field tied for first place. The Braves win, 8-7, on a Bill Bruton RBI in the eighth inning. Joe Adcock hits his 13th homer against the Dodgers, tying the major league record of Jimmie Foxx and Hank Sauer for the most against one opponent in a season. Milwaukees' Bobby Thomson is out trying to steal home and gets fined $100 for going without a signal.

SEPTEMBER 13:

Warren Spahn beats the Phillies, 4-3, in 12 innings, for his 200th career win. The Braves win the nightcap, 3-2, in 13. Hank Aaron drives in the winning runs in both games, and now the Braves lead the second-place Dodgers by a full two games.

SEPTEMBER 14:

In Detroit, Yogi Berra hits a homer against Jim Bunning. It is the 237th home run of his career, surpassing Charles "Gabby" Hartnett and setting a major league record for catchers. Starter Don Larsen pitches a four-hitter, and the Yankees go on to beat the Tigers, 5-1.

SEPTEMBER 18:

Mickey Mantle hits an 11th-inning home run today against Chicago's Billy Pierce for his 50th of the year, and the Yankees clinch the pennant with a 3-2 victory. Mantle is the eighth player in major league history to reach the 50-homer mark. Whitey Ford wins his 19th.

SEPTEMBER 21:

Batting left-handed, Mickey Mantle hits a 450- to 500-foot homer off Frank Sullivan at Fenway Park that strikes the back wall in center field, within a foot of clearing the ballpark. It is his 51st of the season. The Yankees bang out 15 hits and receive nine walks, and Boston commits five errors. But New York strands a major league record 20 runners and loses, 13-7. Billy Klaus bats in five runs for Boston. The winning pitcher is George Susce; Bob Turley gets the loss.

SEPTEMBER 25:

Sal "The Barber" Maglie, now of the Dodgers, no-hits the Phillies, 5-0, at Ebbets Field. The 39-year-old right-hander walks two and strikes out three; the Dodgers make no errors. The losing pitcher is Jack Meyer. Maglie's masterpiece keeps the Dodgers in the thick of a three-way pennant race with the Braves and Redlegs.

SEPTEMBER 26:

The Indians' Herb Score strikes out 12 Athletics and wins his 20th of the season. Vic Wertz hits four doubles – tying a major league record – and drives in five runs in the 8-4 win.

SEPTEMBER 29:

In conflict with general manager Hank Greenberg over concerns that the Indians are a "dull" team, manager Al Lopez announces he will not return as manager for the 1957 season.

Authors Donald Dewey and Nicholas Acocella have another version of Lopez's resignation. According to their version, third baseman Al Rosen, playing with a broken finger, is subjected to innuendo in the press that he is being allowed to play at less than par just because both he and Hank Greenberg are Jewish. He also is derided by fans for leaving a game when his nose is broken. It is disgust over these incidents that leads to the resignation of Lopez, and Rosen's retirement after the season at age 32.

SEPTEMBER 30:

The Dodgers top the Pirates, 8-6, to beat out the Braves for the NL pennant. Don Newcombe records his 27th win; Duke Snider and Edmundo "Sandy" Amoros each hit two home runs.

At Yankee Stadium, Mickey Mantle is hitless in one at-bat as a pinch hitter, but sews up the AL Triple Crown with a batting average of .353, 52 homers, and 130 RBI. He is the fourth major leaguer to accomplish the feat; Ted Williams was the last, in 1942. Yogi Berra hits his 30th homer of the season, but the Red Sox and Dave Sisler win, 7-4, in 10 innings. Tom Morgan gets the loss.

In Philadelphia, Robin Roberts sets a major league record

HISTORY

Bob Feller retires at the end of the season. With nearly four years out for service with the navy during World War II, Feller spent 18 years with the Indians, compiling a record of 266-162 with a 3.25 ERA and 2,581 strikeouts. He faded to 4-4 in 1955 and 0-4 this season.

CULTURE

***Bang the Drum Slowly*, a novel by Mark Harris, tells the story of Henry "Author" Wiggen and his dying battery mate, Bruce Pearson. Also published this year, Harris's *Ticket for a Seamstitch* is about Wiggen, too.**

> "No, why should I?"
> — *Don Larsen, when asked if he ever tires of talking about his World Series perfect game*

CULTURE

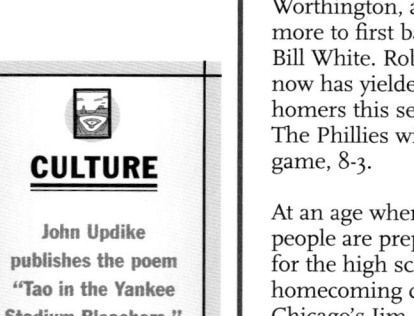

John Updike publishes the poem "Tao in the Yankee Stadium Bleachers."

he would rather not have. He serves up a gopher ball to the Giants' pitcher, Al Worthington, and two more to first baseman Bill White. Roberts now has yielded 46 homers this season. The Phillies win the game, 8-3.

At an age when most people are preparing for the high school homecoming dance, Chicago's Jim Derrington becomes the youngest pitcher in this century to start a major league game. Derrington, 16 years and 10 months old, starts for the White Sox against the Athletics. He pitches six innings, allowing nine hits, walking six, and fanning three. He singles once in two at-bats, becoming the youngest player to hit safely in an AL game. But he is the losing pitcher in a 7-6 Kansas City victory.

Derrington pitches in 20 games in 1957, compiling an 0-1 record, with a 4.86 ERA. He goes to the minors and is finished before he is 18 years old. His major league record is 0-2, with a 5.23 ERA.

OCTOBER 1:

The Briggs heirs sell their stock in the Detroit Tigers for $5.5 million to a syndicate of radio/television executives headed by John Fetzer, Fred Knorr, and Kenyon Brown. Knorr will become the team's president.

REGULAR SEASON WRAP-UP:

The Yankees hit an AL record 183 home runs and finish the season at 97-57, nine games ahead of the Indians. Manager Casey Stengel's charges are led by Triple Crown-winner Mickey Mantle. Yogi Berra has 30 home runs and 95 RBI; Bill Skowron, 23 round-trippers and 90 RBIs; Gil McDougald bats .311. Whitey Ford is the ace at 19-6.

Under Walter Alston, the Dodgers repeat as NL champions with a record of 93-61, one game in front of the Braves and two ahead of the Redlegs. Don Newcombe anchors Brooklyn's staff with a glittering 27-7 record. Duke Snider bats .292 with 43 home runs and 101 RBI. Gil Hodges has 32 homers; Carl Furillo, 21; and Roy Campanella, 20.

The third-place Redlegs tie the major league record of the 1947 Giants with 221 homers in this season. Rookie Frank Robinson has 38, Wally Post, 36; Ted Kluszewski, 35; David "Gus" Bell, 29; and Ed Bailey, 28.

OCTOBER 3:

World Series, game one. The Dodgers and Yankees face off in the World Series for the sixth time in 10 years. At Ebbets Field, the Yankees are out for revenge after last year's defeat, but the Dodgers pick up where they left off. Behind nine-hit pitching by Sal Maglie, Brooklyn wins, 6-3. Gil Hodges hits a two-run homer and Jackie Robinson has a solo shot. Mantle has a two-run round-tripper for the Yankees and Billy Martin adds a solo home run. Whitey Ford is charged with the loss.

OCTOBER 5:

World Series, game two. Today the Dodgers steamroll the Yankees, 13-8, at Ebbets Field as the Yankees blow a 6-0 lead and send a record seven pitchers to the mound. The game takes three hours and 26 minutes to play, the longest nine-inning game in series history. Duke Snider hits a three-run homer; Berra hits a grand slam. The winning pitcher is reliever Don Bessent; Tom Morgan gets the loss.

OCTOBER 6:

World Series, game three. At Yankee Stadium, Whitey Ford keeps the Yankees breathing with a 5-3, eight-inning victory. Enos Slaughter brings the Yankees back from a 2-1 deficit with a three-run homer in the sixth. Billy Martin also homers for New York. The losing pitcher is starter Roger Craig.

OCTOBER 7:

World Series, game four. Tom Sturdivant knots the series with a six-hit complete-game, 6-2 win at Yankee Stadium. Mickey Mantle hits a bases-empty home run in the sixth and Hank Bauer a two-run clout in the seventh. Starter Carl Erskine gets the loss.

OCTOBER 8:

World Series, game five. In the bottom of the ninth with two out, Dale Mitchell is now all that stands between Yankees' pitcher Don Larsen and a perfect game, as well as the first no-hitter in series history. On his 97th pitch of the game, Larsen catches Mitchell look-

OCTOBER 8
The Yankees' Don Larsen throws a perfect game against the Dodgers in the World Series.

OCTOBER 10
With a 9-0 blanking of the Dodgers, the Yankees win the World Championship.

ing and NL umpire Ralph "Babe" Pinelli, behind the plate for the last time in his career, calls it a strike. Pandemonium erupts in the stadium; Yogi Berra charges Larsen and leaps into his arms. Almost lost in the excitement is the fact that the Yankees are now one game up in the series after the 2-0 victory. Mantle is the supporting hero today with a fourth-inning homer off losing pitcher Sal Maglie and a back-hand running catch in deep left center field to preserve Larsen's masterpiece.

A reporter supposedly asks Don Larsen, "Is that the best game you ever pitched?" New York journalist Joe Trimble writes: "The imperfect man pitched the perfect game."

The Cardinals release catcher Walker Cooper (.265 in 40 games) and pitcher Jim Konstanty (1-1, 4.65 ERA). Cooper will be a St. Louis coach next season.

OCTOBER 9:

World Series, game six. Clem Labine isn't perfect but he holds the Yankees scoreless at Ebbets Field for a 1-0, 10-inning win, to tie the series. Enos Slaughter misjudges a two-out Jackie Robinson fly ball, turning it into the game-winning hit. Bob Turley gets the loss despite yielding only four hits.

DISTINGUISHED POET MARIANNE MOORE, A DEVOTED DODGERS FAN, WRITES "HOMETOWN PIECE FOR MESSRS. ALSTON AND REESE." HER POEM, WHICH APPEARS IN THE *NEW YORK HERALD-TRIBUNE* ON OCTOBER 3, CELEBRATES BROOKLYN'S WORLD SERIES VICTORY AND CONCLUDES:
"YOU'VE GOT PLENTY:
JACKIE ROBINSON
AND CAMPY AND BIG NEWK,
AND DODGERDOM AGAIN
WATCHING EVERYTHING YOU DO.
YOU WON LAST YEAR. COME ON."

OCTOBER 10:

World Series, game seven. Yankee power asserts itself in a 9-0 blowout at Ebbets Field. A pair of two-run homers by Yogi Berra, a bases-loaded blast by Bill Skowron, and a bases-empty home run by Elston Howard, combined with a complete-game three-hitter by Johnny Kucks, bring the championship back to the Bronx. Starter Don Newcombe gets the loss. Yogi Berra finishes the series with a .360 average, three homers, and 10 RBI. Mickey Mantle hits only .250 but has three homers of his own and six RBI. Enos Slaughter bats .350 with four RBI. Gil Hodges leads Brooklyn with .304. But despite the outstanding hitting, the 1956 World Series always will belong to Don Larsen.

POST-SEASON

OCTOBER 11:

Dodgers' owner Walter O'Malley minimizes the chances of

CULTURE

"I Love Mickey" is recorded by Teresa Brewer, with an assist by Mickey Mantle. "The Ballad of Don Larsen" is recorded by Red River Dave McEnery.

CULTURE

On television, *Bang the Drum Slowly*, starring Paul Newman, Albert Salmi, and George Peppard, is based on Mark Harris's novel. *The Life of Mickey Mantle* stars James Olson as the Yankees' star. *The Lou Gehrig Story* stars Wendell Corey as the Iron Horse and Jean Hagen as Eleanor. *The Jackie Jensen Story* stars the major leaguer as himself. *The Comeback* stars former major leaguer Chuck Connors as pitcher Lou Brissie.

moving his team to Los Angeles. He tells the *Los Angeles Times* that the territory belongs to "my good friend Phil Wrigley" and cites attendance concerns and a lack of progress on a stadium. Another owner who has eyes on the West Coast is stymied. The proposed move of the Washington Senators to Los Angeles is rejected. Six days later, Calvin Griffith considers bids from San Francisco and from Louisville, Kentucky.

OCTOBER 29:

Al Lopez is named the manager of the Chicago White Sox for the 1957 season. He will replace Marty Marion, who led the White Sox to a third-place finish at 85-69.

OCTOBER 30:

The Dodgers sell Ebbets Field. Real estate businessman Marvin Kratter purchases the historic ballpark and will lease it back to the Dodgers through the 1959 season before using the site for a housing development.

NOVEMBER 19:

The Philadelphia Phillies trade longtime outfield mainstay Del Ennis (.260, 26 homers, 95 RBI) to the Cardinals for infielders Eldon "Rip" Repulski (.277, 11 homers) and Bobby Morgan (.196).

RICHIE ASHBURN OF THE PHILLIES RECALLS HIS FIRST AT-BAT AGAINST DON DRYSDALE, WHO MAKES HIS MAJOR LEAGUE DEBUT WITH THE BROOKLYN DODGERS IN 1956: "I HAD A GOOD LOOK AT THE FIRST PITCH I EVER SAW FROM DRYSDALE. IF I HAD NOT DUCKED, IT WOULD HAVE HIT ME RIGHT BETWEEN THE EYES."

NOVEMBER 28:

Major "Kerby" Farrell is named manager of the Indians, replacing Al Lopez. Farrell managed the American Association Indianapolis Indians to the Junior World Series championship.

NOVEMBER 29:

New York City mayor Robert F. Wagner sets up a committee to attract an existing major league team. The committee is composed of department store magnate Bernard Gimbel, former Giants' pitcher Clint Blume, former U.S. postmaster general James A. Farley, and attorney Bill Shea. The Redlegs are the group's first choice, followed by the Phillies. But Shea decides a new league is the best option.

DECEMBER 10:

Grace Comiskey, the widow of Charles Comiskey, dies today, leaving the controlling interest in the White Sox to her daughter, Dorothy Rigney.

DECEMBER 13:

There is no joy in Flatbush – or any other part of the New York City borough of Brooklyn. In what once would have been considered unthinkable, the Dodgers trade star shortstop Jackie Robinson (.275, 10 home runs, 12 stolen bases) to the archrival Giants for pitcher Dick Littlefield (4-6, 4.37 ERA with three teams) and $30,000.

DECEMBER 18:

Phil Rizzuto, released by the Yankees earlier in the year, is hired to broadcast games in 1957. He'll team with Mel Allen and Walter "Red" Barber in the broadcast booth.

In O Holy Cow: The Selected Verse of Phil Rizzuto, *a collection of on-air gems from the lips of the longtime broadcaster, Roy Blount Jr. writes an "Introduction to the Rizzuto Poems": If the Scooter ever makes it To the Baseball Hall of Fame, As I believe he should, My own closest brush with diamond Immortality will beThe flu he had once When I interviewed him He got it "from that Coleman," He said, meaning the old Yankee Second-sacker Gerry. And then I came down with it. Score that 4 to 6 to me – one of my greatest sports thrills.*

THE BEST OF 1956

NATIONAL LEAGUE

HITTERS

Batting Average:
Hank Aaron, Milwaukee Braves, .328

Slugging Average:
Edwin "Duke" Snider, Brooklyn Dodgers, .598

Home Runs:
Duke Snider, 43

Runs Batted In:
Stan Musial, St. Louis Cardinals, 109

Hits:
Hank Aaron, 200

Stolen Bases:
Willie Mays, New York Giants, 40

PITCHERS

Wins:
Don Newcombe, Brooklyn Dodgers, 27

Strikeouts:
Sam Jones, Chicago Cubs, 176

Earned Run Average:
Lew Burdette, Milwaukee Braves, 2.70

Winning Percentage:
Don Newcombe, .794

Saves:
Clem Labine, Brooklyn Dodgers, 19

Most Valuable Player:
Don Newcombe, Brooklyn Dodgers

Cy Young Award:
Don Newcombe, Brooklyn Dodgers

Rookie of the Year:
Frank Robinson, Cincinnati Redlegs

AMERICAN LEAGUE

HITTERS

Batting Average:
Mickey Mantle, New York Yankees, .353

Slugging Average:
Mickey Mantle, .705

Home Runs:
Mickey Mantle, 52

Runs Batted In:
Mickey Mantle, 130

Hits:
Harvey Kuenn, Detroit Tigers, 196

Stolen Bases:
Luis Aparicio, Chicago White Sox, 21

PITCHERS

Wins:
Frank Lary, Detroit Tigers, 21

Strikeouts:
Herb Score, Cleveland Indians, 263

Earned Run Average:
Ed "Whitey" Ford, New York Yankees, 2.47

Winning Percentage:
Whitey Ford, .760

Saves:
George Zuverink, Baltimore Orioles, 16

Most Valuable Player:
Mickey Mantle, New York Yankees

Rookie of the Year:
Luis Aparicio, Chicago White Sox

CULTURE

Baseball Magazine folds.

1957

"I have to think of the future and the security of my family."
– *Jackie Robinson, upon retiring*

NEWS

SOVIETS LAUNCH SPUTNIK SATELLITE

Eisenhower outlines doctrine to combat Communism in Middle East

SENATOR JOSEPH McCARTHY DIES

Strom Thurmond filibusters for record 24 hours, 27 minutes

CIGARETTE SMOKING LINKED TO LUNG CANCER

U.S. troops sent to Little Rock, Arkansas, to enforce desegregation at high school

HUMPHREY BOGART, OLIVER HARDY DIE

NBC TELECASTS FIRST VIDEOTAPED PROGRAM

World's longest suspension bridge, over Mackinac Straits, opens

PRE-SEASON

JANUARY 9:

The Indians release Bob Feller, who had announced his retirement at the end of the 1956 season.

JANUARY 22:

In an article in *Look* magazine, Jackie Robinson announces he is retiring from baseball. According to the Hall of Fame Library, Robinson actually retired on January 5. Robinson will become a vice president with the Chock Full O'Nuts food chain. He explains: "I have to think of the future and the security of my family." He asserts that he made his decision before the late 1956 trade that would have sent him to the Giants for pitcher Dick Littlefield and $30,000, but he did not speak at the time because of his deal with *Look*. The trade is canceled.

Robinson takes a parting shot at the Phillies, Red Sox, and Tigers, who still are without black players. Says Robinson: "If 13 major league teams can come up with colored players, why can't the other three?" The Phillies subsequently buy the contract of shortstop John Kennedy from the Kansas City Monarchs.

FEBRUARY 19:

The Yankees obtain third baseman Clete Boyer (.217 in 67 games), pitchers Art Ditmar (12-22, 4.42 ERA), Bobby Shantz (2-7, 4.35 ERA), and Jack McMahan (0-5, 5.04 ERA), along with first baseman Wayne "Footsie" Belardi (.279, six homers) and second baseman Curt Roberts (.177 in 31 games). In return the Athletics receive infielder Billy Hunter (.280 in 39 games), pitchers Walter "Rip" Coleman (3-5, 3.67 ERA), Tom Morgan (6-7, 4.16 ERA), and Maurice "Mickey" McDermott (2-6, 4.24 ERA) plus outfielder Irv Noren (.219 in 26 games) and minor league second baseman Milt Graff.

The Yankees actually receive Roberts on April 4 and Boyer on June 4 – after he has appeared in 10 games without a single at-bat.

FEBRUARY 21:

On the surface it's a swap of minor league franchises, but it has enormous implications for Brooklyn and its fans. Walter O'Malley of the Dodgers trades the territorial rights to Fort Worth in the Texas League and $2.5 million to Phil Wrigley and the Cubs. In return, O'Malley gets the territorial rights to Los Angeles in the Pacific Coast League and the Angels' 22,000-seat Wrigley Field. The exchange clears the way for the Dodgers to leave Brooklyn and relocate in Los Angeles.

FEBRUARY 26:

First baseman-outfielder Carroll "Whitey" Lockman (.260, one homer) returns to the Giants from the Cardinals. In return, St. Louis will receive pitcher Hoyt Wilhelm (4-9, 3.83 ERA).

MARCH 18:

The Red Sox offer $1 million for the Indians' Herb Score.

MARCH 19:

The Indians say no. General manager Hank Greenberg says, "I hesitated because of the size of the offer. But I must reject the offer. Score is going to become one of the greatest southpaws in history."

JANUARY 22
In an article in *Look*, Jackie Robinson announces that he is retiring from baseball.

APRIL 18
Indians' rookie Roger Maris hits his first major league homer – a grand slam.

MARCH 26:

Yankees' manager Casey Stengel has a run-in with a sports photographer for the *St. Petersburg Independent* during an exhibition game against the Dodgers at Al Lang Field in Florida. Stengel is accused of blocking the photographer's view, then kicking and cursing him. Stengel is arrested and released on $50 bail.

MARCH 31:

Never at a loss for words, Ted Williams – in New Orleans – lashes out at the Marine Corps and calls President Harry S. Truman and U.S. Senator Robert F. Taft "gutless politicians."

APRIL 5:

The Brooklyn Dodgers made a deal to obtain five players and $75,000 from the Philadelphia Phillies in exchange for shortstop Humberto "Chico" Fernandez (.227 in 34 games). Going to Brooklyn in the swap are outfielder Elmer Valo (.287, five homers), pitchers Ron Negray (2-3, 4.19 ERA) and Ben Flowers (1-3, 5.98 ERA), plus two minor leaguers – shortstop Mel Geho and first baseman Tim Harkness. Fernandez will end up appearing in 49 games for the Phillies, hitting .262 with five home runs and 51 RBI.

APRIL 15:

Former major league pitcher Jack Coombs dies at age 74 in Palestine, Texas. In 14 years, Coombs was 159-110 with a 2.78 ERA. In 1910 he won 31 games and was 5-0 in three World Series.

APRIL 18:

Indians' rookie Roger Maris hits his first major league homer – a grand slam – in the 11th inning. Cleveland defeats the Tigers, 8-3, in Detroit.

Night baseball has its drawbacks. For the first time in major league history, a power failure halts a game. Tonight's Orioles-Senators game in Washington is suspended after five.

APRIL 22:

The color barrier finally is down in Philadelphia. The

The Brooklyn Dodgers announce the team's move to Los Angeles.

Phillies send John I. Kennedy, who is black, into today's game against the Dodgers. He is inserted as a pinch runner.

APRIL 25:

In Cincinnati, nine walks – four by Moe Drabowsky, three by Jackie Collum, and two by Jim Brosnan – in the fifth inning undo the Cubs and they lose to the Redlegs, 9-5.

APRIL 27:

After Cubs' pitcher Moe Drabowsky is hit on the foot by a pitch, rookie Dick Drott rolls a wheelchair to homeplate, loads his teammate into it, and pushes him to first base. Umpire Stan Landes is not at all amused; he proves it by ejecting Drott.

MAY 7:

A hush falls over the crowd of 18,386 at Cleveland's Municipal Stadium when star left-hander Herb Score is struck in the right eye by a line drive off the bat of the Yankees' Gil McDougald in the first inning. Score is hit so hard, the ball caroms to third baseman Al Smith. Score's eye is severely damaged, he is hemorrhaging and his nose is broken. The pitcher is taken to Lakeside Hospital. Bob Lemon comes in to relieve and the Indians win, 2-1.

Score returns to baseball, but never again is the dominating pitcher he was in 1956 when he won 20 games and struck out 263. He pitches until 1962, leaving with a 55-46 record and an ERA of 3.36. He then becomes a play-by-play broadcaster for the Indians.

MAY 8:

Ted Williams hits three homers against Bob Keegan of the White Sox in Chicago. It is the first time since 1946 that the 38-year-old Williams has connected for three round-trippers in a single game. Boston wins, 4-1.

MAY 16:

A group of Yankees' players attend the Copacabana in New York City to celebrate Billy Martin's 29th birthday but the occasion turns out to be anything but festive. Martin, Mickey Mantle, Whitey Ford, Yogi Berra, Johnny Kucks, and Hank Bauer – along with some of their wives – are seated at a table when a patron approaches. He later charges that he was

RULES CHANGE

The Redlegs' Don Hoak finds a unique way to break up a double play and brings about a rule change. Hoak leads off second base with the Braves in the field. An apparent double-play ball is hit toward second; Hoak fields it and flips it to Braves' shortstop Johnny Logan. He is out but the runner is safe. Under the new rule, both the batter and runner are out when there is willful interference with a batted ball.

IN *MY TURN AT BAT*, TED WILLIAMS WRITES: "I SAID WE HADN'T HALF TRIED TO WIN THE KOREAN WAR... I HAD A FEW WORDS ABOUT THE MARINE CORPS, SOME OF THE CRAP THEY HAD TO TAKE, THE LOUSY EQUIPMENT." HE ADDS: "MR. TRUMAN WAS GREAT ABOUT IT. HE SAID HE ALWAYS ENJOYED WATCHING ME PLAY. HE SAID HE DIDN'T SEE ANYTHING SO BAD IN WHAT I HAD SAID, AND THAT HE HAD SAID A FEW THINGS HIMSELF IN HIS DAY."

assaulted by Bauer in the nightclub's basement in what becomes known as the "Copa incident." The *New York Daily News* headline blares: BAUER IN BRAWL IN COPA. Bauer, Martin, Mantle, Ford, and Berra are fined $1,000; Kucks gets off with $500.

From Baseball: An Illustrated History*: "Martin...was small, scrawny, and unprepossessing...but no antagonist was ever too big for him to curse out or take on – in the schoolyard, on the diamond, or in the saloons... It was less his skill than his spirit, his willingness to do anything it took to win, that made him a Stengel favorite."*

MAY 26:

At Wrigley Field, Cubs' rookie Dick Drott strikes out 15 – including Hank Aaron four times – as Chicago beats the Braves, 7-5.

MAY 27:

NL owners approve the acquisition of territorial rights to Los Angeles by the Dodgers.

MAY 28:

Herb Score today is released from Lakeside Hospital, but is prohibited from working out. He'll make five starts this year.

JUNE 4:

Yankees' superscout Paul Krichell, who knew 'em when he saw 'em, dies at age 74 in New York City. Krichell signed Lou Gehrig, Charlie Keller, Tony Lazzeri, Robert "Red" Rolfe, Mark Koenig, Phil Rizzuto, Whitey Ford, and Vic Raschi. Krichell played two major league seasons – 1911 and 1912 – as a catcher for the Browns, hitting .222.

JUNE 5:

The Dodgers' Don Drysdale pitches his first major league shutout, beating the Cubs, 4-0, at Roosevelt Stadium in Jersey City, New Jersey.

JUNE 9:

At Connie Mack Stadium, Ernie Banks hits a three-run home run against Robin Roberts in the eighth inning. It is Banks's 100th career home run. The Cubs win, 7-3; rookie Dick Drott gets the victory.

JUNE 12:

In Brooklyn, the Braves' Eddie Mathews hits his 200th career homer, however, the Dodgers go on to win the game, 11-9.

The Cardinals' Stan Musial appears in his 823rd consecutive game, surpassing Gus Suhr's record.

JUNE 13:

For the second time this season, Ted Williams hits three homers in a game. Today he victimizes the Indians' Early Wynn and Bob Lemon in Cleveland. Williams is the first player with two three-homer games in a season. Boston wins, 9-3.

Yankees' pitcher Art Ditmar buzzes Larry Doby's head. The ball gets by catcher Elston Howard, and when Ditmar covers the plate, Doby reportedly warns him, "If you ever do that again, I'll stick a knife in your back." Doby then takes a swing at Ditmar and both benches empty. Bill Skowron takes on Doby. White Sox Walt Dropo slugs it out with Yankees' Enos Slaughter, whose jersey ends up getting torn. Finally, just as order is restored after 30 minutes, Billy Martin hears about the remark from Ditmar and attacks Doby. Finally, the Yankees go on to win the game, 4-3.

IN *MY TURN AT BAT*, TED WILLIAMS DESCRIBES THE "REAL CRUX OF BASEBALL...: YOU'RE NOT PLAYING THE CINCINNATI REDS OR THE CLEVELAND INDIANS, YOU'RE PLAYING THAT PITCHER – JOHNNY VANDER MEER, BOB FELLER, BOB LEMON, WHOEVER HE IS – AND HE'S THE GUY YOU CONCENTRATE ON."

TRIVIA

***The High Hard One*, by Kirby Higbe, a former major league pitcher, is published.**

In *My Turn at Bat*, Ted Williams writes: "I came within five hits of .400 that year. What's five hits? I was 39 years old, aging, and aching. There had to be among a season's collection of groundballs at least five leg hits for a younger Ted Williams."

CULTURE

Fear Strikes Out stars Anthony Perkins, as Jimmy Piersall, and Karl Malden. In *The Truth Hurts*, the real Jimmy Piersall says, "He threw a baseball like a girl. I hated the movie."

At Ebbets Field, Don Drysdale plunks Braves' shortstop Johnny Logan in the ribs, triggering a fight. Both are ejected. Carl Sawatski hits a homer to give the Braves an 8-5 victory, moving them into first place and tagging Clem Labine with his first loss in 38 relief appearances.

JUNE 14:

One-time AL batting champion, infielder Billy Goodman (.063 in 18 games) is traded to the Orioles from the Red Sox for pitcher Jose "Mike" Fornieles (2-6).

JUNE 15:

Outfielder-third baseman Bobby Thomson (.236 in 41 games), a Giants' hero for the ages, returns to New York from the Braves. Also coming to the Giants are infielder Danny O'Connell (.235 in 48 games) and pitcher Ray Crone (3-1). The Braves will get second baseman Albert "Red" Schoendienst (.307 in 57 games).

In the aftermath of the "Copacabana incident" and amid speculation that he is a negative influence on Mickey Mantle, Billy Martin (.241 in 43 games) is traded by the Yankees to the Athletics in a six-player transaction. Joining Martin in Kansas City will be shortstop Woody Held (.000 in one game) and minor league outfielder Bob Martyn. Going to the Yankees are pitcher Rinold "Ryne" Duren (0-3, 5.27 ERA), second baseman Milt Graf (.181 in 56 games), and outfielders Harry "Suitcase" Simpson (.296 in 50 games) and Jim Pisoni (.237 in 44 games).

JUNE 16:

Today in Washington, D.C., pitcher Millard "Dixie" Howell of the White Sox hits two home runs during his three and two-thirds innings of relief pitching. Chicago goes on to beat the Senators, 8-6, after taking the opener, 4-2.

JUNE 21:

Less than a month ago, 18-year-old Max "Von" McDaniel was a student at Hollis High School in Oklahoma. Today, he makes his major league debut with a two-hit, 2-0 shutout of the Dodgers in St. Louis. McDaniel, whose older brother Lyndall "Lindy" also is a member of the Cardinals, allows no hits until the sixth inning. Then Jim Gilliam singles and Duke Snider beats out a bunt for Brooklyn's only safeties.

JUNE 28:

After Cincinnati fans stuff the All-Star ballot box, electing eight Redlegs to the starting team, Commissioner Ford Frick "unstuffs" it. He replaces three Redlegs – first baseman George Crowe, center fielder David "Gus" Bell, and right fielder Wally Post – with Stan Musial, Willie Mays, and Hank Aaron, respectively.

JULY 9:

In St. Louis, the AL wins the All-Star Game, 6-5. Cincinnati still has five players on the starting team: Johnny Temple, Don Hoak, Roy McMillan, Frank Robinson, and Ed Bailey and one reserve, Gus Bell. No home runs are hit and the key play in the game is a running catch by Minnie Minoso on Gil Hodges's drive with a runner on in the bottom of the ninth. Jim Bunning is the winner; Curt Simmons gets the loss.

JULY 19:

One of the most popular of all Dodgers is honored at Ebbets Field. On Gil Hodges Day, the first baseman records his 1,000th career RBI and Brooklyn sweeps a doubleheader from the Cubs, 3-0 and 5-3. The Dodgers' John Roseboro hits his first major league homer in the nightcap.

JULY 20:

Duke Snider hits his 300th career homer as the Dodgers – behind Don Drysdale and Clem Labine – beat the Cubs, 7-5.

JULY 22:

Former manager Joe McCarthy, who never played a day in the majors but has a .615 winning percentage, the best of all time, is inducted into the Hall of Fame. He won eight pennants and seven World Series with the Yankees between 1932 and 1943 and won the NL pennant with the Cubs in 1929. Also inducted today is outfielder "Wahoo" Sam Crawford, who played 19 years and hit .309. Crawford played from 1899 to 1917, hit .300 or better 11 times, and is the all-time leader in triples with 312. He appeared in the 1907, 1908, and 1909 World Series with the Tigers.

JULY 28:

Ted Williams collects his 2,300th hit in a four-for-four day

JUNE 16
White Sox reliever Dixie Howell hits two homers in his three and two-thirds innings of work.

AUGUST 1
Brooklyn's Gil Hodges hits the 13th grand slam of his career in a 12-3 win in Chicago.

against the Indians. Williams reached two other landmarks earlier in the month. On July 12, Williams got his 1,600th career RBI; on July 26, he scored his 1,600th run.

Are the McDaniels the new Deans? The Cardinals' Von McDaniel follows his brilliant major league debut with a one-hitter against the Pirates, winning, 4-0. The only hit is Gene Baker's second-inning, two-out double. McDaniel then retires 22 in a row. He strikes out four and picks up his fifth win.

No, the McDaniels are not. Von is 7-5 in his rookie season with a 3.22 ERA. He develops a sore shoulder and his career is over after he appears in only two games in 1958, going 0-0 with a 13.50 ERA. Lindy enjoys a 21-year career; his record is 141-119 with a 3.45 ERA.

JULY 30:

Today in Cincinnati, the Phillies' Ron Northey, signed earlier today as a free agent, smacks a two-run pinch-hit home run in the eighth inning against the Redlegs. It is the ninth pinch-hit homer of his career, tying a major league record. The Phillies win, 8-5.

"LET'S KEEP THE DODGERS IN BROOKLYN," RECORDED BY PHIL FOSTER, WRITTEN BY RAY ROSS, SAM DENOFF, AND BILL PERSKY, CONCLUDES: "SO SEND THE PHILS TO TRENTON, THE GIANTS TO ST. PAUL, BUT KEEP THE DODGERS IN BROOKLYN, THE GREATEST BOROUGH OF ALL!"

AUGUST 1:

In Milwaukee, Pirates' manager Bobby Bragan is ejected. He returns with an orange drink and offers some to the umpires.

AUGUST 1:

Brooklyn's Gil Hodges hits the 13th grand slam homer of his career – an NL record. Today's blast comes off Dick Littlefield in Chicago; the Dodgers win, 12-3.

AUGUST 3:

Two days ago, NL president Warren Giles fined and reprimanded Bobby Bragan for "repeated farcical acts." Today, the Pirates fire their manager. Pittsburgh is 36-67 under Bragan, who will be replaced on an interim basis by Danny Murtaugh.

AUGUST 10:

Mickey Mantle adds Baltimore's Memorial Stadium to the list of sites for his mammoth homers. Today he becomes the first to hit a ball over the center-field hedge, a drive estimated at 460 feet. It is one of Mantle's four hits in a 6-3 victory over the Orioles. Bob Turley gets the win.

AUGUST 19:

The New York Giants board of directors votes 8-1 to move the franchise to San Francisco. The dissenting vote is by M. Donald Grant, a partner in Fahnestock & Co. of Wall Street, representing Mrs. Joan Payson. Voting for the move are three of owner Horace Stoneham's relatives – his son Charles H. Stoneham, his nephew Charles S. "Chub" Feeney, and his brother-in-law Charles Aufderhar. The Giants have been in New York since 1883 and plan to keep the team nickname. President Horace Stoneham tells Frank Graham of the *New York Journal-American*, "I feel bad for the kids. I've seen lots of them at the Polo Grounds. But I haven't seen many of their fathers lately." The Giants drew 629,179 in 1956; in their championship year, 1954, attendance was 1.15 million. They will play at the 22,500-seat Seals Stadium until a new facility is completed.

AUGUST 20:

Bob Keegan of the White Sox no-hits the Senators, 6-0, in Chicago. Keegan walks two and fans one; the White Sox

LEAGUE

In June, Brooklyn Representative Emanuel Cellar reconvenes congressional hearings into baseball. Congressman Torbert MacDonald of Massachusetts proposes a four-year renewable reserve clause, but the players are not in favor of it. Activist Bob Feller wants a five-year limit on the provision.

"Trying to sneak a pitch past Hank Aaron is like trying to sneak a sunrise past a rooster."
– Joe Adcock

make no errors. The game's losing pitcher is Chuck Stobbs.

AUGUST 22:

After tearing a muscle and chipping a bone in his shoulder swinging at a high outside fastball, Stan Musial is sidelined, ending his NL record consecutive game streak.

Actually, Musial gets to add one game to his streak after sitting out today's game. On August 26, the Cardinals complete a game suspended on July 21. Musial appears as a pinch runner, then plays first base in the bottom of the ninth to bring his NL mark to 895 games, topping previous record-holder Gus Suhr by 73 games.

AUGUST 23:

The Monterey, Mexico, team wins the Little League World Series, becoming the first from outside the United States to capture the title.

AUGUST 25:

Warren Spahn beats the Phillies, 7-3, for his 219th career win and sixth place among left-handers. He also hits his 18th career home run, tying him with Lynwood "Schoolboy" Rowe for sixth place all-time among major league pitchers. Bob "Hurricane" Hazle hits a pair of two-run homers for the Braves; he is batting .526 since being called up from Wichita last month.

SEPTEMBER 1:

Today marks the last time in their storied rivalry that the Dodgers will host the Giants at Ebbets Field. Some 18,000 faithful fans turn out for the occasion; the Giants win, 7-5.

Sal "The Barber" Maglie will don his third different New York uniform. The Yankees buy the 40-year-old right-hander from Brooklyn, where he compiled a 6-6 record this season. Maglie previously pitched for the Giants, as well.

SEPTEMBER 3:

At Wrigley Field, Warren Spahn six-hits the Cubs, 8-0. It is Spahn's 41st career shutout, an NL record for left-handed pitchers. The record previously was held by Larry French. Hank Aaron homers for Milwaukee. The losing pitcher is Dick Littlefield.

The Dodgers play their last home game at Jersey City's Roosevelt Park, bowing to the Phillies, 3-2, in 12 innings. Dick Farrell is the game's winning pitcher, while Don Drysdale takes the loss. The Dodgers are 11-4 in their Jersey City games.

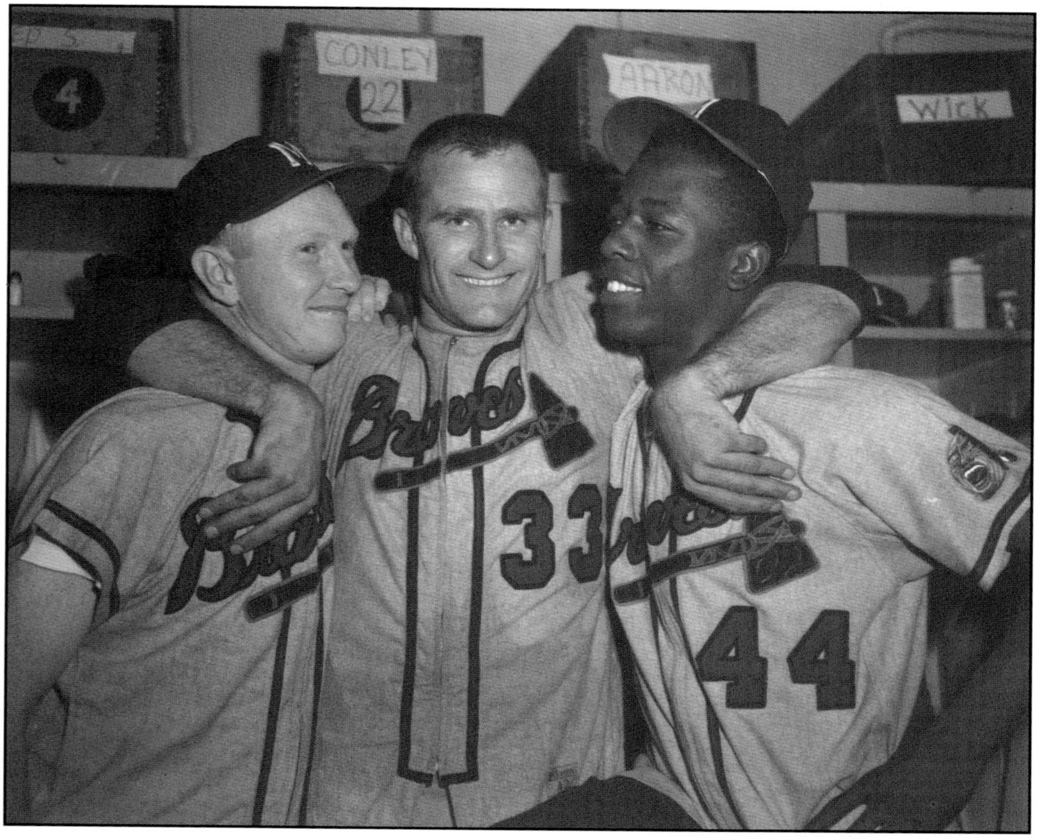

Braves' pitcher Lew Burdette, flanked by Red Schoendienst and Hank Aaron, won three games in the 1957 World Series against the Yankees.

SEPTEMBER 23
Hank Aaron's two-run homer in the 11th gives the Braves a win – and the NL pennant.

SEPTEMBER 29
The Giants play their last game at the Polo Grounds, losing to the Pirates, 9-1.

SEPTEMBER 8:

Now the legendary rivalry plays its last act at the Polo Grounds, where the Giants host the Dodgers for the final time. Willie Mays triples and the Giants win, 3-2.

SEPTEMBER 14:

Ernie Banks hits three straight bases-empty homers against the Pirates at Wrigley Field in the nightcap of a doubleheader. The Cubs win, 7-3, after dropping the opener, 3-1.

At Fenway Park, the Indians' Vic Wertz drives in seven runs in two innings, tying a major league mark. But the Red Sox win the game, 13-10.

SEPTEMBER 16:

The Dodgers come a step closer to a new ballpark – but not in Brooklyn. The Los Angeles City Council okays the sale of 300 acres at Chavez Ravine to the Dodgers. In return, the Dodgers give the $4 million Wrigley Field in Los Angeles to the city and will donate 40 acres at Chavez Ravine for a playground.

SEPTEMBER 21:

Duke Snider hits two homers – his 39th and 40th of the season – against the Phillies' Robin Roberts. Snider ties Ralph Kiner's NL record of 40 round-trippers in five consecutive years. The Dodgers win, 7-3, tagging Roberts with his 22nd defeat of the season.

SEPTEMBER 22:

As the Dodgers prepare to head west, play goes on in Brooklyn. Duke Snider hits two round-trippers today in a 7-3 win over the Phillies. He is the last player to homer in Ebbets Field.

SEPTEMBER 23:

The Yankees, who have been in first place since June 30, clinch another AL pennant.

Hank Aaron drills Billy Muffet's first pitch in the bottom of the 11th inning over the center-field wall for a two-run homer, giving the Braves a 4-2 win over the second-place Cardinals and the NL pennant. It is Aaron's 43rd round-tripper of the season. The winning pitcher is Gene Conley; Muffet gets the loss.

SEPTEMBER 24:

In what will be the last game at Charlie Ebbets's ballpark, the Dodgers' Danny McDevitt blanks the Pirates, 2-0. Bennie McDaniel loses in his major league debut.

Gladys Gooding, the organist at Ebbets Field since 1942, serenades the 6,702 fans with "Auld Lang Syne" and "Say It Isn't So."

Hank Aaron hits a grand slam home run – the first of his career – against Sam Jones of the Cardinals in the first inning today. It is Aaron's 44th homer of the season – giving him the major league title and the 100th of his career. The Braves beat the Cardinals, 6-1.

Ted Williams grounds out against the Senators' Hal Griggs, ending his streak of 16 consecutive at-bats without being retired. Williams's streak began with a pinch-hit home run on September 17. Boston beats the Senators, 2-1, in Washington.

Williams has found a new role – occasional pinch hitter. In eight at-bats, he has three homers, two walks, and a single, a .666 average.

SEPTEMBER 29:

The Giants say good-bye to Coogan's Bluff, playing their last game at the Polo Grounds. They lose, 9-1, to the Pirates. The winning pitcher is Bob Friend; Johnny Antonelli is the loser. Attending on the sad occasion are old-time Giants Carl Hubbell, Richard "Rube" Marquard, George Burns, Larry Doyle, Harry "Moose" McCormick, and Wilfred "Rosy" Ryan. The widow of John J. McGraw says, "It would have broken John's heart." She tells reporters, "The Giants have been my life. Why, I don't know what I'll do with myself."

The Dodgers play for the final time with "Brooklyn" on their chests, losing to the Phillies, 2-1, in Philadelphia. Seth Morehead is the winning pitcher; Roger Craig gets the loss.

At Fenway Park, Ted Williams doubles and singles in two at-bats against the Yankees to finish at .388, becoming the oldest player to win a batting championship. It is the fifth AL batting championship for the 39-year-old Williams.

The Indians fire manager Major "Kerby" Farrell after a 76-77 season and a sixth-place finish. He

TRIVIA

The perennial debate in New York was over the relative abilities of the three center fielders – Willie Mays, Mickey Mantle, and Edwin "Duke" Snider. But for many, the comparison is between Mays and Mantle. Leonard Koppet in *A Thinking Man's Guide to Baseball* wrote: "Only a handful of players, in all of baseball history, have been as important to winning teams, and have been able to contribute as much to eventual victory, rather than statistics, as Mickey Mantle. Willie, on the other hand, I can sum up very simply: he's the best baseball player I ever saw."

"He was the greatest hitter I ever saw..."
– Mickey Mantle, on Ted Williams

will be replaced by Bobby Bragan, dismissed in 1957 by the Pirates with the team at 36-67.

REGULAR SEASON WRAP-UP:

The Yankees and Braves each win their pennant by comfortable margins. The Braves, under Fred Haney, are 95-59, eight ahead of the Cardinals. Hank Aaron hits .322 with 44 homers and 132 RBI. Eddie Mathews has 32 homers and Wes Covington, 21. Red Schoendienst bats .310. Warren Spahn is the top winner with 21-11.

Casey Stengel's Yankees, 98-56, also win the pennant by eight games – over the White Sox. Mickey Mantle is the main batting threat with a .365 average, 34 homers, and 94 RBI. Yogi Berra hits 24 homers and Hank Bauer, 18. Bill Skowron bats .304. The team has no 20-game winners; Tom Sturdivant is 16-6. Ted Williams receives 33 intentional walks – an AL record.

The Braves set a new home attendance mark with 2,215,404; the team has topped the 2 million mark in each of its four seasons in Milwaukee.

OCTOBER 2:

World Series, game one. Whitey Ford five-hits the Braves, 3-1, topping Warren Spahn at Yankee Stadium. The Yankees score twice in the sixth inning, on Andy Carey's RBI single and a squeeze bunt by Jerry Coleman.

OCTOBER 3:

World Series, game two. Lew Burdette bests Bobby Shantz and the Braves beat the Yankees, 4-2. Johnny Logan homers for the Braves; Hank Bauer for the Yankees. The Braves break a 2-2 tie with singles by Joe Adcock, Andy Pafko, and Wes Covington, followed by an error by Tony Kubek.

OCTOBER 5:

World Series, game three. In the first series game ever in Milwaukee, the Yankees capitalize on nine hits to beat the Braves, 12-3. Tony Kubek, a Milwaukee native, hits a three-run homer and a solo shot. Mickey Mantle adds a two-run round-tripper. Don Larsen gets the win in relief of Bob Turley. Bob Buhl lasts only two-thirds of an inning and gets the loss. Hank Aaron has a two-run homer for the losers. The Braves set records by leaving 14 runners on base and by walking 11 Yankees' batters.

OCTOBER 6:

World Series, game four. The Case of the Shoe Polish Stain does in the Yankees. In the bottom of the 10th with New York up, 5-4, and Tommy Byrne pitching, Vernal "Nippy" Jones pinch-hits for Warren Spahn. Jones claims to be hit on the foot by a Byrne pitch and shows a shoe polish stain on the ball to umpire Augie Donatelli, who awards him first base. Johnny Logan doubles to tie the score and Eddie Mathews wins the game with a two-run homer. Spahn gets the win. Bob Grim is charged with the loss. Earlier, Hank Aaron hit a three-run home run and Frank Torre a solo shot for Milwaukee. Elston Howard has a three-run round-tripper for New York.

OCTOBER 7:

World Series, game five. In Milwaukee, Lew Burdette allows seven hits and outduels Whitey Ford, 1-0. The winning run scores in the sixth on two-out singles by Eddie Mathews, Hank Aaron and Joe Adcock. Wes Covington robs Gil McDougald of a homer in the fourth.

OCTOBER 8:

To the surprise of just about no one, Walter O'Malley makes it official – the Dodgers are moving from Brooklyn to Los Angeles. But O'Malley does not attend a press conference at 4 p.m. today at the Waldorf-Astoria Hotel in New York City. Instead, he has a publicity representative read a prepared statement. The relocation was approved by a unanimous vote of stockholders and directors. The team will construct a $10 million, 50,000-seat ballpark at Chavez Ravine. The Dodgers have played in Brooklyn since 1890 and in Ebbets Field since 1913.

OCTOBER 9:

World Series, game six. Back in New York, the Yankees tie the series on Bob Turley's complete-game four-hit, 3-2 victory. Hank Aaron and Hank Bauer match homers in the seventh inning; Frank Torre of the Braves and Yogi Berra – with one on

OCTOBER 10
Lew Burdette blanks the Yankees, 5-0, as the Braves win the World Championship.

NOVEMBER 22
For the second straight year, Mickey Mantle edges out Ted Williams in the AL MVP vote.

– homered earlier. Ernie Johnson loses in relief of Bob Buhl.

OCTOBER 10:

World Series, game seven. Lew Burdette shuts out the Yankees, 5-0, on seven hits for his third Series win, and the World Championship belongs to Milwaukee. Pitching on two days' rest, Burdette has his second straight shutout and becomes the first Series three-game winner since Stan Coveleski in 1920. A Tony Kubek error in the third opens the door for four Braves' runs. The Braves compile a team average of .209. Hank Aaron is the top hitter at .393, with three homers and seven RBIs. Lew Burdette has an 0.67 ERA to go with his three wins. Jerry Coleman hits .364 and Berra .320 for the Yankees.

POST-SEASON

OCTOBER 16:

The Indians' board of directors removes Hank Greenberg as general manager. Under Greenberg, who also is a principal shareholder in the franchise, the Indians were 737-493. In 1957, though, the team finished below .500 for the first time in a decade.

OCTOBER24:

The Redlegs announce they will be staying put in the city of Cincinnati, and will not be moving to Roosevelt Stadium in Jersey City.

NOVEMBER 12:

Frank "Trader" Lane deals himself out of the Cards. After owner August A. Busch Jr. warns that without a pennant in 1958 Lane "would be out on his rump," Lane resigns in the second year of a three-year contract. Bing Devine steps in. Lane replaces Hank Greenberg as manager of the Indians.

NOVEMBER 20:

When the Tigers and Athletics are through dealing, 13 players change addresses. Going to Detroit are second baseman Billy Martin (.251, 10 homers), outfielder Gus Zernial (.236, 27 homers), outfielder Lou Skizas (.245, 18 homers), catcher Tim Thompson (.204 in 81 games), and pitchers Tom Morgan (9-7, 4.64 ERA) and Maurice "Mickey" McDermott (1-4, 5.48 ERA). Kansas City gets outfielders Bill Tuttle (.251, five homers) and Jim Small (.214 in 36 games), pitchers Duane "Duke" Maas (10-14, 3.28 ERA) and John Tsitouris (1-0, 8.10 ERA), catcher Henry "Frank" House (.259, seven homers), and two minor league first basemen – Kent Hadley and Jim McManus.

NOVEMBER 22:

For the second consecutive season, Mickey Mantle is elected the AL's Most Valuable Player, with 233 votes. (Ted Williams got 209.) Mantle hit .365 with 34 homers and 94 RBI. Williams finished at .388 with 38 homers and 87 RBI. One writer has Williams ninth on his ballot; another places him 10th. Mantle is ranked no lower than fourth by any voter.

DECEMBER 3:

The White Sox send outfielder Larry Doby (.288, 14 homers) to the Orioles along with pitcher Jack Harshman (8-8, 4.10 ERA), minor league first baseman-outfielder Jim Marshall, and minor league pitcher Russ Heman. In return, Chicago gets outfielder John "Tito" Francona (.233, seven home runs in 97 games), infielder Billy Goodman (.294, three homers), and pitcher Ray Moore (11-13, 3.72 ERA).

DECEMBER 4:

The Indians send pitcher Early Wynn (14-17, 4.31 ERA) and infielder-outfielder Al Smith (.247, 11 homers) to the White Sox in exchange for outfielder Minnie Minoso (.310, 12 home runs) and infielder Fred Hatfield (.202 in 69 games).

DECEMBER 5:

The Redlegs trade 19-year-old infielder Curt Flood (.333 in three games) and outfielder Joe Taylor (.262, four homers in 33 games) to the Cardinals for pitcher Willard Schmidt (10-3, 4.78 ERA) and minor league pitchers Marty Kutyna and Ted Wieand.

DECEMBER 25:

Rickey Henderson is born in Chicago.

DECEMBER 28:

The Pittsburgh Pirates and Cincinnati Redlegs agree to swap first basemen. Coming to the Pirates is Ted Kluszewski (.268, six home runs in 69 games). In return, Cincinnati will get Dee Fondy (.313, two home runs).

THE BEST OF 1957

National League

HITTERS

Batting Average:
Stan Musial, St. Louis Cardinals, .351

Slugging Average:
Willie Mays, New York Giants, .626

Home Runs:
Hank Aaron, Milwaukee Braves, 44

Runs Batted In:
Hank Aaron, 132

Hits:
Albert "Red" Schoendienst, New York Giants/ Milwaukee Braves, 200

Stolen Bases:
Willie Mays, 38

PITCHERS

Wins:
Warren Spahn, Milwaukee Braves, 21

Strikeouts:
Jack Sanford, Philadelphia Phillies, 188

Earned Run Average:
Johnny Podres, Brooklyn Dodgers, 2.66

Winning Percentage:
Bob Buhl, Milwaukee Braves, .720

Saves:
Clem Labine, Brooklyn Dodgers, 17

Most Valuable Player:
Hank Aaron, Milwaukee Braves

Cy Young Award:
Warren Spahn, Milwaukee Braves

Rookie of the Year:
Jack Sanford, Philadelphia Phillies

American League

HITTERS

Batting Average:
Ted Williams, Boston Red Sox, .388

Slugging Average:
Ted Williams, .731

Home Runs:
Roy Sievers, Washington Senators, 42

Runs Batted In:
Roy Sievers, 114

Hits:
Jacob "Nellie" Fox, Chicago White Sox, 196

Stolen Bases:
Luis Aparicio, Chicago White Sox, 28

PITCHERS

Wins:
Walter "Billy" Pierce, Chicago White Sox; Jim Bunning, Detroit Tigers, 20

Strikeouts:
Early Wynn, Cleveland Indians, 184

Earned Run Average:
Bobby Shantz, New York Yankees, 2.45

Winning Percentage:
Dick Donovan, Chicago White Sox; Tom Sturdivant, New York Yankees, .727

Saves:
Bob Grim, New York Yankees, 19

Most Valuable Player:
Mickey Mantle, New York Yankees

Rookie of the Year:
Tony Kubek, New York Yankees

1958

"It is difficult to see how this sort of thing can catch the public fancy."
– New York Times, *1939, on television*

NEWS

ARKANSAS GOVERNOR DEFIES SUPREME COURT ORDER; REFUSES TO INTEGRATE LITTLE ROCK HIGH SCHOOL

U.S. launches Earth satellite *Explorer I*

Moviegoers enjoy *Vertigo, Gigi, Cat on a Hot Tin Roof*

On television, *The Donna Reed Show, The Andy Williams Show* debut

VLADIMIR NABOKOV PUBLISHES *LOLITA*

Prince Charles becomes Prince of Wales

NIKITA KHRUSHCHEV BECOMES PREMIER OF U.S.S.R.

First atomic sub, *Nautilus*, travels under North Pole

PRE-SEASON

JANUARY 15:

The Yankees sell the television rights to 140 games in 1958 for more than $1 million to WPIX-TV.

JANUARY 23:

The Senators get the long and the short in a trade with the Red Sox. Coming to Washington are six-foot, four-and-a-half-inch, 220-pound first baseman Norm Zauchin (.264, three homers in 52 games) and minor league outfielder Albie Pearson, five feet, five inches, 140 pounds. Boston gets infielder James "Pete" Runnels (.230, two home runs).

JANUARY 28:

The Tigers obtain their first black player, infielder-outfielder Osvaldo "Ozzie" Virgil (.235, four home runs in 96 games) from the San Francisco Giants along with first baseman Gail Harris (.240, nine homers in 90 games). The Giants get infielder Jim Finigan (.270 in 64 games) and $25,000.

At 3:34 a.m., while three-time NL Most Valuable Player Roy Campanella is returning from a television appearance, his car flips over on a slick road in Glen Cove, New York. After the car hits a telephone pole, Campanella, his neck broken, is pinned in the wreckage for a half-hour. He is taken to Community Hospital, where a team of seven surgeons operates on him for four hours and 15 minutes to repair two fractured vertebrae. The prognosis is not good: Campanella is paralyzed from the shoulders down and may never walk again.

JANUARY 29:

Stan Musial signs a $100,000 contract with the Cardinals, making him the highest-salaried player in the NL.

The Indians buy first baseman James "Mickey" Vernon (.241, seven homers), a former two-time AL batting champion, from the Red Sox for the waiver price.

FEBRUARY 6:

Ted Williams becomes the highest-paid player in the history of baseball when he signs a new Red Sox contract for a reported $150,000.

RULES CHANGE

It now will cost a pitcher $50 for the first warning he receives for throwing at a batter.

APRIL 15
The Dodgers and Giants have their first West Coast showdown, in San Francisco.

FEBRUARY 18:

The Tigers acquire pitcher Hank Aguirre (1-1, 5.75 ERA) and catcher Jim Hegan (.216 in 58 games) from the Indians for catcher-outfielder J.W. Porter (.250 in 58 games) and left-handed pitcher Hal Woodeshick (0-0, 13.50 ERA in 1956).

FEBRUARY 21:

Alan Trammell is born in Garden Grove, California.

MARCH 20:

The Yankees sell long-time first baseman Joe Collins (.201 in 79 games) to the Phillies. Collins, a lifetime .256 hitter, refuses to report and retires instead.

MARCH 28:

The 1932 NL Most Valuable Player, Chuck Klein, dies in Indianapolis, at age 53. Klein, an outfielder, played 17 years and batted .320 with 300 homers. He won the league's Triple Crown in 1933. In 1930, he batted .386.

APRIL 1:

Outfielder Larry Doby returns to Cleveland, where he broke the AL's color barrier in 1947. Doby (.288, 14 homers) is traded by the Orioles to the Indians along with pitcher Don Ferrarese (1-1, 4.74 ERA). In return, Baltimore gets outfielders Gene Woodling (.321, 19 homers) and Dick Williams (.261, seven homers) plus pitcher Leavitt "Bud" Daley (2-8, 4.43 ERA).

THE SEASON

APRIL 15:

Major league baseball comes to the West Coast. Before 23,448 fans at Seals Stadium in San Francisco, the Giants – now of San Francisco – and the Dodgers – now of Los Angeles – resume their traditional rivalry. Ruben Gomez starts against Don Drysdale. Daryl Spencer and Orlando Cepeda homer for the Giants; Drysdale is KO'd in the fourth inning and San Francisco wins, 8-0.

Herb Score makes his first pitching appearance since May 7, 1957, when he almost was blinded by a line drive. He pitches three innings against the Athletics, fanning six, walking four, and allowing three runs. Kansas City and Ned Garver win, 5-0.

APRIL 17:

In St. Louis, Stan Musial homers against the Cubs to give him 5,045 career total bases, surpassing Mel Ott. Chicago wins, 4-3.

APRIL 18:

The Dodgers-Giants rivalry shifts south. The two teams meet for the first time in the Los Angeles Coliseum – built for the 1932 Olympics – with a crowd of 78,672 on hand. The Giants' Hank Sauer hits two home runs over the 42-foot left-field screen only 250 feet from home; Dick Gray has one for the Dodgers. After San Francisco's Jim Davenport fails to touch third in the ninth inning, the Dodgers win, 6-5. The winning pitcher is Carl Erskine; Al Worthington gets the loss.

In his second start after his eye injury, Herb Score pitches a complete game and records his first win – 7-5 over the Tigers in Detroit.

APRIL 21:

The Red Sox make the least of their opportunities. During today's game they have 16 base runners, strand 13 of them, and lose two on double plays. Their only run is a Ted Williams homer as they lose to the Yankees, 4-1.

APRIL 23:

At the Los Angeles Coliseum, it's two landmarks and one exercise in folly for the Dodgers. Gil Hodges hits his 300th career homer and Harold "Pee Wee" Reese appears in his 2,000th game. Duke Snider injures his arm attempting to throw a baseball out of the coliseum. Some 3,000 miles from his 1951 Shot Heard 'Round the World, Bobby Thomson still is a nemesis to the Dodgers. His double in the ninth inning gives Chicago a 7-6 victory.

APRIL 24:

The Cubs' Lee Walls finds the Los Angeles Coliseum to his liking; he hits three homers and drives in eight runs in a Chicago victory over the Dodgers, 15-2. Gene Fodge gets the win, the only one of his career.

MAY 13:

At Wrigley Field, Stan Musial hits a pinch-hit double to left field in the sixth inning on the sixth pitch from the Cubs' Moe Drabowsky; it is his 3,000th career hit. Musial was on the bench so he would get his landmark hit before his hometown fans, but manager Fred Hutchinson needed his bat today. Musial's double scores Gene Green and the Cardinals win, 5-3. Musial joins Ty Cobb, Tris Speaker, Honus Wagner, Eddie Collins, Napoleon Lajoie, Paul Waner, and Adrian "Cap" Anson in the 3,000 hit "club."

MAY 20:

The Cubs acquire infielder Alvin Dark (.297 in 18 games) from the Cardinals for pitcher Jim Brosnan (3-4).

JUNE 3:

It's official. Voters approve the purchase of property in Chavez Ravine by the Los Angles Dodgers for a new stadium. The referendum passes 345,435 to 321,142.

For the second time in his career, the Yankees' Whitey Ford fans six straight batters. He beats the White Sox, 3-0.

JUNE 4:

Measuring Mickey Mantle home runs may become a full-time job. At Yankee Stadium today, Mantle hits right-handed against Billy Pierce and rockets a homer into the 19th row of the left center-field bleachers, 478 feet from home plate. New York wins, 7-2.

JUNE 6:

And then there was one – the Red Sox. Ozzie Virgil, acquired by the Detroit Tigers on January 28, is recalled from their Charleston farm team and becomes the first black to play for the team. He has one hit today in the Tigers' 11-2 victory over the Senators.

JUNE 15:

The Dodgers break a strong link to their Brooklyn past. They trade former NL Most Valuable Player and Cy Young Award winner Don Newcombe (0-6) to the Redlegs for first baseman Steve Bilko (.264 in 31 games) and pitcher Johnny Klippstein (3-2).

Wade Boggs is born in Omaha.

The Athletics send first baseman Vic Power (.302 in 52 games) and infielder-outfielder Woodie Held (.214 in 47 games) to the Indians. In return, they get outfielder Roger Maris (.225 in 51 games), first baseman Preston Ward (.338 in 48 games) and pitcher Dick Tomanek (2-3).

The Pirates split up the identical O'Brien twins. Eddie remains in Pittsburgh while second baseman Johnny O'Brien (.000 in three games) and third baseman Gene Freese (.167 in 17 games) are shipped to the Cardinals for infielder Dick "Ducky" Schofield (.213 in 39 games).

JUNE 23:

Willie Mays gets his 1,000th career hit today in Milwaukee and the Braves become the first team to drive relief pitchers in from the bullpen. They transport Don McMahon to the mound in the sidecar of a motor scooter. The Braves beat the Giants, 6-0, with Carlton Willey getting the victory in his first major league start.

JUNE 26:

With the Indians 31-36 and trailing the Yankees by 12 games, general manager Frank Lane fires skipper Bobby Bragan and replaces him with Joe Gordon. Lane tells Bragan, "Bobby, I don't know how we're going to get along without you, but starting tomorrow, we're going to try."

JUNE 27:

Billy Pierce of the White Sox comes within a hair's breadth of a perfect game today in Comiskey Park. With two out in the ninth, the Senators send up pinch hitter Ed Fitz Gerald. On the first pitch, he hits an opposite-field looper just fair down the right-field line for a double. Pierce then fans Albie Pearson – his ninth strikeout of the game – for a 3-0, one-hit victory.

JULY 2:

The Indians release their great right-hander Bob Lemon (0-1, 5.33 ERA). In 13 years, all with Cleveland, Lemon was 207-128 with a 3.23 ERA.

The Dodgers draw 66,485 to the Coliseum for today's doubleheader with the Cardinals. In 35 games, Los Angeles now has 1,026,285 in attendance. They lose the opener, 4-2, and take the nightcap, 3-2.

JULY 8:

The 25th anniversary of baseball's All-Star Game is marked at Baltimore's Memorial Stadium, where the AL wins, 4-3, in the first of the contests without an extra-base hit. Pinch hitter Gil

HISTORY

There are no Hall of Fame inductions in 1958.

JULY 25
Whitey Ford blanks the Indians, 6-0, for his third consecutive shutout.

HISTORY

The Baseball Writers Association picks its Silver Anniversary team:

1B
Lou Gehrig
2B
Rogers Hornsby
SS
Honus Wagner
3B
Harold "Pie" Traynor
C
Bill Dickey
OF
Ty Cobb
OF
George Sisler
OF
Babe Ruth
P
Walter Johnson
P
Robert "Lefty" Grove
P
Carl Hubbell
Manager
John McGraw

McDougald drives in Frank Malzone with the winning run in the sixth inning. The AL manages nine hits, the NL four. The winning pitcher is Early Wynn; Bob Friend is charged with the loss.

JULY 9:

Casey Stengel and Mickey Mantle are among the witnesses before the U.S. Senate Subcommittee on Anti-Trust Monopoly. The Senators are taking testimony on a proposed antitrust exemption for sports. Senator William Langer asks Stengel if he intends to keep on monopolizing the World Championship; he gets an answer that is pure Stengelese: "I got a little concern yesterday in the first three innings when I saw the three players I had gotten rid of, and I said when I lost nine what am I going to do and when I had a couple of my players. I thought so great of that did not do so good up to the sixth inning I was more confused but I finally had to go and call on a young man in Baltimore that we don't own and the Yankees don't own him, and he is doing pretty good, and I would actually have to tell you that I think we are more the Greta Garbo type now from success." He continues: "We are being hated, I mean, from the ownership and all, we are being hated. Every sport that gets too great or one individual – but if we made 27 cents and it pays to have a winner at home, why would not you have a good winner in your own park if you were an owner?" Senator Estes Kefauver turns to Mickey Mantle and asks, "Do you have any observations with reference to the application of the antitrust laws to baseball?" Mantle responds: "My views are just about the same as Casey's."

At one point Senator Estes Kefauver says in response to an answer in "Stengelese": "Mr. Stengel, I am not sure that I made my question clear." Stengel replies: "Yes, sir. Well, that's all right. I'm not sure I'm going to answer yours perfectly either."

JULY 19:

The Braves sign pitcher Phil Niekro and assign him to the minor leagues.

JULY 20:

Jim Bunning of the Tigers no-hits the Red Sox, 3-0, at Fenway Park in the opener of a doubleheader. Bunning strikes out 12, walks two, and hits one batter. The Red Sox make no errors. The losing pitcher is Frank Sullivan.

Hoyt Wilhelm's knuckleball is as hard to handle as it is to hit. His Indians batterymate J.W. Porter tries a first baseman's mitt behind the plate. It doesn't help; Porter is charged with four passed balls. The Orioles beat the Indians, 3-2, in 10 innings.

> "IT TAKES NO EFFORT AT ALL TO PITCH A KNUCKLEBALL," SAID HOYT WILHELM ABOUT HIS SIGNATURE PITCH, WHICH HE DEVELOPED ON HIS OWN. "NO WINDUP IS NECESSARY. IT'S SO SIMPLE THAT VERY LITTLE WARM-UP IN THE BULLPEN IS REQUIRED. THAT'S WHY I CAN PITCH SO OFTEN WITHOUT BEING OVERWORKED."

JULY 22:

The Phillies fire Edward "Mayo" Smith with the team at 39-45. His replacement is Eddie Sawyer, who will manage the Phillies for the second time. In his previous go-round he led the team to the 1950 pennant.

JULY 25:

The Yankees' Whitey Ford shuts out the Indians, 6-0. It is Ford's third straight shutout; previously he whitewashed the White Sox and the Athletics. Ford now is 13-4 with six shutouts.

Ted Williams apologizes to the fans in Kansas City for spitting at them on July 23. Williams was fined $250 for his actions.

SEPTEMBER 8
Roberto Clemente's three triples in a 4-1 win over the Reds ties the modern ML record.

JULY 28:

Mickey Mantle hits "switch" homers for the sixth time in his career, pacing the Yankees to a 14-7 win over the Athletics.

JULY 29:

In the third inning in Detroit, Ted Williams smacks a homer off Jim Bunning with the bases loaded. It is his 17th career grand slam homer. With it, he passes Babe Ruth and trails only Lou Gehrig, who had 23 in his career. The Red Sox go on to beat the Tigers, 11-8.

AUGUST 13:

One of baseball's top young sluggers, Rocky Colavito of the Indians, tests his superior outfielder's arm on the mound. He makes his major league pitching debut, relieving against the Tigers in the seventh inning with runners on second and third. Colavito works three innings allowing no hits, striking out one, and issuing three walks. The Tigers win, 3-2, handing the Indians their fifth straight loss.

AUGUST 14:

The Indians' Vic Power, who runs sparingly, steals home twice today against the Tigers. In the eighth inning, Power follows a homer by Rocky Colavito with his first steal, putting the Indians up, 9-7. The Tigers tie the score and, in the 10th with Colavito at bat, Power steals home again giving Cleveland a 10-9 win.

AUGUST 20:

At Wrigley Field, the injury-strapped Cubs run out of catchers. Moe Thatcher is in the hospital, Sammy Taylor is removed for a pinch hitter, and Cal Neeman is ejected. They turn to first baseman Dale Long, who becomes the first left-hander to catch in a major league game since 1902. Long uses his first baseman's mitt behind the plate. The Pirates win the game, 4-2. The Cubs come back to take the nightcap, 5-1.

AUGUST 23:

Gil Hodges sets an NL record with his 14th career grand slam. Dodgers' pitcher Don Drysdale also homers – it is his seventh career round-tripper, tying the NL pitchers' mark of Don Newcombe. The Dodgers trample the Braves, 10-1, at the Los Angeles Coliseum. The Orioles buy pitcher Hoyt Wilhelm (2-7) from the Indians for the waiver price.

SEPTEMBER 1:

In St. Louis, the Cardinals' Wilmer "Vinegar Bend" Mizell sets a record for the most walks in a shutout. Mizell beats the Redlegs, 1-0, while issuing nine bases on balls. Cincinnati wins the nightcap, 9-3.

SEPTEMBER 8:

The Pirates' Roberto Clemente hits three triples, tying a modern major league record held by many players. Pittsburgh beats Cincinnati, 4-1.

SEPTEMBER 11:

Orioles' manager Paul Richard is making the unorthodox routine. Today, he presents a starting lineup for a game with the Athletics that includes three pitchers. Jack Harshman is in left field, Milt Pappas is at second base, and Billy O'Dell is in his customary position on the mound. The Orioles rally in the first and, with two on and two out, he sends Jim Busby and Billy Gardner to bat for Harshman and Pappas. Despite the maneuvering, Kansas City wins, 7-1.

SEPTEMBER 13:

In Milwaukee, Warren Spahn beats the visiting Cardinals, 8-2, for his 20th win of the season. It is Spahn's ninth season with 20 or more wins, a record for left-handed pitchers. Spahn previously was tied with Eddie Plank and Lefty Grove.

SEPTEMBER 14:

After sweeping the Athletics in a doubleheader to wrap up their 24th pennant, the Yankees board a train for Detroit. En route, relief pitcher Rinold "Ryne" Duren mashes a cigar against coach Ralph Houk's face. Houk, a World War II combat veteran, hits him with a backhand blow.

SEPTEMBER 15:

Private eyes are watching the Yankees on the order of general manager George Weiss. Mickey Mantle and Whitey Ford lose their tails, but the gumshoes stay on the trail of Tony Kubek and Bobby Richardson. The Yankees' double-play combination is followed – into the YMCA, where they play Ping-Pong. The story of the great Kubek-Richardson caper

TRIVIA

Damn Yankees **stars Tab Hunter, Gwen Verdon, and Ray Walston in the film version of the Broadway musical about a middle-aged Senators' fan who sells his soul to the devil to win a pennant.**

SEPTEMBER 29
The Phillies' Richie Ashburn has three hits in securing his second NL batting title.

breaks and Weiss becomes the target of ridicule.

George "Snuffy" Stirnweiss dies at age 39 in Newark, New Jersey, in a freak accident. Stirnweiss is on a Jersey Central train that plunges into Newark Bay when a drawbridge is left open. Stirnweiss, an infielder, led the AL in batting with .309 in 1945. In 10 years, he averaged .268 and stole 134 bases.

SEPTEMBER 16:

Orel Hershiser is born in Buffalo, New York.

SEPTEMBER 20:

Knuckleball pitcher Hoyt Wilhelm, picked up on waivers by the Orioles August 23, no-hits the Yankees, 1-0, at Baltimore's Memorial Stadium. It is Wilhelm's third appearance for the Orioles; prior to this season, Wilhelm had been exclusively a reliever. Wilhelm strikes out eight and walks two; the Orioles play errorless ball in the team's first ever no-hitter. Don Larsen is the losing pitcher. Baltimore's Gus Triandos homers against relief pitcher Bobby Shantz for his 30th of the year, tying Yogi Berra's record for catchers.

SEPTEMBER 21:

Warren Spahn wins his 21st game and clinches the Braves' second consecutive pennant. Hank Aaron provides most of the offense in a 6-5 win over the Redlegs with a homer – his 30th of the year – a double, and four RBI.

SEPTEMBER 22:

At Fenway Park, Ted Williams, who is hitless in his last eight at-bats, strikes out and throws his bat. It accidentally hits 60-year-old Gladys Heffernan in the head. Ms. Heffernan, sitting in a box seat, is the housekeeper for Red Sox general manager Joe Cronin. Williams, as is the custom at Fenway, is booed. He checks to see if she is injured and he is comforted by her. At Christmas, Williams sends Ms. Heffernan a $500 diamond watch.

In Philadelphia, Phillies' pitchers fan a major league record 21 Pirates' batters in a 3-2, 14-inning victory. In the 12th and 13th, Jack Meyer sets an all-time mark for relief pitchers by fanning the first six batters he faces.

SEPTEMBER 28:

Ted Williams homers and doubles in four at-bats against the Senators while his teammate James "Pete" Runnels is hitless in his four turns. The 40-year-old Williams has seven hits in his last 11 at-bats and wins the AL batting title with a .328 average, beating out Runnels, who finishes at .322. The Red Sox top the Senators, 6-4.

SEPTEMBER 29:

In Pittsburgh, Richie Ashburn has three hits in four at-bats to wrap up his second NL batting title. The Phillies' outfielder finishes at .350 to Willie Mays's .347. Phillies' pinch hitter Dave Philley doubles while batting for Juan "Pancho" Herrera. It is Philley's eighth straight pinch hit this season, setting a major league record. The Phillies win, 6-4. Willie Mays goes down fighting with three hits in five at-bats in a Giants' 7-2 victory over the Cardinals.

REGULAR SEASON WRAP-UP:

The defending World Champion Braves win the NL pennant by eight games over the Pirates. Managed by Fred Haney, the team finishes at 92-62. Hank Aaron hits .326 with 30 home runs and 95 RBI. Wes Covington bats .330 with 24 home runs and 74 RBI. Eddie Mathews hits 30 homers and drives in 95, while batting .251. The Braves have two 20-game winners – Warren Spahn (22-11) and Lew Burdette (20-10). Casey Stengel's Yankees win their fourth straight pennant with a 92-62 record – 10 games ahead of the White Sox. Mickey Mantle hits .304 with 42 homers and 97 RBI. Norm Siebern bats .300; Yogi Berra has 22 homers and 90 RBI to go with a .266 average. Bob Turley leads the pitchers with a 21-7 record.

OCTOBER 1:

World Series, game one. In Milwaukee, the Yankees and Braves meet in a rematch of the 1957 fall classic. Warren Spahn gets the Braves off to a positive start with an eight-hit, 10-inning, 4-3 win, despite a solo homer by Bill Skowron and a two-run blast by Hank Bauer. The Braves win on singles by Joe Adcock, Del Crandall, and Bill Bruton. Ryne Duren is tagged with the loss in relief of Whitey Ford.

OCTOBER 2:

World Series, game two. The Braves hammer Bob Turley and beat the Yankees, 13-5,

OCTOBER 9
The Yankees win the World Series against the Braves, overcoming a 3-1 games deficit.

on 15 hits, including a solo homer by Bill Bruton and a three-run shot by winning pitcher Lew Burdette. The Braves set a record with a seven-run first. With his complete-game victory today, Burdette now has four consecutive series wins against the Yankees. Mickey Mantle homers twice and Bauer once in a losing effort. Turley gets the loss.

Lew Burdette's mastery over the Yankees in the 1957 and '58 World Series, some said, was because he threw an illegal spitball, which he denied, replying, "I'd love to use it, if I knew how. Burleigh Grimes told me...not to monkey around with it, but to let them think I threw it. That's what I've done."

OCTOBER 4:

World Series, game three. Today in New York, Don Larsen and Hank Bauer end the Yankees' slide with a 4-0 win. Bauer has a two-run home run as well as a two-run single to account for all the scoring in the game. Ryne Duren saves Larsen's win with two innings of scoreless relief. Bob Rush gets the loss.

OCTOBER 5:

World Series, game four. Milwaukee moves to within a game of its second straight championship with a 3-0 Warren Spahn two-hitter at Yankee Stadium. Norm Siebern misplays two balls in the left-field sun at Yankee Stadium, leading to a pair of runs. Spahn stops Hank Bauer's 17-game series hitting streak. Whitey Ford gets the loss.

OCTOBER 6:

World Series, game five. The Yankees face Lew Burdette, who has mastered them in two series. Their last gasp turns into a sigh of relief. Behind Bob Turley's five-hit pitching, the Yankees beat the Braves, 7-0, in New York. Gil McDougald gets the Yankees off with a solo homer in the third inning and a six-run seventh puts the game away.

OCTOBER 8:

World Series, game six. Gil McDougald homers and Bill Skowron hits an RBI single to give the Yankees a 4-3 victory in 10 innings in Milwaukee, knotting the Series. With the tying run at third and two out, Bob Turley comes out of the bullpen to snuff Frank Torre. Hank Bauer resumes his Series hitting with a homer in the first. The winning pitcher is Ryne Duren; Warren Spahn gets the loss.

OCTOBER 9:

World Series, game seven. The Yankees are World Champions again, defeating their nemesis Lew Burdette, 6-2, in Milwaukee. It is the first time since the Pirates in 1925 that a team has come back from a 3-1 deficit to win the Series. The Yankees break a 2-2 tie in the eighth with two out on an Elston Howard single and a three-run homer by Bill Skowron. Bob Turley gets the win with six and two-thirds innings of work in relief of Don Larsen. Burdette gets the loss. Hank Bauer hits .323 with four homers and eight RBI. Mickey Mantle, Gil McDougald, and Bill Skowron have two homers each. Hank Aaron hits .333 for the Braves. Last year's hero, Lew Burdette, is only 1-2 with a 5.64 ERA.

POST-SEASON

OCTOBER 16:

The Cleveland Indians, being wooed by Minneapolis and Houston, will stay in Cleveland, according to team owner William Daley.

OCTOBER 28:

Construction begins on the new ballpark for the Giants in San Francisco. The rocks in the area are said to resemble candlesticks.

NOVEMBER 5:

Paul Richards is replaced as general manager of the Orioles by Lee MacPhail. Richards, who led Baltimore to a 74-79 record and a sixth-place finish last season, will continue as the team's manager.

NOVEMBER 13:

Preliminary plans for a new baseball circuit – to be known as the Continental League – are announced today by New York City mayor Robert F. Wagner. With the departure of the Dodgers and Giants for the West Coast, New York has no NL franchise.

NOVEMBER 17:

Former major league pitcher Mort Cooper dies at age 45 in Little Rock, Arkansas. Cooper pitched for 11 years, compiling a record of 128-75 with

LEAGUE

During 1958, Brooklyn Congressman Emmanual Cellar introduces a bill that would bring all sports under antitrust laws, with exemptions that are "reasonably necessary" for "competitive practices." No progress is reported on the bill.

"They've taken my playing record off and put my managerial record on."
– Sparky Anderson, on why he likes his 1974 baseball card

TRIVIA

Burgess Fitzpatrick publishes *Casey's Redemption*, in which the grandson of Casey (who struck out in "Casey at the Bat") redeems the family name.

a 2.97 ERA. A three-time 20-game winner, Cooper had his best season in 1942 with the Cardinals; he was 22-7 with a 1.78 ERA and 10 shutouts.

NOVEMBER 18:

After an unsuccessful bid to gain control of the Indians, minority owners Hank Greenberg and Charles and Andrew Baker sell their shares for $800,000 to Bill Daley and the majority stockholders.

NOVEMBER 20:

The Indians acquire infielder Billy Martin (.255, seven homers) and pitcher Alva "Al" Cicotte (3-4, 4.06 ERA) from the Tigers for pitchers Don Mossi (7-8, 3.90 ERA) and Ray Narleski (13-10, 4.07 ERA) plus infielder Oswaldo "Ossie" Alvarez (.209 in 87 games with Washington).

Al Cicotte is the grand-nephew of the disgraced Black Sox pitcher Eddie Cicotte.

NOVEMBER 21:

Hall of Fame outfielder Mel Ott dies at age 49 in New Orleans, after being injured in an automobile accident caused by a drunk driver. Ott played 22 years, all with the New York Giants, batting .304, hitting 511 homers, and amassing 1,861 RBI. He was inducted into the Hall of Fame in 1951.

NOVEMBER 28:

Carl Yastrzemski, a 19-year-old outfielder from Long Island, New York, is signed by the Red Sox for a reported bonus of $100,000.

DECEMBER 2:

The Indians acquire unpredictable outfielder Jim Piersall (.237, eight homers) from the Red Sox for first baseman Vic Wertz (.279, three homers in 25 games) and outfielder Gary Geiger (.231).

The Indians trade second baseman Bobby Avila (.253, five homers), the AL's 1954 batting champion, to the Orioles for minor league pitcher Russ Heman and $30,000.

DECEMBER 3:

The Phillies send pitcher Jack Sanford (10-13, 4.44 ERA) to the Giants for pitcher Ruben Gomez (10-12, 4.38 ERA) and catcher Valmy Thomas (.259, three home runs in 63 games). The Phillies also trade outfielder Chuck Essegian (.246, five homers in 39 games) to the Cardinals for shortstop Ruben Amaro (.224 in 40 games).

DECEMBER 8:

Tris Speaker, regarded by many as the greatest center fielder of all time, dies at age 70 of a heart attack in Lake Whitney, Texas. Speaker, known as the Grey Eagle, played for 22 years in the major leagues, compiling a .345 lifetime batting average with an all-time high 792 doubles among his 3,514 hits. He was elected to the Hall of Fame in 1937. Speaker also managed the Cleveland Indians for eight seasons, leading the team to the 1920 World Championship. Reportedly, his last words were: "My name is Tris Speaker."

DECEMBER 18:

Yet another link to the glory days in Brooklyn is severed. Harold "Pee Wee" Reese, the Dodgers' shortstop for 16 seasons – with four years out of the game for World War II service – retires at the age of 40. Reese has a lifetime batting average of .269 and hit .272 in seven World Series. He will become a Los Angeles coach.

DECEMBER 20:

Following a court fight with the Comiskey family, Bill Veeck – who in previous years had owned both the Cleveland Indians and the St. Louis Browns – and his partners win majority control of the Chicago White Sox.

DECEMBER 23:

The Dodgers trade minor league second baseman George "Sparky" Anderson to the Phillies for outfielder Eldon "Rip" Repulski (.244, 13 home runs in 85 games) and minor league pitchers Jim Golden and Gene Snyder. Anderson, who will go on to make his mark in baseball as the only manager to win World Series titles in both leagues– with Cincinnati's "Big Red Machine" of the mid-1970s and the Detroit Tigers in 1984 – only plays one season in the majors. In 1959, in 152 games for the Phillies, the second- sacker hit .218, with nine doubles, three triples, no home runs, and six steals.

THE BEST OF 1958

National League

HITTERS

Batting Average:
Richie Ashburn, Philadelphia Phillies, .350

Slugging Average:
Ernie Banks, Chicago Cubs, .614

Home Runs:
Ernie Banks, 47

Runs Batted In:
Ernie Banks, 129

Hits:
Richie Ashburn, 215

Stolen Bases:
Willie Mays, San Francisco Giants, 31

PITCHERS

Wins:
Bob Friend, Pittsburgh Pirates;
Warren Spahn, Milwaukee Braves, 22

Strikeouts:
Sam Jones, St. Louis Cardinals, 225

Earned Run Average:
Stu Miller, San Francisco Giants, 2.47

Winning Percentage:
Spahn; Lew Burdette, Milwaukee Braves, .667

Saves:
Roy Face, Pittsburgh Pirates, 20

Most Valuable Player:
Ernie Banks, Chicago Cubs

Rookie of the Year:
Orlando Cepeda, San Francisco Giants

American League

HITTERS

Batting Average:
Ted Williams, Boston Red Sox, .328

Slugging Average:
Rocky Colavito, Cleveland Indians, .620

Home Runs:
Mickey Mantle, New York Yankees, 42

Runs Batted In:
Jackie Jensen, Boston Red Sox, 122

Hits:
Jacob "Nellie" Fox, Chicago White Sox, 187

Stolen Bases:
Luis Aparicio, Chicago White Sox, 29

PITCHERS

Wins:
Bob Turley, New York Yankees, 21

Strikeouts:
Early Wynn, Chicago White Sox, 179

Earned Run Average:
Ed "Whitey" Ford, New York Yankees, 2.01

Winning Percentage:
Bob Turley, .750

Saves:
Ryne Duren, New York Yankees, 20

Most Valuable Player:
Jackie Jensen, Boston Red Sox

Cy Young Award:
Bob Turley, New York Yankees

Rookie of the Year:
Albie Pearson, Washington Senators

LEAGUE

Before baseball's winter meetings in December, AL president Will Harridge announces he will be retiring. Harridge, 72, has been on the job for more than 27 years.

Angeles
53
Angeles
1

1959

"The trick against Drysdale is to hit him before he hits you."
– *Orlando Cepeda*

NEWS

SOVIET UNMANNED SPACECRAFT REACHES MOON

Vice President Nixon visits U.S.S.R.; engages in "Kitchen Debate" with Khrushchev

Typhoon kills more than 3,000 in Japan

Alaska becomes 49th state; Hawaii is 50th

KHRUSHCHEV VISITS U.S.

Iowa plane crash kills Buddy Holly, Richie Valens, "Big Bopper"

JAZZ GREAT BILLIE HOLIDAY DIES

***LADY CHATTERLEY'S LOVER* BANNED FROM U.S. MAIL**

U.S. RECOGNIZES NEW CUBAN GOVERNMENT

Architect Frank Lloyd Wright dies

Quiz show "fix" scandal rocks TV world

PRE-SEASON

JANUARY 15:

Joe Cronin, general manager of the Red Sox, is okayed by the AL screening committee to become the league's president, succeeding Will Harridge. Stanley "Bucky" Harris will be Boston's new general manager.

JANUARY 30:

The Reds acquire slugging outfielder Frank J. Thomas (.281, 35 homers, 109 RBI), infielder-outfielder Jim Pendleton (.333 in three games), outfielder Johnny Powers (.183, two homers in 57 games), and pitcher Charles "Whammy" Douglas (3-3, 3.26 ERA in 1957) from the Pirates. In return, Pittsburgh gets pitcher Harvey Haddix (8-7, 3.52 ERA), infielder Don Hoak (.261, six homers), and catcher Forrest "Smoky" Burgess (.283, six home runs in 99 games).

JANUARY 31:

At the Commodore Hotel in New York City, 52-year-old Joe Cronin is officially elected to a seven-year term as AL president. He is the first former player to hold the position and plans to move the league's headquarters to Boston. Outgoing Will Harridge, who retired, is named chairman of the board.

FEBRUARY 7:

Hall of Fame infielder Napoleon "Larry" Lajoie dies of pneumonia at age 84 in Daytona Beach, Florida. Inducted into the Hall of Fame in 1937, Lajoie played 21 years and batted .338 with 3,244 hits, including 658 doubles. Lajoie managed Cleveland from 1905 to 1909 and never appeared in a World Series, either as player or a manager.

FEBRUARY 28:

Mickey Mantle ends his one-day holdout in St. Petersburg, Florida, signing a contract for $72,000 plus a $2,000 bonus. Mantle was seeking $85,000. General manager George Weiss wanted to cut Mantle by $10,000 to $60,000.

MARCH 10:

After winning control of the White Sox late in 1958, Bill Veeck, Hank Greenberg, and Arthur Allyn buy out the interests of Dorothy Rigney, the granddaughter of original owner

RULES CHANGE

Interleague trading is okay for a three-and-a-half-week period beginning November 21 to coincide with baseball's winter meetings.

LEAGUE

The Cincinnati Redlegs go back to being the plain old Reds again.

The Dodgers celebrate their 1959 World Series win over the White Sox in six games.

LEAGUE

In February, the players oust their lawyer, J. Norman Lewis, and replace him with Judge Robert C. Cannon, who will advise them on baseball law. He is the son of Raymond J. Cannon, a onetime Wisconsin Congressman who tried to unionize the players in 1920.

HISTORY

Between July 28, 1957, and May 10 of this year, the Yankees' Yogi Berra plays 148 games behind the plate without committing an error.

Charles Comiskey and the wife of former Chicago pitcher Johnny Rigney. Her brother, Chuck Comiskey, still holds a sizable minority share of the team.

MARCH 17:

Howard Ehmke dies of spinal meningitis in Philadelphia at age 64. Ehmke was 166-166 with a 3.75 ERA in 15 years, but he is best remembered for his 13-strikeout, 3-1 victory as the surprise starter for the Athletics in the opening game of the 1929 World Series.

MARCH 21:

The Indians trade outfielder Larry Doby (.283, 13 homers in 89 games) away for the second time. Doby goes to the Tigers for outfielder-first baseman John "Tito" Francona (.254, one homer in 86 games).

THE SEASON

APRIL 10:

On opening day in Detroit, Jacob "Nellie" Fox of the White Sox, who had no homers last year, hits a big one with a runner on base in the 14th inning to beat the Tigers, 9-7. Fox earlier had three singles and a double; he collects seven RBI for the day – one-seventh of his total in 1958.

On April 10, the Red Sox send infielder Elijah "Pumpsie" Green to their Minneapolis Millers farm team in the American Association. Boston remains the only major league team that never has had a black player.

The National Association for the Advancement of Colored People charges the Red Sox with discrimination and initiates an investigation into the team's policies.

The Barber has given his last shave. Sal Maglie is released by the Cardinals, ending his 10-year major league career. Maglie, who was suspended from baseball from 1946 to 1949 for jumping briefly to the Mexican League, leaves with a 119-62 career record and a 3.15 ERA.

APRIL 11:

Early Wynn of the White Sox seven-hits the Tigers, 5-3, for his 250th career victory.

The Braves obtain first baseman James "Mickey" Vernon (.293, eight home runs) from the Indians for pitcher Humberto Robinson (2-4, 3.02 ERA)

APRIL 16:

In Milwaukee, the Phillies' Dave Philley extends his record consecutive pinch hit streak to nine when he connects in today's 7-3 loss to the Braves. Philley had eight of the hits in his streak last season.

APRIL 21:

Mickey Mantle hits the 250th homer of his career in an 11-4 win over the Senators in Washington.

APRIL 22:

In Washington, D.C., the Yankees' Whitey Ford pitches 14 innings, striking out 15 Senators. Bill Skowron's home run gives Ford and the Yankees a 1-0 win.

The White Sox score 11 runs in the seventh inning against the Athletics, but they don't exactly knock the cover off the ball. With only one hit plus 10 walks, three Kansas City errors, and one hit batter, Chicago tallies only two earned runs in the frame and wins the game, 20-6. Bob Shaw gets the win; Leavitt "Bud" Daley, who pitches only one and two-thirds innings, gets the loss.

APRIL 26:

Reds' pitcher Willard Schmidt becomes the first player to be hit twice by a pitch in one inning. The following inning he is hit a third time – on the hand by a shot off the bat of Johnny Logan – and has to leave the game. The Reds and Braves use 14 pitchers before Cincinnati wins the game, 11-10.

MAY 1:

In Chicago, 39-year-old Early Wynn does everything but sell peanuts between innings. He pitches a one-hitter against the Red Sox, fanning 14, and hits a double and a homer to win the game, 1-0.

MAY 3:

Charley Maxwell welcomes new Tigers' manager Jimmy Dykes with a home run barrage. Maxwell ties an AL record with four consecutive homers in a doubleheader, hitting one in the opener and three in the nightcap against the visiting Yankees. The Tigers sweep the two games, 4-2 and 8-2. Dykes replaces Bill Norman,

MAY 19
A 120-foot home run by Orioles' pitcher Billy O'Dell beats the White Sox, 2-1.

who had the Tigers off to a 2-15 start.

MAY 7:

Roy Campanella is saluted by 93,103 fans – the largest baseball crowd ever assembled – on a night in his honor at the Los Angeles Coliseum. Campanella, who was paralyzed in an automobile accident before the Dodgers began playing on the West Coast, is wheeled to second base, where he cries and tells the crowd, "This is something I'll never forget. I thank God I'm here living to be able to see it; it's a wonderful thing." In a charity exhibition game that follows the ceremonies, the Yankees top the Dodgers, 6-2. Los Angeles's share, estimated at between $50,000 and $75,000, will help the financially strapped Campanella; the Yankees' share goes to other charities.

MAY 10:

Relief pitchers Lindy McDaniel of the Cardinals and Elmer Singleton of the Cubs trade wins and losses in a doubleheader today in St. Louis. In game one, Singleton gets the 10-9 win and McDaniel the loss. In the second game, McDaniel returns the favor and gets the win, 8-7, while Singleton is the losing pitcher.

MAY 13:

Larry Doby and Bill Veeck, the man who signed him as the AL's first black player in 1947, are reunited in Chicago. The White Sox buy Doby (.218 in 18 games) from the Tigers for $30,000.

MAY 19:

A 120-foot home run by a pitcher wins a ball game for the Orioles. Billy O'Dell hits a fly ball off rival pitcher Billy Pierce that bounces off the right-field foul line and over the head of outfielder Al Smith. O'Dell has an inside-the-park homer with Billy Gardner scoring ahead of him for a 2-1 win over the White Sox.

MAY 20:

Despite a two-run homer by Mickey Mantle, Yankee-killer Frank Lary and the Tigers beat New York, 13-6. The Yankees fall to last place for the first time since May 1940.

MAY 22:

The Orioles' Hoyt Wilhelm almost no-hits the Yankees again, but Jerry Lumpe's eighth-inning single breaks up the bid. The Orioles win, 5-0.

MAY 26:

Hall of Famer pitcher Big Ed Walsh dies at age 78 in Pompano Beach, Florida. Walsh pitched for 14 years, compiling a 195-126 record and the lowest

Dodgers' catcher Roy Campanella was saluted by 93,103 fans in L.A.

MAY 26
Pirates' pitcher Harvey Haddix throws 12 perfect innings, but loses, 1-0, to the Braves.

ERA ever – 1.82. In 1908 he won 40 games for the White Sox and six times had an ERA lower than 2.00. He was 2-0 in the 1906 World Series and was inducted into the Hall of Fame in 1946.

The Pirates' Harvey Haddix turns in one of the most remarkable pitching performances in history and ends up with a loss. Haddix pitches a perfect game for 12 innings against the Braves, but Pittsburgh is unable to provide him with a run. In the top of the 13th, Felix Mantilla reaches first on a throwing error by Don Hoak. After he is sacrificed to second and Hank Aaron is intentionally walked, Joe Adcock hits one over the right center-field fence. It is an apparent home run, but Adcock is called out for passing a base runner during the celebration – after the winning run scores. Adcock gets credit for a double, and Haddix, who retired 36 batters in a row, loses, 1-0. Lew Burdette, who yields 12 hits, gets the win.

The Yankees get pitcher Ralph Terry (2-4) and infielder-outfielder Hector Lopez (.281 in 36 games) from the A's for pitchers Johnny Kucks (0-1) and Tom Sturdivant (0-2) and infielder Jerry Lumpe (.222 in 18 games).

MAY 28:

Baltimore's Hoyt Wilhelm continues to baffle the Yankees with his knuckleball. For the second time in six days, he shuts out New York, winning both games by the same score – 5-0.

JUNE 2:

Ted Williams doubles to center field against Ray Herbert of the Athletics for his 2,500th career hit. However, Kansas City beats Boston, 5-3.

Gnats go nuts in Chicago. Swarms of the flying insects cause a 28-minute delay in the Orioles-White Sox game. A variety of methods – including fire, water, and smoke bombs – fail to chase them off. Finally fireworks clear the field; the Orioles and Hoyt Wilhelm go on to win the game, 3-2.

Owner Bill Veeck tells the press: "It takes all winter to train them and now... poof... one lousy bomb and they're all blown up."

JUNE 6:

Following the departure of shortstop Granny Hamner in May, the Phillies trade another of the 1950 Whiz Kids, Willie "Puddin' Head" Jones (.269 in 47 games). He joins Hamner on the Indians. Coming to Philadelphia is outfielder Jim Bolger (.000 in eight games) and cash.

JUNE 7:

Hoyt Wilhelm of the Orioles pitches his third straight shutout and wins his ninth consecutive game. He lowers his ERA to a measly 0.996.

JUNE 8:

The Cardinals and Reds swap pitchers. Jim Brosnan (1-3) goes to Cincinnati. Hal Jeffcoat heads for St. Louis.

JUNE 10:

Rocky Colavito of the Indians slams his way into the record books with four consecutive home runs against the Orioles

Ernie Banks was named the NL MVP for the second straight year in 1959.

JUNE 21
Stan Musial breaks Honus Wagner's NL record with his 653rd career double.

today at Baltimore's Memorial Stadium. After a first-inning walk, Colavito hits a two-run homer in the third against Jerry Walker. In the fifth he homers with the bases empty, and in the sixth with two on, both against Arnie Portocarrero. And in the ninth he hits a solo home run against Ernie Johnson. Colavito is one of six players with four homers in a game, but joins Lou Gehrig as the only ones to do it consecutively. He also ties a record held by many with four extra-base hits in a single game. Colavito drives in six runs and the Indians win, 11-8. Billy Martin and Minnie Minoso also homer for Cleveland. The winning pitcher is Gary Bell; the losing pitcher is Walker.

JUNE 12:

Mike McCormick of the Giants pitches an abbreviated no-hitter against the Phillies with an assist from the weather. With the Giants ahead, 3-0, in Philadelphia, in the bottom of the sixth inning, McCormick walks two and gives up a single – the first hit – to Richie Ashburn. But rain halts the game, washing out the walks and Ashburn's hit; McCormick is given credit for a five-inning no-hitter.

JUNE 14:

Ernie Banks hits a homer – the 200th of his career – against Carlton Willey of the Braves in the seventh inning at Wrigley Field. The Cubs and Dick Drott win, 6-0.

JUNE 21:

Stan Musial doubles twice – the 652nd and 653rd of his career – topping the NL mark set by Honus Wagner. The Cardinals and Pirates split a doubleheader in St. Louis.

JUNE 22:

In Los Angeles, Sandy Koufax fans 16 Phillies in a 6-2 Dodgers' victory.

JUNE 28:

U.S. Senator Estes Kefauver of Tennessee brings to the Senate floor an antitrust bill that would affect baseball, but it is voted down.

JUNE 30:

A disputed call by the official scorer costs the Giants' Sam Jones a no-hitter. A grounder that eludes shortstop Andre Rodgers is called a hit for the Dodgers' Jim Gilliam and is the only safety against Jones in a 2-0 Giants' win at the Los Angeles Coliseum.

It starts routinely enough with a fourth-inning walk to Stan Musial by the Cubs' Bob Anderson. But the 3-1 pitch gets away from catcher Sammy Taylor. As Taylor and Anderson argue with umpire Vic Delmore, claiming the ball hit the bat, Musial heads for second base. The Cubs' batboy throws the ball to field announcer Pat Pieper. Cubs' third baseman Alvin Dark grabs that ball from Pieper and throws it to second. Umpire Delmore gives Anderson a new ball and he throws that to second too. Shortstop Ernie Banks takes Dark's throw and tags Musial while Anderson's peg goes

Knuckleballer Hoyt Wilhelm came close to a no-hitter against the Yankees on May 22.

into center field. Delmore calls Musial out at second while Al Barlick says he is safe at first. In a 10-minute argument, Cardinals' manager Solly Hemus demands an interference call on the batboy while the Cubs' manager, Bob Scheffing, claims the ball hit Musial's bat and should be strike two. Musial finally is determined to be out because he was tagged with the "original" ball. The Cardinals win anyway, 4-1, negating a protest by Hemus.

CULTURE

The Wonderful Country's star Robert Mitchum, Julie London, and Leroy "Satchel" Paige as a cavalry sergeant.

TRIVIA

"Ko, or a Season on Earth," by Kenneth Koch, is a poem about baseball.

JULY 3:

The Indians' Herb Score, on the comeback trail, strikes out 14 in an 8-4 victory over the Athletics.

The Red Sox, 31-42, fire manager Mike "Pinky" Higgins. Coach Rudy York will handle the team on an interim basis.

JULY 4:

Billy Jurges is named the new manager of the Red Sox. Rudy York was 0-1 as the interim skipper.

JULY 7:

In the first of this year's two All-Star Games, the NL wins, 5-4, at Forbes Field. A Hank Aaron single and a Willie Mays triple provide the tying and go-ahead runs in the eighth. The AL's Al Kaline and the NL's Eddie Mathews hit home runs. Starter Don Drysdale pitches three perfect innings and Johnny Antonelli gets the win. Whitey Ford is the losing pitcher.

BOB STEVENS OF THE *SAN FRANCISCO CHRONICLE* WRITES OF MAYS'S TRIPLE: "HARVEY KUENN GAVE IT AN HONEST PURSUIT, BUT THE ONLY CENTER FIELDER IN BASEBALL WHO COULD HAVE CAUGHT IT HIT IT."

JULY 9:

In Milwaukee, the Braves' Roger Craig three-hits the Braves for 11 innings on only 88 pitches in a 4-3 Los Angeles win. The Dodgers win the game when Wally Moon triples and Eldon "Rip" Repulski singles him home. Norm Larker hit a home run earlier in the game.

JULY 20:

Outfielder Zack Wheat is the only 1959 inductee into the Hall of Fame. Wheat played 19 seasons, all but the last with Brooklyn. He compiled a batting average of .317 and led the league with .335 in 1918.

JULY 21:

Twelve-plus years after Jackie Robinson's historic debut with the Dodgers, the Red Sox finally put a black player on the field. Elijah "Pumpsie" Green, recalled from Minneapolis in the American Association, is inserted as a pinch runner and remains in the game to play shortstop for one inning. The Red Sox are the last team in the majors to break the color line.

JULY 27:

New York attorney William A. Shea announces the formation of the Continental League and reports it will have franchises in New York City, Houston, Toronto, Denver, and Minneapolis-St. Paul and is considering 11 or more other cities. Shea, who had tried to get a major league team into New York to replace the departed Dodgers and Giants, says Branch Rickey will be offered the presidency of the new circuit. Franchise owners of the original teams are investing $2.5 to $3 million plus costs of stadium construction. According to Shea, the organizer of the league, the original teams have $50,000 on deposit in the circuit's treasury.

JULY 30:

The Giants' 21-year-old first baseman Willie "Stretch" McCovey breaks in with a bang. He hits two triples against the Phillies' Robin Roberts and adds two singles in four at-bats as San Francisco beats the Phillies, 7-2.

In Cincinnati, the Cardinals' 23-year-old rookie right-hander Bob Gibson records his first major league win with a 1-0 victory over the Reds.

AUGUST 2:

The Giants' Willie McCovey homers against Ron Kline of the visiting Pirates; it is his first major league round-tripper.

AUGUST 3:

The AL gains a split for the year, winning the season's second All-Star Game, 5-3, at the Los Angeles Coliseum. Yogi Berra's two-run homer against Don Drysdale in the third puts the AL ahead for good. Frank Malzone and Rocky Colavito also homer for the AL. Frank Robinson and Jim Gilliam hit round-trippers for the NL. The winning pitcher is Jerry Walker; Drysdale gets the loss.

AUGUST 4:

At Fenway Park, Pumpsie Green of the Red Sox leads off with a triple against the Athletics' John Tsitouris in a 4-1 Boston victory.

AUGUST 6:

Hoyt Wilhelm of the Orioles pitches a masterpiece in relief. Baltimore's Billy O'Dell and Chicago's Billy Pierce battle to a 1-1 tie into the ninth. Wilhelm comes in for O'Dell and pitches eight and two-thirds innings of no-hit ball before allowing a hit. The game is called after 18 innings because of a midnight curfew.

At Wrigley Field, Cubs' outfielder Billy Williams makes his major league debut against the Phillies. Williams is hitless in four at-bats, but drives in a run in Chicago's 4-2 victory.

AUGUST 11:

Al Kaline singles against Ken McBride of the White Sox in the seventh inning for his 1,000th career hit. The Tigers win, 8-1.

AUGUST 13:

At Wrigley Field, the Cubs and Giants play a three-hour, 50-minute game – the longest nine-inning game ever. Chicago rookie George Altman has five hits in six at-bats, including two homers. Alvin Dark hits a grand slam; Dale Long and Ton Taylor also homer for the Cubs, who win, 20-9.

AUGUST 25:

First baseman-outfielder Harry Simpson is headed for his third team of the season. After hitting .187 in 38 games for the White Sox, Simpson is traded – along with minor league infielder Bob Sagers – to the Pirates for first baseman Ted Kluszewski (.262 in 60 games).

AUGUST 26:

Rocky Colavito's league-leading 38th homer of the year gives the Indians their eighth victory in a row, 5-4, over the visiting Yankees. Jim Perry gets the win.

AUGUST 30:

At Forbes Field, Pirates' reliever Elroy Face is shaky, but wins his 17th straight game of the year and his 22nd over two seasons. Face comes on in the 10th with the score tied, 5-5. He yields a homer to the Phillies' Ed Bouchee, but the Pirates come back with two runs in the bottom of the inning to win for Face. Al Lopez and his White Sox take a major step toward the AL pennant with a doubleheader victory – 6-3 and 9-4 – and a four-game sweep of the Indians. Chicago is now in first place by five and a half games with 24 to play.

AUGUST 31:

The Dodgers' Sandy Koufax ties Bob Feller's 1938 major league single game strikeout record, when he fans 18 Giants today before a crowd of 82,074 at the Los Angeles Coliseum. Koufax strikes out 15 of the last 17 batters he faces. Wally Moon hits a three-run homer in the bottom of the ninth to give the Dodgers a 5-2 win.

SEPTEMBER 2:

In Milwaukee, the Braves' Albert "Red" Schoendienst makes his return to baseball after being sidelined with tuberculosis. Schoendienst pinch hits against the Phillies and grounds out.

Harvey Haddix was almost perfect on May 26.

"No one feels baseball better than Yogi Berra... He is a masterpiece of a ballplayer."
– Sportswriter Robert Creamer

LEAGUE

The major leagues get a caution from a powerful antitrust voice in Washington, D.C. Senator Estes Kefauver warns that the attitudes of organized baseball toward the Continental League will be closely monitored.

Schoendienst appears in 5 games, going hitless in 3 at-bats. He is a part-time player through the 1963 season, when he retires.

SEPTEMBER 12:

The Dodgers score two runs in the bottom of the ninth inning at the Los Angeles Coliseum to pin a 5-4 defeat on Pirates' reliever Roy Face – his first after 17 straight wins this season and 22 over the last two years. Face relieves Bob Friend with the Pirates up, 4-3, in the eighth and retires the side. But in the ninth, Jim Gilliam hits an RBI triple and scores on a Charlie Neal single. Face hadn't lost a game since May 30, 1958. The winning pitcher is Chuck Churn. The Dodgers go on to win the nightcap, 4-0.

Enos "Country" Slaughter makes the final stop in his 19-year career. He is purchased for the waiver price by the Braves after hitting .172 in 74 games for the Yankees this year.

SEPTEMBER 15:

For the seventh time in his career, Mickey Mantle hits "switch" home runs. Batting right-handed against Billy Pierce of the White Sox, Mantle hits a two-run home run. When Bob Shaw relieves for Chicago, Mantle hits a left-handed round-tripper. The home runs are his 30th and 31st of the season, but New York loses, 4-3, at Yankee Stadium.

SEPTEMBER 18:

Joe Gordon has his fill of disputes with general manager Frank Lane and quits as manager of the Indians. One of the points of contention is the platooning of Billy Martin and Jim Piersall. The Indians are in second place at 89-65, five games behind the Chicago White Sox.

Ryne Sandberg is born in Spokane, Washington.

SEPTEMBER 19:

Yogi gets a day at Yankee Stadium. The catcher, now in his 14th year with the franchise, donates $9,800 to Columbia University for a "Yogi Berra scholarship." He receives a wristwatch from Joe DiMaggio and a station wagon from the Yankees' owners. The Yankees beat the Red Sox, 3-1, with Berra hitless. Whitey Ford pitches a four-hitter for his 15th win.

SEPTEMBER 22:

In Cleveland, the White Sox defeat the Indians, 4-2, to wrap up the AL pennant, their first in 40 years. With the bases loaded in the bottom of the ninth and Gerry Staley pitching, Vic Power lines into a double play. Jungle Jim Rivera and Al Smith homer for Chicago; Early Wynn is the winning pitcher.

In St. Louis, the Dodgers use a record nine pinch hitters – including Frank "Hondo" Howard, who hits a 420-foot three-run homer in the ninth – but come up short, 11-10. The Cardinals use a single pinch hitter, Stan Musial, who singles in the third. Gil Hodges has a home run for the Dodgers; the Cardinals' Hal R. Smith and Curt Flood also hit round-trippers. The winning pitcher is Marshall "Sheriff" Bridges; Clarence "Chuck" Churn is credited with the loss.

Here's how the Dodgers' pinch hitters fare: Herman "Tommy" Davis strikes out, Don Demeter and Carl Furillo fly out, Joe Pignatano walks, Chuck Essegian doubles, Ron Fairly and Sandy Amoros ground out, Eldon "Rip" Repulski singles, and Frank Howard homers.

SEPTEMBER 23:

Cleveland general manager Frank Lane calls a press conference to announce his new manager. He is expected to introduce Leo Durocher as Joe Gordon's replacement. After he says, "Bring in Leo," it is not Durocher who steps out but... Joe Gordon. Lane reveals he has signed Gordon to a new two-year contract, which includes a $10,000 raise.

SEPTEMBER 26:

The Giants' Sam Jones, who lost a no-hitter earlier this year on a disputed scoring decision, pitches an abbreviated version today in St. Louis. He beats the Cardinals, 4-0, allowing no hits in a game called after seven innings by umpire Frank Dascoli because of rain. It is the Giants' second "mini" no-hitter of the season. Mike McCormick had a five-inning no-hitter on June 12. Jones walks two and strikes out five. Wilmer "Vinegar Bend" Mizell gets the loss. Willie Mays hits his 34th homer of the season, and

SEPTEMBER 15
For the seventh time in his career, Mickey Mantle hits "switch" home runs.

OCTOBER 4
In the first World Series game in Los Angeles, Don Drysdale beats the White Sox, 3-1.

Willie McCovey raps his 13th. The Giants are one and a half games behind the Dodgers and Braves.

Eight years after his Shot Heard 'Round the World, Bobby Thomson – now a Cub – continues to haunt the Dodgers. He has four hits in four at-bats today and Alvin Dark hits a three-run homer to beat Los Angeles, 12-2, at Wrigley Field, and prevent the Dodgers from wrapping up the pennant. Dave Hillman gets the win; Johnny Podres is the loser.

The Braves stay in the race with a 3-2 win over the Phillies. With the score tied in the eighth, Eddie Mathews and Hank Aaron single and the winning run scores on Bobby Avila's ground ball.

SEPTEMBER 27:

Los Angeles and Milwaukee end the regular season in a tie for the NL pennant as the Dodgers beat the Cubs, 7-1, in Chicago, and the Braves top the visiting Phillies, 5-2, on five unearned runs. The Giants, with a chance to make it a three-way tie, drop a doubleheader to St. Louis.

SEPTEMBER 28:

Charlie Grimm becomes the Cubs' manager for the third time. He replaces Bob Scheffing, who compiled a 74-80 record and finished fifth. Grimm won pennants with Chicago in 1935 and 1945.

The Dodgers and Braves meet in a best-of-three playoff. In Milwaukee, with the score tied, 2-2, Johnny Roseboro of the Dodgers homers against losing pitcher Carlton Willey for the winning run. Rookie Larry Sherry pitches seven and two-thirds innings of shutout relief and gets the win.

SEPTEMBER 29:

At the Coliseum, the Dodgers beat the Braves, 6-5, in 12 innings, for the NL pennant. Short stop Felix Mantilla's wild throw on Carl Furillo's ground ball scores Gil Hodges with the winning run after Los Angeles had tied the game with a three-run, ninth-inning rally against Lew Burdette. The Dodgers' Charlie Neal and the Braves' Eddie Mathews homer. Stan Williams gets the victory; Bob Rush is charged with the loss.

REGULAR SEASON WRAP-UP:

Under Al Lopez, the White Sox compile a 94-60 record, beating the Indians by five games. Jacob "Nellie" Fox is the leading hitter, at .306. Sherman Lollar provides much of the power with 22 homers. Early Wynn tops the pitchers at 22-10. The Dodgers, managed by Walter Alston, are 88-68, two games over the Braves by virtue of their playoff sweep. Duke Snider hits .308 with 23 homers and 88 RBI. Wally Moon finishes at .302 with 19 homers. Gil Hodges with 25 and Charlie Neal with 19 are the other power hitters. Don Drysdale has the best pitching record, 17-13. The Dodgers draw 2,071,045 for the season.

OCTOBER 1:

World Series, game one. After waiting for the Dodgers to complete their playoff against the Braves, the White Sox host Los Angeles at Comiskey Park. It is the first postseason appearance for the franchise since the notorious 1919 Black Sox Series. Paced by a pair of two-run homers and five RBI by Ted Kluszewski and strong pitching by Early Wynn, Chicago beats the Dodgers and Roger Craig, 11-0. Wynn fans six.

OCTOBER 2:

World Series, game two. In Chicago, the Dodgers rebound, 4-3, on a two-out pinch-hit homer by Chuck Essegian and two by Charlie Neal – one with a runner on. Johnny Podres is the winner; Bob Shaw takes the loss.

OCTOBER 4:

World Series, game three. In the first-ever Series game in Los Angeles, Don Drysdale beats Chicago, 3-1. Carl Furillo provides the punch with a bases-loaded single in the seventh inning. Dick Donovan is the losing pitcher. Attendance is a staggering 92,394.

OCTOBER 5:

World Series, game four. In Los Angeles, the Dodgers top the White Sox, 5-4. Chicago's Sherman Lollar hits a three-run homer in the top of the seventh, but Gil Hodges's solo round-tripper is the winning run. Larry Sherry is the winning pitcher in relief of Roger Craig; Gerry Staley is tagged with the game's loss. Attendance is 92,650.

HISTORY

The Indians' John "Tito" Francona finishes with the highest average in the AL – .363. But he has only 399 official at-bats – one short of the required total – and Harvey Kuenn at .353 is the AL batting champion. The rule is later changed, but not in time to benefit Francona.

> "If you don't get on first, you can't score a run."
> – *Enos "Country" Slaughter*

HISTORY

Second baseman George "Sparky" Anderson completes his one and only major league season, appearing in 152 games for the Phillies and batting .218 with no homers and 34 RBI.

OCTOBER 6:

World Series, game five. In Los Angeles, the White Sox come back with a 1-0 victory. Bob Shaw is the winning pitcher with relief help from Billy Pierce and Dick Donovan. Sandy Koufax gets the loss. A great running catch by Jungle Jim Rivera on Charlie Neal snuffs a seventh-inning Dodgers' rally. The winning run scores on a Sherman Lollar double-play ground ball. Attendance is a record 92,706.

OCTOBER 8:

World Series, game six. In Chicago, Larry Sherry beats Early Wynn and the White Sox, 9-3, to win the World Series. The Dodgers build an 8-0 lead and hang on despite Ted Kluszewski's three-run homer in the fourth. Larry Sherry pitches five and two-thirds scoreless innings in relief of Johnny Podres and gets the win. Duke Snider and Wally Moon hit two-run homers for Los Angeles and Chuck Essegian hits a pinch-hit solo homer, joining Yogi Berra as the only player with a pair in Series play. Early Wynn gets the loss. Larry Sherry has two wins and two saves with an ERA of 0.71. Gil Hodges hits .391 and Charlie Neal .370 for the Dodgers. Ted Kluszewski hits .391 with three homers and 10 RBI for Chicago.

POST-SEASON

OCTOBER 13:

The Braves release two veterans – outfielder Enos "Country" Slaughter and first baseman James "Mickey" Vernon. Slaughter, who hit .171 this season, ends his 19-year career with a .300 average. Vernon, who led the AL in batting in 1946 and 1953, hit .220 in 74 games in 1959.

OCTOBER 19:

The U.S. Supreme Court upholds the validity of the sale of Chavez Ravine by the city of Los Angeles to the Dodgers.

Claude "Lefty" Williams, banned for life as one of the Black Sox eight, dies today of Hodgkin's disease at age 66 in Laguna Beach, California. Williams, after accepting money to dump the 1919 World Series, lost three games and compiled a 6.61 ERA. In his seven-year career he was 82-48 with a 3.13 ERA. He was a 20-game winner in both 1919 and 1920.

On the day the tarnished Lefty Williams dies, an emerging Chicago idol, Ernie Banks of the Cubs, is named the NL's Most Valuable Player for the second straight year, the first player in history to earn that distinction. Banks hit .304, with 45 home runs and 143 RBI.

NOVEMBER 21:

In the first transaction on the first day of interleague trading, the Red Sox send first baseman-outfielder Dick Gernert (.262, 11 homers) to the Cubs for first baseman-outfielder Jim Marshall (.252, 11 homers) and pitcher Dave Hillman (8-11, 3.53 ERA).

DECEMBER 1:

The Red Sox acquire outfielder-third baseman Bobby Thomson (.259, 11 home runs) from the Cubs for pitcher Al Scholl (2-5, 5.37 ERA).

DECEMBER 6:

The White Sox obtain outfielder Minnie Minoso (.302, 21 homers, 92 RBI), catcher Dick Brown (.220, five homers in 48 games), and pitchers Don Ferrarese (5-3, 3.20 ERA) and Jake Striker (1-0, 2.70 ERA) from the Indians. Cleveland gets first baseman Norm Cash (.240 in 58 games), infielder-outfielder John Phillips (.264, five homers), and catcher Johnny Romano (.294 in 53 games).

DECEMBER 11:

The Yankees obtain outfielder Roger Maris (.273, 16 homers), infielder Joe DeMaestri (.244, six homers), and first baseman Kent Hadley (.253, 10 home runs) from the A's for Hank Bauer (.238, nine homers), pitcher Don Larsen (6-7, 4.33 ERA), outfielder Norm Siebern (.270, 11 homers), and first baseman Marv Throneberry (.240, eight homers in 80 games).

"Sunny" Jim Bottomley, who drove in an ML record 12 runs on August 16, 1924, dies at age 59 in St. Louis. He played 16 years in the majors and hit .310. He twice led the NL in RBI and played in four World Series with the Cardinals.

DECEMBER 15:

The first interleague trading period ends; 30 players are traded.

DECEMBER 24:

The Braves sign 20-year-old outfielder Ricardo "Rico" Carty.

"I'm 49 and I want to live to be 50."
– Eddie Sawyer, on retiring as the Phillies' manager after one game

APRIL 12
The Giants' West Coast home, Candlestick Park, opens with a 3-1 win over St. Louis.

APRIL 14:

After an opening day 9-4 loss to the Reds in Cincinnati, Phillies' manager Eddie Sawyer quits. Sawyer led the Phillies to the 1950 pennant and returned to the helm in 1958. He has two comments: "There wasn't any one thing, just a lot of things"; and "I'm 49 and I want to live to be 50." Coach Andy Cohen takes over for the Phillies home opener, a night game against the Braves. Philadelphia wins the game, 5-4, in 10 innings.

APRIL 15:

Gene Mauch, who has been managing the Minneapolis Millers in the American Association, is named the new skipper of the Phillies today.

The Continental League New York Mets pick Charles Hurth as their first general manager. He was president of the Southern Association.

APRIL 17:

Indians general manager Frank "Trader" Lane pulls a shocker, trading the AL's home run champion for its batting leader. Going to the Tigers is the popular 26-year-old outfielder Rocky Colavito (.257, 42 homers, 111 RBI). In return the Indians get the 29-year-old outfielder-infielder Harvey Kuenn (.353, nine homers, 71 RBI).

APRIL 18:

The Indians give up on Herb Score (9-11, 4.71 ERA), who seemed a sure shot for Cooperstown until an eye injury in 1957. Cleveland sends the left-hander to the Chicago White Sox for pitcher Arnold "Barry" Latman (8-5, 3.75 ERA).

On opening day in Washington, D.C., Camilo Pascual of the Senators strikes out 15 Red Sox and wins, 10-1. In his first at-bat, Ted Williams hits a 500-foot home run – the 493rd homer of his career – tying Lou Gehrig.

APRIL 19:

At Fenway Park, Roger Maris makes his debut in a Yankees' uniform, with four hits – including two homers – and four RBI. Bill Skowron also has four hits for New York in an 8-4 victory.

In Cleveland, the Tigers beat the Indians, 4-2, in 15 innings – the longest opening day game ever. Pete Burnside gets the win with four innings of relief. Jim "Mudcat" Grant, who works three and a third innings, is charged with the loss.

The Giants host the Dodgers at Candlestick Park for the first time. Los Angeles scores three runs in the ninth and Johnny Podres beats San Francisco, 4-0.

MAY 1:

In Chicago, Al Smith hits a homer off Jim Bunning of the visiting Tigers, setting off Bill Veeck's new $300,000 exploding scoreboard. The White Sox win two, 6-3 and 5-2.

MAY 4:

After 17 games, Lou Boudreau leaves the Cubs' broadcast booth to become the team's manager. Charlie Grimm, who gets Chicago off to a 6-11 start, leaves the dugout to replace Boudreau behind the microphone. Under their new skipper, Dick Ellsworth and the Cubs beat the Pirates, 5-1.

MAY 9:

Tony Gwynn is born in Los Angeles. In 22 years, he'll make his major league debut in nearby San Diego.

MAY 13:

Pirates' shortstop Dick Groat raps out six hits – three doubles and three singles – against the Braves in Milwaukee. Pittsburgh wins, 8-2.

MAY 15:

Two days after being acquired in a trade with the Phillies, Don Cardwell makes his first start for the Cubs and no-hits the Cardinals, 4-0, at Wrigley Field in game two of a doubleheader. Cardwell walks Alex Grammas in the first inning; no other Cardinal reaches base, and seven go down on strikes. It is the first no-hitter against St. Louis since 1919. The last batter, Joe Cunningham, hits a sinking liner to left field that is snatched by Walt Moryn. Lindy McDaniel gets the loss. In the opener, two homers by Ken Boyer help the Cardinals to a 6-1 win.

MAY 27:

At Yankee Stadium, Orioles' catcher Clint Courtney comes out to handle knuckleballer Hoy Wilhelm with an oversized mitt designed by manager Paul Richards. In games Wilhelm pitches, Courtney and the Orioles' other catch-

HISTORY

In the 1950s, the decade just ended, eight percent of the major league players were black. But eight of the 10 NL Most Valuable Player Awards went to African-Americans. Roy Campanella won three times, Ernie Banks twice, and Willie Mays, Don Newcombe, and Hank Aaron once each.

George Weiss's credo: "There is no such thing as second place. Either you're first or you're nothing."

TRIVIA

The formerly cordial relationship between Ty Cobb and Ted Williams ends during a 1960 conversation about Rogers Hornsby and his place in baseball history. To make a point, Williams notes that Hornsby's .424 season topped Cobb's best. Cobb shouts: "Get away from me! And don't come back!" He never speaks to Williams again.

ers Myron "Joe" Ginsberg and Gus Triandos, already have 11 passed balls in 1960 after 38 last season. Since there is no rule restricting the size of a catcher's mitt, Richards is trying one 50 percent bigger than the standard. Courtney has no passed balls and the Orioles beat the Yankees, 3-2. The "Richards mitt" is later banned.

MAY 28:

Yankees' manager Casey Stengel is hospitalized with a virus and fever. Coach Ralph Houk will handle the ballclub in his absence.

MAY 30:

After a Memorial Day doubleheader, fans charge Mickey Mantle, trying to swipe his cap and glove. Mantle is punched in the jaw but is not seriously injured. The Yankees lose the opener to Washington, 2-1, and come back to take the nightcap, 3-2.

JUNE 8:

Casey Stengel is back, but he retains the lineup changes made by interim manager Ralph Houk: Clete Boyer is at third base, Hector Lopez is in left field, Art Ditmar is in the starting rotation, and Johnny Blanchard is sharing the catching. Bob Turley three-hits the White Sox and Mickey Mantle hits two homers in a 6-0 Yankees' win.

STAN MUSIAL ONCE SAID: "THE FIRST PRINCIPLE OF CONTRACT NEGOTIATIONS IS, DON'T REMIND THEM OF WHAT YOU DID IN THE PAST. TELL THEM WHAT YOU'RE GOING TO DO IN THE FUTURE."

JUNE 17:

In Chicago, Clete Boyer homers and his Yankees' teammates react with their own fireworks in a mockery of Bill Veeck's $300,000 exploding scoreboard. Led by Casey Stengel, the Yankees march around holding sparklers in the air.

Ted Williams, 41 years old and in his 19th year – with two interruptions for military service that remove four and a half seasons from his career – hits his 500th home run. He becomes the fourth player to reach that level. Williams hits his landmark homer against Wynn Hawkins of the Indians in Cleveland and it clears the left centerfield fence. The Red Sox win, 3-1.

JUNE 18:

Today Tom Sheehan replaces Bill Rigney as manager of the Giants. Rigney is dismissed with the team at 33-25. At 66 years and two months old, Sheehan, a part-time scout, is the oldest rookie manager ever.

JUNE 28:

It's a close call for the game of baseball in Washington, D.C. By only four votes, the Senate fails to pass a bill introduced by Senator Estes Kefauver that would have made the sport subject to current antitrust regulations.

JUNE 29:

The Cleveland Indians buy pitcher Don Newcombe (4-6) from the Reds.

JULY 3:

In St. Louis, the Braves' Hank Aaron homers against the Cardinals' Ron Kline in the seventh inning. It is Aaron's 200th career home run.

JULY 4:

Mickey Mantle homers against Hal Woodeshick of the Senators in a 9-8 Yankees' loss. It is the 300th home run of Mantle's career and he is the 18th player to reach that mark.

The Orioles sign outfielder-third baseman Bobby Thomson, who was hitting .263 in 40 games with the Boston Red Sox.

Thomson plays three games with Baltimore and retires. He leaves

JUNE 17
Ted Williams, 41, hits his 500th career home run in a 3-1 Red Sox win over the Indians.

JULY 19
Juan Marichal, 22, makes his debut with the Giants, throwing a one-hit shutout.

baseball with a .270 average over 15 years and 264 homers – none as big as the one that gave the Giants the 1951 pennant.

JULY 11:

Today in Kansas City, behind three shutout innings by Bob Friend and heavy hitting by Willie Mays, the NL beats the AL, 5-3, in the first of this year's two All-Star Games. Roy Face relieves with the bases loaded in the fifth and gets Luis Aparacio on an inning-ending double play. Willie Mays has a single, double, and triple. Ernie Banks and Del Crandell homer for the NL; Al Kaline for the AL. Friend gets the win; Bill Monboquette is the losing pitcher.

JULY 13:

The National League sweeps both of this year's All-Star Games, the second today with a 6-0 win at Yankee Stadium. The Senior Circuit attack includes home runs by Eddie Mathews, Willie Mays – one of his three hits – Ken Boyer, and a pinch-hit round-tripper by Stan Musial. The winning pitcher is starter Vernon Law of the Pirates; theYankees' Whitey Ford is the game's losing pitcher.

JULY 17:

In the opener of a doubleheader against the Reds, the Pirates' Dick Groat gets his 1,000th career hit.

JULY 19:

The Giants' 22-year-old right-hander Juan Marichal makes his major league debut with a one-hit, 2-0 victory against the Phillies at Candlestick Park. Marichal fans 12 and allows no hits until rookie Clay Dalrymple's two-out pinch-hit single in the eighth inning.

JULY 23:

The shift didn't work, so now the Indians' Jimmy Piersall comes up with a different approach to stop Boston's unstoppable Ted Williams. In the eighth inning, Piersall runs back and forth between his center-field position and left trying to distract Williams. Piersall gets ejected from the game for his efforts, and Cleveland manager Joe Gordon follows him to the clubhouse, after arguing the case too strenuously at the end of the inning. Mike de la Hoz hits his first major league home run for Cleveland and Jim Perry is the winning pitcher in the victory, 4-2.

AUGUST 2:

The Continental League will have a place in the history books but not in the record books. A year after its formation, it reaches an agreement with the majors and will disband without playing a game. The eight teams unanimously accept an arrangement allowing four of its franchises to be absorbed into the existing structure of the NL and AL – expanding them from eight to 10 teams each. Expansion is targeted for 1961 but will take place no later than 1962. The Continental League ran into difficulty when it did not reach agreement with minor league teams on territorial compensation and other money issues.

AUGUST 3:

Is Frank "Trader" Lane of the Indians running out of players to swap? Today he trades his manager Joe Gordon to the Tigers for their manager Jimmy Dykes. According to reports, the trade began with a tongue-in-cheek remark on April 17 by Tigers' general manager Bill DeWitt to Lane when they were arranging the Rocky Colavito-for-Harvey Kuenn transaction. The 63-year-old Dykes has the Tigers in sixth place with a 44-52 record, 11 ½ games behind the first-place Yankees. Under Gordon, age 45, the Indians are 49-46, six games behind. Says Dykes: "I've been around baseball a long time, but I've never seen anything like this."

AUGUST 4:

In Cincinnati, Billy Martin of the Reds, reacting to a pitch behind his head, throws his bat at Jim Brewer's head, charges the mound, and punches the Cubs' pitcher, who allegedly had called him a "little dago son of a bitch." Brewer's right cheekbone is shattered and his eyeball socket is depressed. In baseball, Ernie Banks homers and the Cubs win the game, 5-3.

The hot-headed Martin is levied a $500 fine by the league's front office and given a five-day suspension. Brewer spends two months in the hospital undergoing two operations and misses the entire season. The Cubs file a suit against Martin for $1 million, but eventually drop it. Brewer pursues the case for six years and wins $10,000 after a trial.

EQUIPMENT

Bill Veeck puts the names of his players on the backs of the White Sox uniforms. In his autobiography, Veeck explains he instituted the concept "under the obviously misguided notion that the fans might want to know who they were." He notes that "protests came in from every other team in the league."

HISTORY

Ted Williams hits safely in a season opener for the 14th consecutive year. In those 14 games, Williams has a .449 batting average with seven doubles, one triple, and three homers, batting in 14 runs and scoring nine times.

LEAGUE

Reportedly, Gene Autry comes to the AL owners meeting seeking broadcasting opportunities and goes home as the owner of an expansion franchise. AL president Joe Cronin notes, "We would be silly not to move into Los Angeles."

AUGUST 10:

In Cleveland, Ted Williams homers off Barry Latman in the fifth inning for his 512th career round-tripper to move past Mel Ott into sole possession of fourth place on the all-time list. In the sixth, he smacks his 513th – this time against Johnny Klippstein. The Red Sox win, 6-1. After the game, Williams announces that he will retire at the end of the season.

AUGUST 14:

Hall of Famer Fred Clarke dies at age 87 in Winfield, Kansas. Clarke played in the majors for 21 years, compiling a .312 average and hitting 220 triples – the seventh highest total of all time. He also managed for 19 years, leading the Pirates to four first-place finishes, as well as one World Championship.

AUGUST 17:

The *Sporting News* names Boston's Ted Williams the Player of the Decade (1950s).

AUGUST 18:

The Braves' Lew Burdette no-hits the Phillies, 1-0, in Milwaukee; a hit batter is the only base runner. Burdette strikes out three. Gene Conley is the losing pitcher.

IN *MY TURN AT BAT*, TED WILLIAMS WRITES, "NOBODY KNEW THIS, BUT THE YANKEES TRIED TO HIRE ME TO PLAY ONE MORE YEAR IN 1961." HE STATES THAT CO-OWNER DAN TOPPING OFFERED TO PAY HIM $125,000 TO "STRICTLY PINCH HIT." WILLIAMS ADDS, "I WASN'T INTERESTED. I WAS NEVER GOING TO HIT ANOTHER BALL IN A BIG LEAGUE PARK."

AUGUST 20:

Against the Orioles, Ted Williams is walked for the 2,000th time in his major league career.

AUGUST 24:

Cal Ripken Jr. is born in Havre de Grace, Maryland.

AUGUST 28:

The White Sox' Ted Kluszewski loses a home run because his teammates Earl Torgeson and Floyd Robinson are warming up outside the bullpen area in Baltimore. As it goes, Kluszewski, batting in the top of the eighth against Milt Pappas, hits an apparent three-run homer to put his team ahead, 4-3. But third base umpire Ed Hurley notices the location of the two White Sox players and calls time before the pitch.

AUGUST 30:

Pete Runnels of the Red Sox enjoys a nine-hit day in a doubleheader with the Tigers. In the opener, Runnels has a double and five singles in seven at-bats. His two-base hit drives in

In his autobiography, Ted Williams writes that his goal was "to have people say, "There goes Ted Williams, the greatest hitter who ever lived."

the winning run in the 15th inning. Runnels then adds three more hits in the nightcap.

SEPTEMBER 2:

And if there's a grandson, Ted Williams probably will hit him, too. Williams, who homered off Thornton Lee, hits one off his son, Don Lee, of the Senators today. But Washington sweeps Boston, 5-1 and 3-2.

SEPTEMBER 10:

For the third time in his career, Mickey Mantle hits a ball over the right-field roof at Tiger Stadium. Today's drive – off Paul Foytack in the seventh – carries past Trumbell Avenue and lands in a parking lot. The Yankees win, 5-1.

SEPTEMBER 16:

Warren Spahn, 39 years old, pitches his first no-hitter, beating the Phillies, 4-0. Spahn strikes out 15 and walks two; the Braves make no errors. The last batter, Bobby Malkmus, hits the ball off Spahn's glove. It caroms to shortstop Johnny Logan, who throws to Joe Adcock to end the game and preserve Spahn's no-hitter. The losing pitcher is John Buzhardt. It is the second time this season a Braves' pitcher has no-hit the Phillies. Spahn's season record is now 20-9, the 11th time in 16 years he has won at least 20 games.

SEPTEMBER 17:

The Orioles' Clint Courtney becomes the first catcher ever with two career unassisted double plays. But the Yankees win, 5-3.

SEPTEMBER 17:

The Yankees beat the Orioles twice, 7-3 and 2-0, before a crowd of 53,876 at Yankee Stadium to complete a four-game sweep in a key series. The Yankees began the four-game set leading Baltimore by .001. Whitey Ford got the Yankees moving on September 16 when he beat Steve Barber, 4-2.

SEPTEMBER 20:

Carroll Hardy has the distinction of pinch-hitting for one of baseball's greatest players ever. After Boston's Ted Williams is injured fouling a ball off his ankle in the first inning today, Hardy bats for him and lines into a double play against Hal Brown of the Browns. In 1958, as a member of the Indians, Hardy had pinch-hit a three-run home run for Roger Maris.

SEPTEMBER 25:

The Pirates lose to the Braves today, 4-2, in Milwaukee, but the Cubs still beat the Cardinals, giving Pittsburgh its first NL pennant in 33 years. Behind Ralph Terry, the Yankees beat the Red Sox, 4-3, to wrap up their 25th pennant and the 10th for manager Casey Stengel. Then comes the really bad news: Red Sox owner Tom Yawkey makes it official – Ted Williams is retiring.

SEPTEMBER 28:

The Kid, now 42 years old, says good-bye to his fans and his foes at Fenway Park. Ted Williams, who originally said he would retire at the end of the season, decides to bow out three games

HISTORY

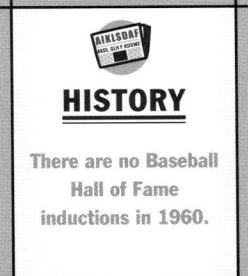

There are no Baseball Hall of Fame inductions in 1960.

Ted Williams goes out with a bang – a homer.

In answer to a question, Ty Cobb states he could hit .300 against modern pitchers, then adds: "You've got to remember – I'm 73."

LEAGUE

The NL will admit teams from Houston and New York. The AL shifts from the original agreement and takes in a new Los Angeles team and a replacement team in Washington instead of two from the Continental League.

earlier. After being robbed of a home run by Al Pilarcik of the Orioles in right center field, Williams comes to the plate for the last time in the eighth inning. He catches a 1-1 pitch from Jack Fisher and hits it out for his 521st – and final – career home run. The fans stand and chant: "We want Ted," but, true to form, he does not emerge from the dugout. ("I couldn't," he explains later.) Carroll Hardy replaces Williams in left field in the top of the ninth, and the career of the man who was perhaps baseball's greatest pure hitter is over. With the Red Sox out of the pennant race, Williams will go fishing in Maine while the team travels to New York for its final games of the season.

Williams finishes his 19-year career with a .344 lifetime average. He is the last man to hit .400 in the majors and ranks third all-time in homers, behind Babe Ruth and Jimmie Foxx. After the game he says, "I've gone as far as I can."

OCTOBER 2:

The Yankees finish the regular season on a roll, beating the Red Sox, 8-7, for their 15th straight victory.

In what will be the last game for this Senators team, they lose to the Orioles, 2-0. Milt Pappas is the winning pitcher; Pedro Ramos gets the loss.

OCTOBER 3:

The Detroit Tigers, who had traded to get manager Joe Gordon in August, fire him today. Detroit was 26-31 under Gordon and finished in sixth place in the AL.

REGULAR SEASON WRAP-UP:

The Yankees win their 10th AL flag in 12 years under Casey Stengel. New York finishes at 97-57, eight games ahead of the Orioles. Roger Maris hits 39 homers with 112 RBI and bats .283. Mickey Mantle hits .275, but has 40 homers and 94 RBI. Bill Skowron hits 26 round-trippers. Art Ditmar is the club's top winner at 15-9.

Danny Murtaugh's Pirates finish at 95-59, seven over the Braves. Shortstop Dick Groat is the NL's top hitter at .325. Groat is one of only three shortstops to lead the NL in batting; the others are Honus Wagner and Joseph "Arky" Vaughan. Roberto Clemente hits .314 with 16 homers and 94 RBI. Dick Stuart has 23 homers. Vernon Law is the staff's ace with a record of 20-9. Reliever Elroy Face has 24 saves.

George Crowe of the Cardinals hits four pinch-hit homers this season, giving him a major league record 14 for his career. The Dodgers set an NL attendance record with 2,253,887, topping the 1957 Braves.

OCTOBER 5:

World Series, game one. At Forbes Field, the Yankees bang out 13 hits – including a solo homer by Roger Maris and a two-run blast by Elston Howard, but lose the opener, 6-4. Bill Mazeroski's two-run homer in the fourth is the key blow for the Pirates. Vernon Law gets the win with a save by Roy Face; Art Ditmar, the first of four Yankees' pitchers, gets the loss.

OCTOBER 6:

World Series, game two. Yesterday, 13 hits weren't enough for the Yankees; today they have 19 – to the Pirates' 13 – and win, 16-3. Mickey Mantle is New York's big gun with two-run and three-run homers and five RBIs. Bob Turley goes eight and a third for the win, with a save from Bobby Shantz. Bob Friend, the first of six Pittsburgh hurlers, gets the loss.

OCTOBER 8:

World Series, game three. At Yankee Stadium, New York continues its assault on Pirates' pitching with 16 hits and Whitey Ford hurls a complete-game four-hitter for a 10-0 win. Mantle homers again with a runner on and Bobby Richardson hits a grand slam, driving in a record six runs in the game. The Pirates again use six pitchers; starter Wilmer "Vinegar Bend" Mizell is tagged with the loss.

OCTOBER 9:

World Series, game four. Vernon Law – with a save from Roy Face – quiets the Yankees' bats today in New York for a 3-2 victory. The Pirates score three in the fifth to offset a homer by Bill Skowron. Law has a clutch double; Face sets down eight in a row. Ralph Terry is the losing pitcher.

OCTOBER 10:

World Series, game five. The Yankees trail the Series after losing at home today, 5-2, on strong pitching by

OCTOBER 13
The Pirates win the World Series over the Yankees on Bill Mazeroski's home run.

OCTOBER 18
Casey Stengel, who led the Yankees to seven World Championships, is fired as manager.

Harvey Haddix and two and two-thirds innings of no-hit relief from Roy Face, who gets another save. Roger Maris homers for the Yankees with the bases empty; starter Art Dirmar is credited with the loss.

OCTOBER 11:

Today John Fetzer announces that he is buying out Kenyon Grown and becoming the majority stockholder in the Tigers.

OCTOBER 12:

World Series, game six. The Yankees find Forbes Field to their liking. They pound out 17 hits in support of Whitey Ford, who limits the Pirates to seven hits in a complete game, 12-0 win. There are no homers in the game, but Bobby Richardson hits two triples and raises his RBI total to a record 12. Once again the Pirates use six pitchers; starter Bob Friend gets tagged with the loss.

OCTOBER 13:

World Series, game seven. At Forbes Field, Bill Mazeroski's bases-empty homer in the bottom of the ninth gives the Pirates a 10-9 win and their first World Championship in 35 years. It is the first World Series to end with a homer. The game turns in the bottom of the eighth on a bad-bounce ground ball. The Yankees enter the inning up, 7-4, when Virdon's grounder hits shortstop Tony Kubek in the throat, opening the door to a five-run inning including a three-run homer by Hal W. Smith off Jim Coates. The Yankees tie the game in the top of the ninth, thereby setting the stage perfectly for Mazeroski's dramatic home run. Harvey Haddix gets the win with an inning of relief. Ralph Terry gets the loss. Bill Skowron and Berra had homered earlier for the Yankees; Glenn "Rocky" Nelson had one for the Pirates. The Pirates are out-scored 27-55 and their pitchers compile a 7.11 ERA. Series hero Bill Mazeroski hits .320 with two homers and five RBI. Roberto Clemente bats .310. Roy Face has three saves in the Pirates' four wins. Mickey Mantle hits .400 with three homers and 11 RBI; Bobby Richardson bats .367 with 12 RBI; Bill Skowron hits .375, Tony Kubek .333, and Yogi Berra .318. Whitey Ford wins two games, both shutouts.

CASEY STENGEL TELLS NEW YORK SPORTSWRITER DICK YOUNG: "THEY EXAMINED ALL MY ORGANS. SOME OF THEM ARE QUITE REMARKABLE AND OTHERS ARE NOT SO GOOD. A LOT OF MUSEUMS ARE BIDDING FOR THEM."

POST-SEASON

OCTOBER 17:

NL owners meet in Chicago's Sheraton Blackstone Hotel and agree on expansion to 10 teams for 1962 with "unanimous enthusiasm"; new franchises will be added in New York and Houston. The New York group is composed of Mrs. Charles Shipman Payson, M. Donald Grant, Dwight Davis Jr., G. H. Walker Jr., and William Simpson. The Houston franchise is owned by Craig F. Cullinan, Judge Roy Hofheinz, R.E. Smith, K.S. "Bud" Adams, and George Kirksey. The Houston group will construct a $14.5 million stadium in Harris City. The New York team will play in a 55,000-seat ballpark to be constructed in Flushing, New York.

OCTOBER 18:

Casey Stengel, the man who brought the Yankees 10 pennants and seven World Championships, is sacked today by the Yankees' brass. The announcement is made by co-owners Dan Topping and Del Webb at the Savoy Hotel in New York. Topping says, "You are retiring of your

TRIVIA

"Dream of a Baseball Star," a poem by Gregory Corso, is published.

Bill Mazeroski's ninth-inning homer wins the World Series for the Pirates over the Yankees.

11
5

ATES
16
40
42

"I'll never make the mistake of being 70 years old again."
–Casey Stengel

LEAGUE

A poignant and remarkable chapter in baseball history ends when the Negro American League, the last of the major black circuits, disbands after the 1960 season. With the doors open for blacks in the major leagues, the talent pool for the Negro Leagues has steadily diminished, and interest along with it. The Negro National League had been absorbed into the Negro American League in 1949.

own volition, aren't you, Mr. Stengel?" Stengel responds: "Boys, I'm not retiring; I've just been fired." He adds: "I commenced winning pennants when I came here, but I didn't commence getting any younger. They told me my services were no longer desired, because they wanted to put in a youth program as an advance way of keeping the club going. I'll never make the mistake of being 70 years old again." Ralph Houk, 41, and a coach with the club since 1958, will manage the Yankees in 1961. He was a reserve catcher for the team from 1947 to 1954.

OCTOBER 26:

The major league landscape keeps shifting. The AL, meeting at the Savoy Hilton in New York, approves expansion to 10 teams. They okay Calvin Griffith's shift of the Washington Senators to the Minneapolis-St. Paul area. They give the green light to a new team in Los Angeles and one to replace the Senators in Washington, D.C. – all for the 1961 season. The new Washington team is backed by retired lieutenant general Elwood R. "Pete" Quesada, chief of the Federal Aeronautics Agency. Western film and recording star Gene Autry is awarded the California franchise. The "old" Senators, to be renamed, will play in Metropolitan Stadium, which is being expanded from 22,000 to 40,000 seats. An all-new Washington Stadium, with a capacity of 40,000, is under construction.

NOVEMBER 2:

George Weiss, one of the more successful but hardly the most beloved executives in baseball, retires as general manager of the Yankees – with a little push from ownership. Weiss spent 29 years with the organization, rising from farm director to general manager. The Yankees won 19 pennants during that period. Weiss, who will be replaced by Roy Hamey, will serves as an adviser to the Yankees.

NOVEMBER 3:

Hall of Famer infielder Rhoderick "Bobby" Wallace dies today in Torrance, California, one day before his 87th birthday. Wallace, primarily a shortstop, played 25 years from 1894 to 1918, batting .266. He also managed for three years. He was inducted into the Hall of Fame in 1953.

NOVEMBER 17:

The American League approves General Elwood R. "Pete" Quesada's bid for the Washington, D.C., expansion franchise.

NOVEMBER 19:

James "Mickey" Vernon will manage the "new" Senators.

NOVEMBER 21:

Bob Scheffing is signed to a two-year contract as manager of the Detroit Tigers. He replaces Joe Gordon, who replaced Jimmy Dykes.

DECEMBER 3:

The Giants obtain outfielder-infielder Harvey Kuenn (.308, nine home runs) from the Indians for outfielder Willie Kirkland (.252, 21 homers) and pitcher Johnny Antonelli (6-7, 3.77 ERA).

The Reds sell infielder Billy Martin (.246, three home runs) to the Braves.

DECEMBER 14:

In Boston, the American League holds its free-agent draft for the new Washington and Los Angeles franchises. Los Angeles opens the session by picking New York Yankees' pitcher Eli Grba; Washington then selects New York's pitcher Bobby Shantz. Among the other players selected by Washington are Gene Woodling, Willie Tasby, Dale Long, Dick Donovan, Johnny Klippstein, Dave Sisler, Tom Sturdivant, and Pete Burnside. Los Angeles's list of draftees include Ted Kluszewski, Bob Cerv, Eddie Yost, Ned Garver, Bob Rodgers, Jim Fregosi, Albie Pearson, and Steve Bilko. In total, Los Angeles spends $2,150,000 for 309 players, while the Washington owners face a price tag of $2,175,000 for 31.

DECEMBER 20:

Charles O. Finley purchases 52 percent of the Kansas City Athletics franchise for the reported price of $2 million from the heirs of the late owner, Arnold Johnson, who passed away in March.

OCTOBER 26
AL owners approve expansion franchises in Washington, DC, and Minneapolis-St. Paul.

NOVEMBER 2
George Weiss retires as GM of the New York Yankees, after 29 years with the organization.

THE BEST OF 1960

NATIONAL LEAGUE

HITTERS

Batting Average:
Dick Groat, Pittsburgh Pirates, .325

Slugging Average:
Frank Robinson, Cincinnati Reds, .595

Home Runs:
Ernie Banks, Chicago Cubs, 41

Runs Batted In:
Hank Aaron, Milwaukee Braves, 126

Hits:
Willie Mays, San Francisco Giants, 190

Stolen Bases:
Maury Wills, Los Angeles Dodgers, 50

PITCHERS

Wins:
Ernie Broglio, St. Louis Cardinals;
Warren Spahn, Milwaukee Braves, 21

Strikeouts:
Don Drysdale, Los Angeles Dodgers, 246

Earned Run Average:
Mike McCormick, San Francisco Giants, 2.70

Winning Percentage:
Ernie Broglio, .700

Saves:
Lindy McDaniel, St. Louis Cardinals, 26

Most Valuable Player:
Dick Groat, Pittsburgh Pirates

Cy Young Award:
Vernon Law, Pittsburgh Pirates

Rookie of the Year:
Frank Howard, Los Angeles Dodgers

AMERICAN LEAGUE

HITTERS

Batting Average:
James "Pete" Runnels, Boston Red Sox, .320

Slugging Average:
Roger Maris, New York Yankees, .581

Home Runs:
Mickey Mantle, New York Yankees, 40

Runs Batted In:
Roger Maris, 112

Hits:
Orestes "Minnie" Minoso, Chicago White Sox, 184

Stolen Bases:
Luis Aparicio, Chicago White Sox, 51

PITCHERS

Wins:
Chuck Estrada, Baltimore Orioles;
Jim Perry, Cleveland Indians, 18

Strikeouts:
Jim Bunning, Detroit Tigers, 201

Earned Run Average:
Frank Baumann, Chicago White Sox, 2.67

Winning Percentage:
Jim Perry, .643

Saves:
Johnny Klippstein, Cleveland Indians;
Mike Fornieles, Boston Red Sox, 14

Most Valuable Player:
Roger Maris, New York Yankees

Rookie of the Year:
Ron Hansen, Baltimore Orioles

CULTURE

Jim Brosnan, a Cincinnati Reds pitcher, publishes *The Long Season.*

1961

"He pitched his game. Cool. Crafty. Nerves of steel."
– *Mickey Mantle, on Whitey Ford*

NEWS

DISTRICT OF COLUMBIA GAINS RIGHT TO VOTE

ANTI-CASTRO REBELS MEET DISASTER AT CUBA'S BAY OF PIGS

FREEDOM RIDERS TAKE BUS TOUR OF SOUTH TO FIGHT SEGREGATION

USSR's Yuri Gagarin Orbits Earth

ALAN B. SHEPARD IS AMERICA'S FIRST MAN IN SPACE

Kennedy, Khrushchev hold summit meeting in Vienna

ERNEST HEMINGWAY DIES

***The Wide World of Sports* makes its television debut**

PRE-SEASON

JANUARY 1:

Detroit's home field, formerly known as Briggs Stadium, officially becomes Tigers Stadium.

JANUARY 3:

Frank "Trader" Lane becomes the new general manager and executive vice president of the Kansas City Athletics. To accept the new post, Lane resigns as general manager of the Cleveland Indians – where he engineered the controversial trade of Rocky Colavito to Detroit for Harvey Kuenn in 1960.

JANUARY 5:

Strained relationships between the United States and Cuba could keep leading Cuban players currently on major league rosters from returning to their teams for the 1961 season. Among the affected players are such stars as Minnie Minoso of the Chicago White Sox and Camilo Pascual and Pedro Ramos of the Minnesota Twins.

JANUARY 6:

The Cuban players will be able to play in the United States for the 1961 season according to a "high-ranking" foreign ministry official in Cuba.

JANUARY 9:

Leo Durocher signs as a coach for the Dodgers, managed by Walter Alston. The 54-year-old Durocher, who won two pennants with the Giants and one with the Brooklyn Dodgers, will receive less than half of his managerial salary and will wear number 2, the number he wore as a player and manager.

JANUARY 12:

The New York Yankees sign Yogi Berra to a new one-year contract estimated at $52,000.

Cubs' owner Philip K. Wrigley signs Charlie Grimm and Verlon Walker as his sixth and seventh coaches. Wrigley plans to play the season with a staff of eight coaches functioning in place of a manager. Other members of the coaching staff are Rip Collins, Harry Craft, Vedie Himsl, Goldie Holt, Elvin Tappe, and Bobby Adams.

JANUARY 14:

Richie Ashburn, who spent the previous 12 seasons with the Phillies, is signed to be an "ex-officio" member of the Cubs' "management team." He also will be a regular outfielder for his new team.

JANUARY 16:

The Yankees sign Mickey Mantle to a new contract for an estimated $75,000. Pitcher Early Wynn, 41 years old, signs with the White Sox.

JANUARY 19:

Don Newcombe, once one of the most overpowering pitchers in baseball, is released by the Indians, ending his career. Newcombe, a winner of the Rookie of the Year, Cy Young, and Most Valuable Player Awards, was 2-3 with the Indians and 6-9 overall last season. In his 10-year career, Newcombe was 149-90 with a 3.56 ERA.

JANUARY 20:

Kansas City's owner, Charles O. Finley, orders the famous elephant emblem removed from the game uniforms of the Athletics. Finley explains that he is responding to "semi-serious" complaints from Kansas City Democrats – including some city councilmen. Yet the pachyderm will rise again.

JANUARY 19
Veteran pitcher Don Newcombe – 149-90, 3.56 ERA in 10 years – is released by Cleveland.

JANUARY 20
Athletics' owner Charlie Finley orders the famed elephant removed from A's uniforms.

JANUARY 24:

Only three weeks after becoming general manager of the Athletics, Frank "Trader" Lane lives up to his reputation with a five-for-two deal. He sends outfielders Dorrel "Whitey" Herzog (.266, eight homers in 83 games) and Russ Snyder (.260, four homers) to the Orioles for first baseman Bob Boyd (.317 in 71 games), outfielder Al Pilarcik (.247, four homers), infielder James "Wayne" Causey (not in the majors in 1960), and minor league pitcher Jim Archer. Catcher Clint Courtney is originally part of the trade, but is sent back to the Orioles on April 15.

JANUARY 25:

The Cardinals sign Stan Musial to a $75,000 contract, bringing his aggregate earnings for his 20-year career to an estimated $1,128,177. Warren Spahn signs with the Braves for the same amount.

The Reds trade Joe Nuxhall (1-8, 4.42 ERA), who debuted with the team as a 15-year-old in 1944, to the Athletics for pitchers John Tsitouris (0-2, 6.55 ERA) and Johnny Briggs (4-4, 6.42 ERA.

JANUARY 30:

Roger Maris, the AL's Most Valuable Player, signs a new Yankees' contract worth a reported $36,000 for the 1961 season.

FEBRUARY 1:

Yankees' president Dan Topping announces his intention to have all of the team in one hotel during spring training in St. Petersburg, Florida. The Yankees' black players had been staying in separate facilities because of segregation laws. Concerns about segregated accommodations also are being voiced by the Orioles and White Sox.

FEBRUARY 9:

The Giants sign Willie Mays for $85,000, the largest contract in major league baseball.

FEBRUARY 16:

Hall of Fame pitcher Clarence "Dazzy" Vance dies in Homosassa Springs, Florida, at age 69. Elected to the Hall of Fame in 1955, Vance was 197-140 with an ERA of 3.24 in 16 years. He led the National League in strikeouts for seven consecutive years with the Dodgers.

Vance was famous for sporting a tattered, whitened shirtsleeve on the days he pitched. Rube Bressler, a pitcher turned first baseman/outfielder and, at the end of his career, a teammate of Vance's, recalled: "You couldn't hit him on Monday. He'd cut the sleeve of his undershirt to the elbow, you know, and on that part of it he'd use lye to make it white, and the rest he didn't care how dirty it was. Then he'd pitch overhand, out of the apartment houses in the background at Ebbets Field. Between the bleached sleeve of his undershirt waving and the Monday wash hanging out to dry – the diapers and undies and sheets flapping on the clothesline – you lost the ball entirely. He threw balls by me I never even saw."

FEBRUARY 20:

One more color barrier is broken in baseball today. Emmett Ashford becomes the first black umpire in the major leagues when he is hired by the American League to call games for the 1961 season.

MARCH 9:

The New York Yankees announce they will move to Fort Lauderdale for spring training by 1963 at the latest. Co-owners Dan Topping and Del Webb also state that the new NL franchise in New York should play its home games in the Polo Grounds rather than Yankee Stadium. A stadium for the new team – as yet unnamed – is unlikely to be ready for the 1962 season.

MARCH 14:

Kirby Puckett is born in Chicago.

Former Yankees' general manager George Weiss is named president of the NL's as-yet-unnamed team in New York.

MARCH 15:

The Cardinals reacquire second baseman Albert "Red" Schoendienst, signing him as a free agent. Last season with the Braves, he hit .257 in 68 games.

MARCH 16:

New York State approves a bond issue for the construction of a 55,000-seat stadium in Flushing Meadow near the site of the 1939-40 World's Fair for the new NL team.

CULTURE

"Twelve Perfect Innings: A Pretty Good Game," a poem by Weldon Myers, recounts Harvey Haddix's 1959 12-inning perfect performance.

Joe Trimble of the *New York Daily News* asks Roger Maris if he thinks he can break Babe Ruth's record. Maris retorts, "How should I know?"

CULTURE

A duo of baseball songs: "The First Baseball Game," written by Don Raye and Gene DePaul; and "Goodnight, Little Leaguer," written by Dorcas Cochran and Russ Black, are recorded by Nat King Cole.

MARCH 19:

Boston rookie Carl Yastrzemski (known as Mr. Y.) will start in left field for the Red Sox, replacing Ted Williams.

MARCH 29:

Today the Phillies sell Connie Mack Stadium. The 52-year-old ballpark, once known as Shibe Field, showcased such Hall of Famers as Lefty Grove, Al Simmons, and Jimmy Foxx. The stadium's new owners are likely to raze the aging facility.

APRIL 6:

Vadie Himsl, a former pitcher who never played or managed in the major leagues, is named the Chicago Cubs' first "head coach." The 44-year-old Himsl is expected to hold his post for "about two weeks" and then will be replaced by another "member of the coaching board."

THE SEASON

APRIL 10:

The AL's expansion team in Washington, D.C., debuts in traditional Senator fashion, that is, losing its opening day game, 4-3, to the White Sox, with President John F. Kennedy among the 26,725 in attendance. Roy Sievers hits a homer and drives in the winning run with a sacrifice fly.

A distinguished group of politicos joined President Kennedy in his field box as he threw out the first ball. To his right was Vice President Lyndon Johnson, to his left was Senator Mike Mansfield. Directly behind him were Senators Hubert Humphrey and Everett Dirksen and baseball commissioner Ford Frick.

APRIL 11:

The Minnesota Twins, formerly the Washington Senators, win their first game, defeating New York, 6-0, at Yankee Stadium.

The AL's second new team, the Los Angeles Angels, wins its first game, 7-2, over the Orioles in Baltimore. Ted Kluszewski, once one of the NL's most feared sluggers, hits two homers for the Angels and drives in five runs. Bob Cerv also homers for Los Angeles. Eli Grba gets the win; Milt Pappas is the loser.

In his first major league at-bat, Carl Yastrzemski singles against the Athletics' Ray Herbert. He then strikes out twice and grounds out twice as Kansas City beats the Red Sox, 5-2, on a cold, damp day at Fenway Park.

APRIL 13:

Outfielder-infielder Dick Williams (.288, 12 homers) becomes an Oriole for the third time when he is traded by the Athletics to Baltimore along with pitcher Dick Hall (8-13, 4.05 ERA). In return, Kansas City gets pitcher Jerry Walker (3-4, 3.74 ERA) and outfielder Chuck Essegian (.000 in one game).

APRIL 21:

Major league baseball debuts in Minnesota, with the visiting Senators beating the host Twins, 5-3.

APRIL 22:

New York's Governor Nelson A. Rockefeller signs a bill permitting New York City to build a 55,000-seat stadium in Flushing Meadow, Queens, for its new NL team.

APRIL 27:

Gabe Paul is named general manager of the Cleveland Indians, replacing outgoing skipper Frank Lane.

APRIL 28:

Forty-year-old Warren Spahn of the Braves no-hits the Giants, 1-0, in Milwaukee. It is Spahn's second no-hitter and his 290th victory. He strikes out nine and allows the Giants two base runners – via walks – who are erased by double plays. Hank Aaron's single in the first inning accounts for the game's only run. Sam Jones is the losing pitcher.

APRIL 30:

In his 1,234th major league game, Willie Mays hits four home runs in a 14-4 win over the Braves in Milwaukee. Mays, who hits homers in the first, third, sixth, and eighth innings, becomes the ninth player in history to accomplish the feat. His bid for a record-breaking fifth fails to materialize as he waits on deck while the third out in the Giants' ninth is made. Until today Mays had been hitless in seven at-bats against the Braves. Jose Pagan homers twice for the Giants; Billy Loes is the winning pitcher.

Loes was with the Dodgers when Gil Hodges hit four homers and when Joe Adcock had four for Milwaukee

APRIL 28
Braves' pitcher Warren Spahn, 40, no-hits the Giants, 1-0, for his second career no-hitter.

MAY 8
The new National League franchise in New York will be called the Mets.

against them. He also was a member of the Orioles when Rocky Colavito had his four homers for the Indians.

Outfielder Jackie Jensen, who sat out 1960 and rejoined the Red Sox for this season, retires again.

MAY 8:

The new NL team in New York will be called the Mets. Fans were asked to vote by mail, and the name was selected from a list of finalists that included Burros, Skyliners, Rebels, and Skyscrapers.

Jackie Jensen is back with the Red Sox after "unretiring" again.

MAY 9:

"Diamond" Jim Gentile of the Orioles hits bases-loaded home runs in two successive innings – a major league first. His grand slammers come off Twins' pitchers Pedro Ramos and Paul Giel in Minnesota in the first and second innings, respectively. The Orioles win the game, 13-5. Only Tony Lazzeri (1936), Jim Tabor (1939), and Jimmy Foxx (1946) hit two grand slam home runs in a single game, but not in successive innings. Gentile also has a sacrifice in the game, giving him a total of nine RBI.

White Sox pitcher Herb Score two-hits his former Indian teammates, 4-2. Jim Piersall's triple and Johnny Temple's single are the only hits.

MAY 12:

During a Tigers-Yankees game, Detroit outfielder Rocky Colavito, who was raised in the Bronx, climbs into the Yankee Stadium stands to assist his father, Rocco Sr., who is in an altercation with a fan. Colavito is ejected from the game but the Tigers win anyway, 4-3. He later explains, "What would you do if you saw someone belting your 60-year-old father? I'd do it again." The Tigers win the game on a home run by pitcher Frank Lary. Bill Monboquette of the Red Sox fans 17 Senators today.

MAY 13:

Yesterday's fight and ejection have no effect on Rocky Colavito's performance at Yankee Stadium today. He connects for two home runs and two singles, driving in four runs as the Tigers beat New York by a score of 8-3.

NEW YORK DAILY NEWS' TOUGH COLUMNIST DICK YOUNG TURNS ALMOST POETIC TO DESCRIBE MARIS'S AT-BATS ON SEPTEMBER 19: "HERE IN THE MONUMENTAL TOWN WHERE BABE RUTH WAS BORN, THE CHAUVINIST WIND TONIGHT WHIPPED UP TO A PROUD FURY TO PROTECT BABE'S HOMER RECORD. THE MISTY ADVANCE GUSTS OF HURRICANE ESTHER BLEW HARD FROM RIGHT AND INTO THE FACE OF ROGER MARIS, LEAVING HIM HOMERLESS IN NINE AT-BATS."

HISTORY

Only four people associated with baseball attend Ty Cobb's funeral: Gordon "Mickey" Cochrane, who played with him on the Athletics; former White Sox catcher Ray Schalk; fellow Georgian and former pitcher George "Nap" Rucker; and director of the Hall of Fame, Sid Keener. According to sportswriter Fred Lieb, Cobb, near death, told comedian-actor Joe E. Brown: "Joe, I do indeed think I would have done some things different. And, if I had, I would have had more friends."

JUNE 25
Baltimore wins a 14-inning game vs. the Angels featuring a record 16 pitchers.

TRIVIA

Candlestick Park is earning a reputation as a tough place to play baseball. In the ninth inning of a July 11 game, with the NL leading 3-2, AL runners on second and third and Rocky Colavito batting, the wind blows Stu Miller off the mound as he goes into his windup and he is called for a balk.

MAY 17:

More than one month into the 1961 season, the Yankees' Roger Maris is mired in a slump with a .208 batting average and only four home runs.

MAY 28:

Is the 1961 baseball livelier? The debate is fueled when AL teams hit 27 home runs in a single day – in seven games. The old mark of 26 was set by the NL in eight games on May 30, 1956. That same day AL players hit 24.

MAY 31:

Carroll Hardy pinch-hits today for Carl Yastrzemski in the eighth inning of today's game and bunts for a single against the Yankees' Luis Arroyo. He becomes the only player to pinch-hit for Ted Williams and Yastrzemski. New York wins, 7-6.

JUNE 8:

Lew Krausse Jr., an 18-year-old pitcher, receives what is reportedly the largest bonus ever paid – $125,000 – from the Athletics. The youngster, who struck out 24 batters in a single game and pitched 18 no-hitters in high school, was signed on the recommendation of Kansas City Athletics' scout Lew Krausse Sr., who happens to be his father. The Braves hit four consecutive home runs – a major league record – but lose the game to the Reds in Cincinnati, 10-8. Eddie Mathews, Hank Aaron, Joe Adcock, and Frank Thomas comprise the quartet of home run hitters in the seventh inning.

JUNE 10:

The *New York Times* reports from Los Angeles that Sandy Koufax finally "has zeroed in on home plate." Known as Sandy the Scatter Arm, Koufax has walked only 33 while striking out 79 in 82 1/3 innings and is 8-2 with the Dodgers.

JUNE 12:

Bill Veeck, the quintessential promotional genius, leaves major league baseball. The 48-year-old Veeck, whose health is impaired by a leg injury suffered in the South Pacific during World War II, sells his interest in the White Sox to partner Arthur C. Allyn. Chuck Comiskey retains 46 percent of the team.

Jackie Jensen's fear of flying gets the best of him and he refuses to fly with the Red Sox to Detroit. He travels by train instead.

JUNE 16:

Lew Krausse Jr. makes his major league debut for Kansas City, three-hitting the Angeles, 4-0.

JUNE 18:

Eddie Gaedel, the midget who was hired by Bill Veeck to pinch-hit for the St. Louis Browns in one game in 1951, dies in Chicago 10 days after his 36th birthday.

Bob Cain, who had walked Gaedel in his one major league at-bat, attends his funeral. He is the only person from the world of baseball at the service.

JUNE 23:

Ernie Banks is out today with an injured knee, ending his consecutive-game streak at 717. Banks began his streak on August 26, 1956. The visiting Braves win, 5-3.

JUNE 25:

The Orioles and Angels use an ML record 16 pitchers – eight apiece – in a 14-inning game won by Baltimore on a Ron Hansen homer.

JUNE 27:

At a meeting in Chicago, officials of NL teams agree that the franchises for 1962 – in New York and Houston – will draw their rosters from a pool of players made available by the eight present clubs.

JUNE 28:

Commissioner Ford Frick welcomes Houston into the NL in ceremonies at Busch Stadium honoring Dickie Kerr, the pitcher who won two World Series games for the 1919 Chicago "Black Sox."

JULY 11:

The NL beats the AL, 5-4, in the first of the season's two All-Star Games. Playing in San Francisco, Willie Mays doubles in the bottom of the 10th inning and Roberto Clemente singles him home with the winning run. Harmon Killebrew homers for the AL; George Altman for the NL. The winning pitcher is Stu Miller; Hoyt Wilhelm is the losing pitcher.

JULY 17:

Ty Cobb, whose lifetime average of .367 is the highest ever, dies at age 74 in Emory University

JULY 25
Roger Maris, with four home runs, is 27 games ahead of Babe Ruth's 60-homer pace.

Hospital in Atlanta. The Georgia Peach led the AL in batting a record 12 times. The cause of his death is listed as prostate cancer, diabetes, and heart disease.

JULY 18:

As Yankees' sluggers Roger Maris and Mickey Mantle pursue Babe Ruth's single season home run record, Commissioner Ford Frick announces that the Bambino's record of 60 can be broken only within 154 games. According to Frick, a player who tops 60 after 154 games would have a "distinctive mark" in the record books. Maris currently is 19 games ahead of Ruth's 1927 pace and Mantle is eight games up.

The Cardinals' Bill White hits a homer, two triples, and a double in today's twinbill against the Cubs, giving him 14 hits in 18 at-bats against Chicago in two days. White's feat ties a record by Ty Cobb, who died yesterday. He also bats in six runs in the two days. White began his tear yesterday with four hits in five at-bats in each game of a doubleheader, won by St. Louis, 10-6 and 8-5. The Cardinals also win both of today's games by scores of 8-3 and 7-5.

WHITEY FORD ALWAYS HAD A SENSE OF HUMOR. IN MANY OF HIS MAJOR LEAGUE-LEADING 25 WINS, THE LEFT-HANDER WENT SEVEN INNINGS AND WAS RELIEVED BY LUIS ARROYO, THE YANKEE'S ACE RELIEF PITCHER. HERE'S HOW ARROYO DESCRIBED THE CY YOUNG AWARD CEREMONY HONORING FORD'S 1961 PITCHING ACCOMPLISHMENTS: "WHITEY SAID HE HAD A NINE-MINUTE SPEECH. HE WAS GOING TO TALK FOR THE FIRST SEVEN MINUTES AND LET ME DO THE LAST TWO. AND THAT'S WHAT HE DID."

JULY 24:

Outfielders Max Carey and William Hamilton are inducted into the Hall of Fame. Carey played 20 seasons (1910-1929) with the Pirates and Dodgers, batting .285. He led the NL in stolen bases 10 times and amassed a career total of 738. In 1932 and 1933, he managed the Dodgers to third- and sixth-place finishes. Hamilton, known as Sliding Billy, played from 1888 through 1901 with Kansas City (American Association), the Phillies, and the Braves. He compiled a lifetime batting average of .344, leading the league twice. He hit .399 (fifth to Hugh Duffy's all-time high .438) in 1894 and led the NL in batting the previous season with a .380 mark. Like Carey, a speedster on the bases, he topped the league in stolen bases seven times.

JULY 25:

New York slugger Roger Maris hits four home runs today in a doubleheader against the Chicago White Sox. The Yankees go on to win both games by scores of 5-1 and 12-0. Maris is now a full 27 games ahead of Babe Ruth's record pace, when Ruth hit 60 home runs.

TRIVIA

Richie Ashburn is in the Cubs' lineup as Warren Spahn spins his 300th win. Ashburn, then with the Phillies, also was on the field when Spahn won his 100th and 200th games.

Mickey Mantle on the ball debate: "Maybe the players now are livelier."

EQUIPMENT

AL president Joe Cronin and NL president Warren C. Giles order tests to determine if the 1961 baseball is livelier.

JULY 26:

Mickey Mantle hits his 39th home run in a Yankees' 5-2 win over the White Sox in New York to move 22 games ahead of Babe Ruth. Roger Maris, 23 games ahead of Ruth's pace, goes hitless in three at-bats and remains at 40 home runs.

JULY 31:

The season's second All-Star Game is halted by rain at Boston's Fenway Park after nine innings and ends as a 1-1 tie. Rocky Colavito homers in the first inning and Bill White drives in a run in the sixth on an infield hit to account for all the scoring. AL starter Jim Bunning pitches three perfect innings, repeating his 1957 feat. He is the only starting pitcher to hurl three perfect innings in two All-Star Games.

AUGUST 1:

Player representatives meet in Boston today and approve the continuation of two All-Star Games – the proceeds of which go to the players' retirement fund – because "the public wants two." They also address the issue of segregated housing in Florida during spring training. The players' attorney says, "There might be more certain clubs can do," but adds that baseball must respect local laws.

AUGUST 10:

The NL dismisses umpire Frank Dascoli. League president Warren C. Giles asserts that the on-field integrity and impartiality of Dascoli, who has umpired in the league since 1948, are not in question. Dascoli had complained frequently that the League did not back its umpires. Giles states that Dascoli's off-field remarks "makes his continued employment incompatible with the best interests of our umpiring staff, our office and the League." According to the *New York Times*, Dascoli has been "a center of controversy among players, managers, fans and league officials."

AUGUST 11:

Braves pitcher Warren Spahn wins the 300th game of his career, 2-1, over the Cubs in Milwaukee. Spahn pitches a complete game, giving up six hits and one walk, while striking out five. He becomes the 13th major league pitcher to reach 300 wins.

AUGUST 14:

The *New York Times* turns to a firm of consulting chemists and engineers to determine if the 1961 baseball has been "juiced up." Technologists at Foster D. Snell Inc. of New York City "subject balls to surgical dissection, battering rams and other tests." The conclusion? "The 1961 ball is slightly larger, slightly lighter and slightly livelier than one 1927 ball... The effect of these differences cannot be estimated in the absence of the quantity of test samples." The *Times* headline reads:

IS THE '61 BALL LIVELIER THAN THE RUTHIAN VARIETY? MAYBE YES AND MAYBE NO.

And the debate rages on.

AUGUST 19:

Reds' manager Fred Hutchinson tries technology to relay his signals from the bench to his third base coach Reggie Otero. Hutchinson equips Otero with a shortwave receiver, but gives up on the experiment in the first inning when his instructions are heard over the press box public address system and by the fans sitting in that area.

AUGUST 20:

The Phillies lose their 23rd straight game – a modern major league record. The Phillies reach the low-water mark with a 5-2 loss to the Braves in the opener of a twin-bill in Milwaukee. Philadelphia is one short of Cleveland's consecutive loss string in 1899. The Braves' victory is their 10th straight. In the nightcap, the Phillies break their losing streak with a 7-4 victory on John Buzhardt's nine-hitter. Buzhardt was the winning pitcher in the last Phillies' win, which was on July 28.

With tests on the baseball inconclusive, the *New York Times* turns to the bats. Joseph M. Sheehan concludes that players are taking "heavier swings with lighter bats." The legendary Satchel Paige pitches for the West against the East in the Negro American League All-Star Game in Yankee Stadium. Paige, whose age may be anywhere from 52 to 60, pitches three innings as the West wins 7-1 and is named the game's Most Valuable Player.

AUGUST 22:

Roger Maris hits his 50th home run earlier than any player in his-

AUGUST 11
Warren Spahn spins his 300th career game, 2-1, over the Cubs in Milwaukee.

SEPTEMBER 11
Mickey Mantle, with three fewer homers than Maris's 56, is injured for the rest of the year.

tory. He is now 14 games ahead of Babe Ruth's record pace. Number 50 is hit against the Angels' Ken McBride in Los Angeles, but New York loses, 4-3. Kansas City owner Charles O. Finley accuses his general manager Frank Lane of "spreading harmful rumors about the team" and fires him only seven months and two days after hiring him.

AUGUST 24:

New York Governor Nelson A. Rockefeller, who hasn't attended a Yankees' game since 1958, bets three barrels of his state's apples against one barrel of Michigan apples put up by Governor John B. Swainson on the outcome of the pennant race.

AUGUST 29:

Paul Richards resigns as manager of the Baltimore Orioles and is expected to become the general manager of the NL's new Houston Colts. Chalmer "Luman" Harris will take over the 78-57 Orioles.

SEPTEMBER 2:

The current issue of the *Sporting News* reports that Ty Cobb's estate is worth at least $11.78 million.

SEPTEMBER 3:

Mickey Mantle hits his 49th and 50th home runs at Yankee Stadium, despite a strained muscle in his left forearm. Roger Maris singles in four at-bats and the Yankees defeat the Tigers, 8-5.

SEPTEMBER 6:

Roger Maris hits his 54th home run in an 8-0 Yankee win over the Senators in New York.

Warren Spahn strikes out Charlie Smith for the final out as the Braves beat the Phillies, 1-0. The strikeout is Spahn's 100th of the year for the 15th straight season, breaking his own record. It is also his 306th win, the most by an NL left-hander in one league.

SEPTEMBER 9:

With Jim "Mudcat" Grant on the mound for the Cleveland Indians, Roger Maris connects for his 56th home run. The Yankees beat the Indians, 8-7, in New York.

SEPTEMBER 11:

Mickey Mantle, who trails Maris's 56 home runs by three, receives a shot for the flu. The needle strikes a bone and Mantle develops an infection in his side that will limit his action for the rest of the season and into the World Series.

SEPTEMBER 15:

In the first game of a doubleheader in Detroit, Yogi Berra, Bill "Moose" Skowron, and Clete Boyer homer to give the Yankees a major league record 223 for the season, breaking a mark held by the 1947 New York Giants and the 1956 Cincinnati Reds.

Sandy Koufax strikes out 10 Braves in Los Angeles. Koufax brings his season total to 243, breaking the NL record for left-handed pitchers. The previous record holder was the New York Giants' Richard "Rube" Marquard, who fanned 237 in 1911. The Dodgers win the game, 11-2.

SEPTEMBER 19:

Roger Maris, with 58 home runs, fails to connect in games 152 and 153 – a doubleheader at Baltimore's Memorial Stadium.

SEPTEMBER 20:

The Yankees beat the Orioles, 4-2, in Baltimore, clinching the pennant. Roger Maris hits his 59th home run in the third inning off Milt Pappas. His bid for number 60, a long drive off Oriole's pitcher Dick Hall, goes foul by about 10 feet. In his last at-bat in this, the 154th game of the season, Maris hits a checked swing bouncer back to Hoyt Wilhelm and is thrown out.

The fan who catches Maris's 59th homer, Bob Reitz, asks for $2,500. After ascertaining that Reitz will keep the ball without the money, Maris tells him, "Good luck to you then."

SEPTEMBER 21:

Commissioner Ford Frick clarifies his ruling on Babe Ruth's record. If Roger Maris surpasses 60 home runs in the remaining eight games, it will be recorded as a season high for a 162-game schedule. Maris will not be credited with breaking Ruth's record. The commissioner adds there will be no star or asterisk in the record book. "I never said it," he asserts.

SEPTEMBER 22:

The Baltimore Orioles' Jim Gentile hits a grand slam home run against Don Larsen of the Chicago White Sox. It is Gentile's fifth of the season, tying Ernie Banks's major league record.

TRIVIA

According to reports from Tel Aviv, Israeli radio is broadcasting updates on the Maris-Mantle home run race as a regular part of its news programs.

The Tigers' Norm Cash (.361, 41 homers, 132 RBI) on his career-best year: "I owe my success to expansion pitching, a short right-field fence and my hollow bats."

Mickey Mantle (left) and Roger Maris have fans cheering for home runs.

SEPTEMBER 24:

Warren Spahn continues his own assault on the record books. In Milwaukee, he beats the Cubs to become the fourth pitcher in major league history to win 20 or more games 12 times. His 8-0, two-hit victory brings his career total to 308, tying Charles "Hoss" Radbourn for 10th place, and he moves to fourth place among major league strikeout leaders.

SEPTEMBER 26:

In the third inning, Roger Maris hits his 60th home run off Jack Fisher of the Orioles, on a 2-2 pitch. The ball lands in the third deck at Yankee Stadium. In the crowd of 19,401 is Mrs. Claire Ruth, the widow of the Bambino.

A 6-3 Cincinnati victory over the Cubs in Chicago, combined with an 8-0 loss by the Dodgers to the Pirates in Pittsburgh, clinches the NL pennant for the Reds.

SEPTEMBER 27:

Sandy Koufax fans Pancho Herrera in the sixth and Bobby Gene Smith in the eighth to record his 268th and 269th strikeouts of the season, setting an NL record. The previous mark of 267 was established by Christy Mathewson in 1903. The Dodgers beat the Phillies, 2-1.

SEPTEMBER 29:

The Mets name 71-year-old Casey Stengel as their manager for the 1962 season. Stengel, who spent the 1961 season out of baseball after being released by the Yankees, insists on and receives a one-year contract. At the press conference, he refers to his new team as the "Knickerbockers" and tells reporters, "You can say I'm happy to be going back to the Polar [sic] Grounds."

OCTOBER 1:

Roger Maris hits his 61st home run to pass Babe Ruth. The landmark blast comes at Yankee Stadium in the fourth inning against Tracy Stallard of the Red Sox. The home run also is the Yankees' 240th as a team, setting a new major league mark. The Yankees win the game, 1-0.

The Chicago Cubs, who finished 60-94 in seventh place with two managers in 1960, improve to 64 and 90 under the

SEPTEMBER 27
Sandy Koufax sets a new NL record with his 269th strikeout of the season.

OCTOBER 1
On the last day of the season, Roger Maris sets a new home run record – 61.

leadership of eight coaches. But they still finish in seventh place in the eight-team NL – 29 games behind the Cincinnati Reds.

OCTOBER 2:

Coach Mel McGaha is named the Indians' manager for the 1962 season. The Indians were 78-83 last season and finished in fifth place in the AL.

OCTOBER 3:

Pennsylvania State Supreme Court Judge Michael A. Musmano urges the Cincinnati Reds to change their name. In a letter to Reds' manager Fred Hutchinson, he describes himself as a "foe of communism" who is "grieved to the core" by the name. However, he extends his best wishes to the Reds for the World Series.

REGULAR SEASON WRAP-UP:

The Yankees are the runaway winners in the AL in Ralph Houk's first year as manager. New York compiles a 109-53 record, beating the Tigers by eight games. Roger Maris, with 61 home runs, 142 RBI, and a .269 batting average, teams with Mickey Mantle – .317, 54 homers (the most ever by a switch hitter), and 128 RBI – to give the Yankees an awesome one-two punch. There is power throughout the lineup as well: Bill Skowron has 28 homers, Yogi Berra 22, and Elston Howard 21. Whitey Ford is a sparkling 25-4 and reliever Luis Arroyo sets a major league record with 29 saves.

> IN 61 BY TONY KUBEK AND TERRY PLUTO, MICKEY MANTLE TALKS ABOUT HIS TEAMMATE ROGER MARIS: "I WAS ASKED THE OTHER DAY WHO WAS THE BEST ALL-AROUND PLAYER I'D SEEN, AND I SAID ROGER. I REALLY BELIEVE THAT THE 61 HOMERS WAS THE GREATEST FEAT IN BASEBALL HISTORY."

The Reds, managed by Fred Hutchinson, finish 93-61, four games ahead of the Dodgers, and have power of their own. Frank Robinson hits .323, with 37 homers and 124 RBI. Vada Pinson bats .343 with 16 homers and 87 RBI. Wally Post and Gene Freese hit 26 round-trippers each and Wally Post adds 20. Joey Jay is the big winner at 21-10.

The Orioles' Dave Philley sets a major league season record with 24 pinch hits; in 1958 he had 18 in the National League.

OCTOBER 4:

World Series, game one. Whitey Ford two-hits the Reds, 2-0, at Yankee Stadium for his record eighth Series win. The Yankees' runs score on homers by Elston Howard and Bill Skowron. Bobby Richardson has three of New York's six hits.

OCTOBER 5:

World Series, game 2. Joey Jay beats the Yankees, 6-2, in New York, allowing only 4 hits. Gordy Coleman homers for Cincinnati; Yogi Berra for New York. Ralph Terry is charged with the loss. Jimmy Piersall (.322, six homers) is coming to Washington. The Senators obtain the volatile outfielder from the Indians for pitcher Dick Donovan (10-10 with a league-leading 2.40 ERA), catcher-outfielder Gene Green (.280, 10 homers), and infielder Jim Mahoney (.241 in 43 games).

OCTOBER 7:

World Series, game three. At Crosley Field the Yankees score single runs in the 7th, 8th, and 9th innings to edge the Reds, 3-2. Johnny Blanchard's pinch-hit homer ties the game in the 8th and Roger Maris's round-tripper wins it in the 9th. Luis Arroyo gets the win with 2 innings of shutout relief. Bob Purkey gets the loss.

OCTOBER 8:

World Series, game 4. Whitey Ford pitches 5 scoreless innings before injuring his ankle. He brings his scoreless streak to 32, topping Babe Ruth's Series' mark. Jim

TRIVIA

Maris's 61st home run ball lands in Box 163D, Section 33 in the right-field stands, where it is retrieved by Sal Durante, a 19-year-old fan from Coney Island. Durante wins a trip to Sacramento, where a restaurateur will give him $5,000 for the ball and a trip to the Seattle World's Fair.

Coates finishes the game and the Yankees win, 7-0. The Reds manage only five hits. Jim O'Toole is charged with the loss.

OCTOBER 9:

World Series, game 5. Despite the absence of the injured Mickey Mantle and Yogi Berra, the Yankees win, 13-5, in Cincinnati to take the World Series 4 games to one. Ralph Houk becomes the third manager in history to win the championship in his first year, joining Bucky Harris of the Washington Senators (1924) and Eddie Dyer of the St.Louis Cardinals (1946) in the exclusive circle. The Yankees bang out 15 hits – including a two-run homer by Johnny Blanchard and a three-run shot by Hector Lopez, who has five RBIs. Frank Robinson and Wally Post homer for the Reds. The winning pitcher is Leavitt "Bud" Daley in relief of Ralph Terry; Joey Jay, who lasts two-thirds of an inning, gets the loss. Whitey Ford, 2-0 and a 0.00 ERA, is named outstanding player. Bobby Richardson hits .391; Bill Skowron, .353 with five RBI. Roger Maris finishes at .105 with 1 homer and two RBI; the injured Mickey Mantle has one hit in only 6 at-bats. Wally Post hits .333 for the Reds.

POST-SEASON

OCTOBER 10:

In Cincinnati, the new Houston Colts and New York Mets take only three and a half hours to select players for their 1962 rosters, spending $3.65 million for 45 choices. Among the Mets' choices are pitcher Roger Craig, first baseman Gil Hodges, pitcher Jay Hook, infielders Don Zimmer and Felix Mantilla, catcher Chris Cannizaro, and outfielders Lee Walls, Joe Christopher, and Jim Hickman. Houston's selections include infielders Joe Amalfitano and Bob Lillis; pitchers Bobby Shantz, Sam Jones, and Dick Farrell; catcher Hal Smith; outfielder Al Spangler; and first baseman Dick Gernert. In 1962, the Colts will go 64-96, while the Mets set the record for single-season futility, with 120 losses on the year.

Whitey Ford is 2-0 in the World Series, with a 0.00 ERA.

OCTOBER 9
The Yankees win the World Series vs. the Reds, four games to one.

NOVEMBER 15
Roger Maris edges out teammate Mickey Mantle for the AL MVP Award.

OCTOBER 11:

The Dodgers sign manager Walter Alston to a one-year contract. Alston has managed the team since 1954 on a series of one-year pacts.

OCTOBER 15:

Major league baseballs are being tested at the Massachusetts Institute of Technology to determine if the 1961 ball is a livelier model.

Ground is broken for the New York Mets' stadium in Flushing Meadow Park in Queens. The new facility will seat 55,000 and has the potential for an additional 25,000 seats and a plastic protective dome.

OCTOBER 16:

The very last of the 1950 Phillies Whiz Kids is gone from Philadelphia. The Phillies sell pitcher Robin Roberts (1-10, 5.85 ERA) to the Orioles.

NOVEMBER 8:

The Chicago White Sox today solve their controversial spring training segregation problems by buying a hotel in Sarasota, Florida, to accommodate all their players, black and white.

HALL OF FAME PITCHER DIZZY DEAN ON THE "LIVELY" BALL, "HOLD IT IN YOUR HAND AND YOU CAN FEEL ITS HEART BEATING."

NOVEMBER 14:

John Fetzer buys out the Fred Knorr estate and becomes the sole owner of the Tigers.

NOVEMBER 15:

Roger Maris of the New York Yankees is the AL's Most Valuable Player, edging out his teammate Mickey Mantle by 4 votes.

DECEMBER 30:

The Giants acquire pitchers Billy Pierce (10-9, 3.80 ERA) and Don Larsen (not in the majors in 1961) from the White Sox for pitchers Eddie Fisher (0-2, 5.35 ERA) and Dom Zanni (1-0, 3.95 ERA), first baseman Bob Farley (.100 in 13 games), and a player to be named later (minor league pitcher Verle Tiefenthaler, who joins Chicago on August 17, 1962).

DECEMBER 1:

Two is better than one. The American and National Leagues approve the continuation of two All-Star Games for the 1962 season. The AL wants a return to one game after next season; the NL favors continuation of the present two-game system.

DECEMBER 8:

The Chicago Cubs sell outfielder Richie Ashburn (.257) to the New York Mets.

DECEMBER 13:

Mickey Mantle signs an $82,000 contract for the 1962 season.

DECEMBER 15:

William Ellsworth "Dummy" Hoy dies in Cincinnati at the age of 99. Hoy, a deaf-mute from birth, played 14 seasons in the major leagues, beginning in 1888 with Washington, which was then in the NL. Hoy, who threw out the first ball for game three of this year's World Series in Cincinnati, set a major league outfielding record with three assists in a single inning. He was the oldest living former major leaguer.

Change is blowing in the Windy City. It is announced that the Comiskey family will be out of baseball for the first time in 60 years. The reason is that the Comiskeys have sold their 46 percent interest in the Chicago White Sox to an 11-person management group. It is estimated that the sale of the ballclub will net the family $3.3 million.

HISTORY

In this record-breaking year Roger Maris drew no intentional walks. Many baseball experts attribute that statistical oddity to the fact that Mickey Mantle batted fourth behind Maris and was the more feared slugger of the two.

TRIVIA

On October 10, the day after the final World Series game, a full-page ad for Camel Cigarettes appears in the *New York Times* saluting the Yankees' victory. The ad pictures Yankees' stars Roger Maris, Yogi Berra, Whitey Ford, and Bill Skowron with cigarettes in their hands.

THE BEST OF 1961

NATIONAL LEAGUE

HITTERS

Batting Average:
Roberto Clemente, Pittsburgh Pirates, .351

Slugging Average:
Frank Robinson, Cincinnati Reds, .611

Home Runs:
Orlando Cepeda, San Francisco Giants, 46

Runs Batted In:
Orlando Cepeda, 142

Hits:
Vada Pinson, Cincinnati Reds, 208

Stolen Bases:
Maury Wills, Los Angeles Dodgers, 35

PITCHERS

Wins:
Joey Jay, Cincinnati Reds; Warren Spahn, Milwaukee Braves, 21

Strikeouts:
Sandy Koufax, Los Angeles Dodgers, 269

Earned Run Average:
Warren Spahn, 3.02

Winning Percentage:
Johnny Podres, Los Angeles Dodgers, .783

Saves:
Stu Miller, San Francisco Giants; Roy Face, Pittsburgh Pirates, 17

Most Valuable Player:
Frank Robinson, Cincinnati Reds

Rookie of the Year:
Billy Williams, Chicago Cubs

AMERICAN LEAGUE

HITTERS

Batting Average:
Norm Cash, Detroit Tigers, .361

Slugging Average:
Mickey Mantle, New York Yankees, .687

Home Runs:
Roger Maris, New York Yankees, 61

Runs Batted In:
Roger Maris; Jim Gentile, Baltimore Orioles, 141

Hits:
Norm Cash, 193

Stolen Bases:
Luis Aparicio, Chicago White Sox, 53

PITCHERS

Wins:
Ed "Whitey" Ford, New York Yankees, 25

Strikeouts:
Camilo Pascual, Minnesota Twins, 221

Earned Run Average:
Dick Donovan, Washington Senators, 2.40

Winning Percentage:
Whitey Ford, .862.

Saves:
Luis Arroyo, New York Yankees, 29

Most Valuable Player:
Roger Maris, New York Yankees

Cy Young Award:
Whitey Ford, New York Yankees

Rookie of the Year:
Don Schwall, Boston Red Sox

1962

"... If Mr. Hornsby takes care of his ballclub..., I'll take care of mine."
– *Yankees' manager Ralph Houk*

NEWS

U.S., SOVIETS FACE OFF OVER MISSILES IN CUBA; WEAPONS WITHDRAWN AFTER KENNEDY ORDERS BLOCKADE

JOHN GLENN ORBITS EARTH IN SPACE CAPSULE

Poll tax banned

SUPREME COURT BANS OFFICIAL SCHOOL PRAYER

VIOLENCE AT UNIVERSITY OF MISSISSIPPI OVER ADMISSION OF BLACK STUDENT JAMES MEREDITH

Marilyn Monroe, William Faulkner die

Rachel Carson's environmental treatice, *The Silent Spring*, is published

Sam Walton opens first Wal-Mart

PRE-SEASON

JANUARY 22:

This time he means it. Outfielder Jackie Jensen, who retired and returned several times since 1960, calls it quits for good today. Jensen, a three-time AL RBI leader, completes his 11-year career with a .279 average and 199 homers. Last season, he hit .263 with 13 homers and 66 RBI.

FEBRUARY 19:

The Mets preview their uniforms, which include Dodger blue, Giant orange, and Yankees' pinstripes.

MARCH 22

Roger Maris declines to pose with Hall of Famer Rogers Hornsby, who had criticized him in *My War with Baseball*. Hornsby, a Mets' coach, responds by calling Maris a "bush leaguer" and saying: "I've posed with some real major leaguers, not bush leaguers like he is. He couldn't carry my bat. He didn't hit in two years what I hit in one."

The following day, Yankees' manager Ralph Houk defends Roger Maris at a press conference and says, "I think it'll be swell if Mr. Hornsby takes care of his ballclub and I'll take care of mine."

THE SEASON

APRIL 9:

On opening day in their new $20 million District of Columbia Stadium, the Senators beat the Tigers, 4-1, behind Bennie Daniels's five-hitter. Bob Johnson hits a two-run homer for Washington. The ceremonial first pitch is thrown out by President John F. Kennedy.

APRIL 10:

The Houston Colt .45s, one of the NL's two new teams, debut at Colt Stadium with an opening day 11-2 win over the Cubs before a crowd of 25,271. Roman Mejias paces Houston with a pair of three-run homers and Hal W. Smith also has a round-tripper. Ernie Banks homers for the Cubs against starter and winner Bobby Shantz.

After four years at the Los Angeles Coliseum, the Dodgers inaugurate their new Dodger Stadium at Chavez Ravine. A crowd of 52,564 turns out for the event. Kay O'Malley, wife of the Dodger owner, throws out the first ball in the

LEAGUE

John "Buck" O'Neil becomes baseball's first black coach, joining the staff of the Cubs for the 1962 season. Since 1956, the Negro Leagues' star has been scouting for Chicago, and among his recommendations were Ernie Banks and Lou Brock.

"If I'd known I was gonna pitch a no-hitter today, I would have gotten a haircut."
– Angels' rookie pitcher Bo Belinsky

HISTORY

In his three and a half seasons in the NL, Jack Hamilton never serves up a home run to Hank Aaron.

Casey's Mets have an inauspicious debut.

$18-million ballpark. The Reds' Wally Post's three-run homer in the seventh inning breaks a 3-3 tie and the Reds win, 6-3. Johnny Podres is the losing pitcher.

APRIL 11:

New York Mets debut in St. Louis, losing to the Cardinals 11-4. The day began badly for the team when 16 players were stuck in the Chase Hotel elevator for 20 minutes. And the signs continue to be bad when starting pitcher Roger Craig drops the ball during his stretch in the third inning and is called for a balk, scoring Bill White from third with the first run ever against the Mets. Gil Hodges and Charlie Neal homer for New York; Craig gets the loss. The winning pitcher is Larry Jackson.

APRIL 12:

Pete Richert of the Dodgers has a memorable major league debut. He comes out of the bullpen to relieve Stan Williams and strikes out the first six Reds batters he faces. Four of those strikeouts come in the third inning when catcher Johnny Roseboro muffs a third strike to Gordy Coleman. Richert's third-inning victims are Frank Robinson, Coleman, Wally Post, and Johnny Edwards. The Dodgers win, 11-7.

APRIL 13:

The Yankees no longer have New York to themselves. After four years, the Big Apple is a two-team town as the Mets play their home debut at the venerable Polo Grounds. A total of 12,447 turn out to welcome the NL's new entry, but the Mets bow, 4-3, to the Pirates despite a home run by Frank J. Thomas. The winning pitcher is Tom Sturdivant; Sherman Jones gets the loss. Pirates' rookie Willie Stargell homers.

In Chicago, Stan Musial scores for the 1,860th time of his career, surpassing the NL record for career runs sets by Mel Ott. The Cardinals win, 7-4.

APRIL 18:

At Wrigley Field in Chicago, Ernie Banks – moved from his familiar shortstop postion to first base – homers against Dick Farrell of the Colt .45s in the 10th inning. It is Banks's 300th career home run and wins the game, 3-2. Dick Ellsworth gets the victory.

APRIL 22:

At Forbes Field, the Pirates beat the Mets, 4-3, extending two record streaks. Pittsburgh's victory is their 10th in a row — tying the Dodgers' 1955 major league record for the start of the season. The Mets' loss is their ninth in a row, equaling the all-time mark at the outset of a year. The co-holders with the Mets are the 1918 Dodgers and the 1919 Braves. Bill Mazeroski's eighth-inning triple produces the winning run, hanging the loss on Sherman Jones.

APRIL 23:

The Mets get off the schneid, winning their first game after nine straight losses to start the season. They beat the Pirates soundly, 9-1, on the five-hit pitching of Jay Hook – the first Mets pitcher with a win. Hook helps his own cause with a two-run single in the second; Bobby Gene Smith drives in two more with an eighth-inning triple. New York also snaps the Pirates' record-tying winning streak. Tom Sturdivant is the game's losing pitcher.

APRIL 24:

At Wrigley Field, Sandy Koufax ties the major league record

APRIL 11
A day after the Colt .45s debut in Houston, the Mets begin play in St. Louis.

MAY 21
The Dodgers host the Giants for the first time at new Dodger Stadium, winning, 8-1.

by fanning 18 Cubs in a 10-2 victory. Koufax previously struck out 18 in a game in 1959.

APRIL 26:

The Braves' Tommie Aaron, Hank's younger brother, hits his first major league homer – against Jack Hamilton – in a 10-4 Milwaukee victory over the Phillies.

APRIL 29:

In the opener of a twinbill at the Polo Grounds, left-hander Al Jackson pitches the first-ever Mets shutout, beating the Phillies, 8-0. Jackson allows eight hits and benefits from a seven-run fourth inning. Art Mahaffey gets the loss. In the nightcap, the Phillies win, 10-2, behind Bobby Locke, ending the Mets' two-game winning streak.

MAY 5:

For the first time in 23 years, the White Sox have one owner, and he is Arthur Allyn, who today buys the remaining 46 percent of the team.

The Angels' madcap rookie Robert "Bo" Belinsky shows some skills to go with his clowning. He no-hits the visiting Orioles, 2-0, striking out nine and walking four. The Angels make one error. Steve Barber gets the loss. It is the first no-hitter in the AL since 1958.

Bo Belinsky: "If I'd known I was gonna pitch a no-hitter today, I would have gotten a haircut." Daniel Okrent and Steve Wulf write in Baseball Anecdotes*: "As his teammates rushed out of the dugout, and the home crowd went wild, Belinsky pointed to the stands and said to his catcher, Buck Rodgers, 'Hey, look at the blonde.'"*

MAY 6:

The Yankees beat the Senators, 8-0, with Mickey Mantle hitting home runs left-handed and right-handed for the ninth time in his career.

MAY 9:

The Orioles' Brooks Robinson hits a grand slam homer against the Athletics. Robinson had a grand slam in his last game on May 6 and becomes one of five AL players to hit bases-loaded homers in back-to-back games.

The Mets acquire first baseman Marv Throneberry (.000 in nine games) from the Orioles for catcher Hobie Landrith (.289) and a cash payment.

CLETE BOYER OF THE YANKEES RECALLS BATTING AGAINST THE GIANTS WITH WILLIE MAYS IN CENTER FIELD: "I SAID TO MYSELF TWO THINGS. THE FIRST THING I SAID WAS, 'HELLO, DOUBLE!' THE SECOND THING I SAID WAS ... 'HE'S OUT THERE."

MAY 11:

In St. Louis, the Cardinals' Minnie Minoso fractures his skull and breaks his wrist when he runs into the outfield wall in a game against the Los Angeles Dodgers.

MAY 19:

At Dodger Stadium, the Cardinals' Stan Musial singles against Ron Perranoski in the ninth inning, It is the 3,431st career safety for the 41-year-old Musial, who surpasses Honus Wagner as the NL's all-time hit leader. St. Louis wins, 8-1.

MAY 20:

In Philadelphia, rookie Ken Hubbs of the Cubs has eight hits in eight at-bats in today's doubleheader. In game one, the Cubs win, 6-4; Hubbs has three singles in three at-bats. Cal Koonce gets the win. Hubbs has five singles in five trips to the plate in the nightcap, an 11-2 win for Chicago and Bob Buhl.

MAY 21:

In their first-ever meeting at the new Dodger Stadium, Los Angeles beats the Giants, 8-1, with Sandy Koufax fanning 10. Tommy Davis knocks in three runs.

HISTORY

One of Charley Finley's innovations in the 1960s is hiring a woman - Betty Caywood - to do color commentary on broadcasts of Athletics' games. Ms. Caywood, the first female to regularly announce baseball games, airs reports from the dugouts and stands.

The 1962 Dodgers are not an offensive powerhouse. According to one story, Don Drysdale was granted a night off and received a call informing him that teammate Sandy Koufax had pitched a no-hitter. Drysdale's response: "Did he win?"

TRIVIA

Washington Post **sports editor Shirley Povich is listed in *Who's Who in American Women,* which reprints his biography verbatim from *Who's Who in America,* including the fact that he is married to Ethel Friedman.**

MAY 22:

With an injured Mickey Mantle out of the lineup, Roger Maris, who had no intentional walks last season, gets four today plus an "unintentional" base on balls. Whitey Ford no-hits the White Sox for seven innings before leaving with back spasms. Reliever Jim Coates yields a ninth-inning hit to Bob Rodgers; the Yankees go on to win, 2-1, in 12.

MAY 26:

In Los Angeles, the Dodgers' Sandy Koufax fans 16 Phillies in a 6-3 win. It is the second time in his career that Koufax has retired 16 Phillies on strikes; the last time was June 22, 1959.

At Yankee Stadium, the Tigers' Al Kaline preserves Detroit's 2-1 win with a diving catch of Elston Howard's line drive for the last out of the game. But it is a costly putout; Kaline suffers a broken right collarbone. Hank Aguirre is the game's winning pitcher.

MAY 28:

In Chicago, Warren Spahn loses a four-hitter to the Cubs, 2-1. It is the 200th loss of Spahn's career.

MAY 29:

At Wrigley Field, Ernie Banks hits three consecutive homers, and his teammates Billy Williams, Bob Will, and George Altman chip in with one each, but it's not enough. The Braves beat the Cubs, 11-9, in 10 innings.

JUNE 8:

The Mets, behind Jay Hook, beat the Cubs, 4-3, in the first game of a doubleheader, ending their 17-game losing streak. The elation is brief, however, as Chicago comes back in the nightcap with a 3-2 win.

JUNE 11:

John "Boog" Powell of the Orioles is carried out on a stretcher after being beaned by Leavitt "Bud" Daley in the fourth inning of today's game at Yankee Stadium. In the bottom of the frame, Robin Roberts – known for his pinpoint control – "shaves" Roger Maris and then a fight breaks out. Baltimore's manager Billy Hitchcock and Yankees' skipper Ralph Houk are both ejected from the game. With a save by Hoyt Wilhelm, Roberts gets his first American League win, by a score of 5-3.

JUNE 12:

Brothers Hank and Tommie Aaron homer — for the first time in the same game — as the Braves spank the Dodgers, 15-2, in Milwaukee. Hank hits his home run in the second against Phil Ortega; Tommie in the eighth off Ed Roebuck.

JUNE 16:

After missing nearly a month and 30 games because of knee and thigh injuries, Mickey Mantle limps to the plate as a pinch hitter and belts a 450-foot three-run homer against Gary Bell. The Cleveland crowd of 72,000 gives Mantle an ovation that chokes him up. The Indians win the game, 10-9.

JUNE 17:

In the opener of a twinbill, the Cubs' Lou Brock deposits a pitch from Al Jackson into the center-field bleachers at the Polo Grounds, a drive of some 480 feet. The only other player to hit a homer into that section of the ballpark was Joe Adcock in 1953. The Cubs win, 8-7, and take the nightcap, 4-3, on a ninth-inning homer by Ron Santo. In the opener, the Mets' Marv Throneberry hits an apparent triple, driving in two runs. But he is called out for missing second base. Casey Stengel comes out to argue and is told by third base coach Harry "Cookie" Lavagetto, "Don't argue, Case. He missed first base, too."

JUNE 18:

The Braves' Hank Aaron becomes the second player in two days and the third in history to homer into the center-field bleachers at the Polo Grounds. Aaron hits his round-tripper with the bases loaded against the Mets' Jay Hook. The Braves win the game, 7-1.

JUNE 22:

Almost every game means a new record for Stan Musial. Today, against the Phillies, he becomes the major leagues' all-time leader in total bases with 5,864.

The Orioles' John "Boog" Powell becomes the first player in major league history to clear the center-field hedges at Baltimore's Memorial Stadium. Powell hits his homer — estimated at 469 feet — off Don Schwall of the Red Sox in the seventh inning of a nightcap. Baltimore wins the game, 4-3.

MAY 26
For the second time in his career, Dodgers' pitcher Sandy Koufax strikes out 16 Phillies.

JUNE 22
Boog Powell is the first to hit a ball over the center-field hedges at Memorial Stadium.

JUNE 24:

In Detroit, some seven hours after the first pitch, Yankees' outfielder Jack Reed hits a two-run homer into the left-field seats against Phil Regan to give the Yankees a 9-7 victory in 22 innings. It is the longest game – in time – ever in the major leagues. Jerry Casale holds the Yankees scoreless for 19 innings but is not involved in the decision. Jim Bouton, with seven shutout innings, gets the victory. Bobby Richardson sets an AL record with 11 at-bats. Yogi Berra, 37 years old, catches the full game for New York and has three hits in 10 at-bats.

Reed plays three seasons with the Yankees, batting .233 in limited action. His home run today is the only one of his brief career.

JUNE 26:

At Fenway Park, Earl Wilson no-hits the Angels, 2-0, and hits a 400-foot-plus homer. It is the first AL no-hitter by a black pitcher. Wilson fans five and walks four; the Red Sox play errorless ball. Bo Belinsky, who no-hit Baltimore in his last start, is the losing pitcher today.

MANAGER CASEY STENGEL TALKS ABOUT HIS LINEUP PRIOR TO THE METS' OPENING DAY: "AND IN LEFT FIELD, IN LEFT FIELD WE HAVE A SPLENDID MAN AND HE KNOWS HOW TO DO IT. HE'S BEEN AROUND AND HE SWINGS THE BAT THERE IN LEFT FIELD AND HE KNOWS WHAT TO DO. HE'S GOT A BIG FAMILY AND HE WANTS TO PROVIDE FOR THEM, AND HE'S A FINE OUTSTANDING PLAYER, THE FELLA IN LEFT FIELD. YOU CAN BE SURE HE'LL BE READY WHEN THE BELL RINGS – AND THAT'S HIS NAME, BELL!"

JUNE 27:

In Pittsburgh, the Mets' Richie Ashburn singles in the fourth inning against Bob Friend. It is Ashburn's 2,500th career hit, and he is the 39th player in history to reach that level. The Pirates win the game, 6-5, in 10 innings.

The Mets sign 17-year-old first baseman Ed Kranepool from James Monroe High School in the Bronx, New York, for an $85,000 bonus.

JUNE 28:

Hall of Fame catcher Gordon "Mickey" Cochrane dies at age 59 in Lake Forest, Illinois. Cochrane batted .320 in 13 major league seasons and appeared in five World Series. His playing career was cut short when his skull was fractured by a pitch in 1937. He was the Tigers' manager for seven seasons, winning two AL pennants and one World Championship. He was inducted into the Hall of Fame in 1947.

JUNE 29:

The New York Mets milk Dodgers' pitchers for 16 walks and win today's game, 10-4. Jay Hook is the winning pitcher.

CULTURE

The film *Safe at Home* stars Mickey Mantle, Roger Maris, and William Frawley.

"This guy didn't just come to play. He came to beat ya."
– Leo Durocher, on Jackie Robinson

HISTORY

After his record 61-homer season in 1961, Roger Maris hits 33 round-trippers and bats only .174 in the World Series. As Mickey Mantle becomes more popular with fans, Maris becomes the target of greater abuse. He comments: "Sometimes I wish I never hit those 61 home runs. All I want is to be treated like any other player."

JUNE 30:

The Mets get five more walks today, but nothing else from Sandy Koufax. The Dodger left hander no-hits New York, 5-0, at Dodger Stadium. It is the first no-hitter for Koufax, who fans 13 – including the first three batters of the game on nine pitches. The Dodgers play errorless ball behind him. Bob L. Miller gets the loss.

JULY 1:

The White Sox hit a major league record three sacrifice flies in one inning. In the fifth inning of the nightcap of a double-header against the Indians, pitcher Juan Pizarro hits a fly to right that is dropped by Gene Green, allowing a runner to score from third. Pizzaro gets credit for a sacrifice fly. Later in the inning, Jacob "Nellie" Fox flies to Green, who again drops the ball with the same result. On his third try, Green holds on to a fly — hit by Al Smith — but a third run scores. All told, Chicago scores six runs in the frame and wins, 7-6.

JULY 2:

In Los Angeles, the Dodgers' Johnny Podres fans eight straight Phillies, tying a major league record held by a number of pitchers. The Dodgers win, 5-1, in the opener of a doubleheader and then take the nightcap, 4-0, behind Stan Williams' pitching.

JULY 6:

Mickey Mantle, who homered in his last two at-bats on July 4, hits another pair in his first trips to the plate today against Camilo Pascual in Minnesota. Mantle ties a major league mark with four consecutive round-trippers, and his seven in 12 at-bats matches Ralph Kiner's performance of the feat in 1947. The Yankees win, 7-5.

At the Polo Grounds, Mets fans have something to cheer about. Gil Hodges homers against the Cardinals; it is the 370th of his career, placing him behind only Jimmie Foxx among right-handed hitters. Ralph Kiner, now a Mets' broadcaster, falls to third place with 369. The Mets win the game, 10-3.

JULY 7:

The Cardinals' Stan Musial hits an eighth-inning home run against Mets' pircher Craig Anderson to beat New York, 3-2, at the Polo Grounds.

JULY 8:

Stan Musial homers in his first three at-bats today — in the first and fourth against Jay Hook and in the seventh against Willard Hunter – putting him in the record books with many major leaguers who have hit four in a row over two games. In the eighth inning Musial is fanned by Bob L. Miller. The Cardinals beat the Mets, 15-1, at the Polo Grounds.

JULY 10:

The NL wins the season's first All-Star Game, 3-1, at District of Columbia Stadium. Maury Wills, who has a single, a stolen base, and two of the NL's three runs, gets the first Arch Ward Trophy, named for the game's founder. Roberto Clemente has three hits. Juan Marichal gets the win; Camilo Pascual is charged with the loss.

JULY 12:

In Milwaukee, Hank and Tommie Aaron hit home runs in the ninth inning against the Cardinals; they are the first brothers to homer in the same frame since Lloyd and Paul Waner in 1938. Tommie pinch-hits for pitcher Claude Raymond with one out and touches Larry Jackson for a round-tripper. Hank hits a grand slam against Lindy McDaniel to win the game, 8-6. Eddie Mathews also belts a home run for the Braves.

JULY 14:

Unfortunately for Ralph Branca, it is 11 years too late and it doesn't count anyway. In the New York Mets' first Old-Timers' Game, reliever Ralph Branca faces Bobby Thomson, the man who hit the historic 1951 home run against him to give the Giants the 1951 pennant. This time Branca gets Thomson out on a fly ball to center field. In the real game itself, the Dodgers smash the Mets, 17-0.

JULY 17:

The Dodgers hold their collective breath as Sandy Koufax experiences numbness in his pitching hand and is replaced after one inning against the Reds in Cincinnati. The Reds win the game, 7-5.

JULY 18:

Two swings equal eight runs for the Twins in the first inning against the Indians. Minnesota sluggers Bob Allison and Harmon

Killebrew each hit grand slam home runs in an 11-run rally at Metropolitan Stadium. They are the first AL teammates to accomplish the feat in an inning. The Twins romp over Cleveland by a score of 14-3.

JULY 20:

Mickey Mantle launches another moon shot into the third deck of the left-field stands, a rare feat for anyone, in Yankee Stadium against Steve Hamilton with a runner on. Mantle also has two singles in a 3-2 Yankees' victory over the Senators.

JULY 22:

The Chicago White Sox Floyd Robinson is six for six – all singles – in a 7-3 victory over the Boston Red Sox.

JULY 23:

Jackie Robinson, Bob Feller, Bill McKechnie, and Edd Roush are inducted into the Hall of Fame. Robinson, who broke the modern color line in 1947, was one of baseball's most fiery and exciting players. In his 10-year career, he hit .311 and stole 197 bases. He played in six World Series. Growing up on a farm, Feller developed arm strength that enabled him to throw in excess of 100 miles per hour. In 18 years he was 266-162, with 2,581 strikeouts and 46 shutouts. Roush, now 69, played the outfield for 18 years, hitting .323 and twice leading the NL in batting. McKechnie, 75 years old, is in the Hall of Fame on his managerial credentials. In 25 years, he won pennants with three different teams – the Pirates in 1925, the Cardinals in 1928, and the Reds in 1939 and 1940. His 1925 Pirates and 1940 Reds also won the World Series. As a player, McKechnie batted .251 in 11 years.

Leo Durocher once said of Jackie Robinson: "This guy didn't just come to play. He came to beat ya."

JULY 25:

In St. Louis, Stan Musial hits a two-run homer in a 5-2 loss to the Dodgers. He now has 1,862 RBI in his career, passing Mel Ott for the NL record.

JULY 26:

When the Red Sox team bus stalls in traffic for 15 minutes near the George Washington Bridge en route from Yankee Stadium to Newark Airport, pitcher Gene Conley and infielder Elijah "Pumpsie" Green get off and disappear. The Red Sox were on their way out of New York after a 13-3 loss to the Yankees

CULTURE

Danny Kaye performs the song "D-O-D-G-E-R-S Song (Oh, Really? No, O'Malley)."

Willie McCovey's bat comes up big in the World Series.

> "How could he be exptected to remember where the bases are? He gets on so infrequently."
> – *Sportswriter Jack Lang, on Marv Throneberry*

CULTURE

Flashing Spikes, based on a novel by Frank O'Rourke and starring James Stewart, Jack Warden, and Don Drysdale, airs on television.

in which Conley was KO'd in an eight-run, third-inning rally.

The New York Daily News finds a cabdriver who took Conley to Idlewild Airport, where he was refused passage on El Al Airlines to Israel because he had no passport. Conley makes his way home, turning up in Foxboro, Massachusetts, after 68 hours. He is fined $1,500. Green returns to the team after 27 hours and is slapped with a $1,000 fine.

Braves left-hander Warren Spahn hits a home run off the Mets' Craig Anderson in a 6-1 win for Milwaukee. It is Spahn's 31st career home run, the most ever by an NL pitcher. Spahn surpasses nineteenth-century pitcher Happy Jack Stivetts. The game also marks the Mets' 11th straight defeat.

JULY 29:

Burt Shotton dies at age 77 in Lake Wales, Florida. Shotton played outfield for 14 major league seasons, hitting .270, but is best remembered for his 11 years as a manager. Four of those years were spent at the helm of the Dodgers, winning two pennants. He also managed the Phillies and Reds.

JULY 30:

At Wrigley Field, Pete Runnels, Leon "Daddy Wags" Wagner (with one on), and Rocky Colavito (with two on) homer for the AL in a 9-4 victory in the second of the season's All-Star Games. The winning pitcher is Ray Herbert; Art Mahaffey is the loser.

AUGUST 1:

Bill Monboquette of the Red Sox no-hits the White Sox, 1-0, at Comiskey Park. Lu Clinton drives in Jim Pagliaroni in the eighth inning with the game's only run. Monboquette strikes out seven and walks one (Al Smith in the second, Chicago's only base runner); the Red Sox play errorless ball. Early Wynn is the losing pitcher. It is the second no-hitter by a Boston pitcher this year; Earl Wilson pitched one on June 26.

AUGUST 3:

At the Polo Grounds, Frank J. Thomas hits two home runs today against the Reds, tying a major league record with six home runs over three straight games. Thomas had a grand slam on August 1. Clarence "Choo Choo" Coleman, Charlie Neal, and Marv Throneberry also homer for New York, but the Reds win the game, 8-6.

AUGUST 4:

Roger Clemens is born in Dayton.

AUGUST 11:

The Giants beat the Dodgers, 5-4, ending Don Drysdale's winning streak at 11 in a game marked by a controversy over the field conditions. Los Angeles claims that the field at Candlestick Park was intentionally soaked to handicap Maury Wills's baserunning.

AUGUST 14:

Hank and Tommie Aaron homer in the same game for the third time this season. In Cincinnati, Tommie connects against Johnny Klippstein in the 6th; it is his eighth round-tripper of the year. Hank hits his 45th of the season against Ted Wills of the Reds in the seventh inning. Milwaukee wins, 5-4.

AUGUST 18:

The Cardinals' Minnie Minoso returns to action for the first time since July 18, when he fractured his skull and broke his wrist running into an outfield fence. Today in the nightcap, he is hit by a pitch by the Mets' Craig Anderson in the sixth and suffers a broken bone in his forearm. Earlier, Minoso had a homer and double. St. Louis sweeps, 7-4 and 10-0.

AUGUST 19:

The Yankees' Mickey Mantle and Elston Howard put on a demonstration of power in a 21-7 win over the Athletics. Howard hits two homers and drives in eight runs. Mantle has a grand slam home run, drives in seven runs, and shows he still can run by stealing two bases.

AUGUST 26:

The Twins' Jack Kralick no-hits the Athletics, 1-0, at Metropolitan Stadium in Minnesota. Kralick throws only 97 pitches, striking out three and allowing only one base runner – a ninth-inning walk to George Alusik. The losing pitcher is Bill Fischer. Kralick's no-hitter is the fifth in the majors in three and a half months.

SEPTEMBER 2:

Stan Musial pinch-hits for Bobby Shantz and singles against Al Jackson of the Mets. It is Musial's 3,516 career hit, putting

SEPTEMBER 2
Stan Musial's single leaves him second all-time in hits, behind only Ty Cobb.

SEPTEMBER 17
Warren Spahn's victory over the Dodgers gives him 324 career wins, the most ever by a lefty.

him ahead of Tris Speaker and second only to Ty Cobb. Musial now holds 41 major league records — one for every year of his age. The Mets win the game, 4-3.

SEPTEMBER 7:

Maury Wills steals four bases against the Pirates at Dodger Stadium, setting an NL record with 82 for the season. The Pirates win, 10-1.

SEPTEMBER 10:

Mickey Mantle returns from a rib injury and homers with the bases empty against Hank Aguirre in Detroit. It is the 400th home run of Mantle's career. Ralph Terry wins his 21st game on a Hector Lopez pinch-hit single in the ninth inning.

SEPTEMBER 11:

Yogi Berra reaches a landmark of his own. His 10th-inning homer in Detroit is the 350th of his career. The Yankees and Jim Bouton win the game, 8-7.

SEPTEMBER 12:

The Senators' Tom Cheney strikes out 21 Orioles in 16 innings – a major league record for extra-inning games. Washington wins, 2-1, in Memorial Stadium in Baltimore. Cheney has 13 strikeouts in nine innings; he adds two in the 10th, two in the 11th, two in the 14th, one in the 15th, and one in the 16th. John "Boog" Powell is the only Oriole Cheney fails to fan. He no-hits Baltimore from the eighth through the 16th, allowing 10 hits overall. A home run by Marion "Bud" Zipfel wins the game and gives Cheney his sixth victory against eight losses. The losing pitcher is Dick Hall.

SEPTEMBER 17:

The Braves' Warren Spahn defeats the Dodgers and Pete Richert, 2-1, for his 324th career victory, the most ever by a left-handed pitcher.

SEPTEMBER 18:

American League owners meet in Kansas City and turn down a proposal from Charles O. Finley of Kansas City for expansion into the Dallas-Fort Worth area.

SEPTEMBER 20:

In Detroit, the Tigers' Al Kaline hits a two-run homer in the fifth inning against starter Jim Kaat of the Twins. It is Kaline's 1,500th career hit. The Tigers win the game, 5-1.

SEPTEMBER 21:

Sandy Koufax returns to the mound after a long layoff because of a circulatory disorder in his pitching hand and is KO'd by the Cardinals in the first inning of the contest.

SEPTEMBER 22:

The Mets keep rolling – downhill. At the Polo Grounds, they are defeated, 9-2, by the Cubs for their 116th loss of the year – a modern NL record. The 1935 Braves with 115 losses were the previous record holders. Al Jackson loses his 20th of the season.

SEPTEMBER 23:

At Busch Stadium, The Dodgers' Maury Wills singles, then steals second base and third to tie Ty Cobb's modern record of 96 stolen bases in a single season, set in 1915. In the seventh inning, with Jim Gilliam at bat and Larry Jackson on the mound, Wills steals yet another base when Carl Sawatski's throw gets past Dal Maxvil. Wills sets a new mark of 97. The Cardinals beat the Dodgers, 12-2. Jackson gets the win; Don Drysdale is charged with his eighth loss of the season against 25 wins.

SEPTEMBER 25:

At Yankee Stadium, New York, behind Whitey Ford, beats the Senators, 8-3, to wrap up another pennant — Ralph Houk's second in his two years as the club's manager.

The Dodgers' Ed Roebuck loses, 3-2, to the Houston Colt .45s in 10 innings. It is his first loss in 60 appearances over a two-year period.

SEPTEMBER 26:

The Braves beat Roger Craig and the Mets, 6-3. The Mets now own the modern major league record for the most losses in a season – 118. The only team to lose more were the Cleveland Spiders, who dropped 134 games back in 1899.

SEPTEMBER 29:

In Milwaukee, the Braves and Warren Spahn beat the Pirates, 4-3. It is Spahn's 327th career win, the most ever by a left-handed pitcher.

SEPTEMBER 30:

Los Angeles loses to the visiting Cardinals, 1-0, on a Gene Oliver home run in the ninth inning.

LEAGUE

In November, owners and players agree to return to one All-Star Game a year beginning in 1963. There have been two since 1959.

"The Mets have shown me ways to lose I never knew existed."
– *Casey Stengel*

The Giants beat the Houston Colt .45s at Candlestick Park, 2-1, on a Willie Mays home run against Dick "Turk" Farrell in the eighth inning. Earlier, the hometown fans had booed Mays. The Dodgers and Giants end the season in a tie, necessitating a playoff series.

The season ends mercifully and expectedly for the Mets. They drop their 120th game of the season (against only 40 wins) by losing to the Cubs, 5-1. They finish 60 ½ games out of first place. Bob Buhl gets the win; Willard Hunter is the losing pitcher. Added to the ignominy is an eighth-inning triple play. With Richie Ashburn on first and Sammy Drake on second, Joe Pignatano hits a popup toward rightfield. Second baseman Ken Hubbs makes the catch, throws to first baseman Ernie Banks, who relays to shortstop Andre Rodgers for 3 outs. The triple play rings down the curtain on the playing careers of Ashburn, Drake, and Pignatano.

Casey Stengel: "When I go back in my mind to our play in 1962, I just wonder how we ever got to win 40 games." He also said, "Imagine, 40 games! I won with this club what I used to lose!"

Maury Wills's season is stacked with stolen bases.

OCTOBER 3:

At Dodger Stadium, San Francisco scores four runs in the eighth inning and beats Los Angeles, 6-4, to take the best of three playoff and the NL pennant on the 11th anniversary of Bobby Thomson's home run. Don Larsen gets the win in relief of Juan Marichal. Ed Roebuck, who replaces Johnny Podres, gets the loss. Maury Wills steals three bases today to bring his major league record total to 104 in 165 games.

REGULAR SEASON WRAP-UP:

The Giants, with a playoff win over the Dodgers, finish at 103-62, a game ahead of Los Angeles. Alvin Dark's team is led by Willie Mays with a .304 average, 49 homers, and 141 RBI. Orlando Cepeda bats .306 with 35 homers

SEPTEMBER 30
The Mets finish their inaugural season with a record-setting 120 losses vs. 40 wins.

OCTOBER 16
Ralph Terry one-hits the Giants in game seven, and the Yankees win the World Series.

and 114 RBI; Felipe Alou, .316 with 25 homers and 98 RBI. Veteran Harvey Kuenn hits .304. Jack Sanford at 24-7 leads the pitching staff.

The Yankees, under Ralph Houk, are 96-66, five games ahead of the Twins. Mickey Mantle hits .321 with 30 homers and 89 RBI. Roger Maris has 33 homers and 100 RBI with a .256 average. Bill Skowron (23 home runs), Elston Howard (21), and Tom Tresh (20) provide additional power. Bobby Richardson bats .302, and Ralph Terry tops the pitching staff with a 23-12 win-loss record.

Pirates' relief pitcher Elroy Face sets an NL record with 28 saves. Pitcher Bob Buhl of the Cubs is hitless in 70 at-bats, a major league mark. The Dodgers set a major league attendance record – 2,755,184.

OCTOBER 4:

World Series, game one. The Giants and Yankees resume an old rivalry, only in a new setting – San Francisco. Whitey Ford scatters 10 hits and Clete Boyer hits a seventh-inning homer to give the Yankees a 6-2 win. The Giants score a run in the first, snapping Ford's scoreless Series streak at 33 innings, but he wins his 10th post-season game. Billy O'Dell gets the loss.

OCTOBER 5:

World Series, game two. Jack Sanford three-hits the Yankees, 2-0. Willie McCovey homers in the seventh inning against the losing pitcher, Ralph Terry.

Second baseman Red Schoendienst (.301 in 89 games) is released as a player by the Cardinals and will join the team's coaching staff for 1963.

OCTOBER 7:

World Series, game three. In New York, Bill Stafford four-hits the Giants and the Yankees win, 3-2. Ed Bailey hits a two-run home run for San Francisco. Billy Pierce gets the loss.

OCTOBER 8:

World Series, game four. Former Yankees' World Series hero Don Larsen pitches a third of an inning of relief and gets the victory in a 7-3 Giants' win today at Yankee Stadium. Jim Coates, who also pitches one-third of a frame, gets the loss. Chuck Hiller becomes the first NL player with a Series grand slam when he homers off Marshall Bridges in the seventh inning. Tom Haller also homers, with a runner on.

OCTOBER 10:

World Series, game five. Tom Tresh hits a three-run homer in the bottom of the eighth against Jack Sanford, and Ralph Terry goes all the way as the Yankees win at home, 5-3. Jose Pagan homers for San Francisco. Sanford gets the loss despite striking out 10.

OCTOBER 15:

World Series, game six. After three days of steady rain in San Francisco, the Series resumes and Billy Pierce holds the Yankees to three hits in a 5-2 victory. Whitey Ford gets the loss. Roger Maris has a solo homer for the Yankees; Orlando Cepeda bangs out three hits for the victorious Giants.

OCTOBER 16:

World Series, game seven. Ralph Terry hurls a four-hit shutout to beat Jack Sanford and the Giants, 1-0, making Ralph Houk the only manager with World Championships in his first two seasons. With two runners on base and two outs in the bottom of the ninth, Willie McCovey hits a liner that has trouble written on it. But second baseman Bobby Richardson snares it to end the game and the Series. The Yankees' big guns are relatively silent: Mickey Mantle, Roger Maris, and Elston Howard all hit below .200, and Maris has the trio's only homer. Tom Tresh at .321 (one homer and four RBI) and Clete Boyer at .310 are New York's top bats. Ralph Terry has a 1.80 ERA to go with his 2-1 performance. Jose Pagan hits .368 for the Giants; Mays finishes at .250 with no home runs and one RBI.

POST-SEASON

OCTOBER 17:

The Chicgo Cubs acquire pitchers Larry Jackson (16-11, 3.75) and Lindy McDaniel (3-10, 4.12 ERA) along with catcher Jimmy Schaffer (.242 in 70 games) in a deal with the St. Louis Cardinals. On the return end of the bargain, the Cardinals obtain outfielder George Altman (.318, 22 home runs, 74 RBI), pitcher Don Cardwell (7-16, 4.92 ERA) and catcher Morris "Moe" Thacker (.187 in 65 games).

CULTURE

***My War With Baseball*, by Rogers Hornsby and Bill Surface, is published.**

"Thou shalt not steal, I mean defensively. On offense, indeed thou shall steal and thou must."
– *Branch Rickey*

OCTOBER 29:

The Cardinals sign 80-year-old Branch Rickey as a special consultant on player matters. It marks a return to the Cardinals for Rickey, 20 years after he left St. Louis to go to the Dodgers. He has been officially inactive since his departure from Pittsburgh in 1955, but was involved with the short-lived Continental League.

NOVEMBER 1:

The Houston Colt .45s sign 19-year-old free-agent second baseman Joe Morgan.

NOVEMBER 16:

Lou Perini sells the Braves to a group including general manager John McHale, insurance executive William Bartholomay, and five others. Bartholomay becomes chairman of the board.

NOVEMBER 19:

Today the St. Louis Cardinals swing a deal to acquire shortstop Dick Groat (.294) and pitcher Diomedes Olivo (5-1, 2.77 ERA) from the Pittsburgh Pirates for pitcher Don Cardwell (7-16, 4.92 ERA) and infielder Julio Gotay (.255). Groat will lead the league with 43 doubles in 1963.

NOVEMBER 20:

A group headed by Gabe Paul buys the Cleveland Indians from William Daley.

Dr. Strangeglove goes to Fenway. The Red Sox acquire first baseman Dick Stuart (.228, 16 homers) and pitcher Jack Lamabe (3-1, 2.88 ERA) from the Pirates for pitcher Don Schwall (9-15, 4.94 ERA) and catcher Jim Pagliaroni (.258, 11 home runs in 90 games).

NOVEMBER 26:

The Red Sox trade AL batting champion James "Pete" Runnels (.376, 10 homers), an infielder, to the Colt .45s for outfielder Roman Mejias (.286, 24 home runs).
The Yankees trade their regular first baseman Bill "Moose" Skowron (.270, 23 homers, 80 RBI) to the Dodgers for pitcher Stan Williams (14-12, 4.46 ERA).

The Baltimore Orioles draft 18-year-old outfielder Paul Blair from the New York Mets organization. The Orioles also trade catcher Gus Triandos (.159 in 66 games) and outfielder Dorrel "Whitey" Herzog (.266 in 99 games) to the Detroit Tigers for catcher Dick Brown (.241, 12 home runs).

NOVEMBER 27:

The Indians acquire first baseman Joe Adcock (.248, 29 homers) and pitcher Jack Curtis (4-6, 4.04 ERA) from the Braves for pitcher Frank Funk (2-1, 3.24 ERA) and outfielders Don Dillard (.230, five homers in 95 games) and Ty Cline (.248).

DECEMBER 7:

Former pitcher Louis "Bobo" Newsom dies at age 55 in Orlando, Florida. Newsom is one of only two pitchers with 200 victories and more losses than wins. He finished his 20-year career with a 211-222 record and a 3.98 ERA. Traded repeatedly, Newsom played four times with the Senators, three times with the Browns, and twice each with the Dodgers and Athletics – among other teams.

One baseball writer said of Newsom: "He was as tough as shoe leather, as unlucky as an old maid, as colorful as a treeful of owls, and about the friendliest fellow you'd ever want to meet." The Hartsville, South Carolina, native was unpredictable, too, winning 20 games three times in his career, and losing 20 three times.

DECEMBER 11:

The New York Mets and Boston Red Sox pull off a deal today. Elijah "Pumpsie" Green (.231 in 56 games) – who is the first black player for the Red Sox – is traded to the Mets along with pitcher Tracy Stallard (0-0) and minor league infielder Al Moran. In return, Boston gets infielder-outfielder Felix Mantilla (.275, 11 home runs).

DECEMBER 15:

The Baltimore Orioles and San Francicso Giants swap pitchers and catchers today. Going to Baltimore are right-handed reliever Stu Miller (5-8, 19 saves, 4.12 ERA) and left-handed starting pitcher Mike McCormick (5-5, 5.38 ERA) along with catcher John Orsino (.271, 18 games). San Francisco obtains right-handed starter Jack Fisher (7-9, 5.09 ERA) and lefty starter Billy Hoeft (4-8, 4.59 ERA), plus catcher Jim Coker (.000 in three ML at-bats). Next season, Miller appears in a league-high 71 games and leads the majors with 27 saves. Orsino is also a solid contributor in Baltimore, appearing in 109 games behind the plate and hitting .272.

OCTOBER 29
Branch Rickey, at age 80, is brought back to the Cardinals as a special consultant.

NOVEMBER 1
The Houston Colt .45s sign 19-year-old free agent second baseman Joe Morgan.

THE BEST OF 1962

NATIONAL LEAGUE

HITTERS

Batting Average:
Herman "Tommy" Davis, Los Angeles Dodgers, .346

Slugging Average:
Frank Robinson, Cincinnati Reds, .624

Home Runs:
Willie Mays, San Francisco Giants, 49

Runs Batted In:
Tommy Davis, 153

Hits:
Tommy Davis, 230

Stolen Bases:
Maury Wills, Los Angeles Dodgers, 104

PITCHERS

Wins:
Don Drysdale, Los Angeles Dodgers, 25

Strikeouts:
Don Drysdale, 232

Earned Run Average:
Sandy Koufax, Los Angeles Dodgers, 2.54

Winning Percentage:
Bob Purkey, Cincinnati Reds, .821

Saves:
Roy Face, Pittsburgh Pirates, 28

Most Valuable Player:
Maury Wills, Los Angeles Dodgers

Cy Young Award:
Don Drysdale, Los Angeles Dodgers

Rookie of the Year:
Ken Hubbs, Chicago Cubs

AMERICAN LEAGUE

HITTERS

Batting Average:
James "Pete" Runnels, Boston Red Sox, .326

Slugging Average:
Mickey Mantle, New York Yankees, .605

Home Runs:
Harmon Killebrew, Minnesota Twins, 48

Runs Batted In:
Harmon Killebrew, 126

Hits:
Bobby Richardson, New York Yankees, 209

Stolen Bases:
Luis Aparicio, Chicago White Sox, 31

PITCHERS

Wins:
Ralph Terry, New York Yankees, 23

Strikeouts:
Camilo Pascual, Minnesota Twins, 206

Earned Run Average:
Hank Aguirre, Detroit Tigers, 2.21

Winning Percentage:
Ray Herbert, Chicago White Sox, .690

Saves:
Dick Radatz, Boston Red Sox, 24

Most Valuable Player:
Mickey Mantle, New York Yankees

Rookie of the Year:
Tom Tresh, New York Yankees

1963

APRIL 1
No foolin' – the Duke's back. Former Brooklyn Dodger Duke Snider signs with the Mets.

NEWS

JOHN F. KENNEDY ASSASSINATED IN DALLAS; LYNDON B. JOHNSON BECOMES PRESIDENT

Soviet Valentina Tereshkova is first woman in space

SOUTH VIETNAMESE ARMY TAKES CONTROL OF GOVERNMENT

129 DIE IN *THRESHER* NUCLEAR SUB DISASTER

MEDGAR EVERS ASSASSINATED IN MISSISSIPPI

MARTIN LUTHER KING DELIVERS "I HAVE A DREAM" SPEECH TO 200,000 IN WASHINGTON FREEDOM MARCH

University of Alabama desegregated with aid of federal troops

BIRMINGHAM CHURCH BOMBING KILLS FOUR BLACK CHILDREN

ROBERT FROST DIES

PRE-SEASON

JANUARY 5:

Hall of Famer Rogers Hornsby dies of a heart attack and stroke at age 66 in Chicago. Hornsby hit .400 three times, including 1924 when he batted .424 — the highest average ever by a modern player. His lifetime batting average of .358, compiled over 23 years, is the second-highest ever and his .577 slugging average ranks seventh all-time.

Rogers Hornsby's single-minded commitment to the game was legendary. He once said: "People ask me what I do in the winter when there's no baseball. I'll tell you what I do. I stare out the window and wait for spring."

JANUARY 8:

Funeral services are held today for Rogers Hornsby in Chicago. Unlike Ty Cobb's funeral, today's service is attended by a number of baseball figures, including AL president Will Harridge, Hall of Fame director Sid Keener, and former players and managers Clarence "Pants" Rowland, Lou Boudreau, Charles "Gabby" Hartnett, Ted Lyons, Ray Schalk, and Elvin Tappe. Hornsby will be buried in Austin, Texas, on January 10.

JANUARY 14:

Baltimore obtains the left side of an infield — shortstop Luis Aparicio (.241, seven homers) and third baseman Al Smith (.292, 16 homers) – from the White Sox for pitcher Hoyt Wilhelm (7-10, 1.94 ERA, 15 saves), outfielder Pete Ward .143 in eight games), shortstop Ron Hansen (.173 in 71 games), and outfielder Dave Nicholson (.173, nine homers in 97 games).

JANUARY 29:

The Washington Senators are sold by General Elwood R. "Pete" Quesada and his partners to James H. Johnston, James H. Lemon, and George M. Bunker, who become the team's majority owners.

The first modern major leaguer to play with eyeglasses, Lee Meadows, dies at age 68 in Daytona Beach, Florida. Known as Specs, he pitched in the majors from 1915 through 1929 with the Cardinals, Phillies, and Pirates, compiling a 188-180 record with a 3.38 ERA. In 1926 he won 20 games for Pittsburgh.

FEBRUARY 4:

Flushing Meadows Stadium – home of the New York Mets – officially becomes William A. Shea Municipal Stadium through a bill signed today by New York City Mayor Robert F. Wagner.

FEBRUARY 27:

With a $100,000 contract in his pocket, Mickey Mantle reports to the Yankees' spring training camp.

FEBRUARY 28:

Eppa Rixey dies at age 71 in Terrace Park, Ohio, a month and a day after being elected to the Hall of Fame. Rixey, known as Eppa Jephtha, pitched for 21 years with the Phillies and Reds, winning 266 and losing 251. His career ERA was 3.15. In 1922, Rixey led NL pitchers with 25 wins. That season he pitched 313 ⅓ innings.

APRIL 1:

The Duke of Flatbush returns to New York City. Duke Snider, the former star of the Brooklyn Dodgers, is

"I stare out the window and wait for spring."
– *Rogers Hornsby, on the off-season*

APRIL 13
The Reds' Pete Rose gets his first major league hit – a triple – against the Pirates.

purchased from Los Angeles by the Mets for $40,000. Snider, who spent 16 years with the Dodgers in two cities, hit .278 last year in 80 games.

APRIL 8:

The Detroit Tigers acquire 20-year-old right-hander Denny McLain on waivers from the White Sox system. McLain appears in three games for the Tigers in 1963, going 2-1 with a 4.29 ERA.

APRIL 10:

Retired Air Force Colonel Robert V. Whitlow becomes "athletic director" of the Cubs in another experiment by the team's owner Philip K. Wrigley. It is the first time a major league team has had an athletic director.

THE SEASON

APRIL 11:

Duke Snider registers his first home run as a New York Met after belting 389 homers during his previous years with the Brooklyn and Los Angeles Dodgers. Today's round-tripper is hit off the Atlanta Braves' starter Warren Spahn. Despite the Duke's long ball, the Mets lose, 6-1.

Pete Rose of the Reds gets his first major league hit – a triple – off pitcher Bob Friend of the Pirates.

APRIL 19:

At the Polo Grounds, Hank Aaron hits his 300th career home run. The landmark round-tripper comes against the Mets' Roger Craig.

APRIL 28:

Hall of Fame umpire Tom Connolly dies. Connolly, inducted into the Hall of Fame in 1953, worked in the NL from 1898 to 1900 and in the AL from 1901 to 1931. Appointed chief of staff of AL umpires after the 1931 season, he worked until he was 83 and then served on the rules committee.

MAY 3:

San Francisco's Willie Mays is honored with a night at the Polo Grounds, the scene of many of his greatest moments. A total of 49,431 fans turn out to cheer Mays, but the spotlight falls on another old New York center fielder, Duke Snider, who hits two home runs for his new team, the Mets. The Giants go on to win the game, 5-3.

Dickie Kerr, the honest 1919 White Sox pitcher, dies today in Houston at age 64. While eight of his teammates were involved in a fix, Kerr was pitching his heart out in the World Series against the Reds and won two games. He later was disciplined by Commissioner Kenesaw Mountain Landis for a minor infraction not directly connected to the Black Sox scandal. He was out of baseball in 1922, 1923, and 1924, and returned briefly in 1925.

Asked to name the greatest pitcher of all time, 1970s-80s pitcher Bill "Spaceman" Lee selects Dickie Kerr of the Black Sox. "Had to be," says Lee. "He won two World Series games when eight guys on his team were trying to lose."

The Braves' Bob Shaw commits three balks in the third inning and five for the game – a major league record – as the Cubs beat Atlanta, 5-3. Shaw walks Billy Williams, who scores on the three balks. Shaw is ejected in the fifth for arguing.

MAY 8:

In St. Louis, Stan Musial hits a home run in an 11-5 loss to the Dodgers. It is Stan the Man's

Lefty Sandy Koufax is nearly unhittable.

Juan Marichal gets a good angle on hitters.

1,357th career extra-base hit. With that, Musial tops Babe Ruth's long-held major league record.

MAY 11:

Sandy Koufax no-hits San Francisco, 8-0, in Los Angeles. The Giants' only base-runner is Ed Bailey, who draws an eighth-inning walk with one out. Harvey Kuenn bounces back to Koufax to end the game. Koufax strikes out four. The losing pitcher is Bob G. Miller.

MAY 17:

Don Nottebart of the Colt .45s no-hits the Phillies today, 4-1, in Houston. Only 8,223 fans are at hand to see Nottebart handle the Phillies in two hours and 12 minutes. Nottebart walks three and strikes out eight. Don Hoak's sacrifice fly in the fifth inning leads to an unearned run for Philadelphia. Jack Hamilton is the game's losing pitcher.

MAY 21:

The Reds' Jim Maloney strikes out eight straight Milwaukee Braves – 16 for the game – on the way to a 2-0 victory.

MAY 22:

Mickey Mantle, batting left-handed in Yankee Stadium against Bill Fischer of the Athletics, opens the 11th inning with a home run off the third tier of Yankee Stadium, 374 feet from home plate. It just misses going out of the stadium, and Professor J.E. McDonald, a senior physicist at the University of Arizona, estimates it would have traveled 620 feet

MAY 11
Sandy Koufax no-hits the Giants, 8-0, and just misses a perfect game, with one walk.

JUNE 15
Juan Marichal of the Giants twirls a 1-0 no-hitter against the Houston Colt .45s.

if it hadn't hit the right-field facade. Mantle describes it as "the hardest ball I ever hit." Mantle's homer wins the game, 8-7.

Gil Hodges is named manager today of the Senators, replacing Mickey Vernon. Hodges played with the Mets, hitting .227 in 11 games. The Senators are 14-26 so far this season under Vernon after losing 101 games last year.

MAY 23:

The Senators sell outfielder Jim Piersall (.245 in 29 games) to the Mets. The transaction is linked to the signing of Gil Hodges (.227 in 11 games) as Washington's manager.

JUNE 5:

Mickey Mantle breaks his left foot when his spikes become entangled in a wire fence while he is going after a shot off the bat of Brooks Robinson at Memorial Stadium in Baltimore. He also damages ligaments and cartilage in his knee. Some Baltimore fans cheer Mantle's injury. Mantle is sidelined for 61 games as a result of the injury.

JUNE 9:

In baseball's first-ever Sunday night game, the Houston Colt .45s beat the San Francisco Giants, 3-0, at the Colt Stadium. The game is scheduled at night because of the intense daytime heat in Houston, and 17,437 turn up. Dick "Turk" Farrell and Hal "Skinny" Brown combine for the Houston shutout, which is the Giants' seventh straight loss.

At Wrigley Field Ernie Banks smacks three homers – two against Sandy Koufax – but the visiting Dodgers beat the Cubs, 11-8.

JUNE 14:

Former Dodgers' center fielder and idol of Brooklyn Duke Snider hits his 400th career home run. It comes against Bob Purkey of the Reds in a 10-3 Mets' win at Crosley Field.

JUNE 15:

Giants right-hander Juan Marichal no-hits the visiting Houston Colt .45s, 1-0, at Candlestick Park. In the first no-hitter for the Giants since Carl Hubbell in 1929 and the first by a Latino in the major leagues, Marichal strikes out five, walks two, faces 29 batters, and throws only 89 pitches. It also is Marichal's sixth consecutive win and 10th of the season.

The losing pitcher, Dick Drott, gives the Giants only three hits, but the eighth inning is his downfall – Jim Davenport and Chuck Hiller hit back-to-back doubles for the Giants' only run. For Houston, Al Spangler walks in the fifth inning and Bob Aspromonte in the seventh inning.

The Cardinals obtain pitcher Lew Burdette (6-5) from the Braves for catcher-first baseman Gene Oliver (.225 in 39 games) and minor league pitcher Bob Sadowski. Burdette was the Braves hero in the 1957 World Series when he was 3-0 with a 0.67 ERA.

JUNE 19:

At Fenway Park, the Tigers' William "Gates" Brown homers against Don Heffner, becoming the first black player to hit a round-tripper in his first major league at-bat.

JUNE 21:

Today the Cleveland Indians sign free-agent pitcher Early Wynn (7-15, 4.46 ERA with the Chicago White Sox in 1961). When he joins the Tribe, Wynn is just one victory short of 300 for his major league career.

JUNE 23:

Mets' outfielder Jim Piersall writes his own chapter in the zany history of the team. He runs backwards around the bases after hitting his 100th career home run off Phillies pitcher Dallas Green, who is not at all amused. Piersall's home run comes in the third inning of the opener of a Polo Grounds doubleheader. The Mets win both games, 5-0 and 4-1.

After the game, Piersall explains: "That way I can see where I've been. I always know where I'm going." Manager Casey Stengel has a different reaction: "There's room for only one clown on this team."

JUNE 26:

Negro Leagues infielder Jud Wilson today dies at the age of 64 in Washington, D.C. Wilson, who hit .408 in 1927, was a ferocious competitor known as Boojum – supposedly for the sound his hits made hitting outfield fences. In 24 years, he batted .347 and primarily played first base.

JUNE 28:

Frank "Home Run" Baker dies of a stroke in Trappe, Maryland,

TRIVIA

Willie Mays bats in the neighborhood of .700 against the Yankees' Whitey Ford. When Ford fails to make this year's All-Star team, he wires Mays: "Dear Willie – Sorry – Whitey."

HISTORY

Injuries took their toll on the Yankees M&M combination. Collectively, Mickey Mantle and Roger Maris appeared in 155 games and managed only 484 at-bats. Mantle appeared in only 65 games, hitting .314 with 15 home runs and 35 RBI. Maris played in 90 games; his average was .269 with 23 home runs and 53 RBI. In 1961, the two combined for 115 home runs and 270 RBI.

at age 77. Inducted into the Hall of Fame in 1955, Baker played 13 years with the Athletics and Yankees, hitting .307 with 96 home runs and 1,013 RBI. Despite his low home run total – by today's standards – Baker was a power hitter in his day, leading the AL in homers four times and hitting two in 1911 World Series.

JULY 2:

In an old-fashioned pitching duel at Candlestick Park, San Francisco's Juan Marichal beats Milwaukee and Warren Spahn, 1-0, in 16 innings on a Willie Mays home run. Spahn goes 15 1/3, allowing nine hits and only one walk. Marichal yields eight hits and strikes out 10. The game takes four hours and 10 minutes to play.

JULY 9:

The NL wins the All-Star Game, 5-3, at Cleveland. The game marks Stan Musial's record 24th appearance; he lines out as a pinch hitter in the fifth. The NL is paced by Willie Mays, who drives in two runs and robs Joe Pepitone of an extra-base hit. The winning pitcher is Larry Jackson; Jim Bunning is tagged with the loss.

JULY 11:

The Yankees' Roger Maris is hospitalized for surgery on rectal fissures. Maris, who hit his historic 61 home runs in 1961 and 33 last year, misses a total of 72 games in 1963. His home run production falls to 23 and his RBI total to 53.

JULY 13:

Early Wynn of the Indians wins his 300th career game in Kansas City in his eighth try for the coveted mark. The 43-year-old righthander goes five innings in a 7-4 win and gets four innings of relief help from Jerry Walker in the second game of a doubleheader. Moe Drabowsky takes the loss. Wynn gave up all three runs in the fifth. He gave up six hits, struck out three, and walked three in his stint. He now has a career total of 1,765 walks, the most ever, surpassing Bob Feller's 1,764. Wynn, who began his major league career in 1939 and overcame eight seasons with the Senators, becomes the 14th pitcher to reach 300. He and Warren Spahn are the only active players at that mark. The A's took the opener, 6-5; John Wyatt was the winning pitcher.

JULY 19:

Roy Sievers of the Phillies hits his 300th career home run with one out and one on in the ninth inning against Roger Craig of the Mets. The Phillies win, 2-1, on the Sievers home run; Craig loses his 13th straight.

JULY 22:

The New York Mets now have only one clown. The team releases outfielder Jim Piersall, who was hitting .194 in 40 games with the team.

Casey Stengel had conflicting feelings about Piersall, whom he described as "the greatest defensive outfielder I ever saw." On another occasion he said: "He's great but you gotta play him in a cage."

JULY 26:

In Houston, the Mets add to their unwanted major league record by losing their 21st consecutive road game. The Colt .45s beat the Mets, 1-0, on a combined five-hitter by Bob Bruce and Hal Woodeshick. The loser is Roger Craig, his 16th straight. John Bateman's eighth-inning home run is the game's only tally. Yesterday, the Mets bowed to the Colt .45s, 7-3, to set the major league record on a grand slam home run by Bob Aspromonte off the loser, Tracy Stallard. Dick "Turk" Farrell was the winner.

JULY 31:

The Indians become the first AL team to hit four consecutive home runs. The round-trippers are hit in the nightcap of a twinbill off the Angels' Paul Foytack with two out in the sixth inning by Woodie Held, pitcher Pedro Ramos, Tito Francona, and Larry Brown. The Indians were trailing, 5-1, at home, before the homer barrage; they win 9-5. Pedro Ramos, who hits another home run today, is the winning pitcher and strikes out 15. The Indians won the opener, 1-0, behind Arnold "Barry" Latman. Fred Whitfield's home run is the only run in that game.

AUGUST 4:

Mickey Mantle returns as a pinch hitter in the second game of a doubleheader at Yankee Stadium and hits a seventh-inning home run against the Orioles. Mantle's 410-foot home run into left field off the second pitch from left-hander George Brunert ties the score at 10-10.

JULY 2
Juan Marichal and Warren Spahn battle in a 16-inning tilt, won by the Giants, 1-0.

AUGUST 21
The Pirates' Jerry Lynch sets a major league record with his 15th career pinch-hit homer.

Says Mantle: "The ovation actually chilled me." The Yankees go on to win 11-10 in 10 innings. The Yankees lost the opener, 7-2.

While Yankee fans are cheering Mantle in New York, Mets fans are groaning over pitcher Roger Craig in Milwaukee. The hapless Mets' hurler ties an NL record with his 18th straight loss, bowing to the Braves, 2-1. Craig is the main culprit in the loss; his wild pickoff throw to first base enables Lou Klimchock to score all the way with the game's winning run.

AUGUST 5:

John Clarkson, Elmer Flick, Sam Rice, and Eppa Rixey are inducted into the Hall of Fame. Clarkson, who died in 1909, pitched for 12 seasons from 1882 to 1894. He compiled a lifetime record of 326-177 with a 2.81 ERA, 485 complete games, 1,978 strikeouts, and 37 shutouts. In 1885, he was 53-16 with a 1.85 ERA and in 1889, 49-19. Flick, an outfielder and great all-around player, spent 13 seasons in the majors, batting .313, hitting 166 triples, and stealing 334 bases. He hit .300 or better in eight seasons, and in 1905 with the Cleveland Naps, he led the AL in batting with .306. He split his career with the Phillies and Cleveland. Rice played for 20 years – 19 with the Senators and one with the Indians – compiling a lifetime average of .322 with 351 stolen bases and 184 triples. An outfielder, he hit .300 or better 15 times and batted .302 in three World Series. Rixey, who died earlier this year, was a six-foot, five-inch left-hander who compiled a 266-251 record with a 3.15 ERA and 39 shutouts over a 21-year career with the Phillies and Reds. He appeared in the 1915 World Series with Philadelphia.

According to Paul Dickson, Rixey's reaction to his election to the Hall of Fame was: "They're really scraping the bottom of the barrel, aren't they?" He once visited the Hall of Fame and sent postcards that read, "I finally made it to Cooperstown – for one day."

AUGUST 7:

In Detroit, the Tigers play errorless ball in beating the Red Sox, 5-4. It is the 12th game in a row for the Tigers without an error – a major league record. Al Kaline's three-run homer in the seventh inning against Dick Radatz wins the game.

AUGUST 9:

With an opportunity to set a major league record for consecutive losses, Roger Craig does something he has been unable to do since April 29 – he wins a game. Craig can thank teammate Jim Hickman. The Mets' outfielder hits a two-out, bases-loaded home run off the Cubs' pitcher Lindy McDaniel in the bottom of the ninth to give the Mets a 7-3 win at the Polo Grounds. Frank J. Thomas of the Mets had homered earlier. Craig comes up one short of the major league record set by the Philadelphia Athletics' Jack Nabors in 1916. Craig is now 3-20, 13-44 in two seasons with New York. The game's losing pitcher is Paul Toth.

AUGUST 12:

Stan "The Man" Musial announces he will retire at the end of the season, his 22nd in the major leagues. Musial, who will join the Cardinals' front office, breaks the news at the team's annual picnic.

AUGUST 13:

Warren Spahn fans the Dodgers' Al Ferrara in the ninth for a career total of 2,382 strikeouts, the most ever for a left-handed pitcher. The previous record holder was Rube Waddell, who set the mark in 1910.

AUGUST 21:

Jerry Lynch sets a major league record with his 15th career pinch-hit home run. Today's round-tripper gives the Pirates a 7-6 win over the Cubs.

AUGUST 23:

When Warren Spahn steps on the mound today for the Braves, he sets an NL record for most starts – 601 – topping the previous mark set by the great pitcher Grover Cleveland Alexander. Earlier in the day, Spahn appeared before the cameras as a German sergeant for an episode of the TV series *Combat*. Milwaukee beats the Dodgers, 6-1.

AUGUST 25:

There's lots of breeze as the Red Sox meet the Indians in a doubleheader. A total of 17 Boston players and 27 Indians fan in the two games. Boston wins the opener, 8-3; Bill Monboquette of the Red Sox fans 11. The Indians win the nightcap in 15 innings on a single by John "Tito" Francona; Bob Heffner of Cleveland strikes out 12.

HISTORY

John Paciorek injures his back and never again plays in the major leagues. *The Baseball Encyclopedia* records his lifetime batting average as 1.000. His brother Tom enjoyed an 18-year career and a lifetime batting average of .282. A third brother, Jim, played one season with Milwaukee, appearing in 48 games and batting .228.

"For the Washington Senators, the worst time of the year is the baseball season."
– *Sportswriter Roger Kahn*

TRIVIA

In the *50th Anniversary Hall of Fame Yearbook*, historian Lee Allen wrote: "[Elmer] Flick reported with a bat that he had turned out for himself on a lathe and kept in a canvas bag."

AUGUST 27:

At Candlestick Park, Willie Mays reaches another career milestone. In the third inning with the bases empty, he blasts a home run against the Cardinals' Curt Simmons. It is Mays's 400th career four-bagger. The Giants win the game, 7-2.

AUGUST 28:

For the second straight day, the Senators-Twins game that was scheduled for Washington, D.C., is canceled because of the massive civil rights march in the nation's capital. Jackie Robinson is among the participants in the demonstration.

AUGUST 29:

After two postponements, the Senators and Twins play a doubleheader in Washington. Despite the cancellation of batting practice because of rain, the Twins hit 12 home runs. In the opener, won by the Twins, 14-2, they hit a major league-tying eight. Harmon Killebrew and Vic Power have two each; Bernie Allen, Bob Allison, Jimmie Hall, and Rich Rollins, one apiece. In the nightcap, they hit four more.

In *Jackie Robinson: A Biography*, author Arnold Rampersad writes of the March on Washington: "To Jack...the day was an unparalleled triumph. Instead of fights and rioting that some predicted, the mood was one of self-confidence and shared humanity. 'I have never been so proud to be a Negro,' he wrote. 'I have never been so proud to be an American.' The sight of thousands of blacks and whites marching together for a common cause stirred him: 'One had to be deeply moved as (one) stood, watching Negroes and whites, marching hand in hand, singing songs of freedom,' he wrote. He was proud, too, of his family. Jack watched (his wife) Rachel's eyes moisten as, spellbound, she listened to Dr. King's 'I Have a Dream' oration."

AUGUST 27
Willie Mays connects for his 400th career homer in a 7-2 Giants win over the Cardinals.

SEPTEMBER 6
The Alous – Felipe, Jesus, Matty – are the first brother trio to play in the same outfield.

SEPTEMBER 2:

Yogi Berra homers at Yankee Stadium against Kansas City's Moe Drabowsky. It is Berra's 358th career round-tripper and will be the last of his career.

SEPTEMBER 6:

In Washington, the Senators beat the Indians, 7-2 – a game of small consequence except that it is the 100,000th played in the major leagues.

SEPTEMBER 8:

Improved with age: At Philadelphia's Connie Mack Stadium, 42-year-old Warren Spahn and the Braves beat the Phillies 3-2. It is Spahn's 20th win of the season, a feat he has accomplished 13 times, tying him with Christy Mathewson for the modern NL record. (The record for the most 20-win seasons belongs to the American League's Cy Young with 16.) Spahn, who moves to 20-5 for the season, now has 347 career wins. Today he hurls a complete game, allowing nine hits, with no walks and no strikeouts. Gene Oliver's two-run home run in the top of the eighth inning provides the winning margin in the game.

SEPTEMBER 10:

Randy Johnson is born in Walnut Creek, California.

In a baseball first, the Alou brothers make all three outs for the Giants in the eighth inning of a game against the Mets. Felipe is retired as the lead-off hitter; Jesus and Matty as pinch hitters. The Mets win, 4-2.

SEPTEMBER 15:

The Alou brothers accomplish something that eluded the three DiMaggio brothers. Playing in today's game for San Francisco against the Mets, the Alous – Felipe, Jesus, and Matty – become the first three siblings to appear in the same outfield together.

SEPTEMBER 16:

Johnny Niggeling, who had several effective seasons as a pitcher in the 1940s, hangs himself in Le Mars, Iowa. His best season was 1942 when he was 15-11 with a 2.66 ERA for the Browns.

SEPTEMBER 18:

In Los Angeles, 24-year-old Steve Barber beats the Angels, 3-1, to become the Orioles' first-ever 20-game win- ner. Barber gets relief help from Dick Hall.

In the fourth inning, Jim Hickman of the Mets hits the last home run in the last two hours and 14 minutes of baseball ever at the storied Polo Grounds, with only 1,752 fans attending. The Phillies, behind Chris Short's complete game, win the game, 5-1. Craig Anderson takes the loss. Bobby Wine's two-run triple is the big hit for Philadelphia. Ted Schreiber of the Mets hits into a double play to end the game. The Mets will move to their new home in Flushing, New York, next season, and the Polo Grounds will be demolished.

SEPTEMBER 21:

Cecil Fielder is born in Los Angeles.

SEPTEMBER 25:

Today the Cardinals announce they will retire Stan Musial's number 6. He will become a vice president of the team.

SEPTEMBER 27:

The Orioles' Stu Miller relieves and earns a save against the visiting Tigers, setting a pair of AL records in the process – 71 appearances and 59 games finished. He also records his 26th save of the year. Baltimore wins, 5-2.

Youth will be served at Colt Stadium in Houston. Manager Harry Craft starts an all-rookie lineup against the Mets. The starters average 19 years, four months old, and before third-year outfielder Carl Warwick enters the game, 15 rookies appear. The Mets win the game, 10-3, behind their "grizzled" 28-year-old pitcher Al Jackson.

Here is Harry Craft's all-rookie lineup: BrockDavis, LF; Jimmy Wynn, CF; Aaron Pointer, RF; Rusty Staub, 1B; Joe Morgan, 2B; Glenn Vaughan, 3B; Sonny Jackson, SS; Jerry Grote, C; and Jay Dahl, P. This is 17-year-old Dahl's only big league appearance.

SEPTEMBER 28:

The Los Angeles Dodgers' Tommy Davis gets two hits in a 12-3 loss today to the Philadelphia Phillies. The two hits enable Davis to finish the season at .326, winning the NL batting title. At 24 years old, he becomes the youngest player in NL history to win two consecutive batting championships.

CULTURE

"Our Old Home Team" is recorded by Nat King Cole.

"I will always remember this day. For me it is both a great joy and a great sorrow. It is a joy because of this wonderful day for me, and it is a farewell."
– Stan Musial, at Busch Stadium for his final game

RULES

On January 26, the Major League Rules Committee increases the strike zone. It now will be delineated by the top of the shoulders and the bottom of the knees – the same dimensions it was in the 1950s. In practice, the strike zone has contracted over the years.

SEPTEMBER 29:

St. Louis says goodbye to its hero, Stan Musial. For his final game in a Cardinals uniform, 27,576 fans show up at Busch Stadium. In pre-game ceremonies, Stan the Man tells them: "I will always remember this day. For me it is both a great joy and a great sorrow. It is a joy because of this wonderful day for me, and it is a farewell."

In his first at-bat, Musial is fanned by the Reds' Jim Maloney. Then in the fourth, he singles past second baseman Pete Rose for the first hit of the game. In the sixth, he singles to drive in the first run of the game. It is his 3,630th hit and 1,951st RBI. Musial has identical career hit totals at home and on the road – 1,815. His final career average is .331. After Musial reaches first, Gary Kolb comes in t o run for him and the curtain falls on a singular career. The Cardinals go on to win the game, 3-2, in 14 innings.

Hank Aaron hits his 44th home run of the season, enabling him to tie the Giants' Willie McCovey for the NL title. Each of the sluggers wears number 44.

A brief, bright light flickers for Houston. Outfielder John Paciorek makes his major league debut with three singles in three at-bats, a walk, three RBI, and three runs scored as the Colt .45s beat the Mets, 13-4.

REGULAR SEASON WRAP-UP:

Without a .300 hitter, Ralph Houk's New York Yankees win the pennant with 104 victories, 10 1/2 games ahead of the White Sox. Elston Howard leads the team with .287. Howard (28), Joe Pepitone (27), Tom Tresh (25), and Roger Maris (23) are the top home run hitters. Whitey Ford leads the staff with a 24-7 record.

The Dodgers, managed by Walter Alston, are built around the arms of Sandy Koufax (25-5, 1.88 ERA, 306 strikeouts) and Don Drysdale (19-7, 2.63 ERA, 251 strikeouts). Tommy Davis (.326, 16 homers, 88 RBI) and Frank "Hondo" Howard (.273, 28 homers, 64 RBI) are the main offensive threats on the club.

Dick Stuart of the Red Sox hits 42 homers and drives in 188 runs; he is the first with 40 round-trippers and 100 RBI in each league. Dave Nicholson of the White Sox strikes out a record 175 times. The 1963 season ends with each league totaling the lowest composite batting averages since 1910. AL hitters combine for .247; the NL is even worse – .245.

OCTOBER 2:

World Series, game one. In New York, the Dodgers beat the Yankees, 5-2. Sandy Koufax fans a World Series record 15 batters in a complete game six-hitter. Yankee pitchers Whitey Ford, Stan Williams, and Steve Hamilton strike out 10 Dodgers – the 25 total also constitutes a record. John Roseboro hits a three-run homer in the second off Ford – who is charged with the loss – giving Koufax all the support he needs. Tom Tresh accounts for the Yankee runs with a two-run home run.

OCTOBER 3:

World Series, game two. In New York, Johnny Podres goes eight and a third to beat the Yankees, 4-1. Ron Perranoski pitches the last two-thirds. Willie Davis doubles to drive in two runs in the first inning when Roger Maris slips in right field. Bill Skowron homers for Los Angeles. The contest's losing pitcher is Al Downing.

OCTOBER 4:

World Series, game three. In Los Angeles, Don Drysdale's three-hitter beats the Yankees and Jim Bouton, 1-0. Drysdale strikes out nine batters and walks one in his complete game performance. The only run of the game comes early: Tommy Davis singles in Jim Gilliam in the first.

OCTOBER 6:

World Series, game four. In Los Angeles, Sandy Koufax goes the distance to beat the Yankees, 2-1, and the Dodgers sweep New York for the first time. Whitey Ford pitches well in defeat but is done in when Joe Pepitone loses the ball against the background of the crowd on a throw from Clete Boyer in the third inning. Willie Davis's sacrifice fly then scores Jim Gilliam with what becomes the winning run. Koufax completes the Series with two victories and 23 strikeouts and is named MVP. Tommy Davis bats .400 and Bill Skowron, playing against his former

OCTOBER 6
The Dodgers complete a sweep of the Yankees in the World Series behind Sandy Koufax.

NOVEMBER 7
Yankees' catcher Elston Howard is the first black player to win the AL MVP Award.

teammates, .385. The Yankees top hitter is Elston Howard at .333.

POST-SEASON

OCTOBER 12:

The Polo Grounds is the site for one more baseball contest – the Hispanic All-Star Game, which features Minnie Minoso, Tony Oliva, Roberto Clemente, Luis Aparicio, and Vic Power. The NL beats the AL, 5-2. Al McBean is the winning pitcher; Pedro Ramos is charged with the loss. Juan Marichal fans six in four innings of work.

OCTOBER 14:

After he gets his 300th victory, Early Wynn is released by the Indians and will become a coach for the team.

OCTOBER 24:

New York manager Ralph Houk turns over the reins of the Yankees to Yogi Berra and becomes the team's general manager, replacing Roy Hamey, who is retiring. Houk won three pennants and two World Series in three years. Says Berra, "I've been with the Yankees 17 years, watching games and learning. You can see a lot by observing."

YOGI BERRA ON SANDY KOUFAX: "I CAN SEE HOW HE WON 25 GAMES, BUT WHAT I CAN'T UNDERSTAND IS HOW HE LOST FIVE."

NOVEMBER 4:

Roger Craig, coming off a nightmare 5-22 season with the Mets, makes his getaway. He is traded today to the first-division Cardinals for outfielder George Altman (.274, nine homers) and minor league pitcher Bill Wakefield.

NOVEMBER 7:

Elston Howard, the first black to play for the Yankees, becomes the first black Most Valuable Player in American League history. The catcher appeared in 135 games and hit .287, with 28 home runs and 85 RBI.

NOVEMBER 18:

Detroit trades outfielder Rocky Colavito (.271, 22 homers, 91 RBI) and pitcher Bob Anderson (2-7, 5.02 ERA) plus $50,000 to the Kansas City Athletics for second baseman Jerry Lumpe (.271, five home runs) and pitchers Ed Rakow (9-10, 3.92 ERA) and Dave Wickersham (12-15, 4.09 ERA).

DECEMBER 3:

The Giants break up the Alou brothers. They send outfielder Felipe Alou (.281, 20 homers), pitcher Billy Hoeft (2-0, 4.44 ERA), catcher Ed Bailey (.263, 21 homers), and infielder Ernie Bowman (.184 in 81 games) to the Braves. In return, the Giants receive catcher Del Crandall (.201 in 86 games) and pitchers Bob Shaw (7-11, 2.66 ERA) and Bob Hendley (9-9, 3.93 ERA).

DECEMBER 4:

The Detroit Tigers remain active in the off-season trading market. This time they send their pitcher Jim Bunning (12-13, 3.88 ERA) and catcher Gus Triandos (.239, 14 home runs) to the Philadelphia Phillies for outfielder Don Demeter (.258, 22 homers) and pitcher Jack Hamilton (2-1, 5.40 ERA).

DECEMBER 10:

Chicago says goodbye to an old friend today. The White Sox send veteran second baseman Jacob "Nellie" Fox (.260), who has been with the Windy City ballclub for 14 major league seasons, to the Houston Colt .45s in exchange for pitcher Jim Golden (0-1, 5.68 ERA) and minor league hurler Danny Murphy plus cash. Fox will appear in 133 games for Houston in 1964 (.265) and only 21 in his final year.

"Show me a guy who can't pitch inside and I'll show you a loser."
– *Sandy Koufax*

THE BEST OF 1963

NATIONAL LEAGUE

HITTERS

Batting Average:
Herman "Tommy" Davis, Los Angeles Dodgers, .326

Slugging Average:
Hank Aaron, Milwaukee Braves, .586

Home Runs:
Willie McCovey, San Francisco Giants; Aaron, 44

Runs Batted In:
Hank Aaron, 130

Hits:
Vada Pinson, Cincinnati Reds, 204

Stolen Bases:
Maury Wills, Los Angeles Dodgers, 40

PITCHERS

Wins:
Sandy Koufax, Los Angeles Dodgers;
Juan Marichal, San Francisco Giants, 25

Strikeouts:
Sandy Koufax, 306

Earned Run Average:
Sandy Koufax, 1.88

Winning Percentage:
Ron Perranoski, Los Angeles Dodgers, .842

Saves:
Lindy McDaniel, Chicago Cubs, 22

Most Valuable Player:
Sandy Koufax, Los Angeles Dodgers

Cy Young Award:
Sandy Koufax, Los Angeles Dodgers

Rookie of the Year:
Pete Rose, Cincinnati Reds

AMERICAN LEAGUE

HITTERS

Batting Average:
Carl Yastrzemski, Boston Red Sox, .321

Slugging Average:
Harmon Killebrew, Minnesota Twins, .555

Home Runs:
Harmon Killebrew, 45

Runs Batted In:
Dick Stuart, Boston Red Sox, 118

Hits:
Carl Yastrzemski, 183

Stolen Bases:
Luis Aparicio, Baltimore Orioles, 40

PITCHERS

Wins:
Ed "Whitey" Ford, 24

Strikeouts:
Camilo Pascual, Minnesota Twins, 202

Earned Run Average:
Gary Peters, Chicago White Sox, 2.33

Winning Percentage:
Whitey Ford, .774

Saves:
Stu Miller, Baltimore Orioles, 27

Most Valuable Player:
Elston Howard, New York Yankees

Rookie of the Year:
Gary Peters, Chicago White Sox

1964

"The first game I ever saw was at the Polo Grounds. It was like seeing Oz."
– *Pitcher John Curtis*

NEWS

LYNDON JOHNSON BEATS BARRY GOLDWATER IN LANDSLIDE

Martin Luther King receives Nobel Peace Prize

OSWALD ACTED ALONE, SAYS WARREN COMMISSION

SIX DIE IN HARLEM RIOTS IN NEW YORK

President Johnson signs Civil Rights Act

ALASKAN EARTHQUAKE KILLS 114

BEATLES TOUR AMERICA

DOUGLAS MACARTHUR DIES

WORLD'S LONGEST SUSPENSION BRIDGE – VERRAZANO-NARROWS – OPENS IN NEW YORK

North Vietnam reportedly attacks USS *Maddox* in Gulf of Tonkin; U.S. retaliates

THREE CIVIL RIGHTS WORKERS SLAIN IN MISSISSIPPI

SURGEON GENERAL WARNS OF HEALTH DANGERS FROM CIGARETTES

PRE-SEASON

JANUARY 6:

The AL brass rejects Charles O. Finley's bid to move the Athletics from Kansas City to Louisville, Kentucky.

JANUARY 23:

Warren Spahn signs an $85,000 contract with the Braves for 1964, becoming baseball's highest paid pitcher.

FEBRUARY 15:

Ken Hubbs dies in a plane crash in Utah Lake, Utah. Hubbs was returning from a Brigham Young University basketball tournament when his Cessna 172 crashed on a frozen lake near Provo. Hubbs, who had his license only two weeks, was piloting the plane despite bad weather and poor visibility. Also dying in the accident is 23-year-old Dennis Doyle. Hubbs, the regular second baseman for the Cubs, was the 1962 NL Rookie of the Year.

APRIL 1:

In Tucson, Arizona, where the Indians are in spring training, manager George "Birdie" Tebbetts is hospitalized with a heart attack. George Strickland will be named the team's interim manager.

APRIL 8:

Jim Umbricht, a pitcher for the Colt .45s, dies of cancer in Houston, at the age of 33. Umbricht was 4-3 last season and 9-5 in five years with the Pittsburgh Pirates and Houston.

APRIL 9:

The Braves send Milwaukee-born catcher Bob Uecker (.250 in 13 games) to the Cardinals for outfielder Gary Kolb (.271 in 75 games) and catcher Jim Coker (.200 in four games with the Giants).

APRIL 10:

The legendary Polo Grounds, the site of 14 World Series and countless feats of baseball greatness, is razed to make room for a housing project.

APRIL 11:

Bret Saberhagen is born in Chicago Heights, Illinois.

THE SEASON

APRIL 14:

Sandy Koufax goes all the way in his only opening day start, allowing no walks and

LEAGUE

Manager Alvin Dark appoints Willie Mays captain of the Giants. Mays is the first African-American player to hold a team captaincy.

Miller Huggins, as manager of the Yankees, once noted: "A manager has his cards dealt him and he must play them."

CULTURE

"Dandy Sandy," recorded by Jimmy Durante, written by Jackie Barnett and Sammy Fain, is a song about Sandy Koufax.

beating the Cardinals, 4-0, at Dodger Stadium. Frank Howard homers for Los Angeles.

APRIL 16:

Shea Stadium is dedicated in Flushing Meadows, New York. William A. Shea, after whom the $25 million ballpark is named, "christens" it by pouring water from the Harlem River (near the Polo Grounds) and the Gowanus Canal (near Ebbetts Field) on the infield.

Says Casey Stengel of Shea Stadium: "Lovely, just lovely. The park is lovelier than my team."

APRIL 17:

The New York Mets inaugurate their new ballpark in Flushing, Queens, with 48,736 fans on hand, but Shea Stadium is no more conducive to victory than the Polo Grounds. The visiting Pittsburgh Pirates beat New York, 4-3. The first hit in the stadium is a second-inning home run by the Bucs' Willie Stargell against Jack Fisher. The first Mets' hit is a Tim Harkness single in the third against Bob Friend, the game's winning pitcher. Ed Bauta gets the loss in relief of Fisher.

APRIL 20:

Former Cardinals' manager Eddie Dyer dies at age 63 in Houston. Dyer won the World Series in 1946, the first of five years he managed St. Louis. He finished second three times and fifth once. When he was offered a one-year contract after the 1950 season, he permanently left baseball for the business world. Dyer pitched for six years with the Cardinals, with a record of 15-15 and a 4.75 ERA.

APRIL 21:

At Wrigley Field, the Pirates beat the Cubs, 8-5; every run scores on a homer. Homering for the Cubs are Jimmy Stewart, Ron Santo, Andre Rodgers, Billy Cowan, and Billy Williams. For the Pirates, the home run hitters are Jim Pagliaroni and Gene Freese, with three-run homers, and Roberto Clemente and Dick "Ducky" Schofield.

Outfielder Edwin "Duke" Snider (.243, 14 homers) is sold by the Mets to the Giants.

APRIL 22:

In St. Louis, an elbow injury kayoes Sandy Koufax, and the Cardinals beat the Dodgers, 7-6. Charlie James, Carl Warwick, and Bill White homer for St. Louis. Frank Howard slams a 460-foot homer and Willie Davis adds one of his own for the Dodgers.

APRIL 23:

At Colt Stadium, knuckleball pitcher Ken Johnson of the Colt .45s becomes the first ever to lose a game without yielding a hit. Johnson holds his former team, the Reds, hitless through eight, walking two and allowing only three balls out of the infield. In the ninth, with one out, he throws wildly on a Pete Rose bunt. Rose takes second on the error and moves to third on an infield out. Second baseman Jacob "Nellie" Fox misplays a grounder by Vada Pinson, and Rose scores the game's only run. Joe Nuxhall, who allows only five hits, shuts down the Colt .45s in the bottom of the ninth to defeat Johnson. Previously, eight pitchers have allowed hits after nine innings of no-hit ball; Johnson is the first to lose a true no-hitter.

APRIL 24:

In Minnesota, the Tigers' Mickey Lolich pitches his first major league shutout, three-hitting the Twins, 5-0, and fanning seven. Jerry Lumpe bats in three runs.

MAY 2:

At Kansas City, the Twins hit four consecutive homers in the 11th inning in a 7-3 win over the Athletics. Minnesota is the third team to accomplish the feat. The home runs are hit by Tony Oliva, Bob Allison, Jimmie Hall, and Harmon Killebrew.

MAY 4:

In Milwaukee, even 73-year-old Casey Stengel gets into this one. He and 23-year-old Dennis Menke of the Braves tangle during a brawl triggered by a collision at home plate between the Mets' Ron Hunt – who is called out – and catcher Ed Bailey. Hunt, who represented the tying run, throws Bailey to the ground and the melee begins. The Braves win the game, 2-1.

It must be the full moon. While Casey Stengel is fighting a player one-third his age, a beanball war erupts today in the Cardinals-Phillies game in St. Louis. In the third inning, the Cardinals' Bob Gibson buzzes

MAY 5
With a shutout of the Mets, Warren Spahn has blanked every team in the NL.

Phillies pitcher Dennis Bennett with two straight pitches. In the bottom of the fourth, reliever Jack Baldschun hits Gibson, who throws his bat underhanded in the direction of the mound. Home plate umpire Doug Harvey ejects Gibson, but the Cardinals win the game on 14 hits, 9-2.

MAY 5:

The Braves' Warren Spahn whitewashes the Mets, 6-0. The venerable lefthander now has shut out every NL team at least once in his career.

MAY 19:

The Cardinals' Ernie Broglio throws a record-tying three wild pitches in a single inning as St. Louis loses the game to the Chicago Cubs, 7-4.

MAY 20:

In San Francisco, the Phillies defeat the Giants, 7-4, ending Juan Marichal's 12-game winning streak. Philadelphia's Johnny Callison has a home run and four singles in five at-bats in the victory.

MAY 24:

Harmon Killebrew of the Twins muscles a 471-foot home run against the Orioles' Milt Pappas today at Memorial Stadium. The baseball soars over the hedge in left center field and is the longest ever at the ballpark. Baltimore wins the game, 7-6.

MAY 25:

Ground is broken for the Cardinals' new stadium in St. Louis. The facility is expected to be ready in time for the 1966 season.

MAY 26:

At Wrigley Field, it's a rare case of Mets' muscles. Dick A. Smith has five hits, Ron Hunt four, and Charley Smith hits a homer and drives in five runs in a 19-1 New York victory. Jack Fisher backs the heavy hitting with a four-hitter.

The Mets' feeble performance and today's offensive outburst, give rise to a joke: "The Mets scored 19 runs today." "Really? Did they win?"

MAY 30:

The New York Yankees' killer is moving to the National League. The Tigers sell sore-armed pitcher Frank Lary (0-2), a two-time 20 game-winner, to the New York Mets.

MAY 31:

The Mets and Giants play the longest doubleheader in major league history – nine hours and 52 minutes – at Shea Stadium. In the opener, Juan Marichal beats Al Jackson and the Mets, 5-3. The nightcap lasts 23 innings – seven hours and 23 minutes – making it the longest game, measured by time played. It features a triple play in the 14th inning, when Orlando Cepeda lines out to Mets' shortstop Roy McMillan, who steps on second base to double up Jesus Alou and throws to Ed Kranepool at first to retire Willie Mays. Del Crandall's double and Jesus Alou's infield hit give the Giants an 8-6 win. Gaylord Perry gets the win; Galen Cisco is charged with the loss. The teams also set a record for the most innings played in one day – 32. The doubleheader begins with 57,037 fans in attendance; by the end of game two, the crowd has dwindled to fewer than 10,000.

Mets' Ed Kranepool, recalled from the Buffalo Bisons where he had played in a doubleheader yesterday, drives all night to make the game. He says, "I wanted it to go a little longer. That way, I could always say that I played in a game that started in May and ended in June."

JUNE 4:

Sandy Koufax no-hits the Phillies, 3-0, striking out 12 hitters today at Connie Mack Stadium in Philadelphia. Koufax joins Bob Feller as the only modern-era pitchers with three career no-hitters. Larry Corcoran and Cy Young also pitched three. Koufax yields only one walk, faces 27 batters, and allows only four balls out of the infield. All of the Dodgers' runs score on Frank Howard's three-run homer in the seventh inning against Chris Short.

JUNE 15:

The Cardinals obtain outfielder Lou Brock (.251 in 52 games) and pitchers Jack Spring (1-0) and Paul Toth (0-2) from the Cubs for pitchers Ernie Broglio (3-5) and Bobby Shantz (1-3) plus outfielder Doug Clemens (.205 in 33 games).

JUNE 21:

Jim Bunning of the Phillies celebrates Father's Day by pitching the first

EQUIPMENT

The Athletics' Ken Harrelson is the first player to wear batting gloves in a game.

JULY 18
Pete Rose powers the Reds' 14-4 demolition of the Phillies with his first career grand slam.

AUGUST 9
The Phillies' Jim Bunning, who no-hit the Mets on Father's Day, shuts them out.

HISTORY

While Jim Bunning becomes the first modern pitcher with no-hitters in each league (he pitched his first in 1958 for the Tigers), Gus Triandos is the first to catch one in both circuits. He was behind the plate for Hoyt Wilhelm's classic against the Yankees in 1958.

regular-season perfect game in 42 years, a 6-0 gem against the Mets today at Shea Stadium. Bunning needs only 86 pitches; the last is a strike to pinch hitter John Stephenson, the 10th to be fanned by Bunning. The last regular perfect game was pitched by Charlie Robertson in 1922; Don Larsen threw one in the 1956 World Series. In the nightcap, Rick Wise three-hits the Mets, 8-2. The Mets tie an NL record by managing only three hits in a doubleheader.

JUNE 24:

The Angels invest a staggering $300,000 in bonuses on two players. They sign University of Wisconsin outfielder Rick Reichardt for $200,000 and catcher Tom Egan, a Whittier, California, high school catcher for $100,000.

JULY 4:

The Kansas City Athletics' Manny Jiminez misses a chance for a fourth consecutive home run when today's game is called after nine innings with the score tied, 6-6, so a scheduled Independence Day fireworks demonstration can proceed as planned.

JULY 7:

The NL wins the All-Star Game on a three-run homer by Johnny Callison in the bottom of the ninth inning at Shea Stadium. Billy Williams and Ken Boyer previously had homered for the Nationals. Juan Marichal gets the win; Dick Radatz is the losing pitcher.

JULY 10:

The Giants' Jesus Alou has six consecutive hits – five singles and a home run – in a 10-3 victory over the Cubs in Chicago.

JULY 12:

Hank Aaron gets his 2,000th career hit in a 6-2 Milwaukee victory over the visiting Phillies in the nightcap of a double-header. The Braves win the opener, 4-3.

JULY 16:

President Lyndon B. Johnson signs a bill granting Little League baseball a Congressional Charter of Federal Incorporation. The Little League is the only sport with a congressional charter.

JULY 17:

Pay TV comes to baseball. Subscription Television offers the first pay cablecast of baseball – the Dodgers-Cubs game tonight in Los Angeles. The Dodgers win, 3-2, behind Don Drysdale, who strikes out 10. Robin Roberts provides his fans with a flashback – scattering 11 hits but yielding no runs – as he beats the Tigers, 5-0, for the Orioles.

> RICHIE ASHBURN, THE PHILLIES' CENTERFIELDER, ONCE OBSERVED OF KOUFAX: "EITHER HE THROWS THE FASTEST BALL I'VE EVER SEEN OR I'M GOING BLIND." ON ANOTHER OCCASION, PHILLIES MANAGER GENE MAUCH WAS ASKED IF HE RANKED KOUFAX AS THE TOP LEFT-HANDER HE'D EVER SEEN. HE REPLIED: "HE WAS THE BEST RIGHT-HANDER, TOO."

JULY 18:

In Cincinnati, the Reds' Pete Rose hits a fifth-inning grand slam homer – the first of his career – in a 14-4 victory over the Phillies.

JULY 23:

If beginnings are careers, Kansas City's Dagoberto "Bert" Campaneris is destined for his own corner in the Hall of Fame. On the first major league pitch he sees, the 22-year-old Campaneris hits a homer off Jim Kaat. Campaneris homers again in the seventh inning as the A's beat the Twins, 4-3, in 11.

JULY 24:

Barry Bonds is born in Riverside, California.

JULY 27:

Luke Appling, Urban "Red" Faber, Burleigh Grimes, Miller

Huggins, Tim Keefe, Heinie Manush, and John Montgomery Ward are inducted into the Hall of Fame. Appling, one of the very best-hitting shortstops of all time, played 20 years for the White Sox, batting .310. He led the AL in batting in 1936 with .388 and again in 1943 at .328. He hit .300 or better in 16 seasons. Faber also spent 20 years with the White Sox, compiling a 254-213 record with a 3.15 ERA, 30 shutouts, and 274 complete games. He led the AL in ERA twice and was 3-1 with a 2.33 ERA in the 1917 World Series. Grimes, who was the last legal spitball pitcher, had a 19-year major league career. He was 270-212 with a 3.53 ERA, 35 shutouts, and 314 complete games. He twice led the NL in victories – in 1921 with Brooklyn and in 1928 with Pittsburgh. He won 20 games or more five times and appeared in four World Series. Huggins, who stood five feet, six and a half inches and weighed 140, played second base for 13 years with the Cardinals and Reds, batting a respectable .265 with 324 stolen bases. But it is as the manager of the Yankees that he is celebrated. From 1918 to 1929, he led the team to six pennants and four World Series championships. He also managed the Cardinals for five years. Huggins, who was an attorney and a graduate of the University of Cincinnati Law School, died in 1929 while skipper of the Yankees. Keefe, who died in 1933, pitched from 1880 to 1893. In his 14 seasons, he was 342-225 with a 2.62 ERA, 557 complete games (third best all-time), and 40 shutouts. Manush, an outfielder, played 17 major league seasons and batted .330. While with the Tigers in 1926, he led the AL in batting with .378, one of 11 seasons in which he hit .300 or better. He also batted .378 for the 1928 Cardinals. Monte Ward was an attorney and the founder of the Players League. He was an infielder, outfielder, and pitcher. In 17 seasons – from 1878 to 1894 – he batted .275 and stole 504 bases. In seven years as a pitcher, he was 165-100 with a 2.10 ERA, 25 shutouts, and 244 complete games. Ward, who also managed in the NL and Players League, passed away in 1925.

According to The Ballplayers: *"It was said Grimes's idea of an intentional pass was four pitches at the batter's head." Grimes himself once said: "Why is it there are so many nice guys interested in baseball? Not me. I was a real bastard when I played."*

AUGUST 9:

In Philadelphia, Jim Bunning is perfect again against the Mets – until the fifth inning. On the heels of his perfect game against New York on June 21, Bunning retires every Met he faces until Joe Christopher beats out a bunt with two out in the fifth. Bunning and the Phillies win, 6-0.

AUGUST 11:

Hank Aaron hits his 362nd career home run, passing Joe DiMaggio on the all-time list. Milwaukee goes on to beat visiting Houston, 9-6.

AUGUST 12:

For the 10th time in his career – a major league record – Mickey Mantle hits "switch" homers in a game. Batting left-handed against Ray Herbert of the White Sox, Mantle rockets a ball into straightaway center field at Yankee Stadium. It carries over the 461-foot marker, clears a 22-foot background screen, and lands 15 rows into the bleachers – 502 feet from the plate. Mantle, back after missing three days with a groin pull, says, "I didn't hit it all that good." Later in the game, he hits a right-handed drive into right field. The Yankees win, 7-3; rookie Mel Stottlemyre gets a complete-game victory in his major league debut.

AUGUST 14:

By a vote of 8-2, AL owners approve a proposed sale of 80 percent of the New York Yankees to the Columbia Broadcasting System. The Angels, unhappy with their lease arrangement at Dodger Stadium, get the okay to move to Anaheim. Also in August, Commissioner Ford Frick officially notifies major league owners of his intention to step down at the end of this term – which is his third seven-year stint.

AUGUST 16:

Curt Flood of the Cardinals has eight consecutive hits in a doubleheader against the Dodgers in Los Angeles. But the Cardinals manage only a split. Sandy Koufax pitches

LEAGUE

Major league attendance is a record 21,280,341.

a seven-hitter in the opening game; Los Angeles wins, 3-0. In the nightcap, Curt Simmons limits the Dodgers to six hits and St. Louis wins the contest by a score of 4-0.

AUGUST 17:

Oscar "Happy" Felsch, one of the eight Black Sox banned from baseball for life, passes away five days before his 73rd birthday in Milwaukee. An outfielder, Felsch had a six-year batting average of .293. He hit .192 and made two errors in the fixed 1919 World Series.

AUGUST 20:

Yankees' reserve infielder Phil Linz becomes the world's most infamous harmonica player. After New York loses to the White Sox, 5-0 – its

From *Baseball: The Biographical Encyclopedia*: "Felsch's personality was described as easygoing, which may account for his nickname. He never finished elementary school, but had speed to burn and a good aptitude for batting. In 1917, he was at the top of the baseball world. He hit .308 with 102 RBI to lead Chicago to the pennant, its first since 1906. In the World Series, Felsch batted .273 as the White Sox beat the New York Giants in six games. His home run in the fourth inning of game one gave Chicago a 2-0 lead, and moundsman Eddie Cicotte made it stand up for a 2-1 victory. At that point, Felsch was 26 years old, a centerfielder with an arm that could cut down base runners, and a .300 hitter for the best team in baseball. It all disappeared very quickly."

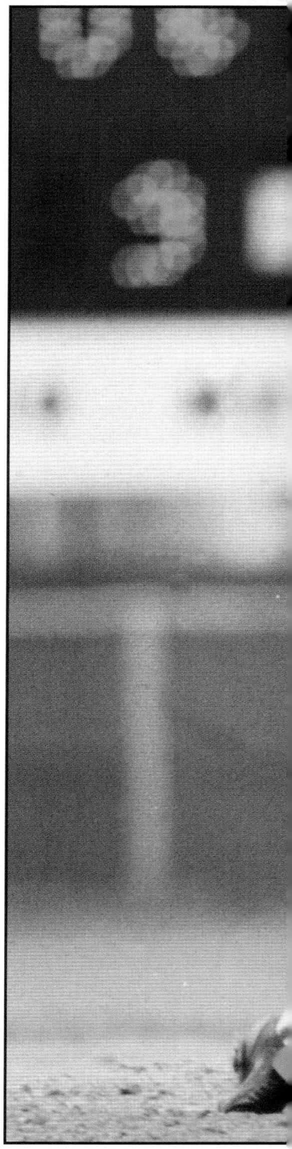

fourth straight defeat – Linz begins playing "Mary Had a Little Lamb" in the back of the team bus to O'Hare Airport. Manager Yogi Berra tells Linz to stop, but he keeps on playing. Berra goes to the back of the bus and knocks the harmonica away. Coach Frank Crosetti, with the Yankees 33 years, calls it the "first case of open defiance by a player." Linz is later fined $200.

Here's Linz's version of what happened as reported by the New York Daily News*: "It was pretty somber... Yogi yells, 'Hey Linz, shove that right up your - - -.' I didn't hear him, so I asked Mickey [Mantle] what Yogi had said and Mick said, 'He said play it louder.' So I did. Yogi went berserk and came charging to the back of the bus, enraged. Mick couldn't stop laughing."*

St. Louis fireballer Bob Gibson was 2-1 in the 1964 World Series, including a win over the Yankees in the Series-clinching Game 7

Cardinals' manager Johnny Keane, on any thought of lifting Bob Gibson from game seven of the World Series: "I never considered taking him out. I had a commitment to his heart."

AUGUST 29:

In game one of a doubleheader against the Red Sox, Mickey Mantle hits his 447th career home run, off Earl Wilson. In the nightcap, he fans to tie Babe Ruth's career record of 1,330. It also is Elston Howard Night.

AUGUST 31:

Groundbreaking ceremonies take place for the Angels' new stadium in Anaheim. The ballpark will be on State College Blvd. in Orange County, just 35 miles south of Los Angeles.

SEPTEMBER 1:

Masanori Murakami, a left-handed pitcher, makes a memorable debut today with the Giants, becoming the first Japanese-born player to appear in the U.S. major leagues. He shuts out the Mets in his one inning of relief, but New York wins the game, 4-1.

Murakami appears in 54 games for the Giants in 1964 and 1965, compiling a 5-1 record with a 3.43 ERA, in 89.1 innings of work and just one start, before he is pressured by the Japanese government to return home.

SEPTEMBER 12:

The Orioles' Frank Bertaina and the Athletics' Bob Meyer match one-hitters. Baltimore wins the game, 1-0, giving Bertaina his first major league victory.

SEPTEMBER 13:

The Cardinals become the second modern team to score in every inning (the 1923 Giants were the first) in a 15-2 win over the Cubs at Wrigley Field. Julian Javier and Lou Brock homer for St. Louis; the winning pitcher is Curt Simmons. Dick Ellsworth is the game's losing pitcher.

SEPTEMBER 17:

Mickey Mantle reaches two career landmarks in today's game against the visiting Angels. He smacks his 450th career homer (31st of the season) and collects his 2,000th hit (three today). The Yankees win the game, 6-2.

SEPTEMBER 30:

In a Fenway Park doubleheader, the Indians' Luis Tiant and Sudden Sam McDowell combine for 17 strikeouts, giving Cleveland an AL record of 1,129 for the season. Tiant pitches a four-hitter in the opener, won by the Indians, 5-0. McDowell pitches a 3-0, seven-hit win in the nightcap.

OCTOBER 3:

The Yankees beat the visiting Indians, 8-3, on five runs in the bottom of the eighth, to wrap up the AL pennant. Pete Mikkelsen gets the victory in relief.

OCTOBER 4:

On the last day of the season, the Cardinals win the NL pennant with an 11-5 victory over the Mets while the Phillies, behind Jim Bunning, are beating the Reds, 10-0. St. Louis's Bob Gibson gets the win in relief of Curt Simmons. Galen Cisco is the Mets' losing pitcher. Bill White drives in the winning runs with a two-run homer in the sixth. Curt Flood also hits a home run for the Cardinals. Herman Franks is named manager of the Giants, replacing Alvin Dark. The Giants finished fourth in the National League with a 90-72 record. Dark had been the focal point of controversy following his reported derogatory remarks about Latin and black players in July.

REGULAR SEASON WRAP-UP:

The Cardinals win one of the NL's closest pennant races ever, 93-69. The Phillies and Reds tie for second at 92-70, one game behind St. Louis; three games separate the top four teams. Johnny Keane's team is led by Ken Boyer, with a .295 average, 24 homers, and 119 RBI, and Bill White, who bats .303 with 21 homers and 102 RBI. Lou Brock bats .348 and Curt Flood .311. Ray Sadecki (20-11) and Bob Gibson (19-12, 245 strikeouts) top the pitching staff.

The Yankees win their fifth AL pennant in a row under three different managers. It also is their 14th in 16 years. Managed by Yogi Berra, the Yankees finish at 99-63, one game ahead of the White Sox by virtue of a 22-6 record in September. It is New York's 39th straight winning season, a streak that began in 1926. Mickey Mantle hits .303 with 35 homers and 111 RBI. Elston Howard hits 15 home runs and drives in 84 runs with a .313 batting average. Roger Maris dips to 26 homers. Jim Bouton is the staff's top winner with an 18-13 record.

SEPTEMBER 17
Mickey Mantle smacks career homer 450 and picks up his 2000th career hit.

OCTOBER 15
Bob Gibson and the Cardinals win game seven of the Series against the Yankees.

The Orioles' Brooks Robinson leads the AL in four defensive categories including fielding average – .972. Athletics' pitcher John Wyatt appears in a record 81 games. Tony Oliva of the Minnesota Twins is the first rookie to lead the AL in hitting.

OCTOBER 7:

World Series, game one. In St. Louis, each team has 12 hits, but the Cardinals make more of theirs in a 9-5 win. St. Louis rallies from a two-run deficit with a four-run sixth. Mike Shannon's two-run homer, Carl Warwick's pinch-hit single, and Curt Flood's triple are the key blows. Ray Sadecki gets the win; Whitey Ford is charged with the loss. Tom Tresh has a two-run home run for New York.

OCTOBER 8:

World Series, game two. Rookie Mel Stottlemyre pitches a complete game and limits the Cardinals to seven hits in an 8-3 win in St. Louis. Phil Linz substitutes a bat for his harmonica and hits a solo home run. Bob Gibson gets the loss; the Yankees score four runs in the ninth inning after he is replaced by a pinch hitter.

OCTOBER 10:

World Series, game three: At Yankee Stadium, Mickey Mantle leads off the ninth inning with a home run on the first pitch into the upper deck in right field to beat the Cardinals and Barney Schultz, 2-1. It is Mantle's 16th World Series homer – topping Babe Ruth's record, set in 1932. Jim Bouton pitches a complete game six-hitter for the victory.

OCTOBER 11:

World Series, game four. The Yankees seem in control with a 3-0 lead in the fifth when Ken Boyer hits a grand slam homer – the second by an NL player in World Series play. The Cards win, 4-3, with reliever Roger Craig getting the win. Al Downing is charged with the loss.

OCTOBER 12:

World Series, game five. Bob Gibson pitches 10 innings, holding the Yankees to six hits, and his catcher Tim McCarver hits a three-run home run in the 10th to give the Cardinals a 5-2 win at Yankee Stadium. In the ninth, Tom Tresh sent the game into extra innings with a two-run homer.

OCTOBER 14:

World Series, game six. Mickey Mantle and Roger Maris lead the Yankees to an 8-3 win with back-to-back homers against Curt Simmons

OCTOBER 15:

World Series, game seven. Bob Gibson withstands three Yankees' homers, going the distance for a 7-5 Cardinals' win and the World Championship. Mickey Mantle hits a three-run homer, Phil Linz has a solo shot. Ken Boyer homers in the seventh and New York's Clete Boyer in the ninth, becoming the first brothers to hit round-trippers in the same Series game. Lou Brock also has a home run. Mel Stottlemyre gets the loss. Tim McCarver leads all regulars with .478; Lou Brock bats .300 – each has five RBI. Ken Boyer has two homers and bats in six runs. Bob Gibson, with two wins, fans 31 in 27 innings. Second baseman Bobby Richardson knocks out a record 13 hits and has a .406 batting average for New York. Mickey Mantle bats .333 and supplies plenty of firepower, unloading for three home runs and driving in eight runs in the losing effort.

POST-SEASON

OCTOBER 16:

Upset with front office changes, including the firing of general manager Bing Devine, Cardinals' manager Johnny Keane announces his resignation one day after winning the World Series. Keane, who also is troubled by rumors that he was to be replaced by Leo Durocher, dated his letter of resignation September 28, but gives it to Cards owner August A. Busch Jr. today.

After just one year and an AL pennant, Yogi Berra is fired as Yankees' manager.

OCTOBER 19:

Albert "Red" Schoendienst is the Cardinals' new manager, replacing Johnny Keane. St. Louis also drops its baseball consultant, Branch Rickey, who had been earning $65,000 a year. In Pittsburgh, Harry "The Hat" Walker is named the new manager of the Pirates. He will replace Danny Murtaugh, who is stepping down because of poor health. The Pirates finished in seventh place with a record of 80-82. In a not-so-

"Isn't it odd that in the communications field you seem to have the biggest breakdown in communications of any business."
– Announcer Mel Allen

subtle game of managerial musical chairs, Johnny Keane is appointed the new manager of the New York Yankees, replacing Yogi Berra.

OCTOBER 21:

The Braves' directors vote to seek permission to move the team from Milwaukee to Atlanta in time for the 1965 season. Ground was broken on April 15 for a 57,500-seat ballpark. To be known as the Atlanta-Fulton County Stadium, the new facility presently is under construction.

NOVEMBER 4:

The Columbia Broadcasting System officially announces it is buying 80 percent of the Yankees from owners Dan Topping and Del Webb. CBS will pay $11.2 million for baseball's most successful team. During Topping and Webb's 20 years of ownership, the Yankees won 15 AL pennants and 10 World Series.

NOVEMBER 7:

In a special meeting in Phoenix, Arizona, NL owners approve the move of the Braves to Atlanta. However, the team will be required to remain in Milwaukee through the 1965 season. It will be the second move for the franchise, which is in the final year of its lease in Milwaukee. In 1953, the Braves moved from their original home in Boston to Milwaukee. In its first years in Milwaukee, the Braves broke attendance records; they now are claiming operating losses of $500,000 last season.

NOVEMBER 12:

Fred Hutchinson dies of cancer at age 45 in Bradenton, Florida. In 10 years as a Tiger pitcher, he was 95-71 with a 3.73 ERA. He managed for 12 years, leading the 1961 Reds to the pennant.

NOVEMBER 17:

The Mets, who already have ex-Yankees' manager Casey Stengel and former general-manager George Weiss, sign Yogi Berra to a two-year contract as a coach.

NOVEMBER 23:

The New York Mets buy baseball's winningest left-handeditcher, Warren Spahn (6-13, 5.29 ERA), now 43, from the Braves. Spahn is4-12 and then dealt to the Giants in 1965.

NOVEMBER 29:

The Phillies acquire good-hit, no-field first baseman Dick Stuart (.279, 33 home runs, 114 RBI) from the Red Sox for pitcher Dennis Bennett (12-14, 3.68 ERA).

DECEMBER 1:

The Houston Colt .45s, who will move to their new Astrodome ballpark for the 1965 season, officially change their name to the Houston Astros.

DECEMBER 3:

Robert "Bo" Belinsky (9-8, 2.86 ERA) says goodbye to Hollywood and actresses Ann-Margret, Mamie Van Doren, Connie Stevens, and Tina Louise. The playboy pitcher is traded by the Angels to the Phillies for minor league pitcher Rudy May and first baseman John "Costen" Shockley (.229 in 11 games).

DECEMBER 4:

The Senators and Dodgers engineer a blockbuster trade. Going to Washington are outfielder Frank "Hondo" Howard (.226, 24 homers), pitchers Phil Ortega (7-9, 4.00 ERA) and Pete Richert (2-3, 4.15 ERA), infielder Ken McMullen (.209 in 24 games), and minor league first baseman Dick Nen. In return, Los Angeles gets pitcher Claude Osteen (15-13, 3.33 ERA), infielder John Kennedy (.230, seven homers), and $100,000.

DECEMBER 14:

Pitcher Roger Craig (7-9, 3.25 ERA), who lost 55 games over the last three seasons, is traded to the Reds along with outfielder Charlie James (.223, five homers in 88 games). In return, the Cardinals get pitcher Bob Purkey (11-9, 3.04 ERA).

DECEMBER 15:

The American Broadcasting System will pay the major leagues $12.2 million for the rights to broadcast 27 games a season for the next two seasons.

DECEMBER 17:

The New York Yankees fire their longtime radio and TV voice, Mel Allen, one of baseball's legendary broadcasters. Allen popularized the "going, going, gone" call for home runs and noted unusual events with a mellifluous "How about that?"

NOVEMBER 7
The National League approves the move of the Braves from Milwaukee to Atlanta.

DECEMBER 17
"Going, going, gone!" Yankees' longtime announcer Mel Allen is fired.

THE BEST OF 1964

NATIONAL LEAGUE

HITTERS

Batting Average:
Roberto Clemente, Pittsburgh Pirates, .339

Slugging Average:
Willie Mays, San Francisco Giants, .607

Home Runs:
Willie Mays, 47

Runs Batted In:
Ken Boyer, St. Louis Cardinals, 119

Hits:
Roberto Clemente; Curt Flood, St. Louis Cardinals, 211

Stolen Bases:
Maury Wills, Los Angeles Dodgers, 53

PITCHERS

Wins:
Larry Jackson, Chicago Cubs, 24

Strikeouts:
Bob Veale, Pittsburgh Pirates, 250

Earned Run Average:
Sandy Koufax, Los Angeles Dodgers, 1.74

Winning Percentage:
Sandy Koufax, .792

Saves:
Hal Woodeshick, Houston Colt .45s, 23

Most Valuable Player:
Ken Boyer, St. Louis Cardinals

Rookie of the Year:
Dick Allen, Philadelphia Phillies

AMERICAN LEAGUE

HITTERS

Batting Average:
Tony Oliva, Minnesota Twins, .323

Slugging Average:
John "Boog" Powell, Baltimore Orioles, .606

Home Runs:
Harmon Killebrew, Minnesota Twins, 49

Runs Batted In:
Brooks Robinson, Baltimore Orioles, 118

Hits:
Tony Oliva, 217

Stolen Bases:
Luis Aparicio, Baltimore Orioles, 57

PITCHERS

Wins:
Gary Peters, Chicago White Sox; Dean Chance, Los Angeles Angels, 20

Strikeouts:
Al Downing, New York Yankees, 217

Earned Run Average:
Dean Chance, 1.65

Winning Percentage:
Wally Bunker, Baltimore Orioles, .792

Saves:
Dick Radatz, Boston Red Sox, 29

Most Valuable Player:
Brooks Robinson, Baltimore Orioles

Cy Young Award:
Dean Chance, Los Angeles Angels

Rookie of the Year:
Tony Oliva, Minnesota Twins

1965

"This is a tough yard for a hitter when the air-conditioning is blowing in."
– Bob Boone, on the Astrodome

NEWS

FIRST U.S. COMBAT TROOPS TO VIETNAM

MARTIN LUTHER KING LEADS CIVIL RIGHTS MARCHES IN SELMA AND MONTGOMERY

DEMONSTRATORS PROTEST U.S. INVOLVEMENT IN VIETNAM

PRESIDENT LYNDON JOHNSON SIGNS VOTING RIGHTS ACT

Winston Churchill, Adlai Stevenson, Nat King Cole, Stan Laurel die

Riots in Watts section of Los Angeles

MALCOLM X ASSASSINATED

Massive power outage darkens Northeast

ST. LOUIS GATEWAY ARCH COMPLETED

HEALTH WARNINGS APPEAR ON CIGARETTE PACKS

Pope Paul VI visits New York

42 die in airline collision over Connecticut

Medicare bill passes in Congress

PRE-SEASON

JANUARY 7:

Retired Air Force Colonel Robert V. Whitlow leaves the post of athletic director for the Cubs. Whitlow was appointed to the position in 1963 in one of owner Philip K. Wrigley's experiments.

JANUARY 11:

Former major league first baseman Wally Pipp dies at age 71 in Grand Rapids, Michigan. Pipp, who played 15 years – 12 with the Yankees – and hit .281, is best remembered as the player whose headache in 1925 gave Lou Gehrig the opportunity to become a starter for the Yankees and go on to set an ML record for consecutive games played.

JANUARY 20:

Chicago, Cleveland, and Kansas City complete a three-cornered trade. Returning to the Indians after five years is outfielder Rocky Colavito (.274, 34 homers, 102 RBI) along with catcher Camilo Carreon (.274 in 37 games). The White Sox get catcher Johnny "Honey" Romano (.241, 19 homers), pitcher Tommy John (2-9, 3.91 ERA), and outfielder Tommie Agee (.167 in 13 games). Pitcher Fred Talbot (4-5, 3.70 ERA) and outfielders Mike Hershberger (.230) and Jim Landis (.208) end up with the Kansas City Athletics.

FEBRUARY 18:

Elston Howard, the AL's Most Valuable Player in 1963, signs a new Yankees' contract for $70,000, making him the highest paid catcher of all time. Howard hit .313 with 15 homers and 84 RBI last season.

MARCH 1:

Del Webb sells his remaining 10 percent share of the Yankees to CBS for $1.4 million. CBS now owns 90 percent of the team; the other 10 percent is controlled by Dan Topping.

MARCH 5:

One of baseball's fieriest competitors, John Leonard Roosevelt "Pepper" Martin, dies at age 61 in McAlester, Oklahoma. Known as the Wild Hoss of the Osage, Martin played 13 years with the Cardinals, batting .298 and leading the NL in stolen bases three times. Martin, primarily an outfielder, saved his best for post-season play. In three World Series, he hit an all-time high .418, compiled the sixth-best slugging average – .636 – and stole seven bases.

MARCH 6:

Former major league catcher Wally Schang dies at age 75 in St. Louis. In 1916, Schang became the first major leaguer to hit "switch" homers in one game. In 19 years he batted .284 and appeared in six World Series.

MARCH 19:

John "Pop" Lloyd, who played in the Negro Leagues for 24 years and batted .353, dies at the age of 79 today in Atlantic City, New Jersey.

APRIL 9:

President Lyndon B. Johnson and Texas Governor John Connally are among 47,876 on hand for the opening of the Astrodome and an exhibition game between the Astros and the Yankees. Mickey Mantle has the first indoor hit in major league history – a first-inning single – and the first home run – a 400-foot drive in the seventh. The Astros win the game, 2-1, in 12 innings.

APRIL 9
The Houston Astrodome opens with an exhibition game win by the Yankees, 2-1.

MAY 14
Carl Yastrzemski hits for the cyle and drives in five in a 12-8 Red Sox win over Detroit.

THE SEASON

APRIL 12:

Baseball moves indoors. In the first regular season game at Houston's Astrodome, the Phillies beat the Astros on Dick Allen's two-run homer in the third inning off Bob Bruce. Chris Short gets the 2-0 victory.

At Wrigley Field, the Cardinals' Steve Carlton makes his major league debut, issuing a walk in the 11th inning of a game that ends in a 10-10 tie in 11 innings.

APRIL 20:

Warren Spahn, now pitching for the Mets, fans John Kennedy of the Dodgers for his 2,501st career strikeout and the final out in a 3-2 win. Spahn will be 44 years old in three days.

APRIL 27:

The Mets activate coach Yogi Berra. After losing to Houston, 3-2, in their first game at the Astrodome, the Mets complain about playing conditions – specifically the air conditioning, which allegedly blows cold air toward home for visitors and is reversed when the Astros bat. In the ninth inning, left fielder Joe Christopher loses a ball hit by Eddie Kasko for a two-run double.

APRIL 28:

Mets' broadcaster Lindsey Nelson provides a new perspective on baseball. He ascends in a gondola to the apex of the Astrodome, a height of 208 feet above the playing surface, and delivers play-by-play of the seventh and eighth innings plus color commentary from his perch. Nelson is linked by walkie-talkie to his broadcast partners Ralph Kiner and Bob Murphy. The gondola, under ground rules, is "in play," but it is not hit. The Astros win the game, 12-9.

MAY 1:

Yogi Berra makes his playing debut for the Mets as a pinch hitter in the eighth inning of today's game in Cincinnati against the Reds. Berra faces Sammy Ellis and grounds out to first baseman Gordy Coleman. The Reds win, 9-2.

Berra appears in four games for the Mets – two behind the plate – and has two singles in nine at-bats for a .222 batting average.

MAY 2:

In the nightcap of a doubleheader against the Phillies, Hank Aaron hits a homer against the Phillies' Bo Belinsky; it is the 368th of his career. Eddie Mathews has 378, enabling the two Braves to surpass the NL record of Duke Snider and Gil Hodges for the most homers by teammates. The Braves win, 10-7.

MAY 5:

The Phillies' Jim Bunning pitches and bats the Mets to a 1-0 defeat. Bunning homers for the game's only run and wins his sixth consecutive complete game. Warren Spahn gets the loss for New York.

MAY 8:

Springfield and Elmira of the Eastern League play the longest professional baseball game ever – 27 innings. Elmira wins the game, which surpasses the 1920 26-inning Boston-Brooklyn contest.

MAY 13:

Angels' rookie Dick Wantz dies at the age of 25 in Inglewood, California, after emergency surgery. Wantz, who pitched one inning for the Angels on opening day, was diagnosed with a brain tumor.

MAY 14:

Against the Tigers at Fenway Park, Carl Yastrzemski hits for the cycle – including his fifth and sixth homers of the year – drives in five runs, and scores twice. But Boston loses to Detroit, 12-8, in 10 innings. Willie Horton of the Tigers hits two homers. Terry Fox gets the win; Dick Radatz is the loser.

CULTURE

Two baseball novels are published: *Today's Game* by Martin Quigley and *Voices of a Summer Day* by Irwin Shaw.

Houston's new Astrodome is an indoor wonder to behold.

Sandy Koufax says, "I became a good pitcher when I stopped trying to make them miss the ball and started trying to make them hit it."

LEAGUE

In April, after pressure from Commissioner Ford Frick, the Nankai Hawks of the Pacific League in Japan acknowledge a "grave mistake" in trying to prevent Masanori Murakami from playing with the Giants after the 1964 season. Murakami, who pitched nine innings last season, will be able to play with San Francisco in 1965. The Hawks originally had claimed he was in the U.S. on only a one-year lease.

MAY 17:

Yogi Berra is deactivated as a player and returns to full-time coaching for the Mets.

MAY 23:

The comedy of errors continues for the Mets in their fourth year. After turning a routine fly ball into a three-run triple, then popping out, Ron Swoboda puts his foot through his batting helmet and cannot dislodge it.

MAY 25:

The National Brewery Co. buys 64,000 shares of the Orioles from Joseph Iglehart. Brewery chairman Jerold Hoffberger assumes the same position with the Baltimore Orioles.

MAY 29:

The Phillies' Dick Allen launches a 529-foot, first-inning home run over the left center field roof at Connie Mack Stadium against Larry Jackson. The Phillies beat the Chicago Cubs, 4-2.

JUNE 8:

Baseball's first free-agent draft is held in the Hotel Commodore in New York City, with 20 teams picking 320 players. The first pick, by the Athletics, is Arizona State University outfielder Rick Monday. Going second, to the Mets, is 19-year-old left-handed high school pitcher Leslie Rohr. Among the other picks are two 17-year-olds – Billy Conigliaro by the Red Sox and Bernardo Carbo by the Reds. The draft will be conducted every June and January and teams select in the reverse order of their league standing.

JUNE 14:

Jim Maloney of the Reds no-hits the Mets until the 11th inning, when Johnny Lewis hits a leadoff homer to give New York a 1-0 win. Maloney strikes out a record-tying 18 and allows only one walk. The Mets' Larry Bearnarth relieves Frank Lary, pitches three innings, and gets the win.

JUNE 15:

Today In Detroit, Denny McLain comes out of the bullpen and promptly strikes out the first seven Red Sox batters he faces. McLain works six and two-thirds and strikes out 15; the Tigers win, 6-5, and Bill Freehan ties a major league record for catchers with 19 putouts. The Atlanta Braves' third baseman Eddie Mathews collects his 2,000th career hit in a 12-7 Braves' victory.

JUNE 20:

Al Kaline singles in two runs against the Athletics, giving him 1,000 career RBI. The Tigers rally from an eight-run deficit in the second inning to win the game, 12-8, for their eighth consecutive victory. Kansas City ends the streak in the nightcap.

JUNE 22:

Mickey Mantle's injury-plagued career is winding down – injury-plagued. The Yankees' star seriously injures a hamstring as the Yankees beat the Athletics, 4-2, after losing the opener of a doubleheader, 6-2. Mantle will be out of action for three weeks.

JUNE 28:

The New York Mets sign 18-year-old right-handed pitcher Lynn Nolan Ryan.

Ryan would join the Mets after just one year in the minors. In his book Kings of the Hill, *Ryan writes comically of his first encounter with the club: "When I walked into my first major league clubhouse in early September 1966, the scene actually startled me. I was 19, with high school and a year of minor league ball behind me, and I had never seen players smoking cigars. That was about all they were doing, that and playing cards and answering their fan mail by sailing letters into the nearest trash can. These were the New York Mets, the last of the lovable, comical, pie-in-the-face Mets, and – I say this with no disrespect – the strangest collection of athletes you can imagine. It was as if someone had taken a truck to a union hall and picked up a load of day workers."*

JULY 10:

In the aftermath of his fight last week with teammate Dick Allen, first baseman-outfielder Frank J. Thomas (.260 in 35 games) is sold by the Phillies to the Astros.

JULY 13:

In the All-Star Game the NL beats the AL, 6-5, in Metropolitan Stadium in Minnesota. Sandy Koufax is the winning pitcher and "Sudden Sam" McDowell takes the loss. Willie Mays,

JUNE 8
The Athletics select Rick Monday as the first pick in the first-ever amateur draft.

JULY 20
Yankee Mel Stottlemyre is the first pitcher in 55 years with an inside-the-park home run.

Joe Torre, Willie Stargell, Dick McAuliffe, and Harmon Killebrew hit home runs in the game, but a single by Ron Santo in the seventh inning drives in the winning run. AL manager Al Lopez falls to 0-5 in All-Star competition, the worst record ever.

JULY 20:

Sometimes he hits too. Sandy Koufax singles in a run in the ninth inning to defeat the Astros, 3-2. Koufax allows three hits and fans 10 in ringing up his 11th straight victory.

It's a good day for pitchers with the bat. The Yankees' Mel Stottlemyre becomes the first pitcher in 55 years to hit an inside-the-park grand slam homer. Stottlemyre does it against the Red Sox in a 6-3 win.

JULY 22:

The Giants sign Warren Spahn (4-12), who was cut by the New York Mets earlier this month.

JULY 25:

Some time after midnight this morning, Casey Stengel breaks his left hip getting out of a car after the Mets' Annual Old-Timers' Dinner in New York City.

Forest "Smoky" Burgess of the White Sox collects his 108th career pinch hit – a major league record. Johnny "Honey" Romano hits a grand slam homer in a victory over the Tigers.

JULY 26:

James "Pud" Galvin is the sole inductee into the Hall of Fame in 1965. Pitching from 1879 to 1892, Galvin won an astonishing 361 games while losing 308, with an ERA of 2.87. He pitched 5,941 1/3 innings and 639 complete games. In both 1883 and 1884 he won 46 games. Galvin passed away in 1902.

Casey Stengel, who will be 75 in four days, undergoes hip joint replacement. Coach Wes Westrum will manage the Mets for the remainder of the season.

AUGUST 8:

The Reds hammer visiting Los Angeles, 18-0; it is the worst margin of defeat ever for the Dodgers. The Reds bang out 20 hits – 10 for extra bases – and Jim Maloney holds the Dodgers to only four hits. Don Drysdale does heavy damage to his earned run average, yielding six runs in two innings. Nick Wilhite and Mike Kekich give up five each.

AUGUST 9:

In Houston, Robin Roberts – acquired by the Astros after his release by the Orioles – pitches his first NL shutout since

Harmon Killebrew's 25 homers power the Twins to the World Seris.

September 10, 1961. Roberts holds his old team, the Phillies, to four hits, and wins the game, 8-0.

AUGUST 18:

Hank Aaron launches a tremendous drive off Curt Simmons onto the pavilion roof in Busch Stadium in St. Louis, but all he has to show for it is a frustrating out. Cardinals' catcher Bob Uecker convinces home plate umpire Chris Pelekoudas that Aaron stepped beyond the batter's box and he is called out, negating the apparent home run. The Braves win, 6-2.

AUGUST 19:

If at first you don't succeed... Jim Maloney, who had a no-hitter broken up in the 11th inning on June 14 and lost, pitches another hitless game and wins this one in 10 innings. Maloney beats the Cubs, 1-0, at Wrigley Field, despite wildness. He walks 10, hits one batter, and strikes out 12; the Reds make one error. Larry Jackson is the game's losing pitcher. In the nightcap, the Cubs rebound, 5-4, on a pair of home runs hit off the bats of Billy Williams and Don Landrum.

REPORTEDLY, IN SPRING TRAINING CASEY STENGEL IS ASKED WHAT PEOPLE HIS AGE THINK OF MODERN PLAYERS. HE RESPONDS, "HOW THE HELL SHOULD I KNOW? MOST OF THE PEOPLE MY AGE ARE DEAD."

AUGUST 22:

It's conflict today at Candlestick. In the third inning of today's Dodgers-Giants faceoff, with Los Angeles ahead, 2-1, some bad blood between the two teams boils over. Two days ago, Dodger Maury Wills was accused of hitting the mitt of Giants catcher Tom Haller with his bat. Matty Alou then hit Dodgers catcher Johnny Roseboro's mask with his stick, and the Dodgers' catcher buzzed his head with a throw to the mound. Today's hostilities begin with Giants pitcher Juan Marichal dusting Maury Wills and Ron Fairly. When Marichal comes to bat, Dodgers pitcher Sandy Koufax throws two inside pitches, and Roseboro comes close to Marichal's head with the return throw. Marichal claims his ear was nicked with the ball. After an exchange of words, Marichal then hits Roseboro in the head twice with his bat. Koufax tries to separate them, but a 15-minute brawl breaks out, including Dodger Bob L. Miller versus Marichal and Alou. The Giants' Rigoberto "Tito" Fuentes arms himself with a bat. Dodgers manager Walter Alston and the Giants' Willie Mays fear Roseboro has lost an eye. Mays leads Roseboro into the dugout while chief umpire Shag Crawford grabs Marichal, who is dragged off the field. When the game resumes, Ron Herbel replaces Marichal and Jeff Torborg substitutes for Roseboro. Willie Mays hits a three-run homer off Koufax for a 4-3 Giants' win.

Marichal is fined $1,750 and suspended for eight games. Roseboro has a concussion and a two-inch cut, but his eye is okay. He files suit against Marichal, but eventually drops it. In time Marichal says, "I feel sorry that I used the bat."

AUGUST 25:

Archibald "Moonlight" Graham dies in Chisholm, Minnesota, at age 88. Graham appeared in the outfield for one game with the Giants in 1905 without batting or handling a chance.

The magical major league story of Moonlight Graham is recounted in W.P. Kinsella's exemplary novel Shoeless Joe *and in the film version,* Field of Dreams.

HISTORY

On June 20, Jay Dahl, 19 years old, dies in an automobile crash in Salisbury, North Carolina. No active or former major leaguer died at a younger age. Dahl appeared in only one game – on September 27, 1963 – when the Astros fielded an all-rookie lineup against the Mets. He pitched two and two-thirds innings, allowing seven hits and compiling a 16.88 ERA, and was charged with the loss.

AUGUST 29:

Hall of Fame outfielder Paul "Big Poison" Waner dies at age 62 in Sarasota, Florida. He is survived by his younger brother, Lloyd "Little Poison" Waner. In 20 years, Waner batted .333 with 603 doubles and 190 triples. He led the NL in batting three times, with a personal high of .380 in 1927.

Willie Mays homers against Jack Fisher of the Mets for his 17th in August. Mays breaks Ralph Kiner's NL record for home runs in a month, set in September 1949. It also is Mays' 41st homer of the season. The Giants beat the Mets, 8-3, at Shea Stadium today.

Ron Hansen of the White Sox ties a major league record for shortstops with 28 chances in a doubleheader. In game one, Hansen handles 18 – tying an AL record – and Chicago beats Boston, 3-2, in 14 innings. Hansen has 10 more chances in the White Sox 3-2 win in the nightcap.

AUGUST 30:

At the Essex House in New York City, the Mets announce the retirement of Casey Stengel. Interim manager Wes Westrum will take over the team full time. Stengel tells the media: "If I can't run out there and take a pitcher out, I'm not capable of continuing as manager." Stengel, who completes a 56-year career as player and manager, is the only skipper the Mets have had in their four-year existence. Under Stengel, they are 175-404 and finished last each year. It is a far cry from Stengel's career with the Yankees; in 12 years he was 1,149-696, with 10 pennants and seven World Series wins.

SEPTEMBER 2:

At Shea Stadium, the Mets retire Casey Stengel's number 37, which will be displayed in a glass case at the ballpark. Stengel observes, "I'd like to see them give the number 37 to some young player so it can go on and do some good for the Mets. I hope they don't put a mummy in the glass case."

At Wrigley Field in Chicago today, Ernie Banks hits a three-run home run in the third inning against the St. Louis Cardinals' Curt Simmons. It is the 400th home run of Banks's career. It also provides Bob Hendley and the Cubs with a 5-3 victory.

> METS' SCOUT JOHN "RED" MURFF ON 18-YEAR-OLD HIGH SCHOOL PITCHER NOLAN RYAN: "HAS THE BEST ARM I'VE EVER SEEN IN MY LIFE. COULD BE A REAL POWER PITCHER SOME DAY."

SEPTEMBER 5:

In the first inning in Cincinnati, the Phillies' Dick Stuart hits his ninth career grand slam home run. He adds a two-run homer in the seventh, but the Reds win the game, 10-9.

SEPTEMBER 8:

Bert Campaneris of the Athletics demonstrates unprecedented versatility by playing all nine positions in today's game against the Angels. Campaneris opens at his customary position, shortstop, then switches to second base in the second inning. In successive frames, he plays third base, left field, center field, right field – where he makes an error – and first base. In the eighth inning, he takes the mound; the first batter he faces is none other than his cousin, Jose Cardenal, who promptly pops up. Campaneris allows just one run on a hit and two walks. Then he dons the catcher's "tools of ignorance" for the ninth inning. But he injures his shoulder in a collision at the plate and is replaced by Rene Lachemann. He is hitless in three at-bats. The Angels win the game, 5-3, in 13 innings.

TRIVIA

Officially known as Harris County Domed Stadium, the $31.6-million Astrodome has three and a half acres of "Tiffany Bermuda grass" and a roof with 4,796 panes of clear glass to help it grow. The stadium also features a 474-foot (half an acre) scoreboard and measures 208 feet (18 stories) from the playing surface to the top of the dome. Air-conditioning keeps the temperature at 72 degrees for every game.

SEPTEMBER 13
Willie Mays goes deep and becomes the fifth member of baseball's 500 home runs club.

HISTORY

In a 1995 poll of members of the Society for American Baseball Research to select the greatest game ever pitched, the September 9 Koufax-Hendley duel finished first.

SEPTEMBER 9:

Dodger left-hander Sandy Koufax pitches a perfect 1-0 game against the Cubs in Los Angeles. He becomes the first modern pitcher with four career no-hitters. Koufax is at his overpowering best, striking out 14 and allowing only seven balls out of the infield. He fans the final six batters and seven of the last nine. The Dodgers score their run in the fifth without a hit on a wild throw by catcher Chris Krug. Bob Hendley is good enough to win most games, allowing only one hit – a seventh-inning bloop double by Lou Johnson.

SEPTEMBER 10:

The Phillies' 21-year-old Ferguson Jenkins makes his major league debut with four and a third innings of relief against the Cardinals. The Phillies win, 5-4, in 12 innings; it is their 10,000th game of the century, not counting ties.

SEPTEMBER 13:

Willie Mays becomes the fifth member of baseball's 500 Club. The Say Hey Kid hits his 500th career home run today against Don Nottebart in the Astrodome. The Giants win, 5-1.

SEPTEMBER 16:

The Red Sox Dave Morehead no-hits the Indians, 2-0, at Fenway Park. The 23-year-old righthander allows one walk – to Rocky Colavito – and fans eight; Boston makes no errors. Lee Thomas homers for Boston. Luis Tiant gets the loss. After the game, Mike "Pinky" Higgins is fired as general manager of the Boston Red Sox and replaced by Dick O'Connell.

The AL hires Emmett L. Ashford, who will become the first African- American umpire in major league history. Ashford is coming to the AL from the Pacific Coast League. Now 46 years old, he began calling balls and strikes in 1951 in the Southwest International League and subsequently worked in the Arizona-Texas and Western International Leagues.

SEPTEMBER 18:

Mickey Mantle is saluted by 50,180 fans at Yankee Stadium on the 2,000th game of his career and his day. A total of $32,000 is raised for research on Hodgkins disease, which killed his father, Mutt Mantle. The Detroit Tigers beat the Yankees, 2-1, in 10 innings.

SEPTEMBER 20:

Baseball has another bat episode. The Tigers' Larry Sherry brushes back Indians' second baseman Pedro Gonzalez, who comes after the pitcher with a bat. The Tigers win the game, 5-4, in 14 innings. Gonzalez is fined $500 and suspended for the remainder of the season.

OCTOBER 2:

With 13 strikeouts today, Sandy Koufax ends the season with a major league record 382, topping Bob Feller's previous mark of 348 in 1948. The Dodgers beat the Braves, 3-1, on a Lou Johnson home run, wrapping up the NL pennant.

The Phillies' Chris Short strikes out 18 Mets in 15 innings of game two of a twi-night doubleheader at Shea Stadium. Because of a 1 a.m. curfew, the contest ends at 0-0 after 18 innings, the longest scoreless night game ever. Earlier, Jim Bunning pitched his seventh shutout of the season, beating the Mets, 6-0.

OCTOBER 3:

Batting against Bill McCool of the Reds in the fourth inning at Candlestick Park, Willie Mays homers. It is his major league-leading 52nd of the year and the 505th of his career. He is six behind Mel Ott for the all-time Giants' record. San Francisco wins the game, 6-3.

The Indians' Rocky Colavito is the first major league outfielder to play a 162-game schedule without making an error. Colavito flawlessly handles 274 chances, while hitting 26 homers. Steve Barber of the Orioles bests Sudden Sam McDowell of the Indians, 2-1. McDowell finishes the season with 325 strikeouts.

At Forbes Field, the Cubs execute a triple play against the Pirates in the fifth inning; it is their third of the season, tying a major league record. Bill Faul was on the mound for all three.

In their last game as a Milwaukee team, the Braves are beaten by the Dodgers, 3-0, in Los Angeles. Bob L. Miller gets the win; Bob Sadowski is the losing pitcher.

At Comiskey Park, the home of the Chicago White Sox, pitcher Eddie Fisher sets an American League record by appearing in his 82nd game of the season.

OCTOBER 14
Sandy Koufax shuts out the Twins in game seven, and the Dodgers win the World Series.

REGULAR SEASON WRAP-UP:

The Dodgers, under Walter Alston, are 97-65, two games over the Giants in the NL. Los Angeles is a team built on pitching and speed with little power. Sandy Koufax is a spectacular 26-8 with a 2.04 ERA; Don Drysdale is 22-12 with a 2.77 ERA. The team has no .300 hitters; Maury Wills is tops at .286 with a major league-leading 94 stolen bases. Jim Lefebvre and Lou Johnson each have 12 homers. The Dodgers' .245 team average is the lowest of any NL pennant winner.

Under Sam Mele, the Twins are 97-65 and finish seven games ahead of the White Sox. Tony Oliva is the AL's top hitter with a .321 average. No other Twin hits .300. But the team has power: Harmon Killebrew hits 25 homers, Bob Allison 23, and Don Mincher 22. Jim "Mudcat" Grant is the leading pitcher at 21-7.

The Yankees finish under .500 (77-85) in sixth place. Mickey Mantle plays in only 122 games and Roger Maris in 46. Tony Conigliaro of Boston, at age 20, is the AL's youngest-ever home run leader. Cubs' pitcher Ted Abernathy appears in a record 84 games, surpassing the 1964 mark set by Kansas City's John Wyatt.

OCTOBER 6:

World Series, game one. In Minnesota, Sandy Koufax sits out the opener because it is the Jewish high holy day of Yom Kippur. The Twins beat his replacement, Don Drysdale, on Jim "Mudcat" Grant's complete-game one-hitter and a six-run third, 8-2. Ron Fairly of the Dodgers and the Twins' Don Mincher and Zoilo "Zorro" Versalles hit home runs.

Grant, who was born in Florida, got his nickname in 1954 from a teammate in the minors who thought Grant was from Mississippi, known as the "Mudcat State."

OCTOBER 7:

World Series, game two. At Minnesota, the Twins go up two games to none on Jim Kaat's complete game seven-hitter. The final score is 5-1 and Los Angeles starter Sandy Koufax takes the loss.

OCTOBER 9:

World Series, game three. In Los Angeles, the Dodgers rebound on Claude Osteen's five-hit complete-game shutout, 4-0. Johnny Roseboro singles in two runs in the fourth. Camilo Pascual is the losing pitcher.

OCTOBER 10:

World Series, game four. In Los Angeles, the Dodgers tie the Series with a 7-2 win on Don Drysdale's complete-game five-hitter. The losing pitcher is Mudcat Grant. The game features home runs by Harmon Killebrew and Tony Oliva of the Twins, and Maurice "Wes" Parker and Lou Johnson of the victorious Dodgers.

OCTOBER 11:

World Series, game five. In Los Angeles, the Dodgers make it three in a row on Sandy Koufax's four-hit complete-game shutout. Koufax strikes out 10 in a 7-0 victory. Maury Wills has two doubles and two singles. Jim Kaat is the losing pitcher.

OCTOBER 13:

World Series, game six. The Twins win, 5-1, to tie the World Series. Mudcat Grant hits a three-run homer and goes all the way, allowing the Dodgers six hits. The Twins make the most of their six hits with Grant's round-tripper and a two-run homer by Bob Allison. Ron Fairly has a solo homer for L.A. The losing pitcher is Claude Osteen.

OCTOBER 14:

World Series, game seven. In Minnesota, Sandy Koufax comes through with a three-hit, complete game 2-0 win to give the Dodgers the World Championship. Koufax strikes out 10 and lowers his Series ERA to 0.38. The losing pitcher is Jim Kaat. Lou Johnson homers for the Dodgers. Ron Fairly leads all hitters with a .379 clip, two homers, and six RBI. Maury Wills bats .367 and steals three bases. For the Twins, Harmon Killebrew and Zoilo Versalles are the top hitters at .286. Walter Alston sets an NL record with four World Series championships.

POST-SEASON

OCTOBER 25:

The Lip lands in the Windy City. Today Leo Durocher, 60 years old, is named the manager of the Chicago Cubs for the 1966 season. The Cubs finished in eighth place this season with a record of 72-90.

HISTORY

The career of the great left-hander Warren Spahn comes to a close after 21 major league seasons. Spahn retires with a record of 363-245 and an ERA of 3.09. He ranks sixth all-time with 63 shutouts and is a 13-time 20-game winner. In 1965, Spahn split the season between the Mets and the Giants, compiling a 7-16 record and a 4.01 ERA.

NOVEMBER 3 Sandy Koufax becomes the first three-time winner of the Cy Young Award.

DECEMBER 9 Branch Rickey, the man who brought Jackie Robinson the Dodgers, dies at 83.

LEAGUE

After the Astros finish 65-97 in ninth place, owner Roy Hofheinz fires general manager Paul Richards and skipper Chalmer "Luman" Harris. When someone says Judge Hofheinz is his own worst enemy, Richards retorts, "Not while I'm alive he isn't."

OCTOBER 27:

The Phillies obtain first baseman Bill White (.289, 24 homers, 73 RBI), shortstop Dick Groat (.254), and catcher Bob Uecker (.228 in 53 games) from the Cardinals for outfielder Alex Johnson (.294, eight homers in 97 games), pitcher Art Mahaffey (2-5, 6.21 ERA), and catcher Pat Corrales (.224 in 63 games).

OCTOBER 29:

Hall of Famer Bill McKechnie dies at age 79 in Bradenton, Florida. McKechnie managed in the majors for 25 years, winning pennants with three different teams – the Pirates, Cardinals, and Reds. He was inducted into the Hall of Fame three years ago.

NOVEMBER 3:

Sandy Koufax is named the Cy Young Award winner, becoming the first three-time recipient.

NOVEMBER 17:

Baseball owners select retired Air Force Lieutenant General William D. Eckert as baseball commissioner to succeed Ford Frick. The general is elected by a vote of 20-0 and gets a seven-year contract. A graduate of West Point and Harvard Business School, the 56-year-old Eckert retired in 1961 after 35 years in the Air Force and is a former fighter pilot. AL president Joe Cronin gets a seven-year

Sportswriter Larry Fox of the New York World-Telegram & Sun *comments, "They've done it. They've chosen the Unknown Soldier."*

OUTGOING COMMISSIONER FORD FRICK GETS LESS THAN HIGH MARKS FROM SPORTSWRITER RED SMITH: "AS NATIONAL LEAGUE PRESIDENT, HE'D OFTEN SAY, 'THAT'S NOT MY JURISDICTION.' AS COMMISSIONER, HE'D SAY JUST AS FREQUENTLY, "IT'S A LEAGUE MATTER.'"

NOVEMBER 18:

Wes Westrum, who was 19-48 as the Mets interim manager in 1965, will pilot the team in 1966.

NOVEMBER 28:

Matt Williams is born in Bishop, California.

NOVEMBER 29:

The Yankees trade utilityman Phil Linz (.207), who once said, "You can't get rich sitting on a bench – but I'm giving it a try." He goes to the Phillies for shortstop Ruben Amaro (.212).

DECEMBER 1:

The Athletics obtain minor league first baseman outfielder Joe Rudi and catcher Phil Roof (.162 in 52 games) from the Indians for outfielder Jim Landis (.239) and minor league pitcher Jim Rittwage.

DECEMBER 9:

Former NL Most Valuable Player Frank Robinson (.296, 33 homers, 113 RBI) goes to the Orioles from the Reds. In exchange for the outfielder, Cincinnati receives pitchers Milt Pappas (13-9, 2.60 ERA) and Jack Baldschun (who went to Baltimore from the Phillies in a December 6 trade) along with outfielder Dick Simpson (.222 in eight games). Reds' president Bill DeWitt on why he traded Robinson, "We feel he's an old 30."

Baseball's mahatma, Branch Rickey, who broke the modern major leagues' color barrier by signing Jackie Robinson in 1947, dies in Columbia, Missouri, at 83.

Red Smith of the New York Herald-Tribune *wrote: "To say that Branch Rickey has the finest mind ever brought to the game of baseball is to damn with the faintest of praise, like describing Isaac Stern as a fiddler... He was a giant among pygmies. If his goal had been the Supreme Court of the United States... he would have been a giant on the bench."*

THE BEST OF 1965

NATIONAL LEAGUE

HITTERS

Batting Average:
Roberto Clemente, Pittsburgh Pirates, .329

Slugging Average:
Willie Mays, San Francisco Giants, .645

Home Runs:
Willie Mays, 52

Runs Batted In:
Deron Johnson, Cincinnati Reds, 130

Hits:
Pete Rose, Cincinnati Reds, 209

Stolen Bases:
Maury Wills, Los Angeles Dodgers, 94

PITCHERS

Wins:
Sandy Koufax, Los Angeles Dodgers, 26

Strikeouts:
Sandy Koufax, 382

Earned Run Average:
Sandy Koufax, 2.04

Winning Percentage:
Sandy Koufax, .765

Saves:
Ted Abernathy, Chicago Cubs, 31

Most Valuable Player:
Willie Mays, San Francisco Giants

Cy Young Award:
Sandy Koufax, Los Angeles Dodgers

Rookie of the Year:
Jim Lefebvre, Los Angeles Dodgers

AMERICAN LEAGUE

HITTERS

Batting Average:
Tony Oliva, Minnesota Twins, .321

Slugging Average:
Carl Yastrzemski, Boston Red Sox, .536

Home Runs:
Tony Conigliaro, Boston Red Sox, 32

Runs Batted In:
Rocky Colavito, Cleveland Indians, 108

Hits:
Tony Oliva, 185

Stolen Bases:
Bert Campaneris, Kansas City Athletics, 51

PITCHERS

Wins:
Jim "Mudcat" Grant, Minnesota Twins, 21

Strikeouts:
Sam McDowell, Cleveland Indians, 325

Earned Run Average:
Sam McDowell, 2.18

Winning Percentage:
Jim Grant, .750

Saves:
Ron Kline, Washington Senators, 29

Most Valuable Player:
Zoilo Versalles, Minnesota Twins

Rookie of the Year:
Curt Blefary, Baltimore Orioles

1966

"Baseball is both the greatest and worst thing that ever happend to me."
– Indians' pitcher Sam McDowell

NEWS

VIETNAM WAR ESCALATES

13 KILLED, 31 WOUNDED BY SNIPER IN TEXAS UNIVERSITY TOWER

Medicare introduced

JAMES MEREDITH SHOT ON CIVIL RIGHTS MARCH

MANNED SPACEFLIGHTS GEMINI 8, 9, 10, 11, AND 12 LAUNCHED

WALT DISNEY DIES

Michael DeBakey performs first human heart transplant

THUNDERBALL, STARRING SEAN CONNERY, BRINGS JAMES BOND TO THE MOVIES

The National Oranization for Women (NOW) is formed

STAR TREK BEGINS AIRING ON TELEVISION

PRE-SEASON

FEBRUARY 24:

The Braves today sign University of Southern California right-handed pitcher George Thomas "Tom" Seaver for a $50,000 bonus.

FEBRUARY 28:

Sandy Koufax and Don Drysdale begin an unprecedented joint holdout against the Dodgers. They are seeking a joint three-year pact for $1 million and say they will share the money.

Paramount Pictures announces that Sandy Koufax and Don Drysdale have been signed to appear in the movie *Warning Shot*, a police drama with David Janssen.

MARCH 2:

Commissioner William Eckert voids the Braves' contract with Tom Seaver because signing a college player during his college season is against the rules.

MARCH 5:

Marvin J. Miller, economist and negotiator for the United Steelworkers, will be executive director of the Major League Players, Association. He is elected by a vote of 489-136, with most of the negatives coming from managers, coaches, and trainers.

MARCH 25:

Tom Glavine is born in Concord, Massachusetts.

MARCH 30:

The Koufax-Drysdale holdout ends and, with it, their fledgling movie careers. At a Los Angeles press conference, general manager E.J. "Buzzy" Bavasi announces the signing but does not disclose specific numbers. Koufax is estimated to be getting $120,000 and Drysdale $105,000, making them the highest paid teammates in history. Meanwhile, Paramount Pictures releases them from their movie contract.

APRIL 3:

Commissioner William Eckert holds a drawing to determine whether the Mets, the Indians, or the Phillies – teams who agree to match the Braves' original $40,000 offer – will win the right to sign USC pitcher Tom Seaver. The commissioner picks a name from a hat, and the Mets come up lucky. The Mets waste no time in signing their prize. They land Seaver for a $50,000 bonus and assign him to AAA Jacksonville in the International League.

Revenge is sweet, even if it's only in spring training. In his first at-bat against Juan Marichal since the Giants' pitcher assaulted him with a bat, Dodger catcher Johnny Roseboro hits a three-run, inside-the-park home run in the second inning. The Dodgers win, 8-4, in Phoenix, Arizona.

THE SEASON

APRIL 11:

The major leagues' first African-American umpire, Emmett Ashford, makes his debut on opening day in Washington, D.C., where the Senators are hosting the Indians. Ashford was signed late last year to work AL games. The Indians win, 5-2.

APRIL 12:

Today major league baseball comes to the South. The transplanted Braves make their debut in Atlanta before 50,671 fans at the $18-million Fulton County Stadium. Prior to the game, a parade draws

APRIL 12
The Braves debut at Atlanta's Fulton County Stadium, but lose to the Pirates, 3-2.

APRIL 28
The Indians beat the Angels, 2-1, for their AL-record 10th straight win to start the season.

250,000 fans along Peachtree Street. The Braves, wearing their uniforms, ride in convertibles, accompanied by floats and bands. But the day belongs to the Pirates' Willie Stargell, whose second homer of the game, a two-run shot in the top of the 13th inning, gives his team a 3-2 win. The Braves score both of their runs on home runs by Joe Torre. Jim Pagliaroni homers for the Pirates. The winning pitcher is Don Schwall; Tony Cloninger gets the loss.

Not a very warm welcome to the American League. In his first at-bat in an Orioles uniform, Frank Robinson is hit by a pitch from Earl Wilson of the Boston Red Sox. Brooks Robinson follows with sweet revenge – a homer. Baltimore wins the game when Jim Lonborg walks in the winning run in the 13th inning.

APRIL 14:

Greg Maddux is born in San Angelo, Texas.

APRIL 15:

Sam McDowell of the Indians whiffs 10 in 5 2/3 innings; the Indians win, 8-7 in 12 innings.

APRIL 16:

Indians' starting pitcher Gary Bell strikes out 13 Red Sox batters and winning pitcher Bob Allen adds three for a team total of 16 today. With 17 Ks yesterday – including 10 by Sam McDowell – Cleveland's pitchers ring up an AL record of 33 for two games. The Indians win, 3-2, in the 10th on a Jim Landis hit.

APRIL 18:

The "Tiffany Bermuda grass" in the infield at the Astrodome has been replaced by Astroturf, an artificial playing surface. The outfield will be done later this season. In the first regular season game ever played on Astroturf, the Dodgers beat Houston, 6-3. Don Sutton gets his first major league win. Robin Roberts gets the loss.

APRIL 19:

It's a tough debut in California today. In their first game in their new ballpark, Anaheim Stadium, before a crowd of 31,660, the Angels lose to the Chicago White Sox, 3-1. Tommy John gets the win; Chicago's Marcelino Lopez is charged with the loss.

APRIL 20:

Hank Aaron hits his first homer in an Atlanta uniform – against Ray Culp of the Phillies – and in the ninth inning smacks his 400th career round-tripper, against Bo Belinsky. The Braves win, 8-1.

APRIL 21:

The Cubs acquire pitcher Ferguson Jenkins (0-0) along with outfielder Adolfo Phillips (.000 in two games) and first baseman-outfielder John Herrnstein (.100 in four games) from the Phillies for pitchers Bob Buhl (0-0) and Larry Jackson (0-2).

APRIL 24:

The Giants' Willie Mays homers in a 4-2 win over the Astros in Houston. It is the 511th of his career, tying him with Mel Ott for the most ever by an NL player. It also is Mays's sixth of the season.

APRIL 28:

Cleveland continues its strong start. Today the Indians beat the California Angels, 2-1, for their 10th consecutive victory to begin the season – which is an American League record. Wilfred "Sonny" Siebert is the winning pitcher.

MAY 1:

The Indians' Sudden Sam McDowell one-hits the White Sox, 1-0. It is the second consecutive one-hitter for McDowell; he is the fourth ever to accomplish the feat. The only hit is a Don Buford single in the third inning. Tommy John gets the loss. McDowell is now 4-0 with a 1.55 ERA and 49 strikeouts in 40 2/3 innings.

MAY 4:

At Candlestick Park, Willie Mays homers off the Dodgers' Claude Osteen in a 6-1 Giants' win. It is Mays's 512th career home run, putting him in fourth place all-time, ahead of Mel Ott. He needs 20 more to tie Jimmie Foxx for the most round-trippers by a right-handed hitter.

MAY 7:

With the New York Yankees off to a miserable 4-16 start, their manager, Johnny Keane, is given the hook. Part-owner Dan Topping moves general manager Ralph Houk back to the dugout to replace Keane. Under Keane, the Yankees finished 77-85 last season in sixth place, 25 games behind the pennant-winning Twins.

HISTORY

As 60-year-old Leo Durocher prepares to debut as skipper of the Cubs, 10 of his alumni are currently managers in the major leagues: Bobby Bragan (Braves), Alvin Dark (Athletics), Charlie Dressen (Tigers), Herman Franks (Giants), Billy Herman (Red Sox), Gil Hodges (Senators), Gene Mauch (Phillies), Bill Rigney (Angels), Eddie Stanky (White Sox), and Wes Westrum (Mets).

Dick "Richie" Allen on Astroturf: "If horses can't eat it, I don't want to play on it."

Frank Robinson adusts nicely to the AL.

MAY 8:

The Orioles' Frank Robinson mashes a Luis Tiant pitch over the left-field wall at the 451-foot marker and out of the ballpark – an estimated 541 feet from home. The Orioles win, 8-3.

In the last game at the old Busch Stadium (formerly Sportsman's Park) after 78 years, the Giants beat the Cardinals, 10-5. Willie Mays hits the last homer ever in the ballpark. After the game, groundskeeper Bill Stocksick, who set the original home plate in 1909, digs up the current version. It then is flown by helicopter to the new Busch Memorial Stadium, where Stan Musial and Joan Nolan – Miss Redbird of 1966 – plant it.

The 1961 NL home run leader, first baseman Orlando Cepeda (.286 in 19 games), is sent by the Giants to the Cardinals for pitcher Ray Sadecki (2-1). Cepeda, the Baby Bull, appeared in only 33 games in 1965 because of a knee injury.

MAY 10:

After 12-plus years in a Dodger uniform, pitcher Johnny Podres (0-0), a hero of the 1955 World Series, is sold to the Tigers.

MAY 12:

In the first game at Busch Memorial Stadium in St. Louis, the Cardinals defeat the visiting Braves, 4-3, in 12 innings despite two homers by Felipe Alou. Lou Brock drives in the winning run with a 12th-inning single.

MAY 16:

Tigers' manager Charlie Dressen suffers his second heart attack in two years. Coach Bob Swift is named acting manager.

MAY 26:

At Candlestick Park, the Giants' Juan Marichal pitches all 14 innings to defeat the visiting Phillies by a score of 1-0.

MAY 29:

At Wrigley Field, for the second straight day, the Cubs' Ron Santo beats the Atlanta Braves with a home run in extra innings. Today his 10th-inning round-tripper gives Chicago a 3-2 win. Yesterday, he hit a three-run homer in the 12th for an 8-5 victory.

JUNE 7:

The Mets have the first overall pick in the free agent draft and select 17-year-old catcher Steve Chilcott. The Athletics, picking second, take 20-year-old Arizona State University outfielder Reginald Martinez Jackson.

JUNE 8:

Senators' second baseman Bob "Rabbit" Saverine has a day to forget, going hitless

MAY 26
Giants' workhorse Juan Marichal pitches all 14 innings of a 1-0 win over the Phillies.

JUNE 11
Ernie Banks ties an ML record with three triples in an 8-2 Cubs win at the Astrodome.

in 12 at-bats in a doubleheader against the Orioles. He matches the unenviable record set by the Cardinals' Albert "Red" Schoendienst – also a second sacker – in the 1947 season.

JUNE 9:

It's five homers and a near-miss in the Twins' assault on the record book. Playing against the visiting Athletics at Metropolitan Stadium, the Twins trail, 4-3, in the seventh inning. Kansas City's Jim "Catfish" Hunter walks Earl Battey and yields homers to Rich Rollins and Zoilo Versalles. Paul Lindblad comes out of the bullpen and retires Hilario "Sandy" Valdespino and serves up home runs to Tony Oliva and Don Mincher. John Wyatt relieves and Harmon Killebrew greets him with the fifth homer of the inning, tying the 1939 major league record of the Giants. Jimmie Hall then cracks a drive that hits the top of the wall and just misses going out. Killebrew had an earlier round-tripper in a 9-4 win for Minnesota.

JUNE 10:

The Indians' Sonny Siebert no-hits the Senators, 2-0, in Cleveland. It is the first no-hitter by an Indians' pitcher in 15 years. Siebert strikes out seven and walks one; Cleveland makes one error. Phil Ortega gets the loss.

> HALL OF FAME MANAGER JOE MCCARTHY, WHO KNEW TED WILLIAMS FROM BOTH SIDES OF THE DIAMOND, ONCE SAID: "HE COULD AFFECT A GAME JUST BY BEING IN THE ON-DECK CIRCLE. THE PITCHER WOULD KEEP LOOKING OVER AT HIM AND WORRYING ABOUT HIM. THERE NEVER WAS ANOTHER HITTER LIKE TED." JOE DIMAGGIO CLAIMED: "TED WILLIAMS WAS THE BEST HITTER I EVER SAW. THERE WAS NOBODY LIKE HIM."

JUNE 11:

Ernie Banks finds indoor baseball to his liking. The Cubs' first baseman ties a major league record with three triples in today's 8-2 win over Houston at the Astrodome.

JUNE 15:

In St. Louis, the Cardinals' Bob Gibson three-hits the Pirates, 1-0, for his 100th career win.

JUNE 21:

Hank Aaron hits his 24th homer in June, tying the record for the most ever in that month. Aaron hits the round-tripper in a 4-1 win over the visiting Phillies.

JUNE 26:

In Anaheim, the Orioles pound out 20 hits – including five by Russ Snyder – in a 12-7 win over the Angels. John "Boog" Powell drives in four runs on the day.

JULY 2:

In Washington, D.C., Mickey Mantle hits two solo home runs

CULTURE

In *The Great Baseball Mystery: The 1919 World Series*, a new book by Victor Luhrs, the author contends the Reds would have won the fixed World Series anyway. *The Glory of Their Times* by Lawerence S. Ritter is also published.

After the All-Star Game, Casey Stengel is asked his opinion of Busch Memorial Stadium. He replies: "Well, it certainly holds the heat very well."

TRIVIA

One of Athletics' owner Charles O. Finley's gimmicks is a mechanical rabbit that pops out of the ground near home plate with baseballs for the home plate umpire. The rabbit later moves with the Athletics from Kansas City to Oakland.

against starter Mike McCormick. It is his third two-homer game in the last five days; Mantle hit a pair against the Red Sox on June 28 and again on June 29. Despite Mantle's power display, the Senators win today's game, 10-4.

JULY 3:

It's a grand feat. Tony Cloninger of the Braves becomes the first NL pitcher to hit two grand slam home runs in a single game. He adds a single and knocks in nine runs in a 17-3 win over San Francisco at Candlestick Park. In the first inning, Cloninger homers over the centerfield fence against Bob Priddy. In the fourth, he hits a opposite-field homer to right against Ray Sadecki. Big days with the bat are not new for Cloninger; on June 16, he hit two homers and drove in five runs against the New York Mets. He has now driven in 18 runs over his last four ball games. Cloninger's teammates Joe Torre, Rico Carty, and Hank Aaron also connect for home runs. In the losing effort, Sadecki and Tom Haller hit round-trippers for the Giants. The losing pitcher in the game is Joe Gibbon.

JULY 4:

Casey a Tiger? Joe Fall of the *Detroit Free Press* reports rumors that 75-year-old Casey Stengel will come out of retirement to manage the Tigers. Both the team and the Old Perfessor deny the story.

At Wrigley Field, the Cubs' Ron Santo extends his consecutive game hitting streak to 28 in the opener of a doubleheader. The Pirates beat the Cubs, 7-5. In the nightcap the news is better for the Cubs, but worse for Santo. His hitting streak is snapped, but Chicago wins the game, 6-4.

JULY 6:

John "Boog" Powell of the Orioles drives in 11 runs in a doubleheader against the Athletics, tying a major league mark. Powell does his major damage in the opener, hitting two homers – including a grand slam – two doubles, and a sacrifice fly for seven RBI. Baltimore wins, 11-0. In the nightcap, he drives in four more.

JULY 8:

At Yankee Stadium, Mickey Mantle homers against Dick Bosman and Jim Hannan of the Senators. Mantle has now hit two homers in a game four times in 11 days. But the day ends badly for Mantle; he tears a hamstring muscle trying to score from second base on a wild pitch. The teams split.

JULY 9:

Astroturf is finally installed in the Astrodome outfield.

JULY 12:

The NL beats the AL, 2-1, in 10 innings on a single by Maury Wills, in the All-Star Game at Busch Memorial Stadium, where the temperature hits 105 degrees. The winning pitcher is Gaylord Perry; Pete Richert gets the loss.

JULY 13:

Tiger manager Bob Swift, filling in for the ailing Charlie Dressen, is himself stricken by a stomach ailment and hospitalized. Coach Frank Skaff becomes the acting manager. Under Dressen and Swift, the Tigers' record is 48-35.

JULY 15:

Acting Tiger manager Frank Skaff makes an unorthodox move and it pays off. With two out in the bottom of the ninth and the score tied, 5-5, he sends pitcher Earl Wilson in to pinch-hit against the Orioles' Stu Miller. Wilson hits a three-run homer for a Tigers' victory.

JULY 20:

Against the Reds at Wrigley Field, Ernie Banks reaches the 2,000-hit plateau. Cincinnati wins the game, 5-4.

JULY 22:

At Candlestick Park, the Giants' Gaylord Perry whiffs 15 Phillies en route to a 4-1 victory.

JULY 25:

Ted Williams and Casey Stengel are inducted into the Hall of Fame. Williams, the last major leaguer to hit .400, retired after 19 years with a .344 average, 521 homers, 1,839 RBI, and a .634 slugging percentage. Stengel won an unprecedented 10 pennants and seven World Series with the Yankees. The five-year waiting period was waived for Stengel, now five days short of 76 years old.

Ted Williams uses part of his induction speech to send a message: "I hope that someday Satchel Paige and Josh Gibson will be voted

JULY 3
The Braves' Tony Cloninger is the first NL pitcher to hit two grand slams in one game.

AUGUST 15
At Fenway, the Orioles' Boog Powell launches three homers over the Green Monster.

into the Hall of Fame as symbols of the great Negro players who are not here only because they weren't given the chance."

JULY 27:

With Sandy Koufax and Jim Bunning on the mound, it didn't figure to be a good day for hitters at Dodger Stadium – and it isn't. In 11 innings, Koufax strikes out 16 Phillies and allows four hits; Bunning fans 12 Dodgers, yielding six safeties. Los Angeles wins, 2-1, in 12 innings. Neither starter is involved in the decision.

JULY 29:

Mickey Mantle homers against Bruce Howard of the White Sox; it is his 494th career round-tripper and he passes Lou Gehrig for sixth place on the all-time list. The Yankees and Al Downing beat Chicago, 2-1.

AUGUST 10:

Tigers' manager Charlie Dressen, sidelined with a heart ailment since early this season, dies at age 67 in Detroit. Dressen managed for 16 years with the Reds, Dodgers, Senators, and Braves; the acme of his career were pennants with Brooklyn in 1952 and 1953. He also played in the majors as an infielder, batting .272 in eight years.

AUGUST 12:

Cincinnati's Art Shamsky makes a late but memorable entrance into today's game against the Pirates at Crosley Field. With Pittsburgh ahead by a 7-6 score, Shamsky comes to bat for the first time and greets Al McBean with a two-run homer. Stargell's homer puts the Pirates back up in the 10th. But in the bottom of the frame, Shamsky hits his second homer of the game, with the bases empty, against Elroy Face. In the bottom of the 11th, Shamsky does it again – walloping a two-run round-tripper against Billy O'Dell. The Pirates go on to win the game with three in the 13th – including a two-run single by Manny Mota—14-11. With 11 homers, the Pirates and Reds set an ML record for two teams in one game. Besides Stargell and Shamsky, the home run hitters are the Reds' Bob Bailey (two), Deron Johnson, and Pete Rose; and the Pirates Jesse Gonder, Roberto Clemente, and, finally, Jerry Lynch.

AUGUST 13:

The Indians have a new principal owner. Vernon Stouffer, the 64-year-old chief executive officer of the Stouffer Food Corporation, buys out Gabe Paul for $8 million. Indians fans get some good news; the franchise will remain in Cleveland.

AUGUST 14:

After being idle yesterday, Art Shamsky hits a pinch-hit two-run homer today off the Pirates' Vernon Law. It is Shamsky's fourth straight round-tripper, which ties a major league record.

AUGUST 15:

The Orioles left-handed slugger John "Boog" Powell hits three opposite-field homers over the left-field Green Monster at Fenway Park. Powell has 13 total bases in the game, won by Baltimore, 4-2, in 11 innings.

AUGUST 17:

Willie Mays homers against Ray Washburn of the Cardinals. It is his 535th career home run, putting him second only to Babe Ruth on the all-time list. Mays, who had been tied with Jimmie Fox, now holds the record for homers by a righthanded batter. The Giants win, 4-3.

AUGUST 22:

A tragedy is averted today when Andy Etchebarren saves teammate Frank Robinson from drowning at an Orioles' pool party.

AUGUST 25:

Albert Belle is born in Shreveport.

AUGUST 26:

Aggravated by cartoons shown on the Astrodome scoreboard targeting him, Cubs' manager Leo Durocher rips the dugout telephone off the wall during the ninth inning of the game and hurls it onto the playing field. Bob Aspromonte hits a grand slam homer against Cal Koonce and the Astros beat the Cubs, 7-4 – and Durocher gets billed for the telephone.

AUGUST 29:

The Detroit Tigers' Denny McLain wins his 16th start of the season, even though he doesn't do it the easy way. He throws 229 pitches, walks nine, and allows eight hits. However, he strikes out 11 in a 6-3 victory over the Baltimore Orioles.

TRIVIA

When Marvin Miller assumes the leadership of the Players' Association, its treasury contains $5,400 and its only property is a file cabinet.

HISTORY

John "Boog" Powell of the Orioles becomes the first player to appear in both the Little League World Series and the-major-league World Series.

SEPTEMBER 2:

If only he could face them in every start. The Phillies' Jim Bunning beats the Mets, 6-0. Bunning now has won eight out of eight against New York – all complete games, including five shutouts. He has allowed the Mets a total of four runs. At Forbes Field, Roberto Clemente homers against the Cubs for his 2,000th career hit. He also bats in his 101st run of the year in a 7-2 win.

SEPTEMBER 3:

The Pirates' Willie Stargell hits a home run against Robin Roberts of the Cubs. It is the 505th "gopher" ball thrown by Roberts – a major league record.

SEPTEMBER 4:

Attendance is only 18,670 in Cincinnati for a game with the Dodgers, but it enables Los Angeles to become the first team with 2 million in combined road/home attendance. The Dodgers beat the Reds, 8-6, on Jim Lefebvre's two-run homer.

SEPTEMBER 7:

The Giants meet the Dodgers in Los Angeles in their last contest of the season, trailing by one and a half games. In the top of the 12th, with the score tied, 2-2, and two out, a limping Willie Mays walks and then scores from first on a single into right field by rookie Frank Johnson. The Giants hold on for the victory.

IN HIS HALL OF FAME INDUCTION SPEECH, STENGEL SAYS, "I WANT TO THANK MY PARENTS FOR LETTING ME PLAY BASEBALL, AND I'M THANKFUL I HAD BASEBALL KNUCKLES AND COULDN'T BECOME A DENTIST."

SEPTEMBER 11:

Nolan Ryan makes his major league debut with the Mets, working two innings against the Braves, allowing a hit and a run while fanning three. Atlanta wins, 8-3, in New York.

SEPTEMBER 12:

The Dodgers' Ron Perranoski comes out of the bullpen and fans six Cardinals in a row in the fifth and sixth innings, tying an NL record. The Dodgers win, 3-2.

SEPTEMBER 15:

The Orioles' Tom Phoebus makes his major league debut, four-hitting the visiting Angels and striking out eight batters for a 2-0 victory.

SEPTEMBER 18:

Indians' pitchers continue to mow down opposing batters. In a game against the Tigers today in Detroit, Sam McDowell, John O'Donoghue, and Luis Tiant strike out 19 in nine innings. Cleveland has 21 for the game in a 6-5, 10-inning victory. The Tigers do some tough pitching as well, striking out a total of 10 Cleveland hitters.

SEPTEMBER 19:

Dan Topping sells his remaining 10 percent interest in the New York Yankees to the moguls at Columbia Broadcasting System for $1.4 million. CBS ends up paying a total of $14 million for full control of the team.

SEPTEMBER 20:

Tom Phoebus is making it look easy. The Orioles' right-hander pitches his second shutout in two major league starts, beating the Athletics, 4-0. Phoebus is the fourth AL pitcher and the eighth in the major leagues to record two shutouts in his first two games. Frank Robinson hits a two-run homer – his 47th round-tripper of this season.

The Tiffany Network takes over in the Bronx today. CBS executive Mike Burke replaces Dan Topping as president of the New York Yankees. It is decided, though that Ralph Houk will remain as manager.

SEPTEMBER 22
The Orioles clinch the AL pennant behind Jim Palmer's 6-1 gem against the Athletics.

OCTOBER 2
Sandy Koufax's victory over the Phillies – his last win ever – gives the Dodgers the NL flag.

SEPTEMBER 22:

Jim Palmer five-hits the Athletics, 6-1, in Kansas City to clinch the AL pennant for the Orioles, the first for the franchise since 1944, when they were the St. Louis Browns. Frank Robinson and Brooks Robinson have two RBI each.

It is more than a gathering and less than a crowd at Yankee Stadium. The depths to which baseball's greatest franchise has fallen is reflected in today's pathetic home attendance of 413 for a game with the White Sox. Chicago wins it, 4-1.

Sportscaster Red Barber has a WPIX-TV camera scan some of the 66,587 unoccupied seats at Yankee Stadium. The action is generally regarded as the reason Barber is dismissed at the end of the season. Howard Berk, a former Yankees' vice president, asserts the dismissal was because of Barber's announcing style.

SEPTEMBER 28:

He's got their number. The Cardinals' starter Larry Jaster whitewashes the Dodgers, 2-0; it is his fifth shutout against Los Angeles in five starts this year, tying an NL record. In 45 innings of work, he has limited the Dodgers to 24 singles. Between his first and second victories against Los Angeles, Jaster was sent to the minors and spent six weeks with Tulsa. Overall his record is 11-5 with a 3.26 ERA.

OCTOBER 2:

With Sandy Koufax's 6-3 victory over the Phillies in the nightcap of today's doubleheader, the Dodgers clinch their second consecutive NL pennant. Koufax records his 27th win of the season – and his last ever. In the opener, the Phillies beat Don Drysdale by a score of 4-3.

OCTOBER 3:

Edward "Mayo" Smith is signed to a two-year contract as manager of the Tigers, who finished third at 88-74 last season.

REGULAR SEASON WRAP-UP:

The Orioles win the AL pennant with a 97-63 record under Hank Bauer, finishing nine games ahead of the Twins. The pop in the lineup comes from Triple Crown winner Frank Robinson (.316, 49 homers, 122 RBI), backed by Boog Powell (.287, 34 homers, 109 RBI) and Brooks Robinson (.269, 23 homers, 100 RBI). Russ Snyder bats .306. The team has no 20-game winners; Jim Palmer is 15-10.

Under Walter Alston, the Dodgers win their second straight NL pennant with a record of 95-67, one and a half games ahead of the Giants. Los Angeles has no .300 hitters. Sandy Koufax has a dream year: 27-9 with a 1.73 ERA. Ron Fairly is the leading hitter with a .284 average and 11 homers. Jim Lefebvre hits 24 homers and drives in 74 runs; Lou Johnson has 17 homers and 73 RBI.

Rookie Jim Nash of the Athletics compiles a 12-1 record (.923 winning percentage). Matty Alou of the Pirates bats .342 for the NL title, beating out the Braves' Felipe Alou, who hits .327; they are the first brothers to finish first and second in a batting race.

OCTOBER 5:

World Series, game one. At Dodger Stadium, Moe Drabowsky comes out of the bullpen to hold Los Angeles to one hit, striking out 11 – including six in a row. Baltimore wins, 5-2. Frank Robinson and Brooks Robinson hit back-to-back homers in the first inning against losing pitcher Don Drysdale. Jim Lefebvre homers for the Dodgers.

OCTOBER 6:

World Series, game two. Jim Palmer four-hits the Dodgers, 6-0. Los Angeles makes six errors – including three in a row in the fifth by centerfielder Willie Davis – behind their losing pitcher, Sandy Koufax. Davis's misplays break a scoreless tie and enable the Orioles to tack on three runs.

OCTOBER 7:

The Phillies release veteran outfielder-infielder Harvey Kuenn (.296 in 89 games). Kuenn completes his 15-year career with a .303 average. In 1959 he led the AL in batting with a .353 average.

OCTOBER 8:

World Series, game three. In the first Series game ever in Baltimore, the Orioles' Wally Bunker and Dodgers' Claude Osteen lock up in a classic pitching duel. Bunker prevails, 1-0, on Paul Blair's fifth-inning, 430-foot

HISTORY

Over the last four years, Koufax is 97–27, including 27–9 in 1966. He pitches four no-hitters, wins three Cy Young Awards, and tops the NL in ERA five straight years. He holds the single season strikeout record – 382 in 1965 – and compiles an 0.95 ERA in World Series play. In his 12-year career, he is 165–87 with a 2.76 ERA, 40 shutouts, and 2,396 strikeouts.

OCTOBER 9
Frank Robinson's homer is all the Orioles need to sweep the Dodgers in the Series.

Sudden Sam McDowell is a one-hitter wonder.

homer. Bunker allows six hits; Osteen yields only three hits, but is charged with the game's loss.

OCTOBER 9:

World Series, game four. With 54,458 on hand at Memorial Stadium, the Orioles beat the Dodgers, 1-0, behind Dave McNally's four-hitter and sweep the World Series. Don Drysdale, who is tagged with the loss, allows only four hits, but one is a Frank Robinson fourth-inning homer that wins the game and the championship. The Orioles' staff has a 0.50 ERA and renders the Dodgers scoreless for 33 straight innings. Dodger pitchers allow 2.65 earned runs. Boog Powell bats .357. Frank Robinson hits two homers and bats in three runs. Lou Johnson is the Dodgers' top batter at .267.

POST-SEASON

OCTOBER 12:

The Chicago White Sox and Pittsburgh Pirates swap left-handed pitchers today. Chicago gets Wilbur Wood (1-1, 3.16 ERA in 1965). Going to Pittsburgh in the deal is Juan Pizarro (8-6, 3.76 ERA).

OCTOBER 17:

Bob Swift, who twice filled in for the late Charlie Dressen as Tigers' manager, dies at age 51 of lung cancer in Detroit. A former catcher who hit .231 in 14 years, Swift was 24-18 with Detroit in 1965 and 32-25 this past season.

NOVEMBER 8:

The Orioles' Frank Robinson is unanimously voted the AL's Most Valuable Player, becoming the first player to win the honor in both leagues since the Baseball Writers Association took it over in 1931. His teammates Brooks Robinson and Boog Powell finish second and third. Robinson, who won the AL's Triple Crown, was the NL's MVP in 1961 as a member of the Reds.

NOVEMBER 14:

Mets' president George Weiss, who has been with the team since its first season in 1961, retires. Bing Devine succeeds him and will be general manager, as well.

NOVEMBER 18:

The most dominating pitcher of his time, Sandy Koufax, announces his retirement at the age of 30. Speaking at a press conference in Los Angeles, the Dodger left-hander cites his arthritic pitching elbow and concerns about permanent disability. Koufax, who first experienced trouble three years ago, is placed on the voluntarily retired list and forgoes his $125,000 salary.

Koufax says, "I've had too many shots and taken too many pills because of my arm trouble. I don't want to take a chance of disabling myself. I don't regret for one minute the 12 years I spent in baseball, but I could regret one season too many."

NOVEMBER 29:

The Yankees trade their great gloveman, third baseman Clete Boyer (.240, 14 homers), to the Braves for outfielder Bill Robinson (.273 in six games) and pitcher Federico "Chi Chi" Olivo (5-4, 4.23 ERA).

The Dodgers send outfielder Herman "Tommy" Davis (.313, three homers), a two-time NL batting champion, to the Mets along with outfielder Derrell Griffith (.067 in 23 games). In return, Los Angeles obtains infielder Ron Hunt (.288, 3 homers) and outfielder Jim Hickman (.238, 4 home runs in 58 games).

DECEMBER 1:

Shortstop Maury Wills (.273, 38 stolen bases), who left the team during a tour of Japan, claiming a knee injury, and then was found playing the banjo in a nightclub in Hawaii, is traded to the Pirates. Los Angeles receives outfielder-third baseman Bob Bailey (.279, 13 home runs) and infielder Gene Michael (.152 in 309 games).

DECEMBER 8:

The man who broke Babe Ruth's single-season home run record today becomes a Cardinal. The New York Yankees trade outfielder Roger Maris (.233, 13 home runs), who hit 61 homers in 1961, to St. Louis. In return, the Yankees get the much-traveled infielder Charley Smith (.266, 10 homers).

DECEMBER 12:

The United States Supreme Court today declines to hear a lawsuit brought by the state of Wisconsin to prohibit the move of the Milwaukee Braves to Atlanta – after the fact, as they've been there since April.

Eddie Mathews, recalling his playing days in Milwaukee: "You know, I never had a cross word with anybody in 15 years in Milwaukee. Everybody had fun. We'd get to the park two, three hours early, sit around two, three hours after the game. Boy, that was enjoyable".

DECEMBER 13:

The San Francisco Giants obtain pitcher Mike McCormick (11-14, 3.46 ERA) from the Washington Senators in exchange for pitcher Bob Priddy (6-3, 3.96 ERA) and outfielder-infielder Charles "Cap" Peterson (.237 in 89 games).

DECEMBER 31:

The Braves trade Eddie Mathews (.250, 16 homers), who has been a fixture at third base for 15 years, to the Astros. Going to Houston along with Mathews are pitcher Arnold Umbach (0-2, 3.10 ERA) and infielder-outfielder Santos "Sandy" Alomar (.091 in 31 games). Atlanta gets outfielder Dave Nicholson (.246, 10 homers) and pitcher Bob Bruce (3-13, 5.34 ERA) in exchange.

Mathews is the only player to appear with the Braves in all three of their cities. He plays in Boston in 1952, in Milwaukee from 1953 to 1965, and in Atlanta this past season. He spends most of the 1967 season with the Astros – hitting .238 in 101 games and playing first base in more than half of those – before being dealt again, this time to the Detroit Tigers, where he finishes his 17-year career in 1968.

THE BEST OF 1966

NATIONAL LEAGUE

HITTERS

Batting Average:
Matty Alou, Pittsburgh Pirates, .342

Slugging Average:
Dick Allen, Philadelphia Phillies, .632

Home Runs:
Hank Aaron, Atlanta Braves, 44

Runs Batted In:
Hank Aaron, 127

Hits:
Felipe Alou, Atlanta Braves, 218

Stolen Bases:
Lou Brock, St. Louis Cardinals, 74

PITCHERS

Wins:
Sandy Koufax, Los Angeles Dodgers, 27

Strikeouts:
Sandy Koufax, 317

Earned Run Average:
Sandy Koufax, 1.73

Winning Percentage:
Juan Marichal, San Francisco Giants, .806

Saves:
Phil Regan, Los Angeles Dodgers, 21

Most Valuable Player:
Roberto Clemente, Pittsburgh Pirates

Cy Young Award:
Sandy Koufax, Los Angeles Dodgers

Rookie of the Year:
Tommy Helms, Cincinnati Reds

AMERICAN LEAGUE

HITTERS

Batting Average:
Frank Robinson, Baltimore Orioles, .316

Slugging Average:
Frank Robinson, .637

Home Runs:
Frank Robinson, 49

Runs Batted In:
Frank Robinson, 122

Hits:
Tony Oliva, Minnesota Twins, 191

Stolen Bases:
Bert Campaneris, Kansas City Athletics, 52

PITCHERS

Wins:
Jim Kaat, Minnesota Twins, 25

Strikeouts:
Sam McDowell, Cleveland Indians, 225

Earned Run Average:
Gary Peters, Chicago White Sox, 1.98

Winning Percentage:
Wilfred "Sonny" Siebert, Cleveland Indians, .667

Saves:
Jack Aker, Kansas City Athletics, 32

Most Valuable Player:
Frank Robinson, Baltimore Orioles

Rookie of the Year:
Tommie Agee, Chicago White Sox

1967

"I think about it all day. And I dream about it at night."
– Carl Yastrzemski, on baseball

NEWS

U.S. LAUNCHES FIRST AIR STRIKES ON HANOI

In New York City, hundreds of thousands protest Vietnam War

26 die in Newark race riots; 43 in Detroit disorder

TEAMSTER BOSS JIMMY HOFFA GOES TO PRISON

Three astronauts die in launching pad fire at Cape Kennedy

Thurgood Marshall first African-American on Supreme Court

ANTI-WAR MARCH IN WASHINGTON

Jack Ruby, killer of Lee Harvey Oswald, dies

LBJ, SOVIET PREMIER KOSYGIN MEET IN NEW JERSEY

Poets Carl Sandburg, Langston Hughes die

***At the movies,* Guess Who's Coming to Dinner?, The Graduate, Bonnie and Clyde, In the Heat of the Night, Cool Hand Luke, The Dirty Dozen**

PRE-SEASON

JANUARY 6:

A heart attack kills Johnny Keane at age 55 in his Houston home. Keane had managed the 1964 Cardinals to the World Championship. Most recently a special assignment scout for the Angels, he managed the Cardinals for four years and the Yankees for one and a fraction seasons. Keane never played major league baseball, however.

JANUARY 23:

Stan Musial is named general manager of the Cardinals, replacing Bob Howsam, who resigned to join the Cincinnati Reds.

The Red Sox report they have received an offer of $500,000 from the Athletics for 22-year-old outfielder Tony Conigliaro (.265, 28 homers, 93 RBI).

JANUARY 30:

Team president Mike Burke announces that Yankee Stadium, the House That Ruth Built, will get a $1.5-million facelift.

FEBRUARY 23:

Hank Aaron gets a $100,000 contract from the Braves. Last season he led the NL in homers with 44 and RBI with 127 while batting .279.

MARCH 4:

Wilber "Bullet" Rogan dies in Kansas City, Missouri, at the age of 77. Rogan starred with the Kansas City Monarchs in the Negro League. He was 113-45 as a pitcher and batted .343 in his 18-year major league career – including more than .400 twice.

THE SEASON

APRIL 10:

On opening day in Washington, D.C., Mickey Mantle plays first base for the first time and pitcher Mel Stottlemyre two-hits the Senators, 8-0. Bill Robinson and Elston Howard homer.

APRIL 13:

Tom Seaver, the pitching phenom out of the University of Southern California, makes his major league debut with the New York Mets at Shea Stadium. The 22-year-old right-hander pitches five and a third innings against the Pirates, yielding six hits, two earned runs, and four walks, and striking out eight. The Mets win, 3-2, but Seaver is not in-volved in the decision.

CULTURE

The television version of the Broadway musical *Damn Yankees*, starring Lee Remick, Phil Silvers, and Jerry Lanning, with Joe Garagiola, airs.

MAY 9
Nines are wild as Roger Maris, number 9, hits his first NL homer right to Seat 9, Row 9.

TRIVIA

During a May 20 game, the Orioles' madcap Moe Drabowsky rings up the telephone in the Athletics' bullpen, imitates Kansas City manager Alvin Dark's voice, and orders the relievers to begin warming up. Athletics' pitcher Jim Nash, who is working on a two-hitter, rages on the mound when he sees the action in the bullpen and thinks he is going to be replaced.

APRIL 14:

At Yankee Stadium, left-hander Bill Rohr makes his major league debut for the Red Sox, no-hitting New York for eight and two-thirds innings. Elston Howard's two-strike single busts up the no-hitter, but Boston wins, 3-0, beating Whitey Ford.

Rohr wins only one more game in 1967. He is 1-0 for the Indians in 1968 and finishes his brief major league career at age 22 with a two-year record of 3-3 with a 5.64 ERA.

APRIL 19:

In Chicago, Whitey Ford beats Tommy John and the White Sox, 3-0, for his 235th career win and his 45th and final shutout. The Yankees move into first place.

APRIL 20:

Tom Seaver beats the Chicago Cubs, 6-1, at Shea Stadium for his first major league victory. He allows eight hits and no walks, while striking out five batters in seven and two-thirds innings of work. The Mets' Herman "Tommy" Davis hits a home run against Chicago pitcher Curt Simmons.

APRIL 21:

Today's Dodgers-Cardinals game in Los Angeles is postponed because of rain. It is the first rainout after 737 games played at Dodger Stadium.

APRIL 29:

At Yankee Stadium, Whitey Ford beats Tommy John and the White Sox, 11-2, for the second time in 10 days. It is Ford's 236th career win and his last.

APRIL 30:

Orioles' pitchers Steve Barber and Stu Miller combine to no-hit the Tigers, but Baltimore loses, 2-1, in the opener of a double-header in Detroit. Barber is plagued by wildness, but carries a 1-0 lead into the ninth inning. He walks Norm Cash and Ray Oyler. Tiger pitcher Earl Wilson sacrifices and Willie Horton fouls out. Within one out of a no-hitter and victory, Barber throws a wild pitch, scoring the tying run. He then walks Mickey Stanley and is replaced by Stu Miller. Don Wert grounds to Luis Aparicio, but Mark Belanger drops the throw at second base for what would have been the final out and Oyler scores with the winning run. Winning pitcher Earl Wilson and Fred Gladding combine to hold the Orioles to only two hits. The Tigers win the night-cap as well, 6-4.

MAY 5:

At Fenway Park, Carl Yastrzemski homers against the Orioles' Eddie Fisher. It is his 100th career homer.

MAY 9:

Nine is today's lucky number for Roger Maris of the Cardinals. Playing against the Pirates in Pittsburgh, Maris – who wears number 9 – hits his first NL home run on the ninth day of the month and it lands in Seat 9, in Row 9.

MAY 14:

In the seventh inning at Yankee Stadium, Mickey Mantle, batting left-handed, hits a Stu Miller 3-2 pitch into the lower right-field stands. It is his 500th career round-tripper and provides the Yankees with a 6-5 victory over Baltimore. Mantle is the sixth player to reach 500 homers. Horace "Dooley" Womack gets the win.

MAY 15:

The Dodgers' Phil "The Vulture" Regan loses for the first time in 71 appearances – more than a year. Bob Aspromonte of the Astros hits a two-run triple in the 10th inning to defeat Regan and the Dodgers, 5-3.

John Smoltz is born in Detroit.

MAY 16:

The Dodgers release Edmundo "Sandy" Amoros, one of the heroes of Brooklyn's 1955 World Series win. The 37-year-old Amoros, who last played in the majors in 1960, was signed on May 5 so he could qualify for a pension.

MAY 17:

The Orioles and Red Sox play long ball with 10 home runs in a 12-8 Baltimore victory. In the seventh inning, the Orioles' Andy Etchebarren, Sam Bowens, John "Boog" Powell, and Davey Johnson homer. Paul Blair, Frank Robinson, and Brooks Robinson also hit round-trippers for Baltimore. Carl Yastrzemski has two and Don Demeter one for Boston. The winning pitcher is Bill Dillman; the Orioles' Galen Cisco is pinned with the loss.

MAY 20:

At Wrigley Field, the Cubs score every which way en route to

MAY 30
The Yankees' longtime ace Whitey Ford retires with a career record of 236-109 and 2.75 ERA.

a 20-3 win and Dodgers' pitcher Don Drysdale waves a white towel in surrender. Randy Hundley has a grand slam homer, Adolfo Phillips drives in six runs, Glenn Becker hits an inside-the-park round-tripper, and Ted Savage steals home. Ken Holtzman, who reports for army service tomorrow, is the winning pitcher.

MAY 21:

His great career winding down, Whitey Ford lasts only an inning against the Detroit Tigers because of a sore elbow.

MAY 30:

Whitey Ford calls it a career. With the retirement of Sandy Koufax last November and now Ford, baseball has lost two of its greatest left-handed pitchers. Troubled by a bone spur in his pitching elbow, Ford is only 2-4 but has a 1.64 ERA. His .690 career winning percentage is the highest of any modern pitcher with 200 or more wins. Ford finishes with a 236-106 record, a 2.75 ERA, and 10 Series wins.

JUNE 4:

Cardinals' centerfielder Curt Flood drops a fly ball in a game against the Cubs at Busch Stadium, ending his NL record of 227 consecutive games and 568 chances without an error.

JUNE 6:

Catcher Bob Uecker (.171 in 18 games) is traded by the Phillies to the Atlanta Braves. Philadelphia gets catcher-first baseman-outfielder Gene Oliver (.196 in 17 games).

JUNE 11:

Adolfo Phillips homers three times, Randy Hundley twice, and Ernie Banks and Ron Santo once each as the Cubs hammer the Mets, 18-9, in the second game of a doubleheader at Wrigley Field. The Mets homer three times; the combined 11 ties a major league record set by the Tigers and Yankees in 1950. The Cubs also won the opener, 5-3. In that game, Phillips had a home run and Ted Savage stole home.

JUNE 12:

Batting against Dick Farrell of the Phillies in the eighth inning, Hank Aaron singles to left for his 2,500th major league hit. Philadelphia wins the game at home, 7-4. In Washington, D.C., the Senators beat the White Sox, 6-5, in a 22-inning contest that lasts six hours and 38 minutes, the longest night game ever in the American League.

JUNE 17:

In Detroit, the Tigers and Athletics play a nine hour and five minute doubleheader – and split the two games. In the opening contest, which is delayed by rain, the Tigers win, 7-6. The nightcap, a 19-inning affair, is won by the Athletics, 6-5, on a Dave Duncan homer.

JUNE 18:

The Astros' Don Wilson no-hits the Braves, 2-0, in Houston. Wilson fans 15 and walks three; the Astros play errorless baseball. Phil Niekro is charged with the loss.

JUNE 21:

Things get ugly at Yankee Stadium. Yankees' pitcher Thad Tillotson hits Joey Foy of the Red Sox in the head and Jim Lonborg retaliates by hitting Tillotson. The Yankees' pitcher throws at

CULTURE

***The Bedfellow*, a novel by Eliot Asinof, is about a black former major league player who is at a crossroads in his life.**

Carl Yastrzemski is the last Triple Crown winner.

HISTORY

In 1967, outfielder Carroll Hardy completes his eight-year major league career with a .225 lifetime average and 17 home runs. Yet he was the only man ever to pinch-hit for Ted Williams (in 1960) and also batted for Roger Maris and Carl Yastrzemski. Hardy played professional football with the San Francisco 49ers in 1955.

Lonborg. In the next inning, Dick Howser is hit in the head by Lonborg. It takes a dozen security officers to break up the ensuing brawl. Boston manager Dick Williams and Yankees' coaches Frank Crosetti and Loren Babe all get warnings from the umpires. (Ralph Houk had been ejected earlier for arguing.) The Red Sox go on to win the game, 8-1. In San Francisco, Braves' catcher Bob Uecker hits a grand slam homer and drives in five runs in a 9-2 win over the Giants.

JUNE 27:

The Orioles' Frank Robinson suffers a concussion when his head hits the knee of White Sox second baseman Al Weis. Robinson will be out for a month; Weis fares worse – he will miss the remainder of the season.

Another American League superstar, Al Kaline of the Detroit Tigers, suffers a disabling injury, but this one is self-inflicted. The normally placid Kaline is fanned by the Indians' Sudden Sam McDowell and breaks his right hand jamming his bat into the rack. Kaline will be sidelined for 28 days. He returns to finish at .308 with 25 homers.

PLAYER-TURNED-BROADCASTER BOB UECKER RECALLS, "THE HIGHLIGHT OF MY BASEBALL CAREER CAME IN PHILADELPHIA'S CONNIE MACK STADIUM WHEN I SAW A FAN FALL OUT OF THE UPPER DECK. WHEN HE GOT UP AND WALKED AWAY, THE CROWD BOOED."

JUNE 30:

In the nightcap of a doubleheader, Phillies' utility player Octavio "Cookie" Rojas pitches a scoreless ninth inning in a 12-3 Giants' victory. With the Phillies since 1963, the versatile Rojas now has played all nine positions.

JULY 3:

In Atlanta, the Cubs and Braves explode for five homers in the first inning – a major league record for any frame. In the top of the first, Billy Williams, Ron Santo, and Randy Hundley hit homers; the Braves come back with round-trippers by Rico Carty and Felipe Alou. Carty adds another later in the game and the Cubs' Glenn Beckert hits a three-run shot. The Cubs and Ray Culp win, 12-6.

JULY 4:

In the opener of a doubleheader in Minnesota, Mickey Mantle homers twice against Jim "Mudcat" Grant – his 511th and 512th career round-trippers – tying and passing Mel Ott. Mantle now trails only Babe Ruth, Willie Mays, Jimmie Foxx, and Ted Williams. The Twins win twice, 8-3 and 7-6.

JULY 9:

Dick Allen of the Phillies hits a pitch from Nelson Briles of the Cardinals over the centerfield fence between the flagpole and stands in Connie Mack Stadium. He is the first to homer to that spot since the height of the fence was increased to 32 feet. The Phillies win, 4-3.

JULY 11:

Tony Perez of the Reds ends the longest All-Star Game in history with a 15th-inning home run off Jim "Catfish" Hunter, giving the NL a 2-1 victory in Anaheim Stadium. Despite Perez's home run, the game is a showcase for pitching. The NL's Ferguson Jenkins strikes out seven hitters, tying a record held by Carl Hubbell and Johnny Vander Meer. Five pitchers for the AL allow no walks, and a total of 30 batters for both teams are retired on strikes. Dick Allen and Brooks Robinson also homer in the game.

JULY 14:

Eddie Mathews of the Astros homers against Juan Marichal in the fourth inning today at Candlestick Park. It is Mathews's 500th career home run; he is the seventh in

JULY 3
The Cubs and Braves combine for five first-inning homers – a major league record.

JULY 11
The Reds' Tony Perez ends the longest-ever All-Star Game with a 15th-inning home run.

history to reach that plateau and the second this season. Houston goes on to win the game, 8-6.

JULY 15:

Cardinals' pitcher Bob Gibson suffers a broken leg when he is hit by a line drive off the bat of the Pirates' Roberto Clemente in the fourth inning of today's game in St. Louis. The Pirates win the game, 6-4.

JULY 21:

Hall of Famer Jimmie Foxx chokes to death on a piece of meat in his brother's home in Miami. He was 59 years old. In 20 years, Foxx hit 534 homers and compiled .325 batting and .609 slugging averages along with 1,921 RBI. Elected to the Hall of Fame in 1951, Foxx hit .344 and compiled a .609 slugging average playing in three World Series.

JULY 22:

The Braves use a major league record five relief pitchers in the ninth inning against the Cardinals in St. Louis. Coming out of the bullpen are Ken Johnson, Ramon Hernandez, Claude Raymond, Dick Kelley, and Cecil Upshaw. Atlanta hangs on, 5-4.

JULY 24:

Branch Rickey, famed for bringing Jackie Robinson to the major leagues; Charles "Red" Ruffing; and Lloyd "Little Poison" Waner are inducted into the Hall of Fame. Rickey, the creator of baseball's farm system, was a major league player and manager, but is remembered most for his leadership in breaking down the modern color line in the major leagues. Ruffing pitched 22 years, compiling a 273-225 record with a 3.80 ERA, winning 20 games four times. In seven World Series he was 7-2 with a 2.63 ERA. Waner, an outfielder, played 18 years and hit .316. He hit .300 or better 11 times, with a high of .355 in 1927, his rookie season. He is the younger brother of Hall of Famer Paul "Big Poison" Waner.

In I Never Had It Made, *Jackie Robinson said of Branch Rickey: "I realized how much our relationship had deepened after I left baseball. It was that later relationship that made me feel almost as if I had lost my own father. Branch Rickey, especially after I was no longer in the sports spotlight, treated me like a son."*

JULY 25:

Today's Tigers-Orioles game is postponed because of racial rioting on the streets in Detroit. The games scheduled for tomorrow and the following day will be shifted to Baltimore.

JULY 29:

The Indians trade outfielder Rocky Colavito (.241 in 63 games) to the White Sox for outfielder Jim King (.120 in 23 games with Chicago) and infielder Marv Staehle (.111 in 32 games).

AUGUST 3:

Catcher-outfielder-first baseman Elston Howard (.196 in 66 games), who in 1955 became the first black to play for the Yankees, is traded to the Red Sox for pitcher Pete Magrini (0-1, 9.82 ERA in 1966) and minor league pitcher Ron Klimkowski.

AUGUST 5:

Today the Minnesota Twins' Dean Chance pitches five perfect innings against the Boston Red Sox, but rain halts the game. Minnesota's 2-0 win counts, but Chance's feat is listed under "No Hits Allowed, Less Than 9 Innings." Chance finishes the season at 20-14, with 18 complete games.

AUGUST 6:

Brooks Robinson of the Orioles sets a major league record by hitting into a triple play for the fourth time in his career.

AUGUST 17:

The Tigers acquire third baseman-first baseman Eddie Mathews (.238 in 101 games) from the Astros for pitcher Fred Gladding (6-4, 1.99 ERA, 12 saves) and a cash payment.

AUGUST 18:

In the fourth inning at Fenway Park, Angels' pitcher Jack Hamilton hits Tony Conigliaro in the face with a pitch, breaking his cheekbone and sending bone fragments into his left eye. The 22-year-old Conigliaro is carried off the field and taken to Boston's Santa Maria Hospital.

Conigliaro, who was batting .287 with 20 homers and 67 RBI in 20 games, misses all of the 1968 season. He returns in 1969, but has a problem with his eyesight for the remainder of his career.

AUGUST 19:

A's owner Charles O. Finley, embroiled in a clash with his

CULTURE

In "Mrs. Robinson," a song from the 1967 film *The Graduate*, Simon and Garfunkel ask a question that is destined to become a catchphrase of our culture: "Where have you gone, Joe DiMaggio? Our nation turns its lonely eyes to you."

Athletics' players, suspends pitcher Lew Krausse for conduct unbecoming a major league player.

AUGUST 20:

Charles O. Finley, expected to offer manager Alvin Dark a two-year contract, instead fires him for "losing control of his players." Luke Appling is installed as interim skipper. Dark read a letter from the players accusing Finley of using clubhouse informers and undermining team morale. Finley says, "this compels me to withhold the announcement of a two-year Dark contract until further consideration." The owner has averaged a manager a year since 1960.

AUGUST 24:

The Phillies' Dick Allen cuts his right hand when a headlight breaks while he is pushing a car. Allen, who was hitting .307 with 23 homers and 117 RBI, is lost for the rest of the season.

AUGUST 25:

The Twins' Dean Chance, who pitched a mini-perfect game on August 5, hurls a nine-inning, 2-1, no-hitter today against the Indians in Minnesota in the nightcap of a twi-night doubleheader. Chance walks five and fans nine batters. The Indians score their run on two walks, an error, and a wild pitch in the first inning. The Twins score on a Harmon Killebrew single in the second and a balk by losing pitcher Wilfred "Sonny" Siebert in the sixth. The Twins also win the opener, 6-5.

AUGUST 28:

Outfielder-first baseman Ken Harrelson, cut by Charles O. Finley on August 18 for calling the Athletics' owner "detrimental to baseball" and refusing to retract the statement, is signed by the Red Sox. Harrelson, who is getting an estimated $150,000 package, will replace the injured Tony Conigliaro. Harrelson is hitting .275 (.305 in 61 games with the Athletics and .203 in 26 with the Washington Senators).

AUGUST 29:

Bert Campaneris of the Athletics ties a modern major league record with three triples in a game, but Kansas City bows to the Indians, 9-8, in 10 innings.

SEPTEMBER 10:

Joel Horlen of the White Sox no-hits the visiting Tigers, 6-0, in the opener of a doubleheader. Horlen strikes out four and allows no walks; Chicago makes one error. The losing pitcher is Joe Sparma.

SEPTEMBER 17:

Athletics' rookie Reggie Jackson homers against Jim Weaver of the Angels in Anaheim. It is Jackson's first major league round-tripper.

SEPTEMBER 18:

In Philadelphia, Bob Gibson three-hits the Phillies, 5-1, to clinch the NL pennant for the Cardinals. The game marks Gibson's return from a broken leg suffered 52 days ago.

SEPTEMBER 21:

After two years at the helm, Wes Westrum – who replaced Casey Stengel – resigns as manager of the Mets. He will be replaced, on an interim basis for the final 11 games of the season, by coach Francis "Salty" Parker. The Mets finished ninth in 1966 and are in last place this year with a 57-94 record.

SEPTEMBER 27:

Luckless Jim Bunning of the Phillies loses, 1-0, in 11 innings to the Houston Astros. It is Bunning's fifth 1-0 loss this season. He finishes at 17-15.

OCTOBER 1:

Jim Lonborg beats the visiting Twins, 6-3, in the last game of the year and the Angels beat the Tigers, 8-5, to give the Red Sox the AL pennant – their first since 1948. Lonborg allows seven hits and four walks and strikes out five for his 22nd win of the year. Dean Chance gets the loss. Carl Yastrzemski has four hits – including a double – and two RBI in four at-bats. In the final two weeks of the season, he hits .522 with five homers and 16 RBI. The Indians fire manager Joe Adcock after just one season. The Indians are in eighth place with a record of 75-87, their worst since 1914.

OCTOBER 2:

Alvin Dark is named the manager of the Cleveland Indians for the 1968 season.

Ground is broken for the Phillies' new stadium in Philadelphia.

REGULAR SEASON WRAP-UP:

The Cardinals, under Albert "Red" Schoendienst, win the NL pennant with a record of 101-60, 10 1/2 games ahead of the Giants. Orlando Cepeda hits .325 with 25 homers and 111 RBIs. Curt Flood bats

HISTORY

The playing career of one of baseball's strange characters, Jimmy Piersall, comes to an end in 1967 after he is hitless in three at-bats with the Angels. An able outfielder who hit .272 in a 17-year career, Piersall detailed his emotional turmoil in *Fear Strikes Out,* which was made into a movie and a TV film. His on-field antics, including a fistfight with the Yankees' Billy Martin, often obscured his ability.

.335 and Lou Brock .299 with 52 steals. Bob Gibson misses 52 days with a broken leg and finishes 13-7. The top winner is Dick Hughes at 16-6.

The Red Sox, in ninth place last season, compile a 92-70 record under Dick Williams and beat Detroit by a game in the AL. Outfielder Carl Yastrzemski hits .326, 44 homers and 121 RBI. George Scott bats .303 with 19 homers. Jim Lonborg tops the pitching staff with a 22-9 record.

The Minnesota Twins are the first major league team ever with three pitchers at 200-plus strikeouts for the season – Dean Chance, 220, Jim Kaat has 211, and Dave Boswell finishes with 204.

OCTOBER 4:

World Series, game one. Bob Gibson six-hits the Red Sox and fans 10 in a 2-1 victory for the Cardinals at Fenway Park. Boston pitcher Jose Santiago homers in his first at-bat, but gets tagged with the loss. Lou Brock has four hits in his four at-bats and steals two bases.

OCTOBER 5:

World Series, game two. Carl Yastrzemski and Jim Lonborg even the Series for Boston with a 5-0 win at Fenway Park. Lonborg allows one hit – a two-out double by Julian Javier in the eighth inning. Yastrzemski hits a solo homer and a three-run homer. Dick Hughes is tagged with the loss.

OCTOBER 7:

World Series, game three. At Busch Stadium, Nelson Briles goes all the way, limiting Boston to seven hits in a 5-2 victory. Mike Shannon hits a two-run homer for St. Louis; Reggie Smith homers with no one on for Boston. Gary Bell is the game's losing pitcher.

OCTOBER 8:

World Series, game four. Bob Gibson five-hits Boston, 6-0, at Busch Stadium. He strikes out six and allows only one walk. St. Louis puts the game away early with a four-run first and a two-run second. Jose Santiago is the losing pitcher for the second time in the Series.

OCTOBER 9:

World Series, game five. Jim Lonborg outpitches Steve Carlton and the Red Sox win, 3-1, in St. Louis. Lonborg goes the distance, allowing three hits, striking out four, and walking none. He loses his shutout on a Roger Maris solo home run in the bottom of the ninth. Elston Howard drives in the winning run in the top of the ninth with a bases-loaded single.

OCTOBER 11:

World Series, game six. Back at Fenway Park, the Red Sox hit four homers to beat the Cardinals, 8-4. In the fourth inning, Boston sets a Series record with three homers – by Carl Yastrzemski, Reggie Smith, and Rico Petrocelli (his second of the game). The winning pitcher is John Wyatt, the fourth of Boston's five pitchers. The Cardinals use eight pitchers; Jack Lamabe gets the loss.

Gil Hodges is named manager of the Mets, replacing interim

Orlando Cepeda is the NL's first unanimous NL MVP.

> "Bob Gibson is the luckiest pitcher I ever saw. He always pitches when the other team doesn't score any runs."
> – *Cardinals' catcher Tim McCarver*

skipper Salty Parker. Under Wes Westrum and Parker the Mets finished last place with a 61-101 record.

OCTOBER 12:

World Series, game seven. Bob Gibson three-hits the Red Sox, 7-2, and the Cardinals are the World Champions. Gibson helps his own cause with a homer and strikes out 10 Red Sox while issuing only three walks. Julian Javier hits a three-run homer for St. Louis. Jim Lonborg goes six innings and gets the loss. Gibson finishes the Fall Classic with three complete-game wins, a 1.00 ERA, and 26 strikeouts in 27 innings. Lou Brock has 12 hits, a .414 average, and seven stolen bases. Roger Maris hits .385 and bats in seven runs. Carl Yastrzemski hits .400 with three homers and five RBI.

POST-SEASON

OCTOBER 18:

In an 11-plus-hour meeting at the Continental Plaza Hotel in Chicago, AL owners approve Charles O. Finley's transfer of his Athletics from Kansas City to Oakland in time for the 1968 season. The AL also approves expansion "no later than 1971," under which Kansas City will get a new team and Seattle will be awarded a franchise. In 1969, both leagues will have two divisions and post-season playoffs for the pennant.

NOVEMBER 7:

The Cardinals' Orlando Cepeda is the first-ever unanimous Most Valuable Player selection in the history of the NL.

NOVEMBER 27:

The Mets send pitcher Bill Denehy (1-7, 4.70 ERA) and $100,000 to the Senators for the rights to manager Gil Hodges. The former Dodgers' star led Washington to a 76-85 record and tied for sixth place in the AL this past season.

NOVEMBER 28:

The Twins trade shortstop Zoilo Versalles (.200, six homers), the 1965 AL MVP, and pitcher Jim "Mudcat" Grant (4-6, 4.72 ERA) to the Dodgers. In return, Minnesota gets catcher Johnny Roseboro (.272, four homers) and pitchers Ron Perranoski (6-7, 3.18 ERA) and Bob L. Miller (2-9, 4.31 ERA).

NOVEMBER 29:

The White Sox reacquire outstanding shortstop Luis Aparicio (.233, four homers) five years after trading him away. Coming to Chicago from Baltimore with Aparicio are outfielder Russ Snyder (.236, four homers) and minor league first baseman John Matias. In return, the Orioles acquire outfielder-infielder Don Buford (.241, four homers) and starting pitcher Bruce Howard (3-10, 3.43 ERA) and Roger Nelson (0-1, 1.29 ERA in his rookie season).

DECEMBER 1:

The NL unanimously votes to add two more teams by 1971. Earlier this year, the AL approved expansion by 1971 with the addition of a Seattle franchise and a new Kansas City team. The NL is looking at applications from the cities of Milwaukee, Dallas-Fort Worth, Montreal, Toronto, Buffalo, and San Diego. The league's owners hire John J. Gaherin, president of the New York City Publishers Association. He will lead the Major League Baseball Players Relations Committee, which is composed of the league presidents and three owners from each circuit.

DECEMBER 5:

The Cardinals' Stan Musial, the only general manager with a World Series winner in his first year, resigns his position but will remain with the team as senior vice president and consultant. Musial became general manager last year. Bing Devine leaves the New York Mets to succeed Musial.

DECEMBER 15:

Today the Pittsburgh Pirates obtain veteran right-handed pitcher Jim Bunning (17-15, 2.29 ERA) from the Philadelphia Phillies in exchange for pitcher Woodie Fryman (3-8, 4.05 ERA), minor league infielder Don Money, and minor league pitchers Bill Laxton and Hal Clem.

DECEMBER 27:

Jim Lonborg, who won a league-leading 22 games this season for Boston Red Sox, undergoes surgery on torn ligaments in his left knee at Santa Maria Hospital. Lonborg was injured in a skiing mishap back on December 23 at a resort in Heaven Valley, California.

LEAGUE

U.S. Senator Stuart Symington of Missouri threatens Federal legislation and calls A's owner Charles O. Finley, "one of the most disreputable characters ever to enter the American sports scene." And he has more "kind" words for the departing Athletics: "Oakland is the luckiest city since Hiroshima."

OCTOBER 12
Bob Gibson wins his third Series game vs. the Red Sox, and the Cardinals are champs.

OCTOBER 18
American League owners okay the move of the Kansas City Athletics to Oakland.

THE BEST OF 1967

NATIONAL LEAGUE

HITTERS

Batting Average:
Roberto Clemente, Pittsburgh Pirates, .357

Slugging Average:
Hank Aaron, Atlanta Braves, .573

Home Runs:
Hank Aaron, 39

Runs Batted In:
Orlando Cepeda, St. Louis Cardinals, 111

Hits:
Roberto Clemente, 209

Stolen Bases:
Lou Brock, St. Louis Cardinals, 52

PITCHERS

Wins:
Mike McCormick, San Francisco Giants, 22

Strikeouts:
Jim Bunning, Philadelphia Phillies, 253

Earned Run Average:
Phil Niekro, Atlanta Braves, 1.87

Winning Percentage:
Dick Hughes, St. Louis Cardinals, .727

Saves:
Ted Abernathy, Cincinnati Reds, 28

Most Valuable Player:
Orlando Cepeda, St. Louis Cardinals

Cy Young Award:
Mike McCormick, San Francisco Giants

Rookie of the Year:
Tom Seaver, New York Mets

AMERICAN LEAGUE

HITTERS

Batting Average:
Carl Yastrzemski, Boston Red Sox, .326

Slugging Average:
Carl Yastrzemski, .622

Home Runs:
Carl Yastrzemski; Harmon Killebrew, Minnesota Twins, 44

Runs Batted In:
Carl Yastrzemski, 121

Hits:
Carl Yastrzemski, 189

Stolen Bases:
Bert Campaneris, Kansas City Athletics, 55

PITCHERS

Wins:
Earl Wilson, Detroit Tigers; Jim Lonborg, Boston Red Sox, 22

Strikeouts:
Jim Lonborg, 246

Earned Run Average:
Joel Horlen, Chicago White Sox, 2.06

Winning Percentage:
Joel Horlen, .731

Saves:
Minervino "Minnie" Rojas, California Angels, 27

Most Valuable Player:
Carl Yastrzemski, Boston Red Sox

Cy Young Award:
Jim Lonborg, Boston Red Sox

Rookie of the Year:
Rod Carew, Minnesota Twins

HISTORY

Making their major league debuts in 1967 are four future Hall of Famers: Tom Seaver, Johnny Bench, Rod Carew, and Reggie Jackson.

1968

"Winning isn't the only thing. But wanting to is."
– *Jim "Catfish" Hunter*

NEWS

MARTIN LUTHER KING ASSASSINATED IN TENNESSEE

ROBERT KENNEDY ASSASSINATED IN CALIFORNIA

Violence in Chicago streets during Democratic Convention

NIXON DEFEATS HUMPHREY FOR THE PRESIDENCY

Soviet Union occupies Czechoslovakia

U.S. ASTRONAUTS ORBIT THE MOON

North Korea seizes USS *Pueblo*

Jacqueline Kennedy marries Aristotle Onassis

JOHN STEINBECK, HELEN KELLER DIE

***APOLLO 7* ORBITS EARTH FOR 11 DAYS**

2001: A Space Odyssey *stars a computer named HAL*

PRE-SEASON

FEBRUARY 5:

Roberto Alomar, the son of White Sox infielder Santos "Sandy" Alomar, is born in Ponce, Puerto Rico.

FEBRUARY 21:

The owners' Players Relations Committee and the Players consistency Association sign the first ever "basic agreement." Among its provisions are an increase of minimum salaries to $10,000 and a formal grievance procedure. Both sides also agree to further study of the reserve clause.

MARCH 21:

The AL's new Kansas City franchise announces it will be known as the Royals.

MARCH 31:

Seattle, the AL's second new team, announces its nickname – the Pilots.

THE SEASON

APRIL 15:

In Houston, the Astros beat the Mets, 1-0, in 24 innings and six hours and six minutes – the longest shutout and night game ever. With Les Rohr on the mound for New York in the bottom of the 24th, Norm Miller singles and goes to second base on a balk. Jim Wynn receives an intentional walk. John Bateman follows with another base on balls. After that, Bob Aspromonte's ground ball, looking like a sure double play, goes rolling through the legs of shortstop Al Weis, scoring Miller with the winning run. The winning pitcher is Wade Blasingame; Rohr gets the loss.

APRIL 17:

The Athletics play their first game in Oakland-Alameda Coliseum, bowing to the Orioles, 4-1, on a Dave McNally two-hitter. Lew Krausse is credited with the loss.

APRIL 18:

In his 2,000th major league game, the Tigers' Al Kaline hits his 305th career homer. The Tigers win their sixth straight, 5-0, with Joe Sparma seven-hitting the Indians.

APRIL 19:

Mets' right-hander Nolan Ryan fans three Dodger batters on nine pitches in the third inning of today's game, but Los Angeles wins, 3-2.

APRIL 27:

The Orioles' Tom Phoebus no-hits the Red Sox, 6-0, in Baltimore. Phoebus strikes out nine and walks three; the Orioles play errorless ball. Brooks Robinson makes a diving catch of Rico Petrocelli's eighth-inning line drive to preserve the no-hitter. The game's losing pitcher is Gary Waslewski.

MAY 1:

"Sudden" Sam McDowell of the Indians and Johnny "Blue Moon" Odom of the Athletics both start hot. McDowell never cools off. Odom retires the first 15 Indians' batters, but the Indians reach him for a run in the sixth and two more in the seventh. McDowell three-hits Oakland, striking out 16 and winning, 3-0.

MAY 6:

At Yankee Stadium, Mickey Mantle touches Sam McDowell for a homer – the 522nd of his career, putting him ahead of Ted Williams into fourth place. But the game otherwise belongs to McDowell, who fans 14 and hits a two-run double for a 3-2 win. McDowell sets an AL

APRIL 17
The Athletics debut in Oakland with a 4-1 loss to the Baltimore Orioles.

MAY 8
The A's Catfish Hunter, just 22, pitches a perfect game against the Twins.

record with 30 strikeouts in two games and has 63 in 45 1/3 innings. The game is marked by a fistfight between the Yankees' Gene Michael and the Indians' Tony Horton; both are ejected.

MAY 8:

Jim "Catfish" Hunter of the Athletics pitches a perfect game against the Twins in Oakland. The 22-year-old Hunter is overpowering, fanning 11 and allowing only five balls out of the infield in a 4-0 victory. Hunter also has three hits and three RBI. It is the 10th perfect game ever and the first in the AL since Charlie Robertson of the White Sox in 1922. Hunter finishes the ninth by getting Johnny Roseboro to ground out, then fanning Bruce Look and Rich Reese, on a 3-2 pitch. Dave Boswell is the losing pitcher.

MAY 12:

Luis Tiant wields his whitewash brush for the fourth consecutive time, beating the Orioles, 2-0, in the opener of a doubleheader. Tiant now is 5-2. In the nightcap, Stan Williams of Cleveland beats Baltimore, 4-1.

MAY 14:

At Shea Stadium, a young and promising pitcher named Nolan Ryan strikes out 14 Reds and wins, 3-2, for the Mets.

MAY 15:

In the first of nine "home" games in Milwaukee, the White Sox lose to the Angels, 4-2, before a crowd of 23,403. The winning pitcher is George Brunet; Bob Locker gets the loss.

MAY 17:

Luis Tiant shuts out the Orioles for five innings, extending his scoreless inning streak to 41. But in the sixth John "Boog" Powell homers for Baltimore with two on, ending Tiant's skein, and the Orioles go on to win, 6-2.

MAY 18:

At Tiger Stadium, six-foot, seven-inch, 250-pound Frank "Hondo" Howard of the Senators homers twice in an 8-4 Washington win. Howard now has 10 homers in six games, breaking a record jointly held by Roger Maris, Willie Mays, George Kelly, and Walker Cooper. He also ties an AL record by homering in six consecutive games.

Both of today's round-trippers are smashed against Mickey Lolich, and are his 16th and 17th of the season. The Tigers' Al Kaline homers off Steve Jones for his 307th career round-tripper.

The Pirates' Bill Mazeroski sets an NL record for second basemen by playing in his 392nd consecutive game.

MAY 25:

Lew Krausse of the Athletics hits Al Kaline with a pitch and breaks his arm. The Tigers' outfielder-first baseman will be out of action for more than a month.

MAY 26:

A day after the Detroit Tigers' Al Kaline is sidelined by a pitched ball, the Oakland Athletics' pitcher, Jack Aker, hits Jim Northrup of the Tigers in the head. A 15-minute fight breaks out; Northrup is injured in the melee and has to leave the game. Oakland goes on to win, 7-6, in 10 innings.

A steady diet of perfect Catfish leaves the Twins feeling hitless.

Don Drysdale pitches 58 2/3 scoreless innings.

MAY 27:

After 10 hours of discussion and 16 secret ballots in Chicago, NL owners okay the entry of Montreal and San Diego to the circuit for next year. The new NL teams will debut at the same time as the AL's Kansas City and Seattle entries. Montreal and San Diego beat out Buffalo, Milwaukee, and Dallas-Fort Worth; they pay an entry fee of $10 million and will spend $6 million each to purchase 30 players from existing teams. San Diego, headed by former Dodger executive E.J. "Buzzy" Bavasi, will play in a new 45,000-seat stadium already built. Montreal, owned by a seven-person syndicate headed by financier Jean-Louis Levesque, has promised to construct a domed stadium.

Eddie Mathews of the Tigers homers against Sammy Ellis of the Angels in Anaheim. It is Mathews's 512th – and last – career home run. Detroit wins, 4-1.

Jeff Bagwell is born in Boston.

Frank "The Big Hurt" Thomas is born in Columbus, Georgia.

MAY 28:

The AL will have a different look next season. The league announces it will play in two divisions in 1969. Baltimore, Boston, Cleveland, Detroit, New York, and Washington will be the East. California, Chicago, Kansas City, Minnesota, Oakland, and Seattle will comprise the West.

MAY 29:

The Tigers' Denny McLain four-hits the Angels, 3-0, and fans 13 for his eighth win of the season.

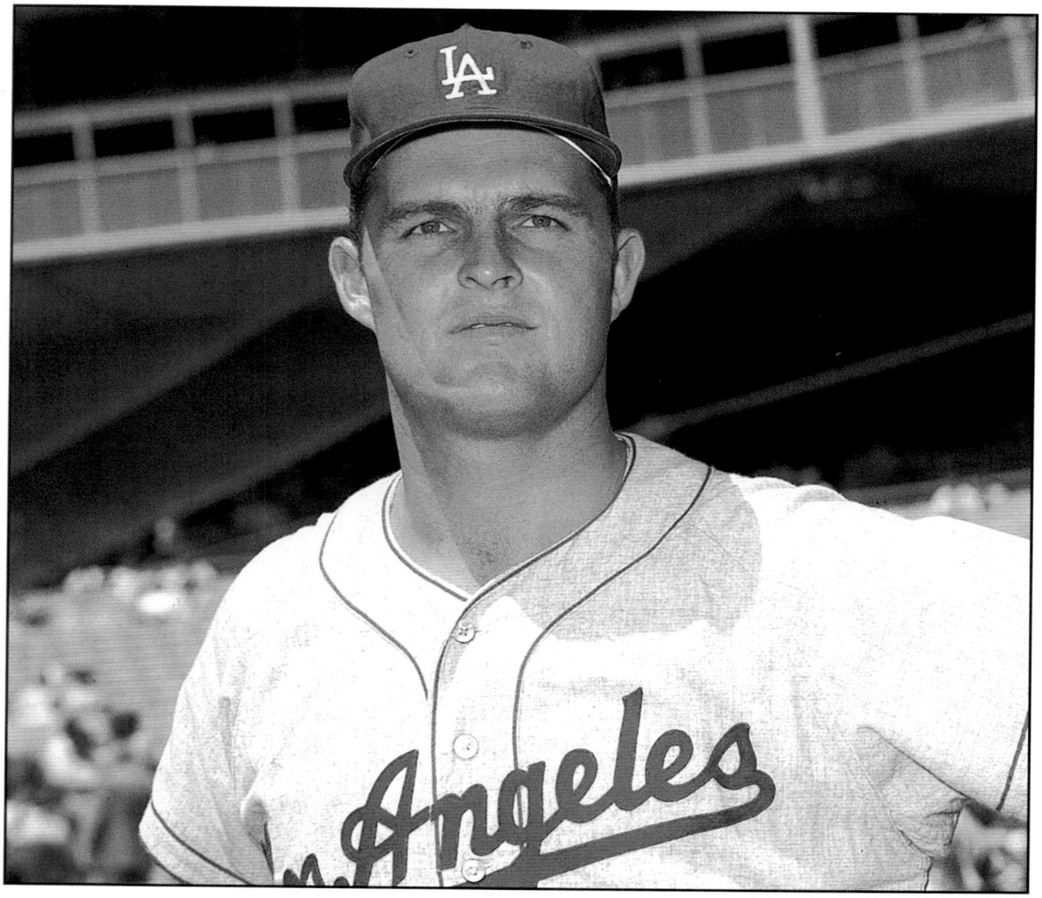

MAY 31:

Don Drysdale gets by with a little help from his friends – Rule 6.08b and home-plate umpire Harry Wendlestedt, who is familiar with it. In the ninth inning against the Giants, Drysdale is working on his fifth straight shutout. With the bases loaded, he hits Dick Dietz with a pitch, ostensibly forcing in a run that will end his scoreless inning streak. But Wendlestedt rules that Dietz made no effort to avoid the pitch. The runner – Willie McCovey – is returned to third, Dietz continues to bat and flies out. Drysdale proceeds to retire the side and the Dodgers win, 3-0.

JUNE 1:

The Cardinals' Joe Hoerner comes out of the bullpen to fan the last six Mets in a 6-5 victory, tying the

JUNE 8
Don Drysdale's record 58 2/3 scoreless innings end when the Phillies break through.

JUNE 25
Giants' rookie Bobby Bonds makes the most of his major league debut – a grand slam.

NL record for relief pitchers. He also gets the win when Mike Shannon hits a 10th-inning home run.

JUNE 4:

Don Drysdale shuts out the Pirates, 5-0, at Dodger Stadium for his sixth straight shutout, extending his string of scoreless innings to 54.

JUNE 8:

Don Drysdale's major league record scoreless inning streak ends today at 58 2/3 when the Phillies' Howie Bedell hits a sacrifice fly scoring Tony Taylor in the fifth inning at Dodger Stadium. In the third inning, Drysdale topped 1913 Walter Johnson's major league mark of 55 2/3. At the end of the inning, Philadelphia manager Gene Mauch demands that umpire Augie Donatelli inspect Drysdale for "moisture." Drysdale is warned that if he touches the back of his head, he will be automatically ejected from the game. In the fourth inning, Mauch is out to complain again. Drysdale began his streak on May 14, with a 1-0 whitewashing of the Chicago Cubs. The Dodgers win the game, 5-3.

JUNE 14:

In Cleveland, Ken Harrelson of the Red Sox homers three times consecutively – twice off Luis Tiant and once against Eddie Fisher. Harrelson also drives in all of Boston's runs in a 7-2 victory.

JUNE 15:

Hall of Fame outfielder Sam Crawford dies today at age 88 in Hollywood. A lifetime .309 hitter and the all-time leader in triples with 312, Crawford was inducted into the Hall of Fame in 1957.

JUNE 24:

In Cleveland, the Tigers' Jim Northrup hits grand slams in the fifth and sixth innings against the Indians' Eddie Fisher and Billy Rohr in a 14-3 Detroit win. Northrup began the day by striking out with the bases loaded. Denny McLain gets the win, his 13th. The game's losing pitcher is Mike Paul.

JUNE 25:

The Giants' Bobby Bonds hits a bases-loaded homer off Dodger pitcher Jack Purdin in the sixth inning, becoming the first player since Bill Duggleby in 1898 to make his major league debut with a grand slam. The 22-year-old outfielder was called up yesterday from the Pacific Coast League, where he was hitting .367. He is hitless in his other two at-bats. The Giants win, 9-0; Ray Sadecki is the winner, Claude Osteen gets the loss.

JUNE 26:

In the opener of a doubleheader in St. Louis, Bob Gibson beats the Pirates, 5-0, recording his fifth consecutive shutout. In the nightcap, the Cardinals end Maury Wills's 24-game hitting streak, but the Pirates win, 3-1.

JUNE 29:

Jim Northrup of the Tigers hits a bases-loaded home run against the White Sox in a 5-2 win. It is his third grand slam home run in less than a week. Denny McLain picks up his 14th win of the year.

JULY 1:

Bob Gibson's run at the consecutive scoreless inning record of 58 2/3 – set by Don Drysdale earlier this year – ends in the first inning today when his wild pitch enables Len Gabrielson to score. Gibson strung together 48 2/3 shutout innings. He gets some solace by beating the Dodgers, 5-1.

JULY 3:

Denny McLain keeps mowing down AL hitters. Today he limits the Angels to four hits and strikes out 15 in a 5-2 victory – his 15th of the season. Norm Cash, Willie Horton, and Dick Tracewski homer for the Tigers.

Luis Tiant, the Indians' crafty right-hander, spins a gem, striking out 19 batters while walking none in a 1-0, 10-inning win over the Twins. Tiant allows six hits and wins his 13th – with seven shutouts.

JULY 7:

The Tigers are rolling and the rest of the AL is eating their dust. In the opener of a doubleheader today, Denny McLain pitches a five-hitter, beating the Athletics, 5-4, for his 16th win. In the nightcap, the Tigers take a 7-6 decision. At the All-Star Game break, they lead second-place Cleveland by nine and a half games.

JULY 9:

Two firsts at the All-Star Game: the NL beats the AL in the

CULTURE

"(Love Is Like a) Baseball Game" is recorded by the Intruders, a quartet from Philadelphia. It is written by Kenny Gamble and Leon Huff.

JULY 14
With a long ball against the Giants, Hank Aaron joins the elite 500-home run club.

LEAGUE

The Major League Players Association signs a baseball card contract with Topps reportedly worth "several million." "

first-ever 1-0 game. And for the first time the game is played indoors – at Houston's Astrodome. Willie Mays scores on a double-play ball by Willie McCovey in the first inning for the game's only run. Don Drysdale is the winning pitcher; Tom Seaver strikes out five batters in his two innings of work. Luis Tiant gets the loss.

JULY 10:

At a four-and-a-half-hour joint session on uniformity for the 1969 season, both leagues accept the recommendations of baseball's executive council. Each will have two divisions of six teams – a format the AL already approved; the schedule will consist of 162 games in a 25-week season; play will commence on April 7 and end on October 2, and divisional playoffs will be best-of-five faceoffs.

JULY 11:

First base coach Earl Weaver is named Baltimore Orioles' manager, succeeding Hank Bauer, who had the team at 43-37.

JULY 12:

In Minnesota, Tigers' ace Denny McLain three-hits the Twins, 5-1, for his 17th win. Sam McDowell of the Indians fans 15 Athletics in a 6-3 win in Oakland.The White Sox fire manager Eddie Stanky (34-45). Les Moss will handle the team on an interim basis until Al Lopez returns from retirement for his second stint as Chicago's skipper.

JULY 14:

Hank Aaron hits his 500th home run – against the Giants' Mike McCormick – becoming the eighth player in history to reach that level. Aaron's three-run, 400-foot shot over the left center-field fence also is his 2,700th career hit and his 19th homer of the season. It gives Atlanta a 4-2 win and occurs one year to the day that Aaron's former teammate, Eddie Mathews, hit his 500th homer. Bill Bartholomay, president of the Braves, presents Aaron with a trophy.

Don Wilson of the Astros fans 18 Reds in a 6-1 win in the second game of a doubleheader. He ties the record for most strikeouts in a nine-inning game.

JULY 22:

Three outfielders, Hazen "Kiki" Cuyler, Leon "Goose" Goslin, and Joe "Ducky" Medwick, are inducted into the Hall of Fame. Cuyler played for 18 years, batting .321 with a high of .360 in 1929. He led the NL in stolen bases four times and appeared in three World Series. Cuyler died in 1950. In his 18-year career, Goslin hit .316, leading the AL in batting with .379 in 1928. He appeared in five World Series. Medwick played for 17 years and compiled a .324 lifetime average. He led the NL in batting in 1937 with .374, was the home run leader once and the RBI champ three times. He played in two World Series.

JULY 23:

Al Lopez, back as White Sox manager for less than two weeks, has an emergency appendectomy. Les Moss will again handle the team.

Lopez, who was 6-5 before taking ill, misses 34 games; Moss compiles a record of 12-22 in his absence.

JULY 24:

Two days before his 45th birthday, Hoyt Wilhelm comes out of the White Sox bullpen to relieve Tommy John in the ninth inning and retires the Athletics on six pitches. But Oakland wins, 1-0. It is the 907th game for Wilhelm, surpassing Cy Young's record.He is the losing pitcher in the nightcap, which Chicago drops, 2-1.

JULY 27:

It's still July and Denny McLain has 20 wins. The Tiger right-hander three-hits the Orioles, 9-0, to reach the milestone. Detroit raps out five homers: two by Willie Horton and one each by Al Kaline, Don Wert, and Dick McAuliffe.

JULY 29:

Senators shortstop Ron Hansen becomes the eighth player in history to execute an unassisted triple play; it is the first in 41 years. It also is the fifth in AL history; all have involved Cleveland. Hansen turns the triple killing on a line drive to Cleveland's Joe Azcue in the first inning today with runners on first and second. Hansen's day is not all bright; he fans four times against Sam McDowell and Washington loses, 10-1. George Culver of the Reds no-hits the visiting Phillies, 6-1. He strikes out four and walks five, and Cincinnati makes three errors. The Phillies score an

AUGUST 16
Denny McClain's 4-0 win over the Red Sox is the Tigers' pitcher's 25th of the season.

unearned run in the second inning. Chris Short is the game's losing pitcher.

JULY 31:

The Tigers' Denny McLain fans Ron Hansen twice today. Hansen now has fanned in six consecutive at-bats.

AUGUST 1:

Ron Hansen breaks his strikeout streak with a walk and follows with a grand slam homer against Detroit's Pat Dobson.

AUGUST 2:

Three days after executing an unassisted triple play, shortstop Ron Hansen (.185 in 86 games) is traded by the Senators to the White Sox for infielder Tim Cullen (.200 in 72 games). Cullen and Hansen were traded in the opposite direction as part of a February 13 transaction between Washington and Chicago. They are the only players to be traded for each other twice in a single season. Hansen finishes at .230, Cullen, .2.72.

AUGUST 4:

St. Louis honors Stan Musial. In pre-game ceremonies held in 93-degree heat, a 10-foot bronze statue of Stan the Man is unveiled outside Busch Stadium. Some 47,000 are on hand for the game, won by the Cubs, 6-5, on a Lee Elia pinch-hit single in the 13th inning.

AUGUST 5:

Roger Maris, the man who has broken Babe Ruth's single season home run record, is calling it a career. The Cardinals' outfielder, a two-time AL Most Valuable Player, will retire at the end of the current season.

AUGUST 10:

At Yankee Stadium, Mickey Mantle homers twice against the Twins' Jim Merritt for both of New York's runs in a 3-2 loss. The round-trippers are the 530th and 531st of his career, but only his 12th and 13th of the season. It is the 36th and final time Mantle hits a pair of homers in a game.

AUGUST 16:

Denny McLain rings up his 25th. The Tigers' right-hander seven-hits the Red Sox, 4-0, and is not 16-0 on the road.

AUGUST 19:

In Philadelphia, it's power pitcher against power hitter and Bob Gibson wins. The Cardinals' right-hander fans Phillies' slugger Dick Allen four times in a 2-0 victory. Allen sets an undesirable major league record with four strikeouts in seven different games.

The Cardinals' Bob Gibson defeats the Phillies and Woodie Fryman, 2-0, for his 15th consecutive victory.

AUGUST 22:

Mickey Mantle today comes off the bench to pinch-hit against the Twins' Jim Merritt and hits his 534th homer, tying Jimmie Foxx for third place on the all-time list. Mantle's round-tripper is the Yankees' only run in Merritt's three-hit, 3-1 win.

White Sox pitcher Tommy John throws too close to the head of the Tigers' Dick McAuliffe and pays a steep price. McAuliffe wrestles him to the ground, and John tears a ligament in his pitching shoulder. McAuliffe is suspended for five days and fined $250.

AUGUST 25:

Today Rocky Colavito, signed by the Yankees after 40 games with the Dodgers, takes a turn on the mound in his native Bronx. The rifle-armed outfielder pitches two and two-thirds innings of relief against the Tigers and allows his former teammates one hit, two walks, and no runs, while striking out one. He hits a home run and gets credit for the victory. Daryl Patterson is the loser. It is the second time Colavito has pitched. In 1958 with the Indians, he held the Tigers hitless for three innings.

AUGUST 26:

Yesterday outfielder Rocky Colavito, today shortstop it's Gene Michael, tomorrow – who? In the nightcap of a doubleheader at Yankee Stadium, Michael pitches three innings against the Angels. He allows five hits and no earned runs, striking out three and issuing no walks. California wins, 10-2.

The White Sox complete their nine-game "home" schedule in Milwaukee the way they began it – with a loss. Detroit dumps Chicago, 3-0, behind Earl Wilson. Cisco Carlos gets the loss. Today's attendance is 42,808; the total for nine games is 265,452.

AUGUST 29:

The NL expansion San Diego Padres select Preston Gomez to be the ballclub's first manager.

LEAGUE

The AL East is Baltimore, Boston, Cleveland, Detroit, New York, and Washington. The AL West is California, Chicago, Kansas City, Minnesota, Oakland, and Seattle. The NL East is Chicago, Montreal, New York, Philadelphia, Pittsburgh, and St. Louis. The NL West is Atlanta, Cincinnati, Houston, Los Angeles, San Diego, and San Francisco.

TRIVIA

Before game five of the World Series, Jose Feliciano sings "The Star Spangled Banner" with a Latin lilt and sparks a controversy.

AUGUST 31:

Relief pitcher Elroy Face (2-4), who spent all his 15 major league years in a Pirates' uniform, is sold to the Tigers.

Hideo Nomo is born in Osaka, Japan.

SEPTEMBER 1:

Denny McLain starts a third-inning triple play en route to beating the Orioles, 7-3, for his 27th win of the season.

SEPTEMBER 5:

Gene Mauch is picked to be the first manager of the expansion Montreal Expos.

SEPTEMBER 6:

Denny McLain wins his 28th, a nine-hit, 8-3 victory over the Twins. McLain strikes out 12. Willie Horton drives in five runs for Detroit with his 32nd homer of the season and a double.

Rico Carty of the Atlanta Braves is released from a Florida hospital after 163 days of treatment for tuberculosis.

SEPTEMBER 10:

Denny McLain is within an eyelash of a coveted 30-win season. He beats the Angels today, 7-2, yielding eight hits and striking out 12. He backs up his strong pitching with his bat – hitting a triple and two singles and driving in two runs.

Billy Williams wallops the Mets. The Cubs' outfielder hits three home runs for all Chicago's runs in a 3-1 win. Williams homered twice yesterday, giving him five in his last two games. Bill Hands gets the win.

SEPTEMBER 11:

Hank Aaron plays first base for the first time in his major league career, but it doesn't affect his hitting. Aaron cracks a homer against Juan Marichal – his 27th of the season – and collects two other hits in a Braves' victory. Aaron passes Jimmie Foxx and is now eighth all-time in total bases. Pat Jarvis gets credit for the 3-1 win.

Cubs' pitcher Ferguson Jenkins has the grounds for a nonsupport suit. He loses his fifth 1-0 game of the season – a major league record. The winning pitcher at Wrigley Field is Jim McAndrew of the Mets.

SEPTEMBER 12:

Former major league pitcher Don Rudolph is killed in a truck accident in Granada Hills, California, at age 37. Rudolph had pitched six years with the White Sox, Reds, Indians, and the Senators, compiling an 18-32 record with a 4.00 ERA. Rudolph was married to stripper Patti Waggin, the "Coed With the Educated Torso," and was her manager and publicist as well. Because of his wife, he was the target of stinging bench jockeying, which may have affected his mound performance.

SEPTEMBER 13:

At Shea Stadium, lefty Jerry Koosman pitches a 2-0 shutout against the Pirates. It is his seventh of the season, tying the NL rookie record held by Irving Young (1905), George McQuillan (1908), and Grover Cleveland Alexander (1911). The game also marks the Mets' 67th win, the most ever for the franchise.

SEPTEMBER 14:

Detroit's Denny McLain becomes baseball's first 30-game winner since Dizzy Dean in 1934 and the first AL pitcher since Lefty Grove in 1931 when he beats the visiting Athletics, 5-4, before a crowd of 44,087. The Tigers score twice in the bottom of the ninth to give McLain the victory, despite two homers by Oakland's Reggie Jackson. Willie Horton singles in the winner. McLain allows six hits, walks one, and strikes out 10 to improve his record to 30-5. Diego Segui gets the loss.

SEPTEMBER 15:

The Cardinals clinch the NL pennant with a 7-4 win over the Astros in Houston. Roger Maris hits his 275th – and last – career homer. Curt Flood has five hits.

SEPTEMBER 17:

Don Wert singles for the Detroit Tigers with the bases loaded and two out in the bottom of the ninth inning to beat the Yankees, 2-1, giving the Tigers the American League pennant. It is the first for Detroit since 1945. Joe Sparma gets the victory with a complete-game five-hitter. At Candlestick Park, the Giants' Gaylord Perry no-hits the Cardinals, 1-0. Perry throws 101 pitches, walking two and striking out nine; the Giants make one error. Ron Hunt's homer in the first inning against Cardinals' starter Bob Gibson – who allows only four hits and fans 10 – is the game's only run.

SEPTEMBER 14
Detroit's Denny McClain is the first 30-game winner since Dizzy Dean in 1934.

SEPTEMBER 20
Mickey Mantle hits his 536th – and his last – career home run off Boston's Jim Lonborg.

SEPTEMBER 18:

Today, for the second consecutive day, Candlestick Park is the scene of a no-hitter. Today it is the Cardinals' Ray Washburn who no-hits the Giants, 2-0. Washburn labors, throwing 138 pitches and walking five batters. But he strikes out eight and the Cardinals play errorless ball behind him. Mike Shannon and Curt Flood drive in St. Louis's runs. The losing pitcher is Bobby Bolin.

SEPTEMBER 19:

On the way to his 31st victory of the season, Denny McLain throws a belt-high fat one to Mickey Mantle, which the Yankees' slugger hits into the upper deck for his 535th career home run. Mantle passes Jimmie Foxx for the third spot on the all-time list. It is Mantle's first homer in nearly a month. The Tigers win, 6-2. Afterward McLain says, "Thanks for what? I make mistakes all the time."

Madison Square Garden boxing matchmaker Harry Markson has a fascinating take on the situation. "When a guy has bought 534 drinks in the same saloon, he's entitled to one on the house."

BASEBALL'S RULES COMMITTEE MEETS IN SAN FRANCISCO AND COMES UP WITH A BARREL OF CHANGES DESIGNED TO STEP UP THE OFFENSE. AMONG THE MODIFICATIONS: THE PITCHER'S MOUND WILL BE LOWERED FROM 15 INCHES TO 10 INCHES; THE STRIKE ZONE WILL BE DECREASED (PRESENTLY FROM THE SHOULDERS-TO-KNEES, IT WILL BECOME ARMPITS-TO-TOP-OF-KNEES); TIGHTER ENFORCEMENT AGAINST ILLEGAL PITCHES (UMPIRES WILL HAVE THE POWER TO EJECT PITCHERS CAUGHT USING FOREIGN SUBSTANCES); ENFORCEMENT OF LAST YEAR'S RULE – A PITCHER WHO PUTS HIS HAND TO MOUTH ON THE MOUND WILL BE CALLED FOR AN AUTOMATIC BALL. EXTRA-INNING TIES NOW WILL BE RESUMED FROM THE POINT OF THE INTERRUPTION; PREVIOUSLY THEY WERE STARTED OVER AND REPLAYED. A COMMITTEE IS APPOINTED TO STUDY ARTIFICIAL SURFACES.

SEPTEMBER 20:

At Yankee Stadium, Mickey Mantle circles the bases at his home park for the last time when he hits a third-inning solo home run against Jim Lonborg of the Red Sox. It is Mantle's 536th career round-tripper – and his last. Boston wins the game, 4-3.

SEPTEMBER 22:

Minnesota's Cesar Tovar matches Bert Campaneris's 1965 demonstration of versatility by playing all nine positions against the Athletics. The first batter Tovar faces as he takes the mound in the first inning is Campaneris, who fouls out. He then fans Reggie Jackson, walks Danny Cater, and gets Sal Bando on a foul. Tom Hall relieves Tovar and gets the 2-1 win.

SEPTEMBER 25:

Following manager Gil Hodges's "mild" heart attack yesterday, Albert "Rube" Walker is appointed acting skipper of the New York Mets for the rest of the season. Hodges is expected to return in time for the 1969 season. Indeed, he's back for three more.

HISTORY

The Bob Gibson-Denny McLain matchup marks the first time two Cy Young Award winners oppose each other in the World Series. At the time of the game, the awards have not yet been announced.

"If I ever made a mistake inside, all right, but the outside [of the plate] is mine and don't you forget it."
– Bob Gibson

Denny McClain wins 31 games – plus the AL Cy Young and MVP awards.

SEPTEMBER 27:

Bob Gibson beats the visiting Astros, 1-0, for his 22nd win and his 13th shutout, the most in the NL since 1916. Gibson has a minuscule 1.12 ERA, the second lowest ever in the NL. Sam McDowell four-hits the Orioles and fans 11 to finish the season with a major league-leading 283 strikeouts. Despite his high strikeout total and a sparkling 1.81 ERA, McDowell's season record is only 15-14.

SEPTEMBER 28:

At Fenway Park, Mickey Mantle makes his last appearance in a regulation game. He is hitless in one at-bat

SEPTEMBER 27
Bob Gibson's 1-0 win over the Astros is his 22nd of the season and 13th shutout.

OCTOBER 10
Mickey Lolich beats Bob Gibson in game seven to give the Tigers the Series vs. St. Louis.

and is replaced by Andy Kosco, who hits a homer to win the game, 4-3. Mantle finishes the season with a .237 batting average and 18 homers, and he drives in 54 runs.

SEPTEMBER 29:

At Shea Stadium, Dick Allen of the Phillies drives in seven runs with three home runs – including a grand slam – in a 10-3 victory.

SEPTEMBER 30:

Satchel Paige is released by the Braves. He was signed on August 11 and placed on Atlanta's 40-man roster so he could qualify for a major league pension. Paige, who last played in the majors in 1965, made no appearances for the Braves. He will be an Atlanta coach next season.

REGULAR SEASON WRAP-UP:

Both pennant winners ride the strong right arms of their ace pitchers to the World Series. Behind Denny McLain's 31-6, 1.96 ERA, and 336 innings, the Tigers finish at 103-59, 12 games ahead of Baltimore in the AL, under manager Edward "Mayo" Smith. Mickey Lolich compiles a 17-9 mark. Willie Horton is the big gun with 36 homers, 85 RBI, and a .285 average. Norm Cash and Bill Freehan each have 25 home runs. Dick McAuliffe plays in 151 games without grounding into a double play – an AL record.

With Bob Gibson at 22-9 and a 1.12 ERA (and 13 shutouts), the Cardinals under manager Albert "Red" Schoendienst finish 97-65, nine games ahead of the Giants in the NL. Curt Flood has the top average – .301. Lou Brock steals 62 bases and Orlando Cepeda hits 16 home runs.

Batting averages plummet in both leagues: AL teams bat .230; the NL average is .243. The White Sox Wilbur Wood pitches in 88 games, topping the 1965 mark set by the Cubs' Ted Abernathy. His teammate Hoyt Wilhelm appears in 72 games, bringing his career total to a record 937.

OCTOBER 2:

World Series, game one. Bob Gibson pitches a masterpiece: a five-hit shutout with 17 strikeouts as the Cardinals defeat the Tigers, 4-0, in St. Louis. In the ninth inning, Gibson fans Al Kaline; then strikes out Norm Cash for his 16th, breaking Sandy Koufax's Series record; and gets Willie Horton on a called third strike to end the game. Lou Brock homers for the Cardinals. Denny McLain takes the loss.

OCTOBER 3:

World Series, game two. Mickey Lolich six-hits the Cardinals and hits his first major league home run in an 8-1 victory in St. Louis. Willie Horton and Norm Cash also hit home runs as the Tigers even the series. The losing pitcher is Nelson Briles.

OCTOBER 5:

World Series, game three. In Detroit, Tim McCarver and Orlando Cepeda hit a pair of three-run home runs and Lou Brock steals three bases in a 7-3 Cardinals' victory. Ray Washburn gets the win; the game's losing pitcher is Earl Wilson. Al Kaline and Dick McAuliffe have homers for Detroit.

OCTOBER 6:

World Series, game four. In a rematch of game one, Bob Gibson and Denny McLain are the starting pitchers in Detroit. Gibson pitches a five-hitter, striking out 10 and homering in a 10-1 win. It is his seventh straight series victory, a record. McLain lasts only two and two-thirds innings and gets the loss. Lou Brock homers for St. Louis; Jim Northrup for the Tigers.

OCTOBER 7:

World Series, game five. Mickey Lolich wins his second complete game, 5-3; the big hit is an Al Kaline single with the bases loaded in the seventh inning. Orlando Cepeda hits his second three-run homer of the Series. The losing pitcher is Joe Hoerner in relief of starter Nelson Briles.

OCTOBER 9:

World Series, game six. Back in St. Louis, Denny McLain gets his first Series win, scattering nine hits in a 13-1 victory. The Tigers score 10 times in the third inning; Jim Northrup's grand slam keys the rally. Al Kaline also homers. Ray Washburn is the losing pitcher.

OCTOBER 10:

World Series, game seven. An outfield misplay, combined with five-hit pitching by Mickey Lolich, gives the Tigers a 4-1 win and the World

HISTORY

Bob Gibson wins the NL Most Valuable Player and Cy Young Awards; Denny McLain gets both honors in the AL. It is the first time pitchers sweep the four awards.

> "Lots of guys have a good belly and a bad arm, but I've got a bad belly and a good arm."
> – *Tigers' pitcher Mickey Lolich*

CULTURE

Robert Coover publishes his novel The *Universal Baseball Association, Inc., J. Henry Waugh, Prop.*

Championship. Lolich and Bob Gibson are locked in a scoreless duel going into the seventh. With two out, Norm Cash and Willie Horton single. Curt Flood misjudges a Jim Northrup drive; it carries over his head and is ruled a triple, scoring two runs. In the sixth, left-hander Lolich picks Lou Brock and Flood off first base, choking off a rally. Mike Shannon homers for St. Louis; Bob Gibson gets the loss. Norm Cash at .385 with a homer and five RBI and Al Kaline, .379 with two homers and eight RBI, lead the Tigers' hitters. Northrup also has eight RBI with two homers. Mickey Lolich wins three games and has an ERA of 1.67. Lou Brock hits .464 on 13 hits and steals seven bases. Bob Gibson finishes at 2-1 with a 1.67 ERA.

POST-SEASON

OCTOBER 11:

The Cardinals obtain outfielder Vada Pinson (.271) from the Reds for outfielder Bobby Tolan (.230, five homers in 92 games) and pitcher Wayne Granger (4-2, 2.25 ERA). The Cardinals also trade catcher Johnny Edwards (.239 in 85 games) and minor league receiver Tommie Smith to the Houston Astros for pitcher Dave Giusti (11-14, 3.19 ERA) and catcher Dave Adlesh (.181 in 39 games).

OCTOBER 14:

The major leagues hold their expansion draft, with the new San Diego, Montreal, Kansas City, and Seattle franchises electing players for their 1969 rosters. Among those selected are: Montreal – Maury Wills, Manny Mota, Jesus Alou, Jim "Mudcat" Grant, Bill Stoneman, and Larry Jackson; San Diego – Ollie "Downtown" Brown, Nate Colbert, Clarence "Cito" Gaston, Dick Selma, and Al McBean; Kansas City – Hoyt Wilhelm, Moe Drabowsky, Dick Drago, Joe Foy, Jerry Adair, and Jim Rooker; Seattle – Don Mincher, Tommy Harper, Tommy Davis, Lou Piniella, Gary Bell, and Mike Hegan.

OCTOBER 29:

The Red Sox release catcher Elston Howard (.241, five homers in 71 games). Howard, the Yankees' first black player, played 14 years and had a .274 average. He also appeared in 10 World Series and was the AL's Most Valuable Player in 1963.

NOVEMBER 3:

Vern Stephens, a hard-hitting shortstop, dies in Long Beach, California, at age 48. In 15 years, he compiled a .286 batting average and hit 247 homers. He was the AL's home run leader in 1945 and three times was tops in RBI. Stephens jumped to the Mexican League but returned after just a few days, avoiding suspension.

DECEMBER 3:

Robert E. Short buys the majority interest in the Washington Senators.

For the second time in the last two months, the Cardinals obtain pitcher Dave Giusti n a trade. In between Giusti was selected by the Padres in the expansion draft from the list of unprotected St. Louis players. Today, St. Louis sends outfielder-infielder Ed Spiezo (.157 in 29 games), outfielder Ron Davis (.203), minor league catcher Danny Breedon, and minor league pitcher Phil Knuckles to San Diego in a deal to reacquire Giusti.

DECEMBER 4:

The Orioles send outfielder Curt Blefary (.200, 15 homers) and minor league first baseman John Mason to the Astros for pitcher Mike Cuellar (8-11, 2.74 ERA), minor league shortstop Enzo Hernandez, and minor league infielder Elijah Johnson.

DECEMBER 6:

The major league owners ask for and receive the resignation of Commissioner William Eckert with three years to go on his contract. The National League's attorney, Bowie Kuhn, is appointed interim commissioner.

DECEMBER 12:

Right-handed relief pitcher Hoyt Wilhelm (4-4, 1.73 ERA, 12 saves) is sent to the California Angels by the Kansas City Royals in exchange for catcher-outfielder-infielder Ed Kirkpatrick (.230 in 89 games) and minor league catcher Dennis Paepke.

DECEMBER 15:

It seems that blood is not thicker than water in the world of baseball. Al Campanis of the Los Angeles Dodgers trades his own son, catcher Jimmy Campanis (.091 in four major league games), to the Montreal Expos in exchange for two minor league players.

OCTOBER 29
Elston Howard's 14-year career ends when he's released by the Red Sox.

DECEMBER 6
Commissioner William Eckert resigns and Bowie Kuhn is name interim commish.

THE BEST OF 1968

NATIONAL LEAGUE

HITTERS

Batting Average:
Pete Rose, Cincinnati Reds, .335

Slugging Average:
Willie McCovey, San Francisco Giants, .545

Home Runs:
Willie McCovey, 36

Runs Batted In:
Willie McCovey, 105

Hits:
Pete Rose; Felipe Alou, Atlanta Braves, 210

Stolen Bases:
Lou Brock, St. Louis Cardinals, 62

PITCHERS

Wins:
Juan Marichal, San Francisco Giants, 26

Strikeouts:
Bob Gibson, St. Louis Cardinals, 268

Earned Run Average:
Bob Gibson, 1.12

Winning Percentage:
Steve Blass, Pittsburgh Pirates, .750

Saves:
Phil Regan, Los Angeles Dodgers/ Chicago Cubs, 25

Most Valuable Player:
Bob Gibson, St. Louis Cardinals

Cy Young Award:
Bob Gibson, St. Louis Cardinals

Rookie of the Year:
Johnny Bench, Cincinnati Reds

AMERICAN LEAGUE

HITTERS

Batting Average:
Carl Yastrzemski, Boston Red Sox, .301

Slugging Average:
Frank Howard, Washington Senators, .552

Home Runs:
Frank Howard, 44

Runs Batted In:
Ken Harrelson, Boston Red Sox, 109

Hits:
Bert Campaneris, Oakland Athletics, 177

Stolen Bases:
Bert Campaneris, 62

PITCHERS

Wins:
Denny McLain, Detroit Tigers, 31

Strikeouts:
Sam McDowell, Cleveland Indians, 283

Earned Run Average:
Luis Tiant, Cleveland Indians, 1.60

Winning Percentage:
Denny McLain, .838

Saves:
Al Worthington, Minnesota Twins, 18

Most Valuable Player:
Denny McLain, Detroit Tigers

Cy Young Award:
Denny McLain, Detroit Tigers

Rookie of the Year:
Stan Bahnsen, New York Yankees

1969

"I can't play anymore... I have to quit."
– *Mickey Mantle*

NEWS

NEIL ARMSTRONG IS FIRST MAN TO WALK ON THE MOON

Former President Eisenhower dies at age 78

250,000 IN WASHINGTON ANTI-WAR MARCH

Vietnamese civilians massacred by U.S. troops at My Lai

ACTRESS SHARON TATE, EIGHT OTHERS SLAIN BY CHARLES MANSON CULT

TED KENNEDY PLEADS GUILTY IN CHAPPAQUIDICK CAR ACCIDENT THAT KILLS MARY JO KOPECHNE

400,000 GATHER AT WOODSTOCK FOR MUSIC FESTIVAL

Qaddafi in power in Libya following coup

HURRICANE CAMILLE KILLS 400; DAMAGE ESTIMATED AT $1 BILLION

VIETNAMESE LEADER HO CHI MINH DIES

Chicago Seven go on trial

JUDY GARLAND, JACK KEROUAC DIE

PRE-SEASON

JANUARY 18:

Ted Williams is named manager of the Washington Senators. He replaces Jim Lemon after the Senators' 65-96 last-place finish in 1968. Reportedly, Williams signs a five-year contract with an annual salary of $75,000, plus 10 percent of the team's stock. The 50-year-old Williams says, "I can only tell you from the heart I am happy to be here."

JANUARY 22:

The Montreal Expos make their first major trade, acquiring first-baseman Daniel "Rusty" Staub (.291, six homers) from the Astros. Houston receives outfielder Jesus Alou (.263), first baseman Donn Clendenon (.257, 17 home runs, 87 RBI), pitchers Jack Billingham (3-0, 2.14 ERA) and Drannon "Skip" Guinn (0-0, 3.60 ERA), as well as a $100,000 payment.

JANUARY 24:

Former major league pitcher Tom Zachary dies in Burlington, North Carolina, at age 72. In death as in life, Zachary is remembered for yielding Babe Ruth's record homer. The *New York Times* headline reads: TOM ZACHARY, PITCHER, IS DEAD; SERVED RUTH'S 60TH HOME RUN.

FEBRUARY 4:

At Bal Harbour, Florida, 42-year-old attorney Bowie Kuhn is unanimously elected baseball commissioner pro tem. He gets a one-year term at $100,000. Kuhn is elected after a deadlock between the two leading candidates, Mike Burke of the Yankees and Charles "Chub" Feeney of the Giants. Kuhn's law firm has handled the NL's legal affairs since 1950.

FEBRUARY 25:

There will be no baseball strike in 1969. Today the Players, Association's executive council accepts a proposal from the major league ballclub owners that includes a number of improvements to the ML pension plan. Qualification for a pension is dropped from five to four years. Also, the age of eligibility is lowered from 50 years old to 45, and the benefits are enhanced. The team owners also will increase their contribution to the plan over the next three seasons.

FEBRUARY 26:

Carl Yastrzemski signs a $130,000 contract for 1969, becoming the highest paid AL player in history. Last season, he led the league in batting with .301 – the lowest ever – hit 23 home runs, and drove in 74 runs.

MARCH 1:

Mickey Mantle announces he is retiring from baseball. Mantle will end his career with a record of remarkable achievements, but one that still falls far short of his initial promise – principally because of his endless injuries. In his 18 years, Mantle batted .298 with 536 home runs, 1,734 walks, and 1,710 strikeouts. He appeared in 65 World Series games, hitting 18 home runs and batting in 40 runs.

Mantle tells the news media at a Fort Lauderdale, Florida, press conference: "I can't play anymore. I can't hit the ball when I need to. I can't steal second when I need to. I can't go from first to third when I need to. I can't score from second when I need to. I have to quit." Last season, Mantle hit .237 with 18 home runs and 54 RBI in 144 games.

MARCH 1
Yankees' slugger Mickey Mantle retires, ending his remarkable 18-year career.

APRIL 14
In the first regular-season ML game played outside the U.S., the Expos beat the Cards..

MARCH 14:

Henry "Heinie" Zimmerman, banned from baseball for life in 1919 for allegedly trying to fix games, dies today at age 82 in New York City. Zimmerman, a Triple Crown winner with the Chicago Cubs in 1912, played 13 years and hit .295.

MARCH 17:

Atlanta acquires first baseman Orlando Cepeda (.248, 16 homers), the 1967 NL Most Valuable Player, from the Cardinals in return for catcher-first baseman Joe Torre (.271, 10 homers).

MARCH 21:

Mike "Pinky" Higgins, a major league third baseman and manager, dies at age 59 in Dallas. Higgins played 18 years, batting .292 with a high of .330 in 1934. He managed the Red Sox for eight years, never finishing higher than third place.

THE SEASON

APRIL 7:

On opening day, Don Drysdale's first two pitches are smacked for homers by Pete Rose and Bobby Tolan of the Reds. Drysdale settles down, and the Dodgers win, 3-2.

APRIL 8:

The Montreal Expos make their debut, meeting the Mets at Shea Stadium. Jose "Coco" Laboy hits a three-run homer against Canadian-born Ron Taylor in a four-run eighth-inning rally; the Expos take an 11-6 lead. Don "Duffy" Dyer hits a three-run pinch-hit homer in the ninth; the Mets rally for four runs but fall short, 11-10. Don Shaw gets the win.

Jack Murphy Stadium (named after a popular sportswriter) in San Diego is dedicated. In the opening game the Padres beat the visiting Astros, 2-1, with 23,370 attending. Third baseman Ed Spiezio homers in the fifth inning against Don Wilson. The blast is his first major league hit and the first safety for the Padres.

The Seattle Pilots make their American League debut a winning one, defeating the Angels, 4-3, in Anaheim. The Pilots score four runs in the top of the first; the big blows are a Tommy Harper double and a Mike Hegan home run against Jim McGlothlin. Seattle's Jerry McNertney has two RBI. Marty Pattin is the winning pitcher.

Tony Conigliaro is back in the Red Sox lineup for the first time since his beaning in 1967. Conigliaro starts in right field and connects for a two-run homer in the 10th inning on a 2-2 pitch from the Orioles' Pete Richert. Frank Robinson hits a game-tying homer for Baltimore in the 10th. Conigliaro walks in the 12th and scores on a Dalton Jones sacrifice fly for a 5-4 Boston win. Boston's Juan Pizzaro is the first major league pitcher to be credited with a save – the new scoring statistic – when he relieves Bill Landis in the 12th inning against the Orioles and preserves the Red Sox win.

APRIL 9:

At Wrigley Field, the Cubs' Billy Williams hits four consecutive doubles in an 11-3 victory over the Phillies. Bill Hands gets the win.

The Twins' Rod Carew steals home in the fifth inning against Kansas City. Carew leads off with a double and moves on to third. With Roger Nelson pitching to Graig Nettles, Carew beats the second pitch to the plate and completes his first career steal of home.

In Washington, D.C., Ted Williams debuts as manager of the Senators with an 8-4 opening day loss to the Yankees.

APRIL 11:

With Mount Rainier in the background, 17,850 turn up at Sicks Stadium for the first major league game in Seattle. Gary Bell and the Pilots beat the visiting White Sox, 7-0. Don Mincher hits his second homer of the young year and drives in two runs.

APRIL 13:

Jim Palmer of the Orioles, coming back from two years of arm woe, four-hits the Washington Senators, 2-0. Palmer was 3-1 in 1967 and was out of the majors, rehabbing his arm in 1968.

APRIL 14:

In the first regular season major league baseball game played outside the United States, the Montreal Expos beat the Cardinals, 8-7, at Parc Jarry before a crowd of 29,184 fans, plus some 200 journalists. There has been no baseball in Montreal since 1961 when the Dodgers' Montreal AAA farm team last played. The players are

RULES

The save for relief pitchers becomes an official major league statistic.

MAY 13
The Cubs' Ernie Banks records his 1,500th career RBI as he drives in seven runs.

LEAGUE

Donn Clendenon refuses to join the Astros; the Expos send Billingham, Guinn, and cash to Houston in his stead on April 8

introduced in both French and English. Mack Jones of the Expos hits a three-run homer and a two-run triple to pace the Montreal attack. Charles "Dal" Maxvill has a grand slam homer for the Cardinals in the seven-run fourth. The winning pitcher is Dan McGinn in relief. Gary Waslewski is tagged with the loss.

APRIL 16:

At the Astrodome, Hank Aaron homers against Denny LeMaster. It is the 512th of his career, tying him with his former teammate Eddie Mathews for sixth place on the all-time list.

APRIL 17:

The Expos' Bill Stoneman no-hits the Phillies, 7-0, at Connie Mack Stadium. Stoneman strikes out eight and walks five; Montreal commits no errors. The losing pitcher is Jerry Johnson.

APRIL 19:

In Minnesota, Rod Carew steals home for the second time this season. With two out, the Twins behind, 5-4, to the Angels and Harmon Killebrew at bat, Carew beats the throw home.

MICKEY MANTLE REFLECTS ON ONE ASPECT OF HIS CAREER: "DURING MY 18 YEARS I CAME TO BAT ALMOST 10,000 TIMES. I STRUCK OUT ABOUT 1,700 TIMES AND I WALKED MAYBE 1,800 TIMES. YOU FIGURE A BALLPLAYER WILL AVERAGE ABOUT 500 AT-BATS A SEASON. THAT MEANS I PLAYED SEVEN YEARS WITHOUT EVER HITTING THE BALL."

APRIL 20:

Boston pitcher Ray Jarvis is a loser at the plate, but a winner on the mound. He fans five times in a row against the Indians, but is the winning pitcher in a 9-4 Red Sox victory.

APRIL 23:

On the 30th anniversary of his first major league homer, Ted Williams returns to Fenway Park as the manager of the Senators and his new team wins, 9-3.

For the second straight year, the White Sox will be playing a slate of "home" games in Milwaukee. In today's contest – the first of 11 – Chicago beats the Angels, 7-1, behind Gary Peters. George Brunet gets the loss. Official attendance is only 8,565.

APRIL 28:

Hank Aaron hits his 513th career homer, passing Eddie Mathews and taking sole possession of the sixth spot all-time. Atlanta beats visiting Houston, 12-1.

APRIL 30:

At Crosley Field, Jim Maloney of the Reds no-hits the Astros, 10-0. It is the second career no-hitter for Maloney, who strikes out 13 batters and walks five. The Reds play errorless ball. Bobby Tolan wields the big bat with three hits and four RBI. Wade Blasingame gets the loss.

With Seattle's Darrell Brandon pitching and Rich Reese at bat, the Twins execute a rare triple steal. Rod Carew, the lead runner, is credited with his third steal of home this season when he slides away from Larry Haney's tag.

MAY 1:

It's back-to-back no-hitters at Crosley Field. One day after Jim Maloney no-hit the Astros, Houston's Don Wilson returns the favor in a 4-0 classic. Wilson walks six and strikes out 15; the Astros make one error. It is the second career no-hitter for Wilson. Only nine days ago, the Reds mauled the Astros and Wilson, 14-0. Dennis Menke drives in two runs and Doug Rader hits a solo homer. Jim Merritt gets the loss. It is the second time no-hitters have been pitched on consecutive days in one ballpark. In 1968, the Giants' Gaylord Perry and the Cardinals' Ray

JUNE 4
Twins' speedster Rod Carew gets his fifth steal of home on the season.

Washburn accomplished the feat at Candlestick Park.

MAY 3:

Al Lopez ends his career again when he resigns as manager of the White Sox after an 8-9 start. He will be replaced by coach Don Gutteridge.

MAY 4:

Bob Oliver of the Kansas City Royals is the first AL player in seven years to have six hits in six at-bats. Oliver hits a homer, a double, and four singles against the California Angels.

With the help of an NL record seven double plays, the Astros beat the Giants, 3-1, in Houston. First baseman Curt Blefary sets a new major league mark by participating in all seven; shortstop Denis Menke and second baseman Joe Morgan are involved in five.

MAY 5:

Eddie Cicotte, banned for life from baseball for his role in the 1919 Black Sox, scandal, dies at age 84 in Detroit. Cicotte took $10,000 to participate in throwing the World Series to the Reds; he was 1-2 with an ERA of 2.91 and didn't have it when it counted. In his 14-year career, Cicotte was 208-149 with a 2.37 ERA. He led the AL in victories twice.

Among Cicotte's comments on his role in the fixing scandal are: "I done it for the wife and kiddies," and "I have played a crooked game and I have lost."

MAY 6:

In St. Louis, Bob Gibson five-hits the Giants, 3-0, for his 150th career win.

MAY 13:

At Wrigley Field, Ernie Banks drives in seven runs – among them his 1,500th career RBI – in a 19-0 blowout over the Padres. Dick Selma gets the victory.

MAY 17:

Former White Sox' manager Clarence "Pants" Rowland dies today at age 90 in a Chicago rest home. Rowland managed the White Sox from 1915 to 1918, leading the team to a World Series victory over the Giants in 1917. He never played major league baseball.

MAY 18:

In the third inning against the Tigers, Rod Carew swipes home for the fourth time this season. Trailing 2-0, Carew on first and Cesar Tovar on second execute a double steal; Tovar follows by stealing home, with Carew remaining on second. Carew then steals third and beats Mickey Lolich's next pitch home with the tying run. Carew becomes the first base runner in 28 years to steal his way around the bases.

MAY 22:

In Atlanta against the Mets, Hank Aaron hits his 519th career homer. He passes Ted Williams in lifetime extra bases. He then singles for his 2,480th hit, passing Charlie Gehringer. He also comes to bat for the 9,015th time – the most ever. The Braves win, 15-3.

MAY 23:

In Detroit, the Tigers' Mickey Lolich fans 16 Angels' batters and Mickey Stanley hits a grand slam homer for a 6-3 win.

MAY 24:

In San Diego, Ernie Banks hits a grand slam home run against Jack Baldschun in a 7-5 Cubs' victory. It is the 12th – and last – of Banks's career.

MAY 26:

In Atlanta, Hank Aaron hits his 500th career double. He joins Babe Ruth and Ted Williams as the only players with 500 homers and 500 two-base hits. During the game the tent that houses the Braves' mascot, Chief Noc-a-homa, catches fire.

JUNE 1:

In Philadelphia, Dick Allen homers in his fifth consecutive game, however the Dodgers beat the Phillies, 12-4.

JUNE 4:

With Rod Carew coming home against relief pitcher Lindy McDaniel and rookie catcher John Ellis, the Twins pull off a triple steal against the Yankees in the bottom of the eighth.

It is the second triple steal for Minnesota this season and Rod Carew's fifth steal of home this season.

JUNE 8:

On the second Mickey Mantle Day in four years, the Yankees retire their former star's number 7 as 60,096 cheer in the ballpark where he once heard boos. Mantle says, "Playing 18 years in Yankee

EQUIPMENT

The White Sox install an Astroturf infield at Comiskey Park.

Stadium for you folks was the best thing that could ever happen to a ballplayer." The Yankees then sweep a doubleheader from the White Sox, 3-1, and 11-2.

HISTORY

In baseball's "centennial year," Babe Ruth is selected the Greatest Player Ever and Joe DiMaggio the Greatest Living Player.

JUNE 9:

The Tigers' Mickey Lolich fans 16 Pilots, but Seattle wins, 3-2, in 10 innings. Lolich, who leaves after nine, is not involved in the decision. A pinch-hit single by Don Mincher ties the score and Tomas "Gus" Gil's sacrifice fly drives in the winning run. Marty Pattin wins his sixth game; Pat Dobson is the loser.

JUNE 11:

Infielder Maury Wills (.222 in 47 games) returns to the Dodgers, three years after he was sent to the Pirates. Wills is traded by Montreal to Los Angeles along with outfielder Manny Mota (.315 in 31 games). In return, the Expos get outfielder-first baseman Ron Fairly (.219 in 30 games) and infielder Paul Popovich (.200 in 28 games).

JUNE 14:

Reggie Jackson has 10 RBI with two home runs, a double, and two singles in a 21-7 A's win over Boston.

SPORTS ILLUSTRATED REPORTS AN ON-AIR CONVERSATION BETWEEN YANKEE BROADCASTERS PHIL RIZZUTO AND JERRY COLEMAN, WHO ARE SELECTING AN ALL-TIME YANKEES' ALL-STAR TEAM. COLEMAN PICKS MICKEY MANTLE IN LEFT FIELD, JOE DIMAGGIO IN CENTER, AND ROGER MARIS IN RIGHT. RIZZUTO COUNTERS: "I'LL GO ALONG WITH YOU ON MANTLE AND DIMAGGIO, JERRY, BUT I'VE GOT TO SAY CHARLIE KELLER IN RIGHT." COMMENTS *SPORTS ILLUSTRATED:* "WHATEVER HAPPENED TO THAT FAT FELLOW WHO USED TO PLAY RIGHT FIELD FOR THE YANKS? HIT A LOT OF HOME RUNS ONCE."

JUNE 15:

First baseman Donn Clendenon (.240 in 38 games), who refused to report to Houston in a transaction earlier this year, is sent to the Mets. In return the Expos receive infielder Kevin Collins (.150 in 16 games) and minor league pitchers Steve Renko, Bill Carden, and Dave Colon.

JUNE 16:

The White Sox play a "home" game in Milwaukee County Stadium, beating the Pilots, 8-3, before 13,133 fans. Chicago scores all its runs in the first three innings against Mike Marshall and Bob Locker.

Against the Angels and pitcher Tom Murphy, Twins Rod Carew and Tony Oliva execute back-to-back double steals. On the second double steal, Carew comes home. It is his sixth homer of the season.

JUNE 24:

Dick Allen fails to show for a twi-night doubleheader against the Mets in New York and is suspended by Phillies manager Bob Skinner until July 20.

According to writer-researcher Craig R.

JUNE 28
The Dodgers score 10 runs in the third on the way to a 19-0 blanking of the Padres.

JULY 9
Mets' pitcher Tom Seaver comes up just a single short of a perfect game.

Wright, it seems that Allen had forgotten the starting time had been moved up and learned on the radio that he was late and suspended.

JUNE 28:

In the most one-sided shutout ever in the NL, the Dodgers wallop the Padres, 19-0, on 17 hits. The Dodgers break the game open early with 10 runs in the third inning. Don Drysdale gets the win.

JUNE 29:

At Wrigley Field, Billy Williams sets an NL record on this day. A crowd of 41,060 is on hand as Williams appears in his 895th and 896th consecutive games, breaking Stan Musial's NL record. Williams has five hits as the Cubs sweep the Cardinals, 3-1 and 12-1.

JUNE 29:

In Washington, D.C., the Red Sox set a record by using five pitchers in the ninth inning while losing to the Senators, 5-4.

JULY 2:

Reds' pitchers hit five Braves batters – the most in this century – but the only pitcher ejected is Milt Pappas, for yelling at the umpires. Gerry Arrigo hits Hank Aaron and Felix Milan; Pedro Ramos gets Milan, Bob Aspromonte, and Clete Boyer. The umpires issue no warnings. The Braves win, 9-4.

JULY 4:

The Pirates' Willie Stargell sends a pitch from Mets' starter Tom Seaver over the right-field roof and out of Forbes Field, but the Mets win, 11-6.

JULY 8:

Robert "Red" Rolfe dies at the age of 60 in Gifford, New Hampshire. The third baseman played for the Yankees for 10 years, compiling a .289 average and hitting .284 in six World Series. He managed the Detroit Tigers from 1949 to 1952.

Bill "Rough" Carrigan, who managed the Red Sox to World Championship in 1915 and 1916, dies in Lewiston, Maine, at age 85. Carrigan, a catcher, also played 10 years in the majors, batting .257.

JULY 9:

The Dodgers' Manny Mota fails in his bid to tie the NL record for hits over three consecutive games. He gets three today, after eight yesterday in a doubleheader, but comes up one short of Milt Stock and Stan Musial, who had 12. The Dodgers beat the Braves, 3-1.

At Shea Stadium before a crowd of 50,709, Tom Seaver takes a perfect game against the Cubs into the ninth inning. With one out, Jimmy Qualls singles to left centerfield. Seaver settles for a one-hitter and a 4-0 victory. Ken Holtzman gets the loss.

JULY 14:

At Wrigley Field, Bill Hands tops Tom Seaver and the visiting Mets, 1-0. Billy Williams's RBI single in the sixth inning gives the Cubs the game's only run. The Cubs are in first place by five and a half games.

Rod Carew is a base-stealing batting champ.

JULY 25
Hank Aaron hits his 536th career home run in an 8-7 Braves win over the Expos.

JULY 16:

Rod Carew steals home again – for the seventh time, tying Pete Reiser's 1946 total. Today's steal comes in the bottom of the third inning against Jerry Nyman and the White Sox. With the Twins up 5-2, bases loaded, and John Roseboro at bat, Carew comes home and catcher Don Pavletich fails to hold the ball. Minnesota wins, 6-3.

JULY 17:

In Minnesota, pitcher Jim Kaat's golden glove turns to lead. The AL's top fielding pitcher for seven consecutive years commits three errors and yields three unearned runs to the White Sox. But he and the Twins win anyway, 8-5.

It's the Case of the Catcher With Two Gloves. Orioles' receiver Clay Dalrymple has a fielder's glove in his back pocket and a catcher's mitt on his hand. He intends to use the mitt for pitches and the glove for plays. The umpires say no.

JULY 18:

In Cleveland, left fielder Willie Horton bats and fields the Tigers to a 4-0 win over the Indians. Horton hits a two-run homer and ties an AL record for outfielders with 11 putouts. Denny McLain racks up his 14th victory of the season.

JULY 23:

In Washington, D.C., the NL wins its seventh straight All-Star Game, 9-3. Willie McCovey is the hitting star with a two-run and a solo home run. Johnny Bench also homers for the NL; Bill Freehan and Frank Howard for the AL. Steve Carlton gets the win; the losing pitcher is Mel Stottlemyre.

JULY 25:

Hank Aaron hits his 536th homer today, tying him with Mickey Mantle. Earlier, Aaron doubled for his 2,900th career hit. The Expos top the Braves, 8-7.

JULY 27:

Jim Hardin of the Orioles enjoys a laugher. He limits the White Sox to two hits while his teammates pound out 20 safeties for 39 total bases. Baltimore wins, 17-0.

Cubs' manager Leo Durocher visits his son at a Wisconsin camp and ends up in hot water at home. Durocher takes off – without permission – during a game at Wrigley Field with the Cubs leading. Someone apparently tips off a reporter and the Cubs claim Durocher was "ill."

Durocher fails to show the following day and owner Phil Wrigley threatens to dismiss the fiery manager.

JULY 28:

Roy Campanella, Stan Musial, Stan Coveleski, and Waite Hoyt are inducted into the Hall of Fame. Musial played 22 seasons with the Cardinals, hitting .331 with a .559 slugging average, 475 homers, 1,951 RBI, and 725 doubles. He appeared in four World Series. Roy Campanella's career was cut short when he was paralyzed in a January 1958 auto accident. He played 10 years – all with the Dodgers, batting .276 with 242 homers. He appeared in five World Series with the Dodgers. Stan Coveleski won three games and compiled an 0.67 ERA in the 1920 World Series. In his 14-year career, he was 215-142 with a 2.88 ERA and won 20 games five times. Hoyt pitched 21 years, compiling a 237-182 record with an ERA of 3.59. He pitched in seven World Series.

When Coveleski and Hoyt were elected to the Hall on February 2, 1969, former baseball Commissioner Ford Frick said, "We wanted to elect them while they are still around to smell the roses."

JULY 30:

At Shea Stadium, in the ninth inning of the first game in a doubleheader, Denis Menke hits a grand slam homer against Cal Koonce and Jim Wynn smacks a bases-loaded shot against Ron Taylor; Houston wins, 16-3. In the third inning of the nightcap, Mets' manager Gil Hodges leaves the dugout and goes out to left field to remove Cleon Jones for not hustling. The Astros score 10 runs in the inning and beat New York, 11-5.

The Orioles' Dave McNally beats the Royals, 4-2, for his 15th consecutive victory this season against no losses. McNally has won 17 in a row over two seasons.

AUGUST 1:

Boston Red Sox manager Dick Williams fines outfielder Carl Yastrzemski $500 and benches him for today's ball game for not hustling.

AUGUST 16
Bob Gibson sets an NL record by reaching 200 strikeouts for the seventh straight year.

AUGUST 3:

In Minnesota, the Twins beat Dave McNally, 5-2, ending his consecutive game winning streak at 15 (17 over two seasons) and handing him his first loss of the year. A pinch-hit grand slam by Rich Reese in the seventh defeats McNally. Jim Kaat is the winning pitcher.

AUGUST 5:

Today Willie Stargell becomes the first player to hit a home run out of Dodger Stadium when he muscles a 506-foot drive over the right-field pavilion against Alan Foster. The Pirates beat the Dodgers, 11-3.

AUGUST 10:

Twins' manager Billy Martin kayoes his own pitcher Dave Boswell outside a Detroit restaurant. The trouble began earlier in the day when coach Art Fowler reported that Boswell had not run the required laps. At 11:30 P.M., Boswell declares himself out to "get that squealer Fowler." Teammate Bob Allison tries to play peacemaker, but Martin, 41, goes after the 24-year-old Boswell, hitting him in the stomach and head, inflicting a 20-stitch wound. Billy Martin cuts his right hand in the fracas.

AUGUST 11:

Troubled by shoulder problems, Dodger right-hander Don Drysdale announces his retirement. Drysdale, the last Dodger who had played with the team in Brooklyn, is 5-4 with a 4.43 ERA this season. In his 14-year career, all spent with the Dodgers, he is 209-166, with a 2.95 ERA and 49 shutouts. He led the league in strikeouts three times and teamed up with Sandy Koufax to give Los Angeles one of the most potent lefty-righty pitching combinations ever. Drysdale appeared in five World Series.

AUGUST 13:

The Orioles' Jim Palmer no-hits the Athletics, 8-0, in Baltimore. This is the second start for Palmer after coming off the disabled list four days ago. He strikes out eight and walks six; the Orioles make two errors. Brooks Robinson hits a homer. The losing pitcher is Chuck Dobson. Denny McLain beats the Angels, 3-0, for his 18th win and eighth shutout of the season. Jim Northrup homers.

Bowie Kuhn gets a seven-year contract from major league owners as baseball commissioner. Since February, he has been serving on a temporary basis.

AUGUST 15:

The Dodgers acquire pitcher Jim Bunning (10-9) from the Pirates for two minor leaguers – infielder Chuck Goggin and outfielder Ron Mitchell.

AUGUST 16:

Bob Gibson raises his season strikeout total to 200 in an 8-1 Cardinals victory in Atlanta. Gibson has fanned 200 or more seven times – which is an NL record.

AUGUST 17:

In Oakland, the Tigers support Denny McLain with six homers as he wins his 19th of the season, 9-4. Al Kaline hits two round-trippers and Mickey Stanley, Don Wert, Tom Tresh, and Jim Northrup one each.

AUGUST 19:

Ken Holtzman of the Chicago Cubs no-hits the Braves, 3-0, at Wrigley Field today. Holtzman, who walks three and has no strikeouts, has a close call in the seventh inning when Billy Williams catches Hank Aaron's fly ball in deep left field. In his autobiography, Aaron writes that the wind held up the ball and Williams told him it was five or six rows into the bleachers when it was blown back into play. Ron Santo provides all the Chicago runs with a three-run round-tripper.

Today John "Swede" Hollison, the last surviving pitcher who had worked from the rectangular pitching box set 50 feet from home plate, dies at age 99 in Chicago. Hollison pitched four innings for the 1892 Chicago Colts in the NL, allowing one hit and no walks and striking out two. His lifetime record is 0-0 with a 2.25 ERA.

AUGUST 24:

The Mets beat the Dodgers, 7-4, completing a home stand in which they won nine games and now trail the Cubs by five. Cal Koonce gets the win; Don Sutton is charged with the loss.

SEPTEMBER 4:

The Padres' Dick Kelly and Gary Ross end Willie Davis's 31-game hitting streak, the longest in the majors in

CULTURE

***The Year Boston Won the Pennant*, a play by John Ford Noonan, stars Roy Scheider.**

Tom Seaver is the amazin' Mets' ace.

"When I'm hitting, the ball comes up to the plate like a basketball. You can see the stitches and the writing on the ball."
– *Rod Carew*

LEAGUE

In 1969, the American Civil Liberties Union demands more equality in the Hall of Fame. According to historian John Holway, commissioner Bowie Kuhn's attorney informed him that Cooperstown is a private club and is not covered under interstate commerce or federal civil rights laws.

20 years. Al Ferrara bats in all three runs in the Padres' 3-0 win over the Dodgers.

SEPTEMBER 5:

Billy Williams of the Cubs duplicates the 1903 feat of Norman "Kid" Elberfeld by getting all his team's hits. Elberfeld, playing with the New York Highlanders, had all singles. Williams hits two homers and two doubles, drives in and scores all Chicago's runs in a 9-2 loss to the Pirates. Winning pitcher Steve Blass has four hits of his own, including a three-run homer. Manny Sanguillen also homers for the Pirates. Ken Holtzman is the losing pitcher.

SEPTEMBER 7:

The Mets, one-time doormats of the NL, are red hot. Behind Nolan Ryan, they beat the Phillies, 9-3. The victory is the 18th in their last 24 games and moves them to within two and a half games of the Cubs, who have won only eight of their last 18.

SEPTEMBER 8:

The gap is closing. A crowd of 43,274 at Shea Stadium sees the Mets edge the Cubs, 3-2, behind Jerry Koosman's 13-strikeout pitching. Tommy Agee hits a two-run home run in the third and scores the winning run in the sixth. Bill Hands is the losing pitcher. The Cubs' first-place lead is now only one and a half games.

SEPTEMBER 9:

The Mets make it two for two in their mini-series with the Cubs. Tom Seaver pitches a five-hitter; Donn Clendenon and Art Shamsky homer; the Mets win, 7-1, and trail Chicago by only a half game. Ferguson Jenkins is the game's losing pitcher.

SEPTEMBER 10:

The Mets sweep a doubleheader from the Expos, 3-2, in 12 innings and 7-1, at Shea Stadium, while the Cubs are losing to the Phillies, 6-2. The Mets move into first place for the first time ever – with a one-game lead over Chicago.

Hank Aaron hits his 40th homer of the season in an 8-4 Braves victory. Aaron ties Willie Mays's NL record of 40 or more homers six times. Aaron sets a major league record with 300 or more total bases in 14 seasons.

In Chicago, Rod Carew is cut down trying to steal home, pitcher Tommy John throwing to catcher Don Pavletich.

Kansas City manager Joe Gordon sets a major league record by using 27 players in a nine-inning game. All the substituting is for naught; the Angels beat the Royals, 11-4. Andy Messersmith gets the win; the losing pitcher is Bill Butler.

SEPTEMBER 11:

The Cubs drop their eighth straight game – a 4-3 loss to the Phillies – while the Mets and Gary Gentry are beating the Expos, 4-0. With the win New York increases its lead over Chicago to two games.

SEPTEMBER 12:

In Pittsburgh, Jerry Koosman and Don Cardwell record the New York Mets' first-ever double shutout and up their lead over the Cubs to two and a half games. Each game ends with a 1-0 victory; each pitcher drives in the winning run.

SEPTEMBER 13:

In Pittsburgh, Tom Seaver registers his 22nd win and Ron Swoboda hits a grand slam homer to give the Mets their 10th straight win, 5-2. The Mets now hold first place by three and a half games.

SEPTEMBER 15:

Steve Carlton fans Frank "Tug" McGraw, Derrel "Bud" Harrelson and Amos Otis of the Mets in the ninth inning today at Busch Stadium for his 17th, 18th, and 19th strikeouts of the game – a major league record. But Carlton and St. Louis lose the game, 4-3, on a pair of two-run homers by Ron Swoboda. Carlton, who walks only two, surpasses the previous mark of 18 Ks by Sandy Koufax, Bob Feller, and Don Wilson. He strikes out the side in the first, second, fourth, and ninth innings.

Carlton, in the days when he was talking for the record, tells the New York Times: *"It was the best stuff I ever had. When I had nine strikeouts, I decided to go all the way. But it cost me the game because I started to challenge every batter."*

SEPTEMBER 17:

Hank Aaron's 12th inning homer beats the Dodgers, 6-5, and moves the Braves into first place in the NL West.

SEPTEMBER 15
The Phillies' Steve Carlton sets a major league record by striking out 19 Mets.

SEPTEMBER 24
The amazing Mets, a ninth-place team last season, clinch the NL East title.

SEPTEMBER 20:

The Pirates' Bob Moose no-hits the Mets, 4-0, at Shea Stadium. Moose strikes out six and walks three; the Pirates commit no errors. Moose improves his season record to 12-3. Gary Gentry is charged with the loss.

SEPTEMBER 21:

The Mets rebound after yesterday's no-hitter loss and sweep the Pirates, 5-3, and 6-1, at Shea Stadium. New York's "magic number" – the combined Mets' victories and Cubs' losses needed to clinch the division – is just four.

Today in Minnesota, Harmon Killebrew hits his 45th and 46th homers of the season, but a homer in the top of the ninth by John Kennedy of the Pilots gives Seattle a 4-3 win and prevents the Twins from clinching the AL West. Seattle's Tommy Harper steals his 72nd and 73rd bases.

SEPTEMBER 22:

Willie Mays hits a seventh-inning pinch-hit home run against Padres' rookie Mike Corkins at Jack Murphy Stadium. It is Mays's 600th career homer; he now trails only Babe Ruth with 714. The ball lands in the left centerfield pavilion and is returned to him. Mays, batting for George Foster, also breaks a 2-2 tie with his round-tripper – the 13th of the season – and the Giants win, 4-2.

According to Charles Einstein, Corkins asks Padres' manager Preston Gomez: "Why'd it have to be me?" Gomez replies: "Son, there've been 599 before you."

Tom Seaver wins his 24th game, topping the Cardinals, 3-1, and the Mets edge closer to the NL East title.

SEPTEMBER 23:

At Wrigley Field, against the Cardinals, Ernie Banks of the Cubs singles for his 2,500th career hit.

At Fenway Park, Carl Yastrzemski homers against Mel Stottlemyre of the Yankees; it is Yaz's 200th career round-tripper. Boston wins the game, 8-3.

In Houston, the Braves and George Stone beat the Astros and Jim Bouton, 10-2. Atlanta takes over first place in the NL West.

The Mets, a ninth-place team last season, clinch at least a tie for the NL East title, when Ron Swoboda's 11th-inning single scores Bud Harreleson with the winning run in a 3-2 victory over the St. Louis Cardinals.

SEPTEMBER 24:

Mets rookie Gary Gentry four-hits the Cardinals, Donn Clendenon hits two homers, Ed Charles adds another, and New York wins, 6-0, clinching the NL East. A crowd of 54,928 fans witness the amazing one-year turnaround that brings Gil Hodges's team the first-ever divisional title in baseball history. The losing pitcher is Steve Carlton.

John Allyn buys the White Sox from his brother Arthur Allyn Jr. today. The team will not be moved to Milwaukee, but will remain in Chicago.

SEPTEMBER 26:

In Seattle, Rod Carew takes off for home with two out and Claude "Skip" Lockwood pitching. Carew's slide knocks down the home plate umpire, Jim Honochick. He gets to his feet and calls Carew out on what would have been his eighth steal of home this season. Carew flings his helmet and then is ejected.

In the last of 11 "home" games in Milwaukee, the White Sox bow to the Royals, 5-3. Moe Drabowsky is the winning pitcher; Joel Horlen gets the loss. Attendance today is 9,587; the year's total in Milwaukee is 196,712. Beginning in 1970, Milwaukee will have an AL expansion team and the White Sox will play all their home ball games in Chicago.

SEPTEMBER 27:

Even with the Eastern Division title clinched, the Mets keep the heat on. Tom Seaver wins his 25th of the season and 10th straight, beating the Phillies, 1-0.

SEPTEMBER 28:

The Minnesota Twins clinch the American League West Division title today with a 5-2 win over the Seattle Pilots in the opening game of a doubleheader in Seattle.

The Braves' Hank Aaron's RBI today against the San Diego Padres gives Hammerin' Hank 100 for the season. It is the 14th time Aaron has batted in at least 100 runs, a major league record. The Braves win, 4-2.

HISTORY

Pilots' catcher Jerry McNertney later acknowledges he never tagged Carew in that September 26 game. According to sports historian Ron Marshall, the Society for American Baseball Research in 1991 determined that the record actually was eight by Ty Cobb in 1912. Consequently, Carew and Reiser are tied for second place.

"He's so good that blind people come to the park just to hear him pitch."
– Reggie Jackson, on Tom Seaver

HISTORY

Hoyt Wilhelm of the Angels is the first pitcher in history with 200 career saves.

SEPTEMBER 29:

Rico Petrocelli of the Red Sox hits his 40th homer today, setting an AL record for shortstops. Ernie Banks holds the major league mark with 47. Boston beats the Senators, 8-5, in Washington, D.C.

The Miracle Mets reach 100 wins, beating the Cubs, 6-5, in 12 innings.

SEPTEMBER 30:

In Atlanta, Rico Carty's seventh-inning sacrifice fly drives in the winning run in a 3-2 Braves' victory over the Reds, clinching the Western Division title. It is Atlanta's 10th victory in a row. Phil Niekro is the winning pitcher and the team's closer, Hoyt Wilhelm, picks up another save.

Hank Thompson, the first black to play for the St. Louis Browns, dies at the age of 43 in Fresno, California. Thompson, an infielder-outfielder, played in the major leagues for nine seasons, hitting .267. He appeared in two World Series with the Giants.

It's too little, too late for Leo Durocher's Cubs. Chicago beats the visiting Mets, but ends up eight games behind. The Mets finish at 100-62 on the strength of 38 victories in 49 games since August 14.

OCTOBER 2:

Only 5,473 turn up for the final game of the season in Seattle, where the Pilots lose, 3-1, to the Athletics. Jim Roland gets the win; Steve Barber is charged with the loss – the 98th of the season for the Pilots. The game marks the end of the team's one-year stay in Seattle. The Pilots total attendance is only 677,944 and the team finishes in last place.

REGULAR SEASON WRAP-UP:

The Mets go from ninth place to a divisional title, with a 100-62 record, and the NL pennant. Gil Hodges's team bats .242, the lowest ever for a pennant-winner. Tom Seaver at 25-7 with a 2.21 ERA is the team's leading pitcher. Cleon Jones bats .340; Tommie Agee hits 26 homers and bats .271.

Earl Weaver's Orioles are 109-53 in the AL. Boog Powell bats .304 with 37 homers and 121 RBI. Frank Robinson finishes at .308, with 32 homers and 100 RBI. Brooks Robinson hits 23 homers and drives in 84 runs; Paul Blair bats in 76 with 26 homers. The team has two 20-game winners – Mike Cuellar (23-11) and Dave McNally (20-7).

The Giants' Bobby Bonds, with 32 homers and 45 stolen bases, becomes the fourth player in the 30-30 Club. He also sets a major league record by striking out 187 times. Astros' pitchers set a major league record with 1,221 strikeouts and are the second team ever with three pitchers who have 200 or more – Don Wilson, 235; Larry Dierker, 232; and Tom Griffin, 200. The Twins' Harmon Killebrew walks a league-leading 145 times. Wayne Granger of the Reds pitches in 90 games, surpassing Wilbur Wood's 1968 mark of 88.

OCTOBER 4:

NLCS, game one. The Mets and Tom Seaver beat Phil Niekro and the Braves, 9-5, in Atlanta. Tony Gonzalez and Hank Aaron homer for the Braves. The Mets win the game with a five-run eighth inning.

ALCS, game one. In Baltimore, the Orioles beat the Twins, 4-3, in 12 innings. Frank Robinson, Mark Belanger, and Boog Powell homer for the Orioles; Tony Oliva for the Twins. Mark Belanger scores the winning run on a two-out suicide squeeze by Paul Blair. The winning pitcher is Dick Hall; the loser is Ron Perranoski.

OCTOBER 5:

ALCS, game two. In Baltimore, in an 11-inning pitching classic, the Orioles win 1-0, on Curt Motten's pinch-hit RBI single. Dave McNally goes all the way for Baltimore, allowing only three hits and fanning 10. Dave Boswell, who is relieved in the 11th by Ron Perranoski, is the losing pitcher.

NLCS, game two. The Mets use 13 hits to beat the Braves, 11-6, in Atlanta. Tommie Agee, Ken Boswell, and Cleon Jones hit two-run homers for the Mets; Hank Aaron hits a three-run home run for Atlanta. The winning pitcher is Ron Taylor in relief. Ron Reed is the game's losing pitcher.

OCTOBER 6:

ALCS, game three. In Minnesota, Jim Palmer, behind an 18-hit Orioles' attack, pitches a complete game and wins, 11-2, for the AL pennant. The losing pitcher is Bob L. Miller.

OCTOBER 6 The Mets and Orioles sweep their respective LCS and will meet in the World Series.

OCTOBER 16 The Miracle Mets win game five, 5-3, for the franchise's first World Championship.

Baltimore's Paul Blair hits the game's only home run, adds two doubles, and drives in five runs.

NLCS, game three. The Mets sweep the Braves, 7-4, at Shea Stadium for the NL pennant. Three Mets homers by Tommie Agee (solo), Ken Boswell (one on), and Wayne Garrett (one on) offset two-run homers by Atlanta's Hank Aaron and Orlando Cepeda. Nolan Ryan gets the win with seven innings of three-hit relief. Pat Jarvis is the losing pitcher.

OCTOBER 7:

The Cardinals and Phillies complete a major trade. St. Louis acquires first baseman Dick Allen (.288, 32 homers, 89 RBI), infielder Octavio "Cookie" Rojas (.228, four homers), and pitcher Jerry Johnson (6-13, 4.29 ERA). In return, Philadelphia gets outfielder Curt Flood (.285, four homers), catcher Tom McCarver (.260, seven homers), pitcher Joe Hoerner (2-3, 2.89 ERA), and outfielder Byron Browne (.226 in 22 games).

OCTOBER 9:

George "Sparky" Anderson, who was a coach with the Padres this season, is named the manager of the Reds. Under Dave Bristol, Cincinnati was 89-73 and finished third in the NL West last season.

Former major league infielder Don Hoak dies in Pittsburgh at age 41, of a heart attack, after chasing car thieves. Hoak batted .265 in 11 years and was known for his aggressive play.

DICK ALLEN, WHO IS THE PERSONIFICATION OF A MAN WHO MARCHED TO HIS OWN DRUMMER, ONCE SAID: "BASEBALL IS A FORM OF SLAVERY. ONCE YOU STEP OUT OF BOUNDS, THAT'S IT. THEY'LL DO EVERYTHING POSSIBLE TO DESTROY YOUR SOUL."

OCTOBER 11:

World Series, game one. In Baltimore, the Orioles' Mike Cuellar six-hits the Mets and Don Buford homers off the second pitch of the game from Mets' starter Tom Seaver, the losing pitcher, for a 4-1 win.

OCTOBER 12:

World Series, game two. The Mets' starter Jerry Koosman allows just two hits and Ron Taylor pitches the final one-third of an inning as New York tops the Orioles, 2-1. Koosman pitches six no-hit innings. Donn Clendenon connects for a home run and the Mets win on an RBI single off the bat of Al Weis in the ninth inning. Baltimore's Dave McNally goes all the way, allowing six hits, but nonetheless is the losing pitcher.

OCTOBER 14:

World Series, game three. At Shea Stadium, Gary Gentry and Nolan Ryan combine to shut out the Orioles, 5-0. Centerfielder Tommy Agee homers and makes two great catches – in the fourth inning on an Elrod Hendricks drive with two on and in the seventh with the bases-loaded on a Paul Blair shot. Ed Kranepool also homers for the Mets. The winning pitcher is Gentry; Jim Palmer gets the loss.

OCTOBER 15:

World Series, game four. Tom Seaver and the Mets beat the Orioles, 2-1, in 10 innings. Once again, a great outfield play saves the game – this time by right fielder Ron Swoboda on a Brooks Robinson drive with runners on first and third in the ninth. In the tenth, Rod Gaspar runs for Jerry Grote, who had doubled, and scores the winning run on a throwing error by pitcher Pete Richert. Donn Clendenon hits a home run for the Mets. The loser is Dick Hall in relief.

OCTOBER 16:

World Series, game five. The Mets complete their Miracle of 1969. Jerry

LEAGUE

At the owners' winter meeting in Bal Harbour, Florida, Charles S. "Chub" Feeney is unanimously elected NL president, succeeding Warren Giles, who is retiring.

"I certainly agree with you that you, as a human being, are not a piece of property to be bought and sold."
– Commissioner Bowie Kuhn to Curt Flood

Koosman five-hits Baltimore for a 5-3 victory and the World Championship. After a two-run home run by the Orioles' starting pitcher Dave McNally and a solo homer by Frank Robinson, the Mets tie the game on a two-run round-tripper by Donn Clendenon and a bases-empty homer by Al Weis. The Mets win it in the eighth on doubles by Cleon Jones and Ron Swoboda off losing pitcher Eddie Watt. Al Weis hits .455, Ron Swoboda .400, and Donn Clendenon .357 with three homers to lead the Mets' offense. Mets' pitchers compile a 1.80 ERA. Jerry Koosman is 2-0 with a 2.04 ERA. Boog Powell is Baltimore's top hitter at only .263. Mike Cuellar is 1-0 with a 1.13 ERA.

POST-SEASON

OCTOBER 25:

Jackie Robinson fires another salvo in the baseball centennial controversy – this time at former manager Casey Stengel. He tells Will Grimsley of the Associated Press: "They voted Casey the greatest living manager. That's...a joke. The only thing a manager has to do is relate to the players. Who did Casey ever relate to? Nobody but himself."

OCTOBER 29:

The Phillies sign pitcher Jim Bunning (13-10, 3.69 ERA) following his release by the Dodgers. Bunning pitched for Philadelphia from 1964 to 1967.

NOVEMBER 15:

Billy Southworth dies at age 76 in Columbus, Ohio. He managed the Cardinals and Braves for 13 years, compiling the fifth-best winning percentage of all time – .597. Southworth won three pennants and two World Series with St. Louis and one NL pennant with the Braves. His playing career lasted 13 years and he batted .297, appearing in two World Series and hitting .333.

NOVEMBER 21:

George "Ken" Griffey Jr. is born in Donora, Pennsylvania, the birthplace of Hall of Famer Stan Musial.

DECEMBER 3:

The champion New York Mets trade their outfielder Amos Otis (.151 in 48 games) and pitcher Bob Johnson (0-0) to the Royals for infielder-outfielder Joe Foy (.262, 11 homers).

DECEMBER 4:

The Yankees trade first baseman Joe Pepitone (.242, 27 homers) to the Astros for outfielder-first baseman Curt Blefary (.253, 12 homers). Pitcher Joe Niekro (8-18, 3.70 ERA) goes to the Tigers from the Padres for pitcher Pat Dobson (5-10, 3.60 ERA) and infielder Dave Campbell (.103 in 32 games).

DECEMBER 7:

Francis "Lefty" O'Doul dies in San Francisco at the age of 72. O'Doul played 11 years, batting .349. He twice led the NL in batting with a high of .398 in 1929 with the Phillies. Before becoming a full-time outfielder, O'Doul was a nondescript pitcher, compiling a 1-1 record with a 4.87 ERA between the years 1919 to 1923.

DECEMBER 10:

The Minnesota Twins obtain a pair of pitchers – Luis Tiant (9-20, 3.71 ERA) and Stan Williams (6-14, 3.94 ERA) – from the Indians for pitchers Dean Chance (5-4, 2.95 ERA) and Bob L. Miller (5-5, 3.02 ERA) along with outfielder Ted Uhlaender (.273, eight homers) and third baseman Graig Nettles (.222, seven homers in 96 games).

DECEMBER 24:

Curt Flood refuses to report to Philadelphia after being traded on October 7. He writes to new Commissioner Bowie Kuhn: "After 12 years in the Major Leagues, I do not feel that I am a piece of property to be bought and sold irrespective my wishes. I believe that any system which produces that result violates my basic rights as a citizen and is inconsistent with the laws of the United States and of the several States. It is my desire to play baseball in 1970, and I am capable of playing. I have received a contract offer from the Philadelphia club, but I believe I have the right to consider offers from other clubs before making any decisions. I, therefore, request that you make known to all Major League clubs my feelings on this matter, and advise them of my availability for the 1970 season."

Commissioner Bowie Kuhn responds: "I certainly agree with you that you, as a human being, are not a piece of property to be bought and sold. That is fundamental in our society and I think obvious. However, I cannot see its applicability to the situation at hand."

DECEMBER 4
The Yankees trade popular first baseman Joe Pepitone to the Houston Astros.

DECEMBER 24
Curt Flood refuses a trade to the Phillies, setting of the battle for free agency

THE BEST OF 1969

NATIONAL LEAGUE

HITTERS

Batting Average:
Pete Rose, Cincinnati Reds, .348

Slugging Average:
Willie McCovey, San Francisco Giants, .656

Home Runs:
Willie McCovey, 45

Runs Batted In:
Willie McCovey, 126

Hits:
Matty Alou, Pittsburgh Pirates, 231

Stolen Bases:
Lou Brock, St. Louis Cardinals, 53

PITCHERS

Wins:
Tom Seaver, New York Mets, 25

Strikeouts:
Ferguson Jenkins, Chicago Cubs, 273

Earned Run Average:
Juan Marichal, San Francisco Giants, 2.10

Winning Percentage:
Tom Seaver, .781

Saves:
Fred Gladding, Houston Astros, 29

Most Valuable Player:
Willie McCovey, San Francisco Giants

Cy Young Award:
Tom Seaver, New York Mets

Rookie of the Year:
Ted Sizemore, Los Angeles Dodgers

AMERICAN LEAGUE

HITTERS

Batting Average:
Rod Carew, Minnesota Twins, .332

Slugging Average:
Reggie Jackson, Oakland Athletics, .608

Home Runs:
Harmon Killebrew, Minnesota Twins, 49

Runs Batted In:
Harmon Killebrew, 140

Hits:
Tony Oliva, Minnesota Twins, 197

Stolen Bases:
Tommy Harper, Seattle Pilots, 73

PITCHERS

Wins:
Denny McLain, Detroit Tigers, 24

Strikeouts:
Sam McDowell, Cleveland Indians, 279

Earned Run Average:
Dick Bosman, Washington Senators, 2.19

Winning Percentage:
Jim Palmer, Baltimore Orioles, .800

Saves:
Ron Perranoski, Minnesota Twins, 31

Most Valuable Player:
Harmon Killebrew, Minnesota Twins

Cy Young Award:
Mike Cuellar, Baltimore Orioles;
Denny McLain, Detroit Tigers

Rookie of the Year:
Lou Piniella, Kansas City Royals

LEAGUE

In December the Players' Association executive board meets in Puerto Rico and team representatives vote unanimously to support Curt Flood's suit against baseball and to pay his legal fees.

1970

"Greatest Living Player in baseball's centennial year..."
– Joe DiMaggio's Yankee Stadium plaque

NEWS

U.S. INVADES CAMBODIA

Terrorists blow up TWA plane in Jordan

FOUR STUDENTS KILLED BY NATIONAL GUARD AT KENT STATE ANTI-WAR DEMONSTRATION

Chicago Seven acquitted of conspiracy

Postal Workers Go on Strike

VOTING AGE LOWERED TO 18

CIGARETTE ADVERTISING BANNED FROM TV, RADIO

***Monday Night Football* debuts on television**

126 RUNNERS COMPETE IN FIRST NEW YORK CITY MARATHON

Janis Joplin, Jimi Hendrix die

PRE-SEASON

JANUARY 14:

Mets' general manager Johnny Murphy dies of a heart attack at age 61 in New York City. Murphy was one of the first and most successful relief pitchers. In 13 years – all but one with the Yankees – he compiled a 93-53 record with a 3.50 ERA and 107 saves. His best year was 1941, when he was 8-3 with a 1.98 ERA and 15 saves. He was 2-0 with a 1.10 ERA in six World Series. He is replaced by Bob Scheffing.

Vernon "Lefty" Gomez once was asked how many games he expected to win. His response was: "Ask Murphy."

JANUARY 17:

Baseball faces perhaps its most dangerous legal challenge when Curt Flood files a $4.1 million suit in federal court against Commissioner Bowie Kuhn, the presidents of the AL and NL, and 24 team owners, charging that the reserve system is "slavery." Flood, who has the support of the Players Association, gave up a $90,000 salary by retiring and refusing to join the Philadelphia Phillies. According to authors Lee Lowenfish and Tony Lupien, before the trial begins, Flood is telephoned by Monte Irvin, who is Commissioner Bowie Kuhn's assistant. He claims, "...the commissioner was willing to concede to Flood half his December request. He was free to attempt to arrange a deal with any National League club and not damage his litigation. Flood realized that if he accepted the offer, his case would likely end... Flood turned down the last-minute offer."

FEBRUARY 5:

Rudy York dies at the age of 56 in Rome, Georgia. In 13 years, the first baseman hit .275 with 277 homers. He led the AL in homers in 1943, and four times he hit 30 or more in a season.

FEBRUARY 13:

Commissioner Bowie Kuhn announces that he is investigating the off-field activities of Detroit Tigers' pitcher Denny McLain.

FEBRUARY 17:

Sports Illustrated reports on Denny McLain's alleged involvement with bookmaking activities and his association with mobsters. On February 19, after a five-and-a-half-hour meeting with McLain, Commissioner Bowie Kuhn announces that, effective April 1, the pitcher is suspended indefinitely for bookmaking activities.

MARCH 15:

Thanks, Dad. Peter O'Malley becomes president of the Dodgers when his father Walter J. O'Malley moves up to the new post of chairman of the board. At age 32, Peter O'Malley is baseball's youngest team president.

MARCH 18:

In an exhibition game, the Indians and Pilots test a livelier baseball designated X-5. The Pilots win, 19-14, in a game with 34 hits. The Indians' Jack Heidemann hits two home runs and teammate Jack Ford has a grand slam. The ball is reputedly 5 percent livelier; Indians, pitcher Sudden Sam McDowell claims the figure is 100 percent.

APRIL 1:

One day after federal bankruptcy court referee Sidney C. Volinn okays the sale, automobile dealer Allen "Bud" Selig and his investment group buy the Seattle Pilots for

FEBRUARY 17
Tigers' pitcher Denny McClain is suspended from baseball for bookmaking activities.

APRIL 21
The Reds and Braves combine for 10 home runs in a 13-8 Cincinnati win.

$10.8 million. A purchase agreement was signed on March 8. Seattle has the dubious distinction of having the shortest franchise in major league history – one year. But it was time enough to lose $1 million. The team will be moved to Milwaukee and become the Brewers. Milwaukee had an AL franchise in 1901, but the team moved to St. Louis in 1902 as the Browns.

Denny McLain begins a three-month suspension handed down by Commissioner Bowie Kuhn for his involvement in Detroit bookmaking.

THE SEASON

APRIL 7:

American League baseball comes back to Milwaukee after 69 years. At County Stadium, 37,237 turn out to see the new Brewers lose to the visiting Angels, 12-0, on a four-hitter by Andy Messersmith.

APRIL 8:

The Phillies receive two minor leaguers outfielder first baseman Willie Montanez and pitcher Bob Browning – as replacements for Curt Flood, who refused to report to the Phillies in the aftermath of his October 7, 1969, trade from the St. Louis Cardinals.

APRIL 10:

The Phillies inaugurate their new $52 million ballpark – Veterans Stadium – with a 4-1 win over the Expos. A crowd of 55,352 attends the opening of the ballpark, located at the corner of Broad and Pattison Streets in South Philadelphia. Jim Bunning gets the win with a save from Joe Hoerner. Don Money homers for the Phillies in the bottom of the sixth. The losing pitcher is Bill Stoneman.

APRIL 11:

In Chicago, the Brewers beat the White Sox, 8-4, on four runs in the ninth inning, for their first win. Danny Walton has two homers for Milwaukee and John O'Donoghue gets the win in relief.

APRIL 12:

Plaques honoring Joe DiMaggio and Mickey Mantle are dedicated today in centerfield of Yankee Stadium. DiMaggio's plaque recalls his 56-game hitting streak and reads: "Greatest Living Player in baseball's centennial year in recognition of his singular excellence and for his legacy of greatness." Mantle is described as, "A magnificent Yankee... the most popular player of his era in recognition of his true greatness in the Yankees' tradition and for his unequaled courage..."

> "IF YOU COULD MASTER HITTING BY THINKING OR BY SIMPLY LEARNING THE TECHNIQUE, YOU'D HAVE A LOT OF 50-YEAR-OLD .300 HITTERS STILL AROUND."
> – Joe DiMaggio

APRIL 18:

At Shea Stadium, Nolan Ryan yields a leadoff single to the Phillies' Denny Doyle. It is the only safety Ryan gives up as he strikes out 15 en route to a 7-0 win.

APRIL 21:

The hills are alive with the sound of homers. The Reds and Braves combine for 10; Cincinnati ties an NL record with six players connecting. Bernie Carbo hits two and Pete Rose, Bobby Tolan, Johnny Bench, Dave Concepcion, and Tony Perez hit one each. Felix Milan, Orlando Cepeda, and Rico Carty hit round-trippers for Atlanta. The Reds win, 13-8.

APRIL 22:

Tom Terrific ties Lefty. Only one season after Steve Carlton fanned a record 19 in one game, Tom Seaver of the Mets ties his mark. In a 2-1 victory over the Padres at Shea Stadium, Seaver

LEAGUE

In May the second basic agreement is signed; it recognizes the Major League Baseball Players Association as "the sole and exclusive bargaining agent for all Major League Players." The minimum salary for 1970 is raised to $12,000 and will go to $15,000 by 1972. Grievances will be arbitrated and maximum salary reductions are established at 20 percent – 30 percent over two years. The reserve clause is not addressed.

APRIL 26
Cardinals' ace Bob Gibson strikes out 15 Reds and gives up just five hits in a 4-1 win.

records his third straight win this season and his 13th dating back to last year. He also sets a major league record by fanning 10 straight batters. Seaver allows two hits – a second inning homer by Al Ferrara and a fourth inning Dave Campbell single – and walks two. He ends the game by retiring the last 16 batters in a row. Mike Corkins gets the loss. Catcher Jerry Grote has 20 putouts, a major league record.

APRIL 26:

The Cardinals' Bob Gibson fans 15 Reds – including six in a row – and allows only five hits in a 4-1 victory.

APRIL 27:

The Angels trade outfielder Rich Reichardt (.167 in nine games), the recipient of a $200,000 bonus in 1964, to the Senators along with infielder Aurelio Rodriguez (.270 in 17 games). In return, they get third baseman Ken McMullen (.203 in 15 games).

APRIL 29:

Glove man becomes bat man. Paul Blair of the Orioles hits three homers against the White Sox in an 18-2 Baltimore win.

APRIL 30:

In Atlanta, the Cubs' Billy Williams plays in his 1,000th consecutive game. The Braves top Chicago, 9-2.

MAY 6:

The Indians' Sam McDowell fans 15 White Sox batters – 13 in the first six innings – but Chicago wins the game, 2-1, on a Carlos May homer in the ninth inning.

MAY 7:

The Dodgers' Wes Parker hits for the cycle, and his triple in the 10th beats the New York Mets, 7-4.

MAY 10:

Hoyt Wilhelm comes out of the bullpen for the Atlanta Braves and becomes the first pitcher to appear in 1,000 games. The Braves lose to the Cardinals, 6-5.

MAY 11:

Tom Seaver's 16-game winning streak – over two seasons – ends at the hands of the Expos and Dan McGinn, who three-hits the Mets, 3-0.

In Anaheim, Ray Culp of the Red Sox starts strong – fanning Santos "Sandy" Alomar, Roger Repoz, Ray Oyler, Jim Fregosi, Alex Johnson, and Jim Spencer in a row – but is not involved in the decision. But he does tie an AL record. The Angels win the game, 2-1, in 16 innings.

MAY 12:

In the second inning at Wrigley Field, Ernie Banks drives a pitch from Atlanta's Pat Jarvis into the left-field bleachers for his 500th career home run. The ball bounces back on the field. Rico Carty retrieves it and gives it to Banks who tips his cap to the 5,264 fans. Banks is the ninth ML player to reach 500, the first shortstop, and the only Cub. Billy Williams also homers and Ron Santo wins the game, 4-3, with an RBI single in the 11th.

MAY 15:

Rico Carty of the Braves hits safely in his 31st consecutive game. He is batting .451 in the streak. Atlanta downs Cincinnati, 3-1.

In Philadelphia, Mike Compton singles in the third inning for the only hit against Tom Seaver in a 4-0 Mets' victory. Seaver fans 15 Phillies.

MAY 17:

In the second game of a Crosley Field doubleheader, 37-year-old Hank Aaron gets a first-inning infield hit against Wayne Simpson, becoming the ninth player in major league history with 3,000 hits. In

APRIL 29
The Orioles' Paul Blair clubs three home runs in an 18-2 assault on the White Sox.

MAY 12
Ernie Banks becomes the ninth major leaguer to hit 500 career home runs.

the third, Aaron cracks his 570th career home run, with a runner on base. The Reds outlast the Braves, however, for a 7-6 victory.

JUNE 1:

Jim Bouton gets a public spanking for writing Ball Four from Commissioner Bowie Kuhn, who calls the book "detrimental to baseball."

JUNE 5:

Al Kaline singles against Johnny "Blue Moon" Odom in the fifth inning for his 2,500th career hit. The Athletics beat the visiting Tigers, 4-2.

Brooks Robinson steals the World Series show.

JUNE 20
The Orioles' Brooks Robinson's 2,000th career hit is a three-run homer vs. the Tigers.

NL MVP Johnny Bench proves his worth at the plate – and behind it.

JUNE 12:

Despite issuing eight walks, Dock Ellis of the Pirates no-hits the Padres, 2-0, in San Diego. Willie Stargell hits two homers for all the game's runs. Ellis strikes out six – including Ed Spiezio to end the game. The Pirates play errorless ball and second baseman Bill Mazeroski makes a great catch of Ramon Webster's liner to save the no-hitter.

A controversial character, Ellis had a stormy relationship with the fans and press (an article about him was titled "Ellis Probably Most Unpopular Buc of All Time"), but was accepted in the clubhouse. His Pittsburgh teammates enjoyed his offbeat humor, as well as his 47 wins from 1970 to 1972.

JUNE 20:

The Orioles' Brooks Robinson hits a three-run homer against the Senators' Joe Coleman in the fifth inning today. It is Robinson's 2,000th career hit. Baltimore wins the game, 5-4.

JUNE 21:

Tigers' shortstop Cesar Gutierrez, a lifetime .215 hitter, singles six times and doubles once in seven at-bats against the Indians. He has three infield hits, scores three times, and drives in a run. Gutierrez, who wears uniform number 7, is the first modern major leaguer to enjoy a seven-for-seven day. Gutierrez's accomplishment overshadows heavy home run hitting. For the Tigers, Jim Northrop hits two and Al Kaline and Mickey Stanley one each. Tony Horton, Chuck Hinton, and Ted Uhlaender homer for the Indians. The Tigers win the game, 9-8, in 12 innings. Tom Timmerman is the winning pitcher; Phil Hennigan is tagged with the loss.

In 1971, Gutierrez has just seven hits for his entire season (38 games).

JUNE 24:

Yankees' outfielder Bobby Murcer hits four consecutive homers in a doubleheader against the Indians. Murcer homers in the ninth inning of the opener and then three consecutive times in the nightcap – with a walk in between. The Yankees win the second game, 5-4, after dropping game one, 7-2. Another historic ballpark will fall under the wrecker's ball. The Reds and Giants meet today in the last major league game ever at Crosley Field, which was opened in 1912. The Reds' Johnny Bench and Lee May homer in the bottom of the eighth to beat Juan Marichal, 5-4. After the game, home plate is flown by helicopter to the Reds' new home, Riverfront Stadium.

JUNE 25:

To prevent Bobby Murcer from setting a record for consecutive homers, the Indians' manager, Alvin Dark, calls all the pitches himself from the dugout and relays them to pitcher Steve Dunning. Murcer gets

JUNE 21
Light-hitting Tigers' shortstop Cesar Gutierrez goes 7-for-7 against the Indians.

JUNE 24
The Yankees' Bobby Murcer hits four consecutive homers in a doubleheader.

no good pitches to hit, walking three times and popping up with a 3-1 count.

JUNE 26:

It's two swings, two homers, and eight RBI for the Orioles' Frank Robinson, who becomes the seventh major leaguer with two grand slams in a game. Robinson connects in the fifth inning against the Senators' Joe Coleman and in the sixth off Joe Grzenda. Don Buford also homers for Baltimore; Rick Reichardt has a round-tripper for the Senators. The Orioles win the game, 12-2, in Washington. Dave McNally gets the win; Coleman is charged with the loss.

JUNE 28:

Baseball says good-bye to another old ball park. Today's doubleheader between the Pirates and the Cubs marks the last games at Forbes Field, opened in 1909. With 40,918 fans attending, the Pirates leave in style, sweeping Chicago, 3-2 and 4-1. Al Oliver hits the last-ever homer at Forbes.

JUNE 30:

Cincinnati's new Riverfront Stadium is just another ballpark for the Braves' Hank Aaron. Aaron inaugurates Riverfront – which features "wall-to-wall Astroturf" – with a home run in the very first inning against the Reds' Jim McGlothlin. Atlanta wins the game, 8-2. Attendance is 51,050.

GEORGE F. WILL, IN *BASEBALL: AN ILLUSTRATED HISTORY*, FONDLY RECALLS BYGONE BALLPARKS: "TO GO TO A GAME IN SPORTSMAN'S PARK IN ST. LOUIS, OR CROSLEY FIELD IN CINCINNATI, OR FORBES FIELD IN PITTSBURGH, OR SHIBE PARK IN PHILADELPHIA WAS TO EXPERIENCE BASEBALL INTIMATELY, AND TO BE MARINATED IN A SENSE OF MANY SUMMERS LINGERING IN THE ATMOSPHERE."

JULY 1:

Detroit's Denny McLain returns from his three-month suspension, pitches five and a third innings against the Yankees, but is not involved in the decision.

JULY 2:

Indians' catcher Ray Fosse extends his consecutive game hitting streak to 23 with a homer against the Orioles. Teammate Tony Horton hits for the cycle, and his ninth-inning home run gives Baltimore and Dennis Higgins a win, 10-9.

JULY 3:

Clyde Wright of the Angels no-hits the Athletics, 4-0, in Anaheim. Wright throws only 98 pitches, striking out one and walking three; California commits no errors. Ken McMullen's third-inning home run gives Wright all the support he needs. The game ends when Felipe Alou hits into a

TRIVIA

Carlos May wears his birthday on his back. His uniform reads: "May 17."

JUNE 30
The Reds' new Riverfront Stadium opens, and Hank Aaron greets it with a homer.

TRIVIA

In its 61-year history, Forbes Field never was the site of a no-hitter. The closest was Bob Moose's effort in 1968; a soft single with two out in the eighth spoiled the bid. Moose finished with a two-hitter.

double play. The losing pitcher is Chuck Dobson, who also was on the short end of Jim Palmer's 1969 no-hitter.

JULY 6:

Indians' manager Alvin Dark shuffles well and pitcher Sam McDowell goes from the mound to second base and back again. With two out in the 8th inning, runners on second and third, and right-handed slugger Frank Howard coming to bat, Dark brings in Dean Chance. Instead of removing the left-handed McDowell, he sends him to second. Second baseman Eddie Leon replaces third baseman Graig Nettles. Howard is walked intentionally. Rick Reichardt then grounds to Leon, who throws to McDowell at second base for the third out. McDowell returns to the mound for the 9th inning and picks up his 12th win of the season, 6-4.

JULY 7:

The Indians honor their former shortstop with Lou Boudreau Day. His number is retired and a street is renamed Lou Boudreau Boulevard. The Senators tarnish the day by beating the Indians, 9-3.

JULY 8:

The Giants' Jim Ray Hart becomes the first NL player since Fred Merkle in 1911 to drive in six runs in one inning. Hart also hits for the cycle in a 13-0 win over Atlanta.

JULY 11:

The Braves' Orlando Cepeda collects his 2,000th career hit as Atlanta loses to the visiting Reds, 7-6.

JULY 14:

Pete Rose crashes into catcher Ray Fosse in the bottom of the 14th and scores the winning run for the NL in a 5-4 All-Star Game today at Cincinnati's Riverfront Stadium. Fosse suffers a badly injured shoulder as a result of the collision. The NL had tied the score in the ninth, and Jim Hickman's single to center drives in Rose with the winning run. The Giants' Gaylord Perry and the Twins' Jim Perry become the first brothers to pitch in the All-Star Game. The NL's Dick Dietz hits the game's only homer. Claude Osteen gets the win; Clyde Wright is tagged with the loss. The game is the first since 1957 in which the fans chose the players.

JULY 16:

The Pirates open their new 50,000 seat, Astroturf-ed Three Rivers Stadium, located at the confluence of the Monongahela, Allegheny, and Ohio Rivers. A crowd of 48,846 attends the opening game, won by the Reds, 3-2. The Pirates introduce knit uniforms, replacing the traditional heavy flannels.

JULY 18:

The Giants' Willie Mays gets his 3,000th career hit, a two-out single in the second inning against Montreal's Mike Wegener. The Giants win the game, 10-1, at Candlestick Park with 28,879 on hand.

JULY 20:

The Dodgers' Bill Singer no-hits the Phillies, 5-0, in Los Angeles. He strikes out 10 and issues no walks; the Dodgers commit two errors. Woodie Fryman is the losing pitcher.

JULY 21:

San Diego manager Preston Gomez makes a controversial move. With his team behind, 1-0, he sends in Clarence "Cito" Gaston to pinch-hit for Clay Kirby, although the pitcher has been no-hitting the visiting New York Mets for eight innings. The Padres fail to score and then the Mets add two more runs against reliever Jack Baldschun for a 3-0 victory. Jim McAndrew gets the win.

JULY 23:

Pitcher Jim Lonborg, still struggling after tearing up his knee in a December 1967 ski accident, is sent down to AAA Louisville by the Boston Red Sox.

JULY 24:

Pittsburgh Pirates' fans salute their right fielder on Roberto Clemente Night at Three Rivers Stadium. Clemente doesn't disappoint, treating them to a sliding catch on a Denis Menke foul in the ninth inning and the Pirates beat the Astros, 11-0.

JULY 26:

While the Reds' Johnny Bench is hitting three consecutive home runs off Cardinals' pitcher Steve Carlton in Cincinnati, the Braves' Orlando Cepeda is duplicating the feat against the Cubs in Chicago. Atlanta beats Chicago, 8-3, while the Reds top the Cards by a score of 12-5.

JULY 14
Pete Rose slides home with the All-Star Game winner, taking out Ray Fosse in the process.

AUGUST 23
For the second straight day, Roberto Clemente has five hits in Pirates' wins over the Dodgers.

JULY 27:

Lou Boudreau, Earle Combs, former NL president and baseball Commissioner Ford Frick, and Jesse "Pop" Haines are inducted into the Hall of Fame. Frick, a former journalist, was president of the NL from 1935 to 1951 and commissioner of baseball from 1951 to 1965. Boudreau, a shortstop, played 15 years, hitting .295. He led the AL in batting in 1944 with .327 and had a personal high average of .355 in 1948. Combs, overshadowed by his teammates Babe Ruth and Lou Gehrig, played center field for the Yankees for 12 years, hitting .325 with 154 triples. His highest average was .356 in 1927 and he batted .350 in four World Series. Haines pitched 19 years – all but one with the Cardinals – compiling a 210-158 record with a 3.64 ERA. He had a 3-1 record in four World Series.

Lou Boudreau tells the fans: "I'm really humbled by this because I never considered myself a superstar like Williams, DiMaggio, or Aaron." He adds: "This is reaching the top... I feel that my life is fulfilled now."

AUGUST 1:

Willie Stargell ties a major league record – held by several players – when he collects five extra-base hits in Atlanta. Stargell hits two homers and three doubles as the Pirates beat the Braves, 20-10. The teams combine for five homers in the seventh inning – tying another major league mark. Bob Robertson, Stargell, and Jose Pagan connect in the top of the inning. Hank Aaron and Rico Carty respond by hitting a pair of round-trippers for the Braves.

AUGUST 8:

Nearly 10 years after firing him, the New York Yankees honor 79-year-old Casey Stengel at Old-Timers' Day. A crowd of 47,914 is on hand at Yankee Stadium as Stengel's number 37 is retired. Whitey Ford and Yogi Berra present Stengel with his uniform. The Orioles then defeat the Yankees, 4-2.

AUGUST 11:

The Phillies' Jim Bunning beats the Astros, 6-5, for his 100th NL win. He now has 100 victories in each league. Cy Young recorded 200 in each league.

AUGUST 12:

Judge Irving Ben Cooper rules against Curt Flood in his antitrust suit. The judge says, "Decisions of the Supreme Court are not lightly overruled... We find no general or widespread disregard of the extremely important position the player occupies... Clearly the preponderance of credible proof does not favor elimination of the reserve clause." The judge says changes in the reserve clause should be made through negotiation and he denies Flood damages. Flood's attorney, former U.S. Supreme Court Justice Arthur Goldberg, files for an appeal.

AUGUST 22:

The Pirates' Roberto Clemente has five hits in seven at-bats today, scoring once and batting in a run in a 2-1, 16-inning victory over the Dodgers in Los Angeles.

AUGUST 23:

For the second straight day, Roberto Clemente has 5 hits; the Pirates rout the Dodgers, 11-0, in Los Angeles. Clemente ties a modern NL record with 10 hits in 2 games, collecting 8 singles, a double, and a home run.

AUGUST 28:

The Tigers' Denny McLain dumps a pail of ice water on Jim Hawkins of the *Detroit Free Press* and Watson Spoelstra of the *Detroit News.* McLain is suspended for a week and fined $500 a day by Detroit general manager Jim Campbell.

AUGUST 30:

The Indians and Angels tie a major league record when nine players homer in today's game. For the Angels, Alex Johnson, Jay Johnstone, Bill Voss, Santos "Sandy" Alomar, and Ken McMullen connect. Chuck Hinton, Graig Nettles, Vada Pinson, and Ray Fosse home run for the Indians. California wins the game, 10-9, on a pair of wild pitches by Dennis Higgins.

SEPTEMBER 3:

Billy Williams's consecutive game streak ends at 1,117 when he benches himself today because he is "pooped." The Cubs' outfielder will later explain: "I'm tired, that's all it is." With the White Sox at 49-87, manager Don Gutteridge is fired. Bill Adair will handle the team on

Hank Aaron comments: "It took me 17 years to get 3,000 hits in baseball. I did it in one afternoon on the golf course."

HISTORY

The Reds' Wayne Granger records a major-league-record 35 saves.

an interim basis until September 15 when the Pacific Coast League season ends and Chuck Tanner, manager of the Hawaii Islanders, can take over the club.

SEPTEMBER 9:

Denny McLain, still under suspension, is informed by Commissioner Bowie Kuhn that he will not be permitted to return this season. McLain is receiving the additional discipline for carrying a gun and violating the terms of his probation agreement.

SEPTEMBER 21:

In Oakland today, the Athletics' 21-year-old left-hander Vida Blue no-hits the Twins, 6-0. He walks one and strikes out nine; Oakland plays errorless ball. The losing pitcher is Jim Perry.

The Cubs buy pitcher Hoyt Wilhelm (6-4) from the Braves for the waiver price.

SEPTEMBER 22:

The Twins clinch the AL West today with a 5-3 victory over the Athletics in Oakland.

The Brewers' Tommy Harper hits a two-run homer in the seventh inning against the Angels. It is his 30th home run of the season. Harper, who has 38 stolen bases, joins Ken Williams, Willie Mays, Hank Aaron, and Bobby Bonds in the exclusive 30-30 "club." Milwaukee and Marty Pattin win the game, 4-2.

SEPTEMBER 27:

Behind Dock Ellis, the Pirates beat the Mets, 2-1, at Three Rivers Stadium to complete a three-game sweep and clinch the NL East. Dave Giusti gets the save.

OCTOBER 1:

The Phillies beat the Expos, 2-1, in 10 innings, in the last game ever at Connie Mack Stadium – formerly Shibe Park. A crowd of 31,822 attends today's game won by Dick Selma. Howie Reed gets the loss. The ballpark was opened in 1909 and was the home of the Athletics until their move to Kansas City after the 1954 season. In what is becoming a tradition, home plate is moved to the new facility, Veterans Stadium. After Oscar Gamble drives in Tim McCarver with the winning run, the fans run wild, ripping the stadium apart, and a farewell ceremony is canceled. Montreal was able to tie the game when fans interfered with the Phillies' left fielder Ron Stone as he tried to make a catch. Earlier, fans received slats from the seats as souvenirs, but threw them and used them as weapons.

After grounding out in the first inning, the Angels' Alex Johnson singles against the visiting White Sox in the third and fifth to win the AL batting title. He edges Boston's Carl Yastrzemski .3289 to .3286, the closest margin since George Kell beat out Ted Williams in 1949.

Tigers' pitcher John Hiller ties an AL record by fanning seven in a row in a 1-0 victory over the Indians.

REGULAR SEASON WRAP-UP:

The Reds, managed by George "Sparky" Anderson, compile a 102-60 record in the NL and field an awesome offensive lineup. Johnny Bench bats .293 with 45 homers and 148 RBI. Tony Perez (.317, 40 homers, 129 RBI), Pete Rose (.316, 15 homers), Bobby Tolan (.316, 16 homers), Lee May (34 homers and 94 RBI), and Bernie Carbo (.310, 21 homers) are the other big guns. Jim Merritt tops the pitching staff with a 20-12 record. Earl Weaver's Orioles go into the ALCS with a 108-54 regular season record in the AL. The team has three 20-game winners – Mike Cuellar (24-8), Dave McNally (24-9), and Jim Palmer (20-10). Boog Powell hits. 297 with 35 homers and 114 RBI. Frank Robinson finishes at .306 with 25 homers and 78 RBI; third baseman Brooks Robinson hits .276 with 18 home runs and 94 RBI.

Tony (26) and Billy Conigliaro (18) of the Red Sox combine for 54 homers – the most in a season by brothers.
The Cardinals' Vic Davalillo ties Dave Philley's major league mark with 24 pinch hits.

OCTOBER 3:

Major league umpires stage a strike. The six assigned to work the opening game of the NLCS against the Reds in Pittsburgh are outside the ballpark picketing while four minor league officials work the game itself. Today at Bloomington, Minnesota, where the Twins are hosting the Orioles in the ALCS, there are no pickets, but minor league umpires work the game. The major league umpires are

SEPTEMBER 21
Oakland's Vida Blue, just 21, no-hits the Twins, 6-0, walking one and fanning nine.

OCTOBER 5
Johnny Bench homers for the Reds as they sweep the Pirates in the NLCS.

seeking an increase from $2,500 to $5,000 for playoff games and from $6,500 to $10,000 for the World Series. The owners are offering $3,000 and $7,000 respectively.

NLCS, game one. Inside Three Rivers Stadium, Gary Nolan of the Reds pitches nine shutout innings and beats the Pirates, 3-0, on three runs in the 10th. Lee May hits a two-run double against losing pitcher Dock Ellis. Clay Carroll gets the save.

ALCS, game one. In Minnesota, with a crew of minor league umpires calling the game, the Orioles bomb the Twins, 10-6, with home runs by pitcher Mike Cuellar – with the bases loaded – Don Buford, and John "Boog" Powell. Harmon Killebrew homers for the Twins. Cuellar gets the win; Jim Perry the loss.

OCTOBER 4:

Umpires end their strike after one day and accept a four-year deal with escalating pay for post-season and World Series games. NLCS, game two. In Pittsburgh, the Reds make it two in a row with a 3-1 win. Jim Merritt gets the victory with a save by reliever Don Gullett. Bobby Tolan hits a solo home run. The losing pitcher is Luke Walker.

ALCS, game two. In Minnesota, Dave McNally allows six hits and the Orioles pound out 13 hits for an 11-3 victory. Davey Johnson hits a solo blow for Baltimore. Harmon Killebrew and Tony Oliva connect for the Twins. The losing pitcher is Tom Hall.

OCTOBER 5:

NLCS, game three. In Cincinnati, the Reds beat the Pirates, 3-2, to sweep the playoffs and win the NL pennant. Tony Perez and Johnny Bench homer; Bobby Tolan's single in the eighth drives in the winner. Milt Wilcox gets the win in relief of starter Tony Cloninger; Bob Moose is charged with the loss.

ALCS, game three. In Baltimore, the Orioles win, 6-1, to sweep the Twins and win the American League pennant for the second straight year. Jim Palmer goes all the way for the O's, limiting Minnesota to just seven hits. Davey Johnson homers and Brooks Robinson has three hits. The losing pitcher is Jim Kaat. The Cardinals trade infielder-outfielder Dick Allen (.279, 34 home runs, 101 RBI) to the Dodgers today for infielder Ted Sizemore (.306 in 96 games) and catcher Bob Stinson (.000 in three at-bats).

OCTOBER 9:

The Tigers give up on trouble-prone Denny McLain, who for two years was the dominant pitcher in the league. They send McLain (3-5, 4.65 ERA) along with infielder Don Wert (.218, six homers), third baseman-outfielder Elliott Maddox (.248), and pitcher Norm McRae (0-0, 2.90 ERA) to the Senators. In return, Detroit gets shortstop Ed Brinkman (.262), third baseman Aurelio Rodriguez (.249, 19 homers), and a pair of starting pitchers, Joe Coleman (8-12, 3.58 ERA) and Jim Hannan (9-11, 4.01 ERA).

OCTOBER 10:

World Series, game one. At Riverfront Stadium, a Series game is played on artificial turf for the first time. Jim Palmer gets relief help from Pete Richert to beat the Reds, 4-3. The Reds break on top, 3-0, but Boog Powell hits a two-run homer and Elrod Hendricks and Brooks Robinson add solo shots for Baltimore's runs. Gary Nolan is the game's losing pitcher.

OCTOBER 11:

World Series, game two. Boog Powell homers and Elrod Hendricks drives in two runs with a double as the Orioles overcome another 3-0 deficit to beat the Reds, 6-5. Johnny Bench and Bobby Tolan homer for Cincinnati. The winning pitcher is Tom Phoebus in relief of Mike Cuellar. Milt Wilcox gets the loss.

The Red Sox trade outfielder Tony Conigliaro (.266, 36 homers, 116 RBI), catcher Gerry Moses (.263 in 92 games), and pitcher Ray Jarvis (0-1, 3.94 ERA) to the Angels; Boston gets pitcher Ken Tatum (7-4, 2.93 ERA), outfielder Jarvis Tatum (.238 in 75 games), and infielder Doug Griffin (.127 in 18 games).

OCTOBER 13:

World Series, game three. In Baltimore, Dave McNally scatters nine hits and whacks a bases-loaded homer in the sixth inning – the first pitcher in Series history with a grand slam – in a 9-3 win. Frank Robinson and Don Buford also

LEAGUE

The Players Association and the owners' Player Relations Committee meet. Jim Bouton facetiously suggests that the reserve clause end at age 65. NL attorney Louis Carroll responds: "No, next thing you'll be asking for is a 55 limit."

> "He came thousands of miles for this and he may never get this close again."
> – *Sparky Anderson, on Series pinch-hitter Pat Corrales*

homer for Baltimore, and Brooks Robinson has a two-run double. The losing pitcher is Cincinnati's starter, Tony Cloninger.

OCTOBER 14:

World Series, game four. The Reds stay alive in Baltimore on a three-run homer by Lee May in the eighth inning. Clay Carroll gets the win, 6-5. Eddie Watt is charged with the loss. Pete Rose also homers for the Reds; Brooks Robinson hits a solo shot for Baltimore. The Reds' victory snaps the Orioles' 17-game winning streak that began with 11 in the regular season.

OCTOBER 15:

World Series, game five. Mike Cuellar pitches a complete-game six-hitter, Frank Robinson hits a two-run homer, Merv Rettenmund also homers, and the Orioles win, 9-3, for the World Championship. Jim Merritt gets the loss. Brooks Robinson hits .429 with six RBI and is named the Series' MVP. Paul Blair hits .474. Lee May bats .389 with eight RBI in a losing cause.

In the ninth inning, Reds' manager Sparky Anderson sends Pat Corrales to bat for Hal McRae, regarded as a more dangerous hitter. Anderson explains: "Why? This Series is the dream of every man in baseball. He came thousands of miles for this and he may never get this close again. I think there will be more for him, but I couldn't forget him." Corrales does not hit safely and never gets another chance to play in the Series.

POST-SEASON

NOVEMBER 3:

Curt Flood ends his retirement and accepts the offer of owner Bob Short to play for the Senators. In exchange for Flood, who hit .285 in 1969, Washington today sends three players to the Phillies. They are first baseman–outfielder Greg Goossen (.241 in 42 games), outfielder Gene Martin (.364 in nine games in 1968), and minor league pitcher Jeff Terpko.

NOVEMBER 5:

Former pitcher Charlie Root dies today at age 71 in Hollister, California. Best known for serving up the "called" home run to Babe Ruth in the 1932 World Series, Root pitched for 17 years and was 201-160 with a 3.58 ERA.

NOVEMBER 30:

The Braves reacquire relief pitcher Hoyt Wilhelm (6-5, 3.40 ERA, 13 saves) from the Cubs for minor league first baseman Hal Breeden.

DECEMBER 1:

The Boston Red Sox acquire shortstop Luis Aparicio (.313, five home runs) from the Chicago White Sox in exchange for infielder Mike Andrews (.253, 17 homers) and shortstop Luis Alvarado (.224 in 59 games).

DECEMBER 11:

Rico Carty, who was the National League's top hitter with a .366 batting average in 1970, breaks his leg in a collision with Matty Alou in a Dominican League winter-ball game. As a result, Carty will miss the entire 1971 season. He was hospitalized for 163 days with tuberculosis and missed all of 1968.

DECEMBER 15:

The Cincinnati Reds trade right-handed pitcher Jim Maloney (0-1, 11.12 ERA), a two-time 20-game winner and the author of two no-hitters, to the California Angels for lefty pitcher Greg Garrett (5-6, 2.64 ERA).

OCTOBER 15
The Orioles beat the Reds in game five of the World Series, 9-3, to clinch the world title.

NOVEMBER 3
Curt Flood ends his retirement and accepts an offer to play for the Washington Senators.

THE BEST OF 1970

NATIONAL LEAGUE

HITTERS

Batting Average:
Rico Carty, Atlanta Braves, .366

Slugging Average:
Willie McCovey, San Francisco Giants, .612

Home Runs:
Johnny Bench, Cincinnati Reds, 45

Runs Batted In:
Johnny Bench, 148

Hits:
Billy Williams, Chicago Cubs;
Pete Rose, Cincinnati Reds, 205

Stolen Bases:
Bobby Tolan, Cincinnati Reds, 57

PITCHERS

Wins:
Bob Gibson, St. Louis Cardinals;
Gaylord Perry, San Francisco Giants, 23

Strikeouts:
Tom Seaver, New York Mets, 283

Earned Run Average:
Tom Seaver, 2.81

Winning Percentage:
Bob Gibson, .767

Saves:
Wayne Granger, Cincinnati Reds, 35

Most Valuable Player:
Johnny Bench, Cincinnati Reds

Cy Young Award:
Bob Gibson, St. Louis Cardinals

Rookie of the Year:
Carl Morton, Montreal Expos

AMERICAN LEAGUE

HITTERS

Batting Average:
Alex Johnson, California Angels, .329

Slugging Average:
Carl Yastrzemski, Boston Red Sox, .592

Home Runs:
Frank Howard, Washington Senators, 44

Runs Batted In:
Frank Howard, 126

Hits:
Tony Oliva, Minnesota Twins, 204

Stolen Bases:
Bert Campaneris, Oakland Athletics, 42

PITCHERS

Wins:
Jim Perry, Minnesota Twins;
Dave McNally, Baltimore Orioles;
Mike Cuellar, Baltimore Orioles, 24

Strikeouts:
Sam McDowell, Cleveland Indians, 304

Earned Run Average:
Diego Segui, Oakland Athletics, 2.56

Winning Percentage:
Mike Cuellar, .750

Saves:
Ron Perranoski, Minnesota Twins, 34

Most Valuable Player:
John "Boog" Powell, Baltimore Orioles

Cy Young Award:
Jim Perry, Minnesota Twins

Rookie of the Year:
Thurman Munson, New York Yankees

1971

"To me, baseball means money, and that's all I care about."
– *Vida Blue*

NEWS

U.S. REDUCES TROOP STRENGTH IN VIETNAM

THOMAS E. DEWEY, LOUIS ARMSTRONG DIE

Inmates riot at prison in Attica, N.Y.

CHARLES MANSON, ACCOMPLICES CONVICTED OF MURDER OF SHARON TATE, SIX OTHERS

Walt Disney World opens in Florida

MUHAMMAD ALI'S DRAFT EVASION CONVICTION OVERTURNED BY SUPREME COURT

Moviegoers enjoy *The French Connection*, *Shaft*

All in the Family *makes its television debut*

FDA approves soft contact lenses

PRE-SEASON

JANUARY 9:

Hall of Fame outfielder Elmer Flick dies in Bedford, Ohio, two days before his 95th birthday. He led the AL in batting with .306 in 1905, hit .300 or better eight times, and had 334 career stolen bases. He was inducted into the Hall of Fame in 1963.

JANUARY 11:

Tigers' pitcher John Hiller suffers a life-threatening heart attack in his Duluth, Minnesota, home. The 27-year-old left-hander was 6-6 with a 3.03 ERA in 1970.

FEBRUARY 4:

Blacks who played in the old Negro Leagues will have a separate section in baseball's Hall of Fame, according to baseball Commissioner Bowie Kuhn.

FEBRUARY 17:

Carl Yastrzemski of the Red Sox signs a three-year, $500,000 contract, becoming the highest-paid player in ML history.

APRIL 4:

Carl Mays dies at the age of 79 in El Cajon, California. Mays pitched for 15 years, compiling a 208-126 record with a 2.92 ERA and batted .268. He is associated with baseball's most noted tragedy. In 1920, Mays, then with the Yankees, fatally injured the Indians' Ray Chapman when he hit him in the head with a pitch.

FORMER BASEBALL HALL OF FAME HISTORIAN LEE ALLEN RECALLED ELMER FLICK: "FLICK REPORTED WITH A BAT THAT HE HAD TURNED OUT FOR HIMSELF ON A LATHE AND KEPT IN A CANVAS BAG."

THE SEASON

APRIL 5:

Washington, D.C., the traditional site of major league baseball's opening day, hosts what will be its last one. A crowd of 45,061 turns out to see the Senators beat Oakland, 8-0, on a Dick Bosman six-hitter at Robert F. Kennedy Stadium. Vida Blue takes the loss. The Senators' Frank Howard and Mike Epstein drive in two runs each. Master Sergeant Daniel Pitzer, a POW in Vietnam, throws out the first ball.

APRIL 7:

Three judges of the Circuit Court of Appeals uphold Judge Irving Ben Cooper's dismissal of Curt Flood's anti-trust suit against baseball.

APRIL 10:

In the first game ever in their new Veterans Stadium, the Phillies

FEBRUARY 17
Carl Yastrzemski signs a three-year, $500,000 contract to become the ML's highest paid.

APRIL 27
The Pirates' Willie Stargell hits his 11th homer in April, setting a one-month record.

beat the Expos, 4-1. The largest crowd in Philadelphia baseball history – 55,352 – turns out for the game. Jim Bunning gets the win with a save by Joe Hoerner, and Bill Stoneman takes the loss. The Phillies' Don Money hits a home run.

APRIL 21:

Willie Stargell rocks the Braves with three homers in a 10-2 win in Pittsburgh. It is the second time this season – the first was on April 10 – and the fourth in his career that Stargell has hit three round-trippers in a single game.

APRIL 27:

At Three Rivers Stadium Willie Stargell homers against the Dodgers. It is his 11th in April, a major league record for that month. But the Dodgers go on to win the game, 7-5.

On the first pitch to him from Gaylord Perry in the third inning, Hank Aaron hits a 350-foot homer over the left-field fence, scoring Ralph Garr ahead of him. It is Aaron's 600th career home run, a level previously attained only by Babe Ruth and Willie Mays. It also is Aaron's eighth of the season, making this his best April ever. In the first inning, Aaron hit his 542nd double – the eighth-most in ML history. The visiting Giants win the game, 6-5, on Willie Mays's RBI single, his fourth hit of the game.

MAY 3:

A time-out at Shea Stadium costs the Cubs a potential win against the Mets. With the score tied, 2-2, in the top of the ninth, the Cubs have bases loaded. Third base umpire Stan Landes calls a balk on Mets' relief pitcher Frank "Tug" McGraw. But home plate umpire Mel Steiner had called time out. McGraw gets another chance and works out of the inning. Tommie Agee's pinch-hit single in the bottom of the 11th inning wins it for New York, 2-1.

MAY 6:

Today the National Broadcasting Company pays $72 million for a four-year baseball TV package. For each year from 1972 to 1976, NBC will telecast 10 Monday night games, 26 Saturday afternoon contests, the All-Star Game, the respective League Championship Series, and the World Series. All weekday World Series games will be aired at night. Each team will realize $750,000 per year via the deal. NBC beat out ABC and CBS for the contract.

MAY 11:

Indians' pitcher Steve Dunning hits a grand slam homer against the Athletics' Diego Segui. The Indians go on to win the game, 7-5. Dunning does not get credit for the victory – it goes to Phil Hennigan – but he is the last AL pitcher to hit a bases-loaded home run.

MAY 12:

Hall of Fame outfielder Henry "Heinie" Manush dies at age 69 in Sarasota, Florida. Manush played 17 years, batting .330. He was the AL batting champion in 1926 with .378 and hit .300 or better 11 times. He was inducted into the Hall of Fame in 1964.

MAY 15:

Three days after the death of Heinie Manush – whom he battled for the 1928 AL batting title – Hall of Fame outfielder Leon "Goose" Goslin dies in Bridgeton, New Jersey, at age 70. In 18 major league seasons, Goslin batted .316 with 248 homers. He hit .300 or more 11 times and led the AL in 1928 with a .379 average. He played in five World Series, hitting seven homers. Goslin was inducted into the Hall of Fame in 1968.

At Wrigley Field, Billy Williams hits his 300th career homer in a 6-4 Cubs' win over the Padres.

MAY 17:

Two days after being released by the Braves without pitching for them, Luis Tiant is signed by the Red Sox. He was 7-3 with a 3.39 ERA in 1970 with the Twins.

MAY 20:

Negro Leagues star Martin Dihigo dies three days before his 65th birthday in Cienfuegos, Cuba. An infielder, outfielder, pitcher, and manager, Dihigo batted an estimated .319 in 12 years. He hit .421 in 1926 with the Cuban Stars and .408 in 1930 playing with the Stars of Cuba.

MAY 26:

Former 20-game winner Camilo Pascual returns to the Indians after some heavy-duty traveling. Pascual appeared in 10 games for the Dodgers last

EQUIPMENT

Batting helmets are now mandatory in the major leagues.

TRIVIA

All teams have ball boys to retrieve foul shots. Charles O. Finley hires the sport's first ball girls. They are 14-year-old Sheryl Lawrence and 13-year-old Debbi Sivyer, who later becomes the entrepreneur of Mrs. Field's Cookies.

Ted Williams receives the Brotherhood Award from Howard University. In his acceptance speech, he says of his baseball career: "A chill goes up my back when I think I might have been denied this if I had been black."

CULTURE

The Boys of Summer, by Roger Kahn, is a memorable book about the Dodgers of the 1950s.

season (0-0, 2.56 ERA), then was signed by the Indians on April 5, sold to the Padres on May 22, and sent back to Cleveland today.

The Dodgers' Maury Wills' gets his 2,000th career hit in a game against the Giants in Los Angeles. The Giants score twice in the ninth to win, 6-4.

MAY 29:

Nolan Ryan of the Mets strikes out 16 San Diego Padres in nine innings; New York wins, 2-1.

JUNE 3:

The Cubs' Ken Holtzman no-hits the Reds, 1-0, at Riverfront Stadium. In his second career no-hitter, the lefty walks four and strikes out six, while his teammates play errorless ball. Holtzman also scores the game's only run on a single by Glenn Beckert in the third. He retires the last 10 batters, fanning Tommy Helms and Lee May for the final outs. Holtzman is the first pitcher in modern Cubs' history with two no-hitters.

JUNE 12:

The Giants manage only one hit against Clay Kirby of the San Diego Padres, but it is enough. After Kirby retires 21 batters in a row, Willie McCovey hits a two-run homer to give San Francisco a 2-1 victory.

JUNE 15:

Roberto Clemente is the latest to have a play designated the "greatest catch ever made." Playing in the Astrodome, the Pirates' right fielder, running all-out, hauls in a liner off the bat of Bob Watson and crashes into the wall. He holds on to the ball, preserving a 3-0 victory for Pittsburgh.

JUNE 16:

At Wrigley Field, the Cubs' Don Kessinger has six hits – five singles and a double – in six at-bats as Chicago beats the Cardinals, 7-6, in 10 innings.

JUNE 19:

It's another victory for the owners and another defeat for Curt Flood. The U.S. Supreme Court upholds federal court judge Irving Ben Cooper in his denial of an injunction and damages to Flood.

JUNE 21:

Mike Lum, Hal King, Hank Aaron, and Darrell Evans homer in the eighth inning. The Braves are the 13th NL team to have five home runs in a single inning.

JUNE 23:

The Phillies' Rick Wise enjoys a career day. He no-hits the Reds, 4-0, in Cincinnati, hits two homers, and drives in three runs. He is the first to hit two homers while pitching a no-hitter. The only base runner for the Reds is Dave Concepcion, who walks in the sixth. Wise throws only 95 pitches, fanning three; the Phillies make no errors. Ross Grimsley is the losing pitcher.

JUNE 29:

Tom Seaver fans Willie Montanez in the seventh inning of today's game against the Phillies for his 1,000th career strikeout. Jerry Grote, Cleon Jones, and Ed Kranepool homer to give New York and Seaver a 3-0 victory.

JULY 7:

Negro Leagues players will have full membership in the Hall of Fame, not a separate wing as previously announced by Commissioner Bowie Kuhn. The announcement is made today by Kuhn and Paul Kirk, president of the Hall of Fame.

JULY 8:

The Orioles' Frank Robinson hits a three-run home run against Horacio Pina of the Senators; it is his 2,500th career hit. Baltimore beats Washington, 7-3, with Mike Cuellar picking up his 11th straight win and the 13th in his last 14 decisions.

JULY 9:

There's no place to go but up for the Braves' 20-year-old rookie shortstop Leo Foster. He commits an error on the first ball ever hit to him and in his first at-bat hits into a double play. But it gets worse. In the 7th inning he hits into a triple play.

Baseball life doesn't improve all that much for Foster. He plays five years with the Braves and Mets, hitting .198 with two homers.

The Athletics beat the Angels, 1-0, in a 20-inning marathon. It is the longest shutout ever in the AL.

JULY 10:

At Three Rivers Stadium, Willie Stargell homers against the Braves in a 5-4 victory. It is Stargell's 30th of the year and his 10th against the Braves.

JUNE 3
Ken Holtzman of the Cubs no-hits the Reds, 1-0, for his second career no-hitter.

AUGUST 10
Harmon Killebrew's long ball vs. the Orioles is the 500th of the slugger's career.

JULY 11:

Tony Conigliaro of the Angels holds a 5:00 A.M. press conference to announce he is retiring. Until he was beaned in 1967, Conigliaro was one of baseball's brightest young prospects. He is hitting .222 with four homers this season.

Deron Johnson of the Phillies hits three consecutive homers today in a 11-5 victory over the Expos. Johnson homered in his last at-bat yesterday, giving him four straight in two games.

Turmoil swells around the Red Sox after Billy Conigliaro accuses Carl Yastrzemski of being responsible for the trade of his brother, Tony C. Reggie Smith refuses to play with Billy Conigliaro and owner Tom Yawkey vows action on the matter. Conigliaro later apologizes.

JULY 13:

The AL breaks its eight-game All-Star Game losing streak with a 6-4 home run derby victory at Tiger Stadium. Reggie Jackson hits the light towers on the right-field roof; Frank Robinson and Harmon Killebrew also homer for the AL. Johnny Bench, Hank Aaron, and Roberto Clemente connect for the NL. Aaron's is his first in All-Star play; Robinson becomes the first to hit homers for each league. Vida Blue gets the win; Dock Ellis is the losing pitcher. It is the AL's first win since 1962.

JULY 21:

At Wrigley Field, Ernie Banks homers against the Mets in a 11-7 victory. It is the 511th career home run for Banks, tying him with Mel Ott.

JULY 28:

Brooks Robinson, winner of 11 straight Golden Glove Awards, commits three errors in the sixth inning of today's game against the Athletics. But Frank Robinson wins the game with a three-run homer in the ninth inning.

AUGUST 4:

The Cardinals' Bob Gibson registers his 200th career victory, beating the Giants, 7-2, in St. Louis.

AUGUST 9:

Dave Bancroft, Jake Beckley, Charles "Chick" Hafey, Harry Hooper, Joe Kelley, Richard "Rube" Marquard, Leroy "Satchel" Paige, and George Weiss are inducted into the Hall of Fame. Bancroft, a slick-fielding shortstop and a switch hitter, batted .279 in 16 years and appeared in four World Series. Beckley, who died in 1918, played 20 years at first base, batted .308, and is fourth in triples with 243. He batted .300 or better 13 times, with a high of .343 in 1894. Hafey, an outfielder with an extraordinary throwing arm, was the NL's top hitter in 1931 with a .349 average with St. Louis. He hit .300 nine times and has a career average of .317. Hooper, a strong-armed outfielder, played 18 years, batting .281, and never led the league in anything. His top average was .328 in 1924. He appeared in four World Series. Kelley, who died in 1943, was an outfielder who hit .317 in 17 years. He had 194 triples and 443 stolen bases – including 87 in 1896. Marquard pitched 18 years, compiling a 201-177 record with a 3.08 ERA with 1,593 strikeouts. He was a 20-game winner three times and appeared in five World Series. Satchel Paige, regarded by many as the greatest pitcher of all time, played only briefly in the majors. In six years, he was 28-31 with a 3.29 ERA and pitched in one World Series. Estimates of his career statistics include: 250 teams, 2,500 games, 2,000 wins, 100 no-hitters. Weiss was associated with the Yankees from 1932 to 1960. During those 29 years, the team won 19 pennants and 15 World Series.

AUGUST 10:

Today in Minnesota, Harmon Killebrew connects against Mike Cuellar of the Orioles in the first inning for his 500th career homer. Later in the game, the Twins' slugger hits his 501st, but Baltimore wins, 4-3, in 10 innings.

AUGUST 14:

The Cardinals' Bob Gibson no-hits the Pirates, 11-0, in Pittsburgh. Gibson strikes out 10 and walks three; the Cardinals make no errors. Gibson also drives in three of the St. Louis runs. Center fielder Jose Cruz runs down Milt May's 400-foot drive in the seventh inning and third baseman Joe Torre makes an outstanding play to preserve Gibson's first-ever no-hitter. Bob Johnson is the losing pitcher.

HISTORY

After 15 games with the Senators, hitting .200, Curt Flood leaves the team and flies to Spain. He sends a 22-word telegram to owner Bob Short: "I tried. A year and a half is too much. Very serious problems mounting every day. Thanks for your confidence and understanding." Flood, who spent 1970 in Denmark out of baseball, reportedly is having financial problems.

"I am the proudest man on the face of the earth today."
– *Satchel Paige*

ERNIE BANKS IS WONDERFULLY SUMMED UP IN *BASEBALL: AN ILLUSTRATED HISTORY* BY GEOFFREY WARD AND KEN BURNS: "ERNIE BANKS, SHORTSTOP (AND LATER FIRST BASEMAN) FOR THE CHICAGO CUBS, WOULD HIT 47 HOME RUNS ONE SEASON, MORE THAN ANY OTHER SHORTSTOP HAS EVER HIT, AND SLAMMED OVER 20 HOME RUNS IN 13 SEASONS. HE WON ANOTHER KIND OF IMMORTALITY FOR THE INFECTIOUS ENTHUSIASM HE BROUGHT TO DAILY PLAY EVEN WHEN, AS WAS USUALLY THE CASE WITH THE CUBS DURING HIS TIME, VICTORY SEEMED WILDLY IMPLAUSIBLE. IT WAS ERNIE BANKS WHO SAID, 'WHAT A GREAT DAY FOR BASEBALL, LET'S PLAY TWO.'"

AUGUST 17:

Two durable stars reach hitting landmarks on the same day. The Cubs' Billy Williams collects his 2,000th career hit in a 5-4 loss to the Braves. And, in Pittsburgh, the Pirates' Bill Mazeroski gets his 2,000th hit in a 6-5 loss to the Astros.

AUGUST 24:

Ernie Banks hits his 512th – and final – career home run. Banks connects in the first inning against Jim McGlothlin of the Reds in Wrigley Field. The Cubs win, 5-4.

AUGUST 28:

Phillies' pitcher Rick Wise hits a homer in the fifth and a grand slam in the seventh in a 7-3 win over the Giants – tying an ML record for pitchers with two homers in a game twice in a year.

AUGUST 29:

Hank Aaron drives in his 100th run of the season and establishes an NL record with 100 or more RBI for 11 seasons. The Braves beat the Cubs, 5-4.

AUGUST 30:

According to owner Tom Yawkey, the entire Red Sox roster is available for trades.

SEPTEMBER 1:

Twenty-four years after Dodger Jackie Robinson's major league debut, the Pirates become the first major league team to field an all-black lineup. Starting for Pittsburgh today against the Expos in Montreal's Parc Jarry are Al Oliver (1B), Rennie Stennet (2B), Jackie Hernandez (SS), Dave Cash (3B), Willie Stargell (LF), Gene Clines (CF), Roberto Clemente (RF), Manny Sanguillen (C), and Dock Ellis (P). The Pirates win, 8-4.

SEPTEMBER 2:

In the box score it's a blast, although in reality Cesar Cedeno's inside-the-park grand slam travels only 200 feet on the fly. The Dodgers' right fielder, Bill Buckner, and second baseman Jim Lefebvre collide chasing Cedeno's fly ball and the Astros' outfielder circles the bases. Houston beats Los Angeles, 9-3.

SEPTEMBER 3:

Leo Durocher is not the first manager to win a vote of confidence from his club's owner, but he may be the only one who gets it in a newspaper ad. Owner Philip K. Wrigley buys space to criticize the anti-Leo faction on the Cubs; it reads in part: "The Dump Durocher Clique might as well give up... P.S. If only we could find more team players like Ernie Banks."

SEPTEMBER 5:

The Astros' six-foot, eight-inch right-hander J.R. Richard makes his major league debut, striking out 15 Giants, tying a record set by Karl Spooner in his first game in 1954. The Astros win, 5-3.

SEPTEMBER 8:

Amos Otis of the Kansas City Royals bedevils the Brewers and catcher Darrell Porter. Otis steals five bases and scores on a wild throw by Porter to give Kansas City a 4-3 victory.

SEPTEMBER 13:

In the opener of a doubleheader against the Detroit Tigers in Baltimore today, the Orioles' Frank Robinson hits his 499th career home run in a 9-1 victory. Dave McNally rings up his 13th straight win. In the nightcap, Robinson connects for a three-run home run in the ninth inning against Fred Scherman for his 500th round-tripper. But the Tigers win,

SEPTEMBER 5
J.R. Richard makes his ML debut with the Astros, striking out 15 Giants in a 5-3 win.

SEPTEMBER 26
Ernie Banks plays his 2,528th – and final – game, retiring with 512 career home runs.

10-5. The home runs also are Robinson's 24th and 25th of this season.

SEPTEMBER 14:

In Cincinnati, Hank Aaron hits a homer and drives in five runs. Aaron now has a career total of 1,953 RBI, surpassing Stan Musial as the all-time NL leader. The Braves win the game, 5-2.

SEPTEMBER 20:

In Boston, the AL holds a 13-hour meeting and, by a 10-2 vote, approves the Washington Senators' move to the Dallas–Fort Worth area of Texas. Baltimore and Chicago cast the dissenting votes. The AL attaches conditions to the move: the stadium at Arlington must be enlarged from 22,000 to 25,000 seats in 1972 and to 45,000 seats in 1973. In addition, compensation must be paid to the Texas League franchise presently playing in the stadium. The vote effectively ends 71 years of baseball in the nation's capital. Bowie Kuhn calls it "a sad day for Washington."

SEPTEMBER 21:

With a 5-0 victory over the Yankees today, the Orioles' pitcher Dave McNally wins 20 games for the fourth consecutive season.

At Wrigley Field, Ron Santo of the Cubs hits his 300th career home run – off Tom Seaver – and Burt Hooten shuts out the Mets, 3-0.

SEPTEMBER 24:

The Orioles sweep a doubleheader from the Indians and two more Baltimore pitchers win their 20th games of the season. In the opening game, Mike Cuellar beats Cleveland, 9-3. In the nightcap, Pat Dobson pitches a 7-0 shutout.

SEPTEMBER 26:

Jim Palmer three-hits the Indians, 5-0, and hits an RBI double for his 20th win of the season. The Orioles now have four 20-game winners, equaling the 1920 White Sox quartet of Urban "Red" Faber, Claude "Lefty" Williams, Dickie Kerr, and Ed Cicotte.

Ernie Banks, one of the most popular players of all time, says good-bye to Chicago and to baseball. In his 2,528th game, he singles in the first inning against the Phillies' Ken Reynolds for his 2,583rd hit. He finishes his 19-year career with a batting average of .274 and 512 home runs. The Phillies win the game, 5-1.

At Shea Stadium, Tom Seaver pitches his third career one-hitter, beating the Pirates, 3-1. Vic Davalillo's 7th inning single is Pittsburgh's only safety.

SEPTEMBER 29:

When Montreal's Ron Hunt is plunked by Milt Pappas of the Cubs, it is the 50th time this season he has been hit by a pitch – a major league record. The Expos win the game, 6-5.

SEPTEMBER 30:

In Washington, D.C., the second incarnation of the Senators plays its final game prior to the shift of the franchise to Texas. With a 7-5 lead against the Yankees in the ninth inning and two out, the Senators find a new way to lose. Many of the 14,460 fans in attendance run out of the stands and rip up the field, digging for souvenirs. Chief umpire Jim Honochick declares a forfeit and awards the Yankees a 9-0 win. The victory gives the Yankees an 82-80 record, enabling them to top .500. The Senators end their major league history with a 63-96 season.

At Shea Stadium, the Mets' Tom Seaver fans Luis Melendez of the Cardinals in the seventh inning. It is Seaver's 284th strikeout of the season, breaking his own NL record for right-handed pitchers. The Mets win the game, 6-1.

REGULAR SEASON WRAP-UP:

The Orioles under Earl Weaver win their third straight AL pennant, finishing the regular season at 101-57. It also is their third straight year with 100 or more wins. Baltimore has an overpowering pitching staff with four 20-game winners – Dave McNally (21-5), Pat Dobson (20-8), Mike Cuellar (20-9), and Jim Palmer (20-9). Merv Rettenmund at .318 has the team's top average. Frank Robinson bats .272 with 28 homers and 99 RBI. Boog Powell hits 22 homers; Brooks Robinson, 20; and Don Buford, 19.

Danny Murtaugh's Pirates have a regular season record of 97-65 and win their second NL pennant in a row. Roberto Clemente bats .341 with 13 homers and 86 RBI. Willie Stargell tops the NL with 48 home runs, bats .295, and drives in 125 runs.

The Athletics' Vida Blue strikes out 301 and is the first to fan 300 and not lead his

HISTORY

The Braves' Hank Aaron drives in 118 runs; it is the 11th time he has had 100 or more RBI – an NL record.

HISTORY

The Senators produced stars like Walter Johnson, won the World Series in 1924 and two other AL pennants – in 1925 and 1933. But they were identified mainly with failure. Sportswriter Charles Dryden said: "Washington – first in war, first in peace, last in the American League."

Jim Palmer is a 20-game winner for the Orioles.

league; the honor goes to the Tigers' Mickey Lolich with 308. Denny McLain, who in 1968 and 1969 won 55 games, is now the AL's big loser with 22 for the Senators.

OCTOBER 1:

Cleveland shipbuilder George Steinbrenner and former Indians third baseman Al Rosen make a bid to buy the Indians. Currently under consideration is the scheduling of 30 games in New Orleans, but Steinbrenner says he will keep the ballclub in Cleveland.

OCTOBER 2:

NLCS, game one. In San Francisco, the Giants' Gaylord Perry goes all the way, allowing the Pirates nine hits in a 5-4 win. Willie McCovey and Tito Fuentes provide the offense with two-run homers in the fifth inning. Steve Blass gets the loss.

OCTOBER 3:

ALCS, game one. In Baltimore, the Orioles erupt for four runs in the bottom of the seventh inning against starter Vida Blue and win the game, 5-3. Paul Blair's two-run double is the big blow. Dave McNally gets the win with a save by Eddie Watt.

NLCS, game two. Bob Robertson homers three times and Ty Clines goes deep once as the Pirates bomb the Giants, 9-4. Robertson also doubles, driving in 5 runs for the game. Willie Mays homers for San Francisco. Dock Ellis is the winning pitcher; John Cumberland is charged with the loss.

OCTOBER 4:

ALCS, game two. It's power and pitching for Baltimore in a 5-1 victory today over the Oakland Athletics. Jim "Catfish" Hunter allows only seven hits, but four of them are homers: two by Boog Powell (a two-run shot and a solo shot) and one each by Elrod Hendricks and Brooks Robinson. Mike Cuellar goes the distance and scatters six hits for the win.

OCTOBER 5:

NLCS, game three. At Three Rivers Stadium today, Bob Robertson homers again and Richie Hebner's eighth inning round-tripper against starter Juan Marichal gives Pittsburgh a 2-1 win. Bob Johnson gets the win with a save by Dave Giusti. Marichal, who allows only four hits, is the loser.

ALCS, game three. Jim Palmer goes the distance, despite yielding two homers to Reggie Jackson and one to Sal Bando, to beat the Athletics, 5-3, and capture the AL pennant for the Orioles. Brooks Robinson's bases-loaded single is the key hit for Baltimore. The losing pitcher is Diego Segui.

OCTOBER 6:

NLCS, game four. The Pirates beat the Giants, 9-5 in Pittsburgh to win the NL pennant. Richie Hebner and Al Oliver hit three-run homers and Bruce Kison pitches four and two-thirds scoreless innings for the win. Willie McCovey has a three-run homer and Chris Speier a solo shot for the Giants.

The 1964 Cy Young Award winner, Dean Chance (4-6, 3.50 ERA), is unconditionally released by the Tigers, ending his 11-year career. A two-time 20-game winner, the 30-year-old Chance has a lifetime record of 128-115 with a 2.92 ERA.

OCTOBER 9:

World Series, game one. Dave McNally three-hits the Pirates, 5-3, in Baltimore, with home run support from Frank Robinson, Merv Rettenmund – a three-run blast – and Don Buford. The losing pitcher is Dock Ellis.

OCTOBER 11:

World Series, game two. Jim Palmer makes it two in a row, with an eight-hit, 11-3 Orioles' win. The Pirates' runs come in the eighth on a homer by Richie Hebner. The Orioles hit 14 singles, three by Brooks Robinson, who also walks twice and ties a Series record, reaching base five straight times.

The Red Sox and Brewers complete a 10-player trade. Going to Milwaukee are pitchers Jim Lonborg (10-7, 4.13 ERA) and Ken Brett (0-3, 5.34 ERA), outfielders Billy Conigliaro (.262, 11 homers) and Joe Lahoud (.215, 14 homers), first baseman George "Boomer" Scott (.263, 24 homers), and catcher-infielder Don Pavletich (.259 in 14 games). Headed for Boston are pitchers Marty Pattin (14-14, 3.12 ERA) and Lew Krausse (8-12, 2.95 ERA), outfielder Tommy Harper (.258), and minor league outfielder Pat Skrable.

OCTOBER 12:

World Series, game three. In Pittsburgh for the first time, Steve Blass three-hits

22

Dick Allen says: " I once loved this game. But after being traded four times, I realized that it's nothing but a business. I treat my horses better than the owners treat us. It's a shame they've destroyed my love for the game."

HISTORY

Ron Santo and Leo Durocher are at the center of the commotion. During batting practice, Durocher tells the slumping Santo, "I didn't want to bring this up, but the only reason the Cubs are giving you a Ron Santo Day is that you asked Holland [the team's general manager] for one because Banks and Williams had one." Santo tries to throttle the manager, but is restrained by his teammates.

the Orioles, striking out eight, and Bob Robertson hits a three-run homer in the seventh for a 5-1 victory. Frank Robinson hits a solo home run for Baltimore, and Mike Cuellar gets the loss.

OCTOBER 13:

World Series, game four. In the first World Series night game, Roberto Clemente gets three hits and leads the Pirates to a 4-3 win over the Orioles at Three Rivers Stadium before a crowd of 51,378. Milt May's fifth inning pinch-hit single drives in the winning run. Bruce Kison gets the win in relief; Eddie Watt is the losing pitcher.

OCTOBER 14:

World Series, game five. Nelson Briles pitches brilliantly, allowing the Orioles only two hits in a complete game, and wins, 4-0. He also drives in a run and Bob Robertson cracks another home run. Roberto Clemente extends his Series hitting streak to 12 games. The losing pitcher is Dave McNally.

OCTOBER 16:

World Series, game six. Today, back in Baltimore, the Orioles edge the Pirates, 3-2, in 10 innings. Brooks Robinson scores Frank Robinson with a sacrifice fly for the win. Roberto Clemente and Don Buford hit homers. Dave McNally ends the game with the bases loaded and picks up the win. Bob L. Miller is charged with the loss.

OCTOBER 17:

World Series, game seven. Steve Blass limits the Orioles to four hits and Roberto Clemente homers to give the Pirates a 2-1 win and the World Championship. Willie Stargell scores the winning run on a Jose Pagan double in the eighth. Mike Cuellar gets the loss. Clemente, the Series' Most Valuable Player, hits .414 with two homers. Manny Sanguillen bats .379. Despite a .240 average, Bob Robertson has two homers and five RBI. Steve Blass wins two games, allowing two earned runs in 18 innings. Brooks Robinson bats .318 for the Orioles.

POST-SEASON

OCTOBER 28:

Indians' owner Vernon Stouffer and general manager Gabe Paul head to New Orleans to investigate the possibility of playing ball games in the Crescent City in 1972.

NOVEMBER 23:

Bill Virdon has a hard act to follow. He is named Pirates' manager, replacing Danny Murtaugh, who retired after winning the 1971 World Series.

Owner Robert E. Short announces today that the former Washington Senators will now be known as the Texas Rangers.

NOVEMBER 29:

The Athletics obtain pitcher Ken Holtzman (9-15, 4.48 ERA) from the Cubs for outfielder Rick Monday (.245, 18 home runs).

The Reds trade first baseman Lee May (.278, 39 homers, 98 RBI) to the Astros, along with infielder Tommy Helms (.258, three homers) and outfielder-infielder Jimmy Stewart (.232 in 80 games). In return, Cincinnati gets second baseman Joe Morgan (.256, 13 homers), outfielder Cesar Geronimo (.220 in 94 games), infielder Denis Menke (.246), pitcher Jack Billingham (10-16, 3.39 ERA), and minor league outfielder Ed Armbrister.

The Giants trade pitcher Gaylord Perry (16-12, 2.76 ERA) and shortstop Frank Duffy (.182, 34 games) to the Indians for pitcher Sam McDowell (13-17, 3.39 ERA, 192 strikeouts).

DECEMBER 2:

The Orioles trade former AL and NL Most Valuable Player outfielder Frank Robinson (.281, 28 homers, 99 RBI) to the Dodgers along with pitcher Pete Richert (3-5, 3.50 ERA). In return, Baltimore gets pitchers Doyle Alexander (6-6, 3.82 ERA) and Bob O'Brien (2-2, 3.00 ERA), minor league catcher Sergio Robles, and minor league outfielder Royle Stillman.

The Dodgers send first baseman Dick Allen (.295, 23 homers, 90 RBI) to the White Sox for pitcher Tommy John (13-16, 3.62 ERA) and infielder Steve Huntz (.209 in 35 games). Chicago also acquires pitcher Stan Bahnsen (14-12, 3.35 ERA) from the Yankees for infielder Rich McKinney (.271, eight homers).

DECEMBER 10:

The Mets trade Nolan Ryan (10-14, 3.97 ERA, 137 strikeouts) and Don Rose (0-0, 0.00 ERA), outfielder Leroy Stanton, and catcher Francisco Estrada to the Angels for infielder Jim Fregosi (.233).

OCTOBER 17
The Pirates take game seven, 2-1, and win the World Series vs. the Baltimore Orioles.

DECEMBER 10
The Mets trade pitcher Nolan Ryan and two others to the Angels for infielder Jim Fregosi.

THE BEST OF 1971

National League

HITTERS

Batting Average:
Joe Torre, St. Louis Cardinals, .363

Slugging Average:
Hank Aaron, Atlanta Braves, .669

Home Runs:
Willie Stargell, Pittsburgh Pirates, 48

Runs Batted In:
Joe Torre, 137

Hits:
Joe Torre, 230

Stolen Bases:
Lou Brock, St. Louis Cardinals, 64

PITCHERS

Wins:
Ferguson Jenkins, Chicago Cubs, 24

Strikeouts:
Tom Seaver, New York Mets, 289

Earned Run Average:
Tom Seaver, 1.76

Winning Percentage:
Don Gullet, Cincinnati Reds, .727

Saves:
Dave Giusti, Pittsburgh Pirates, 30

Most Valuable Player:
Joe Torre, St. Louis Cardinals

Cy Young Award:
Ferguson Jenkins, Chicago Cubs

Rookie of the Year:
Earl Williams, Atlanta Braves

American League

HITTERS

Batting Average:
Tony Oliva, Minnesota Twins, .337

Slugging Average:
Tony Oliva, .546

Home Runs:
Bill Melton, Chicago White Sox, 33

Runs Batted In:
Harmon Killebrew, Minnesota Twins, 119

Hits:
Cesar Tovar, Minnesota Twins, 204

Stolen Bases:
Amos Otis, Kansas City Royals, 52

PITCHERS

Wins:
Mickey Lolich, Detroit Tigers, 25

Strikeouts:
Mickey Lolich, 308

Earned Run Average:
Vida Blue, Oakland Athletics, 1.82

Winning Percentage:
Dave McNally, Baltimore Orioles, .808

Saves:
Ken Sanders, Milwaukee Brewers, 31

Most Valuable Player:
Vida Blue, Oakland Athletics

Cy Young Award:
Vida Blue, Oakland Athletics

Rookie of the Year:
Chris Chambliss, Cleveland Indians

1972

"Lefty" – Steve Carlton – is right on all season.

NEWS

NIXON DEFEATS McGOVERN FOR PRESIDENCY

U.S. GROUND TROOPS LEAVE VIETNAM

Nixon visits China, Soviet Union

SALT treaty signed, limiting nuclear weapons development

GEORGE WALLACE SHOT

FIVE ARRESTED IN WATERGATE BURGLARY

SUPREME COURT FINDS DEATH PENALTY UNCONSTITUTIONAL

HURRICANE AGNES KILLS 127 ON EAST COAST

BOMBING OF NORTH VIETNAM RESUMES

EARTHQUAKE DEVASTATES NICARAGUA

***Life* magazine folds**

PRE-SEASON

JANUARY 27:

Yankees' president Lee MacPhail says the team is likely to play its home games in Shea Stadium while Yankee Stadium is being renovated.

FEBRUARY 16:

Tom Seaver signs a new Mets contract, reportedly for the sum of $120,000. At age 27, Seaver is the youngest player to reach a six-figure annual salary. Seaver was 20-10 last season with a 1.76 ERA and 289 strikeouts.

FEBRUARY 28:

The Phillies acquire pitcher Steve Carlton (20-9, 3.56 ERA, 172 strikeouts) from the Cardinals for pitcher Rick Wise (17-14, 2.88 ERA, 155 strikeouts).

FEBRUARY 29:

Hank Aaron signs a new three-year, $600,000 contract with the Braves. He becomes the first ML player to earn $200,000 a season.

MARCH 4:

The sad odyssey of pitcher Denny McLain (10-22, 4.27 ERA) continues. Texas sends baseball's last 30-game winner to Oakland for pitcher Jim Panther (0-1, 10.50 ERA) and minor league pitcher Don Stanhouse.

MARCH 11:

Hall of Fame outfielder Zack Wheat dies in Sedalia, Missouri, at age 83. Inducted into the Hall of Fame alone in 1959, Wheat played 19 years – 18 with Brooklyn – and batted .317. He led the NL in 1918 with a .335 average and batted .300 or more 14 times. He played in a pair of World Series for Brooklyn.

MARCH 16:

For the second time in five days, a Hall of Famer dies. Harold "Pie" Traynor passes away at age 72 in Pittsburgh, where he played 17 years and managed for six with the Pirates. Primarily a third baseman, Traynor compiled a .320 lifetime average. He hit .300 10 times with a high of .366 in 1930. Traynor appeared in two World Series.

The Athletics' Vida Blue (24-8, 1.82 ERA, 301 strikeouts) says no to the contract offered by owner Charles O. Finley. The 22-year-old left-hander says he will work for a company that makes bathroom fixtures instead of playing baseball.

MARCH 22:

The American League approves the sale of the Cleveland Indians by Vernon Stouffer for $9.7 million to a group headed by Nick Mileti. On March 8, Mileti's previous bid had been rejected and he returns with more solid financing. Included in the new ownership group are Bing and Dudley Blossom, Howard Metzenbaum, and Richard Miller. Mileti also owns the pro basketball Cleveland Cavaliers and the Cleveland Barons hockey team.

Today the New York Yankees acquire relief pitcher Albert "Sparky" Lyle (6-4, 2.77 ERA, 16 saves) from the Red Sox for outfielder-infielder Danny Cater (.276, four homers).

APRIL 1:

Today was the day baseball expected to hear that the cities of Cleveland and New Orleans would "share" baseball's Indians. Instead, Nick Mileti, who purchased the ballclub on March 22, becomes the team's president – and quickly drops the two-city plan developed last July.

32

Marvin Miller, executive director of the Players Association on the strike: "Money is not the issue. The real issue is the owners' attempt to punish the players for having the audacity not to settle and for having the audacity not to crawl."

TRIVIA

Moe Berg, who held degrees from New York University and Princeton, may well be the only .243 hitter to have two full-length biographies written about him. *Moe Berg: Athlete, Scholar, Spy,* by Louis Kaufman, Barbara Fitzgerald, and Tom Sewell, is published in 1974. Nicholas Dawidoff's *The Catcher Was a Spy: The Mysterious Life of Moe Berg* is issued in 1995.

APRIL 2:

After golfing with coaches Joe Pignatano, Albert "Rube" Walker, and Eddie Yost, Mets' manager Gil Hodges suffers his second heart attack and dies in West Palm Beach, Florida. Hodges would have been 48 in two days. He led the 1969 Mets to the World Championship. Previously he served nine years as the Senators' manager. Hodges spent 18 years as a player with the Dodgers and Mets and was a particular favorite of New York fans. He compiled a lifetime average of .273 with 370 home runs and 1,274 RBI and played in seven World Series.

APRIL 5:

The Montreal Expos send outfielder Rusty Staub (.311, 19 home runs, 97 RBIs), often known as "Le Grande Orange" in Montreal for his red hair, to the New York Mets. In return, the Expos get outfielder Ken Singleton (.245, 13 homers), first baseman-outfielder Mike Jorgensen (.220, five homers in 45 games), and infielder Tim "Crazy Horse" Foli (.226 in 97 games). Staub will end up having two stints in New York.

APRIL 6:

Baseball experiences its first general strike. The major issue is an increase in the players' pension fund.

Following the funeral of Gil Hodges, the Mets announce they have signed Yogi Berra to a two-year contract as manager.

APRIL 11:

The owners and the players agree on a $500,000 increase in pension fund payments and it appears the strike is over. But a new issue surfaces to keep it going – paying players because of the games missed during the work stoppage.

APRIL 13:

Commissioner Bowie Kuhn and Marvin Miller of the Players Association announce the end of the strike. The 86 games missed will not be made up and some teams will play only 153 games, eliminating the issue of pay for missed contests. The settlement comes on the heels of two days of owner meetings in Chicago. Play resumes with 12 games tomorrow.

APRIL 15:

Reggie Jackson of the Athletics becomes the first major leaguer with a mustache since Wally Schang of the Athletics in 1914. The Dodgers' Stanley "Frenchy" Bordagaray showed up at spring training in 1936 with a mustache but was asked to shave it off.

THE SEASON

APRIL 16:

On a frigid day at Wrigley Field, the Cubs' Burt Hooten no-hits the Phillies, 4-0. Hooten strikes out seven and walks seven; the Cubs play errorless ball. The losing pitcher is Dick Selma.

APRIL 21:

In the first game in Arlington Stadium in Texas, the Rangers beat the visiting Angels, 7-6. Arlington Mayor Tom Vandergriff throws out the first ball and AL president Joe Cronin is among the crowd of 20,105. In the first inning, Frank Howard homers for Texas. The winning pitcher is Dick Bosman, with a save by Paul Lindblad.

MAY 11:

The Giants' legend Willie Mays is coming back to New York. The Mets acquire the 41-year-old Mays (.184 in 19 games) from the Giants for pitcher Charlie Williams (5-6, 4.80 ERA in 1971) and, reportedly, $50,000.

In Willie's Time, Charles Einstein says he asked the former Giants' owner Horace Stoneham in 1978 how much money the Giants received for Mays. Einstein writes: "I'm not wholly sure why, but his answer stunned me. He said, 'There was no money.' 'None?' 'None. Do you think I was going to give him up for money?'"

Tom Seaver beats the Dodgers, 2-1, at Shea Stadium; it is his 100th career victory. Los Angeles wins the nightcap, 6-4.

MAY 12:

In Minnesota, the Brewers and Twins battle 21 innings to a 3-3 standoff when the game is suspended because of a 1 A.M. curfew. A two-run single in the seventh by the Brewers' Tommie Reynolds ties the game at 3 apiece.

MAY 13:

The Brewers and Twins resume the suspended game. Mike Ferraro wins it with an RBI single in the top of the 22nd inning; the game takes five hours and 47 minutes to complete. Jim Colborn

APRIL 6
Baseball experiences its first general strike by members of the Players Association.

MAY 26
Hammerin' Hank Aaron connects vs. the Giants for his 646th career homer and 3,300th hit.

gets the win. The two teams then go 15 innings in the regularly scheduled contest with the Twins winning, 5-4. Ferraro, the hero of the suspended game, homers in the top of the 15th to give Milwaukee the lead. But Eric Soderholm hits a two-out homer off Jim Slaton to win the game. The teams set an AL record with 37 innings in consecutive games and play a total of nine hours and 23 minutes to achieve a split.

MAY 14:

The clock is turned back – if only for a moment. In his New York Mets' debut before 35,505 at Shea Stadium, Willie Mays connects for a home run against his former Giants' teammate Don Carrithers to give New York a 5-4 win. It is the 646th career home run for Mays, who bats leadoff and walks in his first turn.

MAY 16:

Today at Veterans Stadium, the Philadelphia Phillies' only run in an 8-1 loss to the Cubs is a memorable one. In the fourth inning, Greg Luzinski launches a monstrous, 500-foot home run into the centerfield stands.

JACK KAVANAUGH, AUTHOR OF *WALTER JOHNSON, A LIFE*, WRITES: "AN UNDUE INFLUENCE LATER ON THE SELECTIONS OF THE VETERANS COMMITTEE BY THE PERSUASIVE FRANK FRISCH MIGHT HAVE HAD MORE TO DO WITH SO MANY 1924 GIANTS ENDING UP IN COOPERSTOWN THAN THEIR RECORDS SUPPORTED, BUT FRISCH SWUNG THE PORTAL FOR HIS INFIELD MATES AND ROSS YOUNG'S, TOO."

MAY 21:

In Philadelphia, the "old Mays magic" is back. For the second time in a week, the Mets' Willie Mays hits a game-winning homer in a 4-3 victory over the Phillies. Tom Seaver is the winning pitcher. It is the 11th straight victory for the Mets, who are in first place in the NL East by six games.

MAY 26:

In Atlanta, Hank Aaron hits his 646th career home run – it also is his 3,300th hit – as the Braves top the Giants, 9-4.

MAY 29:

One of the most mysterious and intriguing personalities in baseball history, Morris "Moe" Berg, dies in Belleville, New Jersey, at age 70. Berg, an attorney, linguist, mathematician, scholar, and spy, played in only 662 games in his 15-year career, batting .243 with six homers. His best year was 1929, when he hit .288 in 106 games. Berg spied on the Japanese military during a major league tour in the 1930s and also was involved in atomic espionage for the U.S. It was said: "He can speak 12 languages, but can't hit in any of them."

LEAGUE

In May, eight games into the season, Vida Blue gives up bathroom fixtures and picks up a baseball. He accepts Charles O. Finley's offer, reportedly $63,000.

William "Judy" Johnson on one of his Pittsburgh Crawfords teammates: "If Josh Gibson had been in the big leagues in his prime, Babe Ruth and Hank Aaron would still be chasing him for the home run record."

JUNE 4:

The Los Angeles Dodgers retire three uniform numbers today: number 32, worn by Sandy Koufax; number 39, worn by Roy Campanella; and number 42, worn by Jackie Robinson. Following ceremonies at Dodger Stadium, the Cardinals and Bob Gibson put a damper on the day by blanking Los Angeles by a score of 4-0.

JUNE 9:

Delphia "Del" Bissonette, a former major league first baseman and manager, shoots himself to death at age 72 in Augusta, Maine. Bissonette played five years with the Dodgers, batting .305, with a high of .336 in 1930. As a rookie in 1928, he hit 25 homers. Bissonette managed the 1945 Milwaukee Braves to a sixth-place finish.

JUNE 10:

In Philadelphia, Hank Aaron hits his 14th career grand slam – and his 649th home run – against Wayne Twitchell in a 15-3 Braves' victory. Aaron now trails only Babe Ruth on the all-time home run list.

JUNE 18:

Athletics' owner Charles O. Finley declares today Mustache Day. Earlier, he had offered $300 to each of his players who grew a mustache by Father's Day.

JUNE 19:

The U.S. Supreme Court votes 5-3 against Curt Flood in his suit against baseball. Baseball's 1922 anti-trust exemption will continue, but Justice Harry A. Blackmun, voting with the majority, calls it an "aberration" and an "anomaly."

The A's Gene Tenace goes deep four times in the World Series.

JUNE 18
Today, according to A's quirky owner Charlie Finley, is Mustache Day.

JUNE 19
The U.S. Supreme Court votes 5-3 against Curt Flood's suit against baseball.

However, he asserts it can be changed only by Congress or collective bargaining. William O. Douglas, Thurgood Marshall, and William F. Brennan dissent. The majority, in addition to Blackmun, is composed of Chief Justice Warren E. Burger, Byron R. White, Potter Stewart, and William F. Rehnquist. Lewis F. Powell does not participate in the opinion. Baseball is the only sport with such an exemption.

JUNE 21:

At Fenway Park, Rico Petrocelli is involved in a statistical oddity; he is credited with six RBI on one hit. He hits a grand slam homer and drives in two additional runs with sacrifice flies. The Red Sox beat the Rangers, 10-9.

JUNE 24:

After three years of lawsuits culminating in a January court ruling that waived the height minimum for umpires, Bernice Gera makes her debut in a New York–Penn League game. When she steps on the field for the day's contest between the Auburn Phillies and the Geneva Rangers, she becomes the first female umpire in professional baseball. But the five-foot, two-inch, Queens, New York, resident is quickly embroiled in a dispute. In the fourth inning she is the subject of a tirade from Auburn manager Nolan Campbell over a call, and she quits after the game.

BUCK LEONARD RECALLS: "I WAS IN COOPERSTOWN THE DAY SATCHEL PAIGE WAS INDUCTED, AND I STAYED AWAKE ALMOST ALL THAT NIGHT THINKING ABOUT IT... I ALWAYS WANTED TO GO UP THERE TO COOPERSTOWN. YOU FELT LIKE YOU HAD A REASON, BECAUSE IT'S THE HOME OF BASEBALL, BUT YOU DIDN'T HAVE A SPECIAL REASON. WE NEVER THOUGHT WE'D GET IN THE HALL OF FAME. WE THOUGHT THE WAY WE WERE PLAYING WAS THE WAY IT WAS GOING TO CONTINUE. I NEVER HAD ANY DREAM IT WOULD COME. BUT THAT NIGHT I FELT LIKE I WAS PART OF IT AT LAST."

JUNE 29:

Three months after acquiring pitcher Denny McLain (1-2 in five games) in a trade, the Athletics trade him to the Atlanta Braves for outfielder Orlando Cepeda (.298 in 28 games).

JULY 2:

Willie McCovey of the Giants hits his 14th career grand slam. He now shares the NL record with Gil Hodges and Hank Aaron. The Giants down the Dodgers, 9-3.

JULY 3:

At the Astrodome, Hank Aaron hits a three-run homer in a 13-9 Braves victory. His three RBI raise his career total to 2,000, the most by any NL player.

JULY 4:

At Shea Stadium, Leron Lee of the Padres singles with one out in the ninth, breaking up Tom Seaver's no-hitter. It is

CULTURE

Baseball is the subject in *The Summer Game*, by Roger Angell, and *Runner Mack*, a novel by Barry Beckham.

July 8, 1972

Lefty Gomez was known for his biting wit, as well as his blazing fastball. He once said: "The secret of my success was clean living and a fast outfield." After he went 12-15 in 1935, Yankees' owner Colonel Jacob Ruppert wanted to cut his salary from $20,000 to $7,500. Gomez told him: "You keep the salary, I'll take the cut."

TRIVIA

Sandy Koufax, whose baseball experience at Brooklyn's Lafayette High School was limited, was a questionable prospect for the major leagues because of his wild pitching. After trying out for the Giants, he was told by catcher Bobby Hofman: "Make sure you get a good college education, kid, 'cause you won't make it in the majors." He also failed to get an offer from the Pirates and reportedly was signed by the Dodgers – for a $14,000 bonus – only after a journalist threatened to tell the Yankees about him.

the only hit off Seaver in a 2-0 victory. The Padres win the nightcap by a 4-2 margin.

JULY 8:

Tigers' pitcher John Hiller, sidelined since a January 1971 heart attack, returns to the club's active roster.

JULY 9:

For the second time in less than 10 days, the Angels' Nolan Ryan fans 16 batters in a game. Today's victims are the Red Sox; eight go down in a row in the first, second (on nine pitches), and third innings. California wins, 3-0. On July 1, Ryan struck out 16 Athletics in nine innings.

JULY 10:

The Phillies' general manager, Paul Owens, replaces manager Frank Lucchesi – with himself. Owens takes over the 26-50 team for the remainder of the season.

JULY 11:

The Cardinals find a way to stop Hank Aaron; they walk him a major-league-record five times. But Atlanta wins the game, 5-4.

In Chicago, the Cubs' Billy Williams has eight hits in a doubleheader against the Astros, but Chicago manages only a split. In the opening game, Williams has a homer and two singles in three at-bats; Houston wins, 6-5. In the nightcap, Williams has another homer, a double, and three singles in five at-bats and the Cubs triumph, 9-5.

JULY 14:

Catcher Tom Haller takes his position behind the plate for the Tigers. Looking over his shoulder is his brother, home plate umpire Bill Haller. It is the first time ever in major league history that an umpire works a game in which his brother catches. The Royals edge the Tigers, 1-0.

JULY 21:

In his first game in San Francisco since his trade to the Mets, Willie Mays connects off Jim Barr for his 650th career home run. The Mets win, 3-1.

JULY 22:

Prior to today's game with the Pirates in Pittsburgh, Reds' catcher Johnny Bench and pitcher Wayne Simpson get calls in their hotel room from someone identifying himself as "Louie." He offers them $2,000 for a "fat pitch" to Pittsburgh's hurler Bob Robertson. Simpson reports the incident to manager Sparky Anderson, but an investigation turns up no further information. The Reds win the game, 6-3.

JULY 24:

With the Cubs' season record at 46-44, Leo Durocher resigns and is replaced as manager by Carroll "Whitey" Lockman.

JULY 25:

In Atlanta, Joe Morgan singles in Nate Colbert in the bottom of the 10th and the NL wins the All-Star Game, 4-3. Hank Aaron for the NL and Octavio "Cookie" Rojas of the AL hit two-run homers. The winning pitcher is Frank "Tug" McGraw; the loser is Dave McNally. The NL has won all seven of the extra-inning All-Star Games.

JULY 31:

Dick Allen of the Chicago White Sox becomes the first major league player since 1950 with two inside-the-park home runs in a single game. Allen connects in the first inning with two on and again in the fifth inning with one runner on base as the Pale Hose beat Minnesota, 8-1.

AUGUST 1:

Nate Colbert goes to town in Atlanta, hitting five homers, driving in 13 runs in a doubleheader, and totaling 22 total bases. The Padres' first baseman, who came into today's games with a .233 average, sets one record – most RBI in a twin bill – and ties Stan Musial's major league mark for homers in a doubleheader. In the opener, Colbert hits a first inning, three-run homer against Ron Scheuler and in the seventh connects with the bases empty off Mike McQueen. He also drives in a run with one of his two singles. San Diego wins, 9-0. The winning pitcher is Clay Kirby; Scheuler gets the loss. In the nightcap, Colbert hits a second-inning grand slam off Pat Jarvis, a seventh-inning two-run round-tripper against Jim Hardin, and a two-run blast in the ninth off Cecil Upshaw. The Padres sweep the Braves, 11-7. Ed Acosta is the winning pitcher; Tom Kelley gets the loss.

In New York, the Mets score a run in the fourth inning off the Phillies' Steve Carlton, ending his scoreless innings streak at 30. It is the only run of the game for the Mets;

JULY 9
For the second time in less than 10 days, Nolan Ryan strikes out 16 batters in a game.

JULY 31
Dick Allen is the first player since 1950 with two inside-the-park homers in one game.

they lose, 4-1. In the opener, the Mets edged the Phillies, 3-2, in 18 innings.

AUGUST 7:

The Hall of Fame inducts eight: Lawrence "Yogi" Berra, Josh Gibson, Vernon "Lefty" Gomez, former AL president Will Harridge, Sandy Koufax, Walter "Buck" Leonard, Early Wynn, and Ross Youngs. Yogi Berra, presently manager of the Mets, is a three-time AL MVP. A catcher and occasional outfielder, he hit .285 with 358 homers over 19 seasons and played in 14 World Series with the Yankees, hitting 12 homers. Josh Gibson, a catcher in the Negro Leagues, played from 1930 to 1946, hitting 900 plus home runs and batting more than .350. He hit .400 in several seasons and in 1938 and 1939 had slugging averages over 1.000. Gibson once hit a 580 foot home run in Yankee Stadium. He died in 1947. Lefty Gomez pitched 13 years with the Yankees and one with the Senators, compiling a lifetime 189-102 record with an ERA of 3.34. In five World Series with the Yankees, he is 6-0, with an ERA of 2.86; his winning percentage of 1.000 will remain a record. Will Harridge, who died last year, served as president of the AL from 1931 to 1958. In his 12 years with the Dodgers, Sandy Koufax overcame initial wildness to record 165 wins against 87 losses with a 2.76 ERA, 2,396 strikeouts (better than one per inning), and 40 shutouts. In World Series play, he compiled an ERA of 0.95, two shutouts, and 61 strikeouts in 57 innings. Buck Leonard, a first baseman, played 15 years with the Homestead Grays, batting .328 with 69 homers. Early Wynn, despite eight seasons with the pitiful Washington Senators, compiled 300 victories, winning 20 games or more five times. Ross Youngs, who died in 1927 at age 30, hit .322 in 10 years as an outfielder with the Giants. He played in four World Series.

In an echo of a remark he made on Yogi Berra Night 25 years ago in St. Louis, Berra tells the Hall of Fame induction audience: "I guess the first thing I ought to say is that I thank everybody for making this day necessary."

The bickering Boston Red Sox are at it again. Catcher Carlton Fisk criticizes teammates Carl Yastrzemski and Reggie Smith for lack of leadership and not hustling on the field.

AUGUST 8:

The Yankees will remain in the House That Ruth Built through the year 2002. The team will sign a 30-year lease, effective in 1976, with New York City to continue to play at Yankee Stadium in the Bronx. The city had acquired the facility under a condemnation process. The Yankees then beat the Tigers, 4-2.

Twenty-two Reds batters are fanned by Dodger pitchers – including 13 by Tommy John – but Cincinnati makes its hits count, winning, 2-1, in 19 innings. Los Angeles catcher Steve Yeager handles 22 chances and makes 22 putouts, both which are NL marks.

AUGUST 9:

Ted Simmons of the Cardinals, who is the first ever to play most of a season without a contract, signs today for $75,000 through the 1973 campaign.

AUGUST 13:

In Detroit, the Tigers go into a doubleheader against the Indians on a four-game losing streak. Manager Billy Martin decides to pull his lineup from a hat. He comes up with Norm Cash (1B), Jim Northrup (RF), Willie Horton (LF), Ed Brinkman (SS), Tony Taylor (2B), Duane "Duke" Sims (C), Mickey Stanley (CF), Aurelio Rodriguez (3B), and Woodie Fryman (P). The Tigers win, 3-2, then drop the nightcap, 9-2.

Former Yankees and Mets executive George Weiss dies at age 78. Weiss, inducted into the Hall of Fame in 1971, was associated with the Yankees from 1932 to 1960 – a period in which they won 19 pennants and 15 World Series – and guided the New York Mets in their formative years.

AUGUST 21:

The Braves beat the Phillies and Steve Carlton, 2-1, in 11 innings, ending his consecutive game winning streak at 15.

AUGUST 26:

At Wrigley Field, the Cubs' Ron Santo collects his 2,000th career hit. Billy Williams hits two homers, driving in four runs, and the Cubs beat the Giants, 10-9, in 10 innings.

TRIVIA

As an eight-year-old in St. Louis, Nate Colbert saw the May 2, 1954, doubleheader in which Stan Musial hit five homers, drove in 12 runs, and had 21 total bases.

"There's not enough mustard in the world to cover that hot dog."
– Darold Knowles, on Reggie Jackson

Roberto Clemente is a player of destiny.

AUGUST 27:

In the opener of a doubleheader, Willie Horton homers in the 11th inning to give the Tigers a 5-3 victory over the Twins. In the nightcap, an 11th-inning homer by Aurelio Rodriguez produces a 1-0 Detroit win. The Tigers also won yesterday on an 11th-inning round-tripper off the bat of Aurelio Rodriguez.

Houston Astros' owner Judge Roy Hofheinz fires manager Harry Walker and replaces him with Leo Durocher, because he will be "able to whip the horses down the final stretch." Houston was 67-54 under Walker and 1-0 under interim skipper Francis "Salty" Parker.

According to Baseball: The Biographical Encyclopedia, *"...Houston players as a whole had a problem dealing with Walker. In 1972, with the team in second place, they openly revolted." Under Durocher, the Astros remained runners-up to the Reds, but at 84-69, enjoyed their first-ever winning season. Walker finished his career in '73 as a batting instructor for the Cardinals.*

SEPTEMBER 2:

Today at Chicago's Wrigley Field, Milt Pappas of the Cubs is one pitch away from throwing a perfect game with a 1-2 count on San Diego Padres' pinch hitter Larry Stahl. Pappas throws three balls in a row, walking Stahl, and spoiling the perfect game. He then retires pinch hitter Garry Jestadt on a popup for a no-hitter. The Cubs win the game, 8-0, with Pappas fanning six Padres. Opposing pitcher Mike Caldwell takes the loss.

SEPTEMBER 3:

Steve Carlton of the Phillies whitewashes the Braves in Atlanta, 8-0, for his eighth shutout of the season. Henry Aaron singles in the first inning for the 6,135th total base of his career, passing Stan Musial.

SEPTEMBER 8:

Ferguson Jenkins beats the Phillies, 4-3, in Philadelphia for his 20th win of the season. It is the sixth straight year the Cubs' right-hander has won 10 or more games.

SEPTEMBER 9:

With today's 10-inning, 2-1 victory over the Red Sox, the Indians' Gaylord Perry becomes the sixth pitcher with 20 wins in each league. Perry won 23 with the Giants in 1970. This game's losing pitcher is Gary Peters.

SEPTEMBER 12:

The Angels' Nolan Ryan strikes out 15 Rangers in a 3-0, nine-inning victory.

SEPTEMBER 16:

In Philadelphia, Mike Schmidt, the Phillies' third baseman, connects against Balor Moore of the Expos for his first major league home run.

SEPTEMBER 3
Phillies' Steve Carlton blanks the Braves, 8-0, for his eighth shutout of the season.

SEPTEMBER 30
Roberto Clemente's double is his 3,000th – and last – hit of his 18-year career.

Cubs' pitcher Burt Hooten smacks a grand slam against Tom Seaver. The Cubs collect 15 walks in the game – five for Elrod Hendricks – and hammer the Mets, 18-5.

SEPTEMBER 19:

You may not be able to tell the players even with a scorecard. The Athletics and White Sox use a record 51 players in an extra-inning game. Oakland exhausts its 30-man roster and uses pitchers Jim "Catfish" Hunter as a pinch hitter and Vida Blue as a pinch runner. The White Sox finally prevail, 8-7, in 15 innings with Rich "Goose" Gossage getting the win. Gary Waslewski is charged with the loss. Ed Herrmann and Luis Alvarado home run for Chicago; Dave Duncan and Jorge Orta for Oakland. The teams also use 10 pinch hitters. Two days ago, Chicago and Oakland used 14 pinch hitters in a 15-inning game.

SEPTEMBER 30:

Today at Three Rivers Stadium, Roberto Clemente doubles to left centerfield off the Mets' Jon Matlack. It is Clemente's 3,000th – and last – career hit. Bill Mazeroski pinch hits for Clemente in what would have been his final at-bat and the Pirates win, 5-0. Clemente joins Ty Cobb, Stan Musial, Tris Speaker, Honus Wagner, Hank Aaron, Eddie Collins, Napoleon Lajoie, Willie Mays, Paul Waner, and Adrian "Cap" Anson in the 3,000-hit "club."

Nolan Ryan continues to blow away AL batters. Today, the Angels' right-hander fans 17 Twins in a nine-inning game. California wins the contest, 3-2.

Today Ted Williams announces he is stepping down as manager of the Rangers. Texas finishes last in the AL West with a 54-100 record in 1972. Dorrel "Whitey" Herzog will replace him at the helm.

OCTOBER 2:

Despite issuing seven walks, the Expos' Bill Stoneman no-hits the Mets, 7-0, at Parc Jarry. It is the second career no-hitter for Stoneman, who strikes out nine. The Expos make no errors. Jim McAndrew is tagged with the loss.

OCTOBER 3:

Orioles' pitcher Roric Harrison homers against the Indians' Ray Lamb in the sixth inning in the second game of a double-header. It is the last regular season home run by a pitcher in the AL, which switches to the designated hitter rule next season. Baltimore wins the game, 4-3.

Detroit's slugger Al Kaline singles in the winning run and the Tigers beat the Boston Red Sox, 3-1, to win the AL East. Woodie Fryman gets the win; Luis Tiant is the losing pitcher. Because of games missed during the players' strike, the Tigers play one more game than the Red Sox. With one more win, they beat out Boston by a half-game to capture the AL East flag.

The Phillies bang out six home runs and Steve Carlton beats the Cubs, 11-1, at Wrigley Field for his 27th win of the year.

OCTOBER 4:

Yankees' rookie Larry Gowell doubles off Jim Lonborg of the Red Sox, becoming the last pitcher to hit safely in a regular season AL game before the implementation of the designated-hitter rule. It also proves to be Gowell's only hit in his two-game career in the major leagues.

REGULAR SEASON WRAP-UP:

The Oakland Athletics, managed by Dick Williams, are 93-62 in the regular season in the AL. Starter Jim "Catfish" Hunter is the top pitcher at 21-7 with a 2.04 ERA. Rollie Fingers has 21 saves. Joe Rudi bats .305 with 19 homers and 75 RBI. Reggie Jackson finishes at .265 with 25 homers and 75 RBI. Mike Epstein has 26 home runs; speedy Bert Campaneris racks up 52 stolen bases.

Sparky Anderson's Cincinnati Reds are 95-59 in the National League. Catcher Johnny Bench bats .270 with 40 home runs and 125 RBI; Pete Rose hits .307, and second baseman Joe Morgan homers 16 times. The leading pitcher is Gary Nolan with a 15-5 record.

OCTOBER 7:

NLCS, game one. In Pittsburgh today, the Pirates, behind Steve Blass, beat the Reds, 5-1. Al Oliver hits a two-run homer for Pittsburgh; Joe Morgan has a solo shot for Cincinnati.

ALCS, game one. In Oakland, the Athletics beat the Tigers, 3-2, in 12 innings on a throwing error by out-

TRIVIA

Ted Williams once was trying to improve the hitting of Dick Billings (who had a .227 lifetime average). He asks the catcher-infielder if he'd ever read Williams's book on hitting. Billings responds: "No. But I could read a book on medicine and it wouldn't help make me a surgeon either."

"Every time I look at my pocketbook, I see Jackie Robinson."
– Willie Mays

HISTORY

Steve Carlton (27-10) is the only pitcher to win the Cy Young Award with a last-place team. He accounted for nearly 46 percent of Philadelphia's wins.

fielder Al Kaline, who had put Detroit ahead with a home run in the top of the frame. Rollie Fingers gets the win in relief; starter Mickey Lolich is the losing pitcher. Norm Cash smacks a home run for Detroit.

OCTOBER 8:

NLCS, game two. The Reds score four runs in the first inning and kayo losing pitcher Bob Moose en route to a 5-3 victory in Pittsburgh. Joe Morgan homers for Cincinnati. The winning pitcher is Tom Hall in relief of Jack Billingham.

ALCS, game two. Johnny "Blue Moon" Odom three-hits the Tigers, 5-0, to even the playoff. The game turns ugly in the seventh inning when Detroit's Lerrin LaGrow hits Bert Campaneris in the ankle with a pitch. Campaneris gets up and throws his bat at LaGrow and the benches empty, with manager Billy Martin leading the Tigers' charge. The umpires restrain Martin; LaGrow and Campaneris are ejected. Woodie Fryman gets the loss.

Campaneris is fined $500 and suspended for the remainder of the ALCS and for the first seven games of the 1973 season. But he will be permitted to play in the World Series, should Oakland win the AL pennant.

One of the best tributes to Jackie Robinson came before his death from teammate Harold "Pee Wee" Reese: "Thinking about the things that happened, I don't know any other ball player who could have done what he did. To be able to hit with everybody yelling at him... To do what he did has got to be the most tremendous thing I've ever seen in sports."

OCTOBER 9:

Hall of Fame shortstop Dave Bancroft dies in Superior, Wisconsin, at age 81. Elected to the Hall in 1971, Bancroft hit .279 in 16 seasons and appeared in four World Series. He managed the Braves from 1924 to 1927.

NLCS, game three. Manny Sanguillen homers and drives in the winning run as the Pirates beat the Reds, 3-2, today in Cincinnati. Bruce Kison gets the victory in relief of Nelson Briles. The losing pitcher is Clay Carroll.

OCTOBER 10:

NLCS, game four. Ross Grimsley two-hits the Pirates, 7-1, losing his shutout on a Roberto Clemente home run at Riverfront Stadium. Dock Ellis gets the defeat.

ALCS, game three. Joe Coleman pitches a seven-hit shutout, striking out a record 14 batters in a 3-0 Tiger win at home. Bill Freehan homers. Starter Ken Holtzman is the losing pitcher.

OCTOBER 11
The Reds rally for two runs in the bottom of the ninth vs. the Pirates to win the NLCS.

OCTOBER 22
The Athletics nip the Reds, 3-2, in game seven to take the World Series.

OCTOBER 11:

NLCS, game five. The Cincinnati Reds win the National League pennant by scoring two runs in the bottom of the ninth for a 4-3 victory at Riverfront Stadium. Johnny Bench ties the game with a home run and Bob Moose's wild pitch scores the winning run. Cesar Geronimo had hit a home run earlier for Cincinnati. Clay Carroll gets the win with an inning of scoreless relief. Dave Giusti is charged with the game's loss.

ALCS, game four. Jim Northrup singles in the winning run as the Tigers beat the Athletics, 4-3, in 10 innings. Mike Epstein homers for Oakland; Dick McAuliffe for Detroit. The winning pitcher is John Hiller with a third of an inning of relief. Joe Horlen takes the loss.

OCTOBER 12:

ALCS, game five. In Detroit, the Athletics edge the Tigers, 2-1, to take the AL pennant. Blue Moon Odom gets the win with four innings of relief help from Vida Blue. Woodie Fryman gets the loss. Oakland scores the winning run in the fourth on a Gene Tenace two-out single scoring George Hendrick.

OCTOBER 14:

World Series, game one. In Cincinnati, the Athletics' Gene Tenace hits two-run and solo homers in his first two at-bats – a Series first. Oakland beats the Reds, 3-2. Ken Holtzman gets the win with a save from Vida Blue. Gary Nolan takes the loss.

OCTOBER 15:

World Series, game two. Jim "Catfish" Hunter pitches eight and two-thirds innings of strong pitching and gets a save from Rollie Fingers as the Athletics win their second straight, 2-1. Joe Rudi homers and saves the game with an outstanding catch in the ninth inning. The losing pitcher is Ross Grimsley.

OCTOBER 18:

World Series, game three. In Oakland, Jack Billingham and Clay Carroll combine to whitewash the Athletics, 1-0, on four hits. Billingham gets the win. Blue Moon Odom allows only three hits and fans 11, but gets a loss for his efforts. Dick Williams employs unusual strategy with Rollie Fingers pitching to Johnny Bench on a 3-2 count and runners on second and third in the eighth. Williams goes to the mound and points to first base, creating the impression Bench will get an intentional fourth ball. Catcher Gene Tenace also signals for a walk. Instead, Fingers throws a strike and fans Bench.

OCTOBER 19:

World Series, game four. The Athletics beat the Reds, 3-2, on two runs in the bottom of the ninth. Angel Manguel drives in the winner and Gene Tenace has a homer. Rollie Fingers gets the win with an inning of relief. Clay Carroll is the losing pitcher.

OCTOBER 20:

World Series, game five. Pete Rose, who homered on the first pitch of the game from Catfish Hunter, singles in the winning run in the top of the ninth. The Reds win, 5-4; Ross Grimsley gets credit for the victory. Denis Menke homers for Cincinnati; Gene Tenace has a three-run round-tripper for Oakland. The losing pitcher is Rollie Fingers.

The Braves obtain pitcher Tom Phoebus (3-4, 4.04 ERA) from the Cubs for infielder Tony LaRussa (.133 in 32 games in 1971).

OCTOBER 21:

World Series, game six. Johnny Bench homers, Bobby Tolan and Cesar Geronimo drive in two runs each, and the Reds rough up four different Oakland pitchers, 8-1. Ross Grimsley gets the win in relief of Gary Nolan. Starter Vida Blue is charged with the loss.

OCTOBER 22:

World Series, game seven. Gene Tenace drives in two runs with two hits and the Athletics beat the Reds, 3-2, today in Cincinnati to win the World Championship. Catfish Hunter gets the win with two and two-thirds innings of relief. Pedro Borbon is tagged with the loss. The Series is marked by six one-run ball games. Gene Tenace ties a Series record with four homers and drives in nine runs while batting .348. Tony Perez hits .435 for the Reds.

POST-SEASON

OCTOBER 24:

Jackie Robinson, to whose name always will be appended "the man who broke modern baseball's color line in 1947," dies of a heart attack today in Stamford, Connecticut, at age

HISTORY

Rod Carew of the Twins becomes the first AL player to lead the league in batting without hitting a home run.

NOVEMBER 27
The Dodgers trade outfielder Frank Robinson to the California Angels.

53. Robinson was suffering from diabetes and was nearly blind at the time of his death. Robinson, inducted into the Hall of Fame in 1962, was one of baseball's most ferocious competitors and one of its most exciting performers. Few, if any, players were subjected to the cruel and indecent hazing Robinson received in his early years. In 10 major league seasons, he batted .311 while stealing 197 bases. He played in six World Series with the Dodgers.

Roger Kahn wrote in The Boys of Summer: *"If one can be certain of anything in baseball, it is that we shall not look upon his like again." Publicist Irving Rudd, according to Kahn, says, "... If there's a God, Jackie's up there now and he's ripped off his cap and he's kicking dirt with his spikes and he's hollering, 'What a lousy decision. I shoulda been safe. I was only 53!'"*

OCTOBER 27:

The Atlanta Braves send Rico Carty (.277, six homers in 86 games), a former National League batting champion, to the Rangers for pitcher Jim Panther (5-9, 4.12 ERA).

NOVEMBER 22:

Ruly Carpenter replaces his father, Bob Carpenter, as president of the Philadelphia Phillies.

NOVEMBER 27:

The New York Yankees send outfielders Charlie Spikes (.147 in 14 games) and Rusty Torres, second baseman Jerry Kenney (.210 in 50 games), and catcher-first baseman John Ellis (.294, five home runs in 52 games) to the Cleveland Indians for third baseman Graig Nettles (.253, 17 homers) and catcher Gerry Moses (.220 in 52 games).

NOVEMBER 28:

Outfielder Frank Robinson (.251, 19 homers) is traded by the Los Angeles Dodgers to the California Angels along with infielders Billy Grabarkewitz (.167, four home runs in 53 games) and Bobby Valentine (.274) and pitchers Bill Singer (6-16, 3.67 ERA) and Mike Strahler (-12, 3.26 ERA). In exchange, the Dodgers obtain pitcher Andy Messersmith (8-11, 2.81 ERA) and third baseman Ken McMullen (.269, nine home runs).

NOVEMBER 30:

The Braves acquire pitcher Pat Dobson (16-18, 2.65 ERA), second baseman Davey Johnson (.221, five homers), pitcher Roric Harrison (3-4, 2.30 ERA), and catcher Johnny Oates (.261, four homers in 85 games) from the Orioles. In return, Baltimore gets catcher-infielder Earl Williams (.258, 28 homers, 87 RBI) and minor league infielder Taylor Duncan.

The Reds trade outfielder Hal McRae (.278, five homers in 61 games) and pitcher Wayne Simpson (8-5, 4.14 ERA) to the Royals for outfielder Richie Scheinblum (.300, eight homers) and pitcher Roger Nelson (11-6, 2.08 ERA).

DECEMBER 10:

The AL approves the use of a "designated hitter," a player who will bat in place of the pitcher but not field a position, on a three-year trial basis.

DECEMBER 20:

Hall of Fame catcher Charles "Gabby" Hartnett dies in Park Ridge, Illinois, on his 72nd birthday. Inducted into the Hall of Fame in 1955, Hartnett hit .297 in 20 years. He managed the Cubs from 1939 to 1940, leading them to the NL pennant in his first year.

DECEMBER 31:

One of baseball's genuine superstars, Roberto Clemente, is killed when the DC-7 in which he is flying relief supplies to the victims of the recent Nicaraguan earthquake crashes in the Atlantic Ocean a mile from San Juan, Puerto Rico. The four-time NL batting champion was only 38 years old.

John Sayles, the writer and director, whose film work includes Eight Men Out, *which documents the 1919 Black Sox scandal, commented on Roberto Clemente: "I never thought about being a writer as I grew up; a writer wasn't something to be. An outfielder was something to be. Most of what I know about style I learned from Roberto Clemente."*

Said Clemente once himself: "I want to be remembered as a ballplayer who gave all he had to give.

On another occasion, he remarked, in an eerily prophetic way: "When I wake up in the morning, I pray I am still asleep."

DECEMBER 10
The American League approves the use of a "designated hitter" on a trial basis.

DECEMBER 31
Roberto Clemente, 38, is killed in an airplane crash near San Juan, Puerto Rico.

THE BEST OF 1972

NATIONAL LEAGUE

HITTERS

Batting Average:
Billy Williams, Chicago Cubs, .333

Slugging Average:
Billy Williams, .606

Home Runs:
Johnny Bench, Cincinnati Reds, 40

Runs Batted In:
Johnny Bench, 125

Hits:
Pete Rose, Cincinnati Reds, 198

Stolen Bases:
Lou Brock, St. Louis Cardinals, 63

PITCHERS

Wins:
Steve Carlton, Philadelphia Phillies, 27

Strikeouts:
Steve Carlton, 310

Earned Run Average:
Steve Carlton, 1.97

Winning Percentage:
Gary Nolan, Cincinnati Reds, .750

Saves:
Clay Carroll, Cincinnati Reds, 37

Most Valuable Player:
Johnny Bench, Cincinnati Reds

Cy Young Award:
Steve Carlton, Philadelphia Phillies

Rookie of the Year:
Jon Matlack, New York Mets

AMERICAN LEAGUE

HITTERS

Batting Average:
Rod Carew, Minnesota Twins, .318

Slugging Average:
Dick Allen, Chicago White Sox, .603

Home Runs:
Dick Allen, 37

Runs Batted In:
Dick Allen, 113

Hits:
Joe Rudi, Oakland Athletics, 181

Stolen Bases:
Bert Campaneris, Oakland Athletics, 52

PITCHERS

Wins:
Gaylord Perry, Cleveland Indians;
Wilbur Wood, Chicago White Sox, 24

Strikeouts:
Nolan Ryan, California Angels, 329

Earned Run Average:
Luis Tiant, Boston Red Sox, 1.91

Winning Percentage:
Jim "Catfish" Hunter, Oakland Athletics, .750

Saves:
Albert "Sparky" Lyle, New York Yankees, 35

Most Valuable Player:
Dick Allen, Chicago White Sox

Cy Young Award:
Gaylord Perry, Cleveland Indians

Rookie of the Year:
Carlton Fisk, Boston Red Sox

1973

NEWS

SEVEN GUILTY IN CONTINUING WATERGATE SCANDAL

Impeachment resolutions introduced against President Nixon

TAX EVASION CHARGES CAUSE VICE PRESIDENT SPIRO T. AGNEW TO RESIGN; GERALD FORD REPLACES HIM

FORMER PRESIDENT LYNDON B. JOHNSON DIES AT AGE 64

VIETNAM PEACE PACT SIGNED

Chicago Seven convicted of contempt

World's tallest building – Sears Tower in Chicago – is completed

U.S. LAUNCHES SKYLAB SPACE STATION

HENRY KISSINGER, LE DUC THO SHARE NOBEL PEACE PRIZE

George Foreman knocks out Joe Frazier for heavyweight title

PRE-SEASON

JANUARY 3:

A group of 17 investors led by Cleveland shipbuilder George Steinbrenner purchases the New York Yankees from the Columbia Broadcasting System for $10 million. Steinbrenner reportedly will own 30 percent of the team. CBS gets some $4 million less for the team than it originally paid.

JANUARY 11:

At a joint meeting of owners, all 24 approve the use of a designated hitter in the AL starting this season in a three-year experiment. It is the first time since 1901 that the AL and NL will play under different rules. The owners also refer the possibility of interleague play to a committee for study.

Of the designated hitter rule, Commissioner Bowie Kuhn says: "I hope it works. I would have preferred that both leagues did it. But if it's successful in one, then I hope the National follows suit."

JANUARY 18:

One week after the rule change is approved, the Red Sox become the first team to sign a designated hitter – one-time NL Most Valuable Player Orlando Cepeda. He hit a combined .287 with four homers in 37 games with the Braves and the Athletics last season.

FAMOUS LAST WORDS. AT A PRESS CONFERENCE ANNOUNCING HIS PURCHASE OF THE YANKEES, GEORGE STEINBRENNER PLEDGES: "WE PLAN ABSENTEE OWNERSHIP AS FAR AS RUNNING THE YANKEES IS CONCERNED. WE'RE NOT GOING TO PRETEND WE'RE SOMETHING WE AREN'T. I'LL STICK TO BUILDING SHIPS."

FEBRUARY 1:

The Orioles sell outfielder Don Buford (.206, five homers) to Japan's Fukuoka Lions.

FEBRUARY 25:

The owners and players reach a new basic agreement. A key provision is a new "10 and five rule"; players in the majors for 10 years and with their present team for five will be able to veto trades. Minimum player salary will be increased to $16,000 in 1975 and salary disputes will be arbitrated. Each side will submit its best offer, and the arbitrator will pick one or the other with no compromise. The agreement will also enable spring training to begin; the owners, fearful of a strike, had threatened to keep the camps closed.

MARCH 5:

Yankees Fritz Peterson and Mike Kekich shock the baseball world and provide standup comics with a wealth

MARCH 20
The late Roberto Clemente is voted into the Hall of Fame in a special election.

APRIL 6
Ron Blomberg of the Yankees, the first-ever designated hitter, walks in his first at-bat.

of material. It is revealed today that the two pitchers have switched families, swapping wives, children, and dogs. Susanne Kekich will take up housekeeping with Fritz Peterson, and Marilyn Peterson will join Mike Kekich.

MARCH 11:

Manager Yogi Berra fines Willie Mays for being absent without authorization from the Mets' spring training camp.

MARCH 12:

Hall of Fame infielder Frankie Frisch dies today in Wilmington, Delaware, at the age of 74, of cardiac arrest as a result of an automobile accident last month. Known as the Fordham Flash, Frisch was inducted into the Hall of Fame in 1947. In 19 years, he hit .316 and stole 419 bases. As player-manager, he led the Cardinals to the 1934 World Championship and appeared in seven other Fall Classics.

MARCH 20:

Eleven weeks after his death in a plane crash, Roberto Clemente is voted into the Hall of Fame in a special election, without the required five-year waiting period. Clemente, whose .317 lifetime batting average is the highest by any right-handed batter since World War II, becomes the first Latin American in Cooperstown. He receives 93 percent of the 424 ballots cast and is the first to be chosen in a special election. In 1939, Lou Gehrig was elected by acclamation.

Bowie Kuhn on Roberto Clemente: "He had about him a touch of royalty." Roger Angell on Clemente, "He played a kind of baseball that none of us had ever seen before..."

MARCH 26:

Hall of Fame first baseman George Sisler dies in Richmond Heights, Missouri, two days after his 80th birthday. In 15 major league seasons, Sisler compiled a lifetime average of .340 and stole 375 bases. He led the AL in batting in 1920 with .407 and in 1922 with .420. His 1920 total of 257 hits remains a major league record. Sisler never appeared in a World Series. He also managed the St. Louis Browns from 1924 to 1926. Among his survivors are his sons Dick and Dave, both former major league players.

MARCH 27:

The Braves unconditionally release pitcher Denny McLain two days before his 29th birthday, ending a career that burned brightly but briefly. McLain's record last season was 4-7 with a 6.39 ERA for the Athletics and Braves. In 10 years, he was 131-92 with a 3.39 ERA and 1,282 strikeouts.

Pitcher Jim Perry is the first player to approve his own trade under the new "10 and five" rule. The Twins send Perry (13-16, 3.34 ERA) to the Tigers for minor league pitcher Dan Fife and cash.

THE SEASON

APRIL 6:

At Fenway Park, Ron Blomberg of the Yankees faces Luis Tiant and becomes the AL's first-ever designated hitter. Blomberg walks with the bases loaded; he has a single in three official at-bats in the game, won by the Red Sox, 15-6. Orlando Cepeda, Boston's designated hitter, is hitless in six trips to the plate.

The Pirates retire Roberto Clemente's number 21 in a pregame ceremony at Three Rivers Stadium attended by 51,695. The Pirates then beat the Cardinals, 7-5.

On opening night in Oakland, the Twins' Tony Oliva hits a first-inning pitch from Jim "Catfish" Hunter for a two-run homer. Oliva becomes the first designated hitter to hit a round-tripper. Minnesota wins, 8-3.

APRIL 9:

The Yankees mark the golden anniversary of the Stadium with 82-year-old Bob Shawkey, the winning pitcher on opening day in 1923, throwing out the first ball. The Yankees have no Shawkey on their roster today. They settle for Fred "Fritz" Peterson, who loses to the Indians, 3-1.

APRIL 10:

In 39-degree weather, a crowd of 39,476 attends the first game at the new Royals Stadium, part of the Harry S Truman Sports Complex; Kansas City beats the Rangers, 12-1. John Mayberry and Jeff Burroughs homer. The winning pitcher is Paul Splittorff; Pete Broberg gets the loss.

APRIL 27:

The Royals' Steve Busby no-hits the Tigers, 3-0, in Detroit.

Ron Blomberg ushers in the designated-hitter era.

Yankees' general manager Lee MacPhail says of the Peterson-Kekich affair: "We may have to call off family day."

Nolan Ryan throws two no-hitters this year.

Busby strikes out four and walks six; Kansas City commits no errors. The losing pitcher is Jim Perry, who also was on the short end of Vida Blue's 1970 no-hitter.

APRIL 29:

Yankees' president Mike Burke resigns and will return his part ownership in the team. Gabe Paul becomes chief executive officer for the new Steinbrenner regime.

MAY 4:

In Philadelphia, the Phillies beat the Braves, 5-4, in a 20-inning game that lasts five hours and 16 minutes. The Braves strand 27 runners, a major league record for extra innings. Ralph Garr of Atlanta ties a major league mark with 11 plate appearances.

MAY 8:

Cubs' manager Carroll "Whitey" Lockman gets thumbed in the third inning and coach Ernie Banks completes the game for him. It is the first time a black has managed in a major league game. The Cubs edge the Padres, 3-2. The Pirates' Willie Stargell, who, in 1969 was the first to hit a ball out of Dodger Stadium, does it again – this time off Andy Messersmith. The Dodgers overcome Stargell's blast to win the game, 7-4.

MAY 13:

A sore shoulder puts the Mets' 42-year-old Willie Mays on the disabled list.

MAY 15:

The Angels' Nolan Ryan no-hits the Royals, 3-0, in Kansas City. Ryan fans 12 and walks three, while California makes no errors. Jeff Torborg, who caught Sandy Koufax's final no-hitter in September 1965, is behind the plate for Ryan today. The losing pitcher is Bruce Del Canton.

No, he is not Ted Williams and it's not the "Boudreau shift," but the Pirates' Dave Cash faces a five-man infield when he comes to bat against the Expos in the bottom half of the 11th. Manager Gene Mauch's strategy fails; Cash singles in the winning run in Pittsburgh's 9-8 victory at Three Rivers Stadium.

MAY 18:

The Cubs' Glenn Beckert extends his consecutive game hitting streak to 26 as Chicago beats the Phillies, 9-2. In 1968, Beckert had a 27-game hitting streak.

MAY 24:

The Red Sox keep battling – each other. A clubhouse brawl follows an on-field fight between outfielder Reggie Smith and pitcher Bill Lee.

MAY 29:

Tom Seaver has pop in his bat and pop in his fastball. He three-hits the Giants, fanning 16, and hits his sixth career homer in a 5-2 Mets' victory.

MAY 31:

The Cubs beat the Astros, 16-8, at

JULY 3
Pitchers Jim and Gaylord Perry are the first brothers to face each other in the AL.

JULY 15
Nolan Ryan is only the second pitcher ever to throw two no-hitters in a single season.

Wrigley Field on 10 unearned runs in the first inning. A two-out error by Houston third baseman Doug Rader opens up the floodgates.

JUNE 12:

In the aftermath of the wife-swapping affair, pitcher Mike Kekich (1-1) is traded by the Yankees to the Indians for pitcher Lowell Palmer (0-0).

JUNE 19:

Pete Rose gets his 2,000th hit, a single, against the Giants. Against the Braves, Dodger Willie Davis homers for his 2,000th hit.

JUNE 23:

In Pittsburgh, the Mets' Willie Mays collects his 3,252nd career safety, giving him seventh place on the all-time hit parade. The Pirates beat the Mets, 3-2, in 10 innings.

In Montreal, the Phillies' Ken Brett homers in a 7-2 win over the Expos. Brett now has round-trippers in four consecutive games – a major league record for pitchers. Brett previously homered on June 9 against the Padres, in a 4-1 win; on June 13, against the Dodgers, in a 16-3 triumph, and on June 18, against the Mets, in a 9-6 victory.

In the nightcap of a doubleheader, the Dodgers infield of Steve Garvey (1B), Davey Lopes (2B), Bill Russell (SS), and Ron Cey (3B) debuts in Philadelphia in a 16-3 loss. The four infielders will play together for eight and a half years, which sets a major league record.

JUNE 27:

David Clyde, the Texas Rangers' 18-year-old, $125,000 "bonus baby," makes his major league debut at Arlington Stadium. Clyde, signed as a high school student in Houston, pitches five innings against the Twins, yielding only one hit – a homer to Mike Adams – and striking out eight batters. Clyde gets credit for the 4-3 win; Jim Kaat is charged with the loss.

JULY 2:

Hall of Fame outfielder Charles "Chick" Hafey dies at the age of 70 in Calistoga, California. Inducted into the Hall of Fame in 1971, Hafey hit .317 in 13 years and led the NL with .349 in 1931.

The Detroit Tigers sign outfielder Ron LeFlore, recently paroled from prison.

JULY 3:

It's brother versus brother on the mound for the first time in an AL regular season game when Jim Perry of the Tigers and Gaylord Perry of the Indians face off in Cleveland. Sparked by Norm Cash's two home runs, Detroit hands Cleveland its seventh consecutive loss, 5-4. Jim Perry is not involved in the decision; Ed Farmer gets the win. Gaylord Perry is charged with the loss.

JULY 9:

After Mets' chairman of the board M. Donald Grant addresses his last place team on believing in themselves, pitcher Frank "Tug" McGraw says, "He's right! He's right! Just believe! You gotta believe! You gotta believe!" And the Mets' battle cry is born. New York then beats the visiting Astros, 2-1, on a Felix Millan single in the 12th inning.

JULY 11:

The Tigers' leadoff hitter Jim Northrup hits two home runs and bats in eight runs in a 14-2 win over the Rangers. Northrup scores for the 500th time in his career and bats in his 500th run.

The player the Mets obtained for Nolan Ryan will now be his teammate in Texas. New York sells infielder Jim Fregosi (.234 in 45 games) to the Rangers today.

In San Diego, the Pirates' Willie Stargell hits his 302nd career home run in a 10-2 pasting of the Padres. Stargell thus passes Ralph Kiner as Pittsburgh's top all-time home run hitter.

JULY 15:

Nolan Ryan no-hits the Tigers, 6-0, in Detroit, walking four and striking out 17 – including eight in a row. It is Ryan's second no-hitter of the season, and improving his record to 11-11. Ryan, 26 years old, joins Johnny Vander Meer, Allie Reynolds, and Virgil Trucks as the only pitchers with two no-hitters in a season. In the sixth inning after fanning twice, Norm Cash brings a furniture leg to the plate, but umpire Ron Luciano makes him use a bat. Cash pops up. Eddie Brinkman, is Ryan's 17th victim. The loser is Jim Perry. Twice this season and three times in his career, Perry has been on the losing end of no-hitters.

CULTURE

A spate of baseball novels are published: *The Bingo Long Traveling All-Stars and Motor Kings* by William Brashler, about black barnstorming teams; *The Great American Novel* by Philip Roth; *Babe Ruth Caught in a Snowstorm* by John Alexander Graham; *Sam's Legacy* by Jay Neugeboren.

JULY
24
Bobby Bonds homers and doubles to lead the NL to a 7-1 win in the All-Star Game.

JULY 19:

A contrast in pitching styles produces a classic duel. Fireballing Nolan Ryan of the Rangers faces crafty Mike Cuellar of the Orioles. Ryan strikes out 13 and carries a no-hitter into the eighth when Mark Belanger singles. Cuellar strikes out 12, pitching a complete game and getting a 3-1 victory when Terry Crowley hits a two-run double off Dave Sells in the 11th.

JULY 20:

Wilbur Wood's attempted Iron Man feat turns to slag. The White Sox left-hander starts both games of a doubleheader against the Yankees in New York, is kayoed twice, and is tagged with two losses, 12-2 and 7-0.

JULY 21:

Hank Aaron closes in on Babe Ruth's once unapproachable career home run record. In the third inning in Atlanta, he hits a 1-1 fastball for his 700th home run – a 400foot drive into the left center-field bleachers with one on against Philadelphia's Ken Brett. The ball is retrieved by 18-year-old Robert Winborne, who gets 700 silver dollars for returning it. Aaron, now 39, was five months old when Babe Ruth hit his 700th round-tripper. The Braves lose, 8-4.

STAN MUSIAL ONCE OBSERVED OF WARREN SPAHN, WHO PITCHED UNTIL HE WAS 44: "I DON'T THINK WARREN SPAHN WILL EVER GET INTO THE HALL OF FAME. HE'LL NEVER STOP PITCHING."

JULY 24:

The NL, paced by Bobby Bonds's home run and double, beats the AL, 7-1, in Kansas City. Johnny Bench hits a solo homer and Willie Davis a two-run homer for the NL. In his last All-Star at-bat, Willie Mays is fanned by Albert "Sparky" Lyle on three pitches. The winning pitcher is Rick Wise; Bert Blyleven gets the loss. A total of 54 players make it into the game.

JULY 30:

The Rangers' Jim Bibby no-hits the Athletics, 6-0, in Oakland. He strikes out 13 and walks six; Texas plays errorless ball. The losing pitcher is Vida Blue.

At Wrigley Field, the Cardinals' Lou Brock walks against Rick Reuschel and steals second. It is his 600th career stolen base. He then scores on a Tim McCarver hit, but it is St. Louis's only run as the Cubs beat Bob Gibson, 3-1.

AUGUST 1:

The AL's premier catchers, the Yankees' Thurman Munson and Carlton Fisk of the Red Sox, duke it out at Fenway Park. In the top of the ninth with the score tied, Munson barrels into Fisk while trying to score from third on a missed bunt by Gene Michael, igniting the fight. In the bottom of the frame, Mario Guerrero singles off Sparky Lyle to give Boston a 3-2 win.

AUGUST 4:

The Brewers' Johnny Briggs bangs out six consecutive hits – two doubles and four singles – in a 9-4 victory over the Indians.

AUGUST 5:

In Atlanta, Phil Niekro no-hits the Padres, 9-0, walking three and fanning four. The Braves make two errors. The losing pitcher is Steve Arlin. Niekro is the first Atlanta pitcher with a no-hitter.

A doubleheader loss to the Cardinals, 3-2 and 4-1, at Shea Stadium seems to bury the Mets in last place in the NL East. After today's double defeat, New York is 48-60, 11 1/2 games out of first place.

AUGUST 6:

Roberto Clemente, William Evans, Monford "Monte"

AUGUST 17
The Mets' Willie Mays hits his 660th – and final – career homer, off the Reds' Don Gullett.

Irvin, George Kelly, Warren Spahn, and Michael "Smiling Mickey" Welch are inducted into the Hall of Fame. Clemente hit .317 in 18 years – all with the Pirates. An outstanding outfielder, he led the NL in batting four times, hit .300 or better 13 times, and had 240 career homers. He had a .362 batting average in two World Series. Evans umpired in the AL from 1906 to 1927 and once had a fist-fight with Ty Cobb under the stands. He died in 1956. Irvin came to the majors at the age of 30, one of the first blacks signed after Jackie Robinson. He played for eight seasons, batting .293. The outfielder hit .458 in the 1951 World Series. In seven years in the Negro Leagues – mostly with the Newark Eagles – he hit .345. Kelly, a first baseman known as Highpockets, was an outstanding fielder. In 16 years, he batted .297 and had six consecutive .300 seasons. He appeared in two World Series. Spahn, in a 21-year career, won 363 games while losing 245 and compiled an ERA of 3.09. He pitched 5,243 2/3 innings and recorded 63 shutouts. He appeared in three World Series. Welch, who died in 1941, compiled a 308-209 record with a 2.71 ERA, pitching for the Troy Trojans and the New York Giants for 13 years. In 1885, he was 44-11 with a 1.66 ERA. He won 30 games three times and 20 games five times.

AUGUST 7:

Maybe it's a reward for his no-hitter. The Braves buy Phil Niekro's younger brother Joe from the Detroit Tigers, uniting the two for the first time in the majors. Joe did not appear for the Tigers in 1972; last season he was 3-2, with a 3.83 ERA.

AUGUST 10:

The Mets are still breathing. Less than a week ago, they were 11 1/2 games out of first. Today, after beating the Giants and Juan Marichal, 7-1, they narrow the gap to seven and a half.

AUGUST 15:

The White Sox buy pitcher Jim Kaat (11-12) from the Twins for the waiver price.

AUGUST 17:

Willie Mays of the Mets homers against the Reds' Don Gullett at Shea Stadium. It is Mays's 660th – and final – career homer. The Mets lose, 2-1, and remain in last place, seven and a half back.

AUGUST 29:

Jerry Koosman beats the Padres, 3-0, and the Mets climb out of last place, just five and a half back. New York had occupied the cellar in the NL East since June 25.

Willie Mays goes out in World Series style.

SEPTEMBER 8
Six days after being fired as manager of the Tigers, Billy Martin is hired by the Rangers.

TRIVIA

Tigers' pitcher Bill Slayback and play-by-play announcer Ernie Harwell write the song "Move Over Babe (Here Comes Henry)." "There Used to Be a Ballpark," written by Joe Raposo, is recorded by Frank Sinatra.

AUGUST 30:

The Mets' respite from the NL East cellar was brief. New York is back in the basement after losing, 1-0, in 10 innings to the St. Louis Cardinals on a Jose Cruz single.

AUGUST 31:

The Mets bounce back up with a 6-4 win over the Cardinals in 10 innings today.

SEPTEMBER 2:

The Tigers fire manager Billy Martin, who had been under a three-day suspension. Martin admitted instructing two of his pitchers, Joe Coleman and Fred Scherman, to throw spitballs against the Indians. Martin was angry because he believed Cleveland's Gaylord Perry was "loading up" the ball. Coach Joe Schultz takes over as manager of the 71-63 Tigers.

SEPTEMBER 3:

Hank Aaron ties another Babe Ruth mark. He hits two homers today – the 707th and 708th of his career. The second ties the Bambino for the most in one league.

SEPTEMBER 6:

The Yankees unload their two Alou brothers. They sell Felipe (.236 in 93 games) to the Expos and Matty (.296 in 123 games) to the Cardinals.

SEPTEMBER 7:

The Mets sweep the Expos in a twi-night doubleheader in Montreal. After a 1-0, win, Jerry Koosman has his shutout inning string of 21 2/3 broken by a Bob Bailey RBI single. The Mets win the game, 4-2, in 15.

SEPTEMBER 8:

Billy Martin is not unemployed long. The Rangers hire him as manager. Martin will take over from interim manager Del Wilbur (1-1), who replaced the recently fired Whitey Herzog, for the final 23 games and for the 1974 season. Owner Bob Short explains: "If my mother were managing the Rangers and I had the opportunity to hire Billy Martin, I'd fire my mother."

SEPTEMBER 12:

The New York Mets' late-season surge continues. They move within two and a half games of the first-place Pirates with a 3-2 win over the Phillies in Philadelphia. Starting pitcher Jon Matlack gets the win with a save from reliever Tug McGraw.

SEPTEMBER 16:

Despite a 4-3 win over the Cardinals at Shea Stadium, the Mets remain two and a half behind the Pirates with 13 games to play. They win today on a squeeze bunt by Jerry Grote; Tug McGraw gets the victory.

SEPTEMBER 17:

Move over Babe, Henry really is coming. Hank Aaron hits his 711th career homer in a home game against the Padres. Teammate Davey Johnson hits his 42nd of the season, tying Rogers Hornsby's major league season record for second basemen. Carl Morton 10-hits San Diego, 7-0.

The Mets' mission looks more impossible. They lose to the Pirates, 10-3, at Three Rivers Stadium, falling three and a half back with 12 games to go. Home runs by Willie Stargell and Richie Hebner kayo Tom Seaver, who yields seven runs in three innings of work.

SEPTEMBER 18:

The Mets stave off disaster at Three Rivers Stadium. New York comes back from a 4-1 deficit in the ninth to beat the Pirates, 6-5, keeping their title hopes alive. Don Hahn's two-run single gives the Mets the lead; they are two and a half out of first.

SEPTEMBER 19:

The Braves' Davey Johnson hits his 43rd homer of the year, setting a single season mark for second basemen. Previously, he was tied with Rogers Hornsby. Johnson's round-tripper is Atlanta's only run in a 4-1 loss to the Los Angeles Dodgers.

Frank Robinson of the Angels homers against the Rangers at Arlington Stadium. With that, Robinson now has at least one home run in every one of the 32 major league ballparks.

SEPTEMBER 20:

Is there another miracle in the making for the Mets? At Shea Stadium they beat the Pirates, 4-3, in 13 innings to edge within a half-game of first place. The Mets catch a break in the top of the 13th when a Dave Augustine drive against Ray Sadecki hits the edge of the left-field wall and bounces into Cleon Jones's glove. Jones throws to Wayne Garrett, whose relay gets Richie Zisk at the plate. Ron Hodges wins the game with a

SEPTEMBER 19
Frank Robinson's homer gives him at least one in all 32 major league parks.

OCTOBER 1
The 1973 edition of the Miracle Mets beats the Cubs, 6-4, and wins the NL East title.

solid single, scoring John Milner from second base.

Willie Mays, arguably the best all-around player in history, announces that he will retire at the end of the season.

SEPTEMBER 21:

Believe. The Mets beat the Pirates, 10-2, behind Tom Seaver's five-hitter. It is New York's fourth victory in five games against Pittsburgh, and they move into first place with a 77-77 record. John Milner, Wayne Garrett, and Rusty Staub each hit home runs for the Mets.

SEPTEMBER 22:

In Detroit, Tigers' relief pitcher John Hiller pitches shutout ball for three and two-thirds innings against the Boston Red Sox in a 5-1 victory. Hiller gets credit for his 38th save of the season, a major league record.

Al Bumbry hits three triples, tying a modern major league mark and leading the Orioles to a 7-1 victory over Milwaukee for the NL East title. Doyle Alexander gets the win.

Jon Matlack four-hits the Cardinals, 2-0, and the Mets lead the NL East by a full game with seven to play.

SEPTEMBER 25:

A sellout crowd at Shea Stadium salutes its longtime hero Willie Mays – the Say Hey Kid – as his career comes to a close. The 42-year-old Mays, who is hitting only .211 with six homers, says, "In my heart, I am a sad man. Just to hear you cheer like this for me and not be able to do anything about it makes me a very sad man. This is my farewell. You don't know what is going on inside of me tonight." The Mets beat the Expos, 2-1, behind Jerry Koosman. With five games left, New York leads the NL East by one and a half.

SEPTEMBER 27:

On his last pitch of the season, the Rangers' Nolan Ryan fans Rich Reese of the Twins in the 11th inning at Anaheim. Reese becomes Ryan's 383rd strikeout of the season, a major league record. In the eighth, Ryan fanned Steve Brye to tie the previous record holder, Sandy Koufax, at 382. The 26-year-old Ryan gets a four-minute ovation from the Anaheim crowd. California wins the game, 5-4, giving Ryan his 21st win of the season.

SEPTEMBER 29:

Hank Aaron homers against the Astros' Jerry Reuss for his 713th career homer – one behind Babe Ruth's once unassailable record. It also is Aaron's 40th of the season, making the Braves the first team in history with three 40-homer players. Davey Johnson now has 43 and Darrell Evans 41. At 39, Aaron is the oldest major league player ever to hit 40 round-trippers in a season.

SEPTEMBER 30:

After today's 8-5 loss to the Detroit Tigers – a game attended by 32,000 – Yankee Stadium's gates are shut until the 1976 season. The House That Ruth Built will be renovated and the Yankees will play their home games at Shea Stadium. The Yankees make additional news – that manager Ralph Houk will resign after an 80-82 record and a fourth-place finish in the AL East.

OCTOBER 1:

At Wrigley Field, the 1973 version of the Miracle Mets beats the Cubs, 6-4, to win the NL East. Tom Seaver gets the win, finishing the season at 19-10. Tug McGraw gets credit for his 25th save. Cleon Jones homers. Burt Hooten gets the loss. The scheduled nightcap, now not necessary, is not played.

Renovation begins on Yankee Stadium. Home plate is presented to Mrs. Babe Ruth; first base to Mrs. Lou Gehrig.

REGULAR SEASON WRAP-UP:

The mighty Oakland Athletics, managed by Dick Williams, finishes at 94-68 in the regular season in the AL, and brings three 20-game winners and a power-packed lineup to the Series. Catfish Hunter is 21-5; Ken Holtzman, 21-13; and Vida Blue, 20-9. Rollie Fingers adds 22 saves. Reggie Jackson bats .293 with 32 homers and 117 RBI. Sal Bando hits 29 homers, Gene Tenace, 24; and DH Deron Johnson, 19.

The "miracle" in the Mets' pennant is apparent from their lineup. Yogi Berra's team, which finishes at 82-79 in the NL, has no .300 hitters and little power, and only one of its top three pitchers – Tom Seaver at 19-10 – has a winning record. Felix Millan is the top average hitter at .290. Rusty Staub has 15

HISTORY

The Giants' Bobby Bonds hits a major-league-record 11 leadoff homers.

CULTURE

The Mark Harris novel *Bang the Drum Slowly* is made into a movie starring Robert DeNiro and Michael Moriarty.

homers with his .279 average. John Milner bats .235 with a team-leading 23 homers. Wayne Garrett adds 16 round-trippers.

HISTORY

Art Williams becomes the first African-American umpire in the NL.

OCTOBER 6:

NLCS, game one. In Cincinnati, Johnny Bench homers on a 1-0 pitch in the ninth inning to beat Tom Seaver and the Mets, 2-1. Pete Rose's eighth-inning homer had tied the game. Seaver allows only six hits, fans 13, and doubles in the Mets' only run, but gets the loss. Pedro Borbon gets the win with one inning of relief work.

ALCS, game one. In Baltimore, Jim Palmer pitches a five-hit complete game, defeating the Oakland Athletics, 6-0. The Orioles get off early with a four-run first inning, kayoing starter Vida Blue after only two-thirds of an inning of work.

OCTOBER 7:

NLCS, game two. Jon Matlack two-hits the Reds, fanning nine, in a 5-0 Mets' victory. Rusty Staub homers for New York in the fourth; Andy Kosko has both Cincinnati hits. Don Gullett is the losing pitcher.

ALCS, game two. Jim "Catfish" Hunter, backed by four home runs and a save by Rollie Fingers, beats the Orioles, 6-3. Sal Bando homers twice – once with a runner on; Joe Rudi and Bert Campaneris add solo round-trippers. The game's losing pitcher is Dave McNally.

OCTOBER 8:

NLCS, game three. At Shea Stadium, Jerry Koosman eight-hits the Reds and Rusty Staub homers twice – once with a runner on – for a 9-2 victory. Denis Menke homers for Cincinnati; Ross Grimsley is the losing pitcher. In the fifth inning, with Pete Rose on first, Joe Morgan grounds to first baseman John Milner. Rose, in an attempt to break up a double play, slides hard into Mets' shortstop Bud Harrelson, then pushes and grapples with him. Their actions trigger a dugout-clearing brawl, with both teams spilling out onto the field. Pedro Borbon and Lee "Buzz" Capra go at it. Rose becomes the target of a junk and bottle barrage. The Reds leave the field and the Mets' fans are warned of a possible forfeit. Seaver, Willie Mays, Cleon Jones, and Yogi Berra calm the crowd, and the game resumes. Rose says, "I'll be honest, I was trying to knock him into left field."

OCTOBER 9:

ALCS, game three. In Oakland today, Ken Holtzman outduels Mike Cuellar in an 11-inning classic won by the Athletics, 2-1, on a Bert Campaneris home run. Holtzman allows only three hits; Cuellar four.

NLCS, game four. The Reds tie the playoffs today on a Pete Rose homer in the 12th inning against losing pitcher Harry Parker for a 2-1 victory. Clay Carroll gets the win in relief; Pedro Borbon is credited with a save. Tony Perez homers in the seventh inning.

Pete Rose (left) and Bud Harrelson battle on the base paths in the NLCS.

OCTOBER 9
Game three of the ALCS between the A's and O's ends on an 11th-inning homer by the A's.

OCTOBER 21
The Athletics win the World Series, taking game seven from the Miracle Mets, 5-2.

OCTOBER 10:

NLCS, game five. The believing continues. Tom Seaver, with a save from Tug McGraw, tops the Reds, 7-2, and the Mets win the NL pennant. Jack Billingham is tagged with the loss. Once again the Mets flirt with a forfeit as fans come out onto the field on several occasions.

ALCS, game four. Bobby Grich of the Orioles homers in the eighth inning with no one on to give the Orioles a 5-4 win and knot the playoffs. Earlier, Andy Etchebarren hit a three-run round-tripper for Baltimore. Grant Jackson gets the win in relief. Rollie Fingers takes the loss.

OCTOBER 11:

ALCS, game five. Catfish Hunter's five-hit shutout beats the Orioles, 5-0, and gives Oakland its second straight AL pennant. Doyle Alexander is charged with the loss.

The Tigers sign Ralph Houk to a three-year managerial contract. He replaces interim manager Joe Schultz.

OCTOBER 13:

World Series, game one. The Fall Classic opens in Oakland with the Athletics beating the Mets, 2-1, on two unearned runs in the third inning. Felix Millan's misplay of a Bert Campaneris grounder scores Ken Holtzman, who had doubled, and Joe Rudi singles in the second run. The winning pitcher is Holtzman with a save by Darold Knowles. Jon Matlack is the losing pitcher.

OCTOBER 14:

World Series, game two. The Mets and Athletics use a record 11 pitchers before New York prevails, 10-7, in 12 innings, in Oakland. Two errors by second baseman Mike Andrews open the door for a four-run Mets rally. Willie Mays's single – his last major league hit – puts the Mets ahead. The winning pitcher is Tug McGraw; the loser, Rollie Fingers. Cleon Jones and Wayne Garrett hit homers for New York.

Mays apparently conned pitcher Rollie Fingers and catcher Ray Fosse into throwing him a fast-ball by pretending he couldn't see the first pitch – a slider.

OCTOBER 15:

Oakland A's owner Charles O. Finley tries to remove Mike Andrews from his World Series roster by putting him on the disabled list. Finley gets Andrews to sign a statement claiming he has an injured shoulder.

OCTOBER 16:

World Series, game three. Prior to today's Series game at Shea Stadium, Oakland Athletics' manager Dick Williams tells reporters he will not be returning in 1974. Oakland then goes on to beat the Mets, 3-2, in 11 innings on a Bert Campaneris RBI single against losing pitcher Harry Parker. Tom Seaver works eight strong innings, fanning 12. Paul Lindblad gets the win in relief duty. Wayne Garrett of the Mets has the game's only home run.

OCTOBER 17:

World Series, game four. Today at Shea Stadium, the Mets even the Series on strong pitching by Jon Matlack and Ray Sadecki in a 6-1 win. Rusty Staub hits a three-run homer and three singles, driving in five. Ken Holtzman, who lasts only a third of an inning, is the loser. In the eighth inning, Mike Andrews – reinstated by baseball Commissioner Bowie Kuhn – pinch hits for Horacio Pina. The New York crowd cheers him for three minutes and gives him another round of applause after he grounds out.

OCTOBER 18:

World Series, game five. Jerry Koosman and Tug McGraw limit the Athletics to only three hits, while the Mets make the most of their seven, in a 2-0 win in New York. Koosman gets the win; Vida Blue is the losing pitcher.

OCTOBER 20:

World Series, game six. The A's Catfish Hunter outpitches Tom Seaver for a 3-1 Oakland victory. Reggie Jackson doubles in the first and third innings for two RBI and scores once. Rollie Fingers retires the Mets in order in the ninth for a save.

OCTOBER 21:

World Series, game seven. Reggie Jackson and Bert Campaneris connect for two-run homers and the Athletics beat the Mets, 5-2, for their second straight World Championship. Ken Holtzman gets the win with a save from Darold Knowles, who becomes the first pitcher to appear in

HISTORY

At age 42, Willie Mays becomes the oldest player not pitching to appear in a World Series game.

OCTOBER 25
The San Francisco Giants trade first baseman Willie McCovey to the Padres.

DECEMBER 21
AL president Joe Cronin voids a deal for Dick Williams to manage the New York Yankees.

all seven games of a World Series. The losing pitcher is Jon Matlack. The A's Dick Williams makes it official after the game – he is quitting as Oakland's manager. Joe Rudi leads Oakland's hitters with a .333 average and four RBI; Reggie Jackson hits .310 and drives in six. Rollie Fingers (0.66, two saves) and Darold Knowles (0.00, two saves) dominate from the bullpen. Rusty Staub tops all hitters with .423 and six RBI.

POST-SEASON

OCTOBER 25:

The Rangers obtain pitcher Ferguson Jenkins (14-16, 3.89 ERA) from the Cubs for third baseman Bill "Mad Dog" Madlock (.351 in 21 games) and infielder Vic Harris (.249, eight homers).

The Giants trade away slugging first baseman Willie McCovey (.266, 29 home runs, 75 RBI) and outfielder Bernard Williams (.191, three homers in 46 games in 1972) to the Padres for pitcher Mike Caldwell (5-14, 3.74 ERA).

The Tigers release DH–first baseman Frank Howard (.256, 12 home runs in 85 games). It's the end of the trail for the six-foot, seven-inch Hondo, after 16 years in which he hit .273 with 382 homers and 1,119 RBI. With the Senators in 1968 and 1970, Howard led the AL in homers with 44. He hit .300 in the 1963 World Series with the Dodgers.

OCTOBER 26:

Red Sox outfielder Reggie Smith, who demanded a trade, gets his wish. Boston sends Smith (.303, 21 homers) and pitcher Ken Tatum (0-0, 9.00 ERA) to the Cardinals for pitcher Rick Wise (16-12, 3.37 ERA) and outfielder Bernie Carbo (.286, eight home runs). The Cardinals also acquire pitcher Wilfred "Sonny" Siebert (7-12, 4.06 ERA) from the Texas Rangers for outfielder Cirilio "Tommy" Cruz (three games, no at bats).

OCTOBER 28:

Athletics' owner Charles O. Finley is slapped with a $7,000 fine for his dealings with Mike Andrews after game two of the World Series.

NOVEMBER 3:

Pete Rose and Bud Harrelson are fined $250 each and Pedro Borbon $150 for their roles in the October 8 bench-clearing brawl that occured during the Mets-Reds playoff game at Shea Stadium.

DECEMBER 4:

Cubs' third baseman Ron Santo becomes the first player to refuse a trade under the new "ten and five" rule adopted February 25. Four veteran players – Jim Perry, Jim Kaat, Willie McCovey, and Dick McAuliffe – approved their trades.

DECEMBER 5:

Montreal gets outfielder Willie Davis (.285, 16 homers, 77 RBI, 17 stolen bases) from the Dodgers for relief pitcher Mike Marshall (14-11, 2.66 ERA, and an NL-leading 31 saves).

DECEMBER 7:

The Boston Red Sox have a busy day on the trade front. They buy pitcher Juan Marichal (11-15, 3.79 ERA) from the Giants for $100,000. And they ship pitchers John Curtis (13-13, 3.58 ERA), Lynn McGlothen (1-2, 8.22 ERA), and Mike Garman (0-0, 5.32 ERA) to the Cardinals for pitchers Reggie Cleveland (14-10, 3.01 ERA) and Diego Segui (7-6, 2.78 ERA, 17 saves), plus infielder Terry Hughes (.214 in 11 games). The Royals send outfielder Lou Piniella (.250, nine homers) and pitcher Ken Wright (6-5, 4.89 ERA) to the Yankees for pitcher Lindy McDaniel (12-6, 2.86 ERA, 10 saves).

DECEMBER 11:

Ron Santo, who previously vetoed a trade to the Angels, accepts a deal that sends him to the White Sox. In return for Santo (.267, 20 home runs, 77 RBI), the Cubs received pitchers Steve Stone (6-11, 4.24 ERA), Ken Frailing (0-0, 1.96 ERA), and Jim Kremmel (0-2, 9.00 ERA), plus minor league catcher Steve Swisher.

DECEMBER 18:

Dick Williams, who led the Athletics to World Series wins in 1972 and 1973, is signed as Yankees' manager. Williams leaves Oakland after problems with owner Charles O. Finley.

DECEMBER 21:

AL president Joe Cronin, finding Dick Williams is still legally bound to the A's, voids his new contract with the Yankees. He also determines that Ralph Houk is free to go to the Tigers.

THE BEST OF 1973

NATIONAL LEAGUE

HITTERS

Batting Average:
Pete Rose, Cincinnati Reds, .338

Slugging Average:
Willie Stargell, Pittsburgh Pirates, .646

Home Runs:
Willie Stargell, 44

Runs Batted In:
Willie Stargell, 119

Hits:
Pete Rose, 230

Stolen Bases:
Lou Brock, St. Louis Cardinals, 70

PITCHERS

Wins:
Ron Bryant, San Francisco Giants, 24

Strikeouts:
Tom Seaver, New York Mets, 251

Earned Run Average:
Tom Seaver, 2.08

Winning Percentage:
Tommy John, Los Angeles Dodgers, .696

Saves:
Mike Marshall, Montreal Expos, 31

Most Valuable Player:
Pete Rose, Cincinnati Reds

Cy Young Award:
Tom Seaver, New York Mets

Rookie of the Year:
Gary Matthews, San Francisco Giants

AMERICAN LEAGUE

HITTERS

Batting Average:
Rod Carew, Minnesota Twins, .350

Slugging Average:
Reggie Jackson, Oakland Athletics, .531

Home Runs:
Reggie Jackson, 32

Runs Batted In:
Reggie Jackson, 117

Hits:
Rod Carew, 203

Stolen Bases:
Tommy Harper, Boston Red Sox, 54

PITCHERS

Wins:
Wilbur Wood, Chicago White Sox, 24

Strikeouts:
Nolan Ryan, California Angels, 383

Earned Run Average:
Jim Palmer, Baltimore Orioles, 2.40

Winning Percentage:
Jim "Catfish" Hunter, Oakland Athletics, .808

Saves:
John Hiller, Detroit Tigers, 38

Most Valuable Player:
Reggie Jackson, Oakland Athletics

Cy Young Award:
Jim Palmer, Baltimore Orioles

Rookie of the Year:
Al Bumbry, Baltimore Orioles

CULTURE

Poet Lawrence Ferlinghetti publishes "Baseball Canto."

1974

Hank Aaron celebrates home run number 715.

NEWS

RICHARD NIXON RESIGNS IN WAKE OF WATERGATE SCANDAL AND POSSIBILITY OF IMPEACHMENT

Gerald Ford becomes president; names Nelson Rockefeller his vice president

FORD PARDONS NIXON

Patricia Hearst kidnapped

CIVIL WAR SHIP *MONITOR* FOUND OFF NORTH CAROLINA

Charles Lindbergh dies

Dreyfus offers money-market funds for small investors

CHRIS EVERT AND JIMMY CONNORS WIN AT WIMBLEDON

U.S. GOVERNMENT SETS NATIONAL SPEED LIMIT AT 55 MPH

Heimlich Maneuver developed

PRE-SEASON

JANUARY 1:

Lee MacPhail is the new AL president, replacing Joe Cronin, who retires after 15 years in office.

JANUARY 3:

Bill Virdon, who led the Pirates to the NL East title in 1972, is named manager of the Yankees.

JANUARY 25:

Ray Kroc, founder of McDonald's restaurants, buys the San Diego Padres from C. Arnholt Smith for $12 million. As a result of the purchase, the Padres will remain in San Diego instead of being moved to Washington, D.C.

FEBRUARY 11:

Twins' pitcher Dick Woodson becomes the first player to settle a salary dispute through the new binding arbitration process. Woodson, who was 10-8 last season and 32-29 in four years, seeks $29,000; the Twins offer $23,000. Harry H. Platt, a Detroit attorney, selects Woodson's figure. Woodson is one of 48 players to file for arbitration.

FEBRUARY 21:

The Mets' Tom Seaver signs a new contract for $172,500, becoming the highest paid player ever.

MARCH 11:

Commissioner Bowie Kuhn vetoes the Braves' plan to have Hank Aaron sit out the opening three-game series in Cincinnati so he can break Babe Ruth's career home run record at home in Atlanta. Kuhn insists Aaron must play in at least two games at Riverfront Stadium.

MARCH 19:

The Yankees, Tigers, and Indians complete a three-way trade. The Tigers get catcher Gerry Moses (.254 in 21 games). Going to the Yankees are outfielder Walt Williams (.289, eight homers), pitcher Ed Farmer (3-2, 4.91 ERA), and minor league pitcher Rick Sawyer. Pitcher Jim Perry (14-13, 4.03 ERA) joins his brother Gaylord in the Cleveland bullpen.

MARCH 26:

The Red Sox clean house. Orlando Cepeda (.289, 20 homers, 86 RBI), the first DH ever signed, veteran shortstop Luis Aparicio (.271), and pitcher Bobby Bolin (3-4, 2.72 ERA) all are released today. Aparicio, a classy fielder, finishes his 18-year career with a .262 average and 506 stolen bases.

THE SEASON

APRIL 4:

On his first swing of his season, Hank Aaron hits a 3-1 pitch from the Reds' Jack Billingham with Ralph Garr and Mike Lum on base for his 714th career homer, tying the all-time mark set by Babe Ruth. After his teammates come onto the field to congratulate him, Aaron goes into the stands to hug his wife Billye, and his father. The largest opening day crowd in Reds' history – 52,124 – packs Riverfront Stadium to see Aaron make history. The Reds win the game, 7-6, on a Pete Rose double in the 11th with two out.

APRIL 5:

Former major league outfielder Fred Snodgrass dies in Ventura, California, at age 86. Snodgrass, like many others, is remembered for a misplay despite a solid career. In the 1912 World Series playing for the Giants, he dropped a

small caption to go here
small caption

APRIL 8
In Atlanta, Hank Aaron hits his 715th career home run, breaking Babe Ruth's record.

HISTORY

Charles O. Finley signs record-holding sprinter Herb Washington as a "designated runner." Washington, who has not played baseball since high school, will be used exclusively as a pinch runner. Washington appears in 92 games in 1974 without batting; he steals 29 bases and scores 29 times.

fly ball, opening the door for a Red Sox rally. Largely forgotten is the outstanding catch he made on the next play. In nine years Snodgrass batted .275 – with a high of .321 in 1910 – and stole 215 bases.

APRIL 6:

After 51 consecutive opening days at Yankee Stadium, the Yankees' "home" opener takes place at Shea Stadium with a crowd of 20,744 on hand. Graig Nettles hits a two-run homer and Mel Stottlemyre pitches New York to a 6-1 victory.

APRIL 8:

At Fulton County Stadium in Atlanta, a crowd of 53,775 anticipates it will see history made tonight. After walking in his first at-bat, Hank Aaron steps in to face the Dodgers' left-hander Al Downing in the fourth inning with two out and Darrell Evans on base. He connects on a 1-0 pitch and sends it into the left centerfield bullpen for his 715th home run. Aaron breaks the "unbreakable" record – surpassing Babe Ruth's 714 lifetime home runs. Atlanta sportscaster Milo Hamilton makes the call: "That ball is gonna beee – OUTA HERE! IT'S GONE! IT'S 715! There's a new home run champion of all time! And it's Henry Aaron!" With skyrockets bursting in the background, Aaron is hugged by his teammates. Atlanta relief pitcher Tom House, who caught the ball in the bullpen, hands it to him, saying, "Hammer, here it is!" The scoreboard flashes: "715. You were there. You fans here at Atlanta Stadium have just witnessed the great, if not the greatest, moment in recorded sports history." Lost in the celebration is the fact that Aaron has just scored his 2,063rd run – tying Willie Mays's NL record. The Braves win the game, 7-4.

HENRY AARON OBSERVES: "BABE RUTH WILL ALWAYS BE NUMBER ONE. BEFORE I BROKE HIS HOME RUN RECORD, IT WAS THE GREATEST OF ALL. THEN I BROKE IT AND SUDDENLY THE GREATEST RECORD IS JOE DIMAGGIO'S HITTING STREAK."

A notable absence from the game in Atlanta is baseball Commissioner Bowie Kuhn, who is in Cleveland for the Indians' opening day against Milwaukee and a speach at the Wahoo Club. That game is snowed out. In his autobiography, Aaron notes that Kuhn was not in Cincinnati in 1972 for his 3,000th hit and did not send him a congratulatory telegram for his 700th homer.

APRIL 9:

On opening day in San Diego, a crowd of 39,083 is watching the Padres get mauled by the Astros, 9-2 in the eighth inning. Ray Kroc, who has owned the team for four games, doesn't like what he sees. He takes over the public address microphone and tells the crowd, "Ladies and gentlemen, I suffer with you." At that point a streaker dashes onto the field, interrupting Kroc, who says, "Throw him in jail." Then he continues, "I've never seen such stupid baseball in my life." Later, he adds, "The streaker just added gas to the fire." Kroc has cause for despair; the Padres previously lost 8-0, 8-0, and 9-2 to the Dodgers.

APRIL 26:

The record-breaking is not over for Henry Aaron. Today he hits his 15th career grand slam home run, passing Gil Hodges and Willie McCovey for the NL mark. The Braves go on to beat the Cubs, 9-3.

APRIL 27:

The Yankees trade family-swapper Fred "Fritz" Peterson (0-0) and three other pitchers – Steve Kline (2-2), Fred Beene (0-0), and Tom Buskey (0-1) to the Indians. In return, New York gets first baseman Chris

JUNE 1
The Dodgers' Ron Cey drives in seven runs in a 10-0 victory over the Cubs at Wrigley Field.

Chambliss (.328 in 17 games) plus pitchers Dick "Dirt" Tidrow (1-3) and Cecil Upshaw (0-1).

APRIL 30:

At Fenway Park, Nolan Ryan of the Angels strikes out 19 Red Sox batters in nine innings in a 4-2 victory. In a frightening moment, he hits second baseman Doug Griffin in the head with his fastball. Griffin will be sidelined for two months.

MAY 1:

The Dodgers beat the Mets, 2-1, in 14 innings, despite a heroic effort by Tom Seaver. In 12 innings, Seaver yields only three hits and strikes out 16. Steve Garvey drives in the winning run for Los Angeles off Harry Parker in the 14th inning.

Tom Seaver's style is described in The Sporting News Selects Baseball's Greatest Players: *"Seaver literally exploded off the mound, driving hard toward the hitter with powerful legs and a well-muscled, 210-pound body. He looked like a locomotive bursting from a tunnel. The delivery was compact and so low that Seaver's right leg would drag the ground during his follow-through. He was overpowering, a strikeout pitcher who...topped 200 strikeouts in nine consecutive seasons. But he also was a craftsman who would set up hitters with different-speed fastballs and other well-placed off-speed pitches."*

MAY 29:

An investment group headed by Bradford G. Corbett buys the Texas Rangers from Robert E. Short.

JUNE 1:

Ron Cey homers in the second inning and drives in seven runs in a 10-0 Dodger victory over the Cubs in Wrigley Field. Los Angeles third base coach Tommy Lasorda is miked for NBC's *Game of the Week* and the audience hears him call Cey's home run.

The always loquacious Lasorda once said of his upbeat coaching style: "I motivate players through communication...I started in the minor leagues. I used to hug my players when they did something well. That's my enthusiasm. That's my personality. I jump with joy when we win."

"THEY EXPECT AN UMPIRE TO BE PERFECT ON OPENING DAY AND TO IMPROVE AS THE SEASON GOES ON."

– Umpire Nestor Chylak

Tom Seaver said of Nolan Ryan in his 1992 book, Great Moments in Baseball, *written with Marty Appel: "...I suspect that there will be no problem filling up his plaque in Cooperstown five years after he retires. He has simply been one of the most remarkable American athletes ever, at the end of his career seemingly reaching immortal status, right there with Cy Young, Christy Mathewson, Walter Johnson, Lefty Grove, Bob Feller, Warren Spahn, and Sandy Koufax." Indeed, Ryan was inducted into the Hall of Fame in 1999 – his first year of eligibility.*

Reggie is summed up in The Sporting News Selects Baseball's Greatest Players: *"He was charming and belligerent; cocky and self-effacing; articulate and crude; enigmatic and straightforward. You didn't just watch Reggie Jackson, you experienced him. The love/hate bond that fans, players, and owners formed with the complex, often-contradictory kid from Wyncote, Pa., lasted 21 years, surviving 563 home runs and at least that many well-publicized tantrums.... The bot-*

HISTORY

To avoid the circulation of fraudulent baseballs after Hank Aaron breaks Babe Ruth's record, an ingenious marking system has been in use since homer number 710. Each authentic ball has a set of numbers and a diamond that can be seen only under fluorescent light.

JUNE 5
Hank Aaron hits his 16th career grand slam homer as the Braves beat the Phillies, 7-3.

CULTURE

A television biography of Roy Campanella, *It's Good to Be Alive*, stars Paul Winfield and Ruby Dee as his wife, Ruthie.

tom line on Jackson was drama – and emotion, which he kept up front for all the paying customers to see."

JUNE 5:

Henry Aaron hits his 16th career grand slam homer as the Braves top the Phillies, 7-3, in Philadelphia.

Athletics' teammates Reggie Jackson and Billy North slug it out, but the principal casualty is catcher Ray Fosse. Attempting to be the peacemaker, Fosse incurs a crushed disc in his neck, which requires surgery, and will miss the rest of the season.

JUNE 7:

A faulty popcorn machine causes a fire in right field at Comiskey Park. Fans evacuate onto the field and the game with the Red Sox is delayed more than an hour. When play resumes, Chicago beats Boston, 8-6, on a Dick Allen homer.

JUNE 10:

Mike Schmidt of the Phillies hits a first-inning pitch from Claude Osteen off the public address speaker in the Astrodome, 117 feet above the playing surface and more than 300 feet from home plate. Under the ground rules, the ball is in play. Neither Larry Bowa nor Dave Cash, who were on base, score, and Schmidt gets credit for a single.

JUNE 12:

Little League Baseball announces that girls are now allowed to participate.

JUNE 14:

Nolan Ryan fans 19 Red Sox batters in 12 innings of work; he gets Cecil Cooper six straight times. Denny Doyle's RBI double in the 15th inning off Luis Tiant gives the Angels a 4-3 win.

JUNE 18:

In Baltimore, the Orioles' Bobby Grich hits three consecutive home runs in a 10-1 victory over the Twins. Ross Grimsley is the winning pitcher.

JUNE 19:

Kansas City's Steve Busby no-hits the Milwaukee Brewers, 2-0, in Milwaukee. It is Busby's second no-hit game in 14 months. He strikes out three and issues a second inning walk to George Scott – the Brewers' only runner. The losing pitcher is Clyde Wright.

JIM MURRAY WRITES IN THE *LOS ANGELES TIMES*: "WELL, WE'RE ALL 120 YEARS OLDER TODAY. DIZZY DEAN IS DEAD AND 1934 IS GONE FOREVER. ANOTHER PART OF OUR YOUTH HAS FLED... DIZZY DIED THE OTHER DAY AT THE AGE OF 11 OR 12. THE LITTLE BOY IN ALL OF US DIED WITH HIM... DIZZY DEAN. IT'S IMPOSSIBLE TO SAY WITHOUT A SMILE. BUT, THEN, WHO WANTS TO TRY? IF I KNOW DIZ, HE'LL BE CALLING GOD 'PODNER' SOMEPLACE TODAY... HE MIGHT HAVE BEEN WHAT BASEBALL'S ALL ABOUT."

JUNE 29
Lou Brock gets his 700th career stolen base as the Cardinals beat the Cubs, 11-2.

JULY 17
Cardinals' ace Bob Gibson records his 3,000th career strikeout.

JUNE 20:

At Wrigley Field, Rick Reuschel of the Cubs puts runners on base in every inning, but manages a 12-hit shutout, beating the Pirates, 3-0.

JUNE 27:

In Cleveland, the Indians' Jim Perry wins the 200th game of his career with a 2-1 victory over the Indians.

JUNE 29:

At Wrigley Field, Lou Brock gets his 700th career stolen base in the first inning today against the Cubs. It also is his 65th of the season. Brock is in select company; the only other players with 700 or more stolen bases are Ty Cobb (892), Eddie Collins (743), Max Carey (738), and Honus Wagner (701). The Cardinals beat the Cubs, 11-2.

JULY 1:

After going 2-2, interim manager Whitey Herzog – who has replaced fired Bobby Winkles – hands over the managerial reins of the Angels to Dick Williams, who led the Athletics to two consecutive World Series championships.

JULY 8:

In Oakland, the Indians' Gaylord Perry seeks his 16th consecutive victory to tie an AL record. Opposing him is Vida Blue. In the 10th inning with the score tied 3-3, Claudell Washington defeats Perry and Cleveland with a triple.

Yankees' shortstop Jim Mason hits four doubles, tying a major league record, as New York beats the Rangers, 12-5, in Texas today.

JULY 16:

Texas manager Billy Martin is fined and suspended for ordering his pitchers to throw at Brewers' batters. Martin defends his action, calling it a retaliation against Milwaukee for throwing at Toby Harrah. He states, "I had to protect him to keep peace in the family."

JULY 17:

In St. Louis, Bob Gibson fans Cesar Geronimo of the Reds in the second inning for his 3,000th career strikeout. Baseball Hall of Famer Walter Johnson is the only other pitcher with 3,000 strikeouts. The Reds win, 6-4.

On the same day that a current great Cardinals' right-hander is setting a career landmark, a past hero of St. Louis baseball is passing on. Hall of Fame pitcher, one-of-a-kind sportscaster, and all-around colorful character Dizzy Dean dies at age 64 in Reno, Nevada, after suffering a heart attack. Dean pitched for 12 years, compiling a 150-83 record, with a 3.02 ERA. In 1934, he was 30-7 with a 2.66 ERA. He won two games for the Cardinals in the 1934 World Series and he pitched for the Cubs in the 1938 Fall Classic.

JULY 19:

Dick Bosman of the Indians no-hits the Athletics, 4-0, in Cleveland. Bosman, who fans four, loses a perfect game on his own throwing error in the fourth inning. Dave Hamilton is the game's losing pitcher.

JULY 20:

On Hank Aaron Day in Atlanta, he plays in his 3,034th game, tying him with Ty Cobb for the most ever. The Braves lose, 7-6, in 11 innings.

JULY 23:

In Pittsburgh, the NL tops the AL, 7-2, for its 11th victory in the last dozen All-Star Games. Reggie Smith homers and Steve Garvey has a double and single for the NL. Ken Brett gets the win; Luis Tiant is charged with the loss. Baltimore Orioles' third baseman Brooks Robinson, normally a winner, sets a record by appearing on the losing team 15 times in All-Star play.

JULY 25:

Carl Yastrzemski homers against the Tigers' Mickey Lolich; it is the 300th of Yaz's career.

JULY 29:

The Tigers bomb the Indians' Fritz Peterson in the first inning with consecutive home runs by Al Kaline, Bill Freehan, and Mickey Stanley. Ralph Houk brings Steve Kline out of the bullpen, but before the inning is over he serves up a home run to Ed Brinkman. The Tigers win the game, 8-2.

In San Diego, Henry Aaron hits his 727th and 728th career homers in a 5-2 win over the Padres. It is the 62nd time Aaron has hit two round-trippers in a game and the pair are his 14th and 15th of the season. The 29 score-

TRIVIA

"Hey Hank I Know You're Gonna Do It," a song about Hank Aaron, written by Mark Barkan and Donald Oriolo, is recorded by Pirates' pitcher Nelson Briles.

AUGUST 12
Angels' fireballer Nolan Ryan strikes out 19 Red Sox, tying the major league record.

Lou Brock had 938 career stolen bases.

less innings string by Braves' pitchers is ended when the Padres score two runs against Phil Niekro in the ninth frame.

AUGUST 7:

The Tigers send two longtime stalwarts packing. Outfielder Jim Northrup (.237 in 97 games) is sold to the Expos. First baseman Norm Cash (.228, seven home runs in 53 games) is released, ending his career. In 17 years, Cash won an AL batting title and compiled a lifetime average of .271 with 377 homers.

AUGUST 12:

The Hall of Fame inducts James "Cool Papa" Bell, Sunny Jim Bottomley, umpire John "Jocko" Conlan, Ed "Whitey" Ford, Mickey Mantle, and Samuel Thompson. Bell, known for his blazing speed, reportedly once stole 175 bases in a season. He spent 20 years in the Negro Leagues, playing some 940 games and batting .337. In 1951, at the age of 48, he was offered a contract with the St. Louis Browns but declined. Bottomley, who died in 1959, played for 16 years, hitting .310 with 219 homers. The first baseman batted .371 in 1923 and hit .300 or better eight other times. Conlan was an NL umpire from 1941 to 1965. Ford, a left-hander, known as The Chairman of the Board, pitched for 16 years, compiling a 236-106 record with an ERA of 2.75 and 45 shutouts. In 11 World Series, he was 10-8 with a 2.71 ERA. Mantle, Ford's teammate and close friend, combined power and speed but consistently was hampered by serious injuries. In 18 years, he batted .298

SEPTEMBER 10
Lou Brock sets a new major league record with his 105th stolen base of the season.

with 536 homers and 1,509 RBI. He was the AL's Triple Crown winner in 1956 and hit 18 home runs in 12 World Series. Thompson, who died in 1922, was an outfielder who played 15 years and batted .331. In 1894, he hit .404 and topped .300 eight times. He led the NL with a .372 average in 1887 with the Detroit Wolverines.

Cool Papa Bell says at his Hall of Fame induction, "There were a lot of great ones in the Negro Leagues. We – Satchel, Irvin, Campy, Leonard, and myself – were the lucky ones. I'm thanking God for letting me smell the roses while I'm still living."

The Angels' Nolan Ryan fans 19 Red Sox in a 4-2 victory in Anaheim. In nine innings, Ryan allows seven hits and two walks. His 19 strikeouts equal the major league mark set by Steve Carlton in 1969 and Tom Seaver in 1970 and break Bob Feller's 1938 AL record of 18. He also ties the major league record for strikeouts in two consecutive games – 32 – set by Luis Tiant. Ryan now has 15 wins and 260 strikeouts.

AUGUST 20:

Nolan Ryan's fastball is clocked by infrared radar at 100.9 miles per hour on two pitches to Ron LeFlore. Bob Feller threw the previously fastest timed pitch – 98.6 in 1946. Ryan fans 19 Tigers in 11 innings, but his pitching heroics are in vain; Detroit and Mickey Lolich win, 1-0.

Davey Lopes puts up big numbers at Wrigley Field. The Dodger second baseman collects 15 total bases on three home runs, a double, and a single to lead Los Angeles over the Cubs, 18-8. The Dodgers as a team have 48 total bases.

AUGUST 24:

Four days ago it was his bat; today it is his legs. The Dodgers' Davey Lopes steals five bases against the Cardinals, tying an NL record set by Dan McGann of the New York Giants in 1904. Don Sutton beats St. Louis, 3-0.

AUGUST 27:

At Shea Stadium, the Mets' Benny Ayala homers against the Astros' Tom Griffin in his first major league at-bat. He is the first NLer in 13 years to debut with a round-tripper. The Mets win, 4-2.

SEPTEMBER 1:

For the fourth time in his career, the Cardinals' Lou Brock steals four bases in a game. Today's thefts – against the Giants in San Francisco – are his 95th, 96th, 97th, and 98th of the season. The Cardinals win the game, 8-1.

Oakland's Gene Tenace ties a 1930 record set by John "Bud" Clancy of the White Sox by playing nine innings at first base without having a fielding chance.

SEPTEMBER 10:

In St. Louis, Lou Brock singles in the seventh inning against the Phillies' Dick Ruthven and, after one pitch and two pickoff attempts, steals second, beating catcher Bob Boone's throw. It is his record-breaking 105th stolen base of the season. Both teams come out to second base to congratulate Brock in an 11-minute celebration. Brock had stolen his 104th base in the first inning. The Phillies go on to beat the Cardinals, 8-2, with Ruthven getting the win. Mike Schmidt hits his 35th homer.

HALL OF FAME PITCHER SATCHEL PAIGE ON COOL PAPA BELL'S SPEED: "ONE DAY, WHEN I WAS PITCHIN' TO COOL, HE DRILLED ONE RIGHT THROUGH MY LEGS AND WAS HIT IN THE BACK BY HIS OWN GROUND BALL WHEN HE SLID INTO SECOND." WHEN HE WAS IN HIS 40S, BELL PLAYED AN EXHIBITION GAME AGAINST A TEAM OF MAJOR LEAGUERS – INCLUDING PITCHER BOB LEMON AND CATCHER ROY PARTEE OF THE INDIANS – AND SCORED FROM FIRST BASE ON A SACRIFICE BUNT.

SEPTEMBER 12
The Cardinals beat the Mets, 4-3, in a 25-inning game that began the night before.

SEPTEMBER 28
Nolan Ryan notches his third career no-hitter in a 4-0 Angels win over the Twins.

SEPTEMBER 12:

The Mets and the Cardinals conclude a game at 3:13 this morning that began last night at 8 p.m, with St. Louis winning it, 4-3, in 25 innings. The winning run scores when Mets' pitcher Hank Webb commits a throwing error and Arnold "Bake" McBride scores from first base. Attendance at the start was 13,460 but only 1,500 remained for the finish. The teams use 50 players, including 13 pitchers. The winning pitcher is Wilfred "Sonny" Siebert; Webb gets the loss.

Outfielder Frank Robinson (.251 in 129 games) is traded by the Angels to the Indians. California receives catcher Ken Suarez (.248 in 93 games in 1973) and outfielder Rosendo "Rusty" Torres (.187 in 108 games).
In Detroit, the Tigers' John Hiller picks up his 17th win of the season – all out of the bullpen, breaking Dick Radatz' 1964 record. Tom Veryzer homers into the left-field upper deck off Tom Murphy of the Brewers for a 9-7 victory in 10 innings.

SEPTEMBER 13:

With 16 games left to play, Dick Allen of the White Sox announces he is retiring. Allen has been playing with a bad shoulder and back and hit only .214 over the last three weeks.

Rumors have persisted through the years that Allen was really trying to force a trade. Former Chicago general manager Roland Hemond told baseball historian Craig R. Wright it was not the case: "He was very sincere about retiring."

SEPTEMBER 15:

In Baltimore, Gaylord Perry of the Indians celebrates his 36th birthday by blowing away the Orioles, 1-0, for his 20th win of the season. Ross Grimsley gets the loss.

SEPTEMBER 17:

Lou Brock continues to run almost at will against NL pitchers and catchers. Today, against the Pirates in Pittsburgh, he steals his 109th base of the season. In the September 20 issue of *The Christian Science Monitor,* Reggie Jackson says, "When you've played this game for 10 years, gone to bat 7,000 times and gotten 2,000 hits, do you know what that really means? It mean you've gone zero for 5,000!"

LOU BROCK, ON THE MINDSET OF A BASE STEALER: "YOU KNOW YOU'RE ALWAYS ON THE VERGE OF DISASTER...IF YOU'RE THROWN OUT, YOU COULD BE WIPING OUT A POTENTIAL RALLY. BUT YOU HAVE TO FIGURE THAT YOU'LL STEAL FOUR OUT OF FIVE TIMES. AND IF THEY CATCH YOU, WELL THEN THEY OWE YOU FOUR."

SEPTEMBER 24:

At Memorial Stadium in his hometown of Baltimore, the Tigers' Al Kaline doubles down the right-field line off Dave McNally in the fourth inning for his 3,000th career hit. Kaline is the 12th player to reach the 3,000 level. Baltimore beats Detroit, 5-4.

SEPTEMBER 25:

The Dodgers' Tommy John undergoes revolutionary surgery on his pitching arm after rupturing a ligament during a July 17 game against the Expos. Dr. Frank Jobe takes a tendon from John's right arm and transplants it into his left. John was 13-3 at the time of his injury.

SEPTEMBER 27:

There's turmoil in the Cleveland clubhouse. Frank Robinson and Gaylord Perry confront each other over a story in which the pitcher is quoted as saying he deserves more money than Robinson. And then Indians' manager Ken Aspromonte tells his team he will not be returning next season.

SEPTEMBER 28:

The Angels' Nolan Ryan no-hits the Twins, 4-0, today at

OCTOBER 3
Frank Robinson becomes the major leagues' first African-American manager.

Anaheim. He is the sixth pitcher in history with three career no-hitters; the others are Sandy Koufax – who has four – Bob Feller, Jim Maloney, Larry Corcoran, and Cy Young. Ryan walks eight and fans 15, bringing his season's strikeout total to 367. He also improves his won-lost mark to 22-16. The losing pitcher is Joe Decker.

The Dodgers' Andy Messersmith beats the Padres for his 209th win of the season. He is the 14th pitcher in history to win 20 in each league.

SEPTEMBER 29:

Only the end of the season stops Lou Brock. The Cardinal speedster steals his 118th – and final – base of the year in a 7-5 win against the Cubs in Chicago.

OCTOBER 1:

The Dodgers beat the Astros, 8-5, behind Don Sutton to win the NL West. Sutton picks up his 19th win and pitcher Mike Marshall appears in his major league record 106th game.

OCTOBER 2:

Tigers' outfielder Al Kaline announces his retirement. Baseball's quiet superstar played 22 years – all with Detroit – appearing in 2,834 games, batting .297 with 3,007 hits and 399 homers. He appeared in one World Series, in 1968, batting .379.

With the NL East at stake for the Pirates, they go into the ninth inning trailing the Cubs, 4-2. With Manny Sanguillen on third base, Rick Reuschel pitching, and pinch hitter Bob Robertson at bat, a third strike gets by catcher Steve Swisher. His throw then hits Robertson, allowing Sanguillen to score the tying run, putting the game into extra innings. Later in the game, Sanguillen's slow roller to third baseman Bill Madlock scores Al Oliver, and the Pirates capture the NL East flag.

In what will be his last NL at-bat, Henry Aaron homers off Rawly Eastwick of the Reds. It is his 733rd career homer and his 3,600th hit. Atlanta wins the game, 13-0.

OCTOBER 3:

Another barrier falls. Twenty-seven years after Jackie Robinson debuted with the Dodgers, baseball has its first African-American manager. Frank Robinson is signed to a one-year, $175,000 contract by the Indians. The announcement is made by general manager Phil Seghi at a press conference held at Municipal Stadium. Seghi reads a congratulatory telegram from President Gerald Ford. In attendance are Commissioner Bowie Kuhn and AL president Lee MacPhail. Kuhn says, "We got something done that we should have done before." Robinson replaces Ken Aspromonte, who led Cleveland to a 77-85 record and a fourth-place finish in the AL East last year. The 39-year-old Robinson expects to play next season and becomes the team's ninth player-manager and its 28th skipper.

Frank Robinson says, "If I had one wish in the world today, it would be that Jackie Robinson could be here to see this happen."

REGULAR SEASON WRAP-UP:

New manager Alvin Dark leads the Athletics to their third straight World Series. Oakland, 90-72 in the regular season in the AL, has no .300 hitter among its regulars but plenty of power. Reggie Jackson hits .289 with 29 homers and 93 RBI. Gene Tenace (.211, 26 home runs, 73 RBI), Sal Bando (.243, 22 homers, 103 RBI), and Joe Rudi (.293, 22 home runs, 99 RBI) are the team's other main long-ball threats. Catfish Hunter is 25-12. Rollie Fingers appears in 76 games and has 18 saves.

Under Walter Alston, the Dodgers go 102-60. Steve Garvey is the team leader with a .312 average, 21 homers, and 111 RBI. Bill Buckner bats .314. Jimmy Wynn has 32 homers and 108 RBI; Ron Cey has 18 home runs. Andy Messersmith has a 20-6 record and a 2.59 ERA. Mike Marshall pitches in 106 games and has 15 wins and 21 saves.

Two outstanding Red Sox rookies – Fred Lynn (.419, two homers in 15 games) and Jim Rice (.269, one homer in 24 games) – make their major league debuts this season. Lynn will be named MVP and Rookie of the Year.

OCTOBER 5:

NLCS, game one. Don Sutton four-hits the Pirates at Three Rivers Stadium and Jimmy Wynn, Joe

Says Hank Aaron: "I don't want them to forget Babe Ruth. I just want them to remember me."

TRIVIA

Four of the five games in the 1974 World Series end in 3-2 scores.

Ferguson, and Davey Lopes drive in the runs in a 3-2 Dodger victory. The losing pitcher is Jerry Reuss.

ALCS, game one. Mike Cuellar scatters nine hits and Paul Blair, Brooks Robinson, and Bobby Grich each hit home runs to give Baltimore a 6-3 win over the Athletics in Oakland. Catfish Hunter gets the loss.

OCTOBER 6:

NLCS, game two. The Dodgers make it two in a row in Pittsburgh, with a 5-2 win. Ron Cey is the big gun with a home run, two doubles, and a single. Andy Messersmith gets the win with two innings of relief from Mike Marshall. Dave Giusti is tagged with the game's loss.

ALCS, game two. Ken Holtzman five-hits the Orioles, 5-0, to even the playoffs. Holtzman gets offensive support from Ray Fosse with a three-run homer and Sal Bando with a solo round-tripper. Dave McNally gets the loss.

OCTOBER 8:

NLCS, game three. The Pirates stay alive as Bruce Kison and Ramon Hernandez combine to shut out the Dodgers, 7-0, in Los Angeles. Richie Hebner homers with one on and Willie Stargell connects for a three-run round-tripper. The losing pitcher is Doug Rau.

ALCS, game three. The scene shifts to Baltimore, where Vida Blue out duels Jim Palmer, allowing only two hits in a 1-0 Oakland victory. Sal Bando homers for the game's lone run. Blue strikes out seven and walks none. Palmer allows only four hits, but gets the loss.

OCTOBER 9:

NLCS, game four. The Dodgers win the NL pennant today with a 12-1 thumping of the Pirates in Los Angeles. The Dodgers bang out 12 hits – including two home runs by Steve Garvey, who bats in four runs. Willie Stargell homers for Pittsburgh's only score. Don Sutton gets the win; Jerry Reuss is the game's losing pitcher.

ALCS, game four. The Athletics edge the Orioles, 2-1, today in Baltimore, to win the AL pennant. Oakland has only one hit, but Orioles' pitchers issue 11 walks – nine by Mike Cuellar. Reggie Jackson doubles in Sal Bando in the seventh for the victory. Catfish Hunter gets the win; Cuellar is charged with the loss.

OCTOBER 12:

World Series, game one. The All-West Coast Series opens in Los Angeles, with the Athletics beating the Dodgers, 3-2, on a second-inning home run off the bat of Reggie Jackson. Rollie Fingers gets the win in relief of Ken Holtzman; Andy Messersmith is charged with the loss. Jimmy Wynn homers for the Dodgers.

OCTOBER 13:

World Series, game two. Los Angeles pitchers Don Sutton and Mike Marshall combine to limit the Oakland Athletics' batters to six hits in a 3-2 Dodgers' victory. Sutton gets the win, Marshall a save. Vida Blue gets the loss, yielding six hits, including a two-run home run hit by Joe Ferguson in the game's sixth inning.

Hall of Fame outfielder Edgar "Sam" Rice dies in Rossmor, Maryland, at age 84. Inducted into the Hall of Fame in 1963, Rice played 20 years – 19 with the Senators – batting .322. He hit .300 or better in 14 full seasons, with a high of .350. He played in three World Series. In game three in 1925 he made a controversial catch on the Pirate's Earl Smith.

The Mets acquire first baseman-third baseman Joe Torre (.282, 11 homers) from the Cardinals for pitchers Ray Sadecki (8-8, 3.48 ERA) and Tommy Moore (0-1, 10.80 ERA in 1973.)

OCTOBER 15:

World Series, game three. Despite solo homers by Bill Buckner and Willie Crawford of the Dodgers, the Athletics win, 3-2, in Oakland. Catfish Hunter gets the win with a save by Rollie Fingers. Al Downing is the loser.

OCTOBER 16:

World Series, game four. Ken Holtzman homers and pitches seven and two-thirds strong innings to get the win in a 5-2 victory over the Dodgers in Oakland. Rollie Fingers gets a save. The losing pitcher is Andy Messersmith. Jim Holt has a pinch-hit two-run single.

OCTOBER 17:

World Series, game five. The Athletics beat the Dodgers, 3-2, on Joe Rudi's seventh inning home run

OCTOBER 17
The A's take game five of the World Series from the Dodgers to win the Championship.

NOVEMBER 2
Hank Aaron and Japan's homer king Sadaharu Oh begin a home run contest in Tokyo.

to win the World Championship. Ray Fosse had homered earlier. The winning pitcher is Johnny "Blue Moon" Odom. Mike Marshall gets the loss. Rollie Fingers has three saves and a win. Bert Campaneris is Oakland's top hitter with .353; Joe Rudi has a homer and four RBI to go with his .333 average. Steve Garvey tops all hitters with a .381 average.

POST-SEASON

OCTOBER 22:

The Yankees and Giants swap outfielders in what is reportedly the first ever one-for-one trade of $100,000 players. Going to San Francisco is Bobby Murcer (.274, 10 homers, 88 RBI). New York receives Bobby Bonds (.256, 21 homers, 71 RBI, 41 stolen bases).

OCTOBER 23:

The Cubs trade their longtime outfield star Billy Williams (.280, 16 homers) to the Athletics for second baseman Manny Trillo (.152 in 21 games) and pitchers Darold Knowles (3-3, 4.25 ERA) and Bob Locker (10-6, 2.55 ERA in 1973).

NOVEMBER 2:

Henry Aaron meets Japanese home run champion Sadaharu Oh in a contest in Korakuen Stadium in Tokyo. Each player is given 20 swings against the pitching of Mets' coach Joe Pignatano. Oh hits nine into the seats. Aaron, batting without spiked shoes, hits 10 on 18 swings and skips the final two.

NOVEMBER 6:

The contents of a letter written on July 26, 1965, by the late Sam Rice to Paul S. Kerr, president of the Hall of Fame, are revealed today. The handwritten letter, to be opened only after Rice's death, concerns his controversial catch in the 1925 World Series. It reads: "It was a cold and windy day – the rightfield bleachers were crowded with people in overcoats and wrapped in blankets, the ball was a line drive headed for the bleachers toward right center. I turned slightly to my right and had the ball in view all the way, going at top speed and about 15 feet from the bleachers jumped as high as I could and back handed and the ball hit the center of the pocket in glove (I had a death grip on it). I hit the ground about five feet from the barrier about four feet high in front of the bleachers with all the brakes on but couldn't stop so I tried to jump it to land in the crowd but my feet hit the barrier about a foot from top and I toppled over on my stomach into first row of bleachers. I hit my Adam's apple on something, which sort of knocked me out for a few seconds, but McNeely arrived about that time and grabbed me by the shirt and pulled me out. I remember trotting back towards the infield still carrying the ball for about halfway and then tossed it toward the pitcher's mound. (How I have wished many times I had kept it.) At no time did I lose possession of the ball." It is signed "Sam" Rice.

NOVEMBER 10:

Today Norman E. Budesheim, a resident of Silver Spring, Maryland, who, as a 17-year-old, was in the first row of the bleachers when Sam Rice made his controversial catch, writes to Paul Kerr of the Hall of Fame with his account of the event: "I caught Sam full across the chest and arms as did my friend. When Sam went out of the park he had the ball in his glove definitely. However, upon hitting us, he definitely dropped the ball. I wish to emphasize he rolled off our laps and was flat on the ground in the tight space between our legs and feet and the barrier and I frantically trying to get the ball – me to give it to him and he to get it himself naturally... Sam beat me to the ball. When Sam says 'at no time did I lose possession of the ball,' he is generally and literally correct, in that I never got it and he had it under control so to speak but not necessarily in his glove without interruption."

Walter Johnson biographer Jack Kavanagh concludes that the letter "verified Sam Rice's account and accepted the truth as deemed by the outfielder."

Ben Paschal, who had batted for both Babe Ruth and Lou Gehrig, dies at age 79 in Charlotte, North Carolina. An outfielder with a .309 lifetime average in his eight-year career, Paschal hit for Ruth on April 12, 1927, after Ruth fanned twice and took ill. Paschal singled against the Athletics' Lefty Grove in an 8-3 Yankees' opening day win. He pinch-hit

LEAGUE

While Aaron is in Japan, the Braves trade him – home run record and all – to the Brewers at his own request. Aaron wants to play for Milwaukee so he can become a DH and limit outfield play on his 40-year-old legs. In return, the Braves get outfielder Dave May (.226, 10 homers) and minor league pitcher Roger Alexander. Aaron hit .268 with 20 home runs and 69 RBI this past season.

DECEMBER 3
Dick Allen is traded from the Chicago White Sox to the Atlanta Braves.

DECEMBER 31
A's ace Catfish Hunter, earlier declared a free agent, signs a deal with the Yankees.

three times for Lou Gehrig in 1925. He struck out on June 18, sacrificed on June 23, and grounded out on August 2.

NOVEMBER 28:

George Steinbrenner is benched for two years. Commissioner Bowie Kuhn suspends the principal owner of the Yankees after Steinbrenner is convicted in federal court of making illegal contributions to the reelection campaign of Richard Nixon.

DECEMBER 3:

Dick Allen (.301, 32 homers, 88 RBI) is traded by the White Sox to the Braves for a player to be named later and cash.

On May 15, 1975, Jim Essian is sent to the White Sox to complete the trade.

The inspirational leader of the 1973 Miracle Mets, pitcher Frank "Tug" McGraw, is traded to the Phillies along with outfielders Don Hahn (.251, four homers) and Dave Schneck (.205, five home runs in 93 games). In return, New York gets outfielder Del Unser (.264, 11 homers), pitcher Mac Scarce (3-8, 5.01 ERA), and catcher John Stearns (.500 in two at-bats).

TOMMY JOHN SAYS OF HIS REVOLUTIONARY ARM SURGERY: "WHEN THEY OPERATED, I TOLD THEM TO PUT IN A KOUFAX FASTBALL. THEY DID – BUT IT WAS MRS. KOUFAX'S."

The Orioles acquire first baseman Lee May (.268, 24 home runs, 85 RBI) and minor league outfielder Jay Schlueter from the Astros for infielder-outfielder Enos Cabell (.241 in 80 games) and minor league infielder Rob Andrews.

DECEMBER 4:

The Orioles obtain outfielder Ken Singleton (.276, nine homers) and pitcher Mike Torrez (15-8, 3.58 ERA) from the Expos for pitcher Dave McNally (16-10, 3.58 ERA), outfielder Rich Coggins (.243, four homers), and minor league pitcher Bill Kirkpatrick. The Expos also acquire pitcher Woodie Fryman (6-9, 4.31 ERA) from the Tigers for pitcher Tom Walker (4-5, 3.82 ERA) and catcher Terry Humphrey (.192 in 20 games).

DECEMBER 13:

Arbitrator Peter Seitz agrees with Jim "Catfish" Hunter's contention that Athletics' owner Charles O. Finley has breached his contract with the pitcher. Seitz declares that Hunter is now a free agent.

DECEMBER 16:

The Braves release pitcher Lew Krausse (4-3, 4.16 ERA), thus ending his 12-year major league career. Krausse, who was signed for a $125,000 bonus in 1961, compiles a 6891 record, with a 4.00 ERA and only five shutouts.

DECEMBER 18:

Hall of Fame outfielder Harry Hooper dies at the age of 87 in Santa Cruz, California. Admitted to the Hall in 1971, Hooper had a lifetime average of .281 for 17 years.

DECEMBER 31:

The Yankees win the bidding war for 1974 Cy Young Award winner Catfish Hunter (25-12, 2.49 ERA, six shutouts), signing him to a five-year, $3.75 million contract. In his last four seasons with the A's, Hunter has won 21, 21, 21, and 25 games.

THE BEST OF 1974

NATIONAL LEAGUE

HITTERS

Batting Average:
Ralph Garr, Atlanta Braves, .353

Slugging Average:
Mike Schmidt, Philadelphia Phillies, .546

Home Runs:
Mike Schmidt, 36

Runs Batted In:
Johnny Bench, Cincinnati Reds, 129

Hits:
Ralph Garr, 214

Stolen Bases:
Lou Brock, St. Louis Cardinals, 118

PITCHERS

Wins:
Andy Messersmith, Los Angeles Dodgers; Phil Niekro, Atlanta Braves, 20

Strikeouts:
Steve Carlton, Philadelphia Phillies, 240

Earned Run Average:
Lee "Buzz" Capra, Atlanta Braves, 2.28

Winning Percentage:
Andy Messersmith, .769

Saves:
Mike Marshall, Los Angeles Dodgers, 21

Most Valuable Player:
Steve Garvey, Los Angeles Dodgers

Cy Young Award:
Mike Marshall, Los Angeles Dodgers

Rookie of the Year:
Arnold "Bake" McBride, St. Louis Cardinals

AMERICAN LEAGUE

HITTERS

Batting Average:
Rod Carew, Minnesota Twins, .364

Slugging Average:
Dick Allen, Chicago White Sox, .563

Home Runs:
Dick Allen, 32

Runs Batted In:
Jeff Burroughs, Texas Rangers, 118

Hits:
Rod Carew, 218

Stolen Bases:
Bill North, Oakland Athletics, 54

PITCHERS

Wins:
Jim "Catfish" Hunter, Oakland Athletics; Ferguson Jenkins, Texas Rangers, 25

Strikeouts:
Nolan Ryan, California Angels, 367

Earned Run Average:
"Catfish" Hunter, 2.49

Winning Percentage:
Mike Cuellar, Baltimore Orioles, .688

Saves:
Terry Forster, Chicago White Sox, 24

Most Valuable Player:
Jeff Burroughs, Texas Rangers

Cy Young Award:
Jim "Catfish" Hunter, Oakland Athletics

Rookie of the Year:
Mike Hargrove, Texas Rangers

1975

NEWS

SOUTH VIETNAM FALLS TO NORTH VIETNAM

Terrorists bomb historic Fraunces Tavern in New York

CAMBODIA SEIZES USS *MAYAGUEZ*; CREW FREED IN MILITARY OPERATION

President Gerald Ford escapes two assassination attempts

WOMEN MAY ENTER ARMED SERVICES ACADEMIES

New York's La Guardia Airport bombed; 11 killed

PATTY HEARST CAPTURED

Jimmy Hoffa disappears

GALAXY 8 BILLION LIGHT YEARS FROM EARTH IS DISCOVERED

U.S. AND SOVIET UNION IN JOINT SPACE VENTURE

PRE-SEASON

JANUARY 5:

The Astros' Don Wilson dies of carbon monoxide poisoning at age 29. He is found in his 1972 Thunderbird in the garage of his home; the ignition is on and the gas gauge reads empty. Carbon monoxide fumes penetrate his home, killing his five-year-old son. His nine-year-old daughter is comatose and his wife is in fair condition. Wilson, who pitched two no-hitters in his career, was 11-13 with a 3.07 ERA last season. Lifetime, he was 104-91.

FEBRUARY 25:

The Orioles trade first baseman-DH John "Boog" Powell (.265, 12 homers) and pitcher Don Hood (1-1, 3.47) to the Indians for catcher Dave Duncan (.200, 16 homers) and minor league outfielder Al McGrew.

FEBRUARY 28:

The Giants sell outfielder-infielder Dave Kingman (.223, 18 homers, 125 strikeouts) to the New York Mets for $125,000.

MARCH 21:

Hall of Fame outfielder Joe "Ducky" Medwick dies at age 63 in St. Petersburg, Florida. Medwick played for 17 years, hitting .324 with 205 homers. He won the NL's Triple Crown in 1937 with a .374 batting average, 31 homers, and 154 RBI. He was inducted into the Baseball Hall of Fame in 1968.

MARCH 27:

Citing the "inconvenience and emotional strain" on part-time players, Indians' reserve infielder-outfielder John Lowenstein asks for a raise. He hit .240 last season in 140 games.

MARCH 29:

Mel Stottlemyre (6-7, 3.58 ERA), who pitched valiantly through some of the Yankees' worst seasons, is given his unconditional release. Stottlemyre, suffering from a torn rotator cuff, pitched 11 seasons, compiling a 164-139 record with a 2.97 ERA and 40 shutouts.

APRIL 6:

The Astros buy pitcher Joe Niekro (3-2, 3.56 ERA) from the Braves for $35,000.

THE SEASON

APRIL 8:

In Cleveland, with an opening day crowd of 56,204 on hand, baseball's first black manager, Frank Robinson, makes his debut at the helm of the Indians. Rachel Robinson, the widow of Jackie Robinson, throws out the first ball. The Indians beat the Yankees, 5-3. Robinson hits a first-inning homer – the 575th of his career – off George "Doc" Medich. John "Boog" Powell also homers for the Indians and drives in two runs. Gaylord Perry gets the win – the 199th of his career.

One year to the day after hitting his 715th career homer, Henry Aaron debuts in a Milwaukee Brewer uniform, at Fenway Park. Aaron is hitless in three at bats in his first-ever AL game, won by Boston, 5-2. Tony Conigliaro is back in a Red Sox uniform for the first time since 1971; he collects one hit in four at-bats.

APRIL 11:

In Milwaukee, Henry Aaron singles against Jim Perry in the sixth for his first AL hit and drives in a run in

APRIL 26
The Phillies' Mike Schmidt ties an ML record with his 11th homer hit in April.

MAY 7
Dick Allen, traded to the Braves in December, is now dealt to the Phillies.

the Brewers' 6-2 win over the Indians. A crowd of 48,160 braves 37-degree temperature to witness the moment.
In the Yankees' last "home" opener as tenants at Shea Stadium, Jim "Catfish" Hunter makes his debut in pinstripes, losing 5-3 to the Tigers. The Yankees lose an opportunity for victory when Bobby Bonds – who had singled and doubled – strikes out with the bases loaded. The game is marked by an anti-war demonstration.

APRIL 18:

Hank Aaron homers against the Indians' Gaylord Perry in a 5-1 Milwaukee win. It is Aaron's first in the AL and the 734th of his career. Pete Broberg gets the win.

APRIL 26:

In Philadelphia, Mike Schmidt homers twice in a 10-9 win over the Reds. The two round-trippers are Schmidt's 10th and 11th in April, tying a major league record for the month.

APRIL 29:

The Yankees execute a major league record-tying six double plays against the Indians, but lose, 3-1, on a Don Hood four-hitter.

MAY 1:

Henry Aaron singles against the Tigers' Vern Ruhle scoring Sixto Lezcano and registering his 2,210th career RBI. In the fifth, he doubles driving in Robin Yount, tying Babe Ruth's career record 2,211 RBI. He finishes the game with four hits as the Brewers beat the Tigers, 17-3, on 17 hits.

Indians' player-manager Frank Robinson tears a tendon in his left shoulder in a 7-6 loss to the Red Sox.

MAY 4:

At 12:32 P.M. today, Houston's Bob Watson crosses the plate on a three-run homer by Milt May off the Giants' John Montefusco at Candlestick Park, scoring the major leagues' one millionth run. Watson beats the Reds' Dave Concepcion by seconds for the honor. The Astros and Giants split a doubleheader.

The Giants obtain first baseman Willie Montanez (.286 in 21 games) from the Phillies for outfielder Garry Maddox (.135 in 17 games).

MAY 7:

Five days after getting permission from the Braves to negotiate with first baseman Dick Allen (.301, 32 homers, 88 RBI last season), the Phillies obtain him in a trade with Atlanta. Coming to Philadelphia with Allen is catcher Johnny Oates (.222 in eight games). The Braves get catcher Jim Essian (1.000 in one at bat), minor league outfielder Barry Bonnell, and cash.

MAY 9:

Henry Aaron homers in a five-run seventh inning to beat the Royals, 7-1, for Ed Sprague. Milwaukee now leads the AL East by one and a half games.

MAY 14:

Mets' chairman M. Donald Grant fines outfielder Cleon Jones $2,000 for "betraying the image of the club." Jones was arrested on charges of indecent exposure in St. Petersburg, Florida, but the charges were eventually dropped because of insubstantial evidence.

MAY 17:

In Philadelphia, the Phillies top the Braves, 9-8. Gene Garber gets his third win in three consecutive games, tying a major league record for relief pitchers.

MAY 22:

Hall of Fame pitcher Robert Moses "Lefty" Grove dies today in Norwalk, Ohio, at age 75. The hot-tempered Grove pitched for 17 years in the majors with the Athletics and Red Sox, compiling a record of 300-141 with a 3.06 ERA, 2,266 strikeouts, and 35 shutouts. Inducted into the Hall of Fame in 1947, Grove had appeared in three World Series and was 4-2, with a 1.75 ERA.

JUNE 1:

Nolan Ryan pitches his fourth career no-hitter, tying Sandy Koufax for the major league record. Ryan walks four and strikes out nine, beating the Orioles, 1-0, today in Anaheim. The Angels make one error. The no-hitter also marks Ryan's 100th career victory. Ross Grimsley gets the loss.

JUNE 3:

Two days after tying Stan Musial on the all-time hit list, Henry Aaron takes sole possession of second place with his 3,631st career safety. The Brewers beat the Athletics, 5-4, on a

HISTORY

Orioles' third baseman Brooks Robinson wins his 16th Gold Glove – the most of any fielder.

LEAGUE

A Charles O. Finley experiment ends this month when the Athletics release "designated runner" Herb Washington. In two seasons, the world-class sprinter never batted, appeared in 105 games, scored 33 runs, and stole 31 bases in 48 attempts.

JUNE 18
Red Sox rookie phenom Fred Lynn has 10 RBI, with three homers, a triple, and a single.

Fred Lynn is the AL's MVP and Rookie of the Year.

wild pitch by Jim Todd. Billy Champion gets the win.

JUNE 6:

Nolan Ryan fails in his bid for a second consecutive no-hitter when Henry Aaron singles with two out in the sixth inning. Ryan yields one more hit – an eighth inning single by George Scott – and the Angels beat the Brewers, 6-0.

JUNE 9:

The Dodgers top the one million mark in home attendance in only 27 games. The previous best were the 1948 Indians, who took 28 games to reach the mark.

JUNE 10:

Ceremonies at Shea Stadium honoring the U.S. Army's 200th birthday have unexpected consequences. As the Yankees prepare to meet Nolan Ryan and the Angels with 37,793 fans on hand, the Fort Hamilton 26th Army Band and its ceremonial gun battery take the field. Two 75mm artillery pieces fire a 21-gun salute to the accompaniment of smoke and the sound of breaking glass. When the air clears, there is a hole in the centerfield fence and other damage to the area. The fence is repaired and Chris Chambliss hits a two-run homer to defeat Ryan, 6-4.

JUNE 12:

Billy Williams of the Athletics hits his 400th career homer and Henry Aaron connects for the first time in Milwaukee since July 20, 1965. The Brewers win the game, 9-7.

JUNE 13:

The Rangers send three pitchers and $100,000 to the Indians for pitcher Gaylord Perry (6-9). In addition to the cash, Cleveland gets Jim Bibby (2-6), Jackie Brown (5-5), and Rick Waits, who made no appearances in the majors to date.

JUNE 14:

Tony Conigliaro, attempting a comeback after three seasons out of baseball, gets an ultimatum from the Red Sox: report to Pawtucket in the minor leagues or be released.

JUNE 16:

Clint Courtney, the first major league catcher to wear eyeglasses, dies at age 48 in Rochester, New York. Known as Scrap Iron, the combative Courtney played 11 seasons and hit .268.

JUNE 18:

Fred Lynn knocks in 10 runs on three homers, a triple, and a single as his Red Sox rout the Tigers, 15-1, in Detroit. The Red Sox's rookie outfielder hits a first-inning two-run homer against Joe Coleman, smacks a three-run shot off Coleman in the second, and connects for another three-run round-tripper against Tom Walker in the ninth. In between home runs, he has a two-run triple and an infield single. His 16 total bases tie an AL record. Lynn is hitting .352 and leads the AL with 50 RBI.

JULY 1:

The belief that no one gets hurt in baseball fights is fractured – literally. In San Diego, the Dodgers' Willie Crawford takes exception to a pitch from Bill Greif and goes after him. In the ensuing melee, Los Angeles catcher Joe Ferguson gets a fractured arm. The Padres win the game, 10-1.

JULY 2:

In Detroit, Don Baylor of the Orioles homers three consecutive times today in a 13-5 win over the Tigers. Baylor homered last night in his final at-bat against the Red Sox, putting him in the record book with a number of other players.

JULY 15:

The NL beats the AL, 6-3, in the All-Star Game, played this year in Milwaukee. Dodgers' teammates Steve Garvey and Jimmy Wynn hit back-to-back homers in the second inning and Bill Madlock has a bases-loaded single. Carl Yastrzemski has a three-run home run for the AL. The winning pitcher is Jon Matlack; Catfish Hunter gets the loss.

JULY 18:

The other stellar Red Sox rookie, Jim Rice, hits a home run at Fenway Park that owner Tom Yawkey describes as the longest he's ever seen. Rice's shot clears the centerfield wall; he is the sixth player to put a ball out in that section of Fenway. Boston beats the Royals, 9-3.

JULY 21:

In New York, the Mets' Joe Torre has a day to forget. Playing against the Astros, he ties a major league

LEAGUE

In July, the owners hold their summer meeting in Milwaukee and elect Commissioner Bowie Kuhn to a seven-year term.

"I don't play cards, I don't play golf, and I don't go to the picture show. All that's left is baseball."
– *Casey Stengel*

record by hitting into four consecutive double plays – each with Felix Millan on base. The only other players with the distinction are Leon "Goose" Goslin in 1934 and Mike Kreevich in 1939. Despite homers by Rusty Staub and Dave Kingman, Houston and Ken Forsch win the game, 6-2.

JULY 23:

Dodgers' pinch hitters Willie Crawford and Lee Lacey each homer in the ninth inning of today's game against the Cardinals, tying a major league record set in 1963 by Los Angeles' Frank Howard and Bill Skowron. Despite the success of Crawford and Lacy, St. Louis wins the game, 5-4.

JULY 24:

Tom Seaver fans Dan Driessen of the Reds in the second inning for his 2,000th career strikeout. The Reds win, 2-1.

The Royals fire manager Jack McKeon (50-46) and replace him with Dorrel "Whitey" Herzog.

AUGUST 1:

With the Yankees at 53-51, Billy Martin replaces current manager Bill Virdon. The announcement is made at Old-Timers' Day at Shea Stadium, where the Yankees beat the Indians, 5-3.

AUGUST 6:

The 56-53 Mets fire manager Yogi Berra and replace him with Roy McMillan.

AUGUST 9:

With the Mets' left-hander pitcher Jerry Koosman on the mound at Shea Stadium, Davey Lopes of the Dodgers steals his 32nd straight base, breaking Max Carey's major league record. Lopes also has two hits and scores twice in a 2-0 Los Angeles victory.

AUGUST 15:

A doubleheader means a double ejection for Orioles' manager Earl Weaver. He is thumbed during the opener and again before the start of the nightcap – both times he's run by umpire Ron Luciano.

The feud between Weaver and Luciano reached almost Olympic proportions. Luciano wrote in his book, The Umpire Strikes Back: *"We got along slightly better than Hugh Hefner and the Moral Majority."*

AUGUST 16:

It takes an outstanding pitching job by Ray Bare for the Tigers to snap their 19-game losing streak. Bare two-hits the Angels in Anaheim and the Tigers win, 8-0, avoiding a tie for the most consecutive losses ever in the AL.

AUGUST 18:

Earl Averill, Stanley "Bucky" Harris, Billy Herman, William "Judy" Johnson, and Ralph Kiner are inducted into the Hall of Fame. Averill, an outfielder, played 13 years and hit .318. He batted .300 or better eight times with a high of .378 in 1936 and played in one World Series. Harris was known as the Boy Wonder. He had managed the Senators to two pennants and a World Championship; with the Yankees he won one World Series. As a second baseman, he played for 12 years and averaged .274. Herman, an infielder, played 15 years and hit .304 with a high of .341 in 1935. He batted .300 or higher eight times and appeared in four World Series. Judy Johnson starred as a shortstop and third baseman in the Negro Leagues for 18 years, hitting an estimated .301. Connie Mack, the Grand Old Man of Baseball, once told Johnson: "If you were a white boy, you could name your own price." Johnson was a coach and scout and helped to bring Dick Allen to the majors. Sportswriter Arthur Daley described Kiner as "Huckleberry Finn in a baseball uniform." An outfielder, Kiner had a brief but spectacular career. In 10 years, he hit 369 homers and has the best home run-at-bat ratio in history. He batted only .279, but led the NL in round-trippers for seven consecutive years, hitting 51 in 1947 and 54 in 1949.

The 73-year-old Earl Averill says, "My disagreement with how Hall of Fame elections are held and who is elected is not based on bitterness, that I had to wait 34 years after retirement to receive this honor. It is based on the fact that statistics alone are not enough to gain a player such recognition. What rights does anyone have to ignore cold hard facts in favor of looking for some intangible item to keep a person out of Cooperstown?" He adds, "There's no meaning to this honor if you're not alive."

AUGUST 9
The Dodgers' Davey Lopes steals his 32nd straight base, setting a new ML record.

SEPTEMBER 16
Rennie Stennett is the first modern player to get seven hits in a nine-inning game.

AUGUST 20:

In Pittsburgh, the Pirates beat the Giants, 3-1, giving manager Danny Murtaugh his 1,000th career win.

Yogi Berra, fired two weeks ago as Mets' manager, is added to the Yankees' coaching staff.

AUGUST 21:

The career of Tony Conigliaro, once filled with limitless promise, comes to an end. Injuries, beginning with a near-fatal beaning in 1967, take their toll on Tony C., who is hitting .123 in 21 games for the Red Sox. In eight major league seasons, he hit .264 with 166 homers. In 1964, his rookie season, he hit .290 with 24 home runs and led the AL with 32 round-trippers the following season. Conigliaro is only 30 years old.

At Wrigley Field, the Cubs' Rick Reuschel pitches six and a third innings of shutout ball against the Dodgers. His brother, Paul Reuschel finishes up with two and two-thirds scoreless innings. The Cubs win, 7-0, and the Reuschels become the first brothers to combine for a shutout.

CASEY STENGEL ONCE WAS ASKED ABOUT THE BEST MANAGER HE EVER SAW. HE REPLIED, "I WAS THE BEST MANAGER I EVER SAW AND I TELL PEOPLE THAT TO SHUT 'EM UP AND ALSO BECAUSE I BELIEVE IT."

AUGUST 23:

The Angels' Nolan Ryan undergoes surgery on his pitching elbow.

AUGUST 24:

The Giants' Ed Halicki no-hits the Mets, 6-0, in the nightcap of a doubleheader at Candlestick Park. Halicki strikes out 10 and walks two; the Giants make one error. Craig Swan gets the loss. It is the fifth time in 14 years that the Mets have been the victims of no-hitters. The Mets won the opener, 9-5, on a grand slam homer hit by Dave Kingman.

In St. Louis, with Carl Morton of the Braves pitching and Biff Pocoroba catching, Lou Brock steals his 800th base. St. Louis wins the game, 6-2.

Gary Carter cuts down the Dodgers' Davey Lopes trying to steal in the 12th inning. The Expos' catcher ends Lopes' string of 38 consecutive stolen bases, a major league record set with a seventh inning theft. Mike Marshall yields three runs in the 14th and Montreal beats Los Angeles, 5-2.

SEPTEMBER 1:

At Shea Stadium, Tom Seaver fans the Pirates' Manny Sanguillen in the seventh inning. It is Seaver's 200th strikeout of the season and he is the first pitcher to record 200 or more for eight consecutive years. The Mets win, 3-0, and Seaver chalks up his 20th win.

SEPTEMBER 16:

Pirates' second baseman Rennie Stennett becomes the first modern baseball player with seven hits in a nine-inning game. The Pirates roll over the Cubs, 22-0, in Chicago; it is the most one-sided shutout ever. Stennett collects a triple, two doubles, and four singles, scoring five times, in seven at-bats. He also hits safely twice in the first and again in the fifth innings. After an eighth-inning triple, Stennett is lifted for a pinch hitter. He began the game hitting .278; he exits at .287. The last player with seven hits in nine innings was Wilbert Robinson in 1892 with Baltimore. The Pirates bang out 24 safeties – including homers by Willie Stargell, Dave Parker, and Richie Hebner – and everyone in the lineup hits and scores. The winning pitcher is John

CULTURE

Some heavy hitters record baseball songs. "Catfish," written by Bob Dylan and Jacques Levy, and recorded by Joe Cocker, is about Yankee pitcher Jim "Catfish" Hunter. Paul Simon records "Night Game."

SEPTEMBER 18
Harmon Killebrew, now with the A's, hits his 573rd career homer, against his old team.

Candelaria; Rick Reuschel – who works a third of an inning, allowing six hits and eight runs – gets the loss.

SEPTEMBER 17:

Rennie Stennett gets three hits in five at-bats against the Phillies; he ties a major league record with 10 hits over two consecutive games. The Pirates win, 9-1.

SEPTEMBER 18:

Playing in his old ballpark in a new uniform, the Athletics' Harmon Killebrew homers against the Twins' Eddie Bane. It is Killebrew's 573rd – and last – career home run.

SEPTEMBER 21:

In Detroit, Red Sox rookie Jim Rice is hit by a pitch from Vern Ruhle and suffers a broken left hand. Rice, who was hitting .309 with 22 home runs and 102 RBI, will be lost to Boston for the remainder of the season. The Red Sox win the game, 6-5.

SEPTEMBER 22:

A statistical oddity: brothers Gaylord Perry of the Rangers and Jim Perry of the Athletics on this day have identical career won-loss records: 215-174.

SEPTEMBER 23:

Randy Jones of the Padres beats the Dodgers, 6-4, to become the first 20-game winner in the history of the San Diego franchise.

SEPTEMBER 24:

It's a near-miss for the Mets' Tom Seaver at Wrigley Field. The right-hander allows no hits until two out in the ninth inning, when Joe Wallis singles. Chicago wins, 1-0, in 11 innings, defeating Claude "Skip" Lockwood.

SEPTEMBER 26:

The Dodgers' Burt Hooten beats the Astros, 3-2, in Los Angeles, for his 12th consecutive win. J.R. Richard gets the loss.

SEPTEMBER 27:

The Yankees sweep a doubleheader from the Orioles, giving the Red Sox the AL East title.

SEPTEMBER 28:

In the first four-pitcher no-hitter in history, Vida Blue, Glenn Abbott, Paul Lindblad, and Rollie Fingers beat the Angels, 5-0, in Oakland. Blue pitches five innings, walking two – the game's only base runners. Abbott and Lindblad pitch one frame each. Rollie Fingers finishes up with two no-hit innings, getting pinch hitter Mickey Rivers on a grounder for the final out. Reggie Jackson hits two homers and drives in three runs. Gary Ross gets the loss.

Two hours before the last game of the season, the Brewers fire manager Del Crandall with the team in fifth place in the AL East, at 67-94. He is replaced at the helm by Harvey Kuenn, who manages the team to a 7-0 win on a Larry Anderson five-hitter. Darrell Porter homers.

SEPTEMBER 29:

Charles Dillon "Casey" Stengel dies of cancer at age 85 in Glendale, California. Inducted into the Hall of Fame in 1966, Stengel compiled a managerial record that is unlikely ever to be equaled. In 12 years as the skipper of the Yankees, he won 10 pennants, seven World Championships – five in a row – finished second once and third once. After being fired by the Yankees, he was the manager of the Mets for their first four years. He also managed the Dodgers and Braves. In 14 years as a player, Stengel batted .284; in three World Series, he hit .393.

Stengel biographer Robert W. Creamer reports that after the funeral, Richie Ashburn, who played for Stengel on the Mets, said, "Don't shed any tears for Casey. He wouldn't want you to. He loved life and he loved laughter. He loved people and above all he loved baseball. He was the happiest man I've ever seen."

OCTOBER 1:

Larry MacPhail dies in Miami at the age of 85. One of baseball's great innovators, MacPhail was the father of night baseball, and the first to have his teams travel on commercial airlines. He was general manager of the Reds from 1934 to 1936 and the Dodgers from 1938 to 1942. He then became part of the Yankees' ownership group, remaining with the franchise through 1947. Among his survivors is the AL's president, Lee MacPhail, his son.

REGULAR SEASON WRAP-UP:

Cincinnati's Big Red Machine, managed by George "Sparky" Anderson, rolls over the NL with a 108-54

SEPTEMBER 27
The Yankees' double-header sweep of the Orioles gives the Red Sox the AL East title.

SEPTEMBER 28
A quartet of Oakland pitchers combine for the first-ever four-pitcher no-hitter.

record. The cogs in this big wheel are Joe Morgan (.327, 17 homers, 94 RBI), Tony Perez (.282, 20 homers, 109 RBI), Pete Rose (.317), Ken Griffey (.305), George Foster (.300, 23 homers), and Johnny Bench (.283, 28 homers, 100 RBI). The pitching staff has three 15-game winners – Gary Nolan, Jack Billingham, and Don Gullet. Rawly Eastwick gets credit for 22 saves.

Managed by Darrell Johnson, the Red Sox compile a 95-65 regular season record in the AL. Fred Lynn (.331, 21 homers, 105 RBI) and Jim Rice (.309, 22 homers, 102 RBI) are the mainstays, with support from Carlton Fisk (.331) and Cecil

Carlton Fisk's bat and body language help force a game seven in the World Series.

OCTOBER 7
The Red Sox and Reds sweep their respective LCS and will face off in the World Series.

HISTORY

Fred Lynn of the Red Sox becomes the first major leaguer to win both the Rookie of the Year and the Most Valuable Player Awards for the same season. Lynn hits .331 with 21 homers and 105 RBI.

LEAGUE

After the owners' defeat in the Messersmith-McNally case, Athletics' owner Charles O. Finley suggests that teams make all their players free agents at the end of each year.

Cooper (.311). The top winner is Rick Wise at 19-12. Dick Drago has 15 saves.

OCTOBER 4:

ALCS, game one. At Fenway Park, Luis Tiant three-hits the Athletics, 7-1, striking out 8 and issuing 3 walks. Fred Lynn drives in 2 runs with a double. Ken Holtzman is the losing pitcher.

NLCS, game 1. At Riverfront Stadium, Don Gullet pitches and hits the Reds to an 8-3 victory over the Pirates. Gullet scatters 8 hits, homers and singles, and drives in 3 runs. The game's losing pitcher is Jerry Reuss.

Joan Whitney Payson, principal owner of the New York Mets, dies today at the age of 72. Her heirs will eventually sell the club to Nelson Doubleday and Fred Wilpon.

OCTOBER 5:

ALCS, game 2. The Red Sox make it two in a row at Fenway Park today, beating Oakland, 6-3. Reggie Cleveland gets the win with a save by Dick Drago. Carl Yastrzemski hits a two-run homer, and Rico Petrocelli has a solo shot. Reggie Jackson homers for the A's with a runner on. The loser is Rollie Fingers, in relief.

> THE DODGERS' WALTER ALSTON, WHO MANAGED ANDY MESSERSMITH THIS PAST SEASON, SAYS, "IF HE WINS THIS CASE, BASEBALL IS DEAD."

NLCS, game two. The Reds beat the Pirates, 6-1, on strong pitching by Fred Norman and Rawly Eastwick, plus heavy hitting by Tony Perez. Jim Rooker gets the loss. Perez has a two-run homer, a single, and three RBI.

OCTOBER 7:

ALCS, game three. The Red Sox sweep the Athletics, 5-3, in Oakland and win the AL pennant. Rick Wise gets the win with a save by Dick Drago. Ken Holtzman is charged with the loss.

NLCS, game three. The Reds beat the Pirates, 5-3, in Pittsburgh to complete a three-game sweep and win the NL pennant. Rawly Eastwick gets the victory in relief. Pete Rose has a two-run homer and Dave Concepcion a solo round-tripper for Cincinnati. Al Oliver homers with one on for Pittsburgh. Pirates' starter John Candelaria fans 14, but is not involved in the game's decision; Ramon Hernandez is tagged with the loss.

OCTOBER 11:

World Series, game one. At Fenway Park, the Red Sox score six times in the sixth inning and Boston's veteran starter Luis Tiant pitches a five-hitter for a 6-0 Red Sox win over the Reds. Don Gullet is the losing pitcher. Attendance is 35,205.

OCTOBER 12:

World Series, game two. Rain during the seventh inning holds up today's game at Fenway Park. The Reds go on to score two runs in the top of the ninth to beat the Red Sox, 3-2. Dave Concepcion drives in Johnny Bench with a single, steals second, and scores the winning run on a double by Ken Griffey. Rawly Eastwick gets the win; Dick Drago is charged with the loss.

OCTOBER 13:

Charles "Swede" Risberg, one of the players with the 1919 Chicago Black Sox, dies on his 81st birthday in Red Bluff, California. Risberg played shortstop in the tainted 1919 World Series, batting .080 and committing four errors. In his four regular seasons in the major leagues, all spent with the White Sox, he hit .243. He was banned from baseball for life by Commissioner Landis for his role in the Series fix.

OCTOBER 21
Carlton Fisk hits one of the most dramatic home runs in World Series history.

OCTOBER 22
Joe Morgan's RBI single in the ninth gives the Reds the win – and the World Championship.

OCTOBER 14:

World Series, game three. In Cincinnati, the Reds beat the Red Sox, 6-5, in 10 innings. Boston comes back from a 5-1 deficit to lose in a controversial 10th inning. With Cesar Geronimo on, pinch hitter Ed Armbrister bunts. Boston catcher Carlton Fisk bumps into him, then throws into centerfield, advancing Geronimo to third and Armbrister to second. The Red Sox claim interference, but umpire Larry Barnett says it was unintentional and the play stands. After a walk to Pete Rose and a strikeout, Joe Morgan singles in Concepcion with the winning run. The winning pitcher is Rawly Eastwick; Jim Willoughby gets the loss. The game features homers by Cincinnati's Johnny Bench, Concepcion, and Geronimo, and Boston's Fisk, Bernie Carbo, and Dwight "Dewey" Evans (with a runner on).

OCTOBER 15:

World Series, game four. Luis Tiant is unsteady but tough as he allows nine hits on 163 pitches, pitching a 5-4 complete game victory. Boston gets 11 hits against four Cincinnati pitchers. The losing pitcher is starter Fred Norman.

OCTOBER 16:

World Series, game five. Tony Perez homers twice – once with two on – and drives in four runs as the Reds beat the Red Sox, 6-2, in the final series game in Cincinnati. Don Gullet gets the win with a save by Rawly Eastwick. Boston starter Reggie Cleveland is the losing pitcher.

OCTOBER 18:

The Boston Globe reports the left-field wall at Fenway-Park – the infamous Green Monster – is not 315 feet from home plate as previously believed, but only 304 feet. To circumvent Red Sox officials, author George Sullivan and Art Keefe measured the distance prior to the Red Sox-Athletics ALCS meeting using aerial photography and computers and came up with 304.779 feet.

OCTOBER 21:

World Series, game six. After a four-day rain delay, the series resumes with an epic 12-inning battle at Fenway Park. Carlton Fisk homers off the left-field foul pole to give the Red Sox a come-from-behind, 7-6 win, evening the series. Pinch hitter Bernie Carbo had tied the score for Boston with a three-run homer in the eighth. Fred Lynn has a three-run homer. Cesar Geronimo hits one for the Reds. Rick Wise gets the win in relief. Pat Darcy, Cincinnati's eighth pitcher of the game, is charged with the loss.

OCTOBER 22:

World Series, game seven. Joe Morgan's two-out soft single in the top of the ninth inning drives in Ken Griffey with the winning run in a 4-3 Reds' victory for the World Championship. The Reds had rallied from a 3-0 deficit with the help of a two-run homer by Tony Perez. Clay Carroll gets the win; Jim Burton is charged with the loss. It is Cincinnati's first World Series title since 1940. Pete Rose leads the Reds' hitters with .370; Tony Perez has three homers and seven RBI. Carl Yastrzemski hits .310 for Boston. The Curse of the Bambino continues.

POST-SEASON

OCTOBER 30:

The Braves, who finished fifth in the NL West, make a change. They fire the chimpanzee who has been sweeping the bases after the fifth inning of home games and return it to the circus.

NOVEMBER 17:

The Rangers trade pitcher Ferguson Jenkins (17-18, 3.93 ERA) to the Red Sox for outfielder Juan Beniquez (.291 in 78 games), pitcher Steve Barr (0-1, 2.57 ERA) and minor league pitcher Craig Skok.

The Dodgers obtain outfielder Johnnie "Dusty" Baker (.261, 19 homers, 72 RBI) and first baseman-third baseman James "Ed" Goodson (.208 in 86 games) from the Braves for outfielder Jimmy "The Toy Cannon" Wynn (.248, 18 homers), infielder-outfielders Lee Lacy (.314, 7 homers) and Tom Paciorek (.193 in 62 games), and infielder Jerry Royster (.250 in 13 games).

NOVEMBER 21:

A three-man arbitration panel begins hearing the case of Dave McNally of the Expos and Andy Messersmith of the Dodgers at Barbizon Plaza Hotel in New York City. Neither pitcher signed his 1975 contract, opting

CULTURE

Leo Durocher publishes *Nice Guys Finish Last.* And in *Mortal Stakes,* by Robert B. Parker, private eye Spenser investigates a possible fix involving the Red Sox.

"You mean players might have to be paid what they are worth?"
– Players Association's attorney Richard Moss

instead to test the free-agent system. Messersmith claims he has completed his option year and should be a free agent. McNally, who was traded to Montreal by Baltimore in December 1974, retired after appearing in 11 games for the Expos. The panel is composed of Marvin Miller, executive director of the Major League Baseball Players Association; John Gaherin representing the owners; and chairman Peter Seitz, who has 20 years of professional arbitration experience.

During the hearing, Players Association attorney Richard Moss asks, "You mean players might have to be paid what they are worth?" AL president Lee MacPhail responds, "No. They might have to be paid more than they are worth."

DECEMBER 1:

Former major league second baseman Jacob "Nellie" Fox dies of cancer in Baltimore, at age 47. An overlooked candidate for the Hall of Fame, Fox played 19 years with the Athletics, White Sox, and Astros, hitting .288. He batted .300 or better six times in his career and led the AL in hits four times. He appeared in the 1959 World Series, batting .375.

The Messersmith-McNally hearing that began on November 21 ends. The ruling is still to come.

DECEMBER 10:

One week after rejecting Bill Veeck's bid to buy the White Sox and requiring additional capitalization of $1.2 million, the AL approves his purchase of the team from John Allyn.

The Phillies acquire 37-year-old pitcher Jim Kaat (20-14, 3.11 ERA) and minor league shortstop Mike Buskey from the White Sox for pitcher Dick Ruthven (2-2, 4.17 ERA), outfielder-infielder Alan Banister (.262 in 24 games), and minor league pitcher Roy Thomas.

DECEMBER 11:

It's a big day in the player market for the Yankees. They send pitcher George "Doc" Medich (16-16, 3.50 ERA) to the Pirates for infielder Willie Randolph (.164 in 30 games) plus pitchers Dock Ellis (8-9, 3.79 ERA) and Ken Brett (9-5, 3.36 ERA). They also trade outfielder Bobby Bonds (.270, 32 homers, 85 RBI, 30 stolen bases) to the Angels in return for outfielder Mickey Rivers (.284 plus a league-leading 70 stolen bases and 13 triples) and pitcher Ed Figueroa (16-13, 2.91 ERA).

DECEMBER 12:

The Mets trade Daniel "Rusty" Staub (.282, 19 homers, 105 RBI) and minor league pitcher Bill Laxton to the Tigers for pitcher Mickey Lolich (12-18, 3.78 ERA) and outfielder Billy Baldwin (.221, four homers in 30 games).

DECEMBER 17:

Paul Richards is named the new manager of the White Sox. He succeeds Chuck Tanner, who is the new Athletics manager, replacing Alvin Dark.

DECEMBER 23:

In a 61-page decision, arbitrator Peter Seitz rules that Andy Messersmith and Dave McNally are free agents and now may play for the highest bidder. The case is a victory for the Players Association and a serious blow to baseball's reserve clause.

DECEMBER 28:

The owners fire arbitrator Peter Seitz, whose ruling made free agents of Andy Messersmith and Dave McNally.

DECEMBER 31:

The basic agreement between the owners and players expires.

Writes David Q. Voigt in Total Baseball: *"Certainly the implications of this 'Seitz decision' were far-reaching. The decision effectively circumvented the long-established reserve clause which had recently been tested by player Curt Flood before the U.S. Supreme Court... In 1972, the court rejected Flood's appeal..., but the court's ruling suggested that the players might overturn the reserve clause by means of collective bargaining. And when the owners failed to overturn the Seitz decision on legal appeal, they staged a lockout of spring training camps in 1976, claiming that the latest basic agreement had expired with no new labor contract in place. However, a compromise reached by the embattled players and owners allowed the 1976 playing season to open on time. And... negotiations produced a basic agreement."*

DECEMBER 10
The AL approves Bill Veeck's purchase of the Chicago White Sox from John Allyn.

DECEMBER 31
The basic agreement between the teams' owners and the players expires.

THE BEST OF 1975

NATIONAL LEAGUE

HITTERS

Batting Average:
Bill Madlock, Chicago Cubs, .354

Slugging Average:
Dave Parker, Pittsburgh Pirates, .541

Home Runs:
Mike Schmidt, Philadelphia Phillies, 38

Runs Batted In:
Greg Luzinski, Philadelphia Phillies, 120

Hits:
Dave Cash, Philadelphia Phillies, 213

Stolen Bases:
Davey Lopes, Los Angeles Dodgers, 77

PITCHERS

Wins:
Tom Seaver, New York Mets, 22

Strikeouts:
Tom Seaver, 243

Earned Run Average:
Randy Jones, San Diego Padres, 2.24

Winning Percentage:
Don Gullet, Cincinnati Reds, .789

Saves:
Rawly Eastwick, Cincinnati Reds; Al Hrabosky, St. Louis Cardinals, 22

Most Valuable Player:
Joe Morgan, Cincinnati Reds

Cy Young Award:
Tom Seaver, New York Mets

Rookie of the Year:
John Montefusco, San Francisco Giants

AMERICAN LEAGUE

HITTERS

Batting Average:
Rod Carew, Minnesota Twins, .359

Slugging Average:
Fred Lynn, Boston Red Sox, .566

Home Runs:
Reggie Jackson, Oakland Athletics; George Scott, Milwaukee Brewers, 36

Runs Batted In:
George Scott, 109

Hits:
George Brett, Kansas City Royals, 195

Stolen Bases:
John "Mickey" Rivers, California Angels, 70

PITCHERS

Wins:
Jim Palmer, Baltimore Orioles; Jim "Catfish" Hunter, New York Yankees, 23

Strikeouts:
Frank Tanana, California Angels, 269

Earned Run Average:
Jim Palmer, 2.09

Winning Percentage:
Mike Torrez, Baltimore Orioles, .690

Saves:
Rich "Goose" Gossage, Chicago White Sox, 26

Most Valuable Player:
Fred Lynn, Boston Red Sox

Cy Young Award:
Jim Palmer, Baltimore Orioles

Rookie of the Year:
Fred Lynn, Boston Red Sox

1976

"If you're going to burn the flag, don't do it in front of me."
– *Rick Monday, to demonstrators*

NEWS

JIMMY CARTER ELECTED PRESIDENT, DEFEATING GERALD FORD

U.S. celebrates bicentennial

Chicago's controversial Mayor Richard Daley dies

U.S., SOVIETS SIGN NUCLEAR TEST AGREEMENT

TETON DAM IN IDAHO COLLAPSES, KILLING 14

Concorde service begins between U.S. and Europe

Barbara Walters is first female news anchor

PATTY HEARST CONVICTED IN 1974 BANK HEIST

Legionnaire's Disease kills 29 in Philadelphia

UNMANNED *VIKING 1* LANDS ON MARS

PRE-SEASON

JANUARY 6:

Broadcasting magnate Ted Turner announces he is buying the Braves from the Atlanta-Lasalle Corporation, headed by Bill Bartholomay, for $11 million. The NL owners unanimously approve the sale on January 14.

FEBRUARY 6:

The AL grants a new franchise in Seattle to an investment group including the film star Danny Kaye. The team will begin play in 1977. Other partners are Stanley Golub, Walter Schoenfeld, Lester Smith, James Stilwell Jr., and James Walsh.

MARCH 1:

With the absence of a new basic agreement, major league owners lock the players out of spring training.

MARCH 2:

After 57 years, the ownership of the Giants passes from the Stoneham family. Financier Robert A. Lurie and Bud Herseth, an Arizona cattle rancher, buy the team from Horace C. Stoneham, enabling the Giants to remain in San Francisco. Prior to the intervention of San Francisco Mayor George Moscone, it appeared the team would be sold to the Labatt's Breweries and moved to Canada. Mayor Moscone says, "Bobby Thomson lives!"

MARCH 16:

The owners take another hit in the Messersmith-McNally case. Missouri federal judge John W. Oliver finds the owners' position on the reserve clause "ludicrous" and states, "Congress did not entrust this court or any other court with the responsibility of looking out for our national pastime."

MARCH 17:

Commissioner Bowie Kuhn overrules the owners and ends the spring training lockout.

MARCH 22:

The groundskeeper for the Angels finds 500 marijuana plants growing in the outfield of Anaheim Stadium. The suspicion is that they were planted by attendees at a recent concert by the rock group The Who.

MARCH 26:

The AL approves expansion into Toronto, awarding a franchise to Imperials Trust, Ltd., Labatt's Breweries, and the Canadian Imperial Bank of Commerce.

APRIL 2:

The Athletics trade two of the stars of its championship teams. Going to Baltimore are outfielder Reggie Jackson (.253, 36 home runs, 104 RBI, 17 stolen bases) and pitcher Ken Holtzman (18-14, 3.14 ERA), along with minor league pitcher Bill Van Bommell. In return, Oakland gets outfielder Don Baylor (.282, 25 home runs, 76 RBI, and 32 stolen bases) plus pitchers Mike Torrez (20-9, 3.06 ERA) and Paul Mitchell (3-0, 3.63 ERA).

APRIL 6:

After a five-week holdout, Tom Seaver (22-9, 2.38 ERA, 243 strikeouts, five shutouts) signs a three-year contract with the Mets at $600,000 per year.

THE SEASON

APRIL 10:

Free-agent pitcher Andy Messersmith (19-14, 2.28 ERA, 213 strikeouts, seven shutouts) signs a "lifetime" contract with the Braves. Messersmith,

APRIL 15
Mets' slugger Dave Kingman smashes a home run estimated to travel 550 feet.

declared a free agent last December by arbitrator Peter Seitz, reportedly inks for three years at $1.75 million with renewal clauses. Messersmith reaches agreement with the Braves in San Diego, where he was in conversation with the Padres. New Braves' owner Ted Turner says Messersmith will "never be traded... will be a Brave as long as I am."

A time-out costs the Brewers a victory in Milwaukee. In the bottom of the ninth, with the Yankees winning, 9-6, Don Money hits a home run against Albert "Sparky" Lyle. But Yankees' first baseman Chris Chambliss had called time-out and the play is negated. Lyle then gets Money on a fly ball and New York wins the game, 9-7.

APRIL 15:

The newly renovated Yankee Stadium is dedicated in ceremonies attended by Mrs. Babe Ruth, Mrs. Lou Gehrig, Joe DiMaggio, Mickey Mantle, Whitey Ford, Don Larsen, and former heavyweight champion Joe Louis. Eighty-five-year-old Bob Shawkey, who pitched a three-hitter when Yankee Stadium opened in 1923, throws out the first ball. The Yankees come back from a 4-0 deficit to beat the Twins, 11-4. Dick Tidrow gets the win in relief. The $3 million-plus scoreboard doesn't work.

The Mets' Dave Kingman hits a homer – estimated at 550 feet – at Wrigley Field in a 10-8 New York victory.

APRIL 17:

At Wrigley Field, Mike Schmidt of the Phillies hits four consecutive home runs and a single, batting in eight runs for a 10-inning, 18-16 victory for the Phillies. Schmidt is the eighth modern player with four in a game. He also is the only NL player to hit four consecutively in one game. Aided by a 20-mile-per-hour wind blowing out, Schmidt victimizes brothers Rick and Paul Reuschel. He hits a two-run homer in the fifth, a solo homer in the seventh, a three-run blast in the eighth, and a game-winning two-run round-tripper in the 10th. Obscured by Schmidt's heroics is Philadelphia's comeback from a 13-2 deficit. Also homering in the game are Garry Maddox and Bob Boone for the Phillies and Steve Swisher and Rick Monday of the Cubs. The winning pitcher is Frank "Tug" McGraw; Darold Knowles gets the loss.

Thurman Munson is named the Yankees' first captain since Lou Gehrig. He then hits a homer in a 10-0 victory over the Twins.

APRIL 25:

At Dodger Stadium, Cubs' centerfielder Rick Monday makes headlines when he stops a flag burning. In the fourth inning a man and a youngster come onto the field and try to set fire to an American flag in front of left fielder Jose Cardenal when Monday intervenes. He says, "I saw the clowns come on the field and I thought they were out to prance around. But they began spreading out the flag like it was a picnic blanket." He adds, "If you're going to burn the flag, don't do it in front of me. I've been to too many veterans' hospitals and seen too many broken bodies of guys who tried to protect it..."

APRIL 26:

The Mets' Mickey Lolich, who had 207 wins in the AL, gets his first in the NL, beating the Dodgers, 3-1.

MAY 2:

One day short of his 56th birthday, Dan Bankhead, the major leagues' first black pitcher, dies in Houston. In three seasons with the Dodgers, Bankhead was 9-5 with a 6.52 ERA. He homered in his first at-bat for Brooklyn. Prior to joining the Dodgers, he played in the Negro Leagues with the Birmingham Black Barons, the Cleveland Buckeyes, and the Memphis Red Sox.

In San Francisco, the Cubs' Jose Cardenal drives in the winning run in a 6-5 win over the Giants. Cardenal has six hits – including a homer and double – and drives in four runs.

MAY 4:

Rick Monday Day is celebrated at Wrigley Field, honoring the Cubs' centerfielder for stopping a flag burning at Dodger Stadium on April 25. Among those honoring Monday for his intervention are President Gerald Ford and Commissioner Bowie Kuhn.

MAY 13:

Maybe it was bad luck dust. The Indians dress "ball girl" Debbie Berndt in a

EQUIPMENT

Bill Veeck has the Astroturf removed from the Comiskey Park infield and replaced with the real stuff. It was installed by the previous owners for the 1969 season.

LEAGUE

After signing Andy Messersmith, Ted Turner nicknames him Channel and issues uniform number 17 to him. Each time Messersmith takes the field with "Channel 17" on his back, he is promoting the Turner-owned Braves TV superstation. NL president Chub Feeney puts an end to the stunt.

MAY 15
Tigers' pitcher Mark "Big Bird" Fidrych makes – and wins – his first major league start.

MVP Joe Morgan sparks the Big Red Machine.

white "fairy godmother" gown. After she sprinkles Rick Manning with "fairy dust," the centerfielder misplays one ball into a triple and commits a three-base error. Cleveland ends up losing the game to the Boston Red Sox by a score of 7-5.

MAY 15:

In Detroit, Tiger pitcher Mark "The Bird" Fidrych makes his first major league start and two-hits the Indians, 2-1. Fidrych previously appeared twice in relief.

MAY 20:

At Yankee Stadium, another New York-Boston brawl has long-term consequences. The fight starts when Lou Piniella crashes into Red Sox catcher Carlton Fisk in a play at the plate. The dugouts empty and pitcher Bill "Spaceman" Lee becomes the target of the Yankees. Mickey Rivers hits him in the back o f the head; Graig Nettles lifts him and slams him – shoulder first – into the ground. Lee has torn ligaments in his pitching shoulder and a black eye; he is sidelined for an extended period. He yells at Nettles, "How could you do this to me? I played ball with your brother Jimmy in Alaska." When the game resumes, Boston wins, 8-2. Carl Yastrzemski hits two homers. He had three yesterday against the Tigers, tying a major league mark with five in two games.

MAY 21:

When the major league umpires refuse to cross a vendors' picket line at Three Rivers Stadium in Pittsburgh, an amateur crew works the Pirates-Cubs game.

MAY 28:

Yankees' pitchers Ed Figueroa and Felix "Tippy" Martinez end the 30-game hitting streak of the Tigers' Ron LeFlore, holding him hitless in four at-bats.

MAY 29:

In the seventh inning of today's game at the Astrodome, Houston pitcher Joe Niekro ties the game with his first – and only major – league home run. The victim is his brother Phil, pitching for the Braves. The Astros go on to win, 4-3; Joe gets the win, Phil takes the loss.

MAY 30:

Hall of Fame outfielder Max Carey, who was born Maximilian Carnarius, dies at age 86 in Miami. Carey played 20 seasons, batting .285 and stealing 738 bases. He led the NL in stolen bases 10 times, with a high of 61 in 1913. He managed the Dodgers in 1932 and 1933.

MAY 31:

Another new owner takes over the public address microphone.

MAY 29
Houston knuckleballer Joe Niekro hits his first and only major league home run.

In Atlanta, after an error sets up six-runs for the Padres in the eighth inning, Braves' boss Ted Turner tells the crowd, "Nobody's going to leave here a loser tonight. If the Braves don't win, I want you people to come back tomorrow night as my guests. We're going to be in big league baseball for a long, long time, and we appreciate your support." He wins cheers from the 2,994 fans. San Diego wins, 10-7.

JUNE 1:

In Detroit, Tigers' relief pitcher John Hiller wins both ends of a doubleheader against the Milwaukee Brewers, 8-7 and 6-5. Milwaukee's Eduardo Rodriguez loses twice. Hiller was sidelined by a heart attack in 1971.

JUNE 11:

Jim Konstanty, the NL's 1950 Most Valuable Player, dies in Oneonta, New York, at age 59. A bespectacled relief pitcher, Konstanty enjoyed a career year in 1950 with the Phillies' Whiz Kids. He appeared in 74 games, was 16-7 with an ERA of 2.66 and 22 saves. He lost a heartbreaking 1-0 game to the Yankees in the opener of the World Series. In his career, Konstanty was 66-48, with a 3.46 ERA and 74 saves.

JUNE 15:

Charles O. Finley sells two of his Athletics' stars – outfielder-first baseman-DH Joe Rudi and relief pitcher Rollie Fingers – to the Red Sox for $1 million each. The Red Sox are playing in Oakland; Boston manager Darrell Johnson does not play Rudi and Fingers against the A's. Finley also attempts to sell A's pitcher Vida Blue to the Yankees for $1.5 million.

Says Finley: "I'm disappointed with the necessity of having to make these sales. But I just refused to let these players drive me into bankruptcy with their astronomical salary demands."

Rain causes the postponement of a game in a domed stadium. It happens today for the first time when the Astros-Pirates ball game in the Astro-dome is canceled because 10 inches of rain in Houston keeps the umpires, fans, and stadium staff from reaching the ballpark. The playing field, however, remains dry.

The Yankees and Orioles complete a five-for-five trade. Coming to New York are pitchers Ken Holtzman (5-4), Doyle Alexander (3-4), and Grant Jackson (1-1); catcher Elrod Hendricks (.139 in 28 games), and minor league pitcher Jimmy Freeman. Baltimore receives pitchers Felix "Tippy" Martinez (2-0), Dave Pagan (1-1), and Rudy May (4-3); catcher Rick Dempsey (.119 in 21 games), and minor league pitcher Scott McGregor.

JUNE 16:

Commissioner Bowie Kuhn warns the Red Sox and Yankees not to use the players they obtained from the Athletics until he concludes an investigation into the transactions.

JUNE 18:

Not so fast, you guys! Nobody's going anywhere. Baseball Commissioner Bowie Kuhn negates Charles O. Finley's sale of Vida Blue to the Yankees and Joe Rudi and Rollie Fingers to the Red Sox. All three will be eligible for free agency at the end of the 1976 season; none play for their "new" teams while awaiting the commissioner's decision.

Kuhn expresses his concern about the Athletics' ability to remain a competitive team, saying, "While I am aware that there have been cash sales of player contracts in the past, there has been no instance in my judgment which had the potential for harm to our game."

Henry Aaron homers in the top of the ninth inning to give the Brewers a 3-2 win over the Athletics. It is Aaron's 750th career home run and his third in six days.

JUNE 22:

Randy Jones of the Padres walks leadoff hitter Marc Hill in the eighth inning to end his streak of issuing no walks in 68 innings. Jones ties a record set by Christy Mathewson 63 years ago. The Padres beat the Giants, 4-2.

JUNE 23:

Former pitcher and umpire Lon Warneke dies at the age of 67 in Hot Springs, Arkansas. Known as The Arkansas Hummingbird, Warneke pitched for

CULTURE

At the movies, *The Bad News Bears* stars Walter Matthau and Tatum O'Neal; *The Bingo Long Traveling All-Stars and Motor Kings* stars Billy Dee Williams, James Earl Jones, and Richard Pryor.

RULES

The designated hitter is being used in World Series played in even years. The Reds' Dan Driessen becomes the first National League DH when he comes to bat in the second inning and flies out.

JULY 20
Hank Aaron hits his 755th home run – which is also the last of his career.

JULY 28
White Sox's pitchers Blue Moon Odom and Francisco Barrios no-hit the A's.

TRIVIA

According to Hank Aaron's autobiography, the 755th home run ball is retrieved by Dick Arndt of the grounds crew. He refuses to return it and is fired. Aaron writes that he calls Arndt "every few years" and has offered up to $10,000 for the ball – to no avail.

15 years with the Cardinals and Cubs, compiling a 193-121 record with a 3.18 ERA and 31 shutouts. He appeared in two World Series. After retiring as a ball player, he umpired in the NL from 1949 to 1955.

JUNE 26:

He could have left his glove in the clubhouse. Rangers' shortstop Toby Harrah plays all 18 innings of today's doubleheader against the White Sox, and has no batted balls hit to him.

JUNE 29:

Mickey Lolich of the Mets pitches his first NL and 40th career shutout, beating the Cardinals, 2-0.

JULY 3:

In the first morning game in the history of Comiskey Park, the visiting Rangers beat the White Sox, 3-0.

JULY 4:

The Phillies Tim McCarver hits a grand slam home run, but is called out for passing teammate Garry Maddox on the bases. The Phillies beat the Pirates anyway, 10-5.

JULY 6:

In Anaheim, Indians' player-manager Frank Robinson hits the 586th – and final – home run of his career. The pitcher is the Angels' Isidro "Sid" Monge.

JULY 9:

The sole owner of the Boston Red Sox, Tom Yawkey, dies at age 73 of leukemia in New England Baptist Hospital. Yawkey owned the team for 44 years. The Red Sox won the AL pennant in 1946, 1967, and last year, but failed to bring Yawkey the World Series he coveted. The team will be inherited by his widow, Jean Yawkey.

Larry Dierker of the Astros no-hits the Expos, 6-0, in Houston. Dierker fans eight and walks four. Houston plays error-free ball. The losing pitcher is Don Stanhouse.

JULY 12:

The owners and players sign a new basic agreement, which includes a modification to the reserve clause and a free-agent reentry draft to be held in November. Players now will become free agents after five years. Clubs will select players for whom they wish to bid. A team may select as many players as they want; players may be drafted only 12 times. Undrafted players are free to deal with any teams. Negotiation rights to players may be returned by teams. Seven owners vote against the new agreement.

JULY 13:

With five Reds in the lineup, the NL wins this year's All-Star Game, 7-1, played at Veterans Stadium in Philadelphia. One of those Reds, George Foster, hits a three-run homer and is named the game's MVP. Cesar Cedeno also homers for the NL, Fred Lynn for the AL. It is the NL's fifth straight win. The winning pitcher is Randy Jones; the losing pitcher, Mark Fidrych. President Gerald Ford is among the 63,974 in attendance.

JULY 16:

In Detroit, Tigers' rookie Mark "The Bird" Fidrych goes 11 innings to beat the Athletics, 1-0.

JULY 17:

The man with the string of 23 one-year managerial contracts, Walter Alston of the Dodgers, wins his 2,000th game. Los Angeles beats the visiting Cubs, 5-4, behind Rick Rhoden, who is now 9-0.

JULY 20:

Henry Aaron homers against the Angels' Dick Drago in a 6-2 Brewers' win. It is his 755th – and last – career home run and his 10th of the season.

JULY 21:

Hall of Fame outfielder Earle Combs dies at age 77 in Richmond, Kentucky. Combs, known as the Kentucky Colonel, was inducted into the Hall of Fame in 1970. He spent his entire career – 12 years – with the Yankees, batting .325 with 154 triples. He batted .300 or better nine times with a high of .356 in 1927.

JULY 27:

Yankees' pitcher Dock Ellis hits Reggie Jackson of the Orioles in the face with a fastball, shattering his eyeglasses. Ellis asks the umpire, "Is he dead?" Later, he explains: "I owed him one." Ellis apparently is referring to Jackson pumping his fists after a homer off him five years ago in the 1971 All-Star Game.

Ferguson Jenkins of the Red Sox beats the Indians, 8-7, for his 200th career victory.

AUGUST 25
The Yankees outduel the Twins, 5-4, in a five-hour, 36 minute, 19-inning marathon.

JULY 28:

Johnny "Blue Moon" Odom and Francisco Barrios of the White Sox pitch a combined no-hitter against the Athletics at Oakland, winning 2-1. Odom goes five innings, yielding nine walks. Barrios pitches the final four frames, issuing two walks. The losing pitcher is Paul Lindblad.

AUGUST 8:

The White Sox make a fashion statement, but no one is quite sure what they are saying. Chicago plays the first game of today's doubleheader against the Royals wearing navy-blue Bermuda shorts and white tops. Chicago wins the game, 5-2.

AUGUST 9:

The Pirates six-foot, seven-inch left-hander, John Candelaria, no-hits the Dodgers, 2-0, in Pittsburgh. The Candy Man strikes out seven and walks one; the Pirates commit two errors. It is the first ever no-hitter against Los Angeles. Doug Rau is the losing pitcher.

Oscar Charleston, Roger Connor, Cal Hubbard, Bob Lemon, Fred Lindstrom, and Robin Roberts are inducted into the Hall of Fame. Charleston, who died in 1954, is regarded by many as the greatest of the Negro League stars. For power, speed, and fielding he was compared favorably with Babe Ruth, Ty Cobb, and Tris Speaker. An outfielder, he played 26 years, batting .350. In 1932, he was player-manager of the Pittsburgh Crawfords – whose lineup included Satchel Paige, Josh Gibson, and William "Judy" Johnson – and batted .363. Connor, who died in 1931, was a first baseman for 18 years, hitting .317 with 233 triples. He hit .300 or better 11 times and led the NL in 1885 with .371. In 1890 he was the top home run hitter in the Players League with 13. Hubbard was an AL umpire from 1936 to 1951. He then served for 15 years as the league's supervisor of umpires. Hubbard is the only man to be inducted into the baseball, college football, and professional football halls of fame. Bob Lemon pitched for 13 years with the Indians, compiling a 207-128 record with a 3.23 ERA and 31 shutouts. A good-hitting pitcher who began his career as a third baseman-outfielder, he won 20 games or more seven times and played in two World Series. Fred Lindstrom is another outstanding player perhaps best remembered for two misplays – balls that bounced over his head in the 1924 World Series, enabling the Senators to win the championship. An outfielder and third baseman, Lindstrom hit .311 in 13 years with a high of .379 in 1930. He hit .300 or better seven times and played in two World Series. Roberts, a workhorse with an overpowering fastball and pinpoint control, pitched for 19 years, compiling a 286-245 record and a 3.41 ERA, 45 shutouts, and 2,357 strikeouts. He appeared in one World Series.

MINNIE MINOSO SAYS OF HIS FANS: "IT'S BEEN MANY YEARS SINCE I FACED PITCHING LIKE THIS. I HOPE THEY FORGIVE ME."

AUGUST 24:

Seattle's new team will be known as the Mariners. The name is selected from 15,000 entries in a contest, and was suggested by Roger Szmodis of Bellevue, Washington.

AUGUST 25:

In New York, the Yankees and Twins battle for five hours and 36 minutes, and 19 innings, until Mickey Rivers singles in Oscar Gamble with the winning run. The final is 5-4 and Grant

HISTORY

While in the NL, Hank Aaron feasted on Don Drysdale, hitting 17 roundtrippers against the Dodger righthander. No pitcher yielded more to Bad Henry. The Aarons combine for the most career homers ever by brothers – 768. Henry has 755; Tommie, 13.

CULTURE

Basbeball lovers are reading *Journal of Leo Smith: Story of a Nineteenth Century Shortstop* by Randolph Linthurts and *The Sensuous Southpaw* by Paul R. Rothweiler.

SEPTEMBER 3
Mets' ace Tom Seaver reaches 200 strikeouts for the ninth straight time in his career.

CULTURE

***Ball Four*, a short-lived CBS television series based on Jim Bouton's book, stars the author and Jack Somack. "Ball Four" by Harry Chapin is the theme song for the series.**

Jackson gets the victory. The Twins score all their runs in the second inning and are shut out for the next 17. Willie Randolph of the Yankees sets an AL record for extra innings with 13 assists and 20 chances at second base.

AUGUST 30:

At Fenway Park, Jim Rice homers for the Red Sox in the fifth inning against the Rangers. It is Boston's 100th homer of the season, marking the 31st consecutive time they have reached the century mark. The Red Sox beat the Rangers, 11-3.

The Athletics buy first baseman Willie McCovey (.203 in 71 games) from the Padres.

SEPTEMBER 1:

Red Sox's pitcher Ferguson Jenkins tears his Achilles tendon while covering first base in the fifth inning of a game against the Rangers.

SEPTEMBER 3:

At Shea Stadium, Tom Seaver fans Tommy Hutton of the Phillies in the seventh inning of today's 1-0 New York victory. Hutton is Seaver's 200th strikeout victim of the season – the ninth straight year the Mets' right-hander has reached that mark.

SEPTEMBER 6:

In San Diego, Steve Yeager is in the on-deck circle with teammate Bill Russell at the plate. Russell's bat breaks and nine pieces puncture Yeager's throat, narrowly missing his windpipe and artery. The Dodgers win the game, 4-1.

SEPTEMBER 10:

California's Nolan Ryan strikes out 18 White Sox hitters in a nine-inning, 3-2 victory.

SEPTEMBER 11:

The White Sox's Minnie Minoso, age 53, becomes a four-decade player when he makes his first appearance in the major leagues today since 1964, going hitless in three at-bats as a designated hitter against the Angels. California wins the game, 7-3.

With the Yankees 12 1/2 games ahead in the AL East, manager Billy Martin gets a three-year contract extension.

SEPTEMBER 12:

Minnie Minoso's "comeback" is in its second day.

> TOMMY LASORDA IS THE CONSUMMATE DODGER. HE SAYS, "I BLEED DODGER BLUE, AND WHEN I DIE, I'M GOING TO THE BIG DODGER IN THE SKY." GAYLORD PERRY ONCE COMMENTED, "WAIT UNTIL TOMMY MEETS THE LORD AND FINDS OUT THAT HE'S WEARING PINSTRIPES."

Appearing as a DH against the Angels, he singles off Isidro "Sid" Monge of the Angels to become the oldest player to hit safely in the major leagues. The White Sox win, 2-1.

SEPTEMBER 14:

Pitcher Dennis Martinez makes his debut with the Orioles, becoming the first player born in Nicaragua to appear in the major leagues. Martinez strikes out the first three Tigers he faces, pitches five and two-thirds scoreless innings, and gets credit for the 9-7 win.

SEPTEMBER 18:

In Baltimore, where he played on four pennant-winning teams, Indians' player-manager Frank Robinson bats for the last time in his illustrious career today. Robinson goes out on a positive note, hitting a pinch-hit single against Rudy May.

SEPTEMBER 25:

The Yankees put an end to a six-game losing streak with a 10-6 win over the Tigers to wrap up the AL East. Doyle Alexander gets the victory.

Hall of Fame pitcher Urban "Red" Faber dies at age 88 in

SEPTEMBER 11
Minnie Minoso of the White Sox, at 53, becomes a four-decade player, going 0-for-3.

SEPTEMBER 29
Tommy Lasorda is named to succeed Walter Alston as the Dodgers' manager.

Chicago, Illinois. Elected to the hall in 1964, Faber pitched for 20 years – all with the White Sox – with a record of 254-213 and an ERA of 3.15. He won three games in the 1917 World Series.

SEPTEMBER 26:

In Montreal, Jim Lonborg pitches a four-hitter and Greg Luzinski hits a three-run homer in the sixth inning to give the Phillies a 4-1 victory and the NL East title. The Expos' Dan Warthen is the losing pitcher.

SEPTEMBER 27:

After 23 years, seven pennants, and four World Series championships, 64-year-old Dodger manager Walter Alston is retiring. Alston, who began with Brooklyn in 1954, leaves with a record of 2,040-1,613. The team will be managed by third base coach Tom Lasorda for the final four games.

SEPTEMBER 29:

The Giants' John "The Count" Montefusco no-hits the Braves, 9-0, at Candlestick Park. Montefusco strikes out four and walks one; the Giants are errorless behind him. The losing pitcher is Jamie Easterly. Montefusco's no-hitter is the third in the NL this season.

Tom Lasorda is named to succeed Walter Alston as the team's manager for 1977. Lasorda, in the Dodger tradition, gets a one-year contract. The Dodgers were second in the NL West with a record of 92-70 last season.

OCTOBER 1:

The Royals clinch the AL West despite a 4-3 loss to the Twins because the Angels defeat the Athletics, 2-0.

OCTOBER 2:

In Milwaukee, Tigers' rookie Mark "The Bird" Fidrych beats the Brewers, 4-1, for his 19th win of the year. Jim Slaton is the losing pitcher.

OCTOBER 3:

In Detroit, with Dave Roberts pitching, DH Henry Aaron comes to bat in the sixth inning for the last time in the major leagues. The 42-year-old Aaron gets an infield hit – the 3,771st safety of his career – and gives way for pinch runner Jim Gantner. Aaron leaves baseball with a barrel of records, most notably 755 lifetime home runs and 2,297 RBI. The Brewers lose, 5-2, and only 6,858 are on hand to see Aaron in his 3,298th game.

On the last day of the season, Cubs third baseman Bill "Mad Dog" Madlock goes four for four against the Expos to edge out Ken Griffey of the

Mark Fidrych grips a league-low 2.34 ERA.

Outfielder Roy White places a Yankees' cap on Reggie Jackson's head at a press conference at the Americana Hotel in New York City. Jackson tells reporters, "I didn't come to New York to become a star. I brought my star with me."

TRIVIA

Mark Fidrych is the latest in a line of odd-ball pitchers. He talks to the ball, manicures the mound, shakes hands with his fielders, and resembles *Sesame Street*'s Big Bird. After a base hit, he refuses to use the same ball, explaining, "Well, the ball had a hit in it, so I want it to get back in the ball bag and goof around with the other balls in there. Maybe it'll learn some sense and come out as a pop-up next time."

Reds for the NL batting title. Madlock finishes at .339; Griffey bats .336.

George Brett beats out teammate Hal McRae for the AL batting championship with a controversial inside-the-park homer. The two Royals' stars enter the ninth with McRae leading .333 to .332. Brett flies to left field where the Twins' Steve Brye misplays the ball and it takes an artificial turf bounce over his head, giving Brett a round-tripper. McRae grounds out to short, finishing at .332 to Brett's .333. McRae has angry words for Twins' manager Gene Mauch, accusing him of instructing Brye to let the ball drop. Mauch denies any such thing, maintaining he "would never, never do anything to harm the integrity of baseball." Brye says he made a "mistake by playing too deep." The Twins win the game, 5-3.

REGULAR SEASON WRAP-UP:

Sparky Anderson's Big Red Machine compiles a regular season record of 102-60 in the NL. The intimidating lineup is led by Joe Morgan (.320, 27 homers, 111 RBI, 60 stolen bases) and includes Ken Griffey (.336), Pete Rose (.323), George Foster (.306, 29 homers, 121 RBI), Tony Perez (19 homers, 91 RBI), Johnny Bench (16 homers), and Cesar Geronimo (.307). The team has no 20-game winners; Gary Nolan is 15-9, Rawly Eastwick records 26 saves.

The Yankees, managed by Billy Martin, have a 97-62 regular season mark in the AL. Catcher Thurman Munson is the team leader with a .302 batting average, 17 homers, and 105 RBI. Graig Nettles has 32 homers and 93 RBI; Oscar Gamble and Chris Chambliss each hit 17 homers. Ed Figueroa is the top starter at 19-10; Albert "Sparky" Lyle has 23 saves.

OCTOBER 8:

Roy Hartsfield is named the first manager of the Toronto Blue Jays, who will begin play in the AL East next season.

OCTOBER 9:

NLCS, game one. A crowd of 62,240 is in attendance today in Philadelphia to watch the Reds double up the Phillies, 6-3. Cincinnati's Don Gullett is the winning pitcher, allowing two hits in eight innings. Lefty Steve Carlton takes the loss. George Foster of the Reds smacks a home run.

ALCS, game one. In Kansas City, Catfish Hunter five-hits the Royals and the Yankees win, 4-1. Two George Brett errors in the first result in two Yankees' runs against losing pitcher Larry Gura.

Pirates' pitcher Bob Moose is killed in an automobile accident in Martin's Ferry, Ohio, on the way to a party for his 29th birthday. Five years ago today, Moose was pitching three and two-thirds innings of relief against the Orioles in the World Series. In 10 years with the Pirates, Moose was 76-71, with a 3.50 ERA. Last season he was 3-9 with a 3.70 ERA.

OCTOBER 10:

NLCS, game two. In Philadelphia, the Reds make it two in a row with a 6-2 win over the Phillies, despite Jim Lonborg's no-hit pitching for five innings. The Reds break the game open with four runs in the sixth. The winning pitcher is Pat Zachry; Lonborg takes the loss.

ALCS, game two. In Kansas City, the Royals come back to beat the Yankees, 7-3. Tom Poquette and John "Buck" Martinez each drive in two runs. The winning pitcher is Paul Splittorff, in relief of Dennis Leonard. Ed Figueroa is the losing pitcher.

OCTOBER 12:

NLCS, game three. The scene shifts to Cincinnati, but the result is the same. The Reds beat Philadelphia, 7-6, with a three-run ninth, to sweep the playoffs and win the NL pennant. Rawly Eastwick, who relieves in the eighth inning, is the winner; Gene Garber gets the loss. George Foster and Johnny Bench homer back-to-back for the Big Red Machine in the ninth-inning rally.

ACLS, game three. In New York, the Yankees win, 5-3, before a stadium crowd of 56,808. Dock Ellis gets the win with ninth-inning relief help from Sparky Lyle and a two-run homer by Chris Chambliss. The losing pitcher is Andy Hassler.

OCTOBER 13:

ALCS, game four. In New York, the Royals win, 7-4, defeating Catfish Hunter. Little

OCTOBER 21
Cincinnati's Big Red Machine completes a four-game World Series sweep of the Yankees.

Freddie Patek drives in three runs. Doug Bird earns the win in relief of Larry Gura. Graig Nettles homers twice for three of New York's runs.

OCTOBER 14:

ALCS, game five. At Yankee Stadium, with the score tied, 6-6, in the bottom of the ninth inning, Chris Chambliss homers off relief pitcher Mark Litell to give the Yankees a 7-6 win and the AL pennant. The winner is Dick Tidrow, who pitched a scoreless ninth inning. Earlier, John Mayberry and George Brett hit home runs for the Royals.

OCTOBER 16:

World Series, game one. In Cincinnati, the Reds make the Yankees' first World Series game in 12 years a losing one. Don Gullet allows five hits in seven and a third innings and Pedro Borbon closes out New York, 5-1. Doyle Alexander gets the loss. Joe Morgan hits a solo homer for the Reds; Tony Perez has three hits.

OCTOBER 17:

World Series, game two. A ninth-inning throwing error by shortstop Fred Stanley enables the Reds to come from behind to defeat the Yankees and Catfish Hunter, 4-3. Tony Perez drives in Ken Griffey with the game's winning run. Jack Billingham gets the win in relief of Fred Norman.

OCTOBER 19:

World Series, game three. The DH rule pays big dividends for the Reds today. Dan Driessen has three hits – including a homer in Cincinnati's 6-2 win. Pat Zachry picks up the win with a save supplied by Will McEnaney. Dock Ellis is charged with the loss. Jim Mason hits a solo homer for the Yankees.

OCTOBER 21:

World Series, game four. Cincinnati's catcher Johnny Bench hits two-run and three-run homers to lead the Reds to a 7-2 win and a World Championship sweep. Gary Nolan gets the win with a save by Will McEnaney; Ed Figueroa is charged with the loss. Bench finishes the Series with a .533 average, two homers, and six RBI. George Foster bats .429, Joe Morgan, .333, and Tony Perez, .313. Thurman Munson is valiant in defeat, going 9-for-. 17 – a .529 average.

POST-SEASON

NOVEMER 4:

At New York City's Plaza Hotel, baseball holds its first free-agent re-entry draft to work out bargaining rights for 26 players. A total of 13 teams participates in the proceedings and 24 players are selected. The first chosen is Bobby Grich of the Orioles. The Athletics' Gene Tenace is selected by 12 teams – the most of any player. The White Sox pick the most players for the purposes of negotiation – 18. The new system was established under the new basic agreement between the owners and players.

NOVEMBER 5:

Another day, another draft at the Plaza Hotel. The AL conducts its expansion draft to provide 30 players each for its new Toronto and Seattle franchises, at a cost of $5.25 million per team. Among the players chosen by Toronto are Bob Bailor, Jim Clancy, Rico Carty, Pete Vukovich, Bill Singer, Doug Ault, Ernie Whitt, Garth Iorg, and Dave Lemanczyk. Seattle's draft picks include Ruppert Jones and Gary Wheelock.

The Pirates get a new manager but it costs them a player and $100,000. Chuck Tanner is released from his contract with the Athletics to manage Pittsburgh. In return, Oakland gets catcher Manny Sanguillen (.290, two homers) and the cash. Tanner was 87-74 with Oakland, good for a second-place finish in the AL West. He replaces Danny Murtaugh, who is retiring. The Pirates were 92-70, in second place in the National League East.

NOVEMBER 6:

Relief pitcher Bill Campbell (17-5, 3.01 ERA, 20 saves) is the first of the free agents to sign a contract. He inks a deal with the Red Sox rumored to be worth between $1 million and $1.05 million over four or five years. Campbell was with the Twins last season.

NOVEMBER 17:

The Ranger sign free-agent shortstop Bert Campaneris (.256, 54 stolen bases). He played last season with Oakland.

NOVEMBER 18:

The Yankees sign free-agent pitcher Don Gullet (11-3, 3.00 ERA), who was with

LEAGUE

In less than a month, Oakland loses four stars to free agency – Bert Campaneris, Sal Bando, Gene Tenace, and Rollie Fingers.

New York's Thurman Munson scored on this play from Game 4 of the World Series, but Cincinnati swept the Yankees.

BENCH
5

NOVEMBER 29
The Yankees sign the A's free-agent outfielder Reggie Jackson to a five-year deal.

DECEMBER 16
The Cincinnati Reds trade first baseman Tony Perez to the Montreal Expos.

the World Champion Reds last season. Gullet reportedly will earn $2 million over the next six years.

NOVEMBER 19:

The Indians sign free-agent pitcher Wayne Garland (20-7, 2.68 ERA, 4 shutouts) to a 10-year, $2.5 million contract. Garland played with the Orioles last season. Wayne Garland's mother tells him, "You're not worth it."

The Brewers sign free-agent infielder Sal Bando (.240, 27 homers, 84 RBI). Bando was with the Athletics last season.

NOVEMBER 24:

The Angels ink infielder Bobby Grich (.266, 13 home runs, 14 stolen bases).

NOVEMBER 29:

The Yankees sign free-agent outfielder Reggie Jackson (.277, 27 homers, 91 RBI, 28 stolen bases). Jackson, who was being sought by 13 teams, gets $2.9 million over five years.

DECEMBER 1:

George Earnshaw dies in Little Rock, Arkansas, at age 76. A pitcher, Earnshaw was the right-handed complement to Lefty Grove with the Athletics from 1929 to 1931. In that period he won 21 games or more three times. Lifetime, he was 127-93 with a 4.38 ERA and appeared in three World Series.

DECEMBER 2:

Danny Murtaugh, who retired as Pirates' manager after the 1976 season, dies of a heart attack at age 59 in Chester, Pennsylvania. Murtaugh managed Pittsburgh for 15 years, winning five pennants and two World Championships – in 1960 and 1971. He compiled a 1,115-950 record. Murtaugh played nine major league seasons as an infielder, batting .254.

DECEMBER 7:

The Mariners make their first-ever trade, acquiring shortstop Craig Reynolds (.250 in seven games) and minor league infielder Jimmy Sexton from the Pirates for pitcher Grant Jackson (7-1, 2.54 ERA).

DECEMBER 9:

The Braves send five players and $250,000 to the Rangers for outfielder Jeff Burroughs (.237, 18 homers, 86 RBI). Texas receives the outfielders Ken Henderson (.262, 13 homers) and Dave May (.215, three homers), along with pitchers Carl Morton (4-9, 4.18 ERA) and Adrian Devine (5-6, 3.21 ERA, nine saves), plus the cash.

DECEMBER 10:

The Indians get first baseman Andre Thornton (.196, 11 homers in 96 games) from the Expos for pitcher Jackie Brown (9-11, 4.25 ERA).

The Pirates obtain pitchers Rich "Goose" Gossage (9-17, 3.94 ERA) and Terry Forster (2-12, 4.38 ERA) from the White Sox for outfielder Richie Zisk (.289, 21 homers, 89 RBI) and minor league pitcher Silvio Martinez.

Rangers' infielder Danny Thompson dies of leukemia at age 29 in Rochester, Minnesota. Traded by the Twins to the Rangers on June 1, Thompson appeared in only 98 games in 1976, batting .222. In seven major league seasons, he hit .248.

DECEMBER 14:

The Padres sign two Athletics mainstays as free agents – catcher-first baseman-third baseman Gene Tenace (.249, 22 homers) and pitcher Rollie Fingers (13-11, 2.47 ERA, 20 saves).

DECEMBER 16:

The Reds trade first baseman Tony Perez (.260, 19 homers, 91 RBI) and pitcher Will McEnaney (2-6, 4.88 ERA, seven saves) to the Expos. In return, they get pitchers Woodie Fryman (13-13, 3.37 ERA) and Dale Murray (4-9, 3.26 ERA, 13 saves). The Big Red Machine, ranked in many circles as one of the greatest teams of all time, reaches its zenith in 1976. The trade of Perez – part of the nucleus, along with Johnny Bench, Joe Morgan, and Pete Rose – marks the end of the Reds' dominance of the decade. The team will finish in second place the next two seasons, then its architect, George "Sparky" Anderson, will be replaced after the 1978 campaign by John McNamara. He will lead them back to the top of the NL West in 1979 – even if without Pete Rose, who's signed with the Phillies – but by then the family-friendly Pittsburgh Pirates have taken over the league's mantle. They will sweep the Reds in the NLCS.

THE BEST OF 1976

NATIONAL LEAGUE

HITTERS

Batting Average:
Bill Madlock, Chicago Cubs, .339

Slugging Average:
Joe Morgan, Cincinnati Reds, .576

Home Runs:
Mike Schmidt, Philadelphia Phillies, 38

Runs Batted In:
George Foster, Cincinnati Reds, 121

Hits:
Pete Rose, Cincinnati Reds, 215

Stolen Bases:
Davey Lopes, Los Angeles Dodgers, 63

PITCHERS

Wins:
Randy Jones, San Diego Padres, 22

Strikeouts:
Tom Seaver, New York Mets, 235

Earned Run Average:
John Denny, St. Louis Cardinals, 2.52

Winning Percentage:
Steve Carlton, Philadelphia Phillies, .741

Saves:
Rawly Eastwick, Cincinnati Reds, 26

Most Valuable Player:
Joe Morgan, Cincinnati Reds

Cy Young Award:
Randy Jones, San Diego Padres

Rookie of the Year:
Pat Zachry, Cincinnati Reds;
Clarence "Butch" Metzger, San Diego Padres

AMERICAN LEAGUE

HITTERS

Batting Average:
George Brett, Kansas City Royals, .333

Slugging Average:
Reggie Jackson, Baltimore Orioles, .502

Home Runs:
Graig Nettles, New York Yankees, 32

Runs Batted In:
Lee May, Baltimore Orioles, 109

Hits:
George Brett, Kansas City Royals, 215

Stolen Bases:
Bill North, Oakland Athletics, 75

PITCHERS

Wins:
Jim Palmer, Baltimore Orioles, 22

Strikeouts:
Nolan Ryan, California Angels, 327

Earned Run Average:
Mark Fidrych, Detroit Tigers, 2.34

Winning Percentage:
Bill Campbell, Minnesota Twins, .773

Saves:
Albert "Sparky" Lyle, New York Yankees, 23

Most Valuable Player:
Thurman Munson, New York Yankees

Cy Young Award:
Jim Palmer, Baltimore Orioles

Rookie of the Year:
Mark "The Bird" Fidrych, Detroit Tigers

1977

"If I played there, they'd name a candy bar after me."
– Reggie Jackson, on New York

NEWS

PRESIDENT CARTER PARDONS VIETNAM DRAFT RESISTERS

BLACKOUT DARKENS NEW YORK CITY FOR TWO DAYS

Space shuttle *Enterprise* takes first flight

JOHNSTOWN, PENNSYLVANIA, FLOOD KILLS 76

FARMERS STAGE NATIONWIDE STRIKE

IN FIRST U.S. EXECUTION IN 10 YEARS, GARY GILMORE DIES BEFORE FIRING SQUAD

Treaty signed to give Panama control of canal by 2000

BING CROSBY, GROUCHO MARX DIE

SON OF SAM MURDERS IN NEW YORK

Star Wars *makes its movie debut*

Woody Allen's Annie Hall win Academy Award for Best Picture

PRE-SEASON

JANUARY 1:

Brewers' pitcher Danny Frisella is killed when his dune buggy overturns in Phoenix, Arizona. Frisella, 30 years old, was 5-2 last year with a 3.13 ERA. In his 10-year career, he was 34-40 with a 3.32 ERA.

JANUARY 3:

Mary Shane becomes the first female TV play-by-play announcer when she is signed by the White Sox for the 1977 season.

JANUARY 6:

The Giants sign free-agent first baseman Willie McCovey (.204, seven homers in 82 games), who played 15 years for San Francisco before being traded to the Padres. McCovey split last season between San Diego and Oakland.

In baseball's second tragedy in less than a week, the California Angels' 23-year-old shortstop Mike Miley is killed in a Baton Rouge, Louisiana, automobile accident. In two abbreviated seasons with the Angels, the right-handed Miley batted .176 in 84 games, with four home runs and 30 RBI.

JANUARY 11:

The Los Angeles Dodgers obtain outfielder Rick Monday (.272, 32 home runs, 77 RBI) and pitcher Mike Garman (2-4, 4.97 ERA) from the Chicago Cubs for outfielder Bill Buckner (.301, seven home runs, 60 RBI), shortstop Ivan DeJesus (.171 in 22 games), and minor league pitcher Jeff Albert.

JANUARY 3
The White Sox hire announcer Mary Shane, who is the first woman to call games on TV.

JANUARY 6
The Giants bring back Willie McCovey, who had spent 15 years in San Francisco.

FEBRUARY 11:

The Cubs trade third baseman Bill Madlock (.339, 15 homers, 84 RBI, 15 stolen bases), the NL batting champion for the past two years, to the Giants, along with infielder Rob Sperring (.258 in 43 games). In return, they get outfielder Bobby Murcer (.259, 23 homers, 90 RBI, 12 stolen bases), infielder Steve Ontiveros (.187 in 59 games) and minor league pitcher Andy Muhlstock.

MARCH 15:

The Pirates acquire second baseman Phil Garner (.261, eight homers) and pitcher Chris Batton (0-0, 9.00 ERA) from the Athletics. In return, Oakland gets outfielder Tony Armas (.333 in four games), pitchers Dave Giusti (5-4, 4.32 ERA, six saves),

Reggie Jackson thrice stirs the Yankees.

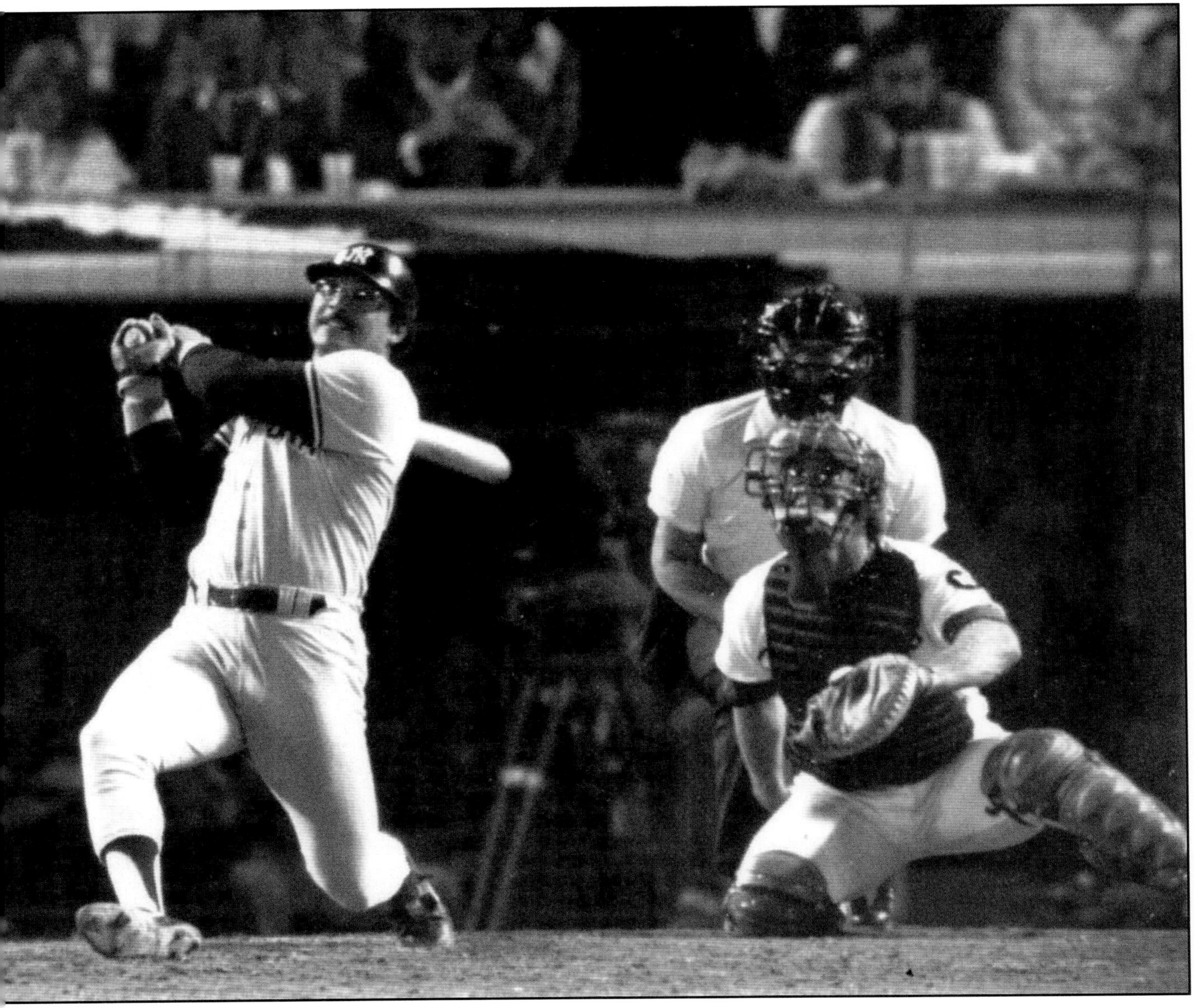

Says Ted Turner: "Managing isn't all that difficult. Just score more runs than the other guy."

CULTURE

Bleacher Bums, a comedy by several authors about Cubs' fans, makes it to the stage.

George "Doc" Medich (8-11, 3.51 ERA), Doug Bair (0-0, 5.68 ERA), and Rick Langford (0-1, 6.26 ERA) along with minor league outfielder Mitchell Page.

MARCH 21:

Tigers' pitcher Mark "The Bird" Fidrych tears the cartilage in his left knee and will require surgery.

MARCH 26:

Infielder Rico Petrocelli (.213 in 85 games) is released by the Red Sox after 13 years in which he batted .251 with 210 homers – including 40 in 1969.

MARCH 28:

Rangers' infielder Lenny Randle, 28 years old, punches out Texas Rangers 50-year-old manager Frank Lucchesi after being benched. Lucchesi's cheekbone is shattered and he will need plastic surgery. Randle is arrested a month later and plea bargains a $1,000 fine and the payment of Lucchesi's medical expenses. The Rangers also fine Randle $10,000, suspend him, and then release him. Randle signs with the Mets.

APRIL 4:

The Pirates acquire outfielder Mike Easler (.241 in 21 games) from the Angels for minor league pitcher Randy Sealy.

APRIL 5:

The Yankees acquire shortstop Bucky Dent (.246) from the White Sox for outfielder-DH Oscar Gamble (.232, 17 homers) and the minor league pitchers LaMarr Hoyt and Bob Polinsky plus $200,000 in cash.

THE SEASON

APRIL 6

The Mariners make their major league debut with a 7-0 loss to the Angels before a crowd of 57,762 at the Kingdome in Seattle.

APRIL 7:

In the first game ever played at Toronto's Exhibition Stadium, the Blue Jays beat the White Sox, 9-5. Attendance is 44,649 despite frigid weather and snow. The honor of the first AL home run on Canadian soil goes to Richie Zisk of the White Sox, but the hitting star is Blue Jays' first baseman Doug Ault, who hits a homer in the first inning against Ken Brett and adds a two-run shot in the third, plus an RBI single in the eighth. Al Woods of Toronto hits a pinch-hit homer in his first major league at-bat. Toronto comes back from a 4-1 deficit to win, 9-5. The winning pitcher is Jerry Johnson. The loser is Brett.

Tommy Lasorda debuts as Dodgers' manager with a 5-1 victory over the Giants in Los Angeles. Don Sutton gets the win.

APRIL 10:

At Fenway Park, the Indians rally for 13 runs – nine unearned – in the eighth inning to beat the Red Sox, 19-9. Boston stages a rally of its own – tallying six in the bottom of the frame – but falls short. The combined 19 runs is a major league record for two teams in one inning.

Juan Bernhardt hits the first homer in Mariners' history – against Frank Tanana of the Angels in the first inning at the Kingdome. The Angels go on to win the game, 12-5.

APRIL 12:

Philip K. Wrigley, owner of the Cubs, dies at age 82 in Elkhorn, Wisconsin. His son, William, inherits the team.

APRIL 15:

Olympic Stadium in Montreal is the third new ballpark – all domed – to be inaugurated this season. In the opening game, the Phillies defeat the Expos, 7-2, behind Steve Carlton. Ellis Valentine homers for both Montreal runs. Attendance is 57,592.

The Braves retire Henry Aaron's number 44, making the home run king the first player to have his number retired by two teams. The Brewers did so last season. After the ceremony, Jeff Burroughs makes his Braves' debut with a two-run homer in a 4-3 victory.

APRIL 17:

In Atlanta, after Bob Watson of the Astros scores on a passed ball in a close play, the instant replay on the scoreboard fires up the crowd and the umpires walk off the field. They return only after a Braves' official assures them there will be no more instant replays of close calls. The Braves win the contest, 5-4.

APRIL 22:

Sixteen games into their history, the Mariners have their first triple play. In the Kingdome, Darrell

MAY
9
The AL's two new expansion teams, the Mariners and Blue Jays, meet for the first time.

Porter of the Royals grounds to shortstop Craig Reynolds, forcing Amos Otis. The throw to first baseman Danny Meyer beats Porter. Meyer then throws to catcher Alfred "Skip" Jutze to get John Mayberry trying to score from third base.

APRIL 25:

It's Reggie against the Baltimore boo-birds at Memorial Stadium. Apparently angry that Reggie Jackson left their team to sign with the Yankees, Orioles rooters hang him in effigy and throw objects at him. Jackson responds with two doubles and a game-winning home run in a 9-6 Yankees win, the team's sixth straight.

APRIL 29:

Short a starting pitcher, Yankees' manager Billy Martin presses Ron Guidry into service against the Mariners in Seattle. Guidry, who has only one major league start in two seasons, pitches eight shutout innings and gets relief help from Albert "Sparky" Lyle. The Yankees win, 3-0.

APRIL 30:

The Dodgers' Ron Cey homers to drive in a run in the seventh against the Expos – it is his major league record 29th RBI of the month. The Dodgers win, 6-4, and are 17-3 starting the season under new manager Tom Lasorda.

WHITE SOX'S MANAGER BOB LEMON SAYS, "I CAN'T WAIT TO GET THE PAPERS EVERY DAY AND READ WHAT'S GOING ON WITH THE YANKEES. IT'S LIKE *MARY HARTMAN, MARY HARTMAN*."

MAY 5:

As part of a promotion for the new Reggie, Reggie, Reggie candy bar, fans at Yankee Stadium get free samples. They throw them on the field, forcing the game to be halted so the grounds crew can clear them away.

MAY 9:

The AL's two new expansion teams meet for the first time; the Blue Jays beat the Mariners by a score of 12-4.

MAY 11:

During a 16-game losing streak, Braves' owner Ted Turner sends manager Dave Bristol on a 10-day scouting assignment and steps in to manage the team. Under Turner the losing streak is extended to 17 with a 2-1 loss to the Pirates.

MAY 12:

NL president Charles "Chub" Feeney invokes Rule 20, Section A. Turner cannot continue to run the team on the field because managers and players may not own a financial interest in teams. Vern Benson steps in for one game and does what Ted Turner and Dave Bristol couldn't – he ends the losing streak. The Braves beat Pittsburgh, 6-1, and manager Bristol resumes managing.

MAY 14:

In Kansas City, the Royals' Jim Colborn no-hits the Rangers. He strikes out six and issues one base on balls; Kansas City makes no errors. The losing pitcher is Tommy Boggs.

MAY 17:

The Cubs play long ball, banging out seven home runs – including three in an inning twice – in a 23-6 thrashing of the visiting Pirates. Larry Biitner, Steve Ontiveros, and Gene Clines start things off with round-trippers in the third inning. Biitner, Jerry Morales, and Bobby Murcer homer consecutively in the fifth, and Dave Rosello homers in the 8th.

The Padres trade last season's NL Rookie of the Year, pitcher

TRIVIA

SABR-ite Russ Lake points out that Steinbrenner's list generated additional controversy because – with one exception – it was the same as one created in 1974 by Gabe Paul for Yankees' manager Bill Virdon. Paul was upset with its use by Steinbrenner – who added the seventh requirement specifically for Martin.

Charles O. Finley is quoted in the *Los Angeles Times*: "We run our club like a pawn shop – we buy, we trade, we sell."

TRIVIA

Comiskey Park organist Nancy Faust plays "Na Na Hey Hey Kiss Him Goodbye" after a White Sox home run against the Royals. The taunting refrain catches on with fans around the country and is heard in virtually every sports arena.

Clarence "Butch" Metzger (0-0) to the Cardinals for pitcher John D'Acquisto (0-0) and infielder Pat Scanlon (.185 in 11 games in 1976).

MAY 22:

In the opener of a doubleheader, the Red Sox hit six homers to down the Brewers, 14-10 at Fenway Park. Milwaukee has five round-trippers. The two teams match a major league record set by the Tigers and Yankees in 1950 and equaled by Cubs and Mets in 1967. The Red Sox's bats are silent in the nightcap; starter Eddie Rodriguez beats them, 6-0.

MAY 23:

Sport Magazine publishes a story by Robert Ward in today's issue in which Reggie Jackson is quoted as saying, "I'm the straw that stirs the drink. It all comes back to me. Maybe I should say me and Munson but really he doesn't enter into it... Munson thinks he can be the straw that stirs the drink but he can only stir it bad." Later, at Yankee Stadium, Jackson homers and avoids his teammates. In the eighth inning he misplays a single into a double, leading to the winning run in a 4-3 win by the Red Sox.

MAY 29:

Chris Chambliss hits a two-run home run against the White Sox and, as Thurman Munson scores ahead of him, the Yankees' captain snubs Reggie Jackson. The Yankees win the game, 5-3, behind Ed Figueroa.

MAY 30:

Cleveland Indians' right-hander Dennis Eckersley no-hits the Angels, 1-0, today in Cleveland. Eckersley fans 12 and walks one; the Indians play error-free baseball. The losing pitcher is Frank Tanana. In his last start, Eckersley no-hit the Mariners for seven and two-thirds innings and ended up with a 2-1 win in 12 innings.

At Fenway Park, Yankees' catcher Thurman Munson relents and shakes Reggie Jackson's hand after "the straw" homers. Mike Torrez beats the Red Sox, 5-4.

MAY 31:

First baseman Joe Torre is appointed manager of the Mets, replacing Joe Frazier, who was fired with the team off to a 15-30 start.

JUNE 1:

Dennis Eckersley is within six outs of Cy Young's record for consecutive no-hit innings when Ruppert Jones homers in the fifth inning. Eckersley had put together a string of 22 1/3 no-hit innings. The Indians beat the Mariners, 7-1.

JUNE 5:

On Old-Timers Day, the Dodgers honor their manager of 23 years, Walter Alston, by retiring his number, 24. Alston himself retired after last season. The Dodgers then beat Doug Rau and the Padres, 4-2.

JUNE 6:

In Kansas City, the Red Sox's players reach two landmarks in a 1-0 victory over the Royals. Luis Tiant registers his 100th Red Sox victory. And Carl Yastrzemski receives his 1,452nd base on balls, tying Jimmie Foxx for the 10th spot.

JUNE 7:

Tom Seaver fans Dan Driessen in the seventh inning for his 2,397th career strikeout, passing Sandy Koufax for the 23rd spot on the all-time list. Seaver beats the Reds, 8-0, in what will be his last game at Shea Stadium as a Met until 1983.

JUNE 8:

The Angels' Nolan Ryan fans 19 Blue Jays in 10 innings; California wins the game, 2-1.

JUNE 9:

At Fenway Park, Carl Yastrzemski doubles against the Orioles; it is the 500th two-bagger of his career.

JUNE 12:

Tom Seaver, in his last game in a Mets' uniform, beats Houston, 3-1, in the Astrodome.

JUNE 13:

Ferguson Jenkins of the Red Sox registers his 2,397th career strikeout, passing Sandy Koufax for the 23rd spot on the all-time list. Boston beats Chicago, 5-4, in 10 innings.

JUNE 15:

In a busy day on the player market, the Mets pull off a shocker, trading the best pitcher in their history and one of the most formidable ever, Tom Seaver (7-3), to the Reds. In return, the Mets get pitcher Pat Zachry (3-7), infielder Doug Flynn

MAY 22
With six Red Sox homers and five by the Brewers, a single-game record is matched.

JUNE 8
The Angels' Nolan Ryan strikes out 19 Blue Jays in a 10-inning, 2-1 California win.

(.250 in 36 games), and minor league outfielders Steve Henderson and Dan Norman. The Mets also send outfielder-first baseman Dave Kingman (.209 in 58 games) to the Padres for infielder Bobby Valentine (.179) and pitcher Paul Siebert (0-0). And, in a third deal, they acquire infielder-outfielder Joel Youngblood (.185 in 25 games) from the Cardinals for infielder Mike Phillips (.209 in 38 games).

JUNE 18:

Network television cameras give a national audience an inside look at the turmoil in the Yankees. Against Boston in Fenway Park, Reggie Jackson plays a soft Jim Rice hit into a double. Manager Billy Martin replaces Jackson with Paul Blair. In the dugout, Jackson goes after Martin and the two have to be separated by Yankees' coaches Elston Howard and Yogi Berra.

Mets manager Joe Torre (.176 in 26 games) retires as a player. In 18 years, Torre batted .297 with 252 homers. In 1971, with the Cardinals, he led the NL in batting with a .363 average.

SAID JOE TORRE OF THE LATE-NIGHT AFTEREFFECTS OF WINNING – AND LOSING – WHILE AT THE HELM WITH THE METS: "WHEN WE LOSE, I CAN'T SLEEP AT NIGHT. WHEN WE WIN, I CAN'T SLEEP AT NIGHT. BUT WHEN YOU WIN, YOU WAKE UP FEELING BETTER." HE ALSO HAD SOME SAGE WORDS ON THE DIFFERENCE BETWEEN WINNING AS A PLAYER AND MANAGER: "BEING A WINNER AS A PLAYER IS GETTING THE MOST FROM YOUR ABILITY. BEING A WINNER AS A MANAGER IS NOT GETTING FIRED."

JUNE 19:

The Red Sox swing and home run records fall at Fenway Park. In beating the Yankees, 11-1, Denny Doyle, Bernie Carbo, Jim Rice, and Carl Yastrzemski homer. The Red Sox now have 21 over five consecutive games, 18 over four straight games, and 16 in three successive games (sweeping the Yankees).

The Indians are 26-31 in fourth place in the AL East and Frank Robinson pays the price. Cleveland fires baseball's first black manager and replaces him with coach Jeff Torborg.

JUNE 20:

In Baltimore, Butch Hobson homers against the Orioles, giving the Red Sox 22 homers over six consecutive games, another major league record. Rick Wise pitches a two-hitter and fans 10 in a 4-0 win.

JUNE 21:

Jim Rice and George Scott homer for the Red Sox in Baltimore, extending Boston's major league record to 24 round-trippers in seven straight games. Luis Tiant backs the heavy hit-

CULTURE

In James F. Donohueís unusual novel, *Spitballs and Holy Water*, Babe Ruth is struck out by a black nun.

JULY
4
On Independence Day, the Red Sox liberate eight baseballs from Fenway Park.

ting with solid pitching; he two-hits the Orioles, 7-0.

JUNE 22:

The Red Sox continue to shatter home run records. Today Boston's George Scott, Jim Rice, Carlton Fisk (twice), and Butch Hobson homer against Jim Palmer. The Red Sox now have 29 round-trippers in eight consecutive games. They top the Orioles, 7-4, for their 12th win in 13 games.

The Rangers fire manager Frank Lucchesi with the team at 31-31. Former Cardinals and White Sox skipper Eddie Stanky will take over.

JUNE 23:

Will it ever end? At Baltimore, Butch Hobson homers, giving the Red Sox 30 in nine consecutive games. Boston wins the game, 7-3.

With new manager Eddie Stanky in charge, the Rangers beat the Twins, 10-8, in Minnesota. After the game, Stanky announces he is quitting to return to his previous job as coach of the University of South Alabama baseball team. The 60-year-old Stanky explains: "After the excitement calmed down, I started getting lonesome and homesick." Connie Ryan will handle the team on an interim basis.

JUNE 28:

Billy Hunter is named the new manager of the Rangers, replacing interim skipper Connie Ryan, who was 2-4 in his tenure.

JULY 4:

At Fenway Park, the Red Sox hit a major league record-tying eight homers to beat the Blue Jays, 9-6, and end a nine-game losing streak. In the eighth inning, Fred Lynn, Jim Rice, Carl Yastrzemski, and George Scott connect. Lynn, Scott Butch Hobson and Bernie Carbo account for the other four homers in the game.

JULY 8:

In Pittsburgh, two superstars are injured in a brawl between the Pirates and Reds that begins when Pittsburgh pitcher Bruce Kison hits Mike Schmidt. Both benches empty, and in the ensuing melee, Schmidt dislocates a finger. Willie Stargell, acting in the role of peacemaker, suffers a pinched nerve in his left elbow.

JULY 10:

In Milwaukee, the Red Sox tie a major league record by stranding 20 in 11 innings. But they score when they need to, beating the Brewers, 8-5.

JULY 11:

The Great Blackout in the Northeast interrupts the Mets-Cubs game at Shea Stadium with Chicago ahead, 2-1 in the sixth.

JULY 14:

A fifth-inning single by Carl Yastrzemski against the Indians' Al Fitzmorris gives him 2,655 career hits, surpassing Ted Williams's lifetime total. Boston wins, 7-4.

JULY 19:

The NL wins the All-Star Game, 7-5, at Yankee Stadium. Joe Morgan, Steve Garvey, and Greg Luzinski homer for the NL, George Scott for the AL. Don Sutton gets the win; Jim Palmer, who gives up four runs in the first, is tagged with the loss.

JULY 21:

Luis Tiant of the Red Sox fans the Indians' Rico Carty in the fourth inning for his 2,000th career strikeout as Boston wins the game, 11-4.

JULY 25:

George Steinbrenner issues his seven requirements for manager Billy Martin. The standards by which Martin will be judged are:
1. Won-lost record.
2. Does he work hard enough?
3. Is he emotionally equipped to lead the men under him?
4. Is he organized?
5. Is he prepared?
6. Does he understand human nature?
7. Is he honorable?

JULY 29:

In Pittsburgh, the Braves' Gaylord Perry opens up the sixth inning by striking out Dave Parker and Bill Robinson. After Al Oliver doubles, he fans Rennie Stennet, who takes first base on a passed ball. Perry then whiffs Omar Moreno for his fourth strikeout of the inning, a major league record held by 14 others. Perry wins his 10th game of the season, 5-3.

AUGUST 1:

Willie McCovey hits his 18th – and final – career grand slam home run, an NL record. Lou Gehrig

LEAGUE

In March, federal court judge Frank McGarr finds that Commissioner Bowie Kuhn acted within his powers when he canceled Charles O. Finley's sale of three stars to the Red Sox and Yankees for $3.5 million.

AUGUST 8
The Cubs' longtime shortstop, Ernie Banks, is inducted into the Hall of Fame.

AUGUST 17
The Phillies' luck runs out as their 13-game win streak ends with a 13-0 loss to the Expos.

holds the major league mark with 23. The Giants beat the Expos, 9-2.

The Rangers and White Sox play the longest night game in AL history – three hours and 56 minutes. They fall one minute short of the record for the longest nine-inning game ever in the league. Texas wins, 11-6.

AUGUST 5:

A crowd of 36,833 sees the Mariners beat the Yankees, 5-3, putting Seattle's season attendance over 1,000,000.

AUGUST 8:

Ernie Banks, Martin Dihigo, John Lloyd, Al Lopez, Amos Rusie, and Joe Sewell are inducted into the Hall of Fame. Banks, one of baseball's most upbeat personalities, played shortstop and first base for the Cubs for 19 years. He compiled a .274 average with 512 homers. He twice led the NL in homers and in RBI, and hit 40 or more homers in five seasons. Banks never had the opportunity to display his talents in a World Series. Martin Dihigo, an outstanding pitcher and hitter, is the only player elected to halls of fame in three countries – Cuba, Mexico, and now the United States. The Cuban-born Dihigo was voted the all-time best second baseman in black baseball. He was 218-106 as a pitcher; his incomplete hitting statistics include a .302 batting average and 130 home runs. Dihigo died in 1971. Pop Lloyd played shortstop for 24 years and was described by Babe Ruth as the greatest player anywhere. Lloyd, who died in 1964, overshadowed Ty Cobb in a 1910 exhibition series in Cuba and hit .353 in 24 years in the Negro Leagues. He hit .400 several times. Al Lopez won pennants with the Indians in 1954 and the White Sox in 1959 in 17 years as a manager. He also had 10 second-place finishes. Lopez caught for 19 years in the majors, hitting .261. Amos Rusie, a pitcher, was also known as the Hoosier Thunderbolt, and his overpowering speed is regarded as the reason the mound was moved back to 60 feet, 6 inches. In 10 years, he was 246-174 with a 3.07 ERA and 1,934 strikeouts. Sewell won 30 games or more four times and 20 or more four times. In 1894, he was 36-13 with a 2.78 ERA. Rusie died in 1942. Sewell, an infielder, played with the Indians and Yankees, hitting .312 in 14 years with 436 doubles. He hit .300 or better 10 times, with a high of .353 in 1923.

Ernie Banks tells the Cooperstown audience, "I once read that success depends on the talents God gave you and also on the people who believe in you. This honor belongs to those people who believed in me – my parents, my wife and children, and those individuals such as Monte Irvin and Cool Papa Bell, who helped teach me. And then, of course, there are the fans."

AUGUST 9:

The Blue Jays beat the Twins, 6-2, before a crowd of 23,450, putting Toronto's home attendance for 50 games at 1,219,551 – a new record for an expansion team.

AUGUST 15:

Jim Rice of the Red Sox hits a third-inning double to right field, giving him 20-plus home runs, 20-plus doubles and 10-plus triples. Only four players since World War II have reached that "triple-double" – Charlie Keller in 1946, Joe DiMaggio in 1950, and Mickey Mantle in 1955. Boston tops Kansas City in the game, 5-3.

AUGUST 17:

The Phillies are hammered by the Expos, 13-0, ending their winning streak at 13, their longest since 1892.

AUGUST 21:

A crowd of 46,265 turns out at Shea Stadium for Tom Seaver's return in a Reds' uniform. Seaver strikes out 11 of his former Mets' teammates, allows six hits and beats Jerry Koosman, 5-1.

AUGUST 27:

At spacious Yankee Stadium today, the Rangers' Toby Harrah and Elliott "Bump" Wills hit back-to-back, inside-the-park home runs on consecutive pitches in the seventh inning from the Yankees' Ken Clay. Texas wins, 8-2.

In a 7-5 win over the Twins at Fenway Park, Tommy Helms and Butch Hobson hit back-to-back homers today for the Red Sox. It is the 15th time this season that Boston

HISTORY

In the series in which he played against Ty Cobb, Pop Lloyd put the tag on the Georgia Peach three times at second base. And he came prepared, wearing metal shin guards under his uniform to protect him from Cobb's spikes. Honus Wagner once said, "I am honored to have John Lloyd called the Black Wagner. It is a privilege to have been compared with him."

AUGUST 29
With number 893, Lou Brock ties Ty Cobb's career stolen base record.

SEPTEMBER 10
The neophyte Blue Jays hand the Yankees a 19-3 pasting, their worst loss in 50 years.

TRIVIA

Dusty Baker's October 2 home run supposedly results in the birth of the high five. His Dodgers' teammate Glenn Burke is in the on-deck circle when Baker connects. As Baker passes by, Burke raises his hand and Baker slaps it – a high five.

players have hit consecutive home runs, tying a major league record.

AUGUST 28:

The Dodgers' Steve Garvey hits two home runs – including a grand slam – and three doubles and Don Sutton pitches a shutout in an 11-0 victory over the Cardinals. Garvey ties a major league record with five extra base hits in a game.

AUGUST 29:

In San Diego, Lou Brock leads off the game with a base on balls from Dave Freisleben and steals second base on the first pitch to tie the career record of 893 set by Ty Cobb. In the seventh inning with Frisleben pitching, Brock reaches on a fielder's choice and steals second for a major league record. He is presented with second base as a memento. It took Cobb 3,033 games to reach 893; Brock accomplished it in 2,376. Brock also holds the single season mark with 118 in 1974. San Diego wins the game, though, 4-3.

The Angels' Nolan Ryan fans 11 Orioles today, giving him 300 in a season for the fifth time. Baltimore beats California, 6-1.

HUB KITTLE DESCRIBES BRUCE SUTTER'S SPLIT-FINGER FASTBALL: "AS HE COMES OVER AND DOWN WITH VERY FAST ARM ACTION, JUST LIKE HIS FASTBALL, THE BALL SQUIRTS OUT WITH SINKER SPIN FROM HIS THUMB. THE BALL COMES IN LOOKING LIKE A STRAIGHT FASTBALL WITH A VELOCITY AROUND 85 MILES AN HOUR. AS IT GETS TO THE PLATE, IT JUST SEEMS TO SIT, LIKE AN AIRPLANE COMING IN FOR A LANDING."

Indians' second baseman Duane Kuiper homers against Steve Stone of the White Sox. It is the first for Kuiper in 1,382 at-bats and four seasons. Teammates Andre Thornton and Bruce Bochte homer back-to-back and Cleveland wins the game, 9-2.

Kuiper plays 12 years, coming to bat 3,379 times. Today's homer is the only one of his career. He does hit a respectable .271.

SEPTEMBER 3:

Sadaharu Oh hits his 756th career home run with the Yomiuri Giants of Tokyo in the Japan Central League. Oh's historic shot carries 328 feet into the right-field stands of Korakuen Stadium in Tokyo in the bottom of the third with the bases empty off Yasumiro Suzuki. The Giants beat the Yakult Swallows, 8-1.

SEPTEMBER 8:

At Wrigley Field, the Cubs' Bruce Sutter comes out of the bullpen to fan eight straight Expos, tying an NL record for relief pitchers. Chicago beats Montreal, 3-2.

For the 16th time this season, Red Sox batters hit back-to-back homers, breaking the major league record set by the Twins in 1964. Today's long ball hitters are Carlton Fisk and George Scott against the Blue Jays' pitchers in Toronto.

SEPTEMBER 10:

The young Blue Jays soar against the Yankees with a 19-3 victory in New York. It is the worst defeat for the Yankees in more than 50 years. The principal damage is done by Roy Howell, who hits two homers, two doubles and a single, driving in nine runs.

SEPTEMBER 11:

Gary Matthews, Biff Pocoraba, and Pat Rockett execute a triple steal for the Braves against the Padres. Atlanta wins the game, 7-3.

SEPTEMBER 15:

In San Diego, Braves' catcher Dale Murphy hits his first two major league homers. He connects for the second in the top of the 10th in an 8-7 Atlanta win.

The Orioles forfeit today's game to the Blue Jays in Toronto,

SEPTEMBER 23
The Reds' George Foster becomes the fifth NLer to hit 50 homers in a season.

9-0, when O's manager Earl Weaver removes his team from the playing field in the fifth inning. Weaver is angry when umpire Marty Springstead will not order the removal of a tarpaulin in the Blue Jays bullpen, which the manager claims is dangerous to his fielders. Baltimore was trailing, 4-0, at the time.

SEPTEMBER 16:

The Mariners beat the Royals, 4-1, ending Kansas City's 16-game winning streak which began back on August 31.

The Mets and Cubs resume playing their July 13 game, which was interrupted by the Northeast's Great Blackout. The Cubs and Ray Burris win the game, 4-3.

SEPTEMBER 17:

The Dodgers and the visiting Braves draw 52,527, giving Los Angeles a major league record season attendance of 2,756,464.

SEPTEMBER 22:

The Rangers' Bert Blyleven no-hits the Angels, 6-0, in Anaheim. Blyleven strikes out seven and walks one; Texas makes no errors. The losing pitcher is Paul Hartzell.

SEPTEMBER 23:

In Atlanta, the Reds' George Foster connects against Lee "Buzz" Capra for his 50th homer of the season. Foster is the fifth player in NL history to hit 50. The others are Hack Wilson, Ralph Kiner, Johnny Mize, and Willie Mays. The Reds beat the Braves, 5-1.

In Anaheim, the Royals, behind Dennis Leonard, defeat the Angels, 7-3, to clinch the AL West.

SEPTEMBER 26:

Former major league catcher Ernie Lombardi dies at age 69 in Santa Cruz, California. One of baseball's hardest hitters and slowest runners, he played for 17 years, hitting .306 with 190 homers. He was the NL's batting champion in 1938 with .342 and in 1942 with .330. Lombardi appeared in two World Series with the Reds.

SEPTEMBER 27:

In Chicago, the Phillies beat the Cubs, 15-9, to win their second consecutive NL East title. Larry Christenson hits a grand slam homer in the seventh inning and is the winning pitcher. Mike Schmidt connects for his 38th of the season. The losing pitcher is Bill Bonham.

SEPTEMBER 29:

Executors of Tom Yawkey's estate pick a 13-member group to buy the Red Sox. The group includes team vice president Haywood Sullivan, former trainer Edward "Buddy" LeRoux, and the Harry M. Stevens Co. The sale price is $16 million, pending AL approval.

SEPTEMBER 30:

In the eighth inning of the opener of a doubleheader, Lou Brock steals second base against the Mets. It is the 900th career stolen base for Brock and 35th of the season. The Cardinals win the game, 7-2.

OCTOBER 1:

While the New York Yankees wait out a nearly three-hour rain delay today, the Baltimore Orioles beat the Boston Red Sox, giving New York the AL East flag. The Yankees eventually play their game, losing to the Detroit Tigers, 10-7.

OCTOBER 2:

In his last at-bat of the season, Johnnie "Dusty" Baker hits a sixth-inning home run against the Astros' J.R. Richard. It is Baker's 30th home run. He joins teammates Steve Garvey (33), Reggie Smith (32), and Ron Cey (30) in making the Dodgers the first team in history to have four players with 30 or more round-trippers. The Astros go on to win the game, 6-3.

Pirates' relief pitchers Kent Tekulve and Rich "Goose" Gossage each appear for the 72nd time as Pittsburgh beats the Cubs, 3-2. Willie Stargell ends the game at .338 to top the National League.

REGULAR SEASON WRAP-UP:

Billy Martin's New York Yankees just hit the century mark, going 100-61 in the regular season in the American League. With no 20-game winner among his starting pitchers, Sparky Lyle excels out of the bullpen with a 13-5 record, a 2.17 ERA, and 26 saves. The offense comes from Reggie Jackson (.286, 32 homers, 110 RBI), Thurman

LEAGUE

Despite a record of 54-107, the Blue Jays register a home attendance of 1,701,052 in their first year in the majors. The Mariners draw 1,338,511, the most ever for a U.S. expansion team.

OCTOBER 9
The Yankees beat the Royals in the ALCS and will meet the Dodgers in the World Series.

LEAGUE

According to authors Don Dewey and Nicholas Acocella, a media guide cover negated a trade and changed recent baseball history. Prior to the start of the 1977 season, the Blue Jays agreed to a trade that would send pitcher Bill Singer to the Yankees for little-used lefthander Ron Guidry. Toronto then realized Singer was on the cover of their 1977 media guide and, wanting to avoid embarrassment, decided to keep him. Singer is 2-8 in 1977 and retires after the season. Guidry compiles a 16-7, 2.82 ERA year and goes on to become a dominant pitcher for the Yankees.

Munson (.308, 18 homers, 100 RBI), Lou Piniella (.330), Mickey Rivers (.326), Chris Chambliss (17 homers), and Graig Nettles (.255, 37 homers, 107 RBI).

Tom Lasorda wins the National League pennant in his first full season as Dodgers' manager; Los Angeles compiles a 98-64 regular season mark. The Dodgers feature four 30-home run hitters, and Tommy John is the team's pitching leader (20-7).

The Red Sox set numerous home run records during the season and lead the AL with 213, but finish tied for second in their division, two and a half games behind the Yankees. The Padres' Gene Richards steals 56 bases, a major league rookie record.

OCTOBER 4:

NLCS, game one. In Los Angeles, the Phillies beat the Dodgers, 7-5, despite a grand slam home run by Los Angeles's Ron Cey. Greg Luzinski hits a two-run homer for the Phillies; Arnold "Bake" McBride, Larry Bowa, and Mike Schmidt single for two runs in the ninth. The winning pitcher is Gene Garber in relief of Steve Carlton. Elias Sosa takes the loss.

OCTOBER 5:

ALCS, game one. In New York, the Royals beat the Yankees, 7-2, behind Paul Splittorff with relief help from Doug Bird. Hal McRae, John Mayberry, and Al Cowens home run for the Royals. Thurman Munson hits a round-tripper for New York. Don Gullett is the losing pitcher.

NLCS, game two. In Los Angeles, the Dodgers bounce back, 7-1, behind a complete-game nine-hitter by Don Sutton. Dusty Baker paces the Dodger attack with a grand slam home run off Jim Lonborg with the score tied, 1-1, in the fourth. Bake McBride homers for Philadelphia. Lonborg is the losing pitcher.

OCTOBER 6:

ALCS, game two. In New York, Ron Guidry three-hits the Royals and the Yankees win, 6-2, with the help of a home run by Cliff Johnson. The losing pitcher is starter Andy Hassler. Guidry goes all the way for the win.

OCTOBER 7:

NLCS, game three. In Philadelphia, 63,719 see the Dodgers win their second straight, 6-5. The Dodgers score three runs with two out in the top of the ninth to win the game. Los Angeles's fifth pitcher of the game, Clarence "Lance" Rautzhan, gets the win. Gene Garber is charged with the loss.

ALCS, game three. In Kansas City, the Royals beat the Yankees on Dennis Leonard's complete-game four-hitter. Hal McRae has two doubles and scores a pair of runs. Mike Torrez is the losing pitcher.

OCTOBER 8:

NLCS, game four. In Philadelphia, the Dodgers win the NL pennant on a 4-1 complete-game victory by Tommy John, who scatters seven hits. Johnnie "Dusty" Baker hits a second-inning, two-run homer off losing pitcher Steve Carlton.

ALCS, game four. In Kansas City, the Yankees knot the playoffs with a 6-4 victory today. Albert "Sparky" Lyle, who comes on in the fourth and completes the game, is the winning pitcher. Mickey Rivers has four hits for New York. Royals' starter Larry Gura is the game's losing pitcher

OCTOBER 9:

ALCS, game five. In Kansas City. For the second straight year the ALCS between the Yankees and the Royals goes down to the wire, and again New York prevails. Going into the ninth, the Royals lead, 3-2, behind strong pitching from Dennis Leonard. The Yankees score three runs, Sparky Lyle holds the Royals in the bottom of the ninth, and New York wins, 5-3, for its second straight pennant. Lyle gets the win, Leonard the loss.

OCTOBER 11:

World Series, game one. At Yankee Stadium, Paul Blair singles in Willie Randolph – who had doubled – with the winning run in the bottom of the 12th. Randolph previously had homered in the Yankees' 4-3 win. Sparky Lyle gets the win with three and two-thirds innings in relief of starter Don Gullett. The losing pitcher is Rick Rhoden.

OCTOBER 12:

World Series, game two. The Dodgers rebound, 6-1, on a

OCTOBER 18
Reggie Jackson hits three straight homers to lead the Yanks to the World Championship.

NOVEMBER 22
Bobby Cox is signed as manager of the Atlanta Braves, replacing Dave Bristol.

five-hit complete game hurled by Burt Hooten. Ron Cey and Reggie Smith hit two-run homers; Steve Yeager and Steve Garvey have solo shots. Jim "Catfish" Hunter gets the loss.

OCTOBER 14:

World Series, game three. In Los Angeles, Mike Torrez overcomes a three-run homer by Dusty Baker to gain a 5-3 win. Mickey Rivers paces the Yankees with three hits, including two doubles. Tommy John gets the loss.

OCTOBER 15:

World Series, game four. Ron Guidry strikes out seven and yields four hits – including a two-run homer to Davey Lopes – to beat the Dodgers, 4-2. Reggie Jackson has a solo homer and a double. Doug Rau is credited with the loss.

OCTOBER 16:

World Series, game five. The Dodgers unload on four Yankees' pitchers, banging out 13 hits in a 10-4 win. Steve Yeager has a three-run homer and four RBI, Reggie Smith homers with a man on, and Dusty Baker collects three hits. Don Sutton goes all the way, allowing nine hits, for the win. Reggie Jackson and Thurman Munson hit bases-empty home runs for New York. Starter Don Gullett gets the loss.

OCTOBER 17:

Hall of Fame umpire Cal Hubbard dies today at the age of 77. Hubbard, who also was supervisor of American League umpires, was inducted into the Hall last year. A fine all-around athlete, Hubbard was also a member of the College and Professional Football Halls of Fame.

OCTOBER 18:

World Series, game six. Reggie Jackson puts on a stirring show with three consecutive homers and five RBI as the Yankees beat the Dodgers, 8-4, in New York for the World Championship. It is the first World Series title for the Yankees since 1962. Jackson hits a two-run homer into the right-field seats in the fourth inning against Burt Hooten; another two-run round-tripper into right field against Elias Sosa in the fifth, and a leadoff bases-empty homer in the eighth into center field off Charlie Hough. Chris Chambliss adds a two-run shot of his own; Reggie Smith hits a homer for the Dodgers. Mike Torrez goes all the way, giving up nine hits, for the win. Hooten gets the loss. Reggie Jackson hits five Series home runs and bats .450 with eight RBI. Thurman Munson bats .320 with a homer and three RBI. Steve Garvey leads Los Angeles hitters with a .375 batting average.

POST-SEASON

NOVEMBER 8:

Hall of Famer Stanley "Bucky" Harris dies today in Bethesda, Maryland, on his 81st birthday. Enshrined in the Hall of Fame in 1975, Harris was a major league manager for 29 years, winning three pennants and a pair of World Championships, with the Senators and Yankees. He played second base for 12 years, batting .274.

NOVEMBER 9:

The Texas Rangers sign free-agent outfielder-designated hitter Richie Zisk (.290, 30 home runs, 101 RBI) to a 10-year, $2.3 million deal. Zisk had played with the Chicago White Sox this season.

NOVEMBER 17:

Free-agent outfielder-DH Larry Hisle (.302, 28 home runs, 119 RBI) signs with the Brewers. Last season with the Twins, Hisle led the AL in RBI.

NOVEMBER 21:

The Angels sign free-agent outfielder Lyman Bostock (.336, 14 homers, 16 stolen bases). Bostock, the son of former Negro League star Lyman Bostock Sr., played last season with the Minnesota Twins.

NOVEMBER 22:

Bobby Cox is signed as the manager of the Braves, replacing Dave Bristol. Atlanta was 61-101 and last in the NL West.

The Dodgers sign their first free agent – pitcher Terry Forster (6-4, 4.45 ERA), who spent last season with the Pirates.

NOVEMBER 23:

The Yankees sign free-agent relief pitcher Rich "Goose" Gossage (11-9, 1.62 ERA, 26 saves) to a $2.75-million, six-year contract. Gossage was with the Pittsburgh Pirates last season.

The Red Sox sign two free-agent pitchers – Mike Torrez (17-

CULTURE

At the movies, *The Bad News Bears in Breaking Training* stars William Devane and Jackie Earle Haley.

NOVEMBER 30
The Chicago Cubs sign free-agent veteran slugger Dave Kingman.

DECEMBER 14
Future Hall of Fame pitcher Ferguson Jenkins is traded back to the Rangers.

TRIVIA

In the movie *Oh, God,* George Burns in the title role utters the line, "My last miracle was the '69 Mets."

13, 3.92 ERA, two shutouts) and Dick Drago (6-4, 3.41 ERA). The 31-year-old Torrez split last season between the Oakland Athletics and New York Yankees; he gets a seven-year, $2.5 million deal from Boston. Drago was with he Angels and Orioles. Torrez will go 16-13 the next two seasons in Boston, with an ERA of 3.96 in 1978 and 4.50 in '79.

NOVEMBER 24:

Edward "Mayo" Smith, who managed the 1968 Detroit Tigers to the World Championship, dies at age 62 in Boynton Beach, Florida. In his nine-year career, Smith also managed the Phillies and Reds. His playing career consisted of only 73 games in 1945 with the Phillies; he batted .212.

NOVEMBER 28:

Bob Meusel, who played in the Yankees' outfield with Hall of Famers Babe Ruth and Earle Combs, dies at age 81 in Downey, California. Known as Long Bob, he played for 11 years – all but one with the Yankees – batting .309 with 156 home runs. Meusel hit .300 seven times, with a high of .337 in 1927. In 1925, he led the AL in homers with 33, beating out Ruth. Meusel appeared in six World Series, opposing his brother Emil "Irish" Meusel of the Giants three times. Irish Meusel died in 1963.

NOVEMBER 30:

The Chicago Cubs sign free-agent outfielder-infielder Dave Kingman (.221, 26 home runs, 78 RBI). Kingman, who first came into the major leagues in 1971, has played with the New York Mets, San Diego Padres, California Angels, and New York Yankees in 1977. He will stick with the Cubs for three years.

DECEMBER 5:

In the midst of the free-agent signings, two teams pull off a trade: the Chicago White Sox acquire outfielder-DH Bobby Bonds (.264, 37 homers, 115 RBI, 41 stolen bases), outfielder Thad Bosley (.297 in 58 games), and minor league pitcher Richard Dotson from the California Angels. In return, California acquires catcher-outfielder-DH Brian Downing (.284, four homers in 77 games) and pitchers Chris Knapp (12-7, 4.81 ERA) and Dave Frost (1-1, 3.00 ERA).

DECEMBER 7:

Well, he wasn't traded. Pitcher Andy Messersmith (5-4, 4.41 ERA), the player Braves' owner Ted Turner said last year would "never be traded... will be a Brave as long as I am," is sold to the Yankees.

DECEMBER 8:

Because of questions raised regarding the financing of the deal, the American League holds up approval of the $16-million sale of the Boston Red Sox to a 13-member group.

DECEMBER 9:

The Detroit Tigers pull off a deal, trading outfielder Ben Oglivie (.262, 21 home runs) to the Milwaukee Brewers for a pair of pitchers, Jim Slaton (10-14, 3.58 ERA) and Rich Folkers (0-1, 4.50 ERA).

DECEMBER 14:

The veteran right-handed pitcher and future Hall of Famer Ferguson Jenkins (10-10, 3.68 ERA) returns to the Texas Rangers in a trade with the Boston Red Sox. In return, Boston gets pitcher John Poloni (1-0, 6.43 ERA) and cash. Fergie will go 18-8, with a 3.04 ERA with the Rangers in '78.

"THE THING ABOUT REGGIE IS THAT YOU KNOW HE'S GOING TO PRODUCE. AND IF HE DOESN'T, HE'S GOING TO TALK ENOUGH TO MAKE PEOPLE THINK HE'S GOING TO PRODUCE."
– REGGIE JACKSON'S YANKEES' TEAMMATE, HALL OF FAME PITCHER JIM "CATFISH" HUNTER

THE BEST OF 1977

NATIONAL LEAGUE

HITTERS

Batting Average:
Dave Parker, Pittsburgh Pirates, .338

Slugging Average:
George Foster, Cincinnati Reds, .631

Home Runs:
George Foster, 52

Runs Batted In:
George Foster, 149

Hits:
Dave Parker, 215

Stolen Bases:
Frank Taveras, Pittsburgh Pirates, 70

PITCHERS

Wins:
Steve Carlton, Philadelphia Phillies, 23

Strikeouts:
Phil Niekro, Atlanta Braves, 262

Earned Run Average:
John Candelaria, Pittsburgh Pirates, 2.34

Winning Percentage:
John Candelaria, .800

Saves:
Rollie Fingers, San Diego Padres, 35

Most Valuable Player:
George Foster, Cincinnati Reds

Cy Young Award:
Steve Carlton, Philadelphia Phillies

Rookie of the Year:
Andre Dawson, Montreal Expos

AMERICAN LEAGUE

HITTERS

Batting Average:
Rod Carew, Minnesota Twins, .388

Slugging Average:
Jim Rice, Boston Red Sox, .593

Home Runs:
Jim Rice, 39

Runs Batted In:
Larry Hisle, Minnesota Twins, 119

Hits:
Rod Carew, 239

Stolen Bases:
Freddie Patek, Kansas City Royals, 53

PITCHERS

Wins:
Dennis Leonard, Kansas City Royals;
Dave Goltz, Minnesota Twins;
Jim Palmer, Baltimore Orioles, 20

Strikeouts:
Nolan Ryan, California Angels, 341

Earned Run Average:
Frank Tanana, California Angels, 2.54

Winning Percentage:
Paul Splittorff, Kansas City Royals, .727

Saves:
Bill Campbell, Boston Red Sox, 31

Most Valuable Player:
Rod Carew, Minnesota Twins

Cy Young Award:
Albert "Sparky" Lyle, New York Yankees

Rookie of the Year:
Eddie Murray, Baltimore Orioles

1978

Ron Guidry is in Cy Young form.

NEWS

CAMP DAVID PEACE CONFERENCE ON MIDDLE EAST IS CONVENED

JIM JONES, 900 CULT MEMBERS DIE IN BIZARRE SUICIDE RITUAL AFTER MURDER OF CONGRESSMAN LEO RYAN

Love Canal toxic waste site in New York evacuated

HUBERT H. HUMPHREY DIES

WEST VIRGINIA NUCLEAR PLANT ACCIDENT KILLS 51 WORKERS

Jimmy Carter tours Europe, Middle East

San Francisco Mayor George Moscone, City Supervisor Harvey Milk assassinated

JOHN D. ROCKEFELLER DIES

PANAMA CANAL TREATY RATIFIED

FIRST "TEST-TUBE BABY," LOUISE BROWN, IS BORN IN LONDON

PRE-SEASON

JANUARY 3:

Hall of Fame manager Joe McCarthy dies at age 90 on his farm near Buffalo, New York. McCarthy, who never played major league baseball, managed for 24 years, compiling the highest winning percentage of all time – .615. He won one pennant with the Cubs in 1929. He became manager of the Yankees in 1931 and won eight pennants and seven World Series. He also managed the Red Sox for three seasons. McCarthy was inducted into the Hall of Fame in 1952.

JANUARY 20:

George Bamberger is hired as manager of the Brewers, who finished sixth in the AL East last year with a record of 67-95.

JANUARY 25:

The Padres obtain pitcher Gaylord Perry (15-12, 3.37 ERA) from the Rangers for pitcher Dave Tomlin (4-4, 3.00 ERA) and $125,000.

JANUARY 30:

Commissioner Bowie Kuhn voids another of Charles O. Finley's deals. This one would have sent pitcher Vida Blue to the Reds for minor league first baseman Dave Revering and $1.75 million. Finley had ignored Kuhn's directive that he be consulted on any transaction involving $400,000 or more.

FEBRUARY 3:

The Cleveland Indians are bought by F.J. "Steve" O'Neill.

FEBRUARY 25:

Charlie Finley still must keep Vida Blue, but he does get Dave Revering. He acquires the first baseman and cash from the Reds for relief pitcher Doug Bair (4-6, 3.47 ERA, eight saves).

MARCH 15:

Charlie Finley tries again. This time he trades Vida Blue to the Giants for seven players and $390,000 – $10,000 below the amount subject to Commissioner Bowie Kuhn's approval. In return for Blue, Oakland gets catcher Gary Alexander (.303, five homers in 51 games), outfielder-first baseman Gary Thomasson (.256, 17 homers), infielder-DH Mario Guerrero (.283 in 86 games), pitcher Dave Heaverlo (5-1, 2.55 ERA), and minor league pitchers Alan Wirth, John Henry Johnson, and Phil Huffman.

MARCH 16:

Yankees' pitcher Andy Messersmith, attempting to come back from arm troubles in 1977, falls and separates his shoulder during an exhibition game.

MARCH 19:

The *New York Times* reports that the cost for renovating Yankee Stadium is up to $95.6 million and that it would have cost $48.8 million to rebuild the ballpark.

MARCH 21:

Roger Craig is appointed the new manager of the Padres, who were 69-93 in fifth place in the NL West under three managers – John McNamara, Bob Skinner (one game), and Alvin Dark, who is fired 17 days before the start of the 1978 season.

According to historian David L. Porter, Dark was fired "because of a player revolt, his failure to communicate with the front office, and his unwillingness to designate authority to his pitching, hitting, and other coaches."

The Yankees' Mickey Rivers says: "Me and George and Billy are two of a kind."

LEAGUE

In April, the score is Bowie Kuhn, 2; Charlie Finley, 0. The U.S. District Court of Appeals upholds the 1977 decision of federal judge Frank McGarr, who supported the commissioner's revocation of the trade of three Oakland stars. Finley had claimed Kuhn exceeded his authority.

MARCH 30:

The Red Sox acquire pitcher Dennis Eckersley (14-13, 3.53 ERA, 191 strikeouts) and catcher Fred Kendall (.249) from the Indians for pitchers Rick Wise (11-5, 4.78 ERA) and Mike Paxton (10-5, 3.83 ERA) along with designated hitter Ted Cox (.362 in 13 games) and catcher Baudilio "Bo" Diaz (.000 in one at-bat).

THE SEASON

APRIL 8:

Former baseball commissioner Ford Frick dies at age 79 in Bronxville, New York.

APRIL 13:

Mickey Mantle and Roger Maris are reunited at Yankee Stadium for the raising of the 1977 championship banner prior to the home opener, attended by 44,567. It is the first time in more than 11 years that Maris has been in the ballpark. Reggie Jackson hits a three-run homer off Wilbur Wood in the first, and Ron Guidry beats the White Sox, 4-2.

APRIL 14:

Former major league second baseman and manager Joe Gordon dies at the age of 63 in Sacramento, California. The smooth-fielding, good-hitting Gordon was the AL's Most Valuable Player in 1942, when he hit .322 with 18 homers and 103 RBI. He holds the AL career record – 246 – and the season record – 32 – for homers by a second baseman. In 11 years, he hit .268 and played in six World Series.

APRIL 16:

The Cardinals' Bob Forsch no-hits the Phillies, 5-0, in St. Louis – the first in the city in 54 years. Forsch has an anxious moment in the eighth inning when Garry Maddox hits a ball that goes under the glove of third baseman Ken Reitz. Official scorer Neal Russo of the St. Louis Post-Dispatch takes 10 seconds and makes the call – an error. Forsch strikes out three and walks two. Randy Lerch is the losing pitcher.

MAY 5:

Today at Riverfront Stadium, the Reds' Pete Rose singles to left field against Steve Rogers of the Expos in the fifth inning for his 3,000th career hit. He is the 13th player in history to reach that mark. A crowd of 37,823 give Rose a five-minute ovation and a brief ceremony ensues. Earlier, Rose collected his 2,999th hit when Rogers mishandled a ball in the third inning. The official scorer was cheered by the fans when the "hit" sign was posted. Rose, age 37, reached 3,000 hits faster than any player in history. The only sour note of the day is the Reds' 4-3 loss.

In California, Wayne Garland, the Indians' $10 million free-agent pitcher, undergoes surgery by Dr. Frank Jobe for a rotator cuff injury. After a 13-19 record last season, Garland started only six games in 1978 and had a record of 2-3.

MAY 6:

In Pittsburgh, the Dodgers' Lee Lacy hits his second consecutive pinch-hit homer, tying a major league record. Lacy hit the first on May 2. The Pirates beat the Dodgers, 3-2.

MAY 8:

First there was the "Boudreau shift," now it's the "Herzog shift." In a night game at Fenway Park against the Royals, Jim Rice steps up to bat and finds he is facing four outfielders, with no one at the normal second base position. The defensive lineup is the brainchild of Kansas City manager Dorrel "Whitey" Herzog. Rice lines out but gets a base hit in his next at-bat. Carl Yastrzemski and Fred Lynn homer in an 8-4 Boston victory. Bob Stanley gets the win; Dennis Leonard is the losing pitcher.

MAY 13:

In Montreal, the Atlanta Braves' Phil Niekro registers his 2,000th career strikeout. But the Expos win on a Steve Rogers three-hitter.

MAY 14:

The Cubs beat the Dodgers, 10-7, in Los Angeles on a three-run homer by Dave Kingman in the top of the 15th inning. Kingman has three home runs, a single, and eight RBI in the game. After the game, Los Angeles manager Tommy Lasorda launches into an obscene tirade to reporters. In 1976, while with the Mets, Kingman had three homers and eight RBI against the Dodgers.

MAY 16:

The Rangers acquire outfielder-DH Bobby Bonds (.278 in 26 games) from the

APRIL 16
Bob Forsch tosses St. Louis's first no-hitter in 54 years, blanking the Phillies, 5-0.

JUNE 17
Ron Guidry sets an AL record for lefties by striking out 18 Angels in a 4-0 Yankees' win.

White Sox for outfielders Claudell Washington (.167 in 12 games) and Rosendo "Rusty" Torres, who has not played in 1978.

MAY 17:

Lee Lacey becomes the first major leaguer to hit pinch-hit home runs in three consecutive at-bats as the Dodgers down the Pirates, 10-1.

MAY 20:

Willie Stargell makes sure his 407th career home run is one to remember. The Pirates' star launches a 535-foot skyrocket against the Expos' Wayne Twitchell in Olympic Stadium. It is the longest ever in that ballpark and ties Stargell with Edwin "Duke" Snider on the all-time home run list. The Pirates win the game, 6-0.

MAY 23:

The AL okays the sale of the Red Sox for a reported $20.5 million to an investment group that includes Mrs. Jean Yawkey, widow of the sole owner Tom Yawkey; former Red Sox catcher Haywood Sullivan; and one-time team trainer Buddy LeRoux. The AL previously had rejected a purchase proposal. The new one gives a more important role to Mrs. Yawkey – who will be team president – and her husband's estate.

MAY 25:

At Dodger Stadium, seven Los Angeles players – Johnnie "Dusty" Baker, pitcher Rick Sutcliffe, Steve Garvey, Gary Thomasson, Joe Ferguson, Derrel Thomas, and Davey Lopes – homer in a 17-6 thrashing of the Reds.

MAY 28:

The Orioles' Jim Palmer beats Mike Paxton and the visiting Indians, 3-0. It is Palmer's 200th career victory.

JUNE 3:

In Philadelphia, the Phillies' Davey Johnson hits a pinch-hit grand slam homer off Terry Forster with one out in the ninth to beat the Dodgers, 5-1. It is Johnson's second of the year. Gene Freese in 1959 is the only other player with two pinch-hit grand slams in a season. Johnson hit his first on April 30 off Bob Shirley of the Padres in the fifth inning, tying a game the Phillies went on to win the game, 11-4.

METS' PITCHER TOM SEAVER ONCE REMARKED: "A GOOD PROFESSIONAL ATHLETE MUST HAVE THE LOVE OF A LITTLE BOY. AND THE GOOD PLAYERS FEEL THE KIND OF LOVE FOR THE GAME THAT THEY DID WHEN THEY WERE LITTLE LEAGUERS."

It's pitchers on parade at Wrigley Field. The Braves and Cubs tie a major league record by using seven pitchers each in a game won by Chicago, 8-6.

JUNE 4:

The Orioles select high school senior Cal Ripken Jr. in the second round of today's draft. An 18-year-old from Aberdeen, Maryland, Ripken is a pitcher-outfielder. He hit .492 and was 7-2 with an ERA of 0.70.

JUNE 16:

Tom Seaver of the Reds no-hits the Cardinals, 4-0, at Riverfront Stadium. It is the first career no-hitter for Seaver, who strikes out three and walks three, while Cincinnati is error-free. Seaver has had three other attempts at throwing a no-hitter broken up in the ninth inning. The game's losing pitcher is John Denny.

JUNE 17:

At Yankee Stadium, Ron Guidry strikes out 18 Angels in a 4-0 victory, setting an American League record for left-handed pitchers. It is the 11th straight win for Guidry against no losses – and his 15 strikeouts come in the first six innings.

At his Hall of Fame induction, Eddie Mathews describes himself as "just a beat-up old third baseman." He describes how he developed his batting style, with his mother pitching to him as a youngster: "If I hit one up the middle, close to my mother, I'd have some extra chores to do. My mother was instrumental in making me a pull hitter."

Bill "Spaceman" Lee returns to the Red Sox after a one-day protest over the sale of Bernie Carbo to the Indians. The Red Sox win their ninth straight, 5-4, beating the Mariners in Fenway Park. Bob Stanley is the winning pitcher.

JUNE 26:

At Yankee Stadium, the Red Sox and Dennis Eckersley beat New York, 4-1, and extend their first place lead to nine and a half games.

His pitchers can't stop the Blue Jays, so Orioles' manager Earl Weaver looks to his position players. He throws outfielder Larry Harlow and catcher Elrod Hendricks into the game. Harlow lasts a third of an inning, allowing five runs. Hendricks fares better; he works two and a third, allowing one hit and no runs. Toronto rakes Baltimore for 24 hits and wins, 24-10.

JUNE 27:

Dennis Kinney of the Padres becomes the only pitcher in major league history to give up two pinch-hit grand slam homers in the same season. Today, Jack Clark of the Giants connects against Kinney. And on May 6, when he was pitching for the Indians, he served up the first, to Merv Rettenmund of the Angels.

JUNE 30:

In the opener of a doubleheader, the Giants' Willie McCovey hits Jamie Easterly's two-strike pitch in the second inning over the left-field fence at Fulton County Stadium in Atlanta for his 500th career home run. In the sixth inning, Mike Ivie of the Giants hits a pinch-hit grand slam home run – his second of the season – against Dave Campbell. He is the third in history and the second this season to accomplish the feat. Ivie previously pinch-hit a grand slam against Don Sutton of the Dodgers on May 28. The Braves sweep today's doubleheader, 10-9 and then 10-5.

The White Sox fire manager Bob Lemon (34-40). Coach Larry Doby replaces him and becomes baseball's second African-American manager.

On the White Sox's roster is reserve catcher Larry Doby Johnson, named after the AL's first black player.

THE YANKEES FINE THURMAN MUNSON, GRAIG NETTLES, ALBERT "SPARKY" LYLE, AND MICKEY RIVERS $500 EACH FOR FAILING TO ATTEND A CHARITY LUNCHEON. NETTLES SAYS, "IF THIS CLUB WANTS SOMEBODY TO PLAY THIRD BASE, THEY'VE GOT ME. IF THEY WANT SOMEBODY TO GO TO LUNCHEONS, THEY SHOULD HIRE GEORGE JESSEL."

JULY 2:

Ron Guidry beats the Tigers, 3-2, in the opener of a doubleheader, to run his record to 13-0. Gary Thomasson's two-out, three-run homer gives the Yankees the nightcap, 5-2.

JULY 4:

The Mets sell pitcher Butch Metzger (1-3, 6.57 ERA) to the Philadelphia Phillies.

Metzger makes no appearances for the Phillies and his brief major league career comes to an end. In 1976, Metzger was 11-4, with a 2.92 ERA and 16 saves; he was the co-winner of the NL's Rookie of the Year Award. But he is short-circuited by arm trouble and ends his five years with an 18-9 record and a 3.74 ERA.

JULY 7:

A crowd of 40,210 turn out in Milwaukee to see the Brewers beat the Yankees, 6-0, snapping Ron Guidry's winning streak at 13. Larry Hisle has a homer and four RBI; Sixto Lezcano also hits a round-tripper for the Brewers. Mike Caldwell gets the win.

JULY 11:

Dodger first baseman Steve Garvey becomes the first two-time All-

JUNE 30
In Atlanta, the Giants' Willie McCovey joins the elite 500 career home run club.

Star Game Most Valuable Player when his single and triple lead the NL to a 7-3 win over the AL at Jack Murphy Stadium in San Diego. Bruce Sutter gets the win; Rich "Goose" Gossage is charged with the loss.

JULY 13:

It's not exactly a "Let's win one for the Gipper" speech. With the Yankees fading fast, owner George Steinbrenner and his manager, Billy Martin, meet. Steinbrenner then tells the team, "I'm not going to lie down and die like a dog, and neither are you."

JULY 14:

Thumb me and I'll sue. After Don Sutton is ejected by umpire Doug Harvey for tampering with the ball in today's 4-1 loss to the Cardinals in St. Louis, the Dodger right-hander threatens to sue. Harvey found three doctored balls; Sutton claims the umpire is interfering with his ability to earn a living.

Sutton escapes with a warning from NL president Charles "Chub" Feeney.

JULY 16:

Ex-Yankee Larry Gura beats New York, 3-1. It is the Yankees' eighth loss in their last 10 games; they now are in fourth place, 13 games behind the first-place Red Sox.

JULY 17:

Billy Martin and Reggie Jackson are involved in another dispute – this time over a bunt. In the bottom of the 10th inning, Yankees' third base coach Dick Howser tells Jackson – in words not signs – that the sacrifice bunt sign is off and he is to hit away. Jackson bunts a two-strike pitch anyway, fouls it off, and is out on strikes. The Yankees fail to score and the Royals win the game, 9-7, in 11 innings. Martin suspends Jackson for five days.

In Baltimore, Rangers' pitcher George "Doc" Medich saves a 61-year-old fan who suffers a heart attack. Medich, a medical student administers heart massage until the paramedics arrive.

JULY 19:

The Yankees begin the day in Minnesota in fourth place in the AL East, trailing first-place Boston by 14 games. Ed Figueroa pitches a six-hitter and the Yankees beat the Twins, 2-0.

JULY 23:

Steve Carlton of the Phillies beats the visiting Astros, 13-2, for his 200th career win.

The Yankees beat the White Sox, 3-1, behind Ed Figueroa and Goose Gossage, to move within 10 games of first-place Boston. At O'Hare Airport after the game, manager Billy Martin tells reporters that Reggie Jackson and owner George Steinbrenner "deserve each other. One's a born liar, the other's convicted."

JULY 24:

At Shea Stadium Pete Rose singles against Pat Zachry, extending his consecutive game hitting streak to 37. Rose is now tied with Tommy Holmes for the NL record. The Reds win, 5-3; Zachry breaks his foot kicking the dugout steps when he is removed from the game.

In the nightcap of a doubleheader in Minnesota, Carl Yastrzemski drives in Fred Lynn with a sixth-inning single off Geoff Zahn. It is Yastrzemski's 1,500th career RBI. The Red Sox win, 4-2, on a three-run homer by Carlton Fisk. The Twins won the opening game, 5-4.

Billy Martin resigns as manager of the Yankees for the first time, with the team at 52-42. Dick Howser fills in today and loses to the Royals in Kansas City, 5-2.

JULY 25:

Bob Lemon is named to replace Billy Martin as manager of the Yankees. Lemon, who was a Cleveland teammate of club president Al Rosen, says, "I don't think Boston has won it yet. It could be interesting." The Yankees then beat the Red Sox, 4-0, on Ron Guidry's six-hitter. It is Boston's sixth loss in seven games; they lead the AL East by nine and a half.

Pete Rose singles against Mets' pitcher Craig Swan in the third inning to set an NL consecutive game hitting record of 38. The Mets, however, win the game, 9-2, at Shea Stadium.

JULY 26:

Pete Rose doubles in the fifth inning at Shea Stadium against Nino Espinosa to extend his NL record hitting streak to 39 games. The Mets win the game, 12-3.

While the Yankees are beating the Indians, 3-1, on a Lou Piniella

CULTURE

In the movies, baseball is the theme in *The Bad News Bears Go to Japan*, starring Tony Curtis and Jackie Earle Haley, and *Here Come the Tigers*, starring Richard Lincoln.

AUGUST 1
Pete Rose's hitting streak ends at 44 games, as the Braves beat the Reds, 16-4.

Boston's Jim Rice is the major's home run king.

three-run homer in the ninth at Yankee Stadium, owner George Steinbrenner and former manager Billy Martin are having a secret meeting.

JULY 29:

It is Old-Timers' Day at Yankee Stadium and public address announcer Bob Sheppard stuns the crowd: "Managing the Yankees in the 1980 season and hopefully many seasons after that will be Number One, Billy Martin." A seven-minute ovation greets Martin as he emerges from the Yankees' dugout. Under current manager Bob Lemon, who is a lame duck after only four days, the Yankees beat the Twins, 7-3.

JULY 30:

In Atlanta, the Expos' Larry Parish hits three homers in a row in three consecutive innings – the third, fourth, and fifth. Montreal beats the Braves, 19-0. He is the third major league hitter to accomplish the feat.

JULY 31:

Pete Rose leads off the sixth inning with a single off Phil Niekro of the Braves to extend his consecutive game hitting streak to 44, tying Wee Willie Keeler's NL single-season record, but still 12 shy of Joe DiMaggio's major league mark. The Reds win, 3-2.

AUGUST 1:

Pete Rose's consecutive-game hitting streak is ended at 44 today by Atlanta Braves pitchers Larry McWilliams and Gene Garber in a game he begins with a walk and ends with a strikeout. In between he lines out to the pitcher in the second, grounds out in the fifth, and lines into a seventh-inning double play. Rose began his streak on June 14 and hit .385 with 70 hits in the 44 games. The Braves beat the Reds, 16-4.

AUGUST 3:

At Yankee Stadium, the Red Sox regain momentum with a 7-5 victory in the completion of last night's game – suspended by a 1 A.M. curfew – and an 8-1 victory in the regularly scheduled game. The Red Sox, who had lost 11 of their last 13, leave New York six ahead of the Brewers and eight and a half games ahead of the Yankees.

AUGUST 5:

Hall of Fame pitcher Jesse "Pop" Haines dies in Dayton, Ohio, at age 85. Haines pitched for 19 years – all but one with the Cardinals – compiling a record of 210-158 with an ERA of 3.64. He appeared in four World Series and had a 31 record with a 1.67 ERA. Haines was inducted into the Hall of Fame in 1970.

AUGUST 8:

Eddie Mathews, Adrian "Addie" Joss, and Leland "Larry" MacPhail are inducted into the Hall of Fame. Joss, who died in 1911 while still an active player, pitched nine years, compiling a 160-97 record. His lifetime ERA of 1.88 is baseball's second best. Joss pitched a perfect game in 1908, completed 234 of the 260 games he started, won 20 games or more four times and had an ERA of 2.00 or less five times. The Veterans Committee waived its 10-year eligibility rule to elect Joss. MacPhail, an executive with the Reds, Dodgers, and Yankees, was known for his tempestuous personality and innovative spirit. He introduced night baseball, corporate and season ticket plans, stadium clubs, female ushers, and continuous radio coverage. He also created Old-Timers' Day, promoted TV coverage, and was the first to fly his teams regularly. On the other side of the coin, he dragged his heels on integrating baseball. Eddie Mathews, a third baseman and first baseman, played for the Braves in three home cities. In 17 years, he batted .271 with 512 homers and 1,453 RBI. He twice led the NL in homers, hitting 40 or more in a season four times and 30 or more six times. He played in three World Series. Ty Cobb once said of Mathews: "I've only known three or four perfect swings in my time. This lad has one of them."

AUGUST 16:

In Anaheim, Luis Tiant of the Red Sox beats the Angels, 4-2, to gain his 200th career victory.

AUGUST 20:

Steve Garvey takes exception to remarks made by his Dodgers' teammate Don Sutton, and the two scrap in the Shea Stadium clubhouse before today's game. The Dodgers beat the Mets, 5-4.

Sutton explains: "I know you won't believe this. We had a slight disagreement. I couldn't

LEAGUE

In August, major league umpires strike for better benefits. Amateur crews call 13 games before a judge issues a restraining order and sends the regular umpires back to work.

Catfish Hunter on Reggie Jackson: "[He'd] give you the shirt off his back. Of course, he'd call a press conference to announce it."

CULTURE

Baseball fans have much to watch on television: *A Love Affair: The Eleanor and Lou Gehrig Story* stars Edward Herrmann and Blythe Danner; *One in a Million: The Ron LeFlore Story* stars LeVar Burton and Madge Sinclair, with Billy Martin, Al Kaline, Norm Cash, and Bill Freehan.

convince Garvey that the Southeastern Conference is as good as the Big Ten."

AUGUST 22:

The Tigers' Ron LeFlore steals his AL record 27th consecutive base in a streak that began on July 16. Detroit downs Minnesota, 7-3.

AUGUST 27:

The Reds' Joe Morgan hits his 200th career homer in a 7-1 loss to the Cubs. He is the first player with 200 homers and 500 stolen bases.

SEPTEMBER 1:

Orioles' right-hander Sammy Stewart takes the mound for the first time in the major leagues and proceeds to fan seven straight White Sox batters – Jorge Orta, Chet Lemon, Thad Bosley, Mike Colbern, Kevin Bell, Claudell Washington, and Greg Pryor. Baltimore wins the contest, 3-0.

SEPTEMBER 3:

In Pittsburgh, Willie Stargell collects his 2,000th career hit – against Craig Skok of the Braves in the ninth inning. Dale Berra homers in the ninth and the Pirates win, 6-3.

THE ECCENTRIC RED SOX PITCHER BILL "SPACEMAN" LEE OBSERVES, "WE WERE THREE AND A HALF GAMES OUT AND FADING FAST, ABOUT TO GO DOWN IN INFAMY WITH THE '64 PHILLIES AND THE '67 EGYPTIANS."

The Yankees beat the Mariners, 4-3, closing to within five and a half of the Red Sox. Goose Gossage comes out of the bullpen with runners on second and third and takes only 11 pitches to fan the side.

John Stearns of the Mets steals his 23rd base of the season, tying the NL mark for catchers set by Johnny Kling of the Cubs in 1902. The Mets beat the Dodgers, 8-5.

SEPTEMBER 5:

At Wrigley Field, Cubs' manager Herman Franks and Expos' skipper Dick Williams use 45 players in a nine-inning game – the most ever. They tie another record by using 14 pitchers. Montreal prevails, 10-8; Wayne Twitchell, the fifth of eight Expos' pitchers, gets the win. Bruce Sutter, the fifth of six for the Cubs, is charged with the loss. The game includes homers by Montreal's Ellis Valentine and Larry Parrish and Chicago's Dave Kingman.

SEPTEMBER 7:

In Boston, the Red Sox and Yankees begin a four-game series that may determine the AL East title. The Yankees get off first, pounding out 21 hits in a 15-3 victory. Second-sacker Willie Randolph has three hits and drives in five runs. Thurman Munson and Roy White also have three hits each. The winning pitcher is Ken Clay, in relief of Catfish Hunter, who left with a strained groin. Mike Torrez gets the loss.

The record is all John Stearns's. The Mets catcher steals a base for the 24th time this year – the most ever by an NL catcher. New York beats Montreal, 9-4.

SEPTEMBER 8:

The Yankees hammer the Red Sox again, 13-2 on 17 hits, at Fenway Park. Reggie Jackson and Lou Piniella homer. Jim Beattie gets the win with a third of an inning of relief help from Ron Davis. Jim Wright is the game's losing pitcher.

SEPTEMBER 9:

Ron Guidry two-hits the Red Sox, 7-0, at Fenway Park today, improving his season record to a gaudy 21-2. It is the first shutout by a left-hander in Fenway since Ken Holtzman's four years ago. Rick Burleson and Jim

AUGUST 27
The Reds' Joe Morgan becomes the first player with 200 homers and 500 stolen bases.

SEPTEMBER 24
Ron Guidry tosses his third two-hitter in his last four starts, beating the Indians, 4-0.

Rice single for Boston's only hits. Dennis Eckersley is the losing pitcher.

SEPTEMBER 10:

The Yankees, who came to Boston trailing the Red Sox by four games, leave town tied for first in the AL East. New York wins today, 7-4, completing a four game sweep – their first at Fenway Park since 1943. Ed Figueroa gets the win with three innings of relief help from Goose Gossage. Bobby Sprowl is charged with the loss. In the four games, the Yankees collected 67 hits and scored 42 runs. The team was 14 games behind the Red Sox on July 19.

SEPTEMBER 14:

When the Royals' Amos Otis finishes circling the bases after a homer against Oakland's Bob Lacey, among those he finds waiting to shake his hand is the Athletics' pitcher. Lacey says, "Nobody ever hit one of my change-ups like that before. That's the way it's supposed to be."

SEPTEMBER 15:

At Yankee Stadium, Ron Guidry again two-hits the Red Sox, 4-0, running his record to 22-2. It is his second two-hitter against Boston in six days. Rick Burleson – who had one of Boston's two hits against Guidry on September 9 – and Fred Lynn have the only safeties today. Chris Chambliss and Graig Nettles homer for New York. Luis Tiant is tagged with the game's loss.

In Los Angeles, Don Sutton beats the Braves, 5-0; Lee Lacy hits a two-run homer; the game draws 47,188. The Dodgers' season attendance is now 3,011,368; they are the first team to top 3 million.

SEPTEMBER 16:

At Yankee Stadium, Mickey Rivers's ninth-inning sacrifice fly gives the Yankees and Catfish Hunter a 3-2 win. Reggie Jackson hits his 23rd homer of the season. The Yankees now lead Boston by three and a half games. Mike Torrez gets the loss despite Jim Rice's 41st round-tripper of the season.

Big Bill Foster, who pitched in the Negro Leagues for 15 years, compiling a 137-62 record, dies today in Lorman, Mississippi, at age 74. Foster was regarded as one of the best left-handed pitchers in the history of the Negro Leagues .

SEPTEMBER 17:

Carl Yastrzemski homers while Dennis Eckersley and Bob Stanley hold the Yankees to four hits in a 7-3 victory in New York. It is the first Boston win after six straight losses to the Yankees. Jim Beattie gets the loss. The Yankees lead the Red Sox by two and a half games.

SEPTEMBER 23:

Angels' outfielder Lyman Bostock is killed by a shotgun blast in an automobile driven by his uncle, at Fifth Avenue and Jackson Street in Gary, Indiana. Sadly, Bostock is the innocent victim of a domestic dispute. The murderer, Leonard Smith, intended to kill his wife, but instead shot Bostock in the temple with a .410 gauge shotgun. Bostock was 27 years old and a .311 hitter in four major league seasons. Earlier in the day he had two hits in four at-bats against the White Sox in Chicago.

SEPTEMBER 24:

In Cleveland, Ron Guidry pitches a two-hitter – his third in four starts – and the Yankees beat the Indians, 4-0. It is Guidry's ninth shutout of the season, tying Babe Ruth's AL record for left-handed pitchers, and his record is now 23-3. Duane Kuiper has both of Cleveland's hits. The Yankees are one game up on the Boston Red Sox.

Bob Welch five-hits the Padres, 4-0, and the Dodgers are the NL West champions.

SEPTEMBER 26:

Locker rooms are no longer a strictly male province – at least not in New York. U.S. District Court Judge Constance Baker Motley rules that women sportswriters cannot be barred from the locker rooms of New York teams.

In Lady in the Locker Room, *baseball writer Susan Fornoff noted: "(*Sports Illustrated*) had sued (the New York Yankees) on (SI's Melissa) Ludtke's behalf because she had been denied equal access at Yankee Stadium in the 1977 postseason. Oh, she was allowed to watch Reggie Jackson hit all of those home runs. She just wasn't allowed to go into the clubhouse to talk to him about them."*

TRIVIA

In music, "Baseball Card Lover" is recorded by Rockin' Richie Ray. "(I Used to Be a) Brooklyn Dodger," recorded by Dion DiMucci, is written by DiMucci, Dan Beck, M. Tiernan, and R. Steele. Meat Loaf records "Paradise by the Dashboard Light," with a play-by-play by Phil Rizzuto in the background; the song is written by J. Steinman.

OCTOBER 2
In a one-game playoff for the AL East, Bucky Dent's homer leads the Yankees to a 5-4 win.

HISTORY

George Foster of the Reds leads the NL in RBI (120) for the third consecutive time – only Babe Ruth, Ty Cobb, Honus Wagner, Rogers Hornsby, and Joe Medwick previously accomplished that feat.

Larry Gura and the Royals defeat the visiting Mariners, 4-1, to clinch the AL West.

SEPTEMBER 28:

The Astros' J.R. Richard racks up his 303rd strikeout of the season, the most ever by an NL right-hander. Houston beats Atlanta, 4-3.

SEPTEMBER 29:

Jim Rice doubles and singles against the Blue Jays at Fenway Park, giving the right-handed slugger 400 total bases for the season. He becomes the first AL player to reach that level since Joe DiMaggio in 1937. The Red Sox win the game, 11-0, for Bob Stanley. Jim Clancy gets the loss.

SEPTEMBER 30:

In Pittsburgh, the Phillies snap the Pirates' 24-game home winning streak with a 10-8 victory and clinch their third straight NL East title. Winning pitcher Randy Lerch hits two home runs and Greg Luzinski connects for his 35th of the season. Willie Stargell hits his 28th for Pittsburgh. Grant Jackson gets the loss.

The Yankees and Ed Figueroa beat the Indians, 7-0; New York holds a one-game lead in the AL East. Figueroa gets his 20th win of the season; he is the first native-born Puerto Rican to win 20.

OCTOBER 1:

One of baseball's most dramatic races takes another twist. On the final day of the season, the Red Sox win their eighth in a row, beating the Blue Jays, 5-0, on a Rick Waits five-hitter in Fenway Park, while the Yankees are losing, 9-2, to the Indians in New York. The Red Sox and Yankees end the regular season tied at 99-63 and will meet in a one-game playoff.

OCTOBER 2:

At Fenway Park, the Yankees and Red Sox meet in a one-game playoff to decide the AL pennant. Bucky Dent is an unlikely hero, driving a Mike Torrez pitch over the Green Monster in left field for a three-run homer. The Yankees' two other runs result from a Reggie Jackson homer and a Thurman Munson RBI. With New York up, 5-4, in the ninth and Rick Burleson on first base, Jerry Remy lifts a fly to Lou Piniella in left field. Piniella loses the ball in the sun, but fakes the catch and Burleson holds at second. He moves to third on a Jim Rice drive to right for the second out. Gossage then gets Carl Yastrzemski on a popup in foul territory to third baseman Graig Nettles. The Yankees win, 5-4, Ron Guidry registers his 25th victory, and the Yankees are the AL East champions.

REGULAR SEASON WRAP-UP:

The Dodgers win their second NL pennant in two years under Tom Lasorda, finishing with a regular season mark of 95-67. Steve Garvey bats .316 with 21 homers and 113 RBI. Reggie Smith hits 29 homers; Ron Cey, 23; and Rick Monday, 19. Burt Hooten leads the starters with 19-10 and a 2.71 ERA; the closer, Terry Forster, records 22 saves.

After Bob Lemon takes over in late July, the Yankees are 48-20 to overtake the Red Sox in one of baseball's great comebacks. The Yankees finish at 100-63. Ron Guidry has a memorable season: He is 25-3 with an .893 winning percentage (the highest ever for a 20-game winner) and a 1.74 ERA. Ed Figueroa is 20-9, and Goose Gossage has 27 saves. The top batter is Lou Piniella at .314. Reggie Jackson and Graig Nettles have 27 home runs each. Bobby Bonds – who split the season between the White Sox and Rangers, and ended it by being traded to the Indians – hits 31 homers and steals 43 bases; he is the first player in the 30-30 club five times.

Joe Morgan plays 91 games without an error at second base for the Reds.

OCTOBER 3:

ALCS, game one. In Kansas City, the Yankees and Royals face off for the AL pennant for the third straight year. New York breaks out on top on a 7-1 combined two-hitter by winning pitcher Jim Beattie and reliever Ken Clay. The losing pitcher is Dennis Leonard. Reggie Jackson hits a three-run homer in the eighth inning.

OCTOBER 4:

NLCS, game one. In Philadelphia, last year's division winners, the Dodgers and Phillies, are rematched for the 1978 pennant. With 63,460 on hand, the Dodgers win, 9-5, behind two home runs, a triple, and

OCTOBER 10
In game one of the World Series, the Dodgers pound the Yankees, 11-5.

four RBI by Steve Garvey, and round-trippers by Davey Lopes and Ron Cey. Jerry Martin homers for Philadelphia. The winning pitcher is Bob Welch in relief of starter Burt Hooten. The loser is Larry Christenson.

ALCS, game two. In Kansas City, the Royals bomb three Yankees' pitchers for 16 hits in a 10-4 win. Larry Gura gets the win; Ed Figueroa the loss. Little Freddie Patek hits the game's only home run.

OCTOBER 5:

NLCS, game two. In Philadelphia, the Dodgers win again, 4-0, on a complete-game four-hitter by starter Tommy John. Phillies' starter Dick Ruthven is the losing pitcher. Davey Lopes hits his second home run in two games as well as a triple and single for three RBI.

OCTOBER 6:

ALCS, game three. In New York, Goose Gossage, in relief of Catfish Hunter, gets the victory in a 6-5 game, despite three solo homers by George Brett. Doug Bird is tagged with the loss. For the Yanks, Reggie Jackson and Thurman Munson each hit two-run homers.
NLCS, game three. Today in Los Angeles, the Phillies strike back against the Dodgers, with a 9-4 win on a complete game performance by Steve Carlton, who helps his cause by hitting a homer. Other homers are hit by Greg Luzinski and Steve Garvey. The losing pitcher is Dodger starter Don Sutton.

OCTOBER 7:

ALCS, game four. In New York, with 54,356 attending, the Yankees win their third consecutive pennant with a 2-1 victory over the Royals. Ron Guidry, with ninth-inning help from Goose Gossage, gets the win. Dennis Leonard is the hard-luck loser, going nine innings and yielding only four hits. It's just unfortunate for Leonard that two are home runs – by Graig Nettles and the sixth-inning game-winner by Roy White.

NLCS, game four. Before a hometown crowd of 55,124, the Los Angeles Dodgers win their second straight pennant, beating the Phillies, 4-3, in 10 innings. Bill Russell drives in Ron Cey for the winning run. An error by Garry Maddox on Dusty Baker's line drive sets the stage for Russell's heroics. Terry Forster gets the win with one inning of scoreless relief. Tug McGraw is charged with the loss. Ron Cey and Steve Garvey (his fourth of the playoffs) hit home runs for the Dodgers; Bake McBride and Greg Luzinski for the Phillies.

OCTOBER 8:

One day after his Dodgers win the NL pennant and nine days before his 50th birthday, coach Jim "Junior" Gilliam dies of a cerebral hemorrhage in Inglewood, California. Gilliam was a Los Angeles coach at the time of his death. Gilliam, who played all 14 years of his major league career in a Dodger uniform, had a lifetime average of .265 with a high of .300 in 1956. Prior to joining Brooklyn in 1953, he played Negro League ball with the Baltimore Elite Giants. Gilliam appeared in seven World Series and is the only Dodger to play on four World Championship teams.

OCTOBER 10:

World Series, game one. In Los Angeles, the Dodgers hammer four Yankees' pitchers for 15 hits in an 11-5 victory. Davey Lopes connects for two- and three-run homers, and Dusty Baker adds a solo shot. Reggie Jackson has a bases-empty round-tripper for New York. The winning pitcher is Tommy John; Ed Figueroa gets the game's loss.

OCTOBER 11:

World Series, game two. Ron Cey hits a three-run homer and an RBI single as the Dodgers make it two in a row with a 4-3 win over Catfish Hunter. The Yankees squander 11 hits; Burt Hooten gets the win with a save from Bob Welch, who fans Reggie Jackson in the ninth inning.

OCTOBER 13:

World Series, game three. Ron Guidry is not sharp – yielding eight hits and seven walks – but he's good enough to go the distance, beating the LA Dodgers, 5-1, at Yankee Stadium. Roy White's homer and Graig Nettles's outstanding defense boost Guidry and the Yankees. Don Sutton is the losing pitcher.

OCTOBER 14:

World Series, game four. With two out, Lou Piniella singles

HISTORY

Brian Doyle's .438 Series batting average is 246 points higher than his regular season mark.

OCTOBER 17
The Yankees win game six of the Series, 7-2, for the club's 22nd World Championship.

CULTURE

In books, Merritt Clifton publishes *A Baseball Classic.* In *The Screwball King Murder* by Kin Platt, private eye Max Roper investigates the murder of a Dodgers' pitcher.

in Roy White with the winning run in the bottom of the 10th, enabling the Yankees to square the series with a 4-3 win. All of Los Angeles's runs come on a fifth-inning, three-run homer by Reggie Smith. The winning pitcher is Goose Gossage; Bob Welch gets the loss.

OCTOBER 15:

World Series, game five. The Yankees bang out 18 hits – without a homer – to beat the Dodgers, 12-2. Brian Doyle – playing in place of injured second baseman Willie Randolph – Mickey Rivers, and Bucky Dent have three hits each. Jim Beattie gets the victory with his first-ever complete game. Burt Hooten is the loser.

OCTOBER 17:

World Series, game six. The Yankees win their 22nd World Championship with a 7-2 victory behind winning pitcher Catfish Hunter and Goose Gossage. Reggie Jackson homers for New York, Davey Lopes for Los Angeles. Brian Doyle and Bucky Dent continue their hot hitting with three safeties apiece. Don Sutton gets the loss. Series MVP Bucky Dent hits .417 with seven RBI. Substitute Brian Doyle bats .438. Reggie Jackson weighs in with .391, two homers, and eight RBI. Thurman Munson hits .320 and Mickey Rivers, .333. Bill Russell of the Dodgers leads all hitters in the Series with .423. Davey Lopes has three homers, seven RBI.

POST-SEASON

OCTOBER 19:

Shortstop Don Kessinger is named player-manager of the White Sox. Under Bob Lemon and Larry Doby, Chicago was 71-90 in fifth place in the AL West.

NOVEMBER 10:

The Yankees acquire minor league pitchers Dave Righetti, Mike Griffin, and Greg Jemison; outfielder Juan Beniquez (.260, 11 homers); and pitcher Paul Mirabella (3-2, 5.79 ERA) from the Rangers. In return, Texas gets pitchers Sparky Lyle (9-3, 3.47 ERA, nine saves), Larry McCall (1-1, 5.63 ERA), and Dave Rajsich (0-0, 4.05 ERA); catcher Mike Heath (.228 in 33 games); and shortstop Domingo Ramos.

NOVEMBER 13:

The Yankees sign free-agent pitcher Luis Tiant (13-8, 3.31 ERA, five shutouts) to a two-year contract today, estimated at $875,000. Tiant will become a Latin American scout for New York when he retires. Tiant was with the Red Sox this past season.

NOVEMBER 21:

The Yankees sign free-agent pitcher Tommy John (17-10, 3.30 ERA) to a five-year, $1 million contract. John was with the Dodgers last season.

DECEMBER 5:

At a press conference in Orlando, Florida, the Phillies announce the signing of 37-year-old free-agent Pete Rose (.302, seven homers, 51 doubles) to a four-year, $3.2 million contract, making him baseball's highest-paid player. Rose, the NL's 1973 Most Valuable Player, has hit .300 or better 13 times in 16 years and three times led the NL in batting. At one point, the Phillies withdrew from the bidding but came up with a new and successful proposal. Among the teams who met with Rose as he traveled around the country listening to offers were the Braves, Mets, Pirates, and Royals. In 1979, Rose hits .331, with 208 hits, 40 doubles, and 90 runs scored. He will remain in the game through 1986.

DECEMBER 7:

The Spaceman heads north. The Expos obtain pitcher Bill Lee (10-10, 3.46 ERA) from the Red Sox for infielder-DH Stan Papi (.230 in 67 games). He goes 16-10 with a 3.04 ERA next season, but then tails off considerably before retiring after the 1982 season.

DECEMBER 8:

After 12 years in a Mets' uniform, pitcher Jerry Koosman (3-15, 3.75 ERA) is traded to the Twins for a pair of minor league pitchers, Jesse Orosco and Greg Field.

DECEMBER 20:

Willard Mullin, honored in 1971 as the Sports Cartoonist of the Century, dies in Corpus Christi, Texas, today at the age of 76. Mullin, who worked for the *New York World-Telegram* for 32 years, was best known for his creation of the Brooklyn Dodgers' lovable "Bum."

DECEMBER 5
The Phillies sign 37-year-old free agent Pete Rose to a four-year contract.

DECEMBER 7
Bill Lee – the Spaceman – blasts off from Boston and lands in Montreal.

THE BEST OF 1978

NATIONAL LEAGUE

HITTERS

Batting Average:
Dave Parker, Pittsburgh Pirates, .334

Slugging Average:
Dave Parker, .585

Home Runs:
George Foster, Cincinnati Reds, 40

Runs Batted In:
George Foster, 120

Hits:
Steve Garvey, Los Angeles Dodgers, 202

Stolen Bases:
Omar Moreno, Pittsburgh Pirates, 71

PITCHERS

Wins:
Gaylord Perry, San Diego Padres, 21

Strikeouts:
J.R. Richard, Houston Astros, 303

Earned Run Average:
Craig Swan, New York Mets, 2.43

Winning Percentage:
Gaylord Perry, .778

Saves:
Rollie Fingers, San Diego Padres, 37

Most Valuable Player:
Dave Parker, Pittsburgh Pirates

Cy Young Award:
Gaylord Perry, San Diego Padres

Rookie of the Year:
Bob Horner, Atlanta Braves

AMERICAN LEAGUE

HITTERS

Batting Average:
Rod Carew, Minnesota Twins, .333

Slugging Average:
Jim Rice, Boston Red Sox, .600

Home Runs:
Jim Rice, 46

Runs Batted In:
Jim Rice, 139

Hits:
Jim Rice, 213

Stolen Bases:
Ron LeFlore, Detroit Tigers, 68

PITCHERS

Wins:
Ron Guidry, New York Yankees, 25

Strikeouts:
Nolan Ryan, California Angels, 260

Earned Run Average:
Ron Guidry, 1.74

Winning Percentage:
Ron Guidry, .893

Saves:
Rich "Goose" Gossage, New York Yankees, 27

Most Valuable Player:
Jim Rice, Boston Red Sox

Cy Young Award:
Ron Guidry, New York Yankees

Rookie of the Year:
Lou Whitaker, Detroit Tigers

1979

NEWS

Carter, Brezhnev sign SALT II

U.S., China establish full diplomatic relations

SHAH OVERTHROWN IN IRAN; AYATOLLAH RUHOLLAH KHOMEINI TAKES CONTROL

IRAN SEIZES U.S. EMBASSY, TAKES AMERICANS HOSTAGE

ISRAEL-EGYPT PEACE TREATY SIGNED

John Wayne, Richard Rodgers, Nelson A. Rockefeller die

WHO FANS RUN WILD; 11 DIE AT RIVERFRONT STADIUM CONCERT

POPE JOHN PAUL II VISITS U.S.

HURRICANE FREDERIC HITS GULF COAST, CAUSES $1.5 BILLION IN DAMAGE, KILLS EIGHT

Nuclear power plant accident at Three Mile Island in Pennsylvania

PRE-SEASON

JANUARY 1:

Lorinda de Roulet replaces M. Donald Grant as chairman of the board of the Mets.

JANUARY 8:

Outfielder-DH Jim Rice (.315, 46 homers, 139 RBI), 25 years old, becomes the highest salaried player in baseball. He signs a seven-year contract with the Red Sox estimated to be worth between $5.2 and $6 million and said to include a $1 million bonus. Rice, who had won the AL MVP Award in 1978, was widely regarded as the league's most feared hitter. "I've never heard a bat louder than his," said Ken Harrelson. "You hear it going through the strike zone and the sound is unmistakable. It goes 'vump.' That's when he misses."

FEBRUARY 6:

AL batting champion Rod Carew (.333, five homers, 27 stolen bases) is traded by the Twins to the Angels for outfielder Ken Landreaux (.223, five homers in 93 games), pitcher Paul Hartzell (6-10, 3.44 ERA, six saves) and two minor leaguers – pitcher Brad Havens and infielder-catcher Dave Engle. Carew, who led the AL in batting six times, was in the option year of his contract with Minnesota with no agreement.

MARCH 9:

Commissioner Bowie Kuhn decrees that all reporters – regardless of gender – will have equal access to all major league teams' locker rooms.

MARCH 10:

At 10:01 a.m. Doris Kearns Goodwin becomes the first female in the Red Sox clubhouse in Winter Haven, Florida. Boston had opened its facilities to all media in accordance with the commissioner's decree. No players are present when Ms. Goodwin enters.

MARCH 29:

Former Indians' first baseman Luscious "Luke" Easter is murdered in Euclid, Ohio, in a robbery after cashing payroll checks for TRW, Inc., his employer. Easter was 63 years old. After two seasons with the Homestead Grays in the Negro League, he came to the majors in 1949 at the age of 34. In six years he hit .274 with 93 homers. The six foot, four-and-a-half-inch, 240-pound Easter demonstrated his enormous power in 1952 when he hit 31 home runs.

According to historian Jules Tygiel, Easter called August 4, 1921, "his baseball birthday" and hinted he might be five, or perhaps 10 years older.

THE SEASON

APRIL 5:

The Orioles defeat the visiting White Sox, 5-3, giving Earl Weaver his 1,000th victory as a manager in the major league .

APRIL 7:

Ken Forsch of the Astros no-hits the Braves, 6-0, in Houston. He and Bob Forsch are the first brothers to throw no-hitters. Bob pitched his last year. In today's game, Ken strikes out five and walks two; Houston makes no errors. The losing pitcher is Larry McWilliams.

APRIL 9:

In Atlanta, following a 9-4 loss to the Reds, the Braves' Barry Bonnell bars two female sportswriters from the clubhouse.

APRIL 19:

What starts as banter between teammates in the Yankees' clubhouse turns into a fist-fight between relief pitcher Rich "Goose" Gossage and catcher-DH Cliff Johnson. Gossage ends up with a thumb injury that will sideline him until July 9.

APRIL 21:

In Toronto, the umpires' labor dispute threatens the Tigers-Blue Jays game. The grounds crew, concession workers, and electricians refuse to cross the umpires' picket line. Acting in what they describe as the "best interest of the fans," the umpires remove the pickets and the game proceeds with substitute umpires. The Tigers may wish it hadn't; the Blue Jays win, 5-4.

APRIL 24:

What was the call? At Shea Stadium, where the Mets are hosting the Giants, scab umpires confer for 28 minutes, change their call twice, and then make a compromise decision. Mets' manager Joe Torre and Giants' skipper Joe Altobelli both file official protests. The commotion begins with Richie Hebner on first base and Frank Taveras on third for the Mets. Lee Mazzilli flies to Jack Clark, who catches the ball, tries to throw, and drops it. Taveras tags up and scores. Hebner is tagged out by Bill Madlock at second base. High school umpire Phil Lospitaliere calls it a double play. When Torre argues, the crew reverses the call and puts Mazzilli and Hebner on base. Joe Altobelli challenges that decision and the umpires – Lospitaliere, Dave Pallone, Merrill Hadry, and Jerry Loeber – leave the field to confer. When they return, they have a new call: Mazzilli is out because Clark caught the ball and Hebner is safe because of the confusion caused by the umpires. The Mets win the game, 10-3, and Mike Scott gets the first major league victory of his career.

MAY 1:

In Pittsburgh, the Braves' Phil Niekro seven-hits the Pirates, 5-2, for his 200th major league win. Gary Matthews homers in the ninth to break a tie and Atlanta adds two insurance runs to give Niekro his landmark victory.

Frank Taveras fans five times, tying a major league record for a nine-inning game, and his Mets lose to the Padres, 10-5.

MAY 9:

With substitute umpires at work in Atlanta, two brawls break out after four batters are hit by pitches. The Pirates win, 17-9, but Pittsburgh manager Chuck Tanner and Atlanta skipper Bobby Cox file protests.

Substitute umpires, chapter two. Scab home plate umpire Rich Reed, working his first major league game, tosses Indians' manager Jeff Torborg for protesting a balk call with two out in the ninth and the bases loaded. The Indians beat the Brewers, 8-7.

Substitute umpires, chapter three. At the Astrodome, minor league umpire Dave Pallone rules that Cardinals' shortstop Garry Templeton missed second base on a force play. The St. Louis players respond by throwing helmets and bats onto the field. Pallone ejects everyone on the bench.

Substitute umpires, chapter four: At Fenway Park, Angels' manager Jim Fregosi is thumbed for protesting after Don Baylor is called out for running outside the third base line. Baylor was called safe by the third base umpire but overruled by the minor leaguer behind the plate.

MAY 17:

The 45-day umpires' strike is settled after 14 hours of negotiations. The umps get an average $7,000 pay increase, a hike in maximum salaries from $40,000 to $50,000 after 20 years, two weeks of vacation during the season, and improved pension benefits. Both leagues will hire an extra crew to accommodate vacations. The league presidents add some of the scab umpires to the regular roster. In Boston, where the Yankees are meeting the Red Sox, the regular umpires get an ovation when they take the field.

With an 18-mph wind blowing out, Wrigley Field is the site of another home run barrage. The Phillies beat the Cubs, 23-22, in a game that includes 11 homers and 50 hits. The Cubs blow a 21-9 lead, and a 10th-inning round-tripper by Mike Schmidt – his second of the game – against

CULTURE

On television, *The Kid From Leftfield*, starring Gary Coleman and Robert Guillaume, is a remake of the 1953 movie.

Sportswriter Maury Allen once wrote: "There are 499 Major League ballplayers. Then there's Willie Mays."

Bruce Sutter gives Philadelphia the victory. It is the highest scoring game since August 25, 1922, when the Cubs beat the Phillies, 26-23. Dave Kingman of the Cubs has three homers and six RBI; teammates Bill Buckner (a grand slam), Steve Ontiveros, and Jerry Martin also homer. In addition to Schmidt's two, the Phillies get homers from Bob Boone, Garry Maddox, and pitcher Randy Lerch. The winner is Rawly Eastwick, who actually manages two shutout innings amid all of the slugging. The game takes four hours and three minutes to play.

MAY 21:

That's why there's a Mendoza line. The Mariners smack out 15 hits in a 12-7 win over the Royals. The only Seattle player without a safety is Mario Mendoza.

MAY 31:

The Tigers' Pat Underwood makes his major league debut against the Blue Jays. Taking the mound against him is his older brother, Tom. The Tigers win, 1-0, with Pat yielding three hits in eight and a third innings of work for the win. Tom goes all the way, giving up six hits and getting the loss Jerry Morales's eighth-inning homer is the game's only run.

JUNE 5:

At the Kingdome, the Mariners' Willie Horton hits a long drive that appears to be headed for the upper deck for his 300th career home run. Instead it hits a speaker, which is a single under the ground rules.

JUNE 6:

It took a day longer, but Seattle's Willie Horton gets his 300th home run; he is the 43rd player to reach that level. The Mariners go on to nip the Tigers, 4-3.

JUNE 9:

Nolan Ryan of the Angels continues to mow 'em down. He fans 16 Tigers today in a 9-1 victory. It is the 21st time in his career that he has struck out 15 or more batters in a game.

JUNE 12:

The Tigers, at 27-26, fire manager Dick Moss and replace him with George "Sparky" Anderson, former skipper and architect of Cincinnati's Big Red Machine. Dick Tracewski will handle the team for two games until Anderson arrives on June 14.

JUNE 15:

In the aftermath of the clubhouse fight that injured ace reliever Goose Gossage, the Yankees trade catcher-DH Cliff "Healthcliff" Johnson (.266 in 28 games) to the Indians for pitcher Don Hood (1-0).

JUNE 18:

It isn't quite 1980 – the year Billy Martin was to return as Yankees' manager – but he's in and Bob Lemon is out. Lemon, who led the Yankees to their miracle pennant and a World Series championship last season, has the team in fourth place at 34-31 and is fired by owner George Steinbrenner

The underrated Hal Trosky dies at age 66 in Cedar Rapids, Iowa. The former major league outfielder played 11 seasons, hitting .302 with 228 homers. In 1936, he hit 42 homers and led the AL with 162 RBI.

JUNE 26:

Outfielder Bobby Murcer (.258 in 58 games), now 33 years old, returns to New York, where he debuted in 1965. In return for Murcer, the Yankees send the Cubs minor league pitcher Paul Semall and cash.

JUNE 28:

The Pirates acquire infielder Bill "Mad Dog" Madlock (.261 in 69 games), a two-time NL batting champion, along with pitcher Dave Roberts (0-2) and infielder Lenny Randle (no appearances). In return, they send the Giants pitchers Ed Whitson (2-3) and Al Holland (0-0, 9.00 ERA in 1977) and minor league pitcher Fred Breining.

JULY 6:

The Dodgers buy the contract of pitcher Fernando Valenzuela from Puebla in the Mexican League for $120,000. Valenzuela, a left-hander, is assigned to Lodi in the California League.

JULY 10:

The Phillies' Del Unser hits a pinch-hit homer – his third in three consecutive at-bats – tying a record set by the Dodgers' Lee Lacy last season. Unser had pinch-hit round-trippers on July 5 and June 30. The Phillies top the Padres, 6-5.

JULY 12
Disco Demolition Night at Comiskey goes up in smoke as the crowd gets too rowdy.

AUGUST 2
Yankees' catcher Thurman Munson dies when the plane he's piloting crashes.

JULY 12:

Another ballpark promotion backfires. It's Disco Demolition Night at Comiskey Park. The promotion was initiated by WLUO-FM disc jockey Steve Dahl with the involvement of Mike Veeck, son of owner Bill Veeck Jr. Fans who bring in disco records receive a ticket to the doubleheader with the Tigers for 98 cents. Some 50,000 adolescents turn up with records, which are to be burned in a bonfire between games. But rowdiness begins with discs being thrown onto the field during the first game, won by the Tigers, 4-1. Between games, a swarm estimated at between 5,000 and 7,000 refuses to leave the field despite pleas from owner Bill Veeck. After a delay of one hour and sixteen minutes, umpire-in-chief Dave Phillips decides the field is unplayable and calls the game.

JULY 13:

AL president Lee MacPhail awards the Tigers a 9-0 forfeit over the White Sox as a consequence of yesterday's Disco Demolition Night turned debacle.

JULY 17:

The NL wins the All-Star Game for the eighth straight time. In Seattle's Kingdome, Lee Mazzilli, who homered to tie the score in the eighth, walks with the bases loaded in the ninth for the winning run in a 7-6 game. Fred Lynn has a two-run homer for the AL. The winning pitcher is Bruce Sutter; Jim Kern is charged with the game's loss.

JULY 20:

The Tigers trade DH Daniel "Rusty" Staub (.236 in 68 games), who held out in the spring, to the Expos for minor league catcher Randy Schafer and cash. Staub played in Montreal from 1969 to 1971 and was a popular figure with fans, who liked to call him *Le Grande Orange.*

JULY 23:

The Orioles' Felix "Tippy" Martinez pitches seven and two-thirds innings of perfect relief in a 7-4 win over the Athletics on a grand slam by Harold "Pat" Kelly.

JULY 24:

At Fenway Park, Carl Yastrzemski hits a seventh-inning homer against the Athletics' Mike Morgan. It is the 400th career home run for the Red Sox star.

JULY 28:

At Shea Stadium, the Cubs' Dave Kingman hits three homers, giving him five in the last two games, tying a record established by Adrian "Cap" Anson in 1884 and equaled by several others. Kingman also had three homers in a game on May 17. Despite Kingman's barrage, the Mets win the game, 6-4.

AUGUST 1:

The ever-benevolent George Steinbrenner trades Mickey Rivers (.287 in 74 games) to the Rangers, explaining, "We had to get him out of the New York environment. He's just a sweet, sweet kid." Going to Texas with Rivers are three minor league pitchers – Bob Polinsky, Neil Mersch, and Mark Softy. Coming into the New York environment are outfielder-DH Oscar Gamble (.335 in 64 games), minor league pitchers Ray Fontenot and Gene Nelson, and minor league third baseman Amos Lewis.

AUGUST 2:

Tragedy strikes the Yankees. Team captain Thurman Munson is killed when the private plane he is piloting crashes outside Canton, Ohio. Munson, 32 years old, was trying to land his Cessna Citation twin-engine jet on a trip home during an off-day. The plane hits treetops and crashes 200 feet short of the runway at Akron-Canton Airport. Two passengers survive the accident. The Yankees' catcher was a three-time Golden Glove winner who had a lifetime batting average of .292. The 1976 AL MVP and a seven-time All-Star, he hit above .300 and drove in more than 100 runs for three straight seasons. His lifetime post-season batting average was .357, including a .529 mark in the 1976 World Series.

AUGUST 3:

After the full team attends Thurman Munson's funeral in Ohio, the Yankees fly to New York to play the Orioles. A crowd of 51,151 pays its respects to the late Yankees' captain, who is eulogized by New York's Terence Cardinal Cooke. The scoreboard reads:

CULTURE

It's a good year for baseball in books: *The Seventh Babe,* a novel by Jerome Charyn, is about a white player on a black barnstorming team; *It Looked Like For Ever* is the final volume in the Henry Wiggen quartet by Mark Harris; *Long Gone,* by Paul Hemphill, is a novel about minor league life in the South; *The Last Great Season* is a roman a clef about the 1941-42 Dodgers by Donald Honig.

"When they hit it, I catch it; when they throw it, I hit it."
– *Willie Mays*

HISTORY

Pete Rose, now with the Phillies, collects 208 hits, the 10th time he has had 200 or more in a season, breaking another Ty Cobb record (nine years).

"Our captain and leader has not left us. Today, tomorrow, this year and next our endeavors will reflect our love and admiration for him." After a 10-minute standing ovation, the Yankees take the field, but no one occupies the catcher's spot. Jerry Narron ultimately goes behind the plate. Bobby Murcer, one of Munson's close friends, hits a three-run homer to propel the Yankees to a 5-4 win over the Orioles.

AUGUST 4:

A knuckleball is hard to hit and catch; sometimes it's also hard to throw. Today is one of those times for Braves' pitcher Phil Niekro at the Astrodome. He uncorks six wild pitches in the game – tying J.R. Richard's 1979 major league record – and four in one inning – equaling Walter Johnson's mark in 1914. Only 10 days ago, Niekro threw four wild pitches in a game. The Astros win the game, 6-2, and also take the nightcap, 4-3.

AUGUST 5:

Willie Mays, Lewis "Hack" Wilson, and Warren G. Giles are inducted into the Hall of Fame. Mays, the Say Hey Kid, played 22 years, hit 660 home runs, drove in 1,903 runs, scored 2,062 times, hit .302, and compiled a .557 slugging average, while setting new standards for fielding prowess. Wilson, who died in 1948, played for 12 years, hitting .304 with 244 homers. He blazed brightly and faded quickly, with a peak in 1930 of .356, 56 home runs, and an all-time record 190 RBI. But by 1934 – his final year, he had crashed to .245 with six homers and 30 RBI as a part-time player. He hit .300 five times and was a four-time home run champion. Wilson died a pauper's death in 1948. Giles served from 1951 to 1969 as president of the NL. Previously, he was president of the Reds from 1948 to 1951. He died earlier this year.

The secret of Willie Mays' greatness? "When they hit it, I catch it; when they throw it, I hit it." Sportswriter Maury Allen once wrote: "There are 499 Major League ballplayers. Then there's Willie Mays."

AUGUST 9:

Walter O'Malley, the man who took the Dodgers out of Brooklyn, dies at the Mayo Clinic in Rochester, Minnesota. O'Malley, 75, was the owner and chairman of the board of the team at the time of his death.

Walter O'Malley: "Baseball isn't a business, it's more like a disease."

AUGUST 10:

The Dodgers' hurler Don Sutton beats the Giants, 9-0, at Candlestick Park for the 50th shutout of his pitching career.

AUGUST 13:

In St. Louis, Lou Brock singles in the first inning against Dennis Lamp for his 2,999th career base hit. In the fourth inning, he becomes the 14th player to reach the coveted 3,000-hit mark when he hits a line drive single off Lamp's hand. The Cardinals beat the Cubs and Lamp, 3-2, in a 10-innings affair.

AUGUST 21:

Jeffrey Leonard of the Astros steps up to the plate in the ninth inning, beginning one of the oddest and longest at-bats ever. Leonard flies out against the Mets' Pete Falcone, apparently ending the game. But the out is nullified because New York shortstop Frank Taveras had called time out. This time Leonard singles, but no sooner reaches first than the umpires call him back to the plate because Mets' first baseman Ed Kranepool had not been in position when Falcone pitched. Houston manager Bill Virdon protests the game and Leonard flies out again, ending the contest with an apparent 5-0 victory by New York.

AUGUST 22:

After NL president Charles "Chub" Feeney upholds Houston's protest, yesterday's game resumes with Jeffrey Leonard on first – the result of the single in his second at-bat in yesterday's ninth inning. Kevin Kobel relieves Pete Falcone to pitch to Jose Cruz and retires him on the ground ball, ending the game with the same result – a 5-0 Mets' victory.

AUGUST 29:

In Minnesota, the Orioles' switch hitter Eddie Murray hits three consecutive homers in a 7-4 win over the Twins.

With his pitchers getting shelled by the Royals, Brewers' manager George Bamberger turns to

AUGUST 5
Willie Mays and Hack Wilson are inducted into the Baseball Hall of Fame.

AUGUST 13
The Cardinals' Lou Brock becomes the 14th major leaguer with 3,000 career hits.

SEPTEMBER 28
Gary Templeton is the first player to have 100 hits from each side of the plate in a season.

his everyday players – infielders Sal Bando and Jim Gantner and catcher John "Buck" Martinez. Bando works three innings, giving up three hits and two earned runs. Gantner pitches one inning, allowing only two hits and not a single earned run. Martinez pitches one inning, walks one, yields one hit and one earned run. The Royals win, 18-8.

SEPTEMBER 2:

The Dodgers' Manny Mota delivers a pinch hit against the Cubs in the eighth inning of today's game in Los Angeles. It is the 145th of his career, tying Forrest "Smoky" Burgess for the major league record. Davey Lopes's grand slam in the ninth gives the Dodgers a 6-2 victory.

SEPTEMBER 4:

Norman Thomas "Turkey" Stearnes dies in Detroit, Michigan, at the age of 78. Stearnes was an outfielder with the Detroit Stars of the Negro National League in the 1920s and hit 140 homers in 585 games. In 1932 and 1933 he led the Chicago American Giants to championships in the Negro National League.

SEPTEMBER 5:

After his 18 consecutive losses, Athletics' pitcher Matt Keough five-hits the Brewers, 9-5, striking out five hitters and getting a boost from Dwayne Murphy's homer and four RBI. It is Keough's first victory since September 1, 1978. Mike Caldwell gets the loss. Keough's 14 losses to begin the season equals the major league mark set by Joe Harris of the Red Sox in 1906. The crowd of 1,172 fans chants, "Keough, Keough, Keough."

SEPTEMBER 12:

At Fenway Park, Carl Yastrzemski singles to right field against Jim Beattie for his 3,000th career hit. Yaz, who is retiring at the end of the year, is honored in a 15-minute ceremony near first base while a Fenway Park crowd of 34,337 cheers him. He is the 14th player – the second this season – to reach the 3,000-hit mark. He also is the first AL player with 3,000 hits and 400 home runs; Henry Aaron and Willie Mays accomplished it in the NL. Boston beats New York, 9-2.

SEPTEMBER 15:

In a 10-2 victory over the Orioles today in Baltimore, Bob Watson of the Boston Red Sox becomes the first major leaguer to hit for the cycle in each league. Watson previously did so with the Astros on June 24, 1977.

SEPTEMBER 16:

The old order gives way to the new at Yankee Stadium. On Catfish Hunter Day, the 33-year-old pitcher, who will retire at the end of the season, tells his fans, "Three people I wish were here today... Clyde Kluttz, the scout who signed me... My dad... and... Thurman Munson... Three guys who got me where I am today and I miss them." Then 20-year-old left-hander Dave Righetti makes his major league debut, but is not involved in the decision, an 8-4 loss to the Tigers.

SEPTEMBER 22:

Lou Brock ties Billy Hamilton's career "record" of 937 stolen bases when he swipes second base in the fourth inning against the Mets. When Hamilton played, 1888 to 1901, stolen bases were credited more liberally, and his official total is 915.

SEPTEMBER 23:

Lou Brock now holds the undisputed major league record – official or unofficial – for career stolen bases. Brock steals second base today in the fifth inning against the Mets at Shea Stadium, bringing his lifetime total to 938. The 40-year-old Brock broke Ty Cobb's mark of 892 in 1977. The Cardinals beat the Mets, 7-4.

SEPTEMBER 25:

In Anaheim, Jim Fregosi's Angels, behind Frank Tanana, beat the Royals, 4-1, and wrap up the American League East with an 88-74 record.

SEPTEMBER 26:

Phil Niekro beats the Astros, 9-4, for his 20th win of the season. He is the first NL pitcher since Irv Young (20-21) in 1905 with 20 wins and 20 losses. Phil Niekro finishes at 21-20; Joe Niekro finishes at 21-11 with Houston. They are the first brothers to win 20 games in the same season.

SEPTEMBER 28:

Garry Templeton of the Cardinals, a switch hitter, has three hits against the Mets, becoming the first major leaguer with 100 safeties from each side of the plate in one season. Templeton batted only

TRIVIA

Rotisserie baseball – a fantasy pastime for would-be managers based on the actual day-to-day performance of real life major leaguers – is born. Writer Daniel Okrent draws up the first set of rules.

OCTOBER 17
The Pirates beat the Orioles in game seven of the World Series to clinch the title.

SAMPLES OF JERRY COLEMAN'S BROADCASTING MALAPROPISMS AND GOOFS: "WINFIELD GOES BACK TO THE WALL. HE HITS HIS HEAD ON THE WALL, AND IT ROLLS OFF! IT'S ROLLING ALL THE WAY BACK TO SECOND BASE! THIS IS A TERRIBLE THING FOR THE PADRES!" AND: "THEY THROW WINFIELD OUT AT SECOND AND HE'S SAFE." AND: "ON THE MOUND IS RANDY JONES, THE LEFT-HANDER WITH THE KARL MARX HAIRDO."

right-handed in his last nine games to improve his chances of setting the record.

SEPTEMBER 29:

Houston's J.R. Richard fans 11 Dodgers to set an NL record for right-handed pitchers – 313 strikeouts in a season. He tops his own 1978 mark by 10. Richard allows only five hits in beating Los Angeles, 3-0. One of the Dodgers' five safeties is a pinch hit by Manny Mota, setting a career record of 146.

OCTOBER 1:

The San Diego Padres name their broadcaster Jerry Coleman as the team's new manager for 1980, replacing Roger Craig. The Padres were 68-93, finishing fifth in the NL West.

Books could be written on Jerry Coleman's broadcasting malapropisms and other goofs. Some samples: "Winfield goes back to the wall. He hits his head on the wall, and it rolls off! It's rolling all the way back to second base! This is a terrible thing for the Padres!" and "They throw Winfield out at second and he's safe," and "On the mound is Randy Jones, the left-hander with the Karl Marx hairdo" and "McCovey swings and misses and it's fouled back."

REGULAR SEASON WRAP-UP:

Chuck Tanner's Pirates are an offensive machine with a team slugging average of .416. The team finishes 98-64 in the regular season. Willie Stargell (.281, 32 homers, 82 RBI) and Dave Parker (.310, 25 homers, 94 RBI) are a potent one-two punch. Bill Madlock bats .328; Bill Robinson has 24 homers and 75 RBI. The strength of the pitching staff is the bullpen, with Kent Tekulve's 31 saves and 94 appearances. Grant Jackson has 14 saves. John Candelaria leads the starters with a 14-9 record.

Under Earl Weaver, the Orioles are 102-57 in the regular season. Mike Flanagan is the top starter at 23-9. Eddie Murray (.295, 25 homers, 99 RBI) and Ken Singleton (.295, 35 homers, 111 RBI) are the big bats. Gary Roenicke has 25 homers and DH Lee May, 19. Pete Rose of the Phillies collects 208 hits, the 10th time he has had 200 or more in a season, breaking another Ty Cobb record (nine years). Mike Marshall, now with the Twins, sets an AL mark by pitching in 90 games. Willie Wilson of the Royals steals 96 bases, the most in the AL since Ty Cobb's 96 in 1915.

OCTOBER 2:

NLCS, game one. In Cincinnati, Willie Stargell hits a three-run homer in the top of the 11th to give the Pirates a 5-2 victory over the Reds. Grant Jackson gets the win; Tom Hume is charged with the loss. Phil Garner homers for Pittsburgh in the third; George Foster has a two-run round-tripper in the fourth.

OCTOBER 3:

ALCS, game one. The Orioles top the Angels, 6-3, on John Lowenstein's pinch-hit three-run homer in the 10th inning in Baltimore. Don Stanhouse, in relief of Jim Palmer, gets the win; John Montague, who relieved Nolan Ryan, gets the loss. Dan Ford homers for California.

NLCS, game two. Dave Parker's single drives in the winner in a Pirates' 3-2 win in 10 innings. Don Robinson, who is Pittsburgh's sixth pitcher of the game, gets the win. Doug Bair gets the loss.

OCTOBER 4:

ALCS, game two. In Baltimore, the Orioles outlast California, 9-8. The winning pitcher is Mike Flanagan with one-third inning of relief from Don Stanhouse. Eddie Murray has a three-run homer and an RBI single for the Orioles. Dan Ford homers for the Angels. Dave Frost takes the loss.

OCTOBER 5:

NLCS, game three. In Pittsburgh, behind Bert Blyleven's eight-hit complete game, the Pirates sweep the Reds with a 7-1 victory and take the NL pennant. Bill Madlock and Willie Stargell hit home runs for the Pirates; Johnny Bench connects for the Reds. The losing pitcher in the game is starter Pete LaCoss.
ALCS, game three. In California, the Angels win their first playoff game, 4-3, on Larry Harlow's RBI double in the bottom of the ninth. Don Baylor hits a home run for California. The winning pitcher is Don Aase in relief of Frank Tanana. Don Stanhouse, in relief of Dennis Martinez, gets the loss.

OCTOBER 23
The tempestuous Billy Martin gets into a fight with a marshmallow salesman.

OCTOBER 6:

ALCS, game four. In California, Scott McGregor's six-hit shutout beats the Angels, 8-0, and gives the Orioles the AL pennant. The losing pitcher is Chris Knapp. The big blow for Baltimore is a three-run homer by Harold "Pat" Kelly.

OCTOBER 10:

World Series, game one. The World Series begins a day late because of rain and today is wet and cold, but the Orioles' bats are hot, bashing the Pirates for five runs in the first inning. Doug DeCinces sends a ball deep for a two-run homer and Mike Flanagan scatters 11 hits in pitching a 5-4 complete game victory. Willie Stargell has a solo homer for the Pirates. Pittsburgh pitcher Bruce Kison is charged with the game's loss.

OCTOBER 11:

World Series, game two. The Pirates rebound with a 3-2 victory. Manny Sanguillen drives in the winning run with a ninth-inning two-out single, scoring Ed Ott. Don Robinson gets the win in relief with a save by Kent Tekulve. Don Stanhouse is the loser. Eddie Murray homers with no one on for Baltimore.

OCTOBER 12:

World Series, game three. After a 67-minute rain delay at Three Rivers Stadium, the Orioles use 13 hits – including a two-run homer by Benigno "Benny" Ayala – to beat the Pirates, 8-4. Alfonso "Kiki" Garcia has four hits, including a three-run triple. Scott McGregor goes the distance, yielding nine hits for the win. John Candelaria gets the loss in relief.

OCTOBER 13:

World Series, game four. The Pirates out-hit the Orioles 17 to 12, but still lose the game, 9-6. Baltimore scores six runs in the eighth inning, with pinch hitters John Lowenstein and Terry Crowley delivering two-run doubles. Willie Stargell hits a home run for Pittsburgh. The winning pitcher is Tim Stoddard; Kent Tekulve gets the game's loss.

OCTOBER 14:

World Series, game five. The Pirates battle back, banging 13 hits today for a 7-1 victory in Pittsburgh. Bert Blyleven gets the victory with four innings of scoreless relief; starter Mike Flanagan gets the loss. Crazy Horse and Mad Dog – Tim Foli and Bill Madlock – pace the offense. Madlock has four hits; Foli drives in three runs.

OCTOBER 16:

World Series, game six. Playing back in Baltimore, the Pirates even the Series on a combined 4-0 shutout by winning starting pitcher John Candelaria and reliever Kent Tekulve. Jim Palmer gets the loss. Omar Moreno picks up three hits.

OCTOBER 17:

World Series, game seven. Willie Stargell hits a two-run homer in the sixth inning to put the Pirates ahead for good in a 4-1 victory for the World Championship. Grant Jackson gets the win in relief. Scott McGregor is tagged with the loss. Rich Dauer homers for Baltimore. Pittsburgh puts on a potent offensive display, averaging 12 hits a game and batting .323. Five Pirates – Willie Stargell, Omar Moreno, Tim Foli, Dave Parker, and Phil Garner – have 10 or more hits in the series. Garner bats .500, Stargell .400 with his team's only three homers and seven RBI. Kent Tekulve picks up three saves. Baltimore's top hitters are Kiko Garcia at .400 and Ken Singleton with .357.

POST-SEASON

OCTOBER 20:

Cy Slapnicka, the scout who signed Hall of Famer Bob Feller, dies in Cedar Rapids, Iowa, at the age of 93. Slapnicka's own major league career was limited to 10 games in two years with a lifetime pitching record of 1-6. He also was an executive of the Indians from 1935 to 1941.

OCTOBER 23:

In Bloomington, Minnesota, Billy Martin punches out 52-year-old marshmallow salesman Joseph W. Cooper, who said the Yankees' skipper didn't deserve the Manager of the Year Award. Martin bets him $300 to a penny on the outcome of a fight between the two. He blocks the 200-pound Cooper's left, crosses with a right, and inflicts a cut on his opponent's lip that requires 20 stitches.

OCTOBER 28
For the second time in 15 months, George Steinbrenner fires Billy Martin.

NOVEMBER 19
The Houston Astros sign strikeout king and future Hall of Famer Nolan Ryan.

OCTOBER 28:

For the second time in 15 months, George Steinbrenner fires Billy Martin as Yankees' manager. Replacing Martin is former major leaguer Dick Howser, who has been the baseball coach at Florida State University.

OCTOBER 29:

The same year he is inducted into the Hall of Fame, Willie Mays severs all ties to baseball after signing a contract with the Bally Corporation, which is involved in legalized gambling in Atlantic City, New Jersey. Commissioner Bowie Kuhn had warned Mays and Mickey Mantle that they could not work for companies with gambling interests and remain a part of baseball.

NOVEMBER 1:

The Yankees trade Chris Chambliss, the hero of their 1976 ALCS victory. New York obtains catcher Rick Cerone (.239, seven homers), pitcher Tom Underwood (9-16, 3.69 ERA), and outfielder-DH Ted Wilborn (.000 in 12 at-bats) from the Blue Jays. In return, the Yankees send Toronto first baseman-DH Chambliss (.280, 18 homers), infielder Damaso Garcia (.263 in 11 games), and pitcher Paul Mirabella (0-4, 9.00 ERA). And the Yankees are busy in the front office, as well. With Dick Howser attending, the team holds a press conference to announce Gene Michael as its new general manager.

NOVEMBER 8:

The Yankees sign two free agents – pitcher Rudy May (10-3, 2.30 ERA) and first baseman-DH Bob Watson (.303, 16 homers). May spent last season with the Expos; Watson split the year between the Astros and Red Sox.

NOVEMBER 13:

Willie Stargell of the Pirates and Keith Hernandez of the Cardinals are named the first ever co-MVPs. Hernandez hit .344; Stargell hit 32 homers and drove in 82 runs.

NOVEMBER 15:

Pitcher Dave Goltz (14-13, 4.16 ERA), the first free agent to be selected by the maximum 13 teams in the first round of the draft, is signed by the Dodgers to a six-year, $3-million contract. He pitched for the Twins last season.

NOVEMBER 17:

The Dodgers throw an additional handful of millions at another free-agent pitcher. Today they sign Don Stanhouse (7-3, 2.84 ERA, 21 saves) to a $2.1-million deal. Last year, Stanhouse pitched for Baltimore.

Rotisserie baseball – a fantasy pastime for would-be managers based on the actual day-to-day performance of real life major leaguers – is born. Writer Daniel Okrent draws up the first set of rules.

NOVEMBER 18:

Former major league pitcher Freddie Fitzsimmons dies at age 78 in Yucca Valley, California. Known as Fat Freddie, he was a solid performer for 19 years with the Giants and Dodgers, compiling a 217-146 record with a 3.51 ERA and 29 shutouts. His best season was 1928, when he was 20-9 with New York. Fitzsimmons managed the Phillies from 1943 to 1945.

NOVEMBER 19:

The Astros sign baseball's most overpowering pitcher, Nolan Ryan (16-14, 3.59 ERA, 223 strike-outs, and a league-leading five shutouts) for $1 million. Ryan was with the Angels for the 1979 season.

The Padres pay $1.95 million to free-agent pitcher Rick Wise (15-10, 3.72 ERA), who was with the Indians this past season.

NOVEMBER 26:

The Padres sign free-agent pitcher John Curtis (10-9, 4.17 ERA) for $1.75 million. Curtis was with the Giants this past season.

DECEMBER 5:

The Blue Jays trade Chris Chambliss to the Braves before he plays a game in Toronto. Heading south with Chambliss is infielder Luis Gomez (.239 in 59 games). The Blue Jays get outfielder-third baseman Barry Bonnell (.259, 12 homers), pitcher Joey McLaughlin (5-3, 2.48 ERA, five saves), and shortstop Pat.

THE BEST OF 1979

NATIONAL LEAGUE

HITTERS

Batting Average:
Keith Hernandez, St. Louis Cardinals, .344

Slugging Average:
Dave Kingman, Chicago Cubs, .613

Home Runs:
Dave Kingman, 48

Runs Batted In:
Dave Winfield, San Diego Padres, 118

Hits:
Garry Templeton, St. Louis Cardinals, 211

Stolen Bases:
Omar Moreno, Pittsburgh Pirates, 77

PITCHERS

Wins:
Joe Niekro, Houston Astros;
Phil Niekro, Atlanta Braves, 21

Strikeouts:
J.R. Richard, Houston Astros, 313

Earned Run Average:
Richard, 2.71

Winning Percentage:
Tom Seaver, Cincinnati Reds, .727

Saves:
Bruce Sutter, Chicago Cubs, 37

Most Valuable Player:
Keith Hernandez, St. Louis Cardinals;
Willie Stargell, Pittsburgh Pirates

Cy Young Award:
Bruce Sutter, Chicago Cubs

Rookie of the Year:
Rick Sutcliffe, Los Angeles Dodgers

AMERICAN LEAGUE

HITTERS

Batting Average:
Fred Lynn, Boston Red Sox, .333

Slugging Average:
Fred Lynn, .637

Home Runs:
Gorman Thomas, Milwaukee Brewers, 45

Runs Batted In:
Don Baylor, California Angels, 139

Hits:
George Brett, Kansas City Royals, 212

Stolen Bases:
Willie Wilson, Kansas City Royals, 83

PITCHERS

Wins:
Mike Flanagan, Baltimore Orioles, 23

Strikeouts:
Nolan Ryan, California Angels, 223

Earned Run Average:
Ron Guidry, New York Yankees, 2.78

Winning Percentage:
Mike Caldwell, Milwaukee Brewers, .727

Saves:
Mike Marshall, Minnesota Twins, 32

Most Valuable Player:
Don Baylor, California Angels

Cy Young Award:
Mike Flanagan, Baltimore Orioles

Rookie of the Year:
Alfredo Griffin, Toronto Blue Jays;
John Castino, Minnesota Twins

1980

"George Brett could get good wood on an aspirin."
– *Royals' manager Jim Frey*

NEWS

SOVIETS INVADE AFGHANISTAN

U.S. MISSION TO RESCUE HOSTAGES IN IRAN FAILS

JOHN LENNON SLAIN BY CRAZED FAN

FBI ABSCAM PROBE IMPLICATES 32 PUBLIC OFFICIALS IN CORRUPTION

15 DIE IN ERUPTION OF MOUNT ST. HELENS VOLCANO IN WASHINGTON

U.S. WITHDRAWS FROM SUMMER OLYMPICS TO PROTEST AFGHAN INVASION

Ronald Reagan is elected president, defeating incumbent Jimmy Carter

ROBERT DENIRO WINS BEST ACTOR ACADEMY AWARD FOR HIS ROLE IN *RAGING BULL*

TED TURNER LAUNCHES CABLE NEWS NETWORK

PRE-SEASON

JANUARY 24:

Publisher Nelson Doubleday and real estate magnate Fred Wilpon – Sandy Koufax's teammate at Lafayette High School in Brooklyn – buy the Mets from the Payson family after a three-month "auction." The price is estimated to be a record $21.1 to $21.3 million.

The National League will approve the sale two weeks later.

JANUARY 28:

Henry Aaron will not accept an award for his 715th home run from Commissioner Bowie Kuhn. Aaron is displeased with baseball's treatment of its retired black players.

FEBRUARY 15:

The Texas Rangers obtain 41-year-old right-handed pitcher Gaylord Perry (12-11, 3.05 ERA), infielder Thomas "Tucker" Ashford (.245 in 75 games in 1978), and minor league pitcher Joe Carroll from the San Diego Padres for first baseman Willie Montanez (.256, 13 home runs, 71 RBIs). Perry, a five-time 20-game winner, will be traded to the Yankees later in the season.

MARCH 1:

The Philadelphia Phillies trade left-handed pitcher Randy Lerch (10-13, 3.74 ERA) to the Milwaukee Brewers for designated hitter-outfielder Dick Davis (.271, four homers). Lerch is 4-14 in 1980.

APRIL 1:

The players walk out of spring training camps, negating the final eight games of the pre-season schedule. The players are reacting to lack of a new basic agreement, which is stalled by the issue of free agency. They will return for the start of the season, but will strike on May 23 if no agreement is reached.

THE SEASON

APRIL 9:

The Reds' George Foster hits a two-run homer against the Braves' Phil Niekro in a 9-0 victory. Foster is the first major leaguer to get credit for a "game-winning RBI." Frank Pastore limits the Braves to three hits.

In Seattle at night, Ted Cox of the Mariners is the first AL player with an official game-winning RBI. His two-run

RULES

The major leagues introduce a new official statistic – the game-winning RBI. This is the run batted in that gives the winning team a lead that it never relinqushes.

HISTORY

With baseball gone from Washington, D.C., an eight-foot high plaque honoring Walter Johnson, unveiled by President Harry S. Truman in 1947 at Griffith Stadium, is now moved to Walter Johnson High School in Bethesda, Maryland.

← George Brett is regal at his third base position.

APRIL 12
The Brewers' Cecil Cooper and Don Money hit grand slam homers in the same inning.

CULTURE

In the theater, *Lady of the Diamond*, about a female major league pitcher, stars Christine Baranski and John Goodman.

HISTORY

In 1974, Cesar Geronimo – at bat for Nolan Ryan's 3,000th career strikeout this season – was the victim of Bob Gibson's 3,000th career strikeout, as well. He explains: "I was just in the right place at the right time."

double against the Blue Jays' Dave Lemanczyk puts the Mariners ahead in a game they win, 8-6.

APRIL 12:

Cecil Cooper and Don Money of the Brewers become the fourth teammates in history to hit grand slam homers in the same inning. Cooper hits his against Mike Torrez; Money connects off Chuck Rainey. The Brewers beat the Red Sox, 18-1; Larry Sorenson is the winning pitcher.

APRIL 21:

Joe Page, a bullpen mainstay on the 1947 and 1949 Yankees' championship teams and a prototype of the modern reliever, dies at age 62 in Latrobe, Pennsylvania. In eight seasons, Page was 57-49 with a 3.53 ERA and 76 saves.

APRIL 29:

After six years, Bradford G. Corbett sells the majority interest in the Rangers to oilman H.E. "Eddie" Chiles.

The Brewers bang out seven home runs and beat the Indians, 14-1. Ben Oglivie and Sal Bando connect twice; Larry Hisle, Sixto Lezcano, and Paul Molitor once each. Oglivie also has five RBI. The winning pitcher is Bill Travers.

MAY 3:

Willie McCovey of the Giants homers against the Expos' Scott Sanderson in Montreal. It is McCovey's 521st – and last – career home run. The Giants win, 3-2.

The Rangers' Ferguson Jenkins beats the Orioles, 3-2, in Arlington for his 100th AL win. He joins Cy Young, Jim Bunning, and Gaylord Perry as the only pitchers to win 100 games in each league.

MAY 4:

In Toronto, the Blue Jays' Otto Velez wrecks Indians' pitching in a doubleheader sweep, 9-8 and 7-2, banging out three homers and tying an AL record with 10 RBI.

Mike Squires of the Chicago White Sox, normally a first baseman, becomes the first left-handed catcher in major league history since Dale Long of the Chicago Cubs in 1958. Squires works behind the plate in the ninth inning of today's 11-1 loss to the Brewers. He will have one more game at catcher this year.

MAY 23:

At 5:10 A.M. in New York City, 10 hours before the strike deadline, players and owners reach agreement on all but one issue – free-agent compensation. The owners want to increase the compensation to teams that lose free agents; the players are opposed. Both sides agree to table the issue for the present and address it again next year.

MAY 30:

The Tigers' 37-year-old relief pitcher John Hiller, who came back from a major heart attack in 1971, announces his retirement to Detroit fans during the third inning of today's game against the Angels. Hiller pitched 12 years, appearing in 545 games and compiling an 87-76 record with a 2.83 ERA and 125 saves. In 1973, he had a 1.44 ERA and a league-leading 38 saves. The Tigers go on to win the ball game, by a score of 12-1, on a pair of home runs hit by infielder Richie Hebner and one each by Lance Parrish, Kirk Gibson, and Stan Papi. Right-handed starter Milt Wilcox is the winning pitcher.

MAY 31:

Scott McGregor and the Orioles hold Ken Landreaux hitless in four at bats, ending his consecutive game hitting streak at 31. Baltimore beats Minnesota, 11-1.

JUNE 1:

Hall of Fame pitcher Richard "Rube" Marquard dies at age 90 in Baltimore. Marquard pitched 18 years with the Giants, Dodgers, Reds, and Braves, compiling a 201-177 record with a 3.08 ERA, 1,593 strikeouts, and 30 shutouts. He played in five World Series and was inducted into the Hall of Fame in 1971.

Because there are questions about his true date of birth, it is speculated that Marquard actually was 93 years old.

JUNE 3:

With the overall first pick in the free-agent draft, the New York Mets select 18-year-old Darryl Strawberry, a left-handed hitting outfielder from Los Angeles.

JUNE 6:

The Yankees' pitcher Tommy John beats the Mariners, 3-0, in Seattle, for his 200th major league win.

JUNE 3
In the free-agent draft, the Mets pick 18-year-old outfielder Darryl Strawberry.

JULY 4
Nolan Ryan records his 3,000th career strikeout, fanning the Reds' Cesar Geronimo.

Brewers' manager George Bamberger returns to the team after undergoing coronary bypass surgery. Under interim manager Bob "Buck" Rodgers, Milwaukee was 26-21.

JUNE 9:

Dorrel "Whitey" Herzog replaces Ken Boyer as manager of the Cardinals. St. Louis is off to an 18-33 start this season.

Herzog manages the Cardinals for 11 years. At one point in his tenure, elderly owner August Busch tells him he has a lifetime contract. Herzog responds: "Whose lifetime – mine or yours?"

JUNE 20:

Freddie Patek, the Angels' five-foot, five-inch, 148 pound shortstop, hits three homers against the Red Sox in a 20-3 California victory at Fenway Park. Patek is the smallest player ever to hit three round-trippers in a single ball game.

See you in court. Bad blood between White Sox's pitcher Ed Farmer and Tigers' outfielder Al Cowens leads to a brawl in Chicago. Last year Farmer had broken Cowens's jaw with a pitch. Today, after grounding to short, Cowens heads for the mound instead of first base. Farmer promises criminal action. The Tigers win in 11 innings, 5-3.

JUNE 21:

AL president Lee MacPhail suspends Al Cowens for seven days for his attack on Ed Farmer yesterday in Chicago.

JUNE 25:

The Tigers capitalize on 15 hits and 14 walks to beat the Indians, 13-3, in Cleveland. Every Tiger starter bats in at least one run. Detroit extends its winning streak to seven games, and winning pitcher Milt Wilcox pitches his sixth consecutive complete game.

JUNE 27:

The Dodgers' Jerry Reuss no-hits the Giants, 8-0, at Candlestick Park. San Francisco's only base runner results from an error by shortstop Bill Russell. Reuss fans two. Vida Blue gets the loss.

JULY 4:

Nolan Ryan of the Astros fans the Reds' Cesar Geronimo in the second inning for his 3,000th career strikeout. Ryan is the fourth pitcher to reach the 3,000 plateau. The Reds beat the Astros, 8-1.

In Los Angeles, Reggie Smith hits the Dodgers' 7,000th home run in the NL, and Don Sutton registers his 52nd career shutout, beating the Giants, 4-0.

JULY 6:

At Three Rivers Stadium, the Pirates beat the visiting Cubs, 5-4, in a 20-inning, game of five hours and 31 minutes. Cubs relief pitchers allow no hits for 12 1/3 innings beginning in the eighth, but it is not enough for a victory.

The Dodgers retire Duke Snider's number 4 at ceremonies during Old-Timers' Day, but the archrival Giants win the regularly scheduled game, by a score of 7-4.

JULY 11:

The New York Mets sign their number one draft pick, Darryl Strawberry.

JULY 14:

The Orioles' Eddie Murray is out of the lineup today, ending his consecutive game streak at 444. Murray will miss four games after being struck in the eye by a George Brett ground ball.

JULY 26:

The Orioles' Steve Stone beats the Brewers and Mike Caldwell, 4-1, for his 14th consecutive win.

According to Daniel Okrent and Steve Wulf, Stone – who goes on to win the Cy Young Award – throws curves 60 percent of the time. Stone's rationale: "I knew it would ruin my arm, but one year of 25 and 7 is worth five years of 15 and 15."

The Dodgers' Reggie Smith, leading the NL in batting with .322, injures his shoulder and will miss the remainder of the season. Adding insult to injury, the visiting Cubs beat the Dodgers, 5-3.

JULY 27:

The Bengals and A's shake things up today in California. Earthquake tremors rock the upper deck and press box at Oakland Coliseum during a Tigers-Athletics doubleheader attended by 44,093 trembling fans. The Tigers win the opener, 4-2; the Athletics take the nightcap, 4-0.

AUGUST
3
Al Kaline and Duke Snider are among the inductees into the Hall of Fame.

Mike Schmidt's bat powers the Phillies.

JULY 28:

In the bottom of the seventh, the Expos' Ron LeFlore steals his 62nd base of the season, then is picked off while reading the scoreboard. The Expos beat the Reds, 5-4.

JULY 30:

Houston pitcher J.R. Richard suffers a stroke during a workout at the Astrodome and undergoes surgery to correct a blocked artery in his neck. Richard became dizzy while throwing a baseball and was rushed by ambulance to the hospital, where a blood clot was discovered behind his right collarbone in a main artery. Richard had been complaining of arm fatigue amid rumors of emotional causes for his distress. He had been hospitalized for four days in July for tests.

LOS ANGELES TIMES COLUMNIST JIM MURRAY ONCE WROTE: "(CHARLIE) FINLEY IS A SELF-MADE MAN WHO WORSHIPS HIS CREATOR."

AUGUST 3:

Al Kaline, Chuck Klein, Duke Snider, and Tom Yawkey are inducted into the Hall of Fame. Kaline played 22 years, all with the Tigers, batting .297 with 399 homers and 1,583 RBI. He hit .300 or better nine times and led the AL with .340 in 1955. Kaline, who broke into the majors at age 19, appeared in one World Series. Klein, who died in 1958, played 17 years in the NL, batting .320 with 300 homers and 1,202 RBI. He hit .300 or more nine times – seven times consecutively – and was the NL's home run champion in four

AUGUST 4
Maury Wills becomes the major leagues' third black manager, taking over the Mariners.

AUGUST 23
The ever-controversial Charlie Finley sells his Oakland Athletics for $12.7 million.

seasons. In 1933, he hit .368 with 20 homers and 120 RBI. Klein appeared in one World Series. Snider hit .295 with 407 round-trippers and 1,333 RBI in 18 years. He led the NL with 43 homers in 1956 and hit 40 or more for five straight years. Snider was a .300 hitter seven times and appeared in six World Series. Yawkey was the sole owner of the Red Sox for 44 years, after purchasing the team at the age of 30 for $1.5 million. His teams won three pennants – in 1946, 1967, and 1975 – but never fulfilled his dream of a World Series Championship. Yawkey died in 1976.

In his induction speech, Duke Snider recalls: "We wept... When they tore down Ebbets Field, they tore down a little piece of me." He also uses the occasion to remember his teammate, Jackie Robinson: "The greatest competitor I've ever seen; I've seen him beat a team with his bat, his ball, his glove, his feet, and in a game in Chicago one time, with his mouth."

AUGUST 4:

Former Dodger Maury Wills becomes baseball's third black manager when he replaces the Mariners' Darrell Johnson, fired with the team at 39-65.

AUGUST 11:

At Yankee Stadium, Reggie Jackson hits his 400th career home run in a 3-1 victory over the White Sox. Aurelio Rodriguez, purchased from the Padres a week ago and subbing at third for Graig Nettles, who has hepatitis, wins the game with a two-run homer in the bottom of the ninth. Rudy May pitches a four-hitter and gets the victory.

AUGUST 12:

Mark "The Bird" Fidrych, attempting a comeback, struggles through eight innings against the Red Sox, yielding 11 hits and five runs in a 5-4 loss in Detroit.

AUGUST 14:

The Yankees acquire 41-year-old pitcher Gaylord Perry (6-9) from the Rangers for pitcher Ken Clay (1-7, 5.42 ERA in 1979) and minor league outfielder Marvin Thompson.

AUGUST 19:

In Texas, Jon Matlack and the Rangers hold George Brett hitless in three at-bats, ending his consecutive game hitting streak at 30. In his final turn, Brett bounces out to first baseman Pat Putnam. During his streak, Brett hit .467 with six homers and 42 RBI. The Royals beat the Rangers, 4-3.

AUGUST 20:

The Yankees' Bob Watson triples off the centerfield speaker at the Kingdome in Seattle. Yesterday, Watson doubled off the left centerfield speakers.

AUGUST 22:

Edward DeBartolo Sr. reaches an agreement to purchase the White Sox from Bill Veeck for $20 million.

The AL turns down DeBartolo because he has interests in horse racing.

AUGUST 23:

Charles O. Finley, one of baseball's most controversial personalities and a creative owner, sells his Oakland Athletics for $12.7 million to Walter Haas, Wally Haas (his son), and Roy Eisenhardt (Haas's son-in-law). The new owners are the heads of Levi Strauss and Co. The departure of Finley ends his ongoing feud with Commissioner Bowie Kuhn and numerous others in the baseball establishment. Finley had railed against escalating salaries and advocated the use of the DH and yellow baseballs. He introduced flamboyant uniforms, offbeat promotions, the designated runner, and a mule named Charlie O. He also had a predilection for making up colorful nicknames. He dubbed Jim Hunter "Catfish" – for no particular reason.

When Finley tried to get Vida Blue to use "True" as a first name, the pitcher responded: "If he thinks it's such a great name, why doesn't he call himself True O. Finley?"

AUGUST 25:

Rangers' pitcher Ferguson Jenkins is arrested in Toronto when marijuana, cocaine, and hashish are found stashed in his suitcase.

AUGUST 26:

At Shea Stadium, Padres' pitchers issue six intentional walks to the Mets – a new major league record. Claudell Washington, who homered twice, gets three of the walks, an NL record. Willie Montanez wins

HISTORY

Rick Honeycutt becomes the first pitcher since the Browns' Nelson Potter in 1944 to be suspended for doctoring a ball. Honeycutt is slapped with a 10-day suspension and a $250 fine.

SEPTEMBER 10
Expos' pitcher Bill Gullickson sets a rookie record by striking out 18 batters.

OCTOBER 4
The White Sox's Minnie Minoso becomes the second MLer to play in five different decades.

LEAGUE

For the first time ever, all 12 NL teams top 1 million in attendance.

the game for San Diego, 8-6, with an 18th inning single.

AUGUST 27:

Cardinals' minor league pitching coach Hub Kittle takes the pitcher's mound for Springfield against Iowa. At six months past his 63rd birthday, he reputedly is the oldest player ever in organized baseball. Kittle retires Iowa in the first on two flies and a groundout. He throws one pitch in the second and leaves the game.

AUGUST 29:

After 73 games, Whitey Herzog assumes the post of general manager for the Cardinals and Albert "Red" Schoendienst becomes the interim manager of the team. St. Louis was 38-35 under Herzog.

Under Schoendienst, the Cardinals are 18-19 and finish fourth in the NL East. Herzog returns to the dugout for the 1981 season.

SEPTEMBER 1:

In Detroit during the exchange of lineups at home plate, Ed Farmer of the White Sox and Al Cowens of the Tigers shake hands – as the crowd cheers – and end the feud that triggered a brawl last season.

SEPTEMBER 5:

George Brett of the Royals has one hit in four at-bats against the Indians, falling below .400 for the final time in his bid to become the first player since Ted Williams in 1941 to reach that mark.

SEPTEMBER 7:

George Bamberger, the Brewers' only winning manager in their history and the 1978 Manager of the Year, retires. Since June 6, when he returned to action after heart surgery, the team is 47-45. Bamberger will be replaced by Bob "Buck" Rodgers, who handled the team in his absence. In Bamberger's last game, the Rangers beat the Brewers, 7-2. He leaves with the team tied for fourth, 13 1/2 games behind the Yankees.

SEPTEMBER 8:

Commissioner Bowie Kuhn suspends Rangers' pitcher Ferguson Jenkins for the remainder of the season for refusing to cooperate with the investigation into his arrest on drug charges in Toronto on August 25. The Players Association files a grievance against the commissioner for the suspension.

SEPTEMBER 10:

In Montreal, the Expos' Bill Gullickson fans 18 Cubs, setting a major league strikeout record for rookie pitchers. The Expos win the game, 4-2.

SEPTEMBER 12:

The comeback attempt of Mark "The Bird" Fidrych continues to go poorly. He starts against the Indians today in Cleveland, but has to leave because of shoulder pain after only six pitches. Detroit wins, 6-3.

SEPTEMBER 17:

Dennis Leonard whitewashes the visiting Angels, 5-0, and the Royals wrap up the AL West title.

SEPTEMBER 22:

Ferguson Jenkins's suspension is overturned by a three-man arbitration panel. As expected, Marvin Miller, executive director of the Players Association, supports Jenkins's grievance against Commissioner Bowie Kuhn. And, equally as expected, Ray Grebey, director of the owners' Players Relations Committee, upholds Kuhn. The tie-breaking vote belongs to arbitrator Raymond Goetz, a University of Kansas law professor, who rules the commissioner's powers over players is not as sweeping as it is over the owners. Ferguson goes to trial on drug possession charges on December 18.

SEPTEMBER 24:

Manny Mota of the Dodgers adds to his record career pinch-hit total with his 148th today as Los Angeles defeats the visiting Giants, 5-4, in 12 innings. The Dodgers top the 3 million mark in attendance.

SEPTEMBER 30:

Umpire Bill Kunkel catches the Mariners' Rick Honeycutt attempting to doctor a baseball. Honeycutt has a thumbtack hidden under a Band-Aid on his glove hand in the third inning of a game against the Royals. Honeycutt is ejected from the game. He explains: "What I did was stupid and... I'd never do it again. I never wanted this to happen. I didn't know the consequences. Besides, I'd only scratched three

"Besides, I'd only scratched three balls that night and none of them did anything."
– *Mariners' pitcher Rick Honeycutt*

balls that night and none of them did anything."

Playing against the White Sox, Rickey Henderson breaks Ty Cobb's single-season stolen base record of 96. Henderson completes the game with 98 steals.

OCTOBER 4:

At Yankee Stadium, the Yankees beat the Tigers, 5-2, in the first game of a double-header, to clinch the AL East title. Reggie Jackson hits a three-run homer – his 41st of the season and his third in three games.

In Milwaukee, Rickey Henderson steals his 100th and final base of the season.

At Comiskey Park, 57-year-old Saturnino "Minnie" Minoso becomes the second major league player in history to appear in games in five decades. Minoso pinch-hits – unsuccessfully – against the Angels in his first game since 1976. He made his debut back in 1949 with the Indians. The only other player whose career spanned five decades is Nick Altrock, who pitched from 1898 to 1924. The White Sox win today's game, 4-2; LaMarr Hoyt is the winning pitcher and Ed Farmer gets his 30th save of the year.

Minoso is hitless as a pinch hitter against the Angels the following day and ends his 17-year career with a batting average of .298, 186 homers, and 205 stolen bases.

OCTOBER 5:

Earl Weaver's Orioles beat the Indians, 7-1, for their 100th win of the year. But it's only good enough for second place in the AL East, where the Yankees win 103. It is the second consecutive 100-win season for Baltimore. Scott McGregor gets his 20th win; 19-game winner Len Barker is the losing pitcher for Cleveland.

In the eighth inning against the Phillies, the Expos' Ron LeFlore pinch-runs for Bobby Ramos. He steals second and third for a total of 97 to top the NL; he is the only player to lead both leagues. In 1978 with the Tigers he swiped 68 bases.

OCTOBER 6:

After the Dodgers sweep the Astros in a three game series – 3-2, 2-1 and 4-3 – the teams end up at 92-70, tied for first place in the NL West, necessitating a one-game playoff. Behind Joe Niekro, Houston wins, 7-1, to capture the division title.

REGULAR SEASON WRAP-UP:

Jim Frey's Royals head into their first World Series with a regular season record of 97-65 in the AL. George Brett brings a phenomenal .390 average with 24 homers and 118 RBI. Willie Aikens has 20 homers and 98 RBI to go with a .278 average. Willie Wilson hits .326 and steals 79 bases. Dennis Leonard is the ace of the staff at 20-11. Dan Quisenberry appears in 75 games and has 33 saves to his credit.

The Phillies, managed by George "Dallas" Green, have a regular season record of 91-71 in the NL. Mike Schmidt hits .286 with 48 homers and 121 RBI. Arnold "Bake" McBride bats .309; Greg Luzinski hits 19 homers despite a .228 average. Steve Carlton leads the starters with a 24-9 record; Tug McGraw picks up 20 saves on the season.

The Padres are the first team to have three players with 50 or more stolen bases: Gene Richards (61), Ozzie Smith (57), and Jerry Mumphrey (52). The team has 239.

OCTOBER 7:

NLCS, game one. In Philadelphia, before a crowd of 65,277, Steve Carlton and the Phillies beat Houston and Ken Forsch, 3-1. Greg Luzinski hits a two-run homer for the winners. Frank "Tug" McGraw gets a save.

OCTOBER 8:

ALCS, game one. For the fourth time in five years, it's the Yankees versus the Royals for the AL pennant, and Kansas City still is seeking its first pennant. Today they start in high gear at home with a 7-2 win on Larry Gura's complete game. The Yankees' loser is Ron Guidry. George Brett homers for the Royals and Frank White has three hits and two RBI. The Yankees get round-trippers from Rick Cerone and Lou Piniella.

NLCS, game two. In Philadelphia, the Astros score four times in the top of the 10th to beat the Phillies, 7-4, and tie the playoffs. Dave Bergman's two-run triple is the key hit in the inning. The winning pitcher is Frank LaCorte, who

OCTOBER 12
Garry Maddox's RBI double in the 10th inning wins the NLCS for the Phillies.

relieves in the ninth. Ron Reed is the losing pitcher.

OCTOBER 9:

ALCS, game two. In Kansas City, Dennis Leonard, with ninth-inning relief from Dan Quisenberry, beats the Yankees, 3-2, despite a Graig Nettles home run. Willie Wilson has a two-run triple for the Royals. Rudy May takes the loss for New York.

OCTOBER 10:

NLCS, game three. In Houston, Joe Morgan triples and Denny Walling drives him in with a sacrifice fly to give the Astros a 1-0 win in 11 innings. Joe Niekro pitches 10 scoreless innings for Houston, but it is Dave Smith with one inning of relief who gets the victory. Tug McGraw, who comes on in the eighth inning is the loser.

ALCS, game three. With their backs to the wall, the Yankees return to New York in a must-win game. They don't. The Royals win and take their first-ever AL pennant. Dan Quisenberry, in relief of starter Paul Splittorff, gets the 4-2 win. Goose Gossage, in relief of Tommy John, is the loser.

TOM YAWKEY, THE LATE OWNER OF THE BOSTON RED SOX, ONCE EXPLAINED HIS GENEROSITY TO HIS PLAYERS: "LISTEN, IF TRYING TO TREAT THE PLAYERS AS HUMAN BEINGS IS SPOILING THEM, THEN I SPOIL THEM. BUT I WAS BROUGHT UP TO TREAT A HUMAN BEING AS A HUMAN BEING UNTIL HE PROVES UNWORTHY OF HIMSELF."

The Royals are boosted by home runs from Frank White and George Brett – with two on.

OCTOBER 11:

NLCS, game four. In Philadelphia, the Phillies beat Houston, 5-3, in 10 innings. Warren Brusstar, the fifth of six different Philadelphia pitchers, is the winner, Joe Sambito gets the loss in relief. Greg Luzinski and Manny Trillo hit back-to-back doubles in the 10th-inning rally.

OCTOBER 12:

NLCS, game five. In Houston today, Philadelphia beats the Astros, 8-7, in 10 innings and wins the NL pennant. It is the fourth straight extra-inning game in the playoffs and it is decided on a Garry Maddox double driving in Del Unser. Dick Ruthven, the Phillies' sixth pitcher of the game, gets the win. Frank LaCorte is charged with the loss.

OCTOBER 14:

World Series, game one. In Philadelphia, the Phillies beat the Royals, 7-6, despite three two-run home runs – two by Willie Aikens and one by Amos Otis. The winner is rookie Bob

OCTOBER 21
The Phillies are World Champions after beating the Royals in game six of the Series.

NOVEMBER 21
Despite leading the Yankees to a 103-59 record, manager Dick Howser is fired.

Walk, with relief help from Tug McGraw. The loser is Dennis Leonard. Bake McBride hits a three-run home run for Philadelphia.

J.R. Richard, who is paralyzed on his left side as a result of a stroke on July 30, undergoes 18 hours of bypass surgery for a clotted shoulder artery today.

Richard, the pitcher with a 100-mph fastball, never appears again in the majors. He completes his too-brief 10-year career with a 101-71 record, an ERA of 3.15, 1,493 strikeouts, and 19 shutouts.

OCTOBER 15:

World Series, game two. In Philadelphia, Steve Carlton and the Phillies top the Royals, 6-4. With doubles by pinch hitter Del Unser and Mike Schmidt, Philadelphia scores four in the eighth inning against losing pitcher Dan Quisenberry, in relief of Larry Gura.

OCTOBER 17:

World Series, game three. In Kansas City, the Royals bounce back. Willie Aikens singles in Willie Wilson with the winning run in the bottom of the 10th inning for a 4-3 victory. Dan Quisenberry, the loser in game two, gets the win in relief. Tug McGraw is the loser. Mike Schmidt, George Brett, and Amos Otis hit home runs.

OCTOBER 18:

World Series, game four. Willie Aikens hits a solo homer against Larry Christenson and a two-run shot off Dickie Noles as the Royals top the Phillies, 5-3, in Kansas City. Aikens is the first player ever with a pair of two-homer games in the Series. The winning pitcher is Dennis Leonard; Christenson is the losing pitcher.

OCTOBER 19:

World Series, game five. In Kansas City, the Phillies win another one-run game, 4-3, on Manny Trillo's RBI single. Tug McGraw is the game's winner; Dan Quisenberry gets the loss. After he loads the bases on walks, McGraw strikes out Jose Cardenal to end the game. The Phillies' Mike Schmidt hits a two-run home run and Amos Otis gets his third – a solo shot – of the Series.

OCTOBER 21:

World Series, game six. In Philadelphia, before a crowd of 65,838, the Phillies become World Champions, beating the Royals 4-1. Steve Carlton is the winner with seven strikeouts in seven innings. He gets two innings of three-hit relief help from Tug McGraw. Mike Schmidt drives in two runs. Rich Gale is the Royals' starter and loser. The hitting star of the Series, in a losing cause, is Willie Aikens with four homers, eight RBI, and a .400 batting average. MVP Mike Schmidt hits .381 with two homers and seven RBI for the World Champions. Steve Carlton is 2-0 and Tug McGraw is credited with two saves.

POST-SEASON

OCTOBER 27:

Ralph Houk becomes the 35th manager in the history of the Red Sox. With the Yankees, Houk won three pennants and two World Series in his first three years as a manager. He also was the skipper of the Tigers for five years. Boston finished 83-77 for a fourth-place finish in the AL East last season.

NOVEMBER 17:

The Braves sign free-agent outfielder Claudell Washington (.278, 11 homers, 21 stolen bases) to a five-year contract estimated to be worth almost $5 million. Washington split last season between the White Sox and Mets.

NOVEMBER 21:

Despite leading the Yankees to a 103-59 season mark, Yankees' manager Dick Howser is fired by George Steinbrenner. Howser's "sin" apparently was losing the ALCS to Kansas City in three straight games. Howser, who will be replaced by Gene Michael, becomes the team's director of southeast scouting. Michael's front office responsibilities will be split by Cedric Tallis and Bill Bergesch.

DECEMBER 4:

The Astros sign free-agent pitcher Don Sutton (13-5, an NL-best 2.21 ERA, and two shutouts). Sutton spent the past 15 years with the Dodgers.

DECEMBER 6:

The White Sox sign free-agent outfielder Ron LeFlore (.257, four homers, 97

DECEMBER 15
The Yankees sign Padres' outfielder Dave Winfield to a 10-year contract.

stolen bases). He was with the Expos for the 1980 season.

DECEMBER 8:

The Cardinals and Padres complete an 11-player trade. St. Louis gets pitchers Rollie Fingers (11-9, 2.80 ERA, 23 saves) and Bob Shirley (11-12, 3.55 ERA, seven saves), along with catcher/first baseman Gene Tenace (.222, 17 homers) and minor league catcher Bob Geren. Heading for San Diego are catchers Terry Kennedy (.254, four homers in 84 games) and Steve Swisher (.250 in 18 games), infielder Mike Phillips (.234 in 63 games), and pitchers John Littlefield (5-5, 3.14 ERA, nine saves), John Urrea (4-1, 3.46 ERA, three saves), Kim Seaman (3-2, 3.38 ERA, four saves), and Al Olmstead (1-1, 2.83 ERA).

DECEMBER 9:

The Cubs trade pitcher Bruce Sutter (5-8, 2.65 ERA and an NL-best 28 saves) to the Cardinals for first baseman-outfielder Leon Durham (.271, eight homers in 96 games), third baseman Ken Reitz (.270, eight homers), and third baseman Tye Waller (.083 in five games). The Cardinals also release outfielder Bobby Bonds (.203, five homers, 15 stolen bases in 86 games).

DECEMBER 10:

The Red Sox acquire third baseman Carney Lansford (.261, 15 homers, 80 RBI, 14 stolen bases), outfielder-DH Rick Miller (.274), and pitcher Mark Clear (11-11, 3.31 ERA, nine saves) from the Angels for two veterans – shortstop Rick Burleson (.278, eight homers, 12 stolen bases) and Clell "Butch" Hobson (.228, 11 home runs in 93 games).

DECEMBER 12:

The Brewers obtain catcher-outfielder Ted Simmons (.303, 21 homers, 98 RBI) and pitchers Rollie Fingers (11-9, 2.80 ERA, 23 saves) and Pete Vukovich (12-9, 3.41 ERA) from the Cardinals. In return, St. Louis gets outfielder Sixto Lezcano (.229, 18 homers), pitchers Larry Sorenson (12-10, 3.67 ERA) and Dave LaPoint (1-0, 6.00 ERA), and minor league outfielder David Green.

The Mariners and Rangers engineer an 11-player swap. Texas gets pitcher Rick Honeycutt (10-17, 3.95 ERA), catcher Larry Cox (.202, four homers), infielder Mario Mendoza (.245), DH Willie Horton (.221, eight homers in 97 games), and outfielder-DH Leon Roberts (.251, 10 homers). Heading for Seattle are DH-outfielder Richie Zisk (.290, 19 homers, 77 RBI), infielder Rick Auerbach (.333 in 24 games), pitchers Brian Allard (0-1, 5.79 ERA), Ken Clay (2-3, 4.60 ERA), and Jerry Don Gleaton (0-0, 2.57 ERA), and minor league pitcher Steve Finch.

DECEMBER 14:

Elston Howard, who broke the Yankees longstanding color line in 1955 and was the AL's first black Most Valuable Player, dies at age 51 in New York City. Howard played for 14 seasons, batting .274 with 167 homers. He was an outstanding defensive catcher who also played the outfield and first base; in 1961 he batted .348. Howard was a nine-time All-Star and played in 10 World Series.

DECEMBER 15:

The Yankees sign free-agent outfielder Dave Winfield (.262, 20 homers, 87 RBI, 23 stolen bases) to 10-year contract – with incentives – estimated at between $13 and $25 million. Winfield, who spent the last eight seasons with the Padres, becomes the highest paid athlete in the history of team sports.

The Mets acquire 1976 Cy Young Award-winner Randy Jones (5-13, 3.92 ERA, three shutouts) from the Padres for pitcher John Pacella (3-4, 5.14 ERA) and infielder Jose Moreno (.196, two home runs in 37 games).

DECEMBER 18:

Ferguson Jenkins's trial for drug possession begins in Toronto today.

DECEMBER 31:

Bob Shawkey dies in the Veterans Administration Hospital in Syracuse, New York, at age 90. Shawkey pitched for 15 years with a 198-150 record, a 3.09 ERA, and 33 shutouts. He won 20 games or more four times and played in five World Series. He managed the Yankees to a third-place finish in 1930. Shawkey had the distinction of pitching the first game ever at Yankee Stadium in 1923. And in 1976, he threw out the first ball at renovated Yankee Stadium.

TRIVIA

With the questions about Satchel Paige's true birthday, is it possible that he, not Hub Kittle, was the oldest to play in organized baseball? Probably not. Paige was perhaps 50 when he pitched his last game in the majors in 1965.

"If I ever die, I want to die in Chicago."
– Minnie Minoso

THE BEST OF 1980

NATIONAL LEAGUE

HITTERS

Batting Average:
Bill Buckner, Chicago Cubs, .324

Slugging Average:
Mike Schmidt, Philadelphia Phillies, .624

Home Runs:
Mike Schmidt, 48

Runs Batted In:
Mike Schmidt, 121

Hits:
Steve Garvey, Los Angeles Dodgers, 200

Stolen Bases:
Ron LeFlore, Montreal Expos, 97

PITCHERS

Wins:
Steve Carlton, Philadelphia Phillies, 24

Strikeouts:
Steve Carlton, 286

Earned Run Average:
Don Sutton, Los Angeles Dodgers, 2.21

Winning Percentage:
Jim Bibby, Pittsburgh Pirates, .760

Saves:
Bruce Sutter, Chicago Cubs, 28

Most Valuable Player:
Mike Schmidt, Philadelphia Phillies

Cy Young Award:
Steve Carlton, Philadelphia Phillies

Rookie of the Year:
Steve Howe, Los Angeles Dodgers

AMERICAN LEAGUE

HITTERS

Batting Average:
George Brett, Kansas City Royals, .390

Slugging Average:
George Brett, .664

Home Runs:
Reggie Jackson, New York Yankees; Ben Oglivie, Milwaukee Brewers, 41

Runs Batted In:
Cecil Cooper, Milwaukee Brewers, 122

Hits:
Willie Wilson, Kansas City Royals, 230

Stolen Bases:
Rickey Henderson, Oakland Athletics, 100

PITCHERS

Wins:
Steve Stone, Baltimore Orioles, 25

Strikeouts:
Len Barker, Cleveland Indians, 187

Earned Run Average:
Rudy May, New York Yankees, 2.47

Winning Percentage:
Steve Stone, .781

Saves:
Rich "Goose" Gossage, New York Yankees; Dan Quisenberry, Kansas City Royals, 33

Most Valuable Player:
George Brett, Kansas City Royals

Cy Young Award:
Steve Stone, Baltimore Orioles

Rookie of the Year:
Joe Charboneau, Cleveland Indians

PUMA

1981

NEWS

IRAN RELEASES 52 AMERICAN HOSTAGES AFTER 444 DAYS

RONALD REAGAN WOUNDED IN ASSASSINATION ATTEMPT

America's *Columbia* space shuttle, world's first reusable spacecraft, orbits Earth

SANDRA DAY O'CONNOR BECOMES FIRST WOMAN ON SUPREME COURT

AIDS IS IDENTIFIED

POPE JOHN PAUL II SURVIVES ASSASSINATION ATTEMPT

Israel bombs Iraqi nuclear reactor

EGYPT'S PRESIDENT ANWAR SADAT IS ASSASSINATED

MS-DOS developed by Microsoft

PRE-SEASON

JANUARY 6:

The Minnesota Twins offer reinstatement to pitcher Mike Marshall in settlement of his grievance against the team. Marshall, who will receive his 1981 salary of $300,000 whether or not he plays, charged the Twins with releasing him because of his union activities.

The owners of the Indians call off the sale of the team to a group of New York investors. An agreement in principle for the sale had been reached on October 30, 1980.

JANUARY 8:

The board of directors of the White Sox approve the sale of the team to a group of local investors headed by real estate investor Jerry Reinsdorf and television executive Eddie Einhorn. The sale price is $20 million. The transaction is approved three weeks later.

JANUARY 12:

Pitcher Gaylord Perry (10-13, 3.67 ERA) is signed by the Braves to a one-year contract. The *Atlanta Journal* reports his salary will be $300,000. Perry, 42 years old, is 11 wins short of 300. He split last season between the Rangers and the Yankees.

JANUARY 14:

Frank Robinson is named the new manager of the Giants, the first black pilot in the NL. He replaces Dave Bristol, who was 75-86 in fifth place in the NL West last season.

JANUARY 23:

The Red Sox trade centerfielder Fred Lynn (.301, 12 homers) and pitcher Steve Renko (9-9, 4.20 ERA) to the Angels for outfielder-first-baseman-DH Joe Rudi (.237, 16 homers) plus pitchers Frank Tanana (11-12, 4.15 ERA) and Jim Dorsey (1-2, 9.00 ERA). Lynn, who was engaged in an arbitration proceeding against Boston, was sought by the Yankees to play outfield between Dave Winfield and Reggie Jackson. The Angels are expected to pay Lynn $1 million per season.

JANUARY 29:

Real estate developer George Argyros buys 80 percent of the Seattle Mariners for $10.4 million. Entertainer Danny

CULTURE

***Casey*, a one-man show starring Charles Durning as Casey Stengel, airs on television.**

Things are looking up for the Dodgers with the arrival of rookie phenom Fernando Valenzuela.

"I think one thing is clear. The owners have decided to instigate a strike."
– Marvin Miller

Kaye and three other owners will each retain 5 percent of the franchise.

FEBRUARY 4:

All charges are dismissed against Dr. Patrick A. Mazza, who had been accused of illegally prescribing amphetamines to seven members of the Philadelphia Phillies. Mazza testified he did supply pep pills to the players at their request. At the hearing, only Randy Lerch admitted taking amphetamines.

FEBRUARY 6:

Pitcher Ferguson Jenkins will not be suspended for his 1980 drug conviction in Canada. Jenkins issues a public apology and, under the terms of an agreement with baseball Commissioner Bowie Kuhn, will donate $10,000 to drug education programs for youngsters. Kuhn also announces that all major league teams will be required to begin drug abuse programs by the start of the season.

FEBRUARY 12:

After a contract dispute with the Boston Red Sox, catcher Carlton Fisk is declared a free agent. Fisk, who has been with the Red Sox since 1969, is seeking a five-year, $3.5-million contract with protection against trades or being cut. The Red Sox have counter-offered a four-year, $2.5-million deal.

FEBRUARY 20:

Ray Grebey, director of player relations for the baseball owners, announces the implementation of rules for compensation to teams who lose players to free agency. Currently teams that lose free agents are compensated with an amateur draft choice. The announcement gets a strong response from Marvin Miller, executive director of the Major League Baseball Players Association: "I think one thing is clear. The owners have decided to instigate a strike."

FEBRUARY 23:

Tigers outfielder Steve Kemp wins his arbitration case against the team. Kemp is awarded a $600,000 salary; the Tigers had offered $360,000. Two years ago, Kemp earned $75,000 per year.

FEBRUARY 25:

May 29 is set as the strike deadline by the major league players if the issue of free-agent compensation is not satisfactorily resolved.

YANKEES' OUTFIELDER REGGIE JACKSON, UPSET OVER CONTRACT NEGOTIATIONS, DESCRIBES HIMSELF AS A "WALKING KEG OF DYNAMITE," ADDING, "I SO MUCH WANT A CONFRONTATION, I CAN'T WAIT FOR IT TO HAPPEN." HE HINTS THAT 1981 WILL BE HIS LAST SEASON WITH THE YANKEES.

FEBRUARY 28:

They're playing traveling music again for Dave Kingman (.278, 18 home runs in 81 games). The outfielder-first baseman is reacquired by the Mets from the Cubs for outfielder Steve Henderson (.290, eight homers, 23 stolen bases). Since breaking into the majors in 1971, Kingman has played with the Giants, Mets, Padres, Angels, Yankees, and Cubs.

MARCH 6:

Owner Ruly Carpenter announces he will sell the World Champion Phillies. The team had been purchased by the Carpenter family in 1943. Carpenter attributes his decision to "some deeply ingrained philosophical differences between the Carpenter family and some of the other owners to how baseball should be conducted... It's been a dramatic escalation in salaries and what I'm saying now enough is enough." Carpenter played a role in the escalating salaries; in 1978, he gave free-agent Pete Rose a four-year, $3.2 million contract. The Phillies'

MARCH 16
It is reported that the average player's salary has risen to $185,000 a year.

APRIL 9
Fernando Valenzuela, in his major league debut, five-hits the Astros for a 2-0 Dodgers' win.

owner said he did not blame Marvin Miller, executive director of the Major League Baseball Players Association. "But I can fault my peers for giving and will include myself," Carpenter said.

MARCH 13:

The California Angels' Rick Burleson becomes the highest-paid shortstop in history when he signs a six-year, $4.2-million contract. But the 29-year-old Burleson is only the third highest-paid Angels' player – behind both Fred Lynn and Rod Carew.

MARCH 16:

The *New York Times* reports that the average major league salary for 1981 is an estimated $185,000. In 1976, the figure was $51,000, and last year it was $143,756. Ticket prices to ball games in the same period have increased from an average of $3.45 to $4.53.

MARCH 17:

Paul "Daffy" Dean dies at age 67 in Springdale, Arkansas. The younger brother of Dizzy Dean, he won 19 games in each of his first two seasons with the Cardinals before developing arm troubles. In 1934, his rookie season, he pitched a no-hitter against the Brooklyn Dodgers. In his nine-year career, he was 50-34 with a 3.75 ERA.

MARCH 18:

New York Yankees owner George Steinbrenner calls Reggie Jackson "a four-year-old running into a corner and having a tantrum."

Catcher Carlton Fisk (.289, 18 homers) changes his Sox from Red to White. He signs with Chicago after three weeks on the free-agent market and receives a five-year, $2.9-million contract.

MARCH 25:

The Phillies acquire outfielder Gary "Sarge" Matthews (.278, 19 homers, 75 RBI) from the Braves for pitcher Bob Walk (11-7, 4.56 ERA). Walk, a rookie last season, was 1-0 in the 1980 World Series.

MARCH 29:

Describing his quest as "an almost impossible dream," New York State Senator Thomas J. Bartosiewicz asks the Los Angeles Dodgers to approve a new major league franchise in Brooklyn. Bartosiewicz is introducing legislation for a new Ebbets Field and proposes to call his suggested new team the Brooklyn Dodgers.

APRIL 1:

As President Ronald Reagan recovers from wounds received yesterday in an assassination attempt, the White House cancels his April 8 opening day appearance at the Phillies-Reds game in Cincinnati. The president was to throw out the first ball.
The Tigers option their colorful pitcher Mark "The Bird" Fidrych to the minor leagues. At age 26, Fidrych's career appears to be over because of lingering arm trouble.

APRIL 3:

The Jason Thompson trade is canceled. Some 20 hours of negotiations by telephone to restructure the trade or modify the purchase price are unsuccessful and Thompson will remain in Pittsburgh.

THE SEASON

APRIL 9:

Los Angeles Dodgers rookie left-hander Fernando Valenzuela five-hits the visiting Houston Astros, 2-0, in his first major league start.

APRIL 13:

A baseball strike begins today – but not one that involves the major league players. In Jeffersonville, Indiana, 330 workers go on strike against the Hillerich & Bradsby Co. baseball bat plant. The company is famous as the manufacturer of Louisville Sluggers, and supplies an estimated 90 percent of major league bats.

APRIL 18:

Cincinnati Reds pitcher Tom Seaver fans Keith Hernandez of the Cardinals in the fifth inning in Cincinnati to record his 3,000th career strikeout. The Reds lose, 10-4. Seaver, 36, joins Walter Johnson, Gaylord Perry, Bob Gibson, and Nolan Ryan as the only pitchers to strike out 3,000.

In the International League, Pawtucket and Rochester are involved in the longest game in the history of organized baseball. The game begins today and is suspended at 4:07 a.m. after 32 grueling

CULTURE

In books, fans enjoy *The Seventh Game,* a novel by Roger Kahn with a World Series background, and *The Man Who Brought the Dodgers Back to Brooklyn* by David Ritz – obviously a work of fiction.

CULTURE

On May 31, ABC broadcasts *Don't Look Back*, based on the life of Leroy "Satchel" Paige. The TV movie stars Louis Gossett Jr. as Paige, Beverly Todd, and Ossie Davis. Ernie Barnes plays Josh Gibson and Clifton Davis is James "Cool Papa" Bell. Paige is the technical consultant. The title is taken from Paige's sixth rule of staying young: "Don't look back. Something might be gaining on you."

innings, with the score tied at 2-2. The two teams complete the day having played eight hours and seven minutes. In June, nine weeks later, the game is resumed and, after only 18 minutes, Dave Koza of Pawtucket singles off Steve Grilli for a 3-2 win. The total playing time is eight hours and 25 minutes, a professional record. Bob Ojeda gets the win; Grilli is the loser.

Among the participants in the marathon game are Wade Boggs for Pawtucket, who has four hits in 12 at-bats, and Rochester's Cal Ripken Jr., with two safeties in 13 plate appearances.

APRIL 19:

The Athletics win their 11th straight – against no defeats, the best start ever in modern baseball. They defeat the Mariners, 6-1.

APRIL 22:

Orioles pitcher Dennis Martinez is struck in the eye with a beer bottle as he stands near the bat rack during a rain delay in a game at Chicago's Comiskey Park. Four stitches are required to close the wound.

APRIL 27:

Oakland Athletics manager Billy Martin calls on umpires to measure the batter's box at Seattle's Kingdome. Martin claims Seattle's Tom Paciorek was out of what should have been the batter's box when hitting against curveball pitcher Rick Langford. Then the umpires find the box is actually seven feet long instead of the required six feet. According to the groundskeeper, he was ordered by Mariners manager Maury Wills to make the change. The A's win the game, 7-4.

Pittsburgh's Mayor Richard Caliguiri files a federal law suit against the city of New Orleans and the Louisiana Superdome. The suit seeks to prevent the defendants from luring the Pirates away from their home city. Major league baseball has been played in Pittsburgh since 1882 and the franchise has been part of the NL since 1887. Since moving from Forbes Field to Three Rivers Stadium in 1970, the Pirates report losses of $7 million and the team is suing the Stadium Authority to nullify the Three Rivers lease, which still has 30 years to run.

APRIL 28:

Maury Wills is suspended for two games for "doctoring the batter's box." Wills claims to be shocked and dumbfounded and maintains it was inches, not a foot.

APRIL 29:

Lefty strikes again... and again... and again. Pitcher Steve Carlton of the Phillies strikes out Montreal's Tim Raines, Jerry Manuel, and then Tim Wallach in the first inning to record his 3,000th career strikeout. He fans six more Phillies in the game, which Philadelphia wins, 6-2, at home.

MAY 3:

The Expos score with two out in the eighth inning, ending Fernando Valenzuela's scoreless inning streak at 36. But the Dodgers win the game, 6-1, and Valenzuela improves his record to 6-0.

MAY 4:

Yankees reliever Ron Davis strikes out eight straight Athletics batters, tying Nolan Ryan's AL record. The Yankees win, 4-2.

MAY 6:

Montreal's Mike Gates, Tim Raines, and Tim Wallach hit back-to-back-to-back triples in the ninth inning of today's 13-5 loss to the Padres.

MAY 10:

The Expos' Charlie Lea no-hits San Francisco in Montreal. A native of Orleans, France, Lea is the first French-born pitcher to throw a no-hitter. He strikes out eight Giants and walks four for a 4-0 win. Montreal plays errorless ball. Ed Whitson gets the loss.

Pete Rose of the Phillies singles and triples to tie Henry Aaron for second on the all-time NL hit list with 3,600. (Stan Musial holds the NL record with 3,630 and Ty Cobb the major league mark – 4,191.) The Phillies still manage to lose the game, 8-4, to the Padres in Philadelphia.

MAY 14:

The Dodgers' Fernando Valenzuela beats the Expos, 3-2, to run his record to 8-0. He ties what is believed to be a major league rookie record set by Dave "Boo" Ferriss of the Red Sox in 1945.

Kansas City's George Brett, hobbled by a sprained ankle, swings a crutch at a

MAY 4
Yankees' reliever Ron Davis strikes out eight A's in a row, tying Nolan Ryan's AL mark.

MAY 15
Indians' pitcher Len Barker records a perfect game against the Blue Jays.

news photographer who is trying to get his picture after a 3-2 loss to the Rangers.

MAY 15:

The Indians' Len Barker pitches a perfect game against the Blue Jays, winning, 3-0, in Cleveland on a misty, 47-degree day. Barker also strikes out 11. It is the first major league perfect game since Catfish Hunter's in 1968 against Minnesota and the 11th in major league history. The losing pitcher is Luis Leal.

MAY 18:

The Phillies beat the Dodgers' 20-year-old rookie pitcher Fernando Valenzuela, 4-0, ending his winning streak at eight and handing him his very first major league loss.

MAY 19:

Facing a May 29 strike deadline, representatives of the owners and players begin three days of scheduled negotiations.

MAY 25:

Ranger Bill Stein hits a pinch-hit single off Doug Corbett in the bottom of the ninth to beat the Twins, 4-3, in Arlington, Texas. It is Stein's seventh consecutive pinch hit, an AL record. The previous record was set in 1964 by Bob Johnson of the Orioles. The major league record is nine by Dave Philley of the Phillies over the 1958-59 seasons.

FOLLOWING THE YANKEES' DEFEAT IN THE WORLD SERIES, OWNER GEORGE STEINBRENNER SAYS: "I WANT TO SINCERELY APOLOGIZE TO THE PEOPLE OF NEW YORK AND TO THE FANS OF THE NEW YORK YANKEES EVERYWHERE FOR THE PERFORMANCE OF THE YANKEE TEAM IN THE WORLD SERIES. I ALSO WANT TO ASSURE YOU THAT WE WILL BE AT WORK IMMEDIATELY TO PREPARE FOR 1982." HE ALSO CONGRATULATES THE DODGERS.

MAY 26:

A National Labor Relations Board lawyer accuses the baseball owners of not bargaining in good faith and seeks a federal injunction to make the owners provide financial data the players are seeking.

MAY 27:

In the second strange controversy in Seattle in the past month, Mariners third baseman Lenny Randle is accused by home plate umpire Larry McCoy of trying to blow a slow roller into foul territory. Randle drops to all fours and blows on a ball hit along the third base foul line by Kansas City's Amos Otis. "I didn't blow on it," Randle explains, "I used the power of suggestion. I yelled at it, 'Go foul, go foul!'" Umpire McCoy calls the ball foul but reverses his decision after Royals manager Jim Frey complains.

MAY 28:

In U.S. District Court in Manhattan, both sides agree to extend the strike deadline. The strike now can occur as early as June 4 of this year or as late as June 1, 1982.

MAY 29:

The Expos acquire pitcher Jeff Reardon (1-0) and outfielder Dan Norman (no appearances in 1981) from the New York Mets for outfielder Ellis Valentine (.211 in 22 games).

JUNE 1:

AL president Lee MacPhail suspends Athletics manager Billy Martin for a week and fines him $1,000 for bumping umpire Terry Cooney and throwing two handfuls of dirt at him during a May 29 game against Toronto.

No progress is today reported in the strike negotiations.

JUNE 2:

After three days, Oakland manager Billy Martin is allowed to return to the Athletics' dugout while he appeals his week's suspension.

JUNE 4:

The Cubs purchase outfielder Bobby Bonds (.203, five homers, 15 stolen

LEAGUE

Baseball Commissioner Bowie Kuhn announces baseball will have a split season, and details a complex playoff arrangement.

TRIVIA

Stanford University's junior quarterback John Elway is signed by the Yankees to a one-year minor league contract. When not playing football, Elway is an outfielder; he hit .316 in the past college season.

"We have been meeting most of the day, we have accomplished nothing. The strike is on."
– Marvin Miller

bases in 86 games) from the Rangers. In his first play as a Cub, he breaks a finger fielding a ball hit by the Pirates' Tim Foli in Pittsburgh and will be in a cast for at least three weeks.

JUNE 5:

Federal mediator Kenneth E. Moffett reports on the strike negotiations: "Nothing happened. We couldn't get going."

JUNE 7:

The Cardinals obtain pitcher Joaquin Andujar (2-3) from the Astros for outfielder Tony Scott (.227 in 45 games). St. Louis also sells pitcher George Frazier (1-4, 1.61 ERA in 1980) to the Yankees.

Mariners Julio Cruz ties a major league record for second basemen when he handles 18 chances in nine innings without an error. He handles one more in extra innings as Seattle beats the Indians, 5-4, at the Kingdome.

JUNE 10:

Philadelphia's Pete Rose singles against Nolan Ryan of the Astros in his first at-bat to tie Stan Musial's NL record for career hits – 3,630. Ryan then strikes out Rose three times, but the Phillies top the Astros, 5-4.

An injunction that would have postponed free-agent compensation – the key issue in the negotiations – for a year is denied by a federal judge. The National Labor Relations Board had filed for the injunction on behalf of the players. The judge declares, "There is no reasonable cause to believe that an unfair labor practice has been committed."

JUNE 11:

A black day for baseball fans. Marvin Miller announces: "We have been meet-

Gary Carter goes deep in the All-Star Game and in the playoffs.

JUNE 10
Pete Rose's single ties him with Stan Musial for most career hits in the NL – 3,630.

JUNE 11
Unable to reach an agreement with owners, major league players go on strike.

ing most of the day, we have accomplished nothing. The strike is on." It is the third play stoppage in 10 years, but the first during the regular season.

As the clock winds down on the season, the Mariners' Julio Cruz steals his 32nd consecutive base in an 8-2 victory over the Orioles.

JUNE 12:

Baseball players' strike, day one. The first game "struck out" would have matched the San Diego Padres against the Chicago Cubs at Wrigley Field's friendly confines. Twelve other games are canceled today.

JUNE 14:

The *New York Times* reports: "It became apparent yesterday that there is no rush among the owners to become any more directly involved in the dispute with the players than they were before the strike began."

JUNE 16:

Strike talks resume in an atmosphere that is not considered optimistic. A participant on the players' side tells the *New York Times*: "This thing is going off the cliff... this is a next-season situation."

The *Chicago Tribune* buys the Chicago Cubs from William Wrigley for $20.5 million. The transaction, which includes Wrigley Field, ends the Wrigley family's involvement, which began in 1916. The current Wrigley's grandfather, also William, became a minority shareholder in 1921. His son, Philip K. Wrigley, became a major shareholder in 1932. When he died in 1977, his son assumed control of the team.

JUNE 18:

With a record 87 games canceled, strike talks resume.

JUNE 19:

Relations between the owners and the players worsen and talks again break down. Kenneth E. Moffett says, "It's kind of stupid just to be going through a charade of getting together on a regular basis when there's no movement as far as the parties are concerned."

JUNE 22:

The strike is now 11 days old. Despite the dispute, business goes on. The Phillies sign Steve Carlton (24-9, 2.34 ERA, 286 strikeouts, three shutouts) to a $3 million, four-year contract, including incentive clauses. The left-hander had been earning $400,000 per year.

JULY 1:

After 19 days and the cancellation of 237 games, negotiators for both sides agree to try again. The Players Association files default notices on behalf of eight players who say they should be receiving their salaries. Their teams have 10 days to respond or the players will be free agents. Additional defaults may be filed.

Marvin Miller, rarely at a loss for words, says, "The gap between us is so wide it defies my vocabulary to define it." Miller's remark comes after three and a half hours of negotiations, with another meeting scheduled for tomorrow. The owners have reduced the maximum number of free agents for whom compensation will be mandated and have settled the default claims of two players.

Miller regains his powers of speech to describe the owners' new offer: "[It] assumes a player is a piece of property and they own him."

The man described as the "dean of American baseball writers," Dan Daniel, dies at age 91 in Pompano Beach, Florida. Daniel covered the sport for more than 50 years.

JULY 4:

For the first time in this century, there is no major league baseball played on Independence Day. Meanwhile, in the ninth negotiating session, the players reject management's latest offer, which included a maximum number of premium free agents for whom compensation would be required.

Claiming it was part of his compensation, the Braves take back the 1981 Continental Mark VI they were providing to pitcher Phil Niekro. They also reclaim outfielder Ed Miller's 1980 BMW. The Braves say the automobiles will be returned after the strike is settled.

JULY 10:

Players agree to a new proposal put forth by mediator Kenneth Moffett but the owners reject it,

LEAGUE

What was the price of the strike? A total of 713 games were canceled. The players lost some $28 million in salary. Approximately $116 million – including concession revenues – was lost by the owners. They received $44 million in strike insurance, for a net loss of $72 million.

New York Daily Mirror columnist Dan Parker once wrote: "Your arm is gone, your legs likewise; But not your eyes, Mize, not your eyes."

CULTURE

During the strike, Terry Cashman's song "Talkin' Baseball" (also known as "Willie, Mickey and the Duke") is released. Inspired by a photograph of Willie Mays, Mickey Mantle, Duke Snider, and Joe DiMaggio, Cashman strikes a nostalgic chord in baseball fans with lyrics like, "The Whiz Kids had won it, Bobby Thomson had done it, and Yogi read the comics all the while."

saying it "eliminates two-thirds of any compensation for ranking free agents." They offer a counter-proposal. The All-Star Game is officially postponed.

JULY 11:

The *New York Times* reports that major league cities have lost millions of dollars due to the baseball strike. It cites as an example Cleveland, which was to host the All-Star Game on July 14 and had anticipated 75,000 fans spending $2.6 million. In New York City, each baseball game pumps $50,000 to $100,000 into the economy. In Baltimore, Detroit, and Philadelphia, baseball accounts for approximately $10,000 a day. Negotiations collapse after seven hours of talks on Friday night and Saturday morning. The owners' chief negotiator, Ray Grebey, charges that Marvin Miller wrote the proposal put forward by arbitrator Moffett. Moffett says, "It's getting very nasty in there."

JULY 16:

The players propose binding arbitration to settle the strike. The owners reject the proposal and Kenneth Moffett schedules no further meetings.

JULY 20:

The talks move from New York City to Washington, D.C., and U.S. Secretary of Labor Raymond J. Donovan steps in.

JULY 21:

Despite Secretary of Labor Raymond J. Donovan's participation in strike talks, there is no reason for optimism. At his request, a news blackout goes into effect.

JULY 22:

For the first time, owners and players meet face to face in secret session. The meeting, which brings together the players' negotiating committee and the owners' board of directors, lasts 90 minutes. The regular bargaining teams are scheduled to resume their next round of meetings tomorrow.

JULY 23:

After four days of meetings, the talks collapse yet again. The strike is now six weeks old and 500 games have been lost. No further talks are scheduled until the middle of next week.

JULY 27:

The players' representatives of all 26 teams voice unanimous support for their negotiators in a Chicago meeting attended by more than 50 players.

JULY 30:

Back in New York, talks resume and the *New York Times* reports the two sides are on the "verge of a settlement."

JULY 31:

The strike ends with an early morning settlement after a 12-hour negotiating session. The season will resume with the All-Star Game in Cleveland, now rescheduled for August 9; regular season games will start the following day. The two sides agree to a pool free-agent compensation system that will give teams that lose ranking free agents a player and an amateur draft pick. The collective bargaining agreement also is lengthened under the agreement. The negotiations were so bitter that Marvin Miller refuses to pose for a photo with Ray Grebey. Miller also announces he will retire after fifteen years as executive director of the Players Association.

AUGUST 1:

Ray Kroc, owner of the San Diego Padres, announces he will give away all 50,000 seats to his team's August 10 home game against the Atlanta Braves at Jack Murphy Stadium. The gesture amounts to a $250,000 loss in ticket revenue. The Atlanta Braves will be paid their normal visitor's share.

AUGUST 2:

Andrew "Rube" Foster, Bob Gibson, and Johnny Mize are inducted into the Baseball Hall of Fame. Foster was the driving force in the formation of the Negro National Baseball League in 1920. A right-handed pitcher, he played for such teams as the Waco Yellow Jackets, the Chicago Union Giants, the Cuban X Giants, and the Chicago American Giants. He died in 1930 and is represented at the Hall of Fame ceremonies by his son Earl. Bob Gibson, an overpowering right-handed pitcher, won both the NL's Most Valuable Player Award and its Cy Young Award in 1968 and was a repeat Cy Young win-

JULY 31
The players' strike ends, with baseball set to resume August 9 with the All-Star Game.

AUGUST 9
The NL wins the All-Star Game, 5-4, largely on a pair of homers from Gary Carter.

ner in 1970. He spent 17 years in the major leagues, all with the St. Louis Cardinals, winning 251 games – including 56 shutouts – striking out 3,117, and compiling an ERA of 2.91. He was 7-2 in World Series play with an ERA of 1.89. Mize, a lifetime .312 hitter with 359 homers and 1,337 RBI in 15 major league seasons, was reputed to have so keen an eye for the strike zone that umpires were reluctant to call a pitch he took anything other than a ball. Mize played with the Cardinals, Giants, and Yankees, finishing his career as one of the best pinch-hitters in the game. He appeared in five World Series.

According to Tim McCarver, who caught him, "Bob Gibson is the luckiest pitcher I ever saw. He always pitches when the other team doesn't score any runs." He also recalls "one time going out to the mound to talk with Bob Gibson. He told me to get back behind the batter, that the only thing I knew about pitching was that it was hard to hit."

AUGUST 9:

The All-Star Game is finally played, and the NL wins it, 5-4, before 72,086 fans in Cleveland, the largest crowd ever for the contest. A record 56 players participate and Montreal's Gary Carter, with two home runs, is the game's outstanding player. Dave Parker, Mike Schmidt, and Ken Singleton also homer. The winning pitcher is Jerry Reuss; Tommy John gets the loss. It's the NL's 10th straight All-Star win.

IN 1907, *CHICAGO INTER-OCEAN* WROTE: "RUBE FOSTER IS A PITCHER WITH THE TRICKS OF RUSIE AND WITH THE COOLNESS AND DELIBERATION OF A CY YOUNG. WHAT DOES THAT MAKE HIM? WHY, THE GREATEST PITCHER IN THE COUNTRY; THAT IS WHAT THE GREATEST BASEBALL PLAYERS OF WHITE PERSUASION THAT HAVE GONE AGAINST HIM SAY." HONUS WAGNER CALLED FOSTER: "THE SMARTEST PITCHER I HAVE EVER SEEN IN ALL MY YEARS OF BASEBALL."

AUGUST 10:

Baseball's regular season resumes. Philadelphia's Pete Rose singles off Mark Littell of the Cardinals in the eighth inning to break Stan Musial's career hit mark with 3,631. Musial, who is in attendance, congratulates Rose from his box seat.

Seattle's Julio Cruz fails in his bid to set the AL consecutive stolen base record when he is out on a disputed call in the seventh inning. Cruz remains tied with Willie Wilson at 32. The Mariners beat the Angels, 5-4, at the Seattle Kingdome.

AUGUST 20:

Bowie Kuhn states that his previously announced playoff system "had some warts, but no integrity warts." He announces a revised system: The top team in the first half of the season in each division will play the top team in the second half in a best-of-five series. If a team wins both halves, it will play the team with the second-best record for both halves. The first-half winners are the Phillies, Dodgers, Yankees, and Athletics.

AUGUST 25:

At Three Rivers Stadium, Reggie Smith – who is not in the lineup – warns Pirates pitcher Pascual Perez to stop throwing at the Dodgers. After the half-inning Smith, Perez, and their teams engage in a 10-minute fight in the runway behind the Pittsburgh dugout. There are no injuries and no ejections. The Dodgers win, 9-7.

AUGUST 28:

Yankees manager Gene Michael reports that owner George Steinbrenner is threatening to fire him. Says Michael: "I don't know how serious it is, but I don't like it. It's not fair that he criticizes me and threatens to fire me all the time. I'd rather he do it than talk about it. I told him exactly that today – don't wait." To

CULTURE

In the theater, *The First* is a musical starring David Alan Grier as Jackie Robinson, Lonette McKee as Rachel Robinson, and David Huddleston as Branch Rickey. *The Amazin' Casey Stengel, Or Can't Anybody Here Speak This Game?* stars Paul Dooley in the title role.

"I don't know how serious it is, but I don't like it. It's not fair that he criticizes me and threatens to fire me all the time."
– Yankees' manager Gene Michael, on George Steinbrenner

CULTURE

Steve Goodman's song, "A Dying Cub Fan's Last Request," is released.

which Steinbrenner responds: "Any discussions I have with my managers are not public."

AUGUST 29:

Oakland manager Billy Martin drops the appeal of his suspension for bumping and throwing dirt at umpire Terry Cooney on May 29. Martin apologizes to the umpire, as well.

AUGUST 30:

Jim Frey is fired as manager by the Royals and replaced by former Yankees skipper Dick Howser. The Royals are 10-11 since the end of the strike.

AUGUST 31:

NL president Charles "Chub" Feeney fines umpires Nick Colosi ($500) and Frank Pulli ($300) for getting into a shoving match with a TV crew and breaking a camera after an August 24 game between the Phillies and the Braves.

Cardinals shortstop Garry Templeton, who made obscene gestures to fans during an August 26 game against the Giants in St. Louis's Busch Stadium, is hospitalized for psychiatric observation. He previously was fined $5,000 and placed on the disabled list. Templeton will return to the action on September 15.

SEPTEMBER 6:

The LA Dodgers' Fernando Valenzuela ties an NL rookie record held by four others when he registers his seventh shutout of the season, beating the Cardinals, 5-0. It is his 12th win of the season.

Despite finishing in first place in the pre-strike half of the season, Gene Michael is fired as Yankees manager by owner George Steinbrenner and replaced with Bob Lemon. The sixth man to manage the Yankees since 1973, Lemon returns to the team that he managed for parts of the 1978 and 1979 seasons.

SEPTEMBER 15:

The bizarre career of Jimmy Piersall takes a new twist. The White Sox report that the announcer was suspended last week and will not be reinstated during this season for making "derogatory remarks" about players' wives.

SEPTEMBER 20:

Three Twins – Gary Gaetti, Kent Hrbek, and Tim Laudner – make their major league debuts today. Each smacks a homer as the Twins top the Royals, 7-2.

SEPTEMBER 21:

Steve Carlton whiffs the Expos' Andre Dawson in the third inning for his 3,118th strikeout, surpassing Bob Gibson as the NL record holder. Carlton fans 11 other Expos in Montreal although Philadelphia loses the game, 1-0, in 17 innings. Carlton is now fourth on the all-time strikeout list. Walter Johnson leads with 3,508, followed by active players Gaylord Perry and Nolan Ryan.

SEPTEMBER 26:

Houston's Nolan Ryan no-hits the Dodgers in the Astrodome, 5-0, becoming the first pitcher to hurl five in his career. Ryan previously was tied with the Dodgers' Sandy Koufax with four. Ryan, who also has seven career one-hitters, struck out 11 Dodgers and walked three. The Astros commit no errors. The losing pitcher is Ted Power.

OCTOBER 3:

Montreal beats the Mets, 5-4, at Shea Stadium to win the NL East's second half title. It is the first title ever for Canada after 13 years of major league baseball.

The Astros win the NL West's second-half pennant when the Reds lose to the Braves, 4-3, at home. Under the complex system devised after the strike, the Reds do not make post-season playoffs despite having a 66-42 record for the full season, the best in the NL.

The Brewers beat the Detroit Tigers, 2-1, in Milwaukee today to win the AL East second-half title.

OCTOBER 4:

Hall of Fame outfielder-infielder Freddie Lindstrom dies in Chicago, at age 75. Inducted into the Hall of Fame in 1976, Lindstrom played 13 years, batting .311. His best season was 1930, when he hit .379 with the Giants. He appeared in two World Series.

OCTOBER 5:

The Royals win the AL West second half title with a 9-0 win over the Indians in Cleveland.

Gaylord Perry, just three games short of 300 career wins,

SEPTEMBER 6
Yankees manager Gene Michael is fired and replaced by Bob Lemon.

OCTOBER 3
By defeating the Mets, 5-4, the Expos become Canada's first baseball team to win a title.

is released by the Braves after an 8-9 season with a 3.93 ERA.

REGULAR SEASON WRAP-UP:

In the strike-abbreviated, split season, Tommy Lasorda's Dodgers are 63-47 overall in the NL. Johnnie "Dusty" Baker hits .315 with 11 homers. Pedro Guerrero bats .300 with 12 round-trippers. Fernando Valenzuela is the top winner with a 13-7 record.

Bob Lemon, who took over as manager with 25 games left in the season, leads the Yankees into the World Series with an overall 59-48 record in the AL. Ron Guidry is the big winner at 11-5. Jerry Mumphrey bats .307. Dave Winfield finishes with a .293 average, 13 homers, and 68 RBI. Reggie Jackson and Graig Nettles hit 15 home runs apiece.

The strike drastically affects season totals, but perhaps nowhere is the impact greater than in San Diego, where Joe Lefebvre leads the team in home runs with only eight.

OCTOBER 6:

NL Western Division Playoff, game one. In Houston, Nolan Ryan two-hits the Dodgers, 3-1. Alan Ashby hits a two-run homer in the ninth to win the game. Steve Garvey homers for the Dodgers' run. The losing pitcher is Dave Stewart in a relief appearance.

AL Western Division Playoff, game one. In Kansas City, Mike Norris pitches a four-hitter and the Athletics beat the Royals, 4-0. Greg Gross hits a three-run homer and Dwayne Murphy a solo shot to account for all of Oakland's runs. Dennis Leonard is charged with the loss.

OCTOBER 7:

NL Eastern Division Playoff, game one. In Montreal, Steve Rogers beats Steve Carlton and the Phillies, 3-1, with a save by Jeff Reardon. Keith Moreland hits a home run for Philadelphia.

NL Western Division Playoff, game two. Denny Walling's two-out pinch hit single with the bases loaded gives the Astros a 1-0 win over the Dodgers in 11 innings. Joe Sambito gets the win, pitching in relief. Dave Stewart is the losing pitcher for the second consecutive game.

AL Eastern Division Playoff, game one. In New York, Oscar Gamble hits a two-run homer to pace the Yankees to a 5-3 win over the Brewers in Milwaukee. Ron Davis gets the win with a save from Rich "Goose" Gossage. Bryan "Moose" Haas is tagged with the loss.

AL Western Division Playoff, game two. Tony Armas's RBI double in the eighth and Steve McCatty's 10-hit complete game pitching give Oakland a 2-1 win. Mike Jones is the game's losing pitcher.

OCTOBER 8:

NL Eastern Division Playoff, game two. Gary Carter hits a two-run homer while winning pitcher Bill Gullickson and Jeff Reardon limit the Phillies to six hits in a 3-1 Expos victory. The losing pitcher is Dick Ruthven.

AL Eastern Division Playoff, game two. Lou Piniella homers with the bases empty and Reggie Jackson clouts a two-run shot for the Yankees' runs in a 3-0 win in Milwaukee. Starter Dave Righetti, with relief help from Ron Davis and Goose Gossage, is the winning pitcher. The losing pitcher is Mike Caldwell.

OCTOBER 9:

NL Eastern Division Playoff, game three. The Phillies collect 13 hits – including three by Gary Matthews – to beat the Expos, 6-2, in Philadelphia. Larry Christenson gets the win; Ray Burris is the loser.

NL Western Division Playoff, game three. In Los Angeles, the Dodgers' behind Burt Hooten's three-hitter, beat the Astros, 6-1. Steve Garvey homers for Los Angeles; Art Howe for Houston. The losing pitcher is Bob Knepper.

AL Eastern Division Playoff, game three. The Brewers beat the Yankees, 5-3, in New York thanks to a Ted Simmons two-run homer and a Paul Molitor tie-breaking round-tripper with the bases empty in the eighth inning. Rollie Fingers gets the win with three innings of relief. Tommy John gets the loss.

AL Western Division Playoff, game three. The first-half winners, the Athletics, beat the Royals, 4-1, to sweep the Western Division Playoff.

OCTOBER 19
Rick Monday's ninth-inning homer sends the Dodgers to the World Series vs. the Yankees.

OCTOBER 28
The Dodgers win the World Series, defeating the Yankees, four games to two.

James "Rick" Langford gets the win; Larry Gura is charged with the loss. Dave McKay homers for the Athletics.

OCTOBER 10:

NL Eastern Division Playoff, game four. George Vukovich's pinch-hit home run in the bottom of the 10th off losing pitcher Jeff Reardon gives the Phillies a 6-5 win and ties the playoff. Previously, Mike Schmidt hit a two-run round-tripper and Gary Matthews connected with the bases empty. Gary Carter homers for Montreal. The winning pitcher is Frank "Tug" McGraw.

NL Western Division Playoff, game four. Fernando Valenzuela four-hits the Astros and beats Vern Ruhle – who also yields four hits – 2-1. Pedro Guerrero homers for Los Angeles and Bill Russell drives in Los Angeles's second run with a single.

AL Eastern Division Playoff, game four. The Yankees lose to the Brewers, 2-1, in New York. Pete Vukovich gets the win; Rick Reuschel is charged with the loss. Ben Oglivie's two-out double in the fourth is the key hit for Milwaukee. After the game, owner George Steinbrenner lashes out at his team, criticizing "stupid baserunning" and saying, "Now we'll see who the players are who deserve to be in the playoffs... which of these players don't deserve to be Yankees."

OCTOBER 11:

NL Eastern Division Playoff, game five. In Philadelphia today, starter Steve Rogers six-hits the Phillies, 3-0, to clinch the NL East for the Expos. Rogers helps his own cause with two hits and two RBI, beating Steve Carlton.

NL Western Division Playoff, game five. Jerry Reuss pitches a complete-game five-hitter, beating the Astros and Nolan Ryan, 4-0, and the Dodgers win the NL West. Steve Garvey has a triple and a single.

AL Eastern Division Playoff, game five. Today the Yankees rebound to defeat Milwaukee, 7-3, in New York to take the first Eastern Division championship. The Yankees have 13 hits – including a two-run homer by Reggie Jackson and solo drives by Oscar Gamble and Rick Cerone. Gorman Thomas homers for Milwaukee. The winning pitcher is Dave Righetti in relief; Goose Gossage is credited with a save. Moose Haas is tagged with the loss.

OCTOBER 13:

NLCS, game one. In Los Angeles, Pedro Guerrero hits a three-run homer and Mike Scioscia connects with the bases empty to lead the Dodgers to a 5-1 win over the Expos in Los Angeles. Burt Hooten gets the win; Bill Gullickson is charged with the loss.

ALCS, game one. At Yankee Stadium, Tommy John – with relief help from Ron Davis and Goose Gossage – beats the Athletics, 3-1. The losing pitcher is Mike Norris. All of New York's runs score on a first-inning three-run double off the bat of Graig Nettles.

OCTOBER 14:

NLCS, game two. Ray Burris pitches a five-hits complete-game, 3-0 victory in Los Angeles. Tim Raines accounts for three of Montreal's 10 hits as they defeat Fernando Valenzuela.

ALCS, game two. The Yankees pound out 10 hits – including two-run homers by Graig Nettles and Lou Piniella – to beat the Athletics, 13-3. The winning pitcher is George Frazier with five and two-thirds innings of relief. Steve McCatty gets the loss

The *New York Times* reports that the White Sox will join other Chicago professional teams – including the hockey Black Hawks and the basketball Bulls – in Sportsvision, a pay-TV venture. The White Sox are expected to charge approximately $260 per year for their games.

OCTOBER 15:

ALCS, game three. The Yankees score three runs in the ninth inning to beat the Athletics, 4-0, and sweep the ALCS, three games to none, for the AL pennant. Winning pitcher Dave Righetti, Ron Davis, and Goose Gossage combine to shut out Oakland, 4-0, on five hits. Willie Randolph has a solo home run. Matt Keough gets the loss. At a victory party, outfielder Reggie Jackson and third baseman Graig Nettles exchange angry words and scuffle.

OCTOBER 16:

NLCS, game three. Steve Rogers's seven-hit pitching and Jerry White's three-run

"There are three types of baseball players – those who make things happen, those who watch it happen, and those who wonder what happens."
– Dodgers manager Tommy Lasorda

homer add up to a 4-1 Expos win in Montreal. Jerry Reuss is tagged with the game's loss.

OCTOBER 17:

NLCS, game four. The Dodgers knot the playoffs with a 7-1 victory today in Montreal. Steve Garvey hits a two-run homer and Burt Hooten goes seven and a third innings for the win. Bill Gullickson is tagged with the loss.

OCTOBER 19:

NLCS, game five. In Montreal, Rick Monday hits a two-out home run in the ninth inning to give the Dodgers the NL pennant with a 2-1 win over the Expos. Fernando Valenzuela gets the win with a save by Bob Welch. The losing pitcher is Steve Rogers in relief.

OCTOBER 20:

George Bamberger is named the New York Mets' new manager, replacing Joe Torre. The Mets were 41-62 in fifth place in the NL East under Torre.

World Series, game one. The World Series opens in New York, marking the 11th championship meeting between the Yankees and Dodgers; the Yankees lead with eight World Series crowns against the Dodgers. New York wins the opener, 5-3, behind Ron Guidry, who gets relief help from the Ron Davis-Goose Gossage bullpen combination. Bob Watson homers with two on in the first for the Yankees; Steve Yeager hits a solo shot for Los Angeles. The losing pitcher is Jerry Reuss.

OCTOBER 21:

World Series, game two. Tommy John pitches seven shutout innings against his old team and Goose Gossage finishes up for a 3-0 New York victory. Bob Watson has two hits and drives in a run. The game's losing pitcher is Dodgers starter Burt Hooten.

In one of the more short-sighted deals ever, the New York Yankees trade minor league outfielder Willie McGee to the Cardinals for pitcher Bob Sykes (2-0, 4.62 ERA).

OCTOBER 23:

World Series, game three. Playing at home, the Dodgers record their first win of the series, 5-4. Fernando Valenzuela goes the route, allowing nine hits and seven walks. Reliever George Frazier gets the loss. Ron Cey hits a three-run homer for the Dodgers; Bob Watson connects with the bases empty and Rick Cerone with one on for the Yankees.

OCTOBER 24:

World Series, game four. The Dodgers edge the Yankees, 8-7, to tie the Series. Jay Johnstone hits a pinch-hit two-run homer for Los Angeles; Willie Randolph and Reggie Jackson homer with no one on for the Yankees. Steve Howe, the fifth Dodger pitcher, gets the win. New York reliever George Frazier loses his second straight.

OCTOBER 25:

World Series, game five. Ron Guidry throws two bad pitches and they cost him the game, 2-1. In the seventh inning, he serves up back-to-back homers to Pedro Guerrero and Steve Yeager, giving Jerry Reuss all the runs he needs. Reuss allows five hits for the win; Guidry gives up four.

Pete Reiser dies at the age of 62 in Palm Springs, California. An outfielder of exceptional promise, Reiser hit .343 with the Brooklyn Dodgers in 1941, his first full major league season. He was hitting .350 in 1942 when he crashed into the center-field wall in St. Louis, the first of 11 such collisions. As a result of that first injury, Reiser suffered from headaches and dizziness for the rest of his career, still finishing with a lifetime average of .295.

OCTOBER 28:

World Series, game six. The Dodgers beat the Yankees, 9-2, in New York to take the World Series, four games to two. The Dodgers have 13 hits, including a solo homer by Pedro Guerrero, who has five RBI. The winning pitcher is starter Burt Hooten, with relief from Steve Howe. Yankees reliever George Frazier is charged with his third consecutive defeat, tying a series mark. Steve Garvey hits .417; Pedro Guerrero knocks in seven runs and hits two homers, while batting .333. Lou Piniella bats .438 to lead all hitters, and Bob Watson has two homers and seven RBI in a losing cause.

"You want me to call the Mayflower moving men? I don't think it looks good for me."
– *Reggie Jackson*

POST-SEASON

OCTOBER 29:

A group of investors assembled by Phillies executive vice president Bill Giles buys the team for $30.175 million. The largest investor is Taft Broadcasting Co. of Cincinnati, which pays $15 million for "slightly less than 50 percent." The Carpenter family, which sold the Phillies, originally purchased the team 38 years ago for $500,000.

NOVEMBER 2:

Yankees outfielder Reggie Jackson becomes a free agent. He is one of 10 – including Bert Campaneris of the Angels – to declare today, bringing the total to 30. Jackson was a member of the Class of '76, the major league's first free agents.

NOVEMBER 4:

Outfielder Ken Griffey (.311, two homers, 34 RBI, 12 stolen bases), 31 years old, is acquired today by the Yankees from the Reds for minor league pitchers Brian Ryder and Fred Toliver. Reggie Jackson tells the *New York Times*, "Wow! ... That's unreal. You want me to call the Mayflower moving men?... I don't think it looks good for me."

NOVEMBER 18:

Dick Williams, who won two World Series with the Athletics and one pennant with the Red Sox, is named the new manager of the San Diego Padres. He replaces Frank Howard. The Padres finished the season in last place in the National League West with a 41-69 record.

NOVEMBER 20:

In a three-way trade, the Cardinals acquire outfielder Lonnie Smith (.324, 21 stolen bases in 62 games). The Indians obtain pitchers Lary Sorensen (7-7, 3.28 ERA), Silvio Martinez (2-5, 3.99 ERA), and Scott Munninghoff (0-0, 7.20 in 1980). Going to the Phillies is catcher Baudilio "Bo" Diaz (.313, seven homers in 63 games).

NOVEMBER 20:

Tommy Lasorda signs his seventh one-year contract to manage the Los Angeles Dodgers, this season's World Champions.

DECEMBER 7:

Baseball lost $25 million in 1980, according to Commissioner Bowie Kuhn, speaking at the 80th annual business meeting, attended by 1,600 major and minor league officials, in Hollywood, Florida. He states that the 1981 records are not ready, but that reports about baseball's finances are "disturbing." Retiring Players Association representative Marvin Miller responds in the *New York Times*: "We don't even know how they arrive at what is a loss or profit. 'I lost money last week.' What does that mean? It's basically meaningless. You can make statements that are not backed up, so let him make them." Kuhn also promises that there will be no split season in 1982.

DECEMBER 8:

George Steinbrenner surprises the baseball world by re-signing manager Bob Lemon for the 1982 season.

The Cubs sign free-agent Ferguson Jenkins (5-8, 4.50 ERA), who spent the past four years with the Rangers. Jenkins pitched for Chicago from 1966 through 1973.

DECEMBER 9:

The Boss – New York Yankees' owner George Steinbrenner – is up to his old tricks once again. This time around he announces that Gene Michael, fired as the Yankees' manager during this past year, will nonetheless pilot the team for the 1983, 1984, and 1985 seasons. Yesterday, Steinbrenner had announced that Bob Lemon would be the club's 1982 manager.

The World Champion Los Angeles Dodgers today trade right-handed pitcher Rick Sutcliffe (2-2, 4.02 ERA) and second baseman Jack Perconte (.222 in eight games) to the Cleveland Indians for outfielder-DH Jorge Orta (.272, five home runs in 88 games) and two minor leaguers – pitcher Larry White and catcher Jack Fimple.

DECEMBER 21:

The Philadelphia Phillies sign their All-Star third baseman Mike Schmidt to a new six-year contract reportedly worth $1.2 million per season. In 1981, Schmidt led the major leagues in home runs (31), RBI (91), and slugging percentage (.644). He hit .316 on the year.

THE BEST OF 1981

NATIONAL LEAGUE

HITTERS

Batting Average:
Bill Madlock, Pittsburgh Pirates, .341

Slugging Average:
Mike Schmidt, Philadelphia Phillies, .644

Home Runs:
Mike Schmidt, 31

Runs Batted In:
Mike Schmidt, 91

Hits:
Pete Rose, Philadelphia Phillies, 140

Stolen Bases:
Tim Raines, Montreal Expos, 71

PITCHERS

Wins:
Tom Seaver, Cincinnati Reds, 14

Strikeouts:
Fernando Valenzuela, Los Angeles Dodgers, 180

Earned Run Average:
Nolan Ryan, Houston Astros, 1.69

Winning Percentage:
Tom Seaver, .875

Saves:
Bruce Sutter, St. Louis Cardinals, 25

Most Valuable Player:
Mike Schmidt, Philadelphia Phillies

Cy Young Award:
Fernando Valenzuela, Los Angeles Dodgers

Rookie of the Year:
Fernando Valenzuela, Los Angeles Dodgers

AMERICAN LEAGUE

HITTERS

Batting Average:
Carney Lansford, Boston Red Sox, .336

Slugging Average:
Bobby Grich, California Angels, .543

Home Runs:
Grich; Eddie Murray, Baltimore Orioles; Dwight Evans, Boston Red Sox; Tony Armas, Oakland Athletics, 22

Runs Batted In:
Eddie Murray, 78

Hits:
Rickey Henderson, Oakland Athletics, 135

Stolen Bases:
Rickey Henderson, 56

PITCHERS

Wins:
Pete Vuckovich, Milwaukee Brewers; Dennis Martinez, Baltimore Orioles; Steve McCatty, Oakland Athletics; Jack Morris, Detroit Tigers, 14

Strikeouts:
Len Barker, Cleveland Indians, 127

Earned Run Average:
Steve McCatty, 2.32

Winning Percentage:
Pete Vuckovich, .778

Saves:
Rollie Fingers, Milwaukee Brewers, 28

Most Valuable Player:
Rollie Fingers, Milwaukee Brewers

Cy Young Award:
Rollie Fingers, Milwaukee Brewers

Rookie of the Year:
Dave Righetti, New York Yankees

1982

NEWS

MARTIAL LAW DECLARED IN POLAND

Israel invades Lebanon

U.S. PEACEKEEPING FORCES IN LEBANON

78 die when airliner plunges into Potomac

POISONED TYLENOL KILLS SEVEN

LARGEST CASH HEIST EVER NETS $9.8 MILLION

JOHN HINCKLEY NOT GUILTY BY REASON OF INSANITY IN REAGAN SHOOTING

BRITAIN, ARGENTINA GO TO WAR OVER FALKLAND ISLANDS

BARNEY CLARK IS FIRST ARTIFICIAL HEART RECIPIENT

MONACO'S PRINCESS GRACE, ONE-TIME U.S. FILM ACTRESS, KILLED IN AUTOMOBILE ACCIDENT

PRE-SEASON

JANUARY 22:

Free-agent Reggie Jackson (.237, 15 homers, 54 RBI in 94 games) is signed by the Angels to a four-year contract estimated at $1 million per year plus an attendance bonus. The Yankees made no effort to retain "the straw that stirs the drink."

JANUARY 27:

The Cubs acquire infielder Ryne Sandberg (.167 in 13 games) and shortstop Larry Bowa (.283, 16 stolen bases) from the Phillies for shortstop Ivan DeJesus (.194, 21 stolen bases).

JANUARY 29:

Graig Nettles is not superstitious and accepts the Yankees' captaincy. Lou Gehrig and Thurman Munson, the Yankees' last two captains, both died prematurely.

The Indians release pitcher Wayne Garland (3-7, 5.79 ERA). Garland was signed by Cleveland to a 10-year, $2.5 million contract in 1976. In 1978, he underwent surgery for a torn rotator cuff and won only 28 games in five seasons for the Indians. He leaves baseball with a 55-66 record with a 3.89 ERA in nine years.

FEBRUARY 8:

The Dodgers trade their longtime second baseman Davey Lopes (.206, five homers, 20 stolen bases in 58 games) to Oakland for minor league second baseman Lance Hudson.

FEBRUARY 10:

The Mets get Reds' slugging outfielder George Foster (.295, 22 homers, 90 RBI) in return for catcher-infielder Alex Trevino (.262 in 59 games) and pitchers Jim Kern (1-2, 2.70 ERA, six saves) and Greg A. Harris (3-5, 4.43 ERA). Foster hit 52 home runs in 1977.

FEBRUARY 11:

St. Louis and San Diego swap shortstops. The Cardinals get Ozzie Smith (.222, 22 stolen bases); the Padres obtain Garry Templeton (.288 in 80 games).

The swap of Smith for Templeton, which gives the Cardinals a Hall of Fame-caliber shortstop, is just one part of a three-stage deal. On December 10, 1981, the Padres send pitcher Steve Mura (5-14, 4.27 ERA) to the Cardinals for outfielder Sixto Lezcano (.266, 5 homers in 72 games). On February 19, 1982, pitcher Al Olmsted (1-1, 2.83 ERA in 1980) is sent by San Diego to St. Louis for pitcher Luis DeLeon (0-1, 2.40 ERA).

FEBRUARY 17:

Former major league umpire Nestor Chylak dies at the age of 59 in Dunmore, Pennsylvania. Chylak umpired in the AL from 1954 to 1978. In 1972 he had received the Umpire of the Year Award.

George Steinbrenner tells the world, "Bob Lemon's going to be our manager all year. You can bet on it. I don't care if we come in last. I swear on my heart he'll be the manager all season."

MARCH 24:

The Dodgers automatically renew their pitcher Fernando Valenzuela's contract when he ends his three-week holdout and reports for spring training at Vero Beach, Florida. The disgruntled pitcher, however, does not sign the new contract.

MARCH 27:

Gaylord Perry (8-9, 3.93 ERA) will get his chance for 300 victories. The 43-year-old right-hander, who has 297 career wins, is signed to a one-year contract by the Mariners. Perry was released by the Braves after last season.

APRIL 1:

The Mets trade popular outfielder Lee Mazzilli (.228, six homers, 17 stolen bases in 95 games) to the Texas Rangers for two minor league pitchers – Ron Darling and Charles "Walt" Terrell.

THE SEASON

APRIL 6:

In the first game played under the canopy in the new $68 million Hubert H. Humphrey Metrodome in Minnesota, the Mariners beat the Twins, 11-7, with 52,279 in attendance. There are five home runs in the game. The new facility, the only air-supported dome in baseball, is dedicated by Muriel Humphrey, the widow of the former vice president and U.S. Senator.

APRIL 9:

Former White Sox pitcher Francisco Barrios dies of a heroin overdose in Hermosillo, Mexico, at age 28. Barrios, released by Chicago after going 1-3 with a 4.00 ERA in eight games in 1981, was arrested last June for cocaine possession and entered a rehabilitation program. In seven years he was 38-38 with a 4.15 ERA; his best season was 1977 when his record was 14-7.

APRIL 10:

After 500 tons of snow are removed from the playing field at Municipal Stadium in Cleveland, you might expect to see the Browns and

CULTURE

***Shoeless Joe*, by W.P. Kinsella, is about an Iowan who builds a diamond in his cornfield, where the Black Sox and other assorted ghosts play baseball. It's not just a sports book, but a major American novel.**

Rickey Henderson sets a new stolen base records.

President Ronald Reagan says to Gaylord Perry, "I know it's just an ugly rumor that you and I are the only people alive who saw Abner Doubleday throw the first pitch out."

TRIVIA

Some members of the Society for American Baseball Research say the "Mendoza" line actually was named for infielder Cristobal "Minnie" Mendoza, who appeared in 16 games for the 1970 Twins and has three hits in 16 at-bats for a .188 average. SABR-ite Tom Zucco claims the "Mendoza line" remark did not originate with George Brett.

Cowboys. But 62,443 hardy fans brave a wind-chill factor of 17 degrees to watch the Indians play the Rangers. Behind Charlie Hough, Texas wins, 8-3. Rick Waits gets the loss.

APRIL 22:

The Reds, behind pitchers Bruce Berenyi and Tom Hume, six-hit the Braves at Fulton County Stadium in Atlanta. The 2-1 Reds victory ends Atlanta's NL record 13-game win streak (to open a season). With Bob Walk pitching, the Braves led 1-0 until the Reds scored twice in the fifth inning. Braves first baseman Chris Chambliss took the end of the winning streak philosophically: "We didn't expect to go 162-0."

APRIL 25:

With their season only 14 games old, the New York Yankees fire their manager, Bob Lemon, and replace him with Gene Michael. The firing comes at Yankee Stadium after New York beats the Tigers, 3-1, to bring the season record to 6-8. Lemon, in George Steinbrenner fashion, will be reassigned to scouting duties for the club.

APRIL 26:

In the eighth inning of the opener of a doubleheader in Comiskey Park, Wade Boggs of the Red Sox singles off Rich Dotson for his first major league hit. Boston beats Chicago, 3-2.

MAY 2:

Steve Garvey keeps his consecutive game streak alive at 968 by appearing as a pinch hitter today against Montreal at Dodger Stadium. Garvey fans on four pitches from Steve Rogers and the Expos win, 13-1.

MAY 6:

Gaylord Perry beats the Yankees, 7-3, before 27,369 at the Kingdome for his 300th career win. Perry, now in his 21st major league season, gives up nine hits and walks four but hangs on to become the 15th pitcher to reach the 300-win mark. The losing pitcher is Doyle Alexander.

MAY 17:

Fred "Dixie" Walker, known as the People's Cherce when he was playing for the Dodgers, dies of cancer in Birmingham, Alabama, at age 71. In 18 years he compiled a .306 average. His best season was 1944 when he was the NL batting champion with a .357 average. Walker played eight years in Brooklyn, but was traded to the Pirates in December 1947. A Southerner, he objected to playing with Jackie Robinson and circulated a petition against him. But, according to historian Jules Tygiel, "Walker, despite his distaste for integration, never went out of his way to be unpleasant to Robinson, who later described him as a man of 'innate fairness.'"

MAY 24:

Maybe if it had been a homer... After going hitless in his previous 20 appearances as a pinch hitter, Jay Johnstone of the Dodgers doubles against the Pirates. When he returns to the bench, manager Tommy Lasorda informs him that he has been released. The Pirates win, 9-3.

MAY 25:

In San Diego, the Cubs' Ferguson Jenkins fans Garry Templeton for his 3,000th career strikeout; he is the seventh player to attain that record. But the Padres beat the Cubs and Jenkins, 2-1.

JUNE 1:

Bob "Buck" Rodgers, who led the Brewers to the AL Eastern Division playoffs last season, is fired and replaced by Harvey Kuenn. Milwaukee's record is 23-24.

JUNE 3:

Recurring tendinitis halts the career of the AL's 1980 Cy Young Award-winner, Steve Stone of the Orioles. The 34-year-old Stone was 4-7 last season with an ERA of 4.57 and has not played in 1982. He completes his 11-year career with a record of 107-93 with a 3.96 ERA. His best season was 1980, when he was 25-7.

JUNE 5:

Robin Yount, Cecil Cooper, and Ben Oglivie homer consecutively in the seventh inning of today's 11-3 win over the Athletics. Ted Simmons and Gorman Thomas also homer in the game. It is the second time this season that Milwaukee has hit three homers in a row. On May 28, Cooper, Don Money, and Thomas accomplished the home run feat.

JUNE 6:

The Indians' 11-game winning streak dies in Toronto, 5-1, on a four-hitter by Dave Stieb of the Blue Jays. Lary Sorenson takes the loss in a crisply played one-hour, 47-minute game. Cleveland wins the second game, 7-5, behind Ed Glynn.

JUNE 7:

A crowd of 44,714 at Dodger Stadium salutes Steve Garvey as he appears in his 1,000th consecutive game. He is the fifth player to reach that mark. Garvey goes hitless in four at-bats as the visiting Braves beat Los Angeles, 4-3, on a three-run homer by Dale Murphy in the seventh inning.

JUNE 8:

Leroy "Satchel" Paige dies in Kansas City, Missouri. According to official records Paige would have been 76 on July 7, but he gave many differing accounts of his age and he may have been older. Paige played in the Negro Leagues during his prime baseball years. Reputedly, he could throw faster than any of his contemporaries in the majors. In 1948, at age 42, he finally was signed by the Indians and was 6-1 with a 2.48 ERA. He also pitched with the Browns and Kansas City, completing his career at age 49.

PAIGE WAS THE STUFF OF WHICH LEGENDS ARE MADE. RALEIGH "BIZ" MACKEY, A GREAT NEGRO LEAGUES CATCHER, STATED, "I'VE HEARD ABOUT SATCHEL THROWING PITCHES THAT WASN'T HIT BUT THAT NEVER SHOWED UP IN THE CATCHER'S MITT NONETHELESS. THEY SAY THE CATCHER, THE UMPIRE, AND THE BAT BOYS LOOKED ALL OVER FOR THAT BALL, BUT IT WAS GONE. NOW HOW DO YOU ACCOUNT FOR THAT?"

In 1969 Dizzy Dean told Rex Lardner in Sport Magazine, *"I know who's the best pitcher I ever seen and it's old Satchel Paige, that big lanky colored boy... My fastball looks like a change of pace alongside that little pistol bullet old Satchel shoots up to the plate... Satchel Paige, with those long arms of his, is my idea of the pitcher with the greatest stuff I ever saw."*

JUNE 14:

Mario Mendoza is released by the Texas Rangers. A lifetime .215 hitter, Mendoza is at .118 at the time of his release. He has the dubious distinction of inspiring the phrase "Mendoza line." (The Mendoza line is the figurative boundary in the batting averages between those batters hitting above and below .200.) George Brett, Kansas City's slugger, says, "The first thing I look for in the Sunday papers is to see who's below the Mendoza line."

JUNE 20:

The Phillies' Pete Rose becomes the fifth player in major league history to play in 3,000 games and extends his consecutive game streak to 523. The Phillies lose to the Pirates in Pittsburgh, 3-1.

JUNE 22:

Pete Rose doubles against the Cardinals' John Stuper in the third inning to pass Henry Aaron and move into second place on the all-time hit list with 3,772. The Cardinals win the game, 3-2, in St. Louis. Rose predicts, "I should make it sometime before the All-Star game in 1984."

JULY 7:

Former major leaguer Jumping Joe Dugan dies at age 85 in Norwood, Massachusetts. Dugan was the Yankees' third baseman from 1922 to 1928, appearing in five World Series. He also played with the Athletics, Red Sox, Braves, and Tigers, compiling a lifetime average of .280 in 14 years.

JULY 10:

Larry Parrish of the Rangers hits a grand slam homer in the first inning against Milt Wilcox in a 6-5 win over the Tigers. It is Parrish's third in a week, tying a major league record set by Lou Gehrig in 1931 and tied by Jim

TRIVIA

The Metrodome roof requires 250,000 cubic feet of air pressure per minute to remain inflated. The facility was not a favorite of Billy Martin. In 1985, he tells the *Sporting News*, "This place stinks. It's a shame a great guy like HHH had to be named after it."

CULTURE

Two poems celebrate baseball: "The Abominable Baseball Bat" by X.J. Kennedy and "The Ball Game" by Robert Creeley.

Northrup in 1968. Parrish hit his other bases-loaded homers on July 4 and July 7.

JULY 13:

In the first All-Star Game played outside the United States, the NL beats the AL for the 11th straight time, 4-1, in Montreal's Olympic Stadium. Dave Concepcion hits a two-run home run. The winning pitcher is Steve Rogers of the hometown Expos; Dennis Eckersley is tagged with the loss.

JULY 14:

Baseball's one-time Golden Boy, Jackie Jensen, dies at age 55 in Charlottesville, Virginia. Jensen, whose career was curtailed by a flying phobia, played 11 years with the Yankees, Senators, and Red Sox, batting .279 with 199 homers. In 1956, with the Red Sox, he hit .315 with 20 home runs. In 1955, the outfielder led the AL in RBI with 116.

JULY 19:

The Padres' 22-year-old outfielder Tony Gwynn makes his major league debut against the Phillies and has two hits.

A new dimension is added to Old-Timers' games. Today, at Robert F. Kennedy Stadium in downtown Washington, D.C., the AL wins the first Old-Timers' All-Star Game, 7-2. Luke Appling, 75 years old, homers for the winners against 61-year-old Warren Spahn before a crowd of some 29,000.

After the game, Appling says, "I'm sure glad the season is over."

JULY 22:

Hall of Fame outfielder Lloyd "Little Poison" Waner dies at age 76 in Oklahoma City. Inducted into the hall in 1967, Waner hit .316 in 18 years. His older brother, Paul "Big Poison" Waner, also a Hall of Famer, died in 1965.

JULY 30:

The Braves return mascot Chief Noc-a-homa to his teepee in the left-field stands. After removing him to add 235 seats to Atlanta's stadium, the Braves lost 19 of 21 games.

JULY 31:

Yankees' starting pitcher Tommy John and team executive Bill Bergesch almost come to blows over the left-hander's use in a game today as a relief pitcher.

AUGUST 1:

Hank Aaron, former baseball commissioner A.B. "Happy" Chandler, Travis "Stonewall" Jackson, and Frank Robinson are inducted into the Hall of Fame. Aaron, who ranks first in career homers with 755 and RBI with 2,297, played 23 seasons and batted .305. He hit .300 or better 14 times and led the NL in homers and RBI four times. He appeared in two World Series, batting .364. Chandler, a former governor of Kentucky and U.S. senator, served as baseball commissioner from 1945 to 1951. It had been during Chandler's tenure that baseball's racial barriers came down. Robinson, who won the Most Valuable Player Awards in both leagues, played for 21 years, batting .294. The former outfielder ranks fourth in career homers with 586 and batted in 1,812 runs. He was the AL's Triple Crown winner in 1966 and played in five World Series. Robinson is the only player with 200-plus homers in each league and, with Rusty Staub, holds the record for homers in the most stadiums – 32. Jackson played 15 seasons for the New York Giants, mostly at shortstop. He batted .291 with 135 homers and played in four World Series.

Frank Robinson says: "I don't see anyone playing in the major leagues today who combines both the talent and the intensity that I had. I always tried to do the best. I knew I couldn't always be the best, but I tried to be. I expect that of my players today and of my kids. My wife says I shouldn't expect that of my children, but I don't think that's asking too much."

AUGUST 2:

The U.S. Postal Service issues a Jackie Robinson stamp as part of its Black Heritage series. Robinson is the first African-American player to appear on a U.S. postage stamp.

AUGUST 3:

Some 34,000 fans at Yankee Stadium get free tickets for sitting through a doubleheader loss to the White Sox, 1-0 and 14-2. Yankees' pitcher George Frazier sits down on the mound while public address announcer Bob Sheppard reads the offer by owner

JULY 19
In his major league debut, the Padres' rookie Tony Gwynn has two hits.

AUGUST 8
The Angels' Doug DeCinces hits three homers in a game – as he did five days ago.

HAPPY CHANDLER TELLS THE COOPERSTOWN CELEBRANTS, "I FELT I WAS DOING WHAT JUSTICE AND MERCY REQUIRED. I KNEW ONE DAY I WOULD HAVE TO FACE MY MAKER AND HE WOULD ASK ME WHY I DIDN'T LET THIS BLACK MAN PLAY BASEBALL. IF I SAID IT WAS BECAUSE HE WAS BLACK, I DIDN'T THINK HE WOULD FEEL THAT WAS A SATISFACTORY ANSWER."

George Steinbrenner. After the doubleheader, the Yankees make another managerial change. Gene Michael, who took over for Bob Lemon after 14 games, is himself replaced by Clyde King. New York is 44-42 under Michael, 50-50 overall.

AUGUST 4:

He wasn't in two places at the same time, but he came pretty close. In an unique series of circumstances, Joel Youngblood becomes the first player in major league history to hit safely for two teams in two different cities on the very same day. Youngblood's day begins normally enough; he starts in centerfield for the Mets against the Cubs in Chicago. In the third inning, he hits a two-run single against Ferguson Jenkins. He then is informed that he has been traded to the Expos for pitcher Tom Gorman (1-0). Youngblood, who is batting .257 in 80 games, flies to Philadelphia, where Montreal is facing the Phillies. He is inserted into right field for defensive reasons in the fifth inning and singles against Steve Carlton in his only at-bat. The Mets win their game, 7-4; the Expos lose their game, 5-4.

AUGUST 6:

The Giants' Jack Clark and Reggie Smith homer twice back-to-back in today's 7-6 win over the Houston Astros.

At Yankee Stadium, New York left-hander Dave LaRoche introduces "La Lob," his version of the blooper pitch. LaRoche fans the Rangers' Lamar Johnson with the gimmick pitch in a 6-0 Yankees' victory.

AUGUST 8:

The Angels' Doug DeCinces hits three homers – two solo shots and a two-run blast – against the Mariners in a 9-5 California victory. DeCinces had also three round-trippers back on August 3.

The Yankees trade the hero of the 1978 AL playoff, shortstop Russell "Bucky" Dent (.169 in 59 games) to the Rangers for outfielder Lee Mazzilli (.241 in 58 games).

AUGUST 11:

The Minnesota Twins' Terry Felton suffers his 13th consecutive loss of the season today. The beleaguered pitcher is now 0-13 on the season and 0-16 in his two-year career in the major leagues.

AUGUST 14:

The Phillies' Pete Rose sets a major league record for at-bats when he steps up to the plate for the first time today against the Expos. He flies out to left. Rose now has batted 12,635 times, surpassing the previous record holder Hank Aaron. Rose is two for five as Philadelphia wins the game, 15-11.

AUGUST 18:

In today's *Houston Post*, Hall of Fame pitcher Waite Hoyt, who pitched against Ty Cobb and broadcast Reds' games while Pete Rose was in Cincinnati, evaluates the two, "As far as skills are concerned, there is no comparison... Cobb was so brilliant with his bat manipulation that it would be impossible to describe the things he could do..."

Pete Rose isn't done just yet with his assault on major league baseball's record books. Today he breaks another one of Hank Aaron's longevity records. Rose makes his 13,941st plate appear-

HISTORY

After three years, the Blue Jays' Danny Ainge leaves baseball with a lifetime average of .220 to concentrate on his professional basketball career. When asked what he threw to get Ainge out, Orioles' pitcher Felix "Tippy" Martinez responds, "Strikes." Ainge will go on to have a stellar career playing for the Boston Celtics and playing and coaching for the Phoenix Suns.

"Gaylor Perry is a very honorable man. He only calls for the spitter when he needs it."
– Gabe Paul, Cleveland Indians president

ance. Rose is hit by a pitch and is hitless in six official at-bats as the Phillies go on to beat Houston, 5-3, in extra innings.

AUGUST 21:

The Brewers' Rollie Fingers gets credit for a save today as Milwaukee tops Seattle, 3-2. Fingers becomes the first player ever with 300 saves in his career.

AUGUST 23:

Caught! After 21 years of suspicion, in the seventh inning of today's game against the Boston Red Sox, umpires finally catch Gaylord Perry with a foreign substance on the baseball, and the Seattle Mariners' right-hander is ejected for the first time in his major league career. Boston wins the game, 4-3.

AUGUST 27:

After he is walked by George "Doc" Medich with two out in the third inning in Milwaukee, Rickey Henderson beats out a Ted Simmons's throw and steals second base. It is his 119th stolen base of the season, topping Lou Brock's record. Henderson takes second base out of the ground and holds it aloft. Participating in a brief ceremony are Brock and AL president Lee MacPhail. When the game resumes, Henderson keeps on running: he steals second again in the sixth inning, then second and third in the eighth, ending the game with 122. But Jim Gantner's two-run single in the eighth

HISTORY

The Mets' Dave Kingman has the lowest batting average ever (.204) for a home run champion (37). The Royals' Hal McRae sets a record for DHs with 133 RBI.

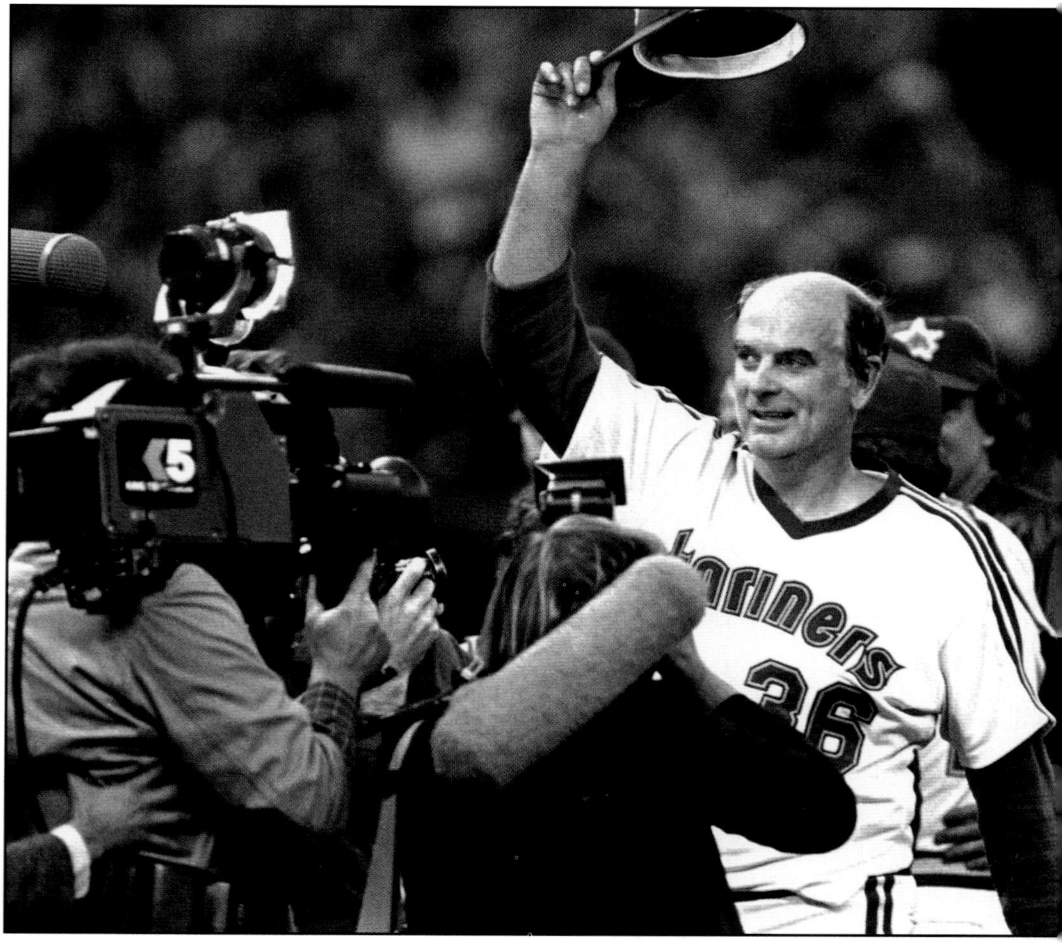

Gaylord Perry caps off another 100-Ks season.

AUGUST 27
With his 119th stolen base, Rickey Henderson sets a new single-season record.

AUGUST 29
Gaylord Perry records his 100th strikeout of the season, the 18th time he's done it.

gives Medich and the Brewers a 5-4 victory over Henderson's Oakland Athletics.

Henderson finishes the season with 130 stolen bases – an all-time high; he also is caught stealing a record 42 times

AUGUST 29:

Gaylord Perry records his 100th strikeout of the season. It is the 18th time he has fanned at least 100 batters in a single season, which ties him with Walter Johnson and Cy Young. Perry has a total of four today in a 6-2 Mariners win over the Detroit Tigers.

AUGUST 30:

The Milwaukee Brewers acquire pitcher Don Sutton (13-8) from the Astros for outfielder Kevin Bass (.000 in 18 games), pitcher Frank DePino (no appearances), minor league pitcher Mike Maddux, plus a cash payment.

SEPTEMBER 7:

Former NL Most Valuable Player Ken Boyer dies at age 51 of lung cancer in St. Louis. Boyer played 15 years, mostly at third base, hitting .287 with 282 home runs. He also managed the Cardinals from 1978 to 1980. Boyer was MVP in 1964 when he batted .295 with 24 homers and a league-leading 119 RBI. He is survived by his brothers, former major leaguers Cloyd and Clete Boyer.

SEPTEMBER 8:

The Yankees' Dave Winfield hits his 30th homer of the season as the Yankees end the Orioles' 10-game winning streak, 10-5. Winfield becomes the ninth player ever with 30 round-trippers in each league. He hit 34 home runs in 1979 for the Padres.

SEPTEMBER 12:

For the third time this season, the Brewers bang out back-to-back-to-back home runs. In the third inning today, Cecil Cooper, Ted Simmons, and Ben Oglivie connect for Milwaukee, but the Yankees win, 9-8.

SEPTEMBER 29:

Monty Stratton dies in Greenville, Texas, at age 70. Stratton was 15-5 in 1937 and 15-9 in 1938 with the White Sox. In 1938, his leg was amputated following a hunting accident and he returned to pitch in a charity game between the White Sox and Cubs for his benefit in 1939 at Comiskey Park. Stratton subsequently pitched one season in the East Texas League, where he was 18-8. His story was told – more or less – in the 1949 motion picture *The Stratton Story*, starring James Stewart in the title role, along with June Allyson.

SEPTEMBER 30:

Steve Garvey plays in his 1,104th consecutive game, placing him third on the all-time list, and collects three hits in what will be his last game in a Dodger uniform. Los Angeles beats Atlanta, 10-3 and sets a major league attendance mark of 3,608,881.

OCTOBER 3:

On the last day of the season, the Brewers and the Orioles are tied for first place in

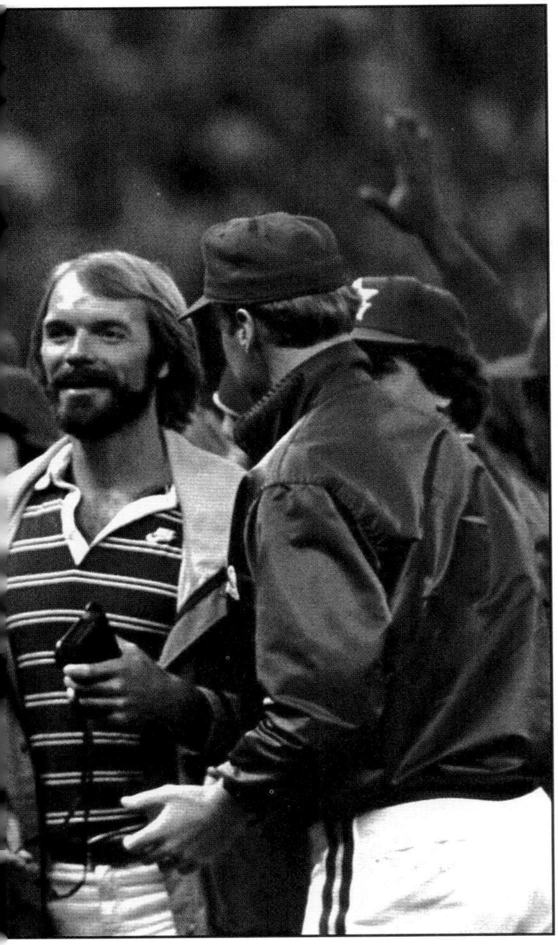

HISTORY

Steve Carlton of the Phillies becomes the first pitcher to win four Cy Young Awards.

"We're going to hang our heads high."
– Harvey Kuenn, after a Series loss to the Cardinals

TRIVIA

According to Hank Aaron, it was Dodgers pitchers Sandy Koufax and Don Drysdale who hung the "Bad Henry" nickname on him. Mickey Mantle said of the man who topped Babe Ruth: "As far as I'm concerned, Aaron is the best ball player of my era."

the AL East. Milwaukee, loser of three straight to Baltimore, wins the game, 10-2, and the division by just a single game. Newly acquired from the Astros, Don Sutton gets the win; Jim Palmer takes the loss. It is the last game for Orioles' manager Earl Weaver, who receives a 45-minute series of ovations from a crowd of 51,642. In his 15 years at the helm of the Orioles, Weaver won four pennants and one World Series.

In 1983, Scott McGreggor recalls Weaver: "He cussed so awful last year. I finally told him I wasn't going to sit beside him because the Lord was going to strike him dead if he kept talking like that, and I didn't want to be there when it happened."

REGULAR SEASON WRAP-UP:

Harvey Kuenn's Brewers, who finish at 95-67, are a power-packed team that leads the AL with 216 homers. Known as Harvey's Wallbangers, the Brewers have a triple punch composed of Robin Yount (.331, 29 homers, 114 RBI), Cecil Cooper (.313, 32 homers, 121 RBI), and Paul Molitor (.302, 19 homers, 71 RBI). Additional power comes from Gorman Thomas (.245, 39 homers, 112 RBI), Ben Oglivie (.244, 34 homers, 102 RBI), and Ted Simmons (.269, 23 homers, 97 RBI). The top winner is Pete Vukovich at 18-6; Rollie Fingers has 20 saves on the year.

HANK AARON STATES: "I'M PROUD TO BE STANDING WHERE JACKIE ROBINSON, ROY CAMPANELLA, AND OTHERS MADE IT POSSIBLE FOR PLAYERS LIKE FRANK ROBINSON AND MYSELF TO PROVE THAT A MAN'S ABILITY IS LIMITED ONLY BY HIS LACK OF OPPORTUNITY."

Dorrel "Whitey" Herzog's Cardinals finish the regular season at 92-70 in the NL. Lonnie Smith is the top average hitter at .307. George Hendrick hits .282 with 19 homers and 104 RBI. Rookie Willie McGee bats .296. The team has a pair of 15-game winners – Bob Forsch and Joaquin Andujar. Jim Kaat (5-3, 4.08 ERA) completes his record 24th season in the majors in a career spanning four decades. Bruce Sutter leads the NL with 36 saves.

OCTOBER 5:

ALCS, game one. In California with 64,406 on hand, the Angels beat the Brewers, 8-3, with Tommy John, recently traded from the Yankees, spinning a complete-game seven-hitter and Don Baylor driving in a record five runs. The losing pitcher is Mike Caldwell. Fred Lynn has a solo homer for California; Gorman Thomas connects with a runner on for Milwaukee.

OCTOBER 6:

ALCS, game two. In California, the Angels win again, 4-2. Bruce Kison, the winner with a five-hitter, and losing pitcher Pete Vukovich both pitch complete games. Reggie Jackson homers in the fourth inning with no one on. Paul Molitor spoils Kison's shutout with a two-run, inside-the-park homer in the fifth.

OCTOBER 7:

NLCS, game one. In St. Louis, Bob Forsch three-hits the Braves, 7-0, and his teammates collect 13 hits to beat Pascual Perez. The Cardinals benefited from a washout of yesterday's game in the fifth inning with the Braves ahead, 1-0.

OCTOBER 8:

ALCS, game three. In Milwaukee, the Brewers win, 5-3, on strong pitching by winner Don Sutton with a save by Pete Ladd. Geoff Zahn gets the loss. Paul Molitor hits a two-run homer for the Brewers; Bob Boone has a solo shot for the Angels.

OCTOBER 20
The Cardinals beat the Brewers in game seven of the World Series for their ninth world title.

NOVEMBER 1
Bowie Kuhn is out as baseball commissioner when the owners fail to renew his contract.

OCTOBER 9:

NLCS, game two. After another rain cancellation, the Cardinals make it two straight with a 4-3 win at home. Ken Oberkfell drives in the winning run with a single off reliever Gene Garber in the bottom of the ninth. Bruce Sutter is the winning pitcher; Garber gets the loss.

ALCS, game four. In Milwaukee, the Brewers overcome a grand slam homer by the Angels' Don Baylor to even the playoffs with a 9-5 win. Reserve outfielder Mark Brouhard has three hits – including a two-run homer – three RBI, and four runs. The winning pitcher is Bryan "Moose" Haas, with a save from Jim Slaton. The loser Tommy John.

OCTOBER 10:

NLCS, game three. The Cardinals beat the Braves, 6-2, in Atlanta to sweep the NLCS and take their first pennant in 14 years. Willie McGee has a solo homer and a triple. Joaquin Andujar gets the win with a save by Bruce Sutter. Rick Camp is charged with the loss.

ALCS, game five. In Milwaukee, the Brewers win their third straight, 4-3, on Cecil Cooper's single in the seventh, for their first AL pennant. Helped by a Ben Oglivie home run, Bob McClure is the winning pitcher. The loser is Luis Sanchez. Don Baylor finishes the ALCS with 10 RBI; Fred Lynn has 10 hits in 18 at-bats for the Angels.

OCTOBER 12:

World Series, game one. In St. Louis, Mike Caldwell limits the Cardinals to just three hits while the Brewers are banging out 17 in a 10-0 victory. Paul Molitor is the first ever with five hits in a Series game; Robin Yount adds four and Ted Simmons has a solo home run. Bob Forsch is the losing pitcher.

OCTOBER 13:

World Series, game two. The Cardinals tie the Series with a 5-4 victory in St. Louis. Reliever Pete Ladd walks Steve Braun on four pitches, forcing in George Hendrick with the winning run. The winning pitcher is Bruce Sutter; Bob McClure gets the loss. Ted Simmons homers for Milwaukee.

OCTOBER 15:

World Series, game three. Willie McGee connects for a three-run homer and a solo blast to lead the Cardinals past the Brewers, 6-2, in Milwaukee. He also sparkles in the field as Joaquin Andujar gets the win, with a save by Bruce Sutter. The losing pitcher is Pete Vukovich. Cecil Cooper has a two-run homer for Milwaukee.

OCTOBER 16:

World Series, game four. The Brewers use 10 hits to beat the Cardinals, 7-5, in Milwaukee. Jim Slaton gets the win in relief of Moose Haas, with a save by Bob McClure. The losing pitcher is Doug Bair.

OCTOBER 17:

World Series, game five. The Brewers beat the Cardinals, 6-4. Robin Yount has four hits – including a solo home run – to become the first ever to do so twice in the Series. Mike Caldwell gets the victory, with a save from Bob McClure. Bob Forsch is the losing pitcher.

OCTOBER 19:

World Series, game six. In a game delayed by rain for two and a half hours, the Cardinals pound the Brewers, 13-1, on 12 hits to knot the Series. Keith Hernandez and Darrell Porter hit two-run homers; Dane Iorg has a triple and a pair of doubles. John Stuper goes all the way, allowing four hits, for the win. Don Sutton gets the loss. Milwaukee commits four errors.

OCTOBER 20:

World Series, game seven. Joaquin Andujar, with a save by Bruce Sutter, beats the Brewers, 6-3, and the Cardinals have their ninth World Championship. St. Louis puts the game away with a three-run sixth. Ben Oglivie hits a home run for Milwaukee; Bob McClure gets the loss. George Hendrick and Lonnie Smith lead the Cardinal regulars with .321 averages. Keith Hernandez bats in eight runs. Joaquin Andujar is 2-0 with a 1.35 ERA. Robin Yount hits .414 with six RBI in a losing cause.

POST-SEASON

NOVEMBER 1:

After 14 years as baseball commissioner, Bowie Kuhn gets bounced by the major league owners, when the renewal of his

"Instead of looking like the American flag, I look like a taco."
– former Dodger Steve Garvey, on his new Padres uniform

contract is blocked by five NL clubs. Kuhn needs nine of 12 NL votes and 10 of 14 from the AL. He receives 11 in the AL, but only seven in the NL. The opposition reportedly is spearheaded by Nelson Doubleday of the New York Mets and August A. Busch of the Cardinals. George Steinbrenner of the Yankees, Eddie Chiles of the Rangers, and George Argyros of the Mariners also oppose his rehiring. Among Kuhn's supporters are Ted Turner of the Braves, John McMullen of the Astros, and William Williams of the Reds. Vendettas and the desire for stronger business ties are said to be behind the ouster of Kuhn, whose term expires in August.

NOVEMBER 3:

Ray Fisher, introduced at Old-Timers' Day at Yankee Stadium this past season, dies at age 95 in Ann Arbor, Michigan. Fisher was 100-94 in 10 seasons, with a 2.82 ERA and 19 career shutouts. He pitched for the Yankees and Reds and appeared in the 1919 World Series. Fisher was banned from baseball in 1921 in one of Commissioner Kenesaw Mountain Landis's inexplicable and unjustified actions.

NOVEMBER 4:

Mike Ferraro gets a two-year contract to manage the Indians after Billy Martin, who was fired by the Athletics, turns down a $1 million offer. The Indians were 78-84 in sixth place in the AL East under Dave Garcia.

NOVEMBER 11:

Manager Tommy Lasorda, whose Los Angeles Dodgers finished second in the NL West with an 88-74 record, signs his eighth one-year contract with the club.

DECEMBER 1:

The Yankees sign free-agent designated hitter Don Baylor (.263, 24 home runs, 93 RBI). Baylor was with the California Angels in 1982.

DECEMBER 6:

The Athletics obtain third baseman Carney Lansford (.301, 11 homers), outfielder Garry Hancock (.000 in 11 games), and minor league pitcher Jerry King from the Red Sox in exchange for outfielder-DH Tony Armas (.233, 28 homers, 89 RBI) and catcher-DH-infielder Jeff Newman (.199, six home runs in 72 games).

DECEMBER 9:

The Blue Jays acquire minor league first baseman Fred McGriff, outfielder Dave Collins (.253, three homers, 13 stolen bases), and pitcher Mike Morgan (7-11, 4.37 ERA) plus $400,000 from the Yankees for pitcher Dale Murray (8-7, 3.16 ERA, 11 saves) and minor league third baseman Tom Dodd.

The Cleveland Indians trade outfielder-infielder Von Hayes (.250, 14 homers, 82 RBI, 32 stolen bases) to the Phillies for infielder Julio Franco (.276 in 16 games), second baseman Jesus "Manny" Trillo (.271), outfielder George Vukovich (.272, six home runs), pitcher Jay Baller (0-0, 3.38 ERA), and minor league catcher Jerry Willard.

DECEMBER 10:

The Mets trade starting pitcher Mike Scott (7-13, 5.14 ERA) to the Astros for outfielder-first baseman Danny Heep (.237, four home runs in 85 games). Scott goes 10-6, 3.72 in 1983.

DECEMBER 16:

The New York Mets reacquire the greatest pitcher in their franchise's history – Tom Seaver (5-13, 5.50 ERA). In return for Seaver, New York sends pitcher Charlie Puleo (9-9, 4.47 ERA) and two minor leagu- ers – catcher-outfielder Lloyd McClendon and outfielder Jason Felice – to the Cincinnati Reds. Seaver plays just one year with the Mets this time around, going 9-14 with a 3.55 ERA in 1983. He then spends two-plus years with the White Sox before ending his 20-year career with the Red Sox in 1986.

DECEMBER 21:

First baseman Steve Garvey (.282, 16 home runs, 86 RBI) says goodbye to the Los Angeles Dodgers. After 14 years in a Dodgers uniform, Garvey failed to reach agreement with the ballclub last month. Instead, the San Diego Padres give him a five-year, $6.6 million contract. He will enjoy several productive years with the Padres, helping them to the 1984 World Series, before finally retiring in 1987.

DECEMBER 9
Minor league first baseman Fred McGriff is traded by the Yankees to the Blue Jays.

DECEMBER 21
After 14 seasons with the Dodgers, Steve Garvey signs with the San Diego Padres.

THE BEST OF 1982

NATIONAL LEAGUE

HITTERS

Batting Average:
Al Oliver, Montreal Expos, .331

Slugging Average:
Mike Schmidt, Philadelphia Phillies, .547

Home Runs:
Dave Kingman, New York Mets, 37

Runs Batted In:
Al Oliver; Dale Murphy, Atlanta Braves, 109

Hits:
Al Oliver, 204

Stolen Bases:
Tim Raines, Montreal Expos, 78

PITCHERS

Wins:
Steve Carlton, Philadelphia Phillies, 23

Strikeouts:
Steve Carlton, 286

Earned Run Average:
Steve Rogers, Montreal Expos, 2.40

Winning Percentage:
Phil Niekro, Atlanta Braves, .810

Saves:
Bruce Sutter, St. Louis Cardinals, 36

Most Valuable Player:
Dale Murphy, Atlanta Braves

Cy Young Award:
Steve Carlton, Philadelphia Phillies

Rookie of the Year:
Steve Sax, Los Angeles Dodgers

AMERICAN LEAGUE

HITTERS

Batting Average:
Willie Wilson, Kansas City Royals, .332

Slugging Average:
Robin Yount, Milwaukee Brewers, .578

Home Runs:
Reggie Jackson, California Angels; Gorman Thomas, Milwaukee Brewers, 39

Runs Batted In:
Hal McRae, Kansas City Royals, 133

Hits:
Robin Yount, 210

Stolen Bases:
Rickey Henderson, Oakland Athletics, 130

PITCHERS

Wins:
LaMarr Hoyt, Chicago White Sox, 19

Strikeouts:
Floyd Bannister, Seattle Mariners, 209

Earned Run Average:
Rick Sutcliffe, Cleveland Indians, 2.96

Winning Percentage:
Jim Palmer, Baltimore Orioles; Pete Vukovich, Milwaukee Brewers, .750

Saves:
Dan Quisenberry, Kansas City Royals, 35

Most Valuable Player:
Robin Yount, Milwaukee Brewers

Cy Young Award:
Pete Vukovich, Milwaukee Brewers

Rookie of the Year:
Cal Ripken Jr., Baltimore Orioles

CULTURE

Strike Three You're Dead, **is published - a Harvey Blissberg mystery by Richard D. Rosen.**

1983

"He's the manager – until he screws up."
– George Steinbrenner, on Billy Martin

NEWS

U.S. EMBASSY IN LEBANON BOMBED; 63 DIE

237 U.S. MARINES KILLED IN BOMBING OF BEIRUT BARRACKS

Harold Washington becomes Chicago's first black mayor

SALLY RIDE IS FIRST U.S. WOMAN IN SPACE

REAGAN CALLS SOVIET UNION "THE EVIL EMPIRE"

269 DIE WHEN SOVIETS SHOOT DOWN KOREAN AIRLINER

U.S. INVADES GRENADA

Martin Luther King's birthday becomes national holiday

PHILIPPINES OPPOSITION LEADER BENIGNO AQUINO IS ASSISSNATED

***AUSTRALIA II* WINS AMERICA'S CUP, SNAPPING 131-YEAR U.S. RUN**

PRE-SEASON

JANUARY 11:

The Yankees' managerial merry-go-round continues. Billy Martin is named New York Yankees skipper for the third time. He replaces Clyde King, who is transferred to the front office.

JANUARY 20:

Dodger third baseman Ron Cey (.254, 24 homers), who has been with the team since 1971, is traded to the Cubs for two minor leaguers – pitcher Vance Lovelace and outfielder Dan Cataline.

FEBRUARY 5:

The Blue Jays obtain minor league first baseman Cecil Fielder from the Royals for outfielder Leon Roberts (.230, two homers in 71 games).

FEBRUARY 8:

Baseball Commissioner Bowie Kuhn orders Hall of Famer Mickey Mantle to cut all ties to major league baseball. Kuhn takes his unpopular action because Mantle is working in a sports promotion capacity with a casino in Atlantic City, New Jersey. In 1979, Willie Mays, who also is employed by a company involved in legalized gambling in Atlantic City, was the target of similar action by Kuhn.

FEBRUARY 19:

Fernando Valenzuela (19-13, 2.87 ERA, 199 strikeouts) sets an off-the-field major league record. He becomes the first player ever to be awarded $1 million per year through arbitration and now is the third-highest-paid player in baseball.

MARCH 4:

At the Dodgers' Vero Beach, Florida, spring training camp, pitcher Steve Howe reveals he has been chemically dependent but reports he is now free of his cocaine habit.

THE SEASON

APRIL 5:

At Candlestick Park, the Padres beat the Giants, 16-13, in the major league's highest-scoring opening day game in 50 years. Winning pitcher Tim Lollar chips in with three RBI, as does his battery mate Terry Kennedy. Garry Templeton paces the Padres with a home run and four RBI and hiss effort is matched by the Giants' Bob Brenly. Other home runs are hit by San Francisco's Darrell Evans, Max Venable, and Charles "Chili" Davis.

APRIL 7:

The TV rights to major league baseball are now worth an eye-popping $1.2 billion. That's the price ABC and NBC agree to pay to share a one-year contract, and it is more than triple the price of the previous contract. Each major league team will derive some $7 million per year as a result of the deal, which takes effect for the 1984 season. ABC will fork over $575 million for regular season prime time and some Sunday afternoon games. NBC pays $550 million for 30 Saturday afternoon games. The two networks will continue the present system of rotating coverage of the League Championship Series, the World Series, and the All-Star Game. The contract runs through the 1989 season.

APRIL 14:

Talk about bringing the house down. Heavy snows in Minnesota cause the roof of the Twin's Metrodome to deflate,

Dale Murphy is an RBI machine for the Braves.

Braves
3

Walter Alston described his philosophy as, "Look at misfortune the same way you look at success: Don't panic. Do your best and forget the consequences."

CULTURE

Red River Dave McEnery records "Homer, the Seagull Who Loved Baseball," a song about the Dave Winfield incident.

LEAGUE

White Sox president Jerry Reinsdorf is fined $500 for a riddle he asks at the All-Star Game: "How do you know when George Steinbrenner is lying? When his lips are moving."

and today's game with the Angels is postponed.

This is the third time the roof has deflated. Previously the problem occurred on November 19, 1981, and December 1982, both after the baseball season.

APRIL 16:

San Diego's Steve Garvey sets an NL record for consecutive games played – 1,118 – when he appears against his old team, Los Angeles, at Dodger Stadium. The previous record holder was Billy Williams. It is Garvey's first trip back since he signed a free-agent pact with the Padres last December. The Dodgers designate his homecoming as Steve Garvey Weekend, and 50,800 fans turn out. Garvey responds with two hits, but Los Angeles wins its sixth straight, 8-5.

APRIL 27:

Nolan Ryan writes a new chapter in the pitchers' record book when he surpasses Walter Johnson in career strikeouts. In the eighth inning, Ryan strikes out the Expos' Tim Blackwell swinging, to tie Johnson. Then the Astro right-hander gets pinch hitter Brad Mills looking on a 1-2 curveball to break the record. Walter Johnson, who set his record in 1927, took 21 years and 5,923 innings to reach 3,508. Ryan achieved that mark in his 16th year and 3,357 innings.

APRIL 29:

After the Cubs lose, 4-3, to the Dodgers, manager Lee Elia unleashes a tirade against the hometown Chicago fans. Elia rages: "Rip 'em, rip those country suckers like they rip my players. Eighty-five percent of the people in this country work and the other 15 percent come out here and boo my players. It's a playground for them."

MAY 20:

Walter Johnson's career strikeout record is surpassed for the second time in less than a month – this time by Steve Carlton of the Phillies, who fans four Padres for a career total of 3,511. Carlton trails Nolan Ryan, who topped Johnson's mark on April 27, by 10 strikeouts. Visiting San Diego whitewashes Philadelphia, 5-0.

MAY 24:

The Phillies are finding batting against the Dodgers to be an exercise in futility. Behind the four-hit pitching of Alejandro Pena, Los Angeles shuts out Philadelphia for the third consecutive game. Today's score is 3-0. Yesterday Fernando Valenzuela whitewashed the Phillies, 2-0; the day before it was Bob Welch by a 5-0 score.

MAY 25:

A 74-year-old record for wildness is equaled by Pirates pitchers Jim Bibby and Jim Winn who walk seven consecutive Braves batters. It's no surprise that Atlanta wins, 7-0.

MAY 29:

The Dodgers' Steve Howe enters a rehab center in Orange County, California.

In June, after completing 30 days of rehabilitation, Steve Howe is fined $53,867 in salary for missed games. It is the largest fine ever levied.

JUNE 6:

Milwaukee sends outfielder-DH Gorman Thomas (.183 in 46 games) – a two-time AL home run champion – and pitchers Jamie Easterly (0-1) and Ernie Camacho (0-1 in 1981) to the Indians for outfielder Rick Manning (.278 in 50 games) and pitcher Rick Waits (0-1).

JUNE 7:

The Phillies' Steve Carlton pulls ahead of Nolan Ryan in the strikeout sweepstakes. Carlton fans the Cardinals' Lonnie Smith in the third inning for career strikeout 3,522. The Cardinals narrowly win the game, 2-1.

JUNE 11:

The Cardinals' Lonnie Smith enters a drug rehabilitation facility. Prior to the Cardinals' June 9 game, Smith informed manager Dorrel "Whitey" Herzog of his problem. Smith, who was hitting .311, will undergo three weeks of therapy.

JUNE 12:

Ted Simmons of the Brewers singles with the bases loaded in the bottom of the 12th inning to defeat the Yankees, 6-5. It also is a landmark for Simmons – his 2,000th career hit. Tom Tellman gets the win.

JUNE 15:

The Mets get one of baseball's premier first basemen, Keith Hernandez (.284 in 55 games) from the

APRIL 27
Nolan Ryan breaks Walter Johnson's career strikeouts record, with number 3,509.

JULY 4
On the birthday of his country and his Boss, Yankee Dave Righetti no-hits the Red Sox.

Cardinals for pitchers Neil Allen (2-7) and Rick Ownbey (1-3). In 1979, Hernandez led the NL in batting with .344 and was the co-Most Valuable Player.

JUNE 24:

In Milwaukee, Brewers' right-hander Don Sutton fans Alan Bannister in the eighth inning for his 3,000th career strikeout. Sutton is the eighth pitcher to reach that mark. The Brewers beat the Indians, 6-2. Gorman Thomas, traded by the Brewers earlier in the month, is victimized by Sutton three times. Lary Sorenson is credited with the loss.

JUNE 26:

Daniel "Rusty" Staub of the Mets hits a ninth-inning pinch single against the Phillies. It is his eighth straight pinch hit, tying Dave Philley's major league record. The Phillies win the game, 8-4.

JULY 3:

The Rangers generate a mammoth rally in Oakland. In the 15th inning, Texas scores 12 runs on eight hits, four walks, an error, and a wild pitch, to win, 16-4. The explosion begins against A's pitcher Dave Beard, who is relieved by Ben Callahan.

JULY 4:

It's a Yankee-Doodle-Dandy Independence Day as New York's Dave Righetti no-hits visiting Boston, 4-0. It also is the birthday of Yankees owner George Steinbrenner. Righetti's last out is one of the toughest hitters in baseball – Wade Boggs – who strikes out to end the game. Boggs is the ninth strikeout victim for Righetti, who walks four. The Yankees play errorless baseball. The losing pitcher is John Tudor.

At third base for the Yankees is Bert Campaneris, who is

GEORGE BRETT SAYS OF THE PINE TAR INCIDENT: "I'VE NEVER BEEN THAT MAD IN MY WHOLE LIFE."

Dave Righetti renders the Red Sox hitless on the 4th.

HISTORY

Gaylord Perry and Don Sutton have two things in common: They are both 300-game winners and each has been accused of doctoring the ball. Sutton claims when he was introduced to Perry, "he handed me a tube of Vaseline. I thanked him and gave him a sheet of sandpaper."

"Brooks Robinson belongs in a higher league"
– *Pete Rose*

Dan Quisenberry is a record-setting savior.

appearing in his 11th no-hitter – the most of any player.

JULY 6:

In the 50th anniversary All-Star Game, the AL wins, 13-3, ending an 11-game NL winning streak. Fred Lynn hits a grand slam against Atlee Hammaker in a seven-run third inning and Jim Rice adds a solo homer in the frame. Hammaker leaves with ghastly stats: two-thirds of an inning, six hits, seven earned runs, and one walk. But it is starter Mario Soto who is charged with the loss. Dave Stieb is the winning pitcher. The game is played at Chicago's Comiskey Park, site of the first All-Star Game.

JULY 7:

Vic Wertz dies in Detroit, at age 58. A solid 17-year major league player with a lifetime average of .277 with 266 homers, Wertz is best remembered for the line drive he hit to center-field in the Polo Grounds in the 1954 Cleveland-New York World Series, which Giant outfielder Willie Mays turned into one of the greatest catches in post-season history. Wertz overcame polio in 1955 and returned to play in the majors until 1963.

JULY 10:

The Brewers and White Sox play the longest nine-inning game in AL history – four hours, 11 minutes. Ted Simmons's bases-loaded single drives in two runs in a three-run eighth and gives Milwaukee a 12-9 victory. Jim Slaton gets the win.

JULY 18:

Despite the fact that the Phillies are in first place in the NL East with a record of 43-42, manager Pat Corrales is fired and replaced today by the team's general manager, Paul Owens.

Within two weeks, Pat Corrales is hired as the Indians' manager, replacing Mike Ferraro, who led the team to a 40-60 record.

JULY 24:

A game between the Yankees and the Royals becomes the occasion for one of the great controversies in modern baseball – the Pine Tar Incident. At Yankee Stadium, with two out and U.L. Washington on first in the ninth inning, Yankees' reliever Goose Gossage is pitching to protect a 4-3 lead. George Brett hits a home run that puts the Royals ahead, 5-4. But then home plate umpire Tim McClelland calls Brett out because pine tar is found more than 18 inches from the knob of his bat – a rules violation. Brett goes beserk and is restrained. Kansas City manager Dick Howser protests the game.

JULY 27:

The Royals' Gaylord Perry records his 3,500th career strikeout; he is the fourth pitcher to attain that mark. Kansas City beats Cleveland, 5-4.

JULY 24
George Brett's homer against the Yankees is nullified – his bat has too much pine tar on it.

JULY 27
Gaylord Perry becomes the fourth pitcher ever to record 3,500 career strikeouts.

JULY 28:

AL President Lee MacPhail upholds the Royals' protest of the July 24 pine-tar game. MacPhail finds that George Brett's bat was not "altered to improve the distance factor." Brett's homer counts and MacPhail orders the game resumed on August 18 from the point of the dispute – with two out in the top of the ninth inning with the Royals ahead, 5-4.

Comments George Steinbrenner: "If we lose the division race by one game, I'd hate to be Lee MacPhail and living in New York. Maybe he should go house hunting in Kansas City."

JULY 29:

Steve Garvey's consecutive game streak comes to an end at 1,207. He appears in the first game of a doubleheader against Atlanta at Jack Murphy Stadium in San Diego. He gets an infield hit, goes to third, and tries to score on a Pascual Perez wild pitch. He is thrown out, injures his thumb, and has to leave the game, which the Braves win, 2-1. Garvey, who has not missed a game since 1975, is unable to play in the second game. His 1,207 consecutive games put him in third place all time, behind Lou Gehrig's 2,130 and Everett Scott's 1,307.

JULY 31:

Walter Alston, George Kell, Juan Marichal, and Brooks Robinson are inducted into the Hall of Fame. Alston, whose major league career consisted of one hitless at bat in 1936, managed the Dodgers for 23 years, compiling a record of 2,040-1,613. His teams won seven pennants and four World Series. Kell, a superb third baseman, played 15 years, batting .306. He led the AL with .343 in 1949 and nine times batted .300 or better. Kell never appeared in post-season play. Marichal was involved in an ugly incident in 1965 during which he hit Johnny Roseboro with a bat. When Marichal was passed over in the first two years of his eligibility, Roseboro lobbied for the pitcher's election to the hall. In 16 years, Marichal compiled a 243-142 record with a 2.89 ERA, 52 shutouts, and 2,303 strikeouts. He was a 20-game winner six times and pitched in one World Series. Robinson, a 16-time Gold Glove winner known as the Human Vacuum Cleaner, holds most lifetime fielding records for third basemen. In 23 years with the Orioles, he hit .267 with 268 homers. In 1964, he led the league with 118 RBI and in 1970 batted .583 in the World Series. He was the AL's 1964 Most Valuable Player.

"Brooks Robinson belongs in a higher league," says Pete Rose of the third baseman.

AUGUST 4:

Controversy, which seems to be as much a part of the modern Yankees' tradition as their pinstripes, surfaces in a new form. In the middle of the fifth inning of a game with the Blue Jays in Toronto's Exhibition Stadium, New York right fielder Dave Winfield, with a warm-up throw to the ballboy, hits and kills a seagull, which bounces on the artificial surface. Seagulls are on Canada's endangered species list and, as the victim is removed, Winfield takes his cap off and holds it over his heart. For the gesture, he is derided and pelted with debris by the fans. After the game, Winfield is arrested by plainclothes police on criminal charges that could involve a six-month prison sentence and a $500 fine. He is released on $500 bail and must return to court on August 12.

AUGUST 5:

Dave Winfield is off the hook. After talking to the Yankees' star, crown attorney Norman Matusiak decides the seagull's death was accidental. Charges of animal cruelty against Winfield are dropped and the case is closed.

AUGUST 16:

Hall of Fame outfielder Earl Averill dies at the age of 81 in Everett, Washington. Known as the Earl of Snohomish (after his hometown), Averill played 13 years in the major leagues, hitting .318 with 238 RBI. He batted above .300 eight times, with a high of .378 in 1936, and appeared in one World Series. He was inducted into the Hall of Fame in 1975.

AUGUST 18:

The pine-tar game is resumed and takes nine minutes and 41 seconds to conclude. But first there is another incident – the Yankees appeal Brett's home run, saying he missed first

HISTORY

The Royals' Dan Quisenberry sets a major league record with 45 saves.

LEAGUE

In May, George Steinbrenner gets a double dose of discipline. Baseball Commissioner Bowie Kuhn slaps him with a $50,000 fine and AL president Lee MacPhail suspends him for one week. His offense: derogatory remarks about umpires.

Bobby Brown was studying to become a doctor during his Yankees' years. According to one story, he was reading a medical text, *Gray's Anatomy*, while his roommate, Yogi Berra, was finishing a comic book. Berra asked him, "How did yours come out?"

CULTURE

Amiri Baraka writes the poem "The Ball Game."

CULTURE

The movie *Blue Skies Again* stars Harry Hamlin, Mimi Rogers, and Robin Barto as a female softball player with big league baseball ambitions.

and second base. The umpires are prepared and Dave Phillips produces a statement notarized on July 24 confirming Brett touched every base. Then the game resumes. The Royals' Hal MacRae strikes out to end the top of the ninth inning. In the bottom of the ninth, the Yankees are retired in order and lose the game, 5-4.

AUGUST 24:

In the 10th inning of a game against the Blue Jays, Orioles infielder Lenn Sakata is pressed into service as a catcher. Three straight Toronto batters, with no respect for Sakata's arm, take long leads at first base. And left-hander Felix "Tippy" Martinez picks off all three. Sakata hits a homer to win the game for Baltimore, 7-4.

AUGUST 29:

The estate of the late F.J. "Steve" O'Neill assumes ownership of the Indians after his death.

SEPTEMBER 17:

At Comiskey Park, the White Sox beat the Mariners, 4-3, to win the AL Western Division by 20 games – a major league record – over the Royals.

SEPTEMBER 19:

On his 40th birthday, second baseman Joe Morgan demonstrates youthful pop in his bat. He hits two home runs in a four-for-five day as his Phillies beat the Cubs, 7-6.

SEPTEMBER 23:

Steve Carlton records his 300th career victory by defeating the Cardinals, the team that traded him away in 1972. And he does it before 27,266 at St. Louis's Busch Stadium. He is the 16th pitcher in history to win 300. Carlton pitches eight innings, yielding eight hits and striking out 12, as the Phillies win, 6-2, their eighth straight victory. Carlton, who also singles in a run in the first inning, is now 37-12 against his former team.

SEPTEMBER 25:

The Orioles beat the Brewers, 5-1, to clinch the AL East.

SEPTEMBER 26:

The Cardinals' Bob Forsch no-hits the Montreal Expos, 3-0, at Busch Stadium. He is the first Cardinal ever to pitch two no-hitters. Forsch strikes out six and allows no walks; the Cardinals commit one error. The losing pitcher is Steve Rogers.

SEPTEMBER 29:

Athletics rookie Mike Warren – only 22 years old – no-hits the Chicago White Sox in Oakland, 3-0. Warren strikes out five and allows three walks. Oakland commits no errors. The losing pitcher is Britt Burns.

Warren is 5-3 in 1983, but pitches only sparingly over the next two seasons. He completes his three-year major league career at age 24 with a record of 9-13 and an ERA of 5.06.

OCTOBER 2:

The Brewers ask for and receive the resignation of manager Harvey Kuenn, who led the team to the 1982 World Series. Milwaukee beats the Tigers, 7-4, today in the last game of the season to finish in fifth place with a record of 87-75.

REGULAR SEASON WRAP-UP:

Under first-year manager Joe Altobelli, the Orioles are 98-64 in the regular season in the AL. Cal Ripken Jr. (.318, 27 homers, 102 RBI) and Eddie Murray (.306, 33 homers, 111 RBI) drive the offense. Garry Roenicke adds 19 homers and Ken Singleton, 18. Scott McGregor is 18-7; Felix "Tippy" Martinez has 21 saves.

Paul Owens, who took over for Pat Corrales during the season, leads the Phillies to a 90-72 record and the NL pennant. The team has no .300 hitters and no 20-game winner. Mike Schmidt provides the pop with 40 homers and 109 RBI while batting .255. The top average hitter is Garry Maddox at .275. John Denny is 19-6; Al Holland has 25 saves on the year.

The Phillies are not unique – the entire NL has no 20-game winners; with the exception of the strike-shortened 1981 season, it is the first time since 1931. The Expos' Tim "Rock" Raines leads the NL in two speed categories – stolen bases (90) and runs (133). The Blue Jays enjoy the first winning season – 89-73 – in franchise history; they finish nine games behind in fourth place in the AL East.

OCTOBER 4:

NLCS, game one. In Los Angeles, Steve Carlton outpitches

SEPTEMBER 19
On his 40th birthday, Joe Morgan is 4-for-5 with two homers in a 7-6 Phillies' win.

OCTOBER 16
Scott McGregor shuts out the Phillies in game five, and the Orioles win the World Series.

Jerry Reuss and the Phillies win, 1-0, on a Mike Schmidt home run in the first inning. Al Holland gets a save when he retires the Dodgers with the bases loaded in the eighth.

OCTOBER 5:

ALCS, game one. In Baltimore, LaMarr Hoyt and the White Sox beat Scott McGregor and the Orioles, 2-1. Hoyt goes all the way, allowing five hits. He is aided by Rudy Law's three hits.

NLCS, game two. In Los Angeles, Fernando Valenzuela pitches the Dodgers to a 4-1 victory over the Phillies and John Denny. Tom Niedenfuer picks up the save. Pedro Guerrero's two-run triple is the big hit for the Dodgers. Gary Matthews's home run accounts for the Phillies' only score.

OCTOBER 6:

ALCS, game two. In Baltimore today, starting pitcher Mike Boddicker five-hits the White Sox, 4-0, striking out 14 batters, to pull the Orioles even in the playoffs. Floyd Bannister is the losing pitcher. Gary Roenicke hits a two-run home run.

OCTOBER 7:

NLCS, game three. In Los Angeles, the Phillies, behind a four-hitter by Charlie Hudson, top the Dodgers, 7-2. Bob Welch takes the loss. Gary Matthews hits a solo homer for the winners; Mike "Moose" Marshall hits a two-run round-tripper for the Dodgers.

ALCS, game three. In Chicago, behind Mike Flanagan, the Orioles bomb the White Sox, 11-1. Richard Dotson gets the loss. Eddie Murray drives in three runs with a home run.

OCTOBER 8:

ALCS, game four. In Chicago, the Orioles win the AL pennant with a 3-0 victory over the White Sox in 10 innings. Felix "Tippy" Martinez is the winning pitcher; Britt Burns gets the loss. Terry "Tito" Landrum's home run is the big blow in Baltimore's 10th-inning three-run rally.

With 64,494 fans in Veterans Stadium, the Phillies give their rooters something to cheer about – the NL pennant. Steve Carlton beats Jerry Reuss, 7-2. Gary Matthews hits a three-run homer, and teammate Sixto Lezcano connects with one on for the Phillies. Johnnie "Dusty" Baker has a solo round-tripper for Los Angeles.

OCTOBER 10:

Tom Monaghan, the founder of Domino's Pizza, buys the Tigers from John Fetzer.

OCTOBER 11:

World Series, game one. In Baltimore, the Phillies and the Orioles each manage only five hits, but Philadelphia prevails, 2-1. John Denny is the winning pitcher; Scott McGregor gets the loss. Bases-empty home runs produce all the game's runs. Joe Morgan and Garry Maddox connect for the Phillies, Jim Dwyer for the Orioles.

OCTOBER 12:

World Series, game two. In Baltimore, the Orioles ride a three-hitter tossed by Mike Boddicker and a John Lowenstein home run to a 4-1 victory today. Charlie Hudson is the loser for the Phillies.

OCTOBER 13:

Davey Johnson is named manager of the Mets for 1984, replacing interim skipper Frank Howard. New York finished last in the NL East at 68-94 under Howard and George Bamberger. Johnson led the Tidewater Tides to the 1983 AAA World Series championship.

OCTOBER 14:

World Series, game three. Today in Philadelphia, the Orioles win, 3-2, beating Steve Carlton. The winner is Jim Palmer in relief of Mike Flanagan. Dan Ford homers for Baltimore; Gary Matthews and Joe Morgan connect for the Phillies – all with the bases empty. The winning run scores in the seventh inning on an error by Ivan DeJesus.

OCTOBER 15:

World Series, game four. In Philadelphia, 66,947 hometown faithful watch the Orioles beat the Phillies, 5-4. Each team has 10 hits, three by Baltimore's Rich Dauer, who knocks in three runs. The winner is George "Storm" Davis; John Denny gets the loss.

OCTOBER 16:

World Series, game five. In Philadelphia, Scott McGregor shuts

CULTURE

On television, *Bay City Blues*, a series about a minor league team, stars Michael Nouri, Bernie Casey, Ken Olin, and Dennis Franz. *Tiger Town* stars Roy Scheider and Justin Henry, with Sparky Anderson and Ernie Harwell.

"The only real way to know you've been fired is when you arrive at the ballpark and find your name has been scratched from the parking list."
– *Billy Martin*

CULTURE

***Hoopla*, by Harry Stein, is a fact-based fictional account of the Black Sox scandal, focusing on Buck Weaver. *The Celebrant*, by Eric Rolfe Greenberg, is a novel about a Jewish immigrant who makes jewelry and worships Christy Mathewson.**

out the Phillies on five hits. The Orioles win the game, 5-0, and the World Series, four games to one. Eddie Murray hits two home runs and Rick Dempsey, who is named the Series MVP, has one, plus a double. Starting pitcher Scott McGregor gets the win with a complete-game five-hitter. Charlie Hudson is charged with the loss. Dempsey and John Lowenstein lead all hitters with .385. Tippy Martinez records two saves. Pete Rose is Philadelphia's top hitter at .313.

POST-SEASON

OCTOBER 18:

Willie "Puddin' Head" Jones passes away in Cincinnati at age 58. He spent 12 of his 15 major league years with the Phillies and was a mainstay of the 1950 pennant-winning Whiz Kids. That year, he hit .267, with 25 home runs and 88 RBI, and batted .286 in the World Series. Jones, a third baseman, compiled a lifetime record of .258 with 190 homers.

OCTOBER 20:

The Dodgers break a longstanding tradition of one-year contracts for their managers. Since the 1950s and the advent of Walter O'Malley's ownership, Dodger skippers get one-year deals. But today they give the colorful – and highly successful – Tommy Lasorda a three-year, $1 million pact. In nine years at the helm, Lasorda has won three pennants and one World Series.

NOVEMBER 2:

The Dodgers continue their big-spending ways. Just 24 hours before he would have become a free agent, Jerry Reuss (12-11, 2.94 ERA) gets a four-year, $4.25-million contract.

NOVEMBER 15:

Charlie Grimm dies today at age 85 in Scottsdale, Arizona. Known as Jolly Cholly, he played 20 years as a major league first baseman, hitting .290. He also managed for 20 years and led the Chicago Cubs to the World Series in 1932, 1935, and 1945.

NOVEMBER 17:

Three Royals are in major trouble away from the playing field. Willie Wilson, Willie Aikens, and Jerry Martin receive three-month prison sentences for attempting to buy cocaine. U.S. Magistrate J. Milton Sullivant fines Wilson and Aikens $5,000 each and Martin $2,500.

DECEMBER 6:

The Reds reacquire first baseman Tony Perez (.241, six homers in 91 games) from the Phillies in a cash transaction. The former member of the Big Red Machine was traded to the Montreal Expos in 1976, after 13 seasons in Cincinnati.

DECEMBER 7:

The Reds sign free-agent outfielder Dave Parker (.279, 12 home runs, 69 RBIs, 12 stolen bases). Parker spent the last 11 years with the Pirates.

DECEMBER 8:

Cardiologist and former major league infielder Dr. Robert W. Brown is elected president of the AL. Known as Bobby Brown when he played with the Yankees from 1946 to 1954, he hit .279 and batted .439 in four World Series.

The Mets get pitcher Sid Fernandez (0-1, 6.00 ERA) and minor league infielder Ross Jones from the Dodgers for outfielder-infielder Bob Bailor (.250, 18 stolen bases) and pitcher Carlos Diaz (3-1, 2.05 ERA, two saves).

DECEMBER 15:

Commissioner Bowie Kuhn imposes a season-long suspension on troubled Los Angeles Dodgers pitcher Steve Howe for substance abuse. According to Kuhn, Howe will not be permitted to return to major league baseball until he is drug-free. Howe had been suspended indefinitely by the Dodgers in September for leaving the ballclub without permission.

DECEMBER 16:

The ever-controversial Billy Martin is fired as the Yankees' manager and former New York catcher Yogi Berra is hired to replace him. This is Berra's second time around as New York's manager. The Yankees were 91-71 this season and finished in third place under Martin.

DECEMBER 19:

The Detroit Tigers sign free-agent infielder Darrell Evans (.277, 30 homers, 82 RBI). Evans was with the San Francisco Giants in the 1983 season.

OCTOBER 20
The Dodgers reward manager Tommy Lasorda with a three-year contract.

DECEMBER 16
Billy Martin is fired as manager of the Yankees, and replaced by Yogi Berra.

THE BEST OF 1983

NATIONAL LEAGUE

HITTERS

Batting Average:
Bill Madlock, Pittsburgh Pirates, .323

Slugging Average:
Dale Murphy, Atlanta Braves, .540

Home Runs:
Mike Schmidt, Philadelphia Phillies, 40

Runs Batted In:
Dale Murphy, 121

Hits:
Jose Cruz, Houston Astros, 189

Stolen Bases:
Tim Raines, Montreal Expos, 90

PITCHERS

Wins:
John Denny, Philadelphia Phillies, 19

Strikeouts:
Steve Carlton, Philadelphia Phillies, 275

Earned Run Average:
Atlee Hammaker, San Francisco Giants, 2.25

Winning Percentage:
John Denny, .760

Saves:
Lee Smith, Chicago Cubs, 29

Most Valuable Player:
Dale Murphy, Atlanta Braves

Cy Young Award:
John Denny, Philadelphia Phillies

Rookie of the Year:
Darryl Strawberry, New York Mets

Manager of the Year:
Tommy Lasorda, Los Angeles Dodgers

AMERICAN LEAGUE

HITTERS

Batting Average:
Wade Boggs, Boston Red Sox, .361

Slugging Average:
George Brett, Kansas City Royals, .563

Home Runs:
Jim Rice, Boston Red Sox, 39

Runs Batted In:
Jim Rice; Cecil Cooper, Milwaukee Brewers, 126

Hits:
Cal Ripken Jr., Baltimore Orioles, 211

Stolen Bases:
Rickey Henderson, Oakland Athletics, 108

PITCHERS

Wins:
LaMarr Hoyt, Chicago White Sox, 24

Strikeouts:
Jack Morris, Detroit Tigers, 232

Earned Run Average:
Rick Honeycutt, Texas Rangers, 2.42

Winning Percentage:
Richard Dotson, Chicago White Sox, .759

Saves:
Dan Quisenberry, Kansas City Royals, 45

Most Valuable Player:
Cal Ripken Jr., Baltimore Orioles

Cy Young Award:
LaMarr Hoyt, Chicago White Sox

Rookie of the Year:
Ron Kittle, Chicago White Sox

Manager of the Year:
Tony LaRussa, Chicago White Sox

CULTURE

The song "Pine Tar Wars (The Ballad of George Brett)," written by Larry Stewart and Larry Isley, is recorded twice, by C.W. McCall and Red River Dave McEnery.

1984

JANUARY 20
Peter Rose, 42 and once again a free agent, signs with the Montreal Expos.

NEWS

RONALD REAGAN REELECTED PRESIDENT, DEFEATING WALTER MONDALE

DEMOCRAT GERALDINE FERRARO IS FIRST FEMALE VP CANDIDATE FROM A MAJOR PARTY

SENATE REJECTS SCHOOL PRAYER AMENDMENT

U.S. TROOPS LEAVE LEBANON

SIX-YEAR-OLD STORMIE JONES OF TEXAS RECEIVES FIRST HEART AND LIVER TRANSPLANT

4,000 affected by AIDS to date

KATHRYN SULLIVAN IS FIRST U.S. WOMAN TO WALK IN SPACE

BABOON HEART TRANSPLANTED INTO BABY FAE; SHE SURVIVES 30 DAYS

GUNMAN MURDERS 21 AT McDONALD'S IN SAN YSIDRO, CALIFORNIA

PRE-SEASON

JANUARY 6:

The Yankees sign free-agent pitcher Phil Niekro (11-10, 3.97 ERA). The 44-year-old Niekro spent the 1983 season with the Atlanta Braves.

JANUARY 12:

The Padres sign free-agent relief pitcher Rich "Goose" Gossage (13-5, 2.27 ERA, 22 saves). He spent the 1983 season with the Yankees.

JANUARY 14:

Padres' owner Ray Kroc dies at age 81. His widow, Joan Kroc, succeeds him as chairwoman of the board; Ballard Smith becomes the team's president.

JANUARY 20:

Pete Rose will continue his charge on baseball's records from a new home address. The 42-year-old first baseman (.245) is signed as a free agent by the Expos; he played with the Phillies for the past five seasons.

The White Sox claim Tom Seaver (9-14, 3.55 ERA, two shutouts) in the compensation draft after losing free agent pitcher Dennis Lamp (7-7, 3.71 ERA, 15 saves) to the Blue Jays. Seaver spent last season with the Mets, who had reacquired him in a December 1982 trade with the Reds.

MARCH 3:

Peter Ueberroth is elected baseball's sixth commissioner, succeeding Bowie Kuhn, who remains in office until October 1. Ueberroth is president of the Los Angeles Olympic Organizing Committee and will complete that assignment before taking over as commissioner. The 46-year-old will serve for a five-year term. Kuhn's term ended in August of last year but he agreed to remain on the job. Ueberroth apparently learned from Kuhn's bad experience with the owners. As a result of his demands, a simple majority in each league now will reelect the commissioner. Previously, a three-quarter vote was needed. Kuhn was ousted even though he had a simple majority.

MARCH 18:

Charlie Lau, a lifetime .255 batter who became one of the gurus of modern hitting, dies today in Key Colony Beach, Florida, at age 50. A catcher, Lau played 11 years with the Tigers, Brewers, Orioles, Royals, and Braves.

MARCH 20:

Hall of Fame pitcher Stan Coveleski dies in South Bend, Indiana, at age 94. He is best remembered for his 3-0, 0.67 ERA performance for the Indians in the 1920 World Series. In his 14-year career, he was 215-142 with 38 shutouts and a 2.88 ERA. A five-time 20-game winner, Coveleski was inducted into the Hall of Fame in 1969.

MARCH 24:

The Detroit Tigers acquire relief pitcher Guillermo "Willie" Hernandez and first baseman Dave Bergman (.286, six homers in 90 games) from the Phillies for catcher-infielder-outfielder-DH John Wockenfuss (.269, nine homers in 92 games) and outfielder Glenn Wilson (.268, 11 home runs).

MARCH 30:

Graig Nettles (.266, 20 home runs), the Yankees third baseman for the past 11 years, is traded to the Padres for pitcher Dennis Rasmussen

"Managing is getting your players to put out 100 percent year after year."
– *Sparky Anderson*

MARCH 3
Peter Ueberroth is elected baseball's sixth commissioner, replacing Bowie Kuhn.

LEAGUE

They liked what they saw. Two days after he beats them, 9-7 at Comiskey Park, the Mariners acquire relief pitcher Salome Barojas (3-2) from the White Sox for minor league pitchers Gene Nelson and Jerry Don Gleaton.

CULTURE

Baseball books are popular: *The Dixie Association*, a novel by Donald Hays about the fictional Arkansas Reds; *The Cheat*, a mystery novel by Pat Jordan; *Strike Three You're Dead* by Richard D. Rosen, featuring outfielder-turned-private eye Harvey Blissberg; *Things Invisible to See*, a novel by Nancy Willard.

Sparky Anderson's Tigers get off to a quick start.

APRIL 7
Tigers' pitcher Jack Morris throws a no-hitter against the White Sox.

CULTURE

At the movies, *The Natural* stars Robert Redford, Robert Duvall, Glenn Close, and Kim Basinger. Former major leaguer Sibby Sisti appears as an opposing manager. The film is based on the novel by Bernard Malamud.

(0-0, 1.98 ERA) and minor league pitcher Darin Cloninger.

THE SEASON

APRIL 3:

On opening day at Arlington Stadium, the Rangers confiscate the contents of picnic baskets, snacks, and lunches to enforce a ban on incoming food.

APRIL 7:

Jack Morris of the Tigers no-hits the White Sox, 4-0, in Chicago. Morris strikes out eight and walks six; Detroit commits no errors. The losing pitcher is Floyd Bannister.

Dwight Gooden, the Mets' 19-year-old pitching "phenom" makes his major league debut against Houston in the Astrodome. He goes five innings, gives up three hits, one earned run, and two walks, and strikes out five Astros to earn the win in a 3-2 victory.

APRIL 10:

For the second time in his career, LaMarr Hoyt of the White Sox wins 15 consecutive games. His current streak began on July 27 of last season.

SIXTY-SIX-YEAR-OLD BOB FELLER IS ASKED HOW FAST HE STILL CAN PITCH. HE RESPONDS: "I CAN STILL THROW IN THE 70S. AND I CAN THROW IT IN THE 80S IF I DON'T WANT TO COMB MY HAIR FOR A WEEK."

Karl Spooner, whose debut at the end of the 1954 season was one of the most impressive ever, dies at age 52 in Vero Beach, Florida. The left-hander broke in with two shutouts, striking out 27 batters and walking only six. He injured his arm in spring training in 1955 and went on to an 86 season before his career ended.

APRIL 13:

On the 21st anniversary of his first major league safety and on the eve of his 43rd birthday, the Expos' Pete Rose doubles off Jerry Koosman of the Phillies in the fourth inning at Olympic Stadium for his 4,000th career hit. Rose, who is the second player ever to reach the 4,000-hit plateau, gets a three-minute standing ovation from the crowd. The Expos go on to win the game, 5-1.

APRIL 21:

In a game shortened to five innings by rain, the Expos' David Palmer no-hits the Cardinals, 4-0, in St. Louis. Palmer is perfect in his abbreviated pitching gem.

MAY 4:

Over the fence is a homer, but through the ceiling is two bases. In Minnesota's Metrodome, Dave Kingman of the Athletics hits a fly through a drainage hole in the roof. The ball never returns to the playing field and Kingman is awarded a ground-rule double.

MAY 6:

At Arlington Stadium, Texas, Cal Ripken Jr. hits for the cycle and leads the Orioles to a 6-1 victory over the Rangers. Ripken triples in the first, singles in the fifth, doubles in the seventh, and adds a homer in the ninth. He has two RBI and two runs. The winning pitcher is Mike Boddicker, who pitches a five-hitter; Frank Tanana is the losing pitcher.

MAY 8:

Kirby Puckett of the Twins singles against Jim Slaton of the Angels in his first major league at-bat. Puckett goes on to hit safely four times in five at-bats in a 4-0 victory in Anaheim. Puckett is the 12th major leaguer to debut with four hits.

MAY 9:

Harold Baines hits a 420-foot homer in the 25th inning to give the White Sox a 7-6 win over the Brewers at Comiskey Park. It

MAY 9
The White Sox win an AL-record, 25-inning marathon against the Brewers, 7-6.

JULY 4
Yankees' knuckleballer Phil Niekro records his 3,000th career strikeout.

is the AL's longest-ever game by innings and sets a major league time record - eight hours and six minutes. Play was suspended this morning after 17 innings at 1:05 A.M., because of a curfew. Tom Seaver gets the win in relief, then pitches eight and a third innings in today's regularly scheduled game, which Chicago wins, 5-4, in a relatively brisk two hours, nine minutes. Seaver gets the victory. Chuck Porter is charged with the loss in the marathon game. Ben Oglivie has a three-run homer for Milwaukee in the 21st inning.

MAY 16:

Carlton Fisk of the White Sox hits for the cycle in a 7-6 loss to the Royals.

MAY 17:

The Padres' Alan Wiggins steals five bases to tie an NL record held by Davey Lopes (1974), Dan McGann (1904), and Lonnie Smith (1982).

MAY 25:

The Red Sox obtain first baseman-outfielder Bill Buckner (.209 in 21 games) from the Cubs for pitcher Dennis Eckersley (4-4) and minor league infielder Mike Brumley.

MAY 27:

The Toronto Blue Jays' Alfredo Griffin is out of the lineup today, ending his consecutive game streak at 392 – the longest among active players.

JUNE 13:

The Cubs obtain pitchers Rick Sutcliffe (4-5) and George Frazier (3-2), along with catcher-first baseman Ron Hassey (.255 in 48 games), from the Indians for outfielders Joe Carter (.176 in 23 games in 1983) and Mel Hall (.280 in 48 games), pitcher Don Schulze (0-0), and minor league pitcher Darryl Banks.

JUNE 15:

Mariners' rookie Mark Langston fans 12 Rangers - including seven straight. Seattle beats Texas, 4-3 in 10 innings.

JUNE 22:

Calvin Griffith sells his majority interest in the Twins to businessman Carl Pohlad for $32 million. The sale marks the end of 60 years of control of the franchise by the Griffith family.

WAITE HOYT ONCE SAID, "THE SECRET OF SUCCESS AS A PITCHER LIES IN GETTING A JOB WITH THE YANKEES." HE ALSO REMARKED, "A YANKEE PITCHER NEVER SHOULD HOLD OUT BECAUSE HE MIGHT BE TRADED AND THEN HE WOULD HAVE TO PITCH AGAINST THEM."

JUNE 28:

Dwight Evans hits for the cycle – including a game-winning three-run homer in the 11th inning – to pace the Red Sox past the Mariners, 9-6.

JUNE 29:

Montreal's Pete Rose plays in his 3,309th major league game – the most ever. The previous record holder was Carl Yastrzemski. The Expos top Rose's former team, the Cincinnati Reds, 7-3.

JULY 4:

Phil Niekro of the Yankees fans Larry Parrish of the Rangers for his 3,000th career strikeout. Niekro has five for the game.

JULY 14:

Al Schacht, the Clown Prince of Baseball, dies today at the age of 91 in Waterbury, Connecticut. Schacht entertained before countless major and minor league games, including 25 World Series and 18 All-Star Games. Schacht, who wore a top hat and tails over a baseball uniform for his costume, pitched for three seasons with the Washington Senators, compiling a 14-10 career record with a 4.48 ERA.

LEAGUE

Because of a strike by major league umpires, the first game of the NLCS is called by college umpires. The regulars are seeking a pool of $340,000 to be distributed to all umpires, including those not working in post-season games. Currently, each working umpire gets $10,000 for the LCS and $15,000 for the World Series. If the strike is not settled by World Series time, the games will be called by former major league umps.

"They shouldn't try to compare Dwight to Sandy Koufax or Nolan Ryan... They should be comparing the others to Dwight."
– Mets' manager of Dwight Gooden

Dwight Gooden has 267 strikeouts as a rookie.

JULY 23:

The Angels' Mike Witt fans 16 Mariners in a 7-1 victory.

Rollie Fingers of the Brewers records his 216th career save in a 6-4 win over the Yankees. It also is the 23rd of the season for Fingers, who ties Albert "Sparky" Lyle for first place on the all-time list.

JULY 26:

Montreal's Pete Rose hits safely in the 8th inning against the Pirates to tie Cobb in career singles at 3,052. The Expos beat Pittsburgh, 5-4.

JULY 27:

One day after tying Ty Cobb for most career singles, Pete Rose adds another.

AUGUST 5:

Cliff Johnson of the Blue Jays hits his 19th career pinch-hit home run – a major league record. Johnson's round-tripper, hit off Felix "Tippy" Martinez of the Orioles in the eighth inning, enables him to surpass the mark set by Jerry Lynch, who played from 1954 to 1966. Toronto goes on to beat Baltimore by a score of 4-3.

JULY 23
Brewers' closer Rollie Fingers has his 216th career save in a 6-4 win over the Yankees.

AUGUST 16
Pete Rose returns to the Cincinnati Reds, coming back as a player-manager.

AUGUST 12:

Luis Aparicio, Don Drysdale, Rick Ferrell, Harmon Killebrew, and Harold "Pee Wee" Reese are inducted into the Hall of Fame. Aparicio, a shortstop, was described by Bill Veeck as "the best I've ever seen." Aparicio won nine Gold Gloves, batted .262, and stole 506 bases in an 18-year career with the White Sox, Orioles, and Red Sox. A native of Maracibo, Venezuela, he appeared in two World Series. Drysdale, who teamed with Sandy Koufax for one of baseball's toughest-ever right-handedleft-handed pitching duos, was 209-166 with a 2.95 ERA in 14 years. Drysdale set a major league record in 1968 with 58 2/3 consecutive scoreless innings. He was a two-time strikeout leader, recorded a career total of 2,486, Ks and threw 49 shutouts. Drysdale was the 1962 Cy Young Award winner with a 25-9 record and a 2.83 ERA. Ferrell, a catcher, played 18 years – from 1929 to 1947 – with the Browns, Red Sox, and Senators, batting .281. His best year at the plate was 1932, when he hit .315. Killebrew, the AL's Most Valuable Player in 1969, played 22 years, hitting only .256 but slugging 573 home runs. He walked 1,559 times and struck out 1,699 times. Killebrew hit 40 or more homers in a season eight times, led the AL in round-trippers six times and in RBI three times. He appeared in two World Series. Reese, one of the dominant shortstops of his time, played 16 seasons with the Dodgers, batting .269 and stealing 232 bases. He appeared in seven World Series, hitting .277.

It is a beanball war interrupted by a baseball game in Fulton County Stadium, where the Braves meet the Padres. Hostilities begin when Atlanta's Pascual Perez hits Alan Wiggins of the Padres with the first pitch of the game. Ed Whitson of the Padres throws behind Perez when he comes to bat in the second inning. In the fourth inning Whitson "low bridges" Perez for the second time. In the eighth inning, Perez is the target again; this time Craig Lefferts hits him, igniting a 10-minute brawl. In the ninth inning the Padres' Graig Nettles is hit by Donnie Moore, and the benches empty again.

In the aftermath of 16 ejections, umpire John McSherry says, "It took baseball down 50 years, the worst thing I've ever seen in my life."

AUGUST 16:

Pete Rose goes home. The fifth-place Reds acquire the first baseman (.259 in 95 games) from the Expos and name him their manager. He replaces Vern Rapp, who led the team to a 51-70 record. In return for Rose, Montreal receives infielder Tom Lawless (.250 in 43 games). Rose, who is also a native of Cincinnati, spent the first 16 years of his career with the Reds.

Tommie Aaron, the younger brother of Henry Aaron, dies in Atlanta, at age 45. The younger Aaron spent seven years in the major leagues for the Milwaukee and Atlanta Braves, hitting .229 with 13 home runs. At the time of his death, he was a coach with Atlanta.

AUGUST 22:

Dwight Gooden fans nine Padres today to bring his season total to 200. The Mets' right-hander is the 11th pitcher to fan 200 batters in his rookie season.

AUGUST 25:

Hall of Fame pitcher Waite Hoyt dies in Cincinnati, at age 84. In 21 major league seasons, Hoyt was 237-182 with a 3.59 ERA and pitched in seven World Series. His best seasons were with the Yankees, from 1921 into the 1930 season, when he twice was a 20-game winner and won 19 games two times.

SEPTEMBER 7:

Mets' right-hander Dwight Gooden fans Ron Cey of the Cubs in the second inning to set an NL rookie record with 228 strikeouts for the season. He tops the mark set by Grover Cleveland Alexander of the Phillies in 1911. Gooden goes on to one-hit Chicago, 10-0.

Hall of Fame shortstop and former AL president Joe Cronin dies today at the age of 77 in Osterville, Massachusetts. Inducted into the Hall of Fame in 1956, Cronin played 20 years, hitting .301. He managed the Senators and Red Sox for 15 years. Cronin served as president of

HISTORY

The Mets' 19-year-old rookie Dwight "Doc" Gooden sets a major league rookie record with 276 strikeouts.

LEAGUE

Commissioner Peter Ueberroth warns Chicago he will move future playoff games to St. Louis unless lights are installed in Wrigley Field.

> "Who would accept a job with Marge Schott's dog, Ted Turner and George Steinbrenner as your boss?"
> – *New Commissioner Peter Ueberroth*

CULTURE

Baseball inspires two poems by Donald Hall: "The Baseball Players" and "Couplet/Old Timers' Day, Fenway Park, 1 May 1982."

the American League for two terms beginning in 1959.

SEPTEMBER 12:

Dwight Gooden fans 16 Pirates in a 2-0 Mets' victory to run his season total to 247 – a major league rookie record. Herb Score of the Indians set the old mark with 245 in 1955.

SEPTEMBER 17:

On the 17th anniversary of his first major league round-tripper, Reggie Jackson of the Angels homers into the right-field stands on the first pitch from Bud Black of the Royals in the seventh inning at Anaheim. It is Jackson's 500th career homer; he is the 13th player to reach that mark and the first since Willie McCovey in 1978. After a brief ceremony, Kansas City wins the game, 10-1.

Dwight Gooden fans 16 Phillies en route to a 2-1 victory. With 16 against the Pirates on September 12, the Mets' rookie ties a major league record – 32 strikeouts in two games.

SEPTEMBER 20:

The Padres beat the Giants, 5-4, to win the NL West – their first division title ever.

SEPTEMBER 24:

The Cubs win their first title of any kind since 1945, when they take the NL East with a Rick Sutcliffe two-hit, 4-1 victory over the Pirates.

SEPTEMBER 28:

The Cardinals' Bruce Sutter records his 41st save of the season in a 4-1, 10-inning victory over the Cubs at Wrigley Field today. Sutter equals Dan Quisenberry's major league mark, established last season.

Charlie Leibrandt and the Royals top the Athletics, 6-5, in Oakland to capture the AL West title.

SEPTEMBER 30:

Mike Witt of the California Angels pitches a perfect game against the Rangers in Texas. Witt strikes out 10 and the Angels win, 1-0, on an unearned run. Witt retires the last batter, Marvis Foley pinch-hitting for Curtis Wilkerson. He throws only 94 pitches – 70 strikes. It is the first perfect game in the majors since Len Barker's in 1981. Charlie Hough is the losing pitcher.

It's Yankee against Yankee for the American League batting title on the final day of the season, and Don Mattingly, with 4 for 5, prevails over Dave Winfield, who has one hit in four at bats. Mattingly ends the season with .343 to Winfield's .340. Seattle's rookie Mark Langston fans nine White Sox in seven innings, bringing his season total to 204 and giving him the AL strikeout championship. The left-hander beats Chicago, 5-3, for his 17th win on back-to-back homers by two other rookies – Danny Tartabull and Jim Presley.

REGULAR SEASON WRAP-UP:

The Tigers, under George "Sparky" Anderson, are 104-58 in the regular season. The team packs power, leading the AL with 187 homers. Lance Parrish hits 33 homers and drives in 98 runs with a .237 batting average; Kirk Gibson hits .282 with 27 home runs and 91 RBI. The top average hitter is Alan Trammell at .314 with 14 home runs. Jack Morris anchors the pitching staff with a 19-11 record; Guillermo "Willie" Hernandez has 32 saves in 33 opportunities.

Dick Williams's Padres have a regular season record of 92-70 in the NL. The offensive leader is Tony Gwynn with .351 and 213 hits. Kevin McReynolds (.278, 20 homers, 75 RBI) and Graig Nettles (20 homers and a .228 average) add pop to the Padres. First baseman Steve Garvey handles 1,319 chances without an error, becoming the only first baseman in history to play a full season and record a 1.000 fielding average. The top winner is Eric Show at 15-9; Goose Gossage records 25 saves.

OCTOBER 1:

A year after being inducted into the Hall of Fame, Walter Alston dies at age 72 in Oxford, Ohio.

Billy Goodman dies in Sarasota, Florida, at age 58. In 1950, he led the American League in batting with .354. That season Goodman played the outfield and all four infield positions for the Red Sox, becoming the only player without a regular position to win a batting title. He had a .300 lifetime average in 16 seasons.

Peter Ueberroth assumes office as commissioner of baseball today.

SEPTEMBER 30
Angels' pitcher Mike Witt tosses a perfect game against the Texas Rangers.

OCTOBER 9
In game one of the World Series, the Tigers nip the Padres, 3-2, behind Jack Morris.

OCTOBER 2:

NLCS, game one. The Cubs celebrate their return to post-season play with an offensive explosion – five home runs, 16 hits, and a 13-0 win over the Padres in Wrigley field. Rick Sutcliffe goes seven innings for the win and connects for a solo homer. Gary "Sarge" Matthews sets the pace with a two-run and a solo homer; Bob Dernier and Ron Cey also homer. The losing pitcher is Eric Show.

ALCS, game one. In Kansas City, Jack Morris and the Tigers take the opener, 8-1. Alan Trammell, Lance Parrish, and Larry Herndon hit solo homers for the Tigers. Trammell also has a triple and three RBI. Bud Black takes the loss.

OCTOBER 3:

NLCS, game two. At Wrigley Field, the Cubs make it two in a row, 4-2, behind five-hit pitching by Steve Trout and then two innings of hitless relief by Lee Smith. The losing pitcher is Mark Thurmond.

ALCS, game two. In Kansas City, the Tigers win, 5-3, in 11 innings on a two-run double by Johnny Grubb. Kirk Gibson hits a solo homer for the Tigers. The winning pitcher is Aurelio Lopez in relief of Dan Petry. Royals' relief pitcher Dan Quisenberry is tagged with the loss.

OCTOBER 4:

NLCS, game three. Back in San Diego, the Padres beat the Cubs, 7-1, for their first playoff win. Kevin McReynolds hits a three-run homer and Ed Whitson gets the win with relief from Rich "Goose" Gossage. The losing pitcher is Dennis Eckersley.

OCTOBER 5:

ALCS, game three. Before a hometown crowd of 52,168, Milt Wilcox shuts out the Royals, 1-0, on three hits to give the Tigers a three-game sweep and the AL pennant. Charlie Leibrandt takes the loss, despite allowing only three hits in eight innings.

OCTOBER 6:

NLCS, game four. Steve Garvey cracks a two-run homer in the bottom of the ninth to give the Padres a 7-5 win and tie the playoffs. Craig Lefferts, the fifth San Diego pitcher, gets the win; Lee Smith is tagged with the loss. Jody Davis and Leon Durham hit home runs for Chicago.

OCTOBER 7:

Major league umpires are returning to work and will call the final game of the NLCS in San Diego. The umpires end their one-week strike when new baseball Commissioner Peter Ueberroth convinces them – and league officials – to accept binding arbitration to settle the dispute.

NLCS, game five. In San Diego, the Padres score four runs in the seventh inning to beat the Cubs, 6-3, and win their first-ever NL pennant. Craig Lefferts gets the victory in relief. Starter Rick Sutcliffe is charged with the loss. Leon Durham and Jody Davis homer for the losing Cubs.

OCTOBER 9:

World Series, game one. In San Diego, Jack Morris goes all the way, limiting the Padres to six hits for a complete-game, 3-2 Tigers' victory. Larry Herndon's fifth-inning, two-run home run is the big blow for Detroit. Mark Thurmond is charged with the loss.

OCTOBER 10:

World Series, game two. Kurt Bevacqua hits a three-run homer in the fifth to pace the Padres to a 5-3 win in San Diego. The winning pitcher is Andy Hawkins, who allows one hit in five and a third innings in relief of Ed Whitson. Starter Dan Petry gets the loss.

OCTOBER 12:

World Series, game three. In Detroit, the Tigers capitalize on 11 walks and seven hits to beat the Padres, 5-2. Marty Castillo hits a two-run homer in a four-run fourth inning. The winning pitcher is starter Milt Wilcox, with a save from closer Willie Hernandez. Tim Lollar getsthe loss.

OCTOBER 13:

World Series, game four. Jack Morris pitches a five-hitter for a 4-2 win and his second complete game victory of the series. Alan Trammell hits a pair of two-run homers. Eric Show gets the loss. Terry Kennedy homers for the Padres.

Hall of Fame first baseman George "Highpockets" Kelly dies at the age of 89 in Burlingame, California. In 16

TRIVIA

What if? In his first five years in the major leagues, Harmon Killebrew played in only 113 games. He batted only 254 times and connected for 11 homers. In the next 17 years, he hit 562 round-trippers. Where would Killebrew rank among home run hitters if he had been given the opportunity to bat more frequently in those early years?

"I've never met him, but get word back to George that I love him dearly and admire him very much."
– Marge Schott, on George Steinbrenner

CULTURE

***Long Gone*, a made-for-cable movie based on Paul Hemphill's 1979 novel, stars William Peterson.**

years, Kelly batted .297 with 148 homers. In 1921, with the Giants, he led the NL with 21 homers. Kelly was elected to the Hall of Fame in 1973.

OCTOBER 14:

World Series, game five. Kirk Gibson homers twice – with one on and two on – and Larry Parrish adds a solo round-tripper as the Tigers beat the Padres, 8-4, in Detroit to win the World Series. Sparky Anderson becomes the first manager with a World Championship in both leagues. The winning pitcher is Aurelio Lopez in relief; Andy Hawkins is tagged with the loss. Kurt Bevacqua has a solo homer for San Diego. Alan Trammell paces all hitters with a .450 average. He adds two homers and six RBI. Kirk Gibson bats .333 with two homers and seven RBI. Ace Jack Morris has two wins; Willie Hernandez two saves. Kurt Bevacqua bats .412 for San Diego.

POST-SEASON

DECEMBER 6:

The White Sox acquire minor league shortstop Ozzie Guillen, pitcher Tom Lollar (11-13, 3.91 ERA), infielder-outfielder Luis Salazar (.241 in 93 games) and minor league pitcher Bill Long from the Padres for pitcher LaMarr Hoyt (13-18, 4.47 ERA) and two minor league pitchers, Todd Simmons and Kevin Kristan.

DECEMBER 7:

The Braves sign free-agent relief pitcher Bruce Sutter (5-7, 1.54 ERA and a league-leading 45 saves). Sutter was with the Cardinals this past season.

The Brewers trade pitcher Don Sutton (14-12, 3.77 ERA) to the Athletics for pitcher Ray Burris (13-10, 3.15 ERA), minor league pitcher Eric Barry, and a player to be named later.

DECEMBER 8:

The Yankees receive outfielder Rickey Henderson (.293, 16 homers, 66 stolen bases), pitcher Bert Bradley (0-0, 6.48 ERA in 1983), and cash from the Athletics in return for pitchers Jay Howell (9-4, 2.69 ERA, seven saves) and Jose Rijo (2-8, 4.76 ERA, two saves), outfielder Stan Javier (.143 in seven games), and minor league pitchers Eric Plunk and Tim Birtsas.

In their second deal of the day, the Athletics acquire outfielder Dave Collins (.308, 15 triples, 60 stolen bases), shortstop Alfredo Griffin (.241), and cash from the Blue Jays for pitcher Bill Caudill (9-7, 2.71 ERA, 36 saves).

DECEMBER 10:

The Mets acquire catcher Gary Carter (.294, 27 homers, and a league-leading 106 RBI) from the Expos for infielder Hubie Brooks (.283, 16 homers, 73 RBI), catcher Mike R. Fitzgerald (.242), outfielder Herm Winningham (.407 in 14 games), and minor league pitcher Floyd Youmans.

DECEMBER 11:

The Orioles sign free-agent outfielder Fred Lynn (.271, 23 homers, 79 RBI). Lynn spent this past season with the California Angels.

DECEMBER 16:

Debs Garms, who led the NL in batting in 1940 with a .355 average, dies in Glen Rose, Texas, at age 76. An outfielder-infielder, Garms played 12 seasons with the Cardinals, the Bees, and the Pirates, batting .293.

DECEMBER 21:

Today Marge Schott becomes the owner of the Cincinnati Reds.

After Schott, a successful Cincinnati car dealer, accuses the Yankees' George Steinbrenner of "ruining baseball" with his free spending, he fires back: "I'm ruining baseball? The last two years, I've done nothing but sit back. I've watched them take Reggie Jackson from me and I've watched them take Rich Gossage from me last year. I'm spending money?" He continues, "She had better brush up on what's what. I don't even know who she is. But I wouldn't buy a car from her." Says Schott: "I've never met him, but get word back to George that I love him dearly and I admire him very much."

DECEMBER 27:

The New York Yankees sign free-agent starting pitcher Ed Whitson (14-8, 3.24 ERA) to a five-year, $4.4-million contract. Whitson was with the San Diego Padres this past season.

OCTOBER 15
A pair of Kirk Gibson homers pace the Tigers in game five, and Detroit wins the Series.

DECEMBER 10
The New York Mets acquire catcher Gary Carter from the Montreal Expos.

THE BEST OF 1984

NATIONAL LEAGUE

HITTERS

Batting Average:
Tony Gwynn, San Diego Padres, .351

Slugging Average:
Dale Murphy, Atlanta Braves, .547

Home Runs:
Murphy; Mike Schmidt, Philadelphia Phillies, 36

Runs Batted In:
Mike Schmidt; Gary Carter, Montreal Expos, 106

Hits:
Tony Gwynn, 213

Stolen Bases:
Tim Raines, Montreal Expos, 75

PITCHERS

Wins:
Joaquin Andujar, St. Louis Cardinals, 20

Strikeouts:
Dwight Gooden, New York Mets, 276

Earned Run Average:
Alejandro Pena, Los Angeles Dodgers, 2.48

Winning Percentage:
Rick Sutcliffe, Chicago Cubs, .941

Saves:
Bruce Sutter, St. Louis Cardinals, 45

Most Valuable Player:
Ryne Sandberg, Chicago Cubs

Cy Young Award:
Rick Sutcliffe, Chicago Cubs

Rookie of the Year:
Dwight Gooden, New York Mets

Manager of the Year:
Jim Frey, Chicago Cubs

AMERICAN LEAGUE

HITTERS

Batting Average:
Don Mattingly, New York Yankees, .343

Slugging Average:
Harold Baines, Chicago White Sox, .541

Home Runs:
Tony Armas, Boston Red Sox, 43

Runs Batted In:
Tony Armas, 123

Hits:
Don Mattingly, 207

Stolen Bases:
Rickey Henderson, Oakland Athletics, 66

PITCHERS

Wins:
Mike Boddicker, Baltimore Orioles, 20

Strikeouts:
Mark Langston, Seattle Mariners, 204

Earned Run Average:
Mike Boddicker, 2.79

Winning Percentage:
Doyle Alexander, Toronto Blue Jays, .739

Saves:
Dan Quisenberry, Kansas City Royals, 44

Most Valuable Player:
Guillermo "Willie" Hernandez, Detroit Tigers

Cy Young Award:
Guillermo "Willie" Hernandez, Detroit Tigers

Rookie of the Year:
Alvin Davis, Seattle Mariners

Manager of the Year:
George "Sparky" Anderson, Detriot Tigers

CULTURE

In the theater, *The Babe*, a one-character play, stars Max Gail in the title role. *Diamonds* is a musical revue by several composers.

1985

"I'm pleased to welcome back... Willie Mays and Mickey Mantle."
– *Commissioner Peter Ueberroth*

NEWS

REAGAN, GORBACHEV HOLD SUMMIT MEETING IN GENEVA

133 DIE IN DELTA AIRLINES CRASH AT DALLAS/FORT WORTH

U.S. hits South Africa with trade sanctions

WRECK OF THE *TITANIC*, SUNK IN 1912, FOUND NEAR NEWFOUNDLAND

PLO HIJACKS *ACHILLE LAURO*, KILLS 69-YEAR-OLD AMERICAN

HURRICANE JUAN CAUSES $1 BILLION IN DAMAGE

Rock Hudson dies of AIDS; Yul Brynner dies of cancer

REBEL LEADER DANIEL ORTEGA BECOMES PRESIDENT OF NICARAGUA

ANNE TYLER'S THE ACCIDENTAL TOURIST IS PUBLISHED

PRE-SEASON

JANUARY 24:

Pitcher Donnie Moore (4-5, 2.94, 16 saves) goes to the Angels from the Braves as compensation for losing Fred Lynn to Baltimore as a free agent.

The Toronto Blue Jays claim pitcher Tom Henke (1-1, 6.35 ERA) from the Rangers as compensation for losing free-agent designated hitter Cliff Johnson to Texas.

JANUARY 29:

There will be no drug testing clauses in the contracts between individual players and teams; instead a major league-wide joint program will be developed with the Players Association. Earlier in the month the Dodgers had announced drug testing provisions in their new contracts; the existing pact with Bill Russell will remain in effect. So, too, will the agreements signed by members of the Giants.

FEBRUARY 4:

Slugger Greg Luzinski retires after 15 years. Luzinski, a first baseman-outfielder-DH, compiles a lifetime average of .276 with 307 homers and 1,128 RBI with the Phillies and White Sox. With Chicago last year, he hit .238 with 13 home runs.

FEBRUARY 7:

Major league owners approve the purchase of the controlling interest in the Reds by auto dealer Marge Schott. A limited partner since 1981, Schott is purchasing the shares of James and William Williams.

FEBRUARY 21:

Yankees' owner George Steinbrenner gives his manager, Yogi Berra, a vote of confidence in the *New York Times*, "Yogi will be the manager this year. I said the same thing last year; I'm saying it again this year. A bad start will not affect Yogi's status."

MARCH 13:

The *New York Times* reports from Fort Lauderdale, Florida, that major league baseball claims losses of $58 million in 1983. In figures released to the players, the owners predict they will lose $58 million this season. The owners' negotiator Lee MacPhail states: "It is evident that the majority of clubs continue to operate at a significant loss even with the increased television revenue." Players Association representative Donald Fehr tells the *Times* it is difficult to understand the numbers on the owners' chart and adds: "While I don't want to prejudge it, it raises an awful lot of questions."

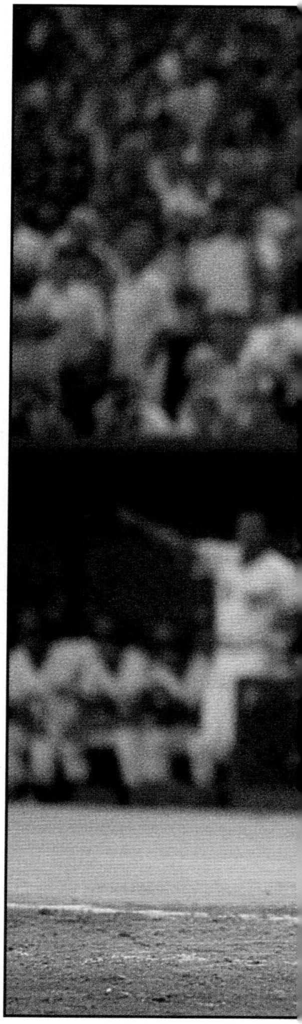

MARCH 25
The Cubs plans to begin night baseball at Wrigley Field are stalled by the courts.

APRIL 1
***Sports Illustrated* concocts the legend of Mets' pitching phenom Sidd Finch.**

MARCH 17:

Speaking today at New York City's Waldorf-Astoria Hotel, new baseball commissioner Peter Ueberroth says, "I'm pleased to welcome back to baseball Willie Mays and Mickey Mantle, effective immediately." The two Hall of Famers had been banned by previous Commissioner Bowie Kuhn because they were employed by companies with ties to legal gambling operations in Atlantic City, New Jersey.

Commissioner Peter Ueberroth says, "The world changes. I don't think we can start dictating who you can play golf with."

MARCH 25:

The Cubs' attempt to bring night baseball to Wrigley Field gets a setback. An Illinois judge finds that state and city laws against night baseball is constitutional. The Cubs had to give up a 1984 home playoff game because of the lack of lights and then instituted suit.

APRIL 1:

Sports Illustrated hits the newsstands with a story about the Mets' phenomenal rookie pitcher Sidd Finch. The pitcher reportedly

With hit number 4,192, Pete Rose is baseball's career hits leader.

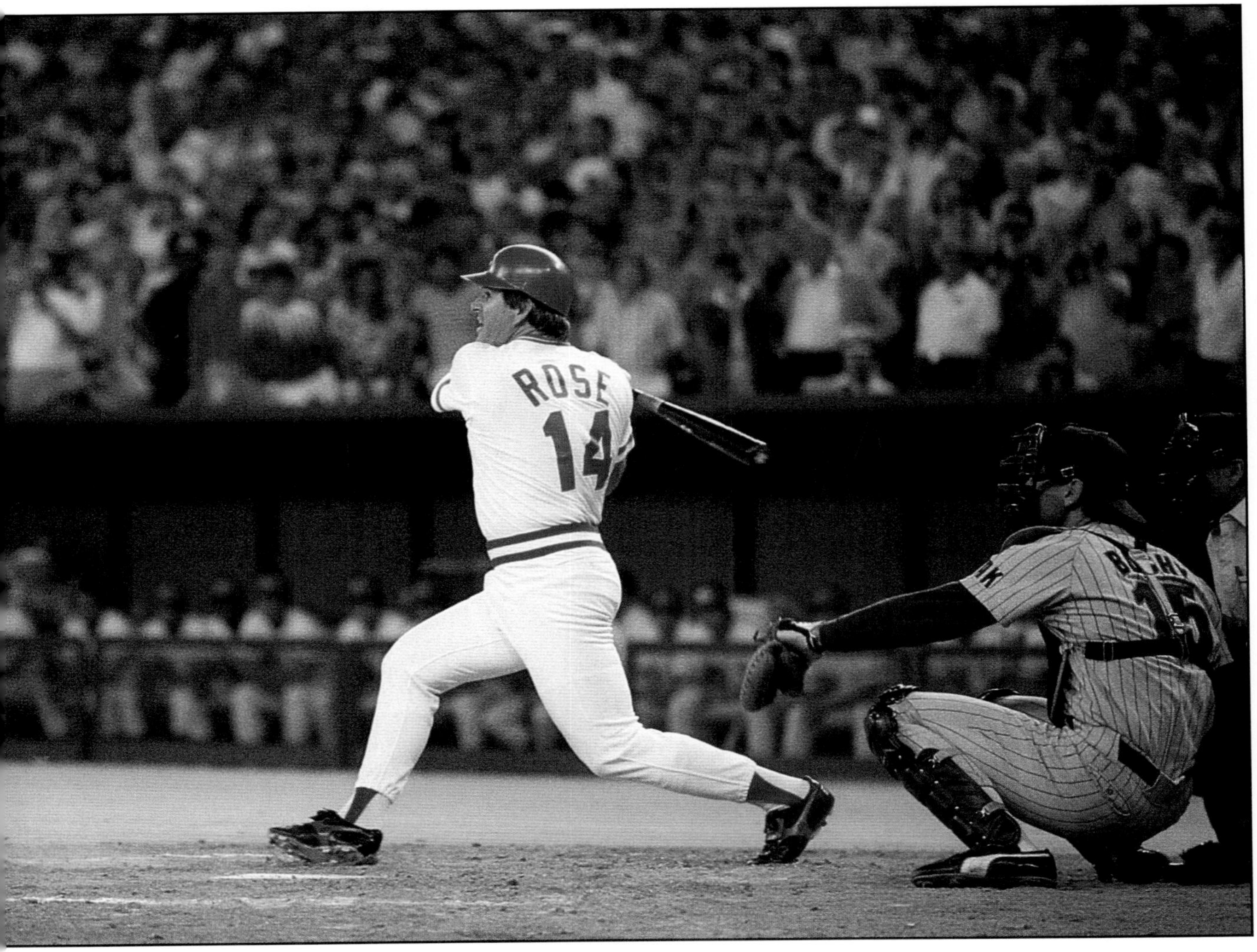

HISTORY

During the 1985 season, Nolan Ryan ties Tom Seaver's major league record of 200 strikeouts per season in 10 seasons.

is a Tibetan Buddhist monk who can throw 168 mph. Readers who are impressed with the description of Finch would do well to check the cover date of the magazine (April 1) and the story's byline (George Plimpton). As it turns out, "The Curious Case of Sidd Finch, Buddhist Pitcher" is an April Fool's joke.

APRIL 3:

Baseball's League Championship Series are altered from a best-of-five to a best-of-seven game format. The new structure is expected to produce $9 million in additional revenues. The ALCS will begin on October 8; the NLCS will begin on October 9. The World Series will start on October 19.

THE SEASON

APRIL 10:

On a third-inning pickoff play against the Rangers, Cal Ripken Jr., playing in his 444th consecutive game, sprains his ankle. Ripken remains in the lineup and post-game X-rays are negative.

APRIL 11:

The Mariners beat the Athletics, 16-4, on the strength of Gorman Thomas's trio of home runs and six runs batted in.

APRIL 13:

The Milwaukee Brewers' nonpariel closer Rollie Fingers records his 217th American League career save, breaking a record set by Albert "Sparky" Lyle. Overall, Fingers now has a major league record 325 saves. Milwaukee beats the Texas Rangers, 6-5. Starting pitcher Bob Gibson is credited with the win and Cecil Cooper bats in two runs.

APRIL 28:

Yankees' petulant owner George Steinbrenner strikes again. Only 16 games into the season and with the New York at 6-10, Yogi Berra is ousted as Yankees' manager and then replaced by – who else? – Billy Martin. This will be Martin's fourth stint as the ballclub's skipper.

Berra vows he never will set foot in Yankee Stadium "as long as he [owner George Steinbrenner] is still there." Berra holds to his vow, shunning Old-Timers' Days, dedications, and other special events. He will eventually reconcile with The Boss in 1999.

"THERE ARE CLOSE TO 11 MILLION UNEMPLOYED AND HALF OF THEM ARE NEW YORK YANKEES' MANAGERS."
– Johnny Carson

MAY 6:

Walter "Kirby" Higbe dies at age 70 in Columbia, South Carolina. A 22-game winner for the Dodgers in 1941, Higbe was 118-101 with a 3.69 ERA in his 12-year career.

MAY 17:

After 990 at-bats without a home run – the longest stretch by a non-pitcher – Mariner second baseman Jack Perconte breaks the ice. He hits a round-tripper at the Kingdome, but the visiting Orioles win the game, 11-3.

MAY 29:

In a case of the TV tail wagging the dog, all this year's World Series games will be played at night because ABC exercises an option in its contract with the major leagues. Until 1971, all series games were played in the daytime. Says Commissioner Peter Ueberroth: "The contract predates me."

JUNE 11:

The Phillies hammer the Mets, 26-7 on 27 hits; it is the worst defeat in the team's history. Von Hayes hits two home runs – including a grand slam – and drives in six runs in a nine-run first inning. No player ever has hit two homers in the opening frame; they are the only round-trippers of the game. The winning pitcher is Charlie Hudson; Tom P. Gorman gets the loss.

JUNE 13:

The Orioles lure 54-year-old Earl Weaver out of retirement to take over as manager. Weaver managed the team for 14 1/2 years, stepping down after the 1982 season. He replaces Joe Altobelli, who was 29-26. Cal Ripken Sr. handled the team for one game, a victory.

JUNE 18:

Commissioner Peter Ueberroth announces a mandatory drug test-

Phillies' shortstop Larry Bowa said of Lou Brock in 1976 to the *New York Times*: "Everybody in the park knows he's going to run and he makes it anyway."

ing program that will begin next month with players and umpires in the minor leagues. In August, major league managers, coaches, trainers, and umpires will be affected. In all, 4,000 will be covered in the program – but not major league players.

JUNE 27:

The Padres trade outfielder Alan Wiggins (.054 in 10 games), who is battling drug addiction, to the Orioles for pitcher Roy Lee Jackson (no appearances to date in 1985) and a player to be named later (pitcher Rich Caldwell on September 16).

JULY 1:

Baseball's oldest stadium, Comiskey Park, celebrates its 75th anniversary with 11 fans who attended its opening in 1910 present today. The Mariners spoil the occasion with a 3-1 win over the White Sox.

JULY 3:

Pitcher Steve Howe is released by the Dodgers after asserting he cannot "effectively handle many of the pressures I have here in the Los Angeles area." Howe, who missed a game on June 30, was suspended in 1984 for cocaine use. He is 1-1 with a 4.91 ERA. Howe subsequently is signed by the Twins for $450,000.

JULY 4:

The Mets beat the Braves, 16-13, in 19 innings, with Keith Hernandez hitting for the cycle. The game – halted twice by rain – ends at 3:55 A.M. on July 5. Scheduled Independence Day fireworks finally are launched at 4:01 A.M. Pitcher Rick Camp, the only Braves player left and a .062 lifetime hitter, homers with two outs in the 18th to tie the game at 12-12. Camp strikes out in the 19th to end the game and is the losing pitcher.

JULY 11:

In Houston today, starter Nolan Ryan of the Houston Astros fans the New York Mets' Danny Heep on three pitches in the sixth inning to become the first pitcher to reach 4,000 strikeouts. The Astros win the game, 4-3, in 12 innings. Bill Doran's fifth hit of the game produces the winning run. Ryan strikes out 11 batters in the eight innings he works and brings his season total of strikeouts to 130.

JULY 16:

In Minnesota, the NL wins the All-Star Game, 6-1. It is the senior circuit's 21st victory in 23 games. The winning pitcher is LaMarr Hoyt; Jack Morris gets the loss. Sparky Anderson – who lost with the NL in 1971 – becomes the first manager with a loss for each league.

JULY 19:

The Cubs, unable to play post-season games in Wrigley Field because there are no lights, turn down an offer to play in the home of the White Sox, Comiskey Park. The team, if it makes the playoffs, will use an NL ballpark.

JULY 23:

Braves pitcher Pascual Perez is suspended indefinitely after he jumps the team following a July 21, 15-10 loss to the Mets in New York. Perez yielded seven runs and seven hits in the game, bringing his ERA to 6.52 with a 1-8 record. According to his agent, Tom Reich, Perez is in a New York City hotel.

JULY 28:

The Hall of Fame inducts Lou Brock, Enos Slaughter, Arky Vaughn, and Hoyt Wilhelm. Brock, who played with the Cubs and Cardinals, batted .293 over 19 years, but was acclaimed as a base stealer; his career total was 938. In 1974, he set the major league season record by stealing 118. Not known for his glove, Brock appeared in three World Series, batting .391 and stealing an all-time high 14 bases. Slaughter, a hard-nosed outfielder known as Country, played 19 years – 13 with the Cardinals. His lifetime average was an even .300 and he was a .300 hitter 10 times. Slaughter appeared in five World Series and batted .291. Vaughn, who drowned in 1952, was a shortstop who hit .318 over 14 years. He batted .300 or better 12 times, with a high of .385 in 1935. Vaughn played for the Pirates and Dodgers, appearing in one World Series for Brooklyn and batting .500. Wilhelm, arguably the greatest knuckleball pitcher of all time, played 21 years, winning 143 and losing 122, with an ERA of 2.52 and 227 saves. He ranks first in games pitched with 1,070 and in relief victories (124). Wilhelm pitched until he was 49 years old and was unconditionally released on nine occasions.

CULTURE

The Thrill of the Grass* is a collection of short stories by W.P. Kinsella, author of *Shoeless Joe.

HISTORY

Before the start of game four of the NLCS, light rain is falling in St. Louis. Cardinals' outfielder Vince Coleman is walking off the field when the 150-foot-long cylinder of the automatic tarpaulin machine begins unrolling. It runs over Coleman's left foot and up his leg, causing a bone chip in his knee and bruises. Coleman is out for the entire post-season. He is replaced in leftfield by Terry "Tito" Landrum, who has four hits and three RBI.

In September, with the Yankees and Blue Jays in a race for the AL East title, New York owner George Steinbrenner laments: "Where is Reggie Jackson? We need a Mr. October or a Mr. September. Winfield is Mr. May. My big guys are not coming through."

CULTURE

The Babe, starring Max Gail as the Bambino, is the TV version of his one-man play.

HISTORY

On the day he sets the career hits record, a tearful Pete Rose is presented with a red Corvette bearing the license plate: PR 4192; it is a gift from the team's owner, Marge Schott.

The Royals celebrate their World Series win.

AUGUST 4
The Angels' Rod Carew, 39, becomes the 16th player in major league history with 3,000 hits.

AUGUST 20
Dwight Gooden is the first NLer with 200 strikeouts in each of his first two seasons.

JULY 29:

Smoky Joe Wood, regarded as one of the hardest throwers of all time, dies at age 95 in a West Haven, Connecticut, convalescent home. Wood's pitching career was shortened by an injury and he came back as an outfielder. Pitching 11 years, for the Red Sox and Indians, he was 116-57 with a 2.03 ERA. In 1912 with Boston, he was 34-5 with a 1.91 ERA and 10 shutouts. He was 3-1 for the Red Sox in the 1912 World Series. He had a lifetime batting average of .283

AUGUST 4:

Batting against Frank Viola of the Twins in the third inning, Rod Carew of the Angels singles for his 3,000th career hit. The 39-year-old Carew spent 12 years with Minnesota and is the 16th player to reach the 3,000 hit plateau. The Angels win the game, 6-5.

While Carew is reaching a hitting landmark, Tom Seaver records his 300th win, beating the Yankees 4-1 on a six-hitter before 54,032 at Yankee Stadium during Phil Rizzuto Day. The 40-year-old Seaver is the 17th pitcher to reach the 300-win mark.

AUGUST 6:

After nine months of negotiations for a new basic agreement lead nowhere, the players strike for the second time in five seasons. The issues include free agency, arbitration, and salary minimums.

AUGUST 7:

After only two days and the cancellation of 25 games, the strike ends. The owners drop their demand for an arbitration salary cap and the players approve an increase in arbitration eligibility from two years to three. Also negotiated is an end to the reentry draft; teams may now negotiate with any free agents. Salary minimums are increased from $40,000 to $50,000. The NL will add two teams to equal the AL's present 14. A new, five-year basic agreement is signed at 10:45 p.m. and play resumes tomorrow.

AUGUST 20:

The Mets' Dwight Gooden retires 16 Giants batters on strikes and becomes the first NLer with 200 strikeouts in each of his first two seasons. The Mets win the game, 3-0.

AUGUST 25:

The Mets' Dwight Gooden beats the Padres, 9-3, for his 20th win of the season. At the age of 20, Gooden is the youngest 20-game winner in baseball history. Until today, Bob Feller — in 1939 – was baseball's youngest 20-game winner. Gooden beats him by one month.

AUGUST 26:

Former major league outfielder Dick Wakefield, considered baseball's first "bonus baby," dies in Wayne County, Michigan, at age 64. Signed out of the University of Michigan for $52,000 and a car, he was a player of enormous – but mostly unfulfilled talent. Wakefield played nine years, hitting .293. In 1944, he batted .355.

AUGUST 29:

Ouch! The Yankees' Don Baylor is hit by a pitch from Kirk McCaskill of the Angels in the first inning of today's game. It is the 190th time in his career he has been hit by a pitch – breaking the AL record of 189 by Minnie Minoso. Ron Hunt holds the major league mark – 243. The Yankees win, 4-0.

AUGUST 31:

The Los Angeles Dodgers acquire third baseman Bill "Mad Dog" Madlock (.251) from the Pittsburgh Pirates for three players to be named later. Madlock has twice been the National League batting champion.

The Pirates receive outfielder R.J. Reynolds (.266) on September 3 and first baseman Sid Bream (.132) and minor league outfielder Cecil Espy on September 9.

SEPTEMBER 6:

The Reds' Pete Rose continues his pursuit of Ty Cobb's career base hit record. Today, against the Cubs, Rose homers against Derek Botelho for his 4,188th hit and then singles in the 6th inning off Reggie Patterson.

SEPTEMBER 8:

Pete Rose singles in the first inning and again in the fifth – both times against the Cubs' Reggie Patterson – to tie Ty Cobb at 4,191 hits. Rose is hitless in his next two at-bats.

LEAGUE

Pittsburgh Associates reaches an agreement in principle with the Galbreath family to purchase the Pirates. As a result, the team will remain in Pittsburgh. The purchasing group is composed of Carnegie-Mellon University, the Aluminum Company of America, Mellon Bank, PNC Financial Corporation, PPG Industries, USX Corporation, Westinghouse Electric Co., Eugene and Raymond Litman, John McConnell, and Harvey M. Walken.

"What they start,
I finish."
– Closer Rollie Fingers

LEAGUE

In June, the Pirates make 20-year-old Barry Bonds their first pick in the free-agent draft. The son of former major leaguer Bobby Bonds, he is the sixth pick overall in the draft.

HISTORY

Reggie Jackson of the Angels strikes out 138 times this season. He is the first player with the dubious distinction of striking out 100 times in 17 consecutive seasons – not counting the strike-shortened 1981 season, in which he went down on strikes "only" 82 times.

SEPTEMBER 9:

The Mariners' Gorman Thomas homers in a 12-inning, 8-7 win over the Indians at the Kingdome. It is Thomas's 250th career round-tripper and his 30th homer of this season.

SEPTEMBER 10:

Keith Hernandez, who testified as an immune witness last week in the Pittsburgh drug trial of Curtis Strong and admitted using cocaine, gets a 30-second standing ovation and flowers – with some boos – from New York fans as he takes the field at Shea Stadium against the St. Louis Cardinals. The Mets win, 5-4; Hernandez has a single.

SEPTEMBER 11:

Fifty-seven years to the day after Ty Cobb played his last game, Pete Rose of the Reds hits a single off San Diego's Eric Show for his 4,192nd hit, breaking the Georgia Peach's career record. Rose collects his historic hit at 8:01 p.m. at Riverfront Stadium. Petey Rose, 15 years old, leads his father's teammates onto the field to salute their 44-year-old teammate. Rose later triples and scores twice in a 2-0 Cincinnati victory.

BURLEIGH GRIMES WAS A TOUGH MAN. ST. LOUIS SPORTSWRITER BOB BROEG ONCE DESCRIBED THE FEUD BETWEEN GRIMES AND FRANKIE FRISCH: "ONE DAY, FRISCH DRAG-BUNTED DOWN THE FIRST BASE LINE AND ACCIDENTALLY SPIKED GRIMES AS THEY RACED TO THE BAG; HE ALMOST SEVERED ONE OF THE TENDONS IN BURLEIGH'S ANKLES, WHICH WOULD HAVE RUINED HIS CAREER. SO SOMETIME LATER, FRISCH, BEFORE A GAME, SAID, '...BURLEIGH, I NEVER MEANT TO DO THAT TO YOU.' BUT THE NEXT TIME FRANKIE CAME UP, BURLEIGH HIT 'IM AND THE WAR WAS ON AGAIN. ON THE WAY DOWN TO FIRST BASE, FRISCH YELLS, '...BURLEIGH, I APOLOGIZED.' AND BURLEIGH SAYS, 'YES, BUT YOU DIDN'T SMILE.'"

SEPTEMBER 12:

Billy Martin gets into a fight with Yankees pitcher Ed Whitson, who'd been having an argument with a guest in a Baltimore hotel. Martin gets kicked and punched and ends up with a broken right arm, bruises, and lacerations. Whitson has a broken rib and a cut lip.

SEPTEMBER 15:

Astros' outfielder Jose Cruz collects his 2,000th career hit in a 2-1 victory over The Padres.

The Yankees acquire Joe Niekro (9-12) from the Astros for minor league pitcher Jim Deshaies and two players to be named later.

On January 1, 1986, Houston receives two minor leaguers – infielder Neder Horta and pitcher Dody Rather – to complete the trade.

SEPTEMBER 16:

The Twins release Steve Howe after he suffers a relapse of his substance abuse problem. Howe was 3-4 with a 5.49 ERA with the Dodgers and Twins. Howe, who

SEPTEMBER 11
Pete Rose breaks Ty Cobb's record and becomes the all-time hits leader, with 4,192.

OCTOBER 6
On the last day of the season, Phil Niekro records his 300th career victory.

has been missing since September 12, admits he used drugs last weekend and will enter a rehabilitation program at St. Mary's Hospital in Minneapolis.

SEPTEMBER 17:

The Brewers' Rollie Fingers works a third of an inning against the Orioles, ending his brilliant major league career. Fingers, 1-6 with a 5.04 ERA and 17 saves this season, finishes his 17 major league seasons with a 114-188 record, a 2.90 ERA, and 341 saves. Baltimore beats Milwaukee, 6-0, today.

SEPTEMBER 20:

After a 14-day trial, Philadelphia caterer Curtis Strong is found guilty of 11 counts of cocaine sale to major league players between 1980 and 1983. Six others are convicted along with Strong and they receive sentences of up to 12 years. Immune witnesses in the trial included major leaguers Keith Hernandez, Lonnie Smith, Dave Parker, Jeffrey Leonard, Dale Berra, John Milner, and Enos Cabell.

SEPTEMBER 24:

At Wrigley Field, the Expos score 12 runs in the fifth inning and beat the Cubs, 17-15. Montreal's big inning features 10 hits, two walks, and one Chicago error. Andre Dawson has a pair of three-run homers and eight RBI in the game; Tim Wallach hits a two-run round-tripper.

SEPTEMBER 28:

Cardinals manager Dorrel "Whitey" Herzog, in an interview in today's *Washington Post*, says 11 Cardinals were "heavy" drug users in the early 1980s. He recalls: "One day in Montreal our pitcher hit an Expo – the guy who might have been the biggest dealer in the league – with a pitch. One of my own infielders comes in and chews out our pitcher on the mound because he's afraid his drug dealer is going to get beaned."

OCTOBER 2:

The Dodgers and Orel Hershiser beat the Braves, 9-3, and win the NL West. Hershiser improves his record to 19-3.

OCTOBER 5:

In Toronto, the Blue Jays beat the Yankees, 5-1, for the AL East title. It is the first ever in their nine-year history. The Cardinals, at Busch Stadium, beat the Cubs, 7-1, to take the NL East. The Royals top the Athletics, 5-4, in Kansas City, to sew up the AL West.

OCTOBER 6:

On the last day of the season, Phil Niekro of the Yankees four-hits the Blue Jays, 8-0, in Toronto to join the circle of 300-game winners. He is the 18th pitcher with 300 victories. At age 46, Niekro also becomes the oldest pitcher to hurl a complete-game shutout. Niekro, who fans Jeff Burroughs on his first knuckleball of the game for the final out, had failed to win his 300th on four previous attempts. Niekro is 16-12 on the season and 300-250 lifetime.

REGULAR SEASON WRAP-UP:

The Cardinals, under Dorrel "Whitey" Herzog, finish at 101-61. Willie McGee is the NL's top hitter at .353 and has 82 RBI. Rookie Vince Coleman – out of the series with an injury – has 100 stolen bases; he's the third NLer to reach that level. Tommy Herr bats .302; Jack Clark hits 22 homers and drives in 87 runs with a .281 average. John Tudor at 21-8 and a 1.93 ERA and Joaquin Andujar, 21-12, lead the staff. Jeff Lahti has 19 saves. Dick Howser's Royals are 91-71 in the AL. At .335, George Brett is the team's only .300 hitter. He also has 30 homers and 112 RBI. Steve Balboni, a .243 hitter, has 36 homers and 88 RBI. Frank White hits 22 homers with a .249 average. Bret Saberhagen is the pitching ace at 20-6 with a 2.87 ERA. Dan Quisenberry registers a league-leading 37 saves.

The Pittsburgh Pirates' Jose DeLeon compiles the worst winning percentage of any 20th-century pitcher with a minimum of 20 decisions – .095 with a 2-19 record. The Reds' Tom Browning becomes the first rookie since 1954 to win 20 games. Pitcher Don Sutton, who split the season between the Athletics and Angels, becomes the first major leaguer to strike out 100 batters or more for 20 consecutive seasons. Darrell Evans of the Tigers is the first to hit 40 home runs in each league. Wade Boggs of the Red Sox collects 240 hits – 187 are singles – the most one-base hits in the AL since 1928, when Heinie Manush had 241 singles.

HISTORY

Dwight Gooden, 20 years old, is the youngest Cy Young Award winner.

LEAGUE

Ex-President Richard M. Nixon, selected earlier this month to arbitrate the pay dispute with major league umpires, makes his decision. The umpires will get a 40 percent increase in pay for League Championship Series. The increase will move the compensation from $12,000 up to $14,000 for the series.

OCTOBER 16
The Royals and Cardinals win their respective LCS and will meet in the I-70 Series.

HISTORY

In February, outfielder Tim Raines of the Expos sets a record with a $1.2-million arbitration salary award. Raines batted .309, with eight homers and 75 stolen bases last season.

LEAGUE

Commissioner Peter Ueberroth and the owners meet in St. Louis and, according to author and agent Randal A. Hendricks, the teams get "exclusive control over the players on its rosters who would become free agents." Hendricks writes: "This was collusion officially born."

OCTOBER 8:

ALCS, game one. In a Toronto night game before 39,115, the Blue Jays beat the Royals, 6-1. Dave Stieb is the winner; Charlie Leibrandt is tagged with the loss. Ernie Whitt and Tony Fernandez each bat in two runs.

OCTOBER 9:

NLCS, game one. The Dodgers beat the Cardinals, 4-1, in Los Angeles. Fernando Valenzuela is the winner, with relief from Tom Niedenfuer. The losing pitcher is Cardinals starter John Tudor.

ALCS, game two. In Toronto, the Blue Jays win again, 6-5, in 10 innings, despite Royals home runs by Willie Wilson and Pat Sheridan. The winning pitcher is reliever Tom Henke; the losing pitcher is Dan Quisenberry. Al Oliver's two-out, two-run single wins the game for Toronto.

OCTOBER 10:

NLCS, game two. The Dodgers make it two in a row with a 13-hit, 8-2 victory. Orel Hershiser goes the distance, allowing eight hits. Joaquin Andujar, the first of five St. Louis pitchers, gets the loss. Greg Brock hits a two-run home run for Los Angeles; every Dodger regular has at least one hit.

OCTOBER 11:

ALCS, game three. In Kansas City, the Royals win their first game of the playoffs, 6-5. Steve Farr gets the victory in relief; Jim Clancy is the loser. George Brett hits two home runs for the Royals, Jim Sundberg, one. Brett is four for four with three RBI and four runs. Jesse Barfield and Rance Mulliniks homer for Toronto.

OCTOBER 12:

NLCS, game three. Today the Cardinals rebound with a 4-2 victory at home, stealing three bases, collecting eight hits, and capitalizing on two Dodger errors. The winning pitcher is Danny Cox; Ken Dayley gets the save. Tommy Herr hits a solo homer for St. Louis. Bob Welch is the losing pitcher.

ALCS, game four. In Kansas City, the Toronto Blue Jays forge ahead, three games to one, on a 3-1 win, scoring all their runs in the ninth inning. Al Oliver hits a two-run pinch-hit double for the victory. Tom Henke gets credit for the win in relief of Dave Stieb; Charlie Leibrandt is the loser.

AFTER HIS RECORD 1961 SEASON, MARIS SAID: "AS A BALLPLAYER, I WOULD BE DELIGHTED TO DO IT AGAIN. AS AN INDIVIDUAL, I DOUBT IF I COULD POSSIBLY GO THROUGH IT AGAIN."

OCTOBER 13:

ALCS, game five. In Kansas City, the Royals top the Blue Jays, 2-0, on a complete-game eight-hitter by Danny Jackson. Jimmy Key takes the loss for Toronto. Lonnie Smith has three hits for Kansas City.

NLCS, game four. The Cardinals pound the Dodgers, 12-2, on 15 hits. St. Louis scores a playoff record nine runs in the second inning to bury Los Angeles. Bill Madlock homers for one of the Dodgers' two runs. The winning pitcher is John Tudor; Jerry Reuss gets the loss.

OCTOBER 14:

NLCS, game five. The Cardinals win, 3-2, on Ozzie Smith's solo homer with one out in the bottom of the ninth. Jeff Lahti, the Cardinals' fourth pitcher of the day, gets the win. Tom Niedenfuer is tagged with the loss. Bill Madlock's homer accounts for both Los Angeles runs.

Today's home run is the first for switch-hitting Ozzie Smith when he's batting left-handed.

OCTOBER 17
George Steinbrenner, not the be outdone by the start of the Series, fires Billy Martin.

OCTOBER 20
In game two of the World Series, the Cards rally for four runs and beat the Royals, 4-2.

OCTOBER 15:

ALCS, game six. In Toronto, the Royals tie the playoffs with a 5-3 victory. Starter Mark Gubicza is the winner with help from a George Brett home run hit in the fifth inning. Doyle Alexander is charged with the loss.

OCTOBER 16:

ALCS, game seven. In Toronto, Kansas City wins, 6-2, for its third victory in a row and the AL pennant. Charlie Leibrandt is the winner in relief of Royals starter Bret Saberhagen. Dave Stieb is the loser. Pat Sheridan homers for the winners.

NLCS, game six. In Los Angeles, the Cardinals beat the Dodgers, 7-5, to win the NL pennant. Jack Clark's three-run homer into the left-field bleachers off losing pitcher Tom Niedenfuer with two out in the ninth gives St. Louis the win. Mike Marshall and Bill Madlock had solo homers for the Dodgers. Todd Worrell gets the win and Ken Dayley records a save.

OCTOBER 17:

George Steinbrenner indulges his taste for making news during the World Series. He fires manager Billy Martin and replaces him with Lou Piniella. The Yankees finished at 97-64 in second place in the AL East. Martin had replaced Yogi Berra after only 16 games.

OCTOBER 19:

World Series, game one. The I-70 Series (nicknamed for the highway linking Kansas City and St. Louis) begins. The visiting Cardinals beat the Royals, 3-1. John Tudor gets the win with a save by Todd Worrell. Starter Danny Jackson is the loser.

OCTOBER 20:

World Series, game two. At Kansas City, the Cardinals win again, 4-2, scoring all their runs in the ninth inning. The winning pitcher is Ken Dayley; the loser Charlie Leibrandt, who was within an out of victory. He then yields hits to Jack Clark and Tito Landrum and a bases-loaded double to Terry Pendleton. For the second consecutive game, there are no home runs.

OCTOBER 22:

World Series, game three. In St. Louis, the Royals record their first win, 6-1, on

Jack Clark hits 22 homers for the Cardinals.

"It would have been a helluva lot more fun if I had never hit those 61 home runs."
– Roger Maris, on the 1961 season

CULTURE

Movie fans can see *The Slugger's Wife*, by Neil Simon, starring Michael O'Keefe and Rebecca DeMornay, and *Brewster's Millions*, starring Richard Pryor as a major league pitcher, and John Candy.

CULTURE

Theatergoers see *Bingo!* a musical based on William Brashler's novel The *Bingo Long Traveling All-Stars and Motor Kings*, starring Norman Matlock and David Winston Barge; and *The Flatbush Faithful* by Gene Nye.

the strong right arm of Bret Saberhagen. He pitches a six-hit complete game, while Joaquin Andujar gets the loss. Frank White hits a homer for the Royals; he also has a double and three RBI.

OCTOBER 23:

World Series, game four. Today in St. Louis, the Cardinals are within one game of winning the Series as a result of today's 3-0 win on a complete-game five-hitter by starting pitcher John Tudor, who fans eight. Harry "Bud" Black takes the loss for Kansas City. Tito Landrum and Willie McGee hit home runs for the Cardinals.

OCTOBER 24:

World Series, game five. In St. Louis, the Royals again stave off disaster on Danny Jackson's 6-0 complete-game, five-hit victory. Willie Wilson's two-run triple in a three-run second inning paces the Royals. Bob Forsch is charged with the loss. Todd Worrell of St. Louis fans six consecutive Royals in two innings, tying a Series record.

OCTOBER 25:

Jimy Williams replaces Bobby Cox as manager of the Blue Jays. Toronto finished in first in the AL East with a 99-62 record last season. Cox will become general manager of the Atlanta Braves.

OCTOBER 26:

World Series, game six. In Kansas City, 41,628 see the Royals continue their amazing comeback and tie the Series at three games apiece – with help from a disputed call at first base in the ninth. Submariner Dan Quisenberry, in relief of Charlie Leibrandt, gets credit for the 2-1 win. Todd Worrell is hit with the loss. In the bottom of the ninth, with the Cardinals ahead, 1-0, umpire Don Denkinger calls Jorge Orta safe at first on a close play. The Royals go on to score twice on pinch hitter Dane Iorg's single for the victory.

OCTOBER 27:

World Series, game seven. The Royals are the first team in history to come back to win the World Championship after losing their first two games at home. Bret Saberhagen pitches a complete game five-hitter, and the Royals win, 11-0. Darryl Motley hits a two-run homer for the winners. John Tudor took the loss in a game in which the Royals bat around in both the third inning and fifth inning. The Cardinals use a record five pitchers in the fateful six-run fifth. Saberhagen, who was 2-0 in the Series with an ERA of 0.50, is named Most Valuable Player. George Brett leads all hitters with .370; teammate Willie Wilson bats .367. Tito Landrum has a .360 average for the Cardinals.

POST-SEASON

NOVEMBER 20:

Jim Leyland becomes the new manager of the Pirates, replacing Chuck Tanner, who was 57-104 with a last-place finish in the National League East.

DECEMBER 6:

Hall of Famer hurler Burleigh Grimes, who was the last legal spitball pitcher, dies at age 92 in Clear Lake, Wisconsin. Grimes pitched in the majors from 1916 through 1934, compiling a 270-212 record with a 3.53 ERA. He was inducted into the Hall of Fame in 1964.

DECEMBER 10:

The Cardinals trade tempestuous pitcher Joaquin Andujar (21-12, 3.40 ERA) to the Athletics for catcher Mike Heath (.250, 13 homers) and pitcher Tim Conroy (0-1, 4.26 ERA).

DECEMBER 14:

Roger Maris, an outstanding outfielder and one of the most-misunderstood baseball player of modern times, dies at age 51 in Houston. A two-time AL Most Valuable Player, Maris compiled a .260 batting average with 275 homers in 12 years. He appeared in seven World Series, batting only .217 with six homers. Of course, Maris will be best remembered for his historic performance in 1961 while playing with the New York Yankees. Maris was locked in a season-long home run battle with teammate Mickey Mantle. The Mick dropped out with an injury late in the season, and then Maris went on to set a new single-season record, with 61 homers, which also broke Babe Ruth's long-standing record of 60 round-trippers.

Of criticism that he broke the record in 161 contests compared to Ruth's 154-game schedule, Maris said, "A season's a season."

OCTOBER 27
The Royals are World Champions, beating the Cardinals in game seven of the Series.

THE BEST OF 1985

NATIONAL LEAGUE

HITTERS

Batting Average:
Willie McGee, St. Louis Cardinals, .353

Slugging Average:
Pedro Guerrero, Los Angeles Dodgers, .577

Home Runs:
Dale Murphy, Atlanta Braves, 37

Runs Batted In:
Dave Parker, Cincinnati Reds, 125

Hits:
Willie McGee, 216

Stolen Bases:
Vince Coleman, St. Louis Cardinals, 110

PITCHERS

Wins:
Dwight "Doc" Gooden, New York Mets, 24

Strikeouts:
Dwight Gooden, 268

Earned Run Average:
Dwight Gooden, 1.53

Winning Percentage:
Orel Hershiser, Los Angeles Dodgers, .864

Saves:
Jeff Reardon, Montreal Expos, 41

Most Valuable Player:
Willie McGee, St. Louis Cardinals

Cy Young Award:
Dwight Gooden, New York Mets

Rookie of the Year:
Vince Coleman, St. Louis Cardinals

Manager of the Year:
Dorrel "Whitey" Herzog, St. Louis Cardinals

AMERICAN LEAGUE

HITTERS

Batting Average:
Wade Boggs, Boston Red Sox, .368

Slugging Average:
George Brett, Kansas City Royals, .585

Home Runs:
Darrell Evans, Detroit Tigers, 40

Runs Batted In:
Don Mattingly, New York Yankees, 145

Hits:
Wade Boggs, 240

Stolen Bases:
Rickey Henderson, New York Yankees, 80

PITCHERS

Wins:
Ron Guidry, New York Yankees, 22

Strikeouts:
Bert Blyleven, Cleveland Indians/Minnesota Twins, 206

Earned Run Average:
Dave Stieb, Toronto Blue Jays, 2.48

Winning Percentage:
Ron Guidry, .786

Saves:
Dan Quisenberry, Kansas City Royals, 37

Most Valuable Player:
Don Mattingly, New York Yankees

Cy Young Award:
Bret Saberhagen, Kansas City Royals

Rookie of the Year:
Ozzie Guillen, Chicago White Sox

Manager of the Year:
Bobby Cox, Toronto Blue Jays

CULTURE

Song-lovers hear "Baseball Dreams" performed by the Naturals, with Mel Allen, the voice of the Yankees, and "Centerfield" by John Fogerty.

1986

"Baseball is a game to be savored rather than taken in gulps."
– *Bill Veeck*

The Rocket's glare helps him to a Cy Young season.

NEWS

SEVEN ASTRONAUTS DIE IN *CHALLENGER* SPACE SHUTTLE EXPLOSION

Reagan, Gorbachev exchange New Year's TV appearances

HAITI'S DUVALIER, PHILIPPINE'S MARCOS OUSTED

U.S. BOMBS LIBYA

SUPREME COURT REAFFIRMS ABORTION RIGHTS

IRAN-CONTRA SCANDAL BREAKS

Cary Grant dies

ELIE WIESEL WINS NOBEL PEACE PRIZE

Four Americans die in terror bombing of TWA plane

OLIVER STONE'S VIETNAM FILM, *PLATOON*, EARNS BEST PICTURE, DIRECTOR OSCARS

Nintendo video games debut

PRE-SEASON

JANUARY 1:

Mike "The Big Bear" Garcia, a mainstay of the Indians' pitching staff throughout the 1950s, dies at age 62 in Fairview Park, Ohio. In 14 years, Garcia was 142-97 with a 3.27 ERA. He twice led the AL in ERA and shutouts.

JANUARY 2:

One of baseball's most astute and zaniest executives, Bill Veeck, dies at age 71 of cardiac arrest at Illinois Masonic Medical Center in Chicago. Veeck, who owned the Browns, White Sox, and Indians, had been in ill health for many years. Among his innovations were an exploding scoreboard and players' names on the backs of their uniforms. He broke the AL color barrier by signing Larry Doby to an Indians' contract in 1947 and brought the legendary Negro Leagues star Satchel Paige to the majors. He also concocted such offbeat stunts as sending a midget in to pinch hit.

JANUARY 8:

Outfielder-DH Kirk Gibson (.287, 29 homers, 97 RBI, 30 stolen bases), who had his bags packed for other parts, opts to remain in Detroit and the Tigers make it worthwhile. Gibson gets a $4-million, three-year contract with a $100,000 attendance bonus.

FEBRUARY 3:

The Baseball Players Association files a grievance, charging the owners with collusion on free agents.

FEBRUARY 14:

The Dodgers' Bill Madlock, fingered by two players as a supplier of amphetamines, gets a Valentine from the commissioner's office. Peter Ueberroth clears him, stating, "Bill Madlock's reputation on and off the field is above reproach."

FEBRUARY 15:

The Dodgers give Fernando Valenzuela (17-10, 2.45 ERA, 211 strikeouts, five shutouts) a three-year, $5.5 million contract, making him the first player with a $2 million-plus annual salary. He tops the Cubs' Rick Sutcliffe, who is earning "only" $1.8 million per season.

FEBRUARY 17:

Hall of Fame pitcher Charles "Red" Ruffing dies at the age of 81 in Mayfield Heights, Ohio. Inducted into the Hall of Fame in 1967, Ruffing pitched for 22 years compiling a 273-225 record with a 3.80 ERA. A good-hitting pitcher, he had a .269 lifetime average. He pitched in seven World Series and was 7-2.

FEBRUARY 27:

A natural gas explosion rocks the clubhouse at the Brewers' Chandler, Arizona, spring training camp. Manager George Bamberger – back with the Brewers – general manager Harry Dalton, catcher Bill Schroeder, pitcher Bill Wegman, and coaches Tony Muser, Herman Starrette, Larry Haney, and Andy Etchebarren are injured. Muser has severe burns and requires skin grafts.

FEBRUARY 28:

Commissioner Peter Ueberroth suspends seven players for drug use. All seven choose to contribute 10 percent of a season's salary to drug abuse programs and perform 100 hours of community service plus agree to random testing. This was one of two alternatives offered by the commissioner; the other was a one-year suspension. Ueberroth

Don Sutton on whether he uses "foreign" substances on the ball: "Not true at all. Vaseline is manufactured right here in the United States of America."

HISTORY

The *New York Times* reports Royals' pitcher Bret Saberhagen is suing Rawlings over an endorsement deal. In a time when mega-bucks are being paid to athletes, Rawlings is compensating Saberhagen with two gloves per season – and the sporting goods company has an option for 10 more years. The 1985 Cy Young Award winner signed the less-than-lucrative contract in March 1983 before his first major league season. He charges Rawlings misrepresented the deal and it is costing him $50,000.

charges that the seven – the Mets' Keith Hernandez; the Yankees' Dale Berra, son of Yogi Berra; the Athletics' Joaquin Andujar; the Giants' Jeffrey Leonard; the Royals' Lonnie Smith; the Dodgers' Enos Cabell; and the Reds' Dave Parker – used drugs or "facilitated the spread of drugs in baseball." Lesser penalties are given to 14 other players.

MARCH 13:

Hal McRae, age 39, and his 18-year-old son, Brian, appear together for the Royals in a pre-season game against the Phillies. Brian singles and steals second against Shane Rawley in the first inning; his dad walks. Kansas City manager Dick Howser describes the event as the Big Mac Attack. Brian is expected to be sent to the minor leagues next week for further seasoning.

MARCH 22:

It's bad news at the Yankees' spring training camp today. Pitcher Britt Burns, an 18-game winner who was obtained in a December trade with the White Sox, is suffering from a degenerative hip condition and will miss the entire season.

The 25-year-old Burns never plays in the majors again, finishing his eight-year career with a 70-60 record and a 3.66 ERA.

MARCH 28:

The Yankees send DH-outfielder-first baseman Don Baylor (.231, 23 homers, 91 RBI) to the Red Sox for DH-outfielder Mike Easler (.262, 16 homers, 74 RBI).

Says Yankees' owner George Steinbrenner: "Baylor's bat will be dead by August." It isn't; Baylor bats only .238, but hits 31 homers and drives in 94 runs.

THE SEASON

APRIL 8:

At the Astrodome, Will Clark makes his major league debut with the Giants and homers against the Astros' Nolan Ryan in his first at bat. He is the 53rd player to hit a round-tripper in-his first turn at the plate.

APRIL 18:

In Milwaukee, the Rangers' Bobby Witt loses a no-hitter without yielding a safety. Witt renders the Brewers hitless through five innings and strikes out 10. But he issues eight walks, throws two wild pitches, and allows two runs. Manager Bobby Valentine removes him and Texas goes on to win, 7-5. Witt not only loses the chance for a no-hitter, he does n't even get the win. It goes to Greg A. Harris. The losing pitcher is Ray Searage. Steve Buechle and Don Slaught both homer for Texas.

APRIL 19:

In Seattle today, the Athletics beat the Mariners, 7-2, and the two teams combine for a record 30 strikeouts. Winning pitcher Jose Rijo, fans 16 Seattle batters; his teammate Bill Mooneyham adds two more. For the Mariners, Mark Langston whiffs five, Bill Swift two, Mike Morgan and Karl Best one each. Except for Alvin Davis of the Mariners, every starter on both teams strikes out at least once. Gorman Thomas and Danny Tartabull of the Mariners are victimized four times.

APRIL 26:

The Twins' game with the visiting Angels is interrupted for nine minutes in the bottom of the seventh when wind tears the inflatable roof off the Metrodome.

A promotion at Arlington Stadium backfires when some in the crowd of 25,499 make the Rangers and the umpires targets of hundreds of the free baseballs during the seventh inning while the visiting Brewers are rallying. Milwaukee wins, 10-2.

APRIL 27:

Former major leaguer Leron Lee sets a career home run record for foreign players in Japan when he hits his 246th today. Lee, the DH for the Lotte Orions in the Pacific League, hits his landmark home run against the Seibu Lions in Miyagi, breaking Clarence Jones's mark. It is his third round-tripper of the season. Lee spent eight years in the majors – most recently with the Dodgers – and began playing in Japan in 1977.

APRIL 29:

Overpowering right-hande pitcher Roger Clemens of the Red Sox strikes out a major league record 20 Mariners in a 3-1 victory at Fenway Park. Clemens allows only three hits and no

APRIL 26
Red Sox power pitcher Roger Clemens strikes out 20 Mariners, a major league record.

walks, and his fastball is clocked at 98 mph. The 23-year-old, who underwent shoulder surgery last year, surpasses the mark set by Steve Carlton in 1969 and matched by Tom Seaver in 1970 and Nolan Ryan in 1974. He throws 138 pitches, fanning every Mariner at least once and getting Phil Bradley four times. Bradley is the 20th victim, going down with two out in the ninth. Dwight Evans hits a homer for the Red Sox; Gorman Thomas for Seattle. The losing pitcher is Mike Moore. Between the fourth and sixth innings, Clemens fans eight straight batters.

MAY 2:

For the second time, the Yankees acquire pitcher Tommy John as a free agent. John, who has been with the Athletics, previously was signed by New York in 1978 from the Dodgers. In 1985, John was 4-10 with a 5.53 ERA with the Angels and the Athletics.

MAY 4:

Paul Richards dies at age 77 in Waxahachie, Texas. Although he hit only .227 in eight years as a major league catcher, Richards made his mark as a manager and general manager, introducing many new concepts to the game, including the oversized mitt for handling knuckleballs.

IN HIS OBITUARY FOR BILL VEECK IN THE *CHICAGO TRIBUNE*, JEROME HOLTZMAN WRITES: "THERE WAS ALSO A MORE SERIOUS SIDE TO MR. VEECK. HE DEVOURED BOOKS WITH AN UNCOMMON HUNGER, OFTEN READING AS MANY AS FIVE A WEEK, AND WAS A CONSTANT CHAMPION OF LIBERAL, AND SOMETIMES UNPOPULAR CAUSES. ALTHOUGH HE HAD A PEG LEG, HE REPEATEDLY REFUSED THE USE OF CRUTCHES, EVEN WHEN HE PARTICIPATED IN THE DAY-LONG CIVIL RIGHTS MARCH IN SELMA, ALA., IN MARCH OF 1965."

MAY 14:

Reds' pitcher John Denny denies he assaulted *Cincinnati Post* writer Bruce Schoenfield prior to a game in Philadelphia. In April, Denny was accused of throwing a bat at a television camera during a game with the Mets.

MAY 15:

More trouble for pitcher Steve Howe. He is banned from playing with the Class A San Jose Bees. Following a "discrepancy" in a May 1 drug test, Commissioner Peter Ueberroth ordered him not to pitch, but he goes five innings today because Al Rosen of the Giants and Pat Gillick of the Blue Jays were on hand. John Johnson, president of the National Association of Professional Baseball Leagues – which governs the minors – says Howe now is ineligible "based on certain information, which was discussed with

LEAGUE

In June, the Giants draft infielder Matt Williams as the third overall pick. Williams previously was drafted – but not signed – by the Mets in June 1983.

LEAGUE

If the Cubs make the playoffs, they will use St. Louis's Busch Stadium as their home field. Because of the absence of lights at Wrigley Field, it cannot be used for the NLCS or World Series.

Mr. Howe regarding his drug rehabilitation efforts."

MAY 28:

Joe Cowley of the White Sox fans the first seven Rangers he faces today, but he lasts only four and two-thirds innings. Texas wins, 6-3, and Cowley gets the loss after yielding six hits, six runs, and a walk. Cowley is the first pitcher since Mickey Welch of the New York Gothams to open a game with seven strikeouts. Today's victims are Oddibe McDowell, Scott Fletcher, Pete O'Brien, Pete Incaviglia, Gary Ward, George Wright, and Steve Buechele. The streak is broken by Orlando Merced, who flies out. The winning pitcher is Ed Correa.

MAY 31:

The Pirates' Barry Bonds doubles against Rick Honeycutt of the Dodgers for his first major league hit.

JUNE 2:

Rod Carew, one of baseball's best pure hitters, retires at the age of 40. Carew, who turned down a chance to play with the Giants, says, "I discovered that there is life after baseball and it's a pretty good life." Carew hit .328 in 19 years, led the AL in batting six times, and topped .300 15 times. Last season, he batted .280 for the Angels.

JUNE 4:

In Atlanta, Barry Bonds of the Pirates homers against the Braves' Craig McMurtry. It is Bonds's first major league round-tripper and one of his four hits in five at-bats today. Pittsburgh beats Atlanta, 12-3.

JUNE 5:

For the first time in his 2,201-game career, Steve Garvey of the Padres is ejected by an umpire. Garvey is tossed by Charlie Williams after a call at home plate.

JUNE 6:

In Milwaukee, Roger Clemens of the Red Sox beats the Brewers, 3-0, to improve his record to 10-0.

JUNE 8:

David Cone makes his major league debut for the Royals, yielding three hits and an earned run to the Brewers in one inning of work.

The Orioles beat the Yankees, 18-9, at Yankee Stadium in the AL's longest nine-inning game ever – four hours, 16 minutes. The teams fall two minutes short of the major league mark. Lee Lacy of the Orioles hits three homers; his teammate Larry Sheets adds another, and Mike Pagliarulo connects for New York. The winning pitcher is Ken Dixon; Ed Whitson gets the loss.

JUNE 9:

Don Sutton of the Angels beats the White Sox and Tom Seaver, 3-0. The two starters represent the most wins, cumulatively – 604 – for opposing pitchers. Before the game begins Sutton has 298 and Seaver 306. The previous high was established on August 26, 1926, when Walter Johnson, with 406 and Urban "Red" Faber with 197, faced off.

A. Bartlett Giamatti, president of Yale University and renaissance scholar, is elected president of the National League today. He will succeed outgoing president Charles "Chub" Feeney. The league gives Giamatti a five-year term. Feeney held the post for 17 years. Giamatti will become the commissioner in 1989.

JUNE 18:

Angels' right-hander Don Sutton reaches the coveted career 300-win mark with a three-hit, 5-1 victory over the Texas Rangers in Anaheim. Sutton, in his 21st year, never has won more than 21 games in a season and is only a one-time 20-game winner. He is the 19th to win 300 and the ninth to do so without pitching a no-hitter. The others are Grover Cleveland Alexander, Charles "Kid" Nichols, Tim Keefe, Steve Carlton, Mickey Welch, Eddie Plank, Lefty Grove, and Early Wynn. The 44-year-old Sutton throws only 85 pitches.

JUNE 20:

The Blue Jays' Cliff Johnson hits a pinch-hit homer against the Tigers. It is the 20th of his career, improving on his own major league record.

JUNE 21:

Roger Clemens beats the Orioles, 7-2, at Fenway Park. He becomes the seventh in history to open a season with 13 consecutive wins.

JUNE 23:

In Philadelphia, the Phillies bombard the Cubs, 19-1, on 20

Nick Peters writes of Willie McCovey in the *Oakland Tribune*: "He did it all despite arthritic knees, a troublesome hip, aching feet and assorted other ailments. He did it in the Candlestick Park cold and despite more intentional walks than any player of his era."

safeties and set an NL record with 15 extra base hits. Juan Samuel hits two homers; teammates Mike Schmidt and Milt Thompson chip in with one apiece. The winning pitcher is Shane Rawley; Jamie Moyer is tagged with the loss.

JUNE 25:

After refusing to retire, four-time Cy Young Award winner Steve Carlton is released by the Phillies. The 41-year-old pitcher is experiencing control and shoulder problems; his record is 4-8 with a 6.18 ERA and he has issued 44 walks in 83 innings.

JUNE 27:

The Toronto Blue Jays' Damaso Garcia doubles four times against the Yankees, tying a major league record held by many other players.

Giants' rookie Robby Thompson sets a major league record when he is caught stealing four times in a 7-6, 12-inning victory over the Reds.

JUNE 28:

There are 600 wins on the mound as the Indians and Angels face off in Anaheim. For the first time in this century, two 300-game winners – Cleveland's Phil Niekro and California's Don Sutton – oppose each other. The Angels win, 9-3, on a six-run eighth inning, but neither starting pitcher is involved in the game's decision.

JUNE 29:

Tom Terrific gets a new address. The White Sox send Tom Seaver (2-6) to the Red Sox for infielder Steve Lyons (.250 in 59 games).

JULY 6:

Bob Horner hits four home runs for the Braves, but Atlanta loses to the visiting Expos, 11-8. Horner ties a major league record. In the second inning, he hits a homer with the bases empty against Andy McGaffigan. He connects against McGaffigan again in the fourth with no one on and in the fifth with two runners on base. In the ninth, he connects for another solo homer – this time against Jeff Reardon. Mitch Webster of Montreal has five hits and three RBI and a homer. His teammates Andre Dawson and Al Newman also connect. Tim Burke gets the win; Zane Smith is the loser.

Steve Carlton makes his debut in a Giants' uniform, two days after joining them. He works three and a third innings, yields three runs to the Cardinals, and leaves the game trailing, 3-0. The Giants go on to win the game, 8-3.

JULY 7:

After being fired by the White Sox and replaced by Doug Rader, Tony LaRussa is appointed manager of the Athletics, replacing Jeff Newman, who was 2-8. Newman, in turn, had replaced Jackie Moore, who compiled a 29-44 record.

JULY 14:

The San Jose Bees ask pitcher Steve Howe – reinstated on June 24 – to enter drug rehabilitation, after test results are "99.9 percent" positive for cocaine. Howe denies any knowledge of drug use, stating, "I'm pondering retirement right now. I really don't know what's going on."

JULY 15:

In Houston, the AL wins the All-Star Game, 3-2. Roger Clemens gets the win; Dwight Gooden is charged with the loss. Fernando Valenzuela equals Carl Hubbell's 1934 feat, fanning five straight. In the fourth, the Dodgers' left-hander whiffs Don Mattingly, Cal Ripken Jr., and Jesse Barfield. In the fifth, he fans Lou Whitaker and Teddy Higuera. Whitaker had a two-run homer off Gooden in the second, and Frank White connects for a solo shot.

JULY 17:

Dennis "Oil Can" Boyd of the Red Sox is hospitalized after being suspended for leaving the team and then threatening the police. Reportedly, Boyd's outburst was triggered by his failure to make the AL All-Star team. Boyd won't return until August.

JULY 22:

The Cubs fire their 28-year-old ball girl, Marla Collins, who posed nude for *Playboy* magazine. Collins had been with the team five years.

JULY 23:

The Pirates obtain outfielder-infielder Bobby Bonilla (.269 in 75 games) from the White Sox for pitcher Jose DeLeon (1-3). Bonilla hits .240 for the Pirates.

CULTURE

***Out!*, by Lawrence Kelly, is a play about the 1919 Black Sox. It stars Michael Countryman as Shoeless Joe Jackson.**

In the 1989 50th Anniversary Hall of Fame Yearbook, former Yankee Tommy Henrich, who played many key games against the Red Sox, recalls: "Bobby Doerr is one of the very few who played the game hard and retired with no enemies."

HISTORY

Vincent "Bo" Jackson, who chose baseball over professional football, plays 25 games as an outfielder and DH for the Royals, batting .207 with two homers. One of his homers is the longest ever at Royals Stadium – a 475-foot blast against Mike Moore of the Mariners. The Auburn All-American and Heisman Trophy winner is earning $1.066 million and says he picked the Royals instead of the National Football League's Tampa Bay Buccaneers because he likes baseball best. He was offered a $7.7 million deal to play pro football.

Heisman Trophy winner Bo Jackson knows baseball.

AUGUST 1
Twins' pitcher Bert Blyleven records his 3,000th career strikeout.

AUGUST 6
In a 13-11 Texas win over Baltimore, a record three grand slam homers are hit.

Hall of Fame pitcher Ted Lyons dies today at the age of 85 in Sulphur, Louisiana. Lyons pitched for 21 seasons with the White Sox, compiling a 260-230 record with a 3.67 ERA.

JULY 27:

What was unique less than a month ago happens again: two 300-game winners are the opposing starters. Don Sutton, who started for the Angels the June 28 faceoff of 300-game winners, is on the mound again. This time he is opposed by Tom Seaver of the Red Sox. Sutton and the Angels win, 3-0.

AUGUST 1:

Bert Blyleven of the Twins records his 3,000th career strikeout as Minnesota defeats the Athletics, 10-1. He is the 10th pitcher to reach the mark.

AUGUST 3:

Bobby Doerr, Ernie Lombardi, and Willie McCovey are inducted into the Hall of Fame. Doerr, a second baseman who spent his career with the Red Sox, batted .288 in 14 years, never hitting below .270 and reaching .300 three times. In 1944, he led the AL in slugging with .528 and hit .409 in his one World Series. Lombardi, a catcher, batted .306 with 190 homers in 17 years, twice leading the NL in batting. He hit .300 or better 10 times, but his hitting was overshadowed by his slowness of foot. Lombardi died in 1977. McCovey played 22 years, hitting 521 home runs and batting .270. A first baseman, he was the NL slugging average leader and home run champion three times. He appeared in one World Series.

Lombardi was bitter about the lack of respect he was accorded and his frequent turndowns for the Hall of Fame. He once said: "If they elected me, I wouldn't show up for the ceremony... All anybody wants to remember about me was that I couldn't run. They still make jokes. Let them make jokes." One of the jokes was that he once was out stretching a double into a single.

AUGUST 6:

One day after recording his 4,000th career strikeout, the Giants' Steve Carlton says he is retiring.

AT FENWAY PARK, RALPH KINER IS BROADCASTING AN EXHIBITION GAME BETWEEN THE METS AND RED SOX WHEN HE RECEIVES WORD OF HANK GREENBERG'S DEATH. KINER, WHO PLAYED ONE SEASON WITH GREENBERG IN PITTSBURGH, TELLS HIS BROADCAST PARTNER, TIM MCCARVER, "THIS IS THE WORST DAY OF MY LIFE. MY DEAREST FRIEND, AND THE MAN WHO WAS LIKE A FATHER TO ME, HANK GREENBERG, HAS DIED."

He fanned the Reds' Eric Davis on a 1-2 pitch to reach the 4,000 plateau. Carlton left the game with two out in the fourth after yielding seven hits, seven runs, and three walks and throwing a wild pitch. The Reds win, 11-6. Carlton, second only to Nolan Ryan in career strikeouts, says, "I realized that I've reached a milestone never before accomplished by a pitcher spending his entire career in one league." He is 1-3 with San Francisco and 4-11 overall this season.

At Baltimore, three grand slam homers are hit in one game for the first time in major league history. The batting fireworks begin with Toby Harrah's bases-loaded blast against the Orioles' Ken Dixon in the second inning to give the Rangers a 6-0 lead. In the bottom of the fourth, Larry Sheets and Jim Dwyer hit grand slams – off Bobby Witt and Jeff Russell – to spark a nine-run Baltimore rally. But Texas wins, 13-11. Also homering in the game are Lee Lacy of the Orioles and Steve Buechle and Pete O'Brien of the Rangers. The winning pitcher is Mitch Williams; Rich Bordi gets the loss.

HISTORY

Vince DiMaggio lived and played in the shadow of his brothers: His .249 lifetime average pales beside Dom's .298 or Joe's .325. But he had a better All-Star Game average than his brothers – 1.000 (three for three) in two games. Joe hit .255 in 11 games and Dom .353 in six games.

Pitcher Kirby Higbe on Hall of Fame inductee Ernie Lombardi: "He was the best hitter I ever saw, including everybody."

TRIVIA

Angels' manager Gene Mauch, regarded as an outstanding baseball brain, now has managed for 25 years without winning a pennant.

AUGUST 11:

At Wrigley Field, the Cubs and Pirates complete a game that had been called because of darkness on April 20. The teams set an NL record by using 17 pitchers. The Cubs establish a major league mark with 10. The Pirates prevail, 10-8, in 17 innings. Bobby Bonds, who drives in the winning run, was in the minor leagues when the game began, as was winning pitcher Barry Jones. Frank DiPino, who was with Houston on April 20, gets the loss. The game features homers by Sid Bream and Steve Kemp of the Pirates and the Cubs' Keith Moreland. Chicago's pitchers are Dennis Eckersley, Jay Baller, Matt Keough, George Frazier, Lee Smith, Dick Ruthven, Rick Sutcliffe, Steve Trout, DePino, and Dave Gumpert. The Pirates use Mike Bielecki, Bob Walk, Jim Winn, Cecilio Guante, Don Robinson, Pat Clements, and Jones.

The Reds' Pete Rose, 45 years old, bangs out five hits in a game for the 10th time in his career – an NL record. He also reaches a record 4,256 career at-bats. It will be Rose's last appearance in a major league lineup. Rose has a double among his five hits and three RBI against the Giants.

Baseball: A Biographical Encyclopedia *summarizes Rose: "...Baseball's 'Charlie Hustle' never did anything halfway in his life. His all-consuming passion for playing serious baseball is legendary. 'I'd walk through hell in a gasoline suit to keep playing baseball,' he once said. Rose...popularized the headfirst slide and would run to first base even on a walk." Rose, in sizing himself up, once said: "Well, I'm not too good a base stealer, and I don't have the strongest arm in the world... But I compensate for it by charging the ball fast and getting rid of it fast. But those aren't weaknesses. I don't have no weaknesses." In* Baseball: An Illustrated History, *he was likened to Ty Cobb: "Rose played with a ferocity unmatched by any of his contemporaries. He stretched doubles into triples, singles into doubles, groundouts into singles. Rose's aggression was infectious, a constant spur to his teammates to try and match it." Of his 1970 All-Star Game-winning slide into catcher Ray Fosse, Rose remarked: "I could never have looked my father in the eye if I hadn't hit Fosse that day."*

AUGUST 12:

In the nightcap of a doubleheader with the Royals, Don Baylor of the Red Sox is hit by a pitch from Harry "Bud" Black. It is a record 25th time Baylor has been hit this season. The previous black-and-blue record holders were Bill Freehan in 1968 and Norman "Kid" Elberfeld in 1911. The Royals win, 6-5.

Steve Carlton, all of six days after retiring, signs with the White Sox, pitches three innings, and is tagged with the loss in a 7-3 victory by the Tigers in Detroit. Carlton strikes out four, to bring his career total to 4,004, but he gives up seven hits and two walks for six runs. Healso is charged with a wild pitch. The winner is Mark Thurmond.

AUGUST 17:

Steve Carlton beats the Brewers, 7-4, for his first AL win and the 320th of his career. Rob Deer homers for Milwaukee.

In Kings of the Hill, *Nolan Ryan said of Carlton: "(His) greatness could be judged not by what he said but by what he did. For eight years he didn't say anything, not to the press. But he would rank high on virtually any classification you can invent. He had one of the superior fastballs. He intimidated hitters. He qualified as a workhorse. He was a prototype left-hander, with a liquid delivery and one of the best pickoff moves in the game. He was too serious to be labeled a character, but he might be fairly described as quirky.... He was a left-handed hitter's nightmare. 'Like drinking coffee through a fork,' said Willie Stargell."*

AUGUST 30:

The Yankees look like the New York Graybeards as they start 43-year-old Tommy John and 41-year-old Joe Niekro in a doubleheader against the Mariners. The oldsters split: John loses, 1-0, and Niekro wins, 3-0. They are the first 40-plus pitchers to start a doubleheader since Sad Sam Jones and Urban "Red" Faber

AUGUST 11
Pete Rose, 45, appears in a major league line-up for the last time – and gets five hits.

AUGUST 17
Steve Carlton, now a Brewers' pitcher, gets his first AL win and 320th of his career.

Fate finds Bill Buckner in this year's World Series.

It is said that after the seventh game of the 1986 World Series against the Mets, Boston was so quiet, you could hear New York screaming.

of the White Sox on August 13, 1933.

SEPTEMBER 3:

In the resumption of a game begun last night, the Astros beat the Cubs, 8-7, in 18 innings at Wrigley. The teams use a major league record 53 players until Billy Hatcher's home run wins the contest after five hours and 14 minutes. Danny Darwin gets the win; Greg Maddux is charged with the loss. Chris Speier, Cleotha "Chico" Walker, and Leon Durham homer for Chicago; Glenn Davis connects for Houston. Starter Nolan Ryan goes seven innings for the Astros, allowing three runs and striking out five.

SEPTEMBER 4:

Hall of Famer Hank Greenberg dies today at age 75 of cancer in Beverly Hills, California. Greenberg played 13 years, hitting .313, with a slugging average of .605 and 331 homers. In four World Series, he batted .318. Inducted into the Hall of Fame in 1956, Greenberg was general manager of the Indians from 1948 to 1957 and vice president of the White Sox from 1959 to 1963. In 1938, he hit 58 homers, tying the major league record for right-handed batters and setting the AL mark.

In his autobiography, Greenberg wrote: "History labels you incorrectly... I should have been remembered for driving in 183 runs, but instead, I'm remembered for a record that I didn't find particularly satisfying."

SEPTEMBER 7:

The Mets defeat the Cubs, 4-2, to wrap up the NL East title. It is the earliest clinching ever in the division.

SEPTEMBER 8:

Orioles' manager Earl Weaver announces he will retire at the end of the season. He begin his second stint as Baltimore's skipper in June 1985. Weaver says, "The best thing is I don't have to answer any more questions. It's all over... That's a relief."

SEPTEMBER 12:

The Minnesota Twins today name Tom Kelly the ballclub's new manager. He replaces Ray Miller, who was 59-80. Kelly will lead them to the World Series in 1987.

SEPTEMBER 19:

Joe Cowley of the White Sox no-hits the Angels, 7-1, in Anaheim. Cowley strikes out eight and walks seven; Chicago makes no errors. The losing pitcher is Kirk McCaskill.

SEPTEMBER 23:

The Astros' Jim Deshaies fans the first eight Dodgers he faces and goes on to win a 2-0, two-hitter.

SEPTEMBER 25:

The Astros' Mike Scott no-hits the Giants, 2-0, at the Astrodome. The victory gives Houston the NL West title over Cincinnati; it is the first time a title is clinched by a no-hitter. Scott strikes out 13 and walks two. The Astros play errorless baseball. The losing pitcher is Juan Berenguer. The 31-year-old Scott, who was taught to throw his split-finger fastball by Giants' manager Roger Craig, is now 18-10.

SEPTEMBER 26:

The Angels beat the Rangers, 8-3, to win the AL West title.

Tom Trebelhorn is named manager of the Brewers today, succeeding George Bamberger, who is retiring after a 71-81 season.

SEPTEMBER 28:

At Fenway Park, the Red Sox take the AL East with a 12-3 victory over the Blue Jays.

SEPTEMBER 29:

Greg Maddux of the Cubs and his brother Mike of the Phillies take the mound against each other. It is the first such meeting since Joe and Phil Niekro in 1982. The Cubs win, 8-3, and Greg gets the victory. Mike, who is tagged with the loss, says, "The last time I faced him, I think it was in the backyard playing Wiffle Ball."

The well-traveled Bert Blyleven, now pitching for the Twins, serves up three home runs to the Indians in a 6-5 victory. Blyleven's total for the season climbs to 49, breaking a major league record of 46 set by Robin Roberts in 1956. Jay Bell, in his first major league at-bat, hits one of the three homers.

OCTOBER 2:

At Fenway Park, Don Mattingly singles in the seventh inning

SEPTEMBER 25
Mike Scott's no-hitter against the Giants gives the Astros the NL West title.

OCTOBER 4
Yankee Dave Righetti closes both ends of a doubleheader, gaining a record 46 saves.

against Bruce Hurst for his 232nd hit of the season – a team record. Earlier Mattingly hit his 52nd double of the season. Mattingly gets a hand from the Fenway Park fans as his batting average climbs to .350 and the Yankees beat the Red Sox, 6-1.

OCTOBER 3:

Vince DiMaggio dies at age 70 in North Hollywood, California, just before he is scheduled to travel to a Connecticut baseball card show and appear with his younger brothers, Joe and Dom. DiMaggio played 10 years in the majors, hitting .249 with 125 home runs.

OCTOBER 4:

In Boston, Dave Righetti saves both games of a double-header to bring his season total to 46 – a new major league record, topping Dan Quisenberry and Bruce Sutter. The Yankees win, 5-3 and 3-1. Teammate Don Mattingly becomes the second player ever with a six-for-six game at Fenway Park, adding to his team record with his 238th hit and 53rd double on the year. Myril Hoag, also a Yankee, was six for six in 1934.

REGULAR SEASON WRAP-UP:

The Boston Red Sox, managed by John McNamara, finish at 96-66. Wade Boggs is the AL's top average hitter at .357. Jim Rice bats .324 with 20 homers and 100 RBI. Don Baylor hits 31 homers and drives in 94 runs. Dwight Evans has 26 home runs and 97 RBI; Bill Buckner weighs in with 18 round-trippers. Roger Clemens is the AL's big winner and ERA leader at 24-4 and 2.48. Bob Stanley records 16 saves. Davey Johnson's Mets finish at 108-54 in the NL. Wally Backman hits a team-best .320; Keith Hernandez bats .310 with 83 RBI. Gary Carter (24 homers, 105 RBI) and Darryl Strawberry (27 homers, 93 RBI) provide power. Dwight Gooden (17-6) and Bob Ojeda (18-5) lead the staff; Roger McDowell records 22 saves, Jesse Orosco has 21. Mike Schmidt – with 37 homers – leads the NL for a record eighth time.

OCTOBER 7:

ALCS, game one. In Boston, the California Angels handle the Boston Red Sox, 8-1, behind starting pitcher Mike Witt's complete game five-hitter. Boston's ace, Roger Clemens, is charged with the loss in his first post-season start.

OCTOBER 8:

NLCS, game one. Mike Scott pitches a complete-game five-hit shutout, defeating the Mets, 1-0, at the Astrodome. Scott ties an NLCS record with 14 strikeouts and Glenn Davis homers for the game's only run off losing pitcher Dwight Gooden. ALCS, game two. At Fenway Park, the Red Sox even the playoffs with a 9-2 win. Bruce Hurst goes all the way, yielding 11 hits, for the win. Kirk McCaskill takes the loss. Three California errors open the door for a three-run Boston rally in the seventh. Wally Joyner of California and Jim Rice of Boston hit home runs.

OCTOBER 9:

NLCS, game two. Bob Ojeda goes the distance, scattering 10 hits in a 5-1 Mets' victory. Nolan Ryan lasts five innings and gets the loss. Keith Hernandez drives in two runs with a fifth-inning triple.

OCTOBER 10:

ALCS, game three. In California, John Candelaria is the winning pitcher; Dennis "Oil Can" Boyd gets the loss. Angels Dick Schofield and Gary Pettis hit home runs for California's 5-3 win.

OCTOBER 11:

NLCS, game three. Darryl Strawberry hits a three-run homer and Lenny Dykstra a two-run round-tripper in the ninth to give the Mets a 6-5 win in New York. Bill Doran goes deep for the Astros. The winning pitcher is Jesse Orosco with two innings of shutout relief. Dave Smith, who pitches only a third of an inning, gets the loss.

ALCS, game four. In Anaheim, the Angels win again, 4-3, on Bobby Grich's RBI single in the 11th inning. Doug Corbett gets the win and Calvin Schiraldi the loss, both in relief appearances. Doug DeCinces homers for the Angels.

OCTOBER 12:

ALCS, game five. In California, with the Red Sox trailing, 5-4, in the ninth and facing elimination, Dave Henderson hits a two-out, two-strike pitch for a home run. In the seventh, Bobby Grich of the Angels hits a ball that goes off Dave Henderson's

CULTURE

On TV, *A Winner Never Quits* stars Keith Carradine as Pete Gray, along with Mare Winningham and Dennis Weaver. Gray, who had one arm, played 77 games in the majors in 1945.

"I can't remember the last time I missed a ground ball. I'll remember that one."
– *Bill Buckner*

glove and over the fence for a homer. The Red Sox go on to win, 7-6 in 11 innings. The losing pitcher is Donnie Moore on a sacrifice fly to Henderson in the top of the 11th. The winning pitcher is Steve Crawford.

NLCS, game four. Mike Scott is tough again, limiting the Mets to only three hits in a complete-game 3-1, victory. Sid Fernandez gets the loss. Alan Ashby hits a two-run homer and Dickie Thon adds a solo shot for all of Houston's runs.

Former AL batting champion Norm Cash falls off a boat and drowns at Beaver Island, Michigan. Cash, age 51, played 17 years, hitting .271 with 377 homers. In 1961 with the Tigers, he led the AL with a .361 batting average; it was his only .300 season.

OCTOBER 14:

NLCS, game five. Mets' catcher Gary Carter singles in the winning run in the bottom of the 12th inning to defeat the Astros and Charlie Kerfeld, 2-1. Jesse Orosco gets the win with two innings in relief of Dwight Gooden. Houston starter Nolan Ryan goes 9 innings, fanning 12 Mets and allowing only 2 hits. ALCS, game six. Back in Boston, the Red Sox make it three in a row with a 10-4 victory. Starter Oil Can Boyd gets the win; Kirk McCaskill the loss. Brian Downing hits a home run. Spike Owen of the Red Sox has four hits

OCTOBER 15:

NLCS, game six. The Mets win a breathtaking 16-inning game, 7-6, at the Astrodome to win the NL pennant. The Mets score three times in the top of the 16th and hold off the Astros when winning pitcher Jesse Orosco fans Kevin Bass with two runners on. Earlier, the Mets sent the game into extra innings with a three-run ninth-inning rally. The losing pitcher is Aurelio Lopez. The game's only homer is hit by Houston's Billy Hatcher.

ALCS, game seven. Coming from a deficit of three games to one, the Red Sox capture the AL pennant with an 8-1 victory at Fenway Park. The Angels commit two costly errors, and seven of Boston's runs are unearned. The winning pitcher is Roger Clemens, aided by home runs from Jim Rice and Dwight Evans. The Angels' John Candelaria is the losing pitcher.

OCTOBER 18:

World Series, game one. Bruce Hurst works eight strong innings, allows four hits, gets a save from Calvin Schiraldi, and beats the Mets, 1-0, in New York today. The game's only run scores in the seventh on an error by second baseman Tim Teufel.

OCTOBER 19:

World Series, game two. Boston amasses 18 hits to pound the Mets, 9-3, at Shea Stadium today. Steve Crawford gets the win with one and two-thirds innings in relief of the starter, Roger Clemens; Mets' starter Dwight Gooden is charged with the loss. Dave Henderson and Dwight Evans each homer for Boston.

OCTOBER 21:

World Series, game three. The Mets bounce back, 7-1, at Fenway Park behind winning pitcher Bob Ojeda, who gets relief help from Roger McDowell. Oil Can Boyd gets the loss. Lenny Dykstra leads off the game with a homer, and the Mets score four in the first.

OCTOBER 22:

World Series, game four. The visiting Mets tie the Series with a 6-2 victory. Winning pitcher Ron Darling allows four hits in seven innings and gets support from two homers by Gary Carter and one by Lenny Dykstra. Jesse Orosco gets a save. The losing pitcher is Boston starter Al Nipper.

OCTOBER 23:

World Series, game five. At Fenway Park, Bruce Hurst scatters 10 hits and pitches a complete-game, 4-2 victory over the Mets. Dwight Gooden gets the loss. Tim Teufel homers for New York.

OCTOBER 25:

World Series, game six. Yes, Virginia, there is a Curse. The Red Sox are on the brink of their first World Championship since 1918. They score twice in the top of the 10th at Shea. The Mets have two out and a runner on when Gary Carter hits a two-strike pitch for a single. Ray Knight singles, scoring Kevin Mitchell. Bob Stanley, who relieves Calvin Schiraldi, uncorks a wild pitch, scoring the tying run. Mookie Wilson then hits a soft grounder to first base-

CULTURE

In books, *The Iowa Baseball Confederacy* by W.P. Kinsella is about an all-star team that plays the 1908 Cubs in an endless game. *The Berenstain Bears Go Out for the Team*, a children's book by Stan and Jan Berenstain, is also published.

OCTOBER 25
The Mets score the winning run in game six of the World Series on Bill Buckner's error.

OCTOBER 27
The Mets' miracle is complete as they rally to win game seven and a World Championship.

man Bill Buckner for what appears to be the final out of the inning; it goes through his legs and the Mets win, 6-5. Rick Aguilera gets the win; Schiraldi is charged with the loss.

OCTOBER 27:

World Series, game seven. The Mets come back from a 3-0 deficit after two innings to beat the Red Sox, 8-5, in New York for the World Championship. Roger McDowell gets the win; Calvin Schiraldi is charged with the loss. Ray Knight and Darryl Strawberry hit solo homers for the Mets; Dwight Evans and Rich Gedman connect for the Red Sox. Knight hits .391 for the Mets; Gary Carter drives in nine runs. Ron Darling compiles a 1.53 ERA and splits his two decisions. Marty Barrett of Boston leads all hitters with a .433 average; Dave Henderson bats .400. Bruce Hurst stars in a losing cause – he is 2-0 with a 1.96 ERA.

POST-SEASON

NOVEMBER 14:

To the victors go the spoils. Partners Nelson Doubleday and Fred Wilpon acquire primary ownership of the World Champion New York Mets today from Doubleday and Company.

NOVEMBER 26:

In a one-sided trade, the Yankees and Pirates trade pitchers for pitchers. New York sends Doug Drabek (7-8, 4.10 ERA), Brian Fisher (9-5, 4.93 ERA) and minor leaguer Logan Easley to Pittsburgh. In return, they receive Rick Rhoden (15-12, 2.84 ERA), Cecilio Guante (5-2, 3.35 ERA) and Pat Clements (0-4, 2.80 ERA)

DECEMBER 2:

Yankees' owner George Steinbrenner talks via telephone with gambler Howard Spira, who claims to have detrimental information about Dave Winfield. The Yankees' outfielder has been involved in an ongoing feud with Steinbrenner. The conversation begins a new, bizarre chapter in the Steinbrenner saga.

DECEMBER 5:

The Illinois General Assembly approves funding legislation for a new stadium across the street from historic Comiskey Park, home of the White Sox for more than 75 years. The vote comes a month after the defeat of a referendum that would have enabled the team to move to suburban Addison

DECEMBER 9:

Commercial real estate developer Richard E. Jacobs and his brother, David H. Jacobs, buy the Indians from the estate of the late F.J. "Steve" O'Neill.

DECEMBER 11:

The Mets and Padres engineer a multiplayer trade. Coming to play in New York are outfielder Kevin McReynolds (.288, 26 homers, 96 RBI), pitcher Gene Walter (2-2, 3.86 ERA), and minor league infielder Adam Ging. Going to San Diego are outfielders Kevin Mitchell (.277, 12 homers, 43 RBI) and Stan Jefferson (.208 in 14 games), along with three minor leaguers – pitchers Kevin Armstrong and Kevin Brown, plus outfielder Shawn Abner.

DECEMBER 30:

In Tampa, Florida, gambler Howard Spira meets with George Steinbrenner and charges Dave Winfield with financial irregularities in the outfielder's charitable foundation. He accuses Winfield of threats and irregular loans.

IN 1988, THE WHITE SOX HALL OF FAME SHORTSTOP LUKE APPLING RECALLED OLD COMISKEY PARK: "THIS PLACE WAS BUILT ON A DUMP. ONE DAY, I DUG UP AN OLD BLUE-AND-WHITE COFFEE CUP OUT AT SHORTSTOP. THEY HAD TO STOP THE GAME AND COME OUT WITH A COUPLE OF SHOVELS OF DIRT."

THE BEST OF 1986

NATIONAL LEAGUE

HITTERS

Batting Average:
Tim Raines, Montreal Expos, .334

Slugging Average:
Mike Schmidt, Philadelphia Phillies, .547

Home Runs:
Mike Schmidt, 37

Runs Batted In:
Mike Schmidt, 119

Hits:
Tony Gwynn, San Diego Padres, 211

Stolen Bases:
Vince Coleman, St. Louis Cardinals, 107

PITCHERS

Wins:
Fernando Valenzuela, Los Angeles Dodgers, 21

Strikeouts:
Mike Scott, Houston Astros-306

Earned Run Average:
Mike Scott, 2.22

Winning Percentage:
Bob Ojeda, New York Mets, .783

Saves:
Todd Worrell, St. Louis Cardinals, 36

Most Valuable Player:
Mike Schmidt, Philadelphia Phillies

Cy Young Award:
Mike Scott, Houston Astros

Rookie of the Year:
Todd Worrell, St. Louis Cardinals

Manager of the Year:
Hal Lanier, Houston Astros

AMERICAN LEAGUE

HITTERS

Batting Average:
Wade Boggs, Boston Red Sox, .357

Slugging Average:
Don Mattingly, New York Yankees, .573

Home Runs:
Jesse Barfield, Toronto Blue Jays, 40

Runs Batted In:
Joe Carter, Cleveland Indians, 121

Hits:
Don Mattingly, 238

Stolen Bases:
Rickey Henderson, New York Yankees, 87

PITCHERS

Wins:
Roger Clemens, Boston Red Sox, 24

Strikeouts:
Mark Langston, Seattle Mariners, 245
Earned Run Average: Roger Clemens, 2.48

Winning Percentage:
Roger Clemens, .857

Saves:
Dave Righetti, New York Yankees, 46

Most Valuable Player:
Roger Clemens, Boston Red Sox

Cy Young Award:
Roger Clemens, Boston Red Sox

Rookie of the Year:
Jose Canseco, Oakland Athletics

Manager of the Year:
John McNamara, Boston Red Sox

1987

"They call him Awesome because it rhymes with Dawson."
– Jerry Pritkin, on Andre Dawson

NEWS

U.S., USSR SIGN ARMS CONTROL PACT

U.S. Navy shells Iranian oil platform to retaliate for attack on freighter

EVANGELIST JIM BAKKER CAUGHT IN SEX SCANDAL

THREE AMERICANS KIDNAPPED IN WEST BEIRUT

AIRLINE CRASH IN DETROIT KILLS 156; FOUR-YEAR-OLD GIRL IS ONLY SURVIVOR

IRAN-CONTRA REPORT BLAMES REAGAN

IRAQI AIR FORCE ATTACKS USS *STARK* IN PERSIAN GULF

TONI MORRISON'S PULITZER PRIZE-WINNING NOVEL *BELOVED* IS PUBLISHED

JOHN HUSTON DIRECTS HIS LAST FILM, *THE DEAD*

WW II NAZI KLAUS BARBIE CONVICTED

PRE-SEASON

JANUARY 9:

George "Twinkletoes" Selkirk, the man who replaced Babe Ruth as Yankees right fielder, passes away in Fort Lauderdale, Florida, at age 79. In nine years with the New York Yankees, Selkirk hit a respectable .290, but his career total of 108 home runs fell 606 short of the Babe.

FEBRUARY 23:

Royals manager Dick Howser, who is battling brain cancer, announces his resignation in Fort Myers, Florida. He will be succeeded by Bill Gardner.

FEBRUARY 25:

LaMarr Hoyt, the AL's 1983 Cy Young Award winner, is banned for the entire season by Commissioner Peter Ueberroth. Hoyt was arrested in October for illegal possession of pills and released on January 7 by the Padres with three years left on his contract. Hoyt recently finished serving 30 days for violation of federal drug laws.

MARCH 3:

Entertainer Danny Kaye, part owner of the Seattle Mariners, dies at age 74 of heart failure in Los Angeles.

MARCH 6:

The Cubs sign free-agent outfielder Andre Dawson for $500,000. Anxious to leave Montreal after 11 years, Dawson reportedly signs a blank contract with Chicago and the team fills in the figure – $500,000. Last season, Dawson hit .284 with 20 home runs and 78 RBI.

MARCH 27:

The Mets obtain pitcher David Cone (0-0, 5.56 ERA) and minor league outfielder Chris Jelic from the Royals for catcher Ed Hearn (.265, four homers in 49 games), pitcher Rick A. Anderson (2-1, 2.72 ERA), and minor league pitcher Mauro Gozzo.

APRIL 1:

The Cardinals get catcher Tony Pena (.288, 10 homers) from the Pirates for outfielder-first baseman Andy Van Slyke (.270, 13 homers, 21 stolen bases), catcher Mike "Spanky" LaValliere (.234), and minor league pitcher Mike Dunne.

LEAGUE

The Major League Players Association files a grievance charging the owners acted "in concert with one another" to restrict salaries. The association cites few offers to free agents in 1985, 1986, and 1987, noting that most free agents returned to their original teams. According to an association study, the 1985 free agents lost between $70 and $90 million.

Orioles
33

Luke Sewell had a pointed answer for those who claimed a baseball cannot be thrown in a curved path: "Isn't it strange that the optical illusion only happens when someone tries to throw a curve ball and never when a fast or straight ball is attempted?"

APRIL 2:

The Mets' Dwight "Doc" Gooden begins a 28-day rehabilitation program at the Smithers Alcoholism and Treatment Center in New York City. The 1985 Cy Young Award winner tested positive for cocaine use.

APRIL 3:

The Athletics acquire pitcher Dennis Eckersley (6-11, 4.57 ERA) and infielder Dan Rohn (.200 in six games) from the Cubs for three minor leaguers – outfielder David Wilder, infielder Brian Guinn, and pitcher Mark Leonette.

The Athletics will put Eckersely, a starting pitcher since coming up to the majors with the Indians in 1975, in the bullpen, where he will become one of baseball's most dominant closers of all time. Wrote Susan Fornoff, who covered the Athletics for the Sacramento Bee, in Lady in the Locker Room: *"Eckersley's antics were colorful, like the vocabulary of words and phrases that were so distinctly his 'Ecktionary,' or, as Peter Gammons called it, 'DialEckt.' There was 'baboomba,' a home run. There was...'iron,' the big money he was making.... There was, now and then, a 'walk-off piece,' a game-winning homer by the opposing team host to send Eckersley and his fellows in the field walking forlornly off to the showers. But normally it was Eckersley who walked off happily, sometimes too happily for his opponents. ...In Cleveland on the Fourth of July, Eckersley angered Ron Washington by his game-ending display of excitement. On the fifth of July, Eckersley sought out Washington before the game and shook hands with him. 'I don't want people thinking I'm a jerk,' Eckersley said. He didn't seem to be a jerk.... He talked, always, about the fear he feels, standing on the mound in the ninth inning with the victory of some other pitcher – probably a good friend – in his charge. I think the emotion he vented was the same that you or I would unleash should we realize, as we sit down to a pile of bills, that, yes, that is a winning lottery ticket at the bottom of the pile. Go ahead, say it: 'YES!' And you, too, could be Dennis Eckersley striking out the side in the ninth."*

THE SEASON

APRIL 13:

After falling behind the Giants, 2-0, in the top of the first, the Padres get homers from their first three batters – Marvell Wynne, Tony Gwynn, and John Kruk – off Roger Mason. The feat sets a major league record.

APRIL 15:

Juan Nieves of the Brewers no-hits the Orioles, 7-0, in Baltimore. It is the first no-hitter ever by a Brewer pitcher. Nieves fans seven and walks five; Milwaukee commits no errors. The losing pitcher is Mike Flanagan. Dale Sveum, Greg Brock, and Glenn Braggs homer for the Brewers.

APRIL 16:

Hall of Fame umpire John "Jocko" Conlan dies in Scottsdale, Arizona, at age 89. Inducted into the Hall of Fame in 1974, Conlan umpired in the AL from 1941 to 1965, working five World Series. Conlan, who wore a polka-dotted bow tie while working, played outfield for the White Sox in 1934 and 1935, batting .263.

APRIL 18:

Philadelphia's Mike Schmidt hits a three-run home run over the left-field fence at Three Rivers Stadium in the ninth inning for his 500th career round-tripper. The historic home run, which puts Schmidt in the company of 13 other players, comes on a 3-0 pitch from the Pirates' Don Robinson. The Pittsburgh crowd – 19,361 in number – cheer Schmidt, and his teammates meet him as he crosses home plate. The Phillies win the game, 8-6.

APRIL 19:

San Francisco's Matt Williams hits his first major league home run. Williams's round-tripper comes against Atlanta's Jeff Dedmon in Candlestick Park.

APRIL 20:

In Chicago, the Brewers beat the White Sox, 5-4, for their 13th straight victory, tying the 1982 Braves for the best start ever. Greg Brock hits a two-run homer and Robin Yount drives in Paul Molitor with the winning

LEAGUE

In June, high school outfielder Ken Griffey Jr. is selected by the Seattle Mariners with the first overall pick in the 1987 amateur draft. He is the son of active major league outfielder Ken Griffey of the Braves. The White Sox, with the fifth overall pick, select pitcher Jack McDowell of Stanford University.

Eddie Murray switches it on for the Orioles.

Baseball Commissioner Peter Ueberroth comments: "Catfish Hunter had the distinction of playing for both Charlie Finley and George Steinbrenner, which is enough in itself to put a player in the Hall of Fame."

LEAGUE

Major league attendance reaches a record 52,029,664.

HISTORY

Mark McGwire ends the season with a league-leading 49 homers.

---

run in the seventh inning. Chuck Crim gets the victory.

APRIL 21:

The White Sox end the Brewers' winning streak, 7-1. Joel Davis gets the win; Mike Ciardi is charged with the game's loss.

APRIL 25:

The Reds' Eric Davis sets a major league record when he fans for the ninth consecutive time. Davis is victimized three times by Nolan Ryan – who has 11 strikeouts for the game – and once each by relievers Larry Andersen and Dave Smith in a 3-0, 10-inning Cincinnati win over Houston. Davis, who is hitting .371, struck out four straight times in 11 innings yesterday. Sandy Koufax fanned 12 straight times in 1955, but Davis sets a record for consecutive strikeouts in two extra-inning games.

The Tigers' Billy Bean hits safely four times – including two doubles – in his major league debut. He is the 13th player ever to accomplish the feat.

MAY 9:

The Orioles' switch-hitting first baseman Eddie Murray hits home runs from both sides of the plate as Baltimore beats the White Sox, 15-6, at Comiskey Park. With "switch" home runs yesterday, Murray is the first ever to hit home runs left- and right-handed in two consecutive games.

MAY 14:

Luke Sewell dies at age 86 in Akron, Ohio. He was the manager of the 1945 St. Louis Browns, the franchise's only pennant winner. In his 10-year career as a manager, Sewell was 606-644; as a player, the catcher's lifetime batting average was .259 for 20 years.

MAY 20:

The Brewers, who opened the season with a record-tying winning streak, begin the day with a 12-game losing streak. But, on homers by Cecil Cooper, Greg Brock, and Robin Yount, and the pitching of Juan Nieves, they defeat the White Sox, 5-1, to end their winless slide.

MAY 30:

The Reds' Eric Davis has a record to be proud of in May. He establishes an NL mark with three grand slam home runs in a single month. He hits the record-breaker in the third inning today against the Pirates' Dorn Taylor in a 6-2 Reds victory in Pittsburgh. Davis's 19 home runs for April and May also set a new NL record. He is batting .355.

JUNE 1:

Phil Niekro and the Indians beat the Tigers, 9-6. As a result, he and his brother Joe of the Twins are now the winningest pitching brothers in major league history. Their total of 530 combined victories surpasses the previous mark held by Gaylord and Jim Perry.

JUNE 3:

At Wrigley Field, the Cubs claw the Astros, 22-7, in a game featuring three grand slam homers. It is the second time in major league history and the first in the NL that three bases-loaded homers have been hit in one game. Billy Hatcher of the Astros and Brian Dayett and Keith Moreland of the Cubs hit the grand slams. Moreland hits a second round-tripper in the game. Also reaching the seats are Bill Doran of Houston and Chicago's Ryne Sandberg, Andre Dawson, and Jim Sundberg. Rick Sutcliffe gets the win; Bob Knepper, who yields nine earned runs in one inning, is charged with the loss.

JUNE 5:

Doc Gooden returns to the New York Mets after participating in a substance abuse program.

JUNE 6:

The Twins acquire pitcher Joe Niekro (3-4) from the Yankees for catcher-DH Mark Salas (.378 in 22 games).

JUNE 17:

Dick Howser dies of brain cancer at age 51 in St. Luke's Hospital in Kansas City, Missouri. Howser was first diagnosed in July 1986. As an infielder, Howser played for eight years, batting .248. After leading the Yankees to 103 wins in 1980, he was fired by owner George Steinbrenner. He subsequently managed the 1985 Royals to a World Series championship.

George Steinbrenner says: "Firing Dick Howser [at the time it was described as a reassignment] and not re-signing Reggie [Jackson] were the two biggest mistakes I ever made with the Yankees."

MAY 9
Orioles' slugger Eddie Murray has "switch" homers for the second day in a row.

JULY 18
The Yankees' Don Mattingly ties an ML record by homering in his 8th straight game.

JUNE 21:

It's bombs away in the AL. Teams in the junior circuit set a major league record with 30 homers in a single day – in eight games. The Tigers lead the way with five. NL teams hit 14 homers in six games.

JUNE 22:

On the day another class act, Fred Astaire, dies, Tom Seaver announces his retirement from baseball. Seaver spent the last 16 days trying to come back with the Mets, but decides his career is over. A three-time Cy Young Award winner with a record of 311-205, Seaver declares, "I can say for the rest of my life, I got every ounce out of it."

JUNE 27:

The Athletics beat the Indians, 13-3, paced by rookie Mark McGwire's three homers, five RBI, and five runs scored.

JUNE 28:

Mark McGwire bombs the Indians again – with two homers, two RBI, and two runs. Steve Ontiveros pitches a shutout and Oakland wins, 10-0. McGwire is the first rookie to hit five homers in two games. He is the second "freshman" to score nine times in two games; Baldomero "Mel" Almada in 1937 was the first to do so.

Don Baylor of the visiting Red Sox is hit by a pitch from the Yankees' Rick Rhoden. It is the 244th time Baylor has been hit; he surpasses the career mark of Ron Hunt.

JULY 4:

The Giants acquire outfielder-infielder Kevin Mitchell (.245 in 62 games) and pitchers Craig Lefferts (2-2) and Dave Dravecky (3-7) from the Padres. In return, San Diego obtains infielder Chris Brown (.242 in 38 games) and pitchers Mark Davis (4-5), Keith Comstock (2-0), and Mark Grant (1-2).

JULY 5:

Mark McGwire of the Athletics becomes the first rookie to reach 30 home runs prior to the All-Star Game, when he connects in a 6-3 win over the Red Sox. His teammate Jose Canseco hits two round-trippers of his own.

JULY 7:

Eric Show of the Padres hits Andre Dawson of the Cubs with a pitch, precipitating a brawl. Dawson requires 24 stitches.

JULY 14:

The NL defeats the AL, 2-0, on a two-out, two-run triple by Tim Raines in the 13th inning in Oakland. The winning pitcher is Lee Smith; the losing pitcher is Jay Howell. The NL is 8-0 in extra-inning All-Star Games.

The Royals' Vincent "Bo" Jackson announces that he will play football for the NFL's Los Angeles Raiders in addition to major league baseball. Jackson, who will report to the Raiders after the baseball season, signs a five-year contract to pursue what he calls a "hobby." The hobby pays well – he will receive $500,000 for eight games plus a $1 million signing bonus. He is making some $300,000 with the Royals. Last year, the Tampa Bay Buccaneers offered Jackson a $7.6-million deal.

JULY 17:

The Yankees' Don Mattingly homers against Paul Kilgus of Texas, making him the first AL player and the second major leaguer with round-trippers in seven straight games. The Yankees win, 8-4.

JULY 18:

Don Mattingly ties Dale Long's 1956 major league record by homering in his eighth consecutive game. Mattingly's historic shot comes off a 2-0 pitch from the Rangers' Jose Guzman in the fourth inning and clears the left centerfield fence at Arlington Stadium. It is his 18th of the season. Mattingly is called out of the dugout by the 41,871 fans, who give him a ovation. Mattingly has 10 homers during the eight-game streak, which began on July 8. Texas goes on to win the game, 7-2.

JULY 19:

Don Mattingly has two hits – including a double – in four at-bats, but no homers today against the Rangers, and his streak ends.

JULY 20:

The Russians are claiming they invented baseball. In the *New York Times* Bill Keller, reporting from Moscow, quotes a Russian sportswriter who asserts that baseball is derived from the ancient Russian

TRIVIA

Cal and Billy Ripken are the first brothers to be managed by their father in the major leagues.

"Basketball is really my game. Problem was the other kids got bigger and quicker and I stayed short and slow."
– Indiana native Don Mattingly

HISTORY

After hitting only .220 with 15 homers for the Athletics, 41-year-old Reggie Jackson retires. The colorful and controversial Jackson leaves the game after 21 years with 563 homers, 1,702 RBI, and a .262 batting average. He holds first place in strikeouts, with 2,597. In five World Series, Jackson batted .357, compiled the all-time best slugging average – .755 – and hit 10 homers.

game of lapta. According to the journalist, Sergei Shachin writing in Izvestia, the game was brought to California by Russian immigrants. And, he adds that the best players are Cubans. Aleksandr V. Kalivod, chief of the baseball department of the State Committee on Sports, says nyet; he asserts: "I doubt there is evidence in history that lapta was the basis of baseball. Baseball is quite new to us."

JULY 26:

Ray Dandridge, Jim "Catfish" Hunter, and Billy Williams are inducted into the Hall of Fame. Dandridge, who played in the Negro and Mexican Leagues, was a third baseman-shortstop who batted .322. He played with the Giants' farm team in Minneapolis, batting .363 in one season and winning the American Association's Most Valuable Player Award. Roy Campanella said of him: "I never saw anyone better as a fielder." Hunter, dubbed "Catfish" by Oakland owner Charles O. Finley, who liked colorful nicknames, pitched 15 years in the majors with the Athletics and Yankees. He was the first of the big-dollar free agents and compiled a 244-166 record with a 3.26 ERA, 42 shutouts, 3,448 1/3 innings pitched, and 2,012 strikeouts. In six World Series, he was 5-3. Williams, an outfielder, played 18 years – 16 with the Cubs. He batted .290 with 426 homers and led the NL in batting in 1972 with a .333 average. He appeared in one World Series.

JULY 27:

Hall of Fame shortstop Travis Jackson dies in Waldo, Arkansas, at age 83. Jackson batted .291 in 15 seasons – all with the New York Giants – and appeared in four World Series. He was inducted into the Hall of Fame in 1982.

JULY 31:

One of baseball's best left-handers of all time, Steve Carlton (5-9), goes from the Indians to the Twins for minor league pitcher Jeff Perry. Carlton has 328 career victories.

Another year, another study on whether baseballs are livelier than in the past. The Science and Aeronautics Department of the University of Missouri-Rolla spent two weeks comparing the 1987 and 1985 balls. The conclusion: the 1987 ball is no livelier. According to the *New York Times*, the researchers found a minimal difference attributed to the storage and age of the 1985 baseballs, but the 1987 version was "totally within the parameters of major league standards."

AUGUST 2:

Kevin Seitzer has a big day with his bat as the Royals pound out 20 hits to beat the Red Sox, 13-5. Seitzer has two homers – among his six hits in six at-bats – and seven RBI.

In Cincinnati, Eric Davis homers against the Giants to give the Reds a 5-4 win. Davis becomes the seventh player with 30 home runs and 30 stolen bases. No one ever has reached the 30-30 mark earlier in the season.

AUGUST 3:

Gotcha! Joe Niekro of the Twins is caught with the goods in the fourth inning of today's game with the Angels. When umpires Tim Tschida and Dave Palermo suspect he is doctoring the ball, they instruct him to empty his pockets; Niekro turns away and a 5-inch emery board falls to the mound. Niekro is ejected and five balls are sent as evidence to AL president Dr. Bobby Brown. The Twins win, 11-3. Brown slaps Niekro with a 10-game suspension.

AUGUST 6:

Steve Howe's contract is purchased by the Rangers after he pitches for Class AAA Oklahoma City. On July 12, he was signed by Texas to a minor league contract, despite failing a drug test with the San Jose Bees in the California League. Howe also pitched for the Tabasco Gonaderos in the Mexican League. Commissioner Peter Ueberroth fines the Rangers $250,000 for signing Howe without approval.

AUGUST 11:

In Seattle, Mark McGwire of the Athletics homers in the seventh inning against Mike Moore. It is his 38th round-tripper of the year, breaking the AL rookie record set by the Indians' Al Rosen in 1950. The Oakland Athletics lose to the Mariners, 8-2.

AUGUST 12:

The Braves acquire minor league pitcher John Smoltz from the

AUGUST 2
The Royals' Kevin Seitzer goes 6-for-6 with two homers in a 16-5 win over Boston.

AUGUST 14
A's slugger Mark McGwire connects for his rookie-record 39th homer of the season.

Tigers for veteran pitcher Doyle Alexander (5-10).

The Pirates trade pitcher Rick Reuschel (8-6) to the Giants for pitcher Jeff D. Robinson (6-8) and minor league pitcher Scott Medvin.

AUGUST 14:

The A's, Mark McGwire hits a two-run homer off Don Sutton of the Angels in the sixth inning today – his 39th of the year, setting a major league rookie record. McGwire surpasses the mark set by Wally Berger in 1930 and matched by Frank Robinson in 1956. Oakland goes on to win the game, 7-6, in 12 innings.

AUGUST 16:

Paul Molitor of the Brewers has two hits against the Orioles, extending his hitting streak to 31 consecutive games. Chuck Crim and Milwaukee win the game, 6-2.

Montreal's speedy Tim Raines hits for the cycle and has five hits in five at-bats as the Expos beat the Pirates, 10-7.

AUGUST 17:

Reggie Jackson of the Athletics homers against Mike Witt of the Angels. It is Jackson's 563rd – and last – career homer. It also is his 15th home run of the season.

AUGUST 19:

Paul Molitor's hitting streak is extended to 34 games with four hits – including a homer – against the Indians. Molitor's streak now is the 11th longest in major league history. The Brewers, behind Juan Nieves, win, 13-2.

AUGUST 25:

Paul Molitor singles against Don Gordon in the sixth inning – his only hit in four at-bats against the Indians; his consecutive game hitting streak reaches 39. Milwaukee, behind Juan Nieves, beats Cleveland, 10-9.

AUGUST 26:

Joe DiMaggio's record 56-game streak is safe. Paul Molitor is held hitless in five at-bats by Indians' rookie John Farrell; his hitting streak is snapped at 39 games – the longest since Pete Rose's 44 in 1978. He fans, grounds out three times, and reaches base on an error. He is on deck in the 10th when teammate Rick Manning drives in Mike Felder with the winning run off reliever Doug Jones. Teddy Higuera gets the 1-0 win in 10. Molitor had 68 hits and hit .415 in the streak, which began back on July 16 against the Angels.

SEPTEMBER 8:

The *New York Times* publishes two "exposes" by science writer James Gleick. The first explains why a knuckleball dances, the other deals with why there is a proliferation of homers in the major leagues. Gleick, after consulting with research scientists, reveals they "are focusing on the role of the baseball's stitches in creating turbulence in the airflow, and they calculate that, under certain conditions, the knuckleball undergoes an aerodynamic 'crisis' that warps its trajectory in mid-flight." Stitches are at the heart of the home run outbreak as well. Gleick quotes Joel W. Hollenberg of the Cooper Union School of Engineering: "It appears there's a different stitch roughness on the newer baseballs and that's reflected in the drag data we have. If the stitch roughness is greater, that will contribute to lower drag."

Kirby Puckett is the Twins' spark plug.

SEPTEMBER 9:

The Astros' Nolan Ryan fans 16 Giants in eight innings in Houston. Ryan strikes out 10 of the last 12 and five in a row to end the game, a 4-2 victory. He also drives in Kevin Bass with the game-winner in the second inning. It is the highest strikeout total for Ryan in the NL; he now has 226 in 176 innings. He also raises his career total to 4,503 and has fanned 10 or more 172 times.

SEPTEMBER 11:

With a stolen base today in the fourth inning against the

> "What the hell, he couldn't have hit a 20-run homer!"
> – *Cal Ripken Sr., on Cal Ripken Jr.*

LEAGUE

The Rookie of the Year Award is renamed the Jackie Robinson Award. The name change applies to both leagues.

Cardinals, the Mets' Howard Johnson becomes the first NL infielder with 30 homers and 30 stolen bases in a season. Johnson has hit 34 round-trippers. The Cardinals win, 6-4, in 10 innings.

SEPTEMBER 14:

At Exhibition Stadium in Toronto, the Blue Jays become the first major league team to hit 10 home runs in a game as they bomb the Orioles, 18-3. Ernie Whitt connects three times, George Bell and Rance Mulliniks twice each, and Lloyd Mosely, Rob Ducey, and Fred McGriff once. Mike L. Hart homers for Baltimore. The combined 11 homers tie a two-team major league record. The previous team record of eight was set by the Yankees in 1939 and equaled by other teams. Jim Clancy gets the win; Ken Dixon is charged with the loss.

Orioles manager Cal Ripken Sr. removes shortstop Cal Ripken Jr. from today's game, ending a string of 8,243 innings. The streak encompasses five seasons and 908 games. Ripken Sr. explains: "What the hell, he couldn't have hit a 20-run homer!"

SEPTEMBER 21:

Sachio Kinugasa, known as the Lou Gehrig of Japan, announces he will retire at the end of the season. The 40-year-old third baseman for the Hiroshima Carp in the Central League plays in his 2,192nd consecutive game today, appearing against the Yomiuri Giants.

Arbitrator Thomas T. Roberts rules that baseball's owners colluded against the 1985 free-agent players, restricting their movement and weakening their bargaining position. Roberts finds that teams used a database and did not pursue free agents unless there was no interest by the original clubs, "in itself a strong indication of concerted action." He cites the case of Kirk Gibson as an example: "The interest of the Royals in Kirk Gibson suddenly cooled... after meetings among owners and general managers." Those who re-signed with their original teams will be free agents again if they so wish. The grievance charges involving 1986 free agents are being examined by another arbitrator.

SEPTEMBER 22:

Wade Boggs collects his 200th hit of the season. It is the fifth straight year the Red Sox third baseman has reached the 200-hit plateau, tying a major league record held by Al Simmons, Charlie Gehringer, and Chuck Klein. In June, Boggs had a 25-game hitting streak. The Tigers win today's game, 8-5.

SEPTEMBER 28:

The Twins beat the Rangers, 5-3, in Texas and clinch the AL West Division, their first title in 17 years.

Giants pitcher Don Robinson hits an eighth-inning homer to beat the Padres, 5-4, and sew up the NL West crown for San Francisco. It is the Giants' first title in 16 years.

SEPTEMBER 29:

Don Mattingly hits a grand slam home run against Bruce Hurst of the Red Sox. It is his sixth of the season, a major league record. Prior to the 1987 season, Mattingly had none.

OCTOBER 1:

The Cardinals defeat the Expos, 8-2, for the NL East crown, their third in six years.

OCTOBER 2:

Padres rookie Benito Santiago doubles in the first inning on a 2-2 delivery from Fernando Valenzuela of the Dodgers, extending his consecutive game hitting streak to 34. Santiago is one for three, raising his average to .301 for the season and .351 during the streak. Los Angeles wins 10-3.

Orel Hershiser and the Dodgers end Santiago's streak at 34.

OCTOBER 4:

The Tigers beat the Blue Jays, 1-0, on a Frank Tanana six-hitter to win the AL East title. The Blue Jays lost seven straight in the final week of the season, enabling the Tigers to win the crown.

REGULAR SEASON WRAP-UP:

The Twins, under Tom Kelly, finish at 85-77 in the AL. The team is power-packed: Kent Hrbek has 34 home runs; Tom Brunansky, 32; Gary Gaetti, 31; and Kirby Puckett, 28. Puckett also leads the team in batting at .332. Frank Viola, with 17 victories, is the big winner. Jeff Reardon accounts for 31 saves.

SEPTEMBER 11
The Mets' Howard Johnson is the first NL infielder with 30 homers and 30 steals in a season.

SEPTEMBER 29
Don Mattingly sets a major league record with his sixth grand slam of the season.

The Cardinals, managed by Dorrel "Whitey" Herzog, compile a 95-67 record in the NL. Ozzie Smith leads the regulars with a .303 average, followed by Vince Coleman at .289 with 109 stolen bases. Willie McGee bats in 105 runs. Jack Clark is the power hitter with 35 homers and 106 RBI along with a .286 batting average. The team has no 20-game winners; three pitchers – Danny Cox, Greg Mathews, and Bob Forsch – win 11 games each. Todd Worrell has 33 saves.

Darryl Strawberry and Howard Johnson of the Mets become the first teammates with 30 homers and 30 stolen bases apiece. Nolan Ryan of the Astros records 270 strikeouts, setting a major league record by topping 200 for the 11th time.

OCTOBER 6:

NLCS, game one. In St. Louis, the Cardinals beat the Giants, 5-3. Winning pitcher Greg Mathews limits San Francisco to four hits in seven innings and bats in two runs. Ken Dayley gets the save. The losing pitcher is Rick Reuschel. Jeffrey Leonard homers for the Giants.

OCTOBER 7:

ALCS, game one. In Minnesota, the Twins beat the Tigers, 8-5. Each team has 10 hits and two home runs. Gary Gaetti connects twice for the Twins; Mike Heath and Kirk Gibson once each for the Tigers. The winning pitcher is Jeff Reardon; the loser is Doyle Alexander.

NLCS, game two. Dave Dravecky pitches a two-hitter and the Giants win, 5-0. Will Clark homers with one on and Jeffrey Leonard hits a solo round-tripper. John Tudor gets the loss.

OCTOBER 8:

ALCS, game two. In Minnesota, the Twins win their second straight, 6-3, despite homers by Chet Lemon and Lou Whitaker of the Tigers. Kent Hrbek hits a solo round-tripper for the Twins. The winning pitcher is Bert Blyleven; Jack Morris is charged with the loss.

OCTOBER 9:

NLCS, game three. At Candlestick Park, the Giants score in the bottom of the ninth to beat the Cardinals, 6-5. Bob Forsch gets the win in relief; Todd Worrell is credited with a save. The losing pitcher is Don Robinson. Jim Lindeman hits a two-run homer and bats in three runs. Jeffrey Leonard and Harry Spilman homer for San Francisco.

OCTOBER 10:

ALCS, game three. In Detroit, before a hometown crowd of 49,730, the Tigers win, 7-6. The winning pitcher is Mike Henneman in relief of Walt Terrell. Pat Sheridan homers for the Tigers; Greg Gagne and Tom Brunansky for the Twins. Jeff Reardon gets the loss.

NLCS, game four. The Giants, behind Mike Krukow's complete-game, nine-hitter, beat the St. Louis Cardinals, 4-2. Danny Cox goes nine, allows nine hits, and gets the loss. The Giants score all their runs on homers: a two-run shot by Jeffrey Leonard – his fourth of the NLCS – and solo shots by Robby Thompson and Bob Brenly.

OCTOBER 11:

ALCS, game four. In Detroit, the Twins win, 5-3, on home runs by Kirby Puckett and Greg Gagne. The winning pitcher is Frank Viola; Frank Tanana takes the loss.

NLCS, game five. The Giants win, 6-3, with reliever Joe Price getting the win on five innings of one-hit pitching. Bob Forsch, the second of four Cardinals pitchers, is tagged with the loss. Kevin Mitchell hits a homer for San Francisco.

OCTOBER 12:

ALCS, game five. In Detroit, 47,448 see the Twins win the AL pennant with a 9-5 victory over the Tigers. Tom Brunansky homers for the Twins; the winning pitcher is Bert Blyleven. Matt Nokes and Chet Lemon homer for the Tigers; Doyle Alexander gets the game's loss.

OCTOBER 13:

NLCS, game six. Three Cardinals pitchers limit the visiting Giants to six hits in a 1-0 St. Louis victory. Starter John Tudor gets the win with relief from Todd Worrell and a save by Ken Dayley. The game's only run scores on a triple by Tony Pena and a sacrifice fly by Jose Oquendo in the second inning. Giants starter Dave Dravecky is charged with the loss.

CULTURE

In the theater, *Fences*, a Pulitzer Prize-winning drama by August Wilson, stars James Earl Jones as a former Negro Leagues star.

OCTOBER 17
For the first time, a World Series game is played indoors, as the Twins and Cards meet.

OCTOBER 25
The Minnesota Twins win game seven, 4-2, to claim their first-ever World Championship.

OCTOBER 14:

NLCS, game seven. Before their hometown fans, Danny Cox eight-hits the Giants, a 6-0 shutout, and the Cardinals win the NL pennant. Jose Oquendo provides the big blow, a three-run homer in the second. The losing pitcher is Atlee Hammaker.

OCTOBER 17:

World Series, game one. For the first time in history, a World Series game is played inside at Minnesota's Metrodome, where the Twins maul the St. Louis Cardinals, 11-1, before a crowd of 55,171. The Twins' 11 hits include a bases-loaded home run by Dan Gladden and a two-run blast by Steve Lombardozzi. Frank Viola is the winning pitcher, allowing 5 hits in eight innings; Joe Magrane is the loser.

OCTOBER 18:

World Series, game two. At Minnesota, the Twins make it two in a row with an 8-4 win. Bert Blyleven gets the win; Danny Cox is charged with the loss. Gary Gaetti and Tim Laudner hit home runs for the Twins. Minnesota scores six runs in the fourth; the big blow is Randy Bush's bases-loaded double.

OCTOBER 19:

Billy Martin becomes Yankee manager for the fifth time, replacing Lou Piniella, who, in turn, succeeds Woody Woodward as the team's general manager. Woodward resigns his post. Under Piniella, the Yankees were 89-73 and finished fourth in the AL East.

OCTOBER 20:

World Series, game three. In St. Louis, the Cardinals win, 3-1, on strong pitching by John Tudor, who limits the Twins to five hits in seven innings. Todd Worrell finishes up for the save. Vince Coleman has a two-run double. Juan Berenguer is the loser.

OCTOBER 21:

World Series, game four. In St. Louis, the Cardinals even the Series with a 7-2 win. The winning pitcher is Bob Forsch; the loser, Frank Viola. Tom Lawless of the Cardinals and Greg Gagne of the Twins hit home runs.

OCTOBER 22:

World Series, game five. In St. Louis, the Cardinals win their third straight game, 4-2. The winning pitcher is Danny Cox; Todd Worrell gets a save. The loser is Bert Blyleven. St. Louis's Curt Ford delivers a bases-loaded single in the sixth inning.

Sachio Kinugasa of the Hiroshima Carp in the Central League in Japan plays in his 2,215th consecutive game. A third baseman, Kinugasa fashions his streak from October 19, 1970.

OCTOBER 24:

World Series, game six. Back in the friendly confines of the Metrodome, the Twins beat the Cardinals, 11-5, to even the Series. Kent Hrbek and Don Baylor homer for the Twins; Tommy Herr for the Cardinals. The winning pitcher is Dan Schatzeder; the loser, John Tudor.

OCTOBER 25:

World Series, game seven. In Minnesota, the Metrodome is a wall of sound as 55,376 fans cheer the Twins to a 4-2 win over the Cardinals and their first-ever World Championship. Frank Viola, with relief help in the ninth inning from Jeff Reardon, earns the win. Danny Cox, who relieves Joe Magrane, is charged with the loss. Playing time is three hours and four minutes. Viola (2-1, 3.72 ERA) is named the Most Valuable Player. Kirby Puckett hits .357 and Dan Gladden drives in seven runs for Minnesota. Cardinal Tony Pena bats .409.

POST-SEASON

OCTOBER 31:

Eight U.S. Senators look into baseball expansion.

NOVEMBER 6:

The Reds get pitcher Danny Jackson (9-18, 4.02 ERA) and minor league shortstop Angel Salazar from the Royals for pitcher Ted Power (10-13, 4.50 ERA) and shortstop Kurt Stilwell (.258).

DECEMBER 1:

The Giants sign free-agent outfielder Brett Butler (.295, nine homers, 33 stolen bases), who spent last season with the Indians.

DECEMBER 8:

The Cubs trade relief pitcher Lee Smith (4-10, 3.12 ERA, 36 saves) to the Red Sox for pitchers Calvin Schiraldi (8-5, 4.41 ERA) and Al Nipper (11-12, 5.43 ERA).

THE BEST OF 1987

NATIONAL LEAGUE

HITTERS

Batting Average:
Tony Gwynn, San Diego Padres, .370

Slugging Average:
Jack Clark, St. Louis Cardinals, .597

Home Runs:
Andre Dawson, Chicago Cubs, 49

Runs Batted In:
Andre Dawson, 137

Hits:
Tony Gwynn, 218

Stolen Bases:
Vince Coleman, St. Louis Cardinals, 109

PITCHERS

Wins:
Rick Sutcliffe, Chicago Cubs, 18

Strikeouts:
Nolan Ryan, Houston Astros, 270

Earned Run Average:
Nolan Ryan, 2.76

Winning Percentage:
Dwight Gooden, New York Mets, .682

Saves:
Steve Bedrosian, Philadelphia Phillies, 40

Most Valuable Player:
Andre Dawson, Chicago Cubs

Cy Young Award:
Steve Bedrosian, Philadelphia Phillies

Rookie of the Year:
Benito Santiago, San Diego Padres

Manager of the Year:
Bob "Buck" Rodgers, Montreal Expos

AMERICAN LEAGUE

HITTERS

Batting Average:
Wade Boggs, Boston Red Sox, .363

Slugging Average:
Mark McGwire, Oakland Athletics, .618

Home Runs:
Mark McGwire, 49

Runs Batted In:
George Bell, Toronto Blue Jays, 134

Hits:
Kirby Puckett, Minnesota Twins; Kevin Seitzer, Kansas City Royals, 207

Stolen Bases:
Harold Reynolds, Seattle Mariners, 60

PITCHERS

Wins:
Dave Stewart, Oakland Athletics; Roger Clemens, Boston Red Sox, 20

Strikeouts:
Mark Langston, Seattle Mariners, 262

Earned Run Average:
Jimmy Key, Toronto Blue Jays, 2.76

Winning Percentage:
Roger Clemens, .690

Saves:
Tom Henke, Toronto Blue Jays, 34

Most Valuable Player:
George Bell, Toronto Blue Jays

Cy Young Award:
Roger Clemens, Boston Red Sox

Rookie of the Year:
Mark McGwire, Oakland Athletics

Manager of the Year:
George "Sparky" Anderson, Detroit Tigers

CULTURE

On television, *Long Gone*, based on Paul Hemphill's novel, stars William L. Peterson and Virginia Madsen.

1988

"Don't ever bet against the Dodgers' pitching and Kirk Gibson."
– Giants' manager Roger Craig

NEWS

PRESIDENT REAGAN VISITS THE SOVIET UNION

Iran-Iraq war ends

GEORGE BUSH DEFEATS MICHAEL DUKAKIS FOR PRESIDENCY

PANAMA'S GENERAL NORIEGA INDICTED BY U.S. FOR DRUG SMUGGLING

U.S. TROOPS SENT TO HONDURAS

Sandanistas, Contras agree to truce in Nicaragua

SALMAN RUSHDIE'S *THE SATANIC VERSES* PUBLISHED

Dustin Hoffman is Best Actor for *Rain Man*

Leveraged buyout of R.J. Reynolds-Nabisco: $30 billion

PRE-SEASON

JANUARY 8:

Pitcher Joaquin Andujar (3-5, 6.08 ERA) returns to the Astros, signing a free-agent contract. Andujar, who spent last season with the Athletics, was with Houston from 1976 into the 1981 season.

JANUARY 15:

The life of former Cy Young Award winner LaMarr Hoyt continues its downward spiral. He is sentenced to one year in prison in Montgomery, Pennsylvania, for parole violation on drug charges. He served 45 days last year and faces other charges in South Carolina.

JANUARY 17:

The Rangers, who were fined last year for signing pitcher Steve Howe, cut the left-hander after he fails yet another drug test. Howe was 3-3 with a 4.31 ERA last season.

JANUARY 29:

Outfielder Kirk Gibson (.277, 24 homers, 79 RBI) takes advantage of arbitrator Thomas T. Roberts's September 22 ruling. He signs a three-year, $4.5 million deal with the Dodgers. Gibson was with the Detroit Tigers in 1987.

FEBRUARY 12:

The Padres send pitchers Rich "Goose" Gossage (5-4, 3.12 ERA, 11 saves) and Ray Hayward (0-0, 16.50 ERA) to the Cubs for third baseman-first baseman Keith Moreland (.266, 27 home runs, 88 RBI) and infielder Mike Brumley (.202 in 39 games).

FEBRUARY 23:

Chicago's Board of Alderman okay lights for Wrigley Field. By a vote of 29-19 they repeal the anti-noise laws that had kept Wrigley the only major league ballpark without lights. The major league owners put pressure on the city and promised Chicago the 1990 All-Star Game if lights were approved. The Cubs will play eight night games this coming season and 18 per year until 2002.

FEBRUARY 28:

Former AL batting champion Harvey Kuenn dies at age 57 in Peoria, Arizona. In 15 seasons he hit .303; his best year was 1959 with .353. Kuenn managed the Milwaukee Brewers for three seasons, winning the pennant in the 1982 season.

MARCH 3:

Kirk Gibson walks out of the Dodgers' Vero Beach, Florida, training camp before his debut. All business when it comes to baseball, Gibson is angered when teammate Jesse Orosco plays a practical joke on him by putting eyeblack in his cap. Gibson returns the following day.

MARCH 21:

Hall of Fame outfielder Edd Roush dies at age 94 in Bradenton, Florida. Roush, inducted into the hall in 1962, played 18 years, batting .321. He led the NL in batting for the Reds in 1917 and 1919, with averages of .341 and .321 respectively.

MARCH 28:

Former major league pitcher Vic Raschi, the Springfield Rifle, dies at age 69 in Groveland, New York. In 10 years, Raschi was 132-66 with a 3.72 ERA. In six World Series with the Yankees, he was 5-3. Raschi was on the

Jose Canseco bashes 42 homers and is the MVP.

Billy Martin, who now has been fired five times by Yankees' owner George Steinbrenner, asks, "How many times can a man have his heart broken?"

mound when Hank Aaron hit the first of his record 755 major league home runs.

MARCH 29:

Former NL home run champion Ted Kluszewski dies at age 63 of an apparent heart attack today in Cincinnati, Ohio. Kluszewski was so muscular in his playing days, he had to cut away his uniform sleeves. He played 15 seasons, mostly with the Reds, batting .298 with 279 home runs. From 1953 to 1956, he hit 40, 49, 47, and 35 round-trippers. He appeared in the 1959 World Series for the White Sox, batting .391 with three home runs and 10 RBI.

THE SEASON

APRIL 4:

George Bell of the Blue Jays hits three homers against Bret Saberhagen of the Royals; he is the first major leaguer to accomplish the feat on opening day. Toronto goes on to beat Kansas City, 5-3.

APRIL 13:

Jose Canseco of the Athletics hits the first ever home run off the second deck facade in left field at the Kingdome. The Athletics beat the Mariners, 12-7

APRIL 20:

New Yankee Jack Clark, acquired as a free agent from the Cardinals, hits his first home run of the season. It is the Yankees' 10,001st, and they are the first major league team ever to reach that level.

Fans gather at Tiger Stadium, ring the historic Detroit ballpark, and give it a "hug" on its 76th birthday. It is part of a protest against Mayor Coleman A. Young, who is advocating that the stadium be razed and replaced with a domed facility.

APRIL 22:

Roberto Alomar, son of former major leaguer Sandy Alomar, makes his major league debut with the Padres and singles against Nolan Ryan of the visiting Astros.

APRIL 29:

After beginning the season with 21 consecutive losses, the Orioles win for the first time in 1988, beating the White Sox, 9-0. Mark Williamson and Dave Schmidt combine to hold Chicago to four hits. The Orioles' losing streak is the longest in AL history. The 1906 Boston Pilgrims and the 1914 and 1943 Philadelphia Athletics each lost 20 in a row. Frank Robinson is now the Orioles' manager; Cal Ripken Sr. was fired after the first six losses.

APRIL 30:

At Cincinnati's Riverfront Stadium, Reds manager Pete Rose pushes Dave Pallone after the umpire makes a late call at first base in a game with the Mets. During the ensuing argument, Pallone accidentally pokes Rose in the face and gets two shoves in return. The Mets win the game, 6-5. Two days later, the NL's President A. Bartlett Giamatti suspends Pete Rose for 20 days and imposes a $10,000 fine on him.

MAY 14:

Cardinals utilityman Jose Oquendo yields a two-out, two-run double to the Braves' Ken Griffey in the 19th inning; Atlanta beats St. Louis, 7-5. Oquendo is tagged with the loss and becomes the first non-pitcher in 20 years to be involved in a pitching decision.

JUNE 23:

The Yankees' managerial merry-go-round makes another rotation. When it stops, Billy Martin is out. Lou Piniella, who had been replaced by Martin, is named to succeed him. The Yankees presently have a 40-28 record.

JUNE 25:

Orioles shortstop Cal Ripken Jr. starts at shortstop against the Red Sox; it is his 1,000th consecutive game – the sixth longest streak in baseball history. Boston beats Baltimore, 10-3.

JUNE 30:

At midnight, the Illinois General Assembly passes an amended stadium bill that will keep the White Sox in Chicago.

JULY 4:

Umpire Lee Weyer suffers a fatal heart attack at age 51 in San Mateo, California. An umpire since 1963, he called yesterday's Cubs-Giants game at Candlestick Park.

JULY 9:

The Giants use five homers to beat the Cardinals, 21-2. Ernest Riles hits the

While visiting the Pirates' spring training camp in the early part of this decade, Edd Roush was asked about Babe Ruth. He responded: "Babe Ruth. I knew Ruth. Left-handed hitter. Hit a lot of home runs. Used to be a pitcher."

fifth San Francisco round-tripper, which also is the 10,000th inthe franchise's 106-year history.

JULY 12:

In Cincinnati, the AL wins the All-Star Game, 2-1 on two RBI by Terry Steinbach. The catcher drives in one run with a third-inning homer and the second with a sacrifice fly in the fourth. Starter Frank Viola gets the victory; Dwight Gooden is tagged with the loss.

JULY 18:

Mariners pitcher Gene Walker commits four balks, tying an AL record for a nine-inning game.

JULY 21:

In a classic "What were they thinking?" trade, the Yankees send two minor leaguers – outfielder Jay Buhner and pitcher Rich Balabon – and a player to be named later to the Mariners for DH-first baseman Ken Phelps (.284 in 72 games).

JULY 29:

The Orioles trade former 20-game winner Mike Boddicker (6-12) to the Red Sox for outfielder Brady Anderson (.230 in 41 games) and minor league pitcher Curt Schilling. The right-handed Schilling will blossom several years later when he's dealt to the Phillies.

JULY 30:

Cincinnati Reds reliever John Franco is credited with his 13th save of the month – which establishes a major league record – in a 2-0 victory over the Padres. The previous record holders were Bruce Sutter, Albert "Sparky" Lyle, and Bob Stanley with 12.

JULY 31:

Willie Stargell is the only 1988 inductee into the Baseball Hall of Fame. Stargell played 21 years – all with the Pittsburgh Pirates – batting .282 with 475 home runs and 1,540 RBI. An outfielder-first baseman, he led the NL in slugging average in 1974 with .646 and twice was the Senior Circuit's home run champion. Stargell played in two World Series, batting .315.

Pittsburgh Pirates Manager Chuck Tanner once told Time *magazine: "Having Willie Stargell on your ballclub is like having a diamond ring on your finger."*

"IT'S SUPPOSED TO BE FUN. THE MAN SAYS 'PLAY BALL,' NOT 'WORK BALL,' YOU KNOW."

– *Willie Stargell*

AUGUST 3:

The Angels sign University of Michigan pitcher Jim Abbott, a member of the U.S. Olympic baseball team. Abbott was born without a right hand.

AUGUST 8:

Harry Grossman, a 91-year-old Cubs fan, gets the honor of throwing the switch lighting 74-year-old Wrigley Field for the first time. Wrigley,

Wade Boggs is the majors' top hitter.

Reported dialogue between manager Tony LaRussa and Jose Canseco: LaRussa: "How did you do in school?" Canseco: "Not so good. But I learned the new math. Forty home runs plus 40 steals equals 1.6 million dollars."

which was the last major league ballpark without illumination, is bathed in light from 540 lights in six banks on the roof as the Cubs take the field to meet the Phillies in their first-ever night game. But heavy thunderstorms wipe out the contest after three and a half innings.

AUGUST 9:

The Cubs try night baseball again at Wrigley Field after last night's rainout. This time they succeed. With 500 journalists and 36,399 fans on hand, Chicago beats the visiting Mets, 6-4.

Cubs reliever Rich "Goose" Gossage records his 300th career save.

AUGUST 12:

The Red Sox beat the Tigers, 9-4, at Fenway Park for their 23rd consecutive home victory – an AL record. The previous record was held by the 1931 Philadelphia Athletics, with 22 straight victories notched at home.

AUGUST 19:

Jay Buhner debuts at Yankee Stadium in a Mariners' uniform and becomes the first right-handed hitter and the fourth player in history to hit a home run into the centerfield stands. Buhner's blast – with one on – carries an estimated 450 feet.

AUGUST 30:

Phillies reliever Kent Tekulve pitches two innings in a 7-5 victory over the Giants. He becomes the second pitcher ever to appear in 1,000 games; Hall of Famer Hoyt Wilhelm is the first.

AUGUST 31:

Arbitrator George Nicolau finds that the owners are again in collusion and have violated the collective bargaining agreement. This time the decision focuses on the 1986 free agents. It is the third time the owners have been cited. In January, a similar ruling was issued affecting the 1985 free agents. The owners restricted the movement of free agents and acted in concert to keep a lid on salaries.

Outfielder Fred Lynn (.252 in 87 games), acquired by the Tigers from the Orioles, can't make it to his new team by midnight. Under current rules, he is ineligible for post-season play with Detroit. In return for Lynn, Baltimore receives three minor leaguers – catcher Chris Hoiles and pitchers Robinson Garces and Cesar Mejia.

Tigers general manager Bill Lajoie decides to tell the truth about Lynn's reporting time, instead of claiming the outfielder arrived before midnight. The Tigers, nevertheless, fail to make the playoffs and thus Lynn's eligibility becomes a non-issue.

SEPTEMBER 9:

Braves relief pitcher Bruce Sutter is credited with his 300th career save.

SEPTEMBER 16:

At Riverfront Stadium in Cincinnati, the Reds' Tom Browning pitches a 1-0 rain-delayed perfect game against the Dodgers. The 28-year-old left-hander throws 102 pitches and fans seven. It is the NL's first perfect nine-inning game in 23 years. Cincinnati scores the game's only run in the sixth inning on a throwing error. Browning fans Tracy Woodson – batting for losing pitcher Tim Belcher – to end the game.

In Montreal, at their annual meeting, the owners unanimously elect NL president A. Bartlett Giamatti to a five-year term as commissioner of baseball. He replaces Peter V. Ueberroth, who declined a second term. Giamatti will begin serving in April 1989, before Ueberroth's term expires. Giamatti, who served two years as NL president, will hire a businessman to assist him in his new position.

SEPTEMBER 17:

Twins reliever Jeff Reardon comes in to pitch the ninth inning of a 3-1 victory over the White Sox and records his 40th save – in 47 opportunities – of the season. He is the first pitcher with 40 saves in each of the two leagues. With the Expos in 1985, Reardon was credited with 41.

SEPTEMBER 19:

In Oakland, the Athletics beat the Twins, 5-3, to take the AL West crown.

SEPTEMBER 20:

In Toronto, Wade Boggs of the Red Sox hits a groundball single to left field in the fourth inning. It is his 200th hit of the season, and he becomes the first player in the 20th

SEPTEMBER 20
Wade Boggs becomes the first 20th-century player with 200 hits in six straight seasons.

SEPTEMBER 23
Jose Canseco is the first player ever with 40 homers and 40 steals in a single season.

SEPTEMBER 28
Dodgers' pitcher Orel Hershiser extends his shutout streak to 59 innings.

century to reach that level in six consecutive seasons. Boggs, who is three for three with two walks, raises his average to .362 and joins Lou Gehrig as the only major leaguers with three straight seasons of 200 hits and 100 walks. The Red Sox beat the Blue Jays, 13-2.

Tony Gwynn, an eight-time batting champion with the San Diego Padres, once said of Boggs, who won five batting crowns: "He's a truly amazing hitter. He rarely swings at bad pitches, he's very selective, he gets good pitches to hit, and nine times out of 10, he hits it hard. He's unbelievable."

SEPTEMBER 22:

The Mets win their eighth straight, beating the Phillies, 3-1, and taking the NL East title.

SEPTEMBER 23:

The Athletics' Jose Canseco steals his 39th and 40th bases and hits his 41st home run in a 9-8, 14-inning victory over the Brewers in Milwaukee. He becomes the first player to hit 40 home runs and steal 40 bases in the same season. Canseco's 39th follows a first-inning single. He bunts safely in the fifth and then steals second again.

Mickey Mantle's reaction: "If I had known they were going to make such a big deal out of 40-40, I would have done it two or three times myself."

SEPTEMBER 24:

Pascual Perez of the Expos pitches a five-inning no-hitter against the Phillies. Montreal wins, 1-0.

SEPTEMBER 28:

The Dodgers' Orel Hershiser pitches 10 shutout innings against the Padres to extend his string of shutout innings to 59, breaking Don Drysdale's major league record. Hershiser gets an assist from umpire Paul Runge, who calls interference on a run-scoring double play, preserving the streak. The Padres go on to win the game, 2-1, in 16 innings. Hershiser began his streak on August 30 with four shutout innings in Montreal. He next beat the Braves, 3-0; the Reds, 5-0; the Braves, 1-0; the Astros, 1-0; and the Giants, 3-0.

SEPTEMBER 30:

Despite losing to the Indians, 4-2, the Red Sox wrap up the AL East when the Brewers drop a 7-1 decision to the Oakland Athletics.

In Toronto, the Blue Jays' Dave Stieb one-hits the Orioles, 4-0. He becomes the sixth modern player to pitch consecutive one-hitters. Jim Traber spoils Stieb's no-hit bid with a single. On September 24, Julio Franco of the Indians singled with two out in the ninth against Stieb. Toronto won that game, 1-0.

REGULAR SEASON WRAP-UP:

Oakland, under Tony LaRussa, finishes the regular season at 104-58 in the AL. The big bats are Jose Canseco (.307, 42 homers, 124 RBI, 40 stolen bases), Mark McGwire (.260, 32 homers, 99 RBI), and Dave Henderson (.304, 24 homers, 94 RBI). Dave Stewart is the ace of the staff with a 21-12 record; Dennis Eckersley has a league-leading 45 saves on the year.

The Dodgers, managed by Tommy Lasorda, are 94-67 in the NL. Kirk Gibson is the main offensive threat with a .290 batting average, 25 home runs, and 76 RBI. Mike "Moose" Marshall bats .270 with 20 homers and 82 RBI. Orel Hershiser anchors the pitching staff with a 23-8 record and a 2.26 ERA. Jay Howell records 21 saves. The Yankees' Rickey Henderson has 93 stolen bases. The Twins become the first AL team to top 3 million in attendance.

OCTOBER 4:

NLCS, game one. In Los Angeles, the Mets strike first with a 3-2 victory over the Dodgers. Randy Myers gets the win with two innings in relief of starter Dwight Gooden. Orel Hershiser holds the Mets scoreless until the ninth, extending his consecutive shutout innings – begun in the regular season – to 67. Darryl Strawberry's double breaks the streak. Gary Carter doubles in the winning run with two out, making a loser of relief pitcher Jay Howell.

OCTOBER 5:

ALCS, game one. At Fenway Park, the visiting Athletics beat the Red Sox, 2-1, on Rickey Henderson's RBI single in the eighth. The hit makes

HISTORY

During the regular season, the Dodgers dropped 10 of 11 games against the Mets.

a loser of Bruce Hurst, who goes the route, allowing only six hits. Three Oakland pitchers limit the Red Sox to six hits; Rick Honeycutt gets the win, Dennis Eckersley the save. Jose Canseco homers for Oakland's other run. NLCS, game two. The Los Angeles Dodgers tie the playoff with a 6-3 win behind starting pitcher Tim Belcher, who gets the win and strikes out 10. Alejandro Peña is credited with a save. The losing pitcher is the Mets' starter, David Cone. Keith Hernandez smacks a two-run homer for New York.

RULES

Following the 1988 season, the game-winning RBI is dropped as an official statistic.

OCTOBER 6:

ALCS, game two. Jose Canseco's two-run homer and Walt Weiss' ninth-inning RBI single pace the Athletics to a 4-3 victory. Gene Nelson gets the win in relief; Dennis Eckersley earns a save. Rich Gedman hits a home run for Boston and Lee Smith is charged with the loss.

OCTOBER 7:

Fiery Dallas Green is hired by tempestuous George Steinbrenner as Yankees manager for the 1989 season. He replaces Lou Piniella, who took over for Billy Martin 68 games into the season. Martin had the Yankees at 40-28; Piniella led the team to a 45-48 finish. The Yankees finished in fifth place in the AL East. Steinbrenner promises Green will be around for the full 1989 season.

OCTOBER 8:

NLCS, game three. The Mets capitalize on a five-run eighth inning at home in Shea Stadium to beat the Dodgers, 8-4. Randy Myers, the

Orel Hershiser shuts down the opposition.

OCTOBER 5
Walt Weiss's ninth-inning RBI wins game two of the ALCS vs. the Red Sox, 4-3.

OCTOBER 15
Kirk Gibson comes off the bench to hit a game winner in game one of the World Series.

third of four New York pitchers, gets the win; Alejandro Pena is charged with the loss. Jay Howell, who relieves starter Orel Hershiser in the eighth, is ejected when pine tar is found on his glove. Howell is suspended for three games; after an appeal his penalty is reduced to two games.

ALCS, game three. In Oakland, the Athletics beat the Boston Red Sox in a slugfest, 10-6. Oakland notches 15 safeties – including four homers; Boston, 12. The winning pitcher, in relief, is Gene Nelson – the second of six Oakland pitchers. Dennis Eckersley gets a save. Boston starter Mike Boddicker is charged with the loss. Homering for the Athletics are Mark McGwire, Carney Lansford, Ron Hassey, and Rickey Henderson. Mike Greenwell homers for Boston.

OCTOBER 10:

ALCS, game four. It's a sweep and the AL pennant for Oakland. The Athletics, with a homer by Jose Canseco and strong pitching, beat the Red Sox, 4-1. Starter Dave Stewart gets the win; Dennis Eckersley gets the save – his fourth in four games. The losing pitcher is Bruce Hurst.

> NBC'S BOB COSTAS'S OBSERVATION OF KIRK GIBSON'S GAME-WINNING HOMER: "...THE SPONTANEOUS OUTPOURING OF EMOTION AND THIS RELEASE OF TENSION AS HE MADE HIS WAY AROUND THE BASES WAS ONE OF THE GREATEST THINGS I'VE EVER SEEN IN BASEBALL."

NLCS, game four. Kirk Gibson homers in the top of the 12th and Alejandro Peña retires the Mets in the home half of the inning; the Dodgers win, 5-4, at Shea Stadium. Pena gets the win; Roger McDowell is charged with the loss. Los Angeles's Mike Scioscia sent the game into extra innings with a two-run homer off starter Dwight Gooden in the ninth. Darryl Strawberry and Kevin McReynolds have homers for the Mets.

OCTOBER 10:

NLCS, game five. Kirk Gibson strikes again. The Dodgers outfielder cracks a three-run homer in the fifth inning, pacing Los Angeles to a 7-4 victory. Dodgers starter Tim Belcher is the game's winning pitcher; Brian Holton records a save. New York starter Sid Fernandez is credited with the loss. Lenny Dykstra launches a three-run round-tripper for New York.

OCTOBER 11:

NLCS, game six. The Mets, behind winner David Cone's complete-game five-hitter, beat the Dodgers, 5-1, in Los Angeles. Kevin McReynolds has four hits – including a two-run homer – and three RBI. Dodger starter Tim Leary absorbs the loss.

OCTOBER 12:

NLCS, game seven. Orel Hershiser goes all the way, limiting the Mets to five hits. Los Angeles wins the game, 6-0, and the NL pennant. The losing pitcher is Ron Darling, who lasts only one inning.

OCTOBER 15:

World Series, game one. In an all-West Coast Series, the Dodgers host the Athletics in Los Angeles. Kirk Gibson limps off the bench to pinch hit with two out in the bottom of the ninth and the Dodgers trailing, 4-3. He cracks a two-run homer off reliever Dennis Eckersley, giving the Dodgers a dramatic 5-4 victory. Alejandro Pena gets the win. Earlier, Jose Canseco had a grand slam for Oakland; Mickey Hatcher homered with one on for Los Angeles.

OCTOBER 16:

World Series, game two. Orel Hershiser spins a complete-

LEAGUE

In December, major league baseball signs a four-year, $1.05 billion television deal with the Columbia Broadcasting System.

Kirk Gibson hits a Series homer for the ages.

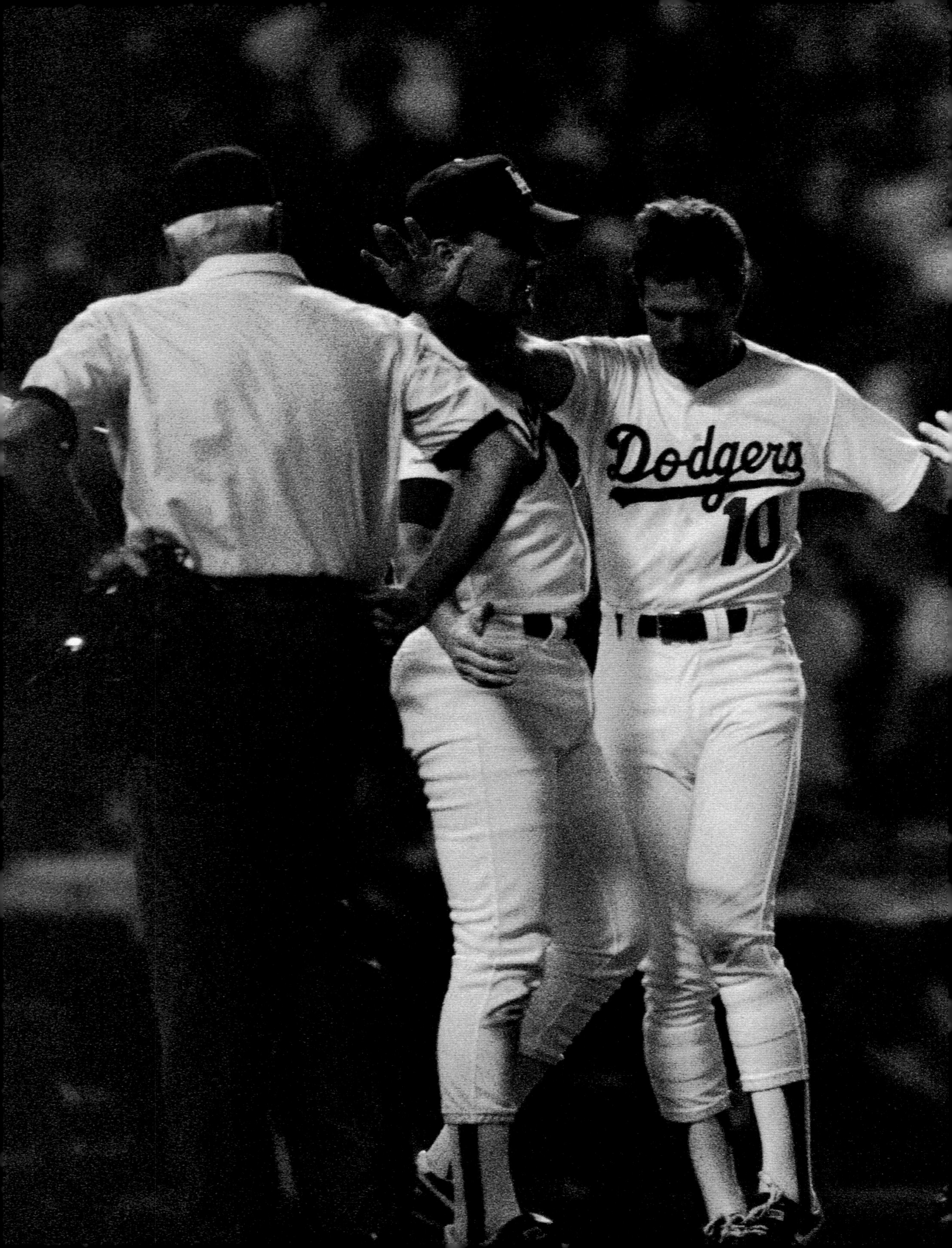
Dodgers
10

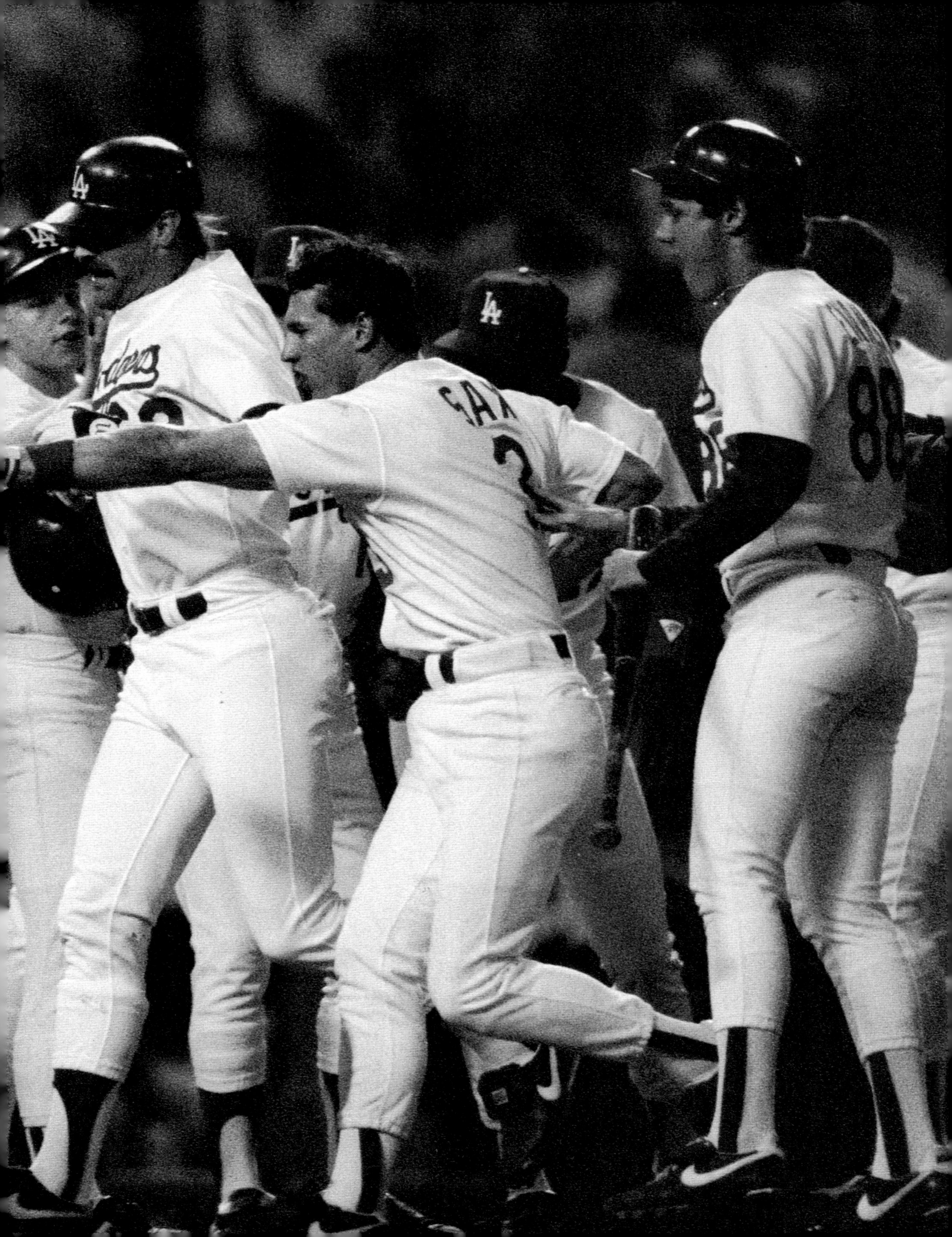
SAX
88

"Like driving, the name of the game is to get home safe."
– *Tommy Lasorda*

CULTURE

At the movies, *Bull Durham* stars Kevin Costner, Tim Robbins, and Susan Sarandon, along with baseball clown Max Patkin; it's a story about the minor leagues. *Eight Men Out*, based on Eliot Asinof's book about the Black Sox, stars D.B. Sweeney, John Cusack, Charlie Sheen, and David Strathairn. *Stealing Home*, about a minor leaguer, stars Mark Harmon and Jodie Foster.

game three-hitter, beating the Athletics, 6-0. A three-run homer by Mike Marshall in the fifth is all the help Hershiser – who has three hits himself – needs. Dave Parker has all of Oakland's safeties. The losing pitcher is George "Storm" Davis.

OCTOBER 18:

World Series, game three. The scene shifts north to Oakland, and the Athletics respond with a 2-1 victory on Mark McGwire's solo home run in the bottom of the ninth. The fourth Oakland pitcher of the game – Rick Honeycutt – gets the win. Reliever Jay Howell is tagged with the loss.

OCTOBER 19:

World Series, game four. Tim Belcher gets the victory and Jay Howell a save as the Dodgers beat the Athletics, 4-3, to move within one game of the championship. Oakland starter Dave Stewart gets the loss.

OCTOBER 20:

World Series, game five. Behind Orel Hershiser's complete-game four-hitter, the Dodgers beat the Athletics, 5-2, and win the World Championship. Hershiser gets support from two-run homers by Mickey Hatcher and Mike Davis. The losing pitcher is Storm Davis. Hershiser, 2-0 with a 1.00 ERA, is the Series' Most Valuable Player. Mickey Hatcher bats .368 with two homers and five RBI. Kirk Gibson's dramatic at-bat in game one is his only 1988 Series appearance. Terry Steinbach hits .364 for Oakland.

POST-SEASON

OCTOBER 24:

Fourteen members of the free-agent "class" of 1986 are freed by arbitrator George Nicolau after the owners were again found – on August 31 – to be in collusion. The list is composed of Tim Raines (who re-signed with the Expos for $6.3 million over three years), Claudell Washington, Ron Guidry, Willie Randolph, Brian Downing, Bob Boone, Ernie Whitt, Rich Gedman, Alan Ashby, Jim Clancy, Doyle Alexander, Ken Dayley, Roy Smith, and Dave Concep-cion. They have until December 16 to sign with a new team, rejoin their old clubs, or remain free agents.

NOVEMBER 21:

Hall of Fame pitcher Carl Hubbell, known for his screwball, dies today in Scottsdale, Arizona, at age 85 of head and chest injuries suffered in an automobile accident. In 16 years with the Giants, he was 253-154 with a 2.97 ERA and 1,678 strikeouts. He twice was the NL's Most Valuable Player. In three World Series, Hubbell was 4-2 with a 1.79 ERA. He was inducted into the Hall of Fame in 1947.

DECEMBER 4:

The Dodgers acquire first baseman Eddie Murray (.284, 28 homers, 84 RBI) from the Orioles for pitchers Brian Holton (7-3, 1.70 ERA) and Ken Howell (0-1, 6.39 ERA), plus minor league infielder Juan Bell.

DECEMBER 5:

The Rangers acquire outfielder-first baseman Rafael Palmeiro (.307, eight homers) and pitchers Jamie Moyer (9-15, 3.48 ERA) and Drew Hall (1-1, 7.66 ERA) from the Cubs for pitchers Mitch "Wild Thing" Williams (2-7, 4.63 ERA, 18 saves), Paul Kilgus (12-15, 4.16 ERA), and Steve Wilson (0-0, 5.87 ERA); infielder Curtis Wilkerson (.293), and two minor leaguers – infielder Luis Benitez and Pablo Delgado.

DECEMBER 6:

Agnes Neil Williams, the widow of attorney and Orioles owner Edward Bennett Williams – who died in August – sells the team for $70 million. The purchaser is a syndicate that includes Eli Jacobs, R. Sargent Shriver, and Larry Lucchino.

The Rangers acquire infielder-DH Julio Franco (.303, 10 homers, 25 stolen bases) from the Indians for outfielder-DH Oddibe McDowell (.247, six homers, 33 stolen bases), first baseman-DH Pete O'Brien (.272, 16 homers), and infielder Jerry Browne (.229 in 73 games).

DECEMBER 8:

The Padres, who today lost Andy Hawkins to the Yankees, sign another free-agent pitcher, Bruce Hurst (18-6, 3.66 ERA), who was with the Red Sox in 1988. Hurst gets a three-year, $5.25 million deal from San Diego.

OCTOBER 20
The Dodgers beat the Athletics, 5-2, in game five to capture the World Series.

THE BEST OF 1988

NATIONAL LEAGUE

HITTERS

Batting Average:
Tony Gwynn, San Diego Padres, .313

Slugging Average:
Darryl Strawberry, New York Mets, .545

Home Runs:
Darryl Strawberry, 39

Runs Batted In:
Will Clark, San Francisco Giants, 109

Hits:
Andres Galarraga, Montreal Expos, 184

Stolen Bases:
Vince Coleman, St. Louis Cardinals, 81

PITCHERS

Wins:
Danny Jackson, Cincinnati Reds; Orel Hershiser, Los Angeles Dodgers, 23

Strikeouts:
Nolan Ryan, Houston Astros, 228

Earned Run Average:
Joe Magrane, St. Louis Cardinals, 2.18

Winning Percentage:
David Cone, New York Mets, .870

Saves:
John Franco, Cincinnati Reds, 39

Most Valuable Player:
Kirk Gibson, Los Angeles Dodgers

Cy Young Award:
Orel Hershiser, Los Angeles Dodgers

Rookie of the Year:
Chris Sabo, Cincinnati Reds

Manager of the Year:
Tom Lasorda, Los Angeles Dodgers

AMERICAN LEAGUE

HITTERS

Batting Average:
Wade Boggs, Boston Red Sox, .366

Slugging Average:
Jose Canseco, Oakland Athletics, .569

Home Runs:
Jose Canseco, 42

Runs Batted In:
Jose Canseco, 124

Hits:
Kirby Puckett, Minnesota Twins, 234

Stolen Bases:
Rickey Henderson, New York Yankees, 93

PITCHERS

Wins:
Frank Viola, Minnesota Twins, 24

Strikeouts:
Roger Clemens, Boston Red Sox, 291

Earned Run Average:
Allan Anderson, Minnesota Twins; Teddy Higuera, Milwaukee Brewers, 2.45

Winning Percentage:
Frank Viola, .774

Saves:
Dennis Eckersley, Oakland Athletics, 45

Most Valuable Player:
Jose Canseco, Oakland Athletics

Cy Young Award:
Frank Viola, Minnesota Twins

Rookie of the Year:
Walt Weiss, Oakland Athletics

Manager of the Year:
Tony LaRussa, Oakland Athletics

CULTURE

***The Eight Corners of the World*, a novel by by Gordon Weaver, includes a fictionalized account of the 1935 major league baseball tour to Japan and Moe Berg's activities as an American spy. *The Further Adventures of Slugger McBatt*, by W.P. Kinsella, is a book of short stories. *Saturday Night Dead*, by Richard D. Rosen, is another mystery featuring private eye and former major leaguer Harvey Blissberg.**

1989

"I'm the kind of guy who doesn't let up."
– *Dave Stewart*

NEWS

TWO LIBYAN JETS SHOT DOWN BY U.S. NAVY PLANES

MAJOR EARTHQUAKE HITS SAN FRANCISCO AREA

JAPAN'S EMPEROR HIROHITO DIES

SERIAL KILLER TED BUNDY EXECUTED IN FLORIDA

LUCILLE BALL, LAURENCE OLIVIER, BETTE DAVIS DIE

IRAN'S AYATOLLAH KHOMEINI DIES

HURRICANE HUGO RIPS NORTH, SOUTH CAROLINA, KILLING 10 AND CAUSING EXTENSIVE DAMAGE

BERLIN WALL COMES DOWN

Communists ousted in Czech and Polish elections

UPRISING IN ROMANIA TOPPLES COMMUNIST GOVERNMENT

PRE-SEASON

JANUARY 5:

On the heels of the recently-announced $1.1 billion CBS television deal, outgoing commissioner Peter Ueberroth announces a $400 million, four-year contract with ESPN for the cable rights to 175 games a season and a $50 million, four-year radio pact with CBS.

JANUARY 9:

Hall of Famer Bill Terry, who hit .401 in 1930, dies in Jacksonville, Florida, at age 92. A first baseman, Terry played 14 years with the New York Giants, compiling a lifetime batting average of .341 with 154 homers. He batted .300 or better for 10 consecutive seasons and appeared in three World Series, hitting .295. Terry also managed the Giants for three years, leading the team to three pennants and one World Series Championship. Terry was inducted into the Hall of Fame in 1954.

Terry once said the secret of his hitting success is "confidence, my boy, confidence." He added, "What I mean is that if you want to accomplish something, you must have confidence in your method of doing it."

JANUARY 21:

Carl Furillo, a rifle-armed right fielder for the Dodgers from 1946 through 1960, dies in Stony Creek Mills, Pennsylvania, at age 66. Furillo, the NL's batting champion in 1953 with a .344 average, compiled a lifetime mark of .299 and appeared in seven World Series.

JANUARY 22:

Willie "Devil" Wells, Negro Leagues shortstop, dies in Austin Texas, at age 80. In some 20 years, Wells batted .328 and was regarded as the best at his position in the 1930s and 1940s.

FEBRUARY 3:

Former major league first baseman and broadcaster Bill White becomes the president of the NL, succeeding A. Bartlett Giamatti. White is the highest ranking black executive ever in sports. He played 13 years and batted .286 with 202 homers.

FEBRUARY 9:

Red Sox third baseman Wade Boggs challenges the $6 million "palimony" suit brought by Margo Adams, with whom he had a four-year affair. Boggs has admitted Adams accompanied him on Red Sox road trips.

FEBRUARY 15:

The Red Sox sign pitcher Roger Clemens (18-12, 2.93 ERA, 291 strikeouts, eight shutouts) to a three-year, $7.5 million contract. It is baseball's highest salary.

FEBRUARY 16:

One day after signing his new contract, Red Sox pitcher Roger Clemens no longer is baseball's highest paid. Orel Hershiser, the 1988 World Series Most Valuable Player, signs a $7.9 million, three-year contract, and he becomes the highest paid. Hershiser gets a $1.1 million signing bonus. The *New York Times* reports 21 major league players are making $2 million a year or more.

FEBRUARY 17:

Hall of Fame pitcher Vernon "Lefty" Gomez dies at age 80 in Greenbrae, California. Gomez, also known as Goofy, pitched for 14 years, compiling a 189-102 record with a 3.34 ERA. He twice was the AL's big winner

FEBRUARY 16
Pitcher Orel Hershiser signs a $7.9 million, three-year contract, the richest to date.

FEBRUARY 20
Commissioner Peter Ueberroth meets with Pete Rose to discuss Rose's gambling habits.

After a shaky start, the Oakland Athletics sweep the cross-Bay rival San Francisco Giants in the World Series. A's pitcher Dave Stewart is 2-0 with a 1.69 ERA – and the Series MVP.

and was 6-0 with an ERA of 2.86 in five World Series for the Yankees. He was inducted into the Hall of Fame in 1972.

FEBRUARY 20:

Reds' manager Pete Rose meets with outgoing Commissioner Peter Ueberroth and his replacement, A. Bartlett Giamatti. It is a command performance for Rose, who is questioned about betting on baseball.

FEBRUARY 27:

Blue Jays' draftee John Olerud undergoes surgery to remove a brain aneurysm. Olerud collapsed on January 11 after working out at Washington State University. He was drafted by Toronto last June.

MARCH 2:

Mets' outfielder Darryl Strawberry throws a punch at his teammate, first baseman Keith Hernandez, during the team's photo session at their Port St. Lucie, Florida, spring training camp. Before the scuffle, the two stars argue about remarks concerning salaries as they take their places in the front row. Strawberry then leaves spring training camp and threatens to miss the entire season unless the team renegotiates his contract, which pays him $1.4 million this season. His agent Eric Goldschmidt says, "He's underpaid." Strawberry tells the *New York Times*: "I'm going. I don't know when I'll be back. When I feel like it, I guess. I'll be back one day."

Strawberry returns two days later after being fined and says he will play two seasons more with the Mets and then leave. After meeting with team psychiatrist Dr. Alan Lans, Strawberry and Hernandez shake hands.

MARCH 18:

Eddie Chiles sells the controlling interest in the Texas Rangers to an investor group of 30 limited partners led by George W. Bush – son of President Bush – and Edward W. "Rusty" Rose.

MARCH 20:

Commissioner Peter Ueberroth announces he "has been conducting a full investigation into serious allegations" about Reds' manager Pete Rose.

MARCH 27:

Sports Illustrated reports details of Pete Rose's gambling activities. The maga-

CULTURE

***Field of Dreams*, the film version of W.P. Kinsella's modern classic novel *Shoeless Joe*, stars Kevin Costner, Amy Madigan, Ray Liotta, James Earl Jones, and Burt Lancaster. *Major League* stars Tom Berenger, Charlie Sheen, and Corbin Bernsen as members of the Cleveland Indians.**

Says Steve Wulf of *Sports Illustrated* about the fight between Strawberry and Hernandez: "Right-fielder Darryl Strawberry finally hit his cutoff man."

zine alleges that, from the dugout in Cincinnati's Riverfront Stadium, Rose gave hand signals about his bets to an associate.

APRIL 1:

A. Bartlett Giamatti takes over as baseball commissioner, becoming the seventh to hold the position.

THE SEASON

APRIL 3:

Ken Griffey Jr., the youngest major league player at 19, hits the first pitch he sees – off the Athletics' Dave Stewart – for a double to left center field at the Oakland-Alameda Coliseum. The Athletics win the game, 3-2. Griffey and his father – Ken Sr. of the Reds – are the first father and son to play in the majors at the same time.

APRIL 12:

The Rangers' Nolan Ryan strikes out 15 Brewers in an 8-1, one-hit victory. Ryan allows two walks and serves up an eighth-inning single to Terry Francona. His career strikeout total now is 4,798. Bill Wegman is the losing pitcher.

APRIL 18:

Commissioner A. Bartlett Giamatti contacts federal judge Carl Rubin, who is sentencing Ron Peters on drug charges. Peters was described by *Sports Illustrated* as Pete Rose's bookie. Giamatti writes that Peters has provided "critical sworn testimony about Mr. Rose and his associates... I am satisfied Mr. Peters has been candid, forthright and truthful with my special counsel."

APRIL 26:

With his first four-hit game plus three RBI, Ken Griffey Jr. leads the Mariners to a 7-6 victory over the Blue Jays. Griffey wins the game with a two-run homer off David Wells.

APRIL 30:

In Texas, before a crowd of 40,429, two right-handed fireballers face off in an old-fashioned pitchers' duel. Going into the eighth, the Red Sox and Roger Clemens lead the Rangers and Nolan Ryan, 1-0. With one on, Rafael Palmeiro catches a Clemens' pitch and parks it over the wall and just inside the right-field foul pole. Texas wins, 2-1. Ryan fans 11; Clemens strikes out six Rangers.

MAY 2:

The Phillies' Mike Schmidt homers against Jim Deshaies of the visiting Astros. It is Schmidt's 548th career home run – and his last.

MAY 4:

The Blue Jays' Junior Felix becomes the 53rd major leaguer to homer in his first at-bat. Felix connects against starter Kirk McCaskill in the third inning, although the Angels beat the Blue Jays, 3-2, in a 10-inning affair.

MAY 7:

With Beau Comiskey – the great-great-grandson of original White Sox owner Charles Comiskey – Chicago mayor Richard M. Daley, and Illinois governor James Thompson participating, ground is broken for the new Comiskey Park.

MAY 13:

The Twins' Kirby Puckett doubles four times against the visiting Toronto Blue Jays at the Metrodome. Puckett ties a record held by many others.

MAY 14:

Pirates' first baseman-outfielder Benny Distefano comes in to catch in the ninth inning of a game against the Braves and becomes the first left-handed receiver in the majors in nine years. Mike Squires of the White Sox in 1980 and Dale Long of the Cubs in 1958 were the last two southpaws to catch. The Braves win, 5-2.

Sportswriter Gerald Eskenazi reports in the *New York Times* that baseball memorabilia has now become a $1 billion-plus business.

MAY 15:

The Blue Jays fire Jimy Williams and name Clarence "Cito" Gaston acting manager. Under Williams, Toronto was 12-24.

MAY 23:

After being fanned in his previous six at-bats against Nolan Ryan, Vincent "Bo" Jackson of the Royals launches a monster drive – 461 feet. It is believed to be the longest homer ever at Arlington Stadium.

MAY 25:

The Mariners and Expos engineer a major trade involving

APRIL 3
Rookie Ken Griffey Jr. hits the first major league pitch he sees for a double.

five pitchers. Going to Seattle are six-foot, 10-inch left-hander Randy Johnson (0-4), Brian Holman (1-2), and Gene Harris (1-1). Montreal receives Mark Langston (4-5) – who led the AL in strikeouts in 1984, 1986, and 1987 – and a player to be named later. Pitcher Mike Campbell (1-2) goes to the Expos on July 31, 1989, to complete the trade.

MAY 28:

In their last game ever at Exhibition Stadium in Toronto, the Blue Jays beat the White Sox, 7-5, in 10 innings on a George Bell homer. The winning pitcher is Tom Henke; Bobby Thigpen gets the loss. In 1977, in the first game ever played at Exhibition, the Blue Jays topped the White Sox by a score of 9-5.

MAY 31:

Sixteen days after being named the Blue Jays' interim manager, Cito Gaston gets the job permanently.

JUNE 2:

The Phillies obtain first baseman-outfielder John Kruk (.184 in 31 games) and outfielder-infielder Randy Ready (.254 in 28 games) from the Padres for outfielder-third baseman Donald "Chris" James (.207 in 45 games).

JUNE 3:

In Seattle, Nolan Ryan of the Rangers one-hits the Mariners, 6-1, and fans 11. Harold Reynolds leads off the game with a single for the Mariners' only hit. Ryan allows only two walks in his complete-game victory. His career strikeout total climbs to 4,875, and he has 100 for the season. He now has fanned 10 or more batters in 188 games, a major league record. On April 23, Ryan carried a no-hitter into the ninth inning against the Blue Jays; Nelson Liriano spoiled that bid with a one-out triple.

In Houston, the Astros and Dodgers battle for 22 innings and seven hours, 14 minutes – the longest night game ever in the NL. The game ends after midnight when Rafael Ramirez of Houston singles in the winning run; the final is 5-4. The length of the contest creates player shortages: the Dodgers end up with pitcher Fernando Valenzuela at first base, first sacker Eddie Murray at third, and infielder Jeff Hamilton pitching. The teams begin a second game at 1:35 a.m. and struggle through 13 more innings, with the Astros winning again, 7-6.

JUNE 5:

The new home of the Blue Jays, Toronto's SkyDome, opens with a crowd of 48,378 on hand. The stadium, which took three years to build at a cost estimated between $375 million and $425 million, features a $100 million retractable roof, a hotel behind centerfield, the largest scoreboard in baseball (four stories high and 115 feet wide), 420,000 lights, four McDonald's eateries, an 800-seat restaurant, a theatre, and a swimming pool. The seating capacity is 50,516. The first batter, Paul Molitor, singles against Toronto's Jimmy Key, and the Brewers go on to spoil the inaugural with a 5-3 victory. Glenn Braggs hits a two-run homer for Milwaukee after the Blue Jays' Fred McGriff connects in the second inning with the first round-tripper in the SkyDome.

JUNE 14:

Hall of Famer William "Judy" Johnson dies in Wilmington, Delaware. A Negro Leagues third baseman, shortstop, and manager who batted .301 in 18 seasons, Johnson was inducted into the Baseball Hall of Fame in 1975.

There is a disagreement about Judy Johnson's age at the time of his death. The New York Times *and the* Baseball Encyclopedia *record it as 89;* The Negro Leagues Book *lists him as 79.*

JUNE 18:

The Mets ship outfielder Lenny "Nails" Dykstra (.270 in five games) and pitcher Roger McDowell (1-5) plus a player to be named later to the Phillies for infielder-outfielder Juan Samuel (.246 in 51 games). The player to be named later is minor league pitcher Tom Edens, who joins Philadelphia on July 26.

JUNE 19:

Pete Rose institutes a suit against Commissioner A. Bartlett Giamatti, major league baseball, and the Reds. Rose maintains Giamatti cannot fairly judge him and wants to have a jury trial.

TRIVIA

President Ronald Reagan, a former sportscaster, does one inning of color commentary on the national telecast of the All-Star Game.

Johnny Bench's Hall of Fame plaque notes that he "redefined standards by which catchers are measured."

HISTORY

In July, the Cardinals' Vince Coleman steals his 50th consecutive base, a streak compiled over two seasons. His streak ends when Nelson Santovenia of the Expos throws him out.

JUNE 21:

FBI sources tell Murray Chass of the *New York Times* they are in possession of betting sheets in Pete Rose's handwriting and with his fingerprints. The material records bets Rose made on the Reds. Rose claims the slips are forgeries.

Rickey Henderson (.247 in 65 games) returns to the Athletics from the Yankees. Oakland sends New York pitchers Eric Plunk (1-1) and Greg Cadaret (0-0) plus outfielder Luis Polonia (.286 in 59 games).

JUNE 25:

The Mets become the second team ever to play a nine-inning game without an assist. The 1945 Indians were the only other team to manage the feat. The Mets beat the Phillies, 5-1.

JUNE 27:

In Baltimore, the Orioles, managed by Frank Robinson, face the Blue Jays with Cito Gaston at the helm. It is the first time in the majors that two black managers oppose each other. The Orioles win the game, 16-6.

JULY 5:

The Mariners' Ken Griffey Jr. hits a pair of 400-foot-plus homers in a 7-3 victory over the Twins. Pitcher Gene Harris records his first major league victory.

JULY 11:

In Anaheim, the AL downs the NL, 5-3 in the All-Star Game; Vincent "Bo" Jackson and Wade Boggs hit back-to-back homers in the first inning. Nolan Ryan, age 42, becomes the oldest pitcher with an All-Star Game victory; John Smoltz is tagged with the loss. It is the first All-Star Game in which the DH is used.

JULY 12:

Yankees' left-hander Ron Guidry retires. Struggling to regain his form after elbow surgery last year, Guidry is only 2-3 with a 4.18 ERA. In 14 years with New York, he is 170-91 with a 3.29 ERA and 1,778 strikeouts. A three-time 20-game winner, Guidry enjoyed his best season in 1978 when he was 25-3 with a 1.74 ERA and nine shutouts. In three World Series, he compiled a 3-1 record and an ERA of 1.69.

JULY 17:

At Comiskey Park, Carlton Fisk of the White Sox hits safely against the Yankees for his 2,000th career hit.

JULY 18:

Donnie Moore, the 35-year-old former Angels' pitcher, shoots his wife, Tonya, and then kills himself with a .44 pistol in Anaheim, California. Moore's suicide is attributed to lingering depression over the homer he yielded to Dave Henderson of the Red Sox in the 1986 ALCS, dashing the Angels' pennant hopes. Moore was with the AAA Omaha Royals this season. Tonya survives the shooting.

JULY 19:

Cleveland Indians outfielder Joe Carter ties Lou Gehrig's AL record with three home runs in a game four times. He also drives in six runs to lead his team to a 10-1 win over the Twins at Minnesota. Carter had two round-trippers yesterday and, on June 24, had three in a game. Albert Belle hits his first major league homer off Randy St. Claire.

JULY 23:

Johnny Bench, Albert "Red" Schoendienst, Carl Yastrzemski, and former umpire Al Barlick are inducted into the Hall of Fame. Bench, regarded by many as the greatest catcher of all time, played 17 years with the Reds, batting .267 with 389 homers. He led the NL three times in RBI and twice in homers. He appeared in four World Series, batting .279. Schoendienst, primarily a second baseman, played 19 years with the Cardinals, Giants, and Braves. He batted .289 with a high of .342 in 1953. In three World Series, he had a .269 average. Yastrzemski played 23 years, appearing in 3,308 games, all with the Red Sox. The outfielder compiled a lifetime average of .285 with 452 homers and 1,844 RBI. He led the AL in batting three times and in homers once. He hit .352 in two World Series. Barlick umped for four decades in the NL, working seven World Series and retiring after the 1970 season.

JULY 31:

The Twins trade left-hander Frank Viola (8-12) to the Mets for pitchers Rick Aguilera

JULY 11
In the All-Star Game, Bo Jackson and Wade Boggs hit back-to-back home runs.

JULY 19
Joe Carter ties Lou Gehrig's AL mark with three homers in a game four times.

(6-6), David West (0-2), and Kevin Tapani (0-0); minor league pitcher Tim Drummond, and a player to be named later. Minor league pitcher Jack Savage joins Minnesota on October 16, completing the trade.

The Mets make a second trade, sending popular outfielder William "Mookie" Wilson (.205 in 80 games) to the Blue Jays for pitcher Jeff Musselman (0-1) and minor league pitcher Mike Brady.

AUGUST 3:

The Reds set a major league record with 16 hits – 12 singles – in the first inning of today's game against the visiting Astros. The barrage produces 14 runs and Cincinnati goes on to an 18-2 victory. Jim Clancy and Bob Forsch of Houston surrender two hits each to seven Reds in the frame. Clancy, who faces seven hitters without recording an out, gets the loss. Forsch goes seven innings, allowing 18 hits and 10 runs. Tom Browning is the winning pitcher. Ken Griffey, Rolando Roomes, and Jeff Reed homer for Cincinnati. Glenn Davis connects for the Astros.

LEFTY GOMEZ RETAINED HIS SENSE OF HUMOR UNTIL THE END. HIS WIFE, JUNE O'DEA GOMEZ, TOLD THE *WASHINGTON POST*: "IN THE HOSPITAL, ABOUT A WEEK BEFORE HE DIED, THE DOCTOR LEANED OVER HIS BED AND SAID, 'LEFTY, PICTURE YOURSELF ON THE MOUND AND RATE THE PAIN FROM 1 TO 10.' AND LEFTY LOOKED AT HIM AND SAID, 'WHO'S HITTING, DOC?'"

AUGUST 4:

The Blue Jays' Dave Stieb is an out away from a perfect game when disappointment strikes in the form of Yankees' outfielder Roberto Kelly, who doubles on a 2-0 slider to spoil the bid. Steve Sax then singles and Stieb must settle for a two-hitter and a 2-1 victory in the SkyDome. The losing pitcher is Clay Parker.

AUGUST 10:

Giants' pitcher Dave Dravecky returns after surgery for removal of a cancer on his pitching arm and beats the Reds, 4-3, at Candlestick Park. Dravecky goes seven innings and allows just one hit.

AUGUST 15:

Dave Dravecky's pitching arm breaks with a sound audible throughout Olympic Stadium in Montreal as he is delivering a pitch in the sixth inning against the Expos. He drops to the ground and is carried off the playing field, suffering a stress fracture of the humerus. The pitcher, who underwent surgery in 1988 for cancer in his pitching arm, had allowed only three hits and was shutting out the Expos when disaster struck. The Giants go on to win, 3-2, and Dravecky gets credit for the victory. On August 17, the *New York Times* reports that doctors had warned Dravecky of the possibility of such a fracture. He retires with a lifetime win-loss record of 64-57.

The Rangers get 13 hits and don't score; the Mariners manage only one, score twice and win, 2-0. Brian Holman and Mike Schooler of Seattle combine to shut out Texas. Rangers' pitcher Charlie Hough yields two runs on a single hit and is credited with the loss.

AUGUST 18:

The full season promised to Dallas Green when he became the Yankees' manager last October ends today when he is fired by owner George Steinbrenner after a series of clashes. The straw that is assumed to have broken Steinbrenner's back is Green's reference to him as "manager George." With the Yankees at 56-65, Bucky Dent assumes the ballclub's helm.

The Orioles' Cal Ripken Jr. plays in his 1,208th consecutive game. He now is in third place, after passing Steve Garvey.

HISTORY

No pitcher besides Nolan Ryan has even come close to 5,000 strikeouts. The next best record is Steve Carlton, with 4,136.

"I have an obligation to try to mend the breaks of baseball."
– Commissioner Bart Giamatti

HISTORY

The Dowd Report says Rose bet on Reds' games 52 times in 1987, wagering a minimum of $10,000 a day. It also alleges he borrowed $47,000 from a drug dealer. The report was compiled by attorney John Dowd.

AUGUST 20:

The Mets' Howard Johnson homers in a 5-4 loss to the Dodgers. It is Johnson's 30th round-tripper of the year, and he also has 30 stolen bases. Along with Bobby Bonds and Willie Mays, he is the only two-time member of the 30-30 "club."

AUGUST 22:

Forty-two-year-old Nolan Ryan of the Rangers goes where no pitcher has gone before. At Arlington Stadium with 42,869 fans cheering him on, he strikes out the Athletics' Rickey Henderson in the fifth inning with a 96-mph fastball for his 5,000th career strikeout. Ryan begins the game needing six to reach the exalted mark. In the first inning he fans Jose Canseco; he gets Dave Henderson and Tony Phillips in the second, and Henderson and Ron Hassey in the third. He finishes the night with 5,007, but Texas loses, 2-0.

AUGUST 23:

The Dodgers beat the Expos, 1-0, in a six-hour, 15-minute, 22-inning game in Montreal. The game ends on a Rick Dempsey homer off Dennis Martinez. The game had apparently ended in the 16th when Larry Walker scored on a sacrifice fly, but the Montreal run was wiped out on appeal. Two umpires on their way to the locker room were recalled and the game resumed. John Wetteland gets the victory.

AUGUST 24:

Commissioner A. Bartlett Giamatti releases details of an agreement Pete Rose has signed that permanently bans him from baseball, although he is eligible to apply for reinstatement in one year. He tells the press that, on the basis of his investigator's report, "I have concluded that he bet on baseball." Rose also agrees that he will not challenge the decision on reinstatement and he drops his lawsuits. He acknowledges that Giamatti was fair. In return, the commissioner issues the following satement: "Nothing in this statement shall be deemed either an admission or a denial by Peter Edward Rose of the allegation that he bet on any major league baseball game."

Giamatti says: "The matter of Mr. Rose is now closed. Let no one think it did not hurt baseball. That hurt will pass, however, as the great glory of the game asserts itself and a resilient institution goes forward. Let it also be clear that no individual is superior to the game."

SEPTEMBER 1:

At 4:30 p.m., baseball commissioner A. Bartlett Giamatti dies of a heart attack at age 51, while vacationing at his summer cottage in Martha's Vineyard, Massachusetts. He and Kenesaw Mountain Landis are the only commissioners to die while in office. He said of his role: "I have an obligation to try to mend the breaks in baseball – financial, technological, and social."

Bart Giamatti, who had a lifelong love of baseball, in 1977 wrote in Yale Alumni Magazine*: "It breaks your heart. It is designed to break your heart. The game begins in the spring, when everything else begins again, and it blossoms in the summer, filling the afternoons and evenings, and then as soon as the chill rains come, it stops and leaves you to face the fall alone."*

SEPTEMBER 3:

In Toronto, John Olerud, who underwent surgery in February to repair a brain aneurysm, makes his major league debut as a defensive replacement at first base for the Blue Jays. He then singles against German Gonzales of the Twins for his first major league hit.

Truett "Rip" Sewell, the inventor of the "eephus" pitch, dies in Plant City, Florida, at 82. The eephus was a blooper pitch, and Sewell is perhaps best remembered for the mammoth homer Ted Williams hit off it in the 1946 All-Star Game. Sewell pitched 13 years, compiling a 143-97 record with a 3.48 ERA. In 1943, he led the NL with 21 wins.

SEPTEMBER 13:

Fay Vincent Jr., a 51-year-old attorney and former chairman and CEO of Columbia Pictures, is elected to serve the unfinished four and a half years of the late A. Bartlett Giamatti's term as baseball commissioner. Vincent was Giamatti's deputy commissioner.

SEPTEMBER 26:

The Cubs beat the Expos today, 3-2, in Montreal to wrap up the NL East title. It is Chicago's first title since 1984.

AUGUST 22
Nolan Ryan, 42, fans Rickey Henderson to record his 5,000th career strikeout.

SEPTEMBER 1
A week after banning Pete Rose from baseball, Commissioner Bart Giamatti dies.

SEPTEMBER 27:

The Athletics beat the Rangers today, 5-0, in Oakland, winning the AL West title.

The Giants lose to the Dodgers, 1-0, in Los Angeles, but win the NL West when the Reds top the Padres, 2-1, in 13 innings.

SEPTEMBER 29:

August Anheuser "Gussie" Busch Jr., owner of the Cardinals, dies at age 90 in suburban St. Louis. Busch owned the team for 36 years, from 1953 until today.

SEPTEMBER 30:

In Toronto, Cito Gaston's Blue Jays beat the Orioles, 4-3, to wrap up their second AL East title in the last five years.

REGULAR SEASON WRAP-UP:

Tony LaRussa's Athletics finish the regular season with a 99-63 record in the AL. Carney Lansford is the team's top average hitter at .336. Mark McGwire hits 33 homers and drives in 95 runs with a .231 average. Dave Parker adds 22 homers and 97 RBI. Rickey Henderson bats .294 and steals 77 bases. Dave Stewart leads the staff at 21-9; Dennis Eckersley records 33 saves.

The Giants, managed by Roger Craig, are 92-70. Kevin Mitchell leads the NL in homers (47) and RBI (125) and bats .291. Will Clark bats .333 with 23 homers and 111 RBI. The team has no 20-game winner. Rick Reuschel is 17-8. Craig Lefferts has 20 saves; fellow closer Steve Bedrosian, 17. The Giants will meet Cubs in the NLCS.

OCTOBER 3:

ALCS, game one. In Oakland today, the Athletics behind Dave Stewart beat the Blue Jays, 7-3. A critical error by Toronto second baseman Nelson Liriano along with homers by Dave Henderson and Mark McGwire are instrumental in Oakland's victory. Dave Stieb gets the loss; Ernie Whitt homers for the losers.

OCTOBER 4:

NLCS, game one. At Wrigley Field, the Giants use 13 hits to

HISTORY

Wade Boggs of the Red Sox adds to his own major league record with 200 hits for the seventh consecutive season.

The World Series between the Giants and A's is disrupted by a serious earthquake.

MR.SUB
328
BLUE JAYS
THE NEXT GENERATION

MR SUB
375
328
THE NEXT GENERATION
AMERICAN LEAGUE

hammer the Cubs, 11-3. Will Clark does the major damage with a four-for-four day – including a grand slam and a solo homer – and five RBI. Kevin Mitchell adds a three-run round-tripper and starter Scott Garrelts gets the win. Greg Maddux takes the loss. Mark Grace and Ryne Sandberg homer for Chicago. ALCS, game two. Dave Parker homers, Rickey Henderson steals four bases, and Mark McGwire has an RBI double to give Mike Moore and the Athletics a 6-3 victory. Todd Stottlemyre is charged with the loss.

OCTOBER 5:

NLCS, game two. Despite three Giants' homers – by Kevin Mitchell, Matt Williams, and Robby Thompson – the Cubs prevail, 9-5. Jerome Walton has two hits in a six-run 1st inning by Chicago. The winning pitcher is Les Lancaster, with four innings of relief. Starter Rick Reuschel is charged with the loss.

Radio magnate Jeff Smulyan of Emmis Broadcasting Company and his partners – Michael Browning and the Morgan Stanley Group, Inc., of New York City – complete the purchase of the Mariners from George Argyros. The new owners, who reached an agreement to buy the team in August, won approval in September. They will retain general manager William "Woody" Woodward and manager Jim Lefebvre.

OCTOBER 6:

ALCS, game three. In Toronto, the Blue Jays break the ice with a 7-3 win, coming from behind with a four-run fourth inning. Toronto had lost five consecutive ALCS games prior to tonight. Jimmy Key gets the win; George "Storm" Davis is charged with loss. Dave Parker homers for Oakland.

OCTOBER 7:

NLCS, game three. At Candlestick Park, the Giants win, 5-4, on Robby Thompson's seventh-inning home run with a runner on. Don Robinson, the third of six San Francisco pitchers, gets the win. Les Lancaster is charged with the loss.

ALCS, game four. Rickey Henderson hits a pair of two-run homers and Jose Canseco adds a solo shot to lead the Athletics past the Blue Jays, 6-5. Bob Welch gets the win with a save by Dennis Eckersley. Mike Flanagan is the losing pitcher.

OCTOBER 8:

NLCS, game four. Matt Williams's solo homer paces the Giants to a 6-4 win, with Kelly Downs getting the victory. Steve Wilson is the game's losing pitcher. Steve Bedrosian fans Andre Dawson on three pitches with the bases loaded to end the game and earn a save. Luis Salazar homers for the losing Cubs.

ALCS, game five. The Athletics overcome home runs by Lloyd Moseby and George Bell to beat the Blue Jays, 4-3, wrapping up the AL pennant. The winning pitcher is Dave Stewart; Dennis Eckersley pitches the final inning and gets a save. The losing pitcher is Jays' starter Dave Stieb. Rickey Henderson hits .400 with a 1.000 slugging average and a record eight stolen bases.

OCTOBER 9:

NLCS, game five. At home today in San Francisco, the Giants top the Cubs, 3-2, to win the NL pennant. Will Clark's bases-loaded single in the bottom of the eighth puts the Giants up for good. Mike Bielecki gets the win; Rick Reuschel is tagged with the loss. Clark hits .650 and is named the NLCS Most Valuable Player.

OCTOBER 14:

World Series, game one. In the West Coast equivalent of a Subway Series, Bay Area rivals, the Giants and Athletics, face off in Oakland. Behind Dave Stewart's complete-game five-hitter, the Athletics win, 5-0. Dave Parker and Walt Weiss homer. Scott Garrelts gets the loss.

OCTOBER 15:

World Series, game two. Terry Steinbach hits a three-run homer and Mike Moore beats the Giants, 5-1. San Francisco manages four hits and starter Rick Reuschel is tagged with the loss.

OCTOBER 17:

At 5:04 P.M. – 20 minutes before game three is scheduled to begin – an earthquake rocks Candlestick Park, jolting the crowd of some 58,000. Measuring 6.9 on the Richter scale, the quake shakes the stadium and knocks out power. Players move onto the field, sig-

←

Toronto's new SkyDome has a retractable roof.

OCTOBER 17
Game two of the World Series at Candlestick Park is abruptly halted by an earthquake.

OCTOBER 28
Finally, the Series is back on, and the A's complete a sweep with a 9-6 victory.

naling to their families to leave stands. The ballpark is evacuated and the game postponed.

OCTOBER 27:

World Series, game three. As the San Francisco area continues to work toward recovery from the effects of the October 17 major earthquake, baseball resumes. The Series originally was to pick up on October 24, but was postponed again. The Athletics pick up where they left off on October 15 – beating the Giants. Oakland uses 14 hits – including two homers by Dave Henderson and one each from Tony Phillips, Jose Canseco, and Carney Lansford – to fashion a 13-7 victory. The winning pitcher is Dave Stewart, who works seven innings. Matt Williams and Bill Bathe hit round-trippers for San Francisco. Starter Scott Garrelts is tagged with the loss.

OCTOBER 28:

World Series, game four. The Athletics sweep the Giants with a 9-6 victory and capture the World Championship. Oakland carves out an 8-0 lead and Mike Moore pitches seven innings for the win. Rickey Henderson homers for Oakland; Kevin Mitchell and Greg Litton connect for San Francisco. The losing pitcher is Don Robinson. Dave Stewart is 2-0 with a 1.69 ERA and wins the Series' Most Valuable Player Award. He also becomes the first pitcher with two wins each in the League Championship and World Series. Rickey Henderson bats .474 and steals three bases. Carney Lansford hits .438. Terry Steinbach drives in seven runs. The leading hitter for the Giants is Kevin Mitchell at .294.

POST-SEASON

NOVEMBER 1:

The Senior Professional Baseball Association begins play in Florida. The league is composed of the Gold Coast Suns, managed by Earl Weaver, with Luis Tiant, Ed Figueroa, Stan Bahnsen, Bert Campaneris, and Paul Blair; the Bradenton Explorers, managed by Clete Boyer, with Bruce Kison, Willie Aikens, Al Cowens, Hal McRae, and Al Oliver; the Winter Haven Super Sox, managed by Bill "Spaceman" Lee, who also will pitch, with Ferguson Jenkins, Rick Wise, Cecil Cooper, Bernie Carbo, and Mike Cuellar; the Fort Myers Sun Sox, managed by Pat Dobson, with Dennis Leonard, Dan Driessen, Dave Collins, Amos Otis, and Wayne Garland; the St. Petersburg Pelicans, managed by Bobby Toland, with Dock Ellis, John Matlack, Bake McBride, Al Holland, and Steve Henderson; the West Palm Beach Tropics, managed by Dick Williams, with Rollie Fingers, Toby Harrah, Dave Kingman, Mickey Rivers, and Lee Lacy; the St. Lucie Legends, managed by Graig Nettles, who also will play, with Vida Blue, Ross Grimsley, Oscar Gamble, Bobby Bonds, and George Foster; and the Orlando Juice, managed by William "Gates" Brown, with Bill Madlock, U.L. Washington, Jose Cruz, Ken Landreaux, and Sixto Lezcano.

NOVEMBER 13:

Jim Rice, who had been feuding with manager Joe M. Morgan, is released by the Red Sox. In 1988, the two had engaged in a shoving match after Morgan replaced Rice with a pinch hitter. Rice, who batted only .234 with three homers in 1989, completes his 16-year career – all in a Red Sox uniform – with a .298 average, 382 homers, and 1,451 career RBI.

NOVEMBER 17:

The Royals reward ace pitcher Bret Saberhagen with a three-year contract reportedly worth some $2.96 million. Saberhagen led the AL with victories (23-6) and ERA (2.16) this past season.

NOVEMBER 20:

Robin Yount of the Brewers is named the AL's Most Valuable Player. Yount, an outfielder-DH, is the second two-position player to be elected MVP.

NOVEMBER 22:

The Twins sign outfielder Kirby Puckett, the AL batting champion, to a three-year contract worth $3 million per season. Puckett, who hit .339 with 9 homers and 85 RBI for Minnesota, is the first ever to earn $3 million per year.

NOVEMBER 28:

On the day the owners and the Players Association begin negotiating a new collective bargaining agreement, outfielder Rickey Henderson

CULTURE

The book *Casey on the Loose*, by Frank Deford, reworks the famous poem "Casey at the Bat." with a different ending by Frank Deford. *Beanball: Murder at the World Series* is by Tom Seaver, with Herb Resnicow. *Strike Zone*, a mystery by David Nighbert, features former pitcher William "Bull" Cochran. *Dead Pull Hitter*, another mystery, is by Alison Gordon.

Former Texas Rangers owner to Billy Martin: "One of three things is going to happen to you. You're either going to kill somebody, somebody is going to kill you, or you're going to kill yourself."

(.274, 12 homers, 77 stolen bases) re-signs with the Athletics. He receives a multi-year deal worth $3 million per season. He was traded back to Oakland by the Yankees in mid-season.

DECEMBER 4:

At the winter meetings, new commissioner Fay Vincent tells the owners: "Bart [Giamatti] had a singular skill as a public speaker. He spoke well because he thought so well. But I point out to you that the most often quoted remark of Bart's brief tenure as commissioner was a very simple declarative sentence. That sentence is the cornerstone on which I will build my own administration. Bart said very simply, 'No one is bigger than the game.' I repeat today what Bart said in August, no one – no player, no executive, no owner, no commissioner, no umpire – is bigger than the game."

DECEMBER 6:

The Mets acquire a relief pitcher – John Franco (4-8, 3.12 ERA, 32 saves) – along with minor league outfielder Don Brown. In return, they send reliever Randy Myers (7-4, 2.35 ERA, 24 saves) and minor league pitcher Kip Gross to the Reds.

The Indians send outfielder-first baseman Joe Carter (.243, 35 homers, 105 RBI, 13 stolen bases) to the Padres for catcher Sandy Alomar Jr. (.211 in seven games), outfielder-third baseman Chris James (.243, 13 homers), and minor league infielder Carlos Baerga.

DECEMBER 8:

The Angels sign free-agent pitcher Mark Langston, who was 4-5 with Seattle and 12-9 with Montreal this past season.

DECEMBER 11:

This year's NL Cy Young Award winner, Mark Davis (4-3, 1.85 ERA, 44 saves), is signed as a free agent by the Royals. Davis was with the San Diego Padres in 1989.

On paper, this signing was a no-brainer. In reality, it was less than a triumph. Davis was 2-7 in 1990 with a 5.11 ERA and only six saves. In 1991, he saved only one game and was traded to the Braves in 1992.

DECEMBER 12:

Multiple drug offender Steve Howe writes to Commissioner Fay Vincent, assuring him: "I have a responsibility to myself, my family, and to baseball and to the fans to conduct myself in a manner that promotes strong morals and good sportsmanship. If I cannot do that by remaining clean and sober, then I myself will walk away from the game."

The Yankees obtain pitcher Tim Leary (8-14, 3.52 ERA) and outfielder Van Snider (.143 in eight games) from the Reds for outfielder-first baseman-DH Hal Morris (.278 in 15 games) and minor league pitcher Rodney Imes.

DECEMBER 13:

Pam Postema and seven male umpires are released from AAA minor league contracts because there is no interest by the major leagues in their services. Postema has been umpiring for 13 years and called major league games in spring training for two years. The 35-year-old tells the Associated Press, "The only thing it said was that I ejected too many people... This is just outrageous. I doubt I'll have anything else to do with baseball. I wanted to be an umpire."

DECEMBER 25:

Billy Martin dies at age 61 in an automobile accident in Johnson City, New York. Martin is a passenger in a pickup truck that skids off the road and down a 300-foot embankment. At the time of his death, he was a member of the Yankees' front office. In 16 years as pilot of the Yankees (five times), Tigers, Rangers, Twins, and Athletics, he won 1,253 games, producing five first-place teams and one World Champion – the 1977 Yankees. His playing career spanned 11 years, and he batted .257.

"He's the kind of guy you'd like to kill if he's playing for the other team," Cleveland general manager Frank Lane said of Martin in 1959, "but you'd like 10 of him on your side."

Martin himself, during one of his five different stints as manager of the Yankees, once said: "All I know is, I pass people on the street these days, and they don't know whether to say hello or to say goodbye." Another time he remarked: "When I get through managing, I'm going to open up a kindergarten."

DECEMBER 6
The Mets acquire lefty reliever – and Brooklyn native – John Franco from the Reds.

DECEMBER 25
Much-traveled manager and former Yankee Billy Martin dies in a car accident.

THE BEST OF 1989

NATIONAL LEAGUE

HITTERS

Batting Average:
Tony Gwynn, San Diego Padres, .336

Slugging Average:
Kevin Mitchell, San Francisco Giants, .635

Home Runs:
Kevin Mitchell, 47

Runs Batted In:
Kevin Mitchell, 125

Hits:
Tony Gwynn, 203

Stolen Bases:
Vince Coleman, St. Louis Cardinals, 65

PITCHERS

Wins:
Mike Scott, Houston Astros, 20

Strikeouts:
Jose DeLeon, St. Louis Cardinals, 201

Earned Run Average:
Scott Garrelts, San Francisco Giants, 2.28

Winning Percentage:
Mike Bielecki, Chicago Cubs, .720

Saves:
Mark Davis, San Diego Padres, 44

Most Valuable Player:
Kevin Mitchell, San Francisco Giants

Cy Young Award:
Mark Davis, San Diego Padres

Rookie of the Year:
Jerome Walton, Chicago Cubs

Manager of the Year:
Don Zimmer, Chicago Cubs

AMERICAN LEAGUE

HITTERS

Batting Average:
Kirby Puckett, Minnesota Twins, .339

Slugging Average:
Ruben Sierra, Texas Rangers, .543

Home Runs:
Fred McGriff, Toronto Blue Jays, 36

Runs Batted In:
Ruben Sierra, 119

Hits:
Kirby Puckett, 215

Stolen Bases:
Rickey Henderson, New York Yankees/ Oakland Athletics, 77

PITCHERS

Wins:
Bret Saberhagen, Kansas City Royals, 23

Strikeouts:
Nolan Ryan, Texas Rangers, 301

Earned Run
Average: Bret Saberhagen, 2.16

Winning Percentage:
Bret Saberhagen, .793

Saves:
Jeff Russell, Texas Rangers, 38

Most Valuable Player:
Robin Yount, Milwaukee Brewers

Cy Young Award:
Bret Saberhagen, Kansas City Royals

Rookie of the Year:
Gregg Olson, Baltimore Orioles

Manager of the Year:
Frank Robinson, Baltimore Orioles

1990

NEWS

Iraq Invades Kuwait; U.S., Allies send armed forces to Persian Gulf

MARGARET THATCHER RESIGNS AS BRITISH PRIME MINISTER

GERMANY REUNIFIED

NELSON MANDELA OUT OF SOUTH AFRICAN PRISON AFTER 27 YEARS

FINANCIER MICHAEL MILKEN GOES TO JAIL FOR ILLEGAL JUNK BOND DEALS

THE SIMPSONS MAKE THEIR TELEVISION DEBUT

FIRST MCDONALD'S OPENS IN SOVIET UNION

US POPULATIONS 248,709,873

HOLLYWOOD MOURNS GRETA GARBO, SAMMY DAVIS, JR.

MAJOR FLAW IN HUBBLE

PRE-SEASON

JANUARY 7:

Horace C. Stoneham, who was principal owner and president of the Giants for 40 years, dies at age 86 in Scottsdale, Arizona. Stoneham sold the team in 1976 and had been retired for 13 years. He became president of the New York Giants in 1936, when his father, Charles A. Stoneham, died.

JANUARY 8:

George Steinbrenner pays gambler Howard Spira $40,000 by check for derogatory information about Dave Winfield. Spira insists on an additional $110,000 and Steinbrenner contacts the FBI.

How come there are only nine guys on the field? Former University of Michigan football coach G. E. "Bo" Schembechler is named president of the Detroit Tigers.

JANUARY 17:

Pitcher Dave Stewart, the Most Valuable Player in last season's World Series, is rewarded by the Athletics with a new contract worth $3.5 million per year. Stewart was 21-9 with a 3.32 ERA.

JANUARY 22:

Will Clark of the Giants becomes baseball's first $4 million man. He signs a four-year, $15-million contract, which will pay him an average of $3.5 million per season. Al Rosen, the team's general manager, says, "He plays like a Hall of Famer and he should be paid like one." Last season, Clark batted .333 with 23 homers and 111 RBI.

FEBRUARY 3:

Darryl Strawberry is admitted to the Smithers Alcoholism and Treatment Center in New York City for what the Mets describe as an "alcohol problem." Strawberry recently was arrested when his wife charged he threatened her with a gun.

FEBRUARY 9:

The owners warn they will not open spring training camps if there is no new basic agreement with the players.

FEBRUARY 15:

The owners make good on their threat, and the news is bad. Spring training camps will not open tomorrow as the owners institute their third lockout of players. Previously, camps were closed in 1973 and 1976. The lockout is blamed on the absence of a basic agreement and an unresolved dispute over salary arbitration. The two sides engage in four and a half hours of negotiations in New York City.

FEBRUARY 22:

The owners drop their proposals on arbitration and minimum salaries, but training camps remain closed.

FEBRUARY 24:

Former major leaguer Tony Conigliaro dies in Salem, Massachusetts, at age 45. Conigliaro, once a promising young star, had suffered a heart attack some years ago and was incapacitated. His eyesight and career were impaired when he was beaned in 1967. He played for eight seasons, batting .264 with 166 homers. In 1965, he led the AL in homers with 32.

MARCH 6:

Hall of Fame shortstop Joe Sewell dies at age 91 in Mobile, Alabama. In 14 major

In February, Yankee owner George Steinbrenner pledges, "Bucky Dent will be the manager all year. I'm very strong on loyalties."

league seasons with the Indians and Yankees, Sewell batted .312. He appeared in two World Series.

MARCH 10:

Spring training camps remain closed for the 24th day, making this the longest lockout ever. In 1976, then-commissioner Bowie Kuhn ordered the training camps open after a 23-day lockout. No negotiations are scheduled in the present dispute.

MARCH 18:

Owners and players announce a settlement of the dispute that created a spring training lockout. Camps will open on March 20 and the season will begin one week late, on April 9. Teams will try to make up lost games on open dates and with double headers. Expectations are that the season will consist of a minimum of 158 games.

MARCH 23:

Gambler Howard Spira is arrested for extorting money from Yankee owner George Steinbrenner. Spira's

Andre Dawson steals it all for the Cubs.

LEAGUE

The season actually is extended by three days to accommodate 162 games. Playoffs begin on October 4; the World Series on October 16.

HISTORY

Steve Howe, suspended from baseball four times, gets the okay from commissioner Fay Vincent to play in the minors, but he must participate in a drug aftercare program. Howe remains ineligible to play in the majors until 1991.

APRIL 20
Pete Rose pleads guilty to tax evasion.

CULTURE

If I Never Get Back by Darryl Brock is a time travel book in which the hero teams up with the 1869 Cincinnati Red Stockings. *The Year I Owned the Yankees*, obviously a work of fiction, is written by Sparky Lyle with David Fisher; the former relief pitcher is the new boss of his old team. *No Fun on Sunday*, another novel, is written by Frederick Manfred.

apartment in the Bronx, New York, was raided by the FBI and tapes were confiscated. Steinbrenner paid Spira $40,000 in January.

From Baseball: A Biographical Encyclopedia: *"Steinbrenner provided various reasons for the payment to Spira, one of which was, 'I did it out of the goodness of my heart. No other reason.' (Spira's mother had cancer.) Another of his justifications: 'You don't know what it's like when you've got a guy out there calling and threatening to kill people in your family.'... Shortly thereafter, Spira was convicted of extortion."*

APRIL 6:

The much-traveled and much-disciplined Steve Howe, now 32 years old, signs with the Salinas Spurs of the Class A California League.

Cecil Fielder finishes the season with 51 home runs.

APRIL 7:

It's deja vu in the Bay Area. An earthquake rumbles through San Francisco while the Giants and Athletics are playing an exhibition game at Candlestick Park.

THE SEASON

APRIL 9:

Ken Griffey Jr. of the Mariners opens in midseason form, collecting four hits–including a homer–in five at-bats and driving in three runs. Seattle beats California, 7-4, in Anaheim.

Delino DeShields of the Expos becomes the 14th major leaguer to make his debut with a four-hit game. DeShields has three singles and a double.

APRIL 11:

Angels' pitchers Mark Langston and Mike Witt combine to no-hit the Mariners, 1-0, in Anaheim. Langston is making his debut in a California uniform after being signed as a free agent in December 1989. He works seven innings, walking four and fanning three. Witt pitches the final three, striking out two and

MAY 29
Rickey Henderson bests Ty Cobb's AL stolen base record

JUNE 6
George Steinbrenner fired Bucky Dent

issuing no bases on balls. Dante Bichette drives in the game's only run. The Angels commit one error. The losing pitcher is Gary Eave.

APRIL 20:

Pete Rose pleads guilty to two felony counts of filing false tax returns. Rose understated his income by $354,698–earned at baseball card shows–on his 1985 and 1987 returns.

The Mariners' Brian Holman pitches eight and two-thirds perfect innings against the Athletics in Oakland. Pinch hitter Ken Phelps spoils Holman's bid for baseball immortality with a home run. Holman then strikes out Rickey Henderson to win the game, 6-1.

APRIL 26:

Old man Ryan, he just keeps rolling along. Now 43 years old, Nolan Ryan of the Rangers throws another one-hitter, fans 16 White Sox batters, and wins, 1-0, in Texas. Ryan ties Bob Feller's major league record with 12 career one-hitters and records his 293rd career victory. Ron Kittle's second-inning, checked-swing single just past first baseman Rafael Palmeiro is Chicago's only safety. Ryan now has 58 career shutouts, and has fanned 10 or more 200 times, and 15 or more 24 times.

APRIL 30:

A front page story in the *New York Times* by Gerald Eskenazi discusses the information revolution and the proliferation of esoteric baseball statistics; the headline asks: HOW MUCH IS ENOUGH?

MAY 4:

The Cardinals acquire relief pitcher Lee Smith (2-1) from the Red Sox for outfielder Tom Brunansky (.158 in 19 games).

MAY 11:

Outfielder-DH Dave Winfield (.213 in 20 games), who has been embroiled in a multiyear war of nerves with Yankee owner George Steinbrenner, is traded to California. In return, New York receives pitcher Mike Witt (0-3).

MAY 22:

The Cubs' Andre Dawson sets a major league record when he is intentionally walked by the Reds five times. The strategy backfires when Dawson receives the fifth of the walks in the bottom of the 16th and the next batter, Dave Clark, singles in the winning run in a 2-1 victory. Cincinnati pitchers issue seven walks overall. The previous record for intentional walks was jointly held by Roger Maris and Garry Templeton.

MAY 23:

Charlie Keller, who teamed with Joe DiMaggio and Tommy Henrich to give the Yankee's one of baseball's all-time great outfields, dies at age 73 in Frederick, Maryland. Known as King Kong, a name he reportedly despised, Keller played 13 years in the majors, batting .286 with 189 homers. He particularly excelled in World Series play, compiling .306 batting and .611 slugging averages in four fall classics.

MAY 29:

In today's game against the Blue Jays, Rickey Henderson gets the 893rd stolen base of his career, topping Ty Cobb's AL record. Henderson doubles and reaches the landmark with a steal of third with two out in the sixth off catcher Greg Myers. Henderson pulls the base out of the ground to mark the occasion. But the Athletics lose, 2-1. David Wells gets the win; Dave Stewart is charged with the loss.

Davey Johnson is out as manager of the 20-22 Mets. He is replaced by Derrel "Bud" Harrelson.

JUNE 2:

The Mariners' six-foot, 10-inch Randy Johnson no-hits the Tigers, 2-0, at the Kingdome. It is the first no-hitter in Seattle's history. Johnson fans eight and walks six; Seattle makes one error. The losing pitcher is Jeff Robinson.

JUNE 4:

In Los Angeles, Dodgers' pitcher Ramon Martinez fans 18 and limits the Braves to two hits in a 6-0 victory. Martinez strikes out 14 of the first 19 batters and gets Jeff Blauser with one out in the eighth for his 18th. Tom Glavine, the losing pitcher, fans six Dodgers.

JUNE 6:

Russell "Bucky" Dent joins the ever-increasing list of ex-Yankee managers when he is

LEAGUE

The NL announces it will expand from 12 to 14 teams in 1993. The two new franchises will be announced next season.

JUNE 11
Nolan Ryan pitches his sixth no-hitter

HISTORY

Nolan Ryan is the fourth oldest pitcher– behind Phil Niekro, Gaylord Perry, and Early Wynn– to win 300.

fired today and replaced by Carl "Stump" Merrill. Under Dent, the team was 18-31.

JUNE 11:

Nolan Ryan of the Rangers pitches his record sixth career no-hitter, beating the Athletics, 5-0, in Oakland. Ryan fans 14 and walks two; Texas commits no errors. The losing pitcher is Scott Sanderson. Ryan, 43 years old, had been on the disabled list with a bad back. He is the first pitcher with six no-hitters, the oldest to throw one, and the only pitcher to do so with three different teams.

JUNE 12:

The Orioles' Cal Ripken Jr. extends his consecutive game streak to 1,308 when he takes the field for today's contest with the Brewers at Memorial Stadium in Baltimore. Ripken takes over second place in the record books, moving past Everett Scott and trailing only Lou Gehrig at 2,130. Ripken has been in the Orioles' lineup without interruption since May 20, 1982. His string of 8,243 consecutive innings played ended in 1987 when he was replaced by a pinch hitter.

> JOE MORGAN ON HIS ELECTION, "I TAKE MY VOTE AS A SALUTE TO THE LITTLE GUY, THE ONE WHO DOESN'T HIT 500 HOME RUNS. I WAS ONE OF THE GUYS THAT DID ALL THEY COULD TO WIN. I'M PROUD OF ALL MY STATS, BUT I DON'T THINK I EVER GOT ONE FOR JOE MORGAN. IF I STOLE A BASE, IT WAS TO HELP US WIN A GAME, AND I LIKE TO THINK THAT'S WHAT MADE ME A LITTLE SPECIAL."

JUNE 13:

At their meeting in Cleveland, major league owners unanimously approve the sale of the Padres by Joan Kroc to television producer Tom Werner and a syndicate of 14 other Southern California businessmen. The purchase price is estimated at $90 million.

JUNE 15:

The strange case of Shufflin' Phil Douglas, banned from baseball by then-commissioner Kenesaw Mountain Landis in 1922, takes another turn. After petitions signed in Tennessee–where Douglas died in 1952–are presented to Commissioner Fay Vincent, word comes down–no reinstatement. Vincent's deputy, Steve Greenberg, says, "The resurrection of the Phil Douglas case today would be inappropriate. The events surrounding the matter cannot be recreated in sufficient detail to provide an adequate basis to review Commissioner Landis's decision. Commissioner Vincent cannot substitute his judgment nearly 70 years after the fact for the judgment of a commissioner with a reputation for the highest degree of integrity." The petitioners say they will take the case to court.

JUNE 19:

A new claimant for the birthplace of baseball surfaces when New Jersey Governor Jim Florio signs a proclamation from the state legislature declaring Hoboken as the place where America's national pastime originated. The proclamation cites a June 19, 1846, game between the New York Nine and the New York Knickerbockers at the Elysian Fields as the first. Attending the ceremonies is 35-year-old Alexander Cartwright IV, the great-great-grandson of the man who wrote the first rules.

JUNE 27:

The Brewers' Dave Parker collects his 2,500th career hit. Jose Canseco of the Athletics becomes baseball's top paid player–for the moment–when he signs a five-year, $23.5 million contract.

JUNE 29:

Records fall as Oakland's Dave Stewart no-hits the

JULY 1
Andy Hawkins pitches a no hitter, and still loses.

JULY 30
George Steinbrenner is banned from baseball "for life."

Blue Jays, 5-0, in Toronto and the Dodgers' Fernando Valenzuela pitches a 6-0 no-hitter against the Cardinals in Los Angeles. It is the first time in the 20th century that two complete-game no-hitters were pitched on the same date and the first time ever that pitchers in each league threw no-hitters on the same date. Stewart strikes out 12 and walks three in his game. Oakland makes no errors. The losing pitcher is John Cerutti. Valenzuela strikes out seven and walks three. The Dodgers make one error. Jose DeLeon gets the loss.

JULY 1:

In Chicago, the Yankees' Andy Hawkins pitches a no-hitter–and loses. With two out in the eighth and no score, Sammy Sosa reaches first base on a throwing error by third baseman Mike Blowers. Ozzie Guillen and Lance Johnson walk. Robin Ventura's fly ball is dropped by Jim Leyritz in left field for a two-base error. Right fielder Jesse Barfield drops Ivan Calderon's fly for another error, and the White Sox win, 4-0. Hawkins walks five and strikes out three.

Houston's Ken Johnson is the only other pitcher in history to lose a no-hitter; he was defeated, 1-0, by the Reds in 1964.

JULY 10:

At Wrigley Field, the AL wins the All-Star Game, 2-0, on a seventh-inning two-run double by Julio Franco. Six AL pitchers allow a total of only two hits; Bret Saberhagen gets the victory. Jeff Brantley is charged with the loss.

JULY 12:

At Yankee Stadium, Melido Perez of the White Sox pitches an abbreviated no-hitter, beating New York, 8-0. The game is called in the middle of the seventh inning because of rain.

JULY 15:

The Royals' Vincent "Bo" Jackson hits three homers–including the 100th of his career–against the Yankees. His big day turns sour when he separates his shoulder trying to catch Deion Sanders's inside-the-park home run.

JULY 17:

The Twins execute two triple plays in one game–a baseball first–but lose to the Red Sox, 1-0, at Fenway Park. Both triple killings are started by third baseman Gary Gaetti and involve second baseman Al Newman and first baseman Kent Hrbek. The game also features a major league record 10 double plays–six by the Twins.

JULY 18:

Strike three. A third collusion decision is handed down–by arbitrator George Nicolau–and it favors the players over the owners. While Nicolau was determining the second collusion grievance case–which the owners also lost–all 26 of the "lords of baseball" knew of the existence of a databank to monitor 1987 salary offers.

JULY 19:

Pete Rose gets five months in prison, three more in a treatment center, a $50,000 fine, and 1,000 hours of community service from U.S. district judge Arthur Spiegel after pleading guilty to income tax evasion. Rose will not appeal.

JULY 25:

According to comic actress Roseanne Barr, her off-key, wailing rendition of The Star-Spangled Banner –complete with spitting on the ground and grabbing her crotch–is a "joke on the players." But many people fail to see the humor in the performance before the Padres-Reds game at Jack Murphy Stadium in San Diego; the critics include President George Bush. Barr's husband, Tom Arnold, says, "She did the best she could. That's the way she sings." She was invited to "sing" by Padres' chairman Tom Werner, who also is executive producer of her television show, *Roseanne*.

JULY 30:

The Boss gets the boot. Baseball commissioner Fay Vincent puts George Steinbrenner on the permanently ineligible list for conduct "not in the best interests of baseball." Steinbrenner gets the "life ban" for his role in the Dave Winfield-Howard Spira case. Steinbrenner had a three-year association with Spira and paid the known gambler $40,000 for detrimental information on Dave Winfield. Steinbrenner is the first AL owner banned as a disciplinary action, and he

CULTURE

On television, The Court Martial of Jackie Robinson stars Andre Braughter as Robinson and Stan Shaw as Joe Louis. Ruby Dee, who played Robinson's wife, Rachel, in the 1950 film The Jackie Robinson Story, portrays his mother in this cable television production. The film focuses on Robinson's military experiences and his days with the Kansas City Monarchs.

Jim Palmer once was asked how long an injury would keep him out and he responded, "Two weeks, maybe three. You never know with psychosomatic injuries."

HISTORY

Willie McGee of the Athletics in the American League leads the National League in batting with a .335 average. Despite being traded by the Cardinals in August, McGee had enough at-bats to qualify for the NL title. It is the first time a player has led a league in batting while playing in the other circuit.

cannot be involved in the operation of the team. Commissioner Vincent reports he was "able to evaluate a pattern of behavior that borders on the bizarre."

Newsweek magazine, published today, describes Steinbrenner as the "Most Hated Man in Baseball."

JULY 31:

Nolan Ryan of the Rangers becomes the 20th and newest member of baseball's 300 Club. The right-hander, 43 years and six months old and in his 24th season, defeats the Brewers, 11-3, at Milwaukee's County Stadium for his 300th career win. Ryan strikes out eight and walks three in seven and two-thirds innings of work before a crowd of 55,097. He allows three runs–only one earned–and is relieved by Brad Arnsberg. The losing pitcher is Chris Bosio. Julio Franco's grand slam homer is the key hit for Texas.

AUGUST 3:

The Braves trade their long-time star outfielder Dale Murphy (.232 in 97 games) and pitcher Ira "Tommy" Greene (1-0) to the Phillies for pitcher Jeff Parrett (4-9), outfielder Jim Vatcher (.261 in 36 games), and minor league shortstop Victor Rosario. Murphy led the NL in homers in 1984 and 1985. Greene and Vatcher switch teams on August 9; Rosario joins Atlanta on September 4.

AUGUST 6:

Joe Morgan and Jim Palmer are inducted into the Hall of Fame. Morgan, a second baseman, played 22 years, batting .271 with 689 stolen bases and 268 homers. He won back-to-back NL Most Valuable Player Awards in 1975 and 1976 and hit double figures in homers 13 times. His lifetime total of 1,865 walks ranks behind only Babe Ruth and Ted Williams. Morgan appeared in four World Series–three with the Reds. Palmer pitched for 19 years, all with the Orioles. He compiled a lifetime record of 268-152 with a 2.86 ERA and 53 shutouts. He was a 20-game winner eight times and won the AL's Cy Young Award three times–in 1973, 1975, and 1976. He was 4-2 in six World Series.

Earl Weaver on Jim Palmer's many injuries, "The Chinese tell time by The Year of the Horse or The Year of the Dragon. I tell time by The Year of the Back and The Year of the Elbow. This year it's the Year of the Ulnar Nerve. Someone once asked me if I had any physical incapacities of my own... 'Sure I do,' I said. 'One big one: Jim Palmer.'"

AUGUST 8:

The final, sad chapter in the Pete Rose case is played out as he reports to the federal work camp at Marion, Illinois, to serve his three-month sentence for income tax evasion. Rose was given a delay so that he could recuperate from knee surgery and reports two days before the court-ordered deadline.

The Expos acquire outfielder Moises Alou–the son of former major leaguer Felipe Alou, pitcher Scott Ruskin (2-2), and minor league infielder Willie Greene from the Pirates for pitcher Zane Smith (6-7). Alou, who is hitting .200 in two games, actually goes to Montreal on August 16.

AUGUST 10:

Harry "Cookie" Lavagetto, whose double with two out in the ninth inning broke up Bill Bevens's no-hitter in the 1947 World Series, dies at age 77 in Orinda, California. In a 10-year career with the Pirates and Dodgers, he hit .269. Lavagetto appeared with Brooklyn in the 1941 and 1947 World Series.

AUGUST 14:

The Blue Jays' George Bell hits three sacrifice flies against the White Sox, tying a major league record.

AUGUST 15:

The Athletics' Mark McGwire hits a grand-slam homer in the 10th inning of a 6-2 victory over the Red Sox. It is his 30th round-tripper of the season, and he becomes the first to reach that level in each of his first four seasons.

The Phillies' Terry Mulholland no-hits the visiting Giants, his former team, 6-0, at Veterans Stadium. Mulholland walks none and fans eight. The Phillies commit one error. The losing pitcher is Don Robinson

AUGUST 17:

In the opener of a double header in Texas, Nolan Ryan of the Rangers throws 10 shutout innings against the White

AUGUST 31
Ken Griffey Sr. and Jr. debut as a father-and-son team.

SEPTEMBER 22
Andre Dawson steals his 300th base.

Sox, fanning 15 and allowing three hits and no walks. Kenny Rogers gets the win in relief on a Ruben Sierra RBI single in the 13th. In the nightcap, Carlton Fisk of the White Sox homers off Charlie Hough. It is the 328th of his career, a major league record for catchers, surpassing Johnny Bench's mark. Chicago wins the game, 4-2.

AUGUST 28:

The Cubs' Ryne Sandberg homers in a 5-2 victory over the Astros. It is his 30th of the season, and he is the first second baseman to reach that level in successive seasons.

AUGUST 29:

The Cardinals trade outfielder Willie McGee (.335) to the Athletics for outfielder Felix Jose (.264 in 101 games) plus two minor leaguers–third baseman Stan Royer and pitcher Darryl Green.

AUGUST 31:

Ken Griffey Sr., 40 years old, and Ken Griffey Jr., 20 years old, become the first father and son to play together in the majors. Each hits a first-inning single and each has one hit in four at-bats, as their Mariners beat the Royals, 5-2. Griffey Sr. plays left field and bats second; Junior is in center field and hits third.

The Astros acquire minor league first baseman Jeff Bagwell from the Red Sox for pitcher Larry Andersen (5-2).

SEPTEMBER 2:

Dave Stieb of the Blue Jays no-hits the Indians, 3-0, in Cleveland. He throws 122 pitches, striking out nine and walking four; Toronto plays errorless ball. Jerry Browne flies to Junior Felix for the final out. Fred McGriff backs Stieb with two homers. The losing pitcher is Harry "Bud" Black. Stieb pitched five one-hitters in less than a year, losing no-hit bids with two out in the ninth twice in 1988. In 1989, he was one out away from a perfect game against the Yankees when Roberto Kelly doubled. Stieb's is the ninth no-hitter in the majors this season - a record. There were seven in the majors in 1908 and 1917.

SEPTEMBER 3:

At Comiskey Park, White Sox reliever Bobby Thigpen is credited with a save against the Royals. It is his 47th of the season, a major league record.

SEPTEMBER 13:

With George Steinbrenner permanently banned from baseball, theatre magnate and the Yankee's limited partner Robert E. Nederlander is named managing general partner of the team.

SEPTEMBER 14:

In Anaheim, the Griffeys write a new entry in father-and-son baseball. They become the first to hit back-to-back homers in the majors. In the first inning, Ken Griffey Sr. connects on an 0-2 pitch and sends the ball into center field. Junior smacks a 3-0 pitch also into center. Both homers are struck off the Angels' Kirk McCaskill.

SEPTEMBER 22:

Against the Mets today, after a walk from Ron Darling, the Cubs' Andre Dawson records the 300th stolen base of his career. It puts Dawson in a club that has one other member - Willie Mays. They are the only players in major league history with 2,000 hits, 300 homers, and 300 stolen bases. The Mets mar Dawson's day by beating the Cubs, 11-5, in Chicago.

SEPTEMBER 25:

The Athletics win their third straight AL West title with a 5-0 victory over the Royals.

SEPTEMBER 29:

A Dodger loss to the Giants gives the Reds the NL West.

SEPTEMBER 30:

In the last game ever at Comiskey Park–the oldest stadium in the majors–the White Sox defeat the

Jose Rio clinched the World Series for the Reds.

OCTOBER 10
The Athletics sweep the Red Sox for the AL pennant.

Mariners, 2-1. Next year the White Sox will play at a new Comiskey Park across the street from the historic one, which opened in 1910. The White Sox record at the ballpark is 3,0244-2,926 for a .508 percentage.

Chuck Comiskey, grandson of the team's original owner, Charles Comiskey, tells USA Today, "Nothing is forever. The ballpark has served us well. It deserves a rest."

The Pirates defeat the Cardinals, 2-0, for the NL East title.

OCTOBER 2:

Joe McIlvaine is named general manager of the Padres, replacing Jack McKeon, who was fired on September 21.

OCTOBER 3:

Cecil Fielder of the Tigers connects with two men on base in the eighth inning against Alan Mills of the Yankees at Yankee Stadium. It is Fielder's 51st homer of the year. In the fourth, he connected against Steve Adkins for his 50th, becoming the first major leaguer since George Foster in 1977 to reach that mark. He is the 11th major leaguer with 50 and the second Tiger; Hank Greenberg had 58 in 1938. The Tigers win, 10-3.

The Red Sox are the AL East champions by virtue of a 3-1 victory over the White Sox.

OCTOBER 4:

NLCS, game one. In Cincinnati, the Pirates win, 4-3, when Andy Van Slyke's drive in the seventh inning is mishandled by left fielder Eric Davis and goes for a double. Sid Bream has a two-run homer for Pittsburgh. Bob Walk is the winning pitcher; Ted Power gets a save. Cincinnati's Norm Charlton is charged with the loss.

OCTOBER 5:

NLCS, game two. The Reds, behind combined six-hit pitching by winner Tom Browning and relievers Rob Dibble and Randy Myers, win, 2-1. Paul O'Neill drives in both of Cincinnati's runs; Pittsburgh scores on a fifth-inning homer by Jose Lind. Doug Drabek pitches a complete game, but gets the loss.

OCTOBER 6:

ALCS, game one. Dave Stewart–with a save from Dennis Eckersley–defeats the Red Sox, 9-1, at Fenway Park. Oakland puts the game away with seven runs in the top of the ninth inning. Larry Andersen gets the loss for Boston. Wade Boggs hits a solo home run.

OCTOBER 7:

ALCS, game two. Oakland makes it two in a row with a 4-1 victory. Bob Welch picks up the win with a save by Dennis Eckersley. Greg Harris is charged with the loss. DH Harold Baines has three RBI.

OCTOBER 8:

NLCS, game three. The Reds' Mariano Duncan has a three-run homer and four RBI, leading his team to a 6-3 victory in Pittsburgh. Billy Hatcher also homers for Cincinnati. Danny Jackson gets the win with a save by Randy Myers. Zane Smith is charged with the loss.

OCTOBER 9:

NLCS, game four. Paul O'Neill and Chris Sabo homer for the Reds in a 5-3 win over the Pirates. Jose Rijo is the winning pitcher with a save from Rob Dibble. Bob Walk gets the loss. Jay Bell homers for Pittsburgh.

ALCS, game three. In Oakland, the Athletics continue to manhandle the Red Sox, defeating them today, 4-1. Mike Moore gets the win with another save by Dennis Eckersley. Mike Boddicker, who goes all the way for the Red Sox, gets the loss. Substitute second baseman Willie Randolph has two singles and two RBI.

OCTOBER 10:

NLCS, game five. Doug Drabek pitches eight and a third strong innings and Bob Patterson gets a save as the Pirates bounce back with a 3-2 win. Tom Browning gets the loss.

ALCS, game four. The Athletics sweep the Red Sox with a 3-1 win and take the AL pennant. Dave Stewart gets the victory; Rick Honeycutt is credited with a save. The losing pitcher is starter Roger Clemens, who is ejected in the second inning by home plate umpire Terry Cooney.

OCTOBER 20
The Reds sweep the Athletics for the World Series.

OCTOBER 12:

NLCS, game six. Back home, the Reds top the Pirates, 2-1, to take the NL pennant. Danny Jackson, winning pitcher Norm Charlton, and Randy Myers–who gets a save–allow only one Pirate hit, a Carmelo Martinez double. Ron Oester scores the winning run on a seventh-inning single by pinch hitter Luis Quinones. Zane Smith is charged with the loss.

REGULAR SEASON WRAP-UP:

Under manager Lou Piniella, the Reds finish the regular season at 91-71 in the NL. Mariano Duncan (.306) and Barry Larkin (.301) are the top regulars. Chris Sabo has 25 homers and 71 RBI; Eric Davis hits 24 and drives in 86 runs. The team has no 20-game winners; Tom Browning leads the staff with a 115-9 record. Randy Myers has 31 saves.

The Athletics, managed by Tony LaRussa, are 103-59 in the AL. Rickey Henderson is the top average hitter at .325 with 28 homers and 65 stolen bases. Mark McGwire hits 39 homers and drives in 108 runs; Jose Canseco has 37 homers and 101 RBI. Dave Henderson adds 20 round-trippers. Bob Welch is 27-6 with a 2.95 ERA; Dave Stewart compiles a 22-11 record with a 2.56 ERA. Dennis Eckersley has 48 saves.
The Orioles' Cal Ripken Jr. sets a major league fielding record for shortstops by playing in 161 games and committing only three errors for a .996 fielding average. He also plays in 95 straight games without a miscue. Cubs' second baseman Ryne Sandberg plays 123 consecutive games over two seasons without an error
Bobby Thigpen of the White Sox sets a major league record for saves with 57.

OCTOBER 16:

World Series, game one. In Cincinnati, winning pitcher Jose Rijo, Rob Dibble, and Randy Myers combine to shut out the Athletics, 7-0. Eric Davis gives the Reds all the runs they will need with a two-run homer in the first inning. Dave Stewart takes the loss.

OCTOBER 17:

World Series, game two. The Reds make it two in a row with a 5-4 win on Joe Oliver's RBI single in the bottom of the 10th inning. Reliever Rob Dibble gets the win; Dennis Eckersley is charged with the loss. Jose Canseco hits a solo homer for Oakland. Billy Hatcher has four safeties, setting a series record with seven consecutive hits.

OCTOBER 19:

World Series, game three. In Oakland, the Reds bang out 14 hits and defeat the Athletics, 8-3. Chris Sabo has two homers for Cincinnati; Harold Baines and Rickey Henderson connect for Oakland. Starter Tom Browning gets the victory with relief from Rob Dibble and Randy Myers. Mike Moore is tagged with the loss.

OCTOBER 20:

World Series, game four. It's a sweep and the World Championship for the Reds as they defeat the Athletics, 2-1, behind Jose Rijo with a save from Randy Myers. Hal Morris's sacrifice fly in the eighth inning drives in the winning run. Dave Stewart goes all the way for the hard luck loss. Rijo is 2-0 with an 0.59 ERA and is named the Most Valuable Player of the series. Billy Hatcher hits a sizzling .750 and teammate Chris Sabo hits .563 with five RBI. Barry Larkin finishes at .353 and Joe Oliver .333. Rickey

Bobby Thigpen pitches for the White Sox, who played their last game at the old Comiskey Park.

DECEMBER 5
Toronto trades Joe Carter and Roberto Alomar to San Diego for Fred McGriff and Tony Fernandez.

TRIVIA

Paul Snyder, scouting director for the Braves, is demoted when he argues that Larry "Chipper" Jones is the best player in this year's draft. Much of the "conventional wisdom" identifies pitcher Todd Van Poppel as the number one selection.

Henderson bats .333 for the losing Athletics.

POST-SEASON

OCTOBER 21:

After manager Tony La Russa decides to bench Jose Canseco for game four of the World Series, he gets an earful. Canseco's wife, Esther, calls the manager a punk.

NOVEMBER 8:

The Dodgers sign free-agent outfielder Darryl Strawberry (.277, 37 homers, 110 RBI) to a five-year, $20.25 million contract. Strawberry was with the Mets for the 1990 season.

NOVEMBER 15:

AL president Robert "Bobby" Brown suspends Red Sox pitcher Roger Clemens for five days and fines him $10,000 for his conduct during the ALCS.

NOVEMBER 23:

Reds' catcher Baudilio "Bo" Diaz is killed when a satellite dish he is installing on his home in Caracas, Venezuela, falls on him. Diaz, who was 37 years old, batted .255 in his 13-year career. In 1983, he hit .333 for the Phillies in the World Series.

DECEMBER 1:

The Royals sign free-agent outfielder Kirk Gibson (.260, eight homers in 89 games), who played for the Dodgers this year.

DECEMBER 3:

Free-agent outfielder Willie Wilson (.290, 24 stolen bases) is signed by the Athletics. Wilson spent the past 15 seasons with the Royals and was the AL batting champion in 1982.

DECEMBER 5:

The Blue Jays and Padres complete a major trade. Going to Toronto are outfielder-first baseman Joe Carter (.232, 24 homers, 115 RBI, 22 stolen bases) and second baseman-shortstop Roberto Alomar (.287, six homers, 24 stolen bases). In return, San Diego gets first baseman-DH Fred McGriff (.300, 35 homers, 88 RBI) and shortstop Octavio "Tony" Fernandez (.276, 26 stolen bases, and an AL-leading 17 triples).

The Mets sign speedy free-agent outfielder Vince Coleman (.292, six homers, 77 stolen bases) to a four-year, $12 million contract. With the Cardinals in 1990, he has led the NL in stolen bases for six consecutive seasons.

The Giants trade relief pitcher Steve Bedrosian (9-9, 4.20 ERA, 17 saves) to the Twins for minor league pitcher Johnny Ard and a player to be named later. On December 18, San Francisco gets minor league pitcher Jimmy Williams, completing the transaction.

DECEMBER 7:

Murray Chass reports in today's New York Times that the Players Association will receive $280 million in settlement of three grievance cases in which the owners were found to be in collusion against free-agent players. A total of 15 players who were free agents in 1987 will be allowed to sell their services to any teams.

DECEMBER 10:

Free-agent pitcher Eric Show (6-8, 5.76 ERA) is signed by the Athletics. Show was with the Padres last season.

DECEMBER 15:

The Dodgers acquire free-agent outfielder Brett Butler (.309, 51 stolen bases and a league-leading 192 hits), who was with the Giants this past season.

DECEMBER 18:

The NL announces its "nominees" for expansion: South Florida, Tampa, St. Petersburg, Orlando, Denver, Buffalo, and Washington, D.C.

DECEMBER 20:

Free-agent pitcher Charlie Hough (12-12, 4.07 ERA), with the Rangers in 1990, is signed by the White Sox.

DECEMBER 26:

The Senior Professional Baseball Association goes out of business during its second season. Because of trouble within the ownership, the Fort Myers team cancels its games and the five other clubs vote to follow suit midway into its 56-game schedule.

THE BEST OF 1990

NATIONAL LEAGUE

HITTERS

Batting Average:
Willie McGee, St. Louis Cardinals, .335

Slugging Average:
Barry Bonds, Pittsburgh Pirates, .565

Home Runs:
Ryne Sandberg, Chicago Cubs, 40

Runs Batted In:
Matt Williams, San Francisco Giants, 122

Hits:
Len Dykstra, Philadelphia Phillies; Brett Butler, San Francisco Giants, 192

Stolen Bases:
Vince Coleman, St. Louis Cardinals, 77

PITCHERS

Wins:
Doug Drabek, Pittsburgh Pirates, 22

Strikeouts:
David Cone, New York Mets, 233

Earned Run Average:
Danny Darwin, Houston Astros, 2.21

Winning Percentage:
Doug Drabek, .786

Saves:
John Franco, New York Mets, 33

Most Valuable Player:
Barry Bonds, Pittsburgh Pirates

Cy Young Award:
Doug Drabek, Pittsburgh Pirates

Rookie of the Year:
David Justice, Atlanta Braves

Manager of the Year:
Jim Leyland, Pittsburgh Pirates

AMERICAN LEAGUE

HITTERS

Batting Average:
George Brett, Kansas City Royals, .329

Slugging Average:
Cecil Fielder, Detroit Tigers, .592

Home Runs:
Cecil Fielder, 51

Runs Batted In:
Cecil Fielder, 132

Hits:
Rafael Palmeiro, Texas Rangers, 191

Stolen Bases:
Rickey Henderson, Oakland Athletics, 65

PITCHERS

Wins:
Bob Welch, Oakland Athletics, 27

Strikeouts:
Nolan Ryan, Texas Rangers, 232

Earned Run Average:
Roger Clemens, Boston Red Sox, 1.93

Winning Percentage:
Bob Welch, .818

Saves:
Bobby Thigpen, Chicago White Sox, 57

Most Valuable Player:
Rickey Henderson, Oakland Athletics

Cy Young Award:
Bob Welch, Oakland Athletics

Rookie of the Year:
Sandy Alomar Jr., Cleveland Indians

Manager of the Year:
Jeff Torborg, Chicago White Sox

1991

NEWS

U.S. AND ALLIES OVERWHELM IRAQI ARMY IN OPERATION DESERT STORM

CONGRESS APPROVES BRADY GUN CONTROL BILL

L.A. police beat Rodney King after high-speed chase

CLARENCE THOMAS NOMINATED TO REPLACE THURGOOD MARSHALL ON SUPREME COURT

JEFFREY DAHMER CHARGED WITH WISCONSIN SERIAL KILLINGS

PAN AM AIRLINES BANKRUPT

BASKETBALL LEGEND MAGIC JOHNSON ANNOUNCES HE IS HIV-POSITIVE

ISRAELIS, PALESTINIANS BEGIN PEACE TALKS

U.S.S.R. DISINTEGRATES AS PRESIDENT GORBACHEV RESIGNS

LAST U.S. HOSTAGES FREED FROM LEBANON

PRE-SEASON

JANUARY 3:

Hall of Fame shortstop Luke "Old Aches and Pains" Appling dies at age 83 in Cumming, Georgia. He played for the White Sox for 20 years, hitting .310 and leading the AL in batting in 1936 with .388 and in 1943 with .328. Appling, who never made it to the World Series, was inducted into the Hall of Fame in 1964.

JANUARY 6:

Former major league outfielder-infielder Alan Wiggins dies of AIDS in Los Angeles, at age 32. Wiggins, whose career was shortened by drug problems, played seven years with the Padres and Orioles, batting .259 with 242 stolen bases. In the 1984 World Series, he batted .364 for San Diego. In 1984, he tied an NL record with five stolen bases in one game.

JANUARY 10:

Pete Rose, released from prison on January 1, faces another setback. A special panel recommends that eligibility rules for the Hall of Fame be changed to bar anyone who is permanently ineligible for baseball. If the recommendation is adopted, Rose cannot be on the ballot.

JANUARY 25:

Former major league outfielder Walter "Hoot" Evers dies in Houston, at age 69. Evers played 12 seasons – with the Tigers, Red Sox, Giants, Orioles and Indians – batting .278. From 1948 to 1950, he hit .300 or better for three straight seasons.

FEBRUARY 4:

The board of directors of the Hall of Fame votes unanimously that Pete Rose is ineligible as long as he is banned from baseball. Rose would be a certain inductee if his baseball records were the only consideration.

FEBRUARY 6:

Dale Long, who set a major league record in 1956 with homers in eight consecutive games, dies at age 64 in Palm Coast, Florida. Long hit .267 in 10 years and in 1958 appeared in two games as a left-handed catcher.

FEBRUARY 7:

James "Cool Papa" Bell, the Negro Leagues star elected to the Hall of Fame in 1974, dies at age 87 in St. Louis. An outfielder from 1922 to 1946, Bell batted .337 and was an estimated 10-7 on the mound. He was known for his blazing speed. At the age of 48, he turned down a chance to play with the St. Louis Browns.

FEBRUARY 8:

Roger Clemens of the Red Sox gets a contract extension for four years at $21,521,000, making him baseball's highest-paid player. Clemens, who was 21-6 with a 1.93 ERA last season, could end up with $26,021,000 over five years.

FEBRUARY 14:

Doug Drabek of the Pirates gets a Valentine's Day present – a record salary arbitration award. The 1990 Cy Young Award winner, who was 22-6 with a 2.76 ERA and three shutouts, will receive $3.35 million for 1991.

FEBRUARY 18:

Lightning does not strike the Pirates for a second and third time. According to Murray Chass in today's *New York Times,* Pittsburgh was

According to *The Ballplayers*, in 1946 while with the Homestead Grays, Cool Papa Bell "deliberately forfeited the batting title to Monte Irvin to enhance Irvin's chance to follow [Jackie] Robinson to the majors."

Dan Gladden of the Twins scores to win the World Series.

FEBRUARY 21
226 players are making $1 million or more.

TRIVIA

Comiskey Park is a $137 million symmetrical facility with an old-fashioned facade, a real grass playing surface, 90 skyboxes, and a 140-foot by 80-foot centerfield scoreboard.

the winner in salary arbitration cases involving stars Barry Bonds and Bobby Bonilla. Bonds, the NL's Most Valuable Player, will receive $2.3 million, not the $3.25 million he was seeking. And Bonilla will have to settle for $2.4 million instead of $3.475 million.

FEBRUARY 21:

The baseball salary list is released and it reveals that 226 players are making $1 million or more; 31 are at $3 million or above. Darryl Strawberry of the Dodgers heads the list, with $3.8 million for the season.

MARCH 9:

Pete Rose is back on the memorabilia-show circuit, appearing at New York City's Roosevelt Hotel, where he is selling autographs for between $20 and $50.

MARCH 12:

Hall of Fame pitcher Jim Palmer, 45 years old, tears a hamstring at spring training camp in Clearwater, Florida, ending his attempt at a comeback with the Orioles. Palmer pitched two innings against the Red Sox yesterday. He will return to broadcasting.

MARCH 14:

The Angels acquire well-traveled DH-first baseman Dave Parker (.289, 21 homers, 92 RBI) from the Brewers for outfielder Dante Bichette (.255, 15 homers, 53 RBIs).

Parker now is teamed with veteran Dave Winfield, who comments, "You're going to hear pitchers saying, 'Nobody told me there'd be Daves like this.'"

MARCH 15:

The Royals release outfielder-DH Vincent "Bo" Jackson (.272, 28 homers, 78 RBI). On January 13, he injured his hip playing football for the NFL's Raiders against the Bengals, and the orthopedist's report indicates he cannot play baseball this year or, perhaps, ever. Jackson is paid $391,484.25 in termination money. All teams passed on him when he was placed on the waiver list.

MARCH 20:

Phillies' outfielder Lenny Dykstra is put on probation for a year after he admits to losing $78,000 playing poker at the home of Herbert Kelso, who has been accused of illegal gambling.

APRIL 1:

The Mets shell out $15.45 million over three years to retain pitcher Dwight Gooden, who was 19-7 with a 3.83 ERA. Al Harazin, the team's executive vice president, says, "He is the heart and soul of the club."

APRIL 2:

AL president Dr. Bobby Brown upholds the $10,000 fine and five-game suspension of Roger Clemens for his ejection from game four of last year's ALCS. He says, "There is not a special set of rules and regulations for superstars or award winners."

APRIL 3:

The White Sox take a gamble, signing the injured Bo Jackson to a contract. Jackson gets a guaranteed salary of $700,000 plus options.

THE SEASON

APRIL 15:

Willie Randolph, now of the Brewers, collects his 2,000th career hit in a 7-2 loss to the Orioles in Milwaukee.

APRIL 18:

The new Comiskey Park opens with the White Sox hosting the Tigers before a sellout crowd of 42,191, including Vice President Dan Quayle, Illinois Governor James R. Thompson – who throws out the first ball – Chicago mayor Richard M. Daley, and Commissioner Fay Vincent. The Tigers spoil the day by crushing Chicago, 16-0. Cecil Fielder hits a third-inning home run against losing pitcher Jack McDowell. Frank Tanana gets the win and Jerry Don Gleaton is credited with a save. Rob Deer and Tony Phillips also homer for Detroit.

APRIL 20:

William "Bucky" Walters dies one day after his 82nd birthday in Abington, Pennsylvania. Walters made the successful switch from third baseman to pitcher, winning 20 games three times and compiling a 198-160 record, with a 3.30 ERA. He was 2-2 in two World Series for the Reds.

APRIL 22:

In the first night game at the new

APRIL 22
The first night game is played at the new Comiskey Park.

Comiskey Park, the White Sox beat the Orioles, 8-7. Frank Thomas hits the first home team round-tripper in the new ballpark.

APRIL 28:

Reds' pitcher Ron Dibble angrily fires a baseball into the stands at Riverfront Stadium; it strikes a teacher, Meg Porter. Dibble apologizes two days later. He is suspended for three games and fined $1,000.

MAY 1:

On Arlington Appreciation Night in Texas, Nolan Ryan of the Rangers no-hits the best-hitting team in the majors, the Blue Jays, 3-0, striking out 16 batters and walking only two. It is the unprecedented seventh career no-hitter for Ryan, who strikes out Roberto Alomar to end the game. Texas makes no errors. At age 44, Ryan is the oldest pitcher to throw a no-hitter.

On the day Nolan Ryan is adding to his pitching records, the Athletics' Rickey Henderson reaches a base running landmark. In the fourth inning at Oakland Coliseum, Henderson steals third base on Yankee pitcher Tim Leary and catcher Matt Nokes. It is the 939th career steal for Henderson, eclipsing Lou Brock's mark. Henderson pulls the base out of the ground and holds it over his head as 36,139 cheer. Bobbie Henderson rewards her son with a hug. Oakland wins the game, 7-4.

Brock comes onto the field to congratulate the new recordholder. In 1982, Henderson broke Brock's single season record with 130 steals.

The Brewers beat the White Sox, 10-9, in 19 innings in Milwaukee on a Willie Randolph single. The game, which takes six hours and five minutes to compete, is the longest since Milwaukee and Chicago went 25 innings in 1984. The winning pitcher is Don August; Wayne Edwards gets the loss.

MAY 6:

Phillies' stars Lenny Dykstra and Darren Daulton are injured in a one-car automobile accident in Radnor, Pennsylvania, while returning from a bachelor party for teammate John Kruk. Dykstra, who was driving his 1991 Mercedes, suffers broken ribs, cheekbone and collarbone. Daulton's left eye socket is fractured. Dysktra is on the disabled list from May 6 to July 15; Daulton from May 6 to May 21.

MAY 7:

Darryl Strawberry returns to Shea Stadium in a Dodger uniform with mixed results. Many in the crowd of 49,118 boo the former Mets' star, who hits a two-run homer off Frank Viola and later bounces out to third with two runners on to end the game. New York wins, 6-5.

MAY 20:

Two-time AL batting champion James "Pete" Runnels dies at age 63 in Pasadena, Texas. Runnels compiled a .291 average over 14 years and played all four infield positions. He managed the Red Sox to a ninth-place finish in 1966.

Red Sox reliever Jeff Reardon gets credit for his 300th career save in a 3-0 victory over the Brewers. Steve Lyons and Jack Clark homer for Boston.

MAY 23:

The Phillies' Ira "Tommy" Greene no-hits the Expos, 2-0, in Montreal. Greene strikes out 10 and walks seven. Philadelphia commits no errors. The losing pitcher is Dennis "Oil Can" Boyd.

JUNE 6:

Commissioner Fay Vincent decides that the AL will receive 22 percent of the $190 million in expansion fees for the new NL franchises. In return for the unprecedented cut, the AL will provide the same number of players as the NL for the expansion draft.

JUNE 10:

And the winners are – Denver and South Florida. Commissioner Fay Vincent announces the two locations as the choices of baseball's expansion committee. The new franchises will fork over fees of $95 million each to join the NL for the 1993 season. The selection process took six years and developed six finalists – Buffalo; Washington, D.C.; St. Petersburg-Tampa; Orlando; and the winning locations. The NL had been a 12-team circuit since 1969. The two new franchises will put the senior circuit on equal footing with the AL, which has had 14 teams since 1979.

HISTORY

The Hall of Fame librarian, Bil Deane, finds a clipping from the *Gazette of Delhi*, New York, dated July 13, 1825. It reads, "A CHALLENGE The undersigned challenge an equal number of persons of any town in the county of Delaware to meet them at any time at the house of Edward B. Chace to play the game of BASS-BALL, for the sum of one dollar each per game."

LEAGUE

NL owners unanimously approve the selections of South Florida and Denver as the new expansion franchises. The South Florida franchise goes to H. Wayne Huizenga, chairman and CEO of Blockbuster Entertainment Corporation and owner of the National Hockey League Florida Panthers, National Football League Miami Dolphins, and Joe Robbie Stadium.

JUNE 11:

Tiger Stadium, the target for possible demolition, is listed by the National Trust for Historical Preservation as one of the 11 most "endangered historic places." The ballpark was opened in 1901 as Bennett Field and rebuilt in 1912. The National Trust states, "This landmark is a symbol of stability for a city that has suffered major social, political, and economic upheavals of 20th-century life."

JUNE 14:

At a press conference today, the original owners of the Expos – Charles Bronfman, Hugh Hallward and Lorne Webster – announce the sale of the team to the Montreal Baseball and Co. Limited Partnership, headed by Claude R. Brochu.

JUNE 15:

Former baseball commissioner A.B. "Happy" Chandler dies of a heart attack at age 92 in his home in Versailles, Kentucky. Chandler, a U.S. Senator and governor of Kentucky, was elected commissioner in 1945, serving one term before being ousted by the

Rickey Henderson passed Lou Brock's stolen base record.

THE ATHLETICS COMMEMORATE THE RECORD BY PRESENTING RICKEY HENDERSON WITH A NEW AUTOMOBILE. HE RESPONDS, "I'D RATHER HAVE A MERCEDES, BUT I GUESS A PORSCHE MAKES A NICE SUMMER CAR."

owners. Chandler supported Branch Rickey's decision to hire Jackie Robinson in 1947, breaking baseball's color barrier. He also suspended Dodgers' manager Leo Durocher prior to that season for conduct detrimental to baseball. Chandler was elected to the Hall of Fame in 1982.

JUNE 16:

The Braves' Otis Nixon steals six bases against the Expos, setting a modern NL record and tying the major league mark set by Eddie Collins of the Athletics in 1912. Nixon also has three hits, but Montreal wins, 7-6.

JUNE 18:

Dave Dravecky's physical woes continue. The former Padres' and Giants' pitcher has his left arm amputated at Memorial Sloan-Kettering Hospital in New York City. The 35-year-old Dravecky has undergone three operations for cancer and made a courageous comeback that ended when he broke his arm pitching. The new surgery is being performed because of chronic infection and nerve damage, and doctors state there is the likelihood of cancer.

JUNE 24:

The Angels' Dave Winfield, at 39 years, eight months, and 23 days old, is the oldest player ever to get five hits in a game. He hits for the cycle in a 9-4 California victory over the Royals in Kansas City. Winfield also had a five-hit game against the Twins in April.

JULY 1:

The White Sox and Bobby Thigpen beat the Twins in Minnesota, 5-4. It is the 7,000th win in the history of the White Sox franchise. Carl Willis gets the loss.

JULY 5:

The Angels release Fernando Valenzuela after an abnormal cardiogram. The 30-year-old left-hander is 0-2 with a 12.15 ERA.

JULY 6:

Mike Hargrove is named manager of the 25-52 Indians, replacing John McNamara.

JULY 7:

In Arlington, Nolan Ryan of the Rangers sits down seven straight Angels on strikes and carries a no-hitter into the eighth inning, when another "senior citizen," Dave Winfield, singles. Ryan goes eight and two-thirds innings, yields only two hits, and fans 14 for a 7-0 victory. He had a perfect game until issuing a walk to Luis Polonia in the seventh. The losing pitcher is Chuck Finley.
AL umpire Steve Palermo is shot and seriously wounded trying to stop a holdup outside Campisi's Egyptian restaurant in Dallas at 1 a.m. Palermo has been in the majors since 1977.

Palermo makes a partial recovery from the resulting paralysis from the waist down. He works as a broadcaster and talks about someday returning to umpiring.

JULY 9:

The AL takes the All-Star Game, 4-2, in Toronto. Cal Ripken gets the AL off and running with a three-run homer against former teammate Dennis Martinez in the third inning. Jimmy Key gets the win; Martinez is tagged with the loss. Andre Dawson homers for the NL.
Tony LaRussa becomes the first manager with three straight wins.

JULY 14:

The Athletics beat the Orioles, 3-2, in 11 innings, giving manager Tony LaRussa his 1,000th career victory. He is the 40th manager to reach that level.

JULY 18:

Nolan Ryan, 44 years old, signs with the Rangers for another season and will receive $4 million in 1992. The right-hander has 307 career wins and 5,431 strikeouts.

JULY 21:

Rod Carew, Ferguson Jenkins, Tony Lazzeri, Gaylord Perry, and Bill Veeck are inducted into the Hall of Fame. Carew batted .328 in his 19-year career with the Twins and Angels. Born in Panama, Carew was a six-time AL batting champion – with a high of .388 in 1977 – and hit .300 or better for 15 consecutive years. He was also the AL's Most Valuable Player in 1977 and stole 353 bases in his career. The infielder never appeared in a World Series. Jenkins, Canadian-born, pitched 19 years, compiling a 284-226

HISTORY

Ron Hassey, who catches Dennis Martinez's perfect game, also was behind the plate for the Indians when Len Barker pitched a perfect game on May 15, 1981.

Bill Veeck wrote in his autobiography, "If I returned to baseball tomorrow, won 10 straight pennants and left all the old attendance records moldering in the dust, I would still be remembered, in the end, as the man who sent a midget up to bat."

TRIVIA

The *New York Times* notes on August 16 that owner George Steinbrenner – in his first year – gave manager Ralph Houk a list of players who were to get haircuts. Houk ignored it.

RULES

Baseball's Committee on Statistical Accuracy's definition of a no-hitter is accepted by major league baseball: "one in which a pitcher – or pitchers – completes a game of nine innings or more without allowing a hit." Other games – abbreviated no-hitters or those lost in extra innings will be regarded as "notable achievements and will be listed separately."

record with a 3.34 ERA. He was the NL's 1971 Cy Young Award winner. His career statistics include 3,192 strikeouts, 49 shutouts, and seven 20-win seasons. In 1971 he was the NL's top winner, and led the AL in 1974. Like Carew, he never played in a World Series. Lazzeri, who died in 1946, played 14 years — 12 with the Yankees — and saw plenty of post-season action. He appeared in seven World Series, batting .262. Primarily a second baseman, Lazzeri compiled a lifetime average of .292 with 178 homers and had five .300 seasons. Perry won the 1972 AL Cy Young Award and the NL's in 1978. In 22 years, he was 314-265 with a 3.10 ERA, five 20-win seasons, and 3,534 career strikeouts. In the 1971 World Series, he was 1-1 for the Giants. Veeck, who died in 1986, owned the Indians, Browns, and White Sox. He was an innovator, a showman, and one of baseball's most colorful characters.

> DISCUSSING FELLOW HALL OF FAMER ROD CAREW, GAYLORD PERRY TOLD *NEWSWEEK* IN 1977, "GREASEBALL, GREASEBALL, GREASEBALL. THAT'S ALL I THROW HIM, AND HE STILL HITS THEM. HE'S THE ONLY PLAYER IN BASEBALL WHO CONSISTENTLY HITS MY GREASE. HE SEES THE BALL SO WELL, I GUESS HE CAN PICK OUT THE DRY SIDE."

JULY 23:

Ken Griffey Jr. of the Mariners homers with the bases loaded in the ninth inning off Lee Guetterman at Yankee Stadium. It is the first grand slam of his career, and Seattle defeats New York, 6-1. Randy Johnson, who fans nine, gets the win. Scott Kamieniecki is charged with the loss.

JULY 25:

The Mariners' Jay Buhner hits the longest homer ever — 479 feet over the bullpen in left centerfield — in the renovated Yankee Stadium. He connects off Wade Taylor with a runner on in the first inning. The Mariners win, 6-3.

JULY 28:

This time the Dodgers don't get off the hook. Dennis Martinez of the visiting Expos pitches a perfect game, beating Los Angeles, 2-0. Martinez throws only 96 pitches, 66 of them strikes, and fans five. It is the 13th perfect game in baseball history. Losing pitcher Mike Morgan is masterful, yielding his first hit in the sixth to Ron Hassey. Montreal scores twice in the seventh on two Dodger errors and a Larry Walker triple. Martinez improves his season record to 11-6.

JULY 29:

Yankee fans escalate their war on Oakland's Jose Canseco. In May, after he was seen leaving Madonna's apartment in the early morning, he was serenaded at Yankee Stadium with *"Like a Virgin"* and had a confrontation with one fan. Today, the incidents are more serious: Canseco is bombarded from the right-field stands with baseballs, paper cups, a transistor radio, and an inflatable doll.

JULY 30:

In Milwaukee, the Brewers' Paul Molitor singles against Bret Saberhagen of the Royals. It is the 2,000th career hit for Molitor.

AUGUST 11:

In only his first start for the White Sox and his second major league game, rookie Wilson Alvarez no-hits the Orioles, 7-0, in Baltimore. Alvarez fans seven and walks five; Chicago commits two errors. The losing pitcher is Dave Johnson.

AUGUST 13:

In Milwaukee, Paul Molitor of the Brewers hits a two-out, three-run homer in the ninth inning off Blue Jays' reliever Tom Henke for a 5-4 win. The loss snaps Henke's string of 25

JULY 23
Ken Griffey Jr. hits first career grand slam.

AUGUST 14
Dave Winfield gets his 400th career home run.

saves. Chuck Crim gets the win.

AUGUST 14:

In the fourth inning in Minnesota, Dave Winfield of the Angels drives a 1-2 pitch from the Twins' David West over the left-field fence for his 400th career homer; he is the 23rd major leaguer to reach the mark. It also is Winfield's 22nd of the year. California beats Minnesota, 7-4; Kirk McCaskill gets the victory.

Fred McGriff of the Padres homers off the Astros' Jim Deshaies in the first inning; he becomes the fourth player in NL history with grand-slam homers in consecutive games. McGriff's round-tripper provides San Diego with all their runs in a 4-1 victory. The winning pitcher is Dennis Rasmussen.

AUGUST 15:

Don Mattingly, who was named the Yankees' 10th captain on February 28, is benched today by manager Carl "Stump" Merrill for refusing to get a haircut. He also is fined $250, with $100 added for each day his locks remain unshorn. Also warned to get their hair cut are Pascual Perez, Matt Nokes, and Steve Farr. The Yankees beat the Royals, 4-1.

AUGUST 26:

Bret Saberhagen of the Royals no-hits the White Sox, 7-0, in Chicago. Saberhagen strikes out five and walks two. Chicago makes one error. Charlie Hough is charged with the loss.

SEPTEMBER 4:

Baseball's Committee on Statistical Accuracy decides the qualification – or asterisk – on Roger Maris's 1961 record 61 homers is removed. Previously, Commissioner Fay Vincent said, "I'm inclined to support the single record thesis, and that is that Maris hit more home runs in a season than anyone else."

The Mets' pitching staff suffers a double blow. Dwight Gooden (13-7, 3.60 ERA) is out for the season and may require shoulder surgery. And left-hander Sid Fernandez (1-3, 2.86 ERA) will undergo arthroscopy on his left knee.

SEPTEMBER 5:

Bo Jackson has two hits for the White Sox and drives in three runs in an 11-2 victory against the visiting Royals, his former team. They are the first hits for Jackson – who fans twice – since his comeback.

SEPTEMBER 13:

A 55-ton slab of concrete falls onto the playing field at Olympic Stadium in Montreal. No one is injured, but the ballpark is expected to be closed for a minimum of five days and the Expos will have to move at least four home games.

SEPTEMBER 16:

Otis Nixon of the Braves is suspended for 60 days after testing positive for cocaine, and will be ineligible for post season play. Nixon avoids a more severe penalty because of his previous good conduct.

SEPTEMBER 18:

Tony Gwynn of the Padres undergoes arthroscopic surgery on his left knee and is finished for the season. Gwynn has a final 1991 average of .325.

SEPTEMBER 22:

The Pirates wrap up the NL East title.

SEPTEMBER 24:

The Mets' Howard Johnson hits a two-run homer to right field in the fourth inning; it is his 37th of the season, setting an NL record for switch hitters. But the Pirates defeat the Mets, 10-8.

SEPTEMBER 29:

The Twins clinch the AL West while losing to the Blue Jays, 2-1, in Toronto. The second-place White Sox are eliminated when they lose, 2-1, to the Mariners.

OCTOBER 2:

The Blue Jays beat the Angels, 6-5, at the SkyDome in Toronto to wrap up the AL East title.

In a 6-4 victory over the Expos, the Cardinals' Lee Smith is credited with his 47th save of the season – an NL record.

Attorney William A. Shea, the driving force in bringing NL baseball back to New York after the move west by the Dodgers and Giants, dies at age 84 in New York City of complications from a stroke. Shea Stadium, home of the New York Mets, is named in his honor.

OCTOBER 5:

The Braves win, 5-2, over the Astros and sew up the NL West.

CULTURE

Babe Ruth, **a made-for-TV movie, stars Stephen Lang in the title role, Bruce Weitz as Miller Huggins, and Donald Moffat. It is based, in part, on Robert Creamer's biography. Lang, tutored by Hall of Famer Rod Carew, had the most realistic swing of the three fictional Babe Ruths.**

OCTOBER
7
Leo Durocher dies at age 86.

LEAGUE

The Blue Jays set a major league attendance record with 4,001,527.

HISTORY

The Orioles' Cal Ripken Jr. becomes the first AL shortstop to hit .300 with 30-plus homers and 100-plus RBI; he finishes with .323, 34, and 114.

OCTOBER 6:

In Philadelphia, David Cone of the Mets fans 19 Phillies in a 7-0 victory, tying the NL strikeout mark jointly held by Steve Carlton and Tom Seaver. The losing pitcher is Andy Ashby.

REGULAR SEASON WRAP-UP:

Both pennant winners were last-place teams in 1990. The Twins, managed by Tom Kelly, are 95-67 in the AL. Kirby Puckett leads the offense with .319, 15 homers, and 89 RBI. Shane Mack bats .310. Charles "Chili" Davis has 29 homers; Kent Hrbek, 20. Scott Erickson at 20-8 and Jack Morris at 18-12 lead the staff. Rick Aguilera has 42 saves.

The Braves under Bobby Cox are 94-68. Terry Pendleton at .319 is the NL's top hitter. He also has 22 homers and 86 RBI. Ron Gant has 32 homers and 105 RBI. David Justice adds 21 round-trippers. Tom Glavine is the NL's top winner at 20-11 with a 2.55 ERA. Steve Avery is 18-8. Juan Berenguer has 17 saves; Alejandro Pena, 11.

OCTOBER 7:

On the eve of the start of post-season play, one of baseball's legendary managers, Leo Durocher, dies at age 86 in Palm Springs, California. Durocher registered 2,008 regular season wins in 24 years and led the Dodgers to the 1941 pennant and the Giants to the 1951 and 1954 NL pennants. His 1954 team swept the favored Indians in four games for the World Championship. Durocher also managed the Cubs and Astros. As a player, he spent 17 years in the majors with the Yankees, Reds, Cardinals, and Dodgers, batting .247 in regular season play and .241 in two World Series. In his will Durocher instructs his heirs not to allow his posthumous election to the Hall of Fame.

According to Pete Hamill, in 1947 when a group of Dodgers presented Durocher with a petition protesting the presence of Jackie Robinson on the team, Durocher had a blunt response: "I'll tell you what you can do with that petition. You can wipe your #! with it. I don't care if the guy is yellow or black, or if he has stripes like a #!%*-ing zebra. I'm the manager of the team and I say he plays. I'll play an elephant if he can do the job."*

OCTOBER 8:

ALCS, game one. In Minnesota, the Twins beat the Blue Jays, 5-4. Jack Morris is the winning pitcher, with a save from Rick Aguilera. Tom Candiotti is the loser. The Blue Jays commit three errors.

OCTOBER 9:

NLCS, game one. In Pittsburgh, the Pirates beat the Braves, 5-1. After six shutout innings, winning pitcher Doug Drabek leaves the game with a hamstring injury; Bob Walk pitches the final three and gets a save. The losing pitcher is starter Tom Glavine. Pittsburgh's Andy Van Slyke homers and doubles; David Justice hits a round-tripper for Atlanta.

ALCS, game two. Toronto tops the Twins, 5-2, behind winner Juan Guzman, with a save from Duane Ward. Kevin Tapani is charged with the loss. Devon White scores three times; Joe Carter and Kelly Gruber have two RBI each.

OCTOBER 10:

NLCS, game two. Steve Avery and Alejandro Pena baffle the Pirates' lineup, in a 1-0 victory. Glavine gets the win; Pena a save.

OCTOBER 11:

ALCS, game three. In Toronto, the Twins win, 3-2, on a pinch-hit homer by Mike Pagliarulo in the top of the 10th. Mark Guthrie gets the win in relief; Rick Aguilera registers a save. Mike Timlin is the losing pitcher.

OCTOBER 12:

NLCS, game three. In Atlanta, the Braves wallop the Pirates, 10-3. Starter John Smoltz gets the win, and Alejandro Pena is credited with a save. The losing pitcher is John Smiley. Orlando Merced and Jay Bell have solo homers for the Pirates.

ALCS, game four. The Twins win, 9-3, behind Jack Morris, with relief help from Steve Bedrosian in the ninth. Todd Stottlemyre takes the loss.

OCTOBER 13:

ALCS, game five. In Toronto, the Twins win the AL pennant with an 8-5 victory over the Blue Jays. David West is the winning pitcher in relief. Duane Ward takes the loss. Kirby

"How you play the game is for college boys. When you're playing for money, winning is the only thing that matters. Show me a good loser in professional sports, and I'll show you an idiot." – *Leo Durocher*

Puckett, for the second straight game, hits the only home run, and he is named the ALCS Most Valuable Player.

OCTOBER 14:

NLCS, game four. Mike LaValliere hits a pinch-hit single driving in Andy Van Slyke with the winning run in the top of the 10th; the Pirates win, 3-2. Stan Belinda gets credit for the victory; Kent Mercker gets the loss.

OCTOBER 15:

NLCS, game five. The Pirates get a pitching gem from winner Zane Smith and a save from reliever Roger Mason as they beat the Braves, 1-0. Jose Lind drives in the winning run with a fifth-inning single. The losing pitcher is starter Tom Glavine.

OCTOBER 16:

NLCS, game six. In Pittsburgh, Steve Avery shuts out the Pirates for eight innings, and Alejandro Pena finishes up the 1-0 victory. Greg Olson's two-out double scores Ron Gant in the top of the ninth for the game's only run.

OCTOBER 17:

NLCS, game seven. John Smoltz pitches a complete-game-six hitter, defeating the Pirates, 4-0, for the NL pennant. It is the first pennant for the Braves since moving to Atlanta. John Smiley gets the loss. Brian Hunter hits a two-run homer and an RBI double.

OCTOBER 19:

World Series, game one. In Minnesota, the Twins, paced by a three-run homer by Greg Gagne and a solo shot from Kent Hrbek, beat Atlanta, 5-2. The winning pitcher is Jack Morris; Charlie Leibrandt is the loser. Attendance at the Metrodome is 55,108.

OCTOBER 20:

World Series, game two. The Twins make it two in a row with a 3-2 win on rookie Scott Leius's solo homer in the bottom of the eighth. Chili Davis also connects for Minnesota. The winning pitcher is Kevin Tapani, with a save by Rick Aguilera. Tom Glavine, who pitches a complete game four-hitter, is the loser.

OCTOBER 22:

World Series, game three. In Atlanta, 50,878 turn out to see the Braves beat the Twins, 5-4, in 12 innings on Mark Lemke's two-out single scoring David Justice. Former Blue Jay Jim Clancy, the Braves' sixth pitcher, gets the win. The Twins' seventh pitcher, Rick Aguilera, is the loser. David Justice and Lonnie Smith hit home runs for the Braves. Kirby Puckett and Chili Davis connect for the Twins.

OCTOBER 23:

World Series, game four. The Braves win, 3-2, on Jerry Willard's sacrifice fly, which scores Mark Lemke in the bottom of the ninth. William "Mike" Stanton is the winner in relief. Twins, reliever Mark Guthrie gets the loss. Terry Pendleton and Lonnie Smith homer for the Braves; Mike Pagliarulo for the Twins.

OCTOBER 24:

World Series, game five. The Braves make it three in a row, punishing Minnesota's pitching staff, 14-5, on 17 hits. The winner is Tom Glavine, the first of five Braves' pitchers. Starter Kevin Tapani, followed by four others, gets the loss. David Justice – who has five RBI – Lonnie Smith, and Brian Hunter homer for the Braves. Smith ties a series record with homers in three straight games.

OCTOBER 26:

World Series, game six. The Twins come home facing elimination. But, with wall-to-wall sound at the Metrodome from 55,155 fans, they knot the series with a 4-3 win in 11 innings on Kirby Puckett's home run. Puckett has three hits and three RBI. Reliever Rick Aguilera is the winning pitcher. Charlie Leibrandt, one of the hard-luck pitchers of post-season play, gets the loss. Terry Pendleton homers for the Braves.

OCTOBER 27:

World Series, game seven. In Minnesota, after nine and a half scoreless innings, the Twins break the deadlock on a Gene Larkin pinch hit for a 1-0 win and the World Series Championship. The winning pitcher is Jack Morris, who pitches all 10 innings and allows the Braves only seven hits. Alejandro Pena, who relieved starter John Smoltz in the ninth, is the loser. Morris, 2-0 with a 1.17 ERA, is the series' Most Valuable Player. Brian Harper

CULTURE

Basbeball is big in the mystery market. *Murder in Wrigley Field* by Crabbe Evers (a pseudonym for William Brashler and Reinder Van Til), is a mystery novel focusing on former sportswriter Duffy Hose and his niece Petrinella "Petey" Biggers. Also published this year are *Murderer's Row* and *Bleeding Dodger Blue* by Crabbe Evers, *Safe at Home* by Alison Gordon, *Suicide Squeeze* by David Everson, and *Dead End Game*, a Lieutenant Joe Dante mystery by Christopher Newman.

OCTOBER 27
The Twins win the World Series in game seven, after 9 ½ scoreless innings

HISTORY

Lonnie Smith of the Braves becomes the first player to appear in the World Series for four different teams. He previously was with the Phillies in 1980, the Cardinals in 1982, and the Royals in 1985.

leads the Twins in batting, with a .381 average. Kirby Puckett has two homers and four RBI. Scott Leius bats .357. Mark Lemke of the Braves leads all hitters with .417.

POST-SEASON

OCTOBER 29:

Another Yankees' manager bites the dust. Despite enforcing a haircut edict on Don Mattingly, Stump Merrill, who guided the Yankees to a 71-91 record and a fifth-place finish in the AL East, is out. Third base coach William "Buck" Showalter, who was fired himself 22 days ago, replaces him. At 35 years old, Showalter is the youngest manager in the majors.

OCTOBER 30:

Groundbreaking ceremonies are held in Arlington, Texas, for the Rangers' new ballpark.

OCTOBER 31:

John Labatt Limited becomes 90 percent owner of the Blue Jays by purchasing the shares of Imperial Trust. The remaining 10 percent of the team is retained by Canadian Imperial Bank of Commerce.

NOVEMBER 25:

The Cardinals acquire first baseman Andres "Big Cat" Galarraga (.219, nine homers) from the Expos for pitcher Ken Hill (11-10, 3.57 ERA).

NOVEMBER 27:

The Mets sign free-agent first baseman Eddie Murray (.260, 19 homers, 96 RBI). The switch-hitting Murray was with the Dodgers last season.

NOVEMBER 28:

Olympia Stadium in Montreal, closed on September 13 when a slab of concrete fell, is now deemed safe to reopen.

DECEMBER 2:

Bobby Bonilla (.302, 18 homers, 100 RBI), becomes the highest-paid athlete in team sports. The Mets sign the free-agent outfielder-third baseman-first baseman to a $29 million five-year contract. Bonilla has been with the Pirates for the past five seasons.

DECEMBER 9:

Free-agent first baseman Wally Joyner (.301, 21 homers, 96 RBI) is signed by the Royals. Joyner has been with the Angels for the past six years.

DECEMBER 10:

The Indians acquire outfielder-first baseman Kenny Lofton (.203 in 20 games) and infielder Dave Rohde (.122 in 29 games) from the Astros for pitcher Willie Blair (2-3, 6.75 ERA) and catcher Eddie Taubensee (.242 in 26 games).

DECEMBER 11:

The Mets acquire two-time AL Cy Young Award winner Bret Saberhagen (13-8, 3.07 ERA, two shutouts) and infielder-outfielder Bill Pecota (.286) from the Royals for infielder Gregg Jefferies (.272, nine homers, 26 stolen bases), outfielder Kevin McReynolds (.259, 16 homers, 74 RBI), and infielder-outfielder Keith Miller (.280 in 98 games).

The Giants send outfielder-first baseman Kevin Mitchell (.256, 27 homers, 69 RBI) and pitcher Mike Remlinger (2-1, 4.37 ERA) to the Mariners for three pitchers – Bill C. Swift (1-2, 1.99 ERA, 17 saves), Mike R. Jackson (7-7, 3.25 ERA, 14 saves), and Dave Burba (2-2, 3.68 ERA).

DECEMBER 12:

Former major leaguer Ken Keltner, whose play at third base for the Indians helped snap Joe DiMaggio's record hitting streak at 56 games in 1941, dies at age 75 in Milwaukee, of a heart attack. Keltner played 13 seasons – 12 with the Indians, one with the Red Sox – batting .276 with 163 homers. He hit .325 in 1939 and had 31 homers in 1948.

DECEMBER 18:

The Blue Jays sign free-agent pitcher Jack Morris (18-12, 3.43 ERA, two shutouts), who spent the 1991 season with the Twins. Morris was 2-0 with a 1.17 ERA for Minnesota in the World Series.

DECEMBER 19:

The Blue Jays sign another veteran free agent – DH-outfielder Dave Winfield (.262, 28 homers, 86 RBI) – who was with the Angels last season.

The Orioles sign free-agent pitcher Rick Sutcliffe (6-5, 4.10 ERA), who was with the Cubs last season. He was the NL's 1984 Cy Young Award winner.

Steve Howe, who has a $600,000 contract with the Yankees, is arrested in Kalispell, Montana, for attempting to buy a gram of cocaine.

THE BEST OF 1991

NATIONAL LEAGUE

HITTERS

Batting Average:
Terry Pendleton, Atlanta Braves, .319

Slugging Average:
Will Clark, San Francisco Giants, .536

Home Runs:
Howard Johnson, New York Mets, 38
Runs Batted In:
Howard Johnson, 117

Hits:
Terry Pendleton, 187

Stolen Bases:
Marquis Grissom, Montreal Expos, 76

PITCHERS

Wins:
John Smiley, Pittsburgh Pirates;
Tom Glavine, Atlanta Braves, 20

Strikeouts:
David Cone, New York Mets, 241

Earned Run Average:
Dennis Martinez, Montreal Expos, 2.39

Winning Percentage:
John Smiley; Jose Rijo, Cincinnati Reds, .714

Saves:
Lee Smith, St. Louis Cardinals, 47

Most Valuable Player:
Terry Pendleton, Atlanta Braves

Cy Young Award:
Tom Glavine, Atlanta Braves

Rookie of the Year:
Jeff Bagwell, Houston Astros

Manager of the Year:
Bobby Cox, Atlanta Braves

AMERICAN LEAGUE

HITTERS

Batting Average:
Julio Franco, Texas Rangers, .341

Slugging Average:
Danny Tartabull, Kansas City Royals, .593

Home Runs:
Jose Canseco, Oakland Athletics;
Cecil Fielder, Detroit Tigers, 44

Runs Batted In:
Cecil Fielder, 133

Hits:
Paul Molitor, Milwaukee Brewers, 216

Stolen Bases:
Rickey Henderson, Oakland Athletics, 58

PITCHERS

Wins:
Scott Erickson, Minnesota Twins;
Bill Gullickson, Detroit Tigers, 20

Strikeouts:
Roger Clemens, Boston Red Sox, 241

Earned Run Average:
Roger Clemens, 2.62

Winning Percentage:
Scott Erickson, .714

Saves:
Bryan Harvey, California Angels, 46

Most Valuable Player:
Cal Ripken Jr., Baltimore Orioles

Cy Young Award:
Roger Clemens, Boston Red Sox

Rookie of the Year:
Chuck Knoblauch, Minnesota Twins

Manager of the Year:
Tom Kelly, Minnesota Twins

TRIVIA

A rare 1910 Honus Wagner baseball card – one of only 40 known to be in existence – goes at a Sotheby's auction for $451,000. The buyers are hockey great Wayne Gretzky of the Los Angeles Kings and the Kings' owner Bruce McNall.

1992

NEWS

Bill Clinton defeats George Bush and Ross Perot for presidency

POLICE ACQUITTED IN RODNEY KING BEATING; 52 DIE IN SUBSEQUENT RIOTS

BOXER MIKE TYSON CONVICTED OF RAPE

Macy's, TWA file for bankruptcy

PANAMA'S NORIEGA SENTENCED TO 40 YEARS IN U.S. PRISON

SILICONE BREAST IMPLANTS CAUSE HEALTH SCARE

PRESIDENT BUSH PARDONS SIX OFFICIALS CONVICTED IN IRAN-CONTRA SCANDAL

U.S. SENDS TROOPS TO SOMALIA

MARLENE DIETRICH DIES

U.S. NAVY ROCKED BY TAILHOOK SEX SCANDAL

PRE-SEASON

JANUARY 2:

The Red Sox sign free-agent pitcher Frank Viola (13-15, 3.97 ERA), who spent the 1991 season with the Mets.

JANUARY 6:

The Yankees sign free-agent outfielder-DH Danilo "Danny" Tartabull (.316, 31 homers, 100 RBI and an AL top .593 slugging average), who spent the 1991 season with the Royals.

JANUARY 15:

The U.S. Attorney decides Steve Howe will be charged with a misdemeanor rather than a felony for attempting to buy a gram of cocaine in Montana for $100 last December. In a written statement, the Yankees' pitcher acknowledges he wanted cocaine "one last time" before spring training.

JANUARY 19:

The Reds' All-Star shortstop Barry Larkin (.302, 20 homers, 69 RBI, 24 stolen bases) re-signs for a $25.6 million, five-year deal.

JANUARY 28:

Tigers' first baseman Cecil Fielder gets the biggest one-year salary ever – $4.5 million. Fielder's salary represents 19 percent of Detroit's total team payroll. He hit .261 last season but led the AL in homers with 44 and in RBI with 133.

JANUARY 31:

The Pirates re-sign Barry Bonds (.292, 25 homers, 116 RBI, 43 stolen bases) to a one-year contract worth $4.7 million. In addition, Bonds will have hotel suites in San Diego, Los Angeles, and San Francisco. Bonds was the NL's Most Valuable Player in 1990.

FEBRUARY 26:

Jean Yawkey dies at age 83 in Massachusetts General Hospital in Boston, six days after suffering a stroke. The widow of Tom Yawkey, she had been the majority owner of the Red Sox since 1976. She has no survivors; for the first time since 1933 the Red Sox will be owned by someone other than a Yawkey.

MARCH 2:

Baseball has another new highest-paid player. The honor now belongs to Cubs' second baseman Ryne Sandberg (.291, 26 homers, 100 RBIs, 22 stolen bases), who signs a four-year contract extension worth $7.1 million per season. For the one year remaining on his existing contract, Sandberg will receive a paltry $2.1 million.

MARCH 5:

Yankee pitcher Pascual Perez reportedly fails a drug test and gets a one-year suspension. Perez appeared in only 14 games last year, compiling a 2-4 record with a 3.18 ERA.

MARCH 10:

The Pirates acquire outfielder-DH Kirk Gibson (.236, 16 homers, 18 stolen bases) from the Royals for pitcher Neal Heaton (3-3, 4.33 ERA).

MARCH 17:

The Twins acquire the NL's top winner in 1991, pitcher John Smiley (20-8, 3.08 ERA), from the Pirates for pitcher Denny Neagle (0-1, 4.05 ERA) and minor league outfielder Midre Cummings.

Blue Jays' catcher Pat Borders draws a bead on a pop up.

LEAGUE

The lockout lasted 32 days — the second longest in history. Lost games will be made up on open dates and in double headers.

A small caption to go with the cut-out image.

MARCH 18:

Twelve hours of negotiations in New York City produce an agreement ending an owners' lockout and giving the green light to the start of the 1992 season — one week late. Under a compromise, 17 percent of players with between two and three years of major league service will be eligible for arbitration. Minimum salaries will be hiked to $100,000, and contributions to the players' pension fund will be increased.

MARCH 20:

Spring training camps open.

MARCH 23:

NL president Bill White will step down when his term expires on March 31, 1993. A league spokesperson says, "He doesn't want another."

MARCH 27:

The Padres acquire third baseman-DH Gary Sheffield (.194 in 50 games) and minor league pitcher Geoff Kellogg from the Brewers for pitcher Ricky Bones (4-6, 4.83 ERA) plus two minor leaguers — infielder Jose Valentin and outfielder Matt Mieske.

MARCH 30:

The Cubs and White Sox make a crosstown trade. Going to the Cubs are outfielder Sammy Sosa (.203, 10 homers) and pitcher Ken Patterson (3-0, 2.83 ERA). The White Sox receive outfielder George Bell (.285, 25 homers, 86 RBI).

THE SEASON

APRIL 6:

A crowd of 44,568, including President George Bush, is on hand as the Orioles inaugurate their new stadium, Oriole Park at Camden Yards. Rick Sutcliffe gets Baltimore off to a winning start with a 2-0 five-hitter against the Indians. Charles Nagy is charged with the loss. The new ballpark is built in old-fashioned style with irregular dimensions and a 94-year-old brick warehouse behind right field. It also features a 25 foot scoreboard in the right-field wall.

Jack Morris takes the mound for his new team, the Blue Jays, and sets a major league record with his 13th consecutive opening day start. He surpasses the record shared by Tom Seaver and Robin Roberts. Morris goes all the way, allowing five hits, and defeats the Tigers, 4-2, in Detroit. He fans seven and walks three.

APRIL 12:

In Cleveland, Matt Young and Roger Clemens of the Red Sox limit the Indians to two hits in a double header, breaking the major league record of three set by Paul and Dizzy Dean in 1934 and equaled by Dave "Boo" Ferriss and Emmett O'Neill of the Red Sox in 1945. But the Red Sox manage only a split. In the opener, Young pitches eight innings of no-hit ball, but loses, 2-1. Seven walks help to cost Young credit for a no-hitter. In the first inning, Cleveland's Kenny Lofton walks, steals second and third, then scores on an error by shortstop Luis Rivera. Mark Lewis and Lofton walk in the third; Lewis scores on a ground-

MAY 1 Rickey Henderson steals his 1,000th base.

MAY 23 Eddie Murray drives in his 1,500th run.

ball out. Charles Nagy goes seven innings for the win; Brad Arnsberg gets a save. In the nightcap, Clemens two-hits the Indians, winning, 3-0.

APRIL 16:

A lineup mistake costs the Mariners the use of a DH in today's game against the White Sox. The lineup card submitted by manager Bill Plummer lists two first basemen — Tino Martinez and Pete O'Brien. Under the rules, the pitcher must bat. Chicago wins, 5-4. But before Rich DeLucia comes to the plate in the third inning, Plummer sends in pinch hitter Dave Cochrane, who doubles.

MAY 1:

In Detroit, Rickey Henderson of the Athletics doubles in the third inning and steals third base. It is the 1,000th stolen base of his career and comes one year to the day after he stole his 939th to break Lou Brock's major league record. The Athletics beat the Tigers, 7-6, on a Mark McGwire home run.

MAY 2:

After a pre-game salute to the stars of the old Negro Leagues, the White Sox take the field for a game against the Rangers at Comiskey Park wearing the caps of the Chicago American Giants.

MAY 3:

Eddie Murray, now of the Mets, hits an opposite-field homer batting left-handed against Marv Freeman of the Braves in the eighth inning. It is Murray's 400th career home run, putting him in second place among active players and number two all time among switch hitters (behind Mickey Mantle). The Mets win, 7-0.

MAY 21:

At 1:47 a.m., en route from the Bronx to Baltimore, the Angels' team bus goes out of control on the New Jersey turnpike near Deptford Township, about 20 miles from Philadelphia, and crashes into trees. Manager Bob "Buck" Rodgers has elbow, rib, and knee injuries, and will be sidelined for a minimum of two months. First baseman Alvin Davis has a bruised kidney; 10 others, including Rod Carew, are slightly injured. Coach John Wathan will handle the team in Rodgers's absence.

MAY 22:

Felipe Alou replaces Tom Runnels as manager of the Expos. Under Runnels, Montreal was 17-0.

MAY 23:

Three weeks after hitting his 400th career homer, Eddie Murray of the Mets drives in his 1,500th run with a third-inning single in San Francisco. Murray, who is two for five today, now ranks second among active players in RBI. Bobby Bonilla has four hits, including a homer, and the Mets beat the Giants, 6-3.

MAY 30:

The Orioles' Cal Ripken Jr. extends his consecutive game streak to 1,620 — the equivalent of 10 seasons.

The Yankees' Scott Sanderson beats the Brewers, 8-1, and becomes the ninth pitcher in history with victories over all 26 major league teams.

The others are Doyle Alexander, Rich "Goose" Gossage, Tommy John, Gaylord Perry, Nolan Ryan, Don Sutton, Mike Torrez, and Rick Wise.

JUNE 4:

Bobby Bonilla gets a rough reception from Pittsburgh fans when he returns in the uniform of the Mets. In addition to being booed, Bonilla gets hit with a golf ball and wears a batting helmet onto the field in the bottom of the eighth inning. It is a bad day all around for Bonilla — he is hitless in four at-bats and the Mets lose, 7-2.

JUNE 6:

With two RBI today against the Pirates, the Mets' Eddie Murray surpasses Mickey Mantle with 1,510 career RBIs — the most ever by a switch hitter.

JUNE 8:

In a Montana court, Yankee pitcher Steve Howe pleads guilty to attempting to purchase cocaine on December 19, 1991. The left-hander, who has a history of substance abuse going back to 1982, is suspended indefinitely from baseball.

JUNE 9:

The Players Association comes to the defense of Steve

HISTORY

When 45-year-old Nolan Ryan takes the mound for the Rangers on opening day, he begins his 26th season in the major leagues, tying Tommy John's longevity record.

LEAGUE

Murray Chass reports on baseball salaries in the *New York Times*. The average is now $1 million, up 22 percent from $890,844 in 1991. The top team average belongs to the Mets — a record $1,711,615.

CULTURE

***A League of Their Own*, a fictional film account of the wartime All-American Girls Professional Baseball League, stars Tom Hanks, Geena Davis, and Madonna. *The Babe* stars John Goodman as Babe Ruth, and Kelly McGillis. Mr. Baseball stars Tom Selleck.**

Barry Bonds, re-signed by the Pirates, smiles over his $4.7 million contract.

Howe. Charging that the suspension of Howe by Commissioner Fay Vincent was "without just cause within the meaning of the basic agreement," the association files a grievance.

JUNE 11:

Major league owners approve the sale of the Mariners by Jeff Smulyan to the Baseball Club of Seattle, L.P. Videogame manufacturer Nintendo owns 49 percent of the consortium purchasing the team.

JUNE 15:

Former major league pitcher Ed Lopat dies at age 73 of pancreatic cancer in Darien, Connecticut. Lopat, born Edmund Walter Lopatynaski in New York City, pitched 12 years, compiling a 166-112 record and a 3.21 ERA. He was a mainstay of the Yankees' pitching staff from 1948 to 1954, appearing in five World Series with a 4-1 record and a 2.60 ERA.

JUNE 24:

Commissioner Fay Vincent hits Steve Howe again — hard — banning him from baseball permanently. Vincent says the pitch-

JULY 6
Commissioner Fay Vincent orders realignment of NL for 1993 season.

er "has finally extinguished his opportunities to play major league baseball." Players Association representative Eugene Orza contends the suspension is without just cause.

JUNE 30:

The Athletics' Dennis Eckersley records his 26th consecutive save this season in a 5-4, 11-inning victory over the Mariners. He tops Tom Henke's mark and now has 30 straight saves over two seasons.

JULY 1:

Commissioner Fay Vincent threatens to suspend Yankees' manager Buck Showalter, general manager Gene Michael, and vice president of baseball operations Jack Lawn for testifying on behalf of pitcher Steve Howe. Vincent is holding hearings on Howe's alleged violation of baseball's drug policies. Also appearing for Howe were his teammates Don Mattingly and Matt Nokes.

JULY 6:

Commissioner Fay Vincent orders a realignment of NL teams for the 1993 season. Under Vincent's plan, which more closely conforms to geographic reality, the Atlanta Braves and Cincinnati Reds will move to the Eastern Division; the Chicago Cubs and St. Louis Cardinals would shift to the Western Division. The plan is criticized by the Cubs, Dodgers, Reds, and NL president Bill White, who calls it a violation of the league's constitution.

JULY 14:

The AL wallops the NL, 13-6 on 19 hits in the All-Star Game played this year in San Diego. Ken Griffey Jr. has three hits – including a solo homer – and two RBI. Ruben Sierra hits a two-run homer for the AL. The winning pitcher is starter Kevin Brown; Tom Glavine gets the loss. Will Clark homers for the NL.

The Indians obtain pitcher Jose Mesa (3-8, 5.19 ERA) from the Orioles for minor league outfielder Kyle Washington.

JULY 21:

Mark Davis (1-3), the 1989 NL Cy Young Award winner, is traded by the Royals to the Braves for pitcher Juan Berenguer (3-1).

JULY 23:

U.S. district judge Suzanne B. Conlon responds to a suit by the Cubs and finds commissioner Fay Vincent exceeded his authority in ordering a realignment of the NL. She temporarily blocks the move.

> IN 1976, TOM SEAVER TOLD THE *NEW YORK TIMES*, "IN BASEBALL, MY THEORY IS TO STRIVE FOR CONSISTENCY, NOT WORRY ABOUT THE NUMBERS. IF YOU DWELL ON STATISTICS, YOU GET SHORTSIGHTED; IF YOU AIM FOR CONSISTENCY, THE NUMBERS WILL BE THERE AT THE END. MY JOB ISN'T TO STRIKE GUYS OUT; IT'S TO GET THEM OUT, SOMETIMES BY STRIKING THEM OUT."

JULY 24:

Commissioner Fay Vincent okays the return of suspended Yankee's owner George Steinbrenner to baseball on March 1, 1993.

AUGUST 2:

Roland "Rollie" Fingers, Bill McGowan, Hal Newhouser, and George Thomas "Tom" Seaver are inducted into the Hall of Fame. Fingers, regarded by some experts as the greatest relief pitcher of all time, recorded 341 saves in 17 years with the Athletics, Padres, and Brewers. He compiled a 114-118 record — 107 wins in relief — with a 2.90 ERA in 944 games. In 1981, Fingers — who wore a handlebar mustache — was both the Most Valuable Player and the Cy Young Award winner in the AL. He led the AL in saves twice and the NL once. In three World Series with Oakland, he was 2-2, with a 1.35 ERA and four saves. Bill McGowan, who died in 1954, umpired in the AL for 16 1/2

HISTORY

Juan Gonzalez of the Rangers, with 43 homers, becomes the major league's youngest home run champion. Gonzalez, at 22 years, 11 months, and 19 days old, is 46 days younger than Joe DiMaggio in 1937.

AUGUST 31
A's trade two-time AL home run king Jose Canesco to the Texas Rangers.

HISTORY

Deion Sanders's plan to become the first athlete to play in two separate professional sporting events on the same day is foiled by Braves manager Bobby Cox. Sanders plays a 1 p.m. National Football League game with the Atlanta Falcons against the Dolphins in Miami. With CBS camera crews following him, Sanders flies a charter plane to Pittsburgh for tonight's game, which begins at 8:37 p.m. But Cox keeps his player on the bench. When broadcaster Tim McCarver criticizes Sanders, Neon Deion dumps ice water on him three times.

years — from 1925 to 1954 — handling 2,541 consecutive games. He also called four All-Star Games — including the first — and eight World Series. Newhouser is the only pitcher to win consecutive Most Valuable Player Awards. He accomplished the feat in 1944 and 1945 with the Tigers. Despite a record of 207-150 with an ERA of 3.06 and four 20-win seasons with Detroit and Cleveland, the left-hander often does not receive his due because three of his best seasons were during the war years. Newhouser's top year was 1944, when he was 29-9 with a 2.22 ERA. Seaver, known as Tom Terrific, received 98 percent of the ballots — 425 out of 430 — the highest vote ever for the Hall of Fame. A three-time NL Cy Young Award winner (1969, 1973, and 1975), he was 311-205 with a 2.86 ERA, 61 shutouts, and 3,640 strikeouts in a 20-year career. Seaver pitched for the Mets, Reds, White Sox, and Red Sox and won 20 games or more five times. In two World Series with the Mets, he was 1-2. Seaver was the NL strikeout leader five times in the 70s.

ROLLIE FINGERS ONCE OBSERVED, "IN 1971 I HAD 17 SAVES AND GOT A RAISE. IN 1985 I HAD 17 SAVES AND GOT RELEASED."

AUGUST 4:

At a Manhattan auction, actor Charlie Sheen pays $85,000 for the ball hit by the Mets' Mookie Wilson through the legs of Red Sox first baseman Bill Buckner in game six of the 1986 World Series. Ty Cobb's 1924 uniform goes for $160,000 and Tom Seaver's uniform top gets $50,000.

AUGUST 17:

Kevin Gross of the Dodgers no-hits the Giants, 2-0, in Los Angeles. Gross fans six and walks two; the Dodgers are error-free. Francisco Oliveras gets the loss.

AUGUST 18:

In Missoula, Montana, Steve Howe gets a $1,000 fine and three years on probation for attempting to buy cocaine. Magistrate Bart Erickson describes it as "a real tragedy."

AUGUST 19:

Bret Boone debuts for the Mariners at second base, making his family the first with three generations in the major leagues. Grandfather Ray, an infielder, played from 1948 through 1960. Bob Boone, Ray's son and Bret's father, was a major league catcher for 19 years, from 1972 to 1990. Bret singles in his first at-bat and goes one for four.

AUGUST 23:

Clearwater is the scene of a double no-hitter in a Class A Florida State League game. The Clearwater Phillies and Andy Carter top the Winter Haven Red Sox and Scott Bakum, 1-0. Clearwater scores on two walks and two sacrifice bunts in the seventh inning. It is believed to be the first double no-hitter in the minors in 40 years.

AUGUST 24:

The Orioles sign their shortstop Cal Ripken Jr. to a new five-year, $30.5 million contract.

AUGUST 27:

The Blue Jays acquire pitcher David Cone (13-7) from the Mets for infielder Jeff Kent (.240 in 65 games) and minor league outfielder Ryan Thompson.

AUGUST 28:

The Brewers bang out 31 hits — 26 singles — and trounce the Blue Jays, 22-2. Only the 1932 Indians had more hits in one game.

AUGUST 31:

The Athletics trade two-time AL home run king Jose Canseco (.246, 22 homers, 72 RBI) to the Rangers. In return for the 28-year-old outfielder, Oakland receives outfielder Ruben Sierra (.278, 14 homers, 70 RBI) — who is sidelined with the chicken pox — along with pitcher Bobby Witt (9-13, 4.46 ERA) and reliever Jeff Russell (2-3, 1.91 ERA, 28 saves), plus cash.

SEPTEMBER 2:

Trucking magnate Jerry McMorris, mining and trucking entrepreneur Oren Benton, and refrigerated food executive Charles Monfort — all Coloradans — acquire 100 percent ownership of the Rockies.

SEPTEMBER 9
Brewer's Robin Yount belts his 3,000th hit.

SEPTEMBER 3:

The owners vote 18-9 — with one abstention — calling for the resignation of Commissioner Fay Vincent. The leaders of the anti-Vincent faction are Jerry Reinsdorf of the White Sox, Allan "Bud" Selig of the Brewers, Stanton Cook of the Cubs, and Peter O'Malley of the Dodgers. The Mets support Vincent; the Yankees want his removal.

SEPTEMBER 5:

Hall of Fame second baseman Billy Herman dies in West Palm Beach, Florida, at age 83. Herman played 15 years, batting .304, and appeared in three World Series with the Cubs and one with the Dodgers. He was inducted into the Hall of Fame in 1975.

SEPTEMBER 6:

Mariners' pitcher Mike Schooler serves up his fourth grand-slam homer of the year, a major league record. Today's blast is hit by Carlos Martinez of the Indians. The Seattle staff now has allowed 10 this season, also a major league mark. Despite Jay Buhner's two homers, Seattle loses, 12-7, in Cleveland. Albert Belle has a three-run round-tripper for the winners.

SEPTEMBER 7:

Commissioner Fay Vincent, who had declared, "I will not resign — ever!" changes his mind six days before the end of his third year in office. Vincent states he is stepping down "in the best interests of baseball..." He adds, "I've concluded that resignation — not litigation — should be my final act as commissioner."

He tells Murray Chass of the New York Times, *"If I'm the last commissioner, that's a sad thing."*

SEPTEMBER 8:

Danny Tartabull of the Yankees has a five-for-five day with two homers, a double, 12 total bases, and nine RBI. The Yankees beat the Orioles, 16-4, in Baltimore. Scott Sanderson is the winning pitcher; Arthur Rhodes gets the loss.

SEPTEMBER 9:

Robin Yount of the Brewers becomes the 17th major leaguer to reach the 3,000-hit plateau. After going hitless in three at-bats, Yount drives a pitch from the Indians' Jose Mesa into right centerfield at Milwaukee's County Stadium for his historic hit. The scoreboard flashes a retrospective look at Yount's career and lists the 16 other players with 3,000, and Yount is saluted by 47,589 fans. Yount, who will be 37 on September 16, is the third youngest with 3,000 hits and the first to reach that level since Rod Carew in 1985. The Indians win the game, 5-4. Yount, Jim Gantner, and Paul Molitor now have a combined total of 6,340 hits — the most by any teammates.

Allan H. "Bud" Selig is chosen as chairman of the major league's executive council. In effect, he becomes the acting or interim commissioner. Selig also is the owner of the Brewers.

SEPTEMBER 11:

Cal Ripken Jr. twists his right ankle hitting a double against the Brewers in his 1,713rd consecutive game. He remains in the game.

SEPTEMBER 17:

Reds' manager Lou Piniella and his relief pitcher Rob Dibble get into a wrestling match in the clubhouse in front of the other players and TV cameras. The confrontation follows a 3-2 Reds' victory over the Braves in which Piniella used reliever Steve Foster instead of Dibble. Piniella told reporters it was because Dibble had a tight shoulder. Dibble maintains his shoulder is okay. He uses an obscenity for Piniella, who calls him a liar, and the fight is on. The two are separated by players and coaches. Piniella and Dibble meet with owner Marge Schott and general manager Bob Quinn. Dibble apologizes and is not suspended.

SEPTEMBER 20:

At Pittsburgh's Three Rivers Stadium, Phillies' second baseman Mickey Morandini executes an unassisted triple play in the sixth inning of today's game against the Pirates. With runners on first and second, Jeff King lines to Morandini, who steps on second to force Andy Van Slyke, then tags Barry Bonds. Pittsburgh wins anyway, 3-2. It is the ninth unassisted triple play and the first in the NL since 1927, when the Cubs'

CULTURE

More baseball mysteries this year: *The Plot to Kill Jackie Robinson* by Donald Honig, featuring sportswriter Joe Tinker; *All the Dead Heroes* by Steven Wilcox; and *Squeeze Play* by David Nighbert.

LEAGUE

The *New York Times* reports that 262 players now are earning $1 million a year or more. In 1991, the number was 223.

Jimmy Cooney — who died in 1991 — executed one against the Pirates.

SEPTEMBER 23:

Bernice Gera, the first female professional umpire, dies at age 61 of kidney cancer in Pembroke Pines, Florida. After a five-year legal battle, Gera umpired a 1972 Class A New York-Penn League game between the Geneva Rangers and the Auburn Phillies. She resigned after that one contest.

SEPTEMBER 24:

In Baltimore, Dave Winfield of the Blue Jays hits his 23rd homer of the season and, at age 40, becomes the oldest major leaguer ever with 100 or more RBI. Winfield hits a homer and a two-run double to bring his season total to 103. The Blue Jays beat the Orioles, 8-2.

With Commissioner Fay Vincent out, his NL realignment plan is not far behind. The Cubs withdraw their lawsuit; acting commissioner Bud Selig and his executive council scrap realignment.

SEPTEMBER 27:

The Mariners' Randy Johnson fans 18 Rangers in only eight innings, tying the AL record for left-handed pitchers set by Ron Guidry. Johnson is not involved in the final decision. Nolan Ryan, who starts for Texas, fans five in eight innings. The Rangers win the game, 3-2. Matt Whiteside gets the win; the losing pitcher is Jeff Nelson.

The Pirates beat the Mets, 4-2, to take the NL East title.

SEPTEMBER 28:

The idle Athletics clinch the AL West when the second-place Twins lose to the White Sox.

SEPTEMBER 29:

A 6-0 victory over the Giants gives the Braves the NL West title.

SEPTEMBER 30:

On the first pitch to him from the Angels' Tim Fortugno in the seventh inning, George Brett of the Royals singles past second baseman Ken Oberkfell for his 3,000th career hit. Brett, who had a sore shoulder and missed the two previous games, doubled in the first inning and singled in the second and fifth. In the ninth, he reaches on an error. Brett is the 18th major leaguer to reach 3,000 hits. The Royals win, 4-0.

OCTOBER 3:

The Blue Jays, behind the pitching of Juan Guzman, beat the Tigers, 3-1, to clinch their third AL East title in four years.

REGULAR SEASON WRAP-UP:

The Blue Jays, managed by Clarence "Cito" Gaston, are the first Canadian team in the World Series. Toronto is 96-66 in the regular season in the AL. Roberto Alomar is the team's top hitter at .310. Joe Carter, at .264, hits 34 homers and drives in 119 runs. Dave Winfield (.290, 26 homers, 108 RBI), John Olerud (.184, 16 homers, 66 RBI) and Candy Maldonado (.272, 20 homers, 66 RBI), add punch to the lineup. Jack Morris is the big winner at 21-6. Tom Henke records 34 saves.

Atlanta, under Bobby Cox, is 98-64 in the NL. The top average hitter is Terry Pendleton at .311, with 21 homers and 105 RBI. David Justice hits 21 homers and drives in 72 runs with a .256 average. Ron Gant has 17 homers and 80 RBI. Tom Glavine is the NL's top winner (20-8). Alejandro Peña has 15 saves.

OCTOBER 6:

NLCS, game one. John Smoltz allows four hits in eight innings and the Braves beat the Pirates, 5-1, in Atlanta. Starter Doug Drabek is charged with the loss. Jeff Blauser hits a solo homer in the fifth for Atlanta. Jose Lind homers in the eighth for Pittsburgh's only run.

OCTOBER 7:

ALCS, game one. At Toronto, the Athletics top the Blue Jays, 4-3, in a game with five home runs — with a ninth-inning shot from Harold Baines providing the winning run. Also connecting for Oakland are Mark McGwire and Terry Steinbach, consecutively in the second. Pat Borders and Dave Winfield find the seats for Toronto. Jeff Russell is the winning pitcher in relief. Starter Jack Morris goes all the way and gets the loss.

NLCS, game two. Paced by Ron Gant's grand slam in the fifth, the Braves pound the Pirates, 13-5, on 14 hits. Starter Steve Avery gets the win with relief help by four teammates.

SEPTEMBER 24
Dave Winfield, at age 40, becomes the oldest major leaguer to hit 100 or more RBI.

OCTOBER 16
Groundbreaking ceremonies are held at the site for Coors Field, the future home for the new Colorado franchise.

Pirates' starter Danny Jackson is tagged with the loss.

OCTOBER 8:

ALCS, game two. Winning pitcher David Cone pitches eight strong innings, Tom Henke gets a save, and the Blue Jays score three times on four hits for a 3-1 victory. Mike Moore is charged with the loss. The big blow is a two-run homer by Kelly Gruber in the fifth. Gruber also has a double.

OCTOBER 9:

NLCS, game three. The Pirates win for the first time, 3-2, at home behind a complete game five-hitter by Tim Wakefield. Andy Van Slyke's seventh-inning sacrifice fly scores Gary Redus with the winning run. All of Atlanta's scoring results from solo homers by Sid Bream and Ron Gant. Don Slaught connects with the bases loaded for the Pirates. Starter Tom Glavine gets the loss.

OCTOBER 10:

NLCS, game four. The Braves move to within a game of the pennant with a 6-4 win. Otis Nixon leads the Atlanta 11-hit attack with four safeties and two RBI. John Smoltz gets the win with a save from Jeff Reardon. Pittsburgh starter Doug Drabek is the losing pitcher.

ALCS, game three. In Oakland, the Blue Jays — with homers by Roberto Alomar and Candido "Candy" Maldonado — top the Athletics, 7-5. Juan Guzman gets the win; Tom Henke is awarded a save. The losing pitcher is starter Ron Darling.

From "Pizza, pizza" to "Baseball, baseball." The Tigers change hands — from one pizza manufacturer to another. Mike Ilitch of Little Caesar's buys the team from Tom Monaghan of Domino's.

OCTOBER 11:

NLCS, game four. Bob Walk three-hits the Braves, 3-1, in Pittsburgh, and the Pirates remain alive. Steve Avery lasts a third of an inning and is charged with the loss. The Pirates give Walk all the support he needs with a four-run first inning.

ALCS, game four. Pat Borders's sacrifice fly scores Derek Bell in the top of the 11th and the Blue Jays win, 7-6, to move one game from their first-ever pennant. The winning pitcher is reliever Duane Ward; Tom Henke gets his third straight save. Kelly Downs gets the loss. John Olerud and Roberto Alomar homer for Toronto.

OCTOBER 12:

ALCS, game five. Dave Stewart keeps the Athletics alive with a complete-game, seven-hit, 6-2 victory. Ruben Sierra hits a two-run homer for Oakland. David Cone gets the loss and Dave Winfield homers for the Blue Jays.

OCTOBER 13:

NLCS, game six. The Pirates flex their muscles with a 13-hit, 13-4 win in Atlanta to tie the playoff. Tim Wakefield goes all the way, allowing nine hits, and gets the win. Starter Tom Glavine is the losing pitcher. Barry Bonds hits a solo homer and Jay Bell connects for a three-run round-tripper for Pittsburgh. David Justice hits two home runs for Atlanta.

OCTOBER 14:

ALCS, game six. Juan Guzman goes seven innings, striking out eight and allows only five hits for a 9-2 win and the AL pennant for the Blue Jays before a hometown crowd of 51,335. Joe Carter hits a two-run homer and Candy Maldonado adds a three-run blast. Mike Moore is charged with the loss.

NLCS, game seven. Pinch hitter Francisco Cabrera singles with two out in the bottom of the ninth to drive in the tying and winning runs, and the Braves defeat the Pirates, 3-2, for the NL pennant. Atlanta uses five pitchers; the last, Jeff Reardon gets the victory. Starter Doug Drabek loses for the third time in the NLCS.

OCTOBER 16:

Groundbreaking ceremonies are held today on 20th and Blake Streets in Denver, the site for Coors Field, the future home ballpark for the new Colorado franchise.

OCTOBER 17:

World Series, game one. On a four-hit complete game by Tom Glavine, the Braves beat the Blue Jays, 3-1, in Atlanta. Damon Berryhill, a .228 hitter in the regular season, drives in all of Atlanta's runs

LEAGUE

Terry Cooney, the umpire who stirred controversy by ejecting Roger Clemens of the Red Sox in the 1990 ALCS, will not be returning. His name does not appear on the list of AL umpires for the 1993 season.

Walter "Red" Barber once said he "didn't broadcast with a Brooklyn accent, but I did broadcast with a Brooklyn heart."

with a three-run homer in the sixth. Joe Carter has a solo round-tripper in the fourth. The losing pitcher is Jack Morris.

OCTOBER 18:

World Series, game two. Ed Sprague connects for a two-run, pinch-hit homer off reliever Jeff Reardon in the top of the ninth, and Toronto evens the series with a 5-4 win. The winner is Duane Ward, the fourth of five Blue Jay pitchers. Tom Henke gets a save.

OCTOBER 20:

World Series, game three. At home in the SkyDome, the Blue Jays beat the Braves, 3-2, on Candy Maldonado's bases-loaded single in the bottom of the ninth. Reliever Duane Ward gets the win; Steve Avery works the first eight and is tagged with the loss. Joe Carter and Kelly Gruber hit solo homers for the Blue Jays.

OCTOBER 21:

World Series, game four. Jimmy Key and Tom Glavine duel in Toronto. The Blue Jays and Key win, 2-1, to move within a game of the World Championship. Tom Henke gets a save. Glavine is the loser. Pat Borders homers for Toronto, and Devon White drives in the second run with a single in the seventh.

OCTOBER 22:

World Series, game five. John Smoltz and William "Mike" Stanton limit the Blue Jays to six hits in a 7-2 Braves' win in Toronto. Smoltz is the winner; Stanton is credited with a save. Lonnie Smith homers with the bases loaded, and David Justice adds a solo round-tripper for Atlanta. Jack Morris gets the loss.

One of baseball's greatest — and its most distinctive — broadcasting voices is silenced. Walter "Red" Barber dies at age 84 in Tallahassee, Florida, of complications from surgery he underwent on October 10 for an intestinal blockage. Barber began his career in 1934, broadcasting a Reds-Cubs game, the first major league contest he'd ever seen. He moved from the Reds to Brooklyn in 1939, where his voice was strongly identified with Dodger baseball, and he added many colorful phrases to the language of the game. He also broadcast the first televised baseball game on August 26, 1939. He left the Dodgers to join the Yankees' broadcast crew.

In 1978, Barber and Mel Allen were the first broadcasters inducted into the Hall of Fame.

OCTOBER 23:

Rene Lachemann is named the first manager of the expansion Florida Marlins. Lachemann, who previously managed the Mariners and the Brewers, gets a three-year contract. He appoints his older brother, Marcel Lachemann, as the team's pitching coach.

OCTOBER 24:

World Series, game six. The World Championship pennant for America's pastime flies in Canada. The visiting Blue Jays take today's game, 4-3, in 11 innings, to win the World Series. The hero is veteran Dave Winfield, whose two-run double in the top of the 11th gives Toronto its winning margin. Jimmy Key, the sixth Toronto pitcher, gets the win; he is relieved by Mike Timlin, who gets a save. The Braves' fifth pitcher of the game, Charlie Leibrandt, is the loser. Candy Maldonado has a solo homer. Pat Borders hits .450 for the Blue Jays. Joe Carter hits two homers. Jimmy Key records two wins with a 1.00 ERA, and Tom Henke picks up two saves. Lonnie Smith has five RBI for the Braves, despite a .167 average.

POST-SEASON

OCTOBER 27:

Former major leaguer Don Baylor is named the first manager of the Colorado Rockies. Baylor will become baseball's fourth active black manager. The others are Cito Gaston of the Blue Jays, Hal McRae of the Royals, and Felipe Alou of the Expos.

NOVEMBER 3:

The Yankees and Reds swap outfielders. Going to New York is Paul O'Neill (.246, 14 homers, 66 RBI); Cincinnati gets Roberto Kelly (.272, 10 homers, 28 stolen bases) plus minor league first baseman Joe DeBerry.

NOVEMBER 9:

Lou Piniella, who led the 1990 Reds to the World Championship, is named manager of the Mariners. Piniella gets a three-year contract. Coming to Seattle with Piniella

OCTOBER 24
The Blue Jays become first Canadian team to win the World Series.

OCTOBER 27
Don Baylor is named the first manager of the Colorado Rockies.

as batting coach is Ken Griffey Sr., who will be reunited with his son. Last year under Bill Plummer, Seattle was 64-98 and finished last in the AL West.

Drayton McLane Jr., a grocery distribution magnate, officially becomes owner of the Astros. McLane purchased the team from John McMullen for $115 million.

NOVEMBER 10:

The owners turn thumbs down on the relocation of the Giants from San Francisco to St. Petersburg, Florida. The move would be a $115 million transaction, some $15 million more than the best offer to keep the team in San Francisco.

NOVEMBER 12:

In folklore, a cat has nine lives, but how many does a troubled pitcher have? The answer appears to be more than seven. Arbitrator George Nicolau overturns the suspension of Yankee' left-hander Steve Howe because it was too severe. (The Players Association had filed a grievance on Howe's behalf.) Howe claims his substance abuse problems stem from hyperactivity as a child. Nicolau rules that Howe's future contracts must include drug testing and that another failure will lead to life expulsion. The pitcher is re-signed by the Yankees.

Former baseball commissioner Fay Vincent, who imposed the ban, says, "It's like saying you've had seven chances, but eight is the right number."

NOVEMBER 16:

The Rockies sign free-agent first baseman Andres Galarraga (.243, 10 homers in 95 games). Galarraga was with the Cardinals this past season.

NOVEMBER 17:

Baseball holds an expansion draft to stock the rosters of the NL's two new teams. A total of 72 players are selected by the two teams. Among those selected by Colorado are David Nied, Charlie Hayes, Jody Reed, Joe Girardi, Andy Ashby, and Vinny Castilla. Florida's selections include Nigel Wilson, Chuck Carr, Brian Harvey, Jeff Conine, Danny Jackson, and Junior Felix.

The Reds send pitcher Norm Charlton (4-2, 2.99 ERA, 26 saves) to the Mariners in return for outfielder-DH Kevin Mitchell (.286, nine homers).

NOVEMBER 20:

Controversy swirls around Reds' owner Marge Schott, who is accused of using racial epithets and possessing a Nazi armband.

Schott is described in Baseball: A Biographical Encyclopedia*: "A sixth-generation Cincinnatian, Schott inherited her husband's local business empire when he died in 1968. She became an astute businesswoman herself, becoming the first woman ever to own a major metropolitan-area General Motors dealership. She became a limited partner of the Reds in 1981 before taking controlling interest of the team four years later. Living alone in her big house with her St. Bernard, Schottzie, Schott adopted the Reds as her family."*

NOVEMBER 30:

The Reds sign free-agent pitcher John Smiley (16-9, 3.21 ERA), who was with the Twins this past season.

DECEMBER 1:

The Astros sign free-agent pitcher Doug Drabek (15-11, 2.77 ERA, four shutouts), the NL's 1990 Cy Young Award winner. Drabek was with the Pirates this past season.

DECEMBER 4:

Kirby Puckett (.329, 19 homers, 100 RBI) signs a new contract with the Twins; it calls for $30 million over five years.

DECEMBER 7:

Meeting in Louisville, Kentucky, owners vote 15-13 to reopen the collective bargaining agreement with the players. They will focus on free agency, salary arbitration, and salary minimums.

After 15 years with the Brewers, DH-first baseman Paul Molitor (.320, 12 homers, 89 RBI, 31 stolen bases) leaves to sign a free-agent contract with the Blue Jays.

DECEMBER 8:

The Giants pluck one of the game's premier players, outfielder Barry Bonds (.311, 34 homers, 103 RBI, 39 stolen bases) and

DECEMBER
9
The Braves sign 1992 NL Cy Young Award winner Greg maddux.

TRIVIA

A baseball that may or may not be the one Babe Ruth hit for his record 60th home run in 1927 fetches $200,000 at a San Francisco auction. The winning bid is telephoned in from Atlanta. The Hall of Fame claims it has the authentic ball, which was caught by Joe Former and sold for $100. That baseball was acquired by the Hall in 1964.

make him baseball's highest-paid player — $43.75 million over six years. For all seven years of his career, Bonds has been with the Pirates.

David Cone (17-10, 2.81 ERA, five shutouts, 261 strikeouts) acquired in a late-season trade by the Blue Jays, is signed as a free agent by the Royals. He gets a three-year contract worth $18 million, making him the game's highest-paid pitcher. Cone split the 1992 season between the Mets and the Blue Jays.

Another veteran leaves his team for free agency. Shortstop Greg Gagne (.246, seven homers) signs with the Royals after 10 years with the Twins.

The Blue Jays sign free-agent pitcher Dave Stewart (12-10, 3.66 ERA), who spent the past six seasons with the Athletics.

Pitcher Dave Stieb (4-6, 5.04 ERA), who has spent his entire 14-year career in Toronto, signs a free-agent contract with the White Sox.

While other headline players are changing addresses today, one free agent stays home. Outfielder-DH-first baseman Joe Carter (.264, 34 homers, 119 RBI) re-signs with the Blue Jays.

The Federal Mediation and Conciliation Service and the New York State Mediation Board receive an ominous notice from baseball's owners — after 60 days they may lock out the players.

DECEMBER 9:

The Braves pick a plum, signing the 1992 NL Cy Young Award winner, Greg Maddux, to a free-agent contract. Maddux, who spent the first seven years of his career with the Cubs, says no to a Yankees' offer of $34 million in favor of $28 million from Atlanta. Reportedly, Atlanta makes Maddux a "take it or leave it" offer. Last season, he was 20-11 with a 2.18 ERA and four shutouts for Chicago.

"There's no secrets," said Greg Maddux of his craft. "To pitch, you have to do two things. You have to locate your fastball and change speeds. That's all you have to do. If you can do those two things, you can pitch." Maddux will prove to the Braves that he can pitch, going 20-10 with 267 strikeouts, and a 2.36 ERA in his first season with the club – plenty enough to earn his second of four straight Cy Young Awards.

DECEMBER 10:

The Yankees, who failed in their bid to sign Greg Maddux, ink free-agent pitcher Jimmy Key (13-13, 3.53 ERA, two shutouts), who was with the Blue Jays for all nine years of his career.

DECEMBER 15:

One of baseball's top hitters, third baseman Wade Boggs (.259, seven homers), signs a free-agent contract with the Yankees. He comes to New York from Boston, where he played for 11 years and five times led the AL in batting.

DECEMBER 16:

Johnnie "Dusty" Baker is named manager of the Giants, replacing Roger Craig. San Francisco was 72-90, in fifth place in the NL West in 1992.

DECEMBER 17:

DH-outfielder Dave Winfield (290, 26 homers, 108 RBI) goes home to Minnesota. The Twins sign the St. Paul native to a free-agent contract.

DECEMBER 28:

Former major league pitcher Sal "The Barber" Maglie dies from complications of pneumonia at age 75 in a Niagara Falls, New York, nursing home. Maglie suffered a stroke five years ago. Maglie, who pitched for all three New York teams, compiled a 10-year record of 119-62 with a 3.15 ERA. He was 23-6 with a 2.93 ERA for the Giants in 1951 and pitched in three World Series. Maglie once explained his mound philosophy, "When I'm pitching I figure the plate is mine, and I don't like anybody getting too close to it."

THE BEST OF 1992

NATIONAL LEAGUE

HITTERS

Batting Average:
Gary Sheffield, San Diego Padres, .330

Slugging Average:
Barry Bonds, Pittsburgh Pirates, .624

Home Runs:
Fred McGriff, San Diego Padres, 35

Runs Batted In:
Darren Daulton, Philadelphia Phillies, 109

Hits:
Andy Van Slyke, Pittsburgh Pirates;
Terry Pendleton, Atlanta Braves, 199

Stolen Bases:
Marquis Grissom, Montreal Expos, 78

PITCHERS

Wins:
Tom Glavine, Atlanta Braves;
Greg Maddux, Chicago Cubs, 20

Strikeouts:
John Smoltz, Atlanta Braves, 215

Earned Run Average:
Bill Swift, San Francisco Giants, 2.08

Winning Percentage:
Bob Tewksbury,
St. Louis Cardinals, .762

Saves:
Lee Smith, St. Louis Cardinals, 43

Most Valuable Player:
Barry Bonds, Pittsburgh Pirates

Cy Young Award:
Greg Maddux, Chicago Cubs

Rookie of the Year:
Eric Karros, Los Angeles Dodgers

Manager of the Year:
Jim Leyland, Pittsburgh Pirates

AMERICAN LEAGUE

HITTERS

Batting Average:
Edgar Martinez, Seattle Mariners, .343

Slugging Average:
Mark McGwire, Oakland Athletics, .585

Home Runs:
Juan Gonzalez, Texas Rangers, 43

Runs Batted In:
Cecil Fielder, Detroit Tigers, 124

Hits:
Kirby Puckett, Minnesota Twins, 210

Stolen Bases:
Kenny Lofton, Cleveland Indians, 66

PITCHERS

Wins:
Jack Morris, Toronto Blue Jays;
Kevin Brown, Texas Rangers, 21

Strikeouts:
Randy Johnson, Seattle Mariners, 241

Earned Run Average:
Roger Clemens, Boston Red Sox, 2.41

Winning Percentage:
Mike Mussina, Baltimore Orioles, .783

Saves:
Dennis Eckersley,
Oakland Athletics, 51

Most Valuable Player:
Dennis Eckersley, Oakland Athletics

Cy Young Award:
Dennis Eckersley, Oakland Athletics

Rookie of the Year:
Pat Listach, Milwaukee Brewers

Manager of the Year:
Tony LaRussa, Oakland Athletics

1993

Toronto wins the World Series on a Joe Carter home run.

NEWS

TERRORIST BOMB EXPLODES AT WORLD TRADE CENTER IN NEW YORK CITY

FEDERAL AGENTS RAID COMPOUND IN WACO, TEXAS; 72 BRANCH DAVIDIAN FOLLOWERS OF DAVID KORESH DIE

FIRST LADY HILLARY RODHAM CLINTON HEADS HEALTH REFORM TASK FORCE

Mississippi flood ravages parts of eight states

Janet Reno becomes first female U.S. attorney general

RABIN AND ARAFAT SIGN HISTORIC PEACE ACCORD

ARMED FORCES BEGIN "DON'T ASK, DON'T TELL" POLICY FOR GAYS

JAZZ GREAT DIZZY GILLESPIE DIES

PRE-SEASON

JANUARY 7:

The Tigers' Cecil Fielder holds the transient title of baseball's highest paid. Detroit signs the slugging first baseman to a five-year, $36 million contract. Fielder gets a $10 million signing bonus.

JANUARY 12:

The Giants will remain in San Francisco. Peter A. Magowan, chairman of Safeway, and a local group buy the team from Robert A. Lurie. The new owners will not move the team to Tampa Bay.

JANUARY 13:

Richard Ravitch, president of the owners' Player Relations Committee, is urging that there be no player lockout during negotiations, which begin today. Says Ravitch, "I will recommend to the owners that under all circumstances baseball should be played in 1993."

JANUARY 21:

Hall of Fame second baseman Charlie Gehringer dies in a nursing home in Bloomfield Hills, Michigan, at age 89. Gehringer suffered a stroke last month. In his 19-year career – all with the Tigers – he batted .320 with a high of .371 in 1937.

JANUARY 25:

Player reps and Richard Ravitch meet for four and a half hours.

FEBRUARY 3:

Reds' owner Marge Schott is slapped with a $25,000 fine and banned from the day-to-day operations of her team for a year. She remains the Reds' general partner. Baseball's executive council finds Schott used the "most base and demeaning type of ethnic and racial stereotyping." Among her alleged remarks is describing Reds' outfielder Eric Davis in a derogatory statement.

FEBRUARY 11:

Nolan Ryan of the Rangers will pitch one final season – his 27th – at the age of 46.

FEBRUARY 12:

The Cardinals obtain infielder-DH Gregg Jefferies (.285, 10 homers, 75 RBIs, 19 stolen bases) and minor league outfielder Ed Gerald from the Royals for outfielder Felix Jose (.295, 14 homers, 75 RBI, 28 stolen bases) and infielder-outfielder Craig Wilson (.311 in 61 games).

FEBRUARY 17:

The owners decide that revenue sharing and a salary cap will be linked.

MARCH 1:

George Steinbrenner resumes his role as general partner of the Yankees after having been banned for his dealings with gambler Howard Spira.

MARCH 4:

U.S. Senator Howard Metzenbaum will introduce a bill to end baseball's 71-year-old antitrust exemption. The Ohio Democrat says, "Baseball is big business. It's a billion-and-a-half-dollar business, and it doesn't deserve any special treatment under our antitrust laws."

MARCH 7:

The focus of the Yankees' new ad campaign to sell tickets is not Don Mattingly. It is not new Yankees Jimmy Key or Paul O'Neill. It is owner George Steinbrenner.

The Giants hire Sherry Davis as the Candlestick

29
Phillies

LEAGUE

Bronx borough president Fernando Ferrer charges that Yankees' owner George Steinbrenner is under-reporting home attendance to justify moving the team to another location.

Park public address announcer. A legal secretary, she is the first female to hold the position in a major league ballpark.

MARCH 22:

Tragedy strikes the Indians during spring training. Pitchers Steve Olin and Tim Crews are killed and Bob Ojeda is badly injured when the motorboat from which they were fishing strikes a pier on Little Lake Nellie in Florida. Olin is only 27; Crews, 31.

MARCH 31:

Bill White resigns as NL president, but will remain in office until March 1994. White was the first ever African-American league president.

APRIL 3:

The Rockies sign free-agent outfielder Dale Murphy (.161 in 18 games). Murphy, who has 398 career homers, spent last season with the Phillies.

THE SEASON

APRIL 5:

The Marlins make their NL debut before 42,334 at Joe Robbie Stadium in Miami, beating the Dodgers, 6-3. Hall of Famer Joe DiMaggio throws out the first ball. Jeff Conine has four hits in four at-bats, and Walt Weiss clouts a three-run triple in the second inning for Miami. Tim Wallach homers for the Dodgers. Charlie Hough fans four and gets the win with a save from Bryan Harvey. Orel Hershiser is tagged with the loss.

The Rockies open on the road, losing their first NL game to the Mets, 3-0, at Shea Stadium. Dwight Gooden pitches a complete-game four-hitter for the victory. David Nied gets the loss. Andres Galarraga leads off the second inning with Colorado's first-ever hit. Bobby Bonilla homers for the Mets.

While President Bill Clinton throws out the first ball at the Orioles-Rangers game in Baltimore, First Lady Hillary Rodham Clinton, a longtime Cubs' fan, does the honors at Wrigley Field for a game with the Braves. Both home teams lose.

APRIL 8:

In Cleveland, the Indians' Carlos Baerga does something that eluded even Mickey Mantle – he becomes the first major leaguer to switch hit homers in one inning. Baerga connects against a pair of Yankee Steves – Howe and Farr – in a nine-run seventh inning. The Indians win, 15-5.

APRIL 9:

Major league baseball comes to Colorado. The Rockies play their first home game at Mile High Stadium, with a record crowd of 80,227 on hand. Capacity at the ballpark is 76,037. The previous attendance record – 78,672 – was set by the Dodgers in a game against San Francisco on April 18, 1958. The hometown fans go away happy as the Rockies beat the Expos, 11-4, behind winning pitcher Bryn Smith. Eric Young and Charlie Hayes homer for Colorado; Mike Lansing connects for Montreal. The losing pitcher is Kent Bottenfield.

Vincent "Bo" Jackson, in his first game after hip replacement and in his White Sox debut, homers on his first swing. Jackson becomes the first to play in the major leagues with an artificial hip. Brewers' outfielder Darryl Hamilton sets an AL record when he handles his 541st consecutive chance without an error.

APRIL 11:

Baseball's millionaire population is decreasing – sort of. Murray Chass reports in the *New York Times* that the number of players earning $1 million or more dropped to 262 from 269 last year. However, there has been a 45 percent increase in those at $3 million and above.

APRIL 18:

In San Francisco, Barry Bonds doubles off the Braves' William "Mike" Stanton. It is Bonds's 1,000th career hit.

APRIL 22:

The Mariners' Chris Bosio no-hits the Red Sox, 7-0, at the Kingdome. He walks the first two batters to open the game, then throws a double-play ball. He then goes on to retire the next 26 Red Sox in a row. Joe Hesketh gets the loss.

APRIL 30:

Brewers' pitcher Graeme Lloyd becomes the first

APRIL 8
Carlos Baerga is the first to switch hit homers in one inning.

MAY 13
George Brett hits his 300th career home run.

Australian to win a major league game. Lloyd was born on April 9, 1967, in Geelong, Australia.

MAY 13:

In a game marred by a brawl, George Brett of the Royals homers off the Indians' Mark Clark; it is the 300th round-tripper of his career. Brett, who will be 40 tomorrow, joins Henry Aaron, Stan Musial, Carl Yastrzemski, Willie Mays, and Al Kaline as the only players with 300 homers and 3,000 hits. The Indians' Albert Belle charges the mound after the Royals' Hippolito Pichardo hits him with a pitch and triggers a brawl. The Royals win the game, 7-3. Belle is slapped with a three-game suspension.

MAY 14:

In Cincinnati, the Rockies' Jay Gainer hits the first major league pitch he sees for a home run. The first baseman is the 12th major leaguer and fifth NLer to accomplish the feat. Kevin Mitchell offsets Gainer's effort with four hits – including a homer – in four at-bats and Cincinnati wins, 13-5.

MAY 17:

In Texas, Mike Blowers of the Mariners hits a grand-slam homer today against the Rangers' Craig Lefferts in a 16-9 Seattle victory. Blowers hit a bases-loaded homer yesterday against Bobby Witt at Oakland. Today's blast makes him the 13th major leaguer with grand slams in consecutive games. The Mariners bang out 23 hits in today's game.

MAY 19:

George "Dallas" Green replaces Jeff Torborg as manager of the Mets. The team is 13-25.

MAY 24:

With the Reds at 20-24, rookie manager Tony Perez is fired and replaced by Davey Johnson, who led the 1986 Mets to the World Championship.

MAY 26:

The Rangers' Jose Canseco imitates old-time outfielder Babe Herman. During today's game against the Indians, Carlos Martinez lifts a fly ball into right field. It bounces off Canseco's head and into the stands for a home run. The Indians beat the Rangers, 7-6.

MAY 27:

One of baseball's quiet stars, Dale Murphy, calls it quits after 18 years. Murphy was hitting only .143 in 26 games for the Colorado Rockies. Murphy leaves baseball with a .265 average, 398 homers, and 1,266 RBI. He twice led the NL in slugging average and home runs and led once in RBI. From 1976 until midway through the 1990 season, he was an outfielder for the Braves.

MAY 28:

For the first time since 1925, two 3,000-hit players face off when the Royals' George Brett and the Brewers' Robin Yount take the field today. But there are no fireworks from the two stars. Yount gets one hit in four at-bats; Brett is hitless in three. The Brewers win, 5-1.

MAY 29:

The misadventures of Jose Canseco continue. He convinces manager Kevin Kennedy to allow him to pitch and he pitches the eighth inning against the Red Sox today at Fenway Park. Canseco yields three runs, two hits, and three walks on 33 pitches in a 15-1 loss.

JUNE 6:

A brawl in Baltimore between the Orioles and Mariners endangers Cal Ripken Jr.'s consecutive game streak. Players from both teams fight for 20 minutes and Ripken, in his 1,790th consecutive game, strains his right knee. He remains in the game, but Mariners Chris Bosio, Mackey Sasser, Bill Haselman, and Norm Charlton are ejected. Their manager, Lou Piniella, follows them to the clubhouse for arguing about the ejections.

Ripken plays the next day despite a painful swollen knee. He later comments, "It was the closest I've come to not playing."

JUNE 9:

The Padres pick 29-year-old Randy Smith as their vice president of baseball operations and general manager. Smith is the youngest general manager in the history of baseball. He is the son of longtime baseball executive Tal Smith.

LEAGUE

The trade of Gary Sheffield triggers a class action lawsuit against the Padres. Season ticket holders Stephen Schreiner and Paul and Nancy Marshall claim they were deceived by the ball club when president Dick Freeman sent a letter in November promising Sheffield and other stars would not be traded. On August 23, the suit is dropped when the Padres agree to a change in the refund policy and donate 1,000 tickets to charity.

JULY 3
Don Drysdale dies at age 56.

JUNE 15:

The acorn never falls very far from the oak. Ken Griffey Jr. of the Mariners connects off the Royals' Billy Brewer. It is his 100th career homer, and at age 23, Griffey becomes the sixth youngest to reach that level. Only Mel Ott, Tony Conigliaro, Eddie Mathews, Johnny Bench, and Henry Aaron hit 100 at a younger age.

JUNE 22:

On a night in his honor at Comiskey Park, Carlton Fisk of the White Sox, 45 years old, catches in his 2,226th major league game, surpassing Bob Boone's major league record. Fisk is hitless in two at-bats, but Chicago beats Texas, 3-2.

JUNE 23:

The Mariners' Jay Buhner hits for the cycle in a 14-inning victory over the Athletics at the Kingdome. Buhner smacks a grand-slam homer in the first, a double in the second, a single in the fifth, and a triple in the 14th. He is the first Seattle player to accomplish the feat.

JUNE 24:

The Marlins obtain outfielder Gary Sheffield (.295 in 68 games), the NL's 1992 batting champion, and pitcher Rich Rodriguez (2-3) from the Padres for pitcher Trevor Hoffman (2-2) plus minor league pitchers Andres Berumen and Jose Marrtinez.

JUNE 26:

Hall of Fame catcher Roy Campanella dies of a heart attack at age 71 in Woodland Hills, California. Campanella, one of the most popular Dodgers ever, was paralyzed and left wheelchair-bound by an automobile accident in 1958.

Campanella played 10 years — all with the Brooklyn Dodgers — batting .276 with 242 homers and winning three NL Most Valuable Player awards. He appeared in five World Series.

JUNE 28:

Jose Canseco's brief attempt at a pitching career has serious consequences. During the one inning he threw against Boston last month, he injured his arm and now faces ligament transplant surgery. Canseco appears in only 60 games in the 1993 season.

JULY 3:

Hall of Fame pitcher Don Drysdale dies of a heart attack in a Montreal hotel room at age 56. He was traveling with the Dodgers as a broadcaster at the time of his death.

One of the most intimidating right-handers of his era, Drysdale was 209-166 with a 2.95 ERA, 49 shutouts, and 2,486 strikeouts in his 14 years with the Dodgers. He was inducted into the Hall of Fame in 1984.

JULY 7:

Former major league outfielder Ben Chapman, remembered more for his savage and racist

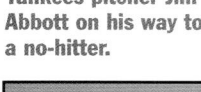

Yankees pitcher Jim Abbott on his way to a no-hitter.

"You have to have a lot of the little boy in you to play baseball for a living."
– *Roy Campanella*

bench jockeying of Jackie Robinson in 1947 than for his considerable baseball skills, dies at age 84 in Hoover, Alabama, of a heart attack. In 15 years, Chapman batted .302 and stole 287 bases.

Mets' pitcher Bret Saberhagen throws a firecracker under a table near reporters at Shea Stadium. Later, he is unapologetic, saying, "It was a practical joke. If the reporters can't take it, forget them."

JULY 14:

In Baltimore, the AL wins the All-Star Game, 9-3. Kirby Puckett, Roberto Alomar, and Gary Sheffield hit home runs. The winning pitcher is Jack McDowell; John Burkett gets the loss.

JULY 15:

Cal Ripken Jr. of the Orioles homers in the sixth inning against the Twins' Scott Erickson in Baltimore. It is Ripken's 278th home run as a shortstop, a major league record. The previous mark was held by the Cubs' Ernie Banks. The Orioles win, 5-3.

JULY 18:

The Braves acquire first baseman Fred McGriff (.275 in 83 games) from the Padres for two minor leaguers - outfielder Melvin Nieves and pitcher Donnie Elliott.

KEN GRIFFEY JR.'S MONSTROUS, RECORD-TYING HOMER ON JULY 28 WAS RECALLED BY GEOFFREY WARD AND KEN BURNS IN *BASEBALL: AN ILLUSTRATED HISTORY*: "...HE SLAMMED A 404-FOOT HOMER RUN THAT CAROMED OFF THE THIRD DECK OF THE KINGDOME... HE WAS JUST 23. 'I'M IN AWE JUST LIKE YOU GUYS ARE,' HIS FATHER SAID. 'I'M A VERY PROUD DAD.'"

JULY 24:

In Los Angeles, the Dodgers beat the Mets, 5-4, and Anthony Young loses his major league record 27th straight.

Following the game, Mets' outfielder Vince Coleman throws a firecracker from a parked car at fans seeking his autograph. The blast injures a one-year-old child, an 11-year-old youngster, and a 33-year-old woman. Coleman will be charged with a felony.

JULY 28:

The Mariners' Ken Griffey Jr. homers into right field against Willie Banks of the Twins. Griffey now has hit round-trippers in eight consecutive games, tying the major league record set by Dale Long in 1956 and equaled by Don Mattingly in 1987. But Griffey's homer is Seattle's only run in a 5-1 loss.

The Mets' Anthony Young ends his major league record 27-game losing streak when he beats

LEAGUE

U.S. district judge John Padova rules that baseball team owners are subject to federal antitrust laws and refuses to dismiss a suit by Vincent Piazza and Vincent Tirendi. The two plaintiffs claim they were stymied in their 1992 bid to buy the Giants and they want to overturn the antitrust exemption.

JULY 28
Ken Griffey Jr. has eight homers in eight games.

CULTURE

At the movies, *Rookie of the Year* stars Thomas Ian Nicholas, Gary Busey, and Eddie Bracken; with Barry Bonds, Bobby Bonilla, and Pedro Guerrero. In it, a broken arm turns a youngster into an unhittable pitcher.

the Marlins in relief, 5-4.

JULY 29:

Ken Griffey's home run streak ends at eight as the Mariners beat the Twins, 4-3.

JULY 31:

The Blue Jays acquire outfielder Rickey Henderson (.327 in 90 games) from the Athletics for two minor leaguers – pitcher Steve Karsay and outfielder Jose Herrera.

AUGUST 1:

Reggie Jackson is inducted into the Baseball Hall of Fame. Jackson, one of the most flamboyant players of recent times, played 21 years, batting .262 with 563 homers – the sixth most in history – with 1,702 RBI and an all-time high 2,597 strikeouts. Jackson, an outfielder-DH, saved some of his best performances for postseason play. He appeared in five World Series with the Athletics and Yankees, batting .357, with the highest slugging average in history – .755. He also hit 10 homers and drove in 24 runs.

Royals owner Ewing Kauffman dies at age 76 of bone cancer in Mission Hills, Kansas. In 1968, Kauffman, the founder of a drug company, bought the rights to an expansion team in Kansas City and has owned the Royals ever since. On July 2, Royals Stadium was renamed Kauffman Stadium in his honor.

AUGUST 2:

Blue Jays' first baseman John Olerud goes into a four-game series with the Yankees in New York, batting .402. He has one hit in four at-bats, dipping to an even .400 as the Blue Jays win, 4-0. Stadium fans boo throughout "O Canada," the Canadian national anthem and chant, "USA, USA" at the Toronto players.

The Cubs beat the Pirates, 12-10, at Wrigley Field in a game marked by seven home runs and a brawl. Homering for the Cubs are Steve Buechele, Doug Jennings, and Sammy Sosa. Carlos Garcia hits two for Pittsburgh, and teammates Al Martin and Lloyd McLendon hit one apiece. Violence erupts in the sixth inning. Cubs' pitcher Bob Scanlan hits Carlos Guerra and the Pirates' Blas Minor retaliates by throwing at Mark Grace in the bottom of the inning, triggering a fight. Scanlan, the winning pitcher; Minor, who gets the loss; and Martin are ejected.

IN 1974, REGGIE JACKSON TOLD *TIME* MAGAZINE, "I'D RATHER HIT THAN HAVE SEX. TO HIT IS TO SHOW STRENGTH... GOD, DO I LOVE TO HIT THAT LITTLE ROUND SUMBITCH OUT OF THE PARK AND MAKE 'EM SAY WOW!"

AUGUST 3:

The batting average of Blue Jays' first baseman John Olerud dips below .400 for the first time this season.

AUGUST 4:

The Padres' Tony Gwynn collects six hits against the Giants; it is the fourth time this season he has five or more hits in a game, tying a major league record. The mark was set by Wee Willie Keeler in 1897 and equaled by Ty Cobb in 1922 and Stan Musial in 1948.

How do you hit a legend? Robin Ventura of the White Sox has no hesitation. After a pitch he regards as too close, he attacks Nolan Ryan, gets the 46-year-old right-hander in a headlock, and punches him six times. Ventura is ejected and suspended for two games.

Vince Coleman's "practical joke" is getting expensive. The Mets' outfielder, under indictment on felony charges for throwing a firecracker at fans in Los Angeles in July, goes on

AUGUST 9
A revenue-sharing plan is rejected by baseball's team owners.

AUGUST 12
Owners pledge there will be no lock-out in 1994.

unpaid leave from the team to prepare for his trial.

AUGUST 6:

In Colorado, Tony Gwynn of the Padres singles off Bruce Ruffin of the Rockies in the sixth inning; it is his 2,000th career safety. Gwynn is the 193rd major leaguer to reach the 2,000-hit mark. He raises his average to .348.

AUGUST 7:

Bob Ojeda, who survived a spring training boating accident that killed two of his Indians' teammates, returns to action. He receives a standing ovation from Baltimore fans when he enters the game in the fourth inning. Ojeda pitches two frames, giving up four hits — including a homer to Cal Ripken Jr. — two runs (one earned), no walks; he strikes out one. The Orioles beat the Indians, 8-6.

AUGUST 9:

The major league owners meet with their labor negotiator Richard Ravitch in Kohler, Wisconsin, and are presented with a revenue-sharing plan. With only 18 of the necessary 21 owners favoring it, the plan fails to win approval.

AUGUST 10:

Mets' pitcher Bret Saberhagen admits he was the one who sprayed bleach from a water gun on three reporters on July 27. The pitcher, who maintained his innocence until now, says he was aiming at Mets' employees, not the journalists, and says, "I am sorry for the accident and the failure to come forward." Saberhagen currently is on the disabled list. As part of his "apology," Saberhagen donates $15,384.61 – one day's pay – to the Eye Research Foundation, a charity chosen by the New York Baseball Writers Association.

AUGUST 12:

There will be no lockout by owners during the 1994 season. Owners, who failed to agree on revenue-sharing, also state they will not unilaterally alter the present collective bargaining agreement.

The Boss bites back. George Steinbrenner hires the accounting firm of Coopers & Lybrand to rebut charges by Bronx borough president Fernando Ferrer that he is under-reporting attendance. Steinbrenner says, "If he continues to accuse us of 'fudging the numbers,' he will drive us out of the Bronx."

AUGUST 14:

After nine games with the Blue Jays wearing number 9, newly acquired Rickey Henderson decides he wants his old number instead, but it already is being worn by Turner Ward. Henderson solves the problem by buying it from Ward, reportedly for $25,000.

The price of numbers has escalated. In 1989, when he joined the Yankees, Henderson convinced Ron Hassey to give him number 24 by buying the catcher a set of golf clubs and a new suit.

AUGUST 23:

Joe Carter of the Blue Jays hits three homers against the Indians at Toronto's SkyDome. It is the fifth time in his career that he has hit three in a game and sets an AL record. The major league record is held by Johnny Mize at six. The Indians win, 9-8. Jeremy Hernandez gets the win; Mark Eichhorn is charged with the loss.

AUGUST 26:

Co-owner Fred Wilpon announces that Vince Coleman will remain on "administrative leave" for the rest of the season, but he is through as a Met. Wilpon states, "He might have good stats this year. We don't want him on this team."

AUGUST 28:

The Rangers' Nolan Ryan, who injured a rib cage muscle against Baltimore, goes on the disabled list for the third time this season. The great right-hander is 5-3 with a 4.53 ERA this season.

Will he wear Blue Suede Spikes? The Mets sign Kirk Presley, chosen eighth in this year's amateur draft, for $960,000. He is a cousin of the late Elvis Presley.

AUGUST 29:

The Pirates pay homage to two great Negro Leagues teams that played in Pittsburgh. They unfurl Homestead Grays and Pittsburgh Crawfords banners in the upper deck of

LEAGUE

The realignment of the AL was announced last week. The Baltimore Orioles, Boston Red Sox, Detroit Tigers, New York Yankees, and Toronto Blue Jays make up the East. The Central Division will be the Chicago White Sox, Cleveland Indians, Kansas City Royals, Milwaukee Brewers, and Minnesota Twins. The West comprises the California Angels, Oakland Athletics, Seattle Mariners, and Texas Rangers.

SEPTEMBER 16
Dave Winfield gets his 3,000th career hit

HISTORY

For the first time in 100 years, teammates finish 1-2-3 in batting. John Olerud of the Blue Jays, who flirted with .400 during the season, leads the AL in batting with .363. Paul Molitor is the runner-up at .332. And teammate Roberto Alomar, with three hits in five at-bats on October 3 against the Orioles, finishes third with a .326 average. In 1893, Phillies' teammates Billy Hamilton (.380), Sam Thompson (.370), and Ed Delahanty (.368) were the NL's top three batters.

Three Rivers Stadium, where they will fly permanently. Participating in the ceremonies are former Negro Leagues players Wilmer Fields, Robert Gaston, Harold Tinker, Bill Pope, Walter Hughes, and Allie Tompkins.

AUGUST 31:

Tim Raines of the White Sox enjoys a big day on the bases and at bat at Yankee Stadium. He records the 744th stolen base of his career – placing him fourth on the all-time list – and switch hits home runs in an 11-3 Chicago victory. Raines connects off losing pitcher Sterling Hitchcock in the fifth and against Rich Monteleone in the ninth. Frank Thomas hits his 37th homer of the season for the White Sox; Wilson Alvarez is the winning pitcher.

SEPTEMBER 4:

At Yankee Stadium, Jim Abbott no-hits the visiting Indians, 4-0. Abbott strikes out three and issues five walks. Randy Velarde homers for the Yankees in the sixth inning. Bob Milacki is charged with the loss.

SEPTEMBER 7:

Mark Whiten of the Cardinals ties Sunny Jim Bottomley's 1924 major league record by batting in 12 runs in one game. Whiten, who had nine homers and 43 runs all of last season, hits four homers in the second game of today's double header against the Reds in Cincinnati. The Cardinals win the game, 15-2. Whiten knocked in one run in the opener, tying Nate Colbert's RBI mark of 13 in a doubleheader, set 21 years ago. He hits a first-inning grand slam against starter and loser Larry Luebbers, a pair of three-run homers – in the sixth and seventh – off Mike Anderson, and a two-run clout off Rob Dibble in the ninth.

SEPTEMBER 8:

The Astros' Darryl Kile no-hits the Mets, 7-1, in Houston. Kile, who fans nine, walks Jeff McKnight in the fourth inning. McKnight moves to third on a wild pitch and scores when Jeff Bagwell throws wildly. Replays show that the pitch actually hit the batter, Joe Orsulak. Andujar Cedeno and Ken Caminiti homer for Houston. The losing pitcher is Frank Tanana.

SEPTEMBER 12:

On Nolan Ryan Appreciation Day in Arlington, Texas, the great right-hander is saluted by pitching greats Sandy Koufax and Gaylord Perry, Angels' owner Gene Autry, Roger Clemens of the Red Sox, and the catchers for six of his no-hitters. Ryan goes five and two-thirds against the Twins, yielding four hits, four runs, and five walks while fanning three. The Twins beat the Rangers, 4-2.

Tony Gwynn undergoes arthroscopic surgery on his left knee and will be lost to the Padres for the remainder of the season. He last played on September 5 in Atlanta and concludes his season with a .358 average.

Another star is lost for the season today. In Philadelphia, Astros' first baseman Jeff Bagwell is hit by a pitch from the Phillies' Ben Rivera. The ball breaks the fifth metacarpal bone in Bagwell's left hand, and he will miss the rest of the season. The injury ends Bagwell's consecutive game streak at 304. He finishes his season with a .320 average, 20 homers, and 88 RBI.

SEPTEMBER 15:

The realignment of the NL into three divisions is announced today. The last obstacle was removed when the Pirates dropped their objections to the plan. The East will comprise the Atlanta Braves, Florida Marlins, Montreal Expos, New York Mets, and Philadelphia Phillies. In the Central Division will be the Chicago Cubs, Cincinnati Reds, Houston Astros, Pittsburgh Pirates, and St. Louis Cardinals. The West will consist of the Colorado Rockies, Los Angeles Dodgers, San Diego Padres, and San Francisco Giants.

SEPTEMBER 16:

Dave Winfield of the Twins singles to left field off Dennis Eckersley of the Athletics at the Metrodome. It is Winfield's 3,000th career hit; he is the 19th to reach that mark. It is the second hit of the game for Winfield, who will be 42 years old in three weeks. In the seventh inning,

SEPTEMBER 22
Nolan Ryan pitches his last game.

SEPTEMBER 25
George Brett retires after 20 years with the Royals

he beats out a ball that bounced off home plate. The Twins top the Athletics, 5-4.

SEPTEMBER 17:

There's gold in them thar hills. The Rockies top 4 million in attendance in 71 home games. Today, behind David Nied, Colorado beats the Dodgers, 12-3.

The Yankees acquire veteran left-handed pitcher Frank Viola (7-15) from the Mets for minor league pitcher Kenny Greer.

The Expos' Curtis Pride, mostly deaf, gets his first major league hit – a double – against the Phillies in Montreal. He also drives in two runs.

SEPTEMBER 18:

The Yankees beat the Red Sox on an "extra out" in the ninth inning at Yankee Stadium. With two out in the ninth, New York catcher Mike Stanley apparently flies out. But umpire Tim Welke waves off the play because a fan is on the field. Given another chance, Stanley singles. Don Mattingly then drives in two runs with another single and the Yankees win, 4-3. Bob Wickman gets the win; Greg Harris is charged with the loss. The Red Sox protest the game, but the AL disallows it.

SEPTEMBER 22:

The great Nolan Ryan makes his last appearance in a major league game, and it is not a memorable one. The 46-year-old right-hander yields a grand slam to Dann Howitt of the Mariners, throws two pitches to Dave Magadan, and leaves the game with a torn ligament in his pitching elbow. The Mariners beat the Rangers, 7-4.

Ryan leaves baseball after a 27-year career during which he set or tied 53 major league records. He finishes with a 324-292 record and a 3.19 ERA, and is baseball's all-time strikeout leader with 5,714. SABR-ite Charles Blahous points out that Ryan held opposing batters to the lowest batting average of any pitcher ever.

SEPTEMBER 25:

George Brett retires after 20 years, all with the Royals. He leaves with a lifetime average of .305, 665 doubles, 317 homers and three batting titles.

Brett, who was the AL's Most Valuable Player in 1980 when he hit .390, says, "The game became a job. It wasn't a game anymore. And baseball shouldn't be treated that way."

SEPTEMBER 26:

Randy Johnson of the Mariners fans Ruben Sierra of the Athletics in the 9th inning; it is his 300th strikeout of the season. Johnson is the 12th pitcher in the 20th century to fan 300 in a single season.

The Rockies set an attendance record, reaching 4,483,350 while beating the visiting Reds, 12-7, with two homers by Eric Young.

SEPTEMBER 27:

Both AL divisional titles are clinched today. The Blue Jays beat the Brewers, 2-0, to take the AL East. And the White Sox, on a three-run homer by Bo Jackson, top the Mariners, 4-2, for the AL West.

SEPTEMBER 28:

Mariano Duncan's grand slam homer paces the Phillies to a 10-7 victory over the Pirates and the NL East title. The Expos' Dennis Martinez beats the Marlins, 3-2, for his 100th NL win. He becomes the seventh pitcher ever to win 100 games in each league.

SEPTEMBER 30:

The Phillies suffer their first shutout in 174 games, losing today to the Pirates, 5-0. It is the longest streak without being whitewashed by an NL team in this century. The previous best was the Pirates, 1924 to 1925, who went 150 games. The major league record is held by the Yankees – 308 games – between August 1931 and August 1933. In today's game, the Phillies – who clinched the NL East on September 28 – are blanked by Tim Wakefield, and Tommy Greene gets the loss. The last time Philadelphia was blanked, it also was at the hands of the Pirates – and Doug Drabek – on September 19, 1992.

A plaque is placed within 50 feet of what was home plate at the home of the New York Highlanders in Hilltop Park, located on Fort Washington Avenue off 165th Street in Manhattan. The

HISTORY

Lenny Dykstra is the first major leaguer in 30 years to lead his circuit in hits (194) and walks (129).

Major League Baseball comes to Colorado with the April 9 home opener at Mile High Stadium in Denver.

ROCKIES
Rocky Mountain News
22
BANK ONE
Coca-Cola
Coors
KING Soopers
Jeep
Dodge
Eagle
Your ALL-STAR Team
Office DEPOT
COORS FIELD

USWEST
EVEREN
McDonald's
UNITED AIRLINES
COLORADO ROCKIES

OCTOBER 5
Bob Watson becomes baseball's first black general manager.

ceremony commemorates the 90th anniversary of the AL in New York and is attended by 102-year-old Chester "Red" Hoff, who played in Hilltop Park for the Highlanders.

The location now is the garden of Columbia Presbyterian Medical Center.

OCTOBER 2:

The NL's other expansion team, the Florida Marlins, also does well at the gate. Today's game attracts 43,210 to put the team over 3 million for the season.

OCTOBER 3:

The Braves beat the Rockies, 5-3, for their 104th win of the season. The Dodgers beat the Giants, 12-1, giving Atlanta the NL West title. San Francisco finishes second despite 103 victories.

In the last game at Arlington Stadium in Texas, after 22 years, the Royals beat the Rangers, 4-1, with a crowd of 41,039 on hand. Gary Gaetti homers for the Royals and Kevin Appier gets the win, with a save by Jeff Montgomery. The losing pitcher is Steve Dreyer.

REGULAR SEASON WRAP-UP:

The Blue Jays, under Clarence "Cito" Gaston, win their second straight AL pennant with a regular season record of 95-67. The lineup features four big bats: AL batting champion John Olerud (.363, 24 homers, 107 RBI), Paul Molitor (.332, 22 homers, 111 RBI), Roberto Alomar (.326, 17 homers, 93 RBI), and Joe Carter (.254, 33 homers, 121 RBI). Tony Fernandez hits .306. The top pitcher is Pat Hentgen at 19-9. Duane Ward has 45 saves.

The Phillies, managed by Jim Fregosi, finish at 97-65 in the NL. John Kruk bats .316 with 14 homers and 85 RBI; Lenny Dykstra finishes at .305 with 19 homers and 66 RBI. Darren Daulton with 24 homers and 89 RBI, Dave Hollins with 19 round-trippers, and reserve outfielder Pete Incaviglia – who has 24 home runs and drives in 89 runs – provide additional power. Curt Schilling and Tommy Greene have 16 wins apiece; Mitch Williams records 43 saves.

OCTOBER 4:

The AL owners unanimously approve the sale of the Orioles to labor attorney Peter Angelos and his partners by Eli Jacobs for $173 million. Angelos's partners include best-selling author Tom Clancy, filmmaker Barry Levinson, sportscaster Jim McKay, and tennis star Pam Shriver.

OCTOBER 5:

Former major leaguer Bob Watson is named general manager of the Astros. Watson is baseball's first black to hold that post in the major leagues.

ALCS, game one. In Chicago, Paul Molitor has four hits including a two-run homer as the Blue Jays beat the White Sox, 7-3, on 17 safeties. Ed Sprague also has four hits, including a triple; John Olerud hits a two-run double. Juan Guzman is the winning pitcher; Jack McDowell, the loser.

OCTOBER 6:

ALCS, game two. In Chicago, behind Dave Stewart, the Blue Jays make it 2 in a row over the White Sox, 3-1. Duane Ward gets a save. Young Alex Fernandez takes the loss.

NLCS, game one. In Philadelphia, the Braves begin their quest for a third straight pennant, but Kim Batiste singles in John Kruk and the Phillies edge Atlanta, 4-3, in ten innings. Mitch Williams gets the win in relief; Greg McMichael is the losing pitcher. Philadelphia's Pete Incaviglia hits the game's only home run.

OCTOBER 7:

NLCS, game two. In Philadelphia, Atlanta hammers the Phillies, 14-3, on 16 hits. Atlanta's 14 runs are an LCS record. Fred McGriff, Jeff Blauser, Terry Pendleton, and Damon Berryhill homer for the Braves, and Greg Maddux gets the victory. Dave Hollins and Len Dykstra connect for the Phillies. Tommy Greene, the Phils' starting pitcher, is the loser.

OCTOBER 8:

ALCS, game three. In Toronto, Wilson Alvarez pitches a complete-game seven-hitter and the White Sox win their first playoff game, 6-1. Ellis Burks and Lance Johnson have two RBI each and Tim Raines has four hits. Pat Hentgen is the loser.

OCTOBER 10
Game four of the NLCS is a 2-1 pitchers' duel that the Phillies win.

OCTOBER 20
Game four of the World Series is a 15-14 slugger's duel that the Blue Jays win.

OCTOBER 9:

NLCS, game three. In Atlanta, the Braves continue their heavy hitting and beat Philadelphia, 9-4. The Phillies' John Kruk hits the only home run, but Atlanta gets 12 hits, including a two-run double by David Justice. Tom Glavine is the winning pitcher. Terry Mulholland gets the loss.

ALCS, game four. In Toronto, Tim Belcher and the White Sox tie the playoffs with a 7-4 win. Lance Johnson homers with one on and hits a two-run triple; Frank Thomas adds a solo round-tripper. Todd Stottlemyre is the losing pitcher.

OCTOBER 10:

NLCS, game four. In Atlanta today, the pitchers take center stage and Danny Jackson outduels John Smoltz for a 2-1 Phillies' victory. Mitch Williams gets a save. Jackson drives in the winning run with a fourth inning single.

ALCS, game five. In Toronto, despite homers by Ellis Burks and Robin Ventura, the Blue Jays win, 5-3. Roberto Alomar leads the Toronto attack with three hits. Juan Guzman is the winner; Jack McDowell is tagged with the loss.

OCTOBER 11:

NLCS, game five. In Atlanta, the Phillies beat the Braves, 4-3, in 10 innings on Lenny Dykstra's homer off Mark Wohlers. Mitch Williams is credited with the win in relief. Darren Daulton also homers for the Phillies.

OCTOBER 12:

ALCS, game six. In Chicago, the Blue Jays beat the White Sox, 6-3, behind winning pitcher Dave Stewart, and capture the AL pennant. Duane Ward gets a save. Alex Fernandez suffers his second loss of the ALCS. Devon White homers for the Blue Jays; Warren Newson connects for the White Sox. Stewart is now 8-0 in ALCS play.

OCTOBER 13:

NLCS, game six: Tommy Greene goes seven innings and Mitch Williams gets a save as the Phillies beat the Braves, 6-3, for the NL pennant. The losing pitcher is Greg Maddux. Dave Hollins hits a two-run homer and teammates Darren Daulton and Mickey Morandini drive in two runs each to account for all of Philadelphia's runs. Jeff Blauser homers for Atlanta.

OCTOBER 16:

World Series, game one. In Toronto, the Blue Jays down the Phillies, 8-5, on home runs by Devon White and John Olerud. Al Leiter is the winning pitcher with two and two-thirds innings of middle relief; starter Curt Schilling is the loser. Duane Ward gets a save.

OCTOBER 17:

World Series, game two. Terry Mulholland, aided by home runs from Jim Eisenreich – with two on – and Lenny Dykstra, beats the Blue Jays, 6-4. Mitch Williams gets the save. Joe Carter homers for Toronto, and starter Dave Stewart gets the loss.

OCTOBER 19:

World Series, game three. In Philadelphia, after a 72-minute holdup for rain, Toronto uses 13 hits – including a solo homer and a two-run triple by Paul Molitor – to top the Phillies, 10-3. Pat Hentgen is the winner; Danny Jackson suffers the loss. Milt Thompson hits a homer for Philadelphia.

OCTOBER 20:

World Series, game four. It's the sluggers' showcase in Philadelphia, as the Blue Jays prevail, 15-14, in a four-hour, 14-minute contest. Devon White's two-run triple in the eighth caps a six-run rally and gives Toronto the edge. Tony Castillo, the third of five Blue Jays' pitchers, gets the victory. Mitch Williams is tagged with the loss. Lenny Dykstra hits a pair of two-run homers and Darren Daulton adds another for Philadelphia. The winners total 17 hits; the Phillies 14.

OCTOBER 21:

World Series, game five. After 32 base hits in yesterday's game, the pitchers silence the hitters in Philadelphia. Curt Schilling pitches a five-hit complete game, beating the Blue Jays, 2-0. Kevin Stocker's second-inning double drives in Darren Daulton with the winning run. Juan Guzman takes the loss.

OCTOBER 23:

World Series, game six. Back in Toronto

CULTURE

More baseball mysteries: *Sometimes You See It Coming*, a novel by Kevin Baker about a mysterious major league slugger; *Fear in Fenway* by Crabbe Evers; *Last Man Out* by Donald Honig; and *Night Game*, a Kate Henry mystery by Alison Gordon.

NOVEMBER 19
The Expos trade Delino DeShields to the Dodgers for Pedro Martinez.

DECEMBER 31
Baseball's collective bargaining agreement expires.

with 52,195 on hand, Joe Carter sends a Mitch Williams pitch over the left-field fence with two on in the bottom of the ninth to give the Blue Jays a dramatic 8-6 victory and the World Series. Duane Ward wins the clincher in relief; Williams gets the loss. Len Dykstra homers for the Phillies, and Paul Molitor hits one out for the Blue Jays. Paul Molitor hits .500 with two homers and eight RBI; Roberto Alomar bats .480 and drives in six runs. Joe Carter has two home runs and eight RBI. Duane Ward is 1-0 with an ERA of 1.93 and two saves. John Kruk (.348), Lenny Dykstra (.348, four homers, eight RBI), and Mariano Duncan at .345 provide the offense for the Phillies.

POST-SEASON

NOVEMBER 3:

Indians' pitcher Cliff Young dies in a truck crash in Willis, Texas. Young, 29, is the third Cleveland pitcher to die in an accident this year. Young was 3-3 with a 4.62 ERA.

NOVEMBER 5:

The White Sox decline to pick up the option on Bo Jackson for 1994. Instead, they pay him $150,000 in termination money and save between $2.41 and $3.75 million in salary. Playing with an artificial hip, Jackson batted .232 with 16 homers and 45 RBIs in 85 games.

NOVEMBER 12:

Hall of Fame catcher Bill Dickey dies at age 86 in a Little Rock, Arkansas, nursing home. In 17 years – all with the Yankees – Dickey batted .313 with 202 homers and appeared in eight World Series. He was inducted into the Hall of Fame in 1954.

NOVEMBER 19:

The Expos acquire pitcher Pedro Martinez (10-5, 2.61 ERA) from the Dodgers for outfielder Delino DeShields (.295, 43 stolen bases).

NOVEMBER 22:

The Rangers obtain one of baseball's premier first basemen, Will Clark (.283, 14 homers, 73 RBI). For all of his eight years in the majors, Clark has played for the Giants.

NOVEMBER 26:

The last of the Cardinals' Gas House Gang, Burgess Whitehead, dies at age 83 of a heart attack in Windsor, North Carolina. A reserve on the 1934 St. Louis World Championship team, Whitehead played nine years and batted .266.

DECEMBER 2:

The Indians sign free-agent first baseman Eddie Murray, who spent the past season with the Mets, hitting .285 with 27 homers and 100 RBI.

Mitch "Wild Thing" Williams (3-7, 3.34 ERA), who recorded 43 regular season saves but failed the Phillies in the World Series, is shipped to the Astros for pitchers Doug Jones (4-10, 4.54 ERA, 26 saves) and Jeff Juden (0-1, 5.40 ERA).

DECEMBER 9:

Left-hander Randy Johnson gets a new contract from the Mariners, which will bring him $20.25 million over four years. Johnson was 19-8 with a 3.24 ERA and a major league-leading 308 strikeouts in 1993.

DECEMBER 12:

The Orioles sign free-agent Rafael Palmeiro (.295, 37 homers, 105 RBI). He spent this past season with the Rangers.

DECEMBER 17:

Rickey Henderson (.289, 21 homers, 59 RBI, 53 stolen bases) returns to the Athletics, signing a two-year, $8.6 million contract.

DECEMBER 18:

Top Yankees' pitching prospect Brien Taylor injures a shoulder in a fight near his home in Beaufort, North Carolina, and will require surgery. He will miss the entire 1994 season and his future is in doubt. Taylor — whose fastball has been timed at 95 mph — signed for a $1.55 million bonus in 1991 and was 13-7 with a 3.48 ERA and 150 strikeouts at the Yankees' Class AA Albany farm team.

DECEMBER 31:

Baseball's collective bargaining agreement runs out with no agreement for a new one.

THE BEST OF 1993

NATIONAL LEAGUE

HITTERS

Batting Average:
Andres Galarraga, Colorado Rockies, .370

Slugging Average:
Barry Bonds, San Francisco Giants, .677

Home Runs:
Barry Bonds, - 46

Runs Batted In:
Barry Bonds, - 123

Hits:
Lenny Dykstra, Philadelphia Phillies, 194

Stolen Bases:
Chuck Carr, Florida Marlins, 58

PITCHERS

Wins:
John Burkett, San Francisco Giants;
Tom Glavine, Atlanta Braves, 22

Strikeouts:
Jose Rijo, Cincinnati Reds, 227

Earned Run Average:
Greg Maddux, Atlanta Braves, 2.36

Winning Percentage:
Mark Portugal, Houston Astros, .818

Saves:
Randy Myers, Chicago Cubs, 53

Most Valuable Player:
Barry Bonds, San Francisco Giants

Cy Young Award:
Greg Maddux, Atlanta Braves

Rookie of the Year:
Mike Piazza, Los Angeles Dodgers

Manager of the Year:
Johnnie "Dusty" Baker, San Francisco Giants

AMERICAN LEAGUE

HITTERS

Batting Average:
John Olerud, Toronto Blue Jays, .363

Slugging Average:
Juan Gonzalez, Texas Rangers, .632

Home Runs:
Juan Gonzalez, - 46

Runs Batted In:
Albert Belle, Cleveland Indians, 129

Hits:
Paul Molitor, Toronto Blue Jays, 211

Stolen Bases:
Kenny Lofton, Cleveland Indians, 70

PITCHERS

Wins:
Jack McDowell, Chicago White Sox, 22

Strikeouts:
Randy Johnson, Seattle Mariners, 308

Earned Run Average:
Kevin Appier, Kansas City Royals, 2.56

Winning Percentage:
Jimmy Key, New York Yankees, .750

Saves:
Jeff Montgomery, Kansas City Royals;
Duane Ward, Toronto Blue Jays, 45

Most Valuable Player:
Frank Thomas, Chicago White Sox

Cy Young Award:
Jack McDowell, Chicago White Sox

Rookie of the Year:
Tim Salmon, California Angels

Manager of the Year:
Gene Lamont, Chicago White Sox

1994

NEWS

RICHARD M. NIXON DIES AT AGE 81

Jacqueline Kennedy Onassis dies at age 64

RONALD REAGAN AFFLICTED WITH ALZHEIMER'S DISEASE

NELSON MANDELA ELECTED PRESIDENT OF SOUTH AFRICA

YITZHAK RABIN, YASSIR ARAFAT SHARE NOBEL PEACE PRIZE

UP TO 500,000 DIE IN RWANDA CIVIL WAR

Los Angeles earthquake kills 61

132 DIE IN USAIR JET CRASH IN PITTSBURGH

MOSCOW MOLE IN CIA ARRESTED

O. J. SIMPSON CHARGED WITH DOUBLE MURDERS

WHITEWATER FINDINGS FAVOR WHITE HOUSE

N. Y. RANGERS WIN HOCKEY"S STANLEY CUP

PRE-SEASON

JANUARY 5:

Mets' co-owner Fred Wilpon is true to his word. After he promised that Vince Coleman would never again play for the team, New York sends Coleman (.279, 38 stolen bases in 92 games) to the Royals for former Met outfielder Kevin McReynolds (.245, 11 homers).

JANUARY 6:

The owners meet at the Hyatt Regency in Rosemont, Illinois, and fall one vote short of approving the revenue-sharing plan developed by their negotiator Richard Ravitch.

Yankee owner George Steinbrenner expresses his opinion of revenue sharing to Hal Bodley of *USA Today*, "We have to decide if these cities that are struggling should really have teams...This is basically socialism at work."

JANUARY 9:

Harvey Haddix, who pitched 12 perfect innings in a 1959 game and lost in the 13th, dies at age 68 of emphysema in Springfield, Ohio. Haddix pitched 14 years in the majors, compiling a record of 136-113, with an ERA of 3.63. He was a 20-game winner for the Cardinals in 1953.

JANUARY 10:

Charles "Chub" Feeney, former NL president, dies of a heart attack at age 72 in San Francisco. Feeney was the grandson of New York Giants' owner Charles C. Stoneham and was the team's general manager. He also served as president of the Padres. Feeney was NL president from 1969 to 1986.

JANUARY 17:

In Fort Lauderdale, Florida, after several unsuccessful attempts to reach an agreement on a revenue-sharing plan, the major league owners approve a new proposal from Cardinals' president Stuart Meyer, 28-0. Teams will be divided into three classes: high, middle, and low revenue. A team can move from one category to another from year to year.

JANUARY 19:

The owners make the prospects of a labor settlement more difficult. They amend the major league agreement,

CULTURE

Terry Cashman salutes Michael Jordan's quest for the major leagues with *Good Enough to Dream*.

LEAGUE

Labor strife is in the air – again. Owners approve a revenue plan that is keyed to a salary cap – which needs player approval. The plan would allot $59 million to those characterized as low-revenue franchises.

←

Michael Jordon steps to the plate.

Their new manager Tom Trebelhorn observes, "The last time the Cubs won the World Series was in 1908. The last time they were in one was 1945. Hey, any team can have a bad century."

EQUIPMENT

In April, the Royals announce they will replace the artificial surface in their Kauffman Stadium with real grass in time for the 1995 season.

giving complete power to the commissioner on labor negotiations. The commissioner will have the authority to hire and supervise a negotiator. Allan "Bud" Selig, owner of the Brewers, will continue to function as interim commissioner. In addition, a 75 percent vote will be required to approve future collective bargaining issues if there is a strike. Previously a majority, with a minimum of five teams in each league, was needed to reach an agreement.

FEBRUARY 7:

Michael Jordan, arguably the greatest basketball player of all time, decides to try his skills at baseball. Jordan, who last played baseball in his junior year of high school, signs a minor league contract with the White Sox. After spring training with Chicago, he will go to the minor league team in Nashville.

FEBRUARY 11:

Baseball draws new rules for the commissioner, who previously could act broadly in the "best interests of baseball." He now loses his power to affect the World Series, post-season play, expansion, and the sale of franchises. He also no longer can apply the "best interests of baseball" rule to collective bargaining. In practice, he will be unable to end a lockout the way Bowie Kuhn did in 1976.

The owners, in a press release, claim they have "enhanced the authority and independence of the baseball commissioner." Acting commissioner Allan "Bud" Selig comments, "I think overall the office is clearly strengthened."

Next stop: Cooperstown. After 21 years in the majors – all with the Brewers – Robin Yount retires at the age of 38. One of baseball's quiet superstars, Yount is a two-time AL Most Valuable Player. His lifetime statistics include a .285 batting average with 251 homers and 3,142 hits. He began his career as an 18-year-old shortstop, later playing the outfield and appearing as a DH.

FEBRUARY 12:

Hall of Famer Ray Dandridge dies at age 80 in Palm Bay, Florida. A Negro Leagues star from 1933 to 1953, Dandridge was an infielder and batted .322. He was inducted into the Hall of Fame in 1987.

FEBRUARY 15:

Ila Borders becomes the first female to pitch in a college game. Appearing for Southern California College of Cosa Mesa, she five-hits Claremont-Mudd-Scripps, 12-1, yielding three walks and striking out two.

MARCH 1:

Leonard Coleman is elected president of the NL, succeeding Bill White. A former banker and public official, the 45-year-old Coleman has been executive director of market development for major league baseball. He also succeeds White as baseball's highest-ranking black executive.

MARCH 3:

It's a new round of trouble for Darryl Strawberry. He is under investigation by the Internal Revenue Service and the U.S. Attorney's Office for allegedly failing to report income of $300,000-plus earned at autograph and memorabilia shows.

MARCH 4:

Basketball superstar Michael Jordan bats for the first time in a major league uniform, facing Rangers' pitcher Darren Oliver in a spring training game. The would-be White Sox hits back to Oliver, who tags him out.

MARCH 7:

Talks resume between owners' representative Richard Ravitch and some 75 players in Tampa, Florida.

MARCH 9:

Phillies' first baseman-outfielder John Kruk is diagnosed with testicular cancer and will undergo surgery in Lakeland, Florida. Doctors expect Kruk to recover completely.

MARCH 10:

Longtime major league umpire Jim Honochick dies at age 75. He umped in the AL from 1949 to 1973, handling six World Series. After retiring, Honochick appeared in Lite Beer commercials, uttering, "Hey, you're Boog Powell" to the former Orioles' star.

MARCH 16:

Former major league pitcher Eric Show dies at age 37 of

FEBRUARY 15
Ila Borders becomes the first female to pitch in a college game.

APRIL 8
The Dodgers' Chan Ho Park becomes the first Korean player in the major leagues.

unknown causes at the Rancho L'Abri Drug and Alcohol treatment center in Dulzura, California, near San Diego. Show was in the facility for treatment of cocaine, alcohol, and heroin use. He pitched 10 years with the Padres and one with the Athletics, compiling a 101-80 record with a 3.66 ERA.

MARCH 18:

The Braves release outfielder Ron Gant, who broke his leg in a motorcycle accident. Gant had been signed to a $5 million contract. By cutting him prior to a contractual deadline, Atlanta is obliged to pay him "only" $900,000. In June, he will sign with the Reds.

MARCH 21:

U.S. Senator Howard Metzenbaum holds a two-and-a-half-hour hearing in Tampa, Florida, on baseball's antitrust exemption. Metzenbaum observes, "You don't have to be a genius, you don't have to be a Philadelphia lawyer, you don't have to be a Supreme Court justice to understand that under this new agreement you have denigrated the position of the commissioner." Acting commissioner Bud Selig disagrees, "That man has as much authority in this industry as any human being in the United States of America... He has more authority in those areas than he ever had in the past." Metzenbaum, a Democrat from Ohio, responds, "I say BS."

MARCH 30:

In Phoenix, Richard Ravitch speaks again, but his audience is smaller. This time he addresses approximately 50 players.

MARCH 31:

Anthony Young (11-6, 3.77 ERA), holder of an unenviable record – most consecutive losses – is traded by the Mets to the Cubs for shortstop Jose Vizcaino (.287, four homers, 54 RBI, 12 stolen bases).

THE SEASON

APRIL 4:

Jacobs Field opens in Cleveland with 41,259 on hand to see the Indians beat the Mariners, 4-3. Eddie Murray homers for Cleveland; Eric Anthony reaches the seats for Seattle. The winning pitcher is Eric Plunk in relief of Dennis Martinez; Kevin King takes the loss.

Cubs' rookie Karl Rhodes has an auspicious debut; he homers in each of his first three major league at-bats against the Mets' Dwight Gooden. He is the first ever to accomplish the feat. Each of Rhodes's homers is hit with the bases empty and sails into the left-centerfield bleachers at Wrigley Field. He also has a single off John Franco. But the Mets win the game, 12-8, and Gooden gets the victory. The losing pitcher is Mike Morgan.

The Dodgers place outfielder Darryl Strawberry on the disabled list because of a substance abuse problem. Strawberry, who failed to show for the team's final exhibition game, will enter a drug rehabilitation program.

APRIL 8:

The Braves' Kent Mercker no-hits Los Angeles, 6-0, at Dodger Stadium. Mercker fans 10 and walks four; his teammates make no errors. Fred McGriff, David Justice, and Terry Pendleton homer for Atlanta. The losing pitcher is Pedro Astacio. Mercker was part of a three-pitcher, combined no-hitter on September 11, 1991. The Dodgers' Chan Ho Park comes out of the bullpen in the ninth, bows to the umpire, and becomes the first Korean player to appear in the major leagues. He yields one hit, two runs, and two walks, fanning two.

Darryl Strawberry enters the Betty Ford Clinic in Rancho Mirage, California, for 18 days of treatment.

APRIL 9:

The Blue Jays' Paul Molitor singles in the ninth inning against Bobby Thigpen of the visiting Mariners; it is his 2,500th career hit. Molitor enjoys a 3-4 day and the Blue Jays win, 8-6, on a two-run homer by Joe Carter, offsetting a pair of 400-foot round-trippers by the Mariners' Ken Griffey Jr.

APRIL 10:

Basketball great Michael Jordan singles in the third and seventh innings for the AA Birmingham Barons against the Knoxville Smokies. They are his first two professional safeties.

APRIL 11:

In the first regular season game at the Ballpark at Arlington,

HISTORY

At Fenway Park in Boston, Leslie Sterling becomes the AL's first female public address announcer.

LEAGUE

Baseball begins the 1994 season with three divisions in each league, the first major structural change in 25 years.

The Cleveland Indians' Jacobs Field.

375
325
JACOBS FIELD
BROWNS

CULTURE

It's a big year for baseball movies. *Cobb* stars Tommy Lee Jones as Ty Cobb and Robert Wuhl as sportswriter Al Stump, with Roger Clemens as a Philadelphia Athletics' pitcher. *Little Big League* stars Luke Edwards as a 12-year-old who inherits the Minnesota Twins, and features Ken Griffey Jr., Leon "Bull" Durham, Kevin Elster, Mickey Tettleton, Sandy Alomar Jr., Carlos Baerga, Randy Johnson, Rafael Palmeiro, Tim Raines, Paul O'Neill, Lou Piniella, Ivan Rodriguez, and Alex Fernandez. *Angels in the Outfield*, a remake of the 1951 film, stars Danny Glover, with Mitchell Paige and Carney Lansford. *Major League II* stars Charlie Sheen, Tom Berenger, and Corbin Bernsen, with Bob Uecker and Steve Yeager. *The Scout* stars Albert Brooks, Brendan Fraser, and Dianne Wiest, with Bret Saberhagen, Bobby Murcer, Steve Garvey, Tim McCarver, Reggie Smith, Keith Hernandez, and Ozzie Smith.

the Brewers beat the Rangers, 4-3.

APRIL 18:

Mickey Mantle discusses his longtime problem with alcohol and his rehabilitation at the Betty Ford Clinic in the current issue of *Sports Illustrated.*

APRIL 27:

Scott Erickson of the Twins no-hits the Brewers, 6-0, facing 31 batters. He strikes out five, walks four, and hits one batter. It is the first no-hitter ever in the 13-year history of the Metrodome and the first for the Twins in 27 years. Kent Hrbek hits a home run. The losing pitcher is Jaime Navarro.

MAY 3:

The *New York Times* reports today that 708 home runs were hit in April — 210 more than in the comparable period in 1993. It quotes a representative of Rawlings as saying that the specifications and materials, as well as the manufacturing and testing processes, have not changed since 1976, when the company began making major league balls.

MAY 17:

Marcel Lachemann is named manager of the Angels, replacing Bob "Buck" Rodgers, who was 16-23. Lachemann's brother, Rene, is the manager of the Marlins. Bobby Knoop was 1-1 as interim manager.

MAY 18:

Marge Schott is at it again. The Reds' owner tells the Ohio County Treasurers Association, "Only fruits wear earrings." She then explains to the *Cincinnati Enquirer*, "I was raised to believe that men wearing earrings are fruity. I guess things have changed since then." She then asserts that her remarks were misconstrued.

MAY 22:

The New York Times publishes a poignant story by Dave Anderson on 75-year-old Ted Williams and his battle against the effects of a stroke. Williams's passion for hitting and his ambition to be the best ever still burn. He tells Anderson about a hospital experience, "I'm half asleep. I dream I'm in spring training working with the young Red Sox hitters like I did for years. But somehow Randy Johnson is out there on the mound, the big left-hander with Seattle...Now with Johnson out there, all the Red Sox are saying, "Why don't you go up there and take a few cuts?" I tell them, "I haven't hit in years and I just had a stroke and I can't see too well,' but they keep teasing me and I say, "Yeah, I'll do it.' But as I'm walking to home plate, I'm thinking, `I'm not going to try to pull this guy because he can really throw.' The first pitch, he laid one right in there. I pushed at it. Line drive through the box for a base hit."

MAY 23:

Richard Ravitch keeps talking — but his proposals are likely to fall on deaf ears. Today he advocates the elimination of trade restrictions, of termination pay, and of giving credit for major league service to players who are called up from the minors in September.

MAY 24:

Cal Ripken Jr. hits his 300th career homer.

MAY 25:

The Dodgers unconditionally release Darryl Strawberry.

Dodgers' manager Tommy Lasorda discusses Darryl Strawberry on a cable-television show and tells the interviewer, "You're wrong. Darryl Strawberry is not a dog. A dog is loyal and runs hard after balls."

MAY 27:

In Milwaukee, the Brewers end their 14-game losing streak with a 5-2 victory over the Mariners on a three-run homer by B. J. Surhoff in the eighth inning. Cal Eldred gets the win; Bill Risley is charged with the loss.

MAY 28:

In St. Paul, Minnesota, before a crowd of 3,954, the Silver Bullets beat the Richfield Rockets, 7-5, in what is believed to be the first victory by a women's professional team over a squad of all males. The Rockets are an amateur team composed of men 35 years old or older. Lee Ann Ketcham fans 14 for the Silver Bullets, and Stacy Sunny has three RBI.

MAY 30:

Giants' centerfielder Darren Lewis gets his first error in 392 consecutive games. It is the longest error-free

MAY 24
Cal Ripkin Jr. hits his 300th career homer.

JUNE 28
Dwight Gooden is suspended after failing two random drug tests.

string for any player in any position. Montreal beats San Francisco, 7-3.

JUNE 7:

The Blue Jays defeat the White Sox and Wilson Alvarez, 9-5, at Comiskey Park, ending the pitcher's 15-game winning streak, which began on August 24, 1993. Alvarez lasts three innings, yielding eight hits – including a Roberto Alomar home run – and four runs. The winning pitcher is Pat Hentgen.

JUNE 8:

The AL owners unanimously elect Gene Budig to a five-year term as their president. Budig, the chancellor at the University of Kansas, replaces Dr. Bobby Brown, who held the post for 10 years. Budig also headed the University of Virginia and Illinois State.

JUNE 13:

The Cubs' Ryne Sandberg rocks baseball by announcing his retirement. Sandberg, batting .239 with five homers, is giving up $16 million in guaranteed salary. He explains, "I didn't have what I felt I needed to go on the field every day and live up to the standards I set for myself." Sandberg, a second baseman, is 34 years old.

JUNE 14:

The owners propose that players split revenues 50-50 in exchange for a salary cap, the elimination of arbitration, and lowering the eligibility for free agency to four years (from six) with provisions.

JUNE 19:

The Giants are the latest team to gamble that Darryl Strawberry's talent will outweigh his problems. They sign Strawberry, who finished a drug rehabilitation program at the Betty Ford Center in Rancho Mirage, California, six weeks ago, to a free-agent contract. The 32-year-old Strawberry was released by the Dodgers on May 25.

JUNE 22:

John Franco of the Mets records his 17th save of the season, bringing his career total to 253.

JUNE 23:

Oakland's Bobby Witt comes within an umpire's call of a no-hitter today against the Royals in Oakland. In the sixth inning with one out and Witt pitching a perfect game, umpire Gary Cederstrom calls Greg Gagne safe at first on a ground ball. TV replays show Gagne was out. Witt ends up with a 4-0 win and a one-hitter; David Cone gets the loss.

Former major leaguer Marv Throneberry dies of cancer at age 60 in Fisherville, Tennessee. Throneberry, who became the symbol for the ineptitude of the early Mets, was a first baseman who had excellent minor league power stats, but who hit only .237 with 53 homers in the majors.

JUNE 28:

Mets' pitcher Dwight Gooden is hit with a 60-day suspension without pay for violating the terms of his drug aftercare program. Gooden reportedly failed two random drug tests. He issues an apology. In 1987, Gooden underwent treatment at New York City's Smithers Institute.

Fernando Valenzuela, regarded as washed up by the Dodgers and Angels, returns in a Phillies' uniform. The left-hander works six innings against the Marlins, giving up six hits, one unearned run, and two walks while fanning one. The Marlins win, 2-1. Jeff Mutis gets the win; Paul Quantrill gets the loss.

JULY 1:

Ken Griffey Jr. of the Mariners records 32 homers by the end of June, the most in history for that time period.

JULY 3:

Forty-seven years after Larry Doby broke the AL color line, the Indians get around to retiring his uniform number, 14.

Bobby Witt of the Athletics beats the Red Sox, 10-0, at Fenway Park for his third consecutive shutout. Witt, who now has a string of 27 scoreless innings, previously whitewashed the Royals on June 23 and the Angels on June 28. Chris Nabholz gets the loss.

JULY 11:

The Pirates unveil a $300,000 statue of their late star Roberto Clemente outside Three Rivers Stadium.

JULY 12:

In Pittsburgh, Moises Alou doubles in Tony Gwynn in the 10th inning to give the NL

TRIVIA

The Lachemanns become the first brothers to manage in the major leagues at the same time since 1879, when Harry and George Wright managed the Providence Grays and the Boston Beaneaters, respectively.

Leo Durocher once explained his approach to baseball: "If I were playing third base and my mother were rounding third with the run that was going to beat us, I'd trip her. Oh, I'd pick her up and brush her off and say, 'Sorry, Mom,' but nobody beats me."

HISTORY

Despite the strike-shortened season - 113 games – Frank Thomas of the White Sox becomes the third player ever to hit .300 with 20-plus homers and 100 RBI, 100 walks, and 100 runs in four straight seasons. The others were Ted Williams from 1946 to 1949 and Lou Gehrig – who accomplished the feat twice – from 1929 to 1932 and again from 1934 to 1937.

an 8-7 victory in the All-Star Game, ending the AL's six-game winning streak. Marquis Grissom and Fred McGriff homer. The winning pitcher is Doug Jones; Jason Bere gets the loss. Walter "Buck" Leonard, a star of the old Negro Leagues and now 86 years old, is the honorary captain of the NL All-Stars.

JULY 14:

Cesar Tovar dies at age 54 in Caracas, Venezuela. He is one of two major leaguers to play all nine positions in a game. Born in Caracas, Tovar played 12 years in the majors, batting .278 with 226 stolen bases. In 1971, he hit .311 for the Twins and led the AL with 204 hits. He appeared in three World Series, batting .250.

After the *New York Times* publishes a remark by Yankees' manager Buck Showalter critical of Mariners' star Ken Griffey Jr. for wearing his cap backward, Seattle's players all turn theirs around before a game with visiting New York. Showalter explains he didn't know the comment would be published and it was something he "wouldn't say publicly." He adds, "I have a lot of respect for him... We all learn from things we say and don't intend to hurt anybody." Griffey says, "I'm happy. I'm not going to change for one person. I've had it on this way since I was a kid." The Yankees win the game, 13-8. Griffey is two for five.

The Giants down the Expos, 8-3, in Montreal, with Darryl Strawberry connecting for a grand slam – his first homer in more than a year. Harry "Bud" Black gets the win. Pedro Martinez is charged with the loss.

JULY 16:

The Indians' Dennis Martinez whitewashes the White Sox, 2-0, on four hits at Comiskey Park. It is Martinez's 25th career shutout.

JULY 18:

The players turn down the salary cap that was proposed to them on June 14. They offer a counterproposal: salary minimums to be upped to $200,000 (from $175,000), arbitration after two years, and elimination of certain restrictions on free agency.

ROCKIES' MANAGER DON BAYLOR POSES A QUESTION WITHOUT AN ANSWER TO MURRAY CHASS OF THE *NEW YORK TIMES*: "WHY WOULD YOU WANT TO CORK A BAT WHEN THEY TALK ABOUT THE BALL BEING JUICED? HOW FAR DO YOU WANT IT TO GO? YOU HAVE TO CLEAR THE FENCE, BUT THEY WANT TO CLEAR THE CONCESSION STANDS."

The Indians' Albert Belle is suspended by AL president Bobby Brown for 10 days for using a corked bat. Belle's bat was confiscated by the umpires following a July 14 game against the White Sox. On July 27, Belle drops his appeal of the suspension and it is reduced to six days plus a $7,000 fine.

In Philadelphia, Barry Bonds of the Giants homers off the Phillies' Shawn Boskie. It is Bonds's 250th career homer.

In Houston, the Astros tie an NL record for comebacks in a game against the visiting Cardinals. Down 11-0 at one point, Houston rallies with 11 runs in the 6th inning and wins, 15-12. Jeff Bagwell homers for Houston; Gregg Jefferies for St. Louis. The winning pitcher is Mike Hampton; Brian Eversgerd gets the loss.

JULY 19:

It's not the sky that's falling, but part of the ceiling at the Kingdome in Seattle. Four tiles fall to the field and halt today's game between the Mariners and the Orioles. It is the first postponement at the Kingdome.

JULY 16
The Indians' Dennis Martinez pitches his 25th career shutout.

JULY 31
Steve Carlton, Leo Durocher, and Phil Rizzuto are inducted into Hall of Fame.

The roof problems at the Kingdome make a permanent road team of the Mariners.

JULY 22:

Dwight Gooden is admitted to California's Betty Ford Center for treatment of substance abuse.

JULY 25:

The Mariners' press agents and their computers are busy comparing not apples and oranges but home runs and mountains. They determine that Ken Griffey's 36 homers – which average 406 feet – if piled end-to-end would be taller than Mount Rainier in Washington. Griffey's homers add up to 14,645 feet; Mount Rainier measures 14,410 feet.

Before tonight's game, new Giant Darryl Strawberry and Dodgers' manager Tommy Lasorda make peace – sort of. Strawberry shakes hands with Lasorda during batting practice and gets a hug in return. Lasorda, according to the Associated Press, says, "It's good to see you. I hope everything goes well for you. Good luck to you. Take care of yourself." Tonight, Strawberry is hitless in four at-bats and the Dodgers win, 10-5.

Earlier in the week, Lasorda complained, "It's an almost unbelievable situation. We paid him. He's got our money and he's out here now trying to beat us, the same guys who were feeding him. Crazy game, isn't it?"

JULY 27:

Tigers' manager Sparky Anderson is now tied for fourth place on the all-time win list with Joe McCarthy, at 2,126. Anderson reaches the lofty position when Detroit beats visiting Seattle, 3-1, on Travis Fryman's two-run homer. Mike Moore allows two hits in eight innings for the victory; Randy Johnson is charged with the loss.

Richard Ravitch, the negotiator for the owners, disposes of the players' proposals.

The Marlins' 46-year-old pitcher, Charlie Hough, goes on the disabled list because of a hip ailment. The oldest player in baseball, Hough is not expected to return to action and eventually needs a hip replacement. In 25 years, Hough was 216-216 with a 3.75 ERA.

JULY 28:

In Texas, the Rangers' Kenny Rogers pitches a perfect game, defeating the visiting Angels, 4-0. Rogers strikes out eight in the 11th regular season perfect game in history.

The Players Association executive board unanimously approves August 12 as the date for a strike. Donald Fehr of the Players Association says at a press conference, "A strike is a last resort. I want to emphasize that. No one wants to play more than the players do."

JULY 31:

Steve Carlton, Leo Durocher, and Phil Rizzuto are inducted into the Hall of Fame, which now has 219 members, of whom 55 are living. Acting commissioner Bud Selig, for the second straight year, is not in attendance. Carlton pitched 24 years - mostly with the Cardinals and Phillies - compiling a 329-244 record with a 3.22 ERA, 4,136 strikeouts, and 55 shutouts. He won 20 games or more six times with a best of 27-10 in 1972. He also led the NL in strikeouts five times with a high of 310 in 1971. Carlton was 2-2 in four World Series. Durocher, who had expressed a desire not to be posthumously inducted into the Hall of Fame, is represented by his son Christopher. He managed for 24 years with a record of 2,008-1,709, winning pennants with the Brooklyn Dodgers in 1941 and the New York Giants in 1951. His 1954 Giants swept the Indians in four games for the World Championship. Durocher died in 1991. As a player, Durocher spent 17 seasons in the majors, batting .247 and appearing in the 1928 World Series with the Yankees and the 1934 fall classic with the Cardinals. Rizzuto was the Yankees' shortstop from 1941 to 1956, with time out for Navy service during World War II. He batted .273 with a high of .324 in 1950, when he was the AL's Most Valuable Player. Presently a Yankee broadcaster, he appeared in nine World Series with New York.

Acting commissioner Bud Selig later explains his absence to Ira Berkow of the New York Times: *"Well, it fell on the day after my 60th birthday and I had functions in town here [Milwaukee]. And*

LEAGUE

Hostilities between the owners and players heat up. Owners withhold $7.8 million they are obligated to pay to the players' pension and benefit plans.

Phil Rizzuto, passed over in many votes for enshrinement in Cooperstown, finally realizes his dream. On one occasion, he said, "I'll take any way to get into the Hall of Fame. If they want a batboy, I'll go as a batboy."

HISTORY

Barry Bonds of the Giants and former major leaguer Bobby Bonds now have the most combined homers of any father and son – 591 through 1994. Barry has accounted for 259; his father, 332. They are second to Maury and Elliott "Bump" Wills in stolen bases. The Wills duo has 782; Barry and Bobby Bonds, 770.

I don't remember why I missed the year before. But I love that weekend and I've been there before."

AUGUST 1:

Cal Ripken Jr. becomes the second player in history to appear in 2,000 consecutive games. The active player with the next most consecutive games is Jeff Conine of the Marlins, at 267. Ripken plays in his landmark game against the Twins in Minnesota and is hitless in four at-bats. The Orioles, behind Arthur Rhodes, beat the Twins, 1-0.

At Fenway Park, the Blue Jays' Joe Carter cracks a two-run homer against Steve Farr of the Red Sox. It is Carter's 300th career round-tripper.

At Candlestick Park, Matt Williams of the Giants homers against the Reds' Erik Hanson. It is Williams's 200th career home run.

AUGUST 5:

In Houston, the Astros' Jeff Bagwell has three hits in four at-bats – including a homer and a double – and drives in five runs in a 12-4 victory over the Giants. Bagwell leads the NL with 112 RBI, has 38 homers, and is batting .370 with 71 extra-base hits.

AUGUST 6:

The Mariners beat the Royals, 11-2, ending Kansas City's 14-game winning streak. Edgar Martinez hits a three-run homer and Reggie Jefferson drives in three runs for Seattle. The winning pitcher is Tim Davis; Mark Gubicza gets the loss. The Royals last lost on June 22.

AUGUST 10:

In Houston, Astros' first baseman Jeff Bagwell is struck on the left hand by a pitch from San Diego's Andy Benes that fractures the fourth metacarpal bone. In September of last year, Bagwell was sidelined with a broken fifth metacarpal bone in the same hand after being struck by a pitch.

Talks between the players and owners break off, and a strike appears to be inevitable.

AUGUST 11:

As players take the field for today's games, it appears fans are seeing the last baseball to be played for the foreseeable future.

The Mariners beat the Athletics, 8-1, in Oakland. The contest ends at approximately 1 a.m. EDT and may be the final game of the year.

AUGUST 12:

Nobody blinks, major league players go on strike, and there are no games today. It is the third work stoppage in the past 23 years. The dispute focuses on a salary cap, free agency, salary arbitration, and minimum salaries.

President Bill Clinton urges a settlement, saying, "There are a lot of little kids out there who want to see this season come to a close and there are a lot of not-so-little kids out there who know that this is the most exciting baseball season in 40 years."

AUGUST 17:

Two construction workers are killed when their basket on a construction crane plummets 250 feet to the floor of the Kingdome in Seattle. A third man is injured when the basket hits the cab of a crane. The workers were involved in repairing the roof of the Kingdome after acoustic tiles fell last month.

AUGUST 18:

Owners accede to federal mediators and will meet at the bargaining table with player reps. In the meantime, Representative Jack Brooks of Texas warns of congressional hearings on baseball's anti-trust exemption. Brooks states that the exemption "has contributed to a recurring pattern of strikes, lock-outs and bad faith collective bargaining that makes the labor disputes in the auto, steel, or coal industries look like the epitome of harmonious dialogue."

AUGUST 22:

Acting commissioner Bud Selig announces his lineup for negotiations: Bill Bartholomay and Stan Kasten of the Braves, Paul Beeston of the Blue Jays, David Glass of the Royals, John Harrington of the Red Sox, Andy MacPhail of the Twins, Drayton McLane of the Astros, Jerry McMorris of the Rockies, Stuart Meyer of the Cardinals, David Montgomery of the Phillies, Jerry Reinsdorf of the White Sox, and Wendy Selig-Prieb of

AUGUST 12
Major league players go on strike.

SEPTEMBER 14
Owners cancel baseball season.

the Brewers. The 12 owners and/or executives will "assist" negotiator Richard Ravitch. Both sides agree to meet tomorrow – for the first time since August 12.

AUGUST 25:

No progress is reported as two days of negotiations conclude in New York. No new meetings are scheduled. A total of 181 games have been lost due to the strike.

AUGUST 31:

Three and a half hours with federal mediators produce no progress, and no further talks are on tap between owners and players in the strike, which is going into its fourth week.

DH-outfielder Dave Winfield (.252, 10 homers in 77 games) is sold by the Twins to the Indians. Winfield leads all active players with 3,088 career hits.

SEPTEMBER 2:

September 9 is the tentative deadline for canceling the season if there is no new agreement, according to acting commissioner Bud Selig. Yesterday, Selig raised the possibility that he might join the negotiations.

U.S. Secretary of Labor Robert Reich raps both sides, saying baseball is "becoming a symbol of national greed." He tells Mutual-NBC Radio, "If the parties don't want to resolve their dispute, well, then unfortunately, they're going to have to stew in their own juice."

SEPTEMBER 5:

Hank Aguirre dies at age 62 of complications of prostate cancer in Detroit. A native of Mexico, Aguirre played with the Indians, Tigers, Dodgers, and Cubs, with a career record of 75-72 and a 3.25 ERA. He was one of the worst hitters in the game, with a lifetime average of .085. His career year was 1962 with the Tigers, when he was 16-8 and has the AL's best ERA - 2.21.

SEPTEMBER 7:

Bargaining resumes in New York with secret meetings held between management and union representatives.

SEPTEMBER 8:

A proposal for a 1 1/2 percent tax on payrolls and revenues of the 16 largest franchises and a plan for sharing 25 percent of gate receipts is put on the table by the union. Under its plan, the money would be allotted to the teams with the lowest revenues and payrolls.

SEPTEMBER 9:

One day after receiving the players' tax proposal, the owners reject it.

SEPTEMBER 14:

The unbelievable becomes reality. The baseball season is canceled by the owners after 34 days of the players' strike. For the first time since 1903, there will be no World Series. The owners vote 26-2 to take the drastic step; the only dissenting votes are cast by Peter Angelos of the Orioles and Marge Schott of the Reds.

POST-SEASON

SEPTEMBER 15:

The Mets get word they'd rather not hear. Dwight Gooden is in violation of his aftercare program for substance abuse.

SEPTEMBER 23:

Barry Bonds undergoes surgery to remove bone chips from his right elbow.

OCTOBER 14:

Bud Selig and Donald Fehr meet with President Bill Clinton at the White House. Labor Secretary Robert Reich gives W. J. Usery the unenviable assignment of mediating the baseball strike.

NOVEMBER 1:

Plans are announced for a new United League, which will compete with the existing major leagues. The new league is the brainchild of agent Dick Moss, Texas congressman John Bryant, and former New York congressman Bob Mrazek. According to the founders, the United League expects to put teams in six to eight cities.

NOVEMBER 4:

If there is a 1995 season, Dwight Gooden of the Mets will not be playing. The right-hander receives a season-long suspension for violating his substance abuse aftercare program. Gooden, who was in treatment at the Betty Ford Center in California from July 22 to August 14 of this year, reportedly has continued to test positive for cocaine.

CULTURE

Babseball lives on in the book world. *How George Radbourn Saved Baseball*, written and illustrated by David Shannon, is a fable about a nine-year-old living in a time when the sport is illegal. *Brittle Innings* is a novel by Michael Bishop about minor league baseball and a supernatural creature. *Hitting Into the Wind* is a collection of short stories by Bill Meissner. *The Elements of Hitting* is novel by Matthew F. Jones. *Strike Zone* is novel by Jim Bouton and Eliot Asinof. And in mysteries, *Tigers Burning* is by Crabbe Evers, *Murder at Fenway Park* is by Troy Soos and features Red Sox rookie Mickey Rawlings, and *Drover and the Designated Hitter* is by Bill Granger.

DECEMBER 8
Daryll Strawberry and his agent are indicted for failing to report income from autograph sales.

NOVEMBER 10:

In Rye Brook, New York, negotiations begin anew between the parties to the baseball strike.

NOVEMBER 17:

If it looks like a cap and sounds like a cap... Owners present a new proposal. Described as a tax proposal, it serves the same purpose as a cap.

DECEMBER 5:

He doesn't wear spikes, but if he did he would be hanging them up. Richard Ravitch will step down as negotiator for the owners on December 31 when his contract runs out.

DECEMBER 8:

Darryl Strawberry and his agent, Eric Goldschmidt, are indicted for allegedly failing to report $500,000 in income derived from the sale of autographs at baseball card shows between 1986 and 1990.

DECEMBER 9:

The Red Sox acquire outfielder Jose Canseco (.282, 31 homers, 90 RBI) from the Rangers for outfielder Otis Nixon (.274, 42 stolen bases) and third baseman Luis Ortiz (.167 in seven games).

DECEMBER 13:

The Angels sign free-agent relief pitcher Lee Smith (1-4, 3.29, and a major league-leading 33 saves). He was with the Orioles last season and has 434 career saves.

DECEMBER 14:

Owners are the target of a National Labor Relations Board complaint for withholding payment of $7.8 million to the players' pension fund on August 1.

The Yankees acquire pitcher Jack McDowell (10-9, 3.73 ERA), the 1993 AL Cy Young Award winner, from the White Sox for minor league pitcher Keith Heberling and a player to be named later.

The Phillies sign free agent Gregg Jefferies (.325, 12 homers), who spent the 1994 season with the Cardinals.

DECEMBER 22:

Once again, negotiations break off with no progress. With the break in negotiations the 1995 season's start is in jeopardy.

DECEMBER 23:

It's now nuclear warfare. The owners unilaterally implement a salary cap after declaring a negotiations impasse.

DECEMBER 27:

The National Labor Relations Board receives charges of unfair labor practices from both sides.

Former major league pitcher Allie Reynolds dies at age 79 in Oklahoma City. Reynolds pitched for 13 years with the Indians and Yankees, compiling a 182-107 record with a 3.30 ERA. He enjoyed his best years with the Yankees, building a 7-2 record in six World Series. He was a 20-game winner in 1952 when he led the AL with a 2.06 ERA. The previous year he became the first AL pitcher with two no-hitters in single season.

DECEMBER 28:

The Astros and Padres complete a 12-player trade, the largest in the majors since a November 20, 1957, transaction between Detroit and Kansas City. Going to Houston are outfielder Derek Bell (.311, 14 homers, 24 stolen bases), infielder Ricky Gutierrez (.240 in 90 games), pitcher Pedro Martinez (3-2, 2.90 ERA), outfielder Phil Plantier (.220, 18 homers in 96 games), and infielder Craig Shipley (.333 in 81 games). San Diego receives third baseman Ken Caminiti (.283, 18 homers, 75 RBI), shortstop Andujar Cedeno (.263 in 98 games), outfielder Steve Finley (.276, 11 homers in 94 games), infielder Roberto Petagine (.000 in eight games), pitcher Brian Williams (6-5, 5.74 ERA), and a player to be named later.

Minor league pitcher Sean Fesh goes to the Padres on May 1, 1995, to complete the deal.

TRIVIA

John C. Freed of the *New York Times* feeds the statistics for the interrupted season into a computer and comes up with projections on how things might have been without a strike. Among the results: Matt Williams would have reached 60 homers; Tony Gwynn's batting average would be .394, and Jimmy Key's final pitching mark would be 25-6.

DECEMBER 27
The National Labor Relations Board receives charges of unfair labor practices from players and owners.

THE BEST OF 1994

NATIONAL LEAGUE

HITTERS

Batting Average:
Tony Gwynn, San Diego Padres, .394

Slugging Average:
Jeff Bagwell, Houston Astros, .750

Home Runs:
Matt Williams, San Francisco Giants, 43

Runs Batted In:
Jeff Bagwell, 116

Hits:
Tony Gwynn, 165

Stolen Bases:
Craig Biggio, Houston Astros, 39

PITCHERS

Wins:
Ken Hill, Montreal Expos;
Greg Maddux, Atlanta Braves, 16

Strikeouts:
Andy Benes, San Diego Padres, 189

Earned Run Average:
Greg Maddux, 1.56

Winning Percentage:
Bret Saberhagen, New York Mets, .778

Saves:
John Franco, New York Mets, 30

Most Valuable Player:
Jeff Bagwell, Houston Astros

Cy Young Award:
Greg Maddux, Atlanta Braves

Rookie of the Year:
Raul Mondesi, Los Angeles Dodgers

Manager of the Year:
Felipe Alou, Montreal Expos

AMERICAN LEAGUE

HITTERS

Batting Average:
Paul O'Neill, New York Yankees, .359

Slugging Average:
Frank Thomas, Chicago White Sox, .729

Home Runs:
Ken Griffey Jr., Seattle Mariners, 40

Runs Batted In:
Kirby Puckett, Minnesota Twins, 112

Hits:
Kenny Lofton, Cleveland Indians, 160

Stolen Bases:
Kenny Lofton, 60

PITCHERS

Wins:
Jimmy Key, New York Yankees, 17

Strikeouts:
Randy Johnson, Seattle Mariners, 204

Earned Run Average:
Steve Ontiveros, Oakland Athletics, 2.65

Winning Percentage:
Jason Bere, Chicago White Sox, .857

Saves:
Lee Smith, Baltimore Orioles, 33

Most Valuable Player:
Frank Thomas, Chicago White Sox

Cy Young Award:
David Cone, Kansas City Royals

Rookie of the Year:
Bob Hamelin, Kansas City Royals

Manager of the Year:
William "Buck" Showalter, New York Yankees

1995

NEWS

ISRAELI PRIME MINISTER RABIN ASSASSINATED

TERRORIST BOMB KILLS 167 IN OKLAHOMA CITY

BOSNIAN PEACE ACCORD SIGNED; U.S. TROOPS SERVE AS PEACEKEEPERS

JAPANESE EARTHQUAKE KILLS 5,000

NERVE GAS TERROR ATTACK KILLS 11, INJURES 5,000 ON TOKYO SUBWAY

O. J. SIMPSON ACQUITTED OF MURDER CHARGES

CHRISTOPHER REEVE PARALYZED IN HORSEBACK RIDING ACCIDENT

SHOWDOWN IN CONGRESS LEADS TO SHUTDOWN OF GOVERNMENT

PRE-SEASON

JANUARY 1:

There are no players; now there are no umpires either. Major league baseball owners lock out the 64 American and National League umpires.

JANUARY 4:

Five bills aimed at settling the baseball strike are introduced in Congress. Among the provisions are a repeal of the antitrust exemption and binding arbitration.

Acting commissioner Bud Selig responds, "This is the kind of thing that has to be settled by negotiation. The end of the exemption doesn't mean the end of the strike."

JANUARY 5:

All 835 unsigned players are now free agents because owners unilaterally changed the uniform contract, according to players' union chief Donald Fehr.

JANUARY 9:

The owners claim 835 unsigned players are not free agents. Donald Fehr meets with 63 Latin American major leaguers in San Juan, Puerto Rico, to address rumors that they would be strikebreakers. Says Blue Jays' pitcher Juan Guzman, "Everybody's still together."

JANUARY 10:

The owners take another hit – this one for collusion damages for actions in 1986 and 1987. Arbitrator Thomas Roberts awards $9,708,756 to 11 players. The big winners are Rod Carew, who gets $782,036 for 1986, and Dave Kingman, who is awarded $829,850 for 1987.

JANUARY 13:

The use of replacement players for both spring exhibition and regular season games is okayed by baseball's executive council. Spring training starts February 16, and acting commissioner Bud Selig says, "We are committed to playing the 1995 season and will do so with the best players willing to play." Retired players will be among the replacements who will make $628.42 per day during the season.

JANUARY 18:

Former major league umpire Ron Luciano dies at age 57 in Endicott, New York, an apparent suicide. Luciano, one of the game's most colorful characters, umped in the AL for 11 years, wrote *The Umpire Strikes Back* and three other books, and also worked as an NBC commentator. His feuds with then Orioles' manager Earl Weaver were among the most heated in history.

Umpire Ken Kaiser, who worked with him for seven years, tells the Associated Press, "He was a classic. There was only one Luciano."

Former big league pitcher Phil Niekro, 54, claims he has been contacted by an NL team about becoming a replacement player. According to Niekro, the unidentified team also inquired about his 50-year-old brother Joe.

JANUARY 19:

There is a serious crack in the solidarity of the owners. Orioles' owner Peter Angelos, himself a prominent labor attorney, reaffirms a January 14 Associated Press story – his team will not use replacement players.

A concern in Baltimore is Cal Ripken Jr.'s consecutive game streak, which will end when

JANUARY 10
Collusion damages totaling $9,708,756 are to be paid by owners to 11 players.

JANUARY 26
President Clinton warns owners and players: "resume bargaining."

and if the season begins and there is a replacement player in his spot. Angelos says, "My position hasn't changed. The use of so-called replacement players would stigmatize the game." He concludes, "We have a special problem in Baltimore with the Cal Ripken streak...one that we certainly will do everything to avoid harming."

JANUARY 23:

Stories published today reveal that former major league pitcher J. R. Richard, whose career was ended by a stroke in 1980, is homeless, broke, works part-time, and sometimes lives under a freeway overpass in Houston. Richard, age 44, once earned $850,000 a year and seemed like a sure shot for the Hall of Fame; now he says he has only $20. Former teammates Jimmy Wynn, Bob Watson, and Enos Cabell are trying to help Richard rebuild his life.

Former major league pitcher Saul Rogovin, who went on to become a New York City high school English teacher at age 56 after working as a liquor salesman, dies at 71. He had a career record of 48-48 and led the AL with a 2.78 ERA in 1951.

JANUARY 26:

Both sides in the strike get the word from President Bill Clinton: resume bargaining. And reach an agreement by February 6.

FEBRUARY 1:

Faced with another National Labor Relations Board complaint – this time that they illegally imposed a salary cap – owners revoke it and agree to return to the old agreement. After 40 days of silence, talks resume. Owners substitute a luxury tax proposal for a salary cap.

FEBRUARY 6:

President Clinton's deadline expires with no resolution of the impasse. Richard Ravitch, who has been negotiating for the owners, charges union leaders with misleading players, saying, "These kids were not being told the truth."

It may take a Babe Ruth to restore baseball to respectability

Tom Glavine tosses a one-hitter as the Braves win their first World Series.

RULES

Beginning July 12, breaks between innings will be cut by 40 seconds, and batters will not be permitted to routinely step out of the box between pitches. The changes are designed to speed up games.

HISTORY

Babe Ruth's 100th birthday is observed with a scholarly symposium at Hofstra University in New York. The three-day event, held April 27, 28, and 29, is titled "Baseball and the Sultan of Swat."

LEAGUE

The player hardest hit by the strike is the Giants' Barry Bonds. If the stoppage continues into the regular season, Bonds is out $42,350 a day. Cecil Fielder of the Tigers stands to lose $39,344 per day. Frank Thomas of the White Sox is next at $39,071.

TRIVIA

Every cloud has a silver marketing opportunity; Rawlings finds a way to unload 5,000 balls it manufactured for the World Series that wasn't. For only $29.95, baseball fans can buy the Official 1994 World Series ball, being merchandised as "the most sought after World Series Baseball ever!"

in the eyes of the fans. Today marks the 100th anniversary of the birth of the Babe, the man who helped baseball survive the Black Sox scandal. In Baltimore, his granddaughters join a Bambino look-alike at a celebration at the three-story row house that was his birthplace.

Darryl Strawberry is suspended for 60 days for violation of baseball's drug policy and his own aftercare program. And he receives a second blow when he is released by the Giants.

FEBRUARY 7:

A trip to Washington and the White House produces no results. President Clinton's call for binding arbitration is rejected by the owners.

FEBRUARY 9:

It's strike three for Darryl Strawberry – at least for the present. He pleads guilty to income tax evasion and will spend three months in prison, in addition to paying back taxes, interest, and penalties.

FEBRUARY 13:

The Dodgers sign Hideo Nomo, an all-star in Japan's Pacific League, for a reported $2 million bonus. Nomo pitched the past four seasons with the Kintetsu Buffaloes, compiling a 78-46 record with a 3.15 ERA and 1,204 strikeouts.

FEBRUARY 14:

The new United League, announced on November 1, 1994, plans to begin play in 1996 with franchises in Los Angeles, New Orleans, New York, San Juan (Puerto Rico), Vancouver (British Columbia), and Washington, D.C. One possibility is a franchise in Brooklyn, which has been without baseball since the Dodgers departed in 1957. Other locations under consideration are New England; Mexico; Florida; Portland, Oregon; Columbus, Ohio; San Antonio, Texas; Sacramento, California; and Honolulu. Start-up costs are expected to be approximately $20 million.

FEBRUARY 15:

According to a story in *Florida Today*, the Lords of Baseball are pressuring Little League teams who use major league nicknames to pay fees – $6 per player – for the rights. Acting commissioner Bud Selig notes that the majors contribute in excess of $1 million to youth baseball.

FEBRUARY 16:

In Orlando, Florida, some 260 players meet and discuss remarks by the Phillies' Lenny Dykstra, which were interpreted as meaning he might become a strikebreaker. Afterward, Donald Fehr tells reporters, "There are 1,000 players out there and you're focusing on just one. Lenny has never suggested to me or anyone else that he would act contrary to the opinion of the majority of other people."

FEBRUARY 17:

Stating that "there ain't no place in our game for replacement players," the Tigers' venerable manager Sparky Anderson says no to managing them and is put on an involuntary leave of absence. Anderson, 60, and the fourth-winningest manager ever, adds, "There ain't enough money in the world to buy my integrity." The Orioles, too, are taking a stand: general manager Roland Hemond announces Baltimore will not play in exhibition games against replacement players.

FEBRUARY 19:

The Blue Jays assign manager Cito Gaston and his coaching staff, along with trainers and equipment men, to work with minor league players – all season if necessary – so they will not have to deal with replacement players. General manager Gord Ash explains, "Quite simply, we feel this is the best way to preserve our team atmosphere."

FEBRUARY 23:

Kevin Mitchell, who hit .326 with 30 homers for the Reds last season, is heading for Japan. The NL's 1989 MVP is signing with the Daiei Hawks.

MARCH 1:

In Tempe, Arizona, replacement players in Angels' uniforms play against Arizona State University. It is the first time since 1912 that replacement players appear in a game. Approximately 350 fans – some with paper bags over their heads – are on hand for the exhibition game.

FEBRUARY 17
Tigers' manager Sparky Anderson refuses to manage replacement players.

MARCH 10
Michael Jordan announces his retirement from baseball and returns to the NBA.

MARCH 2:

The Reds and Indians engineer the first trade of replacement players. The Reds, who found themselves shorthanded when 23 left camp, get former major leaguer Barbaro Garbey and four others in return for "future considerations."

MARCH 3:

A bunch of guys in Yankee uniforms lose to make-believe Braves, 8-2, in Fort Lauderdale, Florida, after losing yesterday to ersatz Dodgers, 11-3.

Owner George Steinbrenner complains about the imbalance in "talent" between teams. Says Steinbrenner, "If those teams loaded up because their general managers knew what was happening because they were on the inside, then I'm going to raise real hell...Our guys might have been asleep at the switch."

MARCH 4:

With opening day scheduled for April 4, hope for a settlement of the strike dims as talks between players and owners break down in Scottsdale, Arizona.

MARCH 9:

Owners meeting at Palm Beach, Florida, vote 28-0 to admit two new teams – the Tampa Bay Devil Rays and the Arizona Diamondbacks – for the 1998 season. The expansion fee is $130 million per franchise. The new teams will be assigned to leagues in January 1997. The principal owner of the Diamondbacks is Jerry Colangelo, who also owns the Phoenix Suns in the National Basketball Association. Vince Naimoli is the owner of the Devil Rays. The major league owners do not vote on the use of replacement players for the regular season should the strike remain unsettled. Mediator William J. Usery – who reportedly is getting $60,000 a month underwritten by both sides – instructs the owners to make their best offer and do it soon.

MARCH 10:

The Michael Jordan experiment ends. With a White Sox deadline for reporting to minor league spring training camp facing him, basketball's greatest player announces he is giving up baseball and returning to the hard-

Hideo Nomo winds up for the Dodgers.

TRIVIA

The *Boston Globe*'s Dan Shaugnessy measures the distance from home plate to the Green Monster – the left-field wall – in Fenway Park and substantiates a longtime rumor: It is closer than the official measurement. As a result of Shaugnessy's field work, the Red Sox change the marker down the left-field line from 315 feet to 310 feet. The sports columnist, who had an assistant and a 100-foot tape measure, actually calculates the distance as 309 feet, three inches. "I could be a couple of inches off, but it's damn close to that." In 1975, the Red Sox denied the *Globe* permission to measure, and the newspaper attempted to use aerial photographs.

wood. Jordan says, "The labor dispute has made it increasingly difficult to continue my development at a rate that meets my standards."

MARCH 13:

Negro Leagues' star Leon Day dies at age 78 of heart failure in Baltimore, just six days after being voted into the baseball Hall of Fame. Monte Irvin, himself a Hall of Famer, says, "Leon was as good as Satchel Paige, as good as any pitcher who ever lived..." Day, who used a no-windup delivery, once fanned 18 batters in a 1942 game.

MARCH 14:

The National Labor Relations Board issues a complaint against the owners, charging violation of labor laws. It is the third such complaint in three months.

The players' union warns it will not settle the dispute if replacement players are used in the regular season and the game results are not voided. Players Association representative Gene Orza says, "You can take it to the bank that scab games will not count in the

"IT CAN'T BE A COINCIDENCE THAT THE FIRST TIME A WOMAN GOT TO SAY SOMETHING IN THE BASEBALL STRIKE WAS THE FIRST TIME ANY OF THIS NONSENSE STARTED TO GET SORTED OUT."
– *David Hinckley*, New York Daily News

standings once this strike is settled...this is a line in the sand."

MARCH 20:

The remainder of the Orioles' spring training games are canceled because of the team's refusal to use replacement players.

MARCH 21:

After two days of meetings between Bud Selig and Donald Fehr, neither reports any progress. At the same time, the Maryland House of Delegates approves legislation to bar teams playing at Camden Yards from using replacement players.

MARCH 25:

Dave Shotkoski, a 30-year-old replacement pitcher for the Braves, is shot and killed in a robbery attempt near the team's hotel in West Palm Beach, Florida.

MARCH 27:

National Labor Relations Board General Counsel Fred Feinstein files for an injunction to restore previous work rules to the game.

MARCH 29:

Players vote to return to work, if a U.S. District Court judge supports the National Labor Relations Board's unfair labor practices complaint against the owners. Players Association head Don Fehr announces, "If the prior terms and conditions of employment are restored effectively by the injunction, the players will return to work." Rockies' boss Jerry McMorris is leaning toward a lockout if there is no negotiated settlement and Yankee owner George Steinbrenner warns Fehr to "give our offer serious consideration...He has to know that we will open the season with replacement players." By a vote of 26-2, the owners support the use of replacement players; Steinbrenner changes his vote from no to yes. The Blue Jays and Orioles are the two dissenting franchises.

Terry Moore, who teamed with Stan Musial and Enos Slaughter to give the Cardinals one of baseball's premier outfields, dies in Collinsville, Illinois, at age 82. Moore played 11 years, batted .280, and was a superb fielder.

MARCH 31:

After a two-and-a-half-hour hearing, U.S. District Judge Sonia

APRIL 2
The longest strike in pro sports history ends as owners accept players' offer to return.

Sotomayor takes 15 minutes to issue a preliminary injunction that requires baseball owners to comply with the expired collective bargaining agreement. Her ruling is a major victory for the players. Owners will meet tomorrow in Chicago to decide on a response.

APRIL 1:

Tonight's opening game between the Marlins and Mets – with replacement players – is postponed. Owners appeal Judge Sotomayor's decision.

APRIL 2:

The longest strike in pro sports history – 234 days – will end as baseball owners today accept the players' offer to return. The season originally would have begun today. Players will begin reporting to spring training camps on April 5 on a voluntary basis and the season will begin on April 26. Teams will play 144 games instead of 162. The strike began last August 12 and caused the cancellation of 52 days of the 1994 regular season and the World Series. Replacement players were released yesterday.

APRIL 3:

Tiger's manager Sparky Anderson resumes his post, stating, "I can look in the mirror now."

Dennis Eckersley inks a one-year contract with the Athletics; he is the first player to sign a contract since December 22, 1994.

APRIL 4:

The request by owners to stay Judge Sotomayor's injunction is denied by the Second U.S. Court of Appeals. Chief Judge Jon O. Newman tells the owners' lawyer, "What will it take to persuade you that your position is wrong? Do you want to hear it from Judge Sotomayor or from us? When you're telling us that the injunction is stopping you from negotiating a collective bargaining agreement, you're telling us something that isn't so."

Out of the spotlight, the other labor dispute continues as a four-hour meeting between umpires and owners goes nowhere.

APRIL 5:

The Expos send pitcher Ken Hill (16-5, 3.32 ERA), the NL's top winner in the shortened 1994 season, to the Cardinals for pitcher Bryan Eversgerd (2-3, 4.52 ERA) along with two minor leaguers – pitcher Kirk Bullinger and outfielder Darond Stovall. They continue to unload payroll by sending reliever John Wetteland (4-6, 2.83 ERA, 25 saves) to the Yankees for minor league outfielder Fernando Seguignol, a player to be named later, and an undisclosed amount of cash.

APRIL 6:

The Royals trade pitcher David Cone (16-5, 2.94 ERA) to Toronto for three minor leaguers – infielder Chris Stynes, outfielder Tony Medrano, and pitcher David Sinnes.

APRIL 7:

The Marlins sign free-agent infielder Terry Pendleton (.252 in 77 games), the NL's 1991 Most Valuable Player. Pendleton was with the Braves last season.

APRIL 8:

The Rockies spend $34 million to sign free agents Larry Walker and Bill Swift. Swift was 8-7 with the Giants last season; Walker hit .322 and 19 homers for the Expos.

The Indians sign free agent Orel Hershiser (6-6, 3.79 ERA), who spent the past 12 years with the Dodgers, to a one-year contract reportedly worth $1.5 million.

APRIL 9:

Bob Allison, a slugging outfielder with the Senators and Twins in the late 1950s and 1960s, dies at age 60 in Rio Verde, Arizona. In 13 years, Allison hit .255 with 256 homers and was the 1959 AL Rookie of the Year.

APRIL 16:

Boston's Jose Canseco lends his presence and support to locked-out major league umpires. The Red Sox slugger joins eight umpires on the picket line before an exhibition game with the Rangers in Fort Myers, Florida. Canseco explains, "You saw what the game was like without the real players. It's going to be the same thing without the real umpires."

APRIL 18:

Veteran pitcher Jack Morris calls it quits after 17 years and a

LEAGUE

The Seattle Mariners will be the only major league team wearing a commemorative patch on their uniforms to mark the 75th anniversary of the Negro Leagues.

HISTORY

In April, Richard "Goose" Gossage, one of the most intimidating relief pitchers ever, retires after 22 years. His career record is 124-107, with a 3.01 ERA and 310 saves.

LEAGUE

Financial World **estimates the value of the Yankees at $185 million – the most valuable franchise in major league baseball.**

LEAGUE

The Associated Press reports that Memorial Day crowds are down 21.5 percent from 1994 in major league baseball parks.

LEAGUE

In the 234-day strike, owners lost revenue estimated at between $800 and $900 million; players lost some $350 million in salary, and fans were deprived of 921 regular season games plus the playoffs and World Series.

254-186 career record. Morris was with the Reds this spring.

APRIL 20:

It won't heal old wounds, but it's a gesture in the right direction. Los Angeles Dodgers' president Peter O'Malley donates the Brooklyn Dodgers' 1955 World Championship banner to the borough in which it was won. The banner will be displayed tonight by the Brooklyn Historical Society. It was O'Malley's father, Walter, who took the Dodgers to the West Coast in 1957. Peter O'Malley says, "The flag belongs in Brooklyn."

Sportswriter Stan Isaacs and three other journalists "confiscated" the Dodger's banner in 1959 and lent it to the Hall of Fame. According to Isaacs, the hall refused to return it when the Brooklyn Historical Society opened in 1989. Isaacs tells New York Newsday, *"I guess you need the Dodger clout. It's back in Brooklyn, and that's what I'm happy about."*

APRIL 24:

Darryl Strawberry cops a break. After being convicted on tax evasion charges, he is sentenced to six months of home confinement and must pay the government $350,000 in back taxes. More good news for Strawberry: He may play baseball.

THE SEASON

APRIL 25:

After a strike that lasted 234 days, big league baseball is back. The first game since the strike began on August 12, 1994, matches the Dodgers against the Marlins in Florida with 42,125 on hand. The Dodgers win, 8-7, but the game is played with replacement umpires as the regular arbiters continue to be locked out. Ramon Martinez gets the win; the loser is John Burkett.

Money continues to flow after a strike about escalating player salaries. The Braves today sign outfielder Marquis Grissom to a one-year, $4.9 million contract.

APRIL 26:

Opening day in Pittsburgh is disrupted. Fans, protesting the strike and the on-field performance of the Pirates, throw wooden sticks onto the playing field, holding up action for 17 minutes. The sticks were part of the souvenir flags given away in a promotion. Montreal wins the game, 6-2.

Reds' owner Marge Schott defies Cincinnati's no-smoking ordinance, which bans smoking in seats at Riverfront Stadium. Schott sits in the front row puffing away as the Cubs beat the Reds, 7-1, in an opening day game.

APRIL 28:

The Ontario Labor Board says no to replacement umpires for Blue Jays' home games, effective next week. Under Ontario law, replacement workers may not be used during a strike or lockout.

When the Giants open at home today, they are playing in a familiar ball park with a new name. After a computer company agrees to pay $4 million over four years to the city of San Francisco, Candlestick Park is rechristened 3Com Stadium. The facility originally was named after Candlestick Point near the Stadium.

The Associated Press reports the reaction of one fan, Jerry Flaherty: "What's next, Burger King Park?"

MAY 1:

Owners end the umpires' lockout after reaching a five-year agreement today. The deal is reported to involve a 4.5 percent increase in pay this year. The umps will return to work on May 3.

MAY 2:

Hideo Nomo of the Dodgers becomes the first Japanese-born player to appear in the major leagues since 1964. The 26-year-old Nomo pitches five innings against the Giants in San Francisco, yielding a hit, four walks, and no runs, while fanning seven. When Nomo departs the game is scoreless; the Giants go on to win, 4-3, in 15.

Opening day at Tiger Stadium is marred when fans charge out onto the field and others throw bottles at Indians' centerfielder Kenny Lofton. Tigers' manager Sparky Anderson characterizes it as the "worst thing I've ever seen. These weren't fans. They were just people trying to be malicious." Some twenty fans of the 39,398 in attendance are apprehended; Cleveland goes on to win the game, 11-1.

APRIL 28
The Giants' Candlestick Park is rechristened 3Com Park

MAY 2
Hideo Nomo of the Dodgers becomes the first Japanese-born player to appear in major leagues since 1964.

LOS ANGELES DODGERS' PRESIDENT PETER O'MALLEY RETURNS THE 1955 WORLD CHAMPIONSHIP BANNER: "THE FLAG BELONGS IN BROOKLYN."

MAY 5:

During the seventh-inning stretch of today's Cubs-Astros game at Wrigley Field, a fan shakes the ashes of his late father from the left-field bleachers onto the warning track. The fan, acting on his father's last wishes, is escorted from Wrigley for throwing things onto the field. Says Cubs' official Mike Hill, "He was asked to leave the park, which he did because he had accomplished what he came to do."

MAY 7:

Gus Bell, father of former big leaguer Buddy Bell and grandfather of Indians' infielder David Bell, dies at age 66. Gus Bell played 15 seasons in the NL and was a .281 career hitter.

MAY 9:

The Indians tie a major league record by scoring eight runs before any outs are recorded in the first inning. The rally features three homers – a grand slam by Paul Sorrento, a leadoff shot by Kenny Lofton, and a two-run round-tripper by Carlos Baerga. Orel Hershiser gets the win in the 10-0 rout of the Royals. Doug Linton takes the loss.

MAY 10:

So how come nobody's laughing? A *Hartford Courant* columnist reports (ostensibly as a joke) that Cal Ripken was injured in a series of ludicrous accidents and will be unable to face the Red Sox at Fenway tomorrow. Orioles' manager Phil Regan says, "I think it's sick and stupid."

MAY 12:

Free agent John Kruk signs with the White Sox. Last year with the Phillies, Kruk hit .302 in 75 games; his career average is an even .300.

MAY 18:

The Walt Disney Co. buys 25 percent of the Angels, to become the managing partner of the team. The company also has the option of buying the rest of the team six months after the death of owner Gene Autry.

MAY 19:

Despite the absence of a collective bargaining agreement, players agree to an All-Star Game on July 11 in Arlington, Texas. The agreement follows settlement by the owners of an unfair labor practice complaint for not paying $7.8 million due in benefits last summer. The owners now will fork over $8.2 million before June 1.

MAY 23:

The Expos trade outfielder Roberto Kelly (.274) and relief pitcher Joey Eischen (0-0) to the Dodgers for outfielder Henry Rodriguez (.263) and infielder Jeff Treadway (.118).

MAY 24:

At Comiskey Park, it takes the White Sox and Rangers seven hours and 39 minutes to play an 18-inning double-header, making it the longest twin bill in major league history. At the end of the day, the teams split the two games. Chicago scores five times in the bottom of the eighth for a 10-8 win in the four-hour, one minute opener. The Rangers tally seven times in the third inning to win the three-hour, 38-minute nightcap, 13-6. Chicago pitchers walk 17 and the Rangers 15 in the two games. The double-header begins with 19,368 in the stands; seven hours and 37 minutes later, only hundreds witness the last out. The longest previous regulation double-header was a six-hour, 50-minute twin bill played by Detroit and Kansas City on July 23, 1961.

MAY 26:

In Seattle, Ken Griffey Jr. makes a spectacular catch off a Kevin Bass drive in the seventh inning of tonight's game, but plays a steep price when he hits the wall, breaking his left wrist. Orioles' manager Phil Regan calls it "probably the greatest catch I've ever seen." Griffey will require surgery and is expected to miss at least three months. Prior to the injury, Griffey hit his seventh homer of the year in an 8-3 Mariners' win.

LEAGUE

The Colorado Silver Bullets, a women's pro team that plays against men, applies to the National Association of Professional Baseball Leagues for Class A status with the aim of applying for a minor league franchise in the future. The team is managed by former major league pitcher Phil Niekro, with his brother Joe as pitching coach. In February, Martina Navratilova's agent told the *Atlanta Journal-Constitution* the tennis great wants to try out for first base or the outfield. No follow-up is reported. In July, the Silver Bullets' record fall to 7-24 on the season.

CULTURE

***Past the Bleachers*, a television movie, stars Richard Dean Anderson, Barnard Hughes, Glynnis O'Connor, and Grayson Fricke as a mute Little League player.**

Kirk Gibson's battered body continues to generate power. The Tiger DH, who turns 38 in two days, hits his fourth homer in four days in the bottom of the ninth today to give Detroit an 8-7 win over Chicago. It is Gibson's sixth round-tripper of the year.

MAY 28:

At Tiger Stadium, Detroit and Chicago set two slugging records: most combined homers by two major league teams (12) and most extra-base hits ever in an AL game (21). The White Sox win the slugfest. For the Tigers, Cecil Fielder, Chad Curtis, and Kirk Gibson homer twice, as does Ron Karkovice of Chicago, setting another AL record (most players with two) and tying the major league mark. Other Chicago players reaching the seats are Ray Durham, Craig Grebeck, and Frank Thomas. Lou Whitaker homers for Detroit. Scott Radinsky, the fourth of five Chicago pitchers, gets the 14-12 win; Wedsel "Buddy" Groom is tagged with the loss for the Tigers.

MAY 29:

The Marlins' Chris Hammond hits a grand slam against the Astros, becoming the first pitcher to accomplish that feat in the major leagues since Bob Forsch in 1986. The Marlins win the game, 9-7.

MAY 30:

New York City detectives recover a uniform worn by Babe Ruth in 1924 and in *Pride of the Yankees* in 1942. The uniform was stolen from the trunk of a car on May 23 and recovered when the thief tried to sell it back to the collector who owned it. The uniform consists of a size 50 shirt and size 44 pants; estimates of its value range from $10,000 to $50,000. A 1952 Mickey Mantle card estimated at $7,500 is not recovered.

Glenn Burke, the first major leaguer to publicly declare he was a homosexual, dies at age 42 in San Leandro, California, of complications of AIDS. Burke, an outfielder with the Dodgers and Athletics, batted .237 in four-plus seasons in the majors in the 1970s.

Cincinnati business executives and Reds' owner Marge Schott will explore building a new baseball stadium next door to Riverfront Stadium. The Reds have played at Riverfront since 1970 and share the facility with the National Football League's Cincinnati Bengals. "There are lots of places that would want the Cincinnati Reds," Schott warns.

MAY 31:

The Yankees, picked by many to win the AL pennant but mired in last place, finish a 1-8 West Coast road trip, putting a major dent in their pennant hopes. The final game of the trip goes to Seattle today, 11-9, and is punctuated by Yankee Jim Leyritz's being hit in the face by a pitch from fireballer Randy Johnson. But instead of extra practice, more time in front of the mirror is the order of the day. Manager Buck Showalter tells his team that goatees must go – the word is believed to have come from owner George Steinbrenner. Among those affected by the edict are captain Don Mattingly – who was involved in a 1991 haircut controversy – and pitchers Jack McDowell and John Wetteland.

JUNE 3:

Pedro Martinez of the Expos throws nine perfect innings against the Padres, yielding a double to the 28th batter – Leon "Bip" Roberts – on a 1-1 pitch in the 10th inning in San Diego. Martinez is then relieved by Mel Rojas. Montreal wins, 1-0, on an RBI single by Jeff Treadway off Brian Williams in the top of the 10th. Martinez gets credit for the victory, but not a no-hitter or a perfect game under rules amended in 1991.

JUNE 6:

Today is consecutive game number 472 for Buck Showalter as Yankees manager. He surpasses Billy Martin for the longest unbroken tenure under George Steinbrenner's ownership.

JUNE 8:

Mickey Mantle receives a liver transplant in Dallas.

JUNE 9:

The AL's 1965 Most Valuable Player, Zoilo Versalles, dies in Bloomington, Minnesota, at age 55 of hardening of the arteries. In 1965, Versalles led the Twins to the AL pennant while leading the league in doubles, triples, and runs, and batting .273. In 12 major league seasons the shortstop hit .242.

JUNE 19
The Yankees sign Darryl Strawberry to a one-year contract.

JUNE 30
The Indians' Eddie Murray gets his 3,000th hit.

JUNE 10:

In Baltimore, Orioles' rookie third baseman Jeff Manto homers in the second inning against Mike Bielecki of the Angels. Manto's round-tripper is his fourth in four consecutive at-bats, tying Johnny Blanchard's 1961 major league record. After a walk, Manto flies out in the sixth to end his streak. Baltimore, behind Ben McDonald, wins, 6-2.

JUNE 11:

Mark McGwire homers with the bases empty in three consecutive at-bats today against Zane Smith of the Red Sox. McGwire had two round-trippers yesterday, tying the major league mark for homers in consecutive games. The Athletics win today's contest, 8-1. Todd Stottlemyre gets the victory.

JUNE 12:

Beginning today, baseball fans are able to dial a toll-free number to cast votes for the All-Star Game. Fans also are able to vote on-line by computer.

JUNE 14:

Hideo Nomo strikes out 15 Pirates in eight innings in Pittsburgh as the Dodgers win, 8-5. Mike Piazza hits two homers for Los Angeles.

Giants' third baseman Mike Benjamin, subbing for Matt Williams -- who has a broken bone in his right foot – goes six for seven and drives in the winner in a 4-3, 13-inning win against the Cubs in Chicago. Benjamin also sets a major league record with 14 hits in three games. Steve Mintz gets the win; Anthony Young is charged with the loss.

JUNE 15:

The Cardinals' Ray Lankford may be the only player ever to get a fireworks display for a double. Playing at home in Busch Stadium, Lankford hits an eighth-inning drive off the right-field wall. Lankford had homered in the fifth and the scoreboard operator assumes this ball too will carry out and sets off the display. The Cardinals beat the Padres, 2-1.

JUNE 19:

The Yankees sign Darryl Strawberry to a one-year contract at a salary that could go as high as $775,000. Strawberry, who last played in 1994 for the Giants and hit .239, is serving a 60-day suspension for substance abuse.

JUNE 20:

In Anaheim, Lee Smith preserves the Angels' 3-2 win over the Royals to set a major league record with 18 saves in 18 opportunities.

Lee Smith's streak ends on June 28 when he gives up three runs to Texas.

JUNE 22:

Two 30-pound, eight-feet by two-and-a-half-feet acoustic panels fall from the roof of the Toronto SkyDome into the stands, injuring seven people during the seventh inning of today's Blue Jays-Brewers game. The game goes on despite the mishap and the Brewers win, 9-0, behind rookie Steve Sparks.

JUNE 25:

The Marlins' David Weathers loses a shot at a no-hitter when he is hit. Batting in the sixth inning after holding the Reds hitless for five, Weathers is struck on his pitching hand by a Tim Pugh fastball and has to leave the game. He is replaced by Terry Mathews, who allows three hits the rest of the way as Florida wins, 5-1.

In San Diego, the Rockies' Andres Galarraga hits home runs in the sixth, seventh, and eighth innings, becoming the fourth major leaguer with homers in three consecutive innings. His third home run of the game travels an estimated 455 feet. Galarraga has seven RBI as well, as Colorado beats the Padres, 11-3.

JUNE 29:

Dwight Gooden, under suspension for substance abuse, will not be permitted to return to baseball this season, according to a story in the *New York Times*. The 30-year-old Gooden has been working out in St. Petersburg, Florida, in hopes of playing in 1995.

JUNE 30:

Eddie Murray of the Indians singles against Mike Trombley of the Twins in the sixth inning for his 3,000th career hit. He is the 20th major leaguer to reach the plateau; one of them is his Indians teammate Dave Winfield. The 39-year-old Murray joins Pete Rose as the only

HISTORY

Pedro Martinez and Harvey Haddix (1959) are the only major league pitchers to pitch perfect games beyond nine innings. Haddix lost his masterpiece and the game in the thirteenth inning. When Haddix's experience is related today to Martinez, he says, "Oh, that's tough. But I still don't know who he is."

LEAGUE

According to an Associated Press report, 61 players who filed for arbitration this season received an average of 80 percent in raises – the lowest since 1989. Last year the average raise was 95 percent.

switch-hitters to reach the mark. The Indians win, 4-1, in Minnesota.

Murray and Winfield are not the first teammates with 3,000 hits. The 1928 Philadelphia A's had three – Ty Cobb, Tris Speaker, and Eddie Collins.

JULY 1:

The 1996 baseball season will begin on Sunday night, March 31, with the White Sox facing the Mariners in Seattle. It is the earliest season start ever. Because of the expanded playoff system, without a March start the World Series would be played in November. Under the new schedule, game seven of the 1996 World Series – barring postponements – will be played on October 27.

JULY 2:

It's the spotlight to the disabled list for the Indians' Eddie Murray. He leaves today's game in the fifth inning with two broken ribs incurred when he is tagged by Twins' catcher Matt Walbeck while sliding into home in the third. Before leaving the game, Murray had a single and double and drove in a run. The Indians win, 7-0.

Police arrest a 31-year-old woman and confiscate a .22 caliber pistol from her at the SkyDome Hotel in Toronto. She is charged with threatening to kill the Blue Jays' Roberto Alomar because she was unable to "establish a relationship" with him.

JULY 5:

The Dodgers' Hideo Nomo and the Braves' John Smoltz strike out 22 batters in a pitchers' duel won by Atlanta, 4-1, with three runs in the bottom of the ninth. Neither pitcher is involved in the final decision. Smoltz goes eight innings and strikes out 12; Nomo works seven and strikes out 10, allowing only two hits. A three-run homer by the Braves' Chipper Jones off Rudy Seanez is the margin of victory.

JULY 6:

One of baseball's best relievers, Rick Aguilera (1-1, 2.52 ERA, 12 saves), is acquired by the Red Sox from the Twins for pitcher Frankie Rodriguez and a player to be named later.

Atlanta's Greg Maddux shuts out the Dodgers, 1-0, and extends his "walkless" streak to 49 innings. Fred McGriff's RBI single in the bottom of the ninth scores the winning run.

JULY 7:

Randy Johnson strikes out 13 Indians as the Mariners win, 5-3, in Cleveland. It is the eighth time this year Johnson has reached double figures in strikeouts in a game. Johnson, who once struggled for control of his awesome fastball, walks none and allows only eight hits in a complete game outing. Edgar Martinez hits a homer.

JULY 8:

The Blue Jays' David Cone hits Mark McGwire of the Athletics in the head in the third inning of game one of a doubleheader in Oakland, precipitating a bench-clearing episode. It is the second time in less than a week that McGwire has been hit by a pitch, and the ninth of the young season. Today's beaning drops him to his knees; he leaves the field under his own power but does not play in game two. Two Oakland pitchers – Doug Johns and Mike Harkey – are ejected for throwing at batters and, after Toronto's Joe Carter is hit in the seventh, the benches empty again with no punches thrown. The Blue Jays win the game 9-6, with Cone getting the win.

JULY 11:

At the Ballpark in Arlington, the NL wins the All-Star Game, 3-2, on an eighth-inning pinch-hit home run by the Marlin's Jeff Conine. Conine, who was selected but did not play in last year's game, becomes the 10th player to homer on his first All-Star at-bat, and is the game's MVP. Frank Thomas hits a two-run homer for the AL; Craig Biggio and Mike Piazza connect for the NL. Hideo Nomo starts for the Nationals; the winning pitcher is Heathcliff Slocumb. Steve Ontiveros is tagged with the loss.

Strange as it seems, Frank Thomas's homer was the 139th in All-Star history but the first by a White Sox player. In addition to Jeff Conine, the nine others who homered in their first All-Star Game at-bats are Max West, 1940; Walter "Hoot" Evers, 1948; Jim Gilliam, 1959; George Altman, 1961; Johnny Bench, 1969; Dick Dietz, 1970; Lee Mazzilli, 1979; Terry

JULY 15
The Mariners' Randy Johnson reaches double figures in strikeouts for the eighth time this season

JULY 23
1989 World Series MVP Dave Stewart retires.

Steinbach, 1988; and Vincent "Bo" Jackson, 1989.

JULY 12:

Montreal pitcher Ugueth Urtain Urbina beats the Cubs in his first major league start. He is the only player in history with the initials U.U.U.

JULY 14:

The Dodgers' Ramon Martinez no-hits the Marlins, 7-0, in Los Angeles. Martinez allows only one base runner – on an eighth-inning walk to Tommy Gregg – and strikes out eight. The losing pitcher is John Burkett.

The strike may be ended but the bitterness lingers on. Padres' general manager Randy Smith gets an earful when he tells the team he is recalling former replacement player Ira Smith from the minors. Pitcher Andy Ashby describes the move as "bad karma" and Smith instead calls up Archi Cianfrocco, who refused to become a replacement player and remained in minor league camp in the spring.

JULY 15:

Randy Johnson strikes out 16 and allows only three hits from Toronto in pitching the Mariners to a 3-0 win in Seattle. Johnson is now 10-1 with 168 strikeouts.

The Yankees sign 19-year-old catcher-outfielder Michael Munson and assign him to their Class A Tampa farm team in the Gulf Coast League. He is the son of Yankee captain and catcher Thurman Munson, who died in a 1979 plane crash.

JULY 17:

They're never too young – or too huge. Two Australian pitchers – six-foot, five-inch, 190-pound Matthew Gourlay and six-foot, three-inch, 180-pound Chad Needle – both not yet 16 years old – are signed by the Toronto Blue Jays for 1996.

In Chicago, the Mets' heralded pitcher Jason Isringhausen makes his major league debut against the Cubs. He retires the first 10 batters he faces, goes seven innings, allowing two hits, two walks, and two earned runs while striking out six, but is not involved in the decision. The Mets win the game, 7-2, with five runs in the ninth, and Jerry DiPoto is credited with the win.

JULY 18:

Dave Andrews, the public address announcer for the minor league Abilene Prairie Dogs is ejected by the umpire. Andrews's offense: after Abilene manager Charlie Kerfeld is ejected, Andrews reads a commercial for Lenscrafters, an eyeglasses chain. Andrews claims it was coincidence, but he is fined $50. Fans raise money to pay his fine and donate the excess cash to a charity for the visually impaired.

JULY 21:

The Indians' Dennis Martinez, a 40-year-old grandfather, pitches a complete game six-hitter to beat Oakland, 6-1. For Martinez, who strikes out six and walks three, it is the ninth win of the season without a loss. Homers – by Albert Belle, Manny Ramirez, and Tony Pena – help Cleveland defeat Todd Stottlemyre.

JULY 23:

Dave Stewart, who transformed his career from journeyman pitcher to ace of the Athletics on the 1988-90 World Series teams, calls it quits. The 37-year-old Stewart retires with a record of 168-129. He was the Most Valuable Player of the 1989 World Series, but this year struggled at 3-7 with a 6.89 ERA.

Warfare continues in Chicago between the Brewers and White Sox. Yesterday, managers Terry Bevington of Chicago and Phil Garner of the Brewers got into a brawl. Today Brewers' relief pitcher Jamie McAndrew is ejected by umpire Mike Reilly for hitting Craig Grebeck in the side in the bottom of the eighth. McAndrew was responding to events in the top of the inning, when Chicago's Kirk McCaskill threw at Kevin Seitzer's head before walking him. According to reports, the White Sox regard Seitzer as the instigator in yesterday's brawl. In baseball, Chicago wins, 11-6, with a three-run homer by Lyle Mouton and the pitching of Jim Abbott.

JULY 27:

The Cardinals send pitcher Ken Hill (6-7, 5.06 ERA) to the Indians for three minor leaguers: third baseman David Bell,

TRIVIA

A 15-foot mural depicting the 1955 World Series win by the Brooklyn Dodgers, painted by a Bronx-bred artist, is unveiled at the Brooklyn Diner in Manhattan. The representation of Ebbets Field contains several errors: the celebrated "Hit Sign, Win Suit" sign is in the wrong place, the scoreboard is omitted, and right-field bleachers are painted in (there were none). Later in the year, the owner of the diner announces the mural will be removed and replaced.

JULY 28
The Yankees acquire pitcher David Cone in trade with Toronto Blue Jays.

pitcher Rick Heiserman, and catcher Pepe McNeal.

Hall of Fame catcher Rick Ferrell dies at age 89 in Troy, Michigan, of arrhythmia. Farrell and his younger brother, pitcher Wes, were a successful battery with the Red Sox and Senators and spent many years as on-field opponents. In 1931, Rick, then with the Browns, almost broke up his brother's no-hit bid with an eighth-inning grounder against the Indians that was scored an error. The last surviving player from the first All-Star Game in 1933, Ferrell was elected to the Hall of Fame in 1984.

It's a rare mea culpa from an umpire. Dale Scott, who called the Royals' Wally Joyner safe at home with the winning run in a 6-5 victory against the Yankees, acknowledges after the game that he was wrong. Says Scott, "I looked at it numerous times from numerous angles and apparently I missed the play. It happens. I'm not happy about it, but today is a new day."

JULY 28:

The Yankees obtain pitcher David Cone (9-6, 3.14 ERA) from Toronto for minor league pitchers Marty Janzen, Jason Jarvis, and Mike Gordon. In addition, designated hitter-outfielder Danny Tartabull (.224 in 59 games), in disfavor with the Yankees front office and fans, is traded to the Athletics for designated hitter-outfielder Ruben Sierra (.265 in 70 games) – in manager Tony LaRussa's doghouse – and minor leaguer pitcher Jason Beverlin.

The Orioles acquire Bobby Bonilla (.325, 18 homers, 53 RBI) and a player to be named later (pitcher Jimmy Williams) from the Mets for two outfielders, minor leaguer Alex Ochoa and Damon Buford (.063 in 24 games).

JULY 30:

Two former Philadelphia Phillies – third baseman Mike Schmidt and outfielder Richie Ashburn – Negro League star Leon Day; the first NL president William A. Hulbert; and turn-of-the-century pitcher Vic Willis are inducted into the Hall of Fame. Schmidt played 18 years, batting .267 with 548 homers and 1,595 RBI and three times was the NL's Most Valuable Player. He led the NL in home runs eight times, with a high of 48 in 1980, and appeared in two World Series. Ashburn, an outstanding contact hitter with little power, compiled a .308 average over 15 seasons – 12 with the Phillies. He batted .300 or better nine times and twice led the NL in hitting. He played in one World Series. Day pitched with the Baltimore Black Sox, the Brooklyn Eagles, and – for most of his career – the Newark Eagles. He also played two seasons in Mexico. His unofficial record is 67-29. He also was a good-hitting pitcher with a .288 lifetime average. Hulbert, who died in 1882, became the NL's president in 1877 and played a key role in curtailing gambling, drinking, and fixed baseball games. Willis pitched 13 seasons, from 1898 to 1910, compiling a 248-204 record, with a 2.63 ERA and 50 shutouts. He was a 20-game winner eight times and appeared in the 1909 World Series for the Pirates.

Speaking before 20,000 spectators, Mike Schmidt warns, "Our game has reached a crossroads. I don't believe we can survive unless players and owners are one...If we make the fans number one, they will come." Richie Ashburn echoes Schmidt's sentiments, "Let's get this mess straightened out. We're sitting here without a commissioner. I can't believe it."

Jeff Bagwell, the 1994 National League MVP, is hit by a pitch by San Diego's Brian Williams in the fourth inning of today's game and suffers a fracture of the fourth metacarpal bone in his left hand. It is an identical injury to the one he suffered last year when he was hit by the Padres' Andy Benes. Bagwell will miss up to four weeks. The Astros go on to win the game, 7-1 behind Doug Drabek's pitching.

Following an 8-3 Angels win over the Brewers in Milwaukee, California's Chili Davis is charged with disorderly conduct for allegedly slapping a fan who was taunting him. Davis is accused of leaving the on-deck circle in the third inning and poking the fan in the face with his finger. Witnesses claim Davis accosted the wrong man.

The Dodgers' rookie Hideo Nomo wins his eighth game of the

HISTORY

Wade Boggs gets his 2,500th base hit in 7,482 at-bats – 616 fewer than Pete Rose, who needed 8,098 to reach that plateau.

Braves' ace Greg Maddux wins the Cy Young Award.

Calling him baseball's greatest third baseman, statistician/author Bill James says, "If Mike Schmidt hit .320, he would have been the best player who ever lived."

CULTURE

In *The New York Yanquis*, a novel by Bill Granger, the team's owner hires 24 Cubans as replacement players. Baseball is still hot in the mystery genre, as well: *The Fan* by Peter Abrahams involves the Red Sox; *Murder at Ebbets Field* by Troy Soos; *Shutout* by David Nighbert.

season with an assist from a manicurist. In his last start, Nomo was forced to leave because of a cracked fingernail. It was repaired with acrylic bonding, and Nomo was effective today, limiting the Reds to five hits and a run in eight innings while fanning 11. The Dodgers win, 5-4.

JULY 31:

John Kruk singles in the first inning today against the Orioles in Baltimore, and when the White Sox are retired, he retires as well. The 34-year-old is replaced by pinch-hitter Frank Thomas in the third and after the game states, "The desire to compete at this level is gone. When that happens, it's time to go." Kruk had informed his teammates of his intentions yesterday, but wanted to officially step down with a hit. He was hitting .308 this season and leaves with a lifetime batting average of .300. Last year he was treated for testicular cancer. The Orioles win the game, 8-3.

The Rockies acquire pitcher Bret Saberhagen (5-5) from the Mets for minor league pitchers Juan Acevedo and Arnold Gooch.

AUGUST 1:

The sports world is saddened to learn through a videotaped message – aired today – that Mickey Mantle's cancer has spread from his liver to his lungs. Mantle left the hospital after his liver transplant on June 28.

AUGUST 3:

By a 9-8 vote, the Senate Judiciary Committee – for the first time in history – sends a bill calling for the partial repeal of baseball's anti-trust exemption to the full Senate.

AUGUST 5:

Former major league manager and outfielder Harry Craft dies in Conroe, Texas, at age 80. Craft had two firsts in his managerial career: he was Mickey Mantle's first minor league skipper and he was the first pilot of the Houston Colt .45s. Craft also managed Roger Maris with the Kansas City Athletics.

As part of an economy campaign, Reds' owner Marge Schott orders her press office to reduce the daily game notes distributed to the press at home games. At today's game against Philadelphia, journalists received one page of notes instead of the previous five. The Associated Press reports that the team will save $3.45 per game, or less than $100 for the remainder of the season.

AUGUST 8:

Tim Wakefield wins his ninth straight game – and 13th of the year – as the Red Sox beat the Indians, 5-1, in Boston. One of the six hits yielded by Wakefield is a home run to Eddie Murray – the 472nd of his career. Mark Clark is the losing pitcher.

AUGUST 9:

George Nicolau, who has been baseball's impartial arbitrator since 1986, is fired by major league owners.

AUGUST 10:

It's Ball Day at Dodger Stadium, a crowd of 53,361 is on hand for the game, but it's anything but a ball for the home team. The visiting Cardinals are awarded a 2-1 forfeit by chief umpire Jim Quick with one out in the bottom of the ninth when fans begin bombarding the field with more than 200 of the balls they received as a promotional giveaway when they entered the ballpark. Umpire crew chief Bob Davidson says, "We gave them three chances. Three strikes and you're out."

He adds, "The whole thing was Tom Lasorda's fault. He instigated the crowd, waving his arms. He has himself to blame, absolutely." Lasorda responds, "How did I instigate it? I was talking to [ump] Jim Quick. All I was asking was why he threw my players out...that is a real crime for these guys to try to put that blame on me."

AUGUST 11:

One of baseball's fiercest competitors, 38-year-old Kirk Gibson, hangs up his spikes. He issues a written statement declaring he is "being traded to his family." Gibson, the hero for the Dodgers in the 1988 World Series, played 17 years and batted .268. His 1995 average is .260. Also retiring today is 1987 NL Cy Young winner Steve Bedrosian, who is 1-2 with Atlanta this season. His lifetime record is 76-79.

AUGUST 12:

The Dodgers, aided by a rare call, beat the Pirates, 11-10, in 11 innings in Los Angeles. In the bottom of the 11th, with Roberto Kelly the runner at third, Mitch

AUGUST 13
Mickey Mantle dies in Dallas.

AUGUST 20
The Indians' Jose Mesa sets a major league record by notching his 37th save in his 37th opportunity.

Webster swings at a pitch in the dirt and Pittsburgh's rookie catcher Angelo Encarnacion fields it with his mask. Tommy Lasorda appeals to the umpires, citing Rule 7.05(d), which awards two bases to a runner if a fielder uses his mask to touch a thrown ball. Kelly is allowed to score from third for the Dodger's victory.

AUGUST 13:

Hall of Famer Mickey Mantle, a longtime alcoholic who only recently entered treatment, dies today of liver cancer at age 63 in Dallas. Hampered throughout his career by a bone disease and a series of serious injuries, Mantle gritted it out for 18 years, batting .298 with 536 homers and 1,509 RBI. He was the AL's Triple Crown winner in 1956, led the circuit in homers four times, and was selected Most Valuable Player three times.

AUGUST 15:

Mickey Mantle's funeral in Dallas is attended by some 1,200 people. Pallbearers are his teammates Johnny Blanchard, Yogi Berra, Bill Skowron, Whitey Ford, and Bobby Murcer. Another teammate, Bobby Richardson, delivers the sermon, and country singer Roy Clark sings "Yesterday When I Was Young."

Mantle is eulogized by sportscaster Bob Costas, who tells the mourners, "I just hope God has a place for him where he can run again. Where he can play practical jokes on his teammates and smile that boyish smile, 'cause God knows, no one's perfect. And God knows there's something special about heroes."

The Reds' Reggie Sanders slams home runs in his first three at-bats at Riverfront Stadium in an 11-3 win over the visiting Rockies. The first two homers come off Bryan Rekar; the third against David Nied. Sanders is hitless in his next two at-bats and misses the major league record held by 12 players.

AUGUST 17:

The United League, still a paper entity, announces a 20-year TV deal with Liberty Sports, a subsidiary of the largest U.S. cable operator, TCI. The deal includes regular-season regional cablecasts of 30 to 40 games plus postseason coverage and revenue sharing of the proceeds among the eight franchises. The United League is slated to begin play in March 1996 with a 154-game schedule.

AUGUST 18:

Hall of Fame shortstop Phil Rizzuto retires as a Yankee broadcaster – a job he has held for 39 years. Reportedly, Rizzuto is motivated by the refusal of New York station WPIX-TV to allow him to miss a game to attend Mickey Mantle's funeral.

Rizzuto returns to the booth for the '96 season.

The Indians' Jose Mesa records his 36th save in 36 opportunities in a 7-5 win over the Brewers in Cleveland. Mesa ties Dennis Eckersley's 1992 major league record for consecutive saves in one season without a blown opportunity. Albert Belle paces the offense with a homer and a double. Mark Clark gets the win; Rickey Bones is tagged with the loss.

AUGUST 20:

Cleveland's relief ace Jose Mesa records his 37th save in 37 opportunities – a major league record. After the Indians score five in the bottom of the eighth to lead the Brewers, 8-5, Mesa pitches a scoreless ninth for the save.

Von McDaniel dies at age 56 in Hollis, Oklahoma, after a heart attack and stroke. McDaniel and his brother, Lindy, were mainstays of the Cardinals' pitching staff in 1957 – Von's rookie year. He was 7-5 with a 3.22 ERA, but pitched only two more games in the majors.

The Giants' Matt Williams, who has been on the disabled list since breaking his foot on June 3, homers into the upper deck at Veterans Stadium in his first start. But the Phillies beat San Francisco, 8-7, in 10 innings. Williams also plays superbly in the field.

AUGUST 23:

Wade Boggs hits a sixth-inning, RBI, pinch-hit single against Don Wengert of Oakland for his historic 2,500th hit. But the Athletics beat the visiting Yankees, 2-1.

AUGUST 25:

In Cleveland, the Indians beat the Tigers, 6-5, on a

HISTORY

How impressive is Cal Ripken's Iron Man feat? From the time Ripken began his streak in 1982 through June of this year, teams have used the disabled list 3,501 times.

Yogi Berra remembers Mickey Mantle, "He could run, throw and hit. There's no telling how good he'd have been with two good legs."

LEAGUE

Creaking joints: Among the replacement players are former major leaguers Dennis "Oil Can" Boyd (age 35), Lenny Randle (46), Pedro Borbon Sr. (48), Rudy Arias (37), Guillermo Hernandez (40), Kevin Hickey (39), and Todd Cruz (39 – a grandfather). But two players for the women's team Colorado Silver Bullets – pitcher Ann Williams and infielder Shannon Mitchem – are cut by the Mets after one day at Port St. Lucie, Florida.

Sandy Alomar homer with one out in the bottom of the ninth, but their ace reliever, Jose Mesa, blows a save for the first time in 39 opportunities.

AUGUST 26:

Greg Maddux beats the Cubs, 7-2, in Chicago to tie a major league record – 16 consecutive road victories. Maddux last lost on the road to Montreal on June 17, 1994. Maddux shares the record with Denny McLain, Cal McLish, and Rich Dotson.

AUGUST 27:

New York Times sports columnist Robert Lipsyte recommends that Cal Ripken "do the right thing, to sit out a game before September 6, when he is expected to break Lou Gehrig's record..." He echoes suggestions by Hall of Famer Mike Schmidt and media personality Larry King that Ripken tie the record and bench himself. It is the second time Lipsyte has made the suggestion.

AUGUST 31:

The Braves' Greg Maddux six-hits the Astros, 5-2, in Atlanta for his 13th win of the season. Maddux is now 15-2 and has allowed only three runs in the past 25 innings. Atlanta's offense is paced by a home run by Chipper Jones in the seventh inning.

SEPTEMBER 4:

Robin Ventura of the White Sox hits two grand slam home runs in a 14-3 victory over Texas. Ventura – whose grand slams come in the fourth inning against Dennis Cook and in the fifth against Danny Darwin – becomes the eighth player ever with two grand slams in a game. Ventura also knocks in eight runs.

SEPTEMBER 5:

Cal Ripken Jr. ties the record many in baseball regarded as unbreakable. When he takes the field tonight in Baltimore, Ripken appears in his 2,130th consecutive game, equaling Lou Gehrig's Iron Man streak. "I don't know how everyone else feels," says Ripken, "but I'm exhausted." The 48,804 fans at Camden Yards give Ripken a five-minute standing ovation.

In Atlanta, the Braves' Greg Maddux shuts out the Cardinals 1-0, for the second time in 17 days by the same score. Maddux goes all the way for the 10th time this season, yields seven hits, and strikes out eight without a walk. His record improves to 16-2. A Fred McGriff home run in the second inning against losing pitcher Tom Urbani is the only run of the game.

The Brewers' John Jaha hits a grand slam homer in the first inning today against the Twins. It is Milwaukee's 10th grand slam of the season, tying the major league record set by Detroit in 1938 and equaled by the 1987 Yankees. Minnesota wins, 9-6.

SEPTEMBER 6:

Cal Ripken Jr. stands alone in the record book as baseball's new Iron Man with 2,131 consecutive games. A crowd of 46,000 – including President Bill Clinton, Vice President Al Gore, and Hall of Famers Joe DiMaggio and Frank Robinson – is on hand in Baltimore to see Ripken pass Lou Gehrig's long-standing mark. But the record is official only when the game is official – after four and a half innings are completed. His teammates Bobby Bonilla and Rafael Palmeiro get Ripken to take a lap around the ballpark. As he passes the visitors' dugout, some of the Angels come out to hug him. Ripken stops to give his uniform shirt to his wife, Kelly, to high-five his two-year-old son, Ryan, and to kiss his five-year-old daughter, Rachel. The game resumes after a 22-minute delay, and Ripken enhances the occasion with his 15th home run of the year, off a 3-0 pitch from Shawn Boskie in the sixth. The Orioles and Matt Mussina go on to win, 4-2. Ripken comments, "Today seemed like it was a little more relaxing than yesterday." Joe DiMaggio observes, "Well, that goes to prove that even the greatest records are made to be broken."

It took the 35-year-old Ripkin more than 13 years to set the new record; he began his streak on May 30, 1982, in Baltimore against the Blue Jays. Gehrig's streak began on June 1, 1925, and ended on April 30, 1939.

SEPTEMBER 8:

The Indians wrap up the AL Central Division title with a 3-2 victory over the Orioles. In 1991, the Indians lost 105 games; this season,

SEPTEMBER 6
Cal Ripken Jr. breaks Lou Gehrig's consecutive game record.

SEPTEMBER 19
The Indians' Albert Belle hits three home runs, giving him five in two consecutive games.

they win the title in their 123rd game – the quickest in major league history.

The NL comes down hard with suspensions against the Reds and Astros for a bench-clearing brawl on September 5. Cincinnati pitcher Xavier Hernandez will sit out eight games; Ron Gant, four; and manager Davey Johnson, two. Houston manager Terry Collins is slapped with a two-day suspension; pitcher Doug Drabek and catcher Pat Borders, five apiece.

SEPTEMBER 14:

The sale of the Athletics by Walter A. Haas Jr. and his family to businessmen Steven Schott and Ken Hoffman for $85 million is approved unanimously by major league owners. A provision of the sale is that the team remains in Oakland. The Haas family bought the Athletics in 1980 from Charles O. Finley for $12.7 million.

SEPTEMBER 19:

The Indians' Albert Belle smacks three homers today against the White Sox, giving him five home runs in two consecutive games and tying a major league mark. Belle shares the record with 16 other major leaguers. Belle leads off the sixth, eighth, and ninth innings with home runs in today's 8-2 win. He now has 44 homers. Charles Nagy is the beneficiary of Belle's slugging and ups his record to 15-5.

In Boston, the Red Sox top the Brewers, 5-3, to clinch a tie for the AL.

SEPTEMBER 20:

Walter A. Haas Jr., who last week sold the Athletics, dies in Oakland, California, at age 79 of cancer. Haas also was chairman of the board of Levi Strauss & Company.

SEPTEMBER 21:

The Reds win the NL Central Division title when the Padres beat the Dodgers, 5-1, in Los Angeles. Because of the complex structure of baseball's new playoff system, Cincinnati is unaware of its victory until notification comes from the Elias Sports Bureau.

Tony Cuccinello, who lost the 1945 AL batting title by one point to George Stirnweiss, dies today in Tampa, Florida, at age 87. An infielder, he hit .300 five times in his 15-year career.

SEPTEMBER 23:

Donald Fehr, executive director of the Players Association, tells baseball fans they "should have no doubt that this season will be completed and a new World Series champion crowned," despite the absence of a basic agreement with the owners. Acting commissioner Bud Selig responds, "I was confident that neither party would interrupt this season, but I'm delighted with Don's statement."

SEPTEMBER 28:

A fan picks the wrong player to mess with. At Wrigley Field, a spectator runs onto the field and charges the Cubs' Randy Myers after the pitcher yields an eighth-inning, two-run homer to the Astros' James Mouton. The six-foot, one-inch, 230-pound Myers, a martial-arts expert, knocks the fan down with a forearm and pins him to the ground until his teammates come to his aid. The fan is charged with assault and disorderly conduct. Cubs shortstop Shawon Dunston says, "I was afraid Randy was going to snap his neck. I know Randy. He's into martial arts and he will hurt you." The Cubs beat the Astros, 12-11, when the game resumes.

In Minneapolis, the Twins' Kirby Puckett suffers a broken jaw when he is struck by a Dennis Martinez fastball in the first inning. Twins' pitcher Frank Rodriguez says, "I've never seen that much blood on a baseball field – ever. It was scary." Martinez, who describes Puckett as one of his best friends, says, "It's the worst I've ever felt in my life." Cleveland goes on to beat the Twins, 12-4.

SEPTEMBER 29:

The Mariners come from behind to beat the Rangers in Texas, 4-3, and clinch a tie for the AL West title. Seattle's victory is its 15th in the past 16 games. Bobby Ayala is the winning pitcher; the loser is Ed Vosberg.

Baseball's owners suffer another blow when a three-judge panel of the second U.S. District Court of Appeals unanimously finds that the Player Relations Committee acted illegally in its attempt to eliminate free agency, salary

HISTORY

Three major playoff records are set in the Mariners-Yankees series: most home runs by two teams (22), most home runs by a player (Ken Griffey, Seattle – 5), and consecutive strikeouts (David Cone, Yankees – 5)

Cal Ripken tells columnist Pat O'Brien, "When I came up in 1981, I sat in the dugout for the first time and watched. I said to myself, 'If I ever get a chance to play, I'm never coming out.'"

RULES

The new television contract contains a provision for expanding playoff rounds to the best-four-of-seven format in 1997.

arbitration, and other provisions of the bargaining agreement.

SEPTEMBER 30:

In Cleveland, Albert Belle hits his 50th homer of the season as the Indians beat the Royals, 3-2, in 10 innings. Belle's homer – his 17th of September, tying Babe Ruth's record for the month – comes off Melvin Bunch and ties the game at 2-2. Carlos Baerga wins it with an RBI single off loser Jeff Montgomery. Alan Embree is the winner.

OCTOBER 2:

Behind Randy Johnson's complete game three-hitter, the Mariners beat the Angels, 9-1, in Seattle to win the AL West title. Johnson walks one and fans 12 in besting Mark Langston. The only run against Johnson is a Tony Phillips homer in the ninth.

Sparky Anderson resigns as Tigers' manager after 17 years. He led Detroit to a World Championship in 1984 and an AL East title in 1987. Although he is the winningest manager in Tiger's history, Anderson managed a 60-84 record this season.

REGULAR SEASON WRAP-UP:

Manager Bobby Cox leads the Braves to a 90-54 record in the NL. Paced by pitcher Greg Maddux (19-2, 1.63 ERA), the Atlanta staff includes Tom Glavine (16-7), John Smoltz (12-7), and reliever Mark Wohlers (25 saves.) The main offensive threats are Fred McGriff (.280, 27 homers, 93 RBI), Chipper Jones (.265, 23 homers, 86 RBI), David Justice (.253, 24 homers, 78 RBI), and Ryan Klesko (.329, 23 homers, 70 RBI).

Mike Hargrove's Indians compile a 100-44 regular season mark in the AL and are ranked by some observers as one of the best teams of all time. The controversial Albert Belle provides the punch with a .317 batting average, 50 homers, and 126 RBI. He is backed by five other .300 hitters – Eddie Murray (.323), Carlos Baerga (.314), Jim Thome (.314), Kenny Lofton (.310) – who also steals 54 bases – and Manny Ramirez (.308). Orel Hershiser and Charles Nagy have 16 wins each; Jose Mesa comes out of the bullpen with a league-leading 46 saves.

OCTOBER 3:

In game one of the NL Division Series, Cincinnati beats Los Angeles, 7-2. Reds' ace Jose Rijo, out of the playoffs because of August 22 elbow surgery, was refused a place on the team's chartered plane to Los Angeles by owner Marge Schott.

In an NL Division Series game, Atlanta tops Colorado, 5-4.

In New York, in the first game of the AL Division Series, the Yankees beat Seattle, 9-6.

In the first game of the AL Division Series, Cleveland edges Boston, 5-4, in 13 innings.

OCTOBER 4:

Cincinnati edges Los Angeles, 5-4, in an NL Division Series game. Dave Burba gets the win; Al Osuna is charged with the loss. Eric Karros has two homers for the Dodgers; Reggie Sanders, one for the Reds.

In Colorado, the Braves take a two-games-to-none lead over the Rockies with a 7-4 win today in the NL Division Series. Alejandro Pena gets the win in relief, with a save by Mark Wohlers. Mike Munoz is tagged with the loss. The game features home runs by Larry Walker of the Rockies and Marquis Grissom of the Braves.

In Cleveland, the Indians shut out Boston 4-0 behind the pitching of Orel Hershiser, who yields only three hits in seven and a third innings. Erik Hanson takes the loss. Attendance is 44,264.

OCTOBER 5:

Jim Leyritz hits a two-run home run in the bottom of the 15th at Yankee Stadium to give the Yankees a 7-5 win over the Mariners and a 2-0 lead in the playoffs. Mariano Rivera gets the win; Tim Belcher is the losing pitcher. Paul O'Neill and Don Mattingly homer for the Yankees, and Ken Griffey Jr. and Vince Coleman for Seattle.

OCTOBER 7:

Colorado beats Atlanta, 7-3, in 10 innings to stay alive in the playoffs.

The Mariners knot the playoff at two games apiece with an 11-8 win over the

SEPTEMBER 30
The Indian's Albert Belle ties Babe Ruth's record for homers in month of September.

OCTOBER 8
The Seattle Mariners win AL divisional playoffs, the fourth team to come back from a two-game deficit.

Yankees at the Kingdome. The Mariners forge ahead with a five-run eighth and withstand a Yankee two-run rally in the ninth for the victory. Relief pitcher Norm Charlton, who pitches only two-thirds of an inning, is the winner; Yankee reliever John Wetteland is charged with the loss. The game is marked by a home run barrage: the Mariners' Edgar Martinez has two and Ken Griffey Jr. and Jay Buhner, one each. Paul O'Neill homers for New York.

OCTOBER 8:

In Atlanta, the Braves beat the Rockies, 10-4, to capture their NL divisional playoff series. Atlanta ace Greg Maddux gets the win; Bret Saberhagen is charged with the loss. Atlanta's Fred McGriff homers twice; Dante Bichette and Vinnie Castilla connect for Colorado.

The dramatic AL divisional playoffs end – dramatically – when Edgar Martinez doubles in two runs against Jack McDowell to give the Mariners a 6-5, 11-inning victory over the Yankees at the Kingdome. In a see-saw game, the Yankees had scored a run against Randy Johnson in the top of the 11th to take the lead. Johnson, normally a starter, enters the game in the ninth and gets the win; McDowell takes the loss. The Mariners, only the fourth team ever to come back from a two-game deficit in a best-of-five playoff, will meet the Indians for the AL pennant.

OCTOBER 10:

Agreement is reached today for the sale of the Pirates to Kevin McClatchy and partners for $85 million. The Pirates' board unanimously approves the sale; major league baseball's okay is pending.

Yankees' owner George Steinbrenner is fined $50,000 by AL president Gene Budig for criticizing the umpiring in the New York-Seattle playoff series. In 22 years, Stein- brenner has been fined more than $600,000.

Says Steinbrenner, "It seems that everyone else can speak without being fined, but not me."

NLCS, game one. In Cincinnati, the Braves edge the Reds, 2-1, in 11 innings. Mark Wohlers gets the win in relief of Tom Glavine and Alejandro Pena. The losing pitcher is Mike Jackson. Atlanta scores the winning run in the top of the 11th on a single by Mike Devereaux.

ALCS, game one. Behind strong pitching by 22-year-old rookie Bob Wolcott, the Mariners beat the Indians, 3-2, in Seattle's Kingdome. The Mariners score all their runs on a two-run, second-inning homer by Mike Blowers and a seventh inning RBI double by Luis Sojo. Wolcott yields a home run to Albert Belle. Dennis Martinez is charged with the loss.

OCTOBER 11:

NLCS, game two. In Cincinnati, the Braves win another extra-inning game, beating the Reds, 6-2, in 10 innings. With the score tied in the final frame, Mark Portugal wild pitches in one run and then serves up a three-run homer to Javier Lopez. The winning pitcher is Greg McMichael; Portugal is charged with the loss.

ALCS, game two. In Seattle, paced by Manny Ramirez' four for four – including two solo homers – Cleveland wins, 5-2. Orel Hershiser gets the victory; Tim Belcher is charged with the loss. The Mariners score both of their runs on homers – by Ken Griffey Jr. and Jay Buhner.

OCTOBER 13:

NLCS, game three. Friday the 13th is no jinx for Atlanta as they continue to roll over the Reds, winning, 5-2. Greg Maddux gets the victory, allowing one run in eight innings. The losing pitcher is David Wells. Chipper Jones and Charlie O'Brien homer for Atlanta.

ALCS, game three. Seattle wins, 5-2, in 11 innings, with Jay Buhner's second home run of the game the big blow. The winning pitcher is Norm Charlton, who pitches three innings in relief of Randy Johnson. Reliever Julian Tavarez takes the loss for Cleveland.

OCTOBER 14:

NLCS, game four. The Braves win the NL pennant by defeating Cincinnati today, 6-0, and sweeping the championship faceoff. Steve Avery

LEAGUE

For some, the faceoff between the Indians and the Braves is the politically incorrect World Series. Before game one, Native Americans picket Atlanta-Fulton County Stadium to protest the use of American Indian symbols and mascots. Protesters carry signs reading, "Racist Mascots Must Go" and "Indians Are People, Not Mascots."

Paul Richards once said of Mickey Mantle: "This man hit 53 homers and did everything else he did on one leg."

LEAGUE

A total of 241 homers are hit in the Rockies' Coors Field in its first season, following 120 last year at Mile High Stadium. Theories range from the high altitude in Denver to the size of the ballparks. Mike Downey of the *Los Angeles Times* comments, "We wouldn't want to dampen the enthusiasm of Colorado's many new fans, but wonder if any would like to attend a real major league game?" Bob Kravitz of the *Rocky Mountain News* adds, "Kindergarten children who play T-ball could clear any fence in left, right or center. Coors Field isn't baseball. Coors Field is baseball lite."

pitches six outstanding innings for Atlanta, allowing only two hits and fanning six. Pete Schourek takes the loss for the Reds. Mike Devereaux hits a three-run homer during a five-run seventh inning that breaks the game open for the Braves.

ALCS, game four. In Cleveland, Ken Hill, with relief help from three Indians' pitchers, shuts out the Mariners 7-0. Hill yields five hits in seven innings, and Mariners' starter Andy Benes takes the loss. Eddie Murray and Jim Thome hit home runs.

OCTOBER 15:

ALCS, game five. In Cleveland, the Indians beat the Mariners, 3-2, with Jim Thome homering.

OCTOBER 16:

The Yankees sign the talented but troubled Dwight "Doc" Gooden to a three-year contract. Gooden, who has been on suspension for violations of his substance abuse program, receives one guaranteed year at $1 million and could earn in excess of $6 million over the life of the contract.

OCTOBER 17:

ALCS, game six. In Seattle, the Indians, behind 40-year-old Dennis Martinez – relieved by Julian Tavarez and Jose Mesa – defeat the Mariners and Randy Johnson, 40, to win the AL pennant. Carlos Baerga homers for Cleveland.

OCTOBER 21:

Former major league outfielder Vada Pinson dies at age 57 in Oakland, California, following a stroke. Pinson spent 11 years with the Cincinnati Reds, batting .286. He is one of six players with 250 homers and 300 stolen bases.

World Series, game one. Behind a two-hitter by Greg Maddux, the Braves beat Cleveland, 3-2, in Atlanta. Orel Hershiser gives up two runs in the seventh en route to the loss. Fred McGriff paces the Braves' attack with a solo homer in the second inning. The Indians' fleet-footed centerfielder Kenny Lofton steals two bases in the first inning, becoming the first player since Babe Ruth in 1921 to accomplish the feat in the World Series.

OCTOBER 22:

World Series, game two. The Braves make it two straight with a 4-3 win on the strength of a two-run homer by catcher Javier Lopez in the sixth inning. Tom Glavine is the winning pitcher; Mark Wohlers records a save. Dennis Martinez takes the loss, and Eddie Murray has a two-run homer for the losers.

OCTOBER 23:

The Cardinals hire Tony LaRussa as their manager. LaRussa, who replaces Mike Jorgenson, guided Oakland to one World Series title and three pennants. He signs a two-year pact estimated at $1.5 million per season.

The Yankees name Bob Watson as general manager, replacing Gene Michael. He had been general manager of the Astros.

The King County Council today approves plans for a new $320 million stadium for the Mariners. The new facility will include natural grass and a retractable roof and will enable Seattle to keep its baseball team from moving to another city.

OCTOBER 24:

World Series, game three. In an 11-inning contest in Cleveland, Eddie Murray singles in Alvaro Espinoza to give the Indians a 7-6 win. The winning pitcher is Jose Mesa, who pitches three shutout innings. Alejandro Pena takes the loss. Fred McGriff and Ryan Klesko of Atlanta have the game's only home runs.

OCTOBER 25:

Anheuser-Busch, which has owned the Cardinals for 42 years, plans to sell the team. The Cardinals reportedly lost $12 million in the 1995 season. A spokesperson says the goal is to find a new owner who will keep the team in St. Louis. Anheuser-Busch bought the Cardinals for $2.5 million from Fred Saigh in 1953.

World Series, game four. In Cleveland, the Braves take a commanding three-games – to one lead on a 5-2 win today. Steve Avery, who allows three hits in six innings, is the winning pitcher. Cleveland starter Ken Hill takes the loss. The game features home runs by the Indians' Albert Belle and Manny Ramirez, and the Braves' Ryan Klesko.

OCTOBER 23
The Yankees name Bob Watson as general manager.

OCTOBER 28
The Braves win their first World Series since moving to Atlanta.

OCTOBER 26:

World Series, game five. In Cleveland, with relief help from Jose Mesa, Orel Hershiser pitches the Indians to a 5-4 win. Greg Maddux takes the loss. Albert Belle and Jim Thome homer for Cleveland; Luis Polonia and Ryan Klesko for the Braves.

OCTOBER 28:

World Series, game six. Playing before their hometown fans, the Braves win their first World Series since moving to Atlanta by beating Cleveland, 1-0, on a combined one-hitter by Tom Glavine and Mark Wohlers. David Justice homers in the sixth inning for the game's only run. The Braves become the first team to win the World Series representing three different cities. As the Boston Braves they won in 1914, and as the Milwaukee Braves in 1957. Glavine pitches eight innings for the win. Jim Poole, who relieves Dennis Martinez, takes the loss.

POST-SEASON

OCTOBER 30:

Davey Johnson, who led the Reds to the NL West title, signs a three-year contract to manage the Orioles. He succeeds Phil Regan. The Reds replace Johnson with Ray Knight, who gets a two-year pact.

OCTOBER 31:

Ryne Sandberg, who stunned Cubs fans when he retired last season in the middle of a four-year $28.4 million contract, announces he will return for the 1996 season. The 36-year-old, 10-time All-Star second baseman signs a one-year contract.

NOVEMBER 1:

Paul Molitor gets a $1 million buyout from the Blue Jays, who opt not to pay him $4 million for next season. Molitor becomes a free agent tomorrow. He will join the Twins by the end of the year.

NOVEMBER 2:

Joe Torre is named the new Yankees manager, replacing Buck Showalter. Torre's appointment marks the 20th managerial change in the 23 seasons George Steinbrenner has owned the team. The 55-year-old former player last managed in the majors in 1984 with the Braves. He also managed the Cardinals and the Mets.

NOVEMBER 7:

Baseball signs a $1.7 billion, five-year television deal with Fox, NBC, ESPN, and Liberty Media. Each team will get $12 million per season, and the full post-season schedule will again be available on national television.

NOVEMBER 9:

The Dodgers' Hideo Nomo is named the NL Rookie of the Year. Nomo, 27 years old, is the first Japanese player to win a major American baseball award. He compiled a 13-6 record with an ERA of 2.54 and led the NL with 236 strikeouts.

NOVEMBER 10:

The rumored move of the Astros to Virginia is on hold – at least for one more season. Faced with a turndown from baseball's other owners, Drayton McLane Jr. announces he will keep the Astros in Houston for the 1996 season. The team was rumored to be on the verge of sale to a group of Virginia investors.

NOVEMBER 13:

Atlanta's Greg Maddux wins an unprecedented fourth straight NL Cy Young Award. Maddux, the unanimous choice, joins Steve Carlton as the only pitcher with four Cy Young Awards. Maddux, only 29 years old, was 19-2 in 1995 with an ERA of 1.63. Maddux is the first pitcher since Walter Johnson in 1918-19 to have an ERA lower than 1.80 for two straight seasons.

The Players Relations Committee today releases information on team payrolls to the general managers at baseball's annual meetings in Scottsdale, Arizona. The statistics show the Yankees with the top payroll – $54,889,849. Second are the Reds with $46,763,886. The World Champion Braves rank fourth at $46,423,444, and the AL pennant-winners, the Indians, are sixth, with a payroll of $39,088,500. The lowest major league payroll belongs to the Expos – $12,956,557.

NOVEMBER 15:

The Arizona Diamondbacks – a team that will not begin play until 1998 – sign Buck Showalter to a seven-year contract as their manager. Showalter's

TRIVIA

Artistic errors aren't limited to the Brooklyn Dodgers. A nine-foot bronze statue of Babe Ruth erected outside Oriole Park at Camden Yards is authentic in all details – except one. The left-handed Babe is depicted holding a right-hander's glove

Representing Leon Day is his widow, Geraldine, who asks for the admission of more Negro Leagues stars to the Hall: "I pray one day it will be made right."

TRIVIA

Babe who? Pompano Beach, Florida, police report that two boys – ages 13 and 14 – who stole a baseball autographed by Babe Ruth threw it into a garbage Dumpster. The ball, valued at $6,000, was among some $45,000 worth of memorabilia stolen from a baseball-card store. By the time police got to the Dumpster, the contents had been emptied and the ball was not retrieved.

Cal Ripkin Jr. celebrates his consecutive game streak.

contract is reported to be worth between $6 and $7 million. Which league Arizona will play in is yet to be determined.
In Scottsdale, Arizona, players and owners meet in formal negotiations for the first time since March 30. The owners present a proposal to the players which, according to the *New York Times*, calls for "a floating payroll tax based on club revenues."

NOVEMBER 21:

Don Mattingly, one of the most popular Yankees of all time and the team captain, retires – or does he? The 35-year-old Mattingly informs the Yankees not to plan on him for the 1996 season. He leaves open the possibility that he will return – to the Yankees or another team. Once one of baseball's most feared hitters, Mattingly suffered from back problems that diminished his power, but he remained one of the game's finest-fielding first basemen. This season he batted .288 with seven homers and 49 RBI. His career average is .307 with 222 homers and 1,099 RBI.

The Marlins sign 33-year-old free-agent outfielder Devon White to a three-year, $9.9 million contract. White played for Toronto in 1995, batting .283, his career high. He is a seven-time Gold Glove winner.

NOVEMBER 28:

According to figures released today by the Players Association, the Yankee's average salary this past season was a record $2,000,271. However, the average major league salary dropped by 5 percent to $1,110,766. The lowest was the Expos at $750,840.

NOVEMBER 29:

Pat Gillick, who was general manager of the Blue Jays' 1992 and 1993 World Championship teams, ends a short retirement and becomes general manager of the Orioles.

NOVEMBER 30:

The strange, brief Yankee career of Darryl Strawberry seemingly comes to an end. New York buys out Strawberry's for $175,000 and releases him when the team is denied a second extension on exercising an option for 1996 at $1.8 million. Strawberry appeared in only 32 games for the Yankees, batting .276 with three homers.

The Dodgers sign free-agent shortstop Greg Gagne to a one-year contract reportedly worth $2.6 million. With Kansas City last season, Gagne, age 34, hit .256.

DECEMBER 1:

Hall of Famer Duke Snider is sentenced to two years' probation and fined $5,000 for failing to pay taxes on money he earned at card shows and signing autographs. Snider and fellow Hall of Famer Willie McCovey pleaded guilty to tax fraud conspiracy last summer. Other former major leaguers are reportedly being investigated.

DECEMBER 2:

Michael Stirn, the fan who caught Cal Ripken's home run ball the night the Oriole star tied the consecutive game record, sells it to a Maryland businessman at auction for $41,736.

DECEMBER 4:

The *New York Daily News* reports that Hank Aaron, Ernie Banks, Reggie Jackson, Harmon Killebrew, the late Mickey Mantle, Frank Robinson, and Mike Schmidt "are among the stars believed to have dodged the tax man."

DECEMBER 6:

Billy Bruton, who starred on the Braves during the 1950s and also played with the Tigers, dies in Marshallton, Delaware, at age 69 after suffering a heart attack. Bruton's career average was .273; he led the NL in stolen bases for three straight seasons.

DECEMBER 7:

First baseman Tino Martinez crams a lifetime of memories into a single day. Martinez is traded from Seattle to the Yankees; signs a five-year, $20.25 million contract with his new team, and his wife gives birth to a daughter, their third child. Martinez hit .293 last season with 31 homers and 111 RBI. In exchange for the All-Star, the Mariners get pitcher Sterling Hitchcock (11-10, 4.70 ERA) and third baseman Russell Davis (.276). Going to New York with Martinez are relief pitcher Jeff Nelson (7-3, 2.17

Orioles
8

DECEMBER 14 The Indians sign free-agent pitcher Jack McDowell.

DECEMBER 21 Free agent David Cone re-signs with Yankees.

ERA) and minor league pitcher Jim Mecir.

Today also is a big day for signings with many players joining new teams. Among those inked are Eddie Murray, Manny Ramirez, Orel Hershiser, and Julio Franco (Indians); Fernando Valenzuela (Padres); Otis Nixon (Blue Jays); and Phil Plantier (Tigers).

DECEMBER 14:

The Indians sign free-agent pitcher Jack McDowell (15-10, 3.93 ERA) to a two-year contract. McDowell was with the Yankees in 1995.

Free-agent outfielder Lance Johnson (.306, 40 stolen bases, and a league-leading 186 hits) signs with the Mets in a two-year deal reportedly worth between $5 and $6 million.

Sportswriter Al Stump dies at age 79 in Newport Beach, California. Stump worked with the ferocious Ty Cobb on *My Life in Baseball: The True Record* and was the author of *Cobb: A Biography*.

DECEMBER 21:

Free agent David Cone (18-8, 3.57 ERA) re-signs with the Yankees and becomes a rich pitcher, receiving a three-year, $18 million contract. Earlier, the Orioles sign free-agent second baseman Roberto Alomar (.300, 13 homers, 30 stolen bases) to a three-year, $18 million pact.

The Royals trade first baseman Wally Joyner (.310, 12 homers, 83 RBI) to the Padres for infielder-outfielder Bip Roberts (.304, 20 stolen bases). The Royals also lose free-agent pitcher Tom Gordon (12-12, 4.43 ERA), who signs with the Red Sox. Gordon inks a three-year deal; he will earn $2.9 million per year for the first two seasons and $3.1 million in the third.

DECEMBER 22:

Anheuser-Busch agrees to sell the Cardinals for $150 million to an investment group – including businessman William DeWitt Jr., lawyer Frederick Hanser, and banker Andrew Baur – that agrees to keep the team in St. Louis. The price tag is the second highest for any major league team.

DECEMBER 23:

The Cardinals sign two free agents – pitcher Andy Benes (11-9, 4.76 ERA) and outfielder Ron Gant (.276, 29 homers, 88 RBI, 23 stolen bases). Benes, who will be teamed with his brother, Alan, also a pitcher, split last season between the Padres and Mariners. Gant was with the Reds.

DECEMBER 27:

Hall of Fame umpire Al Barlick dies at age 80 in Springfield, Illinois. Barlick, a National League ump from 1940 to 1972, was reputed to have the loudest ball-strike call in baseball.

THE BEST OF 1995

NATIONAL LEAGUE

HITTERS

Batting Average:
Tony Gwynn, San Diego Padres, .368

Slugging Average:
Dante Bichette, Colorado Rockies, .620

Home Runs:
Dante Bichette, 40

Runs Batted In:
Dante Bichette, 128

Hits:
Dante Bichette; Tony Gwynn, 197

Stolen Bases:
Quilvio Veras, Florida Marlins, 56

PITCHERS

Wins:
Greg Maddux, Atlanta Braves, 19

Strikeouts:
Hideo Nomo, Los Angeles Dodgers, 236

Earned Run Average:
Greg Maddux, 1.63

Winning Percentage:
Greg Maddux, .905

Saves:
Randy Myers, Chicago Cubs, 38

Most Valuable Player:
Barry Larkin, Cincinnati Reds

Cy Young Award:
Greg Maddux, Atlanta Braves

Rookie of the Year:
Hideo Nomo, Los Angeles Dodgers

Manager of the Year:
Don Baylor, Colorado Rockies

AMERICAN LEAGUE

HITTERS

Batting Average:
Edgar Martinez, Seattle Mariners, .356

Slugging Average:
Albert Belle, Cleveland Indians, .690

Home Runs:
Albert Belle, 50

Runs Batted In:
Albert Belle, 126

Hits:
Lance Johnson, Chicago White Sox, 186

Stolen Bases:
Kenny Lofton, Cleveland Indians, 54

PITCHERS

Wins:
Mike Mussina, Baltimore Orioles, 19

Strikeouts:
Randy Johnson, Seattle Mariners, 294

Earned Run Average:
Randy Johnson, 2.48

Winning Percentage:
Randy Johnson, .900

Saves:
Jose Mesa, Cleveland Indians, 46

Most Valuable Player:
Maurice "Mo" Vaughn, Boston Red Sox

Cy Young Award:
Randy Johnson, Seattle Mariners

Rookie of the Year:
Marty Cordova, Minnesota Twins

Manager of the Year:
Lou Piniella, Seattle Mariners

1996

NEWS

PRESIDENT BILL CLINTON REELECTED, DEFEATING BOB DOLE

TWA FLIGHT 800 EXPLODES OFF LONG ISLAND, KILLING 230

UNABOMBER SUSPECT CAPTURED BY FEDERAL OFFICIALS

O.J. SIMPSON FACES CIVIL TRIAL IN MURDER OF HIS WIFE AND HER FRIEND

RAPPER TUPAC SHAKUR SHOT TO DEATH IN LAS VEGAS

THE DOW JONES TOPS 6,500

JAZZ GREAT, ELLA FITZGERALD, DIES

MIAMI DOLPHINS' COACH, DON SHULA RETIRES

OLYMPICS CELEBRATES ITS CENTENARY IN ATLANTA

THE U.S. DEFEAT CANADA TO WIN WORLD CUP OF HOCKEY

PRE-SEASON

JANUARY 2:

Reds' Shortstop Barry Larkin (.315, 15 homers, 66 RBI, 51 stolen bases), the NL's Most Valuable Player, signs a $16.5 million, three-year contract extension.

JANUARY 8:

For the seventh time in history, the Baseball Writers Association of America fails to select an eligible player for the Hall of Fame. Among those snubbed are a pair of 300-game winners — Phil Niekro and Don Sutton.

JANUARY 30:

Cardinals' shortstop Ozzie Smith gives something back to his alma mater. He donates $1 million to Cal Poly-San Luis Obispo — which he attended from 1974 to 1977 — for an athletic complex, including Ozzie Smith Stadium.

JANUARY 31:

The Mariners make Ken Griffey Jr. (.258, 17 homers, 42 RBI) the highest paid baseball player ever with a four-year, $34 million contract. Injuries limited him to 72 games in 1995, but in seven years he has 189 homers and a .302 average.

FEBRUARY 7:

Dave Winfield retires at age 44 with 3,110 hits, 465 homers, 1,833 RBI and a .283 average. Last season — his 22nd in the majors — he was with the Indians.

FEBRUARY 19:

One of the most controversial owners of modern times, Charles O. Finley, dies at 77 in Chicago of heart disease. He left baseball after selling the Athletics following the 1980 season.

THE SEASON

MARCH 31:

In Seattle, the Mariners and White Sox meet in the earliest major league opening day in history. Alex Rodriguez wins the game, 3-2, with a one-out, 12th-inning RBI single. Randy Johnson fans fourteen in twelve innings of work; twenty-one Chicago batters strike out in the game. Frank Thomas accounts for all of the White Sox' scoring with a two-run homer. The winning pitcher is Edwin Hurtado; Bill Simas gets the loss. AL umps are no longer the "men in blue"; their uniforms now include red and navy shirts.

Rodriguez's sudden impact was documented in Baseball: A Biographical Encyclopedia: *"If Ernie Banks spoke the first word on what a power-hitting shortstop might accomplish, Alex Rodriguez might have the final say. Banks hit 40-plus home runs in four consecutive seasons, from 1957-1960, between the ages of 26 and 29. Rodriguez reached the 40-mark twice by age 24."*

Opening day in Cincinnati is marred by tragedy. Home plate umpire John McSherry collapses and dies after calling seven pitches at the start of the Reds-Expos game attended by 53,000 fans. The 51-year-old McSherry, in his 26th year of umpiring, is the first on-the-field fatality in baseball since 1920.

APRIL 6:

Chan Ho Park of the Dodgers defeats the

Yankees' reliever John Wetteland celebrates World Series victory.

25

RULES

The Lords of Baseball increase the size of the strike zone, but it may be hard to tell the difference. Beginning with spring training it will extend to the top of the knee. Previously, it began at the hollow beneath the kneecap. The upper boundary — from a point midway between the top of the shoulder and the top of the belt line — is unchanged.

Cubs, 3-1, at Wrigley Field, becoming the first Korean-born pitcher to record a major league win. Park throws six shutout innings in relief of Ramon Martinez for the win. The loser is Jaime Navarro.

APRIL 8:

The NL announces that 325-pound umpire Eric Gregg has been granted a leave of absence so he can enter a weight loss program.

APRIL 11:

The Padres beat the visiting Braves, 2-1, ending Greg Maddux's major league record of eighteen consecutive road victories. Maddux last lost an away game on June 27, 1994, in Montreal. Today's winner is Alan Ashby.

APRIL 19:

The Rangers ruin the visiting Orioles, 26-7; it is the most runs by an AL team in 41 years. Paced by Kevin Elster's grand slam, Texas stages the biggest eighth inning rally ever in the majors — 16 runs. The Rangers send 19 batters to the plate in the eighth; eight hit safely and eight walk. The game features a homer and six RBIs by Juan Gonzalez, two four-baggers by Dean Palmer and a solo shot by Will Clark. The winning pitcher is Dennis Cook; Kent Mercker gets the loss.

APRIL 24:

At Tiger Stadium, the Twins maul seven pitchers and win, 24-11. The 24 runs represent the most against Detroit in 84 years — since a team of amateurs lost to the Philadelphia Athletics in 1912. Greg Myers and Paul Molitor each drive in six runs.

APRIL 26:

Former major league pitcher Milt Gaston dies at 100 in Hyannis, Massachusetts. Gaston, who played from 1924 to 1934 with a record of 97-164, was the eighth former major leaguer to live to 100. He played with seventeen Hall of Fame players and managers — the most ever.

APRIL 27:

Barry Bonds homers twice today against the visiting Marlins, bringing his career total to 300. Bonds joins his father, Bobby, Willie Mays, and Andre Dawson as the only players with 300 roundtrippers and 300 stolen bases. The Giants and Mark Leiter win, 6-3, but Bonds is ejected for arguing a third strike call in the sixth.

MAY 2:

At 9: 04 p.m., an earthquake measuring 4.8 on the Richter Scale rocks Seattle for 30 seconds, halting the Mariners-Indians game during the seventh inning, with Cleveland leading, 6-3. The game is resumed the following night and the Indians go on to win, 6-4.

MAY 5:

The Reds' owner tells an ESPN interviewer that Hitler "was good in the beginning but he went too far." The inevitable apology from Marge Schott: "Sometimes I do not always express myself well, as in this instance."

MAY 7:

Brett Butler of the Dodgers is diagnosed with throat cancer and will undergo surgery later this month. The malignancy was discovered during a tonsillectomy in Atlanta. Butler chewed tobacco early in his career.

MAY 10:

With his career in jeopardy, Yankee ace David Cone undergoes surgery in New York to remove an aneurysm in his pitching arm.

MAY 11:

Al Leiter of the Marlins pitches an 11-0 no-hitter against the Rockies in Miami. It is the first ever by a Marlins' pitcher. Leiter fans six, walks two and hits a batter. His teammates play error-free ball. The losing pitcher is Mark Thompson.

MAY 14:

Dwight "Doc" Gooden of the Yankees no-hits the visiting Mariners, 2-0. The 31-year-old fans five and walks six; the Yankees commit one error. Tino Martinez drives in the winning run against Sterling Hitchcock with a sixth inning sacrifice fly.

MAY 31:

The Brewers and Indians engage in a bench-clearing brawl in Milwaukee after Cleveland's 6-foot-2 Albert Belle flattens 5-foot-9 second baseman Fernando Vina with a forearm blow in the eighth inning. Vina has a bruised nose and a cut mouth. Indians' pitcher Julian Tavarez throws umpire Joe Brinkman to the

MAY 2
An earthquake delays the Mariners-Indians game.

JUNE 14
Cal Ripken Jr. breaks the world record for consecutive games played.

ground during the melee. Belle was hit by pitches in the 8th and 9th innings. Tavarez retaliated by hitting Mike Matheny. When play is resumed, the Indians coast to a 10-4 win. After the game Belle says, "I wasn't going to get mad; we're going to get even."

Belle and Tavarez are suspended for five days each. In six seasons, Belle has been slapped with five suspensions. AL president Gene Budig reduces the penalties to three games each, stating, "What Albert Belle did crossed the line and it was wrong...he not only threatened injury to another player, but also led to the later disruption of the game. I find the personal conduct and contact by Mr. Belle...crossed the line of good, clean and tough baseball." Belle claimed he was trying to break up a double play. Budig eventually settles on a two-day suspension and a $25,000 fine.

JUNE 1:

Hostilities between the Brewers and Indians continue today in Milwaukee. After Kenny Lofton leads off with a double, he shoves Fernando Vina on a pickoff play at second. Both benches empty, but no punches are thrown. Vina explains, "We started jawing and we almost went at it." The Brewers win the game, 2-1.

JUNE 4:

Pamela Davis reportedly becomes the first woman to pitch for a major league farm team in modern times when she takes the mound for the Class AA Jacksonville Suns against the visiting Australian Olympic team. The 21-year-old throws an inning of scoreless relief in a 7-2 Jacksonville win.

A starter for the Colorado Silver Bullets all-woman team, she says, "I think I proved women can pitch. I felt really good out there."

JUNE 6:

The White Sox execute a triple play at Fenway Park, but John Valentin hits for the cycle to pace the Red Sox to a 7-4 win. It is the first time since a July 1, 1931, meeting between the Cubs and Phillies that a game has featured both a triple play and "the cycle."

JUNE 8:

C. Arnolt Smith, the Padres' first owner, dies at 97 in Del Mar, California. Smith, who sold the team to Ray Kroc in 1973, brought major league baseball to San Diego in 1969.

JUNE 9:

The White Sox hold Roberto Alomar hitless in four at bats, ending his 22-game hitting streak. Chicago wins, 12-10, completing a three-game sweep over Baltimore.

JUNE 12:

Marge Schott is forced to relinquish day-to-day control of the Reds because of her continual use of offensive remarks. The controversial 67-year-old will retain her majority ownership in the team. John Allen, the team's controller, will run the team.

JUNE 14:

Cal Ripken Jr. breaks the world record for consecutive games played — 2,215 — when he appears in tonight's contest against the Royals. He tops the mark set by Japan's Sachio Kinugasa in 1987. Kinugasa was in the stands last night when Ripken tied the record. Ripken is hitless in four at-bats as visiting Baltimore beats Kansas City, 6-1.

JUNE 16:

The long-time voice of the Yankees, Mel Allen, dies at 83 in Greenwich, Connecticut. He and the late Red Barber were the first broadcasters inducted into the Baseball Hall of Fame. Allen called Yankee games from 1939 to 1964 and also narrated the television show *This Week in Baseball*. He was fired by New York following the 1964 season.

JUNE 19:

John Smoltz defeats the visiting Padres, 5-1, for his 14th consecutive victory. Smoltz, who improves his season record to 14-1, pitches a complete game, allowing only two hits and no walks while fanning eight. Chipper Jones homers for Atlanta.

JUNE 19:

Cardinals' shortstop Ozzie Smith announces that he will retire at the end of the season. The 41-year-old has played in the majors for 19 seasons but is mostly a backup this year. He is hitting only .199 in 44 games.

JUNE 24:

Two days after being released by the Yankees, lefthanded

LEAGUE

Interleague play is approved for the 1997 season by major league baseball's executive council. If the details are ironed out, teams from each league will play against those in the corresponding division. Acting commissioner Bud Selig warns that interleague play must be okayed by the Players Association through collective bargaining.

> "The world is not over now... I loved the game. I thought I played the game with respect."
> – *Kirby Puckett*

pitcher Steve Howe is involved in what may be the final chapter of his troubled career. Port Authority police arrest Howe when they find a loaded .357 Magnum in his luggage at John F. Kennedy International Airport before he boards a plane for his home in Montana. Howe claims the weapon belongs to his wife. He was 0-1 with a 6.35 ERA this season. In November, Howe pleads guilty to a misdemeanor and receives three years of probation and 150 hours of community service.

JUNE 25:

Mark McGwire of the Athletics homers to left field off Omar Olivares in the second inning of today's game against the Tigers. It's his 300th career roundtripper; he is the 73rd player to reach that level. McGwire adds another homer — also against Olivares — in the seventh, but the visiting Tigers win, 10-8, on Bobby Higginson's fifth RBI.

JUNE 26:

Yankee pitcher David Cone begins his comeback attempt after surgery for an aneurysm, with 12 pitches at Yankee Stadium.

JUNE 27:

A cameraman for WGN in Chicago accuses Albert Belle of throwing a drink at him in the seventh inning of a game with the White Sox, after the Indians' slugger is removed for a pinch hitter.

JUNE 28:

The visiting Athletics pound out eight homers among their 17 hits as they crush the Angels, 18-2. Connecting are Mark McGwire, Scott Brosius (twice), Geronimo Berroa (bases loaded), Jason Giambi, Terry Steinbach, Ernie Young, and Jose Herrara.

JUNE 29:

After going four for four against the Royals yesterday to extend his consecutive game hitting streak to 23 games, Marty Cordova is held hitless in four at bats by Mark Gubicza. But Minnesota wins the game, 5-2, in Kansas City.

Jason Giambi, Terry Steinbach, and Geronimo Berroa homer against the Angels, giving the Athletics 18 roundtrippers in four games, tying a major league record set by the Red Sox in 1977. Visiting Oakland wins the game, 11-9.

JULY 3:

Cecil Fielder of the Tigers, who stole the first base of his 11-year career on April 2, adds another one today as Detroit beats visiting Milwaukee, 8-5.

JULY 5:

Detroit clears a hurdle in its quest for a new ballpark when the Michigan Court of Appeals rules against the Tiger Stadium Fan Club, which was seeking to prohibit the use of state funds for a stadium. The new ballpark is slated for construction eight blocks away from the current one.

JULY 6:

Darryl Strawberry gets another comeback chance. Two days after signing him to a minor league contract, the Yankees announce they are recalling Strawberry from the Columbus Clippers. Strawberry hit three homers in two games with the Class AAA team. Previously, he was with the St. Paul Saints in the independent Northern League, where he batted .435 and hit 18 homers. His signing comes 10 days after Yankee general manager Bob Watson declared that Strawberry didn't fit in with the team.

JULY 7:

The dubious distinction of being the first manager fired this season goes to the Marlins' Rene Lachemann. The team was 40-47 and in fourth place in the NL East. Marlins' vice president John Boles, who has no major league experience and has not managed at any level in 10 years, replaces Lachemann.

JULY 9:

The NL wins the All-Star game, 6-0, at Philadelphia's Veterans Stadium. The winning pitcher is Atlanta's John Smoltz; Charles Nagy of Cleveland gets the loss. Ken Caminiti and Mike Piazza homer for the Senior Circuit.

JULY 12:

One of baseball's nice guys, Kirby Puckett, announces he is retiring effective immediately. Puckett has been inactive since the beginning of the season because of glaucoma in his right eye. In 12 seasons with the Twins, the outfielder batted .318 with 207 homers and 1,085 RBI; he was a

Paul Richards once said of Mantle: "This man hit 53 homers and did everything else he did on one leg."

10-time all-star. In 1988, Puckett compiled a .356 batting average, 24 homers and 121 RBI. He says, "The world is not over now... I loved the game. I thought I played the game with respect." In October, he is honored with the Roberto Clemente Man of the Year Award for sportsmanship, community involvement and contributions to his team and the sport.

JULY 14:

Ken Griffey Jr. returns to action after 15 days on the disabled list because of a broken bone in his right wrist and leads the Mariners to an 8-0 victory over the Angels in Seattle. Griffey hits a two-run homer and an RBI double.

In Baltimore, the Yankees top the Orioles, 4-1, behind Andy Pettitte to complete a four-game sweep. John Wetteland records a save for New York. Scott Erickson is charged with the loss as the Yankees now lead Baltimore by 10 games.

JULY 15:

A Cal Ripken streak ends, but it's not the big one. Ripken, who has appeared in 2,216 as the Orioles' starting shortstop, is shifted to third base by manager Davey Johnson after the team loses five straight. Ripken's consecutive game streak remains intact at 2,243. Playing short is Manny Alexander. Ripken handles four chances without an error, is hitless in four trips to the plate; the Orioles beat the visiting Blue Jays, 8-6.

JULY 25:

Mark McGwire drills a 488-foot home run into the seventh row of the fifth deck at Toronto's SkyDome. It is believed to be the longest ever in that ballpark. But the Athletics bow to the Blue Jays, 4-3, on Joe Carter's ninth inning, two-out, two-run homer.

JULY 26:

Mark McGwire hits a pinch-hit homer in the eighth against the Blue Jays in Toronto, giving him roundtrippers in four straight games and bringing his season total to 38. Ernie Young's ninth inning two-run homer wins for the Athletics, 5-3.

JULY 27:

Joe Carter hits a 483-foot home run, becoming only the third player ever to reach the fifth deck at the SkyDome. Carter's three-run roundtripper leads the Blue Jays past the Athletics, 6-4. It is Carter's 25th home run of the season.

JULY 28:

Darryl Strawberry, in his comeback with the Yankees, reaches a personal milestone — his 300th career home run. Strawberry connects with a runner on in the bottom of the ninth against Jason Jacome to give New York a 3-2 win over the Royals.

The Marlins and Al Leiter hold John Flaherty of the Padres hitless in three at bats, ending his consecutive game hitting streak at 27.

Flaherty's streak was the second best ever by a catcher. Benito Santiago, then a Padre, had a 34-game streak in 1987. Leiter improves his record to 11-0 as San Diego prevails, 8-2.

JULY 29:

Tommy Lasorda announces he is retiring as manager of the Dodgers. The 68-year-old Lasorda, who underwent an angioplasty on June 26 after suffering a heart attack earlier this year, will become a team vice president. Besides Lasorda, only Connie Mack, John McGraw and Walter Alston managed for 20 or more years. Coach Bill Russell will replace him.

JULY 30:

The Reds acquire outfielder Kevin Mitchell (.304, two homers, 13 RBI), the 1989 NL Most Valuable Player, from the Red Sox for two minor leaguers — pitcher Brad Tweedlie and infielder Roberto Mejia. The Reds also sell outfielder Eric Anthony (.244, eight homers, 13 RBI) to the Astros.

JULY 31:

The Tigers send their slugging first baseman-DH Cecil Fielder (.248, 26 homers, 80 RBI) to the Yankees for outfielder-DH Ruben Sierra (.258, 11 homers, 52 RBI) and minor league pitching prospect Matt Drews, grandson of former major leaguer Karl Drews. In a second transaction, the Yankees acquire pitcher David Weathers (2-2, 4.54 ERA) from the Marlins for pitcher Mark Hutton (0-2, 5.04 ERA).

The Brewers send outfielder-DH Greg Vaughn (.280, 31 homers, 95 RBI) and a player to be named

CULTURE

***The Fan*, the film version of Peter Abrahams's novel, stars Robert DeNiro as a stalker obsessed with a Giants' player, portrayed by Wesley Snipes.**

"I have nothing against the bunt – in its place. But most of the time that place is in the bottom of a long-forgotten closet." – *Earl Weaver*

HISTORY

The Astros retire Nolan Ryan's number, making him the first major leaguer to be so honored by three teams. Ryan's number was retired by the Angels in 1992 and this year by the Rangers.

later to the Padres for pitchers Bryce Florie (2-2, 401 ERA) and Ron Villone (1-1. 2.95 ERA) along with outfielder Marc Newfield (.251).

Chris Sabo of the Reds is slapped with a seven-game suspension for using a corked bat. NL president Leonard Coleman also fines the team $25,000. Sabo maintains the bat wasn't his.

AUGUST 4:

Jim Bunning, Earl Weaver, Bill Foster and Ned Hanlon are inducted into the Baseball Hall of Fame. Bunning, now a Republican Congressman from Kentucky, compiled a 224-184 record with a 3.27 ERA over 17 years. Bunning, who pitched a no-hitter for the Tigers in 1958 and a perfect game for the Phillies in 1964, today is applauded by his nine children and 28 grandchildren. Weaver, who never played in the majors, managed the Baltimore Orioles for 17 years with a 1,480-1,060 record. He won four pennants and led the team to the 1970 World Championship. Foster, a Negro Leagues star and the younger half-brother of Hall of Famer Andrew "Rube" Foster, pitched 15 years mostly with the Chicago American Giants. His record was 137-62. Foster died in 1978. He is represented by his son, also named Bill, who says, "Dad, you made it." Hanlon, who died in 1937, managed 19 years from 1889 to 1907 and had a record of 1,313-1,164. He was the skipper of the old Baltimore Orioles for eight seasons and also managed in Pittsburgh, Brooklyn, and Cincinnati. He played outfield for 13 major league seasons, batting .260.

Weaver applied a basic philosophy to winning ball games: pitching, defense, and the three-run homer. "I have nothing against the bunt – in its place," he said. "But most of the time that place is in the bottom of a long-forgotten closet."

AUGUST 6:

Darryl Strawberry provides a bittersweet taste of what-might-have-been when he cracks three homers off Kevin Tapani of the White Sox at Yankee Stadium. The Yankees win, 9-2, behind strong pitching from Kenny Rogers. Strawberry has four RBIs.
After a 20-day, 17-game road trip necessitated by the 1996 Olympic Games, the Braves return to Atlanta and defeat the Phillies, 10-4. On the road, the Braves were 9-8.

The second half of the Lachemann "brother act" leaves the majors. Marcel Lachemann quits as the manager of the 52-59, last place Angels. John McNamara will fill in for the remainder of the season.

AUGUST 8:

Darryl Strawberry continues his hot hitting with two more home runs in an 8-4 Yankee victory over the White Sox in New York. Strawberry has homered five times in his last nine at-bats and has eight RBI in three games.

AUGUST 11:

Pitcher Kris Benson of Clemson University and the U.S. Olympic team becomes the highest paid draft choice ever when he gets a $2 million signing bonus from the Pirates.

AUGUST 12:

Mark McGwire, who missed 30 games this season, hits his 40th and 41st homers in an 11-1 trouncing of the Twins in Minnesota. His Oakland teammate, Geronimo Berroa, hits three roundtrippers, becoming the 10th player in history with three homers in a game twice in the same season.

AUGUST 13:

Both benches empty as the Expos and Astros brawl in the third inning at Montreal's Olympic Stadium. The fight begins when Houston's Danny Darwin hits Henry Rodriguez on the right hip with a pitch. The action is seen as retaliation because Rodriguez slowly circled the bases after hitting a two-run homer in the second. Rodriguez charges the mound and, in the melee, Moises Alou throws a helmet that strikes Astros' manager Terry Collins in the face, inflicting a four-inch wound above his lip. The Expos win the game, 8-1. Suspensions are handed down to Rodriguez, Alou, David Segui and Jeff Juden of Montreal and Darwin and John Cangelosi of Houston.

AUGUST 14:

Jim Abbott is sent to the minor leagues by the Angels after strug-

AUGUST 16
The Mets and Padres play the first regular season game outside of U.S. or Canada — in Mexico.

AUGUST 20
The Rangers end their error less streak at 15 games.

gling to a 1-15 record with a 7.79 ERA. The 28-year-old Abbott, who will play in the minors for the first time in his career, was born without a right hand. During the off-season, Abbott had signed a three-year, $7.8 million dollar pact with the Angels.

Marlins' outfielder Andre Dawson announces he will retire at the end of the season. The 42-year-old, in his 21st major league season, has knee troubles.

AUGUST 15:

The Associated Press reports that settlement of baseball's ongoing labor dispute is being held up because at least seven owners are opposed to giving players service time for the 75 days wiped out by the 1995 strike.

AUGUST 16:

The Mets and Padres meet in a new setting — Monterey, Mexico, marking the first regular season major league game to be played outside the U.S. or Canada. The Padres, playing as the home team, win, 15-10, before 23,699 fans. Game 2 goes to the Mets, 7-3, with attendance at 20,873. San Diego wins the final game of the series, 8-0; attendance is 22,810. Mexican-born Fernando Valenzuela gets the win.

John Smoltz of the Braves beats the Pirates in Atlanta to become the major's first 20-game winner this season. Smoltz fans six, raising his major league-leading total to 217 and allows only seven hits. Mark Wohlers records a save.

AUGUST 20:

Shortstop Kevin Elster drops a throw and the Rangers' errorless streak ends at 15 games — an AL record. Texas also loses the game to Cleveland, 10-4. The major league record is held by the 1992 Cardinals.

Sammy Sosa, the NL's leading home run hitter with 40, will be lost to the Cubs for at least a month. Sosa suffered a fracture at the juncture of his right hand and wrist when he was hit by a pitch from Mark Hutton of the Marlins in the first inning of today's game. Sosa's consecutive game streak, 304, also comes to an end. It was the third longest current streak after Cal Ripken's and Barry Bond's.

AUGUST 21:

David Cone begins an astonishing comeback from aneurysm surgery. Pitching for the Yankees' Class AA farm team, the Norwich Navigators, Cone faces 16 batters and fans seven with a fastball that reaches 90 mph. He also yields a homer and an unearned run as Norwich bows to the Binghamton Mets, 5-2.

AUGUST 23:

The Yankees acquire pitcher Graeme Lloyd (2-4, 2.82 ERA) and infielder Pat Listach (.240, one homer, 33 RBI) from the Brewers for outfielder Gerald Williams (.270, five homers, 30 RBI) and pitcher Bob Wickman (4-1, 4.67 ERA).

The trade has implications for the rest of the regular season. The Yankees learn that Listach has a broken right foot and Lloyd has a damaged pitching elbow. Milwaukee then sends New York pitcher Ricky Bones and a player to be named later as compensation. Listach is returned to Milwaukee in October.

AUGUST 25:

At Fenway Park, Ken Griffey Jr. smacks his 40th homer, but the Mariners lose to the Red Sox, 8-5. Griffey and Alex Rodriguez homer back-to-back in the eighth. It is the 17th time this season Seattle players have hit consecutive homers, a major league record. Troy O'Leary and Jeff Frye homer back-to-back in the fourth for the winners.

The Mariners' fireballer Randy Johnson (5-0, 3.67 ERA), last year's AL Cy Young Award-winner, will miss the remainder of the season because of a bulging disc in his back. Johnson was on the disabled list from May 12 until August 6, when he returned to the team and was assigned bullpen duty. He has played in only 14 games.

A strained left hamstring sidelines Barry Bonds of the Giants, ending his consecutive game streak at 357.

AUGUST 26:

With the Mets at 59-72 and mired near the bottom of the NL East, the team fires manager Dallas Green. He is replaced by Bobby Valentine.

AUGUST 28:

The Braves, already pitcher-rich, acquire another first-rate

SEPTEMBER 2
Mike Greenwell of the Red Sox has 9 RBI in a single game.

SEPTEMBER 6
Eddie Murray has his 500th career homer and 3,000th hit.

pitcher — Danny Neagle (14-6, 3.05 ERA). In return Atlanta sends Pittsburgh two minor leaguers — first baseman Ron Wright and outfielder Corey Pointer — plus a player to be named later. The trade is the result of orders from Pirates' new owner Kevin McClatchy to deal established players for young prospects.

The heated rivalry between the Yankees and Mariners boils over. After Tim Davis dusts New York's Paul O'Neill in the eighth inning, the outfielder and Seattle catcher John Marzano exchange heated words. Marzano pushes O'Neill who starts punching and both benches empty. When order is restored O'Neill and Darryl Strawberry of the Yankees are ejected along with Marzano, Chris Bosio and Bobby Ayala of the Mariners. In the bottom of the inning, Yankee pitcher Jeff Nelson is ejected after he hits Joey Cora with a pitch. The Mariners win the game, 10-2.

AUGUST 29:

The Orioles, seeking additional right-handed power for the home stretch, acquire third baseman Todd Zeile (.268, 20 homers, 42 RBI) and outfielder Pete Incaviglia (.234, 16 homers, 42 RBI) from the Phillies for two players to be named later.

In the first matchup between brothers since 1988, Ramon Martinez of the Dodgers takes the mound against Pedro Martinez of the Expos in Montreal. Pedro goes nine innings, allowing six hits and fanning 12, but loses, 2-1. Ramon strikes out seven, allows only three hits and gets credit for the victory with a save from Todd Worrell.

AUGUST 30:

The Yankees reacquire third baseman Charlie Hayes (.248, 10 homers, 62 RBI), who played for them in 1992. In return, the Pirates get a player to be named later.

SEPTEMBER 2:

Yankee David Cone, whose career was in jeopardy because of an aneurysm less than four months ago, returns to the mound in storybook fashion, pitching seven innings against the Athletics in Oakland, allowing no hits and no runs. In his first start since May 2, Cone gets credit for a 5-0 victory, throwing only 85 pitches. He fans six and allows three walks. Reliever Mariano Rivera yields an infield single by Jose Herrara in the ninth inning.

Manager Joe Torre explains why he lifted Cone, "I didn't want the no-hitter dictating my decision. There's no question I made the right decision."

Mike Greenwell of the Red Sox drives in all of his team's runs in a 9-8 victory over the Mariners in Seattle. Greenwell breaks the previous major league record of eight set by George Kelly of the New York Giants in 1924 and tied by Bob Johnson of the Philadelphia Athletics in 1938. Greenwell accomplishes the feat with four of his team's seven hits — a two-run homer, a grand slam, a two-run double and a game-winning single in the 10th. Seattle's Alex Rodriguez hits his 35th homer of the season.

SEPTEMBER 4:

Ellsworth "Babe" Dahlgren, who replaced Lou Gehrig at first base in 1939, dies at 84 in Arcadia, California. Dahlgren, who played 12 seasons with eight teams and batted .261, once said, "I'm just glad to be remembered at all."

SEPTEMBER 6:

At Baltimore's Camden Yards, Eddie Murray connects against Felipe Lira of the visiting Tigers in the seventh inning for his 500th career homer. Murray becomes the 15th player in history to join the "500 Club." He is the first to reach 500 since Mike Schmidt in 1987. The switch-hitting Murray has 357 homers left-handed and 143 from the right side of the plate. He also is one of only three players with 500 homers and 3,000 hits; Willie Mays and Hank Aaron are the others. Murray's homer ties the game, but the Tigers go on to win, 5-4, in 12.

Brett Butler, fighting throat cancer, makes a dramatic return with the Dodgers, walking and scoring the winning run in a 2-1 victory over the Pirates in Los Angeles. The 39-year-old has undergone two operations and 32 radiation treatments.

SEPTEMBER 7:

John Smoltz registers his 21st win of the season as the Braves

TRIVIA

In his column in the October 6 *New York Daily News*, Bill Gallo reports that the classic line attributed to Joe Trimble describing the 1956 perfect World Series game by Don Larsen — "Yesterday the imperfect man pitched the perfect game" — was actually written by sportswriter Dick Young. According to Gallo's account, Young typed out the sentence in 20 seconds when Trimble was stuck for a lead.

SEPTEMBER 16
Paul Molitor has his 3,000th hit and 200th season hit.

beat the Mets, 6-1, in Atlanta. He pitches a complete game, allowing seven hits and striking out 13. Jermaine Dye and Javier Lopez homer for Atlanta. Bobby Jones gets the loss.

SEPTEMBER 10:

Brett Butler's courageous comeback from throat cancer ends for the season — and perhaps forever — when he suffers a broken hand while bunting in the fourth inning against the visiting Reds. Butler is struck on the left hand by a pitch from Giovanni Carrara, which is called a foul ball by homeplate umpire Bill Hohn. The Dodgers win, 5-4.

SEPTEMBER 12:

Yankees' outfielder Bernie Williams, blossoming into a genuine superstar, drives in eight runs on two homers and a single in a 12-3 win over the Tigers in Detroit. Williams is batting .300 with 26 roundtrippers and 91 RBI. David Cone works seven innings for his sixth win of the season.

Ellis Burks of the Rockies steals his 30th base, becoming the 19th player in history with 30 stolen bases and 30 homers. Burks connected for his 37th roundtripper of the season with two on in the first against losing pitcher John Smoltz as Colorado topped visiting Atlanta, 16-8.

SEPTEMBER 13:

He may look like a hockey goalie, but underneath the cage-like mask, it's veteran Charlie O'Brien of the Blue Jays. O'Brien introduces a new wrinkle in equipment — a hockey-style catcher's mask that protects the sides, top and back of his head and offers improved peripheral vision. The new gear costs some $1,200 and weighs 47.9 ounces; the standard mask is 38 or 39.

SEPTEMBER 14:

Mark McGwire becomes the 13th player to hit 50 homers in a season when he connects off Chad Ogea in the first inning with a runner on. But, the Athletics lose, 9-8, to the Indians in the nightcap of a double-header in Cleveland. McGwire, hampered by injuries, has appeared in only 119 of his team's 150 games. Albert Belle bashes his 46th of the year in the game. In the opener, also won by Cleveland, 9-2, McGwire hit his 49th, matching his personal best set in 1987.

At Shea Stadium, Todd Hundley of the Mets hits his 41st homer of the season, setting a new major league record for catchers. The previous mark was set by the late Roy Campanella in 1953. Hundley's landmark four-bagger comes in the seventh inning on an 0-2 pitch from Greg McMichael of the Braves with two on. The Mets win the game, 6-5, in 12 innings.

SEPTEMBER 15:

Mark Parent hits a three-run homer in the third inning off Todd Van Poppel of the Tigers, giving the Orioles 241 homers for the season — a major league record. Brady Anderson hits his 46th of the season, Cal Ripken connects twice and Bobby Bonilla bangs a grand slam in a 16-6 victory. Baltimore finishes the game with a total of 243; the previous record was held by the 1961 Yankees.

Barry Bonds is closing in on his father, Bobby. The younger Bonds steals his 30th base today to go with his 39 homers. He is now a four-time member of the "30-30" Club; his father accomplished the feat a record five times. Barry's landmark steal comes in the fifth inning of the nightcap with the visiting Pirates' Rich Loiselle on the mound and Keith Osik behind the plate. Pittsburgh wins the game, 11-9, in 10 innings.

SEPTEMBER 16:

Paul Molitor of the Twins becomes the 21st major leaguer with 3,000 career hits. Molitor, 40 years old, collects his landmark safety — a fifth inning triple off Jose Rosado — in a 6-5 loss to the Royals in Kansas City. In the seventh, Molitor gets his third hit of the game — a single off Bob Scanlan. He adds a sacrifice fly and an RBI to his night's work. He is the first major leaguer with 200 hits in the same season he reached 3,000 hits. His teammate Chuck Knoblauch records his 1,000th career hit in the game.

SEPTEMBER 17:

Hideo Nomo accomplishes what many baseball experts regarded as impossible; he pitches a no-hitter in batter-friend-

TRIVIA

Paul Molitor's 3,000th hit comes exactly three years to the day that Dave Winfield collected his. Both players were born in St. Paul, attended the University of Minnesota and played for the Twins at the tail end of their careers.

Presidential candidate Bob Dole salutes Hideo Nomo's achievment, stating "The Brooklyn Dodgers had a no-hitter last night."

HISTORY

Greg Vaughn, traded from the Brewers to the Padres in midseason, becomes the first player with 100 RBI in the same season playing in two leagues. He finishes with 117.

ly Coors Field. The 28-year-old, Japanese righthander walks four and ends the game by fanning his eighth — Ellis Burks. The Los Angeles Dodgers play errorless ball, beating Colorado, 9-0. Bill Swift is the loser.

Jim Leyland, regarded as one of baseball's best, announces he will step down as manager of the Pirates at the end of the season. Twice the NL Manager of the Year, he won three Division titles. The 51-year-old has been frustrated by the team's failure to keep stars like Barry Bonds, Bobby Bonilla, Doug Drabek, and Denny Neagle. Leyland plans to seek a new position with a pennant contender.

SEPTEMBER 18:

Red Sox' righthander Roger Clemens fans 20 Tigers to tie his own major league mark. Clemens set the record on April 29, 1986, against the Mariners. Tonight, in Detroit, he limits the Tigers to four hits en route to a 4-0 victory. Clemens records his 20th strikeout in the ninth, fanning Travis Fryman, swinging. Utilizing pinpoint control — no walks — Clemens whiffs every Tiger, victimizing Fryman four times and Tony Clark three. He now is 10-12 on the season and has 2,562 career strikeouts.

The Yankees drive another nail into the Orioles' coffin with a 3-2 victory. Rookie Ruben Rivera bats in the winning run in the 10th.

SEPTEMBER 19:

Baseball still has no labor agreement. The owners' chief labor negotiator, Randy Levine, and the Players Association leader, Donald Fehr, meet in New York without completing a prospective settlement.

SEPTEMBER 21:

In the first inning in Chicago, Frank Thomas hits his 40th home run, but strikes out with two on in the seventh as the Twins top the White Sox, 4-3. Thomas has 10 roundtrippers in his last 11 games and has reached the 40-homer mark three times in his seven-year career.

The International Baseball Association approves the participation of professional baseball players in the next summer Olympic Games, to be played in Sydney, Australia, in 2000.

SEPTEMBER 22:

Mark McGwire reaches two milestones against the Mariners in Seattle. He hits two roundtrippers in the fifth inning — a solo 473-foot shot off Bob Wolcott and a 481-foot grand slam against Matt Wagner — bringing his season total to 52. No player since Roger Maris hit 60 in 1961 has had as many homers. And, McGwire becomes the 30th major leaguer ever to homer twice in an inning. Oakland outlasts Seattle, 13-11.

In the opener of a double-header, Barry Larkin of the Reds homers against the Cardinals' Donovan Osborne, giving him 30 for the season. He is the first shortstop ever with 30 roundtrippers and 30 stolen bases in the same season. Howard Johnson, then with the Mets, is the only other infielder in the "30-30 Club." The Reds sweep the visiting Cardinals, 6-3, and, 6-0.

The Braves clinch the NL East title with an 8-2 win over the visiting Expos. John Smoltz works eight innings, allowing 5 hits and fanning 10 for his 23rd win. Atlanta will be appearing in post-season play for the fifth time in the last 6 years.

SEPTEMBER 24:

The Cardinals defeat the Pirates, 7-1, in Pittsburgh to wrap up the NL Central title. Gary Gaetti homers for the winners and Andy Benes gets the win, his 18th of the season.

Dan Jones of Towson, Maryland, sells Eddie Murray's 500th home run ball to the founder of Psychic Friends Network, Michael Lasky. The price originally was reported to be a record $500,000, but in reality Lasky is forking over $280,000 which will be put into a 20-year annuity.

The Murray ball, which ends up in Baltimore's Babe Ruth Museum, is not the most expensive piece of sports memorabilia to change hands this month. On September 21, Christie's Fine Art Auctioneers sold a 1910 T-206 Honus Wagner baseball card to an anonymous buyer for more than $580,000.

SEPTEMBER 25:

The Yankees bash the visiting Brewers, 19-2, on 20 hits to wrap up the AL East title. Tino Martinez drives in five runs with three hits including a home

SEPTEMBER 16
Roger Clemens strikes out 20 in a single game to tie his own record.

SEPTEMBER 22
Barry Larkin records 30 homers and 30 stolen bases in the same season.

run. Tim Raines also homers for New York. The winner is David Cone, who allows four hits and two runs while fanning six in six innings. The Yankees win the nightcap as well, 6-2.

SEPTEMBER 26:

Terry Steinbach hits a sixth inning inside-the-park homer against Jaimie Moyer of Seattle, giving the Athletics their 241st roundtripper of the season. Oakland is the second team this season to top the Yankees' 1961 record. The Athletics also win the game, 7-5. The Seattle Mariners subsequently top the 240 mark as well.

Leading the onslaught for the A's is Mark McGwire, who is rapidly establishing himself among the game's most prodigious long-ball hitters – right there with Babe Ruth and Hank Aaron. He will play in 130 games in '96, during which he hits a team-best 52 homers and ties the record he'd set the year before with one home run every 8.13 at-bats. He also becomes only the 14th player in history to hit 50 or more homers in a season – and the first to do it in fewer than 600 plate appearances.

FROM THE SPORTING NEWS SELECTS BASEBALL'S 100 GREATEST PLAYERS: "(MARK) MCGWIRE... IS A HOME RUN WAITING TO HAPPEN. HE DOESN'T JUST HIT THE BALL OUT OF THE PARK WITH QUIET CONSISTENCY – HE HITS SEAT-SEEKING MISSILES THAT GENERALLY REGISTER 450 FEET OR MORE ON BASEBALL'S TAPE MEASURE."

SEPTEMBER 29:

Hal Morris ends the season with his 29-game consecutive-hitting streak intact – the longest in the majors this season – with a single against Eric Ludwick of the Cardinals in the first.

REGULAR SEASON WRAP-UP:

The Yankees, managed by the quiet and professional Joe Torre, finish the regular season at 92-70 in the AL. They are led by three young players — outfielder Bernie Williams (.305, 29 homers, 102 RBI), rookie shortstop Derek Jeter (.314, 10 homers, 78 RBI), and pitcher Andy Pettitte (21-8, 3.87 ERA) — along with first baseman Tino Martinez (.292, 25 homers, 117 RBI). Mariano Duncan hits .340 and Paul O'Neill chips in at .302. Cecil Fielder and Darryl Strawberry, both acquired during the season, provide punch. The bullpen is anchored by Mariano Rivera (8-3, 2.09 ERA, five saves) and John Wetteland (2-3, 2.83 ERA, 43 saves).

Under Bobby Cox, the Braves finish at 96-66 in the NL and boast a fearsome starting staff. John Smoltz emerges as the ace with a 24-8 record, a 2.94 ERA and 276 strikeouts. Tom Glavine is 15-10 with a 2.98 and Greg Maddux in an "off year" is 15-11, with a 2.72 ERA. Chipper Jones bats .309 with 30 homers and 110 RBI, followed by Marquis Grissom at .308 with 23 homers and 74 RBI. Fred McGriff adds 28 homers and 107 RBI to his .295 average. Ryan Klesko (34 homers) and Javier Lopez (23 homers) are additional sources of power.

A major league record 17 players hit 40 or more homers in 1996, topping the previous mark of eight established in 1961. Lance Johnson of the Mets is the first player to lead both the NL and AL in hits.

SEPTEMBER 30:

Two managers — Kevin Kennedy of the Red Sox and Jim Fregosi of the Phillies — are fired. Boston finished third in the AL East at 85-77. Philadelphia, 67-95, was last in the NL East.

OCTOBER 1:

NL Division Series. The Cardinals break on top with a 3-1 win over the Padres in St. Louis. Gary Gaetti's

HISTORY

For the fourth time ever, two players top the 50-homer mark in a season. Mark McGwire of the Athletics with 52 and Brady Anderson of the Orioles with 50 join Hank Greenberg and Jimmie Foxx (1938), Ralph Kiner and Johnny Mize (1947) and teammates Roger Maris and Mickey Mantle (1961) in the record book. In his previous best home run season, 1992, Anderson hit 21 and had 72 for his career starting this season.

The Yankees' Derek Jeter is Rookie of the Year.

HISTORY

On October 5, umpire John Hirschbeck accepts Roberto Alomar's apology, stating, in part, "I wish to state publicly that I forgive Roberto Alomar for his actions. I am sure that he wishes as much as I do that this incident had never occurred...I ask everyone who loves baseball...to join us in reconciling our differences, and in restoring mutual respect in and for the great game of baseball." Alomar responds, in part, "I hope this puts everything behind us. I hope I can meet with him and his family to tell him how sorry I was that this happened."

first inning homer off losing pitcher Joey Hamilton accounts for all of St. Louis' runs. Todd Stottlemyre gets the win.

AL Division Series. The visiting Rangers top the Yankees, 6-2. John Burkett gets the win. Juan Gonzalez and Dean Palmer homer in the fourth off loser David Cone.

AL Division Series. In a game delayed 17 minutes because the umpires arrived late after postponing a boycott, Baltimore hammers the visiting Indians, 10-4. The umpires threatened a boycott to protest the failure of AL president Gene Budig to punish Roberto Alomar immediately. Replacement umpires were on hand in three playoff cities but were not needed. Bobby Bonilla hits a grand slam. David Wells gets the victory; Charles Nagy is charged with the loss.

OCTOBER 2:

NL Division Series. The Braves edge the Dodgers, 2-1, in 10 innings in Los Angeles. John Smoltz goes nine innings, allowing four hits for the win. Javier Lopez' homer against reliever Antonio Osuna provides the winning run.

AL Division Series. The Yankees pull even with a 12-inning, 5-4, victory over the visiting Rangers. Derek Jeter, who opened the 10th with a single, scores the winning run when third baseman Dean Palmer throws away Charlie Hayes' sacrifice bunt attempt. Brian Boehringer gets the win in relief; Mike Stanton is charged with the loss.

AL Division Series. The Orioles go up two games to none with a 7-4 victory over the Indians in Baltimore. Cal Ripken Jr. scores the winning run on a throwing error by catcher Sandy Alomar in the eighth inning. Armando Benitez gets the win with a save from Randy Myers. Eric Plunk is the loser.

OCTOBER 3:

NL Division Series. In St. Louis, the Cardinals top the Padres, 5-4, to lead two games to none. Brian Jordan scores the winning run from third when Tom Pagnozzi's nubber bounces off pitcher Trevor Hoffman's glove. Rick Honeycutt, 44 years old, gets the win with a save from Dennis Eckersley, who is 42 today.

NL Division Series. The Braves edge the Dodgers, 3-2, in Los Angeles on solo homers by Fred McGriff, Ryan Klesko and Jermaine Dye. Greg Maddux works seven innings, allowing three hits for the win. Ismael Valdes gets the loss.

Gene Lamont is named manager of the Pirates, succeeding Jim Leyland. The 49-year-old Lamont faces a major personnel problem: new owner Kevin McClatchy has decreed a reduction of $18 million in player payroll for 1997.

OCTOBER 4:

From the broadcast booth to the dugout. Former major league pitcher Larry Dierker, who has been the color analyst for the Astros, is named the team's field manager. He is the 12th manager in the team's history since it began play in 1962.

AL Division Series. Albert Belle bashes a grand slam homer in the seventh inning in Cleveland, to pacing the Indians to a 9-4 win over the Orioles. Paul Assenmacher gets the victory in relief; Jesse Orosco is charged with the loss. Manny Ramirez also homers for Cleveland; B. J. Surhoff has a roundtripper for Baltimore.

AL Division Series. In game three, the visiting Yankees come from behind, scoring twice in the ninth for a 2-1 victory over the Rangers. Mariano Duncan's single scores Tim Raines with the lead run, making a losing pitcher of Darren Oliver. Jeff Nelson gets the win in relief. Juan Gonzalez hits his fourth home run of the series in a losing effort; Bernie Williams reaches the seats for New York.

Jim Leyland signs a five-year contract to manage the Marlins. The former Pirates' manager selected Florida over the White Sox, Red Sox and Angels. Reportedly, he will earn some $1.5 million a year. Says the 51-year-old, "It blows my mind. I was in baseball 18 years before I made $20,000."

While Leyland is getting rich, Terry Collins is getting fired by the Astros after an 82-80 season and a second place finish in the NL Central Division. He is replaced by the team's color analyst and former major league pitcher Larry Dierker.

P72
DEREK JETER
LOUISVILLE SLUGGER

OCTOBER 9
The Yankees win game one of the ALCS on a fan interference play.

HISTORY

Bob Watson of the Yankees becomes the first African-American general manager to guide a team to a World Series championship.

In Philadelphia, U. S. District Judge Edmund W. Ludwig prevents major league umpires from striking during the playoff games to protest the "Roberto Alomar incident." The umpires have a no-strike clause in their contract and Judge Ludwig explains, "To not grant an injunction would cause irreparable harm to the ballclubs." But, he adds, "I agree with much of the arguments made on behalf of the umpires...I understand their authority and dignity is at stake. These umpires are the best. In a way, it is a compliment to them to issue the restraining order."

Acting commissioner Bud Selig states, "We're going to have a summit meeting in November, after the World Series, to establish codes of conduct so the Roberto Alomar incident never happens again."

In another courtroom, former major league outfielder Sam Jethroe, has his suit to obtain pension benefits dismissed by a U. S. District Judge Sean McLaughlin. Jethroe, now 79, was the NL Rookie of the Year in 1950 at the age of 33. Under existing rules, he is not eligible for a pension or medical benefits despite three-plus years in the majors. Since 1980, players qualify after only one day.

OCTOBER 5:

AL Division Series. In Texas, Bernie Williams homers twice and the Yankees rope the Rangers, 6-4, to take their series three games to one. Cecil Fielder's RBI single in the seventh breaks a 4-4 tie and negates a homer by the Rangers' Juan Gonzalez — his record tying fifth of the series. David Weathers gets the win with a save from John Wetteland. Roger Pavlik is the loser.

NL Division Series. The Braves top the Dodgers, 5-2, in Atlanta to sweep their playoff series. Tom Glavine gets the win and hits a key double in a fourth inning rally. Chipper Jones homers for the winners. Hideo Nomo is the losing pitcher.

NL Division Series. Brian Jordan homers with one on in the ninth to give the Cardinals a 7-5 victory and a sweep of the Padres. T. J. Mathews gets the win with a save by Dennis Eckersley. Trevor Hoffman is the loser.

AL Division Series. Roberto Alomar, who might have been serving a suspension instead of playing ball, homers for the Orioles against Jose Mesa, giving his team a 4-3, 12-inning win over the Indians in Cleveland. Baltimore moves into the ALCS to face the Yankees. Alomar had tied the game with a two-out RBI single in the ninth off Mesa. Armando Benitez gets the victory; Mesa is the loser.

OCTOBER 9:

ALCS, game one. Bernie Williams connects on a 1-1 fastball from Randy Myers in the bottom of the 11th to give the Yankees a 5-4 win over the Orioles. But Williams' heroics are overshadowed by a 12-year-old who reaches over the left-field fence in the eighth inning, interfering with Baltimore right-fielder Tony Tarasco's attempt to catch a drive off the bat of Derek Jeter. It is ruled a homer, enabling the Yankees to tie the game, 4-4. Mariano Rivera, New York's fourth pitcher, gets the win; Myers is the loser. Brady Anderson and Rafael Palmeiro homer for the Orioles.

The New York media make a hero of the youngster — Jeffrey Maier of Old Tappan, New Jersey — despite the fact that he interfered illegally with play. The boy appears on news and talk shows, is characterized as a "Yankee hero" and arrives at Yankee Stadium for the next game in a limousine, the guest of a local tabloid.

NLCS, game one. The Braves beat the Cardinals, 4-2, in Atlanta. John Smoltz gets the win with a save from Mark Wohlers; reliever Mark Petkovsek is the losing pitcher.

OCTOBER 10:

NLCS, game two. The Cardinals, on a five-run seventh inning, defeat the Braves, 8-3, in Atlanta. Gary Gaetti hits a grand slam for St. Louis; Marquis Grissom connects for Atlanta. Todd Stottlemyre allows four hits in three innings for the win; Greg Maddux is charged with the loss.

ALCS, game two. Baltimore beats the Yankees in New York, 5-3, tying the playoffs. The key hit is Rafael Palmeiro's two-run homer in the seventh off reliever and loser Dave Nelson, breaking a 2-2 tie. David

"These umpires are the best. In a way, it is a compliment to them to issue the restraining order."
– District judge Edmund W. Ludwig

Wells gets the victory. David Cone, starts for the Yankees, allowing five hits and five walks, while fanning five in six innings.

OCTOBER 11:

ALCS, game three. After AL president Gene Budig denies the Orioles protest over game one, Baltimore bows to the visiting Yankees, 5-2. Budig says, "The Orioles are mistaken in their attempt to characterize the play in question as involving anything other than an umpire's judgment." Winning pitcher Jimmy Key works eight strong innings, allowing three hits. Matt Mussina gets the loss. The Yankees four-run eighth, including a Cecil Fielder homer — gives them another come from behind win.

OCTOBER 12:

ALCS, game four. The Yankees edge closer to their first AL pennant in 15 years with an 8-4 win over the Orioles in Baltimore; they now lead three games to one. Darryl Strawberry homers twice; teammates Bernie Williams and Paul O'Neill connect once each. David Weathers gets the win; Rocky Coppinger the loss.

NLCS, game three. The Cardinals make it two in a row, beating the Braves, 3-2, in St. Louis. Ron Gant homers twice against his former teammates; both blows are struck off starter and loser Tom Glavine. Donovan Osborne gets the victory.

OCTOBER 13:

ALCS, game five. The visiting Yankees oust the Orioles and take the AL pennant with a 6-4 win. New York builds its victory on a six-run third inning marked by a solo homer by Jim Leyritz, a three-run blast by Cecil Fielder and a 448-foot drive by Darryl Strawberry. Winner Andy Pettitte allows three hits in eight innings. Scott Erickson gets the loss. Baltimore wastes four-baggers by Todd Zeile, Bobby Bonilla and Eddie Murray.

NLCS, game four. In St. Louis, the Cardinals nip the Braves, 4-2, to move within a game of the NL pennant. Brian Jordan homers for the winners and Dennis Eckersley, with an inning and a third of hitless relief, is credited with the victory. Greg McMichael is charged with the loss. Mark Lemke and Ryan Klesko homer for Atlanta.

OCTOBER 14:

NLCS game five. The Braves bounce back – big time – with a 14-0 blowout of the Cardinals on an LCS record 22 hits. John Smoltz gets the win; Todd Stottlemyre is tagged with the loss. Fred McGriff homers and bats in three runs; Javier Lopez also has a roundtripper. The Series now shifts to Atlanta.

OCTOBER 16:

NLCS game six. Playing before a home crowd in excess of 52,000, the Braves knot the Series with a 3-1 victory. Greg Maddux gets the win; Alan Benes is charged with the loss.

OCTOBER 17:

NLCS, game seven. The Braves crush the Cardinals, 15-0, to take the NL pennant. Fred McGriff, Javier Lopez, and Andruw Jones homer as the Braves parlay 17 hits and strong pitching by winner Tom Glavine into the pennant. Donovan Osborne gets the loss.

OCTOBER 20:

World Series, game one. After the winds and rain of a nor'easter cause a one-day delay, the Braves blow out the Yankees, 12-1, in New York. Andruw Jones, 19 years old, becomes the youngest player to homer in World Series history when he connects with a runner on in the second inning against loser Andy Pettitte. Mickey Mantle was 20 when he established the previous record. For good measure, Jones hits a three-run roundtripper in the third off Brian Boehringer. The Braves collect 13 hits to support strong pitching by John Smoltz, who no-hits New York for five innings and gets the win.

OCTOBER 21:

World Series, game two. The Braves head home up two games to none after trouncing the Yankees, 4-0, tonight. Greg Maddux shows his old form with eight innings of six-hit ball. He strikes out three and issues no walks. Mark Wohlers relieves in the ninth and fans the side. The major damage is inflicted by Fred McGriff with two hits and three RBI. He now has a major league record 15 RBI in this year's post-season play. Jimmy Key gets the loss.

TRIVIA

Despite the matchup of the Braves — "America's team" — and the Yankees — arguably sports' greatest franchise — the 1996 World Series is the third least-watched in history and the lowest in terms of percentage of television sets in use.

"It wasn't about money."
– Albert Belle, on his five-year, $55 million contract.

TRIVIA

Watching game five from his bed at Columbia-Presbyterian medical center in New York is Joe Torre's number one fan — his brother Frank. A former major leaguer himself, Frank is recuperating from heart transplant surgery.

OCTOBER 22:

World Series, game three. The Yankees strike back, beating the Braves on their home field, 5-2. David Cone works six innings, allowing four hits and a run for the victory, with a save from John Wetteland. Tom Glavine is charged with the loss. Bernie Williams homers and drives in three runs for New York.

OCTOBER 23:

World Series, game four. The Yankees even the Series with a dramatic two-run rally in the 10th for an 8-6 victory. Jim Leyritz ties the game with a homer against Mark Wohlers in the eighth as the Braves blow a 6-0 lead. New York scores twice in the 10th — on a bases loaded walk and an error. Graeme Lloyd gets the victory with another save from John Wetteland. Steve Avery, the fifth of six Atlanta pitchers gets the loss. Fred McGriff has a homer for Atlanta.

The 1954 AL Rookie of the Year, Bob Grim, dies of a heart attack at 66 after throwing snowballs with children in his Shawnee, Kansas, neighborhood. He was 20-6 in 1954, his debut season with the Yankees. Grim compiled a career record of 61-41 with a 3.61 ERA.

OCTOBER 24:

World Series, game five. In 1864 Yankee General William Tecumseh Sherman left Atlanta in flames. In 1996, the Yankees baseball team leaves the City and its baseball team in a state of shock. With a nailbiting 1-0 victory today, the Bronx Bombers head home one game from the championship after a sweep of the three contests in Atlanta. The game's only run comes in the fourth on a Cecil Fielder double scoring Charlie Hayes. Andy Pettitte allows five hits in eight-and-a-third innings; John Wetteland finishes up and earns a save. John Smoltz allows four hits and fans 10 in eight and is the hardluck loser.

OCTOBER 26:

World Series, game six. After 18 years, the World Championship banner flies over Yankee Stadium again. The Yankees win their fourth straight against the Braves, in a 3-2 nail-biter, scoring all of their runs in the third, with Joe Girardi's RBI triple the key hit. Starter Jimmie Key allows five hits in seven and two-thirds innings and gets the win with a save by John Wetteland. Greg Maddux is charged with the loss. Wetteland, with four saves and a 2.08 ERA, is the Series' Most Valuable Player. Marquis Grissom bats .444 for the losing Braves. Cecil Fielder leads the Yankees with a .391 average. Teammates Darryl Strawberry and Derek Jeter each drive in six runs. During the celebration, Wade Boggs takes a victory lap around the ballpark riding on a horse behind a mounted New York City police officer.

The Yankees won every post-season road game en route to their 23rd championship. But there is a question clouding the celebration — will George Steinbrenner move the Yankees out of their historic home in the Bronx?

POST-SEASON

OCTOBER 28:

Three veterans change addresses. The Reds acquire outfielder-DH Ruben Sierra (.247, 12 homers, 78 RBI) from the Tigers for two minor leaguers — outfielder Decomba Conner and pitcher Ben Bailey. It is Sierra's fourth trade in 11 years. And, the Angels obtain pitcher Mark Gubicza (4-12, 5.13 ERA) from the Royals for DH Chili Davis (.292, 28 homers, 95 RBI). Albert Belle of the Indians is one of 17 players filing for free agency.

OCTOBER 29:

Former major league pitcher Ewell "The Whip" Blackwell dies at 74 of cancer in Hendersonville, North Carolina. On June 22, 1947, Blackwell yielded a one out single in the ninth to Eddie Stanky of the Dodgers, ending his bid for a second straight no-hitter. He pitched a June 18 no-hitter against the Braves.

OCTOBER 30:

Terry Francona is named manager of the Phillies, replacing Jim Fregosi. The 37-year-old Francona was the team's third base coach this past season.

OCTOBER 31:

Cuba issues a warning to players who may be thinking of defecting to the United States. The Government suspends three top stars because they were involved with a Cuban-American sports agent. The affected players are shortstop German Mesa, pitcher Orlando "El Duque" Hernandez, and catcher Alberto Hernandez.

Despite Cuba's crackdown, on November 4 four more of its players defect during a baseball tournament in Mexico.

NOVEMBER 2:

Toni Stone, the first female to play professional baseball at a big league level, dies of heart failure at 75 in Alameda, California. Stone played second base with the Indianapolis Clowns in the Negro Leagues in 1953 and later with the Kansas City Monarchs. At the time of her debut, she was listed as 22, but was really 32. She played in men's amateur leagues until she was 60.

NOVEMBER 4:

Terry Collins, 47 years old, is named the new skipper of the Angels.

NOVEMBER 6:

When is an agreement not an agreement? When the Lords of Baseball need to ratify it. There is still no peace in the ongoing war between management and players. The owners reject the collective bargaining agreement by a tally of 18-12; 23 votes were needed for ratification. The agreement was reached by owners' negotiator Randy Levine and the head of the players' union, Donald Fehr. Acting commissioner Bud Selig asserts Levine never reached an agreement with the union. Says Randy Levine, "I was hired to reach an agreement with Don Fehr. I did." An attempt to make the rejection unanimous fails, and the owners will seek concessions from the players. Donald Fehr and the Players Association say "no." According to the *New York Times*, Levine is expected to resign his position.

NOVEMBER 13:

With a .326 batting average, 40 homers, and 139 RBIs, third baseman Ken Caminiti becomes the first San Diego Padre to be named MVP. He is also only the fourth player to win the award unanimously, following Jeff Bagwell (1994), Mike Schmidt (1980) and Orlando Cepeda (1967).

The Giants trade slugging third baseman Matt Williams (.302, 22 homers, 85 RBI in 105 games) to the Indians for infielders Jeff Kent and Jose Vizcaino along with pitcher Julian Tavarez (4-7, 5.36 ERA). The two infielders split the 1996 season between the Mets and the Indians. Kent batted .290 with New York and .265 with Cleveland; Vizcaino's averages were .303 and .285.

NOVEMBER 19:

"It wasn't about money," says the tempestuous Albert Belle after he becomes the highest-paid player in the game by signing at five-year, $55 million contract with the White Sox. Playing with the Indians last season, Belle batted .311 with 48 homers and a league-leading 148 RBI.

Jimy Williams becomes manager of the Red Sox. Williams compiled a three-plus season record of 281-241 with the Blue Jays. He replaces Kevin Kennedy.

The California Angels change their logo and their name; henceforth they are the Anaheim Angels.

NOVEMBER 25:

Another money record falls after a month. Tampa Bay signs Waynesboro, Pennsylvania, high school pitcher for a record $10.2 million bonus. The 18-year-

Tony Gwynn of the Padres gets the NL batting crown, hitting .353.

NOVEMBER 27
The owners finally approve a collective bargaining agreement.

DECEMBER 13
Roger Clemens turns down the Yankees for a deal with the Blue Jays.

HISTORY

One day after shortstop Derek Jeter of the Yankees is selected as the AL's Rookie of the Year, outfielder Todd Hollandsworth of the Dodgers wins the honor in the NL. Hollandsworth is the fifth Dodger in a row to be named Rookie of the Year. Previously selected were: Eric Karros, Mike Piazza, Raul Mondesi, and Hideo Nomo.

old had a 0.65 ERA. White tops Travis Lee who was signed last month by Arizona for a "mere" $10 million.

NOVEMBER 27:

The owners reverse course yet again. By a vote of 26-4 they approve the collective bargaining agreement, which includes a 2.5 percent payroll tax on the 1996 and 1997 rosters. Included in the agreement is a revenue sharing provision with the 13 highest earning teams funding the 13 lowest (Colorado and Florida, the newest teams, are exempt for two years). In 1997 and 1998, there will be a "luxury tax" of 35 percent for teams with payrolls of $51 million or more. In 1999, the tax will drop to 34 percent and there will be none for the 2000 and 2001 seasons. Dissenting votes are cast by four AL teams — Chicago, Cleveland, Kansas City, and Oakland. Murray Chass of the *New York Times* calls Randy Levine, the owners' chief executive, the "MVP."

The Mets trade first baseman Rico Brogna (.255, seven homers in 55 games) to the Phillies for pitchers Ricardo Jordan (2-2, 1.80 ERA) and Toby Borland (7-3, 4.07 ERA). In a separate transaction, the Mets acquire pitcher Armando Reynoso (8-9, 4.96 ERA) from the Rockies for pitcher Jerry DiPoto (7-2, 4.19 ERA).

DECEMBER 5:

Jim Leyritz, who batted .375 with a clutch homer in the 1996 World Series, is traded by the Yankees to the Angels for players to be named later. In 88 regular season games, Leyritz batted .264 with seven homers and 40 RBI.

In return for Leyritz, the Yankees receive two minor leaguers — third baseman Ryan Kane and pitcher Jeremy Blevins.

DECEMBER 6:

Atlanta and Seattle swap pitchers. Sterling Hitchcock (13-9, 5.35 ERA) goes to the Braves; Scott Sanders (9-5, 3.38 ERA) to the Mariners.

DECEMBER 8:

Two days after becoming a free agent, pitcher Jimmy Key signs a two-year, $7.8 million contract with the Orioles. Key also will receive $80 thousand in living expenses. With the Yankees this past season, he was 12-11 with an ERA of 4.68.

DECEMBER 12:

Moises Alou (.281, 21 homers, 96 RBI) leaves his manager father and the Expos to sign a five-year, $15 million contract with the Florida Marlins.

DECEMBER 13:

Cy Young Award-winner Roger Clemens turns down $32 million of George Steinbrenner's money to sign a $24.75 million, three-year deal with the Blue Jays. Clemens slumped to 10-13 with a 3.63 ERA this past season for the Red Sox. Pittsburgh and Kansas City complete a five-player deal, and four are named Jeff. The Pirates ship two key players — third baseman Jeff King (.271, 30 homers, 111 RBI) and shortstop Jay Bell (.250, 13 homers, 71 RBI) to the Royals for four players: third baseman Joe Randa and three pitchers named Jeff: Granger, Martin, and Wallace. Granger was 0-0 with a 6.61 ERA; Martin and Wallace have no major league experience.

DECEMBER 15:

Yankee relief ace John Wetteland, the 1996 World series MVP, signs a four-year, $23 million contract with the Rangers. During the regular season, Wetteland was 2-3 with a 2.83 ERA and a league-leading 43 saves. In the World Series, he saved all four Yankee victories and compiled a 2.08 ERA.

DECEMBER 17:

The free-living David Wells gets fitted for pinstripes. The left-hander signs a three-year contract with New York worth $13.5 million. With the Orioles this season, Wells was 11-14 with a 3.99 ERA and has a career record of 90-75.

DECEMBER 18:

In perhaps his last stop before Cooperstown and the Hall of Fame. Eddie Murray signs on with the Angels. Murray has 501 career homers and 3,218 safeties (11th among the all-time hit leaders). With the Orioles in 1996, he batted .260 with 22 homers and 79 RBI.

DECEMBER 20:

The Mets obtain first baseman John Olerud (.274, 18 homers, 61 RBI), the AL's 1993 batting champion, from the Blue Jays for minor league pitcher Robert Preston.

DECEMBER 17
The Yankees get David Wells from the Orioles.

THE BEST OF 1996

NATIONAL LEAGUE

HITTERS

Batting Average:
Tony Gwynn, San Diego Padres, .353

Slugging Average:
Ellis Burks, Colorado Rockies, .639

Home Runs:
Andres Galarraga, Colorado Rockies, 47

Runs Batted In:
Andres Galarraga, 150

Hits:
Lance Johnson, New York Mets, 227

Stolen Bases:
Eric Young, Colorado Rockies, 53

PITCHERS

Wins:
John Smoltz, Atlanta Braves, 24

Strikeouts:
John Smoltz, 276

Earned Run Average:
Kevin Brown, Florida Marlins, 1.89

Winning Percentage:
John Smoltz, .750

Saves:
Jeff Brantley, Cincinnati Reds; Todd Worrell, Los Angeles Dodgers, 44

Most Valuable Player:
Ken Caminiti, San Diego Padres

Cy Young Award:
John Smoltz, Atlanta Braves

Rookie of the Year:
Todd Hollandsworth, Los Angeles Dodgers

Manager of the Year:
Bruce Bochy, San Diego Padres

AMERICAN LEAGUE

HITTERS

Batting Average:
Alex Rodriguez, Seattle Mariners, .358

Slugging Average:
Mark McGwire, Oakland Athletics, .730

Home Runs:
Mark McGwire, 52

Runs Batted In:
Albert Belle, Cleveland Indians, 148

Hits:
Paul Molitor, Minnesota Twins, 225

Stolen Bases:
Kenny Lofton, Cleveland Indians, 75

PITCHERS

Wins:
Andy Pettitte, New York Yankees, 21

Strikeouts:
Roger Clemens, Boston Red Sox, 257

Earned Run Average:
Juan Guzman, Toronto Blue Jays, 2.93

Winning Percentage:
Jamie Moyer, Boston Red Sox/ Seattle Mariners, .813

Saves:
John Wetteland, New York Yankees, 43

Most Valuable Player:
Juan Gonzales, Texas Rangers

Cy Young Award:
Pat Hentgen, Toronto Blue Jays

Rookie of the Year:
Derek Jeter, New York Yankees

Manager of the Year:
Johnny Oates, Texas Rangers; Joe Torre, New York Yankees

1997

NEWS

AN ADULT SHEEP IS CLONED BY SCOTTISH SCIENTISTS

Unmanned U.S. spacecraft lands on Mars

EL NIÑO UNSETTLES WEATHER WORLDWIDE

TIMOTHY MCVEIGH CONVICTED OF MURDER FOR 1995 OKLAHOMA CITY BOMBING; SENTENCED TO DEATH

Diana, Princess of Wales, dies in auto accident

NOBEL LAUREATE MOTHER TERESA DIES

21-YEAR-OLD TIGER WOODS IS YOUNGEST EVER TO WIN U.S. MASTERS TOURNAMENT

GIANNI VERSACE MURDERED OUTSIDE HIS SOUTH BEACH MANSION

PRE-SEASON

JANUARY 11:

Former AL umpire Jerry Neudecker, whose chest protector is in the Baseball Hall of Fame, dies at 66 in Fort Walton Beach, Florida. Neudecker was the last major league umpire to wear the balloon chest protector, which was replaced by more effective protection; a "grandfathering" arrangement in the rules permitted him to continue waering it.

JANUARY 15:

The Padres establish a working relationship with the Chiba Lotte Mariners baseball team in Japan. The arrangement includes the exclusive negotiating rights to pitcher Hideki Irabu, a 27-year-old right-hander who averaged a strikeout per inning in his nine-year career.

The Yankees object to the Padres-Chibe Lotte agreement and indicate they may protest, launching a long, convoluted battle for the rights to Irabu.

JANUARY 19:

The owners, in attempt to redress an old injustice, create a pension plan that covers 90 black players who either were not in the majors long enough to qualify for a pension or were unable to play in the majors because of the color line. The plan will cost the owners $10 million and will provide each of the players with approximately $10,000 a year. Among those covered are Sam Jethroe, the first black to play for the Boston Braves; Buck O'Neill; and Lyman Bostick Sr. The owners study possible expansion of the pension plan to include players who retired before the color barriers came down, in 1947.

JANUARY 20:

Curt Flood, whose landmark lawsuit changed the business of baseball forever and brought about free agency, dies of throat cancer at 59 in Los Angeles, California. Flood, an outfielder, played 15 years with the Reds, Cardinals, and Washington Senators. His lifetime average was .293.

Earlier in the year, on the first day of the 105th Congress, Representative John Conyers (D-MI) paid tribute to Flood when he used the outfielder's uniform number – 21 – on an antitrust bill. Said Conyers, "We all owe a debt of gratitude for his willingness to challenge the baseball oligarchy." The bill, HR 21, would remove baseball's antitrust exemption.

JANUARY 22:

"Donnie Baseball" hangs up his spikes after a 14-year career. Yankees' first baseman Don Mattingly, once considered a sure thing for the Hall of Fame until he was plagued by chronic injuries, leaves with a .307 lifetime batting average, 222 homers, and 1,099 RBI.

Mattingly, considered one of the game's finest fielders, led the AL in batting in 1984 with a .343 average.

JANUARY 27:

Outfielder-DH Jose Canseco returns to the Athletics from the Red Sox for pitcher John Wasdin (8-7, 5.96 ERA) and cash. Canseco appeared in only 96 games in Boston, hitting .289 with 28 homers and 82 RBI.

FEBRUARY 14:

Orioles' pitcher Matt Mussina (19-11, 4.81 ERA) gets the highest

Mariners' manager Lou Piniella says of Ken Griffey Jr., his star, "He's the best player I've ever seen."

one-year salary ever – $6.8 million – in a case that seemed headed for arbitration.

FEBRUARY 25:

Cal Abrams dies of a heart attack at 72 in Tamarac, Florida. Abrams, a native of Brooklyn, was a Dodgers' outfielder for more than three seasons and is best remembered as the Dodger runner thrown out at the plate in the final season game that gave the Phillies the 1950 NL pennant. Abrams, who will be buried in his number 18 Dodger uniform, also played for the Reds, Pirates, Orioles, and White Sox, compiling a .269 average.

Roger Clemens wins 21 games for the Blue Jays.

FEBRUARY 27:

The Major League Baseball Executive Council rules that the Padres are the only team that can negotiate with Japanese pitching star Hideki Irabu.

FEBRUARY 28:

Federal District Court Judge Lewis Kaplan rules in New York that Bud Selig, who has been running baseball for more than four years, is not the commissioner. Legally, he is only chairman of the Executive Council, because he has not been appointed or elected to the commissioner's post. The ruling comes in a suit by a minor league team for territorial compensation from the Florida Marlins.

"There is a vacancy in the commissioner's office," says the judge, echoing the opinion of many in the sport.

MARCH 2:

The Yankees conclude a $90-$95 million, 10-year sponsorship deal with Adidas. The deal is negotiated by the Yankees without the involvement of Major League Baseball. A portion of the proceeds will be given to charity. According to Richard Sandomir of *the New York Times,* the deal "places the Yankees on a possible collision course with Major League Baseball Enterprises."

MARCH 15:

The five-year collective bargaining agreement is signed by both the owners and the players' representatives. Bud Selig – who may or may not be "acting" commissioner – says, "This marks the beginning of a true renaissance and golden era for the game."

MARCH 25:

The Braves send outfielders David Justice (.321, six homers, 25 RBI in 40 games) and Marquis Grissom (.308, 23, homers, 74 RBI) to the Indians for the best leadoff batter in baseball, Kenny Lofton (.317, 75 stolen bases), and relief pitcher Alan Embree (1-1, 6.39 ERA).

MARCH 27:

The Braves make their second trade in three days, shipping

HISTORY

Rangers' catcher Ivan "Pudge" Rodriguez is signed to the highest one-year contract ever – $6.65 million. In 1996, Rodriguez hit .300 with 19 homers and 86 RBI.

LEAGUE

Compensating for the early opening day, schedule-makers have slated 10 of 12 of the April 1 games in either warm-weather cities or domed stadia.

CULTURE

The season begins with two ballparks renamed to reflect their commerical backers: the stadium formerly known as Oakland-Alameda County Coliseum is now UMAX, and the Angels' home park, Anaheim Stadium, is now Edison International.

outfielder Jermaine Dye (.281, 12 homers, 37 RBI) and minor league pitcher Jamie Walker to the Royals for outfielder Michael Tucker (.260, 12 homers, 53 RBI) and infielder Keith Lockhart (.273, seven homers, 55 RBI).

MARCH 30:

Will they be drinking warm beer and eating bangers and mash? Beginning April 1, British television viewers will be able to see American major league baseball every Sunday and Wednesday at midnight. The games, beginning with the Mets visiting the Padres on April 1, will be aired on Channel 5, Britain's new third commercial channel.

THE SEASON

APRIL 1:

Ken Griffey Jr. makes his presence felt with home runs in his first two at-bats of the season against losing pitcher David Cone, as the Mariners down the Yankees, 4-2. Griffey has three RBI and Russ Davis also homers off Cone. Jeff Fassero gets the win.

The Padres down the Mets in San Diego, 12-2, with an 11-run sixth inning. Highlighting the monster rally are consecutive homers by Chris Gomez, Rickey Henderson, and Quilvio Veras – all off Pete Harnisch. Oddly, Harnisch escapes the loss; it is charged to Yorkis Perez, who arrived from the minors 30 minutes before game time. Joey Hamilton gets the win.

The Marlins successfully debut $89 million worth of new talent, beating the Cubs, 4-2, in Miami. Moises Alou, one of their new stars, slams a 388-foot homer and Kevin Brown limits Chicago to one hit in seven innings. Terry Mulholland is the loser.

APRIL 2:

Tino Martinez cracks three homers to lead the Yankees to a 16-2 win against the Mariners. Martinez is the 16th Yankee with three round-trippers in a game. Andy Pettitte is the winning pitcher; Scott Sanders takes the loss.

Gary Sheffield (.314, 42 homers, 120 RBI) of the Marlins gets a six-year contract extension worth $61 million. Cal Ripken, the Orioles iron man, gets two years with an option for a third and $15.1 million in guaranteed salary.

APRIL 3:

Big Mac is on the board. Mark McGwire connects off Orel Hershiser in a 5-4 win over the Indians in Oakland. McGwire adds a double and Geronimo Berroa hits his second round-tripper in two days for the Athletics. The winning pitcher is Richie Lewis; Eric Plunk is tagged with the loss.

APRIL 4:

The Braves open at their new Turner Field (named after the team's owner) with a 5-4 victory over the Cubs. Michael Tucker hits his first home run in the third inning. Brad Clontz gets the win; Terry Adams is the loser.

APRIL 5:

Another superstar gets a contract extension. The Padres' Tony Gwynn signs a three-year pact worth $12.6 million, guaranteeing he will be with the team through the year 2000, when he will be 40 years old. One of baseball's quiet heroes, Gwynn has a lifetime average of .337.

APRIL 6:

At the Kingdome, Ken Griffey Jr. slams a home run for the third consecutive day as the Mariners top the Red Sox, 8-7, in 10. Griffey now has five roundtrippers in five games. Alex Rodriguez also homers for Seattle.

The Braves top the Cubs, 4-0, in only one hour, 47 minutes, the shortest game in the majors in five years. Greg Maddux limits Chicago to three hits in eight innings. Terry Mulholland gets the loss. The Braves also win, 11-5, in the conclusion of a game suspended last night.

The visiting Cardinals lose to the Astros, 3-2, falling to 0-6, their worst start in 106 seasons. Jeff Bagwell provides the winning margin with a two-run double in the eighth inning. The Cardinals and Cubs are the only teams without victories in the young season.

APRIL 7:

Roberto Alomar returns after a five-game suspension for spitting on an umpire last season, and is introduced to a chorus of boos from a Kansas City crowd of 40,052. But the boos turn to cheers when he makes an outstanding catch in the second inning. The home crowd goes home happy, as the Royals beat Alomar's Orioles, 6-5.

APRIL 8:

At Wrigley Field, the Cubs blow a lead and lose to the Marlins, 5-3, lowering their record to 0-7 – the team's worst start in 122 years. The Cubs are done in by a two-out, two-run double in the seventh by Charles Johnson. Steve Trachsel gets the loss and falls to 0-2; Al Leiter is the winner, improving to 2-0. Florida is now 6-1, the best record in the majors.

APRIL 10:

Deion Sanders alters his Reds' uniform as a tribute to Jackie Robinson and gets a warning from NL senior vice president Katy Feeney. Neon Deion, who cut the sleeves off his uniform and wore his pants knee-length after seeing Robinson's picture on a Wheaties box, says, "I'm just trying to honor a man who has given a lot to this game."

The next day, Sanders' Cincinnati teammates decide to emulate his alterations so the team's uniforms are indeed uniform, circumventing Feeney's decree.

RACHEL ROBINSON TELLS THE CROWD – MORE THAN DOUBLE THE ATTENDANCE AT EBBETS FIELD FOR ROBINSON'S DEBUT – "THIS ANNIVERSARY HAS GIVEN US AN OPPORTUNITY AS A NATION TO CELEBRATE TOGETHER THE TRIUMPHS OF THE PAST AND THE SOCIAL PROGRESS THAT HAS OCCURRED. IT HAS ALSO GIVEN US AN OPPORTUNITY TO ASSESS THE CHALLENGES OF THE PRESENT. IT IS MY PASSIONATE HOPE THAT WE CAN TAKE THIS REAWAKENED FEELING OF UNITY AND USE IT AS A DRIVING FORCE SO THAT EACH OF US CAN RECOMMIT TO EQUAL OPPORTUNITY FOR ALL AMERICANS."

APRIL 11:

Mark McGwire unloads a 464-foot homer into the centerfield section of Yankee Stadium to defeat New York, 3-1. Big Mac's mammoth blast comes off a Mariano Rivera fastball in the ninth inning; he is only the 13th player to reach that section of the stadium.

APRIL 13:

If they played every day, the Braves might be 162-0 and the Cubs 0-162. Atlanta deals Chicago yet another loss at Wrigley Field, 6-4. The Cubs commit three errors and fall to 0-10, tying Atlanta's 1988 low mark. The all-time NL record – 0-11 – was set by the Detroit Wolverines in 1884. The major league record is 0-21, by the 1988 Orioles.

APRIL 15:

A crowd of 54,047 packs Shea Stadium to mark the 50th anniversary of Jackie Robinson's major league debut with the Brooklyn Dodgers. Commissioner Bud Selig announces that Robinson's number, 42, will be permanently retired on all major league teams. Jesse Robinson

HISTORY

Regrets are on the way–more than 50 years late. Whitey Eckstein, city commissioner of Sanford, Florida, is working on an apology to Jackie Robinson for what he describes as "a stain on our soul." Eckstein is referring to action by city officials when Robinson appeared with the Montreal Royals in an exhibition game against the Brooklyn Dodgers. The Sanford chief of police arrived at the game after Robinson had played two innings and ordered him off the field. "It was a bad thing," Eckstein says. "We shouldn't have done it. We need to make it right with the Jackie Robinson family."

The crowd at Shea Stadium in New York honors the 50th anniversary of Jackie Robinson's Dodger debut.

PAN AM
GAGNE
SHARP
FROM SHARP MINDS COME SHARP PRODUCTS
The New Dodge
14
41
358
BUD LIGHT
371
GAP
396
PRIORITY MAIL
1947
50
BREAKING BARRIERS

FINLAY
WICKED COOL SPORTS STUFF.
THE SPORTS AUTHORITY
He was the handsome, heroic giant of our youth who taught us determination, taught us perseverance and, finally, he taught us justice.
Budweiser
DODGERS
METS
BALL STRIKE OUT
GREG GAGNE
AVG HR RBI
Armitron
DODGERS
METS
IT'S A NEW YORK THING. DEMAND IT!
CHASE
diet Coke
396
371
358
GAP
NEW YORK METS

APRIL 20
The Cubs finally win one, breaking their losing streak at 14 games.

APRIL 25
The Indians connect for eight home runs against the Brewers.

APRIL 30
Joe Torre manages the Yankees to his 1,000th win.

LEAGUE

The St. Paul Saints – a promotion-minded minor league team – invite a woman to training camp. She is pitcher Ila Borders, who was 4-5 with a 5.22 ERA for Whittier College.

HISTORY

Rangers' catcher Ivan "Pudge" Rodriguez is signed to the highest one-year contract ever – $6.65 million. In 1996, Rodriguez hit .300 with 19 homers and 86 RBI.

Simms, Jackie Robinson's grandson, throws out the ceremonial first pitch. Looking on are President Bill Clinton, Rachel Robinson (Jackie Robinson's widow), Branch Rickey III (president of the American Association and grandson of the Brooklyn Dodgers' executive who brought Robinson to the majors), Ralph Branca, Joe Black, Larry Doby (the AL's first black player), Frank Robinson (baseball's first black manager), Lou Brock, Sandy Koufax, and Reggie Jackson. Umpiring behind the plate is Eric Gregg, the highest-ranking African-American official in all of pro sports.

In a game that is almost anticlimactic, the Mets top the Dodgers, 5-0. Armando Reynoso is the winner; Ismael Valdes gets the loss.

How low can they go? The Cubs lose again in Wrigley Field, this time to the Rockies, 10-7. Colorado hits five homers with Larry Walker connecting twice and winning pitcher Mark Thompson, Quinton McCracken, and Dante Bichette once each. Kevin Foster is charged with the loss. Chicago is now 0-11, the worst NL start in this century.

APRIL 20:

It's bad news and then some good for the Cubs. After extending their record losing streak to 14 with an 8-2 drubbing by the Mets, Chicago comes back to take the nightcap, 4-3, at Shea Stadium.

Mark McGwire becomes the fourth player in history to homer over the left-field roof at Tigers Stadium. McGwire's homer, his sixth of the season, is hit off Brian Moehler. But Detroit wins the game, 9-2.

APRIL 22:

George Steinbrenner gets his man – the six-foot, three-inch, 240-pound Japanese righthander Hideki Irabu. After Irabu refuses to negotiate with any team other than the Yankees, the Padres trade the negotiating rights to Irabu along with three minor leaguers – second baseman Homer Bush and outfielders Gordon Amerson and Vernon Maxwell – to New York. In return, San Diego receives $3 million and two minor leaguers – outfielder Ruben Rivera and pitcher Rafael Medina. The deal requires the approval of baseball's executive council.

Irabu reportedly throws in the 94 to 97 mph range and has been compared to Roger Clemens and Nolan Ryan.

The principals in last year's spitting incident, Roberto Alomar and umpire John Hirschbeck, shake hands in Baltimore prior to a 3-2 Orioles victory against the White Sox. Alomar approaches Hirschbeck, who is umpiring at first, before the game.

APRIL 25:

In Milwaukee, Cleveland's bats are booming. The Indians connect for eight home runs – a team record – routing the Brewers, 11-4. Matt Williams homers three times; David Justice, twice, and Sandy Alomar, Manny Ramirez, and Chad Curtis, once each. Three Brewers – Dave Nilsson, Jeromy Burnitz, and John Jaha – also homer, tying a major league record for the most round-trippers in a nine-inning game. Orel Hershiser is the winner; Scott Karl gets the loss.

APRIL 26:

Matt Williams follows yesterday's three-homer outburst with two more today, tying a major league record, but the Brewers beat the visiting Indians, 9-8.

APRIL 30:

Yankees' manager Joe Torre gets his 1,000th career win as the Yankees edge the Mariners, 3-2. Bobby Cox and Tony LaRussa are the only other active managers with 1,000 victories.

The tape-measure crew is working overtime at Jacobs Field, where Mark McGwire hits a 485-foot home run off Orel Hershiser in the third inning and follows with a 459-foot shot off losing pitcher Jose Mesa in the 10th. The Athletics beat the Indians, 11-9, with Billy Taylor getting the victory.

Larry Walker homers for Colorado to tie an NL record – 11 round-trippers in the month of April. His average is now .456. The Rockies top the Cubs, 11-5, in Colorado.

MAY 1:

Pedro Martinez continues his dominating pitching. The Expos'

MAY 8
The Brewers beat the Athletics in the longest nine-inning game ever.

MAY 25
Ken Griffey Jr. and Mark McGwire keep pounding out the home runs.

right-hander three-hits the Astros, 4-0, fanning nine. Martinez now has 25 consecutive shutout innings and a dazzling ERA of 0.31. Darrin Fletcher provides the offensive spark with a homer and an RBI double.

MAY 6:

Frank Robinson, baseball's first black manager, returns to the game as director of baseball operations for the six-team Arizona Fall League and as a consultant to the commissioner for special projects. The Hall of Famer has been out of baseball since the end of 1995.

MAY 8:

The Brewers beat the visiting Athletics, 1-0. The game takes three hours, 20 minutes to play, making it the longest nine-inning contest in major league history (topping the May 17, 1988, face-off between the Mets and the Padres). Jeff Cirillo's single in the seventh scores Jeromy Burnitz for the only run.

Mike Lansing hits two homers and Henry Rodriguez connects for a grand slam as the Expos bury the Giants, 19-3. Montreal scores 13 runs in the sixth and 17 players bat, setting an NL record and tying the major league mark. Jeff Juden improves to 3-0.

MAY 12:

Jimmy Key of the Orioles ups his record to 7-0 with a 5-1 win over the Athletics. Key gives up no walks and fans none as he lowers his ERA to 1.82. Key has the best record in the majors.

MAY 13:

George Steinbrenner gets slapped with yet another suspension. This time he is booted from baseball's executive committee for "blatant" violation of the Major League Agreement. Steinbrenner also is removed from baseball's important realignment committee. The suspension stems from his deal with Adidas and an antitrust suit the Yankees' principal owner filed against baseball.

Eddie Murray plays in his 3,000th game.

MAY 18:

Pedro Martinez ups his record to 7-0 with a 7-4 win over the Dodgers in Montreal. Martinez works seven innings, strikes out seven, and yields three earned runs. His ERA climbs from 0.70 to 1.20. Mike Lansing has five hits, including a homer for the winners.

Sammy Sosa homers twice to lead the Cubs to a 5-2 victory over the Giants at Wrigley Field. Sosa now has 100 homers with the Cubs, placing him 10th on the team's all-time leader list.

MAY 21:

Roger Clemens' 200th career win is a gem. The big right-hander beats the Yankees in New York, 4-1, yielding only four hits and striking out 12 in eight innings. Clemens is now 8-0 with a 1.86 ERA; his career record is 200-111.

The sad story of Lorenzo "Piper" Davis comes to an end when the one-time Negro Leagues star and manager dies at 79 of a heart attack in Birmingham, Alabama. As skipper of the Birmingham Black Barons, Davis helped to develop Willie Mays. As in infielder, Davis played in the Negro Leagues with such superstars as Satchel Paige, Josh Gibson, and Cool Papa Bell.

Davis was on the verge of a career breakthrough when, in 1950, he was the first black player signed by the Red Sox. He was assigned to a Class A team, and although leading the club in batting average, homers, RBI, and stolen bases, he was cut. The official explanation? "Economical reasons." Bad grammar, and a worse excuse.

MAY 23:

In the NL, Pedro Martinez racks up his eighth win against no losses, as the Expos beat the Pirates, 4-1. Martinez allows five hits and fans 12, including nine of the first 13 batters he faces.

The Indians beat the Orioles and hand Jimmy Key his first defeat of the season. Led by David Justice and Manny Ramirez with three hits each, Cleveland wins its sixth straight. Justice is now batting .384.

MAY 25:

"Junior" Griffey collects homer number 22, a first inning blast against the Royals' Glenden Rusch. But Chili Davis' round-tripper in the bottom of the 11th gives the Royals a 4-3 win over the Mariners.

Mark McGwire continues to pound the

LEAGUE

The Yankees have the major leagues' top payroll – in excess of $58 million.

LEAGUE

In the anniversary year of Jackie Robinson's debut in the major leagues, a commemorative baseball will be used by every team in its home opener.

MAY 26
Sammy Sosa and Tony Womack hit-inside-the park homers in the same innings.

JUNE 10
Kevin Brown of the Marlins no-hits the Giants.

RULES

Interleague play is being conducted following fairly complicated rules. Eastern and Central Division teams will play 15 interleague games, but Western Division teams will play 16. There will be 214 interleague games total played between June 12 and June 18, between June 30 and July 3, and between August 28 and September 3. The DH rule will be in force in AL ballparks, but not in NL stadiums. NL umpires will work in their league's home parks and AL umpires in AL parks. Statistics and records compiled during interleague play will be counted just as they would in any other game.

ball, but he is being overshadowed by Ken Griffey. McGwire connects for his 16th against Bob Tewksbury in a 7-6 Athletics loss in Minneapolis.

MAY 26:

Sammy Sosa hits an inside-the-park homer in the top of the sixth, and the Pirates' Tony Womack responds with one of his own in the bottom of the inning. It is the first time since 1976 that opposing players have hit inside-the-parkers in the same inning. Chicago wins the game, 2-1.

MAY 28:

Pedro Martinez is tagged with his first loss of the season, courtesy of the Mets. New York downs Montreal, 7-0, behind Bobby Jones' four-hit complete game. Jones improves to 9-2. Carlos Baerga homers for New York and Martinez is now 8-1.

MAY 31:

Andres Galarraga clouts one of the longest homers in baseball history - a 529-foot grand slam off the Marlins' Kevin Brown- in the fourth inning and the Rockies win, 8-4. In the eighth inning, Florida reliever Dennis Cook hits Galarraga in the elbow and the slugger is ejected for charging the mound.

Mickey Mantle's 565-foot shot is generally accepted as the longest homer ever.

Roger Clemens improves to 10-0 as the Blue Jays beat the Athletics, 13-3. Clemens allows eight hits in eight innings.

JUNE 7:

The Royals' Chili Davis homers from both sides of the plate for the 10th time in his career, placing him one shy of the major league record set by Eddie Murray. Davis' round-trippers comes in the fifth inning batting right-handed against the Rangers' Darren Oliver, and in the sixth batting lefty against Matt Whiteside. Kansas City beats visiting Texas, 10-4.

JUNE 10:

Kevin Brown of the Marlins pitches a 9-0 no-hitter against the Giants in San Francisco. Only a two-out, 1-2 fastball that hits Marvin Bernard keeps Brown from pitching a perfect game. Brown strikes out seven and walks none, using only 99 pitches for his masterpiece. Charlie Johnson hits a two-run homer in the seventh against losing pitcher William Van Landingham, who carries his own no-hitter into the seventh inning.

JUNE 11:

The Cardinals' Alan Benes retires Tony Gwynn three times and reliever Mark Petkovsek fans the Padres' hitting star in the seventh inning, ending his consecutive game hitting streak at 20. Gwynn finishes the game with a .402 batting average. The visiting Cardinals beat the Padres, 8-3.

JUNE 11:

The Mariners beat the Blue Jays and Roger Clemens, 5-1, ending the big right-hander's winning streak at 11. The big blow is Ken Griffey Jr.'s two-run double. Clemens still leads the Al with a 1.94 ERA.

JUNE 12:

In the first interleague game, the visiting Giants beat the Rangers, 4-3. Stan Javier homers in the first inning against losing pitcher Darren Oliver. Mark Gardner gets the victory. Hall of Famers Willie Mays and Nolan Ryan throw out ceremonial first pitches to mark the historic event.

JUNE 13:

Cancer strikes another major leaguer. Orioles' outfielder Eric Davis, 35, will undergo surgery for colon cancer. Davis may miss the rest of the season, but his surgeons express confidence that he will make a full recovery. Davis was signed by Baltimore as a free agent and is hitting .302 with seven homers and 21 RBI.

JUNE 16:

In the first intra-city interleague games, the visiting Mets beat the Yankees, 6-0, behind Dave Mlicki, and the Cubs beat White Sox, 8-3, at Comiskey Stadium in their first game since the 1906 World Series (other than exhibition contests).

JUNE 17:

The Red Sox lose slugger Mo Vaughn for up to six weeks as he undergoes knee surgery. Vaughn injured his knee in a play at the plate two days ago. He is batting .335 with 20 homer, and 45 RBI.

JUNE 18:

Dennis Martinez, an outstanding major league pitcher for 21 seasons, retires. Known as "El

JUNE 12 The first interleague game is played between the Giants and the Rangers.

JUNE 20 Ken Griffey Jr. hits his 28th homer.

JUNE 24 Mark McGwire smacks home run number 27.

Presidente," Martinez compiled a career record of 241-187. He has been struggling to regain his form with the Mariners, but was released in May after compiling a 1-5 record with an ERA of 7.71.

On July 28, 1991, while with Montreal, El Presidente pitched a perfect game against the Dodgers. Martinez also played for the Orioles and the Indians.

JUNE 20:

Ken Griffey Jr. smacks his major league-leading 28th homer of the season – a fifth-inning grand slam against Bobby Witt of the Rangers in Texas. The Mariners win the game, 5-4. Griffey leads the AL in RBI with 76.

Aaron Boone, grandson of Ray Boone, son of Bob Boone and brother of Bret Boone, – all major leaguers – has a mixed debut with the Reds. Boone, called up from Indianapolis to replace his brother Bret, who was demoted to the AAA team, drives in the winning run as visiting Cincinnati tops St. Louis, 4-2. But after being tagged out in a play at the plate in the sixth inning, Boone slams his batting helmet to the ground and is ejected by umpire Gary Darling. Aaron was hitting .270 in the minors; Brett had a .205 average in the majors.

Luis Gonzales of the Astros singles to extend his hitting streak to 23 games. Houston defeats visiting Chicago, 7-3.

JUNE 21:

Larry Walker and Andres Galarraga both hit their 21st homers as the Rockies rout the Padres, 9-4, in San Diego. Walker is currently batting a torrid .415.

JUNE 24:

Mark McGwire raps out home run number 27 – measured at 538 feet – off losing pitcher Randy Johnson. The visiting Athletics top the Mariners, 4-1. McGwire now has 57 RBI on the season.

One-time Cy Young Award and 30-game winner Denny McLain continues on the road to ruin, beginning a 97-month sentence in a Pennsylvania federal prison. In May, he was convicted of conspiracy, mail fraud, money laundering, and theft of pension plan funds. The 53-year-old previously was in prison on racketeering, gambling, and drug charges. He was released from that sentence in 1987.

JUNE 25:

Ken Griffey Jr. strains his right hamstring in a 9-4 Mariners victory over the Athletics at the Kingdome and is listed as day-to-day. Griffey is the majors' leading home run hitter with 29, and is ahead of Roger Maris's 1961 record pace.

JUNE 27:

The Cubs make Sammy Sosa the third-highest-paid player with a four-year, $42.5 million deal. Only Barry Bonds and Albert Belle out-earn the Cubs' star.

JUNE 28:

Bizarre doings at Yankee Stadium. New York starter David Wells takes the mound wearing a cap said to be Babe Ruth's. The eccentric left-hander reputedly paid $35,000 for the hat, but it remains on his head for only a half inning – in which he allows no hits and one run to the Indians. When manager Joe Torre spots the cap, he orders Wells to remove it and the left-hander gets shelled for eight hits and four more runs in three innings of work. The Indians bounce the Yankees, 12-8, on 19 hits. Kenny Rogers, wearing a regulation cap, gets the loss.

JUNE 30:

It's civil war – baseball style – in Canada as the Toronto Blue Jays entertain the Montreal Expos. For the first time since World War II, when it became customary to play "The Star-Spangled Banner" before every ballgame, the U.S. national anthem is not heard. Instead the anthem is "O, Canada." Pedro Martinez proceeds to stifle the Blue Jays, 2-1, fanning 10 and yielding only three hits. Pat Hentgen gets the loss. Both pitchers go the distance.

The Orioles become the first major league team to sign an African-born player. He is 18-year-old outfielder Ntema Ndungidi, who was born in Zaire but has lived in Montreal since the age of three. He gets a $500,000 contract.

JULY 1:

Randy Myers registers his 300th career

LEAGUE

Baseball's chief honcho, Bud Selig, decrees that there will be no more distribution of free baseballs to fans before the games, after an incident involving his own team, the Brewers. Selig's action comes after fans in a crowd of 42,893 in Milwaukee throw free baseballs onto the field, causing three delays, a protest by the visiting Rangers, and the threat of a forfeit. Milwaukee eventually prevails, with Cal Eldred getting the win. Selig's act prevents free baseball promotions at seven games this week.

Of his "race" with Tino Martinez, Big Mac tells the Associated Press, "Who really cares? Why would that be such a big deal at this point? Why would it matter? I don't play this game for individual accomplishments."

TRIVIA

Writer and former minor league pitcher Pat Jordan, 56 years old, pitches for the Waterbury Spirit in the Northeast League. He becomes the oldest pitcher in a professional game in almost 20 years. Although no precise records are kept for this category, Hub Kittle, who pitched one inning of minor league ball in 1980 at the age of 63, is believed to be the oldest. Hall of Famer Satchel Paige may have been 59 when he appeared for the Kansas City Athletics in 1965. He holds the unofficial major league record.

save as the Orioles beat the Phillies, 4-1. Myers is the third reliever ever with 300 saves.

JULY 5:

One day after a blockbuster trade that would have brought Greg Vaughn to the Yankees from the Padres, the deal is called off because the slugger apparently has a tear in his right rotator cuff. In the now-dead deal, minor league pitchers Kerry Taylor and Chris Clark would have joined Vaughn in New York. The Padres would have received pitcher Kenny Rogers, infielder Mariano Duncan, and minor league pitcher Kevin Henthorne.

JULY 6:

Roger Clemens blanks the Yankees, 2-0, on four hits, earning his 13th win (against only three losses), fanning 10, and lowering his ERA to 1.69.

JULY 8:

AL pitchers limit the NL to three hits for a 3-1 victory in the All-Star Game, played this year in at Cleveland's Jacobs Field. All runs are scored off homers. Edgar Martinez connects with the bases empty off Greg Maddux, and Sandy Alomar hits a two-run four-bagger against losing pitcher Shawn Estes. Javier "Javvy" Lopez takes winning pitcher Jose Rosado deep for the only NL run. Mariano Rivera earns a save with a hitless inning.

JULY 9:

The Royals, 48-58, fire manager Bob Boone and replace him with Cubs' hitting coach Tony Muser. Boone's overall record with Kansas City was 181-206.

JULY 10:

Hideki Irabu wins his first major league game as the Yankees down the Tigers, 10-3, in Detroit. The Japanese right-hander works six and two-thirds innings, allowing 5 hits and 4 walks, while fanning nine.

JULY 11:

Tino Martinez connects for his 30th home run, and winning pitcher Andy Pettitte extends his scoreless inning streak to 22 as the Yankees shut out the Tigers, 3-0, in New York. Pettitte works seven innings; Mariano Rivera records his 28th save.

It's turnabout time as Tony Gwynn out-hits Larry Walker. Gwynn of the Padres has four hits in five at-bats including two homers, boosts his average to .3988, and takes a microscopic lead in the batting race. Walker is held to a single in four at-bats and falls to .3987, but his Rockies top the Padres, 6-5.

A minor league legend passes on. Joe Hauser, who twice hit 60 or more homers in the minor leagues, dies at 98 in Sheboygan, Wisconsin. Hauser hit 63 homers with the Baltimore Orioles of the International League in 1930 and 69 with the Minneapolis Millers of the American Association in 1933. He came up to the majors in 1922 with the Philadelphia Athletics, hit 24 homers in 1925 – second to Babe Ruth's 46 – but a broken kneecap sustained in spring training of 1925 curtailed his career.

JULY 12:

Two pitchers, 10 innings, one no-hitter. The Pirates' Francisco Cordova and Ricardo Rincon combine to close down the Astros, 3-0.

JULY 14:

Bloomberg News Service reports that the Cuban national baseball team has cancelled a U.S. trip because officials are worried about defections. Cuban teams have been playing in the U.S. since 1986 and the current squad was scheduled to begin an eight-game series tomorrow. At least 12 Cuban players have defected to date.

JULY 15:

The Athletics face the Mariners and Mark McGwire outslugs Ken Griffey Jr. Big Mac homers off Jamie Moyer for his 32nd of the year, collects a double and a single and drives in four (bringing his RBI total to 75); Griffey is limited to two singles. McGwire now has 361 career homers, tying him with Joe DiMaggio for 42nd on the all-time leader list.

Lee Smith, the all-time career saves leader with 478, announces his retirement. The 39-year-old Smith was 0-1 with five saves and a 5.82 ERA with the Expos. Smith pitched in the majors for 17 years, beginning in 1980.

JULY 16:

Mark McGwire passes Joe DiMaggio on the all-time home run list

JULY 16 Tino Martinez hits his 33rd home run.

JULY 16 Mark McGwire hits home run number 33 and 34

JULY 31 McGwire is traded to the Cardinals for three pitchers.

when he bangs out two more today in an 11-3 win over the visiting Royals. They are McGwire's 33rd and 34th of the season - topping the Yankees' Tino Martinez for the major league lead – and up his career total to 363.

Tino Martinez keeps the heat on with two more homers – number 32 and number 33 – in an 11-5 win over the White Sox in Chicago.

General manager Joe McIlvaine, generally regarded as the architect of the Mets' resurgence, evident in their 51-41 record, is fired and replaced by his assistant, Steve Philips.

JULY 21:

The Phillies trade catcher Darren Daulton (.264, 11 homers, 42 RBI) to the Marlins for outfielder Billy McMillon (.111 in 13 games).

JULY 22:

Paul Beeston, president and chief executive officer of the Blue Jays, is named baseball's chief operating officer.

JULY 25:

Ken Griffey Jr. ends a 60 at-bat homer drought, connecting against David Wells in New York, as the Mariners top the Yankees, 8-1. It is Griffey's 31st homer of the year.

The Reds fire manager Ray Knight and replace him on an interim basis with 66-year-old Jack McKeon, who becomes the oldest current manager. The Reds were 43-56 under Knight this season. The change has no immediate impact on the teams' fortunes; the Reds lose to the Braves, 7-3, in Cincinnati. Jeff Blauser hits a grand slam – Atlanta's ninth of the season, tying a major league record.

JULY 28:

The Yankees send their $12.5 million pitcher Hideki Irabu to their Class AAA Columbus minor league team. Irabu is 2-2 with a 7.97 ERA.

The New York Times *publishes an editorial on Irabu's demotion, noting, "Not Nolan Ryan, at Least for Now."*

JULY 31:

It's Big Mac to the Golden Arches as Mark McGwire, arguably baseball's premier slugger, changes uniforms. In a blockbuster deal, the Athletics send first baseman McGwire (.284, 34 homers, 81 RBI) to the NL and the Cardinals for pitcher T. J. Matthews (4-4, 2.15 ERA) and two minor league pitchers – Eric Ludwick and Blake Stein.

The Giants acquire pitchers Wilson Alvarez (9-8, 3.03 ERA), Danny Darwin (4-8, 4.13 ERA), and Roberto Hernandez (5-1, 2.44 ERA, 27 saves) from the White Sox for six minor leaguers – shortstop Mike Caruso, outfielder Brian Manning, and pitchers Lorenzo Barcelo, Keith Foulke, Bob Lowry, and Ken Vining.

AUGUST 2:

The Cubs' star second baseman, Ryne Sandberg, announces he will retire at the end of the season. He then hits two homers and drives in three runs to lead Chicago past visiting Los Angeles, 5-1.

AUGUST 3:

With 35 members in attendance, the National Baseball Hall of Fame inducts pitcher Phil Niekro, Negro Leagues star Willie Wells, manager Tom Lasorda, and infielder Jacob "Nellie" Fox. Niekro is currently managing the Silver Bullets, a women's professional team, and many Silver Bullet players are present. Niekro, a knuckleballer, pitched 24 years with the Braves, Yankees, Indians, and Blue Jays, compiling a 318-274 record and an ERA of 3.35. He was a five-time All-Star and pitched a no-hitter against San Diego on August 5, 1973. Nellie Fox died in 1975 and his widow, Joanne, is at the ceremony. Fox played 19 years with the Philadelphia Athletics, the White

TRIVIA

A total of 19 percent of players on opening-day rosters – are foreign-born, hailing from 147 countries. The Dominican Republic, with 57, leads the list.

Livan Hernandez of the Marlins is World Series MVP.

Stella Wells tells the Cooperstown audience that another Negro Leagues great, Cool Papa Bell, informed her that he was going to ask that he be replaced by Willie Wells in the Hall of Fame. She adds, "Well, I hope you and Dad are smiling down on us because the Antelope is in."

LEAGUE

The first round of interleague play is judged to be a success. Attendance for the games is up 35 percent with records set in Chicago, New York, and Seattle. Cumulatively, the 84 games attracted 2,933,407 fans, with the Mariners the top home attraction. The AL won 48 games to the NL's 36. The Red Sox, Giants, and Expos were the most successful on the field at 5-1; the Angels, Cardinals, Padres, Phillies, and Tigers were 1-5. Rusty Greer of the Rangers hit .591; The Royals' Jeff King and the Dodgers' Eric Karros hit four homers each.

Sox, and the Astros, batting .288 and winning the AL's Most Valuable Player Award in 1959. He struck out only 216 times in 9,232 at-bats. Wells, who died in 1989, is represented by his daughter, Stella. He played shortstop for 20 years with the St. Louis Stars, the Chicago American Giants, and the Newark Eagles, batting .331. In 1929, he hit 27 homers in only 88 games and in 1930, he hit .403. Lasorda managed the Dodgers for 20 years, beginning in 1977. Along with Connie Mack, John McGraw, and Walter Alston, he is the only man to manage the same team for 20 or more years. He compiled a 1,599-1,439 record, winning eight NL West titles, four NL pennants, and two World Series championships.

AUGUST 7:

The Rocket notches his major league-leading 17th win, a 4-0 victory over the visiting Indians. Roger Clemens allows only five hits and three walks, fans 10, and lowers his ERA to 1.69. It is his 40th career shutout.

Ken Griffey Jr. homers against Scott Eyre and the Mariners beat the White Sox, 3-2, in Seattle. It is Griffey's 34th of the season and he raises his RBI total to 103.

AUGUST 8:

Randy Johnson whiffs 19 as Seattle beats Chicago, 5-0. He is the first pitcher to strike out 19 batters twice in one season. Johnson allows five hits and walks three. His win-loss record improves to 16-3 and his ERA to 2.35.

The Mets and Cubs complete a six-player deal. Going to New York are 30-year-old relief pitchers Mel Rojas (0-4, 4.42 ERA, 13 saves) and Turk Wendell (3-5, 4.20 ERA, four saves) and switch-hitting outfielder Brian McRae (.240, six homers, 28 RBI). In return, Chicago gets outfielder Lance Johnson (.297, one homer, 21 RBI), infielder Manny Alexander (.248, two homers, 15 RBI), and pitcher Mark Clark (8-7, 4.25 ERA).

McRae makes his Mets debut with 3 hits in 4 at-bats, two runs scored, and a running catch in centerfield. The Mets top the Astros, 6-1, behind Brian Bohanon.

Mark McGwire hits his first NL homer as the Cardinals down the visiting Phillies, 6-1. McGwire's homer comes off Mark Leiter in the first inning.

AUGUST 9:

Pedro Martinez records his major league-leading 12th complete game, four-hitting the visiting Giants, 2-1. He fans eight and walks two. The Expos ace is now 14-5 with an ERA of 1.72

A Mariners rookie makes his major league debut in Seattle and almost pitches his way into the record books. Ken Cloude has a perfect game in the sixth and a no-hitter into the seventh, but ends up with a loss, when Chicago tops Seattle, 5-2. Dave Martinez's leadoff single in the seventh ends Cloude's dream.

David Wells and the Yankees defeat Brad Radke and the Twins, 4-1, ending the pitcher's winning streak at 12.

AUGUST 10:

The Braves re-sign their pitching ace, Greg Maddux, to a five-year, guaranteed $11.5 million contract, making him baseball's highest-paid player. He squeezes past the Giants' Barry Bonds for the honor–by $50,000. To date this season, Maddux is 15-3 with a 2.36 ERA.

AUGUST 12:

Roger Clemens and the Blue Jays fell the Twins, 9-1, in Toronto. Clemens fans 13, allows 8 hits, walks one, and becomes the majors' first 18-game winner this season, while lowering his ERA to 1.66 – also a major league best. Clemens also boosts his career strikeout mark to 2,805, the 12th best in history.

AUGUST 13:

Sammy Sosa hits his 26th home run of the season as the Cubs beat the Giants, 6-5, in San Francisco. Sosa also hits a two-run double. After Jeff Kent is hit with a pitch by winning pitcher Jeremi Gonzalez, the Giants' second baseman and Cubs' catcher Tyler Houston get into a wrestling match and are ejected.

Anaheim obtains 38-year-old outfielder Rickey Henderson (.274, six homers,27 RBI, 29 stolen bases) from the Padres for three minor leaguers – pitchers Ryan Hancock and Stevenson Agosto

AUGUST 8
Randy Johnson strikes out 19 for the second time this season.

AUGUST 9
Pedro Martinez four-hits the Giants in his 12th complete game

plus a player to be named later. Henderson is the all-time stolen base leader with 1,215.

Former Brooklyn Dodgers' pitcher Rex Barney, who no-hit the Giants in 1948, dies at 72 in Baltimore, Maryland. Barney was the public address announcer for the Orioles for the past 25 years. Barney, known for outstanding "stuff" and control problems, was 35-31 with an ERA of 4.34 for his six-year career with Brooklyn.

In a touching tribute to Barney, no public address announcer works the Orioles home game against the Athletics.

AUGUST 16:

Greg Maddux – aided by Fred McGriff's two-run homer – tops the Cardinals, 5-3, in St. Louis. The Braves' right-hander survives a three-run opening frame by the Cardinals and is now 16-3. Matt Morris gets the loss.

AUGUST 17:

Ken Griffey Jr. hits his 39th and 40th homers of the season in the opener of a twin bill against the White Sox in Chicago. Griffey raises his season RBI total to 114.

The Marlins' Moises Alou hits his 100th career homer – a three-run blast off losing pitcher Steve Cooke – and drives in 5 runs in a 10-2 win over the visiting Pirates.

AUGUST 18:

Billy McMillon and Mike Lieberthal each hit grand slam home runs as the Phillies flatten the Giants, 12-3, in Philadelphia. They are the first Phillies teammates to hit grand slams in the same game in 75 years.

AUGUST 22:

Big Mac launches two super-sized homers–his 40th and 41st. The Cardinals top the Marlins, 7-3, in Florida and Mark McGwire assumes the major league leadership in home runs. The first of today's shots – off Tony Saunders – measures some 500 feet; the second – against Robb Nen – travels approximately 462 feet.

AUGUST 23:

Ken Griffey Jr. hits his 41st homer, but the visiting Yankees marinate the Mariners, 10-8, on Paul O'Neill's two-run double in the 11th inning.

"EVERY MISTAKE I THROW, (GRIFFEY) HITS A HOME RUN. THAT DOESN'T SEEM FAIR. HE CAN AT LEAST MIX IN A DOUBLE EVERY ONCE IN A WHILE."
– David Cone

AUGUST 27:

Mike Piazza hits his 30th and 31st homers of the season and drives in six runs to lead the Dodgers past the Pirates in Pittsburgh, 9-5. Piazza becomes the first Dodger since Duke Snider to register thirty homers or more in three successive years. Dennis Reyes gets the win.

AUGUST 28:

Two Colorado records are set today as the Rockies beat the Mariners, 9-5. In the sixth inning, Rockies' first baseman Andres Galarraga launches a 487-foot homer – the longest in the history of Coors Field and his 35th of the season. He is cheered by a crowd of 50,269, the largest in Rockies' history. Junior Griffey is hitless in three official at-bats.

AUGUST 30:

Mets' pitcher Pete Harnisch levels a blast at manager Bobby Valentine. Harnisch, who returned to the team earlier this month after recovering from depression, and Valentine had clashed earlier in the team's Baltimore

LEAGUE

Salary arbitration this year proves profitable for the players, although only one of the five arbitrated cases is won by a player; overall the 80 eligible for arbitration received 154 percent in salary increases – the most ever. The previous high was 113 percent in 1981; in 1996 the figure was 71 percent. The sole winner of the five argued cases was pitcher Tim Wakefield of the Red Sox, who was awarded $2.5 million. Boston had offered $1.55 million.

Mets manager Bobby Valentine says of catcher Todd Hundley (who is fighting injuries and family illnesses), "I think he doesn't sleep enough." Hundley responds, "I don't get paid enough to have a relationship with that guy."

HISTORY

Mark McGwire joins Babe Ruth as the only player with back-to-back 50-homer seasons. Five other players have hit 50 homers twice – (four times), Jimmie Foxx, Mickey Mantle, Willie Mays, and Ralph Kiner.

LEAGUE

Ila Borders, the first woman to pitch in the minor leagues, completes her season with Duluth-Superior Dukes in the Northern League. Borders was traded to the Dukes by the St. Paul Saints. Her pitching stats: 14 1/3 innings in 15 games, no wins or losses, 11 strikeouts, nine walks, 24 hits, and a 7.53 ERA. Says Borders, "It was a dream, basically."

hotel. Almost incidentally, the Mets beat the Orioles, 13-6.

The following day Harnisch (0-1, 8.06 ERA) is traded to the Brewers for minor league outfielder Donnie Moore.

The Marlins top the Blue Jays, 4-1, in Toronto, giving Alex Fernandez his 17th win of the year. The Florida pitcher allows three hits in eight innings, with Robb Nen earning a save. Chris Carpenter gets the loss.

AUGUST 31:

Less than a month after Andres Galarraga hit the longest homer in Coors Field history, teammate Larry Walker tops him. Walker slams a 493-foot home run – one of his two on the day – in a 10-4 win over the Athletics. Walker now has 40.

SEPTEMBER 1:

It's numbers 45 and 46 for Ken Griffey Jr. as his Mariners beat the Padres, 9-6. Griffey adds a double and a single to his 2 round-trippers and drives in four runs, bringing his season RBI total to 126.

A controversy brews in Boston. Steve Avery, who needs to make 18 starts to earn a $3.9 million bonus in 1998, is removed from the starting line-up by manager Jimy Williams and sent to the bullpen. Avery has made 17 starts and is 6-6.

The Associated Press reports Avery's reaction: "It seems to me like they're saying, 'You're better off elsewhere next year.' That's fine."

SEPTEMBER 4:

Ken Griffey intensifies his pursuit of Roger Maris's home run record. In Minneapolis, Griffey connects twice for his 47th and 48th of the year as the Mariners beat the Twins, 9-6.

At his current pace, Griffey would hit 55, falling short of Maris's 61.

SEPTEMBER 5:

The troubled Steve Howe is back in court – this time in Kalispell, Montana. Howe, who has been pitching in the independent Northern League, pleads not guilty to drunk driving charges in connection with an August 19 motorcycle accident.

SEPTEMBER 7:

Ken Griffey Jr. moves to within 11 homers of Roger Maris's record when he connects for home run number 50 against winning pitcher Bob Tewksbury in the fourth inning of today's 9-6 loss to the Twins in Minneapolis. Griffey has seven homers in his past six games.

In Colorado, Mark McGwire hits his 14th NL homer – off Pedro Astacio. It is Big Mac's 48th overall – two behind Griffey.

Roger Clemens records his 21st win and another complete game – his ninth – as the Blue Jays beat the Rangers, 4-0, in Toronto. Clemens allows only two-hits and no walks and fans 14. It is the 12th time this season he has fanned 10 or more batters and the 80th in his illustrious career. Clemens finishes the game with a 1.85 ERA.

SEPTEMBER 8:

In Kansas City, Ken Griffey Jr. is limited to a single and the Royals top the Mariners, 9-2. Chili Davis hits his 29th for Kansas City.

SEPTEMBER 9:

Hall of Fame outfielder Richie Ashburn dies at 70 in New York City. Ashburn played 15 years in the majors – 12 with the Phillies, two with the Cubs, and one with the Mets – batting .308 with only 29 homers. A two-time batting champion, Ashburn was a broadcaster for the Phillies at the time of his death.

SEPTEMBER 10:

In San Francisco, Mark McGwire hits a 446-foot third-inning homer off Shawn Estes. It is McGwire's 50th of the season and 16th since coming to the NL. Despite McGwire's heroics, the Giants beat the Cardinals, 7-6.

SEPTEMBER 12:

If Pete Rose applies for reinstatement to baseball, his effort appears doomed to failure. Citing "two high-ranking baseball officials," Murray Chass of the *New York Times* reports that acting commissioner Bud Selig will "never recommend to the ruling executive council that Rose be reinstated."

Marlins' rookie Livan Hernandez is on the short end of a 1-0 score against the Giants and is tagged with his first career defeat. He is now 9-1.

SEPTEMBER 20
Nomar Garciaparra is the first Red Sox rookie with 200 hits since 1942.

SEPTEMBER 22
Ken Griffey Jr. smacks his 54th and 55th home runs.

SEPTEMBER 13:

Strange doings in the bullpen as the Mets top the visiting Expos, 9-6, in 11 innings. Mets' general manager Steve Phillips is watching the game on television when he sees a familiar face sitting next to another familiar face. The first face belongs to Mets' reliever Corey Lidle. The second is his twin brother, Kevin, who is with the Tigers and about to be released, but is wearing a Mets' uniform. The irate Phillips has the trespassing Lidle removed from the bullpen. But did he eject the right one?

SEPTEMBER 14:

Mark McGwire connects against Joey Hamilton of the Padres in the sixth inning in St. Louis for his 51st homer of the season, one short of his personal best. He has now hit 17 homers in 37 games in a Cardinals' uniform. The Cardinals win, 10-4.

SEPTEMBER 15:

The Orioles top the visiting Indians, 6-5, in the first game of a twin bill to capture a playoff spot, but the spotlight is on Eric Davis. The Baltimore right-fielder is back in the lineup for the first time since June when he underwent surgery for colon cancer. Davis is hitless in three at-bats, but gets several standing ovations and says after the game, "That was the best rehabilitation I could ever have had."

SEPTEMBER 16:

Mark McGwire decides he likes St. Louis and signs a three-year, $28.5 million contract with the Cardinals, making him the sixth-highest-paid player in the game. Big Mac celebrates by cracking his 52nd homer in a 7-6 loss to the visiting Dodgers.

The Phillies' Curt Schilling fans Edgardo Alfonzo of the visiting Mets in the fourth inning for his 300th strikeout of the season. He is the 13th pitcher ever to achieve that mark.

SEPTEMBER 17:

Mark McGwire hits his 53rd homer of the season as the Cardinals outslug the Cubs, 12-9, at Wrigley Field. McGwire has 11 games left in which to overtake Roger Maris. The Astros' Jeff Bagwell hits his 41st homer in an 8-4 win over the Pirates in Pittsburgh.
Randy Johnson (17-4, 2.25 ERA, 272 strikeouts) will be in a Mariner uniform for at least one more season as the team exercises its option on the fireballing lefty.

SEPTEMBER 19:

Mark McGwire homers in Pittsburgh to set a new major league record, but it is not Roger Maris's coveted 61. Big Mac becomes the first major leaguer to hit 20 round-trippers in each league in the same season. Today's clout is his 20th in a Cardinals' uniform and his 54th of the season. St. Louis edges Pittsburgh, 6-5, in 11 innings.

Ken Griffey Jr. homers – his 53rd – and the Mariners top the Athletics, 9-4, in Oakland.

SEPTEMBER 20:

Nomar Garciaparra has a single in five at-bats and becomes the first Red Sox rookie with 200 hits since Johnny Pesky in 1942. The White Sox top the Red Sox, 6-4, at Fenway Park.

SEPTEMBER 21:

In Kansas City, the Indians' John Smiley breaks his pitching arm throwing a curve while warming up in the bullpen. The left-hander has been on the disabled list since August 30 because of tendonitis in his shoulder.

Smiley's career ends at 32 after 12 seasons. He is 126-103 with a 3.80 ERA.

SEPTEMBER 22:

Ken Griffey powers past Mark McGwire and takes aim at Roger Maris, with his 54th and 55th home runs. Griffey connects twice off losing pitcher Eric Ludwick of the Athletics – in the fourth inning and again in the fifth. Griffey boosts his RBI total to 145 and the visiting Mariners win, 4-2.

Eddie Sawyer, who managed the 1950 Phillies Whiz Kids to a World Series, dies in Phoenixville, Pennsylvania, at 87. The pennant was the first in 35 years for the Phillies, but they were swept by the Yankees in the Series. Sawyer had a master's degree from Cornell University and was a member of Phi Beta Kappa. He managed the Phillies until June 1952 and returned to the helm in July 1958. He quit one game into the 1960 season. In

HISTORY

Charlie Johnson, Florida's catcher, sets a major league record when he plays his 160th game without an error. He also tops an NL mark previously held by Earl Grace – 110 consecutive games in one season without an error.

So what else is new? Seattle manager Lou Piniella tells the media, "Junior can hit them."

HISTORY

In Colorado, where the Rockies beat the Dodgers, 13-9, Larry Walker sits out the game with 49 homers, eliminating the possibility of a first – three players with 50 or more homers in the same season.

eight years, he compiled a 390-423 record.

SEPTEMBER 23:

Kevin Brown and the Marlins beat the Expos, 6-3, in Montreal, enabling Florida to clinch a playoff spot. Brown improves his season's record to 16-8.

SEPTEMBER 24:

Mark McGwire hits number 55 – with 1 on in the 5th against Dave Burba of the Reds. Big Mac moves within 6 of the major league record, but the Cardinals lose, 5-4, in St. Louis.

Ken Griffey Jr. is hitless in three at-bats in the leadoff spot against the Angels. He takes himself out of the game for a pinch hitter in the eighth inning. The Mariners win the game.

The Orioles beat the Blue Jays, 9-3, to wrap up the AL East title. Prior to the game, the Blue Jays fire manager Cito Gaston, who led the team to World Series victories in 1992 and 1993. Toronto is in last place in the AL East, with a 72-85 record. Pitching coach Mel Queen will handle the team for the final five games.

SEPTEMBER 25:

Pedro Martinez fans Florida's Kurt Abbott in the fourth inning for his 300th strikeout of the year. Martinez goes on to defeat the Marlins, 3-2, in Montreal, allowing four hits and a run in seven innings, He walks four and whiffs nine to bring his season total to 305. He sets a franchise record and is the 14th pitcher this century with 300 strikeouts or more in a season.

Joe Carter wears fired manager Cito Gaston's number–43–and homers to help the Blue Jays top the Orioles, 4-3, in Toronto. It is Carter's 21st homerun of the year and the 203rd of his career.

Jimy Williams sends Steve Avery to the mound against the Tigers, enabling the pitcher to earn his $3.9 million bonus by making 18 starts this season. Avery allows two hits and no runs in five innings.

SEPTEMBER 26:

Ken Griffey Jr. – six homers behind Roger Maris with three games to go – takes himself out of the lineup for today's game against the Athletics. Says Griffey, "Do I have a chance to break the record? I've got six bombs to go and there ain't no way I'm going to break it."

He adds, "The record's not important. What's important is getting the trophy with all the flags on it."

Mark McGwire stays in the lineup but gets no closer to Roger Maris. Big Mac is homerless and hitless in three at-bats and the Cardinals lose to the Cubs, 5-2, in St. Louis. He and Griffey remain tied at 55 homers. It is the seventh straight loss for St. Louis and McGwire has failed to homer in six of those contests.

Curt Schilling fans Devon White leading off the game and sets an NL record for strikeouts for a right-hander – 314. Schilling whiffs five more batters and then gets ejected for hitting a batter in the eighth inning. The Phillies top the Marlins, 5-3, for Schilling's 17th win.

SEPTEMBER 27:

The home run race heats up again, but it may be too late for the all-time record. In St. Louis, Mark McGwire connects twice – number 56 and number 57 – but he will need four tomorrow to surpass Roger Maris. McGwire now stands in fifth place for homers in a single season. He says of his chances, "There's nothing to shoot for. What's there to shoot for? If I get a hit I get a hit. That's the way it goes." The Cardinals club the Cubs, 12-4.

Ken Griffey Jr. hits his 56th – with the bases empty – against Brad Rigby of the Athletics. He also raises his RBI total to 147. Seattle wins, 9-3, at home and Randy Johnson earns his 20th, working two shutout innings in relief and fanning three. He becomes the Mariners' first 20-game winner and the 49th pitcher to register 2,000 career strikeouts.

The Giants, in the cellar last season, defeat the Padres, 6-1, in San Francisco, to clinch the NL West title.

SEPTEMBER 28:

Mark McGwire finishes with a flourish and 58 homers. McGwire earns a place – but not THE place – in the record books when he slams an 0-2 pitch from Steve Trachsel of the visiting Cubs

SEPTEMBER 27
Ken griffey Jr. hits his last homer of the season–number 56.

SEPTEMBER 28
Mark McGwire finishes his season with 58 home runs.

some 414 feet into straightaway center. The blow ties the record for righthanded hitters set by Jimmie Foxx in 1932 and tied by Hank Greenberg in 1938. It also is the third-highest total ever. The Cardinals win the otherwise meaningless game, 2-1.

Junior Griffey is one for two with no homers as the visiting Athletics beat the Mariners, 9-7. Griffey's teammate Jay Buhner finishes with 40 homers, giving the duo the third-highest combined homer total. Only the Yankees' famous hitting combos – Roger Maris-Mickey Mantle (115 in 1961) and Babe Ruth-Lou Gehrig (107 in 1927) – hit more.

Roger Clemens fans eight in eight-and a third innings, bringing his season strikeout total to a career high 212 and earning him his fourth AL strikeout title. The Blue Jays edge the Red Sox, 3-2, in Toronto, but Clemens does not figure in the decision. The win goes to Dan Plesac in relief. Tom Gordon gets the loss.

Brett Butler, who returned to the majors after surviving cancer in 1996, plays his last game for the Dodgers and hits a two-run triple in four at-bats in a 13-9 loss to the Rockies in Colorado. Butler, 40 years old, played 17 seasons and batted .290, with 558 stolen bases. Teammate Mike Piazza homers twice for a season's total of 40.

The Yankees, behind Hideki Irabu, top the Tigers, 7-2, and move into the playoffs on the strength of five straight wins.

REGULAR SEASON WRAP-UP:

The Indians, under Mike Hargrove, finish the regular season with an 86-75 record in the AL and boast a lineup with three regulars hitting above .300 and three driving in 100 runs or more. David Justice leads Cleveland with a .329 average, 33 homers, and 101 RBI. Manny Ramirez bats .328 with 26 homers and 88 RBI; Sandy Alomar finishes at .324 with 21 homers and 83 RBI. They are supported by Jim Thome (.286, 40 homers and 102 RBI) and Matt Williams (.263, 32 homers, 105 RBI). Charles Nagy (15-11, 4.28 ERA) and veteran Orel Hershiser (14-6, 4.47 ERA) are the top starting pitchers with Jose Mesa (16 save Mike Jackson (15 saves, 3.24 ERA).

Despite 101 wins, the Braves go home and the 92-70 Marlins move on to the World Series for the NL. Managed by Jim Leyland, Florida fields a lineup featuring no hitters with more than 23 homers and only one with 100 or more RBI. The big gun is Moises Alou (.292, 23 homers, 115 RBI), followed by Mets and Orioles cast-off Bobby Bonilla (.297, 17 homers, 96 RBI) and a pair of .250 hitters with power – Gary Sheffield (21 homers, 71 RBI) and Charles Johnson (19 homers, 63 RBI). Pitchers include Kevin Brown (16-8, 2.69 ERA) and rookie Livan Hernandez (9-3, 3.18 ERA), and the bullpen ace is Robb Nen (9-3, 3.89 ERA, 35 saves).

The season is marked by power hitting, and the most powerful of all is Mark McGwire. He finishes the season with 34 homers in the AL; 24 in only 51 games in the NL. Ken Griffey Jr. slams 56 round-trippers. Almost obscured in the homer frenzy are Griffey's other stats – 185 hits, 125 runs, 147 RBI, and a .304 average. Red Sox rookie shortstop Nomar Garciaparra, batting from the leadoff spot, hits .306, with 200 hits, 30 homers, and 98 RBI.

The Mariners' Randy Johnson and the Blue Jays' Roger Clemens demonstrate that a pitcher can still dominate in this era of offense, and Pedro Martinez of the Expos emerges as a potential new mound superstar.

SEPTEMBER 30:

NL Division Series. Florida beats visiting San Francisco, 2-1, in a game highlighted by outstanding pitching by the Marlins' Kevin Brown and the Giants' Kirk Reuter, although neither figures in the final decision. Bill Mueller homers for the visitors and Charles Johnson for Florida, but the game-winning hit is Edgar Renteria's single in the bottom of the ninth. The winning pitcher is Dennis Cook; Julian Tavarez gets the loss.

AL Division Series. The Yankees overcome a five-run first inning by the visiting Indians and prevail, 8-6. New York sends Orel Hershiser to the showers with sixth-inning successive

HISTORY

Murray Chass of *the* New York Times reports that Pete Rose has made "his first formal attempt at a comeback" – reinstatement to baseball. According to Chass, acting commissioner Bud Selig responds that Rose's request "will be handled in due course."

OCTOBER 3
The Marlins and Braves sweep their divisions to play for th NL pennant.

homers by Tim Raines, Derek Jeter, and Paul O'Neill. Tino Martinez also homers and Sandy Alomar connects for Cleveland. The winning pitcher is Ramiro Mendoza. Eric Plunk gets the loss.

NL Division Series. Behind a complete-game seven-hitter by Greg Maddux, the Braves nip the visiting Astros, 2-1. Darryl Kile allows only two hits in seven innings and drives in his team's only run, but he gets the loss. A sacrifice fly and a Ryan Klesko homer account for all of Atlanta's runs.

OCTOBER 1:

NL Division Series. Florida wins another squeaker, 7-6, at home. Moises Alou singles in Gary Sheffield in the bottom of the ninth. Livan Hernandez gets the win in relief; Robb Nen is tagged with the loss. Brian Johnson of the Giants and Bobby Bonilla of the Marlins homer.

AL Division Series. In Seattle, the Orioles beat Randy Johnson and the Mariners, 9-3. Matt Mussina gets the win for the Orioles. The game features five homers: Geronimo Berroa and Chris Hoiles for Baltimore; Edgar Martinez, Jay Buhner, and Alex Rodriguez for Seattle.

NL Division Series. In Atlanta, the Braves work five Houston pitchers for 10 hits in a 13-3 victory. Jeff Blauser homers for the Braves and winning pitcher Tom Glavine gets a key hit in the three-run third inning. The losing pitcher is Mike Hampton.

OCTOBER 2:

AL Division Series. In New York, Jaret Wright, a 21-year-old rookie, gets help from three relief pitchers to down the Yankees, 7-5, and even up the playoffs. Andy Pettitte gets the loss. Matt Williams homers for Cleveland and Derek Jeter for New York.

AL Division Series. The Orioles top the Mariners in Seattle again, 9-3, the same score as in game one. Scott Erickson works six-and two thirds innings for the win; Jamie Moyer, who injures his elbow and leaves in the fifth inning with his team in the lead, is charged with the loss. Baltimore gets homers from Harold Baines and Brady Anderson.

OCTOBER 3:

NL Division Series. Behind Alex Fernandez, the visiting Marlins sweep the Giants, 6-2. Jeff Kent's two homers account for all of the Giants' scoring; Devon White clouts a grand slam for the winners. Wilson Alvarez is saddled with the loss.

NL Division Series. In Houston, the Braves sweep the Astros with a 4-1 win. John Smoltz pitches a three-hit complete game with 11 strikeouts, for his 10th career playoff victory. Chipper Jones homers off losing pitcher Shane Reynolds in the first inning. Chuck Carr's seventh-inning homer is too little too late.

OCTOBER 4:

AL Division Series. The Mariners avoid a sweep in Baltimore, topping the Orioles, 4-2, behind strong pitching from Jeff Fassero. Aided by homers from Jay Buhner and Paul Sorrento and RBI from Roberto Kelly and Ken Griffey Jr., Fassero limits Baltimore to three hits in eight innings. Jimmy Key gets the loss.

AL Division Series. In Cleveland, David Wells allows the Indians only five hits for a complete-game, 6-1, victory. He walks none and strikes out one, besting Charles Nagy. Paul O'Neill hits a grand slam against reliever Chad Ogea in the fourth inning, one of only four Yankees' hits.

OCTOBER 5:

AL Division Series. The Indians nip the Yankees, 3-2, to knot the series in Cleveland. Veterans Dwight Gooden for New York and Orel Hershiser for Cleveland are the starters but neither is involved in the decision. Mike Jackson gets the win and Ramiro Mendoza – New York's sixth pitcher of the game – is the loser. David Justice and Sandy Alomar homer for the winners.

AL Division Series. Matt Mussina outduels Randy Johnson, allowing only two hits in seven innings, to close out the Mariners, 3-1. Edgar Martinez homers in the second for Seattle's only run; Jeff Reboulet and Geronimo Berroa connect for the Orioles.

OCTOBER 6:

AL Division Series. There will be no World Series repeat

OCTOBER 11
The Indians top the Orioles, despite Matt Mussina's 15 strikeouts.

OCTOBER 12
Livan Hernandez holds the Braves to just three hits in his complete game.

for the Yankees. Jaret Wright beats the Bombers for the second time, 4-3, at Jacobs Field, with relief help from three pitchers. Andy Pettitte gets the loss – his second of the series. Manny Ramirez hits a clutch third-inning double, driving in two runs. The Yankees rally in the ninth, but Jose Mesa closes out the game.

Johnny Vander Meer, the only pitcher in major league history with back-to-back no-hitters, dies at 82 in Tampa, Florida. Vander Meer accomplished the feat in 1938 as a member of the Reds, no-hitting the Braves, 3-0, on June 11, and the Brooklyn Dodgers, 6-0, on June 15. He was only 23 at the time. Vander Meer pitched for 13 years –11 with Cincinnati and one each with the Cubs and Indians – and compiled a 119-121 record with an ERA of 3.44.

OCTOBER 7:

NLCS game one. The Marlins continue their unlikely drive toward the NL pennant with a 5-3 win over the Braves in Atlanta. Florida scores five unearned runs to defeat Braves' ace Greg Maddux; Kevin Brown gets the victory. Chipper Jones and Ryan Klesko homer for the losers.

OCTOBER 8:

ALCS game one. Scott Erickson holds the hard-hitting Indians to 4 hits in 8 innings and Randy Myers earns a save as Baltimore takes game one at home, 3-0. Chad Ogea is charged with the loss. Brady Anderson and Roberto Alomar contribute homers for the Orioles.

NLCS game two. Behind strong pitching from winner Tom Glavine, the Braves knot the series with a 7-1 win against visiting Florida. Losing pitcher Alex Fernandez leaves the game in the third with an injury. For the second consecutive game, Chipper Jones and Ryan Klesko homer for Atlanta.

OCTOBER 9:

NLCS game two. Cal Ripken Jr. and Manny Ramirez match two-run homers, but Marquis Grissom's three-run round-tripper in the eighth inning off losing pitcher Armando Benitez gives the Indians a 5-4 win over the Orioles. Paul Assenmacher the fourth of six Indian pitchers gets the win.

OCTOBER 10:

NLCS game three. Back home, the Marlins top the Braves, 5-2, paced by a Gary Sheffield homer and a three-run double from Charles Johnson. Rookie Livan Hernandez gets the victory in relief; Atlanta starter John Smoltz is the losing pitcher.

OCTOBER 11:

NLCS game four. Denny Neagle pitches a complete-game four-hitter and the Braves top the Marlins, 4-0. It is the first complete game in the NLCS in five years. Al Leiter gets the loss. Jeff Blauser homers for the Braves.

ALCS game three. The scene shifts to Cleveland and the Indians top the Orioles, 2-1, on a bizarre play at the plate. With Marquis Grissom on third base in the bottom of the 12th, Omar Vizquel attempts to bunt and misses the ball. But calling to mind shades of Mickey Owen, Orioles' catcher Lenny Webster fails to hold on to the ball. Apparently believing the pitch was fouled, he does not chase it and Grissom scores the winning run. The Orioles waste an LCS record 15-strikeout performance by Matt Mussina. Randy Meyers, Baltimore's sixth pitcher of the game gets the loss. Eric Plunk, the seventh Indians' pitcher, gets the win.

OCTOBER 12:

NLCS game five. In Florida, Livan Hernandez dazzles the Braves, 2-1, allowing only three hits in a complete-game performance. He fans 15 Braves, matching the LCS record set only yesterday by Matt Mussina. In the seventh inning, Jeff Conine singles in Bobby Bonilla with the winning run; it is one of only four hits allowed by losing pitcher Greg Maddux. Michael Tucker's second-inning homer accounts for Atlanta's only run.

ALCS game four. At Jacobs Field, the Indians bang out 13 hits to the Orioles 12 and win, 8-7. Jose Mesa gets the win in relief; Alan Mills is the loser. Sandy Alomar's ninth-inning single scores Manny Ramirez and wins the game.

LEAGUE

The face of baseball will undergo an unprecedented change. For the first time in history, a team will be moved from one league to the other. Peter Magowan, owner of the Giants, abstains, but all the other owners approve the switch. Either the Royals, Brewers, or Twins will move from the AL Central to the NL Central. After the realignment, the NL will have 16 teams and the AL 14.

OCTOBER 26
The Marlins win the World Series after only five years as a franchise.

HISTORY

Roger Clemens becomes the first pitcher to win Cy Young Award four times.

CULTURE

***Joe Torre: Curveballs Along the Way*, a biographical made-for-television movie about the Yankees' manager and his strong family ties, stars Paul Sorvino as Torre, Robert Loggia as his brother Frank, and Barbara Williams as Ali Torre. Isaiah Washington plays Dwight Gooden and Kenneth Walsh is George Steinbrenner.**

Alomar and Ramirez previously had homered. Brady Anderson, Harold Baines, and Rafael Palmeiro connect for Baltimore.

OCTOBER 13:

ALCS game five. Scott Kamieniecki bests Chad Ogea and the Orioles stay alive with a 4-2 win. Baltimore's Eric Davis adds another chapter to his comeback from cancer with a homer.

OCTOBER 14:

NLCS game six. In Atlanta, Kevin Brown goes all the way, scattering 11 hits as the Marlins beat the Braves, 7-4, and win the NL pennant, after only five years as a franchise. Tom Glavine gets the loss after yielding four runs in the first. Bobby Bonilla has three RBI for Florida.

OCTOBER 15:

ALCS game six. An unlikely hero leads the Indians into the World Series and negates another classic pitching performance by Matt Mussina. Tony Fernandez, playing in place of injured second baseman Leon "Bip" Roberts, homers off Armando Benitez in the top of the 11th to give the Indians a 1-0 victory. Mussina had allowed only two hits in his eight innings of work but Baltimore leaves 14 on base. Brian Anderson gets the win in relief. Mussina finishes the series with a postseason record 41 strikeouts, compiled in his four starts.

OCTOBER 18:

World Series, game one. In Florida, the Marlins draw first blood with a 7-4 victory over the Indians. The Florida attack is paced by back-to-back fifth-nning homers by Moises Alou and Charles Johnson off losing pitcher Orel Hershiser. Manny Ramirez and Jim Thome homer in a losing cause. Livan Hernandez gets the victory with relief help from Dennis Cook, Jay Powell, and Robb Nen.

OCTOBER 19:

World Series, game two. Behind winning pitcher Chad Ogea – with relief from Mike Jackson and Jose Mesa – the Indians tie the Series with a 6-1 win. Sandy Alomar's homer is among 14 Cleveland hits. Alomar and Bip Roberts drive in two runs each. Kevin Brown is the loser.

OCTOBER 21:

World Series, game three. At Jacobs Field, the Marlins outslug the Indians, 14-11, on 16 hits, including three homers. Dennis Cook gets the win in relief; Eric Plunk is charged with the loss. Gary Sheffield, Darren Daulton, and Jim Eisenreich homer for the Marlins; Jim Thome hits one out for Cleveland.

OCTOBER 22:

World Series, game four. The weather is frigid – the coldest in Series history – but Cleveland's bats are hot; the Indians parlay 15 hits into a 10-3 win at home. Jaret Wright gets the victory in a game marked by snow flurries and a wind chill factor of 15 degrees. Manny Ramirez and Matt Williams homer for the winners; Moises Alou for Florida. The losing pitcher is Tony Saunders.

OCTOBER 23:

World Series, game five. Behind winning pitcher Livan Hernandez, the Marlins bang out 15 hits and nip the Indians, 8-7, at Jacobs Field. The big hit for Florida is Moises Alou's three-run homer off losing pitcher Orel Hershiser. It is Alou's third of the Series and his second off Hershiser. Sandy Alomar hits a fourbagger for the losing Indians.

OCTOBER 25:

World Series, game six. Cleveland roars back in Florida with a 4-1 victory for Chad Ogea. Kevin Brown gets the loss. Ogea aids his cause with two hits, two RBI, and a run.

OCTOBER 26:

World Series, game seven. The Marlins are the improbable champions of baseball, following a 3-2, 11-inning win before a home crowd of 67,204. Edgar Renteria singles with the bases loaded and two out to win the game. Jay Powell, the sixth Florida pitcher, gets the win; Charles Nagy, Cleveland's sixth pitcher gets the loss. Bobby Bonilla homers for the victors. The Series MVP is Cuban-born Livan Hernandez who is 2-0 with a 5.27 ERA. Moises Alou leads the Florida starters with a .321 average three homers and three RBI. Bobby Bonilla also connects for three homers. For the Indians, Tony

NOVEMBER 7
The Devil Rays sign the Marlins' pitching coach as manager.

NOVEMBER 18
The Marlins dismantle their winning team in the expansion draft.

Fernandez hits .471 and Sandy Alomar, .367 with two homers and 10 RBI.

POST-SEASON

NOVEMBER 2:

Former major league shortstop and manager Roy McMillan dies at 68 in Bonham, Texas. Regarded as one of the best fielders ever at his position, McMillan played 16 seasons with the Reds, Milwaukee Braves, and Mets, batting .243.

Eddie Stanky once said of McMillan, "Hitting a ball toward Roy is like hitting it down a sewer." After his playing days, McMillan managed Mets for part of the 1975 season.

NOVEMBER 5:

Davey Johnson resigns as skipper of the Orioles just before he is named AL Manager of the Year. Johnson's resignation stems from a number of disputes with owner Peter Angelos. One of the most serious was the result of $10,500 in fines Johnson imposed on Roberto Alomar. He had Alomar pay the money to a foundation. Because Johnson's wife is a managing director of the foundation, Angelos objected.

According to Murray Chass of The New York Times, Johnson offered to resign if Angelos agreed not to stop him from landing another job for next season. "In a reply less than three hours later," Chass writes, "Angelos accepted Johnson's resignation and told him he was free to take a job elsewhere."

The Brewers will move from the AL Central to the NL Central for the 1998 season. The move was announced today by baseball's executive council. Milwaukee will be competing with Chicago, Cincinnati, Houston, Pittsburgh, and St. Louis in the NL Central. The shift will produce changes in the AL as well: the Tigers move from the AL East to replace the Brewers in the AL Central and the new Tampa Bay Devil Rays will compete in the AL East.

NOVEMBER 7:

The Yankees trade pitcher Kenny Rogers (6-7, 5.65 ERA) to the Athletics for utility infielder Scott Brosius (.203, 11 homers, 41 RBI). New York, disappointed in the left-hander's performance, will absorb $5 million of his $20 million contract.

The Tampa Bay Devil Rays have no players yet, but today they sign a manager. He is Larry Rothschild. The 43-year-old was pitching coach for the World Champion Marlins and has never been a manager, but is an experienced coach.

NOVEMBER 11:

The Marlins trade the hitting star of their World Series team, Moises Alou (.292, 23 homers, 115 RBI), to the Astros for pitchers Oscar Henriquez (0-1, 4.50 ERA) and Manuel Barrios (0-0, 12.00 ERA) plus a player to be named later.

NOVEMBER 16:

Former major league pitcher Russ Meyer dies at 74 in Oglesby, Illinois. He pitched for 13 seasons with the Cubs, Phillies, Brooklyn Dodgers, Reds, Red Sox, and Kansas City Athletics, compiling a 94-73 record with a 3.99 ERA. He was known as "The Mad Monk" and "Rowdy" because of his explosive temper.

NOVEMBER 17:

Before the expansion draft, the soon-to-be Diamondbacks sign their first player – free agent Jay Bell (.291, 21 homers, 92 RBI). The 31-year-old shortstop, who played with the Royals this past season, gets a five-year, $34 million contract.

NOVEMBER 18:

The major leagues hold the fifth expansion draft. The Tampa Bay Devil Rays select first – pitcher Tony Saunders of the Marlins. The Arizona Diamondbacks then choose pitcher Brian Anderson of the Indians. Tampa Bay follows up with outfielder Quinton McCracken of the Rockies, outfielder Bob Abreu of the Astros, second baseman Miguel Cairo of the Cubs, and outfielder Rich Butler of the Blue Jays as their next four picks. The Diamondbacks complete their top five choices with pitcher Jeff Suppan of the Red Sox, third baseman Gabe Alvarez of the Padres, catcher Jorge Fabregas of the White Sox, and outfielder Karim Garcia of the

LEAGUE

Perhaps the biggest plum in the expansion draft falls into the hands of the Red Sox. Boston obtains pitcher Pedro Martinez, a 26-year-old right-hander (17-8, 1.90 ERA, 305 strikeouts), from the always cash-strapped Expos for minor league pitcher Carl Pavano and a player to be named later.

DECEMBER 10
Pedro Martinez becomes baseball's highest-paid player.

LEAGUE

The Marlins, the only expansion team to win the World Series in only five years, have a payroll of $89 million.

Dodgers. Each team selects 35 players.

The draft spawns a feeding frenzy, with the Marlins leading the majors in shedding payroll. Florida sends outfielder Devon White (.245, six homers, 34 RBI), who will earn $3.5 million next season, to the new Diamondbacks for minor league pitcher Jesus Martinez, the brother of Pedro and Ramon. The Marlins also ship ace reliever Robb Nen (9-3, 35 saves, 3.89 ERA) to the Giants for three minor league pitchers. Nen has three years at $14.5 remaining on his contract. The Expos trade second baseman Mike Lansing (281, 20 homers, 70 RBI) to the Rockies for three minor leaguers and the Braves ship first baseman Fred McGriff (.277, 22 homers, 97 RBI) to Tampa Bay for a player to be named later.

NOVEMBER 27:

Hall of Famer Walter Fenner "Buck" Leonard, known as "the black Lou Gehrig," dies at the age of 90 in Rocky Mount, North Carolina, where he was born. Leonard starred for the Homestead Grays from 1934 to 1950 and batted an estimated .328 He hit .320 in five Negro Leagues World Series. Leonard was inducted into the Hall of Fame in 1972 along with his Homestead Grays teammate Josh Gibson.

DECEMBER 1:

The Indians send slugging third baseman Matt Williams (.263, 32 homers, 105 RBI) to the Arizona Diamondbacks for third baseman Travis Fryman (.274, 22 homers, 102 RBI) and pitcher Tom Martin 5-3, 12.89 ERA with Houston). Fryman had been obtained by Arizona from Detroit in an earlier trade for infielder Gabe Alvarez, pitcher Matt Drews, and infielder Joe Randa.

Matt Williams gets a five-year contract extension worth $45 million.

DECEMBER 2:

Former major league pitcher and pro basketball player Steve Hamilton dies at 62 in Morehead, Kentucky. The six-foot, seven-inch Hamilton, who pitched for 12 years with the Indians, Washington Senators, White Sox, Yankees, San Francisco Giants, and Cubs, from 1961 to 1972, was known primarily for a blooper-like pitch he called "the Folly Floater." Mostly pitching in relief, he was 40-31 with an ERA of 3.05 and 42 saves.

DECEMBER 3:

Vic Lombardi, who pitched three seasons each for the Brooklyn Dodgers and the Pittsburgh Pirates, dies at 75 in Fresno, California. He compiled a 50-51 record with an ERA of 3.68.

DECEMBER 8:

The Indians sign Kenny Lofton (.333, 27 stolen bases) as a free agent and complete a five-player deal with the Brewers. Traded to the Indians are pitchers Ben McDonald (8-7, 4.06 ERA), Mike Fetters (1-5, 3.45 ERA), and Ron Villone (1-0, 3.42 ERA); going to Milwaukee are outfielder Marquis Grissom (.262, 12 homers, 22 stolen bases) and pitcher Jeff Juden (11-5, 4.22 ERA with the Expos; 0-1, 5.46 ERA with the Indians). Fetters is then traded to the Athletics for pitcher Steve Karsay (3-12, 5.77 ERA). Grissom and Lofton were key figures in a March trade between the Indians and Braves. Cleveland also signs free agent Dwight Gooden (9-5, 4.91 ERA), who spent 1997 with the Yankees.

DECEMBER 10:

NL Cy Young Award winner Pedro Martinez becomes baseball's highest-paid player when he signs a $75 million, six-year contract with the Red Sox. Although the total dollar amount is less than the $80 million contract between the White Sox and Frank Thomas, Martinez will average $12.5 million a year – $1 million more than the average salary of Greg Maddux.

DECEMBER 15:

The Marlins continue to dismantle their championship team, sending pitcher Kevin Brown (16-8, 2.69 ERA) to the Padres for three minor leaguers – outfielder Derrek Lee and pitchers Rafael Medina and Steve Hoff.

DECEMBER 15
The Marlins continue to dismantle their World Series team.

THE BEST OF 1997

NATIONAL LEAGUE

HITTERS

Batting Average:
Tony Gwynn, San Diego Padres, .372

Slugging Average:
Larry Walker, Colorado Rockies, .720

Home Runs:
Larry Walker, 49

Runs Batted In:
Andres Galarraga, Colorado Rockies, 140

Hits:
Tony Gwynn, 220

Stolen Bases:
Tony Womack, Pittsburgh Pirates, 60

PITCHERS

Wins:
Denny Neagle, Atlanta Braves, 20

Strikeouts:
Curt Schilling, Philadelphia Phillies, 319

Earned Run Average:
Pedro Martinez, Montreal Expos, 1.90

Winning Percentage:
Greg Maddux, Atlanta Braves, .826

Saves:
Jeff Shaw, Cincinnati Reds, 42

Most Valuable Player:
Larry Walker, Colorado Rockies

Cy Young Award:
Pedro Martinez, Montreal Expos

Rookie of the Year:
Scott Rolen, Philadelphia Phillies

Manager of the Year:
Dusty Baker, New York Giants

AMERICAN LEAGUE

HITTERS

Batting Average:
Frank Thomas, Chicago White Sox, .347

Slugging Average:
Ken Griffey Jr., Seattle Mariners, .646

Home Runs:
Ken Griffey Jr., 56

Runs Batted In:
Ken Griffey Jr., 147

Hits:
Nomar Garciaparra, Boston Red Sox, 209

Stolen Bases:
Brian Hunter, Detroit Tigers, 74

PITCHERS

Wins:
Roger Clemens, Toronto Blue Jays, 21

Strikeouts:
Roger Clemens, 292

Earned Run Average:
Roger Clemens, 205

Winning Percentage:
Randy Johnson, Seattle Mariners, .833

Saves:
Randy Myers, Baltimore Orioles, 45

Most Valuable Player:
Ken Griffey Jr., Seattle Mariners

Cy Young Award:
Roger Clemens, Toronto Blue Jays

Rookie of the Year:
Nomar Garciaparra, Boston Red Sox

Manager of the Year:
Davey Johnson, Baltimore Orioles

CULTURE

Snow in August by Pete Hamill, is a novel about life in Brooklyn in the 1940s, with baseball themes. ***The Year of the Buffalo: A Novel of Love and Minor League Baseball*** by Marshall J. Cook is also published, as are two mysteries featuring fictional infielder Mickey Rawlings: ***Hunting a Detroit Tiger*** and ***Murder at Wrigley Field***, both by Troy Soos.

1998

"I'm not toally happy with everything I've done, but on balance, I'll stand on the record"
– *George Steinbrenner*

NEWS

PRESIDENT CLINTON IMPEACHED IN SCANDAL INVOLVING SEXUAL LIAISON WITH WHITE HOUSE INTERN, BUT HOUSE WILL NOT CONVICT

SENATOR JOHN GLENN SUCCESSFULLY COMPLETES SPACE SHUTTLE MISSION AT AGE 77

Viagra, a drug to treat impotence, introduced

U.S. EMBASSY IN KENYA BOMBED

A LAW BANNING THE POSSESSION OF ALL HANDGUNS GOES INTO EFFECT IN BRITAIN

BABY SPECIALIST DR. SPOCK DIES

10,000 PEOPLE LOG ON TO WATCH THE FIRST BIRTH SHOWN ON THE INTERNET

76 MILLION VIEWERS TUNE IN FOR LAST *SEINFELD* EPISODE

GEORGE GERSHWIN WINS POSTHUMOUS PULITZER PRIZE

FRANK SINATRA DIES AT AGE 82

PRE-SEASON

JANUARY 4:

The *New York Times* notes the 25th anniversary of the purchase of the Yankees by a group headed by George Steinbrenner. Boss George tells Murray Chass, "I'm not totally happy with everything I've done, but on balance, I'll stand on the record." In Steinbrenner's quartercentury, the Yankees have compiled the best record in baseball – 2,131 wins against 1,788 losses for a .544 winning percentage. The team won three World Series and five pennants. Steinbrenner has employed 15 general managers and 21 managers; he has been suspended three times and fined on seven occasions.

JANUARY 17:

The Cubs sign free-agent reliever Rod Beck (7-4, 3.47 ERA, 37 saves) to a one-year, $3.5 million contract – a bargain. Beck pitched with the Giants last season, earning $250,000 less than he will make with Chicago.

JANUARY 19:

Two Hall of Famers come to the aid of Shoeless Joe Jackson, banned from baseball for his role in the 1920 Black Sox scandal. Ted Williams and Bob Feller submit a petition to acting commissioner Bud Selig and the Hall of Fame, urging that Jackson be cleared and removed from the Hall of Fame ineligible list so the Veterans Committee can consider his candidacy. Williams says, "I want baseball to right an injustice."

JANUARY 22:

The Athletics sign outfielder Rickey Henderson (.248, 45 stolen bases), the all-time stolen base leader with 1,231, to a one-year contract. The 39-year-old Henderson returns to the A's for his fourth tour of duty; he has spent 12 of his 19 major league seasons with the team. He spent last season in California with the Padres and the Angels.

FEBRUARY 3:

Bob Watson resigns as general manager of the Yankees and is replaced by his 30-year-old assistant, Brian Cashman. Watson was the 17th general manager in George Steinbrenner's 25 years as owner.

Mark McGwire watches one of his 70 homers sail into the stands.

LEAGUE

The *New York Times* reports that the Orioles now have the highest payroll in the major leagues – $70,408,134. The Yankees, usually the symbol of salary excess, are in second at $63,159,901. The Marlins, after an intense salary "dumping" campaign, are in 20th place with $33,434,000. Last year the Florida payroll was $53.5 million. Bringing up the rear – 30th place – are the Expos with only $9,202,000. They are the only team below the $10 million mark. Last year Montreal was at $18.4 million.

The Diamondbacks sign free-agent pitcher Andy Benes (10-7, 3.10 ERA) to a three-year contract reportedly worth $18 million. He spent last season with the Cardinals.

FEBRUARY 6:

The New York teams acquire key players. The Mets add left-hander Al Leiter (11-9, 4.34 ERA) and infielder Ralph Milliard (.200 in eight games) from the Marlins for three minor leaguers — pitchers Jesus Sanchez and A. J. Burnett and outfielder Robert Stratton. Leiter is the sixth-highest-salaried member of the champion Marlins to be dealt away. The Yankees obtain four-time All-Star second baseman Chuck Knoblauch (.291, nine homers, 58 RBI) for $3 million and four minor leaguers – pitchers Eric Milton and Danny Mota, infielder Cristian Guzman, and outfielder Brian Buchanan.

FEBRUARY 18:

The Yankees re-sign their centerfielder, Bernie Williams (.328, 21 homers, 100 RBI), to a one-year, $8.25 million pact, an increase of almost 60 percent. The team and its star reach the agreement on the day of scheduled salary arbitration.

Baseball loses one of its most distinctive voices. Harry Caray, the voice of the Chicago Cubs, dies at 78 in Rancho Mirage, California. At various times prior to joining the Cubs in 1982, Caray announced for the Cardinals, the Oakland Athletics, and the White Sox. He is a member of the broadcasters' wing of the Hall of Fame. Caray's son Skip and his grandson Chip also are baseball broadcasters.

MARCH 6:

The Yankees sign 28-year-old Cuban defector Orlando Hernandez to a four-year, $6.6 million contract. The pitcher known as "El Duque" is the older brother of Livan Hernandez of the Marlins (the MVP of last year's World Series).

MARCH 12:

Ben McDonald, traded to the Indians last December 8 for Marquis Grissom, is returned to the Brewers because he has a damaged rotator cuff. Instead, Cleveland receives minor league pitcher Mark Watson. According to the Brewers' general manager, the revised trade was made "in good faith."

MARCH 17:

Beanballs are blooming in the spring. After Yankees' pitcher Hideki Irabu hits shortstop Alex Gonzalez of the Blue Jays in the fifth inning, Roger Clemens grazes New York shortstop Derek Jeter in the bottom of the frame. It is the fourth beanball incident involving the Yankees during spring training.

MARCH 19:

The Lords of Baseball approve the sale of the Los Angeles Dodgers to media mogul Rupert Murdoch and his Fox Group for a record price estimated at $350 million. Ted Turner, owner of the Braves and a vocal opponent of the sale, dissents, as do the White Sox. The Mets abstain.

Murdoch obtains the team – and Dodger Stadium – from Peter O'Malley, whose family has owned the team since 1950, when it was in Brooklyn. The Dodgers were the last of the family-owned major league franchises.

THE SEASON

MARCH 31:

Mark McGwire picks up where he left off in 1997; Big Mac homers with the bases–loaded in the fifth against Ramon Martinez. The Cardinals down the visiting Dodgers, 6-0.

At home in Tropicana Field, the AL Devil Rays bow to the Tigers, 11-6. Playing in his hometown, Wade Boggs hits a two-run homer in the sixth – the first in team history – off winning pitcher Justin Thompson. Luis Gonzalez homers for the Tigers. Wilson Alvarez gets the loss. Attendance is 45,369.

In their home stadium, Bank One Ballpark, the NL Diamondbacks are drilled by the Rockies, 9-2. Travis Lee's single in the second is the first hit in for Arizona and in the fifth he connects off Darryl Kile for the franchise's first homer. Vinny Castilla connects twice for the winners. Kile gets the victory; Andy Benes takes the loss. Attendance is 47,484.

MARCH 31
Mark Mcgwire hits his first home run of the season.

APRIL 4
Sammy Sosa breaks the ice with his first homer of the year.

Milwaukee past and Milwaukee present come face to face today — and the past prevails. The Braves — who once made their home in Milwaukee — best the present occupants, the Brewers, 2-1, in Atlanta. The game also marks the first game in the NL for the Brewers after 28 years in the AL.

Ken Griffey Jr. homers, but Kenny Lofton connects twice and the Indians edge the Mariners in Seattle, 10-9. Also homering for Seattle are Jay Buhner, Russ Davis, and Edgar Martinez. Sandy Alomar connects for Cleveland

Roger Clemens and the Blue Jays down the Twins, 3-2, in Toronto. Clemens allows only two hits in seven innings.

The visiting Padres pound the Reds, 10-2, and Cincinnati's Calvin "Pokey" Reese ties an opening-day record with four errors at shortstop. Kevin Brown records the win.

Cal Ripken Jr. hits his eighth career grand slam and the Orioles crush the Royals, 10-1, in Baltimore. Scott Erickson limits Kansas City to four hits and registers his 100th career win.

APRIL 1:

Vinny Castilla hits his third homer of the young season and the Rockies, behind John Thomson's three-hit pitching beat the Diamondbacks, 6-0, in Arizona. Mark Clark fans 11 and allows only four hits in seven innings as the Cubs beat the Marlins, 10-3, in Florida. Felix Heredia is charged with the loss.

APRIL 2:

Mark McGwire hits a three-run homer in the bottom of the 12th off Frank Lankford to give his Cardinals an 8-5 win over the Dodgers. It is McGwire's second of the season. The game takes four hours and six minutes, and each team uses all of its position players.

APRIL 4:

Mark McGwire victimizes another Padres' pitcher – Don Wengert – with two runners on for his fourth homer of the season.

The Cubs' Sammy Sosa breaks the ice with his first homer of the season – against Marc Valdes of the Montreal Expos.

APRIL 5:

In his major league debut, Eric Milton pitches six shutout innings and gains his first career win, 10-1, over the visiting Royals.

APRIL 6:

The Yankees are off to a staggering start. Tonight they are blanked by the Mariners and Jamie Moyer, 8-0, in Seattle. Alex Rodriguez homers off Andy Pettitte, who drops to 0-2.

Former major league pitcher John Wyatt dies at 62 in Omaha, Nebraska. Wyatt, who won the sixth game of the 1967 World Series for the Red Sox, pitched for nine years, compiling a 42-44 record and a 3.47 ERA. He spent most of his career with the Kansas City Athletics. He also pitched for the Yankees and Tigers.

APRIL 7:

The Cardinals outhit the Rockies, 12-11, in Colorado, but Mark McGwire is homerless for the first time in five games.

Roger Clemens walks two and retires no one in the first inning and leaves with a strained right groin. The Twins go on to pound the Blue Jays, 12-2, in Minnesota and Clemens takes the loss.

The Milwaukee Brewers, in their first NL home game, top Montreal, 6-4. It is the first time in 33 years – when the Braves left the city – that an NL game is played in Milwaukee. Home run king and Hall of Famer Hank Aaron, who played here for both the Braves and the Brewers, throws out the ceremonial first ball.

APRIL 8:

The once mighty Marlins are floundering. Florida loses its eighth straight, 9-5, to the Phillies in Philadelphia.

APRIL 10:

It's a football score, but baseball – after a fashion – is the game. Before 56,717 fans (the largest regular season crowd in Yankee Stadium since 1976) New York tops the Athletics, 17-13. It is the most runs in a game in the 75-year history of Yankee Stadium. The A's score all their runs in two innings – five in the second and eight in the fifth-and

HISTORY

The Tampa Bay Devil Rays and the Arizona Diamondbacks make their debut and share a common fate – opening day losses.

TRIVIA

El Duque and his common-law wife left Cuba on a 20-foot sailboat. Shipwrecked in the Caribbean, they spent several cold December days on a deserted island before being rescued by the Coast Guard.

LEAGUE

The Marlins to date have disposed of 16 players and reduced their payroll from $53.3 million at the end of the World Series to $24 million after the May 15 deals.

Sammy Sosa shows his home run swing.

match the Yankees with 16 hits. Each team commits two errors; the Yankees draw 12 walks, the A's six.

Despite all of the scoring, there is only one homer – by Tino Martinez, who also has five RBI.

The Marlins drop their ninth straight, losing this time to the Pirates, 4-1, in Pittsburgh. Florida falls to 1-8, the worst start ever by a World Series champion.

Randy Johnson strikes out 15 Red Sox and allows only two hits in eight innings, but the Red Sox beat the Mariners, 9-7, on Mo Vaughn's ninth-inning grand slam against Paul Spoljaric.

APRIL 11:

Sammy Sosa homers – his second of the year – off Anthony Telford – but the visiting Cubs lose to the Expos on Vladimir Guerrero's RBI double in the bottom of the 10th.

Pedro Martinez mows down the Mariners, 5-0, in Boston for his second win. He goes the distance, allowing two hits and striking out 12.

In San Francisco, Mark McGwire reaches a personal milestone, but it is not for home runs. Big Mac registers the 1,000th run batted in of his career – as the result of a bases-loaded walk in the seventh inning of a 7-2 victory over the Giants. He is hitless in his four other trips to the plate.

APRIL 14:

McGwire is on the rampage after an eight-game dry spell. He homers three times today – in the third, fifth-and eighth innings. He raises his season's total to seven and has 22 RBI. His victims today are Barry Manuel and Jeff Suppan (two).

Matt Williams connects for the first gram-slam homer in Diamondbacks history, but St. Louis wins, 15-5.

Kevin Milwood fans 13 and allows only one hit in a 6-0 complete-game win over the Pirates in Atlanta. Jermaine Allensworth's one-out, fifth-inning double spoils the no-hit bid.

APRIL 26:

Juan Gonzalez connects for two homers and drives in four runs to lead the Rangers over the Royals, 11-4, in Kansas City. Gonzalez now has 32 RBI for the month of April; he needs two to tie Tino Martinez's record.

McGWIRE SAYS, "I'M EXCITED FOR SAMMY." SOSA SAYS, "THIS IS THE MARK McGWIRE SHOW. IF I GET THERE FIRST, GOD BLESS AMERICA."

Vinny Castilla homers twice, doubles, and bats in five runs as the Rockies beat the Braves and Greg Maddux, 7-6, in Atlanta. Maddux uncharacteristically yields 10 hits and six runs in only five innings; it is his worst performance since June 7, 1996.

Moises Alou wreaks havoc on his father's team with a homer and five RBI as the Astros crush the Expos, 15-0, in Montreal. It is the sixth time in his career that he has had five RBI in a game.

Curt Schilling fans Mark McGwire three times, strikes out 10 other batters, and the Phillies beat the Cardinals, 9-3.

Longtime executive Gabe Paul dies at 88 in Tampa, Florida. Paul began in baseball at the age of 10 as a batboy for the minor league Rochester Red Wings, and ended his career in 1984 when he resigned as general manager of the Indians. In between, he was the general

CUBS

MAY 8
Mark McGwire hits his 400th career home run.

HISTORY

In 1921, it took Babe Ruth 91 games, and in 1961, Roger Maris needed 96 games to reach the plateau Mark McGwire hit in just 90 games.

HISTORY

Mark McGwire has now homered in all 29 major league ballparks.

manager of the Reds and Yankees, building championship teams for teams. He also was a consultant to the fledgling Houston franchise. Paul was responsible for the purchase of the Yankees by George Steinbrenner.

APRIL 27:

The Yankees improve to 15-5 with a 1-0 win over the Blue Jays in New York. Andy Pettitte earns his fourth win. Tino Martinez's third-inning sacrifice fly with the bases loaded generates the game's only run and makes a loser of Roger Clemens.

APRIL 29:

Despite Ken Griffey Jr.'s ninth homer, the Yankees top the Mariners, 8-5, in New York.

APRIL 30:

Rolando Arrojo three-hits the Twins, 2-0, in Minnesota. It is his first career complete game and the first in the brief history of the Devil Rays. Todd Walker gets all three hits off Arrojo.

MAY 1:

The Tigers pound the Mariners, 17-3, in Seattle. Detroit raps out 20 hits, including two homers by Bobby Higginson.

Rod Beck of the Cubs is today's victim as Mark McGwire connects for 12th of the season. By McGwire standards this is a "puny" homer – only 362 feet.

MAY 2:

Rick Helling of the Rangers subdues the Red Sox, 7-6, in Boston to become the majors' first six-game winner. Helling also becomes the first Texas pitcher to win his first six starts.

MAY 4:

Vinny Castilla hits his 14th homer and the Rockies pummel the Phillies, 11-2, in Philadelphia. Castilla currently leads the majors in homers.

Keith Lockhart connects, giving the Braves homers in 16 consecutive games. Kevin Millwood holds the visiting Dodgers to four hits and Atlanta wins, 4-2.

MAY 5:

Ken Griffey Jr. hits his 13th homer and the Mariners slam the White Sox, 8-1, in Seattle.

MAY 6:

Cubs rookie Kerry Wood pitches himself into the record books alongside Roger Clemens when he strikes out 20 Astros today at Wrigley Field. The 20-year-old with a 100 mile-an-hour fastball is only the second pitcher ever with 20 strikeouts in a nine-inning game. In only his fifth major league start, Wood allows only one hit and walks none. His bid for a perfect game is spoiled by Ricky Guitierrez's leadoff single in the third. In the first, fifth, seventh, and eighth, Wood strikes out the side.

Roger Clemens has accomplished the feat twice – in 1986 and in 1996.

MAY 8:

Mark McGwire hits his 400th career homer and 13th of the season; the historic blow comes off a Rick Reed 0-2 fastball. Mets fans do get to cheer the home team, though; Brian McRae's three-run homer in the fourth leads the Mets to a 9-2 victory.

MAY 9:

For the 21st consecutive game an Atlanta player homers. Today it is Chipper Jones who connects with the bases loaded in the seventh against Dan Miceli. The Braves and Kevin Millwood beat the visiting Padres, 6-4.

MAY 10:

The Braves extend their consecutive-game home run streak to 22 – with an exclamation point. Javy Lopez, Andres Galarraga, Andruw Jones, and Ryan Klesko all reach the seats as Atlanta tops the Padres, 8-5, in Atlanta.

Ken Griffey Jr. is heating up. The Mariners' star hits his 15th homer – in the eighth off Toronto's Dan Plesac – and leads the majors.

MAY 11:

Andruw Jones connects twice and Andres Galarraga once; the visiting Braves defeat the Reds, 8-1, and extend their home run streak to 23 games. Greg Maddux registers his fifth win.

Todd Stottlemyre fans 13, allows only two hits, and beats the Brewers, 7-0, in St. Louis. Mark McGwire walks twice and is

MAY 12
Cardinals' manager Tonay LaRussa gets his 1,500th career win.

MAY 17
The Yankees' David Wells pitches a perfect game.

hitless in two official at-bats.

Kerry Wood fans 13 and wins his fourth game as the Cubs down the Diamondbacks, 4-2, in Arizona. The fireball rookie allows five hits and one run – a homer by Kelly Stinnett – in 7 innings.

MAY 12:

Mark McGwire launches a 527-foot space shot against the Brewers' Paul Wagner with 2 runners on in the 5th. It is the longest home run in the 32-year history of St. Louis's Busch Stadium and the 14th of the season for the slugger. However, it is not the longest of Big Mac's career – that distinction belongs to a 538-foot drive last June while with the Athletics.

The Cardinals give manager Tony LaRussa his 1,500th win when Delino DeShields singles in Dave Howard in the 10th inning.

The Braves tie an NL record – homers in 24 consecutive games – when Andres Galarraga connects for his 15th of the season. The Braves win, 5-1, over the Reds in Cincinnati.

The Yankees continue to roll, defeating the Royals, 3-2, in New York. The Yankees are now 25-7. David Wells gets the win; Mariano Rivera earns a save.

MAY 13:

Ryan Klesko hits one out with a runner on in the sixth off John Frascatore and the Braves set an NL record for homering in consecutive games – 25. Tom Glavine and the Braves beat the Cardinals in St. Louis, 10-2.

MAY 15:

The Marlins ship out four more members of their 1997 World Championship team. Florida sends outfielder Gary Sheffield (.272, six homers, 28 RBI), third baseman Bobby Bonilla (.278, four homers, 15 RBI), catcher Charles Johnson (.221, seven homers, 23 RBI), outfielder-first baseman Jim Eisenreich (.250, one homer, seven RBI), and pitcher Manuel Barrios (0-0, 3.38 ERA in two games) to the Dodgers for catcher Mike Piazza (.282, nine homers, 30 RBI) and third baseman Todd Zeile (.253, seven homers, 27 RBI).

The New York Times *notes that nearly $100 million worth of players were exchanged today: "Never has there been a trade involving the amount of money covered in the players' contracts."*

In St. Louis, after one out in the first, the Marlins rap out nine straight hits, score seven times and defeat the Cardinals and rookie pitcher Brady Raggio, 8-7. On the bench, awaiting completion of the blockbuster trade, are the three players ticketed for Los Angeles.

After having its consecutive-game homer streak ended at 25 games by St. Louis, the Braves are banging the ball out of the park again. Eddie Perez connects twice off losing pitcher Jose Lima and the Braves top the Astros, 3-2. Denny Neagle gets the win with a save by Dennis "El Presidente" Martinez.

MAY 16:

Mark McGwire breaks his own distance record with his 16th homer of the season – estimated at 545 feet. Big Mac unloads against Livan Hernandez in the bottom of the seventh, tying him with Vinny Castilla for the major league lead and setting a Busch Stadium record.

In Cincinnati, Sammy Sosa connects for his eighth homer and the Cubs edge the Reds, 5-4.

MAY 17:

Yankees' left-hander David Wells becomes the 15th pitcher in history to pitch a perfect game. He pitches his masterpiece at Yankee Stadium, defeating the Twin, 4-0, and fanning 11 along the way.

The only other Yankee to pitch a perfect game was Don Larsen in the 1956 World Series. The last in the majors was Kenny Rogers, then of the Texas Rangers, in 1998. Wells also becomes the 10th Yankee pitcher to throw a complete no-hitter game.

MAY 18:

Mark McGwire rocks Jesus Sanchez of the Marlins with a 478-foot homer at Busch Stadium; it is his major league-leading 17th. But, paced by newly acquired Mike Piazza's two run triple, the Marlins beat the Cardinals, 7-3.

On Mark McGwire's heels is Ken Griffey Jr., who slams his

TRIVIA

Family is the theme of the 69th All-Star Game: With his homer, Barry Bonds and his father, Bobby, join the Griffeys as the only two father-son teams to homer in All-Star Games. And Bret Boone and his father, Bob, are the sixth father and son to play in All-Star contests. The others are Moises and Felipe Alou, Barry and Bobby Bonds, the Griffeys, and the Alomars – sons Sandy Jr. and Roberto and father Sandy Sr.

MAY 19
Mark McGwire homers three times against the Phillies.

LEAGUE

Banned for some 30 years because of anger over his tell-all book *Ball Four*, Jim Bouton returns to Yankee Stadium to appear in the Old-Timers Day game.

HISTORY

Also honored in Cooperstown are pioneering African-American journalist Sam Lacy and Jaime Jarin, the Spanish-language announcer for the Los Angeles Dodgers. Lacy, 94 years old, is still a working writer and editor.

16th today in a 9-4 win over the Blue Jays and Roger Clemens in Toronto. Clemens is cuffed for 10 hits and nine earned runs in five innings. It is the most earned runs he has given up in seven years.

MAY 19:

McGwire homers, McGwire homers, McGwire homers. Big Mac connects three times – his 18th, 19th, and 20th of the season – in Philadelphia. He hits his first two off Tyler Green and the third off Wayne Gomes.

The Yankees and Orioles brawl in New York, after Baltimore's Armando Benitez hits Tino Martinez in the back with a fastball. This immediately follows Bernie Williams's three-run homer with two out in the eighth, and is taken by the Yankees as deliberate. Darryl Strawberry leads the Yankee charge, landing a punch to Benitez' face. When calm is restored, Benitez's is ejected and even some of his teammates are critical of his actions. Strawberry and teammates Graeme Lloyd and Jeff Nelson also are ejected, along with the Orioles' Alan Mills. The Yankees win the game, 9-5.

In the aftermath of the fight, AL president Gene Budig suspends Benitez for eight games, Strawberry and Lloyd for three games each, and Nelson and Mills for two games each. Says Budig, "The severity of the discipline reflects the gravity of the offenses. Mr. Benitez not only intentionally threw at Martinez, but the location of the pitch was extremely dangerous and could have seriously injured the player." Several days later, Benitez issues an apology to Tino Martinez and to his own teammates.

Woody Williams flirts with a no-hitter, but has to settle for a 3-1 win over the Devil Rays in Toronto. Williams holds Tampa Bay hitless until the eighth, when Kevin Stocker singles.

MAY 20:

The Yankees take their revenge on the field, beating the Orioles again, 9-6. Martinez is on the bench as a result of his injury last night. And despite being instructed by manager Joe Torre to refrain from throwing at batters, Hideki Irabu plunks two Orioles.

Pedro Martinez rings up his fifth win – against no defeats – beating the White Sox in Boston, 6-2. His ERA is now a sparkling 1.74.
Mark McGwire takes a day off and his replacement, Gary Gaetti, hits two two-run homers, as the visiting Cardinals beat the Phillies, 8-5

Kevin Tapani pitches a complete-game two-hitter, fanning nine, and tops the Dodgers, 5-0, in Chicago.

MAY 22:

Only a week after being traded from Los Angeles to Florida, catcher Mike Piazza is packing his bags for New York and bringing his $8 million-a-year salary and his .331 lifetime batting average with him. The All-Star is exchanged for three minor leaguers – outfielder Preston Wilson and pitchers Ed Yarnall and Geoff Goetz, the Mets' top draft choice last year.

Piazza was in Florida long enough to appear in five games and, come to bat 18 times with five hits and five RBI.

Colorado's Larry Walker hits two singles and extends his hitting streak to 17 games. The Rockies edge the Reds, 3-2, in Cincinnati.

MAY 23:

After slamming his 22nd and 23rd homers today at home, Mark McGwire is on pace for 79. He connects today with the bases empty in the fourth off Rich Rodriguez, and a 477-foot bomb with two on in the fifth against losing pitcher John Johnstone.

The Yankees pound out 15 hits and defeat the Red Sox, 12-3, at Fenway Park. David Wells gets his sixth win. The Yankees have a .762 winning percentage.

MAY 24:

In St. Louis, Mark McGwire victimizes Giants' reliever Robb Nen with a 12th inning homer-his 24th round-tripper of the season. McGwire's homer ties the game, but the Giants take no chances with Big Mac in the 14th – he is intentionally walked by Jim Poole. San Francisco goes on to win, 9-6, in 17 innings. Barry Bonds homers for the Giants – his 11th. McGwire ties Ken Griffey Jr.'s major league record for most homers at the end of May.

JULY
5
Roger Clemens records his 3,000th career strikeout.

The Yankees defeat the red Sox, 14-4, in Fenway Park and are on pace to win an unprecedented 124 games. David Cone records his sixth win. Johnson and Griffey add up to victory. The Mariners defeat the Devil Rays, 3-1, in Seattle. Randy Johnson pitches a complete game, striking out 15; Ken Griffey Jr. slams a 425-foot homer – his 18th – off losing pitcher Dennis Springer.

MAY 25:

Sammy Sosa reaches the seats twice, for his 10th and 11th homers. Mike Cather and Kevin Millwood of Atlanta are today's fall guys.

Pedro Martinez loses for the first time, as the visiting Blue Jays – with Jose Canseco, Jose Cruz, and Shawn Green all homering off the right-hander – win, 7-5.

David Bell his a two-run double to lead the Indians past his father's team, the Tigers, 7-4.

Hideki Irabu has his first shutout as the Yankees streamroller the White Sox, 12-0, in Chicago.

MAY 27:

Sammy Sosa is heating up. The Cubs' slugger connects with one on twice today — off Darrin Winston and Wayne Gomes of the Phillies — for homers 12 and 13. But the Cubs waste Sosa's efforts and lose, 10-5, at Wrigley Field.

The Braves sign catcher Javy Lopez to a three-year, $19.25 million contract extension.

MAY 28:

Alex Rodriguez hits his 20th homer in a 5-2 Mariners victory over the Devil Rays in Tampa Bay. The Seattle shortstop leads the AL in round-trippers.

MAY 30:

Mark McGwire continues to pound the Padres. Today he reaches Andy Ashby for his 30th - a 423-footer with the bases empty.

JULY 1:

The Cubs' Kerry Wood strikes out 13 Diamondbacks and wins his eighth game, 6-4.

Greg Vaughn hits his 28th homer and his Padres beat the A's, 8-4.

JULY 2:

Atlanta Braves ace Greg Maddux whitewashes the Devil Rays, 6-0, for his 12th victory and second straight shutout. Chipper Jones hits his 20th homer. It's number 35 for Ken Griffey Jr. and a 10-3 win over the Rockies for the Mariners.

JULY 3:

Boston's Nomar Garciaparra has three hits, extending his streak to 24 games, in a 15-2 win over the White Sox at Fenway Park.

JULY 4:

The streak is over. Three White Sox pitchers hold Nomar Garciaparra hitless in two official at-bats; Boston wins, 3-0.

It's 60 wins for the Yankees as they top the Orioles again, 4-3, behind Orlando Hernandez.

The Dodgers obtain reliever Jeff Shaw (2-4, 1.81 ERA, 23 saves) from the Dodgers for infielder Paul Konerko (.215, four homers, 16 RBI in 49 games) and pitcher Dennis Reyes (0-4, 4.71 ERA).

JULY 5:

In the third inning, Roger Clemens fans Randy Winn of the Devil Rays to register his 3,000th career strikeout. He is the 11th pitcher to reach that landmark. Clemens fans seven for the game, but is not involved in the decision as the Blue Jays win, 2-1.

JULY 7:

In the All-Star Game, the AL spanks the NL, 13-8, with 19 hits, at Coors Field. The NL collects 12 safeties. Roberto Alomar, who is the game's MVP, homers. Also connecting are Barry Bonds for the NL and Alex Rodriguez for the AL. Bartolo Colon gets the win and Ugueth Urbina is charged with the loss.

JULY 9:

The Yankees and Sammy Sosa pick up where they left off before the All-Star break. Sosa sends a Jeff Juden pitch 432 feet for his 34th homer, but the Cubs, playing in Milwaukee for the first time since 1965, lose to the Brewers, 12-9.

JULY 10:

Sammy Sosa hits his 35th – off Scott Karl. Kerry Wood fans nine, but the Cubs lose again, 6-5, to the Brewers.

Ken Griffey Jr. homers off Chuck

TRIVIA

Leland MacPhail and his father, Larry MacPhail, are the only father-son team in the Hall of Fame.

JULY 12
Mark McGwire hits homers 39 and 40, making him the player who is fastest to reach the 40 plateau

Finley for his 37th, but the Angels win, 5-3.

JULY 11:

Mark McGwire's bat awakens. He connects off Billy Wagner of the Astros for his 38th homer in the bottom of the 11th inning with a runner on, lifting the Cardinals past the Astros, 4-3. McGwire leads Griffey by one homer.

Randy Johnson fans 15 and beats the Angels in Seattle, 2-0. Two days ago Johnson and teammate David Segui had a club-house fight with no apparent winner.

JULY 12:

Mark McGwire reaches 40 homers faster than any other player in history. He connects for two today – off Sean Bergman and Scott Elarton of the Astros – to reach the new plateau in 90 games. McGwire now has 91 RBI. The Cardinals win, 6-4, in St. Louis.

The Braves beat the Marlins, 5-3, for Tom Glavine's 12th win.

Eric Davis, a cancer survivor, hits his 10th career grand slam and collects five RBI as the Orioles beat the visiting Red Sox, 11-7.

JULY 14:

The Yankee Express keeps rolling.
New York tops the Indians in Cleveland, 7-1, for the team's 66th win and Andy Pettitte's 12th.
Ken Griffey Jr. hits his 39th home run and the Mariners top the Rangers, 6-3.

JULY 15:

Andres Galarraga launches two mammoth homers – his 29th and 30th – leading the Braves over the Mets, 12-1, in New York.

The Padres beat the Rockies, 6-2, with Kevin Brown picking up his eigth straight win and 11th on the season.

JULY 16:

Randy Johnson one-hits the Twins, 3-0, in Seattle. Bret Gates's single with one out in the eighth is Minnesota's sole hit. Johnson fans 11.

JULY 17:

It's another pair for Big Mac. Mark McGwire, after being hampered with back spasms, busts out big time with his 41st – against Brian Bohanon – and his 42nd – off Antonio Osuna. He sets a major league record for the most homers by the end of July – and there are still 14 days to go. McGwire also walks twice, bringing his total to 99. The Cardinals beat the Dodgers, 4-1.
Sammy Sosa hits his 36th, against Kirt Ojala in a 6-1 Cubs victory over the Marlins. Sosa had been homerless since July 10.

JULY 20:

McGwire hits number 43 off San Diego's Brian Boehringer with a runner on.

The Yankees go down to the Tigers in New York, 4-3, in 17 innings. It is the fourth loss in 5 games for the Yankees. The Yankees strand 22 runners in the 5 hour, 50 minute contest.

Pitcher Kevin Tapani of the Cubs hits his first career homer and makes it a grand slam. The Cubs beat the Braves, 11-4, and Tapani gets his 11th win.

JULY 21:

Ken Griffey Jr. hits homer number 40 - to lead the AL - and the Mariners beat the Devil Rays, 8-3, in Florida.

JULY 22:

Sammy Sosa homers off Miguel Batista of the Expos for his 37th and the Cubs win, 9-5.

Tom Glavine wins his 14th, topping the Phillies, 14-2. Andres Galarraga raises his home run total to 32 with two today.

The Yankees beat the Tigers, 13-2, in New York; Orlando "El Duque" Hernandez gets his fifth win.

JULY 23:

The Padres beat the Diamondbacks, 3-0, and lead the NL West by 13 games over the Giants.

JULY 25:

Greg Vaughn hits his 37th homer and his Padres beat the Astros, 6-5. Trevor Hoffman ties a major league record when he gets a save in his 41st consecutive opportunity.

JULY 26:

After being held hitless in 16 at-bats, Mark McGwire clubs number 44 off the Rockies' John Thomson in a 3-1 win over the Rockies at Coors Field. McGwire breaks Johnny Mize's team record for home runs in a season.

In Chicago, Sammy Sosa hangs close with his 38th homer – off Rick Reed – and the

LEAGUE

Bud Selig, now officially baseball commissioner, resigns as president and CEO of the Brewers. He is succeeded by his daughter, Wendy Selig-Prieb.

HISTORY

Barry Bonds reaches a milestone. He hits his 400th career homer, becoming the first player ever to reach that number in both home runs and stolen bases.

JULY 31
Pitcher Randy Johnson is dealt to the Houston Astros.

Cubs beat the Mets, 3-1. Kerry Wood gets his 10th win.

Trevor Hoffman blows a save opportunity, ending his streak at 41 and falling short of Rod Beck's major league mark.

Pedro Martinez beats the Blue Jays, 6-3, for his 14th win.

Five baseball immortals are honored at Cooperstown. Inducted today are George Davis, Larry Doby, Bullet Joe Rogan, Don Sutton, and Lee MacPhail. Davis was a turn-of-the-century shortstop. A switch hitter, he batted .295 with the New York Giants and Chicago White Stockings and White Sox during the dead ball era. He had six RBI when the "Hitless Wonders" White Sox beat the Cubs in the 1906 World Series. Davis died in 1940. Larry Doby was the first black player in the AL, following Jackie Robinson into the majors by 11 weeks in 1947. He played for 13 years with the Indians and White Sox (and 18 games with the Tigers), batting .283 with 253 homers. Previously, he starred with the Newark Eagles in the Negro Leagues. Bullet Joe Rogan was a dominant pitcher and an outstanding hitter in the Negro Leagues, helping to lead the Kansas City Monarchs to four championships. His pitching record was 113-45 and he batted .343 in his 18-year career. He also was a manager and an umpire. Rogan died in 1967. Don Sutton won 324 games in his 23-year career with the Dodgers, Astros, Brewers, Athletics, and Angels and fanned 3,574. Leland Stanford "Le" MacPhail was an executive for 45 years with the Yankees and Orioles. During his tenure with New York, the team won seven World Series in 10 years. He also was president of the AL from 1974 to 1983.

Of his historic role, Larry Doby says, "I'll take second. Second ain't all that bad!"

JULY 27:

Sammy Sosa hits number 39 – a grand slam – and number 40, victimizing the Diamondbacks' Willie Blair and Alan Embree.

Wade Boggs of the Devil Rays homers and singles twice against the A's. He now has 2,874 career hits, moving him past Babe Ruth and into 33rd place on the all-time leader list. The Devil Rays win, 11-5.

Former major league outfielder Bill Tuttle dies at 69 in Anoka, Minnesota. After developing mouth cancer, he became a crusader against the use of chewing tobacco. Tuttle played 11 years with the Tigers, the Kansas City Athletics, and the Twins, batting .259 and earning a reputation for his defensive skills.

JULY 28:

Mark McGwire homers to right field off Mike Myers for his 45th of the season, but the Brewers beat the Cardinals in St. Louis, 13-10.

Sammy Sosa stays on McGwire's heels with his 41st, off Bob Wolcott in Arizona. The Cubs lose to the Diamondbacks, 7-5.

JULY 30:

Omar Daal defeats the Cubs, 4-0, becoming the first Diamondback to pitch a complete-game shutout.

Ken Griffey Jr. bangs out his 41st homer – off Dave Burba – but Cleveland tops Seattle, 9-8.
Eric Davis hits two more homers - number 19 and number 20 - and extends his consecutive-game hitting streak to 17 as the Orioles beat the Tigers, 6-4.

The Red Sox obtain Mike Stanley (.240, 22 homers, 47 RBI) from the Blue Jays for two minor leaguers.

JULY 31:

Sammy Sosa clouts number 42 against Jamey Wright of the Rockies, and the Cubs win, 9-1.

The day of the non-waiver trading deadline is marked by a flurry of swaps. The Rangers obtain third baseman Todd Zeile (.291, six homers, 39 RBI) from the Marlins for two minor leaguers - third baseman Jose Santo and pitcher Daniel DeYoung. The Rangers also send pitcher Darren Oliver (6-7, 6.53 ERA) and third baseman Fernando Tatis (.270, three homers, 32 RBI) to the Cardinals for pitcher Todd Stottlemyre (9-9, 3.51 ERA) and shortstop Royce Clayton (.234, four homers, 29 RBI).

The Blue Jays send pitcher Juan Guzman

HISTORY

Amid the excitement of the home run chase, a controversy stirs. An Associated Press reporter sees a bottle of androstenedione – a legal over-the-counter nutritional supplement to enhance the production of testosterone – in Mark McGwire's locker. McGwire admits to using it and a major league spokesman tells AP, "Obviously, if there's more research and it's shown that it's harmful, we'll make people aware." The National Football League and the Olympics currently ban the use of androstenedione. The Cardinals and McGwire issue a statement asserting that it is a "natural substance" with "no proven anabolic steroid effect." The commissioner's office and the players union launch a medical investigation into nutritional supplements.

McGwire is now on pace to hit 75 homers. But, The Associated Press reports, he brushes off talk of a record. "When somebody gets to 50 by September, then it's legitimate to talk about. Right now, I don't think it is."

HISTORY

Richard Sandomir of the *New York Times* reports an anonymous donor has offered $1 million for the 62nd homer ball hit by either Mark McGwire or Sammy Sosa to help "in the continuing search for justice in the 1980 murders of three American nuns and a lay worker in El Salvador."

(6-12, 4.41 ERA) to the Orioles for pitcher Nerio Rodriguez (1-3, 8.05 ERA) and minor league outfielder Shannon Carter. The Mets send outfielder Bernard Gilkey (.227, four homers, 28 RBI), minor league pitcher Nelson Figueroa, and cash to the Diamondbacks for pitcher Willie Blair (4-15, 5.34 ERA), catcher Jorge Fabregas (.199, one homer, 15 RBI), and a player to be named later.

The Giants obtain outfielder Ellis Burks (.286, 16 homers, 54 RBI) from the Rockies for outfielder Darryl Hamilton (.294, one homer, 26 RBI), minor league pitcher James Stoops, and a player to be named later.

The Expos ship pitcher Carlos Perez (7-10, 3.75 ERA), shortstop Mark Grudzielanek (.275, eight homers, 41 RBI), and minor league outfielder Hiram Bocachica to the Dodgers for second baseman Wilton Guerrero (.283, no homers, seven RBI) – who joins his brother Vladimir in Montreal – and three minor leaguers: pitcher Ted Lilly, outfielder Peter Bergeron, and first baseman Jonathan Tucker. The most sought-after player on the block is dealt with just 10 minutes left before the deadline. The Mariners send pitcher Randy Johnson (9-10, 4.33 ERA, 213 strikeouts) to the Astros for two minor leaguers – pitcher Freddy Garcia and infielder Carlos Guillen – and a player to be named later.

AUGUST 1:

Pedro Martinez wins his 15th game as the Red Sox top the Angels, 11-3, in Anaheim.

Tony the Tiger gets into the record book. Detroit's switch-hitting Tony Clark homers from both sides of the plate for the third time this season, setting an AL record. He is one behind Ken Caminiti's major league mark. The Tigers and Brian Moehler blank the Devil Rays, 8-0.

AUGUST 2:

Less than 48 hours after being traded to the Astros, Randy Johnson rings up his first win in his new uniform. He beats the Pirates, 6-2, fanning 12 and allowing six hits.Andy Ashby of the Padres beats the Expos, 4-1, for his 15th win. Roger Clemens strikes out 14, topping the Twins, 6-4, in Minnesota, for his 14th win.

AUGUST 3:

Tony Batista hits the first pinch-hit homer in Diamondbacks' history and Arizona beats the Cubs, 6-5, in Chicago. Sammy Sosa has three hits, with nary a homer among them.

AUGUST 4:

Mike Mussina's bid for a perfect game fails when rookie Frank Catalanotto doubles with two out in the eighth. Mussina settles for a two-hitter and a 4-0 win over the Tigers.

Darryl Strawberry raps out a pinch-hit grand-slam homer in a nine-run ninth as the Yankees top the A's in Oakland for their 80th win.

AUGUST 5:

One contestant resumes the home run chase. While Mark McGwire, in a 24-at-bat homer drought, sits out a game, Sammy Sosa takes Andy Benes of the Diamondbacks long for his 43rd. But Arizona tops Chicago and Kerry Wood, 10-7.

AUGUST 6:

Jack Brickhouse, a baseball broadcaster from 1940 to 1981, dies in Chicago at 82. Brickhouse announced more than 5,000 Cubs and White Sox games during his career.

AUGUST 7:

The Yankees sweep a doubleheader against the Royals in New York, 8-2 and 14-2. The Yankees now have 82 wins and lead the AL East by 17 games.

AUGUST 8:

In a face-to-face meeting in St. Louis, Mark McGwire and Sammy Sosa each take a step forward in the home-run race. McGwire connects against Mark Clark for his 46th, and Sosa takes Rich Croushire long for his 44th. The Cardinals nip the Cubs, 9-8. McGwire had been homerless in 29 at-bats.

AUGUST 9:

The Braves beat the Giants, 7-5, in San Francisco and Dennis "El Presidente" Martinez gets his 244th career victory, making him the winningest Latin American pitcher ever. Andres Galarraga hits his

AUGUST 8
Mark McGwire and Sammy Sosa meet face to face and each homers.

AUGUST 20
Mark McGwire becomes the first player to hit 50 homers in 3 consecutive seasons.

36th homer for Atlanta.

AUGUST 10:

Sammy Sosa draws even with Mark McGwire with two homers today against the Giants. Sosa hits number 45 off Russ Ortiz and number 46 off Chris Brock.

Eric Davis extends his hitting streak to 26 games as his Orioles top the Devil Rays, 2-1.

AUGUST 11:

Mark McGwire inches ahead with his 47th homer of the year – a 464-foot drive in St. Louis off the Mets' Bobby Jones. But the Cardinals lose, 8-3.

AUGUST 12:

Randy Johnson five-hits the Brewers, 3-0, fanning 13 and ringing up his third straight win as an Astro.

Alex Rodriguez hits his 36th homer – and 100th of his career. He is the fourth-youngest player to reach the century mark in homers. Despite the efforts of "A Rod," the Blue Jays sink the Mariners, 11-5.

AUGUST 13:

The Braves' Tom Glavine shuts out the Padres, 5-0, for his 16th win and extends his streak of shutout innings to 23.

AUGUST 14:

Chris Hoiles hits two grand slams as the Orioles rout the Indians, 15-3, in Cleveland. Hoiles is the ninth major leaguer and the first catcher to hit two bases-loaded homers in a single game.

AUGUST 15:

Ken Griffey hits his 42nd homer and his first since July 30. Seattle beats the White Sox, 13-7.

Roger Clemens gets 15 strikeouts and a no decision as the Angels beat the Blue Jays, 6-3.

Andres Galarraga hits a three-run homer – his second in two games – and the Braves beat the Dodgers, 5-3. The "Big Cat" now has 38.

AUGUST 16:

Sammy Sosa ties Mark McGwire with his 47th homer – off Sean Bergman in Houston. Kerry Wood fans 11, but is not involved in the decision. The Cubs win, 2-1.

Five Indians' pitchers shut down Eric Davis, ending his hit streak at thirty games. The Indians beat the Orioles, 5-3.

AUGUST 17:

David Cone wins his 18th as the Yankees top the Royals, 7-1, in Kansas City.

AUGUST 18:

One of the forgotten men in the homer race, Greg Vaughn, hits his 40th as his Padres drop the Marlins, 7-5, in Florida.

Greg Maddux wins his 16th, defeating the Giants, 8-4, in Atlanta.

Mo Vaughn hits his 33rd homer and Pedro Martinez gains his 16th win in the opener of a double-header with the Rangers. The Red Sox sweep with two wins: 4-1 and 5-4.

AUGUST 19:

In another head-to-head meeting – in Chicago – Mark McGwire and Sammy Sosa flex their muscles. McGwire connects against Matt Karchner for his 48th and Terry Mulholland for his 49th, while Sosa homers off Kent Bottenfield for his 48th. St Louis wins, 8-6, in ten innings.

AUGUST 20:

The sleeping giant is wideawake. Playing in New York, Mark McGwire homers in both games of a double-header, bringing his total to 51. McGwire connects off Willie Blair in the opener and Rick Reed in the nightcap. The teams split.

McGwire is the first player to blast 50 homers in three consecutive years.

Curt Schilling is overpowering as he fans 14 and his Phillies beat the Diamondbacks, 11-1.

AUGUST 21:

Sammy Sosa shows that there is gas left in his tank. He slams number 49 with one on off the Giants' Orel Hershiser in Chicago. The Cubs win, 6-5.

AUGUST 22:

With 33 games left in his drive to surpass Roger Maris, Mark McGwire hits his 52nd – off Francisco Cordova in Pittsburgh – and tops Babe Ruth's marks for homers in three consecutive seasons. In the seventh, McGwire's drive falls just short of the centerfield seats. But

HISTORY

On hand to embrace Mark McGwire on his historic day are the four sons and two daughters of the late Roger Maris.

NEW YORK

AUGUST 28
Sammy Sosa keeps pace with Mark McGwire by hitting his 53rd homer.

Pittsburgh pounds the Cardinals, 14-4.

AUGUST 23:

Mark McGwire clouts number 53 in Pittsburgh off Ricardo Rincon, but the Pirates beat the Cardinals, 4-3. Sammy Sosa makes another move. He connects twice off Jose Lima in a 13-3 loss to the Astros. His first drive clears the bleachers in left centerfield and lands on Waveland Avenue. Sosa now has 51 homers.

And still in the hunt is Ken Griffey Jr., who hits his 43rd - off John Snyder - in a 3-2 Mariners' win over the White Sox.

Pedro Martinez wins his 17th, 5-1, against the Twins.

AUGUST 24:

Ken Griffey hits his 44th – off Mike Sirotka – as the Mariners edge the White Sox, 11-10.

Moises Alou homers – his 38th – but Sammy Sosa doesn't, and the Astros annihilate the Cubs, 12-3.

AUGUST 25:

The Rocket is flaming. Roger Clemens fans 18 Royals and allows only three hits in a 3-0 win in Toronto. It is his 16th win.

Kevin Brown wins his 17th for the Padres, downing the Phillies, 5-3.

AUGUST 26:

Sammy Sosa, in a day game, homers against the Reds' Brett Tomko for his 52nd homer. Kerry Wood strikes out 16 for the Cubs and wins his 12th game. Playing at night in St. Louis, Mark McGwire responds with his 54th – off Justin Speier of the Marlins.

The Yankees beat the Angels, 7-6, in the nightcap of a twin bill in New York, ending a four-game slide.

AUGUST 28:

Sammy Sosa bangs out number 53 - off John Thomson of the Rockies at Coors Field.

Randy Johnson fans 15 Pirates, allows only seven hits, and gains his fifth win for the Astros, 2-0.

AUGUST 29:

Umpire Sam Holbrook may be the bravest man in all of baseball. Working behind the plate in St. Louis, he ejects Mark McGwire in the first inning for arguing a called third strike. Holbrook insists he asked manager Tony LaRussa to get McGwire away, saying, "I want to see him get the record as much as anybody."

The Yankees top the Mariners, 11-6, despite Ken Griffey Jr.'s 45th homer; New York clinches a playoff berth and now has 98 wins.

Pedro Martinez defeats the Angels, 6-1, for his 18th victory.

AUGUST 30:

Mark McGwire is back in the lineup against the Braves and smashes a 501-foot homer off Dennis Martinez with two on. McGwire now has 55; he takes his place along with Hack Wilson as the only NL player with 55 in a season.

Sammy Sosa keeps the pressure on, connecting or his 54th in Coors Field against Darryl Kile.

Ken Griffey Jr. cracks two homers against the Yankees, bringing his total to 47, as the Mariners crush New York, 13-3.

Roger Clemens records his third straight shutout, beat-

MARK MCGWIRE, EVER THE GENTLEMAN, SAYS, "I'M RESPONSIBLE FOR IT. . . . DID I CROSS THE LINE? YEAH, I PROBABLY CROSSED THE LINE. I OWN UP TO IT. HE HAD A RIGHT TO THROW ME OUT. I'M NOT ANY BIGGER THAN THE GAME."

LEAGUE

A bill that would remove part of baseball's 76-year antitrust exemption is passed by Congress. Both the owners and the players' union support the bill, and President Bill Clinton is expected to sign it.

Scott Brosius of the Yankees celebrates winning the World Series.

SEPTEMBER 8
Mark McGwire blasts his 62nd homer, beating Roger Maris's record.

TRIVIA

David Bell and Tigers' manager Buddy Bell become the third father-son combo to face each other. The others were Maury and Bump Wills and Moises and Felipe Alou.

ing the Twins, 6-0. It is his 17th win.

AUGUST 31:

They're tied! In Chicago, Sammy Sosa launches his 55th off the Reds' Brett Tomko. Juan Gonzalez of the Rangers hits his 39th homer and drives in seven runs in a 13-2 romp over the Tigers. Gonzalez leads the majors with 143 RBI.

SEPTEMBER 1:

In Miami, Mark McGwire hits his 56th and 57th homers, breaking Hack Wilson's NL single-season mark, set 68 years ago. Big Mac unloads on Livan Hernandez and Donn Pall, and the Cardinals win, 7-1.

David Wells takes a perfect game into the seventh and yields a two-out single to Jason Giambi. He settles for a two-hitter with 13 strikeouts for his 17th win; the Yankees now have 99.

Omar Dall fans 12 – a record for the young Diamondbacks – and beats the Pirates, 4-3.

SEPTEMBER 2:

In an afternoon game at Wrigley Field, Sammy Sosa hits his 56th off Jason Bere of the Reds in a 4-2 win. At night, Mark McGwire responds with two of his own: number 58 (tying his personal high) off the Marlins' Brian Edmonson and number 59 against Rob Stanifer. The Cardinals maul the Marlins, 14-4.

SEPTEMBER 4:

Sammy Sosa slams his 57th today in Pittsburgh off Jason Schmidt. After the series in Pittsburgh, the Cubs move to St. Louis for another chapter in the home run battle.

Mike Piazza celebrates his 30th birthday with his 29th homer. The Mets, behind Al Leiter, beat Tom Glavine and the Braves, 2-1.

SEPTEMBER 5:

Mark McGwire treads where only Babe Ruth and Roger Maris have gone before. In St. Louis, McGwire laces a pitch from the Reds' Dennis Reyes 381 feet to left field for his 60th homer, tying him with Ruth and leaving him one behind Maris.

And in Pittsburgh, the indomitable Sammy Sosa connects off Sean Lawrence for his 58th, tying Hank Greenberg, McGwire, and Jimmie Foxx for the most ever by a right-handed batter.

Ken Griffey Jr. hits his 48th in Seattle and Roger Clemens wins his 18th, beating the Red Sox in Toronto. The courageous Jim Abbott, back from the minors, is the winner as the White Sox drop the Yankees, 9-5, in Chicago. Abbott, who was born without a right hand, last pitched in the majors nearly two years ago.

SEPTEMBER 7:

In St. Louis facing the Cubs, Mark McGwire joins Roger Maris on the 61-home run plateau. Big Mac connects in the first off a Mike Morgan fastball 430 feet for his historic homer. As he crosses the plate, McGwire lifts and hugs his 10-year-old son, Matthew, who arrived 30 minutes before game time. Also in attendance are McGwire's parents; his father, John, is celebrating his 61st birthday today and has 61 homers to remember it by.

SEPTEMBER 8:

Mark McGwire stands alone – the all-time single-season home run champion. McGwire hits the first pitch in the fourth inning from the Cubs' Steve Trachsel 341 feet for his 62nd homer. Once again, McGwire pauses to lift his son in the air and he is embraced by his friendly rival, Sammy Sosa. The ball is retrieved by a member of the Busch Stadium grounds crew, Tim Forneris.

SEPTEMBER 9:

The Yankees beat the Red Sox, 7-5, for their 102nd win and clinch the AL East.

SEPTEMBER 11:

Sammy Sosa keeps swinging and collects his 59th homer – off Bill Pulsipher of the Brewers. He now is in second place for a right-handed hitter and trails only McGwire, Maris, and Ruth for single-season output.

SEPTEMBER 12:

Sammy Sosa draws even with Babe Ruth, slamming his 60th homer today off Valerio De Los Santos of the Brewers.

In Kansas City, Ken Griffey Jr. hits his 51st homer, becoming the third player in history with three consecutive seasons of 50 or more.

SEPTEMBER 23
Sammy Sosa ties McGwire with his 64th and 65th homers.

Randy Johnson fans 11 and beats the Cardinals, 3-2, for his eighth win as an Astro. In the third, he walks Mark McGwire, giving Big Mac 152 on the season.

SEPTEMBER 13:

Can he really do it? Sammy Sosa sends a message: He is still in the home run race. Sosa connects twice today against the Brewers – off Bronswell Patrick for his 61st and Eric Plunk for his 62nd. He is now only one behind McGwire in this incredible contest. McGwire leaves his game today after only 2 at-bats because of back spasms.

SEPTEMBER 14:

Orlando "El Duque" Hernandez outpitches Pedro Martinez, 3-0, for his first career shutout and his 10th win. The Yankees now have 103 victories.

The Braves beat the Phillies, 4-2, to clinch the NL East. Tom Glavine gets his 19th win.

SEPTEMBER 15:

Once again, Mark McGwire rises to the challenge. In St. Louis today, he comes off the bench and bangs out his 63rd homer – off the Pirates' Jason Christensen – in a rare pinch-hitting role.

And the nearly-invisible superstar, Ken Griffey Jr., hits his 52nd homer. The Seattle Mariners' outfielder becomes the fourth youngest player to reach 1,000 career RBI.

SEPTEBER 16:

In San Diego, Sammy Sosa connects for his 63rd – a grand slam off Brian Boehringer.

SEPTEMBER 17:

It's another homer - number 53 – for Mr. Griffey in Oakland. It is his 11th in 23 games.

In yesterday's game, he swiped a base, becoming the third player in history with 20 stolen bases and 50 homers in the same season. The other two are Willie Mays and Brady Anderson.

Chet Hoff, who had been the oldest living former major leaguer, dies in Daytona, Florida, at 107. Hoff made his big-league debut with the New York Highlanders in 1911 and pitched in the majors for four seasons, compiling a 2-4 record with an ERA of 2.49 in 23 games.

SEPTEMBER 18:

Mark McGwire drives a pitch from Brewers' rookie Rafael Roque 417 feet for his 64th homer, putting him one up on Sammy Sosa.

SEPTEMBER 19:

Manny Ramirez of the Indians hits his 44th and 45th homers of the season; he has eight in the past five games, tying a major league record by Frank Howard, who did it twice in 1968.

SEPTEMBER 20:

Mark McGwire hits number 65 in Milwaukee off Scott Karl and loses what might have been another when fans interfere with a ball 392 feet in the left centerfield bleachers. The NL later rules that it is a ground rule double – as called.

SEPTEMBER 21:

Roger Clemens defeats the Orioles, 3-1, striking out 15 and becoming the AL's first 20-game winner.

SEPTEMBER 23:

Sammy Sosa catches Mark McGwire again – hitting his 64th off Rafael Roque and his 65th off Rodney Henderson in Milwaukee.

SEPTEMBER 24:

The Yankees beat the Devil Rays, 5-2, for their 111th win – a team record.

The Red Sox beat the Orioles, 9-6, to clinch a wild card berth. Pedro Martinez gets his 19th win.

SEPTEMBER 25:

And still they battle on. Sammy Sosa connects in the fourth inning against the Astros' Jose Lima for his 66th. Mark McGwire responds with his 66th in the fifth inning against the Expos' Shayne Bennett.

The Yankees beat the Devil Rays, 6-1, for an AL record 112 wins.

SEPTEMBER 26:

Has Big Mac finally put Sammy Sosa in his rearview mirror? In Montreal, Mark McGwire connects twice – off Dustin Hermanson and Kirk Bullinger – for his 67th and 68th homers.

Curt Schilling fans seven Marlins and ends his season with 300 strikeouts.

HISTORY

Scott Brosius, who bats .471 with two homers and six RBI, is the Series MVP.

The Yankees celebrate their 24th World Championship.

18

SEPTEMBER 27
Mark McGwire wraps up his season by hitting his 69th and 70th home runs.

HISTORY

One of baseball's most amazing streaks ends when Cal Ripken Jr. decides not to play – after a record-shattering 2,632 consecutive games. Says the 38-year-old Ripken, "I think the time is right."

SEPTEMBER 27:

In an unbelievable finish to an unbelievable season, Mark McGwire hits two more to finish his dream season with 70 home runs – nine better than the previous record. Today, Big Mac victimizes two rookies – Mike Thurman and Carl Pavano of the Expos – to create an exclusive chapter for himself in baseball's record book.
The Yankees beat the Devil Rays again, 8-3, to end their season with a 114-48 record and a .704 winning percentage.

SEPTEMBER 28:

The Cubs beat the Giants, 5-3, in a one-game playoff for the wild card spot, extending Sammy Sosa's season.

The Rockies, who finished 77-85, fire manager Don Baylor, the only manager the team has ever had.

REGULAR SEASON WRAP-UP:

If commissioner Bud Selig had hired the best Hollywood writers to create a script for restoring interest and excitement to baseball, it is unlikely their effort would have matched the reality of the 1998 season. The drama of a perfect game, 20-strikeout pitching performances, power hitting, the Yankees record-shattering season – all key events – were overshadowed by the titanic home run race between Mark McGwire and Sammy Sosa and the ghosts of Roger Maris and Babe Ruth. The year was also marked by ironies – perhaps none greater than the Braves' failure to make the World Series once again, despite 100 wins.

The Padres, managed by Bruce Bochy,
finish the regular season at 98-64 in the NL. Kevin Brown (18-7, 2.38 ERA), Andy Ashby (17-9, 3.34 ERA), and Sterling Hitchcock (9-7, 3.93 ERA) are the top starters; Trevor Hoffman is the bullpen ace (4-2, 1.48 ERA, 53 saves). Tony Gwynn (.321, 16 homers, 69 RBI), one of baseball's all-time best hitters; Greg Vaughn (.272, 50 homers,119 RBI), a power hitter; and Ken Caminiti (.252, 29 homers, 82 RBI) provide offensive sparks; Jim Leyritz brings a reputation for timely hits, plus World Series experience.

Joe Torre's Yankees run away with the AL, winning 114 games and losing only 48 – a .704 winning percentage. New York fields a balanced team with many role players and no superstars. The pitching staff is anchored by David Cone (20-7, 3.55 ERA), Andy Pettitte (16-11, 4.24 ERA), David Wells (18-4, 3.49 ERA), and Orlando "El Duque" Hernandez (12-4, 3.13 ERA). Mariano Rivera (3-0, 1.91 ERA, 36 saves) is almost unhittable out of the bullpen. The top Yankee offensive weapons are AL batting champion Bernie Williams (.339, 26 homers, 97 RBI), Derek Jeter (.324, 19 homers, 84 RBI), Paul O'Neill (.317, 24 homers, 116 RBI), and Tino Martinez (.281, 28 homers, 123 RBI).

SEPTEMBER 29:

AL Division Series. David Wells, with one inning of relief from Mariano Rivera, beats Texas, 2-0, in New York.

AL Division Series. The visiting Red Sox maul the Indians, 11-3, behind winning pitcher Pedro Martinez and homers from Mo Vaughn (who drives in seven runs) and Nomar Garciaparra. The victory is Boston's first in post-season play after 13 consecutive defeats. Jaret Wright gets the loss. Kenny Lofton and Jim Thome homer for the Indians.

NL Division Series. The visiting Padres, behind Kevin Brown's masterful pitching, top the Astros, 2-1. Brown works eight, allowing two hits and fanning 16. Jim Leyritz's sacrifice fly in the sixth provides San Diego with its first run; Greg Vaughn's eighth-inning homer off losing pitcher Randy Johnson provides the winning margin.

SEPTEMBER 30:

AL Division Series. The Yankees beat the visiting Rangers, 3-1. Shane Spencer and Scott Brosius homer for New York. Andy Pettitte gets the win with relief from Jeff Nelson and Mariano Rivera; Rick Helling is the loser.

NL Division Series. The Cubs, in the playoffs for the first time in nine years, travel to Atlanta and are defeated by the Braves, 7-1. John Smoltz allows only five hits, keeps Sammy Sosa's power in check, and gets the win, with relief from John Rocker and

SEPTEMBER 28
The Cubs defeat the Giants in a one-game playoff for the wild card spot.

Kerry Ligtenberg. Michael Tucker and Ryan Klesko homer for the winners. Mark Clark gets the loss.

AL Division Series. The Indians parlay a five-run second inning into a 9-5 win and knot their series with the Red Sox. Dave Burba enters the game after starter Doc Gooden is ejected – along with manager Mike Hargrove - in the first inning, and gets the victory. Red Sox starter Tim Wakefield gets the loss. David Justice homers for Cleveland.

The Dodgers fire manager Glenn Hoffman, after a 47-41 record as Bill Russell's replacement. Overall, the Dodgers were 83-79.

Former major league relief pitcher Dan Quisenberry dies at 45 in Kansas City, Missouri. A submarine-style pitcher, he compiled a career record of 56-46 with 244 saves — 17th all-time. He pitched for the Royals, the Cardinals, and briefly, the Giants.

OCTOBER 1:

NL Division Series. Houston knots the series with a 5-4 victory; Ricky Gutierrez scores the winning run in the bottom of the ninth on a Bill Spiers single. In the top of the frame, San Diego had forged ahead on a Jim Leyritz two-run homer. Derek Bell homers earlier for Houston and Jeff Bagwell has three RBI. The losing pitcher is Dan Miceli; Billy Wagner gets the victory.

NL Division Series. Chipper Jones delivers a run-scoring hit in the bottom of the 10th inning off losing pitcher Terry Mulholland and the Braves edge the Cubs, 2-1. Kevin Tapani shuts out the Braves until the bottom of the ninth, when Javy Lopez homers with one out to tie the game. Odaliz Perez gets the win; Atlanta starter Tom Glavine sparkles but is relieved after seven with his team trailing.

The Yankees learn that Darryl Strawberry has been diagnosed with colon cancer and will undergo surgery.

Jim Leyland resigns as manager of the Marlins. After leading the team to a World Series championship, Leyland saw the Marlins stripped of their stars in a salary-reduction effort. The Marlins were 54-108 this season.

One week later, Leyland signs a three-year contract to manage the Rockies.

OCTOBER 2:

AL Division Series. The Yankees sweep the Rangers with a 4-0 win in Texas, behind winning pitcher David Cone and relievers Graeme Lloyd, Jeff Nelson, and Mariano Rivera. Paul O'Neill and Shane Spencer homer for the victors in the sixth for all New York's runs. The losing pitcher is Aaron Sele.

Cleveland beats Boston, 4-3, in Boston. Manny Ramirez's homer in the ninth – his second of the game – enables Cleveland to withstand a two-run homer by Nomar Garciaparra in the bottom of the frame. Four of Cleveland's five hits are homers; Jim Thome and Kenny Lofton account for the other two. The winning pitcher is Charles Nagy. Bret Saberhagen is tagged with the loss.

Cowboy film and recording star and part owner of the Angels Gene Autry dies at 91 in Studio City, California.

OCTOBER 3:

AL Division Series. Cleveland rallies for two runs in the eighth on David Justice's double to beat the Red Sox, 2-1, in Boston, and take the series. Nomar Garciaparra's homer gives Boston its lone run. Steve Reed, the third of Cleveland's five pitchers, gets the win. Boston's ace reliever, Tom Gordon, gets the loss.

NL Division Series. The visiting Braves, behind Greg Maddux, win, 6-2, and sweep the Cubs. Maddux delivers a key hit and scores in a five-run, eighth-inning rally. Eddie Perez homers for the winners. Rookie sensation Kerry Wood gets the loss. Despite his 66 regular season homers, Sammy Sosa fails to reach the stands in the series and bats only .182.

NL Division Series. In San Diego, Kevin Brown and Dan Hampton are matched up in a classic pitcher's duel, but neither is involved in the decision. Brown is yanked with the bases loaded in the top of the seventh; game two loser Dan Miceli fans Bill Spiers to end the rally and Jim Leyritz homers in

CULTURE

Thomas Dyja publishes *Play for a Kingdom,* a novel that focuses on Union and Confederate troops playing baseball during the Civil War battle of Spotsylvania. Also published are *Last Days of Summer,* a novel by Steve Kluger; and *The Cincinnati Red Stalkings,* by Troy Soos, the latest in the mystery series featuring the fictional baseball player Mickey Rawlings.

TRIVIA

Of the 15 perfect games so far in the major leagues, two have been pitched by alumni of Point Loma High School in San Diego, California. They are the two Yankees to accomplish the feat: Don Larsen, Class of 1947, and David Wells, Class of 1982.

the bottom of the frame off loser Scott Elarton to give the Padres a 2-1 victory.

OCTOBER 4:

NL Division Series. Two ex-Yankees lead the Padres to a 6-1 victory over the visiting Astros, and San Diego moves forward to the next round. Jim Leyritz hits his third homer of the series and Sterling Hitchcock limits Houston to three hits while fanning 11. Wally Joyner also homers for the winners. Randy Johnson is charged with his second loss of the series.

OCTOBER 6:

ALCS game one. In New York, the Yankees beat the Indians, 7-2, behind David Wells. The Yankees put the game away early – with a five-run first inning. Jorge Posada homers for the winners; Manny Ramirez for the Indians. Starter Jaret Wright gets the loss.

Former major league shortstop Mark Belanger dies at 54 in New York City. The slick-fielding Belanger played 18 seasons – all but one with the Orioles. His lifetime batting average was .228 and he was an eight-time Gold Glove winner

OCTOBER 7:

NLCS game one. Ken Caminiti's 10th-inning homer gives the Padres a 3-2 win over the Braves in Atlanta. Earlier, Andruw Jones homers for Atlanta. The winning pitcher is Trevor Hoffman in relief. The loser is reliever Kerry Ligtenberg.

ALCS game two. The Indians beat the Yankees, 4-1, in New York, with three runs in the 12th, knotting the series. Dave Burba, the sixth of seven Cleveland pitchers, gets the win. Jeff Nelson, the fourth of five Yankee pitchers, gets the loss. A controversial call at first – when Tino Martinez throws Travis Fryman's bunt into the runner's back – leads to a key run in the 12th. While the second baseman, Chuck Knoblauch, argues – in vain – that Fryman was out of the basepath, Enrique Wilson scores the go-ahead run. David Justice homers for Cleveland.

OCTOBER 8:

NLCS game two. Kevin Brown pitches a complete game three-hitter, has two safeties of his own and scores a run as the Padres and the Braves, 3-0, in Atlanta. Tom Glavine gets the loss.

OCTOBER 9:

ALCS game three. The Indians cash in on four homers – three in the fifth – to beat the visiting Yankees, 6-1. Jim Thome connects twice and teammates Manny Ramirez and Mark Whiten once each. Bartolo Colon goes the route, allowing only four hits for the victory. Andy Pettitte is charged with the loss.

OCTOBER 10:

ALCS game four. The Yankees strike back, beating the Indians, 4-0, behind rookie Orlando Hernandez, in Cleveland. Former Yankee Doc Gooden gets the loss. Paul O'Neill hits a home run.

NLCS game three. The Padres beat the Braves, 4-1, in San Diego. Greg Maddux gets the loss; left-hander Sterling Hitchcock wins for the Padres. Tony Gwynn's single in the fifth inning drives in Steve Finley with the winning run.

OCTOBER 11:

ALCS game five. Chili Davis homers and drives in three runs to give the visiting Yankees a 5-3 win over the Indians. David Wells, with relief help from Jeff Nelson and Mariano Rivera, gets the win. Indians' starter Chad Ogea is charged with the loss. Kenny Lofton and Jim Thome homer in a losing cause.

NLCS game four. Andres Galarraga's seventh inning grand slam helps the Braves to stay alive with an 8-3 win over the Padres in San Diego. Javy Lopez also homers for Atlanta; Jim Leyritz connects for the Padres. The winning pitcher is veteran Dennis Martinez in relief. Joey Hamilton is tagged with the loss.

OCTOBER 12:

NLCS game five. Michael Tucker hits a three-run homer in the eighth off Kevin Brown – in a rare relief role – and the Braves nip the Padres, 7-6, in San Diego. Tucker has five RBI. Ken Caminiti, John Vander Wal, and Greg Myers homer for San Diego. The winning pitcher, in relief, is John Rocker. Brown gets the loss.

OCTOBER 21
Yankees sweep Padres to win World Series.

OCTOBER 26
The Mets' Mike Piazza becomes baseball's highest paid player with a new contract.

OCTOBER 13:

ALCS game six. Another AL pennant will fly over Yankee Stadium as New York tops visiting Cleveland, 9-5. A Scott Brosius homer and a key sixth-inning error by Omar Vizquel help the Yankees seal their 35th pennant. David Cone gets the win with relief help from Ramiro Mendoza and Mariano Rivera. Charles Nagy is the loser.

OCTOBER 14:

NLCS game six. The Padres beat the home-standing Braves, 5-0 – scoring all of their runs in the sixth inning – to clinch the NL pennant. Winning pitcher and series MVP Sterling Hitchcock, along with relievers Brian Boehringer, Mark Langston, Joey Hamilton, and Trevor Hoffman, limit the Braves to only two hits. Tom Glavine is the losing pitcher.

OCTOBER 17:

World Series game one. Tino Martinez's grand slam in the seventh off Mark Langston breaks the game open and the Yankees beat the Padres, 9-6, in New York. Earlier in the inning, Chuck Knoblauch homered. The Yankee round-trippers offset two home runs by Greg Vaughn and one by Tony Gwynn. The winning pitcher is David Wells, who gets relief help from Jeff Nelson and Mariano Rivera. San Diego starter Kevin Brown is not involved in the decision; the loss goes to Donne Wall.

OCTOBER 18:

World Series game two. The Yankees make it two in a row with a 9-3 thrashing of the Padres in New York. New York uses 16 hits, including homers by Bernie Williams and Jorge Posada, to take a commanding lead in the Series. Orlando Hernandez gets the win; San Diego starter Andy Ashby is the loser.

OCTOBER 20:

World Series game three. Home cooking doesn't help the Padres. The visiting Yankees, powered by Scott Brosius's two homers, top San Diego, 5-4. Ramiro Mendoza, in relief of starter David Cone and Graeme Lloyd, gets the win. Reliever Trevor Hoffman is the losing pitcher.

OCTOBER 21:

The Yankees complete their dream season by sweeping the Padres with a 3-0 win in San Diego. Winning pitcher Andy Pettitte and relievers Jeff Nelson and Mariano Rivera limit the overmatched Padres to seven hits. Kevin Brown is charged with the loss. Tino Martinez hits .385 with a homer and four RBI, Chuck Knoblauch finishes at .353, and Derek Jeter tallies .353 for the victors. Mariano Rivera records three saves and allows no earned runs and no walks while fanning four. For the Padres, one of the few bright spots is Tony Gwynn – playing in his first series – who hits .500 with a homer and three RBI.

POST SEASON

OCTOBER 23:

After being rejected by Montreal's Felipe Alou, the Dodgers sign Davey Johnson to a three-year contract as their manager. Johnson previously was skipper of the Mets, the Reds, and the Orioles. He won the World Series with the 1986 Mets.

OCTOBER 26:

Mike Piazza (.328, 32 homers, 111 RBI) becomes baseball's highest-paid player when the Mets sign him to a seven-year, $91 million deal.

NOVEMBER 5:

The Yankees sign third baseman Scott Brosius (.300, 19 homers, 98 RBI), the World Series MVP, to a three-year, $15.75 million contract.

NOVEMBER 6:

Henry and H. Wayne Huizenga sell the Marlins to financier John Henry for $150 million, finally ridding themselves of the team.

NOVEMBER 10:

Hall of Fame pitcher Hal Newhouser dies at 77 in Southfield, Michigan. Newhouser pitched for the Tigers and Indians, compiling a 207-150 record over 17 seasons. He is the only pitcher to win two straight MVP Awards – in 1944, when he was 29-9, and 1945, when he was 25-9.

The Braves trade pitcher Denny Neagle (16-11, 3.55 ERA), outfielder Michael

NOVEMBER 19 Sammy Sosa wins the NL MVP Award.

DECEMBER 12 Kevin Brown signs a seven-year, $100 million contract with the Dodgers.

Tucker (.244, 13 homers, 46 RBI), and minor league pitcher Robby Bell to the Reds for second baseman Bret Boone (.266, 24 homers, 95 RBI) and pitcher Mike Remlinger (8-15, 4.82 ERA).

NOVEMBER 11:

The Mets reacquire Bobby Bonilla (.249, 11 homers, 45 RBI) from the Dodgers for relief pitcher Mel Rojas (5-2, 6.05 ERA, two saves).

The Yankees re-sign David Cone (20-7, 3.55 ERA) to a one-year, $8 million contract.

NOVEMBER 19:

Sammy Sosa gets a nice consolation prize – the NL MVP Award. With a .308 batting average, 66 homers, and 158 RBI, Sosa easily outpaces Mark McGwire, who finishes second.

NOVEMBER 20:

Dick Sisler, whose 10th-inning home run against the Dodgers in 1950 gave the Phillies their first pennant in 35 years, dies at 78 in Nashville, Tennessee. Sisler was the son of Hall of Famer George Sisler and the brother of former major league pitcher Dave Sisler. Another brother, George Jr., was president of the International League. An outfielder-first baseman, Dick played eight seasons with the Phillies, Reds, and Cardinals, attaining a lifetime batting average of .276 with 55 homers none more important than his pennant-winning blast.

NOVEMBER 23:

Free-agent outfielder Brian Jordan (.316, 25 homers, 91 RBI, 17 steals) signs with the Braves, reportedly for $40 million over five years. He was with the Cardinals this season.

NOVEMBER 25:

Bernie Williams (.339, 26 homers, 97 RBI), the AL's batting champion, is re-signed by the Yankees to a 7 year pact worth $87.5 million.

The Red Sox lose their slugger, Mo Vaughn (.337, 40 homers, 115 RBI), to the Angels, who give him a six-year, $80 million contract that will pay him a record-setting $13.3 million a year.

NOVEMBER 28:

M. Donald Grant, chairman of the Mets from the team's birth until the end of the 1978 season, dies at 94 in Hobe Sound, Florida. He will be remembered most for ordering the trade of Tom Seaver to the Reds.

NOVEMBER 29:

Longtime Yankee pitching coach Jim Turner dies at 95 in Nashville, Tennessee. He served two stints with New York — from 1949 to 1959 and from 1966 to 1973. In between, he was a coach for the Reds. Turner came to the majors as a player at the age of 33; he pitched 9 years — mostly out of the bullpen — and had a 69-60 record.

NOVEMBER 30:

Another free agent cashes in big time. Randy Johnson signs a four-year, $52.4 million contract with the Diamondbacks. He split last season between the Mariners and the Astros.

DECEMBER 1:

The tempestuous but talented Albert Belle (.328, 49 homers, 152 RBI), who spent the past season with the White Sox, signs a five-year, $65 million pact with the Orioles.

DECEMBER 2:

The Rangers sign Rafael Palmeiro (.296, 43 homers, 121 RBI) to a five-year contract.

DECEMBER 5:

Free agent first baseman Will Clark (.305, 23 homers, 102 RBI) signs a two-year, $11 million contract with the Orioles. He spent last season with the Rangers.

DECEMBER 12:

The richest man in baseball is now pitcher Kevin Brown (18-7, 2.38 ERA), who signs a seven-year, $100 million contract with the Dodgers.

John Moores, owner of the Padres – Brown's 1998 team – says, "It's truly a tragic day for baseball."

THE BEST OF 1998

NATIONAL LEAGUE

HITTERS

Batting Average:
Larry Walker, Colorado Rockies, .363

Slugging Average:
Mark McGwire, St. Louis Cardinals, .752

Home Runs:
Mark McGwire, 70

Runs Batted In:
Mark McGwire, 162

Hits:
Dante Bichette, Colorado Rockies, 219

Stolen Bases:
Tony Womack, Pittsburgh Pirates, 58

PITCHERS

Wins:
Tom Glavine, Atlanta Braves, 20

Strikeouts:
Curt Schilling, Philadelphia Phillies, 300

Earned Run Average:
Greg Maddux, Atlanta Braves, 2.22

Winning Percentage:
John Smoltz, Atlanta Braves, .850

Saves:
Trevor Hoffman, San Diego Padres, 53

Most Valuable Player:
Sammy Sosa, Chicago Cubs

Cy Young Award:
Tom Glavine, Atlanta Braves

Rookie of the Year:
Kerry Wood, Chicago Cubs

Manager of the Year:
Larry Dierker, Houston Astros

AMERICAN LEAGUE

HITTERS

Batting Average:
Bernie Williams, New York Yankees, .339

Slugging Average:
Albert Belle, Chicago White Sox, .655

Home Runs:
Ken Griffey Jr., Seattle Mariners, 56

Runs Batted In:
Juan Gonzalez, Texas Rangers, 157

Hits:
Alex Rodriguez, Seattle Mariners, 213

Stolen Bases:
Rickey Henderson, Oakland Athletics, 66

PITCHERS

Wins:
Roger Clemens, Toronto Blue Jays;
David Cone, New York Yankees;
Rick Helling, Texas Rangers, 20

Strikeouts:
Roger Clemens, 271

Earned Run Average:
Roger Clemens, 2.65

Winning Percentage:
David Wells, New York Yankees, .818

Saves:
Tom Gordon, Boston Red Sox, 46

Most Valuable Player:
Juan Gonzalez, Texas Rangers

Cy Young Award:
Roger Clemens, Toronto Blue Jays

Rookie of the Year:
Ben Grieve, Oakland Athletics

Manager of the Year:
Joe Torre, New York Yankees

1999

"There continued to be an unsettled feeling in camp."
– Blue Jays' general manager Gord Ash, after manager Tim Johnson is axed

NEWS

PRESIDENT BILL CLINTON IS ACQUITTED OF IMPEACHMENT CHARGES AND WILL REMAIN IN OFFICE

JOHN F. KENNEDY JR., WIFE DIE IN PLANE CRASH

Earthquake in Turkey kills 15,000

CIVIL WAR RAGES IN KOSOVO

TWO STUDENTS KILL 13 AT COLUMBINE HIGH SCHOOL IN COLORADO

WORLD TRADE ORGANIZATION MEETING IN SEATTLE DISRUPTED BY PROTESTERS

TWO MARS PROBES FAIL

NATO SUSPENDS BOMBING CAMPAIGN AGAINST YUGOSLAVIA

MICHAEL JORDAN RETIRES

VP AL GORE THROWS IN HAT FOR PRESIDENTIAL RACE

PRE-SEASON

JANUARY 5:

George Steinbrenner and Hall of Famer Yogi Berra end their feud when the Yankees' boss shows up at the Yogi Berra Museum in New Jersey. Berra had disassociated himself from the Yankees and Steinbrenner after being fired as manager 16 games into the 1985 season.

JANUARY 12:

An anonymous bidder pays $3 million at a New York City auction for the ball Mark McGwire hit for his record-shattering 70th home run. The same buyer also buys Sammy Sosa's 66th homer ball for $150,000. The bids are made by telephone.

JANUARY 27:

The Padres re-sign Sterling Hitchcock (9-7, 3.93 ERA) to a $15.5 million, three-year contract, the richest in team history.

FEBRUARY 2:

The Padres trade slugging outfielders Greg Vaughn (.272, 50 homers, 199 RBI) and Mark Sweeney (.234, two homers, 15 RBI) to the Reds for outfielder Reggie Sanders (.268, 14 homers, 59 RBI), infielder Damian Jackson (.316 in 13 games), and minor league pitcher Josh Harris.

FEBRUARY 12:

Jimmy Dudley, who broadcast Indians baseball for 20 years, dies at 89 in Tucson, Arizona. Dudley was a member of the broadcasters' wing of the Hall of Fame.

FEBRUARY 18:

One of the Yankees' most colorful and popular players, David Wells (18-4, 3.49 ERA, 163 strikeouts), is traded to the Blue Jays for five-time Cy Young Award winner Roger Clemens (20-6, 2.65 ERA, 271 strikeouts). Toronto also receives reliever Graeme Lloyd (3-0, 1.67 ERA, no saves) plus infielder Homer Bush (.380 in 45 games).

A shocking announcement of another sort comes from the Braves. The team announces that its popular and hard-hitting first baseman, Andres Galarraga, (.305, 44 homers, 121 RBI), will be sidelined for the season after being diagnosed with cancer in his back. At 37, his life and career hang in the balance.

FEBRUARY 21:

Former major league pitcher Wilmer "Vinegar Bend" Mizell dies at 68 in Kerrville, Texas. After retiring from baseball, Mizell served three terms in Congress, representing a North Carolina district as a Republican. His nickname came from his hometown, Vinegar Bend, Alabama, which had a population of 50 when he was growing up there. Mizell pitched

FEBRUARY 18
The Yankees swap David Wells for pitching giant Roger Clemens.

MARCH 8
"Joltin' Joe" DiMaggio is dead at 84, but his 1941 hitting record lives on.

for the Cardinals, Pirates, and Mets, compiling a 90-88 record with a 3.85 ERA in nine seasons.

MARCH 4:

The Rockies re-sign NL batting champion Larry Walker (.363, 23 homers, 67 RBI) to a six-year, $75 million pact.

MARCH 8:

Joe DiMaggio, who personified all-around excellence in baseball, dies at 84 in Hollywood, Florida. Deemed by many to be baseball's greatest living player, DiMaggio played 13 seasons – all with the Yankees – batting .325 with 361 homers, 1,537 RBI, and 369 strikeouts.

DiMaggio's 56-game hitting streak in 1941 is regarded as one of baseball's unconquerable records.

William Wrigley, chewing-gum magnate and owner of the Cubs, dies at age 66 in Chicago. In 1981, the Wrigley family sold its 80 percent ownership of the team to the Tribune Company for $20.5 million.

The Padres give pitcher Trevor Hoffman (4-2, 1.48 ERA, 53 saves) a four-year contract extension worth $32 million, making him the game's highest-paid reliever.

MARCH 9:

Yankees' manager Joe Torre is diagnosed with prostate cancer. Coach Don Zimmer will handle the team while Torre undergoes treatment.

MARCH 16:

The Cubs announce that Kerry Wood, the NL Rookie of the Year in 1998, will miss the entire 1999 season because of an injury to the elbow of his pitching arm.

Wood undergoes reconstructive "Tommy John" surgery on his elbow, so-called because pitcher Tommy John was among the first to have the procedure – which has since prolonged many pitchers' careers.

MARCH 17:

The Blue Jays fire manager Tim Johnson and replace him with Jim Fregosi. His discharge is the result of untrue

LEAGUE

The Associated Press reports that the average salary for a major leaguer has now reached $1.7 million a year. Murray Chass of the *New York Times* reports that the Yankees' average salary is $3 million per player.

LEAGUE

Commissioner Bud Selig announces that an annual award is being created for the leading hitter in each league, and that it will be named in honor of Hank Aaron. The winners this season will be determined on the basis of hits, homers, and RBI. A panel will determine future recipients.

The Orioles played host to the national team of Cuba (in blue) at Camden Yards.

MARCH 28
The Orioles and Cuban all-stars meet in Havana for first of two matchups.

APRIL 4
27,104 watch the NL season opener – 'Padres vs. Rockies'– in Monterrey, Mexico.

APRIL 10
Clemens, in his Yankees debut, blanks the Tigers, 5-0.

stories he told about combat in Vietnam and about his athletic past. General manager Gord Ash tells Murray Chass of the *New York Times*, "There continued to be an unsettled feeling in camp."

MARCH 24:

George "Birdie" Tebbetts, who spent 53 years in the majors as a player, manager, and scout, dies at 86 in Bradenton, Florida. A catcher, Tebbetts played fourteen years with the Tigers, Red Sox, and Indians, batting .270. As manager of the Reds, the Milwaukee Braves, and the Indians, he compiled a 749-705 record. Tebbetts held a degree in philosophy from Providence College.

MARCH 25:

Another longtime baseball man, Cal Ripken Sr., dies at 63 in Baltimore, Maryland. Ripken, the father of major leaguers Cal Jr. and Billy, was in the Orioles' organization for 36 years as a minor league player and manager, a scout, and a major league coach and manager. During his tenure as Baltimore's skipper, he got to manage both of his sons. The Mets sign 40-year-old pitcher Orel Hershiser (11-10, 4.41 ERA) to a one-year, $2 million contract. Hershiser was with the Giants last season.

MARCH 28:

In a precedent-shattering move, the Orioles travel to Havana to play a team of Cuban all-stars. Baltimore ekes out a 3-2 win in eleven innings. The teams will meet again in Baltimore later this season.

MARCH 31:

Richard Sandomir of the *New York Times* reports the owners are "considering selling small patches of advertising on the uniform sleeves of players as a new way to increase revenue."

THE SEASON

APRIL 4:

It's "Play Ball!" in the major leagues, but opening day is in Monterrey, Mexico, where the NL pennant-winning Padres meet the Rockies. Mexican hero Vinny Castilla has four hits, helping the Rockies to an 8-2 win. Dante Bichette homers for the winners and Darryl Kile gets the win. Andy Ashby gets the loss. Attendance is 27,104.

Hall of Famer Early Wynn, a 300-game winner whose credo was "Every hitter is the enemy," dies at age 79 in Venice, Florida. Wynn pitched for 23 years with the Washington Senators, Cleveland Indians, and Chicago White Sox, compiling a 300-244 record with an ERA of 3.54. He was a five-time 20-game winner and won the AL Cy Young Award in 1959 at the age of 39.

In 1959, the year Wynn enjoys his best season, winning the Cy Young Award with the AL pennant-winning "Go-Go" White Sox, Yankees' manager Casey Stengel tells The Sporting News: *"That Wynn is a pretty tough pitcher. He's got everybody in the league scared. If I had to win one game, I'd have to say I'd want him to go. He knows just about all there is to know about pitching."*

APRIL 5:

It doesn't take Mark McGwire long to pick up where he left off. Big Mac cracks a homer in his first game, against the Brewers' David Weathers. Pedro Martinez finds his groove early as well. He fans nine and beats the Royals, 5-3.

APRIL 9:

Jerold C. Hoffberger, a brewer who owned the Orioles during their heyday, dies at 80 in Baltimore. During Hoffberger's tenure, the team won five AL pennants and two World Series.

APRIL 10:

Roger Clemens makes a great pinstripe debut, defeating the Tigers, 5-0, in New York.

Randy Johnson, in his Arizona debut, fans 15 and six-hits the Braves, 8-3.

Kevin Brown records his first win as the Dodgers down the Rockies 2-0, in Los Angeles.

APRIL 11:

Mark McGwire takes the Reds' Jason Bere long for his second homer of the season. But the Reds down the Cardinals, 4-2.

And, as he did through most of the 1998 season, Sammy Sosa

HISTORY

Umpires are wearing a special patch on their shirts honoring the late Nestor Chylak, the former AL umpire, who will be inducted into the Hall of Fame on July 25.

TRIVIA

Former White Sox minor leaguer Michael Jordan retires from his other sport – professional basketball.

Fernando Tatis of St. Louis slugged two grand slams in one inning against Los Angeles.

Ken Griffey Jr. tells the Associated Press that Ken Griffey Sr. helped get him out of a hitting slump. Says Griffey Jr., "He threw me two pitches in the batting cage and told me exactly what I was doing wrong."

TRIVIA

Jose Jimenez is the first rookie to pitch a no-hitter since Wilson Alvarez in 1991 and the first NL rookie since Burt Hooten in 1972.

HISTORY

The batter's box is an unsafe place at Fenway Park on May 31. Damian Easley ties a major league record when he is hit three times by Red Sox pitchers. The Tigers Matt Anderson is ejected when he hits Mike Stanley with a 3-2 pitch. The Red Sox hold off the Tigers, 8-7.

responds with a home run – his first – off Mike Williams of the Pirates. Pittsburgh tops the visiting Cubs, 9-6.

El Duque comes close. Yankee pitcher Orlando Hernandez is perfect until one out in the seventh inning against the Tigers. Then Gregg Jefferies walks, and one out later Tony Clark singles. The Yankees win, 11-2, in New York.

APRIL 14:

Darryl Strawberry, on the comeback from colon cancer, is arrested in Tampa, Florida, on charges of cocaine possession and soliciting a prostitute.

On May 26, Strawberry pleads no contest and gets 18 months of probation.

APRIL 15:

The Rockies down the Padres, 6-4, at home in Colorado, giving manager Jim Leyland the 1,000th victory of his career.

APRIL 16:

Curt Schilling fans 11, beats the Florida Marlins, 17-3, at Philadelphia's Veteran's Stadium, and improves to 3-0.

APRIL 17:

David Wells and the Blue Jays beat the Orioles, 7-4, and the left-hander ups his record to 3-0. Shawn Green hits his third homer.

APRIL 18:

The Braves pound out 24 hits, routing the Rockies, 20-5, in Colorado. Andruw Jones leads the attack with five hits – including a homer and a triple – and six RBI.

APRIL 20:

Pedro Martinez wins his third "fanning 10" as the Red Sox whitewash the Tigers, 1-0, in Detroit. Troy O'Leary homers for the game's only run.

APRIL 21:

Roger Clemens beats the Rangers, 4-2, for his 17th consecutive win – tying an AL record – and his second of the season.

Jeff Bagwell hits his second, third, and fourth homers of the season and his Astros beat the Cubs, 10-3, in Chicago. Bagwell is now Houston's career leader, with 225.

APRIL 22:

Mike Bordick singles with two out in the eighth, ending Tony Saunders's no-hit bid. It is the Orioles' only hit and the Devil Rays and Saunders win, 1-0.

APRIL 23:

The Cardinals' Fernando Tatis accomplishes something that the greatest sluggers in baseball never did. Playing in Los Angeles, Tatis hits two grand-slam homers in a single inning. He hammers Chan Ho Park of the Dodgers for both grand slams in the third. Tatis, five-feet, ten-inches, 170 pounds, has only 24 career homers and had never before connected with the bases loaded. He also sets a record with eight RBI in a single inning. The Cardinals win, 12-5.

The Yankees and Orlando Hernandez beat the Blue Jays and David Wells, 6-4, in New York.

APRIL 24:

Ken Griffey Jr. homers twice – his fourth and fifth of the year – in a 9-4 Mariners win over the Devil Rays.

APRIL 29:

Ken Griffey Jr. homers twice – including a grand slam in an 11-run fifth inning – and the Mariners maul the Tigers, 22-6, in Seattle. Griffey now has eight homers. Larry Walker continues his hot hitting with two hits and three RBIs in a 6-2 win over the Cardinals in St. Louis.

Last night the Rockies' star hit two homers and drove in eight runs.

MAY 1:

Pedro Martinez strikes out 13 A's in seven innings and wins his fifth game. Troy O'Leary homers for Boston.

The Tigers' Brian Moehler gets caught in the act. Home plate umpire Larry Barnett spots Moehler using sandpaper to doctor the baseball and ejects him. Adding insult to injury, Moehler gets the loss as the Devil Rays beat the Tigers, 4-3.

MAY 2:

A matchup of pitching aces – Kevin Brown of the Dodgers and Curt Schilling of the Phillies – disappoints. Brown gets hammered for six runs in six innings and Philadelphia wins, 12-3. Schilling gets the victory.

MAY 3:

Former Milwaukee Braves' first baseman Joe Adcock dies at 71

APRIL 20
Boston shuts out Detroit, 1-0, thanks to Troy O'Leary's homer.

APRIL 23
The Cardinal's Fernando Tatis hammers two grandslams in one inning.

in Coushatta, Louisiana. Adcock, one of baseball's most powerful hitters, teamed with Hank Aaron and Eddie Mathews for the Braves in the 1950s. Adcock played 17 years with the Reds, Indians, and Angels, as well as the Braves, batting a respectable .277 with 336 homers.

The Blue Jays' Shawn Green hits his eighth homer, teammate Carlos Delgado connects twice, and Toronto outhits the Mariners, 16-10, for David Wells's fourth win.

MAY 3:

The Cuban baseball team exacts revenge on the Orioles, winning the rematch in Baltimore, 12-6. Andy Morales hits a three-run homer for the Cubans.

In 2000, Morales makes his way to the United States via a speedboat. Immigration officials send him back to Cuba, asserting his reasons for defecting were economic and not political.

MAY 4:

Mark McGwire connects in the second inning off Greg Maddux for a grand slam – his sixth homer of the season – and the Cardinals clout the Braves, 9-1, in Atlanta. McGwire has been homerless since April 18. Sammy Sosa is right on his tail, hitting his fifth – off Chuck McElroy of the Rockies.

MAY 5:

John Smoltz and the Braves beat the Cardinals, 12-3. It is the ninth straight win for Smoltz and his fifth of the season.

MAY 7:

Pedro Martinez strikes out 15 in eight innings; the Red Sox hold back the Angels, 6-0.

The Indians use 21 hits – including two David Justice homers – to crush the Devil Rays, 20-11.

MAY 8:

Ken Griffey Jr. hits his 11th homer and the Mariners manhandle the Yankees, 14-5.

MAY 10:

Nomar Garciaparra is a one-man wrecking crew as the Red Sox hammer the Mariners, 12-4, at Fenway Park. The Boston shortstop becomes the 11th major leaguer to hit two grand slams in a game and he drives in 10 runs.

MAY 12:

California's Chuck Finley outpitches New York's David Cone and the Angels beat the Yankees, 1-0. Andy Sheets drives in the lone run in the seventh. Finley strikes out 11, including four in the seventh inning. Pedro Martinez strikes out 15 – for the second consecutive game – while Nomar Garciaparra drives in three runs and extends his consecutive-ame hitting streak to 15. Boston wins, 9-3, and Martinez becomes the season's first seven-game winner.

MAY 13:

The Yankees get blanked again. Four Angels' pitchers hold New York to six hits, and Mo Vaughn homers off Hideki Irabu. Anaheim wins, 2-0

Will this be Ken Griffey's year? Junior slams his 14th homer – the most in the majors – off Scott Service, and the Mariners beat the Royals, 5-1.

MAY 17:

In Florida, Sammy Sosa connects off Ryan Dempster and Braden Looper for his 10th and 11th homers. He has seven in his last 12 games. The Cubs beat the Marlins, 8-1.

MAY 19:

Mark McGwire racks up his ninth homer – off the Padres' Andy Ashby. But Sammy Sosa holds his lead

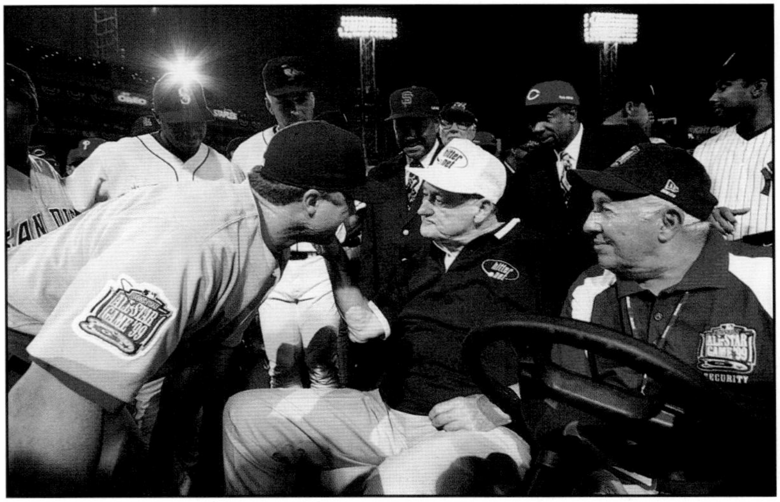

Mark McGwire (left) greets Ted Williams (white hat) at the Team of the Century celebration held at the All-Star Game in Boston.

Branch Rickey once said of Eddie Stanky, known as "The Brat," "He can't run, he can't hit, and he can't throw. But if there's a way to beat the other team, he'll find it."

HISTORY

Jose Canseco is the first player to reach 30 homers with four different teams – Oakland, Texas, Toronto, and Tampa Bay.

LEAGUE

Kenny Rogers (5-3, 4.30 ERA) is back in New York, but this time with the Mets. The left-handed pitcher is acquired from the Athletics for two minor leaguers – pitcher Leoner Vasquez and outfielder Terrence Long.

with his 12th – off the Marlins' Jesus Sanchez.

MAY 20:

Joe Torre returns to the helm and the Yankees, behind Orlando "El Duque" Hernandez, respond with a 3-1 win over the Red Sox at Fenway. Bernie Williams hits his fifth homer.

Mark McGwire hits his 10th – off Sterling Hitchcock. Eric Davis connects twice and Joe McEwing adds a homer of his own in San Diego. The Cardinals top the Padres, 6-4.

Sammy Sosa maintains his lead over McGwire with his 13th off Greg Maddux in Atlanta. The Cubs win, 6-5.

Shawn Green hits his 14th four-bagger and Blue Jays' rookie Roy Halladay shuts out the Tigers, 7-0.

MAY 21:

Jose Canseco of the Devil Rays homers in his fifth consecutive game, in a 10-9 win over the Angels. Canseco has 17 for the season – tops in the majors.

MAY 22:

Roger Clemens beats the White Sox, 10-2, in Chicago, setting an AL record with his 18th consecutive victory. The Yankees' right-hander had been on the disabled list with a left hamstring problem.

MAY 23:

Pedro Martinez and the Red Sox beat the Blue Jays, 10-8, for his seventh consecutive victory.

Call him black-and-blue Brady. Mike Morgan of the Rangers plunks the Orioles' Brady Anderson twice in the same inning. Anderson is the first AL player with that distinction.

MAY 25:

Ken Griffey Jr. slams number 18 – the most in the majors – and the Mariners trample the Twins, 15-5, in Minnesota.

MAY 26:

In Minnesota, Ken Griffey Jr. hits his 19th homer and Edgar Martinez has a grand slam; the Mariners win, 11-3. Griffey is tied with Ralph Kiner for 45th place on the all-time homer list with 369.

MAY 27:

Roger Clemens beats the Red Sox, 3-1, in New York for his 19th straight win. Carl Hubbell and his major league record of 24 are in his sights.

MAY 29:

White Sox player Greg Norton homers for the fifth time in three days and James Baldwin five-hits the Tigers, 7-1.

MAY 30:

Randy Johnson fans 10 Mets and allows five hits as the Diamondbacks bite the Mets, 10-1.

After being hospitalized for 36 hours with an infected leg, Mark McGwire returns to the lineup and keeps the pressure on, slamming his 15th in Chicago, off Terry Adams. But the Cubs beat the Cards, 7-4.

Mo Vaughn hits his 13th for the Angels – his ninth homer in 18 games.

Jose Canseco hits his 19th homer and his Devil Rays beat the Mariners, 15-7.

MAY 31:

Crew chief Frank Pulli and home plate umpire Greg Bonin use video replays to determine whether a drive by Cliff Floyd of the Marlins is a homer or a double. After more than five minutes, the umpires decide the ball struck below the scoreboard, and it is ruled a double. The Marlins protest the game, which they lose, 5-2, to the Cardinals.

The umpires are later admonished for using the video replay.

JUNE 2:

Rafael Palmeiro hits his 15th homer and a two-run double to lead the Rangers to a 7-4 win over the Royals, the team's ninth straight win

JUNE 3:

Sammy Sosa hits Matt Clements for his 19th homer, and the Cubs top the Padres, 7-2.

Mark McGwire hits his 17th – off the Marlins' Alex Fernandez – but leaves the game in the sixth with tightness in his back. The Marlins win, 4-2.

JUNE 4:

In Boston, Pedro Martinez limits the Braves to three hits, strikes out 16, and wins his 11th game, 5-1.

JUNE 5:

The Yankees hand the Mets their eighth

MAY 25 Ken Griffey Jr. leads in homers as he knocks in number 18.

JUNE 5 It's New York against New York in scheduled interleague play.

JUNE 12 The Baseball Hall of Fame turns 60.

straight loss, 6-3, in the interleague "Subway Series."

JUNE 6:

The Mets finally beat the Yankees – and Roger Clemens – 7-2, putting an end to Clemens's consecutive-game winning streak, which had reached 19. Al Leiter gets the win. Mike Piazza hits his 10th homer.

Eddie Stanky, who played on Brooklyn Dodgers, Boston Braves, and New York Giants pennant-winning teams, dies at 83 in Fairhope, Alabama. He also managed the Cardinals and White Sox. Stanky played 11 seasons, batting .268.

JUNE 9:

Jeff Bagwell connects three times for the Astros in a 13-4 win over the White Sox. Bagwell now has 20 home runs.

JUNE 11:

Mets' manager Bobby Valentine is suspended for two games and handed a $5,000 fine by the NL for returning to the Mets' dugout after being ejected from a game on June 9. Valentine showed up in the dugout wearing black glasses and a fake mustache made of eyeblack stickers. On the field, the Red Sox beat the Mets.

Ted Williams throws out the ceremonial first pitch to mark the 60th anniversary of his rookie season.

JUNE 12:

The Baseball Hall of Fame in Cooperstown, New York, marks its 60th anniversary.

The Astros' Jose Lima defeats the Padres, 3-2, giving him 11 wins – tied for the most in the majors.

JUNE 13:

In Atlanta, Cal Ripken Jr. has six hits – including two homers and a double – in six at-bats as the Orioles beat the Braves, 22-1, on 25 hits.

Benny Agbayani homers for the Mets in a 5-4 win over the Red Sox; he now has 10 round-trippers in only 73 at-bats.

In Houston, Astros' manager Larry Dierker has a seizure in the dugout. He is taken to the hospital and the game with the Padres is postponed.

Dierker undergoes a five-and-a-half-hour operation to remove malformed blood vessels in his brain. He recovers and returns to the team.

JUNE 15:

Rickey Henderson (twice), John Olerud, Mike Piazza, Edgardo Alfonso, and Matt Franco homer for the Mets in a 1-3 win over the Reds in Cincinnati. The six home runs are a team record.

JUNE 17:

Roger Clemens strikes out 13 but loses to the Rangers in New York, 4-2.

Kevin Millwood loses his perfect-game bid when Craig Biggio

Boston's Pedro Martinez won pitching's triple crown on his way to the Cy Young Award.

"I don't know how it's portrayed that young kids take it (androstenedione) because of me."
– Mark McGwire, announcing that he's given up the supplement.

LEAGUE

In his remarks, Nolan Ryan thanks Marvin Miller for his role in building the players' union. Many baseball observers believe Marvin Miller deserves enshrinement in the Hall.

singles in the seventh. But the Braves beat the Astros, 8-5.

JUNE 19:

Jose Canseco hits his 27th home run – off Brad Radke of the Twins – in a 4-3 win.

Tampa Bay's Wade Boggs collects his 1,000th career RBI.

Ken Griffey Jr. connects off Dave Burba in Cleveland for his 26th, but the Indians beat the Mariners, 10-6.

JUNE 20:

Pedro Martinez racks up his 13th win, 5-2, fanning 10 Rangers in the process.

David Wells signs an $11.5 million, one-year contract extension with the Blue Jays, then beats the Royals, 2-1, for his eighth win.

JUNE 21:

The Associated Press reports good news: Andres Galarraga, speaking from his native Venezuela, says he expects to complete radiation treatments next month and begin working out with the Braves as early as August.

JUNE 24:

Sammy Sosa hits two two-run homers off the Rockies' Curt Leskanic and Chuck McElroy. They are Sosa's 25th and 26th, and he now leads the NL. The Cubs outslug the Rockies, 12-10.

In Arizona, Mark McGwire homers off Omar Daal for his 23rd in an 8-7 Cardinals loss.

The Mets beat the Marlins, 3-2; it is the team's 14th win in 17 games.

Frank Thomas of the White Sox gets his 1,500th career hit with a third-inning double against the Twins. He is batting .336.

JUNE 25:

Cardinals' rookie Jose Jiminez pitches the first no-hitter of the season, beating Randy Johnson and the Diamondbacks, 1-0, in Arizona. Jiminez fans eight, walks two, and hits a batter. Right-fielder Eric Davis saves the no-hitter with two outstanding catches. Jiminez took a 4-7 record and a 6.79 ERA into the game. Johnson, the hard-luck loser, strikes out 14 and now has 2,500 for his career. An RBI single by Thomas Howard in the ninth produces the game's only run.

Before the end of the season, Jimenez is back in the minors, pitching for the Cardinals' AAA Memphis affiliate.

JUNE 26:

Sammy Sosa hits his 300th career homer – and his 27th of the season – against Robert Person of the Phillies. It's not enough for the Cubs, though; Chicago goes down, 6-2, at Wrigley Field.

At Fenway Park, the Red Sox explode for 11 first-inning runs and Pedro Martinez works five easy innings for his 14th win. Boston bangs out 14 hits and wins, 17-1, over the White Sox.

JUNE 27:

Sammy Sosa is feasting on the Phillies. He connects off Randy Wolf for his 28th, tying him for the major league lead and the Cubs win, 13-7.

In the 1,755th and final game at the Kingdome, Ken Griffey Jr. hits his 27th homer and makes a spectacular catch as the Mariners beat the Rangers, 5-2. Seattle moves into its new $517 stadium, Safeco Field, on July 15.

JUNE 29:

Shannon Stewart's 10th-inning single gives the Blue Jays a 6-5 victory over the Orioles and extends the outfielder's hitting streak to 15 games.

JUNE 30:

In Cincinnati, Randy Johnson strikes out 17 Reds but loses, 2-0, on Dmitri Young's homer and Jeffrey Hammond's single. Ron Villone and Scott Williamson combine to one-hit Arizona.

JULY 1:

The Padres beat the Dodgers, 6-3, for their 13th straight win, but San Diego is only at .500 and trails the first place Giants by 4 1/2 games.

JULY 2:

Mark McGwire hits two – both off Brian Anderson of the Diamondbacks – and now has 25 homers. McGwire's teammate Joe McEwing doubles to extend his hitting streak to 23 games. Despite their efforts, Arizona tops the Cardinals, 9-5.

It is McGwire's 56th multihomer game, tying him with Jimmie Foxx on the all-time leader list.

JULY 2 Mark McGwire slugs two homers in his 56th multihomer game.

JULY 13 Pedro Martinez and the AL take the All-Star Games, 4-1.

Pedro Martinez beats the White Sox, 6-1, for his 15th win.

JULY 3:

The Rockies beat the visiting Padres, 12-10, ending San Diego's 14-game winning streak.

JULY 4:

Mike Sweeney of the Royals drives in two runs, tying an AL record with at least one run batted in 13 straight games. The record was set by Taft Wright in 1941. Kansas City needs both of those runs; the Royals edge the Indians, 10-9.

Toronto's Shawn Green homers twice to reach the 100 career mark. Jose Canseco hits his 30th. The Blue Jays win, 6-3.

Randy Johnson allows four hits and strikes out 12, but Cardinals' rookie Jose Jiminez yields only two hits. The Diamondbacks lose, 1-0.

JULY 9:

Mike Piazza hits a three-run homer – his 18th of the season – off Roger Clemens, and the Mets beat the Yankees, 5-2, at Shea Stadium. Al Leiter gets the win.

JULY 10:

At 3Com Stadium, Mark McGwire slams his 28th – off Russ Ortiz of the Giants – but St. Louis loses, 4-2. It is Big Mac's 485th career homer and he scores his 1,000th run, as well.

Randy Johnson excels again – and loses again. He allows the Athletics three hits and strikes out 11, but one of those hits is a Tim Raines homer and Oakland prevails, 2-0.

The Mets make it two in a row against the Yankees, 9-8, as Mike Piazza homers again.

JULY 11:

The Yankees and Hideki Irabu beat the Mets, 6-3, avoiding a sweep in interleague play.

Jose Canseco, leading the AL with 31 homers, undergoes surgery for a herniated disk and will be out indefinitely. Canseco will miss the All-Star Game after being selected for the first time.

Negro Leagues star Henry Kimbro dies at 87 in Nashville, Tennessee. An outfielder and speed merchant, Kimbro reportedly hit .300 or more for 10 seasons. Playing mostly with the Baltimore Elite Giants, he participated in six East-West All-Star Games. Kimbro, who said he hit a ball out of Briggs Stadium, was too old for the majors when the color barrier came down in 1947.

JULY 13:

At Fenway Park, Pedro Martinez fans the first four batters and the AL wins the All-Star Game, 4-1. It is the AL's third straight win and the ninth in 12 games.

JULY 15:

Sammy Sosa and Mark McGwire homer, but Sosa maintains his lead. Sosa hits his 33rd off the Twins' Bob Wells at Wrigley Field. McGwire's homer is hit off Mike Sirotka of the White Sox and is Big Mac's 29th.

The Braves beat the Yankees, 6-2, and Roger Clemens hears the boos at Yankee Stadium.

JULY 19:

Fernando Tatis continues to demonstrate his newfound power – homering twice today with two on, bringing his season's total to 21. His teammate Mark McGwire misses his second straight day because of a sore back. The Cardinals double up the Twins, 8-4.

JULY 20:

The umpires continue to use strange and ineffective tactics in their labor dispute with Major League Baseball. A week after the umpires submitted their resignations en masse, five of the men in blue want to rescind their letters.

In St. Louis, Mark McGwire drills a pitch from Mike Trombley of the Twins for his 32nd homer. Once again, the Cardinals are defeated, 4-2. Despite McGwire's continued heroics, they are 46-48 in the NL Central.

JULY 22:

Orel Hershiser and the Mets defeat the Expos in Montreal, 7-4. It is Hershiser's 200th career victory, making him the 95th pitcher to reach that landmark. He is 10-7 this season.

At Cinergy Field, Danny Graves serves up Mark McGwire's 33rd homer, and Fernando Tatis hits a pair of two-run homers to bring his total to 23. McGwire has now homered in every stadium in

HISTORY

Hack Wilson's RBI records for 1930 are amended and he now is credited with 191 instead of 190. The correction is made by the baseball commissioner's office after a review of the records by retired Chicago sportswriter Jerome Holtzman and then by a three-man committee. The "missing" run batted in was given to Charlie Grimm instead of Wilson in a July 28 game. Wilson died in 1948.

CULTURE

At the movies, *For Love of the Game* stars Kevin Costner as a 37-year-old pitcher for the Detroit Tigers who is working on a perfect game. Vin Scully, Steve Lyons, and Ricky Ledee are featured.

HISTORY

The Tigers beat the Royals, 8-2, in what will be the last game at Tiger Stadium. The ballpark, built in 1912, will be torn down and the Tigers will play at the new Comerica Park next season.

which he has played. The Cardinals edge the Reds, 6-5.

JULY 23:

Sammy Sosa hammers a Masato Yoshii pitch for his 35th homer, but the Mets win in New York, 5-4.

Look who's right behind Sammy. Mark McGwire hits his 34th – in Colorado off Mike DeJean – to move within one of Sosa. St. Louis wins, 6-4.

Still in the homer hunt is Ken Griffey Jr., who hits his 31st in Minnesota.

JULY 24:

The Yankees bang out 21 hits and defeat the Indians, 21-0, in New York as Hideki Irabu coasts to his seventh victory. Chili Davis has six RBI; he and Scott Brosius homer.

The Marlins send pitcher Livan Hernandez (5-9, 4.76 ERA) – the 1997 World Series MVP – to the Giants for minor league pitchers Jason Grilli and Nathan Bump.

JULY 25:

After hitting his 35th homer – off Pedro Astacio in Colorado – Mark McGwire leaves the game with back pain. He has eight homers in his last 11 games and 12 for the month. The Cardinals win, 6-4.

Ken Griffey, with number 32, and Alex Rodriguez, with number 22, homer back-to-back and the Mariners beat the Twins, 4-3, in Minnesota.

In Cooperstown, New York, the Hall of Fame inducts George Brett, Orlando Cepeda, Nolan Ryan, Robin Yount, Nestor Chylak, Frank Selee, and Joe Williams. Brett played his entire career – from 1973 to 1993 – with the Royals. He is one of only four players with 3,000 hits, 300 homers, and 200 stolen bases. He hit .305 with 317 homers and 1,595 RBI, winning three batting titles. Cepeda, a hard-hitting first baseman, played from 1958 to 1974 with the Giants, Cardinals, Braves, Athletics, Red Sox, and Royals. The NL's unanimous choice MVP in 1967, he batted .297 with 379 homers and 1,365 RBI. Ryan, the all-time strikeout king, pitched for the Mets, Angels, Astros, and Rangers, for 27 seasons – the longest career in history. He compiled a 324-292 record with 5,714 strikeouts and a 3.19 ERA. Like Brett, Yount spent his entire career with one team – the Milwaukee Brewers. In 20 years, he batted .285 with 251 homers and 1,406 hits. He twice was the AL's MVP. Selee, who died in 1909, managed the Boston Beaneaters to an NL pennant in 1891, and under his leadership the team became a great 19th-century dynasty. He also managed the Cubs, where he assembled the Tinkers-to-Evers-to-Chance combination. He won five pennants in 16 seasons. Williams, who died in 1951, was known as "Smoky" because of the velocity of his pitches. He pitched for more than 20 years with the Chicago Leland Giants, the New York Lincoln Giants, the Brooklyn Royal Giants, and the Homestead Grays. He was regarded as one of the Negro Leagues' most dominant pitchers. Chylak, who died in 1982, umpired for 25 seasons and worked five World Series. He was generally regarded as the best AL umpire of his time.

Among those attending today's ceremonies are 80-year-old Ted Williams (in a wheelchair), Willie Mays, and Hank Aaron.

JULY 26:

The Devil Rays and Bobby Witt shut out the Angels, 7-0. It is Anaheim's 11th straight loss.

JULY 27:

Mark McGwire homers again against the Giants – off Kirk Rueter. It McGwire's 37th of the year and his 494th career homer, putting him in 16th place, ahead of Lou Gehrig. And, again, it isn't enough – the Cardinals lose, 2-1.

The umpire labor story gets more complex as 42 umpires try to rescind their resignations after the two leagues hire 25 new umps. Originally some 50 of 66 umpires had submitted letters.

JULY 28:

Sammy Sosa ties Mark McGwire for the major league lead with his 37th homer – hit off Javier Vazquez in Montreal. In San Francisco, McGwire remains tied when he is ejected in the fourth inning for a 10-second argument with plate umpire Greg Bonin over a called third strike.

JULY 29:

The NL drops 13 of the umpires who had

Sammy Sosa says of his back-to-back 60 seasons, "It made me proud of myself. Of all the players to play this game, I'm the first to do it."

submitted their resignations, effective September 2.

JULY 30:

Sammy Sosa homers off Masato Yoshii for his 38th of the year, but the Mets beat the Cubs, 10-9, and move into first place in the NL East. Mike Piazza hits his 21st.

Mark McGwire keeps pace in St. Louis, slamming a sixth inning pitch from Pedro Astacio for his 38th homer. McGwire now has the most homers ever racked up in in five years – 257 – and has connected 11 times in his last 15 games. But the Rockies win, 5-4.

Shawn Green hits his 30th homer and extends his hitting streak to 27 games as his Blue Jays top the Tigers, 8-2.

JULY 31:

The Mets send outfielder Brian McRae (.221) and two minor leaguers – pitcher, pitcher Rigo Beltran and outfielder Thomas Johnson – to the Rockies for outfielder Darryl Hamilton (.303, four homers, 26 RBI) and reliever Chuck McElroy (3-1, 6.20 ERA, no saves).

AUGUST 1:

In St. Louis, Mark McGwire knocks his 40th homer of the season – and the 497th of his career – off Brian Bohanon of the Rockies, but the Cardinals lose another close one, 5-4.

Five Detroit pitchers hold Shawn Green hitless, ending his hitting streak at 30 games. The Blue Jays still get the win, 8-5.

AUGUST 2:

At Busch Stadium, Mark McGwire hits number 41 – off the Padres' Woody Williams – and Sammy Sosa answers with his 41st off the Expos' Dustin Hermanson.

AUGUST 3:

The Mets beat the Brewers, 10-3, and the Pirates down the Braves, 7-1, lifting New York into first in the NL East.

The Blue Jays and Joey Hamilton defeat the Yankees, 3-1.

Arizona's Randy Johnson won the N L Cy Young Award, helped by a career-high 364 strikeouts.

AUGUST 5
Mark McGwire reaches the 500 mark faster than anyone before him.

CULTURE

"The Unnatural," an episode of *The X-Files* about a Negro Leagues star who is really an alien, guest stars M. Emmet Walsh.

The save goes to rookie Billy Koch, bringing his total to 22.

AUGUST 4:

Sammy Sosa hits number 42 off the Expos' Jeremy Powell.

Mark McGwire matches Sosa with his 42nd, hit off the Padres' Donne Wall.

Mark McGwire reports that he has stopped using the controversial but legal supplement androstenedione because "I don't like how it's portrayed that young kids take it because of me. I always discouraged children from taking it."

The Mets come out ahead of the Brewers again, 9-5, to open a two-game lead over the Braves.

AUGUST 5:

Mark McGwire hits his 500th career round-tripper in the third inning in St. Louis off Andy Ashby. In the eighth inning, McGwire connects again off Ashby for his 501st, and 44th of the season. But the Padres win, 10-3.

McGwire has reached the 500 mark faster than any other player in history.

AUGUST 6:

In Montreal, Tony Gwynn lines a first-inning single off Dan Smith for his career 3,000th hit. He is the 22nd player to reach the 3,000-hit level.

Gwynn reached 2,000 hits exactly six years ago to the day, in 1993.

AUGUST 7:

Make that 23. At Tropicana Field in St. Petersburg, Wade Boggs lashes a pitch from the Indians' Chris Haney into the right-field stands for a homer and his 3,000th career hit. Boggs is the first player to reach that plateau with a home run. He points to the sky for his late mother and drops to his knees to kiss home plate.

AUGUST 8:

One-time NL batting champion Harry "The Hat" Walker dies at 80 in Birmingham, Alabama. He was known as "The Hat" because he constantly fidgeted with his cap in the batter's box. Walker played 11 seasons with the Cardinals, Phillies and Reds, batting .296. In 1947, he played with both the Cardinals and Phillies, batting .363, tops in the NL. He was the brother of former major leaguer Dixie Walker.

AUGUST 9:

The Mets lose, 9-2, to the Dodgers and are out of first place.

AUGUST 10:

The Devil Rays send a 3,000-hit player to the mound for the final inning and a third of a 17-1 loss to the Orioles. Wade Boggs allows three hits and a run and strikes out Delino DeShields. Boggs pitched an inning for the Yankees in 1997.

AUGUST 13:

In St. Louis, Mark McGwire homers against two Cubs' pitchers – Kyle Farnsworth and then Rod Beck – for his 45th and 46th of the year, putting him three ahead of Sammy Sosa, who is hitless in two official at-bats.

Manny Ramirez hits his 31st and 32nd homers for the Indians and raises his RBI total to 120.

AUGUST 14:

Mark McGwire and Sammy Sosa match homers in St. Louis as the Cubs beat the Cardinals, 9-7. McGwire's 47th comes off Mirach Bowie; Sosa connects off Darren Oliver for his 44th, keeping the competition hot.

Hall of Fame shortstop Harold "Pee Wee" Reese, who was the mainstay and captain of the great Brooklyn Dodgers teams of the 1950s, dies at 81 in Louisville, Kentucky. Reese, who earned his nickname from a boyhood marbles game, befriended Jackie Robinson during the turbulent days of 1947. In his 16 years on the diamond, he batted .269.

AUGUST 15:

In Detroit, Chuck Finley becomes the first pitcher to strike out four batters in an inning twice in his career. Finley performs the feat today and previously fanned four in a single inning on May 12 of this year. Finley also is the winner as the Angels down the Tigers, 10-2.

Sammy Sosa draws within one homer of Mark McGwire in St. Louis when he smacks two – his 45th and 46th – off Jose Jiminez, while McGwire is held in check by five Cubs' pitchers.

AUGUST 9
The Mets slip out of NL first place with a 9-2 loss to the Dodgers.

SEPTEMBER 4
The Reds crush the Phillies, 22-3, on the strength of nine home runs.

AUGUST 16:

And now they are even. Sammy Sosa homers off Randy Johnson for his 47th.

AUGUST 17:

Ken Griffey Jr. hits his 37th homer – tops in the AL.

AUGUST 18:

In St. Louis, Mark McGwire hits his 48th of the season – off the Phillies' Chad Ogea – and the 505th home run of his career. He is now in 15th place on the all-time list, one ahead of Eddie Murray.

The Mariners beat the Blue Jays, 5-1, for manager Lou Piniella's 1,000th victory.

AUGUST 20:

At Wrigley Field, Sammy Sosa homers twice against Pedro Astacio of the Rockies – his 48th and 49th. But Colorado bombs Chicago, 11-3.

AUGUST 21:

Sammy Sosa is on the rampage. He slams his 50th and 51st homers off John Thomson of the Rockies and the Cubs win, 8-6. He is the fourth player with consecutive 50-plus homer seasons, and he leads McGwire by three.

AUGUST 22:

Playing in New York, Mark McGwire homers – his 49th – off Octavio Dotel and – 50th – off Jeff Tam in the opener of a double-header. Mike Piazza hits his 30th in an 8-7 Mets win. The Cardinals take the nightcap, 7-5.

AUGUST 25:

Shannon Stewart of the Blue Jays singles against the Angels to extend his hitting streak to 23 games.

AUGUST 29:

In Los Angeles, Sammy Sosa is smoking. He raps out his 54th home run off the Dodgers' Darren Dreifort.

Chipper Jones homers against the Cardinals in the 10th to give the Braves their 10th straight victory, 4-3.

AUGUST 31:

In San Diego, Sammy Sosa hits his 55th – off Alan Ashby of the Padres; the Cubs lose, 7-3.

SEPTEMBER 1:

Sammy Sosa's 56th homer – off Sterling Hitchcock – gives the Cubs a 1-0 win over the Padres.

At Busch Stadium in St. Louis, Mark McGwire takes Ryan Dempster downtown for his 52nd homer. The Cardinals win, 9-3

SEPTEMBER 3:

In a day game at Wrigley Field, Sammy Sosa homers off Chan Ho Park of the Dodgers for his 57th.

Playing at night in Milwaukee, Mark McGwire slams his 53rd and 54th home runs – both off Scott Karl. McGwire now has 511 for his career, tying Mel Ott for 15th place.

In Atlanta, Andres Galarraga, recovering from cancer, is in the dugout watching his team take the Diamondbacks, 7-3. He will not return to the lineup this season, but is able to attend games.

SEPTEMBER 4:

The Reds smack an NL record nine homers and stampede the Phillies, 22-3, in Philadelphia. The Reds' home run hitters are Eddie Taubensee (two), Greg Vaughn, Jeffrey Hammonds, Aaron Boone, Dmitri Young, Pokey Reese, Brian Johnson, and Mark Lewis.

Pedro Martinez fans 15 Mariners, allows two hits, and earns his 20th victory, 4-0.

SEPTEMBER 5:

The Reds follow up on yesterday's nine-homer barrage with five more today as they down the Phillies again, 9-7. Today's home run hitters are Jeffrey Hammonds (two), Greg Vaughn, Eddie Taubensee, and Dmitri Young. The 14 round-trippers in two games are a major league record.

Darryl Strawberry, back from his cancer treatment and legal problems, homers for the Yankees in an 8-3 win over the Angels.

SEPTEMBER 6:

Sammy Sosa moves four ahead of Mark McGwire when he pounds out his 58th home run today against the Reds and Juan Guzman. But the Cubs go down, 6-3.

In Seattle, Ken Griffey Jr. hits his 43rd homer – off David Wells of the Blue Jays.

SEPTEMBER 8:

Jeff Bagwell hits his 40th homer as the Astros top the Phillies, 10-2, and Mike

HISTORY

Mark McGwire registers an incredible 135 home runs for the past two seasons – a performance that makes no home run record safe.

SEPTEMBER 18
Sammy Sosa is the first to reach the 60-homer mark in two seasons.

HISTORY

Both houses of the U.S. Congress pass a resolution honoring Hank Aaron. He is saluted for his exploits on the field and for his work helping young children with the Chasing the Dream Foundation. Aaron says, "This is one day I know I'll never forget."

HISTORY

The Yankees win their 25th World Series, the most of any team in any pro sport. In baseball, the Cardinals are a distant second with nine. These Yankees are the first to sweep back-to-back World Series since 1938 and 1939, when that feat also was accomplished by the Yankees.

Hampton picks up his 19th win.

SEPTEMBER 9:

Sammy Sosa is closing in on 60 again. He slugs number 59 off Pete Harnisch of the Reds. Greg Vaughn hits his 36th and the Reds down the Cubs, 5-3.

Hall of Fame pitcher Jim "Catfish" Hunter dies at 53 in Hertford, North Carolina. Hunter, who pitched a perfect game against the Minnesota Twins in 1968, was suffering from ALS, also known as Lou Gehrig's disease. Hunter pitched for the Athletics – in Kansas City and Oakland – and the Yankees, compiling a 224-166 record with an ERA of 3.26. He threw for 20 winning games or more in five consecutive seasons – 1971-1975 – and won the Cy Young Award in 1974.

SEPTEMBER 10:

After 24 homerless at bats, Mark McGwire hits a three-run, eighth-inning homer – number 55 – off Mike Williams of the Pirates.

Boston's Pedro Martinez strikes out 17 Yankees, limits the Bronx Bombers to a homer by Chili Davis, and wins his 21st game, 3-1.

SEPTEMBER 11:

Eric Milton of the Twins no-hits the Angels, 7-0, in Minnesota. The left-hander strikes out 13 and walks only two. Denny Hocking homers for the winners.

Houston's Jose Lima beats the Cubs, 5-3, for his 20th win. He is the first NL pitcher to reach 20 wins this season.

Barry Bonds becomes the 210th player with 2,000 career hits when he doubles in the fourth inning against the Braves.

SEPTEMBER 13:

David Wells defeats the Yankees, 2-1, in Toronto, sending his former team to its fourth straight loss.

Greg Vaughn hits his 38th homer and his Reds beat the Marlins, 7-4, for their seventh straight victory.

Houston's Mike Hampton beats the Phillies, 13-2, for his 20th win.

SEPTEMBER 14:

Ken Griffey Jr. adds to his AL-leading total with his 45th homer.

SEPTEMBER 17:

Mark McGwire hits his 56th – off Jose Lima of the Astros – and passes Ernie Banks and Eddie Mathews on the all-time list. McGwire now has 513 career homers.

SEPTEMBER 18:

Sammy Sosa becomes the first player with 60 or more homers in two seasons. Sosa hits his landmark home run against Jason Bere of the Brewers in Chicago.

SEPTEMBER 19:

Sammy Sosa hits his 61st – off Hideo Nomo of the Brewers – and Mark McGwire takes Chris Holt of the Astros long twice – for his 57th and 58th homers.

SEPTEMBER 20:

Despite 16-miles-an-hour incoming winds and low temperatures at Wrigley Field, Mark McGwire launches a Jon Lieber pitch into the centerfield stands for his 59th homer.

SEPTEMBER 21:

Pedro Martinez strikes out 12 Blue Jays to reach 300 for the season, and he pitches a 3-0 three-hitter for his 22nd win against four losses. The Red Sox' victory eliminates Toronto from postseason play.

SEPTEMBER 22:

Shawn Green hits his 40th home run for the Blue Jays.

SEPTEMBER 23:

The Braves beat the Mets, 6-3, in Atlanta, completing a three-game sweep and boosting their NL East lead to four games.

Roger Clemens and the Yankees beat the White Sox, 5-2, clinching at least a tie for a playoff berth.

SEPTEMBER 24:

Manny Ramirez hits a grand slam and a three-run homer and drives in eight runs, leading the Indians over the Blue Jays, 18-4. Ramirez now has 42 homers and 157 RBI.

SEPTEMBER 25:

Greg Vaughn hits his 43rd homer and the Reds beat the Cardinals, 6-1, to bring the Reds even with the Mets for a wild card berth.

SEPTEMBER 26:

Here comes Big Mac again. Mark McGwire slams his 60th against Scott Sullivan

OCTOBER 3
Big Mac McGwire closes the season with his 65th home run.

OCTOBER 4
The Mets down Cincinnati, 5-0, for a wild card berth.

of the Reds. McGwire joins Babe Ruth and Jimmie Foxx as the only players with 400 homers in 10 years. He also joins Sammy Sosa in an exclusive club of two – they are the only players to hit 60 homers twice. But Pokey Reese hits a three-run homer in the 12th to beat the Cardinals, 7-5.

The Rangers beat the A's, 10-3, to sew up the AL West.

SEPTEMBER 27:

Mark McGwire connects for his 61st homer – off Ron Villone – but the Reds win, 9-7, and continue their drive toward the playoffs.

Pedro Martinez rings up his 23rd win, striking out 12 and downing the Orioles, 5-3.

SEPTEMBER 28:

Sammy Sosa pushes past Mark McGwire once again with his 62nd homer, hit off Anthony Shumaker of the Phillies.

SEPTEMBER 29:

Mark McGwire, who looked to be out of the home run race not long ago, slams two more – his 62nd off Matt Clement in game one of a double - header and his 63rd off Andy Ashby in the nightcap – and passes Sammy Sosa. The Cardinals sweep the Padres.

The Red Sox split a doubleheader with the White Sox, ensuring at least a wild card berth.

OCTOBER 1:

Is Big Mac's power contagious? Fernando Tatis homers off Jon Lieber of the Cubs – it is his 34th of the season. Tatis has never hit more than eight in a season and has a total of only 19 for his three previous years in the majors. Mark McGwire has a single and Sammy Sosa is hitless as the Cubs nip the Cardinals, 3-2.

OCTOBER 2:

With the season dwindling, Mark McGwire moves two up on Sammy Sosa with his 64th homer. With Sosa limited to a single in five at-bats at Busch Stadium, McGwire connects on a pitch from Andy Lorraine to solidify his lead. He also walks three times. The Cubs register a meaningless 6-3 win.

OCTOBER 3:

Mark McGwire finishes another fantastic season with his 65th home run – off Steve Trachsel of the Cubs. Once again Sosa goes where no player has gone – except McGwire – and once again he comes up just short, after hitting his 63rd today off Larry Luebbers.

In another era, Sammy Sosa would have stood at the pinnacle of power hitters. But despite hitting 65 and 63 homers in successive seasons, he finishes second to Mark McGwire twice.

OCTOBER 4:

The Mets and Reds face off in Cincinnati in a playoff game to determine a wild card berth. Edgardo Alfonzo hits a two-run homer off Steve Parris in the first, and the Mets break out on top. Rickey Henderson adds a solo homer and Al Leiter pitches a complete-game two-hitter. The Mets win, 5-0, and head for Arizona to meet the Diamondbacks.

REGULAR SEASON WRAP-UP:

The World Series pits two teams in contention for the title of "Best of the '90s." For the decade, the Braves have the best record, 925-629, for a .595 winning percentage and one World Series win. The Yankees are second, with 851-702 and a .548 winning percentage; they have won two World Series.

The Yankees, managed again by Joe Torre, finish the regular season at 98-64 in the AL and breeze through the playoffs, losing only one game. Bobby Cox's Braves, 103-59 in the NL regular season, have a more difficult playoff journey.

The Yankees have a team batting average of .282, with 193 homers, 104 stolen bases, and an ERA of 4.17. Bernie Williams (.342, 25 homers, 115 RBI) and Derek Jeter (.349, 24 homers, 102 RBI) provide the offensive spark, backed by Chuck Knoblauch (18 homers), Paul O'Neill (.285, 19 homers, 100 RBI), Tino Martinez (28 homers), Chili Davis (19 homers), and Scott Brosius (17 homers). The starting pitchers are Orlando "El Duque" Hernandez (17-9, 4.12 ERA), David Cone (12-9, 3.44 ERA), Roger Clemens (14-10, 4.60 ERA), and Andy Pettitte (14-11, 4.70 ERA). Mariano Rivera (4-3, 1.83 ERA, 45 saves) is the bullpen closer.

The Braves sport a .266 team average, 197 homers, 148 stolen bases, and an

HISTORY

Before World Series game two, the All-Century Team – selected by paper ballot by fansand a review panel – is introduced. On hand are Hank Aaron, Ted Williams, Stan Musial, and many other baseball immortals. But the biggest hand goes to the banned Pete Rose – allowed by Commissioner Bud Selig to participate in this one event. Rose uses the opportunity to promote his case for reinstatement, complaining, "Charles Manson can get a hearing. I hope they don't wait till 2060 to review my case." A greater injustice, in the view of some, is the omission of the late Roberto Clemente from the All-Century Team.

OCTOBER 5
Both New York teams win their first post-season games.

OCTOBER 9
Atlanta advances to the NLCS, knocking out Houston.

LEAGUE

While his father seeks reinstatement to baseball, Pete Rose Jr.'s own dream lives on. The 29-year-old infielder signs a contract to play with the Phillies' AAA Reading minor league team. In the independent Northern League last year, he hit .300 with 15 homers and 53 RBI.

ERA of 3.63. Chipper Jones is Atlanta's top hitter (.319, 45 homers, 110 RBI), backed by Brian Jordan (23 homers, 115 RBI), Andruw Jones (26 homers, 84 RBI), and Ryan Klesko (21 homers, 80 RBI). The pitching staff is led by Greg Maddux (19-9, 3.57 ERA), Kevin Millwood (18-7, 2.68 ERA), Tom Glavine (14-11, 4.12 ERA), and John Smoltz (11-8, 3.19 ERA). The Braves' closer is the tempestuous John Rocker (4-5, 2.49 ERA, 38 saves).

OCTOBER 5:

NL Division Series. Behind Shane Reynolds, the Astros beat Greg Maddux and the Braves, 6-1, in Atlanta. Ken Caminiti hits a three-run homer in the ninth and Houston's rookie Daryle Ward homers earlier. Greg Maddux gets the loss.

NL Division Series. The Mets beat the Diamondbacks, 8-4. Randy Johnson strikes out 13 Mets but gives up seven runs. Edgardo Alfonzo homers twice for New York and bats in five runs. John Olerud connects once. Turk Wendell, the fourth of five Mets pitchers, gets the win.

AL Division Series. The Yankees use pitching and power to pound the Rangers, 8-0, in New York. Orlando "El Duque" Hernandez limits Texas to two hits – both by Ivan Rodriguez – and Bernie Williams drives in six runs with a three-run homer and a double. Derek Jeter has two RBI. Aaron Sele is the loser.

OCTOBER 6:

NL Division Series. Kevin Millwood goes the distance, limiting the Astros to one hit and a run, and the Braves win, 5-1. Ken Caminiti's homer is Houston's only run. Brian Jordan has two RBI for the winners. Jose Lima gets the loss.

NL Division Series. The Diamondbacks beat the Mets, 7-1, in Arizona. Todd Stottlemyre allows four hits and a run, and Steve Finley drives in five runs with two singles. Kenny Rogers takes the loss.

AL Division Series. The Indians beat the Red Sox, 3-2. Jim Thome hits a two-run homer for the Indians and Travis Fryman's single in the bottom of the ninth drives in the winning run. Nomar Garciaparra has a homer and a double, batting in both of Boston's runs. Paul Shuey gets the win; Derek Lowe is the loser.

OCTOBER 7:

AL Division Series. Jim Thome and Harold Baines homer for the Indians, while Charles Nagy holds the Red Sox in check in Cleveland. The Indians win, 11-1. Bret Saberhagen is the losing pitcher.

AL Division Series. Andy Pettitte works seven outstanding innings, allowing one run in seven and a third, and the Yankees down the Rangers again, 3-1, in New York. Juan Gonzalez homers for the Rangers' only run. Rick Helling gets the loss.

The Orioles fire manager Ray Miller, who finished 78-84 with the highest payroll – $78 million – in the majors. Miller was the team's fourth manager in six years.

OCTOBER 8:

NL Division Series. In Houston, Brian Jordan drives in five runs and the Braves beat the Astros, 5-3, in 12 innings. A spectacular play by shortstop Walt Weiss in the 10th cuts down the potential winning run at the plate. John Rocker gets the win in relief; Jay Powell is the loser. Jordan has a homer and doubles in the winning run.

NL Division Series. The Mets, behind Rick Reed, beat the Diamondbacks, 9-2, in New York. John Olerud has two hits and three RBI. The losing pitcher is Omar Daal.

Cardinals' manager Tony LaRussa gets a two-year contract extension. St. Louis was 75-86, 21 1/2 games behind the Astros.

OCTOBER 9:

AL Division Series. The Yankees sweep the Rangers, 3-0, in Texas, behind Roger Clemens's three-hit pitching. Darryl Strawberry's three-run homer in the first inning off loser Esteban Loaiza seals the game early for New York.

NL Division Series. Backup catcher Todd Pratt homers with one on in the bottom of the 10th inning, and the Mets sweep the Diamondbacks, 4-3, moving on to the NL Championship Series. Edgardo Alfonzo homers for New York in the fourth – his third in

OCTOBER 13
The Red Sox and the Yankees square off in ALCS game one.

post-season play. John Franco gets the win in relief; Matt Mantei is the losing pitcher.

AL Division Series. The Red Sox ride a six-run seventh inning to beat the Indians, 9-3, at Fenway Park. John Valentin and Brian Daubach homer for the Red Sox. Derek Lowe, in relief of Pedro Martinez, gets the win. Jaret Wright is charged with the loss.

NL Division Series. The Braves eliminate the Astros, 7-5, in Houston and move onto Atlanta to await the Mets. The Braves pound out 15 hits – but no homers – and John Smoltz gets the win. Ken Caminiti hits his third homer of the series. Shane Reynolds is charged with the loss.

OCTOBER 10:

AL Division Series. Records fall as the Red Sox maul the Indians, 23-7, in Fenway Park. The Red Sox break post-season marks for the most runs and the most hits – 24; John Valentin ties a post-season record for most RBI – seven – and has two homers among his four hits. Jose Offerman and Jason Varitek also homer for Boston. Rich Garces gets the win in relief; Bartolo Colon is the loser. The series will be resolved at tomorrow's game in Cleveland.

OCTOBER 11:

AL Division Series. Troy O'Leary and Pedro Martinez provide the heroics as the Red Sox beat the Indians, 12-8, to win their division series. Martinez, coming off a back injury, works six innings of no-hit relief, strikes out eight and gets the win. O'Leary hits two homers and drives in seven runs. Jim Thome homers twice and Travis Fryman once for the Indians. Cleveland's Paul Shuey gets the loss.

One of baseball's hottest and oldest rivalries – the Yankees and Red Sox – will resume in New York.

OCTOBER 12:

NLCS game one. Behind five-hit pitching by winning pitcher Greg Maddux and two innings of no-hit relief by Mike Remlinger and John Rocker, the Braves beat the visiting Mets, 4-2. Eddie Perez homers for Atlanta. Masato Yoshii gets the loss.

OCTOBER 13:

ALCS game one. Bernie Williams homers in the bottom of the 10th off Rod Beck and Yankees beat the Red Sox, 4-3. Mariano Rivera gets the win in relief of Orlando Hernandez. Scott Brosius also homers for New York.

NLCS game two. In Atlanta, the Braves go up two games to none with a 4-3 victory over the Mets. Kevin Millwood gets the win with a save from John Smoltz. Eddie Perez and Brian Jordan homer off losing pitcher Kenny Rogers.

OCTOBER 14:

ALCS game two. The Yankees make it two in a row, downing the Red Sox, 3-2, in New York. Winning pitcher David Cone allows two runs and strikes out nine in seven innings; Mariano Rivera, the Yankees' sixth pitcher of the game, gets the win. All of Boston's scoring results from a two-run homer by Nomar Garciaparra. Tino Martinez hits a solo homer, and Paul O'Neill's single in the seventh produces the winning run. Ramon Martinez, Pedro's older brother, gets the loss.

The Tigers fire manager Larry Parish and replace him with Phil Garner, who was axed by the Brewers in August. The Tigers were 69-92 this season.

OCTOBER 15:

NLCS game three. The Mets are on the brink of extinction after being shut out by winner Tom Glavine and two relievers, 1-0. Gerald Williams scores from third on a Mike Piazza throwing error in the first inning for the game's only run. Al Leiter is the hard-luck loser. John Rocker gets a save. The Braves beat the Mets, 1-0.

The Indians fire manager Mike Hargrove after a 97-65 year but a disappointing post-season.

OCTOBER 16:

ALCS game three. Pedro Martinez flashes his fastball, the Red Sox flex their muscles, and the Yankees go down, 13-1, at Fenway Park. In a matchup of Red Sox aces past and present, Martinez strikes out 12 Yankees in seven innings of two-hit pitching. Roger Clemens lasts only two innings, getting shelled for five runs and six hits. Boston raps out 21 hits, including homers by Nomar

LEAGUE

A merger between the Yankees and the New Jersey Nets of the National Basketball Association is approved by baseball's owners, who are meeting in Irving, Texas. The new entity will be called Yankee-Nets.

OCTOBER 18
The Yankees win their 36th AL pennant, beating Boston, 6-1.

OCTOBER 19
Atlanta offs the Mets, 10-9, and will advance to the World Series.

Garciaparra, Brian Daubach, and John Valentin. Scott Brosius homers for New York.

NLCS game four. The Mets stay alive – barely – beating the Braves, 3-2, at Shea Stadium. John Olerud – who homered earlier – hits a two-run single in the eighth, giving the Mets and Turk Wendell the win, with a save by Armando Benitez. Mike Remlinger gets the loss. The Braves' runs result from homers by Ryan Klesko and Brian Jordan.

OCTOBER 17:

ALCS game four. Darryl Strawberry and Ricky Ledee homer, Andy Pettitte holds the Red Sox' bats in check, and the Yankees have a 9-2 victory in Boston. Pettitte yields two runs in seven and a third innings, and Mariano Rivera comes on to earn a save. Bret Saberhagen gets the loss.

NLCS game five. Robin Ventura hits a grand slam home run that is officially a single in the bottom of the 15th; two runs score, and the Mets win, 4-3. In the pandemonium that follows Ventura's drive over the right centerfield fence, the Mets' third baseman fails to touch second base, so his hit becomes a single in the box score. Earlier, John Olerud homers off Braves starter Greg Maddux. Octavio Dotel, the 10th New York pitcher, gets the win. Kevin McGlinchy, the sixth Braves pitcher, is charged with the loss. Are the Mets on the verge of yet another miracle?

OCTOBER 18:

ALCS game five. For the 36th time, an AL pennant will fly over Yankee Stadium. At Fenway Park, the Yankees top the Red Sox, 6-1. Derek Jeter cracks a two-run homer in the first, providing all the runs Orlando Hernandez and four other pitchers will need. El Duque works seven innings, yielding a run and five hits. Ramiro Mendoza gets a save. Jorge Posada also homers for New York; Jason Veritek connects for Boston. Kent Mercker is the losing pitcher.

OCTOBER 19:

NLCS game six. The Mets' dream of a pennant and New York City's hopes for a true Subway Series die when Kenny Rogers walks Andruw Jones on a 3-2 pitch with the bases loaded in the 11th inning, bringing home Gerald Williams with the winning run. The Mets, who had rallied from a 5-0, first-inning deficit, lose, 10-9. Russ Springer, Atlanta's sixth pitcher of the night, gets the win. Rogers, the eighth for the Mets, gets the loss. The game's only homer is a first-inning blast by Mike Piazza off John Smoltz.

The Mariners re-sign Edgar Martinez (.337), a two-time batting champion, to a one-year, $5.9 million deal.

OCTOBER 20:

Calvin Griffith, former owner of the Washington Senators and the Minnesota twins, dies at 87 in Melbourne, Florida. Griffith moved the franchise from Washington to Minnesota after the 1960 season. Later in his life, he was castigated for making seemingly racist remarks, and he lost Hall of Famer Rod Carew because of his comments. In 1984, Griffith and his sister sold their 52 percent stake in the Twins to Carl Pohlad.

OCTOBER 23:

World Series, game one. The Yankees break out on top in the Team of the Century Fall Classic, on the strength of Orlando Hernandez's arm plus timely hitting. El Duque works seven innings, allowing the Braves one hit and two walks, while striking out 10 for a 4-1 win. The Yankees use three relievers in the eighth, and Mariano Rivera earns a save. The Yankees score their runs in the eighth on singles by Derek Jeter and Paul O'Neill (two RBI) and a bases-loaded walk to Jim Leyritz from John Rocker. Atlanta's only run is a Chipper Jones homer. Greg Maddux gets the loss.

OCTOBER 24:

World Series, game two. Atlanta's Bobby Cox alters his lineup, but the result is the same – the visiting Yankees rap out 14 hits to beat the Braves, 7-2. It the Yankees' 10th straight win in World Series play. In a contest devoid of home runs, David Cone yields just one hit in seven innings for the win. In effect, the Yankees put the game out of reach with three runs in the first. Bernie Williams has three hits; Tino Martinez drives in two runs. Kevin Millwood gets the loss.

CULTURE

In music, "Ballpark Variations" by Ben Yarmolinsky includes variations on "Take Me Out to the Ballgame" and "The Star-Spangled Banner," with commentary by the composer. "Baseball Songs" by Daniel Sonenberg includes music for Phil Rizzuto's "Prayer for the Captain" (about Thurman Munson) and Dan Quisenberry's "Old (G)love."

OCTOBER 27
The Yankees take game four of the World Series for the Championship.

OCTOBER 26:

World Series, game three. Back in New York, Chad Curtis's leadoff homer in the Mike Remlinger gives the Yankees a dramatic comeback win, 6-5, and a seemingly insurmountable lead in the Series. It is Curtis's second homer of the game. Team-mates Chuck Knoblauch and Tino Martinez also connect as the Yankees' come back from a 5-1 deficit with a 14-hit attack. Mariano Rivera, in relief, gets the win.

OCTOBER 27:

World Series, game four. The Yankees put an exclamation point on Team of the Century, sweeping the Braves in New York with a 4-1 win. New York becomes the first team to win 10 World Series games in a row, and it is the team's 25th World Championship. Roger Clemens fulfills a dream with his first World Series victory, pitching seven and two-thirds innings of four-hit ball. Mariano Rivera earns another save. Jim Leyritz continues his heavy hitting in post-season play with a homer in the eighth; Tino Martinez has two RBI. John Smoltz gets the loss.

RICHARD SANDOMIR OBSERVES IN THE NEW YORK TIMES, "TOGETHER, THE HOME MOVIES PROVIDE TELLING EVIDENCE THAT RUTH'S GESTURES WERE DIRECTED AT THE CUBS' DUGOUT, NOT TO THE OUTFIELD." HE CONCLUDES, "STILL, RUTH MIGHT HAVE GESTURED AND BOASTED TO CHARLIE GRIMM'S CUBS THAT HE WOULD HIT A HOME RUN."

Rivera, with two saves and a 0.00 ERA, is the Series MVP. Scott Brosius bats .375, Derek Jeter .353, and Chuck Knoblauch .313. Tino Martinez drives in three runs and Chad Curtis has two homers. Brett Boone bats .538 in a losing effort.

Jack McKeon, 68 years old, will be back as manager of the Reds after a 96-66 season. He agrees to a one-year contract extension.

On November 10, McKeon is named the NL's Manager of the Year.

Former Warner Brothers studio chief Robert A. Daly is named chairman, CEO, and managing partner of the Dodgers. But in baseball, there are no retakes.

POST-SEASON

OCTOBER 30:

The Rockies trade one of their original players, outfielder Dante Bichette (.298, 34 homers, 133 RBI), to the Reds for outfielder Jeffrey Hammonds (.279, 17 homers, 41 RBI) and Stan Belinda (3-1, 5.27 ERA, two saves).

Max Patkin, billed as the Clown Prince of Baseball, dies at 79 in Paoli, Pennsylvania. He reportedly made more than 4,000 appearances during his career as an entertainer, and was seen in the film *Bull Durham*. Patkin pitched in the minors for the White Sox. His clown routine began during World War II, while he was pitching for a Navy team in Hawaii. He followed Joe DiMaggio around the bases after serving up a homer and imitated the Yankee Clipper's distinctive gait.

Patkin actually was the second Clown Prince of Baseball; Al Schacht, who died in 1984, was the first.

OCTOBER 31:

Don Baylor becomes manager of the Cubs. The Braves' batting coach this past season, he previously managed the Rockies for six years.

NOVEMBER 2:

The Rangers trade two-time AL MVP Juan Gonzalez (.326, 39 homers, 128 RBI), pitcher Danny Patterson (2-0, 5.67 ERA), and catcher Gregg Zaun (.247, one homer, 12 RBI in 43 games) to the

TRIVIA

Nice try, but a curse is a curse. The Red Sox trot out Julia Ruth Stevens, the daughter of Babe Ruth, in an attempt to break the so-called Curse of the Bambino. Some believe that the Curse dates back to the 1919, when Boston sold Ruth to the Yankees. The Red Sox have not won a World Series since. Stevens participates in pre-game ceremonies. She says, "I think that they deserve a break."

NOVEMBER 4
The Indians fetch $320 million from Larry Dolan, a record price for a baseball team.

NOVEMBER 30
Major League umpires reorganize under new union, ousting Richie Phillips.

TRIVIA

Billy Koch, who stands six-foot-three and throws 100 mph, was a premature baby who weighed two pounds and 15 ounces at birth and was given a 40 percent chance of surviving. The *New York Times* reports that during this trip to New York, he visited the doctor and nurse who cared for him as an infant.

Tigers for pitchers Justin Thompson (9-11, 5.11 ERA), Alan Webb (no 1999 record), and Francisco Cordero (2-2, 3.32 ERA); outfielder Gabe Kapler (.245, 18 homers, 49 homers); catcher Bill Haselman (.273, four homers, 14 RBI); and infielder Frank Catalanotto (.276, 11 homers, 35 RBI).

NOVEMBER 3:

Mike Hargrove, who was dismissed a month ago as skipper of the Indians, is signed to manage the Orioles.

NOVEMBER 4:

The Indians are sold by Richard Jacobs to attorney Larry Dolan for $320 million, the highest price ever paid for a baseball team. The new owner is the brother of Charles Dolan, chairman of Cablevision (a New York City area cable service provider) – which owns the New York Rangers hockey team, the New York Knicks basketball team, and Madison Square Garden. Larry Dolan claims his brother and Cablevision are not involved in his purchase and ownership. Davey Lopes signs a three-year contract to manage the Brewers, becoming baseball's fifth current minority manager. He was first base coach for the Padres for the past five years.

NOVEMBER 8:

The Blue Jays trade budding superstar Shawn Green (.309, 42 homers, 123 RBI) to the Dodgers for Raul Mondesi (.253, 33 homers, 99 RBI, 36 stolen bases). The deal is consummated when Green agrees to a six-year contract, averaging $14 million annually. Green, a 26-year-old outfielder, had a 28-game hitting streak last year – the longest in the majors in 1999.

NOVEMBER 11:

Wade Boggs retires after 18 big-league seasons, 3,010 hits, and a lifetime average of .328, compiled with the Red Sox, Yankees, and Devil Rays.

NOVEMBER 15:

The Marlins acquire pitcher Dan Miceli (4-5, 4.46 ERA) from the Padres for their top winner, David Meadows (11-15, 5.60 ERA).

NOVEMBER 16:

The Cardinals acquire three pitchers – former 19-game winner Darryl Kile (8-13, 6.61 ERA), Dave Veres (4-8, 5.14 ERA), and Luther Hackman (1-2, 10.69 ERA) – from the Rockies for pitchers Jose Jimenez (5-14, 5.89 ERA), who pitched a no-hitter this past season; Manny Aybar (4-5, 5.47 ERA); and Rick Croushore (3-7, 4.14 ERA). Colorado also gets minor league infielder Brent Butler.

NOVEMBER 17:

Former Dodgers' catcher Mike Scioscia signs to manage his old team, succeeding Terry Collins. Scioscia has been managing in the minors.

NOVEMBER 18:

Mark McGwire passes up a chance for free agency when he and the Cardinals agree to a $11 million option for 2001.

NOVEMBER 30:

Major league umpires vote, 57-35, to jettison their union, the Major League Umpires Association, and replace it with a new Major League Umpires Independent Organizing Committee. With the vote, the umpires also oust Richie Phillips, their lawyer and chief labor negotiator.

Phillips, who held the job for 21 years, was the engineer of the mass resignation strategy that resulted in the loss of 22 jobs and the hiring of 25 new umpires.

DECEMBER 1:

Former major league second baseman Gene Baker dies at 74 in Davenport, Iowa. In 1953, Baker and shortstop Ernie Banks became the first black players on the Chicago Cubs, and were an outstanding double-play combination for three years. In his eight years with the Cubs and Pirates, Baker batted .265.

DECEMBER 6:

The Mariners sign free-agent first baseman John Olerud (.298, 19 homers, 96 RBI), who spent the 1999 season with the Mets, to a three-year, $20 million pact.

DECEMBER 9:

Former Cardinals third baseman George "Whitey" Kurowski dies at 81 in Shillington, Pennsylvania. The hero of the 1942 World Series, Kurowski played nine major league seasons, batting .286. He hit over .300 three times and was a four-time All-Star. His ninth-nning homer off Red

DECEMBER 17
Ace Orel Hershiser signs a $2 million deal to return to his original team, the Dodgers.

Ruffing of the Yankees in game five gave the Cardinals the World Series championship.

DECEMBER 12:

Free-agent third baseman Todd Zeile (.293, 24 homers, 98 RBI) signs a three-year, $18 million deal with the Mets, who may move him to first base to replace John Olerud. Zeile was with the Rangers last season.

The Cubs trade pitchers Terry Adams (6-3, 4.02 ERA) and Chad Ricketts (no record in 1999), plus a player to be named later, to the Dodgers for pitcher Ismael Valdes (9-14, 3.98 ERA) and second baseman Eric Young (.281, two homers, 41 RBI, 51 stolen bases).

The Phillies obtain pitcher Chris Brock (6-8, 5.58 ERA) from the Giants for catcher Bobby Estalella (.167, no homers, one RBI in nine games).

DECEMBER 13:

In a series of trades involving four teams and nine players, the Rockies trade third baseman Vinny Castillo (.275, 33 homers, 102 RBI) to the Devil Rays for pitcher Rolando Arrojo (7-12, 5.18 ERA) and infielder Aaron Ledesma (.265, no homers, 30 RBI). They also send pitcher Jamey Wright (4-3, 4.87 ERA) and catcher Henry Blanco (.232, six homers, 28 RBI) to the Brewers for third baseman Jeff Cirillo (.326, 15 homers, 88 RBI) and pitcher Scott Karl (11-11, 4.78 ERA). The Athletics ship pitcher Jimmy Haynes (7-12, 6.34 ERA) to the Brewers and get minor league pitcher Justin Miller from the Rockies. Later in the day, the Devil Rays sign free-agent Greg Vaughn (.245, 45 homers, 118 RBI) to a four-year, $34 million contract. Vaughn spent last season with the Reds.

The last four-team trade was in 1985.

Outfielder Chad Curtis (.262, five homers, 24 RBI), who hit two key homers for the Yankees in the 1999 World Series, is traded to the Rangers for minor league pitchers Brandon Knight and Sam Marsonek.

First baseman-outfielder Brant Brown (.232, 16 homers, 58 RBI) is traded by the Pirates to the Marlins for outfielder Bruce Aven (.289, 12 homers, 70 RBI).

DECEMBER 14:

Outfielder-third baseman Wil Cordero (.299, eight homers, 32 RBI in 54 games) signs a three-year, $9 million contract with the Pirates. Last season, Cordero was with the Indians, but was sidelined for three months with a broken wrist.

DECEMBER 16:

The Indians sign free-agent pitcher Steve Finley (12-11, 4.43 ERA) to a three-year, $25 million deal. The left-hander, who spent all 14 of his major league years with the Angels, has a reputation as a Yankee killer with a career mark of 16-9 against the Bronx Bombers.

DECEMBER 17:

After signing a one-year, $2 million deal, pitcher Orel Hershiser (13-12, 4.58 ERA) will be returning to the Dodgers, the team he debuted with in 1983. The 41-year-old right-ander won the 1988 NL Cy Young Award with Los Angeles.

DECEMBER 20:

Reliever Graeme Lloyd (5-3, 3.63 ERA, three saves) signs a three-year, $9 million contract with the Expos, and outfielder Gerald Williams (.275, 17 homers, 68 RBI) is inked by the Devil Rays for $5.75 million over two years. Lloyd spent last season with the Blue Jays; Williams was with the Braves.

The Cardinals acquire second baseman Fernando Viña (.266, one homer, 16 RBI) from the Brewers for pitcher Juan Acevedo (6-8, 5.89 ERA, four saves) and two minor league pitchers to be named later.

DECEMBER 21:

Because they signed third baseman Adrian Beltre when he was underage – their second violation – the Dodgers have their Dominican Republic operations suspended for a year by Commissioner Bud Selig. But the Dodgers get to keep Beltre, who was 15 when he signed.

Left-handed reliever Arthur Rhodes (3-4, 5.43 ERA, three saves) signs a $13 million, four-year deal with the Mariners. Rhodes was with the Orioles for his entire career. Baltimore signs another left-handed reliever – Wedsel "Buddy" Groom (3-2, 5.09 ERA) – to a two-year, $4 million deal. Groom was with the Athletics last season.

TRIVIA

The Associated Press reports that a Chicago tavern owner plans to sell Bill Veeck's wooden leg at auction November 18-19. The family of the former White Sox owner is "appalled." Veeck gave the leg to the bar owner in 1977 when he got a new one. His son, Mike, says, "It's offensive to me. I can't wait to call the I.R.S. and make sure he [the tavern owner] pays the gift tax on it."

Said Cubs' pitcher Burleigh Grimes of Babe Ruth's "called shot":
"Ruth held up his finger to say he had one strike left, and the next thing you know, everybody's saying he called his shot."

David Cone's Yankee teammates carry him off the field after his perfect game, a 6-0 victory over Montreal on July 18.

DECEMBER 22:

Hideki Irabu (11-7, 4.84 ERA), once trumpeted as the second coming of Roger Clemens or even Nolan Ryan, is traded by the Yankees to the Expos for minor league pitcher Jake Westbrook and two players to be named later. In three years with New York, he went 29-20 with a 4.81 ERA.

After failing again to win the World Series, the Braves shake up their team. Going to the Padres are second baseman Bret Boone (.252, 20 homers, 63 RBI), first baseman Ryan Klesko (.297, 21 homers, 80 RBI) and minor league pitcher Jason Shiell. In return the Braves obtain first baseman Wally Joyner (.248, five homers, 43 RBI), second baseman Quilvio Veras (.280, six homers, 41 RBI, 30 stolen bases), and outfielder Reggie Sanders (.285, 26 homers, 72 RBI, 36 stolen bases).

Another kind of player gets another kind of publicity. Jack Curry of the New York Times reports that Melvin Mora of the Mets is in Venezuela trying to locate a young boy who could not find his parents after the disastrous mudslides; the boy may be related to the Mets' outfielder. Mora tells Curry that if they are related he will adopt him, and then says that either way, "I am taking him in for December." Mora's Mets' teammate Edgardo Alfonso also is in Venezuela delivering emergency supplies. A third Met, Roger Cedeno, is loading supplies for the effort in Florida.

THREE DAYS AFTER IRABU'S YANKEES' DEBUT, NEW YORK MAYOR RUDOLPH GIULIANI SAID IN HIS WEEKLY RADIO ADDRESS: "HIDEKI IS THE FIRST PLAYER FROM JAPAN TO WEAR THE PINSTRIPES, AND JOINING THE BRONX BOMBERS WAS THE FULFILLMENT OF A LIFELONG DREAM.... HE CHOSE TO PLAY IN 'THE HOUSE THAT RUTH BUILT' – AND WE ARE VERY GLAD THAT HE DID."

DECEMBER 23:

The Mets land one of baseball's premier young pitchers. In a trade with the Houston Astros, New York acquires Mike Hampton (22-4, 2.90 ERA) and outfielder Derek Bell (.236, 12 homers, 66 RBI), in return for three players: outfielder Roger Cedeno (.313, four homers, 36 RBI, 66 stolen bases), pitcher Octavio Dotel (8-3, 5.38 ERA) – and minor league pitcher Kyle Kessel. Hampton had informed the Astros of his intentions to become a free agent after the 2000 season; the Mets are counting on signing him.

DECEMBER 24:

World Series film footage shot by a Chicago businessman, shows Babe Ruth hitting a homer off the Cubs' Charlie Root in 1932. There has been an ongoing debate about whether or not The Bambino had actually called the shot. This is the second home movie to surface.

The Red Sox add a left-handed pitcher, signing free agent Jeff Fassero (5-14, 7.20 ERA) to a one-year, $2 million deal.

DECEMBER 23
The Mets sign the league leading young pitcher Mike Hampton.

THE BEST OF 1999

NATIONAL LEAGUE

HITTERS

Batting Average:
Larry Walker, Colorado Rockies, .379

Slugging Average:
Larry Walker, .710

Home Runs:
Mark McGwire, St. Louis Cardinals, 65

Runs Batted In:
Mark McGwire, 147

Hits:
Luis Gonzalez, Arizona Diamondbacks, 206

Stolen Bases:
Tony Womack, Arizona Diamondbacks, 72

PITCHERS

Wins:
Mike Hampton, Houston Astros, 22

Strikeouts:
Randy Johnson, Arizona Diamondbacks, 364

Earned Run Average:
Randy Johnson, 2.48

Winning Percentage:
Mike Hampton, .846

Saves:
Ugueth Urbina, Montreal Expos, 41

Most Valuable Player:
Larry "Chipper" Jones, Atlanta Braves

Cy Young Award:
Randy Johnson, Arizona Diamondbacks

Rookie of the Year:
Scott Williamson, Cincinnati Reds

Manager of the Year:
Jack McKeon, Cincinnati Reds

AMERICAN LEAGUE

HITTERS

Batting Average:
Nomar Garciaparra, Boston Red Sox, .357

Slugging Average:
Manny Ramirez, Cleveland Indians, .663

Home Runs:
Ken Griffey Jr., Seattle Mariners, 48

Runs Batted In:
Manny Ramirez, 165

Hits:
Derek Jeter, New York Yankees, 219

Stolen Bases:
Brian L. Hunter, Seattle Mariners, 44

PITCHERS

Wins:
Pedro J. Martinez, Boston Red Sox, 23

Strikeouts:
Pedro Martinez, 313

Earned Run Average:
Pedro Martinez, 2.04

Winning Percentage:
Pedro Martinez, .852

Saves:
Mariano Rivera, New York Yankees, 45

Most Valuable Player:
Ivan Rodriguez, Texas Rangers

Cy Young Award:
Pedro J. Martinez, Boston Red Sox

Rookie of the Year:
Carlos Beltran, Kansas City Royals

Manager of the Year:
Jimy Williams, Boston Red Sox

CULTURE

It's a good year for books about basbeall. *Hanging Curve* by Troy Soos is the latest in the mystery series about fictional infielder Mickey Rawlings. *A Nice Tuesday: A Memoir* is about the experiences of writer and former minor league pitcher Pat Jordan, who, at age 56, returns to play in the Northeast League and becomes the oldest pitcher in a pro game in almost 20 years. *Safe at Second* by Scott Johnson is a young-adult novel about a high school star blinded in one eye by a line drive; Herb Score makes an appearance. *The Mercy Rule* by John T. Lescroat is a legal thriller about a baseball player who becomes a lawyer. The title says it all in the case of *Where They Ain't: The Fabled Life and Untimely Death of the Original Baltimore Orioles, the Team That Gave Birth to Modern Baseball* by Burt Solomon (not the author who wrote the book you are reading now).

02:06PM
PACIFIC BELL
WATERHOUSE
SEGA
Chevron
BUD LIGHT
TULLY'S COFFEE
NORTEL NETWORKS
Panasonic

2000s

PART 4 FOUR

2000

NEWS

BUSH DEFEATS GORE, BECOMES 43RD PRESIDENT

ELIAN GONZALEZ, CUBAN YOUNGSTER RESCUED AT SEA, GOES HOME TO CUBA AFTER EXTENDED LEGAL BATTLE

FEDERAL JUDGE RULES AGAINST MICROSOFT IN ANTITRUST CASE

VLADIMIR PUTIN ASSUMES PRESIDENCY OF RUSSIA

"LOVE BUG" VIRUS DAMAGES MILLIONS OF COMPUTERS

CHARLES SCHULTZ, CREATOR OF *PEANUTS* COMIC STRIP, DIES

HUMAN GENOME IS DECODED

UNDERWATER EXPLOSION ON RUSSIAN SUBMARINE KILLS ENTIRE 118-MAN CREW

PRE-SEASON

JANUARY 4:

Former Mets, Pirates, and Expos first baseman-outfielder John Milner dies at 50 in Atlanta, Georgia. Milner played 12 seasons, batting .249 with 131 homers.

JANUARY 7:

Veteran right-hander Andy Benes, who was 13-12 with a 4.81 ERA pitching for the Arizona Diamondbacks last season, inks an $18 million, three-year contract with the St. Louis Cardinals.

JANUARY 10:

Aaron Sele (18-9, 4.79 ERA), with the Rangers last year, signs a two-year, $15 million contract with the Mariners.

JANUARY 11:

Hall of Famer Bob Lemon dies at the age of 79 in Long Beach, California. The great right-hander compiled a 207-128 record with a 3.23 ERA over 13 seasons with the Indians. He also managed the 1978 Yankees to a World Championship after taking over with the team 10 games out of first. He managed the White Sox and the Royals, as well.

> AFTER SERVING IN WORLD WAR II, BOB LEMON WAS CONVERTED FROM A THIRD BASEMAN TO A PITCHER. SAID TIGERS' CATCHER BIRDIE TEBBETTS: "YOU MAY THINK HE'S A THIRD BASEMAN, BUT I KNOW HE'S A PITCHER. I HIT AGAINST HIM DURING THE WAR IN THE PACIFIC, AND IF I NEVER HAVE TO BAT AGAINST HIM AGAIN IT WILL BE TOO SOON."

JANUARY 12:

The Brewers obtain pitchers Jaime Navarro (8-13, 6.09 ERA) and John Snyder (9-12, 6.68 ERA) from the White Sox for pitcher Cal Eldred (2-8, 7.79 ERA) and shortstop Jose Valentin (.227, 10 homers, 38 RBI).

JANUARY 13:

How much is a losing pitcher worth? A lot. The Devil Rays sign pitcher Steve Trachsel (8-18, 5.56 ERA) to a one-year, $1 million contract.

JANUARY 18:

The Phillies re-sign outfielder Bobby Abreu (.335, 20 home runs, 93 RBI) to a three-year, $14.25 million contract.

JANUARY 25:

New York's baseball teams re-sign two key players. The Mets and Gold Glove shortstop Rey Ordóñez (.258, one homer, 60 RBI) agree to a $19 million, four-year deal. Up in the Bronx, the Yankees ink lefty pitcher Andy Pettitte (14-11, 4.70 ERA) – who was nearly traded last season – to a three-year, $25.5 million contract.

FEBRUARY 10
You *can* go home again: The Reds obtain Ken Griffey Jr. in a trade with the Mariners.

FEBRUARY 3:

Yankees' shortstop Derek Jeter (.349, 24 home runs, 102 RBI), who had been engaged in a drawn-out arbitration process with the club, signs a one-year, $10 million contract.

FEBRUARY 10:

The Reds land baseball's biggest prize, Ken Griffey Jr. (.285, 48 homers, 134 RBI), and pay a relative pittance for him. Griffey, who had vetoed previous trades, goes to his hometown from Seattle for pitcher Brett Tomko (5-7, 4.92 ERA), outfielder Mike Cameron (.256, 21 homers, 66 RBI), and two minor leaguers – pitcher Jake Meyer and infielder Antonio Perez. Griffey signs a nine-year, $116.5 million contract; he will average $12.9 million a year. The 31-year-old outfielder, who has 398 homers in 11 seasons, rejoins his father, who is a coach for the Reds. Says Griffey: "This is something I dreamed about as a little kid."

FEBRUARY 16:

The Red Sox sign outfielder Carl Everett (.325, 25 homers, 108 RBI) to a $21 million, three-year deal. Outfielder Dmitri Young (.300, 14 homers, 56 RBI) accepts a one-year, $1.95 million offer and re-signs with the Reds.

FEBRUARY 17:

The Mets re-sign reliever Armando Benitez (4-3, 1.85 ERA, 22 saves) to a four-year, $22 million pact to be their closer.

FEBRUARY 18:

First baseman Eric Karros (.304, 34 homers, 112 RBI) reups with the Dodgers for a three-year, $24 million deal.

FEBRUARY 22:

After battling back from colon cancer last season, the 37-year-old Yankees' DH Darryl Strawberry tests positive for cocaine. As a multiple offender, six days later he is suspended for one year with no possibility of an earlier return for good behavior. The Major League Players Association does not appeal the suspension. Strawberry previously was suspended on drug charges on February 6, 1995, and April 14, 1999.

FEBRUARY 23:

The Padres acquire outfielder Al Martin (.277, 24 homers, 63 RBI, 20 steals) from the Pirates for outfielder-first baseman John Vander Wal (.272, six homers, 41 RBI) and a pair of minor league pitchers – Jim Sak and Geraldo Padua.

MARCH 3:

The Athletics re-sign 23-year-old outfielder Ben Grieve (.265, 28 home runs, 86 RBI) to a four-year, $13 million pact. Grieve was the 1998 AL Rookie of the Year.

MARCH 7:

Former major league pitcher Jack Sanford dies at 70 in Beckley, West Virginia. Sanford won 16 straight games–the third-longest streak in mod-

Mike Piazza drives the New York Mets' offense.

HISTORY

Pacific Bell Park is located at 24 Willie Mays Plaza and features a nine-foot statue of the Hall of Famer at the main entrance.

The Giants' Barry Bonds aims for McCovey Cove.

ern baseball – for the 1962 NL pennant-winning San Francisco Giants. The NL's Rookie of the Year in 1957, Sanford pitched 12 seasons for the Phillies, Giants, Angels and the Kansas City Athletics, compiling a 137-101 record with a 3.69 ERA.

MARCH 14:

It's an exhibition game the Red Sox probably wish they could bottle and re-open during the regular season. Pedro Martinez and relievers Fernando De La Cruz, Dan Smith, Rheal Cormier, Rich Garces, and Rod Beck combine for a perfect game against the Blue Jays at Fort Myers.

MARCH 18:

The Mets send reliever Jesse Orosco (0-2, 5.34 ERA, one save) to the Cardinals for outfielder-infielder Joe McEwing (.275, nine homers, 44 RBI).

MARCH 23

St. Louis acquires outfielder Jim Edmonds (.250, five homers, 23 RBI in 55 games) from the Anaheim Angels for pitcher Kent Bottenfield (18-7, 3.97 ERA) and minor league second baseman Adam Kennedy.

THE SEASON

MARCH 29:

The Mets open their season at home – but home for the day is in Japan. Playing at the Tokyo Dome in a game that begins at 5:05 a.m. Eastern Time and 4:05 a.m. Central Time, New York bows to the "visiting" Cubs, 5-3, before a crowd of 55,000, including Japan's Crown Prince Naruhito and his wife. Previously, no official baseball game has been played outside of the Americas. Mark Grace and Shane Andrews homer for Chicago; Mike Piazza hits one out for New York. Pitcher Jon Lieber wins, allowing one run in seven innings. Mike Hampton is the loser. Mets' manager Bobby Valentine angers Cubs' skipper Don Baylor when he protests the game with two out in the ninth inning, claiming an irregularity in Chicago's lineup card. Valentine later acknowledges that there is no protest.

MARCH 30:

The Mets, now the "visitors," defeat the Cubs, 5-1, in 11 innings in the final of the two-game series in Japan. Benny Agbayani's pinch-hit grand slam makes winners of the Mets and reliever Dennis Cook.

Brian Hunter (.232, four homers, 34 RBI), who led the AL with 44 steals in '99, is released by the Mariners and signed by the Rockies.

APRIL 3

Andres Galarraga, who missed all of last season with cancer, homers in the seventh inning to give the Braves a 2-0 win over the Rockies in Atlanta. Greg Maddux pitches 7 2/3 shutout innings for the win.

Ken Griffey Jr. is hitless in two at-bats in his debut with the Reds in Cincinnati. The game – against the Brewers – is halted by rain in the sixth inning with the score at 3-3 and will be replayed tomorrow.

MARCH 29
The Mets and Cubs open the major league season in Japan's Tokyo Dome; Chicago wins, 5-3.

APRIL 4:

Hideki Irabu's debut with the Expos is not a success. He lasts only two innings, yields six runs and is the losing pitcher. The visiting Dodgers and Chan Ho Park get a 10-4 win; Gary Sheffield hits a two-run homer.

Pedro Martinez picks up where he left off last season, pitching a two-hitter with 11 strikeouts as the visiting Red Sox beat the Mariners, 2-0.

APRIL 6:

Junior breaks the ice. Ken Griffey Jr. singles home a run in the first – it is his first safety as a Red. Cincinnati beats visiting Milwaukee, 5-1.

APRIL 7:

Alas – gone is the Astrodome as the Astros open their new 42,000-seat Enron Field with a 4-1 loss to the Phillies. It is the first regular-season home game outdoors for the Astros since 1964, when they moved into the enclosed Astrodome. Scott Rolen of the Phillies is the first to homer at Enron. Randy Wolf gets the win; the loser is Octavio Dotel. Enron is the first of three new ballparks to open this season.

Sammy Sosa hits his first home run of the season, Ken Griffey Jr. is hitless in four at-bats, and the Cubs beat the Reds in Cincinnati, 10-6.

The Orioles and Tigers combine for five homers in the fifth – tying a major league record – and Baltimore wins at home, 14-10. Connecting for the Orioles are Charles Johnson and Mike Bordick; for the Tigers, Brad Ausmus, Dean Palmer, and Tony Clark. Johnson now has four home runs and 12 RBI. Also homering for Baltimore are Albert Belle and Cal Ripken Jr. Juan Encarnacion and Wendell Magee connect for Detroit.

APRIL 8:

Mark McGwire shakes off the effects of a bad back and connects for a 424-foot homer off Jim Bruske – his first of the new season; the Cardinals beat the visiting Brewers, 10-8.

Andres Galarraga hits a grand-slam homer as the Braves beat the Giants, 7-5, in Atlanta. Greg Maddux gets the win.

Teammates Manny Ramirez and Jim Thome close in on personal milestones in tandem. Each of the Indians' sluggers connects for his 199th career home run in Tampa Bay. Cleveland wins, 6-4. Steve Trachsel serves up both homers – five pitches apart.

APRIL 9:

Another personal disaster strikes the Yankees. Pitching coach and one-time ace Mel Stottlemyre reveals that he has been diagnosed with a form of bone-marrow cancer. The 58-year-old Stottlemyre will later undergo chemotherapy, but intends to remain with the team. On the field, Roger Clemens gets roughed up and the Mariners drill the visiting Yankees, 9-3.

Pedro Martinez fans 12 and allows five hits in seven and a third innings. Boston beats the Angels in Anaheim, 5-2.

Randy Johnson fans 13 Pirates, allowing only five hits in a complete-game, 1-0 win in Arizona. Johnson is 2-0.

Oakland's new Bash Brothers – who are biological siblings as well – combine for seven RBI in a 14-2 victory over the visiting White Sox. Jason Giambi has a grand slam and drives in five runs. Jeremy Giambi has a triple and two RBI.

Ken Griffey Jr. hits his first NL homer and the Reds beat the visiting Cubs, 8-7, in 11 innings. Sammy Sosa hits a home run for Chicago.

APRIL 10:

Ken Griffey Jr. connects off Rolando Arrojo in Colorado for his 400th career homer. At 30 years old, Griffey is the youngest to reach that plateau. But the Reds go down, 7-5.

APRIL 11:

After 104 years at Tiger Stadium (previously called Navin Field), the Tigers inaugurate their new $300 million, 40,000-seat home, Comerica Park, with a 5-2 victory over the Mariners. A crowd of 39,168 sees Brian Moehler record his first win; the losing pitcher is Freddy Garcia.

The Giants are less successful in the opening of their new $319 million stadium, Pacific Bell Park. Paced by Kevin Elster's three homers, including the first ever in Pacific Bell, the Dodgers record a 6-5 victory before a sellout crowd of

HISTORY

Not everyone thinks playing regular season games in Japan is a good idea. On March 20, Mark McGwire, who was instrumental in rejecting the Cardinals as the Mets' opening-day opponent, tells Murray Chass of the *New York Times*: "I don't think it's in the best interests of the players. You're telling me that we're going to fly two teams over 16-plus hours to play two games? You can't give me a good reason for that. There isn't a good reason. The only reason is money..." McGwire, who signed for less than his market value in 1997, adds: "All of us are well overpaid to play this game of baseball. How much money do you really need? Sometimes it overtakes what you're really here for and I don't think it's right."

APRIL 15
Cal Ripken Jr. becomes the 24th player with 3,000 career hits.

HISTORY

Randy Velarde, who turns an unassisted triple play on May 29, did it before, but it didn't count. In 1995, while in spring training as a member of the Yankees, he pulled off the rare feat against the Dodgers.

HISTORY

Cal Ripken, who hit his 400th career homer last season, is one of only seven players with 3,000 hits and 400 or more round-trippers. The others are Hank Aaron (3,771 hits and 755 homers), Willie Mays, Eddie Murray, Stan Musial, Dave Winfield, and Carl Yastrzemski.

40,930. Barry Bonds, J.T. Snow, and Doug Mirabelli homer for the losers. Chan Ho Park gets the win; the loser is Kirk Rueter.

APRIL 13:

Orlando Hernandez allows the Rangers three hits and an unearned run in eight innings and the Yankees win, 5-1, in New York. The loser is Kenny Rogers.

The Devil Rays purchase pitcher Dwight Gooden (0-0) from the Astros.

Former outfielder-third baseman Stanley "Frenchy" Bordagaray dies at 90 in Ventura, California. One of the game's more colorful characters, he created a stir in 1936 – a time when facial hair was taboo – when he reported to the Dodgers sporting a goatee and mustache. Bordagaray played 11 seasons with the White Sox, Dodgers, Reds, Cardinals, and Yankees, batting .283 with 14 home runs and 270 RBI.

APRIL 14:

Orel Hershiser, pitching with the Dodgers again after five years, tops the Reds, 8-1, in Los Angeles. He allows six hits and a homer by Aaron Boone. Gary Sheffield smacks a homer for the Dodgers.

Frank Thomas hits his third homer of the season and extends his hitting streak to 11 games; the White Sox beat the visiting Angels, 9-4.

APRIL 15:

With three safeties today in Minnesota, Cal Ripken Jr. becomes the 24th player with 3,000 career hits. The landmark hit is a seventh-inning single off Twins' pitcher Hector Carrasco. Ripken also singled in the fourth and fifth innings. Charles Johnson hits his fifth homer and Baltimore wins, 6-4.

Pedro Martinez and the Red Sox beat the Athletics, 14-2, in Boston. Martinez fans nine, allowing five hits in seven innings.

Edgar Martinez makes his 200th career homer a big one. The Mariners' DH hits a grand slam off Pedro Borbon and Seattle beats the Blue Jays, 17-6, in Toronto.

APRIL 16:

Shortstop Alex Rodriguez hits three homers and drives in seven runs in a 19-7 Mariners' triumph over the host Blue Jays. Seattle's Jay Buhner has a home run and five RBI.

APRIL 18:

Robin Ventura hits a grand slam for the Mets – he 14th of his ML career – and Mike Hampton records his first win after three straight losses as the Mets beat the visiting Brewers, 10-7, in New York. Ventura is now tied with Gil Hodges in ninth place for the most career grand slams; Lou Gehrig tops the list with 23.

The Angels outslug the Blue Jays, 16-10, today in Toronto. Anaheim's rookie second baseman Adam Kennedy hits a grand slam, and adds a triple and two singles, driving in eight runs. Jose Cruz Jr., Raul Mondesi, Carlos Delgado, and Craig Grebeck homer for Toronto; Troy Glaus connects on a long ball for the Angels.

The White Sox slam the Mariners, 18-11, in Chicago. An 11-run fourth is highlighted by a three-run homer by Mark Johnson and a two-run blast by Greg Norton.

After completing his reduced sentence, John Rocker returns to the Braves and works a shutout ninth inning, getting a standing ovation from the hometown crowd. The Braves nip the Phillies, 4-3, in 12 on a Brian Jordan homer. If the suspension has mellowed Rocker, it is not immediately evident. According to the Associated Press, after the game Rocker "barks": "Beat it, media. Are you deaf?"

APRIL 19:

Clay Bellinger's 10th-inning homer gives the Yankees their eighth straight win, 5-4, over the Texas Rangers in Arlington.

APRIL 20:

Ken Griffey Jr. breaks a 2-for-17 slump with two long homers – his fourth and fifth of the season – and the Reds beat the Giants, 11-1.

The Chicago Cubs lose to the Expos, 10-6, in Montreal, despite a grand slam and six RBI by Sammy Sosa.

John Rocker registers his first save as the Braves beat the Phillies, 6-4, in Atlanta.

APRIL 21:

In Toronto, the Blue Jays end the Yankees' eight-game winning streak, 8-3.

APRIL 22:

Paced by Derek Bell's six hits in eight at-bats, the Mets sweep the Cubs, 8-3 and 7-6, in New York, which extends their current winning streak to six games.

In Chicago, the White Sox crush the Tigers, 14-6, but ball takes second place to brawl. Hostilities begin when Jeff Weaver of the Tigers hits Carlos Lee. In the seventh, Jim Parque hits Detroit's Dean Palmer in the arm. Palmer charges Parque and the first of the fights begins and ends and begins again. In the ninth, Tanyon Sturtze clips Deivi Cruz of the Tigers; later in the frame Bob Howry of the White Sox hits Shane Halter triggering five more minutes of combat. The umpires eject five Tigers (Doug Brocail, Palmer, Weaver, Rob Fick, and Danny Patterson) and six White Sox (manager Jerry Manuel, coach Joe Nossek, Howry, Bill Simas, Sturtze, and Magglio Ordonez). Chris Singleton of the White Sox has five hits – including a homer – and five RBI.

Barry Bonds hits his 452nd career homer and the Giants beat the Diamondbacks, 8-6, in Arizona. Bonds is now tied with Carl Yastrzemski for 21st place all-time.

Two days after returning from back troubles, Mark McGwire hits his fourth homer of the season, but the Rockies still top the Cardinals, 7-6, at Denver's Coors Field.

APRIL 23:

The visiting Royals lose, 8-5, to the Mariners, on John Olerud's three-run homer in the ninth. It is Kansas City's ninth consecutive loss.

APRIL 24:

Yankees' switch hitters Bernie Williams and Jorge Posada record a baseball first. Each homers twice today – from both sides of the plate – as New York pounds the Blue Jays, 10-7, in Toronto. Williams connects left-handed off Frank Castillo in the first and right-handed against Clayton Andrews in the sixth. Posada hits his lefty home run against Castillo in the second inning and connects right-handed in the fourth off Andrews.

Derek Bell's three-run homer helps the Mets to defeat the Cubs, 15-8, in New York, completing a three-game sweep. Bell has 10 hits in 12 at bats for the series. Mike Hampton gets the win. Sammy Sosa hits his sixth homer.

Mark McGwire hits a homer and teammate Placidio Polancio has a grand slam as the Cardinals beat the Rockies, 6-3, in St. Louis. The Cards now have an NL record 44 homers in April.

Peace prevails today as the Tigers and White Sox face off again. Despite

Ken Griffey Jr. is a hit back in his hometown.

Darin Erstad has an ML-record 48 hits in April.

yielding three homers, James Baldwin wins his third game with no defeats, 9-4.

APRIL 25:

A nationwide protest called by Cuban-Americans has its impact on baseball when a number of players and coaches sit out today's games. The protests are a response to a raid by the Immigration and Naturalization Service to return Elían Gonzáles – an 8 year-old who was rescued at sea off the coast of Florida – to his father in Cuba. In Florida, 10 Marlins (including players Mike Lowell, Alex Fernandez, Vladimir Nuñez, Jesus Sanchez, Antonio Alfonseca, and Danny Bautista; coaches and staff) and three Giants (players Livan Hernandez and Bobby Estalella and coach Carlos Alfonzo) participate in the protest. In Kansas City, the Devil Rays' Jose Canseco sits out his game as do the Mets' shortstop Rey Ordóñez and coach Cookie Rojas. The Yankees' pitcher, Orlando Hernandez, not scheduled to pitch, stays away from the ballpark. All of the protesters – some of whom are not of Cuban ancestry – participate with the consent of management.

In New York, the Reds hammer the Mets, 12-1, ending New York's nine-game winning streak.

Jim Edmonds, Fernando Tatis, and winning pitcher Rick Ankiel homer for the Cardinals, bringing the team's April total to 50, breaking the major league mark set by the 1997 Cleveland Indians. The Cards beat the visiting Brewers, 7-0.

APRIL 27:

On April 27, the *New York Times* reports Hank Aaron's reaction to the work stoppage. He tells James Barron that on the day he hit his 714th career homer in 1974, he was asked "what I would like for my one wish that day. I said I would like to ask for a moment of silence for Dr. Martin Luther King. I was told, 'We are not in the business of politics.'"

Pedro Martinez wins his fourth game against no losses, as Boston defeats the Rangers, 6-3, in Texas, fanning eight and yielding five hits.

Mark McGwire hits his sixth homer and the Cardinals – behind Darryl Kile – defeat the visiting Brewers, 7-2. The Cardinals have homered in 16 consecutive games; McGwire in three straight.

Randy Johnson torments the Phillies for his fifth win against no losses. Johnson fans 11 in six and two-thirds innings, allowing three hits in a 10-2 win in Philadelphia.

APRIL 26:

Ken Griffey Jr. hits his sixth homer and the Reds down the Mets, 2-1, in 12 innings in New York.

Chipper Jones hits a three-run homer and the Braves beat the Dodgers, 6-3, completing a nine-game home stand undefeated.

Frank Robinson comes down hard on the combatants in the April 22 Tigers-White Sox game. At the top of his list are a 15-game suspension to Detroit coach Juan Samuel and eight-game suspensions to Tigers' manager Phil Garner and White Sox manager Jerry Manuel. Seven White Sox and nine Tigers get a total of 82 days in suspensions and nine others are fined.

APRIL 29:

After six straight losses at their new Pacific Bell Park, the Giants top the Expos, 2-1, and Barry Bonds hits ninth homer. The White Sox register their 10th win in 11 games with a 2-1 victory over the Tigers in Detroit. Cal Eldred is the winner.

APRIL 30:

Ace Pedro Martinez makes it 5-0 with a 2-1 victory over the Indians in Cleveland. Martinez limits Cleveland to five hits, while fanning 10, but is ejected in the eighth after plunking Roberto Alomar.

In Chicago, Randy Johnson whiffs 11 and holds the Cubs to five hits and no runs in seven innings. The Diamondbacks win, 6-0, and Johnson gets his sixth win against no defeats.

Thanks to a two-run clout by Mark McGwire and a solo shot by teammate Jim Edmonds, the Cardinals increase their record April total to 55 – tying a 1947 NL record set by the New York Giants for homers in any month. St. Louis defeats the host Phillies, 4-3.

The Angels' Darin Erstad collects two hits, raising his total for the month to 48, breaking a major league record for April set two years ago by the Rockies' Dante Bichette. Erstad is hitting .449. The Angels

HISTORY

The U.S. Olympic baseball team will have a high-profile, high-powered, and high-energy manager – Hall of Famer Tommy Lasorda, who managed the Dodgers for 20 years, leading the team to two World Series championships, four NL pennants, and eight division titles.

Said Phillies catcher Darren Daulton in 1994 of Barry Bonds: "He's the best player in the game, and it's not even close."

HISTORY

Missing from this year's All-Star Game because of injuries is a galaxy of stars bright enough for an All-Star team of their own – Cal Ripken Jr. (whose streak of 16 consecutive All-Star Game starts ends), Alex Rodriguez, Mark McGwire, Ken Griffey Jr., Barry Bonds, Manny Ramirez, Mike Piazza, Greg Maddux, and Pedro Martinez. The Nielsen ratings for NBC's telecast of the game are the lowest since 1967.

beat the Devil Rays, 5-2, in Anaheim.

MAY 1:

Barry Bonds launches a drive out of Pacific Bell Park and into the waters of Willie McCovey Cove of San Francisco Bay. It is the first homer to land in the water beyond the right-field fence of the new stadium. Bonds' clout, his 11th of the season, comes off Rich Rodriguez of the Mets in the sixth with two men on in a 10-3 Giants' victory. Shawn Estes gets the victory.

MAY 2:

The Braves beat the Dodgers, 5-3, in Los Angeles for their 15th consecutive victory. The 1991 Twins were the last team to win 15 straight games.

Kerry Wood, pitching for the first time since reconstructive elbow surgery last year, beats the Astros, 11-1, in Chicago. He goes six innings, yielding three hits and also homers.

MAY 3:

The Rockies pound out 24 hits – a team record – but no home runs en route to a 16-7 win over the Astros in Colorado.

Jose Valentin, Frank Thomas, and Paul Konerko homer back-to-back-to-back in the sixth as the White Sox topple the Blue Jays, 7-3, in Chicago. James Baldwin improves to 5-0.

Major League Baseball suspends Red Sox pitcher Pedro Martinez for five games for hitting the Indians' Roberto Alomar with a pitch on April 30.

The Dodgers beat the Braves and Greg Maddux, 6-4, in Los Angeles, ending Atlanta's winning streak at 15 games.

MAY 4:

Jim Edmonds and Mark McGwire homer back-to-back on two pitches from loser Francisco Cordova and the Cardinals beat the Pirates, 5-0, in St. Louis. McGwire and Edmonds each have 10 homers.

The Giants down the Mets, 7-2, in San Francisco, completing a four-game sweep. Jeff Kent homers for the Giants and Mike Piazza for the Mets.

MAY 5:

In their first NL face-off, Mark McGwire hits his 11th homer, but Ken Griffey Jr. wins the game, 3-2, with his eighth long ball in Cincinnati.

Sammy Sosa hits his 10th homer, but the Pirates beat the Cubs, 4-2. Randy Johnson pitches a five-hitter, fanning 11, and the Diamondbacks beat the Padres, 5-3, in Arizona. Johnson improves to 7-0.

MAY 6:

In New York, Roger Clemens defeats the Orioles, 3-1, for his 250th career win. It also is the Yankees' sixth consecutive victory. Clemens pitches seven innings, yielding four hits.

At Fenway Park, Pedro Martinez fans 17 Devil Rays, allows six hits and a run – and loses. Today, Steve Trachsel is just a little bit better, yielding three hits in nine innings, and Tampa Bay wins, 1-0, on Greg Vaughn's RBI single in the eighth. Martinez' winning streak ends at 13 games; his season record is 5-1.

Curt Schilling allows 11 hits, but pitches a complete-game shutout, beating the Braves, 6-0, for his 100th career victory.

MAY 7:

The Minnesota Twins defeat the visiting Detroit Tigers, 4-0, for manager Tom Kelly's 1,000th career win. Kelly has been at the helm of the Twins since September 1986. He also has 1,092 losses and two World Series Championships.

Kerry Wood rolls seven, but they aren't lucky. In his second start, he is bombed by the Pirates in Chicago. He yields seven hits, seven runs, and seven earned runs; the Pirates win, 11-3.

MAY 8:

Mark McGwire hits his 534th career homer and is now tied with Jimmie Foxx for ninth place on the all-time list. It also is Big Mac's 12th of the season, but it isn't enough as the Giants ground the Cardinals, 6-4, in San Francisco. Bobby Estallela hits two homers for the winners.

Sammy Sosa connects for his 12th and the Cubs defeat the Brewers, 12-11, in 10 innings at Wrigley Field.

MAY 9:

David Wells defeats the Orioles, 6-4, in Toronto for his fifth in a row and his sixth of the season. Carlos Delgado hits his 12th homer, Raul Mondesi connects twice, and Darrin Fletcher also reaches the seats.

MAY 1
Barry Bonds is the first to homer at Pacific Bell Park into Willie McCovey Cove, past right field.

James Baldwin of the White Sox three-hits the host Red Sox, 6-0, for his sixth win against no defeats.

MAY 10:

Splish, splash. Barry Bonds sends two more balls into McCovey Cove – his 13th and 14th homers of the year – and the Giants down the visiting Cardinals, 4-3.

Sammy Sosa connects for number 13 and the Cubs nip the Brewers, 9-8, in Chicago today.

MAY 11:

The Brewers beat the Cubs, 14-8, in the longest nine-inning game in history – four hours 22 minutes. The teams eclipse the mark set by the Orioles and Yankees in 1997. The Brewers use four pitchers, with starter Steve Woodward getting the win. Brian Williams, the third of six Chicago pitchers, gets the loss. Reliever David Weathers brings the game to an end by fanning Sammy Sosa with the bases loaded – the game's 434th pitch. Cubs' catcher Joe Girardi may have a legitimate claim for overtime pay. He also played in the 1997 Yankees-Orioles game.

Not to be outdone by the Oakland Athletics' Giambi brothers, the Boones flex their sibling muscles in Cincinnati. Aaron Boone hits a two-run homer in the bottom of the ninth to give the Reds an 11-9 win over the Padres. Earlier, his brother Bret connects for two – including an inside-the-park homer.

Joe Strong, 37 years old, makes his major league debut for the Marlins, pitching an inning and a third of scoreless relief in a 5-4 win over the Braves. Recalled from the Calgary Cannons in the AAA Pacific Coast League, Strong is the oldest rookie in the majors since 41-year-old Diomedes Olivo of the Pirates in 1960. Another rookie, 23-year-old Jason Grilli gets the victory; he also drives in the winning run. In the fifth, Mike Lowell of the Marlins hits into a triple play.

MAY 12:

Pedro Martinez hurls a two-hitter, fanning 15 and beating the Orioles in Baltimore, 9-0. Martinez now improves to 6-1 with an ERA of 1.01.

Outfielder Jim Edmonds (.394, 11 homers, 28 RBI) signs a six-year contract extension with the Cardinals worth $57 million in total. Edmonds will be donating $1 million to a local charity.

The Devil Rays send outfielder Dave Martinez (.260, one homer, 12 RBI) to the Cubs for relief pitcher Mark Guthrie (2-3, 4.82 ERA).

MAY 13:

Barry Bonds hits his 15th homer, but then leaves the game with a lower-back injury. Adding insult to Bonds' injury, the Rockies beat the Giants, 10-9, in Colorado.

Ken Griffey Jr. hits his 11th and 12th homers. The second – with a runner on in the ninth inning – gives the Reds an 8-7 win over the Astros in Houston

MAY 14:

M.M. ties M.M. Mark McGwire connects twice off Carlos Perez of the visiting Dodgers to pass Jimmie Foxx and tie Mickey Mantle with 536 career homers. He now has 14 for the season. The Cardinals collect 17 hits and defeat the Dodgers, 12-10.

Despite two homers and seven RBI from Henry Rodriguez and five hits and five RBI from Sammy Sosa, the Cubs manage to lose to the Expos, 16-15, in Montreal. In the first inning Montreal executes a triple play on a Rodriguez grounder, but starter Hideki Irabu fails to survive the third.

Jason Giambi homers and drives in three runs to lead the Athletics past the visiting Mariners, 7-2. Giambi leads the majors in homers with 16 and RBI with 46.

MAY 16:

According to an Associated Press story, Roberto Alomar and umpire John Hirschbeck – the principals in the 1996 spitting incident – have become friends. Alomar, his brother Sandy, and Hirschbeck are working together to raise money for research into a rare brain disease that has afflicted two of the umpire's sons, killing one.

Despite allowing only five hits and two runs in eight innings of work and striking out 12 Montreal hitters, Diamondbacks' pitcher Randy Johnson gets no run support and loses to the Expos, 2-0, today at Olympic Stadium; it is the Big Unit's first loss of the season.

LEAGUE

Brett Gray, pitching for the London (Ontario) Werewolves in the independent Frontier League, fans 25 in beating the Chillicothe Paints, 9-1. The minor league strikeout record – 27 – was set by Ron Neccai in 1952.

MAY 21
The Mariners' Rickey Henderson extends his leadoff-homers record with numbers 77 and 78.

TRIVIA

A copy of the 1909 American Tobacco Company T206 Honus Wagner baseball card reportedly sells for $1.1 million through the Internet auction service eBay. Two days later, a baseball autographed by the entire 1919 Black Sox team goes for more than $90,000 on eBay. The ball includes the rare signature of Shoeless Joe Jackson.

MAY 17:

Pedro Martinez shuts out the Blue Jays for seven innings on three hits; the Red Sox bang out 15 hits and win, 8-0, in Toronto. Martinez improves to 7-1.

Bernie Williams hits switch homers – including a grand slam – and drives in five runs, and the Yankees end a five-game losing streak with a 9-4 win over the White Sox in New York. Roger Clemens gets the win.

Four days after being released by the Mets, 41-year-old Rickey Henderson (.219, 5 steals, no homers, 6 RBI) is signed by the Seattle Mariners. In 1986, former Yankees' shortstop and then-broadcaster Tony Kubek said to *The Sporting News*: "(Henderson's) the best leadoff hitter of all time, no question. There has never been a leadoff hitter who matched his combination of on-base percentage, base-stealing ability, and power."

MAY 18:

Mark McGwire is now in sole possession of eighth place on the all-time homer list, passing Mickey Mantle with his 537th, 538th, and 539th homers tonight. McGwire also drives in all seven Cardinals' runs – a personal high – in a 7-2 win over the Phillies.

The Rangers beat the Orioles, 8-7, in Baltimore and John Wetteland gets his 304th save, tying him for 9th all-time.

MAY 19:

Bad back or no bad back, Barry Bonds belts one out. He also drives in three for the Giants today, but the Brewers win, 11-10, in Milwaukee.

MAY 20:

It's a very unhappy birthday – number 37 – for David Wells. The White Sox blow by the Blue Jays and Wells, 6-2, in Toronto. James Baldwin goes the distance for his seventh win without a defeat. The Blue Jays runs result from solo homers by Carlos Delgado-his 13th-and Shannon Stewart.

Rickey Henderson, homerless with the Mets, connects in his first at-bat for the Mariners – his ML record 76th leadoff homer. The Devil Rays win, 4-3, in Seattle.

Mike Matheny, Thomas Howard, and Fernando Vina homer for the Cardinals – the team's season total is now 88. St. Louis beats Pittsburgh, 19-4.

MAY 21:

Mark McGwire hits a two-run homer – it's his 540th career roundtripper – and the Cardinals go on to beat the Pirates, 7-5, in Pittsburgh. It is Big Mac's 18th long ball of the season.

Derek Bell's ninth-inning single off losing pitcher Byung-Hyun Kim scores Joe McEwing, giving the Mets a 7-6 win over the visiting Arizona Diamondbacks. Randy Johnson fans 13 but is not involved in the game's decision. McEwing, Mike Piazza, Robin Ventura, and Edgardo Alfonzo hit home runs for the Mets.

The Giants ride an 11-run 6th inning to a 16-10 win over the Brewers today in Milwaukee. J. T. Snow hits a grand slam for the winners.

It's two leadoff homers in 2 days for Rickey Henderson as his Mariners double up the Devil Rays, 8-4, in Seattle.

MAY 23:

Mark McGwire hits a home run off Ryan Dempster for number 19, Ray Lankford follows with his 8th, and the Cardinals top the Marlins, 10-3, in St. Louis. Jim Edmonds also connects and Darryl Kile wins his 7th

The Blue Jays edge the Red Sox, 3-2, in Boston. For pitcher Pedro Martinez, it's a bad day. He hurls 8 innings, yielding 7 hits – including a homer to Tony Batista – while fanning 7. His ERA goes from 0.90 to 1.19.

Mike Piazza slams a 10th-inning pinch-hit homer off Trevor Hoffman with a runner on, and the Mets beat the host Padres, 5-3. It is Piazza's 13th round-tripper.

Barry Bonds swats his 17th homer, but the Expos beat the Giants, 3-2, in San Francisco.

MAY 24:

Frank Robinson brings down his gavel and 19 Dodgers' players and coaches are suspended for their role in the May 17 brawl with fans at Wrigley Field. All of the combatants also are fined.
For the second consecutive game Mark McGwire and Ray Lankford hit consecutive homers; the Cardinals top the Marlins in St. Louis, 5-1. McGwire's round-tripper is his 20th of

MAY 29
Randy Velarde of the Athletics becomes the 10th player to execute an unassisted triple play.

the season; no player has ever reached that level as quickly. Garrett Stephenson improves to 7-0. Cardinal players now have hit back-to-back homers 14 times.

Andres Galarraga continues his bid for Comeback of the Year with six RBI, as the Braves beat the Brewers, 11-2, on 17 hits in Milwaukee. Galarraga is at .349.

The Giants bang out 18 hits – including Barry Bonds' 18th homer – and defeat the Expos, 18-0, in San Francisco.

MAY 25:

Sammy Sosa hits 2 homers –his 14th and 15th – and the Cubs beat the host Rockies, 6-5. The round-trippers are Sosa's 350th and 351st of his career. He had been homerless for 45 at-bats over 11 games.

David Wells beats the Red Sox in Boston, 11-6, for his 8th win. Carlos Delgado homers – his 15th – for the winners.

Jim Edmonds hits his 15th homer and the Cardinals complete a 3-game sweep of the Marlins today in St. Louis.

Rafael Palmeiro hits his 373rd career homer, tying him with Rocky Colavito for 45th place. His two-run single in the seventh inning gives the Rangers a 5-3 win over the Royals in Kansas City. Ivan "Pudge" Rodriguez has 3 hits on the day to take over the AL batting lead, with a .381 average.

MAY 26:

Jim Edmonds hits his 16th homer of the year, but the Mets and Mike Hampton defeat the Cardinals, 5-2, in St. Louis.

Rickey Henderson hits his third leadoff homer of the season and the Mariners maul the Devil Rays, 11-4, in Tampa Bay.

MAY 28:

Pedro Martinez and Roger Clemens lock horns in a classic pitchers' battle at Yankee Stadium. Martinez prevails when Christopher "Trot" Nixon of the Red Sox hits a two-run homer in the top of the ninth. Martinez allows four hits and a walk, fanning nine. Clemens yields five hits and no walks and strikes out 13.

The Blue Jays beat the Tigers, 12-7, today in Detroit. Toronto's Carlos Delgado hits his 16th and 17th homers of the year. Sammy Sosa hits his 16th home run of the season, Kerry Wood allows three hits and a run in seven strong innings, and the Chicago Cubs beat the host Giants, 4-1.

MAY 29:

Randy Velarde of the Athletics becomes the 10th player to execute an unassisted triple play. Playing 2nd base, he snares a line drive off the bat of Shane Spencer in the sixth, tags Jorge Posada running from first, and steps on second before Tino Martinez makes it back to the bag. The last unassisted triple play was completed by John Valentin of the Red Sox in 1994. The Yankees and Andy Pettitte beat the Athletics, 4-1. Oakland's lone run comes on a Velarde homer in the ninth.

Andres Galarraga's homer – his 13th of the season – with two out in the seventh ends Jon Lieber's no-hit bid and sinks the Cubs, 1-0, at Wrigley Field. Greg Maddux pitches a six-hitter.

Garrett Stephenson pitches a six-hitter and the Cardinals top the host Arizona Diamondbacks, 3-0. Stephenson improves to 8-0. Arizona's Tony Womack extends his hitting streak to 24 games.

Mets' shortstop Rey Ordóñez breaks his left arm applying a backhand tag to F. P. Santangelo on a pick-off attempt at second base. The Dodgers defeat the Mets and Al Leiter, 4-1, in Los Angeles. Ordóñez is lost for the season.

MAY 31:

Randy Johnson fans 10 Cardinals and moves past Cy Young into 15th place on the all-time-leader list with 2,820 Ks. Johnson gets help from a triple play and beats the Cardinals in Phoenix, 6-2. Mark McGwire, whose fourth-inning shallow fly turns the triple play, hits his 21st in the eighth.

David Wells beats the Twins, 4-2, in Toronto for his 150th career victory and ninth of the season. Carlos Delgado hits his 18th homer.

JUNE 1:

Tomokazu Ohka, a 24-year-old pitcher from Japan, pitches a perfect game for the Pawtucket Red Sox in the International League, beating the Charlotte Knights, 2-0, in Rhode Island. He is the third pitcher in the 117-year

HISTORY

A total of 935 homers – an all-time record – are hit in the majors in the month of April.

JUNE 5
The Blue Jays' David Wells's 9-3 win over Atlanta makes him the year's first AL 10-game winner.

history of the IL to accomplish the feat.

JUNE 2:

Former major league infielder, coach, and scout Ellis Clary dies at 85 in Valdosta, Georgia. In four seasons playing with the Washington Senators and St. Louis Browns, he batted .263 with only one homer. He was a member of the 1944 Browns AL pennant-winners.

JUNE 3:

On paper it looked like a classic pitching matchup: two of the most successful pitchers of their era, the Yankees' Roger Clemens and the Braves' Greg Maddux, facing off in Atlanta. Clemens lasts five innings, giving up six hits and four runs. Maddux survives five and two-thirds, yielding 13 hits and seven runs. The Braves beat the Yankees, 11-7, but neither starter is involved in the game's decision.

The Reds roll over the Twins, 9-3, in Cincinnati. Denny Neagle improves to 5-0.

JUNE 4:

Rookie Rick Ankiel fans 11, two Cardinals relievers strike out five more, and Jim Edmonds hits his 17th home run, but the Indians beat the Cardinals, 3-2, in St. Louis. Kenny Lofton and Richie Sexson homer for Cleveland.

Barry Bonds hits his 23rd, Jeff Kent connects twice, and the Giants grind the Athletics, 18-2, on 19 hits in Oakland.

JUNE 5:

Rocker is off to Richmond. The Braves demote the stormy left-hander, assigning him to their International League team. They also smack him with a $5,000 fine. Braves' officials claim the demotion is based on his performance – he has issued 25 bases on balls and yielded 18 hits in just 18 2/3 innings. Brian Jordan calls Rocker "a cancer" on the team.

David Wells and the Blue Jays beat the host Braves, 9-3, making him the AL's first 10-game winner.

Carl Everett's ninth-inning homer downs the Marlins, 3-2, in Florida, ending the Red Sox' five-game losing streak.

Former pitcher Don Liddle dies at 75 in Mount Carmel, Illinois. Liddle had a supporting role in one of baseball's

TRIVIA

On October 1, Shane Halter of the Tigers becomes the fourth player in history – and the second this season – to play all nine positions in a game. The feat was accomplished by Bert Campaneris in 1965, Cesar Tovar in 1968, and Scott Sheldon this season.

OH? IN A JUNE 25 OP-ED PIECE IN THE *NEW YORK TIMES*, HARVARD PROFESSOR OF ZOOLOGY STEPHEN JAY GOULD WRITES ABOUT CHUCK KNOBLAUCH'S THROWING: "KNOBLAUCH'S PROBLEM TAKES THE SAME FORM AS MANY EXCRUCIATING IMPEDIMENTS IN PURELY MENTAL ENTERPRISES WITH WRITER'S BLOCK AS THE MOST OBVIOUS EXAMPLE, WHEN OBSESSION WITH LEARNED RULES OF STYLE AND GRAMMAR IMPEDES THE FLOW OF GOOD PROSE. AND WE SURELY CANNOT DESIGNATE OUR UNBLOCKED MODE AS LESS INTELLECTUAL MERELY BECAUSE WE CANNOT EASILY DESCRIBE ITS DELIGHTS OR PROCEDURES... AND SO, TO CHUCK KNOBLAUCH, A TRULY FINE BALLPLAYER, WE CAN ONLY SAY: THIS TOO WILL PASS."

JUNE 6
The Indians' David Justice hits his 15th homer of the season – and 250th of his career.

JUNE 9
In a Yankees-Mets tilt, Mike Piazza hits a grand slam off Roger Clemens as the Mets win, 12-2.

unforgettable moments. In game one of the 1954 World Series at the Polo Grounds, he delivered the pitch hit by the Indians' Vic Wertz some 450 feet into center-field where it was run down by Willie Mays, in what many regard as the greatest catch ever. Liddle pitched with the Milwaukee Braves, the New York Giants, and the Cardinals for four seasons, going 28-18 with a 3.75 ERA.

JUNE 6:

David Justice hits his 250th career homer, and 15th of the season, as the visiting Indians defeat the Brewers, 4-2.

JUNE 7:

The man who clouted 129 homers over the past two seasons and his manager are in a public dispute. Cubs' manager Don Baylor says that Sammy Sosa should be a more complete ballplayer. Sosa responds, telling Murray Chass of the *New York Times*: "You don't criticize a player who comes here every day and plays hard." He then tells other reporters that Baylor is not treating him "the way I'm supposed to be treated" and he adds that the manager "has got no class."

Despite the dispute, Sosa homers – his 18th – and the Cubs down the visiting Diamondbacks, 9-4. The Cubs' feud triggers a frenzy of trade rumors with Sosa reportedly going to the Yankees, Mets, or Red Sox. Rumors also swirl around the Tigers' unhappy slugger, Juan Gonzalez. Reportedly, the Yankees are in serious discussions on both players.

Carlos Delgado drives in six runs with a grand slam and a two-run homer as the visiting Blue Jays bounce the Braves, 12-8.

JUNE 8:

Pedro Martinez one-hits the Indians for eight innings, walking one and fanning 10, and the Red Sox win, 3-0, in Boston. Carl Everett connects for his 21st homer.

JUNE 9:

Mike Piazza hits a grand slam off Roger Clemens and the visiting Mets trample the Yankees, 12-2. Al Leiter gets his seventh win against one loss. Clemens has allowed two slams in his career, spanning 3,542 innings.

For the second time in two days, David Justice hits a pair of homers. Teammate Richie Sexson also connects twice and the Indians beat the Reds, 7-4, handing Denny Neagle his first loss of the year.

Randy Johnson wins his 10th game, limiting the Angels to three hits and a run in six innings of a 4-1 victory. The Diamondbacks send infielder Andy Fox (.209, one homer, 10 RBI) to the Marlins for outfielder Danny Bautista (.191, four homers, 12 RBI).

JUNE 10:

The Yankees strike back. Jorge Posada hits a three-run, upper-deck homer, teammates Derek Jeter and Paul O'Neill also connect, and the Mets fall, 13-5.

In a battle of homers – Ken Griffey Jr. and Michael Tucker for the Reds; Travis Fryman (two), Kenny Lofton, and Russell Branyan for the Indians – Cleveland prevails, winning, 6-5, at Jacobs Field.

JUNE 11:

Mark McGwire hits number 22 and the Cardinals beat the Tigers, 7-3, in Detroit. It is Big Mac's first homer since May 24 and his first in the new Comerica Park. He now has homered in a record 37 stadia.

JUNE 14:

The encore falls flat. The anticipated rematch between Roger Clemens and Pedro Martinez ends with a 2-1 Yankees victory, but neither starter is involved in the decision. Clemens leaves after one scoreless inning with a strained groin and Martinez departs after six innings and 101 pitches, trailing 1-0. The Red Sox tie the game in the seventh inning on Nomar Garciaparra's homer and the Yankees win it on Tino Martinez's homer off loser Tim Wakefield in the bottom of the frame.

John Rocker is back, but his control isn't. After being recalled because of injuries to the Braves' bullpen, Rocker walks John Vander Wal on four pitches and goes 2-0 to the next batter before leaving. But the Braves beat the host Pirates, 8-4, and Greg Maddux gets his ninth win of the year.

JUNE 15:

Chuck Knoblauch, plagued by a mysterious inability to throw accurately, commits three throwing errors against the White

TRIVIA

On September 6, The Rangers' Scott Sheldon becomes the third player ever to play all nine positions in a game;

JUNE 19
The Yankees pummel the Red Sox, 22-1 – the most lopsided game in the history of their rivalry.

Sox, takes himself out of the ball game, and actually leaves Yankee Stadium. Chicago goes on to trounce the Yankees, 12-3.

JUNE 16:

Chuck Knoblauch returns to the lineup and has no chances at second. The Yankees lose to the White Sox, 3-1, despite David Cone's four-hit pitching over six innings. James Baldwin records his 10th win.

Benny Agbayani leads off today's game with a homer, following a pair of long balls in his last two at-bats last night. He is "limited" to a two-run single in his next turn. The Mets beat the Brewers, 7-1, in Milwaukee, for Al Leiter's eighth win.

In Chicago, as trade rumors continue, Sammy Sosa celebrates the 11th anniversary of his major league debut by recording his 1,002nd career RBI and hitting a bases-loaded triple. The Cubs edge the Expos, 9-8. Vladimir Guerrero hits his 20th.

JUNE 17:

Today the White Sox overcome Bernie Williams' four hits – including his 13th homer – and seven RBI to top the host Yankees in New York, 10-9. Also, Chuck Knoblauch's woes continue as he misfires again and the ball lands in the seats behind third base.

It's number 24 for Mark McGwire and a 4-3 Cardinals' victory over the Dodgers in Los Angeles. Gary Sheffield hits his 20th homer for the losers.

Albert Belle connects off Tim Belcher, giving him homers in four straight games, 10 in his last 14 contests, and 16 for the

The Mets and Cubs open the season in Japan.

JUNE 23
Mark McGwire's 549th career homer puts him in seventh place on the all-time list.

season. But the Angels defeat the host Orioles, 8-3.

Juan Gonzalez, still in a Tigers' uniform, hits a two-run homer in the bottom of the ninth to send the Indians to their sixth straight defeat.

JUNE 18:

The White Sox build on a nine-run first inning to pummel the Yankees, 17-4, and complete a three-game sweep in New York. Jose Valentin hits a grand slam.

Mark McGwire hits his 25th homer, but the Dodgers defeat the Cardinals, 6-3, in Los Angeles.

In San Diego, despite Junior Griffey's 20th four-bagger, the Reds fall to the Padres, 8-7.

And in Chicago, the third of the NL Central sluggers, Sammy Sosa, hits his 20th homer, and his team also loses, 4-3, to the Expos in 11.

JUNE 19:

At Fenway Park, the Yankees bounce back from three losses to the White Sox to humiliate the Red Sox, 22-1, on 19 hits. It is the most one-sided victory in the history of the New York-Boston rivalry.

Five Yankees – Scott Brosius, Felix Jose, Shane Spencer, Derek Jeter, and Jorge Posada – homer.

The White Sox continue their winning ways, downing the Indians, 6-1, in Chicago, for their eighth straight win.

JUNE 20:

The Yankees and Andy Pettitte defeat the seemingly indomitable Pedro Martinez, 3-0, at Fenway Park on bases-empty homers by Paul O'Neill, Bernie Williams, and Derek Jeter.

The Tigers trounce the Blue Jays, 18-6, on 18 hits – including eight homers – in Toronto. Connecting for Detroit and setting a team record are Tony Clark (twice), Juan Gonzalez, Juan Encarnacion, Bobby Higginson, Robert Fick, Rich Becker, and Deivi Cruz.

JUNE 21:

The Cubs' Kerry Wood takes large step on the comeback trail, pitching seven strong innings and beating the Braves, 8-1, in Atlanta. John Rocker pitches one-third of an inning, yielding one hit and five runs, and walking four. His ERA balloons to 5.85.

JUNE 22:

Mark McGwire hits his 548th career homer – a 475-foot drive to centerfield – tying Mike Schmidt for seventh place on the all-time list. Big Mac reaches the landmark in 5,832 at-bats; Schmidt took 8,352. The Cardinals prevail by a score of 11-10.

David Wells beats the Tigers, 7-4, in Toronto; he is the majors' first 12-game winner. Tony Batista hits his 17th and 18th homers of the season for the Blue Jays.

JUNE 23:

Mark McGwire hits number 549 – off Matt Herges – passing Mike Schmidt, and the Cardinals beat the Dodgers, 9-6, in St. Louis. It also is his 27th of the season, tying him with Barry Bonds. For the fourth consecutive game, Gary Sheffield homers for Los Angeles, giving him 25.

Andres Galarraga hits his 18th homer, Jason Marquis wins his first major league game, and John Rocker strikes out the side in the ninth for a save in a 3-2 Braves' win over the visiting Brewers.

Former catcher Bob Tillman dies at 63 in Gallatin, Tennessee. Tillman played with the Red Sox, Yankees, and Braves for nine seasons, batting .232 with 79 homers.

JUNE 24:

Mark McGwire connects off losing pitcher Orel Hershiser for his 28th homer in a 6-1 victory over the visiting Dodgers. Big Mac now has six round-trippers in his last seven games, 103 in 214 games at Busch Stadium, and 550 for his career.

Carlos Delgado hits his 26th – tops in the AL – for Toronto and the Blue Jays beat the visiting Red Sox, 6-4.

JUNE 25:

The Blue Jays beat the Red Sox, 6-5, and handle Pedro Martinez, collecting six hits and five runs in six and two-thirds innings for their fifth straight victory. Toronto wins, 6-5, but Martinez, who fans 10, is not involved in the decision. Carlos Delgado hits a two-run homer, the first off Martinez with a runner on since back in September 1998.

The Giants complete a three-game sweep, downing the Astros, 4-2, in Houston. Winner Russ Ortiz fans 12.

The Braves top the Brewers, 5-4, in

CULTURE

***Havana Heat*, by Darryl Brock, is a novel based on the life of Luther Taylor, who pitched for the New York Giants from 1900 to 1908. In *Castro's Curveball*, by Tim Wendel, set in 1947 Cuba, a former major league catcher tries to convince Fidel Castro to pursue a pitching career with the Washington Senators. *Be the One*, by April Smith, is a thriller about a female scout for a major league team.**

Bill Madden of the *New York Daily News* reports that when Sammy Sosa is informed he had passed Joe DiMaggio on the all-time-homer list, he replies: "Wasn't he the guy whose girlfriend was Marilyn Monroe?"

Atlanta. John Rocker, in relief of starter Kevin Millwood, gets his first victory of the season.

JUNE 26:

Juan Gonzalez will not be wearing pinstripes. The Yankees' deal for the Tigers' slugger falls through.

Ken Griffey Jr. connects for his 23rd and extends his hitting streak to 10 games as the Reds edge the Cardinals, 3-2, in Cincinnati.

JUNE 27:

Ken Griffey Jr. hits two more homers – his 24th and 25th,but Edgar Renteria and Jim Edmonds go long for the Cardinals and St. Louis wins, 4-3, in Cincinnati. Darryl Kile gets his 11th win.

The Devil Rays defeat the Blue Jays, 11-1, and in the process end Toronto's 23-game homer streak.

The bite has gone out of the Bulldog. Tough pitcher Orel Hershiser is waived by the Dodgers after the worst inning of his 18-year career – yielding eight runs to the Padres in a 9-5 loss. The 41-year-old one-time Cy Young Award winner and World Series MVP departs with an ERA of 13.14. Hershiser subsequently retires and goes to work for the Dodgers in what the team describes as "several capacities on and off the field."

JUNE 28:

The Mets beat the visiting Marlins, 6-5, for their seventh straight win. They trail the Braves – their next opponent – by two games.

David Wells rolls on. The left-hander – with help from a Jose Cruz Jr. homer – tops the Devil Rays, 5-2, running his record to 13-2 on a five-hitter.

JUNE 29:

The Yankees make a trade, but it is not the long-discussed deals for Sammy Sosa or Juan Gonzalez. Instead New York acquires outfielder David Justice (.265, 21 homers, 58 RBI) from Cleveland for outfielder Ricky Ledee (.241, seven homers, 31 RBI) and two minor league players to be named later. With the acquisition of Justice, who earns $7 million a year, the Yankee payroll grows to more than $102 million, surpassing its own all-time record.

In New York, before a crowd of 46,998, including an army of police and a host of reporters, the Braves beat the Mets, 6-4. John Rocker comes out of the bullpen – fenced off for security reasons – and pitches a perfect inning, helping to preserve John Burkett's 6-4 win. Andres Galarraga homers – his 19th – off loser Rick Reed. Rocker travels from his Manhattan hotel to Shea Stadium in an unmarked police van.

Sammy Sosa hits his 21st in a 5-4 Chicago loss at Pittsburgh.

Randy Johnson fans 13 and allows five hits and a run in a 7-1 victory over the Astros in Arizona. Johnson's record is now 12-2 with a 1.57 ERA.

Baseball's "enforcer" Frank Robinson gets overruled. Paul Beeston, baseball's chief operating officer, overturns 12 of the 19 suspensions handed down by Robinson after the May 17 brawl between the Dodgers and Cubs' fans.

JUNE 30:

The commotion at Shea Stadium is generated by the Mets' bats in one of the most dramatic comebacks in the team's history. Trailing by 8-1 in the eighth, New York explodes for 10 runs – nine with two out – and goes on to an 11-8 victory. The big blow is Mike Piazza's three-run homer off losing pitcher Terry Mulholland. The Mets' incredible rally is aided by three bases-loaded walks.

Mark McGwire homers off the Astros' Chris Holt. It is his 29th of the year and his 104th at Busch Stadium, breaking teammate Ray Lankford's record. It also is the 551st of his career. The Cardinals go on to win, 5-4.

Frank Thomas hits his 21st and 22nd homers and the White Sox down the Red Sox, 10-4, at Comiskey Park.

The Red Sox acquire third baseman Ed Sprague (.274, 10 homers, 25 RBI) from the Padres for two minor leaguers – infielder Cesar Saba and pitcher Dennis Tankersley.

JULY 1:

In New York, the Mets hammer the Braves, 9-1. Al Leiter fans 12 and bests Greg Maddux for his 100th career win. Mike Piazza, Derek Bell, and Benny Agbayani homer for the winners, who move within a game of first-place Atlanta.

JULY 6
The Cardinals' rookie catcher Keith McDonald becomes the second player ever to homer in his first two at-bats.

JULY 8
The Yankees sweep the Mets in a doubleheader played in two separate ballparks.

The Cardinals' Mark McGwire hits his 30th homer and St. Louis nips the Astros, 10-9, in St. Louis. It marks the 11th time McGwire has hit 30 or more homers in a single season.

JULY 2:

The Braves respond to the pressure, pounding the Mets, 10-2, behind Tom Glavine and earning a split in the four-game series. The Braves leave town the way they came in-two games ahead.

Woody Williams, making his first appearance since surgery for an aneurysm, pitches eight, yielding only one earned run, but his Padres bow to the visiting Rockies, 3-2, in 10. Williams is not involved in the decision.

JULY 3:

David Wells defeats the Orioles, 6-4, in Baltimore, for his 14th win. Carlos Delgado hits his 28th homer for the Blue Jays. The Twins sign pitcher Brad Radke (5-9, 3.95 ERA) to a four-year contract extension reportedly valued at $36 million.

JULY 4:

Jim Edmonds hits his 23rd and 24th homers and drives in four runs as the Cardinals crush the Reds, 14-3, in St Louis, increasing their first-place lead over Cincinnati to a full nine games.

The White Sox 12-game road winning streak ends with a 10-7 defeat at the hands of the Royals. It was the longest streak in the majors since the 1984 Tigers won 17 straight on the road.

Randy Johnson defeats the host Astros, 10-4, for his 13th win. Johnson hurls six innings, striking out eight and yielding four hits – including home runs to Moises Alou and Jeff Bagwell. Jose Lima is tagged with his 13th loss.

JULY 6:

Cardinals' rookie catcher Keith McDonald, who homered in his first major league at-bat yesterday, connects again today. He becomes the second player ever with round-trippers in his first two at-bats; Bob Nieman of the 1951 St. Louis Browns was the first. But the Cardinals lose, 12-6, to the visiting Reds.

Diamondbacks' rookie Geraldo Guzman makes his ML debut with a 2-1 win over the host Astros. Guzman, who left organized baseball in 1990, worked for seven years as a carpenter in the Dominican Republic before signing a minor league contract with Arizona in November, 1999.

JULY 7:

Andres Galarraga continues his miraculous comeback from cancer by clouting his 20th homer in a 5-3 Braves' victory over the Red Sox at Fenway Park.

The Yankees draw first blood with a 2-1 win over the Mets at Shea Stadium. Orlando Hernandez bests Al Leiter.

JULY 8:

In a rare twin bill played in separate ballparks, the Yankees sweep the Mets by 4-2 scores. In the opener, at Shea Stadium, the visiting Yankees win behind Doc Gooden – recalled from the minors. The teams then travel to Yankee Stadium, where starter Roger Clemens, with help from a three-run homer by Chuck Knoblauch, beats Glendon Rusch. The game turns ugly in the second, when Clemens beans Mets' star Mike Piazza, who suffers a concussion. David Wells will go to the All-Star Game as the majors' first and only 15-game winner. The left-hander tops the Expos, 6-3, in Montreal.

Sammy Sosa hits his 22nd homer and Jon Lieber gets his eighth win as the Cubs down the White Sox, 9-2, at Wrigley Field.

JULY 9:

The Mets – without Mike Piazza – salvage the final contest of the four-game series against the Yankees; Mike Hampton bests Andy Pettitte, 2-0, at Shea Stadium.

Nomar Garciaparra hits two homers in a 7-2 Red Sox win over the Braves and ups his average to .389.

Sammy Sosa says no trade. The Cubs' slugger tells Chicago's management he will remain with the team through the end of his current contract, which expires after the 2001 season.

JULY 11:

In the annual All-Star Game, the AL defeats the NL, 6-3, at Turner Field in Atlanta. Shortstop Derek Jeter, with three hits and two RBI, is the MVP; he is the first Yankee to be so honored since the institution

CULTURE

***Cobb*, by Lee Blessing, a 75-minute play that features three Ty Cobbs, representing different stages of his life, plus the ghosts of Babe Ruth and Negro Leagues' star and Hall of Famer Oscar Charleston.**

JULY 17
The Dodgers' slugger Gary Sheffield hits his major league-leading 32nd homer of the season.

of the Award in 1962. Baseball's big winners – David Wells and Randy Johnson – start for their respective teams, but neither figures in the decision. The victory goes to James Baldwin of the White Sox; Al Leiter of the Mets gets the loss. Chipper Jones elates the hometown fans by hitting a third-inning home run off Chicago's Baldwin.

JULY 12:

The Yankees acquire left-hander Denny Neagle (8-2, 3.52 ERA) from the Reds along with minor league outfielder Mike Frank. In return, the Yankees send the Reds four minor leaguers – third baseman Drew Henson and outfielder Jackson Melian plus pitchers Brian Reith and Ed Yarnell.

The Braves obtain pitcher Andy Ashby (4-7, 5.68 ERA) from the Phillies today in exchange for reliever Bruce Chen (4-0, 2.50 ERA) and minor leaguer Jim Osting.

The Colorado Rockies extend the contract of third baseman Jeff Cirillo (.331, nine home runs, 64 RBI). Reportedly, the terms of the deal call for Cirillo to earn $28.5 million through the 2005 season.

JULY 13:

In Boston, Pedro Martinez allows the Mets five hits and two runs in seven innings. The Red Sox win, 4-3; Rich Garces gets the victory.

Carlos Delgado hits his 29th homer and Tony Batista connects twice (number 25 and number 26), but the Blue Jays fall to the Phillies, 8-5, in Toronto. Curt Schilling gets his 100th career win.

JULY 14:

Mike Piazza, showing no ill effects of his beaning, cracks two homers at Fenway Park to lead the Mets past the Red Sox, 6-4.

The Cubs seem to have found a winning combination. Once again, Sammy Sosa homers (number 24), and Jon Lieber gets the victory in a 6-2 win over the Twins in Minnesota.

JULY 15:

In a game marred by an nasty scene between Carl Everett and home-plate umpire Ronald Kulpa, the Red Sox beat the Mets, 6-4, at Fenway Park. Everett is ejected in the second after Kulpa insists he is standing too close to the plate. The Boston slugger rages, bumps the umpire twice, and continues his rampage in the Red Sox' dugout. His replacement, Brian Daubach, wins the game with a three-run homer in the sixth inning off loser Mike Hampton. Ramon Martinez is credited with the win. Randy Johnson fans 12 in seven and a third innings, but is not involved in the decision as the visiting Rangers beat the Diamondbacks, 6-5, in 11 innings.

JULY 16:

Sammy Sosa's two homers lead the Cubs past the host Royals, 10-7. Sosa's round-trippers move him past Joe DiMaggio to 50th on the all-time list.

Carl Everett, still in the Red Sox' lineup while awaiting disciplinary action for his outburst yesterday, hits a two-run homer and makes an outstanding catch. The Red Sox beat the Expos, 5-2, at Fenway Park. Vladimir Guerrero hits his 25th homer of the season for the losers.

Rickey Henderson has three hits in a 6-3 Mariners' win over the Diamondbacks in Arizona. Henderson now has 2,875 career hits, passing Babe Ruth for 35th place.

The Rockies obtain outfielder Robert "Butch" Huskey (.223, five homers, 27 RBI) and second baseman Todd Walker (.234, two homers, eight RBI) from the Twins for minor league first baseman Todd Sears and cash. Both Huskey and Walker were playing in the minor leagues.

JULY 17:

Gary Sheffield hits his major league-leading 32nd home run of the year and the Dodgers top the Pirates, 9-6, in Los Angeles.

Nomar Garciaparra is three-for-three in a 7-3 Red Sox' win over the visiting Expos and raises his batting average to .400.

Less than two weeks ago Cardinals' rookie Keith McDonald homered in his first major league at-bat. Today St. Louis rookie Chris Richard tops his new teammate by homering on the first pitch he sees in the majors. Cardinals Fernando Tatis and Jim Edmonds also connect in an 8-3 victory over the Twins in Minnesota.

JULY 18:

Pedro Martinez fans 12, allows five hits and a run, and beats the Expos, 3-1, in

JULY 18
Denny Neagle, obtained by the Yankees July 12, five-hits the Phillies in a 3-1 New York win.

JULY 22
Omar Vizquel's 95-game errorless streak – the second longest in ML history – ends.

Boston today. It is Martinez's first win since June 8. Nomar Garciaparra has a double in three at-bats, dropping his average to .399.

Denny Neagle pays instant dividends for the Yankees, limiting the Phillies to five hits and a run in eight innings. With Mariano Rivera registering his 22nd save of the year, New York wins at home, 3-1.

JULY 19:

Barry Larkin homers as the Reds down the visiting Astros, 4-0, in Cincinnati. Prior to the game, the Reds indicate they will not re-sign Larkin, who has been with the team for 16 years, and will try to trade him.

The Tigers buy outfielder-first baseman Hal Morris (.222, two homers, six RBI) from the Reds.

The Blue Jays obtain pitcher Esteban Loaiza (5-6, 5.37 ERA) from the Rangers for two minor leaguers – pitcher Darwin Cubrillan and infielder Mike Young.

JULY 20:

Everett is suspended for 10 games and fined a reported $5,000. He subsequently issues an apology to the Boston fans and his teammates.
A two-run homer in the bottom of the ninth by Tony Womack gives the Diamondbacks a 3-2 win over the Cardinals and makes a 15-game winner of Randy Johnson. He hurls a complete game, fanning 11 and yielding six hits. Jeff Kent hits his 24th homer and ups his RBI total to an NL-best 88 as the Giants down the visiting Padres, 7-3.

In Baltimore, Nomar Garciaparra has three hits in the opener of a doubleheader, bringing his average to .403. But he goes hitless in five at-bats in the nightcap and dips to .396. The Red Sox win the opener, 11-7, but the Orioles take the nightcap, 9-4.

JULY 21:

The Orioles, despite two homers by Tony Batista – his 29th and 30th of the season – defeat the Blue Jays, 9-5. It is the first victory for Baltimore on Canadian soil after 20 straight defeats. The Orioles' last win in Canada was also against the Blue Jays – on June 13, 1998. Despite Barry Bonds's 32nd homer, the Dodgers beat the Giants, 6-5, in L.A.

The Yankees continue to trade prospects for established MLers, obtaining outfielder Glenallen Hill (.262, 11 homers, 28 RBI) from the Cubs for minor league pitchers Ben Ford and Ozwaldo Mairena

JULY 22:

After losing to the Braves, 6-3, yesterday in Atlanta, the Mets rebound with a 4-0 victory. Rick Reed earns the win; Greg Maddux gets the loss.

Edgar Martinez hits his 24th homer and runs his RBI total to 93 as his Mariners down the Rangers, 13-5, in Seattle.

After 95 games without an error – the second-longest streak in ML history – Indians' shortstop Omar Vizquel misplays a fifth-inning grounder off the bat of the Twins' Matt Lewton. Minnesota wins, 10-6.

JULY 23:

Catcher Carlton Fisk, second baseman John "Bid" McPhee, first baseman Tony Perez, Negro Leagues outfielder Norman "Turkey" Stearns and manager George "Sparky" Anderson are inducted into the Baseball Hall of Fame. Fisk had 351 career homers – the most by a catcher – and appeared behind the plate in more games than any other major leaguer: 2,226. He played 24 seasons with the Red Sox and White Sox, batting .269. McPhee, who died in 1943, is considered the best at his position in the 19th century. He earned his nickname – Biddy or Bid – because of his small stature. He played 18 seasons – 14 without a fielder's glove – for the Cincinnati Reds, first in the American Association and then the NL, batting .271 and leading the league in fielding eight times. Perez, the first baseman on Cincinnati's "Big Red Machine," batted .279 in 23 seasons with 379 homers and 1,652 RBI; he was a seven-time All-Star. Perez also played with the Expos. Stearnes, who died in 1979, reportedly led the Negro Leagues in homers six times. He played 18 years with the Detroit Stars, the New York Lincoln Giants, the Kansas City Monarchs, and the Chicago American Giants, batting .352 with 181 homers. Anderson played only one major league season, but ranks third in career victories as a manager with 2,194 over 26 years. He is the only manager to

JULY 24
The Rangers' 6-5 loss to the Angels is costly, as Texas loses Pudge Rodriguez for the season.

win World Series championships with both AL and NL teams – the Tigers and Reds. He compiled 17 winning seasons and an overall .545 winning percentage. Turkey Stearnes is the 17th Negro Leagues player inducted into the Hall of Fame. Reds' broadcaster Marty Brennaman is also honored.

After vetoing a trade that would have sent him to the Mets for three top prospects, Reds' veteran shortstop Barry Larkin signs a three-year, $27 million contract extension, keeping him in a Reds uniform through 2003.

Pedro Martinez goes the distance against the White Sox, allowing six hits and no walks while fanning 15. The Red Sox beat the White Sox, 1-0, in Boston, on a Jason Varitek single.

Denny Neagle wins his 100th career game and his second in a New York Yankees' uniform with a complete-game, four-hitter. The Yankees down the visiting Tampa Bay Devil Rays by a score of 5-1.

JULY 24:

The Angels beat the Rangers, 6-5, but Texas loses more than just a game. Catcher "Pudge" Rodriguez, last year's AL MVP, hits his throwing hand on Mo Vaughn's bat in the first inning. Pudge fractures the metacarpal bone and is lost for the season. Rodriguez was batting .347 with 27 home runs and 83 RBI.

JULY 25:

Jay Buhner connects twice to bring his career homer total to 300, but his Mariners lose to the Athletics, 8-7, in Seattle.

Fernando Tatis hits a grand slam, leading the Cardinals to a 7-3 victory over the Diamondbacks and tagging Randy Johnson with his third loss against 15 wins. Garrett Stephenson gets his 11th win.

Ken Griffey Jr. hits his 31st homer, but Jeff Bagwell connects for his 27th, and the Astros beat the Reds, 7-4, in Cincinnati.

JULY 26:

The Phillies trade ace pitcher Curt Schilling (6-6, 3.91 ERA) to the Diamondbacks for outfielder-first baseman Travis Lee (.232, eight homers, 40 RBI) plus pitchers Omar Daal (2-10, 7.22 ERA), Vicente Padilla (2-1, 2.31 ERA), and Nelson Figueroa (0-2, 7.47 ERA). Schilling, who twice has fanned 300 or more batters in a season, joins Randy Johnson, who has accomplished the feat three times.

David Wells becomes this season's first 16-game winner with a five-hit, 8-1, 11-strikeout win over the Indians in Toronto's SkyDome.

The Dodgers, who traded Ismael Valdes (2-4, 5.37 ERA), reacquire him from the Cubs for two minor leaguers – outfielder Jorge Piedra and pitcher Jamie Arnold.

JULY 27:

The Blue Jays defeat the Mariners in Seattle, 7-2; manager Jim Fregosi gets his 1,000th career win.

The Red Sox obtain second baseman Mike Lansing (.258, 11 homers, 43 RBI) plus pitchers Rolando Arrojo (5-9, 6.04 ERA) and Rick Croushore (2-0, 8.74 ERA) and cash from the Rockies for second baseman Jeff Frye (.289, one home run, 13 RBI) and three pitchers: Brian Rose (3-5, 6.11 ERA), John Wasdin (1-3, 5.04 ERA), and minor leaguer Jeff Taglienti.

JULY 28:

The Mets obtain shortstop Mike Bordick (.297, 16 homers, 59 RBI) from the Orioles for shortstop Melvin Mora (.260, six homers, 30 RBI), and three minor leaguers – infielder Mike Kinkade and pitchers Leslie Brea and Pat Gorman. The Mets continue to deal, picking up outfielder Thomas Bubba Trammel (.275, seven homers, 33 RBI) and reliever Rick White (3-6, 3.41 ERA, two saves) from the Devil Rays for two minor leaguers – outfielder Jason Tyner and pitcher Paul Wilson.

The Indians ship outfielder-first baseman Richie Sexson (.256, 14 homers, 44 RBI) and pitchers Paul Rigdon (1-1, 7.64 ERA) and Kane Davis (0-3, 14.73 ERA) plus a player to be named later to the Brewers for pitchers Bob Wickman (2-2, 2.03 ERA, 16 saves), Steve Woodward (1-7, 5.96 ERA), and Jason Bere (6-7, 4.93 ERA). In another deal, Cleveland obtains first baseman David Segui (.336, 11 homers, 57 RBI) from Texas for recently acquired outfielder Ricky Ledee (.236, nine homers, 39 RBI). In a third trade, the Indians get outfielder Wil

JULY 28
As the trading deadline nears, the Mets obtain shortstop Mike Bordick from the Orioles.

JULY 30
Tom Glavine joins Roger Clemens and Greg Maddux as the only active pitchers with 200 wins.

Cordero (.282, 16 homers, 51 RBI), whom they lost to free agency after last season. In return, Cleveland sends third baseman Enrique Wilson (.325, two homers, 12 RBI) and outfielder Alex Ramirez (.286, five homers, 12 RBI) to the Pirates.

The Athletics strengthen their bullpen with the acquisition of Jim Mecir (7-2, 3.08 ERA, one save), along with minor league pitcher Todd Belitz, from the Devil Rays for minor league hurler Jesus Colome and a player to be named later.

On the field, a trade pays quick dividends. Newly acquired Curt Schilling and the Diamondbacks defeat the Marlins, 4-1, in Florida, and Arizona moves into first place in the NL West.

Pedro Martinez fans 11 and allows five hits as the Red Sox down the Athletics, 4-1, in Oakland. Nomar Garciaparra has three hits, including a homer, in four at-bats to finish at .398.

Ken Griffey Jr. hits his 32nd homer – a grand slam – and extends his hitting streak to 19 games in an 8-3 Reds' win over the host Expos. Reds' rookie Elmer Dessens improves to 5-0. Griffey now has hit 14 career grand slams, which ties him with the Mets' Robin Ventura among active players.

Garrett Anderson hits his 30th homer as the Angels come from five down to beat the White Sox in Anaheim, 10-7.

JULY 29:

The Orioles continue to wheel and deal, sending reliever Mike Timlin (2-3, 4.89 ERA, 11 saves) to the Cardinals for first baseman Chris Richard (.125, one homer, one RBI) and minor league pitcher Mark Nussbeck. Later in the day, Baltimore trades catcher Charles Johnson (.294, 21 homers, 55 RBI) and veteran DH Harold Baines (.266, 10 homers, 30 RBI) to the White Sox for catcher Brook Fordyce (.272, five homers, 21 RBI) and three minor league pitchers – Miguel Felix, Juan Figuero, and Jason Lakman.

Wally Joyner hits his 200th career homer and fourth of the year in the Braves' 13-5 win over the Astros.

JULY 30:

Tom Glavine defeats the visiting Astros, 6-3, to join his Atlanta teammate Greg Maddux and the Yankees' Roger Clemens as the only active pitchers with 200 career wins. Glavine is now at 13-5 on the season.

With Sammy Sosa cracking his 32nd homer and Jon Lieber hurling a complete-game four-hitter, the Cubs down the visiting Giants, 3-1.

Randy Johnson fans 11 Marlins and leaves with a one-run lead. but the D'backs lose, 4-3, and he doesn't figure in the decision.

The Phillies acquire starting pitcher Kent Bottenfield (7-8, 5.71 ERA) from the Angels for outfielder

Japan's all-time saves leader, Kazuhiro Sasaki, is the Mariners' new closer.

AUGUST 3
The Giants' Jeff Kent brings his NL-leading RBI total to 96 by driving in six runs.

Ron Gant (.254, 20 homers, 38 RBI).

The Cardinals acquire relief pitcher Jason Christiansen (2-8, 4.97 ERA, one save) from the Pirates for minor league infielder Jack Wilson.

The Giants land reliever Doug Henry (1-3, 4.42 ERA, one save) from the Astros for pitcher Scott Linebrink (0-0, 11.57 ERA in three games).

The Mets got a homer from Mike Bordick yesterday in his first at-bat. Today, new Met Bubba Trammel does the same as the Mets beat the Cardinals, 4-2, to complete a four-game sweep and extend their winning streak to six.

Frank Thomas is back in the swing of things.

JULY 31:

Business is booming at baseball's bazaar on the last day for trades. The Orioles send sought-after outfielder B. J. Surhoff (.292, 13 homers, 57 RBI) and pitcher Gabe Molina (0-0, 9.00 ERA in nine games) to the Braves for pitcher Luis Rivera (1-0, 1.35 ERA in five games), outfielder Trinidad Hubbard (.185, one homer, six RBI), and catcher Fernando Lunar (.185, five RBI).

To back up ailing Mark McGwire, the Cardinals get first baseman Will Clark (.301, nine homers, 28 RBI) from the Orioles for minor leaguer Jose Leon.

The Mariners secure outfielder Al Martin (.306, 11 homers, 27 RBI) from the Padres for third baseman John Mabry (.243, one homer, seven RBI).

The Blue Jays add pitcher Steve Trachsel (3-1, 4.58 ERA) and reliever Mark Guthrie (1-1, 4.50 ERA) for minor leaguer Brent Abernathy and a player to be named later to the Devil Rays.

The Dodgers trade outfielder Todd Hollandsworth (.234, 8 homers, 24 RBI) and two minor leaguers, Kevin Gibb and Randey Dorame, to the Rockies for outfielder Tom Goodwin (.271, five homers, 47 RBI) and cash.

The Padres obtain Jay Witasick (3-8, 5.94 ERA) from the Royals for Brian Meadows (7-8, 5.34 ERA).

The Cubs make two trades. They ship pitcher Scott Downs (4-3, 5.17 ERA) to the Expos for outfielder Rondell White (.307, 11 homers, 54 RBI) and send outfielder Henry Rodriguez (.250, 18 homers, 51 RBI) and cash to the Marlins for two minor leaguers – outfielder-first baseman Ross Gload and pitcher David Noyce.

The Cardinals add a new catcher, Carlos Hernandez (.251, two homers, 25 RBI), and a minor league infielder-outfielder, Nathan Tebbs. In return, they send the Padres reliever Heathcliff Slocumb (2-3, 5.44 ERA, one save) and minor league outfielder Ben Johnson. Hernadez missed all of the 1999 season because of an injury. Somewhere, perhaps in the Big Front Office in the Sky, Frank "Trader" Lane, the general manager who delighted in swapping players, must be smiling. When the day is over, 29 players change uni-

"I got good players, stayed out of their way, let them win a lot, and then just hung around for 26 years."
– Hall of Fame inductee Sparky Anderson

forms in nine deals. In the last four days prior to the trading deadline, 69 players were swapped in 20 transactions. The Orioles give new meaning to housecleaning, trading away five frontline players: catcher Charles Johnson, first baseman Will Clark, shortstop Mike Bordick, outfielder B. J. Surhoff and DH Harold Baines.

The "new look" Orioles defeat the Twins, 6-5, in Baltimore.

The Pirates sign outfielder-first baseman John Vander Wal (.292, 15 homers, 55 RBI) to a two-year, $3.7 million extension.

AUGUST 1:

Mike Mussina one-hits the Twins, 10-0, in Baltimore, fanning 15. The lone Twins' hit is a two-out single by Ron Coomer in the seventh inning.

Mike Cameron hits a leadoff homer off Jeff Fassero in the 19th inning to give the host Mariners a 5-4 win over the Red Sox. Kazuhiro Sasaki gets the victory in the longest game in Mariners' history.

AUGUST 2:

Pedro Martinez rings up his 13th, a five-hitter over the Mariners in Seattle. Martinez fans seven in the 5-2 victory and reduces his ERA to 1.42.

Barry Bonds hits his 34th, but the Giants bow to the Brewers, 6-4, in Milwaukee.

Sammy Sosa hits his 33rd as the Cubs top the Rockies, 3-2.

AUGUST 3:

Jeff Kent homers – his 26th – hits two doubles, and drives in six runs as the host Giants pound the Pirates, 10-2. Kent now leads the NL with 96 RBI.

AUGUST 4:

The Mets KO Randy Johnson in the fourth and beat the Diamondbacks, 6-1, in Arizona. Rick Reed gets the win.

The Phillies trade shortstop Desi Relaford (.221, three homers, 30 RBI) to the Padres for a player to be named later. Yesterday, the Red Sox claimed first baseman Rico Brogna after he was put on waivers by Philadelphia.

AUGUST 5:

Sammy Sosa hits his 34th homer and drives in three runs as the Cubs beat the Padres, 6-3, in San Diego. Sosa has now driven in 100 or more runs for six consecutive seasons.

David Wells becomes the majors' first 17-game winner with an 8-5 win over the Rangers in Toronto.

Frank Thomas hits his 30th homer in the bottom of the 10th off Jason Isringhausen to give the White Sox a 4-3 win over the A's.

Will Clark homers for the third straight game, helping the Cardinals and Garrett Stephenson to a 5-0 win over the Braves.

AUGUST 6:

The Giants execute five double plays in beating the Pirates, 7-1, in San Francisco.

Edgar Martinez homers and doubles for three RBI – bringing his season total to 103 and his Mariners drub the Yankees, 11-1, in New York.

AUGUST 7:

Sammy Sosa hits his 35th homer of the year and the Cubs beat the Dodgers, 7-3, in Los Angeles.

The Yankees continue to stockpile players, adding Jose Canseco (.257, nine homers, 30 RBI) from the Devil Rays on waivers. Canseco becomes the eighth "new" Yankee since June 20, joining David Justice, Denny Neagle, Luis Sojo, Glenallen Hill, Luis Polonia, Jose Vizcaino, and Dwight Gooden.

AUGUST 8:

On two pitches, the Yankees turn a 3-2 deficit into a 4-3 victory over the Athletics in New York. Bernie Williams homers off Jason Isringhausen's first pitch to tie the score. David Justice sends Isringhausen's second pitch out of the park for the win. Mariano Rivera gets the victory.

In a 2-hour, 2-minute game, Ramon Ortiz outpitches his idol, Pedro Martinez, limiting the Red Sox to two hits, in a 2-1 Angels' victory. Martinez allows only three hits and fans nine, but loses his fourth game against 13 wins. Ortiz is 4-2.

Two grand slams, by Jay Buhner and Edgar Martinez, lead the Mariners past the White Sox, 12-4, in the opener of a twin bill. Joel Pineiro, up from the minors, gets the win in his ML debut. Despite Frank Thomas's 31st homer, the Mariners sweep, 7-5. Alex Rodriguez hits his 30th home run for Seattle.

CULTURE

BASEBALL IN MOVIES:
***The Life and Times of Hank Greenberg*, a documentary by Aviva Kempner, follows the Hall of Famer's career and his struggle against anti-Semitism. The film premieres late in 1999 and goes into wider distribution in 2000.**

CULTURE

The American Experience/ Joe DiMaggio: The Hero's Life, a Public Broadcasting System special that presents the Yankee Clipper's strengths and warts; *Greener Grass/Cuba, Baseball and the United States*, a Public Broadcasting System documentary – the title tells it all.

AUGUST 9:

The White Sox crush the Mariners, 19-3, on 24 hits in Chicago. Frank Thomas homers in his first two at-bats – his 32nd and 33rd of the season – and drives in five runs. Also hitting homers for Chicago are Tony Graffanino – a grand slam – and Ray Durham. Earlier this year, Chicago scored 18 runs against Seattle.

Jeff Kent hits a grand slam and drives in four in a 9-3 Giants win over the Brewers in San Francisco. Kent now has 102 RBI and 27 homers.

Ken Griffey Jr. hits his 33rd homer in a 10-6 Reds' win over the Braves today in Cincinnati.

AUGUST 10:

After 15 starts without a victory, Yankees' starter David Cone is back in the win column, beating the Athletics in New York. Cone allows eight hits and two runs while fanning eight in a 12-6 win.

Tony Batista hits his 34th homer – tying him with Frank Thomas for the AL lead – and the Blue Jays bounce the Royals, 15-7, in Kansas City.

AUGUST 11:

Mike Piazza hits a two-run homer and Edgardo Alfonso follows suit as the Mets and Glendon Rusch beat the Giants, 4-1, in New York. Piazza has 31 homers and 97 RBI on the season.

Ken Griffey Jr. hits his 34th homer in a 6-4 Reds' victory over the Cubs in Chicago. Sammy Sosa connects for his 36th homer.

AUGUST 12:

Ken Griffey Jr. doubles in a run in a 3-0 Reds' victory over the host Cubs; it is the fifth straight season in which he has batted in at least 100 runs.

Jason Giambi hits his 30th homer as his Athletics down the Tigers, 9-5, in Oakland today.

Troy Glaus hits his 33rd and 34th homers to lead the Angels past the Yankees, 9-6, in Anaheim.

AUGUST 13:

The Astros' Jeff Bagwell hits his 32nd and 33rd homers and drives in seven runs in a 14-7 win over the host Phillies.

Gary Sheffield leads the ML with his 37th homer as the Dodgers down the Braves, 7-2.

Frank Thomas hits his 35th homer, but John Flaherty's homer in the bottom of the ninth gives the Devil Rays a 5-3 win over the White Sox.

AUGUST 14:

Tom Glavine rings up his 15th win of the year as the Braves beat the Padres, 9-2, in Atlanta.

Sammy Sosa hits his 37th homer, tying Gary Sheffield for the major league lead and his Cubs top the Cardinals, 7-3, at Wrigley Field.

AUGUST 15:

Sammy Sosa forges into the major league lead with his 38th homer of the season, but the Cardinals drop the Cubs, 4-1, at Wrigley Field.

Texas's Gabe Kapler singles to extend his hitting streak to 28 games in a 10-2 loss to the visiting Yankees.

Frank Thomas hits his AL-leading 36th homer and drives in five runs. Teammate Harold Baines matches him with a homer and five RBI as the White Sox wallop the Orioles, 14-4, in Baltimore.

The Angels beat David Wells and the Blue Jays, 8-4, in Toronto. Wells has won two of five since the All-Star break.

AUGUST 16:

Thirty-five is the number of the day. Carlos Delgado homers, his 35th, in the bottom of the ninth to lift the Blue Jays over the Angels, 8-6. Earlier, teammate Tony Batista connects for his 35th. Troy Glaus hits his 35th and Darrin Erstad his 20th in a losing cause. Barry Bonds slams his 35th in a 4-1 Giants victory over the Expos in Montreal and Jeff Bagwell hits his 35th as his Astros nip the Pirates, 11-10, in Houston.

AUGUST 17:

The Braves sign Chipper Jones to a six-year contract reportedly worth $90 million. Jones (.305, 25 homers, 83 RBI) trails only Ken Griffey Jr., Kevin Brown, and Mike Piazza in the salary "race."

Barry Bonds hits his 36th homer as the Giants beat the Expos, 5-4, to complete a three-game sweep.

AUGUST 18:

Sammy Sosa homers twice – number 39 and number 40 – but his round-trippers are the only scores for the

Cubs in an 11-2 loss to the Diamondbacks and Curt Schilling.

Darin Erstad, emerging as one of the game's premier players, beats the Yankees with his glove and bat. The Angels' leftfielder makes a backhanded, diving, game-saving catch on a drive by Jorge Posada in the bottom of the 10th and homers in the 11th to beat New York, 9-8.

AUGUST 19:

Gary Sheffield slams the visiting Mets, 4-1, with his 39th and 40th homers of the year and three RBI. Chan Ho Park gets his 12th victory.

Sammy Sosa's 41st homer drives in two, but it is not enough as the Cubs bow to the Diamondbacks, 11-3. Steve Finley hits his 30th for Arizona.

Pedro Martinez, who has been hampered with a sore shoulder, returns to the mound, allowing the Rangers only three hits while fanning 10 in seven innings. The Red Sox beat the Rangers, 9-0, at Fenway Park.

Frank Thomas hits his AL-leading 38th homer, doubles, and bats in four runs as the White Sox defeat the Devil Rays, 7-0.

Ellis Burks drives in four runs with two homers and Jeff Kent connects for his 28th of the year as the Giants slam the visiting Braves, 12-3.

Manny Ramirez's 13th career grand slam helps the Indians beat the Mariners, 10-4, in Cleveland today.

Jeff Bagwell hits his 36th and 37th homers as the host Astros beat the Brewers, 10-8.

Andy Pettitte wins his 15th, 9-1, over the visiting Angels. Troy Glaus's 36th homer accounts for the losers' only run. David Justice connects twice for New York.

AUGUST 20:

Todd Helton homers (number 31) and doubles to raise his batting average to .398; his Rockies rock the Marlins, 13-4.

Randy Johnson allows four hits and fans 13 for his 16th win – and first since July 20 – 5-4, over the visiting Cubs. Sammy Sosa hits his 42nd homer.

AUGUST 21:

Sammy Sosa is on a long-ball tear. He connects for his 43rd homer of the season in a 5-4 Cubs' loss – their sixth straight – today in Houston. Despite Rafael Palmeiro's 31st homer, the Yankees down the visiting Rangers, 12-3, on homers by Glenallen Hill, Derek Jeter, and Jorge Posada.

Jim Edmonds leads the Cardinals past the Pirates, 7-4, with his 33rd home run. Pittsburgh's Brian Giles hits his 30th.

Todd Helton is a .400 hitter – briefly. In Colorado, the Rockies' star singles in his first two at-bats against the Braves to reach .400. He is hitless in his next two at-bats and drops back to .398. Andruw Jones hits his 27th homer and Chipper Jones his 28th and the Braves win the game, 7-4.

Barry Larkin hits an RBI double in the third against the Phillies for his 2,000th career hit. Larkin is the first shortstop with 2,000 hits in combination with 170 homers and 350 stolen bases. The Reds get the win, 7-4.

AUGUST 22:

Two "position" players take to the mound. In San Diego, with the Mets trailing, 11-1, manager Bobby Valentine sends outfielder Derek Bell, replete with sunglasses, in to pitch the eighth inning. Bell's first pitch is 47 mph; his fastest registers 78 mph. When his stint is over, he has yielded five runs, three hits, and four walks; the Mets are down 16-1 – the game's final score. But in Colorado, with the Rockies running out of players, catcher Brent Mayne-who has never pitched at any level – is sent to the mound in the 12th inning against the Braves. Mayne hurls a shutout inning, the Rockies win, 7-6, and he becomes the first nonpitcher since Rocky Colavito in 1968 – the year of Mayne's birth – to win a major league game. The last NLer to accomplish the feat was Johnny O'Brien of the Pirates in 1956. The game also features a brawl that begins when John Wasdin hits Andres Galarraga in the shoulder in the 11th and the Braves first baseman charges the mound. The loss goes to John Rocker, who tells reporters: "Beat it! I'm not talking."

The Angels' Kent Mercker, sidelined for 80 games after a brain hemorrhage, returns and beats the Red Sox, 11-4, in Boston.

AUGUST 23:

The Braves end Todd Helton's hitting

AUGUST 24
The Mariners' Edgar Martinez homers and drives in his 123rd RBI, but Detroit wins, 10-3.

streak at 14 games and defeat the Rockies, 5-2, in Colorado. Helton's average dips to .393. Greg Maddux gets his 14th win.

Carlos Delgado clouts his 37th and 38th homers, tying Frank Thomas for the AL lead. The Blue Jays edge the Royals, 9-8, in Toronto.

Al Leiter fans 12 Padres en route to his 14th win, a 4-1 Mets victory in San Diego.

Livan Hernandez, backed by Barry Bonds's 38th homer, hurls his second straight shutout and beats the Marlins, 5-0, in San Francisco.

Alex Ochoa of the Reds hits a first-inning grand slam off Phillies' pitcher Bruce Chen in Cincinnati. It is Ochoa's career first, but the 142nd hit in the majors this year, surpassing the record of 141 set in 1966. The Phillies win, 5-4.

AUGUST 24:

Omar Daal of the Phillies faces off against Steve Parris of the Reds, each with 14 losses, in Cincinnati. Parris allows nine hits and two runs and gets his eighth win. Daal yields eight hits and five runs and gets his 15th loss against only three wins.
Pedro Martinez is off his game, allowing eight hits and six runs in eight innings, but the Red Sox down the Royals, 9-7, in K.C.

Edgar Martinez hits his 31st homer and runs his RBI total to 123, but the Mariners fall to the Tigers, 10-3, in Detroit. The Tigers improve to .500.

Martinez, at age 37, is having his most successful offensive season ever, proving why he is one of his era's most potent hitters. Writes Jerry Izenberg in the Seattle Post-Intelligencer: "He would probably be the first to tell you that if Gold Gloves were passports, he couldn't get any farther than Walla Walla.... But put a bat in his hand and Edgar Martinez is golden. He is the Hope Diamond of designated hitters, which figures. He was born to hit. He ought to wear a bell around his neck and carry a sign that says: 'Warning. Pitching to this man may be hazardous to your health, your career, and your ERA – not necessarily in that order.'"

AUGUST 25:

Tom Glavine beats the visiting Cardinals, 7-4, for his 17th win on a three-run homer by Chipper Jones – his 30th.

The Mets rough up Randy Johnson for six runs in two and a third innings and defeat the visiting Diamondbacks, 13-3.

Only a day after reaching the .500 mark, the Tigers are tamed by the Twins, 8-3, in Minnesota and once again have a losing record.

AUGUST 27:

Troy Glaus clouts his 37th homer and Tim Salmon his 30th for the Angels, who become the first team in AL history with four players at or above the 30 mark. Mates Mo Vaughn and Garrett Anderson previously attained that level. Three NL teams have reached that landmark a total of six times. The Angels nip the Indians, 10-9, in Anaheim.

AUGUST 28:

Carlos Delgado continues to mash the baseball, hitting his 39th homer in a 4-2 win over the Angels.

Todd Helton moves closer to the .400 mark; his three hits against the host Phillies raise his average to .397 But the Phillies win, 3-2.

AUGUST 29:

Red Sox ace Pedro Martinez hits Tampa Bay's first batter Gerald Williams, who charges the mound, triggering a brawl. When order is finally restored, Martinez no-hits the Devil Rays until John Flaherty's leadoff hit in the ninth. He fans 13 and gains his 15th victory, 8-0. Eight Devil Rays are ejected in the course of the game – manager Larry Rothschild, two coaches, and five players.

Darin Erstad gets three hits, reaching 200 safeties faster than any player since Joe "Ducky" Medwick 65 years ago. The Angels beat the Blue Jays, 9-4; Troy Glaus (38) and Mo Vaughn (32) homer.

The Mets stop Tony Eusebio's hitting streak at 24 games but lose to the Astros, 11-1, in New York.

AUGUST 30:

Mike Sweeney hits a three-run double, bringing his RBI total to 121 and his Royals beat the Twins, 8-7.

David Wells records his 19th win with help from Tony Batista's

AUGUST 28
Colorado's Todd Helton, still flirting with .400, gets three hits to raise his average to .397.

SEPTEMBER 4
After the Red Sox retire Carlton Fisk's #27, Pedro Martinez fans 11 Mariners for his 16th win.

37th homer in an 11-2 victory in Anaheim.

Randy Johnson hangs up his 17th, a five-hitter with 10 strikeouts over the Expos, 7-0.

Sammy Sosa hits his 44th and 45th and Jon Lieber registers his 12th win as the Cubs down the visiting Padres, 5-1.

Barry Bonds hits his 39th, and the 484th of his career, in a 2-0 win in Pittsburgh.

Tom Glavine gets his 18th win, 5-2, over the visiting Reds, with Andres Galarraga hitting his 25th homer.

AUGUST 31:

Chipper Jones hits his 30th homer, but the Braves lose, 4-3, to the visiting Reds and the Mets move into first place in the NL East by a half game. The Braves finish August 14-15.

SEPTEMBER 1:

It's power versus power and Frank Thomas prevails. The White Sox' slugger slams his 39th in a 9-8 home win over the Angels despite round-trippers by Troy Glaus (39) and Mo Vaughn (34). Matt Ginter, in relief, gets the victory – it's his major league debut. Todd Helton hits his 33rd homer, but it is his only hit in four at-bats, and he drops to .393. The Rockies beat the visiting Brewers, 5-3.

The Giants sign Robb Nen (3-3, 1.58 ERA, 32 saves) to a four-year extension worth $32.5 million, making him the richest closer.

SEPTEMBER 2:

Charles Johnson has a career day with a three-run homer, a three-run double, and 7 RBI as his White Sox bash the visiting Angels, 13-6. Garrett Anderson hits his 32nd homer for the losers.

Jeff Kent hits his 31st in a 13-2 win over the visiting Cubs.

SEPTEMBER 3:

Kenny Lofton steals five bases, scores four times, and bashes a game-winning homer in a 12-11 home win over the Orioles.

Frank Thomas's homer (40) trumps Anaheim's four-baggers and the White Sox beat the visiting Angels, 13-12, despite Troy Glaus' 40th and Tim Salmon's 32nd.

Alex Rodriguez hits his 33rd homer, leading Seattle past the host Red Sox, 5-0. Jim Edmonds's homer in the bottom of the 11th sinks the Mets, 4-3, giving the Cardinals a three-game sweep.

Clyde Sukeforth, who scouted Jackie Robinson for the Brooklyn Dodgers, dies at age 98 in Waldoboro, Maine. Sukeforth, a catcher, played 10 seasons with the Reds and Dodgers, batting .264. But he is best-known for his role in bringing Robinson to the majors; he was the only other participant in the historic meeting at which the Dodgers' Branch Rickey informed Robinson he would be the player to break baseball's color line.

SEPTEMBER 4:

Pedro Martinez fans 11 Mariners and allows only six hits to record his 16th win. Prior to the game, the Red Sox retire Carlton Fisk's number 27.

The visiting A's defeat David Wells and the Blue Jays, 10-0, denying the lefty his 20th win. Another premier AL left-hander, Andy Pettitte, earns his 17th in a 4-3 Yankees' victory in Kansas City.

Barry Bonds hits his 42nd and 43rd and his Giants top the Phillies, 8-5.

Ken Griffey Jr. hits his 37th homer and the host Reds beat Al Leiter and the Mets, 6-2. Mike Piazza connects for his 34th.

SEPTEMBER 5:

David Justice's 35th homer paces the visiting Yankees past the Royals, 10-5, and the revitalized Doc Gooden gets his sixth victory.

In a duel of ace left-handers, Tom Glavine beats Randy Johnson and the Diamondbacks, 5-2, in Atlanta for his 19th win. Chipper Jones hits two home runs off Johnson, who fans 11 but falls to 17-6. Andres Galarraga hits his 26th homer.

SEPTEMBER 6:

Sammy Sosa homes in on a home-run title with his 46th in an 8-5 win over the Rockies in Colorado.

Texas loses to the White Sox, 13-1, with Frank Thomas hitting his 41st homer.

Ken Griffey Jr., heating up, hits his 38th homer and the Reds drop the visiting Mets, 11-8.

The visiting Expos end the Cardinals' six-game winning streak, 7-2, with help from Vladimir

SEPTEMBER 10
Randy Johnson gets career strikeout 3,000, fanning the Marlins' Mark Lowell.

Guerrero's 33rd and 34th homers.

SEPTEMBER 7:

Barry Bonds hits his 44th homer and the Giants keep rolling, with a 13-0 paddling of the visiting Padres.

SEPTEMBER 8:

Sammy Sosa keeps slammin'. Sosa hits his 47th, but the visiting Astros down the Cubs, 13-10.

While Sosa is hitting home runs, Mark McGwire is struggling to overcome injuries. In his first at-bat since injuring his knee on July 7, McGwire strikes out and the Cardinals lose to the Brewers, 6-5, in St. Louis. Cardinals' manager Tony LaRussa, trying to provide at-bats for McGwire, bats him second and lists him at second base, removing him after his first at-bat.

Gary Sheffield strokes his 41st in an 8-5 Dodgers' loss to the Rockies in Colorado.

SEPTEMBER 9:

Andy Pettitte outduels Pedro Martinez and the Yankees beat the Reds Sox, 5-3, in Boston. Scott Brosius's three-run homer in the seventh gives Pettitte his 18th victory.

Richard Hidalgo hits his 34th and 35th homers as Houston routs the Cubs in Chicago, 14-4. The Astros bang out seven homers – in addition to Hidalgo, Tim Bogan and Lance Berkmann connect twice and Daryle Ward once.

The A's Tim Hudson gets his 16th win, a 10-0 two-hitter over the visiting Devil Rays. Jason Giambi hits his 34th home run for Oakland.

SEPTEMBER 10:

On his 37th birthday, Randy Johnson gives himself two gifts, but misses out on a third – a victory. He fans Mark Lowell of the Marlins in the fourth for his 3,000th career strikeout and, with 14 for the game, brings his season total to 300. He joins Hall of Famer Nolan Ryan as the only pitchers with three consecutive 300-strikeout seasons. But Johnson is not involved in the decision and Arizona loses, 4-3, in Florida.

Omar Daal moves closer to a mark he doesn't want – a 20-loss season. Despite allowing only two runs in six innings, Daal is dealt his 18th defeat of the year by left-hander Al Leiter and the Mets, 3-0, in New York.

Ken Griffey Jr. slams his 39th homer in a 6-4 Reds victory in Pittsburgh while Richard Hidalgo stays hot with his 36th and 37th in a 7-6 Astros' win in Chicago.

Sammy Sosa hits his 48th in vain as the Cubs are eliminated from contention.

SEPTEMBER 11:

Frank Thomas hits his AL-leading 42nd homer – a grand slam – and drives in five to boost his RBI total to an ML top 139. The host White Sox trample the Tigers, 10-3.

Sammy Sosa homers again – and the Cubs lose again. Sosa smacks his 49th and the host Reds edge the Cubs, 7-6.

Mark McGwire makes the most of his one at-bat with a homer, his 31st of the season and first since July 1. The Cardinals win, 8-4, in Pittsburgh. Garrett Stephenson gets his 16th win and the Pirates are eliminated from postseason play.

The Giants win a battle of homers, 8-7, in Houston. Barry Bonds (45) and Jeff Kent (32) connect for San Francisco; Jeff Bagwell (42) and Richard Hidalgo (38) go deep for the Astros.

SEPTEMBER 12:

Barry Bonds and Jeff Bagwell continue their home-run duel. Bonds connects for his 46th – tying his career high – and Bagwell for his 43rd. The Giants beat the host Astros again, this time 9-5.

SEPTEMBER 13:

There's life in the old Oriole yet. Cal Ripken Jr., who missed 59 games with back problems, collects four hits in a 9-4 Baltimore victory in Texas.

Greg Maddux hurls his second straight shutout, defeating the visiting Marlins, 4-0, for his 17th victory

Barry Bonds hits his career-high 47th homer and the Giants edge host Houston, 3-2.

SEPTEMBER 14:

Pedro Martinez beats the Indians today in Cleveland, 7-4, for his 17th win. He fans 10 in seven innings. Carl Everett hits his 34th homer for Boston.

Jeff Bagwell connects for his 44th homer and his Astros defeat the visiting Pirates, 8-7.

SEPTEMBER 15:

Mark McGwire hits his 32nd homer – a game-winning pinch hit in the eighth off

SEPTEMBER 15
Sammy Sosa joins Mark McGwire as the only players with three straight 50-homer years.

losing pitcher Jon Lieber while the Cardinals down the Cubs, 3-2, in St. Louis. Teammate Jim Edmonds connects for his 40th – raising his RBI total to 100.

Jason Giambi's 37th homer and seven RBI lead the A's past host Tampa Bay, 17-3.

Rickey Henderson scores twice in Seattle's 10-2 win in Baltimore, bringing his lifetime total to 2,175; he passes Babe Ruth and Hank Aaron on the all-time list and is now second only to Ty Cobb.

Randy Johnson outpitches Tom Glavine for his 18th win, fanning 13 in seven innings, despite Chipper Jones's 33rd homer. Jay Bell's homer gives the host Diamondbacks a 2-1 victory.

Sammy Sosa joins Mark McGwire as the only players in history with three consecutive 50-home run seasons. Babe Ruth hit 50 or more four times, but never three seasons in a row. Yet Sosa achieves and his team doesn't; the Cubs fall to the Cardinals, 7-6, in St. Louis.

SEPTEMBER 17:

Balls continue to fly out of major league parks: Alex Rodriguez hits his 38th long ball in a 3-2 Seattle win in Baltimore; Vladimir Guerrero registers his 38th and 39th in a 5-0 win over the Mets in Montreal; Blue Jays Carlos Delgado (40), Brad Fullmer (32), and Jose Cruz Jr. (31) homer in a 14-1 pounding of the White Sox in Chicago; Manny Ramirez bangs out number 32 and Cleveland clouts the Yankees, 15-4, on 15 hits in New York; Andruw Jones swats his 32nd in a 7-1 Braves' win in Arizona; Jeff Kent reaches 33 – and triples – in a 5-1 Giants' victory in San Diego, Moises Alou hits his 30th and drives in four as the Astros send the visiting Pirates to their ninth straight loss.

SEPTEMBER 18:

Luis Polonia's eighth-inning single ends a no-hit bid by the Indians' Bartolo Colon, who goes on to one-hit the Yankees, 2-0, in New York. Colon, who fans 13, bests Roger Clemens.

The Pirates end their nine-game losing streak with a 6-5 victory in Philadelphia.

Montreal slugger Vladimir Guerrero hits his 40th and 41st homers and the host Expos down the Marlins, 11-4.

Jason Giambi bangs out his 38th in a 12-3 A's romp in Baltimore.

SEPTEMBER 19:

Ken Griffey Jr., out for seven games with a hamstring injury, pinch-hits his 40th homer, but the Reds bow to the Giants in San Francisco. Griffey joins Babe Ruth, Hank Aaron, and Harmon Killebrew as the only players to reach the 40 mark seven times. It is his 438th career four-bagger and ties him with Andre Dawson for 25th place.

SEPTEMBER 20:

The Cardinals clinch the NL Central with an 11-6 win over the visiting Astros and become the first team into the 2000 playoffs. Jim Edmonds hits his 41st homer.

Mike Piazza hits his 36th, Al Leiter wins his 16th and the Mets win, 6-3, over Ton Glavine to salvage one game in their series in Atlanta.

SEPTEMBER 21:

David Wells defeats the Yankees, 3-1, in Toronto for his 20th; Carlos Delgado hits his 41st home run.

Vladimir Guerrero hits his sixth homer in five games – and 43rd of the season – and drives in five runs as the Expos beat the hosting Marlins, 10-3.

SEPTEMBER 22:

Richard Hidalgo keeps hitting, connecting for his 43rd and 44th homers, but the Reds beat the Astros in Houston, 12-5. Hidalgo began the 2000 season with only 24 career home runs – 15 in 1999.

Preston Wilson of the Marlins hits his 30th homer and becomes the 23rd player in ML history with 30 round-trippers and 30 steals in a season. Florida beats host Colorado, 8-4, despite Todd Helton's 37th homer.

SEPTEMBER 23:

The Braves clinch a playoff spot. Greg Maddux records his 19th win in Montreal, 10-0, and extends his shutout streak to 36 ⅓ innings. Reggie Sanders has six RBI.

David Justice hits his 39th and 40th home runs – a career high – and teammates Derek Jeter and Jorge Posada also connect as the Yankees end a six-game losing streak with a 13-8 win over the Tigers at Yankee Stadium.

SEPTEMBER 27
In Sydney, the United States upsets Cuba, 4-0, to capture the Olympic gold medal.

Rafael Palmeiro's 39th homer – the 400th of his career – is wasted as the Angels romp in Texas, 15-4. Palmeiro becomes the 32nd player to reach the 400 mark. Troy Glaus connects for his 42nd and 43rd. Jeff Bagwell hits his 45th with similar results – the Astros fall to the Reds, 6-4, in Cincinnati.

Former third baseman Aurelio Rodriguez, 52, is killed by a car while walking on a Detroit street. Rodriguez, a slick glove man who twice led the AL in fielding, played 17 seasons, mostly with the Tigers and also with the Angels, Senators, Padres, Yankees, White Sox, and Orioles. He batted .237 with 124 homers.

SEPTEMBER 24:

The White Sox clinch the AL Central title with a 6-5 win over the host Twins. It is Chicago's first title since 1993.

Andy Pettitte, with help from Bernie Williams's 30th homer, defeats the visiting Detroit Tigers, 6-3, for his 19th victory.

SEPTEMBER 25:

Tom Glavine defeats the Expos, 6-0, in Montreal for his 20th win. Andruw Jones hits his 34th homer.

Randy Johnson collects his 19th win, 6-4, in Colorado, striking out eight.

Jason Giambi hits his 40th homer and brother Jason Giambi clouts a bases-loaded triple to lead Oakland past visiting Anaheim, 7-5.

SEPTEMBER 26:

The Braves clinch the NL East with a 7-1 win over the Mets in New York. Chipper Jones hits his 35th homer.

Pedro Martinez tops the host White Sox for his 18th win. Nomar Garciaparra hits his 20th homer.

Omar Daal avoids his 20th loss, beating the Cubs, 10-4, at Wrigley Field; he's now 3-19.

Jason Giambi hits his 41st and Tim Hudson notches his 19th win as the Athletics beat the visiting Angels, 10-3.

Todd Helton's 39th home run helps the Rockies push past the visiting Diamondbacks, 7-6; Jim Edmonds hits his 42nd in a 7-1 Cardinals' win in San Diego and Gary Sheffield connects for his 42nd in a 9-0 Dodgers win over the visiting Giants.

SEPTEMBER 27:

The Mets beat the visiting Braves, 6-2, to clinch the NL wild-card spot.

The United States upsets Cuba, 4-0, on a three-hitter by Brewers' draftee Ben Sheets to capture the Olympic gold medal in Sydney, Australia. Tommy Lasorda, the 73-year-old manager of the team, not known for understatement, says: "I managed the Dodgers for 20 years and I had a lot of great moments, but this is the greatest moment of my life."

Jeff Bagwell hits his career-best 46th homer as Houston humbles the Pirates in Pittsburgh, 10-1.

The Yankees continue their tailspin, falling to the Devil Rays, 11-1.

Tony Batista slams his 40th homer and Frank Castillo wins his ninth straight as the Blue Jays blank the host Orioles, 4-0.

Kerry Wood completes his comeback year with a 1-0 victory over the Phillies at

Joe Torre and his Yankees are on top of the baseball world, winning their third straight World Series.

Tommy Lasorda on winning the Olympic gold medal: "I managed the Dodgers for 20 years and I had a lot of great moments, but this is the greatest moment of my life."

Wrigley Field. Wood fans 10. Sammy Sosa singles in Wood with the winning run in the third inning for his 137th RBI.

SEPTEMBER 28:

The Yankees lose again, 11-3, at Tampa Bay and are victimized in a rare double play, with catcher Mike DeFelice – who also hits a three-run homer – recording both outs. Jose Canseco is out at home trying to score on a Tino Martinez hit. After a wild throw, DeFelice also tags Martinez out at the plate.

Too little, too late as the Orioles slam the Blue Jays, 23-1, on 23 hits in Baltimore.

Troy Glaus's 45th homer – in the bottom of the 14th against Scott Service – gives the visiting Angels a 6-3 win in Oakland. Glaus breaks the AL record, previously held by Al Rosen, for most homers hit by a third baseman.

Frank Thomas's 43rd homer isn't enough; the White Sox bow to the Red Sox, 7-6.

Antonio Alfonseca registers his 44th save in the Marlins' 7-4 win over the visiting Expos.

In the last game ever at 48-year-old County Stadium, the Brewers lose to the visiting Reds, 8-1. The Brewers' new Miller Park will open next season.

For the first time in his career, Darryl Kile is a 20-game winner as the Cardinals beat the host Padres, 7-6.

The Mets score three in the fourth off Greg Maddux, ending his shutout streak at 39 1/3 innings, and win, 8-2, at Shea, denying him his 20th victory.

Todd Helton's 40th homer isn't enough; the Diamondbacks beat the Rockies in Colorado, 12-3.

The visiting Giants – with Barry Bonds hitting his 49th homer – beat the Dodgers, 5-3.

SEPTEMBER 29:

The Yankees lose again, 13-2, in Baltimore but back into the AL East title when the Red Sox lose, 8-6, in Tampa Bay. Andy Pettitte fails to win his 20th game and Cal Ripken Jr. hits his 14th.

Jim Thome and Manny Ramirez each hit their 36th homers and the Indians beat the Blue Jays, 8-4.

Troy Glaus collects his 46th in a 9-3 Angels' win over the visiting Mariners and Jason Giambi his 42nd as the Athletics beat the visiting Rangers, 7-5.

Todd Helton hits his 41st in a 4-2 Rockies' win in Atlanta and Gary Sheffield his 43rd as the Dodgers blank the Padres, 3-0, in San Diego.

SEPTEMBER 30:

The Indians remain in the wild-card chase with the Mariners and A's, beating the visiting Blue Jays, 6-5.

Alex Rodriguez boosts his team's postseason hopes with his 39th and 40th homers and seven RBIs in a 21-9 win over the Angels. Edgar Martinez clouts his 37th and Troy Glaus his 47th.

Jason Giambi hits his 43rd as the A's stay in the hunt with a 23-2 rout of the Rangers.

Tom Glavine bags his 21st win and Andruw Jones hits his 36th homer in a 5-2 Braves' win against the visiting Rockies. Jeff Bagwell hits his 47th and the host Astros beat the Brewers, 7-6.

OCTOBER 1:

The Athletics, behind Tim Hudson, beat the Rangers, 3-0, in Texas to clinch the AL West. Hudson wins his 20th. With David Bell hitting a tie-breaking homer and Alex Rodriguez connecting for his 41st round-tripper, the visiting Mariners beat the Angels, 5-2, to wrap up the AL's wild-card berth. Kazuhiro Sasaki gets his 37th save, tying the rookie record set by Todd Worrell in 1986.

Despite Jim Thome's 37th homer and an 11-4 win over the visiting Blue Jays, the Indians fall short and will miss the playoffs for the first time since 1993.

The Yankees finish their season with seven straight losses, 15 of their last 18, bowing today in Baltimore, 7-3.

The Tigers beat the Twins, 12-11, in Detroit. The Pirates play their last game at Three Rivers Stadium, ending as they began – with a loss. Before a crowd of 55,351, the Cubs beat their hosts, 10-9. Three Rivers opened on July 16, 1970, with the Reds defeating the Pirates, 3-2. Next season, the team will play in the new PNC Park, with a capacity of some 38,000.

For the first time since 1942, no manager is fired during the season. But the Phillies waste no time axing

OCTOBER 3
In the NL Division Series, the Cardinals' Rick Ankiel has five wild pitches in the third against the Braves.

their skipper Terry Francona. He is notified of the team's decision prior to today's game, which the Phillies lose, 7-5, in Florida, to finish at 65-97, in last place in the NL East. On the heels of Francona through the exit door are Buck Showalter of the Diamondbacks (85-77, third place), Jack McKeon of the Reds (85-77, second place), Gene Lamont of the Pirates (69-93, fifth place), Davey Johnson of the Dodgers (86-76, second place), and Jim Fregosi of the Blue Jays (83-79, third place).

OCTOBER 3:

AL Division Series. In Seattle, the Mariners defeat the White Sox, 7-4.

In Oakland, the Athletics beat the Yankees, 5-3.

NL Division Series. In St. Louis, the Cardinals beat the Braves, 7-5. Cards' rookie Rick Ankiel has five wild pitches in the third – the first since Bert Cunningham of Buffalo in the Players League in 1890 to hurl five wild pitches in a frame.

OCTOBER 4:

AL Division Series. In Chicago, the Mariners top the White Sox, 5-2.

In Oakland, the Yankees beat the Athletics, 4-0.

NL Division Series. In San Francisco, the Giants beat the Mets, 5-1.

OCTOBER 5:

NL Division Series. In St. Louis, the Cardinals beat the Braves, 10-4.

In San Francisco, the Mets beat the Giants, 5-4, in 10 innings.

OCTOBER 6:

AL Division Series. In Seattle, the Mariners sweep the White Sox with a 2-1 victory.

In New York, the Yankees beat the Athletics, 4-2.

OCTOBER 7:

AL Division Series. In New York, the Athletics beat the Yankees, 11-1.

NL Division Series. In Atlanta, the Cardinals sweep the Braves with a 7-1 victory.

In New York, the Mets beat the Giants, 3-2, in 13 innings.

OCTOBER 8:

NL Division Series. In San Francisco, the Mets, on a Bobby J. Jones one-hitter, beat the Giants, 4-0, to advance to the NL Championship Series.

AL Division Series. In Oakland, the Yankees beat the Athletics, 7-5, to advance to the AL Championship Series.

OCTOBER 10:

ALCS, game one. In 48-degree New York temperatures, so cold the player introductions are canceled, Freddy Garcia and the Mariners down the Yankees and Denny Neagle, 2-0. Alex Rodriguez homers for the winners and Kazuhiro Sasaki gets a save.

OCTOBER 11:

ALCS, game two. Behind Orlando Hernandez, the Yankees strike back, with seven runs in the eighth for a 7-1 victory. Arthur Rhodes takes the loss. Derek Jeter homers for New York.

NLCS, game one. In St. Louis, the Mets ride strong pitching by Mike Hampton to a 6-2 win. Todd Zeile and Jay Payton homer for New York. Darryl Kile gets the loss.

Yankees' owner George Steinbrenner is planning to propose expanding the first round of playoffs from best of five to best of seven.

OCTOBER 12:

NLCS, game two. The Mets nip the Cardinals, 6-5, in St. Louis on a ninth-inning single by Jay Payton, scoring Joe McEwing. Mike Piazza hits a home run for the winners. Reliever Turk Wendell gets the victory; Mike Timlin is charged with the loss.

OCTOBER 13:

ALCS, game three. Andy Pettitte and the Yankees top the Mariners, 8-2, in Seattle, with Tino Martinez and Bernie Williams homering. Mariano Rivera gets the save and extends his playoff shutout-inning streak to 33-1/3, topping Whitey Ford's record. Aaron Sele gets the loss.

OCTOBER 14:

ALCS, game four. Roger Clemens dominates the host Mariners, 5-0, allowing only one hit, Al Martin's leadoff double in the seventh, and fans a record 15. David Justice and Derek Jeter homer.

NLCS, game three. In New York, the Cardinals, behind winning pitcher Andy Benes, bounce back, 8-2. Edgar Renteria drives in two. Rick Reed gets the loss.

OCTOBER 16
The Mets win game five of the NLCS, 7-0, over the Cardinals to advance to the World Series.

OCTOBER 21
The Subway Series opens with a 12-inning marathon, and the Yankees prevail, 4-3.

OCTOBER 15:

ALCS, game five. Freddy Garcia tops the Yankees again, 2-0, with homer help from Edgar Martinez and John Olerud. Denny Neagle is the losing pitcher.

NLCS, game four. The Mets are one game from eliminating the Cardinals with a 10-6 win in New York. Glendon Rusch gets the victory; Darryl Kile is tagged with the loss. Mike Piazza homers for the winners; Will Clark and Jim Edmonds go deep for the losers.

OCTOBER 16:

NLCS, game five. In New York, the Mets wrap up the NL pennant with a 7-0 three-hitter from NLCS MVP Mike Hampton, who fans eight. Pat Hengten is tagged with the loss. Mark McGwire pinch-hits three times in the series, going hitless and drawing one intentional walk.

OCTOBER 17:

ALCS, game six. New York will have its first Subway Series in 44 years, as the Yankees win the AL pennant with a 9-7 victory over the Mariners in New York. Orlando Hernandez gets the victory; Jose Paniagua, the loss. David Justice homers for New York; Alex Rodriguez and Carlos Guillen connect in a losing effort. The Yankees are the first team with three straight pennants since the Oakland Athletics of the 1988-1990 seasons.

END OF SEASON HIGHLIGHTS:

The 14th Subway Series in New York baseball history matches the teams with the fifth-best winning percentage in the AL (the Yankees) and the fourth-best in the NL (the wild-card Mets). Under Joe Torre, the defending champions win the AL East with an 87-74 record. The Yankees have a balanced offense led by Derek Jeter (.339, 15 homers, 73 RBI), Bernie Williams (.307, 30 homers, 121 RBI), David Justice (.286, 41 homers, 188 RBI), Jorge Posada (.287, 28 homers, 86 RBI), and Paul O'Neill (.283, 18 homers, 100 RBI). The pitching staff is anchored by starters Andy Pettitte (19-9, 4.35 ERA), Roger Clemens (13-8, 3.70 ERA), and Orlando Hernandez (12-13, 4.51 ERA), plus closer Mariano Rivera (36 saves, 2.85 ERA). Bobby Valentine's Mets finish at 94-68. The offense is paced by Mike Piazza (.324, 38 homers, 113 RBI), Edgardo Alfonzo (.324, 25 homers, 94 RBI), Todd Zeile (.268, 22 homers, 79 RBI), and Robin Ventura (.232, 24 homers, 84 RBI). Two left-handers, Al Leiter (16-8, 3.20 ERA) and Mike Hampton (15-10, 3.14 ERA), are the aces of the pitching staff, which includes 11-game winners Glendon Rusch and Bobby J. Jones. John Franco (3.40 ERA) and Armando Benitez (41 saves, 2.61 ERA) are the backbone of the bullpen.

OCTOBER 19:

The Cardinals re-sign Darryl Kile (20-9, 3.91 ERA) to a three-year pact at $23 million, with bonus clauses that can boost the pitcher's compensation to $32.55 million over four years.

OCTOBER 20:

Carlos Delgado (.344, 41 homers, 137 RBI) becomes baseball's highest-paid player – for the moment. Delgado is re-signed by the Blue Jays for $68 million over four years, an average salary of $17 million. Delgado and Todd Helton of the Rockies are honored today with the Hank Aaron Award for being the best overall hitters in their respective leagues.

Managers make less, but do okay. The Giants and manager Dusty Baker sign a two-year extension that will pay the skipper $2 million a year, second only to Joe Torre's $3 million.

OCTOBER 21:

World Series, game one. At Yankee Stadium, the longest game in Series history, four hours and 51 minutes, ends when surprise starter Jose Vizcaino singles with two out in the bottom of the 12th, scoring Tino Martinez. Mike Stanton, who pitches two perfect innings in relief, gets the win; Turk Wendell is charged with the loss.

OCTOBER 22:

World Series, game two. Roger Clemens's overpowering pitching is overshadowed by another ugly incident involving Mike Piazza. With two out in the first, Piazza breaks his bat fouling a Clemens pitch. The barrel heads for the Yankees' pitcher, who retrieves it and fires it in the direction of Piazza, who is heading toward first. Both benches empty, but no punches are thrown. The Rocket

OCTOBER 24
The Mets win game three of the Series, 4-2, thanks to Benny Agbayani's two-run double in the eighth.

OCTOBER 26
The Yankees beat the Mets in the Subway Series for their third consecutive World Championship.

goes on to stifle the Mets, allowing two hits and no walks while fanning nine in eight innings. The Yankees withstand round-trippers by Piazza and Jay Payton and a Mets' five-run ninth inning rally for a 6-5 win. Scott Brosius homers for the winners. Mike Hampton takes the loss. Afterward, Clemens offers a number of explanations for his behavior, telling the umpire he thought the bat was the ball. Mets pitcher Al Leiter observes: "Shouldn't he have thrown it to [Yankees' first baseman] Tino?" Following the game, Clemens states: "To be honest with you, I didn't know if it was the bat or the ball." He is fined $50,000 for the episode, tying the highest ever assessed for an offense that does not involve drugs. In 1995, Albert Belle was hit with a $50,000 fine for verbally abusing a reporter during the World Series.

New York City enjoyed its 14th Subway Series.

OCTOBER 23:

The Pirates promote their hitting coach, 41-year-old Lloyd McLendon, to manager. He becomes baseball's fifth current black manager.

OCTOBER 24:

World Series, game three. At Shea, the Mets bounce back with a 4-2 win. Robin Ventura homers for the Mets and Benny Agbayani drives in the lead run with an eighth-inning double to make a winner of veteran John Franco. Two postseason streaks end: Yankees' starter Orlando Hernandez gets his first-ever loss and the Yankees are defeated after 14 consecutive World Series wins.

OCTOBER 25:

World Series, game four. Derek Jeter homers on the first pitch from Bobby J. Jones, and the visiting Yankees never trail, going on to win, 3-2. Jeff Nelson, the third of five Yankees' hurlers, gets the win with a save from Mariano Rivera. Jones is the loser; Mike Piazza homers for the Mets. Jeter also has a triple and teammate Paul O'Neill a three-bagger and single.

OCTOBER 26:

World Series, game five. For the third consecutive year and the 26th time in their 97-year history, the Yankees are the World Series champions. With the score tied at 2-2 in the top of the ninth, another unlikely hero, Luis Sojo, singles to center off starter Al Leiter's 142nd pitch of the game. Jay Peyton's throw hits Jorge Posada as he slides across home plate, allowing Scott Brosius to score the Yankees' fourth run. Mike Stanton, with a perfect eighth, gets the win. Mariano Rivera retires Mike Piazza on a fly to center for the save. Derek Jeter and Bernie Williams homer for the winners; Leiter gets the loss. The Yankees become the first team since the Oakland Athletics of 1972-1974 to record a "threepeat."

Darryl dips to new depths. While his former teammates are celebrating another championship, Darryl Strawberry is in a Tampa, Florida, jail, after leaving a treatment facility without permission and failing a drug test. Earlier this season, he underwent surgery for his recurrence of colon cancer.

The Subway Series may have been a hot attraction in New York, but it earns a dubious distinction across the airwaves – the lowest Nielsen TV ratings ever, beating out the 1998 Yankees-Padres World Series. Derek Jeter is the Series MVP, batting .409 with two homers and two RBI. Teammate Paul O'Neill hits .474, with two triples and two RBI. Mariano Rivera records two saves. For the losing Mets, Todd Zeile hits .400 and Mike Piazza connects for two homers and has four RBI.

THE BEST OF 2000

National League

HITTERS

Batting Average:
Todd Helton, Colorado Rockies, .372

Slugging Average:
Todd Helton, .698

Home Runs:
Sammy Sosa, Chicago Cubs, 50

Runs Batted In:
Todd Helton, 147

Hits:
Todd Helton, 216

Stolen Bases:
Luis Castillo, Florida Marlins, 62

PITCHERS

Wins:
Tom Glavine, Atlanta Braves;
Darryl Kile, St. Louis Cardinals, 20

Strikeouts:
Randy Johnson, Arizona Diamondbacks, 347

Earned Run Average:
Kevin Brown, Los Angeles Dodgers, 2.58

Winning Percentage:
Randy Johnson, .731

Saves:
Antonio Alfonseca,
Florida Marlins, 45

Most Valuable Player:
Jeff Kent, San Francisco Giants

Cy Young Award:
Randy Johnson, Arizona Diamondbacks

Rookie of the Year:
Rafael Furcal, Atlanta Braves

Manager of the Year:
Johnnie "Dusty" Baker, San Francisco Giants

American League

HITTERS

Batting Average:
Nomar Garciaparra, Boston Red Sox, .372

Slugging Average:
Jason Giambi, Oakland Athletics, .647

Home Runs:
Troy Glaus, Anaheim Angels, 47

Runs Batted In:
Mike Sweeney, Kansas City Royals, 144

Hits:
Darin Erstad, Anaheim Angels, 240

Stolen Bases:
Johnny Damon, Kansas City Royals, 46

PITCHERS

Wins:
Tim Hudson, Oakland Athletics;
David Wells, Toronto Blue Jays, 20

Strikeouts:
Pedro Martinez, Boston Red Sox, 284

Earned Run Average:
Pedro Martinez, 1.74

Winning Percentage:
Tim Hudson, .769

Saves:
Todd Jones, Detroit Tigers;
Derek Lowe, Boston Red Sox, 42

Most Valuable Player:
Jason Giambi, Oakland Athletics

Cy Young Award:
Pedro J. Martinez, Boston Red Sox

Rookie of the Year:
Kazuhiro Sasaki, Seattle Mariners

Manager of the Year:
Jerry Manuel, Chicago White Sox

BIBLIOGRAPHY

Aaron, Hank, with Lonnie Wheeler. *I Had a Hammer: The Hank Aaron Story*. HarperCollins, 1991.

Ahrens, Art, and Eddie Gold; ed. by Buck Peden. *Day by Day in Chicago Cubs History*. Leisure, 1982.

Alexander, Charles C. *John McGraw*. Viking, 1988.

Alexander, Charles C. *Rogers Hornsby*. Henry Holt, 1995.

Alexander, Charles C. *Ty Cobb*. Oxford University Press, 1984.

Allen, Lee. *The American League Story – A Colorful and Exciting History*. Hill and Wang, 1962.

Allen, Lee. *The National League Story, the Official History*. Revised edition. Hill and Wang, 1961, 1965.

Allen, Maury. *Where Have You Gone, Joe DiMaggio?* New American Library, 1975.

Asinof, Eliot. *Eight Men Out*. Holt, Rinehart and Winston, 1963.

Bergan, Ronald. *Sports in the Movies*. Proteus, 1982.

Berke, Art, and Paul Schmitt. *This Date in Chicago White Sox History*. Scarborough, Stein and Day, 1982.

Bjarkman, Peter C., ed. *Encyclopedia of Major League Baseball – American League*. Carroll and Graf/Gallen, 1991, 1993.

Bjarkman, Peter C., ed. *Encyclopedia of Major League Baseball – National League*. Carroll and Graf/Gallen, 1991, 1993.

Brown, Gene, ed. *The Complete Book of Baseball, A New York Times Scrapbook History*. Arno/Bobbs-Merrill, 1980.

Bucek, Jeanine, ed. director. *The Baseball Encyclopedia*. 10th ed. Macmillan, 1996.

Carruth, Gorton, and Eugene Ehrlich. *Facts & Dates of American Sports*. Harper and Row, 1988.

Cataneo, David. *Peanuts and Crackerjacks*. Rutledge Hill, 1991.

Clark, Dick, and Larry Lester, eds. *The Negro Leagues Book*. Society for American Baseball Research, 1994.

Connor, Anthony J. *Baseball for the Love of It: Hall of Famers Tell It Like It Was*. Macmillan, 1982.

Creamer, Robert W. *Babe: The Legend Comes to Life*. Simon and Schuster, 1974.

Creamer, Robert W. *Stengel, His Life and Times*. Simon and Schuster, 1984.

D'Agostino, Dennis. *This Date in New York Mets History*. Scarborough/Stein and Day, 1981.

Dewey, Donald, and Nicholas Acocella. *The Biographical History of Baseball*. Carroll and Graf, 1995.

Dickerson, Gary E. *The Cinema of Baseball: Images of America, 1929-1989*. Meckler, 1991.

Dickey, Glenn. *The History of American League Baseball Since 1901*. Stein and Day, 1980.

Dickey, Glenn. *The History of National League Baseball Since 1876*. Stein and Day, 1979.

Dickson, Paul. *Baseball's Greatest Quotations*. Harper Perennial, 1991.

Dittmar, Joseph J. *Baseball's Benchmark Boxscores*. McFarland, 1990.

Eckhouse, Morris. *Day by Day in Cleveland Indians History*. Leisure, 1983.

Eckhouse, Morris, and Carl Mastrocola. *This Date in Pittsburgh Pirates History*. Stein and Day, 1980.

Einstein, Charles. *Willie's Time, A Memoir.* Lippincott, 1979.

Eskenazi, Gerald. *The Lip: A Biography of Leo Durocher*. Morrow, 1993.

Everson, Jeff. *This Date in Milwaukee Braves History*. Everson/Graphic Communications, 1987.

Feller, Bob, and Bill Gilbert. *Now Pitching Bob Feller*. Birch Lane/Carol, 1990.

Fischler, Stan and Shirley. *The Best, Worst and Most Unusual in Sports*. Crowell, 1977.

Gallagher, Mark. *Day by Day in New York Yankees History*. Leisure, 1983.

Gershman, Michael. *Diamonds – The Evolution of the Ballpark*. Houghton Mifflin, 1993.

Gewecke, Cliff. *Day by Day in Dodgers History*. Leisure, 1984.

Gies, Joseph, and Robert H. Shoemaker. *Stars of the Series*. Crowell, 1964, 1965.

Ginsburg, Daniel E. *The Fix Is In: A History of Baseball Gambling and Game Fixing Scandals*. McFarland, 1995.

Goldstein, Richard. *Spartan Seasons: How Baseball Survived the Second World War*. Macmillan, 1980.

Graham, Frank. *The New York Giants*. Putnam's, 1952.

Greenberg, Hank, edited and with an introduction by Ira Berkow. *The Story of My Life*. Times Books, 1989.

Gutman, Dan. *Baseball Babylon*. Penguin, 1992.

Harwell, Ernie, and Fred Smith. *Son of Tiger Trivia*. 1980.

Hawkins, John C. *This Date in Baltimore Orioles and St. Louis Browns History*. Scarborough/Stein and Day, 1983.

Hawkins, John C. *This Date in Detroit Tigers History*. Scarborough/Stein and Day, 1981.

Hendricks, Randal A. *Inside the Strike Zone*. Eakin, 1994.

Honig, Donald. *The American League – An Illustrated History*. Crown, 1983.

Honig, Donald. *Baseball – The Illustrated History of America's Game*. Crown, 1990.

Honig, Donald. *The National League – An Illustrated History. Revised and updated*. Crown, 1983, 1987.

Hynd, Noel. *The Giants of the Polo Grounds*. Doubleday, 1988.

James, Bill. *The Bill James Historical Baseball Abstract*. Villard, 1988.

Kahn, Roger. *How the Weather Was*. Harper & Row, 1973.

Kavanagh, Jack. *Walter Johnson, A Life*. Diamond Communications, 1995.

Kiersh, Edward. *Where Have You Gone, Vince DiMaggio?* Bantam, 1983.

Koppett, Leonard. *A Thinking Man's Guide to Baseball*. Dutton, 1967.

Kubek, Tony, and Terry Pluto. *61*. Macmillan, 1987.

Lansche, Jerry. *Glory Fades Away – The 19th Century* World Series Rediscovered. Taylor, 1991.

Leptich, John, and Dave Baranowski. *This Date in St. Louis Cardinals History*. Scarborough/Stein and Day, 1983.

Lewis, Allen, and Larry Shenk. *This Date in Philadelphia Phillies History*. Scarborough/Stein and Day, 1970.

Lieb, Fred. *Baseball As I Have Known It*. Coward, McCann and Geoghagen, 1977.

Lowenfish, Lee, and Tony Lupien. *The Imperfect Diamond: The Story of Baseball's Reserve System and the Men Who Fought to Change It*. Stein and Day, 1980.

McCue, Andy. *Baseball by the Books: A History and Complete Bibliography of Baseball Fiction*. Brown, 1991.

Mercurio, John A. *Record Profiles of Baseball's Hall of Famers*. Perennial/Harper and Row, 1990.

Moreland, George L. Balldom *The Brittanica of Baseball*. Balldom, 1914.

Mote, James. *Everything Baseball*. Prentice-Hall, 1989.

Nash, Bruce, and Allan Zullo. *The Baseball Hall of Shame*. Wallaby, 1986.

Nash, Bruce, and Allen Zullo. *The Baseball Hall of Shame 2*. Pocket, 1985.

Nemec, David. *Great Baseball Feats, Facts and Firsts*. New American Library, 1987.

The New York Times Book of Baseball History – Major League Highlights From the Pages of the New York Times. Quadrangle/New York Times, 1975.

Okkonen, Marc. *Baseball Memories 1900-1909*. Sterling, 1992.

Okkonen, Marc. *Baseball Memories 1950-1959*. Sterling, 1993.

Okrent, Daniel, and Harris Lewine, eds. *The Ultimate Baseball Book*. Houghton-Mifflin, 1984.

Okrent, Daniel, and Steve Wulf. *Baseball Anecdotes*. Perennial/Harper and Row, 1989.

Onigman, Marc. *This Date in Braves History*. Scarborough/Stein and Day, 1982.

Peary, Danny, ed. *Cult Baseball Players: The Greats, the Flakes, the Weird and the Wonderful*. Fireside Simon and Schuster, 1990.

Peterson, Robert. *Only the Ball Was White*. McGraw-Hill, 1970.

Rader, Benjamin G. *Baseball, a History of America's Game*. University of Illinois Press, 1992.

Rathgeber, Bob. *Cincinnati Reds Scrapbook*. JCP, 1982.

Reichler, Joseph L. *The Baseball Trade Register*. Macmillan, 1984.

Reichler, Joseph L., revised by Ken Samelson. *The Great All-Time Baseball Record Book*. Macmillan, 1981, 1993.

Reidenbaugh, Lowell, compiled by the editors of the Sporting News. *Baseball Hall of Fame Cooperstown*. Arlington House, 1983, 1986, 1988.

Rice, Grantland. *The Tumult and the Shouting "My Life in Sport."* Barnes, 1954.

Robinson, Ray. *Iron Horse: Lou Gehrig in His Time*. Norton, 1990.

Salant, Nathan. *Superstars, Stars and Just Plain Heroes*. Stein and Day, 1982.

Salisbury, Luke. *The Answer is Baseball*. Times Books, 1989.

Schaap, Dick, and Mort Gerberg, eds. *Joy in Mudville*. Doubleday, 1992.

Scheinin, Richard. *Field of Screams*. Norton, 1994.

Seymour, Harold. *Baseball: The Early Years*. Oxford University Press, 1960.

Seymour, Harold. *Baseball: The Golden Years*. Oxford University Press, 1971.

Seymour, Harold. *Baseball: The People's Game*. Oxford University Press, 1990.

Shatzkin, Michael, ed. *The Ballplayers*. Arbor House/Morrow, 1990.

Smith, Ken. *Baseball's Hall of Fame*. Barnes, 1952.

Spalding, Albert G., Samm Coombs, and Bob West eds. *Baseball, America's National Game*. Halo, 1991.

Staten, Vince. *Ol' Diz*. HarperCollins, 1992.

Sullivan, George. *The Picture History of the Boston Red Sox*. Bobbs-Merrill, 1979.

Thorn, John, ed. *The National Pastime*. Warner, 1987.

Thorn, John, and Bob Carroll, eds. *The Whole Baseball Catalogue*. Fireside/Simon and Schuster, 1990.

Twombley, Wells. *200 Years of Sport in America: A Pageant of a Nation at Play*. McGraw-Hill, 1976.

Tygiel, Jules. *Baseball's Great Experiment: Jackie Robinson and His Legacy*. Oxford University Press, 1983.

Veeck, Bill, with Ed Linn. *Veeck – As in Wreck*. Putnam's, 1962.

Voigt, David Quentin. *American Baseball From Gentlemen's Sport to the Commissioner System*. University of Oklahoma Press, 1966.

Voigt, David Quentin. *Baseball An Illustrated History*. Pennsylvania State University Press, 1987.

Walton, Ed. *Red Sox Triumphs and Tragedies*. Scarborough/Stein and Day, 1978.

Walton, Ed. *This Date in Boston Red Sox History*. Scarborough/Stein and Day, 1978.

Ward, Arch, ed. *The Greatest Sport Stories From the Chicago Tribune*. Barnes, 1953.

Ward, Geoffrey C., and Ken Burns, with Paul Robert Walker. *Who Invented the Game?* Knopf, 1994.

Williams, Ted, as told to John Underwood. *My Turn at Bat*. Simon and Schuster, 1969.

INDEX

A

B

C

D

E

F

G

H

K

M

N

O

P

Q

R

S

T

Y

Z

PHOTOGRAPHY CREDITS

The publisher would like to thank the following for their kind permission to reproduce their photographs:

AP/Wide World: 129, 255, 399, 418, 454-455, 485, 496, 575, 606, 658, 672, 722, 735, 739, 767, 787, 853, 858.

Corbis Images: 105, 152, 159, 174, 184, 191, 219, 231, 235, 245, 272, 281, 283, 287, 293, 296, 302, 304, 311, 329, 331, 350, 374, 389, 408, 421, 423, 435, 442, 449, 453, 472, 500, 506, 520, 531, 542, 549, 554, 568, 571, 572, 573, 588-589, 600, 614, 641, 652, 667, 678, 742, 747, 782-783.

Christies: 113.

Dorling Kindersley: 27.

The Library of Congress: 21, 30, 72, 172.

Major League Baseball Photos: 602, 611, 619, 620, 635, 643, 663, 671,687, 691, 699, 700, 714, 719, 730, 736, 752, 762, 774, 779, 801, 806,824, 828, 836, 842, 865, 867, 868, 875, 878, 885, 888, 893, 897, 902,905, 912, 917, 923, 925, 928, 930-931, 935, 941, 942-943, 949, 950, 955,957, 961, 962, 973, 974, 976, 987, 990, 996-997, 1002, 1006-1007, 1017,1019, 1028, 1039, 1043, 1055, 1057, 1063, 1066-1077, 1073, 1086, 1091,1102, 1106-1107, 1113, 1114, 1119, 1121, 1123, 1134, 1139, 1140, 1143,1144, 1152, 1159, 1160, 1168, 1172.

The National Baseball Hall of Fame and Library: 25, 32, 34, 37, 42, 49, 53, 59, 66-67, 77, 85, 87, 94, 118-119, 123, 129, 144, 160, 200, 209, 237, 251, 259, 303, 319, 323, 341, 364, 373, 384, 413.

David Spindel: 29, 33, 69, 98, 120, 124, 223, 252, 414, 457.

Photo research and editing services were provided by the Shoreline Publishing Group, Santa Barbara, California.

ACKNOWLEDGMENTS

Dorling Kindersley would like to thank:
Mandy Earey, Keith Kinsella, Jonathan Bennett, Jill Bunyan, Megan Clayton, Soo Jin Parks, Rahil Briggs and Tim Cain of NewEarthMedia for their fantastic design skills and numerous evenings of burning the midnight oil; Dirk Kaufman for the jacket design; Beth Adelman, Crystal Coble, Chuck Wills, and Craig Zeichner for their additional editorial support; James Buckley, Jr., Editorial Director, Shoreline Publishing Group, for supplying captions; Teri Maurice for indexing a lengthy project in a short time.

And most of all Michelle Baxter, whose commitment, hard work, tolerance, humor, and brilliant organizational skills made the whole thing possible.